KU-189-822

# The Making of Scotland

## A Comprehensive Guide to the Growth of its Cities, Towns and Villages

**Robin Smith**

# The Making of Scotland

## A Comprehensive Guide to the Growth of its Cities, Towns and Villages

**Robin Smith**

EDITOR

Alan Lawson

CONSULTANT

John R Hume

CANONGATE

First published in Great Britain
in 2001 by Canongate Books Ltd
14 High Street, Edinburgh EH1 1TE

10 9 8 7 6 5 4 3 2 1



*British Library Cataloguing-in-Publication Data*
A catalogue record for this book is available upon request from the British Library

ISBN 1 84195 170 6

Typeset by TexturAL, Edinburgh
Printed and bound in Spain by Grafos

www.canongate.net

# Contents

# Illustrations

In the collecting of suitable illustrations for this book, particular assistance has been received from Mike Craig of the George Washington Wilson Collection at Aberdeen University, and from Miriam McDonald and other staff at The Royal Commission on the Ancient and Historical Monuments of Scotland. Special thanks are due to the Royal Commission for waiving reproduction fees. Thanks are also due to the British Geological Survey for waiving fees in respect of their pictures.

Each photograph's source is acknowledged at the end of its caption. The following abbreviations have been used:

GWW: The George Washington Wilson Collection
RCAHMS: The Royal Commission on the Ancient and Historical Monuments of Scotland
SMPC: The StillMovingPicture Company
JRH: John R Hume (consultant). Those credited as RCAHMS/JRH are photographs taken by John R Hume but now in the care of the Royal Commission
RS: Robin Smith (author)
AL: Alan Lawson (editor)

Considerable effort has been made to ascertain and acknowledge the correct source of each illustration, and to make the appropriate payment where required. Any errors or oversights should be notified to the publisher for rectification.

# Preface

## The Origins of this Book

A clerical error in 1948 placed the author, an English conscript soldier, in the Sappers – the Royal Engineers – rather than the infantry. Chance, too, led to a posting to Longmoor Camp in Hampshire to be trained as a *'Clerk Railway C3'*, and to a long night journey north behind toiling steam engines at Easter 1949. As the dawn came up over the North Sea at Berwick upon Tweed he entered a completely new phase of his life. The carriage window revealed rock cuttings, grey stone villages, lush greening cornfields, the stark ruins of Redhouse Castle, Prestonpans pitheads and the red-brick Portobello power station. Emerging from Calton Hill tunnel into Edinburgh's Waverley station, the tall grey cliffs of tenement buildings and the striding arches of North Bridge seemed to dominate the gritty yet stylish city.

A kitbag-encumbered struggle up the 287 steps from platform level brought him to the top floor of the *Scotsman* building. Although converted into a hotel in 2001, in those post-war days this granite-faced edifice still held the Headquarters of Movement Control, Scottish Command – his base for a year. The corner turret afforded a bird's-eye view of Edinburgh's Calton Hill, the shining Forth and distant hills, while elderly tramcars rumbled, screeched and clanged across the North Bridge far below. Scottish maps full of exotic names, talk of railway journeys to distant ports for ferry connections to sprawling islands, became daily companions to work on maintaining Unit records or descending those noisome spiral steps to check *'one prisoner and two escorts'* on to midnight trains to Colchester and the *'glasshouse'*.

In lunch hours a Holyhead friend would join the author to ride the trams to distant suburbs, to cycle among the mining villages of Midlothian or take the Queen's Ferry to Fife. Billeted in Aggie's downmarket hotel on the windy High Street beside the Tron Kirk were other young soldiers from all parts, including assorted memorable characters – a sardonic plumber from Walsall, a honky-tonk pianist and railway fireman from Hull, and the gifted accordionist Alex MacArthur who later became a well-known Scottish dance band leader. We met racing tipster Prince *"Ah Got a Horse"* Monolulu, and housemaid Wee Mary who – having become blonde overnight – departed to try her luck on the streets of London. The Edinburgh Festival was becoming established, and the vast panoply of Scottish scenery and industrial life, plus the soft drizzle encountered on a coach trip to Loch Lomond – so different from the low hills and riversides of his home town of Huntingdon, where the author already had Scottish friends – made a profound and lasting impression.

Later, as a Geography student in Cambridge, he looked in vain for Scottish reports to compare with the central place studies and spatial theories of the German Walter Christaller, then in vogue among economic geographers. So when time allowed he began to collect information on Scotland's towns and villages; the theories didn't fit as they had almost seemed to in East Anglia. Another happy chance led to Liverpool University, Civic Design qualifications and – through a shared joy in Scottish country dancing – his wife Dorothy and her far-flung family. Children and family holidays – many by Motorail and car to the remoter parts of Scotland – punctuated a career in local government planning; this ranged from rural Cambridgeshire and research in busy

Bedfordshire, via housing layouts and property dealings in Northampton and industrial promotion and town centre redevelopment in Scunthorpe, to regional planning in East Anglia.

A career crisis, resolved by the offer of a post as Kirkcaldy's Burgh Planning Officer, gave the opportunity to visit more of Scotland and to research the facilities in Scottish towns. Local government reorganisation in 1974 led to 13 years of rail commuting into central Edinburgh to teach Town, Regional and Transport Planning. Already, reminded by a comment by his banker son-in-law that "urban services must depend on urban economies", he was gathering data on their development. Resistance to the Thatcher regime's retrogressive policies on planning and transport proving futile; early retirement in 1988 seemed an attractive option. So the way was cleared for a further 13 years of hard solo work, culminating in this book, which – like Topsy – just *'growed'*. The author being neither an economic historian nor a Scot, it can only portray facts and reflect views on Scottish cities, towns and villages from the standpoint of a long and varied life. Inevitably, despite the sterling efforts of the editor to make a silk purse out of a sow's ear and to ensure perfection, there will be errors – but that's how it all began!

**Robin Smith**

To Dorothy

*

## Acknowledgements

Innumerable people have kindly provided information, encouragement and assistance of various kinds over many years. My grateful thanks are due firstly to the Connan family of Huntingdon, who in the 1940s inspired a passionate interest in Scotland, and 40 years later to my sons-in-law – Peter Fanning, who gave the germ of the idea for this book, and Julian Cable, who, despite his own busy life, has freely helped with computing problems. Helena and John Butler also gave programming help in the 1980s. Margaret Wilkes, Diana Webster and other staff of the National Library of Scotland map room have revealed a wealth of historic sources. Mrs Irene Thomas read and commented on a very early draft of the text, and Dr Ken Allardyce read and commented on intermediate drafts.

Publication has only been achieved with the help of many other people across Scotland, including those who have answered local questions, members of the staff of Historic Scotland, and photographic archive holders. Among publishers who gave advice, encouragement and introductions (even though, for various reasons, they could not themselves bring the work to fruition) thanks are due to James Campbell of Caledonian Books, Mrs Jill Dick of Scottish Cultural Press, and particularly Dr Keith Whittles of Whittles Publishers and Hugh Andrew of Birlinn Limited.

A special debt of gratitude is owed to Jamie Byng of Canongate for his boldness in taking on the publication of such a weighty tome. Alan Lawson, as editor of what began as an overlong and insufficiently focused text, has given unstinting effort, provided valuable criticism and updating information, and been unafraid to bully the author when necessary. John Hume's active role as consultant has led to many corrections being made, interesting snippets of information being added, and an extensive personal and professional photographic archive being opened for use. He and Alan Lawson have been responsible for illustrating the book – no mean task in itself, and one which I could not have found the time to undertake.

Finally, my wife Dorothy and daughters Katharine and Alison have provided sustenance, help, encouragement and forbearance over the many years that this project has been in gestation. I owe Dorothy more than I can ever convey.

**Robin Smith**
Kirkcaldy
June 2001

# Current Local Authorities (since 1996)

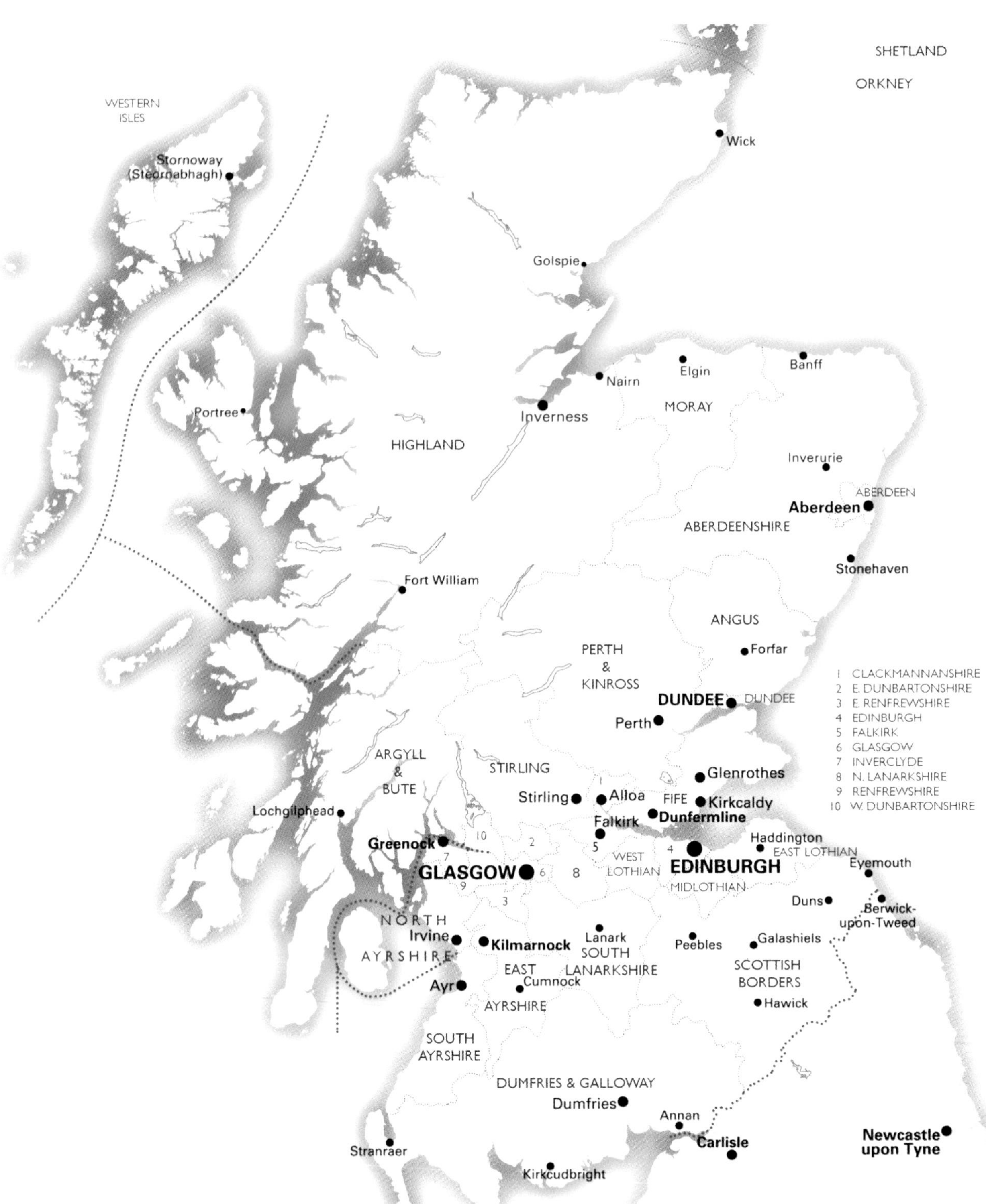


*(Detailed map of Orkney, p. 989; of Shetland, p. 990)*

# Older local authority names and regional names

(Detailed map of Orkney, p. 989; of Shetland, p. 990)

# Reader's Guide

This Guide • explains how to find an entry (major or minor) • describes how to use the detailed maps (at the back of the book) • details the heading information and the text of an entry • provides information on some of the older maps regularly referred to • notes the various surveys of Scotland mentioned and finally • provides useful lists of important individuals, organisations, and technical terms which occur throughout the book.

## HISTORICAL OVERVIEW

To gain a general picture of the major influences in the country's development, read *Scotland's Development: An Historical Overview* which follows this Reader's Guide; it is sectionalised in date order and by theme for those who need quick general information.

## BIBLIOGRAPHY

The Bibliography (p.948) provides a list of the main works used in compiling the book, many of which are referred to in the text.

## FINDING AN ENTRY

**Main entries**: There are 1285 main entries in the book – cities, suburbs, towns, villages and localities; they are arranged in alphabetical order. Many of them incorporate nearby and/or secondary places in their title – e.g., OAKLEY, Carnock & Comrie.

**Cities and suburbs**: Because the cities and many of the larger towns are conglomerations of smaller places which at first developed more or less independently, the stories of many places now considered *suburbs* are separate main entries in the book – e.g., Corstorphine (Edinburgh), Gorbals (Glasgow), Mannofield (Aberdeen), and Lochee (Dundee).

The full list of places being treated as suburbs are to be found under the heading for the larger place of which they are now part – e.g., DUNDEE, Suburbs: *Baldovan, Broughty Ferry, Craigie, Invergowrie & Lochee.*

This should clarify the complexity of city growth, and also help those readers seeking a quick guide to the present-day character of a particular locality within a large urban area.

**City centres** and related inner areas alone comprise the latter part of each article on a city or those larger towns with complex histories such as Kilmarnock, Kirkcaldy and Stirling.

**Also see:** Where there are one or more places very closely related to a main entry, their names appear under the heading information as 'Also see' – e.g., Greenock: Also see Gourock, Port Glasgow & Spango Valley.

**Minor entries, and the Index:** To find a particular place which is not represented by a *main* entry, consult the **Index**, in which a further 3800 names of smaller places, districts, castles, mills, abbeys and other features are listed, showing the main entries in which they are mentioned. The names of historic provinces and island groups lead to appropriate local histories.

## READING AN ENTRY

### Heading Information

**Description:** Each main-entry heading includes a ***short description*** of the place, giving an indication of its general location and its size or nature – e.g., Small Berwickshire village, or S-E. suburb of Edinburgh.

**Place-names**: Due to the recurring changes to our local government structure (1975 and 1996), the names used to describe places and regions are now a mixture of modern administrative names and older 'regional' names, and this diversity is reflected in the terms used in the book. The two maps which immediately precede this Reader's Guide show (1) the latest local government boundaries and names, and (2) older names which are used in the text.

**Population**: An indicative ***population*** figure is also given, though due to difficulties in reconciling functional areas and census data boundaries, and the long time elapsed since the 1991 census, these figures should be used with caution. Where available, census *'locality'* populations are given; for many rural places, it is the populations of small areas (parishes or parts of parishes in which they lie) that are given. City centre and suburb populations are generally based on postcode data. Historic populations from 1901 onwards are derived from census sources; some 19th century data may also be so. In a few cases population figures are not given – either because they are unpopulated or (conversely) because they have grown so fast in recent years as to be very difficult to assess.

**Map references**: Map numbers and co-ordinates are given for the ***detailed maps*** at the end of the book. These maps – prepared in Bishopbriggs by the famed mapmakers Bartholomew's – mark the names of practically every place which has its own main entry, plus other significant features. The 16 sheets cover the whole of Scotland at about 1:600,000 (9 miles to 1 inch); Glasgow and Edinburgh and their environs also appear at about 1:180,000 (3 miles to 1 inch), and the Central Belt which lies between them at about 1:270,000 (4.25 miles to 1 inch). Many maps overlap to ensure a broader picture.

For those wishing to follow the text on the ground, the current ***Ordnance Survey*** 1:50,000 *'Landranger'* sheet number and grid reference (to the nearest kilometre) are also shown.

### The Text of an Entry

Each article emphasises the origins (where known) of the place, its evolving functions, the work of its people, and links between places. Within the text, cross-references to other entries appear where appropriate.

**Historical sequence** is broadly maintained within each article. For all but the smallest places, sub-headings are used – indicating the main contents of that paragraph, and sometimes allowing particular industries and special topics to be described outwith the strict chronological order.

**Units of measurement:** To meet the needs of the younger generation, the *metric* system of measurement is principally used. The approximate equivalents are:
8 km = 5 miles;    1500 metres = one mile
1 metric tonne = 1 ton;    1 hectare (ha) = 2.5 acres.

**Quotations employed:** For the earlier periods, many short *quotations* from contemporary accounts are used (given in italics). Brief notes about these many 'investigators, commentators and travellers' are given towards the end of this Reader's Guide. (The quotes have been slightly adapted in some cases to make for easier reading; those wishing to find the originals should consult the Bibliography.) Many of these writers are featured in P Hume Brown's book *Early Travellers in Scotland.*

***Murray's Handbook* (1894):** This Handbook (or Guide) is much referred to in the text, principally giving assessments of hotels, but often giving a broader view of a place. The 1894 edition (published by John Murray, London, and by Oliver & Boyd, Edinburgh) was the 6th edition; it described itself as "re-cast, and in a great measure re-written, due to the extension of the railways and the greater facilities for travelling". It was clearly meant as a comprehensive guide for tourists. It was re-published in 1971 by David St John Thomas, who described it as "a vivid if relatively brief portrait of the country".

## SURVEYS OF SCOTLAND

A number of different surveys are referred to in the text. The principal ones are described here:

**Medieval Population**, around year 1250: 600,000 *(Registrar-General's 1947 estimate).*

**Webster's Population Survey** (1755). Dr Alexander Webster obtained head counts from all parish ministers in Scotland and totalled them at 1.265 million.

**First Statistical Account** (1791–99), inspired by Sir John Sinclair of Ulbster (born 1754), reported on the condition of every parish in Scotland. The data was obtained from Church of Scotland ministers, and included population, housing, economic activity, welfare, natural features and much else; it was collated by Robert Heron *(see New Galloway)* and edited by Sir John Sinclair.

**Second Statistical Account** (1830s, published 1845), a less well known repeat of the 1790s study.

**Third Statistical Account** (1950s–1990s), an attempt to repeat the work of the First and Second Statistical Accounts.

**Decennial Censuses** (1801–2001), which count and analyse all people resident in or present in Scotland. These are held every 10th year (except 1941, plus a 10% sample in 1966).

Totals (million):

| | |
|---|---|
| 1801: 1.608 | 1951: 5.096 |
| 1851: 2.289 | 1971: 5.229 |
| 1901: 4.472 | 1991: 4.962 |

*(At time of going to press, the 2001 census results were not yet available.)*

## OLDER MAPS

In many of the entries, the early existence and/or condition of a place is described by reference to early maps – especially to those drawn by Timothy Pont (around the year 1600), and by William Roy (around 1750). Maps produced by other map makers have also been consulted and are referred to in places; these are briefly described in the list of 'Map Makers and Illustrators' later in this Reader's Guide.

Immediately following, however, are descriptions in greater detail of the work of Gough, Pont, Roy, and the early (c. 1890) editions of the OS maps.

**The Gough Map:** This ancient manuscript map of Britain, found in the Bodleian Library in the 18th century by Tom Martin, bought by Richard Gough and reproduced by (e.g.) P Hume Brown, is reckoned by modern scholars to date from around 1360 (on the basis of its detailed English coverage). Probably a compilation produced in London, its creator must have used out of date material for Scotland, whose historians think it is of 13th century date. The author believes its Scottish content goes back to around 1230 (based on checking the included placenames and their charter dates). Its reliance on Latin and the dedication of Arbroath Abbey suggest its originator was a monk.

**Timothy Pont**, from Fife, was born around 1560, graduated from St Andrews University, and eventually became Minister of Dunnet. Meantime, from 1583 to about 1596, Pont (who had some private means) *"unaided, travelled afoot over the whole kingdom, sketching and naming innumerable settlements"* (Robert Gordon). His originals are untriangulated, not to scale, and show few trackways. After his death, c.1615, James VI saved his sketches, but hid them! In the 1630s Lord Scotstarvit *(see Ceres)* arranged for their publication, through Robert Gordon and his son from 1641. Pont's maps became the major input to Blaeu's *Atlas Novus*, a fascinating source of information on early Scotland, including its mills and bridges.

*Pont's map of 'Maimor' (Lochaber), c.1600.* *(The National Library Map Room)*

The *'Maimor'* (*Lochaber*) map reproduced here is the best of the originals that survive; West is at the top. Note the sites of Fort William at *'Achaintour'*, and of Kinlochleven at *'Kean-Loch-moir'*; what is now North Ballachulish appears as *'Balecheules'*. The best sheets were discarded after engraving by Blaeu; the others we have are fragmentary, faint and often so small or overdrawn as to be obscure *(see Stone, 1989 and 1991, in the Bibliography).*

**William Roy**, surveyor, quartermaster, soldier and antiquary, was born near Carluke in 1726, the son of an estate factor. He worked for the Post Office, and was then engaged to sketch-map mainland Scotland at 1:36000 as a Military Survey from 1747 to1755. He started alone on the north half of Scotland, with Paul Sandby as draughtsman; the map of *Edinburgh and Leith* reproduced here at a reduced scale was among the later output of 1752–55, when he had several survey teams covering southern Scotland. Note the (unnamed) Nor' Loch covering the site of Princes Street Gardens; the New Town had not been commenced, though Bruntsfield had already been laid out. *'Deanmills'* appears on the dissected portion to the west. Restalrig was a separate village, and the site of Portobello was heathland. Roy was granted an army commission, recommended the foundation of the Ordnance Survey in 1766, and after a memorable career oversaw its commencement in England in 1784 (see O'Donoghue, in the Bibliography).

**The Ordnance Survey of Scotland:** This followed after the survey of England; trigonometrical work started at Balmedie *(q.v.)* in 1817 (see Greenwood, in the Map Makers list). The detail was originally mainly surveyed in the third quarter of the 19th century, and published *inter alia* as a standard series of maps of Scotland at 1:63360 *('One-Inch')* scale, completed in 1880. The revised edition of the 1890s (excluding the outer islands) was republished in the 1980s by Caledonian Books of Collieston, Aberdeenshire. The section reproduced here – showing Leslie, Markinch, Coaltown of Balgonie, Thornton and Kinglassie – embraces the site of Glenrothes, whose planners adopted the old farm names for the various neighbourhoods on which the provision of housing

*Roy's 1750s map of Edinburgh and Leith (and surrounding area).* *(The British Library)*

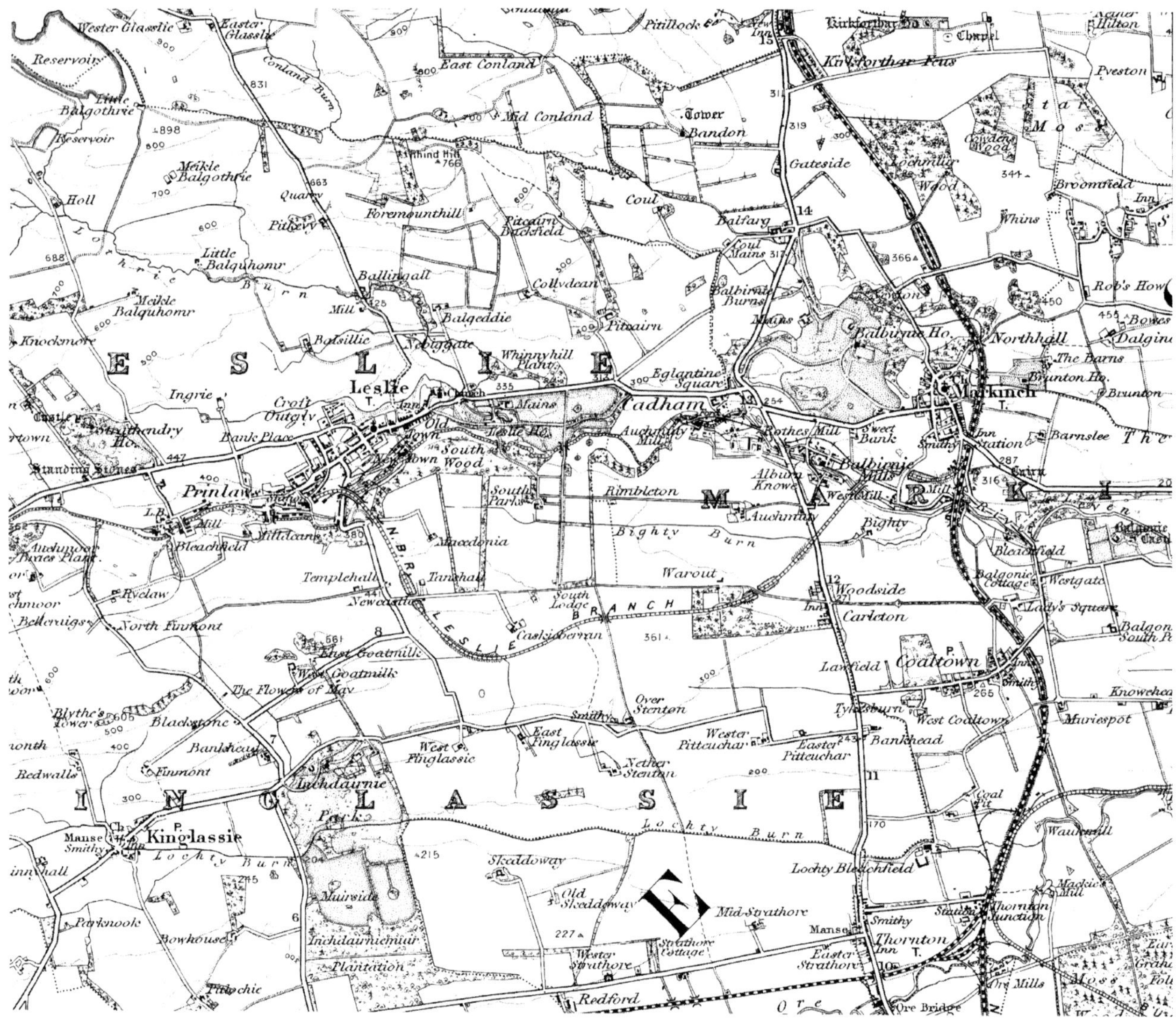


*A section of an 1890s OS map of central Fife.*

and facilities was based. The *'One-Inch'* scale was further revised at irregular intervals and went through seven series, being replaced from 1973 by the 1:50000 *'Landranger'* maps referred to in the article headings, which are now electronically updated and reprinted at frequent intervals. The Ordnance Survey also issues maps at many other scales and for special purposes.

## EXPLANATORY LISTS

Below are a series of explanatory lists of names commonly recurring in the book. *People* are divided into four groups:

- Map Makers & Illustrators
- Investigators, Commentators and Travellers
- Major Constructors, Architects, Engineers and Planners
- Other Influential People

These are followed by a list of *Key Organisations*, and finally there are lists of *Textile Terms* and *Mining Terms*.

*(These lists are for general guidance only and make no claim to be exhaustive.)*

## MAP MAKERS AND ILLUSTRATORS

**Adair, John D,** eminent Scottish map maker, died 1722; from 1683 he charted the Forth and mapped Clackmannan; also made charts for the Scots Parliament in 1686–1703 covering the Orkneys, Western Isles, west coast, etc.

**Adams, Ian H,** Edinburgh lecturer and author; in the 1970s he mapped locations of Scottish Burghs, gasworks, etc. *(see Bibliography).*

**Ainslie, John,** surveyor, born Jedburgh 1745; respected maker of maps of Scottish counties, and of all Scotland in 1782–89.

**d'Arfeville, Nicolay,** published the first reasonably reliable chart of Scottish waters in 1583 (in Paris).

**Arrowsmith, Aaron,** cartographer, born Winston, Durham 1750; worked for John Cary; mapped India, North America, World and in 1807 published a 4-sheet map of Scotland: (*see Haldane*, below).

**Bacon, George W,** geographer and publisher of *Popular Atlas & Gazetteer of the British Isles,* based on Ordnance Survey, London 1896.

**Blaeu, Johannes,** engraver & publisher of *Atlas Novus*, Vol. 5, with 49 plates of Scotland (Amsterdam, 1654), based on the work of Pont and the Gordons *(see Bibliography).*

**Camden, William,** traveller, antiquarian and teacher, born London 1551; wrote *Britannia* in Latin and included a map of Scotland in the 1607 edition; the 1610 and later editions are in English.

**Cary, John,** maker of map of southern and central Scotland, 1803.

**Fowler, William,** surveyor, see Greenwood.

**Gordon, James,** born c.1615 (son of Robert Gordon), cartographer, and minister of Rothiemay; mapped Edinburgh and Aberdeen; updated certain Pont maps for Blaeu.

**Gordon, Robert,** map maker, of Straloch, born Kinmundy, Aberdeenshire 1580; first graduate of Marischal College Aberdeen; updated Pont's maps for publication by Blaeu (father of James Gordon).

**Gough, Richard,** mariner and antiquary, born London 1735; purchaser from Tom Martin's estate of crude early map of Britain *(see Martin, and also earlier in this Guide under 'Older Maps')*; he revised Camden's *Britannia* for republication in 1789.

**Greenwood, Christopher,** London surveyor, in 1817–30 used the national trigonometrical survey as frame for detailed county maps of Berwickshire, East and Mid Lothian, and Fife with Kinross at 1:63 360 scale; Fife & Kinross map published with William Fowler & Thomas Sharp, 1828 and republished 1992 by Wychwood Editions. He also mapped many counties in England and Wales until the appearance of OS maps ended his business.

**Haldane, A R B,** well-known Scottish researcher and author, reproduced amended version of Arrowsmith's map of roads built by the Commissioners of Highland Roads and Bridges 1803–1828 *(see Bibliography).*

**Hay, G D,** illustrator of industrial history *(see Bibliography).*

**Hondius, Joost,** map engraver, born Flanders 1563; worked in London and in Amsterdam with Mercator; engraved Pont's map of Lothian; died 1611.

**Huddart, Captain Joseph,** master mariner, boatbuilder, hydrographer; born Cumberland 1741; charted the Hebrides 1788–91; later became a rope manufacturer.

**Keppie, Lawrence,** curator (Archaeology), Hunterian Museum, Glasgow, produced maps of Roman roads, forts and campaigns in Scotland *(see Bibliography).*

**Kitchin, Thomas,** little-known maker of map of Haddingtonshire 1750.

**McGibbon, David,** born 1831, architectural historian; with Thomas Ross he produced eight volumes of fine drawings and descriptions of Scottish castles, tower houses, early mansions and churches in two series.

**Mackenzie, Murdoch,** hydrographer, born in Orkney in 1712; surveyed the Orkneys in 1742–48, and in 1748–69 charted the Hebridean seas for the Admiralty.

**Martin, Tom,** born Thetford 1697; lawyer and antiquary, discoverer of ancient map in Bodleian Library, Oxford, later acquired by Gough (above).

**Mercator, Gerhard,** atlas maker, born Flanders 1512; published 107-map world atlas 1585–95, including distorted but detailed general map of Scotland 1595.

**Naismith, Robert J,** architect, senior partner of Sir Frank Mears of Edinburgh; made a location map of Scotland's planned villages and lavishly illustrated Scottish rural buildings *(see Bibliography).*

**Ordnance Survey of Scotland,** see earlier under 'Older Maps'.

**Paris, Matthew,** monk, historian and chronicler, illustrator and map maker, born c. 1200, d. 1259.

**Pont, Timothy,** map maker, see earlier under 'Older Maps'.

**Ptolemy,** of Alexandria, mapped tribes and places of Britain c.140 AD.

**Ross, Thomas,** born 1839, architectural historian, see McGibbon above.

**Roy, William,** surveyor, see earlier under 'Older Maps'.

**Sandby, Paul,** mid 18th century Scottish water colourist and draughtsman, re-drew the Roy maps from field sheets as a permanent record for the Hanoverian government.

**Sharp, Thomas,** see Greenwood.

**Silver, Owen,** PhD, of St Andrews, has mapped turnpike and other roads in Scotland, especially in Fife *(see Bibliography).*

**Stell, Geoffrey P,** born Keighley 1944; Head of Architecture, Royal Commission on the Ancient and Historical Monuments of Scotland; illustrator of industrial history (*see Bibliography*, under Hay).

**Taylor, William,** has mapped the military roads in Scotland *(see Bibliography).*

**Wightman, Andy,** forester, researcher and author, maker of maps of modern Scottish land ownership *(see Bibliography).*

## INVESTIGATORS, COMMENTATORS AND TRAVELLERS

[ Writings by many of the people in this list are featured in P Hume Brown's book *Early Travellers in Scotland.* ]

**Ayala, Dom Pedro de,** Ambassador of Spain to James IV, visited Scotland in 1498.

**Barnard, Alfred,** journalist; toured all distilleries in 1886 *(see Bibliography).*

**Beaugue, Jean de,** French soldier and war historian, visited eastern Scotland 1548–49.

**Beveridge, David,** writer on Clackmannan and West Fife 1888 *(see Bibliography).*

**Boswell, James,** of Auchinleck, (1740–95), landowner, author; companion to and biographer of Dr Samuel Johnson *(see Bibliography).*

**Bremner, David,** Edinburgh writer and editor, reported in detail on Scottish industries 1868–69 (originally for *The Scotsman) (see Bibliography).*

**Brereton, Sir William,** Cheshire gentleman, visited southern Scotland in 1636; later a Cromwellian general.

**Brome, Rev James,** (Church of England) visited south-east and central Scotland in 1669.

**Brown, Peter Hume,** historian, born Haddington 1850; collated reports of early travellers in Scotland, extensively quoted in this volume *(see Bibliography).*

**Carlyle, Alexander,** born 1722; minister and author, toured parts of Scotland *(see Bibliography).*

**Chambers, Robert,** born Peebles 1802; author, publisher and bookseller, walked through and wrote about Scotland in the 1820s *(see Bibliography)*, and researched and wrote the *Traditions of Edinburgh.*

**Cobbett, William,** (1763–1835), English reformer and author, toured in Scotland in 1832 *(see Bibliography).*

**Defoe, Daniel,** author and inquirer, born London 1660; visited Scotland repeatedly in early 18th century *(see Bibliography).*

**Fontane, T,** German travel writer, visited Scotland in 1858 *(see Bibliography).*

**Franck, Richard,** well-known angler, Cromwellian trooper and jocular writer, toured in Scotland in 1656.

**Froissart, Jean,** French priest, historian and traveller, visited Scotland c.1360.

**Hardying, John,** antiquary spy for Henrys V and VI of England, toured Scotland about 1415; produced military guide to Scotland in doggerel verse.

**Heron, Robert,** teacher, author, born New Galloway *(q.v.)* 1764; collated the First Statistical Account for Sir Robert Sinclair, and travelled and wrote of Scotland, particularly the west *(see Bibliography).*

**Martin, Martin,** born Skye c.1660, author and traveller in the Hebrides *(see Bibliography).*

**Monro, Dean,** active 1549, clergyman and author on the Western Islands *(see Bibliography).*

**Morer, Rev Thomas,** Church of England parish priest (London), visited south and central Scotland in 1689; after the Union became chaplain to a Scottish regiment.

**Morison, Fynes,** Cambridge law graduate, visited and wrote of south-east Scotland and Fife in 1598.

**Murray, John,** born 1808, third in a long dynasty of London publishers of that name; author of *Handbook for Scotland* whose 1890s revision is extensively quoted in this book *(see Bibliography).*

**Perlin, Estienne,** French ecclesiastic, visited and wrote of Scotland in 1551–52.

**Pratt, J B,** minister and author, active in Buchan in 1858.

**Ray, John,** self-made Cambridge don and naturalist, visited and wrote of south-east and central Scotland about 1662.

**Rocheford, Jorevin de,** French traveller and author, visited and wrote of south-east and central Scotland about 1661.

**Rohan, Henri Duc de,** French Huguenot soldier and politician, visited and wrote of south-east and central Scotland in 1600.

**Somers, Robert,** Minister and writer, toured from Edinburgh to the Highlands, Skye and Mull in 1847 *(see Bibliography).*

**Southey, Robert,** poet, author and traveller, born 1774, friend of Thomas Telford.

**Taylor, John,** 'water-poet' to James VI and I; visited areas of Scotland in 1618.

**Tucker, Thomas,** *'Register'* to the Commissioners for the Excise in England, explored and reported on Scottish ports for the Commonwealth government in 1655.

**Wordsworth, Dorothy,** sister of poet William Wordsworth, toured southern and central Scotland with him in 1803 *(see Bibliography).*

## MAJOR CONSTRUCTORS, ARCHITECTS, ENGINEERS & PLANNERS

**Adam, James,** architect, younger brother of Robert, born Kirkcaldy 1732.

**Adam, Robert,** famous architect and interior designer, son of William, born Kirkcaldy *(q.v.)* 1728.

**Adam, William,** master mason and architect, born Kirkcaldy *(q.v.)* 1684 *(and see Kelty).*

**Arroll, Sir William,** engineer and bridge contractor, born Houston *(q.v.)* 1839 *(and see Bridgeton).*

**Bruce, Sir William,** of Balcaskie, architect, born 1630 *(see Pittenweem).*

**Bryce, David,** architect, born Edinburgh *(q.v.)* 1803.

**Burn, William,** architect, born Edinburgh *(q.v.)* 1789.

**Caulfeild, William,** military engineer and gourmet, of Irish extraction, died 1767; from 1732 supervised the building and repair of military roads in Scotland, greatly extending Wade's road system by some 1300km between 1743 and 1761 *(see Wade below, and Taylor W in the Bibliography).*

**Dale, David,** textile entrepreneur, born Stewarton *(q.v.)* 1739.

**Geddes, Sir Patrick,** pioneer town planner and author, born Perth *(q.v.)* 1854.

**Grieve, Sir Robert,** town and regional planner and administrator, born 1910 Maryhill *(q.v.).*

**Hamilton, Thomas,** architect, born 1784, son of Glasgow builder, worked Edinburgh *(q.v.).*

**Knox, John (I),** see next section.

**Knox, John (II),** bookseller, philanthropist and protagonist of Scottish regional development, born Scotland mid 18th century, worked from London.

**Lorimer, Sir Robert,** architect, born 1864 *(see Pittenweem).*

**Mitchell, Joseph,** born Forres *(q.v.)* 1803, civil engineer, road surveyor under Telford, and builder of much of Highland Railway.

**Mylne, John,** dynasty of Dundee architects *(see Carnoustie)*: father d. 1621, son d. 1657 & grandson born 1611.

**Rennie, John,** architect and bridge engineer, born East Linton *(q.v.)* 1761 *(and see Kelso).*

**Smeaton, John,** early 18th century engineer *(see Perth & Peterhead).*

**Stevenson, Alan,** lighthouse builder, born Edinburgh 1807 – son of Robert *(see Tiree).*

**Stevenson, David,** younger son of Robert, lighthouse builder and manager, born 1815.

**Stevenson, Robert,** lighthouse builder, born Glasgow *(q.v.)* 1772 *(see Arbroath).*

**Telford, Thomas,** stonemason, architect and civil engineer, born Westerkirk 1757 *(see Langholm)*; County Surveyor of Shropshire, engineer to the Commissioners for Highland Roads & Bridges and for the Caledonian Canal, first President of the Institution of Civil Engineers.

**Tindall, Frank,** mid 20th century town planner, County Planner for East Lothian, pioneer of urban conservation in Scotland.

**Wade, General George,** military engineer, from 1724 to 1736 laid out and supervised the building of a T-shaped system of military roads in the central Highlands *(see Caulfeild, above).*

**Young, James,** chemist and industrialist, pioneer of Scottish Shale Oil industry, born Glasgow *(q.v.)* 1811 *(and see Bathgate).*

## OTHER INFLUENTIAL PEOPLE

**Bell, Henry,** millwright and steamship pioneer, born Torphichen 1767 *(q.v.).*

**Bruce, Robert,** King of Scots and victor of Bannockburn, born Turnberry 1264 *(see Maidens).*

**Canmore, Malcolm,** King of Scots, born c.1031, unifier of Scotland *(see Dunfermline).*

**Carnegie, Andrew,** born Dunfermline 1835, became USA railroad manager, steelmaster and famed philanthropist, founded 2811 libraries *(see also Clashmore & Dunfermline).*

**David I,** born 1084, King of Scots 1124–53; founder of Scottish coinage, the system of Royal Burghs, and many religious houses.

**Hardie, Keir,** born Legbranock 1856, newspaper editor and pioneer of the Labour movement in Scotland *(see Newhouse).*

**Knox, John (I),** minister and reformer, born Haddington c.1513 *(q.v.).*

**Knox, John (II),** see previous section.

**Logan, William,** civil engineering contractor, bridge builder and aviation pioneer, born c. 1925 *(see Muir of Ord).*

**McAlpine, Sir Robert,** civil engineering contractor and pioneer builder in concrete, born Newarthill *(q.v.)* 1847 *(and see Glenfinnan).*

**McIntyre, David,** aviation pioneer, born Troon 1905 *(q.v.).*

**Morrison, Sir Murray,** pioneer of Aluminium Industry and Hydro Power in Scotland, born c. 1873 *(see Foyers).*

**Murdoch, William,** born Lugar 1754, pioneer of gas lighting *(see Cumnock).*

**Napier, David,** marine engineer, born Glasgow *(q.v.)* 1790.

**Scott, Sir Walter,** lawyer and author, born Edinburgh 1771 *(see Galashiels).*

**Smith, Adam,** author and pioneer Economist, born Kirkcaldy *(q.v.)* 1723.

**Wallace, Sir William,** born Elderslie *(q.v.)* 1270, patriot and warrior.

**Watt, James,** instrument maker, scientist and entrepreneur, born Greenock *(q.v.)* 1736.

## KEY ORGANISATIONS

**Board of Trustees,** *see* Commissioners and Trustees.

**Commissioners and Trustees for Improving Fisheries and Manufactures in Scotland,** commonly known as the Board of Trustees; established in 1727 (initially for six years), it particularly encouraged the linen industry up to 1819.

**Commissioners for Northern Lights,** *see* Northern Lighthouse Board.

**Commissioners of Supply in the Highland Counties,** administered roads from 1862 until local government took over at various dates around 1890.

**Crofters' Commission (1),** established under the Crofters' Holdings Act of 1886, worked until 1911 to safeguard the interests of crofters versus landlords, then being superseded by a Land Court.

**Crofters' Commission (2),** established 1955 with similar powers to the above; made its headquarters in Inverness.

**Forfeited Estates Commissioners** were set up to take over the lands of Jacobite lairds of the 1745 rebellion. From 1755 they extended existing villages – e.g. Beauly and Callander – to resettle demobilised soldiers, and also expanded Muthill, Thornhill, Balquhidder and Strathyre; but their scheme at Ullapool failed. The last forfeited estates were restored to their owners in 1784.

**Forestry Commission,** established in 1919 to plant and harvest a system of national softwood forests (the aim of 715,000ha throughout Britain by 2000 was well exceeded). Very active in the west Highlands and southern uplands. About 1950 the Commission established three new *'villages'* at Ae, Glen Trool, and Dalavich to service their programmes; later they built houses for workers in existing villages.

**Highland Roads & Bridges (Commissioners for),** set up in 1803 by Act of Parliament to administer new road construction in backward areas with a 50% subsidy; adjoining proprietors had to agree the desirability of projects and find half the cost *(see Telford, Thomas, and Haldane in the Bibliography)*. Ended in 1862 in favour of Commissioners of Supply.

**Highlands & Islands Development Board (HIDB),** set up in 1965 as a grant-making body, it made its headquarters in Inverness. *Inter alia* created a hotel on the Isle of Barra *(see Castlebay)*. Superseded by Highlands & Islands Enterprise and local agencies.

**Napier Commission,** early 1880s body to consider and recommend on the parlous state of the crofting counties; led to the Crofters' Holdings Act of 1886.

**Northern Lighthouse Board (NLB),** or Commissioners for Northern Lights, set up in 1786, with initial remit to provide four lighthouses: Mull of Kintyre, Scalpay Point, Kinnaird Head and North Ronaldsay *(see Stevenson, Robert)*.

**North of Scotland Hydro-Electricity Board,** created by Act of 1943 (which, uniquely, passed without a Commons debate) to create a system of (largely) water-driven power stations and transmission lines in northern Scotland. Early schemes were: (1) Loch Sloy; (2) Tummel–Garry (very contentious, approved in 1945); (3) Conon Basin. Many of the civil engineering works were designed by Sir Alexander Gibb & Partners *(see Olivier in the Bibliography)*. Privatised in the 1990s as Scottish Hydro.

## TEXTILE TERMS

**Buckram,** a coarse open-wove fabric stiffened with size.

**Calico,** plain cotton cloth of Indian type.

**Cambric,** fine white linen, of a type from Cambrai/Kamerijk; a cotton substitute.

**Carding,** combing of wool or flax.

**Check,** fabric woven in a pattern of small squares.

**Diaper,** linen or cotton cloth with square or diamond pattern.

**Dowlas,** coarse linen cloth, after Doulas in Brittany.

**Drugget,** coarse woollen fabric, woven and felted.

**Duck,** a fine canvas fabric for uniforms and small sails.

**Fulling,** the scouring and thickening of fabric in a fulling-mill.

**Gauze,** thin, transparent fabric.

**Gingham,** fabric woven of coloured yarns in stripes or checks in Malaysian style.

**Heckling,** the combing out of flax or hemp fibres.

**Heddle,** frame with eyeletted cords or wires to control warp threads in weaving.

**Hessian,** a coarse cloth made of jute; used in sacking or covering bales, etc.

**Hucks,** short for Huckaback(s), linen or cotton towelling with raised humps.

**Inkle,** broad linen tape of Dutch type.

**Kersey,** coarse woollen cloth, of the type from Kersey in Suffolk.

**Lappet,** a small flap or a head-dress with flaps.

**Lawn,** a fine linen or cotton similar to Cambric, of the type from Laon near Rheims.

**Linen,** a fabric made from flax.

**Madras,** a fine cotton fabric, perhaps gaudily printed, of the type from Madras.

**Muslin,** fine, soft, plain-woven gauzy cotton fabric, originally from Mesopotamia (Iraq).

**Osnaburg,** a coarse linen, of the type from Osnabruck; similar cotton fabric.

**Pullicate** or **Pulicate,** a coloured or checked handkerchief material named after Pulicat near Madras, and made in Glasgow from 1785.

**Sacking,** a strong open- or close-woven fabric for making sacks, palliasses, etc.

**Sailduck,** a fine sailcloth for making small sails.

**Scribbler, scribbling,** a carding machine or process.

**Serge,** strong twilled fabric.

**Shalloon,** light woollen cloth for coat-linings, of the type from Chalons sur Marne.

**Silesia,** linen cloth of the type from Silesia.

**Spinning,** the process of forming yarn from shorter fibres by drawing and twisting.

**Tamboured,** embroidered on a drum.

**Ticks, ticking,** cloth for mattress-covering.

**Tow,** prepared fibres of flax, hemp or jute.

**Tweed** (originally **tweel**), rough woollen cloth used for sports jackets and country suits.

**Twill,** woven fabric showing diagonal lines.

**Wake, walk, waulk,** to full cloth or yarn; **-mill,** a fulling-mill.

**Warp,** in weaving, the threads running the length of the fabric.

**Weaving,** process of forming fabric from crossing threads.

**Weft,** in weaving, threads crossing the warp.

**Wincey,** cloth with linen or cotton warp and woollen weft.

**Woof,** in weaving, thread for a weft.

**Worsted,** a fine woollen fabric, of the type from Worsted in Norfolk.

**Yarn,** thread formed by spinning.

## MINING TERMS

**Adit,** sloping passage leading into coal workings.

**Bell pit,** a bell-shaped hole in the ground leading down to a coal seam.

**Bing,** a heap of coal waste or *'redd'*; alternatively of burnt shale.

**Cage,** a form of lift raised and lowered in a shaft by a winding engine.

**Cannel,** bituminous coal, often used in the past for making gas and/or oil.

**Day level,** a level passage or drainage adit leading from the surface.

**Dip,** the angle which a coal seam or other stratum makes with horizontal.

**Fireclay,** shaly former mud in which grew plants now forming coal; suitable for making bricks or furnace linings.

**Glance coal,** anthracite or hard coal.

**Lignite,** brown or soft coal, originally peat.

**Longwall,** underground mining by total removal of panels of coal.

**Opencast,** surface mining of coal by earth-moving machinery.

**Outcrop,** line along which the edge of a dipping coal seam intersects the surface.

**Overburden,** in opencasting, the material to be removed to expose coal seams.

**Redd,** non-coal-bearing rock overlying or underlying seams (excludes fireclay or other usable rock), having to be removed in mining – hence waste.

**Room,** a hand-worked area of a coal seam *(see stoop)*.

**Seam,** a layer or stratum of coal, often interleaved with fireclay.

**Shaft,** a vertical access into coal workings.

**Steam coal,** coal suitable for firing furnaces to raise steam.

**Stoop,** a pillar of unworked coal left to support the roof after *'rooms'* have been cleared.

**Whim,** a primitive winding engine, usually horse-powered.

**Winding engine,** used to drive a drum around which the cable is wound when raising cages.

# The Making of Scotland:

## An Historical Overview

The history of individual places must be seen in context; this overview aims to highlight key stages of Scotland's development, mentioning salient events which stimulated its principal centres. Inevitably, compression leads to the omission of some perhaps vital aspects; the reader is asked to be forgiving!

### The Physical Basis

Scotland's settlements take the forms we see today largely because of its high latitude, peninsular nature and complex landforms. The surrounding seas moderate the climate and have played a decisive part – originally in providing food for hunter-gatherers, then for intrepid mariners, invaders, settlers and traders, and for fisherfolk who have exploited – and eventually over-exploited – this fundamental life resource. Scotland's core comprises vast areas of extraordinarily ancient and varied hard rocks, forming dissected areas of glaciated high ground with thin soils, typified by low cloud, severe winds, heavy rainfall and winter snowfall, which create a mountain character at modest altitudes. Around them, especially to the east, are many lowland areas, relatively small in extent and once thickly forested, which are the preferred sites of settlement. Until the mid 20th century almost every leading centre in Scotland was on or within sight of tidewater. The hills hold deposits of lead, silver and zinc, copper, gold, talc, barytes and slates; the lowlands have some iron ore, ample flagstones, freestones, glacial sands and gravels, which have provided many bases for the extractive industries from which Scotland's prosperity and buildings have been largely hewn. Coal seams typically underlain by fireclays are – or were – concentrated in the Central Belt, and beneath the seas lie oil and gas.

### Early Human Settlement

Neolithic, Bronze and Iron Age peoples created Skara Brae – Europe's oldest stone-built settlement, older than the Pyramids or Stonehenge – and innumerable other remains including stone circles, as at Calanais, brochs as at Mousa, hut circles, hill forts and standing stones. But like activities of every kind, these ancient peoples appeared, prospered, and declined – parabolas of change, about which in their case we know only what science can demonstrate. In historic times we look back at a series of overlapping parabolas of development. Roman influence in Scotland is slight, due to the mere 20 years or so (AD 142 to 162) that the legions firmly held the lowlands, then largely Brythonic or Cumbric in population; the Caledonians to the north had proved no pushover. The invaders founded Inveresk, and laid out perhaps 1000 km of roads, some of which were made up; a few underlie modern highways, and one aligns the main street of the early market centre of Biggar. We can also see their earthworks as at Braco, and a fine stone lioness from a fort at Cramond, but very little else. Ptolemy's ancient map showed Forres, and we may guess that Crail and Pathhead in Fife could derive from Roman plans; but about 532 an environmental disaster destroyed the economy, and the large Cumbric hill village at Traprain became deserted.

### The Dark Ages

In the succeeding Dark Ages most surviving people lived in turf huts, and grain growing, cattle and swine herding dominated the economy. The arrival of Columba and other Scots from green Ireland in the later sixth century brought the Gaelic language and Celtic Christianity to Iona; from this and other bridgeheads they colonised Argyll – the *'Coast of the Gael'* – and spread throughout the snow-capped lands they called Alba – *'White'*. The Scots in the west and the already resident Picts to the east, north and south founded such early and varied places as Aberdour, Abernethy, Brechin and Culross, the forts of Dunblane, Dundee, Dunedin (now Edinburgh), Dunkeld and Dunoon; also Dysart, Glasgow, Muthill, Peebles, Pittenweem, St Andrews, Selkirk, Tarves, Turriff and Whithorn. Apart from the names of their provinces we know sadly little of the talented but enigmatic Picts, because they lacked a written language. In the seventh century the Anglians moved north-westwards from Northumbria, establishing nucleated farm villages in the Lothians, such as Coldingham and Haddington. They refounded Edinburgh on its rock, also fortifying and holding a strategic central point, which they named *'Place of Strife'* – now Stirling. From the eighth century the quarrelsome Vikings and very civilised Norse mariners and farmers settled the Northern and Western Isles, established Kirkwall and Stornoway, Dingwall and Tain, and introduced flax growing and linen manufacture, which became a staple trade. Their language, Norn, survived for centuries in Orkney and Shetland but is long extinct.

### Forging the Feudal State of Scotland

Scotland as a state dates from 843 when Kenneth MacAlpine, a violent west coast Scots king, annexed the land of the Picts by treachery at their capital, Old Scone. Some 150 years later a more civilised king, Malcolm II, peacefully inherited the Welsh-speaking lands of Strathclyde, then centred in such places as Coylton and Dumbarton, Glasgow and Govan, Lanark and Linlithgow; he also codified Scots law. About 1065 his great-grandson Malcolm III *'Canmore'* founded Dunfermline as a base from which to regain the lands of Lothian from the Anglians, while his clever young second queen, Margaret – half Hungarian, half Saxon – persuaded him to adopt their language. In the early 12th century a feudal state was established by their sons, especially David I, who peacefully inherited the Welsh-speaking lands of

Strathclyde, then centred in such places as Coylton and Dumbarton, Glasgow and Govan, Lanark and Linlithgow. The operation of the feudal system depended on their Anglo-Norman friends, whom they made barons or *'lairds'*, interlopers who threw up earthen mottes crowned in timber, from which they ruled over the peasantry and the dispossesed previous landholders or thanes.

### State, Burghs and Church – the *'Three Estates'*

From 1119 David and later monarchs chartered Royal Burghs – fixed trading towns, the first being Berwick and Roxburgh; among them were Aberdeen, Ayr, Dumfries, Edinburgh, Elgin, Haddington (where David had his palace), Inverness, Irvine, Montrose, Perth and Rutherglen. Mainly coastal, these places were peopled from the south and the Low Countries, and given monopolies of almost all trades; so they grew and often prospered. Basic rural crafts such as milling being excluded, *'miltons'* such as Rothiemay could still develop. Leith was a special case, being Edinburgh's port by 1134. Royal castles of stone were built in new county centres such as Cupar, Dingwall, Forfar, and Kirkcudbright. These monarchs were Catholics whose hold was assured by the development of an elaborate system of dioceses and parishes with small stone churches, around which grew many *'kirktons'*. France and England supplied priests, monks and the masons who built the great religious monastic houses as at Dunfermline, Jedburgh and Kelso, all established in 1128. Melrose Abbey of 1136 and other Cistercian abbeys found great wealth in sheep and wool, while the abbeys of Newbattle of 1140 and Kilwinning of 1162 developed Prestonpans and Saltcoats respectively, to evaporate salt from sea water. By 1178 abbeys were open at Dryburgh, Paisley, and Arbroath. Later came Beauly in 1230, and New Abbey in 1273.

### Turbulent Times

Each burgh progressed at its own rate, along lines influenced by its location and resources, but all too often held back by aggression from the neighbour state of England, whose claims to the vacant Scottish throne from 1290 – the Wars of Succession – were fiercely resisted by Wallace and the Bruces, with ultimate success at Bannockburn in 1314. Slowly recovering from the Black Death of 1350, Scottish coal and salt production increased, and with the clearance of almost the last natural woodlands, timber buildings and bridges were gradually replaced in stone. In time Roxburgh failed, Berwick was lost to England, and in 1452 Perth yielded to Edinburgh as capital. After difficulties with the Lords of the (Western) Isles, the islands were gradually added to the kingdom, the last being Orkney and Shetland in 1468–69.

### Early Hospitals and Universities in a Backward Economy

Medical treatment was available at Soutra from the 12th century, given by monks more skilled than those in the infirmaries attached to most monasteries; lay hospitals were established at Aberdeen by 1300, and in most larger towns after the Reformation . Iron was made in bloomeries and was sufficient in quantity for most rural needs (as well as swords and daggers), but by 1365 the lack of a more substantial Scottish iron industry was a grave problem in the frequent troubles: a French ally, Froissart, remarked that although Scottish knights and esquires were well mounted, *"there is neither iron to shoe horses, nor leather to make harness, saddles or bridles: all these things come ready made from Flanders by sea; and, should these fail, there is none to be had in the country"*. So it was a good sign when the port of Fraserburgh was chartered in the 15th century, initially for trade. Scotland was early into the field of higher education, St Andrews University dating from 1411; Glasgow dates from 1451, Old Aberdeen from 1494, and Edinburgh University goes back to 1582. Marischal College in Aberdeen was added in 1593.

### Castle Towns, Tower Houses and Palaces

Baronial castles gradually replaced the mottes; around them grew small settlements called castle towns, typically appearing in the 15th century – including Braemar, Hamilton, Alloa (which became a castle town in 1497) and Hawick (confirmed as such in 1511). Huntly was also a milton, Inveraray was also the centre of the late-established county of Argyll, and Kilmarnock became famous for cutlery. When Scotland suffered depredations from that great bully Henry VIII of England, the barons, many owning very modest estates, were required by new laws to build the starkly defensive stone tower houses which now form such a conspicuous part of the Scottish heritage. Meantime in the 13th to 15th centuries bishops used church tithes to build themselves castles or palaces, as at St Andrews, Dornoch and Spynie. The later Scottish monarchs did even better for themselves, building palaces at Linlithgow and Falkland in the 15th and 16th centuries, at Holyrood in 1528, in Stirling from 1540, and at Dunfermline from 1593. So did some major lairds, notably at Hamilton in the 15th century, Dalkeith from 1587, Leslie in the 1660s and Drumlanrig from 1676.

### The Reformation

The mid 16th century Reformation led by John Knox saw the destruction of the power of the medieval Roman church, the dispersal of its Scottish assets, and more sadly the ruin of most of its fine buildings, though fortunately the cathedrals of Aberdeen, Glasgow and Kirkwall survived. On the positive side came peace with England, and the introduction of secular education based in the reformed Presbyterian church and its own parish schools. Former ecclesiastical burghs such as Glasgow and Kirkcaldy gained Royal status and developed more rapidly than hitherto. Leven had a harbour by 1556, and by about 1600 was already larger than Dysart. By the 1580s Galashiels had woollen mills.

### The Union of the Crowns brings Posts

Effective postal services were established when James VI and I inherited the English throne in 1603, and gradually banking services evolved. Lerwick began to develop towards mid-century thanks to intercourse – and wars – with the Dutch. Civil wars delayed most development until the Restoration, but from 1661 Methil grew with a harbour for coal export. Paper-making, sugar-boiling, soap-making, glass-making and woollen manufacture all developed in the late 17th century. Roads slowly replaced the cattle-droving tracks which had already brought importance to market centres at Crieff and Falkirk; Airdrie market was chartered in 1695 and by then Lockerbie had lamb sales. The power of commerce gradually superseded that of the barons, who now built fine mansions, such as Bruce's late 17th century Kinross House; an architectural revolution was set in train from Fife by the Adam family – who were builders and architects. Sandstone for such buildings was quarried at Craigleith, Longannet and Locharbriggs by about 1700.

### The Union of Parliaments and the Rebellions

The contentious Union of the Parliaments in 1707 set Scotland on a course of rapid development from a poor, peripheral peasant economy held back by archaic burghal privileges and appalling internal communications, to a centre of innovation and – for a brief period – an industrial powerhouse. In the remote Highlands, where the old religion and allegiance to the discredited Stewarts remained strong, the uprisings of 1715 and 1745 speeded the extension to the periphery of roads built by soldiers under Wade and Caulfeild, brought an end to feuding as a way of life, and caused William Roy to map the whole mainland for the first time. The government built new forts: Fort William created a town, Fort Augustus a village, and gigantic Fort George became a barracks and eventually a tourist attraction.

### Rural Enlightenment Brings New Villages

New practices revolutionised farming: works were opened to make drainage tiles, and fair trading with proper measures became more important: Whites made weighing machines at Auchtermuchty as early as 1715 – they are still there! As farms in the north-east and elsewhere were consolidated, many displaced tenants were properly housed in stone-built villages such as Archiestown and Stuartfield, rectilinearly planned on green field sites and often given the laird's name; hand-loom weaving was introduced to bring them work. Among these new places, Grantown-on-Spey soon grew into a small town. The *'British Society for Extending the Fisheries'*, founded in 1786 and better known as the British Fisheries Society, promoted fishing settlements in the West Highlands and Islands; of these, Tobermory and Ullapool and especially Pulteneytown (Wick) enjoyed some success.

### City Expansion, Learning, the Press and Health

The cities started a period of rapid expansion when Glasgow's trade with the New World began in 1718; sadly it first flourished in tobacco. From 1655 Edinburgh had a sort of newspaper, but information was long held back by taxation, crude printing techniques and poor distribution. Glasgow's first newspaper began in 1715, and Aberdeen's in 1748. Meantime, learning flourished – and through this *'Enlightenment'* the Scots soon led in many fields, especially geology, physics and medicine. Edinburgh Royal Infirmary dates from 1719, and Woolmanhill at Aberdeen from 1741. In 1776 Adam Smith from Kirkcaldy expounded the basis of market economics in his *'The Wealth of Nations'*. Glasgow gained its first post-Reformation infirmary in 1787, Dundee in 1798 and Perth 1836. Dundee gained a newspaper in 1801, Dumfries and Inverness in 1809, and Perth had one by 1812. Daily papers were established in Glasgow in 1847 and by mid-century in Edinburgh. Papermaking flourished at Bucksburn, Culter, Markinch and Penicuik.

### Steam and the Genesis of an Urban Economy

Power – hitherto derived directly from oxen, horses, wind and running water – was augmented from the early 18th century by on-site steam engines, invented elsewhere but made vastly more efficient from the 1760s, thanks to James Watt from Greenock. Meantime in rural areas generally, more new villages were founded, some soon becoming towns: a very successful new market centre was created at Castle Douglas in 1791, and Lochgilphead also dates from around that time.

### Industrial Brewing and Distilling

Brewing moved from being a home affair under the control of alewives into small breweries, as at Bathgate from 1736, and later to increasingly large centralised breweries as at Alloa and Edinburgh. Maltings were developed, which also served whisky making, as it too moved from domestic-scale stills into licensed distilleries which could be taxed – under the major Excise Act of 1823. Wishaw began in 1825 with a distillery. The thousands of dispersed and untaxed stills in the countryside at places like Balfron, and in city nooks and crannies, were outlawed and hunted down. Grain whisky was cheaply produced from 1833 in Aeneas Coffey's patent stills; blending was introduced to improve the quality of grain whisky, and to eke out the lovingly brewed single malts, which have more recently seen a comeback. In Edinburgh, Alloa (especially), Elgin and elsewhere distillery engineering contributed to urbanisation; new growth points for whatever purpose were established with – or without – charter privileges, and minerals were exploited.

### The Coaching Age

Gaps in the road system were filled piecemeal, and turnpiking – whereby trusts levied tolls for road building – gradually created an adequate main road system. From the mid 18th century the stagecoach became the best method of land transport for those who could afford to ride it, either inside or – more cheaply – outside, stimulating the demand for inns where food, changes of horses and overnight accommodation could be obtained. In 1776 the new Rutherglen Bridge was opened, with a new road connecting to Glasgow; a daily market held there by 1779 created the main street of Bridgeton.

## Canals, Ports and Telford

The Monkland Canal was opened in 1778 to carry coal in horsedrawn boats to Glasgow from pits in the Monklands area, but most of the urbanisation associated with it came later with the iron industry. The Forth & Clyde Canal, built in stages between 1768 and 1790, was much more significant. At its west end – Bowling, on the River Clyde – a brewery was in use by 1772. Maryhill and Port Dundas grew as inland ports on this canal, which met the River Forth at Grangemouth, where new wharves laid out from 1779 soon became Glasgow's eastern trading port. The little Crinan Canal, engineered by John Rennie to enable boats to avoid the perilous passage around Kintyre, was dug in 1793–1801; where it entered Loch Fyne, Ardrishaig grew from its maintenance workshops. From 1805 Donside benefited from the opening of the Aberdeenshire Canal to Port Elphinstone. Meanwhile Thomas Telford, a mason from near Langholm, was becoming the greatest civil engineer of the day, designing and overseeing the construction of roads, bridges, harbours and also of the Caledonian Canal, built between 1803 and 1822, stimulating Inverness, Fort Augustus and Banavie. The Union Canal, opened in 1822, linked Edinburgh with the Forth & Clyde at Falkirk. Dalbeattie is largely a product of the demand for hard rock for harbour construction at Liverpool in the mid 1820s, and Castletown in Caithness developed at the same time to supply paving slabs for city streets.

## Iron and Gas

Iron-making by charcoal as at Taynuilt (Bonawe) was being replaced by coal-fired furnaces, the great Carron Company of 1759 being the exemplar. The Omoa Ironworks created Cleland from 1787; other iron formations were Carmyle (1786), Muirkirk (1788) and Shotts (1802). Many local town gasworks were built from the early 19th century, using a process developed by William Murdoch from Cumnock to make gas for lighting, cooking and heating. In 1829 the hot blast iron-making process was adopted at Carmyle, enabling poorer ores to be used; this created new ironworks centres, most spectacularly at Coatbridge, a place which did not exist until 1828, and also at Coltness from 1836, Glengarnock from 1840, Waterside from 1845 and Lochgelly from 1847. Later, coke was used in iron-making, being a by-product of gas-making (or where its crushing strength was vital, the converse); this spurred the mining of suitable coals around Kilsyth.

## Textiles, Chemicals and Textile Machinery

Cotton printing had entered the Glasgow scene by 1719, and in the mid and late 18th century scientific techniques were widely introduced in textiles, which moved from home spinning and weaving to the factory; linen manufacture was greatly encouraged by the Board of Trustees for Manufactures, becoming very important in the east of Scotland and in the Glasgow area. In 1742, a large bleachfield and calico printworks was established at Pollokshaws, soon the basis for a substantial village. Woollen carpets were made at Bannockburn by 1769. In the 1780s cotton created Alexandria, Barrhead, Catrine, Dalmarnock, Johnstone, New Lanark and Stanley. From 1785 four water-powered cotton mills were constructed at Gatehouse, hitherto just a wayside inn. Linen-making continued to prosper, and became very sophisticated in Dunfermline and Dundee. Charles Macintosh of Glasgow pioneered the use of bleaching powder in the textile industry; this and other chemicals were made at the St Rollox chemical works, founded at Port Dundas in 1798. Textile machinery was made at Anderston and at Arbroath. Scottish cotton manufacture peaked at the time of the American civil war; it never fully recovered from the associated disruption.

## Henry Bell, the Steamship, and Firth of Clyde Villas

Helensburgh was created as a spa in 1776, becoming the base of Henry Bell, whose pioneer steamship *Comet* of 1812 had an immense impact. From this tiny vessel grew the great Clydeside shipbuilding industry of the late 19th and early 20th centuries, which created Clydebank and greatly expanded Port Glasgow. Boiler-making became a technique requiring larger and larger iron plates and tubes, benefiting Bellshill and Renfrew, and marine engineering burgeoned at Aberdeen, Alloa, Anniesland, and so through an alphabet of Scottish centres. Steam ferry services and day cruising opened up the Clyde coast to residential and resort development at such places as Rothesay, Dunoon, Tighnabruaich and Wemyss Bay through the building of numerous piers, near which affluent Scots built villas in spacious grounds long before the English *'Garden City'* movement fostered a pink and green sprawl down south. Ferry services for the Outer Isles brought a pier in 1834 to Lochmaddy, an 1802 fishing village; Tarbert (Harris) grew from a pier of 1840, but Lochboisdale had to wait until about 1880. Cruising on inland lochs, especially Loch Lomond, brought less development (but can still be enjoyed on Loch Katrine on the century-old steamship *Sir Walter Scott*, a product of the once world-famous shipyard of Denny of Dumbarton).

## Railways and their Impact

From the 1820s small companies built railways in the Monklands, on Tayside, and in Midlothian; Edinburgh and Glasgow were linked in 1842 and then rails spread throughout the country. The demand grew for coal, rails and rolling stock; Leith built engines, Wishaw made goods wagons. The railways virtually created suburban Lenzie, Ladybank junction, Kittybrewster, and especially Springburn with its giant complex of locomotive building workshops. They stimulated the quarrying of building stone at Bishopbriggs from 1845, made route centres of Carstairs, Larbert, Perth and Stirling, and brought railway workshops to Barassie, Kilmarnock, Inverness and Inverurie. Each railway opening brought cheaper coal, beer and general merchandise, and provided extractive and industrial opportunities. Coal-mining created Fife towns like Cowdenbeath (from the 1840s) and Lochore (from the 1880s), as well as Kelty and Methil; in Midlothian, Newtongrange was an example. Railways also made major centres more accessible, bringing about a revolution in services, hitherto largely the preserve of the rich. Mergers gradually created five main companies based in Glasgow (2), Edinburgh, Inverness and Aberdeen. In the Edinburgh, Glasgow and Ardrossan areas many competing lines were built, lessening the companies' profitability.

### Bridges, Engineering and Vehicles

The making of bridges from cast-iron segments, and safer riveted bridges of malleable iron, benefited the recently developed railway junction town of Motherwell, and also Dalmarnock. Iron hull plating and, later, steel armour plate for the battleships built on Clydeside, were made at Parkhead Forge, established about 1837. Renfrew cast the iron structure of London's Crystal Palace of 1851, and architectural cast ironworks changed Possil from a mining hamlet in the 1860s. In 1862 James Howden & Co began as marine engineers and ships' boiler-makers in the Gorbals, making stationary steam engines and other plant, in our own time building machines to bore the Channel Tunnel. From 1886 the Weirs made pumps at Cathcart, and Cochrane's were soon fabricating innovative boilers at Annan. At that time steel was taking over for bridges – the Forth Bridge of the 1880s being the culmination – and for ships, rails and locomotives. Steel-making came to be the main objective of most ironworks. Steel components and engines went into lorries, built by Albion from 1904 at Scotstoun, and the cars briefly made from 1906 in Alexandria and at Locharbriggs from 1912. Motherwell became Scotland's most important steel-making centre.

### Jute, Linoleum, Thread and Sewing Machines

From 1835 jute was used for carpet backing, made in Dundee, and was used in ever-increasing amounts for sacks which still dominated the carriage of bulk commodities such as grain and sugar, and the delivery of domestic coal. Kirkcaldy made floorcloth – painted linen – from 1847, and linoleum was made at nearby Pathhead from 1877, at Newburgh (Fife) from 1891 and lastly at Falkland from about 1930. Meantime Paisley grew greatly with Clark and Coats to become by 1883 the world centre of the thread industry, which later totally collapsed in the face of overseas competition. Across the river at Clydebank the USA firm of Singer created Europe's largest factory, making sewing machines from 1884 and once employing 17,000 people.

### Universities, Telegraphs, Telephones, Instruments

Since the Enlightenment, Edinburgh University had been growing mightily, the tiny St Andrews University had begun a slow resurgence, and the two Aberdeen universities had merged in 1860. Glasgow University moved out to Hillhead in 1868–87, and in 1886 Anderson's Institution merged into the predecessor of Strathclyde University. Dundee University had humble origins in 1881. In 1885 Edinburgh's technical Heriot-Watt College was formed by merger. Even so, Victorian higher education was for a small minority; most technical and craft work was imbued through apprenticeships. In 1866 William Thomson (later Lord Kelvin) supervised the laying of the Atlantic telegraph cable, transforming communications. Meantime the battery-powered electric telegraph had become essential to safe and efficient railway working, and (for other reasons) it was Alexander Graham Bell from Edinburgh who invented the telephone in the USA in 1874–76; Glasgow's first telephone exchange opened in 1879. The famed optical instruments manufacturers Barr & Stroud, founded in Partick in 1888, later had very large works at Anniesland.

### Railways Build Hotels and Reach the Periphery

From the mid 19th century the coming of the railways hit coaching inns; many that were remote from stations declined, replaced by the once ubiquitous *'Railway Hotel'*; but some, such as Tweeddale's *Crook Inn*, are still very much alive. Conversely, over half a century the railway companies created great hotels of their own at their terminals in central Glasgow and Edinburgh, and at Ayr, Inverness, Turnberry and finally Gleneagles. In 1894 Aberdeen's five hotels were in the words of Murray's Handbook *"all good and all near the station"*. The late 19th century saw railways reach coastal termini; the line that opened to Stranraer in 1861 stimulated its development as the ferry port for Ireland. Thurso and Wick gained rails in 1874, the well-established steamer port of Oban was at last rail-served from 1880, and new railway ports were created at Kyle of Lochalsh in 1897, and finally at Mallaig in 1901. Fish canning and, later, freezing benefitted Peterhead, Fraserburgh and little Eyemouth – all of which used rail links to transport fish to urban markets.

### Victorian Countryside, Clearances and Dairying

Meantime in the lowland countryside the protective Corn Laws of 1815 had maintained a high demand for labour until their repeal in 1846; at the same time farm mechanisation was moving ahead, from simple fanners and horse mills to reapers and steam-driven threshing drums – all reducing the need for farm *'servants'*. New flour mills opened in the city docklands. Meantime the Highlands and Islands were suffering from ruthless clearances of their indigenous people in order to create more profitable sheep farms and, later, sporting estates devoted to rearing and shooting deer and grouse. Some people were allowed to resettle on tiny crofts on the worst land; others were herded overseas or expected to fish the seas from new coastal villages such as Helmsdale or Bettyhill. Many preferred to settle in the towns, where there were so many new opportunities. More happily, dairying grew with better communications; many remoter areas with rich summer pastures developed creameries for butter and cheese, especially in Ayrshire, Dumfriesshire, Galloway and, later, Orkney. From about 1870 Stranraer made much dairy equipment.

### Fishing by Sail, Steam and Diesel Power

Fishing nets were made by machine at Musselburgh from about 1820; the Wick herring fisheries peaked in the 1860s. Kippering, and coopering (long vital for the drinks industry) were related major employers. In the late 19th century fishing boats powered by oars and sails gave way to steam trawlers and drifters, then to motor vessels of steadily increasing size, exploiting more and more distant waters as inshore and near sea fisheries were depleted. Shellfish survived in favoured areas, and are now a mainstay of many tiny ports.

### Homes, Poorhouses, Asylums and Hospitals

Rich suburbs such as Morningside developed as the cities outgrew their sites, creating independent schools, new churches and, at Giffnock and elsewhere, synagogues; city centres were left overcrowded and their residents relatively poor. *'Poorhouses'* for the indigent were established nationwide, many later becoming geriatric hospitals, and some cottage hospitals were built. Major asylums for those with mental problems were built at Dumfries from 1835, Larbert from 1862, at Lenzie from 1871 for Glasgow patients, Hartwood from 1890 and Hillside and Springfield by 1895. General hospitals were provided in some larger centres such as Paisley and Stirling, and in 1910–25 Europe's largest hospital was built at Stobhill. But only with the National Health Service of the 1940s did the rational distribution of hospital facilities become a central concern, leading to new district general hospitals as at Inverness, Kirkcaldy, Crosshouse, Melrose, Monklands and Halbeath.

### Electric Revolution – Phase 1

From 1894 when Glasgow gained its first power station, electricity was generated centrally, initially at various voltages, primarily by steam, and largely for lighting. By 1901 it was available in Aberdeen, Airdrie, Arbroath, Ayr, Broughty Ferry, Clydebank, Dumfries, Dunblane, Dundee, Edinburgh, Falkirk, Govan, Hamilton, Kirkcaldy, Leith, Montrose, Motherwell, Musselburgh, Newport on Tay, Paisley, Perth, Rothesay and Stirling; most other towns were switched on by 1914.

### Electric Tramways and Buses

Horsedrawn (or steam) trams arrived in the 1870s – and survived at Stirling until 1920; Edinburgh had cable trams from 1884. Electric trams, faster and cleaner, came in a rush from 1898, in turn to Glasgow, Aberdeen, Dundee, Hamilton, Motherwell, Falkirk, Greenock, Dumbarton, Paisley, Kirkcaldy and Leith, and to Kilmarnock and Wemyss in 1904. Dunfermline had them by 1909, and by 1910 tramcars were being built at Motherwell. Most Edinburgh lines went electric only in 1922, speeding suburban growth around Corstorphine and Portobello. As trams reached into the suburbs, shops and tenements rapidly spread along the routes. But maintaining the tracks proved a costly problem under prevailing laws; buses – built (e.g.) by Albion of Scotstoun – were cheaper and more flexible, and most small-town systems closed in the 1930s. Dundee's and Edinburgh's trams survived until 1956, Aberdeen's until 1958 and Glasgow's until 1962; trolleybuses were tried there but soon abandoned. Alexander built bus bodies on a large scale at Larbert from the 1930s, and bus services peaked in the 1950s, then faltering under the private car.

### Ceramics, Deep Mining and Mining Machinery

With coal extraction came accessible fireclay; pottery and sanitary ware was made at Barrhead, Glasgow, Greenock and Kilmarnock in the west, and at Kirkcaldy, Pathhead and Portobello in the east. Furnace linings, made at Glenboig and elsewhere in the Central Belt, were required in great quantities. Bricks, made at or near the pithead more or less as a byproduct, were of too poor a quality for heavy engineering use, though Methil bricks have been used as facings. Up to 1914 the demand for coal grew and grew. As accessible seams became exhausted, deeper shafts were sunk; this meant a demand for steel wire ropes and powerful winding engines, built in various places including Kirkcaldy, Paisley and Kilmarnock. Scottish production peaked in 1913 when sinking began at Polkemmet colliery, vastly expanding Whitburn. As the National Coal Board modernised Britain's many collieries from 1947, Mavor & Coulson of Bridgeton expanded, making coal-cutting equipment and conveyors, as did Anderson Boyes of Motherwell; Beckett & Anderson of Glasgow made mine haulage engines. But pit closures led the three firms to merge about 1970.

### The Shale Oil Industry

The distillation of oil from bituminous shale developed from the mid 19th century very largely in West Lothian, especially around Bathgate, where it was preceded by the refining of cannel coal from the 1850s by *'Paraffin'* Young. Broxburn and Uphall joined in, West Calder gained from 1863, Pumpherston from 1883, and Burntisland from 1884–94. From shale-oil refining grew the huge Grangemouth petrochemical industry, initially relying on imported crude oil, later using North Sea oil. By the mid 1960s the shale oil industry was dead, leaving vast red bings of burnt shale, some of which have since been reclaimed, used in road construction or, as at Dalmeny, hollowed out – to accommodate an oil tank farm!

### Entertainment, Sport – and Threats to Whisky

City parks appeared in the mid 19th century; then golf, football and rugby became popular, and clubs created their own grounds or *'parks'*; the great stadiums such as Hampden and Murrayfield evolved through the 20th century. Theatres which had begun beside Edinburgh as early as 1560, grew only fitfully due to religious taboos, and really blossomed in the late 19th century, only to be largely overtaken by cinemas, ice rinks, dance and snooker halls. Glasgow's *Green's Playhouse* (opened in 1927) was the largest cinema in Europe (4368 seats), and Dundee's 1936 *Playhouse* the second largest; both also had dance-floors. Meantime, over-building of distilleries, economic decline, USA Prohibition and a teetotal prime minister

(Lloyd George) drastically affected the whisky industry; only seven new distilleries were built between 1901 and 1950, and many others were abandoned or mothballed.

### Rosyth Dockyard and War Impacts

Stemming from naval competition with Germany's *'Kaiser Bill'*, Rosyth Dockyard was hastily built from 1903 to 1905. At first aptly called *'Tin Town'*, more permanent naval installations were built in 1909–16. For various reasons, in the 1914–18 war Scotsmen formed a high proportion of Britain's military personnel, and paid a disproportionate price in death and injury for the privilege. The 1939–45 war left a more useful legacy, many military airfields finding a new use, especially in civil aviation.

### Building Moves to Concrete and Council Houses

In the early 20th century limestone burnt in local kilns to make quicklime for building gave way to cement imported from England in sacks and later in bulk containers by rail, sea and road. Concrete became the norm for many structural elements from drainage pipes and foundations to mass concrete bridges, as in the Glenfinnan viaduct; later came reinforced and pre-stressed concrete bridges, beams, columns and lintels, enabling tall flats to be built cheaply. The demand for aggregates grew, including sand and gravel. In the second quarter of the 20th century quarrying moved from hand-cut stones of sizes dictated by the faulting and cleavage-planes of the rock, lovingly laid by skilled masons, to crushed stone aggregates *'reconstructed'* into standard blocks which any competent bricklayer could use to erect walls quickly. This led to the closure of freestone quarries and, when combined with an ever-growing demand for road metal, to the opening of hard rock quarries (some in scenic areas). At Balmullo, Bonawe, Inverkeithing, the Hillfoots and Traprain, such quarrying has irretrievably damaged the landscape. The 1950s council estates such as Drumchapel and Templehall (Kirkcaldy), often brick-built with foam slag inner walls, were harled for weather protection (as some pre-war houses had been also). From the 1960s cement has been hauled by rail and road from Scotland's only cement works at Oxwellmains, near Dunbar.

### Electricity and Accelerating Industrial Change

Renewable resources in the form of hydro-electric generators began to be used at Foyers for aluminium production in 1895, followed at Kinlochleven from 1907 and Fort William in the 1920s; the product is rolled at Falkirk. Meantime in 1911 Nairns built an electric power station for their large Pathhead linoleum works. After the 1914–18 war came larger power stations serving local grids – Dalmarnock, Yoker, Portobello and Braehead. From 1929 the Great Depression hit all industries, shipbuilding and its ancillaries particularly severely; in response the government provided industrial estates, as at Hillington and Newhouse. A large pharmaceuticals plant came to Montrose in 1952. The advent of metal drums and paper sacks severely affected the sack-centred jute industry; from mid-century came palletisation and plastic sacks, and from the 1960s larger lorries and interchangeable containers revolutionised transport. In turn the fork-lift truck killed the multi-storey factory, the sack hoist and the jute industry; some jute firms turned to polypropylene and other man-made plastic fibres.

### Electric Revolution – Standard Universal Power

From 1927 Britain's first distribution grid linked central Scotland's power suppliers; voltages were standardised, and direct drives from steam engines located in factory and farmstead were steadily superseded by electric motors. Large new thermal power stations included Clyde's Mill in 1928, and Bonnybridge. After nationalisation Kincardine (also now vanished) was built from 1952, then Cockenzie, and coal firing culminated in 1962 with the start of the giant Longannet plant, directly fed by its own coal mines. Hydro power for public use had entered in 1927 with the Clyde Valley scheme, followed in the 1930s by schemes in Highland Perthshire and Galloway, and from 1944 covered the whole north under the Hydro Board; the two public monopoly suppliers then gradually wired up the countryside, enabling the mechanised milking parlour. From about 1950 nuclear power was developed, first from Chapelcross, then from Hunterston – troublesome 'A' in 1977–90 and efficient 'B' from 1976; finally from Torness, built in 1978–89. Methil power station (now closed) was built from 1966 to burn coal slurry; those at Inverkip (using oil) and Peterhead (originally gas, now also oil) arrived in the mid 1970s.

### Rural Change Accelerates

Afforestation, largely unknown in Scotland until the early 18th century, was massively expanded from the 1920s by the Forestry Commission, which created some new small and remote villages for their workers, as at Ae and Dalavich. After 1945 farmers abandoned horses and the slow, heavy steam traction engine for tractor-drawn ploughs and implements, and later tractor-mounted machinery, made at Crosshouse from the 1950s. Combine harvesters, pea viners and sophisticated equipment aided many types of crop production, so farm labour demands fell very sharply through the mid 20th century. This led to depopulation and the widespread closure of local services in villages and small towns, as dolefully chronicled in this book.

### Air Services and Airports

Air services had started in the 1920s in a small way, largely developing through the hotbed of innovations in military aviation, but gradually becoming an essential system of public transport. Renfrew's World War I airfield became Glasgow Airport in the late 1940s; it was replaced on a former naval air base at Abbotsinch in 1966. Turnhouse, an RAF field of 1925, became Edinburgh Airport after 1945. A field at Dyce, founded for private flying in 1930, became Aberdeen airport in 1955. Stornoway airfield was started in 1934; Prestwick which began at Monkton in 1935 as a grass field with an aircraft factory, played a transatlantic role in World War II and became an international airport in 1946. Sumburgh was started as a civil airfield in 1937–38; before the 1939–45 war Grangemouth had a very short-lived airport, its site now covered by petrochemical works. Inverness, Kirkwall and Wick airports began on former military airfields in 1946. Dundee airport originated in the 1960s; the many smaller fields include Tingwall in Shetland and the bucolic Fife Airport at Glenrothes, while Barra still famously uses the beach!

**New Towns and New Distilleries**

To cope with the extreme urban congestion in west-central Scotland, and to balance Fife mining expansion, the government sponsored a series of industrial New Towns: East Kilbride (designated in 1947), Glenrothes (1948), Cumbernauld (1956), Livingston (1962) and Irvine (1966). Their planning approach was varied, some centralised, others sprawling; but being children of the motor age, only the first was conceived to exploit railways for regional connection. All have usually thrived; Irvine makes paper and vehicle components, and there are roadborne distribution centres in Cumbernauld and Livingston – which, like Glenrothes, has also become a major centre in electronics and administration. Between 1950 and 1980 came 24 new distilleries and vast bottling plants and bonded warehouses, as at Leven; but due to automation of their processes these have had relatively little employment impact, and some closures have continued, while mothballing serves to keep supply in step with the heavily taxed demand. The great Food Park at Bellshill is a far larger employer.

**After Iron and Steel: Aluminium and Plastic Goods**

Plastic rainwater goods have now largely superseded cast iron rainwater goods; aluminium was tried but found too costly for general use. In turn this has superseded steel in many components, including aircraft, van, and bus bodies and some ships' upperworks. Although the vast Ravenscraig steelworks at Motherwell was built around 1960, and steel still had a place, the end of steel-making in Scotland came in the 1990s, allegedly for political reasons. Perhaps an aberration was the aluminium cylinder block of Scotland's sole venture into mass-produced cars, the Hillman Imp of 1963 from Linwood, a place created by a World War II shadow factory. From 1968 to 1981 a short-lived aluminium smelter operated at Invergordon, for a time employing over 1000 people and creating a small new town at Alness.

**Car-borne Tourism and Other Rural Developments**

From the 1920s the caravan gave new opportunities for tourism in the more scenic and coastal areas; Arisaig and Kinghorn benefited – or suffered. Youth hostels opened from the 1930s, and facilities for car-borne tourists grew from the 1950s, including for a time in the 1970s farm milk bars, and new hotels, some in rural mansions as at Sunlaws, which brought jobs and money back into rural areas. Motorways were built piecemeal from the mid 1960s, but the system still has gaps. New commuting villages include Dalgety Bay from 1962 and Westhill from the mid 1970s, depending on the ever-growing numbers of car commuters; the former now has a railway station. Country parks, as at Strathclyde Park and Lochore Meadows, have transformed areas of mining dereliction. Many new golf courses have been created (making a total of well over 500), and golf tourism has developed strongly. Uthrogle, an ancient Fife milling place, became the site of Europe's largest oat mill; other new activities include bottling spring water, fish farming, especially of salmon in sea lochs and trout in inland stream-fed ponds, deer farming, and ice-cream manufacture, as developed from dairying at Rothienorman in the 1980s.

**Universities – the Third Phase**

After 1945, with a proper system of secondary education at last in place, and student grants available to open up higher education to young people from all walks of life, its expansion began in earnest. Technical institutions were already growing, at Paisley and what is now Fife College in Kirkcaldy. In 1954 St Andrews University fully embraced Dundee's University College; the latter gained its independence in 1967. Following the expansion recommended by the Robbins Report of 1963, Stirling University was founded in 1964. About the same time, University status was granted to the merged colleges of Strathclyde, which opted to stay in Glasgow city centre, and Heriot-Watt College, which regrettably chose a Shangri-la approach *(see Currie)*.

**Railways, Beeching and Industrial Decline**

In the late 1950s a moderate Conservative government poured money into the nationalised railways, which had lacked investment since 1914 and borne the transport burden of two world wars. Sadly, British Railways management lacked imagination, and their poor performance sowed the seeds for the present unsatisfactory state of the railways. This lack of real modernisation influenced the Beeching Plan, brought about by a successor government which included a road-building contractor and, like too many since, saw private profit as more important than public transport. Hence in the 1960s the rationalisation and partial destruction of the rail network was ruthlessly pursued; the Borders, Strathmore and Buchan soon lost every station and most lines. On the plus side the container and Inter-City concepts were advanced, and some electrification took place, but eventually a defective form of privatisation was enforced. For other reasons Scottish shipbuilding had collapsed in the 1960s, and many industrial concerns failed, particularly on Clydeside. The four Scottish Stock Exchanges, one in each city, found it necessary to amalgamate in 1964; Glasgow became the largest branch outside London when all the UK exchanges combined in 1973.

**Opencast Mining**

In the 1960s opencast pits such as Westfield (Fife), requiring a minimal workforce, largely replaced the deep coal mines – of which only Longannet now remains active. The legacy of mining has been bings, subsidence and one-industry settlements; where these are remote from other opportunities – as around Dalmellington – many economic and social problems remain.

### Silicon Glen

From 1946 business machines were made in Lochee by US Company NCR, which later developed into the world's leading maker of Automatic Teller Machines – ATMs. As computers were developed, another USA firm, IBM, opened a factory in 1951 at Spango by Greenock which has become a main centre of that giant of computer makers. The arrival of TV led to the closure of most cinemas, and the new supermarkets hit small shops, especially in rural areas. Factories have been created in Scotland to make all kinds of electronic devices – hence the term *'Silicon Glen'*; among many, the American firm Motorola opened Scotland's first semiconductor plant in East Kilbride in 1969, and Livingston was in electronics from 1974.

### North Sea Oil and Gas

Developed from 1970, North Sea oil revolutionised the Aberdeen area and soon made Dyce the world's busiest helicopter base. Flotta in Orkney became an oil terminal from 1973, and Sullom Voe in north Shetland was developed as a major terminal from 1975. Natural gas from undersea was also exploited, with a landfall at St Fergus from the mid 1970s, and from the early 1980s downstream chemical industries were developed at Mossmorran near Cowdenbeath to process NGL (Natural Gas Liquids). From 1972, oil platform yards were laid out at Stornoway, Methil, Ardersier and Nigg (with a maintenance base at Invergordon); and on a temporary basis elsewhere. Pipe coating has become big business.

### Local Government Centralised; Shopping Dispersed

Two major schemes of local government reorganisation, in 1975 and 1996, destroyed the ancient burghs and replaced them by a much smaller number of regional, district or all-purpose authorities – not always based in the same centres. Early beneficiaries included Cumnock and especially Glenrothes, while Montrose, Rothesay and now all small towns except Lochgilphead and Newtown St Boswells have been losers. Between these two dates, *'Out of Town'* shopping boomed as a result of the Thatcher government's car fixation and admiration for all things American; car traffic was rapidly increased to such fine new centres as Cameron Toll, Parkhead Forge and more recently to South Gyle and Braehead. But road accidents caused by drink and worsened by heavy traffic led to the breathalyser, and the hotel and pub trade had to provide good-quality bar meals or go under in the face of fast-food and soft-drink competition. Another dispersed feature of the 1990s, the Multiplex cinema, has recently led to further losses of older central facilities, as in Kirkcaldy and Inverness.

### The Information Technology Revolution

Rodime, makers of hard disc drives in Glenrothes from 1980, pioneered the 90 mm (3.5") floppy disc *before* IBM adopted it as standard. Mainframe computers and powerful networks have enabled centralisation of data processing and encouraged mergers and takeovers on a worldwide basis; even the Bank of Scotland has finally merged (with the Halifax). Computerisation has reduced the need for local offices for financial services, but has not killed the demand for paper, which in fact remains high and has moved away from account books and wrapping paper towards clay-filled glossy papers for magazine printing. More recently, national telephone call centres have been created in many unlikely spots, including rural centres and former heavy industry towns.

### Higher Education for Half the Population?

As part of a campaign to create a better-educated community – though with little political agreement as to how education should be properly and fairly funded – Paisley College and Aberdeen's Robert Gordon's College were promoted to University status in 1992, the year when a merger created Glasgow Caledonian University. Napier Technical College in Morningside also became a University about that time, and lastly in 1994 Dundee's Abertay University was created by promotion. In 1996 a joint effort by existing institutions created a potential university at Dumfries, and the nascent University of the Highlands & Islands began to come together in the 1990s. Both these last are eagerly exploiting the opportunities for distance learning through telecommunications.

### Renewable Energy, Transport, New Technology

From the 1980s wind generators were installed experimentally at Evie in Orkney, and in the 1990s came the first wind farms, now burgeoning. Chicken waste has been burnt at Westfield to supply the electricity grid since 1999, and from 2000 wave energy has been captured commercially at Portnahaven, though on the smallest scale. Bus and coach services remain important, but car travel and lorry transport dominate, aided by some fine new roads. But apart from electrification to England and on Clydeside, Scotland's rail services had seen a minimum of investment until very recent years. Unlike our European neighbours, Britain still cannot quite determine how to equate cost and benefit between these modes of transport so as to create a *'level playing field'* for environmental gain. Meanwhile, bioscience in the Edinburgh area is one of the present growth sectors of the Scottish economy.

### The Revived Scottish Parliament

In 1998–99 the Scottish Parliament, controversially closed down in 1707, was revived by the *'New Labour'* government in a proper democratic manner, with proportional representation. While many consider that its devolved powers are still too limited, or that the system is needlessly complex, or even that Scotland should leave the UK to take a full place in the European Union, few would disagree that the use of the powers that have been devolved from Westminster presents the opportunity to embrace enlightened development policies that suit Scotland's unique character. The one permanent feature in Scotland's complex story – change – seems set to continue.

# Alphabetical Entries

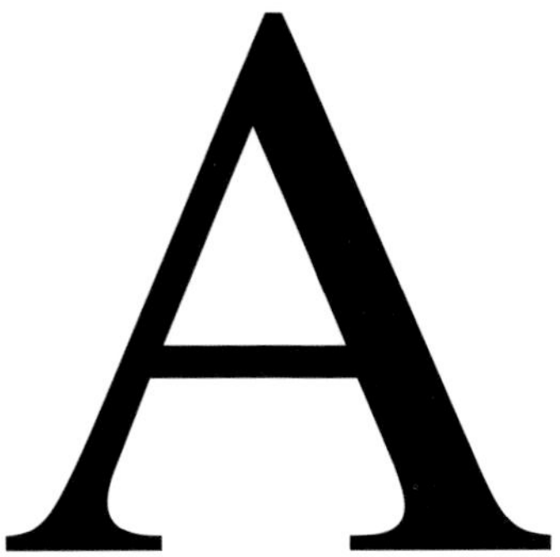

## ABBEY ST BATHANS

**Map 3, B2**

***Borders hamlet,*** *pop. under 100* — OS 67: NT 7562

An ancient hill fort stands above this secluded spot where the Monynut Water joins the Whiteadder Water in a deep and winding valley north of Duns. There St Bathan, a friend of Columba, is claimed to have founded a cell in the sixth century. A small Cistercian nunnery was founded in 1170 by Ada, Countess of Dunbar or March, but made no mark on history until it was burned by Henry VIII's troops in 1544. Some activity remained until 1565 when the building was given to Lord Home. Pont's map of about 1600 showed a well settled area around the *'Kirk of Botthamms'*, and a mill on the Whiteadder above the confluence, but Roy's map of about 1754 showed only the *'Kirk of Abby'*, where a track from Chirnside to the moors to the north crossed the wooded valley.

**Floods, Fish and Afforestation**: A mill had been built on the river below the village by the 1890s, but the valley was always subject to floods, whose levels at the church rose steadily from 2 m around 1880 to 3 m in 1910 and a destructive 5 m in 1948. While the mill still worked as recently as 1963, the only connection with the outside world in the 20th century was on narrow winding byroads. With falling needs for farm labour and the growing flood risk, the resident population decreased steadily from 150 in 1951 to under 100 by 1981, a high percentage of the houses having become second homes, and by then no buses served the one-time village, and the primary school and post office had closed. Besides the tiny ancient church, the public telephone and automatic telephone exchange were practically the only remaining facilities. By 1988 a trout farm braved the threat of floods to exploit the plentiful fresh water, and by 1995 afforestation had begun to clothe the hills to the west. However by then a youth hostel, opened since 1982, served walkers on the Southern Upland Way; they must have been few, for by 2000 it had closed.

## ABERCHIRDER

**Map 10, B2**

***Banff village,*** *pop. 1100* — OS 29: NJ 6252

Two southward-flowing streams enter the River Deveron about 13 km west of Turriff; on the spur between them were Pictish standing stones. Beside the mouth of the western watercourse was the church of Aberchirder, a Cumbric name meaning *'Mouth of the Chirder'*, which had a thanage from about the 11th century. The stream later became known as the Crombie Burn, after Crombie Castle, which was built beside it in the 16th century. At about the same time Carnousie Castle, a Z-plan tower, was built north-east of Netherdale, another early thanage beside the Deveron some 5 km to the east, which has continued as an estate to the present time. Meantime in the 14th century the substantial Kinnairdy Castle, a Crichton property, had risen beside the Burn of Auchintoul where it enters the Deveron 1.5 km downstream of *'Abirkerdir'* Kirk. All these names appeared on Robert Gordon's early 16th century map, as did *'Achintoul'*, 2 km up the eponymous burn.

**Enter Marnoch and Foggieloan**: Later the kirk and parish were renamed Marnoch. The Roy map, made about 1750, showed the House of Auchintoul, about 1 km to the east of which was *Foggy Loan*, a small hamlet or fermtoun on a ridge at an altitude of about 130 metres. Although *Loan* means lane in Scots, the area was still apparently roadless. There were two mills, at Cranna and Auchintoul, and to the south a *'Smiddy-town'*.

**Foggieloan at the Mouth of Nowhere**: The name Aberchirder did not appear on the Roy map, but became an absurd misnomer when formally revived for a new hilltop village founded in 1764 at Foggieloan, the name by which the place was to remain known locally. It was laid out on a rectilinear plan with central square, and by 1797 two annual fairs were held there. Heron in 1799 referred to it as *"the village of Foggeylone, the property of the heirs of General Gordon"*. In the early 19th century the mansion of Mountblairy was built for the Hays beside the River Deveron some 7 km east of Aberchirder. A post office named Aberchirder was open by 1838, and the place later became a police burgh; but the area was never on a railway, and was ignored by Murray's generally exhaustive 1894 *Guide*. A fountain was erected in 1897, and from 1905 buses owned by the Great North of Scotland Railway connected the village to Huntly station. But Mountblairy fell on evil days, was gutted in the 1940s and blown up in the 1950s.

**The Service Village**: Meantime Aberchirder had become quite substantial, with the Marnoch Memorial Hall of 1925, a cottage hospital, a tiny 16 mm cinema, lawyers and a 230-pupil junior secondary school. As centralisation was pursued and car ownership rose, all these *'extras'* were closed between 1951 and 1981. However the area's population remained stable at around a thousand residents. The town council – whose offices were oddly in Banff – built 150 houses before it was eliminated in 1975, and normal village facilities stayed in being. Foggieloan's single hotel of the 1950s had become three by 1981, the *Commercial, Fife Arms* and *New Inn*, none adventurously named; what a missed opportunity! Perhaps officialdom should revert to the correct local etymology by renaming the tiny kirkton of Marnoch as Aberchirder, and recognising Foggieloan as the true and popular name of the more recent hilltop village. A nature trail and picnic area were created; the 1991 resident population of 1075 included many elderly people.

**Modern Foggieloan**: A caravan and camping site noted in the 1980s had vanished by 1999, but the tiny *Old Manse Hotel* at Bridge of Marnoch remained in business. The many local services now include the *Fife Arms*, garages, fire station, primary school, library, health centre, pharmacy, bank, post office, bowling club with modern clubhouse, and at least four varied food shops. A large road haulier is based locally, and although the central square looks forlorn there are recently built houses on the Turriff road. Interesting enterprises include a kitchen fitter and a computer-cut sign service.

## ABERCORN & Hopetoun

**Map 16, C2**

***W. Lothian hamlet,*** *pop. under 100* OS 65: NT 0879

This sheltered place was originally called in Pictish Gaelic Abercurnig, (*'Mouth of the Curnig'*). It lies where the steep valley of a burn enters the south side of the Firth of Forth, 5 km west of the Queensferry narrows. A Columban monastery had been established there, and when in 680 Abercorn lay in Anglian-held territory, it was made the seat of the *'Bishop of the Picts'* by their would-be conqueror King Ecgfrith of Northumbria. However, by 731 the Picts had reoccupied Abercorn and the pretence of the bishopric was soon abandoned. In the 12th century a castle of the Black Douglases was sited on the steep promontory above the mouth of the burn, but this was razed and forfeited in 1455.

**Cashkeeper's Castle...**: The Drummonds had the great tower of Midhope Castle built west of the burn in the 16th century, while the tall narrow Staneyhill Tower was the seat of Sir William Shairp, one-time Royal Cashkeeper; it later became a ruin treated as a folly. Newton of Abercorn some 2 km to the south-east was made a burgh of barony in 1603, and the burn had been bridged by 1612 when both were shown on Hondius' map derived from Pont's work. A parish school opened in 1620.

**...Moneylender's Mansion**: The moneylender John Hope, who wished to move from Winchburgh's Niddry Castle, bought Midhope in 1678. Hopetoun House, designed for him by Sir William Bruce, was built between 1696 and 1730, when it was extended by William Adam into an emparked mansion for Hope, newly ennobled as the Earl of Hopetoun. Like Abercorn itself, Newton became a mere appendage of Hopetoun House. Three quarries at Hopetoun worked variously from 1697, employing 27 in 1902, but had little work after 1908. Midhope Castle was abandoned to ruin around 1950. A primary school later built in open country at Whitequarries, 2 km south-west, soon suffered noise from the adjacent M9 motorway, built between 1971 and 1975. Hopetoun remained intact as a tourist attraction, by 1994 having its own garden centre. Newton with its pub and post office stayed a tiny village, threaded by the increasingly busy A904 between the fast-growing electronics centres of South Queensferry and Linlithgow. In 1993 the *'A'* listed Midhope Castle was re-roofed by the Hopetoun Estates, but it was still unused in 2000.

## ABERDEEN

**Map 10, C3**

***Central area of city,*** *pop. 50,000* OS 38: NJ 9406

Suburbs: *Bridge of Don, Bucksburn, Cove Bay, Cults, Dyce, Mannofield, Mastrick, Old Aberdeen, Westhill & Woodside*

The Royal Burgh of New Aberdeen was founded in the 12th century by King David I, who chose a site on a low hill above the anchorage at the mouth of the River Dee. This offered a more spacious and better sheltered harbour than the mouth of the Don 3 km to the north, on which stood an already ancient religious and trading settlement whose original name would have been *Aberdon*. To maintain the riverine connection the new burgh's name ought really to have been *Aberdee*, but

*Hopetoun House was originally built between 1696 and 1730 for John Hope to designs by William Bruce. To suit the aspirations of the Hope family, it was extended to plans by William Adam from 1830.* *(RCAHMS / JRH)*

*'Aberdeen'* seems to have been a compromise with the older form. Old Aberdeen (as it was officially styled) was known as the *Aulton* to the newcomers, soon called Aberdonians. Mar and Buchan were combined as the Sheriffdom of Aberdeen in 1136.

**The Burgh of New Aberdeen**: Both the burgh and its Church of St Nicholas, a prebend of the bishop of Old Aberdeen, were in being by 1153, and enjoyed speedy success, soon growing into the main trading centre of north-east Scotland. Aberdeen's original, possibly oral, charter was confirmed in writing by William the Lion in 1179; half a century later Alexander II granted it the same constitution as Perth. By then the large church of St Nicholas was nearing or at its final length of 71 m. One of the more important royal mints was in use at Aberdeen by the end of the 12th century; sadly a leper hospice was also needed by 1197. We have no documentary evidence of the town's Royal castle until early in the 13th century, but know that it was strengthened in 1264.

**Markets, Fairs, Religious Houses and Schools**: At first Aberdeen had no fairs, but a merchant guild was active by 1222 when a market was chartered. When the weekly Castlegate market was chartered in 1273 there was already a town council. However in 1289 the equivalent body in Banff made a complaint that the burgh of Montrose was gatecrashing the Aberdeen fair lately set up by Alexander III as a sort of wholesale mart for the benefit of struggling traders in the remote northern burghs. Was it Banff's intervention which ensured the ultimate failure of the Montrose bid? Aberdeen already had a Dominican friary when the burgh was damaged by fire in 1244, and by about 1250 the friars had founded a grammar school; this still exists. Despite a second serious fire in the 1260s, by 1270 a new community of Whitefriars (Carmelites) was also in being and by 1300 there was a *'hospital'*.

**A Good Town exports Wool and Fish**: By 1291 when a tolbooth was built the population may have been about 1000; few though this seems nowadays, Aberdeen was rapidly reaching, and long maintained, a status in Scotland second only to Edinburgh. In 1295 Aberdeen was described as *"a good town"* by one of the soldiers who accompanied the English King Edward I in his Scottish expedition. It then exported cured salmon and other fish, cod being shipped to Flanders where it was known as *abberdaan*. By about 1300 the port of Aberdeen was among the four recognised wool-exporting centres of Scotland; by 1308 it had friendly trading contacts in Germany. Other commodities traded through Aberdeen included hides and other primary products; textile dyeing was practised, and woollen cloth manufactured.

**A Troubled start to the Fourteenth Century**: Aberdeen was the prime centre of resistance to England during the Wars of Independence. The Royal castle, occupied by the English, was consequently razed by Bruce in 1308. In the peaceful aftermath of 1317 the Aberdeen burgh court was moved to regulate the price of bread. The town council became exceptionally keen on record-keeping, and in 1319 Aberdeen was the first burgh to make a fixed payment to the crown while retaining its customs revenues. In the 14th century royal charters were often signed at Aberdeen, though this role faded. In 1326 came yet another fire, but in 1329 the Don was bridged near Old Aberdeen, aiding its landward trade with Buchan. By 1330 Aberdeen's trade was second only to that of Berwick, and customs revenues had climbed from third to second place in Scotland – and then stayed there for centuries. Despite being again devastated by Edward III's troops in 1336, Aberdeen also held second place in Scotland as a wool exporting centre, a position it often held during the succeeding two centuries.

**Before and after the Black Death**: Recovering again, Aberdeen was recognised in 1348 by the German community at Bruges as one of the *'four great towns'* of Scotland (with Edinburgh, Dundee and Perth). By 1350, the year of the Black Death, there were four religious houses; St Nicholas' church was being extended when the pestilence came. Afterwards circumstances were very much harder: though work had been resumed on the church extension by 1360, the quantities of wool exported fell off, and half a century of chaos followed: even Aberdeen's records are scanty. In 1386, said to have been a relatively a good year for trade, only ten ships subject to customs dues entered the harbour!

**Trade and Prosperity Return**: By about 1400 there were several mills, and the population has been estimated at 3000. Although piracy was practised from Aberdeen by the Stewart Earl of Mar in the early 15th century, slowly order returned. There was an established trade with Danzig by 1410, and with Cologne by 1422. In 1415 John Hardyng called Aberdeen *"a goodly city and merchant town"* with *"a goodly port and haven"*. At that period a granite pier was built at Shore Brae, wharves were constructed in stone, and a new Town House was erected.

**Commerce Described**: An annual two-week fair was held, which served the largest hinterland of any of the early Royal Burghs. In 1434 hides and skins were traded in Aberdeen and a little cloth was exported; by 1445 there were 63 guild members and a fairly substantial export trade in wool had again been built up; this remained Aberdeen's main source of customs dues for at least another half century. Rye was imported by 1444, and in 1447 Prussian wheat imported via Leith was sold on the harbourside; the prices of meat, bread and ale were still regulated by the town council. Malt was obtained from Elgin, doubtless among other suppliers. In 1448 Aberdeen had 445 taxpayers and was again one of the three principal towns in Scotland.

**Justice, Religion and Defence**: Although the Burgh of Aberdeen had been refused its own sheriff in 1445, from 1456 a weekly court was held to decide *'small complaints'* regarding trading, and in 1458 Aberdeen joined Edinburgh and Perth as one of the three Supreme Court centres of Scotland. The Saint Thomas's Hospital was established in 1459, and a Franciscan friary was founded in 1469. In 1475 four ships were fitted out locally for naval use, and two years later a blockhouse was built to defend the harbour.

**Trade and Crafts**: Danzig ships were still visiting Aberdeen in 1475, and in 1480 a tailor and hatter was recorded. By 1486 there were at least seven coopers, a long-established trade making salmon barrels for the Dee fisheries, Aberdeen being Scotland's principal source of salmon exports. Although trade was falling, at least two Danzig merchants were still trading in Aberdeen in 1489. In 1493 fish was marketed on Sundays under council control. At that time there was also a busy cattle trade, with Wednesday and Saturday markets. Lambs and cattle were slaughtered in the town, hides were tanned and shoes were made. Red deer horn was crafted into combs and knife handles; wood turning was another local craft.

**Slates, Skins, and Timber**: As permanent buildings multiplied, thatch was no longer favoured and by 1494 slates were being imported. Torry on the south bank of the Dee was made a burgh of barony in 1495; it relied on a ferry to Aberdeen proper. Hides and skins were being shipped to Banff in 1496; in 1499 when John Fitchet was a well-established timber merchant, a return trade in timber was recorded. In 1498 Andrew Cullen of Aberdeen shipped sawn planks to Dundee; his connections and the four Aberdeen ships that traded in the Baltic in 1497 imply a Baltic origin. Street sweeping was organised in 1497, though it seems that no local streets were actually paved until after 1529!

**Scotland's Oldest Business**: The Aberdeen Shore Porters' Society, founded in 1498, was to become Scotland's longest-lasting commercial venture. 1498–99 were bad plague years, restricting trade with Donside and Strathbogie, but by about 1500 the Earls of Huntly were among the rural lairds whose town houses surrounded the Castlegate market place. The council was concerned in 1502 because trade was being conducted outside the gates, and food was short in the winter of 1509. But trade was again rising: from 1508 four men were employed to regulate the markets, and in 1509 there were no fewer than 157 brewers or *alewives* in the town, largely the wives of burgesses. In 1514 Aberdeen still had four friaries, of the Carmelite, Dominican, Franciscan and Trinitarian orders.

**Early Sixteenth Century Trade**: At that time wheat, salt and wine were traded at Aberdeen en route from Leith to destinations throughout the north of Scotland and Orkney. In return sheep and wool from e.g. Turriff were marketed in Aberdeen; skins, hides and barrelled salmon were shipped south to St Andrews, Dundee and Perth, and particularly to Leith for the benefit of growing Edinburgh. By 1520 there was a goldsmith, William Watson. Salmon fishing was still important in the Dee in 1530, involving men based both in Torry and at Footdee, where fish was marketed daily, unregulated by the burgh.

**Bridge and Road Improvements and Industries up to the Reformation**: Aberdeen's first bridge to the south, comprising six well-built arches and promoted by the bishop to replace the ancient ferry at Ferryhill, was built in 1527–29 across the River Dee near Mannofield, well outside the town. In 1529, paving of the muddy streets was commenced. It seems that the road south as far as Cowie (Stonehaven) was also made up with stone, becoming a 'causeway' – but read on to see its parlous state after a century of use. Meantime these improvements facilitated landward trade with the south, hitherto almost exclusively seaborne. Small coal was imported from Dysart for smithing in the 1530s, and there is evidence of brassfounding and ceramics. Aberdeen's share of Scotland's burgh tax revenue was about 16% in 1535. In 1560, the turbulent year of Reformation, the burgh was of course represented in Parliament, but the Carmelite and Dominican friaries were both destroyed. By then there were seven craft guilds, but Aberdeen conducted only a fortieth of Scotland's Baltic trade.

**Marischal College, Post and Portraits**: Freed from Catholic church impositions, trade again built up: by 1566 the tower of St Ninian's Chapel on Castle Hill was used as a lighthouse, the Aberdeen leper house was repaired in 1574, and the first crane was installed at the harbour in 1582. In 1593 Marischal College was founded as a Protestant university in the buildings of the former Franciscan friary by the Earl Marischal of Scotland. By then the town was the centre of a presbytery, and Provost Ross's House was built in the same year; it is now probably the oldest surviving house in Aberdeen. From 1595 Aberdeen had a burgh postal service and a postal connection to Edinburgh, but in that decade Leith's dominance began to make serious inroads in Aberdeen's trade. The population was then around 4000, enough to justify splitting the town into two parishes. George Jamesone, born in the city in 1588, was to become a famous portrait painter of the royalty and nobility.

**The Weaving Trade**: By 1600 weavers were incorporated in the city, earnest of a long association to come; by 1618 Aberdeen drew labour for its plaiding industry from smaller towns. In 1637 the burgh's 569 taxpayers included about 370 members of the merchant guild. Some 75 of the latter traded overseas, many specialising in cloth. The 24 weavers were the town's largest single group of tradesmen, though constituting only a fifth of all trades and having much less prestige than the hammermen. In fact weaving was taught in the House of Correction for three quarters of a century from 1636.

**Granite and Grain, Printing and Water Supply**: The first major granite quarry opened as a source of lintels and window-sills about 1604. Brewing in Aberdeen on an industrial scale also probably dates from that period. A shipyard was established in 1606, some improvements were made to the harbour in 1607–10. In 1621 a windmill was recorded, and tide mills were built at the harbour, though these lasted only two decades; land reclamation around the harbour was begun in 1623. Printing commenced locally in 1622, and in 1623 Aberdeen had 114 craftsmen and about 350 merchants, a number which tended to increase with prosperity; in 1626–27 only 37 people were in receipt of burgh relief. In 1632 a supply of water was piped in from a spring.

**Civil War Destruction, Plague and the Commonwealth**: Aberdeen was the second city in Scotland in 1639, its tax yield about a third of that of Edinburgh with Leith. But in that year five armies in turn occupied the city; it was sacked by the Marquis of Montrose in 1644 when 160 people were killed and the plaiding trade collapsed; to cap it all, bubonic plague struck again in 1646–47, killing a quarter of the population, and many top people fled. But resilient Aberdeen recovered rapidly, and by 1655 Aberdeen was numbered among Scotland's eight Head Ports. Already by 1648 hose was being knitted on frames, though hand knitting continued dominant. General Monk had the town fortified under the Commonwealth about 1651; by that time its population was perhaps 6000.

**A Flourishing City – Pity about the Road South!**: The eloquent Richard Franck, who visited Aberdeen in 1656, was most impressed by this *"flourishing city under the government of well-regulated magistrates"*. It was *"cleanly swept and paved"*, its buildings *"framed with stone and timber"* and the walls *"strengthened with towers and buttresses of stone"*. There was fishing, as well as much trade with the Highlands and overseas. But he travelled a terrible road to the south, *"pointed with rocky stumpy stones, and daubed all over with dingy dirt, that makes it unpassable"*. Gordon later noted that in the 17$^{th}$ century the *"market towns, villages and hamlets of the shires and country nearest neighbouring"* still required licences from Aberdeen town council to *"trade in merchandise either by sea or land"*. By 1661 although some wood and thatch buildings remained, the town was largely built in stone and slate. As well as a music school and town hospital (originally St Thomas's) there were two windmills and many watermills; among these, by 1665 was a bark mill for the tanning industry.

**Famine hits Aberdeenshire**: Posts linked Aberdeen to Edinburgh twice weekly from 1667, and in 1670 the port paid 7% of national customs duties, the third largest share in Scotland. The shipowner Skene who was provost in 1673–83 built himself a fine town house. The market place later named Castle Street was adorned by a Mercat cross from 1686. By the 1690s Aberdeen was for the period quite a large town, with a pollable male population of 3740. Trade was so predominant that little more than a quarter of its workforce was engaged in manufacturing. The Bank of Scotland showed early but abortive interest in Aberdeen with a branch opened in 1696. But in that decade famine killed off a quarter of Aberdeenshire's population, and there was little progress. James Gibbs, born in Aberdeen in 1682, became an architect who found greater opportunities in England, and designed London's church of St Martin in the Fields. From 1703 Aberdeen stocking makers were organised by a company; in 1712 after the Union, woollen cloth and knitted stockings were exported to Germany, Holland, Norway, Portugal and Spain. In 1707 William Black, who had textile interests, established Gilcomston brewery.

**Defoe's Aberdeen**: Defoe writing in the 1720s described *"the third city in Scotland. The people of Aberdeen are universal merchants trading to Holland, France, Hamburg, Norway, Gothenburg, and to the Baltic. The largest and fairest market-place in Scotland; the generality of the citizens' houses are built of stone four story high. They have a very good manufacture of linen, and also of worsted stockings, which they send to England in great quantities, to Holland, and into the north and east seas. They have also a particular export of pork, pickled and barreled, which they chiefly sell to the Dutch. They also export corn and meal from the Firth of Moray, or Cromarty, the corn coming from about Inverness."* Salmon were very plentiful in the Dee, while *"the herring-fishing is a common blessing to all this shore of Scotland"*.

**Textiles and Education**: A further granite quarry was opened at Loanhead in 1730 and by 1733 coarse serges were exported to England and Holland. Despite the setback of a major fire in 1731, Robert Gordon's College, an independent school, was opened in 1732. The Bank of Scotland returned with a second-round branch, opened in 1731 but closed within two years. The Town Hall built in 1734 was designed by William Adam; later college buildings were designed by his more famous son Robert Adam. Woolmanhill infirmary was built in 1741, and by 1745 there were several meal and flour mills.

**Textiles and the Press**: In 1745 a lint mill and a bleachfield attested to linen manufacture, and about that time the Trustees for Manufacture appointed a linen yarn inspector. A second bleachfield was built between 1746 and 1760, together with a printfield which was still operating in 1816. About 1748 Hadden & Green established a large and long-lasting woollen works in the city centre; but eventually they moved out to Garlogie and Old Aberdeen to exploit water power. In 1748 came the first issue of the weekly *Aberdeen Journal*, its first newspaper. The Roy map made about 1750 showed that Aberdeen was irregularly built, except for the large L-shaped market-place containing island developments. Only three roads left the city: northwards to Old Aberdeen, there fanning into four branches; westwards on north Deeside; and south-west to the Bridge of Dee and beyond.

**Granite City: the Pace of Development Quickens**: By 1755 the population was about 15,600 (Webster), and in 1765 according to Alexander Carlyle *"the town begins to be very well built of stone"*. Granite had become the normal building material, at that time hewn from a quarry at Torry, which Roy showed as a hamlet separated from the city by the islands and sandbanks of the Dee, on which no harbour works were shown. Carlyle commended the *"very large and spacious"* market-place, the *"large and handsome"* Town Hall, Gordon's Hospital, the Infirmary and Grammar School; but the state of Marischal College was deplorable, and McGhie's spacious new inn was dirty. The ancient *ports* (gates) were removed in the 1760s to aid the traffic flow, no doubt including many brewers' drays, for the Marischal Street brewery was established in 1765, and Devanha brewery, the longest lasting in the city, rose beside the Ferryhill Burn in 1768. The fiddle-maker Ruddiman flourished around 1772, and by 1773 there were two booksellers, and an inn worthy of the name.

**Banks linked with Linen**: The first Banking Company of Aberdeen lasted only from 1747 to 1753 and had no branches, but by 1765 the British Linen Company had a local agent. The Banking Company in Aberdeen, formed in 1767, had succeeded by 1793 in opening half a dozen branches, in the city and Inverness. The Aberdeen Commercial Banking Company of 1788 briefly had a branch in Arbroath around 1793. John Maberly & Co, London owners of the local Broadford Linen Factory from 1811, had by 1818 established a banking concern with branches in Dundee, Edinburgh, Glasgow and Montrose. In 1824–25 they installed 200 power looms, but in 1832 the firm failed and was absorbed by Richards & Co.

**Slow Coaches**: In 1776 a coastal quarry was opened at Greyhope, making causeway setts for London. By then harbour improvement had become necessary, and Smeaton designed the North Pier, built in 1775–78, which enabled Aberdeen to rank among Britain's top ten ports for coastwise coal imports in the 1780s. The south road must have received attention, for in 1780 a regular wagon service commenced between Aberdeen and Glasgow, though it took six days! In the 1790s stage coaches from Edinburgh still took a remarkable 34 hours.

**Stocking Knitting from Hand to Machine**: By 1770 many outworkers knitted worsted stockings, for which 22 merchants bought and distributed wool. In 1793 912,000 pairs were exported, largely to the Netherlands, and the innovative local Alex Buchan was making knitting frames – leading Heron in 1799 to note that hand knitting of stockings *"has for some years been on the decline, due to the introduction of stocking-looms or frames"*.

**Linen and Cotton Developments**: By 1776 240 looms were in use, making woollens and some linens; in 1787 Gordon, Barron & Co erected a chlorine bleaching works for linens, the first such in Scotland. About 1790 a firm was established to make brown linen sheetings and Osnaburgs; from 1795 it also made sailcloth, widely used by local sailmakers. About 1795 the yarn spun by 10,000 part-time workers in the countryside served 2700 people making linen thread in Aberdeen, both at home and in factories; by 1797 the area had over half Scotland's twist mills for making linen thread. In 1798 Alexander Hadden & Sons built a steam-powered mill at The Green; a second steam-powered cotton mill and the Devanha paper mill were both founded in 1803. But linen continued; in 1806 a bleachfield still operated at Lochhead, and early in the 19th century over 2000 people were still engaged in the area's woollen manufactures.

**Hall's Shipyard and Other Industries**: By 1789 Aberdeen's other industries included quarrying, ropes, bricks and tiles, sawmilling, tanneries, foundries and engineering shops. Three quite significant breweries were at work and a timber merchant was again recorded in 1790, the year that Hall's shipyard was first opened, and Mackinnons began work as millwrights, later specialising in rice and coffee mills. Other industries were developing on Donside just upstream from Old Aberdeen *(see Bucksburn & Woodside)*.

**The Handsome City Replanned**: Four fairs were to be held in 1797, by 1805 a druggist was trading, and the *Aberdeen Chronicle* – a radical newspaper later called the *Aberdeen Free Press* – started in 1806. In 1799 Heron wrote of *"a handsome city, the streets well paved and the houses, in general, lofty and spacious"*; education was given at a *"very neat grammar school"*. The harbour was protected by a *"strong stone pier, lately erected"*. Beside the coasting trade, vessels traded throughout Scandinavia and the Baltic, and southwards as far as Portugal, exporting *"stockings, linen, linen-yarn, salmon, salted pork, grain and oatmeal"*. Under the Aberdeen New Streets Act of 1800, the medieval city was ruthlessly swept away and the modern street pattern including George Street and King Street was expensively created. This effort bankrupted the town council in 1817 and it took until 1825 to regain solvency. Footdee was soon rebuilt as three inward-looking squares of houses for the fisherfolk.

**Transport Improvements**: Aberdeen's importance as a port was recognised by its fishing-boat registry letter, simply 'A', and by one of Scotland's earliest lifeboat stations, opened in 1802. Then, the population was 27,000. By 1817 six small shipyards were in operation, of which Hall's was the largest, building about 20 vessels a year, some of over 400 tons. Calls for a lighthouse came in 1813 when the whaler *Oscar* and 43 crewmen were lost near Girdle Ness, and a battery was built about 1813–15 to protect Aberdeen's trade from American privateers. In 1810–16 the North pier was extended by 300m beyond Smeaton's work. Its designer Thomas Telford inspected it in 1819 with Robert Southey, who noted that coal and lime were imported from Sunderland; he also smelt *"a strong odour of whale oil"*. The city's first steamboat was launched in 1829, over 15 years after the Clyde had pioneered mechanical propulsion.

**Turnpikes, Canal and Coaches**: Meantime between 1795 and 1811 some 500km of new turnpike roads were built in Aberdeenshire. The Aberdeenshire Canal, opened in 1807, connected the city with Inverurie and stimulated Donside industries, but it was 1834 before it was connected to the harbour. By 1830 sixteen road coaches operated from Aberdeen; from 1832 to the 1840s the horse-drawn coach *Defiance* was covering the 208km from Aberdeen to Edinburgh via Perth and Queensferry in 12 to 14 hours. By 1841 the city's population had risen to 63,000.

**Gas, Granite, Food and Drink**: A gasworks concern started in 1818 came into production in 1824, and 1818 also saw the establishment of a granite polishing business by Alexander Macdonald, later joined by Field and then by Leslie. In 1820 the brewery at Ferryhill was joined by the Union Glen distillery, which lasted only until 1855. The Strathdee distillery was built south-west of the city by Henry Ogg in 1821, and William Walker began whisky blending in 1827. By 1825 no fewer than eleven breweries were in production, as well as those in the Aulton; water was piped from Bridge of Dee from 1829. Scotland's first meat cannery was established in the city as early as 1822 by John Moir, later followed by four others, but sugar refining did not last into mid-century.

**Metropolitan Aberdeen**: Chambers wrote that in 1827 Aberdeen was a *"fine city furnished with most of the attributes of a wealthy metropolis"*. Union Street with its 40m arch spanning the Den Burn had been opened in 1811, though it was still incomplete in 1827. *"The harbour has been recently improved by a series of expensive works, and by a pier, running out into the sea, to the amazing length of 367m, constructed of enormous blocks of granite."* John Gibb of Aberdeen built at least four lighthouses designed by Robert Stevenson for the Northern Lighthouse Board between 1825 and 1833, the last being on Girdle Ness.

**Aberdonian Culture, Famous Sons and the Press**: The Music Hall, designed by local architect Archibald Simpson, was originally built as a club in 1820–22, and the Mechanics' Institute was founded in 1824. Sir John Steell who was born in Aberdeen in 1804 became a sculptor, best known for his statue of Scott within the Scott Monument in Edinburgh. George Washington Wilson, born on a Banffshire croft in 1823, became a painter but moved to Aberdeen in 1848 to set up in business as a photographer of people and places; he became perhaps the most famous early Scottish photographer. The imposing St Peter's Roman Catholic School and Orphanage in Constitution Street was built in 1833. The *Aberdeen Herald* newspaper was in weekly publication at least between 1845 and 1853. William Alexander, born in the city in 1826 wrote the well known novel *Johnny Gibb of Gushetneuk* and was for a time the editor of the *Journal's* main competitor, the *Aberdeen Free Press*.

**The Harbour and Whaling 1827–1850**: The harbour was further improved to designs by Telford between 1827 and 1837, creating Trinity Quay and the Upper Dock. There were twenty locally based whaling vessels when the bounty ended in 1824, but by 1834 only a handful of Aberdeen whalers were still at work, and operations soon ceased. A comb factory set up in 1830 by John Stewart with 40 employees was making 9 million combs a year by 1854, possibly of whalebone landed at other ports. Blaikie's Quay was built in 1834 and improved in 1850, and the Victoria Dock was built in 1845–48.

**Bank Mergers**: In 1833 the Aberdeen Commercial Banking Company merged with the National Bank and in 1849 the Glasgow-based Union Bank absorbed the Banking Company in Aberdeen, which had large bad debts from the Banner cotton-mill; but its regional HQ role was retained. In 1825 the Aberdeen Town and County Bank was formed as a joint-stock company. The joint-stock North of Scotland Bank, set up in 1836, grew larger and remained independent until it was acquired by the Midland Bank in 1923; it traded separately until merged with their other subsidiary the Clydesdale in 1950.

**The Combined University of Aberdeen**: In the 1820s Marischal College had nine professors, though its old building was dilapidated. The main block of a new College was erected in 1837–44. In 1860 the two universities finally merged, retaining two-site working in the two still distinct settlements.

*The new front of Marischal College (founded 1593) as completed in 1891 to designs by A. Marshall Mackenzie – then Aberdeen's leading architect. He made full use of local granite to create 'wedding-cake' wallhead decoration on what was described at the time as the largest granite building in the world. (GWW collection)*

Further rebuilding of Marischal College culminated in the frontage of 1906, whose master mason John Morgan completed this, the second largest granite building in the world; but he bankrupted himself in producing its intricate carvings.

**The Clippers: built for Durability and Speed**: In 1845 W Simpson & Co built the 56m iron paddle steamer *Queen*; but this was exceptional, for most Aberdeen builders followed Alexander Hall who in 1839 built the wooden sailing *'clipper'* ship *Scottish Maid*. In 1846 Hall's built the last sailing packet for the Shetland run, the *Matchless*, which plied until 1883, and they continued to build in oak and larch until the 1860s. In 1867 Alex Hall built the sail and steam whaler *Eclipse* for a Peterhead owner; she ultimately became a USSR survey ship until at least 69 years old. From 1867 the distinct firm of Hall Russell used iron hulls. About then Walter Hood & Co built the famous 64m wood and iron clipper *Thermopylae* for the local Thomson shipping line. She once ran about 380 nautical miles in one day, and by averaging 13.75 knots was proved the fastest sailing ship in the world; a record probably never since beaten. In 1867 the three main firms together completed about 12,000 tons of shipping, their 1000 or more employees working a 57-hour week.

**An Electric Locomotive heralds Aberdeen's Steam Railway**: In 1842, a decade before the railway reached Aberdeen, and half a century ahead of his time, Aberdonian Robert Davidson built two tiny battery electric locomotives, perhaps the first in the world; the 5-tonne version achieved 4mph on test at Cowlairs near Glasgow, but the lead batteries were too heavy to be practicable. The arrival in 1850 of the Aberdeen Railway (AR), later part of the Scottish North Eastern Railway (SNER) dealt a mortal blow to the coaching industry. The AR connected from the south to a temporary terminus at Ferryhill, which became Ferryhill Junction when the Deeside Railway opened to that point in 1853. Both services soon moved to the new Guild Street Station, opened in 1854. From 1855 a through coach linked Aberdeen with London Kings Cross via Perth, Stirling and Edinburgh.

**Broken Rails to the North**: From 1853–54 Wordie & Co operated a rail to road cartage depot as sole goods and parcels agents for the Aberdeen Railway and their successors. From 1854 Kittybrewster *(see Woodside)* became the main railway centre of north-east Scotland, with the single-track lines of the Great North of Scotland Railway (GNSR) starting to fan out north-westwards on the line of the old canal. In 1855 the south end of the canal bed was infilled and laid with track, enabling the GNSR to move goods between Kittybrewster and the harbour at Waterloo, where wagons could be exchanged with the AR. The GNSR head office moved from Union Street to Waterloo, which became its passenger terminus in 1856; but relations between the two companies were strained until 1864, and no adequate passenger connection was made between the north and south lines.

**Joining up the Railways**: The Joint Station authorised in 1864 was to be west of Guild Street, adjacent to which the Deeside Railway serving Banchory had built the *'Deeside Yard'*; this company whose line joined the SNER at Ferryhill Junction was leased to the GNSR from 1866. In 1867 with the opening of the Joint Station and the 2.6km Denburn link, built by the SNER, through running from the south became possible; control of the Denburn link passed to the GNSR but in practice all passengers still had to change at the Joint Station, except for the mail trains which were extended to Elgin in 1869, the year when Wordies also became sole carriers to the GNSR; by 1903 they used 339 horses in Aberdeen, their second largest operation.

**Textiles Peak around 1860**: In 1851 Milne, Cruden & Co spun flax by steam power at Gordon's Mills *(see Woodside)* and also for a few years at Spring Gardens. In 1864 the huge Broadford flax and tow mill of Richards & Co had 2175 workers, a calender and adjacent bleachfield; its 16,814 spindles and 428 power looms were driven by 785hp steam engines. In 1869 over 3000 worked in the woollen industry within 20km of the city, and seven or eight firms then made winceys. But another source writing soon afterwards could trace only about 230 power looms and 600 hand looms, for the local textile industry was then entering a long decline *(see also Garlogie and Old Aberdeen)*.

**Mid Nineteenth Century Developments**: By 1852 a racecourse surrounded the Queen's Links, but the city's built-up area spread only 1km from the Union Bridge. In 1861 the long-lasting Northern Co-operative Society was founded. Coachbuilding was a local industry, and the hide market handled over 40,000 hides a year. The harbour was growing busier: around 1850 only 40 fishing boats were at work, but by 1868 there were over 200 boats, more than half of them fishing for herring. Moir's of Aberdeen remained the largest cannery in Scotland in the 1860s, producing over a million kilos of canned foods a year. From 1864 onwards the city's water supplies were drawn from the Dee at Invercanny, 3 km west of Banchory. In 1863 McKinnon & Co of Aberdeen built the Carron bridge in Morayshire, among the last major structures in Scotland to be made of cast iron. John Henderson & Co, founded in 1866, made lifting gear and cableways which were exported worldwide. The striking St Nicholas Church, designed by William Leslie, was built in 1865; a Roman Catholic cathedral was also built. The Albyn School for Girls was founded in 1867, the Bank of Scotland built a new Aberdeen branch office around 1870, and the *Douglas Hotel* was open by 1876.

**Aberdeen's Drinks Industries**: The Strathdee distillery was rebuilt about 1855, and in that year the Ferryhill brewery became the very large *Bon Accord* distillery. By 1878 both William Walker & Sons and Williams & Sons were whisky blenders. By 1886 the number of breweries was down to eight, the site of Cowie's brewery on the quay having become the bonds and bottling plant for the Lochnagar distillery at Balmoral. Three Highland malt distilleries were at work in the city: the *Bon Accord* had just been rebuilt after a disastrous fire; it employed over twenty men producing well over a million litres annually, using Orkney peats and steam power. By 1902 it had been renamed the *North of Scotland*, and remained open until about 1914. The large *Devanha* distillery beside the Dee was long-established, its output a million litres a year, using steam power and water from the city supplies. The *Strathdee* distillery made only 225,000 litres in the same way, also using some water power. However, when the Aberdeen grain distillery was burnt down about 1913 it was not rebuilt.

**Building a Great and Busy City**: The Town House designed by Peddie & Kinnear was built in 1867–74 and from 1876 there was a daily newspaper; the *Aberdeen Evening Express* was first published in 1879. Gray's School of Art was founded in 1883, and a public library opened in 1886. Victoria Park was created in 1871, Union Terrace gardens were laid out in 1877, Duthie Park in 1883, and the promenade too was built about then. A public library – aided by Carnegie money – opened in 1892. On his tour of the British distilleries in 1886 Barnard was delighted with his stay at Aberdeen's *Imperial Hotel*, remarking on Union Street's *"beautiful shops and magnificent buildings"*, and the city's *"noble market buildings"*. Aberdeen was described in 1886 as *"a great and busy city"*. However, cities breed crime, and the Craiginches Prison was opened in 1891. In 1894 the city's five hotels – *Imperial, Palace, Grand, Douglas*, and *Forsyth's Temperance* – were *"all good and all near the station"*.

**Shipping Companies, Coasting Trade and Collision**: J & A Davidson of Aberdeen were established in 1865 as coal, granite and grain merchants, and bought ships to trade to the Baltic and Mediterranean, but in 1888 they settled down to supply the local coal trade by sea, doing so until 1960. In 1872 Hall, Russell & Co built the long-lasting 55 m 632-ton iron coaster SS *Spray* for a West Hartlepool firm; she soon returned to Aberdeen under local coal merchants Ellis & McHardy, founded in 1880, who used her as a collier for 45 years! Aberdeen was still among Britain's top ten ports for coastwise coal imports in 1885, and the Aberdeen Lime Company ran coasting steamers from the 1880s to the 1920s. In 1895 334 lives were lost when the German liner *Elbe* was in collision in the North Sea with a small coaster the SS *Crathie*, owned by William T Moffatt of Aberdeen, which came off lightly. William R Aitken who started in the coasting trade in 1890 owned vessels until 1944, later being taken over by J Cook who traded with the Baltic. In Edwardian days the half dozen vessels in Elsmie & Son's North Eastern Shipping fleet carried coastwise and Continental freight.

**Fishing Intensified**: The Albert Basin was created in 1873–79 by diverting the River Dee, and about then longer and re-sited breakwaters improved the harbour entrance, making it easier for the steam trawlers which in 1882–83 started to exploit, and eventually to decimate, the North Sea's stock of white fish. Their large catches required a new fish wharf, opened in 1888, and in 1889 a covered fish market. Spencer's fish oil plant was set up, and wooden fish-box makers were also busy. In 1907–10 Blaikie's quay was again improved. By 1914 almost 250 steam trawlers were based in Aberdeen, and many fish trains left the city for the south each working day.

**Trams, Trauma and Suburban Trains**: From 1874 horse tramways ran in the city streets, and in 1894 were extended to Bucksburn, the longest route. Meantime because 30 people had drowned in the Torry ferry capsize in 1876, the Victoria Bridge was completed in 1881, linking Torry with the city centre and ousting the ancient ferry. To enable a better train service the Deeside railway line between Ferryhill Junction and Cults was doubled by the GNSR in 1884. From 1887 eight suburban trains a day ran to and from Dyce; so successful were these *'subby'* trains that soon there were 20 each way. In 1894 Aberdeen got an electricity supply, at the cost of pulling down the Dee Village to form the site for the power station. In 1898 the tramways were taken over by the town council and the next year were electrified. Aberdeen was still too compact to support a complex system, even though after major boundary extensions its population in 1901 was over 150,000.

**Late Victorian / Edwardian Entertainment, and Fire Hazard**: In 1872 the 1744-seat *Her Majesty's Theatre* designed by Charles Phipps was built in Guild Street. About 1880 a redundant church was converted into the *Alhambra* music hall, which lasted until 1910. The *Palace*, another makeshift theatre, which opened in 1888 was soon burnt down, but after a full-time city fire service was introduced in 1896 the theatre was rebuilt in 1898 with cramped accommodation for an audience of 3200. Aberdeen's first cinema seems to have opened in 1896, the year that the local Trades Council erected an impressive baronial style meeting hall in Belmont Street, later used as a cinema and warehouse and restored by 1999 as a media centre. Aberdeen Football Club was formed as late as 1903. *His Majesty's Theatre* on Schoolhill was opened in 1906; Schoolhill station, which had been opened in 1893 for the suburban trains just north of the Joint Station, was beside the new theatre, and the GNSR put on evening trains from and to Deeside. The former *Her Majesty's Theatre* closed in 1906, and after internal reconstruction became the *Tivoli Music Hall* in 1910.

**Mixed Fortunes up to 1914**: The large and famous photographic business founded by George Washington Wilson failed in 1907, but its topographic negatives happily survived (a number of which are reproduced in this book). A teacher training centre founded in 1905 later became the College of Education; the new buildings for Marischal College were finally completed in 1906, and in 1906–07 a fine stone-built Head Post Office was built at Crown Street. The Broadford cloth

*Aberdeen harbour from the Municipal Tower in the late 19th century, when the trade of the city was still largely handled by sailing ships, and before it became a leading fishing port.* *(GWW collection)*

works in Maberly Street was enlarged by the Richards Company in 1911–12 with a large four-storey warehouse. Harrott & Co, makers of gloves and hosiery, were established in 1913.

**Railway Prosperity – and the Price of War**: In 1907–08 additional through platforms were added to the station and in 1910 the GNSR bought the adjacent *Station Hotel*. The station was impressively rebuilt in 1913–15 but due to the war was completed only in 1920; with a total of over 3450m of platform faces, it became second in Scotland only to Edinburgh Waverley. By then over 15% of the 609 GNSR staff who had served in the armed forces had lost their lives. New jobs came with the creation during World War I of a railway yard at Craiginches south of Torry, originally for Admiralty traffic. The population of Aberdeenshire as a whole peaked about 1911; but the city continued to grow.

**Granite, Gas and Engineering**: Blaikie Brothers of Aberdeen built the major Speymouth railway viaduct at Garmouth in 1886. The local ironfounders included Harper, and Abernethy of Ferryhill. Up to 1914 locally hewn granite (*see Mannofield and Kemnay*) was being supplemented by large imports of granite from Scandinavia, to be cut and polished for monuments and facings, using machinery manufactured locally by Cassie & Son. In the early 20th century the Seaton Brickworks were in operation, the agricultural engineers R G Garvie & Sons built stationary threshing drums, and D Bruce made chaff cutters; the Bon-Accord Acetylene Gas Company manufactured gas-producing plant, and Barry Henry & Co made internal combustion engines; in 1928 Allan Brothers were in the same business.

**Coasters dominate Aberdeen Shipbuilding**: In 1905 the little-known Aberdeen shipyard of Sir James Laing & Sons built the 11,300 ton *Indrabarah*; unusually large for Aberdeen builders, she later became the naval repair vessel HMS *Cyclops* and lasted until 1947. Alex Hall & Co built coasters, as did John Lewis & Sons – with a series of ten coasters built up to 1925, followed in the 1930s by ten coasters for John Kelly. In 1939 came the last steam collier to be built, their own *SS Mount Battock*, which for many years carried coal for the Aberdeen fishing fleet to a wharf beside the shipyard. In 1931 Hall, Russell & Co built the collier SS *Thrift* for the Northern Co-op Society, in service until 1968, and in 1932 their second coaster named SS *Spray*, for Ellis & McHardy's equally durable successors the Aberdeen Coal & Shipping Company, which took over in 1920. The second Shetland steamer named *St Sunniva* was launched in 1931, and Aberdeen was still among Britain's top ten ports for coastal trade in 1938.

**Fishing Vessels, Fish-guts and Research**: In 1906 Hall Russell were building steam trawlers and Duthie's Torry boatyard produced steam drifters with steel hulls, but this long-established yard closed in 1925. In 1932 Alexander Hall & Co built their 343rd vessel, the last steam drifter in Britain, the *Wilson Line* of Anstruther. An amalgamation of 1928 created Scottish Agricultural Industries, with a fertiliser and fishmeal plant at Sandilands; Isaac Stephenson had a fish glue works at Torry in the mid 20th century. The Torry Research Institute for the fishing industry was opened in 1930. In 1931 C F Wilson of Aberdeen was making fish-gutting machines to a Shetland pattern.

**Rail Cartage under the Grouping**: In 1923 Wordie's GNSR contract passed to the LNER: after 1933 this enabled Wordie's (NE) Ltd with 20 staff to continue trading in private hands. In 1939 when the Waterloo goods station was still busy and congested, the firm's big stables at Rodger's Walk contained about 150 horses and had a provender mill serving the 110 horses in their other ex-GNSR depots by rail, for the firm was very slow to change and owned only 19 motor vehicles. Their Bannermill general warehouse had five floors and a glorious mixture of contents from farm machinery to sacks of grain and tins of pineapple. At that time they carted flour to local bakers from the Caledonian Milling Company. Wordies bought no horses after 1945.

**Press and Entertainment Changes**: Woolworths opened their first local store in 1919, and the BBC's first Aberdeen studio was opened in 1923. In 1922 the *Aberdeen Free Press* was merged with the *Aberdeen Journal* as the *Aberdeen Press & Journal*. The Art Gallery was extended with a museum opened in 1929, as was the Cowdray Hall. The city also became the telephone headquarters for northern Scotland. In 1928 the original flimsy *Beach Pavilion* was replaced by another 750-seat hall of the same name, used for summer revue; so the *Palace* became a cinema in 1929. New swimming baths were built in 1932, and about then the *Beach Ballroom* was built. Jazz and swing caused folk musicians to react: Jeannie Robertson, born in Aberdeen in 1908, became a renowned singer, composer and collector of ballads of the Scottish travelling folk.

**Other Interwar Developments**: Anderson Drive was laid out in the 1920s as a city bypass. Remarkably in 1928, during the Prohibition era, whisky smuggler Samuel Bronfman bought the firm of Joseph Seagram & Sons and Chivas Brothers, then of Aberdeen. About 1930 brewing ceased at the Devanha, last of the city's many breweries. The tramways which had a new depot from 1914, replacing an old barracks, were modernised in 1927–29, though the Torry service was abandoned in 1931. The suburban rail services from Culter and Dyce were also hit by competition from buses and cars, and abandoned in 1937. During the 1930s a new city hospital was built, as were the very respectable Torry or Tullos housing estate and the huge block of council flats at Rosemount Square. But as late as 1936 22% of the city's houses were overcrowded.

**During and after World War II**: From 1940 to 1946 the *Station Hotel* was an Admiralty office, reopening after modernisation in 1950. But the *Palace Hotel*, which had burned down in 1941 was never rebuilt, a department store being erected on its site. Although fishing was badly affected by the war, shipbuilding was given a fillip, employment growing by 150% to a total of 3000 in 1948. The three firms still involved, all combining marine engineering, were Alex Hall & Co, Hall Russell & Co, and John Lewis & Sons. The long-established John Henderson & Co had been building bridges in Sutherland before the war; afterwards they were the largest engineering firm in Aberdeen, making aerial cableways, derricks and mechanical transporters in 1950. Meantime Consolidated Pneumatic Tools had been set up in a wartime factory, but moved to Fraserburgh in the 1980s.

**Post-1945 Shipbuilding sees the end of Steam**: In 1952 Lewis built two steamships for Comben Longstaff of London, but the firm soon abandoned steamships. In 1956 Hall, Russell & Co built and engined the last steam coastal tanker to be built, the 1965-ton bulk bitumen carrier *Esso Preston*, designed to keep its liquid cargo hot, and in 1963–64 built the three vessels which began the car ferry services to the Western Isles. In 1967 sail made a comeback to Lewis of Aberdeen's yard, which built the 45 m 219-ton 3-masted sail training ship *Malcolm Miller*. The three firms' 20 berths also built and repaired trawlers, tugs, and dredgers of up to 4000 tons; but the industry was failing, and within 20 years only struggling Hall Russell was left.

**Services and Entertainment from 1945**: Marks & Spencer had opened their first store in Aberdeen by 1953. In 1949 the city council opened the exposed Balnagask municipal golf course east of Torry. The city's theme song *'The Northern Lights of Aberdeen'* was composed as recently as 1951, by an English couple! In 1960 the *Palace Cinema* was again converted, into a ballroom, and still later became a disco. Grampian TV established its headquarters at Queens Cross and began transmissions in 1961, but in that year the *Beach Pavilion* closed; it became a restaurant in 1963. The *Tivoli* kept variety going until 1966, then becoming a sumptuous bingo hall. The Crown Street post office was modernised and extended in 1965 and in 1972 became Scotland's first mechanised letter office using postcodes. The local daily newspaper publishers moved to new premises at Mastrick about then.

**Industries struggling in the 1960s**: In the early 1960s William Tawse of Aberdeen built the high level dam for the Cruachan pumped storage scheme *(see Dalmally)*. But Aberdeen remained primarily a major fishing port, and generally was not really thriving in the half century up to 1970. This was due to the decline of the local textile industry, which employed under 750 in hosiery and 500 in woollens in 1946, to falling demand for granite in buildings and tombstones, to overfishing of the North Sea, and to the drift of population towards central Scotland with its New Towns.

**Aberdeen Transport thrown off the Rails**: Aberdeen Airport was developing at Dyce *(q.v.)* and British Rail opened a freightliner container terminal in 1966 shortly before Ferryhill locomotive depot closed with the end of steam. But the Aberdeen tramways were closed in 1958, and from the mid 1960s thanks to Marples and Beeching's blinkered approach, all the railways in the region were closed over little more than a decade, save the through route from the south via Aberdeen to Elgin and Inverness. Even this was singled north of Aberdeen station in 1971. Waterloo rail yard was relegated to British Steel traffic, and Aberdeen's extensive suburban developments became entirely reliant on road transport just as the city was about to be revolutionised by the discovery of North Sea Oil in 1970. In 1975 the city boundary was greatly extended to form the new City of Aberdeen district, but the headquarters of the new Grampian Regional Council was located at Mastrick. Despite the loss of its local traffic, by 1978 Aberdeen railway station saw over a million passengers a year. P&O Ferries already operated a fixed ro-ro terminal at Aberdeen for their Shetland services, and a second was opened in 1979. There was also a coastguard station.

**Oil Offices Boom but Harbour Congestion hits Fishing**: In 1982 the fish market was expensively rebuilt, but was hampered by the *'jobs for life'* terms on which its porters were

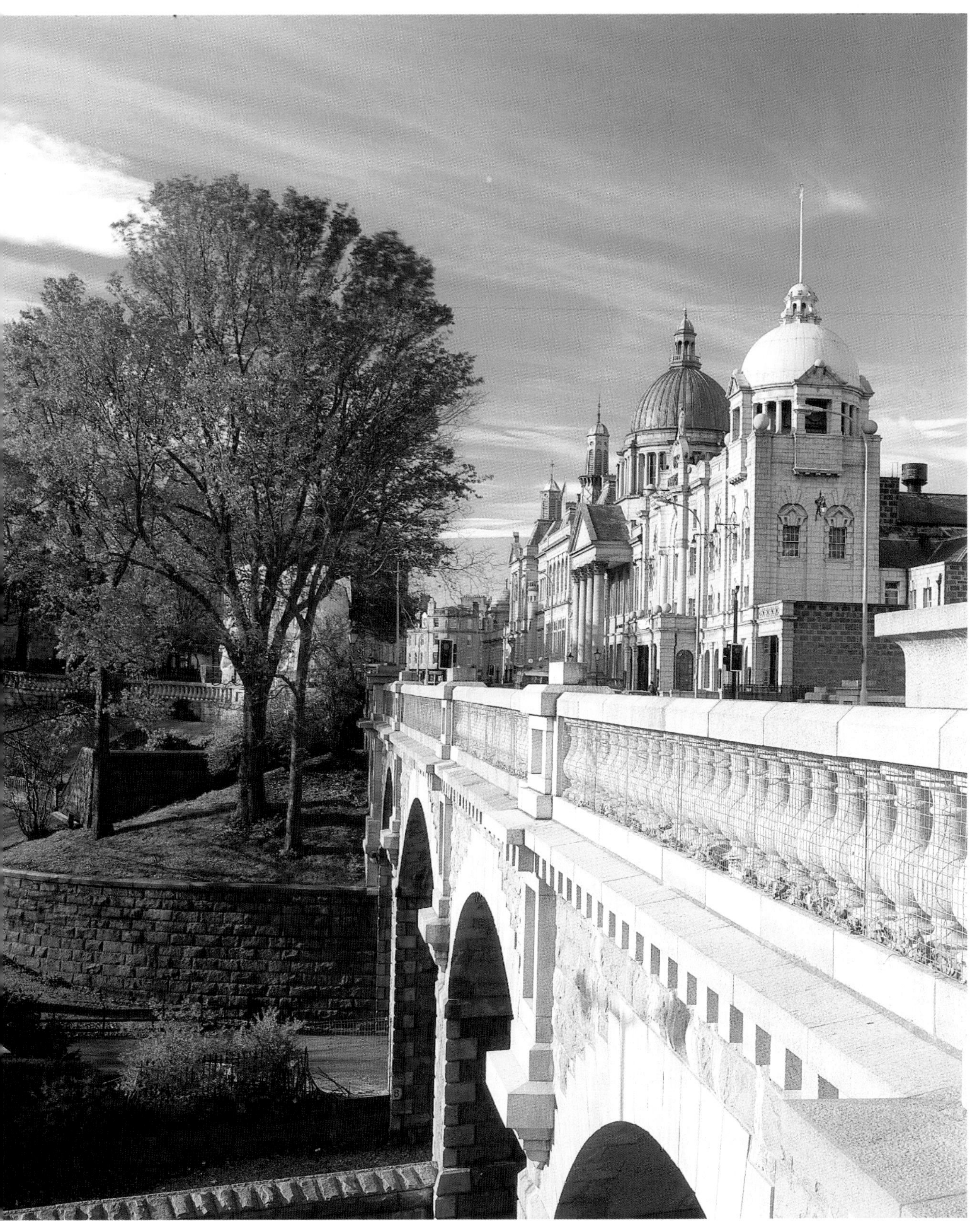

*His Majesty's Theatre, seen from the Rosemount Viaduct. The theatre was designed by Frank Matcham – a noted music-hall architect – and built between 1904 and 1908. Its elaborate interior was refurbished in the early 1980s.* *(SMPC / David Robertson)*

employed. This and harbour congestion caused by the offshore oil industry's numerous service vessels led the fishing industry to shift many of its activities to Peterhead; by 1984 there were only 16 Aberdeen trawlers. Aberdeen's fine municipal art gallery and museum – then probably the leading free attraction north of the Forth – contained a maritime section emphasising fishing, and soon showed models of oil production platforms also. Several major developments took place in the central shopping and business district as well as industrial growth in many surrounding places, especially Dyce and Cove Bay. In 1981 the city centre was more extensive than the whole of the original Royal Burgh. By then about 750 oil-related firms were represented in the enlarged city, and office space was growing at 6% a year. About 1981 the headquarters of the John Wood group, the UK's largest oil servicing industry, was moved from the city centre to the East Tullos estate, where they continued to expand even though the early 1980s saw a setback to the local economy with the low price of oil.

**Hendersons, Shipbuilding and Rubber Depart**: John M Henderson, the well known engineers of Aberdeen, moved their production to Arbroath in 1985 and planned in 1991 to move their head office too. Girdle Ness lighthouse was automated in 1991. The city's last shipyard, Hall Russell, went into receivership in 1988, was taken over by A & P Appledore, and was defunct by 1992. Aberdeen Rubber, which made car components at Tullos by 1983, employed 150 people in 1988; it closed down in 1991 and its operations moved to Donegal. In 1990 about 49,000 people were in oil-related jobs in the district. Problems caused by volatile oil prices led to both closures and responses to overcrowding: the Ben Line subsidiary, Atlantic Drilling of Aberdeen, made 400 workers redundant in depressed 1992, and by 1993 CAM Shipping, responding to growing congestion in Aberdeen harbour, had moved its 36 standby vessels to Montrose.

**Shopping Centres and Headquarter Offices**: Central area redevelopment continued with the Trinity shopping centre, built over the little-used north end of the railway station; it attracted Debenhams and C&A. The St Nicholas shopping centre was built in 1985. By 1989 Aberdeen contained the headquarters of both the North-East River Purification Board and the North of Scotland district of Post Office Counters, and by 1991 also the Hydro-Electric computing centre. In 1993 the head office and main milk processing plant of the large Kennerty Farm Dairies was at West Tullos. Turning to oil headquarters, Amerada Hess set up its HQ in Aberdeen in 1983, and grew to over 300 staff in 1991 *(see Ardersier)*. In 1992 Matthew Hall, lately merged with Press the contractors as AMEX, was creating 200 jobs at a new combined HQ building in the Aberdeen area. By 1991 Aberdeen also had the large HQ office of Britoil, though jobs were threatened by the BP takeover. Conoco which had some 500 workers scattered around the area, decided in 1993 to move its HQ from London to Aberdeen, with a possible transfer of 450 jobs. By 1993 Total Oil too had newly centred its UK offices in Aberdeen, but Shell's Aberdeen HQ at Tullos shed 20% of its 1500 jobs.

**Aberdeen Rail Freight in decline – and New Hope**: In 1983–84 Freightliner wagons ran in passenger trains between Thurso and Aberdeen, but attracted too little traffic to be profitable. The freightliner terminal, closed in 1987 with the others in eastern Scotland, was soon replaced by John G Russell of Gartcosh, who moved a container crane from Kittybrewster to the harbour to distribute containerised coal by road; but this traffic soon dwindled. In 1989 BR's Deeside Yard or *'Guild Street Freight'* still handled 235,000 tonnes of rail freight, including bulk cement, containers, palletised fertilisers, drilling mud, calcium carbonate, starch, china clay, paper, gas oil and hazardous wastes. Although LPG and other petroleum products for local distribution ceased to arrive by rail in 1992, weekly roll-on and container ships sailed to Denmark, Holland and Norway. From 1994 Transrail, a fragment of the former BR freight system, ran a daily *'Enterprise'* freight train between Elgin, Aberdeen, Mossend, Bescot and Wembley, still bringing china clay from Cornwall to Aberdeen. In 1997 the new American-owned EWS (English Welsh & Scottish Railways) started a *'piggyback'* rail service for road trailers between London and Aberdeen, using new skeletal *'Eurospine'* wagons.

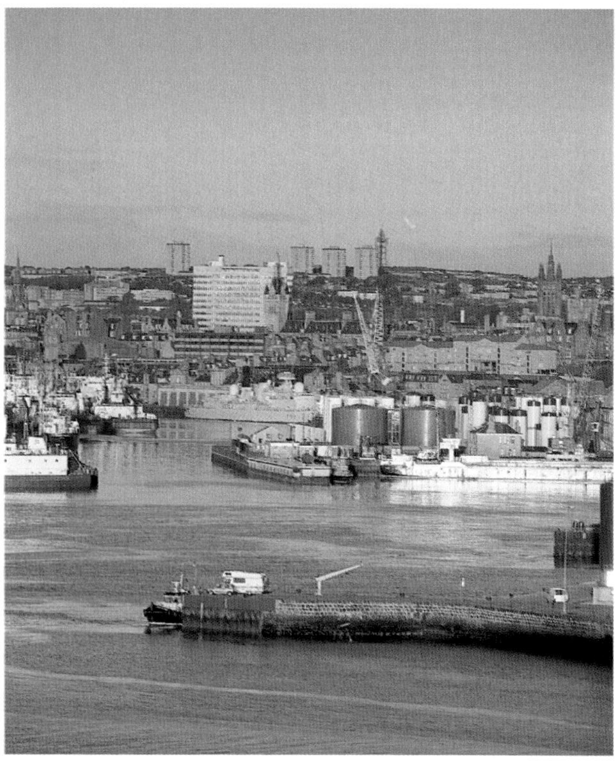

*Aberdeen, harbour and city, seen from Torry, with ships and shore facilities of the North Sea oil industry.* *(SMPC / David Robertson)*

**Public Passenger Transport**: In 1989 1.6 million passengers passed through Aberdeen's partly modernised railway station, though the nearby bus station remained very crude and basic as late as 1999. Inter-City trains were serviced at Clayhills depot, and before privatisation stopped all progress for five years, a suburban rail service was proposed between Inverurie and Stonehaven, with five new stations, including one at Tullos to serve the closely built-up area south of the river. By 1995 Stagecoach of Perth owned Bluebird Buses of Aberdeen, whose 400 vehicles and 700 staff provided public transport in Grampian, Highland, Tayside and Central Regions.

**Massive Central Redevelopments**: A dual carriageway ring round the historic centre was being pieced together by Grampian Region, enabling pedestrianisation of some shopping streets, in progress in 1990 when District Council improvements enabled the weekly retail market which had survived at The Green and Justice Street to move back to the foot of Union Street. In 1990 the huge Bon-Accord Centre with 25,000 m$^2$ of attractively enclosed retail space was opened by the Dutch group Bredero, with District Council help. It drew C&A out of the Trinity Centre and was adjoined by a fine new John Lewis store.

**Marks and Tesco flourish but Nemesis overtakes Norco**: Aberdeen's shopping role was now huge: it performed seventh among 250 British shopping centres in 1991–94 in terms of shop rents and property values. In 1993 Marks & Spencer added a new sales floor to their Aberdeen store, and although Arnotts had vanished, the House of Fraser had opened its own-name department store by 1994. By 1996 there were both Tesco and Tesco Metro stores, but not all retailers had benefited. The Northern Co-op (Norco) who had lately built a new HQ and a large superstore on their 10 ha Berryden site overreached themselves and had to sell this store to Scottish Co-op in 1992, others going to Safeway. In 1993 a retail recession hit its remaining traditional stores and Norco, once Scotland's largest co-op, was liquidated.

**Aberdeen Fish and Food Science in Trouble**: Some 40,000 tonnes of fish was landed in 1992, and in 1993 Aberdeen enjoyed the lowest unemployment rate in Scotland, at a mere 3.5%. In 1997 fish landed included cod, coley, haddock, hake, halibut, ling, monkfish, plaice, skate, sole and whiting. However as fish became scarcer and dearer some small fish processing concerns failed, as did the large and long established road hauliers and fish transporters Charles Alexander & Partners in 1992. In 1995 the government proposed closure of the 100-staff Torry Food Science Laboratory and the transfer of its work to York, and in 1996 110 jobs for disabled people were at risk when the Blindcraft factory was threatened with closure.

**Recreation and Leisure Developments**: The large Beach leisure centre and swimming pool was built in 1988–89; an ice rink was added in 1992. The *Lemon Tree*, a new performing arts venue, opened in 1992. By 1993 the *Satrosphere* in Justice Mill Lane was claimed as Scotland's only 'hands on' science exhibition centre. In 1994 the two remaining cinemas, the *Odeon* and *Cannon*, had seven screens between them, but only occasional concerts used the *Capitol Theatre*. In 1996–97 Scottish Opera was among the users of *His Majesty's Theatre*. The Queens Links Leisure Park opened in 1997 with a 9-screen cinema, restaurants, clubs and some 300 jobs.

**Educational and Medical Developments**: It was about 1960 when Aberdeen College erected a 9-storey slab block in Holburn Street; by 1987 its structure was unsafe and it was vacated, but demolition of this large eyesore was not agreed until 1995. In 1997 Aberdeen Grammar School had 1069 pupils, Harlaw Academy 915 and Torry Academy 451. The independent St Margaret's School for Girls was open at Albyn Place by 1967, with its boarding house at Peterculter, and in 1996 the long-established Albyn School for Girls in Queen's Road had 320 all-age pupils. The independent Robert Gordon's College in Schoolhill admitted girls from 1989. Its senior partner, Robert Gordon's Institute of Technology, kept his famous name when it became a University in 1992, but in 1994 began to move to Mannofield. Biovation, a medical research firm founded in 1994 by Frank Carr, employed 21 people on De-Immunisation technology projects in 2000, when it was sold to the German pharmaceutical combine Merck.

**Historic Buildings Saved**: The large warehouse of the former Richards Broadford Works in Maberly Street was converted in 1995–96 into 51 private dwellings. In 1996 Aberdeen University, mainly based in Old Aberdeen, sold its fine Marischal College building for conversion into a Scandic hotel. Since the mechanised letter office was moving to Altens, the listed former Crown Street post office was for sale in 1996.

**Transport Changes after Regional Government**: In 1996 Aberdeen became a unitary local authority, the demise of Grampian Region again crassly divorcing management of the city from its natural hinterland. But the Aberdeen Shore Porters' Society celebrated 500 years in business in 1998 – over half the city's existence – and its conspicuous juggernauts can still be seen on the road. In 2000 Aberdeen FC were lucky to stay in the Premier League, not due to their performance, but because it was enlarged to 12 clubs! The coastguard station took on duties formerly based in Kirkwall. A new rail freight terminal is planned at Dyce to replace the Guild Street yard in central Aberdeen, where 7.5 ha is proposed for redevelopment for retail, leisure and transport interchange facilities; however the Harbour Board – having provided new roll-on facilities at Matthew's Quay, now with twice-weekly sailings to Amsterdam and also cargo services to Antwerp and Rotterdam – wishes to retain rail access. First Bus has their HQ in the city: they now run 10,000 buses in the UK and employ 50,000 worldwide. The city centre's 4-star hotels include the *Caledonian Thistle* (80 rooms), *Copthorne* (89) and modern *Patio* (124); there is also the central *Grampian* (108 rooms) and a *Travelodge* (95).

## ABERDOUR (Fife) & Inchcolm

**Map 6, B5**

***S. Fife village,*** *pop. 1500*

OS 66: NT 1985

Aberdour is a sheltered spot where the Dour Burn enters the Firth of Forth. Several straight sections of the ancient local road connecting Inverkeithing with Dunearn and Kirkcaldy suggest that the road was possibly of Roman origin. Aberdour's Norman church was first mentioned in 1178, and later

*Inchcolm and its Abbey, with the tourist boat 'Maid of the Forth' in the 1980s. The Abbey was founded by David I; the surviving buildings are mainly of the 13th and 14th centuries.* (RS)

it acquired a Franciscan nunnery. A hermit who lived on Inchcolm, an islet in the Forth 3km south of Aberdour, helped King Alexander I when he was forced ashore there in a storm in 1123; in return the king founded an Augustinian priory on the island. This became an abbey in 1235, and gradually acquired extensive buildings; although sacked in 1542 and 1547, the community survived until 1560.

**Castle and Twin Villages**: Meantime a substantial castle was built at Easter Aberdour in the 14th to 17th centuries for the Douglas family. After their elevation to the Earldom of Morton in 1457, Aberdour became a burgh of barony in 1500; the castle was the home of the 16th century Regent Morton. Pont's map of west Fife, sketched about 1600, shows that by then the Dour Burn had been bridged. By 1629 a school was open, and a fishing harbour was built early in the 18th century. Defoe noted that by the 1720s Regent Morton's property had passed to *"the house of Yester, or Tweeddale"* who had done much *"planting and enclosing"*; but not long after he wrote, the castle was burnt out. The nearby mansion of Aberdour House was apparently soon built as a consequence.

**Shovels for Roadmaking and Quarrying?**: By the time the Roy map was made about 1750 the coastal road between Inverkeithing and Burntisland was clearly marked, and Aberdour which was owned by rival proprietors consisted of the two distinct hamlets, Easter and Wester. By 1757 a post office was open, and by 1797 Aberdour was a post town; by then a short-lived brewery and an ironworking mill making spades and shovels operated. Heron noted in 1799 that it had over 800 inhabitants, and did *"a considerable trade in linen"*, though that industry then faded away. The Earl of Morton's quarry at Hawkcraig produced a hard stone used in early 19th century dock building at Leith, and by 1822 there was another long-lasting sandstone quarrying operation in the Cullaloe Hills 3km north of the village, whose amenities themselves largely survived considerable rock extraction. Aberdour castle ruins remained in existence, to become a draw for modern tourists. By 1827 when Chambers wrote of Aberdour as *"an extremely pleasant little village"*, the newer mansionhouse of Hillside stood in its policies to the north.

**Pleasure Steamers and the first Automatic Lighthouse**: From 1854 pleasure steamers plying out of Leith made Aberdour a favourite destination for Lothian excursionists. Hawkcraig pier was opened about 1865–70 in relatively deep water to facilitate this seasonal traffic, but shallow draught paddle steamers continued to berth at the old stone pier of Wester Aberdour. In summer 1876 the SS *Lord Aberdour* plied to and from the West pier at Leith. The attractive little *Woodside Hotel* was built in 1873, and later enlarged, but the population of the village was still only about 750 in 1891. The Oxcars rocks in the Forth fairway 1.5km south-east of Inchcolm were first illuminated in 1886; only eight years later gas tanks were installed there and the lighthouse became a pioneering automatic operation – by clockwork.

**Railway and Residential Development**: The new Forth Bridge approach line along the shore from Burntisland weaved its way between the two hamlets, and the station which opened in 1890 with its entrances in Wester Aberdour became a pleasantly designed focus for development. Villa building began, and by 1897 when the golf course was opened, the *Aberdour Hotel* was also in use. Silversands, a quiet bay with tree-girt sands just east of the village was already popular by 1900, many decades later becoming an official country park. By 1906 the *Star Hotel* was also open.

**Fortification and Conservation**: Early in World War I a battery for two 233 mm guns was built on a wooded hilltop overlooking Braefoot, and hitherto unspoiled Inchcolm was the most heavily armed of the various Forth islands that were fortified in 1916–17 to protect the Rosyth anchorage. In 1928 the fine panelling and stained glass from RMS *Orontes*, built at Govan and lately broken up at Inverkeithing, was installed in an extension to the *Woodside Hotel*. By 1931 the village population was over 1300. Individual housebuilding continued up to 1939, but the outbreak of war put an end to the steamer trips. In 1898 fifty men worked in the Cullaloe quarries, but they were last exploited in 1948. Although the long-established boatyard continued in work, quarrying at Hawkcraig also ceased.

**Attractions for Tourists**: The village population was some 1500 in 1951, with facilities to match; by 1953 it possessed five hotels, and the harbour was mainly used for yachting. The former mansionhouse of Hillside became a Catholic residential school by 1990. Aberdour lost its post town status in the early 1970s. The quiet tourist found beautiful sheltered coastal walks and the prizewinning gardens of Aberdour's stone-built station, reckoned to be the most attractive in Britain. Small boats provided a summer service from Aberdour to Inchcolm Abbey for a few seasons in the late 1980s.

**The Impact of Braefoot Bay**: Despite fierce opposition from the strong local community, the Braefoot Bay tanker terminal was developed in 1981–83 some 1.5km south-west of the village, to ship propane, butane and natural gasoline fractionated by Shell Expro at Mossmorran *(see Cowdenbeath)*. A broad track passing beneath the railway near Whitehill was filled with ten or more pipelines. The terminal, a major explosion risk, was carefully landscaped. It was owned by Forth Ports, privatised in 1992 (when their *'Authority'* tag was dropped). In the great gales of January 1993 a gas tanker broke from her moorings while loading at Braefoot and with a cargo of butane drifted towards Hawkcraig; she was fortunately brought under control before disaster occurred.

**Top Bankers Commute by Train**: In 1991 Aberdour was an affluent dormitory with 1525 people, containing by far the highest proportion of rail commuters in Scotland, nearly one in four of those at work; the highest proportions in management and administration (almost one in three); and also in banking and finance, at 25%. Aberdour House, for long derelict, became part of a new residential development built in 1991–92. In 1994 and subsequently, Aberdour's beach was among Scotland's cleanest. Hotels in the village include the *Aberdour* and the *Woodside*. The two hamlets still compete annually at football!

## ABERFELDY & Weem — Map 6, A2

***Perthshire small town & hamlet,*** *pop. 1750* — OS 52: NN 8549

The 13th century Kirk of Weem stands at the foot of the steep Weem Hill on the north bank of the upper River Tay; its name derives from the Gaelic for *cave (uamh)*. The great bulk of nearby Castle Menzies dates from 1571; a few years later its facade was sketched in detail by Timothy Pont. His manuscript map also showed a ferry boat crossing the Tay at that point, opposite a mill at Aberfeldy – *'Mouth of the Feldy'* in Pictish Gaelic.

*The bridge over the Tay at Aberfeldy, designed by William Adam and built under his supervision; the finest of the military road bridges, it opened in 1733.* (RS)

**Adam's Tay Bridge and Wade's Military Road**: The monumental high-arched Tay Bridge was designed for the government by William Adam and built under his supervision; it opened in 1733 to carry the new military road, hastily built by troops working westwards past Dull and turning north to Dalnacardoch. By then Weem possessed an inn, which their commander General Wade made his headquarters. The Roy map of about 1750 showed Aberfeldy as a small nucleated place whose only other road led south; Weem Kirk was roadless and surrounded by small hamlets. Aberfeldy's first post office was opened in 1787, the mails going via Dunkeld. In 1797 three annual fairs were scheduled for Kirkton of Weem, and Heron's map of Scotland engraved in 1796 showed *'Weemskirk'* rather than Aberfeldy; however, in 1799 Heron and in 1803 Dorothy Wordsworth called both places *"villages"*.

**Cotton and Whisky**: Heron noted a cotton manufacture in 1799 – a hand-loom weaving factory. From that time Aberfeldy – which had space for development – grew to greater importance than Weem. Illicit stills were replaced in the early 19th century by the tiny Grandtully distillery, over 1 km to the east, built in 1825 and powered by the Cultilloch Burn.

**Railway and Tourism**: The Highland Railway branch line from Ballinluig to Aberfeldy was opened in 1865, and the town acquired a gasworks. It became a minor shopping centre, relying on a tourist trade exploiting its pretty glen, waterfalls, and Adam's historic bridge. In 1886 the Grandtully distillery was the smallest and most primitive in the United Kingdom; its output was only some 22,500 litres of malt whisky. Its owner who worked it with only one helper was resisting proposals for expansion. By 1894 (according to Murray), Aberfeldy was *"a large village, uninteresting in itself"*, but its three hotels included the *"expensive" Breadalbane Arms* and the *"good and comfortable" Weem Hotel*, at which Wade had stayed. The *Palace Hotel* was built in 1899–1902. Meantime a golf club was founded in 1895 and laid out a 9-hole course.

**Whisky and Washing**: Aberfeldy distillery was built in 1896 by John Dewar & Sons (of Perth and the Tullymet distillery), but like many, it closed for a time in the 1930s. The Grandtully operation was last heard of in 1910. Fishers' small laundry, opened in 1900, gradually became the centre of a laundry empire *(see Cupar)*. The last chief of Clan Menzies died in 1918 and the castle, though an ancient monument, became neglected; used in 1939–45 as a Polish Army medical depot, it was derelict by 1970. By the 1950s Aberfeldy's facilities were those of a small town, the mansion of Moness House having become one good hotel among six. Although the next 30 years saw a reversion to the facilities of a large village, by 1981 there were 10 hotels. In 1946 Wordie & Co still operated a small rail to road cartage depot, but the railway was closed completely by Beeching in 1965, the station site going for housing. Machine tools were made in the town around 1970, and the distillery was enlarged to double its capacity in 1973. *(For barytes mines see Tummel Bridge).*

**Education, Food, Drink and Tourism**: Breadalbane Academy was open by 1980; in 1997 it had a roll of 442. By 1981 the water mill was working again as a water-wheel-driven tourist attraction. The massive 16th century tower of Castle Menzies is slowly being restored by a Clan Menzies association; it partly opened to the public in 1980, and its small clan museum was fully opened in 1993. Local initiatives improved the area's facilities: the Recreation Centre which opened in 1984 includes swimming facilities, and by 1985 there was a caravan and camping site. In 1991 when 1750 people lived in Aberfeldy, including a large quite affluent retired element, the distillery was hard at work for United Distillers. In 1993 Tombuie Smokehouse made gourmet products of venison and cheese. The long-established P & J Haggart still manufacture and retail tweeds. The hotels include the *Moness House* (in parkland), the *Guinach*, and the historic *Weem; Farleyer House*, 1 km west of Castle Menzies, was a luxury hotel for several years, but closed in 2001.

## ABERFOYLE & Kinlochard — Map 5, B4

***Village near the Trossachs**, pop. 700* — OS 57: NN 5200

Aberfoyle lies at the foot of the Menteith Hills, on the upper reaches of the River Forth, formerly known as the Abhainn Dhu, which flows from lovely Loch Ard, where there was a prehistoric crannog. Said to have been called *Eperpuill* in the Pictish Gaelic, it was the alleged location of the sixth century fort of Aedan, Prince of the Forth, and had a Dark Age monastery. A market for the sale of bog iron was established thereabouts in the late 15th century. An early bridge was destroyed in 1715, but had been rebuilt as *'Bridge of Aberfoil'* by about 1750. Aberfoyle church and manse were built in 1732–44, but although by then slate quarries had been opened, the Roy map made about 1750 showed a roadless area of scattered hamlets. The Trossachs *(q.v.)* 5 km to the north were opened up by road in the 1760s. Regular fairs were held at Aberfoyle later in the 18th century, but at the start of the 19th century it was still a mere clachan, with an inn and some forestry; Gaelic was still generally spoken. However the coming of good roads changed everything.

**Tourism, Quarries and Railway**: Tourism in the rural Trossachs area immediately quintupled on the publication of Sir Walter Scott's *The Lady of the Lake* in 1810, and by 1838 Aberfoyle had a post office. By 1834 twenty men worked in a slate quarry 3 km north-west of the Kirkton, expanded from 1858 by a company which installed a semicircle of horse-drawn tramway track round the north-east of Craigmore, leading down from what eventually became a complex of four quarries, by way of a steep (12.5%) self-acting inclined plane north-west of the village. In 1882 Aberfoyle became the terminus of a branch railway bringing tourists from the south via Buchlyvie; the station lay virtually over the monastic site. Near the incline was a limestone quarry, and another south-west of Creag Dhubh was linked by a mineral railway to kilns north-east of Aberfoyle.

**More Slate and Golf**: By 1886 the *'Duke's Road'* had been built over the hills to the Trossachs, engineered by Charles Forman of Glasgow (who also laid out the West Highland Railway). With improved transport available, the slate quarry then grew to become the third largest in Scotland, producing 1.4 million slates annually. In 1893 a golf club was founded, which laid out a 9-hole hillside course. The clachan had been rebuilt by 1894, but it was never a burgh despite the *Bailie Nicol Jarvie Hotel* and the two daily horse-drawn coaches which plied to the Trossachs.

**Ocean Billiards and Forest Park**: About 1935 Aberfoyle slate was used by a Kilsyth firm to make the billiard tables for the liner *Queen Mary*. As the demand for roofing slate fell away in the face of cheap mass-produced concrete tiles, the mineral railway from the slate quarries was abandoned in 1947 and the quarries closed in 1958. In 1951 Aberfoyle had a population of about 900 and six hotels, plus the facilities of a typical tourist village; but the railway was closed in that year, the station site becoming a car park. The village subsequently lost its secondary school and chemist. In 1953 the vast Loch Ard Forest covering previously bare hills to the south-west was newly planted; by 1969 it had been designated as the Queen Elizabeth Forest Park. By 1954 the 45-room *Forest Hills Hotel* and a youth hostel were open at beautiful Kinlochard, 6km to the west.

**The Untidy Village of 1975**: In 1975 Aberfoyle was a haphazardly developed one-street tripper centre with a large unsurfaced car park, a seasonal amusement centre, cafes and a tatty ice cream parlour, giving a poor impression likely to deter discerning tourists. But its beautiful surroundings ensured full facilities for visitors, and in season it was busy. One could stay at the *Bailie Nicol Jarvie Hotel*, the *Clachan Hotel, Pavilion Hotel, Rob Roy Motel, Covenanters Inn*, bed & breakfast houses or a residential camp school. Tourists also found gifts and souvenirs, the golf club, information centre, a good tweed shop, craft-shops, the large new *'Trossachs Gift Centre'* and garden shop. Local needs were met by a garage, fire station, two doctors, primary school, bank, post office/general store, Balfron Co-op grocery and other shops, plus a football field and two churches.

**A Tidier Resort**: In 1975 Aberfoyle was transferred from Perthshire to Stirling District in the Central Region. By 1981 its population was down to only 675, and the general services of a small village were supplemented by six hotels, and tourist facilities including a visitor centre at David Marshall Lodge and a caravan site 2 km to the south. But by 1989 the golf course had been extended to 18 holes, and about then the newly built and attractive Scottish Wool Centre was opened, demonstrating hand spinning and weaving among its other tourist facilities. By 1995 Dounans was an all-year Outdoor Education Centre with residential accommodation for 250 students, but by 2000 the youth hostel had closed. The *Forest Hills Hotel*, part of the resort complex at Kinlochard, has 56 rooms and offers various sports facilities.

## ABERLADY

**Map 3, A2**

***E. Lothian village,*** *pop. 850* — OS 66: NT 4680

Probably in the 13th century, and certainly by 1336, there was a Carmelite friary at Luffness, an inlet on the East Lothian coast where a burn falls into a shallow bay some 20km east of Edinburgh. By then a hospital had also been established at Ballencrieff, 3km south-east. In the 14th century Luffness acquired a castle, and at one time had a mill. Nearby Aberlady was the outport of the landlocked burgh of Haddington 8km inland; during the decade of severe scarcity after the Black Death this was a leading source of Scottish customs revenue. Aberlady never became a burgh, its small significance as a port going down as ships gradually increased in size, its customs contribution declining over the next two centuries to around 2% of the total.

**From Shipping to Golfing – and early Dry Rot**: In the 16th century Kilspindie castle was built about 1.5km west of Luffness, but Blaeu's map following Hondius of 1612 showed Ballencrieff and Luffness enclosed, with Aberlady as an inland church plus a line of buildings on the shore. A parish school for Aberlady was founded in 1615, and by 1650 the weavers of Aberlady and Dirleton were competing at golf. By the 1790s the pier was accessible to vessels of only 60–70 tons at the highest spring tides, but Heron in 1799 found a *"village"* of some 400 people. Chambers in the 1820s thought it was a *"little village"* beside which the 18th century Gosford House, *"the seat of the Earl of Wemyss"*, designed by Robert Adam, was about to be pulled down due to extensive dry rot; it was soon rebuilt to house the Duke's art collection, its Adam interiors restored.

**Golf won't make the Railway pay**: Two golf courses originated in 1867, laid out on the links, the Kilspindie to the west of the village and Luffness New to the east. A gasworks was established in 1870. Aberlady had a station on the Gullane branch of the North British Railway, opened in 1898, and by 1901 an inn; but by then the port was dead and the water receded some 2 km at low tide. Aberlady became a quiet residential resort village, but the passenger trains ceased to run in 1932. World War II gave rise to a small Polish hospital, but this was later closed. The population had grown by 1951 to about 1500. The switch to road transport also meant that by 1969 the freight-only railway had been lifted. By 1975 Aberlady Bay was a nature reserve.

**Hotels and Motor Museum**: By 1972 the 13-roomed *Kilspindie House Hotel* was open, and the *Green Craig Hotel* was also open at Harestanes on the coast 2 km to the west. However, the area population had fallen to about 1000, and by 1991 the village alone had 847 residents. The Myreton Motor Museum was established in 1967 some 2 km east of the village, and by 1996 showed a large collection of motor vehicles dating from 1896 to the 1940s. A new golf course was built beside the Kilspindie one in the late 1990s – causing much local disarray! Gosford House was still the prime seat of the Wemyss & March family; an application for housing and 2 golf courses thereby is pending. The *Kilspindie House Hotel* has been doubled in size to 26 rooms.

## ABERLOUR

**Map 10, A2**

***Large Speyside village,*** *pop. 825*

OS 28: NJ 2642

Early in the tenth century St Dunstan baptised the people of central Strathspey in what came to be called *St Drostan's Spring*, which rises on the south bank of the river. A church was built, but no monastery. Pont's map made about 1600 showed *'Abyrlaur'* as a hamlet adjacent to the mouth *(Aber)* of the Lour Burn, which rises from the spring, just downstream of the Kirkton of *'Skeirdustam'*. On Roy's map of the 1750s Aberlour was shown as three dots among other clachans in a totally roadless area, but a post office was opened in 1797.

**Charlestown, Distilling and the Railway**: In 1812 Charles Grant of Wester Elchies built the Aberlour distillery beside the burn on a site previously used for milling, using the water of St Drostan's spring for brewing; but its formal opening was delayed until 1826. Also in 1812 he laid out a new and attractive village, which was chartered as a very late burgh of barony in 1814 under the name of Charlestown. A meal mill and a sawmill were also set up, facilitated by the south Speyside road engineered by Telford, which was apparently complete by about 1815. Benrinnes distillery near Milton of Edinvillie, 3 km to the south, originated in 1835. The Strathspey Railway, later part of the Great North of Scotland, served Aberlour from 1863, giving it a connection to Aberdeen, and from 1866 it was also linked to the south via Boat of Garten. For a time Wordie & Co operated a small rail to road cartage depot.

**A Whisky-dominated Economy**: In 1879 a serious fire hit the original distillery, renamed Aberlour-Glenlivet; it reopened in 1880, its proprietor James Fleming having created *"a perfect model distillery"* (Barnard). In 1886 the distilleries dominated the local economy, both making Highland malt whisky. The Aberlour, which then produced over 360,000 litres per year, had passed to W H Holt & Sons by 1921. The smaller Benrinnes distillery, though continually altered and enlarged, was entirely water-powered in 1886, producing about 225,000 litres annually. Murray called Aberlour *"a thriving little town"* in 1894, though the *Aberlour Hotel* was only *"fair"*. Benrinnes was floated in the boom year 1896, continuing in production in 1902; but the company paid no dividends in 1905–10 and was acquired in 1922 by Buchanan and Dewar's joint subsidiary W P Lowrie of Glasgow.

**Baking, Education and the demise of the Railway**: Joseph Walker established a family bakery in 1898, which put down firm roots. Aberlour House, in the 1890s *"a handsome modern mansion"*, later became a charitable residential school run by the Aberlour Trust until it was closed about 1970. In the 1950s Aberlour was a large village which also possessed a county secondary school; Walker's bakery was growing. The railway was closed to passengers in 1965 and to freight in late 1971 when whisky traffic ceased. By the 1980s the former station had become a cafe and photograph gallery. However, some jobs were created when the attractive modern Glenallachie distillery was built 1 km south of the Aberlour-Glenlivet in 1967–68. In its last years the town council boasted of its bowling, tennis and fishing facilities; in 1975 Aberlour was placed in Moray district.

**Biscuits and Road Haulage Expand**: Walkers' bread, cake, shortbread and oatcake bakery continued to expand. By the 1970s 100 people were employed by the family, and a new 1850 m$^2$ factory built in 1976–77 doubled its floorspace to complete a large modern operation. In 1990 McPhersons Transport of Aberlour was a large road haulage concern, also operating freight depots at Keith and Elgin. Benrinnes distillery was in full production for United Distillers in 1991, producing a dark single malt matured in sweet sherry casks, but struggling to improve the quality of its river-polluting effluent. The same problem affected Glenallachie, closed for a time but reopened in 1989, and also Aberlour (*'Glenlivet'* had been dropped from its title by 1991), which produced a *"subtle"* single malt. Both were owned by Campbell Distilleries, a subsidiary of the French drinks giant Pernod Ricard; the firm had doubled its exports over the period 1987–90.

**Walkers Shortbread and the Prince's Biscuit**: By 1992 Walkers Shortbread Ltd was said to be the largest independent biscuit maker in Britain, under the founders' grandchildren: as its sales and marketing boss said, *"run by bakers not accountants"*. They co-operated with the Duchy of Cornwall to use organic oats and wheat grown at Highgrove to make a cross between oatcakes and wheatmeal biscuits, launched in 1993 as *'Duchy Originals'*. In 1994 between 600 and 700 people were employed, depending on the season, including 30 in a new branch in Elgin. In 1995 using the traditional natural ingredients – flour, sweet cream butter, sugar and salt – Walkers not only made 60% of all the shortbread exported from Scotland, but had become the largest biscuit exporter in Britain, serving over 40 countries: firms that rely on chemical additives please note!

**Village, Tourism and Education**: Meantime despite Walkers' growth, local population decline had been marked: Aberlour had only 821 residents in 1991. However by then a caravan and camping site was open, and by 1994 a museum. By 1994 Aberlour House was back in business as an independent boarding preparatory school, with 100 mixed pupils in 2000. Between 1996 and 2000 Speyside High School at Aberlour, which had 432 pupils, also absorbed 27 pupils from distant Tomintoul, which formerly had its own small secondary school. Some maps still mark Aberlour 'Charlestown of Aberlour'.

## ABERNETHY (Perthshire)

**Map 6, B3**

***Village, s-e. of Perth,*** *pop. 900*

OS 58: NO 1816

A hill fort overlooks the fertile site of Abernethy, which guards the land access to Fife from the north. The *Venicones* had a strong timber fort there in 209 AD, when the Roman troops of Septimus Severus built a small outpost fortress beside the Tay estuary. This may have been known as *Orrea*, later called Carpow, meaning *Fortress Port* in Cumbric. Both port and bath remains of the third century have been found nearby, and its garrison is known to have drunk wine flavoured with horehound for chest complaints. Such a sophisticated settlement 40 km north of the Antonine Wall confirms the strength of the native civilisation.

**Abernethy as a Religious Centre**: Abernethy village, 2 km south-west of Carpow, does not actually lie near the mouth *(Aber)* of any stream, so its name is puzzling. A church existed in the fifth century and a Columban monastery in the sixth. A bishopric was established at Abernethy by the Pictish King Nechtan IV around 715; there is a Pictish symbol stone. The rare round tower at Abernethy is most probably of late eighth or early ninth century origin, for the see was transferred to Dunkeld before 865, when the abbot of Iona re-established

Columban monks at Abernethy. Chambers claimed that medieval Abernethy had *"one of the most extensive Culdee establishments, consisting of a university and a monastery"*. In 1072 a treaty was made at Abernethy between Malcolm Canmore and William I of England, and in the late 12th century the church was granted to the new Arbroath abbey. In 1272 an Augustinian priory was established on the former Culdee site, and by 1400 there was a collegiate church.

**The Burgh that stayed a Village**: Abernethy was chartered as a burgh of barony in 1458. It was called a *"town"* in 1592, but although the parish had a school by 1632, James Gordon's map of Fife, made in 1642, gave Abernethy only slight emphasis. Ferries across the Earn and the Tay connected Carpow with Rhynd and Inchyra by 1647, and shoes were sold at Abernethy market in 1657, but the claim by the generally reliable French traveller Jorevin de Rocheford that it was among the thirteen *"principal towns"* of Scotland in 1661 is not confirmed by other accessible sources.

**Off the Road, on to and off the Railway**: Roy's map surveyed about 1750 did not even accord Abernethy the dignity of upper case lettering. No link was shown into the village from what was then the area's only defined road, connecting from Bridge of Earn by way of the narrow and winding lane over the hills which was still the direct way to Strathmiglo in the 1990s. Abernethy's only early industry of note seems to have been an oil mill, operating nearby in 1775, and although there were two annual fairs in 1797, Heron wrote in 1799 *"the inhabitants of this ancient city, so much decayed, may still amount to about a thousand"*. Chambers noted in 1827 that *"Abernethy is now an insignificant village"*. There was then a ferry at the confluence of the Earn and Tay, but a post office was not established until around 1825. From 1848 to 1955 Abernethy had a station, built by the Edinburgh & Northern Railway on the Burntisland to Perth line; this outlasted the ferries. There was also a gasworks, and by 1893 the *Abernethy Hotel*.

**Productive but Peaceful**: In the 20th century Abernethy remained a village of rather under 1000 people. Despite its long history and highly active farming community there was not very much for the tourist, though by 1974 there was a caravan and camping site. Robert Clow's small but long-established ladies' nightwear factory served prestigious customers, in 1989 including Harrods and Jenners. By then Abernethy had a large depot of West Cumberland Farmers, and a local bakery also serving parts of Fife and Kinross. The village population in 1991 was 895; a sewage disposal works built in 1994–95 enabled some new housing development to continue. Now there's a museum, hotel, pubs, primary school, garage, post office cum shop, bakery, and a new small factory manufacturing Highland dress.

## ABINGTON — Map 2, B2

***Village, Upper Clydesdale,*** *pop. 500* — OS 71 or 72: NS 9323

The Pont map of Upper Clydesdale showed the farms of Over and Nether Abington, where the steep hills crowned by prehistoric forts – of which the nearest is Arbory – fall back to give travellers from Beattock a choice of routes to the north. Roy's survey of about 1754 showed the Clyde Bridge about 3km north of *'Ebbingtone'*, and a road network that was to change little for over 200 years, though the bridge at Abington itself was to appear later. The station which was opened with the new Caledonian Railway in 1847 was described as *'first class'*, i.e. comparable with Beattock and Lockerbie. Abington looked quite significant on the 1895 OS map, with its church, station, post and telegraph office, inn and smithy. Between the wars and after, the LMS-owned Wordie & Co had a rail to road cartage depot, and Abington had a fire station by 1950.

**The Trunk Road Epoch**: As motor traffic grew, Abington provided more services where the A74 trunk road from the south forked to Glasgow and Edinburgh. The *Abington Hotel* had 30 rooms and three AA stars in 1956; then Abington was a post town with the facilities of a typical village, also including a transport cafe, a surviving blacksmith and a doctor; the AA garage with its breakdown service was open day and night. These facilities were also available to the local population of about 625, but some served about 2800 people in all, as far away as Crawford and Wanlockhead.

**After Bypass and Beeching, the Motorway**: By 1964 the A74 bypass was newly open. As the dual carriageways were extended so Abington's significance to road travellers plummeted. As a result of the Beeching plan, the closure of the station took place between 1963, when it had three weekday trains each way, and 1967, when only similarly infrequent buses were available to Lanark, Dumfries and Edinburgh. At the 1971 census 260 people were enumerated in the nearby outdoor centre known as Glengonnar Camp School. By 1981 Abington was no longer a post town, though a post office remained; the facilities of a small village served a total of under 800 people, including the Crawfordjohn and Roberton areas. In the mid 1990s the A74 was converted into a motorway, following the completion by 1992 of a wholly new section of the M74 from Abington to Douglas Mill; a service area and motel were built at its new intersection with the A73/A702. The very oddly named 9-hole *Arbory Brae Hickery Golf Links* is now open; the old *Abington Hotel* has 27 rooms, and *Days Inn* is a 56-roomed lodge.

## ABOYNE, Birse & Glentanar — Map 10, B4

***Large Deeside village,*** *pop. 2050* — OS 37: NO 5298

Aboyne (in Gaelic meaning *The Current*) lies in an exceptionally beautiful area on the north bank of the River Dee nearly 45km west of Aberdeen. Its prehistoric stone circle was later adjoined by a castle, the site of a thanage from about the 11th century; a century later the Forest of Birse to the south became a royal hunting reserve. From about 1242 Aboyne was owned by the Knights of St John *(see Torphichen)*, but by the late 15th century it was a property of the Gordons of Huntly. By about 1600 as Pont's sketch showed, the Water of Tanar which enters the Dee opposite Aboyne had been bridged, but Aboyne itself was not in the mapped area. In the 16th century the tower of Birse Castle was built beside the remote Water of Feugh 9km south of Aboyne.

**Charlestown of Aboyne**: Aboyne Castle was rebuilt about 1671 by Charles, Marquis of Huntly, who obtained a Barony charter in 1676 for a nearby settlement, first known as *Charlestown of Aboyne* (after its founder). The Roy map made about 1750 showed the name in full, relating to a well-defined hamlet on the west bank of the Tarland Burn. It lay on what was then the only road in the area, the north Deeside road, but a bridge had not yet been built across the burn, nor was there a named *'boat'* across the Dee. However, a track led south over the hills to Birse and crossed a 595m pass to Tarfside in Glen Esk.

**Facilities, Bridges, Coaches and Jewels**: An annual fair was being held by 1797, and a post office arrived. In 1828 the River Dee was bridged near Aboyne, giving easy access to Glentanar and the by then little-populated south bank; though the new structure was swept away by the great floods of 1829 it was soon replaced, by a rather flimsy suspension bridge. A jeweller was established in 1850, by which time two daily coaches ran to Banchory, one of which continued to Ballater.

**The Deeside Railway makes a Resort**: In 1859 the Deeside Extension Railway was opened from Banchory to a fine new stone-built station beside the village nucleus at Aboyne, first surmounting a steep grade of 1.4% (1 in 70) to a 186 m summit at Tillychin. It seems that there was as yet no hotel of any size in the village. The line was extended to Ballater in 1866, Aboyne becoming a crossing station, rebuilt about 1890. The Dee suspension bridge failed in 1869 and was replaced by a sturdier third bridge in 1871. Aboyne lost its burgh status in 19th century reorganisations of local government, but due to its situation and the financial contribution of millionaire Sir Cunliffe Brooks, it grew into a large village and minor resort. A golf club was founded in 1883 and laid out an 18-hole parkland course. The noted photographer and ornithological author Seton Gordon was born in Aboyne in 1886.

**Hotel, Electric Power, Phone Centre, Dud Batteries and No Trains**: By 1894 there were monthly livestock markets, and to Murray the *Huntly Arms* was a *"good"* hotel. Around 1900 there was also a railway platform some 1.5 km north-east at the Loch of Aboyne, for winter curling and skating excursionists and summer visitors. A small power station was built in 1914, and in 1924 the substantial War Memorial Hall; the bridge was rebuilt again around 1930. By 1951 Aboyne's population was little more than 1200, but with the facilities of a large village; by virtue of its remoteness, it also became a telephone group centre. Unsuccessful trials in 1958–62 of battery-powered railcars, which more than once broke down in mid-section – causing frantic phone calls from a lineside bed and breakfast house at Heugh-Head – contributed to the railway being closed completely in 1966 under the Beeching cuts; the former station building became shops. Six hotels existed in 1980, and camping and picnic sites were available by 1985.

**Modern Aboyne – Bigger and Warmer!**: By 1991 Aboyne itself had grown to some 2050 people, with an affluent retirement element, new housing estates both east and west, and a new Aboyne Academy, some facilities serving a total population of about 6000. A visitor centre, forest walks and viewpoints had opened up the hilly Forest of Glen Tanar. On exceptional days in June 1994 (28 degrees) and July 1999 (31 degrees), sheltered Aboyne was the warmest place in Britain. To the east at Aboyne Loch is the Aberdeen Water Ski Club, adjoined by a caravan park, with the golf course nearby; 4 km to the west is the small airfield of a gliding club. In 2000 a new Co-op store was built on the site of the long-derelict cattle market. Strachans sell a vast range of goods; various specialist shops opposite the broad central green space include a chemist and outdoor clothing. The well-kept and friendly village has two banks, hospital, police and fire stations, a community centre, the *Huntly Arms Hotel*, restaurants and attractive B&Bs.

## ACHARACLE & Ardtoe — Map 4, C1

***Lochaber village & hamlet,*** *pop. 1200 (area)* OS 40: NM 6767

For centuries the short River Shiel, which outflows from the west end of the 30 km long Loch Shiel, divided the counties of Inverness and Argyll. The compact Castle Tioram was built in 1353 on a tidal islet at the river mouth for Lady Anne MacRuari, divorced wife of the first Lord of the Isles and mother of the founder of Clan Ranald. It was burnt in the 1715 uprising but remains an impressive ruin accessible on foot at low tide. Roy's map made about 1750, the first to detail this remote Jacobite area, showed it well wooded and trackless. In the early 19th century under Telford's guidance, a road was built to open up the area from Corran Ferry via Loch Sunart to reach Acharacle *(in Gaelic 'Field of Noisy Ducks')* at the loch's end, then crossing a new Shiel Bridge about 1810 and wriggling north to end at Kinlochmoidart. A Presbyterian church was later built with government funding, but many Catholic families remained from pre-Reformation times.

**After the Clearances: Steamers and Shellfish**: Clearances were still taking place in the Ardnamurchan peninsula as late as the 1850s. Later a hotel was opened at Shiel Bridge, becoming an anglers' resort. From 1893 there was also a pier which formed the terminus of a steamer service, plying the length of beautiful Loch Shiel to Glenfinnan until at least 1956. Acharacle had a post office by 1913, and by the 1950s was a post town with the commended *Acharacle Hotel*, yet its population – including the hamlet of Mingarrypark north of the river – was little over a hundred. There were however both County and Roman Catholic primary schools – a divisive situation! By 1971 the road had been continued through to Lochailort, and by 1975 the White Fish Authority had moved its shellfish cultivation unit from North Wales to the inconsequential township of Ardtoe, on the coast of sheltered Kentra Bay 6 km north-west of Acharacle, where it also established a farm for cod.

**Clever Halibut**: In that year 1975 the county boundary vanished as the area was unified within the new Lochaber District. The facilities at straggling Acharacle served a widening area, some extending to the whole of the beautiful Ardnamurchan peninsula, and by 1981 catered to the basic needs of some 1200 people. They were approaching those of an average village, with emphasis on tourism and road transport; in 1984 the tiny post office handled local mail sorting and was the base for three vans. By 1989 the researchers of the Sea Fish Marine Unit at Ardtoe were studying halibut farming under the Sea Fish Industry Authority; in 1994 they described this very large predatory food fish as more intelligent than a horse, but dimmer than a dolphin! In 1997 the post office, school and two inns were still open, and there was a museum at Mingarrypark. A proposal of 2000, to rebuild the roofless Castle Tioram as a home, plus a clan museum, was approved by the Highland Council but opposed by Historic Scotland; a public inquiry was pending.

## ACHILTIBUIE & Tanera More — Map 12, A3

***W. Ross small village & island,*** *pop. 100* OS 15: NC 0208

West of the mountains of Coigach and north of Loch Broom lies the long peninsula of *Rubha More*, once part of the scattered county of Cromarty. Badentarbat Bay on its south coast is somewhat sheltered from the west by the Summer Isles, the largest of which is Tanera More, good for grazing. The bay is lined by several crofting townships, some of them named on Blaeu's map of Northern Scotland derived from Gordon's work about 1650, though only *'Killbuy'* appeared in a trackless area on the Roy map made a century later, perhaps representing the ancient chapel near Badenscallie. In 1773 the ship *Hector* took on board at Tanera pier some 200 destitute people from Lochbroom, lured by misrepresentation and destined to be dumped and left to starve without resources in a Nova Scotia forest *(Shaw)*.

**Fish and Smuggling**: In 1784 the British Fisheries Society founded a fishing station on Tanera More, capable for a century of supporting 100 people, who eked out a living by whisky moonlighting and smuggling. Salmon fishing was a 19th century feature. Very late – perhaps around 1900 – a road was built into the area from the main west coast road, connecting near Achiltibuie with the short coastal road linking the tiny townships. Tanera More was abandoned in 1931 but had intermittent residents, including Fraser Darling, there in the role of agricultural improver.

**Tourists and Salmon**: By 1951 only about 75 people lived in the remote area, yet by then the village of Achiltibuie *(Yellow Field)* had a pier, primary school, post office, 11-line telephone exchange and the 16-roomed *Summer Isles Hotel*, which became famous for growing most of its own produce under shelter, also using hydroponics. The Achininver youth hostel stood by the coast 3km to the east and there was also a doctor, though gone by 1978. By 1985 a caravan site was open at Achnahaird Bay, 7km to the north. Tanera More, by then owned by the Framptons of London, was recolonised in the 1980s with a salmon farm filling its bay, and by 1988 held 11 adults and 5 children; in the 1990s it too had a post office. Achiltibuie retains its hotel, post office and primary school, and the Achininver youth hostel is still open in summer.

## ACHNACARRY & Clunes — Map 5, A1

***Settlement, nr Spean Bridge,** pop. 100* — OS 41: NN 1787

At the foot of Glen Cia-aig some 10km north-west of Spean Bridge are waterfalls, *"in spate a splendid sight"* (Bolton). About 1 km to the south, beside the short River Arkaig which flows through a defile lined with attractive woods from beautiful Loch Arkaig into Loch Lochy, stood the ancient home of the Camerons of Locheil. This was burnt out as a result of the 1745 rebellion, but rebuilt for them within half a century into Achnacarry House, described by Alistair Spencer-Nairn as *"a large mansion set in a park"* (in the Gaelic, Achnacarry would mean *Field of the Cia-aig)*. From 1803 Loch Arkaigside contributed its finest trees of fir, ash and birch to the building of the Caledonian Canal by Telford, who laid out a road into the estate. This also lost its people, cleared by Donald Cameron of Locheil between 1782 and 1832, leaving a scattered population of under 100, who were later served by a primary school and post office. Commandos were trained in the area in 1939–45. The population rose somewhat in the late 20th century, enabling the post office to survive, and a museum and forest walks – accessed via Clunes, 3km east – were open by 1997.

## ACHNASHEEN — Map 12, A5

***W. Highlands settlement,** pop. 125* — OS 25: NH 1658

The high moors of Strath Bran, some 150m above sea level, were linked with Poolewe via Kinlochewe by a track passing the site of Achnasheen, aptly translatable as the *'Field of the Rain'*, and in the mid 18th century ending at Bortinicarlach, some 5km west of Loch Achanalt. In the early 1800s Achnasheen became the junction for Telford's very problematic new road, constructed down the defile of Glen Carron to Loch Carron, which left the earlier track near Ledgowan *(Green Nook at the Fork)*. The Achnasheen bridge was built about 1818 and the new road was eventually opened in 1819; however the Poolewe road was not among those improved by the Commissioners.

**The Hotel on the Railway Platform**: The Dingwall & Skye Railway, built to follow the Telford route by the Highland Railway, opened in 1870 with crossing stations at Achanalt and Achnasheen. The latter also served the remote Poolewe area, and for a time Wordie & Co operated a small rail to road cartage depot. By the 1890s what must have been a primitive inn, soon to vanish, stood at Garawgan west of the little Loch Gowan; the modest little railway-owned *Achnasheen Hotel* served passengers very readily as it stood on the eastbound station platform! Up to the mid 20th century Achnasheen station still handled sundries traffic, and its little post office was a *'post town'* or local sorting centre; a primary school served some 300 scattered residents. By 1972 *Ledgowan Lodge* had become a hotel. Despite Beeching's proposal to close the Kyle line, the stations and the Achnasheen passing loop remain open, though only for passengers from 1964; but the *Achnasheen Hotel* was destroyed by fire in 1995 and the site cleared. The school, shop and post office continue in use, plus new cafe at the station; petrol is still for sale at Achanalt. The seasonal *Ledgowan Lodge Hotel* offers 11 rooms.

## ADDIEWELL (or Addiebrownhill) — Map 16, C4

***W. Lothian village,** pop. 1300* — OS 65: NS 9962

*'Adiwel'* in West Lothian, which stands south of the Breich Water and 3km south-west of West Calder, appeared on Pont's map of about 1600. By the 1750s the area was served by roads towards Edinburgh. Taking advantage of the North British Railway's branch line which was opened through Fauldhouse and Whitburn in 1864, mineral railways were laid from West Foulshiels (south of Whitburn) to Addiewell where oil shale workings were opened. There in 1866 James Young's Paraffin Light and Mineral Oil Company built the Addiewell Chemical Works, a major oil distillation plant, managed by Young himself *(see Bathgate)*.

**Young's Addiewell Shale Oil Complex**: By 1869 the Caledonian Railway's new Calder branch passed beside Young's plant, a 30ha sprawl of plant and sidings just east of Addiewell station, believed at that time to be the largest oilworks in the world. It employed over 1000 workers; the retort sheds were 200m long, and the main oil-collecting pipe nearly 1m in diameter. About 35,000m³ of gas was produced daily, some of which was used to heat boilers, the surplus being *'offered'* to Edinburgh and West Calder for street lighting and domestic use. Ammonia was also produced and sold, and candles were made from the wax. By 1869 the related pits – which also supplied the Bathgate works – employed 400 miners; Young's 1400 employees constituted nearly half of all those then at work in the Scottish oil industry. The firm also erected a virtually new settlement at Addiewell, its 360 houses and a school being built of bricks made from local clay and burned on site. Young retired to Wemyss Bay in 1871.

**Culmination and Decline**: By 1873 seven shale mines were open, and at its peak in the 1880s, 2000 people were employed, producing 36 million litres of crude oil. By 1891 Addiewell – also known as Addiebrownhill – had 1700 people and a post office. By then the area was littered with old shafts and shale mines linked by mineral railways; quarries and coal pits extended south-westwards right up the valley of the Woodmuir Burn to a point 5 km south-west of Addiewell. Early in the 20th century a water works and reservoir was built 3 km to the south. Another large rail-connected works was built near Mossend, 2 km south of Young's original works, and more accessible to West Calder. The industry was uneconomic by the 1950s; the Addiewell works were closed and cleared in 1956, its site becoming an industrial estate. By 1971 the last oil works had closed.

**Whisky Bonds and Concrete Pipes**: Addiewell station has survived, served by stopping trains to Edinburgh and Glasgow. By 1975 large bonded warehouses had been lately built nearby; beside them a hotel was open. Stanton & Staveley had developed a works to manufacture concrete pipes, and an industrial estate had also been provided. In 1991 *'Addiebrownhill'* held over 1300 residents, 83% of them living in council housing; 60% of households had no car. Apart from periodic extensions to the bonds (N. British Distillers now employ 70) there had been little development to 1998, but the station, post office and hotel remain open. Addiewell North bing is now a nature reserve.

## AE, Parkgate & The Barony — Map 2, B4

***Dumfriesshire villages,*** *pop. 300* — OS 78: NX 9889

By late Victorian times the emparked mansion of Kirkmichael House stood north of the Water of Ae (pronounced *Eh?)* some 12 km north-north-east of Dumfries; hence the name of the hamlet of Parkgate with its post office and smithy on the Dumfries to Moffat road. The new village of Ae – endowed with the shortest placename in Britain – was built for the Forestry Commission in 1947 4 km west of Parkgate to house workers in the new and extensive Forest of Ae. In 1980 it had a Forestry Commission Management Training Centre and workshops. Though for a time the population of Ae had exceeded 400, by 1981 it was down to some 330, with a post office and primary school. Meantime Kirkmichael House had become in turn the Barony School and the Barony Agricultural College; by 1982 this was unique in Europe in also having a fish farm. Renamed Barony College in 1988, by 1993 it offered courses in all main economic activities of the countryside. Meantime by 1981 William Clark Ltd, engineers of the former Parkgate smithy, handled agricultural and land reclamation equipment. Ae retains its post office/store; an outdoor centre is open at Burnfoot, 2 km to the north.

## AILSA CRAIG — Map 1, B3

***Small island off Ayrshire coast*** — OS 76: NS/NX 0200

Ailsa Craig is a 338 m tall volcanic rock 16 km to the west of Girvan, an almost circular islet 1 km across which on most sides rises sheer from the sea. A castle tower was built there in the 16th century. In 1549 Monro noted that the Ness, a tiny low promontory near the castle, was a white fishing base. Around 1690 Martin noted fishermen living there seasonally in tents, anchoring the boats from which they fished for cod and ling. A gas-lit lighthouse was completed on Ailsa Craig in 1886; for many years curling stones were made from granite quarried on the islet, which later became a bird sanctuary. In 1979 the families of the lightkeepers, by then minding an electric lamp, were based in Girvan, but eventually automation took over. Small inserts of Ailsa Craig granite are still used in modern curling stones *(see Mauchline)*. Boat-trips can be arranged.

## AIRDRIE & Whiterigg — Map 16, A4

***Lanarkshire large town,*** *pop. 37,000* — OS 64: NS 7665
*Suburb: Drumgelloch*

Airdrie stands about 130 m above sea level in the Monklands of north Lanarkshire, 16 km due east of Glasgow. The name Airdrie is said to derive from the Gaelic *Ard Ruith, 'High Pasture'*. The Battle of Airdrie in 577 ensured independence for Strathclyde, but Airdrie's subsequent history could be better documented; it was not shown on Mercator's late 16th century map. However the name appeared four times on Blaeu's mid 17th century atlas which derived from Pont's and Gordon's work, in forms such as *Ardry* and *Ardryhill*, and emphasised symbols were used. Airdrie was held in the 1620s by Sir John Preston. Airdrie market was chartered in 1695, and by the time of Roy's survey of the early 1750s it was a substantial town on a cross plan, with at least six radial roads, and important enough for Roy to name it as the intermediate point of the main road from Glasgow to Edinburgh. Lee End quarry was open to the north, and evidence of coal mining showed both to the west and at Drumgelloch to the east. Turnpiking of the Glasgow to Edinburgh road was completed in 1797.

**Engineering and Weaving**: Dick & Stevenson established the comparatively little known but long-lasting Airdrie Engine Works in 1790. In the 1790s 227 linen weavers were noted in East Monkland, mostly working for Glasgow manufacturers. By 1797 no fewer than five annual fairs were scheduled, and Heron in 1799 noted that *"the village, or town, of Airdrie, regularly built, flourishes from the advantage of coal, and the industry of its inhabitants in various branches of manufacture. It has a weekly market"*. He thought the population was about eighteen hundred. A post office was open by 1802, and in 1816 experiments were made at Airdrie to find the best way to mill flax.

**Burgh and early Railways**: In 1821 Airdrie became almost the last of the many burghs of barony to be chartered; from this time onwards it grew fast. The Town House with its clock tower and spire was built in 1824–26, by which time James Thomson's brewery was at work. By 1824 the Palacecraig coal pit to the south was open, and two years later this was served by the early 4'6" (137 cm) gauge Monkland & Kirkintilloch Railway, which carried coal and passengers, horse-drawn all the way. From 1828 the associated Ballochney Railway, also horse worked and plagued by steep inclines, passed close by on its way from a colliery north-east of Airdrie; its station was at Commonhead. By then the town was known for cotton-weaving.

**Gas, Oil Shale and Through Passengers**: The Airdrie Gas Light Company was set up in 1830 and built its works in Mill Street beside the Fruitfield coal pit. In 1840 the Slamannan Railway opened from a junction with the Ballochney line at Airdriehill near Rawyards; for two years this formed a link in the best (though makeshift) route for passengers from Edinburgh to Glasgow via the Union Canal and Causewayend. By 1842 four daily Garnkirk & Glasgow Railway trains linked Airdrie and Coatbridge rather indirectly with Glasgow, and the Bank of Scotland had an Airdrie branch by about 1843. Oil-shale mines and refineries operated in the area from 1850. Hallcraig Station, built in 1856, was later used only for goods, having been quickly superseded by a new station, Airdrie South on the Bathgate & Coatbridge railway which opened in 1862, later becoming part of the North British system. Already by 1860 Wordie & Co had a modest rail to road cartage depot; by 1903 this needed 12 horses.

**Culture, Entertainment and Expansion**: Airdrie was sufficiently high-lying to be free of the worst smoke from Coatbridge, and became more residential in character. A bowling club was started in 1852 and the local newspaper, the *Airdrie & Coatbridge Advertiser* was founded in 1855. In 1856 Airdrie earned the distinction of opening the first local authority library, and in 1858 came fine classical County Buildings and Courts. The mansionhouse of Arranview, built in 1867, was designed by famous Glasgow architect Alexander *'Greek'* Thomson. A large workingmen's club was founded in 1869, Airdrie golf club originated in 1877 and the *Airdrieonians* FC in 1878. In 1885 the Clarkston and Rawyards areas north and east of Drumgelloch were added to the burgh, but Whiterigg, a hamlet some 1.5 km east of Rawyards, stayed outside; by 1891 it had a population of 640, a station, primary school and post office.

**Castings, Steam Hammers and Wire Ropes**: In 1871 the Airdrie Engine Works built steam hammers, and later under G Inglis & Co manufactured steam winding and haulage engines – and also locomotives – for coal mines. Shields & McNichol established the Sheepford boiler works about 1876; later it passed to Thomas Hudson & Co. In the late 19th century John Martin were ironfounders. Other industries included the Airdrie Light Engineering Works and a wire rope works. In 1886–88 a Caledonian Railway (CR) branch line was built from Newhouse via a triangular junction near the Bellsdyke colliery to a terminus at Graham Street.

**Airdrie in the 1890s: Penalties, Cotton and Racing**: In 1891 some 19,000 people lived in the burgh, which was an important local service centre though it still lacked a hotel; the early *Airdrie Inn* at the Cross had become the *Royal Hotel* by 1914, and later still was called the Royal Buildings. Broomfield Park, a football ground since at least 1871, saw the world's first football penalty kick in 1891 and became the home of Airdrieonians FC in 1892. The Alexandra School was replaced by Airdrie Academy, opened in 1895. By then Airdrie House, a former home of the Hamiltons, stood in modest policies 1 km west of the town near Coatdyke station, and a small racecourse was situated south of Rawyards; however this was soon closed, for a much grander course had opened at Hamilton in 1887. In 1894 Airdrie was described by Murray as *"a busy mining town, dependent on the collieries in the vicinity, and on some cotton works"*. These were substantial, standing beside the former Ballochney railway west of Rawyards; other mineral lines writhed around the area's hillsides.

**Tubes, Trams and Edwardian Entertainment**: The Imperial Tube Works was built in 1898–1900, becoming one of the town's main employers; it made guns and shells in 1914–18. Airdrie's own small electric power station was established in 1899; the Airdrie & Coatbridge tramways opened in 1904 with a terminus in Forrest Street near Motherwell Street. In 1904 the gas company was bought by the town council. The cotton mill was still in operation in 1907, with mainly women workers, and about 1910 the Airdrie Iron Company was making shears for cutting up scrap metal. Beardmore's of Parkhead operated a branch factory at Airdrie during the 1914–18 war. West End Park was laid out in 1909–13 and the Town Hall opened in 1912, named after the local benefactor Sir John Wilson, then of Airdrie House, which became a maternity hospital in 1919. The *Hippodrome Variety Theatre* was created in 1908 from a former market building and indoor fairground. A roller-skating rink built in Graham Street about 1910 was soon converted into the *Pavilion Cinema*.

**Football Cup, Road Rollers and Biscuits**: In 1924 Airdrieonians FC won the Scottish Cup! In 1922 Glasgow Corporation had bought the local tramways and built a link to Baillieston, keeping their fares minimal. Soon trams ran through from Forrest Street to Paisley; a service to Ferguslie Park lasted until about 1940. But by then bus routes competed, also serving Chapelhall, Harthill and Shotts. James Taylor of Wheatholme was a major inter-war baker of bread, cakes and biscuits, delivered by a fleet of lorries, while the little-known firm of Gibb & Hobb of Airdrie were still building steam-driven roadrollers in 1928; one of their locomotives is preserved at Summerlee Heritage Centre.

**Leisure, Crisps and PLUTO**: Sewage disposal works were built in 1928–35 near the Rochsolloch Ironworks. With economic decline, and competition from buses, the rail passenger services to Slamannan and Newhouse ended in 1930. The covered Public Baths were opened in 1935, complete with gymnasium and laundry. In 1938 the *Hippodrome* became the *Rialto Cinema*, and in 1962 a mere bingo hall. The former wire rope works were used for a time to grow mushrooms, but Crimpy Crisps took over the factory in 1938. The Imperial Tube Works made pipes for the Normandy beachhead fuel supply project of 1944, code-named *PLUTO (Pipe Line Under The Ocean)*. Whiterigg had practically vanished by 1954, its school remaining for a year or two.

**Children, Chemicals and Blue Trains**: In 1950 Arranview became a children's home. Boots the Chemists brought a factory to Rawyards in 1949, and the radio manufacturers Pye of Cambridge came to Airdrie in the 1950s. By then Airdrie's facilities were those of a substantial town, and by the 1960s it had almost coalesced physically with its close neighbour Coatbridge. Rail passenger services from Airdrie through Coatbridge to Glasgow and Helensburgh were electrified with *'Blue Trains'* in 1961, but rail services to Bathgate ceased about the time of the tramway closure in 1956. By 1979 the CR station site had been developed with a new bus station and a supermarket.

**Hospital, Fire, Subsidence and Council Houses**: The Airdrie House maternity hospital was closed in 1962 and demolished in 1964, its site being used from 1971 to build the 584-bed Monklands District General Hospital, which opened in 1977. In 1969 the Crimpy Crisps factory went up in smoke. Due to mining subsidence, the same year saw the demolition of the attractive Royal Buildings and the County Buildings, both sites later being redeveloped. By 1972 Airdrie burgh held the dubious distinction of having over 81% of its people living in council housing, more than any other town in Scotland.

**Stresses in Monklands District**: Airdrie lost its burgh status in 1975, becoming part of the Monklands District whose main offices were located in Coatbridge, a sore point because socially Airdrie remained strongly Protestant while later Coatbridge, settled at the time of Irish famines, was still largely Catholic. This made for stresses in the new authority, Airdrie people complaining that all new facilities were located in somewhat larger Coatbridge. In 1981 Airdrie had four small hotels. The rail link through to Bathgate was abandoned in 1982. But Airdrie remained an important local centre, with its rail terminal and bus station, and the new sheriff court served a wide area. In 1987 historic Arranview was converted into flats, but its setting, like its interiors, was lost: for local views see *McCutcheon (1994)*. The town's only purpose-built picture house, the 1100 seater *New Cinema*, was closed about 1970 and later demolished; however, a listed former branch office of the Clydesdale Bank was saved from dereliction in the late 1990s. Remarkably, in 1993 the Gaelic National Mod was held in English-speaking Airdrie, which was also the proud possessor of one of Britain's four public observatories.

**Industrial Airdrie**: In 1989 forgings were produced by British Steel at what they then called the Imperial Finishing Works, where about 1000 people worked; imported pipes prepared at the former Clydesdale Tube Works were still being threaded and finished there in 1992 (although only 250 now employed, as Vallourec). In 1991–95 Pye's successors, the ailing Dutch giant Philips Electrical – locally based in Hamilton – still had a branch factory in Airdrie, making telephones. Coal opencasting, controversially proposed at Drumshangie Moss, 3km north of the town centre in 1992, continues in 2001. In 1993 Boots made cosmetics and toiletries at their Airdrie factory (800 employed), while R Carmichael & Sons produced a liqueur from Scottish malt whisky and cream, marketed as *Heather Cream*. In 1994 Kenneth Ross Knitwear made sweaters on the Victoria Industrial Estate. The swimming pool, rebuilt in the mid 1990s, was renamed after the Labour Party leader John Smith who had died tragically young. More housing had been built north, south and west of the town by 1996. In 1997 Airdrie Academy had 1179 pupils, and St Margaret's High 1416.

**Airdieonians change Home**: From 1989 the rail passenger service was reinstated between Airdrie and Drumgelloch, which in 1991 had a combined rather young population of 37,000. Airdrie was still the centre for the *Airdrie & Coatbridge Advertiser*. After promotion to the Premier League in 1992 an Airdrie match against St Johnstone drew only 3800 spectators to narrow little Broomfield Park, most of whom had to stand. The last match was played there in 1994; the site was sold to Safeway for a supermarket. Plans for a new stadium shared with rivals Albion Rovers of Coatbridge having fallen through, Airdrie went ahead alone. While their new *'Shybery Excelsior'* stadium (also known as New Broomfield) was being built, the team played profitlessly at Cumbernauld, falling into the First Division. There they stayed, and despite playing in their new home by 2000, soon went into receivership. Meantime a 1000-job call centre was opened in 1999, serving firms expanding into Europe. Steel work and distribution also provide numbers of jobs; Monklands Hospital employs 1600. The family-run *Tudor Hotel* offers 20 rooms.

## AIRLIE — Map 6, B2

***Angus small village,*** *pop. 400* — OS 53: NO 2952

Standing stones and other ancient remains adorn the rolling country south-east of the 15th century keep of Airlie Castle, the ancient seat of the Ogilvies. This stood some 7 km north-east of Alyth, on a steep promontory above the confluence of the River Isla, the western boundary of Angus, with the Melgam Water *(see Lintrathen)*. All save the castle gatehouse was ruined by Argyll's men in 1640. A century later the Mill of Airlie turned downstream at Dillavaird; some years later a modest mansion-house was built beside the castle gatehouse for the fifth Earl of Airlie (pronounced by some as *Eroly)*. Lindertis House 5km to the east was built in 1815–16; abandoned in 1955, it became ruinous. The population of the extensive former parish of Airlie, still 630 in 1951, had steadily fallen by 1991 to about 410. It remained entirely rural, with only the most basic of facilities; its post office, known as Craigton, closed around 1980. However, many fine views can be enjoyed from the back road linking Alyth with Kirriemuir.

## AIRTH, Elphinstone & Dunmore — Map 16, B1

***Village, north of Falkirk,*** *pop. 950* — OS 65: NS 9087

Airth on the south shore of the upper Forth estuary had an ancient church, became a Royal Burgh in 1195 and acquired a 13th or 14th century castle. A naval dockyard was established at Pool of Airth, probably in the 15th century; certainly it existed by 1510. However, Airth did not enjoy typical Royal Burgh success; being on a silting river it failed to thrive as a port. Blaeu, following Pont's sketch of about 1600, showed Airth as a small place with a large castle; to the north was the emparked 14th century keep of Elphinstone Castle, later called Airth or Elphinstone Tower. Tucker reported the existence of a coal mine at Airth in 1655, but gave more prominence to Elphinstone, *"a small town, where there is a pretty store of great coal shipped far beyond the seas, although there be never a vessel belong to this place"*. This tiny port was granted a barony charter in 1673 as Elphinstone, but later became known as Dunmore. In the late 17th century Airth still had an active market, and also wind-powered sawmills, but mining seems to have been abandoned.

**Dunmore Park and Pottery**: The Roy map made in the 1750s showed Airth as a substantial place, with several radial roads. Although there was no fair by 1797, Heron noted *"a considerable village, having some shipping, and about 1200 inhabitants"*. By the early 19th century Higginsneuk to the south had become the terminus of a ferry to Kincardine. In 1820 Elphinstone Castle was replaced by the mansion of Dunmore Park. By 1826 Chambers thought of Airth as a *"village"*, and there was no post office as late as 1838. A small faience tile pottery known as Dunmore worked 3km west of Airth, from the early 19th century until Edwardian times; the kiln survived until 1976. South of it from 1885 was the remotely sited Airth station, on the Caledonian Railway's Larbert and Alloa branch; in 1894 Airth was a small village with an inn.

**Coal Mining**: Not long afterwards a new coal mine was sunk some 500 m south of Airth Castle, and was active in 1924 when a mineral railway connected it with Carron. In 1936 the ferry was replaced by the Kincardine Bridge. Meantime the population grew markedly, to some 2000 people in 1951. Three boats based at Dunmore still engaged in anchor-net fishing for sprats in 1955, landing their catches at Alloa. Then decline set in; by 1955 the rail link to the erstwhile colliery had been cut, and by 1963 the passenger trains had been withdrawn. Meantime in 1958 the sinking of a new colliery to exploit a coking coal was begun by the National Coal Board, but falling demand for the product caused the work to be abandoned in 1959.

**Peat and Population Decline; Hotels Flourish**: About 1970 large-scale peat extraction using an extensive tramway system was begun from Letham Moss, 2 km south-west of the village, by Richardson's Moss Litter Company; this continued through the 90s. About 1975 the M9 motorway arrived, linked by a spur to the Bowtrees Farm roundabout 2 km south of the village. By 1977 the 18-roomed *Airth Castle Hotel* was in business, and by 1981 Airth had the facilities of a small village. The shrinking hamlet of Throsk on the Forth bank some 5 km up-river, which had already lost its station and primary school, reeled when its Thermalite factory closed in 1989 and 65 jobs were lost. By 1991 the village population was 940. Although there was little development in the village in the 1990s, by 1999 the *Airth Castle Hotel* had blossomed to four stars, 129 rooms and a country club, and in 1998–99 a new hotel and restaurant was built at the Bowtrees Farm roundabout. The building of pleasure boats is soon to commence at Throsk, by Caledonian Yachts.

## AITH — Map 14, B3

***Township, Shetland,*** *pop. 165* — OS 3: HU 3455

The remote township of Aith or Aithsting stands at the head of a well-sheltered sea loch on the north-western side of the Shetland Mainland. Its Norse name appears on Pont's map of about 1592, but although it gained a post office, roads did not reach Aith until the mid 19th century. In the 1914–18 war, gun emplacements were built on the long uninhabited Isle of Vementry some 8 km north-west of Aith, to protect the anchorage of Swarbacks Minn; a gun still survives *in situ*. A lifeboat station was opened at Aith in 1933 and in the mid 20th century a scattered population of around 200 also had a fishing pier, post office and a small junior secondary school. From 1962 Aith became a rural planning *'holding point'*. In the 1980s Aith's four full-time fishing boats sought queen scallops; other locals fished part-time or tended fish cages off Vementry. By 1994 there was also a marina, and a new primary school had been built; Aith Junior High School, with classes S1-S4, has some 70 pupils.

## ALEXANDRIA & Bonhill — Map 5, B5

***Vale of Leven town,*** *pop. 14,000* — OS 63 & 64: NS 3979

Blaeu's engraving based on Pont's crude and congested map of Lennox made about 1600 showed the Kirk of Bonhill, some 5 km north of Dumbarton on the east bank of the River Leven, an area known as Dalmonach *(Valley of Monks)*. South of Bonhill was *'Kirkmichel'*. On the west bank beside a tributary burn was an emparked house, probably the Place of Bonhill, and just east of this were mills; several modern farm names were shown. The renowned novelist Tobias Smollett, born in the house of Dalquharn in 1721, was the son of the laird of Bonhill. The Roy maps made around 1750 showed a track from Dumbarton to Drymen passing a settlement at the ferry known as *'Bonnille Boat'*, from which a west bank track led north into the Highlands.

**The Founding of Alexandria and the Printworks**: Alexandria began in the 18th century as a single grocer's shop on the west bank of the Leven near *"the old mansion-house of Bon-hill"* (Chambers); it was named after Alexander Smollett, who was also born there. Taking advantage of the plentiful soft water, the Dalmonach printworks were founded in 1786 on the east bank just north of Bonhill, and four years later the Croftingea printworks to the south were established by the Stirlings of Tullichewan *(see Balloch)*. Strathleven House, a classical mansion in a large park also on the east bank, 2 km south of Bonhill, was built in the 18th century for William Cochrane of Kilmarnock.

**Expansion in Textiles, Football and Golf**: The early ferry gave its name to the Ferryfield printworks, open by the 1830s, and in 1836 a suspension bridge was opened to connect Alexandria with the east bank village of Bonhill. A post office was open by 1838; the railway and station opened in 1850, and there was a gasworks. Vale of Leven FC – which played at Millburn Park – enjoyed three periods in the Scottish League between 1893 and 1926. In 1894 Murray noted Alexandria as *"one of several towns that have risen on the banks of the Leven since 1728–68; it has a large trade in bleaching, dyeing and printing, carried on by the Stirlings and the Orr-Ewings"*. With 7800 people in 1891 it was already the largest of these places. By 1903 the Dalmonach printworks was rail-connected. The Vale of Leven golf club originated in 1907, providing an 18-hole course.

**The Industrial Palace of the Argyll Car**: In 1905 Hozier Engineering, a private company founded in Bridgeton in 1901, oddly renamed itself as *Argyll* Motors, building the large but undercapitalised Argyll Motor Works in North Main Street Alexandria, designed by Halley & Neil. Once described as *"the most extraordinary industrial palace in Scotland"*, it was then the largest car plant in Europe, intended to make 2500 cars a year from 1906. But only 1000 Argyll cars were built in 1907, the year that the firm's principal Alexander Govan died from food poisoning; a downturn in business in 1908 ensured that Argyll Motors was liquidated. The factory was not actually closed until 1913, becoming a Naval torpedo factory in World War I.

**The Mid Twentieth Century**: In the 1920s at least two large print works and a dye works continued, though Croftingea later became a bonded warehouse, and in World War II Dalmonach was an artillery barracks. The Vale of Leven Academy was open by 1941 when the Vale took the brunt of the refugees from blitzed Clydebank. By 1950 Alexandria was the local centre for the upper Vale of Leven, with an average range of urban facilities and a population (with Bonhill) of 13,700. From 1961 Alexandria has enjoyed an electric train service to Glasgow. The Vale of Leven Industrial Estate was open by 1963, south of Bonhill and west of Strathleven House, which it later enveloped. However, eventually the once-large textile industries failed. By way of compensation, Barton's new Loch Lomond

*Argyll Motor Works, Alexandria, built in 1905 and described as "the most extraordinary industrial palace in Scotland"; it was then the largest car plant in Europe, but closed in 1913 and became a torpedo factory for the Admiralty (until the 1960s). The remaining frontage block now contains a motor museum.* (JRH)

Highland Malt distillery and bottling plant was built in 1965–66, and through traffic left the old A82 for a dual carriageway bypass, built west of the town in 1969–70.

**Unemployment and Poverty**: Strathleven House was abandoned in the 1970s; it stood forlorn until 1993, but has since been restored. The 20% rise in population between 1951 and 1981, and the many new local facilities such as the new Vale of Leven General Hospital built by 1971 in what had been Tullichewan Park, were not due to industrial growth. Despite the great efforts made to attract industry, success can be measured by such firms as McLaggan Smith Ltd, making ceramic mugs at Jamestown. In 1990 unemployment stood at over twice the UK average, with nearly 4000 jobless people in the Vale. By 1991 the population of Alexandria with Balloch was 14,150; Bonhill had a young population of nearly 10,100. Now the Loch Lomond (Highland Malt) distillery was under a company bearing its own name. The Argyll works site largely went for Wimpey housing while the elaborate, listed administrative block, standing vandalised in 1993, was restored in 1996–97 to hold the classic cars formerly on show at New Lanark, and also some factory outlets.

## ALFORD & Montgarrie

**Map 10, B3**

***Small town & village, Donside,*** *pop. 1400* — OS 37: NJ 5716

Above the Howe of Alford (pronounced *Affud)* – the fertile valley of the River Don some 20km west of Inverurie – stands the stone circle of Old Keig, dating from around 2500 BC. About 20m in diameter, it contains the largest known recumbent stone moved by early man – a 53-tonne megalith 5m-long, originating some 10km away and set as a horizon to match the apogee and perigee of the moon's 18-year cycle. Above it stands a hill fort, and 5km to the south-west near the confluence of the Leochel Burn with the Don is the Kirk of Alford, flanked by two 16th century castles, Balfluig and Asloun.

**The Perfect Castle is Created**: A burgh of barony charter granted in 1594 proved abortive, though by 1618 there was a parish school. Surely the best-known tower house in Scotland is magnificent Craigievar Castle, built in 1610–24 some 7km to the south, its motto *"do not waken sleeping dogs"*. Roy's map of about 1750 showed no village, nor were there any bridges on the four tracks which radiated from Alford Kirk, north via Tullynessle and Clatt, south past Leochel kirk and east–west following the Don to Monymusk and Kildrummy. Apart from fermtouns, the main features were two mansions in modest policies, Haughton and *'Alford'*, the latter seemingly being at Balfluig. Three fairs were scheduled to be held at Alford Kirkton in 1797. A post office first opened in 1802; Telford's early 19th century Bridge of Alford drew to itself an *'emporium'* and a pleasant riverside fishing base, the *Forbes Arms Hotel*; but no village.

**Hotel and Railway Make the Village**: Modern Alford, 2km south-east of the bridge, can be dated to the building in 1850 of the *Haughton Arms Hotel*. Alford station was opened near by in 1859 as the terminus of the Alford Valley Railway (AVR) from Kintore, later a Great North of Scotland Railway branch. The new village which grew along the road beside it seems to have been an unplanned by-product, housing workers in these services and retailing. Montgarrie mill was rebuilt in 1886 (and is still milling oatmeal). In 1891 an ornate drinking fountain was placed outside the hotel, and by 1894 the village had about 500 people. There was a cattle market, and Murray noted the hotel as *"comfortable"*.

**Steam Postie overtaken by Cars**: In 1895 the enterprising Craigievar postman Andrew Lawson built a steam-powered mail cart, soon called the *Craigievar Express*. Alford also had one of the earliest motor garages; locally high levels of car ownership and bus services soon made the passenger trains uneconomic and they ceased to run in 1950. By then Alford's population had grown to 1250, enjoying the facilities of a large village, such as a cinema (which had closed by 1958), agricultural engineers and contractors. The secondary school – now Alford Academy – was still supplemented by secondary classes in primary schools at Montgarrie 2km to the north and Tough, 5km south-east, but these outliers were soon abandoned. Beeching ended the rail freight service in 1966, and by 1971 some garages, banks, a hotel and chemist had closed, and the population had fallen by 12% in 20 years.

**Transport Museum, Rustic Railway, Golf and Skiing**: Evidently North Sea oil prosperity soon penetrated to Alford, which in 1981 was the centre of an extensive area. Lawson's steam car found an honoured place in the Grampian Museum of Transport, founded in Aberdeen as a charity in 1978, and opened in new premises in Alford in 1983 with local government aid. By 1986 a rather rustic miniature railway taking the name of the AVR had been laid, connecting the museum with a caravan site and country park in the Haughton policies. The mart closed around 1985, replaced by a small industrial estate where by 2000 Sciamed made barcode readers and kindred products. Meantime by 1991 new housing had spread on all sides, and the population had recovered quite rapidly to some 1400; Alford golf club had laid out an 18-hole course, and a dry ski slope had also been created. The National Trust for Scotland, which had long managed Craigievar Castle, found that the sheer weight of visitors was damaging its famed plaster ceilings, and in 1995 reduced both its advertising for and the signposting to this attraction. Meantime the local sawmill had closed with a dozen jobs lost, and despite the tourist honeypots the owner of the *Haughton Arms Hotel* – claiming low returns – planned to turn the building into a home for the elderly.

**Facilities Aplenty**: In fact part of the building is still a pub and restaurant under the traditional name, the rest having been intensively developed with shops and flats. A coal merchant at the old goods station, heating engineers, joiners and roofers, garages, a tyre fitter and dry cleaners meet material needs, but the original emporium at Bridge of Alford, already defunct by the 1980s, stands in ruins. However, prosperity and good services are very evident, with a swimming pool, library, children's nursery, police, fire and ambulance stations, and a roads depot. Two supermarkets exist, four banks, and a wide range of shops, including specialists in clothing, sportswear, and camping gear; Alford is almost becoming a town. The tiny *Vale Hotel* and the larger *Forbes Arms* at Bridge of Alford still provide accommodation, but the important and varied Transport Museum is open from April to October only.

## ALLANTON & Hartwood — Map 16, B4

***N. Lanarkshire villages,*** *pop. 1200* — OS 65 or 72: NS 8557

Allanton which lies in the valley of the South Calder Water, some 5 km south of Kirk of Shotts, has been owned by the Steuart family since the mid 15th century. The area was well settled by 1596 when Timothy Pont mapped Strathclyde. The early castle and mill were replaced by the New Mill and Allanton House, built on a new site 1 km to the south. The area was only sketchily mapped by Roy, and stayed rural. Allanton house was enlarged in 1809–20 by James Gillespie Graham; Cobbett who visited in 1832, noted only Sir Henry Steuart's exemplary tree planting, artificial lake and *"very ancient family mansion"*. By 1895 an inn was open east of the crossroads.

**The Railway and Hartwood Asylum**: Meantime Hartwood station, 1 km north of Allanton crossroads, had been provided on the winding Edinburgh to Glasgow line of the Caledonian Railway, opened in 1869. In Murray's 1894 Handbook, a revision, it was simply described as lying in *"a pretty hollow"*, but in 1890–98 the large Hartwood Asylum was built as the district asylum for Lanark, to designs by J Murray of Biggar, and with its own rail connection. In 1906 a sanatorium extended the asylum complex, in 1916 a further block was added, in 1931 came a nurses home to designs by James Lochhead of Hamilton, and finally the Hartwood Hill block, built in 1935.

**The Kingshill Colliery Complex**: A large colliery – Kingshill Nos. 1 & 2 pits, sunk 1 km south-east of the crossroads in the early 20th century – gave rise to the village of Allanton between these points. The sinking of Kingshill No.3 mine was begun in 1946; with shafts 234 m deep it raised coking coal from the Limestone Coal Group for a quarter-century. The population in the area was some 4500 in 1951, served by the facilities of a small village. By 1954 the mines near the village and at Kingshill were linked by a dead-straight 3 km mineral railway, and a line connected with the Morningside railway at Castle Hill Junction, but Allanton House was no more.

**After the Mines the Opencast**: By 1971 the mental hospital had some 1300 inmates. The last part of the mine complex was closed about 1973, leaving for many years an enormous blighted area; the railway to Morningside was closed the next year and there was a swift reduction in population. In 1981 there were 1200 hospital inmates and by 1988 Hartwood was the largest psychiatric hospital in Scotland, but rundown was soon to start. Remarkably, Hartwood station had escaped the Beeching and other cuts. In 1991 Allanton's own population was under 1200. The original Hartwood Hospital was closed in 1997, and the nurses' home – by then used by Bell College of Hamilton – was soon to become redundant. By 1998 the pithead, the bings and most of Redmire Loch had vanished under new woodlands, but vast opencast workings had obliterated all features around Kepplehill Farm to the east.

## ALLOA — Map 16, B1

***Clack'shire main town,*** *pop. 18,850* — OS 58: NS 8892

Alloa whose name may derive from the Gaelic *'lobhar'*, a leper, lies on the tidal River Forth 9 km east of Stirling; a ferry to South Alloa is believed to have operated by the tenth century. Alloa's 27 m tall castle tower, its walls nearly 4 m thick, was begun in 1223. The ferry rights were confirmed by charter in 1363, and in 1365–68 the estate was acquired from the crown by Sir Robert Erskine, whose grandson became Earl of Mar. The title was cancelled before Alloa became the burgh of barony of Alexander, third Lord Erskine, in 1497, but confirmed to his great-grandson, Captain of Stirling Castle, by Queen Mary in 1565. Her son, later James VI, was educated in safe isolation in what was described in 1618 as this *"fair and stately tower"*. Pont's map of Stirlingshire made around 1600 showed *'Alwa'* castle with its park, and a kirk, but no town; though as it lay on the edge of the mapped area this is inconclusive.

**A Pretty Fine Burgh's Coalmining Serfs**: With the discovery of coal in the area, Alloa soon prospered and grew into the principal centre of Clackmannanshire, connected with Stirling by a 16th century bridge across the River Devon at Cambus (*q.v.*). In 1655 Alloa was regarded by Taylor as *"a pretty fine burgh having a fine harbour, and an excellent coal"*; even so it possessed no ships of its own, relying on Dutch vessels for coal shipment. There was an early sawmill, probably for pit props. Mining seems to have degraded Alloa, which was castigated as a *"mean collier village"* in 1689, when many miners were mere serfs, bearing their owners' names on collars riveted round their necks! However, the Earl of Mar was said to have been more enlightened in his treatment. Although brewing was traditionally women's work, Margaret Mitchell was the town's first recorded *'alewife'*, brewing and selling ale in 1694.

**Defoe on the Erskines' contribution to Prosperity**: Early in the 18th century Charles and John Erskine, 5th and 6th Earls of Mar, built on to and adapted the tower into the mansion of

Alloa House; Defoe noted that they had *"beautified the buildings and especially the gardens so completely modern that no appearance of a castle remains"*. John also built a weir 5m high across the Black Devon at Forest Mill; from there a 3km long aqueduct, passing the hamlet of Coalhill Row, fed the reservoir of Gartmorn Dam, 3km east of Alloa, which impounded water for use in driving colliery engines. Another idea of his was for a Forth & Clyde Canal. After his exile and loss of title in 1716 his brother George Erskine evidently worked on the settlement too, for *"The town is pleasant, well built, and full of trade; there is a harbour for shipping, and ships of 300 tons may lie at the wharf. Alloa has a large deal-yard, two saw-mills, large warehouses of naval stores and a rope-walk for making all sorts of ropes and cables for rigging and fitting of ships. Glasgow merchants are erecting warehouses"*, intending to re-export tobacco and sugar brought across country to Alloa. The town was still a major mining centre in 1735 when either George, or John's son Thomas, introduced a water-powered coal hoist.

**Brewing, Glass and Post**: In 1735–36 the grain mill was rebuilt. Its enlarged output fed the town's first large breweries, opened about 1740 and 1760; the Candleriggs Brewery followed in 1774. The Alloa Glass Works Company began work in 1750, when Lady Frances Erskine of Mar brought Bohemian glassworkers to the town. The Roy map of around 1750 showed a large settlement, with three radial roads petering out into tracks to Stirling, to Kinross and to Kincardine, and a ferry to Carsie. Trustees took over the harbour in 1754, soon building a quay and a 10m-wide dry dock. A post office was opened in 1756.

**The Alloa Wagonway and Varied Industries**: A wooden wagonway for coal exports was built by Lady Frances Erskine in 1766–68, passing beneath two streets; it was upgraded with iron plates in 1785. Copper smelting, originally using ore from Bridge of Allan, apparently began in the 1770s, though for some years it was in abeyance. In the mid 18th century a woollen industry also developed, and by 1776 there were already twenty woollen manufacturers employing between them 500 workers using 150 looms, chiefly making *'camblets'* (Bremner). A snuff mill was built about 1775, a millwright was based in Alloa by 1786, and the grain mills were again enlarged late in the century. A shipbuilding yard was established in 1790, a new waulk mill was set up in 1794, and dyewood was ground locally by the 1830s; the British Dyewood & Chemical Company was still active in 1898. By 1780 475 people worked in the largest Alloa mine, and in 1791 520, a quarter of them young children. Another steam engine for the coal industry was erected in 1799 at Backbank.

**Alloa as a Coal Port in the 1790s**: The *'New Town'* was laid out in 1786 to accommodate the growing population. By then there were proper piers on both sides of the river for the ferry, which was then much used by drovers, particularly of cattle from the eastern Highlands to the Falkirk Tryst. In 1797 two fairs were scheduled, and by that time Alloa was also a post town. Heron wrote in 1799, *"The sea port town of Alloa is conveniently situated for the coal trade, has a good harbour, and an excellent dry-dock. A custom-house was here established soon after the Union. Alloa is consequently the resort of all the coal-vessels in the neighbourhood. It has about 7000 tons of shipping, a glass-house, and some other manufactures, which furnish employment for near 5000 inhabitants."* The port's registration letters were 'AA'. The ancient tower was saved when the mansion burned out in 1800; the shell was demolished in 1802, its stone used to build the great wall enclosing the adjacent Kilncraigs Mill. The road to Causewayhead was turnpiked in the same year, and a new parish church was built in 1819.

**Banking and Drinks Industries**: From 1777, the Stirling Banking Company the Paisley Bank, and the Perth Union Banking Company tried branches in the town. Carsebridge distillery was founded by John Bald in 1799, and the Alloa Brewery Company (ABC) was established by Andrew Roy in 1810. There were many 19th century maltings, and by 1825 six breweries, to which was added George Younger's Meadow Brewery, established in 1832. The small Thistle Brewery of 1830 continued in operation outside the various combines which gradually took over many others.

**Alloa as seen by Chambers**: According to Chambers in 1827, *"Alloa is a thriving sea-port and manufacturing town, of above 4000 inhabitants. Besides many other branches of manufacture, brewing is here carried on to a considerable extent; and Alloa Ale is excellent and celebrated."* The glassworks were taken over and extended about 1825 by the Edinburgh, Glasgow & Alloa Glass Company, which built two large stone and brick cones; and a gasworks was set up in 1828. In 1835 two coaches ran daily to Stirling. The estate was returned to the Earls in 1824, and a new mansion of Alloa Park (later known as Alloa House) was built east of the tower in 1834–38. Local mining engineer and geologist Robert Bald, born in 1775, helped Shaftesbury to obtain the Act of 1842 barring women and young people from underground work. One early local newspaper founded in 1841 was the *Alloa Advertiser-Journal*, and by 1852 there were two.

**Patons of Alloa and other big Woollen firms**: John Paton commenced yarn spinning at Kilncraigs mill in 1814, and by 1834 specialised in stocking yarns. Expanded in 1869, it had 300 workers and 17 sets of carding engines spinning various yarns, some going to Dumfries firms. The mills were further extended in the 1880s, and by 1888 J T Paton had built Inglewood on Tullibody Road, described by Beveridge as a *"splendid mansion"*. Thomson Paton engaged Mitchell & Wilson of Edinburgh to design the finely panelled Greenfield House, built in 1892–94. Around 1900 Paton & Baldwin still manufactured knitwear on hand machines. In 1869 the Gaberston Mill of Lambert & Co employed 300 workers spinning and weaving wool into shawls and *'skirtings'*. Keilarsbrae mills were built in stages from 1821 to about 1839; in 1869 the old mill was a small spinning concern run by Henderson's, and the new mill jointly owned by Patons and Lamberts employed nearly 60 people making yarns for hosiery and shawls. At that time too, the Springfield Mill of Thomson Brothers had 220 workers manufacturing fine yarns for shawls, winceys and tweeds.

**Docks and Shipbuilding in the Nineteenth Century**: John Rennie surveyed for dock improvements in 1808. From 1822 the ferry was steam operated, requiring two boats to maintain the service. From 1837 or before, wooden steamboats of up to 32m or more in length were built by J Duncanson, and by 1856 by T Adamson. In 1845 a total of some 18,000 tons of shipping was registered at Alloa. A new dock was built in the 1860s and expanded in 1879–81, enabling the shipment of 175,000 tonnes of coal that year – mostly for exports, which reached a peak around 1895. By 1886 A. Bryce was a marine engineer, and built the machinery for the tiny local ferry steamer *Lord Erskine*. Steel was used locally for hulls by 1905 when Mackay Brothers had a shipyard; steam drifters were still built around 1908.

**Alloa in the Railway Age**: The Stirling & Dunfermline Railway, later part of the North British, reached Alloa by 1850 from the east, and was linked to the Scottish Central (SCR) main line at Stirling in 1852, and from 1850 William Wordie had a rail cartage depot. In 1851 Alloa became the junction for a short branch line to Tillicoultry, which was extended through to Kinross by 1863. In 1865 the SCR's successor the Caledonian Railway started a ferry from South Alloa, which they closed in 1885 when they opened a railway crossing the Forth west of the town by Scotland's largest swing bridge, joining the existing line linking South Alloa with the main line at Larbert *(see Marshall)*. Meantime Rowand Anderson had designed the Episcopal church, built in 1868–73. Alloa Athletic Football Club was formed in 1878 and first played at Recreation Park in 1895. A new post office was built in 1882, and a Paton gifted a fine new public hall to the town in 1888. By then three hotels were open, the *Crown, Royal Oak* and *Victoria*; Alloa was known for ale, glass, woollens and worsteds.

**Late Nineteenth Century Grain Whisky and Brewing**: Carsebridge distillery was converted to produce grain whisky about 1850, and later greatly enlarged; it was still owned in 1876 by John Bald & Co, who in 1877 joined DCL as founder members of this new grain whisky combine. In 1886 the 150 employees at Carsebridge used steam power, water from Gartmorn Dam, and grain imported through Alloa harbour, to produce over 7.7 million litres of grain whisky annually. About 1890 it was equipped for yeast-making. Younger the brewers built the Craigward maltings in 1868, and followed by erecting those at Ward Street in 1897–99. Archibald Arrol took over the ABC in 1895; by the end of the century at least four substantial breweries were at work in the town.

**Coppersmithing for Drinks Industries**: The Alloa Copper Works were re-established around 1805; later under Robert Willison they produced stills to both Coffey and Stein designs, tuns, mashing machines, brewery plant and fittings. By 1886 the Broad Street Engine Works of coppersmiths R G Abercrombie engaged in brewery and distillery engineering, and they also operated a large foundry. By 1894 when it was described by Murray as *"thriving and increasing"* Alloa had an important service role, but only the *Crown* and *Royal Oak* hotels deserved a mention. Alloa House which had again been rebuilt around 1870 was by then surrounded by a large park, as extensive as the tightly-packed town!

*Distillery worms, made in Alloa by R G Abercrombie & Co, being delivered to the Craigellachie distillery in 1997. These worms were placed in tanks of water, and used for condensing the vapours from the stills.* *(JRH)*

**New Industry, Ferries and Mansion House**: About 1901 the expanding population of Clackmannanshire reached a plateau at around 32,000, but Alloa continued to grow. Electric power was provided about 1899, and in 1902 came the works of British Electrical Plant Ltd, who made transformers in 1910. Due to the expansion of local sawmills in 1905, commuting increased so much that the ferry to South Alloa, which had been re-equipped in 1887, required a larger boat, actually supplied in 1911; by 1924 a vehicular steam ferry was in operation. Meantime the Eglinton beer bottling plant was added by Youngers in 1912. Also in 1912 the fine mansion of Gean House was built beside Inglewood on Tullibody Road.

**Italian Entrepreneurs Make Good**: In 1911 Rocco Forte left his Italian mountain village of Monforte and joined relatives to buy and run the Savoy Cafe in Alloa. His eldest son Charles built up from milk bars into a huge catering enterprise after the second world war and eventually bought out the Trust House Hotel chain, rather regrettably taking it downmarket. The major glassworks development at Kelliebank occurred in the 1920s, a period when Carsebridge Distillery was also expanded, becoming one of the largest grain whisky plants in Scotland. A Jeffrey's Forth Shipbuilding Company of Alloa was sixth among British yards in terms of the number of its coasters in service. Shipbreaking started about that time; also, large railway yards were laid out west of the town. The Kilncraigs Mills were greatly extended in 1934–36 and Alloa was among the earlier towns in Scotland to be colonised by Woolworths, then a touchstone of progress; but following the opening of the Kincardine Bridge the ferry was closed in 1939.

**The 1940s and 1950s**: During the 1939–45 war McLeod's yard was building and repairing ships. The Glen Alva textile mills were built in 1947, and in 1951 the Alloa Brewery Company became part of Ind Coope & Allsop. By then the county's population was at its highest total to date, around 37,500; Alloa had stabilised at some 13,500 residents. The town council bought Greenfield House for use as offices in 1952, but regrettably Alloa House was demolished in 1959 and its park also vanished under urban development. Donaldsons' textile works was a large concern by the 1950s, and the extensive Jaeger knitwear factory on Tullibody Road was opened in 1960.

**Closure of the Railways and Port**: About 12 local boats still engaged in anchor-net fishing for sprats in 1955. However, unloading which Grangemouth could do in a day took two days at Alloa, so only one cargo ship a fortnight was entering the docks. In total 20,000 tonnes of Dutch silver sand arrived in a year for the two glassworks, plus a little fertiliser. The railway engine shed was closed in 1966; despite being marked for retention in the Beeching report, Alloa lost all its rail passenger services in 1968. The NCB closed its Alloa workshops in 1967. By that time even obsolete ships were too large to negotiate the channel, so shipbreaking also had to cease; the port failed and was closed in 1970, the railway bridge to Larbert being demolished the next year.

**The 1980s**: In 1979 the Alloa works of United Glass boasted the world's largest bottle-making furnace, and by 1980 a branch of Weir Pumps of Cathcart operated in Alloa. Despite some decline, the town remained the local government centre of what in 1975 had become Clackmannan District. The *Crown* and *Royal Oak* hotels were still in business in 1980, and Alloa was still an important centre for other local facilities. By 1980 the former Forebraes secondary school had become Clackmannan Technical College. Distillery engineering was still carried on in 1983 by the long-established Abercrombie's, and Patons & Baldwins maintained an important presence, including offices. The course of the 18th century wagonway beneath the town centre was a footpath by 1984, and it was appropriate that the Museum had an industrial collection by 1990. By 1988 the large new Lornshill Academy had been built on Tullibody Road; the population in 1991 was nearly 18,850.

**Luxury and a Tower for Tourists**: The grade *'A'* listed Edwardian mansion of The Gean in Tullibody Road was renovated in 1990 as the luxurious *Gean House Hotel*. Adjacent Inglewood, also *'A'* listed, which had been used as a Church of Scotland residential home, stood vacant in large policies in 1993, but by 1997 had been saved for posterity. In 1988 the District Council joined the Earl of Mar & Kellie in an Alloa Tower Building Preservation Trust. Repairs and conservation were followed in 1995 by conversion of the tower into a heritage visitor centre in over 3 ha of newly accessible landscaped grounds, its stable block converted into 12 houses and a tearoom. By 1997 the Alloa Leisure Bowl included a swimming pool.

**New and Broken Glass but no Whisky**: In 1990 new glass was made at the Scottish Central Glass Works from Fife sand, Derbyshire soda-ash and West Midlands limestone. Just five of the 700 workers at United Glass operated the recycling plant, which dealt with all of the 32,000 tonnes of broken glass or *cullet* arising in the year from bottle banks throughout Scotland. Carsebridge, lately the largest grain distillery in Scotland, was closed permanently in 1983. In 1991 Alloa's second division football club played at Recreation Park, described by *Scotland on Sunday* as *"a dreary little place"* with a condemned stand, replaced that year; most of the few spectators did have to! The ground was also used by Glasgow Rangers' reserve teams, drawing bigger gates than Alloa FC, who in 1994 joined the new but lowly Third Division; by 2000 they had earned a First Division place. Meantime by 1992 the railway east of Alloa and the sidings to the west had been closed and lifted.

**Software for Holes in Walls**: In 1993 Strategic Software Solutions was established in Alloa; growing fast, by 2000 they advised NCR on adding new services to ATMs (cash machines), were moving into new headquarters, and hoped to recruit 130 more staff. The Jaeger factory shop was still open in 1994, but by then part of the factory was under Coats Viyella. By 1994 Marshall Construction had large premises, and the adjacent Glen Alva Mills made children's knitwear for chain stores. Alloa had long remained a major brewing centre: Alloa Brewery, by 1992 owned by Allied-Lyons, then employed 250 people brewing lagers and beers; in 1994 the ABC's modern premises also produced *Castlemaine XXXX* and *Skol*, but it closed soon after. The Thistle Brewery was still family-owned in 1994 by Maclay & Co. In 1995 it was also the source of the Williams Brothers' *Fraoch* Heather Ale, a traditional mild Scottish bottled ale brewed on night shifts using heather flowers picked across Scotland by 90 workers; production had tripled in two years. Now the work has been transferred to Strathaven.

**Patons and Brewing end, but Rail Re-born?**: In 1996 tiny Clackmannanshire became an all-purpose local authority, far and away the smallest such unit in Scotland! At that time Alloa Academy had 725 pupils and Lornshill 1015. With Alloa's new-found importance in local government, and under the belated but very welcome national pro-rail policy, reinstatement of the rail passenger service from Stirling to Alloa (proposed by Central Regional Council in 1992) was approved by the Scottish Executive in 2000. The reopening to freight of the whole line linking Stirling with Dunfermline was planned by Railtrack and EWS, with government help. These measures are especially welcome because Maclay's brewery closed in 2000, ending Alloa's long history of brewing, and the last 220 jobs at Patons' large and historic Kilncraigs factory also vanished by the year's end – part of the site to become a new Tesco store (300 jobs), and part for expansion of Clackmannan College. However, in 2000 pickle jars were still made by United Glass for Campbell foods, and 'Pavilions' was one of several business parks accommodating high-tech firms.

## ALMONDBANK, Huntingtower & Pitcairngreen

**Map 6, A3**

***Villages w. of Perth,*** *pop. 1200* OS 58: NO 0626

The great 15th century Ruthven Castle was built for Lord Ruthven beside the Town's Lade, an artificial offshoot of the River Almond, bringing water from some 4 km west of Perth to power the burgh's mills. The castle was still Lord Ruthven's seat in 1560 and was clearly sketched by Timothy Pont about 1600, when it lay in a thickly settled area. Upstream was the Mill of Dunkra, while across a bridge on the opposite bank of the river was the Mill of Pitkairn. Roy's map made about 1750 also showed Pitcairn mill and bridge, but the only road shown connected Perth, the castle (by then renamed *Huntingtower*), and Crieff via the rural parish centre of Tibbermore to the south.

*The Huntingtower bleach works at Tibbermore, near Almondbank, Perthshire – just after closure in 1982. It was one of a number of 18th century bleachworks set up in the Perth area, originally to bleach linen in the open air.* *(JRH)*

**Industrial Development and Planned Village**: In 1794 linen handkerchief printing works were active at Ruthvenfield and Cromwell Park – on a substantial scale by 1799. The large Huntingtower bleachfield of 28ha then processed about 600,000 linear metres of linen a year, and had its own machinery workshops. Almondbank village which lay astride the River Almond some 2 km west of the castle was joined by the attractive late 18th century planned hamlet of Pitcairngreen just to the north, created round another bleachfield by Lord Lynedoch. In 1985 it was described by Wright as *"the most rural in appearance of the planned villages"* of Scotland. In all, the water-power of the Almond turned at least seven mills. In 1799 Heron noted, under Methven parish, *"two paper-mills, and several mills for grain"*. The paper mills were operated by Morrison & Lindsay of Perth, and that at Woodend which had four vats where writing and printing papers were made was still in use under Lindsay in 1832, though it appears to have closed within a few years.

**The Perth, Almond Valley & Methven Railway**: This grandly-titled local railway was opened from Perth to Methven in 1858, with stations south of Almondbank and halts at the Ruthven and Tibbermuir crossings; eventually it reached Crieff. By 1864, though still water-powered and bleaching linen, Huntingtowerfield had been lately re-equipped by W & S Turnbull and was the most important works of its type in the Perth area, giving 150 jobs. At that time J Shield & Co of Perth had a water-powered weaving works with 100 looms at Cromwell Park, where Caird & Co had a yarn bleachfield; and David Lumsden's Pitcairnfield bleachworks employed about 55 people. By 1895 Pitcairngreen had an inn; Almondbank was the main centre, with an inn and post office, while beside the castle was the Ruthvenfield Print Works, and another post office.

**Joining the Navy without Seeing the Sea**: The second world war saw Royal Naval aircraft repair workshops built at Almondbank; though the railway had been closed to passengers in 1951, goods traffic continued until 1967. The population was nearly 1000 in 1951, with the facilities of a small village and an extra primary school; by 1963 an Edwardian mansion in half-timbered style had become the *Huntingtower Hotel*. By 1978 the GR International electronic works and a Department of Transport crane depot used some of the RN sheds; at Huntingtower was an agricultural contractor. In 1978 local services included three food stores, butcher, chip shop, PO, and inn. An enlarged primary school served new private housing, for the population had risen steadily, to about 1200 in 1981 (and 1991), with more facilities, especially garages. Until 1982 Lumsden & Mackenzie were still dyers, bleachers and finishers at *'Huntingtowerfield'*. In 1991 some 425 workers repaired helicopters at the RN workshops, but these were run down to closure in 1993; the 6ha site was bought in 1994 by Bett of Dundee to build 63 houses. The *Huntingtower Hotel* now has 34 rooms.

## ALNESS, Dalmore & Teaninich — Map 9, B3

***Small town, Easter Ross,*** *pop. 5700* — OS 21: NH 6569

The name of Alness on the sheltered north shore of the Cromarty Firth may derive from the Norse *'ness'* for a headland. It had a medieval motte, and in 1621 was a minor port paying under 1.5% of Scotland's Customs dues; a parish school existed by 1628. It became a burgh of barony in 1690, named *Obsdale*. The Dingwall to Tain road, open by 1715, crossed the River Averon by ferry; by the 1750s Alness Kirk stood nearby. The Culcairn linen bleachfield was built between 1746 and 1760, but textiles did not thrive there. Teaninich House was originally built in 1784. Telford bridged the river with an 18 metre arch in 1810 and improved the road. A mill and two distilleries arose: Teaninich in 1817, and Dalmore built in 1839–41, which had its own lengthy pier. The first Alness post office opened in 1839.

**Railway, Electricity and Golf**: The Inverness & Ross-shire Railway's single line reached a station at Alness in 1863 en route to Invergordon. In 1886 when Barnard wrote of Alness as a *"rural village"* the distilleries each made nearly 365,000 litres of malt whisky a year. Dalmore was rail-connected but its proprietors, Mackenzie Brothers, grew their own barley on an adjacent farm. It had been often enlarged, lately by Milnes of Edinburgh, who continued to add equipment up to 1898. By 1886 Teaninich was already electrically lit and had its own telephone system. By 1894 though lacking a hotel Alness was *"a village of considerable size"*, and by 1900 a millwright was at work, which continued until at least 1920. Meantime Alness golf club, founded in 1904, provided a 9-hole course.

**Wartime Developments**: Dalmore distillery was taken over in 1917 as a depot for Admiralty mines, made in USA and brought in by rail from Kyle. Its miles of sidings were laid with track uplifted from the HR's Keith and Buckie branches. RAF Alness on the shore to the south was a cramped World War II base for *'Catalina'* amphibians. By 1951 the usual village facilities were available, serving a population of under 1300. In 1946 Wordie & Co operated a small rail to road cartage depot, but the station was closed to passengers in 1960.

**Massive Expansion for Aluminium and Oil**: 1500 people lived in Alness before the Invergordon smelter 6km to the east opened in 1968. Much new housing was built for workers in the smelter and at the oil platform yard at Nigg; rapid growth of bungalow estates to the east brought the population to some 4000 by 1972. A supermarket, a library and a youth and community centre were built; the station was reopened to passengers in 1973, and Alness Academy opened in 1977. Only tiny industries came to Alness, and the planners' 1970s dream of growth to 18,000 remained just that; but it had gained the facilities of a large village.

**Dreams Unfulfilled? Time will Tell**: The smelter closed in 1981 and growth ceased. Teaninich distillery, much enlarged in the 1960s, closed about 1983, but by 1991 had been reopened by United Distillers. By then the youthful population was 5696, and lacking in higher educational qualifications, but a lengthy A9 bypass had recently been completed to the south. Dalmore, which made a single malt for connoisseurs under Whyte & Mackay, had also been closed for a time. In 1992 Highlands & Islands Enterprise built an advance factory and planned both advance-build offices and a training centre. In 1992 Grants of Dalvey, clock manufacturers, gained an export award; by 1996 they made steel luxury products and expanded to 60 employees. Teaninich House, which had become derelict, was restored in the mid 1990s. By 2000 two supermarkets were open; industry included polythene manufacture, fish-farming, and the Caplich quarries.

## ALTNABREAC

**Map 13, A5**

***Locality, Caithness,*** *pop. v. under 100* OS 11: ND 0045

When what soon became the Highland Railway's north main line from Inverness to Wick was completed in 1874, this very remote station and crossing loop 20km south-west of Georgemas Junction was located amid lochan-strewn moors at an altitude of 150m, beside the Sleach Water (Gaelic *Allt na Breac, 'Stream of Trout')*. Lochdhu Lodge with its prominent tower was built in 1895 some 1.5km to the south, as a hunting lodge for Sinclair of Ulbster. Between the wars a school and post office near the station also served Dalnawillan south of Lochdhu. However, the school had closed by 1958 and the railway loop and goods facilities were closed in 1966; the post office vanished soon after. The Hydro Board built a peat-burning power station nearby about 1970 to exploit an 8500ha bog; but to the delight of nature conservationists it was soon abandoned as a failure, leaving only a ruin. Lochdhu Lodge was – for a time around 1970 – a 16-roomed fishing hotel, and the school was reopened for a time around 1977; but in 1993 the Lodge stood vacant among vast new conifer plantations, which since 1974 had entirely transformed the landscape. Today the few trains each weekday still make request stops at Altnabreac.

## ALTNAHARRA

**Map 12, C2**

***Small village, Sutherland,*** *pop. 100* OS 16: NC 5635

Loch Naver has ancient brochs on either shore, and at its west end in a moorland area some 150m above sea level are the remains of hut circles. Nearby is Altnaharra (Gaelic *Allt na-h-Aire, 'Stream of Watching'*, probably a shepherd's base) near where the road from Lairg to Tongue, completed in 1828, meets a secondary road from Bettyhill. An inn was built there about 1818–20 at an altitude of 85m, using timbers from Farr parish church, recently destroyed by the Sutherland Estates' clearances. By 1840 the area was already served by a penny post and it developed as a tiny angling resort. By the 1950s the inn had become a hotel with 18 rooms, and a post office, telephone exchange and school were in use nearby. By the 1980s the population was about 100. Apart from several experimental Forestry Commission plantations in the area, there's been little recent change.

## ALVA

**Map 16, B1**

***Small town, Clack'shire,*** *pop. 5200* OS 58: NS 8897

In 1260 Cambuskenneth Abbey was given the church of the Hillfoot settlement of Alva, making it for centuries part of Stirlingshire. Alva was weaving woollens by about 1550, plaidings being its first well-known product. Alva House was built 1.5km east of the village around 1650. In 1712 Sir John Erskine of Alva opened a fabulously rich silver mine in the glen above the Kirkton, using miners from Leadhills. The ore was the purest ever found in Britain, bringing wealth to Erskine, who improved the estate and financed a coal-carrying canal connecting the River Devon to the Forth. However, mining soon became intermittent; in later years cobalt was produced, which was used in the Prestonpans china manufactory. In the 1750s Alva was still tiny and roadless. Alva House was altered in 1789 to plans by Robert Adam, though only the churchyard mausoleum he designed for the laird John Johnstone escaped eventual demolition.

**Coal, Iron and Woollen Mills**: The Devon or Furnacebank colliery to the south of Alva was first worked in the mid 18th century, and also provided iron ore for the adjoining Devon Ironworks, established in 1792 and described by Heron in 1799 as *"hewn out of the solid rock, instead of being built"*. He mentioned *"the rapidly increasing village of Newton Shaw"*, which may refer to New Sauchie 3km to the south, or to Devon Village near the colliery. A woollen mill was set up on the tumbling Alva Burn in 1798 by Matthews, making serges and blankets. Coblecrook woollen mill, built by the Drysdales, apparently dated from 1802, Harrower's mill started in 1807 and by 1821 the population of Alva was 1150, still making blankets and serges. The seventh and finest mill, the Strude, began work on handlooms in 1825. From 1829 shawls were also manufactured in Alva, by then one of the three main Hillfoot worsted and woollen centres; its first post office was established around 1825.

**The Railway and Seasonal Textile Work**: Tartans were later produced, but despite all these activities Alva was not a pre-reform burgh, and the eighth (Braehead) woollen mill did not begin work until the mid 19th century. By 1861 the population was nearing 3300, and the railway station – the terminus of a short branch from Cambus – opened in 1863. A gasworks was provided, and the famous textile firm of Todd & Duncan was founded in Alva in 1867. In 1869 nine small spinning mills were largely making yarns for Glasgow firms. Both steam and water power were used, but only some 220 people had steady jobs, for the work was highly seasonal: in the busy months about 1400 people were employed, weaving shawls, handkerchiefs, plaids and shirtings, but at other times jobs had to be sought in the Borders.

**Service Development and the Alloa Coal Company**: Alva golf club was founded in 1891 and provided a 9-hole parkland course. In 1894 Murray noted Alva as *"a thriving town, abounding in woollen mills"*, for the Burnbrae and Ochilvale woollen mills were established late in the 19th century. However, in 1895 Todd & Duncan moved from Alva to Kinross. The Glentana mill was added about 1900; in 1923 it acquired one of the last steam mill engines to be made in Kirkcaldy. The ancient Devon Colliery became the largest mine of the predominantly small-pit Alloa Coal Company, and is said to have remained at work for a longer period than any other large pit in Scotland; it was finally closed about 1964 because the white elephant Glenochil Mine *(see Cambus)* had taken all its remaining coal reserves.

**Goodbye to Trains and Printing**: The population of Alva had passed 4000 by 1951, enjoying facilities typical of a small village, including the little *Johnstone Arms Hotel*; it was around this time that Alva House was demolished. Hodgson's mill already manufactured knitwear, and by 1953 Robert Cunningham & Sons were printing books, though this enterprise later vanished. The railway was closed to passengers in 1954; from that time on, Alva had the general facilities of a large village; by 1972 these included the town council's covered swimming pool. However, this was closed in 1978 and public swimming transferred to Alva Academy's

*The Strude Mill, Alva's finest, was erected in 1825 – probably then the largest hand-loom weaving factory in Scotland. It was converted into flats in the 1980s.* *(RCAHMS / JRH)*

pool, until Tory government cuts controversially ended this in 1997.

**Bobbins, Knitwear and Holes in the Ground**: The Glentana mill was fully electrified in 1979; its old steam engine was retired, and is now preserved in the Museum of Scotland in Edinburgh. With coal mining at an end, the number of hotels in Alva rose remarkably, to five by 1980, the *Alva Glen Hotel* being prominent. By 1988 a woodland park had been created east of the Silver Glen. One mill was by then used for electronics, but a modern factory was used by Interbobbin. In 1990 the Coblecrook mills were operated by Hodgson Knitwear, employing 360 people, including the subsidiary Ochilvale dyeing and finishing mill. A firm of dyers, bleachers and finishers still operated, but the Glentana woollen mills soon closed, being converted to a Mill Trail visitor centre in the early 1990s. By 1991 there were 5200 residents in well-educated Alva. In 1995 Hodgson Knitwear still operated large single storey mills beside the Interbobbin factory. Both Ochilvale and the less well known Berryfield Mill had their own knitwear shops in 1994, when old pit shafts were still a hazard at Devon Village. A nature trail was open in the glen by 1997. The fine Strude Mill still stands, converted to flats.

## ALYTH, Ruthven & Bendochy — Map 6, B2

***Small town, East Perthshire,*** *pop. 2350* — OS 53: NO 2448

Alyth in east Perthshire lies 7 km east of Blairgowrie, at the foot of the hills of the Forest of Alyth; where the River Isla leaves the hills is the attractive waterfall known as Reekie Linn. Alyth had a thanage from about the 11th century, '*A Lith*' in Gaelic meaning *The Strength*. A church was built in the 13th century, and the Crawfords of Finavon obtained a barony burgh charter for Alyth in 1488; it had an early wool market, and a narrow packhorse bridge was built across the Alyth Burn, a tributary of the River Isla, around 1500. However, by 1593 the centre of the local presbytery was at Brigton of Ruthven (pronounced *Rivven*), 4 km to the east, where Pont's map of around 1600 confirms that the Isla was already bridged. He also indicated a village spelled *'Elecht'*, where a parish school existed by 1607. By then Alyth was the cattle market centre for Strath Isla, chosen perhaps because the deeply incised detour in the Isla valley inhibited a market at Ruthven, whereas there was an easy droving route to Alyth from the north over the col at Hill of Loyal; consequently the dates of the fairs at Alyth and Kirkton of Glenisla were linked: a new market cross was erected at Alyth in 1670. Meantime Bendochy parish west of Alyth remained stubbornly rural.

**Brewing, Fairs, Inventions and Linen**: The Roy map surveyed around 1750 showed Alyth as a larger place than Blairgowrie, but located on a dead-end spur from the main hillfoot road linking Blairgowrie to Kirriemuir via the Bridge of Ruthven. Alyth's southwards link to Coupar Angus still involved a ferry at *Boat of Bardmanach* (Bardmoney). The *Losset Inn* dates from 1760, and the clever though crippled inventor James Sandy was born in 1766 in what was to become the *Alyth Hotel*. Alyth brewery was in operation by 1777, and in 1797 Alyth had no fewer than nine fairs, putting it among the top ten stances in Scotland for frequency. Two years later, Heron noted the thousand or more inhabitants *"who are employed chiefly in the manufacture of linen"*, an industry which had apparently begun early in the century.

**Linen Dominates**: Alyth had a post office from 1801, and was connected by road to Meigle and Dundee from 1819. In 1822 Gilbert Sandy owned a small flax spinning mill with 120 spindles; J Taylor & Co had a much larger one at Ruthven with 512. The village also became overshadowed by Blairgowrie, its later – and soon more industrialised – neighbour, and between 1815 and 1825 the Alyth brewery ceased work. The Barony Church was built in 1839–43 to designs by Thomas Hamilton of Edinburgh; at that time, local weavers made about 1.44 million metres of *'webs'* annually. After 1850 Alyth became a police burgh.

**The Railway Epoch**: From 1861 cheaper coal was brought in by rail on a minor branch which the Caledonian laid from Alyth Junction on its Strathmore main line, enabling David Smith & Son to build a 100-loom steam-powered linen weaving factory in 1864. In 1869 the two flax, jute and hemp factories employed 315 workers; from one of these a carpet industry was later to develop. In 1894 Alyth was called by Murray *"a small town with some coarse linen factories"*, but also had two hotels, the *Commercial* and the *Airlie Arms*. In that year the local golf club was founded; James Braid designed a *"delightful"* 18-hole course. By 1904 there was an angling shop. The local linen industry faded away, but carpet manufacture continued and by 1939 a housing estate known as New Alyth had been built on the main road A926.

**Exit the Railway**: In 1951, Alyth's main facilities served some 5000 people, over half of them resident in the village. In 1946 Wordie & Co operated a small rail to road cartage depot, but the railway lost its passenger service in 1951, and rail freight ended in 1965; later the station site became a housing estate. In 1974 Alyth was a large village with about 40 shops, a minor tourist industry and some attributes of a town. These included the *Alyth Gazette & Guardian* – a tiny local newspaper associated with the *Kirriemuir Free Press* – the Forfar Carpets (later *'Florcraft'*) factory, a sawmill and a folk museum; but in 1975 its burgh status vanished. Three small hotels were open in 1980, including the *Lands of Loyal* just north of the village.

**Wimbledon Hedges, but No Carpets**: By 1991 only some 2350 people lived in the village, including a quite affluent retired group. However, by 1999 the Barony Church was becoming derelict, as was the old school which had closed as an auction hall about 1990. In 1996 Belwood Nurseries of Brigton of Ruthven, who already employed 36 people, supplied the hedging for the new No.1 Court at Wimbledon, and moved their 10 headquarters staff from Penicuik. In 1997 the former Trustee Savings Bank was closed and Alyth High School lost its secondary role, becoming primary only; senior pupils had to go to Blairgowrie or even Kirriemuir. About 1996 the carpet factory ceased work, its premises soon taken over by specialist restorers of vintage cars.

**Yet More Golf**: In the mid 1990s the Strathmore Golf Centre had laid out the 18-hole Rannaleroch and 9-hole Leitfy Links courses at Leroch, 3 km from of the town; then the new Glenisla golf course was created beside the original course. Joiners G A Davidson, established in 1953, build kit houses; miniature furniture is made and glass engraved. Alyth still serves as a centre for the surrounding raspberry-growing area, having two banks, a post office, fire station, museum and public library, and about 20 shops.

## AMULREE — Map 6, A3

***Settlement, Perthshire,*** *pop. under 100* — OS 52: NN 9036

About 20 km north of Crieff, General Wade's military road to the Highlands via the Sma' Glen met Strath Bran, which offered an easy route to Dunkeld, while to the west a hill road to Kenmore by Glen Quaich passed Loch Freuchie with its ancient crannog and hut circles. Originally built as a kingshouse, the lonely inn at Amulree *(G. 'Royal Mill')* was noted by Dorothy Wordsworth in 1803. By 1839 there was a post office, and a school and telephone exchange were opened later, but Amulree stands among the moors at an altitude of some 270 m, and never grew into a village. The old *Amulree Hotel* had 14 rooms in the 1970s; both this and the post office stayed open, for Amulree was still in effect a crossroads of touring routes.

## ANCRUM — Map 3, B4

***Small Borders village,*** *pop. under 300* — OS 74: NT 6224

The Roman road called Dere Street cut across the River Teviot about 2 km below its confluence with the Ale Water, above the north bank of which were two ancient forts and a standing stone. By the 12th century a market was being held north of the Ale Water, at what was later called Old Ancrum. Only its cross survived the depredations of Henry VIII's English troops in 1544. When Timothy Pont mapped Teviotdale around 1600, two mills turned on the north bank of the Ale Water between Old Ancrum and the confluence. New Ancrum was a substantial settlement south of the Ale Water on the site of the modern village; this gained a barony charter in 1639 as Nether Ancrum. A bridge just below the confluence gave access to the 16th century Timpendean Tower, on the slopes 1 km south of the river.

**A Village in Quiet Decline**: By the time of Roy's map of about 1754, the emparked Ancrum House had replaced Old Ancrum. In 1799 Heron wrote of Ancrum as a *"village"*. The main road later labelled A68 which deviated west from the Roman line near Lilliardsedge about 5 km north of Ancrum, passed by the village, crossing the Teviot by an 18th century bridge which still remains, though made redundant in the 1930s by a new reinforced concrete structure; meantime by 1893 Ancrum had a post office. By the 1950s about 500 people lived there, served by basic facilities; however, 30% of the population was lost in twenty years, leaving just a small village with a pub and a post office, which has lately closed. Ancrum House was demolished around 1970, leaving its surrounding parkland, but by 1984 the Harestanes Visitor centre was open 1 km east of the village.

## ANNAN, Brydekirk & Chapelcross — Map 2, C5

***Dumfriesshire town**, pop. 8900* — OS 85: NY 1966

Annan lies on the Solway Firth at the mouth of the River Annan, a name which may derive from the same early root as Clackmannan. It had a medieval motte, and apparently became a baronial burgh between 1153 and 1214; but it was omitted from Pryde's list. By the 12th or 13th century a *'hospital'* had been established, and Annan was shown on the Gough map of c.1250. Robert the Bruce built a castle there about 1300. About 1415 John Hardyng wrote that there was a *"very ready way"* from Dumfries to Carlisle; this implies the existence of a regular ferry at Annan by that date, but because Annan was repeatedly devastated in border wars, other early travelling authors seem not to have passed that way.

**From Royal Burgh to 'Decay'**: Annan became a Royal Burgh in 1532, but paid no tax in 1535–56. Even so, Pont's map of about 1610 showed a substantial town. Though no evidence of a river crossing was mapped, at that time there was definitely a ferry at Annan. A parish school was started in 1628, Annan's first post office was opened as early as 1642 on the Carlisle to Ireland route, and it would appear that a river bridge was soon built. However, Annan was not mentioned in Tucker's exhaustive survey of ports in 1655, and the well-aware Defoe was equivocal about Annan in the 1720s, stating that *"the merchants, and men of substance, removed to Dumfries; the town continues, to all appearance, in a state of irrevocable decay"*. Yet he added that *"the bridge is very firm and good, and there is a tolerable good market"*. The Roy map of the 1750s showed Annan to have been a linear settlement with three radial roads (today the A75 east, B724 west and B723 north); a mill stood beside and west of the river mouth.

**Cotton Mill and Bathless Inn**: About 1785 a large cotton mill was built, and Annan had two annual fairs by 1797. Heron noted in 1799 *"this town is very ancient. It contains upwards of 1600 inhabitants, has some trade, and annually exports a considerable quantity of grain"*. In the 1790s the town council bought a large house in the High Street, which became the Academy in 1802, the year that framework knitting was begun locally; it later reverted to a house and shops. The new village at Brydekirk, 4km north-west of Annan, was laid out about 1803 but remained of little note. Dorothy Wordsworth praised the town's varied shop signs in 1803, but found Annan's houses *"large and gloomy"*; in 1812 it was simply observed of Annan's inn, already known as the *Queensberry Arms – "nae baths"*.

**Rapid Growth 1815–25**: According to Chambers, while nothing was left of Bruce's castle by the 1820s, Annan was *"an extremely neat and regularly built town, of about 3000 inhabitants, with two very fine bridges over the Annan; a great part of the town has been built of late years, and it is still increasing in extent and prosperity. The grammar-school of Annan is a distinguished seminary"*. What he referred to as the second bridge was actually a replacement designed by Robert Stevenson, begun in stone about 1821 and opened in 1826. A quay and two jetties for the Liverpool steamers were built about that time; shipbuilding was also carried on, and Cumbrian fisherfolk from Maryport settled in the town.

**Whisky, Banking and the Provost's Gasworks**: The Annandale distillery was built in 1830 by exciseman George Donald, but the only feature of Annan noted by Cobbett, who briefly visited the town in 1832, was the Assembly Room. The imposing Erskine Church was built in 1834–35 to designs by William Gregan. Limestone was still quarried at Kelhead in 1834 and Annan was shipping cattle by 1835, the year when its savings bank was founded. About 1840 the Southern Bank of Scotland, based in Dumfries, built a prominent branch office of red ashlar stone at 73 High Street; merger took it to the Clydesdale in 1858, and it was later a Bank of Scotland branch. A gasworks set up by the town council in 1838 was sited in the provost's garden, since no-one else would have it in their back yard! The local paper, the *Annandale Observer*, was founded in 1857.

**The Grandiose Solway Railway Crossing**: What was shortly to become the Glasgow & South Western Railway opened in 1848, connecting Annan with Gretna and Dumfries; from 1852 there was a link with Glasgow, and Carlisle was reached in 1853. A second line passing Annan was opened by the Solway Junction Railway in 1869. This was intended for the transport of Cumbrian haematite ore to Lanarkshire ironworks, via Kirkbride in Cumbria, crossing the costly 1700-metre long Solway Viaduct. This spidery and vulnerable structure reached the Scottish shore at Seafield; the line served Annan's Shawhill station and from there wound north, ending at a junction on the Caledonian main line at Kirtlebridge. The viaduct – which had cast-iron piers – was smashed by ice floes in 1881, but reopened in 1884.

**Industries, Quarrying and Football**: Meantime the small Annandale distillery had been modernised in 1883, and three years later was operated by a combination of turbine wheel and steam; over 125,000 litres of malt whisky was produced annually, the draff being fed to cattle and pigs. In 1894 the cotton mill and a bacon curing works were both open. However, in that year the Newbie grain mills burned out, and stood in ruins for over half a century. In 1877 Cochrane & Co, engineers of Annan, pioneered the vertical smoke-tube boiler. In the late 19th century Cochranes also worked at Birkenhead, moving to new works at Newbie near Annan in 1902, and by 1925 the firm made boilers in 24 standard sizes for use with ships' donkey engines or for heating the water in public baths. By 1880 a quarry in Permian sandstone at Corsehill, 4km north of Annan, produced fine-grained ornamental and building stone. It had reached a depth of 30m by the early 1900s, employed 241 men in 1916, was still connected to the adjacent railway in 1937, when at least 8 masons were employed, and stayed open until about 1956. Public library facilities started in 1903, with Carnegie money. Solway Star FC of Annan played in the Scottish League for just 3 seasons, 1923–26.

**Exit Whisky, enter Chapelcross**: The distillery and the railway viaduct were both closed in 1921; the viaduct was demolished in 1934. A bus service to Carlisle operated from 1925, and Shawhill station was closed in 1931, when passenger trains ceased to run to Kirtlebridge. Wolsey of Leicester opened a knitwear factory in the 1920s. A wartime RAF base built about 1942 at Chapelcross, some 4km north-east of the town, was selected about 1945 as the site for a nuclear power station built by the government-owned British Nuclear Fuels Ltd (BNFL) and equipped with four Magnox reactors. From 1959 it produced plutonium for the Ministry of Defence, with electricity as a by-product; Tritium for nuclear weapons was produced from about 1977. A waste water pipe was laid in the trackbed of the former railway, discharging its suspect contents into the Solway. Brydekirk expanded with the growth of

*The rolling and welding bay, Cochrane's Boiler works, Newbie, Annan, in the early 1970s. The works was built on the Solway Firth to be served by coastal steamers. Cochrane's is now part of Rolls Royce.* *(JRH)*

Chapelcross, but little of the accommodation provided seems to have been permanent, and by 1971 its population had settled at around 300, with primary school and post office.

**Cinemas, Cans and Cranes**: Annan itself grew from a population of about 6000 in 1951, served by typical urban facilities, including two cinemas, and for years after the second world war a miniature repertory theatre played in the town; however, golfers had to play well out of town on the coast at Powfoot, 6 km west. By 1954, when home refrigerators were a luxury and before frozen foods became general, there was a cannery among whose products were prawns from North Berwick. In 1954 John Boyd & Co of Annan, established in 1947, built the engine turntable which is now the centrepiece in the National Railway Museum at York, and in 1968 constructed the two tall 10-tonne travelling grab cranes for the Burntisland dock bauxite traffic.

**District Headquarters, Chemicals and Chipboard**: In 1975 Annan became the HQ of the extensive but sparsely peopled Annandale & Eskdale District; the local newspaper group was also edited there. Salmon and shrimps were still being caught locally in 1976, but Glaxo's pharmaceuticals factory was built in 1977, relying – like the nuclear industry – on the tides to disperse its questionable effluents in the Solway. The modern Weyroc chipboard mill employed 50 people in 1978. In 1980 Annan had average town facilities, serving (as they had in 1951) a total population of some 17,000. The sheep and cattle market was still active, and the old *Queensberry Arms* had long since acquired enough baths to gain two stars.

**Industry Continues but Traffic Bypassed**: Both Cochrane and Boyd's were acquired by Clarke Chapman Ltd of Glasgow in the 1970s. In 1979 their Thompson Cochrane and John Boyd Crane and Bridge Divisions were still busy, the former at the Newbie Works. By 1985 there was a caravan site; a lengthy bypass which opened in 1989 relieved the town, and the smaller places to the east, of through traffic on the increasingly busy A75 route to Stranraer and Northern Ireland. In 1991 the resident population was 8930. At that time the Ross Young (UB) bakery at Annan was a sizeable operation. In 1990 when Chapelcross employed 640 people, BNFL evaluated its replacement by a new nuclear station; but it was granted a ten-year extension. In 1992 BNFL again proposed a new Pressurised Water Reactor (PWR) at Chapelcross, solely to generate power, with a dam and reservoir in the Forest of Ae to provide cooling water. But this came to nothing, and in 1996 when the newer nuclear stations were being sold off, elderly Chapelcross was again allowed a 10-year life.

**Annan regains Stone but loses Local Government**: In 1994 Annan market was still very busy with sheep and some cattle, while Glaxochem, NFI Combustion and Pinneys (salmon smokers) were still active. In 1995 Cochrane Boilers was a member of the Rolls-Royce industrial power group, who had 1500 Scottish employees in three plants. In 1996 the district council lost its powers to Dumfries & Galloway, sadly ending Annan's independent role in local government after 800 years. Corsehill quarry was reopened in 1981 and still works under the Dunhouse Quarry Company or Onyx Contractors. Glaxo still employed 170 staff. By then riverside *Warmanbie* 2 km to the north was a hotel, but the Erskine Church was empty and awaiting a new user. The *Ladystreet Cinema* was still open. In 2000 there were many derelict properties that gave cause for concern, but Pinneys announced a major expansion, aiming to create 300 to 600 new jobs. The historic *Queensberry Arms* now has 24 en-suite rooms – some improvement on 1812!

## ANNBANK, Auchincruive & Mossblown

**Map 1, C2**

***Ayrshire villages**, pop. 3000* — OS 70: NS 4023

The little-known St Quivox gave his name to a parish beside the incised meanders of the River Ayr about 5 km east of Ayr burgh. By 1560 the mansion of Auchincruive, Lord Cathcart's seat, stood on the cliffy banks of the river in a well-settled area. Timothy Pont's map, made about 1600, named *'Montblawin'* and *'Preuick Mill'*. From 1621 a parish school was open. Roy's map made in the 1750s showed Auchincruive beside a road between Ayr and Mauchline; 2 km to the east was the hamlet of Annbank. In 1764 Richard Oswald bought Auchincruive, opened coal pits and commissioned Robert Adam to redesign Auchincruive House. He must also have built Oswald's Bridge, which crosses the River Ayr nearby.

**Railways, Mining Village and Agricultural Research**: When the Ayr & Mauchline branch of the Glasgow & South Western Railway was opened in 1870, Auchincruive was given a station beside St Quivox church, while Annbank Station was sited where this crossed the main road near Mossblown Farm and Drumley House. From there the single-track line to Cumnock, opened in 1872, diverged to the south, then turning east via Ochiltree, and soon serving industrial Drongan and Rankinston; by 1875 coal from the area was exported by rail through Ayr harbour. A small village of single-storey cottages named Annbank was built some 2 km south of the station, soon gaining a post office. A mineral railway which opened in 1892 diverged west of the station to join the Ayr to Glasgow main line at Monkton. Drumley pit was opened north-east of the station in the 1890s by the Ayr Colliery Company, which built only 36 houses for its workers, hence by 1902 miners from Ayr travelled to work there by special trains; by 1914 Annbank held over 1000 people. The West of Scotland Agricultural College at Auchincruive was founded in 1902 and the Hannah Dairy Research Institute opened in 1928; in 1930 the Oswald family gifted Auchincruive House to the nation and it became the College centrepiece.

**Confusing Collieries, Bricks and Station Village**: By then Auchincruive Colliery had been sunk beside the railway to Monkton. Comprising Shafts 1, 2 & 3, it gained pithead baths around 1933; shafts 4 & 5 formed a completely distinct entity. Another pit – Enterkine 9 & 10 – was sunk west of Neilshill to the north; it supplied fireclay to Annbank brickworks near the church, where 30,000 bricks a day were made, and later took in Drumley shaft, before closing in 1959. By 1951 some 2000 people lived at Annbank, with nearly as many in a new settlement around Annbank Station, which had also gained a cinema, a maternity hospital, a Catholic primary school, a small secondary school and a police station. By 1953 passenger trains had been withdrawn from the Cumnock line and from Annbank station; Auchincruive colliery was closed in 1960.

***'Annbank Station'* becomes Mossblown Village**: By 1971 the cinema had also closed, but 2800 people still lived beside the pointed Drumley bing at Annbank Station. The last pit had closed by 1972 and the Monkton rail connection had been cut; the secondary school had gone by 1977. After the withdrawal of passing passenger trains in 1977 the platforms remained *in situ*, but the settlement beside the former station was formally renamed Mossblown. By 1981 the maternity hospital had also closed, but a few other local services developed at Mossblown, where by 1980 Drumley House was an independent junior boys' school; to the east of this a short-lived hotel was built in the early 1980s. However, only the facilities of a small village were available by 1980.

**Fluctuating Fortunes**: The railway to Mauchline was closed in 1985, but part of the former Cumnock branch remained open to serve Killoch Colliery, whose washery was still used after the pit was closed – so when the Mauchline line was reinstated in 1988 to facilitate opencast coal movements, Annbank reappeared as a junction. By 1991 only 925 people lived at Annbank, which kept its pub and post office, and 2039 at Mossblown; 60% lived in publicly rented housing, though new private housing was soon added. In 1992, as the National College for Food, Land & Environmental Studies, Auchincruive offered a range of courses including farming, aquaculture and food technology; by 1999 the restored Auchincruive House had been renamed Oswald Hall.

## ANNIESLAND & Jordanhill — Map 15, C4

***Suburbs of Glasgow,*** *pop. 15,000* — OS 64: NS 5468

The low ridge west of Partick and south-west of the River Kelvin bore many small settlements when Pont's map of Lennox was made about 1600. These included Jordanhill, perhaps already a mansionhouse, and also Westoun. By the 1750s the Roy map showed the start of a road system in this wholly rural area. About 1790 the Forth & Clyde Canal was opened from Maryhill to Bowling, stepping down through two flights of locks north and west of Knightswood Farm some 6 km from Glasgow. Teacher training was started at the mansion of Jordanhill in its extensive policies in 1828, but little other development took place until the dead-straight Great Western Road was built as a Glasgow radial turnpike in 1838–39. The Gartnavel *Lunatic Asylum* as it was then called (later Gartnavel Royal Hospital) was built in deliberate isolation east of Jordanhill between 1840 and 1843.

**Railway, Iron, Gas and Timber**: The Glasgow, Dumbarton & Helensburgh Railway passed through the area to the north of the canal from 1858, but the nearest station was at Drumchapel. A rail-connected smelter – the Garscube Ironworks – was built beside the canal, but did not flourish, and closed within a few years. In 1871 the Partick, Hillhead & Maryhill Gas Company built the Temple gasworks beside the canal; this was enlarged by Glasgow Corporation in 1893–1900 with two huge gasholders together holding a quarter million $m^3$; when town gas production at the nearby Dawsholm works ceased nearly a century later, these remained in use for storage. In 1874 Robinson, Dunn & Co set up the Temple Sawmills on the canal bank, and some cottages were built in Anniesland Road about 1877; but little other new development existed by 1879. In 1883 the Great Western Steam Laundry was built at Crow Road, the main route south from Anniesland Cross.

**Railway Stations, Bricks and Iron**: The Glasgow City & District Railway, a North British subsidiary, was built through the area on a north–south axis in 1885–86, with a station for many years called Great Western Road; another station was provided in 1887 beside the new triangle of lines laid at Hyndland Junctions 1 km to the south by the associated Glasgow, Yoker & Clydebank Railway. These facilities soon stimulated development on the axis of Crow Road/Bearsden Road. By 1903 Knightswood Rows provided some housing, and brickworks grew up nearby. The smaller Temple Ironworks of William Baird, structural engineer, was founded about 1890 and enlarged in 1913. By 1894 a tramway had been laid to Glasgow; this horse-drawn facility had been electrified by 1911.

**Laundries, Printing and Optical Instruments**: Alexander Kennedy's Castlebank Laundry was erected around 1896, being followed some five years later by Ferrier & Co's Alexandra Park Laundry, which later became a repair garage for W Beardmore & Co, the major engineers. In 1903 the Glasgow University printers, R MacLehose & Co, built a printing factory; this was extended in 1914. The optical instruments manufacturers Barr & Stroud (B&S), founded in Partick in 1888, moved in 1903–06 from Byres Road to their eventually very large Patent Works at Anniesland; this was partly financed by the Bank of Scotland, who opened an Anniesland branch in 1904. About 1913 Gleniffer Motors established the Temple Works, making petrol and paraffin marine engines, followed in 1914 by the conversion of the extensive site of the Garscube Ironworks into the Netherton Works of the Ioco Proofing Company, which made an early form of plastic laminates.

**Knightswood: Social Engineering lacks Lubrication**: The mansion was taken over by Jordanhill College, opened in 1921; later a chocolate factory was built nearby. The placename Anniesland – which did not yet appear on the 1895 *'One-Inch'* OS map – had been added to it by 1925, and in the early 20th century Great Western Road was extended on sweeping curves from Anniesland Cross to Duntocher. The large Glasgow Corporation housing estate of Knightswood to the west of Anniesland, built in the 1920s, was denied a public house; however, the *Boulevard Cinema*, built in 1928, must have been thought harmless, and the Knightswood municipal golf course of 1929 positively beneficial! Bearsden Road was rebuilt across the canal as a major road in 1931–32. Gartnavel Hospital was expanding in the 1930s, and about that time Great Western Road station was renamed Anniesland by the LNER. Dairies, furniture and carbon-paper works also existed. Among private housing developments were the large 11-storey blocks of mansion flats built at *Kelvin Court* in the 1930s; the *Ascot*

*Cinema*, built in 1939, eventually went over to bingo as the *County*.

**From Trams to Blue Trains – and Education Galore**: By 1951 the area reached its maximum population of some 35,000, with the facilities of a small town. Though Glasgow's trams soon vanished, the local railways were effectively electrified in 1961 with *'Blue Train'* stations at Anniesland, Jordanhill and Westerton. The Glasgow University veterinary school moved to new premises on the Garscube Road about 1960, Anniesland College of Further Education was open at Hatfield Drive by 1971, and the newly independent High School of Glasgow moved to a site beside its existing club playing fields at Old Anniesland in 1975–76; the former Drewsteignton School of Bearsden became its junior school. But despite these new activities the population in the area steadily fell to an estimated 16,000 in 1981. By 1988 each leg of Anniesland Cross was a dual carriageway.

**The Peace Dividend? Exit Barr & Stroud**: Barr & Stroud, by the 1980s part of Pilkington Optronics and 50% French-owned, then employed some 2450 people, largely on defence contracts making equipment such as night sights for tanks. In 1990–92 drastic redundancies induced by the ending of the Cold War were forced on them, and in 1992 B&S moved their 800 remaining workers to a new factory at Linthouse, Govan; their departure from Anniesland would enable a major shopping and leisure development to be built there by the GA Property group; a new Safeway superstore opened in 1995.

**Education and Health Services**: In 1991 Jordanhill College was discussing a merger with Strathclyde University; its allied secondary school continued to function, and had 580 pupils in 1997, when Knightswood Secondary had 616. In 1991 the closure of the 1275-bed Gartnavel Royal Hospital was mooted, while the 564-bed General Hospital was to be expanded from 1995 to enable the proposed closure of the Western Infirmary at Partick. In 1992 the independent High School of Glasgow added to the facilities for its 950 mixed pupils aged 3 to 18. By 1994 Knightswood claimed one of the highest proportions of elderly people in Europe, and half the council-built houses had been sold off to their tenants. Controversy arose in 1996 when the Scottish Sports Fund granted major aid from the National Lottery to the co-educational High School, for sports facilities intended also for community use. In the late 1990s Glasgow University's Westerland playing fields were developed for housing, but both Gartnavel hospitals remain in use.

## ANSTRUTHER

**Map 6, C4**

***Small town, south Fife coast,*** *pop. 3000*

OS 59: NO 5603

Also see: *Cellardyke*

The twin villages of Anstruther, often called *Ainster* by the locals, line the shore of the East Neuk of Fife. The undateable and long ruined Dreel Castle at *'East Anster'* was the ancient stronghold of its landowners *"the ancient family, Anstruther of that Ilk"* (Chambers). By 1225 fishing boats were based at the mouth of the Dreel Burn which separates Easter and Wester Anstruther; from there fish was sent to Balmerino Abbey, which from 1318 owned a section of Anstruther Easter. The Abbey promoted it as a fishing base and in the 15th century built a chapel (dedicated to St Ayles), and an abbot's house. Although no burgh had yet been chartered, some overseas trading was recorded under Dysart customs as early as 1480. But development was slow, for the Dreel Burn still had to be forded about 1500.

**Charters, Trade and the Armada Straggler**: The formal history of settlement in Anstruther and nearby Kilrenny is confusing: six separate charters were granted, as burghs of barony and Royal Burghs, between 1540 and 1592 (for clarity, the development of *Cellardyke* and its parent *Kilrenny* are a separate entry). Both the Anstruthers were to acquire harbours; one was certainly complete by 1587, and in 1588 an Armada galleon was befriended there, for the local vessels were by then trading as far afield as Spain. By 1595 a school was open, but in 1621 Anstruther paid under 1.5% of the Scottish Customs dues, whereas Kilrenny with its fishing harbour at Cellardyke paid none.

**Churches and Superstition**: By 1577 there was a reformed church at Anstruther Wester. In 1590–91 the energetic local minister Andrew Melville ensured that Anstruther Easter gained Kilrenny's large new manse; in 1634 a church was built there, dedicated to St Adrian, which in 1641 became the centre of a separate parish, leaving Kilrenny to farming and fishing. Religious superstition reborn under Presbyterianism led in 1643–44 to the cruel slaughter of many local *'witches'*, and many Anstruther fishermen were killed at the Battle of Kilsyth in 1645. The remaining Anstruther fishermen abandoned their Barra and Shetland herring haunts, but were back in Shetland by 1661. Brewing was being carried on commercially in Anstruther by the mid 17th century. Tucker reported in 1655 that the two ports possessed ten vessels of up to 50 tons.

**The 1670 Disaster shifts Trade to Anstruther Easter**: Chambers noted much later that Anstruther *"was much resorted to by vessels from foreign ports, particularly from Holland, which preferred landing their goods here and sending them up to Leith by lighters, to performing that perilous voyage themselves. Occasion was thus given to a system of warehousing; but in 1670 a whole street of warehouses were washed away by the sea from the shore at West Anster"*. Two breakwaters were shown at each of two harbours (presumably East Anster and Cellardyke) on John May's chart of about 1680. It appears likely that some stonework still visible is of that date or older. In the late 1680s the Wester town council petitioned against taxes on grounds of poverty, adding that their burgh was *"past all hope of having trade in time coming"*.

**Anstruther entertains Charles in the Crow's Nest**: By then Dreel Castle had a rooftop addition in which Charles II dined, allegedly remarking *"What a good dinner I've gotten in a Craw's Nest"* – hence the modern hotel name. The Dreel Burn had been bridged by 1700, and a new manse was built at Anstruther Wester in 1703. In 1710 Anstruther Easter was noted by Sir Robert Sibbald as *"well built and populous, of great trade, with good magazines* (storehouses) *and cellars and accommodations for curing of herrings, the staple commodity of this town"*, which had lately sent 30 boats to fish for herring off Lewis and owned 24 ships. He noted of the Anstruthers and Cellardyke *"these three burghs seem to be but one town"*.

**Roads, Smuggling, and the decline of Fishing**: There was a road network in the Kellie area by 1717, and Defoe noted Anstruther in the 1720s as a *"small town"*. A site adjoining the chapel of St Ayles became a boatbuilding yard about 1737. But many Anstruther town councillors were also smugglers, and by 1742 there was a King's Warehouse for the locally corrupt Customs service. Anstruther had a post office by 1744. The Roy survey made around 1750 indicated a single linear settlement, including both Anstruthers and the village of Cellardyke, with the harbours at Anstruther Easter and Cellardyke that were to be such a permanent feature. Besides the coast road, the St Andrews road was indicated, showing the early nodal significance of the Easter burgh. By 1797 Anstruther Easter had three fairs a year and was a post town. Yet Heron wrote in 1799 that *"from the decline of the fisheries, the burghs of East and West Anstruther are become very inconsiderable"*.

**Copper in Australia and Herring in the Forth**: Walter Watson Hughes, born in Anstruther in 1802, had a dubious early career but was eventually to discover copper in Australia's Yorke Peninsula, becoming that new country's wealthiest man; he ended with a knighthood. Rodgers' brewery was still active in 1825. Chambers noted that at *'East Anster'* there was still a tannery and *"a trade of imports from Holland and the Baltic"*; but *'West Anster'* was by 1827 *"altogether a very insignificant place"*. The herring returned to the Forth in vast numbers in 1827, and for a time upwards of 150 boats worked out of Anstruther Easter with its large harbour, or from the small harbour at Cellardyke. The Anstruther fishery office which opened in 1824 registered the locally owned boats, most of which had been built at Leith, but some were locally built by James Henderson. A ships' chandlery and net lofts were formed on the site of the chapel, which was demolished about 1850.

**Steam Packet, Clipper Captain and Newspapers**: From 1845 the Edinburgh & Dundee Steam Packet Company's steamer *Britannia* called regularly at Anstruther, Crail and Elie en route between Dundee and Leith. John Keay, born in the Wester burgh in 1828, captained the famous *Ariel* and in his 90 years was master of many other clipper ships. In 1856 a weekly newspaper, the *East of Fife Record*, began publication at Anstruther. However in 1860 the Custom House was closed, the AR fishing boat registration discontinued and all local vessels, of which a growing number were decked, had to bear Kirkcaldy (KY) registrations.

**Railways and Harbour Grow in a Grim Hole?**: In 1863 the railway from Thornton to Leven and Kilconquhar was extended to Anstruther by the Leven & East Fife Railway Company. A lifeboat station was opened in 1865, and the Easter harbour was considerably enlarged as the Union Harbour around 1868–70 by the Stevensons of Edinburgh; but one of the family, the South Sea minded author Robert Louis, sent there as a young supervisor, found the place a *"grey, grim, sea-beaten hole"*!

**Fisheries Heyday, Boatbuilding and Railway extension**: However, the new harbour became for a time Fife's principal fishing port, with about 220 sailing boats crowding it in the 1880s. Fish used to be carted to the station, and rail-hauled to Methil docks for export, mainly to Germany. In 1878 Anstruther had a bank and in the late 19th century there was a local watchmaker. Waid Academy first opened its doors to pupils aged 10 or more in 1886, but fees had to be paid. Meantime in 1884 the line was further extended from Anstruther to Crail by the North British Railway, eventually reaching St Andrews in 1887; for a time it was busy with fish traffic. Wooden fishing boats were still built on Anstruther quay, including steam drifters around 1900; but little other industry developed.

*A timber boat being built at Anstruther in the 1970s by the yard of Alexander Aitken – which closed soon after.* *(RS)*

**Golf, Hotels and Media**: A golf club, founded in 1890, laid out a 9-hole course between Anstruther and Pittenweem. David Henry, a well known architect in St Andrews, designed Anstruther's imposing Chalmers Memorial Church, built in 1890 – his best work. In 1894 Murray called Anstruther *"a small seaport town"*, with the *Commercial* and *Royal* hotels. By 1917 the Anstruther local paper was the *Coast Burghs Observer*, and had been renamed by 1925 as the *East Fife Observer*; but by 1957 it was no more. Meantime silent films had been shown in the Town Hall from 1912, and *'talkies'* at the *Empire* from 1931; there was also the *Regal* which in 1952 claimed 800 seats but by 1958 only 399!

**Fishing Boats from Steam to Diesel**: Around 1920 most local fishermen lived in the adjacent fishing centre of Cellardyke. Anstruther's fishing community was slow to change, ordering Britain's last steam drifter the *Wilson Line*, built in Aberdeen in 1932. The amalgamation of the three burghs, considered in 1914 to help to pay for yet more harbour works then intended at Anstruther, took place in 1929, acquiring Scotland's longest burgh title: *The Royal Burgh of Kilrenny, Anstruther Easter and Anstruther Wester*! In 1929 also, two of a new breed of 16 m fishing vessels with Gardner diesel engines were launched at their home port of Anstruther, and soon there was an enclosed fish-selling shed. Until the start of war in 1939, potatoes were still carried from Anstruther in German ships.

**Coal from 1945**: Soon after 1945, outcrop coal was mined for a time at Billow Ness, but NCB plans of 1953 for larger workings came to nought. Up to 1955 Alex Aitken of Anstruther built some larger motor vessels over 21 m in length, such as the *Argonaut* and *Brighter Hope*, for local owners intent on seine and great line fishing in more distant waters. In 1951 Anstruther and its immediate neighbours still had small-town facilities and a population of 3300, with a little holiday camp and small factories making waterproof clothing and golf cleeks.

**Drifting away from the Fishing to Tourism**: After 1945 the skippers of the fishing boats largely forsook Anstruther's large harbour for Pittenweem's smaller one, leaving a handful of steam drifters still working. The station still had a crossing loop where coaches were often added to summer trains en route from St Andrews to Edinburgh via the coast – until the whole railway with its small engine shed was closed by Beeching in

1964. Over the years to 1981 both cinemas and the employment exchange also vanished. By way of compensation, in 1965 the 262-year-old manse of Anstruther Wester became the *Craw's Nest Hotel*; another hotel and a scampi processing factory also opened.

**The Scottish Fisheries Museum**: The Scottish Fisheries Museum Trust took over much of the boatyard in 1968 and opened as a museum the following year, opposite the attractive and closely related feature of traditional wooden fishing vessels being built on the open quay beside the lifeboat station; but this industry ceased soon after 1974. The fine Chalmers Church stood empty in 1984, and was soon destroyed by fire. Anstruther remained a quaint small town of some 3154 people in 1991, which with its neighbours Pittenweem and Crail serves the East Neuk. Besides the museum, its three hotels, two caravan sites, pleasure boating and a little summer fair on the pier provide a minor resort role. There is still inshore crustacean fishing.

**Enlarged Museum under Threat**: In 1990 the recently enlarged Scottish Fisheries Museum drew over 38,000 visitors and in 1995 was again enlarged, this time taking in the remaining premises of the former fishing boat builders Smith & Hutton. However, the former North Carr light vessel – which had for some 20 years been on show at the harbour – was then towed away to Dundee for display. By 1994 the *Craw's Nest Hotel* had been extended to 31 rooms. The *Smugglers Inn* still had 9 rooms. By then John Hughes, fish merchant, had built sizeable new premises. A Co-op superstore was built on the north edge of town in 2000, but the future of the famed Fisheries Museum was under threat in 2000 as it could not meet its running costs.

## APPIN, Portnacroish, Port Appin & Creagan

**Map 5, A2**

***Argyllshire villages,*** *pop. 500* — OS 49: NM 9346

This district of low hills and valleys lies on the indented coast of Lorne some 15km north-east of Oban as the crow flies, and is sheltered by the Isle of Lismore; the name Appin signifies *'Abbey Lands'* in Gaelic. Its main settlement Portnacroish – *'Port of the Cross'* – lies beside the shallow inlet of Loch Laich, where in the 15th century the tall keep of Castle Stalker was built on a tiny islet. In the 16th century came Castle Shuna, erected on Shuna, a larger offshore islet which is exposed to the gales of Loch Linnhe and not to be confused with another isle of that name *(q.v.)*; both castles became ruinous. There were also several tiny settlements on the mainland when Pont mapped the area about 1600.

**Ferries and Mansions**: Appin House was built in the 17th century on the coast 2km north of Portnacroish, and by 1733 the Shian Ferry plied across Loch Creran to connect with Benderloch. By about 1750 as the Roy map showed, the mansionhouse of Airds had been built beside Port Appin, from where a ferry plied to Lismore; the area was still somewhat wooded. At that time Airds and the small settlement at Kinlochlaich were also connected by tracks with the ferries at Ballachulish across Loch Leven and at *'Rugave' (Rubha Garve)* crossing Loch Creran 2km above Shian; a track through Strath Appin led up Glen Creran to cross over a 500m col into Glencoe.

**Roads, Steamers and the Ballachulish Railway**: Post offices were opened at Portnacroish in 1775 and at Appin in 1788. In 1803 Dorothy Wordsworth found *"a small village – a few huts and an indifferent inn"*; but there was a school nearby, and miles of *"excellent"* smooth roads built for Lord Tweeddale. By 1846 steamers were calling at Port Appin, and better housing was built in the 19th century. In 1903 the marginal Connel to Ballachulish branch of the Caledonian Railway was opened, with a crossing station named Appin at Portnacroish, where the *Appin Hotel* was sited until about 1960, and a station at Creagan beside Loch Creran, which was crossed by a costly steel truss viaduct. The line which gave fine views throughout was closed in 1966, a victim of the unimaginative Beeching Plan, but the viaduct remained.

**Tourism, Co-operation, Computers and Cut-off**: For some time around 1982 a museum was open at Appin House. In the late 20th century the Appin area contained about 500 residents, and the facilities of a small village. The tiny country inn known as the *Airds Hotel* at Port Appin was gradually improved and enlarged. By 1992 Port Appin's shop was owned by a village co-operative and was the terminus of a privately operated workers' ferry to the Glensanda superquarry *(see Kingairloch)*. The primary school shared its computers with Lismore school, and the largest nursery garden centre in the west Highlands had been developed at Kinlochlaich House. In 1996 both Appin and Port Appin retained post offices (but since closed). The long-disused Creagan viaduct, built to carry trains, was adapted in 1997–98 to carry A828 road traffic, cutting 10km from the distance between Oban and Fort William; already some 5km of the old railway alignment north from Appin House had been incorporated into the improved road. The *Airds Hotel* at Port Appin (closed midwinter) has 12 rooms.

## APPLECROSS

**Map 8, B3**

***W. Highland settlement,*** *pop. under 100* — OS 24: NG 7144

This remote area in Wester Ross possessed an early Christian community, founded by St Maelrubha in 671 and originally named *Abercrossan*. Its Gaelic name is *'A Chomraich'* (The Sanctuary), shown in isolation on Robert Gordon's mid 17th century map and engraved by Blaeu as *'Combrich'*. But Roy's survey of about 1750 showed Applecross House with its enclosed policies and shelterbelts; *'Balmulen'* too already existed (this later became translated as Milton), but the only crofts indicated were inland of the site of the later village.

**The Pass of the Cattle**: As the area had no strategic importance there were no roads until about the mid 19th century, when the 20%-plus zigzags of the 625-metre high Beallach nam Bo (*Pass of the Cattle*), were made up as probably the loftiest public road in Britain. By 1894 a tiny temperance inn was open at Applecross; in those days a mail gig came over the pass from Strathcarron three times a week, winter weather permitting. This inaccessibility led to decline: the former township of Salacher to the north of the village was connected to Applecross only by footpath before it was finally depopulated about 1935. However, two piers were built at Applecross, and as late as 1955 the Stornoway mail steamers used to call there.

**The North Road rounds the Peninsula**: In 1965 the construction of a low-level road to serve the north peninsula was begun at Shieldaig. By 1971 it had reached Arinacrinachd on Loch Torridon with its surviving post office, but was too late to save its school; and by then two more one-time townships, Fernmore and Fernbeg to the west, had been virtually abandoned. Between at least 1963 and 1974 MacBraynes operated a once-daily motor boat between Kyle and a jetty at Toscaig in the south of the Applecross peninsula, but by 1982 this service was no longer listed. Cuaig opposite the Isle of Rona was served by a motor boat from Broadford in Skye until the road reached it around 1974; in 1976 the road finally reached Applecross, whose school was at Camusterrach, 2 km south of Milton.

**Torpedo Testing and Tobacco Lairds**: In 1974 Applecross, which had managed to retain its primary school, became a tiny naval base for torpedo testing, with a handful of jobs. By then the tobacco magnates Wills owned the estate but were in residence for only one month in the year; they were unpopular with the Gaelic-speaking Free Church locals for encouraging holiday homes and *'arty-crafty'* English settlers rather than crofting. The *Applecross Hotel* had only 5 rooms and the resident population was so small that the nearest motor mechanic was 40km away by road. Although Applecross largely faded from the news, it retained its hotel and school, and by 1997 there was a caravan and camping site.

## ARBROATH & St Vigeans — Map 6, C2

***Angus coastal town,*** *pop. 23,500* — OS 54: NO 6441

Arbroath on the sunny coast of eastern Angus had complex religious origins. Its known development began 2 km inland on the banks of the Brothock Burn, at a site occupied by the Picts in the ninth century. There the church of St Vigeans was founded about 1100. Arbirlot, 4km to the west, already possessed an 11th century monastic institution, and in 1170 William de Mowbray built the original Kellie (or Kelly) Castle close by. In 1175 Benedictine monks from Kelso founded a very large Tironensian abbey at the mouth of the Brothock Burn, hence its Pictish Gaelic name *Aberbrothock*, from which the common name was derived. The abbey was chartered in 1178, with an ecclesiastical burgh dependent on the abbey but given its own parish. Abernethy and St Vigeans churches were granted to the abbey by William the Lion; St Vigeans remained the parish church when the abbey was built, using pink sandstone, perhaps quarried near Kellie.

**Occasional National Capital**: Arbroath is known to have had a wooden pier from about 1194, and in 1207 the Abbey's privileged wool trade with England was carried in ships owned by merchants from Dundee and Perth; the monks also had connections in Berwick and by about 1300 ran a *'hospital'*. The choice of Arbroath in 1320 as the gathering place for the Scottish Estates, when they made the important Declaration of Arbroath against Edward II's claims of English suzerainty, implies a safe harbour. It was certainly a fishing port, and in the 14th century was sometimes chosen for the signing of royal charters.

**From a New Harbour to the Reformation**: In 1394 the abbot and townsmen agreed to construct a new harbour of stone and timber. By 1434 minute quantities of cloth were being exported; but the burgh's overseas trade remained insignificant throughout the troubled 15th century. Meantime Kellie Castle was extensively rebuilt in locally quarried pink sandstone. In 1518 Arbroath contained only 200 houses, and in 1535–56 the town council still paid under 1.5% of the total of burgh taxes – but no Customs duties because of its ecclesiastical status. In 1560 its abbey, whose number of monks was only some two dozen, had more appropriated churches than any other in Scotland, amounting to 34 and dominating Angus and Aberdeenshire.

**The Reformation ruins the Abbey**: The Reformation of 1558–60 ended the abbey's function, but its newly imposed head the Commendator sat in Parliament. It left behind what Heron described over two centuries later as *"the magnificent ruins of this superb edifice"*. By 1593 the town had become the centre of a presbytery, and was sufficiently important to be converted to a Royal Burgh in 1599. Pont's manuscript map made around 1600 showed a large square coastal settlement, fronted by ships lying between two piers. Pont sketched Kelly Castle, which was restored in 1679. Meantime, although by 1620 some 1500 people lived in the town and a school was open, in 1639 it ranked only 32nd among Scottish burghs in tax yield. Little further development seems to have taken place during the 17th century, and both trade and the local fishing languished.

**Arbroath Textiles awakened by the Wallaces**: The town was again exporting linens by the 1720s, and the harbour was rebuilt from 1725 in the form of a stone basin whose narrow entrance could be closed by huge planks in times of storm, these improvements being made to accommodate peaks of flax imports. The Wallace family dominated the town in the 1730s as shipowners, agricultural and timber merchants. Wallace, Gardyne & Co started work in 1738, with nearly a hundred hand looms in a large factory. An early thread factory was established in the Abbey House in 1740, and a happy manufacturing error by one local weaver resulted in the first piece of cheap coarse *Osnaburgh* linen, soon a popular product. Brown and white linens (including Osnaburgs) were made locally with great success from 1742 by John Wallace & Co, the number of weavers very soon *"as numerous as all the other trades put together"*.

**Post and the Coast Road**: Arbroath had a post office by about 1745, but the Roy map made about 1750 showed only a coastal road, leading from Dundee to end at the Shore, adjacent to the harbour, for the Brothock then remained unbridged. The town was a compact settlement contained within a rectangular enclosure wholly east of the burn, and aligned on the north–south High Street; he labelled it *'ABERBROTHWICK'*. The coastal road continued to the east, and was made up as far as Montrose in 1750, but there was at that time no defined link inland.

**Linen, Golf and Boats**: The linen industry prospered, and Arbroath had a main linen stamping office by 1760. Sailduck (usually called sailcloth) was also produced by 1765. When Alexander Carlyle visited Arbroath in 1765 he stayed at a *"plain old fashioned"* inn. He found the town *"neat, clean, full of very good new houses"*, with a population between three and four thousand, and nine or ten vessels in its *"commodious"* harbour. It appears that golf was already being played on the links to the west, and that the indoor market building was erected in the late 18th century. In 1779 William Kenny established a boatyard west of the harbour. By 1786 Arbroath had become the principal sailcloth manufacturing centre of Scotland, and also became a port of registry with the code letters AH. The harbour was found to be inadequate in size but otherwise still served well, and no more improvements were made for forty years.

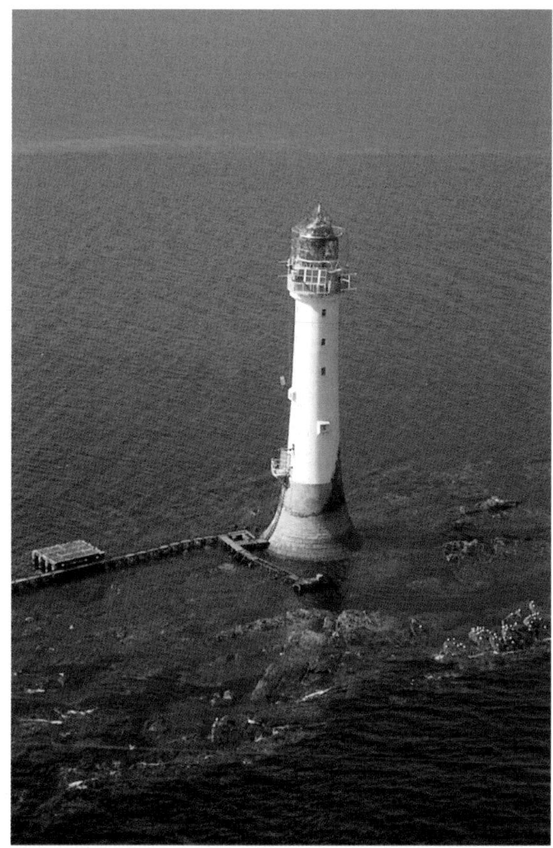

*The 35m-high Bell Rock lighthouse – 18km south-east of Arbroath – was built to designs by John Rennie in 1807–11 under the supervision of engineer Robert Stevenson. It was the first lighthouse built on a rock which was submerged at high tide.* *(JRH)*

**The 1790s busy in Flax**: By 1792 most flax was imported from Russia, and although little thread was still made locally, a million metres of brown and white linen was stamped. The sailcloth was made on nearly 500 hand looms; most went to London, Dundee and Glasgow. Population growth had been rapid for a decade. In 1793 another maker of coarse linens appeared, specialising in making coach seat upholstery material. At that time St Vigeans had 225 weavers, two mills for yarn treatment and a bleachfield. By stages from 1794, Alex Aberdein & Co converted the Inch flour mill on the Brothock into a water-powered flax spinning mill. A new post office was opened in 1793, and three fairs were advertised for 1797. Heron in 1799 called Arbroath *"a considerable town"* with a population of about 5000; its harbour was *"excellent"*.

**Early Banking in Arbroath**: From 1793, the Aberdeen Commercial Banking Company, the Dundee BC, the Dundee New Bank, the Dundee Union BC, and the Montrosse BC had tried local branches. Only 2 survived by the time the homegrown Arbroath BC was formed in 1825. This immediately opened branches in Coupar Angus and Forfar, and was thriving in 1844 when it merged with the Commercial Bank.

**Lighting the Bell Rock**: A lifeboat station was opened at Arbroath in 1803. A major offshore shipping hazard was the jagged Inchcape or Bell Rock, which lies 18km south-east of Arbroath, its ledges 70m by 130m awash even at low water neap tides. It was cleverly conquered under an Act of 1806 by workers led by the Northern Lighthouse Board's engineer Robert Stevenson, who built the massive 35-metre-tall lighthouse there in 1807–11, using 2000 tonnes of stone from the quarries at Rubislaw, Mylnefield and also Craigleith (Edinburgh), cut at Bell Rock Lane in Arbroath *(see Cassells and Munro for full accounts)*. The Signal Tower for communication with the lighthouse – and which was also to house the keepers' families – was built in 1813. The Abbey ruins were taken into government care in 1815 and some of the stonework repaired.

**Textile Mills and Breweries**: Some Arbroath mills were steam driven from 1806; the Brothock linen works had engines by Boulton & Watt, and by Carmichael of Dundee. By 1817 there were 14 flax spinning mills employing in all some 3000 people. Marywell, 3km north of Arbroath, was laid out as a small new settlement in 1819 but remained no more than a hamlet. By 1821 there was a windmill on the low hill west of the town. By then three small breweries were operating in Arbroath and another at St Vigeans; none was apparently large or long-lasting, unlike James Keith's tinsmith and engineering business, founded in 1823.

**Maritime Trade and Lawn Mowers**: Chambers in 1827 thought Arbroath *"an eminently neat and thriving little seaport town; the harbour is neither safe nor spacious, but possesses considerable trade. Arbroath deals largely with Russia, and manufactures a great quantity of sail-cloth, &c"*. Two further local initiatives of 1825 were significant: a gasworks was provided, and Alexander Shanks founded a textile engineering firm. It was he who invented the first effective (horse-drawn) lawnmower in 1842; mowers of various types were manufactured at the Dens Ironworks for well over a century. In 1832 the mill-owners Douglas Fraser & Sons established the Westburn Works where they also made textile machinery.

**The Harbour and Fishing**: Though the town council could not afford to repair storm damage in 1822, and in 1826 there were only three Arbroath-owned boats, in 1827 a slipway was constructed at the east end of the harbour for ship repair. Alexander Stephen – originally from Burghead *(q.v.)* – took over the shipyard from his brother in 1830. Until 1799 the fisherfolk of the 11th century village of Auchmithie 5km along the coast had been serfs of the Earl of Northesk; fishing was re-established in Arbroath in 1830 when they largely abandoned their traditional base for the burgh's better harbour and facilities. The Arbroath Harbour Trust, formed in 1839, brought in representatives of the burgh of Forfar and landed interests, and built a new outer basin in 1841–46. With the coming of the railway in 1838, few further improvements to the harbour were necessary for thirty years. The local newspaper the *Arbroath Herald* was established in 1838.

**Linen, Sailcloth and Buick Automobiles**: The linen industry dipped in 1826, then rose to 1832 when there were four spinning mills in Arbroath with almost 400 workers, and 1173 weavers. St Vigeans had advanced to 12 spinning mills and 1240 workers; in all about 7000 tonnes of flax was spun per year. Lowson started up in 1836, becoming the largest linen firm; by 1838 there were 18 steam flax-spinning mills. Webster & Co still owned a bleachfield; others still worked on the Elliot at Kellyfield, and at Waulk Mill on the Brothock. By 1851 the local flax firms owned over 30,000 spindles, 806 power looms and employed over 4600 people, some of them unhappy: David Buick, born in Arbroath in 1852, left with his parents for the USA. He was to establish the famed Buick car company of Flint, Michigan.

**Pioneers of the Railway Age**: The 5'6" (168 cm) gauge Dundee & Arbroath Railway, promoted by Lord Panmure who owned most of its straight and level right of way, opened in 1838 to a terminus at Lady Loan, beside a rope walk. The next year a horse tramway connected it to the harbour branch of the new Arbroath & Forfar Railway (A&F), which paralleled the oddly named street known as West Grimsby. In 1847–48 the two lines were converted to standard gauge and through running made easy by a new double track laid in a deep cutting through the High Common, with a new station at Keptie Street beside the A&F terminus at Catherine Street. They were also joined to the national system at Forfar, and extended via Guthrie to reach Aberdeen in 1850. From 1854 Wordie & Co operated a rail to road cartage depot at Bell Rock Lane. In 1855 a mineral railway was opened for flagstone traffic from quarries at Carmyllie, diverging from the Dundee line at Elliot Junction, where William Briggs later developed a rail-connected tar works. In 1859–66 four locomotives were built at the local lines' Arbroath works, closed when they were absorbed by the Caledonian Railway in 1866. The railways could be busy: at the June holiday in 1869 over 850 people travelled by rail to both Aberdeen and Dundee, and 344 to Montrose.

**Linen in the 1860s**: In the 1860s the Arbroath Foundry of Munro & Co made stone-cutting and dressing machines on a considerable scale. By 1864 Arbroath was Scotland's second largest linen manufacturing centre. A total of over 30,000 spindles served 836 power looms. In 1867 almost 5000 people worked in 18 flax, jute and hemp works, including the Inch Mill. Of these the largest were owned by Andrew Lowson (1230 workers), Douglas Fraser & Son (640), G & A Gordon (620), D Corsar & Son (560) and Corsar Brothers (440). In prosperous 1867 the Public Halls were built, intended for use as a theatre, which struggled to survive for half a century.

**Development depends on Sailing – Storms Ahead**: The population soared after passing 10,000 in 1851, because textile growth continued: by 1876 there were 34 mills and factories, with 1100 power looms. Though steam was taking over at sea, sailcloth was still the main product, and flax the harbour's main import. The Arbroath golf club, founded in 1877, formalised the long-played links at Elliot into an 18-hole course. In 1887 Colin Grant's big shoe factory had its own currying department and some 700 workers. In 1881 the North British Railway opened a line from St Vigeans Junction to Montrose, and in 1884 Alexander Shanks of the Dens Works – who had built several small railway locomotives – offered to rebuild others. From the opening of the Forth Bridge in 1890, Arbroath (where there was an engine shed) found itself on the East Coast main line; but the Arbroath & Dundee section was jointly owned by the Caledonian, a West Coast concern whose best trains ran via Forfar.

**Utilities, Football and Public Facilities**: A sewerage system was laid in 1872, cleaning up the Brothock Burn, and in 1885 the Arbroath Water Works erected on the Keptie Hills a unique and prominent baronial-style water tower for public supply; just west of this was a skating pond. Patrick Fraser's vast mausoleum was built in 1875–1900, its innumerable figures carved by mason James Peters. Arbroath Football Club was formed in 1878 and first played at seaside Gayfield Park in 1880. The Victoria public park was provided in 1897, and electricity was generated at a local power station built in 1899. In 1898 a public library (Carnegie assisted) was opened in the old building of Arbroath Academy; by 1901 the High School occupied a substantial building in Keptie Road, and the first small building of Arbroath Infirmary had been erected.

**Late Victorian Changes in the Harbour area**: The original Abertay light vessel was built of timber at Arbroath for the Dundee Harbour Trust and stationed in 1877. The inner harbour was slowly rebuilt in the 1870s, and a wet dock was finally opened in 1877; but in 1882 the entrance lock collapsed, resulting in the dock being closed for five years. The shipyard closed in 1881 when Stephens moved to Dundee, but boatyards remained: the decked fishing vessel *Isabella Fortuna*, built at Arbroath in 1890, survived to pay a centenary visit in 1990. By 1891 nearly 146 boats employed over 600 fishermen and boys; the fish processors R R Spink & Sons were established around that time and in 1894 there was a coastguard station. In 1890 a small harbour was built at Auchmithie, where there were at that peak time some 40 boats.

**Busy Railway, Textile and other Industries**: In 1901 the double-tracked goods branch led down to the harbour, where it also served the Arbroath Sawmills beside the Signal Tower. In 1903 Wordie & Co had 71 horses in their Arbroath stables, some hired out to shunt railway wagons at the harbour. By then a four-platform station was in use on the main line; the entrance building on the overbridge was dated 1911. The Lochland Works spun flax and tow, the Stanley spinning mills adjoined the Abbey site, and the Dens Works beside the railway made canvas and sailcloth. The Nursery and Almerieclose mills were owned by David Corsar & Sons, Green's mills and the Baltic flax and jute works were run by Andrew Lowson Ltd, and the Alma Works by the aptly-named flax manufacturers Francis Webster & Sons. There were also tanneries – the Abbey Leather Works. Douglas Fraser & Sons grew hugely from the 1880s in textile machinery manufacture to a workforce of 800 in the 1950s. From 1900 Keith & Blackman specialised in making huge ventilation fans for mines and power stations.

**Holidaying begins**: Despite Arbroath's sands, Black's 1882 tourist guide noted *"little to attract the tourist except its Abbey"*. However, the town developed a modest holiday trade and had four hotels by 1894, the *Imperial, Royal, White Hart* and *Waverley Temperance*; all save the White Hart were still hotels in 1980, when there were 15 in all. Kerr's Miniature Railway was laid out on the sea front in 1935 to the very narrow gauge of 7.25" (184 mm), but relaid for the 1937 season at 10.25" (260 mm), a safer gauge for passenger carrying.

**Motor Mowers, Museum and Textile Trouble**: By 1907 there was little export trade through the harbour. Besides textile machinery and horse-drawn mowers, Alexander Shanks & Sons made both vertical steam engines and later motor mowers, which sold worldwide in the 1920s. The Public Halls were gifted to the town in memory of the son of the Webster textile family, killed in the 1914–18 war, becoming the Webster Memorial Hall and the Arbroath Museum. With the near demise of sail power at sea, a catastrophic decline occurred in the linen industry in the 1920s, though Webster's Alma Works survived. Between the wars Arbroath's seaborne trade was only half that of Montrose, though fishing and curing was busy; *Arbroath Smokies* became well known, and in 1930 a Woolworth store was opened.

**Caravans and Fish Cans**: Kerr's miniature railway was re-opened after the war and by 1951 Arbroath had the facilities of a minor regional centre and a population of almost 20,000. The Signal Tower housed the lighthouse keepers' families until 1955. Declining rail traffic on the Forfar branch caused it to lose its passenger trains in 1955, and it was closed to freight in 1959; the harbour branch was closed in 1963. From its opening in 1961 until 1970, rail freight traffic from Elliot Junction served the Metal Box factory, from which empty cans were carried to Crosse & Blackwell's fish cannery at Peterhead; the rest of the Carmyllie branch was closed in 1965. By 1967 Scotland's largest caravan site had been laid out west of the town. Though Shanks ceased to make mowers in the 1960s, at that time the Royal Bank erected new offices spanning the burn beside the Brothock Bridge.

**Industrial Changes**: The Netherward Works of British Electrometals were electro platers in the 1970s; at that time Don & Low acquired the Abbey Works, which then made cardboard presentation boxes, lined and finely finished. Braemar of Hawick opened a branch knitwear factory about 1974 in an old school. About 1980 it became Macnan Scotland Ltd, and moved to a prominent sandstone mill adjoining the *Arbroath Herald* printing works; in 1994 Macnan was still making ladies' clothing. The Keith & Blackman factory was closed in 1985 due to the Thatcher government's accelerated rundown of the coal industry. In 1979 Giddings & Lewis-Fraser of the Wellgate Works made textile machinery and machine tools; by 1992 they had absorbed both Douglas Fraser and Shanks. Websters still manufactured sailcloth at the Alma Works in 1983; by then it was also used for marquees.

**Town and Harbour in the 1970s**: Arbroath remained an important fishing centre. In 1969 fish selling on the open dockside was replaced by a covered fish market open daily; fish-curing continued. In 1970 the Webster Memorial Hall was improved into a 634-seat theatre, and the museum collections were moved into the Signal Tower in 1974. About 1972 the bus station was moved to a new site and the A92 through the town was radically reconstructed as a dual carriageway, enabling the quite substantial traditional town centre to be attractively pedestrianised by 1979. Moray Firth Maltings, an S&N subsidiary, greatly expanded their plant over several years around 1980, including the world's first circular malting plant, using largely home-grown barley. A new rail grain terminal was opened in 1988, serving the maltings – the connection being by road!

**Enterprise Zone leads to Relocations**: Although in the late 1970s Halliburton opened a factory to make oil equipment, closures had led to high unemployment (15% in 1988) which in turn led to Enterprise zone status, encouraging 23 new firms to move in. John M Henderson, engineers of Aberdeen, moved their production to Arbroath in 1985; in 1993 they made cable reels and winches for offshore work. Premier Brands opened a large new food processing factory north-west of the town in 1989, bringing 475 full-time and 125 part-time jobs, at the cost of closures in Montrose and Fraserburgh. Swankies for fish and Perimax for meat also opened up processing plants, and Armstrong entered to make packaging. By 1990 Tecnomarine Systems of Aberdeen had a design and testing facility at Arbroath for deepwater oil production systems. Low & Duff of Carnoustie opened a branch engineering factory in Arbroath in 1989, and produced chocolate-making machinery. A rapeseed processing plant was opened in 1995.

*Arbroath smokies in preparation: they are smoked and cooked over a fire of hardwood chips.* *(SMPC / Doug Corrance)*

**Silicon Seashore**: In 1990 the Japanese electronics components firm ALPS Electric moved into an advance factory; by 1993 they made video and TV tuners in Arbroath. In 1990 Arbroath also became the HQ of McMillan Video, national dealers in audio-visual equipment, with branches in 5 UK cities. In 1994 the new industrial estate west of the town included several large buildings of PMP. Arbroath Infirmary which had been extended in the Edwardian period and further enlarged in the 1930s, had 95 beds in 1981, providing general hospital, accident and maternity services. A proposal of 1993 to remove A&E facilities from Arbroath to rural Stracathro, over 25km away, was abandoned.

**Leisure Facilities to 1994**: The *Hotel Seaforth*, originally a modest seafront mansionhouse, had been much extended over the years, to about 20 rooms by the 1950s when it boasted three stars. The large 3-storey Victorian mansion of about 20 rooms which had long ago become the *Windmill Hotel* was owned by the sponsors of Arbroath FC. In 1994 the club joined the new lowly third division, but by 2000 were back in the second. Their seaside football ground at Gayfield was one of Scotland's best small *'parks'*. It was adjoined by the extensive covered *'Pleasureland'* entertainment centre; but in 1994 the Tidy Britain Group found the state of Arbroath's beaches *"disappointing"*.

**Problems on Land and at Sea**: Websters, the long-established weavers of sailcloth, called in the receivers in 1992, and in depressed 1993 Giddings & Lewis-Fraser moved most of their foundry to Merseyside, shedding 300 workers and leaving a mere 75 staff. Then in 1994 came a cut by Halliburton, the oil-field equipment manufacturers, reducing their workforce from about 315 to 240. In 1985 some 30 large fishing boats worked out of the harbour, and in 1988 – the year when the Bell Rock was automated – Arbroath's two small boatyards were still busy building fishing vessels. But fish had become so scarce by 1991 that the formerly daily fish market had become an intermittent event, and most Arbroath boats were fishing out of Aberdeen. Those still using the local harbour caught plaice, dabs and prawns but few haddock, so very few locally-caught fish could still be processed into smokies. Yet in 1992 the long-established R R Spink & Sons began to export smokies to France.

**Arbroath in 1994**: In 1994 only Mackay Boatbuilders was still building small fishing vessels in steel, but their repair slipway was still in use. The harbour was still active though far from busy; lobster creels were much in evidence. Meantime by 1989 the Abbeygate shopping centre had been built with its large Co-op food superstore. The recently-built Safeway store nearby and shops in the High Street precinct seemed prosperous enough, but its southern section had many vacancies.

**Historic Survivals, New Factories and New Facilities**: In 1994 the station goods yard was empty, though its track and Victorian crane remained *in situ*; only the two through passenger platforms could be used. Near the station the Angus Training Group, and the smallish Northern Tool & Gear, Keptie Engineering and Pacitti Foods all had quite modern premises. The *Webster Theatre* was still in use for one-night stands of touring productions. The Arbroath Water Works was still a prominent feature, but the former public baths were being converted to housing. The *'Carnaud Metal Box'* factory still stood beside the railway west of the caravan site. Gerrard Brothers' small boatyard closed early in 1995, the year when the *'Miniature Fun World'*, including all-weather tennis courts, was opened at the West Links. The unemployment rate at 14% was already the highest in Tayside when the Dawson Group closed its Pringle Contract Knitwear factory; 220 people, mostly women, joined the jobless. The railway station was extensively reconditioned in 1999. In 2000 a former leisure centre was converted into a large licensed restaurant.

## ARCHIESTOWN — Map 10, A2

***Morayshire hamlet,*** *pop. 200* — OS 28: NJ 2344

In 1758 Grant of Monymusk founded Archiestown on the hitherto roadless Braes of Elchies above the middle River Spey; by 1760 it had been attractively laid out as a weaving centre. A serious fire in 1783 forced rebuilding. Unlike most Strathspey settlements, commercial distilling was never introduced to Archiestown, which lacked a post office until after 1838, and was never directly rail-served. It gained a small hotel, and Speyside Weavers were also still operating in the area in 1970. Archiestown itself remained in 1981 merely a hamlet, its population having halved since 1951 to only about 225; its museum was short lived, and although there was by then a caravan site 3km to the east, the post office closed around 1990. The *Archiestown Hotel* caters for anglers.

## ARDENTINNY — Map 5, A4

***Argyllshire hamlet, L. Long,*** *pop. under 100* — OS 56: NS 1887

The mountainous west shore of Loch Long near the mouth of Glen Finart was trackless when Roy surveyed the area about 1750. However by 1895 it lay on a road from Strone, some 7km to the south, to Whistlefield and Strachur, and had a post and telegraph office and the small *Ardentinny Hotel*. Bolton in 1953 called it *"a small and unspoiled resort"*. There was also a primary school when the nearby hamlet of Glenfinart was developed by the Forestry Commission around 1950, raising the tiny resident population in the area to around 100. The post office had already closed by 1970, and the school was closed about 1986. The purpose-built Outdoor Centre, opened at Ardentinny in 1973 by Renfrewshire County Council, was used by an average of 2000 West of Scotland children a year until its regrettable closure in 1996 due to Tory government finance cuts, with the loss of 16 jobs. The hotel was still open in 1991, and there was a lochside caravan and camping site 3km to the south.

## ARDEONAIG & Ardtalnaig — Map 5, C3

***Hamlets on Loch Tay,*** *pop. 100* — OS 51: NN 6635

Little remains of the 16th century Mains Castle at Ardeonaig, 10km east of Killin on the south shore of Loch Tay; the Roy map of the 1750s showed only trackless hills. However, in 1803 Dorothy Wordsworth recommended the lochside road. A copper mine was worked nearby in the 19th century, with a small sulphuric acid works on the lochside; by 1895 a post office and a hotel stood near the castle. A footpath led over the hills to Comrie and a ferry plied across the loch to a point near Croftvellick. There was also a post office at the Milltown of Ardtalnaig, near the ancient Carn Ban 5km down the lochside. By the 1930s both places had primary schools, and at Ardtalnaig was an early youth hostel and a pier, from which a second passenger ferry had been provided, crossing the loch to Lawers. The 1939–45 war led to sharp decline: by 1951 the two places could muster under 200 residents between them, and only Ardeonaig school was still in use. By 1962 all Ardtalnaig's facilities had closed and both the ferries had vanished; by then only 140 residents remained. Ardeonaig post office ceased to function about 1973 and its school closed around 1980. However, by 1977 the *Ardeonaig Hotel* had 18 rooms. Firbush Outdoor Centre (Edinburgh University) opened around 1980. The youth hostel had closed by 1984, leaving just a hamlet with a hotel.

## ARDERSIER (or Campbelltown) — Map 9, B3

***Village on Moray Firth,*** *pop. 1100* — OS 27: NH 7855

Ardersier is the point on the south shore of the Moray firth where it narrows to confront Chanonry Point in Easter Ross. It became the southern terminus of a ferry, which was already operating in the 13th and 14th centuries when Fortrose Cathedral was being built *(see Rosemarkie)*. Pont's map made about 1600 showed Ardersier church isolated on the Ard, and two mills on the burn to the south. In 1623 its proprietor from

Cawdor was granted a burgh of barony charter under the family name, so for a time Ardersier was known as Campbelltown, though little was actually built. Roy's map made about 1750 retained the name Ardersier, and showed several hamlets in that area on a road which ended at the church.

**Fort George**: In the mid 18th century the Chanonry ferry was the key link in the land route to the far north and was in constant use. This explains the thinking behind the siting of Fort George on the Ard, so as to defend the Moray Firth and its strategic ferry from Jacobites and privateers. Muir states that a fort already existed in 1746, but was *'slighted'* by the Jacobite army. The present vast complex was built (or rebuilt) between 1748 and 1770 as a huge artillery fort, supplied by the Grand Magazine which was intended to hold 2500 barrels of gunpowder; its defended area of 17 ha could hold a garrison of 2000 men. Being within sight of Culloden Muir, it would remind the Highlanders that their days of rebellion against the Hanoverian government were over. The fort was designed by William Skinner and built by workers under William Adam and his son John, successive master masons of Scotland, acting as contractors, with design aid from John's brilliant architect brother Robert Adam; in the 1760s stone for the massive work was quarried at the mouth of Munlochy bay. Saunders *(q.v.)* claimed that it was *"the finest example of 18th century military engineering in the British Isles and one of the outstanding artillery fortifications of Europe"*.

**Fort, Village and Postal Services**: Fort George had a post office from 1760 and was practically complete when visited by Alexander Carlyle in 1765. He described the settlement which stood on the beach nearby as *"a small village, the produce of the fort"*; though as noted above, appreciable settlement in fact predated both barony burgh and fort. When the village post office was first opened in 1792 the name Ardersier was preferred, so avoiding confusion with Campbeltown in Argyll. Ardersier became a junction for the mails, the Ardersier–Chanonry ferry in 1813 still forming the postal connection between the far north, Fortrose and Cromarty and the South mail, which came via Aberdeen and Nairn.

**Nineteenth Century Fishing, Railway and Secrecy**: In 1801 an attempt was made to establish framework knitting, and Chambers in the 1820s called Campbelltown *"a large modern village; a small pier projects from the fort into the sea for the use of the ferry-boats"*. Beach-based fishing was its mainstay until in 1837 the Ardersier fishermen moved a remarkable 40 km eastwards to Hopeman. In 1854 the Inverness & Nairn Railway was opened, with a station 2 km south of Ardersier, but named Fort George. Although the fort was suppressed from 19th century OS maps – the traditional British notion of equating secrecy with security being no new thing – it remained a highly visible entity in obvious military use!

**Rail and Air Developments**: A ferry still operated from the fort to Chanonry well into the 20th century, but had closed by 1953. Meantime in 1899 the Highland Railway had opened a very short branch line from Fort George station (renamed Gollanfield Junction) to Ardersier, ending near the inn. The new station was named Fort George, but was closed to passengers in 1943 and to goods in 1958. However, Gollanfield was served by passenger trains until 1965. Ardersier was still a substantial village of 1450 people in the 1950s, but subsequently its secondary school and that 5 km to the south at Croy were closed, and its population rapidly declined to only a thousand in 1971. The depot and regimental museum of the Seaforth (now Queen's Own) Highlanders at Fort George was modernised in the 1970s.

**Oil Platforms in Boom and Slump**: In 1972 the North Sea oil industry gave rise to the vast platform construction yard of the US firm McDermott, sited 4 km from the village on the less sheltered side of the promontory; one great shed dominated its quayside. By 1980 the Culloden Pottery and restaurant was also well established beside the A96. By then the number of hotels in the village had risen from one to four, and by 1981 its population had again reached 1100. McDermotts increased their workforce to 1800 in 1990, fabricating the huge jacket and piles for Occidental Oil's Saltire platform, and by 1991 to some 3800 when replacing the disaster-struck Piper Alpha platform and building two jackets for the Scott Field of Amerada Hess. After these were completed in 1992 new orders were not found, and in 1993 McDermotts retained just 100 workers on care and maintenance. But by 1995 some 700 workers were again employed at the yard, shortly merged with the Nigg yard under US-owned Barmac, who again had to close it in 1999–2000 with the loss of numerous jobs. The spectacular fort – an impressive sleeping giant cared for by Historic Scotland – is a year-round tourist draw, its Grand Magazine holding the Seafield Collection, a museum of arms.

## ARDGOUR, Corran, Coull & Clovullin **Map 5, A2**

***Lochaber area,*** *pop. 430 (area)* OS 41: NN 0163

By the 15th century a ferry operated across Loch Linnhe at the Corran narrows, between Nether Lochaber and Ardgour and Coull on the isolated Moidart peninsula. In 1542 Coull was bought by the Macleans, Earls of Ardgour; it was shown by Pont who mapped the area about 1600 as *'Chouill'* (Keil), while *'Koul-chenan'* was in Lochaber; both names later applied to mansionhouses. Roy's map of about 1750 showed a road or track paralleling the Lochaber shore, with a spur down to the shore at *'Current of Ardgour'*; westwards from the presumed ferry a track led for 4 km to Sallachan. These ways would not have been properly made up, and it appears that only primitive settlements existed until the mansion of Ardgour House was built for the 12th Earl in 1765.

**After Telford**: In the early 19th century, contractors for the Commissioners of Highland Roads and Bridges completed the lengthy Moidart road, accessed via new ferry slips built to Telford's specifications at Corran and Ardgour; Ardgour House was reconstructed in 1826–30. A post office was opened, possibly at Clovulin *(G. Cloth-mill)* probably in 1833, from which date a daily post operated to Strontian *(q.v.)*. By 1847 the owner Colonel Maclean of Ardgour House was an improving landlord, and by 1848 a pier was recorded. The Corran lighthouse was first lit in 1860; it was eventually automated in 1970. In 1886 Ardgour was regarded as a *"village"*, served by steamers on the Ballachulish to Fort William route. In 1894 the *Ardgour Hotel* was described by Murray as *"plain and comfortable"*. By then the *Corran Inn* was also open on the Lochaber shore.

**The Grass-Grown 'A' Road**: In 1953 the author saw grass growing in the middle of the single-lane A861 north of the ferry; only a few vehicles a day were carried on a turntable ferry boat. Later as the number of vehicles grew it was replaced by a normal *ro-ro* ferry, which avoided a detour for south traffic of some 70 km round the head of Loch Eil. Both the ferry and

*The Corran–Ardgour ferry at the Ardgour slip in 1976, carrying a bus. This ferry still operates, with more modern vessels.* *(RCAHMS / JRH)*

the settlements which adjoined on both sides of the loch developed in the later 20th century with the expanding tourist trade, the growth of Nether Lochaber, and the improvement of the Salen road. Ardgour House in its parkland policies fell vacant in 1988 but was restored about 1996 for holiday use. A floating *'tidal mill'* generator made by IT Power of Hampshire was tried at the Corran narrows in 1993, and generation continues. The former Kylesku ferry *Maid of Glencoull* now works on the Corran ferry. Ardgour retains its hotel and primary school.

## ARDLUI & Inverarnan — Map 5, B3

***Hamlets on Loch Lomond,*** *pop. v. under 100* — OS 56: NN 3115

The droving inn at Inverarnan at the foot of Glen Falloch was a public house to Dorothy Wordsworth in 1803, when there was *"no village, only scattered huts"*. She made nothing of the waterfalls in the vicinity. The inn became the objective when the river was canalised from the head of Loch Lomond in 1847, and a turning basin for the loch steamers was formed there. A small pier was utilised when building the West Highland Railway, opened in 1894 with a crossing station and siding named Ardlui. The *Ardlui Hotel* had 10 rooms in 1954 when the pier on Loch Lomond was still served by circular tours from Glasgow, and some 70 people lived locally. The pier was closed in 1964 and the local population fell still farther, but the hotel and the ancient inn at Inverarnan both remained open. By 1985 there was a caravan site at Ardlui, and by 1993 a marina and a visitor centre had been provided; a passenger ferry plies across the loch in summer to meet the West Highland Way.

## ARDRISHAIG — Map 4, C4

***Argyllshire large village,*** *pop. 1300* — OS 55: NR 8585

Blaeu's atlas made from Pont's sketch maps of around 1600 showed *'Ardrissack'* among other names in South Knapdale parish west of Loch Fyne, but the fair copy of the Roy map showed nothing in this area (a rare but not unique omission). The construction of a coastal road from the site of Lochgilphead to Tarbert, aided by the Commissioners for Forfeited Estates, was completed in 1780. The Crinan Canal, first proposed in 1783 by the wise itinerant bookseller John Knox to enable boats to avoid the perilous passage round Kintyre, was dug in 1793–1801, and engineered by John Rennie. A pier, basin and locks were necessary at Ardrishaig, where it entered Loch Fyne and its maintenance workshops were built. In 1831 the Glendarroch distillery was built beside the canal at the foot of beautiful Glen Darroch, but as late as 1838 there was no post office at Ardrishaig.

**The *'Royal Route'* to the Hebrides**: The tourist potential of the west coast had been realised, and there were steamers direct to Glasgow. From 1839 connections were made with canal trackboats to Crinan for steamers to Oban, Inverness and the Hebrides. By 1842 two sailings operated per week to Glasgow, a journey which by 1844 took little over five hours. Queen Victoria passed through in 1847, so inaugurating a fashionable *'royal route'*. From 1851 Hutcheson steamers built up the service, with the new fast steamer *Mountaineer* from 1852, and from 1855 the larger SS *Iona* served Ardrishaig pier from Gourock, Rothesay and Tarbert. In 1866 a North British Railway steamer service was tried out between Ardrishaig and Helensburgh, but was soon abandoned. In 1878 the *Iona* was replaced by the famous PS *Columba*, then the largest vessel on the Clyde; this service connected with the little coffee-pot boilered steamer *Linnet* which had plied on the canal since 1866; Barnard called this boat *"celebrated, pretty and com-*

*fortable"*. By 1886 when barley was brought in by canal to the distillery, which produced about 365,000 litres of Highland Malt whisky annually, there were two daily return steamer services to the Clyde.

**Hotel, Oil and Soap Opera**: Murray in 1894 referred to the *"fair" Ardrishaig Hotel*, the only local hostelry, Ardrishaig being principally a transfer point. The canal entrance locks were rebuilt in the 1920s. The distillery had been renamed Glenfyne by 1902, freeing the name Glendarroch for use eight decades later by Scottish Television in their soap opera *'Take the High Road'* (filmed on location at Luss); the distillery finally closed in 1937. By 1950 Ardrishaig had some 1100 residents; its general facilities were those of a village and small yachting resort, with five little hotels and two small oil depots. Until the 1960s the canal was used extensively by *'puffers'* carrying barley and coal to the Islay and Jura distilleries, returning with whisky. The steamers which had plied year-round to Gourock were withdrawn in 1970. About then almost all the shops were redeveloped in two new blocks; one might have sufficed!

**Forests and Houses**: In 1976 workaday Ardrishaig had the Crinan Canal office and workshops, a new Shell oil depot, and a Hydro-Electric base. A garage and goods vehicle testing station, Western SMT bus garage and office served road transport. Three hotels and 14 shops meant good village facilities for the area. A fish farm was developed about 1981 and the whole of the hills to the west were afforested. Busy Lochgilphead having little space to expand, new overflow houses were crowding up the hillside at Ardrishaig, bringing its generally well-educated residents to 1315 in 1991, and a new school had been built by 1996. In 1994 a mansion near the harbour became the *Bridge House Hotel*.

## ARDROSSAN

**Map 1, C1**

***Clyde-coast town**, pop. 10,750*

OS 70: NS 2342

The Gaelic placename for this peninsula on the coast of Cunninghame may derive from *Ard-Ros-chrann*, meaning *'height of roses'*, referring to the natural state of the headland. Ardrossan existed by the 13th century and had a 15th century castle, which together with a town on the point appeared on Timothy Pont's map of about 1600. However, there was no school in the parish as late as 1696, and the Roy map of about 1754 featured only the castle. Ardrossan remained unimportant until the Earl of Eglinton built baths in 1806–07, in a successful attempt to establish a resort. Chambers noted two decades later that this *"modern village consisting of neat and commodious houses has become a favourite resort in the season of sea-bathing for the genteel families of Ayrshire"*; but this function long remained tiny by comparison with nearby Saltcoats.

**Crazy Canal and useful Port**: The Earl had also planned to create a port close by, intended to transfer cargoes from overseas to boats plying on the Glasgow, Paisley & Ardrossan Canal, which was surveyed by Telford. He began its construction at the Glasgow end in 1811, seemingly oblivious of an Act of 1809 which enabled the Clyde to be deepened by dredging... which was vigorously pursued and soon showed up the canal as a hare-brained scheme, whose extension was abandoned when it reached Johnstone in 1813. Work on the port consequently ceased in 1815. However, according to Chambers (writing about 1826) the port *"possesses capabilities and advantages superior to all the other numerous harbours in the Firth of Clyde"* for seaborne trade, and development work had been resumed: the 275-m-long pier already built was being supplemented by another on the north side. Ardrossan also became a port of registry, its boats bearing the letters AD; by 1831 it was served by regular steamers.

**Glasgow to London via Ardrossan!**: From 1831 a local coal-carrying railway, the Ardrossan & Johnstone (owned by the canal company), connected Ardrossan with Kilwinning using horse-drawn trains, and from 1833 the port was further extended, acquiring a customs house. A Bank of Scotland branch opened in 1836. Ardrossan soon became an important seaport for the coal and iron industries, with regular steamers to Arran, Belfast and the Isle of Man. By 1838 Ardrossan had a post office, and by the 1840s some 400 handloom weavers were at work in the growing town. The speedy conversion of the primitive railway to standard gauge and steam haulage in July 1840, enabled its connection at Kilwinning to the Glasgow and Ayr line. For the next 8 years this put Ardrossan harbour on the fastest north–south route: from London by rail to Liverpool – or later Fleetwood – thence by steamer to Ardrossan, and by rail to central Scotland. From 1845 there were also steamers to Campbeltown and the Inner Hebrides.

**The remarkable Dugald Drummond**: In 1846 Ardrossan became the last burgh of barony to be chartered, and a gasworks was established. The young Dugald Drummond, born in Ardrossan in 1840, was inspired by the activities of the town's new and substantial engine shed to become a locomotive engineer. He was to design some of the longest-lasting classes of steam locomotives built in Britain, which were built under his direction successively for the North British, Caledonian and London & South Western Railways – the elegant T9 *'Greyhounds'*, were still spinning along west of Salisbury about 1950 to delight the author's eye. The clever and energetic Drummond also established railway engineering works in Govan, and managed the Australasian Locomotive Company in the 1890s.

**The later Nineteenth Century**: A through rail service to England via Carlisle became available in 1848, so the Fleetwood steamers could no longer compete; but steamers still plied to Northern Ireland. A local newspaper, the *Ardrossan & Saltcoats Herald*, was founded in 1853, a lifeboat station was opened in 1869, and Ardrossan became one of the new police burghs in 1877. Its railway was extended to West Kilbride by the Glasgow & South Western Railway (G&SWR) in 1878. A competing line from Glasgow via Uplawmoor reached Ardrossan in 1888 as the Lanarkshire & Ayrshire, completed with the opening of Montgomerie Pier station in 1890. Meantime in 1882 G & J Burns of Glasgow had bought the Ardrossan Shipping Company, which sailed to Belfast. The harbour was expanded in 1886–91; it exported coal and pig-iron, also becoming a fishing port. There was a coastguard station, a secondary school and a commercial hotel by 1894, when Murray called Ardrossan *"a well-built but uninteresting town"*.

**The Coaster Shipyard**: In 1914 steamers from Ardrossan served Arran, Belfast, Douglas and Portrush. Meantime a shipyard, the Ardrossan Dry Dock & Shipbuilding Company (ADDSC), had been in operation since the turn of the century. In 1919–20 they built the 638-ton sister coasters SS *Cromarty Firth* and SS *Pentland Firth*, engined by Beardmore, for Border

Shipping of Glasgow; both were to be lost in the Normandy landings. In 1927 AD DSC was third among British yards in terms of the number of its coasters in service, and in 1930 built a pair of unintentionally slow diesel vessels for MacBrayne's outer islands services, MVs *Lochearn* and *Lochmor*; the yard worked until at least 1953.

**Electricity, Oil Refining and Holidays**: In 1914 the G&SWR still based 55 steam locomotives at Ardrossan, its fourth largest shed, but new forms of power were arriving. Electricity was supplied to the town from the building of a local power station in 1910. An oil refinery was set up in 1927, producing bitumen as a by-product from 1928, by which year shipbreaking was taking place. The lifeboat station was closed in 1930. Passenger trains to Uplawmoor ceased in 1932 – except for excursions, as the town's minor resort function was maintained; in the 1950s Ardrossan's facilities were those of a typical town.

**Decline**: Then decline became evident: the locomotive depot ceased work in 1959, and Montgomerie Pier station was closed in 1966. While one report claimed that the shipyard was derelict by 1975, McCrindle – who built the Kylesku ferry *Maid of Glencoull* – were still listed as shipbuilders and marine engineers in 1979. But the rail connection to the docks was broken with the cessation by 1978 of the coal and iron trade, and by then the ferry to Ireland had ceased. There had also been a general fall in facilities to those of a small town, despite a population growth of 2500 over 30 years. However, vehicular ferries still continued, to Brodick year-round and in summer to Douglas (IoM). There were more small hotels than in the 1950s, even the largest, the *Eglinton Arms*, having only some 15 rooms. In 1991 the population was 10,750.

**Smaller but more Stable in Oil and Timber**: The old dock had been infilled by 1983 but the ro-ro ferries remained, and the rail passenger service to Glasgow from all three stations (Harbour, Town and South Beach) was electrified in 1987. The town continued to spread inland; its former Town Hall has been saved for posterity. However, the *Eglinton Arms* was destroyed by fire in 1990. The one-time refinery was still a major oil depot which retained its rail connection until around 1990, when Glenlight of Ardrossan was Scotland's main coastal shipper of home-grown timber. The firm expanded in 1992 with a major barge to carry roundwood from Kintyre for use at the Irvine paper mill. A new summer ferry service to Douglas was begun in 1994, when privatised Clydeport (formerly the dock authority for the Clyde) ran the ports of Greenock, Glasgow and Ardrossan. Ardrossan Academy is now a large local authority secondary school. There was still a Stagecoach bus depot when the reinstatement of port rail facilities at Ardrossan was announced in 1999; a new terminal is opening in 2001 for the Brodick ferry, and 220 flats are planned nearby.

## ARDUAINE & Craobh Haven — Map 4, C3

***Argyllshire settlements,*** *pop. under 100* — OS 55: NM 7910

The Roy map showed that by about 1750 a track hugged the coast round the promontory of An Cnap some 5 km south-west of Kilmelford, forking at *'Dell'* to pass a cluster of islets a short way off the west coast of the Craignish *(q.v.)* peninsula, including Eilean an Duin with its ancient dun; other duns stood by the shore. In the 19th century the isolated Daill House stood there, about 25 km south of Oban as the crow flies – but a great deal farther by the winding hilly roads. By the 1950s the 12-roomed *Lunga Hotel*, also known as the *Galley of Lorne*, had taken its place, but this closed about 1975. By 1972 the 28-roomed *Loch Melfort Motor Inn* (now *Hotel*) had been built on An Cnap, overlooking Asknish Bay; nearby was a post office and adjacent caravan and camping site. The 8 ha Arduaine gardens were created from 1971 by brothers Harry and Edmund Wright from Essex, who gifted them in 1992 to the National Trust for Scotland.

**The Saga of Craobh Haven**: In 1984–85 a new holiday village bearing the inelegant hybrid name of *'Craobh Haven'* was begun north of the former *Lunga Hotel* by insensitive English developers, who built a 1.5 km road into the 120 ha site. Although Craobh, pronounced *Cruve*, means *'Tree'* in Gaelic, they razed much of the area and used the stone to build causeways linking Eilean Buidhe and Eilean an Duin with the shore, so enclosing a safe anchorage for 60 yachts. Two shops, a mock baronial pub, watersports centre, and riding stables were built. But in 1987 the rash firm failed, and after some controversy under a new owner, insolvency again stopped development in 1991. By 1994 the troubled marina was for enforced sale for at least the second time and only 30 people lived in the new settlement. However, by 1996 a hotel stood on Eilean Buidhe. The *Loch Melfort Hotel* now has 27 rooms.

## ARDWELL — Map 1, B5

***Galloway location,*** *pop. 165* — OS 82: NX 1045

On the east coast of the Rhinns of Galloway some 15 km south of modern Stranraer is a medieval motte, with the scant remains of the early keep of Killaser Castle and the 16th century Auchness Tower. Later Ardwell House was built, and by the 1750s a road followed the coast. By the 1950s a primary school, post office and telephone exchange had been provided, and in the late 20th century came some new development including public conveniences. By 1996 the gardens of Ardwell House had been opened to the public, and a caravan site had been laid out beside the shingly beach.

## ARISAIG — Map 8, B5

***W. Highland coastal village,*** *pop. 300* — OS 40: NM 6686

Arisaig in South Morar was named on the Blaeu atlas of 1654, based on Timothy Pont's survey of about 1600; but on the Roy map made about 1750, only Keppoch and Killindree were identified amongst the area's trackless wastes. The village stands on the rock-infested Loch nan Ceall; its present site gives stupendous distant views of Skye and the Small Isles. At the start of the 19th century Arisaig was the first objective of the Highland Roads Commissioners, whose *'Loch na Gaul road'* became known as *'The Road to the Isles'*. By 1803 a post office and inn had been established at Arisaig, from which an inadequate track continued northwards to Morar.

**Steamers struggle to serve Remote Piers**: By 1847 steamers called on a Portree to Glasgow service, and there was a school and shops; but except for building his mansion of Arisaig House 4 km east of the village, Lord Cranston who owned the immense estate was no improver, and the natural scenery remained unspoiled. In 1886 the steamers plying as far afield as Stornoway and Cape Wrath called only at a pier which had been built at remote Rhumach, a winding 6 km from the inn and village. This inconvenient state of affairs caused adverse comment by Murray in 1894, when steamers still called on a curtailed route from Oban to Gairloch via Tobermory and Portree.

**Arisaig on the Railway**: The single tracked Mallaig Extension Railway which was completed from Fort William in 1901 provided a crossing station at Arisaig village, and the steamer service immediately abandoned the Rhumach pier for the new port facilities established at Mallaig, to which a road – of sorts – was also built. In the early 20th century Arisaig also gained the 9-hole Traigh golf course 4km to the north, the *Arisaig Hotel* was opened, and in the 1930s a croft house north of the village became the *Cnoc-na-Faire Hotel*. Arisaig then had an out of season population of around 300.

**Caravans *ad Nauseam***: Sadly it soon became notorious for the extensive eyesore of the many obtrusive caravan sites which had been spread around the relatively flat Keppoch area to provide cheap holidays, regardless of their impact on a previously unspoilt scene. In 1984 a boatyard offered island cruises, and the local tourist trade was still expanding in 1988. The post office, primary school and the station are still open, and a passenger ferry plies to the Small Isles in summer. Now a hotel, the *Arisaig House* has 12 rooms, similar to the *Arisaig Hotel*. Besides golfing and sailing there are about seven caravan and camping sites to choose from!

## ARMADALE

**Map 16, B3**

***W. Lothian urban area,*** *pop. 9000*

OS 65: NS 9368

A one-time castle at Woodend, beside the Barbauchlaw Burn 5km west of Bathgate, must have stood near the early road running westward from Edinburgh through the Bathgate area. The road was shown on the Pont map of Lothian, made about 1600, but neither the castle nor the name of nearby Armadale appeared. The Roy map of the 1750s showed an unnamed cross-roads on a spur some 170m above sea level 4km west of Bathgate on the Airdrie road. This became the focus round which the poorly documented mining village of Armadale later grew.

**Railway, Mines, Steel Founding and Overcrowding**: Armadale station – on the North British Railway's single track Bathgate & Monkland line which opened in 1861 – was 1.5km south of the village, beyond the hamlet of Bathville. Armadale was constituted a police burgh in 1863, and by 1891 had 3190 people; by 1895 it was surrounded by at least six rail-connected coal pits, that at Woodend also having coke ovens. There was an inn and a post office; at Lower Bathville, 1km east of Bathville proper, was a firebrick works. The area had large late 19th century steel foundries, and also became an oil shale mining centre; in 1911 Armadale had the most overcrowded housing in Scotland. A gasworks was established – or renewed – in 1919. The village population was about 5000 in 1921, when Armadale FC played in the Scottish League from 1921 to 1932. After a small decline to 1931, renewed growth led to nearly 8000 people living in Armadale in 1951, enjoying the facilities of a large village, and with three coal mines and the brickworks open.

**After the Mines and Foundry**: One mine and the railway station were closed about 1954, a second mine by 1971, and the third and last had shut by 1973. Armadale Academy was built west of the village about 1970. The demise of mining led to industrial estates being developed, and by 1972 a hosiery factory had created some local employment for women. Armadale – which lost its local government status in 1975 – remained a large village, supporting non-league football and bowling clubs. In 1981, before the closure of the Bathgate motor works, the population was 9700. The disused railway was lifted in the 1980s. In 1990 it was expected that the foundry, a branch of North British Steel of Bathgate, would be closed with the loss of 300 jobs; by 1994 this industry was extinct in the area.

**Small Firms Struggling and Prospects Dubious**: Some small clothing ventures were short-lived; in 1991 Wilkie Reinforcements employed 70 workers, only a third of the planned capacity of their refurbished plant for preparing steel reinforcing rods for structural concrete. By then the population had fallen to about 8900; few had higher qualifications, and too many of the men were out of work. While not among the most deprived places, Armadale was remote from the powerhouse of West Lothian at Livingston and progress seemed slow. Armadale Academy had 702 pupils in 1997. Bricks are still made at the Etna Works in Lower Bathville, and Ibstock Bricks are also present; Drummond (distribution) employ 100, Mowlem site investigation 50, and knitwear for schools is also produced.

## ARROCHAR & Tarbet

**Map 5, B4**

***Argyllshire villages,*** *pop. 1000*

OS 56: NN 2904

At the northern end of the aptly named Loch Long is a 2km wide isthmus which separates this Clyde sea loch from the upper reaches of the freshwater Loch Lomond. The Gaelic name Tarbet means *'draw-boat'*, but little remains of the 14th century Tarbet Castle which stood on the east side of the isthmus near the northern limits of Lennox, more recently called Dunbartonshire. Pont's map of about 1600 named the castle, and *'Innerriach'* at the location of modern Arrochar. In 1803 Dorothy Wordsworth noted an inscribed stone at the summit of the *Rest and be Thankful* pass west of Arrochar, which attributed the Dumbarton to Inveraray road to *Colonel* Wade's regiment (although probably a re-make job). Then between 1746 and 1750, under Caulfeild's direction, a military road was built up the northern part of Loch Lomondside and beautiful Glen Falloch to Crianlarich, Tarbet becoming the junction point.

**A Laird's House, Inns and the first Tourists**: Roy's contemporary map, which showed both roads, emphasised the Inveraray road and identified the spot where this met Loch Long as *'New Tarbat'*; yet when a post office was sited there about 1750 this was named *'Arrochar'*. By 1773 an inn was open at Tarbet, a *"village"* to Dorothy Wordsworth in 1803, when the inn was *"a well-sized white house, the best in the place"*. Tarbet contained one other stone house, a large thatched dwelling and a few huts; Gaelic and to some extent English were spoken. At Arrochar she saw fishermen's boats, and noted that the Loin Water had been bridged. She dined well at the *New Inn*, which was full up, being *"celebrated as a place of good accommodation for travellers"*; according to Chambers, this was *"originally the mansion-house of the chief of Macfarlane"* (the former feudal superior).

*Inveruglas hydro-electric scheme on the west side of Loch Lomond, built in 1946–50 and the crowning achievement of the North of Scotland Hydro-Electric Board. It is still today the largest hydro scheme in Britain.* *(SMPC / Tom Robertson)*

**Steamer Services and the Three Lochs Tour**: The first steamer on Loch Lomond was the PS *Marion*, which went into service in 1816, making calls near the Tarbet inn; Chambers noted that curricles – light open coaches – were readily available to take passengers over the hill between Arrochar and Tarbet. By 1831 Arrochar itself was served by regular steamers, including in 1853 the Dumbarton Steamboat Company (SC), between 1864 and 1880 the Loch Long & Loch Lomond SC, and in 1885 the Loch Goil & Loch Long SC. Meantime a new church was built at Arrochar in 1849; Arrochar school was actually nearer Tarbet. Arrochar pier was used from 1867 by the *'Three Lochs Tour'* (Lomond, Long and Goil). Tarbet also had a post and telegraph office by 1883. By 1894 its inn had been further promoted to the *"first class" Tarbet Hotel*, still adjoined by a Loch Lomond steamer pier; by then the inn at Arrochar was named by Murray as the *"plain, comfortable" Arrochar Hotel*; steamers from Gourock terminated at the adjacent pier.

**The West Highland Railway**: Arrochar & Tarbet Station was opened in 1894 as a crossing point on the single-line West Highland Railway. Sited on the col between the two villages, it became the railhead for the Inveraray area, and was later also the terminus of a local service from the pier station at Craigendoran; in steam days it had an engine shed. A 9-hole golf course was open at Stuckiedhu by the 1920s, and still open in 1953, but had vanished by 1964.

**Hydro Power and Youth Hostelling**: Meantime in 1946–50 the Hydro-Electricity Board built the Loch Sloy dam, 540m long, to raise the level of Loch Sloy – in the valley of the Inveruglas Water west of Ben Vorlich – by 47m, to a top water level of some 275m, with tunnels feeding a large power station at Inveruglas on the west shore of Loch Lomond, 5km north of Tarbet. Fifty years later this was still Britain's largest capacity hydro-electric station. No permanent settlement followed the Loch Sloy scheme, for such installations can operate virtually unattended. However the hamlet of Succoth, 1km to the north of Arrochar, was developed by the Forestry Commission about the same time. In the 1950s there were still regular steamers between Arrochar and Glasgow, and one of the earliest youth hostels was opened at Ardgartan where the Inveraray road turns up Glen Croe; later caravan and camping sites were developed there.

**Decline after the Steamers**: The population of Arrochar in 1951 was almost 1000 and of Tarbet over 400, but both places shrank steadily to a combined population of under 1150 by 1971. Arrochar pier, still in use in 1963, was closed about 1970. The Loch Lomond steamer *Maid of the Loch* ceased to call at Tarbet pier in 1974, and it closed in 1975; land difficulties delayed its restoration. The combined number of hotels had risen from four to seven, and the facilities of an average village were available.

**Returning to Water, Rail – and Church?**: Tarbet pier was reopened in 1984 for the *Countess Fiona* service. By 1985 a caravan site was open, and two more were added by 1991. In 1990 timber was still despatched by rail from Arrochar, but this traffic was lost by BR in 1991, when the once attractive station building was disused and falling into decay; only the civil engineer used the sidings by 1993. However and passenger trains still called; by 1999 EW&S had regained some timber traffic. The fine listed parish church, largely disused in 1999, was restored in 2000. The *'Loch Long'* youth hostel at Ardgartan is open except in midwinter.

## ASHGILL, Dalserf, Netherburn & Rosebank

**Map 16, A5**

***Lanarkshire villages,*** *pop. 1000* — OS 64 & 72: NS 7950

Dalserf, an old parish centre about 3km to the east of Larkhall on the steep left bank of the River Clyde, opened its school in 1619. The Roy map of about 1754 showed the Hamilton to Lanark road high above; two lanes led down to Dalserf. In the 1820s a quarry at Dalserf provided fine building stone to enlarge Hamilton Palace. A single-line railway from Motherwell to Lesmahagow and Coalburn was opened in 1856 for mineral traffic. Ayr Road Junction, near the Auldton at the top of the hill to the west of Dalserf and 80m above the Clyde, was the divergence of a single line which was opened in 1862 to Cots Castle via Stonehouse. In 1866 the Caledonian Railway introduced passenger trains, and Dalserf station was opened at the junction; the line from Motherwell and Larkhall was doubled. The small *Popinjay Inn*, pleasantly located at Rosebank, was built in a black and white half-timbered style in 1882.

**Mining creates Ashgill and Netherburn**: By 1895 mineral lines connected to small collieries at Castlehill east of the station, and to the south at Shawsburn, where there was also an inn, and a fireclay pit near Harelees. Miners' rows lined the main road at Ashgillhead (later renamed Ashgill), south of which were hamlets at Dunlop Place, and Woodside with its colliery. Bents station, 2km farther south, served the hamlet of Netherburn, later developed with a housing estate, pub and for a time a post office. The Clyde had been bridged below the station at Garrionhaugh, but Dalserf was just a scatter of buildings on the winding riverside road; on this to the south stood the hamlet of Rosebank (on OS 72). In the early 20th century Ashgill developed from the miners' rows to a population of 1540 in 1951, with basic facilities. But by 1953 Dalserf station had been closed to passengers, by 1954 all the mines had been closed, leaving bings as memorials.

**Glasshouses, Hotels and Building Industry**: Glasshouses were a long-standing feature of the area, where both Shawsburn and Dalserf primary schools were open in the 1950s. By 1971 the railways had vanished, the population had fallen to about 1225 and the new M74 motorway formed a clear division between Ashgill and Larkhall. Near the M74 junction at Swinhill was a hostelry, just a pub in 1963, which soon became the *Shawlands Hotel*. In 1991 Ashgill had about 1050 people. By 1996 the hilltop glasshouses had gone, but some more new housing had been added. The *Popinjay*, steadily developed over a century into a hotel, now has 45 rooms, and the *Shawlands Hotel* 21.

## ASHKIRK

**Map 3, A4**

***Borders hamlet,*** *pop. 200* — OS 73: NT 4722

Ashkirk lies in the hill-girt upper valley of the Ale Water, some 6km south of Selkirk as the crow flies; there is an ancient earthwork. A parish school was opened in 1618. The Selkirk to Hawick road (now A7) was open when Roy mapped the area about 1754; both Ashkirk and Synton 2.5km downstream had mills. Neither 19th century industry nor railways ever affected this hill-farming area. In 1951 the school, a post office, garage and telephone exchange served a small village; the parish population was 290, a third had been lost by 1981; by then the post office and school had closed. The 1980s saw the reconstruction of the hilly and winding A7 road in sweeping curves, and although only 177 people lived in the parish by 1991, the improved accessibility must have helped the decision to lay out a golf course west of the hamlet in the mid 1990s.

## ASSYNT & Inchnadamph — Map 12, B3

***Area of Wester Ross,** pop. under 100* — OS 15: NC 2522

This remote moorland area about 15km east of Lochinver is characterised by its strange isolated sandstone peaks, Quinag to the north of Loch Assynt and Suilven and Canisp to the south; to the east it is bounded by the 1000m massif of Ben More Assynt. There are several chambered cairns, and near the loch's eastern end stands the ruined 16th century keep of Ardvreck Castle. Around 1600 Pont noted a mill at nearby Inchnadamph, which he regarded as a kirkton. A new church was built in 1741–43, which Roy noted as the *'Kirk of Strathcromble'*; the area was quite well settled but trackless at the time of his survey about 1750. It did not gain roads through Telford's work for the Commissioners, but Assynt post office was in being by 1829. By the 1890s the road system had assumed its modern form and there was an inn at Inchnadamph. This became known as a fishing resort, and grew into a 26-roomed hotel by the 1950s. Meantime the post office had closed, but the primary school was closed for a decade around 1980 due to the lack of children in a local population of about 50. The hotel and a mountain rescue post remain active. The area remains among the least afforested in mainland Scotland; there is also a large hostel for backpackers.

## ATHELSTANEFORD & East Fortune — Map 3, B2

***E. Lothian small village,** pop. 400* — OS 66: NT 5377

Athelstaneford on the tiny Cogtail or Peffer Burn, 4km north-east of Haddington, bears an Anglian name; both this and *'Fortoun Easter'*, 2km farther north-east, where there was a medieval hospice by 1300, appeared as tiny places on Pont's map of Lothian, made around 1600. Athelstaneford was already a village served by road by the time of the Roy survey of about 1754. In 1799 Heron noted Athelstaneford as a *"village"* of some 400 people, and in 1825 a brewery was recorded. From 1846 wholly rural East Fortune had a station, 5km east of Drem on the North British Railway main line. During the 1914–18 war a site just west of the station was developed as the largest Royal Naval airship base in Scotland, the departure point in 1919 for the vast R34 airship which made the first east to west crossing of the Atlantic *(see Hay & Stell)*. A few years later a tuberculosis sanatorium was built on the former airship base.

**Athelstaneford's Fortune returns to the Air**: In 1939–44 an RAF fighter base was in operation on land adjoining the sanatorium, which was later renamed as East Fortune Hospital. In 1951 Athelstaneford and East Fortune had about 500 people each, but the railway station had been closed to passengers by 1965, and soon vanished altogether. In 1971 East Fortune Hospital still held over 250 people, and in 1981 its 261 beds fulfilled several functions; but by then the combined population of the two settlements was a mere 400, with minimal facilities. The Museum of Flight, part of the National Museums of Scotland, opened on East Fortune airfield in 1975, using one of the original hangars for conservation work. It built up a major collection, including (from 1981) five aircraft from Strathallan. By 1996 the hospital had been closed, soon followed by the post office. However, a former doocot is now a museum celebrating the saltire, the St Andrews Cross flag of Scotland.

## AUCHENBLAE & Fordoun — Map 10, B4

***Mearns villages,** pop. 500* — OS 45: NO 7278

Fordoun stands on the west side of the Luther Water, 1km north of the emergence of this small stream from the hills of Drumtochty Forest into the Howe of the Mearns. In the fifth century Fordoun became a very early Christian settlement, from which St Ternan founded Banchory in the same century. In 934 St Palladius, an Irish bishop, built a chapel; Fordoun church, founded beside it in 1244, consequently became known as *"the mother church of the Mearns"*. John of Fordoun, born in 1330, was one of Scotland's first chroniclers. Fordoun was chartered as a burgh of barony in 1554, a parish school was held by 1609 and *'Fordun'* church was marked on Blaeu's atlas of 1654; but little development followed.

**What's in a Name?**: The Roy map made about 1750 showed a road from the Laurencekirk area via *'Crookyden'* to a mill and the *'Kirk of Fordan'*, just north of which on the east side of the Luther Water was a cluster of hamlets named *'Auchblair'*. Two tracks led north, trending north-east towards Glenbervie. Later in the century Boswell mentioned *"Auchenblae, a wretched place, wild and naked, with a few old houses"*. An annual fair was to be held at Auchenblae in 1797; however, Heron in 1799 mentioned only *"the village of Fordoun"*.

**The New Village and Spinning Mill**: The village of Auchenblae was re-founded in 1795 when a flax spinning mill was built to serve local hand weavers; the linen industry became its principal support. According to Chambers in 1827 *"the small village called the Kirktown of Fordoun"* stood beside the

*The Den Mill at Auchenblae was built as a flax-spinning mill in the mid 19th century, but was converted into a malt whisky distillery in 1896, with 300 local shareholders. It closed in 1926, but the building survives.* *(JRH)*

Luther Water opposite the *"larger village called Auchenblae"*. A post office had opened at Auchenblae by 1838. The mill employed about 50 people; it was re-equipped and returned to production about 1863, though on a reduced scale.

**Railway, Placename transfer, and Whisky**: The name of Fordoun was applied to an Aberdeen Railway station which was opened in 1850 4km south-east of Auchenblae, beside the main Laurencekirk to Aberdeen road, and eventually became attached to the adjoining post office and new settlement. The railway age passed Auchenblae by, and it never became more than a village. The linen mill was rebuilt in 1896 as a malt whisky distillery by a local company; it closed in 1926. The *Fordoun Arms* was open at Auchenblae by 1894, eighty years later being a pleasant small hotel. The 9-hole golf course and the facilities of a small village were available by the 1950s; but Auchenblae had declined in population to a mere 500 by 1991, though its main street still gave a sense of enclosure.

## AUCHENCAIRN — Map 2, A5

***Village on Solway Firth**, pop. 400* — OS 84: NX 7951

The Hass Burn enters a sheltered bay on the Solway coast about 12 km east of Kirkcudbright. The area contains ancient earthworks, and an early fort stood somewhat inland. Orchardton Tower, built in the 15th century 2 km to the north-east of the fort, was emparked when Pont noted the area about 1600; *'Achincairn'* near the burn mouth was one of a few tiny settlements in the little-known parish of Renwick. Heron in 1799 mentioned Auchencairn as a *"village"*. A lifeboat station was opened at Balcary Fishery on the coast 2 km south-east in 1884; though it was closed in 1931, the boathouse survives. The small *Balcary Bay Hotel* was open nearby by 1952, when the local population of over 600 was served by the facilities of a small village, and for a time a sawmill was at work. However, the local roads are very winding, and rural depopulation reduced the number of local residents to under 400 by 1981, although by then the *Olde Smugglers Inn* also offered accommodation. By 1991 the whole of Rerrick parish (which also contains Dundrennan) held only 546 people, little more than half the 1951 figure. The 2 hotels and primary school remain open.

## AUCHENGRAY, Cobbinshaw, Tarbrax & Woolfords — Map 16, C5

***Lanarkshire hamlets**, pop. 300* — OS 65 or 72: NS 9954

There was an early chapel at Auchengray, which stands high at about 260m in Carnwath parish. Its name, together with Haywood and Tarbrax, appeared on Pont's 1596 map of Clydesdale. The Roy map showed little between the Edinburgh to Carnwath road and the developments east of Forth *(q.v.)*. The Bog Burn, headwaters of the Murieston Water over the crest in Lothian, was dammed around 1822 to form Cobbinshaw Reservoir, to ensure water supply to the Union Canal *(see Mid Calder)*, which it still does. The Caledonian Railway opened its line from Carstairs to Edinburgh in 1848, following the shallow valley of the Dippool Water to a summit at Woolfords Cottages near Cobbinshaw station. Another station was provided farther south near Auchengray; 1 km to the north a branch line ran westwards to the coal pits complex and station at Haywood, and so to Wilsontown. From the mid 1860s small shale-pits and oil-works operated intermittently at Cobbinshaw, and 3 km to the east at Tarbrax. By 1895 Auchengray had an inn, a post office, and a brick and tile works.

**Shale-Oil and Problems of Remoteness**: The Tarbrax Oil Company works was rebuilt to use electric power in 1904, the date they were taken over by the Pumpherston *(q.v.)* company. The new owners expanded the village, also building houses at Woolfords, where coal was mined; one unusual pithead building survives. When the Tarbrax works was closed in 1926 the village held 2150 people, but as there was no other work, people rapidly left. Under 300 people remained in 1951; the Tarbrax works had vanished by 1954, leaving former shale bings; coal mining in the Haywood area had also ceased. The Wilsontown branch and Auchengray station were closed by Beeching in 1964. By 1981 each place had under 200 people, but unlike Auchengray with its school, remote Tarbrax retained its post office as late as the 1990s; Woolfords post office had lately closed. The former *King's Inn* had been renamed the *Auchengray Inn* by 1986, when cattle rearing was the most evident enterprise in this area of scattered farms and hamlets; the area to the north was afforested in the late 20th century. Auchengray and Tarbrax retain their pubs. Cobbinshaw Reservoir continues to provide trout fishing.

## AUCHINLECK — Map 1, C2

***Ayrshire village**, pop. 4000* — OS 70/71: NS 5522

Little remains of the two early castles of Auchinleck (anciently pronounced *Affleck*) which stood on the banks of the Lugar Water 4km south of Mauchline. In 1507 a burgh of barony was chartered; some writers claim that the charter was not implemented, for only the Kirk of *'Achirlek'* which stood 5km east of the castle was shown on Pont's map of about 1600. However, a small village which took its name did develop nearby, astride the Mauchline-Cumnock road. In the early 18th century the proprietor Lord Auchinleck, the father of the biographer James Boswell, replaced the later castle by the nearby classical mansion of Auchinleck House. This was still named *'Affleck'* on the Roy map made in the 1750s, when it stood in surrounding policies. The tiny village was overshadowed by Cumnock, only 3km away, until coal was found. Despite its Boswell laird's literary prowess, as late as the 1790s there was not even a local school, although a fair was scheduled at Auchinleck in 1797.

**The Railway**: A railway being pushed south from Kilmarnock passed through Auchinleck to reach the ironmaking town of Muirkirk in 1848. In 1850 Auchinleck became a junction from which the line was extended southwards to form the main line of the Glasgow & South Western, to Dumfries and Carlisle. For a time it possessed an engine shed, but this was closed about 1879, perhaps because local mining activity developed by local man William Walker at Airds Moss *(see Cumnock)* to the north-east of the village had declined; the 1895 OS map showed old pits and a disused ironstone mine among active coal workings.

**Highhouse Colliery**: Activity soon intensified west of the village with the sinking from 1894 of William Baird's Highhouse Colliery *(see Hutton, 1996)*, whose winding engine dated from 1896; but main rope haulage was by *'Old Ben'*, a much-travelled beam engine finely built at Bridgeton in 1790 and still used as recently as 1956, when it was saved for posterity and later moved to the Newtongrange Mining Museum. Meantime the firm built two rows of 48 and 49 passable houses for the workers, who at least had piped water.

**Barony pit and its Chequered History**: The deep Barony Colliery was sunk 2 km west of the village in 1906–1912, and in 1914–15 Bairds built 136 houses in the Dalsalloch Rows, beside the Catrine road. A late gasworks was established in Auchinleck in 1923. Barony Colliery was reconstructed with a third shaft sunk from 1938, and was the largest of the many collieries of the Bairds & Dalmellington Company at vesting date in 1947, working five seams by longwall methods. There were over 5000 people in the area in 1951; by then old shafts littered the moors to the east and the Muirkirk railway carried only minerals, later being cut back by degrees as successive collieries closed. In the 1960s Auchinleck lost its passenger trains, and Auchinleck House was abandoned by the Boswells in 1960. Barony No.3 shaft was completed by the NCB in 1953; it was 625 m deep. Meantime a horrendous collapse of the original two shafts occurred in 1962, and production ceased for four years; but because the colliery was generally successful, though with a smaller output than planned, a fourth shaft was sunk, completed in 1966.

**Experimental Power from Coal Slurry**: Meantime an experimental power station fired by coal slurry was completed beside Barony in 1957. This took years to achieve efficient use of the wet fuel, and it was closed in 1982 *(but see Methil)*. A thousand men worked at Barony in 1977, and another 260 in the elderly Highhouse colliery; but the latter was closed in 1983–84, one set of headgear remaining as a monument amid an industrial estate. A major indoor bowling centre had been opened about 1980, but Auchinleck was disadvantaged, and its general facilities were only those of a village. The railway station was reopened for passengers in 1984, and by 1985 large new premises for Auchinleck Academy had been built north of Dalsalloch.

**Thatcher Faults the Barony**: Barony, the last deep mine at work in Ayrshire and, had 400 miners in 1987, raising 7000 tonnes of coal a week, which apparently moved by road to the Killoch washery. Barony was closed in 1989, due to the discovery of a mere 3 m fault in the only coal face then being worked, which made it impossible to continue to meet the very high output targets set after the miners' strike by the Thatcher regime. So the major investment in shafts, surface installations and people was abandoned and a major era in Ayshire history closed. It left yet another disadvantaged former mining village, with 28% male unemployment among a 1991 population of 4100, few having higher qualifications and many with health problems.

**After the Mines**: Meantime in 1985 Auchinleck House had been acquired by the Scottish Historic Buildings Trust for restoration. The Barony Colliery buildings were proposed for demolition in 1991, but the pithead gear remained prominent in 1992. On the brighter side, a bypass was opened about 1992, a Boswell museum had been created in the old parish church, and there was a caravan site 3 km to the east. The relaying of about 9 km of the Muirkirk branch railway was proposed about that time, to carry coal from opencast workings in the valley of the Gass Water east of Cumnock, through a rail loading point at Powharnel. In 1997 Egger UK announced the building of a chipboard factory at Barony to employ 130 people, with an intended rail siding.

## AUCHLEVEN (or Premnay) & Leslie — Map 10, B3

***Aberdeenshire small villages,*** *pop. 200* — OS 37: NJ 6224

The hills extending westwards from Bennachie in Aberdeenshire bear stone circles and an ancient circular settlement, near which the medieval Premnay Kirk was built beside the Gadie Burn. About 1.5 km upstream was Licklyhead Castle, and 3 km farther west Leslie Castle, two 17th century L-plan tower houses respectively some 4 km south and south-west of Insch. Several of these features appeared on Gordon's map, produced by 1642. The Roy map of about 1750 showed a track linking Clatt and Oyne, beside which stood both Leslie Kirk, some 5 km west of Premnay, and a mansion named *'Likelyhead'*, downstream of which was a mill, probably the Mill of Barnes. Roads were built into the Premnay area, but apart from four water mills near Leslie it escaped the attentions of industrialists and writers alike, remaining entirely agricultural. With a 1951 population of some 420, the village of Auchleven which had grown near Licklyhead had only basic services, including the Premnay primary school and the small *Premnay Hotel*. These surprisingly survived a collapse in the number of local residents to no more than 200 by 1981, partly because the even more rural Leslie, and the hamlet of Duncanstone farther west, came to rely on Premnay school and hotel. By 1995 there was an airstrip 1.5 km to the west, and in 2000 a hardware shop and garage were also open.

## AUCHNAGATT & Arnage — Map 10, C2

***Aberdeenshire small village,*** *pop. 200* — OS 30: NJ 9341

Auchnagatt – in Gaelic *'Field of the Sheaf'*, reflecting its quite good farmland – is a Buchan settlement beside the Ebrie Burn, a tributary of the River Ythan. It was shown on Robert Gordon's map made by about 1642. About 5 km downstream to the south was Arnage Castle, a 17th century Z-plan tower. Roy's map surveyed about 1750 showed a track linking Tanglandford and Old Deer, crossing the valley at Auchnagatt; between there and Arnage were the Mills of Elrick, Inkhorn and the possibly later Towie Mill. The track ultimately became a minor road, crossed at Auchnagatt by the main road from Ellon to New Deer, and by 1858 there was *"a good country inn"* (shown on OS maps as the *Baron's Inn*) and a number of small limestone quarries nearby, one of which was at Annochie.

**The Railway Epoch – and After**: The Great North of Scotland Railway's Buchan branch, built in 1858–61, provided stations near Arnage, and at Auchnagatt where there was also a post and telegraph office. In the 20th century compact Auchnagatt provided the services of a small village to several hamlets within a radius of about 5 km, including Arnage which for a time had its own school. The stations were closed to passengers by Beeching in 1965, and in 1979 the railway was closed to freight and lifted. Surviving facilities included the recently extended *Baron's Hotel* and a coach hirer; but the entire population of this remote and wholly agricultural area fell from about 1375 in 1951 to 975 in 1981, when only some 200 people lived in and near the village. Eventually by 1999 the station site was taken for house building, but in 2000 although the school, a general store with hardware and a post office were still open, the hotel was for sale. Remarkably, a primary school was still open at the remote hamlet of Braeside, 4km south-west.

## AUCHTERARDER — Map 6, A4

***Perthshire small town,** pop. 3300* — OS 58: NN 9412

A castle was built at Auchterarder in Strathearn in the 11th century, but the name was not shown on the probably mid 13th century Gough map, which may have been made prior to its chartering as a Royal Burgh in 1246 – the last of Alexander II's few creations. The town of Auchterarder grew 1 km south of the ancient church. In 1290 its Royal castle became briefly the caput of a sheriffdom, visited by the unwelcome Edward I of England en route from Stirling to Perth in 1295. This was apparently the kiss of death, and as early as 1328 the sheriffdom had been merged into that of Perth. The 14th century keep of Kincardine Castle, 2 km south of the town, was sketched by Pont about 1600 as an elaborate 5-storey tower in its own policies, but the village of Auchterarder was not thriving. It had paid no tax in the period 1535–56 and was ignored by the early travel writers. Timothy Pont showed a mill on the Ruthven Water; it was a scattered or a linear settlement, depending on which of his two sketch maps was viewed! By 1610 the parish had a school; at that period the castle was the stronghold of the Grahams, Earls of Montrose. The twice unlucky little town was burnt down in 1716 for supporting the Highlanders' rebellion.

**Rebuilding Auchterarder and Borland Park**: Auchterarder was rebuilt some time after 1716 as a centre for handloom weaving, with a waulk mill, but was still so insignificant that the military road constructed in 1742 to link Stirling with Perth went by way of Muthill and Crieff. The Roy map of the 1750s saw Auchterarder as an unimportant linear settlement on a secondary road or track linking Greenloaning via Dunning to Bridge of Earn (now B 8062); the direct road to Perth was a later turnpike. Borland Park, a hamlet just west of the town, was a government project for soldiers demobilised after a war in 1763. It soon became a centre for the local hand spinning and weaving of linens. A paper mill was set up at the Waulk mill about 1775, and Auchterarder together with Blackford had about 200 weavers by 1778. A post office was in use by 1777, and the considerable total of five fairs was scheduled for 1797. However Heron, who wrote of nearly 600 inhabitants, described the place in 1799 as *"the village of Auchterarder, once a royal borough"*. Low's brewery, established in 1786, was still open in 1825, and in 1847 James Carr of Milton of Auchterarder was a dyer.

**Auchterarder on the Railway**: The Kincardine Viaduct across the Water of Ruthven was a main feature of the new main line of the Scottish Central (later Caledonian) Railway (SCR) between Stirling and Perth. This opened in 1848, but Auchterarder station was rather inaccessible, being beyond the Ruthven Water; a four-in-hand coach was introduced to link the station with the tourist attraction of Rumbling Bridge. By 1860 Wordie & Co had a rail cartage depot, and about then a brick and tile works was in operation at Millands. Warden noted that by 1864 weaving was locally extinct; but matters soon changed, for in 1869 Bremner noted *"recently-erected power-loom factories"*, one of them evidently the Glenruthven mill.

**Golf and Hotels**: The mansion of Collearn House was built in 1870, and Auchterarder House is also a Victorian baronial mansion; but by 1888 Kincardine Castle was a ruin. Auchterarder golf club, which was founded in 1892, laid out an 18-hole parkland course, which survived the coming of the championship courses at nearby Gleneagles *(q.v.)*. In 1894 there were two hotels, the *Star* and the *Crown*, but Auchterarder was noted by Murray as *"of little importance"*. In 1916 R White & Sons' Glenruthven mill installed a second-hand tandem compound steam engine which originally drove about 100 looms, but later rather fewer.

**Auchterarder Hospital**: In 1928 the St Margaret's Hospital was built under the will of a local donor, and by 1953 Auchterarder's facilities were typical of a small town, including a junior secondary school; *Collearn House* in its extensive gardens had become a hotel, one of seven including the *Crown* and *Ruthven Towers* (which became a nursing-home after 1980). The station was closed to passengers around 1960, though Gleneagles only 3km away stayed open, and in 1978 potatoes were still sent south by rail. But the *"Lang Toun"* (as it was often called for its linear layout) had again been declining, and by 1981 was really only a large village, though with as many as eight hotels and two woollen mills. The hazard of fast through traffic was removed with the opening of the A9 bypass in 1982.

**Quiet without the Traffic**: The Glenruthven mill engine, the last such steamable engine in Scotland, ceased work in 1980, but was happily preserved when the mill was converted to electric power. The mill had been closed by 1990, and was converted into a working museum and exhibition centre by the Auchterarder Heritage Centre Trust; by 1996 it also held the Scottish base of the Woodland Trust, which managed 6500ha of broadleaved and native woodlands. In 1990 the local group practice of five doctors proposed a new health centre related to the hospital. In 1991 about 3550 people lived in Auchterarder and Gleneagles, a high proportion owning their homes outright and many having higher qualifications; housing development continued in the 1990s. In 1997 Auchterarder High School had a roll of 332. The local shops are much patronised by visitors to the great *Gleneagles Hotel*. The smaller, local hotels include the *Auchterarder House*, the *Cairn Lodge*, and the restored *Collearn House*.

## AUCHTERLESS & Towie Barclay — Map 10, B2

***Area of Aberdeenshire,** pop. 700 (area)* — OS 29: NJ 7141

Kirkton of Auchterless in the upper reaches of the Ythan valley was the ancient parish centre of an area of quite good farmland, the Howe of Auchterless. In the 12th century the Barclays built the original Towie Barclay Castle, 4km downstream from the kirkton; when it was rebuilt as a tower in the 16th century a plaque was placed on it, stating that *"Sir Valter Barclay foundit Tollie Mills 1210"*. The area was well settled in 1642, and by about 1750 lay on a track linking Turriff and Oldmeldrum; the Ythan had been bridged near a hamlet at Chapel of Seggat, between the emparked castle and the kirk, where the Newmills had been established and a post office was open by 1798.

**Grassic Gibbon outlasts the Railway**: When the Turriff branch of the Great North of Scotland Railway was opened in 1857, Auchterless station was located close to the castle. An annual fair was still held at the kirkton in 1858. Author James Leslie Mitchell, born in the sprawling parish of Auchterless in 1901, became famous in his short life under the pen name of Lewis Grassic Gibbon as the author of *A Scots Quair* and other books. Up to the 1950s there were two post offices and two schools; that at Kirkton had a secondary class and outlasted the Birkenhills school north of the station, which was itself closed to passengers in 1951. Rail freight survived until 1966; by the 1980s the area was wholly rural, but Towie Barclay Castle has been restored, and Mitchell's name lives on in a small museum.

## AUCHTERMUCHTY & Dunshalt — Map 6, B4

***Fife village,** pop. 2000* — OS 58/59: NO 2311

An ancient settlement and the site of a Roman marching camp lay near the headwaters of the River Eden in the western Howe of Fife. The nearby hamlet of Dunshalt bears a Gaelic name, as does Auchtermuchty (*Upper Pigsty* in Gaelic!), locally known as *Muchty*, which lies astride the tumbling Glassart Burn. It was created a Royal Burgh in 1517; nearby stands the tower house of Myres Castle, built about 1530. Though Auchtermuchty paid no tax in 1535–56, by the mid 16th century King James V was boasting of its many bridges, of which at least two tiny examples survive across the burn. However, although Auchtermuchty had a school by 1570 and was somewhat emphasised on Pont's map of about 1600, only the Eden bridge was shown; James Gordon's 1642 map, made little of 'Muchty.

**Religion, Weighing Machines, Malting and Milling**: John Glas, born in Auchtermuchty in 1695, founded the Christian sect known as Glassites or Sandemanians. John White began weighing machine manufacture in 1715, probably for the grain trade, for Auchtermuchty soon became well known for its maltings. A significant market was active by 1728, the year when the town hall was built, and linen was also woven. Roy's map (made about 1750) showed a small linear village on the area's only road, the line of the modern A91 from Strathmiglo towards Cupar; Cash mill was already at work.

**From Market to Industrial Village**: Between 1766 and 1787 the Perth United Banking Company opened a branch in Auchtermuchty; this passed to the Perth Banking Company in 1787, was closed for a time around 1810 but later reopened. Hutchinson & Drummond were wheelwrights in 1788, and in 1791 nearly half a million metres of linen cloth was hand woven locally. The extreme flatness of the land to the south suggests that it must have been very marshy prior to the agricultural drainage improvements of the 18th century; the road to Falkland was eventually set out across it in 1784. Dealers in linen traded in the town by 1792, and although the Newburgh road was unmade until about 1795, imported flax transhipped from Dundee was brought from there to the local linen weavers. Four fairs were scheduled to take place in 1797, and Heron in 1799 estimated the population at 1100.

**Beer and Whisky**: By 1825 Auchtermuchty was the centre for a penny post for Strathmiglo. Following the collapse of a brewery company which operated only from 1809 to 1813, the Auchtermuchty distillery was established in 1829 by the Bonthrone family, using a spirit still bought from a smuggler! As late as 1843, 700 hand weavers still made linen, and by 1864 Peter Skinner's modern bleachfield employed 30 people. From 1857 'Muchty lay on the branch railway linking Kinross and Ladybank, and at one time had a gasworks. In 1886 the little distillery was powered only by water, and used peats brought all the way from Orkney, to produce a mere 90,000 litres of malt whisky a year.

**Mid Twentieth Century Decline**: The distillery was later confusingly renamed *Stratheden* before it closed in 1926 as a result of US Prohibition. About 1930 its whisky bond was acquired by Arthur Bell & Sons of Perth, who still used it in 1976. Auchtermuchty with the hamlet of Dunshelt had a population of 1800 in the 1950s, with the facilities of a large village, but over the next 30 years these declined very significantly, including closure of the secondary school. The railway station was closed in 1950, but the building survived to be incorporated in the Rippin Structures works in 1967.

**Auchtermuchty in 1976**: This relatively remote village had an unusual group of three engineering firms in 1976 – Rippin, Robert Ferlie & Sons, iron and steel founders who made drain covers, and John White & Son, beam and scale manufacturers. Together they employed 278 people, 93% of them male. Rippin was then among Scotland's largest independent structural engineers. There was also a granary and a woollen mill, but the gasworks had gone. In 1976 the bus service through Auchtermuchty linked Cupar with Kinross; there were 183 pupils in the primary school, but the senior pupils were educated at Cupar. Among the 25 shops were specialists in furniture, antiques and musical instruments; there were two banks, two garages, three hotels and a bowling green. The 4-doctor practice also served Strathmiglo, Falkland and Freuchie. The area population by 1981 was over 2000; there were still three little hotels. By 1983 Whites had branches in Dyce and Glasgow.

**The Industrial Village falters on to TV**: In 1987 22 flats were built by a housing association and Lothian Barley, a subsidiary of Edinburgh-based S&N, took over the mill and grain stores. A small electrode factory was open too. In 1989 Rippin Structures was growing in specialist structural steelwork, with a branch factory at Tayport and an ambitious training programme. But the Gulf War proved fatal to their key exports to the Middle East and the firm closed (their site now a furniture warehouse). In 1991 the village itself held 1932 residents. Barley was milled at Auchtermuchty until 1994, when due to stricter health and safety regulations, Lothian Barley moved to more modern premises at Markinch. In the mid 1990s the unspoiled village centre became familiar to many as the backdrop to ITV's *Doctor Finlay* series. By 1989 McRitchie was making hosiery in a new factory beside the old linen weaving sheds known as Reedieden Works, operated by 1994 by John Ford & Co, who manufacture knitwear and hosiery. John White & Son, one of Scotland's most enduring concerns, still make weighbridges and other computerised weighing systems at Station Road. Myres Castle, recently renovated, is for hire when the owners are not in residence and local hotels include the *Royal*, the *Hollies*, and the *Forest Hills*. Dunshalt retains its primary school, post office and blacksmith, plus a mushroom farm.

## AUCHTERTOOL — Map 6, B4

***Small South Fife village,** pop. 425* — OS 58: NT 2190

Most appropriately named *'Upper Hollows' (Uachdartuill)* in Gaelic, Auchtertool stands among the tumbled hills and hollows drained by the Dronachy and Bottom Burns, about 6 km west of Kirkcaldy. Its church beside the steep and winding path between Dunfermline Abbey and the latter's Abbotshall offshoot was first referred to in the 12th century. Balmuto Castle was built 1.5 km to the south-east in the 15th century; it had enclosed policies when Pont's map was made around 1600. In 1604 a new parish church was built on the hill crest, standing on a mound, perhaps a medieval motte. Pont's map showed the kirk in a well settled area, but recorded no mill. Hallyards Castle, built 1 km to the north in the 16th century, later became ruinous.

**A Burgh for Corn Processing and a Railway for Coal**: It seems that a new mill was set turning about 1617 on the Dronachy Burn below its outflow from the tiny Camilla Loch, for the burgh of barony chartered in that year was named Milton of Auchtertool; a parish school was open by 1621. The mill appeared on James Gordon's map about 1650; in that year a brewery was founded nearby. The Milton was still a very small place in the mid 1750s, when work was begun to make up the path as a road from Crossgates through Auchtertool to Kirkcaldy. The brewery became the Auchtertool distillery in 1845, and in 1886 was thought by Barnard to be *"decidedly quaint and striking"*, though with a substantial cooperage; local barley was used by its proprietor Bartholomew of Kirkcaldy, to produce nearly 400,000 litres of Lowland malt whisky each year. In 1896 a mineral railway to Invertiel, intended for coal export from Cowdenbeath, was opened through the Auchtertool area, passing close to the small colliery once open at Little Raith, and serving a goods depot from 1912 to 1963.

**No Secrets on the Phone, Please!**: In the early 20th century some ten addresses including Balmuto Castle, the manse and the distillery shared one party phone line! The distillery closed in 1927, but malting continued until about 1971. Balbarton, a sadly prominent site beside the former railway, was already the major rubbish tip for Kirkcaldy by 1971, and remained so until 1999. A new housing estate was built about 1975, and the maltings site was developed for housing in 1987; the bonded warehouses near the mill site were demolished in 1990–91. The *Camilla Hotel*, built about 1975, was closed in 1989, soon becoming a nursing home. The area population of 425 was probably higher than for many years. Auchtertool's shop and petrol filling station closed in 1999; the post office was relocated, and the primary school remains in use. Due to the building of the new A92 to the north, all the local roads including the B925 – linking the two largest towns in Fife – remain in their narrow, winding medieval form, both scenically and historically very interesting.

## AULDEARN

**Map 9, C3**

***Small village near Nairn,*** *pop. v. under 100* OS 27: NH 9255

Early settlement 3 km inland from the Moray Firth was clearly encouraged by good farming soil, bringing a stone circle, evidence of Bronze Age occupation, Pictish standing stones and two mottes. The Royal Burgh of Earn (*Erne* being the Sea Eagle) was chartered in 1179, perhaps replacing Moyness, about 4 km to the south-east, which had a thanage from about the 11th century. The chartering of an inland place as a main trade centre must have very soon been recognised as an error of judgement, for *'New Earn'* (Nairn) only 4 km away on the coast, was itself chartered in 1190. In 1204 Nairn became the sheriff caput and ultimately an important centre, so that although there was still a royal castle at Auldearn about 1300, both this and the burgh soon ceased to exist. A parish school was open by 1582, and Pont's map shows that Auldearn had a mill by about 1600, near modern Millhill so probably a windmill; but the place was simply named *'Kirk of Alderin'*.

**On and Off the Road and Railway**: A rather similar name appeared on Roy's map of about 1750, when there was a road westwards to Nairn and Inverness but only a track eastwards to Forres. A new church was built in 1757. In 1769 Pennant found all to the east speaking English, whereas Auldearn people spoke Gaelic until the village was served by the Inverness to Elgin turnpike road. A railway station on the main line of the Inverness & Aberdeen Junction Railway was opened 1.5 km to the north in 1857. Goods and parcels traffic was handled by Wordie & Co as an outpost of Nairn, from which a horse and cart came daily. Auldearn was called a *"village"* by Murray in 1894. The station was a crossing point from 1905 to 1960, but was closed to passengers in 1960 and to goods in 1964. A bypass for the tiny village – with its two hotels and the preserved Boath doocot – was opened in 1987, restoring Auldearn's pleasantness. A Georgian mansion used by the military in the second world war is now the *Boath House Hotel*; a post office is still open.

## AULDGIRTH & Dalswinton

**Map 2, B4**

***Small Dumfriesshire villages,*** *pop. 450* OS 78: NX 9186

Ancient earthworks and the sites of two Roman forts – that at Dalswinton being of first century date – lie east of the River Nith where hills close in some 12 km north-west of Dumfries. The now ruined and undateable keep of Auldgirth Castle was shown emparked on Pont's map of around 1600, as was the Castle of Dalswinton, some 3 km south-east; it was shown as a mansion on the Roy map made about 1754. By then the Dumfries to Sanquhar road followed the River Nith, which by 1799 was spanned by what Heron called a *"fine bridge"*. Dalswinton Mill was built around 1775. Although a *'new village'* founded at Dalswinton about 1780 never grew beyond a hamlet, in 1788 the tiny Dalswinton Loch became known as the site of William Symington's steamboat trials *(see Wanlockhead)*.

**On and Beside the Railway**: The Glasgow, Dumfries & Carlisle Railway opened in 1849 with a station at Auldgirth, the next year becoming part of the Glasgow & South Western. The area remained agricultural, and Dalswinton Mill was re-equipped in 1893. Up to the closure of the station shortly before 1953, Auldgirth's facilities – those of a small village with a 4-roomed inn and 2-doctor practice – served a local population of 350, and to some extent a wide rural area containing in all some 3000 people. But Auldgirth's local population steadily shrank to under 250 by 1981, when Dalswinton had under 200 people. Only about 750 people in all depended on Auldgirth's facilities, which still include the post office, inn and primary school, plus a caravan site 3 km to the south near Ellisland Farm, of Burns' *Tam o' Shanter* fame. Some of Dalswinton Mill's machinery remained until its conversion to a dwelling house in the late 1990s.

## AULTBEA

**Map 8, C1**

***Small Wester Ross village,*** *pop. 200* OS 19: NG 8789

The crofting township of Aultbea in Wester Ross stands on the shore of the sea inlet of Loch Ewe, 8 km north of Poolewe and 4 km from Laide. In 1549 Munro noted that the offshore Isle of

Ewe was wooded. Blaeu's Atlas showed the area well settled by the 1640s, and the Roy map of around 1750 marked several clachans. After the potato famine of 1846 which caused great distress in remote western areas, the *Destitution Road* – a relief project – was built westwards from Braemore near Ullapool via Laide and Aultbea, and completed to Poolewe in 1851. Over 40 people lived on the Isle of Ewe in the 1880s; by then Aultbea had an inn. By the 1930s Drumchork Lodge, later a farmhouse, stood to the south of scattered Aultbea which had a pier, a post office, hotel and two churches; the primary school was 1 km to the west at Bualnaluib on the way to the large township of Mellon Charles.

**Convoys Gather**: The reasonably sheltered deep water of Loch Ewe became a minor naval base during World War II, when Arctic convoys for the USSR would assemble there; a larger pier was built to the south. By the 1950s Aultbea had a resident population of some 225, a little market two days a week, two hotels and a youth hostel, although this had closed by 1984. By 1972 the *Drumchork Lodge Hotel* was open, the population had grown a little and Aultbea had most of the facilities of a small village. Some new development had concentrated there by 1996, and two young families still lived on the farmed Isle of Ewe. There is still a naval refuelling base. The long-established *Aultbea Hotel* and the seasonal *Drumchork Lodge Hotel* continue to serve.

## AVIEMORE & Duthil

**Map 9, C5**

***Large Speyside village,*** *pop. 2200* — OS 36: NH 8912

A stone circle in the ancient Duthil parish shows the early significance of the area where a great rocky bluff or *'Big Face'* (in Gaelic *Aghaidh Mhor)*, juts into Strathspey. Around 1600 Timothy Pont mapped the area down-river from the bluff – part of a hill confusingly called Craigellachie – identifying the nearby settlement as *'Auymoir'*. This became the site of a *'kingshouse'* or inn where the Caulfeild road down Strathspey, built from 1743, branched from Wade's military road to Inverness, completed a few years earlier. Aviemore also had a post office by about 1745. These facilities would account for the emphasis given to the name of the small village shown on Roy's map of about 1750; tracks branched southeast from Inverdruie up the two glens. The area remained an extensive outlier of Moray until at least 1830. From 1836 Aviemore was served by mail coaches, and in 1858 the inn was an active posting station.

**The Highland Railway**: In 1863 a wayside station was opened at Aviemore on the new main line of the Inverness & Perth Junction Railway from Forres to Dunkeld. The hamlet grew into a village from 1892 when the successor Highland Railway opened the direct line from Aviemore to Inverness; a new and impressive station with three through platform faces was built to serve the junction. A hotel was proposed in 1894, and a four-bay stone-built engine shed was opened in 1898.

**The Aviemore Centre**: By 1951 Aviemore had grown to over 1000 people, with typical village facilities plus five hotels, the largest the 30-room 3-star *Cairngorm*. By 1961 there was also a youth hostel. Steam locomotives were based in Aviemore until 1965 when the original main line railway was closed and Aviemore became just a crossing station. The Aviemore Centre was developed from 1964 by Highland Tourist (Cairngorm Development) – the House of Fraser with brewers S&N and Tennent. Starkly designed under the direction of the corrupt architect J G L Poulson, it opened in 1966–67 as a resort village exploiting winter weather, with access to the high Cairngorms by improved roads to and beyond Glenmore *(q.v.)*. Its 4-star 90-room *Strathspey* and 75-room 3-star *Badenoch* hotels, caravan park, *Speyside Theatre*, swimming pool, fishing loch, putting course, karting track, dry ski slope and ice rink – which soon drew curlers from as far afield as Fochabers – were followed in 1971 by the 3-star 103-room *Post House* and in 1973 by squash courts. Later Stakis bought the ugly development. Over the river at Inverdruie came the 133-room 4-star *Coylumbridge Hotel*, open by 1972.

**British Rail hates Strathspey Steam**: In 1973 a preservation society succeeded in reopening the original Highland line to Boat of Garten as the *Strathspey Railway* (SR), Britain's most northerly steam-hauled tourist attraction. Though BR had inherited a fine large station with a spare platform face, their rigidly anti-steam policy forced the SR to build a new station some distance away, to the disadvantage of everyone! Further development by 1977 had brought the *Aviemore Chalets Hotel, Freedom Inn* and *Red McGregor Hotel*. Nearby by 1978 was a trout farm. Although the Aviemore Centre provided about 600 jobs and catered to up to 700,000 visitors a year, up to at least 1978 it generally ran at a loss, proving more popular in summer than winter. In 1978 a new tourist office and new Bank of Scotland premises were prominent.

**Golf, and Houses for the Energetic**: By 1981 Aviemore had ten hotels and the facilities of a large resort village. Aviemore golf club was founded in 1982 and laid out a valley course of 9 holes; about that time the expanding village was bypassed to the west by a new section of the A9. In 1990 *Scotland on Sunday* asserted that *"the worst eyesore in Scotland is commonly said to be the commercial complex at Aviemore"*. Much new housing was already rising around the golf course north-east of the village. In 1991 Aviemore had 2215 residents, and at 58% of all workers, Scotland's highest proportion in catering and distribution; census statistics also revealed a young, fit but not highly-educated population – the location and facilities favour the outdoor type! By 1992 there was a mountain rescue post. About 1992 the Centre was sold to Berkeley de Veer, a Sheffield firm which aroused local ire by felling mature trees on a site where they wished to build a supermarket; they had plans in 1993 for indoor swimming, tennis and larger ice rink facilities.

**Improving the Ambience**: In 1993 consultants for the Regional Council and Moray Badenoch & Strathspey Enterprise recommended improving the ugly ill-planned village as a whole. Proposals included traffic calming, creating a new square centred on the station and *Cairngorm Hotel*, and northwards expansion for up to 650 houses between Dalfaber and Edinkillie. A Tesco store opened in 1996, and by 2000 a new police station was in evidence. The SR trains run to Boat of Garten most days from March to October, using the third platform in the well conserved original station. Sizeable non-tourism ventures include Watt's timber haulage, and Hydrasun (who make components for the offshore industry), plus The Cairngorm Brewery. At Inverdruie is a retail complex, including produce from the Rothiemurchus estate. Hotels include the *Corrour House* (at Inverdruie), *Stakis Coylumbridge* (175 rooms), the *Hilton* (89), the *Freedom Inn* (94), *Highlands* (103) and *Rowan Tree* (at Loch Alvie) – plus guest houses, the youth hostel and a backpackers hostel.

## AVOCH

**Map 9, B3**

***Village in Easter Ross**, pop. 1000*

OS 26/27: NH 7055

Avoch in Easter Ross enjoys a sheltered position at the mouth of the Killen Burn on the inner Moray Firth, 3km west of Fortrose. Above it stand the fragmentary remains of the 12th century Ormond Castle, but tradition has it that the village originated in an Armada galleon wrecked in 1588. No Pont map of the area survives, and Avoch never became a burgh of barony, but it was certainly an early fishing centre, whose kirk dates from 1670. The Roy map made about 1750 showed a mansionhouse at Arkendeith and a coastal hamlet named *'Ach'*, reflecting the local pronunciation *Auch*. In the late 18th century this self-sufficient community wove its own clothes and sailcloth from locally grown flax and hemp. A pier and harbour were built in 1814 to designs by Thomas Telford, but as late as 1838 there was no post office. In 1847, despite famine in the locality among people fleeing from inland clearances for sheep, barley was being exported – the refugees had no means to buy it. Those who found work stayed, for by 1855 there were 160 fishermen and as many as 596 shore workers, including 480 netmakers. Woollen mills were also opened, employing fifty to sixty workers in 1869, with two sets of carding engines; their later history is little known.

**The Railway's brief association**: In 1894, when there was already an inn, a station was opened on the new Fortrose branch of the Highland Railway, where in 1946 Wordie & Co still had a small rail to road cartage depot. The station was closed to passengers in 1951; the goods trains and the tracks vanished in 1960. The small secondary school also soon closed. But over 1000 locals still enjoyed the facilities of a small village. Avoch fishermen thrived into the 1970s, mostly working their 17 vessels out of west coast ports, and also offering sea angling; but by 1985 only one of Avoch's twelve boats worked locally, catching shellfish. Avoch's population had dipped below 1000, but was up again to 1010 in 1991, due no doubt to the new housing inspired by the much greater accessibilty to Inverness introduced by the Kessock bridge. The harbour is now mainly used by pleasure craft.

## AVONBRIDGE

**Map 16, B3**

***Village s. of Falkirk**, pop. 800*

OS 65: NS 9172

An early bridge was thrown across the River Avon about 7km south of Falkirk, just above the point where it ceased to form the border between Stirlingshire and West Lothian; the bridge existed by about 1600, when Pont mapped the area. The settlement of Brigend already stood beside it, and there were mills at Dalwheen upstream of the bridge and at Straith downstream. The Roy map made in the 1750s showed Brigend and the bridge, which by then carried the Airdrie to Linlithgow road. In 1840 the idiosyncratic Slamannan Railway was opened following the north side of the valley, with a station near the bridge. It later became part of the North British Railway (NB) and was brought up to standard gauge. The NB provided another station at Blackstone, 1km farther east, from which a branch line was built south-eastwards to Westfield and Bathgate.

**Brigend, Craigend and Gowanbank**: Brigend, by then known as Avonbridge, attracted fertiliser merchants and seedsmen, and by 1895 there was an inn, post and telegraph office. Blackstone station was an early casualty; by 1955 the railway had been lifted west of what had become merely a goods station at Avonbridge, and by 1971 no tracks remained. In the latter half of the 20th century the population of Avonbridge gradually fell, from 900 in 1951 to 821 in 1991, but it retained the facilities of a small village. About 1965 quarrying commenced west of the village, and by 1977 Craigend Brickworks had been developed there; as Craigend Refractories it is still working. There was little new development in the last quarter of the century, but Gowanbank, an *'A'*-listed mansionhouse 1.5km south of the village, was saved for posterity in the mid 1990s.

## AYR & Alloway

**Map 1, C2**

***Large Clyde coast town**, pop. 48,000*

OS 70: NS 3322

Ayr, known in Gaelic as *Inverayr* because it stands at the mouth of the river of that name, was first mentioned in 1177. By 1197 William the Lion had built a castle there, to protect what was then the south-west edge of settled Scotland against the turbulent revolts of Galloway. Ayr was chartered as a Royal Burgh in 1205, and two years later the sheriffdom of Ayr was created by combining the ancient districts of Cunninghame, Kyle and Carrick. The ancient centre of Alloway beside the River Doon 4km south of Ayr had a motte and was once a distinct barony; its formerly extensive parish was split to form the new parish of Ayr.

**The Burgh Success Story: Bridge, Mansions and Parliaments**: The burgh of Ayr was given the right to hold a weekly Saturday market, and by about 1222 there was a merchant guild; the nine local trade guilds covered textiles, leather, metals, cooperage and the building trades. Shipbuilding was also soon established. In 1230 a Dominican friary was founded by Alexander II, the first for this order in Scotland, and a school or Academy existed at Ayr by 1233. Without stating a source, Chambers wrote of *"the Auld Brig, built as far back as the reign of Alexander III"* (1249–86); this was probably at first of timber construction. He added that Ayr *"contained in days of yore the city mansions of many noble families"*. Before the Black Death, kings signed several Royal charters in the town, which was already important enough to be chosen as the seat of Bruce's Parliament in 1315, held in the friary; Bruce also founded a refuge for lepers.

**Overseas Trade and Herring Fishing**: Ayr contributed to Customs revenue, rising from small payments about 1330 to around 2% of the Scottish total in the 16th and early 17th centuries. Herrings became an important local commodity, and Spanish iron and also wine were soon being imported. Ayr became Scotland's principal west coast port, and until 1372 it held exclusive trading rights over the whole shire. This checked the progress of Irvine and put paid to Prestwick's chances of gaining much importance. Evidence from the Black Death period is scanty, but Newton on Ayr, immediately north of the river, was chartered as a burgh of barony some time between 1314 and 1371; it tended to become the industrial quarter. In the 14th century Ayr merchants often traded through east coast ports, perhaps by using pack animals in the absence of a road connection.

**Wool, Cloth and Hides pay for Stone Structures**: In the 1370s Ayr exported small amounts of wool, then apparently an intermittent trade. Ayr was recorded as a *"town in plentiful and fair country"* by John Hardyng in 1415. The guild court of Ayr was in operation by 1428, and early in the 15th century substantial cloth exports built up. In 1432 Ayr and Irvine were in dispute over hide exports, and Ayr's wool trade became appreciable later in the 15th century. Remarkably for a west coast port, in 1488 Ayr was visited by a Danish ship. A Franciscan friary was founded in 1472. The *Auld Brig of Ayr* was rebuilt in stone over the period 1470–1525. Also of 15th century origin at Alloway are the tower of Newark Castle, and the *Auld Brig o' Doon* a little way to the north. Blaeu's map derived from Pont's work of about 1600 showed both of these features, while making relatively little of Ayr; but numerous bridges were indicated across the intervening burn. A century later the much-travelled Daniel Defoe thought the single arch of the Brig o' Doon *"the largest I ever saw"*.

**The Port of Ayr in the Early Sixteenth Century**: Ayr was evidently a fairly substantial fishing centre by 1511, when herrings were sold there by the barrel. However, its contribution to burgh taxes remained under 1% in 1535, though by 1560 the burgh was sufficiently important to be represented in Parliament. After the Reformation, the site and buildings of the Franciscan friary were granted to the town council in 1567. By 1593 Ayr had become the centre of a presbytery, and the third most important port in Scotland, being described as *"better built than Haddington"*, and having the largest trade on the west coast. Ayr acquired a hospital as early as 1605. Although in 1636 the harbour was said to be *"bare naked"* – i.e. exposed – by then there were malt mills, a brewery and an inn. In 1639 Ayr was the 11th richest centre in Scotland; it gained a post office in 1642 on the Edinburgh–Portpatrick–Ireland route.

**Cromwellian Citadel, Depressed Trade, and Mining for Ireland**: Ayr had one of the five citadels built under the Commonwealth from 1652 to hold down Scotland. A parish church was built on the site of the friary in 1654–55, later becoming known as the *'Auld Kirk'*. From the latter year Ayr was one of the eight official *'head ports'*, with three ships of from 30 to 100 tons, mostly just engaged in coasting trade to Glasgow. Thomas Tucker the customs officer, who had evidently sailed or ridden right round the coast of Scotland spying for the Commonwealth government, wrote in 1655 that the area under Ayr's customs jurisdiction, from Irvine to the Solway, was *"fuller of moors and mosses than good towns or people, and all of it void of trading except the towns of Ayr, Kirkcudbright and Dumfries"*. Ayr harbour was rapidly filling with sand, and trade was further depressed because of troubles in Ireland, though an occasional cargo of coal was sent to Ireland, proving mining nearby.

**Post-Restoration Stagnation**: In 1663 a barony charter was granted to the Citadel of Ayr, called Montgomeriestown after major Ayrshire landowners, but it failed to develop a distinct identity, and only one bastion survived early demolition. The visit of Thomas Morer in 1689 showed that Ayr's traders had still not recovered; he wrote *"now they give way to the success of Glasgow, and choose rather to freight other men's ships, than build any of their own"*. In that year the start of the French wars killed Ayr's chief specialist trade in wines and luxury goods, but at least education was still well organised locally in 1691.

**Decay, Tobacco and Other Trade**: In the 1720s Defoe admired the *"handsome stone bridge of four arches"* in a shrunken town – *"like an old beauty, it shows the ruins of a good face"*. He was as puzzled as the locals as to the *"reason of decay of trade here"*. However, there was *"still a very good market for all sorts of provision"*, and trade was starting to revive following the Union. At Newton on Ayr the Craigie salt pans worked by 1727 and for some years, and agricultural improvements and textile work grew on all sides. In the mid 18th century Ayr was still a customs port, whose several vessels of around 100 tons, able to enter on any tide, imported rice from Georgia and Carolina, and tobacco from Maryland and Virginia. A tobacco warehouse was built by Hunter, Ballantine & Co in 1739 and by 1752 there were four tobacco merchants, also serving Kilmarnock and Mauchline. Some tobacco was re-shipped to the Duke of Atholl's fief in the Isle of Man to evade duties, or legitimately to France, Hamburg, the Baltic and Bergen; other imports included salt, wine, oil and citrus fruit from Portugal. By about 1754 the Roy map showed that six or seven regional roads radiated from the town, where a *Poor House* was erected in 1756.

*The 15th century Alloway Brig carried the road from Ayr to Mayb… It was repaired in 1832 and again in 1977 – as a monument, due t… associations with Burns' famous poem 'Tam o Shanter'.*
*(RCAHMS / J…*

**Culture, Sport and Banking**: Meanwhile culture, industry and sport were taking hold: Scotland's favourite poet Robert Burns was born in Alloway in 1759, and Ayr's first library dated from 1762. J Macadam & Co of Ayr provided banking services between 1763 and 1771, when they merged with the even shorter-lived Ayr Bank, which lasted only from 1769 to 1772, as did Douglas, Heron & Co. These primitive banking firms were replaced by Hunters & Co, formed in 1773. Hunters opened branches in Irvine and Maybole. From 1775 there was also a branch of the Bank of Scotland. From 1770 a racecourse existed south of the town.

**Industry, Mining and Roads**: The Mill Street Tannery was established in 1761; by 1790 it was processing 9000 hides and calfskins annually, using much imported west coast tree bark. In 1770 came James Gibb's soapworks. A colliery was sunk at Newton on Ayr in 1765, had been connected to the harbour by a wagonway by 1775, and was deep enough to require an engine by 1791. By 1776 about a hundred looms and fifteen stocking frames were engaged in wool work. Many Ayrshire roads were being improved under a Turnpike Act of 1767 when John Loudon McAdam, born in Ayr in 1756, was growing up, later to become Britain's best known turnpike manager *(see Muirkirk)*.

**Coal Export and Varied Trade**: From a local Act of 1772, harbour trustees slowly developed the port for the coal export trade, soon reaching 5000 tonnes a year. Around 1777 nearly 300 vessels entered the port annually. Mainly small sloops of about 30 tons, almost all of them British, made round trips to such ports as Campbeltown, Greenock and Port Glasgow; but only 10% were locally owned, and Irvine vessels tended to be larger *(see Graham)*. Oliphant & Co, then Scotland's largest wine merchants, generated much trade. English bottles and fine Spanish salt were also imported, together with Highland cattle, Easdale slates, oats from Galloway and wheat from Fife and Dunbar, carried through the Pentland Firth.

**Coal Mining Problems and Tobacco Leaves**: In 1780 Dr James Campbell, owner of the Newton coal pits, closed them after disputes with the miners; James Taylor reopened them in 1786, and by 1790 some 12,600 tonnes were exported annually. By the 1780s the use of larger vessels ended Ayr's tobacco trade, leaving more local cargoes – including Irish limestone ballast, Baltic timber, charcoal, fish, salt, manure, tar and sugar from the local refinery, which was still open in 1810. What proved to be a weak new bridge of four arches, designed by Robert Adam, was erected across the River Ayr in 1785–88.

**Ayr in the 1790s**: The Citadel and Newton breweries existed by 1795, by which time local shipowners had become more significant and there was a daily mail coach to Edinburgh, and three a week to Glasgow. Four fairs were scheduled in Ayr for 1797; about that time too, a second coal pit was sunk. Heron noted in 1799 that Ayr *"may be considered as the market town to all the adjacent coast. Its chief trade, however, is at present in coals and grain. Its fishery has greatly declined."* With 7000 or so people, a shipyard at Newton and also a rope-work, it was quite an important centre for its time; Ayr Academy was re-established in 1798.

**Fine Shops and Regular Steamers serve the Quality**: A lifeboat station was opened in 1802, and the area's first local newspaper, the *Ayr Advertiser*, was published from 1803. A new grid of streets was laid out about that time in imitation of the New Town of Edinburgh. Large warehouses were built at the harbour in the early 19[th] century, limekilns were established and by 1810 soap was being made in three factories. The *Theatre Royal* was opened in 1812, and County Buildings and a jail were built in 1823. In 1827 Chambers found *"a very handsome town in a flourishing condition: many of the shops are as fine as those of Edinburgh and Glasgow"*. By 1819 there was a daily coach to Glasgow, and from 1821 to 1841 regular steamers gave the same service. The Wellington School was founded in 1836 to educate *'young ladies of quality'*.

**Carpets and Textiles**: A small cotton mill built in Fort Street about 1800 became a woollen carding and spinning mill about ten years later, and was bought about 1821 by James Templeton. He began carpet manufacture in 1827, and by 1832 employed some sixty weavers *(see also Bridgeton)*. By 1840 some 650 hand looms were also in use, concentrated in Newton, where 700 women were engaged in the hand embroidery of muslins. Templeton's nephew expanded the carpet works from 1844, producing yarn for sale to manufacturers in Glasgow and Kidderminster and creating the first large factory in Ayr. About 1860 Reid built a small weaving factory in Russell Street, making winceys and flannels, while Gray's large carpet factory was established in 1867. By 1869 Templetons employed some 500 people, including 150 carpet weavers, and their worsted mills were erected in 1878.

**Banking Change as the Railway Age Arrives**: The Ayrshire Bank opened in 1830 as a joint-stock company (leading to decline in Hunters Bank). In 1845 the Ayrshire Bank was absorbed by the Western Bank of Scotland. Meantime, although a gasworks had been set up in the 1830s, the colliery of 1765 was closed about 1832. Newton soon became the starting point of the Glasgow, Paisley, Kilmarnock & Ayr Railway, opened in 1839 as far as Irvine, and linked through to Glasgow the next year. From the start it had one of Scotland's most important locomotive depots. In 1856 the line was extended to loop round the town and through a new station at Ayr proper, to Girvan in 1860 and Stranraer in the 1870s; the Newton terminus was abandoned to goods only. In 1870 a line was opened eastwards via Annbank *(q.v.)* to Mauchline.

**Consolidation**: From 1860 superphosphates were made at Newton, which was absorbed by Ayr burgh in 1873, and more tanneries were built in the late 19[th] century. Adam's bridge having succumbed to a flood, Ayr acquired a new road bridge in 1878. A second local newspaper, the *Ayrshire Post*, was established in 1880, and the Ayr County Hospital was opened in 1883. Designed by Murdoch, a local architect, it was later much extended. From 1888 Somerset Park was used by Ayr FC, which joined the Scottish League in 1897. In 1910 it absorbed Ayr Parkhouse FC of Beresford Park (a league team in 1903–04) to become Ayr United FC.

**Fullarton, McKnight and Ailsa Shipbuilding**: Fullarton built small vessels from the 1860s, and from 1884 S McKnight & Co were building steel-hulled vessels, including the Clyde steamers *Waverley* of 1885 and *Madge Wildfire* of 1886, as well as coasters and packet-ships. In 1902 Ailsa Shipbuilding of Troon took over McKnight's yard, and in 1903 built the 398-ton coaster SS *Elidir*, engined by Ross & Duncan of Glasgow, for the Dinorwic Quarry Company *(see Waine for her eventful history)*. In 1908 came the 469-ton coaster SS *Ophir*, also engined by Ross & Duncan and in 1924 the SS *Ailsa II* (later *Lady Ailsa*) for Girvan-based passenger services; she was engined by Hall of Aberdeen. In 1927 Ailsa was the leading British firm in terms of the number of its coasters in service, and its yard remained open until 1929, when shipbuilding at Ayr ceased in favour of Troon.

**Shipping and Telephones**: Within two years after the construction of a wet dock in 1883, Ayr had become among Britain's top ten ports for the coastal shipping of coal; it was also a Port of Registry, with the code letters AR. But Glasgow steamer excursions sailed to Ayr only in 1886, the year when the railway passenger station was rebuilt with the substantial *Station Hotel*, and the infant local telephone system was connected up to Kilmarnock and Glasgow for the first time. In the early 20[th] century Rowan & Bain of Ayr provided a regular cargo service on the Clyde.

**Late Victorian Prosperity and Snobbery**: In 1893 the Carnegie library was built, and by 1894, with a population of 24,000 *"though inferior to Kilmarnock in manufactures"*, Ayr was ranked by Murray with Ardrossan and Troon in *"shipping prosperity"*. There were three *"good"* hotels, the *Station*, *Wellington*, and *King's Arms*, the last named also being *"good* *for posting and with stabling for hunters"*. In this boastful heyday of the British Empire, Ayr was evidently one of Scotland's most snobbish places, being *"a provincial capital of considerable social standing and attractions, and a favourite hunting centre"*. In fact Ayr was fortunate to have been near the birthplace of Robert Burns, and had already built up a major resort trade on his name, as well as the racecourse, and the view across the lower Firth of Clyde. But the mentally challenged had been consigned to oblivion in the Ayr District Asylum, 4 km south-east of the town, later renamed as Ailsa Hospital. By then Whitletts, a mining village 2 km out of town on the Mauchline road, had 577 people, a smithy, inn and post office, and later acquired glasshouses.

**Industry and Entertainment in Edwardian Ayr**: A municipal electricity supply was installed in 1896, followed by the introduction of Corporation electric trams in 1901, and a second power station was built in 1914. In order to survive intense competition, the two local brewery companies merged in 1898. Andrew Wright became established in joinery manufacture in 1907. Meantime the thousand-seat *Gaiety Theatre* had been opened in 1902, followed in 1911 by the town council's 1500-seat *Pavilion Theatre*. The racecourse was moved to its present site in 1907–08, the former course later being reconstructed as the Belleisle municipal golf course of 1927; a second such course at Seafield dates from 1930.

**Railway Dominance – and 1920s Decline**: In 1916, 76 steam locomotives were based at Ayr depot, the second most important on the Glasgow & South Western Railway (G&SWR), which in 1919 took over Ayr harbour and its one locomotive. In 1920 the Laird Shipping Company of Ayr, with services to Belfast and Dublin, was bought by Coast Lines of Liverpool. The population of Ayrshire peaked about 1921, and few noteworthy developments occurred in Ayr during the 1920s apart from the installation of an electric coal conveyor at the docks. Remarkably, D & F Reid of Ayr were still manufacturing waterwheels in 1928. However, the closure of the shipyard in 1929, followed by abandonment of the tramways in 1931 and closure of the lifeboat station in 1932 marked the start of a period of rapid change.

**Development of the 1930s and World War II**: In the thirties much private housing was built, especially towards Prestwick, and new county buildings were erected in 1932 on the site of the old jail. Butlin's holiday camp at Heads of Ayr 5 km south-west of the town appears to date originally from 1933. Marks & Spencer came to the town in 1935, and indoor bowling was possible from 1936. The *Odeon Cinema* and the original ice rink were built in 1938. The wartime Ayr RAF station at Whitletts was only 2 km south of the site of Prestwick *(q.v.)* Airport. During the 1939–45 war the former shipbuilding yard was reactivated for ship repair work; in the 1950s the Ayr Engineering & Constructional Company would overhaul Clyde steamers there.

**The early Postwar period**: By the 1950s Ayrshire's population had surpassed its earlier peak, and Ayr remained a major regional centre and minor commercial port. But perhaps its prime function was as a major resort, there being over 50 hotels, and excursion steamers from Ayr harbour were packed. Yet the railway between Ayr and Mauchline was closed to passengers in 1951. After fire damage in 1955 the *Gaiety Theatre* was reconstructed with only 570 seats. In 1957 a Roman Catholic cathedral was built to serve their south-west Scotland diocese. Although railway locomotives ceased to be based in Ayr around 1960, new fishing facilities were developed at the harbour, where a rail connection was maintained.

*The upper harbour of Ayr, with flats built c.1990 on one of the north bank quays. The steeple is the Town Hall's.* (JRH)

**Service Developments and Entrepreneurs**: A third municipal golf course, the Dalmilling, was laid out at Whitletts in 1960, the year when the telephone system acquired STD, and shopping developments took place in the 1960s. Craigie College of Education was established in 1964 and provided with new buildings; unlike others founded at that late date, it remained open through the 1980s. Meanwhile in 1966 a new Technical College was opened. Barr Ltd (founded in Ayr as long ago as 1898) was just a small family building firm until it began to blossom in 1969 under third generation Bill Barr. Another entrepreneur was David Murray, born in Ayr in 1952, who started the trading business of Murray International Metals in Edinburgh in 1974; he went on to build up a major privately-owned company, with a workforce of 3000 by 1995.

**Problems and Closures**: Newton brewery finally succumbed to Tennents in 1963. With the nosedive in Clyde cruising, all passenger steamers ceased to call in 1964, and in 1968 the short branch railway to Butlin's at Heads of Ayr was closed; its station became a caravan site, and by 1972 a youth hostel had been opened. Whitletts air base largely vanished under housing and a trading estate, built in the 1970s and 80s. In 1974 the town faced a crisis when the large carpet factory, which had suffered a takeover, was closed with the loss of over a thousand jobs.

**Don't Swim from Ayr Sands**: With Ayr's growing reliance on general tourism, in 1972 the *Gaiety* became the town's civic theatre, while the *Pavilion* became primarily a dance hall. In the same year an indoor swimming pool was opened: perhaps to encourage its use, the town council's entry in the Municipal Yearbook for that year made remarkably honest reading for a seaside resort, stating *"the sewage is drained into the sea"*! The foul beach saga still had decades to run. A new ice rink replaced the old one in 1974. Ayr lost its county town status in 1975, for the next 20 years merely heading Kyle and Carrick District, but in 1976 the *Gaiety Civic Theatre* and *Odeon Cinema* were both open. At that time Ayr had two bus stations, that serving Western SMT being very run down, as were some shops. However, Tesco had invested heavily, in the very diverse town centre. By 1985 the new Kyle Academy had been lately built east of the town at Holmston, and Queen Margaret Academy had risen at Kincaidston.

**Good News in Electronics**: Mosshill industrial estate, 5 km south-east of the town, was laid out in the 1970s. Among the firms open there by 1979 was the electronics concern Prestwick Circuits, founded in 1969 to make printed circuits. Digital Equipment Scotland, a major American computer company, started an Ayr branch factory in 1980. In 1989 they announced a large development to make a range of computers designed in Scotland, and their factory on the Mosshill Industrial Estate soon became the area's largest employer. By 1992 the new engineering firm EMS was designing and manufacturing innovative products, with a staff of 34.

**Fabrics for Travellers**: By 1979 the Belvidere Mills contained the long-established furnishing fabric manufacturers British Replin Weavers, who then exported only 8% of their output; acquired in 1980 by the Dawson Group, by 1993 exports had risen to 65% of output. In 1990 when the firm gained a Queen's Award for Export it employed 110 workers and claimed 80% of the world market for the special fabrics used in aircraft seats and wall coverings. By 1979 Alex Begg & Co were manufacturing travel rugs and accessories at Viewfield Road; they remained active in 1994.

**Rail Passengers go Electric**: The wagon repair works at Ayr was still open in 1981, and the Falkland shunting yard was to last longer. By 1988 over 500,000 tonnes of Ayrshire coal, mainly opencast, was being exported annually to Ireland through a new hopper at Ayr harbour; after the closure of Barony colliery more coal came from the opencast pits in the Douglas basin, from which three trainloads a day were being shipped late in 1989. In 1991 the harbour was being improved; many Spanish fishing boats were based there, seeking Atlantic hake. By 1995 the Enterprise service of Transrail, a fragment of the former BR freight system, was carrying scrap from Aberdeen to Ayr. Passenger usage of the railway increased by some 40% following electrification between Ayr and Glasgow in 1987 (but this was not extended to Stranraer). The reinstatement of passenger trains on the Ayr–Mauchline line was considered in 1992 before poorly conceived privatisation stopped all rail investment for years.

**Recreation and Retail Services**: Butlins opened the *Wonder West World* water complex at their holiday camp in 1988. In 1989 the Dalblair Arcade and Kyle shopping centres both exceeded 5000 m$^2$. Part of the racecourse, Scotland's most prestigious for both National Hunt and flat racing, was sold to Tesco in 1989 for the erection of a large supermarket, thereby financing improvements to the stands and track, completed in 1992. The 22-lane Ayr Bowl at Millar Road was one of only six tenpin bowling centres in Scotland in 1990. In 1991 Ayr United FC were in the First Division; hampered by their old-fashioned ground at Somerset Park, they were relegated by 1996, but had returned by 2000 (nowdays owned by Bill Barr, whose construction company now has a turnover of £120m a year).

**Losers and Winners**: A new 300-bed hospital was built south of the Ailsa Hospital in 1989–91, so the Ayr County Hospital was closed in 1991; it stood derelict in 1995–97. In 1990 Jones & Campbell of Larbert took over a bankrupt Ayr foundry employing 100 men, but closed it in 1992 due to the recession, and transferred key workers to Larbert. By 1995 James Dickie Forgings of Ayr, makers of drop forgings, were in receivership. But by 1994 Barr Ltd, builders of Heathfield, had become the largest privately-owned construction business in Scotland, with consulting services, eleven quarries, five ready-mixed concrete batching plants and nearly 1000 employees.

**Digits go Round the Clock**: In 1993 the Digital Computer Corporation needed to cut costs due to worldwide losses, and decided to close their even larger Galway plant in 1994, transferring 300 to 400 essential jobs to the Ayr factory (which already employed nearly 1000). In mid 1993 they unveiled the *'Alpha AXP'* personal computer, able to operate at double existing speeds. It was assembled at Ayr using the new AXP chips produced at their South Queensferry plant; in all, over 2000 Scottish jobs were involved. By 1994 Digital employed 1600 people at Ayr, over half of them assembling computers; despite the recession the plant was working round the clock. In 1995 Prestwick Circuits were still expanding in PCBs at both Irvine and Ayr, with a total of 120 new jobs. The TT Group employed 450 in auto industry electronics. Compaq's (Digital) workforce was still 1200 in 2001, producing computers. The livestock market of James Craig Ltd, which claimed in 1989 to be the biggest prime cattle market in Scotland, remains busy with cattle and sheep in 2001.

**Education and Culture**: The *Borderline Theatre* was started in the 1980s in a former church in Newton, symphony concerts were occasionally heard in the Town Hall in 1992, and in 1995 the district council ran both the MacLaurin and Roselle House art galleries. By 1990 Mainholm Academy was open beside the race course. In 1993 Ayr's Craigie teacher training college became part of the new University of Paisley. At that time the long-established independent Wellington School, after at least 150 years of providing only for girls, began to admit boys and in 1996 absorbed Drumley House boys' school at Mossblown.

**Dirty Beaches and a Twisted Tale of Local Government**: The right-wing Kyle & Carrick District Council, which owned an area at Greenan west of Alloway, hoped in 1994 to develop it as a coastal golf course; perhaps they should have given some priority to cleaning their dirty seashore, for in that year the Tidy Britain Group found Ayr beach among Britain's very worst. The twist came in 1996 when water and sewerage were removed from local government by the Tories, who transmogrified Kyle and Carrick into the new unitary local authority of South Ayrshire: the sophisticated electorate responded by depriving them of control! The new cycle network passes a new caravan site opposite Butlin's, through the Greenan area and along the sea front.

**Tourism and Sport take to the UK Ice, and Wood returns to Water**: A new 3-screen audio-visual tourist draw, the 100-seat *Tam o' Shanter Experience*, was opened at the Alloway Burns

Visitor Centre in 1995. A third ice rink was three-quarters built when abandoned about 1990; investment by Bill Barr, head of Barr Construction, enabled its completion in 1996 as the *Centrum Arena*. Its newly-recruited ice hockey team the *'Scottish Eagles'* remarkably became the sole Scottish member of the new UK Superleague. Residential and commercial development has continued to expand the town, especially around Alloway, so that by 1998 the area within the bypass was practically full. In 2000 a competition was held to find a design for the development of 20 hectares of the sea front. A timber terminal is to be created at Ayr harbour, to enable pulpwood from Argyll to return to sea transport instead of lorries, and another terminal to handle Norwegian fertiliser. Among many hotels are the *Fairfield* (41 rooms), the modern *Caledonian* (114), the *Quality* (ex-*Station*, 75), and many smaller, as well as guest houses.

## AYTON

**Map 3, C3**

***Berwickshire village,*** *pop. 560*

OS 67: NT 9261

Ayton's medieval castle was founded in the 12th century, built high above the deep valley of the Eye Water some 10km north-west of Berwick upon Tweed; on the other bank was the church. The castle was destroyed in 1497–98, but replaced by its then owners, the Home family. Although Ayton was never a burgh of barony, an early parish school was established in 1583. By the time that Timothy Pont mapped Berwickshire about 1600, *'Aytoun'* was already a substantial village with a bridge where the Great North Road crossed the Eye Water; farther downstream was a mill. One of Scotland's earliest paper mills was opened at Ayton by William Home in 1693. The Roy map of about 1755 showed a track from Reston to Eyemouth intersecting the main *"road from Edinburgh to Berwick"* at Ayton.

**Timber and Bleaching**: By 1771 a sawmill was in operation, and there was also a bleachfield by the late 18th century. The Berwick to Dunbar coach road was turnpiked in the late 1780s, and in the 1790s the paper mill employed 80 people, making grey paper, presumably for wrappings. A post office opened in 1793 and by 1797 Ayton was a post town. Heron in 1799 noted both the paper and bleaching industries in a village of over 500. By the mid 1820s the bleachfield had been closed, but Cobbett (who passed through in 1832) found *"the beautiful park and gardens of Mr Fordyce and a village of very homely stone houses; but the people seem to look very well"*. A bone mill for fertiliser was set up in the 1830s; unfortunately the castle was burnt out in 1834.

**Railway and Baronial Display**: The North British Railway which opened its winding main line in 1846 provided a wayside station east of the village. The dominant red stone mansion called Ayton Castle was built – or rebuilt around the shell of the second castle – in 1851, to designs by James Gillespie Graham. In 1859 James Shaw of Ayton dealt in McCormick's reapers, and by 1861 a papermaking machine had been installed at the mill, which operated well into the 20th century. The *Red Lion Hotel* was open by 1894, when a lengthy *'old race course'* on Lamberton Moor lay beside the Mordington road, and there was a tiny hospital 1.5km west of the village.

**By-passed by the A1**: In the 1950s Ayton was a substantial village of 600 people with two hotels; it had the peculiarity that its market and early closing days were the same. However the station had been closed by 1963, and Ayton's facilities declined very rapidly over the following 20 years, losing a hotel, veterinary surgeon, doctors, a lawyer, bank, and post town status as well as 20% of its population. The A1 bypass was constructed in 1979–81, removing most through traffic. This stimulated resurgence; the castle was open to the public in summer by 1986, and by 1991 Ayton village had 569 residents. The *Red Lion Hotel* is still going (but the post office isn't).

## BACK, Coll, Vatisker & Tolsta **Map 11, C2**

***Village/townships, E. coast of Lewis,*** *pop. 1160* OS 8: NB4840

This crofting peninsula on the east coast of the Isle of Lewis lies about 10km north-east of Stornoway. All the above settlement names and more can be identified on Blaeu's distorted map of Lewis published in 1654, probably derived from sketchy work by Pont. Little or no mark has been made on history by this area. Tolsta at the north-east corner had 699 people in 1891, while Back had 596. Upper Coll *(G. Col)* was founded after Lever, the soap tycoon laird, abandoned his 1920s experiment in modernising the Isle of Lewis: 42 crofts were created by splitting up his only dairy farm. About 1175 people lived in the Back area by 1951 but it had only the most basic facilities, – a post office, telephone exchange with 10 lines and primary school, all named Back; secondary education was provided at the township schools at Tong, 5km to the south, and at North Tolsta at the end of the road 10km to the north.

**Gaelic Strength**: The Coll pottery which was started in 1970 is still in production, and both a garage and a doctor had appeared nearby by about 1980. By 1973 a new small junior secondary school had been built, which still bore the name Back in 1995 but seems to have been closed. The enumerated population of about 1160, a high proportion owning their homes outright, included many children – and almost 80% who could speak Gaelic, the second highest proportion identified in any locality in Scotland (after Ness).

## BADACHRO **Map 8, B2**

***Settlement, Wester Ross coast,*** *pop. 200* OS 19: NG 7873

On the south side of the Gair Loch of Wester Ross is a series of sheltered bays; the Roy map of about 1750 showed woods and settlement at Shieldaig, but not at Badachro to the west. A road from Achnasheen and Kinlochewe to Gairloch was built around 1843, passing through lovely wooded Kerrysdale, where a bridge was built to give access to Shieldaig Lodge and Badachro. By 1951 tiny Badachro had a post office, inn, clothier, jetty and a primary school, which had closed by 1976; Shieldaig Lodge was a hotel with 16 rooms, and some 150 people lived in the area, where there are several freshwater lochs. Little change was apparent to 1996; a bunkhouse for backpackers is open all year at Badachro, from which the narrow and winding coast road extends west and then south past several expanding clachans, to end at Red Point, a noted viewpoint overlooking a sandy beach.

## BAILLIESTON **Map 15, E5**

***Eastern suburb of Glasgow,*** *pop. 16,000* OS 64: NS 6763

About 10km east of Glasgow the River Clyde is joined by the North Calder Water, already bridged near its mouth by 1596 when Pont mapped the area. Baillieston, 2km north of the bridge, was not shown on Blaeu's version of Pont's map, but Roy's map made about 1754 bore the name, beside what was apparently a farm on the Shettleston to Airdrie road. A post office opened at Baillieston after 1838. A gasworks was set up in 1862, and the Rutherglen to Coatbridge line of the Caledonian Railway (CR) was opened in 1865–66 through a station named Baillieston, at Ellismuir south-east of the village; by the 1890s this had a substantial goods yard, and around 1900 coal was mined nearby. Another station named Mount Vernon was 2km west of Baillieston station. Baillieston never became a burgh, although the OS map for 1895 showed a substantial village with coal pits to the north. Inns were open in Baillieston and the adjoining hamlet of Barrachnie, 1km to the west, whose colliery also made bricks. Nearly 4000 people lived in Baillieston by 1901; Glasgow's electric trams were soon extended to terminate at Martin Crescent. In 1914 a quarry was open near Mount Vernon.

**Garrowhill, Calderpark Zoo and the Motorway Web**: The coal pits around Springhill, just north-west of Baillieston, had closed when in the 1920s the straight Edinburgh Road was built across country north of Baillieston, becoming the A8 and relieving the village of through traffic. Garrowhill to the west was developed from the 1930s by private house builders, with a halt (later a station) on the ex-NB line between Glasgow and Airdrie, which since 1861 had formed a natural northern limit to the area. By 1951 the Baillieston area had a population of 12,000, but with the facilities of a big village, plus a greyhound track. Industries included preserve manufacture and photographic equipment. In 1946 Glasgow's Calderpark Zoo opened to the south, served by a tram terminus at Broomhouse, from where some cars ran across the city to Milngavie. A station to serve the zoo was opened on the ex-NBR Hamilton branch, but this line was closed in 1961, whereas the railway serving Garrowhill was electrified in 1961–62. However, the trams ended then, the ex-CR line was closed to passengers about 1965, and in the 1960s much of Baillieston's surroundings became dominated by the M8, M73 and M74 motorways, including Scotland's own *'Spaghetti Junction'* (Baillieston Interchange). By 1971 the Calderbraes golf course was open near the zoo.

**Calderpark Zoo an Endangered Species?**: From 1975 the area was within Glasgow City District. By 1981 its population had grown to 16,000, and though lacking a hotel it enjoyed the facilities of a small town. By 1979 the large contracting firm Henry Boot had its headquarters at Garrowhill. By 1988 sand and gravel working had destroyed the vestiges of countryside to the south, where in the early 1990s the quarrymasters and landfill company, Patersons of Greenoakhill, lost two-fifths of their site to the M74 extension. Calderpark Zoo, twice nearly closed in the 1980s, was well known in 1991 for its work for several endangered species, and with 140,000 visitors in 1992 hoped to build a tourism centre and 100-room hotel. However, in depressed 1993 the staff had to be cut from 28 to 18. In 1993 diesel passenger trains were reintroduced to the old CR's lately freight-only Whifflet and Glasgow Central line, with new stations at Baillieston (750m west of the original site) and Mount Vernon. In 1994 the site for the Springhill Business Park stood empty south of the M8, and in 1996 the Baillieston Distribution Centre had modern units available. By 1997 the Bannerman High School had 1365 pupils.

## BALALLAN *(Baile Ailein)* & Kershader (Lewis) — Map 11, B2

***Township, Lewis,*** *pop. 500* — OS 14: NB 2820

This straggling crofting township near the head of Loch Eirasort in the vast parish of Lochs lines the Stornoway to Tarbert road for 4km; its history is little known. For most of the 20th century its school, post office and telephone exchange served a fairly stable population of around 500, spread among several townships. By 2000 a remotely situated youth hostel was open all year round, across the loch at Kershader.

## BALBEGGIE, St Martins & Collace — Map 6, B3

***Perthshire village & hamlets,*** *pop. 1000* — OS 53: NO 1729

St Martins, a church beside a burn some 8km north-east of Perth, was evidently of some significance in ancient times, having nearby the earthworks of Cairn Beth, traditionally Macbeth's Castle. Some 6km to the east is the isolated hill fort of Dunsinane, near which is the Kirkton of the small agricultural parish of Collace. Evidently a number of tracks radiated from St Martins church, the probable location of the parish school that was open in 1629. The Perth to Coupar Angus road had been made up when the Roy map of the area was rather sketchily surveyed about 1750 (the church was labelled *'Strickmartin'* on the fair copy). Though Balbeggie which now stands astride the modern alignment of this road over 1 km east of St Martins was not named, the *'Doctor Mill'* stood somewhere in the vicinity.

**Balbeggie ousts St Martins**: By 1895 St Martins possessed a post office and a mansionhouse as well as its mill and smithy. What the Ordnance Survey called a *'first class metalled road'* ran through Balbeggie, by then a small village with a post and telegraph office and an inn. Gradually most of the population and facilities at St Martins shifted to Balbeggie. However, by 1951 the two little places were entering a period of great stability, with a combined population of about 550 and the facilities of a small village, effectively all in Balbeggie – some of these served an additional 1220 people in hamlets within a 5km radius. Although rural depopulation cut the additional population served to only about 700 by 1981, there were by then three hotels, in and 2 km north of Balbeggie. Sadly today the lower slopes of 300m high Dunsinane, one of the two most famous hills in Shakespeare, were still being quarried away. Prominent features are the large premises of Earnvale Tractors and an antique centre; the *Balbeggie Inn*, a garage and at least two shops still serve the locals. Near the hamlet of Kinrossie to the north is a major potato packery.

## BALBLAIR, Resolis & Jemimaville — Map 9, B3

***Hamlets, Easter Ross,*** *pop. 300* — OS 21: NH 7066

Balblair in the Black Isle of Ross was the site of an early chapel in Resolis parish. The westernmost name on the coast of Pont's map of the Tarbat peninsula of Ross was *'Innerbraky'*, modern Invergordon, presumably his landing point from the Innerbrachy ferry which evidently plied across the Cromarty Firth by about 1600. Blaeu's later atlas based on Pont's material depicted *'Ferritoun'* on the south shore west of Balblair; modern maps show this name some 2 km from Balblair. The ferry was certainly operating in 1618, and Richard Franck reported it as *"rugged"* in 1656. Balblair which was chartered as a burgh of barony (also known as Auchmartin) in 1677 was called *'Ferrytown'* on Roy's map surveyed about 1750, evidently having superseded earlier terminals; its road access was then from Fortrose and Cromarty only.

**Enter Jemima Poyntz – Exit the Ferry**: In 1797 Balblair had an annual fair. Ardoch House to the south of Balblair was renamed Poyntzfield in the late 18th century, its laird having married Jemima Poyntz, an East Anglian lady of Dutch extraction. He also founded the new settlement of Jemimaville, named after her, on a coastal site on the Cromarty road left blank on Roy's map. A new 80m pier was built at *'Inverbreackie'* in 1821 and two wooden piers were added in 1857. The ferry was still carrying foot passengers a century later, but Balblair remained a hamlet. By 1974 its hotel had become just a pub, and the ancient ferry, reopened for a time in the 1970s to carry workers to Invergordon, had vanished by 1983, when the Balblair and Jemimaville area with a combined population of about 300 jointly enjoyed the facilities of a small village. By 1998 only one pier remained, and the pub at Balblair is now a private house.

## BALDOVAN, Downfield & Strathmartine — Map 6, B3

***N. Suburbs of Dundee.*** — OS 54: NO 3833

Baldovan stands above the Dighty Water in Strathmartine parish, 4km north of Dundee. Two castles, Powrie from the 15th century and Mains from the 16th, lie to the east, but no burgh of barony was created. On his rough sketch map of about 1600, Pont showed Kirkton of Strathmartine as the tiny place that it remained. To the north was *'Strickmartin Castle'*, and to the west one of the burns was bridged. Another bridge spanned the Dighty west of Mains Castle, then evidently lying on the route from Dundee to Forfar. Kirkton of Tealing, 4km to the north, was probably the location of a parish school founded in 1609. Tullideph Hall was built on the Bank estate in 1625 and replaced in the 18th century by Baldovan House, the mansion of the Ogilvy family; this was enlarged about 1825. Dundee town council owned a grain mill at Baldovan by 1750, and the contemporary Roy map marked the *'Mill of Dronlo'* (Dronley) on the Dundee to Newtyle road; the area to the north was roadless.

**The Development of the Dighty Water**: In 1760 a single yarn mill and one bleachfield stood beside the Dighty Water in Mains parish. But by 1790 its proximity to almost waterless Dundee resulted in this modest stream only some 15 km in length giving power to no fewer than 22 small mills. These included lint mills, for treating linen yarn and cloth, and nine bleachfields employing over 100 people in all, processing cloth made in Dundee. In 1790 a spinning mill was built at Trottick; in 1808 it became a yarn-washing mill for Claverhouse bleachfield. By 1833 there were four bleachfields, two very large; four flax-spinning mills powered by both water and steam, and five yarn-washing plash-mills. In the mid 19th century James Finlayson was a millwright based in the area, but the last flax mill was burned down in 1861. In 1864 the three active bleachfields belonged to Turnbull & Co (Claverhouse), Cargill & Co's *'Dundee'* field, and A J Murdoch & Co (Balmuir) – a new venture. Several plash-mills still worked. In 1895 substantial bleachfields remained at Trottick and Claverhouse.

**Railway and Trams**: Baldovan and Baldragon stations, the latter beside Kirkton of Strathmartine, were connected with the city by the primitive Dundee & Newtyle railway from 1831. The Rosemill goods station 1 km west of Kirkton of Strathmartine was the junction for several very short spur tracks, to the Fallaws and Leoch quarries north of the line which were open by 1898, and Auchray and Rosemill to the south. By 1895 the linear village of Downfield had extended Baldovan along Strathmartine Road towards Dundee, whose Clatto reservoir had been built about 1875 on the hill to the west; there was also an inn. By then Fairmuir Junction, where the improved railway crossed Clepington Road, was the start of a freight line which extended eastwards to Lammerton Terrace. In 1894 steam trams from Dundee trundled up Strathmartine Road to Fairmuir; the tram services were electrified in 1902, but a gap remained between the city and the homes of the 1500 people in the Baldovan area.

**Kingsway, Golf and Skating**: The Kingsway, the Dundee bypass of the 1920s, crossed Strathmartine Road south of Downfield village, whose golf club, founded in 1932, laid out an 18-hole course opened in 1933. The *'Dundee'* Ice Rink was opened beside Kingsway in 1937, and to the north and east Strathmartine Hospital and glasshouses added to the area's diversity. A World War II military airfield at Kirkton of Tealing had been adapted to other uses by 1967. The consequent development of Dundee council estates in the Downfield area brought the local population to over 33,000 by 1951, but with only the facilities of a large village.

**After Trains and Trams**: Buses replaced the trams which were withdrawn in 1955, the year passenger trains ceased. Rail freight to Auchterhouse ended in 1965, in 1967 all freight trains ceased, and by 1969 the entire railway had been lifted. In 1964 the Technical College opened in Old Glamis Road, replacing the central Trades College; a new and very fine 18-hole parkland golf course to the west had enabled building to take place on the old course, and numerous tower blocks were complete. However, by 1981 the population was down to about 25,000. By then most local facilities were those of a typical small town, but professional services were few in this urban area. However, by 1990 the Technical College, renamed Dundee College of Further Education, offered various courses to HNC and HND, and some to professional or postgraduate standards; by 1993–94 it had 3000 full-time and 6000 part-time students. Baldovan House suffered fire damage around 1990 and in 1995 stood derelict, vandalised and for sale. The Claverhouse Industrial Park was undergoing development in 1994.

**The Ice is Cut and Low Yields to Tesco**: The construction of a new head office and warehouse for Scotland's largest grocery retailer, Dundee-based William Low, was begun in 1987 at Baird Avenue, and by 1989 their competitor ASDA had opened a store at Derwent Avenue. In 1990 Canadian tycoon Ron Dixon bought the ice rink, failed to provide the promised new rink by 1992, but demolished the old one in that year and sold its cleared site to Low's, who built another major grocery store, one of a string going as far south as Leicestershire. Low also doubled the size of their base in 1992–93, but being relatively small and only modestly profitable by British supermarket standards, sold out to Tesco in mid 1994. Of 320 staff at Low's head office, only 20 were kept on to maintain Scottish contacts. Low's three Scottish warehouses also found a role, serving 67 Tesco stores in Scotland, including 45 former Low stores, one of these being at Kingsway. In 1996 Tesco re-used the former William Low building by opening Tesco Link, a national customer call centre handling telephone enquiries and Internet orders for Tesco Direct; 150 jobs were created. Lawside Academy has about 750 pupils.

## BALERNO — Map 15, B2

***Village / suburb w. of Edinburgh,*** *pop. 5000* — OS 65: NT 1666

The 16th century L-plan tower of Bavelaw Castle stands on the slopes of the Pentland Hills 4 km south of Balerno, which lies on the Water of Leith 12 km south-west of Edinburgh; a place with a derivative of the name appeared on Blaeu's atlas based on Pont's work of about 1600. The Lindsay family took on the Cockburn estate in 1468, and in 1672 the L-plan mansion of Cockburn House was built for them. Water flowing from the Pentlands played a large part in the later development of the area: a mill existed by the time of Roy's survey of about 1754, by which time the road connecting Edinburgh *'by Crosswoodhill'* with Carnwath and Lanark had been defined, later becoming a turnpike. A paper mill was opened about 1790, and another about 1795. The Malleny flax spinning mills were established on the Bavelaw Burn early in the 19th century, and a leather waulking mill opened about 1810. By 1825 John Hill & Co's Bank Paper Mill was working on the same burn, and Balerno long remained primarily a paper mill village; its first post office was established in 1839.

**Railways, Water, Quarrying and Paper**: A sharply-curving single-track through line of the Caledonian Railway was constructed up the valley, opening from Slateford in 1874 and rejoining the main line to Carstairs at Ravelrig Junction south of Dalmahoy; Balerno goods yard lay south of the station, between Harelaw Road and the river. The *Grey Horse Inn* was open at Balerno by 1895 and two water supply reservoirs – Harelaw (now Harlaw), and the larger Threipmuir – had been impounded in the valley to the south, the treatment works being named Marchbank after a nearby villa. In the 20th century quarrying became another main activity, at first taking place in a crook of the Lanark Road, leaving a wet pit, and later at

Kaimes Hill 3 km to the west, so destroying a hill fort. Trains of basic four-wheel coaches for Balerno branch line services were built at Wishaw as late as 1922; its closure to passengers in 1943 was scarcely surprising, for at that time Balerno was still a small village in terms of facilities. However, the population had grown to 1300 by the 1950s. The railway was closed to freight in 1967, later becoming part of the *'Water of Leith Walkway'*. By 1970 the Bank paper mill employed about 500 people making high quality paper and boards. Mackenzie & Moncur made manhole covers in Edinburgh in the early 20th century, later becoming heating engineers and greenhouse specialists, and by 1977 were consulting engineers based in Balerno.

**Suburbanisation**: By 1963 Marchbank had become a hotel, and by 1973 the National Trust for Scotland owned Malleny House and garden, which it opened as a visitor attraction. Suburban population growth since 1951 had been accelerating, passing 4000 about 1973, and in 1975 Balerno became part of Edinburgh City District. From about that time quarrying also took place on Ravelrig Hill north of the village. In 1981 Balerno was an affluent suburb with the facilities of a large village; estate development had spread extensively south of the village and north of Lanark Road. The large Balerno Community High School was built in the early 1980s on the site of the former goods station; by 1997 it had 885 pupils. The Bank Paper Mill was still open in 1983 – but not today. Balerno Mill made carbonless copy paper, but closed about 1990. By 1991 the Balerno postcode sector held almost 5000 people. The Ravelrig area was developed for housing in the 1990s, and although Marchbank reverted to private dwellings in the late 1990s, the Marchbank treatment works was improved by East of Scotland Water in 1999–2000. Hotels include the *Johnsburn* and *Kestrel*; the old *Grey Horse* pub continues in the pedestrianised main street.

## BALFOUR (Shapinsay) — Map 13, B2

***Island community, Orkney,*** *pop. 325* — OS 6: HY 4716

Off the south coast of the fertile inner Orkney Isle of Shapinsay is the islet of Helliar Holm, which protects a small circular bay called Elwick and has an ancient broch. The baronial mansion named Balfour Castle was begun near Elwick by the Balfour lairds in 1790, and completed to designs by David Bryce in 1848. From improved farms a new road system led to a new pier, where Balfour village was laid out and – in 1883 – the Elwick meal mill was built. The lighthouse on the tidal islet of Helliar Holm was lighted in 1893. The Balfours sold Shapinsay to their tenants in the early 1900s. In the 1950s, when the island population was about 500, most of its fairly basic facilities which included a medical practice were at Balfour, while inland at Crossgate was a 60-pupil primary and junior secondary school. This was later replaced by a new school at Balfour. By the 1970s electricity arrived from Kirkwall by submarine cables, and by 1980 the island's first restaurant with bed and breakfast facilities was open. Due to rural depopulation and roll-on ferries to Kirkwall, introduced in 1990 from a new pier, the school had lost its secondary role by 1995, but survives as a primary; the disused mill still stood. By then about 325 people lived on Shapinsay, which has a heritage centre; Balfour Castle is a luxury hotel.

## BALFRON & Boquhan — Map 5, C4

***W. Stirlingshire village,*** *pop. 1400* — OS 57: NS 5488

In early days Balfron in Strathendrick some 25 km north of Glasgow was a hilltop clachan with a medieval motte, and a kirk 1 km north of the Endrick Water and 60 m above it. Pont's map of about 1600 later engraved by Blaeu showed *'Bafron'*; a mill stood on the Endrick east of the tower of *'Balnadallach'* Castle, and a bridge crossed the Boquhan Burn beside Boquhan Mill, but the Endrick was unbridged. Roy's map of about 1750 showed the *'Kirk of Balphrone'* as a tiny place on a track beside the Endrick Water. About 2 km to the north, various hamlets with the name *'Balfronnen'* were sketched beside the early (pre-1724) military road between Stirling and Dumbarton (later the A811).

**Muslin, Cotton and Wool**: Later the Endrick Water was bridged, and from 1778 Robert Dunmore – of Ballindalloch and the Pollokshaws printfield – built a cotton-spinning mill and muslin factory beside the Endrick for the laird, Buchanan. The tiny kirkton, lately of a mere six or seven families, was expanded on a regular plan in 1789–90. In 1792 Dunmore added the Ballikinrain spinning mill for both cotton and wool – for muslin and carpets respectively – employing about 100 people. The large Endrick Printfield of 1792–93, operated by Monteith, Warren & Co of Glasgow, had a 6 ha bleachfield beside the Endrick, embanked to prevent flooding. The building contained 16 water-powered printing presses, 72 block-printing tables and dyehouses; despite a trade recession the works employed 250 people in 1793.

**New Village, Whisky, *'Greek'* and Gas**: Balfron with its 220 slated 2-storey houses was described in the Old Statistical Account as a *"newly erected village"*, and in 1799 Heron believed Balfron *"village contains upwards of a thousand inhabitants"*. Under the poorly conceived tax legislation of the first quarter of the 19th century, Balfron was also a great centre for illicit whisky stills aimed at the Glasgow trade; the product was smuggled into the city by many ingenious means. A post office opened in 1806, served by a penny post from Glasgow. Balfron was the birthplace in 1817 of Alexander Thomson, who became the outstanding architect known as *'Greek'* Thomson, for his favoured style. He designed several fine neo-classical churches and houses in and around Glasgow. A gasworks was built in the 1830s, but the cotton mill failed, and Balfron never became a burgh. Balfron station was opened in 1882 by a subsidiary of the North British Railway, but it was 2.5 km west of the village, too far away to benefit it, though a separate hamlet with a post office named Balfron Station grew up there.

**From Balfron to the Blenheim**: In 1894 Balfron was described as a *"prettily situated village"* (Murray). This had drawn the manager of the Fairfield shipyard at Govan to live at Balfron; he fathered the Barnwell brothers, aviation pioneers of 1908 *(see Stirling)*. Frank Barnwell went on to design famous warplanes for Bristol Aircraft: the Scout and Fighter of World War I and the later Beaufort and Blenheim which, after his accidental death in 1938, were used in the 1939–45 war. Meantime Balfron had developed as a bus service centre, but passenger trains vanished from Balfron station in 1951 when the population was 1250. Stirling County Council made Balfron their key settlement for the provision of local authority services in the south-west of the county; by 1958 the High School had 290 pupils, and was later enlarged. In 1959 the rail freight services were withdrawn, and the track was soon lifted.

**Too Quiet to be a Small Town?**: Balfron in 1977 had an Alexanders Midland bus garage, the established High School and was strong in regional and district services such as a highways depot, police, fire and ambulance stations, a public library and cleansing garage. Otherwise it had average village facilities, including a bank. Most road traffic could be seen to stop in Balfron, which was, locals said, evenly poised between the pulls of Stirling and Milngavie. There was also the headquarters of a livestock transport business. Little more development had occurred by 1986, apart from a mountain rescue post serving Ben Lomond and the Campsie Fells. By 1991, following some recent housing development, 1400 people lived in Balfron, including many retired people. Essentially Balfron remains a quiet place; its High School now has around 800 pupils.

## BALINTORE & Cadboll — Map 9, C2

***Coastal village, Easter Ross,*** *pop. 1180* — OS 21: NH 8675

The finest of all known Pictish cross slabs was found near the exposed shore of the Tarbat peninsula in Easter Ross, some 3 km east of Fearn Abbey. Nearby stood an ancient chapel with a Pictish stone, and the 14th century keep of Cadboll Castle, which appeared on Blaeu's 1640s map derived from Pont's sketches and Robert Gordon's revisions. Farther south was Shandwick and between them lay Abbotshaven, evidently the settlement known in the Gaelic as *Balintore*, the 'Village with the Tower'. The Roy map made about 1750 showed *'Fishertown'* in this location. Though the castle became ruinous, Hilton of Cadboll developed nearby – oddly named for a place on the shore. All three places became fishing hamlets. Balintore acquired an inn, and a harbour was built in the 1890s; soon a boatbuilder, sailmaker and curing yard operated. Besides fish, the harbour exported grain and potatoes in the early 20th century, when a short pier was also built at Hilton of Cadboll.

**The Impact of Oil**: In 1951 when the population in the area was about 900 there was a tiny hotel, the inn and also a junior secondary school, which soon closed. From 1978, oil from the Beatrice field for processing at Nigg Ferry was brought ashore by pipeline at Shandwick, immediately south of the village. Remarkably, a new Free Church was built in 1980. By 1985 the harbour remained in use only by part-timers trapping lobsters and salmon fishing, together with small pleasure boats. In 1991 Balintore had grown to 1181 people; a high proportion owned their houses outright. W H MacKay & Sons, working by 1979 as structural engineers and steel fabricators at Balmuchy, 3 km north of Balintore, went into receivership in 1995. At Cadboll is the restored *Glenmorangie House*, owned by this famous Tain distillery, which has 9 letting rooms.

## BALIVANISH *(Baile Mhanaich)* — Map 7, A3

***Village, Benbecula,*** *pop. 2500* — OS 22: NF 7755

The ancient roofless church of Saint Columba stands on the windswept west coast of the watery Hebridean island of Benbecula *(G. Beinn na Faoghia)*, noted by Monro in 1549 as belonging to Clanranald of Clandonald. Pont's sketches of around 1600 showed *'Baluannich'* among other names; modern Gaelic uses the form *Baile Mhanaich*, and some spell the English version Balivanich! Some 1.5 km from the church was a 14th century nunnery, named by Martin in 1703 as Bael-nin-Killach (Town of Old Women, properly *Baile nan Cailleach)* but now known in English as Nunton. The isle remained Catholic in 1703 and still belonged to Ranald Macdonald of Benbecula, whose family built Newton House after Ormiclate Castle in South Uist burnt down in 1715.

**Cluny's Clearances**: In 1838 it was among the islands sold by Clanranald to greedy John Gordon of Cluny, whose notorious factor Fleming cleared most of its people by 1851, shipping them off to Canada in a starving condition under a most nefarious resettlement scheme. There was a post office at Nunton but thanks to Cluny, commerce and tourism were almost unknown in this sadly depopulated isle, whose sole access to the outside world was by small boats or by fording tidal shallows to reach North or South Uist. The Crofters Holdings Act of 1886 gave security to the remaining tenants, and by the 1890s inns were open at Creagorry 7 km to the south and Gramsdale some 4 km east of Balivanish; a market stance adjoined the single track road between the two.

**War brings Balivanish to the Fore**: An air ambulance was based in Benbecula before 1939 by Northern & Scottish Airways. During the 1939–45 war a causeway was constructed to link Benbecula with South Uist, and the RAF built an airfield on sandy machair land just north of Balivanish. After 1945 the airfield became a civilian airport of the most basic kind, and Balivanish with fewer than 700 civilians was accepted as the main centre of the island. The RAF returned in 1958 to transform the airfield into the base for its South Uist rocket range, and the two islands' road system was linked to North Uist by causeway in 1960. By 1970 the post office had moved to Balivanish, and by 1976 had been renamed Benbecula and become a *'post town'*. By 1977 the new Western Islands Council had established its Uists sub-office at Balivanish, which also had an office of DAFS (Department of Agriculture and Fisheries for Scotland) and an outpost of the North of Scotland College of Agriculture.

**Western Isles Centre Challenged by English Speakers**: In 1978 RAF personnel and their dependants contributed some 400 monoglot English speakers to the Gaelic-speaking local population, which in 1981 totalled over 900. The other facilities of an average village provided for 2500 scattered people. A processing factory for seafoods including lobsters, crabs, prawns, mussels and salmon was opened in 1986 at Gramsdale, and by 1996 a new community school had been built on the shore at Balivanish. The future of the Royal Artillery missile range was under review in 1994. At that time an air service linked Stornoway, Balivanish and Northbay on Barra. In 1996 Uist Seaweed Processors employed 35 people collecting, washing and milling seaweed for alginates; the plant was then being modernised to process 10,000 tonnes a year for Kelco *(see Benderloch & Girvan)*. From 1999 the RAF radar base was to become remote controlled and 80 jobs would vanish; attempts were being made to sell the many vacant MoD houses.

## BALLACHULISH & Laroch

**Map 5, A2**

***Village, Lochaber,*** *pop. 800* OS 41: NN 0858

In the Gaelic the name Ballachulish means *'Village on the Straits'*, the narrows of Loch Leven, now in Lochaber but whose south side was formerly part of the Lorne district of Argyll. Its history has been made complicated by migration of the name to apply to the distinct settlement of Laroch, 3 km to the east, which already existed by the late 16th century, when it was shown by Pont. His carefully finished map of Lochaber showed *'Balecheules'* as a village on the north side of the strait, but subsequent activity has largely taken place to the south.

**Slate Quarrying and Name Confusion**: The first (West) slate quarry was opened near Laroch about 1697 and worked on a small scale by Stewart, who brought in skilled quarrymen from Easdale. By 1733 a ferry plied across the narrows, and the fair copy of the 1750s Roy map showed a road or track running south-west from the ferry landfall towards Oban. The clachan then known as *'Ballachulich'* straggled from the ferry south-wards up Gleann a'Chaclais. Though the hamlets or clachans of Laroch and Mealmor were shown, no mention was made of the adjacent quarry, and that area was still roadless. So already there were two places called Ballachulish, north and south, and by 1774 Laroch was widely known for its slate quarry, also under the name of Ballachulish! Most slate was shipped from the quarry's own wharf, to Glasgow and southern cities. By then the quarry had three levels, and the waste material was tipped into the sea.

**Second Quarry, new Roads and Huts for Homes**: Work at the West quarry ceased about 1780 in favour of a new East quarry. The road linking the ferry with Glencoe and so via Rannoch Moor to the south was built about 1780, and by 1782 it carried the Glasgow mails. One of the Ballachulish villages had a post office by 1800 (Heron spelled it Bailichelish). The Oban road was also improved, though in 1803 Dorothy Wordsworth found that the Gleann a'Chaclais bridge had been damaged by a flood. Just to the east of this was the inn, *"the ferry-house on the main road up into the Highlands"* which was *"excellent"*. Towards Laroch was *"a slate quarry and many large boats with masts"*. The superintendent occupied *"a substantial plain house, that would have held half a dozen of the common huts"*.

**Steamer Calls**: According to Chambers, in the 1820s Balla-chulish was *"noted for its prodigious quarry of slate"*. By 1849 steamers served 'Ballachulish'; but the names tended to be used loosely, and later services suggest that this could relate to a pier 3 km west of the ferry. In 1863 the West quarry was reopened by a new lessee, Alexander Pitcairn.

*Working faces at East Laroch slate quarry, Ballachulish, in 1974. The terraced system of working, though typical of N. Wales, was rare in Scotland. Hand-worked railways at each level were linked with quays on Loch Leven by a rope-worked incline. The area was landscaped in the 1980s.* *(RCAHMS / JRH)*

**Denying not only Education but the Demon Drink**: Bremner's detailed description in 1869 showed that the East quarry was very large, owned by Tennant of Leeds, who had built a Mechanics' Institute about 1865. The East quarry had its own small harbour and five levels, down to 18m below sea level and up to 90m above. It was served by nearly 10km of tramways, some on steep inclines, which enabled 15 million trimmed slates to be brought down each year for shipping, the waste being tipped into the sea to form two more great banks. Some 400 men and boys were employed. The Gaelic speaking and heavily intermarried population totalled under 2000; though there were three schools *"education is deficient, the boys being sent early to work in the quarry"*, some as young as 8 years. The solace of drink was denied them: Tennant would not permit an inn or pub to serve Laroch.

**Ballachulish in the 1890s**: By 1891 the area's population was about 1800. John Gardner of Glasgow who owned the slate quarries in the 1890s used the coasters *Rob Roy* and *Wharfinger* to carry slates to Glasgow. At that time the western pier enjoyed a service of three passenger steamers a day to Oban and Fort William; the hotel at the ferry was described by Murray in 1894 as *"1st class but expensive"*, while Laroch was *"a straggling village, principally occupied by the quarrymen"*; it had a temperance hotel, and there was another of this persuasion at North Ballachulish.

**The Railway and Seaborne Alumina**: In 1903 a branch of the Caledonian Railway was opened from Connel via a station at Ballachulish Ferry to terminate in the virtual mouth of the grim quarry complex in a station simply named *'Ballachulish'*. A proper vehicle ferry was provided at the narrows from 1912, but could initially only carry three tonnes. John Gardner's successors J & A Gardner bought five new vessels in the 1920s, these including the 362-ton *Saint Aidan* of 1920, the firm also shipping granite from the Bonawe quarry, alumina from Larne to Kinlochleven *(q.v.)* and aluminium ingots from there to other ports.

**The Demise of Rail precedes the new Road Bridge**: However, a new road was opened in 1927 from Invercoe to Kinlochleven, after which rail-borne alumina reached the Kinlochleven works by lorry from Ballachulish. The slate quarry later ceased production, the rail terminal for the aluminium traffic was transferred to the Fort William yard in 1965, and after a short period as a passenger-only branch the railway was closed in 1966, the station building becoming a medical centre. The ferry was closed when the road bridge across Loch Leven was opened in 1975, and the population which had sunk by 20% between 1951 and 1971 had partly recovered to over 800 by 1981. By then Ballachulish had typical village facilities but the deepest quarry was a flooded pit.

**Three Freedoms of the Glens**: Reclamation began at Laroch in 1978 in an effort to improve its prospects, for all recent tourist development had been at or near Glencoe. The new 20-room *Lodge on the Loch Hotel* at Creag Dhu was opened in 1992 with its own pool and leisure centre, and the *Isles of Glencoe Hotel* with its indoor swimming pool followed in 1993. A 20-room extension to the *Ballachulish Hotel* was opened by the same owners in 1995, bringing its total to 54 rooms and further developing this unusual trio, a family-owned hotel group styled the *'Freedom of the Glens'*. The long-established *Loch Leven Hotel* at North Ballachulish has 10 rooms.

## BALLANTRAE

**Map 1, B3**

***Ayrshire coastal village,** pop. 250* — OS 76: NX 0882

In this remote and exposed site at the mouth of the River Stinchar, where Carrick faces the North Channel, evidence of a Mesolithic settlement has been found. Ballantrae's Gaelic name meaning *'Village on the Sands'* shows some local significance by about the 11th century. There was a rich hospice for medieval pilgrims at Ardstinchar, whose castle was built by the Kennedys in the 15th century. Ballantrae became a burgh of barony in 1541. Both village and castle appeared on Pont's map of about 1600. A kind of post office existed as early as 1642, on the Edinburgh–Stranraer–Portpatrick (for Ireland) route, but Tucker in 1655 described Ballantrae as a creek – i.e. a sub-port, and *"a market town, as poor as little"*.

**Roads, Smugglers and Harbour**: The coast road from south of the river to Stranraer was made up by the military early in the 18th century. Roy's map of about 1754 showed a water gap, but whether crossed by ford or ferry was unclear; beside it were the castle – now a ruin – a small irregular settlement, and upstream a mill. A bridge was built in 1770, and there on a knoll to the north-east was also a windmill whose stump survives. Tea, brandy and wine smuggling was rampant locally, for Heron commented in 1799 *"The coast* [of Carrick] *is but thinly inhabited, and the only village is Ballantrae, with only 300 inhabitants"*. Chambers in the 1820s found just a *"village... formerly a great haunt of smugglers"*. A minuscule harbour was built about 1860, and Ballantrae became a port of registration with the letters BA; a lifeboat station was open from 1871 to 1919.

**Fishing falls away and Tourism struggles**: David Bryce designed the large baronial mansion of Glenapp Castle, 2 km to the south-east, built from 1870 for James Hunter. The village had 524 residents in 1891 and remained *"a small fishing port"* in 1894, with the *"small, plain but clean" King's Arms Hotel*. Ballantrae has a vast parish, extending 10km inland, which held 1124 people in 1901. The *King's Arms* was still one of three small hotels open by the 1980s, when some B&B accommodation also served those who enjoyed the spectacular rock scenery along the coast or the remote glens inland. Ballantrae was then a small, windswept and slowly declining village of some 250 people, most of them living in basic Council houses, and only tiny boats could use its ineffective harbour. The parish still had 672 residents in 1991. A site at Auchencrosh, 3km south-east, was proposed in 1994 for the convertor station for the Northern Ireland grid interconnector. At the mouth of the river 1km south is a nature reserve. Glenapp Castle, empty from 1982, has been restored since 1993 as a 17-roomed hotel; the *King's Arms* and *Royal* hotels and the post office are still open.

## BALLATER, Craigendarroch & Glenmuick

**Map 10, A4**

***Deeside village,** pop. 1350* — OS 44: NJ 3695

Ballater lies in Glenmuick parish, 60km west of Aberdeen, where the conical hill known as Craigendarroch punctuates the beautiful valley of the River Dee; in 1309 the estate was owned by the Knights of St John *(see Torphichen)*. South of the river is the 16th century tower of Knock Castle: both Ballater and Knock were named on Blaeu's map, based on Gordon's work of about 1640. North of Craigendarroch is a natural pass, which was followed by the area's first road, eventually labelled the B972. The Roy map of 1750 showed that Ballater was then a tiny hamlet beside this road and east of the pass. Farther east was the Mill of Tullich, and west of the pass the road crossed the Bridge of Gairn. There was apparently no development then on the site of modern Ballater, which lies south of Craigendarroch. The mineral springs of Pannanich Wells, on the south bank of the Dee 3km east of modern Ballater, became known for their diuretic qualities in 1760. A Dee ferry plied until a bridge was built in 1778, but this was swept away about 1798, and the ferry resumed.

**New Village – and Bother with Bridges**: Glenmuick and Ballater church was built in 1798 and a new village was laid out in rectilinear form around it. In 1799 Heron drew attention to the spa where *"a handsome building has been lately erected, for the accommodation of the company who, in the summer season, resort to this place"*. Gaelic was still spoken in the area, though not to the east of it. Telford's Dee bridge was completed in 1809, but it was 1825 before Ballater boasted a post office. Telford's bridge in turn collapsed in the great floods of 1829; again a ferry plied until a wooden bridge was opened, in 1834.

**Marmalade Mansion, Railway and Royals**: Marmalade manufacturer James Keiller of Dundee had the early Victorian mansion of Craigendarroch Lodge built near Bridge of Gairn as a rural retreat. Ballater became very fashionable indeed when Queen Victoria leased and then bought the Balmoral *(q.v.)* estate in 1848–52. The daily horse-drawn coach was replaced in 1866 by three passenger trains when the Deeside Railway, soon to be a branch of the Great North of Scotland (GNSR), was extended to their intended terminus at Ballater, complete with engine shed. The track was laid on a freight-only extension to Bridge of Gairn, but when the unamused Queen bought the Ballochbuie estate with its potential timber traffic, the royal lawyer ensured that the extension was never used.

**Seasonal Resort, Shah and Czar**: The railway stimulated Ballater's growth as an inland resort of villas, largely developed by 1880, the year that the mansion of Darroch Learg was built. However, when the bridge was rebuilt in granite in 1885, only a post cart connected onwards to Braemar, except in *'the season'*. By 1882 the *Invercauld Arms Hotel* was open at the bridge; Murray found it *"good"* in 1894. The station was more grandly rebuilt in 1886; such potentates as the Shah of Persia and in 1896 the Czar of Russia came by rail on their way to Balmoral.

**The Burgh and its Facilities**: Ballater became a police burgh; the golf club, founded in 1892, laid out an 18-hole parkland course. The Victoria Hall and Gordon Institute was built in 1895. The first motor bus owned by the GNSR ran between Braemar and Ballater from 1904, and in 1907 the company took over the three steam lorries of Smart, the local carrier. A tiny power station supplied electricity from 1914, a bus station was built in 1923 and a parade of small shops in 1924. By 1928 a police station, four churches, three tennis courts and the Memorial Hall were in use. By the 1950s the resident population was about 1500, and Ballater had the facilities of a very large village, a youth hostel and no fewer than 16 hotels, including the 12-room, ex-Keiller *Craigendarroch*. In spite of the promotion of *'Royal Deeside'* the unimaginative Beeching, totally indifferent to tourism, closed the railway in 1966. This did not prevent another former mansion becoming the *Darroch Learg Hotel* by 1972, with 17 rooms.

**After the Railway: Decline and Recovery**: Ballater lost its burgh status in 1975 and the cinema, secondary school, a bank, a chemist and principal post office status were lost between 1951 and 1981. By then there were caravan and camping sites as well as 18 hotels, the seven largest of which employed 170 people; but they were generally of much lower star rating than in the 1950s. The resident population had fallen to around 1300. In the 1980s the former station buildings were owned and used by the District Council, and its former restaurant was still used as such. The *Craigendarroch Hotel* gained 4 stars and grew to 44 rooms; its 11ha estate was developed with heavily advertised timeshare holiday lodges, and including among its amenities a dry ski slope. With the building of small housing estates the village population kept stable to 1991, when Ballater's 1362 generally affluent residents included Scotland's highest ratio of men working at home – over 25% of those in work; there was a large retired element. The Victoria Hall was renovated in 1992, incorporating a public library. By 1995 a visitor centre had been created on the Royal estate some 13km south-west of Ballater, at the approaches to picturesque Loch Muick.

**Tourist Mecca?**: The wide range of shops include quality clothing and outdoor gear; facilities include two banks, a Rover car dealer and a Bluebird bus garage. Police and fire stations cover emergencies. The town still has its pleasant open spaces; in 2000 the former railway station building was converted to a tourist office and visitor centre. The adjacent small *'sweetie'* manufacturing firm of Dee Valley Confectioners, established in 1965, may be viewed at work. East of the town the infrastructure for further new housing has appeared, and still farther out is the Tullich sporting fishery. Tourists are also served by the *Darroch Learg* in its wooded grounds, the *'historic'* granite-built *Pannanich Wells*, the lengthy *Loirston House* and the *Balgonie*, plus smaller accommodation and several restaurants – but the youth hostel has closed.

## BALLINDALLOCH & Inveravon — Map 10, A2

***Settlement on Speyside**, pop. 140* — OS 28: NJ 1835

Ballindalloch, which has prehistoric chambered cairns, lies on middle Speyside, where the counties of Moray and Banff once met a detached part of Inverness-shire; its Gaelic name may mean *'village of the blind'*. Ballindalloch Castle was built there in the 15th century, and rebuilt in 1546 by the ancestors of the Macpherson-Grants. It was shown on Pont's map of about 1600 as *'Balnadallach'*, sketched as a tower house. Near the confluence of the River Avon (pronounced *Ann*) with the Spey was the Kirk of *'Innerain'* or Inveravon, in whose parish a school was held by 1633. Roy's map showed that by about 1750 the castle was surrounded by policies, but there were only a few ferm touns in this roadless area. However, Black's Boat was named, so presumably a regular ferry operated there, 2.5km north of the castle.

**Roads and Bridges, Whisky and Railways**: Ballindalloch became a post town, but the area remained wholly rural until in the second decade of the 19th century the Speyside road and Bridge of Avon were built under Telford's direction. Glenfarclas distillery was established on the Green Burn 3km north east of Ballindalloch in 1836: nearby at the junction of a road to Blacksboat Bridge grew the hamlet of Marypark. Around that period the *Tombreak Inn* appeared near the bridge; later this was to be known as the *Dalnashaugh Inn*. In 1863 the Great North of Scotland Railway opened a branch from Aberlour to Boat of Garten, with a station named Ballindalloch at Cragganmore, 2 km to the west where the line crossed the river on a notable wrought-iron viaduct. In the 1860s Glenfarclas distillery was bought by the Grant family.

**Cragganmore Distillery**: Old whisky moonlighters' premises near the railway station were adapted by John Smith to create the Cragganmore distillery in 1869. Peats were brought 5 km to Cragganmore; in 1886 its annual production of 410,000 litres of Highland malt whisky was all distributed by Watson of Dundee. It seems that the distillery was later owned by Pattisons of Leith, prior to their demise in 1898; but it outlived them. The smaller output of J & J Grant's Glenfarclas distillery was about 225,000 litres in 1886, but its quality enabled it to weather prohibition.

**The Twentieth Century's First Distillery**: Ballindalloch Castle operated its own horse-drawn fire engine from 1911; this eventually became a prized exhibit at the Highland Folk Museum at Kingussie. But there were few developments until in 1958–59 the first new Highland malt distillery for 60 years was built at Tormore, 3 km west of Ballindalloch, taking its water from the Achvochkie Burn; its attractive design included workers' houses. However, the railway was closed to passengers in 1965 and to freight in 1968; the station became a hostel. By 1979 the inn sported the title of hotel, but by 1981 the population in the area was only some 140.

**Wood Waste makes High Quality Single Malts**: Cragganmore distillery was hard at it in 1990 under United Distillers, its 1978 product, matured in sherry casks, being sold as a twelve year old single malt liqueur whisky. Tormore was steaming away under Allied. Glenfarclas distillery, run in the early 1990s by John and George Grant, kept its reputation for producing a rich single malt whisky of the highest quality; in 1992 this was sold at 25 years old. The Macpherson-Grants still occupied the castle in 1993, when it was open to the public in summer. By 1994 Tormore distillery had a new 5 mw power plant burning forest waste. The former railway trackbed is now the Speyside Way long-distance path.

## BALLOCH, Arden, Cameron & Inchmurrin

**Map 5, B5**

***Urban area, s. of L. Lomond,*** *pop. 8300* OS 56/63/64: NS 3881

The 14th century keep of Lennox Castle, seat of the powerful Lennox family, was built on Inchmurrin, an island in Loch Lomond; eventually it fell into ruin. Some 5 km to the south the short River Leven flows from the loch, enabling small boats to reach the Firth of Clyde. The Gaelic name Balloch means *'The Pass'*, by implication the place where the river could be crossed. The area was already thickly settled by about 1600, when Pont showed Balloch, Cameron and Stuikroger among other tiny places; south of Balloch two mills stood on east bank tributaries of the Leven.

**Textiles and Mansion Houses**: Woodbank, a mansion built about 1650 for the Lindsays of Stuikroger, was enlarged in the 18th century. A linen bleachfield known as Cameronfield was set up on Loch Lomondside about 1727, and Roy's map of about 1754 showed a *'boat'* or ferry at Balloch. The Levenbank Print Works at Jamestown was established in 1784 by Watson & Arthur. In the 19th century its then owner John Stuart named his new riverside villa Lennoxbank. The replacement for a castle shown on Pont's map was the mansion known as Tullichewan Castle, built in 1808 for the Vale of Leven textile magnate John Stirling; it stood in a large park.

**Balloch and the Tourist Industry**: The first Loch Lomond pleasure steamer, David Napier's PS *Marion*, began to ply in 1816; by 1827 circular steamer tours served Tarbet. From 1850 they started from the new Balloch Pier, the terminus of a new railway from Bowling through Dumbarton and the Vale of Leven. This was eventually connected to Glasgow and became a joint Caledonian and North British enterprise. At *Inverarnan Inn* at the north end of the loch *(see Ardlui)* the steamers connected with coaches for Oban, and scenic coach tours through the central highlands. In 1856 a cross-country line grandly entitled the Forth & Clyde Junction Railway (F&CJR) was opened from Balloch to Buchlyvie and Stirling, but this was neither essential nor scenic and never thrived. By 1858 Balloch had an inn, later called the *Balloch Hotel*, and the steamer *MacGregor* was plying on the Loch.

**The Heyday of Loch Steamers**: In 1883 loch sailings came under the Lochlong & Lochlomond Steamboat Company. By 1894 there were three or four daily services up and down the Loch, and two hotels at Balloch, the *Colquhoun Arms* and the long-lasting *Tullichewan Arms*. By then Arden House stood in its lochside park some 4 km north of Balloch, one of several emparked mansions in the area. Sweeney's Cruises were established in 1895, and by 1908 electric trams competed with the trains between Balloch and Dumbarton. At one time there was a quarry 3 km east of Balloch on the slopes of Blairquhomrie Moor, with a tramway to sidings on the F&CJR near Auchencarroch Farm. In the 1920s the large print-works remained open, but in 1934 the F&CJR lost its passenger trains.

**Cruising for Morale and on the Maid of Loch**: Winter sailings on Loch Lomond ended in 1933, but during the 1939–45 war the four steamers on the loch maintained the only daily excursion service in Scotland, and were full. The *Prince Edward* was broken up in 1955, leaving only small private pleasure craft and the railway-owned *Maid of the Loch* of 1952 – the last paddle steamer built in Europe – to operate on Loch Lomond. By 1953 when a new pier was opened, Balloch was a village in terms of most facilities but also had a riverside restaurant, while Woodbank had been converted into one of half a dozen hotels. Tullichewan Castle was demolished in 1954. There was a minor steam engine shed at Balloch until 1961, when electric trains took over the service. By 1963 the *Lomond Castle Hotel* was open at Arden, and at nearby Auchendennan was a youth hostel. About 1970 a country park was opened at the Victorian mansion called Balloch Castle (already owned by Glasgow City Council), and with the building of large council estates such as Mill of Haldane to relieve congestion in the Vale, dramatic growth occurred in the local population, from 2500 in 1951 to 8000 by 1981. In the late 1970s piers were built on the island of Inchmurrin, enabling erection of the *Inchmurrin Hotel*, open by 1980.

**Downs and Ups in Leisure**: With the decline in the cruising habit the *Maid of the Loch* was withdrawn in 1981, but fortunately not scrapped. Individual water-based recreation grew, but little increase took place in the local facilities. The average star class of the local hotels had fallen by 75%, and the *Woodbank Hotel*, by then called *Hamilton House*, ran down to closure in 1981. Planning permission for residential development around its derelict shell was refused in 1995, and it was further fire damaged in 1996; the remains still stood in 1997. Meantime by 1977 Lennoxbank had become the 21-room *Riverside Motor Inn*, but this was vacated about 1990 and in 1994 the extended building stood derelict. In 1982 the 1936-built diesel vessel *Countess of Breadalbane (see Dalmally)* was brought overland from Finnieston to Loch Lomond in two sections, hull and upperworks, by the Alloa Brewery Company; reassembled and refitted, she served as the *Countess Fiona* until 1990, when her then owners failed and she was left on the slipway until cut up in 1999.

**Loch Lomond Park and Cameron Leisure project**: Balloch Pier and Central stations lost their trains in the 1980s, but trains continued to run to new platforms south of the main road. The town station building was taken over for the new headquarters for the Loch Lomond Park Authority, opened in 1988 with over 8 ha of landscaping along the former railway to the pier at the start of Britain's longest cycleway, connecting Balloch with Glasgow. In 1989–90 Craigendarroch Ltd of Ballater converted the mansion at Cameron on the west shore of the Loch to a 68-room hotel and country club, with an indoor swimming pool, outdoor leisure complex, marina and large and luxurious timeshare holiday chalets, all opened in 1990, plus a golf course in 1991. Less fortunate was the *Lomond Park* (or *Lomond Castle) Hotel*, set alight by its proprietor who was later jailed. In 1991 the Balloch postcode sector held 8266 people.

**Recent Developments**: A new and smaller cruise vessel from the Thames, the reconditioned 19 m *Silver Marlin* which could carry 150 passengers, began to ply in 1992 for Sweeney's Cruises. The Paddle Steamer Preservation Society bought the *Maid of the Loch* for restoration, now progressing. In 1994 the Loch Lomond Marina offered a full service to boat owners. In 1995 Dunbartonshire Enterprise acquired the derelict 39 ha site at Drumkinnon Bay west of Balloch for major tourist developments, wisely including wet weather activities. The 5-star *Cameron House Hotel* has 96 rooms; there's also the historic *Balloch*, and the Arden *('Loch Lomond')* youth hostel.

## BALMACARA

**Map 8, B3**

***W. Highland settlement,*** *pop. 300* — OS 33: NG 8227

The sheltered south-facing Balmacara Bay on the north shore of Loch Alsh was well settled by the mid 18th century, when the Kirk of Lochalsh stood 2 km to the east. In the early 19th century a road was carried along the shore of the loch, swinging inland through the hills to Erbusaig, and by 1897 reaching the new station at Kyle. By the 1950s the National Trust for Scotland owned the vast hilly Balmacara estate, which from here enjoys views of Skye and Glenelg, separated by the narrow hill-girt strait of Kylerhea. The scattered village with over 200 people had a 15-roomed hotel, the old Lochalsh primary school, later replaced, a post office, telephone exchange and doctor. A new road alignment completed by 1974 had halved the distance to Kyle, which became 5 km; a caravan site was open, and afforestation had clothed parts of the once bare hills; this was declared access land by the Forestry Commission. By 1981 the population was nearing 300, and by 1997 a new primary school had been built at Auchtertyre, 1 km east of the kirkton. The *Balmacara Hotel* has 29 rooms.

## BALMEDIE

**Map 10, C3**

***Aberdeenshire village,*** *pop. 1260* — OS 38: NJ 9617

Near the coast some 12 km north of Aberdeen was an ancient church, shown by a tiny symbol on Robert Gordon's map of about 1640, as engraved by Blaeu. By about 1750 the church stood near a track to Ellon, later made up as a main road. In 1817 the Ordnance Survey of Scotland chose the coastal links to lay out its 8 km long base line. By 1894 Balmedie House stood in modest policies; among the area's scattered houses and farms were a hotel and post office near Orrock House, and Balmedie post and telegraph office at the Mill of Eggie. A primary school was built, and by 1951 about 600 people lived in the area; by 1971 this figure had fallen to 500. By 1969 Balmedie House was an Eventide Home and the former hotel a pub; by 1974 a coastal caravan site was open, though this eyesore was later removed in favour of picnic areas.

**The Oil Industry brings Development**: Then came the oil industry, and by 1977 the fall in population had been reversed: the *White Horse Inn* at Balmedie became a hotel with 20 rooms. Garages were open by 1980, and housing estates were built in the 1980s. By 1991 these had raised the population of what was by then a compact dormitory village to 1260. There was a strong bias to managerial and professional work, and there was minimal unemployment. More housing continued to spread southwards, and by 1999 a country park had been created on the links, and a dual carriageway bypassed Balmedie and linked it with Aberdeen.

## BALMERINO, Creich, Gauldry, Flisk & Kilmany

**Map 6, B3**

***N. Fife village & hamlets,*** *pop. 1600 (area)* — OS 59: NO 3524

Hill forts and some remains of 16th century towers adorn the hilly rural parishes of Flisk and Creich, on the Fife side of the Firth of Tay. On a low-lying section of the shore to the east, almost opposite Dundee, stands Balmerino, whose Gaelic name *'Happy Village'* suggests that a settlement existed before its Cistercian abbey was founded about 1226–29 *"by Queen Ermengred, wife of King William of Scotland"* (Defoe). It was colonised by monks from Melrose, who established a ferry to Dundee. Around 1250 they were using wagons to cart building stone from Nydie, about 10 km to the south, across a tidal ford, to build the substantial abbey, whose monks sold sorted wool around 1400. The abbey was torched in 1537, and again burnt down by Henry VIII's English troops on Xmas Day 1547. Once more sacked in 1559, the struggling remnant of the community had only three appropriated churches. Kilmany to the south is another ancient and sparsely peopled parish. Meantime Naughton Castle had been built 1.5 km to the east, but it became ruinous, and was eventually replaced by Naughton House.

**Grain Grown, Milled and Exported**: In 1603 the Abbey ruins were given to Sir James Elphinstone, Lord Balmerino. By Defoe's day they were *"eaten up by time"*, but the ferry was still working in the mid 18th century, though the Roy map showed no roads nearby. The abbey never created a burgh but Balmerino, which had a mill by the late 18th century, was a small port exporting grain. In 1799 Heron did not mention Balmerino hamlet, although he had evidently visited the abbey ruins. New quays were built about 1820, served up to the 1930s by the pleasure steamers which till then linked Perth and Dundee, and a mill still worked in the late 19th century when Gauldry some 2 km to the east was a hamlet with a post office and inn. But by the 1980s when Gauldry had grown into a village of over 400 people with a school, shop, garage and large coach-hirer, Balmerino was purely agricultural, parts of the abbey's remnants (NTS-owned) being used as a farm. However, the derelict Balmerino mill was converted into a house in 1999–2000.

## BALMORAL & Crathie — Map 10, A4

***Deeside locations,** pop. 150* — OS 44: NO 2595

The tower house of Abergeldie Castle, 14 km east of Braemar on Deeside, was built in the 16th century. About 2 km to the west was Crathie Kirk, which existed before 1642, when the area was mapped for Blaeu's atlas by Robert Gordon. The Roy map showed that about 1750 the kirk stood solitary and roadless, though the Crathie Burn had already been bridged above its confluence with the River Dee. *'Balmurrel'* was then a tiny place on the site of the modern castle, on the opposite (south) bank of the Dee just west of the church. The road to Corgarff was built under Caulfeild's direction, including Gairnshiel Bridge, opened in 1751, near which was a mill. The original Lochnagar distillery, named after a lochan 8 km to the south which also gave its name to the 1155 m mountain towering over it, was built north of the river some 2 km south-east of Balmoral in 1825 by a reformed local smuggler, John Robertson, whose whisky's quality became renowned; rebuilt after a fire of 1841, it had closed by 1860. Meantime in 1845 the *'(New) Lochnagar'* distillery was built south of the river. Abergeldie Castle was owned in 1831 by Sir Robert Gordon, whose estate carpenter built the fine early doll's house which was displayed at London's Bethnal Green Museum of Childhood in the 1990s. Crathie post office was open around 1842.

**Balmoral – Majestic Abode of the Royals**: Queen Victoria leased the Balmoral estate in 1848, and among its other attractions the Royals acquired a taste for the Lochnagar whisky from 1850. They bought the estate in 1852, perhaps influenced by being told that its Gaelic name meant *'Majestic Abode'*, and reluctant to be upstaged by a commoner! The small mansion-house known as Balmoral Castle was soon rebuilt on the grand scale as a royal holiday residence. Brunel was appointed to design the unusual river bridge, which opened in 1857 (fully described by Hay & Stell). An inn appeared at Crathie, but the estate remained dedicated to Royal blood sports and relaxation.

**Royal Whisky: Creating and Exploiting Snob Value**: By 1886 the new distillery too held the appellation Royal; its twenty employees used water power, local peat and spring water to produce nearly 300,000 litres of Highland malt whisky annually. A hundred cattle were kept on site, fed on the draff and spent wash, but rather unusually for the period the bottling and storage was carried on at Aberdeen harbour by the lessee John Begg Ltd. Little changed in almost a century within the highly conservative Royal area, until about 1975 the narrow Corgarff road was downgraded to category B, and by 1978 the inn at Inver, 3 km to the west, had closed. In 1989 the distillery's new lessees Guinness – who had taken over DCL – applied snob selling techniques to its best single malt *'Royal Lochnagar'* which, having been repackaged at an astounding £95 a bottle, actually sold more cases than it had done at £15! In 1990 the profits helped to fund a distillery visitor centre, now owned by UDV; but by 1995 Crathie had lost its post office.

## BALMULLO — Map 6, B3

***N. Fife village,** pop. 1100* — OS 59: NO 4221

Despite its Gaelic name, Balmullo – which is sheltered by the hills of north-east Fife – was not shown on either of Blaeu's 17th century maps of Fife. By about 1750 when Roy surveyed the area there was a road between Cupar and Brackmont Mill north of Leuchars, and a mill on the Moonzie Burn. By 1894 a sprawling hamlet had developed astride this road some 2 km west of Leuchars station, served by a post office and smithy. By the mid 20th century over 300 people lived locally, and there was a primary school. By 1952 prominent hard rock quarries producing pink chips for suburban driveways had been opened on the south and east slopes of Lucklaw (the appellation *'Hill'* is redundant), and there were sandpits at Brackmont Mill. In the 1970s after the opening of the Tay road bridge some 10 km to the north, estate development of private houses, mainly detached, quickly raised the population to stabilise at over 1100 in both 1981 and 1991. In the latter year Balmullo was a dormitory, from which many mortgagees commuted by car to management jobs.

## BALQUHIDDER — Map 5, C3

***Small village, Stirlingshire,** pop. 150* — OS 57: NN 5320

Between the steep hill ranges of the Braes of Balquhidder in the central Highlands lies Loch Voil, from which the River Balvag drains east then south into Strathyre. The name derives from the Gaelic *Baile-chuil-tir*, meaning *'the distant farm'*. Unmapped by Pont or Blaeu, the area was a crossroads when the fair copy of Roy's map was made about 1750. Tracks led three ways from Balquhidder Kirk, where the famed insurgent Rob Roy is buried: westwards south of Loch Voil, past the *'Braes of Ballwider'* to Loch Doine, where he died in 1734; north over the 585 m pass of the *'Larig Earne'* to Suie in Glen Dochart; and east past the mansion of *'Stron Slany'* to the site of the *Kingshouse Inn*, to join the north–south track through Strathyre. In 1870 the Callander & Oban Railway opened its first section, placing Balquhidder station near the inn, which Murray found merely *"tolerable"* in 1894. From 1905 to 1951 this rural station boasted an engine shed, two signalboxes and a staff of eight men, being the junction for a marginal line to Comrie, Crieff and Perth. Tree planting soon changed the character of Loch Voil, where by 1954 there was a youth hostel at Stronvar; but this closed in the 1970s following Beeching's closure of the remaining railway in 1965, speeded by a landslide in Glen Ogle. By 1981 some 150 people lived in the Balquhidder area, where there were three small hotels. By 1986 *Balquhidder Lodge*, beside Loch Voil 3 km west of the village, had also become a hotel, and forest walks were encouraged in the area, which also now has the *Monachyle Mhor Hotel* (10 rooms), the 18th century centre of a stalking and fishing estate 6 km west.

## BALTASOUND — Map 14, C1

***Shetland village, Unst,*** *pop. 600* — OS 1: HP 6208

Unst was the most favoured of the Shetland isles among early Norse farming settlers, who founded a score of churches there, though most soon fell into disuse. Its natural centre of gravity is around Balta Sound, a deep inlet on its east coast which is the most northerly natural all-weather refuge for shipping in Scotland, protected from easterly seas by the islet of Balta, and from westerly gales by the 200 m tall ridge of Valla Field. Many settlements were shown at its head on Blaeu's map, engraved by 1628 from Pont's sketches of about 1592. Martin writing in 1703 thought Unst was *"the pleasantest of the Shetland Isles; it has three churches and as many harbours"*, which he did not name. Heron wrote in 1799 that Balta was a *"good road for ships, visited often by the Greenland whale fishers"*. At one time in the early 19[th] century Baltasound was said to have been Britain's largest fishing centre; jetties and piers were built, and on its shores evolved the main centre for Unst.

**The *'Earl of Zetland'* and the Herring Fishery**: In 1877 Baltasound pier became the terminus of the North Isles steamer services from Lerwick via Mossbank, provided by the one sturdy vessel *Earl of Zetland* right up to 1946; a post office arrived in the late 19[th] century. In the peak herring year of 1905, the 46 *'herring stations'* made Baltasound the largest fishing centre in the Shetlands – the main jetty at Springfield even had its own tramway. At one time sealskins were cured. Telephones only reached the north isles in 1936–37, and most herring stations had gone by 1939.

**Holding On till Aircraft could Land**: In the 1950s Baltasound had a scattered population of over 500, served by the facilities of a small village, but including a coach garage, two piers, a doctor, the small Baltasound Junior High school (now S1-S4) and the *Baltasound Hotel*. Shetland planners denied the existence of many villages in their islands, but in 1962 selected Baltasound as a rural planning *'holding point'* to cope with depopulation. By the 1970s electricity arrived from Kirkwall via Yell by submarine cables. By 1973 an airstrip was available, associated with the development of North Sea oil resources; but the steamer service ended in 1975 and the boatbuilding formerly carried on was defunct by 1980. However, by then the population was around 600.

**Modern Baltasound**: Talc has been quarried nearby and exported for many years, for use in roofing felt manufacture. By 1987 the airstrip and North Sea oil helicopter base had been glorified as an Airport, jointly owned by the Shetland Islands Council and Airwork. However good its internal facilities might have been, in 1987 the fairly recent *Hagdale Lodge Hotel* was in external appearance only a cluster of hutments. In the 1990s there were two hotels, and by 1994 a new leisure centre. Traces of gold were found by geologists panning a burn in south-east Unst in 1994; it was hoped that commercial quantities would be located. The *Baltasound Hotel* has 25 rooms.

## BANCHORY, Crathes, Raemoir & Strachan — Map 10, B4

***Deeside town & hamlets,*** *pop. 6250* — OS 38 or 45: NO 6995

In the fifth century Saint Ternan from Fordoun founded a monastery some 25 km up the River Dee from Aberdeen; the name Banchory means *'white cauldron'* in Gaelic, probably referring to a riverbed feature, and the parish is Banchory Ternan. The hilly area to the north became a royal forest or hunting preserve in the 12[th] century, as was Durris Forest to the south-east a century later. The more fertile area was well settled when the important Crathes Castle was built in 1553 some 3 km to the east for Burnett of Leys. This towered over a village when Pont made his sketch map about 1600; to the east was a waulk mill. *'Banchry'* with its church was a significant place; across the Dee was a waulk mill on the Water of Feugh, and farther up towards the very rural parish centre of Strachan was a bridge at Collonach. The Burn of Canny 4 km to the west was bridged, with another mill and a settlement named Bridgend. The Douglas's Z-plan Tilquhillie Castle, now a ruin, had been built in 1575 about 3 km to the south-east, and Raemoir, 4 km to the north, was also named by Pont.

**Mean Houses, Mansion and Market**: When Roy mapped the area about 1750 a substantial village lined the Braemar road. There was no Dee bridge, but a ferry must have linked with the road which led south beside the Water of Feugh. Although Pennant stayed at *"a mean house"* at Banchory in 1769, Raemoir House was rebuilt as a fine mansion in the 18[th] century. Banchory gained a fortnightly market, and had a post office by 1793; three fairs were to be held in 1797. The Bridge of Feugh was open by 1799, and soon after this the Dee itself was bridged nearby. Arbeadie, a new village founded in 1805, soon merged into a greater Banchory.

**Banking, the Bonnie Lass and the Railway**: The Municipal buildings and a Bank of Scotland branch were opened in 1838, by 1842 Banchory was served by no fewer than nine carriers, and a gasworks was set up in 1845. James Scott Skinner, born locally in 1843, became a very famous fiddler and composed such well-known airs as *'Jenny's Bawbee'*, *'The Miller o' Hirn'* and *'The Bonnie Lass o' Bon Accord'*. The Burnett Arms Inn was open by 1853, when the new Deeside Railway replaced the two coaches then plying between Aberdeen and Banchory, and ran excursion trains to the town's *'Annual Gathering and Games'* in September. Royal trains began to use the railway almost at once en route to Balmoral. The company's locomotive depot was built at Banchory, which remained a crossing station when an extension to Aboyne was completed in 1859. By 1857 Banchory had a town band.

**Commuters, Waterworks and Nordrach Sanatorium**: In time Banchory became a fashionable residential settlement for the city of Aberdeen, and also a police burgh. Crathes Castle had a halt from the opening of the railway; it was enlarged as a station in 1863. The Aberdeen City waterworks at Invercanny, 3 km to the west, were first opened in 1864. In 1894 Banchory was called by Murray *"a long neat village with many villas and the very comfortable Burnett Arms Hotel"*. A sanatorium on the open-air principles pioneered at Nordrach in Baden, was built of prefabricated sections and opened in 1900, named *'Nordrach-on-Dee Hospital'*. In 1934 it became the *Glen o' Dee Hotel*, but during World War II reverted to hospital use for army TB cases.

**New Station, Golf, Hotels – and Beeching**: Meantime the station was rebuilt on a larger scale in 1902–03 on a new site some 100 m west of the old, with a bay platform to terminate the suburban trains; new engine and carriage sheds were also provided, the last significant improvements to the Deeside railway. Banchory golf club, founded in 1905, laid out an attractive 18-hole course on the river terraces, still popular. The fairly modern Blackhall Castle south west of Banchory was demolished in 1947, allegedly to prevent it becoming a home for mental patients. By the 1950s Banchory was a small resort town of 2700 people with a youth hostel (closed by 1974) and seven hotels, among them *Raemoir*, its tourist trade aided by Crathes Castle and its gardens, restored over a period by the National Trust for Scotland. The railway which had lost traffic to the roads was closed under the Beeching plan in 1966, its tourist potential unexplored.

**Upmarket Oil Dormitory and Tourist Centre**: The oil-related developments around Aberdeen led to rapid car-based dormitory growth in Banchory in the 1970s and especially the 1980s, and to enlargement of the Aberdeen waterworks around 1980. In 1981, with a population of around 5000, Banchory was still a small town in terms of facilities. The local newspaper, the *Deeside Piper*, was started in 1985 as an offshoot of the *Forfar Dispatch*. By 1990 Norco of Aberdeen had recently built an upmarket superstore which was said to be unique in the Co-operative movement; but in an abortive effort to escape insolvency the firm had to sell it to Safeway in 1992. By then there were 6230 residents, with a markedly dormitory character. Fire destroyed the *Stag Hotel* in Xmas week 1993, and the 78-bed Glen o' Dee convalescent hospital, abandoned in 1989, stood sadly decaying in 1997.

**The Biggest and Best Equipped Village?**: By 1999 a golf driving range, trout fishery and a mountain bike trail had been added to the area's facilities. Professions now include accountants, architect, dentist, banks and travel agents; a wide range of shops augment the Safeway. Services include Banchory Academy and two primary schools, plus a recently-built museum and public library. Industry includes sawmills and a small precast concrete works. New house building still proceeds in various directions and varieties, a modern garden centre supplying their landscaping needs, but most locals still regard busy, bosky Banchory as a *"village"*! A preservation group plans to re-lay 3km of the Deeside Railway between Banchory and Crathes in 2001. Nearby, 'Inchmarlo' golf course is a new facility. Medium-sized hotels include the out of town *Raemoir House*, the partly Georgian *Banchory Lodge*, the Victorian *Tor-na-Coille*, the central *Burnett Arms* and the rebuilt *Stag*; guest houses and B&B signs abound.

## BANFF

**Map 10, B1**

***Moray Firth town**, pop. 4100* — OS 29: NJ 6964

A place named *Bugh* had a thanage from about the 11th century; its association with Banff which lies on the Moray Firth at the mouth of the River Deveron is hypothetical. Banff was mentioned in 1120, and was the caput of a sheriffdom from 1136. This, Scotland's most elongated county, had enclaves of jurisdiction within the Aberdeen sheriffdom and defied all natural boundaries. Before it was extinguished in 1975, Banff town council claimed that it was chartered as a Royal Burgh in 1163. Although a harbour was built in 1175, Banff developed only slowly: in 1289 the council complained that Montrose was gatecrashing the Aberdeen fair that had been set up to benefit the struggling burghs in the far north. However, Banff had a Royal castle by 1295, and Robert I founded a Carmelite friary in 1321. Banff had a customs house from 1390; its medieval mercat cross survives.

**Trade in Primary Products**: Around 1400 Banff was one of the three leading salmon fishing centres of Scotland, and there was soon a small export trade in wool. Later in the century this fell away and was replaced by other commodities such as timber. Banff salmon was re-exported through Aberdeen, while in 1496 hides and skins were being shipped from Aberdeen to Banff, and Gilbert Litster of Banff was shipping tree trunks to an Aberdeen timber merchant. Banff's relative insignificance is clear: in the 15th and 16th centuries it generally paid under 1% of the total of burgh taxes, and in 1535 the tax levied on the burgh was only 7% of that of Aberdeen. Banff made a very small contribution to Customs dues in 1542, and in 1560 its church was an appurtenance of Arbroath Abbey. However, as a sheriff caput the burgh was represented in Parliament. Meantime from about 1500 onwards Inchdrewer Castle, an L-plan tower, was built 5km south-west of the town.

**After the Reformation: Golf and Punishment**: In 1574 the priory was granted to King's College in Old Aberdeen, but the buildings were destroyed. Although its salmon fisheries were being disputed in 1588, by 1593 the town was the centre of a presbytery. In the early 17th century Banff Castle was sold to Sheriff-Clerk Sharp, father of the egregious archbishop of St Andrews. Golf was already taken seriously in the town in 1637, when the theft of golf balls was punishable by death! In 1639 Banff held 21st place among Scottish burghs in terms of tax yield; by then commercial brewing was established in the town.

**Pillage, Bridge and Milling**: In 1645 the Royalist Marquis of Montrose inflicted what Chambers called *"indiscriminate pillage"* in Banff; so much so that in 1655 Tucker noted disdainfully of the port that *"something now and then is brought in from Norway, but their only trade is coasting, except some salmon may happen to be shipped out"*. Banff recovered somewhat, with a Deveron ferry by 1683 – soon replaced by a bridge that was to prove inadequate. In the late 17th century a new Town Mill was erected by Montrose millwrights.

**Duff House built, Bridge lost, Good Tunes composed**: Banff was large enough by 1733 to support an early golf course on the links. The William Adam mansion of Duff House was built for the Earl of Fife from about 1735, dressed stone being brought by sea from the Firth of Forth, but was rejected by the client and still incomplete as late as 1765. John Adam redesigned Banff Castle, much altered in 1749–52 for Lord Deskford, but leaving recognisable walls from the old building. However, the Deveron bridge was washed away shortly before Roy surveyed the area about 1750. Banff was a sprawling settlement with only two radial roads – westwards towards Portsoy, and south via a *'boat'* to Turriff. A post office was open by 1755, the year that Isaac Cooper, a well known composer of folk tunes, was born in Banff.

**Beer, Thread and Economic Recovery**: A new brewery was set up at Seatown around 1750, and a linen bleachfield was built. By the time that Alexander Carlyle visited the town in 1765, a large thread mill with some 50 flax dressers was in operation, much of its output being sent by sea to a Nottingham company. He wrote that Banff *"consists of several streets, is very well built, and may contain 2500 people; this town thrives apace"*. Around 1785 sixty men worked in heckling imported Dutch flax, spun by some 4000 people in the district; the yarn was doubled and twisted in Banff by 200 women and children, and 40 more were engaged in bleaching. The finished thread was still sent to Nottingham and Leicester.

**Port, Commercial Centre and new Bridges**: Boswell found Banff's inn *"indifferent"* in 1773, but the inadequate harbour was improved in the 1770s, and by 1780 grain was being shipped to central Scotland. Banff became a port of registry after 1786 with the letters BF. In 1772 a single arch was built to span the Deveron gorge at Alvah, 4km south of Banff, but did not play a key role in the road system. A new Deveron bridge designed by Smeaton was begun at the river's mouth in 1779, though not completed until 1799, when Heron noted an *"elegant bridge of seven arches"*. Banff's first post office opened in 1792; three fairs were scheduled for 1797. The Aberdeen Banking Company had a branch in the town between at least 1793 and 1825. Heron added that Banff had *"several good streets, a brewery, a manufacture of thread, and another of stockings wrought on frames"*. The harbour was enclosed by a *"well-built neat pier"*, but although *"considerable quantities of salmon are exported"* it was *"liable to be choked up with shifting sands"*. By that time it was claimed that 5000 people in the area were employed in making thread.

**Growth in Fishing and Distilling**: The central *Tolbooth Hotel* was built in 1801. Banff became a major fishing port in the early 19th century, with fish curing from 1815. In that year William Brodie, the sculptor of *'Greyfriars Bobby'* and other well-known Edinburgh statues, was born in Banff. Further harbour improvements were begun in 1816, the half-built pier being inspected in 1819 by its designer Thomas Telford and the poet Robert Southey, who noted the use of *"fine masses of red granite from the Peterhead quarries"*. A bonded warehouse was soon built at the harbour for the Inverboyndie distillery *(see Whitehills)*.

**Clean, Neat, Educated – and Starving**: In 1826 Chambers noted Banff as the *"capital of a small county; old-fashioned, but remarkably clean and neat; may contain 3000 souls, drawing some additional support from a bad harbour and the herring fishery"*. Duff House was *"the seat of the Earl of Fife"*; later it was to be used in turn as a hotel, a sanatorium, POW camp and art gallery. By the 1820s there was a coach service from Aberdeen, and a gasworks was established in 1831. A new entrance lodge to Duff House was built in 1836, followed in 1837 by new buildings for Banff Academy. In 1847 meal was being shipped out of Banff in schooners at a time when local people, their numbers swelled by refugees from the Clearances, were actually starving!

**Railways Don't Meet, and Harbour Silts Up**: Although a county town, Banff was off the rails until 1859 when the Banff, Portsoy & Strathisla Railway, later a branch of the Great North of Scotland, was opened from Grange near Keith, forking at Tillynaught Junction near Portsoy, to a station north of the town. It terminated at a siding on a harbour pier, but about then the river changed its course, causing the harbour to silt up; however, wooden coasters were still built there in the 1860s. Another twisting branch line which opened from Turriff to south of Macduff in 1860 provided a station at Banff Bridge from 1872, the year it finally swung round the coast to reach its objective at Macduff harbour. For a time Wordie & Co had a rail to road cartage depot in Banff, but by 1864 linens were no longer manufactured locally. James Matthews designed a new Courthouse and County Buildings, erected in 1870–71.

**Banff for Bare Discomfort**: In 1886 Alfred Barnard stayed in Banff in a *"bare and comfortless hotel whose name we wish to forget"*; but rather strangely he referred to the little town as *"the most fashionable resort in the north of Scotland"!* The link with Fraserburgh was still made by a horse-drawn coach to Rosehearty as late as 1894, but by about 1909 the coach ran only to Strichen and Brucklay stations, via New Pitsligo. In 1893 over 1200 men were directly employed in the fishing, but its decline was setting in. Perhaps there had been a change in hotel management since 1886, for Murray's Handbook noted the *"very comfortable" Fife Arms Hotel*, and a *"good"* temperance hotel. A public library was started (with Carnegie money) in 1899. The town's population, which was under 4000, was to remain virtually static for a further century.

**More Golf and Hotels but No Trains**: The Duff House golf club, founded in 1909, had by 1913 laid out a fine new 18-hole parkland course beside the river. About then the royal physician Lord Dawson of Penn had a mansionhouse built on the cliffs west of the town, with its own Bridgefoot halt; but by 1963 it had become the 7-room *Links Hotel*. In 1951 the railway from Banff Bridge was closed to passengers, and to freight in 1961. Beeching closed Banff's own passenger station in 1964, though some freight traffic lingered there for another four years; eventually a road was built through the site. In 1972 the town councils of Banff and Macduff jointly maintained a 12ha riverside park; the *Banff Springs Hotel* was built in the mid 1970s, and modern housing spread to south and west.

**From Banffshire to Banff & Buchan**: Banff lost its burgh and county town status in 1975, though in a curious form of bureaucratic compensation it became the strangely peripheral headquarters of the equally illogical Banff & Buchan District, which was created by joining parts of both the Banff and Aberdeen counties; this was definitely a case of the Banff tail wagging the Peterhead dog, and come to that the Broch too! Banff's first building society office was opened in 1978, and in this period new buildings were erected for Banff Academy; the Chalmers Hospital had 80 g.p. beds including maternity wards. The distillery stayed in production until at least 1976, but was again out of use by 1983 and was demolished in 1988. By 1981 Banff was a quiet little resort town, lacking much of interest, though with a dozen small hotels. Although serious fishing was moribund, boatbuilding and yachting survived. Inchdrewer Castle was partly restored in 1971, but stood empty in 1997.

**New Facilities; Duff House Restored**: By 1985 there were caravan and camping sites, and the Deveronside woodland walks were an added attraction. By 1987 a spur road and a 1.5km-long miniature railway of 15" gauge had replaced Banff station and its approaches; but too few people rode on the little trains and by 1989 the line had closed. In 1991 the resident population of Banff was 4110. From 1992 Duff House was restored, becoming in 1995 a major art gallery, an outpost of the National Galleries, in an important joint venture aiming to draw many visitors to the town; its entrance lodge was converted into a tourist office. The golf clubhouse was greatly enlarged. New sewage treatment facilities were constructed in 1995–96, sited at the harbour and built to resemble a traditional warehouse; the surroundings were tarted up. By then Banff had Tesco and Somerfield stores.

**Local Government Ended**: Banff & Buchan district disappeared in 1996, its land and people joining Gordon and Kincardine & Deeside districts in an all-purpose *'Aberdeenshire'* authority – without Aberdeen! This ended Banff's tenaciously held if faintly absurd role as a centre of local government; however a local office remains. Yachts far outnumber fishing boats in the harbour, and the Princess Royal Park offers new sports facilities. The old *Tolbooth Hotel* has closed, but the old hospital and a health centre are open; the primary school has been moved to a new building, leaving a nursery in the old one. The town centre offers a choice of banks, professions and some specialist shops, and Banff still retains a postal delivery office. The *Banff Springs Hotel* has 31 rooms.

## BANKFOOT & Auchtergaven — Map 6, A3

***Perthshire village**, pop. 1000* — OS 53: NO 0635

The valley of the Garry Burn contains several Pictish standing stones and the Kirk of Auchtergaven, which lies 8 km on the Perth side of Dunkeld. Around 1600 the kirkton was called Preestoun, as indicated by Pont in his detailed though now rather illegible map of the parish; it was then a densely settled area, with three mills on the various burns. Auchtergaven or Preestoun was chartered as a burgh of barony in 1681, but remained very rural. The Roy map made around 1750 showed that the original made-up road between Perth and Dunkeld passed well east of the kirk through a hamlet at Barns and across Cairnleith Moss to Byres of Murthly, following the dead straight, probably Roman, alignment which still partly survives as a minor road.

**New Village: Road and Railway from Waterloo to Waterloo**: Though little noted in other respects the parish had the substantial total of five annual fairs by 1797. Telford's improvements of the early 19th century were applied to the winding lane past the kirk, which became the coach road on which Bankfoot was established as a new village in 1815. Hence the name Waterloo for another new hamlet. This lay at the foot of a steep hill 2 km farther north on the new road later labelled A9. Bankfoot acquired a post office about 1831, and by 1895 there was a post and telegraph office, a school and an inn. From 1906 a short light railway built by the Caledonian from a junction at Strathord station on the main line near Luncarty terminated at Bankfoot; but in 1931 buses beat the passenger trains, though a freight service mainly carrying potatoes continued until the line met its Waterloo under Beeching in 1964.

**Highland Sporrans and Historic Cars**: The population declined somewhat over the twenty years to 868 in 1971. The opening of a lengthy A9 bypass, partly on the former rail alignment, passing east of the village of Bankfoot and the hamlet of Waterloo, improved the environment; a new housing estate was built and the population rose. The local facilities which for many years had included two small hotels actually increased to those of a typical village, with about ten shops, a restaurant and caravan site where the station had been. Although located just south of the Highland boundary fault, and in Tayside not the Highland region, in the 1970s Bankfoot also held the curious distinction of making sporrans for the Highland regiments. By 1989 the local facilities had been joined by the Highland Motor Heritage Centre 1 km south of the village. There were 1009 people in 1991, a high proportion owning their homes outright; by 1999 houses had been built on the former caravan site.

## BANKNOCK, Haggs, Longcroft & Castlecary — Map 16, A2

***Stirlingshire villages**, pop. 3700 (total)* — OS 64: NS 7879

The sluggish headwaters of the River Kelvin and the Bonny Water diverge in a shared valley, which cuts west and east through the waist of Scotland between the Kilsyth Hills and the Slamannan plateau at an altitude of under 50 metres. A strategically sited Roman fort south of the valley probably originated in the first century AD. Rebuilt with stone walls and stone-built latrines around 140 AD, it was soon incorporated into the Antonine Wall as one of the only two full-blown forts in this defensive frontier. Little is known of local events until early in the 15th century when Castle Cary was built just south of the fort and 7 km east of Kilsyth. Timothy Pont's map made about 1600 also showed Bankier Mill, which stood about 1.5 km north-west of the castle, its wheel turned by a burn draining the flanks of the Kilsyth Hills. By about 1750, as Roy's map showed, the winding road between Denny and Cumbernauld crossed the Bonny Water by a bridge beside the corn mill; to the north-west was the hamlet of Bankier, and Castle Cary was also accompanied by a small settlement.

**Canal, Limeworks, Distilling, Haggs and Longcroft**: Around 1770 the Forth & Clyde Canal was dug through the low ground between the Slamannan plateau and the Kilsyth Hills, its summit level of about 46 m between the headwaters of the Bonny and the Kelvin being retained by locks near the old mill at Wyndford. After passenger boats were introduced on the canal in 1809, Castlecary became an interchange point with the coaches to Stirling, Alloa, Crieff and Perth; from 1811 Wyndford was the terminus of a passenger boat to Glasgow. To the west a basin served the Netherwood lime works. In 1828 Daniel Macfarlane of Paisley adapted the Bankier corn mill into the Bankier Distillery, east of which the straggling villages of Banknock and Longcroft later grew. By 1895 there was an inn at the hamlet of Haggs just east of the post and telegraph office at Banknock.

**The Railways arrive and Distilling seesaws**: The Edinburgh & Glasgow Railway of 1842 criss-crossed the line of the Antonine Wall near Castlecary station, where William Wordie immediately opened a rail to road cartage depot. The main line of the Caledonian and Scottish Central Railways, opened in 1848, crossed the area from south-west to north-east, the ownership divide being at Castlecary. In 1886, when visited by Barnard, the distillery – owned by John Risk – was being modernised. It used barley from Aberdeenshire and Angus, and peat from the Cumbernauld moors, to produce some 680,000 litres of malt whisky annually; a hundred pigs were fed on the draff. Meantime in 1888 came the single-line Kilsyth & Bonnybridge Joint Railway (K&BJR) which gave Banknock its own station. The Cannerton brickworks grew near Banknock station, and a larger refractory brickworks worked beside the Roman wall east of Castlecary. In 1903 Bankier distillery was bought by James Buchanan & Co; DCL closed it in 1928 but retained it as a maltings until 1968. Meantime the Kilsyth railway was closed to passengers in the 1930s. By 1951 the 1500 local people enjoyed the facilities of a small village; but Castlecary station was closed by 1968.

**Bricks and Joinery but no Canal**: The canal was closed in 1962 to enable a new dual carriageway stretch of the A80 to be readily built to bypass Haggs and Longcroft, and a new hotel was built north of the A803 junction; in the 1970s the part of the A80 north of this point was upgraded to the M80 motorway. However, the small secondary school had gone by 1976. By then Leyland trucks had a small service base at Banknock, abandoned in 1978 for a new site at Falkirk. However, by 1980 there were three small hotels, and the population had risen to over 3000. The G R Stein Castlecary brickworks, open in 1980, was closed and demolished soon afterwards, as was the former distillery, which had vanished by 1988, but the Cannerton brickworks survived. By 1990 Avonside Homes of Castlecary was described as a long-established manufacturer of timber kit houses. By 1991 the combined populations of young but disadvantaged Banknock and older and better-educated Haggs (including Longcroft), separate settlements for the Census, had grown to almost 3700. There was little new development in the 1990s, but in 2000 the A80 carriageways were raised, over the canal, so that boat traffic could resume; this would give tourism a chance to develop in this rather workaday area.

## BANNOCKBURN — Map 16, A1

*S. suburb of Stirling, pop. 5800* — OS 57: NS 8190

The Romans built a substantial road from Camelon towards the northernmost outposts of their empire, crossing the glens of the Pelstream Burn and the Bannock Burn 4 km to the south-east of Stirling. It remained in use as a trackway, just east of which is the Dryfield of Balquhidderock – the probable site where the crucial battle for Scottish independence was fought in 1314. The large army of Edward II of England was defeated by a much smaller force of Scots under Robert Bruce, whose sound tactics were aided by a plentiful supply of the four-spiked iron heel-traps called caltrops, very probably locally made by the St Ninians nailmakers,. These were thrown down in the way and successfully disabled the English cavalry, leaving much of the Sassenach force trapped between the burns to north and south, and the boggy carselands to the east, to be cut down in a ditch by Bruce's men coming from the west.

**Bridges, Mills and Market**: Near the battlefield was Beaton's mill at Milltown, which existed by 1488 when it was the location of James III's assassination. In 1516 the burn was bridged on the way between St Ninians and Plean, the work being paid for by the wealthy Royal tailor, Robert Spittal of Stirling. By about 1600, as the Pont map showed, there were bridges both above and below the place by then named Bannockburn, and at least three mills, for the area was quite thickly settled. Bannockburn House was built for the Rollo family in 1674. After the 1715 rising its owner, then Sir Hugh Paterson, forfeited the estate; but he still lived there, and in 1746 it was briefly used by the Young Pretender. The Roy map surveyed around 1754 indicated dams and mills to the west of the village at *'Chatershall'*, and lower down the burn a dam at Milton. The south-eastern part of the village was then called *'New Market'*.

**Turnpike, Carpets and Coal**: The main road from Stirling to Falkirk was turnpiked in 1752–55. In 1769 Pennant found carpets being made at Bannockburn, possibly in the new large water-powered Skeoch woollen mill of William Wilson, who later provided tiny dwellings for the workers. By the 1790s Skeoch used yarn made in Stirling, and dominated the tartan market. By 1783 17 tiny coal pits surrounded Bannockburn House, and by 1794 were producing 30,000 tonnes of coal a

*The Royal George 4-storey mill at Bannockburn, built around 1822 for wool spinning. It closed many years ago, but has survived, with its top storey used as a Masonic Hall.* (RCAHMS)

year – just five to six tonnes a day each! By 1797 there was an annual fair, and two years later Heron described Bannockburn as a *"manufacturing village"* which with St Ninians *(q.v.)* was *"supposed to contain about 6000 inhabitants"* – more than Stirling itself. In 1819 Spittal's bridge was replaced to a design by Telford.

**The Tartan Craze**: The 4-storey Royal George mills were opened in 1822, when William Wilson installed 14 new looms to meet demands for tartan cloth caused by the visit of George IV, the first Hanoverian monarch audacious enough to visit Scotland; the tourists' craze for tartans had begun. In 1827 Chambers found Bannockburn *"Upper and Lower... a village chiefly remarkable for its manufactories of tartan and carpets"*. In 1832 the Milton Old Mill made woollen yarns on water-powered machinery in very poor conditions.

**Postal Services, Road Haulage and the Railway**: Bannockburn never achieved burgh status. From the 1830s to nationalisation in 1948 Wordie & Co, the Stirling carriers, operated a haulage depot at Bannockburn, serving their Stirling and Glasgow route. By 1841 some of the local coal was being used in the Cambusbarron limeworks. The Scottish Central Railway (SCR) at first decided that Bannockburn was too close to Stirling to need a station on their main line (later part of the Caledonian), but relented, and so from 1848 Bannockburn was served somewhat indirectly by a station near Lower Greenyards.

**Bannockburn's Textile Heyday**: In 1869 William Wilson & Sons of Bannockburn employed about 550 workers spinning, dyeing and weaving wool into carpets, tweeds and tartans, while J & W Wilson's 180 workers manufactured only carpets. Two smaller firms also wove tartans and kiltings. In 1891 Bannockburn had 2000 residents; by that time there was an inn and a small hospital, while an annual cattle and horse fair was still held in June. Goodfellow & Co made lathes for brass finishing around 1900. There were then some seven horse-drawn omnibuses a day to Stirling.

**After Textiles: High School, Monument and Motorway**: The last weaving mills closed in 1924, and the ancient Beaton's Mill was unfortunately burnt down in 1950. During the 20th century Bannockburn grew steadily towards St Ninians, and with the coming of motor buses it is not surprising that the inconveniently sited railway station had been closed by 1953. When the equestrian statue of Robert Bruce was set up in 1964 within the land protected by the National Trust for Scotland as a monument to the great battle, it was close to the Borestone – traditional display site of his Royal standard – but the historic Dryfield of Balquhidderock where the fight probably took place became the playing field of Bannockburn High School. This was built at Hillpark around the time of the population peak of 1971 (some 6000 people). Bannockburn House was vacated about 1960; from about 1973 it adjoined the new M9 motorway interchange at Snabhead south of Bannockburn. This inhibited those seeking gracious living, particularly after the M80 motorway was added a few years later, making the junction vastly complex, so although kept in reasonable condition the House remains unused in its wooded policies.

**Motorway Interchange draws Development**: In 1991 Bannockburn, with 5800 people, was in effect a disadvantaged part of Stirling, and still had merely a village level of facilities. About that time new estates were being erected and an eastern bypass was constructed. The possible reopening of a railway station was considered by Central Regional Council in 1992, but put on hold by the destruction of the council and the Byzantine muddle of rail privatisation created in the last throes of Tory government. Meantime by 1995 much work had been done to create the 24 ha Broadleys Industrial Park near the M9/M80 junction. Although targeted at heavy engineering and distribution, it initially attracted the headquarters of a large group of veterinary practices; meantime in 1994 plans had been lodged by McArthur Glen of the USA and BAA for a discount shopping centre nearby. A 37-roomed *Travelodge* has been built at Snabhead.

## BARASSIE — Map 1, C2

***Ayrshire village / suburb of Troon**, pop. 3000* — OS 70: NS 3233

In 1812 the Duke of Portland's Kilmarnock & Troon Railway (K&T) was opened as a horse-drawn plateway of four-foot gauge. In 1839–40 the Glasgow, Paisley, Kilmarnock & Ayr Railway was opened, crossing the K&T near the coast at Barassie farm, 2 km to the north of Troon. In 1846 the old line was regauged to the standard and realigned so that for a short distance the two companies shared the metals, and a station was opened there. OS maps imply that only one terrace of houses facing the sea was in existence nearby when the Barassie Golf Club's 18-hole course north of the station was founded in 1887.

**Barassie Works and Village**: In 1901 railway carriage and wagon works were established at Barassie by the Glasgow & South Western Railway on a 9 ha site south of the station, between the two railways. After railway grouping in 1923, the new LMS moved carriage repairs from Barassie to St Rollox in 1927–29 in exchange for wagon repairs, and the Barassie works were soon also building steel-bodied wagons. Meanwhile a village grew between the railway and the beach. During the 1939–45 war a short runway was built on the adjacent golf course so that Spitfire fighters repaired at the wagon works could speedily return to the fray. By 1951 Barassie had about 1250 people; more housing was built beside the sea by 1972, and there was a garage, primary school and the small Tower Hotel on Beach Road. With falling rail freight, work on wagons was moved back again to Springburn by BR and the Barassie works was closed in 1972. However, Troon needed more houses, so development continued inland to the A78 road at Muirhead, and by 1981 Barassie had about 3000 residents. In the 1990s the Kilmarnock (Barassie) Golf Club as it was then called, added a 9-hole course. By 1998 the site of the wagon works had been built over by another housing estate, and Barassie was becoming just a part of greater Troon.

## BARGEDDIE, Cuilhill & Drumpark — Map 15, E5

***Lanarkshire urban area**, pop. 2300* — OS 64: NS 7064

In 1596 when Pont mapped the area north of the North Calder Water 6 km west of Airdrie, *'Coolhill'* (indicating coal pits) was named near *'O Balgedie'*. The coal-carrying Monkland Canal, dug between 1772 and 1778, passed through Cuilhill, where coal pits were open when a canal basin was built in 1843 at the north terminus of the tiny Drumpellier Railway, which brought more coal from collieries to the south. The mines were later served by a Caledonian Railway (CR) branch line opened in 1865–66 without a station; Bargeddie station, sited at Cuilhill, stood on a line opened in 1861 linking Coatbridge and Glasgow, later part of the North British (NB). In the 1890s there was an inn near the collieries and a post office near Cuilhill.

**Council Housing and Decline**: The large Drumpark brickworks, opened in the late 19th century, stimulated Bargeddie village – later essentially a Lanarkshire County Council housing estate – to develop between the railways. Bargeddie station was renamed Drumpark by the NB's successor the LNER. By 1951 some 3350 people lived in Bargeddie, with basic facilities and also three doctors. The collieries had closed by 1955 and Drumpark station was shut by Beeching about 1965; the brickworks closed in 1977 but stood derelict for 11 years. Despite the excellent new road links at the junction of the A8/M8 and M73 just to the west, the population shrank steadily, by 1991 being only 2300 – very disadvantaged, for under 2% had higher qualifications; but many had craft jobs in factories, mining and building work. In 1993 diesel passenger trains between Whifflet and Glasgow Central were introduced to the freight-only former CR line, with a new station at Bargeddie. A wind storm which hit a new cinema complex being built at Bargeddie late in 1996 claimed two roofing workers' lives.

## BARGRENNAN & Glentrool

**Map 1, C4**

***Galloway hamlets,*** *pop. 300*

OS 76/77: NX 3576

To the east of the upper River Cree in Galloway are chambered cairns, beyond which rise the rocky hills of The Merrick, where in 1307 at the start of Bruce's campaign to free Scotland from English aggression he successfully ambushed an English force. This skirmish took place beside Loch Trool, source of the Water of Trool, which joins the larger Water of Minnoch. By about 1610 when Timothy Pont mapped Galloway, the River Cree had already been bridged at Brigton, in a well settled area above its confluence with the Water of Minnoch and the now fully silted Loch of Cree. Although a school was established at *'Grennan'* in 1631, Roy's map made about 1754 showed less settlement, but a track traversed the area from Newton Stewart to the Nick o'the Balloch and Ayr. A post office was opened in 1773 at the High Bridge of Cree which had been built at Bargrennan, where the turnpike road to Girvan left the older road, the prefix Bar- evidently referring to a tollbar.

**Afforestation and Glentrool Village**: By 1953 Glentrool had become a National Forest Park, and afforestation was fast expanding in the area; the little *House o' Hill Hotel* was open, and Bargrennan's 150 or so people enjoyed basic facilities. By 1963 the tiny Forestry Commission village of Glentrool had been built 2 km north of Bargrennan, from which the post office was moved to Glentrool about 1968; in 1971 Glentrool contained only 120 people. The extent of afforestation roughly doubled in the 1970s, and by 1981 under 300 people lived in the whole area. By 1985 a visitor centre was open at the park entrance, and caravan sites were available between Glentrool and Bargrennan, and above Loch Trool, 5 km east of Glentrool village. In 1986 the hotel and a rundown village hall were still to be seen at remote Bargrennan, which was by then traversed by the Southern Upland Way. Glentrool primary school was saved from closure in 1997, but its post office has closed since 1998.

## BARR

**Map 1, C3**

***Ayrshire village,*** *pop. 300*

OS 76: NX 2794

About 10 km east of Girvan various tributaries join the River Stinchar, which forms a deep valley through an area of somewhat limited farming value. Pont's map as engraved by Blaeu showed that by around 1600, although there was a remarkable dearth of castles, the area was well settled, with mills on both sides of the unbridged river near Easter and Wester *'Barn'* – the modern Milton. In the 1750s a so-called road led up the valley from Ballantrae, repeatedly crossing the river past the ancient Kirkdominae at Kirkland, to terminate at Barr Kirk, 3 km farther east. In later years road communications were improved, though Barr remained a farming community accessible only by winding lanes. Conditions in the area favour angling, and although in 1951 Barr had a population of about 375, its basic facilities included two small hotels. By 1963 Changue Forest east of Barr had been planted and a small quarry was open 3 km to the north, but this later closed. The parish population slowly shrank to 317 by 1991, but the remoteness of Barr's situation was somewhat relieved by the founding of a medical group practice in the compact village, which had little but angling and walking to draw tourists, and seemed never to make the headlines. Afforestation of the hills to the east continued through the last decades of the century; the post office and the *King's Arms Hotel* are still open.

## BARRHEAD & Arthurlie

**Map 15, B6**

***Renfrewshire town,*** *pop. 17,250*

OS 64: NS 5058

When Timothy Pont surveyed Renfrewshire about 1600, the Levern Water had been bridged in Neilston parish, about 1 km below the emparked house of Arthurlie. On either side of the bridge stood towers marked *'Res'*, perhaps the residences of local gentry enjoying the slopes of the Fereneze Hills. By 1755 the Roy map showed *'Bridgebarr'*, an untidy scatter of buildings around the convergence of four roads on the Levern bridge; Farhouse Mill already existed. A linen bleachfield was built at Arthurlie between 1746 and 1760.

**King Cotton brings Five Pubs for each School and Mill**: Dovecotehall, a large mill of 2464 spindles which opened in 1780, was the first of many local cotton mills; the West Arthurlie bleachworks dated from much the same time. The Fereneze printworks was in action by 1782 and Fereneze cotton mill by 1803. Meantime the Gateside mill was built in 1786, and Cross Arthurlie cotton mill dated from 1791. Heron in 1799 referred to Barrhead as a *"village of upward of four hundred inhabitants"*. A new Fereneze mill was built in 1803, and Barrhead – which was served from 1825 with a penny post from Glasgow – was well on the way to becoming a town, having six schools and no fewer than thirty public houses. In their 1832 letter to Cobbett the local people referred to Barrhead as a *"village"* with a *"burgher (secession) church"*. By the 1830s the six mills in the parish (including Neilston – *q.v.*) employed nearly 1400 people. From the 1840s reservoirs between Barrhead and Newton Mearns supplied the Gorbals with piped water by gravity.

**The Railways and Stoneware Industry**: The Glasgow, Barrhead & Neilston Direct Railway, a Caledonian subsidiary, was opened to Barrhead from the city in 1848; it was extended to Crofthead in 1855. Stoneware manufacture began at the *'Tubal'* works in Barrhead about 1852 and by 1858 a millwright's factory had its own water-powered foundry. About then Barrhead became a police burgh, and 1868 saw the provision of a gasworks. The accessibility of Barrhead was much enhanced in 1873 when the railway was extended to Kilmarnock, becoming part of a joint main line with the Glasgow & South Western Railway (G&SWR), a shorter route for Dumfries and Carlisle than the original line via Dalry.

**Baths before Football**: From 1885 the town was served by the Paisley District Tramways Company, relying on horses. By 1891 the population was 8215. A local newspaper, the *Barrhead News* was first published in 1894, when Murray noted Barrhead as *"a busy manufacturing town"*; by then it had not just pubs but an inn. From 1895 the stoneware factory became widely known for making Shanks' sanitary stoneware and related fittings, and about 1905 Smith & Saunders were producing cast-iron baths and shower units. Meantime in 1901 local football club Arthurlie, who played at Dunterlie Park, joined the Scottish Football League; they resigned in 1929.

**More Railways and Electric Trams**: In 1902 the G&SWR opened a direct line to Paisley, passing through a new station named Barrhead Central, enabling a circular service to Glasgow St Enoch; this lasted only until 1907, because the tramways responded in 1904 with electrification. An electric power station was opened about 1908. The Fereneze golf club and course date from 1904, but a flying school founded in 1911 soon failed. In the Edwardian period John Cochrane had an ironfoundry and engineering works in Barrhead, and a quarry was open in the area from at least 1920. For about 50 years Barrhead was connected into the vast Glasgow tramway system; in the 1930s blue trams ran on reserved track from Spiersbridge to Barrhead and onwards via Paisley to terminate at the Renfrew Ferry, but the local section of the tramways was abandoned in 1957. By 1951 over 13,000 people lived in Barrhead; a further increase of 5000 people took place between then and 1971 with the building of the huge Auchenback estate south-east of the town.

**Industries Various**: By 1971 the huge Shanks plant had been acquired by the Staffordshire based Armitage group. Although population growth ceased, by 1977 the country house style *Dalmeny Park Hotel* was in business with 20 rooms. Meantime by 1976 Gateside mill had become a waterproofing works, and by 1979 the Barrhead Kid Company was manufacturing soft leather, while Crossmill was producing petfoods under Spillers. The railway station was rebuilt in 1978, and Barrhead had average urban facilities in 1980. Up to 1984 Spillers sent some of its output by rail via Paisley, and subsequently via Deanside. In 1992 six trainloads of petfood went southwards from there each week to Wisbech, the wagons returning with empty cans for filling. St Luke's High School was built south of the town around 1980.

**Shanks go Down the Plughole**: By 1991 the population had settled at around 17,250. In 1989 competition from cheap Italian taps led to the closure of the engineering and warehousing sides of Armitage Shanks, with the loss of 280 jobs; the ceramic side with 360 workers remained until depressed 1992, when the firm abandoned Barrhead and withdrew to England. A co-operative of former Shanks workers who established a new company in 1992 were denied the use of the Shanks name and factory, opening at Hillington instead. Meantime the Kid Company was still at work, as was the IMI works – formerly Yorkshire Imperial Metals – making copper tubes, though 90 jobs were lost there in 1992.

**Barrhead Whiskies fill the Shelves**: The glaziers G & J Rae toughened glass for other firms in 1993. Burn Stewart was acquired by its management in 1988 and went public in 1991, becoming Scotland's smallest quoted whisky company; they bought the Ledaig distillery at Tobermory in 1993. In 1994 it had Barrhead headquarters and a blending and bottling plant at East Kilbride; half its revenue came from supplying supermarkets with own-label whiskies, while its own *'Scottish Leader'* blend sold 250,000 cases a year. Neary Construction do cable work for railways and others. In 1994 the Barrhead Sports Centre also presented touring plays, including some by the Royal Shakespeare Company. In 1996 Barrhead which had continued to develop north-westwards joined Eastwood in the small new gerrymandered unitary authority of East Renfrewshire. In 1997 both Barrhead and St Luke's High Schools had some 600 pupils. The *Dalmeny Park Hotel* has 20 rooms.

## BARRHILL

**Map 1, C3**

***Ayrshire village,*** *pop. 300* — OS 76: NX 2382

Pont's map of south Carrick, made around 1600, showed many farm settlements in the valley of the River Duisk some 15 km east of Ballantrae, but Barrhill was not named there, nor on Roy's survey of about 1754, when Kildonnan Kirk stood beside the river in a trackless area. However, at some time a waulk mill was built 2 km upstream, and the Mill Loch to the north proves the existence of another mill 1 km downstream. Eventually a road linked Girvan with Newton Stewart, and a village developed, with a post office by 1900. From 1877 a station on the winding, hilly Girvan & Portpatrick Junction Railway was open 1 km from Barrhill village. By 1951 Barrhill was served by facilities typical of a small village, plus a secondary school and a cattle dealer. The population was some 550.

**Forestry dominates the Landscape**: Although by 1963 the Kildonan convent stood nearby, rural depopulation had cut the number of residents to 400 by 1971, and by 1976 the secondary classes had been moved elsewhere. Barrhill station kept its passenger services, but was closed to freight by Beeching in 1965, just as major afforestation projects were planned in the surrounding area. These have now utterly changed its character, and provide a number of jobs. In 1981 under 350 people remained in the increasingly bosky area, where by 1986 the new *Glen Tachur Hotel* had opened 2 km to the north-west, adjoined by a caravan site. But Barrhill itself was a workaday place with little modern housing and the facilities of a small village; although its bowling green was well kept, in 1986 a derelict church – since demolished – dominated the village centre. The railway station, inn and hotel were still in business in 1996; the post office has since closed.

## BARVAS *(Barabhas)*

**Map 11, C1**

***Township, Lewis,*** *pop. 300* — OS 8: NB 3549

Barvas on the bleak north-western coast of Lewis was described as a *"village"* by Martin around 1700, when it had a parish church. The almost straight glen which leads across the moors to Stornoway formed the simplest route for a road, built in the mid 19th century to join the north-west coast with the island capital. By 1951 crofting Barvas – which lines the main north coast road – had a post office, primary school and telephone exchange, serving some 625 people. Although 45% of the population had gone by 1981, by then two garages were available, and a gallery was open by 1999.

## BATHGATE & Boghall

**Map 16, C3**

***W. Lothian town,*** *pop: 14,000* — OS 65: NS 9768

The name Bathgate was first recorded in 1153 as Batket, meaning *'boar wood'* in Cumbric. In 1316 its castle was gifted by King Robert Bruce to Walter the High Steward, who as Chambers later noted had *"one of his principal residences"* there; but Bathgate was not important enough to be shown by Mercator (1595), or Pont (as engraved by Hondius in 1612), although by then it was served by the Edinburgh–Bathgate–Airdrie–Glasgow road. Bathgate stands at the rather high altitude of 150 metres, not ideal for grain growing, but had a long-established mill by 1663 when it was chartered as a burgh of barony.

**Industry and Balbardie House**: By about 1736 G & J Shaws had built a brewery and maltings, and handloom weaving also developed; the Steelyard was the location where locally woven cloth was weighed. Bathgate appeared on Roy's map of the 1750s as a substantial linear settlement with five radial roads or tracks; the Couston Water was bridged. Glenmavis distillery *(see also Torphichen)* was in production east of Balbardie by 1783. Balbardie House was designed by Robert Adam and built just north of the town for Alex Marjoribanks in 1792–93. In 1797 Bathgate was a major fair stance with seven days scheduled in the year, but for regular employment the 2500 people of the parish apparently relied on the brewery, distillery and a coal mine. Heron in 1799 noted Bathgate as a *"village"* of about 1400 inhabitants, rich in coal, lime and ironstone; but a silver vein (perhaps actually at Torphichen, *q.v.*) was *"too inconsiderable to defray the expense of working"*. A post office was open by 1799.

**Two Ways to Oblivion: Chloroform and Drink**: Bathgate was the birthplace in 1811 of Sir James Young Simpson, noted gynaecologist and discoverer of the use of chloroform. Bathgate Academy was established about 1815 through a local benefactor. In 1824 a gasworks was started and by 1825 a second brewery was in use. In 1826 Bathgate was *"a large and thriving village"* (Chambers).

**Railways save the Day**: Bathgate has a subsequent history of booms and slumps. By 1847 when the Edinburgh & Bathgate Railway arrived in the town from a junction at Ratho the handloom weavers were working for near-starvation wages, but the railway brought access to other work, and by 1851 Bathgate had a population of over 3300. In 1855 a single line was opened to Bathgate by the Monkland Railways from a junction at Blackstone near Avonbridge via Westfield. In 1861–62 the Bathgate & Coatbridge Railway completed a single line to Airdrie, so connecting to Glasgow, and another to Morningside (near Newmains) in 1864. Under the North British Railway, Bathgate was served from 1871 by through trains between Edinburgh and Glasgow.

**The World's first Oil Refinery**: In 1850–51 the Bathgate Chemical Company erected the world's first mineral oil refinery, at Inchcross about 2 km south-west of Bathgate. The works, promoted by Binney, Meldrum and James *'Paraffin'* Young, a Glasgow-born chemist with experience under Tennant, Knox & Co, and in Manchester and London, used a process that had been developed by Young to distil paraffin from bituminous Cannel coal, raised from a pit 1 km to the west at Boghead. In the 1860s – as Bremner fully described – the process he developed also required sulphuric acid and caustic soda. The rail-connected works then had 200 retorts producing paraffin lamp oil, lubricating oil, naptha, and solid paraffin wax for candles; coke and gas for lighting were by-products. Beside the works, which at its peak employed 700 men, grew a small settlement named Durhamtoun. The shale oil works closed in 1884, but the Bathgate sulphuric acid works continued. Smaller pits and oil works nearby, such as those at Torbane and Starlaw, used bituminous shales instead of coal.

**Coal, Steel, Whisky and News**: In the decade to 1861 the population of Bathgate had reached 10,000, and that of West Lothian as a whole rose by 28%. Coal pits, steel foundries and rolling mills were developed on the Balbardie estate, and in 1872 the local newspaper, the *Lothian Courier* was founded. Though the breweries were declining and disappearing, in 1855 a version of the Coffey still was installed at Glenmavis, to make malt whisky, an unusual product for this process. In 1886 the water-powered distillery employed 16 workers, producing some 365,000 litres of malt whisky annually; 65 cattle were fed on the draff and spent wash. The Bathgate golf club and course originated in 1892, and by 1894 Bathgate had grown into the principal service centre in West Lothian. By 1895 the confusingly titled Easton Colliery had been sunk west of Bathgate; mines were open north and south of the town, and they also burrowed beneath its streets and buildings, causing costly subsidence problems.

**From Motor Works to Misery**: In 1901 T Blackwood-Murray and N O Fulton, formerly of the car makers Arrol-Johnston which started in Camlachie, founded their Albion Motor Company, which made vans in Bathgate until 1904. Then having become too successful, the company moved to larger premises at Scotstoun *(see Whiteinch)*. Oil shale working peaked around 1913, but the distillery experienced terminal decline in 1910. Bathgate FC – which played in the Scottish League from 1921 – was ruined by the miners' strike and had to resign in 1929, and in 1930 passenger services ceased on the Newmains line. The downward path of Balbardie House in the 20th century included use as a miners' hostel; it was sadly demolished in 1955, except for the west wing.

**The Speedy Collapse of Mining**: The Whiteside electrical engineering works was opened by Plessey in 1947, and soon enlarged. Coal mining was at its maximum about 1951 when there were 12,000 miners in the West Lothian area; but both the local extractive activities swiftly declined: the Bathgate sulphuric acid works closed in 1956, shale mining ended in 1962, and coal mining at Bathgate ceased around the same period. Railway passenger services to Edinburgh and Glasgow ended in 1956; the large engine shed which served local colliery lines was the last in Scotland to operate steam locomotives in the mid 1960s.

**The Truck and Tractor Plant**: As part of a well-meant but ultimately flawed regional policy, whereby areas already too dependent on decaying industry were fed with yet more marginal and subsidised branch plants, the huge British Motor Corporation (BMC) truck and tractor plant was built in the early 1960s, following heavy government pressure and cash aid. Rail connections were laid in, and by 1964 small lorries were being sent by rail to English destinations. BMC made the GF range of 3.5 to 6.5 tonne commercial vehicles; the by then struggling firm was merged with its rival Leyland in 1968 and the name BMC disappeared from new vehicles in 1970; but the BMC types were still produced. The Bathgate factory also produced the *'Redline'* range from 1972, ranging upwards from Terriers at 6.5 tonnes through Boxers to Mastiffs of up to 28-tonne capacity. Many tractors were also made, and by the mid 1970s over 5000 people worked at the plant.

**Enter Boghall, exit Whiteside**: To house the workers, by 1963 a new settlement had been created at Boghall, east of Bathgate, with basic facilities including two primary schools, four shops and a garage – but no pub. But by 1971 when Boghall held over 2500 people the branch railways had been lifted, and soon only the freight connection to Ratho was maintained. By that time the town's three cinemas had shrunk to one, the 1067-seat *Regal* which in 1958 had also hosted variety performances. The Whiteside Works still produced telegraph condensers about 1970, and made capacitors under Plessey in 1977, but was closed in 1981. The Birniehill abattoir was in use by 1980 at Whitburn Road; in 1994 it was an abattoir and food processing plant, operated by ABP Ltd.

**The Chips are Down**: The new West Lothian District Council, formed in 1974–75, based itself at the Burgh Chambers, but Livingston New Town was eroding Bathgate's service role

*Motorola's mobile phone factory at Bathgate. Its closure was announced in April 2001 – another hard blow for the town. (AL)*

and damaging its prospects for new industry. At its peak the 110,000m² Leyland plant employed some 6500 workers; the later types of vehicles made there bore non-doggy names, and many used Cummins engines from Shotts. But it was claimed to be too far from markets and from the motor parts suppliers in the Midlands to be really profitable, a 3% to 4% cost penalty being incurred on each vehicle. After years of decline, total closure came in 1986, when the last 900 workers making tractors lost their jobs. Bathgate became for a time the UK's tenth most disadvantaged town, but a hiatus in the local output of potato crisps was soon restored by Forth Valley Foods, oddly under the Highlander brand name. In 1991 they were owned by the amazingly named Unichips International of Milan, and still making varied crisps and snacks.

**After Tractors – back to the Railway**: When the Leyland closure became certain, *'BASE'* (Bathgate Area Support for Enterprise) was set up and took various initiatives to restore the local economy, including the reopening of the rail passenger service in 1986, providing better access, especially to job opportunities in central Edinburgh. The service was a great success and was increased. As part of the initiative a new M8 motorway junction for Bathgate was provided about 1991. Most new cars for Scotland were still delivered from Bathgate after arriving by rail from Willesden; this service continued as a daily trainload in 1992, but originating from Birmingham, and in 1994 came a 3-year contract to move cars by rail from Luton.

**Reptile Upturn, and Chips with Everything**: In 1988 the oldest known fossil reptile ever found (340 million years) was spotted in the East Kirkton limestone quarry. In 1989 North British Steel still made steel castings at Balbardie. Ten years of work had changed a large adjacent derelict site into a golf course, leisure complex and indoor bowling centre. A scheme to build a monstrous *'out of town'* shopping centre on the motor works site was rejected, so the town centre was improved as a pedestrian precinct; by 1996 a Tesco store was open. The Regal Cinema had somehow survived, and by 1990 the jobless rate was under 10%. In 1990 a 36ha site at Easter Inch Farm was chosen by Motorola for a new 2000-worker plant to make mobile telephones. In 1991 the TI'KO Computer Corporation was expanding its PC sales base in Bathgate. In 1992 Glacier Vandervell opened a new automotive component and bearing factory at Whitehill, aiming to create 500 jobs; they expanded in 1994.

**Earthworks and Industrial History**: In 1991 Bathgate became the base of the business development arm of West Lothian Enterprise, the local LEC. Also in 1994 West Lothian College of Bathgate had over 7000 students and was planning a new campus at Livingston. A bing was removed in 1991–92 and used to infill Little Boghead for housing; its site was afforested but the old Boghall coal area is now being strip-mined for clay. In 1993 a new landmark called Sawtooth Ramps, designed by Patricia Leighton as seven flat-topped mounds each 11m tall and 41m wide, echoing the seven red shale bings of West Calder, was constructed on part of the Motorola site beside the M8. In 1996 West Lothian District became a new unitary authority, but decided to base itself in Livingston, to Bathgate's disadvantage. By 1998 old cottages had been restored to create the Bennie Museum of local history – much needed, for by then the motor works site had been cleared. Motorola had built up to a workforce of 3000 when in April 2001 they announced the closure of the whole plant, due to their falling sales of mobile phones. But a good range of medium-sized firms employed 50–300 each, and Bathgate remained the centre of the expanding Macdonald Hotels chain. The distinctive *Cairn Hotel* offers 61 rooms.

## BAYHEAD *(Ceann a'Bhaigh)*, Paible & Vallay — Map 7, A2

***Small N. Uist village,*** *pop. 200* — OS 18: NF 7468

The low-lying west coast of North Uist was well settled by the 16th century, but its crofting people left little mark on history. Vallay House on the Isle of Vallay, a tidal island off the north coast some 10km to the north of Bayhead, was built about 1900 for the Dunfermline linen magnate Erskine Beveridge. Bayhead still lacked a village centre when at about the same time the Paible junior secondary school was built there. In the 1950s it had about 100 pupils, and while Bayhead had only about 225 residents, there was also a post office and telephone exchange; crofting and lobster fishing were the economic mainstays. Around 1970 the HIDB backed local tulip production, but the trials were soon abandoned. In 1988 Paible school lost its secondary classes to Lionacleit. Vallay House, disused from the 1950s, stood derelict in 1997.

## BEARSDEN, Killermont & New Kilpatrick — Map 15, C4

***Suburb of Glasgow,*** *pop. 27,800* — OS 64: NS 5472

The Antonine Wall built by the Romans in the mid second century followed irregular hills about 5km north of the lower River Clyde, and was paralleled by a road. A small fort at the place later called Bearsden about 9km north-west of modern Glasgow had turf ramparts, but its stone granaries and bath-house showed the intention of permanence. A section of the road survived to bear the modern name Roman Road. The area was well settled by about 1600, but Bearsden was not named on Pont's map. The *'New Kirk of Kilpatrick'* was built where the road to Drymen crossed the line of the wall near the site of the fort, as shown on Roy's map made about 1754.

**Golf and Railway fuel Development**: The mansionhouse of Killermont was built on the banks of the Kelvin 2 km south-east of the kirk and gave its name to the early Glasgow golf club founded there in 1787. But the village grew round the kirk. In 1863 the Edinburgh & Glasgow Railway opened its Milngavie branch with trains to Glasgow from its Bearsden station just south of the fort site. Being upwind of the city and on pleasant slopes falling south-eastwards to the River Kelvin, Bearsden had distinct amenity advantages as a suburb. Villas were soon built, without regard to archaeology: some, since pulled down, overlay the footings of substantial Roman buildings. To the north the Shaw (or Schaw) Home had been built by 1895. Between 1891 and 1908 two more golf courses were founded, the 9-hole Bearsden and the 18-hole Douglas Park (served by 1903 by a second station, at Hillfoot only 1 km to the east). By 1901 2700 people lived in Bearsden.

**Rapid Suburbanisation**: In 1924 Glasgow's electric trams were extended across 2 km of open countryside from Maryhill to Bearsden, and about 1931 the population passed 5500; a Catholic college was established about that time. Both speculative and individual private estates were rapidly developed in the 1930s, and also Canniesburn Hospital, which opened in 1934. By 1951 there was a population of over 12,000, and the facilities of an average town – but for the lack of a local newspaper of its own. By 1953 the Windyhill golf course was open. The Chesters offered residential management courses from the 1950s, and Bearsden became a late Parliamentary Burgh in 1958. Trams ceased to run to Bearsden and Milngavie in 1956, but the train service was electrified in 1961, and rapid private development continued at some 300 new houses a year, doubling the size of the town in 20 years and infilling the rural gap towards Maryhill and Glasgow. In 1972 Bearsden had four golf courses for 25,000 people and by far the lowest proportion of council housing of any Scottish burgh, at 4%; however, the small *'scheme'* was still being extended, and the council soon provided a major swimming pool and sports complex.

*The Schaw Home, Bearsden's grandest building, built in 1895 as a convalescent home for patients from the Glasgow Royal Infirmary, to designs by Baird and Thomson. It is now the Lynedoch Nursing Home, a private concern.* *(JRH)*

**Bearsden in Maturity**: In 1975 Bearsden became the HQ of a new District including Milngavie. When the High School of Glasgow moved to Partick in 1976, Drewsteignton School of Bearsden became its junior school. The Notre Dame RC teacher training college was moved from Glasgow to new buildings beside the existing RC college in the 1970s; it was renamed St Andrews College in 1981, and later became part of Glasgow University. About then the Schaw Home became a hospital. In 1991 the population was about 27,800, of affluent young well-educated suburban character; but only 8% of the workforce used the electric trains to get to work. The green belt, golf courses, and a primary substation to the west inhibited further growth – except to the north-west, where housebuilding continued into the 1990s. In 1996 Bearsden lost out when the district was joined with Strathkelvin in a new unitary authority for East Dunbartonshire. By then Bearsden Academy had 1278 pupils and Boclair Academy 1114. The Chesters has recently become *'Duns Scotus College'*, a Catholic seminary. The *Premier Lodge* is brand-new.

## BEATTOCK

**Map 2, B3**

***Dumfriesshire village,*** *pop. 500* — OS 78: NT 0802

Beattock lies on the Evan Water, a main headwater of the River Annan. It was for long a strategic location, as shown by the number of hill forts and Roman camps in the vicinity. The Romans built a road through the area for marching from Solway to Clyde, seemingly regardless of steep slopes; their Milton fort dates from the first century. Mottes were raised a thousand years later, but the 13th century Auchen Castle fell into ruin, though the 16th century Lochhouse Tower survived. Beattock which stands in the vast parish of Kirpatrick Juxta was not shown on Pont's maps of around 1600. The Roman line was apparently still a main road, evident on Roy's map made about 1754, when the Moffat to Dumfries road already crossed the Evan Water by a bridge 3 km south of Moffat, and 1 km west of the Roman ford at the foot of the once notorious *'Beattock Bank'*. This remained very adverse to northbound stage coaches even after Thomas Telford had overseen the remaking of much of the Glasgow–Carlisle road early in the 19th century. The new road crossed the Evan at the existing bridge point, beside which Telford designed a *'change house'*, later known as the *Old Brig Inn*. Auchen Castle gave its name to a 19th century mansion 1.5 km farther north.

**Living on the Summit**: In 1847 the Caledonian Railway opened its main line between Carlisle and a temporary terminus at Beattock, which was intended to serve Moffat and was regarded as a *'first class'* station, its building designed by Andrew Heiton of Perth. In 1848 the line was completed throughout to give access to both Glasgow and Edinburgh via Carstairs. Beattock Bank was a formidable obstacle to early steam trains, hence a locomotive depot was established to provide the helper locomotives known as *'bankers'*; these left the trains at Beattock summit signalbox 16 km to the north, where loop lines, crossovers, and a small railway community were established, its primary school actually called Summit.

**Beattock as a Junction**: Following the building of a large hydropathic hotel at Moffat, the short road journey from Beattock was felt to be excessive for its rich and hypochondriac clientele, and from 1883 a locally promoted railway linked

Moffat with the main line at Beattock, where a small village developed to house personnel from the engine shed and junction station; in 1894 the *Refreshment Rooms* appeared to serve as a hotel. A quarry was opened at Coatsgate, 3 km north-west. By 1954, the year when the branch passenger trains were withdrawn, Auchen Castle in its extensive grounds had become the more upmarket of the two local hotels, then having 3 stars, and by 1963 the *Beattock House Hotel* was also open. By 1965 Beattock had been bypassed by a new section of the A74 which was then becoming a dual carriageway.

**Railway Run-down**: The goods branch railway was abandoned as part of the Beeching cuts in 1964. The engine shed was closed with dieselisation in 1967 and the passenger station was also closed in 1972. Summit soon vanished as a settlement, and not surprisingly, Beattock itself shrank in population, to only 725 by 1981 and under 500 by 1991. A gas compressor station was built 3 km to the south. However, by 1980 Beattock had gained a major AA depot, for some years the base for a large fleet of vehicles patrolling the A74 trunk road, upgraded to a motorway in the late 1990s. With the waymarking of the Southern Upland Way an additional caravan park, riding and holiday centre had been provided. Except for continued enlargement of the Coatsgate quarry, little new development had occurred by 1997, but rail timber traffic had resumed by 1999, and in 2000 the Dumfries & Galloway Council decided to press for the reopening of a passenger station to serve Moffat and Beattock. The *Auchen Castle Hotel* has 25 rooms, and there's the smaller *Beattock House*.

## BEAULY, Beaufort, Kiltarlity & Lovat **Map 9, B4**

***Large village w. of Inverness,*** *pop. 1350* OS 26: NH 5246

Several ancient hill forts surround the head of tidewater on the meandering River Beauly in eastern Inverness-shire, an area of early Norman French connections. By the early 12th century the first Beaufort Castle had been erected, and a ferry plied to the north bank. A century later, Lovat Castle was built, also south of the river but closer to its mouth near the Ferry Brae. In 1230 John Bisset of Lovat founded a priory for Valliscaulian monks from Burgundy, who gave its site north of the river the French name Beauly, aptly meaning beautiful place.

**Vacuum after the Reformation**: About 1510 the priory changed its adherence to adopt the Cistercian order, but its red sandstone buildings were ruined as a result of the Reformation, and the site given to the Bishop of Ross in 1634. The ferry continued to ply, but scarcely any settlement seems to have remained, though the name *'Beaulie'* appeared on Blaeu's map drafted by Gordon between 1642 and 1654. Beauly was given formal status as a burgh of barony in 1704, also being known as Lovat or Fraserdale, from the owners of Beaufort Castle, and was allowed to hold several yearly fairs at its mercat cross; however, Roy's map made about 1750 showed no roads and no town, only *'Monastry'*.

**Beautiful Place Revived for Veterans, Whisky, Sawmill and Sheep**: About 1760 the Forfeited Estates Commissioners laid out a new village at Beauly, *"an extreme proper place for erecting a village"* to house demobilised soldiers. Beauly's first post office was opened in 1770, and a distillery was also established late around then, though in 1799 Heron noted only a sawmill, down to which timber was floated in great quantity. By 1807 the clearance of people from inland Ross-shire had created conditions for a sheep market at Beauly, which also became for a time an important cattle market centre, a regular event later moved 4 km north to Muir of Ord. Smeaton had estimated for a bridge at Dunballoch in 1772 but it was not until 1811–14 that the Lovat Bridge was built there under the guidance of Telford, so connecting the North with the rest of Scotland by road for the first time. However, the ferry continued to carry foot passengers until at least 1955. The sawmill was still at work in 1824, and Chambers noted *"the little town of Beauly"*, near which was *"Beaufort Castle, a splendid mansion erected upon the site of the former one, so noted as the residence of the infamous Lovat"*, a great petty tyrant and Jacobite of the '45. The distillery closed in 1830.

**On the Ross-shire Railway**: The Inverness to Dingwall section of the Inverness & Ross-shire (later Highland) Railway was opened in 1862 as a single line, crossing the river on a timber viaduct and taking a great sweeping curve round three sides of the village. Beauly was given a crossing station, where by 1875 Wordie & Co operated a rail to road cartage depot; but only two horses were needed. The Bank of Scotland built a new branch office around 1870 and Beaufort Castle was again rebuilt later in the century. The road bridge was destroyed by floods in 1892 but soon rebuilt, and by 1894 Murray noted that the *"village"* of Beauly had the *"very good"* Lovat Arms Hotel. The timber rail viaduct was replaced in steel in 1909.

**The Trains pass Beauly by**: After 1945 gravel was dug from a pit beside the Lovat bridge. In the 1950s Beauly secondary school had nearly 300 pupils and another 150 were taught at Kiltarlity, some 8 km to the south; the latter had closed by 1976. Rail passenger and goods services were withdrawn from Beauly station in 1960 and 1965 respectively, so trains continued to pass uselessly by this important and still compact service village. A timber yard was still at work in 1972. The priory ruins were open as an Ancient Monument, and five hotels were open in Beauly, including the *Lovat Arms* and *Priory*. From the opening of the Cromarty Firth bridge in 1979 the main north road traffic no longer took the circuitous route through Beauly.

**Camping Galore, but Craftpoint is Sacrificed**: Beauly's population had been steady at around 1250 for decades up to 1981. By 1985 two caravan and camping sites were open nearby, but nothing remained to be seen of Lovat Castle. In 1979 the publicly funded Highland Craftpoint was set up at Beauly to help to develop craft-based industry on a commercial scale. In 1991 the freely usable Craftpoint organisation with 2000 members was replaced by Beauly-based MIS (Made in Scotland), promoted by shareholders including Scottish Enterprise and Highlands & Islands Enterprise; but by 1995 it served only some 500 paying members.

**Tragedy for Frasers, and New Station Approved**: In 1991 Beauly had some 1350 people and Beaufort Castle was still the home of the head of Clan Fraser. The estate's Fanellan Spring was tapped in 1992 by a new water bottling plant, its 120 ha catchment free of farming. But Lovat Mineral Water, hit by excessive competition and recession, was a failure, and combined in 1994 with the tragic deaths of their two sons compelled the Frasers of Lovat to sell off their entire 10,500 ha estate in 1995. Beaufort Castle was bought by Ann Gloag, the Perth *'Stagecoach'* co-entrepreneur with her brother Brian Souter. The reopening of an unmanned station, planned in 1999, was at first stymied when EU funding was refused, but was approved in 2001. The hotels include the *Lovat Arms*, *Priory*, and *Caledonian*. At Kiltarlity is *Brockies Lodge*.

## BEITH & Barrmill — Map 1, C1

***Small Ayrshire town,** pop. 6350* — OS 63: NS 3453

Beith lies in a hollow on a hillside site overlooking Kilbirnie Loch in the Cunninghame district of Ayrshire. It had a medieval motte, and a tower named Hill of Beith was shown on Pont's survey of about 1600. This apparently never gave rise to a burgh, nor was it mentioned by early travellers; though a parish school was founded in 1617, it was ineffective as late as 1696. Beith market existed by 1707, from which date it is known to have traded in woollen cloth, and linen was sold there from 1730. A post office was open by 1715. A linen bleachfield was built between 1746 and 1760; by then quite substantial development had taken place. Beith appeared on the Roy map of the 1750s as a rather spidery medium-sized settlement where five roads met, all still important; the Kilwinning road – the 20th century A737 – was built later to avoid the hills on the more northerly road via Longbar.

**Textiles, Candles, Whisky and Stone**: By 1791 there was a school, and five lint mills and 63 thread-makers, including cotton workers. Between 1788 and 1793 the Paisley Union Banking Company established a branch in Beith, which was a post town by 1797; there was also an annual fair. Two years later, Heron found over 1700 people, *"variously employed in two candle-works, and three distilleries, besides branches of the thread, silk, gauze and muslin manufactures"*; hard freestone was quarried, probably at Border some 2 km south-east of the town. By 1810 there were over 200 weavers, and Beith had grown to some 2000 people; at one time it had a gasworks, but it seems that the distilleries had all gone by 1823.

**Railways and Furniture**: The Glasgow Paisley Kilmarnock & Ayr Railway – which opened through the valley below Beith in 1840 – sited its station inconveniently, about 1.5 km north-west of the village. In 1858 the Pollock brothers built a cabinet works beside the line at the Bark Mill, Kilbirnie Loch; this was sold to Robert Balfour from Glasgow in 1870 when the Pollocks, trading as Beithcraft, opened their new Victoria Cabinet Works in the town. In 1872 Balfour too moved up into the town, and when the Pollocks split up in 1883, Matthew founded Beith's third furniture factory, the Caledonian Works; at one time there were six, making the town Scotland's leading centre in this field. Barrmill, a large hamlet with a long-lasting inn 3 km south-east of Beith, still made linen thread in the mid 19th century. A branch line jointly owned by the Caledonian and Glasgow & South Western Railways was opened in 1873 from Lugton via a station at Barrmill, to a more handily placed terminus named Beith Town; a siding connected this line with Border quarry.

**Education and Football**: In 1891 the population was 4795. Spier's School, an endowed secondary, was opened near the town in 1888, and an Academy provided public secondary education by 1894. The furniture factories were then regarded as *"large"* by Murray; Beith's annual horse fairs were noted and also two hotels, the *Saracen's Head* and *Star*. By the 1890s there was a printfield where the Paisley road crossed the Roebank Burn, and from 1896 there was a golf club, its course on the hills north-east of the town.

**A dull and dirty Industrial Town**: Beith FC survived only three seasons in the Scottish League (1923–26). Bruce Lockhart commented sadly that Beith in the 1930s had *"little to commend it for either beauty or interest"*, and there was no written history of the place. It had a series of chimney stacks belching black smoke from its various works, including rope making and tanning. Beith was bypassed by road to the east in the 1930s, and its original station was an early casualty of rail rationalisation. By 1953 only Beith Town station remained open for passengers. Meantime Border quarry had closed. In the 1950s when the population was about 5370 three furniture factories still worked, but Beith was on the margin between town and village. Some 3 km south of the town at Whitespot was a naval depot *(see Lugton)*.

**Cabinets Close; enter Computers and Whisky**: The branch railway was closed to passengers by Beeching in 1962 and to freight in 1964. Although Barrmill still held 250 people in 1971 its limekilns ceased production in 1972. Despite much development on the south side of the town, a range of facilities closed. Beith's six cabinet works had gradually vanished; one was partly converted to a foundry. The last, Beithcraft, had fitted hotels and ships; in 1976 A H McIntosh *(see Pathhead, Fife)* bought the firm, but orders were few, and its workforce was steadily cut from 120 to only 34 before closure in 1982. However, in 1981 FTS set up a computer factory, and by 1989 a 1300-metre-long strip of double-banked whisky bonds for the Dumbarton distilleries was the most striking new addition on the low ground between the town and Kilbirnie Loch. Although by 1985 practically all land within the bypass had been developed, in 1991 the population was still about 6350. Surprisingly little news has since come out of Beith!

## BELLANOCH & Achnamara — Map 4, C3

***Kintyre hamlets,** pop. under 100* — OS 55: NR 8092

*The 5-span cast-iron Islandadd Bridge, Bellanoch, designed by John Gardner and completed in 1851. This bridge replaced a ferry crossing of the R. Add* *(RCAHMS / JRH)*

Roy's map of about 1750 showed a track which meandered through North Knapdale parish, north-west from Loch Gilp to Bellanoch at the head of Loch Crinan, where it turned south-west to fork down both sides of Loch Sween. Later the tracks became roads, and a new road to the north was built in 1851, crossing the Crinan Canal and the estuary of the River Add by the 5-span cast-iron Islandadd Bridge, designed by John

Gardner. Bellanoch gained a crossroads position; a school and post office followed, but little else. Afforestation after 1918 created the vast Knapdale Forest south of Bellanoch, and the tiny Forestry Commission village of Achnamara, *'Meadow of the sea'*, sited on an inlet at the head of Loch Sween 6 km south of Bellanoch; in the 1950s it had a post office and Kilmichael primary school, but both schools had closed by 1976; in 1994 a heritage centre was proposed in Bellanoch school. For some years an outdoor centre was run nearby by Strathclyde Regional Council; in 1996 its purchase by Glasgow Nautical College from closure-intent Glasgow City Council was attempted. Bellanoch post office is still open.

## BELLSHILL & Mossend — Map 16, A4

***Town, n. of Motherwell,*** *pop. 24,000* — OS 64: NS 7360

East of ancient Bothwell on the River Clyde is a low plateau between the valleys of the North and South Calder Waters. The Clyde, the South Calder and the Shirrel Burn, a tributary of the North Calder, had all been bridged in the vicinity by the time that Timothy Pont mapped the thickly settled area in 1596. The nuclei of *'Bellmill'* and *'Mossid'* stand only about 1 km apart on the original Edinburgh–Glasgow turnpike road of 1753. Bellshill was already a small village when Roy's surveyors mapped the area and its various roads about 1754. Though neither place was important enough to be mentioned by the assiduous Heron in 1799, by about 1825 Bellshill was served by a penny post from Hamilton.

**From Babylon to Railways**: The development of coal mining was encouraged by the pioneering 4'6" (137 cm) gauge coal-carrying Monkland & Kirkintilloch Railway (M&KR) which opened in 1826, and its extension the Ballochney Railway built in 1828, which passed through Mossend from north to south. In 1833 the M&KR built a branch to Rosehall pit, 1 km north of Bellshill. These lines were upgraded to standard gauge when in 1848 a section became part of the new Caledonian Railway's main line between Motherwell (only 3 km to the south) and Stirling, soon connecting to Aberdeen. A gasworks was established at Bellshill in 1863, and at about that time the Glasgow, Bothwell, Hamilton & Coatbridge Railway (later part of the North British) built a line from Coatbridge through Bellshill to Bothwell. In 1869 the Caledonian opened its Glasgow to Edinburgh line via Shotts, giving Bellshill two stations and making Mossend into a major junction for freight. This plus its central location gave an opportunity to Peter D Stirling (PDS) who set up a long-lasting road haulier's business there in 1870.

**Iron, Steel, Coal, Stone – and Football**: In the mid 19th century malleable ironworks were erected at Mossend, being large and important by 1894, when Mossend had a post and telegraph office and an inn; by then development was continuous along the road to Bellshill, where a local newspaper, the *Bellshill Speaker*, was established in 1892. This was by then a substantial place with an inn, surrounded by at least five coal pits, including Rosehall colliery to the north, and one at Lawmuir beside Orbiston Mains to the south; all were rail-connected. Murray noted a *"huge red sandstone quarry"* west of the station, towards Viewpark. East of Mossend lay the shallow Thankerton colliery; by 1899 this was connected by a mineral railway with the Monkland steelworks at Calderbank. Bellshill golf club was founded in 1905 at Douglas Park near Orbiston, and an electric power station was established in 1906. Bellshill never became a burgh and has few famous offspring, though Alex James born in 1902 became the most celebrated Scottish footballer of the 1920s and Matt Busby, born in 1909 became the much acclaimed manager of Manchester United.

**Goodbye Scotland – Hello Corby!**: The malleable ironworks became Beardmore's steel plant and was extended in the 1914–18 war; Scottish iron ores having been exhausted, by 1922 its new owners Stewarts & Lloyds (S&L) received pig iron from Scunthorpe by rail. The works closed about 1930, becoming Colville's engineering works. The Scottish demand for boiler tubes for shipbuilding having collapsed, S&L decided to move much of their operations from the Clydesdale Tube Mill to a new works at Corby on the Northamptonshire iron ore field, opened in 1932 to make iron and steel for scaffolding and water pipes near the expanding market of the south of England. In 1934 a thousand Scottish workers left the Bellshill area for Corby, and a regular and long-lasting coach service was begun to join the two towns. (Steelmaking at Corby ended in 1980, but its associations with Bellshill remained.) Meantime S&L had retained the Clydesdale Tube Mill, where a new melting shop was added during World War II.

**From Mining to Industrial Estates**: Meantime W & H Nelson & Co, founded in 1925, produced electrical switchgear

*Tapping open-hearth furnace, Clydesdale tube works, Bellshill. This melting shop was installed during World War II to make steel ingots for conversion to tubes.* (JRH)

at Bellshill. Though mining had ceased by 1951 except at Lawmuir, Bellshill with a population approaching 22,000 still retained the tube works and the facilities of a typical town. By then Orbiston had been largely developed with housing. Residential development in the Shirrel area east of Rosehall started around 1960 and continued for some twenty years. Access from the dual carriageway Bellshill bypass A725 – built west of the town about 1967 and directly connected to the new M74 – helped to attract businesses to the Bellshill Industrial Estate, which was established about 1970 between the bypass and Bellshill, and for a time actually included a heliport. The last coal mine had closed by 1971, about which time the population peaked at 23,000. In 1975 the area became part of Motherwell district. By 1978 Ferranti had a branch electrical engineering factory in Bellshill, whose local facilities had tended to increase since 1951.

**Scotland's Primary Freight Yard serves Smaller Industries**: Mossend yard was connected to the electrified railway system in 1974, and became the primary rail freight marshalling yard for Scotland, the line to Coatbridge being electrified in 1981. In 1975 British Steel's Clydesdale Tube Mill was fed from an electric arc furnace, another of which was under construction to meet demands from the North Sea oil industry; though with an annual capacity of 127,000 tonnes this was only a quarter the size of most competing plants in Europe. Long-established W & H Nelson were making mining switchgear in 1979, but mining cutbacks hit them hard; in 1991 only 17 workers remained. A lack of investment at the tube works led to losses in 1990 and it was largely closed in 1991, with 1200 employees made redundant by its new privatised owners.

**Chocolate, Milk and Clootie Dumplings**: Many firms were set up in the former Bellshill North Industrial Estate, renamed the Motherwell Food Park in 1985; by 1990 an offshoot of the sausage casing manufacturers Devro of Moodiesburn was open, joined in 1991 by Duncan's Chocolates of Edinburgh, who brought their walnut whip recipes and key staff with them. Although Ross abandoned their frozen food depot in 1988, the building was taken over in 1989 to centralise the dairying activities of Robert Wisemans of East Kilbride, who installed a plant processing 1.5 million litres of milk a week. By 1992 they had absorbed 35 small dairy concerns in ten years, becoming Scotland's largest independent dairy firm. The bakery firm of Scotts Kitchen survived liquidation in 1990–91 to continue making carrot cake for BHS, among other products. The delightfully named *'Clootie Dumpling Jam & Pickle Company'* was established in the Food Park in 1990; in 1994 they supplied the English chain of Waitrose supermarkets among other customers

**Strathclyde Business Park**: The 1991 census showed 21,624 residents in Bellshill. Work started late in 1991 to create the Strathclyde Business Park (SBP) within the Enterprise Zone, on the site of the Rosehall colliery bing. This major 63ha project incorporated the Scottish HQ of Mercury Telecommunications, where in 1993 250 jobs were provided (now 700). In 1994 three medical factories opened there; the HQ of the distillers William Grant (340 jobs), the Lanarkshire Development Agency (LDA), and a hotel and leisure development were also intended features. The SBP entered its second phase in 1995 with five new office buildings, and a second phase was also planned at the Medi Park. By 1996 Levi Strauss had a clothing factory at Bellshill; they still employ 290.

**Road-Rail Depots and Channel Tunnel Rail Freight**: In 1990 the long-established PDS, Scotland's second largest independent road haulier, operated their rail-connected terminal at Bellshill for china clay transhipment. They handled 250,000 tonnes of freight a year for 30 customers, and had a branch at Kirkintilloch. A reverse rail traffic through Mossend was aluminium from Fort William to Tavistock. Among rail traffics carried through Mossend in 1992 was carbon dioxide in tankers, en route from Scottish distilleries to Newton le Willows, and a train on alternate days brought steel products from Scunthorpe and Lackenby. In 1991 work began on 6.5ha of the 150ha of developable land beside the rail yard at Mossend to create the Eurocentral Railfreight Terminal (ERT) for Channel Tunnel (CT) traffic *(for nearby Chunghwa see Newhouse)*.

**Bellshill's Eurocentral opens at Rail Crisis time**: A new train crew depot was opened in 1994, and an adjacent 4.5ha site was to provide a *'freight village'*. ERT was opened for Channel Tunnel traffic in 1994; its two 40-tonne mobile reach-stacker cranes could handle up to 400,000 tonnes of freight a year without gantries. Commercially split from both railways and customers, it had endured severe losses of freight to other modes in the hasty and disruptive privatisation process; but the operators aimed to increase to 25,000 container units a year. The 35 Mossend drivers of Euro-trains were all transferred from BR to Freightliners in 1995. At that time the Lanarkshire Development Agency was pressing ahead with its *'Freight Village'*, now to be of 40ha including a car delivery terminal alongside ERT.

**Mossend Yard under Privatisation Muddle**: Transrail, a fragment of the former BR freight system, were shifting china clay from Cornwall and steel from Sheerness to Mossend yard, and was also about to start carrying marble by rail from Lairg through Mossend to Italy. But Mossend was working at only 40% capacity, and Railtrack's high charges inhibited any further development of rail freight. However, in 1997 the new US-owned private rail freight operators English Welsh & Scottish Railways were to begin a new *'piggyback'* rail service for road trailers between London and Aberdeen calling at Mossend, using new skeletal *'Eurospine'* wagons.

**Other Industrials**: Other distribution companies arrived (each providing several hundred jobs): Parceline, John G Russell (Transport), CPL (coal carriers), and Tibbett & Britten. In 1996 Securicor subsidiary Scottish Express International developed a 7600 m$^2$ warehouse at ERT, and Scottish Power was to move from Moodiesburn into a new 15,000 m$^2$ unit nearby. In 1997 Multi Metals of Bellshill, owned by the Murray Group, supplied the aluminium used by Alexanders of Falkirk in their bus bodies.

**Food Park Thriving at the Millennium**: Safeway's huge 475m-long food distribution centre was built in the early 1990s, nudging adjacent Viewpark. Largely dependent on bar codes, in 2000 it used 130 temperature-controlled vehicles and 240 trailers to serve 162 stores in Scotland and northern England (managed by Salvesen's); 1300 staff worked on 3 shifts. By 2000 Devro-Teepak (200 jobs) was making over 500 million metres of sausage casing a year, exported worldwide; Wiseman's (300) vast plant was computer-controlled and adjoined by a related plastic bottle factory. Warburtons' highly automated bakery made loaves for central Scotland and some English customers, and Scot Trout, co-operatively owned, employed 190 (mainly women) to handle the produce of their 17 trout farms, no less than 80% of Scotland's output, and supplied most of the supermarket chains. Duncan's Chocolates had reverted to private ownership after an unsuccessful takeover and was developing new products to keep their 60 staff busy. Green Meadow Foods had built up over a few years from nothing to 200 workers by making sandwiches on a grand scale, and quality for many firms was monitored by locally based microbiological laboratory MM Livesey & Associates. AorTech employ 140 making high-tech medical components. Bellshill Academy had 749 pupils in 1997 and the Cardinal Newman RC High School 1113. The recent *Stakis Hotel* with 107 rooms is now the *Hilton Strathclyde* (160 jobs); there is also a 40-room *Travel Inn*.

## BELLSQUARRY — Map 16, A4

***Part of Livingston,*** *pop. 1500+* — OS 65: NT 0465

In the 16th century the towers of Linnhouse (or Linhouse) and Murieston Castles were built some 5km south-west of Midcalder, in an area well settled by 1612 on Pont's map of Lothian; Murieston later fell into ruins and became just a farm. By about 1754 when the Roy map was made, the Midcalder to Westcalder road passed north of both castles. The main line of the Caledonian Railway was opened south of the castles in 1848. The company's branch line to Glasgow via Shotts was opened from Midcalder Junction in 1869, with a station at Newpark near Murieston. By 1895 Bellsquarry was a hamlet with a post office and inn, its name probably pre-dating the rail-connected shale pit then open south-east of the station. The shale pit had closed by 1951 when some 215 people lived in the area, also served by a primary school. Newpark station was closed about 1960, but by 1971 the population had risen to about 300, and the village was bypassed in the late 1970s. By 1981 the new industries at Livingston New Town had caused a leap in population to over 1250; a large new housing estate had been begun at Brucefield just west of Bellsquarry. By now so much housing development has taken place in the area over two decades that Bellsquarry is just an insignificant inlier in the sprawling new town.

## BENDERLOCH & Barcaldine — Map 5, A3

***Argyll coastal settlement,*** *pop. 425* — OS 49: NM 9040

Ancient cairns, a stone circle and standing stones on the south shore of Loch Creran, a sheltered inlet off the Firth of Lorne, indicate an important early settlement. In the 16th century a tower house was built to command an isthmus, marked as *'Barkalden'* Castle on Pont's map of Lorne. This showed that around 1600 some parts of the area to the east were well wooded, with placenames implying pig-keeping. By 1733 the coastal track which circled the Benderloch peninsula crossed Loch Creran by the *'Rugave' (Rubha Garbh)* Ferry, 2 km east of the castle. At the time of Roy's survey of about 1750 the woods spread eastwards from the ferry, past the emparked Barcaldine House 3 km farther east, to the head of the loch; this area was trackless. Later the roads round the loch and to the Connel ferry were made up and settlement stabilised.

**Mansion, Unprofitable Railway and Seaweed**: The mansion of Eriska House was built in 1886 on an islet at the mouth of Loch Creran, and linked by a road bridge to Barcaldine. In 1898 the Caledonian Railway began to construct the Connel Bridge so that a branch line could be built through the area to reach Ballachulish. It was opened in 1903 with a station named Benderloch at New Selma, south of the old castle, and a halt near Barcaldine House; to the north Loch Creran was crossed by the rail-only lattice girder Creagan Viaduct. During the 1939–45 war a plant was built by the shore 1 km north of Barcaldine House to process seaweed into alginate. By 1951 the area's scattered population was over 250, served by the facilities of a small village in the New Selma area. By 1954 Eriska House was the luxurious 18-roomed *Isle of Eriska Hotel*, but under Beeching's notorious plan the railway was abandoned in 1966, its scenic potential unexplored and the fine viaduct unused, while road traffic made a 10-km detour round the head of the loch.

**Oysters, Sea Life and Luxury**: By 1977 Scottish Fish Farms had set up an oyster hatchery in the area. In 1978 Alginate Industries expanded their seaweed processing factory, which made a stabiliser for ice cream, mayonnaise, beer and soft drinks; a pier was added. By 1981 the area's population had risen to about 425. By 1985 there were three caravan sites in the area, and by 1990 Barcaldine offered visitors cycleways over its forested hills, plus the attraction and interest of the very misleadingly named *'Oban'* Sea Life Centre, an informative marine aquarium. Around 1990 a substantial housing estate was built at Benderloch, where a hotel was open by 1996. In 1995 Kelco, owners of the alginate plant, became a subsidiary of US-owned Monsanto, who sadly closed it in 1996 with the loss of its 80 jobs. However, a timber mill was at work in 1994. The long-disused Creagan railway viaduct was rebuilt in 1997–98 to carry A828 road traffic, so cutting a 10 km detour from the road between Oban and Fort William. The *Isle of Eriska Hotel* built a new pool and gym in 1995; it has a 6-hole golf course.

## BERNERA MHOR (or Great Bernera) — Map 11, B2

***Lewis island community,*** *pop. 260* — OS 13: NB 1636

Loch Roag on the north-west coast of Lewis is divided into two parts by the relatively low but rocky isle of Bernera Mhor *(G. Bearnaraigh)*. In 1549 the optimistic Dean Monro found it *"inhabited and manured, fertile and fruitful, with many pastures; good for fishing and fuel"*. Around 1700 Martin found four villages on *'Bernera Major'*, where weaving was practised. By the 1880s some 600 people lived on the island; Bernera primary school was built in the tiny central township of Breaclete *(G. Breacleit)*, and by 1892 a post office was open. In 1953 there were under 400 islanders, who soon threatened to dynamite a hillside to create a causeway to the Lewis mainland! These protests led to the construction by 1974 of a prestressed concrete bridge, some 150 m in length, at the place where a standing stone marked the shortest sea crossing. In 1972 a fish processing plant was built at Kirkibost pier, and by 1991 the island – noted for lobster fishing – had 262 residents. By 1999 a museum had been opened beside the school, and the post office had moved into the village.

## BERNERAY *(Bearnaraigh)* — Map 7, A5

***Island off Barra*** — OS 31: NL 5680

Monro noted in 1549 that the remote and steep little isles south of Barra – Berneray, Mingulay, Pabbay, Sandray and *"pretty little"* Flodday – all belonged to the Bishop of the Isles. The southernmost, stark Berneray with its 193 metre tall cliffs, was *"very fertile land, and good for fishing"*! It had certainly been long inhabited. At that time all these isles and some even smaller had a chapel. A lighthouse known as Barra Head, the highest in Scotland at 208 m above the sea, was built from local granite atop Berneray and first illuminated in 1833. In 1881 72 people somehow made a living on the isle, which has no sheltered anchorage; but within 50 years all had left except the lightkeepers. The light was automated in 1980; its characterful cottages are now a private house.

## BERNERAY *(Bearnaraigh)* — Map 7, B2

***W. Isles community, Harris,*** *pop. 150* — OS 18: NF 9281

This fertile sandy island with its white beaches and two hills of gneiss has a standing stone and souterrain. It is much closer to North Uist than to Harris, to which it was linked by ownership in 1614 as MacLeod property. Its rocky but sheltered harbour at Bays Loch *(G. Loch a Bhaigh)* encouraged the MacLeod in 1705 to establish a ferry service linking Berneray with Harris, Skye and offshore islets including Pabbay, 3 km to the north-west. The locals who collected kelp and grew potatoes were evidently healthy, for Angus MacAskill, born on Bernera in 1825, grew to an astonishing 7'9" in height after emigrating to Cape Breton Island. As many as 700 people lived on Berneray in 1841, but clearances halved this within a decade. The population grew again, supporting 3 tiny schools by 1865, and to over 500 people by 1891; a post office was open by 1892. Although each 20th century census up to 1971 showed fewer people, in the 1950s when the population was 186, 22 lines were already connected to its telephone exchange. The school had 40 secondary pupils, including a number from North Uist.

**The Prince and the Causeway**: In the 1970s Berneray's main access was a passenger ferry to Newtonferry, and the school was primary only. In 1980 the *'Gatliff hostel'* and B&B houses were active. The main activities were sheep farming, tweed weaving and lobster fishing. In 1981 there were 134 people, including Pabbay. However in 1985 it was claimed that life was hard, conditions marginal and that sheep were ferried to and from nearby islets in open boats. Only some 100 mainly Gaelic-speaking people still lived on Berneray and there were just 9 pupils in the school. However, about then the Prince of Wales chose a Berneray croft family to let him *'get away from it all'*, and once he had revealed this remarkable fact, interest in the quiet isle with its shop and post office was renewed. A new harbour was built about 1990 and the population stabilised; in 1991 there were 141 residents. By then a vehicle ferry had been provided, and crabs were also fished, for sale in southern Europe. Haswell-Smith noted the feeling of optimism and the *"suburban bungalows"* that had appeared. In 1998–99 a causeway was constructed across the 800 m of shallow water to North Uist. A youth hostel is open all year.

## BERRIEDALE — Map 9, C1

***Caithness coastal settlement,*** *pop. 60* — OS 17: ND 1122

The bleak hills of south Caithness give rise to the twin Berriedale and Langwell Waters, whose steep and sheltered valleys converge shortly before entering the sea. Plentiful ancient remains include an Iron Age broch on Ousdale Head. Around 1500 two castles were built, Berriedale and Langwell; both appeared on Pont's map about a century later when the area was well wooded, but little remains of either. The Roy map of about 1750 showed a coastal track passing Berriedale Castle; by 1769 this was being made up and bridges being built just above the confluence of the rivers. Barnard remarked that at the Ord of Caithness where cliffs rise 100 m above the coast between Berriedale and Helmsdale, the old road was *"a mere path or shelf along the outer edge of the promontory, without any protection from the precipice, so that it could not be passed with safety in a storm"*.

**Telford Bridges and Bottled Water**: Telford reconstructed the road about 1813 for the Commissioners for Highland Roads & Bridges, and in 1826 Chambers noted sheltered Berriedale as *"an inconsiderable hamlet with an inn"*; a century later this had vanished. Langwell House, built near the ruined castle, is apparently of 19th century date. In the late 20th century there were some 60 people in this attractive area, served by a post office and a sub branch bank – remarkable in so small a place. By 1988 *'Caithness Spring'* water was being bottled and carbonated at Berriedale, and by 1996 a llama farm was a tourist attraction.

## BERWICK-UPON-TWEED & Tweedmouth (England) — Map 3, C3

***Town, Northumberland.*** — OS 75: NT 9953

There are good reasons for including Berwick upon Tweed in a gazetteer of Scottish towns for it lies on a high bluff commanding the estuary of the Tweed, one of Scotland's most important rivers (though its natural harbour is troubled by a sandbar). Berwick's name means *"Corn Bay"* in Norse, referring to the fertile Merse for which it was the natural outlet. It was first mentioned in 1095, and in the 12th century a merchant called Knut traded between Berwick and the Orkneys.

**One of Scotland's earliest Burghs**: Two churches, St Laurence and St Mary, existed before the burgh charter. Berwick was one of the first two Scottish Royal Burghs, becoming David I's first capital when for a few years between 1119 and 1124 he ruled only Strathclyde and Northumbria – an area extending southwards to the Tees. Berwick became the caput of a sheriffdom between 1124 and 1139, probably the first place in Scotland to play this role. There must by then have been a ferry between Berwick and its satellite Tweedmouth south of the river, for the churches remained attached to the diocese of Durham even though Berwick soon became the leading port and town in Scotland, with higher property values than elsewhere. Berwick was one of the original *'Four Burghs'* of Scotland which sought to act jointly. By 1212 there was a burgh court, and the burgh's own Holy Trinity church first appears in 13th century records.

**The prosperous Thirteenth Century ends in Dispute**: In the middle of the century the Chronicle of Lanercost described Berwick as *"a rich and populous city"*, and from 1271 there was a very early bridge across the formidable barrier of the Tweed. The famous Statutes of the Guild of Berwick which were drafted between 1249 and 1294 were detailed byelaws, later adopted elsewhere; the Guild merchants then comprised textile workers and provision dealers. The clothing industry was very important in Berwick, and herrings and cod were significant commodities. In the absence of banks, in 1275 the abbot of Kelso was lending money in Berwick in return for rents. By 1286 the burgh had a coroner, in effect its own sheriff. By 1292 Berwick comprised ten or more streets plus the

Royal castle, where the disputed succession led the aggressive English King Edward I to make the fateful choice of the weak Balliol as puppet king rather than admit the independence claims of the strong and popular Bruce. By then the Augustinian, Carmelite, Dominican, Franciscan and Sack friaries comprised the largest such concentration in Scotland, plus a Cistercian nunnery and a Trinitarian hospital, perhaps the hospice or *'Spittal'* at the south end of the bridge, which apparently fell in 1294, replaced by a ferry.

**The Year 1296: from Peak Trade to Butchery and Ruin**: By 1296 the abbeys of Kelso, Melrose and 13 other widely scattered religious houses in eastern Scotland held properties in Berwick, apparently warehouses cum lodgings, and not only pack-horse traffic but monastic carts hauled by draught animals plied between Berwick and such parent abbeys as Melrose and Newbattle, carrying corn, salt, coal and wine, and also wool for export to Flanders. By that time merchants from Cologne were resident in Berwick, and Norwegian ships called. But Edward seized the town in March 1296 and was said to have butchered 8000 inhabitants, a huge number for the period; the Flemings' Red Hall was destroyed. Edward held a parliament among the ashes and then set about building town walls to secure his prize, also strengthening the castle by erecting the White Wall in 1297–98.

**Berwick as a Pawn, though Scotland's busiest Port**: In 1302 Berwick was re-chartered as an English borough. But in 1318 town and castle were recaptured by Bruce, for the new walls were *"so low that a man on the ground could, with a spear, strike another on the wall in the face"* (Barbour). As King Robert I, Bruce had the stone wall raised by 3 m all round the town and installed a strong garrison, who held off the English in 1319. When in 1328 the dying king made peace with England, his infant son David was ceremoniously wed at Berwick to young Edward III's baby sister Joan, but no children came from this marriage. By 1330 Berwick was exporting nearly 300 tonnes of wool annually, a third of the Scottish total, and was the prime source of customs revenue for Scottish kings, who signed three Royal charters there before it was again lost to the English in 1333.

**An international Shuttlecock**: Fortified and re-chartered by each side in turn as it changed hands another ten times in all, and while under English rule having little contact with its natural hinterland, Berwick's decline was inevitable. Its German community was soon persecuted, and by 1371 the justices for Berwickshire permanently met at Coldingham. The wooden bridge built in 1376 to re-establish a passage for vehicles across the Tweed amazingly survived more than another century of strife. In 1455 Berwick's Royal castle was in English hands, but the town was recaptured by the Scots in 1461; a decade later its port paid only about 2% of Scottish Customs dues.

**Berwick lost to Scotland – Forever?**: Berwick finally fell to the English in 1482; later Henry VII built a fort north of the walls. The bridge was described as *"decayed"* in 1513, but in 1514 no fewer than five *'hospitals'* or almshouses were in operation, no doubt all too well supplied with war veterans. Remarkably, the town too had somehow survived: this may be attributed to its highly strategic site, but its prosperity had gone. Earthwork defences were thrown up by the English in 1522–23; but in 1540 their fort at Berwick had a garrison of only 40. After the tyrannical Henry VIII's destructive invasions of 1544–45, Berwick was briefly neutral from 1551, but once the position of the border was finally agreed in 1552 it was administered by England. Berwick's refortification against possible attack by Scots artillery was entrusted by Elizabeth of England in 1558–70 to Sir Richard Lee. By 1569 he had cut the fortified area of the town by a third, but enormously strengthened it on the bastion system. The walls and tunnels topped by massive grassy mounds were not fully completed and were never used, but survived to become tourist attractions (for a plan see Saunders (1989)). The Great North Road, Tweed bridge, castle and town walls were conspicuous features of the compact Berwick seen by Pont when he mapped the area about 1600. As Blaeu's derived map shows, Tweedmouth and *'Spittell'* were then distinct places.

**After the Union of the Crowns: Post Office, Stone Bridge and Inns**: No sooner were Scotland and England united in 1603 under James VI and I than a post office was opened at Berwick on the new Edinburgh–London Royal Mail route, and a market was chartered in 1604. The erection of another bridge (the present Old Bridge) was begun in 1611, though it took 13 years to complete – nearly a year per arch. Sir William Brereton in 1636 wrote that the Crown Inn gave *"good lodging"*, but it was *"a very poor town, many indigent persons and beggars therein"*. The harbour was now a problem, being *"narrow, shallow and barred"*, with only a few fishing boats, though there was an enormous salmon fishery, typically 100 being taken at a draught. By the mid 17th century brewing too was more than just a home activity in Berwick.

**Berwick Old, Decayed – but soon Busy!**: In the 1720s Defoe admired the bridge, a *"noble, stately work of sixteen arches"*, though for some reason he attributed it to Queen Elizabeth I. But the town was *"old, decayed, and neither populous nor rich; the chief trade in corn and salmon"*. Certainly the castle was completely ruined by the time that the Bucks drew their panorama in 1745, but by then the town was evidently well built, and the river was packed with ships. A new Town Hall was erected in 1750–61. Even so, Roy's map made about 1754 showed only the reduced area within the Elizabethan walls built up. Roads led over the bridge and to Edinburgh; the connection to Kelso via Birgham existed too, but as yet no piers or major harbour works had been built.

**Scottish Borderers, a Bank and better Roads**: Barracks erected in the 18th century became the HQ of the King's Own Scottish Borderers (KOSB). By 1760 with agricultural improvements in the Merse, Berwick was rather more prosperous, and its people's old clothes had become a source of rags for local paper mills. A bank was established in 1768, and the town still exported wool, eggs, and salmon. The roads to Kelso and Greenlaw were turnpiked under an Act of 1772; by 1797 Berwick's *Red Inn* was an important staging point on the Edinburgh to London coach service. Four fairs were held annually. Not only was Berwick the only English possession north of the Tweed but the town was also a judicial anomaly – a detached part of County Durham known as Berwick Bounds.

**Trade and the Port of Berwick**: In 1799 Heron noted that the barracks were still in use and that *"this town has a weekly market on Saturdays, and a yearly fair for black cattle and horses. The salmon fishery at the mouth of the river is a great source of commerce. Vast quantities of eggs, also, are exported. The trade is with the port of London. Berwick smacks have long been noted for the punctuality; they now proceed to Leith, and carry on almost the whole naval intercourse between that* *port and London."* As a port of registry from the 1786 Act, Berwick vessels bore the code letters BK. John Rennie was engaged in harbour improvements in 1807, and grain was still being exported in some quantity in 1810; boatbuilding was a significant occupation in that period.

**A Solid Town of Antique Dignity**: A local newspaper, the *Berwick Advertiser*, was founded in 1808; in that year Berwick was selected as a main postal centre. By 1825 there were breweries both in Berwick and in Tweedmouth across the river; including Tweedmouth and Spittal, Berwick had a population of 9000. According to Chambers *"the streets of Berwick are spacious, with a strong cast of antique dignity about them. Most of the shops are elegant. There is a large establishment for soldiers; the castle is now a shapeless ruin, with a deserted wind-mill towering in the centre. The trade of the port is considerable, the salmon caught in the Tweed being the chief export."* A lifeboat station was opened in 1835. However, the local Tweed Bank failed in 1841 due to losses in the whaling trade.

**Railway Links and the Royal Border Bridge**: The North British Railway (NBR) opened to Berwick in 1846, and the Newcastle & Berwick Railway reached Tweedmouth in 1847, a single horse bus at first sufficing to carry all the *'international'* passengers between the two stations. In Victorian times a steam ferry also plied across the river to Tweedmouth and Spittal, so it was a brave decision to fund the major high-level railway viaduct that was needed to join the two rail termini. The so-called Royal Border Bridge of 28 stone arches, each of 18 m span and carrying trains 38 m above the river, was built to designs by Robert Stephenson and opened in 1850. Most of the ruins of Berwick's ancient castle were regrettably obliterated, its site being adopted for the new station, shared by the NB and the newly united York, Newcastle & Berwick (YN&B) Railways. Completion of the east coast railway route brought through trains, leading to soaring numbers of long-distance passengers; the local economy benefited relatively little. The YN&B soon built a branch westwards from Tweedmouth (where there were extensive goods yards and an engine shed), up the Tweed Valley to Kelso, later connected to Newtown St Boswells.

**Local Industries and Hostelries**: A new dock was built at Tweedmouth in 1872–77 and the Border Brewery Company's works were expanded in 1887. The firm of George Black made steam boilers at Tweedmouth, which also acquired various small industries; but new activities in Berwick itself were few. In 1894 the town still had only two hotels; in 1899 the *King's Arms Inn* was preferable to the downmarket *Hen & Chicken*! In the early 20th century Berwick slowly developed as a minor resort and sub-regional shopping centre, with an art gallery and museum.

**A Resort but no longer a Railway Junction**: The station was radically rebuilt in 1927 by the London & North Eastern (LNER), about the time that a second road bridge was thrown across the Tweed to carry the growing traffic on the A1. Shielfield Park at Tweedmouth became the football ground of Berwick Rangers in 1954, its stand second-hand – from Bradford! Buses served a wide area around the town, and by 1965 the branch railway was down to two daily passenger trains between Berwick and St Boswells; these took seven minutes to reverse direction at Tweedmouth! Not surprisingly the line was soon closed and lifted. Tweedmouth engine shed vanished; rail freight ceased in 1994, but sidings remained. Berwick became the rather quiet passenger railhead for the whole of the eastern Borders, but as a port it was by that time of little significance. For mail purposes it was included in the Galashiels (TD) postcode area.

**Modern Berwick develops**: A branch knitwear factory, open under Pringle of Hawick by 1969, became the town's largest employer. Fatstock markets were still important in 1971, by which time Berwick had a population approaching 12,000, but the corn market soon ran down and was closed about 1980. In 1976 a fish processing factory also drew on Eyemouth landings. In 1982 Berwick was bypassed on the west by a new section of the A1. By 1989 its several caravan sites included a holiday centre with indoor and outdoor swimming pools and a ballroom, and some yachts could be seen at Tweedmouth; in 1990 the Maltings Theatre and arts centre was opened, and by 1992 there was a Wine and Spirit Museum. Tweedmouth still had major grain handling and storage facilities in 1991, and Jus-Rol Ltd who produced frozen pastry and vegetables, had a branch factory at Amble; in 1992 Seafresh of Berwick dressed crabs.

**A Foot in Both Camps**: In 1974 the town became the administrative centre of an extensive but sparsely populated local government district running far down into England. In retrospect its severance from Scotland had created a major anomaly, in view of the administrative integrity long attained by most Scottish river basins; advice has had to be available locally on both the legal systems. Berwick is only 92 km from Edinburgh as against 101 km from Newcastle, and a tedious 542 km from London. In the 1990s its long-distance post was apparently sorted in Edinburgh's mechanised letter office and – until privatisation – the town was served by the South of Scotland Electricity Board (later Scottish Power), though by England's Northern Gas. The regimental museum of KOSB added still more Caledonian flavour, and the often struggling Berwick Rangers FC was in the Scottish League; in 1989 their second division ground at Shielfield Park (south of the Tweed!) had roofless stands that could seat little more than a quarter of its capacity crowd of some 5250. For a time in 1992 the club was in receivership, but in 2000 fought back into the Second Division. Until 1994 when Tesco took over William Low the local supermarkets looked both ways, Gateway being English; the bus station harboured several services of both Northumberland Motor Services and Lowland Scottish. When a small new brewery was established, it chose the name *'Border'*.

## BETTYHILL

**Map 12, C1**

***N. Sutherland village,*** *pop. 250* OS 10: NC 7061

By about 1600, when Pont mapped the remote north coast of Sutherland, the Kirk of Farr stood beside the mouth of the River Naver. Pont noted iron being smelted at the Wood of Skell (Skail), 14km up Strathnaver. Evidently charcoal was used, and local ores were identified both at Ben *'Staomny'* (Stumanadh) to the west and beside the *'Allt Skelpigg'* (Skelpig Burn) to the east. This is apparently the earliest reference so far traced to ironmaking in Scotland. By about 1750 an isolated stretch of road had been made along the coast of Farr, between Strathy and Tongue; a new kirk was built near the original site. William Daniell's 18th century aquatint of Invernaver shows that there were already stone houses on the shore at the site of the later pier.

**Controversial Countess Commemorates Herself**: The village of Rossal in Strathnaver was cleared of its people in 1814; in part compensation it was immediately (by 1815) replaced beside Farr Kirk at the mouth of the River Naver by a new crofting and fishing village. This was called Bettyhill by Betty herself, formally known as Elizabeth, the Countess of Sutherland, who had until then turned a blind eye to the ruthless acts of clearance perpetrated on her estates since 1807, and which were to continue until 1821. A post office was open at Bettyhill by 1838; the fishing station, its name anglicised to *'Navermouth'*, acquired a rope walk. Eventually the road was completed through to Thurso, 41 km from Farr as the crow flies; but no railway company ever ventured closer to Bettyhill, which remained a small village, though by the standards of the local area it was from the start a key settlement. The *Bettyhill Inn* was *"good"* to Murray in 1894, when the daily horse-drawn coach averaged under 8 km (5 miles) per hour on its tiring journey from Thurso to Bettyhill and Tongue.

**Scotland's First Electric Lighthouse**: The elaborate but squat and squarely built lighthouse on Strathy Point, 15 km east of Bettyhill, came into use as late as 1958. Though the first in Scotland to be all-electric, it was the last to be built for manned operation; after that date automation ruled, and by 1996 had taken over even at Strathy Point. By 1974 there were caravan and camping sites at Bettyhill, and by 1978 a restaurant, the Strathnaver Crofting Museum and – in anticipation of much planting – the local Forestry Commission HQ. Farr School had been extended and included a secondary class of 10 pupils. In 1989 many of Bettyhill's population used Kinbrace station, 45 km to the south-east, for contact with Inverness and beyond. By 1990 the Strathnaver Museum had industrial exhibits, and in 1996 was claimed to be the only museum commemorating the shameful Scottish clearances. By then Farr High School had 77 pupils.

## BIGGAR

**Map 2, B2**

***Small town, upper Clyde valley,*** *pop. 2000* OS 72: NT 0437

A first glance at a map makes Biggar appear to be in upper Clydesdale, little more than 2 km from an elbow of the River Clyde; but it actually stands on a tributary of the Tweed, the Biggar Burn. Its gap site is therefore strategic and Biggar is an ancient settlement, close to a hill fort and early earthworks. Its main street is on the line of a first century Roman road connecting the upper Clyde Valley with Inveresk, so its reputedly 13th century bridge over the Biggar Burn will not be the first to have stood there. Biggar also acquired a castle motte and a 12th century church; 2 km west at Cormiston was another motte. Biggar was important enough to be shown on the 13th century Gough map. It stands at an altitude of about 215 metres, among the highest places to have aspired to some urban status by the time it was chartered as a burgh of barony in 1451. The parish church was rebuilt in 1545 for Malcolm, Lord Fleming, as the last collegiate foundation in pre-Reformation Scotland.

**After the Reformation**: The area was thickly settled when Timothy Pont made his pictorial sketch map of Clydesdale in 1596; Biggar's name and large church were heavily emphasised, and nearby were a *'Spittel'* and the 16th century tower house of Boghall. A parish school was founded in 1608, and the small parish centre of Coulter or Culter some 4 km to the south gained a school in 1620. A post office was open by 1715. The Roy map of about 1754 showed Biggar as a substantial linear settlement with a mill at its west end, two other mills nearby and radial roads much as today, but the road to the west forded the Clyde at Wolfclyde near Cormiston. By 1797 Biggar was a post town with two annual fairs. A small grain mill and a millwright were active when Heron noted in 1799 *"the town of Biggar, which contains only about 400 inhabitants"*; Coulter was a *"village"*.

**Authorship, Brewing, Railway, Gas and Golf**: John Brown who was born in the town in 1810 became the author of a famous tale of Scots country life, *Rab and his Friends*, and was also the biographer of the child poet, Marjory Fleming of Kirkcaldy. A brewery was open by 1827 when Biggar was according to Chambers *"a neat little town"*, and in 1832 Edinburgh merchant Robert Gray had the elegant villa of Carwood House built 2 km north of the town. The Biggar Gas Light Company works was started in 1839, and at some time the Thistle woollen mill was established. A branch railway from Symington to Biggar and Broughton (*q.v.*) was opened by the Caledonian in 1860. Another station (at Wolfclyde, 2 km southwest) was named after Coulter, which later gained a post office and primary school but remained little more than a hamlet. The striking Cornhill House was built between Coulter and its station in 1868 for Alexander Kay, to French Gothic designs by William Leiper.

**From Peak to Stagnation**: By 1891 the population of Biggar was 1356. By 1894 two hotels were open there, the *Elphinstone Arms* and the *Commercial*, while Biggar was described by Murray as *"a country town of one wide street"*. The Victorian villa of Loaningdale stood just north of Biggar, which acquired a municipal golf course in 1895. The gasworks was re-equipped in 1914. The burgh population reached 1489 in 1921. By 1951 there was a High School, but minimal investment had been made in Biggar for decades due to falling numbers of residents in its rural hinterland, which by then had a total population of only some 5300. However by then the *Hartree Hotel* was open 2 km south of the little town; by 1963 it had been extended to 31 rooms. Carwood House was sadly abandoned to ruin in the 1950s; the railway was closed to passengers before 1953, and for freight in 1966. However, Biggar market continued active.

**Commemorating Gasworks**: When the antiquated gasworks was closed in 1963 it was chosen for preservation by the National Museums for Scotland, who brought in other historic gasworks plant for display *(see Hay & Stell)*. The firm of James A Cuthbertson was founded about 1952, and by 1992 employed 28 people manufacturing snowploughs, gritters and ditcher ploughs. Biggar had risen to a population of 1637 by 1971, but lost its local government burgh status in 1975, becoming part of the Clydesdale district (run from Lanark), with just an area sub-office. Though there had been about eight hotels for many years, by 1981 Biggar's people relied on facilities that had been reduced in many respects – on the margin between a small town and a large village. Greater decline had occurred in remote Douglas, Biggar thereby becoming the main commercial centre for an even more extensive but sparsely peopled area in Strathclyde and the Borders, with a total population around 7000.

**Museums Aplenty and Scotland Direct**: About 1977 the former Thistle woollen mill was taken over by local residents Arthur and Susan Bell, whose *'Scottish Gourmet'* mail order business selling fine foods from all over Scotland had been founded at New Lanark in 1973. By 1992 the Bells' business was called *'Scotland Direct'*, and some 100 people worked at Thistle Mill. In the mid 1980s a caravan and camping site was laid out. Biggar's spacious main street was often fully packed with farmers' and tourists' cars, and the cattle market was still active in 1991 when the town's population was almost 2000, with an elderly retired character. In 1997 Biggar High School had some 600 pupils. Cornhill House, by then a 17-roomed nursing home, closed in 1996, and has since become a hotel. Less lucky Carwood stood a roofless shell by 1999. To the Moat Park Heritage Centre and Gladstone Court Museum were added from 1993 the Brownsbank Cottage Museum, 6km north-east of Biggar, commemorating the work of its most famous occupant, the author Hugh MacDiarmid. Another nascent museum in the town itself was amassing Albion Motors memorabilia, the founders of that company having come from this area. By 1996 Loaningdale, for a time a school, had become an Outdoor Centre.

## BIRSAY (Orkney) — Map 13, B2

***Orkney coastal village,*** *pop. 250* — OS 6: HY 2427

The exposed north-western tip of the Orkney Mainland has a shelly, limey soil ideal for farming, and the natural defensive site on Brough Island which has sea caves was a very early fishing centre. Birsay was a Pictish settlement, with a cluster of remarkable ancient remains, including standing stones – evidence of a chapel from the seventh or eighth centuries. Excavation has shown that glass and lead were cast and bronze jewellery made, before the Vikings came about the year 800; they soon laid out a planned settlement, including a smithy. The Brough was the key centre of the tenth century Norse earldom of Thorfinn the Mighty, who also ruled Shetland, Caithness and Sutherland. By then Birsay was regarded as a small town. The Brough – accessible except at high tide – has the slight remains of a Minster, built between 1014 and 1064; the mainland church has a 12th century origin, but the rise of Kirkwall from 1137 caused stagnation in Birsay.

**Decline, Oppression and Survival**: From 1574 Thorfinn's great house or palace was rebuilt around a large courtyard by the hated Earls of Orkney, Robert and Patrick Stewart; Blaeu's map – probably based on a Pont sketch made about 1592 – emphasised both places. After the oppressors met their end in 1614, the palace became ruinous. Around 1790 the area was known for flax growing and handmade linen manufacture, the earliest accurate maps showing its settlement as being totally scattered. The overshot Boardhouse water mill was erected in 1873 on the short burn flowing seaward from the Loch of Boardhouse; in 1990 it still ground 20 tonnes a year of locally grown bere for bannocks on a one-man basis, and remains open to the public. Meantime by 1967 there was a hotel, but the school was closed in 1975 and Birsay (also called The Barony) had a 1981 population of under 300. In 1995 Swannay Farm 5km to the east was making cheese for direct sale to Tesco. The ruined palace, small hotel and (until recently) a post office were still open, but the repeatedly over-restored church is interesting only for its ancient gravestones.

## BISHOPBRIGGS — Map 15, D4

***Suburb of Glasgow,*** *pop. 24,000* — OS 64: NS 6170

Cadder Roman fort was probably built in the first century AD, almost entirely in timber, on low ground just south of the River Kelvin and about 7km north of the site where Glasgow was later to be founded. The more important Balmuildy fort was erected on a similar site 4km to the west around 140 AD, shortly before the construction of the Antonine Wall, which there crossed the River Kelvin and incorporated both forts. Balmuildy was one of only two forts on this turf barrier to be walled in stone, as were its principal buildings, but unlike Cadder – in Gaelic *Caer-Dur*, the Obstinate Fort – it left no permanent settlement. Pont's map made in 1596 showed a track linking Glasgow with Kirkintilloch; about 5km north of the city's cathedral and 2 km south of Cadder it crossed a small stream, hence perhaps the origin of the name Bishopbriggs, though this was not shown.

**Railway, Quarry and Coal Pits**: By about 1754 when surveyed by Roy, Bishopbriggs was already a hamlet on what had become the Kirkintilloch road. It was served by a station on the Edinburgh & Glasgow Railway which opened in 1842, later merging with the North British. By 1845 fine white or yellowish sandstone suitable for ashlar was being quarried nearby at Huntershill, some of this being moved by rail for use in buildings in Edinburgh's Cockburn Street. In 1854 the workings moved underground, using the *'stoop and room'* technique; 46 men were employed in 1905 but work ceased after a tragic roof collapse in 1907. By the 1890s Bishopbriggs – though still tiny in terms of physical development – was passing the 1000 population mark and had an inn. In 1896 the Carron Company opened the rail-connected Cadder coal pits in the Mavis Valley to the north.

**Suburbanites, Publishers and Government Guests**: Two golf clubs and courses were established, the Bishopbriggs west of the town in 1906 and at Cawder House (Cadder) in 1933, this club now also having the Keir course; plus a municipal course at Littlehill to the south in 1926. By 1911 electric trams joined Bishopbriggs to Glasgow via Springburn, and for many years Kenmure Avenue was the terminus of *'caurs'* to Carnwadric and Crookston. At some time an industrial school was opened. In 1931 Blackies the publishers moved from Glasgow to Westerhill, north-east of Bishopbriggs, leaving their old premises – to their rivals Collins! In the mid 20th century the large timber hutted camp which became Low Moss Prison was built at Cadder, and Keir & Cawdor had brick works at Bishopbriggs; but the coal pits had closed. In 1947 an old mine shaft beside houses collapsed, but developers pressed on and by 1951 Bishopbriggs' population was 10,000, with the facilities of a large village plus a small secondary school, the nucleus of Bishopbriggs High. Sportworks Ltd, founded in 1947, built sports grounds and golf courses, and by 1970 employed 250 people. The trams had vanished by 1962.

**Briefly a Burgh: Suburban Explosion**: Bishopbriggs was among the last few burghs to be designated – in 1964. In 1972 under 18% of its houses were council-owned, being second only to Bearsden among west of Scotland burghs in the dominance of private ownership. In 1975 its brief career was ended by incorporation in the new Strathkelvin District, based in ancient Kirkintilloch. By 1977 Cadder had a railway yard, opposite which a large rail-connected oil depot was built about 1970. In 1983 it received gas oil by rail from Stanlow, but in 1992 daily deliveries came by rail from Grangemouth in 1600-tonne trains. In a bizarre twist, Blackie's works were swallowed by Collins about 1980, but continued in operation. Further large private housing estates raised the population, and the facilities of an average town were enhanced by the opening of a Fine Fare superstore in 1981. By 1986 Bishopbriggs had three High Schools: Bishopbriggs, Thomas Muir and Turnbull, and by 1991 the population was nearing 24,000, of a young suburban character. By 1994 a new shopping centre had been built east of the station, the green gap between Bishopbriggs and Milton had been infilled, and development was pushing towards Robroyston.

**Collins and Murdoch in Trouble; Canal Reopened**: The Collins operation was taken over by Rupert Murdoch, and by 1989 it was very large. In the 1993 recession over 250 manufacturing workers were made redundant to safeguard the remaining 1000 jobs of what was by then named HarperCollins; in 1994 they sold their book production plant at Westerhill, nowdays named Omnia. In 2001, HC's Bartholomews subsidiary *(see Newington)* produced the clear and attractive maps for this book. Meantime in 1995 a second prison was planned near Low Moss, then a low-security prison. In 2000 a new mobile phone factory was announced, with 400 jobs planned. A large retail park had developed close to Westerhill, and the Forth & Clyde Canal was reopened between Bishopbriggs and Kirkintilloch in May 2000.

## BISHOPTON & Rossland — Map 15, A4

***Large dorm. village, Renfrewshire,*** *pop. 5400* OS 64: NS 4371

Overlooking the broadening estuary of the River Clyde about 10 km north-west of Paisley was a second century Roman fort which guarded against infiltration across the Clyde west of the end of the Antonine Wall. Bishopton nearby was a tower house, but little else was noted by Pont, who mapped Renfrewshire about 1600; Formakin Mill dates from the 17th century. By Roy's day around 1754 the tower house had become Bishopton House, a mansion and country estate. Difficulties in tunnelling through the whinstone spur to the east delayed the opening of the Glasgow, Paisley & Greenock Railway in 1841. A station named Bishopton was provided well inland in the vicinity of Rossland (some 2.5 km south-east of Bishopton House), which came to be called Old Bishopton. A hamlet known as Bishopton developed on the main Paisley to Port Glasgow road between these two nuclei, acquiring 323 people by 1891, plus an inn and a post and telegraph office by 1895.

**The Royal Ordnance Factory – not there at all?**: In 1904 the Erskine golf club set out a course beside the Clyde, and Formakin Mill was greatly enlarged by Lorimer in 1908, a turbine generator being added to serve Formakin, a house begun for a Glasgow stockbroker but never completed. In 1937–39 the enormous and sprawling Royal Ordnance Factory (ROF) was established in the level valley of the Dargavel Burn to the south. Though it was quite impossible to hide, being one of the largest industries in Scotland, plainly visible from passing trains and aircraft, it was not shown on OS maps until the 1990s! Old Bishopton House, much altered and extended, became a convent in 1948. By 1951 the area's population was some 2300, with village facilities.

**Electric Trains and the M8 draw Commuters**: With the electrification of the railway in 1967, housing development rapidly filled the space between the station-side community known as Rossland and the main village, and by 1971 the population had reached nearly 4000. In the mid 1970s the M8 motorway was constructed, passing between Bishopton and Erskine and relieving through traffic, but adding little to local accessibility because of the detours required to gain access. By 1981 the unified settlement had facilities approaching those of a large village; substantial areas to the north continued to be developed with new housing in the 1980s. The huge and sprawling ROF was sold off cheaply by the government in 1987, and its new owners British Aerospace, intending asset-stripping, proposed its run-down over three years from 1988 with the loss of all its 1200 jobs (mainly of workers from other and poorer settlements such as Inverclyde)... in spite of the seemingly unique role the plant fulfilled as the alleged sole UK manufacturer of rocket propellant. After a rethink in 1989 some 700 of the jobs were saved.

**Bishopton Prospers, but the ROF to Close**: In 1990 it was revealed that the ROF had an area of 780 hectares, was surrounded by a fence over 16 km long, and contained 35 kilometres of road and an almost unbelievable 96.5 km of rail sidings. In May 1990 this giant white elephant of perhaps 200 hutment workshops was still making and storing explosives, and early in 1991 a hundred more workers were taken on to satisfy the short-term needs of the Gulf war. At that time Bishopton's young resident population of 5394 was well-educated; unemployment was low, and over 70% of households were mortgagees. Formakin House and Mill were converted into houses from 1997; the miller's house was also saved. The ROF, which employed 270 people at the millennium, is now threatened with closure in 2003; the future of the enormous low-lying site is undecided.

## BLACKBURN (Aberdeenshire), Kinaldie & Kinellar — Map 10, B3

***Aberdeenshire villages,*** *pop. 1130* OS 38: NJ 8212

About 4 km south-east of Kintore in an area rich in Pictish standing stones is the parish of Kinellar, its kirkton built on a spur overlooking the Don valley. The area is separated from Aberdeen by the hills of Kirkhill Forest, in the 12th century a royal hunting preserve, but was well settled by the mid 17th century, as shown on Robert Gordon's map. By about 1750 when the Roy map was made, a hill track joining Aberdeen with Kintore passed south of Kinellar Kirk, crossing the Black Burn midway. A distillery set up there in 1821 was among the casualties of the cheap grain whisky introduced in the mid 19th century.

**Quarrying and Commuters**: From 1854 Blackburn was inconveniently served by Kinaldie station, 3 km to the north on the main line of the Great North of Scotland Railway, where a post and telegraph office was opened. However, by 1894 there was also a quarry 1 km east of the hamlet, and a large quarry had been opened in Elrick Hill 2.5 km to the south-east. With the advent of bus services Blackburn slowly but steadily grew, for it was only 13 km from Aberdeen and 7 km from Bucksburn. A primary school was built, and an agricultural contractor was in business by 1951, when Blackburn had a population of 600 and also an inn. Kinaldie station was closed about 1965, and quarry working appears to have ceased in the late 20th century. In 1981 the local facilities were those of a small village, serving over 1000 people in Blackburn and Fintray. By 1985 a large housing estate had been built north of the village, and 1.5 km to the south, college buildings had been erected. The 1991 population had reached 1130, and in the 1990s the local section of the A96 was rebuilt as a dual carriageway, bypassing the village, which continued to grow, mainly as a dormitory.

## BLACKBURN (W. Lothian) — Map 16, C4

***W. Lothian urban area,*** *pop. 5000* — OS 65: NS 9865

The very early Edinburgh–Hamilton road kept to a ridge on the north side of the headwaters of the River Almond. By the time that Pont mapped the area around 1600, Blackburn stood beside the road some 4 km south of Bathgate, and there was a mill nearby. Blackburn gained a post office in 1642 on the Edinburgh–Portpatrick–Ireland route. It appeared on the Roy maps of the 1750s as a tiny settlement; by then the turnpike road through Whitburn (the present A705) had been built, and a village developed near the point where it crossed the Almond, also having a side road to Bathgate. Blackburn House was built about 1760 for the farm improver George Moncrieff, and at some time a cotton mill was erected.

**Mining, Motorway and Motors**: Blackburn was never directly served by rail, and coal mining developed late. With only 814 people in 1891, it had little more than a post office and an inn. The A8 trunk road diversion passing between Blackburn and Bathgate was built in the 1920s. Relatively large mines later surrounded the place, which grew quickly to some 2000 people by 1931 and about 3300 by 1951, though retaining the facilities of a mere hamlet. Whitrigg Colliery, south-west of the village, still open in 1955, was disused by 1963. However, the M8 motorway had been completed by 1971, with a junction only 2 km west of Blackburn, which was also close to the then new works of British Leyland *(see Bathgate)*. Having an intervening industrial estate as well, the population of Blackburn burgeoned, with additional council estates built around 1960 both north and east of the village, peaking at over 7500 in the 1971 census. By that time the facilities had reached those of a typical village, the large St Kentigern's Academy had been built, and a major sewage disposal plant was being completed.

**Discount Clothes and Recycled Furniture**: But the motor works though large was never really economic and the village population rapidly fell back. After the closure of the motor works in 1986 the future of the area rested on Livingston New Town, rapidly growing to the east. Meantime Blackburn House had been abandoned in 1972 and was still derelict in 1997. By 1991 the population was down to around 5000, with sadly deprived characteristics impacting on its many children, and in 1993 the bleak main street was marred by vandalism, vacant shops and a disused hotel. However, by 1994 a Safeway depot had been built adjoining the M8, and the Freeport shopping complex at Westwood was opened in 1996 with 30 units, mainly occupied by major brand names discounting clothes direct from the factory, but also providing some catering and children's recreation. In 1996 Thackwray of Lincoln, who used century-old pine timbers to make hand-crafted furniture, moved their workshops to Blackburn, which could be entering a happier phase. In 1997 St Kentigern's Academy had a roll of 1015.

## BLACKFORD & Tullibardine — Map 6, A4

***Perthshire villages,*** *pop. 575* — OS 58: NN 8909

In 1488 James IV commented favourably on the ale from Blackford in Strathallan, its Ochil Hills spring water being especially pure. Blackford was shown on Pont's map made about 1600, had a parish school by 1613 and became a burgh of barony in 1706, but evidently remained rural. Roy's map made in the mid 18th century showed that there was no road on the present A9 route hereabouts, such traffic as there was between Greenloaning and Auchterarder keeping north of the Allan Water. Eventually a through road (the 20th century A9) was developed under one of the 1771 to 1790 Turnpike Acts.

**Wool and Whisky**: Blackford (together with Auchterarder) had about 200 weavers by 1778, and an annual fair was scheduled for 1797. A woollen carding mill built in 1802 was enlarged into a blanket factory in 1825. Blackford was first recorded as having a distillery in 1798, though its exact site is unknown. Tullibardine, after which the distillery was named, actually lies about 5 km to the north, and has an ancient chapel; a parish school was founded there in 1599, and in the early 18th century Tullibardine was the secondary seat of the Duke of Atholl. A new brewery was opened at Blackford in 1830 but the original distillery closed in 1837, and there was not even a post office by 1838.

**Icy, Dry – and Wet again**: When the main line of the Scottish Central Railway was being built, the Allan Water was diverted for about a kilometre west of the village, to avoid the need to build six bridges; on its opening in 1849, Blackford was given a station. At that time Blackford church was important to the village; by the 1990s it was in ruins. A station which was opened only for curling matches on the adjacent loch was provided in 1851 at Carsebreck, 3 km west of the village; used only 25 times, it lasted until 1935. Meantime both the *Blackford Hotel* and a telegraph office were open by 1894. The *'Gleneagles'* Maltings were built in 1896–98. The smaller brewery closed in 1912, and was eventually converted into the Tullibardine distillery in 1949. By 1951 Blackford had about 700 people and typical village facilities, but its main railway station was closed in 1956, leaving only a troublesome level crossing, while the

*Thompson's Ltd, Brewers & Maltsters, Blackford (Perthshire); these maltings were built in the 1890s, but were converted into flats in the 1980s.* *(JRH)*

professional services of local doctors, lawyers and dentist also vanished.

**Highland Spring Waters the Desert**: The distillery was doubled in size in 1974 by Invergordon Distillers. By 1978, at about the time when Blackford was bypassed, there were nine shops, two hotels, and two pubs. The larger brewery had closed, but its maltings were used until the 1980s, then being converted into flats. In 1979 a water bottling plant was built by Dubai interests to exploit a spring on the Braes of Ogilvie in the Ochil Hills, once used as Blackford's water supply. Fifty people were soon employed filling up to 40 million plastic bottles a year of *'Highland Spring'*. By 1992 *'Highland Spring'* (with 80 employees) was exporting over 300 million litres (300,000 $m^3$) of water a year, and supplied over a third of the supermarket own-label water drunk in the UK. The Tullibardine distillery pressed on, converting more pure water into the *'fire water'* of whisky, for which demand was then also rising, but in 1995 White & Mackay mothballed it, with the loss of about 8 jobs; it may soon be reopened.

**Water Bottles for Babies**: In 1991 the Haldanes' Gleneagles Mineral Waters began to bottle *'Gleneagles Spring'* water; John Hamilton of *'Highland Spring'* fame installed Europe's most modern water-bottling plant in the former Gleneagles Maltings, to exploit two springs capable of yielding 250 tonnes of water an hour. They hoped to employ 150 people, but Gleneagles Spring Water was not a great success. A year later they introduced a baby's water bottle, complete with teat! However, the concern was still making losses in 1995 for its owners Allied Domecq. In 1999 the reopening of the station for passengers and freight was being pressed by Perth & Kinross Council. The old inn is now the *Blackford Hotel*.

## BLACKNESS

**Map 16, C2**

***Settlement on S. side of R. Forth,*** *pop. 375* — OS 65: NT 0479

Blackness, a low promontory on the Forth foreshore 7km west of South Queensferry, had an early chapel of St Ninian, but its first mention in extant records was in 1302 when *'Sea Coal'* was already being taken from Blackness to Linlithgow. A castle was built in the 14th century, and in 1384 Spanish sailors were recorded at Blackness. The landlocked burgh of Linlithgow obtained a charter in 1465 to build a new port or pier at Blackness, which lay 6km from the burgh. The old castle was strongly rebuilt as an artillery fort in 1537–42; this was shown as the prominent but solitary Blackness Castle on Pont's map around 1612. Seamills built about 1608 were still in use in 1642, but had become ruinous by 1722. Although Blackness was once reckoned to be the third most important port in Scotland, in 1655 Tucker wrote that it was *"sometimes reported to have been a town, but now nothing more than three or four pitiful houses, and a piece of an old castle"*. This decay was no doubt due to the rise of Bo'ness, nearer to Linlithgow and blessed with ample coal. Later in the 17th century the otherwise redundant castle was used as a state prison, and for a time to store armaments, but such uses had long ceased by the 1720s.

**Temporary Revival, Vandalism – and *'Hamlet'***: The Roy map of about 1754 showed the castle and a single row of buildings. Eventually an access road was built, and later in the 18th century Blackness was shipping coal, salt, woollen cloth, skins and hides, and its imports included many luxuries. It also re-exported tobacco (landed at Glasgow) to Amsterdam, till this trade was killed by the Forth & Clyde Canal and legislative changes. In 1799 Heron described Blackness as a *"village."* For half a century from 1870 the castle was again an arms depot, then being opened to the public. The creation after 1918 of the Cauldcots Holdings on the road to Bo'ness by the Land Settlement Association seems to have led to the building of a primary school, but the ancient Linlithgow Guildry warehouse, which had survived until the 1960s, was demolished in an act of vandalism, becoming the site for council flats. Blackness still has its school, a pub and the very impressive castle ruin, which has been used as a location for filming *Hamlet*.

## BLACKRIDGE, Bedlormie & Westcraigs

**Map 16, B3**

***W. Lothian village,*** *pop. 1560* — OS 65: NS 8967

Blackridge stands at the high altitude of 190 metres on the Bathgate to Airdrie road 4km west of Armadale, where for a few kilometres the Barbauchlaw Burn, a tributary of the Avon, forms the West Lothian / Lanarkshire boundary. The burn had been bridged by about 1600 when Pont mapped the area, but Blackridge was not named on Blaeu's derived maps. The Roy map made about 1754 was very sketchy in this area, though it showed a road linking Airdrie with Torphichen. North of this on the slopes below Blawhorn Moss stood the ancient buildings of Bedlormie, east of which was Wester Redburn, later called Bedlormie House.

**The Railway and Mining**: From 1862 Westcraigs station beside the road to Harthill was served by the North British Railway's single track Monkland branch. By 1895 nearby Blackridge was a compact village of 800 people, having a post office, inn, smithy and 1km to the east a *'barracks'* – originally a *'berewick'* or granary. Nearby in Lanarkshire, a mine adjoined the railway. By 1899 Westcraigs was the junction for a mineral railway to Shotts, with extensive branches in the Harthill area, to coal pits and coke ovens at Woodend 3km north-east, and to a coal pit near Southrigg Farm. Two quarries were opened to the south-west. By 1901 some 800 people lived locally, rising to 2000 by 1931. In 1923 most passenger trains on the main line served the station. The population peaked around 1951 at some 2500, for quite extensive building of council estates had taken place. But by 1953 only two trains a day stopped at Westcraigs, and by 1955 all the mines were disused except for two on the Woodend line; the quarry south of the station had closed.

**After Mining ceased**: The facilities of a small village and a 120-pupil secondary school remained, but the station closed when passenger trains were withdrawn in 1956. In 1963 the mineral line to Harthill was closed and lifted, and by 1971 little but the bing remained of the major colliery. Other evidence of active mining disappeared in the 1970s; the railway was closed, and lifted in the early 1980s. The secondary school, chemist and inn had also gone, leaving only minimal facilities. However, one large quarry was still active in the late 1980s, and there was again an inn. In 1991 76% of Blackridge's reduced and disadvantaged population of 1560 lived in council houses. By 1998 the Edinburgh to Glasgow cycleway followed the route of the old railway, and despite little recent development the pub remained open; the post office has since closed.

## BLACKWATERFOOT, Shiskine & Machrie — Map 1, B2

***Village on w. coast of Arran,*** *pop. 250* — OS 69: NR 8928

An Iron Age fort, hut circles and a standing stone overlook Drumadoon Bay on the west coast of Arran, at the mouth of the short Black Water; the island's finest prehistoric features are 5km to the north, the stone circles on Machrie Moor and a standing stone on the shores of Machrie Bay. Pont's distorted map of Arran made about 1600 gave prominence to *'Kilmichel'* (Ballymichael) 4km inland, where there must have been an early church, and also *'Shedack'* (Shedog near Shiskine, a ferm toun 2 km inland), Torbeg, and *'Forling'* (Feorline). Martin noted in 1703 that Kilmichael was then a *"village"* with one of Arran's four parish churches, but little non-farm development seems to have occurred until a road was built into the area from Brodick in 1817.

**Coastal, Golfing and Hotel Developments**: Bacon's 19th century atlas named *'Drumodoon village and port'*, but a *"small inn"* on the coast near Feorline was named Blackwaterfoot by 1894. The Shiskine Golf and Tennis Club was founded in 1896, laying out an unusual 12-hole course on the links. In 1901 came the Machrie Bay club which provided a similar 9-hole course there, and a post office was opened at the nearby hamlet of Tormore. By 1951 despite a resident population of only about 400 there were six hotels, including one at Machrie. The various settlements combined provided typical services for a small village. The *Kinloch Hotel* on the coast near the 12-hole golf course was the largest on the island by 1979; it had an indoor swimming pool, by 1992 a squash court and a gymnasium. Another major extension meant 44 rooms, and 40 jobs in summer. Meantime by 1997 Shiskine had an outdoor centre, and an airstrip was proposed in the vicinity.

## BLAIR ATHOLL — Map 6, A2

***Highland Perthshire village,*** *pop. 500* — OS 43: NN 8765

Among the best known of present-day castle towns is Blair Atholl (anciently Athole). In Gaelic *blair* means *'field'*, for it is located on the highest good farmland in Glengarry, the easiest route to the Highlands. There the River Garry is joined by the foaming River Tilt, fed by Cairngorm snows. The great Blair Castle was built nearby from 1269 onwards; in 1560 it was the seat of the powerful Earl of Atholl. Pont's map makes it clear that a Tilt bridge existed by about 1600, by which time the castle was both large and elaborate. By then the Haugh Mill stood on the Banvie Burn near the river, and 2 km west on the south bank of the Garry was the Mill of Invervack; the site of the restored water mill in the modern village goes back only to 1613, and unlike many other castle towns, no burgh of barony charter seems to exist.

**Dukedom, Private Army and Military Roads**: The Earldom was promoted to a Dukedom in 1703, apparently to support the planned Act of Union. Defoe noted in the 1720s *"The Duke of Atholl (being the) lord, I was almost going to say king of the country, can bring above 6000 men together in arms at very little warning"*. In the late 1720s the first road, hastily built by soldiers under General Wade following the 1715 rebellion, reached Blair Atholl on its way to the north by Glen Garry and the bleak 450-metre-high Druimuachdar Pass – anglicised as Drumochter. Another inadequate roadway, laid out by way of Glen Tilt to Braemar about 1760, was never properly metalled.

**Blair Atholl Textiles, Fair and New Village**: In the 1790s local flax was spun by hand into linen yarn, largely sold to pay the rents. An annual fair was scheduled for 1797, and Heron noted Blair Atholl as a *"town"* in 1799, while giving no details. In 1803 Dorothy Wordsworth stayed at what was evidently the only inn, located at Old Blair, for it looked out on *"a part of the town"* near St Bride's churchyard. The inn was *"in an uproar"* after the September Tuesday fair. The Duke's runner carried post to and from Dunkeld until 1808, when a stone bridge replaced a timber structure across the Tilt; the reconstruction of the North Road, under Telford's supervision for the Commissioners of Highland Roads & Bridges, enabled a stage coach service to be introduced between Perth and Inverness. Chambers noted in 1827 *"a recent shift of the road to the south has occasioned a neater village, at the new Bridge of Tilt; and the old house is now seldom resorted to"*. Marble was quarried in Glen Tilt for a time.

**Clearances inhibit Development until the Railway comes**: For many years the new road carried only local mails, the Inverness mails still going via Aberdeen until 1836, when a post office was finally opened at Blair Atholl. Meantime the clearances perpetrated by the Dukes in the early 19th century prevented Blair Atholl from retaining a substantial hinterland population, and when visited by Fontane in 1858 he found *"a little village of 300 inhabitants"*. However, from its opening in 1863 the station became an important operating point on the Inverness & Perth Junction Railway (later Highland – HR) main line, where pilot engines were stabled, ready to be attached to help trains over the Drumochter Pass. Tourism also developed, based on the castle and the beautiful surrounding mountains and forested countryside. Blair Atholl golf club was founded in 1892, laying out a flattish 9-hole course between the railway and the Garry; in 1894 Murray noted two hotels, the *"very good" Atholl Arms* by the station and the *"very fair" Glen Tilt*.

**High Flying?**: From 1907 to 1913 the Marquis of Tullibardine, heir to the 7th Duke, aided the experiments of J W Dunne, a Farnborough aircraft designer, and arranged for the secret development and testing of his primitive military machines, building sheds on a remote plateau on the south side of Glen Tilt 5km from the castle. Meantime between 1900 and 1909 the railway over the pass to Dalwhinnie was doubled section by section to cope with increasing traffic, but was singled by Beeching in 1966, only to be doubled again in the 1970s on account of North Sea oil developments around the Moray Firth.

**Tourism and Television**: In 1978 a garage, basic food and drapery shops were open and estate caravan sites had been laid out; there were still the same two attractive hotels, plus holiday homes. The A9 bypass was built in 1983–84. Blair Castle was a busy tourist honeypot, the interesting water mill was once again at work, and timber chalets were replacing caravans. The bogus but traditionally painted name sign *'Strathblair'* then *in situ* showed the use of the station as a backdrop in a TV series of that name. The Duke's *'private army'* the Atholl Highlanders still existed as a small peaceful body when the estate passed to a family trust in 1996. The HR engine shed still survives, though boarded up and long derelict; the former primary school now holds a folk museum. The long-standing but all too prominent quarry to the south is still active; a new cycle track has recently been built beside the A9 towards Drumochter. Hotels include the fine old *Atholl Arms* (30 rooms) and *Bridge of Tilt* (37); several guest houses are also open.

## BLAIRGOWRIE, Rattray, Rosemount & Kinloch

**Map 6, B2**

***E. Perthshire town,*** *pop. 8000* OS 53: NO 1845

A large medieval motte was raised on the shore of the small east Perthshire loch nowadays spelled Clunie, to protect the north-western approaches to Strathmore from Highland incursions following the line of the Lunan Burn, from Strathtay through the royal hunting forest of Clunie. It was replaced about 1300 by a royal castle known as *'The Peel of Kluny'*, sited on an islet in the loch and rebuilt in the 16th century. This was owned in the late 18th century by the Earl of Airlie, but played no significant role and fell into ruin. Near a stone circle 5 km to the east was Ardblair Castle, a 16th century L-plan tower, and Newton Castle of similar date. Between these castles, near the shallow Loch Drumellie, was the Kirk of Kinloch. Blair Kirk, accompanied by tiny Newton of Blair, stood 2 km east of Ardblair on the right bank of the turbulent River Ericht as it entered Strathmore. Newton was first set up as a market centre, and later chartered in 1634 as a burgh of barony called Blairgowrie.

**Education and Roads**: Rattray stood opposite, on the left bank, and had a parish school by 1606; these places were shown on Pont's map of about 1600. Above Rattray was the *'Milhol'*, and a bridge already spanned the Lornty Burn. Roads which followed the modern A923/926 must have existed before Blairgowrie became the starting point for the early 18th century military road to Braemar, completed by 1724. Roy's survey of about 1750 showed this broadly following the route of the later A93 northwards, though it took the river's west bank above the village, then a small compact place, to cross the Lornty Bridge and Bridge of Cally. North of this it appeared as a mere track. The village of Rattray was very small indeed, though three mills stood downstream of it.

**Linen as a Home Industry**: An early linen stamping office failed, but after reopening in 1785 it dealt with rapidly increasing quantities. By the 1790s there were 100 weavers, and a bleachfield at Rattray. A quarter million metres of linen was stamped in 1792. A post office was opened in 1796 and Blairgowrie immediately became a post town. It had two annual fairs – possibly there was also one at Rattray. Heron in 1799 found two *"villages"*, Blairgowrie with about 400 inhabitants and Rattray probably smaller.

**Adamson, Grimond and other Mills and Activities**: The Meikle flax-spinning mill was erected in 1798. By that year a small lint mill at the Haughs of Rattray below Blairgowrie had been converted to flax spinning. The water-powered Lornty lint mill 1.5 km above the town was in use by 1798 as a flax mill; it was rebuilt in 1814 by David Grimond – later a pioneer in jute – and apparently named Oakbank; with only four spinning frames, its yarn was sent to Dundee. About 1820 Grimond built the Brooklinn mill on its tailrace, and by 1864 his three mills had 2160 spindles and 290 employees (*for an air view see Hay & Stell*). Meantime by 1825 there was a brewery, and a gasworks was established in 1834. Ashbank mill was started about 1836, and by 1839 the steady flow of the Ericht had enabled eleven moderate-sized water-powered mills to be

*A raspberry harvesting machine. The Blairgowrie area has long been famous for soft fruit growing and processing. (SMPC / Niall Benvie)*

in use, *"perched above the rocks of the Ericht"* (Somers); to accommodate the workers a rectilinearly planned extension was added to the town. A Bank of Scotland branch opened about 1840.

**A grubby Baronial Burgh**: In 1848 the critical Somers described Blairgowrie as a *"rising place"*; when the old bridge was swept away in floods in 1847 it was soon replaced. The flax mill owned by Adamson & Leadbetter then employed 400 people. But Somers wrote *"There is a lamentable deficiency in the organisation of rural towns like Blairgowrie. Your burghs of barony, with obsolete charters granted by the obsolete Stuarts, are a species of urban outcasts for which there is no one to care."* Perhaps in response to Somers' strictures, from 1850 police burgh powers could be used to administer small towns. A local newspaper, the *Blairgowrie Advertiser*, was established in 1855, and in that year a branch railway was completed from Coupar Angus on the Strathmore main line. Blairgowrie became locally important as a railhead; by 1864 there was an iron turning mill, and a water turbine was installed at Brooklinn mill about the same time. By 1870 Wordie & Co had a small depot for road to rail cartage.

**Mills in the 1860s**: The Haughs mill had been expanded with 250 power looms into the large partly steam-powered Ericht Works, where by 1864 800 people – half the town's textile workers and all their power loom weavers – were employed by John Adamson. The 11 working mills then contained 13,200 spindles, 250 power looms and 1600 workers; most still processed flax, and only two or three were in jute. The various firms were closely involved with Dundee for supplies and markets. Handloom weaving was almost gone, and yet another mill was under construction at Keathbank. More steam power was added at the Ericht mills, and another waterwheel came into use at Erichtside Works in 1871.

**Golf, Hotels and the Raspberry**: Blairgowrie Golf Club was founded at Rosemount in 1889, and its fine 18-hole course was developed with the zeal that was appropriate in what Murray called *"an industrious town"*. The 1891 population was 3714, plus 2225 in Rattray. By 1894 there was an inn at Bridge of Cally, and Murray noted two *"very fair"* hotels, the *Royal* and *Queens* at Blairgowrie; but its locally grown strawberries went *"chiefly to fill the jam pots of Keiller of Dundee"*. During the 20th century Blairgowrie itself became the strategic canning and freezing centre for the Scottish soft fruit industry, especially raspberries. Flax scutching mills still operated in World War II, and a modest textile industry survived: the mid 19th century Westfield mill long retained its water wheel. The town took over the Mechanics Institute Library in 1937, and continued to provide a normal range of urban facilities, except for the railway which lost its passenger trains in 1955 and was closed entirely in 1965; the station site became an industrial estate.

**From the Mills to the Pistes**: The number of hotels rose from seven in the 1950s to thirteen by the 1980s when there were camping and ski shops, since from the 1960s Blairgowrie benefited from being the nearest town to the Glenshee pistes. In 1975 Blairgowrie became part of Perth & Kinross district. By 1977 a Georgian mansion had become the *Altamount House Hotel*. In 1979 the Smedley fruit and vegetable cannery was closed with the loss of 340 jobs and 75 others were threatened in two local jute mills. The combined population of Blairgowrie and Rosemount rose to 8000 in 1991, when it had many detached houses owned outright by affluent retired people; over one in five of its occupied people walked to work.

**Blairgowrie from Soft Fruit to Software**: Ian Bilsland of Alexandria founded Graphic Information Systems (GIS) at Blairgowrie in 1978, soon finding a niche for the firm's power control system display software and employing 22 people by 1989. In 1990 GIS won a contract covering the entire network of Electricite de France, demonstrating that the relative isolation of small towns need not prevent success as centres of innovation. By 1991 the suburb of Rosemount had expanded, along with Blairgowrie Golf Club, which by then was a large 45-hole complex comprising two 18-hole championship courses (the original and the 1979 Lansdowne) and the old 9-hole *'Wee'* course. In 1993–99 Oakbank Mill stood derelict, but by 1996 there was a Tesco store. Blairgowrie High School had 1081 pupils in 1997. Keathbank mill retains its water wheel, now perhaps Scotland's largest, and is a tourist attraction. Hotels include the *Angus* (81 rooms), the *Kinloch House* (20 rooms, 5km west), and the *Altamount House* (7); *Craighall Castle* 3km to the north also takes guests, and the long-established *Bridge of Cally Hotel* is still open.

## BLAIRINGONE & Solsgirth — **Map 16, C1**

***Locations s-e. of Dollar,*** *pop. v. under 100* — OS 58: NS 9896

Blairingone is on the Alloa to Kinross road, 3km from Dollar on the borders of Clackmannan, Fife and Kinross. It had a coal mine in 1796; however, coal working had ceased by 1888, when two inns were the main features in the area and the hamlet of Blairingone also had a post office. The proximity of the Dollar mine in the early 20th century, and the Solsgirth mine, sunk in the 1960s as part of the Longannet complex, left Blairingone seemingly untouched. About 1980 the post office closed. In the mid 20th century a quarry was open 2 km to the east; this was disused by 1988, but in 1994 a vast opencast coal operation was in progress just east of the small village; this area had been restored by 1997.

## BLAIRS & Ardoe — **Map 10, C3**

***Location s-w. of Aberdeen,*** *pop. 300* — OS 38: NJ 8800

When Roy surveyed lower Deeside about 1750 little development was shown south of the river save the Mill of Ardoe, 7km south-west of Aberdeen. Later, roads were built, and in 1829 the Roman Catholic church opened Blairs College, 1.5km west of the mill, as a seminary for boys, to combat growing Protestant dominance of the Highlands. The little-known Deeside Hydropathic at Heathcot was begun in 1877. In 1878 Ardoe House, a lavish turreted baronial mansion designed to rival Balmoral Castle, was built near the mill for the laird, one Alexander *'Soapy'* Ogston. His family owned the 400ha estate until 1945, resisting other development, so it remained largely rural, and the mill closed. Meantime a new building for Blairs College was erected in 1908.

**Hotel outlives Catholic College**: In 1947 Ardoe House became the 15-room *Ardoe House Hotel*, which after a thin patch in the 1970s recovered and was greatly extended, by the mid 1990s boasting 4 stars and 71 rooms. However, Blairs College was closed about 1986 for lack of pupils, and stood empty and decaying in 1994. In 1993 the Aberdeen Planning Committee approved but the Regional Council rejected, major proposals by two developers to create a new town of over 4000 houses at Banchory Devenick, 8km south of the city. An application for development of the Blairs College site was called in by the Region in 1994. By 1999 the nearby post office had closed for lack of a local community. The *Ardoe House Hotel* has been extended again, now having 112 rooms.

## BLANTYRE — **Map 15, E6**

***Lanarkshire town,*** *pop. 18,500* — OS 64: NS 6857

On the west bank of the River Clyde opposite Bothwell Castle is a narrowing tongue of land between the Clyde and the unhappily named Rotten Calder Water. Blantyre's Augustinian priory, a dependency of Jedburgh, was founded there in the

*Workers' housing at Low Blantyre Mills, which began as water-powered cotton mills on the R. Clyde in 1785. David Livingstone, the African missionary and explorer, was born here in 1813, and these buildings were converted in the 1930s into a memorial to him.* *(JRH)*

first half of the 13th century by Alexander II. The area was thickly settled when Pont sketched the Clyde valley in 1596; he repeated the name Blantyre in three locations, and no fewer than three bridges appeared to span the Rotten Calder beween Calderwood Castle and its mouth. Blantyre or High Blantyre, 3 km south of the priory and 4 km west of Hamilton, was chartered as a burgh of barony in 1598, and in 1599 Walter Stewart, Lord Blantyre took over the former priory. The first parish school dated from 1611. The Roy map of about 1754 showed Blantyre as a small compact place, on a loop off the main road from Hamilton to Glasgow. Other roads led to East Kilbride and Bothwell Bridge.

**The Low Blantyre Cotton Mill**: In 1785 Messrs Dale, Monteith & Bogle established a large water-powered cotton-spinning mill in the shallow gorge at Low Blantyre, some 2 km upstream of the priory and 2.5 km north-east of High Blantyre, driven by water diverted by a weir built across the Clyde. Power-loom weaving and calico printing were added later. By 1799 the mill employed *"upwards of 500 people"* (Heron), housed in a model village on the plateau above; according to the mill manager in 1816 its whole population worked there. William Cobbett who visited in 1832 described Low Blantyre as a *"manufacturing village belonging to Messrs Monteith, with water-wheels wonderful to behold ... the condition of the people appeared to be very good"*.

**David Livingstone and his Times**: In 1813 David Livingstone was born in a one-room mill tenement at Low Blantyre and worked in the mill while improving his education. He became a doctor, the famed explorer of south-central Africa until 1873, and daringly navigated across the Indian Ocean in a river steamer! Meantime, however, there was no post office in Blantyre before the penny post of 1840. A Caledonian Railway (CR) branch from Newton to Hamilton was opened in 1849, with a station near the mill at Low Blantyre; in 1852 a sturdy footbridge, the *'Pay Brig'*, was built across the Clyde to replace the ferry which linked the mill and the dyeworks with Bothwell town. By 1888 an inn also served the works, but they closed in that year; most of the complex later vanished but its great curved weir remained.

**Repeated Pit Disasters at High Blantyre**: Meantime High Blantyre had a post and telegraph office from about 1854, and the hamlet of Auchinraith grew just to the east. In the early 1860s the circuitous Hamilton to Strathaven branch of the CR was built, looping right round High Blantyre in order to gain height. William Dixon opened five pit shafts around the village between 1872 and 1877, by which time some 700 shiftworkers had raised nearly a million tonnes of coal for him; but Blantyre was *"a maze of dirty and intricate ways and byways"*. A methane explosion in October 1877 in No.3 shaft caused Scotland's worst pit disaster, which killed 207 of the 235 miners in one shift. An inquiry revealed sloppy working practices – not fully eradicated when work was resumed; in 1879 another explosion killed 28 miners.

**Railways, Trams and Industry**: From 1883 to 1914 Hunthill Junction beside High Blantyre station was linked to East Kilbride by a single-track branch of the CR which failed to earn its keep. Blantyre (however defined) had 1505 people in 1891. Meantime Stonefield – the area of sprawling development on the Glasgow road which in 1891 had a population of 5581 and included two inns – was described by Murray in 1894 as *"a large workmen's village"*; this became the area's effective centre. An electric power station was opened in 1906, and from that time to 1931 the Lanarkshire Tramways Company served the town. The Clydeside policies of Auchinraith House became a brickworks; in later years concrete products, oils and aerated waters were made in the town, whose coal pits were still active from 1920 to 1945. In 1926 the Blantyre Engineering Company reconstructed the headgear of the Alice pit near Crossgates (Fife).

**Commemorating Livingstone**: In 1929 the David Livingstone Memorial Museum took over the explorer's birthplace. Although much better housing was built, Blantyre remained in the shadow of its larger neighbour Hamilton, and its inns degenerated to pubs, for it seems never to have enjoyed a 20th century hotel. The Clyde footbridge was replaced in 1952 by a new structure (which lasted only 45 years). Around 1950 Rolls-Royce of Hillington established a branch factory at Blantyre, which by then had a population of over 17,500 but had only the facilities of a small town. All the local coal mines had closed by 1963, although Allanshaw's foundry was still active, and the brickworks was still open in the 1970s. In 1981 the A725 elevated dual carriageway linking East Kilbride with the M74 was driven ruthlessly through Auchinraith. In 1991 Blantyre's quite young population was 18,500.

**Combating Poverty after the Coal**: Meantime in 1983 the Clyde-Calders project had set about restoring the landscape and byways of the whole degraded area between Glasgow and Newmains. By 1980 J K Reid printers were at work, now a substantial operation. In 1993 a 47 ha site at Blantyre Park became part of the Lanarkshire Development Agency's Enterprise Zone, later named the Hamilton International Technology Park; the Auchenraith industrial estate had modern units available in 1996. Significant employers now are First Direct financial services (600), CTS backpanel systems (450), and also Dunduff whinstone quarry (280). In 1997 Blantyre High School had 851 pupils. A 1980s ASDA superstore was still open in 2000 but the adjacent redeveloped shopping centre had numerous vacancies. However, there is a modern sports centre, and pleasant open spaces adjoin the original CR station. This is still open near the interesting David Livingstone Centre, including the museum, which was adopted by the National Trust for Scotland in 2000, when a brand new tubular steel footbridge was erected by Barr of Ayr, leading to paths to Bothwell and its ancient castle.

## BLYTH BRIDGE, Drochil & Kirkurd — Map 2, B2

***Village & hamlets, N-W. Borders,*** *pop. 100* — OS 72: NT 1345

Many hill forts and a stone circle at Kirkurd, centre of the area once known as Urd, cluster round this remote area on the Tarth Water, a tributary of the Lyne Water which later joins the Tweed. Near the confluence of Tarth and Lyne is Drochil Castle, a Z-plan structure built from 1578 for the Regent Morton – left incomplete when he was executed in 1581. This was given much more emphasis on Pont's map of Tweeddale than tiny Kirkurd or Blyth, where no bridge was shown, although Millside mill already turned there. By Roy's day around 1754 a road passed Blyth, linking Howgate near Penicuik with the West Linton to Biggar road. Provided with other roads but shunned by the railways, the area remained very rural, its most prominent feature in 1895 being the emparked mansion of Castlecraigs at Kirkurd, whose parish population was 293 in

1901. By then a post office and smithy stood at Knock Knowes, which by 1908 was known as Blyth Bridge. By 1951 it had a primary school, and a telephone exchange was named after the ruined Drochil Castle. By 1970 Castlecraigs had lost its park but Blyth Bridge had a pub; a nearby water-mill became a tea-room, retaining its wheel. Although by 1976 there was a school for the physically handicapped, the primary school was closed in 1985, so the local children have to attend Newlands school at Romanno Bridge. By 1988 the nearest post office was at Dolphinton. By 1991 when the resident population of the parish was 125, Castlecraigs had become a 47-bed alcoholism clinic (Castle Craigs) complete with an indoor heated swimming pool. There is still a pub at Blyth Bridge, and Netherurd House is a Girl Guides centre.

## BOAT OF GARTEN

**Map 9, C5**

***Speyside village,*** *pop. 700*

OS 36: NH 9419

This Speyside locality stands at an altitude of 220m, 8km down the River Spey from Aviemore. *'Gart'* was named on Pont's map made about 1600, but this did not show either a *'boat'* or a ferry; nor did the Roy map of about 1750, which depicted Loch Garten to the east but showed no features on the left bank between *'Balliblair'* (opposite the modern Street of Kincardine) and *'Dashers'* (Deishar). At that time the nearest road was one joining Aviemore with Carr Bridge. Roads had evidently been built to a ferry across the Spey by the time the Inverness & Perth Junction Railway opened its main line from Forres to Dunkeld in 1863, keeping to the west of the river, as a crossing station named Boat of Garten was placed at the ferry approach. In 1866 this became the junction of the Great North of Scotland Railway (GNSR) line to Nethy Bridge, Aberlour, Craigellachie and Keith. The GNSR provided a locomotive shed, and a village developed westwards from the station.

**Road Bridge, Golf – and vanishing Rails**: In 1898 a golf club was founded, which laid out an 18-hole course, and what had by then become a chain ferry was replaced by a wooden road bridge. Although in 1951 Boat of Garten had mills and two substantial hotels, the *Boat* and *Craigard* (between them having 58 rooms and 5 AA stars), the population was under 400, served by the general facilities of a small village. The engine shed had gone before all the area's railways were closed to passengers by Beeching in 1965; and freight services 3 years later.

*A large timber yard near Boat of Garten. (SMPC / Michael Good)*

**The Strathspey Railway Society**: By 1971, following the major tourist developments at Aviemore, the population of the village had risen to almost 500. In 1973 the Strathspey Railway Society, an association of steam preservation enthusiasts which had made the former station their headquarters, reopened the line from Boat of Garten to Aviemore for tourist use; ultimately they aim to extend down the valley to Grantown. A new road bridge was built around 1975. By 1981 the local resident population was approaching 700, served by the facilities of a small village. By 1992 some more housing had been built, a sawmill (employing 50) was active, a caravan and camping site were open and forest walks had been laid out. The Osprey Centre formed at Loch Garten nature reserve is an important local attraction. The long-established *Boat* is one of several hotels.

## BODDAM

**Map 10, C2**

***Village s. of Peterhead,*** *pop. 1450*

OS 30: NK 1342

Boddam stands on the Buchan coast 4km south of Peterhead. Dundonnie, a headland 1km to the south, appears to be named for a Pictish fort, now vanished. Between there and Boddam is a ruined castle built by Keith in the 14th century. Pont's map of about 1600 showed a substantial settlement named *'Bottom'*, then apparently much larger than Peterhead. A century later a tiny Dutch settlement was planted at Boddam by William of Orange, but this failed to grow – the Roy map showed no significant villages in the area in the mid 18th century.

**Boddam lights up the Earl's Harbour**: Buchan Ness lighthouse was built for the Northern Lighthouse Board by John Gibb of Aberdeen to designs by Robert Stevenson, and commissioned in 1827 with the first flashing light in Scotland. Earls Lodge was built in 1840 of pink granite for the laird, the then Prime Minister, the Earl of Aberdeen, who under an Act of Parliament of 1845 largely financed Boddam harbour, built for both fishing and trade. In 1858 Pratt found *"a fishing station rapidly rising in importance, one of the cleanest and most thriving on the east coast. A good pier has been lately erected which has led to a great increase of boats employed both in the white and herring fishing."* In the den west of Boddam was a carding mill.

**Granite**: By then the reddish-pink Peterhead granite had long been quarried in Stirling Hill south of Boddam by Macdonald & Leslie, who employed 80 men; Pratt noted their *"world-wide fame"*. By 1869 the quarry was linked to the harbour by a tramway and was a main supplier to the Aberdeen stone-yards. When the Admiralty decided to form a Harbour of Refuge in Peterhead Bay, by building a huge breakwater, a second quarry was opened in Stirling Hill and a winding mineral railway was constructed to convey blocks of granite down to the base at Burnhaven. By 1894 large quarries were also open at Blackhills or Longhaven, 3km to the south; the latter had a siding on the Boddam branch of the Great North of Scotland railway, opened from Ellon in 1897.

**The Decay of Fishing and the Railways**: Powered fishing boats appeared before the harbour of refuge was ready, and with the decline of fishing, by 1930 there was little need for either the harbour or the branch railway. Passenger trains ceased in 1932, and freight in 1945; eventually houses rose on the station site. In the mid 20th century the large Cold War radar station of RAF Buchan was built on Stirling Hill. The Admiralty railway was closed in 1950. About then a resurgence

*Boddam ('Peterhead') power-station, built by the Hydro Board in the 1970s to use oil, and altered in the early 1990s to take gas also.* *(SMPC / Jim Wedderburn)*

of fishing led to the conversion of an old curing yard into the Highland Seafoods fish processing factory.

**North Sea Oil and the Power Station**: In the 1970s the harbour became a supply base for North Sea oil rigs, and the quay was rebuilt in 1976 to serve the Hydro Board's Peterhead power station just north of the village, built with two oil-fired 660mw generators in 1974–78; two 115mw gas turbines were installed there in 1990–92, when the plant was converted to burn sour gas from the Miller field. To the west was a major grid substation. Although there were only the facilities of a small village, Boddam harbour still supported about 20 lobster boats in the mid 1980s. Buchan Ness lighthouse was automated in 1987, retaining its original lantern. Earls Lodge, by 1977 a small hotel, was burnt out in 1984; its walls still stood in 1997. In 1991 Boddam had 1435 residents. Although the Stirling Hill quarry was still growing, a big scheme to develop the working Blackhill quarry in the cliffs south of Boddam was successfully resisted by nature conservation interests about 1992. Following the ending of the Cold War, RAF Buchan was under threat in 1999. Boddam power station is currently being upgraded.

## BONAR BRIDGE, Ardgay & Invercharron

**Map 9, B2**

***Villages on Kyle of Sutherland,*** *pop. 850* OS 21: NH 6191

Ancient remains including cairns, sculptured stones, hut circles and a broch abound on the sheltered shores around the lengthy sea inlet known as the Kyle of Sutherland; Wester Fearn on the south shore marks the original site of the Premonstratensian religious community, an offshoot from distant Whithorn, which moved to modern Fearn *(q.v.)* between 1338 and 1372. Blaeu's atlas maps showed the area thickly settled by 1654. Ardgay (pronounced *Ardguy*) near Kincardine Kirk – south of the Kyle and some 20km west of Tain – was chartered in 1686 as a burgh of barony, also called Bonarness. Roy's map made about 1750 showed various hamlets beside a track from Tain, which forked up Strath Carron to Amat, and northwards to end at Inverhouse opposite the undateable Castle of Shin; but no routes were shown on the north side. A hamlet near Invercharron House and Bonar was named Ferrytown.

**The Commissioners' Bridges and Roads**: The ironwork for Telford's Bonar Bridge was cast in Wales and erected across the Kyle for the Commissioners in 1811–12; the south bank track was made up, and on the north a connecting road was built eastwards to Dornoch, Golspie, Wick and Thurso. Meantime by 1813 a post office had been opened at Invercharron (Ardgay). Ardgay bridge across the River Carron was built by Alex Muirson in 1818, opening up the hilly area to the north-west; sadly this encouraged Munro of Novar to clear Strath Oykel of its people in 1820. By 1820 the *Balnagown Arms* was open, and became a coaching inn. By 1828 an extensive new village known as Bonar Bridge had grown on the east side of the Kyle opposite Ardgay, and regular cattle markets were being held in the vicinity.

**The Duke's Roundabout Railway**: The circuitousness of the railway to the far north resulted from the then all-powerful third Duke of Sutherland's requirement that the extension of the line from the south, largely built by the Inverness & Ross-Shire Railway, and completed to *'Bonar Bridge'* station at Ardgay in 1864, should enable the opening-up of his estates to the west. An inn was open at Ardgay by 1866, and Wordie & Co established a small rail to road cartage depot. The Sutherland Railway's line was opened in 1868 to Lairg and Golspie, largely at the Duke's expense, crossing the Kyle 5km upstream of Ardgay by the stone-arched Oykell Viaduct, with a 70 metre lattice girder centre span. In 1870 his mother thoughtfully secured stations on both sides of the firth at Culrain and Invershin. The Bonar Bridge was washed away in 1892 and replaced the next year by a new William Arrol structure. By then two hotels were open, the *Ardgay* and *Ardross*.

**Luxury for Duchess, King – and Hostellers**: The Bonar Bridge & Ardgay golf club, founded in 1904, laid out a 9-hole parkland course on the hillside overlooking little Loch Migdale. Another, controversial Dowager Duchess of Sutherland created the huge baronial mansion of Carbisdale Castle, built in 1907–17 by an Ayrshire firm. In 1933 it was bought by Theodore Salvesen, head of the Leith company; King Haakon of Norway was housed there from 1940 during the Nazi occupation of his country. Theodore's son Harold Salvesen gifted the castle to the SYHA in 1945, and it at once opened as Scotland's largest and most luxurious youth hostel; ceilidhs are still held in its magnificent public rooms. The area once held some of the scattered offices of Sutherland county council and had a small secondary school. After 1945 the poorhouse became a hospital; by 1955 a hydro-electric station had been built at Inveran 2 km north of Carbisdale Castle.

**Money for Roads not Rail**: In 1973 a third Bonar Bridge (bowstring type) was built – like the second designed by Crouch & Hogg – for what was then the A9. Bonar Bridge station was renamed Ardgay in 1977; by 1978 Ardgay had a bank, community hall, general merchant, newsagent, butcher, restaurant, the *Lady Ross Hotel*, two garages and new housing; to the east at Ardchronie was a large rock quarry, still growing in the 1990s. The twin settlements were relieved of through traffic when the Dornoch Firth road bridge opened in 1991; at that time they had 840 residents. Both retain their schools and post offices. Culrain and Invershin remain as request stop platforms, used by hostellers; the small *Invershin Hotel* is still open, and petrol is available. Though the jointed track on timber sleepers indicates little recent investment, the few trains taking the winding route to and from the far north can still cross at Ardgay station, and passengers can admire ever-changing views of the beautiful firth. There is still a salmon-fishing station on the Kyle.

## BONCHESTER, Hobkirk & Southdean

**Map 3, B4**

***Borders hamlets,*** *pop. 500* — OS 80: NT 5812

Between Hawick and Jedburgh the Rule Water flows northwards from the Cheviot Hills to the River Teviot; on the summit of nearby Bonchester Hill is a large ancient fort. Various other earthworks exist, such as above ancient Southdean on the Jed Water 4 km south-east, and ancient churches were to be found including, on Pont's map of around 1600, the *'Kirk of Hoppkirch'*; downstream by the *'Hall of Roull'* was what was later known as Hallrule mill. Hobkirk parish school opened in 1619 and Southdean in 1620. Roy's map made about 1754 showed *'Hope Kirk'* (Hobkirk) at the start of a road leading eastwards to fork near Southdean church into two routes crossing the border, one being the present road via Carter Bar. The other, interestingly labelled the *'Wheel Causeway'*, is nowadays a mere footpath, crossing into England at Knox Knowe and so down into Kielder Forest. This and the name Chesters near Southdean may be indications of secondary Roman routeways and settlement.

**Bridge, Forests and Tourism**: Bonchester's early 19th century bridge attracted an inn and post office, and enabled the completion of a skeletal road system. In 1901 552 people lived in Hobkirk parish; rural depopulation was slow, and bottomed out at 473 in 1971, with basic facilities at Bonchester Bridge and a doomed primary school and post office at Southdean. The vast afforestation scheme of Wauchope Forest steadily clothed the hills to the south, and for a time around 1972 *Wolflee*, 3 km south, was a small hotel; although this closed, by 1985 a caravan site was available, by 1991 there were 503 residents and by 1995 a tourist information centre; Bonchester's inn and Hobkirk primary school are still in use, but the post office has recently closed.

## BO'NESS, Kinneil & Grangepans

**Map 16, C2**

***Town on s. side of R. Forth,*** *pop. 14,600* — OS 65: NS 9981

To anchor the east end of the Roman Antonine Wall, two forts were built about 5 km apart, either side of a promontory on the shore of the Firth of Forth. Near one fort was Kinneil, mentioned by Bede in 731. The later burgh of Linlithgow, 5 km inland, discovered coal seams on the shore: the English spy Hardyng mentioned in the early 15th century that its town council had promoted a tidal harbour there, which replaced the ancient port of Blackness. The new port was at first called Borrowstounness, i.e. the Borrow's (or burgh's) town on the *'ness'* (point of land). Three fortified mansions were built in the 16th century. Near the fort sites were Carriden House to the east and Kinneil House to the west, which contains Scotland's best surviving wall and ceiling paintings of the Renaissance; later came Bonhard, 2 km inland. About 1600 when one was a seat of the Duke of Hamilton, Timothy Pont noted two *'Saltcotts'* on the coast; presumably saltmakers lived and worked there.

**Serving Stirling and the Netherlands**: In 1621 Grange near Carriden was granted a barony charter, and also became a salt-making village, being generally known as Grangepans (distinct from Grangemouth). Bo'ness had a parish school from 1630 and acquired a brewery by 1655. Tucker reported in that year that Bo'ness was the port for Stirling, was already *"a mercat town"* and one of the eight head ports for the Scottish Customs, but was still owned by and subservient to the Royal Burgh of Linlithgow. Coal was being dug out *"in great quantities"* for export, mainly in Dutch boats, making Bo'ness the second port in all Scotland (after Leith). Grange was then *"some few houses, some salt-pans and coal-heughs"*. In 1668 Bo'ness was chartered as a burgh of barony under the rich and powerful Duke of Hamilton, who rebuilt and extended Kinneil House in the 1670s. Glasgow interests were weakening the dominance of Linlithgow and Stirling; but by 1684 Bo'ness was Scotland's largest trading port for the Netherlands.

**Bo'ness at the Union**: In 1690 the combined pollable male populations of Bo'ness and Grangepans exceeded 1900, including large merchant and professional elements, indicating a total population of at least 5000. Grangepans eventually became a constituent of Bo'ness. However, by 1699 outcrop coal accessible by primitive techniques had been practically exhausted. Defoe described Bo'ness in the 1720s as *"a long town of one street... it has more ships belong to it than to Edinburgh and Leith put together; yet their trade is declined of late"* which he attributed, perhaps incorrectly, to the diversion of Dutch trade to England since the Union. Thirlestoun Pans were important by 1737, and a mine pump was installed in 1740, enabling coal mining to greater depths. By that time much flax seed was being imported through Bo'ness from Holland and the Baltic for Lanarkshire flax growers. Bo'ness had a post office by 1745, and Bridgeness just east of Grangepans was chartered as a burgh of barony in 1750.

**Harbour Improvements, Iron Ore, Pottery and Whaling**: Bo'ness harbour was improved in three stages between 1744 and 1794, but remained tidal, eventually able to be cleared of silt by the use of a scouring basin. Meantime, iron ore found at Bo'ness in the 1750s was used as the first basis for the Carron (*q.v.*) works. A pottery was founded in 1766, and improved its product under Roebuck of Carron from 1784. Pennant in 1769 mentioned *"Burrowstoneness smoking from its numerous salt-pans and fire-engines – a town enveloped in smoke"*. A ferry plied to Torryburn in Fife from the *"good quay, much frequented by shipping"* which was engaged in the coal trade and also whaling; at its height this involved eight ships and two *'boiling houses'* for rendering down the blubber.

**Famous Names, Shipbuilding and Brewing at Bo'ness**: Around 1770 James Watt worked on the development of his steam engine at Kinneil House for the proprietor of the Kinneil collieries, Dr John Roebuck, who introduced *'long-wall'* mining to Scotland. When Shaw and George Hart were shipbuilders in Bo'ness in the 1780s they took on as an apprentice the young and innovative Henry Bell *(see Port Glasgow, Torphichen and Helensburgh)*; later Hart's son Alex founded a famous shipyard in Grangemouth. By the 1790s the brewery was quite a large enterprise, and Bo'ness was a general cargo port through which 14,000 tons of shipping passed in a year – though an attempt to link it by still water with the Forth & Clyde Canal was abandoned in 1796 as too costly. Heron wrote in 1799, *"Shipbuilding is carried on here to considerable* *extent; this town possesses 25 sail of shipping."* Bridgeness, Benhardpans and Grangepans were all *"villages"*; the latter had a *"coal-work, and makes a good deal of salt"*.

**Post, Copperas and Distilling**: Although there was still an annual fair in Bo'ness in 1797, and it was a post town, the postal service was carried out on an agency basis until 1807 when a proper post office was opened. About 1808 a copperas (ferrous sulphate) works was set up as an offshoot from Lightbody's of Hurlet *(see Nitshill)*. But by then much trade was being diverted to the new canal port of Grangemouth (*q.v.*), and the Bo'ness Custom House was transferred there in 1810. Addisons closed the brewery in 1813, and a third brewing firm lasted only from 1817 to 1842. Chambers in 1827 described Bo'ness as a *"seaport with numerous salt pans... a place of considerable trade"*. Distilling is known to have started in Bo'ness in 1795, but according to Barnard the Bo'ness malt whisky distillery was founded at the Pans Braes by Vannan in 1830. The Fife ferry became steam-powered in 1834 (*see Limekilns*) and a gasworks was established in 1843.

**Railway, Ironworks and Kinneil Colliery**: A steep single track branch from the Edinburgh & Glasgow Railway at Manuel west of Linlithgow was opened down to Bo'ness in 1846, where an engine shed was built, and an ironworks; a foundry was started there in 1856. But although it was Scotland's top coal export port in 1866, Bo'ness was still struggling to keep its general cargo trade, by now only a quarter of 1790; the ferry closed in 1877. However, Kinneil Colliery was sunk in 1880 and a new 3ha dock was built in 1879–81, provided with a new Custom House, enabling the port to clear over 250,000 tons of shipping annually, and remaining Scotland's second coal export port. Baltic timber was imported for pit props and preparation by six sawmills.

**Grain Whisky, Yeast and Ironfounding**: The distillery was still expanding in 1886, powered by steam, employing 40 men to produce nearly 4 million litres of malt whisky a year. It included a yeast factory whose product was shipped to England and Germany. But Barnard (who noted these facts) remarked that *"the collieries and iron works entirely spoil the look of the place"*, which also had earthenware and chemical manure works; the ironworks closed in 1894. James Calder & Co, brewers in Alloa, acquired the distillery in 1873. They enlarged and converted it in 1894 to produce grain whisky, also connecting it to the railway. The population was 5866 in 1891. The West Lothian or Bo'ness golf club was founded in 1892 and laid out its 18-hole course 2 km south of the town. Murray then described Bo'ness as *"a busy seaport town"* with shipbuilding, coal-mining and iron-working. A second foundry began operations in 1900. A public library, with Carnegie aid, began in 1901. In 1911 came the building of the unique circular art nouveau *Hippodrome* cinema, designed by local architect Matthew Steele.

**Collieries continue but the Dock closes**: In 1916 locomotive maintenance was transferred to Polmont; the distillery was sold to DCL in 1921 and distilling ceased about 1925, though bonded stores remained until the 1980s. The slight shipbuilding industry was replaced by shipbreaking, under Thomson & McGregor during the early 1930s. Bo'ness FC even played in the Scottish League from 1921–32. Kinneil continued to raise coal, and even at the economic nadir of 1931, 60,000 tons was exported through Bo'ness; Carriden colliery was still at work in 1947 under the new National Coal Board (NCB). In the 1950s Bo'ness – which at that time still imported timber and broke up obsolete ships – had over 13,500 residents, and typical urban facilities. The dock was closed in 1955, and its gates were welded shut; by 1989 it contained literally nothing but silt.

**Sparling Decline; New Investment Wasted**: The *Hippodrome Cinema* was still open with 711 seats in 1958; less notable but longer lasting in films was the *Star*. Meantime around 1960 the local newspaper the *Bo'ness Journal* was taken over by the *Linlithgowshire Gazette*, and the ancient Bonhard House was sadly demolished in 1962. Sparling fishing from Bo'ness no longer flourished, this pollution-sensitive species declining as mercury pollution from Grangemouth petrochemicals increased; by 1965 it was locally extinct. Kinneil colliery's two new shafts 860m deep were started by the NCB in 1951 to give access to coking coal beneath the Forth to the north and west. Soon the new Alloa Area of the NCB took over, German equipment was installed, and from 1964 the output from Valleyfield in Fife was raised at Kinneil, which was linked under the Forth by a costly new tunnel nearly 6km long; but the pit never reached its target output of 3000 tonnes a day, and was closed in 1983 when some 500 men were employed. In 1975 Bo'ness lost its local government status and was transferred from West Lothian to Falkirk District within the new Central Region, breaking the Linlithgow tie. Not surprisingly some urban facilities also closed, and by 1981 only those of a small town survived.

**Old Trains for New Tourists**: In 1979 the Scottish Railway Preservation Society, which had previously conserved vehicles at Falkirk, moved their headquarters to Bo'ness; they started a working museum of steam on the riverside, recreated a station with the train shed obtained from the original Haymarket station, and began to re-lay track on the branch line. By 1990 they ran trains as far as the Birkhill clay mine *(see Whitecross)* and had relaid a BR connection at Bo'ness Junction near Manuel to enable their historic coaches to be used for rail tours; the line drew 77,000 visitors in the season. In 1993 the two local authorities joined them in establishing the Bo'ness Development Trust, aiming to develop the line and the mine into a full-scale national museum of the Scottish railway industry. Proximity to the growth industries of Grangemouth helped the population to increase slowly; in 1991 the population was 14,595.

**Industries and Problems**: The *'A'* listed Hippodrome, open as a bingo hall as late as 1980, was bought by a heritage trust – but stood awaiting a new use in 2000. In 1989 varied industries worked in wood and metal: Carriden Sawmills of Walker Timber made kit buildings and in 1991 employed some 300 people, including those in satellite depots. The Victorian Custom House had become a computer supplies centre. Braemar Alloys, Kingdom Engineering, Ballantyne's Bo'ness Iron Company and Cochrane's Seaview Ironworks were also active, as was a large road transport yard. However, the Kinneil colliery headgear stood forlorn, and was later demolished; some shops and a former cinema were derelict, as they remain. By 1990 Shieldness Produce Ltd had a chilled food plant at Carriden, packaging vegetables and salads. In 1994 the US-owned Russell Corporation made leisurewear. Some housing development had taken place over the past decade and a Tesco store was open. In 1997 Bo'ness Academy had 950 pupils.

## BONNYBRIDGE & Dennyloanhead — Map 16, B2

***Urban area, w. of Falkirk,** pop. 6000* — OS 65: NS 8280

Above its confluence with the River Carron the Bonny Water was paralleled by the Roman Antonine Wall. By the time that Pont made his map around 1600 a mill had been built on one of its southern tributaries east of Castle Cary, perhaps in the area later called Milnquarter; but no bridge was indicated. By the time of Roy's survey about 1750 there were at least four mills south and west of the *'Bonie Bridge'*, from which four roads radiated; but other settlement was confined to hamlets and farms. Just to the west was *'Turnpike Loanhead'*, later known as Dennyloanhead. From the 1770s the Forth & Clyde Canal also accompanied the little river. The Edinburgh & Glasgow (E&G) Railway opened in 1842, with a station (later called Bonnybridge High) south-east of the village which was developing round the bridge. Then in 1848 came the northern extension of the Caledonian and Scottish Central Railways, which changed companies as it passed under the E&G's viaduct. A link was built to Greenhill (Lower Junction) about 1 km south of Bonnybridge, so connecting Glasgow with Larbert and the north. By 1860 Wordie & Co had a rail cartage depot.

**Ironfounding, Bricks and an Excess of Stations**: From 1871 the village grew with Smith & Wellstood's Columbian ironfoundry; kitchen stoves, well-known as *'ESSE'* – were made there; they soon expanded into Port Dundas *(q.v.)*. From the late 19th century the Caledonian stove works was also in operation, and firebricks were made by Dougall near the former E&G station. Further railway developments resulted in Bonnybridge's fourth railway station, linking into the Caledonian's Denny branch; so the name of little Bonnybridge appeared in no fewer than five different tables in Bradshaw's Railway Guide! By 1901, when both Bonnybridge and Dennyloanhead had post offices and inns, their joint population was about 3000; but burgh status was never attained. At that time Milnquarter was apparently just a farm but later had a chemical works. J G Stein & Co made bricks and Rollo Industries were engineers in the early 20th century; it appears that the Broomside foundry commenced in 1922.

*Smith & Wellstood's Columbian ironfoundry, Bonnybridge. This works was built in 1871 to make 'American' coal-fired cooking stoves. 'ESSE' kitchen stoves were also amongst its products.* *(RCAHMS / JRH)*

**Golf, Needless Deprivation and Knitwear**: A club which laid out a 9-hole golf course was established in 1924. Passenger trains were withdrawn from Bonnybridge's later stations in 1930 and 1935, and the Kilsyth line was lifted before the 1939–45 war. However by 1951 Bonnybridge was a very large industrial village or small town with a power station and primary substation at Carmuirs and a population approaching 8000; development had spread around Milnquarter and nearly reached Greenhill Junction. Despite this the last remaining railway station (the original of 1842) was mindlessly closed by Beeching about 1965, and the secondary school and employment exchange were also closed. The M876 was built as a northern bypass in the late 1960s, and by 1970 *'Campsie Glen'* knitwear was made by a subsidiary of clothing manufacturers Laird-Portch Fashions of East Kilbride. In 1977 Dougall still had two firebrick works south of the main Edinburgh railway. By 1979 E & R Moffat were manufacturing catering equipment and stainless steel sinks at Bonnymuir Works. In 1981 the facilities of Bonnybridge were still those of a large village, by that time having four hotels.

**Cleaning Up**: The Re-Chem incinerator at Bonnybridge became controversial and was closed in 1984 for *"financial reasons"*; anxiety regarding the dangerous pollutants known as PCBs was suspected to be the true cause. The power station had also closed by the 1980s, but about then Chieftain Contracts of Bonnybridge fabricated the large boatbuilding shed for Miller of St Monans, and in 1983 Broomside were still ironfounders. In 1989 Stirling Fibre *(see Gartcosh)* created a new mill to recycle paper; the cause was set back when their waste paper warehouse burned down at New Year 1992. In 1990 Moffats were expanding into Europe, and in 1991–92 when the population was down to some 6000, the reopening of a railway station on the Stirling and Glasgow route was being considered by the doomed Central Regional Council. The former Re-Chem plant was demolished in 1996 and its contaminated site cleaned. By 1998 still more development had occurred at Milnquarter. The reinvigorated Forth & Clyde Canal is to be reopened throughout in 2001.

## BORGUE & Senwick — Map 2, A5

***Small Galloway village,** pop. 250* — OS 83: NX 6348

On the west side of Kirkcudbright bay is a relatively lowland area; Pont's map of around 1610 showed this thickly settled and at its centre, Borgue Kirk. Besides many earthworks along the coast there was the ancient Senwick church, 2 km south-east of Borgue, and the nearby tower of Balmangan Castle, while to the north-west beyond a motte at Barmagachan was the emparked Plunton Castle, both of the 16th century and doomed to relative obscurity, as was the edifice now known as Borgue Old House. Roy's map of about 1754 showed Senwick Mill, but the area was roadless. Borgue remained exclusively agricultural into the 20th century; in 1951 a scattered population of 500 was served by basic facilities and the small *Borgue Hotel*. Though the population was halved over the next twenty years, most of the facilities remained, and the hotel was actually enlarged to 11 rooms. By 1980 *Senwick House* had become a small hotel. By then a caravan and camping site was open at the sandy Brighouse Bay 3 km south of the village, and by 1985 another on the coast to the east. By 1994 the 280 ha Brighouse Bay Holiday Park was Scottish AA Campsite of the Year and had provided its own 9-hole golf course, indoor swimming pool and activity centre offering a wide range of outdoor leisure pursuits. The 2 hotels are still open, but the post office has closed since 1994.

## BORTHWICK & North Middleton — Map 3, A2

***Midlothian hamlets,*** *pop. v. under 100* — OS 66: NT 3759

About 1430 the major keep of Borthwick Castle was built beside the Gore Water, 9 km south-east of Dalkeith; close by was the ancient church of Borthwick parish. Pont's map of around 1600 gave emphasis to *'Borthyick'*, east of which, and perhaps showing where lime for its construction was burned, was the name *'Lymkills'*, possibly that later known as Halflaw Kiln. Middleton House 1.5 km south of Borthwick was built as a mansion in 1710. The Roy map of about 1754 showed an extensive road system in the area around Borthwick. Middleton, 1 km west of the castle, had a post office from 1780 and was a post town by 1797, with an alternate days service on the Edinburgh to Stow route; the village later came to be called North Middleton. The steeply graded Edinburgh & Hawick Railway was built through the area in 1849; the nearest station was at Fushiebridge near Gorebridge.

**Finding a use for Middleton Hall**: Meantime by 1895 a limestone quarry worked near the Middleton North Burn, with a tramway down to limeworks on the road west of the emparked Middleton House, which was finely extended in 1898. In 1951 the area had under 200 people, served by North Middleton post office and Borthwick primary school. The railway was closed in 1969. By 1973 the mansion had become in succession a special school and a refugee camp; by 1975 it was a conference centre known as Middleton Hall. By 1977 the castle was the Borthwick Castle Hotel, and by 1981 the local population had risen to 350. In the 1990s Middleton Hall or House, *'A'* listed, was bought by the government, intended for use as a Prison Service college, but was for some reason then resold at a loss: an odd way to save public money! However, its new owners soon saved it for posterity. By 1996 North Middleton had been bypassed and had lost its post office but did have a pub; the still-active limestone quarry is a lengthy gash.

## BORVE — Map 11, C1

***Lewis townships,*** *pop. 800* — OS 8: NB 4056

On the bleak north-western coast of Lewis some 25 km north of Stornoway are ancient remains and early Christian monuments. Among a cluster of crofting settlements some 9 km to the east of the main road junction at Barvas is Borve *(G. Bhuirgh)*, also known as Five Penny Borve. This gained the more important post office and telephone exchange, whereas the area's primary school was built at Shader *(G. Siadar)* some 2 km to the south-west. By 1951 their combined populations were around 930, falling to around 850 by 1981. However, by then Borve had a doctor, and tourism was developing, with the 6-roomed *Borve House Hotel* from about 1976. By 1999 Borve had a pottery.

## BOTHWELL — Map 15, E6

***Lanarkshire small town,*** *pop. 6500* — OS 64: NS 7058

The great ruined Bothwell Castle on its bluff above the Clyde was built from 1242 by Walter of Moray. Important enough to be shown on the Gough map, the castle then passed from hand to factional hand. In 1301 a giant *'belfry'* or siege tower fabricated in Glasgow for Edward I was carried in pieces to besiege Bothwell Castle, using 30 waggons and a temporary bridge: the stratagem succeeded. After recapture by Bruce half the keep was slighted. The parish church was made collegiate in 1398 by Archibald the Grim, Earl of Douglas, and both castle and church were largely rebuilt for him about 1400, at the same time as the first (and for centuries the only) bridge over the middle Clyde was erected. Sited about 3 km above the castle, it was originally a four-arched structure only 3.6 m wide between parapets. Bothwell Castle had its own sheriff; in the late 15th century it was the seat of the powerful Bothwell family.

**The Burgh in the Shadow of the Bridge**: Pont's map dated 1596 showed *'Bodwal'* Castle emparked, and between it and the *'Clyd brigh'* was a small place named *'Boithwel'*. This was chartered as a burgh of barony in 1602, and a parish school was established in 1612, but the settlement did not attract the attention of early travellers. It was the strategic importance of the bridge that mattered, shown by its defensive gate and by the Battle of Bothwell Brig fought in 1679; by the time of the Roy survey of about 1753 six roads or tracks converged there, including the main road from Edinburgh to Ayrshire. But Bothwell itself, though by that time a medium-sized linear settlement, was apparently mainly agricultural. Dorothy Wordsworth did not mention the settlement in 1803, noting only that the ruin of Bothwell Castle was *"a large and grand pile, of red freestone, harmonising perfectly with the rocks of the river, from which, no doubt, it has been hewn"*. It is possible that the actual quarry lay near Bellshill.

**Concrete Bob's Solid Springboard**: By about 1825 Bothwell was served by a penny post from Hamilton. The bridge was widened in 1826 to 10 metres as part of the improvement of coach roads, while remaining the only Clyde bridge in the vicinity of Hamilton. Bothwell itself grew with fortunate slowness into a large village with sweeping avenues. The signal boxes of the Glasgow, Bothwell, Hamilton & Coatbridge Railway – later part of the North British Railway (NBR) – which opened between Shettleston and Bothwell in 1877, were built by Robert *'Concrete Bob'* McAlpine. Until then he had been a bricklayer's labourer, but his flair and ambition led him to found what one in the business described to the author as an *"expanding contracting firm" (!)* that would go on to build entire railways: the Lanarkshire & Dunbartonshire, Lanarkshire & Ayrshire and the West Highland Extension with its spectacular curved viaducts.

**Railways and Trams yield to the Motorway**: In 1879 the NBR extended their branch to Hamilton; at one time their yard sorted sixty coal and goods trains per day. Uddingston golf club, founded in 1893, laid out a 9-hole course in Bothwell Park; from 1922 it was named after the castle. By 1895 the Caledonian had constructed a spur from its main line at Fallside to a second station. An asylum (mental hospital) was built 1 km north of the town, a gasworks was established, and an electricity generating station was built about 1906. From that time the Lanarkshire Tramways Company served the town, Motherwell and Uddingston, where from 1907 to 1931 they connected with Glasgow *'caurs'*. By 1951 the population was 3180; two small hotels were open. The rail passenger service to Glasgow ended in 1961, and by 1971 the whole local rail system had been lifted, replaced by the M74 motorway with its service station; Bothwell CR station became a factory site.

**Putting the Heart Back**: By 1977 the *Bothwell Lodge Hotel* with its function suite was in business in the village centre, later being renamed the *Bothwell Bridge Hotel*. In 1979 Levi Strauss operated a factory at Bothwell Park and opened another, with 300 new jobs, but growing Bothwell remained a large village; the mental hospital still existed. The Bothwell firm of Bio Medical Systems was developed in the 1980s by Gordon Wright to supply heart-lung machines and heart valves; together with a Cumbernauld plant it employed 150 people by 1990 when they were sold to the American combine 3M. Bothwell had 6542 residents in 1991, with an emphasis on higher qualifications. In 1994 Hewden Stewart plc, a major plant hire group, had its HQ in Bothwell, more recently claimed as a *"conservation village"*. Harte Construction, Haemonetics (medical appliances) and Lynx Parcel Express all employ several hundred. Hotels include the *Bothwell Bridge* (90 rooms), the long-established *Silvertrees* (26) and the modern *Express by Holiday Inn* (120).

## BOTHWELLHAUGH

**Map 15, E6**

***ex-village, Lanarkshire.*** OS 64: NS 7258

Bothwellhaugh stood just above the level of floods where the South Calder Water entered the River Clyde 1 km east of the town of Bothwell. An experiment in progress at nearby Orbiston in 1826, aimed at creating a humanist new settlement for 500 people, was described by Chambers as *"a handsome place"*; but it appears sadly to have failed at an early stage after abuse from the local people who labelled it *'Babylon'*! By 1888 the large Hamilton Palace Colliery had been sunk near Bothwellhaugh, exploiting low sulphur coal, and in that year a village of two-storey houses was built to house the miners, sited on the flood plain itself! By 1895 the mine had been rail connected to the Caledonian Railway's main line.

**The Vanished Village lives on in a Home Movie**: In 1951 1240 people lived in the village of Bothwellhaugh, surrounded by riverside subsidence flashes; but in 1959 exhaustion of the coal reserves led to closure of the mine. In the early 1960s local slater Joe Griffiths made a fascinating cinematic record of village life which is Bothwellhaugh's sole memorial, for by 1971 the bing had been used to raise the nearby stretch of the new M74 above flood level, and by 1979 all traces of the mine headworks and of the village itself had been obliterated, enabling the creation of the north-west corner of Strathclyde Country Park; much of the village site is covered by the artificial Strathclyde Loch. By 2000 the *Holiday Inn* stood beside the M74 junction only 500 m from one-time Bothwellhaugh.

## BOWLING

**Map 15, A4**

***Village on n. side of R. Clyde,*** *pop. 500* OS 64: NS 4473

Bowling lies 5 km east of Dumbarton on the north bank of the tidal River Clyde, where it is most closely approached by the Kilpatrick Hills; the 15th century Dunglass Castle, which originally stood on a small peninsula, controlled access up the river. There were mills both east and west of the castle by about 1600 when Timothy Pont mapped the area, but Bowling was not named. A waterside inn may reflect the location of the ferry shown on the Roy map, made about 1754; this seems to have competed with the Erskine to Old Kilpatrick ferry, but the map also emphasised the significance of the coastal road between Glasgow and Dumbarton. Taking advantage of the pure streams flowing from the hills, a brewery was sited at Littlemill in Bowling, and was in production by 1772 when a maltings was built.

**Canal Port and Rail Terminus**: Bowling was chosen as the Clyde terminus of the Forth & Clyde Canal, opened thanks to Government aid in 1790. It became mainly a transhipment point for coal and iron, but is noteworthy as the site of the trials in 1812 of the pioneer steamship *Comet*. By 1820 the brewery had been converted into the Littlemill distillery, and from 1825 a shipyard was open (owned by Scott & Sons from 1850). The port was improved by constructing a basin in 1848, and in 1850 the isolated Caledonian & Dunbartonshire Railway opened from a terminus at Bowling to Dumbarton and Balloch; this connected with Clyde steamers serving Glasgow and Lochgilphead.

**Railways and Whisky**: In 1858 the Glasgow, Dumbarton & Helensburgh Railway (later a North British branch) was opened between Bowling and the national rail system at Cowlairs on the Edinburgh & Glasgow Railway. This reduced the role of the canal, which was bought by the Caledonian Railway (CR) in 1867. The CR added another basin in the 1880s. In 1875 the distillery was improved and enlarged, employing both steam and water power; in 1886 the peat came from Stornoway and Perthshire, 680,000 litres of Lowland malt whisky being produced; the firm bottled its product in Glasgow. By the 1890s Auchentorlie House stood in a small park west of the village. Murray found the *Sutherland Arms Hotel* open in 1894; Bowling was *"a cheerful and busy-looking village with landing stages, wharves, and a large enclosed dock where Clyde steamers are laid up during the winter"*. From 1896 a duplicate railway to Dumbarton was operated by the CR, adding Bowling to other Clydeside places with two competing stations, here facing each other across the main street.

**Scotts of Bowling**: Among the many small vessels built by Scott & Sons was the ugly but serviceable early motor vessel *Lochinvar* for MacBrayne's Sound of Mull service. In 1927 Scotts was fourth among British yards in terms of the number of its coasters in service. In 1928–31 Scotts built six *'Yewboats'* for John Stewart of Glasgow, such as the 827-ton SS Yewpark, each fitted with war surplus engines. The Scott family's own steam-yacht is now at the Scottish Maritime Museum.

**Yet more Whisky**: Littlemill ceased production about 1929 but was bought in 1931 by the American Duncan G Thomas, who put it back to work, later selling to Barton of Chicago. The ex-CR line through Bowling was closed completely in early British Railways days; but the town's first line survived to be electrified in 1961. By the 1950s Bowling had lost its hotel, and from the deck of a Clyde steamer in 1959 the author noted Scott's as a small struggling shipyard. There was a rail-connected Esso oil depot fed by coastal tankers, but the canal basin was used for yachting.

**Rail Nadir, and Canal Resurgence; Whisky ends**: The canal was severed about 1970, the shipyard was closed in 1979 and Bowling's facilities had declined to a minimal level by 1981. In 1991 when the population was under 500 a pipeline was opened to bring petroleum products from Grangemouth to the Esso storage terminal, from which deliveries were still carried by rail to Oban and Mallaig in 1992; but this traffic was killed off in 1993 by the Tory profit seekers put in to *'manage'* rail freight, and the terminal has now sadly been demolished. In 1966 Bartons opened a new distillery, bonds, and bottling plant at Littlemill, which was producing 1.8 million litres a year in 1967 *(see also Alexandria)*. Still operating to capacity in 1983, it was closed from 1984 to 1989, when it reopened under Gibson International. The distillery ceased work in 1994 and much was demolished, leaving the listed 1772 maltings in need of a new user in 1997. The reopening throughout of the Forth & Clyde and Union Canals, planned for 2001, should provide new opportunities for water-based tourism.

## BOWMORE & Bridgend

**Map 4, B5**

***Villages, Islay,*** *pop. 1000*

OS 60: NR 3160

Monro wrote in 1549 that the Isle of Islay was *"fertile, fruitful, and full of natural grassing, with many great deer (and) many woods; hunting beside every toune"*; it had lead ore and good harbours. Laggan on the sheltered shores of Loch Indal was already emphasised as a very significant place on a map of Timothy Pont who worked around 1600. In 1614 it was chartered as a burgh of barony, now called Bowmore, a name which translates as *'Big Cow'*! The unique Islay Parliament, which originally convened at Finlaggan (*q.v.*), was moved to Bowmore in 1718, and met there until 1843.

**Planned Village, Distillery and Woollens**: Bowmore was replanned in 1767–68 by the laird Daniel Campbell who lived at Islay House by Bridgend, 3 km north of Bowmore. A unique circular church was built, an experiment not adopted elsewhere, and Islay's first legal distillery was licensed in the village in 1779. A single annual fair was held on Islay in 1797; by that time Bowmore was a post town. Two years later, Heron noted of Islay that *"the principal village now is Bowmore, where several neat buildings have lately been erected. This new town has a convenient harbour."* In the 1830s Islay had a dense rural population of 18,000, but this could not be sustained under prevailing conditions and was soon greatly reduced by emigration; in one period of 30 years 5000 people left the island. The early 19th century Bridgend carding mill was superseded by the Islay Woollen Mill across the river, founded by J Christie about 1870; he made hand looms to his own patents and in 1883 set up a spinning, dyeing, blanket and drugget mill *(see Hay & Stell)*.

**Flights of Fancy, Flying Boats and Cheese**: In 1886, the energetic Barnard described Bowmore as *"a town containing 800 inhabitants"*. The distillery was large, producing 900,000 litres of Islay malt whisky annually, and had been owned by W & J Mutter of Glasgow since 1852. It had its own steamship to carry barley from Inverness and Morayshire, while its water supply flowed from the upper River Laggan through a long and winding lade. Barnard stayed at the *"picturesque" Beul-an-Ath Hotel, "the best and only one of any importance in Islay, possessing gardens and grounds of most enchanting loveliness"*; this was at Bridgend. By 1894 the *Black Bull Hotel* was open

*Bowmore from the pier. The village was re-planned in the 1760s, and the unique circular church was built in 1767 by Thomas Spalding for the laird, Daniel Campbell.* *(JRH)*

in Bowmore, but Murray's Handbook remarked archly that although Bowmore was *"the chief village of Islay, Bridgend is a much better place at which to stay"*. By the 1920s Glasgow steamers loaded and unloaded by lighter, due to the shallow water at Bowmore pier, and the service was abandoned about 1937; but in the 1940s the pier was briefly used as a wartime flying boat base. In 1953 Bowmore was described as a fishing village; but it already had the small Islay Cheese Creamery, the island's secondary school, two hotels and two tiny hospitals. By the 1970s it was also the site of Islay's diesel-driven power station, built by the Hydro Board.

**Pottery and Whisky**: By 1977 a pottery was open at Bridgend, near the Newton of Kilmeny primary school. In 1979 Bowmore was the shore station for the lighthouse keepers of Rhinns of Islay and Ruvaal, but the harbour had silted up. By 1980 English speech predominated, but a Gaelic revival was said to be in progress. Bowmore had the facilities of a large village, and was the main shopping centre for Islay, plus five small hotels. In 1981 the island's population was a mere 3500, but over 1000 lived in and around Bowmore. In 1990 the Bridgend mill contained an industrial museum. A new swimming pool had been built by 1992. In the 1990s the energy-efficient distillery welcomed visitors, making a strong and peaty Single Malt, bottled at their Springburn bond by the owners, Morrison Distillers, and sold at ten to twelve years old; in 1994 it was sold to the Japanese firm Suntory. The reopened cheese creamery finally closed in 2000. Though the woollen mill still makes tweeds, the old Bridgend carding mill stood derelict by 1997, and by 2000 the few pupils in the Newton primary school made its future uncertain, though Bowmore's Islay High School has about 250 pupils and its primary school remains open. Hotels include the *Lochside* and the *Bridgend*.

## BRACO, Ardoch & Greenloaning

**Map 6, A4**

***Perthshire villages,*** *pop. 900* OS 57/58: NN 8309

In the first century the Roman legions built a major earth-embanked fort east of the River Knaik, where it left the western hills 15 km north of Stirling. With the smaller forts at Kaims to the north and Glenbank to the south it defended their road beside the Allan Water, which led to Tayside. Later, smaller garrisons built inner banks; by the mid second century it was an outpost north of the Antonine Wall, but was soon deserted. Braco Castle, a 16th century tower, arose 2 km upstream. By 1724 a *'King's Road'* between Stirling and Crieff nearly paralleled the Roman road, crossing the Knaik at Braco, the centre of Ardoch parish. The Roy map of about 1750 showed Ardoch House south of the fort, the tiny village of Braco west of the Knaik bridge, and the Allan bridge 2 km to the south. At the nearby hamlet of Greenloaning the later turnpike road to Perth struck off to the east. Though bypassed, the village was enlarged around 1815, and for a time had cattle fairs.

**The Passing Railway**: The Scottish Central Railway opened in 1848, with a station at Greenloaning, partly built with stone from Ardoch quarry. In 1868 the baronial mansion of Orchill New House was built in large policies 3 km north-east of the village. By 1895 inns were open at both Orchill and Braco, which also had a post and telegraph office: tourism helped its inn to expand into the *Braco Hotel*. Ardoch parish was very stable – it contained 916 people in 1901, and 933 in 1991. In the 1940s Orchill New House was vacated and became farm buildings. The station at Greenloaning had also been closed by 1967, and during the 1970s some housing estates were built at Braco and a small one at Greenloaning, which had a pub. Ardoch House was derelict by 1980. Braco remained a small village in terms of facilities. Orchill Quarry was still worked in 1995, despite Council attempts to end it. In 1997 Orchill New House was restored for residential use. Now known as Ardoch, the fort is among Scotland's most complete Roman features.

## BRAE & Busta

**Map 14, B3**

***Village and hamlet, Shetland,*** *pop. 750* OS 2 or 3: HU 3567

Busta Voe is a sheltered inlet on the north-west coast of the Shetland Mainland, separated from the eastern Sullom Voe by a narrow isthmus. Although Busta House was built in 1588, Pont's map of about 1592 showed no settlement. When in 1712 the salt tax priced foreign fish curers out of the market hitherto dominated by the Dutch, Gifford the laird of Busta House set up a fishing and fish drying centre with a tiny stone-built harbour below his garden, where he optimistically planted trees. These grew into stunted specimens, still a Shetland wonder in 1827. Fishing prospered for some years but Busta remained tiny. The nearby crofting township of Brae had a post office by 1843, one of the first in Shetland; it commanded the new road north, and by 1894 a weekly steamer called at Brae pier.

**Brae overtakes Busta and Trees grow at Gaza**: By the 1950s Brae had garages and a 50-pupil junior secondary school, so in 1962 it was chosen as a rural planning *'holding point'*. In 1957 there was a small mine near the small crofting township of Sullom, 8 km to the north; this soon closed, replaced by a quarry. The steamer service had long ceased when, during the development of the Sullom Voe (*q.v.*) oil terminal around 1980, Brae rapidly grew to a quite large and busy though rather bleak village, with the new Brae High School, a sailing club, health centre and new hotels. Historic *Busta House* had long been a very pleasant hotel, and by 1987 there was a new pier, a new village hall and a few new houses nearby; despite the often fierce winds, an experimental forestry plantation at nearby Gaza had succeeded. In 1991 Brae had 756 residents. The *Busta House Hotel* has 20 rooms; a caravan and camping site is open to the south.

## BRAEMAR

**Map 6, B1**

***Deeside village,*** *pop. 425* OS 43: NO 1591

Castleton of Braemar lies 340 m above sea level where the Clunie Water flowing from the Cairnwell Pass joins the upper Dee. The first of its three castles was Kindrochit, built by Malcolm Canmore in the late 11th century as a hunting lodge, modernised 300 years later and in 1455 still Royal property. Second was a wooden structure atop the 12th century Invernochty motte, raised by a noble brought in by David I. This had rotted away and Kindrochit was already a ruin in 1618 when Taylor visited Braemar, which was then inhabited by *"Irish-speaking"* Highlanders in tartans and plaids, and frequented by nobles in August and September for deer hunting in the large pine forests nearby.

**A Military Role**: The third and last Braemar Castle was built in 1628. Due to its strategic location in the eastern Highlands, the 1715 rising gathered here; afterwards it was used as a barracks, with curtain walls added around it. By 1724 a military road had been built over the Cairnwell Pass from Blairgowrie. At Dalchalmore, 5 km south of Braemar, this crossed Fraser's Bridge, built in 1752 by James Robertson of Dunkeld. South of the *'barrack'* the Roy map marked some 15 dots clustered near the Clunie bridge, representing the huts of *'Castletown'*. Across the Dee was the House of Invercauld, from which six rides radiated through its forested policies. In 1752 the Dee was bridged at Invercauld, 3 km to the east of Castleton, under the direction of Caulfeild whose men also built the Lecht road on to Grantown in 1753–54.

**From Rough Hamlet to Sophistication**: By about 1770 a *"commodious inn"* stood at Castleton, and in 1797 two fairs were scheduled at Braemar, whose first post office opened between 1813 and 1838. A new parish church was built in 1830, and Prince Albert who had bought the Balmoral estate in 1852 later set up a meteorological station. The Linn of Dee bridge – built of Aberdeen granite – was opened 9 km west of Braemar in 1857. The first Invercauld bridge was superseded in 1859, but left in place. The hamlets of Auchindryne west of the Clunie Water and Castleton to the east were joined by a bridge built in 1870. Robert Louis Stevenson wrote Treasure Island in 1881 while staying at Braemar. The *Invercauld Arms Hotel* was open at Castleton by 1882. By 1894 the village had *"changed from a rough Highland hamlet to a tidy watering-place"*. Murray found regular Highland games; the *Fife Arms* and *Invercauld Arms* hotels were *"both first class but expensive; secure rooms beforehand"*. Old Mar Lodge was replaced in 1895 for the Duke of Fife by a new rambling Mar Lodge with a ballroom *'decorated'* by 3000 red deer antlers! An early motor bus of the Great North of Scotland Railway ran from 1904 between the *Fife Arms Hotel* and Ballater station to connect with the trains.

**Tourism and Conservation**: Braemar golf club, founded in 1902, laid out a rather bleak 18-hole riverside course. By the 1950s six hotels and a youth hostel augmented the facilities of a typical village; another youth hostel was open by 1966 at beautiful Inverey, 8 km up-river. The old parish church was converted in the 1950s into the Festival Theatre. Meantime Braemar itself was shrinking, from over 750 residents in 1951 to only about 425 in 1981, losing a hotel, the chemist, secondary schooling and post town status. However a bank, school, garage and grocer remained, while a horncraft shop, woodcarver, four art galleries, five hotels, the youth hostel, a pottery and the golf course served the tourists.

**Base for Walkers, Skiers and Royal Watchers**: In 1994 the *Invercauld Arms* was reopened as a high grade hotel. In 1995 the 31,000 ha Mar Lodge Estate, including Ben Macdhui, was bought by the National Trust for Scotland (NTS), helped by a large grant from the National Lottery; the Lodge was opened to paying guests. By 1996 a heritage centre, mountain rescue post and caravan site had been added to the local facilities. The *Festival Theatre* building, last used in 1990, had been saved for re-use by 1999. The annual Braemar Gathering maintained a permanent circular site for Highland games at Auchendryne, and still drew the Royals. Both youth hostels are still open, Inverey being seasonal; there is also an independent hostel for backpackers.

## BREASCLEIT & Callanish

**Map 11, B2**

***Lewis townships,*** *pop. 500* — OS 8 or 13: NB 2135

Some 5000 years ago the wet and windy Outer Hebrides were naturally forested, but the neolithic peoples who settled on the west coast of Lewis burned and felled the trees to practise agriculture. Their field clearances inadvertently created a wet peat-covered desert seamed with stone walls. They also built several stone circles in this locality, a peninsula in the sheltered Loch Roag some 20 km west of Stornoway. Chief among them are the 47 standing stones of Callanish, in Britain second only to Stonehenge. This famous monument still dominates the area, but by about 2000 BC the people had left.

**Crofting Townships shrink – Fish Meal grows**: Eventually the area was re-settled, though Pont's map of about 1600 marked only *'Breasklet'* (Breascleit). In more modern times a road was made through the area, a pier was built, and a primary school and post office were provided; the crofting township at Callanish *(G. Calanais)* also acquired a pier and post office, and later a mobile bank called fortnightly. There was a combined population of about 750 in 1951, and the standing stones by 1957 were in the care of the state. Lewis Stokfisk Ltd, a new joint Norwegian and HIDB fish drying factory, was already open at Breascleit when in 1978 the Western Islands Council approved the proposal by Vincent of Tampa, Florida, to build a fish meal factory close by, providing 36 jobs; even so the population had shrunk to only 500 by 1981.

**Salmon, Field Studies and Pharmaceuticals**: By 1991 Callanish Ltd, which had defied problems of remoteness to take over one of the Breascleit fish factories, was an eager new chemical company making – from evening primrose and other natural oils – various sophisticated products, used world-wide for clinical trials. By 1994, renamed Callanish Pharmaceuticals, they were a subsidiary of Scotia Pharmaceuticals, which was in receivership in 2001 when it employed about 100 staff. Meantime Edinburgh University Archaeological Research Department had set up a field centre at Callanish Farm in 1985, later adding a visitor centre, opened there in 1995. The Grimersta River, 4 km south of Callanish, long noted for its fine salmon, still provides good catches; there is a good small guest house at Breascleit, but no hotel nearer to the standing stones than Carloway, 8 km to the north.

## BRECHIN

**Map 6, C2**

***Angus town,*** *pop. 7650* — OS 44/45/54; NO 6060

The massive twin Iron Age hill forts of Brown and White Caterthun stand nearly 300 m above sea level on southern outliers of the Grampians. Some 8 km to the south-east in a fertile area of Angus is Brechin castle rock, high on the steep south-facing bank of the River South Esk. Brechin may be named after Brachan, a minor sixth century king of Angus. A Culdee priory and a bishopric existed by the eighth century. By 973 Brechin was being described as the *'great city'*, and its rare round tower is thought to have been built about that time. From about the 11th century Menmuir, 8 km to the north-west, had a thanage. In 1150 King David I granted the bishop the right to hold a weekly market in the *'villa'* or village of Brechin, at that time a unique right outwith a burgh.

**City Plagued and Market Lost**: Brechin became an Ecclesiastical Burgh between around 1171; its cathedral church was built of pink sandstone from the mid 12th century. In the 1260s a Maison Dieu or *'hospital'* for the poor was established, of which vestiges remain, and there was a stone bridge by the 13th century. Brechin's see was jointly held with St Andrews, but the Dean of Brechin was the most powerful churchman in Angus and the Mearns. In 1295 Brechin was again described as a *"city"*, and its castle was a royal stronghold, strengthened during the Wars of Succession but besieged in 1303 when Sir Thomas Maule was governor. Up to about 1350 Brechin was sometimes chosen for the signing of royal charters. A Sunday market was chartered by David II in the mid 14th century, but its trade was hit by the calamity of the Black Death, and by suspension of the market rights due to the wrongful erection of a mercat cross, then permitted only in Royal Burghs. In 1372

*Brechin Cathedral, built of pink sandstone from the mid 12th century. The round tower is one of only two in Scotland, the other being at Aberfeldy. The church was restored and remodelled in 1899–1902 to designs by John Honeyman of Glasgow.* (RS)

Forfar and Montrose joined to prevent Brechin's traders – by then unauthorised – from reopening a market.

**Recovery, Towers, Market and Post**: However, by 1488 Brechin had regained its rights and was again a burgh; in the period 1535–56 it paid between 1.5% and 3% of Scotland's burgh tax revenue. The tower house of Aldbar Castle 3 km south-west of Brechin was built in 1580 by Thomas Lyon of Glamis, and Melgund Castle, another 16th century tower which unlike Aldbar was to survive, rose 3 km farther south-west. The pile of Careston Castle, 6 km to the west, whose sculptured chimneypieces made it one of the great houses of the Scottish Renaissance, was originally built around 1590. By 1593 Brechin was the centre of a presbytery, its market was functioning, and it must also have lain on the Perth to Aberdeen postal route established in 1595.

**Royal Burgh: Poverty, Plague and Panelling**: By 1628 Menmuir had a parish school. Although in 1639 Brechin ranked only 29th among Scottish burghs in tax yield, it became a Royal Burgh as late as 1641. Then in 1647–49 bubonic plague struck again; some two thirds of the population succumbed, and again Brechin languished, for half a century. In 1690–1710 the Earl of Panmure had Brechin Castle remodelled into a mansion with many finely oak-panelled rooms to designs by Alexander Edward, a pupil of Sir James Bruce (*see Kinross*). Defoe described Brechin in the 1720s as *"an ancient town with a castle finely situate"* formerly of the Maules, Earls of Panmure, which had been forfeited following the 1715 uprising. However, in time it was returned to them, and in 1827 Chambers noted it as *"the seat of Mr Maule of Panmure"*.

**Eighteenth Century Roads and Textiles**: The road between Brechin and Dundee was improved in 1736. Roy's map of about 1750 showed roads converging on the bridge from the south and from Forfar; tracks led east to Montrose, west to Kirriemuir, and there was a road labelled *"by Drumlithy to Stonehaven, Aberdeen &c"*. The town was linear, paralleling the river between the formally emparked castle and the bridge, to the east of which was a mill. By then Brechin was a linen yarn sorting centre; a bleachfield was built around 1750, and by 1762 there was a British Linen Company manufacturer. A fine Town House with an Assembly Room was erected in 1788, and a second linen bleachfield constructed. The north arch of the bridge was rebuilt in 1786 and the Mill of Cruick, 4 km north-west of Brechin, was built in 1792 for dressing lint. At that time flax was grown in the district, spun by women and hand-woven by men; the local bleachfields enabled finished cloth to be sold in the Brechin market. A cotton mill existed by 1796 when it was converted for flax spinning. In 1797 the annual fair was still programmed; Heron's guide of 1799 noted *"a manufacture of linen and cotton, and a considerable tannery, in the city or borough"*, whose population was *"computed at five thousand"*. Sadly part of the medieval cathedral was demolished in 1807.

**Postal, Banking and Educational Services**: There had certainly been a local post office by 1743, and by 1797 Brechin was a post town. Early 19th century bank branches were attempted by The Dundee Banking Company, The Dundee New Bank, the Dundee Union Banking Company, and The Montrose Banking Company. The Mechanics' Institute for adult education was established in 1836, funded by Lord Panmure; it was housed – together with three local schools and a library – in a fine building designed by local architect John Henderson and built in 1838–39.

**Brewing, Distilling and Pioneers in Scottish Power Weaving**: The original Brechin Brewery was established in 1790, and by 1825 four such were in operation, including the North brewery; but none of them appears to have lasted into the 20th century. The Brechin (North Port) distillery was established on the Den Burn in 1820 by Guthrie Brothers, and the Glencadam distillery was built in 1825. In 1818 nearly 700,000 m² of linen cloth were stamped in Brechin, for the water-powered East Mill had been built around 1800 for flax spinning, and water-powered looms were installed there in 1810, by several years the earliest in Scotland. The Brechin Gas Company was started in 1834. In 1836 the East Mill was replaced by a new mill built alongside, shortly after Lamb & Scott had erected a mill in 1835 to make canvas and hessians.

**Sidelined by the Railways**: Although it lay on the most direct land route from Perth to Aberdeen, Brechin was spurned by the promoters of the main line railway that was created through Strathmore in 1848; they chose to adapt existing lines to form a rather circuitous but less hilly route through Forfar. However, Brechin was important enough to be made the terminus of a branch built at the same time from the Aberdeen Railway at Dubton near Montrose. Its goods yard became busy handling flax for the mills, and lime, cattle and coal for farm and general use: the Brechin Agricultural & Trading Company built a large warehouse at the station.

**Newspaper, Mansion, Paper and more Bleaching**: Perhaps triggered by these developments, a local newspaper, the *Brechin Advertiser*, was founded in 1848. The well known architect David Bryce designed a sprawling mansion for William Maule, built west of the town in 1853 and immodestly named Maulesden; it was later taken over by Lochee and Forfar textile magnates, while the fine old castle passed to the Dalhousie family. A former spinning-mill beside the South Esk was converted into a paper mill in 1851–52 by Oswald Guthrie & Co; a papermaking machine was installed. The town had grown, the prominent West Church being erected in 1856. James Ireland opened a bleachfield in 1852; in 1864 this had 100 workers who bleached 1900 tonnes of yarn a year, while the Inch bleachfield was almost as large. In 1869 these two large factories processed shirtings and the coarse linen known as *'dowlas'*. Brechin Infirmary was built in 1869.

**Smart and Ireland, Lamb & Scott**: About 1854 J & J Smart built a small powered mill for 48 looms but continued to employ hand weavers; the firm has over the years worked in jute, linen, cotton and synthetics, and is still in operation. A steam powered mill was built adjacent to the East Mill in 1858. Powered by steam and water in 1864 and also under Ireland, the mill employed 400 workers and used 1300 tonnes of flax a year. By 1867 the premises had become *"very extensive"* and were owned by the East Mill Company. By 1864 Lamb & Scott had abandoned their mill to manage 600 hand-loom weavers; however they were then erecting a new mill to contain 300 power looms.

**Other Textile Firms and Town Improvement**: Also in prosperous 1864, D & R Duke were moving from 400 hand looms to a new mill of 308 power looms. One of the new mills was the fine 4-storey Den Burn Works, erected in 1864–71. In 1867 three of the four factories had power looms; in all they employed over 1300 workers, a reduction in numbers from 1840. Most firms made bleached sheetings, dowlas and similar goods. In 1867 a public park was provided; new buildings for Brechin High School were commissioned in 1876. In 1886 both the distilleries used local barley, but the peats and the water supply originated in the Grampians, so their output was classed as Highland malt. The annual production of the Brechin establishment was about 450,000 litres, while the small Glencadam distillery employed only 8 men and a gas engine to produce 180,000 litres, mainly sold in the Glasgow area.

**New Facilities, Restoration and Late Railways**: In the late 19th century the town's population held steady around 10,500. A public library was built in 1891–3. Brechin golf club was founded in 1893 and laid out an upland course on Trinity Muir, providing distant views. By 1895 only 6 holes were playable, but the course was later extended to 18 holes. There were three hotels in the town by 1894, the *Commercial, Dalhousie Arms* and *Crown*; from the last-named, horse-drawn excursions trotted up Glenesk to Lochlee. The railway station became the apex of a triangle when a Caledonian Railway branch was opened from Forfar in 1895, and a further branch line to Edzell was added in 1896, though this regularly carried passengers only until 1931. In 1895 the old town house was replaced by new Municipal Buildings, but the cathedral buildings were restored in 1900–02.

**Radar Pioneer**: Sir Robert Watson Watt, a descendant of James Watt, was born in Brechin in 1892. He was about nine years old when in 1901 the Angus Electric Light & Power Company, established in 1898 – an early date for a small town – first generated power locally for public supply; it's possible that this sparked his lifelong interest in electrical matters, leading to his invention of radar while Superintendent of Radio at the National Physical Laboratory. Brechin's linen and distilling industries were augmented by baking and canning, but the paper makers gave up some time after 1899. Brechin City Football Club was formed in 1906, opened its ground at Glebe Park in 1919 and joined Division Two in 1929. The direct line linking the Forfar and Montrose railways was abandoned in the dark days of 1917, and in 1922 the North Port distillery was acquired by Scottish Malt Distillers. The East Mill closed in 1920, but after two quiet decades it was reopened in 1939 as an offshoot of the Coventry Gauge & Tool Company.

*The Den Burn works, Brechin, built for power-loom linen weaving in 1864 and extended in 1871. It was converted into flats around 1990.* *(JRH)*

**Destroying Railways and Mansions**: By 1951 Brechin had average urban facilities and a population approaching 7500. In 1946 Wordie & Co still operated a small rail to road cartage depot, but the remaining rail passenger services were closed in 1952. Maulesden was demolished in 1963, and Aldbar Castle which had long been expanded into a mansion and owned by the Chalmers family was (most regrettably) burnt down and demolished in 1964. In the 1970s Rank's closed their substantial Brechin bakery. On the credit side, Brechin High School moved to another new building in 1970, and much redevelopment of housing in attractive traditional styles had taken place by the time that the town was freed of A94 trunk road traffic when bypassed about 1975.

**Brechin in 1976**: In 1976 Brechin had a Coopers Fine Fare supermarket, and some specialist shops such as a gunsmith and bookseller, among what was – despite some recent closures – still a good range of shops, except perhaps in the clothing sector. There were connections with Aberdeen – for example the *Press & Journal* sold many copies – as well as with other Angus centres, such as Montrose, whose Co-op had lately joined with Brechin's under a North Angus banner. However, townspeople said they generally looked to Dundee for anything not available locally. Both distilleries were still in production in 1976, all the Glencadam's output going to blenders.

**Industry in Transition**: The rail link which still despatched potatoes to the south in 1978 carried coal and other freight until closure in 1981, but thanks to local intervention the tracks and the architecturally attractive station remained relatively intact. By 1983 the Brechin North Port distillery had also closed, and had been dismantled by 1991, though Glencadam remained open under Ballantines. Meantime by 1976 Matrix Engineering was the town's largest employer, undertaking precision work for the oil industry. Although in 1978–79 the firm cut its workforce by 60, extensive housing estates were being added to the north of the town, some for workers at Edzell Airfield. About that time a riverside caravan site was opened; camping facilities were added later. Urban estate development continued in the 1980s.

**Cannery Problems and Economic Promotion**: Into the 1990s the town was still a significant agricultural and shopping centre; remarkably for a small town, the cinema had become a night club in 1985. Smarts still made linens at the Valley Works in 1989. In 1989 Anglia Canners was expanding at Brechin; but in 1991 the cannery was taken over by Hillsdown Holdings at a time of problems for the raspberry industry, and apparently closed to protect the latter's Forfar plant. In 1990 the town became the home of the North Angus Partnership, a joint body formed to stimulate the area's economy. At the 1991 census the resident population was some 7650, with an elderly slant; at that time Sonoco Industrial Packaging operated from a 1980s works. Brechin City FC – whose ground, Glebe Park, was still bucolic – swung widely in fortunes between the first division in 1993, and the third by 2000.

**New Life for the Railway and the Mills**: In 1993 TI Matrix won orders for locomotive clutches for North America, ensuring the continuance of 170 jobs. Local steam enthusiasts collected locomotives from 1979, obtained a Light Railway order and in 1992 reopened the line for tourists to Bridge of Dun as the *'Caledonian Steam Railway'*; the conserved Brechin station has a rail museum. By 1993 the Hillcrest Housing Association had converted the former Den Burn Works to housing. Some out of town shopping and a visitor centre combined with a garden centre 2 km to the west opened about then, and a US Air Force housing estate was threatened in 1995 by the impending closure of the Edzell Airfield base. There was already considerable dereliction in the historic town centre when Glencadam distillery sadly closed in 2000, but the versatile J & J Smart are still in textiles, and D & R Duke are jute weavers. A country park is now open at Brechin Castle, with a visitor centre devoted to the mysterious Picts, but agribusiness has taken over much of Menmuir. The *Northern Hotel* has 16 rooms.

## BREICH — Map 16, C4

***W. Lothian small village,*** *pop. 400* — OS 65: NS 9660

The Breich Water rises on the moors between the Forth and Clyde basins to flow through West Lothian. The Roy map of about 1754 showed the moorland road between Carluke and Livingston (later the B7015) following the north side of this stream; later a turnpike road from Edinburgh to Wishaw paralleled the south side. The Caledonian Railway's Cleland & Midcalder route was opened in 1869 between this road and the Breich Water; Breich Station – 3 km east of Fauldhouse – enjoyed rail passenger services to both Edinburgh and Glasgow. By 1899 a rail-connected quarry and a coal pit were open on Rashiehill Muir 1.5 km south of the station. By 1955 the older mines and quarry had closed, but a new mine was at work on the same rail link 1 km east of Breich, a compact village of council housing which had replaced scattered miners' rows, and had basic facilities. All mining had ceased by 1963; the mine railway was lifted, but some mine buildings and the bing remains. Meantime the village population was slowly rising past 400, and during the 1970s and 80s the hills to the south were extensively afforested. In 1999 Breich still had a post office, and an inn by the station, which had a morning peak train to Edinburgh and two back; but most trains just sail through.

## BRIDGE OF ALLAN, Airthrey & Stirling University — Map 16, A1

***Small town n. of Stirling,*** *pop. 5000* — OS 57: NS 7997

A vitrified fort stood on a knoll 2 km north-east of the site of Stirling Castle, from which it was separated by the windings of the tidal River Forth; Pictish standing stones on the surrounding Airthrey estate are also of unknown significance. To the east the ancient Logie parish church stood near the Clackmannanshire boundary, and except for a riverside castle mentioned under Menstrie, there was little else of note in Logie parish, at the foot of the western end of the massif of the Ochil Hills and bounded on the west by the River Allan. In 1520 a bridge was built over the Allan 4 km north of Stirling, to replace a ford on the road to Dunblane and Perth; soon afterwards a copper mine was opened in a nearby hill to the east. By 1627 Logie had a school. In 1600 a *'change house'* for horse-drawn vehicles was built beside the bridge, which required reconstruction in 1695. By that time a minor settlement focused on the bridge and took its name; it was surrounded by six other clachans. A meal mill was built near the bridge in 1710, and two inns were built about the same time.

**King's Road, Textiles, Copper and Paper**: Caulfeild chose the bridge as the starting point for the *'King's Road from Stirling to Fort William'*, via Doune and Callander, built under his direction in the period 1743–61. By the mid 18th century flax spinning was a cottage industry in the area; a linen bleachfield was built at Keir between 1746 and 1760. The copper mine was expanded about 1770 and gave rise to Alloa's copper smelting industry. The making of low quality paper began on the Airthrey estate about 1775, and the lairds, the Haldanes of Gleneagles, became so prosperous that a mansionhouse called Airthrey Castle was built, a late work by Robert Adam. This stood in large policies, including a lake, and was much extended in the 19th century. Cotton cloth was made from 1792 and became for a time the principal industry; by 1794 Bridge of Allan also boasted three paper mills, a woollen mill, shoemakers, a tannery, and three corn mills. There was also a small distillery, yet in 1796 only 28 families lived in the busy little settlement.

**Bridge of Allan as a Spa**: The copper mine ceased production in 1807, but in 1813 mineral springs were discovered in its disused workings, which the laird, Sir Robert Abercromby, exploited to create a spa. Its mineral water supply was engineered by Robert Stevenson, and baths and billiard rooms were provided. In 1814 the main road north via Bridge of Allan was turnpiked. Chambers in 1826 thought Bridge of Allan was *"every thing which a village ought to be: straw-roofed cottages, a mill, old inns with entertainment for man and horse, and a row of neat little villas for the fashionables who flock to it in summer"* (30,000 visitors a year, it was said). In 1835 four coaches ran daily to Stirling and Perth, plus four horse-drawn omnibuses to Stirling. Though there was no post office until after the 1840 penny post, a direct stage coach from Glasgow began to run in 1841, a gasworks and the substantial *Philp's Royal Hotel* were begun in 1842, and by 1845 a school existed at Lecropt, 1 km to the west.

**The Railway and New Village**: The Scottish Central Railway serving the village opened between Stirling and Perth in 1848; for a time Wordie & Co operated a small rail to road cartage depot. In 1850 a plan was prepared for the spacious resort village that rapidly developed to a population of 1600. In 1858 Fontane found *"a small village, a privileged summer resort for Edinburgh people"*. The Wallace Monument, designed by Rochead of Glasgow, was built from 1861 on the site of a vitrified fort; its gallery provided a superb view over this pivotal area of Scotland. A quarry was opened to provide building stone, and in 1864 the attractive *Ochil Park Hydropathic* was built (later called the *Allan Water Hotel* and ultimately converted into flats). In that year 1864 Alexander Smith described Bridge of Allan as *"the most fashionable of*

*Airthrey Castle, Bridge of Allan, originally designed by Robert Adam in his castellated style for the Haldane family. The Adam castle (1791) is on the right in this view; the towered addition on the left was added by David Thomson in the late 19th century. Stirling University was built in the grounds of this house from 1967, with offices in the castle. (JRH)*

*Scottish spas"*; by the next year there were 126 lodging houses and five hotels.

**Bridge of Allan as a Sporty Burgh**: The village became a police burgh in 1870, and from 1874 a horse tramway connected it with Stirling. In that period two annual livestock fairs were held. A bacon factory opened in 1879 and a gasworks was set up in 1884. Cold winters saw organised mass skating on the loch at Airthrey, and the new Scottish Lawn Tennis Association held its championships in the town. The Romanesque MacFarlane Museum and public hall was built in 1886–87. In 1888 only three hotels were open – *Philp's Royal, Queens*, and the *Hydro*. In 1894 the burgh was regarded by Murray as *"superior to Stirling as a centre for the tourist"*; the golf club was founded in 1895, and its speedily laid out 9-hole course was opened the same year.

**Decline, Wartime Expedients and Vandalism**: By 1899 development had peaked and the quarry was closed. During the 1914–18 war the village with its many hotels and public halls became a military training centre. The local tramway, the last horse-drawn system in Scotland, was closed and lifted in 1920, and the independent Strathallan School, opened in 1912, rapidly outgrew its site and left the town for Forgandenny in 1920. The spa lingered on until 1941, while during the 1939–45 war Westerton House became a prisoner of war camp and Aithrey Castle was used as a maternity hospital. In 1946 the Airthrey paper mill was closed and a large bottle-closure factory replaced the local cotton mill. The burgh's facilities were by then on the threshold between town and village, its *Royal Hotel* having 3 stars. The old bridge was replaced in 1957–60; sadly for posterity, the historic 438-year old structure was thoughtlessly demolished. But the old meal mill still existed as a shop in 1970 *(see MacLean's excellent local history)*.

**University, Beeching, Bypass, Bottle Caps and Jailbirds**: The University of Stirling, founded in 1964, took over Aithrey Castle and built in its beautiful policies. The University was opened in 1967 and its MacRobert Arts Centre, including a theatre – a facility no longer available in Stirling – was donated by Lady MacRobert *(see Tarland)* and begun in 1968. Ignoring any potential for new University traffic, Beeching closed the railway station in 1965; wiser counsels secured its reopening by 1988. The M9 motorway bypass of the village was built in 1970–71, isolated until 1973 when it was connected to the south. The MacFarlane Museum was vacated in 1978–79; it stood decaying in 1995 when a campaign was mounted to save it. By 1979 United Glass owned UG Closures & Plastics, whose Bridge of Allan factory was claimed to supply Europe's largest range of bottle caps. In 1981 Bridge of Allan's facilities remained marginally urban. It had also gratuitously suffered the building of the new Cornton Vale female prison; in 1995 this held all Scotland's 180 woman inmates.

**Sunrise – and other – Industries**: Wang Computers of Massachusetts opened a PC factory east of the University in

1983, providing 240 jobs until global losses in 1989 caused its removal to Limerick. Compaq of Erskine took over the factory, temporarily creating 125 jobs in service and spares; in 1993 Tandem Computers of California planned a new manufacturing operation there. Galloways, a butchery chain which had become Scotbeef meat processors, with factories in Bridge of Allan and East Kilbride, also expanded in the Gorbals and in 1994 won a contract to supply Marks & Spencer. By 1997 the 60-year-old Airthrey Kerse Dairy of Robert Graham & Sons was also a substantial business, with 100 employees.

**Innovation and Culture**: Meantime in 1985 the University had set up an Aquaculture unit, which in 1990 earned an export award for its worldwide advisory service for fish farming, and the University Innovation Park had run to three phases by 1991; in 1995 a new Textile Technology Centre was opened there. By 1990 the Gannochy National Tennis Centre was also a part of the University, which contributed to the affluent character of its 4864 people in 1991. The MacRobert Arts Centre offers a full cultural programme. The refurbished 158-year-old *Royal Hotel* now has 32 rooms; secondary schooling is at the Wallace High at Causewayhead.

## BRIDGE OF DON — Map 10, C3

***Northern suburb of Aberdeen,*** *pop. 21,000* — OS 38: NJ 9409

By about 1750 three roads fanned out north of the River Don from the historic Bridge of Balgownie north-east of Old Aberdeen. They crossed an entirely rural area west of the remarkably straight coastal links, along which in 1817 the 5-mile-long Ordnance Survey baseline for Scotland was measured. Telford's new Bridge of Don was opened in 1830 downstream of the ancient bridge. In 1866 the Aberdeen golf club moved from the King's Links at Old Aberdeen to links north of the river, where eventually the two 18-hole Balgownie courses were developed. By the 1890s a hamlet then known as Damhead had appeared north of the Telford bridge, with a post office, inn and coastguard station. In 1899 an isolated 3'0" (91 cm) gauge railway was opened, linking Bridge of Don with the new Blackdog brickworks 5 km to the north, supplying bricks to city builders – and from 1902 taking passengers to the new 18-hole links course of the Murcar Golf Club, north of the earlier courses. The brickworks closed in 1924.

**Gordon Barracks**: Trains still carried passengers to the Murcar golf course until 1951 when the population of the area, already known as Bridge of Don, was nearing 1800, with basic facilities plus a small secondary school. The Gordon Barracks were built at Bridge of Don about 1935. In 1963 a new base was opened for the Argyll & Sutherland Highlanders, lately billeted in Stirling Castle, but the Gordon Barracks were abandoned about 1990 and awaited redevelopment in 1997. Meantime city development was overspilling more rapidly, including a golf centre by 1967. By 1971 the population had reached 4300.

**North Sea Oil and Offshore Conference Centre**: With the coming of North Sea oil developments, growth accelerated. By 1979 the US-owned Baker Oil Tools was in production at Woodside Road. A large Fine Fare store was built in the 1970s, the area was transferred to Aberdeen City district in 1975 and by 1981 the population was about 12,000, with the basic facilities of an average village, including two small hotels. In the early 1980s an enormous group of retail discount warehouses appeared, in an area once intended as an industrial estate. The former showground site was developed by the mid 1980s with the Aberdeen Exhibition & Conference Centre, which opened about 1989 for the Offshore Europe exhibitions. By 1994 it included a 300-seat auditorium, a conference hall for 1200 delegates, extensive exhibition space and over 4000 parking spaces. The so-called *Aberdeen Quality Hotel* with 123 rooms was built beside it in 1992–93; this soon became the *Posthouse*.

**Occidental Oil and Industrial Development**: In 1990 the UK headquarters of Occidental Petroleum (Caledonia) was moved from London to a new site with its own sports complex; the firm managed the operation of the Claymore field, Scapa and Flotta oil terminals and the redevelopment of the Piper field following the tragic disaster of 1988. Also in 1990 the Offshore Technology Centre was built to develop and test equipment, and Biocure was developing new therapeutic products. Baker Oil Tools were so busy in 1994 that 3-shift working was imposed on over 100 reluctant employees. In 1994 ABB Vetco Gray at Broadfold Road was expanding as a supplier of engineering services to the oil and gas production industry. In 1997 Bridge of Don Academy had 814 pupils and Oldmachar Academy 1158.

## BRIDGE OF EARN — Map 6, B3

***Village s. of Perth,*** *pop. 2400* — OS 58: NO 1318

Various straight sections of early roads converge in the vicinity of the major obstacle of the River Earn near Dunbarney, some 5 km south of Perth. These probably include alignments of Roman origin, such as those southwards past Balmanno to Kelty (the Old North road), east to Inchyra for Errol and Dundee, and west to Forgandenny for Dunning and Braco. There may have been a Roman bridge, probably of timber. Curiously named Ecclesiamagirdle to the west shows early Christian settlement (*'Eccles'* = Church), but medieval travellers on the North Road from Edinburgh had to ford or be ferried across the Earn.

**Stone Bridge, Castles and Mansions**: The early stone Bridge of Earn, which eventually consisted of six arches, dated from around 1326, and was shown by Mercator on his 1595 map. Another geographical connection came through Sir John Scot who rescued the Pont maps (*see Ceres*); he was born at Knightspottie in Dunbarney parish in 1586. The 16th century tower house of Balmanno, 3 km south at the Kirkton of Dron, was later modernised by Sir Robert Lorimer. About 4 km west of Balmanno is Ecclesiamagirdle House, a 17th century tower. The original Moncrieffe House on the sunny slopes north of the bridge was designed by Sir William Bruce and built in 1679–89 for Thomas Moncrieffe.

**New Village, New Bridge and Pitkeathly Spa**: The Roy map showed that by 1750 a small linear settlement had grown on the main road south of the river, where three other routes converged. A new village named Bridge of Earn was laid out in 1769, and a post office was opened in 1803. The Perth magistrates had the old bridge repaired at the end of the 18th century; two ancient arches remained in position after it was replaced in 1822 by a new, wider and very attractive stone structure. Some 2 km to the west was Pitkeathly, where Chambers commented in 1826 that *"the mineral waters have attracted to this spot an immense number of invalids and others"*. He remarked that they all stayed at *Seton's Inn*. Although a hamlet developed there, Pitkeathly Wells proved a nine days' wonder.

**The Railway and Steamers**: Bridge of Earn station on the Perth branch of the Edinburgh & Northern Railway (later the Edinburgh Perth & Dundee) was opened in 1848; it survived undercutting by a private horse bus to Perth in 1851. From 1892 it was also served by trains on the more direct and scenic North British Railway link through Glenfarg and Cowdenbeath via the Forth Bridge; this provided the shortest but apparently least popular rail route to the Highlands for little over half a century. In 1888 David Beveridge noted *"Balmanno House, the principal mansion of the parish of Dron"*. By 1894 Bridge of Earn was a substantial village, with two smithies and what Murray called the *"very fair" Moncrieffe Arms Hotel*. Although there was also a gasworks, an absence of industry meant that burgh status was never attained; but the village did boast a junior secondary school and the private park of Kilgraston House, long a Grant property. Up to the 1930s pleasure steamers running between Perth and Dundee served a pier; paddle steamers could turn on the proverbial sixpenny piece.

**Bridge of Earn Hospital and the Motorway**: The low-lying site of an 1914–18 army camp east of the village was again developed by mid 1940 into a large hutted general hospital of over 800 beds, thereby dispersing wartime medical services from vulnerable urban centres. It was gradually reduced to under half that size by the 1970s, and became a general and rehabilitation hospital. Average village facilities remained, and in the 1950s when the population was nearing 2000 there was also a Friday market. By 1967 Kilgraston House had become a Catholic boarding school for girls. Moncrieffe House was destroyed by fire in 1957, sadly killing the resident Moncreiffe of that Ilk, and was replaced by a modern house. The railway station was closed by Beeching in 1964, and in 1970 the scenic Glenfarg railway route to Kinross and Cowdenbeath was destroyed to enable the M90 to be built more cheaply. The local authority's junior secondary school was closed by the time that the last fragments of the ancient road bridge were regrettably demolished in 1976.

**Transformed by the M90**: Following the removal of through traffic with the opening of the M90 across a major new bridge in the mid 1970s, the pleasant *Bridge of Earn Hotel* lost much of its passing trade and had to close; it became a residential home about 1980. Other local facilities remained those of a village, including a police station, but much housing development took place at Kintillo to the south from the 1960s onward, taking advantage of the motorway junction. Macspud were notably large potato merchants by 1988. By 1991 the slowly rising population was nearing 2400, of dormitory character, quite fit and well-educated. Tayside Health Board had planned to close Bridge of Earn Hospital in 1985, but it eventually closed in 1997. Meantime house building continued, but no new railway station has appeared.

## BRIDGE OF ORCHY — Map 5, B2

***West Highland settlement**, pop. 60* — OS 50: NN 2939

South of the desolate Moor of Rannoch lies Loch Tulla, from which the River Orchy drains southwards through a deep cleft in the mountains before turning west to Dalmally. Southwards is an easy pass leading to Tyndrum in Strathfillan, which was followed by the military road constructed by Caulfeild's troops in 1751, when the Bridge of Orchy was erected. An inn was also built, which became a stance on the drove road and was visited in 1803 by Dorothy Wordsworth. In the 18th century there was another inn 3km to the north-west at Inveroran near Loch Tulla, which became so well known to anglers that the inn blossomed into a small hotel; *"quiet and cosy"* was Bolton's assessment in 1953.

**The West Highland Railway**: The West Highland Railway which opened in 1894 provided a station near the tiny settlement at Bridge of Orchy, which was the scene of several railway incidents that were entertainingly described in the book by John Thomas. A winding track down the glen to Dalmally was made up as a road, and in 1935 a fast new road was completed across Rannoch Moor. By the 1950s the inn at the bridge had grown into a 12-roomed hotel serving motorists, hikers, climbers and fishermen. In 1984 the tiny settlement on the new West Highland Way hiking route comprised nine houses, the busy hotel with its petrol station, a village hall, church, post office and primary school with half a dozen pupils, still open. The population of about 60 still has the station, served by Scotrail trains, and the *Bridge of Orchy Hotel*.

## BRIDGE OF WEIR, Gryfe & Ranfurly — Map 5, B5

***Renfrewshire small town**, pop. 5050* — OS 63: NS 3965

Gryfe Castle beside the River Gryfe 22 km west of Glasgow must have originated very early, for in the 12th century it was the centre of the Sheriffdom of Gryfe. The title of caput passed to Renfrew at some time between 1396 and 1414, and the area's name was irrevocably changed. Ranfurly Castle was built in the 15th century; by the time that Timothy Pont visited the area about 1600 the bridge of Weir (presumably named from a weir diverting water to an estate watermill) had already been built north of the castle. The Lochar printworks were built near the bridge in 1780, but it appears that the village itself was founded in 1792, the year of opening of the High Gryfe cotton mill, which was duplicated in 1793 by the Low Gryfe. The Gryfe Grove cotton mill was founded in 1822 and yet another in the 1830s.

**Leather, Railways and Golf**: The first post office opened around 1825, and a gasworks was established in 1847. Leather was cured at a tannery in the converted High Gryfe mill, and another leatherworks was built later in the century on the site of the Low Gryfe mill. Bridge of Weir station was the original terminus of a short branch line from Johnstone; extended to Kilmacolm and Greenock by a Glasgow & South Western Railway subsidiary in 1869, its heyday ended in 1889 with the opening of the Caledonian's Gourock extension. Ranfurly acquired two 18-hole golf courses, the Ranfurly (Old) in 1889 and Ranfurly Castle 1905, and the large Ranfurly Church was built in 1891; then Bridge of Weir had 1646 people, rising to 2242 in 1901. Murray noted it in 1894 as *"a small manufacturing village"*, and there was an inn. The Bridge of Weir Leather Company, founded in 1905, began in the 1920s to export leather for use in Ford car seats. The tanning industry's smell problems were overcome, and growth continued in this *"residential and golfing"* place, which by 1951 had over 3000 residents, who enjoyed the facilities of a large village.

**Off the Rails and into Luxury Cars**: The Greenock rail link was cut in 1966, leaving Bridge of Weir on a branch to Kilmacolm. By 1976 the former Lochar printworks was another National Chrome (NC) tannery; the *Gryffe Arms Hotel* was open by 1977, but the small secondary school was closed in

1980 when Gryffe High School opened at Houston. High local car ownership led to a long struggle by the remaining rail commuters to Glasgow wishing to retain the line, followed by its complete closure by the Thatcher government in 1983; by 1994 its right of way was a cycle route. Local firm Teknek, set up in 1976, introduced a machine for cleaning printed circuit boards in 1986, and expanded to employ 37 people by 1990. By 1989 Ranfurly Church had become a sports club; it was converted to flats in 1994–95. Yet another new NC tannery was opened in 1989 (now employing over 100), and in 1991 the town's population was 5151, with an emphasis on higher qualifications and fitness. The Bridge of Weir Leather Company kept up its motor industry links, 95% of its output being exported by 2000, mainly to cover seats in luxury cars including models by Volvo, Saab, Renault and Honda, plus airline and office seating. But the weakness of the Euro led to 100 of its 374 workers being made redundant in 2000.

## BRIDGETON, Dalmarnock & Dennistoun

**Map 15, D5**

*Eastern parts of Glasgow, pop. 30,000* OS 64: NS 6064

Pont's map of Lanarkshire dated 1596 showed *'Burrowfield'*, an estate south-east of Glasgow, separated from the city by the Molendinar Burn, already bridged at two points. The Gallowgate – though not shown by Pont – possibly derived from a Roman road between Bothwellhaugh and Old Kilpatrick; it led east from Glasgow Cross, at first keeping north of the Camlachie Burn which joined the Molendinar near the latter's outfall into the River Clyde. By about 1650 another lane, later to be known as Dalmarnock Road, led south-east from Glasgow, leaving the Gallowgate east of the Molendinar bridge by way of what became the short Ross Street. It then turned east, parallel to the Camlachie Burn; later that section became part of London Road. East of Dalmarnock Road's crossing of the Camlachie Burn was the mansionhouse of Barrowfield. From the entrance to its policies the lane continued to Dalmarnock, an ancient farm beside the loop of the Clyde, where a ford gave access to Rutherglen.

**Coal, Calton and James Watt's Condenser**: By 1723 coal was being mined in the west part of the Barrowfield lands between London Road and Gallowgate; though these workings were, it seems, not very successful they gave rise to the name *'Coal-toun'*, hence Calton. By 1734 Glasgow's growing congestion was such that hand loom weavers were overspilling from the east end of the city to build houses in the adjacent Calton, only a few hundred metres east of Glasgow Cross but outwith the burgh, hence free from guild control. In 1765 while walking on Glasgow Green, an open space on the adjacent riverside, James Watt conceived the key invention that triggered the industrial revolution – the separate condenser for steam engines. From 1790 the Monkland Canal (the modern line of the M8) formed a limit to northwards extension of the Calton.

**Rutherglen Bridge, Bridgeton and Glasgow Green**: In 1776 the new five-arched Rutherglen Bridge was opened, with a new road connecting with Dalmarnock Road at the Camlachie Burn bridge; a daily market was held there by 1779 and this became the main street of Bridgeton, the name which replaced Barrowfield. A large area beside Main Street was laid out soon after 1782 to a grid plan, the original road junction becoming known as Bridgeton Cross, the start of the new London Road. By about 1790 Walkinshaw was manufacturing beam engines in Bridgeton, and lest the locals should revolt French-style, barracks were built in 1795. The low-lying land to the south beside the River Clyde was in common ownership, comprising the Low Green beside Greendyke Street, the High Green eastwards to the crook of the river, and until at least 1782 Gallowgate Green, between the Camlachie Burn and London Road from Ross Street to Tobago Street. In 1814 Glasgow Green was laid out as Europe's first formal public park.

**Weaving, Dyeing and Printing Textiles in Babel**: In 1777 George MacIntosh, father of Charles *(see Port Dundas)* moved his cudbear dye manufactory from Leith to Dunchattan, near Glasgow's Wellpark brewery; to ensure the formula remained secret he employed only Gaelic speakers! In 1785 he joined with David Dale (who owned some Calton coal pits) to bring skilled workers from France, and opened a Turkey Red dyeworks there; this prospered, and was taken over for expansion by Henry Monteith in 1805. In 1787 Dale and Macintosh had also founded cotton mills at Dalmarnock, specialising in muslins and gauzes; maybe Scots was spoken there! Around 1800 the Greenhead brewery was opened on the new London Road, and William Scott's brewery in Barrowfield Road was also in production, but this did not survive into the 20th century.

**Cotton Thread**: Calton became a burgh of barony in 1817; the 2000 or more handloom weavers who constituted 40% of its population still eked out a frugal living. Textile developments included the large Broomward Cotton Spinning Works in Kerr Street and two Mile End works – cotton thread in Rogart Street and a spinning and weaving mill in Fordneuk Street about 1835. Dalmarnock Road was straightened and turnpiked when Dalmarnock Bridge was opened 1200 m east of Rutherglen Bridge in 1821. The Greenhead cotton mill was built in 1823 in what later became Templeton Street; G Grant's first power-loom weaving factory at Graham Square off London Road opened in 1825. There was the Burnbank bleachfield on the Molendinar Burn, 1 km east of Glasgow cathedral and above the Town Mill, and the Barrowfield Weaving Company built a four-storey mill in Broad Street.

**Cobbett, Reform and the Monteith Works**: In 1832 *"The Radical Reformers in the east district of the barony parish of Glasgow, and other villages adjacent"* as they described themselves, wrote to thank William Cobbett, a recent visitor and vocal proponent of the Parliamentary reform of that year. He had noted Bridgeton as Glasgow's *"manufacturing part, with the tall chimneys and the smoke, at the east end of the city, and somewhat separated from it"*. Cobbett visited Henry Monteith & Co's Turkey Red works at Rutherglen Bridge, *"for the dyeing and printing of calicoes and shawls and handkerchiefs upon a scale of prodigious magnitude... the buildings as large as a country town"*. Another source noted that Monteith & Co – still regarded as an innovative concern – employed 500 people at the Barrowfield dyeworks, printing cottons for export.

**Cotton continues to expand**: By 1833 Oswald's six-storey spinning mill at Bridgeton Cross employed nearly 500 people, though in poor working conditions even by the low standards of the day. There was a large spinning and weaving mill in James Street near Bridgeton Cross, and Simpson's had a weaving factory built at nearby John Street. Couper, Walker had a 5-storey mill in Broad Street about 1840; Bogle & Co built a 5-storey cotton spinning factory in Reid Street. The Bartholomews also established two large cotton mills, one in Arcadia Street, the other in Greenhead Street.

**Carpets Galore**: James Templeton and John Quigley established chenille Axminster carpet manufacture at Calton in 1837–39. In 1853 Templeton's foreman John Lyle left to found his own company in Fordneuk Street – the Bloomvale carpet works of 1869. Meantime in 1855 J & J S Templeton built the first part of their Crownpoint Carpet Works in St Marnock Street at Mile End, north-east of Bridgeton Cross, and in 1857 James Templeton & Son took over the Greenhead cotton mill of 1823 as a second carpet factory, where in the late 1860s over 500 mainly male workers made Brussels, chenille Axminster and Wilton carpets; over forty of these people designed bespoke carpets, which were also fitted. One frame was ten metres wide! An offshoot of the firm also had a factory at Mile End with about 200 operatives; there damask and *'window hangings'* were also made, some for Windsor Castle.

**Varied Metals Industries**: After 1830 came Wright's brass foundry in Muslin Street, and Donald's tinsmith's works in Main Street. Murdoch & Aitken built locomotives and other equipment at Melbourne Street: in 1851 they manufactured the twin-beam blast furnace blowing engine which eventually found its way to the Ironbridge museum. Then Glen & Ross founded the Greenhead Engine Works in Arcadia Street – these specialised in making steam hammers,

**Gas, Chemicals and Waterproofs**: In 1843 the City & Suburban Gas Company's gasworks was built in Old Dalmarnock Road; its by-products of tar, ammonia and pitch were bought by George Macintosh's son Charles, the ammonia and naphtha from pitch being used to dissolve rubber for waterproofing clothes, using a sandwich of cloth and rubber. About 1849 the Greenvale Chemical Works in Duke Street made matches and blacking among other products, whilst at Greenhead Street in Calton R & J Dick were processing what was then known as gutta percha, a natural gum akin to rubber but harder.

**Bridgeton and Dennistoun within Glasgow**: From 1845 horse buses plied from Anderston through the city centre to Bridgeton, which was absorbed by Glasgow in 1846. Dennistoun was laid out as an area of superior tenements on the south-facing slopes east of the cathedral and above Duke Street about 1850. A fine classical UP church designed by Peddie & Kinnear was built in Duke Street in 1857–58. Meantime the St Andrews Suspension Bridge designed by Neil Robson was erected in 1853–55 to replace the ferry linking Bridgeton with new factories in Hutchesontown.

**Cotton by Power-loom**: The first power-loom factories in Bridgeton were probably in Graham Square (1825) and Broad Street (about 1829). The Fordneuk power-loom weaving factory in David Street was one of 3 with the same name around mid-century. T & D Wilson's muslin, chenille and tapestry works in Rogart Street were followed by J & P Wilson's lappet and muslin manufacturers – they also built a weaving factory in Marquis Street, as did A & J Paterson a weaving factory in Newhall Street near Rutherglen Bridge. The Craigpark power-loom weaving factory beside the Monkland canal, Paul & Co's power-loom weaving mills in Fielden Street, and McMath & Pridie's weaving factory in Brookside Street all arrived in the 1860s ... as William Hollins & Co, this firm was still making woollen piece goods in 1983.

*Pouring a casting at a Bridgeton brass foundry (John Glover & Sons), which was at work by 1868. It made light castings, and machined them to produce things such as taps and valves. (JRH)*

**Bobbins and Singer Sewing Machines**: An ornate 5-storey *'fireproof'* mill was built in Duke Street in 1849 for thread-makers R F & J Alexander, followed by the Clyde Thread Works in Main Street. Among related industries were a bobbin turning works in Tobago Street, while shuttles and weaving utensils were made at Gibson's Sylvan works in Broad Street. Early Singer pattern sewing machines were apparently made in Glasgow by 1851, this work being continued by R E Simpson & Co in 1860, and by the Singer Manufacturing Company themselves in a factory built in James Street, Bridgeton, in 1871–72; even in its first year this turned out over 1000 machines a week. The firm decided in 1882 to move to Clydebank to enable expansion, leaving Bridgeton in 1884.

**Jute and Linen – Refugees from the East?**: The Baltic Works of W & J Fleming & Co were built in 1858 to spin and weave jute and linen in Baltic Street. Then the Glasgow Jute Company built their own Baltic works nearby. In 1863 a Dundee sacking maker, J Y Adams, built the Dalmarnock flax and jute works in Dunn Street. In 1858–61 the Caledonian Railway built a branch across the Clyde from Rutherglen into the Dalmarnock area; this terminated at London Road Station. The Glasgow Tube Works were built beside the new line in Dalmarnock in 1859 for William Wylie & Co, and the 1860s saw a plethora of industries established in what soon became one of the most intensively developed areas in Scotland.

**Leather and Rubber Belting**: The Pleasance Leather Works (1861) made drive belting, at that time the principal method of power transmission to machines in factories and mills; also hosepipes, and bootlaces – no doubt from the offcuts. Local supplies of leather were assured when Martin & Millar set up their large Glenpark tanning works in Duke Street about 1864. Allied firms were the Clydesdale boot and shoe factory in Elcho Street, the St Ann's 5-storey leather works in John Street, the large Scotia leather works, and later the Albion leather works, which made chrome leather for Army boots. The Greenhead gutta percha factory was expanded when textile belting coated with South American balata latex was manufactured, so competing with leather belting, until then unrivalled.

**Engineering and Foundries of the 1860s**: Important companies included the Crownpoint Boiler Works in St Marnock Street, Farquhar, Knox's engineering works in Crownpoint

Road, and the Crown Point iron foundry in Fielden Street (William Ure). From 1865 Duncan Stewart & Co made plant and machinery for sugar works, textiles and steelworks at their London Road Ironworks in Summer Street; these also built a few steam lorries and eventually covered a wide area. J Glover's Bridgeton Brass Foundry was at work in 1868, and about 1869 the Avon crucible steelworks was built in Glenpark Street.

**Retailing, Education, Trams and Timber**: The employees in these numerous factories had time for little but work and sleep, their food being snatched from local providers such as the Bridgeton Old Victualling & Baking Society, which built its stores and stables in Main Street about 1865. By 1866 there were many inadequate schools in the vicinity, yet only a quarter of the rapidly growing swarms of children received any education; by 1875 about 64,000 people had crowded into the area. Horse trams of the Glasgow Tramway & Omnibus Company first ran to Bridgeton in 1872. More space was released when the barracks closed in 1877.

**Power-looms, Paper, Pottery and Pipes**: Henry Fyfe & Son soon turned to power-loom weaving and built their Broomward mill in Kerr Street about 1867. The Dalmarnock Paper Mills came in 1868. The early Campbellfield (later *'Springburn'*) Pottery made Rockingham ware and white earthenware, as did the later Eagle pottery in Boden Street. The largest clay tobacco pipe factory in Scotland – William Christie's – opened in 1877 at Craignestock Street; 9000 were made per day.

**Templeton brings Venice to Glasgow Green**: Carpet manufacture continued to expand; Lyle's Bloomvale works were frequently extended, as were Templetons' Crownpoint works and Greenhead carpet factory. Another large new building in course of erection for Templeton at Greenhead regrettably collapsed in 1889, killing 29 women in some adjacent weaving sheds. It was rebuilt and completed in 1892 to W Leiper's famous design as a Venetian style block, commonly known as the Doges' Palace, to house spool Axminster carpet-making machines. At various times Templetons operated on at least five sites in Bridgeton *(see also Gorbals)*.

**Bridge Engineering by Arrol from 1868**: William Arrol, born in Houston in 1839 as the fourth son of a poor Renfrewshire cottton spinner, started his working life by patching porridge pots. Highly ingenious, efficient and immensely hardworking, at the age of 29 he set up the Dalmarnock Ironworks at Dunn Street, built in 1868–1871. He was the successful contractor for the Bothwell railway bridge built for the North British in 1875. Arrol's famous engineering establishment specialised in hydraulic machinery, also building steam pumping engines as a sideline, no doubt because they were essential for dewatering the cofferdams used in building bridge foundations.

**Bridgeton Builds Giant Bridges**: Arrol's bridge fabrication works was frequently expanded on a large scale up to 1911, spreading into surrounding streets, employing up to 5000 men on a site of 8ha. The firm built the first Clyde Bridge into Glasgow Central Station, then (as Tancred, Arrol) the unique and gigantic Forth Bridge and the second Tay Rail Bridge. Arrol also built the North Bridge in Edinburgh, and London's famous Tower Bridge with its pair of lifting spans (see *South Queensferry*, *Springburn*, and Anthony Murray's *The Forth Railway Bridge*). No man ever better deserved his knighthood than William Arrol, who died in 1913; as Sir William Arrol & Co his successors completed the major rolling lift bridge carrying both road and rail traffic across the River Trent at Keadby near Scunthorpe, opened in 1916 after overcoming wartime steel shortages.

**Engineering for Drinks, Bicycles, Bedsteads and Tubes**: The Bon Accord Engine Works in Fordneuk Street (soon taken over by Drysdale) made pumps and other hydraulic equipment for the drinks trades, but also for ships; they later moved to Clydebank *(q.v.)*. In 1872–73 the Howe Sewing Machine Company, a rival to Singer, built their enormous triangularly planned works of 74 by 18 bays in Avenue Street; they later also made bicycles. In 1876 Andrew Sharp built his substantial iron bedstead works in Campbellfield Street, including a foundry for casting the cornerpieces and finials. Possibly connected with both the above was E W Neil's tubemaking works at Crown Point, an 18th century house in Fielden Street; but his firm seems to have lasted for only two decades.

**Alexandra Park and new Schools**: By 1879 Alexandra Park and Alexandra Parade had been set out north of Dennistoun, enabling people living far from Glasgow Green to stroll and (weather permitting) sit outdoors in their limited leisure time. The fine buildings of Campbellfield School were erected for nearly 900 pupils in 1878–79 to relieve chronic overcrowding; they served for 90 years. In 1883 came the imposing new 17-classroom secondary school in John Street, in 1926 renamed Tullis Street after its largest firm (the school name did not change).

**The City of Glasgow Union Railway**: In 1870 a joint subsidiary of the Glasgow & South Western (G&SW) and North British (NB) Railways was opened between the latter's Coatbridge line at Gallowgate, and Pollokshields on the G&SW. The line was known as the City of Glasgow Union (CGU); it was extended the next year to terminate at College station, and a line for goods traffic from Bellgrove and Parkhead to Springburn was opened in 1875. A quasi-tunnel was first constructed at Barnhill, over which the Monkland Canal was then diverted. Stations were opened in 1881 at Duke Street and Alexandra Park (later called Alexandra Parade).

**More Dyeworks and Weaving Firms**: The Clyde Dyeworks in Strathclyde Street, John Blackwood's Springfield Road dyeworks and bleaching, and McConnell's Dalmarnock dyeworks in Davidson Street were all large in the 1870s/80s. George Wilson & Co built their Dalmarnock weaving factory in Swanston Street, as well as the River Street power-loom weaving factory. The Burnside Works in Brook Street were similarly employed, as were Renison, McNab's works in Boden Street.

**Spinning, Cotton, Muslin and Carpets**: Important names in textiles from the 1870s included The Clyde Spinning Company's mills in Cotton Street, Scott & McKillop's yarn spinning factory in Campbellfield Street, the Glasgow Cotton Spinners Company (two large yarn spinning mills, in Carstairs Street and Swanston Street), and the Burnside power-loom weaving works. John Brown & Sons built their Barrowfield muslin weaving factory in French Street in 1889, and added new premises in Carstairs Street, their Clutha Weaving Factory. In 1898 the reed and heddle manufacturers Neilson, Davie & Co built works in Savoy Street, and a muslin factory in Muslin Street in 1900. The Broomward Weaving Company's mills in

Bernard Street passed to James Templeton for yet another carpet factory.

**Milling and Baking**: The Calton Grain Mills were built about 1878 for James Kerr & Co, whose name became attached to the street in which they stood. The great Victoria Bread & Biscuit Works of John McFarlane & Sons was built in Wesleyan Street from 1880, extended at roughly five-year intervals to 1895, and about 1911. As Macfarlane, Lang & Co the firm built a large new biscuit factory at Tollcross between the wars; the Victoria Works finally closed about 1977. Other companies included the Dennistoun bakery in Paton Street (Beattie's); Kennyhill Bakery at Roebank Street (McAllister's) and another for John Dunn rose in Abercromby Street in 1906, when W & G Muir opened a ten-oven bakery in Soho Street.

**Timber Products Small and Large**: In 1871 William Gunn built a factory in Dunn Street to make shuttles for power-loom weaving mills, of which there were by then many on all sides. Robert Lyon, was a wright (these days he might be called a timber engineer) who set up workshops in Dunn Street, and another wright, Robert Robinson, built workshops in Arcadia Street. In 1876–77 the cabinetmakers A & J Harper established their oddly named *'Victoria Steam Chair Works'* in Orr Street, extended in 1889; presumably they used steam to bend the wood rather than to drive bath chairs! The Greenhead sawmills of McPhun were in Mill Street. George Taggart & Co converted Wood's mill in James Street to a cabinetmaking works; another cabinet works was erected in 1900 at Reidvale Street for James Inglis.

**Leather and Natural Fibre Industries**: Glasgow's cattle market and slaughterhouse, already open between Gallowgate and Duke Street, gave a plentiful supply of hides for tanning to make footwear, mill drive belting, and harness for the city's countless draught horses. The Scotia Leather Works in Boden Street, Miller's harnessmaking in Campbellfield Street, James Hendry Main Street sheds for making leather belting were important. McFarlane & Co used coconut fibre in matmaking at Barrowfield Street from about 1878. Another fibre then available in abundance was horsehair, which was curled for upholstery stuffing in the Dalmarnock Hair Factory, built in 1881 for D MacNair & Co at Summerfield Street.

**Paint and Chemical Works**: The Barrowfield Oil and Colour Works were founded in French Street by James Storer about 1876. George Walker & Sons' Crown Chemical Works in Reid Street followed the virtually new industry of pharmaceuticals manufacture. Hannay, Gourlay & Hinshelwood built oil and chemical works at Glenpark Street from 1883, gradually expanding into a large plant.

**Horses, Haulage and Tramways**: About 1877 the Glasgow Tramway & Omnibus Company built stables in Tobago Street; as the city's public transport services grew so these were enlarged in 1880, and in 1883 with a car shed and stalls for no fewer than 436 horses. Another major user of horse power was the haulage contractor James Henderson, whose stables for 51 horses were built in Elcho Street in 1890, and yet another was Malcolm Cunningham whose forty horses were given new accommodation in Poplar Street in 1897. After Glasgow Corporation took over the tramlines about 1893, its tramways department built a large depot at Whitevale, and the huge car sheds and stables in Ruby Street which by 1895 could accommodate 386 horses.

**The start of Celtic FC**: David Fulton & Co built their Duke Street Engraving Works in 1878. The wholesale stationers William Tait had the former Mile End cotton mills as their warehouse. The year 1887 saw the foundation by a Catholic monk, Brother Walfrid, of what was to become Celtic Football Club, aiming to raise money for poor relief; in 1888 the successful club moved to a larger *'park'*, appropriately sited at Parkhead.

**Engineering**: In the 1880s John Bennie was a hydraulic and general engineer with his Star Engine Works in Moncur Street; William Bennie & Sons built their City Machinery Stores in James Street (see Milngavie for an odd sequel), David Auld & Sons set up their Whitevale iron foundry in Rowchester Street, and the once well-known firm of Acme Machines manufactured wringers for laundering in a large works at Orr Place from 1886; in 1909 Peter Burt of this firm invented the single-sleeve-valve engine later developed by the Bristol Aeroplane Company. In 1886 John Miller & Co were coppersmiths and brassfounders in Dale Street, making stills, vats, receivers and other distillery equipment; Kerson & Campbell of the Carntyne Foundry made pumps. The machinery hall from the 1888 Glasgow International Exhibition was moved to Strathclyde Street by Penman & Co, becoming their Caledonian boiler works in 1889 (in the 1980s parts of the structure were moved to the Bo'ness & Kinneil Railway). About 1894–97 McCormack & Mills who made wire work for papermaking built the Baltic Works in Dale Street.

**Railways from Queen Street to Bridgeton Central**: The City of Glasgow Union Railway (CGUR) was extended north-westwards in 1883–86, squeezing under Glasgow High Street to join the new east–west underground route of the North British through Queen Street Low Level station, known as the Glasgow City & District Railway. A station was provided where it dived underground at Bellgrove. So as to serve the centre of Bridgeton from the west, a 1400m branch line was built from the station at High Street on the CGUR, also going underground after serving Gallowgate Central station, to emerge in 1892 at Bridgeton Cross Station, a large terminus on the site of Oswald's frightful Dickensian spinning mill. From there services ran as far afield as Balloch and Helensburgh – via the station named Singer which served that one-time Bridgeton firm's huge new works at Clydebank.

**The Glasgow Central Railway**: Between 1888 and 1896 contractors building this Caledonian Railway (CR) protégé burrowed slowly under the south side of the city centre. At a new subsurface station of four platforms at Bridgeton Cross, links converged from their Dalmarnock branch (with a new underground Dalmarnock station) and from Coatbridge and Newton, serving another station named Glasgow Green at the east end of Monteith Row, and also Central Low Level, to emerge in the west of the city. The costly but horribly smoky line opened with frequent steam trains in 1896.

**New Road Bridges and Electric Trams hit the Railways**: Dalmarnock Road bridge was rebuilt in 1889–91, and in 1896 Rutherglen Bridge was replaced by a new structure. After 1898 the tramways were speedily converted to electricity, becoming enormously popular, and the Dalmarnock tram depot was still further expanded up to 1903. The contemporaneous Whitevale tram depot in Rowchester Street was extended four times between 1899 and 1912 to accommodate the new electric cars, and the Dennistoun depot built at Paton Street in 1895–96 was also extended, in 1903–05. The costly, dirty subsurface railways were soon competing in a hopeless struggle for patronage against the cheap and clean surface-running electric trams.

**Alcohol and Tobacco**: To slake the myriad thirsts in the area's expanding industries the Slatefield Brewery was built in Slatefield Street from 1881; then in 1889 came the Anchor Brewery in Davidson Street, Dalmarnock. In 1901 the redundant tramway stables in Tobago Street were converted into a tobacco factory for D & J Macdonald – part of the Imperial Tobacco (IT) combine by 1914.

**Confectionery and Soft Drinks**: In 1886 the confectioners Stewart & Young extended the former Barrowfield weaving factory in Broad Street. Meantime in 1892 G & C Moore built an aerated water factory in Mordaunt Street, followed some years later in 1907 by Joseph Dunn's similar plant in Bankier Street. A new invention, the automatic dispenser, was the basis for the Sweetmeat Automatic Delivery Company's large chocolate works at Stamford Street, built in 1899–1902. The well-known name of Carsons Ltd entered the area in 1902–10 when they built and extended their large chocolate works in Solway Street.

**Milking Machines, Electric Motors and Coal-cutting**: In 1894 Shiels, Elliot & Nelson who made the new milking machines and thermostats built their engineering works at Gateside Street. The electrical engineers Mavor & Coulson built new works in 1896–97 at Broad Street by Bridgeton Cross, making another product then at the cutting edge of technology – industrial motors. This firm also constructed a foundry and made coal-cutting equipment.

**Flirting with Motor Vehicles in the Edwardian Age**: In 1902 Alexander Govan's Hozier Engineering Company began to manufacture his so-called Argyll car in Bridgeton. In 1906, like Singer, he too established big new premises in the west; however his move to Alexandria (*q.v.*) in 1907 proved over-optimistic. Scottish Commercial Cars of Duke Street began as distributors, but then produced nearly 400 rather primitive *'Caledon'* lorries for military use; the firm survived on a limited production of crude 4-tonne commercial lorries till 1926.

**Food Industries and Services**: The misleadingly named Strathclyde Creamery was a margarine factory, built in French Street about 1900. In 1913 a great cold store, with two of its six storeys underground, was erected at Melbourne Street for the Union Cold Storage Company. Blackie & Son the printer and publisher had a warehouse built in Milnbank Street in 1906–12. Alexanders' Duke Street thread mill was converted in 1909 as the *Great Eastern Hote*l, in reality soon a refuge for down and outs. In 1910 a telephone exchange, manually operated in those days, was built in Cubie Street; known by 1951 as the BRI (dgeton) automatic exchange, it had 3600 *'connexions'*.

**Entertainment and Utilities**: In 1911 the imposing Olympia Theatre was opened at Bridgeton Cross; it operated as a music hall until after the 1945 war, but in the 1960s was the ABC *Olympia Cinema*. George Singleton, born in Bridgeton on New Year's Day 1900, became a cinema entrepreneur whose main monument is the *Glasgow Film Theatre*, originally built as his *Cosmo Cinema*. The Dalmarnock gasworks, closed since 1904, was reconstructed in 1914, and in the same year Glasgow Corporation Electricity Department started to build its Dalmarnock Power Station, but this was not completed until after 1918. Eventually the River Clyde above Glasgow Green, where the People's Palace museum and exhibition centre was built, was also bordered by waterworks and sewage disposal works.

*Templeton's carpet factory, designed by W. Leiper and commonly known as the Doges' Palace (after the prestigious Venice building), was erected in 1892. It housed machinery to manufacture Axminster carpets. It is now a centre for small businesses.* *(JRH)*

**During and after World War I**: Gallowgate Central station was closed in 1917. John Thomson & Co, boilermakers, moved from the Gorbals to Dalmarnock in the 1920s. The cotton industry withered from overseas competition, but the demise of many firms during the slump remains to be charted. There were also some expansions, for instance Templetons prospered and twice extended their mills during the 1930s. In 1949 Penman & Co still made Cornish boilers at the Caledonia Works, and Dalmarnock also gained a laundry. Both Mitchell's and Imperial Tobacco (IT) built cigarette factories on adjacent sites at Alexandra Parade, the latter a huge 3–4 storey building completed in 1953 for IT subsidiary WD & HO Wills.

**Congestion, Decay and a Tramcar Bonfire**: By then a huge and congested industrial population of some 110,000 lived in the area's tenements, conveniently near their work, to the city centre, and in many cases actually above the little shops which had made Bridgeton a major local centre. Trams, buses and steam trains gave them ready access to the entire conurbation, but their domestic amenities left much to be desired. Glasgow Green station was closed in 1953, Dalmarnock gasworks in 1956, and Anderson's Atlantic Mills in Baltic Street about 1960. The largely timber-built Dalmarnock tram depot which held 119 cars burned down in 1961, destroying 50 vehicles, but like the 134-tram depot at Dennistoun, its tracks remained in some use until the system closed in 1962. Further closures included Templetons' Broomward and Crownpoint carpet factories in 1967 and the Crownpoint box factory in 1969, when it was the last chip-basket factory in Scotland.

**Railway Changes of the 1960s**: The former NBR lines through Bellgrove and from Bridgeton Cross (renamed Central) via Queen Street Low Level were electrified in 1960. After teething troubles, British Railways' *'Blue Trains'* (which are still running) became so popular by comparison with the smoky former CR line via Central Station that the latter was closed by Beeching in 1964.

**Planners in Clearance Mode**: By then the City Council's clearance policies were masterminded by professionals who at times seemed power crazed. In 1967 they removed *inter alia* the Atlantic mills, Greenvale Chemical Works, St Ann's leather works, Taggarts' cabinet works, the roofless former Dalmarnock tram depot, the old Barrowfield weaving factory and the ruins of the Fordneuk factory in David Street. Even the fine John Street School was ruthlessly demolished in 1968, as were the Calton bobbin works. Most of the large Howe Machine Works, the former Hozier and Baltic works and Dunn's old soft drinks factory bit the dust in 1969.

**The Bridgeton Diaspora**: The Catholic secondary school in Charlotte Street was extended in 1963–65 but vacated as redundant in 1989, for tenements were as much at risk as factories. Bridgeton's people were dispersed all over the city and beyond, most of the families and the less lucky being sent to grim peripheral council estates or struggling Cumbernauld New Town; the lucky ones went to prosperous and well-planned East Kilbride. Only 45,000 residents remained by 1971, and major clearance was continued until 1973. Not without cause, the UP Church in Duke Street became a centre for the homeless in 1975. In retrospect some thinning out of the area was essential – but it was disastrously overdone, leaving desperate social problems. However, a small cluster of four tower blocks at Dalmarnock was the only local example of this regrettable approach to rehousing.

**Poverty, and more Electric Trains**: By 1976 Bridgeton's last yarn spinning mill had become a carton factory and the last brewery was a bottling plant; the exotic former Templeton building at Glasgow Green became the Templeton Business Centre, small units for offices and businesses. Part of the former Howe sewing machine works was in use for furniture manufacture. Also on the brighter side, the Argyle line was relaid and reopened to passengers, bringing electric trains to Dalmarnock and Bridgeton in 1979; but at about the same time the electrified spur to Bridgeton was abandoned. Not surprisingly the local newspaper had closed, for a mere 19,000 people remained in the area by 1981, of disadvantaged character.

**The Saga of Anderson Strathclyde**: As the National Coal Board modernised Britain's many collieries, in 1958 Mavor & Coulson cleared an old mill in Rogart Street to enable expansion. By 1970 the firm employed about 1600 people making coal-cutting equipment, as did Anderson Boyes of Motherwell; Beckett & Anderson of Glasgow made mine haulage engines. But pit closures led the three firms to merge. By 1979 the company was known as Anderson Strathclyde (AS), whose head office and works was at Bridgeton; they also had factories in East Kilbride, Glenrothes, Kirkintilloch and in England. In 1989 as Thatcher accelerated coalfield closures, AS cut their workforce from 510 to 350, and they were soon forced to contract their operations to Motherwell only; in 1992 they closed the Bridgeton plant with the loss of its last 150 jobs.

**The GEAR Scheme, and nearly the end of Arrol's**: Meantime poverty was being offset by Scotland's largest urban renewal initiative, the Scottish Development Agency's *'GEAR'* (Glasgow Eastern Area Renewal) scheme. This created great environmental and housing improvement, and built 100,000 m² of new factory space, creating 3200 new jobs in Calton (and also Shettleston) between 1976 and 1984. Most were in some 150 small firms, a sounder basis for the future than over-reliance on a few large enterprises such as Arrol's great Dalmarnock bridge works, which built the 225-ton Goliath crane used in the late 20th century by shipbuilders Lithgows of Port Glasgow. The works finally closed in 1986; but the structural engineering firm of Sir William Arrol was still in existence in 1995 as a member of the Rolls-Royce industrial power group, who had 1500 Scottish employees in three plants (*see also Annan*). By 1993 *GEAR* had been replaced by a local development company for the East End of Glasgow, and by 1994 the Crownpoint Sports Park had been established south of Gallowgate.

**Cigars Go Out**: Joseph Dunn Bottlers were still making soft drinks at London Road, but in 1990 IT closed the Wills cigar factory at Alexandra Parade with the loss of 530 jobs, due to automation and fewer smokers; it stood vacant in 1999, then being sold for conversion to a call centre. In 1994 the doomed Strathclyde Regional Council proposed a new tram system to link Easterhouse with Maryhill, passing through Riddrie, Bridgeton, Gallowgate and the city centre; but nothing ensued. Not surprisingly, considering the lack of unskilled work in Glasgow, in 1993 Calton had one of its worst drugs problems and in 1994 Scottish Homes intended to rehouse the 150 alcoholic or otherwise problematical residents of the *Great Eastern Hotel* and recondition the building. In 1997 St Mungo's Academy had 906 pupils and Whitehill Secondary 765. The former UP Church, fire damaged in the mid nineties, was rehabilitated in 2000, but the characterful mid-Victorian Greenhead Engine Works in Arcadia Street has recently been replaced by housing. The tall *Bellgrove Hotel*, built in Gallowgate in the 1930s, is now a hostel for the homeless.

## BROADFORD & Breakish — Map 8, B3

***Large village, Skye,*** *pop. 925* — OS 32: NG 6423

Chambered cairns show ancient settlement on the shores of Broadford Bay in the parish of Strathaird, later just called Strath; Monro noted in 1549 that it was owned by a McKinnon. Offshore from Broadford Bay were the wooded islet of Pabay, *"good for fishing, and a main shelter for thieves and cut-throats"*, and the larger Isle of Scalpay, then owned by Maclean of Duart, *"full of deer, with little woods and small tounes, well inhabited and manured, with many coves good for fishing"*. Nowadays Scalpay House is its main feature.

**Courts, Cattle Markets and Steamers**: Broadford, a township on the bay, was mentioned in 1703 by Martin, who noted that Sir Donald MacDonald had been *"keeping a sheriff's court"* there. A cattle tryst was held at Broadford in the late 18th and early 19th centuries. Wheeled vehicles were still novelties on the crofting island when the road to Portree was built for the Commissioners in 1806–12. Broadford was enlarged to settle veterans of the Napoleonic wars, and a distillery was in use from 1816 to 1826, but it was 1833 before a post office was opened. However, in 1847 the *Broadford Inn* gave Somers *"excellent quarters"*. By 1853 steamers on the Oban to Portree service were calling at Broadford, which Murray dismissed in 1894 as *"but a fishing village, with an ugly church, a small pier and a good hotel"*. In the early 20th century Broadford grew into a large straggling village. An early youth hostel was open by 1955 near the long Corry Pier; tourism on Skye built up rapidly to 1964, when a quarter of a million visitors came to the island, most of them passing through Broadford, where by 1971 there was a small hospital.

**Media, Tourism and Flying**: The campaigning *West Highland Free Press* (WHFP), founded in 1972, was originally based 3km away at Breakish township, where an airstrip was also laid out in the 1970s. By 1980 there was a fish farm in Loch Ainort about 10km to the west, beside Luib with its crofting museum; the *Broadford Hotel* had been enlarged to 28 rooms and three smaller hotels were open. In 1981 the area still had only 550 residents. Broadford boasted a small shopping centre, seasonal tourist office, pony trekking, and secondary school. A small industrial estate was laid out in the late 1980s; by 1991 the WHFP – also widely read in the Western Isles – was based there (employing 25), and the resident population had rapidly grown to 925. South of Skulamus, there were there were two caravan sites by 1997, and Broadford also boasted a museum and a *'reptile centre'*. In 1999 an air service was planned between Glasgow and Broadford. Industrial activity includes a fish farm and a fish processing company, and Leith's Ltd (haulage and quarrying). The greatly enlarged *Dunollie Hotel* now has 84 rooms; the youth hostel – and another tiny hostel for backpackers at Breakish – are open for an extended season.

## BRODICK — Map 1, B1

***Main centre, Isle of Arran,*** *pop. 1000* — OS 69: NS 0136

The mountainous Isle of Arran was once part of Cinel Gabran in Dalriada. Its north half is a heavily glaciated granite dome which reaches 874m at Goat Fell, 4km north of Brodick, whose name means *'Broad Bay'* in Norse. Nearby stood four standing stones. A royal castle existed by 1263, already strongly built in stone by 1307 when held by an Englishman, Sir John Hastings. Destroyed in 1406, it was soon replaced by a round tower. In the 1470s most of Arran was given to the first Lord Hamilton; in 1503 his son became Earl of Arran, powerful owner of *'Braizay'* castle, whose round tower survived damage in 1528. Invercloy, a settlement with a Gaelic name on the site of modern Brodick 2 km south of the once royal castle, went under other names at various times. Monro noted in 1549 that Arran was *"full of forests, good for hunting"*. In the 1560s the Earls built a much larger castle including the old tower, using the local red stone. In 1609 the first Marquis of Hamilton became the Isle's Commissioner for Justice.

**English Speakers and Hunting Dukes**: The castle was marked on Pont's map of about 1600, engraved by Blaeu, as the emparked *'Brod wick'*. By then the isle's settlement pattern comprised many small clachans, called *"villages"* by Martin in 1703 when the people on the east already spoke English, those on the west still solely the Gaelic. The great Brodick Castle, which he described, had been further enlarged under Cromwell in 1652. It was used as a summer residence by the Isle's proprietor, the Duke of Hamilton. Only a few coppice woods remained nearby, but about 400 mountain deer served the Dukes for sport, and salmon were caught locally. A walled garden was created beside the castle in 1710, and the settlement began to change.

**Commerce, Clearances – and Benevolence at Last**: By 1745 Brodick had a *'merchant'* and in the 18th century the nearby *Cladach Inn* was the first slated house on the island. In the early 19th century there was a carding mill. A steamer service fed by small boats plied to Glasgow from 1828, and by 1838 a post office was named Brodick. But under orders from the absentee feudal superiors, the 9th and 10th Dukes, their hard-hearted factor John Paterson cleared much of the population off the island in 1829–40, and enclosed its farmland to raise the rents. The castle was again enlarged into a baronial style mansion in 1844 to designs prepared by Gillespie Graham for the 11th Duke, one of the few non-absentee and improving island landlords of the day. A school was open by 1845, and by 1847 there were nine local fishing boats. The good Duke moved the village to Invercloy over the next few years, in 1854–56 providing new school buildings and replacing the Cladach Inn by Invercloy's new *Douglas Hotel*. The steamer pier, built by the estate near the hotel in 1872, became the first main access to the island; but then matters deteriorated.

**Lifting the Dead Hand of a Dissolute Duke**: The absentee 12th Duke's dissolute lifestyle wasted his tenants' earnings. He also resisted building on the island, which was becoming popular as a tourist destination: Murray noted that in 1894 the *"fairly large"* hotel was generally overflowing in summer. The Duke's death in 1895 immediately enabled the puffer *Glencloy* to be built at Brodick from local timber, and development then began in earnest, Invercloy growing into a large village under the name Brodick. A village hall was built in 1895, and in 1897 the Brodick golf club laid out a course. In 1913 the golf club was moved by the estate to a new 18-hole links course between village and castle, and tennis courts were built about 1920. The fine woodland garden with its rhododendrons was begun in 1923. A youth hostel was opened at High Glencloy in the 1930s, and a diesel-powered generating station was built at Brodick in 1933 to replace individual private electricity supplies throughout the island.

**Coasting and Tourism**: From 1946 to 1953 the Arran Sea Transport & Supply Company of Brodick owned the elderly little 20m Denny-built puffer *Arran Rose*, originally the *Garmoyle*. From 1954 steamers to Arran called only at Brodick pier, and side-loading car ferries were introduced (from 1970 stern-loading). From 1958 Brodick Castle was in the care of the National Trust for Scotland and its grounds became a country park. The local newspaper the *Arran Banner* was founded in 1974. Brodick went on growing, to an out of season population nearing 1000, and built up a substantial role as a resort. By 1981 the Heritage Museum and 15 small hotels were open, besides the 25-room *Douglas*.

**Literacy, Fragrancy and Accommodation**: By 1991 when Brodick had 822 residents, the *Arran Banner* had reached a circulation of 3300 and earned itself a place in the Guinness Book of Records as the newspaper *"most read within its circulation area"*. Meantime by 1993 the small firm of Arran Aromatics had expanded to employ 35 people making toiletries, cosmetics and gifts for Boots, the House of Fraser, and Habitat France. By 1994 a permanent library was open in Brodick to supplement the island's mobile library, and by 1997 a mountain rescue post had been established. The *Auchrannie Country House Hotel* had 16 rooms in 1977; by 1994 it included an indoor swimming pool and country club, and has now grown to 28 rooms; there are also the *Invercloy Hotel* and the *Kilmichael Country House*. Brodick also has a wealth of mid-range accommodation. Although the SYHA hostel has closed, two others are open on the island.

## BROOKFIELD

**Map 15, A5**

***Renfrewshire dormitory,*** *pop. 600* — OS 64: NS 4164

This small place in Kilbarchan parish which lies beside the Bridge of Weir road about 1.5km north-west of Johnstone is a creation of the early 20th century. The OS map of 1895 showed Merchiston House as its main feature; to the north was Houston station on the Greenock branch of the Glasgow & South Western Railway. By 1945 four or five roads of incomplete suburban development had appeared, with the name Brookfield, plus a post office. By 1971 the station had been renamed Houston & Crosslee, Merchiston House had become Merchiston Hospital, another residential road had been added and the earlier development had been infilled. By 1981 the hospital had been enlarged to 114 beds, used for male MD patients. The railway was closed in 1983 and soon lifted, but by 1988 the hospital had been further extended and another street of houses had been added to Brookfield, which had 600 residents in 1991, but the post office has recently closed.

## BRORA, Clyne & Loth

**Map 9, C1**

***Small town & hamlets, Sutherland,*** *pop. 1700* — OS 17: NC 9004

Brora (in Gaelic *Brura*) stands at the mouth of the River Brora in a relatively low-lying area on the east coast of Sutherland some 10km north-east of Dunrobin Castle. Ancient remains are common in the upper reaches of the valley, around and especially west of Loch Brora. The village lies near the Kirkton of the vast parish of Clyne. Originally called Inverbrora, it has a long but obscure early history: according to Murray's Handbook, Brora was chartered as a burgh of barony in 1345 by David II (but not until 1601 according to Pryde's list). The earlier date is more likely to be correct, because Brora stands on coal-bearing strata: a 1m thick seam of Jurassic age was exploited in the 16th century to fuel local salt pans. The early port of Brora was already silted up. Blaeu's atlas published in 1654 showed a bridge.

**Pumps, Tracks, Whisky and Salmon**: About 1748 a water-powered engine was installed to drain the mine, though its location did not appear as such on Roy's rather sketchy survey made about 1750, nor did this show a bridge on the coast road (the later A9). A road or track from Brora paralleled the north bank of the river, and from Loth, a coastal parish centre to the north-east, a spur track served Kildonan, only to end in the wilds at Forsinard. Clynelish was shown by Roy as a bold square outline. Was the famous distillery already in existence? Officially it dated only from 1819, established by the controversial Marquis of Stafford, who later became the first Duke of Sutherland. Meantime, Pennant found in 1769 a coal mine already between 13 and 21 metres deep; the river had been bridged, there was a salmon fishery and a saltworks, together with a linen industry established by the Commissioners for the Forfeited Estates. At that time Brora was also an important fishing centre, but this did not last.

**Quarry, Village, Coach Road and Deep Mining**: About 1770 a tramway was laid between the coal mine south of the river and the quay. Heron understood in 1799 that the coal mine did not pay, but noted a quarry; this, the Clynelish sandstone quarry, remained open right through the 19th century, and from it originated the white freestone used to reface Dunrobin Castle. In 1810 the south bank coal-mine was closed and the tramroad was diverted to serve a new mine north of the river. A new village layout was created in 1811, and there was a post office by 1813. A new harbour was built in 1814, at about the time that the north road was being greatly improved by Telford for coaches. Chambers in 1826 found Brora a *"new village, with a good inn, a salt-work, and a mine of coal"*. A new water-powered mine-pumping engine was installed about that time, and later in the century the mine reached a depth of 100 metres.

**Railway and Golf**: The Duke of Sutherland's Railway (later part of the Highland) reached Brora in 1871, crossing the river by a single tall arch; Loth gained a wayside station. An engineering works was founded by the Duke and a pottery and a tile factory were established. The mine was further boosted by transhipping coal from the tram tubs to railway wagons – although the coal was not generally of sufficient quality for use in the distillery, which remained primarily water-powered. In 1886 it produced only 90,000 litres of Highland malt whisky, all for *'private customers'*. Brora golf club was founded in 1889, James Braid laying out an 18-hole course on the sandhills. In 1894 Murray found Brora *"a busy but scattered village"*. In 1899 Andrew Murray of Clynelish quarry employed 30 men; thick clay and sand overburden had to be removed. It appears that by the 1930s the quarry had flooded.

**Textiles and Tourism**: The tramway to the harbour operated only until the 1914 war, which prevented coal shipments. The distillery was rebuilt for Ainslie & Co of Leith in 1896; from 1925 it was wholly owned by DCL, and was closed from 1931 to 1939. In the meantime in 1901 J M Hunter had established woollen manufacture in the former engineering works, also using local coal. By 1913 the Station Hotel had been opened, and in 1946 Wordie & Co had a small rail to road cartage depot. In 1954 when Brora's population was about 1400, the three hotels included the 35-roomed *Links* and smaller *Royal Marine*.

**Another Clynelish sees out the end of Coal**: A second *'Clynelish'* distillery was built on a new site in 1967–68, the old one then being renamed Brora. The coal mine, though small and intermittent, was very long-lasting; it also produced bricks, the coal being overlain by Oxford Clay shales. The mine employed 30 men in the 1950s, but was eventually closed in 1974 due to flooding; at that time Hunters' substantial woollen works employed 130 people, and council housing had been built for workers.

**Service Village**: Loth station closed in the 1960s but Brora survived the Beeching cuts, retained its siding and still had some van traffic in 1978; there were then two garages and a National Carriers depot. Tourist facilities included a restaurant, and shops selling tweeds, guns and rods. Caravan sites were open north of the village at Dalchalm and Loth; near the latter was a sand quarry. Local facilities comprised a very new Clydesdale Bank branch, primary school and post office, plus a dozen or so shops including a supermarket. Local people said they went to Inverness rather than Dingwall for what was unobtainable locally. Two more hotels were open by 1980. The old Brora distillery was closed in 1983. Despite its remoteness Brora was, for the Highlands, a large and industrialised village; in addition to woollens and the new distillery, the brick and tile industry and some inshore fishing remained.

**Modern Brora's Big Factory**: In 1991 the population was 1687 and many owned their homes outright. By 2000, Hunters of Brora, woollen and tweed manufacturers, had built a large and prestigious factory west of the village, but their old works were derelict. Brora boasts a base for mobile business system training, and there are Vauxhall and Ford dealerships, petrol station, and an adapted health centre. Afforestation has begun to cover the hills up-river, but sheep farming, a little crofting and inshore fishing continue to the east around Loth, eked out with caravans. The *Royal Marine* has 22 rooms, an indoor pool, gym and 4-lane curling rink, and the *Links* has 23 rooms.

## BROUGHTON & Calzeat — Map 2, B2

***Peeblesshire village**, pop. 300* — OS 72: NT 1136

About 9km to the east of the upper Clyde, the little Biggar Water flows through an almost flat area, forming a striking gap in the hills, to enter an elbow of the upper Tweed. At an altitude of about 205 metres, Broughton lies to the north of this stream, while Calzeat is to the south. Strategic potential is shown by the various hill forts, for example above the 15th and 16th century castles of Tinnis and Whitslade. Some 3km to the south were the 16th century castles of Drumelzier (pronounced *Drumellyer*), an L-plan tower, and Wrae; according to Chambers, Broughton parish had a total of ten old towers. An ancient church stood at Glenholm 4km south of Broughton, and gained a parish school in 1625; Broughton had to wait another five years. Pont's map made in 1596 also showed a mill just below the *'Kirk of Broditoun'*.

**Coach Roads and hopeful Railway**: Kilbucho 2 km west of Broughton became a burgh of barony about 1650, but failed to develop beyond the milltown shown on Roy's map made about 1754; by then a cluster of hamlets enfolded the ancient Broughton Kirk, and the area's through road system was virtually complete. Broughton post office first opened in 1792. Chambers observed that by 1827 Broughton was *"a thriving village rebuilt in the English fashion by the late James Dickson of Kilbucho"*. In 1860 the Symington, Biggar & Broughton Railway was opened from Symington through Biggar to a temporary terminus named Broughton (at Calzeat: this may explain why this name is now almost forgotten). The line was extended as a branch of the Caledonian close beside the river to Stobo and Peebles in 1864. But the station which had a remarkable three platforms was never busy, serving a local population of around 400; the passenger trains were replaced by buses in 1950, and freight ended entirely with the line's closure in 1966.

**Cashing in on John Buchan**: Meantime the village had become known for its connections with the early 20th century statesman John Buchan, better known as the author of the adventure novels *Greenmantle*, *John McNab* and *The Thirty-Nine Steps*. By the mid century Broughton school had also acquired the secondary classes for upper Tweeddale. As the rural population shrank, Drumelzier's pre-war post office was an early casualty, and by 1976 secondary pupils were being educated elsewhere. However, the *Greenmantle Hotel* was open by 1962, and the Broughton Brewery was opened in 1979. Though the 1981 population of the village was under 300 it continues to serve a wider area with small-village facilities, including its village hall, from which Scottish dance music has been broadcast. Following growing demand for *'Real Ale'* in the 1980s, by 1990 the brewery was selling three bottled ales – Greenmantle, Merlin's and Old Jock Strong Ale – as far afield as London, and employed about 30 people. By 2000 it also made Discovery Ale for Dundee's Discovery Centre, and sold draught to the hotel. The John Buchan Museum, open by 1988, is still an attraction.

## BROUGHTY FERRY — Map 6, C3

***E. Suburb of Dundee**, pop. 17,000+* — OS 54: NO 4630

From early days, and certainly by the year 1425, a ferry operated from Broughty on the Tay coast of Angus to Partan Craigs or *'Portincraig'* in Fife. Broughty Castle, built on the shore in 1498, was rebuilt as an artillery fort in 1548 by the English under Protector Somerset, becoming one of the first defences in Britain on the bastion plan. Some way inland is Claypotts Castle, built in 1569. On his map made about 1600, Timothy Pont named Claypotts and a little place, *'Brugh-Tay'*, but Roy's map, made about 1750, merely indicated tiny settlements at East and West Ferry. Heron in 1799 noted only Broughty Castle, *"a ruinous fort"*.

**New Village, Mills and Shipbuilding**: The settlement of Broughty Ferry as we know it was laid out on a grid street plan by George Hunter about 1801, when it was described as a

*Broughty Castle on the waterfront at Broughty Ferry. Built in the 1490s, it was largely rebuilt in 1861 as a coastal battery. Today it contains a museum of the Dundee whaling industry.* (AL)

fishing village. Nearby on Castle Green was the stone tower of a windmill, which later became a joiner's workshop. Meantime two water-powered mills were built on the Dighty Water just north of Claypotts: William Anderson's Balunie spinning mill had 240 spindles in 1822, and A Ireland & Co's Baldovie mill 192. The nearby Linlathen House was remodelled about 1820. Near the ferry J Adamson set up a shipyard; in 1836 this built the 200-ton wooden paddle steamer *Modern Athens* for the Dundee to Leith service. By 1838 a post office and a lifeboat station had appeared.

**Railway, Train Ferry and Rebuilt Castle**: The early Dundee & Arbroath Railway (D&A) of 1839 created a long-lasting level crossing and one of the earliest platform canopies at Broughty Ferry station (both still extant). The ruined Broughty Castle became a coastguard station in 1841. By 1844 there were three shipyards and also slipways. A short pier was built just west of the Castle by the Edinburgh Perth & Dundee Railway as the terminal for a train ferry, which from 1851 plied to Tayport *(q.v.)*. A single line led to an eastwards-facing junction with the D&A at Panmure Street, just beyond which the later Forfar branch diverged. The E&N used the ground floor of Broughty Castle as a store, until the government rebuilt it in 1855–61 as a small fortress and gun battery with its own harbour.

**Burgh, Suburbanisation and Fishing**: By 1851 the village population was over 2750, and it became a police burgh in 1863; the later Orchar Gallery and Park were named after its first provost, Dundee industrialist James G Orchar. In 1863 the lines in Fife were bought by the North British Railway (NB), who from 1866 shared the D&A with the Caledonian. Further stations were soon opened at Stannergate, West Ferry and Barnhill. Water was piped from the Crombie Reservoir which opened for Dundee supply in 1866, and Broughty Ferry gasworks was set up in 1870. These facilities stimulated the building of large numbers of new private houses, and Broughty became a suburb of Dundee. Another harbour was opened in 1872. Both this and the beach provided bases for a hundred fishing boats before steam trawling started around the turn of the century.

**Steam Ferries and Trams**: Broughty had a local newspaper from 1887, the year the second Tay Bridge opened; a simple steam ferry replaced the train ferry, plying to Tayport nine times a day in 1894, when what Murray described as this *"colony of villa residences of Dundee merchants"* extended in depth for 4km along the south-facing slopes. The population had passed 7400, but in the same year William Kidd wrote of a *"village"* where *"elegant shops have sprung up"*. Around 1900 summer entertainments were held on the beach, and the Tay Steamboat Company gave trips to such places as the Bell Rock, May Island, Perth, Montrose and Arbroath. An electric power station was built in 1900, and from 1905 Broughty Ferry was served by trams to Dundee; trams ran under Barnhill Bridge to Monifieth from 1907.

**Broughty Ferry's own Suburb – and Cattle Floats**: The short-lived burgh was incorporated into Dundee city in 1913, but the steam ferry plied until 1920 and the trams to 1931. As residential development continued, Broughty itself acquired an eastern satellite, Barnhill. A substantial town centre had developed by the 1950s, when there were 5 hotels and the population – including Barnhill – had reached 13,000. However, the passenger trains to Forfar were withdrawn in 1955, and the Forfar line was lifted after freight trains ended in 1967. West Ferry station and Barnhill goods station also closed in that year. Meantime Linlathen House had been demolished in 1958.

**Teacher Training**: There are now 17,250 residents in Broughty Ferry and Barnhill with 8 small to medium sized hotels. A Safeway supermarket now augments the many small, characterful shops in the thriving centre. To the west is the campus of the Northern College of Education. Broughty Castle now contains an interesting whaling museum. The mid 1980s saw the creation by the district council of the 40-ha Linlathen industrial estate, part of the Dundee Enterprise Zone. A cycleway, opened on the former Forfar railway route in 1990, proved very popular. The long-established Grove Academy has around 800 pupils. In 2000 the station platform canopies were to be refurbished. In 2001 Bishopcross Investments proposed a major scheme for 350 houses and many other uses at Panmurefield, between Arbroath Road and the Dighty Water. Major sewerage works are now disrupting the waterfront but enhanced lifeboat facilities are to emerge thereafter.

## BROXBURN & Drumshoreland — Map 16, C3

*W. Lothian small town, pop. 8350* — OS 65: NT 0872

In the 14th century the valley of the River Almond was known as Strathbrock (Badger Vale). The Newbridge to Bathgate road existed by about 1600, when Lothian was mapped by Timothy Pont. The tower of Illieston House was built in the 17th century on the crest of a steep bank 30m above the river, 15km west of Edinburgh. Broxburn some 3km north-west of Illieston did not appear on Pont's map, but had become a small village astride the road by about 1754 when the Roy map was surveyed. From 1822 the Union Canal intersected the road at Broxburn; but there was no post office until 1839. Drumshoreland station, opened on the Bathgate railway in 1849, was 1.5km south of the village, but by 1860 Wordie & Co had a rail cartage depot there. In 1861 the population of Broxburn was 660. Oil shale was found at Broxburn in 1858, and mined locally by Bell, who built retorts and supplied shale to Steel of Wishaw, who also built a refinery there.

**The Broxburn Shale Oil Company**: In 1862 further exploitation and refining was begun by the Broxburn Shale Oil Company; soon there were over 200 retorts on their site. Their Albyn oil-works, re-built from 1877 with new efficient retorts, made the company the strongest in the industry in the 1880s, with 850 workers. Factories making candles and sulphuric acid were soon added, and also a cooperage. The company built 600 houses, and a gasworks to supply the town, so Broxburn overtook nearby Uphall to become the main centre in the area, though it was never a burgh. In 1892 a new oil-works and ammonium sulphate plant opened to the south at Roman Camp. The various works were served by a mineral railway from Broxburn Junction near Winchburgh to Drumshoreland Junction. Murray in 1894 noted oil works *"twice as large as those of Pumpherston"*, and increasingly massive red bings of burnt shale were dotted around the area. By 1901 the population was 7000, including almost 2000 company workers.

**From Oil to Food, Drink and Transformers**: Broxburn United FC briefly played in the Scottish League (1921–26). The A8 trunk road diversion bypassed Broxburn from the 1920s. By the 1950s the population was nearing 8000, the minor town centre being strung out along the original main road. The shale mines and oil works began to close in the mid 1950s, and the final closures – including the sulphuric acid plant – occurred under BP in 1962. Meantime industrial estates were urgently provided: about 1965 the Perth firm of Arthur Bell & Sons moved their cooperage, blending and bottling operations from Leith to a 10ha site at Broxburn's East Mains; by the mid 1970s some 275 people were employed there. By 1977 Parsons Peebles of Granton had a branch at Broxburn, making distribution transformers; there was a Simmers Forbes bakery, an offshoot from Hatton in Aberdeenshire. Golden Wonder's large northern plant made crisps, and by 1980 David Hall was established as a sausage manufacturer.

**Industrial Fluctuations**: By 1989 some 200 workers made Slumberdown duvets, but McIntosh Textiles of Newcastle bought and closed this firm in 1990; Halls took over the modern factory the same year. The Golden Wonder crisp factory had been closed in 1988, but food and drink products are still in the ascendant at Broxburn, where in 1990 Simmers developed a new biscuit factory. By 1991 John Miller & Sons, long established as sweet manufacturers in Newington, had moved into part of the former crisp factory, but some population decline had occurred: about 8350 for Broxburn. In 1992 Munro & Miller engineers, formerly of Sighthill, recruited 90 workers for a plant at East Mains. The whisky blending and bottling plant, owned by Guinness, was operated by United Distillers, but 226 jobs were lost when it was closed in 1993. In 1995 it was bought by Macdonald & Muir of Leith. By 1994 Broxburn Bottlers of East Mains Estate had become independent spirit-blenders and bottlers, greatly expanding their contract production facilities. Vaughan's (engineers), and Campbell's (meat wholesalers) are now medium-sized firms, and Crabbie's Ginger Wine, formerly produced in Leith, is now made in Broxburn. Some new residential and industrial development had been completed by 1998, but of the once-great shale-oil industry only a few workers' cottages and the massive Greendykes Bing remain. Broxburn Academy has around 750 pupils. The Union Canal was reopened between Broxburn's Port Buchan and Ratho in May 2000; will this bring tourist facilities to such a workaday area?

## BRUICHLADDICH & Kilchoman — Map 4, B5

***Small village, Islay,*** *pop. 200* — OS 60: NR 2661

The lonely Kilchoman church stands near an ancient dun and a standing stone on the exposed west coast of the Rhinns of Islay. Some 3km to the north-east is Lochgorm Castle, built by the Clan Donald of Kintyre on an islet in a freshwater loch. Described by Monro in 1549 as a *"strength"*, Lochgorm nowadays seems forgotten except by the Ordnance Survey. The same is true of what was then a parish kirk on the tiny Nave Island, off the coast 15km to the north. However, the more sheltered shores of saltwater Loch Indaal to the south were already well-settled. The coastal distillery at Bruichladdich on Loch Indaal dates from 1881 *(see Hay & Stell (1986))*. By 1886 its annual output of Islay Malt was about 425,000 litres. Barnard noted that it was associated with *"quite an aspiring and tastefully-built village"* and a pier, from which the whisky was shipped on weekly steamers to Glasgow. In the 1890s Murray observed that the only hotel in the village was a temperance establishment!

*Bruichladdich distillery, Islay, built in 1881. Today it's owned by Whyte & Mackay. Like all the other large Islay distilleries, it was designed to be served by coastal shipping.* *(JRH)*

**Overdependence on Distilling**: In Edwardian days passenger steamers occasionally called, and cargo steamers served the pier until at least 1937, but the village which had acquired a primary school and sub-branch bank had ceased to grow appreciably. The distillery was modernised in 1960, when its annual capacity was raised to over 2 million litres by Invergordon Distillers. The village was unusual in having a one-doctor practice which in 1978 served over 1100 patients, though by then the primary school had been closed, and the local population was a mere 200 or so. In 1981 Bruichladdich had small-village facilities, still including a single hotel. In 1991 the distillery was producing a mild single malt whisky; in 1992 its highly matured 1967 output was being sold by Invergordon at 25 years old. In 1995 White & Mackay mothballed the distillery with the loss of some 8 jobs, but it now operates intermittently.

## BUCCLEUCH — Map 3, A4

***Borders location*** — OS 79: NT 3214

Buccleuch, meaning Stag Ravine, lies among steep hills on the Rankle Burn, a tributary of the Tweed some 20km west of Hawick. The motte was the original stronghold of what was to become Scotland's greatest landowning family, the Dukes of Buccleuch *(see Drumlanrig)*; in later years it was replaced by a tower. Robert Chambers, who visited this remote place on his walking tour in 1827, found only *"the remains of a church and burial-ground, a kiln and a mill, besides traces of a large dam which conveyed water to the latter"*. But by 1971 there was nothing worth seeing, and fewer than five houses. By the 1990s the vast Craik Forest had clothed all the hills to the south with conifers.

## BUCHANTY (Glenalmond) & Foulford Map 6, A3

***Perthshire hamlets,*** *pop. 150* OS 52: NN 9328

An ancient hill fort overlooks a deep valley some 20km west of Perth, where the Sma' Glen with its River Almond broadens into Glenalmond, and the Fendoch Burn offers an easy pass into upper Strathearn. During their first attempted conquest of Caledonia about 82–84 AD, the Romans built a timber fort at Fendoch to accommodate some 1000 men; later enlarged, it stood on a moraine and was unusually elongated in plan. Despite the site's significance it was soon abandoned, and the Romans apparently fell back to Braco. Little more is known of the area near the fort until Pont's map of Glenalmond – made about 1600. This showed a bridge spanning the River Almond at *'Buthendy'*, a settlement beside which was a tower house. A mill stood on the south bank between the bridge and the confluence of the Fendoch burn, plus two more on the north bank; one is identifiable as Millrodgie, the other lay below the bridge.

**Stubbornly Rural – plus Golf!**: Roy's map made about 1750 showed hamlets at Buchanty and Millhole; the bridge was then a key link in a trackway which joined Wade's military road from Crieff to the north at Foulford, 4km west of Buchanty, and eventually developed into the modern B8063. But no burgh of barony was chartered in the area, which failed to develop, perhaps due to the rise of the great cattle tryst at Crieff. The 1895 OS map marked the Foulford Inn, and a *'castle'* north of the river at Dunie, no longer in evidence. The ancient bridge and inn survived, but two small undated quarries closed, and depopulation had led to closure of Buchanty primary school by 1976. By 1981 under 150 people lived in this wholly rural area. About 1990 the 9-room *Foulford Inn* created its own 9-hole golf course.

## BUCHLYVIE Map 5, C4

***W. Stirlingshire village,*** *pop. 600* OS 57: NS 5793

Buchlyvie – pronounced and for centuries spelt *'Bucklyvie'* – stands on a small burn 3km south of the River Forth, 22 km west of Stirling. Though not named on Pont's map of about 1600, there was already a *'Miltoun'* in the area, which was then a well-settled part of Lennox. Buchlyvie became a burgh of barony in 1672, and in 1702 the fine Auchentroig House was built 3km west of Buchlyvie for the local laird. From the early 18th century Buchlyvie lay on the military road between Stirling and Dumbarton, the area's only road in the 1750s when the Roy map showed Buchlyvie as a linear settlement. By 1797 four annual fairs were scheduled, and Heron in 1799 estimated *'Bucklyvie'* had 400 to 500 people, some hand loom weaving of muslins, and a *'tanwork'*. Though Buchlyvie and Kippen were in his view the only villages west of Stirling, Buchlyvie failed to develop further, and eventually even these minor industries vanished.

**Railed and Derailed**: From 1856 Buchlyvie, by then in Stirlingshire, had a station on the single-line Forth & Clyde Railway linking Stirling with Balloch; it became a rural junction when the Strathendrick & Aberfoyle Railway was opened in 1882. This too failed to promote growth, and in 1895 Buchlyvie was still a small village with the *Red Lion* and *Crown* inns. The Stirling railway lost its passenger trains in 1934; those on the Aberfoyle line continued until 1951, and freight services to Glasgow lasted until 1959. From 1951 to 1991 the population remained stable at around 600, with the facilities of a small village and an enlarged primary school, though by 1980 only the *Red Lion* was still a hotel. Facilities included two pubs, a police office, garage, bank, five shops, and two doctors. There was a small branch of the agricultural merchants Central Farmers, of Leven. Although Auchentroig primary school closed around 1970, by 1985 Old Auchentroig House had become part of St Patrick's College or Monastery, and by 1999 had been newly restored.

## BUCKHAVEN & Denbeath Map 6, B4

***Small town, S. Fife,*** *pop. 8500* OS 59: NT 3698

According to Chambers the people of Buckhaven on the Fife coast 10km north-east of Kirkcaldy were *"supposed to be descended from the crew of a Brabant vessel wrecked on this part of the coast in the reign of Philip II"*. The small village was quaintly named *'Buckheaven'* on Blaeu's map derived from Pont's work of around 1600. By 1671 Earl David Wemyss owned the Happy mine, a coal level in Denbeath glen a short way inland; but few houses were built there. In the 1720s Defoe saw Buckhaven as a *"miserable row of cottage-like buildings inhabited chiefly, by fishermen, whose business is wholly to catch fresh fish every day in the Firth, and carry them to Leith and Edinburgh markets"*. On the beach were also *"a great many boats of all sizes which every year they fit out for the herring season"*. He concluded oddly *"in general the town is rich"*.

**Antique yet Promiscuous?**: The Roy map of about 1750 showed a small linear settlement on the coast road. There were coal pits some way inland at Cameron by 1791, but Heron noted Buckhaven in 1799 as a *"small fishing town"* of about 600 persons. A small harbour was built about that time. Chambers wrote in 1827 that the Buckhaven folk were still not fully integrated into the Fife community; their *"curious antique fishing village consists in a promiscuous irregular troop of cottages, arranged on the face of a steep promontory"*.

**Baking and Fishing Nets**: The harbour was enlarged by the Board of Fisheries about 1851. Stuart's bakery was founded in 1857 and spread with branch shops around the district. In 1858 John Ireland & Sons established a net factory in Buckhaven; it burned down in 1870 and passed to J & W Stewart of Musselburgh, who built a new net works at Buckhaven in 1878. Meantime William Thomson had set up a net works there in 1870, and eventually Robert Watson of Cellardyke – an oilskin, net and buoy manufacturer – also had a branch factory at Buckhaven.

**The Bowman Coal Pits**: The Muiredge coal pit, located 1km inland, hit hard rock when first sunk in 1856, but was acquired in 1864 by Bowman & Co (B&C) – three keen miners from the Crossgates area – who dug further to 163m and struck productive measures. They opened the pit in 1865, served by a mineral railway to Cameron Bridge. B&C then sank Denbeath colliery on the coast east of the village in 1872–75, served by a railway from Methil, adding another shaft to 270m in 1883–85 to work the Chemiss seam. Meantime in 1879–82 B&C had sunk the Rosie pit between Buckhaven and East Wemyss to a depth of 180m; it had its own hamlet of two-storey houses for miners. By about then B&C employed more miners than any other Fife coal concern, including at the Isabella pit, one of two collieries located to the south and south-east of Cameron Bridge.

**Railways and Mines Beat Fishing**: In 1879–81 a passenger and goods railway was built by the Earl of Wemyss between Thornton and Buckhaven; it was extended to Methil harbour in 1887 and in 1889 became part of the North British system. Although white fish were still caught by line in 1889, by then many Buckhaven men had abandoned fishing for work in the surrounding mines of Methil, Wemyss, and Cameron. By 1895 Buckhaven had an inn. After 1901 the Rosie pit acquired its own rail connection towards Denbeath, using the Wemyss Private Railway (WPR) – its history outlined in *Hutton (1999)*. The WPR then swung east to the Wemyss brickworks and Methil. Buckhaven together with Methil and Innerleven became a police burgh in 1901, soon acquiring a powerful steam fire engine, which was used on occasion as far afield as Lochgelly.

**Wellesley Colliery, Trams and Denbeath**: In 1905 the Wemyss Coal Company (WCC) took over the Bowman concern. They immediately added a Baum washery at the Denbeath colliery, and soon closed the coast road, clearing the coastal hamlet of Links of Buckhaven to accommodate a third shaft to enlarge the colliery, which they renamed Wellesley. The WCC built Wellesley Road to replace the old route and to carry the new electric tramway of the Wemyss & District Tramway Company. From 1904 to 1932 this linked Leven and Buckhaven with Gallatown, transported miners, and for a time operated a through service to Kirkcaldy. From 1905 onwards the WCC also built the 220 houses of the model village of Denbeath to accommodate the miners, many of whom were recruited from the declining Lanarkshire coalfield. The enlarged colliery opened in 1910, working as deep as 475 m using Kirkcaldy-built winding engines. In 1914–18 the WCC opened a central sawmill at Muiredge.

**The End of Fishing and Netmaking**: In 1905 there were still 31 local fishing boats at Buckhaven, which from 1911 had an electricity supply and from 1913 a gasworks, but a belated lifeboat station which opened in 1900 was closed in 1932. A public library started in 1925 (with a new building 10 years later). A new Cameron drift mine to work the Bowhouse seam was created by the WCC in the mid 1930s on the site of the old Isabella pit. The Muiredge pit was closed in 1938, but used as a training centre. In the 1930s Thomsons used 34 netmaking machines and employed 70 people, mainly women, until netmaking ended in 1945. With tipping of coal waste on the beaches the harbour became silted up; fishing had ceased by 1953, and by 1970 the harbour had been infilled.

**Decline of Coal and Railways**: When the National Coal Board took over the WPR's colliery links in 1947 it had some 70 km of lines and served 8 pits. By 1951 – when Buckhaven's population was over 10,000 – its facilities were on the margin between a large village and a small town; the sawmill and bakery continued in use. But the Rosie pit was closed in 1953, the Buckhaven to Wemyss and Thornton rail passenger service (ex-NBR) was withdrawn in 1955, the Cameron mine closed in 1959 and the railway closed in 1963. The Wellesley Colliery's output of 2000 to 3000 tonnes a day declined after 1962, and with the impending exhaustion of its reserves and intense foreign competition, the huge pit was closed in 1967 after almost a century of operation. The WPR followed, closed piecemeal in 1966–70. The colliery was demolished in 1972; the subsequent intensive re-use of the site appears under Methil. However, Buckhaven High School was open, a public library had opened in the 1960s, and shortly afterwards the site of the Muiredge colliery became an industrial estate, aiming to offset all these closures.

**Chemicals, Knitwear and Roof Trusses**: The carpet fibre factory built at Muiredge was itself closed in 1977, the premises being taken over by Johnson Matthey (JM), a major chemicals firm. By 1981 Buckhaven's had problems and its population had fallen to around 8500. In 1980 the major sawmiller James Donaldson of Leven opened a branch at Muiredge to manufacture roof trusses; by 1992 it employed 70 people; by 1989 the JM works had become Courtaulds' Organic Chemicals factory. By 1995 C E Forsyth Ltd were making knitwear at their Glengair factory. The *Rosie Tavern* – long isolated – was closed in 1995, and the nearby Rosie Garage was soon renamed; but Stuart's bakery has many branch outlets, and the other firms remain busy. The large Buckhaven High School has a roll of about 1300.

## BUCKIE, Portessie & Rathven — Map 10, A1

*Moray fishing port, pop. 8450* — OS 28: NJ 4265

From about the 11th century there was a thanage of *'Rathenech'*, which has been equated with Rathven, near the coast of the Moray Firth about 25 km west of Banff. There was a church, and around 1200 a *'hospital'* was established; the annual Peter Fair was held there for at least 700 years. The coastal settlement of Buckie, first mentioned in 1362, lies at the mouth of the Burn of Buckie, 2 km to the west of Rathven, which had a parish school by 1600, the approximate date of Pont's blurred sketch map, on which Buckie was named; fishing there was first recorded in 1692, but it long remained only a beach fishing base. Buckie was shown on the fair copy of the Roy map of about 1750 as *'Buckie Shore'*, then comprising four coastal hamlets, either side of the burn. Roy marked half a dozen buildings beside the sea 2 km to the east of Buckie at Rottensluch, a beach fishing station founded in 1727 by Hay of Rannes, later more happily renamed Portessie, though there was no actual harbour. A road followed the approximate line of the modern A98; no connecting links were shown, but this map was evidently left unfinished.

**Mansion, Fisheries and Muddy Harbour**: The elegant 3-storey Letterfourie House, designed by Robert Adam, was built of pink granite in 1773, overlooking the valley of the Burn of Buckie 4 km inland. Cluny Square was built in 1780, but Buckie lacked a charter and in 1794 there were only ten Buckie boats. Even so, in 1799 Heron regarded Buckie as Banffshire's chief fishing village, with about 700 inhabitants. Buckie was rather late to acquire a post office, around 1825. Nether Buckie harbour was built at Seatown in 1857 by Sir Robert Gordon of Letterfourie, but it was found to silt up rapidly – allegedly with River Spey mud. Despite this a lifeboat station was opened in 1860–61, netmaking by machinery was introduced locally in the 1860s, and in 1867 Buckie was among the top twenty Scottish herring fishing ports and one of the top ten curing centres for white fish. In 1886 Nether Buckie and its harbour was renamed Buckpool.

**Whisky at Inchgower and Golf at Strathlene**: The Inchgower Distillery was built at Rathven in 1870–71 by Alex Wilson, to replace Tochieneal (*see Cullen*). Its water, and that of the town, was supplied from a source at the Hill of Menduff, 4km south-east. In 1886 the whisky writer Barnard wrote that the distillery employed twenty men to produce over 280,000 litres of Highland malt whisky annually; the draff and spent wash fed cattle, sheep and pigs on an associated farm. Meantime the Strathlene golf club, founded in 1877, laid out an 18-hole course on moorland high above the coast east of Portessie.

**Cluny Harbour and the Railways**: The 4ha Cluny harbour, 1km east of the original Buckpool harbour which it effectively replaced, was built by the Cluny Estates in 1876–80, and soon became crowded with fishing boats. A local newspaper, the *Banffshire Advertiser*, started in 1881 when the population was over 4250, with 333 boats and 1330 fishermen; the number of vessels registered grew from 46 in 1880 to 91 by 1884. In 1884 the Highland Railway (HR) opened a winding and hilly branch line from Keith through rustic stations south of Buckie at Enzie, Drybridge and Rathven, to Buckie and Portessie, where it terminated and an engine shed was built; but there was little traffic and it had a short history. The more important coastal loop line of the Great North of Scotland Railway from Elgin, passing beside Buckie harbour to Portessie and Portsoy, was finally opened in May 1886; Portessie became a junction with the HR.

**Buckie Burgh and Harbour Enlargement**: Although a new parish church was built at Enzie in 1886, the urban growth at Buckie then quickened; it became a police burgh in 1888, and by 1891 5849 people lived there, plus 941 in Portessie. In 1894 Murray described Buckie as *"a fishing town of some importance"*, with the *"good" Cluny Hotel*. A gasworks was provided, and although from the 1890s onwards the population of Banffshire as a whole declined, Buckie continued its development. A sawmill was established by Johnstone in 1901, and Gray set up in 1903 what later became the Hamlyn meal mill, able to grind 2000 tonnes a year. In 1900 nearly 500 boats were based at Buckie, whose BCK marking was introduced in 1907, locally replacing BF (Banff). The burgh bought the Cluny harbour in 1908, soon enlarging it to its current size. In 1909 the HR engine shed at Portessie was closed, later becoming a concrete block works. At that time Buckie had the largest fleet of steam drifters in Scotland. By 1915 entertainment was available at the *Palace Cinema*. Although the HR line to Keith was abandoned in 1915, a bus service to Keith was begun in 1926.

**Drifters, Coasters, Coopers and more Golf**: By 1918 and probably long before, Jones' Buckie Slip & Shipyards Ltd was building drifters. In 1921 they launched the 251-ton wooden hulled coaster SS *Torwood*, which they used to carry timber from the firm's Larbert sawmills; it was fitted with an engine built in 1914 by the Rose Street Foundry of Inverness. By then there was a cooperage from which coasters would deliver new or fettled herring barrels to ports such as Lerwick. Inchgower distillery suffered many vicissitudes; closed for a time from 1917, and again from 1930, it was bought by the town council. They sold it in 1936 to Arthur Bell & Co of Perth, who restarted it in 1937; but it was again out of use from 1940 to 1945. Meantime Buckie fishermen successfully weathered the changes from sail to steam to diesel-powered boats, though their numbers gradually dwindled. In 1939 Strathlene golf club moved the HR's wooden station building to its course, where it was used as a clubhouse until 1973. Meantime the Buckpool golf club, founded in 1933, had laid out the town's second 18-hole cliff-top course by 1972.

**Postwar Prosperity despite Death of the Railway**: By the 1950s Buckie had grown into a major local centre. In 1962 G Thomson of Buckie built the hull for a full sized replica of Henry Bell's *Comet* steamship of 1812, for operation on the Clyde 150 years after its first voyage, and for display in Port Glasgow. The railway was closed in 1968 and an oil storage depot was built on its alignment east of the site of Buckie station. By 1972 the town's water supply came from River Spey gravels at Ordiquhish south of Fochabers; the council provided facilities for tennis, bowling and putting. There were three yards for building and repairing fishing vessels, marine and general engineering works, a Thorn Lighting factory, fish and scampi processing factories, and a new abattoir built by Aberdeen Meat Marketing Ltd. A large maltings was built west of Rathven in the 1970s. W & J Cruikshank & Co, formerly of Fraserburgh, made soft drinks in Buckie by 1980.

**Buckie in Moray: Old Harbour Infilled**: Buckie was transferred to Moray district in 1975. In 1981 the town had a normal range of urban facilities. By 1985 Buckie had about 30 mainly deep-sea fishing boats based in the Cluny harbour, catching shellfish up to 200km offshore for sale in the local fish market, where in the 1990s a large modern market was created, to meet new EC regulations. Over 100 boats were registered in 1987, but due to over-exploitation of nearer fish stocks under a third of these actually worked from Buckie, where there was by 1994 a maritime museum; Buckpool harbour had been infilled in the 1970s for use as a park, and a caravan and camping site was open east of Portessie. The Cluny harbour was still busy; Moray Seafoods exported over half its output of fresh and frozen shellfish products, and had a Spanish subsidiary. In the 1990s the former Enzie church was converted into a crematorium.

**Boatbuilding in Crisis**: By 1987 the three local boatbuilders included a leading specialist in carvel-built wooden fishing vessels, erected under cover. Despite a dearth of orders, Jones Buckie Boatyard, associated with nearby Herd & Mackenzie, still built and repaired fishing vessels, ferries, lifeboats, workboats and yachts of up to 45m under cover, in any material from traditional wood to steel, aluminium and GRP. They struggled on till early 1995 when 120 people were employed, but like all Scottish yards were denied EU grants by the remote Tory government, and went into receivership. Some 55 craftsmen lost their jobs, but the remaining 50 workers and the Buckie Shipyard with its tall crane were taken on by Lithgows *(see Port Glasgow)* and continue at work; a naval architect is based nearby. The marine engineers, fishmarket, ice factory, and large scampi processing works all continue in operation.

**Busy not Drifting!**: By 2000 the *'Buckie Drifter'* maritime heritage centre was open by the harbour, its new black-clad exterior belying the interesting exhibits within, and maritime paintings can be seen in the public library gallery. A computer centre adjoins the crowded harbour. There are coastguard and lifeboat stations – the latter with two boats – and a vast range of marine services, dealing in chandlery, fish, fishing gear, ice, marine insurance, oils and lubricants, nets, seafoods, ship painting and weatherwear. Nearby is a builders' merchant. The Forsyth Group has two yards, one inshore with a portal crane, the other of 1000m$^2$ being very new, fabricating giant reels some 10m in diameter for cable- or pipe-laying.

**Busy Buckie Town**: A high proportion of its 8425 residents in 1991 owned their homes outright. Inchgower distillery was producing a light whisky under United Distillers, and distillery engineering was also carried on. Grampian Country Pork employed 150 people in their Buckie plant, processing meat from pigs raised by non-intensive methods *(see Cullen)*. The town centre, which lies alongside but above and distinct from the harbour area, contains a full range of shops and facilities; it has a council office, a variety of banks and churches, Buckie High School (with some 850 pupils), and Buckie Thistle football club. Safeway has now opened a store in the town. The small *Cluny* and *Marine* hotels, pubs, and B&B houses serve the visitor.

## BUCKSBURN, Ashmill, Bankhead & Stoneywood

**Map 10, C3**

***Suburbs to n-w. of Aberdeen,*** *pop. 9000* OS 38: NJ 8909

When Robert Gordon mapped Aberdeenshire for Blaeu's atlas about 1640, various tiny settlements including Ashmill (also known as Auchmill) stood west of the lower River Don, north of its sharp bend 5 km west of Old Aberdeen; Kirkhill, the centre of Newhills parish, is 2 km to the west. In 1762 a new road was built from the city to Kintore, hugging the river before veering west over Tyrebagger Hill; on this road the Ashmill or Bucksburn area (formerly Buxburn) grew as an industrial centre, using the water power of the River Don, which fell some 3 m in each kilometre of its course from Dyce to the sea. In 1770–71 John Boyle, a bookseller, and Richard Hyde, a dyer, set up a paper mill near Stoneywood House, whose name it took; a warehouse for rag collection was established in the city. By 1774 there was also a textile beating mill at Greenburn, on a stream west of Stoneywood. A second Stoneywood Mill was erected by Charles Baird about 1789 for carding and spinning, using English machinery. Mugiemoss paper mill was open by 1800, and the New Stoneywood bleachfield was modernised.

**Canal Locks, Snuff Mills and Stationery**: The opening of the Aberdeenshire Canal from the city's harbour to near Inverurie in 1805 improved the communications on the south bank of the Don, despite its 17 locks. In 1810 Stoneywood snuff mill was acquired by Charles Smith, another papermaker, but a new snuff mill appeared at Mugiemoss in 1817. In 1850 Stoneywood paper mill employed a thousand people, making writing paper from 2500 tonnes of rags a year. For a time Bucksburn had a market stance, though it was never a burgh.

**The Railway, and Envelopes by the Million**: The Great North of Scotland Railway's main line opened in 1854, entirely replacing the canal, whose bed was infilled to lay the track. By 1869 Alexander Pirie & Sons of the great Stoneywood paper mill employed over 2000 workers, for they also owned smaller mills at Woodside, and the Union paper works which made a million envelopes a day, by *"mechanism of the most beautiful construction"* (Bremner). The two mills had 26 beating engines between them; one obtained 500 horsepower from the water flow, and they jointly produced about 65 tonnes of paper per week.

**Granite and Trams**: In the late 19th century the extensive Dancingcairn granite quarries became noted for kerbstones. They remained with Bucksburn when in 1891 the areas to the south were incorporated into the City of Aberdeen. A ferry operated between Stoneywood and Grandhome, but was closed by its quarrelsome proprietor in 1890. Murray's Handbook for 1894 noted *"The vale of the Don is the scene of active industry – paper mills, woollen mills, granite quarries, etc."*. In 1894 there were 550 employees in the great Stoneywood paper mill, their journeys to work being made easier when Bankhead became the terminus of Aberdeen's longest tram route; this was electrified in 1899 by the Aberdeen Suburban Tramways Company. In 1901 the Bucksburn village population was only 2200, so commuting out of the city to the various Donside industries must have been considerable.

**Back to Agriculture**: Craibstone College of Agriculture just west of Bankhead was opened in 1920 by the Development Commission for Rural Areas, and the Rowett Research Institute for agriculture was opened at Bankhead in 1922. The 1930s saw the creation of the ambitious *Argosy Cinema* with its cafe and dance hall complex, and soon after 1945 came the large Twin Spires Creamery, which had its own siding for rail traffic until 1969. By the 1950s nearly 6000 people lived in the Bucksburn area, which had facilities typical of a large village, becoming more urban when the Aberdeenshire County Police HQ was built in the late 1950s. However, the tramway was closed in 1955, the cinema complex failed around 1960, and the station was closed by 1963; but the quarries were still open in 1967.

**The Modern Paper Mills**: In 1970 there were still 1500 employees in the Stoneywood paper mill, which by 1989 (under Wiggins Teape) was switching to gas turbine power. Mugiemoss mill had long made paper sacks; by 1980 it used vast quantities of waste paper to produce them under the Abertay label. By 1989 under Davidson & Sons it was both the largest paperboard mill in Britain, and Scotland's largest supplier of board made entirely from waste paper, its green-ness emphasised by a new effluent treatment plant. Some of its 200,000-tonne annual output was moved by rail, and 40% was exported, largely to France and Germany.

**Nutritional Research and Frozen Chickens**: In 1975 Bucksburn was included in Aberdeen City district; about then a 99-room *Holiday Inn* (later *Sheraton*) was built, incorporating an old meal mill. By 1981 the North East River Purification Board had made its HQ at Mugiemoss Road. With the coming of the Bankhead industrial estate, plus a chicken processing plant and all the North Sea oil development at nearby Dyce *(q.v.)*, the Bucksburn area's population had risen to 8500 by 1981. In that year Grampian Regional Council established a skills training centre, and by 1990 the Rowett was Europe's largest nutritional research centre. Traffic on the main Auchmill Road had become very congested by the 1980s; its reconstruction as a dual carriageway in 1987 changed the area's character quite drastically. In 1992 a new station was being considered at Persley, but rail privatisation by the Major government ended that dream. In 1993–94 Grampian Country Chickens – whose total workforce exceeded 2500 and whose headquarters were at Bucksburn – produced both raw and processed chicken products. Bankhead Academy has 700 pupils. The *Craighaar Hotel* has 55 rooms.

## BUNESSAN

**Map 4, B2**

***Small village, west Mull,*** *pop. 200* OS 48: NM 3821

There is a standing stone about 1.5 km east of Bunessan, which lies at the head of the sheltered inlet of Loch na Lathaich on the north coast of the Ross of Mull, a lengthy peninsula of knobbly hills and lochans, also known as the parish of Kilfinichen & Kilvickeon (which includes Iona). The name Bunessan appeared on Pont's work of about 1600 – and on Huddart's chart of 1791, but little seems known of the place until a post office was opened in 1804. A nearby pier was a calling point for the earliest Glasgow to Stornoway steamers, before the road between east Mull and Fionnphort was built between 1850 and 1880. Subsequently, the steamers making an anticlockwise circuit of Mull continued to call. Murray noted that the inn at Bunessan offered *"comfortable angling quarters"* in 1894. In 1901 the parish held 1529 people, but by 1951 only 800. By then Bunessan – with about 200 local residents – was a post town, with a 30-pupil secondary class in its school, two doctors and the 7-roomed *Argyll Arms Hotel*.

**Decline, Resurgence and Rabbits**: The parish population continued to decline rapidly, to only 585 in 1971. Secondary schoolchildren were sent elsewhere after the 1960s, the steamers ceased to call in 1962, and Bunessan was little more than a hamlet by 1971. However, the passing tourist trade to Iona via the road to Fionnphort had been building up, and by 1981 the population had recovered somewhat to over 200. By 1985 a garage and the local telephone exchange stood by the wooded head of an inlet 4km to the west; nearby Ardfenaig was a former shooting lodge, which had become a small hotel. Bunessan was then a very small village, busy in summer, with two shops, lobster fishing, and a nearby boatyard. Despite serving a wide area of the Ross of Mull, the primary school taught barely 30 children in 1989. However, by 1991, 675 people lived in the parish. By praising the anchorage, Haswell-Smith encouraged yachts to visit Iona, Staffa and the scenic coast of Mull; by 1996 a rabbit farm 2 km to the east was an unusual tourist attraction. Small hotels include the seasonal *Ardfenaig* and seasonal *Assapol* (former manse), plus the central *Argyll Arms*.

## BUNNAHABHAIN — Map 4, B4

***Hamlet, Islay,*** *pop. under 100* — OS 60: NR 4273

The lighthouse of Ruvaal, Rhuvaal, or more correctly Rubha a'Mhail, located at the northern tip of Islay, was first illuminated in 1859 to guard the entrance to the Sound of Islay. In 1881 the Islay Distillery Company of Glasgow built the extraordinarily isolated distillery settlement of Bunnahabhain *(G. 'Fort of the Stream')*, pronounced and now often written as Bonahaven. This occupies a coastal re-entrant at the foot of the Abhainn Araig, a stream rising in the tumbled hills 4km north of Port Askaig. The distillery was very substantially built, together with an iron pier; Barnard wrote *"two large ranges of houses provide ample accommodation for the workmen"*, who numbered around sixty. *"Neat villas"* were provided for the excise officers, and a reading room and primary school were also built. Barley and coal were brought in by chartered steamers; the treasured annual output of some 900,000 litres of Islay malt whisky was shipped out by the weekly MacBrayne steamer.

**Highland Distillers**: In 1887 the owners joined with the Glenrothes-Glenlivet distillery of William Grant as founder members of the Highland Distilleries Company (HD). A post office was provided at Bunnahabhain, and survived along with the other facilities, although in the 20th century the population

*The still house of the Bunnahabhain Distillery, Islay – built on a courtyard plan in 1881–83 by the Islay Distillery Company. (JRH)*

gradually reduced – along with the streamlining of the production process – to an estimated 130 by 1981. The lighthouse was automated in 1986. The primary school, closed in the early 1980s, was converted in 1990 into a training centre for City & Guilds qualifications. The distillery was extended in 1963 from two stills to four, but temporarily closed in 1982–84; when reopened, it produced a single malt matured in sherry casks for sale at twelve years old. In 1991 HD, the producers of the *'Famous Grouse'* blend, still owned Bunnahabhain, as well as Glenrothes-Glenlivet and also Glenglassaugh. The distillery is open to visitors.

## BURGHEAD — Map 9, C3

***Coastal village, Moray,*** *pop. 1500* — OS 28: NJ 1169

From at least the fourth century the Pictish fortress and shrine now called Burghead stood on an exposed promontory on the Moray Firth 13km north-east of Forres. Six ancient carvings found there represent bulls, the key to the cattle-rearing economy of the Dark Ages. There was a deep well within the defences, which were destroyed by fire, probably in the seventh century, when the north passed under Viking rule. Earl Sigurd of Orkney rebuilt a fortress in 889 and Danes refortified it in 1008, but were expelled from Moray by Scottish forces by 1010. Little then seems to be known until Pont's map made about 1600 showed *'The Old Brugh'* apparently devoid of buildings.

**Milling, Malting and Shipbuilding**: A large sheet of water, the Loch of Rossyll, acted as a millpond for coastal mills some 3km south of Burghead, until it became filled with sand; Roseisle which adapted the name became known for malting. The Stephen family began to build ships at Burghead in 1750, though Roy's map made about then showed only a roadless and harbourless hamlet, the end of the promontory still being occupied by an elaborate defensive system of banks and ditches. Heron wrote in 1799 of a *"village"* of some 400 people, *"most of whom follow a seafaring life at a station well adapted for a deep, capacious and safe harbour"*.

**The Rebuilt Burghead and the Railway**: The ancient earthworks were largely obliterated when the harbour and village were built or rebuilt in 1805–10, with new stone granaries designed by Telford. A coastguard station was built in 1807, and fish-curing began in 1817 and grew into a large enterprise. In 1834 Burghead was a fairly substantial fishing port, and the destination of a steamer service from Glasgow via the Caledonian Canal, with calls at Cromarty and Invergordon. By 1830 Alexander Stephen & Sons had moved their shipyard to Arbroath *(q.v.)*. The *Grant Arms* inn was open by 1847, when there were over 40 Burghead fishing boats, but meal was being shipped out despite famine in the north of Scotland. A fertiliser works open in the 1860s probably made superphosphate from imported bones. A branch of the Highland Railway was opened from Alves in 1862. This built up a large traffic, and was extended to Hopeman in 1892; earlier, planked *'sand blowers'* had to be built, angled up from the railside at 45 degrees, to prevent the line being smothered by the shifting sands of the Links; Roseisle Forest later covered the whole sandy area. To Murray in 1894 Burghead, with 1662 people, was *"a watering-place and important fishing village"*, served by the *White Horse Inn*.

**Grain on and off the Rails**: Passenger trains ceased in 1931, but the line stayed open for freight; Wordie & Co had a small cartage depot as late as 1946. In the 1930s the town council bought the harbour, and also built a bowling green and tennis courts. By the 1950s there were four small hotels; junior secondary education for local children was provided at Alves, 7km south. Trains handled grain traffic to and from the silos; in the 1980s the harbour imported grain by coaster, and was still the base for a dozen fishing boats. There was a museum and two caravan and camping sites by 1986. About 1980 a new rail-served maltings with grain silos was built by DCL at Roseisle to feed its Speyside distilleries. In 1992 under pressure from the Major government, British Rail doubled its charges; predictably, United Distillers decided to abandon rail transport. (Burghead's rail link was taken out of use in 2000.) Meantime in 1991 Burghead held 1495 residents, a high proportion owning their homes outright; there was little new development. One of the former Telford granaries, *'A'* listed, has been converted to flats; the other still stands deteriorating.

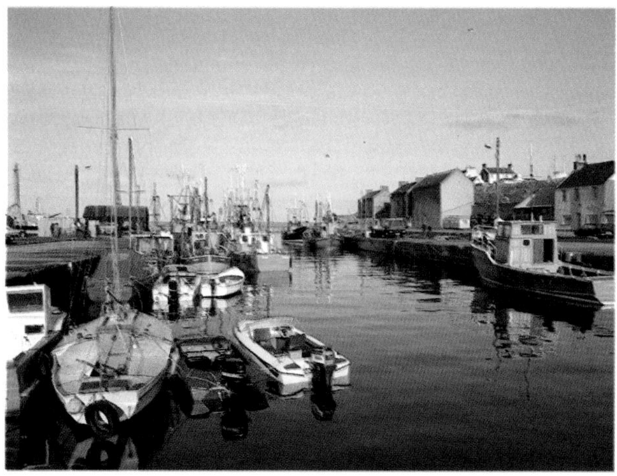

*Burghead harbour, built in 1807–10 to designs by Thomas Telford, largely for shipping corn.* *(JRH)*

## BURNMOUTH — Map 3, C3

***Berwickshire hamlet,*** *pop. v. under 100* — OS 67: NT 9561

Burnmouth lies in a niche at the foot of 100m cliffs, 10km north-west of Berwick upon Tweed, where a small burn forms a steep ravine allowing access to the rocky shore. In Pont's time around 1600 there was a mill at the burn mouth, hence the name. There seems to have been little else until 1830 when a fishing harbour was built. The North British Railway, opened in 1846, provided a station perched at the top of the cliffs; from 1891 this was the junction of a short branch to Eyemouth. The harbour had been enlarged in 1879, and a straggling village developed around these nuclei, linked by a perilous road. The station and branch line were closed in 1962. Eight or nine lobster, crab and white fish boats were based in the harbour in the 1980s; a mixture of holiday houses and fishermen's homes are now served by basic facilities, including a pub and post office. Rail passengers can barely glimpse the village as they pass.

## BURNTISLAND & Newbigging — Map 6, B5

***Town, S. Fife,*** *pop. 6000* — OS 66: NT 2385

The hill fort of Dunearn stands some 200m above sea level and 2km from the south coast of Fife. From its site various straight stretches of early road alignments ran west to Inverkeithing and east to Invertiel via Carlinknowes (a *Caer* placename element). These may represent fragments of a Roman road from Inverkeithing to Crail *(q.v.)*. Barnard wrote that the settlement at the foot of the great hill called The Binn – the present Kirkton – was at first known as Wester Kinghorn; its Old Kirk existed by 1234. The nearby Burntisland Castle was built from 1119 by the Abbots of Dunfermline; David I granted land there as early as 1130. The castle was rebuilt as a massive tower house in the 16th century, and when Burntisland became a Royal Burgh in 1541, a new settlement was founded at the shore close by. Although it paid no tax until after 1556 it soon became renowned as a safe haven, though a parlous fishing centre. Sea mills were soon built, which for three centuries used tidal power to saw timber and to mill grain. Also in 1541 a barony charter was granted to Newbigging, some 1.5km west of the Kirkton, though this remained insignificant. By 1587 a school was open.

**Ferry Disasters**: In 1589 a ferry on a Burntisland–Newhaven voyage sank in a storm, drowning 40 people. The remarkable church – the first post-Reformation church structure in Scotland – dates from 1592–95. It follows a square Dutch model, there being then an active trade with the Low Countries, using vessels of types shown in contemporary paintings on the church gallery. This was the venue in 1601 for the new Church of Scotland's General Assembly, when it resolved to create the King James Bible. A Tolbooth was built at the corner of High Street and Harbour Place in 1616. In 1618 Taylor the waterman-poet met many notable people at Burntisland, called it a *"town"* and noted grain exports. In 1633 a second doomed ferry, the *Blessing of Burntisland*, sank in a storm en route to Leith; some 30 people and the extremely valuable baggage train of Charles I were lost.

**The Attractive Port**: By 1639 Burntisland's meteoric career had brought its tax yield to 80% of that of Kirkcaldy, ranking it 17th among Scottish burghs, a rank it probably never regained. After the civil war, in 1651 Cromwell's troops were asked to help in building quays for the ferry. By 1655 Burntisland was nominally one of the eight head ports of Scotland; but there were only seven local vessels, none exceeding 40 tons and mainly engaged in exporting coal and salt, though neither was apparently produced in the immediate vicinity. Richard Franck waxed lyrical in 1656 about *"the pleasant shores of beautiful Brunt-Island, guarded with rocks that front the harbour and pier"*. The harbour was small but secure, adjoined by a market-place *"facing the ocean; where all or most of her merchants' houses stand"*. The *Star* tavern was established in 1671(still open today). Malt made in Burntisland was exported by the end of the 17th century, and malt mills were working in 1712.

**Defoe's Unhappy Burntisland**: Defoe visited Burntisland, reporting in the 1720s that *"here is a very good harbour which enters as if it had been made by hand into the centre of the town; this is built round it, and the ships lay their broad sides to the very houses"*. However, trade seemed at a low ebb *"the place is unhappy, and must decay yet farther, unless the trade revive, which I do not yet foresee. Here is, however, a manufacture of linen."* Roy's survey of about 1750 showed a large compact settlement on the coast road, its harbour lying to the west of the town and south of the Castle, which was soon to be renamed as *'Rossend'* by one Murdoch Campbell from Skye.

**Burntisland's Industrial Development to 1824**: A post office was opened in 1756. A brewery was built at Grange in 1767, and was converted by Young into an early distillery in 1786. *'Vitriol'* (sulphuric acid) works were in operation at Lammerlaws by the 1790s, foreshadowing the later large chemical industry; they still existed in 1824. A cavernous *'stoop and room'* limestone mine at Newbigging in the hills north-west of the town was operated by the Carron Company from the late 18th century. This mine was connected with the tiny Carron pier by a steeply inclined self-acting mineral railway, and ventilated by fires lit beneath shafts going as deep as 65 m; a new escape tunnel was cut in 1817.

**Golf and Sea Mills**: In 1790 though the ferry piers had decayed there were four ferry boats in use; new quays were built in 1792. The local golfing society was founded in 1797, eventually laying out an 18-hole course on the hills east of the town. Heron in 1799 called Burntisland (with a population of only about 1100) *"a small town, situated under a stupendous rock. It has an excellent harbour, in form of a basin, some shipbuilding, and a sugar-house. Here are two mills employed in making flour, meal and barley. Of these one is erected on the sea, and works about 14 hours a day at all seasons."* These reliable tide mills operated into the early 19th century but then ceased to grind.

**Dung, Refuse and Bathing Machines**: In 1823–24 a fine new manse designed by William Burn was built beside the harbour at Forth Place, and nearby was a tiny dry dock; however, in 1824 the bathing machines on the east sands stood close by a *'dung depot'* at the end of a *'refuse gutter'*! In 1827 Chambers found a *"thriving sea-port, remarkable for having the best harbour in the Firth of Forth. The town is much resorted to as sea-bathing quarters."* In 1834 two whalers were based in Burntisland, and in 1842 an Act of Parliament authorised harbour improvements by the two local lairds, the Gladstones and the Buccleuchs. In 1841 the parish contained some 2200 people, a new Town House was built in 1843.

**The Burntisland and Granton Train Ferry**: When the Edinburgh & Northern Railway came to the town in the mid 1840s, their fine new station building designed by Grainger & Miller was unusual in being built on to the manse at right angles; the latter eventually became the *Forth Hotel*. When in 1848 the line was opened from Burntisland to Kirkcaldy and Cupar, the harbour became the terminal for the new Granton steam ferry; this became the world's first train ferry, the best memorial to that enterprising but slipshod engineer Thomas Bouch, whose novel vessel Leviathan was accessed by sliding double tracks and lifting link spans. She was soon busy with East Coast traffic, for in 1851 a second such ferry was opened across the Tay.

**Mansion Houses, Fishing and Railway Workshops**: The modest mansionhouse of Kingswood was built in 1851 for a sugar planter from Jamaica, on a sheltered site at the foot of the wooded crags on the Kinghorn road. The Italianate villa Greenmount, also destined to become a hotel, was built about the time that Newbigging sandstone quarry was first noted in 1856; by 1896 the quarry employed 30 people. In 1855 23 fishermen still worked out of Burntisland, which was a port of registry with the code BU; they and other fishermen calling at the port were served by a remarkable 189 netmakers, coopers, gutters, packers and vendors. In 1869 a small experimental meat cannery was noted, but this did not seem to thrive, unlike the North British Railway *'workshops'*, a reference to the locomotive depot whose unusual roundhouse was probably built for the opening in 1848.

**Coal Exports, Docks and East Coast Main Line Railway**: With its rail connections into the Fife coalfield via Kirkcaldy, Burntisland soon became known for unmanageably large coal exports. A new harbour was opened in 1860, but was soon found to be inadequate, so the railway company and town council combined to build the enclosed docks, the first of which opened in 1876. The construction of a long sea wall was begun in 1881, enabling the larger East Dock to open in 1901; in all twelve coal hoists were installed. Meantime with the building of the Forth Bridge it was vital that the railway should be extended along the coast to reach Inverkeithing, requiring a steep and sinuous line spanning the High Street on a metal viaduct, which visually divorced the town from its ancient harbour. This line, the Forth Bridge, and the much-adapted station were opened in 1890; the repair works and train ferry service consequently ceased, but a steam passenger ferry continued to operate.

**Quarrying and Shale Oil**: Meantime by 1837 the Grange sandstone quarry had opened near the distillery, and also the Callals quarry; in 1869 these were supplying stone for the

*Bauxite barges in Burntisland harbour. Bauxite was first imported in 1913, and these 'dumb' barges are still used to trans-ship the material from bulk carriers anchored in the Forth; the material is processed in the nearby Alcan alumina factory.* *(JRH)*

repair of St Giles Cathedral and the building of Fettes College (both in Edinburgh). The Newbigging quarry – which raised Carboniferous sandstone from the hillside above the old Carron mine from 1886 to 1939 – supplied the facing stone for Gothenburg Cathedral in Sweden. In 1866 and 1878 oil shale mines were opened at Binnend to the east, accompanied in 1884 by a shale oil works, to which a short but difficult branch railway was built from Kinghorn in 1886–87. Though the industry for a time gave rise to a small village at Binnend, it was very short-lived, closing around 1894. Meantime the Burntisland Co-operative Society had been set up in 1884. In 1886 the quite large distillery used local barley, and had its own gasworks; the output was about 900,000 litres of Lowland Malt.

**Burntisland's Apogee: Resort and Alumina**: The hillfoot mansion of Binn House was built in 1886. By 1891 over 6000 people lived in the town, and by 1892 when the Bowling Club was founded there was a proper golf course and a new recreation ground. By 1894 the small *Forth* and *Royal* hotels were open; in the early 20th century an oil-cake factory worked beside the latter! A public library, with Carnegie assistance, was initiated in 1904. In 1902 Grange quarry had 110 workers, but closed in 1914. An electricity supply was provided in 1911, the peak year for the local coal export trade. The docks remained very busy, because in 1913 the import of bauxite commenced, for conversion into alumina by the works of the North British Aluminium Company, lately built on the site of the former Geds water mill. In 1914 Grange distillery became one of the five founder members of the combine called Scottish Malt Distillers Ltd. But from 1914 the Newbigging quarry worked little stone, and closed in 1937.

**The Ayres buck Decline, but No Whisky**: Wilfred and Amos Ayre, who came from Tyneside, began shipbuilding in 1918 on the site of the early harbour: their Burntisland Shipbuilding Company was an outstandingly successful firm, which launched ten ships in 1932, a depression year when most Scottish yards were silent. In 1936 they built three 1600-ton *'flat iron'* steam colliers, able to pass under London Bridge to serve the new Fulham power station; they were followed in 1939 by the larger *Fulham IV*. Between the wars Burntisland's sandy links remained a minor resort, with an open-air swimming pool, and *Kingswood* became a small hotel in 1930. The coal trade had decreased greatly after the 1914–18 war, affected locally by competition from Methil, though even in the 1930s over half a million tons were exported in an average year. The distillery was closed for ever in 1925, due to American prohibition, and eventually fell into ruin. The Granton ferry was closed in 1940.

**War Stimulates Burntisland Shipyard**: Coal exports died with the second world war, but the capacity of the shipyard was enlarged in 1939, enabling vessels of at least 11,000 tons to be built. The Company bought out the well-known yard of Hall Russell of Aberdeen in 1942. In all, between 1939 and 1945 the yard turned out 69 ships of some 290,000 gross tons, including a merchant aircraft carrier (for both grain and planes) and three Loch Class frigates. In 1958 the shipyard employed 1400 people.

**Decline becomes Endemic and the Yard Closes**: The passenger ferry service to Granton was resumed on a makeshift basis in 1951, using four war surplus tank landing craft, but ended in 1952. The last people left Binnend in 1954, and the settlement vanished. Burntisland's general facilities decreased over the post-war years to little more than those of a large village. However, by 1954 *Greenmount* had become a hotel. The once-important steam locomotive shed lingered on as an outpost of Thornton until the diesel era, then being flattened; British Aluminium (the *'North'* was dropped in 1960) were still using their own steam shunters in 1965. The shipyard whose vessel no. 405 was built in 1963, suffered difficult customers on a 1967 contract, and the yard with its 870 jobs sadly failed in 1968; its last vessel, the 7000 ton cargo vessel *Helen Miller*, was launched in July 1969.

**Rossend Saved by a Whisker**: In 1970 the impressive and historic though roofless Rossend Castle narrowly escaped demolition by the then town council; Binn House was less fortunate, its site soon becoming a housing estate. Meantime the open-air swimming pool had also deteriorated and had to be closed in 1976, just after local government status was – perhaps mercifully – lost to Kirkcaldy District in 1975. The *Forth Hotel* was vacant by about 1975, and was demolished about 20 years later. The castle was luckier, being well restored about 1975 by Robert Hurd & Partners as the HQ of their architectural practice. Intensive activity on the shipyard site was resumed in 1972; under Robb Caledon the western basin was infilled to provide space to build service modules for North Sea oil rigs. Under British Shipbuilders the yard burgeoned to 890 employees; after a takeover by Texaco about 1979, activity on the site became intermittent. The population of the town was still almost 6000 in 1981 and there were about seven small hotels; but the *Greenmount Hotel* burnt out in 1987 – it still stands, roofless. Meantime in the mid 1980s the baronial villa of Starley Hall became a private school.

**Developments in Alumina**: Around 1970 British Aluminium's plant became BA Chemicals employing 400 people. Their research laboratory, formerly in the south of England, was then moved to Burntisland. In 1981 the plant was acquired by Alcan of Canada, and progressively developed. In the late 1980s the firm was the only regular user of the east dock, bringing in up to 300,000 tonnes of bauxite and 15,000 tonnes of caustic soda annually, transhipped into the shallow dock using huge dumb (engineless) barges.

**Burntisland abandons Rail Freight**: Unfortunately about 1987 British Alcan ceased to use British Rail to shunt wagons of bauxite across into the works; the once extensive rail freight facilities became completely disused, and more heavy lorries clogged the narrow streets. Worse, much pink mud residue had to be carried by road for dumping in the one-time oil shale workings. However BA were the town's principal employers, making superfine alumina hydrate, the basis of toothpaste, of some catalysts and ceramics. A 1984 development, fire retardent filler for electric cables, was an expanding line in 1989, output being boosted by 6000 tonnes per year, and some loss of amenity had to be accepted. In 1997 they employed 480 people locally and with world demand steadily growing for the flame retardant alumina powder (also used as a filler in plastics and rubber) the firm was to invest greatly in the *'Superfine'* production plant, keeping 70 construction workers busy over 3 years. However, in 1999 the workforce was cut to 400.

**Stone and Tourism**: Newbigging quarry was briefly reopened in 1980, and again in 1984 by Scottish Natural Stones Ltd to permit the repair of Gothenburg Cathedral, and subsequently its stone was used to face the National Library of Scotland's new annexe in Newington. In the 1980s the west dock was used as a base by a variety of offshore oil concerns, but a major offshore dry dock proposal came to nothing. The *Kingswood Hotel* added a function suite in 1990. Despite some new private housing on the outskirts, including part of the distillery site, there were ugly gaps in the centre, and a one-time cinema was almost derelict in 1989.

**Oil-related Development: Ups and Downs**: In 1990 the fabrication yard, with an area of over 13 ha, was reactivated by the Consafe Engineering (UK) group of Aberdeen, who widened the dock gates in 1991 to accept standard North Sea barges. By then they employed over 300 people, and had built a huge separator column for Coryton oil refinery. In 1993 and 1994 they built two major 1600-tonne living-quarters modules clad in stainless steel for Shell Expro's Brent Bravo and Charlie platforms, giving work to 150 people locally, plus 40 design engineers in Aberdeen. In 1995 they built the Brent Charlie living quarters, followed by an accommodation and control module for the Shell-Esso Brent field, and an 1100-tonne drilling rig; in 1998 700 were employed, but by late 2000 only a skeleton staff remained. Meantime by 1993 the harbour was also the base for the growing operations of Finnish-owned dredging firm Haka UK. Consafe became Bi-Fab after a management buy-out in 2001.

**Two Ferries Lost, but Holidays Popular**: The population in 1991 was 5951. In that year a catamaran was used to reinstate the ferry service to Granton. Despite the awful approaches at both termini it was fairly successful with tourists, but failed to attract the expected commuters from trains and cars, and ceased to operate at the end of the 1992 season. A full-scale search was started in 1992 to locate the sunken ferry of 1633 with its lost Royal treasury: to date without success. In 1995–96, with keen local support, the outgoing Regional Council replaced the open pool with a new covered swimming pool on the same site. A popular holiday trade still flourishes at Burntisland, with a summer funfair. Small hotels include the *Kingswood*, the *Inchview* and *Sands*.

## BURRAVOE (Yell) — Map 14, C2

***Shetland island community**, pop. 200* — OS 2: HU 5279

Burra Voe is a sheltered inlet on the south-eastern tip of the bleak Isle of Yell; Pont's map of about 1592 showed both a settlement and just offshore a ship, implying a useful harbour. The *'Old Haa'* (Hall) was built in 1637, and a new church was built on the site of an ancient kirk in 1828. Regular steamer calls helped to keep a small village in being; by the 1930s it had a school, shop and post office. Steamers ceased to call from 1950, when the local population was about 250, though in 1956 a regular passenger ferry plied from Mossbank to Burravoe, and via Cullivoe to Unst. By 1987 Ulsta *(q.v.)* was the main access point, and the solid pier at Burravoe was disused; but about 25 modern houses had been built nearby. Thanks to Sullom Voe money, the village hall had been enlarged and reconditioned; the post office, shop and school continued, and the Old Haa was a visitor centre. But Yell's population had not grown with oil-related development, rather the reverse.

## BURRAY (Orkney) — Map 13, C3

***Island community, Orkney**, pop. 200* — OS 7: ND 4795

Pont's tiny map of Orkney made about 1592 showed the small island of Burray as having only one settlement (misnamed as St Margaret's Hope). Martin noted in 1703 that in the south of Burray was the ferry to Duncansby in Caithness. In later years a herring station near Westermill on Water Sound (opposite the real St Margaret's Hope on South Ronaldsay) acquired a pier, a primary school, and post office, growing into the village centre of the treeless island. At the start of the 1914–18 war, Scapa Flow – the partly landlocked sea area west of Burray – became a fleet base, and blockships were sunk to form anti-submarine barriers across the sounds north and south of Burray. By 1916 a total of 21 old vessels lay there rusting; among 22 more blockships sunk to reinforce the barriers in 1939–41 was, sadly, the historic *Gondolier* (*see Fort Augustus*).

**Part of the Mainland?**: But one U-boat slipped through, and after the resulting Royal Oak tragedy (*see Kirkwall*) the Churchill causeways (*see Holm*) were built to create permanent barriers and inter-island links; many of the blockships were subsequently removed. Although now within the Orkney Mainland context, Burray lost a third of its people between 1951 and 1971, stabilising by 1981 at little over 200. By the 1970s electricity arrived from Kirkwall by submarine cables. Duncan's, the small but locally important fishing vessel boatyard, had been in the same family for five generations; in 2000 it appeared to be struggling. The remains of some blockships can still be discerned. A sandpit had been opened in the North Links, and a fossil museum had been created north of Westermill. This is now called *'Burray Village'* and still has its basic facilities, including a licensed grocer, plus the former herring station, now converted to a hotel and restaurant. Two garages, and the Scapa Flow Diving Centre at Echnaloch, are also available.

## BURRELTON & Woodside — Map 6, B3

***Perthshire small village**, pop. 600* — OS 53: NO 2037

About 2 km south-west of Coupar Angus in fertile Strathmore, Scotland's largest farming valley, was Keithick, which was granted a barony burgh charter in 1492; its early church was marked on Pont's sketch map of Perth and Angus, made about

1600. This also showed nearby Keithick Mill, beside a burn which entered the River Isla. To the south was *'Cotton of Ireton'* and west of that another illegibly named water mill, probably the Nethermill. By about 1750 – when the Roy map of the Strathmore area was rather sketchily prepared – *the 'New Mill'* stood on a loop track from the Perth to Coupar Angus road, which had been made up on approximately its modern alignment. However Burrelton which later stood astride this new road was not named. A new village named Woodside was laid out immediately to the north in the shape of a triangle, and soon feued off.

**The Railway Comes – and Goes**: In 1848 the Scottish Midland Junction Railway (later the Caledonian main line) was opened between Perth and Forfar; a quarry at Keithick yielded stone for the line's large Cargill bridge, 5 km to the west. A station provided near Keithick mill was at first named Woodside & Burrelton. The former name was dropped because facilities preferred to locate in Burrelton, which by 1895 possessed a village square astride what the Ordnance Survey called the *'first class metalled road'*, an inn, post and telegraph office, a smithy, the Nethermill and a mansionhouse. By 1951 when there was a local sawmill the two places were served by bus and had a combined population of almost 800, with the facilities of a small village, effectively all in Burrelton. The station which by then had only one daily train each way was closed to passengers by the early 1960s.

**Still Rooted in Agriculture**: In 1967 the erstwhile main line was cut back to a mere goods branch to Forfar, and despite the quite recent construction of a great girder bridge carrying it across the improved A94, was closed completely in 1982. By that time although there was an agricultural engineer, and raspberries and chickens were intensively produced in the vicinity, the population of Burrelton including Woodside had fallen to only 650. A primary school, post office, butcher, three inns, a Skoda garage and the agricultural engineer are among the local facilities.

## BUSBY, Clarkston & Stamperland — Map 15, C6

***Glasgow s. suburbs,** pop. 20,500* — OS 64: NS 5757

Busby lies 9 km south of Glasgow beside the White Cart Water, formerly the Lanarkshire/Renfrewshire boundary. Pont's map made in 1596 showed *'Kittokmil'* and Busby; the latter was shown on the Roy map (made about 1754) as a roadless hamlet. In 1765 the mansion of Greenbank House was built 2 km west of Busby, in an area later known as Clarkston. By the late 18th century Kittokmil had been replaced by corn and lint mills called Newmills; then came a cotton mill, built on their site in 1780–81. A second textile mill was in operation by 1791, and limekilns were built at nearby Thorntonhall about the same time. Busby had a paper mill for a period from 1820. A penny post office was open by 1838. From the mid 19th century there was a bleaching and print works, and by 1863 Busby was a *"thriving textile town"* (Thomas).

**The Busby Railway**: On New Year's Day 1866 the locally promoted Busby Railway opened for services to Glasgow via Pollokshaws, and was extended south-east to East Kilbride in 1868; later it became part of the Caledonian system. In 1894 Busby – which then had an inn but a population of under 2000 – was described as *"a manufacturing village"*. Another station had been provided at the hamlet of Clarkston, 1 km north west of Busby, where there was still little else but a smithy in 1895; the hamlet of Sheddens stood between the two places. The large bleaching and print works with its rail connection was stated by Thomas to have closed in 1898, but evidently its use was resumed. Two golf club courses were laid out, the *'Cathcart Castle'* club dating from 1895, and *Williamwood* in 1906.

**Clarkston beats Busby**: In the early 20th century Clarkston and the estate at Stamperland – merely a farm as late as 1925 – were provided with a branch of the great Glasgow electric tramway system. In 1933 the LMS Railway offered travel privileges to new house purchasers at Clarkston *(c.f. Lenzie)*. In the 1930s large private estates were built on all sides of Clarkston, particularly at Netherlee and Stamperland to the north; a small gasworks was approved in 1941, perhaps to serve war industry in the area. By 1951 the combined population had reached 14,000, and Clarkston had become the main centre, having acquired small-town facilities. In 1953 when the incipient *Busby Hotel* was already an inn, the office of a new local newspaper the *Eastwood Mercury and Advertiser* was established. The cotton mills were demolished in the late 1960s. In 1974 an additional title, the *Glasgow South Side News*, was added by its Paisley-based proprietors.

**Disastrous News from Affluent Suburbia**: The combined settlements were never created a burgh; as a result of green belting, by 1971 they had reached a population plateau and held 11,300 residents. In that year a gas explosion in the crowded Clarkston shopping centre sadly killed 20 people and injured 105. Clarkston was incorporated into Eastwood district in 1975, and Busby joined East Kilbride. Tape manufacture continued in Busby in the 1980s. In the early 1980s the National Trust for Scotland acquired the fine Greenbank House, and opened its walled garden to the public. In 1991 the population of this affluent suburban area (including Netherlee and Williamwood) exceeded 20,500; Busby had a youngish, well qualified emphasis. When local government was reorganised in 1996, Busby was transferred from Lanarkshire to join Clarkston in East Renfrewshire. Williamwood High School has around 1300 pupils. The *Busby Hotel* has grown to 32 rooms.

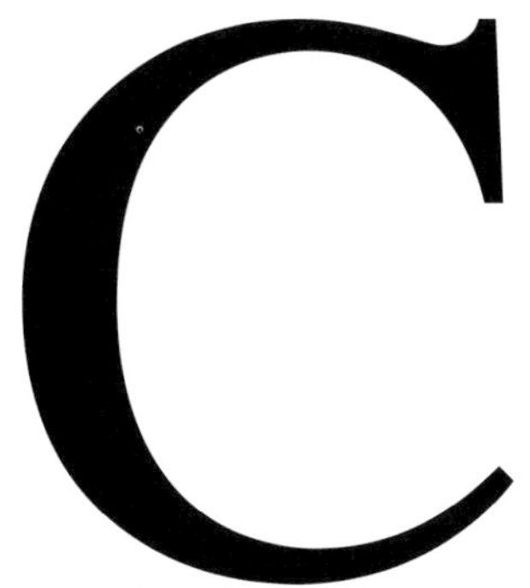

## CAIRNDOW

**Map 5, B4**

***Small Argyllshire village,*** *pop. 150* OS 56: NN 1811

Near the head of the long sea inlet of Loch Fyne, Glen Kinglas leads to the Rest and be Thankful pass and Arrochar. The Butter Bridge in Glen Kinglas was built in 1745 by Dunkeld mason Thomas Clark. It formed a link in Caulfeild's military road between Tarbet and Inveraray, opened round the head of the loch when the sturdy 4-span River Fyne Bridge was completed about 1750. The Roy map then showed two clachans at the foot of Glen Fyne, and another beside the Kirk of Cairndow where the road met the loch. A post office was opened in 1801. An inn was built nearby; this stood almost alone in 1803, when Dorothy Wordsworth wrote that it was *"resorted to by gentlemen in the fishing season"*. By 1827 boats to Inveraray offered an alternative to the road; another road was later built down the south-east side of Loch Fyne to Strachur. The laird of the nearby Ardkinglas estate was a Campbell in 1803. A later laird built an early miniature railway there to entertain his guests; in operation by 1879, it did not outlast the century.

**Mansion, Hotel and Hydro Power**: Murray's Handbook of 1894 found the *Cairndow Inn* which had become the focus of local settlement only *"fair"*, but it was later improved and enlarged to ten rooms. The Noble family commissioned a fine new Ardkinglas House, designed in baronial style by Robert Lorimer and built in 1906–08, equipped with electricity and roofed with Caithness slabs. By 1953 the Clachan hydro-electric generating station had been built near the foot of Glen Fyne, 3 km to the north-east, powered by water impounded by the first pre-stressed concrete dam in Europe – built across the Allt na Lairige a further 8 km upstream – and also supplied from Lochan Shira *(see Inveraray)*. By then the facilities of a small village at Cairndow served nearly 150 residents.

**From Farming to Oysters – and back to Deer?**: In 1981 Cairndow was a small farming village of 120 or so people, with facilities to match. By the 1980s the Strone or Cairndow gardens were open to visitors. In 1975 John Noble, by then the laird of Ardkinglas, began to farm oysters offshore; in 1992 his firm Loch Fyne Oysters had 50 workers, producing 500,000 oysters for Tesco and running three shellfish restaurants, that at Clachan near Cairndow claiming to be the busiest in Britain. In 1993 the 4000 ha Cairndow Estate was bought by Englishman John Turnbull, who evicted the sheep farmers as from 1995 and hoped to turn the hills into a sporting estate for grouse and deer, with more heather and trees. The *Stagecoach Inn* has been extended to 13 rooms.

## CAIRNEYHILL

**Map 16, C2**

***Fife village,*** *pop. 2100* OS 65: NT 0486

The *Caer* element in the name of Cairneyhill might suggest Roman origins but for its absence from the Blaeu maps of Fife. By 1610 the *'Brig of Urquhart'* crossed a burn 2 km east of Torryburn, but the Roy map showed no road there, and it was only in 1753 that the road to Dunfermline alongside which Cairneyhill was to grow was turnpiked. By 1827 it was a weaving hamlet and by 1888 a lengthy *"village"* where a post office, inn and smithy were open by 1895. A very late single track branch of the North British Railway and a station named Cairneyhill were opened in 1906, but buses killed the passenger trains, which ended in 1930; the line stayed open for coal and naval freight. By 1951 nearly 600 people lived locally, with only basic facilities; but once the Forth Road Bridge was opened rapid growth set in, and by 1981 the population had doubled in ten years to 1700, with a second primary school and a garage. By 1991 it was nearing 2100, and a substantial garden centre and some depots had developed; suburbanised Cairneyhill had Scotland's highest proportion of households buying their own homes: 83%! Housing development continued through the 1990s, and by 2000 the *Maltings Hotel* was open.

## CAIRNRYAN

**Map 1, B4**

***Galloway village,*** *pop. 300* OS 82: NX 0668

A medieval motte and the 16th century Craigcaffie Tower mark the southern limits of the hill-girt east coast of sheltered Loch Ryan in western Galloway. The *'Kairn Muleibrugh'* shown on Pont's map of about 1610, as later engraved by Blaeu, implies that Cairnryan was originally a Milton, for which there was certainly more than one convenient stream. Cairnryan was made a burgh of barony in 1701, with the alternative names of Lochryan or Cladahouse. Roy's map made about 1754 showed the mansion of Loch Ryan House, where the coastal road linking Ballantrae and Stranraer swung inland as a steep *'coach road'*, climbing into Carrick over the 200 m-high Haggstone Moor and toppling into Glen App at Dupin. The *'Taxing Stone'* was set up on this road as a toll point.

**Taverns and Highwaymen**: Later a more gently graded road was constructed along the shore and up Glen App. Cairnryan was referred to in 1799 by Heron as *"the village of Cairn, well situated for foreign trade, having an excellent harbour"*; in fact there was merely a pebbly beach. The area was notorious for

*Jetliner leaving Cairnryan for Northern Ireland in the mid 1990s – one of the first of the high-speed ferries which revolutionised the crossing.* (JRH)

robberies in stage-coach days around 1820, when there were nine inns on seven miles of road. The Loch Ryan lighthouse was lit in 1847. About that time Cairnryan nearly became the ferry terminal for Ireland – but the railway reached Stranraer first, and for nearly a century Cairnryan changed but slowly.

**Cairnryan Military Port Surveyed (?)**: From January 1941 Cairnryan became a military port, quickly built by American servicemen in civilian clothes, accessed through a 10km-long railway to a large deepwater jetty some 700m in length at Cairn Point, and connecting with the LMS near Stranraer; many details appear in *Smith D L (1969)*. The present author was required as a conscript Sapper based in Edinburgh in 1949 to draw up a complete diagram of the complex railway system for *'true-to-scale'* reproduction, from sketches on loose sheets of paper comparable in quality to Pont's field sheets, and without even a glimpse of the actual line! Certainly not to scale, but better than nothing, perhaps?

**Dumping Toxins and Scrapping Battleships**: The same careless attitude prevailed between 1945 and 1957, when many thousands of tonnes of chemical warfare agents left over from World War II, including mustard gas shells, were loaded at the military port into landing craft and obsolete ships; simply dumped at sea, largely in or near the deep called Beaufort's Dyke, they were left to decay as a toxic time-bomb. At a nearby quay the battleships HMS *Ramillies* of 29,150 tons and *Valiant* of 32,700 tons were dismantled in 1948–49, the latter as the *Imperieuse*; the hulls were towed to Troon for scrapping.

**Rolling On and Off**: By 1951 under 500 people lived locally, with only basic facilities. About 1952 Loch Ryan Hall, 1.5km south of Loch Ryan House, became a hotel, and a caravan site was laid out nearby. The lighthouse became automatic in 1964. The junction for the military railway was closed in 1962, but Cairnryan made news when the huge aircraft carriers HMS *Eagle* of 54,000 tons, perhaps the largest-ever British fighting vessel, and the 1950s *Ark Royal* of 50,786 tons, were broken up at Cairnryan in 1978–80. By then a caravan site had been laid out. A roll-on terminal rivalling Stranraer had also been opened for the Irish traffic via Larne, and with yachting had given rise to a second hotel; but fewer than 300 residents remained by 1981. In 1990 an Ayrshire company (Barr) proposed a major leisure development to offer 150 jobs on the site of the ship-breaking yard. Cairnryan still had at least two hotels in 1996 when the Larne ferry crossing took 135 minutes; the post office has since closed.

## CALDERCRUIX

**Map 16, A3**

***E. Lanarkshire village,*** *pop. 2300* — OS 65: NS 8267

Caldercruix stands nearly 200 metres above sea level 6km east of Airdrie on the North Calder Water, from whose *'crooks'* or windings its name derives. It appeared as *'Caldercrukis'* on Pont's map made in 1596; Roy's map surveyed about 1754 named a farm on the site *'Crooked Dykes'*, and nearby was Caldermill. A distillery was opened by Reid & Louden in 1827; this was just beyond the eastern end of the Ballochney colliery railway which was opened in 1828. As late as 1838 there was no post office at Caldercruix.

**Paper, Railway, Coal and Water**: A paper mill was founded at Caldercruix in 1848 by T R & G Craig; this may have occupied the buildings of the former distillery. Robert Craig transferred his operations from Newbattle paper mill *(see Newtongrange)* to Caldercruix in 1890. The Glasgow extension of the Edinburgh & Bathgate Railway, linking the valley with Airdrie and Coatbridge, was opened through the area in 1862, passing north of the mill's substantial buildings, to which a siding was laid. A station was provided at Caldercruix, from which mineral lines branched both east and west, serving coal

*The paper mill, Caldercruix, built in 1847 and the reason for the village's construction. Production ended in the 1970s.* (JRH)

pits north and north-west of the hamlet, which had a post office and inn by 1899. The line was then known as the Monklands Branch of the North British Railway, and the extensive Hillend Reservoir had been formed by damming the North Calder Water east of Caldercruix.

**The Decline of Coal and Railways**: By 1951 the old mineral railways had been lifted, but a single coal mine still operated in the valley south of Lilly Loch; the 3200 people of Caldercruix had been largely rehoused into a large estate north of the old centre, which contained only the facilities of a small village, but included a 90-pupil secondary school. The stations were closed about 1954, the paper mill lost its rail connection, and it was out of use by 1980 and soon demolished. The mine was closed sometime between 1963 and 1973. However, in the late 1960s a substantial quarry operated briefly in the Moffat Hills just south of the village.

**After the Purpose had been lost**: Caldercruix had lost its secondary school by 1976 and a third of its 1951 population by 1981 with the facilities of a small village. The lately freight-only railway had been lifted by 1985, and the 1980s saw more clearance than development in this sad outpost of the Monklands. In 1991 Caldercruix still contained almost 2300 people; about 80% of households still rented their homes from public authorities and male unemployment was very high at 23%. By 1998 the former railway formation had been laid out as a long-distance cycle route linking Glasgow with Edinburgh.

## CALGARY

**Map 4, B1**

***Hamlet, Isle of Mull,*** *pop. under 100* — OS 47: NM 3751

The original Calgary, a beautiful sheltered bay on the north west coast of the Isle of Mull, bears a name meaning *'Haven of the Dyke'* after a basalt intrusion to the north. Calgary's people were expelled – or as the saying was *'cleared'* – in 1822 by the Marquis of Northampton. The scattered little Treshnish Isles, some 20km offshore, were inhabited until 1834. In 1883 a senior *'Mountie'*, Col. J F Macleod, who had stayed at Calgary House, took the name to the bleak high plains of Alberta. While the new foundation grew rapidly into a large city, the farming hamlet that was left behind made little mark. Its once-useful pier became derelict in the third quarter of the 20th century, and the local Mornish primary school and Calgary post office closed during the same period, during which the population was well under 100. Only one small boat was to be seen in 1985, beached near the well-kept public toilets. But in 1993 John Murray & Co of Calgary blended Columba Cream, a liqueur of whisky, cream and honey, and by 1996 the *Calgary Farmhouse Hotel* was open.

## CALLANDER

**Map 5, C4**

***W. Stirlingshire small town,*** *pop. 2625* — OS 57: NN 6307

The ancient hill fort of Dunmore and the first century Roman fort of Bochastle were built beside the River Teith, east of Loch Venachar and 20km north-west of Stirling, an area known as Menteith. This was for centuries little-visited and remained a blank on early maps, although beautified by such features as the Bracklinn Falls on the Keltie Water 1.5km east of Callander, whose tower house was the seat of the powerful Livingstone family in the 1430s. A hunting lodge was built beside the river in 1625, but it was not until the 1730s that the Duke of Perth formally established Callander as a settlement. By that time barony charters were no longer regarded as essential, and it appears that none was asked for.

**The King's Road**: Development was rapid, aided by the military road built through the area by Caulfeild after 1743. This connected with Doune by way of the *'Bridge of Kildea' (Keltie)* and continued through the Pass of Leny; the Roy map surveyed about 1750 showed that from *'Loch Lubinich'* it became a track to Strathyre and the north. Callander appeared as a substantial one-street village on this the area's only road. There was also a *"tolerable inn"* by 1755, when Callander was noted as *"becoming a good trading centre"*.

**Resettling Veterans**: The village was expanded by the Forfeited Estates Commissioners resettling soldiers in 1763, when a new inn was built. This was enlarged and improved over 21 years; the River Teith was also bridged. About 1770 a lint mill was erected beside the river at Gartchonzie, 2 km to the east, serving the local weaving trade. Callander acquired a post office in 1793 and had an annual fair by 1797. Two years later Heron enthused that *"the village is remarkable for its singularly beautiful situation, as well as for the neat and regular manner in which it is built. It contains nearly a thousand inhabitants."*

**Minister's Tourist Guide, the Lady and the Lake**: The Falls of Leny to the west and Brack Linn on the Keltie Water east of the village were potentially attractive to tourists, and in 1790 the minister, James Robertson, enterprisingly produced *"a pamphlet descriptive of the neighbourhood of Callander"*. In 1803 Dorothy Wordsworth was given a copy at the *"comfortable"* inn, then the nearest accommodation to the Trossachs; she noted the *"imperfectly cultivated"* area around this *"small town"*. By 1810 the Leith Banking Company had established a branch. In that year came the publication of Sir Walter Scott's novel *The Lady of the Lake*. Tourism to the area rapidly quintupled, and summer coaches soon ran from Stirling to Callander, which by 1826 was – according to Chambers – *"a neat and regular modern village, with an excellent inn"*; they continued to the Trossachs. In 1835 a coach ran daily to Stirling (alternate days in winter).

**Baking, Banking and the Railways**: Donald Campbell starting baking shortbread on a commercial scale in Callander in 1830, and a Bank of Scotland branch was opened about 1840. In 1845 three buses a day ran to Stirling, replaced in 1858 by a local railway from Dunblane, worked by and soon a branch of the Scottish Central Railway. By 1867 the *Dreadnought Hotel* was in being. The Callander & Oban Railway extended the line northwestwards from 1866 by slow degrees to reach Tyndrum in 1873 and Oban in 1880.

**Failed Hydro and Axed Railway**: By 1886 an ill-fated hydropathic establishment had been opened at Palace Road, and Callander golf club, founded in 1890, laid out an 18-hole parkland golf course. In 1894 Callander was characterised by Murray as *"an overgrown village"* with the *"very good" Dreadnought Hotel*. The hydro was being rebuilt after a fire, but eventually ceased to operate. By 1895 Loch Venachar had been regulated by weirs to provide water for Glasgow *(see Trossachs)*. Callander became a police burgh, with gas supplies from 1908. A quiet period followed; in 1939 the hunting lodge of 1625 was converted into the *Roman Camp Hotel*. By the 1950s Callander was a small town amid a vast afforested tourist

*Callander Railway Station, with tourists being transported by horse and carriage in the late 19th century. From 1880 Callander had through trains to Oban as well as the service from Stirling.* *(GWW collection)*

hinterland of mountains and hills. Among its ten hotels was the 3-star *Dreadnought*, by then boasting 71 rooms, but about to enter a long decline in status. Sadly the railway was completely closed by Beeching in 1965, with no thought to how its tourist potential might be exploited.

**Prosperity in a Stirling context**: In 1975 the whole Menteith area was sensibly transferred from Perthshire and merged into the new Stirling District. In 1981, despite the large new McLaren High School south of the river, Callander remained essentially a small town in terms of services, though an important tourist centre with nearly a score of hotels and caravan and camping sites. In 1991 the resident population was about 2625, with an affluent retirement emphasis. Gravel pits near Ballochallan some 3km south-east which marred the area in the 1980s had been afforested by 1993. By 1997 Campbells Butter Shortbread was firmly established in the international tourist market; after 167 years this family firm which used only natural ingredients claimed to be Scotland's oldest bakery business. Small hotels include the *Roman Camp*, the *Bridgend House*, *Dalgair House*, and *Lubnaig*, plus other attractive small hotels and guest houses. An independent hostel is open all year for backpackers.

## CALVINE, Struan & Bruar

**Map 5, C1**

***N. Perthshire hamlets,*** *pop. 400*

OS 42: NN 8065

A medieval motte was raised at Kindrochet, on the point of land where the Errochty Water joins the River Garry just below the Falls of Garry, about 6km west of Blair Castle. General Wade's *'Eye of the Window'* bridge was built in 1728 as part of his military road to the north. This was called the King's Road on the Roy map of about 1750; beside it, below the remarkable Falls of Bruar, stood the huts of Pitagowan, and near the motte on the opposite bank 2 km to the west was *'Strowan'* Kirk. Later a stone bridge was built across the Garry to connect with the Glen Errochty road. But the land was poor and remote; Fontane on tour in 1858 found the area poverty-stricken. The Inverness & Perth Junction Railway (soon part of the Highland Railway main line) was opened in 1863, its stone arched Garry bridge also leaping over the road bridge. A station named Strowan was provided near the church, and by 1895 there was an inn close by.

**Transport proves a Fickle Jade**: By about 1910 the station had been renamed Struan, and was the terminus of a horse-drawn cross-country coach route via Kinloch Rannoch to Rannoch Station on the West Highland line. In 1951 there were only about 150 residents, but the facilities of a small village served in all a scattered population of over 400. Thanks to the poor quality of the busy A9 road at that time, the tiny local garage did a good trade in wreck recovery and crash repairs, as well as running the school bus. Beeching ensured that Struan station was completely closed to goods and passengers in the 1960s. The Clan Donnachie Museum was soon built at Bruar, and by 1980 a second small hotel was open, but by 1985 the tiny village had been bypassed and there was a caravan site beside the inn. The post office has closed since 1996 but a major visitor centre, with specialist shopping, has recently been built at Bruar.

## CAMBUS & Tullibody

**Map 16, B1**

***Clackmannanshire urban area,*** *pop. 6800* OS 58: NS 8594

Cambus lies where the River Devon joins the Forth some 3 km west of Alloa. Tullibody some 1.5 km inland had an ancient church, which was annexed to Alloa in 1600. By 1559 the rich royal tailor Robert Spittal of Stirling had provided the Devon bridge near Tullibody, on the track linking Alloa with Causewayhead. These features were shown on Roy's survey of about 1750, but Tullibody was then simply a mansionhouse designed by John Erskine, 11th Earl of Mar, and built in the early 18th century; other settlement seems scarcely to have existed, though Roy was remarkable for his omissions. By 1791 a woollen manufactory had been introduced near Tullibody House. In 1806 John Moubray converted another mill into the Cambus distillery, which Barnard noted as *"originally a small work"*. The first iron bridge in Scotland was erected beside it at about the same time. By 1815 there was also a brewery, another mill and a harbour, but there was still no post office in the area by 1838.

**The Railway and DCL**: In 1852 the Stirling & Dunfermline Railway was opened through Cambus, which by 1860 had a rail cartage depot of Wordie & Co and in 1863 became the junction for the Alva branch. In 1876 Cambus distillery was owned by Robert Moubray, who in 1877 joined the Distillers Company Ltd (DCL) as a founder member of this new grain whisky combine. By 1886 the distillery was, to use Barnard's word, *"enormous"*, its 60 workers producing over 4 million litres of grain whisky a year through a giant Coffey still. The enterprise was both steam and water-powered, possessed extensive rail sidings and was adjacent to the public wharf. Tullibody was by 1888 *"an irregularly built straggling village"*.

**Can Polluted Water make Pure Whisky?**: Cambus distillery drew all its water from what Barnard disingenuously called *"the Devon, a river of sparkling beauty"*; evidently he could not afford to antagonise the owners, even though the river's upper reaches were polluted by the towns of Dollar, Alva, Tillicoultry and their many mills. Matters had in fact deteriorated when the largest tannery in Scotland was built at Tullibody in 1880 by the Tullises of the St Ann's leather works *(see Bridgeton)*; this large 2-storey brick building – unusually surmounted by two further storeys of timber construction – still survives. To make things worse, the worts were passed through cooling pipes laid in the bed of the river – the same Devon outfall to the Forth that was actually described in Murray's usually squeamish *tourist* guide for 1894 as being *"foul with mill-refuse"*!

**Cambus *'Fire Water'* Proves its Name**: The Braehead golf club of Alloa, founded in 1891, established an 18-hole course on the hill slopes east of Cambus. By 1906 the Cambus product was on the market as a single grain whisky, and from that year was offered at seven years old, matured in wood. A disastrous fire in 1914 put the distillery out of action, and so it remained in 1931 when Tullibody was a small village with little over 800 people. The distillery was restored in 1939, no doubt with both adequate and clean water supplies. With the industrial growth of Alloa, Tullibody had expanded to 3700 people by 1951, though with only minimal facilities.

**The Glenochil Mine Fiasco**: By 1947 the small King o' Muirs colliery was open south of the river and 1 km east of Tullibody, but the coalfield was nearly exhausted. This fact escaped the Coal Board's newly installed bureaucrats, who planned a large new drift mine beside it without seeking advice from the outgoing Alloa Coal Company or geologists. They naively expected to raise 3000 tonnes a day from thin seams, and stoops in already-worked seams (such as the poor quality Coalsnaughton Main). Sinking began at Glenochil in 1952, but exploration efforts became bogged down in arguments over the effects of subsidence on carseland drainage. In 1955 at a depth of 275 m they at last realised the coal reserves were few, scattered and problematical: a complete failure in production, the Glenochil mine was closed in 1962, having also shortened the life of the Devon colliery *(see Alva)* only 2 km away,

**From Pit to Prison**: Glenochil's demise provided a site for the detention centre that took its tarnished name; a new prison for 500 inmates was opened beside it in 1979. Meantime in 1957 the former Knox's brewery at Cambus had been converted into the *'North of Scotland'* or Strathmore grain distillery; but this use ended in the 1980s. Tullibody House was regrettably demolished in 1961, and its site incorporated in the golf course. The passenger station was closed in 1968. The population was around 6800 in 1971, served in 1980 by the facilities of a small village, though including a hotel and chemist. In 1990 molasses was still delivered by rail from Greenock to Cambus, where the original distillery was under DCL's direct successors United Distillers, who in 1993 announced its closure. By 1994 John Tullis & Son, plastics extruders, working in Glasgow in 1979, had taken over the old Tullis tannery at Tullibody. The population remains at about 6800.

## CAMBUSBARRON

**Map 16, A1**

***Village / w. suburb of Stirling,*** *pop. 2000* OS 57: NS7792

Some 3 km south-west of Stirling stand the quarried remains of Gillies Hill, a prominent 170 m limestone crag, an outlier of the Touch Hills. At the foot of Gillies Hill is Cambusbarron, which had Bronze Age and nearby Iron Age remains, notably the dun in Castlehill Wood. Touch was an estate by 1234 and the Chapel of Cambusbarron was visited by Bruce in 1314, but fell into ruin. The tower of Touch was built in the 14th to 16th century (sources differ). Cambusbarron had an early mill, but changed hands frequently and did not appear on Pont's map, made about 1600; the early Cambusbarron House was not very impressive. The mansion of Gartur House, 1 km to the east of Touch, was built in the 17th century for the Murrays of Polmaise Castle, and enlarged and emparked early in the 19th century.

**Lime, Strategic Roads, Whisky and Weaving**: Limestone was quarried on a modest scale near Cambusbarron in the early 18th century and burned to make lime for use on the Blair Drummond estate, using coal carted from Bannockburn. At that time a military road was built to link St Ninians with Dumbarton, with a bridge near Touch, and by 1745 the mansion of Touch House, designed by John Adam, had been built on to the old tower. The Glenmurray Distillery was active from 1741 to 1827, then vanished. Roy's map (made about 1754) showed Cambusbarron as a small village at right angles to the road, 2 km west of St Ninians and 1 km east of Gartur House; from it a track led over the hills to Fintry. A piped water supply from a spring in the Touch Hills was first laid on to Stirling in 1774, and a new Dumbarton Road was built in the early 19th century. Weaving was prevalent in the village; the first small

Hayford Mill was built in 1834, but in 1841 when the population was 657 there were still 120 hand loom weavers.

**Water, Railway, Tramway and Textiles**: The Stirling waterworks were enlarged from 1848, building four successively larger reservoirs in the Touch Hills, the largest in 1881. In 1856 the Forth & Clyde Junction Railway was opened westwards from Stirling, and from this a lengthy siding or tramway was laid up to the Craigend and Murrayshall limeworks; in 1860 there were three working kilns at each, and the latter eventually had a bank of six kilns *(see Hay & Stell)*. The tramway also served the huge 4-storey brick-built Hayford & Parkvale spinning mills just north of the village, which with adjacent weaving sheds were opened in the 1860s by Robert Smith & Son. In 1869 they employed 950 people dyeing, spinning and weaving wool with cotton warps on 530 power looms to make winceys and dress material. The mills raised the population of Cambusbarron to 1230 by 1881. The village had an inn, a school, post and telegraph office and shops by the time the mills closed in 1895–96. Hundreds lost their jobs, and the limeworks closed in 1909.

**Textiles and Limestone Rejuvenated**: A long-desired church was built in 1910, perhaps aided by the reopening in 1909 of the Hayford Mill, whose life was brief. After use as a barracks in 1914–18, the mill became a carpet factory which worked right through the 1930s, later becoming a government storage depot. By 1951 about 1500 people lived at Cambusbarron, conveniently near Stirling by bus or car; so the village had gained few facilities. Limestone was again quarried on a large scale at Gillies Hill from the mid 1950s, but rail freight services ceased in 1957. After 1971 population growth resumed, but Cambusbarron was physically separated from the town by the section of the M9 motorway which opened as a Stirling bypass in 1973. It soon had an active Community Council *(see Paterson, 1980, for a good local history)*, but urban sprawl from Stirling and St Ninians reached to the doors of Cambusbarron by 1985; in 1991 the village was treated by the Census as part of Stirling.

**Derelict Monuments and Ruined Hill mar a Historic Village**: Gartur House was empty and decaying in 1994, but the great Hayford Mill with its weaving sheds to the south still stood, securely blocked off from the world as *'CHHD'*; however, in 2000 it was converted into flats, and low-rise housing was being built around it. In 1994 Tarmac's Murrayshall quarry was still active, part of the crest of Gillies Hill having been most regrettably destroyed. By then the old village school had become a community centre and library, and a small open-air swimming pool adjoined.

## CAMBUSLANG

**Map 15, D6**

***Town s-e. of Glasgow,*** *pop. 14,000* — OS 64: NS 6460

The Kirk Burn joins the River Clyde from the south at the Clyde Ford, 3km east of Rutherglen. The area south of the Clyde was shown on Pont's map, made in 1596, as *'Lang'*; two years later a parish school was founded. About 1730 locally grown flax began to be made by hand into fine linen Hollands, and Cambuslang was large enough by 1742 for a wave of mass *'born-again'* Protestant hysteria to take hold of its simpler inhabitants. Roy's map surveyed about 1754 showed the Hamilton to Rutherglen road, on either side of which were hamlets at Cambuslang Kirk and Cambuslang, served by loop roads and the road to Blantyre. In 1769 Pennant wrote of

*The Clyde Iron Works, Cambuslang, which began in 1786. It was remodelled from the late 1930s to supply pig-iron to the Lanarkshire open-hearth steel industry. The Works closed in 1978.* *(RCAHMS / JRH)*

Cambuslang as a village with handloom linen weavers, *"in a rich and beautiful corn country"*.

**Coal, Co-op, Railway and Dyeworks**: By 1778 coal mining was definitely in progress there, and at some time a shelly ironstone called *'Cambuslang Marble'* was quarried. Around 1790 the weavers changed to making lawns and cambric from yarns sent from Glasgow; David Dale made his country retreat at Rosebank House beside the Clyde. Cambuslang possessed a kind of co-op in the 1830s, and also had a post office by 1838. The Clydesdale Junction Railway, later the main line of the Caledonian Railway (CR), opened in 1849 with a station at Cambuslang, which developed extensively, principally along the main road rather than round the Kirk, but was never granted burgh status. The short-lived Wellshot brewery was built in 1892, and by 1895 a large turkey red dyeworks had been built at Richmond Park, west of Rosebank Street, which by then bridged the Clyde beside Dale's former home and led to Fullarton House. Murray's Handbook ignored Cambuslang in 1894, yet it was a very large village, with an inn at Kirkhill and an estate of villas on Wellshot Hill to the west.

**Football, Golf, Power and Tramcars**: Cambuslang FC lasted for only two seasons in the Scottish League, 1890–92. Golf did better; the small Westburn course of the Cambuslang Golf Club, founded in 1891, was laid out north of the main street, and to the south was the Kirkhill course of 1910. By 1901, when the Steel Company of Scotland was producing a million tonnes of steel a year, much of it in the adjacent Newton area *(see Flemington)*, Cambuslang's population exceeded 12,000. A power station was built from 1903, and by 1910 Glasgow's electric trams terminated at Cambuslang, where the tracks met end-on with the Lanarkshire Tramways to Hamilton and beyond. In 1904 the CR's offshoot, the Lanarkshire & Ayrshire Railway, was opened between Newton and Cathcart, with a station at Kirkhill south of Cambuslang. In the early 20$^{th}$ century Mitchells of Cambuslang made clay-mining and brick-making equipment.

**From Heavy Industry to Vacuum Cleaners**: Heavy industrial development took place in the second quarter of the 20$^{th}$ century across the river west of Carmyle, with railway sidings and attendant waste bings. In 1928 the Clyde Valley Electric Power Company were the operators of the rail-connected Clyde's Mill Power station beside the river (some maps show this as a steel works). By depressed 1931, the year the Hamilton trams vanished, the population in the Cambuslang area *(including Newton, q.v.)* had risen to over 22,000; it still continued to grow, and exceeded 27,000 in 1951. From about 1950 the large new Hoover vacuum-cleaner factory adjoined the large Richmond Park Laundry and dyeworks. Cambuslang then had the facilities of an average town; Woolworths arrived in the 1950s and a basic new shopping centre was built in the 1960s. Though Glasgow trams ceased to run to Cambuslang in 1956, it kept the power station and its key grid substation.

**Two Decades of Decline**: Colliery and industrial closures and population collapse followed, with over a third of the population lost in the twenty years to 1971, while the three cinemas and two local newspapers all failed. In 1975 a rundown Cambuslang was taken over by Glasgow City District. About that time Bridge Street replaced Rosebank Street and the new Clydeford Road bridge was built, leading to Carmyle, and the large new Cathkin High School was erected. By 1981 there had been some population recovery to 21,000, though the area's character was still disadvantaged. The power station was pulled down about 1982, leaving only a peak-load gas turbine generating installation.

**Child Leukaemia, and a Wrong Right Turn?**: In the early 1980s the derelict area north of the river was redeveloped as the Cambuslang Industrial Estate, and efforts were made to improve the area's image and economic prospects. But a shadow lay over the town in 1991–92, for it contained a sixth of all Scotland's cases of child leukaemia: toxic chemical tips were seen as a possible cause. In 1988 the Scottish Development Agency announced a giant scheme, but the Thatcher government compelled them to put their Investment Park up for sale in 1989. Oddly, the *Glasgow* Development Agency still owned a vacant 80ha industrial site in the area in 1995! However, by 1990 Cambuslang College of Further Education was open at Hamilton Road, and in 1991 Cambuslang boasted Scotland's first indoor kart-racing track, of 3700m$^2$.

**A Downsized Hoover goes European**: In 1989 when the US Maytag Corporation bought Hoover, its Cambuslang plant with some 1500 workers was the largest vacuum-cleaner factory in Europe; combined heat and power schemes were to be installed to bring energy savings. The *'free flights'* advertising scandal led to executive sackings in 1993, when only around 1000 workers remained, but the closure of the firm's Dijon plant in France left Cambuslang as Hoover's sole European plant making vacuum cleaners, with 1200 workers. In 1995 Candy of Italy bought out all Hoover's European operations, including Cambuslang; the outcome was that by mid 1996 only 650 jobs remained. The (now) South Lanarkshire College employs 200. The *Travel Inn* at Cambuslang Investment Park has 40 rooms.

## CAMBUS O'MAY

**Map 10, A4**

***Locality, Deeside,*** *pop. 100* — OS 37: NO 4297

The north Deeside road existed by the 1750s; the *Ferry Inn* was built close beside it at Cambus o' May some 4km east of Ballater. In 1865 a corner was cut off the old building to allow the new Deeside Railway to pass between road and inn. Nearby was a ballast pit, and a siding was laid alongside the main road. Goods trains would bring gunpowder for the large granite quarries in Culblean Hill, 3km to the west. The area being very scenic, a passenger station was opened in 1876 to serve an inn, and in 1905 an elegant suspension footbridge was erected across the river. By 1954 the inn was the 18-room *Cambus o' May Hotel*. By 1962 the quarries were out of use, the railway was closed in 1966, but the hotel and post office have stayed in business. By 1995 forest walks had been laid out 2 km to the west.

## CAMELON

**Map 16, B2**

***Urban area w. of Falkirk,*** *pop. 8500* — OS 65: NS 8680

A first century Roman fort once stood on tidewater 2.5km west of Falkirk; the remains of a quay with mooring rings have been found. It became an outpost of the later Antonine Wall with its *'Rough Castle'* to the south. Carmuirs and Tamfourhill existed by about 1600, though Camelon was not named on Pont's map. Roy's survey of about 1754 showed the Bonnybridge and Larbert roads diverging west of Falkirk. It was about there that Camelon grew, spurred by the staircase of locks necessary for the Forth & Clyde (F&C) Canal, constructed around 1770. Rapid development followed, and by 1799 Camelon was notable to Heron as a *"village of near six hundred inhabitants"*.

**Distilling and Canal Interchange**: Stark Brothers built the Camelon distillery, in the early 1800s. The Union Canal, which linked the area with Edinburgh, was opened in 1822 through Scotland's first canal tunnel, of 640m in length south of Falkirk. At its west end south of Camelon was a high-level basin known as Port Maxwell, from which passengers could interchange to Port Downie, west of lock 16 on the F&C. A post office was opened about that time at Camelon, which Chambers in 1826 noted as *"a considerable modern village"*. The Rosebank malt whisky distillery was built on the site of some existing maltings in 1840–42 by James Rankine; it was enlarged three years later.

**The Industrial Revolution at its Worst**: Boys taken from Edinburgh orphanages at an early age were cruelly exploited by a large handmade nailmaking business at Camelon, working a 90-hour week in 1842 while clothed in rags and deformed with rickets, yet expected to make a typical nail on average every 43 seconds. Largely replaced by machines after the 1850s, some of these sad victims remained at the works to make horseshoe nails for the rest of their blighted lives. The Stirlingshire & Midland Junction Railway was opened through Camelon in 1850 to connect Polmont, Falkirk Grahamston, Larbert and Carmuirs, with freight spurs but no passenger station.

**Coal, Tar and Malt**: In 1845 local boatbuilder James Ross began to distil tar from gasworks at Limewharf beside the F&C Canal, a chemicals business which lasted under Scottish Tar Distillers until 1966. The Camelon distillery closed in 1861, becoming maltings for Rosebank, which itself was rebuilt in 1864. By 1886 Rosebank utilised water and steam power in the production of 560,000 litres of Lowland malt whisky a year; water and peat came from local moors, the output being sold in Glasgow and Edinburgh. Barnard noted drily that one William Bastard was an excise officer there! A coal pit was opened to the south, and by 1898 a variety of iron, tar and chemical works had been built beside the canal junction at Tamfourhill and near

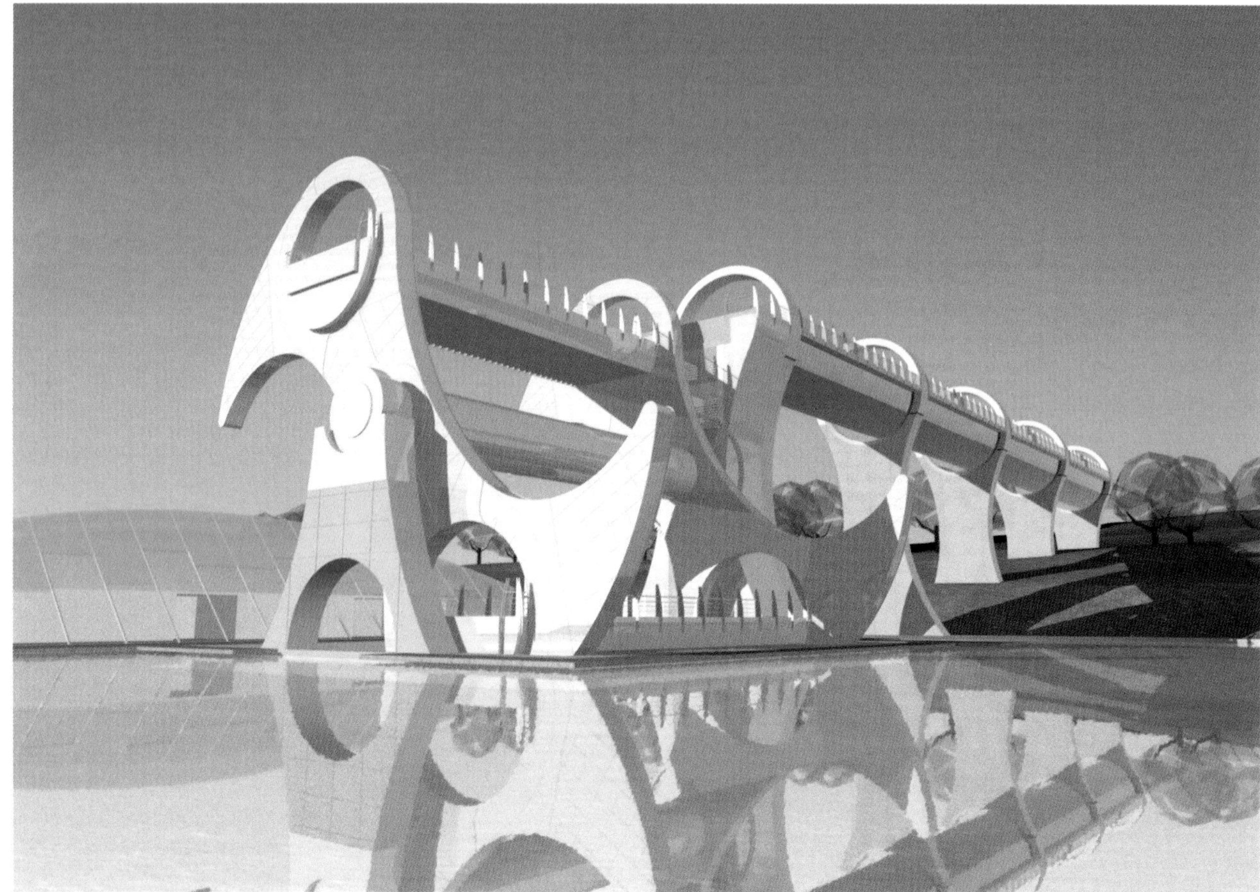

*The Falkirk wheel, to be installed in 2001 to connect the Union and Forth & Clyde canals at Camelon.* *(British Waterways)*

Rough Castle, also being connected to the high-level railway. By about 1910 a passenger station named Camelon had been opened on the line between Grahamston and Carmuirs; west of it was a large iron foundry. Camelon became part of Falkirk Burgh, acquired a small hospital and for a time was served by the Falkirk tramways. Rosebank distillery was one of five founder members of Scottish Malt Distillers Ltd, registered in 1914.

**Golf, Bus Boom and Canal Closure**: The Falkirk Golf Club course was laid out north of Camelon from 1922. Beyond this, and nominally in Camelon, the noted bus entrepreneur Walter Alexander built his central depot and *'Bluebird'* coachworks, around 1930. Being adjacent to Larbert, its story is told there *(q.v.)*. But the Union Canal was closed in 1933 and its locks infilled; the F&C was closed to traffic in 1962. Camelon station was closed about 1965 and the Camelon maltings ceased work in 1968; however, Rosebank distillery remained in production, its dark single malt matured in oloroso sherry casks. Around 1970 the concrete works of J K Miller at Summerford were closed and lay derelict for several years. The large tar works on a 200-ha site at Tamfourhill had badly polluted the soil before it burned down in 1975; new soil was imported, and by 1989 275,000 trees had been planted there. In 1978 a 10,000 $m^2$ extension was approved for Blue Bell Apparel, manufacturers of Wrangler jeans. Though the excellent facilities of Falkirk were close at hand, Camelon – which still had only the facilities of a village – lost a quarter of its 11,000 residents between 1951 and 1981; many disadvantaged people remained.

**Enter Entertainment, Exit Distilling**: Falkirk Sheriff Court was re-sited into new buildings at Camelon in the 1980s, and the Mariner Leisure Centre with its exotic leisure pools and wave machine was opened there in 1985. In 1988 refractories were still made at Camelon; a vast privately owned open-cast coal operation was in progress beside Rough Castle and Bonnyhill to the west in 1987–88, provided with its own rail loading point. The former Rosebank brewery was converted into a hotel in the 1980s, and in 1990 Wimpey Environmental ran their Scottish consultancy service from Rosebank House in Camelon. In 1990 the new GX Superbowl, a tenpin bowling centre, was opened beside the Mariner Centre, and an adjacent new rail passenger station became reality in 1994 – supposedly for a five-year experimental, but it's still there. In 1995 an Indoor Bowling Club also adjoined the Mariner. However, the hospital closed in the late 1980s, and Rosebank distillery was closed by United Distillers in 1993.

**Back to the Water Wheel**: In 1997 the British Waterways Board began its major Millennium Link scheme to reopen the whole of the Forth & Clyde and Union Canals, with investment from the Millennium Commission, European Union, Scottish Enterprise, local authorities and the private sector. The central feature at the canal's reopening in 2001 will be a unique 35 m tall, 28 m-long, 1200-tonne steel revolving boat-lift with two caissons, set in a 100 m diameter basin at the revived canal junction on the Tamfourhill tar-works site south of Camelon. This elegant solution to the perennial problem of locks derives from an abortive German scheme of the early 1900s. Able to lift 600 tonnes or 8 boats at a time, the *'Falkirk Wheel'* – built by Butterley Engineering in Ripley, Derbyshire – should overcome the difference of level in 15 minutes. Reopening the canal at Camelon has also involved the tricky digging of a tunnel under the Antonine Wall and over an abandoned fireclay mine. A transport interchange and visitor centre are being built, and the tourist implications for the Falkirk area are immense.

## CAMERON BRIDGE & Windygates **Map 6, B4**

***Central Fife villages,*** *pop. 1700* OS 59: NO 3500

The site of Cameron House adjoins the end of the long straight road from Kirkcaldy to east Fife known for centuries as the *Standing Stanes Road* (A915). Its name may derive from *Caer Roman* (Roman Camp), by confusion with the Clan Cameron. Another old straight east–west road alignment lies north of the River Leven; beside it some 1.5 km south of Kennoway stands the anciently-named farm of Duniface. Blaeu's map, derived from lost Pont sketches made around 1600, showed Cameron Bridge already spanning the River Leven. It became a key link in the routes from Kirkcaldy to north-east Fife, and by 1679 there was a coach road from the bridge to St Andrews via Ceres. By about 1750 when Roy surveyed Fife, two mills turned beside the Leven east of the bridge. Under Turnpike Acts of the 1790s the area's road system reached nearly its 1980 form; the name *Windygates* may derive from early toll-gates.

**Coal, Spinning, Whisky and Railways**: By 1791 a colliery with an engine was working at Cameron. Downstream of the old Haugh corn mill west of the bridge was the Haugh spinning mill, built in 1794 to spin canvas yarns from flax and tow; its owner George Wilson later installed machinery to spin fine linen yarns, powered by two water wheels. The area was long known for whisky smuggling, and a legitimate malt whisky distillery existed at Cameron Bridge by 1813. In 1824 this water-powered plant was acquired by John Haig, by whom grain distilling was added in 1830; he named his whisky *'Glen Leven'*. The winding single track Leven Railway opened in 1854, with a crossing station at Cameron Bridge, where a new girder road bridge was built across both river and railway. From that point a mineral line laid in 1865 ran east, crossing the river then turning south to serve the Muiredge coal pit, later connecting with other pits at Cameron and Methilhill and with the Wemyss Private Railway.

**The Origins of DCL**: The distillery was owned in 1876 by John Haig & Co, who in 1877 became founder members of a new grain whisky combine better known as DCL. Haigs remained semi-independent, moving blending and bottling from Cameron Bridge to Markinch in the same year. Work ended at the Haugh spinning mill in the early 1880s. By 1886 the Cameron Bridge distillery covered 6 ha, driven by four big water wheels and also steam power. Its varied types of still included pots and Coffey's patent. It had its own yeast factory, gas works, foundry, engineers, cooperage and many rail sidings. Its unusually varied products were of four types including both grain and malt, the annual output nearing 6 million litres. No fewer than 300 passengers used the station on New Year's Day 1889, when goods and passenger traffic was growing. By 1895 Windygates was a substantial village with an inn, and Balcurvie was a hamlet.

**The Drumcaldie interlude and Cameron Hospital**: Bleaching on the Markinch road had ended in 1896, the works being converted into the Drumcaldie distillery, which failed in 1903; it was acquired by DCL in 1907, used as maltings and warehouses for its big neighbour. In 1931 a gasworks was established between Windygates and Kennoway, with a rail connection. Cameron Isolation Hospital for infectious diseases was created around the Victorian Cameron Bridge House in 1939 and enlarged in the 1950s. By 1951 the area had a population of 2300 and a small secondary school. This and the cinema at Windygates subsequently closed, as did the rail passenger service in 1969, by which time the mineral line had vanished; but grain and carbon dioxide traffic to and from the distillery continued by rail. By 1981 with the concentration of new housing in nearby Kennoway, the population had fallen to about 1750; the facilities of Windygates had declined to those of a small village, plus a bowling green.

**Bypasses and the Giant Distillery**: A new Cameron Bridge was built for the bypass which opened to the east in 1987, but the distillery was still accessed across a stone arched bridge. It made *'Cameron Brig'* grain whisky, uniquely sold unblended, and in 1989 it was further enlarged. By 1991 it was under United Distillers, and in 1992 its carbon dioxide by-product was still moved by rail tankers in two trainloads a week to Lancashire and London; the distillery still possessed its own shunting locomotive in 1993. Cameron Bridge House, a listed building, was converted in 1995 by Fife Healthcare into a clinic and offices; Cameron Hospital is still open. In 1995 a diversion of the Markinch road severed the distillery and new private housing east of the old road from the main village to the north, except by way of a rather fine new footbridge. Enlargement of the huge distillery continued in the late 1990s. The long-established *Windygates Hotel* is still open.

## CAMPBELTOWN **Map 1, A2**

***Kintyre (Argyll) town,*** *pop. 5700* OS 68: NR 7220

As early as 503 AD King Fergus I of *Dalriada* (approximately the area of modern Argyll) had his capital at *Dalruadhain* on a sheltered bay on the east coast of the lengthy peninsula of Kintyre, where St Kiarin, tutor of St Columba, had his cell – Kilkerran. Later kings had other ideas; the place sank into near oblivion and bore a variety of names. Around 1500 James IV held a parliament there to emancipate the vassals of the troublesome Macdonalds. Timothy Pont visited the area around 1600; though his map is sadly lost, Blaeu's map based on it showed about ten small places around *'Loch Kilkeran'*.

**Clan Campbell and its Fast Growing Burgh**: Continuing attempts to oust the Macdonalds led in 1607–09 to the erection of Kilkerran Castle by the Campbell 7th Earl of Argyll. Following the fashion of the times he renamed the settlement after his family, licensed a distiller there, and also promoted fishing. By 1630 about 120 boats were based in the new town, and despite its isolation, it soon grew into a significant urban centre – though apparently not chartered as a burgh of barony until 1667. It was promoted to Royal Burgh status in 1700, and a post office was open as early as 1734.

**Trackways, Fishing and Boatbuilding**: Webster's population estimate of about 4600 for 1755 matches Roy's map of about 1750, which showed a large compact settlement with a pier, the Townhead Mill and four local radial roads. One of these linked with Inveraray, though on a very roundabout route via Tayinloan, Castle Sween and Bellanoch; all significant access was evidently by sea, for the roads (or rather tracks) were so poor that there were no carts in the town until 1756. Yet by 1769 Campbeltown was a major commercial fishing centre, and had developed both boatbuilding and also water-powered woollen manufacture, on a burn at Auchaleck.

**Drinks Industries and Coal Carrying**: Commercial brewing began in 1770. A proper road built with help from the Commissioners for the Forfeited Estates connected with the main Scottish system via Tarbert and Carradale from about 1780. A short canal bringing coal from the mines at Machrihanish (*q.v.*) was dug in 1785. Heron (1799) stated that the population was about 5000, with a *"considerable trade, chiefly owing to its being the general rendezvous of the fishing vessels, which annually visit the western coast"*. It was by then a port of registry, with the identification letters CN. Heron did not mention a drinks industry, although by then not only was the brewery in operation but also probably the Hazelburn distillery.

**Banking and more Distilleries**: James Templeton, founder of the Bridgeton (Glasgow) carpet industry, was born in Campbeltown in 1802. Between 1802 and 1810 a branch of the Renfrewshire Banking Company of Greenock was established in the town, but it failed in 1842. In 1818 Campbeltown was the recipient of the last payment made by the Board of Trustees to a Scottish spinning school. In 1815 came the small Campbeltown distillery, founded by John MacTaggart. As a result of the new legislation in 1824, the Lochhead distillery appeared on the site of an ancient mill and smugglers' stills.

**Steamers to Campbeltown**: Steamers served the town from 1816, and its whiskies gained ready access to the Glasgow market when a regular direct steamer service to the city was begun by the Campbeltown & Glasgow Steam Packet Company, founded in 1826. In 1827 Chambers noted Campbeltown as *"a considerable trading and fishing town, with an excellent harbour"*. In the 19th century there were regular sailings to Portrush in Ulster; Ayr and Larne were also briefly served, and schooners were built locally in the 1830s. From 1845 steamers from Ardrossan called in on the way to Port Ellen, Oban, Tobermory and Portree. A lifeboat station was opened in 1861, the first on the west coast north of the Clyde, and by 1867 there were daily steamers to the Clyde, though in 1888 they made many stops en route.

**Campbeltown as the Whisky Capital**: Hazelburn distillery became the largest in the town after enlargement in 1836, and by 1845 no fewer than 17 distilleries had been built there, all steam powered and producing Campbeltown malt whisky, though by 1858 Springburn at least was selling some to Johnnie Walker of Kilmarnock for blending. Campbeltown had become known as the *'Whisky Capital'* – hence the once popular song *'Campbeltown Loch (I wish you were whisky!)'*. There were 21 distilleries in 1885, two-thirds dating from pre-1840. Six of them produced over 500,000 litres a year, and total employment would have been several hundred. (The Scotia and Springbank survived into the present age.)

*Hazelburn Distillery, Campbeltown, which dated from 1836. It closed in 1925, but these warehouses were used until the 1980s.* (JRH

**Gas, Narrow Gauge Railway, Boats and Nets**: A gasworks was set up in 1832; but local coal mining ceased for a time in 1855 and the canal was then infilled. The lighthouse on Island Davaar was first lit in 1854. A local newspaper, the *Campbeltown Courier and Argyllshire Advertiser* was established in 1873. In 1881, when approaching distilling's rather short-lived peak, the population of Campbeltown was around 8000. Though it was never connected by rail with the rest of Scotland, in 1876 a 2'3" (69 cm) gauge mineral railway was laid, linking with a new coal mine at Machrihanish. A boatyard also operated from 1877 at Trench Point, and netmaking was important, allied to the reputation of the area for herring fishing. But other than by sea, communications were extremely slow: in 1886 Tarbert was a six-hour journey by coach. By then the *White Hart Hotel* was open, and in 1894 also the *Argyll Arms*. There was still a daily steamer from the Clyde, and the population by 1901 was over 10,000.

**Distilling enters Decline**: The tiny Longrow distillery had already closed by 1896, but its peaty whisky was long remembered. The railway was extended and converted to carry passengers in 1906 in connection with excursions from Greenock by Turbine Steamers Ltd. The *Royal Hotel* dates from about 1910, and the horse coach to Tarbert was replaced by a bus from 1913. A cinema was open by 1914. The Campbeltown Creamery was opened about 1920, and the Highland distillery (said to have been founded in 1827) also existed by 1921 in Dalaruan Street, east of the little Town corn mill. By then a small infectious diseases hospital was also open.

**Whisky Sinking in a Sea of Problems**: Swingeing increases in the whisky duty imposed by the teetotal Welsh premier Lloyd George trebled its retail price between 1909 and 1921. Despite some ensuing decline and temporary enforced wartime closure, twenty distilleries survived in Campbeltown until 1920, these using local coal mined at Drumlemble, 6 km west. Lochruan distillery which adjoined the Dalintober and Scotia plants was acquired by Buchanan about 1920. It was among the 18 closed after the quality of Campbeltown malts was sacrificed to supply the bootleggers of the US Prohibition period, starting in 1920 and with a final closure in 1934. Even the two that remained – Scotia and Springbank – were inactive for a time. To add to local problems the boatyard closed in 1922, followed by the demise of the railway in 1931–32, due to two competing bus services.

**Scraping By**: Despite this economic collapse a second cinema was in operation by 1934, and air services were started from Machrihanish to Renfrew, while up to 1940 regular railway-owned steamers still plied to Campbeltown from Gourock and Fairlie. World War II saw a naval anti-submarine school formed at Campbeltown in 1940, known as HMS *Nimrod* until its closure in 1946. Steamer calls resumed from 1946 but ceased in 1949, leaving only a few summer cruise visits, by the turbine steamer *Duchess of Hamilton*, known as a good sea boat and consequently well patronised, and later by the *Queen Mary II*. In 1951 Campbeltown had four hotels, including the 40-room *Argyll Arms*, and somehow supported a full range of urban facilities, despite only 7250 residents and a sparsely peopled hinterland; apart from tourists, a total of only some 10,400 people could have been served.

**Hydro Power, Farm Feeds, Cookies and Clothing**: By 1953 the Hydro Board had built the small Lussa hydro power station at Peninver on the Saddell road, 6km north of the town, supplied by an aqueduct from Lussa Loch. Meanwhile Campbeltown suffered an alarming decline in its fishing, and boatbuilding, which had resumed, ceased again in 1960. In the 1970s Campbeltown was the HQ of Kintyre Farmers, co-operative dealers in grain and fodder and suppliers of many services including electrics and plumbing to its 800 members in Kintyre, and in mid Argyll and Cowal through a branch at Lochgilphead. Scallop processing continued in the 1970s. At that time McIlchere Food Products, who also baked in Lesmahagow, made shortbread and oatcakes for export at Campbeltown's Golden Grain Bakery. Campbeltown lost its local government independence in 1975, but about 1980 a 180-job Jaeger clothing factory was opened. In 1981 there were no more than 10,000 residents in the whole area to support Campbeltown's typical urban facilities; growing summer trade helped, for there were now six hotels.

**Restoring Longrow Whisky – and Boatyard Blues**: In 1966 Springbank distillery gave up using local barley for malting, from 1974 buying in all its malt. By 1983 it was one of only two in Scotland to bottle its own single malt whisky, matured in varied sherry casks for flavour. In 1992 the Wrights of Springbank reinstated their old malting floors to recreate the character of the heavily peated Longrow whisky from their defunct competitor next door; they still bottled on site in 1993. Scotia distillery was silent from 1984; in 1989 Gibson International resumed intermittent production as *'Glen Scotia'*. In 1969–70 Lithgows of Port Glasgow re-established a fishing vessel boatyard at Trench Point with four covered slips; it employed over 100 men in 1976, and by 1990 had completed 87 boats in 21 years of operation. At that time said to be one of the last three Scottish yards building small vessels, it had no orders due to reduced fishing quotas, and its 84 workers were laid off for a time; the yard was still open for boat repairs in 1995. Meantime the Island Davaar lighthouse had been automated in 1989.

**A Boost from Wooster**: In 1987 KV Wooster International made an unusual move, leaving the English Enterprise Zone town of Corby for Campbeltown; by 1990 its 36 workers made over 400,000 plastic model aircraft a year, for sale as souvenirs by the world's many airlines. In 1990 some 90 farms sent 35 million litres of milk a year to the Campbeltown Creamery, which employed 46 people making Scottish Cheddar cheese. The town's rather elderly population was 5722 in 1991. In that year the former Hazelburn distillery was converted to business use. Campbeltown's bulk gas supplies arrived by road as LNG (Liquefied Natural Gas), a hazardous substance indeed to carry over Argyll's twisting roads. Although Campbeltown had a local museum, in 1993 the West Highlands & Islands Tourist Board closed the local tourist information office; local leaders found this *"idiotic"* and it was soon reopened. By 1996 there was a heritage centre and a Tesco store, but some dereliction was evident in the town centre and the former Cottage Hospital was a *'building at risk'*. By then Campbeltown Grammar School had 538 pupils.

**Ferries briefly restore an Ulster dimension**: In 1995 Sea Containers gained approval to develop the harbour, by building a new pier 2 km south-east of the town, for a new car ferry service to Ballycastle in Northern Ireland. This started in summer 1997 as the Argyll & Antrim Steam Packet Company, creating 80 summer-only jobs. Sadly these ended with the service in 2000, leading to five of the town's six hotels going up for sale. Efforts to restart the service continue. In 2000 Coats Viyella had recently halved their Scottish workforce, now employing only 400 in Campbeltown and Kilmarnock. In 2001 complete closure at Campbeltown removed the last 160 Jaeger jobs (the town's largest employer). The creamery now makes novelty cheeses under the Inverloch Cheese Company, but financing essential improvements is a problem. Hotels include the substantial 16-room *Royal*, a popular ceilidh venue, and the smaller *Seafield*; there are also guest houses.

## CAMPSIE GLEN (Clachan of Campsie) Map 5, C5

***Strathkelvin hamlet**, pop. 150* OS 64: NS 6179

Campsie Kirk was erected near where the steep Campsie and Fin Glens converge on leaving the 500m hills known as the Campsie Fells. Close by was the 15th century tower of Balcorrach or Ballencleroch, of which little remains. By the time that Pont or Gordon mapped the area around 1610 a mill turned above a bridge in the Fin Glen. Chambers writing in 1827 merely noted Campsie as a *"village"*. A branch of the Edinburgh & Glasgow Railway was extended as a single track from Lennoxtown to Killearn in 1866 and to Aberfoyle in 1882; Campsie Glen station was 1km south of the kirkton, where there was an inn by 1895, and between the two a post office. By 1924 there was a bleach works in the Fin Glen. The passenger trains were withdrawn in 1951 when the population was around 275, and the rails soon vanished, as did the bleach works. The primary school remained in 1977 but by 1981 under 200 people lived locally, though the inn had become the *Campsie Glen Hotel & Restaurant*. Little recent change has been evident.

## CANNA & Sanday, Isles of Map 8, A4

***Small Isles, Inner Hebrides**, pop. 20* OS 39: NG 2705

The hilly Hebridean isle of Canna, 40km west of Mallaig is only 7.5km long; its shallow natural harbour is sheltered by the tidal islet of Sanday. Antiquities include Bronze Age souterrains, ancient forts, a seventh century chapel ruin with an unusual standing stone cross, and Viking burials. Canna was owned by the Abbot of Iona in 1549 when Monro found it *"inhabited and manured, good for corn, fishing and grassing, with a parish kirk and falcon nest"*; but the twin isles were plundered in 1588. In 1703 Martin found the people still

Catholics, under the laird Allan MacDonald. Monro noted the navigational problems caused by the magnetic anomalies of basaltic Compass Hill, which induce compass errors up to 5 km away. Two-thirds of remote Canna's population of about 150 was cleared to Canada by MacNeil in the 1840s, but by 1899 a post office served 40 people.

**The Scholarly Laird**: In 1938 the Gaelic scholar John Lorne Campbell bought the two isles, making Canna House his home. In 1953 the total population was still under 50, but MacBrayne steamers called regularly at Canna pier; cars could not be handled but there was still a church and a tiny school. By 1980 the steamers had gone, and although four passenger ferries from Mallaig called each week there were no tourist facilities. Only sheep, early potatoes and lobster fishing kept a population of just 24; the teacher then moved away to Muck. In 1981 Campbell gifted the twin isles to the National Trust for Scotland; sadly by 1991 Canna's population had shrunk to an unhappy 14. However, the ferry pier was improved in 1992 and a former church became a Gaelic study centre, but the school and post office still serve some 20 people. Canna still has no slipway to enable vehicles on the infrequent Small Isles ferry from Mallaig to embark or disembark.

## CANONBIE & Rowanburn — Map 2, C4

***Dumfriesshire village & hamlet,*** *pop. 1140* — OS 85: NY 3976

Canonbie lies on the Dumfriesshire River Esk only 1 km from the English border, which follows the Liddel Water. It took its name from an Augustinian priory founded near Priorslynn before 1220, by one Turgot de Rosdale. After 300 years of obscurity the monastery was destroyed by the English in 1542. Hollows Tower was built 4 km upstream from the border in the 16th century. *'Kannaby'* appeared on Pont's map of Liddesdale, made about 1610. Remarkably in view of the centuries of well publicised border warfare which had not long ceased, the area was apparently well settled. However, a proper road system was lacking, for when visited by Roy's surveyors about 1753 the *'Boat Bankhead'* ferried passengers to and from England just west of Rowanburnfoot. The *'Kirk of Canonbie'* stood alone east of the river; a ford across the Esk just north of the confluence of the Liddel Water led to the end of the only Scottish road in the area; this followed the west bank of the Esk, where there were some hamlets but no sign of the later village, and linked the area with Langholm.

**Roads, Bridges, Coalmines and Railways**: A new main road between Langholm and Longtown was turnpiked under an Act of 1764, and at about that time the Esk was bridged at Longtown to create the first proper road connection between the west coasts of England and Scotland. By the 1790s the Dukes of Buccleuch had sunk a coal pit with a water-driven drainage engine at Byreburn 3 km north of Canonbie. Canonbie bridge existed by 1827 and the Hollows water-powered grain mill 2 km to the north dated from about the same period, as did the post office. In 1827 Chambers noted that *"Cannobie is a small village, with a handsome new church"*. In 1862 the Border Union Railway was opened along the English side of the Liddel Water, and in 1864 the Langholm branch railway which left the main line at Riddings Junction south of the Bankhead ferry was opened through Rowanburn, where Canonbie station and a coalmine were situated, 1500 metres east of the village. More than one colliery was open by 1894, and lime was quarried in the vicinity. The pit at Rowanburn closed in 1922, but there are substantial coal reserves and the field might eventually be worked again.

**After the Railways the Riverside Inn**: In 1951 the population was about 1450, and Canonbie's facilities were those of a smallish village. The branch railway was closed to passengers in 1964 and freight in 1967, followed in 1969 by the main line, which by 1971 had also vanished north of Riddings. In 1974 the Phillips family created the *Riverside Inn* from a B&B house. Canonbie's character was quite affluent in 1981; there had been little further change in local facilities, and the Hollows mill was still grinding feedstuffs. The A7 bypass was opened in 1985; in 1991 1144 people lived in the village, whose post office is still open; the popular *Riverside Inn* was rated in the 1990s as *'Scotland's best Pub'*!

## CAPPERCLEUCH & St Mary's Loch — Map 3, A4

***Small Borders community,*** *pop. under 100* — OS 73: NT 2423

When Pont mapped Teviotdale about 1600, Yarrow Kirk stood near the head of the valley of the Yarrow Water in the Cappercleuch area, beside the *'Loch of the Lowis'*, as he identified the larger of the pair of lochs. This is now called St Mary's Loch after the dedication of the then *Kirk of Lowis* near the 16th century Dryhope Tower. By about 1754, as Roy's map showed, a road followed the north bank of the Yarrow Water to Dryhope. There it crossed to take the south shore of St Mary's Loch and so over the hills to Moffat; the modern road follows the north shore. It was probably the *Tibbie Shiels Inn* between the lochs that Chambers described in the 1820s as *"lately erected, with halesome and agreeable country fare"*. The *Rodono Hotel* was open by 1933 near the site of the ancient kirk; by the 1950s it had 14 rooms. The remote Megget primary school had closed by the 1970s, enabling the Megget Dam, 3 km west of Cappercleuch, to be built in 1978 for public water supply by Lothian Regional Council, impounding the largest reservoir in south-east Scotland; the dam became a tourist attraction. The *Tibbie Shiels Inn* is in the area where the Southern Upland Way passes by.

## CAPUTH & Spittalfield — Map 6, A2

***Angus hamlets,*** *pop. 500* — OS 53: NO 0940

About 83 AD the Roman legions began to lay out an extensive fortress at Inchtuthil, north of the River Tay some 15 km north of Bertha (Roman Perth). In plan about 500 m square, it was timber built and apparently intended as the main base for the proposed conquest of Caledonia. The remains of a forge, twelve tonnes of nails, and ten iron tyres have been found there. However, trouble in Germany caused a radical change of strategy, and by 87 AD the site had been abandoned.

**Textile Village and Bridges**: The parish centre of Caputh, 4 km west of Inchtuthil and 7 km east of Dunkeld, appeared as a few buildings marked *'Kerath'* on Pont's rough map of about 1600, when Stenton mill was at work; but it made little mark on the Roy map of about 1750, when the area was still roadless. Spittalfield was a planned village, its centrepiece the *'Muckle Hoose'* of 1767, built as a handloom linen factory. In the 1790s Caputh's mainstay was hand spinning and there were 130 local weavers. Spittalfield post office was opened by 1857 and by 1895 there was a school, and a post and telegraph

*The Muckle Hoose at Spittalfield, in Caputh parish; it was built in 1767 – an early instance of bringing hand-loom weavers into a central workshop.* *(RCAHMS / JRH)*

office at Caputh. The Boatlands vehicle ferry was replaced by the *'Iron Bridge'*, built in 1888. A passenger ferry to Murthly Castle plied across the Tay at Dalbeathie 3km west of Caputh in the 1890s and until at least 1903. In 1951 Caputh with its Glendelvine primary school served about 850 people, falling steadily to only about 500 by 1981, when there was still a village hall, post office and licensed grocer at Caputh. Spittalfield had a shop and post office, cricket club, bowling green and two long-standing garages; around 1980 McLennan was a significant motor coach hirer. A small hostel for backpackers is open all year round at Wester Caputh.

## CARBETH

**Map 5, C5**

***Stirlingshire estate,*** *pop. 190* — OS 64: NS 5279

About 3km west of Blanefield is the estate of Carbeth, formerly known as Carbeth Guthrie, on which the *Carbeth Inn* was established in 1816 beside the Glasgow to Drymen road. Carbeth House was an emparked mansion by 1895. In the depression of the 1930s the socially concerned laird Allan Barnes-Graham offered to let out a rough hillside above the inn in plots about 10m square, on which Glaswegians and others might erect weekend chalets or *'huts'*. Eventually over 200 families took advantage of this concession and during the 1930s and 1940s it was a very popular rendezvous for fresh air, and on occasion for escape from the Blitz. By 1983 the estate lay on the West Highland Way. Although it remained in the same family some huts had been removed, many of the tenants were elderly, and the inn was simply a pub. But life was far from peaceful in 2000, as the *'hutters'* were in fierce dispute with the laird.

## CARBOST, Talisker & Portnalong

**Map 8, A3**

***Village & hamlets, Isle of Skye,*** *pop. 500* — OS 32: NG 3831

Talisker on the west coast of Skye was an *"extensive farm"* in 1773 when Boswell and Johnson visited it: prophetically, Boswell wrote *"the water is admirable"*. One suspects he was referring to the *'water of life'*! Once bootlegging had ceased to be the most profitable way to produce whisky, the small Talisker distillery was built at Carbost in 1830. This isolated township, 6km east of Talisker on Loch Harport, had to wait for its post office until after 1838, and remained a small place, but well sheltered; Barnard aptly described it in 1886 as *"a smiling village"*. The distillery had been extended since 1877 and was then powered by a combination of water and steam. Barley was brought to its own pier by puffer, and its modest annual output of some 180,000 litres of best Highland malt whisky was shipped by a weekly steamer to Glasgow. R L Stevenson called it *"the king of drinks"*.

**The new Portnalong**: In 1898 Talisker merged with Dailuaine, and in 1916 Dailuaine-Talisker joined DCL. In 1921, crofters from Lewis and Harris created the township of Portnalong on a little-used peninsula north of Carbost; by 1951 it held some 200 people with a post office, a pier and, by the 1950s, a school with 70 secondary pupils. However, the steamers were withdrawn in 1961, and Portnalong school was run down to primary by 1976 and later closed. Meantime the distillery which had employed 30 crofters in 1964 was linked to the pier by a fat pipe. Though out of production in 1988, it remained the dominant feature of the small but well-equipped village of Carbost, which though it held only some 125 people, had an enlarged school, pub, telephone exchange and post office – the main centre for 550 scattered people. A fish farm began in 1981 at Portnalong, and the distillery was open again throughout the 1990s and welcomed visitors; its whisky was mainly sold as a ten-year-old single malt. Two independent hostels for backpackers are open all year in Portnalong, one being in the old school.

## CARDENDEN, Auchterderran & Dundonald

**Map 6, B4**

***Central Fife villages,*** *pop. 5400* — OS 58: NT 2195

The church which stood below a crag near the River Ore in central Fife was anciently referred to as Herkindora, and later as Auchterderran, meaning *'High Oakwood'*; in 1075 it was given to the Culdees of Loch Leven. Carden Forest to the south was a royal preserve in the time of William the Lion; through this area ran the north–south Pilgrim's Road and the Royal Road between Dunfermline and Falkland. Where these crossed beside the Ore was once a hospice for travellers, later replaced by the Auld House pub. Queen Mary's exclamation *"Champ de fleurs!"* is said to be the origin of the local name Jamphlars.

**Medieval Mills, Mines and Tower**: Pont's sketches of about 1600 showed a mill in the steep tributary valley to the south, incised by a burn which flowed from Loch Gelly into the Ore near *'Achterderans'*, *'Couden'* and *'Spittell Mill'*. Perched above the glen or *den* stood the 16th century Carden Tower; the ancient name Carden means *thicket* in Gaelic, so Cardenden (pronounced with stress on the *last* syllable) means *Thicket Valley*. Shaws Mill stood 1km upstream. Nearby was *'Colheugh Spittel'*, implying coal mining and early almshouses, possibly those where coal was first said to be given as alms to the poor early in the 15th century.

**The Bow Bridges**: The Pilgrim's Road, a winding track linking Burntisland, the holy well at Scotlandwell and Perth, crossed the River Ore 1.5km west of the Kirkton of Auchterderran by the early Bow Bridge, which the heritors had to repair in 1617. South of Auchterderran was the confusingly named Bow Bridge of Bowhill. A school was open at Auchterderran by 1641. Remarkably for that time, the teacher was an Englishman; was this why in 1668 there were only three pupils? In 1702 coal pits were open to the south, and another pit sunk in 1705 was provided with pumping machinery from the outset; the local coal owners were the Goodalls. Not so good was the fate of William Skirving of Auchterderran who was transported to Botany Bay in 1794, merely for advocating universal suffrage! Mining had moved east to Coalden by 1826–27, when Greenwood's map showed there was little else near the kirkton besides farms and two watermills. A bridge crossed the Ore near the church, but there were no turnpike roads in the area. In 1830 a bridge was built on the Torbain road by Ferguson of Raith House. By then the school had 80 pupils.

**Named by the Railway?**: Denend was the sole colliery when in 1848 a branch of the Edinburgh & Northern Railway was built through the area from Thornton Junction to Dunfermline. A station called Cardenden was placed on an embankment near Bowhill Bridge south of Auchterderran. In 1892 the Dundonald Coal Company sank the small Lady Helen shaft. By 1895 numerous old mine workings were shown on the maps, and several small coal pits named Cardenden Colliery were open south of the railway, apparently staffed with Protestant locals from farms. Whether the railway or Cardenden Colliery was the first to use this name is unclear, but in 1894 there was no village or post office named Cardenden. A doctor practised at Auchterderran from 1894.

**Large Scale Mining from 1895**: In 1895 the Bowhill Coal Company started sinking the great Bowhill Nos.1 & 2 collieries north of the River Ore and west of Auchterderran; Field Marshal Earl Haig chaired the company. This created a huge complex with brickworks, extensive rail sidings and its own power station; its mainly Catholic miners came from weaving, and from moribund collieries. Dundonald colliery south of the station was also sunk around the same time as the Bowhill, but even in 1901 the local population was only 715. A brickworks was set up by the coal company to provide materials for a huge *'scheme'* of 532 houses for miners, all complete by 1902. Set out in 19 streets each comprising some 30 dwellings of two apartments and of good quality for the day, they had outside closets, no gardens, and were identified solely by numbers. Despite this characterless start, there developed a village with exceptional enterprise. In 1900 a school was built at Cardenden, used for some 90 years.

**Minto Pit, Village Centre, Golf, and Fife Coal Takeover**: The Minto colliery, sunk from 1903 by the Lochgelly Iron & Coal Company to an eventual depth of 293 m; its pithead was on Brigghills Farm at the foot of the Eliza brae on the road to Lochgelly, only 1 km south-west of the Bowhill shafts. Shops developed along the winding road between kirk and station; Bowhill became the village centre when a branch of the Lochgelly Co-operative Society was built in 1904. In 1904 too a miners' Reading Room and Recreational Centre was built, and also the Higher Grade (secondary) school at Auchterderran. At its peak this had 1500 pupils, and the police station at Jamphlars then boasted a sergeant and 8 constables. Auchterderran Golf Club was founded in 1904 and its good 9-hole course opened in 1906. The *Bowhill Hotel* was also built in 1906, and soon a cinema adjoined. Denend School was added about 1910. In 1909 the Fife Coal Company (FCC) took over the Bowhill company, and owned all the local pits until nationalisation in 1947. So much coal was extracted that a subsidence flash called Jamphlars Pond appeared in 1916.

**Goths, Tragedy and Beta Blockers**: After World War I, semi-detached houses and bungalows were built, along with (in 1924) a *'Gothenburg'* – a pub owned by a Co-operative, an idea promoted by the FCC. In 1931 ten men died in a Bowhill pit accident, but further rapid growth soon followed, and pithead baths were built there in 1936–38, also serving the women who sorted coal on the *'tables'* at the pithead. By 1947 Cardenden provided the facilities of a large village, and its population was nearing 9000 in 1951 when the *Picturedrome* cinema had 875 seats and the *Rex* 550, with variety shows as well as films. Auchterderran secondary school was greatly extended; its swimming pool also served Kirkcaldy till the 1970s. Local man James Black discovered *'beta blockers'* and won a Nobel Prize.

**Council Houses replace Rows and Deep Mines Close**: The miners' rows vanished in the 1950s, replaced by innumerable houses built for Fife County Council, because Cardenden never became a burgh. In 1952 the NCB started sinking Bowhill No.3 shaft to work the Limestone Coal Group, intended to be 840 m deep; but like Glenochil and Rothes it was a nearly complete failure. After 1955 the output of Nos.1 & 2 also declined. The Dundonald colliery had a famous pipe band and was still active in 1954; but it stopped work in 1964, the Bowhill colliery complex was closed in 1965 and the Minto in 1967; only the coal washery remained in use to deal with mountains of coal waste.

**Trains and Opencast keep Wolf from Door**: The pipe band decided to merge with that from Dysart, and the Dundonald site was landscaped in 1977. Meantime the whole countryside to the north was being destroyed by opencasting *(see Lochore)*. In 1979 a tiny firm called Fullview Windows was opened; by 1989 it employed just ten people – small compensation for the hundreds of lost mining jobs! By 1981 the population was down to 6000, but a larger firm making aluminium castings was also at work. By the 1980s Cardenden had a strong home-grown community association, and a peak hour rail service to Cowdenbeath, Dunfermline and Edinburgh. The relative proximity of both Glenrothes and Kirkcaldy helped, and except for cinemas the facilities held up well: by the 1980s Cardenden was *the* place in Fife to buy beds! Auchterderran High School was closed in 1987 *(see Lochgelly)*; its buildings became the Staff Development & Resources Centre for Fife.

**Disadvantaged, but showing Enterprise**: From 1989 a new Fife circular rail service gave an hourly Kirkcaldy connection. The 200-tonne steel girders for the Cardenden Viaduct on the new A92 road which took through traffic out of the village, were fabricated at Glenrothes in 1989. When the Co-op closed their Cardenden shop in 1990, community action soon re-created their own 7-staff grocery store. The population had fallen to under 5400 by 1991, still very disadvantaged. In 1991–97 British Coal won about 1.8 million tonnes of coal by opencasting at *'Westfield Link'* north of Auchterderran, giving 70 jobs, using the rail connection and leaving a hole sufficient to take all the rubbish from central Fife for 70 years. In 1996–99 a smaller area north of Shawsmill was opencasted. By 1995 all the surface buildings of the Bowhill pit had been demolished; the site was levelled to make a playing field. The Cardenden Colliery bing still existed, and the Miners' Reading Room still stood, disused. A 10-year solid waste recycling period is to transform the scarred Jamphlars area from 2001.

## CARDONALD — Map 15, B5

***Suburb, w. of Glasgow,** pop. 35,000* — OS 64: NS 5263

Cardonald lies in a gently rolling area north of the White Cart Water, about 7 km west of Glasgow. Its ancient Cumbric name means *'Donald's Castle'*, and it appeared as a hamlet on Pont's original map of Renfrewshire which was sketched about 1600. By 1642 there was a definite routeway between Glasgow and Paisley, passing north of Cardonald and added by Gordon to Pont's map. There was a road rather than a track in this direction by the time of Roy's survey of about 1754, and development was stimulated by the improvements which resulted from turnpiking this road in the late 18th century.

**Canal, and Railways Curved and Straight**: By 1812 a winding canal north of the White Cart Water was also in use from Glasgow; strangely aimed at Ardrossan, which already enjoyed a sea connection with Glasgow, it got no farther than Johnstone. From 1840 the dead straight Glasgow & Paisley Joint Railway also traversed the area, roughly parallel to the canal about 2 km to the north; but it was only in 1879 that Cardonald station was opened. A second, more sinuous railway was opened by the Glasgow & South Western Railway in 1885 on the line of the one-time canal (the 'Canal' line). In 1895 Cardonald station still lay in open country; to the south was Cardonald post office at the hamlet of Halfwayhouse, which at the time was remarkably bisected by the boundary of Glasgow city. Ross Hall beside the White Cart at Crookston Road was by then the mansion of the Lobnitz family of Renfrew *(q.v.)*. The boilermakers D Cockburn & Son moved from the Gorbals to Cardonald about 1903, and in the 1914–18 war a shell-filling factory was built. Bellahouston and Crookston stations on the Canal line were opened between 1903 and 1909; Mosspark West and Corkerhill stations were added by the LMS after the Grouping of 1923, about the time that the remainder of the area was swallowed by the City of Glasgow.

**Rapid Development for Housing**: While Cardonald attracted private housing in the 1920s, Mosspark was developed with good-quality Glasgow council housing. The more westerly estates, the first called Crookston after the old castle south of the White Cart, were largely built in the 1930s, and the Penilee council housing estate to the north from 1938–40. Meantime Halfwayhouse grew as a local centre, including the *Aldwych Cinema* – one of three strung out along Paisley Road West – which dated from about 1938. In 1938 tramlines were laid from Paisley Road West to Bellahouston Park to serve the Empire Exhibition, but later abandoned, though those on reserved land beside Mosspark Boulevard stayed in use until 1960. Still more stations had been opened, among them Hillington East, actually nearer Cardonald than to the Hillington industrial estate. Around 1950 Rolls-Royce of Hillington opened a branch factory at Cardonald. By 1951 this rapidly-developed area had a population of some 40,000 and the facilities of a small town.

**From Trams to Blue Trains and the Mirror**: Until the tramways closed in 1962 one might travel to Glasgow more cheaply by electric tram than by rail; the former joint railway was electrified in 1967. By 1971 a crematorium had been built at Craigton cemetery. In the 1970s Cardonald College of Further Education was built at Mosspark Drive, but although other facilities in the area had also tended to increase to a more typical urban level, the population had fallen to 35,000 by 1981. By 1991 the Lobnitz mansion had been adapted as the 100-bed Ross Hall private hospital. The Canal railway was closed to passengers in 1983, but surprisingly reopened in 1990 using Sprinter diesel trains, serving stations at Moss Park and Crookston, whose former station building of 1885 had been converted to housing by 1995. In 1990 the Strathclyde Regional Council (SRC) was trying to dispose of a 20 ha problem site in Shieldhall Road, and still owned an industrial estate nearby. In 1994 the Mirror Group newspapers (the *Daily Record* and *Sunday Mail)* moved from Anderston Quay to a new plant at Cardonald. In 1997 Howden *(see Govan)* were still making industrial fans in the former shell-filling factory. The Lourdes Secondary School has 1129 pupils, Penilee Secondary has 815.

## CARDRONA & Horsburgh — Map 3, A3

***Hamlets east of Peebles,** pop. under 100* — OS 73: NT 3039

Hill forts overlook Cardrona south of the River Tweed; its old church stood at Kirkburn, 4 km east of Peebles. In the 16th century two towers were built north of the river, one on an 'L' plan near an ancient *'hospital'* at Horsburgh, and the other at Nether Horsburgh, adjoining which the Pont map of about 1600, as engraved by Blaeu, showed a mill. About the same time another tower rose on a hillside at Cardrona. Roy's survey of about 1754 showed a road following the south bank, with another on the north bank west from Horsburgh Ford. In 1866 the Peebles Railway was extended to Galashiels, crossing the Tweed by viaduct at Horsburgh Ford, where Cardrona station was placed. By 1895 Cardrona House stood in a park below its old tower and another emparked mansion had been built at Kailzie, west of Kirkburn. The mill survived. The area remained wholly rural until after 1963; by then the railway had lately vanished.

**Hotels, new Bridge and Dormitory Growth**: In the 1980s a large hotel was built at Glentress, just north of Horsburgh Castle. In 1989 an ambitious but controversial plan by local farm owner Tom Renwick for housing development at Horsburgh Ford was approved by the Regional Council; far from being self-contained, it regrettably aimed to house long-distance car commuters, but would also include a large hotel and a golf course. Work was not started due to the slump. In 1994 against stiff local opposition the council again approved Renwick's scheme to build a 220-house settlement, a 150-room hotel and a golf course of championship standard. By 1999 a new river bridge, the hotel and a number of houses had been built, and the golf course had been created.

## CARDROSS, Darleith & Kilmahew — Map 5, B5

***Coastal village w. of Dumbarton,** pop. 2000* — OS 63: NS 3477

Cardross on the north shore of the Firth of Clyde, about 5 km north-west of Dumbarton, was the property of the Grahams until 1325 when they moved to Old Montrose, which they had swapped with Robert the Bruce, who died in the early castle of Cardross in 1329; later this vanished. The keep of Darleith was built 2 km north of the kirkton about 1510 by the Darleith family, of whom Lord Darnley was a member. The tower house of Kilmahew, built about the same time, likewise stood aloof, overlooking the Clyde from a distance. At the time of Pont's mapping about 1600, Kilmahew was adjoined by its Kirk, Drumfalloch, *'Achinsaill'* (Auchensail) and a settlement named Achinchry; a mill turned below Wallacetown on the adjacent burn, and – if Pont's map is correct – the area was quite well wooded. Of Cardross there was no sign. Darleith House was expanded into a mansionhouse in 1616, and passed to Yuill of Inveraray; eventually it became dressed as a Georgian mansion. Roy's map of about 1754 marked Cardross Kirk and an adjoining hamlet on the coast road west from Dumbarton.

**Railway, Pioneer Aeronaut and Golf**: From 1858 this road was paralleled by the Glasgow, Dumbarton & Helensburgh Railway, later part of the North British. A station was opened at Cardross, and about 1870 a new mansion named Kilmahew was built near the tower of that name. Only a small village with a mill, post office and inn existed nearby until the end of the 19th century, when it rose to fame due to Percy Pilcher. Born of Scottish parents in Bath in 1867, he was apprenticed at Elder's Fairfield shipyard in Govan, drew plans at the Clydebank yard and became a naval architect. From 1891, inspired by Lilienthal, he and his sister Ella built gliders in his Glasgow home and first flew in them successfully at Cardross. Though he was sadly killed when trying his latest glider in 1899, it survived to be preserved at East Fortune *(see Webster, 1994)*. Meantime the Cardross golf club, founded in 1895, was creating an 18-hole course.

**Air Raids, Electric Trains and Suburban Living**: Despite its lack of industry Cardross was severely bombed in 1941. Ten years later it was still a small village of about 1250 people. The railway was effectively electrified in 1961, triggering new dormitory housebuilding. Meantime the St Peter's Roman Catholic religious training college had been opened at Kilmahew in 1958. In the early 1960s it was greatly enlarged to modernist designs by Glasgow architects to accommodate 100 students, but it could not be heated economically and was closed in 1980. Meantime Darleith House, which had become part of the seminary, was abandoned about 1970. By 1981 Cardross village had grown to nearly 1900 people, with typical village facilities.

**From St Peter's Gate to Hell's Gate?**: About 1984 the RC church turned the Kilmahew buildings into a drugs rehabilitation centre, causing consternation, fear and hatred amongst the staid local residents. In 1991 the population was 1958, well-educated and mainly owner-occupiers. Kilmahew was abandoned by the RC Church by 1991; both estates lay derelict in 2000, their buildings sadly vandalised ruins. The scandalised locals still enjoy the use of their station, post office, pub and 18-hole golf course.

## CARGENBRIDGE & Troqueer

**Map 2, B4**

***Settlement w. of Dumfries,*** *pop. 500* — OS 84: NX 9574

A now lost stone circle and ancient forts or mottes among the low hills in Troqueer parish, 5 km west of Dumfries, marked gaps through which the Cargen Water and the early military road to Portpatrick made their way. In 1688 Troqueer was chartered as a burgh of barony, but no village appeared other than the area now known as Maxwelltown (covered in the Dumfries article). Roy's map of the 1750s marked the Cargenbridge, west of which at Drumsleet the *'lower road'* to Kirkcudbright forked to the south. From 1859 the Glasgow & South Western Railway's Dumfries to Castle Douglas and Kirkcudbright branch also passed through this farming area, though no station was provided; eventually it linked to Stranraer. A primary school was built at Drumsleet.

**Hiding Explosives and the Groundnut Fiasco**: In 1939 a large rail-connected factory was built for the government just west of Cargenbridge, to produce nitro-cellulose and plastics under ICI. In 1949 ICI built fabric research laboratories and a new works on an adjoining site for the manufacture of *'Ardil'* protein fibre from East African groundnuts, part of a notorious colonial government failure; the 1951 revision OS maps showed neither works! Some housing and a new Cargenbridge primary school were built close by. The railway was closed by Beeching in 1965, though the first 5 km remained as a long siding known as the Maxwelltown branch, serving the ICI works, in 1986 home to their Petrochemicals and Plastics Division. This was converted to burn coal and scrap plastic in 1988, but in 1990 the firm cut its workforce by 125 people. By 1994 the plant was known as ICI Films and was making packaging film.

**Pushed off the Rails**: Swingeing increases in rail freight charges imposed in 1993 actually resulted in the regrettable end of rail freight on the line, which however remained in place; its reopening to receive 15,000 tonnes of oil a year is now planned for 2003. Meantime a modern primary school had been opened by 1976, and *Mabie House* among the wooded hills 4 km to the south had become a hotel by 1986. The area remains distinct from Dumfries and has had a steady population of around 500; the factory and school remain open, and by 1997 forest walks and a cycle route had been laid out in Mabie Forest. In 2001 a rail preservation group is seeking to reopen the line westwards towards Dalbeattie.

## CARLOWAY & Garenin

**Map 11, B2**

***Village, Lewis,*** *pop. 400* — OS 8: NB 2042

A large well-preserved broch is the main historical feature of this area on Loch Carloway, an inlet on the west coast of Lewis some 25 km west of Stornoway. Carloway *(G. Carlabhagh)* long remained simply a crofting township. A large concrete pier, perhaps built for wartime use early in the 20th century, was disused by the 1970s. A population of under 600 in 1951 fell to only 400 thirty years later, though the 12-room *Doune Braes Hotel* was open by 1973. By 1981 the local medical group practice was increasingly significant, and the small Harris Tweed works of Donald Macleod Ltd was at work in the 1990s. A street of *'black houses'* at Garenin *(G. Gearrannan)*, 2 km north-west, abandoned in 1973 but the last remaining in Lewis, was restored to use in the 1990s, and a year-round youth hostel was open there by 1999.

## CARLUKE

**Map 16, B5**

***Lanarkshire town,*** *pop. 13,000* — OS 72 or 65: NS 8450

Carluke stands at the rather high altitude of some 200 m, on a plateau about 3 km from the middle reaches of the River Clyde, its site crossed by the Roman road between Bothwell and the camp known as Castledykes east of Lanark. An early church in the area was called Malessok, and Carluke's Cumbric name implies an early fort, but only the name Castlehill remains. Of two 16th century towers, Belstane near the village almost disappeared, but luckier was Waygateshaw House near the river, which has survived intact. Pont's map of Lanarkshire made in 1596 showed Belstane and *'Kirk Karlouck'* surrounded by tiny settlements.

*The Windsor picture-house, Carluke, had 1290 seats, being built in the 1920s with discarded firebricks from local works. It was demolished in the 1980s.* *(JRH)*

**William Roy and his Survey**: Carluke had a parish school from 1620 and in 1662 was chartered as a burgh of barony, also called Kirkstile. Some 2 km to the south-west stood Miltonhead or Meadowhead, the birthplace in 1726 of William Roy, whose military survey of Scotland made around 1750 provided so much material for this book, and who effectively founded the Ordnance Survey. Paul Sandby's fair-copy map-sheets bisected Carluke – perhaps it was taken as an origin – but although this hid the character of the place it did emphasise its great centrality, with no fewer than nine radial roads meeting near the kirk. These included the Roman road; another road or *'causeway'* – which was later partly abandoned – led across Auchterhead Muir north of Blacklaw to Causeyhill and Livingston for Edinburgh, and two others rejoined at Lanark.

**Mansion, Mining, Railway and Preserves**: By then the Carluke area was evidently well cultivated; four annual fairs were scheduled for 1797, and in 1799 Heron described both Carluke and Braidwood, 2 km to the south, as *"rising villages"*. About then a windmill was built; but it was after 1813 when Carluke's first post office was opened. The fine mansionhouse of Milton Lockhart was built on the banks of the Clyde 3 km west of Carluke in 1829–36; designed by William Burn for William Lockhart, it was also the home of John Lockhart, the biographer of Sir Walter Scott. In 1848 the main line of the Caledonian Railway was completed, with stations at Carluke and Braidwood; limestone quarries were opened 2 km east of the latter. A gasworks was erected, and Scott's factory was built in 1878–80 to make jelly. Extractive industries scarred the area by 1895 when there was a small ironworks at Hallcraig 2 km to the west, brick and tile works at Braidwood and at Castlehill (which also had a coal pit), and ironstone and limestone pits to the east at Roadmeetings, Lochknowe and Bashaw, all linked by railways.

**Carluke as a Centre**: Carluke's population was approaching 5000, but it was ignored by Murray's generally comprehensive *Handbook* for 1894. A golf club founded in that year laid out a course west of the station. The *Carluke & Lanark Gazette* was first published in 1906, and after half a century of quiet development Carluke enjoyed the facilities of a small town. The Roadmeetings Infectious Diseases Hospital had been built to the east, extensive glasshouses stood to north and south, and by 1971 the population had grown to 9000. Bricks were made at Roadmeetings in 1980, remarkably by the Glasgow Iron & Steel Company; but the coal mine near Castlehill had gone the way of all Lanarkshire pits, as had Braidwood station.

**Electric Trains; Milton Lockhart to Tokyo**: Electrification of the railway in 1974, with the provision of stopping trains on the Lanark to Glasgow route, stimulated housing development. Regrettably Milton Lockhart House had been largely demolished in 1956, but the derelict remainder was saved in 1987 by being dismantled for re-erection – near Tokyo! By then the quarry too was derelict, and the ironworks had also vanished. However, the 18-hole golf course separated its derelict site from Carluke. In 1976 Carluke still merited an edition of the *Lanark Gazette* and continued to grow steadily, with a population of 11,400 by 1981; but Braidwood had shrunk from 850 in 1951 to only 600, and Roadmeetings Hospital was a 110-bed geriatric unit.

**Suburban Growth**: Fields and glasshouses continued to vanish into suburban estates in the 1980s, when the large new Carluke High School was built, but some glasshouses remained in 1991. By then Carluke's youngish population was nearing 13,000. Renshaw Scott's jam and chocolate factory employs 100, as do McFadyen Glass. The provision of a new swimming pool in 1995 was aided by National Lottery cash. The Castlehill industrial estate had modern units available in 1996. Carluke High School has almost 1400 pupils; the town centre has now been pedestrianised.

## CARMUNNOCK

**Map 15, D6**

***Small village s-e. of Glasgow,*** *pop. 500* OS 64: NS 6057

Carmunnock 4 km south of Rutherglen is an ancient settlement with a Cumbric name, which appeared as *'Kormannoch'* on Pont's map of Lanarkshire dated 1596; a parish school was founded in 1607. By the time of the Roy survey of the mid 18th century, several roads met at the *'Kirk of Kirmunock'*. The first urban-related development of note was the 18-hole Cathkin Braes golf course, opened to the east in 1888. By the late 19th century an inn, smithy, post office, laundry and mill clustered round the church as the nucleus of a village. Railways came no nearer than Busby, but by 1931 a quarry and a Renfrew County Council waterworks fed from small reservoirs had been added. In 1951 just over 1000 people lived locally, with the facilities of a small village. By 1971 there were some small housing estates, but the Glasgow green belt prevented more growth, despite the arrival of the huge Castlemilk housing estate whose edge came within 1 km of the village. By 1981 the population in and around Carmunnock was 1175; however in 1991 there were under 500 people within the tightly-drawn village boundary. A western bypass built in the 1990s removed the through traffic between East Kilbride and Cathcart, leaving a quiet rural enclave.

## CARMYLE

**Map 15, D5**

***S-E. suburb of Glasgow,*** *pop. 7000* OS 64: NS 6561

Carmyle – whose name implies an ancient fort – lies on the north bank of the River Clyde about 6 km south-east of Glasgow. Pont's map of 1596 showed *'Kaermyil'* as a tiny place; across a burn to the west was a bridge giving access to Glasgow. A muslin factory was erected at Carmyle in 1741. Roy's map made about 1754 showed the London road separating Fullarton from Carmyle, then a small nucleated settlement. A linen bleachfield had been added by 1760, and by 1771 textiles were being printed. In the early 19th century a further bleachworks also opened.

**Iron, Coal and the Hot Blast of Progress**: The Clyde Ironworks, an iron-smelting works founded by Thomas Edington at Fullarton Road, was opened in 1786. In 1829 the Clyde Ironworks west of Carmyle Avenue was the first to use the hot blast process, invented by Neilson in the previous year. The Caledonian Railway (CR) branch from Rutherglen to Coatbridge was opened in 1865, with a station at Carmyle. The large Ironworks was rebuilt from 1860. Huge blocks of stone from a Carmyle quarry were used in 1871–72 to build the south abutment of the first Tay Railway Bridge. Carmyle became a railway junction in the 1890s, with the opening of CR link lines to Newton and Bridgeton Cross. In the 1890s a ford still crossed the Clyde to Cambuslang. Both villages had inns by 1901 when there were three coal pits open in the area, at Clyde, Foxley and Kenmuir; these worked into the 1920s.

**A Key Role for the Clyde Ironworks**: The Clyde Ironworks were re-equipped by Colvilles in 1939–40 and again in 1952. By the 1950s the area's population was approaching 6000, and it was extensively built up; a long weir traversed the river above the village centre. But Beeching closed Carmyle station in the early 1960s and the railway to Bridgeton had vanished by 1971; the Clyde Works Colliery was also closed around that time. In 1975 the ironworks still played a key role in the Scottish steel industry, its blast furnaces supplying iron to the newer Clydebridge steel works *(see Rutherglen)* across the river to the west, to Motherwell's Lanarkshire and Dalzell plants, and to remote Glengarnock until the latter's closure in 1978; these recipients of Clyde iron comprised all of Scotland's open hearth steel furnaces, except for modern Ravenscraig. Part of the old Clyde Ironworks site had become the Tollcross foundry; ousted by new plant at Craigneuk, this too closed in 1978.

**Transport Improvements mocked by Decline and Fall of the Iron Industry**: A new river bridge to Cambuslang, together with the Carmyle bypass known as Clydeford Road, were built in the late 1970s. The population was about 7000 by 1981, but local facilities were minimal. By 1986 the railway to Newton had been lifted. Ferguson's chocolate works, established in 1794 at Maryhill, was moved to a Carmyle industrial estate in the early 1980s, but most of the 200-year-old Clyde had been closed and cleared by 1987. The 1991 Census treated Carmyle as part of greater Glasgow. In 1993 diesel passenger train services were reintroduced on the remaining railway, the Glasgow Central to Whifflet route, lately freight-only, with a new station at Carmyle beside the brand new M74 extension; its planned completion from Fullarton Road across the Clyde to meet the existing M8 at Gorbals is still a contentious proposal.

## CARMYLLIE

**Map 6, C2**

***Angus hamlet,*** *pop. 200* — OS 54: NO 5543

Carmyllie and its mill on the Elliot Water 10km WNW of Arbroath existed by 1574 when a parish school was noted, and Pont marked it on his map about 1600, but the Roy map – made about 1750 – noted only *'Kirmley Kirk'* in the centre of a roadless area. However it is known that for several centuries before 1800, local farmers had worked quarries for so-called roofing *'slates'* in a 200m hill on the Earl of Dalhousie's estate at Carmyllie. Some slates were used in Dundee, and others taken by sea to Leith for Edinburgh. This *'Arbroath Pavement'* or ragstone was described by Chambers as *"a peculiar species of stone, which breaks off naturally in 'liths' five inches thick"*.

**Bell's Reaper and the Expansion of Quarrying**: Patrick Bell, born in Carmyllie in 1800, became its minister and there devised the reaping machine, a development that was to revolutionise farming and lead to a great exodus from the land. A quarry at East Hills that was opened by Duncan, Falconer & Co about 1810, soon became so deep that windpumps failed to keep down the water, and a long drainage level was tunnelled about 1830. In the 1840s, up to 14,000$m^3$ of local flagstones were being shipped annually. In 1855 the quarries were connected to the main line at Elliot Junction west of Arbroath by a railway built for the owner, by then a Duke. In 1869 some 150 tonnes a day – at that time a typical trainload – were despatched by rail direct from the quarry floor. Of the 300 workers, most lived in the parish. Their products included widely exported pavings, steps, copings, columns, stone cisterns for bleaching works and tabling in slabs of up to 20 tonnes in weight. Just to the south, Gwynd or Guynd quarry employed about 70 men producing only pavings. In the 1880s one Carmylie quarry sent 50,000 tonnes of stone (mainly by sea) for use in building the Forth Bridge.

**Twentieth Century Decline**: By the 1890s there were three quarries – Latch, Slade and Guynd – and a post office at Redford, but since at least 1869 no public house had been permitted by the Duke, and therefore few new houses were built. A rail passenger service was provided in 1900 to a station at Redford, but this ran only until 1929, for the quarries' production declined as development slowed and concrete slabs replaced hewn paving stones. In 1951 farming predominated: there was an agricultural engineer and an auction mart, but a mere 300 people lived at Carmyllie. Although the quarries had apparently closed by the mid 1950s, the freight railway remained open until 1965. Not surprisingly, the population continued to shrink to a mere 200 or so by 1981, with only the most basic facilities; the primary school at Redford is still open.

## CARNOUSTIE, Downie, Barry, Panmure, East & West Haven

**Map 6, C3**

***Angus coastal town,*** *pop. 10,000* — OS 54: NO 5643

Downie, beside the Pitairlie Burn in Angus, had an ancient souterrain, and a thanage from about the 11th century, while the *Caer* element in the name of Carnoustie at the burn mouth suggests a possible Pictish reference to a Roman fort. The 15th century birthplace of Hector Boece who became the first Principal of Aberdeen University was at Barry, between the two. When about 1600 Pont noted *'Dunie'* as a village, Barry was it seems a bridgepoint in a complex area of settlement, with fermtouns around Monikie Kirk. Farther down the Monikie Burn was the castle of Panmure, built in the 13th century 3km east of Downie, and accompanied by a mill. Another 3km downstream stood the Kirk, Kirkton and Mill of *'Panbryd'*, and also *'Kraig'* Mill. On the coast 1km south of the kirk and between the mouths of the two burns was West Haven, and 2km east of this lay East Haven of Panmure, which was chartered as a burgh of barony in 1540; it too had a mill, but also fished for shellfish and white fish.

**Panmure House, Barry and Weaving**: In 1666 John Mylne built Panmure House, 1 km north-west of the old castle, for George Maule, the 2nd Earl of Panmure *(see Brechin)*. In the 1720s Defoe called it *"the noble palace of Panmure, forfeited in the late rebellion"*. By 1750 what Roy again named Panmuir Castle had shelter-belted policies, which a century later enclosed about 400 ha. Roy's survey showed only one road in the area, following the coast; on it was *'Cornisty'*, a mere hamlet between the Mill of Panbride parish to the east and the village of Barry to the west. However, at that time the Pitairlie Burn appeared to be unbridged. A tall lighthouse was built on Buddon Ness in 1753 by Dundee shipowners. In 1768 a post office was opened at Muirdrum, on the new Dundee to Arbroath turnpike road, 3 km inland. Barry contained about 100 weavers in 1790, using local and imported Riga flax to make high-quality linens. Warden commented that Carnoustie was still *"quite insignificant"* in 1800. In 1812 Lochty Mill was for sale; about then the attractive Barry water mill was built of stone.

**Textile and Railway Development**: George Dow of Panmure gained an award from the Board of Trustees in 1817 for the excellence of his scutching mill operations and improvements. These stimulated local manufacturing, and by 1822 Robert Templeman & Co had built a flax spinning mill with 360 spindles, and John Alexander another with 144. In 1825 West Haven, also called *Newton of Panbride*, was a fishing village with a small brewery. The latter apparently did not survive for long after competition arrived, with the opening at Carnoustie in 1838 of a station on the new railway between Dundee and Arbroath, but the Carnoustie area remained a malting centre. David Henry, born in Carnoustie in 1835, became a well known architect in St Andrews. Carnoustie post office was open by 1840, and in 1842 a coastal bleachfield was at work at Panbridefield. In that year Carnoustie golf club was founded, laying out an 18-hole links course. Panmure House was altered by David Bryce in 1852 to contain some 130 rooms, but after 1874 it was little used outside the hunting season.

**Smieton's Panmure Works and the Abertay Lightship**: The 2500 m$^2$ Panmure Works built in 1857 by James Smieton & Son of Dundee was cited by Warden as *"a perfect model of a power-loom work"*. It was rail-connected; by 1864 216 power looms and over 100 hand looms were at work there, employing 400 people making about five million metres of ducks, pladdings, bleached sheetings and dowlas in a year. The enlightened firm had built houses for its workers and was about to add a Literary Institute, recreation rooms and another 80 houses. So Carnoustie was by 1864 according to Warden *"a very thriving and populous village"* – almost a town. In 1867 Smieton's 400 power looms used a variety of yarns from Angus, Glasgow, France and Ireland, largely jute with either tow or flax, but also hemp and cotton. Hedging his bets, Smieton's 600 workers made over 500 varieties of fabric, perhaps 80 at any one time and totalling over 4 million metres a year in such ranges as drills, checks and stripes, largely for export to the Americas. A smaller factory had some 50 workers. The Abertay light vessel *(see Arbroath)* was stationed by the Dundee Harbour Trust 3 km off Buddon Ness from 1877.

**Golf, Barry Buddon Ranges and more Golf**: The Carnoustie Ladies' golf club was founded in 1873, Simpson's golf shop opened in 1883 and the Caledonia golf club started in 1887. By 1894 Carnoustie was actively promoted as a resort by the Caledonian and North British railway companies which then

*Carnoustie's Golf Hotel, completed in 1999 in time for the return of the Open Championship to the town's famous links.* *(AL)*

jointly owned the line; for a time Wordie & Co ran a rail to road cartage depot. Murray found *"a seaside resort with an excellent golf course"* and two hotels, the *"good" Bruce's* and the *"very fair" Panmure Arms*. There were over 4000 people, a vitriol works, jute machinery works, and the Taymouth Engineering works of Anderson Grice & Co, who then made granite-polishing machinery. A lifeboat station was opened at Buddon Ness in 1894, and in 1895 parts of Barry Links, useless for farming, became the Barry Buddon army firing ranges. An electric power station was built in 1902. The (Barry) Panmure golf club, formerly of Monifieth, laid out an 18-hole course on Buddon Links in 1899, whilst Carnoustie regularly hosted the Open golf championship from 1931 onwards. At that time Winter's Fine Footwear had a factory near the *Bruce Hotel*.

**Dynamiting History**: A fighter airfield of the 1939–45 war was located at Hatton north of East Haven. The Abertay lightship was replaced in 1939 and converted to automatic operation in 1971; meantime the lifeboat station had closed in 1961. By 1951 the area had eleven hotels, 5400 residents, and small-town facilities; an 18-hole municipal golf course was open at Burnside by 1953. The contents of Panmure House were removed to Brechin Castle in 1955; the great house – having proved unsaleable – was regrettably blown up! In the 1960s Anderson-Grice made the two large gantry grabs which fed coal slurry into Methil power station. For some years around 1980 the associated firm Anderson Abrasives Ltd made abrasive wheels at the Taymouth Works. Carnoustie then boasted a high school, three golf courses and three putting courses, as well as 14 hotels, the best being of higher star class than in the 1950s. A second municipal golf course was created at Buddon Links in 1981, the town's fourth 18-hole course! Because Carnoustie was no longer being chosen as a venue for the Open, the erection of a large golfing hotel was agreed in 1988; it was a long time coming! Low & Duff, makers of engineering components, expanded in 1989 and opened a branch factory in Arbroath to gain Enterprise Zone benefits; in 1993 they produced machinery for making chocolates.

**Malt and Yachts, Golf and Guns**: In 1991 when the local population had passed 10,650, the local maltings was sending malted barley in traditional jute sacks to Glenturret distillery near Crieff; in 1992 David Adamson made full-fruit jams; and in 1995 Mackay's Preserves were active (the last makers of marmalade in the Dundee area). A dry Leisure Centre was opened in 1988, the seafront was improved in 1992, and in 1993 the small yacht club had an enclosure on the beach, while the Panmure Works were still in partial use. Barry Buddon had become the largest army range in Scotland by 1978 – a *'Major District Training Area'* of the Ministry of Defence in 1994. By then the Barry water mill had been restored to working order by the National Trust for Scotland to draw summer visitors, and new housing was rising west of the maltings. By 1996 there was a Tesco store, and by 1997 Carnoustie High School had 992 pupils. Meantime David Murray Transport of Carnoustie operated juggernauts.

**Regaining the Open – at a Price**: One of the golf courses now bears the name Dalhousie. The completion in 1999 of Mike Johnston's new 4-star 85-room *Carnoustie Golf Hotel* with its 120 staff enabled the Open Championship to return in that year – won by Aberdeen man Paul Lawrie. But Angus Council had granted the hotelier half the teeing-off times on the local courses on 5 days a week for 35 years, and in 2000 other hostelries were claiming this as a disaster for their trade. Significant hotels in the town include the *Carnoustie Links* and *Carlogie House*.

## CARNWATH — Map 16, C5

***Lanarkshire village,** pop. 1350* — OS 72: NS 9846

Carnwath stands at the high altitude of 220 metres, 2 km north of the remarkable crook in the River Clyde and some 10km east of Lanark. The *Caer-* element in its name suggests a Cumbric fortification, and its 12th century motte was the largest in Lanarkshire; about 2 km to the north stood the 14th century Couthalley Castle. The medieval church was made collegiate in 1424 by Sir Thomas Somerville; Carnwath became his family's burgh of barony in 1451. In 1560 the castle was still the seat of Lord Somerville, but later fell into ruin, and when Pont mapped Clydesdale in 1596 Carnwath was not a large place, though its parish school dates back to 1617. About 4km to the south is Libberton, even smaller, which had a parish school from 1631.

**Road Centre**: By the time of the Roy map, made about 1754, Carnwath had a mill, and the Medwin Water had been bridged on the Libberton road. The combined road from Lanark and Carluke forked at the east end of the linear village, to Edinburgh via Crosswoodhill and to Newbigging, Dunsyre and West Linton. The Glasgow to Peebles road through Carnwath, turnpiked under an Act of 1772, took a more southerly line east of Newbigging (which remained little more than a hamlet 200 years later). Carnwath had a post office from 1786, and by 1797 two annual fairs were scheduled there; it was already a post town with a delivery three times a week from Edinburgh. Heron in 1799 noted about 500 people in the *"village"*, near which were *"sulphureous and chalybeate springs"*, but it did not become a recognised spa; the medieval church was replaced in the early 19th century. Chambers noted in the 1820s *"the village of Carnwath, the capital of a moorland district. Formerly a curious old-fashioned place, now a double line of neat stone-cottages, roofed with slate"*; it had a school.

**Railways and Golf**: A station was opened in 1848 on the Edinburgh branch of the Caledonian Railway from Carstairs Junction and in 1867 another station was opened at Bankhead, 2 km south of Carnwath on the same company's bucolic Dolphinton branch. Industry and police burgh status never appeared, yet its population grew slowly, to 700 in 1891. Carnwath golf club was founded in 1907 and laid out an 18-hole course. The Dolphinton railway had closed by 1953, and Carnwath station was closed by Beeching in the 1960s; only a village level of facilities remained.

**Farming Taught and Pharmaceuticals Proven**: Meantime by 1954 the Kersewell Agricultural School was open 3km to the east, a boarding establishment renamed as a College by 1958. In 1980 Caledonian Peat were excavating the moss, and Carnwath was the headquarters of Wilson's Coaches; it also had the large highways salt depot of Strathclyde Regional Council. The hamlet of Newbigging had a primary school until about the 1960s and still had a post office in 1988. By 1986 a new nucleus of dormitory development had grown at Kame-End on the Peebles road. In 1989 the Scottish Business Enterprise award was won by DAR (Data Analysis & Research) of Carnwath, a *"young and rapidly growing expanding company"* advising pharmaceutical firms. By 1992 DAR employed a hundred people at its Carnwath HQ, doing clinical research, and 25 others at Cambridge.

**Bureaucracy Beaten over Blue Cheese**: Carnwath village contained only some 1350 people in 1991; though many were elderly, the primary school remained open (and still is). Meantime in 1994–95 Humphrey J Errington & Co of Braehead, 6km east of Carnwath in the very rural parish of Walston, employed seven people making *'Lanark Blue'* cheese, over which they fought and won a costly legal battle with the over-zealous public health officials of the doomed Clydesdale District, who had claimed that a hitherto harmless strain of listeria *(type 3b)* found in the cheese was a threat to public health.

## CARRADALE, Dippen & Saddell — Map 1, A1

*Kintyre e. coast village, pop. 575* — OS 68: NR 7938

About the year 1160 a small Cistercian abbey was founded near the mouth of the Saddell Water on the sheltered east coast of Kintyre by Somerled, Lord of the Isles. The community died out in the 15th century, but from 1507 to the Reformation Saddell was the seat of the Bishop of Lismore. About that time the keep of Saddell Castle was built at Port na Cuthaig, 1km south of the abbey. Pont's map made about 1600 marked the parish centre, abbey and castle as *'Sadael'*; north of the stream was *'Plock'*. Six kilometres to the north at the mouth of the Carradale Water stood *'Dupen'*, and on a point 2 km farther east was *'Ard Charadel'*, evidently Aird Castle, which later fell into ruins. Roy's map made about 1750 showed a continuous track along the wooded east coast of south Kintyre, and a bridge across the Carradale Water at Dupen or Dippen, which also became known as Bridgend. By then the mansion of Carradale House had been built. Stone from the former abbey was used to extend Saddell Castle about 1770, but only a tiny farming village existed nearby.

**Steamer Connections**: A post office named Glencarradale was in use by 1841. In the 1850s a ferry to Arran operated from near Aird Castle, but this seems to have been short-lasting, for in 1888 the Glasgow to Campbeltown steamers called at Lochranza, Pirnmill, Carradale and Saddell. The local centre of activity shifted decisively to Aird Carradale, where what Murray called the *"fair" Carradale Inn* was open by 1894. In 1900 the Carradale golf club was founded; it laid out a 9-hole course on a raised beach. By then Carradale had become a small resort and fishing harbour with a pier at the end of a spur road.

**Afforestation and Disaster at Sea**: In 1951, when the population was about 420, two hotels were open plus the usual facilities of a small village. The telephone exchange and Carradale post office were on the main road at Dippen, while the main village had Carradale East post office. By that time the hills of Kintyre were being extensively planted up by the Forestry Commission, whose yard was in Carradale, which gave its name to the forest. The population of Carradale proper fell to under 350 by 1971, but the *Carradale Hotel* acquired two stars and by 1985 there were caravan and camping sites in the vicinity. The golf course was described by Price in 1989 as *"very unsophisticated"*; it still has 9 holes. Meanwhile sea fishing had continued, but tragedy struck Carradale in 1990 when the local fishing vessel *Antares* was accidentally sunk by a British submarine on manoeuvres, with the loss of four lives. In 1992 the former Forestry Commission yard was converted into a visitor centre. The population has risen again, and there has been some recent development.

## CARRBRIDGE — Map 9, C4

*Inverness-shire village, pop. 550* — OS 36: NH 9022

The River Dulnain, a major tributary of the Spey, lies athwart the direct land route from the south to Inverness. Robert Gordon's map of the central Highlands, made about 1643, showed *'Ochterdair'* (perhaps meaning Auchterblair) as the most westerly name on the *'Avon Tulnen'*. The original Carr Bridge was built in 1717 at Lyne of Dalrochney by John Niccelsone, a mason. The military road built about 1730 under General Wade's direction crossed the Dulnain 4km farther west, at a point now known as Sluggan Bridge, before struggling northwards through the summit gorge of Slochd Mor to the upper Findhorn basin.

**Tracks and Roads**: The Roy map made some twenty years later named Wade's route the *'Kings road from Stirling to Inverness'*. A track led eastwards from the early bridge past the hamlets of Lochanchullie and Milltown to the Kirk of Duthil and *'Bridge of Dulcey'*. A branch track from Aviemore crossed a ford to Milltown and on to the Knock of Braemoray, another remote key node in the developing system of roads and tracks. When in the early 19th century Telford reconstructed Wade's crumbling military track into a proper coach road he elected to cross the Dulnain at the older Carr Bridge, where a post office was opened by 1838, and as the settlements coalesced this name became dominant.

**The Highland Railway's Cut-off and Washout**: In 1892 the Highland Railway (HR) opened the first part of its new and shortened main line to the south, at first worked as a branch from Aviemore to a temporary terminal station at Carr Bridge; by 1894 what Murray described as the *"comfortable" Carr Bridge Hotel* attracted visitors to this beautiful area. In 1897–98 the HR extended the line through a rock cutting with a summit of 401 m at Slochd and across a viaduct to Tomatin and Inverness, so greatly reducing the importance of the previous Forres dog-leg. The Baddengorm Burn washout (illustrated in *Nock, 1965)* occurred just north of the station in 1914; five people died and the present steel bridge had to be built.

**Tourist Development**: By 1953 the 55-room *Carr Bridge Hotel* existed, and two other hotels and a 9-hole golf course on river gravels were open; the resident population of Carr Bridge was about 400. The station escaped the Beeching cuts, and tourism grew with the opening of the Austrian Ski School of Karl Fuchs *(see Glenmore)*. The Landmark visitor centre, painfully built practically floating in a bog, and its associated nature trail, opened in 1970. In 1978 two garages, a tweed shop, craft centre and a fish and chip cafe could also be seen. While the Post Office retained the form *Carr Bridge* until at least 1970, nowadays the name is spelt Carrbridge.

**Bypassed but Busy**: The removal of through traffic with the construction of a lengthy new section of the A9 west of the village in the 1970s created a spectacular viaduct over the old road and the railway in the Slochd gorge, and stimulated further development. In 1979 the AA opened a new holiday centre with a swimming pool and 50 lodges at Lochanhully, 1km east of the bridge. The area population crept upwards to reach 550 by 1981, enjoying the facilities of a typical village, which served some 2250 people in a wide area extending from Tomatin to Boat of Garten. By 1990 the Nordic Ski School had been established on the Inverness road, 534 village residents were counted in 1991, and by 1992 the Landmark centre had added a steam-powered sawmill and an adventure playground. By 1999 a riverside mansion had become the *Dalrachney Lodge Hotel*; the *Carrbridge*, the *Fairwinds* and a small bunk-house for backpackers are also open.

## CARRON & Carronshore

**Map 16, B2**

*Urban area n. of Falkirk, pop. 3600* OS 65: NS 8882

The *'Stane House'*, originally probably a Roman temple which was to give its name to Stenhousemuir, stood near the River Carron as it meandered its way to the muddy estuary of the River Forth. It appeared on Timothy Pont's map of about 1600, under its alternative name of *'Arthursund'* (better known as *'Arthur's O'on')*. The map also showed the recently-built but already emparked tower of *'Skemuret'* or Skaithmuir Castle, later called Roughlands, a scatter of farms, and the emparked mansionhouse of Kinnaird where James Bruce was born in 1730; he became famous by exploring the sources of the Nile. By the time of the Roy map survey about 1754, a road led north from Falkirk past farms and Carron placenames, *'Standhouse Mill'* and a single dot labelled *'Stenhousemuir'* to an *'Engine'*, *'Whim'* and *'Collier Row'* north of the river in the vicinity of Kinnaird. Farther west on the north bank were *'sal pans'*; salt water must then have reached farther inland than now.

**Kingpin of the Industrial Revolution**: In 1758 two Englishmen and a Scot founded a company to produce iron by smelting the clayband ironstone lately discovered at Bo'ness: William Cadell was an East Lothian merchant, John Roebuck a scientist and Samuel Garbett an entrepreneur *(see Prestonpans)*. Impressed by the water-power potential of the River Carron, and the ready availability of coal and tidewater, they chose a riverside site some 3km north of Falkirk, where in 1759 they formed the Carron Company, one of the first large firms of the industrial revolution *(for illustrations see Hay & Stell)*.

**Coming on Stream**: The first two coke-using furnaces (1760) were built from English components and used water wheels to create blast, initially making pig iron and castings. The Carron Company employed 615 people in and around the works, including 244 miners in various small pits, some as far afield as Shieldhill. The works' output at that time went principally to Leith, Glasgow, Rutherglen, Bannockburn, Stirling and Northumberland *(for details of operations at that time see Campbell & Dow)*. Soon they were also casting sugar-boiling pans for West Indian sugar plantations; these were made at least as late as the 1870s. Among other products were cast-iron pots, pipes, and by 1771 stoves.

**Vandalism enables rapid Expansion**: Soon Carron had four furnaces, when other concerns had but one. In 1766 too the Carronhall coalmine was opened, connected by wagonway to the ironworks. The Stane House was most regrettably demolished about 1763 by the laird Sir Michael Bruce so that its ashlar stonework could line the Carron Works lade! The water power available was never adequate for the ambitions of the proprietors, and in 1767 James Watt was enlisted to add a steam pump with an 11-metre lift to recirculate 40 tonnes of water a minute to drive the many wheels; apparently the pump castings were made on site.

*The Carron Ironworks, founded in 1758, once led the industrial revolution in Scotland. This view shows the 1890s hand-charged blast furnaces, which operated until about 1963.(RCAHMS / JRH)*

**Pennant on Carron**: When Pennant visited Carron in 1769 he claimed that *"before 1759 there was not a single house, and the country a mere moor"*. Yet by the time of his visit 1200 men were employed, and 100 carts carried goods to Glasgow from Carron wharf, as against *"not three"* as recently as 1750. By Pennant's day a shipping company served the wharf at Carron, satisfying its growing needs for iron ore – which was also shipped through Charlestown from 1765 – and for limestone from Burntisland.

**Carron's Apogee**: In 1773 the firm – by then bossed by Charles Gascoigne, Garbett's manipulative son-in-law – received a Royal charter; still more coal was required, so a new shaft for Kinnaird Colliery was sunk in 1775. The firm also made agricultural implements, and by about 1780 were building Newcomen engines. Soon there were 1600 employees, 18 water wheels and also a blacking works *(Shaw gave a full eye-witness account.)* Following the success of William Symington's boat engine at Dalswinton, the Carron Company built a new engine of his design in 1789 for Miller's first mechanically propelled tug-boat which attained seven knots on the Forth & Clyde Canal in that year, a decade before the more famous *Charlotte Dundas*. This would seem to represent the firm's finest hour in terms of innovation. Carron House was built at Carronshore in the 18th century.

**The Carronade**: A patent cannon, the semi-rifled *'Carronade'* which played a part in the Napoleonic wars, was one of the Carron Company's most renowned products, along with the first devastating shrapnel shell. Heron wrote in 1799 *"the Carron Works are one of the greatest foundries in Europe"*. A hundred tonnes of coal was often burnt in the furnaces in one day, fanned by the water-powered bellows; a great quantity of cannon were *"exported to Russia, Germany and other foreign parts"*.

**Carron Supreme**: Dorothy Wordsworth wrote in 1803 of *"the Carron Ironworks, seen at a distance; – the sky above them was red with a fiery light"*. The firm armed HMS *Victory* in

1805. The works were connected by a tramway to the Forth and Clyde Canal in 1810, and by a canal to Carronshore; later a 5 km canal was cut to Grangemouth. Carron was never a burgh; a co-operative store opened in the 1820s and its first post office, at Carronshore, opened around the same time. Chambers noted in 1827 *"the celebrated CARRON IRON WORKS, the largest manufactory of the kind in the world. All kinds of cast-iron goods are made here; the reflection of the furnaces upon the sky in a cloudy night can be seen at an immense distance, and even the noise of the bellows can be heard a good way off."* Faced by rapidly growing competition, about 1840 a new steam engine was introduced to drive some of the machinery directly. Eventually connected to the railway system, probably in the late 1840s, they made *'Carronade'* guns until 1852.

**Industrial Mammoth**: Water power was still in use in 1868, exploited through a new turbine. Even after a century of intensive and wasteful production some of the raw materials were still able to be mined in the immediate vicinity. There were five blast furnaces and Carron was the largest foundry in Scotland, but Bremner found the firm secretive, its unmodernised premises *"ragged and smoke-begrimed"* and Watt's great engine lay derelict. Production appeared confused and bewildering, casting anything *"from a spittoon to the cylinders of a 200-horsepower engine"*, including much domestic ironware; its reputation then rested mainly on stoves, grates and cooking ranges. Sixteen canal boats, and six steamers, carried its products far afield: by that time there was a dedicated Carron wharf in London for receipt of the company's products.

**Politically Incorrect Company Modernises at Last**: Five villages were considered to be dependent on the works, which in 1868 employed a stable *'Scottish-only'* workforce of nearly 2000 men and boys; the company had recently provided a school. During slumps the works carried on, putting production into stock. New red sandstone offices were provided by the Carron Company in 1876 and four new blast furnaces were built about 1890. These were *"celebrated"* and *"blazing"* in 1894 when the firm's replacement steamer, the SS *Carron* was built at Dundee; in 1907 the company even built a ship at Carron, the SS *Avon*, and up to 1908 they also operated a dozen or more small canal steamers. By then Stenhouse Castle stood in a small park, adjoined by the great pond which served the Carron Works; the population of Carron was nearing 2000. The Mungal foundry at Bainsford was added by the Carron company in 1897.

**Coming Clean**: The Union Chemical Company of Carronshore was set up in 1923 by Robert Ross of Scottish Tar Distillers (at Camelon). Reactivated in 1946 by his son, it grew into Scotland's largest maker of cleaning materials. In 1975 the firm established Scottish Fine Soaps, and by 1979 the two firms shared a 4000 m² factory and employed 150 people, producing toilet soaps and exporting them to over 30 countries.

**Carron Company's Phone Finale**: Most of the red-painted but ill-ventilated and clammy telephone kiosks of the early and mid 20th century – some of which are now listed buildings – were made at Carron, followed by cast iron pillarboxes, gas stoves and baths into the 1970s. The 1890s iron furnaces were eventually closed in 1963, beaten by age and the inexorable advance of technology. Stenhouse Castle was demolished in 1968, and Carron House was largely destroyed by fire; it was a ruin by 1980. The ancient company lingered on towards eventual failure in 1982, when the last 600 jobs were lost. The Carron area had about 3500 people then, but the facilities of a small village.

**Carron Phoenix**: After a management buyout of the failed Carron Company in 1982 it became known as Carron Phoenix, which made Steeline baths and soon built up a strong market position in steel and high-tech composite sinks, with a third of the UK market in 1989, when its production facilities were increased. In 1990 it claimed to be the leading UK producer and exporter of kitchen sinks. At that time the old company's headquarters building with its collection of *'carronades'* still existed, but was to be moved about 30 m to clear space for housing, for although the population in 1991 was still about 3600, Beazer Homes were starting to develop a substantial estate of private houses east of the works. In 1994 Carron Phoenix was bought out by Franke of Germany. By 1998 most of the former ponds west of the works had vanished.

## CARRON & Dailuaine

**Map 10, A2**

***Speyside hamlet**, pop. 150*

OS 28: NJ 2241

Carron lies in a deep valley beside the middle reaches of the River Spey, 5 km west of Aberlour. The site south of the river later occupied by Carron House was probably the place named as *'Koryg'* by Pont about 1600; his sketch map indicated the area as richly wooded. The Roy map showed that it remained remote and roadless in the mid 18th century. Eventually a turnpike was constructed between Aberlour and Ballindalloch; on the north bank a road was built eastwards from Knockando to Wester Elchies, and a bridge connected the two a little west of Carron House; but Carron had no post office until after 1838.

**Dailuaine Distillery and the Railway**: Dailuaine distillery was established on the Carron Burn in 1851 by a Mackenzie. Then came the Great North of Scotland Railway's line from Craigellachie to Grantown, opened in 1863 and crossing the river by a cast-iron arch forming a combined rail and road bridge, one of a select few; Carron station was placed on the north side of the river. The distillery was rebuilt on a much larger scale about 1880–85 to use local Morayshire barley, water and steam power to produce over 700,000 litres of whisky per year; it was for a time the largest Highland Malt distillery and had its own siding connection.

**Imperial Distillery**: Then came the Imperial distillery, founded by Thomas Mackenzie of the Dailuaine-Talisker Company and built on the north bank of the river near the station in 1897. The Carron Warehouse Bonding Company was formed in 1898 by the same agent and others; later a railway halt was opened at Imperial Cottages. In 1916 the owners of Dailuaine-Talisker sold out to a combination of DCL, Dewar, Walker and Lowrie, itself owned by Buchanan! Dailuaine halt was opened there in 1933. By 1951 Carron had a population of almost 300.

**Lost Rails and Modern Carron**: The delightfully located railway which might have been developed as a tourist attraction was instead closed by Beeching in the mid 1960s. It was later converted to a long-distance footpath, the Speyside Way. Meantime the population had shrunk rapidly to a mere 150 people in 1981. The primary school vanished, as did the post office about 1990. Meantime the Imperial distillery was mothballed by DCL about 1983; it was later sold by their successors United Distillers and brought back into production in 1989 by Allied

Lyons. Dailuaine distillery was in full production for United Distillers in 1991, and finding it difficult to avoid discharging polluting effluent.

## CARRON BRIDGE **Map 16, A2**

***W. Stirlingshire locality,*** *pop. under 100* OS 57 or 64: NS 7483

Standing stones mark the head of the upper Carron valley; 3 km to the north-east where the Endrick Water leaves the Fintry Hills is a motte, beside which until the late 20th century stood a ruin known as Sir John de Graham's Castle. When Timothy Pont mapped the area about 1600 he showed this as Dundaff Castle. There was already a mill (now Muirmill) at the high altitude of about 200 metres at the mouth of the Earlsburn, and a little farther down was *'Carron Ford'*. Pont showed no roads, though an *'Old Brigg'* crossed the river near Buckieside some 2 km downstream. From 1695 the Glasgow to Stirling road crossed the river by means of a new bridge sited near the ford, and the old bridge was abandoned; the new bridge was rebuilt in 1715. This *'Carron Bridge'* was shown on the Roy map of about 1754, by which time there was also a road between Fintry and Falkirk. Eventually the main traffic from Glasgow to Stirling transferred to the Denny route, but by 1894 a post office and inn stood beside the Carronbridge. The bridge was rebuilt in 1907 and although the post office had gone by 1955 the inn survived. Meantime by mid century the great Carron Valley Reservoir had been created by two dams – at the east to retain the Carron and at the west to prevent an overspill into Strathendrick – and the previously bare hills around had been afforested.

## CARRONBRIDGE & Durisdeer **Map 2, B3**

***Dumfriesshire (Nithsdale) hamlets,*** *pop. 250* OS 78: NX 8798

North of modern Thornhill, the River Nith traverses a long and very narrow valley. Its tributary the Carron Water rises in the Lowther Hills to the east, and drains a more fertile farming area. At the confluence was a Roman fort. Two medieval mottes adjoin the Carron Water, at Enoch 5 km north-east of Thornhill, the other at Durisdeer being 3 km upstream. A secluded side valley contains the tiny artificial Morton Loch. This was impounded to defend the spectacular late 15th century Morton Castle – once the seat of the powerful family of that name – which it protects on three sides. The first and second Dukes of Queensberry *(see Drumlanrig)* are buried in a splendid mausoleum in Durisdeer Church. The Nithside road between Dumfries and Glasgow, built in 1714–15, crosses the Carron Water near the Roman fort by the Carronbridge. In 1850 a post office was opened at Durisdeer, which also had a mill on the Carron Water. The Glasgow & South Western Railway main line was opened in 1850, the so-called Carronbridge station being at Enoch, due to the devious and costly route dictated by the Buccleuch estate. By the 1950s the extensive area had about 630 people; Durisdeer had gained a primary school and telephone exchange, but the population was falling fast and its post office closed in the 1970s. By the 1960s Carronbridge station had lately closed, but it still had a primary school in 1977. By 1980 only about 270 residents remained in the farming valley. By 1995 even Carronbridge post office had closed, and Morton Castle, one of the most romantically sited ruins in Scotland, is little visited.

## CARRUTHERSTOWN, Dalton & Mouswald **Map 2, B4**

***Small Dumfriesshire villages,*** *pop. 1200* OS 85: NY 1071

About 10 km north-west of Annan between the Kirks of *'Meikle Datoun'* and *'Litil Datoun'* with its motte, was the now vanished *'Datoun Loch'*, which with two attendant mills appeared on Blaeu's map made from Pont's original of around 1610. When Roy mapped the area about 1754 its most conspicuous features were Hoddom Moor, the Kirk of *'Mousall'* and the turnpike road between Annan and Dumfries. Dalton gained a barony charter in 1755. Some 2.5 km south-west of Dalton was the Carrutherstown crossroads, where in 1832 William Cobbett outspokenly noted *"a long scattering village (where) the little Scotchies seem absolutely to swarm"*. By 1895 there was nothing much there but a smithy and a post office. The population of the local area gradually sank, to about 460 by 1981, by which time Dalton primary school had recently closed, leaving just a kirkton; but Carrutherstown itself had grown somewhat and gained the facilities of a small village, including an inn, serving in all some 1250 people. By 1996 Carrutherstown had been bypassed but kept its primary school; its two hotels include the emparked Georgian style, 30-room *Hetland Hall*.

## CARSPHAIRN **Map 2, A4**

***Dumfriesshire hamlet,*** *pop. 180* OS 77: NX 5693

Carsphairn stands solitary on the Stewartry uplands 180 m above sea level, beside a tributary of the Water of Ken. There are prehistoric cairns nearby, and its name suggests a Cumbric fortified place, but its early history is little known. The Pont map of the Stewartry made about 1600 showed only names identifiable with farmsteads: Garryhorn, Knockgray and Carnavel. Carsphairn Kirk had been built between them by the time that the Roy map was surveyed around 1754, standing at the meeting point of tracks from New Galloway and Moniaive to Dalmellington, by way of the two Brigs of Deuch and the Brig of Ken. Robert Heron, a native of New Galloway, writing in 1799 mentioned Carsphairn as a *"village"*, but in 1827 Chambers found it was *"a little clachan; a few scattered houses, with its kirk"*.

**Resource Development more Wind than Winnings**: Lead, copper, silver and zinc were discovered at Woodhead 3 km to the west, and in the 19th century mines were opened; these were apparently closed between 1953 and 1963. By then a hydro power scheme had been built at Kendoon Loch south-east of the tiny village, sadly destroying a picturesque gorge. The population of the area fell from 250 in 1951 to only some 180 by 1981, with minimal village facilities. By 1990 the inn had been closed and the primary school had a roll of only 24 pupils, yet for some arcane reason no new dwellings were permitted by the regional council, merely replacements. By 1997 Scotland's second extensive wind farm, one of Europe's largest, crowned the remote 700 m hills of Carsphairn Forest at the aptly named Windy Standard, 10 km north-east *(see also Douglas)*, and by 1998 a heritage centre was open in the tiny village.

## CARSTAIRS

**Map 16, B5**

***Lanarkshire village,*** *pop. 800* OS 72: NS 9346

Lying 2 km north-east of the first and second century Roman fort of Castledykes and the line of its attendant road is Carstairs; the *Caer-* element in the name suggests a Cumbric fortification, but Carstairs, 6 km east of Lanark, seems not to have played a significant role in history. A parish school was opened in 1619, not long after Timothy Pont made a mess of mapping the Carstairs area. So we have to look to Roy's survey of about 1754 for a glimpse of what was already a sizeable though irregularly formed farming village on the Lanark to Carnwath and Edinburgh road; another road led to Carluke, crossing a bridge at Cowford. Carstairs was chartered as a burgh of barony in 1765, but although having three annual fairs in 1797 it was not important enough to merit a post office until the penny post of 1840.

**From Mansion to Institution**: The mansion of Carstairs House was built in 1821–24 for Henry Monteith to pretentious Tudor Gothic designs by William Burn. It rose beside the Roman road over 1.5 km south of the village, and around it a great park was laid out beside the Clyde. In 1848 the Caledonian Railway placed its station 1250 m east of the village, where most growth took place at the untidy new settlement of Strawfrank (now Carstairs Junction, *q.v.*). However by 1895 there were both an inn and post office at the original compact village. By 1954 the population of Carstairs was under a thousand and Carstairs House had become the St Charles Institution. By 1971 this was a hospital, but was converted into a private nursing home in 1987, under the name Monteith House.

**Road-Rail Conflict**: In 1980 large sandpits were open near Carstairs, which remained a quiet village plus active car dealers; its post office was still open in 1988. Ravenstruther, 1.5 km to the west, had long-standing glasshouses, a post office and a caravan site. A new coal transhipment point was built nearby in 1989 for Derek Crouch, to transfer coal brought by road from opencast workings at Coalburn into rail wagons. In 1992 much coal was despatched by rail to power stations in the north and midlands of England, but the West Coast Main Line still conflicts with the local roads at two level crossings.

## CARSTAIRS JUNCTION

**Map 16, C5**

***Lanarkshire village,*** *pop. 860* OS 72: NS 9545

Some time after Roy mapped the area about 1754, a ferry known as Float was started across the middle River Clyde to link Carnwath with the old parish centre of Pettinain. In 1848 Float gave its name to a station, created near Strawfrank Farm 1250 m east of Carstairs, but west of the triangle where the Caledonian Railway's Glasgow and Edinburgh lines met, north of the new Clyde rail bridge. By 1869 there were railway *'workshops'*, and in 1867 an upland branch railway was opened through to Dolphinton, entering the station – which had been renamed Carstairs – by bridging over one side of what by the 1890s was a double triangular junction. By 1894 the station refreshment rooms also functioned as a hotel. The village of Strawfrank which developed to serve the various rail facilities had a population of 900 in 1901. A road and bridge was built in the 1920s to link Strawfrank with Pettinain, and the ferry closed.

**From Railway Village to a Custodial Role**: After the 1923 Grouping the LMS Railway installed water troughs south of Strawfrank Junction to enable steam-hauled trains to take water without stopping. About then the State Hospital for the criminally insane (an ultra-secure prison) was built on the Carnwath road only 1 km to the east. The decline of local railways under bus competition caused the end of the Dolphinton passenger service in 1933, and by 1955 the whole branch line had been lifted. By 1951 Carstairs and Strawfrank (by then called Carstairs Junction) shared village facilities and had a combined population of 2600, including the hospital inmates. Around 1960 the State Hospital was further expanded with a compound east of the Edinburgh railway. The closure of Carstairs locomotive shed at the end of steam in the late 1960s led to population decline, though the station remained open; in 1974 it became the changeover point where Edinburgh trains left the newly electrified West Coast main line and were coupled to diesels.

**All Trains Electric, but Services Sink**: An inn and post office remained in 1988, as the heavily guarded institution became ever more dominant in the local scene. In 1990 the State Hospital contained 216 dangerously disturbed patients and employed about 400 staff; in 1992 it was transferred to the NHS and in 1993 provided secure psychiatric care for the whole of Scotland and Northern Ireland. Meantime electrification of the Edinburgh line was completed in 1991; with fast through trains replacing the locomotive changeover, and a local population of only 860, the stopping train service was reduced to a token level. In 1994 the last daily train to Edinburgh was withdrawn, but a single service was reinstated later in the year. In 1999 some timber was loaded onto rail at Carstairs Junction, where there is still a base for maintenance of the track and overhead power supply.

## CASTLEBAY (Barra) & Vatersay

**Map 7, A5**

***Main village, & small island,*** *pop. 1325 (total)* OS 31: NL 6698

About 1120 the Clan MacNeil began to build Kiessimul Castle on an islet in a bay on their remote Outer Hebridean Isle of Barra, sheltered by the small offshore island of Vatersay. Monro in 1549 found the largely 15th century Castle *"upon a strengthy crag"*. He believed that Barra was *"a fertile and fruitful isle in corn, abounding in the fishing of keilling, ling and all other white fish, with a parish church named Kilbare"*. Monro also referred to a chapel on Vatersay, which belonged to the Bishop of the Isles and was *"abounding in corn and grass, with good pasturage for sheep and an excellent road* [i.e. anchorage] *for ships that come there to fish"*.

**Dark Deeds**: When Martin visited around 1700, Barra had already abandoned any attempt to adopt Protestantism. The castle, which he described, was still the seat of the MacNeils until 1747 when they left for Eoligarry, but after some seven centuries of use it burned out in 1795. There was no post office on the Catholic island of Barra as late as 1838. Barra and adjacent isles were bought in 1840 by the heartless and greedy absentee laird, Colonel John Gordon of Cluny. Many of Barra's people had been cleared by 1851, with the connivance of his singularly unpleasant factor who sullied the otherwise honourable name of Fleming. Cluny died rich but locally unlamented in 1856.

**After the Clearances the Fishing**: From 1869 James Methuen developed Castlebay – *Bagh A'Chaistell* in Gaelic – as a herring fishing station with packing and curing facilities, soon the base for over 400 small boats. A prominent Church of Scotland was hopefully built in 1892–93. By 1894 a steamer plied to Oban three times a week, and Murray noted the *"good" Castle Bay Hotel*. As late as Edwardian times the bay would be crowded with fishing smacks, and Castlebay became quite a substantial village. A lifeboat station opened in 1931, infilling the huge gap in coverage between Machrihanish and Stornoway. But the over-fishing of herring killed the industry, leaving little but crofting by the 1930s, though the Berneray lightkeepers' families later lived in Castlebay.

**Flying back to the Castle – and Whisky Galore**: With accessibility by air *(see Northbay)* came the American architect Robert L MacNeil who became head of the Clan MacNeill, and began in 1938 to restore the castle as his home. The Isle of Barra was really put on the map by Compton Mackenzie's famous book *Whisky Galore (see Eriskay)*, filmed on the island in 1949 (but called *Tight Little Island* in the USA). By then typical village facilities existed, including three hotels, a secondary school and a population of 600; Gaelic was still the usual local language. By 1971 the population had shrunk rapidly to some 350, but the restoration of the castle was completed in 1970. Around that time submarine cables were laid to bring electricity from South Uist, also extended to Vatersay.

**Tangasdale, Tourism and the Vatersay Link**: By 1976 the 41-room *Isle of Barra Hotel* had been built with major support from the HIDB near a trout loch and white sands at Tangasdale, 3 km north-west of Castlebay, and a perfume factory had been established nearby. In 1979 the current MacNeil, an American lawyer, offered to sell half the island to the occupiers. The population of Castlebay had recovered to some 425 in 1981 and 1325 for the Barra islands cluster. By the 1980s lobster and crab fishing had replaced herrings, and a car ferry had ousted the steamers. Despite a reduction in Castlebay's own hotels to two there were some guest houses, and for its size good shopping facilities, a small hospital, schools and a bank. The causeway forming a fixed road link between Barra and the Isle of Vatersay with its 120 or so beef-rearing and lobster-fishing people was completed in 1990. Boarding at Stornoway for senior pupils ended in 1992 when Castlebay High School was upgraded to sixth-year status; in 1997 it had 103 pupils. The Clan MacNeil museum was also extended. This is within the castle, which is now cared for by Historic Scotland and opened to visitors; however the Church of Scotland building was at risk in 1997. The *Isle of Barra Hotel* at Tangasdale now has 30 rooms.

## CASTLE DOUGLAS & Carlingwark — Map 2, A5

***Galloway small town,** pop. 3700* — OS 84: NX 7662

Early developments in this area of the Stewartry are described under Kelton. Carlingwark, a name implying an early stone building or *'wark'* adjoining Carlingwark Loch, was marked on Pont's map. North of the loch was *'Causayend'*, later spelled Causeway End. This evidence of a paved road east of the Dee implies that Pont's visit to this area was made after the Union of the Crowns, for what appears on modern OS maps as *Old Military Road* was apparently built to facilitate the plantation of Ulster in 1608–10. The Old Bridge of Urr already spanned the Urr Water 6 km north of Causeway End. An inn was open at Carlingwark by 1636. The classical Greenlaw House was built for Robert Gordon in 1741 2 km north-west of Causewayend. The Roy map made about 1754 showed an area of farms and hamlets traversed by the military road; a track from north of Carlingwark led to Old Bridge of Urr. In 1765 the loch level was lowered to enable marl to be dug for manuring farmland, and Carlingwark post office was opened in 1773.

**The New Village**: William Douglas of Penninghame, who – like Kelton Hill's founder – started life as a pedlar *(see Newton Stewart)* and ended with a knighthood, acquired Carlingwark in 1789, and in 1791 obtained a charter for *Castle Douglas* as a very late burgh of barony. He named it after himself in the fashion of the day, and had it laid out to a rectilinear but effective plan more or less on the site of Carlingwark, whose postal address was changed to Castle Douglas in 1792. It made a meteoric start, for around 1793 the Paisley Union Banking Company had a branch there for a time. Castle Douglas was a post town by 1797, with a scheduled fair; the role of Kelton Hill which still had two fairs in that year was apparently soon taken over, and a cotton mill was built at Castle Douglas. Heron's map, engraved in 1796 showed only Carlingwark, but his 1799 text mentioned both the loch, containing *"an inexhaustible treasure of the finest and best shell-marl"*, and also *"the rising village or town of Castle Douglas, having upwards of 700 inhabitants, and several branches of manufacture"*.

**Speedy Success in Industry and Services**: A foundry was at work in the new town early in the 19th century. The large mansion called Gelston Castle, 4 km south, was built of red sandstone for Sir William Douglas about 1805 to designs by Richard Crichton. In 1806 Douglas founded the local Galloway Banking Company, which by 1810 had branches in Dumfries and Kirkcudbright; it went into decline and had to cease trading in 1821, but other banks and facilities rapidly moved in. By 1825 James Hewetson had built a brewery, and in 1827 Chambers noted *"the considerable village of Castle-Douglas, formerly called Carlinwark"* whose 1000 or so people were *"chiefly employed in weaving"*. He overlooked the fast-growing service element; by the 1830s the post office had no fewer than nine sub-offices, and a Bank of Scotland branch opened about 1840. A gasworks was set up in 1843, and the local newspaper the *Galloway News* was established in 1858.

**The Country Railway Junction**: A branch of the Glasgow & South Western Railway from Dumfries was opened in 1859 and was soon extended across the moss at Carlingwark Lane by means of a timber viaduct, opening as a single line through to Kirkcudbright in 1864. The *Douglas Arms Hotel* was open by 1861, the year when Castle Douglas became the junction for the Portpatrick Railway to Stranraer, also single track throughout; but it never became an important rail centre because most trains on both lines ran through to and from Dumfries. By 1894 Castle Douglas was *"a busy country town with a good market"* and the *"commercial, comfortable" Douglas Arms Hotel*. Castle Douglas golf club was formed in 1905 and laid out a 9-hole course. About 1930 the Glenlochar barrage was built across the Dee at Townhead of Greenlaw 4 km north-west of the town as part of the Galloway hydro-electric scheme *(see Tongland)*. Gelston Castle was gutted in 1950 and derelict by 1980, but by the 1950s the compactly developed town was the main local centre of the Stewartry, despite its modest population of only about 3500. It had become a minor tourist centre with a pleasant lochside park and caravan and camping site; by 1953 the out of town mansion of Ernespie had become the 15-roomed *Ernespie House Hotel*.

**Surviving Dr Beeching**: However, the station – and the entire railway system of the Stewartry – were regrettably totally closed by Beeching in 1965, its great tourist potential untapped. Although by 1980 a new school had been built, various other facilities had closed, for a time reducing the town's general status. However, by 1979 Gordon James Engineers were producing dairy utensils and equipment. In 1981 the town had about ten hotels and inns, and was still an important agricultural market; this helped its recovery. Another out of town mansion, Greenlaw House, by then used as a hotel, was less fortunate, being gutted by fire around 1980; it still awaited a new use in 1997.

**Child Leukaemia the Price of War?**: In 1986 Castle Douglas was an attractive high-quality shopping centre with professional services of many kinds, and a swimming pool; it was also virtually unique at the time in having regained a cinema, after both those it once possessed were closed. By 1991, when the town had 3697 residents, the *Galloway News* had combined with a Dumfries paper to become the *Dumfries Galloway News*, though it retained a local office. It was feared in 1993 that the test firing at the Dundrennan *(q.v.)* range in recent years of many shells tipped with depleted uranium was the cause for the Castle Douglas postcode sector now suffering the highest rate of childhood leukaemia in Scotland, and that news of this deplorable practice – recommenced in 2001 – was also damaging the tourist industry.

**Farming and Tourism**: By 1989 Robertson's of Dumfries had opened a branch knitwear factory. By 1990 Castle Douglas had an A75 bypass road, and was the headquarters of the Galloway Cattle Society; Castle Douglas High School has around 500 pupils. Sadly by 2000 little but the finely built walls remained of Gelston House. The Castle Douglas slaughterhouse – the last in south-west Scotland – is to reopen in 2001 under new owners Buccleauch Estates, and Wallets Marts are still active with livestock. The golf course still has only 9 holes; small/medium hotels include the *Douglas Arms, Imperial, King's Arms*, and the *Urr Valley* (2 km north-east).

## CASTLE KENNEDY & Innermessan — Map 1, B4

***Galloway village & hamlet**, pop. 400* — OS 82: NX 1059

At some prehistoric time a cairn was raised in the low-lying area between the Rhinns and Machers of Galloway west of Soulseat Loch, on the south shore of which Fergus, Lord of Galloway, founded the little known Soulseat Abbey in 1148. A medieval motte was raised on the coast at Innermessan, where the Kirclachie Burn entered Loch Ryan. This place gained a charter as a burgh of barony in 1426, accompanied 1 km inland by a large castle of similar date. The charter of more sheltered Stranraer in 1595 ended its development hopes, and the castle became ruinous.

**The Mills of Castle Kennedy**: In 1607 the fifth Earl of Cassilis built the grim tower of Castle Kennedy near an ancient church some 4 km south-east of Innermessan, between the Black and White Lochs. Pont's map of Galloway made about 1610 showed two water mills. One stood on the Soulseat Burn below the former abbey, whose buildings were given little emphasis and later vanished; the other was on the Bishop Burn at *'Bishopston'* near Innermessan. This was marked on the Roy map made about 1754 as the Sand Mill, beside a track linking Stranraer with Cairnryan. Roy also showed the military road built early in the 17th century from Dumfries to Portpatrick, which passed between the Soulseat and White Lochs, throwing off spurs to Castle Kennedy, which had gained fine landscaped policies laid out by the Earl of Stair to embrace the two lochs, then been ruined in the 1715 rebellion.

**The Railway creates a Village**: From 1861 Castle Kennedy had a station on the Portpatrick Railway (later the Portpatrick & Wigtownshire Joint). Castle Kennedy was replaced in 1867 by a new baronial mansion named Lochinch Castle. A small village grew beside the station, and in World War II a military airfield was laid out to the east; it survived seemingly out of use for half a century. Castle Kennedy had a post office and primary school by 1951, serving a scattered population of over 650. But despite some housebuilding near the station, closed by Beeching in the mid 1960s, only 400 people remained by 1981, although by then the small *Eynhallow Hotel* was open. The school and post office survive, and the Castle Kennedy gardens at Soulseat Loch are a visitor attraction beside the Southern Upland Way.

## CASTLEMILK — Map 16, D6

***Urban area w. of Glasgow**, pop. 18,000* — OS 64: NS 6059

A 13th century tower house and its appendages 2 km south of Rutherglen was known until 1579 as *'Castletown of Carmunnock'*, because it lay in Carmunnock parish. About 1460 the tower was rebuilt for the Stuarts of Castlemilk estate south of Lockerbie in Dumfriesshire, who renamed it *'Castlemilk'* in 1579 when they sold their former property and moved to Carmunnock. The castle stood within a network of roads by the time of the Roy survey of the mid 18th century, and was much altered into the mansion of Castlemilk House in 1841 (though retaining *antique* lettering on OS maps). The area was entirely rural as late as 1931.

**The Heavy Hand of Glasgow**: Glasgow Corporation bought the attractive rural estate south of the Burnside to Simshill road in 1935; the remainder was compulsorily acquired in 1938, by which time private suburban housing extended from Croftfoot station in Rutherglen up to this road. The Castlemilk housing estate was commenced in 1953, the tenants at first enjoying what appeared by Glasgow standards to be a quite good environment. The estate was provided with a shopping centre of over 5000 m$^2$, with a swimming pool and facilities, in general those of a large village; but no hotel was permitted. This misguided policy, plus the lack of local workplaces created by a combination of conurbation-wide decline and land-use segregation dogma, inhibited community development; many people drifted back to drink with friends in the Gorbals or Bridgeton at the weekend.

**From High Hopes to Social and Economic Disaster Area**: By 1959 poorly kept houses, poverty and decline were very evident, but worse was to come. For a time Castlemilk House became a children's home, but it was pulled down in 1969. About 1966 Millers opened a large clothing factory, at last providing some local work, though few jobs for men. By 1971 37,000 people lived in the huge scheme, but lack of work took its toll through emigration, and the population had fallen to

*A Castlemilk street, showing typical 1950s tenement blocks – built to house people from the inner city slums of Glasgow.* *(JRH)*

some 29,000 in 1981, by which time Castlemilk had plenty disadvantages. Being surrounded by golf courses, and with its proximity to East Kilbride, it might appear not to have plumbed the depths of deprivation of some of the other overspill schemes.

**Partnership against Deprivation**: However, in 1987 Castlemilk was one of the four downcast estates chosen by the Scottish Office for government-led partnership schemes aimed at securing improvements, and tackling its already endemic drug and alcohol problems. The population had already fallen to about 20,000 when a further blow struck: Millers' factory had passed to Coats Viyella by 1991, when it provided about 500 jobs as *'CV Childrens Wear'*, but the factory was then closed as a result of the slump: politicians and planners alike had utterly failed the local people. By then the lack of so much as a supermarket in the understandably run-down shopping centre also made headlines, only 25 of the 55 units remaining in use. It was inevitable that in 1993 Castlemilk still suffered from appreciable drugs problems. By then a Local Development company for the area was in being; it remained to be seen whether it could change the area's downbeat character. In 1995 with a remaining population of 18,000, the fruits of a five-year regeneration strategy seemed to lie mainly in improved housing and the arts, including a folk festival. In 1997 Castlemilk High School had 664 pupils. The general atmosphere is now better.

## CASTLE SWEEN, Kilmory& Achahoish — Map 4, C4

***Argyll hamlets,*** *pop. 150* — OS 62: NR 7178

Loch Sween on the remote west coast of Knapdale has the ruins of ancient forts, and the source of the hard metamorphic rock known as chloritic schist, from which many medieval and earlier monuments were made by a locally well-developed economy. There is an early chapel at Kilmory Knap, with a fine collection of medieval crosses and grave-slabs; some 5km to the north is the ancient Dun Rostan, now hidden in a wood. On the shore between these points stands the ruined 12th century Castle Sween, one of Scotland's oldest stone castles. This is itself some 16km south of Bellanoch by a narrow winding track, now a road, which was shown on the Roy map of about 1750, when it turned east on a now vanished route to the clachan of Achahoish at the head of Loch Caolisport. In 1852 there was a post office named *'Kilbride Loch Sween'*, a spot now hard to find. In the 1950s tiny Achahoish had a post office, primary school, inn and 6-line telephone exchange. By 1981 this and its inn had closed, but beside Castle Sween was a caravan site. This too had closed by 1997, leaving the primary school at Achahoish as the sole facility of note in this extensive rural area of lumpy hills and part-wooded rocky coasts.

## CASTLETOWN & Kirkton of Olrig — Map 13, B4

***Caithness village,*** *pop. 1000* — OS 12: ND 1967

Castletown on Dunnet Bay, 8km east of Thurso in Caithness, has the ruins of a broch and of an apparently undated castle. Pont's map shows that by about 1600 there was a *'Mylhil'*, implying a windmill, near *'Olric'*, the parish name. Roy's map of about 1750 showed Kirkton of Olrig, Garth and Stanriggill as the main settlements in the area. Olrig House was built by stages in the 18th and 19th centuries. In 1824 James Traill of Rattar near Dunnet *(q.v.)* founded Castletown, laying it out to a regular plan. The village was built of local stone from a new quarry, which worked a stratum of sandstone that can readily be split into flat slabs suitable for paving. By about 1830 the new harbour at Castletown – itself flagstone-built – was shipping out the dressed slabs.

**The Flagstone Industry peaks – and Fails**: Castletown had a post office by 1838, and was noted by Bremner in 1869 as a *"large and thriving village"* with a public hall and several schools. Both water and steam powered Traill's large Castlehill Quarry, where Bremner found some 375 quarry workers and a *'railway'* to the harbour, from which flagstones were shipped as far afield as Argentina; but no connection was ever made to the main rail system. An inn was open by 1894, when – though its population did not reach 1000 – Murray wrote of Castletown as *"a village of considerable size"*. The pavings were then *"prepared by steam-power"*; five coaches ran daily to Thurso and one to Wick. The peak flagstone year was 1902, when over 35,000 tonnes were shipped through the local harbour; but by 1925 the new and easily laid precast concrete paving slabs had killed the natural stone pavings industry. A wartime airfield was built 2 km to the east; in 1940 it was a fighter base. In 1951 the Castletown area still had over 800 people and typical village facilities.

**Frosty Success Grant-aided?**: The firm of Norfrost was started in the mid 1960s, when local TV shop owners Alex and Pat Grant made domestic freezers in their spare bedroom. Moving in 1972 to nissen huts on the village outskirts, but suffering power cuts, they installed their own factory power plant. Remoteness led to other self-sufficiency measures such as jig- and tool-making. Soon Norfrost employed 40 people, standardised, prospered and won awards. Castletown developed with a new small motel, hotel extensions, and new houses, its population passing 1000. The factory was expanded in 1988 by erecting a new shell over the existing sheds, and in 1989 employed 250 people making 5000 freezers a week, largely for export. Business acumen secured a favourable deal on compressors, the most costly component, and a contract for cabinets for Coca-Cola; further expansion was planned.

**Freezers for Mars**: Though the secondary school had closed by 1976, the population held steady, retaining skilled workers made redundant by Dounreay. In 1991 Castletown had 1028

*Windmill tower, Castletown. This windmill drove pumps to drain the Castlehill Flagstone Quarries, founded in the early 19th century by a Mr Traill.* *(JRH)*

residents; a *'Flagstone Trail'* interpretive centre had been created on the site of a former quarry near the harbour. However, in 1993 a US Navy communications base at nearby Murkle which employed some 20 Scottish workers was closed. In 1995 Norfrost again extended the factory to make tumble dryers, and in 1997 when 400 people were employed, Pat Grant announced a 150-job expansion to make still more. Freezers were still in world-wide demand from Mars and Coca-Cola; 75% of output went for export. Meantime in 1996 the fine harbour with its wide quays and slipway was almost disused, but in 2000 Castletown was the base for Cormac, a major livestock haulier. There is a local hotel.

## CATHCART & Holmhead — Map 15, C6

***Suburb of Glasgow,*** *pop. 25,000* — OS 64: NS 5860

The 15th century Cathcart Castle stood in a thickly settled area 5 km south of Glasgow. Nearby was a kirk and a bridge over the White Cart Water, the latter apparently built between 1596 when Timothy Pont surveyed Clydesdale, and the rather later date of his Renfrewshire map; the Netherlee Road bridge was probably rebuilt in 1624. Meantime a parish school was founded in 1603. Nicholas de Champ built the area's first paper mill in 1686–87, followed in 1716 by a second, at Millholme. Roy's map showed that by the 1750s *Holmhead* was a compact medium sized settlement on the main Kilmarnock road, with other radial roads; about 1800 a hump-backed bridge was built across the River Cart.

**Cardboard, Snuff and Coupers' Textiles**: By 1816 a post office was open in Cathcart, served by a penny post from Glasgow. The 17th century meal mill at Cathcart was rebuilt in 1812–14 as a cardboard and snuff mill for Solomon Lindsay from Penicuik. About 1835 the estate spanned the river at Linn Park by a cast-iron bridge leading to the Netherley (or Netherlee) Print and Dye Works 1.5 km to the south. Meantime from 1815 the Millholme mill also ground snuff; from the 1860s under Couper Brothers its product was millboard, while as late as 1870 the Cathcart paper mill was still turned solely by water power. Holmwood, the best known mansion of famous architect Alexander *'Greek'* Thomson, was built in 1857–59 for the Couper brothers, who also funded the Couper Institute, an attractive community building, erected in 1887 to Thomson designs.

**The Weirs and the Caledonian Railway**: In 1886 the marine auxiliary consulting engineers James and George Weir established the Cathcart firm of G & J Weir Ltd, which rapidly developed a substantial works, manufacturing pumps for boiler feed and other purposes. In the same year a subsidiary of the Caledonian (CR), known as the Cathcart District Railway, was opened from Pollokshields East to Cathcart, giving a service to central Glasgow via Queens Park. In 1891 the population of *'Old Cathcart'* was 2511.

**Circle Railway and Trams bring Cathcart into Suburbia**: In 1894 the branch railway was extended, turning sharply back on itself through Pollokshields West to form the Cathcart Circle, a very tightly drawn loop line with a frequent passenger service. Cathcart, though by then a substantial place, was described as a *"village"* by Murray in 1894, when it still lay in Renfrewshire, separated from Langside and Mount Florida by nearly 1 km of open country. But the ribbon of New Cathcart had grown on the road to Netherlee, gaining its own inn, post and telegraph office; to the east of Cathcart stood the mansion of Aikenhead in its large policies. In 1901–02 a new Cart bridge was built to enable Glasgow trams to extend beyond Mount Florida to serve not only Cathcart but the Netherlee Print and Dye Works. The old Millholme Mill closed about 1900 and the snuff mill in 1902, but the latter's 17th century buildings survived. By 1901 the 4ha Weir works was lit by electricity; a public supply was provided from 1906.

**John Brown, more Railways and Industries**: John Brown, born at Muirend in 1901, became a famous naval architect *(see Clydebank)*. In 1903 the Lanarkshire & Ayrshire Railway was completed, diverging south-westwards from Cathcart station through a new station 1 km away at Muirend and serving Whitecraigs and beyond; about 60 years later Beeching cut it back to Neilston. In 1904 a CR connection was opened from Cathcart to their main line at Newton near Cambuslang. New housing had followed better communications, and as the number of upmarket households burgeoned, the Cathcart Laundry was erected about 1905, followed in 1906 by the laundry in Battlefield Road, built for the Misses J & J Walker. From 1913 Wallace, Scott & Co built a notable modern tailoring factory beside the river.

**William Weir, the RAF, and the National Grid**: Cathcart House was built in 1914. Weir's who built major new offices in 1912 and new production facilities in 1913–14 turned plane builders in the 1914–18 war. William Weir, born in 1877, was put in charge of British aircraft production, became Secretary of State for Air at the inauguration of the RAF in 1918 and persuaded Hugh Trenchard to take command of the new service; he was created Lord Eastwood. Later he headed the committee which recommended the creation of the National Grid for electricity, the first part of which was built in central Scotland.

**The Weir Autogyro and Helicopter**: From 1925 William Weir's brother James, born in 1887, conducted research and development of autogyros in conjunction with their inventor, the Spanish aristocrat Cierva, and in 1932 the pumps firm backed this new company financially, enabling them to build their first autogyro and its Douglas-derived engine in 1933. The first Weir helicopter became airborne in 1938, though from 1939 all rotary wing development was diverted to the USA. Later Weirs also aided Frank Whittle's development of the jet engine, and resumed helicopter development between 1945 and 1950, when an accident sadly cost the firm its government support. Weir Pumps built an amenity block in the 1930s; their Holm Foundry and engineering works had become enormous by the end of the 1939–45 war. Macfarlane Engineering of Netherlee Road, founded in 1911 by five brothers, made specialist generators and laboratory electrical equipment by the 1950s and were still active in 1979.

**Inter-war development**: Intensive suburban development was resumed in the 1920s. The Linn Park golf club was founded in 1925, followed by King's Park in 1934. In 1928 the CR's successor, London, Midland & Scottish (LMS), opened a new station at King's Park, only 900 m east of Cathcart on the Newton line, and the *Toledo* cinema with its unique *'atmospheric'* interior was built at Muirend to the south-west in 1933.

**The Time of the Trolleybus**: Trolleybuses took over the Springburn–Mount Florida tram service in 1949, and soon replaced the trams in moving vast numbers of people to and from Hampden Park; the huge Hampden Garage of Glasgow Corporation Transport was also erected. With the building of the Merrylee and Simshill estates, by the 1950s Cathcart contained 24,000 people, who enjoyed the facilities of a town; private house building continued on odd sites. In 1958 Holmwood became a convent; it is now owned by the National Trust for Scotland. The large policies of Aikenhead House became King's Park, and by 1971 the House was a museum.

**Founding an Airline and Controlling the Juice**: In 1961 Frank Thomson from Cathcart founded Caledonian (later British Caledonian) Airlines; this earned him a knighthood, for it grew into a major airline, based at Gatwick by 1988 when it was merged with British Airways. The various railways were electrified in 1962, the electrical control room being located at Cathcart; this was adapted in later years to control all of British Rail's Scottish power supplies. The population peaked about 1971 at over 26,000; by then Langside College of Further Education (FE) was open at Prospecthill Road. A second Cup Final riot at Hampden in 1980 led to a successful legal ban on alcohol at football matches. In that year Cathcart Castle was demolished by its nominal guardians the City Council, which had failed to maintain the structure. By then Cathcart House – formerly the Wallace Scott clothing factory – was the headquarters of the South of Scotland Electricity Board.

**Weir Weather the Slump and Buy their Rivals**: Weir Pumps narrowly survived the 1981 recession, having to sack much of their workforce. Rescued by the Scottish Development Agency, they decided to concentrate on designing and producing specialised pumps, valves and castings, and the Weir Group became successfully re-established. They acquired their Manchester-based rivals Mather & Platt in 1987, slowly running down the latter's Park Works. Thirteen other firms were bought over five years, but Weir kept their head office and works in Cathcart, when 800 worked there in 1990.

**Weir Group and Nuclear Headquarters**: In 1991 the Weir group employed 6000 in all, being Britain's largest manufacturers of pumps, with a predominant export trade in the water industry. The company's markets were almost equally divided five ways, including specialisms in water, oil, power generation, and the desalination equipment for the Middle Eastern market made by Weir Westgarth. In 1992 they won Alaskan oil contracts, and a major contract to supply 60 oilfield pumps and motors to Abu Dhabi. In 1994 Weir installed a computerised machining centre which could operate unattended between shifts. Meantime in 1990 the rump of the former SSEB (now Scottish Power), electricity generators Scottish Nuclear, made their headquarters in Inverlair Avenue, Cathcart; but they were to be merged into their larger English equivalent, Nuclear Electric, before privatisation in the dying days of the Major government.

**All Calls come to Cathcart**: In 1990 the long-disused snuff mill, partly rebuilt in the late 1970s, was converted into three private homes. In 1996 the closure of the Couper Institute, Cathcart's main community centre, was narrowly averted. Cathcart House remained with its gardens within the Cathcart Business Park, which was upgraded in 1995–97 as the 1500-worker operational headquarters of Scottish Power, who opened a new call centre there in 1996, replacing nine district offices; it was to handle some 3 million billing and service enquiries annually. King's Park Secondary School has about 1200 pupils.

## CATRINE

**Map 1, C2**

*Ayrshire village, pop. 2400* OS 70: NS 5325

A waulk mill was in operation on the north bank of the River Ayr 4 km east of Mauchline by the time that Pont sketch-mapped the area about 1600; farther west stood Ballochmyle. By the time of the Roy survey about 1754 there were many ferm touns around, but as yet no road connected to the waulk mill; Catrine House was a mansion by 1786. The other local laird Sir Claude Alexander of Ballochmyle, and his business partner the Glasgow entrepreneur David Dale, greatly developed the mill site in 1787 with a very large water-powered cotton spinning mill, described by J R Hume as *"the finest in Scotland"*. It employed 300 workers and had its own foundry; it was doubled in size in 1790 when a jenny factory and a carding and roving mill were added. A planned industrial village was built, which had a school by about 1795. A brewery (1795) and a corn mill were also built to supply necessities in this still relatively isolated area. Heron wrote in 1799 that about 1400 people lived at Catrine, and commented on *"the elegance of the plan on which the village is built, and the beauty of its situation"*.

**Power Loom Pioneers**: In 1807 the 5-storey spinning mill acquired the first large power loom in Scotland, and by 1814 there were 234 power looms. A bleachworks was added in 1824, and in 1825–27 the mill was equipped with two enormous water wheels, each over 15m in diameter and nearly 4m wide *(see Hay & Stell)*. By 1825 Catrine was served by a penny post from Cumnock, and a branch bank was open by 1845; at that time there were 900 factory textile workers and 120 hand loom weavers.

**Growth and Decline**: In 1894 Murray wrote of *"a village of cotton mills"*, but there was also a hotel and to the east a mansionhouse named Catrinebank. A short and belated branch from the Glasgow & South Western Railway's main line near Mauchline was opened in 1903, and a gasworks was built in 1909. But the railway was closed to passengers in 1943 and the track had been lifted by 1972; the station site became a car park. The giant water wheels were sadly demolished in 1945–47, and replaced by a hydro-electric power station, enabling the mill to be further enlarged in 1950, at that time making cotton sheets and towels. By 1954 Catrinebank had been renamed Daldorch House. The great mill, still working under the name of James Finlay & Co (established in textiles elsewhere about 1755), was burned out in 1963 during demolition. However, the large bleach works remained and have been reused, notably for whisky-blending.

**A Smaller Manufacturing Village**: Despite a hitherto stable population (2681 in 1971), Catrine was also hit by the closure of the coal mines in neighbouring areas; its facilities were reduced between 1951 and 1981 to those of a small village, with the loss of its employment exchange, secondary school and cinema; however the *Old Mill Inn* appropriately stayed open. In 1991 only about 2400 people remained, two-thirds lived in local authority housing and few had higher educational qualifications. By 1998 Daldorch House was a school.

## CATTERLINE, Crawton & Kinneff — Map 10, C4

***Mearns coast hamlets,** pop. 120* — OS 45: NO 8678

Two adjacent small natural harbours on the rocky coast of the Mearns served medieval fishing communities in Kinneff parish: east-facing Catterline 8km south of Cowie dated from the 12th century, and by 1491 the small south-facing Crawton Bay 2 km to the north was used for white fishing. Things changed little until a pier was built at Catterline about 1810, and for a century typically eight or nine boats were based there. In 1813 Crawton had only one boat, but herring fishing enabled this remote community to grow steadily to about 18 cottages, with 13 boats by 1881. The lighthouse built on Tod Head was lit from 1897. However, fishermen found Stonehaven a better harbour for larger boats, and by about 1910 Crawton harbour was out of use; it became completely depopulated in 1927. In 1951 picturesque Catterline with a population of under 200 provided basic services including a primary school, telephone exchange and inn to over 500 people. From 1956 to 1963 artist Joan Eardley lived in Catterline and painted notable seascapes. By 1981 the inn had closed and the population was about 120. By 1985 only a single lobster boat was based there, but salmon were also landed. The lighthouse was automated in 1988.

## CAWDOR & Kilravock — Map 9, C3

***Hamlet near Nairn,** pop. 200* — OS 27: NH 8450

Cawdor lies in a fertile lowland nearly 20km east of Inverness, beside a burn known in Gaelic as the Allt Dearg, a tributary of the River Nairn. Cawdor had a thanage by 1040 when a castle already existed. Despite Shakespeare, Macbeth was not its thane, nor was King Duncan I of Scotland killed within its walls, which were then probably wooden. From the late 12th century when Nairn was founded as a Royal Burgh on tidewater only 7km away, Cawdor's importance was reduced. Cawdor Castle was definitely the home of the Thanes in 1370, and was rebuilt as a stone tower about 1372, its complex ground plan settled before the general preference for right angles spread to the Moray Firth. Further reconstructed in 1454, it was apparently never accompanied by a barony burgh. However, whether officially authorised or not, a little castle town grew beside it. Three kilometres to the west stands Kilravock Castle of 1460.

**Castles, Mills and Poverty**: Pont's map made about 1600 showed both castles, each with its mill; Cantray west of Kilravock also had a mill. A new parish church was built in 1619 and further improvements were made at Cawdor Castle in the 17th century when extensive private parterre gardens were laid out. Roy's map of about 1750 showed the tiny village of Cawdor at the end of a road from Nairn. It was visited in 1765 by Alexander Carlyle, who like Roy called it *Calder*, and found its people worn out by their extreme poverty. In 1769 Pennant noted the large bridge that had lately been built across the Nairn between Cawdor and Kilravock, on the new military road from Cock Bridge to Fort George; this *'White Bridge'* is still in use.

**Whisky and Snowblocks**: By Chambers' day in the 1820s Cawdor Castle was the property of the Campbell Lord Cawdor. Meantime the Royal Brackla distillery had been founded in 1812 by William Fraser at Piperhill, 2 km east of Cawdor. In 1886 it was powered by water and steam, and produced 320,000 litres of Highland malt whisky annually, using only home-grown barley. Coal was stocked on site, because despite being linked to Nairn station by carts hauled by powerful steam traction engines, in winter the distillery was often cut off by snowdrifts which blocked the road for as long as a fortnight. In 1894 Murray described the inn at Cawdor as *"plain"*.

**Cawdor Whisky and Tourism**: With a population of under 300 in 1951, Cawdor had a miniature secondary school and the facilities of a small village; but by the 1980s the school was primary only and the settlement had declined to little more than a hamlet of 200 people; the inn had closed, but by 1980 Kilravock Castle was a guest house. About 1983 Royal Brackla distillery was mothballed by DCL, but by 1991 it had been reopened by a subsidiary of their successors United Distillers, and although most output went for blending it was again producing its smooth single malt; in 1998 it was sold to Dewars. The great castle with its fine contents and gardens, all maintained in perfect order, is opened to the public in summer.

## CELLARDYKE & Kilrenny

**Map 6, C4**

***Fife coastal villages**, pop. 1050*

OS 59: NO 5703

Also see: *Anstruther*

About 3 km from the south shore of the East Neuk of Fife is Pitcorthie, whose name means *'Place of the Standing Stone'*. The ancient church of Kilrenny also stands beside the Gelly Burn, only 1 km from the sea. Saint Ethernan (Adrian), an Irish missionary, lived in a cave at Caiplie 1.5 km east of Kilrenny until he was killed by Vikings in 875. In view of its proximity to ancient Crail, once capital of the Kingdom of Fife, the Culdee name Kilrenny may well derive from the Gaelic *Kil Righinn – 'Church (of the) Princess'* – for it was by 1170 a part of the royal domain of Countess Ada, mother of Malcolm IV.

**Skinfasthaven, Silver Dyke and Silver Darlings**: By 1222 a harbour existed at *'Nether Kilrenny'*, also oddly called Skinfasthaven, a crack in the rocks of the raised beach at the foot of dead cliffs only 1 km east of Anstruther *(q.v.)*. A new church of Kilrenny was dedicated in 1243, and the adjacent estate of Invergelly existed by 1281. In 1452 Bishop Kennedy of St Andrews built a town house beside the pier at Nether Kilrenny. By 1551 there was a mill at Caiplie. Meantime little-used Skinfasthaven was promoted by its laird John Beaton, nephew of the Cardinal, into a fishing port and burgh of regality with a harbour and weekly market. The charter was drawn up by John Lauder, Vicar of Kilrenny in 1543, a loathsome fanatic who helped to achieve George Wishart's ritual murder by the Cardinal. Although a vein of silver ore is geologically improbable there, and there seem to be no records of silver production, by 1579 Skinfasthaven was known by the odd name of Siller Dyke, which as *Silverdyck* appeared on Pont's maps of about 1600. Later spelled Cellardyke, its people became known as Dykers.

**Urban Development and Fateful Storm**: Cellardyke was evidently simply a fishing base, for in 1621 Kilrenny – which had been a Royal Burgh since 1592 – paid none of the Scottish Customs dues. Kilrenny Town Hall was built at Cellardyke in 1624, including a prison cell. In 1623 Innergelly became another of many closely adjoining burghs of barony, but was abortive. In 1641 Kilrenny lost control of Anstruther Easter, which became the centre of a separate parish. However by 1625 there was a parish school at Kilrenny, under which Sillerdyke remained, though its pupils refused to attend there! In 1655 Sillerdyke harbour was utterly destroyed by a storm, and remained unusable in 1668.

**Cellardyke Recovers**: Kilrenny succeeded in withdrawing from Royal Burgh status in 1672, and thus paying less tax, so in the late 17th century it was one of only four parishes in Fife able to maintain a school, and also – after a national appeal – to rebuild Cellardyke harbour. By 1692 there was a maltman, a tailor and even a local doctor; the little port in 1702 had 18 boats; in 1707 there was a cooper. Royal burgh status was regained in 1707, due to a misunderstanding! In 1710 Cellardyke *"commonly called Kilrenny consists of one street and a little harbour"*, the base for 10 white-fishing boats each crewed by six men all year round; at herring time they could muster 20 boats with seven men in each. Many weavers and brewers were busy, and in 1714 *"an old coalpit"* was noted at *'Airdrie Lees'*. Smuggling was rife; around 1725 there were as many as 50 local fishing boats.

**Mansion House, Over-fishing, and the Giant Whale**: Innergelly House which was owned in the 17th century by Sir James Lumsdaine of Swedish fame *(Watson 1986)*, was replaced by a new mansionhouse in 1740. Alex Wood was a local wright and boatbuilder who drowned in 1793, but by then the white fisheries had *"miserably decayed"*, as had the tiny harbour, whose unsafe entrance drowned other boats' crews. Heron writing in 1799 thought the population of Kilrenny was *"about a thousand"*. Although in 1800 seven local boats fished by the great-line method, high seas meant taking refuge elsewhere. By 1812 most locals fished for herring, particularly out of Wick, or joined the whaling: the vast jawbones of the largest Arctic whale ever caught still stood in George Street in the 1980s. Kilrenny's old kirk, having become unsafe, was demolished and replaced in 1806–08.

**From White Fish Boom to Pestilence and Disaster**: White fishing soon returned, and by about 1820 Cellardyke with its cooperages, pickling sheds and smokehouses was the *"cod emporium of Scotland"*. In 1825 over 30 boats and over 200 fishermen were based there, supplying the Glasgow and London markets, and they petitioned for harbour improvements. In 1829 Telford's brilliant aide Joseph Mitchell surveyed its single main pier for improvements and recommended a 38 m extension and a 54 m west pier. Cholera struck Cellardyke in 1832, and the cheaper alterations made by 1833 had actually worsened the little harbour, whose entrance faced into the prevailing winds. The Isle of May was a popular destination for summer pleasure trips – until a tragedy there in 1837 drowned 13 of the 65 passengers on Cellardyke's 11 m (35-foot) boat *Johns*.

**Coal, Crafts and Calamities**: In 1841 quite a wide range of local shopkeepers and craftsmen was recorded in the congested little one-street town, where many houses were crowded with up to 23 people in several families! A new school had been opened for girls and infants. Small outcrops of coal have occasionally been worked in the agricultural hinterland. Thirty Cellardyke men drowned in several marine tragedies in the 1840s; on one occasion 130 local craft, 100 of them herring boats, tried to find safety in the harbour which could hold only 35. Although in 1852 16 men left to seek gold in Australia, by 1855 there were 130 drave boats seeking herring, and in 1857 30 catching white fish; but plans made for a larger harbour at Craignoon between Cellardyke and Anstruther were rejected in favour of the Union Harbour at Anstruther, and some decline then set in; this and a religious revival in 1860 cut trade at the five pubs.

**Fifie Boat, Oilskin Factories and Tea Clipper**: In 1859 Robert Watson set up an oilskin, net and buoy factory which eventually had branches at Newburgh and Buckhaven. Alex Black & Co's Cellardyke Oilskin Factory also made patented canvas buoys for herring nets, and by 1861 Cormack's curing and cod liver oil factory employed 21 people. About 1860 the Cunninghams, local boatbuilders, originated the straight-stemmed *'Fifie'* hull form. From 1860 all local boats were Kirkcaldy registered, and in 1862 the first real improvements in local housing began. In 1866 the *Taeping*, one of a fleet of tea clippers owned by Cellardyke native and ship's captain Alex Rodger, broke the record for a passage from China to London.

**Tragedy in Scotland's Second Fishing Port**: From 1868 the town council, hitherto a byword for corruption, was replaced by a proper democracy; street names were allotted in 1873. In 1875 a great gale damaged the harbour and killed 15 local seamen. In 1878 Sharp & Murray, fish curers and general merchants, commissioned the SS *Onward*, one of the first two steam drifters (the last was built for Anstruther in 1932). By 1881 when Cellardyke at last gained its own church a new school had been built, and in 1882–83 came a new town hall to serve what was then Scotland's second most important fishing port, for 203 Cellardyke boats were registered, crewed by 650 men and boys. By 1884, when the local well-water was condemned for drinking, Duncan & Black had a net factory, and there was even a cricket club; although from that year the fisheries declined, the new railway facilities built at Anstruther did encourage crabbing for London and Lancashire markets.

**The Great Storm precipitates Decline**: A great storm in 1898 wrecked the harbour piers, and even the smaller boats had to follow the larger ones that were already fishing out of Anstruther. Repairs were still proceeding in 1901, causing many Dykers to emigrate to Ontario to fish the Great Lakes. Amalgamation of the three burghs came in 1929 when 438 children crowded the Cellardyke primary school; but by 1946 only 280 attended. The rock-cut swimming pool built by volunteers was opened in 1933 and given the old local name of the Cardinal's Steps.

**No early Holiday at the Camp**: In the second world war Cellardyke's Roger Street suffered bomb damage, and RAF married officers' quarters were built just east of the town; after 1945 they became the Anstruther Holiday Camp. Both Watson's and Martin's still produced protective clothing, while another former oilskin factory in James Street was used to make potato crisps. Even in the 1980s, when the harbour held only a few pleasure craft, some fishing boats still boldly bore the name of Cellardyke as their home port *(for a very full local history see Watson, 1986)*. Cellardyke with its narrow streets remains one of the most traditional of Scottish fishing villages. Local initiative is not dead, for by 1995 East Neuk Outdoors offered a variety of experiences for active young people. Cellardyke primary school was to close as soon as a new school could be built for the Anstruther area.

## CERES, Pitscottie & Tarvit — Map 6, B4

***N. Fife village & hamlets,*** *pop. 1000* — OS 59: NO 4011

Among the hills 4km east of Cupar is Pitscottie, where the Ceres Burn leaves a fertile natural bowl. Its centre at Ceres, where other burns converge, is named after Saint Cyr; locals pronounce it *Sirris*. A tower house on the north-west rim of the bowl was known in 1475 as Inglis-Tarvit after its owner. Robert Lindsay, who wrote *The Chronicles of Scotland, 1436–1565* was born at Ceres about 1532. Pont's map of 1600 noted *'Cyres Mill'*. Craighall, above the den of the Craighall Burn 1km south-east of the kirk, was owned till the late 16th century by the Scotts of Balwearie; Sir Thomas Hope built a new house there about 1600, enlarged by Bruce in 1697–99. Meantime in 1611 the Tarvit estate was bought by the highly cultured and able Perthshire lawyer, educational benefactor, statesman and author Sir John Scot, newly appointed Director of Chancery, for whom the tower was improved in 1627 and renamed Scotstarvit. Scot became Lord Scotstarvit in 1632, soon afterwards rescued the Pont maps from oblivion, and twice visited Amsterdam to arrange for Blaeu to publish them. He also travelled to London on state business 24 times – no mean record for the period *(see Snoddy)*.

**The Burgh of Ceres: Mining, Milling and Weaving**: Ceres became a burgh of barony in 1620, and grew into a large and well-built village. The Blaeu map showed a bridge across the Craighall Burn by 1642, probably the narrow packhorse bridge that still exists. By 1700 bridges had been built both north and south of the village. When the small late 17th century mansion of Wemysshall, designed by Sir William Bruce, was built on a sheltered site 1km east of bleak Scotstarvit, the latter was abandoned. The Roy map of about 1750 showed Ceres at the hub of a fully developed road system, with a mill to the north, and a mining hamlet some 2 km to the east at Callange or Coaltown of Callange, where an engine was in use in 1800. In 1790 much locally grown flax was spun in the parish, woven by 138 hand weavers. Two fairs were to be held at Ceres in 1797.

**Mechanised Textiles**: The roads to Ceres were turnpiked in 1807. In 1825 a bleachfield was established there, and two spinning mills were erected at Pitscottie in 1827. There were many buildings at Coaltown, and 4km south of Ceres the Teasses Mill was working near ruined Craighall; later a third new mansionhouse was built there. Close by were the two limekilns of the Teasses Limeworks. By 1839 around 800 people were making dowlas and sheeting in Ceres, largely it seems for Dysart manufacturers. This *"flourishing place"* must surely have possessed a post office before one was recorded in 1857. In 1864 both Yool's St Ann's bleachworks and James Annan's Pitscottie mill were still busy, the latter having about 50 workers. The mine was still open in 1894 at North Callange, as were the limeworks, bleachfield and an inn. In 1901 the parish population (which included Craigrothie and Pitscottie) was 1545.

**Modern Ceres**: Wemysshall was replaced around 1900 by the mansion called Hill of Tarvit, designed for Sharp, a Dundee jute merchant, by Sir Robert Lorimer; later acquired by the National Trust for Scotland and used as a cancer home, it was open to the public from about 1985. By the mid 20th century the mine and bleachfield had closed and the fairs had become an annual games; in 1951 the parish population was down to 1376 and the village had only 677 people, but an agricultural engineer was at work. Craighall House was pulled down in 1955. Ceres gained the successful Fife Folk Museum, which grew from the 1960s, and a bygone lingerie shop, and retained the general facilities of a small village. Housing development had increased the village population to 987 by 1991. By 1993 Griselda Hill's pottery was making good replicas of the colourful Wemyss Ware *(see Pathhead)*. Ceres keeps its bosky rural charm.

## CHAPELHALL & Calderbank — Map 16, A4

***Lanarkshire villages,*** *pop. 6000* — OS 64: NS 7863

Gartness Mill on the North Calder Water 2 km south-east of Airdrie existed by the 16th century. Pont's map, made in 1596, showed *'Chappell'* on the south bank of the Shotts Burn just above its confluence with the North Calder Water, 1 km below

Gartness Mill; later this became the hamlet of Chapelhall. At the confluence stood The Mains, later the site of Monkland House. Just west of this mansion the Roy map of about 1754 marked *'Clartyholes'*, which can easily be pictured as horribly muddy bell pits from which coal was being extracted against the odds; *'Cherry Wood'* nearby sounds altogether more attractive!

**The Monkland Canal**: The Monkland Canal was started in 1770; surveyed by James Watt, it was dug westwards from the same locality, which became the hamlet of Calderbank. It was intended to convey coals to Glasgow; Watt oversaw the works until it was opened to Barlinnie in 1773; it was later extended to Port Dundas. By 1790 it was owned by the Stirling family, local coal-owners and Glasgow merchants, and extended in 1790–93 to a colliery (Clartyholes?) beside the River Calder, which became its water supply.

**The Monkland Iron & Steel Works**: A small forge established at Calderbank in 1794 was bought in 1804 by the Monkland Steel Company, who made steel from malleable iron, producing files and edge tools. In 1826–31 they built a small ironworks – to make rails – between Monkland House and Calderbank, and another iron-smelting works in 1835. Mineral lines soon connected the two works with numerous coal pits on all sides, but malleable iron became uneconomic in the 1880s and the Chapelhall works were demolished. In 1891 new owners the Calderbank Steel & Coal Company replaced the Calderbank plant by the open-hearth Monkland Steelworks, connected to a branch of the Caledonian Railway which opened through the area in 1888. Both villages – being separated by the steep roadless valley of the North Calder Water – gained stations, and both had inns by 1895, and a total population of 3700.

**The Twentieth Century**: The steelworks were closed and demolished about 1930. A small trading estate was developed about 1938 by the Scottish Industrial Estates Corporation, and the twin villages continued to grow, also being conveniently close to Airdrie and to the Newhouse *(q.v.)* industrial estate. The local railway ceased to carry passengers before 1953, and freight ended in 1966. By 1981, the general facilities of a village were available, plus a Catholic secondary school, which now seems closed. In 1991 about 4400 people lived in Chapelhall which had an inn, and 1700 in Calderbank where there was a pub. By 1992 a bakery simply known as *'The Bakehouse'* was at work on the Chapelhall trading estate; the Chapelhall works site is now a country park, and new Wimpey housing is being built.

## CHIRNSIDE, Hutton & Edrom — Map 3, C3

***Berwickshire village & hamlets,*** *pop. 1250* — OS 67: NT 8756

At a ford across the Whiteadder Water some 13km west of Berwick is Hutton, which had a *'hospital'* by 1300. Chirnside which stands 2 km to the north-west, high above the river, has a 12th century church. By 1593 this had become the centre of a long-lasting presbytery, for although no charters seem to exist to show that the place was ever a burgh, Pont's map made about that time showed many buildings at *'Chirnside toun'*. On the Whiteadder Water stood two mills, one 2 km west of the village already being known as Chirnside Mill, with another just south of the village above the confluence of the Blackadder, on which stood a third mill, opposite the site of the modern village of Allanton and near the long-vanished Blackadder Castle. The emparked tower house of Hutton Hall, today called Hutton Castle, was built in the 16th century. By 1629 Chirnside had a parish school, and Edrom with its ancient church 4km to the west gained one the next year.

**Improved communications**: By the time of Roy's survey about 1754 a bridge by Chirnside Mill was at the convergence of tracks from Cumledge, Chirnside, Reston and Buncle. Under a Turnpike Act of 1772 the Eyemouth–Kelso road was made up; this passed through the village. Blackadder Castle was remodelled as a mansion in the late 18th century by Robert Adam and John Lessels. An annual fair was scheduled at Chirnside in 1797, and Heron in 1799 noted that *"the village of Chirnside contains about 600 inhabitants"*; Hutton, 5km south-east of Chirnside, was a *"village by no means large or populous"*. By 1825 Chirnside had a post office served by a penny post from Duns. Ninewells House was built north of Whiteadder in 1839–41.

**The Paper Mills and Railway**: A paper mill was established at Chirnside Bridge in 1842, and the company built 22 two-roomed houses for its workers on a steep bank. When the Duns branch railway opened in 1849, Edrom and Chirnside had stations, the latter located near the paper mill. For a time wrapping paper was also made at Edington Mill, 5km down-river. In the early 20th century sandstone used to be despatched by horse and cart to Edrom station, over 5km from the quarry 2 km east of Swinton. By 1918 Hutton Castle was the home of retired shipowner William Burrell, who gifted his famed art collection to Glasgow. Although Blackadder was demolished about 1925, Chirnside grew into a large village, where a new school was built in 1938. The Bridge paper mill had 200 employees in 1948, and the population in 1951 exceeded 1200, with average village facilities, plus agricultural engineers. Hutton lost a third of its 200 people in 20 years and its inn soon closed; in 1976 its primary school was *'marginal'*.

**Varied Industries**: Ninewells House was demolished in 1964, a bad year locally, for at that time the railway was closed by Beeching. The secondary school had also gone by 1976, but 130 jobs had recently been created in two new firms, including the very large J B Forrest grain treatment plant and store, west of the paper mill. Chirnside also had a dairy, and retained a good range of small shops in 1989. The paper mill, greatly enlarged by the American firm of Dexter, was making teabag paper in 1988, though in 1990 complaints were laid against it as a river polluter. In 1991 these activities dominated Chirnside, which had 1253 people, with Scotland's highest proportion of plant and machine operatives and of workers in manufacturing industry. By 1993 the factory had been expanded by over 4000m$^2$ and employed over 200 people; as *'Dexter's Non-Woven'* it was also making the paper for surgical gowns. By 1982 Mains House had become a hotel, renamed by 1995 as the *Chirnside Hall Hotel*, and by then further housing had been built, but by 1997 Hutton Castle was a ruin.

## CLACKMANNAN — Map 16, B1

***Large village, Firth of Forth,*** *pop. 3400* — OS 58: NS 9192

Clackmannan stands on a low hilltop above the Black Devon Water, 2 km from the upper Forth estuary. Built round the ancient basalt stone (Gaelic *clach*) of Mannan, known to the Romans, and surely the site of a medieval thanage,

Clackmannan became a sheriff caput between 1147 and 1153; in the latter year it was made a Royal Burgh. A 24m-tall tower house built in the 14th century was later adjoined by the mansion of the Bruces of Clackmannan. After 1497 when Alloa was chartered to exploit a tidewater site for coal exports, Clackmannan lost out, but still held a regular annual fair, even before its re-charter of 1542, and by 1590 there was a grammar school.

**Coal, Salt, Wagonway, Distillery and Squalor**: A major coal mine had long worked west of Clackmannan, by the 1690s being drained by water power from the then great depth of 80 metres. In 1745–46 several local carters took coal to Stirling. By then, as Roy's map showed, Clackmannan was a sizeable one-street village east of its *'castle'*, and had a pier or *Pow* on the Forth. Ferrytown to the south was a hamlet, though no ferry seems documented; south of that, the name Kennet Pans indicated salt evaporation. Forest Mill, 4km to the east on the Black Devon, which had its own school by the 1760s, stayed a mere hamlet. About then a wooden wagonway was laid to the Pow from pits in the Devon valley, enabling coal exports; the Devon ironworks near Alva was connected to this line from 1792. Heron estimated the population of Clackmannan as about 600 in 1799; about then the tower house was abandoned. At that time there was a distillery some 2 km to the south, built by Andrew Haig and worked by Stein & Co 1821–33; but it then vanished. Mining was again recorded near Clackmannan in 1812; by the next year it had a post office, but development stagnated. In the 1820s Chambers found *"a very miserable town; one long, unpaved, straggling, filthy street"*. The sheriffdoms of Kinross and Clackmannan had been combined in 1807, so the county jail had fallen into ruin; oddly, any prisoners were sent to Stirling.

**Clackmannan and the Railway**: Clackmannan station was opened with the new Stirling & Dunfermline Railway in 1852; it was later part of the North British. Patons' woollen mill was set up in 1875, but in 1888 Beveridge found a *"mean and uninteresting"* town, which had lost its county courts; the huge stone remained in place opposite the chief inn. The population in 1891 was 1779. Although regarded as *"a dull place"* by Murray in 1893, both the *Royal Oak* and *County* hotels were open. The wagonway still existed, and bricks and tiles were made beside the railway. Clackmannan FC played 4 seasons in the Scottish League between 1921 and 1926. Passenger trains ceased in 1930, but the line stayed open for goods. Clackmannan's old substandard housing was largely replaced with council housing around 1950. Patons were still mule spinning in 1976, but their works has since closed and been demolished; the distillery building was a ruin by the 1980s. Although the Tower was the only feature of tourist interest in the ancient town, by 1980 it had a third hotel, the *Tower*. By 1991 some 3400 people lived in Clackmannan; few owned their homes outright. The village has since made little news.

## CLASHMORE & Skibo — Map 9, B2

***Sutherland hamlet**, pop. minimal* — OS 21: NH 7489

In the 12th and 13th centuries the bishops of Caithness built their summer castle at Clashmore, overlooking a low-lying area on an inlet of the Dornoch Firth 5km west of their cathedral at Dornoch. Its Gaelic name means *Big Stone*, but the castle was generally known as Skibo, probably from Gaelic *Sgiobal*, a granary. By 1560 the Meikle Ferry (*q.v.*) was plying nearby; Pont's map of about 1600 showed both Skibo and *'Ferrytown'* in a well-settled area, while the Roy map surveyed about 1750 showed Skibo and the *'Ferryhouse'* connected by tracks with Dornoch. There was a cattle market in the 18th century; in 1894 Murray described the *Clashmore Inn* as only *"fair"*. In 1897 Skibo Castle was bought by Andrew Carnegie *(see Dunfermline)* whose extensions transformed it into a vast and magnificently carved and panelled mansion, which stayed in the family until 1982, while Clashmore itself remained a mere hamlet whose post office closed around 1985. A new road bridge was built in 1988–91 somewhat east of the ferry site to shorten the A9. Skibo Castle was bought in 1990 by Peter de Savary, was fully renovated and opened it as the exclusive Carnegie Club in 1994. By 1998 a new golf course had been opened east of the old ferry slip, and not far away was the Dornoch Bridge quarry.

## CLEISH — Map 6, A4

***Kinross-shire hamlet**, pop. 400* — OS 58: NT 0998

Beside the Gairey Water, below the steep rocky escarpment of the Cleish Hills 5km south-west of Kinross, is the church of Cleish, given to Dunfermline Abbey by Alexander I in 1115. There was a mill by 1507, and an L-plan tower house of the 16th century, though the Blaeu maps of the next century showed little but placenames; by 1633 a parish school was open. A stone quarry at work by 1702 was still active in 1834; a new school building was erected in 1734. The tower became ruinous from about 1723, but Nivingston was built in stone on a domestic scale in 1725 as the dower house for the evidently important mill; however, little was made of Cleish on the Roy map of about 1750.

**Quiet Modern Cleish**: Although no railway came nearer than some 4km, the castle was restored about 1850 and a small park was created around it. By 1888 Nivingston too had been enlarged into a mansion, apparently for Thomas Aitken, who was chairman of the Fife Coal Company in 1893. A post office was open by 1901 and the village hall was built in 1928. In the later 20th century the population remained remarkably stable at around 400 because sandpits were at work to the north-west by 1967, and intensive broiler houses augmented the farming backbone of the area. Cleish Mill was extensively adapted as housing in 1999. Nivingston had become a small country house hotel by 1977, since attractively extended into the friendly *Nivingston Hotel*.

## CLELAND, Omoa & Hareshaw — Map 16, A4

***Lanarkshire village**, pop. 2500* — OS 64/65: NS 7958

Pont's map dated 1596 showed several bridges crossing the South Calder Water, and also *'Kneelandtoun'* and *'Kneelandtounhead'*, although many of the placenames were badly misplaced, and Omoa, 8km east of Hamilton, was not named. Meikle Hareshaw to the north had a school from 1605. There were roads in the area when the Roy map was made about 1754, but four sheets met there and it is not easy to draw conclusions. The Omoa ironworks opened in 1789. A coal pit was open by 1793 (probably before that date) and by 1804 the ironworks were linked by wagonway with coal pits at Newarthill.

**Railway Confusion**: In 1833 the Wishaw & Coltness Railway connected the Omoa ironworks into the developing Monklands system, and eventually there was a passenger station there, confusingly named Cleland. The Omoa ironworks closed in 1866. When the Caledonian Railway opened its Glasgow to Edinburgh via Shotts branch in 1869 a second station was opened on the new line only 500m to the north, and named Omoa. In 1894 when new ironworks in the area were owned by Neilsons, brickmaking and freestone quarrying were other industries. Cleland straggled along the road linking the two stations; it had two inns and a post and telegraph ofice, while to the west stood Cleland House in its large policies, but even these were entered by a mineral railway. The later station was still called *Omoa* until after the railway grouping of 1923, to distinguish it from that on the original line (which was not to last many more years); then Omoa was renamed Cleland!

**The End of Cleland's Industry?**: Spoutcroft mine was still open up to 1954, by which time a hospital, brickworks and large whin quarries were active around Auchinlee Farm; but the ironworks had closed and the original railway had been lifted. Cleland then had about 3200 people, and the facilities of a typical village, plus two small secondary schools, which were soon closed. The rail freight service between Chapelhall and Cleland closed in 1966 and by the 1970s the area was littered with the sites of former industries. Cleland had kept most of its facilities, though a small mine near Hareshaw, apparently opened in the 1960s, was disused by 1988. Population decline set in, and by 1991 under 2950 people lived in Cleland. An animal rendering works now occupies the Omoa ironworks site. The new *'Dalziel Park'* Golf course was built in the 1990s at Cleland House, which became the club house. The primary school, post office and the station – originally named Omoa – are still open, but the hospital has recently vanished.

## CLOSEBURN — Map 2, B4

***Small Dumfriesshire village,*** *pop. 300* — OS 78: NX 8992

A medieval motte and bailey stood east of the River Nith about 17km north of Dumfries. The 14th century keep of Closeburn Castle, later modernised, was built 2 km north of this. Pont's map made around 1610 showed *'Closeburn Loch'* between the kirk and castle, which had heavily wooded grounds; later the tiny loch was drained. The Roy map of about 1754 showed both the castle and the *'Old House of Closeburn'* as mansions east of the Dumfries to Sanquhar road. *"Extensive limeworks"* were recorded by Heron in 1799, and an early 19th century woollen mill stayed open until about 1950.

**The Railway makes the Village**: A station on the main road near kirk and castle was provided on the main line of the Glasgow & South Western Railway which opened in 1850, and this became the centre of the tiny village of Closeburn. In 1906 red facing stone was cut at the small Closeburn Quarry, but Waugh noted in 1923 that *"the extensive quarries are now unimportant"*. The station was still open in 1953 when the rather scattered population was about 475, but was subsequently closed. By 1957 the Wallace Hall Academy was a local authority secondary school, but by 1990 this function and name had been transferred to Thornhill's secondary school. In 1980 when the local population was falling towards 300, Martin & Son ran a large garage with a farm machinery business, and a doctor was in practice. Trigony House, an Edwardian hunting lodge, had become a hotel. The *Trigony House Hotel*, the post office cum general store, and the primary school are still open, serving a small village with appreciable new housing development.

## CLOVA & Glendoll — Map 6, B1

***Angus community,*** *pop. under 100* — OS 44: NO 3373

Glen Clova strikes far into the Grampian Mountains from the Angus plain. Clova itself which lies some 25km beyond Kirriemuir had an early religious community and a thanage; but little remains of the 16th century tower of Clova Castle. When Roy made his map about 1750, Clova Kirk stood beside a track labelled *'Road from Killymuir by Glenmuick to Deeside'* which followed the south-west side of the River Clova, nowadays oddly known as the South Esk, before climbing steeply over the glaciated hills at up to 685m; it later became just a footpath, though in the late 20th century much was reinstated for vehicles. By 1955 a youth hostel and later a mountain rescue post at tree-girt Glendoll Lodge, 6km farther up the forking valley, served more energetic visitors to this gloriously remote cul de sac, one of the rockiest areas in the east of Scotland. Meantime the resident population had probably fallen below 100, though now Clova retains a small hotel; the youth hostel is seasonal.

## CLOVENFORDS, Caddonfoot & Peel — Map 3, A3

***Small villages w. of Galashiels,*** *pop. 275* — OS 73: NT 4436

Three towers – Torwoodlee, Whytebank and Windydoors – were built in the 16th century in Caddonfoot parish, the hilly angle between the River Tweed and the Gala Water. By about 1754 the Selkirk to Edinburgh turnpike crossed a road from Innerleithen to Galashiels at Craighalls or Clovenfords, which in 1803 was a single stone house, noted by Dorothy Wordsworth as a modest inn. There was also a smithy before a railway was opened in 1866 between Galashiels and Peebles, with a station at Clovenfords by 1896, and by 1901 there was a hotel and a post and telegraph office.

**The Peel and its General Hospital**: The Peel, a baronial mansion built south of the Tweed in 1904–07 to designs by John Kinross, became an obstetrics hospital about 1939 and Peel General Hospital in 1948; prefabricated buildings were added to bring it to 250 beds, serving the whole Tweed area. In 1951 Clovenfords had some 350 residents, but the station was closed to passengers in 1962 and the line had gone by 1971, when the population was down to 275. The shortage of developable land in Galashiels has led to some housing being built in the 1980s, so that Caddonfoot primary school, marginal in 1976, is still open. A new general hospital was completed near Melrose in 1988; the Peel's accretions were then removed and the *'A'* listed mansion was vacated and put up for sale in 1989; its restoration was still awaited in 1997. Clovenfords post office was active in 1993, but has now closed; the pub remains.

## CLUANIE — Map 8, C4

***Inverness-shire location*** — OS 33: NH 0711

The military *'Road from Bernera to Fort Augustus'* through Glenmoriston was shown on the Roy map, made about 1750. Telford's narrow link south-eastwards over the hills to Glen Loyne and Glen Garry was built in the early 19th century;

where it joined the earlier road at the west end of Loch Cluanie in upper Glenmoriston was built the *Rhiabuie Inn*, later called the *Cluanie Inn*, open by 1896. The whole nature of this very sparsely peopled area was vastly changed by two great dams built by the Hydro-Electric Board between about 1954 and 1961 to feed their new Ceannacroc power station in Glen Moriston, greatly raising the levels of Loch Cluanie and of Loch Loyne in Glen Loyne. The latter blocked Telford's road, the old A87, which was consequently diverted eastwards to join Glenmoriston about 14km farther east, so the inn ceased to stand at a road junction. The isolated *Cluanie Inn* was sold in 1988 as part of the Glenmoriston Estate; it is now *"a haven for climbers"*, with 15 rooms.

## CLYDEBANK & Kilbowie — Map 15, B4

***N. Clyde town**, pop. 29,000* — OS 64: NS 4970

The Garscadden Burn which enters the north side of the tidal River Clyde opposite Renfrew had already been bridged by about 1600, when Timothy Pont mapped the area, for there was a *'Brighouse'*. A short way inland was *'Coulby'* (Kilbowie), and there were also a few farms between the bridge and Dalmuir. The Roy map made about 1754 showed the Glasgow–Dumbarton road as the main feature of the area. The coming of the circuitous Glasgow, Dumbarton & Helensburgh (later North British) Railway to the north bank of the lower Clyde in 1858 enabled the growth of a village near Kilbowie station, 10km west of Glasgow; it had under 1000 people by 1872.

**Thomsons' & Napier's Shipyards**: The Union Bank helped J & G Thomson, who had been persuaded to leave Govan, in their troubled move to a new shipyard which they named Clydebank in 1872–74, and later aided their emergence as a major public company in 1889. The yard being sited opposite the mouth of the Cart Water, longer ships with greater draught could be be launched across the river *(see Whiteinch)*. Thomsons' workers at first commuted daily by steamer from Govan. Thomsons built MacBrayne's flagship, the steel paddle steamer *Columba* in 1878, for their Ardrishaig service; almost 100m long, this was then the longest vessel on the Clyde and was in service until 1936. In 1885 among their many famous ships the same firm built the PS *Grenadier* for the Loch Fyne service. Meantime in 1877 Napier Shanks & Bell (from 1898 Napier & Miller) opened the *'Yoker Old'* shipyard, just within the area of modern Clydebank.

**Linked to USA by Ships and Sewing Machines**: In 1882 the locality – which (after much controversy) took its name of Clydebank from the shipyard – gained a second railway (another North British subsidiary), direct from Partick to Dalmuir, and, more importantly, work began on the enormous Singer sewing machine factory, itself rail connected. This branch of a USA company which had lately been operating in Bridgeton was opened in 1884, and was probably Scotland's first significant example of the reverse colonisation process,

*The Clydebank shipyard, built in 1872–74, gave its name to the later town. Here, light cruisers being fitted out in the 1880s.*
*(John Brown (UCS) collection)*

which began little more than a century after American independence. Its tall tower boasted four 8m diameter clock faces, probably the largest in the world. By 1890 Singer employed some 6000 people, most of whom travelled to work by rail to one of the four stations by then open in Clydebank; the original Kilbowie station was renamed *'Singer'* in a publicity deal. In 1888 Thomson's yard built the first recognisably *'modern'* twin-screw transatlantic liners, the *City of Paris* and *City of New York*, able to make 6-day crossings.

**Burgh, Boilers, Battleships**: By 1886 constant dredging and unplanned development had made the Clyde both *"muddy and odoriferous"*. Clydebank became a police burgh in 1886 and from 1891 had its own local newspaper, the *Clydebank Press*. That year saw the American boilermakers Babcock & Wilcox set up a branch factory within Singer's premises at Kilbowie; having established this toehold in the Clyde market, they moved to new premises at Renfrew in 1895. Meanwhile in 1890–92 Thomson built the 14,000 ton battleship *Ramillies* of the Royal Sovereign class, and in 1895 the battleship HMS *Jupiter* of 14,900 tons and the cruiser HMS *Terrible* of 14,200 tons. The yard was briefly renamed the Clydebank Engineering & Shipbuilding Company (CESC) in 1897–98 when it was building more paddle steamers and cruisers.

**John Brown's for Cruisers and Cunarders**: In 1896 the Caledonian's superfluous subsidiary the Lanarkshire & Dunbartonshire Railway was opened, squeezing round Clydebank by a reverse curve. D & J Tullis moved from Parkhead to Clydebank about 1900 as demand for their laundry machinery rose, largely being destined for luxurious passenger liners. By 1901 Clydebank was a town of 30,000 people. John Brown & Co, steelmasters of Sheffield, took over the CESC shipyard in 1899, and built cruisers. Then came the huge but ill-fated Cunard liner *Lusitania* built in 1904–07, which was sunk by a German submarine off Ireland in 1915 with the loss of almost 1200 lives, leading ultimately to the USA's entry into the War. John Brown later built the huge *Aquitania* of 45,650 tons. Meantime in 1909 the firm had started a subsidiary, Brown-Curtis, to build USA Curtis turbines, and by 1910 the works included an experimental hull-testing tank 122 metres in length, for models themselves up to 6m long.

**Trams, Cinemas and Rothesay Dock Iron Ore**: The erection of an electric power station was begun in 1901, and by 1910 Glasgow's electric trams connected with Clydebank via Partick and Yoker. At Dalmuir trams met more trams for Dumbarton and Balloch, spelling ultimate doom for three of the *five* railway stations then open within 1km of each other: Clydebank, Clydebank Central, Clydebank East, Kilbowie and Singer! In 1906 Napier & Miller moved from the Yoker Old shipyard to Old Kilpatrick to make way for the east end of the new Rothesay Dock, which opened in 1907, handling coal exports and iron ore imports. In the meantime the *Gaiety Theatre* had been opened in 1902; in 1917 it became a cinema, later known as the *Bank*, which was to survive the air raids of 1941, as did the neo-classical Clydebank Library, built in 1912–13 to designs by A McInnes-Gardner (and aided by Carnegie money). The *Cinema Varieties* opened in 1908, being renamed the *Palace* in 1915. The *Empire Theatre* of 1300 seats was opened in 1914; this too became a cinema in 1927. In 1919 the *Pavilion Theatre* of 2000 seats was opened, this being also used as a cinema.

**Battle Cruisers, Submarines and Saints**: The battle cruiser HMS *Tiger* of 28,500 tons was built by John Brown in 1913, followed in 1914 by the 27,500-ton battleship HMS *Barham*. By then the yard had been much enlarged; it built submarines during the 1914–18 war, plus the ill-fated battle-cruisers HMS *Repulse* of 32,000 tons in 1916 and in 1918–20 the fast but lightly armoured *Hood* of 42,100 tons, one of the largest warships ever built in Britain: she was to be sunk by the German battleship *Bismarck* in 1941. In 1919 a brilliant 19-year-old from Cathcart, John Brown – no relation of the owners – became an apprentice at the yard, soon qualifying as a naval architect. An early Clydebank football club played in the Scottish League between 1914 and 1931 when they had to withdraw; Kilbowie Park was laid out for Clydebank Juniors FC in 1939. Meantime between the wars much new housing was built, extending inland around Kilbowie and Radnor Park, and after 1925 to Milton Mains just south of Duntocher.

**Two John Browns Create the Queen of Liners**: The design of a new Cunarder of unprecedented size was begun at John Brown's in 1926, its leading designer under Sir James McNeill being young John Brown! The keel of No. 534 was laid in January 1931, early in the great depression; soon 3640 workers were employed, but the slump stopped work at Christmas 1931, by which time the hull framing was complete; all but 440 were laid off, which put half the town's workforce on the dole. Work was resumed in 1933 with government aid, conditional on a merger with the White Star Line, and the great ship was launched in 1934 as the *Queen Mary (see also Dumbarton)*. Completed in 1936, she made a thousand Atlantic crossings at an average of 31 knots. Bought by the city of Long Beach, California, in 1967, she made her final cruise round the Horn, and her engines were removed; her hull was refitted to form a famed hotel, conference centre and maritime museum, moored in Long Beach harbour. When losing money in 1992 she was put up for sale, but saved for posterity by an appeal. Meantime John Brown had become successively managing director and vice chairman of the firm; as a sprightly 93 year old he visited the famous old liner in 1994, and was finally knighted at the age of 99 in 2000, only months before his death.

**The '*Queen Elizabeth*'**: Meantime Dr Brown had led the works' design team for the similar but ultimately ill-fated *Queen Elizabeth*, which unlike her royal namesake was not to reach her centenary; built in 1936–40, this 32-knot steamer driven by Parsons geared turbines manufactured by Brown's was then the largest passenger ship ever built, of nearly 84,000 gross tons. Withdrawn in 1968, she was burnt out in 1972 while being refitted in Hong Kong as the *Seawise University*. With such giants being hand-riveted, the workplace noise was deafening; and home living conditions for the workers were equally desperate in 1936, when 41% of the houses were overcrowded, almost the worst situation in Scotland. By 1939 Clydebank had a greyhound stadium and at least four cinemas, including the big modern *La Scala* of some 2500 seats.

**Warships Galore**: With the rise of Nazi Germany John Brown's executed a vast amount of Admiralty work in a few years, starting with submarine depot ships, cruisers (including HMS *Fiji* of 8500 tons which was sunk near Crete in 1941), battleships and destroyer depot ships.

**Air Raid Destruction**: Many lives were to be saved by the care taken in 1940 by the renowned planner Robert Grieve *(see Maryhill)* in siting air raid shelters to serve the largest concentrations of people most closely. Two major air raids on Clydeside on successive nights in March 1941 by a total of 440 German bombers, each of which on average dropped a one-tonne or larger high-explosive bomb and numerous incendiaries, hit Clydebank hardest of all. They destroyed 4300 of the town's 12,000 houses, damaged all a few of the remainder and killed some 500 people; 96% of the 55,000 population had to leave the town, where all water supplies were cut for a time. The town library and the old High School were gutted, and the new High School building – then incomplete – was severely damaged, as was Clydebank Central station. Among the losses were two of the four cinemas, the *Palace*, and the *Pavilion*, which burned down in 1942 *(for a graphic account see MacPhail, 1974).*

**Major Industries in the Raids**: John Brown's huge shipyard employed almost 10,000 people before the air raids of 1941, which destroyed its pattern shop and badly damaged the experimental tank and other facilities. Singers' – which then made Sten guns as well as sewing machines – lost its huge timber store by fire in the first raid, together with its foundry, forge, and electric motors department. Sewing machine production was not resumed for some time. D & J Tullis, by that time manufacturers of heavy machine tools, employed 450 people before the air raids, but a direct hit in the machine shop cut production by 30%. Despite blast damage, Dawson & Downie continued to manufacture marine pumps and turbines beside John Brown's at Ferry Road.

**Smaller Factories in the Air Raids of March 1941**: There were by 1941 various lesser-known industries in Clydebank: Arnott Young's metals store was undamaged, and Brockhouse & Co, makers of vehicle parts, got off lightly. Clyde Blowers Ltd which had made boiler cleaning equipment at Livingstone Street from 1936 was damaged but kept working, as did Steedman & McAllister, lifebelt manufacturers. The Aitchison Blair works at Whitecrook, which made small marine engines, was put out of production for two months, and the Strathclyde Hosiery Company factory was completely destroyed.

**Pressing on Regardless to Sea Change**: War damage to major factories was rapidly repaired; work on the aircraft carrier HMS *Indefatigable* of 26,000 tons continued to completion in 1942. The battleship HMS *Vanguard* of 42,500 tons, the largest of all British capital ships, was built at Clydebank in 1944, utilising 38-cm (15-inch) guns left over from World War I; subsequent history made the name of this immediately obsolete vessel seem absurd. The cruiser intended as HMS *Bellerophon* of 9500 tons, laid down by John Brown in 1945, had to be redesigned on the stocks with nuclear warfare in mind, and was not completed until 1955 as HMS *Tiger*, of 12,080 tons.

**Redevelopment and '*Britannia*'**: By 1945 John Brown's yard had five huge slipways, on which its last group of five large passenger ships was built in 1946–49, ending with the 22,000 ton *Rangitane* for the New Zealand Line. The destruction of a third of the town was followed by widespread post-war redevelopment, as befitted a place so committed to national defence and whose Singer works, for a time Europe's largest single factory and the world's largest making sewing machines, employed no fewer than 17,000 people in the 1950s. The pre-war Whitecrook estate was doubled in size, and Drumry and Linnvale were added on either side of the new Drumry station which had opened by 1963, filling the last space between Clydebank and Glasgow's suburbs. In 1953 John Brown designed and the yard built the Royal yacht (and optional naval hospital ship) HMS *Britannia* of 4961 tons; she was to end up as a tourist attraction, for some reason moored in Leith. Gas turbine manufacture became established as an offshoot of Brown-Curtis.

*Singer sewing machine, type 15K, which sold over 19 million between 1885 and 1963. The 'K' refers to Kilbowie, the name of the US-owned factory at Clydebank. With 17,000 employees in the 1950s, it was the largest factory in Europe, but was run down to closure in 1980.* *(JRH)*

**Blue Trains, Goldfish, Turbines and the Final Queen**: In 1960–61 the local railways were electrified and the so-called *Blue Trains* were introduced; but in 1962 the trams stopped. By then Clydebank was once more a major local centre, with facilities including a technical college and two covered swimming pools. Cooling water from Singer's was returned to the Forth & Clyde Canal and provided a warm haven for discarded goldfish, which soon produced a thriving crossbred colony! However, the *Empire Cinema* burned down in 1959 and the *Bank Cinema* was closed in 1961; a surprising 1964 merger between a renewed Clydebank FC and East Stirling FC enabled the former to join the Scottish League, but failed in 1966. By 1969 the Clydebank & District Golf Club had taken over the course at Hardgate *(see Duntocher)*. In the early 1960s John Brown built four Boving pump-turbines – at the time probably the highest-head machines of this type in the world, installed for the pumped storage system within Ben Cruachan. The final sizeable naval vessel built by John Brown of Clydebank was the assault ship HMS *Intrepid* of 12,150 tons in 1964. The large and until then busy yard had handled 202 contracts between the liners *Queen Mary* and its magnificent swansong *Queen Elizabeth II*, built in 1965–69 as No. 736.

**Industrial Disasters Strike Again**: Sadly in 1963 the 80-year-old Singer clock tower was demolished, and after the launch of the *'QE2'* in 1968, John Brown's were in financial difficulties. The workforce was greatly cut on amalgamation with Fairfield of Govan to form the unsuccessful Upper Clyde Shipbuilders, liquidated in 1971; the last launch from the famous yard was the 17,700-ton bulk carrier *Alisa* in October 1972. John Brown Engineering remained at work, making gas turbines for use in the oil industry. Worse was to come, for the vast Singer works – which still employed 13,000 people in 1970 – was steadily run down to a mere 4800 in 1977; the loss-making industrial sewing machine operation was phased out first, so halving the workforce, and the plant was completely closed in 1980. Little iron ore was imported through Rothesay Dock after the General Terminus ore terminal at Gorbals was re-equipped in 1957, and ceased entirely when the Hunterston terminal was opened in 1978; the dock's rail connection was lifted.

**Oil Rigs, New Centre and UIE**: During this black period the Clydebank shipyard re-emerged in 1976 as the oil-rig builders Marathon. In 1978 a large covered shopping mall, the *Clyde Centre* of 65,000 m² and 109 shops, was opened by the District Council which had replaced the burgh in 1975. Thor Ceramics came to Clydebank in 1981. In 1990–91 after surviving near closure, Marathon's successors UIE built the UK's two first entirely automated oil production platforms for BP's Amethyst field off Humberside; in 1992 they completed a 9000-tonne deck for oil production by Amoco in the Lomond field. Various oil platform contracts kept a workforce of around 1000 busy over the next few years.

**Public Enterprise flourishes as Rail Freight dies**: In 1982 Clydebank was declared an Enterprise Zone (EZ) by the government, providing a rates holiday for a ten-year period: some of the lost jobs were replaced by the SDA's successful Business Park on the Singer site, where Scottish Foam started to make packaging in 1983. This and other EZ successes led to greater confidence, and a ten-screen cinema was opened in the town in 1988. By then Radio Clyde had moved from Anderston to Kilbowie Park, which could now seat all Clydebank FC's First Division spectators after a fashion, but was so far from ideal that by 1997 Clydebank and Dumbarton football clubs shared the latter's Boghead ground. For three months in 1988 coal was imported through Rothesay Dock, the rail connection being restored to enable BR to haul it to power stations; but by 1993 the whole Riverside branch was out of use. Meantime Scottish Foam was diversifying to become the first Scottish suppliers of injection mouldings for the computer industry.

**A Different Clydebank**: In 1990 Clydebank College of Further Education offered a variety of HNC/HND courses. In that year the *Clyde Theatre* was opened in part of the former Singer factory. In 1991 when the population was down to some 29,000 and still severely disadvantaged, the Clydesdale Bank, rejuvenated under Australian ownership, built a new computer operations centre at Clydebank (though at the cost of major job losses at its Glasgow centre). By 1991 the *Clydebank Press* had been replaced by the *Clydebank Post*. In 1992 Caledonian Land, owners since 1990 of the former SDA's Clydebank property, built 5000 m² of office space there, and in 1994 the former CR (later Riverside) station building was restored as flats. In 1995 the District Museum occupied the former Town Hall.

**The Fate of John Brown Turbines**: John Brown Engineering gained a Queen's Award for gas turbines in 1990. In 1993 they won an order to build a power station for Malaysia, and in 1994 another to build a gas turbine power station in Morocco. In 1995 the firm which had built over 500 gas turbines in its 29 years of association with their designers GEC, employed 1650 people at Clydebank. Late in 1996 140 jobs were cut as orders for thermal power plant fell away, 130 more jobs went in 1997, and although new owners Kvaerner then reaffirmed their long-term commitment to the plant, they were forced to announce its closure in 2000, with the loss of the last 200 jobs at the former John Brown yard.

**Clydebank Blowing Cold and Hot**: Clyde Blowers was taken over in 1992 in a management buy-out led by Jim McColl; in 1993 as Clyde Blowers the firm acquired a Belgian company and became the largest independent maker of boiler cleaning (soot blowing) equipment in Europe, but had to halve its workforce of 120 until it gained a new order from Japan for equipment for two Philippines power stations. In 1995 the now highly successful firm announced a move to new premises at the Clydebank Industrial Park, incorporating the firm's former Belgian manufacturing operations. At the same time they were about to open a new assembly plant for soot-blowing equipment in Tennessee.

**Combating Closures – by Cutting Local Government?**: Meantime in 1993 Ferry Pickering of Lutterworth had closed its Clydebank carton factory, with the loss of 90 jobs. To offset such losses the Clydebank Business Creation Centre was opened in 1994 by Dunbartonshire Enterprise. The Clydebank Business Park was still well occupied, including the Clydesdale Bank office, and attempts were being made to attract medical technology companies. But in 1996 Clydebank lost out, being combined with most of Dumbarton District in a new unitary authority, West Dunbartonshire. Thor Ceramics – a subsidiary of VRD Europa of Vienna – employed 210 people in 2001, making heavy-duty tubing for use in the steel industry, when a damaging explosion injured 10 employees. Clydebank High School now has around 1100 pupils, St Columba's 1000 and St Andrew's and Braidfield both around 600. By 1999 the modern *Beardmore Hotel* (168 rooms) had appeared; the almost new *Patio Hotel* in the Business Park has 82 rooms. New owners were being sought for Clydebank FC in 2001.

## COALBURN

**Map 2, A2**

***Lanarkshire village**, pop. 1170* — OS 71 or 72: NS 8134

The Coal Burn, a minor tributary of the Douglas Water 5 km south of Lesmahagow, was known for coal by the 16th century, for the name appeared on Pont's map of Clydesdale dated 1596. Extensive mining is implied by *'Collyett'*, *'Hillholes'* and *'Bell's Hole'*, all named on Roy's map made about 1754, by which time a road connected Lesmahagow and Douglas. Pits were open on the moors at Bankend about 4 km from Douglas in 1847, and after much negotiation a lengthy branch of the Caledonian Railway was built from Motherwell via Lesmahagow to reach Bankend in 1856. Over the next forty years the line served three other collieries near Coalburn station, where the passenger trains terminated some 250 m above sea level.

**The Station fosters a Village**: By the 1890s the station was accompanied by a post and telegraph office and an inn, and a scatter of miners' rows named Engine Row, Brick Row, Lime Row etc. Auchlochan colliery was already open 2 km north of the station. By that time the mineral railway had also been extended over 7 km to the south-west, crossing a saddle in the moors and down to the picturesquely named Galawhistle Burn where there was yet another colliery; nearby a final steep branch brought coal down from Spireslack Colliery on the slopes of Hareshaw Hill overlooking Glenbuck *(see also Muirkirk)*. In 1910 Anderson Boyes of Motherwell supplied a coal-cutting machine to Auchlochan colliery; uncovered in 1989, it is preserved at Prestongrange mining museum. Early in the 20th century mines were also opened at Dalquhandy, over 2 km west of Coalburn station.

**Over the Peak**: A peak population of nearly 2300 was reached in 1951 and by then Coalburn was a more compact settlement with a cinema cum dance-hall – though in most respects only village facilities were available. In 1965 the last colliery, Auchlochan, was closed, together with the railway passenger service, and by 1971 the railway had been lifted; the cinema and secondary school had also closed by 1981. With the loss of its main economic basis the population fell steadily, and in 1981 the Coalburn area had only 1500 people and the facilities of a small village; though iron and steel was converted by Coalburn Alloys at Holland Bush Works.

**Problems remain amid the Opencasting**: British Coal promised to build a swimming pool for Coalburn when approval was granted in 1987 for a major opencast coal operation to reclaim the old workings at Dalquhandy west of the village; 15 million tonnes of coal were to be extracted at 4000 tonnes a day from depths down to 90m from the surface, involving moving up to 20 tonnes of spoil to win a tonne of coal. Its vast screening and blending plant was opened as the largest in Britain in 1989; road transport moved the coal to a rail loading point at Ravenstruther near Carstairs, for shipment through Ayr to Kilroot power station in Northern Ireland. In 1991 Coalburn had only 1170 residents; over 70% of its households lived in publicly-rented homes. But ill-health and unemployment were high, and higher qualifications were few. However, its post office survived. Dalquhandy had become the largest opencast mine in Scotland apart from Westfield in Fife, and should continue until 2004. Broken Cross Muir is to be opencasted after Dalquhandy.

## COALTOWN OF BALGONIE — Map 6, B4

***Central Fife village, by Glenrothes,** pop. 850* — OS 59: NT 3099

The hilltop village of Coaltown of Balgonie, south of the River Leven in central Fife, appeared as *'Coltoune'* on both of Timothy Pont's maps of East and West Fife, made about 1600. The medieval Balgonie Castle *(see Milton article)* was omitted, but both this and *'Colton Mill'* appeared on James Gordon's map dated 1645. The long-standing mine workings in the form of *'rooms'* near the castle were already a remarkable 55m deep when in 1731 Landales, the tacksman or agent to Alexander, Earl of Leven, had a new *'water engine'* installed to drain the pit, fed by a new 2km *'colliery lead'*; in 1735 he erected a windpump west of the castle.

**Mining Suspended and Renewed**: In 1738 Landales aimed to dig a second deep sink to 50m below the river level, drained by a second windpump; but the pit was closed by 1743, being too far off the improving road system to remain economic. Work must have resumed nearby on a small scale, for in 1784 Landales' workings in 3m-thick coal were said to be *'recently abandoned'*. In 1785 the Balgonie Colliery was reopened with a more powerful water engine, and the main road to Kirkcaldy, later the A92, was made up by Lord Rothes for his coal carts before it was turnpiked under an Act of 1790.

**The Short Story of the Leven Ironworks**: The discovery of a local seam of iron ore only 40 cm thick led the Earl to build the Leven ironworks just north of the River Leven in 1800–01, its blast furnace(s) powered from a second lade by a 6 or 7m-diameter water wheel, and able to make 30 tonnes of iron a week. However, the operators, William and George Losh from near Newcastle went rapidly bankrupt in 1803; the works reopened but were only operated intermittently until permanently closed in 1815. In 1824 a disappointed Earl David disposed of the Balgonie estate to James Balfour of Whittingham.

**Milling and Textiles**: The Balgonie Corn and Lint Mill employed 13 people in 1813. In 1824 William Russell & Co, its new owners, established the Balgonie Bleachfield beside the Leven, powered by two water wheels. In 1840 its 70 workers bleached nearly 500 tonnes of flax and tow yarns annually, but the works which were active in 1856 later declined. The Balgonie Bleachfield closed during the 1914–18 war and was in ruins by 1968; by the 1980s the buildings had been covered by the mound of a District Council tip.

**The Railway, new Colliery and Hydro Plant**: Meantime the mainline railway built in the 1840s passed under the village street in a cutting and no station was provided. The small Lochtyside coal pit was sunk in 1846, drained by a Cornish beam engine. In 1883–85 the Balgonie Colliery Company sank the Julian coal pit south of the village near the Lochty Burn, connected by rail with Thornton Junction. In 1921–22 they cleaned out one of the former lades and built a turbine house to power the mine pumps. The Lochtyside was superseded by the 1920s Branxton mine; the complex was closed in 1960. The two turbines – which used 7000 litres of water a second to generate enough electricity for 600 homes – were shut down about 1973. Tullis Russell of Markinch reactivated them in 1981, but sold them in 1993 to the Balgonie Power Company of Edinburgh; their output was to be distributed through the National Grid. By then Coaltown was a busy village of 850 people on the fringe of Glenrothes, with garages and depots.

## COATBRIDGE, Gartsherrie & Old Monkland — Map 16, A4

***Lanarkshire large town,** pop. 43,600* — OS 64: NS 7365

Pont's map of Lanarkshire made in 1596 showed that the North Calder Water was already bridged near Carnbroe, an evidently Cumbric settlement on the Monklands plateau, which stands about 100m above sea level some 13km due east of Glasgow. *'Coatdycks'*, *'Wheetflet'* and *'Dunpelder'* (Drumpellier) were named, while near the Kirk of Old Monkland were *'Kirkshawes'* and *'Kirkwood'*. Mining was in progress at Whifflet and Dundyvan by about 1754 when Roy's map was surveyed; it showed the bridge at Carnbroe, and another named *'Kippbrig'* some 2 km north-east of the Kirk of Old Monkland, where the Airdrie to Glasgow road crossed a tributary of the North Calder Water.

**The Monkland Canal and Textiles**: Another bridge was built nearby when the coal-carrying Monkland Canal opened in 1788 between Calderbank and Glasgow, and a basin was formed at Dundyvan; but although there may have been miners' rows there was little else nearby. In the 1790s much flax was grown in West Monkland parish; two scutching mills and two bleachfields served about 400 linen weavers, working under Glasgow manufacturers, and by 1806 a farmer had built a steam flax-mill at nearby Gartsherrie. Heron noted in 1799 *"the village of Old Monkland, near which there are a pottery-work, coal-works, and excellent bleachfields"*.

**Ironworks and Scotland's First Iron Boat**: The Calder Ironworks some 2 km south-east of the various Kipps bridges was promoted in 1800–02 by David Mushet and William Dixon, owner of the Govan colliery, to use local black-band ironstone. The ironworks was connected by wagonway with the Monkland Canal, and like the area in general seems to have developed in an unplanned way. Though iron canal boats had been built in Shropshire since 1787, Scotland's first iron vessel, the Forth & Clyde Canal passenger-boat *Vulcan* of 1818–19, was designed by the elderly Sir John Robison of Edinburgh (who had been a friend of James Watt at Glasgow University), and built by Robert and Thomas Wilson of the adjoining Faskine Ironworks.

**Railways name Coat Bridge – and more Ironworks**: In 1826 the 4'6" (137 cm) gauge Monkland & Kirkintilloch Railway (M&K) was opened as a wagonway, starting at Palacecraig Colliery beside the Calder ironworks, and crossing the Airdrie to Glasgow road by a bridge which from 1828 was known as *Coatbridge*. In 1828–30 William Baird set up the Gartsherrie Ironworks astride a branch of the Monkland Canal under 1 km north of Coatbridge. A self-acting incline brought coal from the company's adjoining pit; ironstone was at first available equally close by. In the 1830s the Summerlee Ironworks was also established beside the canal.

**Fun among the Furnaces?**: Meantime in 1831 the Garnkirk & Glasgow Railway (G&G) formed a connection with the M&K north of Gartsherrie. Further collieries were open at Carnbroe south of the ironworks by 1833, when the M&K was extended southwards by the Wishaw & Coltness Railway, but in 1835 rail *pleasure trips* from Glasgow were advertised only to *"Airdrie, Gartsherrie, and intermediate places"*. The area had ten blast furnaces by 1836. Its earliest post office, opened somewhat to the west by 1838, was at first called *Langloan*, but by 1841 there were 1500 people in the growing village. In 1843 the G&G abandoned their coach service between Gartsherrie and Airdrie, and opened a station named Coatbridge, served by *'engine trains'*.

**Blast Furnaces Galore**: By 1843 the Carnbroe Ironworks were also in blast, for Coatbridge was a phenomenon: by 1846 there were no fewer than 60 blast furnaces around it (about three quarters of those in Scotland), and the Garnkirk & Glasgow Railway was accordingly renamed the *"Glasgow Garnkirk & Coatbridge"*.

**Railways Galore**: The M&K, Slamannan and Ballochney railways amalgamated and were re-gauged in 1847–48 to create the standard gauge Monkland Railways Company, which took over more than 2000 wagons. In 1848 the Caledonian Railway (CR) ran through Coatbridge to form part of its main line to Stirling from the south. There was a station at Whifflet, 1 km to the south. In 1861–62 the Edinburgh & Bathgate Railway (E&B – later North British) opened its Glasgow extension, providing stations at Blairhill, Coatbridge Sunnyside, and Coatdyke (2 km east). In turn, in 1865 the CR opened a line from Rutherglen via Baillieston to Langloan station, turning north to Coatbridge Central where two stations stood side by side. All these railways gave the town remarkable nodality, with shunting yards and at Kipps the E&B repair shops, the first large locomotive running sheds in Scotland.

**The Giant Gartsherrie Ironworks**: William Baird & Co was manufacturing coal-cutting equipment by 1864; by 1869 their Gartsherrie Ironworks had grown by degrees into the largest ironworks in Scotland (and the second largest in Britain), a well-organised enterprise with a workforce of 3200 men and boys. Its sixteen furnaces were provided with hot blast at about 425°C by three beam engines, and produced 100,000 tonnes of pig-iron in a year. Six locomotives moved materials on 80 km of railway track. In the 1860s this works alone burned over

*A colliery haulage engine built by Murray & Paterson of Coatbridge, and used to haul coal trucks underground.* (JRH)

1000 tonnes of coal a day; 95% of this was raised within 1 km of the furnaces.

**Building the Great Pyramid?**: By that time the black-band ironstone, of which over 650 tonnes a day were used, was locally exhausted and had to be crudely calcined at pits within a 30 km radius before being hauled in by rail. Over 260 tonnes of lime and 50 tonnes of red haematite ore were also consumed daily. By 1869 the waste bing at the ironworks was already as large as the Great Pyramid of Egypt! Baird's had built about 500 *"good"* houses for miners at Gartsherrie, mainly of two apartments with a garden. There were also three schools, churches and a co-operative food store serving 700 member families. The firm had 26 furnaces on other sites.

**Dingy Coatbridge becomes a Burgh**: By then Coatbridge was an enormous and extremely grubby village. Among other colourful comments Bremner wrote in 1869, *"From the steeple of the parish church, which stands on a considerable eminence, the flames of fifty blast furnaces may be seen, plus a hundred chimneys of rolling mills, forges and tube works, from which dense clouds of smoke roll over it incessantly, and impart to all the buildings a peculiarly dingy aspect. A coat of black dust overlies everything."* Coatbridge was constituted a police burgh by a special Act. Dunbeth parish church with its tall spire was built in 1872.

**Football, Utilities, Bricks, Bings and Golf**: Albion Rovers Football Club was formed in 1881, the origin of its name being little known. A gasworks was set up in 1877, the CR opened a line from Langloan to Airdrie in 1886 and an electricity supply was available from 1894. In 1891 the population of Coatbridge was 29,917, Coatdyke 1701 and Whifflet 3829. By 1894 they lived in what Murray called this *"large mining town, the centre of a group of blazing iron furnaces surrounded by a network of railways – a desolate, black district, where nature's surface is scarified and loaded with rubbish heaps"*. There were coal pits on all sides except the west, where Drumpellier House remained inviolate, owned at one time by Andrew Stirling who promoted much development in Airdrie; the Drumpellier golf club founded in 1894 laid out a course in its 1 km square park. A Public Library, aided by Carnegie money, began in 1901.

**The Coatbridge Conservator**: Harold Plenderleith, born in the town in 1898 but educated in Dundee, became one of the world's prime conservators, working at the British Museum on historic objects from Tutankhamun's tomb, Ur and Sutton Hoo, writing key textbooks and becoming Director of the International Centre known as Iccrom; he died at a great age in 1997.

**Engineering, Trams and Entertainment**: By 1900 Hudson's Boilerworks fabricated large-diameter tubes. The Airdrie & Coatbridge tramways opened in 1904 with a terminus at Bank Street, Coatbridge, and a 19-car depot. A larger power station was built in 1905, as was the prominent red sandstone Dundyvan Church, designed by Alexander Cullen. Cliftonhill football ground opened in 1919. In 1922 Glasgow Corporation bought the local tramways and built a link to Baillieston; soon trams ran through Coatbridge from Airdrie to Paisley, their fares minimal. A branch of Beardmore's of Parkhead Forge worked at Coatbridge during the 1914–18 war. For many years the town had two variety theatres, the *Empire* (which had become a cinema by 1924) and the *Theatre Royal*, open for half a century. In 1924 Murray & Paterson built a mill to roll the light sections used in the nearby Victoria Mill, and in 1924–26 built the fine pair of steam winding engines installed at Cardowan colliery near Stepps; in the early 20th century Martin Black & Co of the Speedwell Works manufactured wire ropes for use in such situations.

**Decline and Overcrowding**: After 1920, the traumas of Clydeside shipbuilding and falling demand for steel caused much local decline; the old Summerlee Ironworks had outlasted Carnbroe and Langloan, but it was soon demolished. But even in the depths of the depression in 1933, Baird's foundry at Gartsherrie ironworks was still busy, and despite Colvilles' near-monopoly of Scotland, the Scottish Iron & Steel Company remained independent. In 1936 the North British Electric Welding Works was established, making chain cables, but in that year Coatbridge held the unenviable distinction of having the greatest proportion of statutory overcrowding among Scottish burghs, at 45% of all dwellings.

**From Multicoloured Trams to Blue Trains**: After the industrial resurgence of wartime, by 1951 Coatbridge had a population of about 26,700, including Gartsherrie (which had already lost its junction station). Coatbridge was still an important heavy industrial town and also a minor regional service centre; by 1953 the Coatbridge Technical College was operating in Kildonan Street. The Glasgow tramcars left Coatbridge in 1956, except for the many that were destroyed at James Connell's scrapyard around 1958. In 1961 the former NB's line through Sunnyside was electrified to Glasgow and Airdrie, with the introduction of the famed *'Blue Trains'*. The 18-hole Townhead municipal golf course was established in Drumpellier Country Park in 1970. By then a new industrial building stood south of Kirkwood; later enlarged, in 1994 it was the home of Finning Lift Trucks.

**Coatbridge Declines and starts to Recover**: Many losses followed the closure of the once-great Gartsherrie works in 1967: the Rutherglen rail service, the *Coatbridge Leader* newspaper, and most of the half dozen cinemas; by 1980 only the 1500-seat *ABC* was still open, and that too seems to have expired soon after. Over 80% of the houses in Coatbridge were owned by the town council; by 1972 there was also a covered swimming pool. An inner ring road was completed in the 1970s, and Marshalls of Newbridge opened a large chicken-processing plant in 1975. In 1975 Coatbridge became the headquarters of the Monklands District Council (MDC), which included Airdrie. They opened a new sports and leisure centre in 1978.

**Hospital, Snowballs and Superstore**: The one-time Gartsherrie Academy closed, and the tiny Infirmary gave way to the large Monklands General Hospital with 600 beds and a school of nursing which was opened at Coatdyke between Coatbridge and Airdrie in 1977, also serving Cumbernauld. At about the same time one of the earliest ASDA superstores in Scotland was established, and by 1979 John J Lees Ltd were making confectionery such as *'Snowballs'* on a large scale at Newlands Street. In 1981 Coatbridge had a 20,000 population, and by then there was no cinema, theatre or art gallery in the whole of Monklands District. By 1983 Lamberton & Co were machining parts for North Sea oil work, while Tannoy Products had a communication systems factory at Rosehall industrial estate. In the 1980s Coatbridge also benefited from an SDA area project, but Marshall's large chicken packery lost 200 jobs in 1989 as a result of the salmonella scare.The SDA acquired and marketed land for industry and warehousing. A necessary but unattractive local industry recycled car bodies through a crusher.

**Rail Freight Developments**: In 1981 rail electrification was extended from the Mossend yard to the Coatbridge Freightliner container depot (by 1988 was one of only two still remaining in Scotland). It was nonetheless far more important as a container base than Grangemouth and all the other Forth ports put together, for it exchanged nearly 100,000 containers a year on some half dozen daily trains to and from ports in England such as Harwich, as against 50,000 from Glasgow; four gantry cranes were required to shift the great boxes. The Gunnie cement depot at Sunnyside received daily trainloads of Castle cement from Clitheroe, but this traffic was sadly transferred from rail to road in 1993. In mid 1993 an experimental Road-Railer service was tried to London (Stratford).

**A Town of many Stations**: Remarkably, although Langloan had closed, three rail passenger stations remained open in the town, including electrified Blairhill and Sunnyside – though in 1992 Coatbridge Central was carpeted in broken glass, while derelict land and landfill sites north of the town spoke eloquently of its industrial past. A new Whifflet station on the Motherwell line was opened late in 1992, and in 1993 diesel passenger-train services were reintroduced on the Whifflet, Rutherglen and Glasgow Central route, with another new station at Kirkwood, 300 m west of the original Langloan station.

**Culture Returns and the Time Capsule Prospers**: In 1988 culture gaps were filled when the Summerlee Heritage Trust, financed by the Monklands District Council, opened their Summerlee Visitor Park, a *"magnificent museum of industrial and social history over the remains of the Summerlee Ironworks" (Scotland on Sunday)*. Its working exhibits, including one of the Cardowan winding engines, drew 75,000 visitors in 1989, needing 45 staff; the Ironworks Gallery which opened on the site in 1990 was at once *"mobbed"*. A rival attraction in Bank Street sponsored by Monklands Council and opened in 1991 was the thematic Time Capsule, exploiting ice and water for entertainment. In 1991 the resident population of

Coatbridge was about 43,600, still disadvantaged, mainly by poor health. The Quadrant shopping centre opened in 1992 as part of major town centre improvements, and by 1996 a Tesco store was open.

**Football Stumbles, and Research at a Loss**: Meantime something desperately needed to be done at Cliftonhill, the run-down ground where Second Division Albion Rovers struggled to survive despite being allowed to host only 750 spectators in safety, including 500 in the comfort of seating. In 1994 Albion Rovers joined the new lowly Third Division. Plans also fell through to create a new 10,500-seat stadium at Airdrie, to be shared with Airdrieonians. About 1990 the former Mines Rescue Centre became the home of Magnum, a tiny company producing within-computer UPS – uninterruptible power supply gadgets, with nearly 50 highly skilled staff. Scotlab, an expanding medical research firm moved into the town in 1991 and soon employed 40 people. The food manufacturers Lees changed hands in 1991 and 1993, when making losses, but were still producing their popular *'Snowballs'* of marshmallow and coconut for national distribution.

**Blocks enter History but Chickens pack it in**: In 1992 British Coal Enterprise was offering floorspace in its Fountain Business Centre. In 1994 the MSA (safety equipment) works adjoined the M8/A725 junction, and in 1997 concrete blocks manufactured by Paterson of Greenoakhill were used in the reconstruction of New Lanark. Nearly 800 people were employed in 1997 when Marshalls announced the closure of their chicken packery, the remaining work being moved to Newbridge. In 1997, due to the lower production costs of Moroccan factories, Alexandra Workwear of Bristol also intended to close their Coatbridge factory with the loss of 250 jobs, moving the remaining work to Uddingston. Medium-sized employers then were Boots, Lees (with a new factory), Mackinnon (knitwear), Rentokil and Retronix (electronics). Heavy industry included Banks (opencast coal-mining), Shanks (waste & landfill), and Dick's sheet metal works.

**Warehousing, and Local Government**: In 1997 Coatbridge High School had a roll of 767, Columba High 841, Rosehall High 482, St Ambrose High 1114 and St Patrick's High 945; Coatbridge College employed 200. By 1998 although Dunbeth Church had been saved, the gothic Dundyvan Church was long-vacant and deteriorating. In 1996 Monklands District became the central part of the new unitary authority area of *'North Lanarkshire'* (also including Motherwell and Cumbernauld), but Coatbridge did not gain its main headquarters, which went to Motherwell; this led to a new train service being started between the two.

## COCKBURNSPATH & Old Cambus — Map 3, B2

***Berwickshire village**, pop. 500* — OS 67: NT 7771

Cockburnspath – pronounced *Cobberspeth* (so noted Defoe) or *Coppersmith* (according to Chambers!) but locally as *'Copath'*, stands on a plateau above the coastal cliffs of Berwickshire, between the ravine of the Dunglass Burn and the twin gorges of the Heriot Water and Pease Burn. By around 1200 a church and *'hospital'* or hospice had been built above the cliffs at Old Cambus, 3 km to the east, helpful alike for storm-bound pedestrians and horsemen on what was to become the Great North Road, as well as for coasting boatmen unable to round the dreadful cliffs of St Abb's Head. Cockburnspath had an equally old church, and its 15th century castle tower overlooked the Heriot Water.

**The Coaching Burgh and the Geologist**: Pont's map of about 1600 as engraved by Blaeu showed it as a more significant place than most in the Merse, accessed by a short spur from the road, itself unique in the county. In 1603 – immediately after the Union of the Crowns – Cockburnspath gained a post office, a change point on the first mail route between Scotland and England. In 1612 it became a burgh of barony with a chartered market, and an inn was open by 1618 – very likely earlier – as a replacement for the hospice. A parish school was opened in 1619, with another at Old Cambus in 1620. A century later, in 1734, a post office was opened at old Cambus. Meantime Defoe had referred to Cockburnspath as a *"village"*. In the early 1750s, Roy's map showed it as a small nucleated settlement away from the coast-hugging road, on which a bridge already existed. It was at Siccar Point near Old Cambus that the pioneer late 18th century geologist James Hutton identified a great unconformity in the rocks, showing the cycles of erosion and deposition that first implied the earth's vast age *(see Kirriemuir for Lyell's interpretation of Hutton's work).*

**Bridges and Cod Liver Oil**: The Pease was bridged about 1777 some 1.5 km to the east of the village, Heron noticing in 1799 *"a magnificent bridge of four arches"*, while Chambers in the 1820s described a 2-arched bridge some 40 m high with a single lofty pier: had the first bridge fallen? Heron did not mention Cockburnspath; though a fair was still scheduled to take place in 1797, its post office had been transferred to Press Castle near Coldingham, which was on the new and more inland post road by 1827. But in 1832 Cobbett found *"a little village"* with a church. A tiny fishing harbour was built at Cove below Cockburnspath between 1770 and 1831; a cod liver oil factory operated there in the 19th century.

**On and beside the Railway**: The North British Railway served Cockburnspath with a station from 1846; still open in 1923, this had been closed by 1953, many years before Beeching. Meanwhile a school was built in 1872, and by the 1890s the Great North Road had moved inland again, to the present general route of the A1. By the 1950s a coastguard station stood near the village, whose population by then was some 750. By the 1990s Cockburnspath was the eastern terminus of the Southern Upland Way but remained a conservation village, with some 500 people, a post office and inn, a coastguard station and a handful of small fishing boats at Cove. Caravan sites were open at Pease Bay, 2 km to the east, and inland 2 km south of the village, thankfully twice bypassed by costly improvements to the A1.

## COCKENZIE & Port Seton — Map 15, E1

***E. Lothian coastal villages**, pop. 4250* — OS 66: NT 4075

Seton, a little inland from the coast of East Lothian to the east of Prestonpans, had a church by 1242 and became a burgh of barony in 1321. The church was made collegiate in 1492 by George, the fourth Lord Seton, and attractively enlarged by his widow after his death at Flodden in 1513. A so-called golf course played on by Queen Mary existed at Seton in 1567. About 2 km to the west was a natural harbour at Cockenzie, which was chartered as a burgh of barony in 1591 and evidently improved, for Pont's map made around 1600 showed the double breakwaters of *'Cokeny haven'*; inland *'Seatoun'* was prominently shown. Seton had a parish school from 1633.

Chambers observed two centuries later that *"Seton House, erected at the beginning of the 17th century, was by far the most magnificent mansion of its time in Scotland"*. Apparently owned by the Seton Earl of Winton, it suffered for his part in the 1715 uprising, being rebuilt by Robert Adam from 1789 and known as Seton Palace.

**The First Railway in War**: A wagonway carrying coal down from Tranent to Cockenzie, built in 1722, became in the 1745 uprising the first railway to become involved in warfare – the Battle of Prestonpans *(see Thomas (1984))*. The Roy map, made about 1754, showed Cockenzie and only 750m to the east Port Seton, both tiny places; the latter's harbour with its two breakwaters had lately been built for the Earl of Winton. Very belatedly following the example of Prestonpans, in 1784 Port Seton became the site of a salt works developed by Dr Francis Swediaur. By 1797 Cockenzie had an annual fair. In 1799 Heron noted Port Seton as a village with *"a considerable trade in salt and coal. Its inhabitants, with those of Cockenzie, may be about 500, mostly colliers, salt makers, and fishermen"*.

**Improved Harbours, Boats and Yachts**: By 1827 Seton's collegiate church was derelict (but it survives as an Ancient Monument). In 1830 Cockenzie harbour was improved as a coal port. The North British Railway's main line opened in 1846, but the nearest station was at Prestonpans. It passed inland of Seton and under the ancient Cockenzie wagonway, which however closed in 1886. Port Seton harbour was rebuilt in 1879–80, financed by the fishermen themselves with help from the Earl of Wemyss and March. Seton Palace was demolished before 1892. By around 1900 there was a post and telegraph office and an inn; on the coast between Cockenzie and Prestonpans was a colliery. By then Weatherheads *(see Eyemouth)* built wooden drifters at Cockenzie, and later also yachts. In 1937 they built the ocean racing yacht *Dunpelder* for Lord Balfour, but by the 1950s had sold the by then derelict Cockenzie harbour to Samuel White of Cowes, Isle of Wight. However, the boatyard remained open.

**Through the Tramway Era to Caravans**: By the 1920s the Musselburgh Tramways Company operated a route between Port Seton and the Edinburgh boundary, but in 1932 the enterprise was taken over by the Edinburgh Corporation tramways and the section east of Levenhall abandoned. With a combined population of some 3500 in the 1950s the two settlements supported nearly typical village facilities, plus swimming baths and a dance hall; the long-standing caravan park known as Seton Holiday Camp was open by 1954, and had its own post office.

**Mutual Fishermen and the End of Boatbuilding**: In 1951 the Cockenzie & Port Seton Fishermen's Mutual Association was founded, soon providing net-repairing and transport facilities at Port Seton; about 1953 the harbour wall was extended to protect this base for about 24 prawning vessels of around 20m; four more were on order. In those pre-home freezer days part of the catches was sent to Annan for canning. By 1985 the 17 local prawn trawlers actually fished out of Eyemouth, but in 1988 both Cockenzie, and especially Port Seton, still possessed active fishing harbours, and a fish curer. In 1988 the Cockenzie Slip & Boat Yard built the hull for the Falkirk Museum's replica of the *Charlotte Dundas*, but the yard finally closed early in 1995.

**Cockenzie Power Station**: From the 1960s the area was dominated by the towering bulk of the Cockenzie Generating Station, built on the site of the former colliery immediately west of the twin villages; a rail link from the main line served its coal stockyard. The local population rose to nearly 4000 by 1971, and to 4235 in 1991, with a substantial new estate built to the east by 1996. In 1990 the power station provided 520 jobs; in 1992 rail-borne coal was again arriving from the nearby Blindwells opencast quarry. Coal can also arrive by sea, to the large jetty. It was agreed in 1993 that the generating station, owned by Scottish Power, should burn up to 0.8 million tonnes of BC opencast coal a year until 1998. It ran only intermittently in 1994, but with 250 workers in 1997 it was supplied with coal by rail from both Knockshinnoch (opencast) and Monktonhall (deep mined) until the latter's liquidation. Smaller firms nearby involve boat repairing, fish wholesaling and curing, chemical manufacture, and construction.

## COLDINGHAM & St Abbs

**Map 3, C2**

***Berwickshire coastal villages**, pop. 850*

OS 67: NT 9065

A Bronze Age settlement existed on the Buskin Burn 2 km from the North Sea in what later became Berwickshire. A timber-palisaded hill now known as Kirk Hill near modern St Abbs may be the original site of Anglian *Colodaesburg* and its nunnery cum priory, established about 635 AD and later called Coldingham, a very English placename. Soon afterwards a Northumbrian princess named Ebba was shipwrecked on the rocks of the nearby headland. Saved and converted to Christianity she then became a nun, later called *St.Abb*, who from 640 headed the convent; hence St Abb's Head. The building was struck by lightning and burned in 679 AD.

**The Nuns' Bathing Machine**: By 685 the convent had been rebuilt as *"a far famed and stately edifice"*, and Bede in the eighth century described Coldingham as a town *(urbs)*. Apparently it had a roadway, for Chambers – who had an ear for local traditions – wrote in the 1820s that the nuns used to go down to the bay to bathe in a screened chariot – evidently similar in purpose to a Victorian bathing machine! The Danes destroyed the priory in the ninth century. In 1098 a Benedictine priory was re-founded on the same site, described as being in Lothian when King Edgar gave the land to the prior of Durham, so ensuring a continuing English link; in 1100 a church was founded. By the 12th or 13th century a *'hospital'* had been established at nearby Segden.

**Destruction hits Priory and County**: The priory was sacked by King John of England in 1216 but rebuilt soon afterwards, and Coldingham appeared on the Gough map of about 1250. The priory was destroyed yet again in 1314. After reconstruction, and despite the Black Death, Coldingham was the largest settlement in Berwickshire by 1371, having *"hostelries"* and the justices of the shire, who had fled from Berwick. The priory was destroyed for the fifth time about 1430, but was soon rebuilt on a larger scale, and supplied with water through a lead pipe. The 15th century Fast Castle on the cliffs 6km north-west of Coldingham was owned by the Restalrig family. The justices' seat was again moved in 1551, to Duns. In 1560 the Commendator of Coldingham represented the community in Parliament, but the priory suffered partial destruction during the Reformation. It lingered on, but was virtually extinct by 1588, the year after a parish school was founded, and became secular in 1606 under Lord Home; however, Pont's map made about that time showed the priory with much more emphasis than the *'toun'*.

**Barony Burgh in the Coaching Age**: Coldingham was made a burgh of barony in 1638 and for a time appears to have had a minor market. Most of the priory buildings were finally destroyed in 1648, so robbed that the *bedral* (beadle) of the parish remarked in the 1820s that *"there is not a house in the village that has na a kirk stane in't"*. Only two walls of the priory church remained standing, to be incorporated in a rather makeshift parish church in 1662. The village survived to appear on Roy's map as a nucleated settlement on the main coast road – which was the only road in the area in the mid 18th century. The school was open in the 1790s, and an annual fair was scheduled for 1797. Heron observed in 1799 that *"the town of Coldingham contains upwards of 700 inhabitants"*. However from 1768 the post town for Coldingham was at Press Castle, 3 km to the west, by 1799 a staging point for the Edinburgh to London coaches. A post office opened at Coldingham in 1805. A short-lasting brewery was open by 1825 at Coldingham, which Chambers described in 1827 as a *"delightful little village"*.

**St Abbs joins Coldingham**: In 1833–35 a fishing harbour funded by the Edinburgh brewer Usher was built at Coldingham Shore, which was renamed St Abbs; at one time 14 boats were based there. St Abb's Head lighthouse, unusually placed well below the cliff top, was built, and illuminated from 1862. From 1876 it had the first fog siren driven by hot air. The railways passed Coldingham by, but the parish church was restored in the 1850s, and the village had an inn by 1894; the St Abbs lifeboat station was opened in 1911. The *Clachan Hotel* was built in 1928 at Coldingham Bay just east of St Abbs, and a youth hostel was opened there in the 1930s. Coldingham had an agricultural contractor by 1956.

**Light Over and Under the Sea**: When electrified in 1968 the lighthouse became for a decade the single most powerful in Scotland, with a major radio beacon, and until automation in 1993 held a status above all other Scottish lighthouses. Coldingham grew into a significant but quiet resort, with a substantial retired element, three hotels, two caravan and camping sites and a coach garage. A large housing estate was built south-east of the village in the late 1980s. In 1989 St Abbs retained its primary school and remained a very picturesque fishing village, much frequented by sub-aqua clubs from the northern half of Britain; by 1995 it had a visitor centre. The youth hostel is seasonal.

## COLDSTREAM & Birgham

**Map 3, C3**

***Berwickshire village,*** *pop. 1750* — OS 74: NT 8439

At Birgham, 5 km to the west of Coldstream, the English Border as it descends northwards from The Cheviot makes a right-angled turn to follow the River Tweed downstream. This odd alignment seems to date back to at least 1018 when a treaty was signed at Birgham after King Malcolm II had won possession of the Lothians; another treaty made there in 1290 was supposed to re-establish Scotland's independence. But a strategic ford from the village of Cornhill on the Northumbrian bank of the lower River Tweed gave greater importance to Coldstream, on the north bank, and in later centuries Birgham was only a small farming village.

**Lennel, the Hirsel, Priory, Ford and Wars**: Chambers commented that Lennel, about 2 km to the east of Coldstream, was *"the name and kirktown of the parish, before Coldstream existed"*; but the one-time village *"was so completely destroyed in the border wars that the precise site is unknown"*. Coldstream must take its name from the character of the Leet Water, which joins the river near the Hirsel; by about 1143 there was already a church. The 12th century Cistercian Priory or nunnery of Coldstream was founded by Earl Gospatric. There was also an early inn, at which royalty would await low water to cross the river. The ford was used for the invasion of Scotland by the English King Edward I in 1296. By then the priory owned three properties in the burgh of Berwick, but that town's destruction in 1296 and the prolonged wars that followed caused the nuns to leave in 1315.

**Homes, Guards and Ferry Irregular Marriages!**: The final blows in the seemingly endless wars fell in the 1540s, when very little of Coldstream seems to have been left standing. Pont's map made about 1600 showed the emparked mansion of *'Hirsell'* prominently, but only tiny symbols for *'Old Caldstreame'* beside the river and *'New Caldstreame'* some way from it. The Home family acquired the Hirsel in 1611, and Coldstream was made a burgh of barony in 1621 when the priory properties passed to Sir John Hamilton. By 1659 Coldstream was sufficiently important for the famous British regiment of the *Coldstream Guards* to be raised there by General Monk. Roy's map of about 1754 showed Coldstream as a little place laid out as a rough Cross of Lorraine, with roads to east, west and north. The hamlet now known as Lennel was called *Newtown of Coldstream*. A ferry from Cornhill in England was shown by a *'boathouse'* near the site of the later bridge, enabling many irregular marriages of eloping English couples to take place in Coldstream between 1754 and 1857.

**Bridge and Brewery**: The road from Edinburgh was turnpiked under an Act of 1760, and the ford and ferry were replaced by James Smeaton's five-arched Tweed Bridge in 1766. The Hirsel lake was created in the late 18th century. The first post office opened in Coldstream in 1772; by 1797 it was a post town, but the coach staging-point was at Cornhill. Although in 1799 Heron regarded Coldstream – which had two annual fairs – as a *"town"*, it was essentially agricultural, with *"such mechanical employments as the vicinity requires"*; from about 1800 until some time after 1825 Thomas Joppling operated a brewery. A later brewery also failed, though its buildings survived into the 1970s. Maybe better roads brought better beers? From 1822 Coldstream was said to be the first country town in Scotland to set up a penny post in its neighbourhood, including Leitholm.

**Elopements by Coach, and the 23 Gardeners**: In the 1820s Chambers wrote *"of this agreeable and thriving town which, without any assistance from manufactures, seems to subsist chiefly upon the thoroughfare which the Tweed bridge has occasioned. It is resorted to by many imprudent couples for the same purpose which has sent so many to the more celebrated Gretna."* This was evidently to the benefit of the inns, but the marriage trade nearly ended with a change in English law in 1857. Coldstream was never directly served by rail, the nearest station being at Cornhill; and no other industry of consequence appeared. However, in 1870 23 gardeners were employed at the Hirsel, to say nothing of indoor staff. By 1894 Murray saw Coldstream as *"a pleasant, well-built town with very little to* *detain the visitor"*, so perhaps it is unsurprising that it had only one hotel, the *"fair" Newcastle Arms*. There was a ferry from near The Hirsel to Wark.

**Golf and Gas, Paper, Printing and Tourism**: Coldstream kept some commercial importance, acquiring agricultural engineers, and also a gasworks (possibly a replacement) at the unusually late date of 1934. The Hirsel golf club founded in 1948 laid out a 9-hole course in the mansion's park. By 1951 about 1850 people lived in and around Coldstream. Burgh status was lost in 1975, but a paper mill was opened in 1977, producing tissues and packaging. By 1981 there were six hotels, and the Cottage Hospital was a GP acute and maternity unit. By 1983 there was a museum, a caravan site and a tourist information office; Screencraft were specialist colour printers. In 1991 the population was nearly 1750, with a quite affluent retirement emphasis. By 1998 a second museum was open, in what was by then the Hirsel Country Park.

## COLINSBURGH, Kilconquhar, Newburn & Balcarres

**Map 6, C4**

***East Fife villages / hamlets**, pop. 600* OS 59: NO 4703

Kilconquhar (locally pronounced *Kinneuchar*) has a name which dates it as being a Christian foundation of the Dark Ages. Its old church, whose surviving arcade contains Norman work, stands on a mound beside a small loch, a rare feature in east Fife. By 1594 there was a parish school. Some 4km north-west is the ancient ruined church of the tiny rural parish of Newburn. Somewhat inland is Balcarres House, which in part goes back to a tower of 1595 and is overlooked by a crag, perhaps once crowned by an ancient fort, but later the site of a folly. Kilconquhar Castle also dates from the 16th century, and the *Kinneuchar Inn* is ancient too. The linear village of Colinsburgh 1.5km to the north was founded in 1705 by Colin Lindsay, the 3rd Earl of Crawford and Balcarres. Sited astride the road from Largo to Pittenweem, and chartered as a burgh of barony in 1707, its early buildings contain many stones of an almost black volcanic rock. The Roy map showed that by about 1750 there was a mill nearby, and roads linking Colinsburgh in most directions, except apparently to its parochial centre at Kilconquhar!

**Professional Services**: The main east–west road was turnpiked in 1790, and Colinsburgh which already had a lawyer and WS (Writer to the Signet), was a post town by 1797. By then two annual fairs were held there, as well as one at Kilconquhar. The roads to Elie were turnpiked in 1807, and Colinsburgh was the junction for the Elie mails in 1813. By 1827 the secluded mansion of Charleton House in its wooded policies stood north-west of Colinsburgh, which was by then according to Chambers *"a thriving village"*. A surgeon practised in Colinsburgh for fifty years, c.1820–1871.

**Transient Railway and Modern Tourism**: A railway from Leven made its temporary terminal in 1857 at a station a kilometre from Kilconquhar; later the line was extended to Elie and Anstruther. In the late 19th century Colinsburgh had a saddler, and by 1894 both villages possessed hotels or inns. The large and substantial *'Town'* hall at Colinsburgh was built in 1894. Neither place ever attracted industry, though in the 1939–45 war defensive works overlooking the entrance to the Firth of Forth were built on Kincraig Point. Cattle shows lasted at Colinsburgh into the post-war period, but in 1951 the combined populations were little over 750, with average village facilities. The railway was closed by Beeching in 1965, and soon little sign of it was left. With a drop in population to about 600, some other facilities had also gone by 1981. However, a large holiday caravan site at Shell Bay and a 1970s development of timeshare holiday homes at Kilconquhar introduced new activity. By 1992 Charleton House was being run as a conference hotel; the widely acclaimed new Charleton golf courses of 18 and 9 holes were opened in 1994, their parkland setting enhanced by the house.

## COLINTON & Juniper Green

**Map 15, B2**

***Western suburbs of Edinburgh**, pop. 21,000* OS 66: NT 2169

Colinton, which lies on the steep-sided Water of Leith 6km above Edinburgh, has a lengthy but obscure ecclesiastical history going back to the 11th century, and the ruins of the 16th century Colinton Castle. Although the water power of the river was extensively exploited, it was a tiny place when Pont mapped the Lothians about 1600, and never became a burgh. There were mills at Kirkland and Mossie from the 16th century, and West Mill was in use by the late 17th century. By 1651 there was a parish school beside the kirk. Dreghorn Castle was built as a mansion later in that century; it was repeatedly enlarged. Another early mansion was Bonaly (or Bonally) House or Tower, once the home of the judge Lord Cockburn. The Upper Spylaw paper mill was in use from 1681, the first of six such in the area.

**Juniper Green**: Juniper Green less than 2 km up the river from Colinton may take its name from a bleachfield opened about the time of the Union of the Parliaments, while Tipperlin bleachfield was laid out in 1729 with the aid of a government grant. Woodhall mill at Juniper Green was built as a lint mill in the early 18th century, while Denholm's or Curriemuir Mill and the first narrow road bridge were also probably erected in that century. By the time of Roy's survey of about 1754, the road connecting Edinburgh *'by Crosswoodhill'* with Carnwath and Lanark had been defined, later becoming a turnpike.

**Snuff and Paper Mills**: Late in the 18th century the Gillespie brothers from Roslin began to manufacture snuff instead of paper at Upper Spylaw, and sold it in Edinburgh. James Gillespie's will provided the funds to found a school and hospital in the city in 1797. Five more tiny paper mills were founded in the 18th century, though between the six of them they employed fewer than 100 people in the 1790s; grain and snuff mills once operated at East Mill. A post office opened in 1803, and a new school was built in 1815. Woodhall had become a paper and board mill by 1825, and Mossie Mill too was converted into a paper mill in 1838. A church was built at Juniper Green in 1845, at which time Kate's Mill was making paper. There were 5 snuff mills, though later in the century these began to close.

**Oatmeal, Banknotes and Snaky Railway**: Although Hole mill was demolished in 1870, about 1880 Upper Spylaw was converted into a dairy, and about that time Curriemuir was milling Hunter's oatmeal. In 1874 a quite extraordinarily sinuous, and in places steep, single-track branch of the Caledonian Railway was opened up the valley from the main line at Slateford, with stations at Colinton and Juniper Green on its way to Balerno. Some of the paper mills operated in Colinton until at least 1890 when Kate's Mill, then making paper for banknotes, was burned down; the ancient Kirkland mill suffered a similar

*A weir on the Water of Leith just below Colinton. The lade took the water to Kate's Mill – converted from a waulk mill to a paper mill in 1783, and named after the owner's wife. It produced banknotes in the second half of the 19th century.* (AL)

fate in 1916. Scott's porage oats were prepared at the West Mill from 1891 well into the 20th century *(see also Springfield).*

**Suburbs, Reservoirs and Indian Barracks**: In 1891 a new school was necessary, and Colinton and Juniper Green then both had inns and post and telegraph offices. Though at that time still separated from Edinburgh by 3km of open country, suburbanisation began with Baberton golf club, founded at Juniper Green by (and initially for) local residents in 1893, followed only two years later by the Torphin Hill club with its own 18-hole course. The Bonaly, Clubbiedean and Torduff reservoirs on the headwaters of the Braid Burn had been impounded by 1895. Dreghorn Castle became a private school a few years later, subsequently being taken over by the army. Redford Barracks were built in 1909; due to a slight error, a design intended for India was adopted!

**Into the City with Boarding School and Trams**: Craiglockhart Roman Catholic teacher training college was opened in 1918. In the latter year the village became part of the City of Edinburgh, and from then Colinton was served by Edinburgh's trams, forming the terminus for services to Leith and Granton. In 1930 the independent Merchiston Castle School, a boys' boarding establishment, moved from Morningside to new buildings beside Colinton House and the castle ruins. By 1939 Hailes House was a youth hostel. Watt's, last of the five snuff mills, closed about 1940; passenger trains were withdrawn in 1943.

**Suburbanisation and Quarrying**: Colinton had a population of over 13,000 by 1951, though only the general facilities of a large village. The trams vanished in 1955, and in 1955–58 Dreghorn Castle was demolished by the Ministry of Defence, and new barracks erected on its site. The Torphin Hill quarry was an important feature through the second half of the 20th century, but is now disused. By 1970 the youth hostel had gone, the railway had been lifted, and Mossie Mill closed in 1972. By 1981 with continuing suburban development, the local facilities had grown to those of a small town. By 1977 Colinton had acquired the HQ of the Forth River Purification Board (FRPB), and by 1981 contained over 21,000 people; in that year Craiglockhart College was merged into St Andrews at Bearsden *(q.v.)*; in the 1990s the building became part of Napier University. Adjacent to the FRPB was the base of Globespan holidays.

**What makes a school *'Scottish'*?**: In the mid 1980s the A720 City Bypass was driven through the area between Colinton and Juniper Green. In 1989 Redford and Glencorse barracks were jointly the training depot of the Army's Scottish Division. Merchiston Castle School was expanded in the 1980s, and by 1996 had 400 pupils – all boys. The city's Firrhill High School has 800 pupils. By then virtually all space within the bypass had been developed, Baberton was yet another new housing estate and the Bonaly Country Park had been established on the Pentland slopes. There is now a modern 40-room *Travelodge* on the bypass at Dreghorn.

## COLINTRAIVE, Rhubodach & Inverchaolain

**Map 5, A5**

***Argyllshire hamlets,*** *pop. 250* — OS 63: NS 0374

The steep northern shores of the Kyles of Bute, the straits separating the Isle of Bute from Cowal, bear an ancient cairn, while offshore was a fort. The area of Inverchaolain parish was well settled by about 1600 when Pont produced his sketch map; a mill already stood on the Milton Burn. The Roy map showed that by 1750 tracks on both shores led south and east from what was evidently a ferry site near the mouth of the burn. By 1800 a drovers' ferry plied across the Kyles; the cattle were expected to swim, hence the place name which comes from the Gaelic *Caol an t'anaimh*, *'Straits of Swimming'*. The landfall on Bute is known as Rhubodach, *Rubha Bodach* meaning *'Old Woman's Point'*.

**Tourism**: By 1864 Hutcheson steamers served a pier on the north shore at the former Milton, which developed into the small resort village of Colintraive; in 1877 calls were made by the Lochgoil & Lochlong Steamboat Company. By 1894 Murray noted the *"plain" Colintraive Hotel* at the terminal of a regular passenger ferry; there was also a post office, and a single track coastal road led northwards to Springfield and Glendaruel. A car ferry was introduced in 1950. In 1951 about 250 people lived in Colintraive, which by then had a primary school. The population fell to about 175 by 1971, then stabilised, though the school had closed by 1976. In the 1980s a completely new main road was built up the wooded Milton Glen and over a col down to Springfield, leaving the old coast road for local access and pleasure. A post office was open in 1994 (but no more). Today, the *Colintraive Hotel* continues in business, but Rhubodach is merely a slipway from which the ferry operates.

## COLL, Isle of

**Map 4, A1**

***Island, Inner Hebrides,*** *pop. 172* — OS 46: NM 2257

Some 30km out to sea beyond Tobermory on the Sound of Mull lies the long narrow moorland and farming island of Coll, whose name means Hazel. On its exposed western coast are the scant remains of early forts and duns. The solid 14th century Old Breachacha Castle stands on a bay of that name near the island's south-western end, but Martin writing in 1703 noted in the south-east of the isle the *"little castle"* of the resident proprietor, Maclean of Coll; for a time lead was mined nearby. The locals were Protestants, producing barley, oats, cod and ling. In 1750 Hector Maclean the 13th laird had the mansion called Breachacha New Castle built close by the old one, in the shelter of high sandhills.

**Development and Emigration**: The fairly sheltered triangular inlet of Loch Eatharna on the eastern side of the isle became the site for a pier, the starting point of the roads built in the 19th century, and the focus of the tiny village of Arinagour. Originally comprising two terraces each of six cottages, it was built about 1800 by a benevolent Maclean. A post office was opened in 1805. Linen manufacture was fostered and the island population burgeoned, to nearly 1500 by 1841. Emigration was encouraged by the Macleans, but in 1856 they sold out to new Stewart lairds, who soon extended Breachacha Castle. A 5-roomed inn was built at Arinagour. But by 1881 over half Coll's people had been induced to leave. Later, fine cheeses were made, and the harbour became frequented by pleasure sailors; a tiny tourist trade developed. By 1951 the island's population was down to 210, its small-village facilities concentrated at Arinagour where the local bus service was based. This connected three days a week with MacBraynes *'inner islands mail steamer'* to Oban and Lochboisdale via Tobermory and Tiree.

**Coll Cosmetics and quiet Holidays**: A new pier built in 1969 enabled car unloading, by which time the isle's population had fallen below 150. By the 1970s electricity arrived from Scarinish power station on Tiree by submarine cable. In 1975 a cattle farmer's wife, Wendy McKechnie, founded a business to manufacture cosmetics, using only natural products such as lanolin and beeswax; a factory was built with HIDB aid in 1978, when the little firm was already the largest employer on the island. By 1981 the inn had been enlarged into the 9-room *Isle of Coll Hotel* and by 1985 an airstrip had been laid out. In 1986 the Tiree car ferry served Coll, Tobermory, Lochaline and Oban. In that year, mainland electricity was brought to the island for the first time by undersea cable, and by 1991 the population had recovered to 172. Meantime Breachacha New Castle, empty since 1944, had been partly restored in 1968, but stood unused until 1998 when it became holiday homes, as were many of the cottages at Arinagour, where the school and post office are based. The Old Breachacha Castle had also been well restored.

## COLLESSIE

**Map 6, B3**

***East Fife small village,*** *pop. 200* — OS 59: NO 2813

Beween the north Fife hills and the level Howe of Fife 5km east of Auchtermuchty were a standing stone, a tumulus, an ancient chapel and the site of a castle. Pont's map of about 1600 as engraved by Blaeu marked only Collessie Kirk, but by 1631 a parish school was open. By about 1750 the Auchtermuchty to Cupar road passed to the south. By the 1820s the *Trafalgar Inn* stood beside the intersection formed by the road from Freuchie to Newburgh, which climbed through the narrow valley of Collessie Den; cottages clustered round the church on its knoll, and to the south was the emparked mansion of Kinloch House. Collessie was given a station when the Perth branch of the Edinburgh & Northern Railway was opened in 1848 beside the Newburgh road. In 1895 the line had double track, the station had goods facilities, and there was a post and telegraph office.

**Sand and Nature Study**: The inn had closed by 1951 when nearly 450 people still lived in this primarily agricultural area, but there was still a primary school and also a village hall. The railway was later reduced to single track and the station and goods yard were closed in 1955. By then extensive sand and gravel pits were scarring the country to the south. By 1971 the population was only 300 and the post office closed soon afterwards; by 1981 under 200 people were left, though a small new estate of private houses was being added to this picturesque place, where some of Scotland's last few thatched cottages survived. Around 1990 the little Birnie Loch was created from gravel pits as a nature reserve, adjoined in 1999 by the Fife Animal Park and a restaurant. Parts of the over-wide railway bridge remained as prominent skeletons. The village's well-kept Victory Hall (built 1923) survives.

## COLLIESTON, Forvie & Slains

**Map 10, C2**

***Buchan hamlets,*** *pop. 200* — OS 38: NK 0428

The Sands of Forvie on the Buchan coast 10km east of Ellon long ago overwhelmed Forvie village, whose ruined medieval church alone remains. On cliffs 5km to the north stood the first Slains Castle, largely demolished in 1594. Between these landmarks are the Kirkton of Slains – perhaps the site of the parish school opened in 1608 *(but see below)* – and Collieston, both tiny places in the 17th and 18th centuries, as the Blaeu and Roy maps showed. In 1699 Dalgattie or Meikletoun of Slains was chartered as a barony burgh inland from Collieston. Cliff caves made smuggling notorious at Collieston, but in 1750 Roy marked only *'dunes'* at Forvie. About 1800 Collieston was re-founded as a new village beside a cove in the cliffs. However, in 1850 nearly 50 fishermen still worked from an exposed beach at Slains. In 1858 Pratt described Collieston as a *"picturesque fishing village"* and it was also a sea bathing centre *"in spite of its scanty accommodations"*.

**Peak and Decline**: In the 1890s 170 fishermen manned 60 boats, so a pier was built to enclose a small sheltered harbour. As larger vessels were employed they were usually based elsewhere, the locals being left to fish for the small haddock known as Speldings. By 1951 under 400 people lived locally, with the facilities of a hamlet, plus a small hotel which soon closed. The population fell steadily to level off at about 270 in the 1970s. Primary and secondary schooling at Slains – a country school near the Meikle Loch 2 km to the north – was reduced by 1976 to primary only, and soon closed. The coastguard station, open in 1967, had closed by 1985, and many cottages of the local fisherfolk had become holiday homes. Meantime by 1974 the Sands of Forvie had become a nature reserve, whose Forvie Centre was opened near Collieston. There had been remarkably little change by 1999; the post office was still open, and a viewpoint car park had been provided on the cliffs.

## COLLIN, Racks & Torthorwald — Map 2, B4

***Dumfriesshire small villages,** pop. 600* — OS 84: NY 0275

Ancient earthworks flank Torthorwald, about 6km east of Dumfries, from which it was for long separated by the vast trackless wastes of Lochar Moss; like its surroundings, even the 14th century keep of Torthorwald Castle was a blank on the Pont and Blaeu map of Nithsdale. The Roy map of about 1754 showed a road north from Ruthwell and Mouswald, forking at 'Gateside' – modern Collin – north-east to Torthorwald Kirk and Castle, and north-west to a settlement named The Rosken. In 1799 Heron noted both Torthorwald and *'Roocan'* 1km to the west as *"villages"*.

**Roads and Railway Make Collin**: Later, two turnpike roads were built east from Dumfries across the moss, to Torthorwald and to Collin, 2.5km to the south. The latter being on the way to Annan and Carlisle became the more important, and Collin grew accordingly, helped by the station opened in 1848 by the Glasgow, Dumfries & Carlisle Railway at the hamlet of Racks, 2 km to the south. By 1895 Collin held over 600 people, served by basic facilities, with another 150 around the still rural Torthorwald. An hourly bus to Dumfries had forced calls at the station down to one train a day by 1963, and it had been closed by 1968. During the latter half of the 20th century the various areas of Lochar Moss were largely afforested, and in the 1980s an ancient Torthorwald cruck cottage of stone and thatch was restored. By then Collin had a caravan site and three small hotels, plus an inn at Torthorwald, and there had been little change in the population. By 1996 a new housing estate had been added at Greenlea between Collin and Racks. Both villages still have primary schools, but the Collin caravan site has closed. Collin has two 40-roomed hotels, a *Travel Inn* and a *Travelodge*.

## COLLISTON & Letham Grange — Map 6, C2

***Angus hamlet,** pop. 250* — OS 54: NO 6045

Letham Grange, 5km north of Arbroath, was already a mansionhouse at the time of Roy's survey about 1750, when there was little else of note in the area. In later years the turnpike road joining Arbroath to Friockheim passed through Gowanbank, now known as Colliston, which stands 2 km west of Letham Grange (*gowan* = daisy). The Arbroath & Forfar Railway, which from 1838 paralleled the turnpike some 1600m farther east, named its station Colliston after a smaller mansion nearby (now called Colliston Castle). By 1894 Gowanbank post office was adjoined by an inn, and by Colliston West Mill and smithy; Colliston primary school was built nearby, and the renaming process was given a further fillip. Rail passenger services ended in 1955 and freight in 1965; the track was immediately lifted.

**Condor, Commandos and Golfers**: Meantime in 1940 a Royal Naval Air Station (RNAS) was opened 2 km to the south, named HMS *Condor*. Its five runways included a dummy aircraft carrier deck! In 1971 the air station became the HQ of No. 45 Marine Commando as *Royal Marines Condor*. By 1990 ski clubs could use its dry ski slope, and there was also a gliding school. Meantime a new golf course development at Letham Grange, approved in 1979 for local farmer Ken Smith, was started in 1986 when the mansion was converted into the *Letham Grange Hotel*. Expansion work by Japanese interests was delayed by the recession of 1992, but by 1996 two golf courses were open there, one of 18 holes. The *Letham Grange Hotel* now has 41 rooms and has added a curling rink.

## COLMONELL, Carleton & Lendalfoot — Map 1, B3

***Ayrshire village & hamlets,** pop. 400* — OS 76: NX 1485

A prehistoric hill fort crowns Knockdolian, a hill beside the River Stinchar about 4km above its mouth at Ballantrae. About 5km to the north, at Lendalfoot near the coast of Kyle, stands a medieval motte; beside it was built the 15th century keep of Carleton Castle, and nearby was the Carleton Fishery. The substantial Craigneil Castle was also built in the 15th century, standing beside the River Stinchar, 4km east of Knockdolian; Kirkhill Castle on the opposite or north bank beside Colmonell Kirk, and Knockdolian Castle 2 km downstream, were both 16th century towers. Pont's map of Carrick made about 1600, as engraved by Blaeu, showed a well-settled area, with two mills near Knockdolian. A parish school was founded in 1630. The mid 18th century Roy map marked a ford where the south bank road to the west crossed to the north side en route to Pinwherry; later the north bank carried the main road throughout.

**Cattle Shows, Council Houses and Caravans**: Around 1890 cattle shows were a feature of Colmonell, and in 1898 a new Free Church was built to designs by Alex Petrie. By 1951 about 525 people lived in the area, with basic facilities including two small hotels; subsequently the population fell, to about 325 in Colmonell and only 165 in Lendalfoot by 1981, and Lendalfoot's post office and primary school had both closed. When visited in 1986 Colmonell was still accessible only by unimproved roads, but had an estate of council houses, a primary school, a tiny bank, shop and post office, a substantial garage and a small caravan site; Lendalfoot had holiday chalets and a caravan site, and Bennane on the raised beach below the cliffs had permanent caravans and a shop on the coast road. An inn and the post office were still open at Colmonell in 1995 (post office now closed), but the former Free Church was largely disused and deteriorating in 1998.

## COLONSAY & Oronsay (Isles of) — Map 4, B3

***Islands, Inner Hebrides,*** *pop. 100* — OS 61: NR 3994

There are many ancient features such as duns, standing stones and Viking graves on the rolling and fertile Inner Hebridean island of Colonsay, 13 km by 4. Its small lowland neighbour Oronsay has shell mounds, and an ancient dun on its only hill. Once a sanctuary isle, it takes its name from a Celtic priory founded in 563 by St Oran. This was re-founded for Augustinians by a Lord of the Isles about 1340. Dean Monro in 1549 noted Oronsay's *"monastery of canons, convenient havens for Highland galleys, full of hares and fulmars"*. Colonsay was *"a fertile isle good for white fishing"*, and had a parish kirk. Though the priory was abandoned at the Reformation, it appeared as the most prominent feature on Pont's survey of about 1600, when a scattered pattern of a dozen farms was evident.

**Stunted Animals, Emigration and Development**: Martin writing in 1703 noted the strength of the ancient fortification known as Duncoll, and gave many details of the former monastery. But he thought little of the productivity of Colonsay, where the cows, horses and sheep were all *"of a low size"*. The locals spoke only *'Irish'* but were nominally protestants. The Duke of Argyll was the owner until 1700 when McNeil of Knapdale bought the twin isles; in 1722 the family built Colonsay House on an inland site at Kiloran, 1 km from the silver sands of Kiloran Bay. Despite voluntary emigration to America in 1791 a thousand people remained in the 1830s, all tenants of the one laird in Colonsay House; they escaped the clearances, but continued emigration whittled away the population just the same. A steamer pier was built at the tiny settlement of Scalasaig *('Hut by the Sea')*, where the *Colonsay Hotel* was already established by 1894, and Colonsay post office nearby was issued with a date stamp in 1899. Lord Strathcona became laird in 1905 and imported rhododendrons, which have now spread to threaten cattle, sheep and rare species. By 1921 the population was down to 284. As late as the 1950s the Islay mail steamer terminated at Scalasaig pier.

**Golf, Angling and Publishing Stem the Exodus**: The Isle of Colonsay golf course had been laid out by 1953 (by 1995 this had 18 holes). A new ferry pier was built in 1965. In the 1980s Scalasaig was accessed by car ferry from Oban; a postbus circulated round Colonsay three times a week. Its single-track roads, once amazingly given 'A' numbers, were regraded 'B' around 1990; the road access to Oronsay is tidal, and the primary school is still out of the way. With a lack of council housing, the islands' population continued to fall, from about 230 in 1951 to only 106 by 1991. The economy changed when the publishing firm *'House of Lochar'* became in 1995 the first business on the island unrelated to either farming or tourism; it shipped in 13 tonnes of books from Oxford on the ro-ro ferry from Oban, a twice-weekly service (three in summer, when it also serves Port Askaig). Both isles have basic airstrips, and the gardens of Colonsay House are a tourist attraction; the roofless but solid and extensive ruins of Oronsay Priory form part of a large farmstead. A local oyster farmer heads a co-operative which is tackling the rhododendron problem. The sole hotel (sold freehold in 1995) is the *Isle of Colonsay* (11 rooms) – with loch fishing, sea angling and its own craft shop.

## COLVEND, Sandyhills & Portling — Map 2, B5

***Solway Firth hamlets,*** *pop. 200* — OS 84: NX 8854

The stream called Fairgirth Lane, named after the early house of Fairgirth 2 km from its mouth, enters Sandyhills Bay on the coast of the Stewartry south-east of Dalbeattie. On the cliffs at Portling 1.5 km to the west is an ancient earthwork, and still farther west a motte and the nearby Colvend Kirk, only about 1.5 km east of Rockcliffe. Some of these features were accentuated when Pont mapped the well settled area around 1610. The church eventually became the west marker of a very attenuated village some 4 km in length, still virtually off the map so far as Roy's surveyors of the 1750s were concerned. Eventually a coastal road was built.

**Tourism Triumphant**: The rural Colvend golf club, founded in 1896, started a local trend by laying out a 9-hole moorland course near the bay. In the 1950s Colvend had under 200 residents, a school and post office, but the largely farming population reached its nadir of 160 around 1971. By 1980 there was a caravan site at Sandyhills Bay and the *Clonyard House Hotel* was open. In 1986 straggling Colvend also had many B&B signs, two shops, a public hall and a garage. By 1996 a housing estate taking the name Sandyhills had been built 1 km inland of the bay, at the foot of the lately afforested Fairgirth Hill. Coastal development had also enlarged the scattered hamlet of Portling, though its ancient earthwork seemed to have succumbed to the sea. By 2000 the Colvend golf course had been recently enlarged to 18 holes; the *Clonyard House Hotel* has 15 rooms.

## COMRIE & Dalginross — Map 5, C3

***Large W. Perthshire village,*** *pop. 1440* — OS 51: NN 7722

Comrie *(Chomraich in Gaelic)* meaning *'Sanctuary'*, lies some 9 km west of Crieff where the River Earn is joined by the Water of Ruchill from the south and the incised River Lednock from the north; about 1.5 km up the latter stream is the Deil's Cauldron waterfall. A stone circle, tumuli and a first century Roman fort at Dalginross south of the Earn show the early importance of this beautiful locality, which is however subject to occasional mild earthquakes as it stands on the Highland boundary fault. When Pont mapped the area about 1600 the Earn was already crossed by a bridge of four spans just below the Ruchill confluence, linking *'Kombre Kirk'* with Dalginross; 4 km north-west was *'Tonira'* (Dunira). Aberuchill Castle a similar distance south-west was built soon afterwards. Comrie and Inveruchill were chartered as Burghs of Barony in 1682, and a bridge was later built over the River Lednock.

**A Love of Education**: The Roy map indicated Comrie as a hamlet on the east–west road, the tracks south of the Earn soon petering out. Dalginross was laid out as a new village late in the 18th century, but it was very slow to develop. Heron described Comrie as a *"village"* in 1799, by which time there were five stone bridges across the Earn between Loch Earn and Crieff; Linen yarn was extensively made there around 1790, and framework knitting was well established locally by 1802.

Comrie's first post office opened in 1807. Chambers in the 1820s found *"a respectable-looking parish town of above a thousand inhabitants"*. Comrie was noteworthy in 1833 for a fifth of its population attending school, indicating a very young age structure, and possibly adult participation.

**The Railway and Dunira Gardens**: Dunira was rebuilt as a mansionhouse in the mid 19th century by William Burn. The attractive situation in Strathearn led to Comrie becoming a residential centre and summer resort; Comrie golf club was founded in 1891 and laid out what Price called an *"interesting"* 9-hole course. The growing significance of the village justified the opening of a branch of the Caledonian Railway from Crieff as late as 1893. At that time there were two hotels, the *Royal* and *McNeil's*, and also a bank, but Murray found the *"village not interesting in itself"*. In 1901 the railway was extended to St Fillans, and in 1904 to a junction with the Callander & Oban at Lochearnhead. Thomas Mawson designed Dunira's fine gardens, laid out in 1920 for shipowner's son William Macbeth, with a 9-hole private golf course used by the 22 gardeners and other staff; but the mansion was destroyed by fire in 1947, the gardens becoming derelict until restoration began in 2000.

**Hydro Power but No Trains**: After 1945 the Hydro Board built the Lednock dam and power station 8 km north-west of Comrie, also tunnelling to the west to bring more water into the reservoir at a smaller power station. A third hydro station at Dalchonzie, 3 km west of Comrie, is powered by water brought through a tunnel from a weir at the east end of Loch Earn. The costly railway extension was little used and closed completely in 1951, followed by the poorly-used Gleneagles–Crieff–Comrie line in 1964. Comrie's small secondary school had also gone by 1976, and other facilities had somewhat declined.

**Military, Wrinklies and Backpackers**: By the 1980s Comrie offered visitors caravan and camping sites, the Museum of Scottish Tartans, and a Smiddy. In 1991 the 1440 population in Comrie and Dalginross contained many well-educated retired people owning their own homes, Scotland's highest proportion of men over 65, and its second highest of women over 60; but they were remarkably fit! Cultybraggan army camp, 2 km south of Comrie, was in existence by the 1960s, while Tighnablair, farther south (OS 57), gave its name to an extensive danger zone of the Ministry of Defence, including the Ben Clach massif; it was still in use in 1994. In 1992 a new Tulliebannocher golf course was under construction 2 km north-west of the village. Among Comrie's tourist attractions are a fish farm and Earthquake House. The *Royal Hotel* (11 rooms) is one of several hotels; a large backpacker's hostel is open at Braincroft.

## CONDORRAT — Map 16, A3

***Village / suburb of Cumbernauld**, pop. 19,000* — OS 64: NS 7373

The Pont maps failed to cover this area in the detached portion of ancient Lennox between Kirkintilloch and Cumbernauld, within which parish it lay, and the Roy map hardly did it justice. By 1895 the small village of Condorrat, with its smithy, inn and post office, lay in a farming area astride the main road from Glasgow some 5 km from Cumbernauld; to the south was the Luggie Water, on which stood the Wood Mill. The nearest railway, 1.5 km away, had provided no station, and the quarries open north of the village had no rail access. By 1951 the village population exceeded 1000, with two primary schools, post office and an inn, but by 1955 most of the quarries had been closed and become flooded.

**Condorrat within Cumbernauld**: Condorrat was included in the area of Cumbernauld New Town, designated in 1956. It was soon bypassed to enable the A80 from Glasgow to serve the new town centre; for two decades a new length of A73 separated Condorrat village from the developing new town. But by 1979 a new loop road had been laid to enable a very large eastward extension of the village to the A73. By 1981 Condorrat had a chemist, doctor and garage, but no longer an inn. The large St Maurice's High School north of Condorrat was built in the 1980s; in 1997 it had a roll of 1153. By 1988 the extension had been completed with housing, as had the Westfield estate on the other side of the A80 bypass, and an industrial estate which reached to the expanding sewage works beside the Luggie near Mollinsburn. This estate had itself been greatly extended by 1996, and a new loop road north of Westfield presaged yet another extension of housing.

## CONNEL — Map 5, A3

***Argyllshire village**, pop. 800* — OS 49: NM 9134

Connel – the name means *Whirlpool* – holds a strategic position on the west coast, where the tidal rapids of the Falls of Lora bar the mouth of the long Loch Etive; by 1681 this was the location of a ferry. By the 1750s though the ferry was irregular, the Roy map showed Connel as a tiny settlement, with tracks on the lines of the present-day A85 and A828. But in 1803 Dorothy Wordsworth found only one ferry boat, whose service through the tidal rapids was terrifying: *"No open end, or plank, or any other convenience for shipping either horse or carriage"*. She was uncharacteristically rude about the ferrymen, and implied the existence of an inn of sorts north of the ferry: *"We had intended breakfasting if it had been a decent place"*. There was certainly an unremarkable inn there by 1833, but the ferry remained crude until the 1820s, and Connel – then often called *Connel Ferry* – did not have a post office until after 1838.

**The Railway brings the Bridge and Hotel**: Its development as a centre of services really dated from the opening in 1880 of a station on the new Callander & Oban Railway (C&O), a Caledonian (CR) subsidiary; by 1894 this was accompanied

*Connel rail bridge, completed in 1903, was then the second-larg[est] steel cantilever bridge in Britain. It was converted to a road bri[dge] after the Ballachulish branch railway closed in 1965.*
*(RCAHMS / JR)*

by what Murray described as the *"good" Falls of Lora Hotel*. The C&O also built a station some 5 km east of Connel near the Victorian baronial mansion of Achnacloich, designed by John Starforth of Glasgow to overlook Loch Etive. In 1903 Connel became a junction when completion of the remarkable cantilever railway bridge enabled the Ballachulish branch of the CR to be opened. From 1909 occasional road vehicles were carried across on railway wagons; then in 1914 a roadway was laid on the bridge, shared with the infrequent trains for half a century. North Connel acquired a civil airstrip in the 1930s, which was taken over by the RAF in World War II but then returned to general aviation. By 1950 Connel had two hotels and was a village with over 600 people.

**Growth for Tourism**: The station, which had been closed by Beeching in 1965, was very quickly reopened, certainly by autumn 1967, and still called Connel Ferry. The Ballachulish railway was less lucky, being closed completely in 1966; the great bridge was retained for road traffic alone, but its approaches remained difficult until about 1990 when North Connel was bypassed. Population growth reached 800, and there were four hotels; of these *Ossian's Hotel* at North Connel was *"newly built"* in 1979. Achnacloich's fine large garden, developed in the 20th century, was opened to the public from about 1990. In 1990 Connel was a railhead for timber transport to the south, and received oil by rail for the Calmac ferry fleet. But these rail traffics ceased. By 1996 considerable housing developments had taken place at and east of North Connel. Besides the *Falls of Lora Hotel*, (now 30 rooms), there is the *Ards House* and several small seasonal hotels.

*The tollhouse, Conon Bridge – all that is left of Telford's 1809 bridge, which was replaced by a new bridge in the 1950s. (JRH)*

## CONON BRIDGE & Culbokie

**Map 9, B3**

***Villages s. of Dingwall**, pop. 2600*

OS 26: NH 5455

At the western end of the ridge of the Black Isle in Easter Ross are various prehistoric chambered cairns, and north of the River Conon a standing stone. To the south is intriguing but little-known Bishop Kinkell, with the *'Homestead Moat'*, seemingly the great mound of an early castle, known in the 19th century as *'David's Fort'*. In 1582 John Roy Mackenzie bought the estate of Kinkell Clarsach south of the river; there he built Kinkell Castle. Brahan Castle north of the river was built in 1600 as the home of the Stewart Mackenzies of Seaforth, another of the six castles they built in Easter Ross between Fairburn, Leod and Redcastle.

**Maryburgh and Ferintosh Whisky**: Gordonsburgh, north of the River Conon, was chartered as a burgh of barony in 1618; later it became known as Maryburgh, but for centuries grew very little, as did Culbokie (also known as Findon), similarly chartered in 1678, some 7 km to the north-east in the parish of Urquhart & Logie Wester. A distillery at Ferintosh, owned by Duncan Forbes of Culloden, was destroyed by Jacobites in 1689; in compensation the government granted him tax privileges *(see below)*. At the time of Roy's survey about 1750 Kinkell Castle was connected with the outside world by *"a ford"* close to Maryburgh and so by a track to Dingwall; it was reconstructed about 1766. Meantime Conan House was built near Bishop Kinkell in 1758–60 by Sir Alexander Mackenzie of Gairloch. To the east of Kinkell Castle was the Ferintosh estate, but Roy gave no indication of what Heron in 1799 was to call *"the village of Ferrintosh, noted for excellent malt spirits"*.

**The Conon Bridge**: In 1809 when the road to the north from the Kessock Ferry was being constructed for the Commissioners of Highland Roads & Bridges, the 5-arched Conon Bridge was built in stone to a design by Telford, crossing the River Conon close to Maryburgh. About 1814 the new highway built from the Lovat Bridge via Beauly met the Kessock road near the bridgehead. This junction and its octagonal tollhouse formed the node round which a new village grew, originally called Conan, and later Conon Bridge.

**The Demise of Distilling**: Chambers, who walked past in the 1820s, noted only that *"Ferintosh used to be celebrated for its extensive manufacture of whisky. Duncan Forbes, to whom the estate belonged, procured an immunity from tax for the whisky distilled in this part; more was soon distilled here than perhaps in all the rest of the Highlands together, and whisky became generally known everywhere as 'Ferintosh'. When the system had amounted to an insupportible grievance, government bought up the privilege."* Though both Culbokie and Ferintosh had post offices in 1843, and Ferintosh later gave its name to a primary school, it appears that Chambers' use of the word *'extensive'* referred to many dispersed stills, and no formal distillery named Ferintosh was established on the estate *(but see Dingwall).*

**The Railway**: The Inverness & Ross-shire Railway was opened in 1862; *Conan* station lay just south of the masonry viaduct across the Conon. By 1894 Newton of Ferintosh was just a scatter of crofts, but both Conon Bridge and Maryburgh had inns and smithies; in the 20th century these two hamlets grew steadily. Due to its proximity to the Cromarty Firth naval base, the hotel at Conon Bridge was state-owned for half a century until it was sold off about 1975. The two settlements were home to 1450 people in 1951, when there were such facilities as an ambulance station, haulier and agricultural contractor at Conon Bridge; but Brahan Castle was dismantled about 1946–53. The Telford bridge was replaced during the construction of the Dounreay nuclear plant. Conon Bridge station closed in the 1960s. The derelict Kinkell Castle was restored in 1969–70 by Gerald Laing.

**Major Development**: By 1972 a large new fish-freezing plant had been built beside the river, and new housing estates were built to serve aluminium and oil developments at Invergordon and Nigg, requiring a new primary school in 1977. In 1978 Maryburgh also had a school, PO/grocery, and agricultural engineer. By 1981 the population of the twin villages exceeded 2300, with the facilities of a typical village, plus a government surplus store. By 1985 a fast new road route from Inverness via the Kessock Bridge was linked to the west by a new bridge and a bypass road, passing north of the old bridge. By then even the ruins of Brahan Castle had vanished. The two villages, by 1991 named Cononbridge, held almost 2600 residents, and there has been recent bungalow development around the growing village of Culbokie, doubtless encouraged by the easy access to Inverness provided by the Kessock Bridge. A former farmhouse at Easter Kinkell is now the *Kinkell House Hotel.*

## CONTIN & Fairburn

**Map 9, A3**

***Small Easter Ross village,*** *pop. 450* — OS 26: NH 4556

Fairburn Castle, a 16th century tower house of the MacKenzies, was built on a spur between the Rivers Conon and Orrin in Easter Ross. Coul was chartered as a burgh of barony in 1681 about 4km to the north beside the Black Water, a tributary of the Conon; when Roy surveyed the area about 1750, Coul House was already a mansion in its own policies, enjoying fine views. By then Mill Strachan stood a little upstream of Fairburn Castle, near the site of the later Fairburn House, from which a discontinuous track led westwards towards Loch Carron. In 1816 the Black Water was bridged to Telford's designs, near an ancient stone circle at Contin, west of Coul House and below the rugged and picturesque Falls of Rogie. By 1894 Contin had a church, the *Achilty Inn* and a mill, in a setting of wooded hills.

**Power and Tourism from the Rivers**: The Fannich-Orrin power scheme, developed from 1945 by the Hydro-Electric Board, included the 36m tall Aradie Dam on the River Orrin 8km south-west of Contin, which impounded the Orrin Reservoir. From there a 5.4km tunnel feeds water to the Orrin power station, using a head of 225m to turn its single 18,000kW generator, sited on the shore of the newly filled Loch Achonachie on the River Conon. This is itself retained by the 21m tall Meig Dam which gives a 13m head for the adjoining Torr Achilty power station 1.5km from Contin, with its two 7500kW machines. Meantime by 1951 Contin was a village of about 375 people; the *Achilty Inn* was soon enlarged as a 12-room hotel. By 1972 the late Victorian *Craigdarroch Lodge* built by the Mackenzies was a 19-roomed hotel. By 1978 there was also a caravan and camping site, Contin had grown to some 450 residents and *Coul House* had become a hotel, enlarged to 20 rooms; the primary school and post office are still open.

## CORGARFF & Cock Bridge

**Map 10, A3**

***Upper Donside village & hamlet,*** *pop. 200* — OS 37: NJ 2508

Corgarff *('Rough Corrie')* lies in a deep valley on the headwaters of the River Don about 410m above the sea. A tower built as a hunting seat for the Earl of Mar was burned out in 1571 when 27 Forbes clan members were murdered there by Gordon of Auchindoun. Later restored, in 1746 it was occupied by the government for strategic reasons, and fortified with an outer wall. The Roy map of about 1750 labelled it as a *'Barrack'*; across the unbridged river was the Mill of Corgarff. The military road (labelled *'to Nairn')* lately built by Caulfeild's troops climbed over the Lecht pass to Strathavon and Speyside. Eastwards another road led past the fermtoun of *'Caryhole'* (later called Corgarff) to Strathdon, Huntly and Aberdeen. To the south an earlier route from Corgarff was indicated, climbing beside the Cock Burn and over the hills to *'Slioch'*. The road to Braemar starting at Colnabaichin some 4km farther east, shown on modern maps as *'Old Military Road'*, seems to have been built after 1750, as was the Cock Bridge.

**Buses, Tourists and Snow**: The area remained remote, and the barracks were manned against whisky smugglers until the garrison was withdrawn in 1831. From 1907 the GNSR motor bus route from Alford to Bellabeg was extended in summer to Corgarff, which by 1955 was only a tiny straggling village with a school, post office, an inn and a youth hostel. By 1981 the area's population had been halved in thirty years to only 200, and snow blockages of the Lecht road made the only significant news in many years. By 1995 the youth hostel had closed, but there was a museum, and the castle and inn are still open, as is a tiny all-year hostel for backpackers.

## CORNHILL

**Map 10, B1**

***Banffshire village,*** *pop. 450* — OS 29: NJ 5858

Said to date back to the 13th century, the castle or house named on the Blaeu map as Park of Corncairn was rebuilt in the 16th century on the slopes of Corn Hill, some 12 km to the south-west of Banff. To the west was the Kirkton of Ordiquhill, which though chartered as a burgh of barony in 1617 grew little. About 1750 Roy found the area still roadless; the Burn of Boyne turned the *'Uppermill of Park'* just west of Park, and farther down the *'Nethermill of Park'*. Later the burn was paralleled by the Keith to Banff road which bypassed the kirk. Although in 1797 an annual fair was to be held at Cornhill, as late as 1838 there was no post office in the hamlet, where a Free Church was built in 1844.

**Railway and Market**: The Great North of Scotland Railway's branch from Grange to Banff and Portsoy was opened in 1859; Cornhill's simple station was beside the burn. From 1886 it lay on a secondary through route to Elgin, and a regular Thursday cattle market was established beside it; as late as 1909 a horse-drawn coach route still connected to rail-less Aberchirder, 8km south-east. In 1951 an inn, two sub branch banks, post office and 45-line telephone exchange, two garages, a small secondary school, the Hay memorial hall, a seed merchant and remarkably a house furnisher served nearly 500 people.

**Modern Cornhill**: The railway was closed completely in 1968, though the former station yard remained in use by a coal merchant in 1988. The secondary school was no more by 1976, when only 350 residents were left; by 1986 the inn was just a pub. But occasional livestock sales were still held in the 1990s by Aberdeen & Northern Marts. Quantity surveyors and a *Rover* garage and saleroom show the unusual nature of this attractive village, which largely comprises quite modern housing and has a post office, shop and plumber, yet depends on a primary school 2.5km away at Gordonstown, 1km north of the Kirkton of Ordiquhill whose name it bears. The Castle of Park offers self-catering accommodation.

## CORPACH, Banavie, Caol & Annat — Map 5, A1

***Villages n. of Ft. William**, pop. 5,000* — OS 41: NN 1076

Corpach at the western end of the Great Glen existed by about 1600, being the clearest name on Pont's fragmentary map showing Loch Eil. The construction of a road from Fort William to Arisaig was begun in 1795, and in 1803 Banavie became the western construction base for the Caledonian Canal, financed by the government and engineered by Telford to link the Moray Firth with Loch Linnhe. Rubble stone came from a quarry at Banavie itself. The eleven western locks, including eight in the spectacular *'Neptune's Staircase' (see Hay & Stell)*, provided years of building work for masons. To slake their thirsts and those of the many *'navvies'* a brewhouse was built about 1804; for a time up to 1834 a canal worker was allowed to run a temperance inn at Banavie. The canal contractors also built a road north of the canal, from Banavie to the Culross Burn mouth in Loch Lochy, and bridges farther north where Cameron of Lochiel extended the road; in all 56 bridges were built in 16km. In 1820 a ferry sailed between the sea-lock at the canal entrance and Inverlochy near Fort William. The canal was opened in 1822 but soon proved inadequate *(see Cameron, 1994)*.

**Railway and Market**: By 1846 after reconstruction of the canal, regular steamers from Glasgow to Inverness passed through, and tourism began on the *'Road to the isles'*. Murray noted a *"very fair"* hotel at Corpach in 1894, and in 1895 the West Highland Railway opened a 4km branch from Fort William to Banavie to connect with steamers on the canal. Part of this was included in the Mallaig extension railway, opened in 1902 with stations at Corpach and at Banavie with its swing bridge. With both long-established distilling and the later aluminium development between Banavie and Fort William, a village known as Caol (*Narrows* in Gaelic) also developed.

**The Naval Yard and Auction Sales**: A naval repair yard built on the shore in 1942–43 was rail-connected to a new *'rounding loop'* called Camus-na-ha, and the golf course then open to the west was taken over to build 200 concrete houses named Annat village. By 1951 the various townships formed a slowly growing suburb of Fort William, with 1500 people, the facilities of a small village, and the new *'Ben Nevis'* livestock auction mart at Annat. By 1954 the *Achdalieu Hotel* 4km to the west boasted 25 rooms and 3 stars, but closed around 1970, later becoming the Achdalieu Lodge Loch Eil field centre, for sailing and other outdoor activities. Tourism also developed on the canal; a cruiser hirer was established at Banavie by 1976, and by 1980 there was the recently built 12-roomed *Moorings Hotel* at Banavie.

**The Pulp and Paper Mills**: Annat's naval houses were cleared in the 1960s and the site became a caravan park, beside which on the former naval yard the 32ha Wiggins Teape pulp mill was built in 1963–65. The canal's sea lock was lengthened in 1964 to take vessels 62m long, and a wharf with two cranes built for the pulp mill traffic, as it used 10,000 trees a day! Puffers used to bring 80-tonne loads from Mull twice a week, but most came by road. Its six giant digesters – which were built at Leven – were moved to Corpach by sea and canal. They cooked wood chips into pulp, supplied to an adjacent mill – completed in 1966 – making specialised printing papers. At its peak in 1975 the complex employed 930 people, using both Canadian hardwood chips imported through a new pier, and softwood logs from Crianlarich, a daily train carrying 350 tonnes. The mill's half million tonnes a year input was said to provide 3200 forestry jobs, and in the 1970s 25,000 tonnes of pulp a year were exported through the basin, yet its scale – though huge for Lochaber – proved uneconomically small by world standards. In the early 1970s Riddochs, timber merchants of Rothiemay, established at Corpach what was then claimed to be the largest sawmill in the EEC.

**After the Pulp Mill**: The pulp mill was closed in 1980 with the loss of all its 400 jobs and the timber trains, but the paper mill was adapted to work independently. The closure hit Lochaber and the Corpach area (population of 5500) hard. In 1985 Corpach had many B&Bs, a quarry, the timber yard, and some minor industries; the livestock market also remained busy. But the 6ha industrial site intended to replace the pulp mill was still empty at that time. In 1990–92 oil fuel from Grangemouth, and china clay and occasionally starch from north-west England were still delivered daily by rail to the paper mill, by then known as Arjo Wiggins, and paper was despatched by

*A lorryload of wood-chip at Corpach. There's been no pulp mill since 1980, but timber processing continues.*

*(SMPC / Kenny Ferguson)*

rail in containers. But the oil traffic by rail to Corpach ceased in 1993. By 1995 the *'Treasures of the Earth'* Visitor Centre showed gemstones and geology. In 2000 Clydeport established a service with Boyd Brothers to ship locally-felled timber from Corpach quay to Rochester in Kent. Two independent hostels for backpackers are open all year, one being at Farr Cottage Activity Centre.

## CORRIE & Sannox

**Map 1, B1**

***Village & hamlet, Isle of Arran,*** *pop. 275* OS 69: NS 0243

An ancient fort, cairns and standing stones at Sannox on the steep east coast of Arran show its antiquity. Corrie, about 8 km north of Brodick, was named *'Kori-knock-dow'* on Pont's map, made around 1600. It remained an obscure clachan, but a school was open there by 1845. Barytes and some ironstone was mined a short way up Glen Sannox, 3 km to the north-west, from 1840 till about 1862; then the laird, the Duke of Hamilton, closed the mine for amenity reasons. A sandstone quarry was also worked in the 19th century. In 1847 Corrie had a minute harbour and 8 local fishing boats, and a post office was open by 1871. But even in the steamer heyday there was no pier, those ships which called being met by rowing boats.

**Tourist Development outlasts Mining**: The Corrie golf club which was founded in 1892 established a 9-hole hillside course at Sannox; by 1894 there was a hotel at Corrie, a well-wooded location for the period. The barytes mine was reopened about 1920, when a light railway with a balanced incline was laid to connect it to a new pier, from which the material was shipped to Glasgow for paint manufacture, but the mine was worked out in 1938. By the 1950s Corrie had a second equally tiny harbour, and, combined with Sannox, had a population of some 440. Late 20th century afforestation covered the hillsides to the south. A second hotel briefly functioned at Corrie around 1977; by 1981 the *Corrie Hotel* had 19 rooms, and there has been remarkably little change since.

## CORROUR

**Map 5, B2**

***Estate & station, Rannoch Moor*** OS 41: NN 3566

In the 1750s as the rough copy of the Roy map showed, a track led up the river known as the Amhainn Ghuilbinn from Torgulben on Loch Laggan to the head of Loch Ossian, set in the wastes of Rannoch Muir; but with the Clearances this track or footpath faded away. The single-line West Highland Railway was opened across the moor west of Loch Ossian in 1894, with a tiny crossing station, nominally private until 1934, at its bleak summit at Corrour, at a height of 411 m. This encouraged Stirling Maxwell, owner of the vast 19,500ha Corrour estate, to build a shooting lodge at the outfall of the loch, accessed by a tiny private steamer on the loch and a short road link to the station.

**Catering for the Adventurous Tourist**: By 1954 the Loch Ossian Youth Hostel had been opened at the head of the loch, but meantime Corrour Lodge had burned down in 1942 and been replaced by a temporary house. In the late 20th century the track was extended down to the main A86 road near Torgulben, 12 km west of Kinlochlaggan. Remote Corrour escaped the Beeching cuts, but the signal box was closed in 1987 when radio electronic token block signalling was installed. The ex-signalman stayed on, and in 1995 when the estate was for sale, refreshments could still be obtained at the station; by 2000 its buildings had been finely upgraded, with a restaurant, backpackers' bunkhouse and wind turbine; the nearby youth hostel is seasonal. Major new facilities for tourists were under construction in 2000 near the east end of Loch Ossian.

## CORSOCK

**Map 2, A4**

***Village n. of Castle Douglas,*** *pop. 850* OS 84: NX 7576

Some evidence of several ancient settlements, but no medieval castles, are to be found in the valley of the Urr Water, amid the inconsequential hills about 15 km north of Castle Douglas. Pont's map-work of around 1600 showed water mills – now vanished – at both Over and Nether Corsock, while Corsock House was already emparked. A *'Corvaig'* mill was marked on the mid 18th century Roy map, beside the winding track running east from Balmaclellan to Crocketford, then labelled *'Muir Road to Dumfries'* but more recently surfaced and perhaps unjustifiably glorified as the A712. By the 1950s some 300 people lived in an extensive area centred on Corsock, a tiny cluster of cottages which also boasted a church, primary school, inn, post office and telephone exchange. Over a third of the residents were lost within 30 years and the inn became a pub. Meantime extensive afforestation has taken place on the surrounding hills.

## CORSTORPHINE & The Gyle

**Map 15, B2**

***Western suburb of Edinburgh,*** *pop. 21,000* OS 66: NT 2072

Corstorphine, 6 km west of central Edinburgh, lies between a prominent hill and an area that was originally a belt of shallow lakes and marshes; the name – pronounce it as you will – probably derives from the *Cars(e)* or boggy plain of Thorfinn, a Norse settler. By 1128 there was a church (a pendicle of Edinburgh), and a collegiate church was established in 1429 by Sir John Forrester. Corstorphine also possessed a late 14th or 15th century castle, of which nothing remains on the ground. For centuries this was a small farming settlement, whose *Black Bull Inn* was possibly open by 1561, and by about 1600 when Pont mapped the Lothians, Corstorphine stood beside a defined road from Edinburgh, forking to Linlithgow and Airdrie. A school was opened in 1656, and one of Scotland's earliest linen bleachfields was created in 1698.

**Spa and Market, Beer and Cream**: The main Edinburgh to Linlithgow road which passed just north of the village was turnpiked under an Act of 1713. By 1737 a *'physic well'* had given Corstorphine a local reputation as a minor spa, the reason for a *'stage chaise'* running from and to Edinburgh, starting in 1752. Though never a burgh of barony, at one time a regular cattle market was held, and by the 1750s when Roy mapped Scotland, Corstorphine was a linear settlement with four radial routes. By 1777 the loch had been drained, and a short-lasting brewery was open. Heron noted in 1799 that *"the village has long been noted for a preparation from the dairy, well known by the name of Corstophine Cream"*. The first post office at Corstorphine opened in 1804; by 1838 there was a good range of local services.

**The Railway Age**: In 1842 a station was provided 1 km to the south at Saughton on the new Edinburgh & Glasgow Railway; this was renamed *Saughton Junction* when the line to the Forth Bridge was opened in 1890, but Corstorphine was still a totally distinct village in the 1890s; to the west were the farms of North and South Gyle. The large country villa of Beechmount, built in Corstorphine Road by the Bank of Scotland for its Treasurer in 1899, had become within half a century the East of Scotland Radium Research Institute. In 1902 the North British Railway opened a short branch from the main line at Murrayfield to terminate at Corstorphine proper, with a station at Pinkhill and also a halt at Balgreen; fast direct trains connected Corstorphine with Waverley in 11 minutes. A public library (with Carnegie assistance) was opened in 1903.

**Zoo, Trams and Suburbanisation**: In 1909–13 the Royal Zoological Society of Scotland created the *Edinburgh Zoo* on the south-facing hillside above the village. Both the Zoo, and what was later to become the Edinburgh Tapestry Company, founded in 1912, still flourish. Corstorphine was absorbed by the City of Edinburgh in 1920; the *Astoria Cinema* opened in 1930. The city's electric trams reached Corstorphine from Murrayfield in 1923; in 1934 they were extended to North Gyle, where housing development was practically complete by 1939. The Reed carton factory was established in 1934 and the adjacent *Maybury Roadhouse* was built in Art Deco style in 1935–36; the trams were extended along Glasgow Road to Maybury in 1937, the final expansion of this once great transport system.

**Testing Seeds and Moving Traffic on to Rubber Tyres**: By 1949 the Board of Agriculture (later known as DAFS) had established its seed testing station at East Craigs Farm; by 1995 this had become the Scottish Agricultural Science Agency. By 1951 Corstorphine's population had reached 14,000, and a small town centre had become established, including the *Harp Hotel*, later enlarged. In 1954 the clean trams which ran through to Joppa were replaced by polluting buses; the branch railway was closed in 1967 following the Beeching axe, and the station site went for housing. The cinema vanished in 1974, being replaced by a supermarket. Queen Margaret College, with business and health courses, was well established at Clerwood by the 1970s. By the 1970s three new secondary schools were open – Craigmount High, Forrester High and the adjacent St Augustine's RC High.

**Hotel and Office Centre**: Major office development started with the Forestry Commission Headquarters which was moved in 1975 from London to a site opposite the Zoo, and by 1977 the National Coal Board – later renamed British Coal – had a laboratory in Glasgow Road. Large new hotels with over 200 rooms were built: the dominant *Post House* beside the Zoo to the east, and the very plain *Royal Scot* opposite Maybury to the west, which opened in the mid 1970s. Corstorphine was by then of suburban character, with a population of over 21,500, the facilities of an average town and an active set of local societies. The private (BUPA) Murrayfield Hospital on the slopes of Corstorphine Hill was opened in 1984 and enlarged to 60 beds in 1989, while a new Safeway supermarket was opened west of central Corstorphine about 1989. In 1990 the Zoo was the fourth most popular paid visitor attraction in Scotland, far outdoing Calderpark by drawing some 600,000 visitors a year. Across the road was the Barnardo's Scottish HQ, formerly at Drumsheugh. The Reed carton factory was renamed in 1991 as *'SCA Packaging Scotland'*. In 1995 the Scottish Coal Company, new owner of former British Coal assets in Scotland, was based at Glasgow Road.

**South Gyle Station**: A new railway station on the Fife line 1 km west of the old village centre was opened at South Gyle in 1986, but for local trains only. Ferranti of Edinburgh opened a branch at South Gyle in the late 1980s; in 1995 under GEC-Marconi the plant employed some 500 people in air electronics, making such complex items as cockpit displays, and by 2000 had been joined by another, both then under the ownership of BAe.

**Scotland's Instant Banking Centre**: The character of the sprawling South Gyle estate, where housing was built from the late 1980s, was dictated by new office developments which emerged in 1988. These included a 50,000 $m^2$ office block for the Bank of Scotland, and three smaller headquarters buildings housing Murray International Metals, Scottish Brewers and the consulting engineers Blyth & Blyth, who moved from the city centre in 1989. In 1993 the Royal Bank moved its headquarters from the city centre to the huge Drummond House at South Gyle Crescent; it then contained 1400 employees and the most advanced electronic technology. Its foreign exchange and money-market dealing room duplicated the facilities of the Bank's main London dealing room and was unique in Scotland.

**Regional Shopping at South Gyle**: Despite the slump, a metre depth of burnt oil shale infill was spread to enable an enormous 24 ha shopping development to be erected in 1992–93 on the low ground near Maybury, 1 km west of South Gyle station and south of the railway. The Gyle Centre, promoted by the development arm of the city council, opened in 1993, its 280 m-long covered mall of 28,000 $m^2$ containing nearly 70 shops. It was hoped to attract 300,000 shoppers per week. The new major Marks & Spencer store offered the company's full range of merchandise, seven-day opening, and its own free weekly bus services from the Borders and East Lothian, areas which might have benefited from their own more conveniently located branch had the company really had their interests at heart! At the other end was a very large Safeway store; their original store became PC World.

**Cars R Us at The Gyle**: The Gyle Centre's 2700 free parking spaces – as many as a large town centre – were served by Scotland's largest petrol filling station, for most shoppers were

*The new Royal Bank HQ (1993) at Edinburgh Park – one of many such buildings in the large new financial offices development south-west of Corstorphine.* *(AL)*

intended to come by car, many of them using an underpass of the city bypass. Others would hopefully still use the 24 bus routes. By 1997 Craigmount High School had 1300 pupils, Forrester High 960 and St Augustine's RC High 700.

**Edinburgh Park, Broadway Park and Big Hotels**: Construction of the so-called *'Edinburgh Park'* south of the Gyle shopping centre was begun in 1995 with the 28,000 m$^2$ headquarters of insurers Scottish Equitable, moved out in 1998 from St Andrew Square. Much smaller buildings accommodated John Menzies distribution (taken over by W H Smith in 1999) and offices for ICL, who moved from rail-accessible Haymarket premises to the car-only wilds. The HQ of Cala Homes has moved in from Falkirk and Intelligent Finance is also now there, as is a division of Weir's, the Glasgow engineers. S&N decided in 1996 to build two new divisional HQs at Broadway Park, South Gyle. More speculative space was also built, made more attractive by the BT *'Telezone'* which promised assured high-quality telecommunications. In 2000 a David Lloyd Leisure Centre was built on part of the Carrick Knowe public golf course. Remarkably, the original centre of Corstorphine remains very prosperous, with the long-standing 25-room *Harp Hotel*, and a Jaguar car dealer. Meantime the *Forte Posthouse* has been extended into the largest in greater Edinburgh, now with 303 rooms; second largest is the *'Swallow' Royal Scot Hotel*, with 259 rooms.

## CORTACHY, Dykehead & Glenprosen — Map 6, B2

***Angus hamlets**, pop. 300* — OS 44 & 54: NO 3860

Near the River South Esk 6 km north-east of Kirriemuir is a standing stone; nearby is the courtyard castle of Cortachy. Some 2 km down-river is the L-plan tower of Inverquharity Castle, both being of 15th century construction. Pont's detailed map of Glen Clova, made about 1600, named a bridge across the South (or Black) Esk near Inverquharity at now-vanished *'Dalkorky'*. Massive extensions were added to Cortachy Castle in 1870 by David Bryce, but were demolished about 1960. Nearby is the hamlet of Dykehead, where the small *Royal Jubilee Arms Hotel* had been built by 1893. By 1951 Cortachy also had a primary school, a post office, and what was for a country area a busy 53-line telephone exchange. But even including dependent Glenprosen to the north-west the population in the area was only about 260. Closures at agricultural Memus 4 km to the east meant that, despite a fast-falling local population, by 1981 Dykehead's facilities served perhaps 320 people, and the hotel had been enlarged to 11 rooms. By 1984 Memus had a caravan site; a remote primary school in Glenprosen was still open in 1995 (but no longer). The modernised Cortachy Castle still stands in its great private park, almost the whole area being part of the vast Airlie Estate. Dykehead post office has recently closed but Cortachy primary school and the *Royal Jubilee Arms Hotel* are still open.

## COULPORT — Map 5, B4

***Location on L. Long, Argyll*** — OS 56: NS 2187

Coulport is situated deep inside the fiord-like coastline north of the Firth of Clyde, beside sheltered Loch Long. By 1895 it stood at the end of the road which wound around the Rosneath peninsula, and was the terminus of a ferry to the *Ardentinny Hotel* in Cowal. There was never much civilian development, and the ferry closed early in the 20th century, but a telephone exchange existed by 1951, for Coulport had become the site of a Royal Naval Armament Depot (RNAD). More recently a base was built for *'hunter-killer'* and *Polaris* submarines; 2000 jobs were reported in 1982. By 1989 a major facility for the replacement *Trident* submarines on which Britain's safety in the Cold War with the then USSR was supposed to depend was under construction *(see also Faslane)* and new access roads to nameless facilities swept across the hills as far as Loch Lomond. With the collapse of the USSR, by 1993 the workforce at the earlier base was down to 750, of whom nearly half were to be shed within a year, the whole facility to be closed by the millennium. The RNAD was to be the next installation to go, its closure with the loss of 138 jobs being announced in 1995.

## COUPAR ANGUS — Map 6, B2

***Small town, E. Perthshire**, pop. 2200* — OS 53: NO 2240

Coupar Angus lies on a fertile site in Strathmore, to the south of the meandering River Isla. A Roman legion camped there, and from about the 11th century both Coupar Angus and nearby Kettins had thanages. This area was originally part of Angus, and was often called Coupar *in* Angus to distinguish it from Cupar in Fife. Coupar lay on the main routeway from Perth to Aberdeen, and in 1164 an abbey was founded by Cistercians from Melrose. The abbey traded abroad in wool, through Perth and possibly indirectly through Berwick, but about 1225 its property in Berwick was leased to Newbattle Abbey. The church building was dedicated in 1233, and the monks sold sorted wool around 1400.

**Reformation Destruction and Burgh Foundation**: They seem to have had a quietish time until 1559 when the abbey buildings were burned by a reformist mob. In 1560 the abbey still nominally enjoyed six appropriated churches and the Abbot also sat in Parliament, but these privileges were soon ended. The red sandstone ruins were robbed for building stone, and eventually only a single gateway remained. In the 16th century Pitcur Castle, an L-plan tower, was built 4 km south-east of the abbey. By 1581 there was a grammar school, and Pont's map made about 1600 emphasised *'Couper'* as a settlement with substantial buildings. The abbey property was given to James Elphinstone, Lord Coupar in 1606, to whom a burgh of barony was granted in 1607 on the death of the last monk; the buildings later fell into ruin. In 1702 a tall red sandstone tolbooth was built by public subscription, as the *'Prison of the Court of Regality'*. Coupar *in* Angus had a post office by 1730;

*Coupar Angus maltings, the buildings dating from the 18th century and now being part of garage premises. (RCAHMS / JRH)*

its old name remained in use at the time of Roy's survey in the 1750s, when the place was the focus of five radial roads, though still lacking a road connection with Blairgowrie.

**Linen, Banking and Bleaching**: By 1747 John Young was a large linen cloth merchant who supplied yarn and organised weavers. A new linen bleachfield was built between 1746 and 1760. Young's business failed in 1762 but coarse linen manufacture continued, a weaving school being open in 1763, and flax was still extensively grown for many years. Between 1766 and 1787 the Perth United Banking Company opened a branch in Coupar Angus. By 1790 a bleachfield was at work at Balgersho south of the village, together with three at nearby Kettins, and some 200,000m of brown linen and *harn*, a coarse linen fabric for packsheets, was made annually for the English market by the 200 hand weavers in the two parishes.

**Banking and Coaching**: In 1797 there was an annual fair, and Coupar Angus was a post town of some 2000 people. About then red sandstone was used to build a large parish church beside the great abbey's paltry ruins. By 1825 the Perth Union Banking Company had also opened a local branch, and the Arbroath Banking Company immediately opened the third branch bank in the town, then evidently an important centre. In the 1820s Chambers found a *"neat town where there is a considerable linen manufactory, as also a tannery and bleachfield"*. By 1832 the *New Strathmore* was a coaching inn, and by 1844 another carried a coaching name as the *Defiance Hotel.*

**Railways and Power Loom Weaving**: From 1837 Coupar Angus was served by a westward extension of the slow and primitive Dundee & Newtyle Railway (D&NR), but the potato starch mill built in 1840 at Coupar Grange was not near the line. When the Scottish Midland Junction Railway was opened eastwards from Perth in 1848 it joined the upgraded D&NR end-on, as one element in the creation of a main line to Forfar and Aberdeen; to hold down capital costs a level crossing was placed in the town centre. By 1864 the local bleaching works was long extinct, but a small jute industry had developed: John Robertson employed about 300 part-time hand-loom weavers making hessians and coarse linens. A small power-loom works was in the course of erection, and in 1867 three jute, flax and hemp mills had a total of nearly 500 workers. Two hotels were open in 1894, the *Strathmore Arms* and the *Royal*; Murray simply described Coupar Angus as a *"town"*.

**A Junction Station in Perthshire**: For exactly a century from 1855 Coupar Angus was the railway junction for Blairgowrie, and by 1870 Wordie & Co had a small depot for road to rail cartage. When county councils were created twenty years later the burgh of Coupar Angus was transferred to Perthshire. The Victoria Building or Town Hall was erected in 1887, its stone structure some thirty years out of date in style. In 1899 the fastest trains then scheduled in Britain thundered over its level crossing en route between Perth and Forfar, a journey requiring an *average* speed of 60mph.

**Railways and Chickens meet their End**: The jute industry, still alive in the 1930s, had closed by 1951. Then Coupar Angus was a large village with about 2300 people and three small hotels. But in 1955 the Blairgowrie branch railway was closed to passengers, completely closed in 1965. From 1967 even the fast mainline services were routed via Dundee, the Strathmore line being closed to passengers and reduced to a mere freight branch from Stanley to Forfar. Some activity remained at Coupar Angus, where over 30 shops were still open. By 1974 Culross colour printers were long established near the tolbooth, there was a farm machinery depot, and Marshalls of Newbridge had a large new poultry packing works. In 1975 Coupar Angus burgh was extinguished, becoming part of Perth & Kinross District. In 1981, although the secondary school had closed, five small hotels and other farm related industries were open. Rail freight services were withdrawn in 1982 and the track lifted; after this the old village lost its place in the headlines.

**Change for Better, for Worse**: In 1991 the population was still about 2225, generally quite fit and well-educated, as in most rural areas. The mid 1990s saw part of the former railway alignment used to create an internal through-route, and some new housing was erected. In 1997 Marshalls moved some 100 jobs from Coatbridge to their large chicken processing plant at Coupar Angus; by 2000 this was part of Grampian Country Foods. At the other (east) end of the town are the large silos of East of Scotland Farmers, and farther out are vast potato warehouses. Many shops have closed, but several pubs remain, about 15 shops including cafes and a chemist sell a range of necessities, and there is a modern health centre. The former town hall is the public library, four banks are still open, and professions include a solicitor and dentist. W M Culross & Son are still manufacturing stationers and printers. Lamb & Gardiner's large *Ford* garage surrounds the crumbling remains of an 18th century mill and maltings, and there is a rather posh car showroom. Small hotels include the *Moorfield House*, the characterful old *Royal Hotel* and the *Red House Hotel* – recently largely and attractively extended.

## COUSLAND, Carberry & Whitecraig — Map 15, E2

***Villages, Midlothian,*** *pop. 1500* — OS 66: NT 3768

In the 16th century Carberry Tower was built 4km north-east of Dalkeith, one of a cluster of defensive places; nearby was Cousland – a hamlet with an ancient chapel, a limeworks (founded in the 16th century) and a windmill; there was also a large 16th century castle (of which the walls still partially stand). Heron noted in 1799 *"near Cousland are a brickwork and a pottery"*. By 1843 coal was carried to the town of

*Cousland Lime Works sign in the 1970s. The lime works – started in the 16th century – has now finished processing and the site is to be landfilled, but local enthusiasts plan to restore the sign to its former fine condition.* (JRH)

Dalkeith on a private railway from the Duke of Buccleuch's Dalkeith or Carberry colliery, east of Carberry Mains and north of the emparked Tower. Homes for the miners were built in a small square colliery village beside the River Esk, long known as Deantown but eventually renamed Whitecraig after a local farm.

**More Minerals on and off the Rails**: In 1867 a winding branch line was opened by the North British Railway from Monktonhall Junction near Inveresk to Ormiston, passing a station named Smeaton, 1 km west of the Tower, and the Cousland limeworks, where the Chalkieside quarry was open by 1902; both this and the colliery were connected to the new line. The hamlet at Cousland grew to over 250 people and gained a post office and primary school, though buses ended the Smeaton passenger trains in 1933. The Dalkeith mine was reconstructed on a new site about 1953; the old headworks were disused by 1963 and removed by 1971. Meantime in 1965 the railway was cut back to Smeaton, where a coal preparation plant lasted until 1980. The related colliery employed 470 men in 1977, shortly before closure. By 1980 Carberry Towers as it was then known had become a conference centre. In 1991 the population of Whitecraig was 1209. Cousland limeworks are now closed, but Tarmac Concrete and some opencast coal operations exist just west of the neat village at Cousland, where some new housing and a newish primary school can be seen.

## COVE BAY, Nigg & Altens — Map 10, C3

***Villages / dormitories s. of Aberdeen,*** *pop. 5000* OS 38: NJ 9501

Although containing prehistoric cairns, most of the parish of Nigg in the extreme north of the ancient province of Mearns remained rural until recent times, except for Torry, an early satellite of Aberdeen. The Wellington Bridge across the River Dee, and Wellington Road (later A956) were built early in the 19th century to provide a new southern approach to the city. The Aberdeen Railway was built along the top of the coastal cliffs in 1848–50, with a station at the fishing village of Cove, 5 km south of the city centre; at Ness the line swung inland around the end of the 100 km long chain of hills and mountains which separates the Dee valley from Strathmore. In the 1890s the easternmost summit of this ridge was crowned by a belt of woodland; Cove was a small village with a post office, inn and coastguard station, while to the south was a large quarry. Nigg church stood where Wellington Road crossed the ridge, accompanied by another post office and a light scatter of development.

**Cove Shore and Bay**: In later years a breakwater was built to shelter a harbour at Cove Shore, but early in the 20th century the coastguard station and quarry became disused. By 1913 the railway station had been renamed Cove Bay, and the settlement name followed this lead. By the 1950s about 1000 people lived in the area south of the ridge end; but with the station closed about 1960 leaving the facilities of a very small village with a pub.

**North Sea Oil and Altens**: By 1974 a caravan site had been established. In 1975 Cove Bay became part of the City District of Aberdeen, whose rapid growth as the North Sea Oil capital completely changed the area. Large housing estates grew north and west of the village, the main roads were rebuilt, and the enormous Altens industrial estate bridged the gap between Cove Bay and the city; the *Skean Dhu Hotel* had been built there by 1980. Names taken at random show the 1983 nature of Altens: Aberdeen Jig & Tool Company, Container Care, Eastman Hose & Chain, Gardner Cryogenics, Jotun Protective Coatings and many more. In 1990 Hunting Oilfield Services, International Drilling, and Oilfield Chemical Services were in evidence, while in 1991 the Total Oil Marine headquarters at Altens planned to exploit further North Sea oilfields. At that time Cove Bay had 4571 people, evidently including a high proportion of oil industry workers; most were buying their own homes.

**Sorting Post for Aberdeen and the North**: In 1992 Grampian Region and Scotrail considered an Aberdeen suburban rail service to Stonehaven, with a new station at Cove Bay; but rail privatisation prevented any such progress. Meantime the Balmoral Group, pioneered by Shetlander Jimmy Milne, set up new headquarters at Loirston, and in 1994 exported hundreds of tonnes of buoys, tanks, and other heavy-duty plastic products every week. In 1994 the *Skean Dhu Hotel* was upgraded to 4-star standard with 221 rooms as the *Aberdeen Thistle*. In 1995 oil service company Aberdeen R D Engineering of Altens invested in a 60 tonne sheet-metal roller, perhaps the largest in the north of Scotland, used in making large pressure vessels and fabricated structures. In 1996 the Post Office relocated its mechanised letter office (MLO) from central Aberdeen to purpose-built premises at Altens. More housing has been built south of the village, where the *Gordon Hotel* has 25 rooms.

## COVESEA — Map 10, A1

***Moray coast settlement,*** *pop. under 100* OS 28: NJ 1870

Halliman Head on the cliff-bound Moray coast some 8 km to the east of Burghead was named for *'Holy Man'* St Geradine, who is said to have displayed a light there to aid mariners. Covesea to the west was the location of a very early sandstone quarry, which supplied some of the stone used in building the 12th to 14th century cathedral at Old Aberdeen. The Sculptor's Cave may get its name from this period. A barony charter was granted in 1698, at the same time as neighbouring Lossiemouth, but a safe harbour could not readily be provided at exposed Covesea, and its charter came to nothing. The Covesea Skerries lighthouse on Halliman Head was first lighted in 1846 and automated in 1984, the keepers' houses remaining as holiday lets. The area remained rural into the 1990s, but by 2000 the Silver Sands Leisure Park provided 4-star caravanning.

## COWDENBEATH, Lumphinnans & Moss Morran — Map 6, B4

***Central Fife town,*** *pop. 12,000* OS 58: NT 1691

The Kirk of Beath dated back to the 13th century; beside it passed the probably Roman alignment of the Old North Road linking Queensferry with Perth, which was turnpiked in 1753. Beath parish school was built at Cantsdam between the church and Kelty, for Cowdenbeath to the east and Lumphinnans to the north were merely farms. Under an Act of 1809 a very winding but much less hilly route 1 km or so east of the Old North Road was made up for coaches, as fully described by *Silver (1987)*. Scattered development at Cowdenbeath began about 1821; by 1827 a small hamlet and the *Old Inn* had come into being at the junction of the 1810 Act's new turnpike road to Burntisland; the inn was already a change point for horses, used from 1832 to 1845 by the famous stage coach *Defiance (see Gardiner, 1961)*. A bleachfield was built later, where the 1809 road crossed the Gelly Burn.

**Coal and Railways create a Town**: A search for iron ore having revealed coal seams, the first of many small coal mines was open by 1844. The Dunfermline branch of the Edinburgh & Northern Railway, later the North British (NB), opened from Thornton in 1849 with a station near the inn, and a post office opened about the same time. Lumphinnans No.1 pit was sunk from 1852 to raise ironstone, but had more success with coal, and Cowdenbeath rapidly grew into a town of 10,000 people – by then a junction for a rail-line to Kinross. Beveridge noted in 1888 *"a large and populous place, for the most part of recent erection, and mainly dependent on the adjacent collieries"*. Known as *'the town where buildings sink and lean'*, Cowdenbeath became a police burgh in 1890, the year when the NB opened the New station on a new high-level line which crossed over the main street north of the original line, in order to improve the route through Kinross, which was extended to Perth.

**Bricks, Bleaching and Teaching**: Cowdenbeath was simply called *"a colliery centre"* by Murray in 1894: it was then surrounded by mineral railways and the 9 coal pit shafts operated by the Cowdenbeath Coal Company, including the recently sunk 120m deep Mossbeath pit. In 1896 the Fife Coal Company of Leven took them over; Cowdenbeath became their chief sales office. In 1896 Foulford Junction between the Old station and Lumphinnans Junction became the start of a line to Auchtertool and Invertiel; nearby was Newton colliery, and east of the town the Arthur and Foulford pits, the latter having a large brickworks making 20,000 bricks a day in the 1890s. The Gordon colliery, south of Foulford, worked from 1893. The Fife School of Mining was started in 1895, and moved in 1910 to purpose-built premises in the new Beath High School, only to find them affected by subsidence! The school carried on, shored up.

**Bricks, Disaster and Rescue**: There was also a brickworks at Lumphinnans; around 1895 the adjacent Forth Ironworks was replaced by grim miners' rows, and a post office was open there by 1901; despite the surrounding grime, the old bleachfield survived at that time. In 1901 part of the peaty Moss Morran caused a disaster by falling into the long-established Donibristle pit 2 km south of the town; many miners were rescued by heroic efforts, but eight died. The associated pitmen's hamlet of Donibristle *(see also Dalgety Bay)* had a post and telegraph office, but faded away after the pit closed. In 1910 an early Mines Rescue Station was opened in Cowdenbeath by the Fife & Clackmannan Coalowners' Association.

**Tramways and Prosperity**: The Dunfermline Tramways Company opened its electrified main line from Dunfermline in 1909, running via Crossgates and Hill of Beath to its depot at Cowdenbeath, and so to Lochgelly and later Lochore. A small generating station was built in 1910 when the tramway opened a Kelty branch, partly on reserved track – but across a minerally unstable area. Meantime a varied shopping centre grew up. Cowdenbeath Football Club, formed in 1905, had its own ground from 1917 at Central Park, beside the No.7 pit; from 1924 to 1934 they were in the Scottish First Division. The population was so fast-growing, exceeding 14,000 in 1921, that the name *'The Chicago of Fife'* was coined. The *Empire Theatre*, built some years earlier, became a cinema in 1922. In 1924 the Fife Coal Company established their large Central Works and offices in Cowdenbeath, and the impressive Miners' Institute in Broad Street was built in 1925–28.

**Subsidence, Competition and Closure**: The Coal Strike of 1926 hit Cowdenbeath very hard and decline became inevitable. The Kelty line, badly hit by colliery subsidence and bus competition, was closed in 1931 and the rest of the tramway in 1937. Despite emigration, which cut the population to 12,700 by 1931, when the Foulford pit closed, Cowdenbeath still had the worst burghal overcrowding in eastern Scotland; in 1936 40% of its houses exceeded the statutory standard. A new Mining School was opened in Broad Street in 1935. The Gordon pit closed in 1939 but Mossbeath pit was kept going until 1945, one shaft remaining to serve the Mining School. On nationalisation in 1947 the Central Works and Offices employed 750 people; the NCB put them in charge of the whole Fife and Clackmannan coalfield. By 1951 Cowdenbeath had the facilities of a typical town, while large numbers of council houses were replacing the miners' rows.

**The End of Mines and Mining School**: The old Lumphinnans No.1 pit closed in 1957. The Dora pit, south of Lumphinnans, closed in 1959 and Cowdenbeath Colliery was closed in 1960, so the population continued to shrink, though more slowly. By 1960 the *Old Inn* was known as the *Bruce Hotel*. The Kinross and Perth railway was closed in 1970 but a passenger service continued to Dunfermline and Edinburgh. In that year greyhounds and speedway around the football pitch at Central Park gave way to stock-car racing. By 1971 fewer than 12,000 people remained in the town; over 65% of its housing was owned by the council. The Fife Mining School closed in 1976, its work done, but the population stabilised.

**Babies, Glazing and Mossmorran NGL Plant**: By 1977 Babygro of Kirkcaldy had a clothing factory at Old Perth Road and Remploy had works at Kingseat Road. Soon C R Smith of Dunfermline built a large double glazing factory nearby. In the early 1980s Shell Expro built the enormous NGL fractionation plant at Mossmorran, 3km south-east of the town. This splits NGL (Natural Gas Liquids) brought by pipeline from the north of Scotland into natural gasolene, propane, butane and ethane. Much of the ethane is converted into ethylene – the raw material of polythene – by Exxon on an adjoining site; pipelines for ethane and ethylene were laid to Grangemouth, the other products being shipped out through Braefoot Bay *(see Aberdour)*. In the interests of safety the residents of Gray Park, an isolated group of council houses near Mossmorran, were moved to a new estate of the same name at the north end of the town.

**Expansion in Petrochemicals**: Mossmorran soon had only some 400 full-time employees, half under each firm. In 1990–93 a third fractionation module was built, doubling the plant's capacity and giving 700 construction jobs, but bringing Shell Expro's permanent staff to only some 250. Exxon also built a new plant to process propane and butane to produce propylene plastics feedstock; methane was to steam-heat greenhouses, adding in all over 220 permanent jobs. In 1994 Shell built a fourth module at Mossmorran and a third jetty at Braefoot Bay, creating 1000 short-term construction jobs but few permanent

*The pipes leading to Mossmorran, near Cowdenbeath, which connect the plant to Grangemouth refinery complex. The Natural Gas Liquids fractionation plant was built here by Shell Expro in the 1980s.*
*(SMPC / Bob West)*

posts; in 1996 Exxon Chemicals aimed to create 500 new jobs.

**Deprivation, Leisure and Recovery**: The Mossmorran jobs were unsuited to older ex-miners, and by 1987 pockets of severe deprivation in Cowdenbeath were evident to social workers, a trait confirmed by the 1991 census, when the population was 12,126. In 1988 British Coal closed its once great Cowdenbeath workshops and 120 more jobs were lost; in 1990 part of the building went to Redpath Engineering Services for pipe trades, creating up to 110 jobs, and another to Landmark as a furniture distribution depot. In 1990 the new Dora golf course, built for Fife Regional Council, opened on the restored site of the Dora Colliery. A swimming pool was built in the 1980s on the site of St Bede's primary school; a sports hall built in 1994–95 completed the Leisure Centre. In 1989 the passenger trains were extended from Cardenden to form a loop called the *'Fife Circle'*, giving a Kirkcaldy service via Thornton. In 1991 the Fife Coast Laundry, burnt out at Pathhead, reopened in a new factory at Woodend, and in 1992 the Region converted the former Co-op store into a centre for small businesses.

**Baby shrinks, Football fights and Laundry liquidates**: Babygro was sold in 1988 to Robert Lowe of Cheshire, who employed about 185 people in Cowdenbeath; they in turn made losses and sold out. Central Park, also used for stock car racing, was the poor ground of Cowdenbeath's struggling football team; after a particularly disastrous season the main stand burned down in 1992 for the second time in seven years, and Portacabins had to be used as dressing rooms. Demoted in both 1993 and 1994, the club remained in the Third Division in 2000. In 1994 the Keltex Weaving Company who made heavy linens and cotton towels for London Underground and the NHS, installed machinery to avoid sending all their yarn to Lancashire for sizing, an 800km round trip. But in 1995 the Cowdenbeath Laundry was liquidated, and in 1997 J C Gillespie, long established in sheet metal at North End Works, moved to a new factory at Mitchelston (Pathhead). Fife Scottish still has a bus depot, Gordon Greig makes timber windows, and the demolition of several long-derelict buildings in 2000 improved the still-congested High Street. The *Struan Bank Hotel* has 9 rooms.

## COYLTON

**Map 1, C2**

*Ayrshire village, pop. 2000* — OS 70: NS 4119

The traditionally bibulous and fun-loving fourth or fifth century King Cole (*Coellen Guotopauc*, meaning *'Old Cole the Splendid'*) is supposed to have held his musical court beside a stream named after him as the Water of Coyle, a tributary of the River Ayr, 9km east of the latter's mouth. He also gave his name to the province of Kyle or Coila. Ancient earthworks 2 km west of the Water of Coyle might indicate the site of King Cole's palace, though tradition places his grave at Coilsfield House. Then came a millennium of oblivion; though the name of Coyle survived as a parish, the centre of activity in Kyle moved elsewhere. The area's main feature was the 14th century Sundrum Castle, emparked when Pont mapped Kyle about 1600; he regarded Kyle as being bounded by the Rivers Irvine and Doon, but including upper Nithsdale. By then the Water of Coyle had been bridged at *'Brigend'*, 2 km to the north of *'Cultoun'* Kirk. The mid 18th century Roy map showed that the Ayr to Cumnock road still passed the same way, near *'Taybough'* (Trabboch) Mill.

**Slow Development**: The nearest railway with passenger services was opened in 1872, 2 km to the east at Drongan, and by 1902 unspecified mineral workings around Coylton (presumably the early Sundrum colliery shafts) were connected by a very lengthy siding to the Dalmellington branch railway near Dalrymple. By then inns were open at the hamlets of Coylton, New Coylton and Joppa; the latter, some 1.5km to the west, had the post office. After 1947 the new NCB sank a small drift mine (Sundrum 5 & 6) which worked till 1961. By 1951 the homes of some 1400 people were widely scattered around Coylton, enjoying the facilities of a small village, plus a tiny secondary school; Sundrum Castle had become a hotel by 1954.

**Detached Houses in Affluent Coylton**: By 1976 secondary education was provided elsewhere, but the population at Joppa and to some extent New Coylton, by then renamed Hillhead, had continued to grow. By 1987 a caravan site had been added to the north. The 1991 population of the Coylton and Hillhead area was still about 1900, generally quite young and well-educated, served by small-village facilities. By 1998 a leisure centre and further quite substantial areas of new housing had been built. The refurbished *Sundrum Castle* now offers self-catering accommodation.

## CRAIGELLACHIE, Dandaleith & Elchies

**Map 10, A2**

***Small Speyside villages,*** *pop. 500* OS 28: NJ 2945

Pont's map of middle Speyside made about 1600 showed Elchies, its Kirk and Easter Elchies, all west of the River Spey upstream of the cliff called Craigellachie, *(G. Hill of the Rock)*, which rises sheer from its west bank. The tower house of Wester Elchies was built soon after. The Roy map of about 1750 showed a roadless area, with a ferry hamlet, the *'Boat of Fiddich'* east of the river just above the confluence of the River Fiddich, the site of the modern village. In 1813–15 Telford designed and oversaw the erection of the spectacular 46-metre span iron bridge (whose sections were cast in North Wales), erected at the rock for the Commissioners for Highland Roads and Bridges, and connected with Grantown by the south Speyside road *(see Hay & Stell)*.

**Macallan's Whisky and the Railways**: The little Elchies distillery – probably originally an illegal still – high above the west bank of the river nearby, was licensed in 1824 by Alexander Reid; it later bore the famous Macallan name. The first Craigellachie post office was open by 1838, taking over the main role of Mortlach (now Dufftown) for a time. A branch of the Morayshire Railway from Rothes arrived at Dandaleith north of the river in 1858, and in 1863 the Great North of Scotland Railway (GNSR) opened its line from Dufftown to Boat of Garten; Craigellachie became a minor junction linked to Dandaleith for Elgin. By 1886 the distillery, then of *"old-fashioned"* design, made only 180,000 litres of Highland malt whisky a year. There was evidently already a hotel in the *"village, a good hiring-station"* for horse-drawn vehicles; by 1894 Murray found the purpose-built *Craigellachie Hotel "very good"*, and there was a terra cotta works to the south-east.

**Distillery, Brewery and White Horse**: The large Craigellachie distillery was built in 1890–91 by Mackie & Co *(see also Lagavulin)*; in 1909 much of its product went for blending, and by 1927 the firm had been renamed White Horse Distillers. Meantime a brewery had been established in 1895, but it was remote from mass markets and was in production for little more than a decade. One of the area's many Grants made iron ploughs in Craigellachie around 1900, and agricultural engineering continued. Casks and vats for the distilling industry were also made, but Craigellachie never became more than a small village, with around 500 people in the mid 20th century. A 9-hole golf course recorded in 1953 soon vanished, the railway was closed in 1965, and Telford's famous road bridge with its right-angled approach, restored in 1964, was replaced for traffic purposes by a new bridge and approach roads built in 1972, becoming a worthy monument. Craigellachie distillery was more than tripled in size between 1965 and 1975, its new buildings bearing DCL's *'White Horse'* symbol *(see South Queensferry)*; it was busy under United Distillers in 1990. By 1994 Craigellachie boasted a visitor centre.

*The 1815 bridge at Craigellachie, designed by Thomas Telford with ironwork made near Wrexham. It was built as a single steel span to avoid placing a pier in the deep and fast-flowing R. Spey. It carried main-road traffic until 1972.* *(RS)*

**Macallan loses Independence and Jobs**: From 1982 Macallan sold its own single malt, expensively made in small traditional stills and matured in once-filled sherry casks; it was sold at up to 25 years old in 1992. The cooperage, family-run since 1947, was also a tourist attraction by 1994. Macallan Distillers' head office remained at the distillery; in 1994 it sold in bulk to blenders and 80% of its premium single malt went worldwide, especially to Italy and USA. Sherry casks being twelve times dearer than American oak, in 1994 the firm thought of buying its own forest and leasing the casks to sherry producers before using them. However, in 1996 the Macallan was taken over by Highland Distillers, who had their own sales organisation; regarding it as overmanned, they sacked 26 of the 66 workforce, to local consternation. The important Speyside Cooperage still made or repaired about 100,000 varied oaken casks each year, and in 2000 was open to visitors all year round. The *Craigellachie Hotel* has 26 rooms.

## CRAIGHOUSE (Jura)

**Map 4, B4**

***Island community, Inner Hebrides,*** *pop. 200* OS 61: NR 5267

The mountainous Inner Hebridean Isle of Jura, whose name aptly means *"deer island"* in Old Norse, is some 45 km long but only 10 km wide. On and near the coast of its southern half, which rises to 785 m in the central *'pap'* or breast of Beinn an Oir, are various raised beaches and ancient cairns, duns and standing stones. In 1549 Monro noted that Jura was in four ownerships, a *"fine forest for deer, inhabited and manured at the coast side"*, but its *"sometime"* parish kirk was then merely a chapel. Jura people were known for whisky smuggling in the 17th century. The usual access from 1764 or earlier was by ferry from Craignish in mid Argyll, either to Lagg *(q.v.)*, or to Kinuachdrach at the north-east corner. The 27 farms raised many Highland cattle.

**Road, Distillery and Village**: A road was built the entire length of the island from the Feolin (Islay) ferry in 1804–10, making it prudent for the islanders to distil their whisky legally. So the Isle of Jura distillery at Craighouse on the sheltered Bay of Keils was officially built in 1810. By 1831 over 1300 people lived on Jura, but after 1840 many were cleared for sheep. There was no post office on the island until about 1847, reliance being placed on facilities at Port Askaig on Islay. A shop opened in 1861, and in 1865 the lighthouse on the isolated rock of Skervuile, 9 km north-east of Craighouse, was first lit; infrequent steamers served Jura from about 1867. The distillery was extended in 1875 with a turbine water-wheel, to an annual capacity of 820,000 litres of malt whisky, classified as Highland despite its proximity to the distinct Islay malts.

**Enlarged Distillery Underused and the People Vanish**: By 1886 the plant was only working at 35% capacity. There was a weekly steamer from West Loch Tarbert to a *'handsome'* pier at Craighouse, described by Barnard as *"the only place that can be called a village; the workmen's houses form the street"*. The 800 or so remaining islanders lived on dairy produce, potatoes and fish. Apart from deer stalking there was little for tourists, but by 1894 there was an inn at Craighouse. The population went on sinking, to under 400 by 1931, when Jura was largely populated by deer. The distillery was closed down in the early 1900s and became derelict. The Skervuile lighthouse was automated in 1945 and by 1951 the population of Craighouse was under 250; the northern ferry had vanished. Tarbert steamers still called at Craighouse as recently as 1969; but by the 1980s public access was only via a vehicle ferry from Islay (*see Port Askaig*).

**Local Revival: Urbanity in the Wilderness**: By the 1970s electricity arrived via submarine cables which linked Islay with the mainland via Lagg and Keilmore. The distillery was rebuilt due to local initiative in 1960–63, a new warehouse was built in 1972 and the first output was bottled in 1974, evidently selling well, for the plant was doubled in size in 1978. Craighouse, its population down to 150 and with the facilities of a small village, had the last magneto telephone exchange in Britain, its 54 lines being transferred to automatic operation in 1974. As the only appreciable settlement on depopulated Jura, Craighouse itself was urban in socio-economic character in 1981, and had a modest tourist function for cruising boats. In 1992 the delicate *'Isle of Jura'* single malt whisky was released, some of it sold at the remarkable age of 26 years! The population of the entire island was only 196 in 1991. Craighouse still keeps its school, doctor, shop and post office, while the gardens of Jura House at the south end of the isle are a tourist draw. The distillery and the 19-room *Isle of Jura Hotel* are still open all year.

## CRAIGIE (Dundee), Mains, Douglas & Whitfield

**Map 6, B3**

***Northern areas of Dundee,*** *pop. 32,600* — OS 54: NO 4232

A long ridge some 2 km wide extending eastward from Dundee Law separates the valley of the Dighty Water from the Firth of Tay. The keep of Powrie Castle some 5 km north of Dundee was built around 1475 by the Fotheringhams, who replaced it with a small mansionhouse built nearby in the early 17th century. Mains of Fintry Castle was built in 1582 near the Kirkton of Mains; another tower of similar age was Pitkerro. When sketched by Pont about 1600 the Forfar road already bridged the Dighty Water 2 km nearer Dundee. Pont also showed Milton, *'Kragy'* (Craigie) on the ridge, and Whitfield, the latter two probably ferm touns.

**Linen Boom, Railway and Trams**: A linen bleachfield was built at Findrick (Fintry) in the period 1746–60. Roy's map made about 1750 showed two mills on the Dighty between the Forfar and Brechin (now Douglas) roads, and another just to the east. One was the Douglas (or Douglasfield) bleachfield where the first steam-powered calender for cloth finishing was installed in 1797, followed by a Boulton & Watt steam engine built in 1801; in 1819–25 it was owned by William Sandeman. In the late 19th century three other bleachfields – the Claverhouse, Dundee and Balunie – worked on this section of the Dighty Water; farther north on the Brechin road were the hamlets of Whitfield, Drumgeith and Baldovie. Stannergate station near the mansionhouse of Craigie was provided by the Dundee & Arbroath Railway, which opened in 1838. From 1905 trams served the southern edge of the area, routed along Craigie Drive to Broughty Ferry.

**Urbanisation between Tay and Dighty**: Craigiebank, the largest of Dundee's early housing schemes, was begun in 1919, with over 800 houses; other schemes were steadily added, of which the largest was Mid Craigie, lying on the *'country'* side of the Kingsway which was built in the 1920s as a city bypass; schools were included. In 1926 an 18-hole municipal golf course was created on the drumlins of the new Caird Park, around Mains Castle. The trams were withdrawn in 1956, being replaced by buses; by 1951 some 57,000 people lived in the area, a figure which remained fairly constant for thirty years although the originally high occupancy rate had fallen. The huge and monotonous Fintry estate north of the Dighty and the high density Douglas and Angus estates which were built to the east after the second world war merely maintained the population; this remained true even after the building of the Whitfield estate of the 1970s, again north of the Dighty. Linlathen Junior Secondary (later High) School was built off Forfar Road in the 1950s and St Saviour's High School in the 1970s. Powrie Castle was restored in the late 20th century.

**Industries in Growth and Decline**: The 1930s Kingsway East industrial estate was by 1979 the new home of Stewart & Son, Dundee blenders of *'Cream of the Barley'* whisky. Nearby was the Longtown estate. By 1980 Levi Strauss made sports clothing on the Baldovie industrial estate near a large Michelin tyre factory built in the 1970s; it employed 1000 people in 1993 and was to be expanded in 1995. By 1980 Bonar Long were electrical engineers, and Timex *(see Lochee)* had a watchmaking factory at Milton of Craigie; still at work in 1983, it was history by 1993. Meantime in 1990 NI Transformers, a subsidiary of the Swedish-Swiss combine ASEA Brown Boveri, was designing and building the largest types of transformers in growing numbers. In 1991 the newly privatised Scottish Power, muscling in on the former Hydro monopoly, opened one of their superstores on the Longtown estate, and the District Council, which had acquired 25 ha for development as the Claverhouse industrial park, built an advance factory. In 1994 Allied Distillers closed the Stewart & Son bottling plant; nearly 100 jobs were lost. However, about 1994 the D C Thomson offices moved out from the city centre to Kingsway East.

**Tackling Poor Estates and Truancy**: Taken as a whole, the area in the 1980s had only village facilities. By the late 1980s Whitfield suffered from emigration and in 1987 was among the four particularly poor estates in Scotland selected by the government for a partnership scheme, intended to improve housing conditions. The unpopularity of the high-density maisonettes in the Skarne area had led to over 1000 vacant houses, which were to be replaced in the early 1990s by low density housing. Another 350 older and largely vacant flats at Mid Craigie were also to be pulled down, and replaced by houses for sale. In 1995 Linlathen High School had 530 pupils, when they cared to appear, for it had the highest rate of poor attenders in Scotland at 20%, so it was closed the next year. Whitfield High was renamed Braeview Academy, and had 920 pupils in 1997, while Craigie High School had 705 and St Saviour's High 633. In 1996 the City council closed its Baldovie waste incinerator, but Levi Strauss were still busy. By 2000 the Stobswell Ponds off Pitkerro Road were the base for the flourishing Dundee model boat club. A small hostel for backpackers is open all year round at Broughty Ferry Road.

## CRAIGMILLAR — Map 15, C2

***S-E. part of Edinburgh,*** *pop. 12,000* — OS 66: NT 2971

South of the Braid Burn 4 km south-east of Edinburgh is the massive 14th century Craigmillar Castle, which covers some 5000 m$^2$. In 1374 Craigmillar Castle was sold by John de Capella to Sir Simon Preston; the large barmkin was erected in 1427. The castle was built of a pale sandstone extracted from a quarry just to the north, which was also the source of stone for buildings in Edinburgh Castle in 1531. The castle was burned by the English in 1548, and repaired, becoming a favourite residence of Mary Queen of Scots; but it had become rather ruinous by 1827. A nearby settlement which housed her French attendants was called *'Little France'*.

**The Railways**: The bucolic Edinburgh & Dalkeith Railway (E&DR), laid out by James Jardine of Edinburgh to carry coals to the city, was opened through the Niddrie area north of the castle in 1831. In 1884 when the new Edinburgh South Side Suburban Railway was opened by the North British, a proper station named Duddingston & Craigmillar was provided on the new line 1 km north of the castle. By that date the Co-op had established a dairy at the elbow in Niddrie Road (later Niddrie Mains Road) 1 km west of Niddrie House, and margarine was being made there: its *'Craigmillar'* brand name was still in use a century later.

**Multiple Brewery Development**: In 1892 Drybrough's brewery was moved from the Canongate in Edinburgh to a new site near the station, and in 1901 McLachlan established the Castle brewery south of the junction of the two railways. By 1932 there were no fewer than six breweries clustered around the station, all rail connected: the Castle, the Craigmillar, the North British west of the new local park, the Duddingston north of that, and the Pentland brewery. There were several quarries in the area; in 1937, 21 workers were recorded at the Hawkhill Wood quarry, which closed in 1940.

**Council Housing, Biscuits and Buses**: Biscuits were being baked at Craigmillar by the 1920s, and by the 1940s there was also a firework factory just north of the castle. During the 1920s Edinburgh City Council developed the Craigmillar council housing estate, between Duddingston and Niddrie Mains; building was well advanced by 1932. The White House was built as a roadhouse in 1936, but was rather out of character with this industrial area. Remarkably, rather than extending its electric tramways from Newington, Edinburgh Corporation used buses to serve Craigmillar, which was then said to be the second largest brewing centre in Britain, with seven brewery sites still on the map in the late 1940s.

*A brewery at Craigmillar, one of seven which were established in the area from 1890 onwards. In the mid 20th century it was Scotland's largest brewery complex.* *(RCAHMS / JRH)*

**Goodbye Niddrie House and Hello Bison**: In the 1950s the local facilities, on the scale of a small village, were very inadequate to serve the 10,000 people of Craigmillar. Niddrie House was replaced in the 1960s by another City Council housing estate, including two 14-storey blocks built of concrete by Bison using their prefabricated *'Wallframe'* panels. These large housing schemes south of Niddrie Mains Road had raised the population to a peak of 15,000 by 1971. Drybrough's was bought by Watney Mann in 1965; in 1970 they built a new brewery. Although by 1975 there was a caravan site near Little France, in 1981 Craigmillar still had only the facilities of a large village. The population had fallen to 12,500, but despite problems, some community spirit was then expressed through its Festival Society.

**Skittling Bison Blocks and Breweries – enter Fantasy and Infirmary**: The 26-lane Megabowl was opened for tenpin bowling in 1989, located in the Craig Park complex at Newcraighall Road. By 1989 about 120 flats in the two Bison blocks at Niddrie were in so poor a state that they were demolished in 1991, to be replaced by low-rise housing. The Drybrough brewery, still open in 1980, became the Holyrood Business Park in 1990; by 1992 one firm there was called Fantasy Forge, with twenty workers producing war games. The last remaining brewery in Peffermill Road was by 1993 Carlsberg-Tetley Alloa. The long established D S Crawford Ltd, who had taken over the Mackie bakery in Peffermill Road, became bankrupt in 1996; today it's Simmers. In 1994 EU money was intended to be put into the creation of a country park around Craigmillar Castle, but it had also regrettably been decided to build a new Royal Infirmary for Edinburgh at Little France; when building began in 1999 it replaced the caravan site but disrupted the approaches to the castle and damaged its formerly rural surroundings. Sadly in 2000 Craigmillar had three times the national unemployment rate and a reputation for heroin abuse, but much recent building of new houses and a health centre have improved the ambience.

## CRAIGNISH, Ardfern & Kintra — Map 4, C3

***W. Argyll localities,*** *pop. 250* — OS 55: NM 8004

The remote Craignish peninsula on the coast of Lorne is sheltered from the west by the isles of Luing and Shuna. At Kintra, at the head of Loch Craignish, are an ancient fort and standing stones, and at the Kirkton near the end of the peninsula stand the ancient Dun Mhuilig, sculptured stones, and the 16th century tower of Craignish Castle. A ferry plied from the vicinity to Jura from at least 1764 into the 20th century. By 1824 there was a post office at Kintra, but development was gradual. By the 1950s the clachan of Ardfern on Loch Craignish between Kintra and the old Kirkton contained over 100 people, Craignish kirk and primary school, a post office (replacing Kintra) and an inn. By 1985, though the inn had closed, Ardfern had a garage, and a wildlife park had been established in the wooded vicinity. The post office is still open, as is the *Galley of Lorne Inn*. Ardfern is now one of Scotland's most popular yacht havens.

## CRAIGNURE

**Map 4, C2**

***Village, Isle of Mull,*** *pop. 150* OS 49: NM 7137

The great 13th century Duart Castle stands starkly prominent on the eastern tip of the Isle of Mull; Duart means *Black Point* in Gaelic. Dean Monro aptly described it in 1549 as *"a strengthy place, built on a crag at the seaside"*. In 1653 the ship *Swan* sank in a storm while moored close beside the castle, its wreck remaining as a time capsule. Martin reported in 1703 that Duart had been forfeited by Sir John MacLean and transferred to the Duke of Argyll. By the early 19th century a coastal inlet at Craignure, 3 km farther west, was the terminus of a ferry from Ardnacroish (Lismore). Between Duart and Craignure is Torosay, the site of the attractive mansion of Torosay Castle, designed by David Bryce and built in 1855–58. Its tree-sheltered terraced gardens designed by Lorimer were added about 1900. Craignure had a pier by 1894, and by 1900 a post office. In 1911 Sir Fitzroy MacLean bought back his ruined ancestral castle of Duart and restored it, though it remained prey to damp until further work was done in the 1980s.

**Rolling On and Off the Rails at Modern Craignure**: By 1953 a *"trim little inn"* was open at Craignure, which had replaced both Auchnacraig (*q.v.*) and Lochbuie as the terminal of the main Oban to Mull ferry. A starkly ugly new pier was built in 1962–64 for Argyll County Council; its ro-ro service from Oban became the main landing point for the island, and also the coach terminal for the busy Iona tourist connection. Craignure provided several essential services, and tourist development began nearby, including by 1972 the three-star 60-room *Isle of Mull Hotel*, financed by the HIDB and overlooking the pier and a wider, more beautiful scene. The Craignure golf course was reopened in 1979–81. From 1976 David James, then the owner of the very interesting Torosay Castle, promoted the Mull Railway, a short 26 cm gauge passenger-carrying woodland line linking it to the pier. From its opening in 1984 this was the only railway on a Scottish island. In 1992 small vessels owned by Glenlight of Ardrossan shipped logs from the pier; but the firm ceased trading in 1994 and the cargoes were transferred to road and the ro-ro ferries. By 1996 there was a caravan and camping site, as well as the *Craignure Inn*.

## CRAIGO, Logie Pert & Marykirk

**Map 6, C2**

***Angus / Mearns hamlets,*** *pop. 300* OS 45: NO 6864

Across the River North Esk from the ancient parish centre of Marykirk in the Mearns is Craigo, 7 km north of Montrose. Some 2.5 km west is the kirkton of the Angus parish of Logie Pert, near which Gallery House, a finely plastered mansion, was built about 1680 for the Fullertons, fowlers to the medieval kings. The Roy map of about 1750 showed the water-powered *'Mill Craigy'*, linked to Montrose by a track via Kinnaber. Logie bleachfield was established close by about 1760, and as the roads were made up it grew steadily into the 1790s; by then there was also a yarn-cleaning mill. Nearby was the Logie flax spinning mill, at work before 1805 and enlarged in 1835 to employ 130 people; at that time the two textile mills were still water-powered, and both owned by Montrose firms. Meantime in 1814 a major bridge linking the two villages was built in 1814 to designs by Robert Stevenson, better-known for his lighthouses.

**The Railway arrives and passes by: Rural Calm returns**: Craigo was provided with a station on the Aberdeen Railway, opened in 1848 adjacent to the 13-span Craigo Viaduct, originally with timber arches. But the Logie bleachfield had been abandoned by about 1860 for new premises at Hillside *(q.v.)*. Logie mill, also disused for a time, was again busy in 1864 under James Ramsay & Co. Craigo mill had 150 workers and 1800 spindles in 1864, when it was owned by Richards & Co of Montrose, whose adjoining bleachfield then employed 110 people bleaching cloth. But although bleachworks survived to the 1890s, Craigo consisted of tiny hamlets, dependent for its post office on Marykirk, and development then practically ceased. In 1951 over 500 people still lived in the Craigo area, and the school had some secondary classes; but these soon vanished, and the station was closed about 1960. By 1981 the fast-falling rural population thereabouts was little more than 300, with minimal facilities. However, Marykirk with 480 people has retained its inn and post office in 1988, but Logie's primary school and post office have both recently gone.

## CRAIGTOUN & Mount Melville

**Map 6, C3**

***East Fife Park area*** OS 59: NO 4814

The emparked mansion of Mount Melville in the rustic parish of Cameron, 3 km south-west of St Andrews, was a prominent feature of Sharp, Greenwood & Fowler's map of 1826–27; but its small artificial lake came later. By the 1890s there was an inn and post office at the nearby hamlet of Denhead, but these later faded away. From 1887 a station on the St Andrews to Crail railway was named Mount Melville, but it was 1.5 km from the house and was closed to passengers in 1930, though retaining its nameboards until the line was closed in 1965! By 1953 Mount Melville had become the Craigtoun Maternity Hospital, and by 1971 its park was open for leisure use by the public. By 1982 it was a formal country park, with caravan and camping sites; in 1990 it attracted 140,000 visitors. Centralisation of maternity care had led by 1993 to closure of the hospital, which was up for sale; by 2000 the 18-hole Duke's golf course was open in the park.

## CRAIL

**Map 6, C4**

***East Fife coast village,*** *pop. 1450* OS 59: NO 6107

The *Caer* element in the East Fife name Crail *(Caer Regale?)* and its rectangular cliff-top layout suggest Roman origins, as does the line of straight sections of road from Fife Ness, leading westwards past Kellie *(Caer Lee?)* and through modern Colinsburgh to Lundin and Pathhead. Another straight road from Kingsbarns aligns directly on Crail's early church. Crail was a Pictish fishing place, where a nick in the coastal cliffs formed a tiny natural harbour, the nearest mainland port to the small May Isle *(q.v.)*. Between Crail and the May is the Hirst, once a famed herring spawning area, as was the Auld Haikes off Kingsbarns; Crail already exported salt fish in the ninth century.

**Crail Palace and Burgh**: According to Chambers, David I *"had a palace"* at Crail – probably its castle, which perched on a rock dominating the harbour. He also chartered Crail as

*The Golf Hotel, Crail – a typical mid 18th century urban building. The tolbooth tower (behind), showing Low Countries influence, was built in 1517; today it contains a fine local museum.* (JRH)

a Royal Burgh in 1150; perhaps it had been the capital of the ancient Kingdom of Fife, for it became the first caput of the Fife sheriffdom at some time between 1154 and 1178. Markinch *(q.v.)* may have played a role before Cupar was made the caput in 1212–13; by then Crail's church had been enlarged to its ultimate size. Crail properties were still earning good rentals for their St Andrews owners in 1282, but the burgh had little natural hinterland and never appreciably outgrew its early town plan. There was still a royal castle at Crail about 1300; it later passed to another lord, but vestiges remained.

**Fluctuating Fortunes**: Meantime Crail recovered slowly from the hiatus of wars and the Black Death; in 1427–31 it dabbled a little in the wool export trade. In 1471 Crail paid trivial Customs dues, and in the 15th and 16th centuries generally contributed under 1% of the total of burgh taxes. The wool trade was resumed in 1500–1505, and the town was prosperous enough for the building of the tolbooth to start in 1517, the year when the church became collegiate. However, Crail's economy was again at a low ebb when in 1542 nothing was contributed to the exchequer by the local Customs. Meantime Balcomie Castle, a 16th century E-plan tower, had been built just inland of Fife Ness. In 1575, the year after a herring bonanza, five boats were lost at Crail Harbour's ruinous mouth, and repairs were undertaken. The once popular pilgrimage trips to May Isle were banned in 1581. In 1621 Crail still paid under 1.5% of Scotland's Customs dues, and in 1639 it ranked a pitiful 41st among Scottish burghs in tax yield, or about 1% of Edinburgh's trade. Commercial brewers worked in Crail by the mid 17th century.

**Tragedy, Disaster, Golf and Weaving**: Some 90 local men were killed at the Battle of Kilsyth in 1645, and in 1655 30 small vessels sank in the harbour during a storm which badly damaged the pier. The resulting repairs left the harbour in its final modest form, with a breakwater as shown on John May's chart of about 1680. Herring were then being caught from small boats, and in 1695 Crail exported 2400 barrels of fish. Fifeness gained a burgh of barony charter in 1707 but never saw urban development. In the 1720s Defoe described Crail as a *"small town"*; by 1745 it had a post office. By about 1750, as the Roy map showed, Crail still had only the one road, which linked southwards from St Andrews through Crail, there turning west: the route remains the main road 250 years later. But inland from Crail, though roadless, the farmland was apparently generally enclosed by the mid 18th century. The early Crail Golfing Society was founded in 1786, and the *Golf Inn* was open by 1789. From that year subsidies were available for small fishing boats, and the poor state of the harbour was remarked on; but the unusual feature of a tide mill was working by the 1790s. At that time much lint was locally spun into yarn by hand, and local weavers annually made some 35,000m run of various cloths.

**Decay in the Nineteenth Century**: Crail was a post town by 1797, though Heron noted in 1799 that its population was *"only about 1300"*. The traveller James Hall found Crail largely agricultural in 1807, but a brewery was still operating in 1825. Crail was described by Chambers in the 1820s as a town of nearly 2000 people, a *"venerable and decayed burgh which at present possesses no trade"*, its rubbish-strewn main street *"half-covered with rank grass and weeds"*. The little harbour was again repaired in 1825–28, and seems to have enjoyed some success up to about the time when a lifeboat station was opened in 1884, but after this date the fishing declined steadily.

**On the Rails and off the Rocks**: From 1883 Crail was served by the railway which wandered around the coast of east Fife; this stimulated holidays rather than industry, for the line went nowhere near the harbour. In 1889 at the insistence of Trinity House, the Commissioners for Northern Lights marked the North Carr rock 5km north-east of Fife Ness by positioning a lightship nearby. The *Marine Hotel* was built in 1903, but the old King's Mill was demolished in the 1920s and the lifeboat station was closed in 1923; however, a new light-vessel was provided in 1933. Until about 1935 the harbour was still used by small German sailing vessels which brought in timber and shipped potatoes, but thereafter only by crabbing and lobster boats and the occasional small yacht.

**Into the Sky...**: In the 1914–18 war a military airfield was established on the plateau near Fife Ness. In 1940 this field was reactivated and became a Royal Naval Air Service base; like all such it was styled as a ship – HMS *Jackdaw*. In 1944 Crail airfield was the base for No. 827 Squadron, which helped to sink the German battleship *Tirpitz*. The name HMS *Bruce* was adopted in 1947 when it became a naval training establishment. This was closed in 1949, but the Cold War which had already begun in 1948 led to the buildings soon becoming a Russian language school, and consequently they survived remarkably intact.

**...and Under the Ground**: The Cold War also brought about the excavation of a vast underground *'command centre'* (or nuclear funk-hole for the government) in Troy Wood, 5km west of Crail; how on earth did such an exposed location come to be chosen for a top secret installation of this kind? The Bunker, as it was later named, was abandoned in 1983 but was remarkably opened to the public in 1994 as a grotesque tourist attraction, crammed with the now obsolete equipment originally installed there at great cost, and thankfully never used.

**Crail Off the Rails again**: In 1951 Crail was a large stone-built village of 1600 people, with a modest holiday trade served by four hotels. The holiday railway was closed by Beeching in 1964, and later the former station platforms and buildings were incorporated into a specialist water-garden centre. The

North Carr lightship was replaced in 1975 by a light buoy and a low-level automatic fixed light at Fife Ness; the vessel was eventually preserved at Dundee. Burgh status too was lost in 1975. In 1976 Crail was stated to look towards St Andrews and Dundee for services not available locally. The National Trust for Scotland's *'Little Houses'* restoration scheme was a success in Crail, stimulating private owners to follow.

**Modern day Crail**: By 1981 Crail had five hotels, plus other catering facilities. By that time the harbour was only used by tiny pleasure vessels and inshore fishing boats, mainly crabbers. The advent of three caravan and camping sites and more recently a limited amount of new peripheral private housing has fortunately failed to destroy the burgh's unique character, and Crail remains one of the most quietly attractive, extensive and least altered of the early Royal Burghs, the proud possessor of a good local museum. The resident population in 1991 was 1450. Small hotels now include the *Balcomie Links* and the *Croma*, and the Balcomie golf course is just beyond the airfield.

## CRAILING & Nisbet

**Map 3, B4**

***Borders hamlets,*** *pop. 350* — OS 74: NT 6824

Hill forts on Peniel Heugh 6 km north of Jedburgh dominate the extensive rural parish of Crailing, which lies astride the River Teviot between Jedburgh and Kelso. The Roy map showed little in the 1750s apart from a track linking these two towns, on the line of the modern A698. In 1856 a branch of the North British Railway was opened from Roxburgh to Jedburgh, with stations either side of the river, at Nisbet and Jedfoot Bridge. The parish population was 501 in 1901 and still 459 in 1951. Crailing had acquired a parish school and by 1951 had a 57-line telephone exchange, but the post office was at Nisbet. The stations were casualties of the floods of 1948; passenger services were not resumed due to cars and buses, and the line closed to goods in 1968. Population collapse led to closure of the post office around 1973, and the school was later closed. Although in 1991 there were 343 residents, people nowadays have to rely on other places for almost every need.

## CRAMOND & Barnton

**Map 15, B1**

***Villages / suburbs, n-w. of Edinburgh,*** *pop. 17,000*

OS 66: NT 1976

A Roman fort was built about 142 AD on the promontory where the incised River Almond enters the Firth of Forth 6 km west of present-day Edinburgh; its purpose was to guard the eastern flank of the Antonine Wall, and it was at one time a cavalry base. About 208 AD it was recommissioned as an outpost depot, supplied by sea from South Shields. A pottery and craft industries existed, and the place was occupied by Romanised people into the fourth century. The high status of the place is shown by the stone lioness which lay undiscovered in the harbour until the mid 1990s (now in the new Museum of Scotland). In the dark ages Christians claimed the site by placing the village church directly over the centre of the fort. Until the Anglians came in the sixth century the area formed part of Strathclyde, its name consequently deriving from the Welsh Gaelic *Caer Almond*.

**Cramond Brig and King's Cramond**: Though the Roman roads in the area are lost, it is probable that a passenger ferry operated across the Almond to the Dalmeny estate and South Queensferry from at least 1069. By 1178 the Cockle mill was in use, and Cramond Tower existed by 1409. The River Almond was bridged above the village by 1436, though the structure was in timber; the present old *Cramond Brig* dates back at least to 1619, and was possibly built as early as 1500. These bridges improved the largely overland route to Fife via the Queensferry passage, shown on Pont's map-work; this indicated *'Bridgs end'* west of the river. A parish school was opened in 1599 and the House of Kings Cramond was built about 1640. In 1655 Cramond was described as *"a little country village"*; the *Cramond Inn* is dated 1670. By 1707 there were four grain mills, including Peggy's, and the prettily named Fairafar waulk mill.

**Milling and Villas, Iron Mills and Oysters**: A village school was open by about 1725, and in 1765 Carlyle noted the *"many beautiful villas"* standing between Cramond bridge and Barnton House. The Smith & Wright Work Company of Leith took over a former meal mill at Cramond about 1752 as an iron-slitting mill; this was sold in 1759 to the Carron Company which installed water-driven rolling-mills. William Cadell of Carron acquired the iron mill in 1770, using iron bars from elsewhere (probably Carron) as the raw material for nails and rods. He expanded the business into Peggy's mill in 1781 to make barrel hoops, and to Dowie's mill for spade manufacture the following year; about a tonne of coal was burned daily. A harbour built in the 18th century once held *"eleven large boats"* devoted to oyster fishing, but this activity had declined by 1799. Kings Cramond was remodelled by Robert Adam in 1794 for William Ramsay who renamed it Barnton House, replacing an older mansion of that name; it was enlarged in 1810.

**The Demise of Iron; enter Trains and Golf**: In 1799 Heron remarked on *"the village of Cramond of nearly 400 people and with a considerable iron-work which has three forges, two slitting-mills, and two steel furnaces, and employs seven vessels at sea. Much steel is hence exported to India."* Cramond had a post office from 1803, and a new river bridge was built about 1823. The iron and steel business failed in 1860, Peggy's becoming a paper mill, and Dowie's mill a sawmill and furniture factory. By 1880 a sandstone quarry was open in Barnton Park; employing 30 in 1901, it closed in 1916. The Barnton hard rock quarry was opened in the woods beside Queensferry Road early in the 20th century. There was also at one time a maltings. In 1894 a Caledonian Railway branch was opened from Edinburgh's Princes Street Station to terminate at a point just north of the later *Barnton Hotel*, encouraging the Royal Burgess golf club of Musselburgh to move in 1895 to a new course in Barnton Park.

**Suburbanisation Delayed**: The railway failed to draw commuter development, and the area was never served by the Edinburgh tramways. The mills and maltings had all gone by about 1910, and Barnton House was demolished in 1920. But the pleasant surroundings, fashionable golf clubs, motor cars, and new bus services to Edinburgh from the 1920s, led to numerous individual private houses being built in the 1930s. Development was stopped by World War II, and the under-used railway was closed in 1951 when the area had 3300 people and village facilities.

**Army Headquarters and Suburban Housing**: Craigiehall had become the Army's Scottish Command headquarters, and when suburban housing was again permitted, Wimpey Homes established their Scottish office at Barnton Grove. Development particularly in the Clermiston area in the 1960s led by 1971 to the population peaking at about 17,000. Between 1964 and 1972 new buildings were provided at Cramond for the anomalously named *'Dunfermline'* College of Physical Education, and the 50-room *Commodore Hotel* was built on West Marine Drive. The area's character by 1981 was suburban, and small developments continued to be squeezed in. In 2000 the notoriously congested roundabout junction at Barnton was converted to traffic signals. Hotels now include the enlarged *'Quality' Commodore* (86 rooms) and *Barnton Hotel* (50). The passenger ferry still plies across the Almond (fare 50p), and the tidal harbour is used for pleasure boating; the Cramond Inn remains as ever.

## CRAWFORD

**Map 2, B3**

***Small Clydesdale village,*** *pop. 400* — OS 72: NS 9520

Crawford lies in upper Clydesdale at the high altitude of 260 metres, surrounded by traces of ancient settlements. In the first century a Roman fort stood on the east side of the river, on the line of the Roman road from Strathclyde to southern Nithsdale via the Powtrail Water; the fort, though small, had wood-fired ironworks. The first element in the name Crawford may derive from the Brythonic *Caer Ro ('Roman Fort')*. By 1175 the Lindsays, Earls of Crawford, had built a castle, but Crawford became an Ecclesiastical Burgh in 1242; it was shown on the Gough map of the mid 13th century. In 1510 Crawford became a burgh of barony, but paid no tax in 1535–56. Timothy Pont's map, sketched in 1596, showed *'Kraufurd Lyndsay'* as a towering castle and *'Kraufurd'* as a complex settlement on the west bank of the Clyde. But despite its location on the main routeway from Carlisle to Glasgow, Crawford seems to have lost most of its importance by the mid 18th century, for apart from a mill the Roy map implies only a tiny kirkton, and none of the early travellers seems to have noticed it.

**On and Off Rail and Road**: The track to the south was made up as a coach road early in the 19th century, and Crawford gained a coaching and posting hotel. The Caledonian Railway, opened in 1848, provided a wayside station, but little growth followed, and the castle was in ruins by 1894. In the early motor era Crawford profited from its situation on the A74 road, and as a centre for hill walkers; but although by 1951 the population had reached 600, the station was closed by Beeching about 1965, and the improved A74 bypassed the village by 1970. Five hotels remained in 1981, but of lower star class than in the 1950s. The population had fallen to 400 by the 1990s, with the facilities of a small village, at least two inns and a caravan and camping site. By then the A74 had been reconstructed as the M74.

## CRAWFORDJOHN

**Map 2, B2**

***Clydesdale hamlet,*** *pop. 100* — OS 71 or 72: NS 8823

The valley of the Duneaton Water leads down from the Cairn Table hills to join the River Clyde north of Abington. Pont's crude inverted sketch of the waterside area 5km west of Abington as it was around 1600 shows most of its modern farm names, and a large building at Boghouse, later regarded by some as a castle, beside Crawfordjohn Church. A parish school was opened there in 1599, and apparently restarted in 1630. A burgh of barony charter was obtained in 1668, and by the mid 1750s the Roy map was able to show five roads or tracks converging on the kirk. When the roads were metalled and a turnpike was built across the Red Moss some 3km north of the village, to link Abington with Douglas Mill, the direct way to Douglas over Pagie Hill became a footpath.

**The Dual Carriageway 'B' Road**: A water mill was built and a small village grew, which remained so agricultural that the Leadhills road still involved a ford in the late 19th century. By then there was a smithy, and the isolated New Stables stood beside the no longer turnpiked main road. The population of only 160 in 1951, when there were two local inns, continued to fall. About 1970 the A74 gained a second carriageway, but there was no inn at Crawfordjohn, just a primary school, and a post office which closed about 1990. However by 1988 the *Red Moss Hotel* stood on the New Stables site, and a pub was open in the tiny village by 1992. The new M74 having recently opened about 1km to the north, the old road had become the luxuriously overspacious B7078.

## CREAGORRY & Lionacleit

**Map 7, A3**

***Townships, Benbecula.*** *pop: 1100 (area)* — OS 22: NF 7948

This low-lying group of crofting townships with ancient church and castle ruins stands at the south end of Benbecula. It was the starting point of a 7km road, built at the turn of the 19th century to serve a new pier at Port Pheadair, an anchorage sheltered by the uninhabited offshore Isle of Wiay. Completed with government aid in 1896, the remote pier was a white elephant from the start. Creagorry *(G. Creag Ghoraidh)* acquired more centrality in the three Isles of Uist when the causeway to South Uist across the South Ford was built during the 1939–45 war, and more so after North Uist was connected in 1960. In 1951 its tiny 5-room fishing inn, post office and sub-branch bank served a scattered population of around 350. Junior secondary education for 160 pupils was provided at Torlum, 2km north-west, and for 30 at West Gerinish about 7km to the south, but by 1976 both these schools were primary only.

**The Military and School Revolutions**: In 1961 the government built a missile test launching centre on the coast of South Uist some 5km to the south west, beyond the township of Iochdar, served by a new diesel-powered generating station and oil terminal built about the same time by the Hydro Board at Loch Carnan in the north-east of South Uist. By 1969 another short-lived hotel was open at Carnan Iochdar, the causeway head. By 1976, due to the influx of range personnel, new junior secondary classes were held at Iochdar school, one of five primary schools chosen in 1975 by the new Western Islands Council to teach up to *'O'* grade. From then onwards some 50 pupils aged 16–18 were boarded in hostels at Stornoway's Nicholson Institute, rather than near mainland schools as previously; but the strict Presbyterian Sabbath in Lewis was oppressive to many of the Catholics from the southern isles.

**Tourism grows and Education is sorted out at last**: By 1981 some 350 people lived in Creagorry and adjacent townships, some of the facilities serving as many as 1100 people in the surrounding area. The commercial and fishing hotel had been extended to 14 rooms. A crofting museum and silversmith at Lionacleit 3km north of the causeway drew the tourists; a caravan site was open there by 1985. It was a highly significant development when in 1988 the first purpose-built 20th century secondary school in the Uists *(Sgoil Lionacleit)* was opened there, to cater for over 100 pupils from the sixth year upwards, complete with a games hall and public library, bringing the scattered crofting settlements into the village category in terms of facilities, with a hotel.

## CREETOWN, Carsluith & Kirkmabreck

**Map 1, C4**

***Solway Firth villages / hamlets,** pop. 700* OS 83: NX 4758

The ancient Stewartry church of Kirkmabreck stood among the hills inland from the east shore of Wigtown Bay. About 4 km to the north of the kirk on the east bank of the tidal River Cree was *Spittal*, probably the original site of the early ferry to Wigtown, its name referring to a hospice for stranded travellers, founded by 1300. On the shore 2.5 km to the south rose the 15th century tower of Carsluith Castle, near which a corn mill was chartered in 1527. Later the ferry terminus was moved south to Ferrytown of Cree, where the tumbling Moneypool and Balloch burns enter Wigtown Bay. All these places existed by the time that Timothy Pont's map was made about 1610. Ferrytown was stimulated by lying on the early 17th century military road from Dumfries, built for the plantation of Ulster; Barholm Castle, an L-plan tower, was also built around that time 8 km to the south.

**Sand, Water and Mud**: The ferry to Wigtown continued to operate after the River Cree was bridged at Minnigaff in 1745. When the Roy map was surveyed about 1754, *Ferrytown of Cree* was a small close-knit place, south of which stood the mansion of *'Capincarig'* (Cassencarie). For riders with sure-footed horses a *'Ford at Low Water'* connected the hilly road from Dumfries directly to Wigtown. This road was in so bad a state about that time that despite the efforts of a horde of retainers a well-known nobleman's coach became stuck overnight on the Corse of Slakes, 5 km to the east of the ferry. In addition there was a road north which passed *'Spittle'*, whose one-time role was still indicated by the byroad to Wigtown on the opposite bank. Farther north this road bridged the mouth of the Palnure Burn en route to the Cree bridge.

**Textiles and Sea-shells**: Development was spurred when a bleachfield was built at Ferrytown around 1750, and a high-arched bridge was built across the Moneypool Burn in 1769. The name Creetown dates from 1785, when the village was revived by the erection of a small cotton mill for James McCulloch of Barholm, which stood on a bluff overlooking the Cree estuary; a villa designed by Robert Adam for John McCulloch was built there in 1788. Creetown became a burgh of barony in 1791. In 1799 Heron found *"a rising village, containing above 800 inhabitants, and a small port, where there are several sloops constantly employed in carrying sea-shells coastwise or importing coals and lime from Cumberland. The shells are dug from banks without the sea-mark, and are esteemed a valuable manure. Many thousand tons of these are carried off annually."*

**Granite Quarrying and Lead Mining**: Granite was first quarried in the area in the 18th century by Sir Samuel Hannay of Mochrum, to build Kirkdale House some 7 km south-east of Creetown. Heron continued: *"the Bishop of Derry, after seeing the beauty of this house, lately commissioned a large quantity of it to be carried over to Ireland"*. Creetown had a post office from 1801; in the 1820s Chambers found it a *"thriving sea-side village; by crossing the ferry at the village, the traveller enters the County of Wigtown"*. At some time lead mines were opened at Blackcraig, with a lead shot factory which existed until 1839, when it became a farina mill. The Kirkmabreck quarry was opened in grey granite by the Liverpool Dock Trustees about 1832; in 1869 four vessels were still shipping granite blocks to build the vast range of docks at Liverpool. Bagbie quarry was opened in 1864 by Forrest, Wise & Templeton, with a tramway to a pier; by that time the Fell quarry was already operated by the Scottish Granite Company.

**The Railway Age**: The Portpatrick Railway which opened in 1861 served Creetown rather remotely by a station 1.5 km north of the village. Sea-shells were still exported as fertiliser in the mid 19th century, and by the 1890s Creetown was a village of 1000 people, described as *"a small port"*. The pleasant little *Ellangowan Hotel* was built of granite from the local Silver Grey quarries in 1898, and they were still cutting granite blocks for building in 1939, but later mainly produced crushed roadstone. Kirkmabreck and Glebe quarries still made granite setts in 1939. Creetown approximately maintained its population until 1951, but regrettably Barholm villa was demolished in 1960 and the railway was closed by Beeching in 1965, its scenic potential unexploited.

**Decline**: By then Creetown presented a run-down appearance; by 1971 a 10% fall in population had occurred, and by 1981 there had been a serious loss of local facilities including the secondary school, chemist, and post town status; in these terms it was only a small village. In 1975 Creetown was transferred from the Stewartry to Wigtown District. In 1979 concrete products were cast locally, using granite aggregate from the huge quarries at Carsluith – then a hamlet of some 150 people – whose old castle and corn mill could still be seen in the 1990s. But in 1995 Barholm Castle was vacant, ruinous and for sale.

**Into the Age of Tourism**: Meantime in 1971 George and Mary Hinchcliffe had founded the unusual Gem Rock Museum at Creetown, and by the 1980s tourism had grown with two local caravan and camping sites. Quarries were still open at Glebe (Scottish Granite), Glenquicken (Barr's), and Kirkmabreck (Tarmac Roadstone). By 1991 when the population was 692, Barr's Solway Engineering Works stood north of the village, where there were three hotels, two caravan and camping sites, the museum, a restaurant, a well-kept bowling club and eleven varied shops. A serious attempt had lately been made to improve tourism prospects by a concerted policy of redecoration of the village centre. By 1996 Barholm Mains was a tourist attraction. Stake-net fishing for salmon continues at Carsluith, and there is a related smoke-house.

## CRIANLARICH

**Map 5, B3**

***W. Highlands village,** pop. 250* OS 50: NN 3825

In the 16th century the tower of Loch Dochart Castle was built on an islet in Loch Dochart, an expansion of the River Fillan where it forms a dogleg from north to east and is scarcely separated from the head of the south-flowing River Falloch. The military roads from Stirling and Dumbarton, built by Caulfeild's troops around 1750, followed these valleys to converge at the natural route centre of Crianlarich, whose name means *'Low Pass'* in Gaelic; it stands about 160 m above sea level. The roads were combined north-westwards for 7 km before parting again at Tyndrum en route to Taynuilt and to Fort William. A hamlet had grown at Crianlarich by the time of

Roy's survey of about 1750. Though the area had little farming potential, by 1797 an annual fair was scheduled in Strathfillan due to its focal position on droving routes.

**Early Tourism and Railways at Cross Purposes**: The *Crianlarich Hotel* existed by 1840 as a simple house, and by 1850 scenic coach tours connecting Loch Lomond with Killin via Crianlarich were in operation. In 1873 the Caledonian's penurious offspring the Callander & Oban Railway (C&O) was completed up Strathfillan through a station at Crianlarich to a temporary terminus at Tyndrum, as graphically described by John Thomas (1966); the C&O finally reached Oban in 1880. From 1894 the C&O was crossed at Crianlarich by another lengthy single-track line, the North British (NB) affiliate the West Highland Railway (WHR), en route from Glasgow to Fort William. This gave the hamlet the unusual distinction of two stations and for a time an NB engine shed, plus a privately-run tea-room which opened on the WHR station in 1895. In 1897 a connecting line was built to enable through running from Glasgow to Oban, but thanks to pointless rivalry between the companies it was little used until 1949, when the new unified British Railways introduced through trains between Glasgow and Oban.

**Trains and Walkers Meet**: By 1954 when the population was little over 200 a youth hostel was open, and by 1964 a mountain rescue post. In 1962 the celebrated refreshment rooms and the former WHR station building at Crianlarich Upper Station were burned down. In 1965 the original railway from Callander was closed by a landslide shortly before Dr Beeching had intended to abandon it, and all trains for Oban were perforce transferred to the WHR route, diverging or being split from Fort William trains at Crianlarich. After the Corpach pulp mill was completed in 1965, a daily train of 350 tonnes of logs from local forests left from the former C&O yard at Crianlarich, until the mill closed in 1980. In 1981 Crianlarich's general facilities were those of a small village and its population 240; about then it became a stopover point on the long-distance footpath called the West Highland Way.

**Rail Traffic Saved by a Whisker**: By 1990 the timber traffic was moved southwards on rail, for example to the Caledonian paper mill at Irvine, but was then lost by the closure of the Speedfreight network. Fortunately the passenger trains and those serving the aluminium works had survived, the new American owners of rail freight had regained the Crianlarich timber traffic by 1999, and in that year the station was reconditioned and the tearoom reopened. Remarkably, the only significant north–south road, and the only east–west route across the 100km of near wilderness between Balloch and Spean Bridge, pass through tiny Crianlarich, and are still essentially on Caulfeild's alignments. The hotel, plus many B&Bs, is still active, and the youth hostel is open all year except January.

## CRICHTON — Map 15, E3

***Midlothian hamlet,** pop. under 100* — OS 66: NT 3862

An ancient settlement stood above the steep-sided valley of the Tyne Water 7km south-east of Dalkeith; nearby was an early church and a ferm toun. The fine Crichton Castle was built in the 14th century a little to the south; it became the home of William, Lord Crichton, the Chancellor of Scotland, who in 1449 founded a small collegiate church on the hillside between the castle and the ferm toun. In 1581–91 the Earl of Bothwell

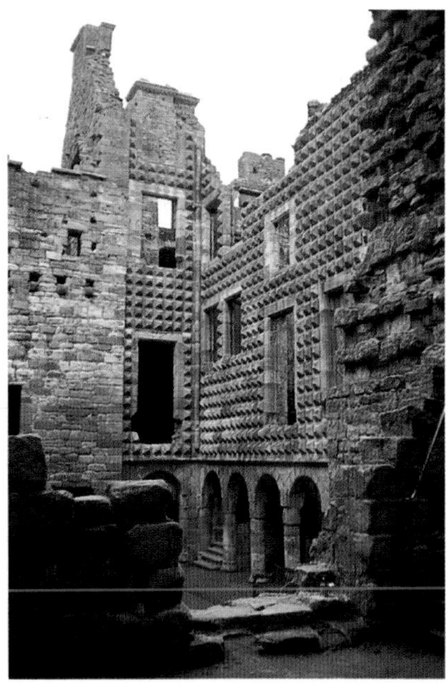

*Crichton Castle, dating back to the 14th century; the courtyard facade of Italianate stonework was added in 1581–91.* (RS)

added the castle's unique courtyard facade of faceted Italianate stonework. The important 16th century tower of Cakemuir Castle was built 4km south-east of Crichton Castle; the latter was shown emparked on Pont's map of Lothian, made about 1600. Crichton gained a parish school in 1627 and became a burgh of barony in 1706, but was not a significant feature on the Roy map of about 1754. Heron noted in 1799 that *"the villages of Crichton and Path-head contain upwards of 450 inhabitants"*. At one time there was a quarry east of the farming hamlet, where a large block of limekilns has survived early 20th century conversion into silo towers. Crichton's ruined castle is very well worth a visit.

## CRIEFF, Monzie & Abercairny — Map 6, A3

***W. Perthshire town,** pop. 6000* — OS 58: NN 8621

Crieff stands on a sunny spur above the River Earn some 25km west of Perth, near the confluence of the Turret Burn. Stone circles nearby, and 3km north-east near the sheltered parish centre of Monzie, show ancient settlement; the Romans camped in the area, and Monzie has hill forts and Pictish standing stones. Strowan some 5km to the west had a thanage from about the 11th century. Crieff's tight medieval street pattern suggests early development, and a carved slab used as a market cross was possibly of tenth to 12th century date. Abercairny 5km east of Crieff came into the ownership of the Morays in the early 14th century, and there it stayed.

**Mills, Bridges and Library**: Pont's manuscript map made around 1600 showed a water mill on the Turret Burn west of Crieff Kirk, and although there was no bridge across the Earn below Comrie, the Pow Water had been bridged at Dollerie to the east of Crieff, implying that the way to Perth was already defined. Craig in the same area was chartered as a burgh of barony in 1626, but came to nothing. Pont marked

Innerpeffray mill, 5 km south-east; nearby was a collegiate church founded in the early 16th century, to which a tiny public library, the first in Scotland, was added in 1691 by Lord Madderty. By 1656 Crieff was also linked by road to Dunblane, crossing the Bridge of Ardoch at Braco, and its own Earn bridge may date from about then; it certainly existed by 1715.

**Burgh and Cattle Tryst, Fire, Banking and Linen**: Crieff became a burgh of barony in 1672, when the *tryst* was chartered. This developed into the key drovers' market for the Highland cattle trade, and by about 1700 Crieff was described as having the largest market in Scotland; some 30,000 cattle passed through in 1723. Lacock of Abercairny, 5 km north-east of Crieff, gained a barony charter in 1706 but never came to much. Crieff recovered quickly from being burnt down in 1716, and according to one account had banking facilities by 1730; there was a post office by 1739. The town was enlarged in the 1730s by its proprietor James Drummond with a planned extension and linen factory; the River Turret was bridged beside the mill.

**Military Roads and Cliphane's Inn**: Crieff lay on what was then the main road from Stirling to Perth, and was made the starting point for the western leg of General Wade's military road system of 1725–1736 (*see Taylor 1976*). In 1743 the road north through the Sma' Glen was made up for carriages, and although part of the town was burnt by the rebels in 1745, the original *Drummond Arms* inn was open by 1746. Roy's survey of about 1750 showed a compact medium-sized settlement grouped about the steep town square, with five radial roads of which three diverged at the bridge. The block of Glen Turret distillery also existed. At that time *Cliphane's Inn* was said to be unusually good by the Highland standards of the day.

**Paper, Tanning and Textiles**: By 1746 Crieff had a skin-dressing trade for pelts brought from the Highlands. The Commissioners for the Forfeited Estates controlled the town from 1752, and about 1763 a paper mill was built with their aid by a local merchant, Patrick Arnot; in 1774 he built a lint mill and also expressed oil. The Commissioners also established the town's first known tannery about 1765. This was a logical development from skin dressing, since many of the ill-bred cattle would be in poor condition after the trek over the hills and be fit only for slaughter; other tanneries were founded later. The Commissioners returned the town to its former owners in 1784; they may have assisted in founding the bleachfield which was erected in 1785, for at that time narrow coarse linens known as scrims were hand-woven locally for the Glasgow market in Crieff, Monzie, and at ancient Fowlis Wester, 6 km east of Crieff. In the early 19th century cotton manufacture supplanted linen.

**Crieff sells fewer Cattle but makes legal Whisky**: The Perth United Banking Company opened a branch in around 1770. However, from about 1765 Crieff's role as the premier cattle market began to be gradually displaced as Falkirk's more famous tryst grew (see Haldane's *The Drove Roads of Scotland*). In 1770 Crieff was described as a *village*, but was still growing because the Glenturret distillery – originally an illicit operation – was licensed in 1775, 2 km to the north-west, and the Milnab mill was erected in 1782. Crieff acquired a brewery in 1791 and a new post office in 1793. At that time, about 100,000 head of cattle were still handled each year. In 1797 the cattle fairs were held at Strowan Murray 3 km west of Crieff, in February and May; Crieff itself also had two annual fairs. Heron in 1799 noted 15 mills along 2 km of the River Turret: *"the town of Crieff, with great annual markets for cattle, and considerable manufactures of various kinds"*.

**The Tryst Declines**: By 1801 Crieff's population was approaching 3000, and continued to increase. In 1804–42 a fine mansion was built on a new site at Abercairny for Charles Moray Stirling, and was extended up to 1869, standing in a huge landscaped park. However by the 1820s Chambers could write of Crieff as *"formerly the scene of a prodigious annual fair, at which the Highlanders attended with sometimes 30,000 head of their black cattle, which were bought by Lowland and English dealers; but this traffic has since been transferred to Falkirk. Crieff is still a thriving town; contains 4000 inhabitants, a favourite summer retreat."* A second brewery was at work by 1825, there was a bark mill by 1837, and three tanneries by about 1840. Fruit jellies were made commercially in the 19th century.

**Education and the Railways**: Morrison's Academy was established as a private secondary school in the 19th century. A local newspaper, the *Strathearn Herald*, was established in 1856, the year the Crieff Junction Railway, engineered by Thomas Bouch, was opened from what is now Gleneagles, and in 1866 a direct line from Perth was completed by another company; two tiny engine sheds were built. Connections westwards were constructed by degrees; Crieff's population was nearing 5000.

**Hydro, Jam, Juice and Golf**: The town hall was open by 1865, by which time the inn was known as the *Drummond Arms Hotel*; the *Crieff Hydropathic*, an enormous 200-roomed hotel, was built in 1867–68. In 1882 the large Strathearn Preserve Works were erected. In 1886 the Glenturret distillery was still entirely water-powered, except of course for heating, and used mainly local barley and peat to produce about 410,000 litres of Highland malt whisky annually. By that time the *Drummond Arms* had been rebuilt on a grander scale, and was considered *"good"* by Murray in 1894; two other smaller hotels were also open. Crieff was *"a thriving town with good shops, and large villas for summer visitors"*; a bowling green and the new golf course of a club founded as recently as 1891 were already available. An electricity generating station was built in 1901, quite early for a small town, followed in 1906 by the 21-bed Crieff Cottage Hospital.

**Decline in the mid Twentieth Century**: Glenturret distillery closed about 1923, putting sixteen men out of work. Abercairny House became a hospital in the 1939–45 war. Crieff had a population of some 5700 in 1951, a recent public library, and at least 20 hotels, with an important shopping centre having almost no chain stores. With ample private transport and buses available in the area, in 1951 the rail connection with Oban was severed, and the passenger trains to Perth withdrawn. The engine shed was closed in 1958, and the surviving uneconomic lines to Comrie and Gleneagles were closed completely in 1964; finally the goods line to Perth closed in 1967. Abercairny House was regrettably demolished in 1960 by Drummond Moray, and replaced by a smaller house. For some years up to 1977 a small theatre on the Ochtertyre estate 3 km west of

*Crieff Hydro – the largest (with 225 rooms and many sports facilities) and most prestigious of Crieff's many hotels – was built in 1868, and is still family-owned and run.* *(Crieff Hydro Hotel)*

Crieff gave public performances. Crieff had a High School by 1980.

**Industries Reawakened for the Tourist**: Glenturret distillery was reopened in 1957 by James Fairlie. The Crieff glassworks was built south of the town in 1964 by Vasart Glass of Perth, with financial aid from the distillers William Teacher & Sons, making ornamental glassware for the tourist trade. In 1980 Stuart Crystal of Stourbridge took over as *'Stuart Strathearn'*. In 1982 their paperweights contained 47% silica sand from Lochaline *(q.v.)*, 33% lead monosilicate from Bootle, 16% potassium carbonate and 4% saltpetre; the mixture was fired by gas in clay pots, and cullet (broken glass) was added. By 1991 a firm known as Perthshire Paperweights had taken over from Stuart's, and glass melting at Crieff ceased, though the works remained open for tourists. About 1972 A W Buchan & Co moved their Thistle Pottery from Portobello *(q.v.)* to modern premises nearby. A substantial restaurant and visitor centre opened near the glassworks about 1984; by then ornamental ironwork was made at a roadside smithy. The lengthy hillside golf course was reconstructed in 1980 to provide both 18- and 9-hole courses. Crieff had a virtually static resident population, and when the modest department store in the town centre burnt down around that time it was not replaced. By 1994 the Penny family of Crieff, proprietors of a small grocery chain, had opened a shopping mall, known as Penny Lane!

**Crieff Hydro and Glenturret for Visitors**: In 1983 the distillery at Glenturret opened its own visitor centre, plus an associated restaurant in 1987. By 1991 only four production workers were necessary, the small distillery using barley malted at Carnoustie to make *'Glen Turret'*, a good single malt, matured in old bourbon casks and sold at between 8 and 21 years of age. In 1991 Crieff had 6023 residents, of a fit and affluent retired character. In 1995 the *Crieff Hydro*, which stood in an estate of 325ha, was still owned by the Leckie family and offered various sports facilities: a golf course, two swimming pools, squash, and riding; it had 225 rooms and employed 250 staff, including 16 chefs. Meantime by 1997 Crieff High School had a roll of 524; Morrison's Academy is still independent. In 1997 a new 44-bed hospital with A&E services was opened to replace the old Cottage Hospital. By 1999 the former preserve works had been converted into about 40 dwellings. As well as the *Hydro*, there are half a dozen hotels, plus many guest houses and B&Bs.

## CRIMOND

**Map 10, C1**

***Buchan village,*** *pop. 876*

OS 30: NK 0556

A prehistoric stone circle and an ancient church lie about 12 km south-east of Fraserburgh in the low-lying Buchan coastal parish of Crimond, which gave its name to a famous hymn tune. *The 'Mill of Krimond'* appeared on Pont's sketch map of around 1600, and by 1601 a parish school was open. Robert Gordon's map showed some scattered development, but the Roy map made about 1750 added little. Later a turnpike road linking Fraserburgh with Peterhead was built past a re-sited church, and a post office was opened. The area remained wholly agricultural until in the 1939–45 war a large military airfield was laid out north-east of the village. Though abandoned soon after 1945, the runways and extensive buildings remained. In 1951 the local farming population was almost 700 and the school had a secondary class. By 1976, when the population had fallen to only 530, the school was primary only. But with the gas development at St Fergus, part of the former airfield became a minor industrial estate; a sizeable housing estate was built south of the village, and by 1981 Crimond was also served by a garage and doctor. Some development continued on the industrial estate in the 1990s, and by 1991 when the population had grown to 876 a visitor centre had been provided for the nature reserve at the Loch of Strathbeg.

## CRINAN

**Map 4, C3**

***Small Mid-Argyll village,*** *pop. 100* OS 55: NR 7894

Loch Crinan, an inlet of the Sound of Jura on the picturesque west coast of Argyll, may derive its name from the tribe of *Creones* noted by Ptolemy about 140 AD. Various prehistoric hill forts were built in the area. The shallow Crinan Canal, engineered by John Rennie, was dug between 1793 and 1801 to connect the Sound with Ardrishaig on Loch Fyne and enable the small sailing vessels of the day to avoid the perilous detour round the Mull of Kintyre. A basin and some of its 15 locks were constructed beside Loch Crinan, which gave the canal its name *(see Hay & Stell, 1986)*. A post office was opened in 1805. The canal was rebuilt and deepened under Telford's guidance in 1811–17; through it in 1819 passed the famous first steamer *Comet*, pioneering a service from Glasgow to Oban and Fort William; later she was wrecked near Craignish Point. By 1825 Crinan had a penny post from Lochgilphead. By 1840 horse-drawn *'trackboats'* worked the canal, connecting by 1848 with steamers plying from an inn at Crinan basin to Tobermory. By 1851 these were owned by Hutcheson, and later by MacBrayne.

**From Steam to Scallops**: From about this time a small chemical works at Crinan Harbour distilled wood to make acetic acid. In 1866 the screw steamboat *Linnet* replaced the trackboats and kept up the service until its end in 1929. Afforestation after 1918 clothed the hills west of Crinan, and the canal entrance locks were rebuilt in the 1920s. By 1956 there was a notable rock garden. Until the 1960s a passenger ferry across the loch shortened the distance to the north for pedestrians to and from Crinan. Meantime the canal basin served some deep-sea fishing boats but became primarily a yacht harbour, beside which the inn had grown by 1981 into a hotel; Crinan Boats had a yard at Fernfield by 1979, still working in 1994. During 1987 about 2000 boats, mainly yachts, passed through the canal to and from Ardrishaig. In the mid 1980s Mike Stewart bought a share in the boatyard and began to raise scallops on the seabed as Scallop Kings, in 1993 obtaining rights to use 100ha of seabed in Loch Crinan. Although forest walks and extensive bike trails had been laid out by 1996, and various new developments had arisen, the Crinan post office had closed, but the 22-room *Crinan Hotel* remains.

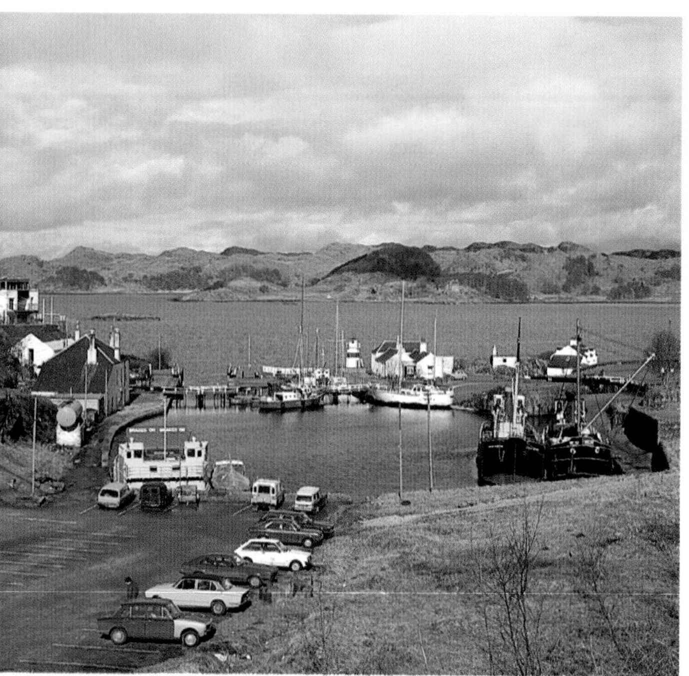

*The Crinan basin, Kintyre, the western terminus of the Crinan Canal – built from 1793 to designs by John Rennie, and upgraded by Telford in 1811–17.* *(JRH)*

## CROCKETFORD (Ninemile Bar) & Kirkpatrick Irongray

**Map 2, B4**

***Dumfriesshire hamlets,*** *pop. 550* OS 84: NX 8372

Ancient cairns stand on the tumbled hills about 14km west of Dumfries, and earthworks and lake dwellings lie in and around the little Milton Loch. The Gaelic name of Auchengibbert Farm appeared on Pont's map of about 1610. The Roy map of about 1754 showed (Bishop) Forest Hill in sparsely peopled Kirkpatrick Irongray parish, and little else but winding tracks. Some of these were later made up as turnpike roads, on which the toll bar nine miles from Dumfries, where the New Galloway road left the main road to the west – later numbered A75 – became the nucleus of the small village of *'Ninemile Bar'*; but except for the hamlet of Shawhead and Glenkiln reservoir, the area remained otherwise deeply rural. By 1951 the facilities of a small village in Crocketford, including two small hotels, served not only some 250 local people but to some extent also another 450 in the Shawhead and Corsock areas. By 1981 rural depopulation had cut these figures to about 200 and 375 respectively, but there was also a caravan and camping site. By 1996 a second caravan site was open; the inn, post office, and tollhouse survive.

## CROFTAMIE

**Map 5, B4**

***W. Stirlingshire small village,*** *pop. 320* OS 54: NS 4786

The rural valley of the Catter Burn, a tributary of the Endrick Water, was followed by the Forth & Clyde Railway, opened in 1856 between Stirling and Balloch. Drymen station was sited 2 km south of Drymen in Kilmaronock parish, just inside Dunbartonshire, near a bridge on the way to Glasgow. By the 1890s a post office was open at Crosshill, 1 km to the west – later moved to Drymen Station, whose name it took – and a villa stood at Endrick Bank to the east. By 1931 this had been renamed as Dalnair House, and the OS map gave the name Croftamie (pronounced *Croftammy*) for the hamlet which had grown round the station and was provided with a primary school; a mill stood south of the stream. Passenger trains were withdrawn from Croftamie in 1934, but freight services lingered until 1959. By 1951 some 400 people lived in the area, a number which fluctuated with the fortunes of Pirniehall Residential School at Crosshill, open in 1977. By 1981 Croftamie had been placed in Stirling District, its post office bore the village name; a small housing estate and a pub had appeared by 1985. The area's population in 1991 was 320.

## CROMARTY

**Map 9, B3**

***Village, Easter Ross,*** *pop. 725* OS 21: NH 7867

Also see: *Nigg Ferry*

Cromarty, which stands on a small flat peninsula at the entrance to the fine natural harbour of the Cromarty Firth, is said to have had a sixth century church; it was known to the Vikings as *Sikkerssand.* Cromarty was chartered as a Royal Burgh in 1264, and in 1264–66 became the caput of a strange sheriffdom comprising six portions scattered across Ross; Chambers called it *"the minced shire"*. There was a royal castle by about 1300, and Cromarty became an important medieval port. In the 15th century there was a *King's Ferry* to Dunskeath (Nigg Ferry). Cromarty's importance waned; by the 16th century it was not a functional Royal Burgh, and paid no tax in 1535–56.

**Education and Linen**: However by 1580 there was a grammar school; Pont sketched the substantial castle and a few other small buildings on his map of about 1600. In 1621 the port paid under 1.5% of Customs dues, and in 1655 Tucker found only *"a little town"* with one tiny vessel, and minor imports of salt; although the grammar school remained in operation, the former castle site had been taken over for a private mansion. By 1672 Cromarty's decline was far advanced, and in 1685 it escaped from its duties as a Royal Burgh. However, a post office opened very early, being noted in 1715. By 1749 master linen spinners were importing flax directly from the Baltic. The Roy map made at that time showed Cromarty as a small linear town with a castle, served only by the coast road from Balblair *(q.v.)*, crossing the *Ferry of Cromarty* to Nigg and then petering out in the marshes around Ankerville.

**Sir George Ross and Herrings fuel Recovery**: Cromarty was bought by Sir George Ross in 1765. The new laird provided a new court house in 1782, and rebuilt the harbour with a new quay in 1785. In 1799 Heron referred to the *"manufacture of coarse cloth, and a considerable coasting-trade in corn, thread, yarn, nails, fish and skins of various sorts"*. A new pier was built in the early 19th century. The quite large brewery, established in 1790 by G & A Ross, lasted until 1825 or later. Chambers observed in the 1820s that Cromarty was *"one of the neatest, cleanest, prettiest towns of the size in Scotland. It is not a royal burgh, though the chief town in the vagrant, incomprehensible county to which it gives its name. The common people of Cromarty are industrious herring-fishers."* In September 1826 he watched 200 women *"cleaning and salting the fish which the innumerable boats were perpetually bringing ashore; while 29 masted vessels lay in the Firth, waiting to convey the full barrels to various ports. Cromarty has a capital harbour, admitting vessels of 400 tons."* The Nigg ferry was working, and a road connected to Tain.

**The Quarryman Geologist**: Most of Ross's sundry enterprises failed to thrive, including the hemp and cloth factories, a ropeworks and a spade and nail factory. Hugh Miller, born in Cromarty in 1802, was educated in a schoolroom that overlooked the harbour mouth. He became in turn quarryman, stonemason, pioneer geologist of the old Red Sandstone and author; in 1834 he became an accountant at the new Cromarty branch of the Commercial Bank. For a time from 1834, steamers plied between Invergordon and Glasgow via the Caledonian Canal, also calling at Cromarty and Burghead; a lighthouse was built at the end of the main street, illuminated from 1846. But once the railways reached Inverness the steamer service died; worse, the sea encroached at Cromarty and the herring fishery failed.

**The County Vanishes but Fishing Recovers**: In 1889 the crazy county was merged with Ross as *Ross & Cromarty*, its base at more accessible Dingwall. Meantime the quay had been extended in 1880, and fishing revived; it was thriving in 1894, with a thousand fishermen and nearly 300 boats, when Murray regarded both the *Cromarty Arms* and *Davidson's* hotels as *"fair"*. The burgh had 1242 residents in 1901. Thanks to Andrew Carnegie, by 1906 the Nigg ferry had a steamboat and a library; by 1909 a steam passenger ferry also plied to Invergordon; a lifeboat station was opened in 1911.

**Fishing Spoilt, Railway Aborted, Town Shrunken**: The local fishing was ended by the use of the Cromarty Firth as a naval base in 1914–18 and by the minefields that protected it. Meanwhile the building of a branch railway from Conon Bridge, begun by the Highland Railway in 1902, had become bogged down in disputes with landowners, and was less than half complete in 1914. The scheme was abandoned in 1918, there being no prospect of a post-war revival of the fishing. By 1931 only about 800 people were left. By 1953 the National Trust for Scotland had opened Hugh Miller's cottage to the public, and the *Royal Hotel* remained open, but Cromarty had shrunk to a mere village. By 1958 the one-time senior secondary school had been downgraded to junior status, and was later closed; the Nigg ferry was abandoned around 1960, the lifeboat station was closed in 1968 and the burgh population was down to only 480 by 1971; like all burghs, Cromarty lost its town council in 1975.

**Oil-related Dormitory Growth**: In the 1970s a small new housing estate was built to accommodate workers from nearby oil-related industries; by then Cromarty was no more than an attractive residential village, its modest tourist trade including some sea angling. The lighthouse was automated in 1985. The 1991 population of the village was 721. The Invergordon ferry still operated in 1987 when the Nigg ferry was reactivated; only the latter still plied in 1998. The brewery has been converted into a study centre, and the hemp and rope works into a pub and housing. Small boats still frequent the harbour, where four prawn-fishing boats were based in 2000, plus Dolphin Ecosse transport boats. There's an Aberdeen University marine research unit, and Thomson & Campbell riflemakers. The 10-roomed *Royal Hotel* serves the town.

## CROOK OF DEVON, Fossoway & Carnbo

**Map 6, A4**

***Village and hamlets, w. of Kinross,*** *pop. 500* OS 58: NO 0300

Carnbo lies on a fragment of the ancient road linking Stirling with St Andrews across the Loch Leven basin. The road's possible Roman origins are suggested by its straightness and the *Caer* element in the Gaelic name Carnbo, literally meaning *'Camp* (or *Castle) of the Cattle'*. About 4 km west of Carnbo the River Devon leaves the Ochil Hills to flow briefly south-east to the site of the ancient church of Fossoway, whose name probably derives from Gaelic *Fasach feidh*, *'Pasture of Deer'* (Beveridge). The river turns sharply west some 2 km downstream at the Crook of Devon, in a way fascinating to students of geomorphology, tumbling into an incised valley before heading towards Stirling. At Aldie, 2 km south-east of the Crook, was a Pictish broch, which was regrettably demolished in 1782. The remote Aldie Castle, near the site of the broch, dates from about 1464.

**Tullibole and Crook of Devon**: Fossoway parish, first mentioned in a charter of 1210, used to be in Perthshire. If the later Roy map is any guide, the *'right fair way with horse and cart to hire'* that by 1415 joined Falkland and Stirling, crossed over the River Devon at the Crook, passing south of the Kirk of Fossoway. This – which stood 1 km west of Middleton Fossoway – was a ruin by the 1890s. The tower called Tullibole Castle was completed in 1608, 2 km east of the Crook, and a market was established; but in 1614 Tullibole was brought under Fossoway parish and in 1615 Crook of Devon or *'New Fossoway'* was chartered as a burgh of barony. Tullibole church was abandoned in 1729 when a new church was erected at Crook; this *'New Kirk of Fossvall'* was shown on Roy's map made about 1750 when Crook and neighbouring Drum were appreciable hamlets. A bridge was built just below Crook in 1767, and soon two mills were turning there. Later there were also two mills at Carnbo. Heron wrote in 1799 of *"the village of Crook"* but there was evidently little of interest. The road to Stirling was turnpiked in 1810. In 1823 John Luke reopened a former lint mill as Fossoway paper mill; it was to remain in use until 1885. Settlement at Fossoway, Crook and Drum was very scattered in 1827, when Carnbo was a hamlet and Tullibole market was still in operation, paying tolls to Inverkeithing; but it later faded out. A very early village library was established in 1839.

**The Railway comes – and goes**: In 1863 a station was opened at Crook on the Devon Valley Railway, built initially from Kinross to Rumbling Bridge *(q.v.)*, which became the temporary terminus. The line was linked through to Alloa in 1871, becoming part of the North British system. In 1894 the *Crook Inn* provided *"angling quarters"*; there were post and telegraph offices. The villages of Crook and Drum, which provided the facilities of a small village, served an area with around 500 people in the second half of the 20th century, but lost their station in 1964 when the railway was closed completely. By 1984 a fish farm and small restaurant had been developed at Crook. The small independent Lendrick Muir School ran from 1946 to 1962, then reopening for *'maladjusted'* children from all over Scotland; in 1993 it provided facilities for children with dyslexia and allied problems, but was soon converted into a conference and holiday centre by the Scripture Union. Meantime a small private housing estate was built at Crook around 1990. Fossoway primary school is still open, but the post office has closed since 1997.

## CROOKSTON & Cowglen — Map 15, B5

***S-W. suburbs of Glasgow,*** *pop. 30,000* — OS 64: NS 5262

Around 1300 a *'hospital'* was built about 7 km west of Glasgow, south of the Levern Water near its confluence with the White Cart. Maybe it was this which Pont labelled *'Old Krukstoun'* on his manuscript map of Renfrewshire made around 1600, for the nearby Crookston Castle (which he sketched as an imposing structure) was built in the 14th century. He also showed two bridges across the Levern. Roads passed through the area by the time that the Roy map was made around 1754. A canal built in 1806–13 wound through the fields between Glasgow and Paisley until in 1885 the Glasgow & South Western Railway (G&SWR) bought, infilled and replaced it with their *'Canal Line'*. The castle was a ruin by the time the Govan District Asylum (later known as Hawkhead Mental Hospital), designed by Malcolm Stark and H & D Barclay, was built on a hilltop nearby in 1893–1908, its prominent campanile water tower dominating the area. A poorhouse was built 500 m to the south-east in the early 20th century, later being extended and renamed as the Crookston Home.

**Corkerhill Depot and Urbanisation**: In 1896–97 the G&SWR built a large locomotive depot at Corkerhill, 2 km east of the castle; in 1897–1900 they added a village of 132 tenement dwellings with a school, shop, library, institution and store, for a population of 600. In 1916 Corkerhill stabled 74 steam locomotives, and after 1923 the LMS built a huge mechanical coaling tower. The large Mosspark municipal housing estate north of Corkerhill was complete by 1931. The Cowglen (Military) Hospital 2 km south-east of the castle was apparently developed in the 1939–45 war. Housebuilding was resumed on a large scale north of Barrhead Road from 1945. With a 1951 population already approaching 20,000, the huge *'Pollok'* estate had no centre, local workplaces being the various hospitals and the locomotive depot, at that time one of the top three in the West of Scotland. Corkerhill railway village was demolished in 1970–71 to make way for a motorway scheme later abandoned; it was replaced a few years later by new housing. By 1980 the imposing Hawkhead Mental Hospital had been renamed Leverndale Hospital, still specialising in mental illness, to avoid confusion with the Hawkhead Hospital for Infectious Diseases in Paisley, only 1.5 km to the west.

**Savings Bank and District Centre**: An enormous office block for the Post Office Savings Bank was built beside the Cowglen Hospital, providing about 2500 largely female jobs by 1971; it was later renamed the National Savings Bank, and about 2000 people still worked there in 1992. In 1973 the City Council proposed a new *'township centre'* of 22,000 m² with a Tesco superstore; this change of plan meant the demolition of 300 post-war council houses so that its development by the new District Council could start in 1977. By the time the centre was open the population which had peaked at nearly 40,000, had fallen back by 1981 to some 30,000. Meantime by 1980 there was a fire station, and two secondary schools had been built nearby, Bellarmine (RC) and Craigbank; by 1994 a leisure centre had been added.

**After the Mental Hospital the Motorway**: More building was done in the 1980s between Old Crookston and the Crookston Home. In 1992 Corkerhill was still a depot for Sprinter trains. By 1991 a 9-hole golf course was open at the 350-bed Leverndale Hospital, which was largely closed in 1991–93 and still a *'building at risk'* in 1995. The controversial extension of the M77 motorway west from Dumbreck Road was built in 1995–96, greatly damaging the belt of woodland which formerly separated the housing from the so-called Pollok Country Park, to the dismay of local people. Bellarmine Secondary School has about 550 pupils, Crookston Castle 690.

## CROSBOST, Liurbost & Ranais — Map 11, C2

***Townships s. of Stornoway,*** *pop. 800* — OS 14: NB 3924

This 6 km-long chain of closely spaced crofts on the north side of Loch Leurbost in Lochs parish some 10 km south of Stornoway appears to have a minimal history. Despite having a population of about 1200 in 1951, only the most basic facilities were available, including junior secondary classes at Liurbost School, which soon ceased. By 1981 although the population had fallen below 900 a garage and doctor were present, and Crosbost or *'Crossbost'* was the base of Lochs Motor Transport. There were still two primary schools in 1996, but little or nothing for the tourist.

## CROSSFORD

**Map 16, B5**

***Village, upper Clyde valley,*** *pop. 600* OS 72: NS 8246

Crossford lies in the deep valley of the River Clyde about 6km below Lanark, just above the confluence of the incised River Nethan. About 3km to the south is a prehistoric hill fort. A powerful local family by 1323 were the Lockharts of Lee Castle 3km to the east, who sired a famous series of lawyers; later their castle or mansion became known as The Lee. Spectacular Craignethan Castle, 1km west of Crossford, was built about 1530 for Sir James Hamilton of Finnart on a promontory above the River Nethan. This very strong encircled anti-artillery tower included a unique vaulted gun-chamber. Two other 16th century castles were built nearby: Hallbar tower of about 1581, near an ancient mill just east of the river, and the defended courtyard of Waygateshaw House a further 1.5km to the north. Craignethan appeared as a prominent emparked tower on Pont's map of 1596.

**Bridge, Mansion and Glasshouses**: The Roy map of about 1754 showed the Nethan bridged at Nethanfoot; but despite Crossford's name a ferry plied there from at least 1720 until about 1785, and again for a time from 1817 until a bridge was built. In the early 19th century a fine South Lodge was built for The Lee. Some way up-river, on a fine site near the Clyde falls, stood Stonebyres castle; much altered from 1840 into a huge baronial pile, it was demolished in 1934. By 1951 Crossford was known for its glasshouses and had almost 1000 people, though its facilities, then still including a secondary class in the village school, also served over 500 more in the sprawling hamlets of Hazelbank and Stonebyres. In 1963 it had both a hotel and an inn, but the population was falling and by 1976 the school had become primary only. By 1981 several motor traders had opened up; the school was still open in 1988. In 1991 Crossford had 591 residents. The long-derelict South Lodge at The Lee was restored as a house in the mid 1990s. Modern vehicular access to the preserved Craignethan Castle is by way of the delightfully named hilltop hamlet of Tillietudlem *(Tilly = knoll)*, also traditionally rich in glasshouses; some survive, as has the intact Hallbar Tower, recently restored for holiday letting. Detached houses are now being built.

## CROSSGATES & Fordell

**Map 6, B4**

***W. Fife village & hamlet,*** *pop. 3400* OS 65: NT1488

Central to the extensive Pictish province of Fothrif and conceivably its ancient capital was the superb defensible site on which the 12th century castle of Fordell now stands, perched above a steep-sided glen incised in a plateau 3km north of the Firth of Forth. Fordell Castle was rebuilt from 1511 onwards by the Hendersons; it was being extended in 1568 when fire damaged both old and new sections. Pont's sketch-maps of about 1600 named Crossgates, 3km north of the castle, *'Mosse Morum'*, and a settlement at *'Fordel Muir'*; however, Crawford's map of Fife made in 1645 named the area *'Forthridge Muirs'*.

**The Mining Industry**: Coal pits were first opened north of the castle in 1596; the name of the hamlet of Coaledge may well denote where the outcrop was first exploited. A day level cut in 1750 led from there to the castle burn to drain the mines; although neglected, it still drains the area. The early coal output mainly went to Inverkeithing in horseback panniers. The Old North Road from Inverkeithing to Perth was built through the area in 1725, and Roy's map (made about 1750) showed a windmill and a *whim* south of Crossgates, accompanied by scattered settlement beside the road. Another miners' village labelled *'Coaltown'* had sprung up south of *'Fordlin'*. The area developed further with the construction of a coal-carrying wagonway – the *'Fordell Railway'* – to St Davids *(q.v.)* on the coast around 1760. In 1756 work was begun to make up the ancient winding pathway between Dunfermline, Auchtertool and Kirkcaldy as a road. Fordell House was built south of the old castle about 1760, and Ansonhill House was built in the late 18th century by an admiral, who named it after his ship.

**Fairs, Quarry and Limeworks**: By the 1790s no fewer than five annual fairs were held at Crossgates, and a post office was opened in 1802. An 1820s map showed six small coal pits, to each of which the wagonway threw off a siding; they continued in operation until at least 1836. A group of colliers' houses stood 2 km north of the ruined castle, and west of them were a quarry and limeworks. By 1838 the Fordell wagonway's wooden rails had been replaced by iron. The Wellington – later William – pit at Crossgates was sunk about 1843, and by 1844 there was another colliery and fireclay works nearby, at Hill of Beath. The western branch of the Edinburgh & Northern Railway (E&NR) from Thornton to Dunfermline was opened in 1849, with a station at Crossgates. The great hall of the castle was restored around 1880 but it was empty in 1888 and again became derelict. Beveridge noted in 1888 that the area was *"dotted with numerous collieries; in the winter season the climate is most inclement, the roads becoming frequently quite impassable from snow, which lies long"* – and this at a modest 120m above the sea.

**Multiple Pits, Manhole Covers and Trams**: The Alice pit near Cuttlehill was sunk from 1880, later connected to the Fordell wagonway. In the 1890s at least six other small Fordell collieries with names such as Lady Anne and George were working in the area. In 1887 the Hill of Beath estate was bought for enlargement by the Fife Coal Company, who built the first *'Gothenburg'* co-operative pub in 1896; the population, including Hill of Beath, had grown to over 3000 by 1901, a year when seven men in one of the Beath mines died from gas poisoning. Fordell sandstone quarry was open by 1878, and employed 15 people in 1907. Wilson Brothers' foundry made cast-iron manhole covers, and a secondary school was provided at Crossgates. From 1909 the Dunfermline Tramways Company linked Dunfermline and Cowdenbeath via Crossgates, but the local facilities remained those of a small village until the system closed in 1937. The Alice pit headgear was reconstructed in 1926, and from 1946 the Henderson mine linked this with the old William pit and the main line railway, enabling the Fordell wagonway to be closed in 1946. The William pit worked until 1950. Crossgates station was closed in 1949; the secondary classes ceased some years later. In 1963 the removal of the bing at Hill of Beath was begun. Fordell House was demolished in 1963, but in the 1960s the castle was restored by the flamboyant Sir Nicholas Fairbairn, long-serving Tory MP for Perth & Kinross.

**Motorway Stimulates Development**: The M90 motorway was opened about 1970, with a junction 1.5km west of Crossgates. In 1977 the Regional Headquarters of the NCB's Opencast Executive was at Crossgates, where despite the prevailing mine closures a rescue centre was opened by their successors British Coal in 1987. This remained the base for a privatised rescue team in 1992, when only the Longannet and Monktonhall collieries were still open, and by 1999 it also specialised in training rescue from confined spaces. The manufacturing joiners John Reid & Sons, at work in Crossgates by 1977, were substantial in 1993. Some 3400 people lived in the area in 1981. By 1977 the Boy Scouts had an activity centre at Fordell Firs, which about 1985 became the organisation's Scottish headquarters. House building resumed in the 1980s north-west of Crossgates, despite various opencast workings (including the site of the one-time George pit); each is being rapidly restored. In 1998 the junction of the M90 and A92 was radically reconstructed and a service area added. Crossgates retains its primary school, medical practice, post office and pubs.

## CROSSHILL

**Map 1, C3**

***Small Ayrshire village,*** *pop. 500* — OS 70 or 76: NS 3206

The burn that drains Maybole joins the Water of Girvan about 4km south of the little town; it powered Bairds Mill, shown on Pont's map of Carrick made around 1600; it was later known as Dalcur Mill. The area was densely settled, but the nearest bridge was some way downstream. By the time that Roy mapped the area (about 1754) the river had been bridged on the Maybole to Newton Stewart road; from the hamlet of Crosshill on the south bank another road led down-river to Dailly. Crosshill was enlarged and rebuilt from about 1808 for handloom weaving. By the 1890s it had a church, inn, smithy and post and telegraph office. In 1951 the population of over 900 had only basic facilities. In 1986 its original humble but solidly built cottages looked to be still in good order; nearby was a caravan and camping site. The population had declined to 526 by 1991; Crosshill with its pub and post office now stands astride a defined cycle route following minor roads.

## CROSSHOUSE & Knockentiber

**Map 1, C1**

***Ayrshire village,*** *pop. 2370* — OS 70: NS 3938

Pont's late $16^{th}$ century map of Cunninghame showed *'Corshouse'* beside a bridge over the Carmel Water, 3km west of Kilmarnock. In the early $17^{th}$ century a tower house known as Busbie Castle was built at nearby Knockentiber. By about 1754, as the Roy map showed, a road between Irvine and Kilmarnock passed the hamlet of Crosshouse, which stood where several lanes met south of the castle.

**Railways, Collieries and Brickworks**: When the Kilmarnock branch of the Glasgow Paisley Kilmarnock & Ayr Railway was opened in 1843, a station sited north of Knockentiber was originally called Busby. When five years later it became the junction for a railway to Irvine, opened in 1848, this was called the *'Busby Branch'*. Shortly becoming part of the Glasgow & South Western Railway, the branch was closed for a while from 1850, but was later reopened and connected to numerous collieries. Crosshouse station was opened in 1872 on the site of the junction. By the 1890s a colliery had been sunk between there and Knockentiber, with others at Busbiehill to the west; yet another colliery was open at Bogside, 1km farther south. Settlement was rather scattered, but at Crosshouse there was an inn and post and telegraph office. Not long afterwards a rail-connected factory was built near the station, to the west of which was established the combined Southook Colliery and Brickworks, which exploited both a 5m seam of fireclay suitable for basin making and a 2m seam containing both coal and fireclay, used to make faience *(see Hutton, 1996)*. On the road to Kilmarnock stood another large brickworks, at Bonnyton, where the mines rescue station for Ayrshire was opened in 1912.

**Tractors come but Trains and Brickworks go**: By 1951 some 2900 people lived in the Crosshouse area, enjoying the facilities of a small village, plus secondary school classes. Other industries developed, including joinery and knitwear, but more especially the large Moorfield works of tractor manufacturers Massey-Ferguson (M-F), which had been established south-east of the village by 1954. But secondary schooling was soon moved elsewhere, and all railway links were closed between 1964 and 1974. The Southook brickworks stopped work in 1971.

**The Massey Crash and Crosshouse Hospital**: The whole district reeled when M-F went into receivership in 1977 with the loss of nearly 2000 jobs, and in 1980 a further 680 jobs were axed from the 22,300$m^2$ works. However, by then Dick Bearings of East Kilbride had a factory at Crosshouse, the motor trade had moved in and the local population had remained remarkably steady. By 1982 the 700-bed Crosshouse General Hospital complex had been completed just east of the village, to serve the whole of Cunninghame. By 1987 a dual carriageway bypass had removed the A71 traffic and the former tractor plant had become an industrial estate, two-thirds let by 1989 by the Kilmarnock Venture Enterprise Trust.

**From Components to Crop Harvesters**: From the M-F collapse had grown the new and vigorous firm of Moorfield Manufacturing, at first making components for earth-moving machinery. In 1990 their 200 workers also made plate safes for autotellers; by 1991 entire whole-crop harvesters were being made. Crosshouse with 2370 residents then looked a vigorous village in terms of facilities, including a small modern hotel. By 1993 the continuing expansion had brought the village medical practice up from three to five doctors in 15 years, but its self-dispensing role was threatened by the opening of a chemist's shop. By 1998 a motel was open adjacent to the extended bypass.

## CROSSMICHAEL & Glenlochar

**Map 2, A5**

***Galloway village & location,*** *pop. 500* — OS 83 or 84: NX 7366

A Roman fort was established beside the River Dee in what later became the Stewartry, 4km north-west of modern Castle Douglas; nearby was a medieval motte, and Townhead Tower, also known as the *Fortalice of Greenlaw*. Pont's map of about 1610 as engraved by Blaeu marked the kirks of Balmaghie and Crossmichael on opposite banks of the river, 2 km upstream. The Roy map of about 1754 showed tracks from the east converging on Crossmichael Kirk, while from Balmaghie the *'Kirk Road'* ran west to Lauriston. A later turnpike road built up the valley intersected the earlier routes at Crossmichael, but the only permanent river bridge was 2 km to the south near the Roman fort, about where Glenlochar primary school was to be built. The Portpatrick Railway opened in 1861 with a station at Crossmichael, where R McGhie later made screw-cutting and drilling machines.

**Hydro Power and Tourism**: The Glenlochar hydro-electric barrage of the Galloway water-power scheme was built at Townhead in the 1930s. A sawmill was at work in 1953 when some 600 people lived in the area, with the facilities of a small village plus the 17-room country house *Culgruff House Hotel*. The entire railway in Stewartry was closed by Beeching in 1965, a hundred people left the area in twenty years, and by 1976 even the post office had closed. However in 1986 there were at least four shops, a garage, the hotel, several B&Bs and a pony trekking stables. By 1996 there was once more a post office, replacing one at Townhead of Greenlaw, and new housing had obliterated the course of the one-time railway.

## CROY

**Map 16, A3**

***Village s. of Kilsyth,*** *pop. 1150* OS 64: NS 7276

The steep and rather isolated Bar Hill, at 155 m the highest of several tumbled wooded eminences south of the headwaters of the River Kelvin, was topped by what was for Caledonia an unusually important Roman fort, dating from the first century Flavian period. This boasted a stone-built *principia* with many columns, a stone-lined well, and left evidence of leather trades; it was later incorporated into the mid second century Antonine Wall, from which the Romans soon withdrew.

**Canals and Railways**: The Forth & Clyde Canal was dug beside the River Kelvin in the late 1760s but the area stayed rural. The Edinburgh & Glasgow Railway, opened in 1842, added Croy station in 1846; a two-horse coach linked it with Kilsyth, some 2.5 km to the north. There was also an inn by 1899, when a lengthy mineral railway left the main line a little to the west, linking coal pits 1.5 km west of the station with Twechar and Kilsyth. Coke ovens were built between the pits, which like many in the west of Scotland employed predominantly Catholic miners of Irish ancestry. East of the station another siding curved north to more coal pits at Nether Croy; by 1905 Smithstone just to the east of Croy was a mining settlement. The stone from a whinstone quarry at Croy was loaded on to barges near the miners' rows at Auchinstarry. The Nether Croy pits had closed by 1924.

**No jobs in a Council-owned Village**: By 1951 nearly 2000 people lived in council housing between the station and Auchinstarry, whose mean housing was demolished; they were served by a Catholic primary school. The larger Gartshore 9/11 Colliery (probably the last in the area) was still active in 1954 but disused by 1971 when the population was 1682; by 1977 Alex Russell Aggregates was exploiting its bing. Another quarry was opened north of Croy in the 1970s. The station stayed open, and in 1991 some 14% of the local workers went to work by train, but a sad 25% of the men were out of work. Of the 1150 people who still lived in Croy, 83% stayed in publicly owned housing. The quarry was disused by 1996; there had been little other external change. However, in 1998 Croy station was rebuilt and became park-and-ride, with a half-hourly service, primarily for Cumbernauld commuters to Glasgow and Edinburgh.

## CRUDEN BAY & Port Erroll

**Map 10, C2**

***Aberdeenshire coastal village,*** *pop. 1700* OS 30: NK 0936

Cruden's name was said by Pratt to derive from the Gaelic *Croch Dain, 'slaughter of Danes'*, being the site of their last battle with the Scots in the early 11th century. Pont's map of around 1600 showed Cruden, 2 km up the Water of Cruden from the east coast of Buchan, as a kirk beside a bridge which led to the Over Mill; downstream of the kirk was the Nether mill, sited in a small ravine. By 1606 a parish school was open. About then the eighth Earl of Erroll built the second magnificent castle called Slains on a cliff top just north of Cruden, named by Pont as Pitskurr. This was about 10 km north of the original castle *(see Collieston)* and near the massive collapsed coastal cave known as the Bullers of Buchan. The second castle was enlarged in 1664 by the 11th Earl. The *'Bishop's Bridge'* was built or rebuilt in 1697 by Bishop Drummond of Brechin, nearer the river mouth, for the Roy map made around 1750 showed that the track south hugged the coast, passing the fishing station of Whinnyfold 3 km to the south.

**Port Erroll or The Ward**: About then the Earl promoted a better fishing base, siting Port Erroll harbour more wisely than the castle, in the inlet of Cruden Bay. Port Erroll had *"clay and slated"* houses in 1769 when visited by Pennant. Although the sprawling castle was admired by Dr Johnson in 1773 it became notorious because nothing would grow on such an exposed site. The very early Port Erroll Golfing Society was founded in 1791, and played on natural links for a century. The castle was reconstructed for the last time in 1836–38 by the 15th Earl. Whinnyfold (locals called it *'Finnyfa')* was still a *"fishing village"* to Pratt in 1858, when to him Port Erroll was *'The Ward'*; by then the *'New Bridge'* had been built near the harbour. However, the coastal track became just a byway, and the castle was eventually abandoned to become a gaunt ruin, though a long-lasting brick and tile works was established just inland. A lifeboat station was opened at Port Erroll in 1877 when the fishing was at its busiest, but the 1891 population was only 490, and in 1894 Murray merely described it as *"a small fishing village"*.

**The Railway Hotel Fiasco**: In 1897 the Great North of Scotland Railway opened a branch line from Ellon to Port Errol and the Boddam granite quarries; blithely ignoring the Earls' castle experience, the company also built the luxurious 55-room *Cruden Bay Hotel* on an almost equally exposed site overlooking the sands of Port Erroll. This was opened in 1899 complete with a golf course and other amenities, plus a 108 cm gauge tramway to the station, where for a time Wordie & Co had a small rail to road cartage depot. The lifeboat station was closed in 1921. Both hotel and railway were a financial disaster once the novelty had worn off, so the railway and tramway were closed to passengers in 1932. In 1939 the *Cruden Bay Hotel* became an army hospital until 1945; unsaleable, it was gradually demolished in 1947–52, leaving only the golf clubhouse near the castle ruins *(see Vallance and Price for two accounts of this story)*. The freight railway was abandoned in 1948.

**Dormitory Development, and Re-Railing**: Cruden Bay retained two unpretentious hotels, but its resident population slumped from over 900 in 1951 to under 700 in 1971. With the coming of oil-related development at Peterhead, the typical village facilities, golfing and sands at Cruden Bay attracted two housing estates, and by 1981 the population was nearly 1700, a figure just exceeded by 1991, when their dormitory character was evident. It also developed further as a resort, with two golf courses, a miniature railway and a caravan and camping site. The brickworks remained in operation in 1983, though closed by 1995, but Port Erroll still pursues its salmon and lobster fishing, while the *Red House Hotel* keeps going.

## CULLEN

**Map 10, B1**

***Large village, Moray coast,*** *pop. 1420* OS 29: NJ 5167

Cullen, whose name means *'holly'*, lies some 17km west of Banff at the mouth of the steep-sided Burn of Deskford; the original village was either at *Invercullen*, or 1km inland. Cullen, which combined fishing and farming, was chartered as a Royal Burgh in 1189, and had a kirk by 1236, but only the motte remains of its early royal castle, described as a *'Manor'* in 1295; this served the royal hunting preserve of Invercullen to the south. The 14th century keep of Findlater Castle was built by the Ogilvies on the cliffs 3km to the east. In the same century Cullen church was rebuilt; it was extended in 1536 and a late college was founded within it in 1543. Though its contribution was rising, in 1535–56 Cullen paid under 1.5% of Scotland's burgh taxes.

**The Findlater Period: Textile Development**: About then Cullen Castle was replaced by Cullen House, an L-plan tower enlarged in 1600 into a mansion for the Ogilvy Earl of Findlater; Findlater Castle then fell into ruin. In 1639 Cullen ranked a mere 38th among Scottish burghs in tax yield, or about 1% of Edinburgh's trade. Despite what Chambers called the *"indiscriminate pillage"* inflicted by Montrose in 1645, Gordon's map then emphasised Cullen. A later Earl of Findlater had Cullen House enlarged in 1711; when President of the Board of Trustees in 1748, the then Earl introduced the linen industry to Cullen. The local speciality was thread-making, and Cullen had become a yarn sorting centre by 1750, when a post office was open. The Roy map of about 1750 showed a long single street running south from the castle site beside the burn and passing immediately east of Cullen House, whose large policies and plantations extended to the west. The area's only road paralleled the coast, passing Rannas (5km west) and Cullen House en route to Portsoy. The burn was already bridged in three places; 2 km upstream was the Mill of Towie and on the shore a dozen buildings were sketched, labelled *'Seatown'*.

**Mechanisation of Textiles**: A new linen bleachfield was built by Lord Deskford in 1752, and was still working in the 1830s. The new mill and village of Lintmill, 2 km to the south, was established between 1760 and 1790 as part of the textile enterprise. Water-powered engines for rubbing and beetling cloth were installed in 1762; in 1769 Pennant found over 100 linen looms, hand operated of course, though the town was *"mean"*. However, there was a *"good inn"* by 1771. Of his visit with Johnson two years later Boswell wrote oddly of Cullen's *"snug, warm, comfortable appearance, though but a very small town and the houses mostly of a poor appearance"*. Framework knitting had begun by 1778 and by 1791 only 65 looms were busy, some making damask. Heron gave Cullen's population as about 1500 in 1799.

**The Rape of the Herring builds New Cullen**: Fish-curing started in 1815, and seven Cullen boats were fishing when harbour works were begun for the Commissioners in 1817. A pier was nearing completion in 1819 when inspected by its designer Thomas Telford with Robert Southey, who noted that 300 barrels of herrings had been caught locally overnight! The poor state of the buildings in the upper town near Cullen House led the Earl of Seafield in 1822–30 to relocate the people into new houses laid out by George MacWilliam beside the Sea-town; the *Seafield Arms Hotel* was built as a central feature. In 1827 Chambers described the *"three various and distinct towns, – the New Town, a tolerably well built place near the sea, with a harbour, – the Auld Town and the Fish Town, a low village, exclusively inhabited by fishermen. Cullen House, the seat of the Earl of Seafield is one of the most princely mansions in the north of Scotland."*

**Whisky for a while, but Fabrics fade**: At Tochieneal beside Lintmill there was once a brickworks, near which in 1822 Alex Wilson built a distillery; but after half a century in production, the family firm moved the equipment in 1871 to a new site at Inchgower by Buckie. Meantime Cullen harbour was enlarged in 1834, a gas works was set up in 1841, and Cullen House was greatly altered by David Bryce in 1858–59. But the local linen trade was failing, and by 1864 both it and the Earldom of Findlater were extinct.

**Clifftop Golf and the Railway Viaducts**: Cullen's interesting coastal 18-hole golf course was established in 1879. In 1884 a branch of the Great North of Scotland Railway was extended from Portsoy to a station at Tochieneal. To avoid the policies of the Earl of Seafield, a director of the rival Highland Railway, a costly series of viaducts was built in 1884–86, bridging over the lower town; the largest had 8 arches. In 1886 Cullen's train service was extended to Buckie and Elgin; for a time Wordie & Co operated a rail to road cartage depot. Fishing boats based in Cullen increased from nine in 1880 to 24 in 1884, when the harbours of Findochty and Portknockie were abandoned. In 1894 the *Seafield Arms Hotel* was *"good"* to Murray.

**Decline and Stabilisation**: In 1929 Cullen voted to become *'dry'* – leading to the cliff-top *Bay Hotel* being built outwith the burgh boundary! In 1951 over 1700 local people enjoyed the facilities of a large village; the population fluctuated over the next 40 years but tended to decline. Tochieneal station was closed in 1964 and the railway was closed completely in 1968; New View Court was built over the station site. Cullen had seven hotels in the 1960s and 70s, but only typical village facilities and little fishing. The burgh offices were in Banff, a remarkable 22 km away, until Cullen was placed in Moray District in the 1975 reorganisation. Cullen House was sold in 1975; about 1990 it was restored and converted into 13 private flats; the grounds are partly accessible at times. Meantime by 1981 only five hotels remained open, plus a caravan site. The population in 1991 was 1420.

**Pigs and Petanque**: The harbour seems solely used by small pleasure boats; a wide range of shops included an antiques specialist utilising a former church. Two banks, a post office, filling station, fire station, police office and primary school are also available. The viaduct still bestrides the main street, and parts of the route have become a walkway. Almost a town, being much too specialised to be a village, Cullen is unable to forget the country, due to the proximity of a vast pig farm! Hotels include the *Cullen Bay Hotel*, the fine large *Seafield Arms*, the small *Bayview* and *Royal Oak* and the villa-type *Elms Guest House*, plus a range of eating houses, pubs and B&Bs. *Petanque* can be played at the *Three Kings*.

## CULLIVOE (Yell) — Map 14, C1

***Shetland island community**, pop. 400* — OS 1: HP 5402

This sheltered inlet of Bluemull Sound, between the islands of Yell and Unst, enjoys probably the best farming soil in Shetland's north isles; the area was already well settled when mapped by Timothy Pont about 1592. In the 19th century Cullivoe became a herring curing station. The simple open craft known as *'sixerns'* – from having six of a crew – had little freeboard, and in a great July storm in 1881, 57 fishermen were lost at sea, mainly from the long-established hamlet of Gloup on a sheltered voe (inlet) some 5km to the west. In 1953 a passenger ferry from Cullivoe was the main access to the island of Unst; later this plied from Gutcher pier, 3km to the south, where the later roll-on ferry terminated. By 1973 a local quarry and gravel pit were both disused. The population of some 200 enjoyed their improving facilities, which by 1981 served some 400 people including Gutcher and Sellafirth. Shellfish and whitefish boats were still based at Cullivoe in 1985–87; by the latter year this small but active place boasted a new village hall, some 20 modern houses, a police station, varied transport facilities and a well-known Scottish dance band.

## CULLODEN, Smithton, Allanfearn & Inshes — Map 9, B4

***Villages e. of Inverness**, pop. 8300* — OS 27: NH 7246

The valley of the River Nairn with its ancient stone remains is separated from the Moray Firth by a long ridge of moors, named on Blaeu's map of 1654 as the *'Mosse of mony lyes'*; northwards are fine views across to the Black Isle and Ben Wyvis as the ground falls away to the coastal plain. In 1745 Culloden House about 6km east of Inverness was the seat of Duncan Forbes, the anti-Jacobite Lord President of the Court of Session. Yet the pretender Charles Stuart stayed there in 1746 before the decisive battle between the Jacobites and Hanoverians on Culloden Muir some 2 km south-east of the house. Roy's map made about 1750 showed a road from Inverness to Nairn, forking at *'Miltown'* to Ardersier; a track crossed the moor to end at Cantry Brig west of Cawdor. Culloden House was rebuilt in 1788 *"in a very elegant style"* (Chambers); but the battlefield was *"a vast tract of table land, covered with heath, over which are scattered a few wretched cottages"*.

**Later hamlets and the Railways**: Early in the 19th century a new road laid out by Telford was built south-eastwards from Inverness to Aviemore, crossing the River Nairn at Craigie Bridge. The hamlet of Balloch, about 1km east of Culloden House, was served from 1855 by the Inverness & Nairn Railway (I&NR). The Cullernie Brickworks was open by 1894 a kilometre to the north. The I&NR's Culloden station was renamed Allanfearn in 1898, when their successor the Highland Railway opened a new station named *'Culloden Moor'* east of the battlefield on its new line to Aviemore. This crossed the 550m-long Culloden Muir Viaduct of 29 arches, the longest overland structure in northern Scotland, built to take a double line, using stone brought from the nearby Leanach quarry by a contractor's railway. A smithy gave rise to a hamlet then named Smithtown.

**Three Nuclei of Development**: In the 1930s the *Drumossie Hotel*, a 40-room roadhouse, was built beside Telford's road (then the A9 trunk road) at Inshes some 2 km south of Smithtown, and by 1951 the homes of some 650 people were scattered around the area. However, both stations were closed to passengers by Beeching in 1965, although the rail-served Highland Bitumens depot remained at Culloden Moor until about 1988, then becoming an oil tank farm. About 1970 the *Drumossie Hotel* was enlarged to over 100 rooms. As the expansion of Inverness speeded up in the 1970s, three housing estates were built, each served by a new primary school, comprising mainly private detached houses at suburban Balloch and Cradlehall. Between these places, contrasting Smithton was largely developed with public authority terraced housing; by 1978 there was also a licensed restaurant and caravan site at Culloden.

**A Major Dormitory for Inverness**: By 1981 a new settlement named Newlands had been built beside the former station, a new dual carriageway had replaced the A9 north of Bogbain and the winding former A96 had given way to a new road inland of the Aberdeen railway. By 1981 the area held nearly 1600 people, a third hotel, a post office and nascent village facilities. By 1990 a large NORCO store had been built at Inshes and by 1992 the Scottish School of Forestry at Balloch was associated with Inverness College. With many new housing developments by 1991, the combined population of these four dormitories was 8068. By 1995 the new Culloden Academy had been built. The Culloden Local Plan of 1994 reserved further housing land at Inshes, Milton of Leys *(q.v.)* and Culloden; as the new city of Inverness explodes with additional activities, further swathes of new detached houses have grown in the area. By 1995 the long-roofless mansion had been lately restored, now being the 23-room *Culloden House Hotel*; the modern *Smithton Hotel* and guest houses are also available.

## CULROSS — Map 16, C2

***Small W. Fife coastal village**, pop. 450* — OS 65: NS 9886

Culross (pronounced *Coorus*), meaning *the Nook in the Point*, stands on the hilly north shore of the upper Firth of Forth. It may have formed part of the Pictish province of Fothrif, and was later in an exclave of Perthshire. It is believed that a Christian community existed as early as the fifth century, and that it educated Glasgow's founding father Saint Mungo or Kentigern. In the eighth century Saint Serf of Dysart also founded a church at Culross, to the west of which was Dunimarle, an ancient fortification. A great Cistercian monastery was founded in 1217 by Malcolm, Earl of Fife, and became famous for the beauty of its manuscripts. For a time around 1310 it was Robert Bruce's refuge from the English. The Order vowed isolation from the world, but the monks sold sorted wool around 1400 and eventually Culross was chartered to the abbot as a burgh of barony in 1490. Dunimarle was rebuilt in the 16th century into a castle; a coal mine sunk about then was abandoned for a time. The early parish church to the west was ruinous by 1560, when the abbey had only three appropriated churches; but its Commendator then sat in Parliament.

**George Bruce, Salt and the Unique Culross Coal Mine**: After the Reformation the Abbey passed to Colville of Cleish in 1569. Mining must have been resumed, for in 1574 there were seven salt pans, but then Sir George Bruce, third son of Edward Bruce of Blairhall, took over as a very enterprising proprietor. He sank the *'Castleland'* pit – the Castle Hill pit was west of the town, a little inland – and from about 1575

*Culross Town House – built in 1626 and the steeple added in 1783. The tiny Town Council's final act in 1975 was to give the building to the NTS. It's now a visitor centre.* *(RS)*

developed a unique undersea coal mine, the Moat pit, which ingeniously worked the poor but shallow Upper Hirst coal by candlelight. It was drained by the *'Egyptian Wheel'*, a chain of 36 buckets powered by three horses. The mine was fully described by Taylor *(see Hume Brown)*, who noted the tiny coal island a little west of the town, created by Bruce about 1590 as a *"circular frame of stone"* (it was only 15 metres across), built at low tide on *"sand mixed with rocks"*. There a pit 12 metres deep and 5 m in diameter was dug to form a second shaft, with a tunnel link to the shore. There was already a grammar school by 1584.

**The Royal Burgh**: George Bruce amassed a great landward estate, becoming known as Lord Bruce of Carnock. He persuaded James VI to grant Culross a Royal Burgh charter in 1588, so authorising coal export, for the islet had a pier. At one time there were 44 salt pans using the local coal, and in the 1590s Culross dominated Scotland's salt exports and was second to Leith in coal; in 1618 Bruce's men made up to 100 tons of salt a week. Between 1597 and 1611 Bruce used the proceeds to build himself a fine town house, known as *'The Palace'* to local people, who themselves built many stone houses. Meantime Edward Lord Bruce, who had been Commendator of Kinloss Abbey, was using Culross Abbey's stone to build his great Abbey House beside the church, begun in 1608; the short-lasting third storey was added in 1670. In 1621 Culross paid high sums in Customs dues, mainly on coal and salt, but the undersea mine was flooded forever in a storm in 1625; George Bruce died soon after, and stone from the wharf was removed to build the pier of Leith.

**Revival after the Flood**: Nonetheless, the town council afforded a Town House, built in 1626; its tower was added in 1783. In 1639 Culross ranked only 30th among Scottish burghs in tax yield, but remained a major salt export port, with some *"fine vessels"* in the 1640s. In 1655 it was known as a brewing and tanning centre. So important was its coal export trade that the *Culross Chalder* was standardised in 1663 as the basis for Scottish coal measurement. Until the 1720s the hammermen of Culross also enjoyed a monopoly in the manufacture of iron cooking girdles, *"the round iron plates on which the people of Scotland bake their coarse barley and oat-bread"* (Chambers). Defoe described Culross in the 1720s as *"A neat and agreeable trading town. Here is a pretty market, a plentiful country behind it and the navigable Firth before it; the coal and the linen manufacture, and plenty of corn."* Around that time George Law was a Culross maltster.

**The Decline of Culross**: Roy's map (surveyed about 1750) showed Culross in very much its 20th century form, with a coastal road from Torryburn connecting westwards to the Kirk of Tulliallan; but no harbour was shown nor any indication of mining, though two piers were in existence by the late 18th century. In 1758 the Bruce family inherited the Earldom of Dundonald. A post office was opened in 1768. The last significant new enterprise at Culross was a works established by Lord Dundonald in 1781 to distil tar from coal, but the mine rapidly became exhausted. Although by 1797 Culross was a post town and still had two annual fairs, it was actually in terminal decline – Heron wrote that *"the Royal Burgh of Culross contains upwards of 1000 inhabitants, but has little or no trade"*. The Georgian mansion Blair Castle was built above the Kincardine road 1.5 km west of Culross.

**Fossils and Quarrying**: Much fine white freestone obtained from the Blair quarries west of the town was used in building the New Town of Edinburgh and London's Drury Lane Theatre; but they were disused by 1888. In 1888 Beveridge described Culross as *"a sort of fossilised town"*, still then part of Perthshire. A visitor found its hotel the *Dundonald Arms* *"snug and comfortable, small but admirably conducted"*; it is still open today.

**Fife finds Culross a Station and a Home**: Water was newly supplied to the village from Glen Sherup in the Ochil Hills, Dunfermline's source; when the anomalous *'Perthshire on Forth'* was extinguished in 1889, this Fife connection may have helped the government to decide to add the area to Fife rather than to adjacent Clackmannanshire. Remarkably, Culross was still described as a *"town"* in 1894. The opening of a very late coastal railway and station by the North British company in 1906 did nothing to reawaken Culross, which shrank to a small and dilapidated village; its passenger trains were withdrawn as early as 1930. Blair Castle, bought by the Fife Coal Company under Charles Carlow for its estate's mineral rights, became in 1927 the Carlow Home for convalescent miners, taking 40 men, extended to 70 in the 1950s.

**Conservation Triumphs – and Hope for Rail**: From 1945 successful conservation work was carried out in Culross by the National Trust for Scotland (NTS), making its steep streets, stone cottages and Bruce's *'Palace'* into a real attraction to tourists. The *Red Lion Inn* became a second small hotel, and the old Town House (conveyed to the NTS as the town council's last act in 1975) soon became an interesting visitor centre. Bruce's islet could still be seen in 1991, and beyond it across the Forth the distant flares of Grangemouth show industrial enterprise in a modern form. For some years the small Inchkeith School has provided independent primary education. In 2000 the reopening to freight of the whole line linking Stirling with Dunfermline was planned by Railtrack and EWS, with government help.

## CULTS, Bieldside, Murtle & Pitfodels **Map 10, C3**

***Suburbs s-w. of Aberdeen,*** *pop. 5200* OS 38: NJ 8903

Pont's rough map of about 1600 named both Cults and the Mill of Pitfodels, on the north bank of the River Dee about 5 km west of Aberdeen. The Roy map made about 1750 showed

*Murtle Mill, Cults, a large water-powered mill of the mid 19th century. It was converted into a hotel around 1970.* *(JRH)*

Cults as a house in policies on the north Deeside road, and accompanied by *'Milltown'*. In 1837 George Morison, minister of Banchory Devenick, had a suspension footbridge erected across the Dee at Cults *(see Hay & Stell 1986)*. The Deeside Railway opened from Aberdeen to Banchory in 1853 with stations at Cults and Murtle. Quiet at first, it was extended by stages to Ballater; by 1884 its new owners were the Great North of Scotland Railway. At that time a ferry to Blairs still plied at Deebank some 1.5km west of Cults, which by then had many villas on its south-facing slopes. A post and telegraph office was open, and Bieldside too had a post office by 1899.

**Frequent Trains, Trams, Golf and Electricity**: In 1894 the GNSR opened closely-spaced stations at Pitfodels and West Cults, and in 1897 added Bieldside station, making 5 stops in all within under 4km, for a new intensive suburban train service; 21 trains a day ran in the 1910s. Private villa building was stimulated by the Deeside Golf Club, founded in 1903, which laid out an 18-hole parkland course beside the station at Bieldside, and also by the electric trams of the Aberdeen Suburban Tramways Company, which linked Bieldside with Mannofield and the city from 1904. Domestic electricity was supplied from a local power station built in 1905. A hydropathic establishment erected at Murtle around that time failed about 1950, and by 1967 had become the 77-bed Tor-na-Dee chest hospital.

**Public Transport Declines but Education Grows**: But with competing buses and private cars the trams were withdrawn in 1927, and the suburban trains were withdrawn in 1937. By 1953 only Cults station remained, with just two weekday trains each way. By then the population was over 2500, with the facilities of a large village. By 1971 a complex of Rudolf Steiner schools had been opened at Bieldside, Camphill, Murtle and Newton Dee. Cults Academy was built about 1960, but the railway was closed by 1966.

**Cults under Oil Pressure**: In 1969 the 67-roomed *Royal Darroch Hotel* was built; useful in the coming oil boom, it was to be ruined by a gas explosion in 1983. By 1971 more housing estates had been completed and the population was nearing 5000, though with green belting any further development was resisted. By 1981 a US-curriculum school had been provided for the children of American oilmen; with 5250 residents, the area was of suburban character. In 1984 the Dee footbridge was largely dismantled. By 1985 a large hospital had been built, almost closing the gap between Cults and Mannofield. Cults Academy had 1111 pupils in 1997, and by 1999 more new housing estates had grown north of Bieldside. Meantime Beechwood House, a mansion on the North Deeside Road, was burnt out in the 1980s; on its 3ha site was built the luxurious *Marcliffe Hotel*, opened in 1993 (42 rooms). Other hotels include the Victorian mansion *Norwood Hall* and the *Cults Hotel*; the converted Bieldside mill is known as the *Waterwheel Toby Hotel*.

## CUMBERNAULD & Abronhill

**Map 16, A3**
***New Town, n-e. of Glasgow,*** *pop. 48,000* — OS 64: NS 7675
Also see: *Condorrat*

The Romans' Antonine Wall crossed the Clyde/Forth watershed between the River Kelvin and the Bonny Water, some 1.5km north of the burnside site that was later occupied by Cumbernauld village. Evidently quite an important place in medieval days, it had a Duke as early as 1170, who also owned property in Kirkintilloch. A small parish church was built in stone around 1225. Cumbernauld was shown on the Gough map of about 1250, and there are slight remains of the ducal castle, which as late as about 1600 was an imposing structure sketched by Timothy Pont. However, the place seems not to have become an early burgh. By about 1754, as the Roy map showed, Cumbernauld had a T-shaped plan, lying in the valley of a small north-eastwards flowing burn, followed by the winding track which joined Glasgow with Denny, another link leading via Dullatur to Kilsyth. Under a Turnpiking Act of 1753 a Glasgow to Edinburgh turnpike was opened through Cumbernauld in 1794. Cumbernauld had a post office by 1813, served by a penny post from Glasgow; remarkably for a settlement draining to the east, it was to retain the Glasgow address rather than becoming a post town.

**A Near Miss for the Railways**: From 1842 Dullatur, 2 km west of Cumbernauld village, had a station on the main Edinburgh to Glasgow line where it sliced through the Roman Wall; from the 1860s sandstone was quarried nearby, employing 71 men in 1903. Cumbernauld station, on the north main line of the Caledonian Railway (CR) which opened in 1848 and followed the valley of the Red Burn by way of Castle Cary, was also over 2 km from the village. By 1895 the latter was sizeable, having an inn and post and telegraph office; to the east lay Cumbernauld House in its extensive park. A fireclay mine was open east of the CR station, and mines also existed at Dullatur, where a golf club founded in 1896 laid out an 18-hole course.

**A Brush with Stockings**: William Clelland of Glasgow had moved his hosiery firm to Cumbernauld by 1904, but labour was lacking, and about 1905 the firm's finishing operations followed the knitting machines to Kilsyth. Dullatur quarry changed from stone to sand in the 1920s and stopped work in the 1930s. By 1951 there had been little major change; some 1500 people lived in Cumbernauld, which had a small secondary school and average village facilities. This essentially agricultural area (including Condorrat) had three post offices and three tiny factories, together employing 71 people in 1956.

**Burroughs Accounts for the New Town**: In 1955 congested Glasgow agreed to subsidise emigrating tenants, so in 1956 a moderate Conservative government designated a new town for Glasgow overspill, to be built around and to the west of Cumbernauld. The large Burroughs accounting machine factory which opened very soon afterwards at Wardpark on the Falkirk road was the town's first new industry; by 1959 it had 1150 employees. By then the NTDC (New Town Development Corporation) had housed 1000 people. From 1961 a local newspaper, the *Cumbernauld News*, was published by the energetic Johnston Press of Falkirk. In 1966 this absorbed the much older *Kilsyth Chronicle*, which continued as an edition. In 1964 a grass airstrip was laid out beside the vast Burroughs factory.

**Spurning Old Cumbernauld and the Railways**: The architect-planners responsible for the New Town's overall plan and phasing regrettably turned their back on all the existing villages, deciding to build a completely new centre – inspired it is said by Italian hill towns – on a hilltop in the middle of nowhere, as described below. The railway stations were also spurned when the early developments were being planned, and about 1965 Dullatur station was closed by Beeching, though Cumbernauld's escaped. Despite its close dependence on Glasgow, Cumbernauld's trains remained steam operated when most surviving Glasgow lines were being electrified.

**Fine Roads and Housing, Ghastly Centre**: On the credit side, some of the earliest housing – for instance at Carbrain – was very innovative and attractive, other groups being terrible! Aided by low car ownership, the new town's ambitious road network which used bridges to separate pedestrians from traffic soon proved very safe in operation. Regardless of climatic factors and the sound precedents set by East Kilbride and Glenrothes, the NTDC proceeded to create a high density town with a temporary hutted centre in an entirely new location on the most exposed hilltop available, 150 metres above sea level, 1.5 km from Cumbernauld village and nearly 1 km from its railway station. Permanent buildings for the town centre were erected in the mid 1960s to a monstrous design which ignored established principles and bankrupted its builder, while creating a gloomy labyrinth of brutal concrete. Surrounded by wastes of mud and high-density housing, it is hardly surprising that the megastructure failed in its struggle to attain the sub-regional status that was attempted for it.

**The Last Burgh of All**: Economically however, Cumbernauld New Town was able to capitalise on its central location in Scotland to become an important warehousing and distribution centre. Cumbernauld was granted burgh status in 1968, the last of all the hundreds to be created; Cumbernauld High School and Greenfaulds High School were open by 1971. National Semiconductor opened a branch plant in 1969, but by 1979 this had been moved to the Spango Valley, where the workforce was already attuned to electronics. However in 1980 Conder Scotland of Wardpark claimed to be the largest manufacturer and exporter of steel-framed buildings in Scotland. A large Woolco store was opened beside the town centre megastructure in the mid 1970s. Palacerigg Country Park, established 4 km east of the town, provided municipal golf from 1975, and later a wildlife collection. In 1977 the Inland Revenue opened a computer centre. In 1978 the 258-seat *Cumbernauld Theatre* was created from a row of cottages in the grounds of Cumbernauld House.

**Protective Clothing but few Jobs**: By 1979 Traditional Weatherwear were making protective clothing; by 1989 this included mackintosh raincoats. Edward Macbean also made foul-weather clothing in the town; acquired in 1994 by the Hollas textile group of Cheshire their protective clothing was supplied to many police forces. Meantime by 1981 Cumbernauld had the facilities of a substantial town; some 22,500 people, three-quarters of them from Glasgow, lived in the central part of the new town and 25,000 more in the entirely new satellite village of Abronhill to the east, and the later private estates around old Condorrat *(q.v.)* to the west. In 1981 52% of Cumbernauld's residents worked outside the town, for Burroughs and the clothing firms could provide only half the jobs they needed. By then Cumbernauld Technical College was in operation south of the new town centre, but there was really little else except warehousing, shops and schools, including Our Lady's RC High School; Abronhill High School was built in the 1980s.

**Struggles in the Eighties**: The innovative Johnston Control Systems had become established by 1983, but troubles deepened when the *Golden Eagle Hotel*, crudely built as part of the town centre megastructure in 1966, had to be demolished in 1982; the Woolco store was closed in the mid 1980s, and the once-great Burroughs factory ceased production in 1987. By 1987 Cumbernauld was the least well-endowed with jobs of all the Scottish New Towns, both absolutely and per head of population, which at 49,500 was actually falling. The unemployment rate was above the high Scottish average, especially for women. It then seemed almost inevitable that Cumbernauld would share the fate of other depressed Glasgow overspill estates, with greater remoteness from the city an added incubus.

**Hinari Comes and Goes**: A remarkably short-lived enterprise was the Hinari television set assembly factory, which despite its name was not Japanese; this opened in 1988 and closed in 1989! Two firms developed in the 1980s by Gordon Wright to supply heart-lung machines and heart valves, with factories in Bothwell and Cumbernauld, employed 150 people between them by 1990 when they were sold to the American combine 3M. Around that time a firm called Allivane (also at Glenrothes) is reputed to have made many artillery shells for sale to Iraq.

**Recovery after 1988**: However, by 1988 the town centre had expanded with the addition of retail warehouses, and in 1989 a new railway station was opened at Greenfaulds, some 1100 m on the Glasgow side of Cumbernauld station. The airstrip was given a hard runway, reopening in 1989 for general aviation as *Cumbernauld Airport* with pilot training, facilities for aircraft hire, and also freight concerns. By 1989 bullish announcements were emanating from the NTDC; it was claimed that local unemployment was now under 10%. A new 18-hole championship-standard golf course designed by Severiano Ballesteros and Dave Thomas had just been completed at Westerwood, where an associated leisure club and hotel were opened in 1991. A local landmark was the Inter-City freight depot (not a railway enterprise). At that time the still relatively young population was 48,762, and the development corporation claimed the town had 600 businesses, but the DC was wound down in 1993–96.

**New Computer and Allied Industries**: By 1989 the Japanese firm OKI had taken over the huge factory on the Burroughs site and employed some 400 people making computer printers. By then Isola Werke were manufacturing computer laminates. Teledyne Incorporated of California opened a factory in 1993

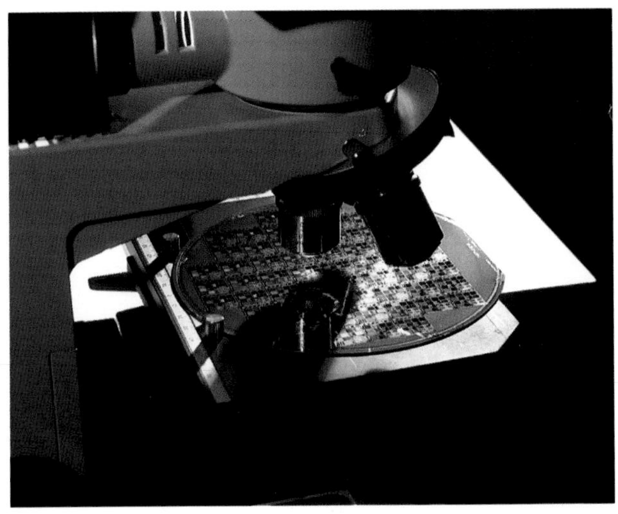

*Computer wafer manufacture – one of Cumbernauld's many high-tech operations.* *(SMPC / Bob West)*

to assemble and test electrical and mechanical products, and 175 jobs were created by Cordata in a new plant to produce PCB's and personal computers. In 1993 Elonex computers also expanded at Cumbernauld. In 1994 Atlantech Technologies Ltd of Westfield Business Park was a young and expanding firm developing software for interactive multimedia networks.

**Other New Developments**: In 1989 Becton Dickinson opened a microbiological production facility, and further new industries expected in 1989 included 300 jobs making transformers for another Japanese firm, and 200 for Tenma producing plastic injection mouldings. In 1991 a new company, Premier Glass Packaging, was established jointly by United Glass *(see Alloa)* and the French firm Verreries de l'Oise, to make speciality etched or decorated drinks bottles in an automated factory of almost 5000 m². In 1993 the town also contained the Co-op Distribution Centre for Scotland, and the large premises of Network Logistics.

**Breezy Broadwood brings Clyde to the Watershed**: By 1993 the town sprawled for 8 km alongside the A80 across the Forth/Clyde watershed, much of it saved from mediocrity by the extensive tree planting. The opening of a new railway curve at Cowlairs in 1993, enabling direct trains to Glasgow Queen Street, so improved Cumbernauld's train service that within a year a 37% increase in ridership had been achieved. Among its last acts, the NTDC built the new 6100-seat Broadwood Stadium at Cumbernauld to accommodate First Division Clyde FC. Early in 1994 this peripatetic club moved in, from their umpteenth temporary base at Hamilton, only to lose to Hamilton Accies in the first match at their windswept new home! Later in 1994 the new stadium – with its health centre and gymnastics school – was also the temporary *'home'* base for Airdrie FC. By 2000 after a thin patch, Clyde FC regained a First Division place.

**Drinks and Golf, but No Council**: In 1995 A G Barr, producer of the famed soft drink *Irn-Bru*, long based in Parkhead, centralised its Scottish production facilities at Cumbernauld, building an efficient new plant in 2000. The town also handled Treasury tax revenues, while the *Cumbernauld Theatre* was still active, and by 1999 had been refurbished. In that year ever-sprawling Cumbernauld lost its role in local government, when with the Monklands it became part of a major new unitary authority area styled *'North Lanarkshire'*, also including Motherwell – which became the HQ (though town planning is now based in Cumbernauld). In 1997 Abronhill High School had about 600 pupils, Cumbernauld High 825, and Greenfaulds High and Our Lady's High just under 1000; Cumbernauld College employs 300. By 2000 OKI employed 900 people making printers, but the strong pound led to 340 redundancies. Other significant employers include Coilcraft (computer components), Greenberg Glass, and distribution firms BOC and Link Logistics. The modern 49-room *Westerwood Hotel* has a country club and a fine golf course.

## CUMINESTOWN (or Auchry) & Monquhitter

**Map 10, B2**

***Buchan village,*** *pop. 500* — OS 29: NJ 8050

The undated Castle of Auchry, home of the Con family, stood at an altitude of nearly 100 metres 6 km east of the Buchan centre of Turriff. It overlooked the valley of the Monquhitter Burn, a name deriving from the Gaelic *'Moine Uachdar'*, meaning *Top of Moor* or *Upper Moor*, and lay just beyond the area of one of Pont's surviving maps. However, Gordon's map showed *'M. Achry'*, implying a mill by about 1650. This was also shown on Roy's map of about 1750, when the *'Kirk of Monwhiter'* stood some 2 km east of the castle, accompanied by *'Achra'* (Auchrie House) in its shelterbelted policies, and also a settlement of about ten buildings; but the area was still roadless.

**The Expanded Village Renamed**: Joseph Cumine of Auchry established an extended settlement with linen manufacture on this site in 1761–63, and a new church was built in 1764; he changed the placename to Cuminestown. The expansion of this existing settlement achieved speedy success, when compared to slower growth by new foundations on greenfield sites, a discovery that was apparently a major influence on landed proprietors *(see Adams)*; would that the mid 20th century planners of Cumbernauld and Livingston had learned the lesson! Cuminestown grew into a fairly substantial village with the delightfully named Mill of Pot, and a post office which was established between 1813 and 1838.

**Stagnation**: Garmond, laid out on rectilinear lines 2 km north of Cuminestown, was noted in 1858 by Pratt as a *"village"*, as was *"long and straggling"* Cuminestown, which was never on a railway and failed to interest the authors of Murray's Handbook for 1894. As late as 1910 when other places enjoyed motor bus services, Cuminestown was still served by a horse-drawn coach linking the stations at Turriff and Maud; the parish church hall was built in 1924. By 1986 Garmond, which had a primary school in the early 20th century, was a mere hamlet. Cuminestown has remained quite a small though busy village, its population shrinking over the forty years 1951–91 to under 500. But its range of shops and activities was quite remarkable: by 1981 it had the *Gordon House Hotel*, and now also the *Commercial Hotel*, a primary school, health centre, post office, garage and tyre services, a road haulier, and a small biscuit manufacturer; near Garmond there is even a small coal merchant.

## CUMMERTREES & Powfoot

**Map 2, B5**

***Solway Firth villages,*** *pop. 740*

OS 85: NY 1466

Cummertrees lies beside the Pow Water in the low-lying carselands 5 km west of Annan, beside what was the main road to Dumfries when the travel writer Alexander Carlyle was born there in 1722. Powfoot on the coast 1 km to the east was once a fishing centre. The Roy map of the 1750s marked Longbrigg Flash on the road to the west, and the mansion of *'Kil Head House'*, 3 km to the north. By 1799 Heron noted limeworks at Kelhead, from whose quarry marble was also excavated. What was shortly to become the Glasgow & South Western Railway opened in 1848, connecting Annan with Dumfries; Cummertrees gained a conveniently sited wayside station. By the 1890s Kil Head had been renamed as Kinmount House. Cummertrees parish had 969 residents in 1901.

**Golf – and Gunpowder?**: The Annan-Powfoot golf club, founded in 1903, laid out an 18-hole seaside course west of the hamlet of Powfoot, which was intended to become a major resort; but it failed to grow, perhaps because about that time Nobel built a large explosives factory immediately to the east. This extensive complex with its rail connection passed to ICI in the twenties, but until recently could not be found on OS maps! By the 1950s the area was served by two post offices, a 78-line telephone exchange, and primary school. There was an inn at Cummertrees, though in the mid 1950s its station was closed to passengers. The *Golf Hotel* at Powfoot was open by 1954 and enlarged in the 1970s, but Powfoot post office closed about 1968, since the resident population of the farming parish was falling fast, to only 725 by 1971. However by 1985 a coastal caravan and camping site was open at Powfoot. In 1989 ICI proposed the closure of its Powfoot explosives factory. Cummertrees parish had 740 residents in 1991. Kinmount House still stands in its vast park, part of the Hoddom estates. A little new development had occurred at Powfoot by 1997; the area still has its post office and rather remote primary school, and the *Golf Hotel* at Powfoot now has 18 rooms.

## CUMNOCK, Lugar & Cronberry

**Map 2, A3**

***Ayrshire town & urban areas,*** *pop. 11,000*

OS 71: NS 5620

Cumnock was anciently of some importance, being shown on the Gough map of the mid 13th century, though hard information is scarce. Some 1.5 km to the west on the south bank of the Lugar Water, a major tributary of the River Ayr, stands the 15th century keep of Taringzean Castle, whose feudal proprietor obtained a burgh of barony charter for Cumnock in 1509. Although early travellers made no mention of the place, and the engraving of Pont's map of about 1600 omitted it, Cumnock had begun to develop into the main centre for the area, for it was shown on the Mercator atlas map of 1595. A parish school was started in 1599, by 1643 there was a struggling grammar school, and Cumnock Mercat cross was erected in 1703.

**Mansion, Mining and the Gas Man**: Taringzean Castle was replaced for the Crichton Earls of Dumfries by the mansion of Dumfries House some 1.5 km farther west, designed by John and Robert Adam and built in 1754. This new mansion appeared on the Roy map surveyed in that or the following year, which showed *'Old Cumnock'* as a medium-sized square settlement at the intersection of the roads connecting Ayr and Ochiltree with Muirkirk, and Sanquhar and New Cumnock with Mauchline via *'Affleck Kirk'* and Howford Bridge. William Murdoch, born in 1754 at Bello Mill near Lugar, grew up with the local mining industry, and developed the process of distillation of coal into gas and coke. Trained by Boulton & Watt, he also designed slide valves for steam engines and built a steam carriage. Meantime by 1771 a local coal mine had reached a sufficient depth to require an engine, a post office was opened in 1782, and a bleachfield was set up in 1785.

**Coaches, Fine Snuff Boxes and Coarse Pots**: By 1797 when daily mail coaches between Glasgow, Kilmarnock, Dumfries and Carlisle passed through Cumnock it was a post town, the centre for Catrine, and had two annual fairs. Yet Heron in 1799 wrote only of some 600 people, adding *"the village of Old Cumnock is neatly built, on a regular plan, with the church in the centre"*. Then came a further boost: from about 1807 fine snuff boxes and by 1810 coarse pottery were being manufactured, and five fairs were being held each year. In 1827 Chambers found it *"a large village known for the making of those peculiar little cabinets known as Cumnock snuff-boxes"*. By then over 100 people were making them from plane-tree wood, *"adorning the lids with drawn devices chaste and beautiful"* and fabricating and fitting the complex *'invisible'* hinges. The famed landscape painter Horatio McCulloch, born in Glasgow in 1805, was in his younger years one of the box decorators. By then Cumnock boasted a town band; a church of unusual design was built in 1831.

**Farm Machinery, Railways – and Cronberry**: A Bank of Scotland branch was opened in 1838 and from about then there was a gasworks. Threshing machines and other farm equipment were built by George McCartney from 1832, and sold widely. The first railway through the town opened in 1850, connecting Glasgow, Kilmarnock and Dumfries and soon forming the main line of the Glasgow & South Western. In 1866 Cumnock became a police burgh and by 1885 had a town hall. A branch line from Ayr was opened in 1872–73 via stations named Skares, 4 km west of the town, and Dumfries House near the mansion only 1 km to the east, its viaduct striding across the valley south of the town to join the Kilmarnock to Muirkirk line near Cronberry station, east of Lugar. Cronberry was already a hamlet built beside the Bello Water in the 1860s by the Eglinton company, by 1895 comprising seven miners' rows, several of them roofed only with tarred felt, a school (later the village hall) and a branch of the Lugar shop; unusually for the day, it had no church. The five mean Carbello Rows were built nearby to serve coal and ironstone mines which worked from 1873 to 1906, and faded in the early 20th century.

**Lugar Ironworks**: In 1866 the great Lugar works of William Baird's Eglinton Iron Company (which eventually had five blast furnaces) was set up 3 km to the east, replacing a smaller works of Wilson & Dunlop at nearby Craigston, where an ironstone pit was open between 1875 and 1890. From the 1850s Airds Moss to the north had been the site of many coal and ironstone pits; after 1870 they were taken over by Baird and linked to the works by mineral railways. Remote Darnconner was a hamlet with a school, and a church built in 1906. The Lugar Institute was built in 1892 beside the company shop to designs by Robert Ingram of Kilmarnock for William Weir, a philanthropic partner in the ironworks company, providing a library and facilities for swimming, games and meetings. By 1894 the *Dumfries Arms Hotel* was open in Cumnock, the Grammar

School (since closed) then being a secondary. Cumnock was noted by Murray in 1894 as a *"town chiefly dependent on the Lugar ironworks"*, where row houses were built and post and telegraph offices were open by 1895. By then the mansion of Logan House stood 2 km east of the town.

**Labour Pioneer as Newspaper Editor**: In 1901, when the burgh population was 3088, a local newspaper, the *Cumnock Chronicle* was established; among its early editors was ex-miner and MP Keir Hardie, originally from Holytown *(also see Hamilton)*, already famed by 1886 as a key founder of the Scottish Miners' Federation, and of the Scottish Labour Party in 1888 and the Independent Labour Party in 1893. By 1902 Baird's Whitehill coal pit had become a large colliery, and gave rise to the company village of Skares, 118 houses in miners' rows, which until the 1950s had a school and post office. Meantime about 1917 a long-lasting barytes mine was opened far up the bleak valley of the Gass Water 10 km to the east, and some workers' cottages were built nearby. Ironmaking ceased at Lugar after the General Strike of 1926, though the coal mines continued, the Eglinton coal-dross briquette works remained on the site, and National Coal Board workshops were added after 1947. A new school was built at Cronberry in 1931 and a public park and outdoor swimming pool were opened at Cumnock in 1936.

**Colliery and Rail Closures**: By 1951 there were three small hotels in Cumnock, including the *Dumfries Arms* and *Royal*, and three junior secondary schools were open, at Cumnock, at Garrallan near Skares and at Glaisnock in the big Netherthird housing estate south-east of the town, which also had a primary school and Craigens post office. But the rail passenger service to Ayr had ceased in 1950, and by 1954 Darnconner had almost vanished, while Logan House had been replaced by a council estate which took its name and gained a post office. Whitehill colliery and its rail links closed in 1966.

**Two Million Shoes a Year**: A large shoe factory making a million pairs a year was opened in 1964 by British Bata; Cumnock also had yarn spinners, and still made farm implements. The station was closed by Beeching about 1965 and by 1972 only the viaduct remained of the Cronberry to Sinclairston line. Logan had been enlarged by 1971 to over 1500 people, with a primary school. Cairnhill colliery, at the end of a short steep branch from the surviving section of the Auchinleck to Muirkirk railway 6 km north-east of Cumnock, still operated as late as 1974. In 1975 the redundant Lugar offices of the National Coal Board became the centre of the new Cumnock & Doon Valley district council, and by 1976 local industries included hosiery and the Cronberry Slag Company's pit. By then there was the modern Cumnock Academy; the town square had been pedestrianised, with new blocks of shops, while five or six large workingmen's clubs provided cabaret and dancing. The council had built a 10-ha sports complex: the fine swimming pool was very popular, with a quarter million admissions in four summer months in 1976.

**Stonefield falls on Stony Ground**: However, by 1977 competition from Ayr had closed the Cumnock cattle market. Problems dogged the Stonefield Vehicles cross-country vehicle plant, which was optimistic in 1978, and in early 1979 employed about 100 people making rough-terrain trucks, but despite SDA support they were in financial trouble and halved the workforce. They were still trying to attract private capital in 1980. By 1979 Monsanto *(see Dundonald)* had a small branch plant in the town, where Gray's Tufted Carpets factory and Cumnock Knitwear were also in production; the latter was still working in 1992. By 1990 St Conval's High School was very well established. In 1981 Cumnock retained its long-established joinery works and had an average town centre, but former mining settlements dominated the area. The Glaisnock shopping centre, built by 1989, exceeded 5000 m$^2$, but the local economy was still weak, and in 1991 unemployment in Cumnock (including the Sanquhar area) was the highest for any travel-to-work area in Scotland, at 17%; by then 9600 people lived in Cumnock, plus some 1200 in Logan. By 1992 a bypass had been newly constructed, a museum and a tourist office were open in the town, and a riverside caravan site had been established, but except for its isolated school, Cronberry had almost vanished, and about then the briquette works closed.

**Fire Engines and Baby Dear**: Emergency One of Cumnock, set up to build fire engines, sold just six in 1990, but over 40 throughout Britain in 1993. In 1992 came further hope when Baby Dear, manufacturers of children's shoes and clothing, moved into Cumnock, and The Sweater Shop aimed to create 200 jobs in a new casual clothing and leisurewear factory by 1995. That year also saw the start of Datum Dynamics, which soon had international customers for its servicing and retooling of printed circuit board factories. A new health centre was built in the mid 1990s. In 1996 the local council disappeared into Kilmarnock's *'East Ayrshire'* authority, led by a mining geologist who preferred job creation to environmental protection; hence large-scale opencasting began at Skares in 1997, despite some local opposition. By 1997 St Conval's High School – though little – was good. The Lugar Institute, at one time used as a dance hall and then a clothing factory, was still vacant and deteriorating in 1998, as was the 1831 church in Tanyard which had been a store. On the brighter side, the long-established *Royal Hotel* (11 rooms) has successfully kept its two stars for many years.

## CUNNINGSBURGH

**Map 14, B4**

***Settlement, Shetland,*** *pop. 700*

OS 4: HU 4329

The Norse name of this sprawling settlement on the east coast of Shetland some 15 km south of Lerwick means *'King's Stronghold'*. The narrow south-facing inlet of Aith Voe provides good shelter for small vessels, and was once an important herring curing centre. Local steatite (soapstone) workings began about 900 under the Vikings: plates, bowls, weights, lamps and other utensils were easily carved from this material, and the industry lasted until about 1550. There was a church at Cunningsburgh well before 1603. The population in 1951 was about 475, with basic facilities, but by 1981 it was nearer 700, local growth being indicated by a second small telephone exchange building beside the old. In 1985 a small jetty was a summer centre for pleasure boating. In 1987 a garage, post office, general store, primary school and playing field were to be seen, and limited housing development was continuing. However by 1994 the primary school had closed.

## CUPAR

*Town, Howe of Fife*, *pop. 7500* **Map 6, B3** OS 59: NO 3714

Cupar on the winding River Eden in the fertile Howe of Fife had an early church, though it lay outside the area of the later town, whose origins are obscure; in 1183 it was recorded as *'Cupre'*. After responsibility for Fothrif was added to the sheriffdom of Fife, the caput was transferred in 1212–13 from peripheral Crail to somewhat more central Cupar, which was chartered as a Royal Burgh before the death of William the Lion in 1214. It seems that about that time a Royal castle was built, for Cupar was shown on the Gough map, probably prepared about the middle of the 13th century. Re-chartered as a Royal Burgh in 1327, Cupar exported wool in the early 14th century, perhaps carried in small boats down the Eden; but exactly where it was transhipped to seagoing vessels is uncertain. A Dominican priory was founded in 1348, only two years before the Black Death, which seems to have struck hard, for the wool export trade seems to have ceased; for many years Cupar made practically no Customs payments, and its contributions always remained slight.

**Wool Trade and Three Estates**: In 1369 Cupar's merchant guild failed to hold its monopoly in staple goods against the more prosperous bishop's burgh of St Andrews, but the wool trade had been resumed by 1400, and seems to have prospered, for a new parish church was built about 1415–29. The peak of Cupar's international trade came about 1427–31, when it held eighth place in Scotland. Cupar merchants were trading with Danzig in 1444; but thereafter the town's international trade declined steadily to nothing. However, by the 16th century a bridge was recorded across the Eden on the road to Pitscottie. In the period 1535–56 Cupar paid between 1.5% and 3% of burgh tax revenue, and in 1560 it was sufficiently important to be represented in Parliament; by 1564 it had a grammar school. The Mount, 4km north-west of Cupar, near the rural Kirk of Moonzie parish, was the birthplace in about 1486 of Sir David Lindsay, poet and author of the influential *Satire of the Thrie Estaites*, which is still performed.

**Exit Castle and Priory: enter Market and Brewery**: Chambers noted that *"the eminent site of the present schools was formerly occupied by a castle"*, demolished in the 16th century; however, the street name *Castlefields* remained. After the Reformation the priory also almost vanished; however, Pont's original map of about 1600 confirmed the Eden bridge, and a *'wakmill'* at *'Cowper of Fyfe'*. By 1593 the town was the centre of a presbytery, and Cupar was known for its farmers' market by 1610. However, Cupar in 1639 held only 22nd place among the burghs in tax yield; by the 1650s brewing was carried on commercially. A post office was in operation by 1715. In the 1720s Defoe noted Cupar as *"the shire town where the public business of the county is all done, and the Earl of Rothes who is hereditary Sheriff keeps his court."*

**Linen Weaving**: A linen manufacturing and bleaching concern set up in 1727 made a shaky start, but the town had an incorporation of weavers by about 1730. With the prevailing agricultural improvements Cupar's market function also became very important, with a Corn Exchange. In 1736 roads were planned to Crail and Newburgh, though only the former was proceeded with. By 1750, as the Roy map showed, there were no fewer than eight roads radiating from Cupar, then a substantial place with two bridges; only the present Newburgh road remained to be added. From 1752 a well-made road existed from Kirkcaldy via the New Inn (near Kirkforthar), through Cupar to the Tay.

**Burnside Mills and the Fairs**: Burnside mills, established in 1774, were still operating in 1988, and a flax mill existed from the 1780s. In the late 18th century Cupar was a busy weaving centre with 223 hand looms, annually weaving half a million metres of a variety of fabrics, some bleached locally at a field on the Eden. By 1797 Cupar was not only a post town but, with twelve fairs a year, was among the four most used fair stances in Scotland; by 1800 all its main radial roads had been turnpiked. It also had a subscription library. In 1799 Heron referred to *"about 3000 inhabitants, many of whom are manufacturers in the bleaching of linen and tanning of leather"*. About 1810, around a million metres of linen was stamped annually.

**Bent Bankers, Prison and Printing**: The Cupar Banking Company was formed in 1802, but retired from business in 1811. More successful at first was the Fife Banking Company, also established in 1802, which had three branches by 1810; in 1825 it failed due to criminal mismanagement. Meantime the imposing County Buildings were erected in 1812–17 to designs by Robert Hutchison. By 1825 Cupar was the centre for a penny post, also serving Leuchars. Cupar Mills also dated from the early 19th century, but were to last far longer. So did the remarkably attractive jail, built about 1825, which was still used as such in 1856 but later became the home of Watts' long-lasting grain merchanting business. A well-known press functioned from 1803 to 1849; its founder Robert Tullis also set up the great Markinch *(q.v.)* paper mills, and Cupar's local newspaper the *Fife Herald* dates back to 1822. In 1825 there were four breweries, but these did not survive into the 20th century.

**Cupar in 1827**: By 1827 there were also two coaching inns, and in that year according to Chambers *"Cupar, being the capital of a productive and wealthy tract of country, is a decidedly prosperous town. It has long sent forth a weekly newspaper; and the editions of the classics printed here by Mr George Tullis are well known internationally for their beautiful and accurate typography. The jail, the school, and the county buildings, are all modern and handsome structures."* By then Tarvit, 1km south-east of the town, had been replaced by the classical mansion of Tarvit House. In 1836 three flax-spinning mills had 236 employees and ten firms employed some 600 weavers. A gasworks was set up in 1839.

**Railway and Golf**: The opening of the Edinburgh & Northern Railway (E&NR) between Cupar and Burntisland in 1847 cut short the coach routes, and Cupar got fine station buildings. In 1850 the line was completed and opened through to Tayport for Broughty Ferry and Dundee by the E&NR's successors the Edinburgh Perth & Dundee Railway. The present Corn Exchange was built in 1861–62. Cupar golf club, founded in 1855, laid out a 9-hole hillside course, its simple layout little altered over the years; but by 2000 a second 9-hole course had been added.

**Textile Mills put out the Banners**: In 1864 Smith, Laing & Co's water-powered Russell Mill contained 2200 spindles, looked after by 200 workers who lived locally in what Bremner styled as *"comfortable houses"*, while William Smith's Cupar Mill employed nearly 100. In 1866 David Martin Stenhouse established the long-lasting Stratheden Linen Mills in Station

Road; they were to specialise in flag and banner making. In 1867 there were 16 textile mills in the wider *'Eden District'*, in all employing over 2000 people. Spinning in Cupar itself ceased about that year, though weaving continued. The Duncan Institute, designed by John Milne of St Andrews, was built in 1869–70.

**Local Government and Sugar Refinery**: The new elected Fife County Council set up in 1889 took over the County Buildings in Cupar where the sheriff court had always sat, though with the prevailing growth of population in west and south Fife, it was already most inconveniently located for the growing majority of industrial Fifers. Bell Baxter High School was founded in 1890, and in 1891 the population was almost 5000, but Cupar's two hotels the *Royal* and *Tontine* were rated *"very fair"* by Murray, and little development of note seems to have occurred for thirty years. Following the Beet Sugar Subsidy Act of 1925, a large beet sugar refining factory was built at Cupar in 1926, the only one ever established in Scotland. Cupar then gained improving urban facilities, and as the county council's importance also grew, it built large office extensions, and the town acquired a telephone group switching centre. Flax scutching mills worked again in World War II. In 1951 the population was about 6000, enjoying a very wide range of services for its size, including Elmwood Agricultural College. D S Honeyman & Co still produced linen beside the station until about 1958.

**Exit Tarvit, Sugar – and the County**: Bell Baxter High School moved into new buildings in 1962, but soon outgrew them, for the town's population was expanding; by 1971 it was about 6900. Tarvit House was regrettably demolished in 1963, but a farm remained. The Corn Exchange was modernised in 1964, by which time a small laundry at Cupar had been acquired by Fishers, originally of Aberfeldy; it was keenly expanded by Donald Fisher. However, the beet sugar factory was closed about 1972, allegedly because of lower sugar content in Scottish beets than those grown in England. In 1974 the newly-elected Fife Regional Council set its face firmly against Cupar, deciding by four votes (in the author's presence) to set up its HQ in Glenrothes New Town (which had cannily offered office premises for let). In 1975 Cupar became the HQ for North East Fife District, to the chagrin of the larger and far more historic centre, St Andrews, which by then had a branch of Cupar's delightfully named law firm Pagan, Osborne & Grace (established in 1789).

**After Seedsmen and Millers: Food, Flats and Vodka**: In 1978 potatoes were still despatched south by rail, but by 1979 Cupar's railway goods yard was empty, and only one firm had set up at the *'Cupar Trading Estate'* (the former beet sugar factory). In 1981 the town's facilities were those of an important local centre, with six small hotels and a large Fife Region vehicle depot. The Watts seed warehouse had closed, but its *'A'* listed building survived, and in 1992 this one-time jail became a restaurant, opened by Michael Short Enterprises of Dundee but still bearing the Watts name. Grain milling seems to have continued until the Cupar Mills of Hamlyn Angus Milling were closed and converted into private housing in 1990. But by then Davaar International blended and bottled whisky and vodka.

**Mending Cars and Cleaning Linen**: The Heggie motor group which started in Cupar in 1972 had built up by 1994 to employ 130 people in five accident repair centres from Dundee to Edinburgh; by 1995 the large and expanding Glenvarigill Garage

*The railway station at Cupar, taken in the 1960s. The station was built in 1847 for the Edinburgh and Northern Railway – an exceptionally fine survivor from that period.* *(RCAHMS / JRH)*

employed ten people on accident repairs alone. Fishers' laundry continued to develop with the tourist hotels it served, and by 1992 had been much extended to become what was claimed to be the largest flat-work laundry north of London, able to process five tonnes of dirty linen an hour! By 1996 Fishers had built a large new laundry on the industrial estate.

**Lorries and Lawyers**: By 1991 when the population had passed 7500, a large road haulage depot was operated by Danskin Distribution, and the livestock market remained busy. Bell Baxter High School acquired a new extension at Westfield Road in 1992 to enable single-site working. By 1993 the old Pagan law firm employed over 100 people and had seven branches in Fife and Tayside. In 1993 the old Edinburgh & Northern Railway granary was converted into a business and training centre. By 1994 the former Honeyman factory was the headquarters of A T Hogg (Fife) Ltd, formerly of Strathmiglo, who for a few years continued to retail footwear and country clothing through five branches.

**After 784 years, just an Area Committee**: In 1995 Cupar was the base for ambulance services throughout north-east Fife, but the former Translink transport depot was for sale. The Major government deprived Cupar of its local government role in 1996 when North East Fife was merged into a new single tier authority. In theory this ended its 784-year role as a centre of local administration; but decentralisation to strong district committees by the new Conservative-free Fife Council largely circumvented this. In 1996 the disused railway goods yard became a car park, and Tesco built a new store near Reekies' garage south of the station. A major development of 358 houses at Ceres Road was completed in the late 1990s. Though it is years since London trains have regularly called there, Cupar retains its wayside railway station, and Houstons still make flags and banners under the Stenhouse name. Wiseman's Dairies opened a distribution centre in 2001, employing 80. Hotels include the *Eden House* (11 rooms); there are good guest houses, and the tiny *Ostler's Close* restaurant.

## CURRIE, Riccarton & Hermiston — Map 15, B2

***Suburb w. of Edinburgh,** pop. 15,000* — OS 65 or 66: NT 1867

The 15th century Lennox Tower stands beside the Water of Leith about 10km south-west of Edinburgh. Riccarton, 2 km to the north, was first built as a tower house in the 16th century. By the time that Timothy Pont mapped the Lothians about 1600, the Lanark road followed the north bank of the river. This was already bridged 1km downstream of Lennox at Currie, on a road from Long Hermiston and Riccarton which led over the Pentland Hills to Glencorse and Roslin. The Roy map of about 1754 showed Currie as a crossroads settlement. Copper was mined in the area for a few years up to 1758, and there was an 18th century church. Kinleith (or Kenleith) paper mills 500m downstream of the bridge originated around 1795. Currie and Hermiston post offices first opened in 1806. In 1823–27 William Burn converted Riccarton tower into a mansion for Sir William Gibson Craig.

**Railways**: Curriehill station on the Caledonian Railway's Edinburgh to Carstairs main line was opened between the village and Riccarton in 1848. In 1874 the same company completed a tortuous single-track suburban branch railway up the valley bottom to stations serving Currie and Balerno. By the 1890s Currie possessed an inn, post and telegraph office, but the one-time road over the Pentlands was no more than a footpath. Passenger trains ceased on the branch in 1943; goods trains survived there until 1967. Curriehill station was closed in 1951.

**Heriot-Watt University and Suburban Growth**: The mansion of Riccarton was demolished in 1956; its site was acquired by the then Midlothian County Council which, in order to attract development and rateable value to its sprawling area, gave it to the newly promoted Heriot-Watt University, then inadequately housed in central Edinburgh. Building began in 1966 and from 1969 teaching departments were transferred stage by stage to this Shangri-La campus, whose first phase was completed in 1974. Student residences were also built, but the campus became almost wholly dependent on the private car for transport; in the 1980s there was a very infrequent bus service. During the 1960s and 1970s much private housing was built around Currie, related both to the new campus and as a suburb of Edinburgh – to whose new City District Currie was transferred in 1975. By 1981 its 15,000 people enjoyed the facilities of a large village. By 1976 the Kinleith Mills had apparently been taken over as a garage.

**Research Park and Conference Centre**: Curriehill station, located between growing Currie and the expanding University, was reopened in 1987, and the latter's very successful science park was extended in 1988–89; by 1989 Syntex alone employed over 250 research scientists. Fermentech, owned in 1994 by Skandigen of Sweden, was making medical products there in 1992; in 1994 its main brewed product was the lubricant *hyaluronic acid*, most useful in eye surgery. In 1993 Inveresk Clinical Research was also engaged in work for the pharmaceutical industry. The Heriot-Watt Edinburgh Conference Centre, developed in 1987–90, was immediately successful; but in 1992 its use of the name was disputed by the proposers of the larger development in central Edinburgh. A better bus service was provided when the University completed its move from the city in the 1990s, and in 1999 East of Scotland Water opened a new laboratory on the research park, named Watermark House. Today Currie High School has around 860 pupils, and the Kinauld Leather Works is still busy above the Water of Leith.

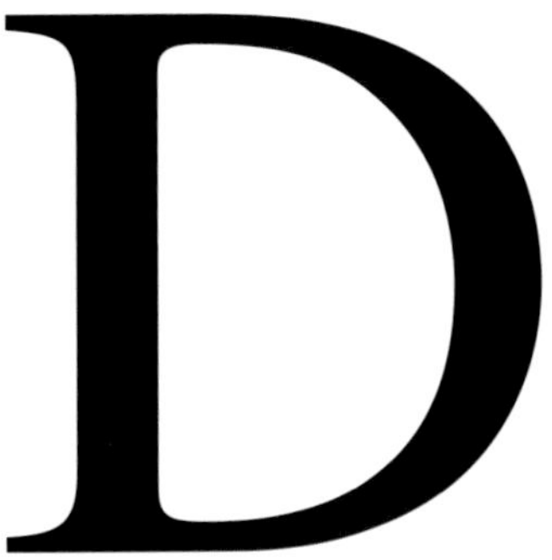

## DAILLY

**Map 1, C3**

*Ayrshire village, pop. 1000* — OS 76: NS 2701

South of the Water of Girvan and about 12 km east of the town at its mouth is the small valley of its tributary the Dobbingstone Burn, where a medieval motte stands on a spur; in the 15th century the stone keep of Kilkerran Castle was built nearby. Midway between Girvan and Maybole, 3 km downstream from Kilkerran on the opposite bank of the Water of Girvan, is the probably later tower of Dalquharran Castle. This was already emparked when Timothy Pont mapped the area about 1600; he also recorded *'Brounstoun'* about 1 km downstream, where in the 17th century the new tower of Brunston Castle rose on a similar site. Opposite to it was *'Makaish Mill'*, but although the area was generally well settled there was much woodland upstream on the site of the present village of Dailly. The Roy map made about 1754 showed a road paralleling the south bank of the Water of Girvan and passing both the *'Old Kirk of Dailly'* and the early 18th century Dailly Kirk opposite Dalquharran. There a new mansion to supersede the old was built on a new site well away from the river bank in 1790, to designs by Robert Adam. Heron wrote of Dailly as a *"village"* in 1799; where this stood he did not say.

**Coal on the Rails and Fire Down the Pits**: A coal pit at Dalquharran which caught fire in 1849 burned for half a century; after the fire had burned itself out, the small Maxwell adit mine dug the coal that remained. The river had been bridged by 1860, when the Glasgow & South Western Railway was opened between Ayr and Girvan, with a station named Dailly near Dalquharran, and another (Kilkerran) at Craigoch, about 4 km upstream, where an acid works was soon built beside the line. In 1895 New Dailly, as the village was still named, had 560 people, a post and telegraph office and a hotel. At least two coal pits named Bargany were open under McHarrie & Couper, one near the station, another 1.5 km west of Brunston Castle. This pit closed in 1908, but was renamed Killochan on reopening under new owners in 1913; in the 1920s the company built miners' housing in Girvan.

**Acid Drops?**: The historic Dalquharran Castle had sadly become ruinous by 1939. In 1951 New Dailly with a population of nearly 1400 had the facilities of a typical village, and the opening of a new Dalquharran adit mine in 1952 led to the primary school being extended. Local decline started when Beeching closed the railway stations to passengers about 1965. Killochan mine employed about 160 men raising and screening coal from two seams, and was still rail-connected until closure in 1967. This accelerated decline; some 65 jobs when the Maxwell closed in 1973, as did the Kilkerran acid works.

**Factory Workers fly from the Farming Village**: In 1986 the village housing was almost all of public authority types; there were several shops, two tiny hotels and a public hall, among the facilities of a typical village. In that year Jim Montgomerie, a local agricultural engineer from Lochwinnoch, flew a successful small autogyro; by 1994 his firm Montgomerie Engineering had built 47 of these unique recreational aircraft, flown from an airstrip at Kilkerran. However, in 1991 only 1007 people lived in Dailly village, with some of the disadvantages of a former mining settlement, but having eight times more farm workers than most localities of its size. By 1996 an 18-hole golf course had been newly laid out at Brunston Castle. At least one hotel, the primary school and the post office remained open.

## DAIRSIE & Kemback

**Map 6, B3**

*N-E. Fife hamlets, pop. 425* — OS 59: NO 4116

Dairsie beside the River Eden, 4 km east of Cupar in North-east Fife, had a thanage by about the 11th century, and there was an early water mill; its late 14th century bridge was restored in 1522. In the 16th century two castles were built, the double tower of Dairsie near the bridge, and 3 km to the north the L-plan tower of Pitcullo. Pont's map of around 1600 showed the *'Newmill of Dairsie'*, the nearby bridge and also a bridge across the Ceres Burn where it tumbled through the gorge of Dura Den at Kemback or Blebo, 1 km to the south.

**Quarrying for St Andrews**: Dairsie's interesting little church dates from 1621–22. St Andrews was largely built of stone from quarries in Blebo Craigs, 1.5 km east of Dairsie Kirk, and in Strathkinness parish 1 km farther east; this source of income may explain why, in the late 17th century, Kemback was one of only four parishes in Fife able to maintain a school. The Roy map of about 1750 showed Dairsie with its church and mill, on a loop from the route linking Cupar with Partan Craigs (Tayport); from the bridge another road, the way for stone carts, led to Strathkinness and St Andrews. Heron wrote in 1799 that *"the situation of the village of Dairsie, on the side of the Eden, is very beautiful"*.

**The New Village: Weaving and Flax Mills**: A new village some 1.5 km to the north was founded in 1790 at Dairsie Muir on the new Cupar to St Andrews turnpike, to house hand-loom weavers; initially it was called *Osnaburgh* after their first product, a coarse linen akin to that made in Osnabruck in Germany.

About then Alex Watson & Son built two flax spinning mills at Blebo on the Ceres Burn to supply them with yarn. In 1839 they built a third and larger flax mill in Dura Den, using a huge 12 m diameter water-wheel in winter and a steam engine in summer; the firm's 4500 spindles were managed by 300 workers, for whom a village of 80 houses had been built. By 1838 Dairsie gave its name to a post office, but the old village and the quarries had almost vanished.

**On and Beside the Railway**: When the new main line of the Edinburgh & Northern Railway opened in 1848, Dairsie station was built near the Lydox flax spinning mill, where in 1864 David Annan still employed about 40 people. By 1901 Dairsie also had an inn and post and telegraph office, but hand-loom weaving had faded away as factory-made linens became cheaper, and it stayed a small village. By the 1950s there was a sawmill, but the station was closed in 1954, and Dairsie became even smaller; its population shrank from around 525 in 1951 to about 425 by 1981 and its facilities also decreased to a very low level. But by 1982 the Clayton caravan park was open 1.5 km east of the pleasant village, and in 1994 the ruined tower of Dairsie Castle was fully repaired and extended as a private house. The fine old stone bridges are still in use; *Todhall House* offers accommodation.

## DALAVICH — Map 5, A4

***Argyllshire hamlet,*** *pop. 200* — OS 55: NM 9612

Midway along the narrow Loch Awe in Argyll is the tiny islet of Innis Chonnell, which in the 13th century was curtain walled to form Ardchonnell Castle, nowadays a dramatic ruin. By about 1750 tracks followed the north-west shore of Loch Awe and also led westwards from Portinnisherrich near the castle, crossing the loch by the *'Ferry of Incherry'* and passing along the south shore of Loch Avich to Kilmelford. Near their intersection at the mouth of the short River Avich was a marble quarry, reported by Heron in 1799. The ferry continued in use, but the rough hilly area was used only for grazing and hunting. From 1876 the Hutcheson steamer *Queen of the Lake* plied on Loch Awe.

**The Start of National Forestry**: In 1907 the Government Office of Woods (later renamed the Forestry Commission), bought the Inverliever estate and soon began the first major public planting scheme in Scotland, known as Inverliever Forest; ultimately, combined with Inverinan Forest to the north, it was to reach nearly 5000 ha. In 1950 the track beside Loch Awe was reconstructed from Ford to Dalavich, where there was a pier, and 37 houses were built by the Commission; the road was improved in 1957, and by 1958 a four-class primary school was open. By 1959 the 50-odd foresters had planted over 1800 ha, and three lorry loads of felled timber went daily to the Ari Mill at Strachur. By then about 200 people, 95% of them said to be from Glasgow, lived in Dalavich, which had a village hall, post office and two shops; twice a week minibuses ran to Oban and Lochgilphead. By 1981 the population was about 220 and the Commission had built holiday chalets; they also laid out the circular *'Two Lochs'* cycle routes. Dalavich post office has closed since 1996.

## DALBEATTIE & Palnackie — Map 2, B5

***Dumfriesshire town & small village,*** *pop. 4400* — OS 84: NX 8361

Butel Castle, a strong 13th century tower with walled enclosure, and a related church now a ruin, stood on the west side of the lengthy tidal creek of the Urr Water near the Solway coast of the Stewartry. As the home of Lady Devorgilla, mother of John Balliol, the castle played a part in the Wars of Succession; later known as Buittle Place, it too fell into ruin. Buittle was chartered as a burgh of barony in 1325, and in the 15th century the round Orchardton Tower was built 6 km to the south. Pont's map, made perhaps as late as 1610, showed this tower emparked. *'Butill'* then comprised a kirk, its mill 4 km to the north, and the name *'Lagann'*, which in later times appeared as two farms. There was a Laird of Dalbeattie in the 17th century, for south of the stream known as Kirkgunzeon Lane stood the *'Mill of Dalbety'*, and on the east bank of the Urr Water was the emparked *'M. Dalbety'*, M here perhaps standing for *'Mansion'*. A parish school for Buittle was founded in 1631. Roy's map made in the 1750s showed no settlement apart from Buittle Place, near which was *'Buthel'* bridge over the Urr Water, carrying the *'Low Road from Kirkcudbright to Dumfries'*. At that time Dalbeattie apparently existed only as a farm called *Little Dalbathy* .

**Industries and the Start of Granite Quarrying**: In 1780 the laird Alexander Copeland developed a water-powered mill on Kirkgunzeon Lane to manufacture paper, and short-lived textile mills also opened late in the 18th century. Heron referred in 1799 to the bridge *"lately erected, of one lofty arch"* (a replacement), for by then Dalbeattie was a *"village"*, and in addition to the paper mill had *"some rising manufactures"*, while to the east *"a mill-stone quarry is worked"*. This may have been the granite quarry that was worked in 1825 by Andrew Newall.

**Quarrying for Liverpool Docks**: At Craignair on the Munches estate a further quarry's *"extensive operations"* were commenced in 1824–25 by the Liverpool Dock Trustees, then constructing Liverpool's Princes Dock and other works. Granite building blocks were at first exported in small vessels at high tide from Craignair Bridge, and within a few months hundreds of men were employed in two quarries. In 1827 Chambers found Dalbeattie *"a village of a peculiar and striking character: the cottages are built of granite. The Water of Urr is navigable for small vessels nearly to the village"*. Dalbeattie's first post office opened about 1825; a forge for farm machinery was established in 1835, and a provender (animal food) mill soon after. A waste slip in 1832 which blocked the quarry's main working face caused a hurried move of operations to Creetown. Quarrying was soon resumed, and Dalbeattie became a police burgh in 1858; the town council immediately established a gasworks.

**The Railway and Thames Embankment**: In 1859 the opening of the Castle Douglas & Dumfries Railway through Dalbeattie enabled local granite to be sent anywhere inland, and by 1869 four quarries were in operation at Craignair, all but one worked by Newalls. The other, which had been opened in 1865 by Shearer, Smith & Co, had its own pier, was rail-connected and employed between 300 and 600 men (depending on demand) cutting blocks for London's Thames Embankment, and making pavings for export from the waste. An *"extensive polishing establishment"* then recently begun was also using quantities of red granite from Mull. In 1871–

74 Dalbeattie granite was used to line the Garvel graving dock in Greenock. A brickworks was in operation in 1869, and the paper mill, still powered only by water in 1870, was mechanised in 1876.

**The only Quarry Town**: The population in 1881 was 3800, and despite a fall to 3100 in 1891, Murray described Dalbeattie in 1894 as *"a thriving town principally dependent on the granite quarries"*, with the *"very fair" Maxwell Arms Hotel*. Dalbeattie granite blocks had gone to build many docks, and monuments, pillars and other artefacts were made of polished granite. Dalbeattie golf club was established in 1897 and laid out a 9-hole moorland course; by 1913 McGeorge of Dumfries had established a textile factory. The King George V Bridge at Glasgow, erected in 1924–28, was faced in Dalbeattie granite; but by 1930 the paper mill had closed. From 1934 Improved Road Constructions Ltd worked granite at six different levels in Craignair Hill, producing building stone, setts and chippings.

**The Munitions Factory**: The 1939–45 war saw the construction of an extensive and explosives production complex, the Edingham Cordite Factory, consisting of about fifty small scattered buildings astride Kirkgunzeon Lane, 2–3 km north-east of the town; this was managed by ICI and had its own railway system connected with the main line. By 1950 Dalbeattie was the only settlement in Scotland to have reached as high as small-town status primarily through quarrying; but the forge had closed, and the armaments complex was derelict by 1965 when the railway was closed.

**Granite Chippings, Industry and Finance**: By 1972 granite quarried at Dalbeattie was mainly crushed for use as road surfacing chips; by then other industries included a creamery, an overall factory, and a radiator manufacturer on part of the Edingham site. By 1980 a new school had been built, and caravan sites were open in the town and at the village of Palnackie near Orchardton (5 km downstream), whose tiny harbour was still active, and to whose school and post office a hotel and telephone exchange had lately been added. But Dalbeattie employment exchange had been closed by 1981. By 1986 the cinema had given up the long struggle to find viability through films and bingo, but a rather remarkable new activity to form a prominent feature in so small a town was a finance company headquarters. In 1991 the population in this little industrial town was 4400, a gain of a thousand in the past forty years, its people living largely in terraced houses – but few were quarrymen. By 1996 there was a local museum, cycle routes were open in Dalbeattie Forest, and more housing was spreading around the town, which by then had a new eastern bypass. Dalbeattie High School has a roll of about 370, the golf course now has 18 holes and the *Pheasant Hotel* provides accommodation.

## DALCROSS, Petty & Inverness Airport **Map 9, B3**

***Locality e. of Inverness,*** *pop. 275* OS 27: NH 7650

About 10 km east of Inverness is a small inlet on the south shore of the inner Moray Firth, above which stood the ancient Petty Church, the burial place of the Mackintosh Lairds of Dalcross, an estate 4 km inland. Nearby is a medieval motte. In the early 17th century a fine L-plan tower house was erected at Dalcross, and the dominating E-plan tower of Stuart Castle arose beside Petty Church. By 1750 when Roy mapped the area it was well served by roads to Inverness, Nairn and Ardersier. The medieval church was replaced on the same site in 1839 by a large new church. When the Inverness & Nairn Railway was opened in 1855, Dalcross station was placed 2 km east of Castle Stuart.

**Into the Air, Timber and Waste**: During the 1939–45 war a military airfield was built north of the station; originally known as Dalcross, it was from 1946 a stop on a Scottish Airways service between Aberdeen and Stornoway. By 1953, despite the preference of Inverness town council for a field close to the town at Longman, it had been renamed Inverness Airport. Petty church was abandoned in 1950, and Beeching closed Dalcross station to passengers about 1965. By 1977 Inverness Airport was accompanied by an industrial estate, where Pasquill Timber Engineering was making trussed rafters, and Nontox, a waste incineration plant, proposed expansion in 1990. In 1993, in addition to varied internal Scottish air services, a regular weekday flight to Manchester was resumed by Business Air. In 1994 the airport had the head office of Highlands & Islands Airports Ltd.

**Timber grows, but off the Rails**: A new subsidised rail siding was laid at Morayhill near Castle Stuart to serve the new Canadian owned works of Highland Forest Products, completed in 1985, to use 160,000 tonnes of timber a year in making Sterling Board, a structural plywood substitute. After sale to Noranda Inc the plant was renamed Norbord Highland (NH), and a 9000 m$^2$ extension was opened in 1994. Manufacturing capacity was doubled, some 70 new jobs added and an extra 200,000 tonnes of timber would be used annually, resulting in around 80 or so jobs elsewhere in the Highlands; but in British Rail's vain search for profit before privatisation, rail transport had priced itself out of NH's market. Petty Church still stood deteriorating in 1995. *Castle Stuart* offers accommodation all year.

## DALGETY BAY & Donibristle **Map 6, B5**

***S. Fife dormitory & ind. estate,*** *pop. 8000* OS 65: NT 1683

The stone-built church of St Bridget beside Dalgety Bay, on the Fife shore of the Firth of Forth, was consecrated in 1244; later work now predominates. In the 14th century Couston Castle (also known as Otterston) was erected 1 km inland of the church, shown as Dalgety Kirk on Pont's 17th century map; the castle was rebuilt about that time. West of the bay was the Donibristle estate with its castle, which in medieval times belonged to Inchcolm Abbey as the abbot's house of St Colme Priory. Shown on a Blaeu map as *'Dunsbirstle'*, it burned down in 1592. The estate was bought in 1593 by Alexander Seton, who became first Earl of Dunfermline in 1605; but he lived mainly at Pinkie.

**The Mansion of the Morays**: Later the Donibristle estate was acquired by the Earls of Moray; Donibristle House was rebuilt in 1719–23 by Alex McGill for the sixth Earl, and part was again rebuilt by William Adam in 1740 as their *"elegant seat" (Heron, 1799)*. By about 1750 the Roy map showed the Aberdour to Inverkeithing road on an inland line, and the ancient church had been abandoned for the new hilltop Kirk of Dalgety; but there was no village. From 1752 the coal-carrying Fordell wagonway passed west of the extensive Donibristle park; the hamlet of Hillend developed near its crossing of the main road. Dalgety Kirk was rebuilt about 1830–35. Chambers, writing in the 1820s, mentioned *"Dunnibrissal House, a large old white building, close upon the shore"*. The core of

Donibristle House again suffered by fire during the mid 19th century, long remaining roofless like the original church.

**The Railway and the Admiralty**: The North British Railway opened its main line beside the main road in 1890, forming the connection between Burntisland and the Forth Bridge approach; but no station was provided at Hillend, which by then possessed an inn. Donibristle had a post office by 1913, but the Donibristle estate was taken over by the Admiralty in World War I as a seaplane base. In 1939 this was reactivated as a Royal Naval Air Station, for a time served by a halt on the railway. Named HMS *Merlin*, this was a Fleet Air Arm aircraft maintenance yard until 1952; then renamed HMS *Cochrane*, it found another naval purpose, until closure in 1959. Returned to civilian use in 1961, it became the Donibristle Industrial Estate. The Marconi electronics factory was among the varied industries established there, alongside what was then the A92 trunk road *('de-trunked'* and re-labelled A921 from the late 1980s).

**Dalgety Bay as *'Exurbia'***: Dalgety Bay was planned in 1962–63 as a new settlement of private houses serving the adjacent industrial estates of Donibristle and Hillend, but also seeking to attract car commuters for Edinburgh to use the new Forth Road Bridge. Fortunately due to the congestion at Barnton and peak hour tailbacks on the bridge this environmentally absurd aim was not entirely successful, many residents preferring to commute by rail from Inverkeithing. By 1981 Dalgety Bay had become a dormitory settlement with a village centre, and was nearing 6000 population; the predominant workplace among many was Edinburgh.

**Electronics, Shopfitting and Station**: By 1977 Bourns (Trimpot) of Hillend were in electrical work; by 1993, they were making potentiometers for a worldwide market. Fortronic's striking new factory was built in 1983–84 at Donibristle Industrial Park; in 1994 owned by the multinational De La Rue, it specialised in the design and supply of electronic payment systems, in which it claimed world leadership. By 1991 there were 7860 residents, of dormitory character. For a number of years the major shopfitting factory of Havelock Europa worked for major shop-chains and banks; in 1994 together with the electronics giant AT&T they refitted entire bank branches. By 1993 Dobbie's of Edinburgh had a garden centre at Dalgety Bay. In 1993 a further large extension of housing up to Hillend was begun, and Hillend itself was bypassed.

**Marconi, Muir and More Electronics**: In 1991 Marconi Simulation (MS) opened a large research and production plant at Donibristle; remarkable success by 1993 had brought 450 jobs, of which 200 were to make new artillery *'imagers'*. By 1993 another Marconi works had become *'GEC-Marconi Avionics'*. In 1992 Rochester Instruments, makers of monitoring and alarm systems, also expanded at Hillend. A new 3700m$^2$ factory for AT&T Global Information Solutions, then at Inverkeithing, opened at the new St Davids *(q.v.)* Business Park in 1994, enabling its expansion from 100 to 250 jobs; a new restaurant opened in 1995, and a new NCR factory in 1996. Meantime in 1994–95 the wings of the ruined mansion of Donibristle were restored by Muir Homes to provide modern dwellings, and the *'A'* listed Donibristle Chapel was also saved for posterity. By 1996 Dalgety Bay had a Tesco store. After 18 years of delay, a new unstaffed station was finally opened at Dalgety Bay in 1998.

## DALKEITH, Eskbank & Newbattle — Map 15, D2

***Midlothian town***, *pop. 11,500* — OS 66: NT 3367

Dalkeith, 10km south-east of Edinburgh, stands on a ridge between the Rivers North and South Esk (a form of *Uisg*, the Gaelic for water). Its own Gaelic name, which aptly enough means *'wooded valley'*, suggests an 11th century origin. About 1km to the south was the Cistercian Abbey of Newbattle, established by David I in 1140; it is believed that the monks quarried coal from outcrops on the Esk bank as early as the 13th century. Dalkeith was first referred to in 1144 and had a castle from about that time, perched on a precipice above the Esk. It was held by the Earl of Douglas in Froissart's day (1360). Chambers heard that the castle *"in time of need was garrisoned by the inhabitants"*.

**Chapel, Mortons' Burgh and Markets**: The abbey was damaged in an English raid of 1385, but repaired; the monks sold sorted wool around 1400. From 1384 Dalkeith had a substantial chapel, an offshoot of Lasswade; Dalkeith became a burgh of barony under Sir James Douglas in 1401. The chapel became a collegiate church in 1406 and gained its own parish in 1467. The Douglas family became the powerful Earls of Morton *(see Aberdour & Thornhill)*. During the same period Dalkeith's grain and wool markets made it the key centre for the area around. Newbattle Abbey which had four appropriated churches was represented in Parliament in 1560, but then its power was stripped; likewise in 1581 Morton lost Dalkeith – and his head.

**Kerr's Abbey, Palace and Slaughterhouses**: In 1587 the abbey became the property of Mark Ker or Kerr, who turned it into a mansionhouse – was later altered on numerous occasions. In 1591 a parish school was opened and Dalkeith had been made the centre of a presbytery. In 1598 Fynes Moryson referred to the Douglas's *'Palace'*, converted from the former castle and shown emparked on Pont's map of Lothian made around 1600. Newbattle had its own school in 1617 and became a barony burgh in 1634. The road from Soutra to Edinburgh was shown crossing the North Esk at Dalkeith. In the 1690s when Dalkeith's pollable male population was nearly 1200 (three quarters that of Perth), and mainly engaged in manufacturing, the town was known for *fleshing* (i.e. slaughtering) for the Edinburgh market, and associated candle making. There was also a richer element among the population.

**Turnpikes and Mansions**: The roads to Edinburgh, Soutra Hill and Galashiels were turnpiked under an Act of 1713, and by the 18th century Dalkeith school was well regarded. Defoe admired the old abbey which had become the fine seat of the Kerrs, Marquesses of Lothian, and even more so the Duchess of Buccleuch's Dalkeith Palace, designed around 1700 by James Smith, which he called *"the finest and largest new built house in Scotland, built upon the foundation of the old castle"*. This was not strictly true, for within the mansion stood a 14th century tower that still survives. Dalkeith itself was *"a pretty large market town, spacious, and well built – great quantities of provisions from the southern countries are bought up here to be carried to Edinburgh market, and sold there"*.

**Carpets, Slated Roofs, Masons, Coaches and Coal**: As early as 1728 carpets were woven locally, and it so happened that from Dalkeith's expertise there developed the great Kilmarnock *(q.v.)* carpet industry. By 1730 a forge or *iron mill* was in operation, and brewing was recorded in 1742, using the town's existing mill for malt. As more permanent houses were built, a Dalkeith slater attained a quite large way of business by 1748. Roy's map of the early 1750s showed an extensive rectangular town, with bridges across both the Esk rivers, and nine radial roads. Regular coaches plied to Edinburgh from 1765, and in 1766 the local Freemasons built a lodge; today this is the oldest such building in the world. The Marquis of Lothian's coal pit at Newbattle was already open on a substantial scale in 1769, and another was in production west of the town at Sheriffhall by 1770. About 200 workers made broadcloths; the Dalhousie bleachfield at Eskbank was at work by 1782. Dalkeith's first post office, opened in 1776, was replaced by a new office in 1793; in 1797 two posts a day were carried between Dalkeith and Edinburgh.

**Great Market, Handsome Bridge and Early Gasworks**: The palace was described by Heron in 1799 as *"a magnificent structure, the seat of the family of Buccleuch. Dalkeith is a considerable place; it contains one very handsome street, besides lanes, and has a great weekly market for corn and oatmeal, and an annual fair for horses and black cattle. Its inhabitants may amount to four thousand. Its manufactures are a tannery, a soap-work, a candle-work, and some tambouring (embroidery). A handsome bridge has lately been built on the great road from Edinburgh to Carlisle"*. This crossed the North Esk on the line of the current A7. However, he commented *"The village of Newbottle seems to be falling fast to decay"*. In 1804 what may have been Scotland's second gasworks was established in Dalkeith – Port Glasgow held first place.

**Banking, Beer and Baron Bailie**: By 1810 the Leith Banking Company had established a branch in the town, and by 1814 John White of the Esk paper mills at Penicuik was also the owner of Dalkeith's Haughhead brewery, a long-lasting enterprise. In Chambers' opinion *" The town is a burgh of barony, under the superiority of the Duke of Buccleuch, and is therefore governed by a baron bailie of his appointment; though of late years, the management of many of the public affairs, has been vested in the hands of a committee of the inhabitants. Dalkeith, next to Edinburgh and Leith, is the most considerable town in Mid-Lothian and is remarkable for the number of its shops"* (most of which sold liquor!). Chambers continued, *"One of the greatest markets in Scotland for grain is held here every Monday and Thursday, on the latter day mostly for meal"*. Dalkeith candles were still a well-known product in the 1820s. Newbattle was a *"small village"* around the church.

**The Edinburgh & Dalkeith Railway**: A new tannery was built in Croft Street in 1835–53, and a branch of the Royal Bank was opened about 1836. By 1843 coal was brought to the town of Dalkeith on a private railway from the Dalkeith colliery near Carberry, and there was also a line from Newtongrange. From 1838 the early horse-drawn Edinburgh & Dalkeith Railway (E&DR), quaintly called the *'innocent railway'* because its promoters were at first lampooned as simpletons, carried both coal and passengers – including *'outside'* riders in stagecoach style – between Dalkeith and St Leonards (Edinburgh).

**The Waverley Route and Mining**: The E&DR was later taken over by the North British, who rebuilt it for steam traction and extended it to Hawick in 1849. Newbattle viaduct, comprising 22 arches of brick and stone, was at 365 m the longest viaduct between Edinburgh and the line's final destination Carlisle, reached in 1862 as the *'Waverley Route'*. In 1867 the Esk Valley Railway was opened to Polton from Esk Valley Junction south of Eskbank. Newbattle colliery was still open in 1869, and mills were built about that time. The 1891 population was almost 7000. In 1894 there were two hotels in Dalkeith, both traditionally named, the *Crosskeys* and *Buck's Head*. An electricity generating station was established in 1901; later the large Dalkeith colliery was sunk 2 km north-east of the town.

**College, Closures – and Concrete Boxes**: The Newbattle golf club was founded in 1934. Newbattle Abbey was gifted to the nation in 1931 by Lord Lothian, and in 1937 opened as an adult residential college. The Dalkeith branch line was closed to passenger trains in 1942, and eventually the station became the site of a bus garage. The brewery was taken over for closure in 1955, and in the 1960s some rather tasteless central area redevelopment was permitted, regrettably destroying much of Dalkeith's character, while leaving its facilities no more than those typical of a market town. Despite being the only rail route still serving Hawick and Galashiels, complete closure of the railway took place in 1969. Meantime Dobbie's large plant nurseries grew 2 km west of Dalkeith.

**Petrol Pumps and Diaries**: In 1961 an industrial estate was provided at Thornybank by the Buccleuch Estates. The electrical engineers Ferranti *(see Granton)* chose this as the site for a large complex of some 23,000 m² of laboratories and production space; in the 1970s forecourt petrol pumps were made, and by 1989 Thornybank was also the company HQ of Ferranti International. Also in the 1960s Charles Letts & Co of London, originators of printed diaries in 1812, had moved their diary printing business to a large new factory at Thornybank, to escape the restrictive practices of London print workers. Newbattle College, by then Scotland's only residential adult education centre, gained extended buildings in 1968. By 1975 a caravan site was open on the A68, 3 km east of Dalkeith.

**Modern Industry and Midlothian HQ**: In 1970 International Computers Ltd (ICL) had leased Dalkeith Palace as a software R&D centre, gradually restoring it; they expanded to a staff of 150 in 1980. The carpet manufacturers Henry Widnell & Stewart, who already had a factory at Eskbank by 1977, moved their headquarters from Bonnyrigg to Dalkeith about 1980. Dalkeith replaced Edinburgh as the headquarters of Midlothian District in 1975. In 1992 Advanced Automation Systems of Korea took over Ferranti Metrology of Dalkeith, and in 1993 were to move the operation to Livingston. In 1994 the new Memory Corporation undertook electronic research at Dalkeith Palace (its sales and marketing were in California). Watco Refrigeration and Watco Design were established in 1976–77 by Clark Watson and Jim Cameron; by 1995 the firm had grown on various local sites into an important importer, supplier and manufacturer of catering, refrigeration, and air-conditioning equipment and shop fittings, with particular connections with Italy.

**Letts Schizophrenic**: During 1989–91 a western bypass was constructed for Eskbank. At Dalkeith Letts, primarily diary producers, employed 500 people in their sole production plant; yet as this sixth generation family firm neared its bicentenary, the HQ functions remained in London. Profits being elusive, in 1992 the family arranged a deal with an American firm to print bibles on new machinery at Dalkeith. Meanwhile by 1986 a nature trail had been laid out in the Palace park, which shortly after became a country park. By 1990 the Royal Scottish Museum's Newbattle store was opened from time to time to display a historic stationary steam engine. By 1991, when the population was over 11,500, the head office of the local newspaper the *Dalkeith Advertiser* was at Bonnyrigg! Though in 1993 the former tannery in Croft Street stood derelict, in 1995 much of it was incorporated into new housing.

**Eskbank Lost – and Found**: Around 1990, Scottish Widows' computer functions moved to Melville Gate near Eskbank. Eskbank's Newbattle College was threatened with closure by the Thatcher government which cynically withdrew its grant in 1989; local authority help staved off closure until 1992, and reopening was achieved in 1995 in association with The Jewel and Esk Valley College at Portobello, one of Scotland's largest further education colleges, offering many vocational subjects. The Dalkeith area is a major educational centre: in 1997 Dalkeith High School had 727 pupils, Newbattle High 790 and St David's RC High 799. By 1996 a Tesco store was open in Dalkeith, whose housing was extending south-eastwards towards Easthouses. In 1996 Midlothian became an all-purpose local authority, further enhancing the town's importance. Borders Transport Futures pressed for the reopening of the rail line from Edinburgh to Galashiels via Eskbank. Although the Dawson Group had a Laidlaw & Fairgrieve woollen factory at Thornybank for some time, this was closed in 2000. However, by then the vast warehouse of Forrest Furnishing was sited nearby.

## DALLAS

**Map 9, C3**

***Morayshire village,*** *pop. 200*

OS 28: NJ 1252

The Kirk of Dallas, in the valley of the River Lossie 11km south-east of Forres, appeared on Pont's map of about 1600, although this did not show the 15th century keep of Tor Castle nearby, of which little remains. In 1680 the circular Dallas Lodge was built, later being known for its gardens. Roy's map, made about 1750, named the Kirktown of Dallas – in a trackless area. Roads were later laid out, the Bridge of Lossie was built and a new village was founded nearby in 1811. This had a small woollen mill (now a house), a post office by 1850 and also an inn, but having given its name to a great American city, the original Dallas remained the tiny centre of an area of farms and forests, whose population shrank from 330 in 1951 to 225 in 1981. Its post office and inn remained open in 1994, but the PO has since gone.

## DALMALLY

**Map 5, A3**

***Argyll village,*** *pop. 400*

OS 50: NN 1627

Dalmally's name means '*Pebbly Valley*', the nature of lower Strath Orchy in Argyll. It had a smithy as early as 1440, serving primitive farming needs and those of the Campbells' 15th century Castle of Kilchurn, whose imposing ruins stand on a peninsula at the head of Loch Awe some 3km to the west. Pont's map of about 1600 showed a church nearby at *'Clachan Dissert'*, but Roy named this the *'Kirk of Glen Orchy'*. By then the tiny nearby clachan of *'Dalmarly'* stood where an east–west track linking Tyndrum and Port Sonachan crossed another joining Inveraray and Bonawe; from a bridge across the River Strae another track led over the 600-metre col into Glen Noe. Duncan Ban MacIntyre, born in Glenorchy in 1724, became well known for his Gaelic poems.

**On the Road**: In 1769 Pennant who had travelled Caulfeild's *"very fine"* military road from Tyndrum, thought Dalmally a well cultivated and fertile spot, with *"a good inn near the village"*, which he called *Glenorchy* after the parish. In 1780 Lord Breadalbane had Dalmally bridge built across the River Orchy, so connecting the Taynuilt road. Heron's account in 1799 mentioned both Glenorchy and Dalmally as *"villages"*. The first Dalmally post office was opened in 1800, its mail carried via Inveraray. Lord Breadalbane had laid out many crofts along the road to the west, north of the river, in the areas later known as Stronmilchan and Edendonich. A new church was built at Dalmally in 1808.

**Steamers, Railway and Hotels**: From 1876 the Hutcheson steamer *Queen of the Lake* sailed on Loch Awe in connection with coaches from Ardrishaig, using a new pier 4km west of Dalmally. The struggling Callander & Oban Railway, opened from Tyndrum in 1877, made its temporary terminus at Dalmally Station. Road coaches extended the service, calling at the pier and continuing to Oban until the line was completed throughout in 1880, with a further station at the pier. Another steamer, the *Countess of Breadalbane*, was added in 1882 by the Earl of that name, sponsor of the *Lochawe Hotel* built near the pier in 1880–81. The hotel at Dalmally was *"very comfortable"* to Murray in 1894 when Dalmally station had a refreshment room; there were *"a P.O. and a couple of shops, numerous scattered houses and cottages, but no village"*.

**From Fresh Water to the Open Sea by Land**: The Caledonian Steam Packet Company bought the steamers in 1922. Their small Denny-built twin-screw diesel vessel, a second *Countess of Breadalbane (see Dumbarton)*, plied on Loch Awe in peacetime years from 1936 till the service ended in 1951; in 1952 she was transported by road to the Clyde for the Holy Loch run, and under other names and owners actually plied the open sea to Staffa and Iona until 1982, when she was moved to Loch Lomond *(see Balloch)*. By the mid 20th century a small cattle market was in use east of Dalmally. About 1960 the *Dalmally Hotel* was doubled in size, and Dalmally retained its station, but Lochawe didn't, despite the nearby youth hostel.

**The Cruachan Hydro Power Scheme**: The Cruachan pumped storage scheme was built some 8km west of Dalmally by the Hydro Electricity Board between 1962 and 1966. Water is retained about 365m above Loch Awe by a dam 46m tall, and fed by two 5m-diameter pressure shafts 457m long to four 100mw pump-turbines built by John Brown of Clydebank, probably the highest-head machines of this type then built. They sit in an impressive 80,000m$^3$ cavern carved deep within Ben Cruachan, accessed by a 1.1km road tunnel from the lochside road. Power is fed through underground transformers and a major substation at the foot of Glen Strae to Windyhill near Glasgow, by a 275 kV transmission line; at times of low demand for current, the flow of the whole system is reversed, and water is pumped up to the top reservoir. The scheme and its visitor centre then required some 50–60 operational staff, who also controlled smaller power stations at Nant (near Kilchrenan) and Inverawe.

**Golf at Last**: In 1981 fewer than 400 people lived in the area, including the Glenview modern estate to the east, and Dalmally's facilities were those of a small tourist village; the reopening of Lochawe station was welcomed in 1985. About 1990 the newly privatised Cruachan plant (but not Nant and Inverawe!) was transferred to Scottish Power because it covered peak load demands that the latter's nuclear stations could not meet. Refurbished in 1990–91, it remains open to visitors. By 1993 a 9-hole golf course had been laid out near the castle (and took its name). Although trains still called, the Dalmally station building stood empty and awaiting demolition. The United Auctions sheep market was still busy in 1994, and rail timber traffic had been resumed by 2000, though the youth hostel had closed. Duncan Ban MacIntyre is commemorated by a nearby hilltop monument.

## DALMELLINGTON

**Map 1, C3**

*Ayrshire large village,* pop. 4000 — OS 77: NS 4805

In medieval times Dalmellington in the deep Doon Valley 25 km south-east of Ayr was part of the wide area called King's Kyle. Pont's sketch map of about 1600 showed the valley well settled, with both Kirk and Castle, and a burgh of barony was chartered in 1607. The Roy map made about 1754 indicated a large hamlet near the end of roads from Ayr and Girvan; the road south served a mill at the outlet of Loch Doon but soon petered out into a track leading across the moors to Carsphairn. Coal pits were indicated north of Camlarg, but apparently working was not on a large scale; the name Sillyhole implies that some sinkings were overoptimistic! Woollen mills existed by 1796, though Heron in 1799 noted only a *"village"* of about 500 people; the *Cross Keys Inn* probably existed by then. In 1827 Chambers noted *"the village is large, neat, and compact, overhung by the singularly lofty motte of the undated castle, surrounded by a deep fosse"*. Dalmellington had a post office by 1838.

**Railways and Coal**: A railway from Ayr which terminated at the village in 1856 was built to serve the so-called Dalmellington ironworks at Waterside *(q.v.)*, some 5 km down the valley; there was a small locomotive shed of what soon became part of the Glasgow & South Western Railway. A company mineral line climbed around Chalmerston Hill, bringing coal down to Waterside from three shallow drift mines, and also from the remote Beoch mine which opened in 1850 and still worked in the 1890s – its site, marked by a remote engine house near Upper Beoch, being among Scotland's highest at 325 m above sea level. North of Dalmellington village the line passed the miners' rows at Craigmark pit, which raised a favourite house coal. In 1894 there were two hotels, the *Eglinton Arms* and *Black Bull*, both with boats on Loch Doon. Murray called Dalmellington *"a neat and compact village"*, but its 1901 population was under 1500. To the south was the extensive estate of Berbeth (later renamed Craigengillan) with its little-known mansion, then emparked.

**Pits proliferate and Bellsbank Housing arrives**: Dalmellington really grew with coal in the early 20th century, when several more collieries were sunk north of the village at Chalmerston and Pennyvenie *(see Hutton, 1996)*; the company built superior houses for miners at Broomknowe around 1910 and at Burnton a decade later. By 1951 only village facilities were available to serve a population of over 5000, including the detached council estate at Bellsbank to the south, which held a growing proportion of the total, including people reluctantly cleared from the friendly if insanitary miners' rows. A high-lying RC church was built above the village to modernist designs in 1961. Minnivey, a steep drift mine, was worked by the National Coal Board from 1954 to 1975; the Scottish

*Pithead gear at Pennyvenie 2/7 colliery, sunk in 1881 by the Dalmellington Iron Co, and seen here after closure in 1978. This was the last coalpit in the Doon Valley.* (JRH)

Industrial Railway Centre (SIRC) was created on its site by the Ayrshire Railway Preservation Group. By then the *Black Bull* had become the *Loch Doon Hotel*. The *Old Cross Keys Inn*, eventually used as a masonic hall, and abandoned about 1950, remarkably still stood in 1994.

**Passenger Trains depart and Pits close**: In 1964 Beeching ended Dalmellington's rail passenger services, but the line stayed open for coal from Beoch until its closure in 1968, subsequently serving only the Pennyvenie complex, the last pit in the Doon valley, where about 250 miners worked on the longwall method in 1977; until closure in 1978–79. By the mid 1980s a wood-window factory, and opencast workings near Upper Beoch, still offered a few jobs. In 1988 a loading point for this coal was opened at Chalmerston, to which the railway was relaid.

**Record Unemployment**: In 1991 if Dalmellington was disadvantaged, as shown by the struggling Doon Academy, Bellsbank's 2040 people had serious problems of poor health, plus the highest male jobless rate in Scotland at a staggering 37%. There was also the highest percentage living in council houses in Scotland, at over 95%. Bellsbank still had its own post office. In Dalmellington village, where only 1600 people lived but many owned their homes outright, the jobless rate was under half as bad. The modern RC church has been derelict for over five years. By 1998 besides the SIRC, which has a fine collection of Scottish industrial locomotives and rolling stock open to the public, another museum was open. Afforestation has clothed all the hills to the east, but a vast hilltop opencast site north of the SIRC has lately been reshaping the 400 m Benbraniachan.

## DALMUIR

**Map 15, B4**

***Urban area n-w. of Clydebank,*** *pop. 15,000* OS 64: NS 4871

Dalmuir, on the north bank of the Clyde 13km north-west of Glasgow, was shown as a small place on Pont's map, made about 1600; there had long been a ferry across the Clyde to Inchinnan. In 1747 Collins opened a paper mill on the steep Cochno Burn, which flows from the rainy Kilpatrick Hills to the Clyde at Dalmuir, but it was still only a tiny settlement on the Glasgow to Dumbarton road. The mill soon made high-quality writing, drawing and printing papers. A linen bleachfield, built between 1746 and 1760, may well have become one of the two printfields near Old Kilpatrick that were mentioned by Heron in 1799; together they employed 600 people. From 1790 Dalmuir also lay beside the new Forth and Clyde Canal, and in 1799 two paper mills were at work, continuing until at least 1832. A post office was open by 1838. In 1858 came the Glasgow, Dumbarton & Helensburgh Railway, which provided a station at Dalmuir; later it became part of the North British system.

**The Beardmore Battleship Yard**: Dalmuir held 940 people in 1891. In 1896 the Caledonian Railway opened a duplicating line. Then in 1905–06 William Beardmore & Co of Parkhead laid out at Dalmuir the biggest shipyard on the Clyde, relocating what had originally been Robert Napier's Govan and Lancefield shipyard and marine engineering works. Beardmore's was Scotland's first specialised building yard for capital ships; the succession of ever larger battleships built there during the arms race with the Kaiser's Germany included HMS *Agamemnon* (16,500 tons) in 1906, *Conqueror* (22,500 tons, 1911), *Benbow* of 25,000 tons in 1913, and *Ramillies* (29,150 tons) in 1916. A lifting bridge, opened in 1915, enabled Glasgow trams to cross the Forth & Clyde Canal; at Dalmuir West they met Dunbartonshire trams for Dumbarton and Balloch.

**Beardmore and the Aircraft Industry**: From 1913 Beardmore's also assembled aircraft in the Dalmuir area. In 1914 they erected big sheds where a total of 487 aircraft were built in 1915–18, including the BE2c, the Beardmore DFW seaplane, and flying boats. Closed for a time, the aircraft factory reopened in 1924 using the Rohrbach patent all-metal stressed-skin construction; their experimental *Inflexible* had the improbably large wingspan of almost 49m (160'). Among their last products in 1929 were two twin-engined *'Inverness'* flying boats and the passenger car for Bennie's Railplane *(see Milngavie)*.

**The Peace Dividend?**: Meantime nobody was buying battleships, and Beardmore's gun plant at Dalmuir was adapted to construct locomotives, such as 2–8–2 steam locomotives for India in 1930; but lorry and bus competition had made the railways poor, and the firm soon became overextended *(see Paisley)*. The last big naval vessel they built was the cruiser HMS *Shropshire* in 1928. With the collapse of demand for ships and locomotives in the slump, the yard was closed about 1931 as the first step in the voluntary rationalisation of the shipbuilding industry. This enabled Arnott Young & Co to open a scrapyard which broke up ships from about 1934, including in 1936 the 72-year old Govan-built steamer *Iona* and the famous paddle steamer *Columba*.

**Rearmament and Air Raids**: By 1939 Dalmuir had become extensively urbanised with houses largely built by Beardmore, as part of Clydebank Burgh, whose sewage – and that from Glasgow's northern outfall – was treated in a large works. The section of Beardmore's known as the diesel works was reactivated about 1939 during the rearmament period, but confined to making heavy armour plate and heat-treating heavy guns. It was two-thirds wrecked in the raids of 1941 *(see Clydebank)*, but recovered normal production in a month. The little-publicised Royal Ordnance Factory at Dalmuir, which employed nearly 1700 people before the air raids, was severely damaged but also soon returned to production. Turner's Asbestos sheeting works largely escaped damage, unlike the lungs of its 260 workers. The *Benbow Hotel*, at the time a men's hostel, was destroyed, and the Dalmuir West area was wrecked, but the *Regal Cinema* survived.

**Rebuilding – and scrapping Battleships**: The devastated area was hastily rebuilt by 1951. Dalmuir's population then exceeded 22,000, but enjoyed only the facilities of a large village. Beardmore's was again reduced to shipbreaking, for the scrapping of major warships resumed at Dalmuir in 1948, starting with the battleship HMS *Queen Elizabeth* of 32,700 tons; HMS *King George V*, of 35,000 tons, was dismantled at Dalmuir in 1959. Shipbreaking continued to1966; Arnott Young ceased trading in 1975.

**Electric Trains attract, but Whisky leaves the Rails**: The railway was successfully electrified in 1961, but the Glasgow trams ended in 1962. The asbestos contamination from delagged pipework and Turner's Asbestos cement works was reduced when the latter closed around 1970. About then a municipal golf course was laid out. Dalmuir station acquired a fifth platform when it became an intermediate terminal and junction for the reactivated Argyle line in 1979, but the 1981 census showed that the population had fallen to 20,500. Subsequently considerable change took place along the waterfront area, where Chivas Regal received trainloads of whisky from Keith for many years. The whole riverside freight line from Clydebank Junction was sadly out of use by the end of 1992, but its track lingered on.

**Talking up the Private Hospital**: In 1991 the population of Clydebank and Dalmuir combined was about 29,000. The asbestos-impregnated site of Turner's works was oddly chosen by Health Care International (HCI), based in Boston (USA), for a private hospital with 250 beds, aiming to treat 3000 mainly overseas patients a year. Scottish Development Agency reports on prospects were ebullient: it was claimed that a specialist industrial park would follow the new hospital, so the public purse paid the cost equivalent of 400 detached houses to clear the poor site and cap the asbestos. Although the NHS would suffer due to HCI creaming off staff, the local planning committee set aside its *'Red Clydeside'* image, and approved this Thatcherite project by a single vote, thanks to HCI's promise to create between 600 and 1800 jobs (even the pessimists were overoptimistic). The new hospital had a remarkable 21 operating theatres, and beside it was built a luxurious hotel for relatives and outpatients. Opened early in 1994, it started very slowly; late that year when only 5% usage had been attained and some NHS work had been taken on in desperation, HCI still employed 400 staff to treat about 20 patients, a situation which could not last: the banks pulled the plug on life-support and the receivers were called in. It was believed at the time that Abu Dhabi interests would buy it and aim to send 2500 Middle Eastern patients a year for heart, cancer and neurosurgery treatment. Known by 1995 as the HCI Medical Centre, the hospital was shortly to treat 300 patients from the Forth Valley Health Board, and it was on similar overflows from the Health Service that it still survives. On a brighter note, the 2001 reopening of the Forth & Clyde Canal will see vessels requiring 3 m headroom passing under busy Dumbarton Road by means of the first *'drop lock'* in the UK.

## DALNACARDOCH & Dalnaspidal — Map 5, C1

***Localities, N. Perthshire*** — OS 42: NN 7270

About 1725 a command hut was established by General Wade at Dalnacardoch in remote Glengarry, some 15 km west of Blair Atholl, where the military roads then under construction by his troops between Crieff and Perth met at an altitude of some 315 m, uniting to cross the 460 m Drumochter Pass. The Garry was bridged by his men in 1730, and in 1732 the hut became an inn, lent importance by its isolation; there was also an early post office, issued with a cancelling stamp in 1839. The inn was still open when Fontane passed that way in 1858. When the railway was built through the area in 1861–63, the station was sited 8 km to the west at Dalnaspidal *(the valley of the hospice)* – then Scotland's highest settlement; the post office transferred to there, where there was also a primary school. The inn soon became a shooting lodge. The station closed in the 1960s. The main road A9 was greatly improved in the 1920s, and radically rebuilt around 1980 with long stretches of dual carriageway; snow gates were installed at Dalnacardoch to keep motorists from venturing over the pass in severe conditions. The historic inn building was restored in 1999.

## DALRY — Map 1, C1

***N. Ayrshire town,** pop. 5700* — OS 63: NS 2949

A medieval motte stands on a spur south of the Rye Water, a tributary of the River Garnock in Cunninghame. Monkcastle and L-plan Blair Castle to the south date from the 16th century, the latter being emphasised on Pont's map of about 1600, where it was shown already emparked: both the Blair estate and the parish ran a school from 1625. *'Kalder'* stood on or near the site of later Dalry, whose development appears to date from a market chartered in 1681. Dalry *(with Stewarton)* is one of the places claimed as the birthplace in 1739 of David Dale, who did so much to mechanise the Scottish textile industry from his Glasgow base. Roy's survey in the early 1750s showed Dalry as a quite substantial place, irregularly developed between the bridges spanning the Rye Water and the Caaf Water, at the end of a road north from Saltcoats via Knockrivoch. Later in the century the large Drakemyre cotton mills were built on the Rye Water, and Heron noted in 1799 *"the village of Dalry contains upwards of 800 inhabitants, employed chiefly in the silk and cotton manufacture"*. A post office was first opened in 1807, and gasworks were set up about 1833.

**Railways, Iron and Woollens**: The main line of the Glasgow Paisley Kilmarnock & Ayr Railway was opened through Dalry in 1839, partly built by local contractors. The Blair ironworks was established in 1839 1 km east of the town, using ores from three ironstone pits around Lambridden, 2 km farther east; in 1882 a pit pony in one of them safely survived a 28-day ordeal when trapped underground by a flood. A branch railway from Blair's works and pits joined the main line south of Dalry Junction, created in 1843 when Dalry became the junction for Kilmarnock. Dalry station grew rapidly until the direct line from Glasgow to Kilmarnock via Stewarton was opened in 1873; its four platforms continued in use. By 1869 Thomas Biggart & Co owned the Bridgend woollen mills, a large 3-storey wool-combing and spinning factory with some 350 workers and 36 carding engines. The Blair ironworks made steel from 1871, and by the 1890s the small Smithstone Colliery 4 km to the south and the Coalheughglen Pit to the east were active. There was a public secondary school in Dalry from 1894, and by 1901 the population of the sprawling settlement was over 5000. Large brickworks surrounded the town.

**After the Ironworks**: The iron and steelworks, still open in 1885 and latterly owned by William Baird & Co, had closed by 1920, though the coal mine beside the River Garnock which had stayed open to feed the Lugar ironworks still employed over 100 men. The works were replaced by a 9-hole golf course, though this had closed by 1963, partly replaced by housing. The Lambridden ironstone pits and the Douglas fire-brick works – drawing raw material from the High Monkcastle clay mine – continued in operation. The population dipped, then rose again to 6600 by 1951, when Dalry had small-town facilities. The Blair 11–12 drift mine, the area's last colliery, employed about 150 men and worked from 1953 to 1969. By 1976 the secondary schools had closed.

**The Roche Plants**: The Swiss company Hoffman la Roche already had a plant in the town before their huge vitamin C works east of Drakemyre was built in 1980–83, soon employing 400 people; its main building is 550 m long. It has kept the rail connection, and an associated coal mine was opened at Girvan. Worsted was still spun at Drakemyre by Hinchcliffe's in 1983. In 1991 there was a population of some 5700 residents. Some housing development continued up to at least 1994, but by then fire had destroyed the roof of the Bridgend mill; it stood derelict in 1998. Although by 1994 its employment had fallen from 800 to 740, the Roche plant was the world's largest producer of vitamin C, and the firm's sole centre for making carotenoid (orange) food colourants, formerly made worldwide. Today, 600 are employed. The small but long-established *Dalry Inn* remains in business.

## DALRY (or St John's Town of Dalry) — Map 2, A4

***Galloway village,** pop. 500* — OS 77: NX 6281

The 11th century castle of Dundeuch was built where the Polmaddy Burn joins the Water of Ken some 40 km north of Kirkcudbright, in the remote and hilly Galloway upland known as the Glenkens. The romantic but undateable island castle of Lochinvar stood 6 km to the south east, and the L-plan tower of Earlstoun Castle was built in the 15th century 4 km south of Dundeuch. Dalry, which stands 3 km farther south on the east bank of the river, was a favoured resort of King James IV in the early 16th century. A well-settled area was mapped by Pont around 1610, by which time the Mill of *'Glenly'* stood opposite the Kirk of *'Darry'* on the west bank of the unbridged river, north of wooded *'Park'*. By then both the Black Water and the Water of Ken had been bridged near Arndarroch, 2 km east of Dundeuch. A parish school was founded in 1626. By the time of Roy's survey about 1754 the Bridge of Ken lay on the track between Moniaive and Carsphairn. Dalry was only the roadless *'St Johns Clachan'*. By 1799 however, Heron used the modern spelling of Dalry for this *"village"*, and in 1827 Chambers found a *"large parish-village"*.

**Hydro-electricity and Tourism**: The population in 1891 was 560, and although remote from railways, in 1894 it nonetheless provided the *"good" Lochinvar Arms Hotel*. The Glenlee power station (PS) of the Galloway water power scheme was built west of the river in the 1930s, fed by water impounded by the great Clatteringshaws Dam 10km south west of Dalry, and other control works; 6km to the north was the Kendoon PS and its artificial loch, and between them Carsfad PS, its loch impounded by a crescentic dam. In the 1950s, although the parish population was only 775, Dalry's remoteness enabled it to possess the facilities of an average village, including a small secondary school, an ironmonger, agricultural engineer, and legal practice. Its beautiful surroundings helped to draw custom to its two substantial hotels – the *Lochinvar*, and (1 km north) the lochside country house *Milton Park Hotel*, plus the *Clachan Inn*. The population gradually fell, and the legal firm withdrew, but Dalry retained its main facilities, and by 1980 a new Dalry Secondary School had been built (now S1-S4). By 1991 the population of the whole parish was only 497. The Southern Upland Way passes through the village, whose post office is still open; there is a new seasonal youth hostel at Kendoon.

## DALRYMPLE

**Map 1, C2**

***Ayrshire village,*** *pop. 1300*

OS 70: NS 3514

Dalrymple lies on the north bank of the River Doon, 8km south of Ayr; Barbieston just upstream once had a castle. The area was already thickly settled when mapped by Pont around 1600; however, there was no bridge to the imposing and emparked 14th century castle of Cassilis, 2 km downstream on the south bank, and Dalrymple failed to draw early travel writers. By about 1754 there was a bridge beside the kirk on the road between Ayr and Straiton, and a side road to Dalmellington; but as late as 1838 there was no post office. From 1856 Dalrymple had a station on the Ayr & Maybole Railway, but this was 1500 metres from the village. In 1891 only some 300 people lived in Dalrymple, west of which extensive waterworks were built; however, in 1951 the population was about 1175. The station was closed sometime between 1953 and 1963, and Dalrymple also lost its hotel. By 1971 the population had risen further to about 1525, with the facilities of a small village, but fell back to about 1300 in 1991. A caravan site closed, replaced by nearby housing; the post office and pub stayed open. In the strange world of repeated local government reorganisations, the conservation village of Dalrymple remains at the end of a long protrusion of East Ayrshire, almost surrounded by South Ayrshire. The *Kirkton Inn* has 11 rooms plus self-catering accommodation.

## DALWHINNIE

**Map 5, C1**

***Upper Speyside small village,*** *pop. 100*

OS 42: NN 6384

Comparatively easy routes converge from the Moray Firth via Strathspey and Glen Truim, and from Lochaber via an easy pass from Loch Laggan, to meet at the head of Glen Truim and take the Drumochter Pass (G. *Druimuachdar)* to Perth and central Scotland. By 1723 Dalwhinnie was a cattle drovers' *valley meeting point* (its Gaelic meaning). Being very bleak, at the high altitude of over 350 metres, a necessary inn was established; on one August day in 1723, eight droves comprising over 1200 beasts passed through Dalwhinnie en route to Crieff. The long deep gash of Loch Ericht, which leads south-westwards, has never found any real significance as a route.

**The Military Roads Meet**: Glen Truim was followed by the military road then being built by General Wade's men from Dunkeld to Inverness, and Dalwhinnie bridge was built across the River Truim about 1728. The construction teams met at Dalwhinnie in 1729, so completing after a primitive fashion the route that is now the A9. North of the inn was the divergence of the General's Corrieyairack Pass road via Laggan. The strategically placed inn was improved in the 1760s by the Commissioners for the Forfeited Estates; Elizabeth Grant found it *"good"* in 1812, when it stood alone. Highland clearances virtually ended the droving trade, and the dangerous Corrieyairack Pass road was abandoned as a route for regular traffic in 1827. Dalwhinnie remained as a small roadside settlement, where in 1858 Fontane found the old tree-girt inn had a walled kitchen garden; later it became the *Dalwhinnie Hotel*.

**The Railway, Desolation and Distilling**: The Inverness & Perth Junction (later Highland) Railway's main line was opened in 1863, its Drumochter summit south of Dalwhinnie becoming the highest point on any main-line railway in Britain, at 452m. The crossing station at Dalwhinnie then became a collecting point for sheep to be taken south by rail. Murray in 1894 called this remote village a *"desolate and solitary spot, protected by a few fir-trees from the cold winds"*, though the *Dalwhinnie Hotel* provided *"good comfortable angling quarters"*. A distillery built in 1897–98 bore the misnomer *Strathspey* in 1902, later taking the village name. It was acquired by an American company in 1912 – hardly in anticipation of Prohibition – and in 1926 fell to DCL. It was seriously fire-damaged in 1934, but reopened in 1938. With the growth of road traffic and winter sports the *Grampian Hotel* was built in the 1930s, and eventually the older hotel was renamed the *Loch Ericht*.

**Developing Hydro Power: the Tummel/Garry Scheme**: The Hydro Electricity Board's complex and extensive Tummel/Garry scheme was begun in 1945. Water diverted from the Edendon Water into Loch an Duin on the headwaters of the River Tromie (in the remote Gaick Forest, over the hills 13km east of Dalwhinnie), was augmented by further diversions enabled by two weirs and a dam, then sent westwards through a

*Dalwhinnie distillery, built in 1897–98 (at the height of the 1890s whisky boom) by the Strathspey Distillery Company Ltd. It was the first distillery to become American-owned.* (JRH)

tunnel to Loch Cuaich. From there it fed through another tunnel to the Cuaich power station, 4 km east of Dalwhinnie distillery, and then passed down an open aqueduct at an altitude of 365 m to Dalwhinnie and Loch Ericht. To the south, Loch Garry was dammed and its waters diverted from Glen Garry through a 7.5 km tunnel to the Loch Ericht power station on the south shore of Loch Ericht. Its exit towards Loch Rannoch, 25 km south-west of Dalwhinnie, was raised with a dam supplying yet another power station *(see Rannoch Station).*

**An Urban Village**: Some new houses were built to serve these developments. Otherwise in 1978 Dalwhinnie consisted of little more than the station, a garage, a large transport cafe, shop and the distillery; the two hotels had lost their 1950s AA stars before the A9 bypass was built about that time. By then (and up to the present) James Buchanan & Co sold Dalwhinnie's single malt whisky at 15 years old. Dalwhinnie had 110 or so residents in 1981. In the 1990s afforestation beside Loch Ericht and to the north reduced the utter desolation of the moors to the north; but beside the Wade bridge to the south is a snow gate, installed to prevent incautious travellers perishing on Drumochter Pass. Outwardly little has changed, the active distillery with its visitor centre (opened in 1992) being well kept; the station, the *Loch Ericht Hotel* and – until recently – the post office remained open.

## DARVEL

**Map 2, A2**

***Ayrshire village,*** *pop. 3750* — OS 71: NS 5637

A first century Roman fort near the conspicuous crag of Loudoun Hill had an unusually large granary, being on a route linking these two grain growing areas. In 1307 the Roman road, still embanked across a bog on the Ayrshire and Lanarkshire border, played a part in the Battle of Loudoun Hill, as described by Barbour. An ancient earthwork adjoins the 15th century keep of Main Castle, 3 km to the south. Darvel, 4 km to the west near the head of the River Irvine, was a mere placename on Pont's map of about 1600; but a whole row of mills led down to Newmilns, 3 km to the west. Darvel was ignored by early literary travellers, but the Roy map made about 1754 showed a tiny settlement astride the valley road.

**From Hand Weaving to Lace Curtains**: Darvel developed in handloom weaving, Heron describing it in 1799 as a *"manufacturing village"* with 60 weavers. Though it had not so much as a post office by 1838 it grew and prospered, survived the collapse of handloom weaving as factories took over, became a police burgh in 1873 and gained a gasworks. The manufacture in Scotland of lace on power looms was begun at Darvel in 1875–76 by Alexander Morton, who brought in a lace-making machine from Nottingham. Stirling, Auld & Co's first factory had meantime been at work from 1877; a second dated from 1881, and Jamieson built a lace and *madras* factory from 1886; but Darvel was ignored by Murray's 1894 Handbook, although it was by then a place of over 2000 people.

**The Railway and Penicillin**: In 1896 the Newmilns branch of the Glasgow & South Western Railway was extended to Darvel, and in 1905 linked eastwards to the Caledonian system and Strathaven. Aird's lace factory was built in 1896; the combined firm of Morton, Aird built yet another lace factory in 1899, and a bleachworks was constructed in 1903. Darvel later also became known for carpet manufacture, the little town's main development occurring before 1930. Alexander Fleming, born at Lochfield Farm north of Darvel in 1881, first observed the action of penicillin in 1928, and named it, but he left its useful development to Florey, Chain and others who shared his Nobel prize. In 1948 Darvel had a population of about 3500, the facilities of a large village and as many as 19 lace and madras factories; but many of these closed during the next 20 years.

**Decline and Stabilisation**: The railway, closed to passengers in 1964, had been lifted by 1970, and Darvel later lost its secondary school and cinemas. The 1903 bleachworks had been derelict for many years when burgh status was lost to Kilmarnock & Loudoun District in 1975, but in 1976 Basford Dyers, Smith & Archibald, the Bonfab and Glen mills, and Stirling, Auld & Co – makers of lace and hosiery – were all still in business. About 35 shops including clothing and jewellery, four pubs and a range of some 20 other outlets served most basic needs. The *Covenanters Hotel*, open in 1980, later closed; it was approved for demolition in 1990. Morton Young & Borland, saved from closure in 1970 by American orders, still made terylene net products in 1983. Darvel's textile industries no longer included carpets, but flourished in the 1980s in such fields as tartans, terylene table covers, woollen hosiery and also textile machinery. In 1990 the lacemakers Smith & Archibald were successfully selling to the USA. Remarkably, by 1991 Darvel had grown to a population of 3760, and had a tourist office; a hotel was still open to the west.

## DAVIDSON'S MAINS, Blackhall, Craigleith & Muirhouse

**Map 15, B1**

***N-W. suburbs of Edinburgh*** — OS 66: NT 2075

By 1511 the first of several sandstone quarries was open at Ravelston some 5 km west of Edinburgh; nearby was an area of excellent farmland, dominated by the 16th century tower of Lauriston and the 17th century Craigcrook Castle. By 1616 a quarry was open at Craigleith, between the castles and the city, and the Maidencraig sandstone quarry at Blackhall was open by 1628. The road from the West Bow of Edinburgh to Cramond Brig, already established in Pont's time around 1600, was soon met by a road from Dean at a place crudely known as *Muttonhole*, where a smithy was open by 1669. In the next year the mansion of Muirhouse was built on the shore of the Firth of Forth some 1.5 km north of Muttonhole, which by the time of Roy's survey about 1754 was a distinct hamlet. In 1776 Muirhouse was acquired by the Davidson family, and eventually the rustic Muttonhole became the respectable Davidson's Mains. Maidencraig quarry worked until around 1800, but by 1855 was flooded.

**Craigleith Quarry prospers, and declines**: In 1795 the fine white sandstone from Craigleith quarry was used to face buildings on the north side of Edinburgh's Charlotte Square. The stone was hard and difficult to dress, but was also used in 1810, to build the top stories of the Bell Rock lighthouse, completed that summer, and in the old building of Edinburgh University. The quarry was at its busiest in the 1820s, when Craigleith stone was hauled down Ferry Road to Leith docks, for export to build the Episcopal cathedral in Aberdeen, and Waterloo Bridge in London. About 1823 the new Queensferry Road bypassed Davidson's Mains, which developed little until a church was built there in 1843 for some dissenters from Cramond; a post office was open by the 1860s. Stone from

Craigleith quarry was later used mainly to make steps, and in 1869 Bremner noted that it had been *"worked out to a great depth"*. The Craigcrook quarry was worked at certain times; Redhall quarry was open by 1850, its free sandstone being used in building Edinburgh's Heriot Row. The Ravelston quarry was still working in the late 1860s, but later many of these great holes filled with water.

**Attempts at Suburban Development**: In 1861 the Caledonian Railway (CR) opened a freight branch to Granton harbour, passing west of Craigleith quarry and the straggling line of large institutions which already demarcated central Edinburgh. These extended from Donaldson's Hospital to the poorhouse which later became the Western General Hospital. In 1879 the Craigleith passenger station was opened on this line, but had failed to stimulate development by 1894, when – apart from Davidson's Mains which by then had a post office and an inn – the area was still rural. At that time Craigleith quarry had 91 workers, but later its working was intermittent.

**The Railway fails but Golf succeeds**: In 1894 CR hope triumphed over experience, and a further short branch was opened from a junction at Craigleith to stations at Barnton Gate (soon renamed Davidson's Mains) and Barnton. Bruntsfield Links golf club moved in 1895 to a course in Barnton Park. Lauriston Castle, enlarged in the 19th century by a wealthy industrialist, was donated to the city about 1910; its grounds became a public park, and the castle a museum including vases and other artefacts made from Derbyshire *'Blue John'* fluorspar. A second quarry worked north of Craigleith, about 1900–1940. The Ravelston quarries employed 28 in 1920, but closed after 1939. The 9-hole Ravelston golf course was established in 1912, offering an inexpensive round. The independent St George's High School for Girls was built at Ravelston early in the 20th century. Otherwise apart from a few schemes – such as the 1935 mansion flats in Ravelston Gardens – low and medium density residential building predominated in this general area, which was extensively developed along a Corporation bus route through Blackhall, extending as far as Silverknowes by 1939.

**Postwar Suburbanisation**: The municipal golf course at Silverknowes was laid out in 1947, the Granton to Cramond foreshore being dedicated as a public park. By 1949 Craigleith quarry had reached a depth of 110m, but was disused. In 1951 the area's population was about 22,250. Cars and buses had not only inhibited tramway construction but led to the early loss of the area's rail services; the Barnton line closed in 1951, Davidson's Mains lost freight services in 1960 and Craigleith station went in 1962. Various estates infilled the remaining rural areas, rapidly raising the population, among them the Muirhouse scheme comprising over 2400 mediocre flatted council dwellings, built in the 1950s and 60s. Meantime the Mary Erskine School took over Ravelston House, and in 1968 the Royal High School was relocated from London Road to East Barnton Avenue; the area's population peaked around 1971 at about 39,000.

**College, Hotels – and the Workless**: The Telford College of Further Education was built at Crewe Toll about 1971. By 1972 the site of the former Craigleith station was adjoined by the 120-room *Esso Hotel*, one of several built in western suburbs towards the airport; it later became the *Crest Hotel*. Meantime by 1981 the area's population was down to about 35,000, and only odd sites remained to be developed. Between 1981 and 1991 Muirhouse lost a third of its population and its rate of unemployment doubled to a depressing 28%; only one in 8 of its dwellings was owner-occupied by 1994, when a plan for action was agreed between interested parties.

**Managing Distilleries, Salmon Farms and Students**: In 1991 Craigcrook Castle was the headquarters of the salmon farmers Marine Harvest. A&E services were controversially withdrawn from the Western General Hospital in 1991. However, in 1992–93 Sainsbury built a 6500m² superstore on the infilled site of Craigleith quarry – leaving a small face exposed – adjacent to the new Craigleith Retail Park. St George's has about 850 on the roll, the Mary Erskine School for Girls 660; city council secondaries are the Royal High School (1100) pupils, and Craigroyston (400). By 1995 Telford College had become one of the largest further education centres in Scotland, with 800 staff and 15,000 students. By 2000 the former *Crest Hotel* had become the *Holiday Inn Garden Court*!

## DAVIOT — Map 9, B4

***Location s-e. of Inverness*** — OS 27: NH 7239

The ancient Dun Davie and a nearby cliff fort above the River Nairn about 7km south-east of Inverness were replaced by the 15th century keep of Daviot Castle, which eventually fell into ruin, itself replaced by Daviot House. General Wade's military road crossed the Nairn about 2km above the nearby Daviot church, but Telford's road, built nearly a century later, came much closer. The road to Stratherrick was probably complete by 1832 when Farr, some 7km farther up Strathnairn, had a post office. By the late 19th century Daviot had a mill, post and telegraph office, inn and smithy.

**Through Traffic conquers All**: For over a year in 1897–98 while the great Nairn Viaduct was under construction to the north, the newly built Daviot station – an inconvenient 2km from the little village – was the northern terminus of the Highland Railway's shortened main line between Aviemore and Inverness. Daviot later acquired a primary school, and the inn was replaced by a 12-roomed hotel. When Beeching closed Daviot station in 1964–65, its accompanying post office was not moved to the village but closed. By 1978 a large quarry was open, providing materials for the sweeping dual carriageways of the new A9, completed about 1980. By then little else but the church and school remained.

## DEANS — Map 16, C3

***Village / suburb of Livingston*** — OS 65: NT 0268

Timothy Pont's map made about 1600 as engraved by Hondius and Blaeu showed the Bathgate to Broxburn road, south of which the name *'Dens'* appeared with a symbol larger than most ferm touns were awarded; but for over a century after the time of Roy's survey the area remained entirely rural. In 1849 the Edinburgh & Bathgate Railway was opened roughly parallel to but well south of the road, at an altitude of almost 150 metres. A country station named Livingston was provided where the line crossed a side road 5km east of Bathgate, but it was about 2.5km from Livingston village by road, and attracted no development. In 1894 Deans was still a farm 1km west of the station, which was surrounded by shelterbelted farmland.

**Oil Works make a Settlement**: Oil shale mining and processing began in the area in 1883, but the main development of oil shale works by the Pumpherston Oil Company took place in 1903–08; the company built 120 good houses north of the station, at a location previously called Upper Barracks (barracks were granaries in Anglian usage), but taking the name Livingston Station. Though substantial, with a red-brick Institute (a public hall with library), and later a school, it seems not to have reached a population of 1000. Deans farm was obliterated by the bing which overshadowed the village. The oil works and station closed by 1953. The works was later demolished, but the line remained open for goods trains. The school closed in 1966.

**The impact of the New Town**: By 1971 the M8 had been opened, passing north of the village, and with the coming of Livingston New Town – designated in 1962 – industrial estates were laid out on either side of the motorway. The village had been renamed Deans before 1975, when it was linked by road to the New Town. Gilbey Vintners, blenders of *'Spey Royal'* whisky by 1938, had moved into Deans by 1977, and the firm of Trunk Trailer was building vehicles there for export. Deans Community High School was built in the mid 1980s; by 1997 it had 762 pupils. With the reopening of the Bathgate railway line to passengers in 1986, the new Livingston North station was opened, some 1200 m east of the original site. By 1989 Torwood Homes were making timber kit houses. By that time Deans appeared as merely part of the sprawling mass of the rather characterless new town.

**NEC beats Japanese Productivity**: In 1982 the Nippon Electric Company of Japan – trading as NEC Semiconductors (UK) Ltd – began the production of chips in the largest Japanese-owned factory in Scotland, at the rapidly expanding industrial estate called Deans West. They were continuing to invest in the plant in 1992, when it was breaking the productivity levels achieved in both Japan and the USA. By 1994 NEC employed 900 people at Deans, and claimed to be the only plant in Europe to combine both wafer fabrication and semiconductor assembly. They then announced their intention to build a new plant to employ a further 430 people. In 1993 Galtronics UK of Deans was making antennas for mobile phones. Another major scheme at Deans in 1995 was the 31 ha Starlaw business park, created by Lothian & Edinburgh Enterprise. By 1998 a minor road had been upgraded as the A779 and connected to the M8 west of Deans to provide a western access to Livingston. North of it is a cycle path, which passes the site where Barracks no longer stands. The old school is now a youth centre and the Institute a community centre. NEC announced yet further expansion plans in 2000, making 1600 jobs in all.

## DEANSTON — Map 5, C4

***Perthshire village**, pop. 375* — OS 57: NN 7101

Deanston on the River Teith near Doune began as a small late 18th century new village planned by Buchanan and Arkwright, serving the large and imposing Adelphi cotton spinning mill, designed by Arkwright and built in 1784–85. Heron wrote in 1799 of a *"village inhabited chiefly by the labouring people belonging to the Adelphi Cotton-work, where upwards of nine hundred persons are employed"*. James Smith, born in this place in 1789, made the innovation of tile drainage in 1823, since so important in agricultural improvement. Meantime the large emparked Lanrick Castle 3 km west of Deanston was built about 1790 for the Haldanes. In 1820–27 the mill was rebuilt

*Deanston cotton-mill, which closed in the early 1960s but was converted into a distillery in 1966 by the Deanston Distillery Co Ltd (and is still in production). The mill building seen here dates from about 1827.* (JRH)

with new water wheels, and became so large that it had its own foundry.

**From Textiles to Whisky**: The same water wheels were still turning in the 1940s, and textile manufacture was continued by James Finlay & Son who made towels. The mill was enlarged in 1950, but closed in 1965. Lanrick Castle was abandoned in 1964, ruinous by 1993 and destroyed by fire in 1994. Deanston had remained a small village, with 360 people in 1971. Meantime in 1965–66 the mill was uniquely converted by a subsidiary of the same firm into the Deanston Highland malt whisky distillery; in 1976 this had the enormous annual capacity of 3.4 million litres – as much as seven or eight of the Campbeltown distilleries of the 1880s. In 1982 the distillery was closed by the Invergordon group; acquired and reopened in 1990 by the Barrhead blending firm of Burn Stewart, who added a by-product plant. It was in full production in 1994 and – like many others – still produced problematical effluents, as well as the Deanston single malt newly offered by Invergordon.

## DECHMONT & Bangour Hospitals — Map 16, C3

***W. Lothian communities**, pop. 800* — OS 65: NT 0470

The Pont map of around 1600 marked the Newbridge to Bathgate road; beside it were settlements at Dechmont and Bangour. By 1895 Dechmont House had been built 4 km south-west of Uphall; a smithy and hamlet named Dechmont stood midway between the two. In 1898–1906 the Edinburgh District Lunacy Board built Bangour Asylum as a series of dispersed architect-designed ashlar-faced villas west of this point; at one time these housed 3000 patients. From 1905 this was linked to the North British Railway west of Uphall Station by a private railway, with a goods and passenger station at the hamlet of Dechmont.

**A General Hospital in Huts**: The Asylum lost its railway in the 1920s and was later renamed as Bangour Village Hospital. From about 1940 it was accompanied by the huge hutted Bangour General Hospital, built on its western side as a wartime precaution to treat city air-raid patients. By 1954 Dechmont had begun to grow as a settlement, and had a post office, primary school, garage and large telephone exchange. By 1971 the M8 had been opened south of the old road; the two hospitals still held nearly 2500 people, and Bangour General Hospital was still fully functioning in the 1970s, but it became redundant with the opening of St Johns Hospital at Livingston in 1989. In 1991 Dechmont's census figures of 1255 were still greatly inflated by 415 hospital residents, resulting in Scotland's highest proportion of women over 60. The General Hospital site had been cleared by 1998 (for sale in 2001), and the Village Hospital – which was already in the process of being vacated in 1995 – was to close by the end of the century, threatening the future of some interesting listed buildings.

## DEERNESS & Toab — Map 13, C2

***Orkney communities**, pop. 750 (area)* — OS 6: HY 5605

An important Pictish broch now known as Dingieshowe guarded the narrow sandy isthmus connecting the fertile and gently graded Deerness peninsula with the Orkney mainland; the enigmatic Iron Age mound of Mine Howe contains a unique corkscrew chamber. Beside a sandy bay on the east coast – the easternmost Orkney landfall for Viking longboats – was a Norse settlement named Skaill, and an early monastery stood 2 km farther north at the Brough of Deerness. In the 11th century a major church – St Andrews – was built with two round towers, but the peninsula then faded into insignificance except for farming based on its good arable land, and eventually the minor village centre of Deerness moved 3 km westwards. In the 1950s St Andrews School near the post office of Toab at Foubister, 2.5 km west of the isthmus, provided junior secondary education for the area, but by 1976 was primary only. By 1997 this and other rural schools, including Deerness, had been replaced by a new community primary school 500 m farther west. A community hall, store, filling station and post office remain in bleak and treeless Deerness, which raises barley, cattle and sheep. A new museum near the monastic site also encourages visitors to see the Mull Head nature reserve and the narrow chasm of a collapsed sea cave, the Gloup – pronounced like *soup*!

## DENHOLM — Map 3, B4

***Borders village**, pop. 600* — OS 80: NT 5618

When Denholm was sketched by Timothy Pont about 1600 it was already a substantial village in Cavers parish; Bedrule, an ancient parish 3 km to the east in the valley of the Rule Water, has a motte, but never developed beyond a rural role. The Roy map surveyed in the early 1750s showed Denholm as an informal square, through which ran the area's only road, linking Hawick with Jedburgh. In 1799 Heron simply referred to Denholm as a *"village"*, but about that time it was re-planned more formally around a spacious green and by 1802 there was a 3-storey stocking mill, still at work in 1844 when it contained 87 knitting frames.

**Learning, Quarrying and Designer Knitwear**: Meantime John Leyden, born locally in 1775, had become a distinguished oriental scholar, and the local education must have been excellent, for Sir James Murray, born in Denholm in 1837, edited the *New English Dictionary*, a massive task. From 1818 to 1870 a quarry was open 1.5 km south of the village. In 1864 a bridge was built across the Teviot. The stocking industry died out about 1900, the mill becoming a private house. Denholm's nearest railway station at Hassendean was 3 km north-west of the village; it too died in the 1960s with the Waverley route. By the 1950s Denholm was a village of almost 800 people, with the *Cross Keys Inn* and a small all-age school, whose secondary classes had been moved elsewhere by 1976, leaving the facilities of a small village. About 1975 Tom Scott began to make designer knitwear, and by 1990 employed some 20 people in this very pleasant place, which by 1991 had only 591 residents. Denholm retains its *Cross Keys Inn* and sub-post office; Scott is now listed as a retailer.

## DENNY & Dunipace — Map 16, A2

***Towns west of Falkirk**, pop. 13,500* — OS 65 & 64: NS 8182

A hill fort stands above the Carron Glen some 10 km west of Falkirk, and nearby Castlerankin dates from the 12th or 13th century. In 1309 the barony of Denny in the valley to the east was one of ten in Scotland owned by the Priory of Torphichen (*q.v.*). Denny had a mill by 1539, shown as a *'Milton'* beside a bridge across the River Carron on Pont's map of about 1600; Denny Kirk also appeared, and just to the north was the 16th century Herbertshire House at Dunipace. The Roy map of about 1754 showed Denny as a substantial linear village on an east–west axis, south-east of the bridge; five roads radiated from it, including one southwards to *'Turnpike Loanhead'* where it met the winding road from Falkirk to Kilsyth.

**Money from Old Rope**: Paper was manufactured, probably from around 1775, but in 1797 neither place possessed a fair, or a carrier to Edinburgh. In 1799 Heron noted in the parish of Dunipace *"a printfield and manufactory for spinning cotton"* but did not name Denny. In 1803 a post office was opened, and to Chambers in 1827 Denny was a *"village"*. By the late 1830s Grays were milling logwood for dyes, and in 1841 the paper mill employed 25 hands making board from old ropes – these being traditionally valueless, did they get their raw materials free of charge?

**Railway, Coal, Iron and Water**: In 1858 a branch of the Caledonian Railway was opened from Larbert junction to Denny, and extended west to Stoneywood in 1860. By then Wordie & Co had a rail cartage depot, soon quite important, with 16 horses in 1861. The Denny foundry started in 1870; among its products were cast-iron fountains. Police burgh status came in 1877, and a gasworks was provided. By 1894 Denny was a *"small manufacturing town"*; both Denny and Dunipace had inns. Rail-connected coal pits – two at Castlerankin and one near Quarter House – were soon closed. The first two must have been shallow workings, for it was found possible by 1895 to create a reservoir – now known as Little Denny – only a few hundred metres to the south; the Drumbowie reservoir was added early in the 20th century.

**More Coal, Iron and Paper**: In 1905 an electric power station was built, the Duncarron foundry was started around then, and by the 1920s the new small Herbertshire colliery was open near the station. The Carrongrove paper works and coating factory opened in 1924, apparently incorporating the old board mill. Among 20th century foundrymen were Cruickshank & Co of

*Carrongrove paper factory at the long-standing papermaking town of Denny; it is still going today. The beaters seen here converted paper pulp and esparto grass into the watery suspension of short fibres from which paper is made.* *(Falkirk Museums)*

the Denny Ironworks and George Paul & Co (later Paul & Maclachlan); the Comelybank Foundry made manhole covers. At nationalisation in 1947 the colliery was working steam coal, anthracite and the poor quality Upper Hirst coal. By 1953 the grounds of Herbertshire House had become a housing estate, and the population was almost 7000. The station had closed to passengers, but the mine was still open; two cinemas augmented the facilities of a large village.

**The Motorway and Glasgow Overspill**: The heavy road traffic between Glasgow and north-east Scotland which wound through the village on the A80 was bypassed by the M80, built in the mid 1960s. About 1960 it was agreed that 500 houses should be built near Denny for Glasgow overspill, to offset local decline. The goods trains ceased to run in 1965, and the Herbertshire colliery had closed by 1971. Between 1971 and 1975 an internal bypass was built round the old town, but rapidly became engulfed by peripheral growth, which included the new Denny High school. Clares Carlton Clothing made workwear from 1974 to 1980, when a lost contract caused closure and about 100 jobs were lost; however, by 1980 a branch of Havelock Manufacturing produced clothing at Denny. James Seddon's clothing factory was closed in 1990; around that time Machan Engineering made reproductions of historic pillarboxes.

**Improving the Mills**: By 1975 the rail connection to the Carrongrove paper mills had been lifted, though they remained large, then employing about 450 people, and the SDA were helping Inveresk to modernise and expand them. Work began in 1979 to restore an area of disused coal bings, rail sidings and sandpits. Both cinemas and the tiny cottage hospital had closed by 1980, but other facilities had increased to small-town level, with three hotels. The Vale Board Mills and both foundries still operated. In the 1980s Denny continued to develop southwards as far as the M876. By 1991 the youngish population of Denny was over 11,000 and of Dunipace 2420.

**The Return of the Salmon**: Carrongrove Mill opened a secondary treatment plant for its effluent in 1991, and salmon then returned to the river after a century of absence. It employed 225 producing paper board for labelling and packaging, and exporting over half its output of *'Gemini'* coated board. With a doubling of pulp prices in 12 months, and falling coal prices, the firm planned in 1995 to recommission a steam turbine, unused for 15 years. Meantime in 1993 Scottish Conservation Projects opened a recycling centre for the Central Region with government support, but six months later dumping of waste paper by Germany caused very low prices for local waste paper, threatening its future. Though the foundries have all closed, Denny remains a substantial industrial town with little of tourist interest.

## DERVAIG

**Map 4, B1**

***Isle of Mull community,*** *pop. 80* OS 47: NM 4352

This area at the head of the sheltered Loch a'Chumhainn in north-west Mull has standing stones and ancient forts; it was still well settled when mapped by Timothy Pont about 1600. Modern Dervaig began as a pleasant one-street farming village of 26 houses, built in 1799 by the MacLeans of Coll, close to the kirk of Kilmore. Later a very sinuous road was built to Tobermory, and an unusual church with a round tower was designed by Peter Chalmers. By 1951 Dervaig had a post office, a tiny hotel and a primary school, but only 70 or so people. The Mull Little Theatre with its mere 38–40 seats was founded in 1965–66 by the Hesketh s, determined optimists, and still survives in use. By 1975 Dervaig had a Forestry Commission sub-office, plus by the 1980s a crofting museum and a second small hotel. Sea angling and boat trips to Staffa were operated from Croig, 5 km to the north-west off the Calgary road. In 1985 Dervaig had a craft shop, newsagent/coffee shop, a large public hall with film shows, a chocolate company, some new bungalows and about 10 A-frame holiday houses. By 1996 forest trails had been laid out; the local facilities remained intact. Small hotels include the *Drumnacroish*, the much-praised *Druimard* (a Victorian villa beside the *Little Theatre*), and the *Bellachroy*.

## DESKFORD

**Map 10, B1**

***Banffshire hamlet,*** *pop. 150* OS 29: NJ 5061

Deskford, nestling in its own valley inland from Cullen in Banffshire, was an ancient settlement, with an interesting kirk of 1551 and a burgh of barony charter dating from 1698. When Roy surveyed the area about 1750, Deskford Kirk stood in a trackless area, but a bleachfield set up about 1752 was the basis for founding a new village about 1760. The Kirktown of Deskford remained a mere hamlet, but nearby Berryhillock gained a corn mill around 1800. The bleachfield failed in 1821, the post office at Berryhillock arrived after 1838, and the agricultural parish was never on a railway. By the 1950s its 415 people were served by the post office and a secondary school for 100 pupils; but depopulation took hold, and the school was closed by the 1970s. By 1991 the parish population was only 158 and about then the post office closed. The old school is now a community centre, but both the ancient church and the characterful old mill are sadly derelict.

## DINGWALL

**Map 9, B3**

***Town, Easter Ross,*** *pop. 5600* OS 26: NH 5559

At the head of the Cromarty Firth is Dingwall, whose Scandinavian name means *'Parliament in the Valley'*. Its little-used Gaelic name of *Inverfeoran* refers to the mouth of the little River Peffery, which leads by an easy pass into Strath Conon and so to the west. Dingwall, alleged birthplace of Macbeth, had a thanage from about the 11th century, was chartered in 1226–27 as a Royal Burgh and by 1259 had a castle, shown on the map by Matthew Paris. About 2 km to the north is the 13th century keep of Tulloch Castle, now a hotel.

**The Sheriffdom of Ross**: From 1265 Dingwall was the caput of the sheriffdom of Ross, a vast and trackless area extending across the whole of northern Scotland and the Minch to include Lewis, but ludicrously intermixed with the then county of Cromarty *(q.v.)*. Dingwall was located on very shallow water and did not thrive as a port; some time after 1306 its judicial role was temporarily ceded to the Sheriff of Inverness. Early travel writers and medieval documents appear to say little about the place, but the castle still existed in 1400 when the earldom of Ross was held by the rebellious Lords of the Isles. Dingwall became dysfunctional as a Royal Burgh, paying no tax in 1535–56; however by 1569 a very early parish school was open. Although in 1621 a small sum was made over in Customs dues, in 1639 Dingwall ranked 43rd among Scottish burghs in tax yield (about 2% of Aberdeen's trade). Blaeu's map – based on work by Pont and Gordon – implies that there was no bridge at Dingwall by 1654, and there was no depiction of substantial settlement. At the time of Thomas Tucker's tour of Scotland in 1655 Dingwall was apparently not worth mentioning as a port; in fact it had no real harbour until the 1720s.

**Recovering in Isolation**: By 1749 master linen spinners were busy in Dingwall, which by 1755 had a linen merchant and a post office. The Roy map of about 1750 showed Dingwall as a substantial one-street town on the High Street axis; but it had no approach roads apart from a single trackway. This started at a marked ford near Maryburgh a short way to the south, appeared to ford the River Peffery, then followed the coast north-eastwards, so leading to Tain and the north; it also connected at Invergordon with the Inverbreackie ferry, which gave access to the east and south of Scotland via Balblair and Chanonry. A ferry plied across the firth to Alcaig from the late 18th century until the 1930s. Dingwall was a post town by 1797, and according to Heron in 1799 had *"about 700 inhabitants. Some linen-yarn is here manufactured; and there is a lint-mill in the neighbourhood of the town"*.

**Dirty Dingwall goes to Law**: Dingwall was connected by road to the rest of Scotland on the completion of the Lovat Bridge over the River Beauly in 1814 and the Conon Bridge at about the same time; a wharf was also built to Telford's design, the river being canalised to give access from tidewater. According to Chambers in 1827 Dingwall was generally less important than Tain, but *"a perfect nest of lawyers; a town which is rather neat, and built in the Dutch fashion and possesses a small harbour. The only fault of Dingwall is its filthiness, every house being provided with its dunghill in front"*. By then Dingwall's medieval castle had vanished; near the shore the former mansion of the powerful family of Ross had been replaced by a new house, and Tulloch Castle became incorporated into an emparked mansion.

**Railway Junction and News**: The largely rural population of Ross-shire, 56,000 in 1801, peaked about 1851 at nearly 83,000, and subsequent slow decline left few growth opportunities for Dingwall to seize. From 1862 the Ross-shire Railway linked Dingwall with Inverness and later the far north. In 1870 it became the junction for the Skye line; these concerns soon joined the Highland Railway (HR). By 1871 Wordie & Co operated a rail to road cartage depot, and in its heyday Dingwall station boasted four platform faces and a small engine shed. The *Ross-shire Journal* was founded in 1875.

**Distilling borrows a Famous Name**: The Ben Wyvis distillery, built in 1879 by D G Ross, was steam powered and rail-connected in 1886, making 725,000 litres of Highland malt whisky annually. In 1894 the *National Hotel* was *"excellent"* to Murray; new county buildings had been erected, and the harbour still existed. A public library started with Carnegie money in 1902. About then James Reid, a millwright and engineer, built large portable threshing drums of the type moved from farm to farm by steam traction engines. By 1922 when owned by DCL's subsidiary DFC, the distillery bore the famous name of Ferintosh *(see Conon Bridge)*, but it was closed in 1926; its original name was later re-used at Invergordon. Ross County football club was founded in 1929, laying out their ground at Victoria Park and establishing a most remarkable Highland League reputation, especially for a town whose population was only 3600 in the 1950s, when little industry remained. However, Dingwall had the facilities of a major local centre, providing some services for up to 32,000 people spread across the Highlands from Portmahomack to Gairloch. Dingwall House was gutted by fire in 1960.

**The Impact of the Oil Industry and Bypass**: Much growth at Dingwall resulted from North Sea Oil development and the short-lived Invergordon smelter; four advance factories were built by the HIDB in 1972. A swimming pool and sports centre was built in 1972–73, simultaneously with extensions to the already large Dingwall Academy and the *National Hotel*. By 1978 the Claymore creamery was open, new shops were under construction, there were at least three garages, a furniture shop, and the Ross County Social Club. Dingwall's increasingly busy High Street obstructed the only main road to the north of Scotland until Fairclough built the new A9 Cromarty Firth bridge in 1977–79. The town's population had risen to 5000 by 1981, but by then its dependent population for specialised facilities had risen to about 55,000. Dingwall's local papers had long ceased to be independently owned, but the *Highland News* series, edited and published in Inverness in 1990, was printed at their Dingwall plant. The Dingwall firm of DMS was then expanding as designers and makers of machine instrumentation systems.

**Local Government falls; Football rises**: When Ross & Cromarty was recast from county to district status in 1975 Dingwall remained the headquarters, and retained its sheriff court; in 1979 Dingwall had become the HQ of the Highland River Purification Board. But in 1996 the district council vanished into the vast unitary Highland Council, nominally ending Dingwall's millennium as a local government centre. Meantime in 1992 Highlands & Islands Enterprise built advance offices in the town, which already held a Hydro-Electric distribution engineering base, and also its northern area power station control centre. The Inverness Auction Mart ran one of its two important livestock markets, active in cattle and sheep in 1996, and Munro's abattoir employs 75. An interesting museum and a pleasant public park were open. In 1994 Ross County FC, which had built a new stand in 1990, was admitted to the Scottish Football League, becoming its most northerly member; a second new stand was built in 1994–95 so that 6500 people could spectate, and the team rapidly worked its way up, joining the first division in 2000.

**Railways Real and Electronic**: The substantial Claymore Creamery was busy in 1995; by 1996 there was a Tesco store, and the weekly *Ross-shire Journal* is produced here. The former HR waiting room was moved 40m in 1997 to enable a new bridge to be built over the railway station. Such is the power of telecommunications to annihilate distance that by mid 1999 a new call centre at Dingwall employed over 200 people dealing with enquiries for Virgin Trains, whose services did not even enter the Highlands! Oil-related firms include structural engineering, under-water surveying, and Maclean electrical suppliers (80 jobs); there's also timber fencing and even printed circuit manufacture. New flats have recently been built beside the railway. *Tulloch Castle* is now a hotel with 19 rooms; the historic *National Hotel* has 51.

*Dingwall station, which began life in 1862, became the junction for the Kyle line in 1870; it once had 4 platforms and a small engine shed. The building seen here was built in 1886.* *(RCAHMS / JRH)*

## DINNET

**Map 10, A4**

***Aberdeenshire hamlet***, *pop. 100* — OS 44: NO 4698

Loch Kinord, 50km west of Aberdeen, contains a prehistoric crannog and has an ancient earthwork on its shores. By about 1750 as the Roy map showed, Dinnet mill – which lies 2km east of the loch – stood beside the Deeside road which linked Aberdeen and Braemar, though both the mill stream and the River Dee were unbridged. When the Dee was eventually bridged nearby, Dinnet gained a crossroads; this became the site of the only intermediate station to be provided when an extension of the Deeside Railway (later part of the Great North of Scotland system) was opened from Aboyne to Ballater in 1866. Once described as being *"in splendid isolation"*, the crossing station attracted a post office, and a school which had a secondary class into the 1950s. By 1954 the 17-room *Profeits Hotel* was open close by; later enlarged and re-named *Glenlewis*, it is now the *Loch Kinord*. The railway was closed completely in 1966. The school had gone by 1976, and the area's population was only about 125 in 1981. Afforestation continued in this already well-wooded area, and by 1995 a visitor centre overlooked tree-girt Loch Kinord; the post office had closed. The Dinnet estate office occupies the old station building; the platforms beside it are overgrown with trees. Adjoining the small hotel is a caravan site and children's playground; the hamlet also has a public hall, tea rooms and a garage.

## DIRLETON

**Map 3, B2**

***Small E. Lothian village,*** *pop. 500* OS 66: NT 5184

Dirleton Castle, a courtyard complex 4km west of North Berwick but some distance inland, was built about 1200 by a de Vaux. In 1444 Sir Walter Haliburton founded a college of priests, placing their chapel within the castle complex. Gardens were laid out around it in the 16th century, and *'Dirltoun'* was a small emparked symbol on Pont's map of about 1600. A burgh of barony was chartered in 1631, and about then a church was built. The castle was slighted by General Monk in 1650; by then the weavers of Aberlady and Dirleton were competing at golf.

**Archerfield and the remote Railway**: The castle's new owners (1663), the Nisbets, soon built the new mansion of Archerfield House nearby; it was altered around 1740, and in 1790 Robert Adam remodelled the interior. But the family continued to develop the castle's grounds and gardens. Roy's map of about 1754 showed a road from Aberlady to North Berwick; *'Dirletoun'* was a small linear settlement on a loop road. In 1827 Chambers waxed lyrical about the resort potential of Dirleton *"village"* and parish, and from 1849 a station named Dirleton was provided 2 km south-east of the village on the North Berwick branch of the North British Railway. By 1894 the *Dirleton Inn* was open, but only *"fair"* to Murray. The population of Dirleton was only 400 in 1931, but bus services and car ownership had developed, and residential growth brought it to nearly 700 by 1951. The ill-sited station – served by only two trains a day – was closed in 1954, while Archerfield House was sadly gutted around 1955 and left vacant.

**Speculation, Dereliction and the Flying Duke**: A bypass was constructed around 1970 and a caravan site was open by 1975; by 1977 the *Open Arms Hotel* was in business as well as the *Castle Inn*. The village population was still under 500 in 1991, and only the facilities of a small village were available. The derelict Archerfield remains the centre of hotel, golfing and residential plans, and Archerfield Home Farm with its private airfield is the base of a well-known engineer, pilot and outspoken animal lover, the current Duke of Hamilton.

## DOLLAR

**Map 16, B1**

***Clackmannanshire small town,*** *pop. 2670* OS 58: NS 9698

The old village of Dollar lies near the foot of the south-facing slopes of the Ochil Hills of Clackmannanshire; high above it a castle perches on a rocky knoll, perhaps the site of a 12th century motte, enjoying an extensive distant view over the upper Forth estuary. Its approach by a narrow and precipitous glen led to the Gaelic name *Doilleir* meaning *'Gloomy Place'*. By the 16th century some of the people of Dollar, a typical castle town, had feudal obligations to supply food, drink and coal to the castle, whose name was anglicised as Gloom; though destroyed in 1466, it was soon rebuilt. In 1489 the name was changed to Castle Campbell after its heiress married the head of that clan, the first Earl of Argyll; for 150 years the Earls used it as their main Lowland seat.

**Bridge, Burgh and Textile Industries**: The active local vicar Thomas Forrest promoted the narrow (under 3 m) bridge, built around 1525 some 2 km to the east on the way to Blairingone. In 1644 the mansion-like castle was slighted and the town burned by Montrose; so the Campbells departed to Inveraray. Consequently Dollar was not chartered as a burgh of barony until 1702, nor did it acquire a significant market. Copper and lead were once mined in the Glen, and a colliery was opened south of the village in 1739. When surveyed by Roy about 1750 a mill stood to the south of the river in the vicinity of Dollarbeg, but Dollar was still a tiny roadless place. A short-lived ironworks existed in the late 18th century, but textiles then replaced mineral working. Two waulk mills were turning by 1790, and 30 men worked in William Haig's extensive bleachfield for Dunfermline linens, established beside the ford to Dollarbeg. Heron in 1799 simply referred to Dollar as a *"village"*.

**Dollar Academy draws the Better-off**: The Dollar to Stirling road was turnpiked in 1810. A woollen mill of about 1805 was replaced in 1818 by a larger integrated mill; the bleachfield was extensively re-equipped in 1823, and was used by the Dunfermline table linen manufacturers as late as 1871. Meantime Dollar Academy was founded in 1818 under the will of John McNab, local boy turned London shipowner, and its classical building was opened in 1820. By 1827 Chambers was noting *"the village of Dollar, remarkable for its academy"*. An endowed school, it offered secondary education to local children of both sexes. Beveridge observed in 1888 that *"multitudes of families, chiefly of the middle classes, have been induced to settle for the educational advantages"*, leading to Dollar's growth into a *"large town with handsome streets"*. This was an overstatement – the 1891 census found just 1807 people!

**Recreation, Railway and Power Station**: Meantime the Dollarbeg ford was replaced by a timber bridge around 1850. About then an easy pathway was blasted through the gorge leading up to the hitherto almost inaccessible castle, and tourists came in growing numbers. From 1869 Dollar was linked with Alloa by the Devon Valley Railway, and in 1871 with Kinross. By 1888 the *Castle Campbell Hotel* was open; in 1894 Murray found this provided *"comfortable"* accommodation.

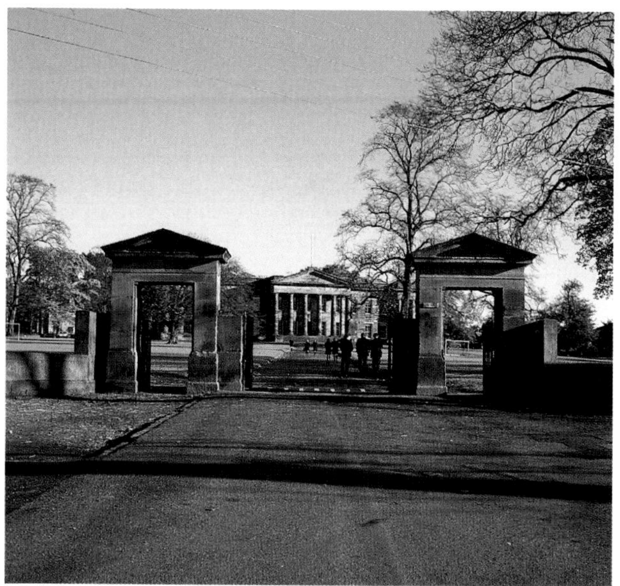

*Dollar Academy, founded in 1818 by local boy made good John McNab 'for the poor of the parish'. The main building dates in part from 1819, and was designed by William Playfair of Edinburgh.* (JRH)

Dollar golf club, founded in 1896, laid out a steep moorland course of 18 holes. In 1901 a power station was built – remarkable for so small a town. The baronial mansion called Dollarbeg Castle was built 2 km to the south-east around that time; in the 1930s it briefly became a holiday centre.

**Coal**: Some time after 1924, Dollar Colliery was sunk east of the town and connected to the railway, but it too was to be short-lived. In 1951 when the population was still around 1600, Dollar's facilities were those of a large village. From about 1956 a drift mine called Dollar No. 4/5 was driven from the former colliery yard; about 1960 it was raising around 2000 tonnes a day from the Upper Hirst seam, for supply to Kincardine power station. When rail passenger services ceased in 1964 the line east of Dollar Mine was abandoned, and the remaining track was lifted on closure of the mine in 1973.

**The Favoured Dormitory**: After wartime use by the RAF, by 1974 Dollarbeg Castle had become a 43-room hotel, but closed in 1980; in 1993 it stood vacant and no longer claimed to be a castle. Meantime despite coal mining, Dollar remained a favoured dormitory village; residential development took place during the 1960s, attracted by the Academy and the pleasant environment, especially the running water of the Dollar Burn in its green centre. Dollar Museum opened in 1988 and moved to larger premises in 1993, featuring the lost Devon Valley Railway. In 1991 the resident population was 2670, of a dormitory character, and more private housing has been built to the east. In 1994 the independent co-educational Dollar Academy had 1100 pupils. The long-established *Castle Campbell Hotel* is one of several in the town.

## DOLPHINTON

**Map 2, B2**

***S-E. Lanarkshire small village,*** *pop. 250* — OS 72: NT 1046

A first century Roman road paralleled the Pentland Hills, connecting the upper Clyde Valley with Inveresk. Pont's map of Tweeddale, drawn about 1600, showed a bridge at *'Dalfindon'* on the Lanarkshire border 6km south-west of West Linton, where this road crossed the Garvald Burn *(Garbh Allt* meaning *'Rough Stream'* in Gaelic) as it tumbled out of the Pentland hills. Dolphinton parish school was founded in 1624. The way between Biggar and West Linton had been made up as a road by about 1754, when Roy mapped the area. In 1864 the overoptimistic Leadburn, Linton & Dolphinton Railway was opened, later part of the North British; from 1867 it formed – in theory – a through route with the almost equally uneconomic branch of the Caledonian Railway from Carstairs Junction, creating twin stations. By 1895 there was a post office; both Garvald House and the emparked Dolphinton House were prominent.

**After the Forlorn Hope Railway**: The population in 1901 was 250. All trains to the east were withdrawn by the LNER in 1933, and the eastern half of the line soon vanished. The Carstairs passenger trains ceased under the LMS in 1945; by 1955 the forlorn line had been lifted. Under 200 people remained in 1951, served by a post office, primary school and telephone exchange. By 1988 the Garvald sandpit was open east of Dolphinton; disused for a time, it is now active and expanding. Meantime although by 1991 there were 234 people, Dolphinton school was agreed for closure in 1992; its post office and Garvald school are still open.

## DORNIE & Kintail

**Map 8, C3**

***Wester Ross small village,*** *pop. 300* — OS 33: NG 8826

Glen Elchaig in Wester Ross holds the almost inaccessible Falls of Glomach, at 113 m the highest in Britain, which tumble down a crack in the mountainside. Some 15 km to the west beside the tidewater of Loch Duich is Dornie, in Kintail parish; on a nearby islet is the hefty 13th century keep of Eilean Donan, featured on the edge of Pont's map made about 1600, on which Dornie did not appear. Nearby Keppoch, a hillside estate 2 km

*Fish-farming in Loch Duich, near Dornie, one of many sites around the West Highland coast-line.* *(Marine Harvest)*

south-east of the castle, gained a baronial burgh charter in 1690, but this came to nothing. Eilean Donan's large castle was almost destroyed in 1719, and Roy's map of about 1750 showed a trackless area; *'Banddoich'* (Bundalloch) was the main township. Telford's Kintail road, a winding single track, was completed along the north shore of Loch Duich by 1821. By then a ferry – which probably carried vehicles – crossed the mouth of Loch Long to Ardelve, and a passenger ferry crossed Loch Duich to Totaig. Dornie still lacked a post office in 1838, and although there was a school, the place was in a sad state due to the clearances and potato famine when seen by Robert Somers in 1847. The *Dornie Inn* was still *"poor"* to Murray in 1894, though Dornie was *"a considerable village"*.

**Rebuilt Castle, Hydro Power and Tourism**: The castle was reconstructed from the ruins in 1912–32 by Farquhar Macrae, and with its curved bridge to the mainland soon became a major tourist draw, so dramatic in situation as to dominate all future views of the area. The Loch Long ferry operated into the 1930s, when Dornie was at last linked to Ardelve by a road bridge. By 1953 there was a small hydro power scheme at Nostie Bridge, 2 km to the west, fed from the Lochalsh Dam, with a submarine cable to the south shore. By 1956 there were two small hotels and Dornie had the facilities of a typical small village. Telford's inadequate though up to then scenically interesting road to the south had become the A87, the main route to Skye. In the 1960s and 70s it underwent major reconstruction, including the cutting off of detours. The population of Dornie, under 200 in 1951, rose to over 300 by 1981; but the Totaig ferry had closed by 1974. By 1977 a caravan and camping site existed, and by 1988 a tourist restaurant. The 1930s bridge was replaced about 1990. The *Dornie Hotel* and the *Loch Duich Hotel* cater for tourists, a tiny bunkhouse for backpackers is open, and another small year-round hostel at Killilan, some 10km to the north-east, beyond the head of Loch Long, lightens the way to the high Falls of Glomach in their spectacular chasm.

## DORNOCH

**Map 9, B2**

***Sutherland small town,*** *pop. 1200* — OS 21: NH 7989

Dornoch, in Gaelic *Doirneagach* meaning *'shingly'*, lies near the north shore of the treacherous Dornoch Firth, in a fairly sheltered area of shingle and sand dunes, and had a Culdee church from the sixth century. Later the Norsemen of Caithness named the area Sutherland, meaning *'southland'*. When King David I created a diocese of Caithness about 1130, a small monastic church was built at Dornoch, which he described as *"Dornoch in Caithness"*; it apparently became the original sheriff caput, with a castle, and may also have been a royal burgh for a time. After its recovery from the Norsemen the bishops actually lived in Caithness proper, but the second bishop was murdered by Norse raiders at Scrabster, and the third by disaffected parishioners at Halkirk!

**Cathedral City**: Bishop Gilbert evidently considered Sutherland a safer part of his diocese in 1224 when he founded Dornoch Cathedral. It seems likely that Dornoch was chartered as an ecclesiastical burgh very early, for as early as 1275 Bishop Archibald wrote of *"my town of Dornoch"*. A bishop's palace was constructed there in the 14th century, its masons building in the same creamy pink sandstone as had been used for the cathedral. When Caithness passed to Wick's civil control, Dornoch became the effective County Town of Sutherland. The Reformation caused its plunder, and the castle-like palace was damaged in 1570; however, Pont's map made around 1600 showed it surrounded by enclosed policies.

**Struggling Royal Burgh**: Despite such problems, by 1588 a grammar school was open, by 1593 the town was the centre of a presbytery and it became a Royal Burgh in 1628. However, in 1639 Dornoch ranked a humble 49th of Scottish burghs in tax rents, the lowest valuation of all those which rendered returns and only half that of the 48th! A post office was in operation by 1715. Roy's map made about 1750 showed only a rather small nucleated settlement whose three roads or tracks led respectively to the Meikle Ferry (*q.v.*), west to Skibo and north to Embo and Skelbo. In 1769 Pennant described Dornoch as *"a small town, half in ruins"*, a phrase repeated by Heron 30 years later. A cattle market was held late in the 18th century, and in 1797 Dornoch was a post town and had six annual fairs. In 1815 Dornoch tolbooth all too briefly held Patrick Sellar, the brutal factor of the Sutherland Estates: the only time he tasted his own medicine.

***'A Miserable Royal Burgh'***: The *Sutherland Arms* was open as a coaching inn by about 1820, but in 1827, according to Chambers, Dornoch had about 500 inhabitants and was *"not touched by either the sea or the post-road. Before the rise of Golspie, it is said to have been much more prosperous; now the thirteen shopkeepers are reduced to four or five. This is, without any exception, the most miserable of all our royal burghs. It is, nevertheless, the county town of Sutherland. The bishop's place is now converted into a county court-room and jail"*.

**Golf wakens the Sleeping City**: Dornoch's population remained at or about 500, and it was even avoided by the meandering Sutherland Railway which was built at the estate's bidding in the 1860s. However, Dornoch golf club was founded in 1877 and in 1886 Tom Morris laid out an 18-hole course. The burgh, which had only 514 people in 1891, was still described as *"insignificant"* by Murray in 1894, but its golf links were excellent, and the *"good" Sutherland Arms Hotel* was open.

**On – and off – the Railway**: A light railway to connect Dornoch with the Mound *(q.v.)* was built with War Office aid as a coast defence measure, and completed in 1902. Its owners, the Highland Railway, built the large *Dornoch Hotel*, opened in 1904 for golfing holidays. Early in the 20th century the bishop's palace was adapted as the *Dornoch Castle Hotel*, the population had reached 725 in 1931, and by 1939 the golf club had added a second 18-hole course. In 1946 Wordie & Co operated a small rail to road cartage depot, but the railway was closed in 1960 and the goods yard became an industrial site. Though Dornoch had only the general facilities of a large village, by 1965 its little Academy had modern buildings, and by 1972 the tiny town had excelled itself by acquiring an aircraft landing strip. In 1975 the remaining County offices passed to the new Sutherland District, which held its meetings in the Carnegie Buildings, which housed two departments.

**Dornoch as Resort**: In 1978 Dornoch was a quiet golfing and residential resort, with a library (built around 1905, with Carnegie aid) and five hotels, of which the *Burghfield House* had 50 rooms, plus several caravan and camping sites, restaurants, holiday bungalows, tennis courts, a craft centre and (for the shooting fraternity) armourers. Small industries included the Dornoch Pottery, Grant's Meats, Balnakeil Sheepskins, and *'Wax Factor'* Candles. In 1991, when there were 1196 residents, many being affluent retired people, the Dornoch Firth road bridge was opened, making the little town much more accessible from the south. Today the small Dornoch 2-year secondary augments Dornoch Primary, and the hotels include the refurbished *Royal Golf* (33 rooms), the baronial *Burghfield House* (34), the historic *Dornoch Castle* (17) and many smaller, plus the *Trenthan Hotel* at Poles, 4km north-west. The *'Royal Dornoch'* golf club has the Championship and Struie courses, both 18 holes.

## DOUGLAS

**Map 2, B2**

***S. Lanarkshire village,*** *pop. 1600* — OS 71 or 72: NS 8330

A reasonably fertile area lies beside the Douglas Water some 13km above Lanark. The foundation of the castle, which was able to command the south western approaches to the Clyde valley, may pre-date the 12th century St Bride's church nearby; it was the original seat of the Black Douglas Earls. Douglas was shown on the Gough map. Its castle was the home of Robert Bruce's stalwart supporter James Douglas, who recovered it from the English in 1307, only to slight it twice, the second time after Clifford of England had refortified it. His castle was destroyed in a siege in 1455, but Douglas became a burgh of barony in 1458, enabling rebuilding by the *"too powerful Earls, who went abroad with a train of 2000 armed men" (Chambers).*

**Leaky-Roofed Burgh and Wild Castle**: Pont's map dated 1596 showed a substantial *'Kirktoun'* and a *'Brigtoun'* near Douglas Castle; a mill stood south of the river some way downstream. The *Sun Inn* was built in 1621, and by 1633 there was a parish school, but in 1662 John Ray wrote that the castle was *"half a mile distant from the town, which though it be a free burgh, and of great antiquity, yet is a pitiful, poor, small place, scarce an house in it which will keep a man dry in a shower of rain"*. But the sad little town survived, though Defoe writing in the 1720s disdained even to mention it, finding the ancient castle *"very ill adapted to the glory of the family whose frequent additions have made it a wild, irregular mass"*.

**Mining, Fire and Mansion**: Roy's map made about 1754 showed Douglas as a large village with roads to Crawfordjohn, Lesmahagow, Douglas Mill and Muirkirk; to the north of the river was *'Collyett'*, doubtless a coal-mining locality. A post office was opened in 1759. The recently burned-out castle was replaced by a new mansion designed by the Adam brothers – largely built in 1757–61 but only completed about 1790. A Turnpike Act of 1772 enabled the existing road from Muirkirk to Douglas and Edinburgh to be properly made up. Douglas Mill, 3km north-east on the main Glasgow to Carlisle road, gained a post office in 1794 and was a post town by 1797, when two annual fairs took place in Douglas.

**Textiles and Bad Roads**: Heron writing in 1799 noted a population of about 700 *"who begin to be employed in the cotton manufacture"*. A post office was opened there in 1802. Dorothy Wordsworth noted in 1803 that the surrounding area was unenclosed corn country, adding *"Douglas Mill is a single house, a large inn, being one of the regular stages between Longtown and Glasgow, and therefore a fair specimen of the best of the country inns of Scotland"*. But the road south to Leadhills was *"very bad"* – the worst section she travelled in the south of Scotland. A wool dyeing mill was in operation by 1813. In 1827 Chambers found a *"pleasant and old-fashioned town with a great annual fair, held in the church-yard"*.

**Not exactly on the Railway**: An ultra-rural branch of the Caledonian Railway was opened from Lanark to Douglas West station in 1864 and extended to Muirkirk in 1873–74; there was also a connection to Lesmahagow. The station was 1.5km to the west, linked in 1894 by a horse bus to the little town whose only respectable inn was the *Douglas Arms*. The so-called *'Douglas'* station stood isolated over 5km from the little town, north of Douglas Mill, at the crossing of what later became the A74; after many decades of travellers being misled, it was renamed *Happendon* after the LMS took over in 1923. The fine 18th century *'castle'* was badly damaged by undermining, but it long survived as a ruin. The guilty Douglas Castle colliery was closed soon after 1955, and the railway was abandoned in 1964.

**From Christmas Trees to Catching the Wind**: A local engineering firm set up in 1969 began to manufacture the oil and gas wellhead equipment known as *Christmas Trees*; today it employs over 100 as Abb Vecto Gray. In spite of the proving of substantial coal reserves at Happendon in 1978, Douglas remained essentially a village, with about half a dozen shops and two inns in 1981. In 1991 the population was over 1600; it contained Scotland's highest proportion of male transport workers, at 20%; many evidently worked for Ramages *(see Glespin)*. In 1992 an inn and a caravan site were open. Scotland's first full-blown wind farm was approved in 1994 for Hagshaw Hill (OS 71), 5km west of Douglas; now complete, its 30 Tri-Gen wind turbines each 32m tall carry 35m span blades *(see also Carsphairn)*. The medieval St Bride's church is open to the public and there is a small museum.

## DOUNBY

**Map 13, B2**

***Orkney village,*** *pop. 350* — OS 6: HY 2920

Dounby in the Orkney Mainland stands on mediocre farmland 8km inland from historic Birsay *(q.v.)*, surrounded by many prehistoric remains. It has few natural advantages, and did not appear on Pont's map which was made about 1592. However, when roads were built in the islands in the late 18th century its crossroads gave centrality, and some non-farm development began. The *'Click Mill'* east of Dounby is a rare horizontal water mill, now restored and open as a tourist attraction. Skeabrae airfield, 2 km west of Dounby, was begun in 1939 for the Royal Naval Air Service, but in 1940 it became an important RAF fighter base. Hard runways and 12 hangars were built; its satellite was Grimsetter *(see Kirkwall)*. Itself downgraded in 1945 to become a satellite of Twatt, Skeabrae was closed in 1949 and sold off in 1957, but its last structure survived until about 1989.

**A Slowly Developing Service Centre**: By the 1950s Dounby with a closely surrounding population of only 400 provided some services to about 2250 people; it had an inn, a market stance and a junior secondary school for 150 pupils, though this soon closed. By 1971 the falling population of the rather scattered village was nearing 300. Decline then ceased and some other facilities were opened, including a garage and a small hotel overlooking the Loch of Harray, reflecting the increasing number of tourists interested in Orkney's unique hoard of archaeology. So by 1981 this little place provided some basic facilities to almost 3000 people within a 9km radius. Small developments continued around Dounby in the 1990s. It now has a sizeable general store, post office and filling station, a modern primary school with a games hall, the tiny *Smithfield Hotel* and a joiner. Harray to the south has the Corrigal Farm Museum, a pottery, shop/post office, restaurant and filling station and a large parish hall. Cattle and grain farming predominate in the treeless countryside around.

## DOUNE

**Map 5, C4**

***Perthshire village,*** *pop. 1200*

OS 57: NN 7201

Also see: *Deanston*

Doune – which had a Roman fort – lies only 10km north-west of Stirling, but became the capital of the Menteith area, later part of Perthshire. Chambers wrote that Doune Castle, sited on a spur between the River Teith and the Ardoch Burn, had been *"the seat of the Earls of Menteith"* and was thought to date back to the 11th century. Doune Castle was greatly enlarged by Murdoch, the second Duke of Albany, about 1395–1400 when as Regent of Scotland he enjoyed great power, and was still a royal property in 1455. The whole area is in Kilmadock parish.

**Duke's Road and Tailor's Bridge**: In 1415 John Hardyng reported that between Doune and Falkland in Fife *"a way ye have right fair, with horse and cart to hire"*; we may guess that this road was built at Albany's bidding, to connect his private stronghold with the royal hunting palace, probably crossing a ford near the later Bridge of Allan. The River Teith remained a serious obstacle until the rich Royal tailor, Robert Spittal of Stirling, arranged for the Doune bridge to be built in 1535, just to deprive a bloody-minded ferryman of a living! Doune became a burgh of barony in 1611, there was a parish school by 1632, and pistols and sporrans were made until the Highland dress was banned.

**King's Road and Post Town**: The Roy map – surveyed about 1750 – showed Doune as a linear settlement on Caulfeild's newly built *'Kings road from Stirling to Fort William'*; from the bridge, other roads led to Gargunnock by fording the River Forth, and via Drip ferry to Stirling. Doune cattle market was started in the 1760s, and a post office first opened in 1793. By 1797 Doune was a post town, and five fairs were scheduled for the year. Two years later, Heron wrote *"the village of Doune is regularly built, and contains nearly a thousand inhabitants"*.

**Turnpike, Railway and Markets**: The Doune to Stirling road was turnpiked in 1812. By 1826 the ruined castle was owned by the Morays. From 1858 there was a station on a branch of the Scottish Central railway from Dunblane to Callander. In 1894 the *"comfortable" Woodside Hotel* served *"a town noted for its fairs of cattle and sheep, driven from the western Highlands"*. But the cattle fairs faded away, and by 1951 Doune was only a village with 2000 people in its immediate area *(including Deanston, q.v.)*, and Beeching closed the railway in 1965.

**Classic Cars and Safari Park**: Meantime in 1953 the then Earl of Moray had started to amass a collection of old cars, and in 1970 opened the Doune motor museum north of the town, soon a substantial attraction. About that time a safari park, unique in Scotland, was established near Blair Drummond, a Victorian mansion which became the site for a Camphill school for handicapped children; a caravan and camping site was laid out. A fair range of shops existed in the 1970s, plus a garage, haulage contractors, four hotels and a gunmaker. However, the local residential population continued to fall, and while the Blair Drummond safari and leisure park flourished, Doune was a quiet village by 1991, its population 1212. The motor museum closed in the late 1990s. A remarkable find in 1999, made during excavations for a new nursery school, was a sophisticated set of Roman surgical instruments. The big ruined castle is a notable tourist attraction; the *Doune Arms* is one of several hotels.

## DOUNREAY

**Map 13, A4**

***Scientific/Industrial area, Caithness***

OS 11: ND 9765

Cairns and standing stones adorn this flat coastal area 13 km west of Thurso. The name Dounreay appeared on the Pont map of about 1600, but it remained no more than farms. By the early 20th century two hamlets had grown nearby, Buldoo on the main coast road having a post office, and inland Achramie with a primary school. Dounreay airfield was one of many temporary bases created during World War II. Its extreme remoteness from cities suited the United Kingdom Atomic Energy Authority (UKAEA), which set up its Experimental Reactor Establishment there in 1954, and began erection of the *'golf ball'* sphere enclosing the experimental Fast Breeder Reactor (FBR); this research project aimed to find cheaper forms of nuclear power. Fuel reprocessing began there in 1958, including overseas customers from 1962, in which year the FBR began to feed the national grid.

**The Deadly Dump**: New residential development was not permitted nearby, but the rapid growth of the staff, locally known as the *'Atomics'*, led instead to the substantial expansion of Thurso, as well as to some development over a wide area of both Caithness and Sutherland. In 1959 a 65 m deep shaft was sunk near the shore to enable excavation of a tunnel, so that low-level nuclear waste could be discharged well out to sea. When the tunnel was complete the shaft became a dump for radioactive debris, including the vile poisons Plutonium and Strontium 90. In 1975 work began on an improved FBR. By 1977 the *'Nuclear Power Development Establishment'* employed some 3500 people, travelling from as far afield as Wick, Melvich and Bettyhill, and had a visitor centre.

**Secrecy covers *'Doomray'***: A small explosion occurred in the dumping shaft in 1977; the resulting radioactive Roman Candle blew out many dangerous particles across the site and beach. Only then did the site director – appointed in 1975 – find out about the dump, and information on the accident was deliberately concealed from the public until 1995; meanwhile the clean-up was left incomplete. Perhaps this was why a sad cluster of child leukaemia victims was found in the area. A longer term threat was posed by the sea, whose steady erosion of the cliffs would need restraint to prevent the shaft being exposed by 2035, to disperse a deadly radioactive cocktail throughout the nearby seas. By 1988 when the prototype FBR was shut down, in favour of the experimental Fast Breeder Reactor, Dounreay also had the premises of Rolls-Royce & Associates, where Pressurised Water Reactor (PWR) plant for Royal Navy submarine engines was designed, developed and tested.

**Fast Breeder meets Premature End?**: In 1989 the government decided to wind down the FBR programme; the staff of 2100 was to be cut by 75% by 1997, posing dire problems for Thurso. To protect jobs, the nuclear establishment set up a pipe descaling plant for North Sea Oil, and also sought more of the profitable reprocessing business from overseas, with some success. In 1992 770 people worked in reprocessing, treating the fuel elements from test reactors and nuclear power stations; uranium was recovered and coated with aluminium to make fresh fuel rods, flown out from the airstrip for use worldwide, to environmental concern. The remaining Plutonium Nitrate was then shipped to Sellafield. Total jobs were down to 1600 before the experimental FBR at Dounreay was shut down in 1994, a seemingly absurd decision by the Major government, as it had just completed its best year! Its generating capacity, which was enough to power the Highlands, was in effect replaced by various new plants in England burning irreplaceable gas.

**Clearing up to take a Lifetime – or More**: Dounreay's research findings were put on ice, and over 300 workers saw their practical expertise junked. Despite this blow, late in 1994 over 1000 people were still employed. In 1995 the US firm Procord took over 140 staff at Dounreay from the UKAEA. In its quest for tax cutting the government also planned to remove the reprocessing subsidy in 1997, but it was the cutting of a power cable during excavation work in 1998 that ended reprocessing; the loss of 570 more jobs would leave only 500 people working on site by 2000. Plans announced that year envisaged that although the waste shaft would be cleared of debris by 2025, decommissioning could take until 2050, with the most radioactive part of the site – the reactor building – barred to general access for perhaps 300 years.

## DREGHORN

**Map 1, C1**

***Large Ayrshire village,*** *pop. 3960* — OS 70: NS 3538

Dreghorn lies between the River Irvine and the Annick Water about 3 km east of Irvine. About 1600 it was shown by Pont as *'Langdreghorn'*, and may have been the source of the coal that was shipped through Irvine by the 1720s. Dreghorn as mapped by Roy in the 1750s was a small linear settlement on the Irvine to Kilmarnock road. In 1845 it was the birthplace of John Boyd Dunlop, who became a veterinary surgeon in Belfast. Its bumpy cobbles rattled his son's tricycle, hence in 1887 he re-invented the pneumatic tyre, in the practical form which was to sweep the board in the 1889 cycle races. It was originally a patent of Thompson in 1846; but it was on Dunlop Rubber Company tyres (and those of his imitators) that the worldwide transport revolution rolled along.

**The Busby Branch Railway and related Coal Pits**: Meantime the Glasgow & South Western Railway built a line between Irvine and Kilmarnock, passing close to Dreghorn. Opened in 1848 as the *'Busby Branch'*, it later became connected to numerous local collieries. However for many years no station seems to have been provided at Dreghorn, although by 1891 this was a large village with 1069 people and an inn. There were by that time rail-connected collieries at Corsehill to the east, Broomlands on the west and Montgomeryfield to the south of the village. Capringstone colliery had been sunk north of the railway and was also linked to it, as was the Bourtreehill Coal Company's pit near Perceton, which became a large brick and fireclay works about 1900.

**Rail Arrival and Sundry Departures**: Dreghorn had acquired a railway station by about 1907, and had grown by 1951 into a place of 2300 people, though apart from secondary schooling it had only the facilities of a small village. Montgomeryfield colliery was the largest and longest lasting in the area, still open in 1954, but soon afterwards only its brickworks remained. Dreghorn station was closed in 1964 and the whole Irvine to Crosshouse railway was abandoned in 1965. Dreghorn continued to grow in population to some 2750 by 1971. Both the brickworks appear to have closed in the early 1970s, and with the growth of Irvine New Town, had been swept away by 1985 with the construction of the A71 Dreghorn bypass. By 1991 Dreghorn had the facilities of an average village, and was on the edge of the new town, with 3960 residents. By then the large new Greenwood Academy had been built; today with 1250 pupils. By 1998 a new crematorium was open east of the village.

## DREM

**Map 3, B2**

***E. Lothian hamlet,*** *pop. under 100* — OS 66: NT 5179

Located in the fertile plains of East Lothian, 6 km north of Haddington, Drem is overlooked by an ancient hill fort called the Chesters, and has slight remains of an early chapel. Labelled *'Dam'* on Pont's late 16th century map, it was erected as a burgh of barony in 1616 and had a parish school from 1629. However, although by the 1750s the Roy map showed the area's road system already well developed, Drem failed to grow beyond a hamlet. When the North British Railway opened its main line in 1846, a station was provided at Drem, which soon became a junction on the opening of the North Berwick branch in 1849–50. Drem also acquired a post and telegraph office, but the school was lost.

**Flying Fighters, Looping Trains and Cooking Turkeys**: By October 1939 a small RAF fighter airfield had been laid out north of the station and west of Fenton Barns; from Drem flew the first fighter to destroy a Nazi aircraft. The airfield was closed after the war. The large intensive turkey farm created in 1948 at Fenton Barns, 2 km north of Drem, soon grew to dominate the tiny local economy. Both Drem station and the North Berwick branch railway narrowly survived the Beeching cuts of the 1960s, to be electrified in 1991. There was a small and shrinking farming settlement of only some 80 people in 1981. At Christmas 1993 growing competition led to the closure of Fenton Barns (Scotland) Ltd, producers of cooked turkey products, with the loss of 40 jobs. To replace this, mushroom growing commenced on a fair scale, and a rural retail park was developed, today with 20 varied outlets; and some poultry processing has recommenced. In 2000 a use was being sought for the vacant building of the unmanned station, which like Drem's quaint post office is still open.

## DRONGAN

**Map 1, C2**

***Ayrshire village,*** *pop. 2900* — OS 70: NS 4418

Timothy Pont mapped Kyle about 1600, showing an emparked place named Drongan, presumably Drongan House, which stands 3 km east of ancient Coylton; the *'Mill of Scheel'* (Shield) was already turning nearby on the Water of Coyle, and soon coal was being raised on the estate. By the mid 18th century – as the Roy map showed – the Ayr to Cumnock road passed near Drongan House, and in the 1770s local pits owned by Mungo Smith raised good quality coal. In 1872 the Glasgow & South Western Railway opened a winding branch line from Annbank to Cumnock; a station named

Drongan was provided not far from the house and the mining village of Taiglum Rows. By 1895 a colliery had been sunk south of Kayshill, and the Drongan Pottery had been opened at Coalhall, where the line crossed the main road near Shieldmains colliery. Drongan was then centred on a village store, post office and smithy at Taiglum, which was sold to Moore & Co with the pit; the area population was about 400. All the children had to walk (or later ride a bus) the 4 km southeast to school at Sinclairston until 1922, when a makeshift infant school was built at Drongan.

**Major Mining leaves its Mark**: The population had risen to 1230 by 1951, mainly rehoused by the council in a compact new settlement south of the station and west of Taiglum, which was then cleared. With the development of bus services, the passenger trains had been withdrawn by 1953, the year that the great Killoch Colliery *(see Ochiltree)* was opened 4 km to the east of Drongan. This led to the by then freight-only railway being diverted to serve it, and to the building of many more council houses at Drongan. However, Shieldmains pit was closed in 1955. By 1981 nearly 3300 people lived in Drongan, though inadequately served by the facilities of a small village. Killoch colliery was closed in 1986, but by 1987 opencasting was in progress between Drongan and Coalhall. By 1991 the population had shrunk to 2900, with twice the national level of male unemployment. But on the brighter side, in 2000 Drongan kept its post office, school and pub.

## DRUMBEG — Map 12, A2

***Sutherland small village,*** *pop. 100* — OS 15: NC 1232

Drumbeg stands somewhat sheltered beside its small loch near the south shore of remote Eddrachilis Bay, according to Roy a trackless and apparently uninhabited area as recently as about 1750. By the late 19th century a road had reached the crofting area from Lochinver and a mail coach ran to Bonar Bridge. By 1940 the scattered clachan had a post and telegraph office, a school, the 10-roomed *Drumbeg Hotel*, and a road to the Kylesku Ferry. A new salmon farm established in 1984–85 brought new families to the tiny but developing village around the hotel; by then there was a doctor, a newly established telephone exchange, a sub-branch bank and perhaps 100 people. In 1993 there was also a fishing school. Ardvar Salmon Farm now employs 25. The post office and the *Drumbeg Hotel* are still open.

## DRUMCHAPEL & Garscadden — Map 15, B4

***N-W. area of Glasgow,*** *pop. 18,000* — OS 64: NS 5271

The area of medieval Lennox south of the Roman wall and 6 km north west of Partick was thickly settled by the late 16th century, when Pont's map showed both *'Chapelton'* and the tower of *'Gartskaden'*, an estate bought by the Colquhouns in 1655. The family had Garscadden House built nearby in 1723, and the tower fell into ruin. The area was wholly rural when Roy's surveyors passed that way 30 years later. Six locks were required on the local section of the Forth & Clyde Canal, completed about 1790, giving a few local jobs, and a brick and tile works was set up just south of the canal. The Glasgow, Dumbarton & Helensburgh Railway (later part of the North British) which opened in 1858 provided a service from a station at Drumchapel. A post and telegraph office was opened around 1900 but, despite mineral workings at Peel Glen, served by a lengthy tramway, Drumchapel remained a tiny village until in 1928–30 Glasgow's Great Western Road (A82) was extended through the area from Anniesland to Duntocher, greatly enhancing road accessibility to the city.

**Drumchapel's Rise and Fall**: Private development began between the new road and the station; a church was built in 1938, and in 1939 Glasgow Corporation bought the Garscadden estate. A tramway extension from Knightswood Cross to Blairdardie was opened in 1949, and in 1950 the Corporation converted Garscadden House into flats; its policies became a park at the centre of the city's first large post-war overspill scheme. A huge housing estate was built very rapidly from early 1951, serving the new Goodyear tyre works and Beattie's large biscuit bakery (west of the early houses) and the new Royal Hospital for Children (to the east); by census day nearly 9000 people already lived in the Drumchapel area. In 1959 vandals regrettably burned down Garscadden House. Drumchapel estate's population alone had reached 34,000 by 1971; by then three secondary schools, a shopping precinct with a Woolworth store, and a swimming pool had been built. But in 1979 poor labour relations and low productivity caused closure of the Goodyear tyre factory, with the loss of 680 jobs. By then Drumchapel possessed most of the facilities of a small town, including a principal post office. In 1981 Drumchapel – which has aptly been called *'Giroland'* – had plenty problems: with the ageing of the first comers and the emigration of young people seeking opportunities elsewhere, by then under 32,000 people still lived in the area.

**Industrial Collapse Complete**: The empty Goodyear tyre factory had become derelict by 1986, and the site was cleared by 1988. A big shopping scheme on the site, including an 8-screen cinema and other leisure and industrial uses, was rejected by the Regional Council in 1988 because of its expected impact on nearby centres. However they allowed a new Gateway supermarket of 7900 m$^2$, open by 1991, and after 2.4 ha of the Goodyear site had been offered in 1994 for the price of a cup of coffee, it was earmarked by B&Q for a DIY store. Meantime in 1988–93 100,000 trees were planted. The bakery, by then known as Fleck's, closed in 1989 with the loss of 300 jobs; this in an area where unemployment already exceeded 20%, even though the estate population had steeply fallen to 19,000 by 1991. Such decline led to the 860-pupil Drumchapel High School being created in 1992, by merging the unacademic Kingsridge and Waverley schools in the buildings of the closed St Pius's RC Secondary. In 1997 it still had a roll of 862.

**Who Pays for Pantomime?**: By 1992 the population of Drumchapel was down to 18,000, under half its 1971 figure, and a local plan proposed to cut down many of the 3- and 4-storey tenements to form houses with gardens. The recently formed Drumchapel Community Organisations Council (DCOC) and the local development company, Drumchapel Opportunities, between them at one time employed over 150 people. The former opened the well-equipped *Mercat Theatre* in 1992 to encourage the arts in this deprived area. Though it ran at 55% capacity and played to full houses during the pantomime season, its parent body DCOC became insolvent in 1994 and collapsed, leading to bank seizures of community facilities; early in 1995 complete closure of the theatre appeared imminent. The extension of the proposed new Glasgow tram service to Drumchapel was considered by Strathclyde Regional Council in 1995 as a means of bringing this forlorn area back into the city's orbit, but the scheme fell with local government reorganisation. Remarkably, a Sainsbury store was opened in 1997.

## DRUMCLOG

**Map 2, A2**

***Lanarkshire small village,*** *pop. 500* OS 71: NS 6439

Above Avondale, in the valley of the Avon Water some 9km south-west of Strathaven, are the Lanarkshire farms of High and Low Drumclog, which stand at altitudes of 260 and 235 metres; they gave their name to a Covenanters battle, fought in 1679. This is commemorated by a monument near High Drumclog, where by 1895 a school had been opened; there was also a post office close by at *'Stobbyside'* (Stobieside), but the wide farming area had not so much as a hamlet. By then there also appears to have been a primary school named Barnock beside the Glengavel Water, near Grouse Lodge some 3km to the south. Early in the 20th century the Caledonian Railway's Strathaven branch was optimistically extended through the valley to the Ayrshire county march, meeting end-on with the Glasgow & South Western Railway's system advancing from Darvel. Passenger services began in 1905, with a station named Drumclog on low ground near the confluence of the Avon with the larger Glengavel Water; the post office moved there and a few houses grew around it. Another station near Gilmourton, 2.5km to the east, was named Ryeland; a creamery there was still a rail user in 1939.

**From Rail to Jail**: The railway's short life was terminated a week after the outbreak of war in 1939 and it was abandoned, as was the school at High Drumclog, though Barnock school survived because it served a very wide area, containing some 600 people. By 1953 the Dungavel Training Centre had been built at Grouse Lodge and the Glengavel Reservoir had been impounded 3km farther south. By 1963 there was also a short-lived post office at Caldermill, between Strathaven and the hamlet of Gilmourton with its school, pub and post office. By 1978 Smith of Drumclog had become a substantial road haulier, but only some 500 people were still around. By 1992 there was a sand and gravel pit at Drumclog; Barnock school and a pub at Gilmourton were open, but the area no longer had a post office. Dungavel had been converted to a small prison, whose intended closure was announced in 1999.

## DRUMGELLOCH, Clarkston & Easter & Wester Moffat

**Map 16, A4**

***Eastern part of Airdrie,*** *pop. 6250* OS 64: NS 7765

When Timothy Pont attempted to map the upland area of Lanarkshire around the North Calder Water in 1596 Drumgelloch was not identified; however, it was clear that the area was well settled and the stream had already been bridged. Roy's survey of about 1754 showed Moffat – later at least a mansionhouse – south of the Airdrie to Avonbridge road, west of *'Caldermill'*. Coal mining was in evidence at that time. It is not known when the Moffat paper mill was established, but by 1848 it was certainly at work on the North Calder Water 1km south of Clarkston, on the main road 2km east of Airdrie.

**Railways, Mines, Quarrying, Coal and Golf**: From 1828 Clarkston was served by a branch of the early Ballochney mineral railway, and an inn was soon open. In 1862 the railway from Edinburgh to Bathgate was extended via Coatbridge to Glasgow, with a station at Clarkston, which formed a linear hamlet with the mining settlement of Drumgelloch; both were added to Airdrie Burgh in 1885. A long, winding siding linked the paper mill with the Bathgate line, crossing a gable by steep 2.5% grades (1 in 40). A quite separate line connected to a coal pit at nearby Gummerscroft, which was closed early in the 20th century. About 1890 the paper mill was greatly extended, and a branch mineral railway served Springbank quarry. Shanks & McEwan of Coatbridge owned the Whinhill Quarry, which from 1915 to 1951 was rail-connected and had its own shunting engine. The Easter Moffat golf club was founded in 1922, and about that time the 58-bed Wester Moffat Hospital replaced the mansionhouse. By 1951 the population had grown to some 5400, but had few facilities, being so close to Airdrie. Clarkston station was closed to passengers in 1956 but both Springbank quarry, by that time very large, and the paper mill remained rail-connected until papermaking ceased in 1964.

**From Paper Mill to Punning Distillery Complex**: The pure water supply from Lady Bell's Moss, 2 km to the east, attracted the US blenders of Inver House whisky, named after the Philadelphia home of the chairman of Publicker Industries. This pun-ridden company, finding whisky supplies hard to obtain, took over Moffat Mills in 1964 for conversion into two distilleries, the Moffat for grain and the short-lived *Glen Flagler* for malt. Both made whisky from 1965, and also *Coldstream Gin* and *Kulov Vodka*. The largest maltings in Europe, a cooperage, major bottling plant and extensive bonded warehouses were soon added. By 1978 when the maltings was sold to Associated British Maltsters the 100ha site was unique in covering every step in spirit production from the raw barley to packaging bottles of gin, vodka and matured whisky brands including *Inver House*, the cheap *MacArthur's* and the 12-year-old *Pinwinnie Royale*, all blends for US consumption, plus *Glenflagler* single malt and also the *Bladnoch (q.v.)* single malt, aimed at the British and European markets.

**Back on the Rails for Passengers**: With some 6500 people in 1981, the Drumgelloch/Clarkston area still had minimal facilities, apart from the large, newly-built Caldervale High School, now with over 1000 pupils. However, in 1989 a new and immediately well-used station named Drumgelloch was opened just west of Clarkston. This extended the Glasgow–Airdrie electric train service along the line lately known as the Inver House branch. By 1991 the Moffat complex produced only grain whisky, but remained in 1993 the head office of Inver House Distillers. The distillery has now been dismantled.

## DRUMLANRIG

**Map 2, B3**

***Estate, Dumfriesshire,*** *pop. under 100* OS 78: NX 8599

Drumlanrig Castle, seat of the Douglases who came to Scotland about 1170, stands west of the middle reaches of the River Nith some 30km above Dumfries; its name means *'Mound (or Motte?) (on) Long Ridge'*. It was built – or rebuilt – in the 14th century, but Tibber's Castle on the nearby riverside was largely destroyed by Bruce in 1311. Pont, who mapped the area about 1610, showed the Mill of Tibbers, and a bridge across the Nith near the emparked Drumlanrig Castle. A parish school was opened in 1619. The castle was rebuilt as a great mansion in 1676–91 to designs by James Smith for William Douglas, third Earl of Queensberry, *"a prodigious land-buyer"*; the locals called it *'The Pink Palace'*. In 1682 Douglas became

Lord High Treasurer of Scotland, and in 1684 the first Duke of Queensberry – but he spent only one night in his rebuilt castle! He also ordered the River Nith to be spanned again – by what Daniel Defoe, who crossed on his visit to Drumlanrig before 1711, described as *"a stately stone bridge"*. Defoe found the country wild, but was greatly impressed by the second Duke's *"fine palace... its gardens so fine, and every thing so truly magnificent"*.

**Poor Communications, but Good for Tourists**: When mapped by Roy about 1754, Drumlanrig Bridge was a key link in the Dumfries to Ayr road; just south of the castle stood the *New Inn*. Drumlanrig had a post office by 1755, but the *New Inn* did not long survive, for a new main road was built east of the Nith. A 1250m-long tunnel 3km to the north was the price the railway had to pay in 1850 for passing through the powerful Duke's lands, for he succeeded in keeping the line well away from the castle and its natural riverside route *(see Carronbridge)*. Drumlanrig, whose estate still comprised about 100 farms in the late 20[th] century, had created no castle town. But its magnificent pile in a large and heavily wooded park is still a ducal home and a prime draw for tourists, who are made to feel welcome and provided with woodland walks, cycle trails and a timber adventure playground.

## DRUMLITHIE, Glenbervie, Fiddes & Mondynes

**Map 10, B4**

***Small Mearns villages,*** *pop. 600* OS 45: NO 7880

Ancient Mondynes with its *Court Stane*, first recorded in 1094, stands beside the Bervie Water at the head of the fertile Howe of the Mearns. An easy pass over the hills 4km east of Mondynes was commanded by the fine 16[th] century tower of the Castle of Fiddes, with its mill and the oddly named Temple of Fiddes. About 1km north of Mondynes, near the point where the headstreams of the little Carron Water create a more difficult pass towards Stonehaven, is Drumlithie, chartered as a barony burgh in 1602. In a more enclosed position 2km to the west is Glenbervie with its early mansionhouse and kirk. Fiddes appeared as 'M(eikle) Fiddes' and 'L.Fiddes' on the Blaeu map, made from Robert Gordon's originals of 1642. The Roy map of about 1750 showed Drumlithie as a village on the trackway from Laurencekirk to Stonehaven; to the south was the Mill of Mondynes. The later turnpike road (now the A94) from Bridge of Mondynes, which for a time had a coaching inn, took a more direct line eastwards, passing 1km south of Drumlithie.

**Beside the Railway**: When the Aberdeen Railway was completed through the pass in 1848 it provided a wayside station close to the village and a *'platform'* at Carmont level crossing, 2.5km to the north. Over 400 people lived in Drumlithie in 1951, when it had good facilities for its size, including Glenbervie school and a small hotel, and served another 650 people within 5km. Both stations were closed to passengers about 1960, and the rail freight service was an early victim of the Beeching cuts, leaving road transport alone to service the area's farming and forestry. By 1981 the village population was down to 260, and the wider rural area whose primary school at Brae of Glenbervie had been closed, held only 420. There had been little new development by 1988, but by 1990 Macphie of Glenbervie was an innovative small foodstuffs firm with a growing export trade.

## DRUMMORE & Kirkmaiden

**Map 1, B5**

***Galloway village & hamlet,*** *pop. 500* OS 82: NX 1336

This remote area on the Rhinns of Galloway 25km south of Stranraer has the remains of a variety of ancient settlements. Above Portankill near the Mull of Galloway was the early church of Saint Medan, after whom the parish of Kirkmaiden was named. Some 10km to the north a medieval motte and fragments of Clanyard Castle stand above Clanyard Bay. Some 3km to the east, above a bay on the sheltered side of the peninsula, is another motte, the *'big mound' (in Gaelic, Drum More)*, near which Drummore Castle was built in the 16[th] century. Pont's map of about 1610 showed a mill at the mouth of the burn below the castle. In 1639 the new church of Kirkmaiden was built on a hilltop 1km west of Drummore, which the Roy map of about 1754 depicted as a small nucleated settlement. It was served by the area's only road, on the line of the modern A716; this already extended south to end at the *'Old Kirk'* near Mull Farm.

**Port and Resort**: The Mull of Galloway lighthouse was designed by Robert Stevenson and first lit in 1830. In the early 19[th] century a breakwater was built to create a tidal harbour at Drummore, from which lime was exported. This implies quarries, coal imports and limekilns, which stood 5km southwest of the village above Portdown Bay, but were evidently not on a large scale. A school was built in 1877, and about the same time a watermill was built, which was still milling grain in 1976. In 1894 Murray referred to the *"comfortable" Small Hotel*, though perhaps this was actually the *Queens*; buses served Drummore from 1907. A coastguard station was open by 1951, when Drummore was a tiny resort and fishing port; the area had a population of over 750, and the 11-room *Queens Hotel* augmented the facilities of a small village. These were supplemented for a time by a primary school near the Mull, and in 1974 by caravan and camping sites both north and south of Drummore, by then regarded as a holiday village. Its population had fallen to under 500 by 1991. By 1996 improvements had been made to the drying harbour, a little development was evident and the post office was still open, but it has since closed and the hotel is just an inn. The long-vacant school was repaired, and for sale in 2000.

## DRUMMUIR, Botriphnie & Towiemore

**Map 10, A2**

***Small villages near Keith,*** *pop. 200* OS 28: NJ 3844

When Robert Gordon revised Pont's sketches for Blaeu's atlas about 1640, *'Drymmoir'* in Botriphnie parish was a tiny place in the trackless upper reaches of Banffshire's Strath Isla. Roy's map made about 1750 showed various ferm touns; by then the new mansion of Drummuir Castle had large policies. The Keith & Dufftown Railway, opened in 1862, placed a station near the castle gate, and a small village with a post office developed alongside the turnpike road nearby. The Towiemore Distillery 2 km north-east of Drummuir was open by 1902, with a rail siding. Towiemore Halt, opened in 1924, stayed open long after the luckless distillery was closed in 1930, becoming only maltings. By 1951 under 300 people lived at Drummuir, declining to around 200 by 1971. The very small secondary school at Botriphnie was downgraded to a primary around 1960, and the railway was closed to passengers in 1968; freight continued for a number of years. By 1992 oatcakes were baked at the Mill of Towie, downstream from the old distillery, but

*Drummuir Castle, built in 1847 for Admiral Duff to designs by James Mackenzie. In the late 1980s it was converted into a trade centre for customers by Justerini & Brooks.* (RCAHMS / JRH)

by 1994 the post office had vanished. The rebuilt Drummuir Castle now has accommodation for trade customers of UDV (United Distillers & Vintners). In 2000 the Keith & Dufftown Railway was reopened by a preservation society, with a diesel passenger service between Dufftown and a temporary terminus at Drummuir; reopening to Keith is planned for 2001.

## DRUMNADROCHIT, Glenurquhart & Lewiston

**Map 9, A4**

***Inverness-shire village & hamlets,*** *pop. 600* OS 26: NH 5029

On the north bank of the 200m deep Loch Ness is a promontory site fortifed since the Iron Age, where the spectacular ruins of the 13th century Castle Urquhart still stand; around 1455 Urquhart was royal property, but was largely rebuilt by Clan Grant after 1509. Timothy Pont's sketchy map of about 1600 also indicated a church and settlement at the foot of Glenurquhart, where the Rivers Enrick and Coiltie share a delta. The castle was blown up after a Jacobite rising in 1689 and left a ruin. The Roy map made about 1750 showed Kilmore Kirk in a wooded area south of the River Enrick, and the ancient St Ninians Chapel north of Urquhart Bay. Between the two were tiny settlements named as *'Shelon Drinnen'* and *'Shilton'*; but there was no track north of the loch, and no information as to settlement in Glenurquhart.

**Planned Village, Bridge and Hotel**: The planned village of Lewiston was created in 1769 on a site between Kilmore Kirk and Urquhart castle. By 1813 the Commissioners for Highland Roads & Bridges had made a through road along the north side of the loch and bridged the River Enrick; a post office named Drumnadrochit *(in Gaelic 'Ridge by the Bridge')* was opened there about 1835. Later in the century a road was built up Glenurquhart, and a primary school was built at Balnain, 6km up the glen. Railways never served the area, though in 1894 the steamer which plied on the loch and the Caledonian Canal called each day at Temple pier, over 2 km away. Despite its relative inaccessibility, the *Drumnadrochit Hotel* was by then rated *"very good"* by Murray.

**Mythical Monster spurs Tourism**: In the 20th century the three villages, including Milton, became a minor central place with a secondary school (now Glen Urquhart High School) and a growing resort role based on exploitation of the fabulous Loch Ness Monster, which very conveniently first appeared in the slump of 1932. By 1953 celtic art was taught locally, and by 1977 the local shops were visibly prosperous and growing. The five hotels in and around the disjointed village included the *Lewiston Arms*, the 65-room *Glenurquhart Lodge* and – 3km west – the seasonal, apparently Edwardian *Polmaily House*. These catered not only for monster researchers, gawpers and castle visitors but served the fishing, walking and pony-trekking recreations available in the area. By 1980 the 18th century Tore meal mill 6km to the west had been restored and opened to the public; by 1982 the oatcake bakery of Highland Pride Foods was at work at Drumnadrochit, and the resident population was over 600.

**Sir Peter's Hoax and the too-Popular Monster**: About that time the famous wildlife artist Sir Peter Scott made news with a drawing of what he called *Nessiteras Rhombopteryx*, a delicious anagram of *'Monster Hoax by Sir Peter S'*. If anything this spurred the public's keen interest in searching for the mythical monster, which by 1992 supported two rival visitor centres drawing over 300,000 people a year. Remarkably they were the most popular commercial attractions in the Highlands, the combination of the gullible and irresponsible resulting in summer conditions that led to the jesting appellation *Drunkendrochit!* No doubt hoping to cash in as well as to inform, Sea Life Centres of Dorset, St Andrews and Barcaldine then proposed a *fresh water* Life Centre at Borlum, devoted to the real wildlife of the great loch; but this has not happened. As well as *Glenurquhart House* and *Polmaily House*, there are B&Bs, and an independent hostel for backpackers.

## DRUMOAK, Durris & Park

**Map 10, B4**

***Ab'shire small village & hamlets,*** *pop. 600* OS 38: NO 7998

Durris parish on the south bank of the River Dee some 15km west of Aberdeen had a thanage from the 11th century, ultimately resulting in a mansionhouse. On a gentle hillside about 2 km north of the river grew the extraordinarily strong keep of Drum Castle, whose almost blank stone walls, nearly 4m thick at the base, date from around 1300. As Pont's map indicated, the Mills of Drum turned by about 1600 where the Burn of Drum, flowing from the shallow Loch of Park, enters the River Dee 5km south-west of the castle; this loch soon silted up. *'Drum-mark'* Kirk already stood on the river bank 3km south-east of the castle. Mathematician and astronomer James Gregory, born at Drumoak in 1638, invented the reflecting principle still in use – e.g. in the Hubble Space Telescope.

**Mansion, Mills and Ferry**: A mansion was built on to Drum Castle in the 17th century to form the House of Drum. This was shown in its policies on Roy's map made about 1750, which also delineated the North Deeside road and the Mill of Drum; the later Mills of Crathes were built a little upstream. The scattered village of Park was to develop on the main road within this triangle of landmarks. At that time the *'Easter Boat'* crossed the Dee from the Mill of Drum to the Kirkton of Durris, which also had a water mill, whence a hill track led south to Auchenblae.

**Three Stations, Two Bridges**: The Deeside Railway, built on the north bank of the river in 1852–53, originally provided three stations; the most westerly, Mills of Drum, was little used and closed in 1863. Drumoak was an early parish library to be set up with Carnegie aid (1893). South of Drum House, was a station named after Park House, the home of Alex Kinloch, a director of the railway. From about 1900 its level crossing led to a toll bridge – first proposed in 1845 and still charging in 1967 – connecting to Durris House. Park Bridge is a fine cast-iron arched structure, made in Aberdeen. The Easter Boat was abandoned when the free Durris Bridge was built 2 km west of Kirkton of Durris. Drum station had little goods traffic and was closed in 1951; Park station lost its freight trains in 1964; Beeching closed the railway completely in 1966.

**Park is Drumoak, Drum a Castle – and a New Castle!**: Drumoak post office and the ancient roofless riverside church survived, and a caravan site was in use at Park by 1974. The House of Drum was bequeathed to the National Trust for Scotland in 1976, and soon opened to the public as Drum Castle. Meantime the scattered population had gradually sunk to under 500 by 1981, though served by the facilities of a small village; but then new housing was built at Park, which became known as Drumoak. A remarkable event in 1988 was the building of Strathieburn Castle near Durris, to a neo-16th century design. By 1999 a further housing estate had been built at Drumoak.

## DRYBURGH — Map 3, B4

***Borders hamlet,*** *pop. 300* — OS 74: NT 5932

In a loop on the north side of the River Tweed 15 km west of Kelso is Dryburgh Abbey, which was founded in 1150 by King David I and Hugh de Moreville, the Constable of Scotland. It was staffed with Premonstratensian monks, the White Canons, from Alnwick in David's Northumberland fiefdom, and linked to Melrose 5 km up-river by the Monk's Ford. Dryburgh Abbey was endowed with land in Lanark and elsewhere; by 1296 it owned properties in Berwick. It was damaged by English attacks in 1322 and 1385, but repaired. Dryburgh became an ecclesiastical burgh in 1526–27. The Abbey was represented in Parliament until 1560 but the Reformation ended its life, though its fine buildings remained relatively intact.

**Mansions, Village and Bridge**: Pont's maps of the Borders made about 1600 showed both *'Drybrugh'* and the 16th century tower of Bemersyde House, 2 km farther north, while *'Martoun tour and Kirk'* 3 km to the east were emphasised. The riverside Jacobean tower house of Old Mertoun was replaced in 1703 by Harden House, designed by Sir William Bruce for the Scotts of Harden. The Roy survey of the mid 1750s showed the lay settlement at Dryburgh as a small nucleated centre from which roads already led to Bemersyde and Mertoun. Dorothy Wordsworth in 1803 noted the *"village"* of Dryburgh, which had no public house; the Tweed still had to be forded on the journey south from the abbey. In 1817 John and Thomas Smith designed an 80 m span chain suspension bridge, the first in Britain, built across the river near Mertoun for the laird, the Earl of Buchan, for whom a baronial mansion of pink sandstone was built at Dryburgh about 1845.

**Tourism and Facilities**: Sir Walter Scott was buried at Dryburgh near his favourite viewpoint, Bemersyde Hill. The 1895 OS map still showed three fords, to Melrose, Newtown and St Boswells; there was a post office at Clint Mains near Harden House, which had been greatly enlarged for the Duke of Bridgwater and renamed Mertoun House, but in the new century it was cut down and restored to designs resembling the original. By 1954 there were 460 residents in the area, a number which later declined somewhat; Mertoun had a primary school and Dryburgh had a post office. The baronial mansion had become the luxurious 32-room *Dryburgh Abbey Hotel*, which has earned many awards. Both the abbey ruins and the gardens at Bemersyde are open to the public.

## DRYMEN, Buchanan & Rowardennan — Map 5, B4

***W. Stirlingshire village & hamlets,*** *pop. 1200* — OS 57: NS 4788

Drymen, pronounced *Drimmen*, lies within the ancient Earldom of Lennox about 15 km north-east of Dumbarton. It stands above the River Endrick, south of which at Catter a medieval motte was raised to command the lowest easy crossing point before the river enters Loch Lomond. Buchanan Castle, 1 km west, was built in the 14th century near the north bank; opposite it rose the probably 15th century tower of Kilmaronock, also called Mains Castle. Despite its 2 m thick walls, this was occupied into the early 18th century, then becoming ruinous. Pont's sketch map of about 1600 showed *'Drumyn Kirk'* on the north bank, and also indicated a bridge; from 1624 a parish school was open. Drymen lay on the military road, built before 1724 to link Dumbarton with Stirling, which crossed the Endrick at the point then still called Catter Boat (after the earlier ferry); from here the Roy maps of 1750 showed a track leading south. *'Drymen in Lenox'* was then a substantial north bank settlement on a north–south axis, but with no other road links. Two plantations sheltered the seat of the Duke of Montrose, which was still known as Buchanan Castle when altered by Robert Adam in 1751 and enlarged by James Playfair in 1789.

**Communications and County change**: A fine stone bridge was built across the Endrick Water in 1765 and a post office was opened in 1798, the mails being carried via Dumbarton. Heron simply referred to Drymen as a *"village"* in 1799. In 1826 the *Rowardennan Inn* was already open at the end of the road 15 km up the lochside, with a ferry to Inverbeg. Buchanan Castle burnt down in 1850, and was replaced in 1852–54 by a new mansion in baronial style bearing the same name, designed by William Burn and built for the Dukes of Montrose 500 m east of the old house. Black's mid 19th century maps bore a note that *"the boundary between Stirling and Dumbarton has been often changed"*; by then Drymen was in Stirlingshire.

**The Railway fails but Golf triumphs**: Drymen was indirectly served by the Forth & Clyde Railway, opened in 1856 between Stirling and Balloch, with a station at Croftamie (*q.v.*) 2 km to the south. By 1895 Balmaha on Loch Lomond 6 km to the west had a steamer pier, and at Drymen was the *Buchanan Arms Hotel*, later noted for its fine gardens. The 9-

hole Strathendrick golf course east of the village was founded in 1901, and Old Buchanan House became the club house for the upmarket 18-hole Buchanan Castle course founded in 1936. However up to this time Drymen village had fewer than 1000 people, and passenger trains were withdrawn in 1934.

**Recreation**: In the 1950s the village facilities, including two hotels, served a sparsely peopled area on the east shores of Loch Lomond, where outdoor recreation was growing. The ferry for Inverbeg still plied in 1954 when Buchanan Castle was vacated, and by 1965 Rowardennan Lodge was a youth hostel, but Balmaha pier was closed in 1971 and its post office vanished about the same time. However, by 1972 the 20-room *Winnock Hotel* was open in traditional buildings at Drymen, and in 1979 the retail magnate Sir Hugh Fraser gifted a small modern library cum tourist office to the village. A third hotel was open by 1980, and the area's scattered population in 1981 was over 1200.

**Recreating the Caledonian Forest**: When the West Highland Way was defined around 1981, it attracted walkers to Drymen, and The Highland Way leisure complex at Balmaha was opened about 1989. The ferry for Inverbeg plied in summer only by 1991, when Drymen village had 844 residents. By 1993 the castle was a roofless shell adjoined by new private housing, but the area remained largely owned by the Duke of Montrose. Village facilities continued to thrive, but tourism dominated, based on three hotels, and horse riding was prominent. In the past five years the Royal Scottish Forestry Society have planted some 400 ha of Cashel Farm at Balmaha with mixed native species, for both demonstration and access purposes. The long-established quality hotels are the *Buchanan Arms* (52 rooms) and the historic *Winnock* (48); the Rowardennan youth hostel is open for a long season.

## DUDDINGSTON

**Map 15, C2**

***Village / eastern suburb of Edinburgh*** — OS 66: NT 2872

The steep volcanic hill known as Arthur's Seat has Bronze Age cultivation terraces. Beside a small glacial loch at its foot, 3 km east of Edinburgh Castle, lies Duddingston, whose Anglian name was first mentioned as the site of a Norman church, built by monks from Kelso about 1143. The ancient *Sheep's Heid Inn* is claimed to date from the 14th century, and was certainly open in 1580. When Pont mapped the area around 1600, *'Wester Duddytoun'* was a small place. It established a parish school in 1630, was chartered as a burgh of barony in 1673, and grew into a village of some 500 people, mainly due to coal mining.

**Coal, Tunnels and Linens**: In later years mining tended to dominate the area; as early as 1720 an engine was in use to drain local coal pits. The Roy map made about 1754 showed *'Diddiston'* as a small village, on a spur road from a mill where the Leith to Dalkeith road crossed the Braid Burn. Duddingston coal pit was sunk in 1745; from 1763 it was deep enough to require an engine. By 1776 two seams were being worked nearly 40 m below sea level, and a tunnel level 5 km long had been excavated to carry away the water to the sea at Joppa saltworks *(see Portobello)*. Around 1792 coarse linens were also woven at Duddingston.

**Mansion, Coal and Suburban Railways**: The classical mansion of Duddingston House was built in 1763 for the Earl of Abercorn, its 80 ha park being added in 1768. The rules of the game of Curling were first formalised in 1804 by the clerk of the Duddingston Curling Society, which used the frozen loch as its rink. The bucolic Edinburgh & Dalkeith Railway (E&DR), laid out by James Jardine of Edinburgh to carry coals to the city, was opened through the area to the south in 1831, and by 1837 Duddingston had a post office. In 1884 when the new Edinburgh South Side Suburban Railway was opened by the North British, incorporating much of the old E&DR route, a proper station was provided 1 km south of the village, named Duddingston & Craigmillar.

**Golf, Nature and Education**: The golf club founded in the park of Duddingston House in 1897 laid out a parkland course which became very well known. The Meadowfield area was developed in the early 20th century, drawing Duddingston into the urban mass of east Edinburgh, though the loch had been declared a nature reserve by 1949. The coal mines had long gone when the Holy Rood secondary school was built in Duddingston park about 1970, now having about 750 pupils. The railway to St Leonards was closed and lifted between 1970 and 1975; eventually its route became a cycleway past Duddingston Loch. By 1975 Duddingston House was a hotel; but in the 1990s it became housing, with more built in its grounds and nearby.

## DUFFTOWN, Mortlach & Cabrach

**Map 10, A2**

***Moray village & hamlets,*** *pop. 1700* — OS 28: NJ 3240

Mortlach lies in Glen Rinnes, the steep valley of the Dullan Water, a short way above its confluence with Glenfiddich. Ptolemy's ancient map named the local cattle-herding tribe as Vacomagi – *Vacca* being Latin for a cow. The tribe may well have given its name to Mar, Moray, and hence to Mortlach, whose name also includes the Gaelic element *lagh*, thus meaning *'law place of Moray'*, for it was once the centre of that Pictish province. Its very early church became the seat of the first bishopric in the North, probably founded before the eighth century, by when it had five associated churches. The parish church of Mortlach, rebuilt in the 13th century, is among the oldest in the north.

**After the Bishops, the Castles and Massacre**: Around 1140 the see was moved to Old Aberdeen. Evidently a monastery remained, for by 1228 a very early parish school was in operation and Balvenie, the 13th century castle of the Comyns some 1.5 km to the north of the kirk, also bears a Gaelic name, meaning *'village of monks' (c.f. Balivanish)*. Some 3 km south-east of Mortlach in upper Glenfiddich is Auchindoun Castle, amidst whose 11th century earthworks was built a 15th century tower. In 1571 it was held by the fierce Adam Gordon, who killed 27 members of the Forbes clan at Corgarff; for his pains his own castle was burnt in 1592 and left an impressive ruin.

**Swedish Field Marshal, Mill, Burgh and Mansion**: Balvenie Castle with its large rectangular courtyard had been extended about 1550, and was the birthplace about 1580 of Sir Alexander Leslie, who uniquely became Field Marshal of Sweden but retired to Balgonie in Fife. Timothy Pont identified a mill just north of this castle in his map made about 1600, probably at Milton of Balvenie, for this place was chartered as a burgh of barony in 1615. Balvenie New House was built in 1724–25 for William Duff of Braco; Roy's military map made about 1750 sketched in only a few other buildings near the *Old Castle*

*Balvenie*. The Kirk of Mortlach then stood alone, and although the area was entirely roadless, it must have been peaceable enough, for the building of military roads was not deemed necessary.

**New Roads create Dufftown and its Whisky**: Later in the 18th century public roads were constructed into the area from the north, and had reached Craigellachie by about 1800. Mortlach had a post office from 1800, but the year 1817 saw the founding of a new settlement on the hillside above it; with the bravado typical of the feudal superior of the day, it was named *Dufftown* by its sponsor the Earl of Fife, one James Duff. Sited between Balvenie and Mortlach, it was well placed for the forthcoming whisky boom from 1823, when Mortlach distillery was among those legalised. But true to its murky history Auchindoun Mill, built around 1850, was the base for a gang of illicit distillers as late as Edwardian times. South-east of Auchindoun a road climbs over a col to the ultra-rural parish of Cabrach on the upper Deveron, and so to Rhynie.

**Railways to the Pacific!**: In 1862 the Keith & Dufftown Railway – a protégé of the Great North of Scotland Railway – opened its line from Keith, curving sharply on a radius of only 275 m to Dufftown station, sited in the valley 1.5 km north of the village, enabling its continuation up Speyside to reach Nethybridge in 1863 and Boat of Garten in 1866. George Stephen, born in Dufftown, became the President of the Bank of Montreal, and was subsequently the President of the famed Canadian Pacific Railway during its planning and construction in the 1880s. By 1863 the Duke of Fife's Kininver limestone quarries were open to the south of the line; by 1902 operations had moved north to the Parkmore limeworks and quarry. The water-powered Mortlach distillery, *"an irregular pile of buildings"*, worked under Gordon & Cowie from 1866. It was making 385,000 litres of malt whisky annually in 1886 when Barnard found Dufftown *"a quaint village, almost aspiring to be a town"*, dominated by the *"large and unsightly gaol which stands in the centre of the square"*.

**Grant's Whisky Galore at Dufftown**: Barnard commented on the *"excellent quality"* of the Mortlach water, and in the whisky boom of the late 19th century the Dufftown area was indeed found to have a particularly favourable combination of water and peat; five distilleries which have survived and intermittently prospered up to the present day were opened there in ten years. The site of Glenfiddich distillery beside Balvenie castle was leased in 1886 by William Grant from the owners of the Mortlach distillery; with the aid of his large family it was built and brought on stream in 1886 using second-hand equipment from Cardow distillery. Its instant success enabled them only five years later to acquire Balvenie Castle and 5 ha of land just across the railway, on which they built the Balvenie distillery with its dam in 1892. By 1896 at least 22 men were employed at Glenfiddich distillery, and by 1902 the extensive but little-publicised Parkmore distillery had been built nearby, but across the railway to the east.

**The Whisky Town**: A local newspaper, the *Dufftown News*, was established in 1894, when Murray rated both the *Fife Arms* and *Commercial* hotels *"good"*. Three more distilleries were being planned: Convalmore was built north of the station in 1894, and Dufftown-Glenlivet was created in 1896 by the conversion of a water-powered sawmill and a meal mill; its water came from the Highlandman's Well in the Conval Hills south-west of the town. Finally in 1897 came the Glendullan distillery beside the Parkmore & Mortlach sidings, which extended 2 km southwards from the quarry. The small but rail-connected Parkmore limeworks stood immediately east of the Bridge of Poolinch, near the ruined Balvenie Castle. The Dufftown Golf Club was founded in 1896, and provided a 9-hole course in undulating parkland on the slopes of Little Conval. By 1902 Dufftown had an auction mart and slaughterhouse.

*Maltings, Mortlach distillery, Dufftown. The distillery began in the 1820s and was extended in 1897 when these maltings were built. The maltings operated until 1968.* *(JRH)*

**Transfers and Closures**: Parkmore distillery was sold in 1923 to Dewars by James Watson & Co of Dundee; though closed in 1931, its buildings remain as warehouses. Convalmore distillery had been acquired in 1906 by James Buchanan & Co, and in 1923 Mortlach distillery was bought by John Walker & Sons. Balvenie New House was razed in 1929. In 1933 Arthur Bell & Sons of Perth bought the Pittyvaich estate, named after a mid 18th century farmhouse, and also the mothballed Dufftown-Glenlivet distillery owned by Mackenzie & Sons of Edinburgh, which they restarted – though it was again out of use due to the second world war in 1940–45. Through the vicissitudes of the distilling trade in the 1914–45 period the Dufftown area continued to rely partly on limestone quarrying for a livelihood.

**The Railway misses a Revival**: However, the whisky trade rapidly revived about 1950, and by 1951 Dufftown had the facilities of a large village, a brand new memorial hall and a population of nearly 2000. About 1957 Grant's Banffshire Copper Works of Dufftown made the spirit safe that was soon installed in Crieff's rejuvenated Glenturret distillery. In 1962 Grants began seriously to export malt whisky, exploiting a market which until then had been dominated by blends, but Glendullan railway siding was closed in 1966 and the line was closed to passengers in 1968. By 1970 output at Bell's three distilleries (one at Dufftown) had been quadrupled in a decade to 8 million proof litres a year.

**Yet more Distilleries**: In 1972 a new distillery with six stills was built at Glendullan by Scottish Malt Distillers; the old distillery, closed in 1985, became maintenance workshops.

Meantime the Pittyvaich-Glenlivet distillery was opened by Bell's in 1974, its capacity 4.5 million proof litres a year; also a dark grains plant to convert both distilleries' waste into cattle food. By then Bells were distilling some 18 million litres of Highland malts a year. In 1975 Chivas added the ultra-modern Allt a'Bhainne distillery, though this was not near the town but on a greenfield site near Ben Rinnes School, 7 km to the south-west. The railway west of Dufftown had been abandoned in 1971, but until 1982 a weekly train still brought in grain; however malt already arrived by road from Burghead and elsewhere. Barrels were still repaired by the coopers Joseph Brown & Sons, and in thirty years from 1955 the substantial limeworks had doubled the excavation left by its quarry.

**Dufftown in 1980**: In 1980 Aberdeen & Northern Marts still ran a cattle market, and two branch banks were open, as were the small hospital and a secondary school (now closed). During the 1970s the cinema was closed and became a cafe, fish and chip and antique shop – a remarkable combination! About two dozen other shops augmented the *Commercial Hotel*, and the *Fife Arms Hotel*. Other facilities included police and fire stations, a garage, and a part-time library.

**Visitors on the Whisky Trail**: Duffown's role as a central place, never really assured, was in decline towards a typical village, hastened by the slump in whisky sales from 1978. In the eighties occasional excursion trains brought trippers to the many distilleries; by 1986 the former jail was a museum. In 1989 over 135,000 people visited William Grant & Sons' showpiece Glenfiddich distillery, still run by a family firm whose HQ was in Glasgow; it produced the pale Glenfiddich whisky.

**Whisky Production at Full Stretch – and afterwards**: In 1990 Grants built a third malt whisky distillery, the Kininvie, at Dufftown, and also had ambitious plans for major expansion of their overworked Balvenie distillery, whose renowned single malt was matured in bourbon casks. The quite modern Pittyvaich distillery was hard at work under the ownership of Bell's (United Distillers), as was Dufftown distillery (both having shed *'Glenlivet'* from their titles). Chivas' Allt-a'Bhainne was busy too, but with recession in 1993 United Distillers mothballed Pittyvaich, and Auchindoun Mill stood empty in 1997. Grants' Glenfiddich Malt was not only unique in the Highlands at that time by being bottled on the premises, but by then claimed no less than half of the world's duty-free whisky sales, and the firm's 18-year old malt *'Glenfiddich Excellence'* won an award at Cannes. In 2000 the Keith & Dufftown Railway was reopened with a diesel passenger service between Dufftown and a temporary terminus at Drummuir; reopening to Keith is planned for 2001.

## DUFFUS — Map 9, C3

***Moray hamlet**, pop. 600* — OS 28: NJ 1768

In the plain of the Laigh of Moray, 2 km south-east of the ancient Duffus Kirk, is the feudal motte of Duffus. This was raised beside Loch Spynie, then an extensive sheet of water, for a noble brought in by David I. In 1303 the stone keep of Duffus castle was built on the motte; a paved road led up to it. Pont's neat map of the Laigh of Moray made about 1600 showed the area densely settled, and full of kirktons; the 17th century Michaelkirk was built as a burial chapel. Heron claimed in 1799 that the streets of the early planned village of Duffus were paved by Cromwellian soldiers. The mansion of Gordonstoun was built 1 km east of the church around 1700; the 1750s Roy map showed it in huge rectangular policies extending about 2.5 km from Duffus Castle to Plewlands, of which the north part had been planted with shelter belts. There were no roads except the short sections already mentioned, but this was soon rectified. Duffus post office was issued with a cancelling stamp in 1845, but railways never arrived.

**Gordonstoun and other Schools**: In 1934 Kurt Hahn moved from Germany with four boy pupils including the future Prince Philip, to board in the great house of Gordonstoun. His independent school soon gained an international reputation and took on more royal pupils. By 1951 some 750 people lived in the area, and there was an inn, but other facilities were minimal. The primary school serving Duffus was known as Keam, whereas Duffus school was at Hopeman! Gordonstoun School's chapel is the old Michaelkirk; there are now some 430 pupils, half of them girls.

## DULL, Coshieville & Keltneyburn — Map 5, C2

***Perthshire hamlets**, pop. 150* — OS 52: NN 8049

It is said that around 500 AD a loop (*dull* in Gaelic) made of leather or textiles broke while being carried through the fertile strath beside the upper River Tay, letting fall relics of St Andrew carried by Eonan, St Columba's biographer. Local standing stones may show the exact location of this trivial event, and a Culdee (Columban church) college was founded at Dull in his memory; its land was held by an abbot. Dull had a thanage from about the 11th century and remained a parish centre of some importance, being shown on the medieval Gough map. The Black Death may have wiped out the settlement, for the energetic cleric Timothy Pont who mapped Tayside about 1600 showed only watercourses in the area between Castle Menzies and the 15th century Comrie Castle at the foot of Glen Lyon.

**Dull on the Road**: Around 1730 a military road was built past Dull by General Wade's men, with a kingshouse at Whitebridge on the way to Tummel Bridge. Roy's map – which showed this route in the style he reserved for carriage roads – also indicated the *'Kirk of Doul'*, west of which a ferry plied to connect with a lochside track to Killin. In 1797 two annual fairs were scheduled for Kirkton of Dull, and the River Lyon was still crossed by a *'boat'* in 1827. Spokes and bobbins were turned at a mill at nearby Camserney in the 1840s. Woollens were made at Keltneyburn Mill, which was eventually converted to housing in 1994; but in the late 20th century apart from the small *Coshieville Hotel* the area remained essentially agricultural, with a scattered population of around 150 and a deer park at Glengolandie.

## DULNAIN BRIDGE — Map 9, C4

***Speyside village**, pop. 250* — OS 36: NH 9924

Glacial action left a clear example of striated rocks near the confluence of the Rivers Dulnain with the central River Spey, a beautiful area which held some early significance, since standing stones were erected nearby. North of the Dulnain was the 13th century royal hunting preserve of Leonach or Leantack, where the courtyard stronghold of Muckrach Castle was built in the 16th century; it later fell into ruin. When Timothy Pont sketched this crofting area about 1600, the Boat of Balliefurth crossed the river near the standing stones. Caulfeild's military road from Aviemore – which crossed the new Dulnain Bridge, first built about 1754, 1 km downstream of the castle – joined another from Forres to Corgarff near the site of later Grantown 5 km to the east. Dulnain Bridge, rebuilt in 1791, was swept away in the great flood of 1829 and again rebuilt in 1830 by Telford's clever aide Joseph Mitchell. In the 1950s Dulnain Bridge was a little village of some 200 people with a primary school, post office, telephone exchange and garage. Although the primary school closed, by 1972 a Victorian shooting-lodge was the *Muckrach Lodge* hotel. By 1980 a second hotel was open, a doctor was practising and the population was nearing 250. A Heather Centre was open by 1992. An Edwardian shooting-lodge is now the *Auchendean Lodge* hotel.

## DUMBARTON

**Map 5, B5**

***Large town, North R. Clyde,*** *pop. 22,000* OS 63/64: NS 3975

The striking 74 m tall rock beside the mouth of the short River Leven, which flows from Loch Lomond to the Clyde, originally bore some variant of the Welsh name *Alcluid*, meaning *'Clyde Rock'*. Hardyng, who visited the area in the early 15th century, found that Dumbarton Rock was even then isolated at high tide. The shallow Leven was fordable, and until the Clyde was dredged in modern times the rock could be reached from the south at low tide by crossing the Dumbuck ford 2 km east of the town, itself overshadowed by the steep 166 m prominence known as Dumbuck. Alcluid lay north of the Romans' Antonine Wall, and was traditionally the birthplace of St Patrick in 387 AD *(but see Old Kilpatrick)*.

**The Ancient Heart of Strathclyde under Repeated Attack**: The dark age kingdom of Strathclyde seems to have been functionally centred on Dumbarton, whose later Gaelic name means *Dun-Briton*, i.e. the British Fortress; though the Northumbrian chronicler Bede's description in 731 translates as *"a strongly fortified British city"*. Alcluid was besieged by an unlikely alliance of Angles and Picts in 756, sacked in 780, and again by Danes from Ireland in 870, when it was evidently quite a large place, *"a great host of prisoners"* being taken. The town was eventually resettled on a site in a meander of the River Leven 1 km north of the rock, but never regained its relative importance, for Strathclyde was merged into Scotland by inheritance early in the 11th century, when many of its leaders fled to Wales.

**Dumbarton in Scotland**: In 1222 Dumbarton became a Scottish Royal Burgh, with a new Royal castle and a merchant guild. However, this was a century after the most important east coast towns had been so recognised. Although herrings were exported, its development was very slow, despite being made the caput of a sheriffdom in 1237. In the early 14th century the rock's impregnability again made it temporarily a key centre while the English held south-east Scotland; the king signed many Royal charters in Dumbarton, which also made some contribution to Customs revenue. The castle, by then built of stone, became a prison under Robert I.

**After the Black Death and Fire**: In 1350 these roles vanished with the Black Death, which seems to have hit the place with devastating ferocity, for little seems to have been recorded until the town was burned down in 1424. Afterwards trade recovered painfully slowly: trivial quantities of cloth were being exported from Dumbarton by 1434, the royal castle was again viable in 1455, and a collegiate church was established in an existing chapel in 1454 by the Duchess of Albany. Commercial growth accelerated: the first mention of a shipyard is for 1487, and in the years 1500–05 Dumbarton had almost as much overseas export trade as Perth, though apart from herrings (where it dominated Scottish exports) the actual quantities were slight; in 1535–56 Dumbarton paid under 1.5% of the total of both Customs and burgh taxes. In 1544 the castle was still intact, having become the centre of the Earldom of Lennox, which later became the split county of Dunbartonshire. Brewing was established in the town by the mid 16th century, and a parish school was started in 1576.

**Post-Reformation Growth and Decline**: Three fairs were held annually by 1600, when the area was thickly covered with tiny settlements. If Pont's map is to be believed, by that time Dumbarton town filled most of the loop in the river, making it some 500 m across; by 1593 it was also the centre of a presbytery. By 1621 the port was very significant, paying between 3% and 10% of Scottish Customs dues, but by 1639 Dumbarton stood 20th in Scottish burgh tax yield – it had only an eighth of Glasgow's riches. In 1655 Dumbarton was according to Tucker *"a small and very poor burgh"* that occasionally imported corn from England or Ireland in a tiny vessel of only sixteen tons.

**Rapid Resurgence**: It is remarkable that by 1666, only six years after the Restoration ended the turmoil and uncertainties, the town possessed five ocean-going ships, including one trading with the West Indies importing sugar, indigo and tobacco. By 1680 Dumbarton had become an important market, but having no bridge over the Leven – which had to be forded or ferried – the town council was petitioning for one to be built; by 1700 a ferry also operated to Erskine, and by 1715 a post office was open, with another from 1717. Apparently Defoe wrote nothing about the town, though the castle was to him *"the most ancient, as well as the most important castle in Scotland"*, perhaps because it was still garrisoned. By about 1730 Dumbarton Grammar School was open. A stone-built bridge across the Leven was finally completed in 1765 as the last link in the military road to the north west. In 1769 Pennant called Dumbarton *"a small but good old town"*, based on spinning and salmon fishing. Later in the century John Napier (the father of David) operated a cannon foundry in Dumbarton, not then the most obvious site for a metal industry, so it was logical that about 1790 the enterprise was moved to Glasgow, and then to Parkhead.

**The Glass Industry**: The Dumbarton to Stirling road was turnpiked in 1794. Five fairs were scheduled to take place in Dumbarton in 1797; two years later, Heron estimated that the population exceeded two thousand, and described it as *"ancient, small, but well built. The Leven is navigable for coasting vessels as far up as the town. About 2000 tons of shipping belong to it. Its principal manufacture is glass"* (this had been established in 1777 and was Scotland's largest, making window glass and bottles in association with Jacob Dixon & Co's brewery) *"but a good deal of thread is also made here. Many of the inhabitants are employed in the neighbouring printfields" (see Renton and Alexandria)*.

**Shipbuilding: McLachlan, Napier and Denny**: Dorothy Wordsworth wrote in 1803 that the inn at Dumbarton had a large dining room but provided *"sorry accommodations"*. She provided a detailed description of the castle, which was even then still garrisoned. The firm of Archibald McLachlan built the very early 27 m wooden paddle-steamer *Dumbarton Castle* in 1815, and in 1816 the first Loch Lomond pleasure steamer PS *Marion*, engined by David Napier. Two years later Napier designed the first open sea steamer, the 25 m PS *Rob Roy*, originally for the Glasgow to Belfast run; Napier made the 30hp engine, but the hull was built by William Denny – famed as a philanthropist and founder of the famous shipbuilding firm – and in 1821 this boat became the first steam ferry across the English Channel.

**From Second Comet to New York Central**: In 1821 another builder, James Lang constructed the *Comet II* of 94 tons for Henry Bell; his maritime career was sadly ended when this vessel collided and sank off Gourock in 1825, with the loss of 70 lives. In 1827 the snobbish Robert Chambers simply dismissed Dumbarton as *"A small town, undistinguished by commerce, and possessing no manufactures except glass-making and shipbuilding"*. A gasworks was established in 1832, Scott & Linton were founded as shipbuilders in 1834, and James Lang was using iron hulls by 1839. William Buchanan, born in Dumbarton in 1830, became a skilled blacksmith, emigrated to the USA, rose to become a locomotive designer, and finally became Superintendent of Motive Power for the prestigious New York Central Railroad.

**Prosperity in the Railway Epoch**: The Caledonian & Dunbartonshire Railway from Bowling to Balloch served the town from 1850, with a tenuous connection to Stirling and beyond from 1856. In 1858 Dumbarton became the junction for the new Helensburgh line, and by 1860 Wordie & Co had a rail cartage depot. Matthew Paul & Co began their marine engineering in 1847, and both Dennystown Forge and shipbuilders Archibald Macmillan & Son were established in 1854. The long-lasting printing firm of McGavigan's was founded at Dumbarton in 1860 *(for its development from 1946 see Kirkintilloch)*. In 1860–63 the baronial mansion of Overtoun House was built 3 km east of Dumbarton for James White, the unscrupulous chemical magnate from Rutherglen, to designs by James Smith of Glasgow. The Dumbarton Co-op and the local newspaper the *Lennox Herald* were established in 1861. The fine Burgh Hall and Library was built in Church Street in 1865–66 to designs by Melvin & Leiper; the building later became the Academy.

***Cutty Sark*, Mansions, First Steel Ship and Experimental Tank**: In 1845 William Denny built the 207 ton iron steamer *Britannia* for the Edinburgh & Dundee Steam Packet Company, and about 1848 the iron-hulled steamer *Waterwitch* for Loch Lomond service. When the glassworks closed about 1850, its site was added to Denny's shipyard. In 1856–58 Peter Denny had Helenslee House built to designs by J T Rochead; so prosperous was his firm that he had John Honeyman radically alter the mansion in 1866–67. In 1869 the enlarged yard had to take over and complete the famous clipper *Cutty Sark*, built from iron and teak by Scott & Linton, who had sadly been bankrupted by the contract. In 1879 Denny's built the first ocean-going merchant vessel with a mild steel hull, the 90m-long *Rotomahana*, for the Union Steamship Company of New Zealand. In 1881 came the *Claymore* for David MacBrayne's West Highland services; she lasted half a century. Denny's pioneer experimental tank for improving hull lines was built between 1879 and 1883, and for a time the firm invested successfully in a steamer service on the Irrawaddy River!

**Chambers Ships, Football and Golf**: By 1881 Dumbarton burgh had a population of 14,172, when Carnegie money helped to start a public library. Another Robert Chambers, who built eleven ships at the Lower Woodyard, including the steel steamer *Chancellor* in 1880 for the Lochlong & Lochlomond Steamboat Company, also operated steamboats in 1879–81. By 1884 the old quay was little used by Clyde steamers, a newish pier south of the Castle Rock being preferred. Dumbarton Football Club was formed in 1872, moving to Boghead Park in 1879 and winning the League in 1892. The golf club was founded in 1888, but Dumbarton was unkindly described by Murray's Handbook in 1894 as a *"thriving but rather dirty town"* with the *"poor" Elephant Hotel*; the ferry was out of use. Away to the east was Dumbuck House. The construction company Babtie began in 1895 (today HQ'd in Glasgow, with 3000 employees).

**Steamers for Stranraer, for Pleasure and Long Life**: William Denny & Brothers built successive ships for the Stranraer to Larne run: the first in 1890 was the steel PS *Princess Victoria*. In 1890–1900 Denny built seven paddlers for Belle Steamers, and about that time also built the renowned 18-knot steamer *Duchess of Hamilton* for the Caledonian Steam Packet Company (CSPC). In 1900 their newly built 115 ton single screw steamer *Sir Walter Scott* began pleasure sailing on Loch Katrine, to which she was transported in sections by barge and dray via Inversnaid, at great cost; 33.5 m long when assembled, her original triple expansion engine was built by Matthew Paul. She celebrated her centenary on the loch in March 2000. The less well known shipyard of Archibald McMillan & Son built the steamer *Clan Macgregor* for the Glasgow-based Clan Line in 1901–02

**Turbine Steamers and Coasters**: In 1901 when Dumbarton's growing population was passing the 20,000 mark, Denny's built the hull of the world's first turbine-driven commercial passenger ship, the screw-propelled TS *King Edward* (Parsons built its turbines); she and her sister TS *Queen Alexandra* sailed between Greenock and Campbeltown. In 1904 Denny built and engined the 100-ton coasters SS *Ailsa* and *Garmoyle* for A McG Leslie of Glasgow. In 1904 the 91 m-long turbine steamer *Princess Maud* was built for the Stranraer run and in 1912 a second, turbine-powered *Princess Victoria*.

**Yachts, Trams – and Helicopters!**: The yacht builders R McAllister & Son built cutters at this time. Dumbarton's first electric power station was built in 1902, and by 1907 the Dumbarton Burgh & County Tramways Company operated electric trams between Dumbuck and Dalreoch Toll on the west bank of the river, where there was also a railway station by 1909. By 1908 Dumbarton and Balloch were linked by tram, and from 1915 Dumbarton trams met those from Glasgow at Dalmuir West. The large Notre Dame Convent with its High School was built in the early 20th century in Cardross Road, beyond the villas of Kirktonhill. In 1905–14 various primitive helicopters were designed by E R Mumford, the Director of Denny's experimental tank; but the 1914–18 war – which kept all the shipyards busy – ended their effective development.

**Successive Slumps: Denny goes Diesel**: After 1921 Dumbarton and the population of its county declined with the shipbuilding slump, plus the collapse of calico printing in the Vale of Leven. Having cut the contract price to the bone to gain the order for the SS *Glen Sannox* (built in 1924–25 for the LMS), in 1926 the Denny family found it expedient to sell

*Dumbarton distillery, built in 1938 by the Canadian concern Hiram Walker. They claimed it was the biggest in the world: it contained grain and malt distilleries, maturing warehouses, and a blending and bottling plant.* (RCAHMS / JRH)

their grand Helenslee House to the independent Keil School *(see Southend)*. Through such measures the Denny yard kept going, launching the TS *King George V* for Williamsons in 1926 – a favourite pleasure ship – and in 1929 built the luxurious 104 m, 2900-ton cross-Channel steamer *Canterbury* for the Southern Railways; this was followed in 1930–31 by the first British diesel-electric ship, the MV *Lochfyne*, for MacBraynes. The less glamorous and innovative McMillan shipyard failed in 1933, but by 1931 Babcock & Wilcox of Renfrew had a tubemaking plant near Dumbuck (east of the town's gasworks), still open in 1958, while marine cranes were built west of the Leven.

**Queens, Princesses and the Welded King**: In 1933 Denny built the TS *Queen Mary* for the Williamson Buchanan line; in 1935 to please the aged King George V, the suffix *'II'* was added to enable a huge new liner to take his consort's name *(see Clydebank)*. In 1931 and 1934 came the Stranraer turbine steamers *Princess Margaret* and a new *Princess Maud*. Ever innovative, during the great Depression Denny's also bought the right to operate the Queens Ferry, for which they built four new paddle ferries over a period, starting in 1934 with *Robert the Bruce*; this 69 m roll-on vessel was the world's first electrically welded ship.

**Over the Sea to Skye and by Land to Loch Awe**: In 1934 Denny also built the TSMV *Lochnevis* for the Skye routes (on which she plied till 1969), and for the LMS one of a pair of paddlers, the rather unreliable *Caledonia*, which ended up as a Thames restaurant from 1970–80; Fairfields built the other. In 1936 Denny prefabricated the 27 m *Countess of Breadalbane*, for erection and launching on Loch Awe. In 1938 Denny built two small motor ships *Ashton* and *Leven* for the CSPC to handle some of the crowds visiting the exhibition at Bellahouston, and also built some 30 coasters for New Zealand over the years.

**Services, Cream, and Whisky for Export**: Overtoun House was gifted to the town in the 1930s, becoming a maternity hospital. The SCWS built a creamery in 1935, and the former McMillan shipyard was soon cleared to build the large Dumbarton Distillery. Intended to produce grain whisky primarily for export, it was opened in 1938 by Canadian-owned Hiram Walker & Sons (Scotland), who claimed it was the largest in the world. In the same complex they also built two Lowland Malt distilleries, the Inverleven and Lomond, and the largest independent whisky blending and bottling plant in Scotland, plus the extensive Strathleven bonded warehouses.

**Flying Boats and Prefabs**: In 1936–37 Denny developed a shadow factory east of the town; its main product from 1939 was the famed Short Sunderland flying boat, of which 242 were built up to 1945. The Academy educated many Clydebank pupils both before and after the raids of 1941, when the very congested town of Dumbarton was more lightly bombed, though it too soon ceased to be a happy place. After 1945 aluminium prefabricated houses were made in the shadow factory until it closed in 1960. In 1951 the burgh population was 23,708. By 1954 the poor *Elephant* seems to have become just a memory, but the *Dumbuck Hotel* had 15 rooms. In the early post-war years, to overcome the housing shortage and congestion, not only was the space within the A82 soon built up in full, including industrial sites at the foot of Dumbuck, but a large peripheral housing scheme was built at Bellsmyre on the lower slopes of Dumbarton Muir. West of the river rose the estates at Brucehill and Castlehill.

**Denny's Decline and Demise**: Denny's built two unlucky ferries named *Princess Victoria* for the Stranraer–Larne run, the 1939 ship with diesel engines and innovative stern carloading being lost in the war, while its sadly underdesigned 1947 replacement foundered in a storm in the North Channel in 1953 with tragic loss of life. Despite this blow, in 1961 they delivered the *Caledonian Princess* for the Stranraer–Larne service; of 3630 gross tons, she was almost 108 m long and able to carry 1400 passengers and over 100 cars. In a desperate bid to stay in business against falling orders and rising foreign competition, Denny's built a hovercraft, delivered in 1963 for Thames service. But with the completion of its last merchant ship, the New Zealand train ferry *Aramoana* of 4228 tons gross, the famous shipyard went into liquidation, and was closed in 1964.

**Dumbarton without Denny**: Dumbarton FC moved a platform canopy from Turnberry station to cover a stand at Boghead Park about 1960. The railway through Dumbarton was electrified in 1961–62, and a new road north of the town was incorporated into the A82 bypass of Alexandria, built 1969–70. Overtoun's hospital use ended in the 1960s when the Vale of Leven hospital was opened at Alexandria. In 1971 the burgh population had reached 25,640. In 1975 the old illogical county of Dunbartonshire was replaced by the much smaller Dumbarton District of Strathclyde Region, but the HQ remained. Hiram Walker became a subsidiary of Allied Distillers, who in the late 1970s built a blending and bottling plant at Kilmalid north of Dumbarton.

**Pictures and Generators**: By 1979 Polaroid UK had opened a factory at the Vale of Leven Industrial Estate, and Aggreko manufactured mobile diesel-electric generators and temperature control equipment. Meantime about 1980 new buildings were provided for the Academy; for a time the old ones became offices. Dumbarton's 1991 population had fallen to 22,000; however, the town had shaken off many of its problems, and in the 1980s and 1990s new housing was creeping up the hillsides north-east of the A82.

**Ups and Downs in Whisky and Football**: In 1990 *'J & B Rare'* was bottled in a new plant beside the A82 in Dumbarton by IDV. The still that had produced the fine Inverleven single malt in the Dumbarton distillery was out of use from 1991, as was the Lomond distillery. In 1991 the Babcock & Wilcox tube works commissioned two new major USA-made spiral finning machines for boiler tube manufacture. However, in that year Strathclyde Sawmills broke its connection with the railway system. In 1993 Hiram Walker's (by then owned by Allied-Lyons), obtained all the malt for their 14 malt and two grain distilleries from their Robert Kilgour maltings in Pathhead (Fife). But in 1995 200 local jobs were shed. In 1990 Dumbarton FC struggled in the second division, their historic but scruffy ground (Scotland's oldest venue) at Boghead Park largely being open terracing; yet from 1997 the ground was shared with Clydebank FC! Their new stadium opened late in 2000.

**Amenities and Local Government**: Robert Napier's first marine engine of 1824 was preserved at Dumbarton as a tourist attraction, and by 1991 Denny's famous testing tank had been restored to working order and public view as part of the Scottish Maritime Museum. Is it too much to hope that – following Dundee's *Discovery* precedent – the famous *Cutty Sark* could perhaps be brought home from Greenwich? The Notre Dame Convent was vacated about 1995, awaited a new user in 1997 and was later burnt out. Meantime in 1996 Clydebank was combined with most of Dumbarton District as a new unitary local authority, 'West Dunbartonshire', owners of the still empty *'A'* listed buildings of the former Academy in Church Street. Overtoun House, still held in the Common Good fund, was impossible for the council to sell due to absurdly archaic legal restrictions, but in 2000 its use as a refuge for single mothers was being negotiated. In 2000, Keil School – down to 189 pupils by 1997 – went out of business. Polaroid's workforce was reduced to 600 in 2001, amidst future worries. Hotels include the *Dumbuck* and a new *Travelodge* at Milton. The RC High School has almost 1500 pupils and Dumbarton Academy has 825.

## DUMFRIES

**Map 2, B4**

***Large S. of Scotland town,*** *pop. 32,000* — OS 84: NX 9776

*Suburb: Locharbriggs*

A wooden plough dating back to around 2000 BC was found in 1994 at the hitherto waterlogged but by then threatened henge known as Pict's Knowe, 4 km south-west of modern Dumfries. The latter's site on the east bank of the River Nith where it meets Solway tidewater was well chosen, forming a centre for the fertile lands to the east, and a defence against raiders from the wilderness of western Galloway; perhaps there was once a Pictish fort or *Dun*. There was already a motte 2 km north of Dumfries when around 1170 a Benedictine nunnery called Lincluden Priory was founded alongside by Uchtred, Lord of Galloway, perhaps to replace an offshoot of a York monastery to whom a sub-king of *'Strathnith'* granted land in *'Dronfres'* in the 1150s.

**Royal Burgh and Capital of Galloway**: In 1186 Dumfries was chartered as a Royal Burgh, so as to colonise and defend the area east of the Nith, newly annexed from Galloway. Western Galloway was added to Scotland on the death of its last Prince in the year 1234, and Dumfries became the caput of a sheriffdom in 1237; for nearly a century its jurisdiction included the Stewartry, and by the end of the 13th century there was a Royal castle. Dumfries also became a market centre, especially for sheep. A bridge was built over the Nith, probably of timber, for it lasted only a few decades; like Dumfries Castle, it has now entirely vanished.

**Greyfriars and Devorgilla's Bridge**: By 1266 a friary had been founded in the town for the new Franciscan order, the Grey Friars. Robert Bruce slew the younger Red Comyn there in 1306. Archibald the Grim, Earl of Douglas and 3rd Lord of Galloway, ejected the nuns from Lincluden Priory in 1389, and had the buildings converted by French craftsmen into a college of priests or *'collegiate church'*. In 1415 nearby Dumfries was described as *"a pretty town plentiful of all good victuals"*. Lady Devorgilla Balliol's bridge over the Nith was built of stone about 1420, originally having 13 arches, and variously rebuilt following floods in 1431–62. There were also mottes 5 km to the west, near which rose the 16th century tower of Hill's Castle, but development was slow, set back by plague and famine in 1439, and the town's contribution to Scotland's burgh taxes was still under 1% in 1535.

**English Occupations**: Dumfries was again set back by being seized repeatedly by the English in 1536, 1542, and 1547. But little lasting damage can have been done, for the town recovered so rapidly in the few years to 1556 that it could pay about twice its 1535 tax contribution. However, in 1570 Dumfries was again occupied by the English for a time.

**Recovery in the late Sixteenth Century**: By 1593 Dumfries was the centre of a presbytery, a burgh post was organised as early as 1599, and the *Globe Inn* was established in 1610. Pont mapped the area about 1610, showing the bridge and *'Brigend'* to the west, *'Castel Dyikes'*, *'Spittell'* and a mill to the south, and to the north the *'Mill of Deskonn'* and the *'Colledge of Lincluden'*. The Nith bridge was partly washed away by floodwaters about 1618, but patched up and reduced to seven arches. Though hitherto unimportant as a port, by 1621 Dumfries was paying between 3% and 10% of Customs duties; the little ships of the day could come up-river to the Dockhead just below the weir. However, famine struck in 1623, when perhaps a sixth of a population of 3000 died; the disruption was enough for pirates to be operating in the Solway in 1630. However, by 1639 Dumfries was the seventh richest centre in Scotland, and traded with England through such ports as Cockermouth in Cumbria; there were about 70 merchants, half of whom operated from *booths*, i.e. primitive shops; some offered a kind of banking service. From 1642 the town had a post office on the new postal route between Carlisle and Ireland.

**Civil War, Decay and Shame**: The Civil War seriously affected Dumfries, which was only 12th in Scotland's modest tax roll of 1649. According to Tucker, in 1655 no ships were based in the Nith, and the official role of head port of south-west Scotland had been transferred to Ayr. He described Dumfries as *"a pretty mercat town, but of little trade, that they have being most part by land, either for Leith or Newcastle"*. Any goods coming by sea were *"usually landed at Kirkcudbright"*. In 1656 it was said that the former town wall of Dumfries was ruinous; Lincluden Abbey also became a ruin. In this period the whole south-west was plagued by baronial feuds, religious hysteria and persecution, robbery and torture: nine women were burned to death for alleged witchcraft in 1659. In that shameful year the town's Wednesday market was first held beside the river at

Whitesands. By 1669 Dumfries' long connection with woollen textiles had begun; cloth manufacture had become noteworthy. The bitter religious wars and local disorders up to 1690 ended its role as a serious competitor to growing Glasgow. However, a grain mill was constructed in 1705, as was the Mid Steeple or Town Hall, designed by Tobias Bachup of Alloa, and also used as a tolbooth or prison.

**Recovery after the Union**: Dumfries was properly connected into the Scottish postal system in 1711, and soon after the Union of 1707 the ancient bridge was partly rebuilt into what Defoe described in the 1720s as *"a very fine stone bridge"*. In the middle of the bridge was a gate, parting *"the two counties of Galloway and Dumfries shire"*. Defoe attributed the end of woollen manufacture in the town to the Union, but added *"Dumfries was always a good town, and full of merchants"* – by which he meant overseas traders. Such trade had increased since 1707, and *"ships of burthen come up close to the quay"*. By 1745 the *Commercial Hotel* (later called the *County*) was open for trade. In 1748 the town council contracted for the building of an early beacon at Southerness, 20km south, but it was at first unlit. There was practically no other industry until another wheat mill was built in 1742; a snuff mill was in operation by about 1750. The first of two 18th century linen bleachfields was built in mid-century, by 1765 the British Linen Company had a local agent, and both a thread mill and a brewery were working by the late 1760s. These water-driven industries resulted in the building of a long-lasting weir across the Nith.

**Eighteenth Century Roads**: Roy's map of the 1750s showed a large town for the time, the present irregular street pattern recognisable and leading to eight radial roads, including two to Kirkcudbright. Outside the town, road bridges had already been built at Cargenbridge and Newbridge, but use of the Moffat road still involved fording streams, as – much more seriously – did the only road connection to England, for the River Esk was still unbridged at Green Ford, south of Sark Bridge on the way to Carlisle. A road was built eastwards across Lochar Moss by the town council about the third quarter of the 18th century. Proper improvement of the roads to Carlisle and Glasgow was arranged in 1788, and in the 1790s a thrice-weekly mail coach commenced running to Edinburgh via Moffat. The New or Buccleuch Street Bridge, designed by Thomas Boyd, was built to improve the road to the Stewartry, leaving the ancient bridge to pedestrians – it still stands.

**Varied Industries**: By 1776 a *"considerable trade in stocking-knitting"* was reported, but the thirty framework knitters working in the town by 1778 were fewer by 1793; however, it began to revive, and Robertsons were established in textiles by 1790. The wheat mill of 1742 was burned down, and replaced by a new corn mill in 1781, by which time there was also a corn merchant. Another old mill was converted in 1778 to a bark mill for the tanning trade: Heron noted in 1799 that Bridge-end, west of the river, was a long-established village of over 1300 people, among whom nearly a hundred made wooden-soled shoes, its *"principal manufacture"*; these were bought by country people. In 1810 this area became the burgh of barony of Maxwelltown.

**Culture in the Southern Capital**: Dalskairth House, 5km south-west of Dumfries, was rebuilt in the later 18th century and twice remodelled. The home of Robert Burns, an exciseman in Dumfries from 1791 to 1796, was preserved as a museum holding his personal relics. The *Playhouse Theatre*, paid for by public subscription, was built in 1792 with about 550 seats, and a prominent Ionic Episcopal church was built in Buccleuch Street in 1817. The two fairs scheduled for 1797 were few for an aspiring town, and Galloway man Heron commented in 1799 that *"Dumfries is the capital of the southern counties – a regular and well-built town, containing about 6000 inhabitants; but has neither foreign trade nor manufactures"*; on the last point he was mistaken.

**Banking, Business and Facilities**: From 1766 various banks opened branches (many short-lived): Johnston, Lawson & Co, The Bank of Scotland (one of the first two branches to be successfully established by them), the Paisley Union Banking Coy, the Dumfries Commercial Banking Company, the Galloway Banking Company of Castle Douglas, and the Dumfries-based Southern Bank of Scotland (eventually part of the Clydesdale). In 1792 a kind of public library was founded, helped by Robert Burns. New buildings were provided for the Academy in 1801. In 1803 Dorothy Wordsworth stayed in a *"tolerably comfortable"* inn; there was a bookseller in Dumfries, which had *"the bustle of a town that seems to be rising up to wealth"*. This was confirmed when it became a main postal route centre in 1808, and a local newspaper was first published in 1809 as the *Dumfries & Galloway Courier*. An early gasworks was set up in 1811 and by 1825 six breweries were in use.

**Hosiery Specialism and the New Quay**: In 1805 William Milligan started a framework knitting business, followed by Robert Scott in 1810. James Dinwiddie began in the hosiery trade in 1829, with a mill at Greenbrae. By 1832 over 300 people in Dumfries and nearby villages were employed in worsted hosiery, making half a million fancy stockings a year, and also knitting woollen underwear. Kingholm Quay, 3km downriver, was rebuilt between 1836 and 1840, helping to justify the status of a Port of Registry with the letters DS. In 1844 about 500 stocking-frames were in use; Milligan, Henderson & Co employed over 100 people, and smaller firms about 200. The largest firm, Scotts, employed 181 hosiers; they had just opened their Kingholm spinning mill, and added an adjacent tweed mill in 1846, both taking advantage of the *'New Quay'* at Kingholm. J & D Robertson, by then long established, started a new hosiery works in 1850.

**Dumfries in 1827**: In 1827, Chambers echoed Heron: *"Dumfries, the capital of the South-Western Province of Scotland, is well and regularly built, with an aspect of great cleanliness"*. Little vessels could still reach the town, which *"has the double advantage of being the residence of the smaller, and what may be called 'dotarial' (i.e.endowed) gentry of the province, and of being a great market town"*. The ruin of Lincluden was *"by far the most attractive and interesting object in the neighbourhood"*, and the castle site had been taken over for the Greyfriars church. Maxwelltown was by then *"an extensive suburban village"* .

**More Facilities 1828–50**: The *King's Arms* hotel was open by 1829, and in 1832 a theatre – probably the *Theatre Royal*– was the venue for a lecture by William Cobbett. In 1834 a new Trades Hall was erected, and in the same year a windmill was converted into a *'camera obscura'* (still in use as part of the town's main museum). In 1835–39 the Crichton Hospital was built east of the New Quay to designs by William Burn, to house the mentally ill; it was extended over the years into a

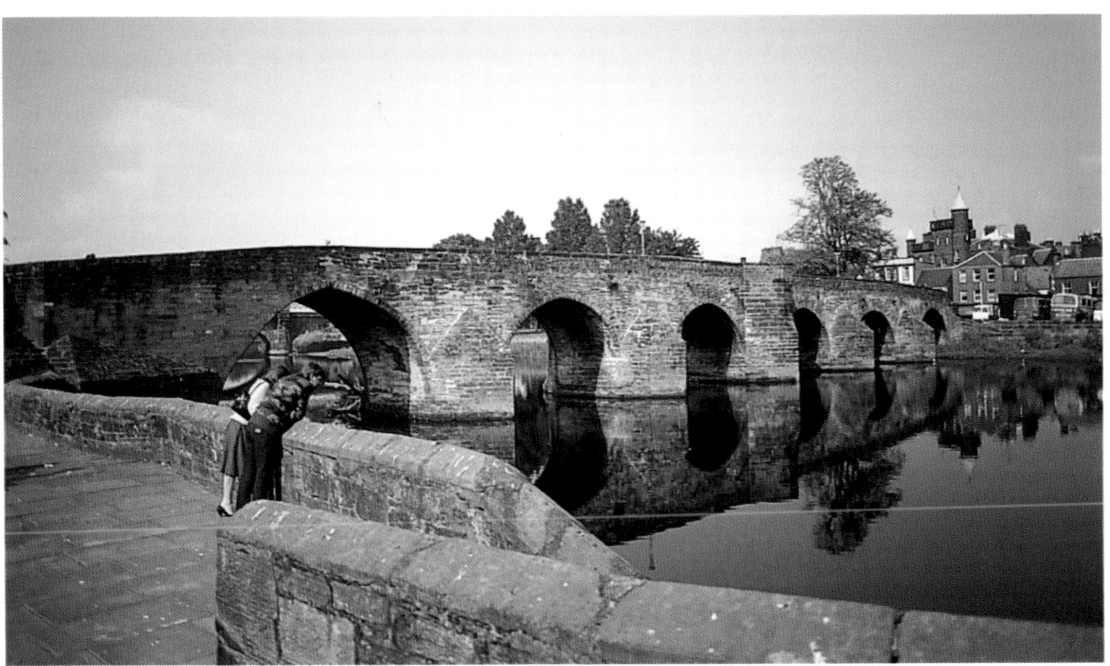

*Devorgilla's Bridge across the River Nith, Dumfries. It was built around 1430, rebuilt in 1620, and shortened to 6 arches in the early 19th century.* *(JRH)*

large complex. This was indeed a sad decline from its original intention of university use, for which funds had been left to the University of Glasgow by Elizabeth Crichton, widow of a former physician to a Governor-General of India, a scheme at that time considered inappropriate by the Chancellor of the University. Meantime literacy was furthered when the *Dumfries & Galloway Standard* was established in 1843, and Dinwiddie's bookshop opened in 1846.

**Hangings and more Hosiery**: The *"large and handsome"* Nithsdale tweed mills were built by Robert Scott in 1856–57, and by 1864 J & A D Grimond of Dundee, for many years manufacturers of linen by hand looms, had added power looms to their Maxwelltown works. The extensive Troqueer tweed mill which employed over 300 people was erected by a relative, Walter Scott, in 1866. In 1868, the year when Dumfries people witnessed Scotland's last public hanging, St Michael's tweed mill was built by J M Henderson. However, by 1869 Milligan was the only firm with power looms for hosiery. By then McGeorge and Halliday both had hosiery mills at Maxwelltown, and Paterson made hosiery at Lochfoot *(q.v.)*. These firms generally drew their yarn from Hawick, Peebles, Alloa and Kinross. In 1879 James Renwick of Hawick joined the frame knitting concerns. In 1881 when the population of Dumfries was 17,100, Robbie McGeorge took over the combined Milligan, Henderson concern, which also made gloves from 1885. Woollens were made on a large scale in the Rosefield Mills opened in 1886. By 1891 Dinwiddie employed 300 people making fine woollen underwear in Dumfries and Maxwelltown.

**Railway Developments**: The Glasgow, Dumfries & Carlisle Railway opened from the Caledonian (CR) main line at Gretna to Dumfries in 1848, reached Closeburn near Thornhill in 1849 and became part of the Glasgow & South Western Railway (G&SWR) on completion of the Glasgow link in 1850. Dumfries became the junction for the G&SWR's Castle Douglas and Kirkcudbright branch in 1859, the route being completed to Stranraer in 1861 by the Portpatrick Railway. In 1863 the CR opened a line from Lockerbie into the G&SWR station, who had established an important engine shed by the 1870s (later housing 45 steam locomotives); freight was more important than passengers in the 1890s, when the town's population was about 18,000. As a last fling of the railway age, a light railway was opened to Moniaive in 1905.

**Ales Fail but Catholic Schools Prosper**: After 1851 more people began to leave the still predominantly farming county – the population on which Dumfries depended then declining for half a century. Another depressing factor was the poor quality of the ales produced by local Dumfries breweries, which failed after the railway brought a greater choice of beverages. But development did not cease, and a suspension footbridge was erected across the Nith in 1875 to benefit workers in the Troqueer woollen mills. In 1874 St Joseph's College was built as a Roman Catholic boys' boarding school (which was to become the largest such in Scotland by the 1950s) and in 1881–84 a Benedictine nunnery and girls' school was built on Corbelly Hill to the west.

**Recreation and Hotels**: After many years of success, by 1876 the *Playhouse Theatre* had been enlarged to seat over 1000 people. The Dumfries & Galloway Golf Club was founded in 1880, followed in 1884 by a 9-hole course at the Crichton Royal Hospital. By 1887 the G&SWR owned the *Station Hotel*, which was *"small, good"* to Murray in 1894, when the *"comfortable" Nithsdale Temperance Hotel* and the *"fair" Commercial* and *King's Arms* hotels were also available. The town had a laundry and retained an important sheep market. New buildings for the Academy were again provided in 1897. The Dumfries & County Golf Club was founded in 1912, the year that the locally financed 1200-seat *Lyceum Theatre* opened to replace the *Playhouse*, which in 1910 had become the silent film *Electric Theatre* – later being used as a roller skating rink and, from the coming of talkies about 1930, as the 470-seat *Electric Cinema*.

**Philosophy, Humour and Growth**: John Macmurray, born in Maxwelltown in 1891, became the influential Professor of Moral Philosophy at Edinburgh University, advising people to find fulfilment through extending family love to action in and for their communities. John Laurie, born in the town in 1897, became a much-loved actor, the Private Fraser of *'Dad's Army'*. In 1899 Dumfries acquired a local electric power station, but adjacent Maxwelltown had to wait for electric light until its own generating station appeared in 1913! Population growth in Dumfriesshire resumed with the new century, for textiles were prospering. By 1906 McGeorge employed 700 workers making gloves and ties, with branches at Sanquhar and (by 1913) also at Dalbeattie and Lochmaben. By 1914 Scotts had abandoned hosiery, but remained in tweeds. The Wolsey (of Leicester) branch hosiery works began operations in 1912 and were enlarged in 1931–34. A glove works opened in 1926, and a dyeing and finishing plant at Troqueer in 1929; by 1932 Robertsons had changed to cashmere knitting.

**Monopoly Lost, Doonhamers Found**: In 1913 the Newbie Games Company of Dumfries patented a board game called *'Brer Fox and Brer Rabbit'*, on which Charles Darrow of the USA later based the hugely successful *'Monopoly'*, without acknowledgement! In 1914 a Georgian mansion became the Moat Brae nursing home. The *Queen of the South* football club (fondly called the *Doonhamers*) was formed by merger in 1919, opening Palmerston Park the same year, and by 1935–36 had reached the First Division of the Scottish League. The St Michael's bridge, the lowest across the Nith, was opened in 1927. In the 1930s the LMS-owned cartage company Wordies bought two local road haulage firms totalling 24 vehicles, Dicksons and Dumfries & Galloway Transport.

**Carnations and Cairndale**: Dumfries prospered despite the slump, for the Carnation condensed milk creamery was established in 1935, and at about the same time the 3-star *Cairndale Hotel* was built, the gourmet base for the author's honeymoon in 1957! Meantime the *Lyceum Theatre* was demolished in 1936, replaced on the same site by a 2000-seat cine-theatre of the same name; the Dumfries Chamber of Trade and Commerce was founded in 1938. With 26,500 people by 1951, plus 1500 staff and inmates in the Crichton Hospital, Dumfries possessed the facilities of a regional centre, augmented in that year by the new Folk Museum in the ancient Bridge House. The one-time *Playhouse Theatre* was closed in 1954 as the *Electric Cinema*, but was saved from demolition in 1959 by an amateur group, the Guild of Players, who successfully reinstated it as a theatre.

**Railway Rundown and Sixties Turmoil**: The Dumfries to Moniaive passenger train service ended in 1943 and the line was disused by 1953; more importantly, the main line to Castle Douglas and Stranraer was closed as unprofitable by Beeching in 1965, though the first 5 km to Cargenbridge remained as a long siding, also serving the Carnation Milk factory in Maxwelltown. The engine shed was closed in 1966 on withdrawal of freight services to Lockerbie, which ended Dumfries' role as a significant junction. In the 1960s clogs were still made in Dumfries, and a government office building of peculiarly awful design was put up, its perpetrators evidently regardless of its surroundings; a new stand was built at Palmerston Park in 1965. In 1967 the textile firm of J & D McGeorge was in trouble, and was acquired in 1968 by the Dawson group *(see Kinross)*. Sadly the second *Lyceum Theatre* failed; it was demolished in 1970.

**Regional Capital and Tourist Centre**: In 1975 Dumfries Burgh and County were replaced by Nithsdale District, and the town also assumed the wider role of capital to the newly merged Dumfries & Galloway Region; it also became the HQ of the Solway River Purification Board. With this boost it continued to develop as a busy and rather congested regional centre, with some 25 hotels of which the leaders were the 44-room *Cairndale* and the 30-room *Station*, and the business hotel the *County*. In 1976 the Canadian firm Kingston Yarn Spinners opened in Dumfries, but moved their 50 jobs to larger premises at Sanquhar in 1979. In 1978 potatoes were still despatched south by rail; by then Penmans made specialist commercial vehicle bodies. The town's population was some 31,000 by 1981, but the Benedictines' girls' school closed in 1982 when St Joseph's became co-educational.

**Shopping, Leisure and Traffic: Mixed Signals**: Marks & Spencer opened a Dumfries branch about 1986, much other shopping development was constructed, and a leisure complex was built in 1989. The lengthy northern bypass for the A75 was opened in 1990, yet the town centre roads remained horribly congested. By 1991 the *Dumfries News* had combined with the Castle Douglas paper to become the *Dumfries & Galloway News*. In 1992 the historic *Theatre Royal* was the oldest working theatre in Scotland. But football was struggling, with Queen of the South FC playing at rundown Palmerston Park. The club leased their car park cheaply to Tesco in 1988 for a superstore, but succeeded in completing a new stand in 1995; in 2000 the team was still stuck in the Second Division.

**Industrial Problems and Dereliction**: Key employers in the area included Carnation (Nestlé) Milk and Robertsons, makers of knitwear since the 18th century. However, by then the fine Rosefield Mills stood derelict, and the Wolsey Knitwear factory was closed by Courtaulds Textiles in 1991 with the loss of 183 jobs. A new factory opened by Dawsons for McGeorge in 1988 employed some 200 people up to its premature closure as a result of the slump of 1992, and also in 1992 a further 200 workers were made redundant from the Nestlé plant. Dalskairth House, which formerly stood in an extensive park, deteriorated from the 1980s and stood unused in 1997. Buccleuch Street church stood long vacant in the 1990s, eventually being converted to a pub!

**Situation saved by Ice and Centralisation?**: Although by 1991 the town's population had risen to 32,000, with new housing spreading on all sides, the newly opened Loreburn shopping centre remained largely unlet and the long-standing Binns store had closed. The Dumfries Enterprise Park had failed to attract any tenants by mid 1993; however, a new Safeway superstore was opened in 1993 at Brooms Road/Lenfield Road and by 1996 a Tesco store was open. New ice-skating facilities were opened in 1992, and in 1996 the *'Dumfries Vikings'* were among the four Scottish ice hockey teams playing in the Northern Premier League. In 1996 the smaller local authorities in Dumfries and Galloway lost all powers to a new unitary authority based in Dumfries; by then tourists had a choice of three museums. By 1998 the town centre had been finely pedestrianised, giving space to admire its historic buildings and attractive shops.

**University Courses after All!**: Times change, and Mrs Crichton would have been greatly pleased to know that in 1996–2000 Glasgow University, the local authority and the local enterprise company adapted part of the Crichton mental hospital as Crichton College. This provides facilities for 600 students, half of them part-time, with special computer teaching links to four parent institutions, also including Paisley University, Bell College of Hamilton and the Dumfries & Galloway College. Dumfries Academy then had 855 pupils, Dumfries High School 1103, Maxwelltown High School 376 and St Joseph's College – by then a council-run secondary school – 636. Local auctioneers Thomson, Roddick & Laurie sold their Dumfries mart – which dealt in 100,000 sheep and 5000 cattle a year – to Cumberland & Dumfriesshire Farmers' Mart of Longtown in 2000. The reopening of the Maxwelltown branch railway to oil traffic is now planned.

## DUNBAR, Belhaven & West Barns — Map 3, B2

*E. Lothian coastal town, pop. 6500* — OS 67: NT 6778

A tiny natural harbour on the exposed coast of East Lothian was protected by a basalt sill, beside which stood a steep defensible rock, fortified as Dunbar – a Gaelic name, but by 650 AD a Northumbrian stronghold. This was re-taken and burned in 849 by the aggressive usurper of the kingdom of the Picts, Scots king Kenneth McAlpin. In 1070 Malcolm Canmore gave the repaired castle to Patrick Cospatrick, a former Earl of Northumberland and first Earl of Dunbar. In 1215 after another burning by the English King John, a convent was founded, and in 1218 a tiny Trinitarian priory was established by Patrick, fifth Earl of Dunbar.

**Burgh Besieged**: Dunbar appeared on the Gough map made around 1250; it was chartered at some time between 1214 and 1314 as a baronial burgh of the earls. In the Wars of Succession the castle was seized and garrisoned by the English until after the Battle of Bannockburn in 1314; when they returned in 1339 the Countess held out against them for five months. After Dunbar was again recovered for Scotland, the port traded with Danzig, and the ninth earl founded Scotland's first collegiate church in 1342, dedicated to the obscure St Bey. After the Black Death of 1350, recovery took a generation. In 1370 Dunbar was re-chartered by the Earl as a burgh of barony, 20 tonnes of wool were exported annually in the mid 1370s, and hides by 1378. In 1415 John Hardyng called Dunbar a *"town"*.

**Royal Burgh Once More against the English**: In 1445, in a third charter, Dunbar became a Royal Burgh. After yet another burning of the town in 1448 by Northumberland's forces, the castle was back in royal hands by 1455. Not surprisingly Dunbar's overseas trade, hitherto mainly wool, fluctuated widely between almost nothing and – for a time in the late 15th century – a significant contribution to Customs revenue. The castle was refortified in 1496–1501, and an outer artillery blockhouse was built in 1523. Although the minuscule contribution to burgh taxes rose, it was still tiny in 1535. The town was yet again burned by the English in 1544 and the thatch was barely back on when it was torched again by the same hands in 1548. So the town was refortified by the French in that same year, when Jean de Beauge wrote that a harbour could easily be made. With the coming of peace this seems to have been done, for in 1560 corn was being exported, and in 1564 a parish school was founded, but the *"handsome strong castle"* of his visit was dismantled in 1566–67 after its defence by Bothwell, ending its chequered history.

**Presbytery and Poverty**: By 1593 Dunbar was the centre of a presbytery; this fact sits uneasily with visitor Fynes Moryson's report of 1598 that the town was *"formerly of some importance, but it lay ruined, and seemed of little moment, as well for the poverty as the small number of inhabitants"*. Timothy Pont mapped the area around 1600; showing West Barns and Belhaven as tiny places; Dunbar was a small settlement at the end of the road from Edinburgh, which crossed the Biel Water 2 km north of the bridge which had already been built at Biel. The map of the Merse made it clear that the road actually continued to Berwick and its bridge.

**Port Recovery and Lighthouse Pioneers**: Dunbar remained a small fishing port, where in 1613 the herring fishery was attended by *"disorder"*, but a herring curing and packing factory was established by Edinburgh merchants about 1615. Taylor in 1618 found a *"town"* which exported grain; brewing was soon a noted local activity. The tiny Town House was built about 1620, and by 1621 the harbour was again contributing to customs duties, though under 1.5% of the Scottish total. The *St George Inn* was founded in 1625, its name a remarkable tribute to the improved relationship with England. Brereton reported in 1636 that there was a *"haven made of great stones piled up"* that could take 100-ton ships at spring tides, *"but not without much hazard"*. In 1636 Alexander Cunningham of West Barns and James Maxwell of Innerwick set up the first proper lighthouse in Scotland on the May Isle *(q.v.)*. Dunbar ranked only 28th in Scottish burgh tax yields in 1639; in 1655 Tucker called it *"a fisher town, famous for herring, with an indifferent good harbour"* but importing little except salt.

**Harbour, Herrings, Witches and Winnowing**: In 1655 work was begun on building the Cromwell Harbour. In 1661 Jorevin de Rocheford called Dunbar a *"village famous for its great fishery of herring and salmon"*. It was in two parts – the fishermen's area, and above it *"a fine large street"*, where to his joy he found a fellow French speaker! In 1669 James Brome found the houses stone built and slated, and a weekly market. The town walls, once strong, had been much damaged in recent years, and it took an age for the town to recover; the Cromwell Harbour was eventually completed about 1730 with a small basin. Dunbar being long prone to brutality and superstition, the last witches were burned nearby as late as 1704, yet in the early 18th century Defoe found *"a handsome well-built town with a great herring-fishery"*; the fish were cured by smoking. James Meikle, born in 1690, and his son Andrew, born in Dunbar in 1719, were innovative millwrights, jointly inventing the winnowing machine *(see Saltoun)*. A post office was opened in 1733; by 1745 Dunbar was again strongly walled and regarded as quite a large town.

**Whales, Roads and Industry**: Whaling commenced from Dunbar in 1752, but this risky business apparently soon ceased. The Roy map of about 1754 showed a coastal road, but indicated that by 1726 Dunbar was already bypassed by the *'great'* road, on roughly the modern line of the A1. This was made up under an Act of 1750, though the road onwards through Berwickshire remained for a long time in a primitive state. However, by 1747 Dunbar had an iron merchant, and in 1761 a coal wharf was provided, evidently intended to receive imports. A bleachfield was laid out in 1758, by 1765 the British

*The Belhaven brewery, Dunbar, started around 1780 and still going strong.* *(JRH)*

Linen Company had a local agent, and woollen manufactures were recorded in 1776.

**More Whales and Beer**: By 1769 when whaling recommenced, corn was being exported through Spotts' harbour granary and the town had an effective school. Knox's brewery was established about 1770, and the uniquely surviving Belhaven Brewery of the Dudgeon brothers began operating about 1780 at the hamlet of that name 1 km west of the harbour. In 1785 another new quay was built, and by 1788 five vessels were engaged in whaling. A fine Customs House was also erected about that time, the High Street was paved, and was lit from 1785 using whale oil. In 1792 two *'Greenland ships'* of 675 tons belonged to the town, plus 16 other small vessels totalling 1500 tons. The grain mills at West Barns, 2 km to the west, already belonged to the town council, and by 1791 flour was being exported. In 1787 Robert Burns on a visit called Dunbar *"a neat town"*.

**Banking, Printing, Whisky and Posts**: The British Linen Bank established a branch in 1788, and in 1795 the town belatedly acquired the first printing press in East Lothian. By 1797 Dunbar was a post town and staging point on the Edinburgh to London coach route, and two fairs were scheduled for the year. A large distillery was built at West Barns in 1798. Heron wrote a full description in 1799: *"Dunbar is a well built town, containing about three thousand inhabitants, a good harbour, and a considerable share of shipping. The fish trade is here carried on very extensively. Grain is also a staple commodity – upwards of 10,000 quarters* [127 tonnes] *have been exported from Dunbar in a year. Two rope-works employ a number of hands and a beginning has been given to the cotton manufacture. Soap and starch are also made."*

**Prosperity and Peculation**: The west pier and a dry dock were constructed about 1800, but Dunbar men abandoned the slaughter of whales in 1804 in favour of fishing in nearer waters; by 1808 a lifeboat was recorded. The East Lothian Banking Company, formed in Dunbar in 1810, at once opened branches in Haddington and Selkirk, but sadly its cashier caused it to fail in 1822. About 1814 a maltings was erected at West Barns, and a third brewery was in use by 1825. In 1819 there were 280 Dunbar boats and 2000 fishermen, plus six foreign-going trading vessels, their registration letters DR. Prosperity enabled the Assembly Rooms to be built in 1822; they later became auction rooms.

**Views of Dunbar around 1830**: The *St George Inn* was rebuilt as a coaching inn in 1828, and in 1832 Cobbett noted that the road from the south was *"very fine and broad, covered in carts all loaded with sacks of corn going to Dunbar, which is a little seaport (though a large town)"*. He admired Lord Lauderdale's *"plain solid"* town house while comparing the opulence of Broxmouth Park just south of the town with the *"very bad-looking houses"* of the *"sort of village"* nearby. A gasworks was set up in 1836, and after 1838 the distillery was converted to a brewery. The Victoria Harbour was added in 1842–44, together with a boat slip, more warehouses and maltings around the same period.

**Conservation Pioneer overcomes the Odds**: In 1848–49 a pious, selfish and brash recruiting sergeant, the father of John Muir (who was born in the town in 1838), emigrated to Wisconsin with his family. There, despite crippling farm labour imposed by his brutal father, John became a brilliant self-taught inventor, observant naturalist and fine writer, the revered pioneer of the world's conservation movement and the founder of the USA national parks system *(see Muir, 1987)*. Meantime the North British Railway opened its main line in

1846 with a station in Dunbar, but passed behind the town and made no connection to the harbour, whose seaborne trade quickly died. The Abbey Church, designed by Thomas Hamilton and built in 1850, eventually became a public hall.

**Drinking, Racing and Golfing Garrison**: Dunbar's first golf course was laid out in 1856 by Tom Morris. Large barracks were built in 1859 when for some reason Dunbar became a garrison town, bringing trade to the Belhaven Brewery. Bielside House at West Barns, designed by Robert Rowand Anderson, was built in 1866 and later enlarged. An engineering works was built near Belhaven in 1878, with a rail connection, and by 1881 the burgh population was 3650. There was a racecourse at West Barns Links by 1894, when Murray unkindly described Dunbar as *"a lifeless town"*; but both the *St George* and *Royal* hotels were open. These were very soon joined by the prominent *Bellevue Hotel*, designed by James Dunn and built in 1896–97, and the *Royal Marine Hotel*, sited on the cliff top.

**Glasgow on Sea**: Although the fishing declined further, the Ordnance Survey established a tidal observatory in 1913 which operated for some years. People on holiday from smoky Glasgow and the cloudy West of Scotland were particularly keen to enjoy East Lothian's good sunshine record, and brought much summer trade. An outdoor pool was built beside the sea for hardy swimmers, and the Winterfield and East golf courses were laid out around 1935. Some 15 hotels were open by the 1950s, when the population was about 4300.

**Cement Dust and Hotel Problems**: From 1963 a white dust hung in the air from the huge Oxwellmains cement works *(see Innerwick)*, only 4 km from the town. Cheap package holidays to Spain were also becoming available, so the local holiday trade began to fail, and the erosion of the hotels' once impressive star gradings began. Barley and malt were still handled by local shipping in the 1950s, and as late as 1963 Belhaven had a rail siding, but the West Barns maltings had closed by 1976 and others were converted to flats; the outdoor bathing pool was removed about 1980. In 1978 potatoes were still despatched south by rail, but all goods traffic soon ceased. Two new housing estates were built east of the town, including one south of the railway, attracting workers at Oxwellmains and Torness nuclear power station *(see Innerwick)*. By 1981 some other small industries had opened.

**Country Park, Nuclear Power and Last Resort**: Having ignored John Muir's achievements for a century, a Trust was eventually formed to further conservation, and his name was given to a Country Park, designated on the coast north-west of West Barns by 1982; in 1994 a John Muir Centre was proposed in Dunbar itself. By then there were several caravan sites north and west of the town. The local hoteliers had found it more profitable to accommodate year-round the many construction workers erecting Torness, than the falling number of seasonal holidaymakers. Its last residents gone, the *Roxburghe Hotel (former Royal Marine)* was vacated about 1988 and demolished about 1995. The *St George Hotel* closed for a time from 1990, and the *Bellevue Hotel* (which burnt out in 1989 while being renovated) has remained a derelict shell. Meantime despite relatively high unemployment, the resident population had risen to 6518 by 1991. William Low had built a large supermarket outside the town centre, whose fine buildings still showed signs of Dunbar's past prosperity.

**Shellfish, Trout and Beer for Export**: By the late 1980s there had been quite a strong resurgence in inshore fishing, mainly for crustaceans, and in 1994 a trout farm and smokery was active at West Barns Farm; but Bielside House was vacant in 1995. Meantime in 1992–93 Belhaven had increased its sales to the generally declining Scottish beer market by 35%, and in 1995 the brewery – which was nearing its annual output capacity of 64,000 barrels – had permission to extend its fermentation and conditioning plant to fill 100,000 barrels, and was developing export markets. It now employs over 100 workers, recently upgraded Blue Circle Cement has 170; Torness has 200+ employees. Major works to improve the appearance of the run-down High Street began in 1995, including the rescue of the *'A'* listed nos 56–60, and a new swimming pool was built on the cliff-top. Dunbar Grammar School has 560 pupils. Some further development south of the railway was started in 2000. About seven small/medium hotels are open, plus guest houses and B&Bs.

## DUNBEATH

**Map 13, B5**

*Caithness village, pop. 325* — OS 11: ND 1629

The steep valley of the little Dunbeath Water cuts into the coastal cliffs of southern Caithness; in the most sheltered area about 2 km inland from its mouth are remains of two Pictish brochs; nearby are ancient settlement sites, a standing stone and chambered cairns. In 1428 Dunbeath Castle, a cliff-top tower house, was built for Sir George Crichton, Lord High Admiral of Scotland, 1 km south of the river's mouth. In 1624 *Inver of Dunbeath* became a burgh of barony; at one time a market was held nearby. A post office was open by 1715. The area was still Gaelic-speaking in the mid 18th century, when the Roy map showed a coastal track and Dunbeath consisted of hamlets. In 1786 John Knox II found *"no roads"* in Caithness, yet by 1797 Dunbeath was a post town.

**Telford, Rocks and the Silver Darlings**: Telford planned Dunbeath bridge, built in 1813 when the road was made up for the Commissioners for Highland Roads & Bridges, and from that year a coaching inn stood nearby. Coaches passing Dunbeath were often pelted with rocks by poor people who had been recently cleared off their ancestral lands by the greedy estate proprietors. However, a pier was built about 1850 and a large fishing industry developed; soon 90 boats were based at Dunbeath, 350 fishermen were employed, there were eight firms of herring curers, an ice-house and a salmon bothy. Neil Gunn, born in Dunbeath in 1891 and the son of a local skipper, became a novelist, writing *"The Silver Darlings"*, set in the era of herring fishing, and much else; but fishing soon faded out.

**Tourism keeps Dunbeath Busy**: Crichton's tower became the site of a Victorian baronial mansion which took its name of Dunbeath Castle. By 1894 Dunbeath boasted what Murray called the *"good" Munro Arms Hotel*, but remained a small village. During World War II there was a battle-training area in the vicinity. By 1974 a caravan site had been laid out near the hotel, and in 1981 when Dunbeath held only 325 residents it was very active and complex in function, with a modern breakwater at Portormin, three boats in full-time lobster fishing, a firm of livestock transporters and a significant tourist industry in the village, plus the Laidhay croft museum and a heritage trail at Balnabruich. About 1990 a tall concrete viaduct of five spans was built to carry the A9 bypass across the river, beside which modest annual Highland Games are still held. The *Dunbeath Hotel* now provides hospitality.

## DUNBLANE

**Map 5, C4**

***Town n. of Stirling,*** *pop. 7400* OS 57: NN 7801

The Roman road from the south to Bertha – Roman Perth – followed the east side of the incised Allan Water, above its confluence with the River Teith. In 602 St Blane, a native of Bute, established a Culdee monastery, perhaps on the site of a Roman fort, 8 km north of Stirling; its related defensive site took his name as Dunblane. A new church was founded there about 1140 by King David I, its red sandstone tower being built just west of the Roman road. In 1233 the bishopric of the small diocese covering Menteith was moved there from Muthill, and the building of Dunblane cathedral was begun, on an axis different from the old tower which it incorporated, which was raised in height. By 1274 Dunblane was a tiny cathedral city, which became a burgh of barony around 1300, but it was overshadowed by Stirling and developed only slowly, though by 1560 the Bishop sat in Parliament.

**Roofless Ruin, and the Pedigree of Keir**: The lead had been stripped from the cathedral nave roof by Edward I, and it fell into disrepair, eventually collapsing in the 16th century. The walled-off chancel remained as the parish church, whose first Protestant minister from 1562 was Robert Pont, father of the famed cartographer Timothy Pont. In the vicinity of Keir some 3 km south of Dunblane stood successively a hill fort, a Norman motte carrying a timber palisade and keep, the 17th century tower of Arnhall Castle, and the mansionhouse of Keir, with its fine Home Farm buildings. Dunblane had become the centre of a presbytery by 1593, and Pont's map showed that by then the Allan had already been bridged in the vicinity of Kippenross, 1 km south of the town, as well as at Bridge of Allan. In 1624 the Dean, James Pearson, built the house which is now the Cathedral Museum.

**The Benevolent Bishop and his Library**: Richard Franck, a jocular traveller, seemed to be in earnest when writing in 1656 that despite its cathedral and the bishop's palace (now vanished), Dunblane was an *"inconsiderable corporation with little or no trade; ale, tobacco and strong waters, are the staple of the town"*; he mentioned *"dirty streets, dirty houses built with stone, low and little"*. Maybe so, but some sturdy 17th century Dunblane houses have lasted up to the present day! Under the will of the erudite Robert Leighton from Montrose, who spoke twelve languages, and was the reluctant but well-liked Episcopal Bishop of Dunblane through the 1660s, he bequeathed his now world famous library of 1400 books to the little town, and money to erect a building to house them.

**Nobility in Town**: Defoe noted in the 1720s that *"the town is pleasantly situated, and tolerably well built, but out of all manner of trade"*. However the nobility were there: Viscount Strathallan lived in Dunblane in 1745. The Roy map showed that by about 1750 the River Allan had been bridged at the foot of the linear town which lined the main and only road between Stirling and Strathearn. Dunblane's first post office opened in 1791; by 1797 it was a post town, and four annual fairs were scheduled. Heron found about 2000 people in a *"village or town rather irregularly built"*. By then the library had gained *"considerable additions"* of volumes, but later it became neglected.

**Rails beat Brewery, but Textiles Thrive**: By 1827 Chambers noted that Dunblane was *"only a pleasant village"*, but elsewhere used the phrase a *"delicious little old city"*. The inn (now the *Stirling Arms*) then stood by the bridge, and a brewery was also open at Bridge End by 1825. The Home Farm buildings on the Keir Estate, an unusual and vast complex designed by David Bryce, were built in 1832 and remodelled in 1856–61. The brewery did not long survive the opening in 1848 of Dunblane station on the Scottish Central Railway's new main line from Stirling to Perth. Ten years later it became the junction for a branch line to Callander, later extended to Oban. At one time there was a gasworks; the Springbank woollen mill was founded in 1851 and extended in 1884. Some 2 km north of Dunblane was a mid 19th century water-powered silk-dyeing mill which was made the basis of the planned community of Ashfield.

**Meteorology Starts in Resurgent Dunblane**: Alexander Buchan, an inspired teacher in Dunblane during the mid 19th century, became famous as the effective founder of the modern science of meteorology, and helped the town to awaken to its opportunities. Trains brought tourists to the large and soon famous hotel known as the *Dunblane Hydropathic*, built on a prominent height and opened in 1878. *The Stirling Arms Hotel* was also in use by 1894, by which time a favoured residential role was becoming marked; but an early golf club appears to have closed. The cathedral was re-roofed in 1890–93, 73% of the cost being borne by Janet Weir, widow of David Wallace of Glassingal; magnificently carved woodwork was installed in the choir in the early 20th century. An electric power station was built in 1900, an early date for a small town. A large boarding school, built north of Dunblane in 1906 for servicemen's children, was named after Queen Victoria. Dunblane New Golf Club was founded in 1923 and laid out an 18-hole parkland course. Wilsons Springbank Mill was re-equipped in 1927, about the time that an internal bypass for north road traffic was built.

**A Dip in the Fortunes**: By 1945 a youth hostel was open, and as late as 1946 Wordie & Co operated a small rail to road cartage depot. In 1954 the *Dunblane Hydro* offered 135 rooms and boasted four AA stars, but for a time it became unfashionable and starless. In the 1950s Dunblane was a small town with under 4000 people, but with train services from Glasgow, Edinburgh, Falkirk and Stirling. These continued, though the lengthy branch railway was closed between Dunblane and Crianlarich in 1965, thanks to low usage, Doctor Beeching and a landslide. Meantime Scottish Churches House, an ecumenical Christian centre, was created in 1961 from a row of condemned cottages east of the Cathedral, incorporating an ancient stone-vaulted cell as its chapel. In 1971, 139 people still lived at Ashfield.

**The Affluent Dormitory leaves Perthshire**: In the early 1970s Dunblane found itself close to the end of the new M9 motorway, bringing high accessibility by car for Edinburgh, Falkirk and Stirling. Faster rail services were introduced from both Edinburgh and Glasgow, and the proximity of the new University of Stirling *(see Bridge of Allan)* to this beautiful situation just clear of the industrial plain of central Scotland, led to Dunblane becoming a fast-growing southwards-looking dormitory. In 1975 it was therefore transferred from rural Perthshire to Stirling District in the Central Region. Dunblane High School was open by 1980. Dunblane was radically changed by the spreading estates of private housing, which brought the 1991 population to 7368, quite fit and very well-educated, with very high proportions of professional and managerial staff – very much a dormitory. Springbank mill closed in the 1980s; part of the building has been incorporated in redeveloping the site for houses. The Leighton Library and its ancient book stock was fully restored in 1989–90, being made available for use worldwide. Keir South Lodge, *'A'* listed, was saved for posterity in the mid 1990s, but Keir Home Farm, also *'A'*, stood vacant and sadly deteriorating in 1997. A western bypass for the busy A9 was newly open by 1993, and by 1996 there was a Tesco store.

**The Hydro Doubled but Tragedy Strikes**: Sand and gravel quarries north of the town were nearing exhaustion in 1997, and expected to become a site for housing. The *Dunblane Hydro* had recovered three stars by 1980, when it was by far the largest of Dunblane's nine hotels (later the *Stakis Dunblane*). But tragedy ensued on 13th March 1996, when 16 Dunblane children aged 4 to 6 and their teacher were massacred in the quiet town's 700-pupil primary school by the crazed gunman Thomas Hamilton, who then killed himself. This terrible event led to a national ban on handguns. In 1997 Dunblane High School had a roll of 772. By 2000 the youth hostel had closed, but the again-renamed *Hilton Dunblane Hydro* and its band leader of 40 years, Jim MacLeod, were both still going strong; some 4km north beyond the hamlet of Kinbuck is the quality mansion of *Cromlix House* hotel.

## DUNDEE

**Map 6, B3**

***City on R. Tay**, pop. 159,000* OS 54: NO 4030

Suburbs: *Baldovan, Broughty Ferry, Craigie, Invergowrie & Lochee*

Dundee, which enjoys a superb south-facing site overlooking the Firth of Tay, may have existed by the second century, when under the Taezali tribe Ptolemy listed *Deeuana*. This may have referred to the vitrified Iron Age fort on the 174m high volcanic neck called Dundee Law; settlement later moved down to the 20m raised beach to facilitate seaborne trade and allow development to spread out. Saint Columba himself *"taught the tribes of Tay"*, though whether at Dundee is unknown. A name more like its present title was first mentioned in 1054. By the time between 1153 and 1182 when Dundee became a burgh with trade guilds it was already a *'town'* and had a church – St Clement's. Its first known charter as a Royal Burgh was probably granted between 1182 and 1191. Although its site had only some 750 mm of rain a year and was short on waterpower, Dundee made good progress, aided by the very fertile land not far away to both east and west. Dudhope Castle, 1 km inland, can be dated back to the 12th century.

**From nowhere to *'Great Town'* in three centuries**: Dundee had a defined harbour by the early 13th century; the High School of Dundee which educated the great Scots patriot William Wallace was founded in 1239, and in 1289 a Franciscan friary (Greyfriars) was founded by Devorgilla Balliol. A Royal castle which existed by 1300 was destroyed in the wars about 1314. Lubeck traders were already visiting Dundee in 1297, and after the wars the town recovered to ship an average of almost 120 tonnes of wool a year around 1330. In 1341 a Dundee *'shipmaster'* was recorded, and David Bruce's charter of 1358 mentioned *"great trade of merchandise"*. Dundee was one of the four *'Great Towns'* of Scotland as known to Bruges merchants in 1348 (with Aberdeen, Edinburgh and Perth), and in the 14th century many royal charters were signed there.

**Decline due to the Black Death**: The Black Death hit Dundee's trade: its Customs payments fell from fourth to sixth place in Scotland, and on average a mere 96 tonnes of wool were shipped annually in the 1370s. Even so, about 1415 Dundee was described by John Hardyng as *"the principal burgh"* north of the Forth. But meantime its share of burgh tax revenue was slowly falling too (from 18% before the Black Death), and by 1427 it was down to fifth among Scottish ports in terms of customs receipts.

**Recovery, Prosperity – and Bogus History**: Cloth was being exported from Dundee by 1434, and the harbour was improved in 1447; this work proved costly to maintain, and about 1467 legislation imposed a duty on ships using the port, for the repair of the harbour. In the 15th century hides, skins and wooden planks were imported from Aberdeen, and Dundee also had a famous body of armourers. There was already a *'hospitalmaster'*, and the towering 50-metre Old Steeple of St Mary's church was built. Hector Boece, born in Dundee in 1465 and locally educated, became the first Principal of Aberdeen University; but his so-called history of Scotland was largely fanciful. Boece noted cloth weaving in Dundee in the early 16th century; the traditional yarn market for the next three centuries was at the Luckenbooths. In 1497 seven Dundee vessels entered Baltic ports, the largest number from any Scottish centre, but soon there was a dip in trade, and by 1535 Dundee paid only 14% of Scotland's burgh taxes.

**Plague and Pillage mar the Fine Town**: By 1540 there were nine craft guilds. A leper house was still in use in 1540, and a further outbreak of plague hit the town in 1544. By 1543 the Blackfriars had a monastery, sacked that year with the Greyfriars by the ardent protestant reformer George Wishart. Such turbulence ensured that the town was walled by 1545; even so, Jean de Beauge wrote in 1548 that Dundee was *"one of the finest towns in Scotland"*. By that time it was known as a centre for the export to the Baltic of locally made cloth of coarse wool, and also hides, skins and fish. But in that year Dundee was pillaged and the leper house became ruinous.

**Wishart Arch and Dudhope Castle**: Poor Wishart was burned at the stake in 1546; after the Reformation the Wishart Arch was built across the Cowgate, a useful monument to his martyrdom. Meantime, in 1560 the burgh was still sufficiently important to be represented in Parliament, but Dundee declined as a port in the 1580s and 1590s as Dutch and French trade shifted to Leith; the population was then probably only around 5000. By 1588 dyers and maltmen were among Dundee's unincorporated trades, and by 1593 the town was the centre of a presbytery. Provost Pearson built a tower house; Timothy Pont's map sketched about 1600 showed *'Dun-Tay'* as a large place dominated by the steeple, and a busy harbour with many ships moored in the Firth, and a mansion on the slopes of the Law: this was Dudhope Castle, home of the Scrymgeours, then hereditary constables of Dundee, who were rebuilding it on a large scale.

**Wine, Watermills and Windmills**: In 1618 grain exports were noted, and in 1621 Dundee paid about 11% of Customs dues and imported 15% of the wine drunk in Scotland. There were six brewers of some size by 1627 and with their help, or in spite of it, the town revived to support about 10,000 people in 1640. Dundee was then the fourth most important Scottish centre, its rents assessed at little less than Glasgow's. By 1641 there were also at least two water mills and a windmill. Dundee was (according to Chambers) *"the residence of six or eight noblemen"*. Among these were the Scrymgeours, but later in the century Dudhope Castle passed to Graham of Claverhouse; its later constables, the Douglases, lived there till about 1792.

**General Monk's Depradations**: A new town wall was hastily built in 1644–45, when the population had burgeoned to over 11,000. When Monk seized and plundered Dundee in 1651, sixty of its hundred ships were in the harbour, which was damaged, and most were sunk in the Tay. However, Dundee quickly recovered from Monk's devastation, for Tucker noted in 1655 that its merchants still owned ten vessels of up to 100 tons, imported goods from Norway, Holland and France, and exported salmon and *'pladding'* – further evidence of textiles, in which the town already specialised in a small way, including bonnetmakers.

**A Very Pretty Town makes Linens**: By 1666 there were malt mills to serve local breweries, and by 1670 the town paid about 7% of Scottish customs dues, making it third equal with Aberdeen port. The suburb of Hilltown became a burgh of barony in 1672, followed in 1707 by Dudhope. Dundee itself acquired a post office in 1689, the year in which Thomas Morer described it as *"a very pretty town furnished with two or three small piers for shipping, and the buildings speak the substance and the riches of the place"*. Linen was made for export before 1700, and by 1707 Dundee already made 1.4 million metres of mainly coarse linens each year. Harbour facilities were again inadequate by then, but permission to tax to improve them was refused, and there was only a single *'shipsmith'* in Dundee in 1720.

**Defoe's Dundee "a City"**: In the 1720s Defoe found *"a pleasant, large, populous city, and well deserves the title of Bonny Dundee, full of stately houses, and large handsome streets, with a large market-place in the middle; it is one of the best trading towns in Scotland, and that as well in foreign business as in manufacture and home trade; there are not a few ships belonging to the place"*. Warehouses and granaries lined the causeway from the town to the *"indifferent harbour"*, but *"the Tay is a large, safe, and good road (anchorage)"*. By the 1720s much linen and corn was shipped to London, corn also going to Amsterdam. Defoe added *"They have a good share of the Norway trade; and as they are concerned in the herring-fishery, they consequently have some east country trade to Danzig, Konigsberg, Riga &c. They send ships also to Sweden, and import iron, copper, tar, pitch, deals, &c."*.

**Textiles and Development to 1750**: Minor development of the harbour began with an Act of 1730, and a new, imposing arcaded Town House with a spire was designed by William Adam and built for the council in the High Street in 1732–34. A bleachfield for coarse linens was also established in 1732, using kelp. The road between Brechin and Dundee was improved in 1736 and that from Forfar in 1739. A yarn sorter was appointed soon after 1740, Andrew Brown was a loomwright by 1741, and despite Dundee's reputation for making poor quality linens, two weaving factories were set up in 1742. The oppressive hereditary jurisdiction of the Dukes of Douglas was bought out in 1747, and better thread-making techniques were learned from Paisley. Coarse linen *Osnaburghs (see Dairsie)* began to be woven locally, gradually replacing woollen plaidings.

**Shedding Light on Transportation**: The harbour improvements had been made to accommodate peaks of flax imports; about 150 tons in 1745, these had grown tenfold by 1795. Meantime in 1753 a group of Dundee shipowners built a lighthouse on Buddon Ness; formally chartered in 1774, they were later known as the Trinity House of Dundee. The Roy map made about 1750 depicted a large settlement for the period, already some 1.5 km long on its east–west axis and 500 m wide, with ribbon development up Bonnet Hill. Five radial roads of sorts linked to Invergowrie, Newtyle and Coupar Angus, Forfar, Brechin and Arbroath; but only a tiny pier and a small square harbour were drawn. In 1752 Kinnears were still making low-grade linen cloth, and Dundee still exported much coarse linen such as sailcloth. Webster's careful population estimate for 1755 was 12,400.

**An Old Town without Beauty or Elegance?**: Another bleaching works arrived in 1756, a main linen stamping office was open by 1760, and by 1762 Neilson's was the largest of all the British Linen Company's manufacturers. By 1772 Charles Raitte was a large linen manufacturer whose firm stamped its own cloth. Some 4 million metres of linen were stamped in 1773, three times the 1707 figure; most was made in the town. In 1778 a Trades Hall was built at the east end of the High Street as a meeting place for the nine incorporated trades (bakers, bonnetmakers, dyers, fleshers, glovers, hammermen, shoemakers, tailors and weavers).

**Whaling, Shipping and Industry**: A whaling vessel was in use by 1754, and four by 1792. By 1777 there was a wet dock and at least two timber yards. Further improvements were made to the harbour before 1790, and by 1792 rope was being made. In 1792 116 vessels belonged to the port, their average tonnage under 74, with crews averaging just 6 men; most were coasters bringing in coal and carrying linens and barley out, but 34 foreign-going ships mainly carried timber and flax from the Baltic. In 1798 a shipping line serving Dundee and Perth was founded and in 1799 the puny local records were broken when a 100-ton ship was built.

**Banking and Buildings Elegant and Odd**: From 1696 bank branches (some short-lived) were attempted by the Bank of Scotland, the British Linen, the Dundee Banking Company (which soon had branches in other towns), the Paisley Banking Company, and the Dundee Commercial Banking Company (later the Dundee New Bank). Turnpike roads opened up Dundee's hinterland in the 1780s and a new post road to Perth was built in the 1790s; but only two annual fairs were scheduled for 1797. About 1787, local works began to make bottles and window glass, employing 100 people by 1791. Heron in 1799 estimated Dundee's population as about 23,000, which seems near the truth. He described in glowing terms this *"large and flourishing town with an excellent harbour, and a great deal of shipping. Some public buildings have lately been erected, that are noticed by strangers as elegant. Among these are the town-house and the new merchant church"* (of St Andrew). Around 1800 a very unusual building was erected near the Wishart Arch, comprising the *John o' Groats* bar, with the Wishart Church on its first floor! An Episcopal church, built about 1800 in such a way as to obstruct the High Street, was to become in 1851 the meeting house of the Dundee Literary Society.

**The start of Jam and Journalism**: Local sugar refining encouraged James Keiller & Son to found a jam factory in the town in 1797; this grew and prospered (but the refinery had gone by 1864). The long-lasting Pleasance brewery was founded in 1809. About 1835 George Mathewson built a tall bonded store in Dock Street. A local newspaper, the *Dundee Perth & Cupar Advertiser*, was established in 1801, when the town's population was 26,000. The *Courier* started up in 1815–16 and the curiously named *Northern Warder* in 1841; the *Courier* incorporated the later *Daily Argus* in 1861.

**Cotton, Sewing Thread and Flax**: In 1779 William Alison & Co began making the sized fabric known as buckram, and around 1789 Dundee manufactured nearly 3 million metres of coarse linens and 650,000m of sailcloth annually (this remained the typical level of production as late as 1807). From about 1790, several small cotton mills were started, and by the end of the century over 1700 people, employed by seven firms, were making coloured sewing thread on 66 twisting-mills; though after a boom in 1802 the industry slowly faded. By 1792 there was also a minor *'hatmaking'* industry, perhaps the traditional bonnetmakers. About then the first small steam-powered flax mill was built in Chapelshade by Fairweather & Marr; it was unsuccessful. Three water-powered waulk mills in the Dens were for sale in 1802, their sites eventually going over to steam, but horse-powered mills persisted for a few years. At that time the flax used was mainly Baltic and English. In 1799 Heron listed Dundee's textile products as cordage, coloured and white thread, osnaburgs, sail-cloth, and buckrams. Tanning, footwear, sugar, tobacco and snuff industries, a foundry and a salt works were also active.

**The Triumph of Steam Spinning**: Three steam flax-spinning mills started in 1798: the small Upper Dens (James Carmichael), Tay Street (Chalmers & Hackney), and East (J & W Brown, 900 spindles by 1822). The first Bell flax mill, built in 1798, had 40 spinning frames but in 1806–07 James Brown erected a larger four-storey Bell Mill in Guthrie Street, installing steam-powered flax spinning machinery made in Leeds; in 1822 it had 1122 spindles. In 1813 the North Dudhope mill (Scott) was started, and from 1816 Indian hemp was used in bagging manufacture. But despite steam spinning, 1500 Dundee women were still spinning by hand in 1820. It was 1821 before Dundee tried powered weaving looms, and many years before these became general, aided by growing local expertise in engine building.

**Civic Improvements**: In 1792 Dudhope Castle was leased from the Douglases for use as a barracks, which it remained until 1880. In 1798 came the opening of the town's first real hospital, the Dundee Infirmary. Dundee had become a Port of Registry, its shipping recognition letters DE. In 1813–15 the town council began work on its final harbour improvements; the main street was also widened, and better access made to the port, whence cartloads of Baltic flax and increasingly of coal made their way uphill to the mills. Progress was aided when a gas supply was provided in 1825. In 1828 the Exchange Coffee House, a fine large meeting house for the local merchants, was built at Shore Terrace.

**Engines, Bridges, Astronomy and Photography**: J & C Carmichael of Ward Foundry in Dundee started up in Guthrie Street about 1810–11, making small two-horsepower steam engines to power hand spinning frames. Gradually their capacity increased, and in 1821 they engined the first steam ferry on the Tay. They did the same for many of the mills, and for a time they also built ships. Another Dundee engineer, John Justice, was fabricating metal bridges by 1824. Thomas Henderson, born in Dundee in 1798, became a famed astronomer, the first to calculate the distance to Alpha Centauri, the nearest star to our sun. James Valentine, born in 1815, became a photographer of landscape and townscape, started in the postcard business in the 1840s and founded the famous Dundee firm.

**Port Development and Whaling**: In 1815 responsibility for the wholly tidal harbour was transferred from the town council to Commissioners including trading and landed interests (and 15 years later to a Harbour Trust). A fine new graving dock for completion in 1820, and a huge floating dock, were inspected in 1819 by their designer Thomas Telford and his friend Robert Southey, who noted the use of spoil in raising adjacent land levels, and that three piers would in Telford's opinion accommodate all the additional trade. By 1822 local shipowners had 158 vessels averaging 105 tons burthen; the town's ten whalers were of up to 400 tons. The bounty to whalers ended in 1824, but while other ports gave up, the industry maintained its hold in Dundee. Nine ships caught a total of 200 of these leviathans a year, about 15% of the British total haul. A steam-powered bone mill for farm fertiliser was opened in 1828; besides livestock bones this would have ground up whalebones unsuited for staymaking.

**Metropolitan Dundee**: The population was nearing 40,000 in the 1820s, the streets being described by Chambers as *"crowded with busy people"*. Dundee buildings were noted for *"tallness and metropolitan character"*, and the town had *"newspapers and lawyers, booksellers and confectioners, the four chief characteristics of a capital"*. There were *"huge manufactories, crowded harbours; within the last few years a prodigious quantity of money has been spent in extending and improving the harbour. The merchants of Dundee, besides a great deal of intercourse with the Continent, have upwards of a dozen smacks sailing perpetually to and from London."*

**Bank Troubles and Mergers**: The Dundee Union Banking Company, set up in 1809, had by 1825 opened branches in Arbroath, Brechin, Forfar and Montrose (later merging with the Western Bank). A branch of John Maberly & Co of Aberdeen was short-lived, as was a second Dundee Commercial Banking Company. The joint-stock Eastern Bank of Scotland was established in Dundee in 1838, later joining with the Clydesdale.

**Coasting Trade and Dock Development**: Steamers were introduced on the Perth run about 1823, the King William IV wet dock replaced the old lower tidal harbour in 1825, and by 1826 19 ships and lighters were owned by the Dundee/Perth concerns. These soon merged, and in 1832 bought two 400-ton steamers to develop the London route. In 1832–34 the tidal harbour was converted into the Earl Grey Dock; but still more quays were needed, and in 1836 a start was made on what was eventually to open in 1875 as the Victoria Dock. Provost Pearson's tower house was used as the Custom House from the late 18th century until the new Custom House was built in 1842–43.

**Small Shipbuilders in Wood and Iron**: By 1815 Provost Riddoch owned a shipyard, and 1826 saw the formation of a shipbuilding co-operative, which lasted a quarter of a century. In 1837 the local firm of Adamson built the 37m wooden paddle steamer *Bonnie Dundee* for the Leith service. The Tay's first iron ship, the paddle steamer *Caledonia*, was built by Carmichaels in 1838, and Borrie built several iron paddlers in 1840; but both these firms soon gave up shipbuilding, and although in 1842 Stephens of Aberdeen acquired a Dundee yard, no more iron ships were built on the Tay for over a decade, and any early advantage was lost.

**Flax Mills, Hand Weaving and the Export Trade**: A flood of small new steam spinning mills had been rising: South Dudhope in 1818 by Davie & Boyack, Ward Road (1820, Henry Blyth), Chapelshade (1821, Bell & Balfour), and Scouringburn (1821, Alex Milne). The peak year of 1822 brought the Anchor (George Gray), Lower Dens (Kinmond & Co), and three in Ward Road (James Hynd, David Lawson and Sharp & Preston). At his new Cowgate (East Port) spinning mill William Shaw also erected the town's first calender for cloth finishing (though one had been at work at Douglasfield since 1797), and the St Roque mill was also set working in 1822. Despite steam spinning, in 1819 the Dundee weavers used hand looms and worked a 14-hour day for low wages, making sacking, bagging, sheeting and sailcloth. Government bounties were paid for linen exports, and in 1828 ships carried linens direct from Dundee to such places as New York, Rio and Mobile.

**Steam Power for Spinning**: In the peak mill-building year of 1822, which also saw the dormant Forfarshire Chamber of Commerce resuscitated in Dundee, some 22 flax-spinning mills were working in the town, with about 2000 employees and almost 8000 spindles; 17 of these mills were steam-operated, many of them engined by Carmichaels. By 1832 some 3000 people were working in flax industries in and around Dundee, and much *'bagging'* for cotton was made in King Street, and exported to the USA. Cotton manufacture continued locally at least as late as 1832, on a small scale.

**Baxter's early Mills**: In 1822 William Baxter & Son of Glamis built their first Dundee flax spinning mill on the Dens Burn. Following the perfection of flax-spinning machinery and when flax was at its cheapest in 1825, a mill twice the size was built farther up the burn by the same firm, by then called Baxter Brothers; about 1830 they provided a school for their workers' children. In 1833 Baxters added a third mill still farther upstream, the *'fireproof'* Upper Dens Mill. The 1830s also saw further town centre improvements, and the ancient Dundee High School's new classical building, at first called the Public Seminaries, was built on the Meadows common land to designs by George Angus in 1832–34.

**Britain's Biggest Linen Centre**: To supply all the new Dundee mills with flax and hemp led to imports through the port growing sixfold between 1820 and 1838; but then they stabilised. Meantime A & D Edward & Co, established in 1828, had built at Scouringburn the 100m-long Logie spinning mill of five storeys. In 1833, a Bank of Scotland branch was opened – by 1896 the Bank's second most important branch for lending. Bank loans facilitated capital projects, including the machine spinning of linen thread, which began in 1832; by 1838 there were no fewer than 36 steam-powered flax spinning mills, with over 70,000 spindles. Dundee had overtaken Leeds as the biggest centre of linen manufacture in Britain.

**Jute, Power Looms, Tobacco and Death**: The Verdant Works in West Henderson's Wynd near the Scouring Burn was built in 1833 for flax spinner David Lindsay. In 1835 it was seen that Indian jute could supplant European flax in making carpet backing and sacks, and by 1839 William Taylor of the Ruthven Mill had discovered that whale oil would soften jute, making it workable. It was first used for coffee bags. Baxter Brothers & Co's new mill at Upper Dens, built in 1836–39, soon employed over 300 workers in power loom weaving. By 1846 the firm operated 11,000 spindles in the Dens mills, and 256 power looms; the burn was dammed to provide boiler feedwater. Tobacco was still cured locally in 1835, going to damage the already parlous health of the locals who slaved long hours in the foul air of the mills: in the 1830s the average lifespan of Dundonians was a horribly short and harsh 32 years, against a mere 45 for Scotland as a whole!

**Pioneer Railway and Lads o' Pairts**: Dundonians built their own early railways and engines. The Dundee & Newtyle (D&N), a crude line on the 4'6" (138 cm) gauge, was opened from Dundee harbour in 1831, enabling Strathmore produce to feed the city more readily; its wagons laden with a return traffic in urban manure were hauled on inclines to surmount the Sidlaws. James Stirling, who owned the Victoria and East foundries, employed Archibald Sturrock, born at Pitreuchie in Angus about 1816, who later laid out Doncaster Locomotive Works. Another Dundonian who was to leave Angus for greener pastures was Charles Thomson Ritchie, born in 1838, who became an MP and achieved fame as the Home Secretary who set up the London County Council and the system of English civil parish councils, comparable to today's community councils in rural Scotland.

**Engines become Stationary**: The radical improvement in transport encouraged expansion in new fields: in 1831 Stewart & Son started a whisky blending business, perhaps encouraged by the prospect of easier delivery of full casks by rail from northern distilleries such as Fettercairn. In 1833–34 James Carmichael & Co branched out to build locomotive engines for the D&N, and also constructed two winding engines for the Edinburgh & Dalkeith Railway's inclined plane. They then concentrated on stationary engines; by the 1860s their typical mill engine was of 100 horsepower. Kinmond, Hutton & Steel of the Wallace foundry at Blackness also built locomotives in the years 1840–51. And from 1845, before railways connected to the south, the Edinburgh & Dundee Steam Packet Company's steamer *Britannia* called regularly at ports in East Fife on its way to and from Leith.

**Rails to Arbroath, Forfar, Perth and the South**: Development on the coastal plain was aided when the Dundee & Arbroath Railway (D&A), isolated like the D&N but well built to the 5'6" (168 cm) gauge, was opened in 1838; a year later a link was opened to Friockheim and Forfar. The D&A's Dundee terminus, later called the East station, was beside Victoria Dock. This early system had to be converted to standard gauge, when in 1849 a tramway was laid along Dock Street by the Dundee Harbour Trustees to connect with the standard gauge Dundee & Perth Railway, whose terminus fronted Union Street (the West Station opened in 1866). This line, whose locomotive works were called Seabraes, was forced to pass seaward of Magdalen Green on reclaimed land; amazingly its rails were not *'fished'* (joined to each other) until after 1863! By 1853 Wordie & Co had a rail cartage depot at Seagate, but their local rivals Mutter Howey were soon taking on North British work as the latter's lines spread into Fife and then Angus.

*A clipper at the jetty, Dundee, in the late 19th century; such ships brought raw jute from Calcutta.* *(GWW collection)*

**Slump and Recovery**: Textiles slumped in 1840, putting half the city's flax spindles out of use for a time, but the industry soon recovered and overspilled to Lochee. In 1840 vessels first arrived directly from India with jute, hemp, linseed, sugar and rice. This was the start of a huge trade in which Gilroy Brothers, whose Tay Works used jute by 1851, had become directly engaged by 1864. However, the railway system connected Dundee with Liverpool from 1848, and the direct export trade to the Americas soon passed to the Mersey. Rail brought cheaper coal, so Baxter's power looms were soon followed by the Dudhope Works, John Laing at Dens Road, The Verdant Works, and Edward's at Logie – which by then had 14,000 spindles. At least 35 other mills having about 56,000 steam-driven spindles were then at work. By 1847 some 9000 tonnes of jute was being used per year.

**Marmalade, Water and Expansion**: James Keiller of Dundee was the first quantity maker of marmalade, entering the London market about 1835; but poor water supplies held back growth. The Dundee (Monikie) Water Act of 1845 enabled the engineer James Leslie to take water from the Crombie Burn to a hilltop settling reservoir at Monikie, and thence by aqueduct and pipeline to serve the city from a reservoir beside Dundee Law. Keiller then made successive extensions to his factory in High Street, using about 300 tonnes of Seville oranges in the winter season to make 1000 tonnes of marmalade. By 1869 his was *"the most extensive confectionery business in Britain"*, with 300 workers – mostly young women – who at other times of year made candied peel, jams, jellies, lozenges and lettered rock in works which (in contrast to the filthy jute mills nearby) had *"an air of cleanliness and order"* (Bremner). Keiller became rich and built a mansion near Ballater.

**Public and Private Developments**: Dundee's *Royal Hotel* was open by 1846. In 1852–55 a second Royal Infirmary arose, a huge foursquare structure of three and four storeys on the high ground adjoining the cable incline of the D&N Railway. In 1853–55 a large new Royal Exchange was erected in Panmure Street to designs by David Bryce, though on poor foundations; it adjoined the *'Jute Shelter'* where trading in jute was carried on, and later became the Chamber of Commerce. About 1853 Dundee's imports of jute were only a third of the amount of flax and hemp, which peaked at about 47,000 tonnes, much of it still brought in by sailing vessels. A boom during the Crimean war of 1854–56 was followed by slump, but the 23 ha Baxter Park donated by Sir David Baxter was laid out on the eastern outskirts of the town from 1859 by Sir Joseph Paxton, designer of the Crystal Palace. Its fine decorative pavilion designed by his son-in-law George Henry Stokes was built in 1863. The Dundee Institute for the Blind was founded in 1865; it moved to Magdalen Green in 1884. Meantime Perth Road saw two new mansions, the banker's baronial *St Helens* of 1850 and the Italianate *Duncarse House*, built on a nearby hill in 1858–60.

**Press Expansion, Trades and Traditions**: By 1851 Dundee had two daily newspapers; then in 1858 came the weekly *People's Journal*, an unusual publication. The *Dundee Advertiser*, daily from 1861, later became a constituent of the *Dundee Courier*, which was bought by D C Thomson & Co in 1905. The weekly *People's Friend*, aimed at women, was started in 1869 (and is still published). Textile merchants still kept to the tradition of doing their business in the street, at Cowgate. Jaffe Brothers, merchants, had recently built a large warehouse there. In 1864 Henry Henderson & Sons were still tanning on a large scale, but Warden listed the lost trades of Dundee: bonnets, bottles, buckles, soap, sugar, and thread. By 1861 the population was over 91,000.

**Jute Dominates Dundee: The Grimond Works**: In the days before pallets and containers the demand for sacks and other coarse textiles seemed insatiable as international trade grew: while in 1855 some 20,000 tons of jute were imported (as the cheapest available fibre) it soon became the mainstay of the frugal but rapidly expanding local textile industries. By 1858 more jute was imported than flax and Russian hemp. The change to jute was speeded by Gilroy Brothers, whose steam-powered Tay Works in Lochee Road had just been extended by a 120m-long 4-storey building, and in the 1860s employed over 2000 people, chiefly making jute products – hessian, sacking and bagging. With a total frontage of 300m by 1869, its latest building of five storeys was then *"by far the largest and most imposing structure in Dundee"*, still processing mainly jute, brought from India in the firm's own vessels.

**Other Large Dundee Mills in the 1860s**: In 1835 J & A D Grimond had established a textile factory; their Bow Bridge spinning mill was built in 1857 and regarded by Warden (who fully described the premises in 1864) as *"perhaps the finest structure of its kind in existence"*. The firm had also added a calender and 136 power looms, while still owning a hand-loom works with 1000 employees. By 1869 Bow Bridge had 2000 employees making cheap carpets, matting and hearthrugs. Brown's Bell Mill of 1806 had been re-equipped to spin and weave jute before it was taken over by O G Miller, who in 1864–69 ran five mills – economically named Arch, Column, East, North and South – containing 17,000 spindles driven by ten steam engines with almost 2000 workers, or *'hands'* as they were called. In 1869 Edward employed 3300 people on power looms, making flax and jute fabrics and damasks. In 1864 W R Morison & Co employed 1700 hands, their long established St Roque mill containing 4000 spindles supplying the 510 power looms in their newer Wallace works. By 1869 the spinning mill had 5000 spindles, and 2100 people were employed. In 1864 Thomson, Shepherd & Briggs employed 2000, 1000 in their Seafield Works. The Constable Works and the Pleasance Mill each had 1000 workers.

**Baxters stay with Linen**: The big exception in the 1860s was Baxter Brothers, who did not use jute in their works at all. They operated an integrated spinning and linen-weaving enterprise making sailcloth, sheeting, dowlas, and ducks under the management of Peter Carmichael. (Bremner gave a graphic account of conditions in their enormous mills in 1869.) On a site of over 8 ha, 4350 employees, mostly female, worked in the world's largest flax and hemp concern, with its own machine shop. Many houses and a large new school for employees and their children had recently been built by the firm. By then 7000 tonnes of flax, plus much hemp, was processed by Baxters each year on 22,000 spindles. The dust in the heckling shops with their primitive ventilation was horrendous: *"so dense is the air that it is almost impossible to distinguish persons at the remote end of a room 30 yards in length"*. Most of the 20 million metres of cloth made each year was sailcloth for the Navy, woven on 1200 power looms driven by 22 steam engines using 300 tonnes of coal a week. Sheeting and towelling were also made, but bleaching in the town was impossible due to the *"smoky atmosphere and scarcity of water"*, because the Monikie scheme was no longer adequate.

**Totals for Textiles**: In 1864 a total of about 70,000 tonnes of fibre, in which jute had acquired the major place, was used in Dundee *(including Lochee)*; some 170,000 spindles and 6700 power looms were driven by 160 steam engines, and 36,000 people were kept busy – still including possibly as many as 5000 hand-loom weavers, a dying trade. No fewer than 61 establishments were listed. Cotton's troubles during the American civil war of 1861–65 stimulated the linen trade from 1862 and activity was high in 1864, when seven public calenders for textile finishing were at work. Jute was used in the war for sandbags, so jute imports rose rapidly, and the towering Lower Dens jute mill was built in 1866. So expansion continued, jute imports reaching nearly 95,000 tons by 1871, all supplies coming from Calcutta.

**Shipbuilding in Dundee from Timber to Iron**: D Livie & Sons of Dundee built boats around 1847 and for much of the century. Meantime changes were transforming the shipbuilding industry. A firm known as John Brown (not connected with the later Clydebank concern of that name) built the Tay's first screw vessel in 1851; the yard had become Brown & Simpson by 1869. In 1856 Alexander Stephen & Sons built their largest ship to date in timber, the *Eastern Monarch* of 1848 tons. Stephens which formerly specialised in wooden whalers, moved on to composite vessels in 1865. In 1856 five other yards were building wooden vessels; but by 1869 only two were doing so. Gourlay Brothers & Co, which developed from the Dundee Foundry, began to build little iron ships in 1854. The other firms active in 1869 were the Tay Shipping Company and the Dundee Shipbuilding Company. Thompson Brothers of Tay Foundry began in marine engineering about 1866, also building a substantial fireproof warehouse in Exchange Street. General engineering included hosiery-knitting machinery, made by T Miln, and mangles made in 1869 by G H & G Nicoll of Bank Street.

**Dundee's Wet Docks**: Besides jute, imports included fertilisers, grain and timber, the latter for ships and for building the hastily erected mills and tenements. Textiles made up 90% of the port's true exports (but in the 1860s coal brought in from Fife for bunkering ships made Dundee appear in statistics as a coal export port). The harbour being crowded with small sailing vessels, two new wet docks were built to take steamships, opened in 1865 (Camperdown) and 1875 (Victoria). But despite railway lines on the quays of the Earl Grey and Victoria docks, and the latter's powerful 90-tonne steam crane on a fixed base, the docks were soon too small to handle the larger steamships that were needed as the jute trade grew.

**A Miscellany of Developments**: The Eastern Necropolis, a burial ground which opened in 1862 (because earlier cemeteries were, not surprisingly, almost full) was soon plastered with monuments – and morbidly regarded as a fine place to visit! Public health was at last recognised as a matter for concern, so the Morgan Hospital was built in 1863–66, becoming an endowed secondary school in 1872. As the premature death rate fell and more hands were required by industry, so a phenomenal population increase of nearly 30,000 – including many Irish – was experienced in the ten years to 1871 *(including Lochee, q.v.)*. This resulted in a Roman Catholic cathedral being built. With major expansion in progress and no public housing provision, Dundee became even more squalidly congested. Dundee had no sewers until 1867. In 1870 the water supplied from Monikie under the 1845 scheme ran dry. As a result a much larger scheme was promoted to bring hill water from Lintrathen *(q.v.)* in Glenisla, nearly 30km northwest of Dundee, and built in 1871–75. Assured supply enabled other drinks industries to start up, such as the Victoria brewery; Ballingall's Park maltings and brewery dated from 1881. Meantime in 1870 the wooden *Alhambra Music Hall* was opened, soon transferring its exotic name to the failed *Theatre Royal* with its 1200 seats.

**Building up to the Tay Bridge Disaster**: In 1877–78 a covered railway link as sinuous as a country lane was built westwards from Camperdown Junction, just east of the East station, through a new Tay Bridge station built in 1876 – designed by Thomas Bouch and using stone from the Bannockburn area – to reach Magdalen Green. There a sea wall some 1220m long and 1.5m thick was built to protect a new goods shed and marshalling yard. From there the line rose through Esplanade passenger station and turned on to the ill-starred Tay railway bridge. Begun in 1871, this high, narrow single-tracked structure designed by Thomas Bouch opened in 1878 to praise by Dundee's uniquely bad poet William McGonagall. Besides the moving trains, its shaky superstructure supported heavy pipes carrying Lintrathen water to north Fife suburbs, but it was underdesigned and poorly built. Its central portion blew down in a great winter gale in December 1879, carrying a train with 75 people to their deaths; a story well retold in John Prebble's *The High Girders*.

**Late Victorian Shopping and Education Facilities**: Meantime local man William Low had started his grocery business in 1868, biscuit manufacture commenced in 1872, and the foodstuffs firm of Watson & Philip was established in 1873. D M Brown's store opened in 1888, incorporating the novelty of a tea room. The imposing Whitehall Street, which replaced slums, was also built in the late 1880s, including Draffen & Jarvie's department store which opened in 1889. In 1869–72 the Albert Institute, designed by Sir Gilbert Scott, was built as a reference library; it was extended in 1873 to incorporate a museum. Bought by the town council in 1879, it was again extended in 1887–89, adding an art gallery to designs by William Alexander. The University College, forerunner of the University of Dundee, was founded in 1881, largely due to the efforts of the Baxter family of Balgavies, and opened in 1883. But despite higher educational advance and its expanding journalism, this great commercial port provided no secondary education to most of its children until Harris Academy was founded in 1885!

**Whaling Peak – and a new Shipyard**: Ten Dundee steamers were whaling by 1873, making it Britain's leading whaling port; at great hardship and risk to crews, whales were cruelly harpooned to obtain the oil used in lamps and for jute processing, and baleen for the corset bones required to crush women's bodies into fashionable hour-glass figures *(see Kirriemuir)*. The Caledon Shipyard, able to build ships of up to 3400 tons, was founded in 1874 by W B Thompson. From 1886 it built coasters for the Clyde Shipping Company of Glasgow, and in 1892 launched the sailing vessel *Lawhill*, one of the last windjammers, for jute shipper Charles Barrie. Such sizeable new businesses needed funding: in 1878 a fine new Clydesdale Bank branch was built behind the Trades Hall, which was demolished as redundant about 1890.

**Restoration of the Fife Rail Link**: When the first Tay Bridge collapsed in 1879, the will and finance was there to rebuild. In 1880–87 a second Tay Bridge designed by W H Barlow was constructed on new foundations and to new double-tracked standards by Tancred, & Co (set up for the purpose by the famed contractor William Arrol). The bridge remarkably incorporated the best surviving girders of the first superstructure – these still carry trains! Meantime in 1885 the Caledonian built new engine sheds in Dundee and opened an imposing new West Station in 1889; the nearby Esplanade was extended around 1900, on land reclaimed by the Dundee Harbour Trust and the railway companies. The new bridge speeded Dundee's overdue growth in services, helping it to usurp much of the regional role of Perth, and to exert a stronger influence over north Fife.

**The Press, Horse and Steam Trams and Recreation**: The *Dundee Evening Telegraph* was published from 1877, the year that the first horse-drawn tram route was introduced; it linked Sinderins with the main Post Office (which later became the office of the *Dundee Courier and Argus*, as it was named in 1897). The tramways were unusual in being worked by steam from 1885. The *Queen's Hotel* was built in 1878, and by about then a permanent circus building had been erected, which became the *Palace Music Hall* in 1893. The promoter of the *Alhambra*, William McFarland, built the 1700-seat *Her Majesty's Theatre*, opened in 1885. This was followed in 1891 by the *People's Palace*, a music hall in Lochee Road.

**Electric City joins St Andrews University**: The association of the University College with St Andrews University which began in 1890 and was complete by 1897 was made easier by the restored railway to Fife. Soon about 300 students attended in Dundee, which was chartered as a City in 1889; by 1891 its population, by then including Lochee, had passed 150,000. In 1893 Dudhope Castle was bought by the new city council, but its occasional use by the army continued. In 1894 Murray listed five hotels, the *Queen's* being *"good"*; two others, including *Lamb's Temperance Hotel* in Reform Street, were committed to sobriety, in itself no guarantee of hostelry quality! Scotland's first central electric power station was authorised in Dundee in 1893, when a generating capacity of 434 kW was provided. The steam tramways which were taken over by the Corporation in 1899 were electrified in 1900–02, including a western route to Ninewells: the central depot was on Lochee Road. With growing power demands, the early generators soon proved inadequate, hence the coal-fired Carolina Port *'A'* power station, opened in 1909 and later converted to oil firing.

**Combating Sickness, Sugar – and Substitute Teeth**: The third Infirmary, of 220 beds, was built in the mid 1880s and later enlarged to 400 beds; King's Cross Hospital was built in 1889 and the Victoria Hospital was opened in 1899. One of the largest flax mills in Dundee proper still employed 4000 people in those days, and Keiller's two factories used 2500 tons of sugar a year (they also had a Guernsey factory so as to evade the sugar tax!). To re-equip the toothless jaws of a city with huge *'sweetie'* manufacturers but very few dentists able to conserve teeth, F H Wright began to manufacture dentures locally in 1898. A new head post office was opened in 1897, followed in 1899 by a large new branch of the Royal Bank, its staff helping to fund the vast jute industry. In 1901 the Dundee Technical Institute became one of the first four Scottish Central Institutions; a teacher training centre opened in 1905.

**Improving the Port**: Following an Act of 1875 the Trinity House of Dundee formed part of the Dundee Harbour Trust, which began in 1881 to construct riverside wharves. In 1893 work was begun on the reclamation of 75ha of land from the river to build a 400m-long eastern wharf. This was open by 1898 and the whole scheme was completed in 1906. By 1912 Caledon had built a new 6-berth shipyard at the eastern wharf. Jute imports, mainly from India, peaked in 1898 at almost 300,000 tons, which by then were all unloaded from steamers at the new riverside quays; at that time the little known Polepark Jute Works, owned by Smith, had its own 10-man fire brigade. James Carmichael & Co had long continued in business as engine builders and millwrights, and by the 1890s were building compound steam engines of advanced design. One supplied in 1899 to Alexander Henderson & Sons' South Dudhope jute works drove 154 looms, four dressing machines and a new 26 kW electrical generator made by Lowdon Brothers & Co, also of Dundee.

***Discovery* and the Apogee of Dundee Shipbuilding**: By the 1890s three Dundee yards were building iron and steel ships. The largest was Gourlay Brothers, also marine engineers, who built tugs by 1889; about 1896 they launched the steel-hulled twin-screw steamer *Hesperus* for the Northern Lighthouse Board, a sturdy vessel which remained at work until 1973. But Gourlay Brothers went bankrupt in 1908. Meantime Panmure, the former Stephens yard, was acquired by the Dundee Shipbuilding Company in 1894. This firm built the Royal Geographical Society's famous ship *Discovery* in 1901; engined by Gourlay Brothers, she became a Royal Research Ship in 1923. The third shipyard was Caird's, on which less information has been widely published, though the Ashton Juteworks was owned by a Caird and the Caird Fountain was built in 1879.

**Dundee's Jute Works at the Peak**: The population of Angus peaked at the 1901 census; in 1904 24% of Dundee houses had over two persons per room. The Blackness Foundry made the looms that were in use at the Hillside Works in 1911. Jute products were among those shipped overseas; the export tonnages in 1910–13 were the highest in the history of the port. To supply industry and homes with enough water, Lintrathen Loch was raised by a further metre in 1911. By then nearly 38,000 people were employed in jute (including the extensive Taybank Works which wove and finished jute products), but only 1100 worked in linen. The Carolina Port fish dock failed to attract a fishing fleet, and whaling – which had declined from the 1890s due to over-exploitation – ceased from Dundee about 1913.

**Recreation Outdoor and Indoor**: From about 1880 Clepington Park north of Dens Road was the base of the Wanderers FC, who played one season (1894–95) in the Scottish League; they were ousted from the park in 1909 by Dundee Hibernian, who renamed it *Tannadice*. Meantime in 1899 an adjacent ground named Dens Park was established by Dundee FC, which was formed in 1893 and originally played at Carolina Port. Dundee greatly improved Dens Park in 1921, and in 1923 the failed Dundee Hibernian became Dundee United. Dundee's first cinema appears to have opened in 1896. The *Gaiety Theatre* was opened in 1903 (being renamed the *Victoria* in 1910). The *Palace* variety theatre succumbed to celluloid in 1912, becoming one of no fewer than 24 picture houses open in the city during its cinema era, including by 1924 the *Empire*. Meantime the *King's Theatre* opened in the Cowgate in 1909; this too became a cinema in 1928. But escapism did not exclude literacy: in 1913, with a stock of over 150,000 books, Dundee's public library service had by far the highest ratio of books per head of any Scottish city; whether largely read for recreation or for self-improvement was not stated. Harris Academy moved to new premises in Perth Road in 1930.

*Bowbridge jute works, Dundee, in the 1970s. This very large works was founded in 1857 by J & A D Grimond, and included the spinning mill seen here. The works were demolished in the 1980s.(JRH)*

**Briggs Bitumen and Batching Oil**: By 1908 William Briggs' Camperdown Refinery made bitumen for marine anti-fouling compounds. In the 1920s the Dundee, Perth & London Shipping Company (DPL) operated the hybrid dry cargo and tanker coaster SS *Broughty* to carry printing ink material from Briggs' refinery to London, returning with batching oil from Briggs to lubricate the spindles of Dundee's jute mills. This was carried in tiny horse-drawn tankers by Wordie & Co, who had a Dundee district office; with some 225 horses in the area as late as 1928, their stables in Dock Street were still busy. DPL also used puffers, including the 20m Denny-built *Garmoyle (see Brodick)* which plied between Perth, Dundee and Leith.

**From 1914 to the Slump**: Through the war and the 1920s Dundee industry remained reasonably busy, though always as a low wage area no longer able to support four breweries. Dundee's Victoria brewery had already closed in 1910, to be followed by Craigie in 1930; meantime in 1923 the whisky blenders James Watson & Co sold their distilleries, mainly to Dewars. As cargo ships grew larger the King George V wharf had to be built from 1913 – twice extended to 1932. Meantime during the 1914–18 war Stannergate became a seaplane base, with slipways and three hangars. From 1919 the city council pioneered housing schemes to relieve congestion and improve living conditions for its 40,000 poorly paid textile workers, who had been badly affected by the crash of 1920 and were by then competing against the near starvation wages of new competitors – the Indian jute workers. The old Town House of 1732 was pulled down to provide a site for the City Square, backed by the great complex of the Caird Hall, which was donated to the city and opened in 1923.

**Dundee Shipbuilding and Jute in the Slump**: In 1923 Carmichael & Co were still manufacturing horizontal steam engines, but Caird's shipyard closed about 1928, the year in which Caledon built paddle steamers, and had a continuing source of orders for coasters about every other year from the Clyde Shipping Company of Glasgow; but by 1936 all the other Dundee shipyards had closed. In 1930 Baxters converted their 1864 foundry into the Eagle jute-spinning mill, but during the slump of 1932 over 70% of the 37,000 jute workers were unemployed. A few jobs came when the small local oil-refining industry was further developed from 1930, and Robert L Fleming founded a sack-making company in 1932. A city observatory on Balgay Hill was opened in Dundee in 1935, a long overdue outcome of the legacy of jute manufacturer John Mills who had died in 1889. But in 1936 24% of Dundee's houses were still seriously overcrowded, and unemployment remained high.

**The Cinema and the Comic enter the Big Time**: The *Alhambra Theatre*, which opened in 1929 of all unlucky years, was soon converted into the *State Cinema*. In 1930 *Her Majesty's Theatre* also became a cinema, the *Majestic*; rebuilt after a fire in 1941, it later became the *Cannon Film Centre*. In 1935 the *Victoria Theatre* likewise became a cinema. The vast Green's *Playhouse Cinema* – with 4126 seats the second largest in Europe – was built in the Nethergate in 1936, complete with a dance floor and cafe. Perhaps this explains why in 1938 the *Palace Cinema* reverted to variety entertainment. Meantime D C Thomson introduced the *Hotspur* comic in 1933, tapping a new vein of childish banality soon very successfully followed up by the famous *Dandy* and *Beano*. Dundee had one of Scotland's first Woolworth stores; the SCWS store was built in 1935, and Marks & Spencer came to the city in 1936.

**World War II, the Demise of Caledon, and Ferry problems**: Dundee's 1939–45 war work included the Caledon-built escort carrier HMS *Activity* of 11,800 tons, launched in 1942, their largest wartime vessel; it was engined by Kincaid. Caledon's last sizeable passenger vessel was its 422nd contract, the 10,000-ton motor ship *Modjokerto* of 1946. Coasters, and two vessels for the Northern Lighthouse Board kept them going; but competition was growing, and the yard closed in 1961. Meantime by 1953 the Dundee Harbour Trust's large vehicle ferries gave a half hourly service to Newport from Craig Pier near Tay Bridge Station, 0700–2200 on weekdays and hourly for a shorter time on Sundays.

**Brewing in Trouble, but Public Services Progress**: By 1947 the daily newspaper was called the *Courier and Advertiser*. The last local breweries, Park and Pleasance, closed in 1964 as the brewing industry centralised. As tenements and redundant mills were cleared, City Council *'schemes'* burgeoned in Hilltown and the suburbs, some still linked by electric trams until 1956. Whereas in 1951 about 30,000 people still lived in the inner city (about 1.5km radius), by 1971 this was down to only 20,000. More houses with baths used more water: an Act of 1964 allowed the City Council to build the Backwater Reservoir to augment Lintrathen Loch. BP opened an oil jetty about 1960, and the efficient oil-fired Carolina Port 'B' power station worked on the waterside beside its older namesake from 1965 to 1982, both then being closed.

**Railway Rationalisation as Jute Falters**: By 1950 there were only 39 firms left in jute, compared with 150 at the industry's height; fierce competition from India was the main cause. Dundee East station was closed by BR in 1959. Dundee's last railway horse carted jute to mills until the mid 1960s when the jute industry was rapidly contracting, destroying the firm of Urquhart Lindsay Robertson Orchar (ULRO) which had made its looms. However, in 1979 the Buist Spinning Company still owned the Stobswell jute spinning works, and a horse-drawn jute cart was seen as recently as the 1990s! The Caledonian engine shed was modernised for diesels in 1962 but demolished in 1989. Its NBR counterpart, long a lowly outpost of Thornton, serviced steam engines until about 1966. In 1965 Beeching sensibly concentrated all remaining services on the main station, Tay Bridge, and the West station was demolished.

**Higher Education, Dundee University and STD**: By 1953 the much-altered Dudhope Castle had been restored to use as a technical school; the teacher training centre became Dundee College of Education in 1959. In 1964 Dundee Trades College moved out to Baldovan. Duncan of Jordanstone College of Art, a Scottish Central Institution, also gained new buildings, next to what had become in 1954 the Queen's College of St Andrews University. Despite having under 2000 students, this became in 1967 the independent University of Dundee. Meantime in 1956 Dundee United FC began to invest heavily at Tannadice, and in 1960 Dundee became the first Scottish city with the facility of STD (Subscriber Trunk Telephone Dialling).

**Logan bridges the Tay and leads Dundee into the Air**: While more road users clogged the ferry, the steamer service to London ceased in 1961. To provide space to build the north approaches to the Tay Road Bridge, the ugly and purposeless Royal Arch, built in stone at the harbourside in 1851, was demolished, and from 1964 the redundant Earl Grey dock (which closed in 1962), the King William dock and the tidal harbour were infilled. Designed by W A Fairhurst, the Tay Road Bridge opened in 1966 with a new approach road across north Fife, and a new 2245m-long 42-span concrete and steel viaduct across the Tay. Its builder was Logan Construction of Muir of Ord, whose boss – Willie Logan of Loganair fame – also persuaded the city council to build the Riverside Airstrip west of the rail bridge. This soon became the base for the aircraft hire firm Aerosport, the Tayside Flying Club, and Tayside Aviation, founded in 1968.

**Theatres and Cinemas Vulnerable to Fire**: A repertory theatre company was active by the 1950s, playing at Ward Road until fire forced a move to a tiny theatre in Lochee Road; but the music halls and many cinemas vanished as television became widely available around 1960. After 1958 the huge *Playhouse Cinema* became the *Mecca* bingo hall, which was so badly damaged by fire in 1995 that it had to be demolished and rebuilt. The *Palace*, which had been renamed the *Theatre Royal* in 1965, had already burned down in 1977; the former *King's Cinema* (later known as the *Gaumont* and later still the *Odeon)* changed to bingo in 1973. The city council took over the *State Cinema* in 1975, and with refurbishment it reverted to its original purpose as the *Whitehall Theatre*; the attractive new *Repertory Theatre* with 450 seats was opened in Tay Street in 1982.

*A worker adjusting polypropylene strings, Dundee, in one of the half-dozen textile companies which have successfully made the transition from jute.* *(Norman Burniston)*

**City Centre Redevelopment: Mixed Success**: Meantime the draughty Overgate Centre was built in 1963–66, including Littlewoods, C&A and Boots stores and a rooftop car park. The much smarter covered three-level Wellgate Centre of 28,000 m$^2$ with branches of BHS (8825 m$^2$) and Tesco, plus 600 parking spaces, was opened in 1977; the adjacent new Central Library opened in 1978. This complex stayed fully let and very busy, but shops in the more westerly Nethergate Centre, also new at that time and connected to the railway station by footbridge, remained unlet and eventually became offices.

**Dundee's Unicorn and the *'City of Discovery'***: In 1968 the hull of the aged wooden frigate HMS *Unicorn*, berthed in the city's otherwise deserted Victoria Dock, was opened to the public. By 1973 a new indoor swimming pool had been built on part of the site of the former Earl Grey Dock; as the Olympia Leisure Centre this comprised by 1994 a complex of swimming pools and water features for all tastes, and also a climbing wall. In 1975 Dundee became the administrative capital of the new Tayside Region, its office block Tay House built on the site of the one-time arch on the waterfront overlooking Fife (!); it also was for 20 years the headquarters of Dundee City District, an area much more extensive than the former Large Burgh or the present City. In 1986 the Antarctic research vessel *Discovery* (see 1901) was returned to the Victoria Dock and opened as a major tourist attraction, so the city's publicists chose the slogan *'City of Discovery'*.

**The Tayside Capital in Transition**: In 1979 Thomas Justice & Sons manufactured and retailed furniture; Levi Strauss operated two jeans factories in the area, but the former Angus Works was converted by the SDA into twelve small factories. A former NCR factory was converted in 1978–79 to house the Valentines greetings card operation; sold by Waddingtons in 1980, it remained in business as art publishers. The former Keiller factory at Albert Square was converted into a new 60-unit shopping centre opened in 1979. About 12,000 or so people then remained within 1.5 km of the city centre. By 1991 the total city population was 159,000.

**The Port of Tay Modernised and Sold – to the Forth!**: In 1979 a ro-ro ferry terminal was built by Dundee Port Authority at the Eastern Wharf, but in 1980 oil tankers could be accepted only of 20,000 tons, and a mere 600 tonnes of grain was exported. In 1985 a second ro-ro facility was opened, but an attempt to establish a ferry service to Europe was abortive. New cranes plus grain handling, storage and drying equipment were installed later, enabling 200,000 tonnes of grain to be exported annually; in 1994 Lothian Barley, a subsidiary of S&N's Moray Firth Maltings, operated grain drying and storage facilities in Dundee. Dredging improved the port to accept 90,000 ton tankers: the Camperdown Refinery, by 1994 owned by the Swedish firm Nynas, cracked Venezuelan crude oil to produce bituminous products. Calls from cruise ships resumed in 1993 after a four-year gap. About 1995 the port of Dundee was sold to the privatised Forth Ports, who in 2000 started to build housing there, and intend to erect a hotel.

**The end of Jute, Jam and Journalism?**: In 1987 William Low began to move its head office to Baldovan, and in 1988 most of James Keiller's remaining interests were sold; marmalade production ceased, and jam production was moved to Manchester. After four years under Alma from Kirkcaldy, *'sweetie'* production ended in 1992. Between 1988 and 1991 Dundee City District Council moved its HQ from the inadequate City Chambers to Dudhope Castle, and by 1993 the Dundee College of Technology Business School had new accommodation there. As tastes changed in newspaper readership, between 1981 and 1991 the circulation of the *Weekly News* declined from about 1.2 million to 0.5 million, and the *People's Journal* – which had once enjoyed the largest circulation of any weekly newspaper in history (400,000 copies in ten regional editions) – was closed in 1990 by the D C Thomson group, who employed 1800 people in 1993. Their *(Dundee) Courier* and other offices were moved out from the city centre to Kingsway East *(see Craigie)*, they expanded into other media and kept their HQ in the Dundee area, the popular *Scots Magazine* being edited in Albert Square in 1999.

**Packaging and Offshore Activity**: Dundee had long been the headquarters of Low & Bonar (L&B), an energetic packaging, plastics and textiles group *(see also Lochee)*; by 1990 they owned 30 plants in the UK, Europe and North America, and opened a large extension to their *'Bonar Teich Flexibles'* plant. In 1989–90 Davy GVA Offshore repaired oil platforms at the former Kestrel Marine shipyard beside the wharf, with a staff of 600–800, but in 1994 it was McGregor Engineering that maintained and repaired oil rigs in the Tay. Stolt Comex Seaway which arrived in 1993 was claimed as the North Sea's largest subsea engineering contractor, and in 1993 Dundee became the base for the world's largest oil-well stimulation ship, the US-owned *Western Renaissance*.

**Valentines leave; Paper Sacks stay a while**: Valentines' factory had closed in 1993 with its last 200 jobs, when card production was moved to Ireland by its owners Hallmark. Jute sacks had vanished too, but Robert L Fleming continued their 60 or more years of paper sack manufacturing near the University; in 1994 huge rolls of paper arrived there from the north via the A92. In 1995 they supplied 80% of the paper packets for the powdered milk market, one in three paper bags for the flour millers, and also sold to the cement and construction industries; but in 1996 the plant became Assidoman Sacks (UK) before closing about 1998. In 1999 the slump in farming hit paper sack maker Agritay, who shed 100 jobs.

**Unfinished Business in Textiles**: A large finishing and dyeing plant for garment fabrics was built in 1989–90 on a riverside site west of the city centre by Tootal and its Japanese partners for the single European market; trading as Dundee Textiles, it provided 240 jobs. In 1989 export-oriented W R Stewart, textile machinery manufacturers, were Britain's last makers of hackles (the combs for flax and hemp processing). The Taybank Works still made textiles about 1990, but the Upper Dens Mill had been converted to housing by 1992. The long-established Riverside Works of J T Inglis & Sons, Textile Proofers, still worked in 1994 but H & A Scott of Tayfield Works, long established in textiles, closed in 1995. In the same year the Sidlaw Group sold off its remaining jute and flax spinning industries and moved its HQ to Edinburgh. Tay Spinners were the last firm still in jute, but half a dozen companies had made the successful transition to polypropylene processing.

**The New Technology Park**: Dundee Technology Park (DTP) was laid out about 1990 between Invergowrie and Ninewells, and with Enterprise Zone benefits soon attracted Richard Lawson, the UK's third largest car delivery firm, to move their HQ from Edinburgh. In 1992 General Accident of Perth moved their London service centre, a major data-processing complex employing 350 people, to a new building at DTP where it created 270 jobs for local people. About that time the Royal Bank and Scottish Power also took up DTP properties, as did US-owned W L Gore *(see Dunfermline)* for their Microwave Cable Assembly Division works.

**Hotels, New Offices and Flying Training**: The *Queen's Hotel* was enlarged and improved in 1990. By 1989 the new *Earl Grey Hotel* had been opened by Stakis on the waterfront, with a casino beside it; in 2000 it became the *Dundee Hilton*. In 1996 Whitbread opened a 40-room *Travel Inn* with a 200-seater restaurant in the waterfront Enterprise Zone. In 1991–92 new city centre offices were built for 240 Inland Revenue staff; Customs and Excise offices were added a few years later. In 1993 General Accident of Perth employed 450 people in their Dundee insurance claims branch. Tayside Aviation built a new maintenance hangar in 1982 with SDA help, and started pilot training at Dyce in 1987; by 1995 they operated 20 aircraft and took over Fife Airport at Glenrothes. In 1992 an air link to Stansted was proposed from the Regional Council's Dundee Airport. In 1999 Brian Souter and Ann Gloag of Perth, founders of Stagecoach, bought tiny Suckling Airways of Cambridge, renamed it Scotairways and started a successful scheduled air service between Dundee and London City Airport, creating 20 jobs. In 2000 they bought small jet airliners to add direct Continental services.

**Shopping Developments**: Norco of Aberdeen had built a superstore at Hilltown by 1991, but it was not a success and in 1993 Norco failed. A Texas store which opened in 1990 on a former railway site at Riverside Drive west of the station did not outlast the firm's demise, unlike an adjacent Tesco store; in addition a Tesco Metro was opened in 1996. In 1991–92, as the city celebrated 800 years since it was for sure a Royal Burgh, an inner relief road was cut along the steep hillside north of the city centre, where the discovery was made in 1991 that air pollution was excessive outside the Wellgate Centre; so central pedestrianisation was soon begun, completed to great benefit in 1994. The Wellgate Centre was fully modernised from 1992; by 1994 Woolworths had moved in, and their former store had become a spacious branch of Menzies (from 1999 W H Smith). The Overgate Centre was also extensively rebuilt from 1992 to 2000 and a large Debenhams department store became the flagship (replacing their makeshift firetrap opposite). Arnotts store remained open as part of the House of Fraser chain.

**Vacancy, Dereliction and Regeneration**: In 1985 the College of Commerce had merged with Kingsway Technical College as Dundee College of Further Education. By 1992 the 8.5 ha University botanic garden at the west end welcomed visitors to its walks and glasshouses; but the nearby Duncarse House, for a time a local authority children's home, was largely vacant by 1993. The fine Exchange Coffee House building, lately used as a pub, shops and printing works by David Winter & Son, was restored in 1994–95, largely as a restaurant. The Dock Street bonded store which had been owned from 1898 by the whisky blenders George Morton & Sons, had also long stood empty by 1993; from 1994 this together with the former *Courier* buildings in Bank Street, the East Port works in Cowgate

*The oldest and the newest in Dundee city centre today: the town's church dominated by the 50-metre high St Mary's Tower (built c.1460), and the recently completed Overgate shopping centre.* *(AL)*

and the *Royal Hotel* in Union Street were all converted into housing with aid from Scottish Homes, providing over 300 units.

**Football Rivalry continues: Stadiums improved**: Dundee still supports two rival football teams based within shouting distance of each other: in 1992 the more successful, Dundee United, could seat only 11% of its Premier League capacity crowd of over 22,000 at Tannadice Park, and planned to develop a 15,000 all-seat stadium. Dundee FC struggled to meet the ground improvement rules, but did erect new stands in the late 1990s at Dens Park. Both were just happy to be in the Premier League in 2000.

**Mapping Leisure and Showing off Dundee's Past**: Close to the railway station was the new domed building of the Discovery Point Heritage Centre, opened in 1993 by the Dundee Heritage Trust to provide a better setting for the RRS *Discovery*. The old North Carr light vessel formerly on show at Anstruther was towed to Dundee for display in 1995. In 1991 the Verdant Spinning Works of the 1830s was bought by Dundee Heritage Trust for restoration into a museum of the jute industry, while the McManus Galleries contained exhibits on local history, art and costume. In 1996 a Vermont firm called Level Nine opened in Dundee, its aim being to extend to Scotland, Britain, Ireland and within two years mainland Europe its Internet program which mapped all hotels and golf courses in detail; this work should create 200 jobs. A warehouse in Nethergate was heavily converted to form a Contemporary Arts Centre, opened in 1999, and it was immediately successful.

**New and Ongoing Industries; Rail Changes**: In 1994 Shield Diagnostics made test kits devised by the University, and Madison Cable announced a new 200-job facility. Torbrex Engineering had opened a new assembly plant in 1993. By 1994 Scottish Soft Fruit Growers, formed in 1990 as the world's largest raspberry company, was processing 40% of the Scottish crop at a plant in Dundee. The Byzantine process of rail privatisation led to the last rail freight facilities being withdrawn in 1994 from Dundee's once busy rail yards. From 1995, due to some uncertainty as to its condition, the bridge was signalled to allow only one passenger train on the high girders at one time, and freight was banned, being diverted via Perth. Railtrack planned to strengthen the structure to carry faster, heavier freight trains (to take growing rail traffic), and repair work by John Mowlem is to take from 2000 to 2003, also enabling 110kmph running.

**Dundee and Abertay Universities**: By 1993 Dundee was the top Scottish university in research grant income per staff member, and was strong in law, accountancy, medicine, dentistry and engineering. Its absorption in 1994 of the adjacent Duncan of Jordanstone College of Art raised student numbers from 5000 to 7000. In 1995 the Wellcome Trust funded the building of a 6-storey laboratory for the University Department of Biochemistry, creating 200 new jobs in biomedical research and making it the fourth largest in the UK. In 1996 the University expanded into Kirkcaldy, taking over its nursing and midwifery school. By 1999 the University's Visual Research Centre was open, built with Scotland's largest lottery grant to date. Meantime in 1994 the fast-growing Dundee College (or Institute) of Technology in its cramped city centre campus had reached the 4000-student mark, enabling it to gain long-coveted status as the University of Abertay, which set about establishing new courses for nursing, and in 1995 completed its new Business school in Dudhope Castle.

**City curtailed, Region destroyed, Rubbish recycled**: In 1996 blatant gerrymandering by the Major government removed Monifieth and very extensive western and northern areas from Dundee City District and placed them in the all-purpose local authorities for Angus and Perth & Kinross. Although the rump of the city gained the same status, the simultaneous destruction of the Tayside Regional Council – whose office block passed to the City Council – and the removal of both water supply and sewerage from local government control, further reduced Dundee's local government significance and prevented coherent planning of this city, which had been so drastically changed in 40 years. At least by 2000 the new council led the way in Scotland by recycling much of the city's rubbish, shaming Fife's dismal performance in this field.

**Pupils attracted, Hospitals dispersed and Port active**: Dundee Royal Infirmary was to close by 1998, and the run-down to eventual closure of the King's Cross acute hospital was announced in 1994, all acute services to move to the Ninewells Hospital overlooking Invergowrie Bay. In 1992 a ro-ro ferry to Eemshaven in Holland was intended, but seems to have come to nothing; however, tankers from Venezuela still dock at Caledon west wharf with oil for the Nynas refinery, and offshore fabrication and maintenance work continues. One-2-One (mobile phones) intend to open a 1000-job call centre in 2002. But decline was still forecast for the area of Greater Dundee, which had seen less suburban development in recent years than Scotland's three larger cities and either Inverness or Livingston. The independent Dundee High School draws its 1140 pupils (including 360 juniors) from a 30-mile radius; the Harris Academy has 1340 pupils. Morgan Academy suffered a serious fire in March 2001. A hotel proposal at Riverside Drive was rejected in 2000, but the Invercarse Hotel (a former Perth Road mansion), continues to attract business and local trade.

## DUNDONALD & Drybridge — Map 1, C1

***Ayrshire village,** pop. 2400* — OS 70: NS 3664

Remains of an ancient *Dun* or vitrified fort survive at Dundonald, 6 km south-east of Irvine. Dundonald Castle was built on a knoll 1 km to the east in the 12th century by Walter Fitzalan, Steward of Scotland under King David I (hence the family name Stewart); it was the home of his descendant Robert Stewart, who became King Robert II in 1390. Little is known until a parish school was founded in 1606. Pont's map made about then showed woodland around *'Aghans'* (Auchans), a tower house 1 km to the west; Dundonald Kirk stood within the park of the prominent Dundonald Castle. This was soon sold to Sir W Cochrane, who obtained a burgh of barony charter for the Kirkton of Dundonald in 1638 and robbed the old castle of materials in 1644 to build a replacement for Auchans. By 1750 a road led northwards to Dreghorn.

**The World's First and most enduring Railway Viaduct**: The very early horse-drawn Kilmarnock & Troon Railway which opened in 1812 provided a station beside the River Irvine 2 km north of the village. The bridge (dated 1811) built on dry land to carry the Dreghorn road across the line was then a most unusual feature, which gave rise to the placename *Drybridge*. Two kilometres farther east was the Laigh Milton Viaduct of four stone arches, which carried the line across the river until 1846, when a diversion made it redundant; though out of use for over 150 years, it most remarkably survives today as the world's oldest railway viaduct.

**Mansion, Militia and Male-only Golf**: Another new mansion called Auchans House was built near the village in the mid 19th century. Meantime a site 3 km to the west became a militia camping ground. A post office and inn existed at Dundonald by 1895; it was a small village, and Drybridge was little more than a mill and the railway station, though it later gained a quite important telephone exchange. In 1892 the Glasgow golf club of Killermont built an 18-hole links course at Gailes, followed in 1897 by the Western Gailes club, 18 holes, at first firmly male chauvinist. In the 1914–18 war a huge barracks called Dundonald Camp was established on the militia site at Gailes. The rail-served Hillhouse whinstone quarry (half-way to Troon), began work some time after 1895 and was already large by 1953; at that time there was a colliery at Gailes and a sawmill at Drybridge. During the 1939–45 war a small airfield was opened at Dundonald as a satellite of Prestwick, but afterwards it soon vanished.

**Nylon and Concrete**: By 1951 Dundonald had a population of over 1100 but few additional facilities; Shewalton Moss 2 km to the west was used as a major tipping site. Gailes station closed after 1953, and Drybridge station was closed in 1969; however, a works built nearby by 1962 had expanded by 1985. In 1966 the large nylon-spinning factory of US-owned Monsanto Textiles was built with government aid north of the village, having 850–900 jobs when it got into difficulties in 1979. Auchans House was pulled down about 1970 and its site was developed for housing, but the old roofless tower remained. By 1981 Dundonald had doubled in size with estate development, but although housing 2750 people it still had only the facilities of a small village – the golf courses excepted. By 1991 the population was down to 2400; by then Dundonald Camp had greatly shrunk. Hillhouse quarry was enormous by 1985 and still producing tarmac and ready mixed concrete; it remained rail-connected in 1997. By 1998 a new leisure centre had been built. The ruined castle, consolidated over a long period, is now open to the public, staffed by volunteers.

## DUNDONNELL — Map 8, C1

***Wester Ross settlement,** pop. 200 (area)* — OS 19: NH 0888

Wester Ross holds the wild and remote mountains of Strathnasheallag Forest, which reaches 1062 metres. To the east, where once was a fragment of the crazy county of Cromarty, is an area regarded as empty when the Roy map was made around 1750. Dundonnell House was built in the 18th century in Strath Beag, a sheltered valley where the Dundonnell River flows into Little Loch Broom. The so-called *Destitution Road* which links Dingwall with Aultbea was built following the potato famine of 1846, and completed in 1851. This road which passes a series of attractive waterfalls alongside the river and the loch gave rise to the tiny *Dundonnell Inn*, open by the 1890s at the head of the loch, just 7 km south-west

*Dundonald (or Hillhouse) quarry, Ayrshire, which began around 1900, pictured in 1921; now very large, and still producing hard stone for the construction industry.* *(British Geological Survey)*

of Ullapool as the seagull flies, but still 40 km by road. In the mid 20th century the tiny township of Badcaul on the coast 7 km to the west had a post office and primary school; Dundonnell had a telephone exchange and post office, plus a youth hostel, open for a time around 1955–61 but closed by 1985; by then Camusnagaul between Dundonnell and Badcaul had a caravan site. Meantime the family-owned inn, progressively enlarged and improved, is now the 28-room *Dundonnell Hotel*, and a small backpackers' hostel is also open at Camusnagaul. There is also some salmon farming and fish-smoking nearby.

## DUNDRENNAN — Map 2, A5

***Galloway small village,*** *pop. 200* — OS 84: NX 7447

Dundrennan lies in a remote sheltered valley in a hilly area 3 km from the coast of the Solway Firth, some 7 km south-east of Kirkcudbright. Its name refers to a fort: a rough count reveals no fewer than 15 prehistoric forts and earthworks within 4 km of the site where in 1142 Fergus, Lord of Galloway, founded a Cistercian abbey. The coastal name Castle Yards is further evidence of fortification. By the late 13th century the abbey owned over 3000 sheep, and the monks sold sorted wool around 1400. The abbey was represented in Parliament in 1560; although it had only two appropriated churches, Chambers wrote much later of its *"magnificent and extensive building"* where in 1568 Queen Mary probably spent her last night in Scotland. The Reformation already in progress caused its downfall and, although still marked as an abbey on Blaeu's map made from Pont's sketch of about 1610, it was secularised to the Earl of Annandale in 1606 and later fell into ruin. The small village which grew nearby in the little-known parish of Rerrick acquired neither burghal status nor any industries save milling, and the 1750s Roy map showed it without roads.

**Shattering the Peace, Risking Health and Leading Decline**: By 1827 Dundrennan had been connected by road to Kirkcudbright and Dalbeattie, but it was never rail-served. In World War II military training took over a wide area of the coast and farms around Corrahill, west of the village; sadly, this danger area with its roofless farms became a permanent feature, and Dunrod school – which stood near Balig Hill – was closed. Although by 1951 the small *Crown & Anchor Hotel* was open in Dundrennan there were under 400 people nearby, and by 1981 little over 200. By 1991 the whole of Rerrick parish (which also contains Auchencairn) held only 546 people, little more than half the 1951 figure. It was feared in 1993 that the test firing at the Dundrennan range in recent years of many shells tipped with depleted uranium was the cause for the Castle Douglas postcode sector now suffering the highest rate of childhood leukaemia in Scotland, and it was clear that this was damaging the local tourist industry. Certainly by 1996 Dundrennan's post office and hotel had gone, leaving just a pub. So although over 100 jobs would be lost following the intended closure of the ranges, announced in 1994, few others would regret their passing. Dundrennan primary school had just 15 pupils in 1997, but has survived a closure proposal.

## DUNECHT (or Waterton) — Map 10, B3

***Small Aberdeenshire village,*** *pop. 350* — OS 38: NJ 7509

Some 20 km west of Aberdeen stands the prominent 274 m Barmekin Hill with its ancient fort, the Barmekin of Echt. Below it in sheltered Housedale, a stone circle stood beside the Kinnernie Burn, a tributary of the Loch of Skene. However, Robert Gordon's 17th century map showed nothing else on the estate of Dunecht. The Roy survey of about 1750 marked a track on the burn's north bank, linking Aberdeen with the remote parish of Tough, crossing a smaller burn by the Bridge of *'Coshie'* (Corskie on later maps). It was later made up as a road; where this crossed a through road between Kintore and Echt was built the small estate village of Waterton of Echt. Dunecht House acquired fine gardens, and Waterton post office opened in 1852; by 1894 a telegraph office and an inn were open. By 1951 the name Dunecht had tended to replace Waterton; it had a falling population of about 425 and the facilities of a small village. By 1955 a large quarry had been opened 2 km to the west in Craiginglow Wood, but some facilities closed. Then around 1980 a golf course was laid out beside Dunecht House, by 1986 a large timber yard was at work, and by 1999 a housing estate had been built. The few services include a garage with shop, post office store and antiques shop.

## DUNFERMLINE — Map 16, C2

***Large W. Fife town****, pop. 45,000* — OS 65: NT 0987

Suburbs: *Cairneyhill, Halbeath, Rosyth & Townhill*

Dunfermline may have been a significant settlement in the Bronze Age. Its site, on a steep knoll above the Lyne Burn, with a long view over the land north of the Forth, was very suited to defence against attackers advancing into Pictland from the west and south, as did both Romans and Angles; a Culdee church stood there from an early date. John of Fordoun described Dunfermline as *"a place, naturally very strongly fortified, surrounded by a dense forest, and guarded by steep rocks"*. Its Gaelic name *Dun Fearam Linn* means *'Fort in the Crook of the Torrent'*. This may well refer to King Malcolm Canmore's tower, a massive circular structure probably built about 1065 when he moved his base from Scone, to give close oversight of his campaign to expel the Northumbrians from Lothian. It was first mentioned in 1070, having become the home of Malcolm's refugee Saxon Queen Margaret, who was Hungarian on her mother's side and displayed great hybrid vigour.

**The Religious Centre of Fothrif**: Queen Margaret founded Dunfermline priory and brought in Benedictines from England to build Holy Trinity church, to which Malcolm III gave the *Shire of Kirkcaladunt* (Kirkcaldy) in 1075. Dunfermline was among the earliest of the Royal Burghs created by their son David I (between 1124 and 1127), and from 1161 to about 1212 Dunfermline actually had a sheriff. David imported more Benedictines from Canterbury, and chartered a new abbey in 1128; its great Norman church (of which the nave still stands) was built over the remains of the Culdee church between 1126 and 1150, and around 1200 a *'hospital'* was also founded. David gave the Abbots rights over *Fothrif (or Fothreve)*, a former Pictish province and later deanery, roughly conterminous with the areas of west and central Fife, and formerly extending to Clackmannan, Kinross and Strathearn. The existence in the vicinity of a noble residence of the Thanes of Fothrif or Fife is confirmed by the location of the name *Thanis Castell* on the ancient Gough map. The doubt arises because for civil purposes Fothrif had already been dismembered: Dunfermline was placed from about 1212 within the sheriffdom of Fife *(see Cupar)*.

**Ecclesiastical Burgh, Coal Mining and Black Death**: Coal mining in Scotland is first recorded in a charter of 1291 to the abbot and convent of Dunfermline, allowing mining in Pittencrieff. A Parliament was held in Dunfermline in 1296, and it was reinstated as an ecclesiastical burgh in 1303, but town and abbey were burned by Edward I of England later that year; in 1304 his troops recovered 53 waggonloads of lead from the Abbey roofs. Occasional royal charters continued to be signed at Dunfermline, and Robert Bruce was buried in the abbey in 1329, but the Black Death struck in 1350. In 1363 Dunfermline became a burgh of regality, but it was long before the town's small importance was regained, with a Tolbooth, a Saturday market and two annual fairs; there was once a horse market, remembered in a street name.

**Trade and Industry**: The monks sold sorted wool around 1400. The Merchant Guild was back in business by 1433, and traded coastally through Limekilns and by 1444 with Danzig, Flanders and other continental areas through Dysart and Leith. Some building was undertaken in stone, including the Abbot's house of about 1460, and by the Halketts who owned the Pitfirrane estate by 1399 and soon built Pitfirrane Tower, 3 km west of the town. Following recovery from a further attack of plague in 1475, a Dunfermline notary was first mentioned in 1478 and weavers in 1491; by that time dyers also plied their trade in the town. Three mills and a grammar school also existed in the 15th century, and barrelled beer was available by 1503. Though the burgh's tiny tax base was rising, in 1535–56 it still paid under 1.5% of the Scottish total.

**Dunfermline after the Reformation: Palace and Problems**: The abbey was *"cast down"* by a mob in 1560 and was *"ruinous and unsafe"* in 1563; Dunfermline must again have been hit hard. The abbey had owned Musselburgh; whereas after the Reformation Alexander Seton, laird of Pinkie, according to one source took over *"most of the temporalities of that abbacy"* and became Earl of Dunfermline. Although James VI granted a return to Royal Burgh status in 1588 and by 1593 Dunfermline was the centre of a presbytery, half its guild members remained illiterate in 1594. The remains of the one-time Abbey guest house were rebuilt as a palace from 1593 for the Queen, Anne of Denmark. Though less important than Stirling, it was certainly a royal residence when the ill-fated Charles I was born there in 1600. In 1618 it was still a *"princely mansion"*, but the last Royal user of the palace was Charles II in 1651; subsequent neglect and stone plunder reduced the building to a single main wall. Meantime in 1611 the first Tower Bridge had been built nearby across the Lyne Burn.

**Conflagration and the Linen Industry**: A thousand or more people lived in the little town by 1624, when another big fire practically destroyed all its thatched cottages: 287 Dunfermline families lost their homes, and in 1639 it ranked only 33rd among Scottish burghs in tax yield. The slow recovery which had begun by the mid 17th century included a brewing industry, and diapers, checks and table linen were woven in the late 17th and early 18th century. As early as 1702 a Dunfermline weaver made a seamless shirt on a loom. About then Sir Robert Sibbald wrote *"the town has a manufacture of Dornick-cloath"* – a stout linen. This probably helped when in 1718–19 damask linen weaving was introduced to Dunfermline by James Blake, a local man who successfully undertook industrial espionage at Drumsheugh in Edinburgh; by 1720 the town was a weaving centre of repute.

**Decayed Town makes Better Linen**: Defoe noted a few years later *"the ancient town of Dunfermline"*. Beside the ruined monastery and palace was *"a decayed town, but the people would be much poorer, if they had not the manufacture of linen for their support, which is carried on with more hands than*

*Dunfermline Abbey, chartered by David I in 1128. One of Scotland's few surviving Norman buildings.* (JRH)

*ordinary, especially for diaper and the better sort of linen"*. A pressure group, the *Dunfermline Weavers' Incorporation*, was in action by 1732. The town council established a bleachfield in 1733, and a post office was in operation by 1743, but for a time progress in linen manufacture was slow, and from about 1749 to 1763 only diaper was produced. Roy's map made about 1750 showed a largish settlement for the day, accompanied by Grange Mills, though with only three radial roads or tracks – to Saline, Kirk of Beath and the port of Inverkeithing; the latter was turnpiked from 1757, together with the road to Torryburn (for Alloa, and by ferry to Bo'ness). A further bleachfield was established in 1763.

**Mining, Metals and More Damask**: In 1768 a coal mine was open at Berrylaw, and by 1769 an iron-beating mill was reported in operation, where spades and shovels were made for use in roadmaking among other purposes (this may in fact refer to the mill near Limekilns, *q.v.*). In 1770 a new bridge and road was built north of the early centre to improve access from the west. Although by 1768 only ten damask weavers were at work, this number then doubled in a decade; expansion was encouraged by the improving roads. Tower Bridge was reconstructed in 1788, and by that year about 900 hand looms were in use, and by 1792 there were 1200. In 1792–93 a flax spinning mill was erected at Brucefield, but was long out of use by 1864.

**Elgin Railway, Posts, Pubs and Pigs**: By 1781 *'Coaltowns'* lay 2.5km north of the town, while the *'Elgin Railway'* – a wooden-railed wagonway – was completed in 1774 from the Elgin Colliery pits at Milesmark north-west of the town, including the James Pit at Coaltown of Pittencrieff which appeared on an 1823 survey. The wagonway followed the line of William Street and Coal Road to cross the burn, then turned sharply west and zigzagged south to Charlestown harbour. Another coal level (an adit mine) was recorded in the Dunfermline area in 1794. By 1797 Dunfermline was a post town, the centre for a penny post serving Torryburn, and its fair stance was very significant on eight days a year. By then no fewer than 101 alehouses supported a brewing industry which produced enough draff to feed 200 pigs. Heron noted in 1799 *"a considerable manufacturing town, and has a good trade in linen goods, particularly diapers. It contains about 5200 inhabitants"*. A gasworks was set up south of the town in 1811. The horse-drawn wagons of the Elgin line (rolling on iron rails from 1804); moved 500 tonnes of coal a day for export by 1821. A fixed engine was installed near Berrylaw in the late 1820s, and by 1832 steam locomotives were in use.

**Churches, Brewers, Bookies and Inns**: Meanwhile a large Church of Scotland building was erected at Queen Anne Street in 1798–1800, and the Abbey church was extended in 1818. In 1825 there were three breweries, but it seems no banks – finance was very late to come to this town of thirsty coal hewers and handloom weavers: there was also a racecourse north of the Crossgates road which must have absorbed many a week's earnings. In 1827 Chambers overlooked this feature and evidence of local poverty when describing this *"ancient and most interesting town, distinguished by its activity and success in linen manufacture. Within the last thirty years its size has been greatly increased by the addition of a large suburb to the west"*, this being enabled by the laird, Chalmers (of *"the neighbouring villa of Pittencrieff")* who had part of the ravine infilled. There were *"two good inns, one new and very handsome, decorated with a spire"*.

**Mean Houses, Jacquard Looms and Sculpture**: The Jacquard loom was introduced in 1824, giving *"an immense impetus to the trade of the town"* (Warden). A school of drawn textile design was established in 1826, and soon 1700 hand weavers were at work. By about 1830 Swan was producing Jacquard mechanisms for hand looms, and around 1835 R Hay of Dunfermline also made Jacquard looms for hand weavers. William Cobbett, who briefly visited Dunfermline in 1832, found an evidently rather poor town, noting its *"manufactory of tablecloths and table-covers, about twelve or fourteen thousand inhabitants, and abundant small and mean houses"*. Amelia Paton, born in the town in 1820, became a very well known sculptress of famous people, and wife of artist and pioneer photographer David Octavius Hill; in later life she was known as Mrs A P Hill.

**A Railway arrives but the Carnegies leave**: In 1834 the Elgin wagonway with its acute bends was improved into a true railway which carried the first fare-paying rail passengers in Fife between Dunfermline and Charlestown, connecting with steamships for Leith and a steam ferry to Bo'ness. The total number of hand looms in Dunfermline had risen to nearly 3000 by 1837, but the first power looms were applied to make table linens about 1845. By then linens were being exported to the United States, and in 1848 William Carnegie, a Dunfermline hand loom weaver, refusing to work in a factory, emigrated to the USA with his family. Among them was his extraordinarily able 13 year old son Andrew, born in 1835, who did not take too long to become *'King Steel'*, the world's richest man – and perhaps its greatest ever benefactor – though he also lived in regal style *(see Clashmore)*.

**Rail Connections to Stirling, South and East**: A prison was built in 1842, and by 1844 another coal mine was in operation. In 1849 the branch of the Edinburgh & Northern Railway very recently opened from Thornton to Crossgates was extended through the former racecourse and the station later known as Dunfermline Upper to Oakley – crossing the earlier Elgin Railway at Elbowend Junction; it later connected to Alloa and Stirling. This gave a new slant to Dunfermline, where in 1858–61 John Whitelaw fabricated 70 sets of railway points and crossings for the Portpatrick Railway, and by 1860 Wordie & Co had a rail cartage depot. In 1877 the wagonway route was replaced by a new and more gently graded railway to Inverkeithing, and extended from there to North Queensferry to give an Edinburgh service by ferry; the former Elgin railway became a mineral branch from the new line.

**Damask Factories: Dewar and Erskine Beveridge**: In 1864 Dunfermline manufactured damasks, table linen etc; several design painters were at work in the town, but hand looms were *"fast disappearing"*. Bleaching was divided between four local fields and the many bleachfields in Perthshire. In 1864 D Dewar, Son & Sons (!) of London and Leslie were building their *'Bothwell'* factory, starting with 470 power looms and over 500 workers. In 1867 over 2400 people worked in the town's five flax, jute and hemp factories. Erskine Beveridge & Co's St Leonards Works then contained over 700 steam-driven power looms; in all they employed some 1500 people. It was the largest concern in Dunfermline, *"a model establishment"*; the firm had run its own school for 300 children for many years. Coarse yarns from Dundee and Kirkcaldy, and finer sorts from Yorkshire and Ireland, were used in a huge single-storey weaving shed of 10,000 m$^2$. This contained 900 Jacquard power looms making about 170,000 m$^2$ of the finest quality white damask table linen every week. Interestingly, most of this was sent to Perth for bleaching, and the firm still employed 180 hand-loom weavers.

**Smaller Works, and the Decline of Hand Weaving**: In 1869 Bremner wrote *"Dunfermline is the chief seat of the manufacture of table linen in Britain – indeed, it may be said, in the World"*. Besides Dewar and Beveridge, three long-established factories were A & H Reid's (two), and Hay & Robertson. Both Alexander's and Inglis had recently erected factories; altogether 2670 power looms were installed. By 1869 Dunfermline's total linen production by all means was some 25 million m$^2$ a year. In 1870 the big St Margaret's linen works was built and hand weaving suffered its death knell; the Dunfermline Foundry Company manufactured power looms for linen weaving around 1885.

**Terra cotta, and the First Carnegie Library**: Meantime in 1852 William Clark had erected *Clark's Music Hall*, combined with an exhibition centre and corn exchange. A local newspaper, the *Dunfermline Press*, was established in 1859. The *St Margaret's Hall*, built in 1878, was a theatre and meeting place with a capacity of 1400. Alexander Wilson & Co, fire-clay manufacturers, made the terra cotta facings for London's vast Royal Albert Hall, built between 1867 and 1871. The City Chambers with their tall clock tower were built in 1876–79 on the site of the old Town Hall – to French Gothic designs by J C Walker. In 1881 when the population was over 17,000 Andrew Carnegie, then aged about 45, donated to his home town both public baths and the buildings – but not the books – of the first of the world's 3000 Carnegie libraries. Dunfermline golf club was founded in 1887 and laid out an 18-hole parkland course at Pitfirrane, whose castle became the clubhouse. Sir Thomas Barclay, born in Dunfermline in 1853, became the prime mover of the *Entente Cordiale*, an inter-governmental accord of 1904 which used the spirit of the *Auld Alliance* to end the traditional enmity between France and England.

**Dunfermline in 1888**: By 1888 the *Spire Inn* and its assembly rooms had been converted into county offices, and a new secondary school had lately been built by public subscription. The hotels in 1888 were the *City Arms* and *Royal*; by 1894 the *Commercial* had been added. Water was by then supplied to the district from Glen Sherup *(see Glendevon)*. At that time the manufacture of table linen was the principal industry, having weathered the *'current depression'*. Erskine Beveridge who lived at St Leonard's Hill still owned the St Leonards factory at the Spital Bridge; it then contained about 1000 power looms, and Matthewson's Bothwell factory in Broad Street was also large. The four other significant firms in linen were Alexander's, Donald's, Walker's, and Hay & Robertson, all sited north of the centre. There was also a cattle market, and *"Provost Walls's grain and flour mills"*. In 1888 Crossford on the road to Pitfirrane was a *"prettily situated village with numerous market gardens"*.

**Mining Hinterland**: Through the later 19th century coal mining had steadily grown in the surrounding area, boosting Dunfermline's population. A crescent of collieries ranged round the town, the main areas of production from west to north-east being (1) Berrylaw, (2) Elgin, (3) Rosebank at Parkneuk, (4) Wellwood and (5) the Townhill *(q.v.)* area. The Rosebank colliery, open by 1893 and owned by John Nimmo & Sons of Glasgow, had six shafts and in 1914 employed 350 workers. From 1890 Dunfermline people could commute to work in Edinburgh on the North British Railway's Perth–Edinburgh through service, via the new Forth Bridge. The town was still extremely compact, filling an inverted triangle of 1500 metres each side.

**From Football and Flea-pit to Opera and Ballet**: Dunfermline Athletic Football Club (the *'Pars'*) was formed from a cricket club at East End Park in 1885. The Canmore golf club established in 1898 located its modest 18-hole course just north of the town, where the original Lauder Technical College was built in 1899. By 1901 the Dunfermline & West Fife hospital had been built just west of the Lower station. Pittencrieff Park was bought and put in trust for the town by Carnegie in 1902. The hopefully named *Opera House* was built in 1903 to seat 1300 people; being unsuccessful it was converted into the *Hippodrome* in 1921, with a mere 900 seats. *Clark's Music Hall* had closed in 1898; after use as a printing works it became the *La Scala* cinema in 1913. This flea pit, derisively known as *'The Scratcher'*, was cleansed by being burnt down in 1924! The famed choreographer Kenneth MacMillan, born in Dunfermline in 1929, earned a knighthood. Meantime a not very successful ice rink was built about 1936–37.

**Electricity, Tramways and Tyre Cord**: William Stevenson & Co made hand wringers in the town around 1905, and by 1912 an enhanced total of ten linen factories employed some 4500 people. A Balfour Beatty subsidiary – the Fife Tramway Light and Power Company (which later also owned the Falkirk tramways) – built the local tramway system of 3'6" (107 cm) gauge, which opened as a single line in 1909 from Townhill to the High Street, whence its main line followed East Port and Halbeath Road to Crossgates, Cowdenbeath and Lochgelly, later reaching Kelty and Lochore, and westwards to Rumblingwell, and finally to Rosyth in 1918; the system eventually boasted 45 cars. Its subsidence-troubled Kelty extension was closed in 1931 and the rest was bought for closure in 1937 by bus operators, the Scottish Motor Traction Group (SMT). The change from tram to bus was aided by the Pilmuir Works of Dunlop Textiles, a large traditional-style mill north of the town centre, re-equipped in the 1920s to make tyre cord.

*The Erskine Beveridge St Leonards Works, a linen mill dating from 1851, and converted into flats in the 1990s.* (JRH)

**After Carnegie, the Admiralty**: After Carnegie's death in 1919 the Memorial beside his birthplace was provided by his widow as a personal museum; he had already donated the town's Library, Museum, Hall, Clinic and swimming pool. Dunfermline fire station was built in 1934–36 to designs by James Shearer. The town also greatly benefited in the first half of the 20th century from the development of the huge naval base at Rosyth *(q.v.)*, and the Admiralty Marine Technology Establishment. With its many naval connections, the town's role in World War II was not well publicised, but the continued presence of numerous naval personnel may explain how the town's four cinemas all managed to remain open until 1970.

**Saratoga, Royal Weddings and Y-Fronts**: By contrast the ice rink was closed about the time the *Hippodrome Theatre* was closed in 1955, becoming a furniture store; its fine interior was later dismantled, shipped to the USA and re-used at a theatre in Saratoga from 1990. Less lucky were the former *St Margaret's Hall*, which was a dance venue when destroyed by fire in 1961, and the ancient Abbot House, rather spoiled by a cheap rebuild in 1963–64. In the 1930s Winterthur Silks of Switzerland took over the Canmore Linen Works; they made the silk fabric used for Princess Elizabeth's wedding dress in 1947 and several dresses for her coronation in 1953. Meantime the linen industry had suffered severely from wartime economies – few servants to starch napkins and tablecloths for the rich – and after the war from less formal eating habits, foreign competition, and the demise of the floating Grand Hotels that were the transatlantic liners. Small compensation that in 1960 Lyle & Scott of Hawick opened a factory employing 400 women and girls to make *Y-fronts*.

**The Forth Road Bridge, and Rail Cuts**: The opening of the Forth Road Bridge in 1964 and the M90 to Perth during the 1970s brought Dunfermline much better accessibility by road, but the town's railways lost out. The engine shed closed with the end of steam about 1967. Alloa and Stirling services ceased in 1968, enabling closure of the Upper station. Kinross and Perth were disconnected in 1970, leaving in operation only the service from Cowdenbeath to Edinburgh, via Dunfermline and Inverkeithing. By 1980 Dunfermline had four High Schools, the Dunfermline, Queen Anne, Woodmill and St Columba's RC.

**Dunfermline for Building, Cards and Cables**: Lauder Technical College moved out to Halbeath about that time, and when the *Regal* and *Kinema (ex Palace)* closed in the 1980s, 3000 cinema seats were lost. However, by 1981 the Dunfermline Building Society had become Scotland's largest, and a large new *VISA* office on the Pitcorthie industrial estate south of the town brought new job opportunities. In 1981 there were 20,000 or more local people; 6 hotels were open, including the 17-room *City*, the modern *King Malcolm* with its 48 rooms, and the *Pitfirrane Arms* at Crossford. The new industrial estate laid out to the south thrived by 1979, when among other firms Gore of the USA had a plant making insulated wires and cables, later producing assemblies for electronics industries. Castleblair Pelts, whose Victoria Works were in Pilmuir Street, had branch factories in Glenrothes and Leven by 1992.

**Kingsgate, Footways and Football**: For many years the steep and tightly developed town centre made it difficult to introduce larger shops, but when the Canmore Works ceased production it was converted into a very large furniture store by Andrew Thomson, furnishers, of James Street. About 1980 Littlewoods opened a new store, and in 1985 not long after troubled Woolworths had closed their quite large two-level store, Marks & Spencer opened their first branch in the town as part of the Kingsgate shopping centre, adjoined by a busy new bus station. Experimental pedestrianisation of the town centre was introduced in 1989, when the erection of six retail warehouses was begun on the site of the former Upper station. About 1989 the swimming pool became the Carnegie Centre for indoor recreation. But Dunfermline FC's East End Park – which had been last upgraded in 1967 – was an uninspiring venue, able to seat only a fifth of its potential 20,000 spectators in 1990, and the team was in and out of the Premier League.

**From Problem Economy to Expanding Industry**: All was not well with the local economy: in 1989 the last of the Erskine Beveridge & Co linen works closed down. In 1989 Dunlop Textiles re-equipped their Pilmuir Works, which then made fabric for all types of tyres from aircraft and earth-moving equipment to motor cycles, and recruited more staff. Shering Weighing, which arrived in 1990, made electronic weighbridges. In 1990 Dutch-owned Philips Circuit Assemblies expanded at Queensferry Road where some 500 people were employed; they added 300 more jobs in 1994. Meantime oil-related TK Valve expanded at Queensferry Road in 1991. In 1992 FMC Subsea Systems expanded their North Sea wellhead-manufacturing plant at Pitreavie industrial park, adding 100 jobs, and by 1994 Aquafire made water-based fire retardants. Due to lack of space at Livingston in 1994, the satellite television company BSkyB developed a huge subscriber management centre on Dunfermline's new Carnegie Campus, employing up to 1000 people.

**Conservation, Closures – and Rail Rebirth?**: Abbot House had been painstakingly restored inside and out under the direction of Elspeth King, using Scottish craftsmen to create fine ironwork, murals and decorative floors; it opened in 1992 as a heritage centre of Dunfermline history. By 1991 Crossford had 2756 residents, and Dunfermline (including Rosyth and Crossgates) 55,083, an increase of 4000 since 1971. The town, now Fife's largest, was hit by 900 job losses from Rosyth in 1991, and the withdrawal of 1000 naval personnel. The 150-job headquarters of the Dunfermline Building Society moved out to the new Pitreavie Business Park at Rosyth in 1992. The completing of the freight line between Dunfermline and Stirling is planned by Railtrack and EWS.

**Hospital Leftovers go to Romania while Hotels proliferate**: With the completion of the Queen Margaret Hospital at Halbeath in 1993, the relatively modern Maternity hospital and the older Dunfermline & West Fife hospital were closed and went for sale. In 1994 the specialised prefabricated building of the latter's A&E unit was dismantled and re-erected nearly 3000km away at the hospital at Tirgu Mures in northern Romania within two weeks, as part of the BBC's breathless *Challenge Anneka* programme, forming that country's first such unit. Milesmark Hospital also closed and was for sale in 1996. Dunfermline was demoted in 1996 to become the centre of a mere area committee of the new unitary Fife Council: a sad comedown for the one-time Scottish capital, which despite setbacks was at that time busier than it had ever been! By then Queen Anne, largest of the three High Schools, had the largest roll in Fife, at 1780, and by 2000 Dunfermline FC had worked its way back into the Scottish Premier League. The wealth of quality hotels now includes the Georgian *Garvock House* at Transy, *King Malcolm* at Queensferry Road, *Pitbauchlie House* (50 rooms) on Aberdour Road, plus *Keavil House* (47) and *Pitfirrane Arms* (38) at Crossford to the west.

## DUNGLASS & Oldhamstocks — Map 3, B2

***E. Lothian hamlets**, pop. 200* — OS 67: NT 7671

Dunglass *(Grey Fort* in Gaelic) stands above the coastal cliffs of East Lothian, north of the ravine of the Dunglass Burn, the traditional boundary with the Merse (Berwickshire). It was probably of 11th century origin, forming a prime defensive base to resist English incursions. In the 14th century the castle was rebuilt in stone, in the 15th century being a property of the powerful Home family of Hume Castle. There was a chapel by 1423, and Sir Alexander Home founded a collegiate church about 1450. Dunglass was chartered to the Homes as a burgh of barony by James IV in 1489. Their castle was sacked by the English in 1532 and 1547, but twice rebuilt – the artillery fort built in 1548 by the English under Protector Somerset being one of the first in Britain to adopt the bastion plan. Oldhamstocks, the parish centre 3km inland, gained a parish school by 1577. Pont's map of about 1600 showed a bridge linking the castle to the Merse, and another where the road from Berwick to Dunbar crossed the burn near its mouth. In 1636 Brereton wrote that Dunglass both *"castle and town"* seemed to be in good repair; however, the castle was blown up in 1640.

**Dunglass as a Mansion**: Over 80 years later, Defoe noted that the hospitable Sir James Hall of Dunglass was an improving laird; by then the castle had been replaced by a mansion-house designed by Richard Crichton, but the village was not mentioned. By the early 1750s, although some woollen manufacture persisted, Roy's map showed Dunglass as a village with the *Castle Dykes*. The Great North Road bridge still existed, and 4km to the north-west the coastal hamlet of Skateraw stood astride the road; but apparently the collegiate church was used as a barn, because Dunglass was shrinking.

**Mansion, Bridges and Water Come and Go**: Dunglass still had a weekly carrier to Edinburgh in 1797, though Heron in 1799 mentioned only *"the fine woods and family seat of Dunglass, the property of Sir James Hall"*, who had Dunglass House picturesquely rebuilt in 1807–13. New bridges have been repeatedly constructed to carry the Great North Road across the burn: about 1780, in 1837, in the 1930s, about 1960 and again in 1991–92! From 1846 the North British Railway also spanned the ravine. By 1901 Dunglass was a mere hamlet. A lifeboat station opened at Skateraw in 1907, but this was closed in 1943. Dunglass House was burnt down and demolished in 1947, the 15th century church, although long ago slighted, now surviving almost alone. By 1971 the shrinking parish of Oldhamstocks held only 184 people, a number which had risen by 1991 to 204; in 1994 Oldhamstocks firm Scottish Border Springs employed ten people, filling 20,000 bottles a day of flavoured water originating from Bransly spring; they now distribute throughout Scotland and in London as *'Clearly Scottish'*.

## DUNKELD & Birnam — Map 6, A2

***Perthshire villages**, pop. 1275* — OS 53: NO 0242

Dunkeld *(G. Dun Coille, 'the fort in the wood')*, in the southern part of the vast mountainous district of Atholl, was a defended Pictish site on the east bank of the River Tay, protected by forested gorges to north and south. King Constantine of the Picts is said to have started a religious foundation there in 729; in the eighth century Dunkeld was also an episcopal centre. Sources differ as to when its later abbey was founded by Culdee monks fleeing from Iona, allegedly with the Stone of Destiny, but it seems to have existed by about 820. Pictland was forcibly merged with Scotia in 843 as the combined state of Alba, so Columba's relics were taken from Iona to Dunkeld in 849, and for the next half century it was the chief religious centre of emergent Scotland. In 865 the abbot of Dunkeld was

*Dunkeld town centre, an area largely conserved by the NTS in the mid 20th century.* *(JRH)*

also *'chief bishop of Fortrui'* – a former Pictish province then based in Abernethy and probably including the Strathearn, Perth, Kinross and Clackmannan areas and maybe Fothrif (central and west Fife), an administrative area which vanished in later centuries. In 870 Dunkeld was also still known as the seat of the *'Bishop of the Picts'*. Although by 906 this prime title had passed to St Andrews, the abbey and the bishopric of Dunkeld survived an attack by Vikings in 903.

**Thanages, Cathedral, Burgh – but no Bridge**: Dalmarnock, about 4km north-west of Dunkeld, had a thanage from about the 11th century, as did Fandowie some 8km up Strath Bran. David I confirmed the bishopric in 1127, but Holy Trinity church was granted to Dunfermline Abbey about 1150. A stone-built Cathedral was begun about 1234, and extended from 1406, though its diocese was small. The adjacent tight-packed little town of Dunkeld was apparently already a burgh of barony by 1511. The bishops having repeatedly failed to build a promised bridge, access across the Tay from famously wooded Birnam in Little Dunkeld parish was still by ferry – yet in 1560 when the cathedral was sacked in mob violence the Bishop sat in Parliament!

**Ferry, Fiddlers and Linen Industry**: By 1593 Dunkeld was the centre of a presbytery, but little growth followed. The sketch map made by Pont about 1600 showed two parallel sagging lines across the Tay below the town. Perhaps these were ropes or chains used to haul the ferry boat, for Blaeu's map published in 1654 and based on recent work by Gordon still showed no bridge, and a ferry was certainly operating in 1678. The first Dunkeld House, erected in 1676–84, is said to be Scotland's earliest brick house. When its first post office was opened in 1689 Dunkeld became one of only some 25 postal centres in Scotland, implying that its great markets and fairs were developing around that time, though set back by another sacking in 1690. Niel Gow, born at Inver near Dunkeld in 1727, became the best known Scottish fiddler and composer of folk airs; his son Nathaniel, born in 1766, followed the same path to fame. A factory making fine linen existed by 1732: in 1769 Pennant found Dunkeld a *"small town"* with a small *"linen manufactory"*. In 1747 a ferry north of the town connected to Inver, on the west bank, where there was already a *"good inn"* and a bridge across the River Braan, as shown on Roy's map of about 1750. This emphasised the north–south road, probably by then made up for coaches, whereas the routes to Amulree and Blairgowrie were shown as tracks. The Inver ferry still plied in 1769.

**Spinning Wheels, and Whey for Tourists**: Local linen production boomed around 1790, by which time there were five lint mills and 160 weavers in Little Dunkeld parish, and by 1796 almost 150,000m of cloth was locally stamped each year. Around then the Perth Banking Company opened a branch in the town; by 1825 the Perth Union Banking Company (a distinct firm) had followed suit. Four fairs were scheduled in 1797, when Dunkeld was a post town, seen by Heron in 1799 as *"the market-town of this part of the Highlands, with some manufacture of linen"*. In 1801 John Lamb was an innovative local wheelwright who had lately improved the details of the spinning wheel. By this time tourism was growing and Dunkeld was becoming a summer resort for *"much genteel company drawn by its romantic situation, and the advantage of drinking goats' whey"*! The Duke of Atholl already opened to the public his much titivated riverside pleasure grounds at the Hermitage, accessed via the Inver ferry, noted by Elizabeth Grant as a *"large flat boat"*, adjoined by a *"little inn"*. Dorothy Wordsworth viewed them in 1803, stating that *"the Duke lived in an ordinary gentleman's house"* beside the ruined abbey, then containing an incongruously modern church. By then there was a road up Strath Braan, beside which were many hamlets.

**The Tay Bridge and Fisher's Inn**: The Tay was eventually spanned by the fine bridge built in 1809 to Telford's designs, with a new approach road cut through the town; bridge traffic was subject to tolls until 1879. As soon as the bridge was finished a *"fine hotel"* (Grant) was opened beside it. In 1827 Chambers noted Dunkeld as a *"town"* with a *"noble bridge"*, remarking *"The principal inn at Dunkeld, kept by Mr Fisher, boasts of the most elegant accommodations, and contains no fewer than 35 bedrooms"*. The second mansion of Dunkeld House was built in the early 19th century, with an ornate gateway complex. The direct mail coaches for Inverness passed through Dunkeld from 1836. A brewery was operating in the High Street in 1825 but did not survive the railway age, and decline in the local linen trade set in: by 1864 it was dead.

**Railway, Insulin and Shipping**: In 1856 the independent Perth & Dunkeld Railway was opened, actually terminating at Birnam (the station, officially styled *'Dunkeld & Birnam'*, is often simply referred to as *'Dunkeld'*). In 1858 Fontane found the *Birnam Hotel "busy with sportsmen"*. In 1863 the Highland Railway's main line was opened from Birnam to Forres, so linking to Inverness and killing the mail coach services. A slate quarry was open by 1869. John MacLeod, who isolated insulin and won a Nobel Prize in 1923, was born near Dunkeld in 1876. Sir Charles Cayzer, the shipping magnate who founded the Glasgow-based Clan Line in 1878, later owned a country estate at Dalguise north-west of Dunkeld. In 1891 the population of the burgh was only 613, yet by 1894 the twin settlements had three hotels, including what Murray classed as the *"very good" Birnam Hotel*, and *"good" Atholl Arms* and *Royal*. Dunkeld golf club, founded in 1910, laid out a rugged 9-hole moorland course. Over the next half century four more hotels were added, including by 1954 the rebuilt mansion of *Dunkeld House*, and a youth hostel also exploited its beautiful situation. But although in 1946 Wordie & Co still had a small rail to road cartage depot, Dunkeld's general importance had declined.

**Conservation, Tourism and Music**: During the 1960s the National Trust for Scotland undertook a major and attractive conservation project on the historic centre, and through traffic on the A9 was bypassed about 1980, to general benefit. In 1988 the *Dunkeld House Hotel* underwent major expansion to 97 rooms, but in 1991 the two villages combined had only 1277 residents, and by 1993 the youth hostel had closed. A new independent weekly boarding school for *'educationally fragile'* children was opened in 1992 at the village of Butterstone about 6km east of Dunkeld. In 1994 a 58km system of footpaths around the little town was opened as a waymarked attraction to tourists. The golf course is now 18 holes (with clubhouse being rebuilt), and the conserved station with its crossing loop retains its low platforms. Hotels include the *Hilton Dunkeld House*, the *Royal Dunkeld*, the *Atholl Arms* and baronial *Birnam House*; among smaller hotels is the *Taybank*, whose musical owner Dougie Maclean runs teaching classes for traditional instruments, as well as running a recording studio at Butterstone. Birnam is now developing a centre to accompany its Beatrix Potter garden (the author having spent family holidays in the neighbourhood).

## DUNLOP — Map 1, C1

***Ayrshire village,*** *pop. 800* — OS 64: NS 4049

Dunlop lies beside the Glazert Burn some 4km north of Stewarton in Cunninghame. Three km west stands the 16th century tower of Aiket Castle, also known as Aiket House. Pont's sketches of around 1600 showed a settlement with a tower. By the 1750s, as the Roy map showed, the small village of Dunlop and its mill lay on a road linking Stewarton and *'Beath'* (Beith). In 1799 Heron noted that Dunlop was celebrated for its *"rich and delicate cheese"*, of which about 65 tonnes was made each year; Cobbett was also impressed by the local cheese in 1832, adding that Dunlop was *"a little village"*.

**Railway, Small Industries and Electromagnetism**: A very conveniently sited station was opened about 1871–73 when the Glasgow Barrhead & Kilmarnock Joint Railway was built. By 1895 Dunlop had an inn, a post and telegraph office, and the closed Hapland mill had reopened; in 1976 this mill still spun yarn for Kilmarnock carpet manufacturers. The district was still noted for cheese in the 1950s, when bacon was cured locally and there was also a timber merchant; the population had slowly grown, enjoying the facilities of a small village. By 1971 762 people lived in Dunlop village, rising to 807 by 1991. In 1992 RFI (Radio Frequency Investigations) moved its small electromagnetic test laboratory to Dunlop, serving the computer industry and intending to create 20 jobs. The village still had its station, post office and pub, but there had been little recent development of note.

## DUNNET, Barrock & Ham — Map 13, B4

***Caithness small communities,*** *pop. low* — OS 12: ND 2271

Dunnet Head in Caithness, the most northerly point on the Scottish mainland, presents a serious hazard to shipping in the stormy Pentland Firth. Dunnet lies on the farming isthmus to the south, being shown on the Roy map of about 1750 as a kirk and hamlet in a roadless area; to the east beyond the small St John's Loch was a long scatter of coastal crofts, and the House of Rattar. In 1824 James Traill of Rattar founded Castletown *(q.v.)*, using its flagstones to build his own tiny port of Ham east of Dunnet. The prominent lighthouse on Dunnet Head was designed by the grandfather of Robert Louis Stevenson, built by James Smith of Inverness and first lit in 1831. A system of narrow roads was laid out, and Dunnet post office was open by 1838–39. By the 1930s a hotel and school had been added; by the mid 20th century, despite having only some 180 residents, a Tuesday market was held at Dunnet, which then had a 20-line telephone exchange; this was later moved 2 km east and renamed Barrock after Barrock House, now home to the Sinclairs. The *Northern Sands Hotel* was open by then. Although Dunnet primary school was closed in the 1960s in favour of the Barrock school, some new housing was to be seen at Dunnet by 1978, when a restaurant, gun shop, filling station and caravan site were open. Recently a museum and visitor centre had been added, and a forest walk laid out in the only woodland in the area, a small modern planting named Dunnet Forest.

## DUNNING — Map 6, A3

***Perthshire village,*** *pop. 750* — OS 58: NO 0214

Dunning in Strathearn about 13km south-west of Perth has a Pictish standing stone, and a Gaelic name indicating fortifications; above it on Rossie Law is a hill fort. Dunning was the centre of a thanage from about the 11th century, and by the 13th a church stood beside the Dunning Burn. A burgh of barony charter was gained in 1511. Pont's map made about 1600 showed *'Dunnyn'* as a cluster of buildings round the towered church, and a bridge across the burn; above this was a mill; *'Kelty'*, 1.5km to the south-west, was already a tower house. A parish school was open by 1610.

**The Rising Village**: By the early 1750s Dunning was a medium-sized village for the period, depicted on the Roy map as *'Dinnin'*; Pitcairn was then a mansionhouse, but a track between Greenloaning, Auchterarder and Bridge of Earn was the only route passing through Dunning. Three fairs were scheduled for 1797, and Heron in 1799 remarked without explanation on the *"rising village of Dunning"*. A post office was opened in 1803, and a brewery existed in 1825; this may have become the distillery which William Eadie ran until sequestration in 1840. A gasworks was set up in 1845 – unusual for a small place distant from coalfields.

**Never quite on the Railway**: The railway came to Strathearn in 1848, but Dunning station was sited 3km away; too far to be useful to the village, which stayed small, though by the 1890s there was an inn. Dunning golf club, founded in 1953, laid out a 9-hole parkland course. By then two hotels were open, though the population was under 1000. The station was closed about 1960 and even with its early satellite Newton of Pitcairns, by 1980 Dunning's facilities were only those of a small village. The *Kippen House Hotel* which opened in a Victorian mansion 1.5km to the south in 1978, was not a success, and by 1990 had become a nursing home. The population had declined to 750 by 1991; the quiet historic character of the village is maintained, and its church is cared for by Historic Scotland.

## DUNNOTTAR

**Map 10, C4**

***Location on Mearns coast*** OS 45: NO 8883

On a tall promontory half detached from the cliffs 25 km south of Aberdeen stand the gaunt ruins of Dunnottar, whose name in Gaelic means *The Castle on the Point*. Irish annals state that it was a Pictish stronghold by 681, and there are Pictish traces on the nearby stack of Dinnacair. The Mearns became a sheriffdom between 1165 and 1178; Dunnottar may have been its caput, because from the 12th century onwards the castle was in the hands of the powerful Keith family. William Keith, the first Earl, erected a strong tower, and the curtain wall was built during the contest between Bruce and Balliol.

**Under and After the Earls Marischal**: The Keith earls were raised in 1457–58 to the lofty status of *Earls Marischal* (Marshal) of Scotland, and more building work was done at Dunnottar, making it very extensive – more of a small town than a typical Scottish castle. In 1560 it was the seat of both the powerful Earl Marischal and the Master of Dunnottar. However in 1562 it seems that the sheriff caput was moved to Kincardine Castle, and the Mearns became Kincardineshire. Dunnottar played a significant part in the story of the saving of the Scottish regalia from the Parliamentarians in 1651 *(Mackie, 1978)*, but by 1685 it was used as a prison. Repairs ceased after the 1715 rising, the site becoming deserted as the new port of Stonehaven gained importance; by 1799 Dunnottar was in ruins, but it became and remains a very striking tourist attraction.

## DUNOON, Kirn & Hunter's Quay

**Map 5, A5**

***Argyllshire small town,*** *pop. 9000* OS 63: NS 1776

Dunoon in Cowal, isolated from the Scottish heartland, enjoys shelter from westerly gales, and long commanded the focal area of the Firth of Clyde. Some way inland is a medieval motte; 2.5 km south of this was built an important 12th century castle, the seat of the Lord High Steward of Scotland. From 1370 this was accompanied by a royal palace, but although still in royal hands in 1455 it was eventually abandoned. Pont's map of about 1600 showed Dunoon castle and church. Dunoon Grammar School – which still exists – was chartered in 1641, yet Roy's map of about 1750 indicated only a hamlet near the castle. This was apparently the terminus of a coastal track between two ferries: one operated between Dunoon and Cloch Point from 1618 to 1820, mainly carrying cattle; the other linked to Rothesay. An annual fair was scheduled for Dunoon in 1797, and in 1799 Heron noted the *"castle and small village of Dunoon"*.

**New Town, Slow Renascence**: Modern Dunoon was planned before 1795 by James Craig, of Edinburgh New Town fame, apparently for the fifth Duke of Argyll, who established a linen factory in the late 18th century. A post office was opened in 1805. In 1810 just before the dawn of the steamship era, Dunoon was already complaining of its lack of a good harbour. In 1813 a ferry to Cloch was introduced from Kirn, 2 km north of the increasingly dilapidated Dunoon Castle. However, a pier had been constructed at Dunoon by 1820; the eastern terminal of the Dunoon to Cloch ferry switched to Gourock in that year. A new timber jetty was built at Dunoon in 1835. Kirn post office was issued with a cancelling stamp about 1840.

**Steamers bring Resort Development**: With the advent of steamers – which by 1842 gave a direct service to Glasgow three days a week – Dunoon and Kirn grew rapidly both as dormitories for the well to do and as day trippers' resorts. From 1852 Dunoon had a gasworks, while from 1851 Dunoon (and by 1864 Kirn) were served by Hutcheson steamers, the forerunners of MacBrayne. Hunter's Quay, 1 km north of Kirn, was built in 1858 and soon attracted settlement. It became the headquarters of the Royal Clyde Yacht Club, founded in 1871 for the owners of smaller vessels ineligible for the Royal Northern Yacht Club of Rothesay. Dunoon became a police burgh in 1868, and in 1871 a local newspaper, the *Dunoon Observer*, was established. In 1877 both Dunoon and Kirn were served by the Lochgoil & Lochlong Steamboat Company (SC), and in 1880 all three had calls by the Lochlong & Lochlomond SC. By 1881 the population was 4700, and Dunoon was called *"a pretty watering-place, its beach crowded with summer visitors"*. From 1889 Gourock could be reached by fast trains from Glasgow, so speedy turbine steamers – soon railway-owned – were put on the Dunoon run, giving it an advantage over other more distant Clyde residential resorts.

**Dunoon for Leisure**: The Cowal golf club was founded in 1890; James Braid laid out its 18-hole parkland course. By 1894 only *"a few steamers"* called at Hunter's Quay, which had a ferry to Strone, but Murray noted Dunoon which by then had 5300 residents as *"one of the most frequented of the Clyde watering-places, where numerous steamers call daily"*. At that time Dunoon had at least two hotels, *McColl's* and the then *"fair" Argyll Arms*. Excursions operated to Inveraray – by horse-drawn coach and steamers on Loch Eck. By 1897 there was a 2-berth pier, and an electric power station was built in 1901. The Pavilion in Castle Gardens was opened for variety shows in 1905; extensive hotel development followed.

**Mid Twentieth Century Improvements**: Between the wars the *Cowal Hotel* of some 30 rooms was a temperance establishment; after 1945 such hostelries were spurned and it became the Argyll County Education Office. *McColl's Hotel* was rebuilt with 80 rooms in the 1930s, gaining 3 stars from the AA, and by 1951 Hunter's Quay had ten hotels and Dunoon as many as fifty, with the facilities of a major local centre and an out of season population of some 11,000. The Pavilion, which burned down in 1949, was eventually replaced by the 1500-seat *Queen's Hall* and theatre, opened in 1958. In the 1960s new buildings were erected for the ancient Grammar School, and by 1972 there was also a modern indoor swimming pool. Meantime through the 1960s to 1980s the hills to the west were almost completely afforested.

**Car Ferries kill Cruising and hit the Hotels**: From 1954 the new car ferry MV *Cowal* made ten return trips a day to Gourock, some also calling at Kirn. From 1972 Western Ferries made its headquarters at Hunter's Quay, and its two second-hand Scandinavian car ferries plied from there to McInroy's Point near Gourock. The collapse of the cruising steamer trade in the 1960s, replaced by the two prosaic competing car ferries, resulted in the closure of a quarter of Dunoon's hotels; by 1972 *McColl's Hotel* had converted many rooms to provide more bathrooms, but despite this had been cut down to 2-star status. Various other facilities closed, leaving what one observer described as *"an obsolete resort, a dowdy town"*.

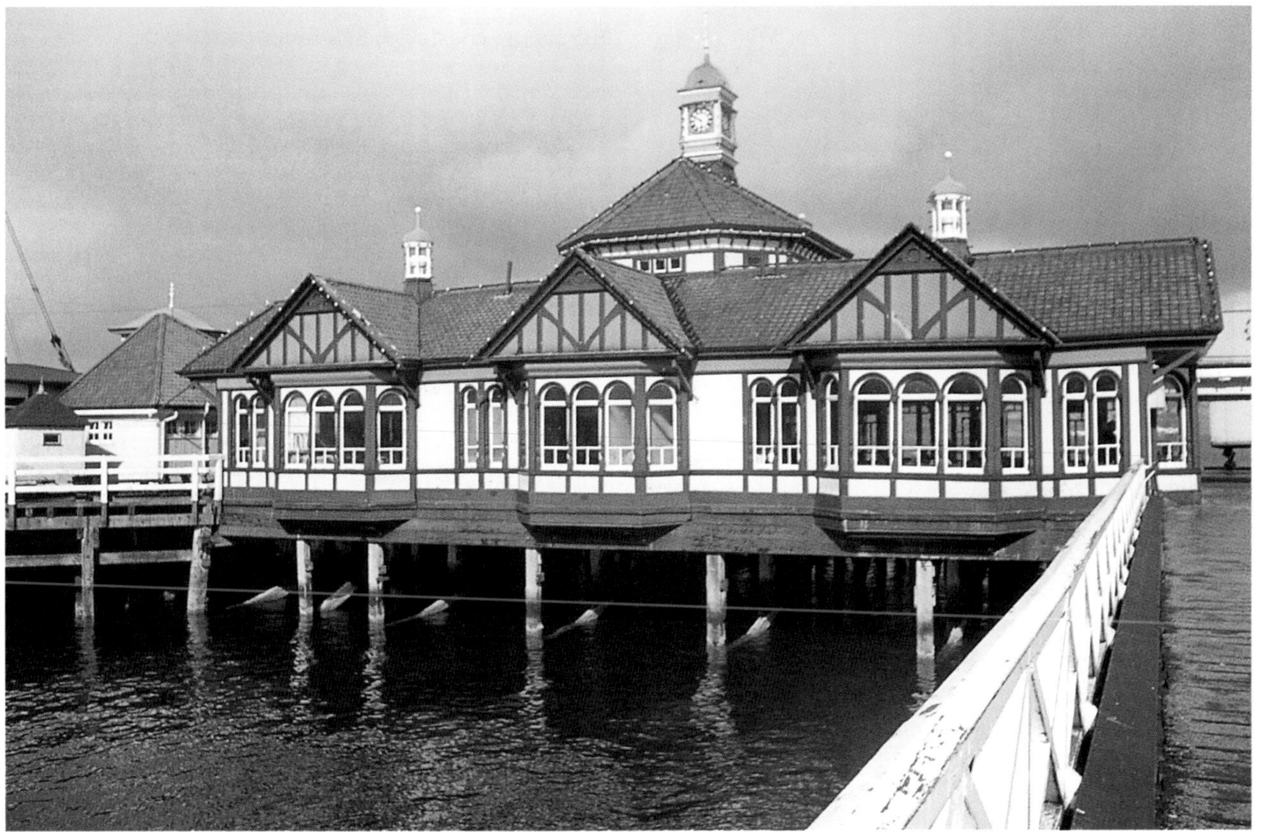

*Dunoon pier building, built in 1896 when the pier was substantially extended by Dunoon Town Council to provide more berths for steamers calling at the resort town.* *(JRH)*

**Dangerous Dependence on the US Navy?**: At that time only 20% of Dunoon's houses belonged to the council, for American families from the Cold War submarine base of the US Navy, established in the Holy Loch in 1961, had made their homes there in large numbers. The resident population had fallen to some 9000 by 1981, with numerous private traders and flats over shops. But this still left 43 hotels, including the 58-room *McColl's*, the smaller *Argyll* and *Queen's* (at Kirn), and the 34-room *Royal Marine* at Hunter's Quay (most having been downgraded in star terms). By 1991 about a quarter of the town's population of 9038 was American, and much of its business and a fifth of its educational life depended on the base; but this was closed in 1992, removing some 800 jobs. Keith Lamanque, an American who had become committed to Scotland, was president of the local Chamber of Commerce and helped to set up a *'Task Force'* to inject new life, and Highlands & Islands Enterprise urgently opened an *'Enterprise Centre'*; despite their optimism 60% of the remaining residents were pensioners, so the town's future looked bleak,

**Houses sell better**: But with removal of the threat of a locally focused Armageddon, house sales rapidly picked up! In 1993 Eikon UK announced a small plant to assemble USA-made computers in the town, initially bringing just 14 new jobs. The Queen's Hall, venue for the 1994 Mod, and the swimming pool, were operated by Gateway Leisure; at that time the *Hafton Hotel* at Hunter's Quay had its own tennis courts and swimming pool. Vehicle ferries still ply from Dunoon to Gourock and from Hunter's Quay to McInroy's Point.

## DUNRAGIT

**Map 1, B4**

***Galloway small village,*** *pop. 400* — OS 82: NX 1557

Ancient earthworks adorn the Galloway hills near Dunragit, which stands on the shores of Luce Bay. Although north of Hadrian's Wall, the departure of the Roman legions from Britain in 410 AD left some Romanised Christians in Galloway. Later described by the Anglo-Saxon Chronicle as the *"South Picts"*, their Romano-Pictish kingdom of Rheged was probably based at Dunragit, 35 km to the north-west of the other known Rheged settlement of Whithorn *(q.v.)*. A relatively peaceful Anglian (Northumbrian) takeover of Rheged by marriage took place about 645 AD. There is a medieval motte, but over the years Dunragit lost its importance to Glenluce and Stranraer. Two tiny places bore the name *'Dunragat'* on Pont's map made about 1610. They soon adjoined the military road that was built early in the 17th century from Dumfries to Portpatrick; this was shown on the Roy map made about 1754, when Dunragit House appeared as an emparked mansion.

**Railway, Cream and Airships**: From 1861 Dunragit had a station on the Portpatrick Railway (later the Portpatrick and Wigtownshire Joint line); Challoch 2 km to the east became a junction in 1877, where the Girvan & Portpatrick Railway (later part of the Glasgow & South Western Railway) converged. The large Wigtownshire Creamery – claimed as the first in Scotland – was established by James McHarrie of Stranraer (with others) in 1882. Dunragit had a post office by 1900. In the 1914–18 war the short-lived RNAS Luce Bay airship station was established 4 km west of Dunragit. Local industry in the mid 20th century included a small quarry and a sawmill. The creamery later passed to Nestlés and was still in use in 1961, though closed by 1975. The station was closed and Challoch ceased to be a junction when the scenic railway to Dumfries was sadly closed by Beeching in 1965. Dunragit's rather scattered population declined steadily between 1951 and 1981 from over 600 to little over 400 *(see also Glenluce)*. However, the facilities of a hamlet were augmented with a hotel by 1977, and by 1991 the former creamery buildings were occupied by AVA Europe. Glenwhan Garden is open to the public, and the school and post office remain in being.

## DUNS, Fogo & Langton **Map 3, B3**

***Berwickshire town & villages,*** *pop. 2400* OS 67 or 74: NT 7853

Duns on the north flank of the Merse of Berwickshire originated as a hill fortress on an eminence 218 m above sea level, later called The Law. Its Gaelic name – until the 20th century pronounced and often spelled with two syllables as *Dunse* – suggests 11th century origin, and the town at the hill foot may well have become an early burgh whose charter was lost, for by the 12th or 13th century a *'hospital'* or almshouse had been opened. At Fogo beside the Blackadder Water 5 km south of Duns was an early Tironensian monastery which soon failed. A Franciscan church school was founded in the 13th century; its noted scholar John Duns Scotus, apparently born in a stone-built house in the old town of Dunse in 1265, argued that religion depended on faith not reason. This evident truth was too controversial for the prejudices of the day, and the pejorative word *'dunce'* was added to the English language in his memory *(see Bearsden)*.

**Dunse at the Hill Foot**: Chambers noted that *"the town originally stretched from the northern border of a lake near Dunse Castle, called the Hen Pow, along the southern skirt of the Law, and covered no part of its present site"*. At an early date the old castle was a property of the Earl of Moray. In 1320 Robert the Bruce had a new castle built, now vanished; the surviving old parts of the castles of Dunse and of Langton (3 km west of Dunse) are dated to the 15th century. Dunse was chartered as a burgh of barony in 1489 by George Hume of Ayton, but little is known of its subsequent history, for it was burnt down by the troops of the tyrannical English King Henry VIII in 1545 (1588 if one was to believe the amazingly misleading plaque to be seen on the site in 1991). The gable stone on the birthplace of Duns Scotus was saved by Hay of Drumelzier as a memorial.

**New Town, Mills and Schools**: The town was quickly rebuilt on a fresh site about 500 m farther south, where it became a successful market centre, and was the county town of Berwickshire from 1551, when it replaced Coldingham (until 1696 when it was itself replaced by Greenlaw). Early travel writers passed it by, and there were apparently no roads or bridges in the area, as shown by the pioneer cartographer Timothy Pont; his sketch map of about 1600 showed the *'Castle and Kirk of Duns'* with many other buildings which formed a line at the foot of the hill, and also straggled up to the top of *'Dunssla'*. Near the emparked Wedderburn Castle 2 km south-east of Duns were two water mills turned by the Langton Burn, and two more upstream to the west; at *'Kymmerjamm'* (Kimmerghame) on the Blackadder Water 4 km south-east of the town was a cluster of three. By 1593 Duns was the centre of a presbytery and parish schools were founded in Duns and Langton in 1600, and at Fogo in 1632.

**Mansions, Industry and Communications**: In the 16th century the Kers built a property 3 km south of Duns; a century later, Nisbet House was built on its site for Sir Alexander Nisbet. This was later altered to designs by Robert Adam, who was also the architect of the new Wedderburn Castle, built by mason James Nisbet of Kelso late in the 18th century. Commercial brewing was carried on by the mid 17th century, but again there is little information about Dunse until a post office was mentioned in 1731 and the Clockmill bleachfield was reported in use by 1745. In 1747 a medicinal spring was discovered; but this failed to make the place an effective spa. The Roy map made about 1754 showed a medium-sized linear settlement at the centre of a system of trackways, including one to Longformacus bridge and Edinburgh, and both east and west on the line of the later A6105 to Chirnside and to Greenlaw; a made road appeared to extend most of the way to Coldstream. Little-known *'Cumorgen'* (Kimmerghame House) was already an emparked mansion (as it remains 250 years later). Much of the town's old castle was incorporated into the mansionhouse now called Duns Castle, a late 18th century Gothic adaptation.

**Ploughs and Paper**: Chambers commented in the 1820s that *"the remains of the former town were only removed from the park round the castle within the recollection of people now in middle age"* (i.e. in the late 18th century). Around 1780 James Small set up a factory *'at Blackadder'* to make iron ploughs of his own design. Dunse was a post town by 1797, when no fewer than six fairs were held annually, putting it in the top thirty stances in Scotland. Heron wrote in 1799 *"this town contains about 2300 inhabitants. It has a good market, a bleachfield, and a small tan-work; there is also a paper-mill in its neighbourhood"*. This was probably the Broomhouse mill, which was transferred to Chirnside in 1842.

**Economic Changes – and Lawyers Aplenty**: Grain mills still turned in the early 19th century, but the bleachfield had closed by the late 1820s. Ainslie's brewery was quite large by 1800; three brewers competed for local custom by 1825, but did not outlast the century. By 1825 the town was the centre for a penny post serving Chirnside and Swinton, and in 1827 Chambers wrote that Dunse was *"The principal town in the County, in respect of size, business, schools; the Town-house is a new structure. Dunse, which contains about 3000 inhabitants, is not a manufacturing town, though deriving considerable employment in the shape of weaving from Glasgow. The finest and largest* [of the four little towns of Berwickshire – Lauder, Greenlaw, Coldstream and Dunse] *it seems to subsist chiefly upon its market, its shops, and its lawyers, who are astonishingly numerous"*. A Bank of Scotland branch opened in 1832, and in 1835 a gasworks was set up. Five years later, clumsy attempts to improve the spa ruined the spring completely.

**Railway Over-Optimism and Pampered Horses**: From 1849 Duns was the terminus of a North British Railway branch line from Reston on the East Coast main line. In 1863 the even more optimistic Berwickshire Railway extended the line across almost empty country to Earlston (and ultimately to Newtown St Boswells). From 1853 Duns again became the county town of Berwickshire, finally replacing Greenlaw, but the county's population peaked in 1861 and Duns entered a long, slow decline. In 1894 Murray thought Duns *"of some importance as a cattle, horse and sheep market"*, but its sole hotel, the *Swan*, was only *"fair"*. By that time Duns was no longer of industrial significance, but in 1898 it acquired a 9-hole golf course. The laird's villa at Manderston, 2.5 km east of the town, was greatly enlarged in the Edwardian decade into a superb mansion with grand terraced gardens, and a stable-block built to luxurious standards.

**Stagnation and Service Development**: The cattle market was closed early in the 20th century, replaced by one beside the main line railway at Reston. Duns was practically overlooked by developers for half a century, and was not helped by the severing of the Newtown rail link by floods in 1948, but did enjoy reasonable facilities in 1951. However, the little surrounding places were shrinking steadily in population and some of the facilities closed, including the remaining railway service to Reston in 1966. However, by then the substantial Berwickshire High School had been recently built west of the town. A few small new firms moved into Duns around 1970, including Clanwood Components, which by 1978 was making kit houses. The Knoll Hospital, planned in 1976, had 39 beds by 1981 for geriatric and GP Acute patients.

**Tourism**: Manderston House was opened to the public after 1979 by Adrian Palmer (of Huntley & Palmer biscuit fame). There were four small hotels in Duns by 1981; by 1983 a museum was open, and Duns Castle was surrounded by a Country Park, later called a nature reserve. Farne Salmon & Trout, a Duns processing works, expanded in 1987, won a Queen's Award for Export in 1991 and opened a branch in the Galashiels area. Duns, with a 1991 population of 2444, is still a pleasant small town; the Berwickshire District HQ remained there until the new Borders Council based in Newtown St Boswells took over all responsibilities in 1996. Duns golf course now has 18 holes, *Duns Castle* offers luxury accommodation for 60 people, and the very grand *'A'* listed Wedderburn Castle, restored in the mid 1990s, can be hired for large parties.

## DUNSCORE — Map 2, B4

***Dumfriesshire small village,*** *pop. 700 (area)* — OS 78: NX 8684

Many ancient earthworks and a motte can be found near Dunscore, which lies in Glencairn some 13 km north-west of Dumfries. Little remains of the 14th century Place of Snade and not much more of the much later Lag Tower, 2 km north-east. A parish school was founded in 1629. When roads were built, Dunscore's topography made it a route focus. A succession of little stations on the Cairn Valley Light Railway served the area from 1905 to 1943; Stepford quarry 3 km to the south was rail connected – the main source of traffic until the line was closed in 1949. In 1951 with a parish population of 1045, some 465 being in or close to the compact village, Dunscore's basic services made it the miniature metropolis of a rather wider area. By 1991 the parish held only 708 residents. Perhaps because tourists found little in the area to interest them, one hotel had closed; however, a doctor was in practice. During the 1990s the large and long-established Stepford quarry was steadily eating into Killyleoch Hill; an inn and post office are still open.

## DUNSTAFFNAGE & Dunbeg — Map 4, C2

***Argyllshire hamlets,*** *pop. 750 (area)* — OS 49: NM 8834

The steep rock of Dustaffnage, standing on a raised beach overlooking the Firth of Lorne on the coast of what is now Argyll, was a readily defended place which, according to legend, became about the year 600 the original capital of the first Scottish kingdom, which grew out of Dalriada. Then called Dun Monaidh, it was abandoned as the capital when Kintyre and the Hebrides fell under Norse control from the eighth century, even before the treacherous Scottish king Kenneth Macalpine assassinated the Pictish leaders and seized their throne and capital Old Scone (*q.v.*) in 843 AD. The present spectacular curtain-walled castle and nearby chapel were built soon after the Norsemen were expelled from the area in 1266, probably by Duncan MacDougall. The strongly defended castle was seized by Robert Bruce in 1312, and remained in use by the Lords of Lorne until a fire in 1810.

**Dunbeg and Marine Research**: Partial restoration of the historic castle and chapel from 1903 created a worthy tourist attraction. In 1924 they stood in isolation, but by 1958 a small settlement known as Dunbeg had been created nearby to serve the Scottish Marine Biological Association's new laboratory. It survived with the loss of some jobs in 1992 as the Natural Environment Research Council's Dunstaffnage Marine Biological Research Laboratory(!), and had its own pier and research vessel. By then the Seawork sailing school and marina was in operation north of the village. In 1994 Seawork of Dunstaffnage was laying mooring blocks in 85 m-deep water in the Red Sea, using a steel raft made by Weldfab of Oban. By 1996 new housing had replaced a caravan site. Today the historic castle is still a visitor attraction, and over 50 work in marine research as one of the 11 colleges of the University of the Highlands & Islands.

## DUNTOCHER, Faifley & Hardgate — Map 15, B4

***Urban area n-w. of Glasgow,*** *pop. 14,000* — OS 64: NS 4972

Duntocher, on the Cochno Water 12 km north-west of Glasgow, probably derives its name from a tiny Roman fort on the Antonine Wall. By about 1600 as the Pont map showed, *'Duntochie'* which originally lay just south of the wall had a bridge and a mill, with another mill downstream at Milton; *'Faichla'* and *'Hartchof'* (Faifley and Hardgate) closely adjoined north of the wall. The Roy map of about 1754 showed an east/west road paralleling the wall, and Duntocher bridge was rebuilt by Lord Blantyre in 1772; by then minor textile manufacture was recorded.

**Dalnottar Ironworks and Textiles**: The Dalnottar Iron Company, founded in 1769 by Glasgow and Newcastle interests, took over the Nether corn mill; it was a forge rather than a smelter. In 1773 two more corn and waulk mills were converted by the iron company as a forge and a slitting mill; by 1799 they had about 275 workers, making malleable iron goods, mainly for export to the New World. Heron mentioned two printfields in Old Kilpatrick parish in 1799, with 600 employees between them; possibly one of these was near Duntocher. A mechanised woollen mill was established in 1785–87 and by the 1790s had 300 workers. After 1813 it was converted to cotton, and after closure of most of the ironworks in 1815 their site too was used for a cotton mill, though spade and shovel manufacture continued.

**Distilling, Spinning and Golf**: Auchentoshan distillery was founded in 1817 by John Bulloch, and Duntocher's first post office dates from the 1813–38 period. The villages were never directly rail-served, and the distillery – which had a chequered history – was still small and rustic in 1886, employing nine people and producing about 225,000 litres of Lowland Malt whisky annually, using water from the Cochno Loch, 3km to the north. Mill dams still existed in 1894 when the villages had two inns, a population of over 2000 and *"a large establishment of spinning mills"*. An infectious diseases hospital was erected, south of which the Hardgate golf club, founded in 1905, laid out a course; by 1969 this had 18 holes and was run by the Clydebank & District club.

**Council Housing, Dams and Problems**: In 1928–30 Glasgow's Great Western Road (the A82) was extended through the area from Anniesland to a point just west of Duntocher. In the 1930s the Strathclyde Hosiery Company was still a large local enterprise, and there was for a time up to 1949 a shuttle service of electric trams to Clydebank. The distillery had survived the slump, only to be bombed in 1941, but was rebuilt; one of the cotton mills became a bakery. By 1945 the Greenside Reservoir had been impounded on the Loch Humphrey Burn to serve the Clydebank Water Works; the rather later Jaw dam had raised the level of Cochno Loch by 1971. Meantime the population of the area had risen to 4400 by the 1950s, when there was also an agricultural engineer. Considerable northwards council housing development – with an associated primary school in the Faifley estate – took place between 1951 and 1971, by which time a major electricity substation had been established east of the village.

**Whisky Visits – in Clydebank**: In 1975 Duntocher became part of Clydebank District, and by 1981 had the facilities of a large village, including four hotels. There were 57 beds in the hospital, which served a variety of specialisms. Auchentoshan distillery was open to visitors looking for an unusual nip; in 1991 it passed to Morrison Distillers. In 1991 the post-war council estate of Faifley had a population of 6087; Duntocher (including Hardgate) had 7882.

## DUNTULM, Hungladder & Kilmaluag — Map 8, A1

***N. Skye locations,** pop. 300 (area)* — OS 23: NG 4174

Near the tip of the long Trotternish peninsula of north Skye are the ruins of an ancient church and of the 15th century Duntulm Castle, perched on a cliff-top crag about 10km north of Uig. Monro noted in 1549 that its master, Donald MacDonald Gorm, who owned Trotternish, was also laird of Sleat in the south of the Isle. Duntulm Castle was abandoned to decay in 1732. A monument was erected at the township of Hungladder, about 3km to the south, in memory of Flora Macdonald, who aided Prince Charles Edward and died in 1790; she was buried there in Kilmuir graveyard. By the 1890s a road had been built from Uig, later extended eastwards through the township of Kilmaluag and around the coast to Staffin. By 1951 there was a coastguard station and a post office; Duntulm Lodge, close beside the ruined castle, had become a hotel, and a doctor was in practice – though like the local primary school and the coastguards this facility was soon lost. By 1980 a group of surviving black houses near Hungladder had been restored as the Skye Cottage Museum; fine-weather visitors can now enjoy picnicking facilities at various cliff-top locations; others go sea angling.

## DUNURE — Map 1, C2

***Small Ayrshire coastal village,** pop. 500* — OS 70: NS 2515

Dunure stands on a steep seaward facing slope 10km south-west of Ayr, above the rocky shore of Carrick. Its 14th century castle was the seat of the powerful Earl of Cassilis in 1560, and emparked by about 1600, when Pont's map showed a mill on the burn to the south; but Dunure was not chartered as a burgh. The Roy map made about 1754 showed a coastal road. Limekilns were built early in the 19th century, and a small fishing harbour was constructed in 1811. In 1906 the Maidens & Dunure Light Railway was opened, with stations at Dunure and at Knoweside 3km to the south, which served a sandy beach and the deceptively inclined section of road at Croy known as the *'Electric Brae'*, making a minor resort. The line did not serve Dunure harbour, and its trains to Ayr and Girvan were withdrawn in 1930, due no doubt to cheaper bus services, but freight continued on the line into the 1950s. Dunure remained a village with a population fluctuating between 600 and 750; its harbour still held a small fishing fleet in the 1980s; by 1987 a caravan site had replaced Knoweside station. At Dunure the occupants of a row of modern luxury villas, built by 1991 in what was still called Station Road, enjoyed a stunning view of the mountains of Arran. Dunure with its spectacular castle ruins – made safe by the Strathclyde Building Preservation Trust – still has its pub and post office.

*Dunure harbour in the mid 1970s, when there was still a small fishing fleet. The harbour was built in 1811, originally for coastal trading as well as fishing.* (JRH)

## DUNVEGAN — Map 8, A3

***Skye village,** pop. 300* — OS 23: NG 2547

The Isle of Skye's early key centre was Dunvegan Castle, which stands beside sheltered waters near the head of the sea loch of that name; it has been held by the MacLeods since about 1200. Although allegedly first built in stone in the ninth century, it largely dates from the 14th to 19th centuries. Monro noted in 1549 that Minginish in the west of Skye and Bracadale in the north-west were owned by MacLeod of Harris, who was based in his castle of Dunvegan, *"a stark strength, built upon a crag"*. The neighbouring pastoral islands such as Isay were *"good for fishing"*.

**Chicken Rents and Piping School**: Although not a sheriff caput, as the feudal administrative centre of the island Dunvegan Castle itself was akin to a little town, absorbing rents

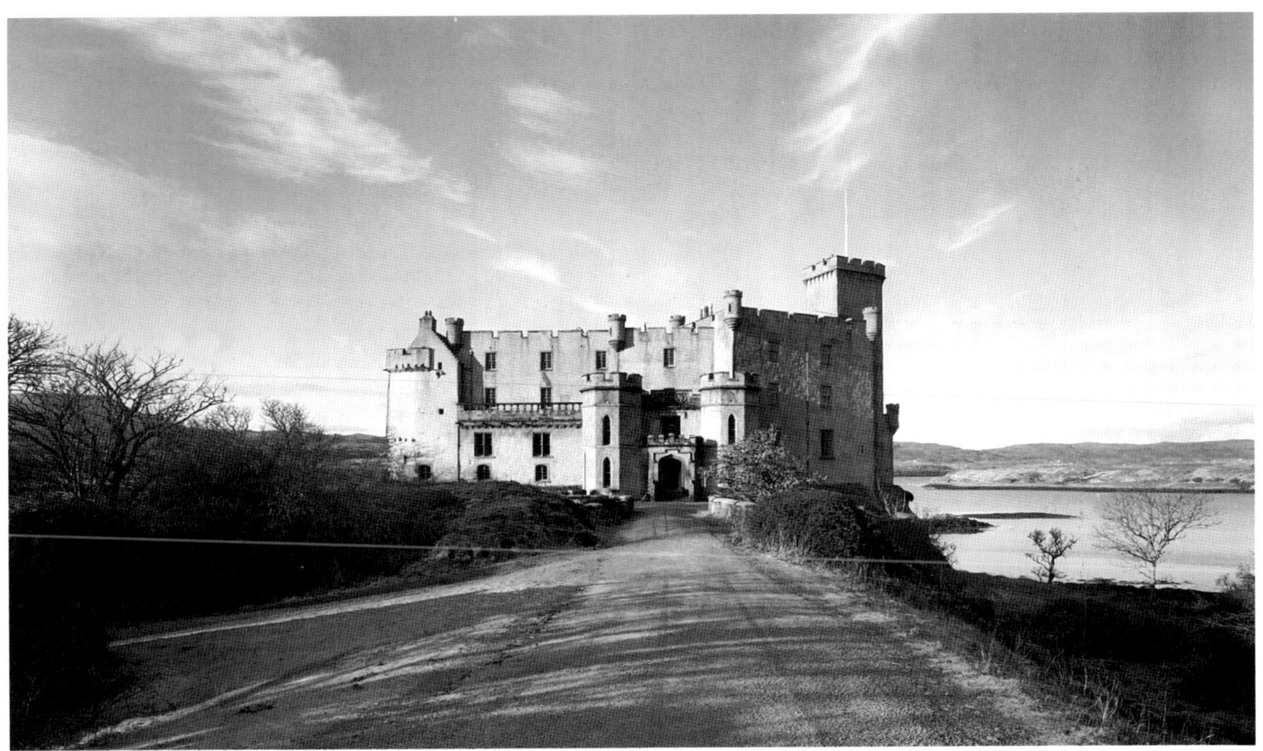

*Dunvegan Castle, largely dating from the 14th century. In 2001, the owner John MacLeod caused controversy when he offered the Cuillins for sale, requiring money to make repairs to the castle (which has origins back in the Dark Ages).* *(JRH)*

in kind to the tune of 9000 hens a year in the 1680s. Martin in 1703 noted Dunvegan church, and the *"good anchorage"* near the castle. In the early 18th century remote Borreraig across the loch was the site of the famous MacCrimmon piping school. As it was not in good farming country, Dunvegan was otherwise no more than a subsistence community based on crofting and fishing: as Boswell found, there was no shop on Skye as recently as 1773, though by that time cattle were sold to drovers to pay cash rents.

**Dunvegan joins the Commercial World**: Dunvegan had a fortnightly post from around 1745, the first settlement in Skye to have such a service. It had a post office by 1755 and was a post town by 1797, with a weekly service via Sconser. The outer isles post for the Uists went to Carinish and later to Lochmaddy via Dunvegan, but apart from a fine Georgian church, the village was insignificant. Chambers noted in the 1820s that Dunvegan Castle, which had been enlarged, was still Skye's *"principal mansion, the seat of the MacLeods, who own the greater part of the isle"*. They were ruthless clearers of tenants in the 1830s, but by 1847 the MacLeod had provided a grocery shop, and was *"also a sheep-farmer, an innkeeper, a coach-proprietor, and a shipowner"* (Somers).

**Clearances, Steamers and Freehold Crofting**: Borreraig was cleared of most of its people in 1852–53 by Macdonald of Sleat. A daily steamer to the Uists called at Dunvegan for a time from 1876, and still plied on that route three times a week in 1894, when Dunvegan had daily steamers to Oban, and an inn; the village was of a fair size, with a small secondary school and later a second small hotel and a golf course. In 1901 the extensive parish of Duirinish – including Waternish and Edinbane – held 3367 people. The remote crofting community of Glendale some 15km west of Dunvegan became uniquely the freeholders of their land following an Edwardian Royal Commission. The lighthouse on Neist Point, 12 km west of Dunvegan as the seagull flies, was first lit in 1909; in 1979 its keepers' families lived at Portree, but it was automated in 1989.

**People Leave; Tourism Develops**: Meantime the parish population had halved by 1951 to only 1592; the steamer services had gone and there was further decline in the 1950s when the golf course vanished. But the piping school was revived in the 1970s. By 1980 the Black House Folk Museum was open at Colbost on the way to Glendale, with its restored water mill and toy museum. In 1981 Dunvegan village was only a small tourist centre with a population little over 300. Its livelihood still largely depends on the castle's opening to visitors, benefiting from recent associated investment in a new restaurant building by the MacLeods; many new bungalows were evident by 1988. But the spectacularly sited castle, though in some part ancient, is surely not the oldest inhabited building in Scotland, as claimed by its latest MacLeod owner *(see Traquair)*. In 2000 his attempt to sell the Cuillin Hills to raise money to improve the castle was highly controversial. The *Three Chimneys* restaurant stands at Colbost.

## DURNESS

**Map 12, B1**

***N-W. Sutherland village,*** *pop. 350*

OS 9: NC 4067

Remote Durness lies near the north-westernmost point of Scotland, Cape Wrath – a name which comes from the Old Norse *'Hvarf'* meaning turning point. It has the ruins of a 12th century church, beside which Pont's map made about 1600 showed two mills and a tower house, several settlements and *'The Smoo'*, the huge and accessible Smoo Cave. Durness was then in the district of Strathnaver, which at that time covered all of northern Sutherland. Smoo Cave was among the few names on the Roy map – made about 1750 – when the area, though well settled, was trackless; Durness Kirk and Mains also stood out. In 1772 most of the 200 people who had scratched a living around the south and east shores of Loch Eriboll, the very deep mountain-girt sea inlet to the east, departed to settle in North Carolina.

**The Lighthouse, Inn and Loch Eriboll Lime**: Cape Wrath lighthouse was built by John Gibb of Aberdeen for the Northern Lighthouse Board to designs by Robert Stevenson, and first lit in 1828. In 1841 Durness was a struggling crofting and fishing community sadly exploited by its head lessee, one James Anderson, but there was already an inn at Durine township. During the 19th century a road was finally built westwards from Tongue to Durness, winding round the head of Loch Eriboll where at that time Lord Reay's men burnt limestone on an islet, Eilean Choraidh. Lime was also quarried, burnt and shipped from Ard Neackie on the east shore, whose long-disused kilns still stand.

**Enterprise and Isolation**: John Mackay, born locally in mid century, worked his way up from cleaning boots to building the Stromness and Stenness Hotels, founding telephone, electricity and bus services, and ending as the owner of a whole chain of hotels. In 1883 another road was completed south-westwards from Durness to Rhiconich near Kinlochbervie; from a ferry at Keoldale another, isolated road was formed, reaching the Cape Wrath lighthouse by 1896. By 1894 a daily coach covered the 90km to Lairg station, and Murray noted Durness as a *"large and straggling village"*. The inn, upgraded as the *Durine Hotel,* was *"very comfortable; good sea-trout fishing"*. But such extreme isolation, even at the end of the 19th century, can also be seen from this note in Murray's Handbook: *"Durness is 20 miles from Tongue for pedestrians, who cross three ferries"*. These were the Tongue ferry across the Kyle of Tongue, Hope Ferry across the short River Hope, and the soon to be closed Heilam passenger ferry across Loch Eriboll from the *Heilam Inn*. In 1901 Durness parish held 870 people.

**Cars and Crafts**: The *Heilam Inn* was already absent by the 1930s, and the Tongue and Hope ferries were eventually replaced by bridges. In 1928 the first motor car reached the remote Cape Wrath lighthouse, and Durness slowly became a resort village of 200 to 250 people, which first had a youth hostel in the 1930s. The parish population was down to 413 by 1951, but the decline then slowed and a doctor was in practice locally by about 1953, when the 10-roomed *Cape Wrath Hotel* was open at Keoldale. The 7-pupil secondary class in the village school had closed by 1974, and for a time there was no youth hostel, but this was replaced by 1984. Meantime a group of RAF hutments from the 1939–45 war had been converted into the Balnakeil craft village.

**Candles, Golf and Killer Whales**: By 1978 there were four hotels, a garage and sub-branch bank in and near Durness. The craft village produced almost every type of craft artefact – with varying degrees of commercial success. The parish population was steady at 354 in 1991. In 1994 the fabrication of full size fibreglass models of killer whales was begun at Durness, these being found highly effective in protecting farmed salmon from grey seals! Balnakeil Craft Village is still active, and there is now a 9-hole golf course. There are several small commended inns with accommodation (some are seasonal); the youth hostel is open in summer only.

## DUROR & Kentallen — Map 5, A2

***Argyllshire village & hamlet,*** *pop. 200* — OS 49: NM 9955

A standing stone in Glen Duror some 9km south-west of the Ballachulish narrows, plus the medieval chapel of Keil on the coast of Loch Linnhe 1.5km farther west, attest to ancient settlement. North-eastwards a col leads to the small inlet of Kentallen Bay. Ardsheal House was built in 1500 on the intervening promontory, overlooking Loch Linnhe. Burnt in the '45, it was rebuilt as a sprawling mansionhouse in 1760. Meantime the Roy map of about 1750 showed a gap in the coastal track where it crossed the River Duror; however, in 1803 Dorothy Wordsworth found at Duror *"a bridge, a mill and some cottages"*, while Kentallen was a *"cluster of huts at the water's edge, with their little fleet of fishing boats at anchor"*. Duror's first post office was opened near the standing stone about 1856; the *Duror Inn* was open by the 1890s.

**Railway Station Hotel**: In 1898–1903 a single-line branch of the Caledonian Railway was built through the area to serve Ballachulish *(q.v*, and see *Thomas, 1966)* with a station at Duror and a crossing station at Kentallen pier; nearby was at one time a quarry for the black granite known as *Kentallenite*, used as a monumental stone. In the 1950s Duror had a telephone exchange, and both places also had post offices and primary schools. Kentallen school was soon closed because the area's population was falling, from about 300 in 1951 to 240 in 1981; meantime the hills to the east were being gradually afforested. The railway was closed in 1966. However, Kentallen station building became a restaurant (now extended into the *Holly Tree Hotel*). Other hotels from the 1970s were the *Duror*, the *Stewart* (in Glen Duror), and the gourmet *Ardsheal House*.

## DYCE & Aberdeen Airport — Map 10, C3

***Suburb n-w. of Aberdeen,*** *pop. 6350* — OS 38: NJ 8812

Stone circles and standing stones remain near Tyrebagger Hill some 10km north-west of Aberdeen; but only the hill appeared on Pont's 16th century map. Gordon's map of 1642 showed Dyce Kirk; but the area was a virtual blank on Roy's map of about 1750. A granite quarry was opened nearby in 1766, and in the late 18th century the River Don was crossed by a new road laid out from Aberdeen to Old Meldrum; this gave off a fork to Kintore (later the B977). The hamlet of Parkhill which grew at this point was a post town by 1797. The Aberdeenshire canal – dug south of the river between Aberdeen and Inverurie – was opened in 1805, and an inn was built beside it on the previously empty Muir of Dyce.

**Dyce Junction and its Village**: The Great North of Scotland Railway's main line to Inverurie and Keith was built in 1852–54, replacing the canal. When the Buchan line was opened in 1861, it diverged from the main line at Dyce Junction; the original Dyce station near Mains was abandoned. Parkhill also had a station until around 1930. Engine sheds and a sleeper creosoting plant were set up at Dyce Junction, where the first feus granted in 1865 were mostly to railway workers. A chemical fertiliser works was established in 1869. In 1887 a suburban train service was introduced to Aberdeen. By 1894 Dyce was definitely a village with a post office, and large quarries of ornamental granite were being worked 2 km to the north-west; to the south was the prophetically named Wellheads Farm. By 1901 the parish population was 1482 and there was a primary school; a library (aided by Carnegie) started in 1906, and by 1921 more shops were open.

**Dyce thrown into the Air**: Dyce airfield was first planned privately in 1930 by Cambridge lawyer, pilot and actor Eric Gandar Dower, opening in 1934. Soon there were weekly flights to Renfrew. Later came routes from Dyce to Wick, Thurso and Stromness, and also to Turnhouse (now Edinburgh Airport) under Allied Airways (Gandar Dower); from 1937 to 1940 this firm and British Airways also provided services from Perth and Dyce to Stavanger and Newcastle. Military use was also made of the airfield, but the suburban train service was abandoned in 1937. A short concrete runway was laid on the hitherto grass airfield in 1938; after war service as a fighter base, by the 1950s there was again a stopping air service to London. The construction of a runway 1830 m long followed in 1952, and Dyce airfield was renamed *Aberdeen Airport* in 1955.

**Bacon Blossoms but Beeching Cuts**: In 1934 Lawson's bacon factory replaced the inn. In 1952 Lawson's employed about 150 workers and a manure works 40. At that time the population of Dyce was 1400, and apart from the airfield only village facilities were available. The Lawson family sold out in 1965 to Unilever, who kept the name. The factory was soon expanding hugely and the population was therefore growing; by 1971 it was nearly 3000. By about 1977 Lawson had 1300 employees, but in 1979 the firm blamed EEC policy when closing their slaughterhouse, which had employed 600 people, leaving only 800 in bacon, pie and sausage making. In 1965, following the Beeching Report, the Buchan branch passenger trains were withdrawn, and Dyce station was closed, so absurdly preventing rail-air connections. The main line from Dyce to Insch was singled in 1969, and from Aberdeen to Dyce in 1971.

**North Sea Oil pulls in the Helicopter Operators**: Meantime as North Sea Oil exploration developed, the hitherto quiet Dyce airport saw its first Bristow helicopter in 1967. Helicopter operators British International (BIH) – a BEA (later British Airways) subsidiary – also came to Dyce in 1967. About 1970 BP established its North Sea Oil exploration HQ in the Aberdeen area; offshore oil was soon proved, and the oil industry quickly made Dyce the world's busiest heliport, multiplying its usage by a factor of 10. Three helicopter bases were built, for Bristow, British Airways and B-Cal; Bond Helicopters, founded in the 1970s, which grew large with little publicity, moved its HQ to Dyce in 1986. These and other oil-associated activities brought rapid local growth between 1969 and 1980, including three large new hotels. The wide range of specialist services required by the oil industry speedily grew on the American model at three industrial estates: Farburn, Kirkhill, and rather oddly (as it was named after the farm) Wellheads, where by 1978 Ferranti Offshore Systems had a small branch factory.

**Dyce limps back to Rail**: A new passenger terminal was opened at the airport in 1977; due to space constraints east of the main runway intersection it had to be sited far from the railway. In 1979 the Buchan branch railway which had triggered

*Helicopters at Dyce; from a start in 1967, the off-shore oil industry made Dyce (Aberdeen Airport) the world's busiest heliport.*
*(SMPC / Ken Paterson)*

the settlement was finally closed to goods. In 1981 Dyce had a population of over 7000, and a small new town centre had been provided. All the new development led to the railway station being reopened in 1984 with an airport bus link; it immediately became the most successful reopening in Scotland, and from the 1990s some trains to and from the south started/terminated there.

**Helicopter Ups and Downs**: Although Bristow operated 24 helicopters on oil service in 1985, in 1986 two-thirds of the activity was curtailed for a time due to a slump in oil prices. As a result British Airways sold BIH to the doomed speculator Robert Maxwell, and B-Cal abandoned its helicopter arm. Airport traffic in 1988 comprised 1.6 million passengers, with one helicopter movement every 15 minutes. A typical Dyce industry, Ramforce welding technologists, was expanding in 1989. By 1991 the population was some 6350.

**Aberdeen Airport booms in the 1990s**: In 1992 over two million passengers used the BAA airport, due to stronger offshore oil-related activity. Meantime an avionics research and development firm known as Caledonian Airborne Systems had developed from its inception in 1988 to 42 staff by 1992, taking over the former BP heliport. In 1993–94 Dyce had the third largest number of aircraft movements in Britain after Heathrow and Gatwick: 116,300! Bristow alone employed 600 people at Dyce in 1993 and BIH had survived Maxwell and had a fleet of 20 helicopters *(see Webster, 1994)*. In 1994 Bond Helicopters of Dyce absorbed Helikopter Service of Stavanger and Clyde Helicopters of Partick into their own fleet to form probably the world's largest civilian helicopter operator.

**Plenty Travellers fill Hotels**: By 1994 the former Lawson meat products factory was known as McIntosh of Dyce. By 1995 the Aberdeen Marriott Leisure Club at Riverview Drive offered a swimming pool among its varied features, but in general the pace of physical development at Dyce had slowed over the last 15 years. In 1997 Dyce Academy had 511 pupils. A new rail-freight terminal for Buchan is to be located at Raiths Farm just north of the airport. The hotels of over 100 rooms include the *Aberdeen Marriott*, the *Thistle*, the *Skean Dhu* and the *Speedbird*.

## DYSART

**Map 6, B4**

***Coastal village / part of Kirkcaldy,*** *pop. 2500* OS 59: NT 3093

St Serf, an eighth century missionary *(see also Culross)*, lived in a cave in the former sea cliff at Dysart on the south coast of Pictish Fothrif; its name was derived from the Latin word *Desertum*, a hermitage. Salmon were at one time fished on the shore, and St Serf's church, built in stone close to the cave, was dedicated in 1245. Heron stated that there was once a priory of black friars at Dysart, but it was its black diamonds that really made the place into a lay settlement. The Dysart Main coal seam, one of the most productive in Scotland and which varied from 4 to 8 metres in thickness, outcropped at the foot of the cliffs just west of the cave, extending inland at right angles to the shore and dipping to the east.

**Coal, Salt and Spanish and Dutch Connections**: Coal mining was already in progress by 1330, when salt was made locally by evaporating sea water over fires of small coal; hides and fish were exported, and an early Dysart man named Thomas was rich enough to endow a pilgrim hospital at Dax in Spain. In 1405 the laird Sir John Sinclair granted a lease for coal mining at Dysart to Sir John Forstar, who worked the Main seam from 1407. Dysart was recorded in 1415 as a *"town"* from which wool was also exported, and was long known as *'Little Holland'* due to its trade links; the steep brae leading up from the harbour was named by Dutch sailors *'het pad'* – meaning *'The Path'*. This name became corrupted to Hot Pot (Wynd), the start of the *"fair ready way"* to Falkland which was noted in 1415, very likely built for the carriage of coals to Regent Albany's new palace there.

**Dysart as a Burgh**: By 1435 Dysart was definitely a Sinclair burgh of barony and by 1444 its merchants were trading with Danzig. The original town records were destroyed in 1446 by a fire which started in a coal working, so the date and nature of Dysart's first burghal trading charter is not known. In 1450 its trade included fish, coal and salt. Customs receipts were first recorded for Dysart in 1480, and the ready removal of outcrop coal from the cliff base soon enhanced a natural rock-girt shelter for small vessels. By then salt was made locally on a large scale, and a Dysart ship carried lime to Aberdeen for building. There must have been a reasonable harbour by 1507, when the town was shipping coal as far as Denmark.

**Market Centre and War Damage**: By 1510, when a market was chartered, Dysart was still Lord Sinclair's burgh of barony, but powerful enough to demand the right to appoint its own bailies. Dysart was trading with Hamburg in 1512 and with Bergen in 1525. Trading profits enabled the building in the early 16th century of St Serf's great church tower. Despite damage inflicted by the English in 1501 and 1522, in 1532 Dysart was taxed at 50% above Kirkcaldy. By 1540 it had two defensive guns and by 1543 there was a mill. Around 1550 Dysart had to supply the government with sailors, labourers and infantrymen. In 1559–60 it was taken and pillaged by the French, cutting its trade by 90%.

**After the Reformation, the Royal Burgh**: By 1571 Dysart had quarrymen and masons, there were no fewer than 16 salt pans, and trade grew; in 1576 the second, solid tolbooth was built. A burgh school was founded in 1579, but in 1584 plague killed 400 local people. However, a Royal charter of 1587 conferred the right to three fair days, and the town was certainly confirmed as a Royal Burgh in 1594, so gaining parliamentary representation. *'Dysert'* was evidently a significant place to Pont, who mapped Fife around 1600, and to James Gordon in 1642, though it then ranked only 31st among Scottish burghs in tax yield.

**Beer and Baggage**: In the early 17th century English beer and fruit, ships' cables, flax and iron were imported. Hides became a principal export, matching the ten oxen and twenty horses that Dysart had to provide in 1617 to move the Royal baggage train across Fife. At that time and for about 150 more years Dysart ships were also smuggling. A *'new harbour'* begun in 1617 may have included the massive stone-built East Pier (most of which which still exists). Grain was exported in 1618, though in 1621 Dysart still paid under 1.5% of Scotland's Customs dues and by 1631 the harbour was full of stones and sand. Even so by 1640 the population was some 1800.

**Plague and Other Disasters**: Despite plague which came again in 1648 and the loss of most of its *"skippers and traffickers"* in the civil wars, four ships of up to 50 tons were still locally owned in 1655, when a severe storm badly damaged the pier and sank 20 small boats in its shelter. In 1656 the tolbooth roof was accidentally blown off by gunpowder, and by 1666 the Scott family had left to seek fortune in Venice. Salt was still made in 1669, but in 1671 the local coal mine was again on fire, and the burgh became bankrupt. By 1691 there were only three ships, no trade and many houses were vacant or ruinous.

**Poverty, Desolation and Fire drives the Laird to England**: Linen manufacture began on a small scale around 1715, but the harbour was still very ruinous. In 1720 riots followed the export of grain when food prices were beyond the people's means, and by 1723 – though the streets were still stone-paved – poverty had removed furniture and glass from most of the houses. In 1724 Defoe found the town in decay, *"a most lamentable object of a miserable, dying corporation; but here is an excellent vein of Scots coal, and the Lord Dysart who resides in England has a good salt-work in the town; there is a small pier or wharf for ships"*; but yet another storm damaged the pier in that year, when there was little other trade; a few *"nailers and hard-ware workers"* were at work. In 1730 a mere 17 Dysart colliers were recorded.

**Shipbuilding and Textiles**: From about 1740 there was a post office, and Dysart House was built in 1748 for the St Clairs. Roy's survey of about 1750 showed Dysart as quite a large settlement for the period, with a harbour and a coastal road. By 1764 when shipbuilding began in Dysart, utilising timber from Germany, the local mines had reached a depth of 46m and were drained by steam pumps. Handloom weaving grew and by the 1770s there were 130 looms in the parish (which included Pathhead, *q.v.)* but in 1770 the town council gave up its common lands to the Sinclairs, and by 1788 the local mines served only the declining salt industry. Then came a remarkable revival. From 1789 there was a twice-weekly ferry to Leith. By then there were some 700 looms in the parish, making checks and ticks from Fife-spun yarns. By 1794 over 100 miners dug 20,000 tonnes of coal a year, much of which was exported to Scandinavia and Holland in exchange for timber; Dysart owned 25 trading vessels, mainly square-rigged and averaging 160 tons, and exported coal and salt, the latter made in eight evaporating pans, hence the name *"Pan Ha'"*. About 1700 people lived in Dysart, though fewer than in Pathhead; 300 children were at school.

**Iron Ore improves Harbour Access**: By 1797 Dysart was a post town, and four fairs were scheduled for the year. In 1799 Heron noted *"a considerable trade in coals; some ships are built. Dysart contains about 1800 inhabitants"*. Local ironstone containing 60% iron was smelted in furnaces located in the long-ruined Priory chapel. Iron ore was also shipped to the Carron works: by 1800 the mines were 90m deep. A new St Serf's Church was built in 1800–02, and Shore Road was laid out in 1807 to make easier access to the harbour, requiring part of old St Serf's to be cut away. In 1811 Dysart had its own linen stamp-master. A steam ferry to Leith started in 1819 and oil street lights were first lit in 1821, but the cattle fair and weekly produce market faded early in the 19th century.

**Whaling too Smelly for the Laird?**: In addition to a hilltop windmill (whose tower has survived to the present day) by 1827 a spinning mill stood on the shore below Edington Place. According to Chambers, Dysart was then a *"town of considerable size full of antique substantial houses, which now possesses only an export trade in coal and salt"*. Chambers cited the *"well-known proverbial expression 'to carry sault to Dysart'"*, comparable to *'Coals to Newcastle'*. In 1829–31 the old quarry at the coastal coal outcrop was converted into an inner harbour basin with gates allowing coal loading at any state of the tide. In 1835, in anticipation of whaling, the town council built an *'Oil House'*, but the Earl prevented its use!

**A Transatlantic Vessel**: By 1839 2088 looms were at work in the wider parish, employing in all some 5500 people and producing about 34 million metres of cloth annually; a gasworks was built in the 1840s. Robert Meldrum built ships in both Dysart harbour and at Burntisland. A successor, John Watt of Dysart, built the barque *St Brycedale* for Swan Brothers of Kirkcaldy; when new in 1866 she sailed for the West Indies. Vessels were still built at the harbour in 1869 and later years, but few early photographs actually show a vessel on the slipway (parts of whose rusty rails can still be seen). Meantime in 1845 Douglas Engineering was established, later becoming Douglas & Grant and in the late 20th century Lewis C Grant.

**From Dysart to Australia**: A high level station was built just north of Dysart by the Edinburgh & Northern Railway, opened in 1847, and soon afterwards the 150m deep Randolph colliery was sunk between the line and the Standing Stane Road by the Earl of Rosslyn's Collieries Ltd, to exploit the two Lower Dysart seams. This encouraged growth in the hamlet of Boreland between Dysart and the colliery. Meantime John McDouall Stuart (pronounced as *Do-All* not Dowel), born in Dysart in 1815, had trained as a surveyor, and emigrated to Australia. Stuart led several transcontinental journeys of exploration on horseback, going northwards from South Australia between 1858 and 1862. His party finally reached the north coast near the site of modern Darwin; then, though sick and near starving, they returned safely across 2650km of arid wastes to Adelaide; this feat made him rightly famous *(see Webster M S, 1958)*.

**Power Spinning and Weaving by Millie and Normand**: In 1856 the *Royal Hotel* was still a posting house. Power looms were at last introduced locally in 1855, making checks and ticks. In 1864 Thomas Millie & Son operated a small spinning mill east of the town, but James Normand & Son then employed nearly 500 people in their steam-powered weaving mill by Dovecote Crescent. Hucks, diapers, and damasks were made. The firm was building an *'extensive spinning-mill'* on an adjacent site and at its peak had about a thousand workers.

**Town Improvements and Frances Colliery**: Town drains were laid in the 1870s and a school board was set up in 1873; in 1876 a Mechanics' Institute was formed. When the Frances (originally *Francis*) Colliery – known locally as the Dubby Pit – was sunk east of the town about 1875, its pit head was sited on the cliff top and a rail connection was laid across the Wemyss Road to the main line. After Normand's death, his linen works continued in production; in 1884 his widow funded the building of the Normand Hall in his memory. Another coastal linen mill near the Frances pit worked intermittently into the 20th century. Meantime Thomas Harrow, who had made linens in Dysart from 1867, owned both power and hand looms in 1889; in 1890 he erected the Munro power loom linen works in Alexander Street near the station.

**Mineral Wealth gambled away**: By 1891 the burgh had some 4000 people, subscription libraries and a town band. In 1890 Dysart House was described as *"the old ancestral home"* of Lord Loughborough, after whom Loughborough Road was named; by then the fourth Earl of Rosslyn was exporting over 50,000 tonnes of coal a year. But he died in 1890 and in 1896 Dysart House was acquired by Sir Michael Nairn from the fifth Earl (a bankrupt gambler).

**Fishing Vessels and the Harbour at its Peak**: A week before the Forth Bridge opened in 1890, Thomson & Co of Dysart launched *"a splendid steam fishing vessel"* for a North Shields firm. In 1895 steps were hewn up to the high-level Sailor's Walk, perched perilously high above the harbour; Dysart had a coastguard station, and the town council employed three pilots to guide vessels in and out of the dock. In 1897 there were 14 small sailing vessels in the port at one time, all taking on board coal from horse-drawn carts; it was exported across the North Sea and to England. Around 1900 a ships' chandler was open, and at some time a tunnel was cut from the quay into the small Lady Blanche pit east of the harbour, from whose coalface coal was brought in trams to the dockside.

**Trams but no Aircraft or Mills**: At the same period the previously unreliable piped water supply was improved. The Dysart Co-op expanded in 1908 with a new fleshing shop. By 1911 there was a chemist's shop, and electricity was available from

*The Frances Colliery and bing above the beach at Dysart, whilst a fishing competition takes place on the shore (1980). The colliery worked from 1875 to 1984; its winding tower of 1918 still stands.* (RS)

that year, enabling an immediate extension of the Kirkcaldy electric tramway system to Dysart Townhead. In 1913 hangars were designed for a proposed military airfield inland from Dysart, but instead flatter Montrose was chosen. Meantime the linen industry was fading; the small Smith's and Terraces' mills and Thomas Harrow's Munro Works all closed within a few years, but for a time bedding was manufactured in the town. Dysart primary school was completed in 1915.

**Golf Clubs, and New Housing**: By 1915 the Munro Works belonged to A G Spalding & Brothers, where despite the Great War 23 male workers still made athletic goods such as golf clubs. For many years a 9-hole golf course was in use near the old windmill tower, but after 1945 this area went for Council housing, which had been built locally from 1921; years later, some were built on the site of the last linen mill, Normand's, which ceased work after the war in 1919, and was demolished in 1928. From 1916 to 1957 the Normand Hall was used as a cinema. From the late 19th century the beach had a bandstand and a cafe, popular with Glasgow holidaymakers until in 1930 the Frances pit bing caught fire and was bulldozed into the sea; this activity, and continued black tipping, ruined the beach.

**Carpets, Council and Cabinet**: James Meikle & Co made carpets in the former Spalding factory in Dysart from 1919. Joseph Westwood – who became a Dysart town councillor in 1912 – progressed to become Secretary of State for Scotland after 1945. In 1922 up to seven ships could still be seen in the harbour any day; small steamships loaded bunker coal at the east pier. In 1923 the Sinclair family sold the local pits to the Fife Coal Company, who built a new washery at the Frances. In 1924 MacAlpines deepened the dock for the town council in a vain effort to regain trade, yet in 1926 striking miners could still hew coal from the harbour bottom at low tide. A Miners' Welfare Institute was built in 1927, but in 1928 the Lady Blanche pit was closed, its upper shaft used as an air vent for the Frances until about 1965.

**Parkland gained but Much Else lost**: About 1928 the Nairn family sold Dysart House to the enclosed Carmelite order, who founded a nunnery there in 1931. The laird's fine coastal policies became the public Ravenscraig Park, presented to the council in 1929, the year when the town council regretfully closed the by then unused dock, and the boatyard also closed. In 1930, Dysart was absorbed by Kirkcaldy burgh; the tramway was closed the next year. By 1955 the harbour was silted up, its timber dock gates rotting and only two fishermen at work. In 1967 Dysart Sailing Club took it over, and the harbour was dredged in the early 1970s.

**Pan Ha' Reconditioned, Carpets move**: In 1968–69 the National Trust for Scotland restored and in part rebuilt the largely derelict Pan Ha' housing. Meantime in 1956 James Meikle & Co had transferred carpet weaving to Kirkcaldy, but in 1967 the firm opened Newlands Mill at their original home, Dysart, which dyed and spun wool for the Kirkcaldy factory. Dysart station was closed to goods in 1965 and to passengers in 1969. In 1967 the NCB closed its Dysart workshops beside the Frances pit, and the Randolph colliery was closed in 1968, although by 1971 the HQ of the Fife Police was located in former NCB offices at the Frances. By then a small bacon factory was in use, and Grubbs still made lemonade, but Meikle's carpet industry failed in 1980. In 1978 the Frances Colliery employed 632 workers; about then it was connected undersea with Kirkcaldy's Seafield colliery.

**Deep Mining ceases at Scotland's Oldest Pit**: In 1984, when employment was down to 500, came the disastrous confrontation between Scargill and Thatcher, and a fire broke out during the miners' final strike, so the whole complex was closed. At least this ended the tipping of coal waste which had for so long damaged the beaches of Dysart and Kirkcaldy. Engineering and financial studies in 1994 showed that any advantage from its coal reserves (offshore from Wemyss, and being only one eighth as sulphurous as English coals), was offset by the problems of wet undersea workings. So in pumping ceased, and by 1999 only a vast wasteland remained, dominated by the rusting (but listed) headgear. Nearby, however, an estate of private houses was being built on the site of a former small oil depot. Opencasting of the former Randolph colliery site, which began in 1999, would remove the last prominent coal bing from the area.

**Home to the Top Historian: Little Left but History**: By 1980 the John McDouall Stuart birthplace had been restored and opened as a museum in his honour, to delight the few Australian visitors. A small firm of precision marine engineers had closed by 1991, but jute machinery and sheet metal computer cabinets were still made by the long-established Lewis C Grant, though in 1996 they completed a move to new premises at Mitchelston (Pathhead). In 1993 the amenity of the harbour area was improved under a joint Fife Enterprise scheme, but the Bank of Scotland closed Dysart's only branch bank, and in 1995 Fife Police moved to new HQ at Glenrothes, leaving their old premises vacant. Also in 1995 the Normand Hall was demolished as unsafe, replaced in 1996 by a public garden; by then the former Miners' Welfare Institute had become the Community Hall. The harbour is now a base for small yachts and shellfish boats. Of all Dysart's industries and trade little remains but the cliff-top sheds of Fife Warehousing, near the former Frances colliery. The long-standing *Royal Hotel* and the well-known *Old Rectory* restaurant are still very much in business.

## EAGLESFIELD & Kirtlebridge

**Map 2, C4**

***Dumfriesshire villages,*** *pop. 900* OS 85: NY 2373

A major circular earthwork marking the site of an ancient settlement stands at Springkell, east of the Kirtle Water about 10km north-west of Gretna; 3km to the south, the Roman road from Carlisle to the Clyde paralleled the wooded Kirtle gorge. Its line passed the much later Robgill Tower and the 16th century Bonshaw Tower, shown on Pont's map of around 1600 as the emparked *'Bonshau Syd'*. To the north of this was *'Kirtil Brig'*, though no bridge was depicted across the Kirtle Water. To the north were the L-plan tower of *'Blacket'* (Blackwood) House, the 16th century Kirkconnel Tower – of which little now remains – the ancient Kirkconnel Church, and a watermill. Roy's map of about 1754 emphasised the already emparked mansion of Springkell House. By then a new road had been laid out south of the Roman alignment, which it left at Newton by Kirkpatrick, and crossing the Kirtle Bridge turned roughly west to Ecclefechan. This alignment was improved under Telford some 50 years later.

**Railwayman Extraordinary**: The Caledonian Railway (CR) main line opened in 1847, Kirtlebridge station being 1.5km west of the bridge, where it also served the hamlet of Eaglesfield. Locally-born James Thompson, who joined the CR as an office boy the moment it opened, rose to be CR General Manager and was knighted in 1897. The single track Solway Junction Railway, which opened in 1869, was originally intended to carry iron ore from Cumbria to Lanarkshire ironworks via the Solway Viaduct *(see Annan)*. It joined the CR main line at Kirtlebridge, which gained a post and telegraph office. By 1895 Eaglesfield had lengthened to 1400m and gained a post office and a smithy. The Annan passenger trains ceased in 1931, and freight lasted only a few years longer. By 1953 some 1050 people lived in the area, which had two primary schools. There was an inn by the railway station, but the latter had been closed by 1963 when the A74 was being widened to dual carriageway, and the two doctors vanished. By 1981 the combined population was down to about 875. When the A74 was rebuilt into a motorway in the 1990s it more effectively separated little Kirtlebridge, with its pub, from the lengthy one-street village of Eaglesfield with its 642 people in 1991, served by a pub and post office. To the east is Springkell in its extensive park.

## EAGLESHAM

**Map 2, A1**

***Renfrewshire village,*** *pop. 3400* OS 64: NS 5751

The remarkably straight road through Eaglesham, a hilly location near the White Cart Water some 13km south of Glasgow, is conceivably a Roman alignment; it points in the general direction of the Roman fort at Bothwellhaugh. The Cumbric word *Eglwys* meaning *'church'* shows that Eaglesham was a very early settlement. Polnoon Castle, a substantial 14th century stronghold of the Montgomery family, probably also bears a Cumbric name. The Pont map of Renfrewshire made about 1600 showed *'Pounuyn Castle'* emparked, and gave prominence to the well-settled *Baronie of Egglisham* with its Kirkton, Kirkland with its bridge, and upstream a mill. Although no road was shown by Pont, and Eaglesham apparently did not become a burgh of barony, a weekly market was held there in the 1670s, and the East Kilbride road existed when the Roy map was surveyed in the 1750s. Beside this road Roy showed a small irregular settlement huddled round the church.

**Planned Village, Cotton and Statuary**: The spacious heart of latter-day Eaglesham was created by the 10th and 11th Earls of Eglinton from 1769, when inwards-looking terraces of cottages

*Weavers' cottages at Eaglesham. The village was laid out in the late 18th century by the 12th Earl of Eglinton, with a water-powered spinning mill in the centre. Hand-loom weavers worked the spun yarn into cloth.* *(JRH)*

overlooking a central green were adventurously laid out on the pronounced hill slopes on either side of the burn. Later in the same century a small cotton mill was erected near the castle by the 12th Earl, followed by a new water-powered cotton spinning mill built astride the burn in 1792. Already by 1799 Heron was impressed by *"the pleasant village of Eaglesham"*. The mill was extended in 1826, relying on the water impounded by two dams above the village. The first post office in Eaglesham opened about the same time, but no railway was ever built into the area. In 1876 the newer cotton mill burned to the ground, never to be replaced. Meantime William Gemmell, born in Eaglesham in 1814, became a joiner and a self-taught sculptor of fine life-sized figures. Eaglesham had an inn by 1896, and Craigmill was an engineering shop in the late 19th century.

**Affluent Suburb conserved, but needs Bypass**: Until the foundation of the Bonnyton golf club in 1957, which laid out an 18-hole course, Eaglesham remained a village of some 2000 people, still focused around its triangular green; thanks to Sir Robert Grieve this had been saved from the tawdry urbanisation of most Central Belt settlements to become an *'outstanding conservation area'*. By 1977 the Lawmuir Residential School was open at the hamlet of Jackton on the East Kilbride road. By 1981 infill and backland estate developments had added to Eaglesham over 1000 extra people and a variety of facilities, while successfully keeping the visual character of the village. The population was 3382 in 1991. Through traffic on the busy B764, still the main road between East Kilbride and Ayrshire, had become a problem by the late 1980s; although by 1996 a roundabout at the top of the village had slowed it down, a bypass was proposed by the new local authority of East Renfrewshire. By 1999 Gemmell's work was displayed at Pillar House. Linn Products, begun in 1972 by its current MD, Ivor Tiefenbrun, now employ 200 in Eaglesham making upmarket audio equipment and home cinema sound systems.

## EARLSTON

**Map 3, B3**

***Borders large village,*** *pop. 1650* — OS 73: NT 5738

The earthen fort of Black Hill above the Leader Water and a standing stone 3 km to the north imply early significance for the area called *'Ercildoune'* or Earlston in Lauderdale. A *'hospital'* or almshouse had been provided by the 13th century; there was another at remote Legerwood, 5 km to the north. The poetic seer Thomas Learmont, called The Rhymer, was the proprietor of an estate and tower at Earlston, for centuries part of the Merse or Berwickshire. Cowdenknowes Castle 1.5 km to the south dates from the 15th century. In 1489, when it was a property of the powerful Bothwell family, Earlston was chartered as a burgh of barony. The peel tower is said to date from the 16th century. The impressive emparked *'Coldinknowes'*, with *'Ersiltoun'* and its Kirk were shown on Pont's map of Lauderdale, made about 1600 and engraved by Blaeu; a mill turned on the opposite bank of the Leader Water below *'Craiksfoorde'*. A parish school was established in 1607.

**Roads, Peace and Presbytery**: Earlston remained obscure until a new church was built in 1736, but it was not – as some imply – a new village. Roy's map of about 1754 showed *'Earls Town'* as a medium sized settlement quite similar in layout to the present day, but road links existed only to the east and south-east. Craigs Ford still crossed the Leader Water, the nearest mill being above the ford on the east bank. A millwright was based in Earlston by 1789, and two fairs were scheduled for 1797. In 1799 Heron referred to *"the town of Earlston"*. By then both the Tweed and the Leader had been bridged near Drygrange, 4 km south of Earlston, and a post office was open by 1813. In 1827 Chambers described Earlston as *"the seat of a Justice of the Peace Court for the ten neighbouring parishes, and was once that of the presbytery of Lauder. It possesses an excellent school, two great annual fairs for cattle, and is a place of considerable trade and manufacture. Though the population does not exceed 1000, there are at least 120 looms employed in the village. There is also a small but promising manufactory of shawl-cloths and ginghams, carried on by the Misses Whale"*. A water-powered woollen mill was built about 1830, and Earlston grew.

**The Railway Era**: In 1863 the North British Railway opened a branch line from Ravenswood near St Boswells to Earlston, then extended it across sparsely-peopled country to complete the route through Duns to Reston in 1865. Little development ensued, and in subsequent local government reform Earlston lost its burgh status. By 1894 it was once more a *"village"* to Murray, though the *Red Lion* was then a hotel. By 1905 there was a specialist draper's shop, Earlston also acquired a secondary school, and a late gasworks was provided in 1919. King's sawmills were opened, and also an agricultural engineering works, extending the buildings of an old mill. The textile mill made woollens and ginghams into the 1950s. In 1948 the railway lost several bridges through severe floods, and Earlston's passenger trains were permanently replaced by buses; the goods trains too had gone by 1966.

**Farm Machinery and Woollens**: Earlston's slowly rising population passed the 1500 mark about 1960, some new textile factory jobs for women were created on the site of the former station about 1970, and in 1975 Earlston was placed in Ettrick & Lauderdale district. It remained a village in terms of most facilities, but had the substantial Earlston High School, plus two firms of agricultural engineers, and Borders Region signposted the *'town centre'*. There was a considerable area of recent housing by 1980. In 1991 Earlston contained only some 1630 people; there has been some further development, and both Pringle's of Hawick, and Yarnwools of Selkirk, had factories on the small industrial estate.

## EASDALE, Ellanabeich & Clachan-Seil (Seil Isle)

**Map 4, C3**

***Argyll island communities,*** *pop. 550* — OS 55: NM 7417

The Earl of Argyll's Isle of Seil was noted by Monro in 1549 as *"good for store and corn"*. The slatey islet of Ellanabeich, just off the exposed west coast of Seil, was labelled with the corruption *'Ylen na Back'* on Blaeu's map, derived from Pont's sketches of around 1600. The production of black slate in the vicinity was believed to have started in the 15th century, with the collection of loose slabs from the shore. Wedges were next utilised to split away blocks of slate from between the tide-marks. Quarrying was certainly active in 1631, beginning at sea level and drained by a sluice at low tide. Around 1750, as Roy's map showed, marble was also quarried on the mainland at Ardmaddy opposite Balvicar, a working which soon faded.

*An Easdale slate quarry in 1904, one of many which were worked in the area from at least the 17th century. (British Geological Survey)*

All this area became part of the vast parish of Kilbrandon & Kilchattan.

**Excavations below Sea Level**: In the 18th century the use of a pump salvaged from a wreck, followed by the installation of a Newcomen pumping engine, enabled excavation at Easdale to continue below the low water mark. Seil was linked to the mainland in 1791–93 by a single arch of 21 m span, designed by Telford and built at Clachan-Seil over a narrow tidewater channel; it came to be called the *'Bridge over the Atlantic'*. The name of the settlement of Easdale on Seil came to be used for the smaller island nearby: Heron described Easdale in 1799 as *"the noted slate island"*. About 1807, when the quarry had reached 15 metres below sea level, a windpump was erected. In 1826 a new steam pump was installed, serving three quarries from which a tramroad linked to new wharves. A new village extension was laid out in the early 19th century, and Easdale post office first opened in 1824.

**Slate Quarries versus the Sea**: About 1841 some of the protective embankments gave way and flooded much of the mainland workings, but the laird – the Marquis of Breadalbane – pressed on, his workers producing about 7 million slates a year through the 1850s. By 1846 steamers on the Oban to Fort William service were calling at Easdale, though as late as the 1860s the Easdale slate was loaded on to a fleet of little sailing vessels of not much over 100 tons. Altogether nearly three-quarters of a million m$^3$ of slate had been extracted before a new company took over in 1867, employing about 300 men at the 50-metre deep Ellanabeich quarry and the 36-metre deep Windmill quarry. The community of 800, of whom 450 lived on the island, were Gaelic speakers and totally dependent on the quarries.

**Overwhelmed by the Ocean – and Devoted to Tourism**: Excessive excavation led to the surrounding protective banks being irretrievably breached by the waves in a November gale in 1881, and quarrying at Ellanabeich was abandoned, in favour of the generally flat islet of Belnahua, 5 km to the south, which also came to be dominated by slate workings to below sea level *(see Hay & Stell)*. The Belnahua workers lived in barracks, whose ruins survive. One of the mainland quarries was nonetheless still open in 1894, and in 1899 there was a school on Ellanabeich, by then holed by at least 8 quarries. With the rise of concrete tiles in the 20th century, Easdale and Ellanabeich became merely a pair of hamlets connected by a passenger ferry; more facilities, including a doctor, were to be found at the ancient kirkton of Balvicar 2 km to the east, where there was another small slate quarry until 1965. By 1978 Seil Island boasted a large tourist shop, *'Highland Arts Studios'*. By 1992 a folk museum had been created on Ellanabeich and by 1996 Clachan-Seil had housing development, Balvicar had a golf course, a garden was open to the public at Easdale, which had retained its post office, and the *Willowburn Hotel* operates at Clachan-Seil.

## EASSIE — Map 6, B2

***Angus hamlet**, pop. 300* — OS 54: NO 3547

Some 4 km west of Glamis Castle in Strathmore is Eassie, which has a very fine Pictish carved stone sheltered in its ancient church. It had a thanage from about the 11th century, now represented by a dry moat around Castleton House, itself built in 1902 to replace an older house on the castle site. When Roy mapped the area about 1750, Eassie Kirk stood on the road between Glamis and Coupar Angus. The early Newtyle & Glamis Railway of 1837, originally a horse-drawn affair extending the Dundee & Newtyle line, was rebuilt in 1848 as part of the main line of a constituent of the Caledonian Railway, and Eassie gained a wayside station. By 1951 a local farming population of 450 was served by basic facilities, but the station had been closed to passengers by 1963, by which time the old church was roofless. Rail goods traffic ceased in 1982, and by then the population had fallen to 300. The railway had vanished by 1987. In 1989 *Castleton House* became a 6-roomed hotel – for sale with its private grounds in 2000.

## EASTERHOUSE, Provan & Garthamlock — Map 15, E5

***Urban area, east Glasgow**, pop. 44,000* — OS 64: NS 6866

In the 15th century the fine Provan Hall was built on a hilltop 7 km east of Glasgow; Bishop Loch was the largest of a nearby chain of lochans. The Roy map of about 1754 also showed Provan Mill, at the end of a road from Glasgow. From 1778 this rural area was traversed by the Monkland Canal, which had lately been dug south of Provan Hall; horses drew the barges laden with coal. A branch of the North British Railway (NB) was opened south of the canal in 1871, linking Glasgow and Coatbridge, with a station named Easterhouse at Swinton, 2 km south-east of the Hall and only 1 km north of Baillieston. By

1895 wagon and tube works had been established beside the canal at Swinton, the nearby hamlet of Maryston had a post office and an inn, and soon a colliery was opened beside the canal at Garthamlock, 1 km west of the Hall.

**A8, Queenslie, Easterhouse and M8**: The area remained largely rural until after the A8 Edinburgh Road was built in the 1920s as a bypass for Shettleston. In the 1940s came the Scottish Industrial Estate Corporation's extensive yet reclusive Queenslie industrial estate. The huge Garthamlock and Easterhouse housing estates were created by Glasgow corporation in the 1950s. A young population was moved out of the city, totalling over 30,000 by 1971. There were secondary schools, but no industries, although the *'Township Centre'* which rather belatedly opened in 1973 provided some of the facilities of a small town: an enclosed shopping centre of over 5000 m$^2$, with library, sports centre, swimming pool, a Woolworth store and supermarkets; but banks, hotels, garages and cinemas notably avoided the area. The once pleasant canal lingered on as a forsaken waterway after closure in the 1960s, until destroyed by the construction of the M8 motorway close beside the Easterhouse estate in 1979–80. This detracted from its scant amenities and sat uneasily with the low car ownership in this already unpopular estate. In 1975 Olivetti built a typewriter factory on the Queenslie estate, where 250 jobs at Weir Pacific Valves were halved in 1979 due to falling demand.

**Poverty, Deprivation – and Opencasting?**: In 1981 the population had thinned out by some 10,000. By 1986 it had the dubious distinction of over 37% male unemployment; it shared with Riddrie the parliamentary constituency with the highest unemployment rate in Scotland. Yet to serve people with all that time on their hands, there was not even a golf course in the area, and opencast coal working proposed at Bishop Loch in 1989 was set to deal its environment yet another blow. It was reported later that year that most of the 44,000 people in and around Easterhouse were living in poverty, served by a single supermarket and one cashpoint. In 1990 the City District Council's housing improvement scheme was said to be having little social spin-off, and an attempt to launch a community radio station as *'East End Radio'* in 1990 attracted only 8000 listeners.

**Body Soap, Clothing – and Drugs**: However, in 1992 a newly formed organisation known as the Greater Easterhouse Development Company engaged staff to help to boost the area's feeble economy, by then aided by the new soapworks set up by the Body Shop chain. In depressed 1993 when the area already had serious drugs problems, Eliot Manufacturing kept 86 people busy making denim goods for major stores, and began to sell knitted denim garments under its own label *Hussy*. A 1994 scheme by the doomed Regional Council to create a new tram system to link Easterhouse to Partick and Maryhill via the city centre was put on hold. Today Lochend Secondary School has about 720 pupils and St Leonard's Secondary 520.

## EAST KILBRIDE & Hairmyres — Map 15, D6

***New Town, south of Glasgow,*** *pop. 70,000* — OS 64: NS 6354

A plateau about 160 m above sea level stands some 11 km south-east of Glasgow Cross; 2 km to the east is the 50 m deep valley of the Rotten Calder Water. East Kilbride had a medieval motte, a 12$^{th}$ century church and an extensive parish, whose school was founded in 1591. Various castles were built in the area: to the north is the 15$^{th}$ century keep of Mains, and beside the motte to the south-east the L-plan tower of Torrance Castle or House, built near the motte in 1570; the Pont map dated 1596 showed a bridge across the river nearby. To the south-west was the oddly named Lickprivick Castle, but this soon fell into ruin. The Peel, an L-plan tower, was built to the west about that time; from 1616 a school was held nearby. East Kilbride was known as a farming village in 1653 when the Society of Friends first met there.

**Barony Burgh and Route Centre**: William Hunter – who was born in the village in 1718 – studied at Glasgow University, became a famous surgeon, and bequeathed Glasgow's Hunterian Museum. Early in the 18$^{th}$ century East Kilbride was chartered as a burgh of barony, entitled to hold a weekly market and four fairs every year. On the Roy map made in the early 1750s, *'Killbryde'* was a compact smallish settlement with the remarkable total for the period of six radial roads: these led (among other places) to Kilmarnock, Rutherglen, Hamilton and Strathaven via the Bridge of Torrance. Shoemaking and muslin weaving became local crafts, and Heron wrote in 1799 of *"the village of Kilbride, where muslins, and cotton counterpanes, bed-covers are made in great perfection"*. By 1825 a cotton mill and a brewery were at work, and a post office was open by 1838.

**Railway, Machinery and Hairmyres Colony**: In 1868 East Kilbride became the terminus of a branch of the Caledonian Railway from Glasgow via Busby; this was optimistically extended to Hamilton in 1883. East Kilbride had a Clydesdale bank branch from 1876 and was *"a small town"* to Murray in 1894, when there was an inn. The East Kilbride golf club was founded in 1900, and laid out a course at Mount Cameron. The Hamilton railway link was a failure, and was closed to passengers in 1924, although a siding to the Mavor & Coulson mining machinery factory at Nerston, 2 km to the north, remained until 1966. Meantime from 1926 Rankin's buses based a fleet of up to 50 vehicles locally, though taken over in 1928 by a Glasgow firm. William Dickie & Sons made water pumps in East Kilbride by 1936. Three kilometres west of the village was the early 20$^{th}$ century Hairmyres Colony, a tuberculosis hospital, complete and having its own station by 1931.

**Hairmyres Hospital and Scotland's first New Town**: The *'colony'* was taken over at the start of the 1939–45 war and hastily transformed into a General Hospital. Agricultural machinery was also produced by 1946, when the three factories provided a total of 380 jobs. The population was 2400, served by the facilities of a large village, including the generous total of 40 shops, and the 280-seat *Picture House* cinema. In 1947 following the Clyde Valley Regional Plan, East Kilbride was designated as Scotland's first New Town, with a target population of 45,000; very soon the Department of Scientific & Industrial Research opened its important National Engineering Laboratory (NEL) at Birniehill, south-east of the village. By 1952 the New Town Development Corporation (NTDC) had geared up to enable rapid growth, and the *East Kilbride News*, a local newspaper established in 1952, recorded its progress.

**Rolls-Royce and a Decade of Growth**: Rolls-Royce of Hillington established a large branch factory for aero engines, opened at Nerston in 1953; among other new projects the V2500 and Tay jet engines were developed there. Hayward Tyler pumps transferred their plant from Edinburgh to Nerston in 1954, as did clothing manufacturers Laird-Portch Fashions from Glasgow, who employed 400 by 1970. In the mid 1950s the US companies Sunbeam Electric, making domestic appliances at Nerston, and Cincinatti Shaper engineering at College Milton industrial estate, north of Hairmyres, arrived; at the same time a Central SMT bus depot was built at Nerston, and Robert Wiseman started a dairy in a former piggery nearby. By the end of 1959 there were 23 new factories providing over 5000 jobs, and the population had reached 27,000.

**Speeding through the Sixties**: G H Barclay started to manufacture machine tools at College Milton in 1962, and from about that time Waterlow's printed the *Radio Times* nearby; by 1970 a factory of STC (Standard Telephones & Cables), and the BBC TV outside broadcast base for Scotland, were close by. The golf course soon vanished under housing estates, being replaced by two new 18-hole courses: the club moved 2 km north to Nerston, and an 18-hole municipal course was opened in 1969 farther out at Torrance House (which in 1996 stood modernised in the Calderglen Country Park). Burgh status was attained – or regained – in 1963, and the most rapid rates of growth in the new town occurred between 1966 and 1970, by which time four secondary schools had been built – Claremont, Duncanrig, Hunter and St Bryde's RC High. Among the large areas of new housing were nine 15-storey blocks of *'executive'* flats.

**The New Town Centre**: The sensible decision had been made in the Master Plan to develop a new town centre within easy walking distance of the old; by 1960 it had been begun and there were over a hundred shops, although its early Plaza shopping centre of over 5000 m$^2$ was rather undistinguished. The town's second hotel, the initially 10-roomed *Stuart*, was open in Cornwall Way by 1963. Alexander Henderson of Glasgow opened a department store in East Kilbride in 1964. Scotland's first Olympic-length indoor swimming pool, a new cinema and the central *Bruce Hotel* opened in 1968, and the rather impressive civic centre was complete by 1970. By then the headquarters of the Clyde River Purification Board stood at Birniehill. The tall office block of the Inland Revenue for Scotland, styled Centre One, was built west of the centre in 1968–70. A Marks & Spencer store opened in 1973.

**Fizz and Chips**: Schweppes began to build a mineral-water plant at College Milton in 1964 to serve the whole of Scotland, and in the same year Wyllie-Young set up close by in plastic injection moulding, making for example the Spirograph drawing toy. In 1966 the USA-owned Dictaphone factory was erected on the new Kelvin industrial estate south of the town, and the American firm Motorola opened Scotland's first semiconductor plant nearby in 1969. By 1970 Lansing Bagnall the electric truck manufacturers, BSR audio engineers, and John Macdonald from Pollokshaws, then making pneumatic tools, were large concerns at College Milton, and numerous other firms were producing (for example) paints and brushes. Rolls-Royce which then employed 3650 people in the town was in financial trouble by 1971, being taken over in the national interest until 1987.

**Reaching Maturity as Sunbeams are extinguished**: East Kilbride which had grown to 63,500 people by 1971 was for long regarded as one of the most successful new towns, and in 1975 it became the headquarters of a District within the new Strathclyde Region. Later arrivals included an Anderson Strathclyde branch engineering factory from Bridgeton, and a firm of meat packers: the total of local jobs peaked in 1978. The population was about 70,000 in 1981. Sunbeam – who had employed 400 in 1970 – had recently closed, and in 1980 some 1600 jobs vanished when Decca shut the factory making record-player decks. In 1981 the government's imposing office block for the Overseas Development Agency headquarters was built at Hairmyres, with some 600 employees by 1989.

**Recession – and Electronics**: Meantime came a recession: by 1983, when a second new municipal golf course was opened at Langlands, decline was becoming evident in the new town as Strathclyde plunged ever deeper into difficulty: 5500 jobs had been lost from East Kilbride in five years, and the estimated population had fallen slightly. Growth was renewed when in 1987 the Japanese firm JVC announced the building of a factory to employ 650 people making colour TV sets. A very large scheme begun in 1988 created a further superstore, the Olympia shopping mall, an ice rink, public library and a 9-screen UCI multiple cinema (open by 1991), and at that time it was hoped to incorporate a newly centralised railway station. In 1991 the town's resident population was about 70,425, and still quite young. In the same year 1991 Victor Technology, part of the USA-owned Tandy Group, opened a plant to make and repair personal computers for the European market, drawing their main processor boards from Wales; 130 jobs were provided, hopefully rising to 250; Matsuki, the Japanese electronics group trading as Panasonic, opened their first Scottish factory in East Kilbride, creating 130 jobs.

**Really Motoring in Electronics**: Meantime in 1989 Motorola had expanded on what they regarded as one of their *'premium manufacturing sites'*; in 1990 (when also starting to develop at Bathgate) they employed 1800 people at East Kilbride. In 1992 further expansion to make tiny chips – so compact that a 5 mm square could contain road maps of the whole UK – was to bring the firm's East Kilbride workforce to 2000. In 1995 Motorola, who claimed that East Kilbride was already Europe's largest silicon-producing centre, rebuilt their Kelvin site to make advanced chips for the Power PC, a joint project with Apple and IBM *(see Spango)*, and also acquired Digital's South Queensferry plant. By 1992 Linn Products (also in Eaglesham) made hi-fi equipment, and the Matsushita Industrial Equipment Company opened a factory to make TV components, about 150 jobs intended. In 1993 printed circuit manufacturers PCI of Singapore set up a factory in the town, expecting 300 jobs, and in 1994 Chicago-based International Components began on a 400-job manufacturing and warehousing complex.

**Closures and Losses**: Problems arose when 170 skilled scientific and technical staff were shed from the NEL, which employed 600 in 1989, under the research-hostile Thatcher regime's privatisation policies, which planned to turn it into the hub of a commercial science park. Anderson Strathclyde of Bridgeton, hit by mining cutbacks engineered by the same government, also announced the closure of their plant in the town in 1989, and the too-successful Wiseman's dairy was to close on moving to new plant at Bellshill. The US-owned Seagate Corporation which had created 220 jobs repairing hard-disc drives decided in 1991 to close the plant, and the computer company AST, US-owned since mid 1993, also closed its local plant in 1994, with 136 jobs lost; the work moved to Limerick.

**Rolls-Royce Roller-coaster**: In 1989 Rolls-Royce were seeking more space at their East Kilbride plant for their R&D and aero engine overhaul operations, but in depressed 1991 –

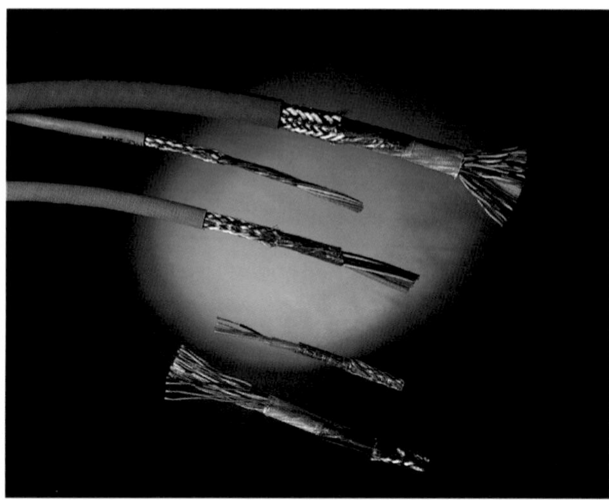

*Computer cables – one of the many high-tech manufacturing industries of East Kilbride.* *(SMPC / Bob West)*

despite this recent expansion – 300 jobs were cut, bringing the firm's Scottish employment total, including the Hillington factory, down to some 4500. In the recession of 1993 220 more of its jobs were lost. Due to defence cutbacks and completion of development of the Trent engine, in 1995 the firm very sadly decided to close its small-engine research and development centre at East Kilbride, with the loss of 600 design engineers and other highly skilled staff. The remaining R&D work was moved to Derby, depriving Scotland of one of its chief centres of excellence. However, 1100 workers remained in the adjacent main UK aero-engine overhaul centre, which in 2001 looked to have secured work for 20 years with a major engine maintenance contract.

**Museum, Golf – and the World's Tallest Fence?**: By 1996 an improved A725 road link north of Calderwood served an emerging northern and western outer bypass road which bounded three new housing estates at Stewartfield and College Milton. By 1990 the John Hastie Museum had an industrial collection. Hairmyres Hospital was being redeveloped, commencing in 1991. The Pro-Range indoor and outdoor golf driving range opened in 1993, its floodlit Astroturf surrounded by an amazing 30m high perimeter fence to allow its use at all times. A major retail development scheme at Stewartsfield was proposed in 1993 and a further 67ha housing site south of the town was approved in 1994. The 18,500m$^2$ Kingsgate Centre opened in 1994, as did Sainsbury's third Scottish store; by 1997 Sainsbury was building a distribution depot for its growing number of Scottish outlets.

**Simple Power and Simple Technology?**: Kelvin South Business Park was developed in 1991–92 with over 50 new units in the range 200 to 300m$^2$. In 1991 the National Wind Turbine Centre was opened on a nearby hilltop, and by 1992 John W Hannay & Co of College Milton were recycling paper and plastics. On the same theme in 1993 an American, Anne Evans, set up EER Europe to build an electricity generating station, to be fuelled by old motor tyres and employing 30 people; but this met with local opposition. In 1996 Simple Technology of California, founded in 1990 by the Moshayedi Brothers, opened its new European headquarters at Peel Park, initially employing 50 people to make computer memory products, but planned to rise to 360 by 1998, also making PC cards, Flash products and undertaking product development for the European and adjacent markets.

**Blending, Bottling and Beefburgers**: In 1994 the Barrhead whisky blending firm of Burn Stewart owned a bottling plant at East Kilbride. Galloways, a butchery chain which had become Scotbeef (meat processors), employing 280, landed a contract to supply Marks & Spencer. In 1994 the Mentholatum Company, manufacturer of medicines and part of a large group, relocated from the south to larger premises in East Kilbride. By 1995 the 31ha site of the NEL, which still employed 250 people, was owned by Scottish Enterprise and the Lanarkshire Development Agency, which renamed it the Scottish Enterprise Technology Park. By 2000 Micron Europe employed 250 people making electrical components, and were to recruit 160 more. Other significant hi-tech employers are Avex Electronics and Clyde Valley Systems (in electronics manufacture), Fuji Electric (semi-conductors), and Smart Modular Technologies (computer memory), plus Field Packaging and Jeyes Chemicals in the 'old economy'. There is now an oil distribution depot at College Milton.

**After the New Town and District, a National Museum**: The NTDC was wound up in 1995, and in 1996 East Kilbride was merged into *'South Lanarkshire'* unitary authority, based in Hamilton – a double blow to the hitherto so successful new town, which by then was 7km across. Its High Schools were the early 1980s Ballerup (657 pupils) and St Andrew's (526), plus the older Claremont (1204), Duncanrig (1040), Hunter (768), and St Bryde's RC (849). The Georgian Kittochside Farm north of College Milton – gifted to the nation by the Reid family, its owners for over 400 years – has now been transformed into the Museum of Scottish Country Life, reopening in 2001 as a working farm run on traditional lines, and replacing the museum at Ingliston. The new Hairmyres Hospital opened in June 2001. The Centre West shopping development by British Land and Stannifer is due for completion in 2002, a Debenhams branch providing 300 jobs is to be its anchor store. There are now at least five sizeable quality hotels, as well as cheaper operations.

## EAST LINTON & Prestonkirk — Map 3, B2

***E. Lothian village**, pop. 1400* — OS 67: NT 5977

Ancient cultures come together here in East Lothian. About 3km north of the Brythonic hill village site on Traprain Law *(q.v.)* is a standing stone, typically Pictish; the nearby place-name Linton shows an intriguing combination of languages, the Anglian *–ton* having been added to the Gaelic *Linn*, referring to the waterfalls on the River Tyne. The 13th century Hailes Castle stands 2km up river, while down-river of the little falls is Preston (*Priest-town*) Kirk, also of 13th century origin. Biel House 4km east of East Linton existed by the 14th century, followed a century later by Whittinghame Castle, 4km to the south. In 1567 Hailes Castle was briefly the home of Queen Mary and Bothwell. A bridge had been built across the river's rocky ledges at the falls by the time that Pont made his sketch map of Lothian about 1600, when it already carried the Edinburgh to Dunbar road. West of Hailes stood the *'Munkmil'*; Preston mill was built in the 17th century. Terraced gardens were laid out at Biel House in 1647 by the

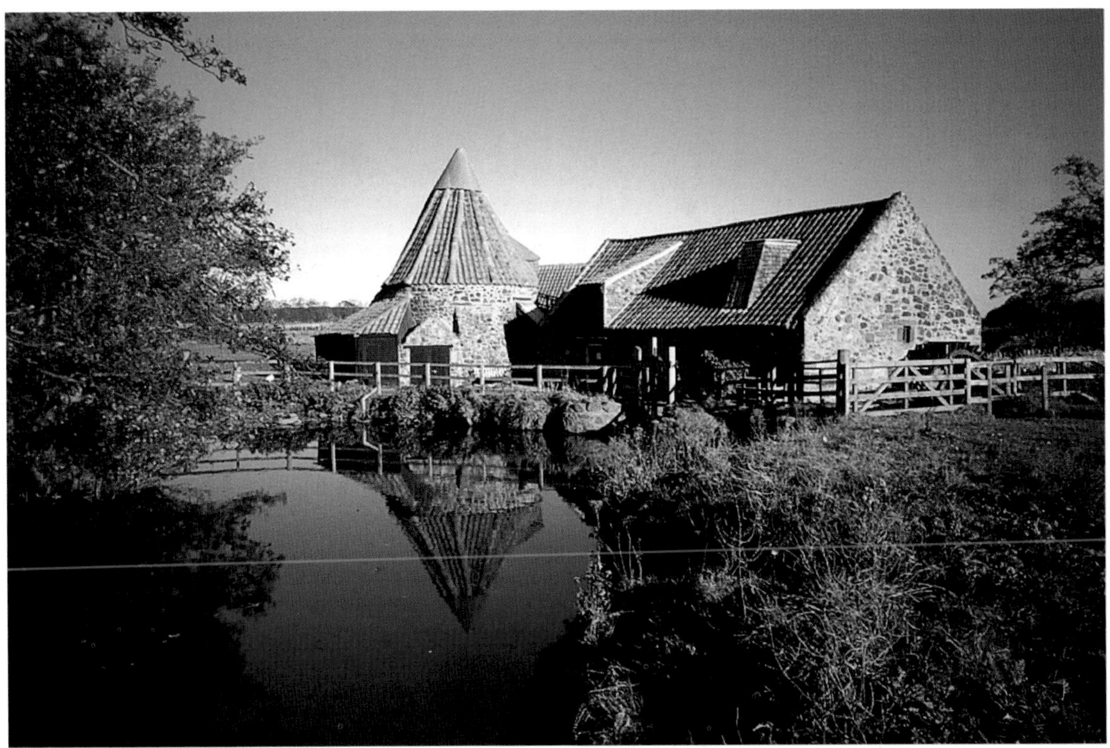

*Preston Mill, East Linton, dating from the 17th century but rebuilt and re-equipped on several occasions. It is now a NTS property.* *(JRH)*

first Lord Belhaven and the mansion was repeatedly enlarged, both in 1760 and in 1814–18, becoming a palatial pile 180m long.

**More Mills, Roads, Woollens and Famous Sons**: In the 1750s the Roy survey showed *Sandy's Mill* opposite the site of the Munkmil; there was another mill between Hailes and the small group of buildings at *Lintoun*. Neither this nor Preston ever became a burgh of barony, though they were already linked by road; from Preston other roads led to Newbyth and Markle. East Linton had woollen manufactures in 1776, and was described as a *"thriving village"* by Heron in 1799; but it was comparatively unimportant, for a post office first opened only in 1801. Chambers noted in 1827 *"the handsome and populous village of Linton"*. Phantassie near East Linton was the birthplace in 1761 of the great civil engineer John Rennie; he started as a millwright and became one of the greatest of the early civil engineers, designing many bridges *(see Kelso)* and the Crinan Canal. John Pettie, born at East Linton in 1839, became a fashionable painter of historical subjects. More notable was Arthur James Balfour, born at Whittinghame Castle in 1848, who became the First Lord of the Admiralty, an Earl, and took a leading part in promoting the controversial state of Israel.

**A Flirtation with Railways**: The North British Railway main line was opened in 1846, with a station beside the village. By 1901 East Linton had a small livestock market, a mill, an inn and a gasworks. At the heyday of railways East Linton had seven passenger trains each way on weekdays. Part of the huge Biel House was demolished about 1952, but the rest was saved. In 1953 the population was some 1550, whose facilities included a library, an agricultural engineer and a typical range of services; but the market was no longer recorded, though its octagonal timber sale ring remains. The station was closed in the mid 1960s.

**Development**: By 1980 the tiny *Harvesters Hotel* had been enlarged to 13 rooms by 1980. A new hard rock quarry was opened about 1979 some 2 km west of the village, to replace that at Traprain. In 1990 the National Trust for Scotland claimed that their Preston Mill was the oldest working water mill in Scotland. The population of East Linton, which had declined to 1350 in 1981, rose again to 1422 in 1991, bringing in a quite affluent retired element, and in 1993–94 a substantial new housing estate was built at the west end of the village. By 1994 Findlay's bottled water from the Lammermuir Hills at Pitcox near Stenton (5 km south-east of East Linton) as *'Presmennan Well'*.

## EASTRIGGS & Dornock

**Map 2, C5**

***Dumfriesshire village,*** *pop. 1900*

OS 85: NY 2466

Timothy Pont's map of around 1600 showed Eastriggs, Dornock and its Kirk as elements in a thickly settled area on a low ridge between the Solway and Nutberry Moss. Dornock parish school was started in 1633. The ridge formed a natural routeway between Annan 5 km to the west and Gretna – followed by a road by the time of the Roy survey of about 1754. A tiny stream draining the moss cut through the ridge between Dornock and Eastriggs, where a water mill was erected. The railway built between Gretna and Dumfries, opened in 1850 as part of the Glasgow & South Western main line, had a station at Dornock; to the east was the hamlet of Lowthertown.

**The Hidden Factory**: A very extensive explosives factory was built south-east of Eastriggs during the 1914–18 war, the area remaining a blank on subsequent OS maps. Dornock station – having become important – was renamed Eastriggs. Eastriggs grew rapidly, but acquired only the facilities of a small village, despite a population in 1951 of almost 1800, which continued to grow slowly to some 1900 in 1991. The lengthy bypass which opened in 1989 had relieved both villages and Annan of the through traffic on the busy A75 route to Northern Ireland. The explosives factory was still rail-connected in 1992, and the MOD still operated its 60 cm gauge railway on the Eastriggs site in 1995. The village pub and post office are still open, and tramways in Nutberry Moss to the north are part of Richardson's peat diggings.

## EAST WEMYSS

**Map 6, B4**

***Fife coastal village,*** *pop. 1750* — OS 59: NT 3497

The cliff-top ruins of the 14th century Macduff's Castle on the south coast of Fife stand on only 2m of rock above the Well Cave, one of several nearby that contain Pictish carvings. They are accessed from the shore close to East Wemyss, whose name derives from *Uamh*, Gaelic for *'Cave'*. Nearby was a medieval quarry and quay, and a village existed by about 1600. Blaeu's map following Pont's originals marked it as *'South Weemis'*: very strange, for it is well north of West Wemyss! From about 1750 linen was woven on a commercial scale, and of very good quality; by 1794 there were 120 looms. A wagonway had been built for the Seventh Earl of Wemyss, leading from a local coal pit, probably north of the ruined castle, to his port of Methil. East Wemyss was noted in 1799 by Heron as a *"village"* of over 500 people.

**Superior Linens, Collieries and Railway**: In 1807 local linen manufacturers won five of the Board of Trustees' eleven prizes for the best Scottish linen fabrics. In the 1820s Chambers found East Wemyss *"perhaps somewhat cleaner and handsomer than the rest of the fishing villages"*. Around 1830 Maw Colliery worked 2 km north-west of the village; it had completely vanished by 1895. Meantime by 1864 G & J Johnston employed about 200 scattered hand weavers, but also had 100 workers in their recently built 200-loom power weaving works, and were soon to replace all the hand weavers. The Fife Coal Company (FCC), formed in 1872, opened the Wellsgreen colliery near the site of Maw in the 1880s. It went down 151m to the Dysart Main seam, and was served by a spur from (the misnamed) *Wemyss Castle* station, on the railway built by the Earl of Wemyss between Thornton and Buckhaven in 1879–81. In 1889 the line which also served the Rosie pit became part of the North British (NB). The 1891 population was 1010.

*The Michael Colliery, sunk by the Wemyss Coal Company from 1892. This one-time model pit was Scotland's largest at nationalisation in 1946. A tragic under-sea fire in 1967 caused nine deaths, and brought immediate closure.* (JRH)

**Michael Colliery, Private Railway and Trams**: The Wemyss Coal Company's large Michael colliery was planned as a model pit, sunk on the coast from 1892–98 to a depth of 245m. It worked the steep Chemiss seam under the sea, but – despite its model village – its railway lines and yards damaged the coastal environment, as did East Wemyss gasworks, sited on the shore 250m east of Macduff's castle. The Wemyss Private Railway (WPR) was promoted by the Wemyss Estate in 1898. This extended northwards from a connection to the NB, collecting spurs from the Earlseat and Cameron pits, also open by 1901, and led eastwards to a triangular junction at Denbeath for coal exports through Methil docks. The WPR had its workshops and central sidings at Scotts Road; other lines from the Michael colliery converged nearby. The many jobs in mining and related railways caused East Wemyss to develop greatly, to 2500 people in 1901. From 1904 until 1932 the Wemyss & District Tramway Company, promoted and partly financed by Randolph Wemyss, linked the village with Leven, and across country to Gallatown (and so to Kirkcaldy).

**Jimmy Shand Music – and Scotland's Biggest Pit**: Jimmy Shand, son of a ploughman turned miner, was born in East Wemyss in 1908; as a highly gifted self-taught musician he created the tradition of accordeon music for Scottish country dancing, and with his talented band became world-famous. He was honoured locally by the name Shand Terrace, and shortly before his death in 2000 was belatedly knighted. In 1928 a third shaft, 540m deep, was sunk at the Michael colliery to work the Lower Dysart seam, and with other improvements completed, nearly 950,000 tonnes were raised annually in 1935 to 1939. In 1946, on the eve of its takeover by the National Coal Board (NCB), the Michael was the largest pit in Scotland; it had a famous pipe band. By 1951 East Wemyss accommodated 3600 people, with the facilities of an average village and extensive (mainly mineral) railways – the WPR and most of the houses by then belonging to the NCB. In 1949–53 the Michael shaft No. 2 was deepened by 288m to the great depth of 830m, then probably the deepest in Scotland, but further investment was neglected by the NCB in favour of the white elephant pits at Rothes and Glenochil.

**Tragic Fire extinguishes Mining**: Wemyss Castle station was closed to passengers in 1955 with the others on the British Rail (ex-NBR) branch, on which freight traffic ceased in 1963. The cinema had already closed, in 1959, the year the Wellsgreen pit with its short-lived drift extension ceased work. Meantime the supposedly long-life Michael colliery's output had declined after 1955 due to underground redevelopment to access its huge undersea reserves; an explosive underground fire in 1967, which sadly caused nine fatalities, caused its immediate closure. The secondary school and chemist at East Wemyss also closed around that time; only 2050 people remained in 1971, and by 1981 further decline had left small-village facilities. The population then stabilised, 1762 residents being counted in 1991. The pumping of water from the former Michael Colliery workings was ended in 1995, and the headgear was immediately demolished. However, large reserves of high quality coal remain under the Firth of Forth. The seaside linen works of G & J Johnston Ltd is still at work, and a substantial private housing scheme is growing west of the village, on a site partly marred by past development.

## ECCLEFECHAN & Middlebie — Map 2, C4

***Dumfriesshire village & hamlet,*** *pop. 850* — OS 85: NY 1974

Ecclefechan, central among many historic localities, stands on low ground near the Mein Water, a tributary of the River Annan. Four kilometres to the north, Burnswark farm adjoins one of Scotland's most spectacular ancient hill forts, which was palisaded about 500 BC. Within some later pre-Roman defences arose a settlement of round huts which was later invested by Roman camps; nearby passed the Roman road from Carlisle into Strathclyde. Near the site of the parish centre of Middlebie, 4 km south-east of Burnswark, this road served the important first and second century Roman fort of *Blatobulgium* or Birrens, which although of under 2 ha in area was also a cavalry base, and eventually acquired as many as six defensive ditches on the uphill side; it contained stone-lined wells and channels among its many cramped stone buildings. The Birrens fort was occupied until about 180 AD and was excavated in 1895, the first modern style *'dig'* of Roman remains in Scotland *(Johnson).*

**Churches, Coaching and Frequent Fairs**: Ecclefechan has a name of Cumbric Christian origin which may go back to the seventh century, though its first known mention was in 1296. Pont's map (made around 1610) showed the Kirk of *'Egilfecchi'*. Kirkconnel Hall dates from 1720. The *Ecclefechan Inn*, built about 1734, later became a coaching inn. The Roy map, made about 1754, showed a linear village astride the road from Carlisle to Lockerbie and the north – then a very poor sort of highway. Road improvements later in the century enabled a fast *'diligence'* to connect Glasgow, Carlisle and London from 1781, and a mail coach on this route passed through from 1788. Ecclefechan was a post town by 1797, and the birthplace in 1795 of the schoolteacher, historian and philosopher Thomas Carlyle. With twelve fairs a year, it was among the four most frequently used fair stances in Scotland. These monthly cattle markets were *"great"* in 1799 when in other respects Ecclefechan was just a *"village of over 500 people"* (Heron). Ecclefechan in 1827 was seen by Chambers as a *"thriving and sweet little post-town, remarkable for its frequent and well-attended markets and fairs"*.

**On the Rail Wayside**: These seem to have faded away by 1847, when a station was opened on the new Caledonian Railway, because from the start this was of the village type labelled *'second class'*, less important than Gretna, Lockerbie or Beattock. In 1894 there was still the inn, later renamed the *Ecclefechan Hotel*; but the village never seems to have acquired any significant industries apart from the small Cleuchbrae Mill, nor did it become a burgh. By the 1950s – with the exception of three hotels and the Carlyle museum – it had only the facilities of a small village, and Ecclefechan railway station was closed by the early 1960s. The village became a backwater when the A74 bypass was opened about 1970; its population reduced slowly to 844 in 1971, then remaining virtually static to 1991. By 1984 a caravan and camping site was open. Today, the village boasts two hotels – the *Ecclefechan* and the *Kirkconnell Hall* – and a post office; the A74 bypass is now a sinuous motorway.

## ECHT — Map 10, B3

***Aberdeenshire village,*** *pop. 200* — OS 38: NJ 7305

Echt lies in a fertile area 20 km due west of Aberdeen, sheltered by the bulky Hill of Fare and 2 km south-east of the Barmkin of Echt, a prominent hill fort. Pont's manuscript map of about 1600 showed Echt as a kirk and a range of buildings in a well-settled area. The Roy map of about 1750 showed a track linking Banchory with Castle Fraser; beside it was Echt kirk – rebuilt as one of Scotland's finest small Georgian churches – and to the south-west was a mansionhouse named Grantsfield, which had vanished by 1894. By then Echt crossroads had a post and telegraph office and an inn. From 1905 motor buses of the Great North of Scotland Railway linked Echt with Peterculter – soon running direct to Aberdeen – and in 1906 the railway also bought up the Echt carrier's steam lorry. By the 1950s a population of 300 had the facilities of a small village; the junior secondary class in the local school soon ceased. Despite a council estate built in the 1960s and the addition of a small garage, the population had declined by 1971 to only about 225. By 1986 the inn was just a pub; there is little recent housing, but the primary school, sports field, post office stores and the old stone village hall remain.

## EDAY, Isle of — Map 13, C2

***Small island, Orkney,*** *pop. 166* — OS 5: HY 5730

Ancient remains abound on the narrow rolling Isle of Eday, some 12 km long. In the 12th century, sandstone from Fersness on Eday was used to build St Magnus' Cathedral in Kirkwall. Off Eday's northern end lies the islet known as the Calf of Eday, which shelters the curving channel of Calfsound. This was described by a note on Blaeu's map (engraved from Pont's originals of around 1592) as *"an excellent good road"* – i.e. an anchorage (emphasised by two ships). Carrick House near Calfsound was built in 1633 for John Stewart, Earl of Orkney. In 1735 Calfsound people owned the 50-ton vessel *James and Jannet* which sailed on the Leith service. By 1841 nearly 1000 people lived on Eday and much peat was shipped out, but within a century the population had halved, primarily agricultural. In the mid 20th century the piers were served by passenger ferries, and primary schools and post offices were open at either end of the island. By 1974 an airstrip had been laid out in the middle. By 1980 the *Eday Hotel* was open and sea angling was available. By 1984 the car ferries between Kirkwall and the other northern isles called at a new pier at Backaland at the south end of the island. The island's population in 1991 was 166, and by 1997 a seasonal youth hostel was open near the airstrip. The northern post office and southern school are still open.

## EDDERTON — Map 9, B2

***Easter Ross small village,*** *pop. 250* — OS 21: NH 7185

A Pictish stone on the coast of the inner Dornoch Firth adjoined the old Kirk of Edderton *('Edardin'* in Blaeu's atlas of 1654); this was replaced in 1743 by the present church. The Roy map made about 1750 showed a track westwards from Tain passing the kirk and hamlet at Edderton, and there was possibly a mansionhouse at Ardmore. Edderton became known as *"the parish of the peats"*, and *"abounded in smuggling bothies"*. A small brewery, probably opened as early as 1749, was officially converted into the Balblair Distillery in 1790. From 1864 Edderton had a station on a constituent of the Highland Railway, though in 1886 Barnard found trains from Tain *"so infrequent that it was impossible to make use of them"* to visit the distillery. This had been rebuilt on a new site about 1870 by Andrew Ross & Son; the *"very small and old-fashioned"* old buildings had been retained as bonded warehouses. Its annual output in 1885 was about 225,000 litres of Highland malt. A parish library commenced in 1900. Edderton station was closed in 1960, for it never served more than a hamlet, with a population around 250 in 1978, when there was a general shop. Balblair distillery, which remained seemingly independent in 1976, was part of the Hiram Walker empire by 1991. In 1994 its Balblair single malt was bottled at ten years old by Gordon & MacPhail of Elgin. Far North road traffic was removed in 1991 by the new Dornoch Firth bridge; there has been little recent development, but an inn and post office remain open.

## EDDLESTON

**Map 3, A3**

***Village n. of Peebles,*** *pop. 500* — OS 73: NT 2447

When Timothy Pont mapped Tweeddale about 1600 there was already a bridge across the Eddleston Water about 7 km north of Peebles, between *'Eddilstane'* Kirk and Darnhall; this former seat of the Murray family, in an area known as the Black Barony, was rebuilt in the 17th century as a turreted four-storey mansion. Pont's map-work also showed two mills, Hatton and Kirkton. An early mansionhouse at Cringletie, 3 km south of Eddleston, was built in 1666. By the time the Roy map was surveyed around 1754, the Edinburgh–Peebles road passed beside Eddleston Kirk. Heron noted Eddleston as *"a pretty populous village"* in 1799, while Chambers in 1827 described it as *"a neat village"* with an annual fair for black cattle and hiring. Neither mentioned the *Horseshoe Inn*, which may well have existed by then (and continues today).

**The Scott Monument and Railway Era**: George Meikle Kemp, born locally in 1794 and the son of a shepherd, became a millwright and taught himself the art of architecture, earning undying fame when in 1838 he won the open design competition for Edinburgh's Scott Monument – though he sadly drowned before it was completed. By then Eddleston had lately acquired a post office; by the 1890s this also boasted a telegraph office and there was still a mill at the Kirkton; the 1891 parish population was 535. The Peebles Railway, which later became a part of the North British system, was opened in 1855 with a station at Eddleston. Cringletie House was demolished about 1861, when a new mansion of pink Dumfries sandstone with lavish oak interiors was built to designs by David Bryce and took its name. It lacked the extensive policies of the mansion of Darnhall, which by 1953 had become the *Black Barony Hotel*. The railway was closed to passengers in 1962 and a few years later the track was lifted.

**Tourism and an Important New College**: Cringletie House became a hotel in 1966. In the late 20th century Eddleston remained a small village with facilities to match and a stable parish population, of 507 in 1991. The *Black Barony Hotel* became the *Barony Castle Hotel*. Whatever the reason, this change was apparently unsuccessful, because the 30-room mansion – complete with swimming pool and leisure complex in 9 ha grounds – was sold in 1995 to become by 1997 the new Scottish Ambulance College. The better-loved *Cringletie House Hotel* continues, as do the primary school and post office, plus the nearby Coweslinn quarry.

## EDINBANE

**Map 8, A2**

***Village, N. Skye,*** *pop. 200* — OS 23: NG 3450

The head of the long sea Loch Greshornish on the north coast of Skye has a waterfall and an ancient broch; it was well settled when Timothy Pont made his crude map around 1600. The crofting township of Edinbane or Edinbain which lies on the road between Portree and Dunvegan gained a large early primary school, an inn and post office. Its remarkable 12-bed Gesto Hospital was founded by a tea planter, Kenneth MacLeod, and later enlarged to 19 beds. In 1951 Edinbain's facilities, in general those of a small village, served some 225 people, a number which fell to about 175 by 1971. Recovery then began, with much afforestation of the hills to the south, and Edinbane was prospering in 1988, with a well-kept council estate and a new village hall. A small venture called Greshornish Shellfish started up in 1990. At that time its tourist facilities included two hotels, restaurant, B&Bs, plus the Marshall Sports Centre and a large pottery-cum-shop. By then the Gesto Hospital catered only for the chronic sick; it was proposed for closure in 1992, angering local opinion, but is still going. There is a caravan site, and *Greshornish House* at the mouth of the loch is a hotel.

## EDINBURGH

**Map 15, C1**

***Capital city (central area)*** — OS 66: NT 2573

Suburbs: *Balerno, Colinton, Corstorphine, Craigmillar, Cramond, Currie, Davidson's Mains, Fairmilehead, Gilmerton, Gorgie, Granton, Leith, Liberton, Morningside, Newington, Portobello, Restalrig & Sighthill*

On either side of a precipitous rock, originally the plug of a large volcano, lay great hollows ground out by ice sheets over 10,000 years ago, and filled by freshwater lochs. This rock, readily defended against attack from the west, north and south, commanded the narrowest part of the Lothian plain between the Pentland Hills and the Firth of Forth. Archaeologists have found on its summit many flint implements dating back at least 3500 years, and in 1990 unearthed hearths and the foundations of timber buildings dating from 1000 BC; evidently an Iron Age stronghold existed on this superb defensive site or *'Crag and Tail'*, now known as Edinburgh Castle Rock. A Roman brooch and remains of fine quality pottery of the late first century AD have been unearthed there, and settlement continued into the second century.

**Bone of Contention between Picts and Anglians**: According to Chambers the rock was *"first mentioned by historians in 452, when it was taken by the Saxons, from the Picts"*; they retook it, but again lost it to the Saxons. It was fortified in the sixth century when briefly held by the Anglian Eidyn, Edwin or Agned, King of Deira; once more recaptured by the Picts, its name became *Din Eidyn* or Dunedin – *Eidyn's Fort*. It was again seized by the Northumbrians under King Oswald about 640 AD, and a Royal defensive work was built there, which became a base for the Anglians' northwards and westwards thrust into Gaeldom, and for holding off Danish attacks. It seems to have been the town of *Guidi* mentioned by Bede in 731. A millennium later, Defoe commented on the castle well of *"prodigious depth"* which provided very good water. This must have been dug at an early date, for the fort was soon adjoined by a tiny settlement on the *'tail'* of higher ground which forms a natural ramp extending eastwards from the protective crag to the low ground of Holyrood. Heron wrote that the first St Giles' Kirk was *"said to have been founded in 854"*.

**Enter the Scots, Holyrood and Canongate**: Edinburgh temporarily fell into Scottish hands about 960 AD, and in 1020 Malcolm II permanently annexed it to Scotland. The fort standing on *"the hill of Agned"* was regarded as a Royal castle by 1093 when Queen Margaret died there; to commemorate her on site, the St Margaret's Chapel was soon built in stone. Her son David as ruler of Lothian and Strathclyde founded Holyrood as an abbey in 1118, granting to it the existing Dean mills on the Water of Leith. St Cuthbert's church was already in existence when he succeeded to the Scottish throne in 1124. In 1128 David created the manor of Coates in Drumsheugh Forest, between mills and castle, and chartered the Canongate between St Giles and the Abbey to the latter as an Ecclesiastical Burgh. Edinburgh's earliest charter dates from 1124, and about 1161 it became the caput of the Lothian sheriffdom. The Royal High School was started in the 12th century, and in 1230 Alexander II founded a large Dominican friary; by about then a *'hospital'* was open. Little development other than horn, antler and bone working has been dated from the 13th century, and Lothian was merely an archdeaconry of St Andrews in 1274.

**Growth, Seizure and Forging Ahead**: From 1296 Edinburgh was held again by the English, and greatly fortified: in 1313 the castle was according to Barbour a *"stronghold wondrous well furnished with men and victual so that it feared no man's might"*. But in 1314 it was besieged by the Scots under Thomas Randolph, Earl of Moray, and boldly recaptured by a force led by William Francis, carrying a short ladder up the rock by a most perilous route. Barbour told how at Bruce's command *"both tower and wall"* were subsequently demolished by undermining. Returned to Scots rule, Edinburgh began to gain rapidly in importance, being one of the original *Four Burghs* which established the Convention of Royal Burghs. Edinburgh's contribution to burgh taxes rose steadily, from 15% in 1326–31, when it was only half that of Aberdeen. The treaty of 1328 in which England reluctantly agreed to Scottish independence was signed in Edinburgh; thus encouraged, in 1329 the town council acquired the port and mills of Leith *(q.v.)*, and immediately overtook troubled Berwick and remote Aberdeen as the principal source of Scottish customs revenue.

**Emerging as Scotland's Capital**: Demolished about 1330 by David II, the castle as Royal property was soon rebuilt, and again fought over. Perth, Stirling, and (on occasion) Forfar had provided the locale for sittings of the Scottish parliament since these resumed in the late 13th century. Before the Black Death Edinburgh was just one among several places where the king signed Royal charters, but afterwards few were signed anywhere but Edinburgh. In 1360 Froissart told of nearly 4000 houses and noted that Edinburgh was already regarded as the capital. By then the castle was the usual residence of the king and was being strengthened in stone. St Giles was first reported as the High Kirk when burned by the English in 1385; it too was promptly rebuilt in stone by 1387.

**Official Capital and Trading Centre**: It was in 1437, the year that the famous 508 mm bore cannon *Mons Meg* was imported from Flanders, that Edinburgh officially deprived more central Perth and Stirling of the title of *Capital of Scotland*. The place was growing rapidly, with Leith soon dominating Scotland's wool trade. Already Edinburgh's trade with Danzig was substantial, that city having a factor resident in Edinburgh. About 1449 the *Cordiners* (shoemakers) of the city were incorporated. Edinburgh was defensively walled in 1450, possessed goldsmiths by 1457 and became one of Scotland's three Supreme Court centres in 1458; as the capital it consequently became Scotland's main legal centre, and from medieval times up to 1707 the town council had sole charge of the standard measure of length, the Scottish Ell (just over a yard). The Greyfriars (Franciscan) friary was founded in 1455–58, but lasted only until 1490; its precinct was used from 1602 for Greyfriars Church. Three collegiate church organisations were set up: Trinity before 1460, St Giles in 1467, and St Mary of the Fields in the early 16th century.

**Trade, Industry, Stone Buildings and the Law**: The skinners and weavers were incorporated by the town council in 1474–75, followed by the Hammermen (smiths) in 1483. By 1477 fifteen specialised markets were held in various parts of the city. By 1485 there was a notary in the Canongate, where stone buildings suitable for subdivision into tenement flats began to appear around that time. A hospital was set up in Leith Wynd in 1479 and another in the Cowgate about 1537. Around 1500 trade was mainly in wool, hides and woolfells, in all of which Edinburgh was increasingly dominant. Printing was brought to the city in 1507 by Walter Chapman and Andrew Myllar. A cannon foundry was at work in the castle by 1508, and after the debacle of Flodden, a larger area was enclosed by the walls in 1513. Fourteen craft guilds were at work by 1523, and in 1528 Holyrood Palace was erected for James V. According to Chambers it was in the 1520s that Edinburgh became *"the seat of the Courts of Justice, then for the first time rendered stationary"*. In 1530 there were as many as 288 alewives (registered home brewers) and by 1533 the *'Society'* quarry was open. From 1535 to 1556 Edinburgh alone contributed over 40% of Scotland's burgh taxation.

**Mid 16th century Prosperity**: In 1544 Holyrood Palace and Abbey were among buildings burned by Henry VIII's troops, but the Palace was soon repaired. In 1558 Edinburgh had a population of about 12,000, including about 367 merchants and 400 craftsmen; there were then 10 bakehouses – each employing up to nine workers, and so breaching the increasingly obsolete craft rules. By 1560 a theatre had been built outside the built-up area at Greenside (Leith Walk) on a site long occupied by recreational activities. In 1560 both the burgh and Holyrood – a very important Cistercian abbey – were represented in Parliament. No fewer than 25 churches were appropriated to the abbey, dominating the Lothians and also including Kirkcudbright. From 1561 Queen Mary based her court at Holyrood and for six years the city resumed rapid growth, its prosperity being shown by the goldsmiths, then ranked among the city's most important trades; there were then at least 31 lawyers in the city.

**War, Reformation, University – and George Heriot**: The melee of Queen Mary's deposition in 1567 led to civil war, in which the Edinburgh printer Thomas Bassenden, like most city people, took her side. The Castle's half-moon battery was built

*A typical northward view down a narrow medieval close off the High Street.* *(JRH)*

in 1574, at which time there were seven mills in Edinburgh. In 1582 the Protestant town council set up the University, the fourth in Scotland, and by 1593 Edinburgh was the centre of a presbytery. It was estimated that in 1583 the city held about 500 merchants and as many craftsmen; half of the latter were tailors. In 1586 the Skinners and the Goldsmiths (the latter until then members of the company of Hammermen) both formed their own companies in Edinburgh; George Heriot, born in Gladsmuir in 1563, became the Royal goldsmith in 1597 and later bequeathed nearly half his large fortune to the city. Meantime the Canongate had become a burgh of barony in 1587, and in 1591 a new tolbooth was built there. It was reckoned in 1592 that the little city contained 8000 people.

**Road Communications about 1600**: The map engraved by Blaeu (after Hondius c.1612, after Pont's originals of about 1600), showed 12 'ways' leading from Edinburgh, clockwise: (1) to Leith; (2) to Musselburgh and the east; (3) to Dalkeith and Lauderdale *(part Roman origins)*; (4) to Lasswade, Heriot and the Gala valley; (5) to Auchendinny and Peebles; (6) to West Linton *(part Roman origins)*; (7) to Currie and *Causewayend* (south of Kirknewton), for Hamilton; (8) to Roseburn, Corstorphine, Livingston and Blackburn; (9, 10) (off route 8) to Bangour (two routes to W. Lothian border); (11) to Linlithgow and Linlithgow Bridge; (12) to Cramond and Queensferry. It is likely that quite lengthy parts of at least some of these ways had been hardened after some permanent fashion, for Causewayend which was near House of Muir some 16km from Edinburgh, still merited a name on Roy's map a century and a half later.

**Edinburgh takes the Industrial Lead**: The Society of Brewers was formed in 1596, and Edinburgh became Scotland's premier brewing centre when in 1598 a common brewhouse was established at Greyfriars. In 1599, twelve city mills were grinding malt and grain. A generation later Brereton called the brewhouse *"vast"*, noting that it supplied the whole city with beer and ale. Apparently less successful was the outcome of the group of Flemings brought in about 1600 to teach broadcloth manufacture. In 1603 William Mayne of Edinburgh made golf clubs for James VI, enabling him to teach the game to his new courtiers in England.

**Union of Crowns: Postal Headquarters and High Buildings**: The headquarters and effective key sorting office of the Scottish Post Office were in Edinburgh from its tiny beginnings in 1603 *(Haldane)*; there was another office in Canongate from the start. Buildings rose to seven storeys by 1618, when the population was around 25,000 and there were about 475 merchants. Buildings were already being converted to new uses: the hospital of 1479 became a workhouse in 1619, where Dutchmen instructed pauper children; but two years later the guild of Tailors were wealthy enough to begin the construction of their Hall in Cowgate. By 1621 Edinburgh and Leith were paying 44% of Scotland's non-wine Customs duty, and 66% of the wine duty. In 1632 the *'Society'* quarry employed 20 men; Parliament House was erected in 1631–41, to designs by James Murray of Kilbaberton. In the 1630s, shortly before Presbyterianism finally took over, St Giles' church became the cathedral of a new Church of Scotland diocese. Some displaced worshippers built the Tron Kirk in 1636–47, to designs by John Mylne Junior.

**The Congested City**: There were 134 tailors in 1636 when Edinburgh acquired the superiority of the Canongate, and there were realistically perhaps 30,000 inhabitants (various sources give estimates from 20,000 to 60,000!). Whatever their number, at around that date David Buchanan commented on the city's extreme congestion. The majority of Edinburgh folk were regarded by the English traveller Brereton in 1636 as *"most sluttish, nasty and slothful"*. Edinburgh, though by far the richest city in Scotland, was undoubtedly a smelly place with no hygiene, poor water and no drains, rewarded by outbreaks of plague from which 20% of the population died. The solidly built Mary King's Close, a warren of rooms abandoned during a plague attack in 1642 or 1645, was later used as a plinth on which to build the City Chambers; it is still accessible by arrangement. Meantime Heriot's Hospital was under construction: building work took from 1628 to 1693!

**Transport, Fire Fighting and Publishing**: In 1636 goods were still dragged on sleds through the steep cobbled streets, but the rich were served by *"some few coaches"*. In 1652 there was a *'journey coach'* to London, at first taking a fortnight. In 1649 the Corporation bought Portsburgh (the West Port area) and had it chartered as a burgh of barony. In 1650 James Colquhoun built an early fire engine for the city, also supplying one to Glasgow; though its feeble hand-pumped jet could surely not reach the top of the 8-storey buildings of 1656. Despite poor transport, congestion and filth, learning was spreading: Andrew Hart was a busy publisher in Edinburgh from 1610 to 1621, probably his most important work being Napier's book of logarithms. The *Mercurius Politicus* – Scotland's first newspaper – appeared in 1655, an edition of a London paper; from 1661 this became more truly Scottish as the *Mercurius Caledonius*, appearing weekly; it was soon renamed the *Kingdom's Intelligencer* and continued for some years.

**Education in the later Seventeenth Century**: The French traveller de Rocheford wrote about 1661 that the University had *"a pretty good library"*. The Advocate's Library (now the National Library of Scotland) was founded in 1680, and the university appointed three professors of medicine in 1685. Heriot's Hospital had become a boys' school by 1689. The

Mary Erskine School for Girls, founded in 1694, was among the first in Britain devoted to teaching girls, very soon followed by three more – in 1695 the Edinburgh Ladies' College (a private day school), the Trades Hospital in 1704 and the Merchants' Hospital in 1707. By 1689 there were 40 booksellers, printers and binders and 46 gold- and silversmiths in Edinburgh, when they were rare elsewhere in Scotland; many armourers also existed. Lawyers made up 62% of the professions in Edinburgh in the 1690s, medicine another 22%, and the city had a near monopoly of wigmaking, then a sign of high class, for by this time the city's unique and lasting combination of culture, snobbery and low life was firmly entrenched.

**City Improvements – and Destruction**: Sir Robert Sibbald, born in the city in 1641, became Geographer-Royal and co-founder of the *physic garden* (forerunner of the Botanical Gardens) planted at Holyrood in 1675. In 1678 the first irregular stage coaches struggled to and from Glasgow, and in 1681 a *lead* pipe at last brought otherwise reasonably pure running water from Comiston. Congestion in the medieval walled city was still growing: the adult pollable population in the late 17th century was over 14,000, with concentrations in manufacturing, professional and merchant categories; the richer elements and nobility were pandered to by over 4000 domestic servants. In 1689 Thomas Morer noted a building near the Parliament House (probably Robertson's Land) that rose to 14 storeys at its underbuilt rear. Holyrood Palace was extended under Charles II and refurbished by James VII in 1687; but the abbey was sacked by a Protestant mob as the unpopular king (known in England as James II) fled to France in 1688.

**Making the Banks and Re-making the Money**: The Bank of Scotland was established by an Act of the Scottish Parliament in 1695. Its first branches were opened in 1696 in Glasgow, Aberdeen, Dundee and Montrose, but they very soon proved to be abortive, and the bank remained centralised in Edinburgh till 1731 and beyond. The Scottish Mint, which melted down and recast the old currency in 1707, was in the Cowgate. John Law, born in Edinburgh in 1671, set up the National Bank of France. The official *Edinburgh Gazette* first appeared in 1699. An estimate by Mackie of some 60,000 people living in the city by 1700 may overstate the congestion, but its squalor was undoubted.

**Famous Sons of the Union**: A hiatus in development followed the loss of its parliamentary role to London in 1707, yet Edinburgh remained unchallenged by Glasgow as Scotland's principal city until much later in the 18th century, its lawyers and businessmen turning from serving the court to the promotion of activities in many other parts of Scotland. Their entrepreneurship was aided as the main radial roads were turnpiked under an Act of 1713. George Drummond, born in the city in 1687, later established the (Royal) Infirmary of Edinburgh. James Short, born locally in 1710, became a well-known maker of astronomical instruments, and in 1739 was the first surveyor of the Orkney Islands. The philosopher David Hume was born in 1711, and James Hutton born in 1726 became the founder of the science of geology. However, his major treatise *"Theory of the Earth"* (1795) was before its time.

**Retail Trade, Marketing and Culture**: Defoe devoted many pages to a lyrical description of the city in the 1720s; only the briefest extracts can be given here. To him the Royal Mile was *"perhaps the largest, longest and finest street not in Britain only, but in the world"*. The tall buildings lining it were by then largely built of free-stone, and patrolled by uniformed town guardsmen; but the centrally situated Tolbooth or prison was *"a miserable hole"*. Defoe noted the weekly sales of woollens, linens, mercery and drapery goods that took place in the Lawnmarket; the West Bow's wholesale traders in *"iron, pitch, tar, oil, hemp, flax, linseed, painters colours, dyes, drugs and woods"* mostly had warehouses in Leith, from which place the road and 6 m-wide *'walkway'* – Leith Walk – were both stone-paved. There were separate markets for herbs and fruits, meal, flesh, poultry, and butter; the Grassmarket also held cattle sales and a weekly horse market. Defoe found a museum at the Surgeons' Hall, and there were numerous churches. Besides divinity and ancient languages, the University already taught history, law and mathematics by 1725. Although the Convention of Royal Burghs and the General Assembly of the Church of Scotland still met in the hilly city, Defoe opined that its fine defensive site also gave *"infinite disadvantages, and scandalous inconveniences"*, particularly a shortage of water and space.

**Better Medicine, Royal Bank and Golf**: The opening of the first Infirmary in 1719 heralded great progress in medicine; in 1725 Provost George Drummond founded the University Medical School. Alexander Munro, born in the city in 1733, was to become the discoverer of the lymphatic and nervous systems. Meantime the Infirmary was chartered as the Royal Infirmary in 1736; two years later it acquired new buildings. The Royal Bank of Scotland – now Scotland's largest company – had been formed in 1727. However, a second attempt in 1731 by the Bank of Scotland to establish branches in Aberdeen, Dundee and Glasgow had failed within two years. Meantime in 1728 came the first circulating library. Golf was played on Bruntsfield Links by 1735, the traditional date of foundation of the Royal Burgess Golfing Society; the Bruntsfield golfing society was formed in 1761. Both now have suburban courses *(see Cramond & Davidson's Mains)*. John Watson's College *"for the sons of decayed merchants"* (Heron) was founded in 1738.

**Printing and Publishing**: The publication known as the *Scots Postman* originated early in the 18th century, while from 1718 there was a second newspaper, the *Edinburgh Evening Courant*; the *Caledonian Mercury* was established in 1720 by Thomas Ruddiman, a printer who was also the keeper of the Advocates' Library. The enduring *Scots Magazine* (now produced in Dundee) was first published in Edinburgh in 1739, and general printing expanded, reaching full professional levels of quality with new firms in 1734. By 1740 there were four printing firms, and Neill & Co, established in 1749, raised the standards still higher; by the 1770s there were 27 competing firms. James Boswell the biographer was born in the city in 1740, and in 1747 a theatre was established at Playhouse Close in the Canongate.

**Textile Trades**: Framework knitters from Haddington worked in Edinburgh by 1706, and linen yarn was long traded, boiled and woven commercially in the city: by 1718 damasks were woven in a workshop at Drumsheugh *(see also Dunfermline)*. By 1728 weaving was thriving beside the Water of Leith, and in 1729 the Board of Trustees settled a colony of French weavers in Picardy Place. By 1733 Edinburgh was also an important centre of woollen manufacture, making *"fine shalloons"*. In 1744 Fountainbridge at the west end of town saw the first premises with six or more looms, and a bleachfield was soon in operation; by then a company was lapping and pressing cloth for the London market. The Picardy Place weavers gave rise to the British Linen Company of 1746, which soon supervised and funded the trade throughout Scotland. In 1750 came a ropery, an unusual textile development for an inland centre. Woollen cloth was still hand beetled in a *'lapping house'* in the 1760s. A yarn staplery was established in 1749 to sort and deal in linen yarn, more linen bleachfields were built from 1746, and the city had a main linen stamping office by 1760. By 1757 a linen weaving works was busy in the Canongate, but this had run down by 1770, and the linen hall established by the Trustees in 1766 was not a great success either, despite being aided by the British Linen Company; by 1770 the latter had switched to banking only, and never looked back, whereas the linen hall closed in 1790.

**Coaches and Coachbuilding**: Coachbuilding began in the city in about 1696. It was re-established on a commercial basis in 1738 by John Home, who had gained experience in London; yet even in 1750 a coach ran only twice a week to Glasgow, in summer only. By 1753 a stage coach provided a service to London, still taking a fortnight en route, yet so quickly were the roads improved that from 1758 a regular wagon service operated to Newcastle and London, taking only a week; the Netherbow Port which obstructed this traffic was demolished in 1764. From 1763 a heavy four-horse coach ran three times a week to Glasgow, becoming daily in 1765. Coachbuilding prospered, for by 1766 coaches were being exported, while George III's state coach was an Edinburgh product that was still in use in 1869. (Despite the later inroads of railways, buses and cars, Edinburgh supported some specialists in coachbuilding until at least 1980.)

**Bells, Brewing and Distilling**: In 1737 John Taylor was a bellfounder *"in the Calton"*. In 1740 Archibald Campbell built the Argyll brewery in the Cowgate, and William Younger's Holyrood brewery at Abbeyhill followed in 1749. By 1750 Drybrough's brewery was also at work in the Canongate. In 1763 the nascent Botanic Garden moved to a larger site on the west side of Leith Walk, to be replaced by Combe Delafield's brewery; yet another brewery was opened in 1765, by James Yates, and the Heriot Brewery was started about 1770. Whisky was popular – too popular in fact – for in 1777 there were eight legal and around 400 illegal distillers in Edinburgh!

**Bursting Point: Squalor, Sin – and Fashion Portraits**: The ancient, filthy, overcrowded city, where in the mid 18th century at least four paper mills had rag stores, was about ready to explode. Perhaps the last straw for living conditions was the major clearance required to fit in the Exchange, designed by John Adam and built in 1753–60; later this became part of the City Chambers. The old city's low life was immortalised when a directory of its brothels and prostitutes was printed in 1775! By then the city had an excessively overcrowded population of 57,000, among them the young James Craig, locally born in 1740, who first became an architect and then the planner of the much needed and extraordinarily successful New Town of Edinburgh. Another talented local lad, the precocious James Donaldson – later of Hospital fame – was born in 1751; in 1764 at the age of only thirteen years he started a significant periodical, the *Edinburgh Advertiser*. Born into the squalor in 1756 – but destined for finer things – was Sir Henry Raeburn, who by the end of the century had become the leading portrait painter of the rich.

**Public Works: Water, Drainage, Posts and Bridges**: A cleaner city was essential: by 1761 cast-iron pipes had been laid to bring pure water from Comiston, 6km to the southwest; this was then pumped up to a reservoir near the Castle, and by 1799 3 million litres a day were available. The stagnant Nor' Loch was drained in 1759–63, and the first North Bridge, designed by Robert Adam and William Mylne, was constructed across the resulting bog in the years 1763–72 to give better access from the High Street to Leith Walk. From 1773 Edinburgh had a penny post, using *'caddies'*. In 1785–86 a ford across the Water of Leith was replaced by a stone bridge known as the Stockbridge, and the South Bridge of nineteen arches – designed by Robert Adam to cross the deep valley of the Cowgate – was built in 1786–88.

**The 1767 *New Town***: Masons, Sawmills and Mound: Meanwhile in 1766 the layout for the famous New Town had been designed for the City Council under the energetic Provost Drummond by the 22 year old James Craig, who also laid out Dunoon, though his career fell into obscurity. When work began on the plateau north of the old Nor' Loch valley in the following year it finally gave the city room to breathe – stone dust, lime, sawdust and paint fumes! Six thousand masons worked on the construction of the New Town for decades, and at least seven water-powered sawmills were soon at work on the Water of Leith to provide carcassing and joinery. Bearford's quarries were open beside the Nor' (or North) Loch through much of the 18th century, but were last heard of in 1770 when an embankment was steadily growing across the valley from spoil excavated in the New Town. A road on its crest – the Mound – was opened in 1781; to either side were left the hollows that in time were to become the sites of Princes Street gardens. But Heron noted in 1799 that despite drainage of the area between the Old and New Towns, *"the morass that remains is still known by the name of the North Loch"*. In that year a post office was opened at Castle Street in the New Town.

**Burgeoning Culture**: Pennant noted that in 1769 there were 600 students in the University, and by 1789 there were almost 1100, including 400 studying medicine. Quickening culture created the pioneer edition of the *Encyclopaedia Britannica*, printed and published in Edinburgh in 1768–71 by Colin MacFarquhar, William Smellie and James Tytler. Printing was of course expanding, with 27 firms of varied quality by the late 1770s. At that time the poet Robert Fergusson (a great influence on Burns) was describing the characters and life of the Old Town, but he died young in 1774, and is buried in the Canongate Churchyard. The prolific author Sir Walter Scott, born in the city in 1771, was soon to keep them extraordinarily busy; another successful local novelist was Susan Ferrier, born in 1782, one of the relatively few Scotswomen of the age who were able to break into a worthwhile career. In 1789 new buildings were commenced for the University by Robert Adam, but in 1794 work was suspended due to the war with France; they were described by Chambers as *"the largest public building in Scotland"* and eventually completed

*An aerial view of the New Town of Edinburgh, laid out in grand style from 1767 onwards to a plan by James Craig, a young local architect.* *(SMPC / Doug Corrance)*

to cheaper designs by Robert Reid and W H Playfair in 1827–34.

**Public Buildings and Banks**: Meantime General Register House, designed by Robert Adam, was built opposite to the north end of the new North Bridge in 1772–74 as the Public Record Office for Scotland. The fine Dundas House on the east side of St Andrews Square was designed by Sir William Chambers and built as a private house for Sir Laurence Dundas in 1771; it became the Excise Office in 1794. The Bank of Scotland head office remained in the Old Town; its first successful branches were started at Dumfries and Kelso in 1774. In 1791 a Bridewell – a prison *"on an improved plan"* – was built on the Calton Hill, in what was later to be named Waterloo Place. Post offices opened in 1793 at Chapel Street near George Square, and in Hanover Street. The first set of Assembly Rooms had been completed by 1799. Heron stated in 1799 that *"new barracks have lately been built on the west side of the castle"*, and that Queen Street was then the most northerly in the city. The last building to Robert Adam's designs was the north side of Charlotte Square, posthumously commenced in 1800.

**Centre of Medical Advance: a Strawberry a day?**: In 1769 the Royal Infirmary had 200 beds; a public dispensary was established by Dr Duncan in 1776, and the Royal Society of Edinburgh was founded in 1789. In 1799 the High School had over 400 pupils, and the Edinburgh Medical School was famous. The Museum of Natural History was a creation of the University's professor of that subject in the early 19th century. Recreation was catered for by the Circus, the Concert Hall, and the *Theatre Royal* which stood in Waterloo Place. As a sidelight on life at the time, Heron observed that the equivalent of over 225,000 *litres* of strawberries were sold in a season in the city and suburbs! He thought that a figure of 85,000 for the population of the same area was an underestimate, so there was an average of three litres of strawberries a head, rich or poor!

**Diverse Industries of the late Eighteenth Century**: Tobacco processing began about 1770 and stationery manufacture in 1780. By 1778 there were also several tanneries around the city, among them Allan Boak's at West Port. The Dean Tannery was started by the Leggets at around the time that Alexander's began footwear manufacture in 1783. With many varied trades and industries, the city's renewed importance was confirmed when the Chamber of Commerce was founded in 1785. A brassfounder named Wall was working in Edinburgh about 1787. Distilling (legal and illegal) continued to flourish: in 1799 Heron noted that *"one of the most extensive distilleries is that erected near Canonmills"*; this had been founded by James Haig about 1780, and worked until about 1840, later becoming a maltings. Meantime in 1815 an unlicensed still was found in an arch under South Bridge, and close by was another, beneath the Tron Kirk!

**Textiles for the Tsarina**: In the 1780s David Foulis was manufacturing Jacquard hand looms, for the fine linen trade was prospering, with about 1500 looms engaged when it peaked about 1788; floorcloth manufacture – heavily painted coarse linen – was established by 1787, but later concentrated into Kirkcaldy. In 1790 the one-time hospital workhouse was converted into a woollen factory by Archibald Macdowal; by 1796 this employed many hands, working with fulling mills and a spinning jenny. At that time blankets were made by Jeeves, and others wove carpets; there was a regular wool market, selling 200 tonnes of wool a year, and the trade concentrated on the top end of the market, making cashmeres and royal gowns which were exported to the Russian empress in 1793. Heron observed in 1799 that *"button manufactories have lately been established and starch has been of late manufactured in great quantities"*. In 1799 Patrick More was calendering and glazing cotton on machinery of his own design, and in 1813 Francis Blair was making linens by water power, probably at Dean village.

**Sedan Chairs and Crane-necked Carriages**: In 1779, 400 sedan chairs still provided the rich with what we would now think of as a third world type *'taxi'* service around the growing city of Edinburgh, for there were only nine hackney carriages for its 70,000 people. From 1783 the journey between Edinburgh and Glasgow took only 12 hours, by combining coach and the Forth & Clyde Canal from Falkirk. In that year an astoundingly large order for a thousand crane-necked carriages for use in Paris was being fulfilled by efficient Edinburgh coachbuilders at about one per day. From 1790 the London coach was greatly speeded and took only two days; in 1797 it used 28 *'stages'* or relays of horses, by any of four routes. From 1792 a light coach ran three days a week between Stirling and Edinburgh. By 1799 the Glasgow coach took 6 hours; by 1814 two coaches plied daily to Stirling. By 1819 there were five daily coaches between Edinburgh and Glasgow, and by 1825 eight Royal Mail coaches and over fifty stage coaches left Edinburgh each day, including ten to Glasgow and six to London. Some of the latter would have crossed the massive Regent Bridge, built in 1816–19 to designs by Archibald Elliot, linking Princes Street more directly with East Lothian. He also designed the elaborate Episcopal church in York Place, built in 1816–18, and the heavily classical Broughton Macdonald church of 1820–21.

**Hotels, Inns and the Union Canal**: In 1799 Heron admired *"the hotels and inns of Edinburgh for elegant accommodation, and ready service"*; in 1803 Dorothy Wordsworth found the White Hart in the unfashionable Grassmarket *"not noisy, and tolerably cheap"*. She was most impressed by the old town, which *"far surpassed all expectation"*. But her further comment that *"a cloud of black smoke overhung the city"* tended to confirm its nickname of *'Auld Reekie'*; it was only in 1817 that coal gas supplies became available, and gradually Edinburgh's direct dependence on coal fires decreased. The old Tolbooth in Waterloo Place was demolished in 1817, replaced by *Johnstone's Hotel*; the *Waterloo Hotel* was open by 1823 and the *Douglas Hotel* by 1845. In 1822 the Union Canal was opened from Camelon near Falkirk to Port Hamilton, a terminal basin east of Gardner's Crescent; another basin – Lochrin – adjoined Fountainbridge.

**Milling, Insurance, Lighthouses and Post**: From about 1800 two flour mills at Dean came into one ownership as Bell's Mills; Greenlands Mill just downstream milled animal provender from around that time until horse transport faded early in the 20th century. The lofty West Mill was built in 1805, and Boag's snuff mill in 1816. The *Scottish Widows* insurance concern was founded in 1815. Thomas Smith, an Edinburgh tinsmith, was the first engineer to the Northern Lighthouse Board from 1786; in the 1820s Smith's works at Greenside was peopled by *"tinsmiths, coppersmiths, brassfounders, blacksmiths and japanners"*. In 1832 the Board set up its long-standing headquarters offices in 84 George Street. Alex Kirkwood & Co of Edinburgh made all the Scottish postal date stamps from 1829 to 1924.

*Croft-an-Righ Brewery, near Hoyrood Palace – one of many breweries in the city in the 19th century.* *(RCAHMS / JRH)*

**Antiquities, Astronomy and Artistry**: About 1800 the National Museum of Antiquities was formed. In 1818 the Edinburgh Astronomical Association founded the Calton Hill Observatory; this moved to Blackford Hill in 1896. The Royal Scottish Academy was also established in 1823, just predating the National Gallery of Scotland. Robert Chambers, travel author about to turn publisher, noted that the School of Arts (Edinburgh College of Art) founded by Leonard Horner in 1821 was *"a huge specimen of Grecian architecture"* erected in 1823–26. The famous sculptor William Calder Marshall was born in Edinburgh in 1813.

**The Publishing Industry**: Thomas Nelson & Sons started printing and publishing in 1798, the *Edinburgh Review* began to offer literary criticism in 1802 and Adam & Charles Black started their famous publishing house in 1806. In 1817 *Blackwood's Magazine* was founded as a monthly and *The Scotsman* first appeared as a newspaper; some time after 1832 this incorporated the older *Caledonian Mercury*. In 1846 another little-known Edinburgh-based newspaper was in publication, the *Scottish Herald*. John Bartholomew entered the map-engraving business soon after 1820. In 1823 Sir D Hunter Blair and J Bruce of Edinburgh, as the Royal printers, produced a finely printed book of Common Prayer – for the Church of England and Ireland! In 1832 William Chambers founded *Chambers' Edinburgh Journal*, and with his brother Robert went on to produce their encyclopaedia, and a Scottish gazetteer; James Thin first sold books in 1848.

**Famous Edinburgh Architects and Bank Designers**: The Bank of Scotland Head Office, designed by Richard Crichton and Robert Reid, was built on a steep site at the head of the Mound in 1802–06; they had 43 branches by 1860.

In 1825 the Royal Bank took over Dundas House from the Excise Office. William Playfair, born locally in 1789, designed many buildings including the Royal Institution, opened on the Mound in 1836, and the Church of Scotland Assembly Hall. William Burn, also born in 1789, drew plans for Camperdown House near Dundee, Falkland House and many fine banks. David Bryce, born in the city in 1803, designed the fine Union Bank office in George Street and the British Linen Bank head office on St Andrew Square, opened in 1851; he also largely redesigned and extended the Bank of Scotland Head Office in 1864–70.

**Early Nineteenth Century Education**: Robert Chambers wrote *"all those families of the nobility and gentry, whose fortunes do not enable them to encounter the expense of a London residence, resort to this city for the enjoyment of society, and the education of their children"*. Not only the rich benefited: the Institution for the Deaf & Dumb, founded in 1810, had a new school built at Henderson Row in 1823–24. Daniel Stewart's Hospital started in 1814, and the Dick Veterinary College in 1823. The Edinburgh Academy for Boys, an independent day school, was founded in 1823 by Sir Walter Scott and others and moved into new premises designed by William Burn at Henderson Row in 1824. In 1827 Heriot's maintained and educated about 180 boys, and John Watson's School of 1825–28, also designed by Burn, rather fewer. The classical Royal High School buildings in Regent Road were designed by Thomas Hamilton and built in 1825–29, this 12th century foundation moving from a site near Surgeon's Hall.

**Modern Athens?**: Chambers wrote that a fancied resemblance *"has caused the city to receive the ridiculous appellation of the 'Modern Athens'"*. There were then said to be about 8000 lawyers in the city (1 in 20 of the population), but under 4000 University members. About 1825 the Royal Botanic Garden moved from Leith Walk to rural Inverleith. In 1826 the new Haymarket Inn marked the city's western limits. Cobbett noted in 1832 the *"fine and well-ordered streets of shops in this beautiful city, and its still more beautiful environs*"; he lectured in the *Adelphi Theatre*, which could seat over a thousand people. In 1832 Telford's four-arched high level Dean Bridge was erected, and the nearby Orphan Hospital was built in 1833. The 6-storey Donaldson's Mill of 1828 later became a warehouse. In 1830 the will of James Donaldson, printer and publisher, established Donaldson's Hospital for the education of the deaf; its buildings, designed by the busy and talented Playfair, rose slowly at West Coates from 1841 to 1851.

**Brewing and Varied Industries**: James Ritchie began to manufacture clocks in 1807; the firm still exists. Maintaining the alcoholic tradition of the city, St Anns brewery at Abbeyhill dated from the early 19th century, and Stein's large Canongate brewery was built in 1800. The Holyrood Brewery was enlarged three times to 1850. In 1825 some 28 breweries were still crammed into the old city centre, particularly the Canongate and Cowgate; James Usher began brewing in Chambers Street in 1831, the Argyll brewery was greatly expanded in that decade, and Barnard's Canongate brewery in 1840; but many soon failed. The Holyrood Glassworks was established in the early 19th century, and in 1820 Craig & Rose *(see Leith)* began to mix paints. By 1827 drug manufacture had also begun. *'Edinburgh Rock'* was first made in 1820, Mackie's shortbread appeared in 1832, and Crawford's started baking biscuits in 1852; but by then sugar refining had failed. Whytock began to weave carpets and damask in George Street in 1807 but moved production to Lasswade in 1840. Meantime the fine linen trade of 1788 was halved by 1822, and production in Edinburgh had ceased by 1869.

**Bankruptcy breeds Accountancy**: The Commercial Bank of Scotland had been formed in Edinburgh in 1810, and by 1825 the ill-fated Maberly of Aberdeen had a branch bank in the capital. By 1827 Midlothian County Hall in the Lawnmarket was *"a modern edifice devoted to the use of several courts connected with the county"*. But the city council went bankrupt in 1833, ruined by the mismanagement of its oligarchs. As more practical financial management came in, the world's first accountants were chartered in Edinburgh. The Edinburgh & Leith Bank and the Dumfries-based Southern Bank of Scotland, both joint-stock banks founded in 1838, merged in 1842, and in 1844 became part of the Edinburgh & Glasgow Bank, which in 1858 was absorbed by the Clydesdale Bank.

**Great Inventors and Scientists of the World**: The Grove House Engine Works of Edinburgh built six steam carriages, designed by John Scott Russell and used in a Glasgow to Paisley service in 1834; they were successful until a boiler explosion rigged by the turnpike trustees destroyed confidence in this novelty. James Syme, born in Edinburgh in 1799, discovered the solvent for rubber which was later patented by the better-known Charles Macintosh. The steam hammer and machine tools were invented by James Nasmyth, born in Edinburgh in 1808. The science of thermo-dynamics was founded by William Rankine, another Edinburgh man born in 1820. Alexander Graham Bell, born in the city in 1847, joined his family in educating the deaf, emigrated to the USA and there almost by accident invented the telephone (1874–76). Another Edinburgh emigré, John Ponton, born in 1842, first proposed telephone exchanges *(see Mackay 1997)*. Brothers Archibald and James Geikie, born in 1835 and 1839, both became famous geologists; Archibald became Director of the Geological Survey.

**Shops and Monuments, Worthy and Unworthy**: By the early 19th century the city had become renowned as a shopping centre; in 1838 came the origins of Jenners' department store in Princes Street (which by about 1912 employed 560 people in imposing premises). Meantime, to cater for the other extreme of society, the turreted Calton Jail was built in 1840, extraordinarily sited almost opposite the Royal High School of 1829. Francis Chantrey designed the huge statue of George IV, erected in George Street in 1831 for no better reason than his being in 1822 the first British monarch to deign to visit Scotland in over a century! In 1840 George Meikle Kemp *(see Eddleston)* designed the ornate Scott Monument, built on Princes Street in 1844–46 to commemorate the author-sheriff. The bronze statue of that arch-Conservative the *'Iron Duke'* of Wellington, produced by the appropriately named sculptor John Steell, was placed at the junction of Princes Street, Leith Street and the Bridges in 1848.

**Edinburgh's Early Railways**: The first line in the area, the Edinburgh & Dalkeith Railway, actually terminated outside the centre at St Leonards *(see Newington)*. The Edinburgh & Glasgow Railway (EGR) opened to a terminus at Haymarket station in 1842; William Wordie immediately opened a rail to road cartage depot there, and by 1869 there was a locomotive depot nearby. Haymarket station's present oddly offset layout came about in 1846, when shallow tunnels were dug and rails laid through Princes Street Gardens to link with the new North British (NB) Railway and Berwick, creating the General Station (the first *'Waverley'*) and the company's HQ *(see Ellis, 1955)*. The Edinburgh Leith & Granton Railway which improved access to Fife and the north was opened in 1847 from a terminus at Canal Street Station (later the site of the Waverley Market). It passed beneath the New Town through the Scotland Street tunnel, so steep at 1 in 27 (almost 4%) as to require cable haulage. The tunnel approached Waverley Station at a right angle, preventing the latter's reconstruction to deal with the more important east–west traffic.

**Railways bring Tourists from England**: The largely English-financed Caledonian Railway (CR) made its original HQ in Edinburgh's George Square from 1845; in 1848 it opened its line to Carstairs, Carlisle and so to London from a makeshift station at Lothian Road. Wordie & Co had a cartage depot there by 1860, and by 1869 the CR had a locomotive shed. The CR created Princes Street Station in 1870 by extending their line up to Princes Street; but its buildings long remained squalid for a city terminal. The Trinity collegiate church was taken down in 1848 to enable improvement of the emerging East Coast main line to England, completed in 1850; the EGR was absorbed by the NB in 1865. In 1854 Alexander Smith noted the already great impact of summer tourism on the city: trains had at last made Edinburgh accessible.

**Public Buildings and Entertainment in the mid Nineteenth Century**: The Assembly Rooms in George Street date from 1843 and the Edinburgh Stock Exchange was opened near St Giles in 1844. The earliest reference to *'zoological gardens'* in the city yet found by the writer is 1848 *(see also Corstorphine)*. The Trades Council was founded in 1849, and St Cuthbert's Co-operative Society in 1859. In 1858 the discerning German traveller Fontane found the 40 year old *Johnstone's Hotel* already decrepit; picturesque closes in the Old Town were filthy, and there were still *"few vehicles on the road"*. In 1863 circuses and plays came to what became the *Queen's Theatre* in Nicolson Street, later called the *Hippodrome*; in 1892 this became the site for the 2000-seat *Empire Palace Theatre*, which in 1896 showed the first cine film to be seen in Scotland. The *Alhambra Music Hall* in Nicolson Street was built about 1863; it failed in 1886 (as the *Royal Princess*). In 1875 the *Gaiety Music Hall* was created in Chambers Street; later known as the *Operetta House*, it was ultimately a cinema.

**Educational and Cultural Development**: Meantime the National Gallery on the Mound had been built in 1850–58. New buildings for Daniel Stewart's, by that time a private boys' school, were erected in 1849–53. Another independent school – Fettes College – was begun in 1868, built of Burntisland stone to designs by Burn and Bryce and opened in 1870 on the north-western edge of the city at Comely Bank. Lansdowne House School for Girls was founded in 1879 by the Misses Fenton and Emerson. The Royal Scottish Museum was established in 1861 as an industrial museum, its main building being opened in 1866. Opposite it in 1872 there commenced the building of the Watt Institution & School of Arts, which merged with George Heriot's in 1885 to form Heriot-Watt College; brewing was one of its earliest subjects – very appropriately, for there was a brewery behind it! Thomas Clouston, born in 1840 in Orkney, became a pioneer in treating mental illness and for 35 years the physician superintendent of the Royal Edinburgh Asylum.

**Telegraphs, Post and Press**: In 1853 the Bank of Scotland head office was connected to London by electric telegraph, and business entered the era of speedy reaction to events. By 1851 three Edinburgh newspapers appeared daily, but *The Scotsman* – which was to outlast them all – became a daily only in 1855. Its presses moved from the High Street to new premises at Cockburn Street in 1860; by 1869 it had nearly 200 full-time employees and sold 30,000 copies a day. When postal pillar boxes came to the city in 1857 they were the first in Scotland. Work began in 1861 on the imposing General Post Office in Waterloo Place, which replaced the *Theatre Royal*. This stood almost above the Scottish Confection and Preserve Works in Calton Road; the old goods station beside it became the site of the GPO yard. Meantime the burgh of Canongate had been fully absorbed into the city in 1856. The Children's Hospital was first opened in 1860, and new buildings for the Royal Infirmary were opened at Lauriston in 1870–79.

**Famous and not so Famous People**: Granville Cunningham, born in Edinburgh about 1847, took a major part in carrying the Canadian Pacific Railway through the Rockies and in building the Toronto and Central London underground railways. The novelist Robert Louis Stevenson, born in Edinburgh in 1850, was a relative of the famous Glaswegian lighthouse engineers. In 1859 two very different authors were born in the city, though both set their novels in England – Sir Arthur Conan Doyle, a doctor whose Sherlock Holmes (based on his Edinburgh professor) became the first heroic sleuth of fiction, and Kenneth Grahame, whose motoring Toad was anything but heroic in *The Wind in the Willows*. Meantime a military career was being determinedly pursued by Douglas Haig, born in the city in 1861, who is better remembered as the Earl Haig who founded the British Legion than for the myriad deaths under his questionable leadership in World War I.

**Printing and Publishing in 1869**: According to Bremner the city's principal industry in the late 1860s was printing and its allied trades: about 5000 people were employed, about half the Scottish total. Newspapers aside, Neill & Co who started up in 1749 were the longest-established printers, and had lately produced the huge 8$^{th}$ edition of the *Encyclopaedia Britannica*. Ballantynes, the printers of Scott's works, had by that time taken over the former Leith Wynd woollen factory (which had started as a hospital in 1479). Thomas Nelson & Sons, founded about 1845, moved into new buildings at Hope Park ten years later and was the largest concern by 1869, combining printing ink manufacture, printing, binding (all by hand) and publishing *"cheap and popular"* works; they employed 440 people, half of them women. W & A K Johnston produced geographical works and banknotes. Adam & Charles Black were both printers and publishers, Bell & Bradfute published legal books, Oliver & Boyd issued the periodical *Edinburgh Almanac* which sold for 150 years, plus juvenile and school books, while other firms specialised in religious publications, in engraving and in bookbinding. James Marr & Co and Miller & Richard were typefounders; the latter was established in 1815, and had over a hundred casting machines in its Nicolson Street works by 1869.

**Fine Industries in 1869**: Edinburgh was Scotland's centre for jewellery, gold and silverware production, mainly in the lanes of the New Town; William Marshall & Co made plate and jewellery, while Mackay, Cunningham & Co were still making elaborate pieces for royalty. In 1862 the Laidlaw brass foundry employed at least 150 workers; by 1869 over 800 brassfounders, a third of the Scottish total, worked in the city. The largest firm was Milne & Son of the Canongate, the principal makers of gas meters in Scotland, with over 350 workers; while James Bertram made papermaking machines at Leith Walk by 1869 *(see also Newington)*. Ford's Holyrood Glassworks was Scotland's *"principal flint-glass manufactory"*, where nearly 200 workers made Edinburgh table crystal, lamp globes and funnels; among smaller firms Ballantine had made stained glass since about 1830, and Millar had begun glass engraving in the late 1850s.

**Other Edinburgh Industries in 1869**: Bremner wrote *"the main thoroughfares of Edinburgh are traversed at frequent intervals by splendid omnibuses"*. These horse-drawn road vehicles of many types were supplied by fourteen coach-building works, *"several of considerable extent"*, of whom the largest were Croall's of York Lane with about 100 workers (who also built early railway rolling stock), and Macrae of Fountainbridge; but none were using quantity production techniques. Over 30,000 hides were sold at the city's hide market, the largest firm of tanners being Allan Boak at West Port near the then cattle market at Lauriston, which opened in the early 18th century and was rebuilt after a fire in the 1860s; they also tanned pigskin and sealskin.

**Yet More Brewing, and Pure Water**: McEwan's Fountain brewery was established in 1856, and around that time the *Croft-an-Righ (King's Farm)* brewery was established near Holyrood House. About 1866 Jeffrey & Co – who had built up every possible cranny in their Heriot Brewery in the Grassmarket – created a rail-connected maltings, cooperage, stores and bottling plant on a new site at Roseburn *"at the extreme west end of the city"*; this marked the western extent of what is now inner Edinburgh. There one wretched lad was required to put *twelve thousand bottles* on to a machine in a ten-hour working day! In 1868 Dunbar's began to make aerated *'mineral'* waters, and it may be no coincidence that in 1869 the Edinburgh Water Trust was formed to improve the city'ssee also supplies. Meantime brewing was developing at Gorgie *(q.v.)*, and even more brewing capacity came with the Roseburn brewery of 1880; at the opposite end of the city the Holyrood brewery was expanded still further by William Younger, and the Abbey brewery was built by Robert Younger in 1896–1900. Meantime Drybrough's brewery had been moved to Craigmillar in 1892, and the old Drumdryden brewery of Taylor Macleod & Co was closed in 1902.

**White Horse Whisky, Distilleries and Engineers**: Mackie & Co named their famous blended whisky after their own *White Horse Inn*, which existed well before 1883 when their records begin, and were very active exporters. In 1881 James Johnstone (of Gleniffer at Elderslie) converted the ancient Dean mills into the Dean distillery, which made about 330,000 litres of Lowland malt whisky annually in 1886; it survived until 1922. By 1886 Alex Mather & Son's Fountainbridge foundry made machinery for distilling, brewing and milling. James Milne & Co were distillery engineers and engine builders between at least 1885 and 1898; they equipped the Dalmore distillery at Alness, and the Fettykil paper mill at Leslie. Vertical steam engines were made at the West End Engine Works.

**Food and other Industries**: In 1869 Alexander Ferguson of East Crosscauseway and Shiels & Son were sweet manufacturers; people first tasted McVitie's biscuits in 1888, and the firm also had a large bakery in Slateford Road. In 1892 their baker Alexander Grant devised the unique recipe for *'Digestive'* biscuits – so successful that the firm moved their bakery from Rose Street to London in 1902. Crawfords, Edinburgh bakers since 1852, were re-established in 1899 and became very well known. Meantime Whytock of carpet fame teamed up in 1875 with Reid, an upholsterer; in 1885 they built a 3-storey cabinet works at Dean village, and the firm still survives. In 1889 Rossleigh entered the transport business with bicycles, later becoming motor engineers. Smith & Nephew began drugs manufacture late in the century. In the same period the Greenlands Mill turned from provender milling to grinding wood flour for the Kirkcaldy linoleum industry; the large Stockbridge mills were destroyed by a flour explosion in 1901.

*Well Court, Dean village, by the Water of Leith in the middle of Edinburgh. This group of model dwellings was built in 1883–86 for John R Findlay, proprietor of 'The Scotsman' newspaper, as a benefaction – and to improve the view from his house in Rothesay Terrace!* *(JRH)*

**Scottish Administration returns to Edinburgh**: By 1885 the Bank of Scotland headquarters building dominated the city centre from the top of The Mound. This matched the emergence of new all-Scotland administrative headquarters in the city, starting with the Fisheries Board in 1882, the Scottish Education Department in 1883, and the Crofters' Commission in 1886 – an activity that might have been more appropriately sited in Oban, or perhaps Glasgow. However, the Scottish Secretary regained a place in the Cabinet in 1892 and the pejorative title *North Britain* (though not as yet the North British Railway) was at last buried!

**Overnight: Mushrooms and Sleeping Cars**: The opening in 1868 of a rail link between Abbeyhill and Trinity by the NB made the steep cable-worked Scotland Street tunnel redundant; by 1889 it was used for mushroom growing. The NB were partners in the first railway sleeping car, introduced in 1873 between Glasgow, Edinburgh Waverley and London. Locomotives for the International Exhibition of Industry, Science and Art – held in The West Meadows in 1886 – reached there on temporary track laid from Lothian Road via the new Melville Drive of 1858. As the city spread, the standard gauge Edinburgh Street Tramways Company (ESTC) introduced horse-drawn vehicles in 1871 on a Haymarket to Leith route. Soon Portobello was served, and in 1881–82 a steam hauled car was tried on this route. Newington was reached by 1886.

**Growing Britain's Greatest Cable Tram System**: The small system of the Edinburgh Northern Tramways Company (ENTC) was built in 1884–88, emulating the new San Francisco cable-drawn trams. Their depot at Henderson Row was also the power station, driving 28 mm diameter endless cables, which from 1888 pulled cars on short distances over steep streets: south to Hanover Street, north to Goldenacre, and from 1890 between Frederick Street and Stockbridge, later extended to Comely Bank. In 1892 the already fragmented public tramways suffered high-handed action by the City Council, the ESTC being foolishly divided up. However, from 1893 an extensive cable tramway system was laid down by a Dick Kerr & Co subsidiary, powered by new engines at new depots at Leith Walk (Shrubhill), where many Edinburgh trams were also to be built, and at Tollcross, the latter erected in 1896–98. Its first route between Braids and Pilrig (Leith Walk) via Princes Street – the spine of the system – opened in 1899. The ENTC was absorbed, routes were added to reach Murrayfield and Gorgie, and in 1900 extended from Newington to Nether Liberton, which required a single haulage cable 10.2 km long! The Mound was served from 1901 and Portobello from 1902, completing 34 km of routes, *"Britain's greatest cable tram system"* (Joyce). From about 1905 Edinburgh trams met those of the electrified Leith system at Pilrig. Finally in 1907 the last horse-drawn route (to Craiglockhart) was converted to cable drive.

**Late Nineteenth Century Stations and Bridges**: Meantime in 1876 Wright Young & Co of Edinburgh made the ironwork for the new NB station of Dundee Tay Bridge. The old Waverley Bridge, built in the 1840s to give access to the NB station, was reconstructed on girders in 1875 to free the track layout beneath of the constraints imposed by stone arches. The NB opened their Edinburgh south side suburban circle in 1884, vying for patronage with the tramways. Belford road bridge opened on the west of the city in 1887, and the Dean footbridge was erected in 1889. In 1890–93 the Caledonian rebuilt its Princes Street station, and the Lothian Road depot was rebuilt in 1892–93 for Wordie & Co's goods only; in 1903 its work required 126 horses. The NB's western routes were revolutionised with the opening of the Forth Bridge in 1890; Waverley station immediately became congested and its reconstruction was begun. The massive second North Bridge with its markedly sloped deck was built in 1894–97, replacing the 1772 structure. Haymarket locomotive depot was rebuilt about 1894 near Roseburn Street, the old site becoming a coal yard.

**Palatial Hotels, Rail Speed and Planned Parenthood**: Princes Street was already lined with at least ten *"good"* hotels, to which were soon added the railways' own rival hotels, the vast *Caledonian*, designed by J M Dick Peddie and George Washington Browne, built in 1893–94 and faced with red Dumfriesshire sandstone, and the *North British* which was completed in 1902, when Waverley Station also achieved its 20th century form, with 4360 m of platform faces in an area of over 7 ha, making it even larger than London's Liverpool Street. Nigel Gresley, who was born in Edinburgh about 1880, designed carriages and engines for the Great Northern Railway of England, and later created the world's fastest steam locomotives, the 126 mph LNER A4 class of 4–6–2; he earned a knighthood.

**Electricity Supplies and Transport Competition**: In 1895 the original power station of the City's Electricity Department was opened beside the Caledonian Railway in Dewar Place, supplemented from 1899 by the Macdonald Road power station. The railways still thrived because although Princes Street was electrically lit from 1895, no tramways were electrified until 1910 when the Edinburgh & District Tramways Company introduced electric cars between Ardmillan Terrace and Slateford. But rail and tram supremacy was to be short, for cars were coming and the city's first primitive motor bus service began in 1898.

**The Press funds the Arts**: The *Evening Dispatch* dated from 1866 and the *Edinburgh Evening News* was founded in 1873. The owner of the *Dispatch* and the *Scotsman*, J R Findlay, donated the large National Portrait Gallery and Museum of Antiquities in York Place, Queen Street, designed by Rowand Anderson and built in 1885–90, to which these institutions moved from the Mound in 1891. Meantime Morrison & Gibb's printing works had been established in 1878; water power was still used to aid bookbinding in the 1870s. A foretaste of future closures came in 1886, with the failure of the *Edinburgh Courant* after 166 years. Above the new Waverley station towered the costly new *Scotsman* building, part faced in polished granite. Waterstons' printing works dates from 1902.

**West End Shopping, Religion, Bathing and Swimming**: Maules department store at the West End of Princes Street was opened in 1872, the year that the Catholic Apostolic Church built the largest of Rowand Anderson's churches, at East London Street; by 1993 it was empty and neglected. The ancient turreted house called Easter Coates Manor was improved by its last owner Sir Patrick Walker, whose daughters funded the building of the adjacent St Mary's Cathedral, designed by Sir George Gilbert Scott as the largest post-Reformation church in Scotland; begun in 1874, it was still slowly approaching completion as late as 1886. The Manor eventually became its choir school. In 1884 the Drumsheugh baths club complex brought indoor swimming and hot baths to well-off people in the west end of the city; fine public baths were built in Infirmary Street in 1885–87, and the Glenogle Road baths followed in 1897. In 1886 with Carnegie's help the city belatedly set about building the central public library, opened in 1890. Jenners burnt down in 1892, but was quickly re-built. The massive combined building for the *Carlton Hotel* and Patrick Thomson's department store was opened on North Bridge in 1900, and large buildings at Tollcross embracing the Methodist Central Hall arose in 1899–1901.

**Culture and Entertainment: People and Places**: In 1886 a permanent circus building was opened in East Fountainbridge; later known as the *Palladium*, it became a cinema in 1911. In 1897 the *New Pavilion* opened in Grove Street; renamed the *Garrick Theatre*, it burnt down in 1921. Meantime Samuel Peploe, whose paintings became internationally regarded, was born in Edinburgh in 1871, Marie Stopes, born in Edinburgh in 1880, was both a fossil hunter who found the oldest flowering plant, and became a fervent advocate of planned parenthood, and George S MacLennan, born in the city in 1884, became a brilliant piper and composer of Scots airs. The 2000-seat *Tivoli Theatre* was opened in St Stephen's Street in 1901; in 1904 it became the *Grand* and by 1920 it was a cinema. The first *Balmoral Hotel* in Princes Street was opened in 1902. The 1500-seat *King's Theatre* was built in 1905–06 of red

Dumfriesshire sandstone on the site of the Drumdryden Brewery at Tollcross. Stockbridge gained a branch library and hall in 1900, with help from Thomas Nelson; in 1911 *St Bernard's Picture Palace*, later called the *Savoy*, was built nearby. The former *Royal Princess* theatre was reopened in 1912 as a cinema, *La Scala*. No doubt it was among those patronised by Alistair Sim, born in Edinburgh in 1900, who later became a much-loved character in British films. The Usher Hall was built in 1911–14.

**Educational Developments**: The striking Torphichen Street School, designed by Robert Wilson, was built in the West End in 1886. In 1901 the University appointed its first Professor of Scottish History; by then the Royal High School – frowning at the new buildings at North Bridge from its cliff-top across the void – had 350 pupils. Moray House, tucked away in the Canongate below, became a teacher training centre in 1905. The cattle market at Lauriston was moved to Gorgie, replaced by Edinburgh College of Art's pompous new building, begun in 1907. Before the 1914–18 war St George's School for Girls, founded in 1888, moved into new buildings at Garscube Terrace, designed by A P B Paul.

**Banks, Biscuits, Tanks and Distilleries**: Bank of Scotland absorbed the Inverness-based Caledonian Bank in 1907 in order to expand. By 1910 it had 169 branches, but had no female employees until 1916. After 1918, branches were opened at a rate of five a year, the total reaching 266 in 1939. An unusual industry from Edwardian times was the Waverley Biscuit factory of the Italians Zaccardelli Cervi & Co, founded in 1909, which (aided by the fact that Italy was an ally in World War I) was still active in 1992 manufacturing ice cream wafers, cones and allied products. In 1916–18 some of the newly invented army tanks were built by Brown Brothers of the Rosebank Iron Works in Broughton Road, who later specialised in hydraulic engineering. Following Lloyd George's interference and US Prohibition, the Dean distillery went into liquidation in 1922 and was acquired for closure by Scottish Malt Distillers, becoming bonded warehouses.

**Buses, Cars, and New Town Commerce**: As motor buses came into general use in the 1920s, large bus garages were built around 1930, tucked away in both Green Street and New Street. The city's first traffic signals were installed at the top of Broughton Street in 1928. Developing bus services and rising car ownership enabled commuting from lower density suburban housing, which attracted better-off people; as they moved out, the originally residential New Town gradually took over much of the Old Town's commercial role. In those days Edinburgh's snobbish and conservative shopping centre long resisted the entry of chain stores, though Boots the Chemists opened their first branch in the city at about that time, and by the late 1930s Woolworths were trading in a spacious new store opposite the *North British Hotel*. Binns' store at the West End was built in 1934, replacing Maules, while the St Cuthbert's Co-operative store near unfashionable Tollcross was extended in 1937. The HQ of the Edinburgh Savings Bank was built in Hanover Street in 1939.

**Edinburgh, Leith and Tramway Electrification**: The city, which had always dominated the port of Leith, was allowed to absorb the latter's local government and electric tramways

*Andrew Carnegie – probably the world's greatest benefactor – at the ceremony to lay the foundation stone of Edinburgh's Central Library on George IV Bridge, in 1887. The building was designed in French Renaissance style by George Washington Browne, and was completed in 1890.* *(Edinburgh City Libraries)*

*St Andrews House, built in 1936–39 as the administrative home of the Scottish Office, to designs by Thomas S Tait.*

in 1920. The tramway leases having expired in 1919, the City Corporation took over the 20-route, 200-car cable tramway. Finding the original cable station at Henderson Row worn out, it was closed in 1921, its service temporarily replaced by buses using the same depot. The system was transformed in 1922–23 by much faster electric traction. After the Portobello route was electrified in 1923 the cable power stations became mere depots. George Street had trams from 1925, the trams (like the other traffic) having to swerve around the statues. Some routes were extended, but the Annandale Street bus garage near Shrubhill was opened in 1926 and Henderson Row then became the police garage. Industries in dated premises included D & J McCallum of Picardy Place which exported blended whisky to India in the 1930s, but Bowaters opened new works at Pilrig.

**Culture, Education and Entertainment**: The National Library of Scotland was formed from the Advocates' Library in 1925; its new buildings on George IV Bridge, designed by Reginald Fairlie, were begun in 1934 but, due to the war, not opened until 1956. George Watson's College moved out of the city centre to Colinton Road *(see Morningside)* in 1932. About that time the *Palladium Cinema* was again converted, this time becoming a 960-seat theatre. The huge *Playhouse Cinema* with 3200 seats was completed shortly before the second world war. About 1932 Edinburgh became briefly the headquarters of BBC Scotland, which moved from Glasgow but returned west to Hillhead about 1935.

**Better Administrative Headquarters for Scotland**: The original St Andrews House, designed by Thomas Tait, was opened in 1939 on the commanding site in Waterloo Place formerly occupied by the Calton jail, enabling the decentralisation of more Scottish Office work from Whitehall. The North of Scotland Hydro-Electricity Board was created in 1943, its headquarters oddly placed in Edinburgh, outwith the Board's area of supply! The castle (and upper floors of the *Scotsman* building where the author worked in Army movement control in 1949–50) bustled with Army HQ activity during and after World War II.

**Director Dialling, Fire and Famous Sons**: Such developments in a growing administrative centre put severe pressure on Edinburgh's telephone system, still connecting automatic exchanges manually: in 1951 the two central exchanges alone had over 9500 lines between them. The phones were radically upgraded by the all-city dialling of the Director system introduced gradually from 1946, presaging the later trunk dialling. In the same year the *Theatre Royal* in Leith Street, the fifth theatre on the site, caught fire – as had all its predecessors – but this time there was to be no rebuilding, and the site was sold to the RC church. Hamish Munro, born in Edinburgh in 1915, became a prolific research scientist in nutritional and allied fields, and a professor at MIT. Dougal Haston, born in the city in 1940, later climbed the north face of the Eiger and was the first to ascend the south-west face of Mount Everest.

**Buses beat Trams to New Housing Schemes**: Private tenement blocks were still being built in the Comely Bank area in the 1930s, but more homes were desperately needed. In 1936 17% of Edinburgh houses were overcrowded – although the other three cities of Scotland and most large towns on Clydeside were even worse. At their peak in 1946–47 the Edinburgh electric trams carried 16 million passengers a month, and in

1949 the author happily rode each line to its terminus. New overspill housing estates were built, such as Craigmillar and Pilton. Sadly, although the clean trams gave highly convenient access to the city centre for the majority, they still ran in the middle of the road (just as in San Francisco where cable trams still survive to delight tourists). This arrangement obstructed the newly acquired cars of the decision-makers, who opted for cheaper, flexible but polluting buses wherever possible.

**Decentralisation speeds Demise of the Trams**: At the 1951 census some 72,500 people still lived within a mile of the Bank of Scotland HQ. The two suburban steam railway systems were failing from bus and car competition, and were closed piecemeal between 1942 and 1967; the Scotland Street railway goods depot lasted until the latter date. The tramway system was deliberately run down from 1950; cars from the Manchester system were acquired cheaply to replace worn-out vehicles, the Comely Bank service was closed in 1952 and despite the public outcry the whole system was closed in 1956, replaced by buses *(for a fine illustrated account see Twidale).* Tollcross tram depot was taken over by buses (until its closure in 1969).

**Banking and Brewing Reorganises**: By 1952 though the Bank of Scotland (BoS) Head Office was subsiding due to poor foundations, they took over the Glasgow-based Union Bank of Scotland in 1952–55; combined they had 453 branches. In 1959 their first computer was installed. New branches were then being opened at three per year, while over twice as many were being closed. Then in 1968–69 the Royal Bank took over the National Commercial Bank of Scotland. In 1959 William Younger of Canongate joined with McEwans of the Fountain Brewery to form Scottish Brewers; within a year or two they had absorbed the Newcastle Breweries to form S&N. The extensive New Fountain Brewery, which contained its own laboratories, was erected in 1976 by S&N; their St Anns brewery was dismantled in 1979, and running down continued at cramped Canongate; in 1988 they closed the merged Abbey and Holyrood breweries.

**Shopping and Service Changes from 1945**: Marks & Spencer finally opened their first Edinburgh store in Princes Street in 1957, and much redevelopment of shopping blocks took place towards the east end of the street. The Infirmary Street Baths survived fire damage in 1960, and in 1963 the *Evening Despatch* and the *Edinburgh Evening News* merged. In 1963 the big *Empire Theatre* became a mere bingo hall, the *Savoy (or Tudor) Cinema* at Stockbridge closed in 1966, and the *Palladium Theatre* failed in 1968, becoming a discotheque. In 1968 the historic Grassmarket became sadly disfigured by the brutal bulk of the Mountbatten Building of Heriot-Watt, a year before the new university's gradual move to outlying Riccarton was begun. The Royal High School was moved out to a site near Davidson's Mains in 1968; from 1969 to 1975 their old building was a City art gallery. About 1980 Lansdowne House school for girls was absorbed by St George's.

**Redevelopment, Explosion and Bank Expansion**: Meantime the St James Centre, planned in 1964 for a large site at Leith Street, was completed in 1970, including the great block of government offices called New St Andrews House, the large *King James Hotel* and the St James shopping centre, including the important John Lewis department store which drew shoppers from the whole of east central Scotland. By 1972 a youth hostel was open at Eglinton Crescent. Bell's mills were destroyed in 1972 by a violent dust explosion, and replaced by the *Dragonara Hotel*; the West Mills were converted to flats in 1973. By 1977 the Scottish Provident Institution head office was in St Andrew Square. From 1966 the Bank of Scotland had set out to connect with Europe, absorbing the Edinburgh-based British Linen Bank in 1969 and funding North Sea oil development, including BP's Forties Field. (In 1977 the name *'British Linen Bank'* was revived for a merchant banking subsidiary.) About 1980 the former Brunswick goods yard was replaced by the GPO's new Mechanised Letter Office, one of only four in Scotland.

**Local Entrepreneurs of the 1970s**: In 1971 successful local businessman Tom Farmer, aged 29, started *'Kwik-Fit'*. By 1995 its 800 branches fitted motor tyres and exhausts in Britain, Eire, Belgium and Holland and employed some 5000 people; it was still based in Edinburgh until sold about 1999. David Murray from Ayr started to trade as Murray International Metals in Edinburgh in 1974, dealing in aluminium wire and moving on to steel. Recovering from the loss of both legs in an accident, he built up a major privately owned company, its subsidiaries including Mimtec of Gourock and Livingston and, from 1988, Rangers FC. It had a workforce of 3000 in 1995.

**Edinburgh reverts to Lothian's Capital**: In 1974 a new headquarters for Lothian & Borders police was opened in Fettes Avenue, and in 1975 the new Lothian Regional Council located its HQ in a new office block on George IV Bridge, the city council being demoted to a district without education or highways powers. The Convention of Royal Burghs, oldest of all Scottish bodies, was reconstituted as COSLA *(Convention of Scottish Local Authorities)*, keeping its tiny headquarters at Rosebery House at Haymarket. Debenhams opened a new store in Princes Street in 1980. The site of the Waverley covered market, demolished in 1973, was redeveloped as an inward-looking speciality shopping mall of the same name, opened in 1984 (but by 2000 renamed *Princes Mall).* Meantime the Royal Insurance group could not expand their HQ operations in Edinburgh's conserved George Street, and therefore moved to Glasgow about 1981. Eighty years of housing decentralisation left 37,500 residents in the core area of Edinburgh in the 1981 census. By then perhaps the most striking statistic about the city as a whole – with its 400,000-plus population – was its high proportion of people with higher educational qualifications.

**Devolution Aborted**: About 1975 the Labour government bought premises in Market Street for the City Council to develop as a City Art Centre, so as to release the former Royal High School building as the seat of a Scottish Assembly. But this was left empty by the failure of the government's devolution proposals in 1979, and was followed by a change to the autocratic Thatcher regime. Their short-termism and strong London centralisation for a time caused Edinburgh office development to sink to a low ebb.

**Cultural Development from 1984**: In 1984 the old buildings of John Watson's College in Belford Road were reopened as the Scottish National Gallery of Modern Art, which moved from Inverleith House. Scotsman Publications, by 1981 owned by Thomson Regional Newspapers, launched the weekly *Scotland on Sunday* in 1988: it did better than its parent. In 1990 Edinburgh Castle and Holyrood Palace were respectively first and eighth among Scotland's paid tourist attractions, with over a million and 300,000 visitors, the free City Art Centre in Market Street also being highly popular. By 1991 Huntly House Museum had industrial collections, as of course had the National Museum of Scotland in Chambers Street, where an extension announced in 1990 was built on the adjacent site (previously public gardens). The Infirmary Street Baths remained in partial use until 1996. In 1996 the Scottish United Services Museum was on two separate sites within Edinburgh Castle; a single site was planned.

**District Council takes Theatres to its Heart**: Meantime the *Palladium* discotheque, once a theatre, fell to the demolition gangs in 1984 and by 1989 the *Caley Cinema* had become a nightclub. But about 1985 the District Council refurbished the *King's Theatre*, which they had owned since 1969. In 1990 after decades of dithering they bought the bingo hall which had once been Scotland's first cinema, the former *Empire Theatre* in Nicolson Street, for radical conversion in 1993–94 into the hitherto elusive opera house, styled the *Festival Theatre*, with facilities for the largest operatic and other performances; its stage claimed to be the largest in the UK at 864 m$^2$, and incorporated the original auditorium to seat 1900 people. Saltire Court, a major traditional-style office block built on a long-derelict site in Castle Terrace, was completed in 1991, including the new *Traverse Theatre*; in 1993 it was sold to Abu Dhabi interests. The *King's, Playhouse* and *Royal Lyceum* Theatres continued. In 1995 the Festival organisers acquired Pugin's Gothic *'Highland Tolbooth'* at the head of the Royal Mile for conversion into a year-round Festival Centre including retail and catering facilities, opened in 1999 as *'The Hub'*, and now a popular venue. The Usher Hall was refurbished in 2000.

**No House Coal by Rail; Passenger Trains Electric**: British Rail electrified the East Coast Main Line and extended the wires through the city to Carstairs, and in 1991, as a recession bit, electric trains began to run from London to Edinburgh in four hours, many of them optimistically continuing to Glasgow Central via Carstairs and vice versa. 1993 saw the lifting of the tracks in the former Haymarket coal yard, city users having finally abandoned the solid fuel heating that had contributed smoke to the smelly city's nickname of *'Auld Reekie'*. The last surviving Motorail service, to Bristol, was sadly withdrawn in 1995, and the planned daily Eurostar train to Paris never materialised.

**Head Offices Old and New**: Bell Lawrie White, the stockbroking arm of Hill Samuel, had its UK head office in Edinburgh in 1990, as did John Menzies, which with about 300 outlets was one of Britain's largest retail groups. The Morrison Construction Group, then one of the largest privately owned building firms, also had its headquarters in the West End. The Ben Line, transport operators, were also headquartered in Edinburgh. Chambers, the directory and reference publisher of Annandale Street, was first taken over by Harraps, but by 1994 had become a subsidiary of Larousse plc. The Johnston Newspaper Group of Falkirk had an Edinburgh office by 1981; by 1994 the company had moved its head office to the city, and owned some 70 titles.

**Conservation and Lack of Space cause Relocation**: In the late 1980s financial services were still the fastest growing users of city floorspace. Both the Bank of Scotland on the Mound and the Royal Bank at St Andrew Square had also found these locations hidebound by controls aimed at maintaining the city's architectural character as a tourist mecca, and consequently inadequate for expansion. So they built offices at the remote and boring South Gyle *(see Corstorphine)*. In the 1990s Heriot-Watt University completed its move to its Green Belt Shangri-La at Riccarton. In 1990–93 the newly privatised (North of Scotland) Hydro Electric plc undertook a logical move of its head office from Edinburgh to Perth, within its area of supply. In 1992 four small insurance companies still had headquarters in the city or at Newington. The much larger Scottish Equitable employed 1250 in Edinburgh and Leith, but moved their HQ to the so-called *'Edinburgh Park'* at South Gyle; their St Andrew Square offices remained empty for some years. ICL also moved from their rail-accessible Haymarket offices to larger premises in the outer suburbs. In 1995 the Scottish Tourist Board, based in Edinburgh, moved part of their operations to Inverness.

**Centralisation versus Decentralisation**: Donaldson's Mill was restored as flats in the early 1990s, but the Torphichen Street School building was unused in 1995. In 1992 Scottish Natural Heritage was formed by the controversial merger of the Countryside Commission for Scotland with the Nature Conservancy Council's Scottish arm; the HQ would initially remain split between Battleby *(see Luncarty)* and Edinburgh. In 1994 the former Heriot-Watt University buildings in Chambers Street were reopened after reconstruction as the city's Sheriff Court, its 16 courtrooms drawing together cases previously heard in various locations around the city. Edinburgh Royal Infirmary was under pressure as a result of the controversial withdrawal of A&E services from the Western General Hospital in 1992; the construction of new buildings for the famous hospital on a greenfield site at Little France *(see Craigmillar)* began in the late 1990s. The small Chalmers Hospital at Lauriston was to close by the end of the century. In the late 1990s James Ritchie & Son, clock manufacturers and precision engineers, moved their production to Livingston, although their Broughton Street shop maintained their 190 years' presence in the city.

**Office Development to Counteract Departures**: Following a 1992 report showing an excess of old offices to let, but a shortfall of 100,000 m$^2$ of modern high class office floorspace in the city centre, several major schemes were built west of Haymarket station and elsewhere. In 1993 the Sea Fish Industry Authority, formerly the White Fish Authority, moved into new offices from its long-standing address in Young Street. In expectation of continued growth, in 1988 a 2.8 ha site in Morrison Street (originally the Union Canal terminus of Port Hamilton) was cleared of the Dickensian Saint Cuthbert's Co-op depot, and was excavated in 1989 ready for a large office development. Depression and receivership followed in 1991, leaving a water-filled hole. But in 1993 Scottish Widows – whose headquarters were at Newington, and 90% of whose insurance business was done south of the border – took an option on the site, seeking permission for up to 65,000 m$^2$ of office space for its 2000 Scottish employees and intending a further 1500 jobs in five years. In the event only 42,000 m$^2$ was completed at Port Hamilton in 1995, but Scottish Widows moved in nonetheless.

**Lothian Road's Financial Area**: In 1989 Standard Life, with long-established headquarters in George Street, claimed to be Europe's largest mutual life assurance company, and was still expanding in 1990 with over 18,000 m$^2$ of new offices at Canonmills. But by 1995 they had decided to consolidate from

20 sites to just one imposing new edifice of 31,000 m$^2$ already under construction on the site of the former Princes Street Station in Lothian Road. Another 18,500 m$^2$ of speculative office space was also appearing nearby, although by 1995 the city centre was, in the words of *The Scotsman, "awash with unoccupied commercial buildings"*. In 1996 the Exchange Plaza on Lothian Road was the largest office scheme under construction in the city centre.

**Head Offices for Textiles, Food and Drinks**: In 1992 Charlotte Square was still the headquarters of the Dawson International Group, with a textile workforce of 12,000, half of them in the USA. Among its brands were Braemar, Pringle and Ballantyne, and its manufacturing arm included Todd & Duncan and Laidlaw & Fairgrieve *(see Hawick, Innerleithen, Kinross, Selkirk & Walkerburn)*. In 1993 Astra Clinical Research, which was owned by a Swedish pharmaceutical company, were recruiting for their expanding ethical operation at the Beaverbank office park in Logie Green Road. In 1994 the salmon farmers Marine Harvest, owned by a New Jersey holding company but whose small HQ were in Edinburgh, employed some 400 people in the West Highlands, and some in Chile. It was then sold to the London based Booker plc. The head office of Scottish & Newcastle (S&N) was still at Holyrood, having dropped *'Breweries'* from the title (since its acquisitions had been diverse, including the Dutch Center Parcs leisure group). In 1995 expanding S&N acquired the large English brewers Courage.

**Hotel Developments**: The 300-room *Sheraton Hotel* on the site of a CR railway yard in Lothian Road was built in 1982. The former *North British Hotel* was slowly gutted, excessively luxuriously refitted, and reopened in 1991 as the 220-room 5-star *Balmoral Hotel*; but its transient owners Norfolk Capital and Queen's Moat became insolvent in 1992 and the Bank of Scotland took over, with management by Forte. In 1991 the century-old 47-room *Palace Hotel* at Castle Street was destroyed by fire, whilst a *Holiday Inn* proposed to be built above a recently erected car stack in the deep hollow at Greenside was abandoned in the recession of 1992, as was the large conference centre proposed nearby, beaten to the post by others. Consequently the 238-room *Scandic Crown Hotel*, owned and built by Danes, and erected on a long-vacant site in the lower High Street in 1989–90 to a stone-faced design aping medieval castles, was known by 1996 as the *Holiday Inn Crowne Plaza*.

**Varied Developments of the 1990s**: In 1990 work began on the Great Mosque at Potterrow for the growing Muslim community. The tall rimmed rotunda of the Edinburgh International Conference Centre, designed by Terry Farrell, was built at long rundown Morrison Street in 1992–96 for Lothian & Edinburgh Enterprise. Its revolving interior was arranged to provide either one hall of 1200 seats or three of 600, 300 and 300. In 1994 the city council proposed a 5-storey budget hotel for a vacant site opposite. By 1999 four independent hostels in central Edinburgh provided over 400 beds for backpackers. In the mid 1990s, Fettes College remained a co-educational independent school for 500 pupils; it still stood in its own vast estate of 34 ha. The nearby Edinburgh Academy had 835 pupils – only a token 30 were girls, all in the sixth form. In the early 1990s a Safeway store was opened at Comelybank, and William Low did likewise at Broughton; but in 1991 the huge St Cuthbert's Co-op store in Bread Street finally closed its doors. The threat of further closures due to the vast peripheral shopping development at Gyle was real, but Frasers department store, the one-time Binns, was still open at the west end of Princes Street, and more upmarket Jenners near the centre; at the east end the major John Lewis Partnership store, enlarged around 1990, still anchors the St James Centre. By 1996 a Tesco Metro store was open, and in 2000 Debenhams proposed a new store.

**Rapid Transit and Heritage Schemes**: Before their disbandment in 1996, Lothian Regional Council had proposed a rapid transit scheme – including reopening the long-disused Scotland Street rail tunnel, first opened in 1847 – aiming to improve north–south access to the city centre while still keeping its historic character, on which tourism and its draw as a head office location largely depend. In 1994 they proposed a segregated busway linking the city centre with the airport via the new East Park business centre; but either a proper rail link or a travolator from a new station on the Fife line would be better. Nothing has happened on the ground so far. In 1996 UNESCO declared central Edinburgh a World Heritage Site, the only such urban site in Britain apart from Bath. But to allow it to work properly while keeping an apparent historic character, compromises have to be made – for instance reproduction buildings, and the setts relaid in 1993–94 to modern patterns to enable the Royal Mile's long overdue traffic-calming.

**Communications Developments in the 1990s**: Spider, founded in 1983 by five redundant executives from ICL Dalkeith to produce computer networking applications, employed 250 people by 1995 in ISDN technology, including 70 research and development staff in Edinburgh. Spider was then sold to Shiva Systems of Massachusetts, a firm of similar size. In 1990 British Telecom began to instal an enhanced electronic exchange network using fibre optic cables for the heart of the city, complemented by an SDA initiative to develop Edinburgh as an international *'teleport'*, a centre of information infrastructure and services. The updated telephone system became fully digital from late 1994. In 1994 Edinburgh University (which had some 14,000 full-time students) landed another key facility, the European supercomputer, able to perform 40 billion calculations per second! Another new facility, the European Call Centre opened in mid 1995 by McQueen Ltd, expected to employ 200 workers answering software and computing enquiries from Europe; these were to include 80 people who had already been recruited from abroad for their multilingual skills.

***Oriana* kept Steady, but Local Government Upset**: In 1996 the former Shrubhill tramcar depot site at Leith Walk was still in use as a bus depot by Lothian Transport. By the 1990s most of Edinburgh's once thriving industries had moved to outlying areas, but Brown Brothers, who by 1977 were hydraulic engineers at the Rosebank Works, were still active in 1993 when they made the stabilisers for P&O's new cruise liner *Oriana*, built on the River Ems in Germany. In 1996 Edinburgh City District became once more a unitary authority, but the Regional Council was controversially abolished, water and sewerage being transferred to a new undemocratic East of Scotland Water Board, while its remaining functions (except police and fire) in East, Mid and West Lothian were given to much weaker new unitary authorities for those areas.

**The Scottish Parliament Back in Action**: In 1997 Broughton High School had 1010 pupils, Drummond Community High 386 and St Thomas of Aquin's RC 650. New housing

*The Clydesdale Bank's 1990s building on Lothian Road – part of Edinburgh's new financial centre.* *(AL)*

was built in 1997 on the site at Croft-an-Righ immediately north of Holyrood House. To the south is the *'Dynamic Earth'* permanent exhibition, a Millennium project built with Lottery aid and opened in 1999, is set deep in a mausoleum-like structure, covered in steps, ramps and a striking tent-like roof; it soon became very popular. The Scottish Parliament, restored with limited devolved powers in 1998–99, was given the site of the Abbey and Holyrood breweries for its new and controversial building, rising in 2000–02 and to be faced in Kemnay granite; meantime the Parliament has met in the Church of Scotland Assembly Hall. The new Scottish Poetry Library is part of a new 4 ha *'William Younger Centre'* on another part of the old Canongate industrial site. The *Scotsman* newspaper moved its offices from North Bridge to new premises built at Holyrood in 1998–99; its great old building was being converted into a hotel during 2000–2001.

**Westminster Takeovers and Waverley Schemes**: In 1999 Scottish Widows was taken over by Lloyds TSB, and the Scottish Provident Institution of Edinburgh was bought out by Abbey National in 2000, ending yet another mutual business. But in a bold move, in 2000 the Royal Bank succeeded in taking over the ailing London-based National Westminster Bank, almost twice its size. The Bank of Scotland merged with the Halifax in 2001 (as HBOS). In 2000 redevelopment of the shores of the Lochrin canal basin with 90 flats, offices and shops was proposed by British Waterways and Miller Developments. Although new shops had been built on the Waverley station concourse in 1999, the extensive ridge and furrow glass roofs over one of Britain's principal stations leaked, and were not regularly repaired by Railtrack. From 2000 Scotrail speeded up and doubled the frequency of its Glasgow–Edinburgh passenger trains to four per hour. Although Glasgow's huge new Buchanan Galleries could thereby very readily draw on a majority of Scotland's population, a hearing into controversial plans to build yet another shopping mall, over the main platforms of Waverley Station, was held in 2000; until the last minute the city council was opposed. The former Head Post Office, *'A'* listed but vacant for 5 years, may soon be renovated for shopping and provided with a lift access to the station. Haymarket is still the major Scotrail maintenance depot, and much-needed passenger lifts are to be added at Haymarket station.

**Hosting the World**: In 1998 the *Tailors Hall* of 1621 was converted into a 42-roomed hotel, the brutal Mountbatten building in Grassmarket has been replaced by the *Apex International* (175 rooms), and a new *Travel Inn* has recently been built in Morrison Street. The city centre's most prestigious hotels may be summarised as the 5-star *Caley*, *Balmoral* (186 rooms) and *Sheraton Grand* (260), the 4-star *Bonham* (48), *Carlton* (185), *Channings* (46), *George* (195), *Hilton* (144), *Holyrood* (157, built 1999), *Howard* (15), *King James* (143), *Roxburghe* (197) and *Royal Terrace* (108). There are many other hotels, of which quite a few are recently opened, including of the budget type. Most Edinburgh suburbs also have good hotels; the two largest hotels in greater Edinburgh are nearer the airport, at Corstorphine *(q.v.)*. At the west end of the city centre is the Eglinton youth hostel.

## EDZELL & Tarfside

**Map 6, C1**

***Angus village & hamlet,*** *pop. 750*

OS 44/45; NO 6069

Edzell's large Norman motte – now known as the Castle Hillock – was thrown up beside the West Water below its emergence from the Grampian Mountains. Some 5 km farther downstream the West Water joins the River North Esk (*Uisge* in Gaelic, which simply means *Water)* while the place name – locally pronounced *'Aigle'* – very possibly derives from Gaelic *Aigeal*, meaning *'Shingly'*, describing an adjacent ford. *Aberlethnot*, an 11th century thanage, was perhaps nearer to Lethnot Mill farther up the valley of the West Water. Another such thanage, *Newdosk*, could relate to Invermark Castle, a 14th century keep far up Glenesk, in which Gaelic was still spoken as late as 1618. Close by the motte of Edzell arose the fine late 15th century Edzell Castle, by 1560 the seat of the Earl of Crawford and Master Lindsay. This powerful family had a minor burgh of barony chartered in 1588, a contemporary plan of which survives. Pont's map, made about 1600, showed *"a great park of firs about and benorth Edzell castle"*, although not its notable walled garden, created by Sir David Lindsay in 1604.

**Fords and Bridges**: Pont also showed the English name Slateford, clearly intended to distinguish this crossing of the North Esk from the already named ford. Corn and waulk mills stood farther south, while below the confluence with the West Water was the *'North Water Brigg'*. The extensive Wood of Dalbog, and Dalbog mill, lay west of the river 3 km to the north; on the opposite bank was Keny mill, and lower down stood the tower of Arnhall in its park. A charcoal iron smelter operated at Dalbog around 1678 – apparently a short-lasting venture; at one time local iron ore was also smelted at remote Tarfside far to the north-west in Lochlee parish, Glenesk. In 1732 Gannachie Bridge was thrown across the ravine of the North Esk 2 km to the north of Slateford; in the 1790s Heron saw it as *"a singular curiosity, both from its situation and construction"*. The Roy map, surveyed about 1750, nevertheless showed no roads north of that from Brechin to Fettercairn via the *'Bridge of Inglismaldie'* (i.e. North Water Bridge). Within the crook in the river was *'Newmill'* and just west of it the main settlement, the small village of Slateford. Between there and the castle – which was named as *'Eagle'* – was the hamlet of Mains; the parish church stood alone to the west of the castle.

**Slateford becomes the Tourist's Edzell**: The castle was abandoned to ruin in 1764 but is now a fine attraction, its garden maintained by Historic Scotland. The parish church of Lethnot was rebuilt in 1819 on a new site at Slateford, which was extended in 1839 by the laird, Lord Panmure, on a spacious plan, and formally renamed Edzell. The fishing in the area was good, so two small hotels were built; excursions were offered to Lochlee. The Dalhousie Arch across the main street was built in 1887 in memory of the 13th Earl of Dalhousie; both the *Eagle Hotel* and especially the *Panmure Arms* were enlarged in the late 19th century. The latter was *"very comfortable"* by 1894, when Murray called Edzell *"a neat little village, suitable for staying at, with a golf course"*. In 1895 a club was founded, which replaced this bleak facility which had only 5 holes, by something much better – an 18-hole parkland course designed by James Braid. The prominent Inglis Memorial Hall, designed by C & L Ower of Dundee, and the *Glenesk Hotel* both opened in 1898; contemporary photographs show the little town's very substantially built High Street stonework still cleanly new, and its trees few.

**The Railway reaches Edzell – Too Late!**: Edzell acquired a gasworks with its very late Caledonian Railway station in 1896; for a time 5-coach trains were run, and Wordie & Co operated a small rail to road cartage depot. But being inconveniently located at the end of a secondary branch from the loop of branches serving Brechin, closure to passengers came early, in 1931; road transport enabled Edzell to continue as a minor inland resort and service village. Electricity arrived late, in 1936. Rail freight was abandoned by Beeching in 1964, the station site going for housing. In 1970 the former junior secondary school became primary only, and the population was 658 in 1971. By 1980 there were three medium-sized hotels: the *Central, Glenesk*, and *Panmure Arms*. By 1991 Edzell had grown to 747 people, but remains quietly pleasant, with occasional livestock markets; distant Tarfside has a primary school, post office and the Retreat folk museum, shop and cafe. A driving range and *'golf academy'* have been added to the golf course; a garage is still open, and shops include a post office, café, chemist, two grocers, a newsagent and a gallery.

## EDZELL AIRFIELD

**Map 6, C1**

***Airfield, Mearns***

OS 45: NO 6269

A 1939–45 war airfield east of the River North Esk in the Howe of the Mearns was named after the nearby Angus village of Edzell. During the Cold War period, apparently around 1960, a completely new settlement was developed there to serve a US Navy submarine surveillance and satellite communications base. With a population of 735 in 1971 it had no civilian existence of its own, but its closure, begun in 1995, meant the loss of 275 civilian jobs as well as the 700 military personnel, with severe implications for the surrounding settlements, especially Brechin with its US housing estate. The base with its sports centre and sewage works was acquired with the aim of recreational use.

## EGILSAY, Isle of

**Map 13, B2**

***Small Orkney island,*** *pop. 50*

OS 5 or 6: HY 4630

The small Orkney isle of Egilsay *('Church Isle')* which lies 20km north of Kirkwall had a chapel and probably also a monastery by 1117, when the pious Earl Magnus was martyred there. The church of St Magnus with its fine round tower was soon built in his memory, and became the seat of a bishop for a period around 1135–40. While its importance did not last, the church was still used into the 19th century. The population was around 200 by 1801; a harbour was built at Skaill and a school and post office were provided. But apart from the tower the church eventually became a roofless ruin, and the mainly farming population had fallen to just 39 by 1971. However by 1989 a daily ro-ro ferry plied from Kirkwall, Rousay and Wyre to a new pier in the Skaill Tang harbour, and the roads were extended. Egilsay was soon largely repopulated by incomers, among them escapees from the south of England; by then the primary school had 11 pupils, and the 1991 census found 46 residents.

## EIGG, Isle of

**Map 8, A5**

***Hebridean island (Small Isles),*** *pop. 60*

OS 39: NM 4884

This small inner Hebridean isle is dominated by a miniature mountain, the 393m Sgurr, whose columnar lava cliffs are almost perpendicular. There was an early monastery where St Donan and all his monks were killed by Vikings in 617. Eigg, which became a MacDonald property in 1309, was noted by Monro in 1549 as *"very good for sheep, with a haven for Highland boats, and a parish kirk"* – commemoratively named Kildonan. In 1577 nearly 400 MacDonalds who had taken refuge in a cave were suffocated by their tribal enemies the MacLeods of Harris. Martin noted in 1703 that the isle belonged in part to Allan MacDonald of Moidart, mentioning *"the village on the south coast"* and that the local people were Gaelic-speaking Catholics, some of whom had fought at Killiecrankie. Siding with the Jacobites caused the sacking of the unlucky island in the 1745 rebellion.

**Lairds Good and Bad**: In 1829 Eigg was sold to an unsympathetic Aberdeen professor, who cleared half the people. There was nothing but crofting when from 1893 the new owner Lawrence Thompson built piers at relatively sheltered Galmisdale, and stimulated development; a road crossed the central col to Cleadale in the north-west. The Lodge was built in 1926–27 in Italianate style for the next lairds, the Runcimans, but by 1951 only some 85 people lived on Eigg, whose 14 telephones were connected to the Mallaig exchange. By 1953 the island had a resident doctor. But with fluctuating ownerships, ageing, and depopulation only 69 people remained in 1971 and the centrally sited school served only two children; by 1975 the population had rapidly shrunk to only 40.

**Making things Hum at *'Islington on Sea'***: Eigg was sold in 1975 to Keith Schellenberg, an English sportsman and laird of Huntly. He built five chalets, introduced pony trekking and sailing dinghies, and in 1976 converted Kildonan Farm to a guest house and craft centre. Access was by private motor vessels, and a new STD telephone exchange and doctor's surgery were built in 1979. By then all electricity was locally generated, there were 7 schoolchildren, and a shop at the post office. By 1981 some 80 people lived on Eigg. But meantime crofting was almost dead, the lack of a good harbour left fishing moribund, and even lobsters were rare. Afforestation of the centre of the island was begun, but the laird's big schemes were not profitable and the craft shop closed. By 1984 when the guest houses gave up, most of the laird's cottages were either derelict or had been restored as holiday homes; the population was down to 60, but there was still a tea room. The doctor retired in 1989, but was replaced, and by 1994 incomers had brought the highly diverse population back up to about 75, described in one newspaper as *"Islington on Sea"*. Bed and breakfast accommodation was available.

**Yet another Impossible Laird – the Last!**: In 1995 the island (whose school was still open) was bought by German architect and artist Marlin Eckhard-Maruma, whose daydreams of development were ended by bankruptcy in 1996; he even sold off the island's cattle, and the former *Galmisdale Inn* stood derelict in 1997. In that year the Isle of Eigg Heritage Trust, formed by the 63 remaining residents, with aid from Highland Council and the Scottish Wildlife Trust, finally bought Eigg from Maruma's creditors. This ended *'top down'* control of this unique isle, where by 1999 the trust were renovating old houses and building new ones. In 2000 Calmac withdrew its last passenger-only ferry, the MV *Lochmor*, replacing it on the Mallaig and Small Isles service by the 14-car roll-on vessel MV *Lochnevis*, allowing supplies to reach the islands without reloading – except Eigg, which still has a jetty but no slipway. The long-standing doctor's practice has Britain's smallest list, the 125 Small Isles patients. A backpackers' hostel is open all year at Cleadale.

## ELDERSLIE, Thorn & Glenpatrick

**Map 15, A5**

***Renfrewshire urban area,*** *pop. 5300*

OS 64: NS 4463

Elderslie, 4km west of Paisley, was noted by Chambers as *"the paternal seat of William Wallace"*, the famous Scots patriot who was born about 1270. Roy's map made about 1754 showed a road from Paisley to Beith which crossed the Old Patrick Water, a burn flowing through the hamlet of Elderslie. The isolated Glenpatrick paper mill was built on this stream in 1815, 1km to the south, and the so-called Gleniffer distillery was built close by in 1833–34. Meantime in 1832 Cobbett had dined at Elderslie, the seat of Mr Spiers in its *"well-wooded park"*. Stations were opened on the new Glasgow, Paisley, Kilmarnock & Ayr Railway in 1840 east of Elderslie, and for Johnstone west of Thorn, 1km west of Elderslie, where the Johnstone road diverged; by 1860 a village had grown there too. About 1860 the Glenpatrick paper mill was converted into the Patrickbank Print Works. The *"old fashioned and quaintly built"* Gleniffer distillery made about 320,000 litres of malt whisky annually in 1886; about 1890 it was renamed as *Glenpatrick*, but was closed permanently in 1894.

**Trams, Golf and Carpets**: From about 1905 Paisley's new electric trams ran through Elderslie to Johnstone and Kilbarchan. Elderslie gained an all-age school and a post office, and its golf club was founded in 1908. The role of the Glenpatrick mill changed again, for around 1920 the Bank of Scotland funded heavy investment there by A F Stoddard & Co, carpet manufacturers. The trams between Kilbarchan and the 47-car Elderslie depot were withdrawn in the 1930s; the depot closed with all the Paisley area services in 1957 and was sold off. Beeching closed the station in the mid 1960s despite the huge new Linwood motor works close by. By that time Elderslie – whose school, now primary only, bore the name of Wallace – had practically coalesced with Johnstone. However, in 1991 its population was 5286, socially balanced and almost unchanged in total since 1971. Stoddard Sekers Carpets at Glenpatrick were still a large and innovative concern in 1992, when they acquired BMK of Kilmarnock. In 1996 they concentrated Axminster carpet production at Elderslie under the *'Stoddard Templeton'* brand; Kilmarnock was retained as their only other factory. The golf course now has 18 holes.

## ELGIN

**Map 10, A1**

***Moray large town,*** *pop. 19,000* — OS 28: NJ 2163

The former Pictish province of Moray was centred on the fertile plain of the Laigh of Moray, later renowned for corn and flax growing. Its early bishopric was later removed from Mortlach to Old Aberdeen. King Duncan lost his life to Macbeth in 1040 in a battle at Pitgaveney, 2 km north-east of Elgin, but the site of the 11th century Moray thanage of Kilmalemnock is unknown. However, by 1115 turbulent Moray again had a bishop. Elgin which now lies on an inland site where an early ferry crossed the little River Lossie may well have been on tidewater when it was chartered as a Royal Burgh by David I in 1136. St Giles' church was established there before or during his reign. From about 1150 Moray had a sheriff, but he seems to have been a mobile official, because the region was not effectively part of Scotland until Malcolm IV won a victory at Urquhart in 1160, and cattle-stealing long remained the way of life of the unconquered Highland clans to the west, as noted in many reports.

**Spynie Palace – by the Sea?**: The Diocese of Moray embraced Inverness and long retained exclaves in upper Strathspey and Strathavon; it had no fixed see until 1210, when the then bishop David Stewart settled at Spynie, a parish centre 3 km north of Elgin. There he built his palace on the south shore of what was then an extensive sea loch at least 7 km long, later cut off by the sandspit growing west from the Spey mouth. In the 15th century the palace was rebuilt as a strong six storey tower house. As shown on Pont's late 16th century map, the loch then extended from about the modern Waterton near Duffus, all the way to Oakenhead by Lossiemouth; but over the centuries it gradually silted up. The church authorities soon realised the importance of having the cathedral in a burgh, so in 1224 Bishop (or Dean) Andrew settled on Elgin as the site, and started to build a fine stone cathedral.

**Struggles to develop Trade and Industry**: Elgin likewise became the caput of the sheriffdom between 1225 and 1232; the Royal castle was probably built about that time. A Dominican friary was founded in 1234 by Alexander II, and *'hospitals'* were also built in the 13th and 14th centuries. There is archaeological evidence of early woollen textile industries and of smithies and copper founding, and barrels may have been made, for old ones were used to line wells. Elgin made a slow start in trade and suffered seemingly endless setbacks, including in 1270 further warlike attempts to regain local independence from Scotland. However, a Franciscan friary was founded about 1281 by William, Earl of Ross.

**Castle on the Hill and Residence in the Town**: A traveller with the invading English army of Edward I in 1295 said there was *"a good castle and a good town"*, which he rather obscurely referred to as *"the city of Deigm"*. He probably found a stout timber castle on the Lady Hill, where a building still stood 300 years later, to be shown on Pont's map. Although this had the status of a royal castle about 1300, it seems not to have been rebuilt in stone and all traces later vanished. Instead, medieval royal visitors would lodge in the town at Thunderton House, like the cathedral built in New Red Sandstone. This was hewn either 3 km to the west in Quarrywood, so marked

*Elgin Cathedral, built from New Red Sandstone in 1224, was rebuilt after being burned by the Wolf of Badenoch in 1390. The lead from the roof was removed in 1567 by the Regent Moray to help pay for his army, but the ship carrying it for sale sank. The central tower collapsed in 1711.* (RCAHMS / JRH)

by Pont, at Rosebrae still farther west, or at Cuttieshillock. The tragedy of the wars was followed in 1350 by the catastrophe of the Black Death. Elgin contributed practically no Customs payments until the late 14th century, and few later.

**Elgin versus the Highlanders**: In 1390 Elgin suffered arson at the hands of the notorious *Wolf of Badenoch* (Alexander Stewart, a son of Robert II), whose base was a 13th century curtain-walled castle secure on an islet in the remote Lochindorb, 40km to the south-west. He *"burnt the city, the parish church, another religious house called Maison Dieu, 18 houses of the canons, and the cathedral"* (Chambers). Thieving Highlanders made yet another incursion in 1402. In 1406–14 the Franciscan friary was rebuilt, and the magnificent cathedral was repaired and completed with its glass windows by about 1420; the central tower and spire was 60m tall. The L-plan tower called the Bishop's House, and the Convent of Mercy in Abbey Street, were also built in the 15th century. Spynie obtained a barony charter in 1451, but this failed, with still more trouble from raiding Highlanders in 1452. In the late 15th century Elgin was a barony of the powerful Murray family, but suffered even more decay than Forres, being taxed at only half the value of the latter town in 1485. However, malt was produced in the 15th century on a sufficient scale to export it to Aberdeen, and by 1535 the burgh was paying rather more tax than Forres, though under 1.5% of the Scottish total.

**Reformation and Ruin**: Despite the recurrent destruction, there were six religious houses in the city by the time of the Reformation, including the surviving friary of the Observants, founded before 1494. Those seeking peace of mind were to be sadly disappointed, for Regent Murray removed the lead from the cathedral roof in 1567–68, so destining one of Scotland's finest buildings to ruin. However, by 1593 Elgin had become the centre of a presbytery. Pont's map made about 1600 showed Sheriffmill. Though the cathedral was roofless, its three steeples still stood in 1618. As Elgin revived, the *Bow Brig* was built between 1630 and 1635, and by 1639 the burgh was the 15th richest centre in Scotland in tax yield. But in 1645 Montrose inflicted *"indiscriminate pillage"* in the town. Spynie palace was abandoned after the last bishop died there in 1686.

**Home from Home for Highland Gents**: After the civil war commercial brewing developed, with a large public brewery at Oldmills; by 1688 the *Red Lion Inn* was open, and malting had become the largest local industry. A post office was opened in 1669 on a new Aberdeen–Inverness postal route. In 1698 the town council established a port at Lossiemouth *(q.v.)*. A bank was founded in 1703, one of the first outside the big cities. A new post office was opened at Elgin in 1711, the year of the sorry collapse of the cathedral's central tower and spire. Defoe noted in the 1720s that *"as the country around is rich and pleasant, so here are a great many rich inhabitants, and in the town of Elgin in particular; for the gentlemen leave their highland habitations in the winter and come and live here for the diversion of the place and plenty of provisions"*.

**Textiles, Bridges and Travellers' Reports**: Elgin had one of the ten spinning schools established about 1730; a bleachfield was in operation by 1745, and by 1755 the town had a linen merchant, and also a grammar school. Roy's survey of about 1750 showed Elgin as a large one-street town on the area's sole road, which ran east and west from Forres by the Kirk of Alves and the *'Kirk of Longbride'* (Lhanbryde). There were no bridges on this route, but one spanned the Lossie at nearby Sheriff Mill, though no road appeared to connect it to the town! The *'Bishops Mills'* were also marked. In 1765 Alexander Carlyle found the agriculture around Elgin better than around Fochabers, the inn *"very good"* and Elgin *"a pretty enough town"*; but he asserted that it was devoid of industry. That the going was still hard was confirmed by Pennant; writing of his tour in 1769, he remarked that by comparison with Aberdeenshire and Banffshire eastern Moray was unimproved, the cottages merely of turf. Elgin he regarded as *"a good town"* but *"excepting its great cattle fairs, has little trade"*; the parish population was around 5000. In 1771 Elgin's long-established *Red Lion Inn* was said to be *"good"*, but two years later Boswell was more critical.

**Tanning, Thread and Fairs**: At that time the urge to develop was again stirring in Elgin. By the 1770s Elgin was importing oak bark from upper Speyside for its tanning industry, and by about 1775 thread mills worked in the town; in 1776 large quantities of woollen yarn were made for the Glasgow and London markets. A bleachfield was built in 1785, and by the 1790s linen yarns were also being exported, and woven into cloth by the town's 70 hand weavers. The College brewery was established by Young in 1784, the Aberdeen Banking Company had a branch in the town between at least 1793 and 1825, and in 1797 five fairs were scheduled. In the 1790s George Brown of Elgin surveyed many road lines north and west of the Great Glen, and in the next decade was the valuer for the construction of the Caledonian Canal. Heron in 1799 wrote of Elgin *"this ancient city contains between three and four thousand inhabitants"*.

**Johnston's Mills, Whisky, and Better Agriculture**: A large water-powered thread mill existed in 1800; integrated and long-lasting woollen mills were set up by Johnston in 1797, and by 1807 these too were a large concern. Spynie quarry – just west of the palace – provided the Permian sandstone for the Fochabers bridge of 1806. By 1811 there were two daily mail coaches between Aberdeen and Inverness, and another daily coach plied between Elgin and Aberdeen. Legal whisky production, which was to play so large a part in the subsequent growth of the Elgin area, began at the Linkwood distillery which was established in 1821 2 km south-east of the town. In 1824 came the Miltonduff distillery, 5km to the south-west, rebuilt from smugglers' stills which were moved into a former monastic brewhouse. Like many other distilleries in the area this later adopted the geographically misleading suffix *Glenlivet*, referring to the character of the whisky for marketing advantage. Throughout Moray and adjoining counties agricultural improvement – including *"draining, planting and enclosing"* – was late to start, and still at its height in the 1820s. Chambers thought Elgin *"a delightful old-fashioned city, having been a place of residence for the gentry of the province, many of whose houses are still pointed out"*. He added *"Elgin possesses a distinguished brewery"*.

**Pauper provides Public Services**: Chambers mentioned an *"infirmary and dispensary"* – Grey's Hospital, designed by James Gillespie, which opened in 1819, having been established under the will of Dr Alexander Gray, a native of Elgin – and the County Buildings, a *"modern structure"*. The *'pale sandstone'* used was apparently local (though whether from Quarrywood or Spynie was not stated): *"a considerable quantity was lately exported for the building of the new London*

*Bridge"*. Andrew Anderson – a unique man, locally born as a pauper, yet having the drive to become a Lieutenant-General in the East India Company – established his Institute in 1830. This remarkably combined a school with an old people's home! Elgin's gasworks dated from the same year, and the town's museum was purpose-built in 1836. By 1856 a water-powered sawmill was in operation at Dean's Haugh.

**Railway Rivalry**: In 1852 Elgin was linked to its port of Lossiemouth by the isolated Morayshire Railway; the wooden sheds of its makeshift terminal station east of Moss Street were in use for fifty years. Two rival companies were involved in the town from 1858, when the Inverness & Aberdeen Junction Railway (I&AJR) extended its Inverness to Nairn line through a separate station west of Moss Street to meet the Great North of Scotland Railway (GNSR) at Keith. This completed the rail route of its title, but the first Inverness to Aberdeen trains took almost four hours en route. A link between the stations was provided at Elgin. The I&AJR became part of the Highland (HR) in 1865; meantime by 1860 Wordie & Co operated a rail to road cartage depot.

**The Longest Train Journey in Britain**: In 1861 the Morayshire Railway opened a second line from its original terminus, crossing over the HR to reach Longmorn and Rothes to the south; in 1863 this local company was taken over by the GNSR. Through coaches in the mail trains from London Euston to Aberdeen were extended to Elgin in 1869, making a journey of almost 1000km, easily the longest in Britain. Few people used them and the through service to Elgin ceased in 1873, but through coaches were reinstated in 1911 between Elgin and Edinburgh. Elgin became still more important as a railway centre when a further GNSR line to Buckie and the coast of Banffshire was completed in 1886, leaving the Lossiemouth line at Lossie Junction, 2 km north.

**Nets, Newspapers and Nuns**: Although the population of Moray began to decline after 1861, Elgin continued to grow; one cause was the introduction to the town in the 1860s of netmaking by machinery. The local newspaper, the *Northern Scot*, was established in 1880. In the 1880s the *"venerable" Gordon Arms* was the principal posting (horse hiring) hostelry in the district. In 1891 the former Greyfriars site was adopted by a convent and was finely restored in 1896 by John Kinross, incorporating the ruined church of the Convent of Mercy in Abbey Street. A public library commenced about then. By 1894 Elgin had nearly 8000 people; Murray noted it as *"neat, pleasant and somewhat busy"*, with four hotels, the *"very good" Station* and the *"good" Gordon Arms, Palace* and *City*.

**Distillery Expansion runs riot**: Meantime in 1873 Linkwood distillery had been rebuilt by William Brown, to produce 225,000 litres of Highland malt whisky a year. At that time Miltonduff distillery used Orkney peats and water power; its ten workers produced about 350,000 litres of Highland malt whisky. Gordon & MacPhail of Elgin were established as whisky blenders in 1895. Such a welter of new distillery development occurred in the area at that time as was never seen before except at Campbeltown, or anywhere at all since. The Glen Moray-Glenlivet, later owned by Macdonald & Muir of Leith, was started up in 1897 on the site of a brewery. (For other new distilleries south of Elgin see the Longmorn article.)

**Railway, Bricks, Golf and Engineering**: From 1889 Elgin was the headquarters of the Moray & Nairn joint County Council. By 1894 the Morayshire brickworks were active at Lochside, 3 km north of the town; by 1955 only its water-filled pits remained. The town's growing importance must have justified the fine new stone station building erected by the GNSR in 1902. Elgin golf club was a late foundation for so important a centre, dating only from 1906, though its good 18-hole parkland course was apparently well worth the wait. In the early 20th century the Newmill Ironworks manufactured cast-iron grids and other distillery components, and G Souter & Sons, Engineers of Greyfriars Foundry, made stationary internal combustion engines in the 1910s.

**Distilling in the Teetotal Doldrums**: It is hardly surprising that Elgin acquired distillery engineering and HQ offices, and that it was the location where Highland Malt distillers met in 1909 to protest against the hated anti-drink budget of the teetotal – though in some other ways immoderate – Welsh chancellor Lloyd George. Glenmoray and Linkwood-Glenlivet distilleries were in difficulties in 1910; the Glenmoray company ceased distilling and sought winding up in 1912 but was denied this. Also in difficulties about 1910 was Glenlossie, which was acquired in 1919 by Scottish Malt Distillers Ltd. Elgin was still a key barley market in 1915, though the last surviving brewery closed around then.

**Transport Centre and the Longest Sleep**: When bus services came to be developed in the 1920s, Elgin became one of Scotland's largest country bus centres, HQ of the Scottish General (Northern) Omnibus Company. But in 1931 Alexander of Falkirk bought the bus firm, and in 1936 the distillers Hiram Walker of Canada acquired George Ballantine & Son, including their Miltonduff distillery. Elgin was served from 1923 to 1939 by a sleeping car from Lossiemouth to London King's Cross, almost a thousand kilometres!

**Growing Population, Shrinking Railways**: By 1951 Morayshire was growing again and Elgin had over 12,000 people, a modern sheriff court and what was then the sign of a vigorous town centre, a Woolworth store. By 1957 Elgin's *Northern Scot* was a major weekly newspaper with offshoots in Forres and Grantown; by 1961, a daily inflow of some 1600 commuters showed how important Elgin had become. It was still *"neat, pleasant and somewhat busy"* when the author first visited in the mid 1960s, but its pleasantness was to be somewhat eroded by traffic and sprawl, due to the town's quite rapid growth. In the 1960s the engine shed, the line to Lossiemouth, the lines to Buckie and the coast, and also to Keith via Rothes and Craigellachie, were closed. However, the goods yard remained active, and in 1978 potatoes were still sent south by rail.

**Elgin in the 1970s**: The 1930s youth hostel was closed soon after 1968, and a small new shopping precinct that had been built by 1970 was at first slow to let. By then Elgin had a modern town hall, a bus station, a covered swimming pool, a large community centre, and the HQ of Scottish Malt Products. Concrete products were made, and by 1979 Riddochs of Rothiemay, timber merchants, had moved to Elgin, where the Elgin City Sawmills were also at work. The long-established James Johnston & Co of Newmill made scarves and other woollen piece goods. The manufacture of oil industry components and telecommunication instruments developed in the 1970s.

**The Moray District Council – and Elgin to Penzance**: In 1975 Elgin lost burgh and county-town status, in compensation becoming the headquarters of the enlarged Moray district.

It was re-emerging as a prime commercial and significant further educational centre, gaining the encouragement of the Grampian regional planners. In the mid 1970s the new 45-room *Eight Acres Hotel* was built as the largest of sixteen in the town, including the 26-room former *Station Hotel*, renamed the *Laichmoray*. In 1984–85 a daily passenger train ran through between Elgin and Penzance, once more giving Britain's longest run! The former GNSR station buildings were listed, and it was planned in the 1980s to convert them into a business centre. In 1990 a small but convenient new station building was opened at the one-time HR platforms.

**Major Shopping Developments**: By 1980 Elgin was the undisputed prime centre for specialist shopping between Aberdeen and Inverness, and in the early eighties Britain's most northerly superstore was built in the town centre by William Low (Tesco from 1994), soon followed by a peripheral ASDA. A recent retail warehouse park at Springfield was developed further in 1991 when the population was 19,027. A 200-job food superstore for Aberdeen-based Norco was also built at that time, taking in the site of the earlier unsuccessful Greyfriars development; but Norco too became insolvent and sold the store to Safeway in 1992. The St Giles Centre, a 28-shop central mall and multi-storey car park, was opened in 1991 but the early take-up of units was slow.

**Other Facilities Prospering**: Health and professional services were also very significant, and a motor museum was open near the town's attractive park. In 1989 the Moray College of Further Education offered a range of business-related courses to HNC/HND level; by 1997 Elgin Academy had 1000 pupils and Elgin High School 600. In 1993 a four-year extension programme was commenced for Gray's Hospital, upgrading its status and bringing 180 new permanent jobs to the town by 1997. The cattle market owned by Aberdeen & Northern Marts remained active in 1996, dealing in beasts from a wide area. Fun pools and ice discos in *"the most modern and varied leisure centre in the Highlands"* augmented the conventional swimming pool and Moray ice rink, where a brand new ice-hockey team – the Moray Dolphins – was founded in 1994.

**Industry in the 1990s**: Johnston's of Newmill had their own dyeworks, wove cashmere (from Outer Mongolia) and lambswool for men's suitings, scarves, and rugs; they owned a Hawick knitwear factory by 1991. In 1991 United Distillers had their laboratory in Elgin; the Glen Moray and Miltonduff distilleries had lost their inappropriate *'Glenlivet'* suffix. Linkwood still made a dark, strong single malt whisky, matured in sherry casks. Gordon & MacPhail, who celebrated their centenary in 1995, bottled Balblair malt whisky from Edderton, *'Old Pulteney'* from Wick, blended a regimental whisky for the KOSB (King's Own Scottish Borderers) and also supplied a range of malt whiskies for connoisseurs. Walkers of Aberlour opened a small factory in Elgin in 1994, its 30 workers making shortbread cookies for Disney! By then Elgin also had the HQ of Moray Badenoch & Strathspey Enterprise.

**Rail Freight struggling**: In 1988 McPherson's Transport of Aberlour installed a rail-mounted crane to move whisky containers on and off trains to and from the Coatbridge terminal. Government stores still arrived by rail for RAF Kinloss near Forres, and carbon dioxide produced as a by-product at the numerous distilleries was also shipped out, by rail tankers. Today potatoes, timber and pulpwood still leave Elgin by rail.

**Tourists see Spynie and Moray regains Independence**: By 1995 an Elgin architectural practice was Scotland's oldest. Spynie quarry was open for building stone in the mid 1990s, under Moray Stone Cutters *(see also Hopeman)*. After 21 years of restoration by Historic Scotland, Spynie Palace was opened to visitors in 1994. In 1996 a new public garden of over 1 ha was opened, stocked so far as the climate would allow with all the plants mentioned in the Bible! By then the Old Mills – still powered by water – could also be visited, as could the Cashmere Centre. In 1996 Moray District became a unitary authority, taking over major responsibilities from the former Grampian Regional Council: this restored Elgin's traditional status in local government. In 2000 Elgin FC was at last admitted from the Highland League to the Scottish League, starting in the Third Division. Besides the Elgin Museum with its science emphasis, the Moray Motor Museum shows an extensive display of vintage cars. Robertson's are major construction employers in the town, and Northern Fabricators include distillery equipment amongst their metal-work. Johnston's – still family-owned – now employ 500, run a mill shop, and have added luxury furnishings to their range. Medium-sized hotels include the *Laichmoray*, *Mansefield House*, and the *Mansion House*; the leisure complex of the *Eight Acres* offers indoor swimming, there is a *Travel Inn* (40), smaller hotels and guest houses, and a tiny hostel for backpackers is open all year.

## ELIE & Earlsferry

**Map 6, C4**

***Fife coast village**, pop. 900*

OS 59: NO 4900

The East Fife placename Ardross is said to derive from *Ardrach*, the Gaelic word for a ferryboat, *"from the establishment of a ferry here by Macduff Earl of Fife"* about 1050 (Heron); Ardross may have been chartered as early as 1070. By 1300 the Earls, who also owned lands in East Lothian, had built a hospice there for southern pilgrims to St Andrews; they still operated a ferry to North Berwick 200 years later. Under the anglicised name Earlsferry the settlement became a burgh of barony in 1541 and was promoted to a Royal Burgh in 1589. Its close neighbour Elie, which had a large though shallow natural harbour, gained only a baronial charter, granted in 1598, but had a parish school by 1600.

**Slavery builds Elie**: Sir John Scot wrote that in 1626 Sir William Scot of Ardross held Elie on the *"slavery tithes of the Lord of Balcarres"*. But Balcarres provided Elie church, built in 1639, and *'Ely'* was shown with much greater emphasis than Earlsferry on Blaeu's map dated 1645, which derived from James Gordon's visit. Elie had two vessels in 1655 and by that time exported grain, though the large isolated granary on the quayside may be of rather later date. In the late 17th century Elie was one of only four parishes in Fife able to maintain a school. Even so, in 1696 Elie petitioned the Privy Council for help in repairing its ruinous harbour. By then the ferry was extinct, but a number of the 17th century buildings have survived. Roy's map of about 1750 showed Earlsferry and Elie as distinct places linked to Pittenweem by road, but the great storm of 1766 filled Earlsferry's harbour forever with blown sand, drowned seven Earlsferry fishermen from one boat, and left it a mere suburb of Elie. James Horsburgh, born locally in 1762, became the Hydrographer to the East India Company.

**Textiles and Trains**: A lint mill was working at Elie by 1761, and the construction of a bleachfield was subsidised in 1762; the Yarn Field dyed yarn specifically for Kirkcaldy checks. In the 1770s the road from Elie to St Andrews was completed, and from 1794 *'Ely'* post office was open; by 1797 Elie was a post town. *"The village of Ely contains about 500 inhabitants"*, wrote Heron in 1799; its harbour was *"good"*. By mid-century James Waddell was Town Clerk of Earlsferry, probably a near sinecure of a post, which he retained for some 50 years! Elie harbour was rebuilt with massive igneous stonework about 1855; but itremained rather exposed from the west. In 1863 a station was opened on the railway from Thornton Junction to Anstruther. Earlsferry & Elie Golf Club was founded in 1858, apparently dividing in two in 1875; two links courses resulted, of 18 and 9 holes.

**Elie and Earlsferry as Resorts**: By the 1880s steamers from Leith brought Edinburgh holidaymakers to Elie's fine sands; there were two hotels by 1894, Murray noting the *"good" Marine* and the *"fair" Victoria.* A late Victorian baronial style mansion built for a wealthy Edinburgh surgeon became the *Golf Hotel* in the 1920s. The North Berwick ferry service was revived for a few years up to 1914, with a Leith connection, but the Forth steamer trade withered and died in the 1920s. However, by the 1950s the number of hotels had grown to nine, mainly small, donkeys carried children along the beach and there was a golf club maker. Then came cheap package holidays in the sun, the railway was closed in 1964 and the prosperity of the hotels steadily dwindled. The mansion of Elie House had become a convent by 1969. The twin settlements became a retirement centre and minor resort with two golf courses – the Earlsferry Thistle and Golf House – and the facilities of a large village. The *Marine Hotel* burned down in 1983, leaving only three. The population was 903 in 1991; by then the harbour was used mainly for yachting. A small number of new houses was built in the 1990s, when many older houses were second homes.

## ELLON & Logie Buchan — Map 10, C2

***Aberdeenshire town,*** *pop. 8600* — OS 30: NJ 9530

Ellon stands on the north bank of the River Ythan at the head of tidewater some 25 km north of Aberdeen. Islets in the river suggest that the placename derives from the Gaelic *Eileann*, meaning island. A tenth or 11th century monastery at Ellon became associated from the 12th century with Kinloss Abbey. Ellon had a medieval motte, where by 1206 the Thane or Earl of Buchan held head courts three times a year, and the Knights Hospitallers had lands by 1345. Esslemont castle 2 km to the west was built in the 14th century. Besides the ford and possible ferry at Ellon, a ferry operated from ancient times at the Boat of Fechil or Waterton some 2 km to the east; the Kirkton of Logie Buchan parish lies on the south bank 2 km farther east. By 1387 Ellon had a parish church, and Ellon castle was built there in the 16th century, replacing the early Kermucks castle.

**Education and Organisation**: Pont's sketchy and much altered map, probably made as late as 1601, showed the Kirk of Ellon, which by 1602 had a school and was the centre of a presbytery. The map, intriguingly, showed a bridge and a ladder-like formation that might represent a *'causeway'* or made road for several kilometres to the north-east past Wester Burness to Arnage and Coldwells – the alignment later adopted for the Peterhead turnpike. However, Gordon's 17th century map showed neither bridge nor causeway. Yet another castle arose at Waterton in the 17th century. A market was in being by about 1700, and Ellon became a burgh of barony in 1707. A post office was open by 1715; in 1721 Ellon was described as a *"village pleasantly situated"*, and in 1725 as a *"town"* with a school.

**Windmill, Textiles and Coach**: The Roy map (surveyed about 1750) showed Ellon as a compact settlement; to the west stood Meikle Mill. Four tracks radiated on broadly north to south and south-west to north-east axes. A threshing windmill erected beside the way at Hilton still survives. In 1778 the parish was known for the home spinning and weaving of wool, and for knitting stockings which Aberdeen's traders in knitwear would export. By 1773 there was an inn, and a new church was built in 1777. Four annual fairs were scheduled for 1797, but Heron still regarded Ellon as a *"village"* in 1799. A bridge must have been built by 1811, when Ellon was served by a daily coach between Aberdeen and Peterhead. In 1851 Ellon Castle was torn down and rebuilt as a mansion with wooded policies.

**A Thriving Market Centre in 1858**: Pratt described Ellon in 1858 as a *"thriving and rapidly increasing village"*. It was in fact already functioning as a town, having five churches, three schools and, being a market centre and fishing resort, three inns: *"the New Inn, lately erected, containing excellent accommodations; the Town Hall forming part of the design; the Buchan Hotel, at the northern extremity of the bridge, also a commodious and comfortable house of entertainment; and the old and well-frequented Commercial Inn"*. There were *"three Banking Houses, a Post Office, and many excellent shops. Markets are held fortnightly, and also fairs; an extensive business is transacted in these markets, in cattle, grain, coals, lime, bone-dust &c"*. Mitchell & Rae had a large granary and agricultural merchants business at the Meadows of Waterton 2 km east of Ellon, using lighters to transport *"corn, coal, lime, and bone-dust"* to and from Newburgh. Near a waulkmill site at the mouth of the Burn of Forvie 3 km to the east was a tile works opened in 1834 *"at which drainage tiles were first made north of the Tay"* (Pratt).

**A Quiet Century beside the Buchan Railway**: In 1861 a station was opened at Ellon on the main stem of the Great North of Scotland Railway's Buchan line from Dyce to Maud, Fraserburgh and Peterhead. By 1894 Ellon was regarded by Murray as a *"town"* with two *"good"* hotels, the *New* and *Station*. In 1897 Ellon became the junction for the ill-fated Cruden Bay and Boddam branch line, which was closed by degrees between 1932 and 1950. Meantime a local power station had been provided in 1914, Ellon Castle was again rebuilt in 1920, and the McDonald golf club was founded in 1927, laying out a 9-hole course. The main railway was regrettably closed to passengers by Beeching in 1965, and to freight in 1979.

**Oil Dormitory and Ostriches**: The population of Ellon (2263 in 1971) was said to have tripled in five years from 1972, with residential development for the oil industry and a new industrial estate. Sea & Land Pipelines Ltd, established in 1978, aimed to employ 150 people. A number of new companies were attracted in the 1980s, and the golf course had been extended to 18 holes by 1989. By 1991 the town's population was 8627, young, fit and well-educated; the fine Meadows sports complex had been created and an eastern bypass had been built, its bridge replacing the Waterton passenger ferry. Norco of Aberdeen had built a superstore, but in 1992 this regional co-op sold it to Safeway, hoping (in vain) to escape insolvency. By 1997 Ellon Academy had 1630 pupils, the largest roll in the new Aberdeenshire. A controversial scheme for an ostrich abattoir was approved in 1996. By 1999 the route of the former railway was a long distance path, the *'Formartine & Buchan Way'*, and still more housing had been built north of the town.

## ELPHIN, Ledmore & Altnacealgach — Map 12, B3

***Village & hamlets, Sutherland,*** *pop. under 100* OS 15: NC 2111

Standing about 150 m above sea level on the borders of Sutherland and Wester Ross, this remote moorland area near the distinctive isolated mountain called Cul Mor has various prehistoric remains. The Roy map of about 1750 depicted the knobbly and trackless terrain, in which the long narrow Loch *Meaty* (Veyatie) and smaller tributary lochs nearby are the main features. In the mid 19th century roads were built from Ullapool, Kylestrome and Lairg, meeting at a junction named Ledmore. By the 1890s the delightfully named clachan of Elphin some 4 km to the west was on the map, and a lochside inn was open at Altnacealgach, 2 km to the east. By the 1930s there was a primary school and post office at exposed Elphin. By 1951 about 70 people lived in the area, and *Altnacealgach* was a hotel, as was *Drumrunie Lodge*, on the Ullapool road 10 km south-west of Elphin, for a period around 1953. By 1976 the school had closed, but Elphin had an automatic telephone exchange. About then a marble quarry was opened 5 km north-east of Elphin, and rapidly grew; in the 1990s the Ledmore North quarry was worked for coloured building stone by Ledmore Marble Ltd, who from 1995 exported the product to Italy by rail through Lairg. By 1998 the striking viewpoint at Knockan south of Elphin had added a visitor centre to its direction finder; Elphin post office has closed, but the primary school has reopened. Nowadays hill walking is among the few activities in this area; *Altnacealgach* is now a motel, and forestry is spreading around it.

## ELPHINSTONE — Map 15, E2

***E. Lothian village,*** *pop. 700* OS 66: NT 3970

On a plateau some 5 km east of Musselburgh stood an early chapel, and nearby was built the major 14th century keep of Elphinstone Tower, in 1560 the seat of Lord Elphinstone. Pont's map of about 1600 showed it emparked, with an accompanying mill on a headwater of the Lothian River Tyne. A school was opened in 1624. Roy's map made about 1754 showed Elphinstone as a small village on an east–west road, with other roads to Musselburgh and Prestonpans. By 1894 a mineral railway from Ormiston served a small colliery at Fleets Farm between Tranent and *'North Elphingstone'*; Elphinstone proper was a tiny village with a post office. Coal mining persisted into the mid 20th century, but had ceased by 1963. Elphinstone Tower, dangerous due to undermining, was demolished about 1964. By 1981 Elphinstone's 750 people enjoyed minimal local facilities. In 1993 Inveresk Research International, a subsidiary of the Swiss SGS Group working for the pharmaceutical and chemicals industries, was expanding its quite recently established Elphinstone Research Centre at the former Fleets Farm. By 1996 there had been a little new development around the village; its post office is still open.

## ELVANFOOT — Map 2, B3

***S. Lanarkshire hamlet,*** *pop. 100* OS 78: NS 9517

The headwaters of the River Clyde include the Clydes Burn which flows from Beattock Summit, and the Powtrail Water which provides a route to Nithsdale. Ancient settlements and earthworks abound, and Roman roads from the south followed both streams, meeting in the vicinity of Elvanfoot, where the little Elvan Water flows into the River Clyde from the west. About 4 km upstream to the south the Daer Water joins the Powtrail Water to form the Clyde. The turnpike road (later the A74), and the Caledonian Railway's main line which opened in 1848, both followed the Clydes Burn route. The first station north of the summmit was at Elvanfoot, which became a larger hamlet. From 1901 Elvanfoot station was the junction for the light railway to Leadhills and Wanlockhead, an uneconomic venture which failed to revive lead mining and was closed in 1939.

**The Daer Reservoir**: In 1951 Elvanfoot's population was about 100 and its post office and few other facilities served some 250 people in all, a number cut to a mere 140 by 1981. Meantime a 750 m-long dam had been built across the Daer Water south of the Daer & Powtrail primary school, at Wintercleugh 8 km south of Elvanfoot, impounding a large reservoir some 40 m deep, opened in 1956. Elvanfoot station, which had two trains per day each way in 1963, was closed about 1965; the school was still open in 1976. But the school closed, and recently the post office also; the nearby A74 has become a motorway.

## EMBO & Skelbo — Map 9, B2

***East coast hamlets, Sutherland,*** *pop. 300* OS 21: NH 8192

Embo lies on poor low-lying farmland near the sandy coast about 3 km north of Dornoch. Landward is the 14th century tower of Skelbo Castle, built for the Lords of Duffus on a motte or eminence. The Roy map made about 1750 showed the mansion of Embo House to the east of a track linking Dornoch and Skelbo; to the west was a straggle of huts. A new fishing village was laid out in the early 19th century to resettle the victims of clearances, Embo pier being built on a coastal reef; by 1845 it had 42 inshore fishing boats. The village was again rebuilt about 700 m north of the pier, and gained a school and post office. A lifeboat station which opened in 1886 lasted only until 1904. When the Highland Railway opened its late branch to Dornoch as a light railway in 1902, a handily sited station was provided; but the line was closed completely in 1960. For a time around 1953 the village hall was used as a 16 mm cinema. By 1975 a caravan and camping park spread along the shore, serving a small but popular yachting and water-skiing centre. The pier had been extended by 1983, but Embo's few remaining fishermen used better and less exposed harbours. By 1980 *Grannie's Hielan' Hame* was a hotel! In 1996 Skelbo Castle, a scant ruin in need of restoration, was sold by Michael Alexander to Russian businessman Mikhail Debouar. The vast caravan site was then owned by a Newcastle company.

## EREDINE — Map 5, A4

***Argyllshire settlement, L. Awe,*** *pop. under 100.* OS 55: NM 9609

The 1750s Roy map showed a track running northwards over the hills from the Furnace area, ending at *During* (now Durran) on the east shore of Loch Awe. By the 1890s this was a tiny road, ungated and unmetalled, but a proper lochside road from Ford to Cladich passed the farm of Eredine 2 km to the north, which stood between two belts of lochside woodlands. By the 1920s a pier had been built at Eredine, but the ancient hill road was only a footpath. In mid century the Forestry Commission *(see Dalavich)* took over the whole area to plant the vast Eredine Forest, which they based on a small new settlement which took the name of the farm opposite, but remains a mere hamlet. A forestry road follows part of the line of the ancient track.

## ERISKAY

**Map 7, A4**

***Small Western Isles island,*** *pop. 175* OS 31: NF 7811

The small, hilly and infertile island of Eriskay lies between Barra and South Uist. Monro in 1549 noted that Eriskay belonged to MacNeil of Barra, and was *"inhabited and manured, with a daily gotten abundance of good fish"*. Pont's tiny map made around 1600 showed only a single settlement. Martin noted *"excellent cod and ling"* in 1703. The Reformation had bypassed Eriskay, whose 80 or so largely Catholic crofters were augmented after 1838 by 400 other poor souls lately cleared from their ancestral islands by the avaricious new laird Gordon of Cluny. They were allowed to resettle because even sheep would not have been profitable on Eriskay, and survived into the 20th century by fishing from the tiny north-facing harbour and jetty at Haun (a Norse word meaning *Haven).*

**Whisky Galore, but Islet no More**: It was looted whisky, comprising many of the 264,000 bottles which were aboard the SS *Politician* when she went aground in the Sound of Eriskay in 1941, that sent 19 islanders to prison, but also inspired Compton Mackenzie's famous comic novel *'Whisky Galore'*. The island – which was bought by a syndicate in 1960 – had by then a post office, telephone exchange, and a school – including a secondary class as late as 1976 – but little for the tourist. In 1981 the young crofting population of 219 owned five trawlers catching prawns and white fish; home knitting was sold through a co-operative. A ro-ro ferry soon replaced the long-established passenger ferry to Saltavik Bay in South Uist. The primary school at Haun served 50 children, the co-operative shop was locally owned, and a pub was opened in 1988, but Eriskay's population was only 179 in 1991. Prawns and lobsters are still fished, but only 19 children attended the school in 1997. A lengthy causeway link to South Uist was opened late in 2000.

## ERROL

**Map 6, B3**

***Village in Carse of Gowrie,*** *pop. 1100* OS 53: NO 2523

Errol stands on a low hill 1 km from the shores of the Firth of Tay in the fertile Carse of Gowrie, midway between Perth and Dundee; it was served by an early ferry from Lindores Abbey in Fife. The Earldom of Errol was created in 1452, and Errol evidently gained some early importance as a market centre, for Pont's unfortunately cramped and smudged map made about 1600 showed it as the largest place in the area, with its name in capitals. He also sketched the imposing battlemented 16th century Megginch Castle, 2 km to the north. Errol had a parish school by 1626 and was chartered as a burgh of barony in 1648.

**Stuck in the Mud**: By 1746 brown linens were being produced for the British Linen Company. The Megginch area had been enclosed by the time Roy's map was made about 1750. *'The Carse Road'* (as Roy labelled it) was one of Scotland's most notoriously muddy coaching roads; it linked Perth and Dundee via Errol, which was a stopping place, so there was evidently an inn at the small village, beside which stood the House of Errol in its policies; a mill turned at the Pow of Errol. The Carse of Gowrie turnpike, later the A85, was opened in 1790 some 3 km distant and the coaches abandoned Errol. Heron in 1799 called it a *"village"* with a population of about 800; Errol's first post office was opened in 1801. In 1831 the extensive parish contained nearly 3000 people, of whom 1200 lived in the village; but the population then fell steadily.

**Too Far from the Railway?**: Six road coaches a day joined Dundee and Perth when the Dundee & Perth Railway Company was promoted by Lord Kinnaird of Rossie Priory. The station was built about 1.5 km north of Errol in 1847; the villagers had advocated a site at Inchcoonans, 2 km farther west – but no nearer to the village! A short freight branch laid to the turnpike at East (or North) Inchmichael, opened in 1849, failed to attract traffic and was closed in 1852; it became a road, now B958. Those best placed to know deny the claim that there was ever a branch line to the village itself. Between at least 1860 and 1890 the rail-connected bone manure works of the Errol Chemical Company stood east of the station. A blacksmith shop grew into a modest iron foundry under John Doe & Sons, who manufactured farm machinery from the 1860s. In 1859 Errol had a Girls' Industrial School, and by 1860 both Highland Games and whippet races were held.

**Bricks, Pipes and Horse Droppings**: In 1894 the village possessed an inn, and had a mill at Port Allen, from which a ferry to Newburgh continued to operate up to 1914. By 1894 Alexander Fraser ran Errol Brickworks, which had its own narrow gauge railway system. Farmers used to spread horse manure swept up from Perth streets, which was received by rail at Inchcoonans until after 1945. The whippet races were popular in Edwardian days when a dozen trains each way called at Errol station with its staff of nine; goods traffic then included farm machinery, coal, seed potatoes, hay, grain in sacks, cattle and horses. From 1902 shuttle buses connected the station and village, and bus services to Perth started in 1924; John Doe & Sons started to deal in tractors. Errol military airfield, built since 1939 and used for advanced pilot training, was abortively selected by the government in 1946 as the civil aviation airport for Dundee and Perth (though disused, its runways – the longest being 1450 m – survived, and some small businesses are now based there). By the 1950s the market was a thing of the past, though in terms of facilities Errol was still a large village, with a population of nearly 1500. By 1981 the secondary school and cinema had closed; the facilities of a typical village remained.

**Heritage Station where No Trains stop**: Errol station was closed to freight in 1975 and to passenger trains in 1985, but survived almost intact. Though its coal merchants and cartage service had long gone, the signal box remained in use to work or supervise the various level crossings in the central Carse, and the listed station building was reopened in 1990 by the Errol Station Trust as a railway heritage centre *(see Beech, 1993)*. Some new housing was added in the 1980s, but in 1991 only 1110 residents were counted. By 1994 the Cairn o' Mhor Winery at East Inchmichael made an elderflower drink, and now produce a wide variety of fruit wines. Fraser's still make tile drainage pipes.

## ERSKINE — Map 15, A4

***Renfrewshire developments**, pop. 13,000* — OS 64: NS 4572

Blaeu's engraved version of Pont's original map showed a substantial emparked tower at Erskine beside the tidal River Clyde, but indicated no Clyde ferries. By about 1700 the *'West Ferry'* connected the Erskine area with Dumbarton. The Roy map of about 1754 showed a ferry, and a *'Ferry House'* on the south bank, with road connections to the Renfrew–Port Glasgow road. A passenger ferry plied to Old Kilpatrick in 1777, for which new quays were built in 1778. A parish church was built in 1813, about the time that Lord Blantyre had a replacement Erskine House built in a large park overlooking the River Clyde. A century later, as a result of the first world war, Erskine House became a permanent hospital, originally for limbless ex-servicemen, and later for all seriously disabled ex-service men and women. A New Town proposal for Erskine in the 1946 Clyde Valley Regional Plan was not then adopted.

**Erskine Bridge, New Village and Hotel**: The stayed girder Erskine Bridge with its approach roads was built in 1971–72, replacing what had long been a vehicular ferry. At the same time work began in 1971 to develop by private enterprise a large new suburban *'village'* east of Erskine. The winding lane known as the A726 was rapidly replaced by a new road. This was laid out with three roundabout accesses to the burgeoning estates and to the 200-room *Esso Hotel* which opened in 1972 beside the Clyde just east of the new bridge; by 1979 as the *Euro Crest* it could cater for conferences for 700 people. By then a large area of housing had been built at Bargarran.

**Enter the AA**: In 1974 the Automobile Association's Scottish HQ were moved from Glasgow to the lately improved Erskine Harbour. More housing was being rapidly built at Craigends, Park Mains and Freeland. By 1981 some 10,000 people lived in the dormitory area; by then Erskine had village facilities, plus the new Park Mains High School by 1988, when housing extended as far as Inchinnan. The large Bridgewater shopping centre of over 5000 m$^2$ was open by 1989. In 1991 about 13,000 people lived locally, 61% of households buying their homes, many in terraced blocks. Erskine Hospital was extended in 1991, and replaced by new buildings in the late 1990s.

**Expansion from Texas, Taiwan and Germany**: Compaq Computers of Texas opened a big plant on the waterfront at Erskine in 1988; this was doubled in size with their European headquarters by 1993, when the company employed 1000 people in the area; a further 250 jobs on two new production lines, for the first time making printed circuit boards, were added in 1994. After further growth, Compaq planned to add 200 jobs in 1997, bringing its total employees to over 2000. In 1994 part of one of the four available business sites had been taken by Foxconn UK, a subsidiary of Hon Hai of Taiwan. In 1996 the German firm EBT Technologies began to build a factory on the Rashielee Business Park, intending to manufacture speciality lighting products for the electronics industry. But in 1996 the AA decided to close its Erskine call centre, centralising the work into four centres in England. Erskine Pine, bedroom furniture makers, are based at the Hospital, but in 2001 Compaq announced closure, with 700 job losses. The Park Mains High School has over 1500 pupils, the largest roll in the new Renfrew authority. The hotel, now called the *Erskine Bridge*, has 177 rooms and indoor swimming; Erskine House is expected to become a hotel.

## ESKDALEMUIR — Map 2, C3

***Dumfriesshire community**, pop. 200* — OS 79: NY 2597

The great prehistoric hill fort known as Castle O'er, many other ancient earthworks and a Roman fort were built on various sites near the White Esk, one of the headwaters of the River Esk which flows through Langholm some 25 km to the south-east. This remote area of hill farms had a kirk known as Eskdale, which – when Roy surveyed the region about 1754 – stood at the head of a track from Langholm. Roads were eventually made up connecting with Langholm, Lockerbie and Selkirk. Although the area's wet climate and narrow valleys precluded much development, a climatological observatory at an altitude of about 235 m was opened 5 km north of the kirk in 1908.

**Afforestation and a Tibetan Refuge**: Eskdalemuir had acquired a school, post office and telephone exchange by 1951, when the area's population was 360, and a seismological station, open by 1962, was created 3 km north of the observatory near the head of the valley. The surrounding hills were widely afforested in the mid 20$^{th}$ century to form the Eskdalemuir and Castle O'er Forests, and by 1980 little Eskdalemuir, despite a third of its population having vanished, had acquired the small *Hartmanor Hotel*. By 1997 the Samye-Ling Tibetan Centre was well established at Johnstone, 2 km to the north, but the locals found this peaceful Buddhist home from home no replacement for their lost post office!

## ETTRICK (Ramsaycleugh) — Map 3, A4

***Tweeddale settlement**, pop. under 100* — OS 79: NT 2714

The remote area of Ettrick Forest some 25 km south-west of Selkirk was a royal forest in the 12$^{th}$ century, but had been fairly well settled by about 1600, when *'Rampsbycleuch'* on the left bank of the upper River Ettrick was marked as a tiny settlement on Pont's map of Tweeddale. Above it stood *'New Kirk'*, but there was no sign of a village or mansionhouse, although Chambers later asserted that Ettrick Kirkton *"was in ancient times the site of a strength called Ettrick House, around which there was a village that contained 53 fire-houses at the time of the Revolution"*. This count of houses with hearths was presumably in 1688, because about 1700 the laird James Anderson of Tushielaw (5 km north-east) evicted the tenants to form a site for the mansion of Ettrick Hall – *"built on the ruins of the poor"*, said a local poet.

**Poetry, Afforestation and Caravanning**: The church was labelled *'Etrick'* by Roy about 1754, when a track joining Selkirk and Moffat followed the north bank of the river, which was unbridged. The poet James Hogg, *'The Ettrick Shepherd'*, was born nearby in the late 18$^{th}$ century. By 1827 Ettrick House had vanished in its turn, but the kirk had lately been rebuilt, *"with its little hamlet"*. Though the track became a through road to Moffat, and the *Tushielaw Inn* became well known, in the 20$^{th}$ century continuing depopulation had reduced Ettrick Kirkton to only some 65 residents by 1981. Between 1960 and 1985 the whole of the hilly area to the south was afforested, and by 1984 caravan sites had been laid out south of the school, and near the post office (now closed) at Hopehouse, 3 km downstream. The Southern Upland Way approaches within 1.5 km of the church and primary school, whilst the *Tushielaw Inn* offers service.

## ETTRICKBRIDGE (End) & Kirkhope **Map 3, A4**

***Borders small village,*** *pop. 150* OS 73: NT 3824

Kirkhope Tower was built in the 16th century north of the Ettrick Water, 10km above Selkirk. When Pont mapped Tweeddale about 1600, there were settlements at the parish centre of Kirkhope, and at Howford on the opposite bank; Pont's map also included a few other tiny places. About 1754 Roy or his surveyors found that the south bank road from Selkirk ended at Howford Mills; crossing the ford, travellers to and from Moffat would follow a track, for the most part on the north bank of the unbridged river. A bridge must have been built near the mills soon afterwards, and eventually the track was upgraded into a through road to Moffat; in 1827 Chambers noted that *'Ettrick-Brig-End'* was a *"considerable village"*. Though no railway ever served the area and the mill faded away, the small *Ettrick Shaws Lodge Hotel* was opened 1.5km up-river, and by 1951 some 300 people lived in the vicinity of the bridge, served by very limited facilities. Twentieth century rural depopulation further reduced Ettrick Bridge End to only some 170 people by 1981. In 1984 there was a one-teacher primary school with 25 pupils, a shop/sub-post-office, two craft potteries, a strong community spirit, a community bus and a well-used village hall. The post office and the school remain, along with the quality *Ettrickshaws Hotel* and the old-established *Cross Keys Inn*.

## EVANTON **Map 9, B3**

***Easter Ross village,*** *pop. 1225* OS 21: NH 6066

Pont's map of greater Moray, made around 1600, later added to by Gordon, named Fowlis in Kiltearn parish of Easter Ross, 7km north-east of Dingwall. About 1750 as Roy's map showed, there were three hamlets at nearby Culcairn, where the coastal track crossed the furious Allt Graad (the River Glass) and the River Sgitheach (pronounced *Skiach*), which despite its harsh name is a gentler watercourse. South of the latter's minor ferry point is the 18th century tower house of Foulis Castle – seat of The Munro. In 1797 another laird's mansion at Novar, north of the Glass, acted as a post town, with a mail service on alternate days. The Struie road was built in 1810–11, leading from Novar over the hills to Bonar Bridge.

**New Village, Railway Stations and Distillery**: The laird, Evan Fraser of Balernie, having cleared inland straths for sheep, created the new village of Evanton at Culcairn between the two rivers on the newly rebuilt coast road. He named it after himself in 1810 with the immodesty so typical of the Highland lairds of the day. However what became the Novar Estates were not the sole landowners in the area, for in 1827 Chambers mentioned *"Sir Hector Monro of Foulis, the proprietor of Ben Wyvis"*. The *Novar Arms* was built in the 1850s as a coaching inn. Evanton, and what was again spelled Fowlis, were served from 1863 by separate stations on the Inverness & Ross-shire Railway, later part of the Highland. Evanton was simply a *"village"* to Murray in 1894. The Glen Skiach distillery, built on the Foulis estate in 1896, seems to have been a victim of US Prohibition, and sank from view in 1926.

**Fleet Air Arm flies In and Out, and Stations close**: A Fleet Air Arm airfield with hangars was built 2km to the east in the 1920s, and was regraded about 1943 as an aircraft maintenance yard; but it had been closed by 1948. However, in 1946 Wordie & Co operated a small rail to road cartage depot. By the 1950s Evanton was a substantial village of 800 people with the *Novar Arms Hotel*, an agricultural engineer and a mill, but soon lost its secondary school. The two stations were closed in 1960; the railway remained open for through trains. The Novar Estates operated a timber yard, but by 1971 the population was under 700.

**Road Bridge arrives but Oil Boom flops**: About 1971 the Ross & Cromarty County Council converted part of the former airfield to an industrial site to serve the oil boom; the over-ambitious planners expected a population of 4000 by 1981. Although by 1978 the industrial site contained Black Hawk North Sea Oil services, a BOC gases depot, wool growers' depot, steel scrapyard and fencemakers, and appreciable population growth had occurred during the ten years that the ill-fated Invergordon smelter was open, in 1981 the actual population of Evanton was little over 1100 and its facilities were those of a typical village, with two grocers, a garage, and a restaurant.

**Bypass, Windpower, Disaster Relief and Tourism**: Meantime the Cromarty Firth had been spanned south of Evanton by the new A9 viaduct on 67 twin concrete piers, which opened in 1979 together with a village bypass. By 1983 there was a caravan and camping site, and in 1991 the population was 1225. Some development continued round the village, where by 1998 an inn was open; a 1200m-long jetty had been constructed from the former airfield into the deep water, and several oil-related engineering companies operated out of the Deephaven Industrial Park, with Isleburn employing 160. Large old hangars now hold the depot of Blythswood International Relief Aid. A firm called Knockrash grows soft fruit under cover. A very large and originally controversial wind farm at Bendeallt, some 8km inland, was approved in 1996 and completed within two years. Accommodation is available at the *Novar Arms Hotel*, and also at *Foulis Castle*; at Foulis Point is the *'Clanland Visitor Centre'* shop and restaurant, and a small bunkhouse for backpackers is open all year round at the Black Rock Caravan Park.

## EVIE & Rendall **Map 13, B2**

***Orkney communities,*** *pop. 500* OS 6: HY 3625

At least seven Iron Age or Pictish circular stone towers, each with its surrounding complex and tightly packed huddle of round stone houses, were spread along a 10km section of the relatively fertile north coast of the Orkney mainland. Central among these is the well-preserved Broch of Gurness or Aikerness, skilfully built of old red sandstone in the first century AD, which stands on the peninsula of Aiker Ness opposite the isle of Rousay. The Picts also erected a standing stone 2 km to the south. Another huge Broch mound at Burgar 3km to the west contained rich Pictish silver and amber. Later came the medieval Peter's Kirk for Evie parish, and a Norse meeting point or Tingwall farther south in Rendall parish, offshore from which was the islet of Gairsay, site of the 16th century courtyard castle of Langskaill. The area was well settled when sketch mapped on a very small scale by Pont about 1592.

**Scattered Settlements catch Fish and Wind**: Farms scattered along the early 19th century coast road tended to cluster into four hamlets: Costa with its former school; Stenso or Georth at the junction of the road to Dounby, which acquired a pier and Evie post office; Redland; and Woodwick with the one-time Helicliff Mill. The population looking to Evie with its medical practice exceeded 900 in 1951, but fell over 20 years to nearer 500. However, by 1974 Tingwall's small stone pier had recently become the terminus of a passenger ferry to Rousay, soon upgraded to roll-on operation. By 1985 lobster boats were based there, and in 2000 boats from Kirkwall, Wick, Buckie and farther afield were seen; in the Bay of Isbister is a fish farm. Redland has Evie's modern primary *'community school'*, and a restaurant is the main tourist facility for visitors to the excavated broch and ancient settlement. Of three experimental wind turbines erected in the early 1980s on the 160m Burgar Hill 2 km west of Stenso, only one remained by September 2000, an ugly inactive white elephant on its giant concrete tower, awaiting imminent demolition. Also a failure was an interpretation centre for the extensive nature reserve, built close by around 1990, but now deserted; two brand new, tall and elegant aerogenerators turned silently on the hilltops to the south.

## EYEMOUTH

**Map 3, C2**

***Berwickshire coastal town,*** *pop. 3500* — OS 67: NT 9464

Eyemouth in Berwickshire stands beside the natural harbour formed by the mouth of the Eye Water. First mentioned as a hamlet around 1200, it is known to have been a fishing centre since 1298. Barracks built and earthworks thrown up by the English in 1548 were superseded a decade later by superior French fortifications at *'Gunsgreene'*, opposite which Pont's map of about 1600 showed a few buildings and a mill. In 1594 a parish school was established, and in 1597 Eyemouth was created a Free Port and burgh of barony. By 1608 a notary, the egregious George Sprott, was in practice there, and by 1621 the harbour, partly built in pudding stone from the French fortifications, admitted to importing a little wine, though contributing under 1.5% of Scotland's other customs duties.

**Boatbuilding and the Smuggling Trade**: Around 1655 Tucker the Cromwellian Customs investigator reported Eyemouth as a *"creek"* with a prohibited trade in hides and wool; the present Gunsgreen emplacement apparently dates from that time. By the 1690s a third of the manufacturing workforce in Eyemouth was engaged in boat and cask building, the latter for either salt herrings or illicit drink. Defoe noted that the Eye Water had been bridged by the early 18th century, when Eyemouth was *"a good fishing town, and some fishing vessels belong to it; for such it is a good harbour, and for little else"*. It seems that Tucker and Defoe were dissembling here, for by then a vast smuggling trade existed, due to the high Customs duties on tea, silks, gin and brandy. Big armed ships were used, and port development was inhibited since they used small boats to ferry their illicit cargoes to remote bays. Such smuggling plus growing legitimate trade enabled Eyemouth, the nearest Scottish port to the continent of Europe, to develop by the 1750s into a medium-sized village with as many as four roads radiating from the quayside, opposite which stood the imposing Gunsgreen House, designed by William Adam; smuggled tea was stored in its roof space! Sloops and barques were built on the beach, and by 1765 the British Linen Company had a local agent.

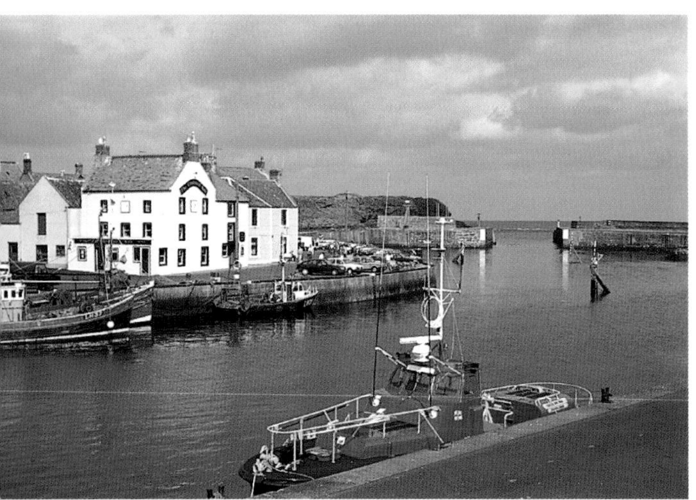

*The harbour, Eyemouth, showing the lifeboat and the pub in 1989. Fishing has been based here since the 13th century.* (RS)

**Harbour, Fish Barrels, Grain and Milling**: John Smeaton designed a breakwater to protect a proper harbour with warehouses for legitimate goods, and also a new bridge – all constructed in 1768–70; the Chirnside road was turnpiked under an Act of 1772. Eyemouth gained its first post office in 1793; at that time grain, sheep and cattle were exported, and there were two fairs per year. In 1799 Heron observed *"the town of Eyemouth contains about a thousand inhabitants, and carries on a considerable trade for its size. It is a small port, where there is a tolerable harbour, and sometimes a good herring fishery"*. Fishing and fish curing grew, with a sawmill for barrel staves built about 1820, which also incorporated threshing machinery and a bark mill for tanning. The Auld Kirk was built in 1812. In 1827 Chambers described Eyemouth as *"a goodly sea-port village whose inhabitants principally subsist by fishing; and there are several prosperous establishments for the curing of herrings. The port has also considerable trade in exporting the grain produced in the fertile fields of the Merse"*.

**Eyemouth Fisheries hit Disaster**: By 1841 new granaries had been built, with a grain mill; a gas works was established in 1845. In 1853 nearly 100,000 barrels of herrings were landed by 166 vessels, 48 of which were local. The first fully-decked fishing vessel was built at Eyemouth in 1854; about then Weatherhead started boatbuilding at the head of tidewater. By 1867 Eyemouth had become Scotland's fourth busiest herring port, visited by almost 700 vessels, and with 135 coopers on shore making fish barrels. A lifeboat station was opened in 1876, and Eyemouth golf club, founded in 1880, laid out a compact 9-hole course at Gunsgreen. By 1881 Eyemouth had nearly 3000 people, and a major harbour extension had been approved, but in that year 20 of its 48 fishing boats, with about 190 fishermen, were lost in a single storm.

**The Town's Railway – and from Herring to Shellfish**: This led the government to switch its harbour-building money to Peterhead in 1882, but Eyemouth rapidly recovered from tragedy, and the harbour was extended on more modest lines in 1885–87. A benefactor helped the *"town"* (as it was to be called by Murray in 1894) to build its own branch railway, opened in 1891 to connect with the North British main line at Burnmouth; the *Home Arms* was then a hotel. In the 1930s most tourists stayed in B&Bs, and herrings were fished intermittently. Quiet Eyemouth suffered in the floods of 1948 which washed away a pier of the railway viaduct, though this was replaced. Just a big village in terms of facilities, Eyemouth had a secondary school and three hotels by the 1950s, when the population was about 2400. By then the long-established fishing boat and yacht builders William Weatherhead & Sons also owned a yard at Cockenzie.

**Processing Industries**: Following a change in subsidy arrangements in 1955, the harbour was reconstructed in 1964–65 and a new fish-selling shed provided, operating daily. So, despite the closure of the railway in 1962, Eyemouth grew into the main Borders port for shrimping and shellfish. The Eyemouth industrial estate was the site of two fish-processing firms established around 1970 (Scot Supreme and Coastal) and also attracted cold storage and marine radio specialists. A fresh vegetable-freezing plant was opened about 1975 by the East Lothian & Borders Association of Growers (hence '*ELBA*') to freeze vegetables including broad beans, carrots, cauliflowers, peas, sprouts, swedes and turnips; some types must be frozen within 90 minutes of harvesting. At that time Eyemouth claimed to be mainly a fishing community; the harbour was very busy, with up to 50 boats in at one time. Scampi was caught for hotels, herrings were landed, and kippering had revived. By 1979 a small textile-printing concern had been established. It was proposed in 1978 to provide a seawater supply for process industries on the industrial estate, where in 1979 Stuart-Shell Ltd planned to build a 200-worker seafood processing factory.

**Expansion**: The demand for new housing was considerable, and substantial developments to the west brought Eyemouth's population to some 3500 in 1981, including about 400 fishermen. It had also enjoyed some growth in professional services and tourism, the golf course having recently been extended to 18 holes; by 1982 a new road link had removed Coldingham traffic from the vicinity of the High School campus. In 1981 the Auld Kirk became Eyemouth Museum, soon a prizewinner. Around 1985 Eyemouth still had about 50 fishing boats, and two further fish-processors began work in 1986 (Scotfresh and Salvesens). Martin's modern bakery and a branch of Border Lairds seafoods (of Amble in Northumberland) started up around the same date.

**Tradition and Modernisation**: Tradition died hard in Eyemouth: in 1989 wooden fishing vessels were still being built, and the tiny cinema was still showing films, though it was closed by its Kelso owner in 1992 due to the fishing recession. In 1991 the population had settled around 3475. By 1993 John Burgon, shellfish processor in Eyemouth, had renovated his premises to new EU standards, and by 1995 the road approaches from the south had been recast. By 1996 the 1840s granary had been converted into flats. At that time 47 fishing boats based in Eyemouth caught haddock, cod and whiting, and new harbour works first proposed in 1987 were about to start; a new fish market and ice plant were opened in 2000. The small *Ship Hotel* remains in business.

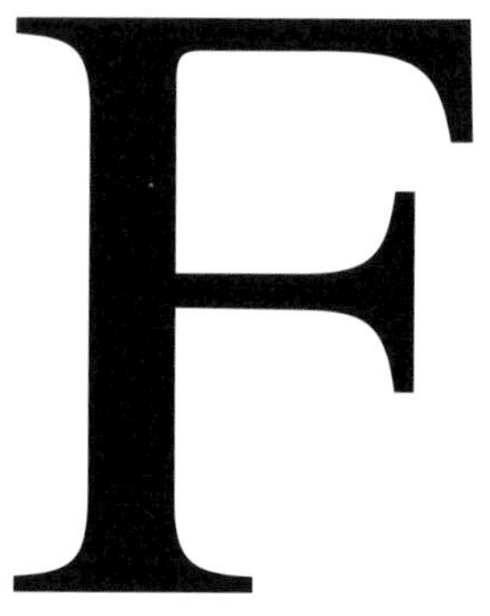

## FAIR ISLE

**Map 14**

***Small Island s. of Shetland,*** *pop. under 100* OS 4: HZ 2074

Fair Isle, an exposed cliff-girt slab of sandstone only about 5 km by 2 km, lies about 40 km south west of the Shetland Isles, of which it forms an administrative part. Its Old Norse name means *Remote* or possibly *Peaceful*; the former is more apt, considering the weather. There are several ancient burial mounds, but Timothy Pont's maps made around 1592 as later engraved by Blaeu showed no features on their outline of the grassy island. Eventually it became well known for its elaborately patterned hand knitwear, and by 1861 the population reached 380. Although a third of the people soon left for Nova Scotia, a school was built in 1880 and two lighthouses were first lit in 1892, Fair Isle North and South. A winding lane between them also served two piers, at both the North Haven and the South Harbour; a post office was opened.

**New facilities arrive**: A redundant wartime naval camp near the North Haven was reopened in 1948 as a bird observatory. Fair Isle was acquired by the National Trust for Scotland in 1954; there were then about 80 residents, with 12 telephone connections. By 1966 the post office, school, coastguard lookout and rescue hut were located at Stonybreck, near the south harbour. The observatory was rebuilt in 1969, including a hostel. By 1971 the population had fallen to only 65, but by 1973 a 550 m landing strip had been laid out and by 1978 a modest revival had begun. The school then contained 15 pupils, while the total population was about 70. From 1980 dances were held in a new school hall, paid for from oil revenues through the Islands Council. The islanders were connected through North Haven with Grutness (Sumburgh) by their own boat, the *Good Shepherd*, and by air with Kirkwall and Tingwall; sea angling was available. The North lighthouse was automated in 1981; keepers on the South one could enjoy their home-made golf course until the very end of manned lights in the early 1990s. In 1991 the population was 67. A new breakwater was built in 1992, improving the North Haven and enabling a summer vehicle ferry to ply to Lerwick. In 1994, by which time there was a museum, special protection was accorded to the isle's birds.

## FAIRLIE

**Map 1, B1**

***Ayrshire village,*** *pop. 1500* OS 63: NS 2055

Near the Cunninghame coast stands the 12th to 16th century keep of the Clan Hunter's Hunterston Castle, and 3 km to the north is Fairlie Castle, whose English name means *Beautiful Meadow*. Allegedly built in 1521, this must have been a date of alteration, for Pont described it as *"a strong tower, very ancient, beautified with orchards and gardens"*. Remarkably, it was overshadowed on his map of about 1600 by the emparked house of Southannan; offshore was the small Fairlie Island. Fairlie was chartered as a burgh of barony in 1601. The Roy map of about 1754 showed it as a linear village on the coast road, and it was known for fishing.

**Boatyards, Pier, Railway and Steamers**: William Fife's boatyard, founded in 1800, built sloops about 1832; the Fairlie pier was built in 1802 and the Fairlie Slip Dock was established as a boatyard in 1812 to build fishing vessels, and later clipper ships and yachts. But Fairlie had no post office until after 1838. In 1880 a Glasgow & South Western Railway branch was opened to a temporary terminus at Fairlie, and extended in 1882 through a tunnel beneath the main street to the pier with its station, which seems to have incorporated the former island. In subsequent summers, through trains from Glasgow connected with ferry steamers to Millport, and for a time to Arran and Campbeltown. The railway was extended north to Largs in 1885, and a small engine shed was opened at Fairlie, whose fine village school was built in 1887. By 1894 the *Fairlie Hotel* was open to exploit the sandy beach; Sir Robert Lorimer restored Hunterston Castle. In 1908 the long-established yacht designers and builders William Fife & Son created the 23 m cutter *Shamrock* for the rich Glasgow grocer Thomas Lipton, as an unsuccessful challenger for the Americas Cup. Some housing was built in the early 20th century, but the LMS Railway closed their engine shed about 1930. By 1951 Fairlie was a typical resort village with two small hotels and about 1000 residents; Clyde steamers used Fairlie pier until 1972, when it became an Admiralty facility, still rail-served.

**The Hunterston Development Complex**: In the 1960s the previously unspoilt character of the area began to be changed irrevocably by large scale industrialisation. By 1971 the Hunterston *'A'* Magnox nuclear power station had been built only 4 km from the centre of Fairlie. Proving troublesome to commission, it only became fully operational in 1977, but its hot water was used to aid the farming of turbot from about 1979. Then in 1973–78 came the Hunterston coal and ore terminal, built for the British Steel Corporation south of Fairlie. It was opened in 1979, comprising a 443m-long deepwater jetty with reception pier and ore conveyor, a single-track branch railway 6km in length (from a new junction and high-level loading plant near Kilrusken) to low-level coal and ore sidings at the waterside, and two direct reduction plants – which were never used, despite their combined annual ore pelleting capacity of 800,000 tonnes. An unrelated development, a literally *'offshore'* yard 800m in length, was constructed in the sea off Hunterston Sands in the 1970s and connected to the mainland near Hunterston House by a causeway; this costly facility built oil platforms from steel for a short time; although disused thereafter, it was once more in use in 1994.

**Hunterston *'B'* boasts of its Efficiency**: By 1989 Hunterston *'B'*, an Advanced Gas-cooled Reactor (AGR) begun in 1975, had become the world's most efficient nuclear power station. In spite of the industrial impacts, in 1981 Fairlie itself had three hotels and was becoming more of a dormitory than a village in character. The railway was electrified in 1987, and by 1991 the population had grown to 1516. Hunterston *'A'* power station was closed on economic grounds in 1990, having produced power for only 26 years; the associated turbot production was moved to the naturally warm waters off Spain. In 1992, when Scottish Nuclear was still considering whether to modernise and recommission the *'A'* reactor, the combined nuclear site was reputed to employ 1000 people, many of them defuelling the station. This work, completed in 1994, removed 99.99% of the radioactivity from the reactor; the flasks of spent fuel went by rail to Sellafield for reprocessing.

**From Iron Ore to Coal**: Until mid 1992 the coal and iron imports for the doomed Ravenscraig steelworks were handled through the Hunterston terminal; after closure by the privatised British Steel it was briefly used to receive 0.6 million tonnes of coal for despatch by rail to Cockenzie and Longannet power stations. The rail link became disused in 1993, but was left in position. Nucor Steel of the USA then considered building a small steelworks at the former ore terminal, but by late 1994 this had been sold by British Steel to privatised Clydeport (formerly the Clyde dock authority and operator of the ports of Ardrossan, Greenock and Glasgow), and the rail link was reopened for coal traffic in 1997. In 2001 Clydeport boasted of the coal terminal's efficiency. Meantime the old village school, replaced by a new building in the 1990s, stood vacant in 1997.

## FAIRMILEHEAD

**Map 15, C2**

***S. Edinburgh suburb**, pop. 10,000* — OS 66: NT 2468

When Timothy Pont mapped the Lothians about 1600, Hillend at the foot of the Pentland Hills 5km south of Edinburgh city centre was a hamlet on the road to Biggar. Fairmilehead was not named on Blaeu's version of his map, and the Roy survey of about 1754 added little here of consequence. From 1761 Edinburgh's water supplies were augmented from springs at the nearby hamlet of Swanston. The classical mansion of Comiston House was built in 1815 for Lord Provost Forrest and enlarged in 1842.

**Golf, Golf, Golf – and Trams**: Mortonhall golf club was founded in 1892, and the steep Lothianburn golf course was laid out in 1893, when Fairmilehead was just a crossroads and there was no urban development south of the Braid Burn. Hillend Park was bequeathed to the City Council and opened in 1924, and the private Swanston golf club was formed in 1927, laying out the area's third 18-hole course; though Lothianburn was rebuilt to challenge it, the Mortonhall course remained the favourite – and in the 1980s the dearest to play. In 1936 the city's electric trams reached Fairmilehead from Braids, terminating at Frogston Road. Private housing development, mainly bungalows for the better off, followed from Morningside up to Fairmilehead. The Fairmilehead church of 1938 was among the few facilities provided to serve this new suburb, and the Princess Margaret Rose children's hospital was also built in the 1930s.

**Year-round Skiing for a Growing Suburb**: By 1951 the population was approaching 5000, but the trams vanished about 1955. In 1964 an artificial ski slope was laid out in an all too prominent position on the hills overlooking the city; in the 1980s this was said to be the largest such facility in Europe, and it soon had flood-lighting as well. By 1981 the population of Fairmilehead exceeded 10,000, of suburban character, but only village facilities were available locally. Personal mobility was generally so high that this was no hardship, and was further aided by the City Bypass, opened by stages south of Fairmilehead in the mid to late 1980s. This was followed by the opening of a Safeway superstore at Hunter's Tryst in 1990. Meantime in the 1970s Comiston House was used as the *Pentland Hills Hotel*; unfortunately renamed in the 1980s as the *Caiystane Park Hotel*, it stood empty in the middle of a new housing development until in the mid 1990s it was finally restored to flats by Miller Homes. By 1996 the *'New Swanston'* housing estate had infilled from Hunter's Tryst to the bypass.

## FALKIRK & Callendar

**Map 16, B2**

***Large town, central Scotland**, pop. 45,000* — OS 65: NS 8879

Suburbs: *Camelon, Carron, Laurieston*

Falkirk lies between the Slamannan plateau and the upper Firth of Forth, on the most level route between Edinburgh and Glasgow. It adjoins Camelon, where the Roman road to Stirling diverged from the Antonine Wall, which was built of turf in 142–43 AD. The area was part of Strathclyde during the Dark Ages; Falkirk had an early lay abbot, and a church was said by Chambers to have been built in 1057 by Malcolm Canmore. First mentioned under its Cumbric name of *Eglesbreth ('Speckled Church')* about 1120, its directly translated name of Falkirk often appeared in old documents, for its church was an appurtenance of Holyrood Abbey. East of the town beside fragments of the Roman Wall was Callendar, which had a thanage from about the 11th century; its 14th century castle was the seat of Lord Livingstone. A small mansion called Callendar Castle (or House) was built for his family in the early 16th century; Pont's map made about 1600 showed it as a tall and imposing tower in a park. To the north stood a water mill. *'Fakirk'* appeared on Pont's map as a substantial but huddled town, which gained a parish school in 1594 – shortly before its late charter as a burgh of barony in 1600. Falkirk had *'lodgings'* by 1636, cloth was made by 1661 and the first post office opened in 1689. Falkirk's second post office opened in 1716, and the town was a main yarn market by the 1730s; Aitken's brewery was set up in 1740.

**Falkirk Tryst**: Meantime from about 1710 the town became the nominal centre for the Falkirk Tryst, which gradually replaced Crieff as the major seasonal cattle market in Scotland (see Haldane's *The Drove Roads of Scotland*). The Roy map of about 1754 made it clear that the Tryst was then actually held on the site of the modern village of Shieldhill, over 3 km south of the town; at some time it moved to Rough Castle. Roy's map showed Falkirk as an already large but compact place with six radial roads, including the old partly Roman route to Stirling via Larbert bridge. In 1752 the post roads to Edinburgh, Kilsyth and Stirling were turnpiked, but as late as 1777 the Edinburgh horse post had to ford streams near Falkirk. By 1767 the printing and publishing business of F Johnston was in existence. Falkirk was described by Pennant in 1769 as *"a large ill built town, supported by the great fairs for black cattle from the Highlands"*. At that time 24,000 head were sold there each year; some went for immediate slaughter, and a tannery was the natural outcome. When the Forth & Clyde Canal was built in the 1770s the animals balked at crossing the bridges, so the tryst was moved again, to nearby Stenhousemuir *(see Larbert)*.

**Banking, Mining, Canal, Fairs and Flour**: In 1761 the Carron *(q.v.)* Company employed 68 coal miners at Callendar. Two coal levels were open near the town by the time the eastern end of the Forth & Clyde (F&C) Canal was completed through its northern outskirts at Bainsford in 1773; Heron called this *"Briansford, a populous village"*. The British Linen Bank was represented in Falkirk by 1767, the *Cross Keys Inn* was in use by 1785 and the Falkirk Banking Company was set up in 1787. This maintained a branch in Glasgow throughout its independent career – unusual for a small-town bank; the firm retired from business in 1826. The short-lasting Falkirk Union Banking Company traded between 1803 and its failure in 1816; it too had a Glasgow branch. A Bank of Scotland branch was opened in Falkirk in 1825. In the 1790s Falkirk had about ten fair days each year. There were at least two breweries, seven flour mills and a paper mill by 1799, when Heron wrote of *"a considerable town"* of about 4000 people. In September 1803 Dorothy Wordsworth found *"no beds in the inns at Falkirk – every room taken up by the people come to the fair, the road being covered all along with horsemen and cattle"*; among them was a Highland drover she had met at Kingshouse in Glencoe eleven days previously. She *"lodged in a neat clean private house"*.

**The Union Canal and its Tunnel**: In 1809 the F&C canal company had a boatyard at Falkirk where Hugh & Robert Baird built trackboats. From 1822 the Union Canal (UC) linked Edinburgh with Falkirk, joining the F&C at Lock 16 near Camelon; south of the town it passed through a 640 m tunnel to Glen village, the only such work in Scotland, enforced to avoid traversing the grounds of Callendar House. The canal passage between Glasgow, Falkirk and Edinburgh took twelve hours. About then the population passed 8000 and the town's five breweries included Aitken's, which was to become one of the largest in Scotland. According to Chambers, in 1827 Falkirk was *"the capital of a district containing 30,000 inhabitants, and possesses a great deal of inland trade. Remarkable for its four annual cattle-markets known by the term 'Falkirk Trysts' and decidedly prosperous, it also has a few manufactures"*. A gasworks was set up in 1829, and by the 1830s two corn mills had been converted to sawmills.

**Iron Works, Railways, Carriers and News**: Meantime in 1819 men from the Carron Works had established the Falkirk Iron Works, starting in a small way beside the F&C Canal. Taken over by Kennard in 1848, the Works was developed into the second largest foundry in Scotland, with 3 ha of buildings; it made railway chairs and a wide range of high-quality structural and domestic cast-iron goods for export. From 1842 the Edinburgh & Glasgow Railway (E&G) served Falkirk High station, rather outside the town to the south; this was the base for a rail to road cartage depot run by William Wordie of Stirling. In 1845 Falkirk's local newspaper the *Herald* was founded by the long-established Johnston Press. The important Stirlingshire & Midland Junction Railway (S&MJR) was opened in 1850 to connect the E&G at Polmont through Falkirk Grahamston to the Scottish Central at a triangular junction at Carmuirs (East and West) 1 km south of Larbert. In 1860 Grahamston became a junction for a line to Grangemouth town and docks; by then Wordie & Co also had a rail cartage depot at Grahamston. Springfield goods yard dated from about 1870.

*Aitken's brewery, Falkirk, dating from 1740. It was once amongst the largest in Scotland, with a major export trade by the late 19th century. It operated until 1960.* *(RCAHMS / JRH)*

**Falkirk casts Guns and the Crumlin Viaduct**: Meantime the Abbots ironworks and foundry had been opened beside the canal east of Bainsford in 1856. In 1857 one Falkirk foundry cast the sections for the famous Crumlin Viaduct in South Wales. The Grahamston Ironworks was founded in 1868; four similar works, also on canalside sites, made largely firegrates and stoves; they soon employed a total of 600 men. By 1867 P Taylor was making engines for small steamboats. The Falkirk Iron Works had turned to armaments in the Crimean war; by 1869 its 900 workers made over 300 tonnes of castings each week. The so-called *'Camelon'* ironworks, well east of Camelon proper, dated from 1872, and the Castlelaurie ironworks opened at Bainsford in 1875.

**Drinks Industries – the Start of Barrs**: Aitken's brewery was enlarged in 1866 and 1878, developing a major export trade. The family firm of Barr was founded in Falkirk in 1830 as corkcutters by Robert Barr, an Ayrshire man whose son Robert F Barr made aerated waters from 1880. He moved the company HQ and most activities to Parkhead (Glasgow) in 1887 to enable expansion – a wise choice that led to the growth of one of Scotland's most successful consumer industries. Eventually in 1959 the Falkirk firm was rejoined with the main company.

Meantime the Earls of Linlithgow lived at Callendar House, which was vastly expanded in the French style to designs by Wardrop and Reid in 1869–77.

**Falkirk as a Regional Centre**: Resulting from its role as a centre for communications, Falkirk became also the principal regional service centre between Edinburgh and Glasgow. The Bank of Scotland built a new branch office around 1870. Another local newspaper, the *Falkirk Mail*, was founded in 1886; for a time there were three such publications in the town, while the *Linlithgowshire Gazette* was established in 1891 as an offshoot of the *Falkirk Herald*. Falkirk Football Club *('The Bairns')* was formed in 1876, locating centrally at Brockville, and East Stirlingshire FC a decade or so later. In 1883 James Ross & Co, chemical manufacturers of Falkirk, built an oil-works at Philpston *(q.v.)*. By 1894 the population of this *"busy town"* was about 20,000, and there were two hotels, the *Red Lion* and *Crown*, but its main preoccupations were industrial (*see I H Adams, map, p. 96*). By 1898 a lengthy goods branch from Camelon served the Carron Works and its pits. Falkirk had outgrown its site, and the villages of Camelon, Laurieston, and Polmont had developed into suburbs, including Falkirk-related activities.

**Falkirk Tramways soon fall to Buses**: A power station had been completed south of the town centre by 1901, and in 1901–05 an unusual 10-km circular tramway was opened, its electric cars of 4'0" (122-cm) gauge passing through Bainsford, Carron, Larbert and Camelon; they carried many parcels as well as passengers. But by about 1919 William Alexander the bus entrepreneur had made Falkirk his key route focus *(see Camelon & Larbert)*. This competition badly affected the tramway, which was bought up by SMT buses in 1936 and closed; the Union Canal had closed in 1933.

**Developments in Services and Industry**: A public library service started (with Carnegie aid) after 1896. In 1901 a redundant church was converted into a cinema, the *Electric Theatre*, later renamed the *Empire*. The very large 2200-seat *Grand Theatre* was opened in 1903; in 1929 it too was converted into a cinema, later becoming the *Cannon*. In 1921 lowly East Stirlingshire FC opened Firs Park; Falkirk FC built Brockville's main stand in 1928. The originally quite small Royal Infirmary was opened in 1931. Marks & Spencer opened a branch in the town in 1936, the Co-operative Society's department store was built in 1937 and the ice rink was opened in 1938. Meantime the Falkirk golf club, formed in 1922, had laid out its course at Camelon *(q.v.)*. An SCWS creamery was added to the range of industries at Bainsford, Aitkens installed a new beer-bottling plant in 1930, and a fire-brick works was active by the 1930s. The war had led to the opening of the vast British Aluminium Company (BAC) rolling mill of some 100,000 m$^2$. After World War II, Bison Floors made concrete products at Matthews works, but Aitken's brewery was taken over for closure by United Breweries in 1960.

**More Regional Facilities**: By 1955 the small hospital had been enlarged into a major infirmary. By then Falkirk had become one of Scotland's principal regional centres, with a large range of facilities of every kind, including by 1972 a swimming pool. However, the *Roxy Cinema/Theatre*, formerly the *Empire* and the town's only theatre, was closed in 1958; demolished in 1961, by 1977 its site in Silver Row had been used for the erection of the 29-room *Metropolitan Hotel*. Meantime the 55-room *Park Hotel* opened about 1972. The Callendar Riggs shopping centre built in the 1960s proved unsatisfactory and lasted only 20 years. A sewage disposal works was built about 1970. In 1972 63% of all houses in the burgh were owned by the town council, the highest proportion in any Scottish regional centre.

**Railways Preserved and Newspapers Centred**: In the 1970s BAC made sheet aluminium for aircraft, and the Lossie Hydraulic Company made trawling gear. About 1961 the Scottish Railway Preservation Society (SRPS) began to conserve historic rail vehicles, moving about 1964 to Wallace Street in Falkirk, one of the few Scottish centres whose passenger services were untouched by Beeching's closures. The SRPS eventually saved some 60 vehicles, and first operated its annual programme of rail excursions in 1970; its move to Bo'ness *(q.v.)* began in 1979. The *Falkirk Mail* ceased publication in 1962, vanquished by the *Falkirk Herald*, whose owners Johnston & Co went from strength to strength. They acquired Kirkcaldy's Fife Free Press group in 1970, and a string of English papers from 1978 onwards. By 1981 Johnston's owned four other titles in the area and also had an Edinburgh office. Johnston Brothers remained a family-owned business until becoming a plc in 1988, and by 1990 had over 2000 employees producing 56 weekly papers. By 1994 the HQ of Johnston Press plc had moved to Edinburgh; but they still operated from Falkirk.

**Falkirk District and Further Education**: In 1975 when Stirlingshire was enlarged, becoming Central Region, Falkirk became the centre of one of Scotland's most populous local government districts. The Technical College, built on Grangemouth Road around 1960, had been promoted to a College of Technology by 1989, but Callendar Park College of Education, opened only in 1964, was abruptly shut down in 1981 by the government. Grahamston station was rebuilt on spartan lines in the 1980s.

**Falkirk's Developing Shopping Centre**: In 1986–89 the town centre became a pedestrian precinct, claimed as the longest in the UK, with extra free parking and the first town centre manager in Scotland. At that time three major new shopping developments were under construction. The large Howgate Centre, with bigger and better Marks & Spencer and Woolworths stores, opened in 1990, and though slow to let at first, its 33 shops drew five million shoppers in 1991, many of them from Cumbernauld. It was 70% filled by 1992. Meantime in 1991 new ASDA and Tesco stores had opened at Grahams Road, but Callendar Square – a replacement for the Callendar Riggs – was only part-built by 1990 when the English contractors, Rush & Tompkins, went into receivership. Work was later resumed and the specialist shopping centre with its 3-level atrium finally opened in 1993–94. A second Tesco store and a retail park were built in 1995–96 near Grahamston Station.

**Commerce at West Mains and Callendar**: The West Mains Industrial Estate of 28 ha was opened by the District Council in 1979, its first occupant being DAF trucks' large sales and servicing depot, followed in 1988 by ASDA's Scottish food distribution depot with 200 jobs; this was expanded in 1991. In 1991 the Forum office complex, built over remains of the Roman wall, was opened at Callendar Business Park by the Central Regional Council, initially accommodating the HQ of another housing firm, Cala Homes (now in Edinburgh's Gyle), and an Inland Revenue office with around 250 jobs. A new building erected from 1992 on the Callander Business Park was to become the home of the government's controversial Child Support Agency, with perhaps another 500 jobs. The Trade Development Centre at Callendar Business Park opened early in 1995 to provide information to would-be exporters; by then the park was 85% let.

**Iron fails and Clothing shrinks**: The Grahamston Iron Company made cast-iron manhole covers in the 1970s, cast-iron stoves in 1983, and was still making domestic solid fuel back-boilers in 1990, though in 1992 50 jobs were lost there and by 1999 it had ceased work. By 1990 Beazer Homes of Falkirk had become one of Scotland's largest firms of housebuilders. In 1992 the Bison concrete products works was busy, as was Marshall's building block factory. (Marshall's pavings are still active in 2001). In 1981 BAC with its rolling mill was taken over by Alcan of Canada. The clothing manufacturers James Seddon closed in 1990, with the loss of a thousand jobs in Falkirk and elsewhere. While in 1994 the Wrangler jeans factory employed about 800 people, by 2000 at least half of these had gone.

**Recreation and Leisure**: The Falkirk museum having been particularly active in collecting industrial items, in 1990 part of Callendar Park was planned to become a pleasure park and tramways museum; the sprawling historic Callendar House was gradually refurbished as the area's main museum, a job nearing completion by 1999. In 1991 the population – including Camelon – was 35,600. Falkirk is the smallest town in Scotland to field two league football teams: Falkirk FC played in the Premier League for odd seasons in the 1990s, but in 2000 near-bankruptcy prevented improvement of Brockville Park to meet its new standards, and the club were denied promotion from the First Division. East Stirling(shire) FC's Firs Park Stadium, was a poor ground in 1990; in 1994 the team joined the new lowly Third Division, where they still play.

**Education and Local Government**: In 1992 Central Regional Council proposed a rail station at Laurieston, but privatisation halted this desirable scheme. The Parklands Business Park was developed in 1993 to include a 70-room hotel; meantime Falkirk College of Technology offered 12 HND courses and served over 8000 students. In 1995 the District Council, whose successor took over all local authority functions for the same area in 1996, planned a new national indoor athletics centre, seeking National Lottery aid. In 1997 Falkirk High School had 1390 pupils, Graeme's High 1435, St Mungo's High 825 and Woodlands High 509. In 2000 Falkirk Council opened five new schools, financed under the controversial Private Finance Initiative scheme. Falkirk was still expanding with new housing, and the large Town Hall is still used for major events. The old 85-bed Loch Green Hospital for the elderly was closed in 1997.

**Canal Prospects, Art and Accommodation**: The intended reopening of the whole Forth & Clyde/Union Canal system in 2001 *(see Camelon)* must surely help to create a pleasure boating industry in Falkirk, with its long canal frontages and enticing tunnel, though in 1999, while the channel was being cleaned out in readiness, a series of gardens in Ewing Avenue slid into the water! In 2000 the council opened the new Park Art Gallery in converted buildings in Callendar Park. Accommodation is provided by the refurbished *Park Lodge* (55 rooms), the *Comfort Inn* (33), and various guest houses.

## FALKLAND & Kilgour

**Map 6, B4**

***Fife village,*** *pop. 1200* — OS 59: NO 2507

The original Dark Age parish church of Kilgour stood near the head of the Eden valley, below the ancient hill fort of Maiden Castle on the steep Lomond Hills. Falkland, similarly sited but 3km east of the church, had a thanage from around 1100. Its name is probably Old English and supposed to mean *'Falcon-land'*, for it was in stag and boar hunting country where in the 12th or 13th century the Macduff Earls of Fife built themselves a hunting tower or castle. It may well have been the ruthless Regent Albany who had appropriated this as royal property by 1402; however acquired – by fair means or foul – it was reconstructed as a royal hunting palace. That this big building job must have required properly made roads was confirmed in John Hardyng's doggerel description of Scotland in 1415, which mentioned the *"fair ready way"* which existed from Falkland to Dysart, while from Falkland to Doune (Albany's baronial home) lay a way *"right fair, with horse and cart to hire"*.

**Anyone for Royal Tennis?**: The higgledy-piggledy village which grew up at the castle gates was apparently a burgh of barony (though not included in Pryde's list) before it was promoted to a Royal Burgh, chartered in 1458. A church was built there, but at first there can have been little else of a permanent nature, for with Falkland's flour being ground at the water-powered King's Mill, the burgh paid no tax in 1535–56. As part of the major reconstruction of the palace for James V by the French master mason Nicholas Roy, a fine Royal Tennis court was built in 1539, now the oldest such in the world. About 1540 the masons were transferred to Stirling to build another palace there.

**The Decline and Ruin of the Palace**: Palace maintenance must have been neglected after James V's untimely death at Falkland in 1542, but a school was open by 1589. Although described by Fynes Moryson in 1598 as an *"old building and almost ready to fall"*, the Palace was again used as a base for hunting by James VI into the early 17th century when, as Pont's map of about 1600 showed, Falkland Wood extended over 2 km northwards, almost to Cash and Newmyres. Kilgour church still existed, and Falkland itself was by then a substantial village. A new burgh church and tolbooth were erected about 1620–30, and maltings were built at Newton of Falkland 1 km to the east. The Great Hall of the palace, last used as such by Charles I in 1650, lost its roof in 1654, burned by Cromwellian troops. Though it remained Crown property, this damage was not repaired. However the Simsons, hereditary falconers to the Scottish Crown, still lived at Falkland in the 18th century.

**After the Royals the Linen trade – and Road Improvements**: Falkland became a centre for hand weaving of linens; there was a horse market, and in 1663 the ancient road from Falkland to Kirkcaldy and Kinghorn was still suitable for coaches. Chambers noted that before the Jurisdiction Act of 1748, Falkland was *"the seat of a court which had a civil power over nearly the whole of Fife, and which caused the constant residence of eight or ten men of business"*; it must have rivalled Cupar. So the post office known to have been in operation by 1752 was probably opened much earlier. In the period 1748–53 the road to Strathmiglo was made up and the Kirkcaldy road further improved. At the time of Roy's survey about 1750, Cash mill was in use, but it seems that by then only a track led

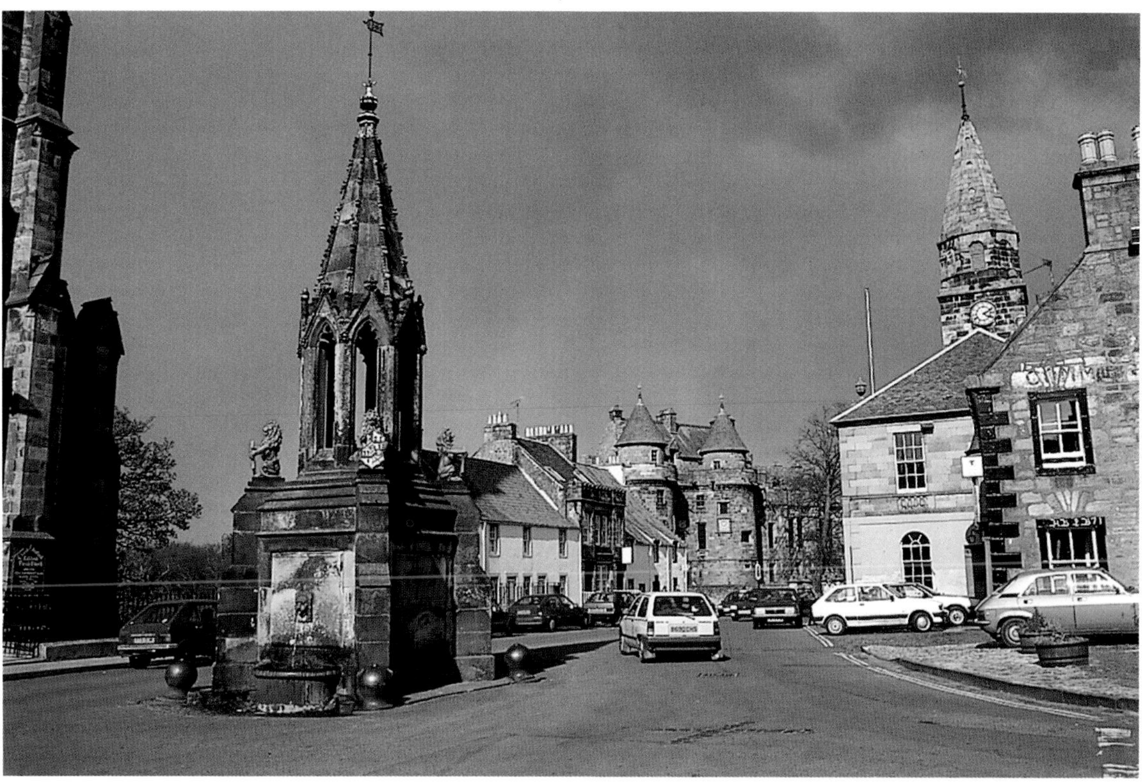

*The centre of Falkland in 1989, showing church (left), Bruce fountain (centre), palace (centre, in distance), and tolbooth (right). There was a Royal Palace here from around 1400, and the twin-towered gatehouse was completed in 1541 for James V. The Town House (tolbooth) dates from 1801, and the parish church from 1850.* (RS)

westwards to Kinross. However, there was a road to Kennoway, from which the Cupar road could be joined at Freuchie. Most Falkland linen was already taken to Auchtermuchty for sale, probably by horse or mule, for the direct road to *'Muchty* was not set out until 1784.

**Falkland Ale, Water and Linen**: Piped water was supplied as early as 1781, and about the same time a brewery was opened at Newton of Falkland, whose population was given by Heron as some 200. In 1792 there were 231 weavers in Falkland and Freuchie, making chiefly coarse linen, sold through Auchtermuchty and Cupar. By 1797 Falkland was also a post town, where seven annual fairs were scheduled to take place. This was a large number for so small a *"town with some linen manufacture"* and a population which Heron in 1799 estimated at about 1000, *"many of whom are employed in agriculture"*. A new town hall was built in 1801 on the site of the tolbooth, and about then the King's Mill became a wood bobbin turning factory. The Palace fell into ruin around 1790, but restoration was begun in 1823 by Mr Bruce. By about 1825 Falkland's penny post also served the Balmalcolm and Kettle area. In 1827 Chambers visited what he called *"this most primitive and curious old burgh, nestling in all its aboriginal thatch and irregularity with unpaved streets, a complete and last-remaining specimen of the Scottish burgh of the 16th century. The people mostly subsisting by the humble trade of weaving; the principal inn of the burgh"* then adjoining the Palace gable. Remarkably the only newspapers then circulating in Falkland were said to be the *Courant* and *Scotsman*, both from Edinburgh.

**Malting, Power-loom Weaving and Linoleum**: The nearest railway station, 4km to the east at *'Falkland Road'*, was opened in 1847. New maltings were built at Newton around 1850 by Alex Bonthrone & Sons, but the 800 handloom weavers at work in 1851 rapidly declined after about 1860, when John Scott built the small St Johns spinning mill and power-loom linen factory at the top of the town. The Pleasance linen factory was also open by the time a branch of the British Linen Bank was built in 1880. In 1885 solicitors were in practice, a gasworks had been constructed, and a house built in 1607 had become the *Bruce Arms Inn*; the *Commercial Hotel* was also open. From 1887 onwards further restoration of the ruined Palace was done for the Crichton-Stewarts, who became its hereditary keepers. In 1891 404 people were busy on power-looms, only 20 still using hand looms, and by 1894 there were said to be several linen spinning mills, though Falkland was still *"a quiet village"*. Electricity was available from 1911. The St Johns linen mill became a floorcloth works about 1900, was acquired by the Scottish Co-operative Wholesale Society in 1920, and greatly extended into a tall and extremely ugly linoleum factory about 1930; this closed in 1966.

**Decisive action by the National Trust for Scotland**: Falkland House, a mansion built about 1840, became a Catholic residential school about 1945. The bobbin factory was still open in 1937, but like the malting and brewing industries had ceased work by 1968. The National Trust for Scotland took over management of the Palace in 1952; they recreated its fine garden, drawing in an important tourist trade, served by cafes and craft shops. When the Pleasance linen works closed in

1974, its site was soon redeveloped for housing. In 1976 Falkland looked mainly southwards to Glenrothes and Kirkcaldy; a chemist and two shops of the Markinch Co-operative Society were open. By 1988 Smith Anderson of Leslie owned the St Johns works, where they made bags from paper and plastic. Between 1982 and 1986 a 9-hole golf course was laid out, and in 1990 the Palace drew 67,000 visitors, for whom a large car park had been created on poorly accessed back land. In 1991 the population was about 1200, and Falkland has kept most of its medieval character. By 1999 the restoration of the Newton maltings as housing was well advanced, and the *Bruce Arms* had been renamed the *Hunting Lodge*. The former *Commercial* has long been the *Covenanter*; The former youth hostel is now a backpackers' hostel, open in summer only.

## FARNELL & Kinnaird

**Map 6, C2**

***Angus hamlets,*** *pop. 200* — OS 54: NO 6255

Farnell stands in a sheltered farming valley beside the little Pow Burn, 5km south-east of Brechin. Kinnaird Castle was built in 1405, 2km north-east of Farnell, whose own tower, Farnell Castle, rose in the 16th century. By about 1750 when Roy surveyed the area, Kinnaird was emparked and the burn had been bridged at Farnell, but no road links were shown. They appeared during the next century, and when in 1848 the first section of the Aberdeen Railway was opened, the handily located station was oddly named *Farnell Road*. The railway failed to stimulate development, though by 1894 Farnell had a post office and a mill. By then the greatly extended Kinnaird Castle stood in a vast deer park of some 525ha and had its own mill on the River South Esk. The station was already down to one passenger train each way per day in 1953 and was soon closed; the line was abandoned in 1967, when two mills still stood beside the burn. The population which had been over 400 in 1951 shrank steadily to only 250 by 1981. In the 1990s Kinnaird Castle's great policies remained a very private walled area, of which only the centre was still a deer park.

## FASLANE & Shandon

**Map 5, B4**

***Location on Gareloch, Firth of Clyde*** — OS 56: NS 2588

The 12th century castle of Faslane stood beside the sheltered Gare Loch, an arm of the Clyde; nearby was the ancient St Michael's Chapel. Little remains of either, both being unnamed on Pont's map-work of around 1600, but a lochside track was implied by the Roy map of about 1750. Later a pier was built at Shandon, where a small villa settlement grew up; Shandon House was built in 1849, and Robert Napier had West Shandon House erected in 1858. The large *Shandon Hydropathic* hotel, open by 1879, had its own golf course by 1913. The population of Shandon was 559 in 1891.

**The Railway and Military Port**: The single-line West Highland Railway (WHR), an offshoot of the North British, was opened in 1894, passing along the braes above the loch. A crossing station was opened at Shandon, in 1930 used on average by only three passengers a day! The large Faslane military port was built early in the 1939–45 war adjacent to Shandon, and opened in 1942 with a 2-km waterfront and extensive rail sidings, which handled 100 loaded wagons a day to and from the WHR until 1945. The Clyde submarine base was named HMS *Neptune* after World War II; it included the Faslane complex, barracks for 1750 sailors, and the Royal Naval Armament Depot at Coulport on Loch Long. West Shandon House vanished about 1958–60.

**Scrap from Battleships and Liners; Port for Polaris**: Faslane scrapped a series of obsolete naval vessels: the battle cruiser HMS *Renown* of 32,000 tons was cut up there in 1948, together with the battleships HMS *Resolution* and HMS *Malaya*. Shipbreaking was carried on by 1950 by the British Iron & Steel Corporation, and later by Metal Industries Ltd. The very large battleship *Vanguard* (42,500 tons), probably the largest of all British capital ships, was broken up in 1960. Far from turning swords into ploughshares, in the 1960s HMS *Neptune* became the base of the controversial *Polaris* submarine fleet, welcomed by the 1800 people who worked there in 1979, though hated and feared by the anti-nuclear lobby.

**Cutting up Aircraft Carriers**: By 1959 Timbacraft was refitting small vessels, but around then the *Shandon Hydro* was closed: its fate was to become part of the Clyde submarine base. Three aircraft carriers were scrapped at Faslane in the 1960s, ending with the huge carrier HMS *Victorious* of 35,500 tons in 1969. To make even more space for military activities the main road between Shandon and north of Garelochhead was moved to a new location up the hillside.

**The Nuclear Stance Renewed**: In the mid 20th century Shandon House was used as a remand home known as St Andrew's School; by 1993 it was long derelict and still held by the dead hand of the Ministry of Defence. The Polaris type vessels were all replaced by 1996, and in 1989 a gigantic submarine lift was being built for their even more potent 150m-long, 16,000-ton *Trident* successors. The troublesome structure was not yet ready by 1992; the ending of the Cold War left Westminster still in thrall to Washington and the cripplingly costly concept of nuclear deterrence – to the despair of the long-standing Peace Group camped at the gate. In 1996 the naval HQ for northern Britain was moved from Pitreavie to Faslane, and with them a squadron of minehunters from the doomed Rosyth base.

## FAULDHOUSE

**Map 16, B4**

***W. Lothian large village,*** *pop. 4700* — OS 65: NS 9360

Fauldhouse lies about 230 metres above sea level on the eastern edge of the moors which separate the Forth and Clyde basins. There the Breich Water traverses the south-western tip of West Lothian, some 6km east of modern Shotts. In the early 14th century Fauldhouse – which then produced butter and cheese – was owned by Torphichen Priory. It appeared on Pont's map of about 1600, as a small place labelled *'Falas'*. The Roy map made in the 1750s apparently omitted Fauldhouse but showed its origin, a moorland road between Carluke and Livingston. There was later a water-powered corn mill, but no post office until after 1838.

**Oil from Shale**: Industrial growth began in the 1850s, when Gray worked oil shale at Calderhall for distillation at the Levenseat oil works, 1.5km south-east of the kirk. A minor branch of the North British Railway (NB) was opened between Bathgate and Wishaw in 1864, with a station at Fauldhouse, where from 1869 it was crossed by the Caledonian Railway's Cleland and Midcalder route; the latter still provides rail passenger services to both Edinburgh and Glasgow. The mineral workings were connected to both railways. At some time Fauldhouse acquired a gasworks, and in 1894 there was also an inn. The coal and ironstone mines and limestone quarries were connected by a veritable maze of mineral railways; Fauldhouse had a population of 2800 in 1901. By 1897 a sandstone quarry at Braehead was worked, soon employing 57 men; the quarry closed in 1937.

**Decay, Isolation and Unemployment**: Despite much growth in population, in 1951 its 5000 people still had to make do with the facilities of a village, and were surrounded by the scars of short-term mineral working. Its last two mines had already closed by 1954, and the former NB line and derelict mineral railways had been lifted by 1963. However, the unassuming Greenburn golf course was laid out from 1953. Only the location of Fauldhouse within reach of alternative jobs in the central belt can have enabled its relative stability in size and facilities to be maintained over the 1951–81 period. Between 1973 and 1988 a very large quarry was started at Leven Seat to the south, plus extensive afforestation and removal of some industrial dereliction. In 1991 4690 people lived locally, but with 17% male unemployment. There has been little recent development.

## FEARN & Hill of Fearn

**Map 9, B2**

***Easter Ross village,*** *pop. 450* — OS 21: NH 8377

A monastic settlement was founded in the dark ages in the flat area of Easter Ross between the Cromarty and Dornoch Firths, 7 km south-east of Tain. Between 1338 and 1372 a Premonstratensian religious community from Wester Fearn (near Bonar Bridge) built and moved into an abbey on the ancient site. The nearby Lochslin castle was also built in the 14th century. The abbey was extended until 1545, and in 1560 its Abbot sat in Parliament. The monks disappeared with the Reformation, but the abbey and castle were clearly shown by Pont who mapped the area about 1600. Two mills turned nearby, while bridges at Ankerville, and apparently also at Calrossie, implied a regular routeway between the Cromarty ferry and Tain.

**Railways and Tatties**: The abbey chapel became known as the Kirk of Fearn; its roof sadly collapsed in 1742 with numerous fatalities, but was restored. A short way to the west, the Roy map of about 1750 marked the roadless hamlet of *Meikle Allan*, later called Hill of Fearn, and eventually the main centre. Heron in 1799 noted that *"near the village of Fearn are the ruins of an abbey"*. The area was eventually supplied with roads, Fearn post office was opened in 1839, and the single-track Ross-shire Railway opened in 1864 with a crossing station called Fearn, nearly 2 km west of Hill of Fearn, plus Nigg station – 2 km towards Dingwall. By 1875 Wordie & Co operated a rail to road cartage depot at Fearn station, which handled heavy seasonal potato traffic, and also fish from Portmahomack; Wordies' horses were here superseded by motors in 1934.

**Fearn by Air and Rail**: In World War II an RAF (later Fleet Air Arm) airfield was built south of the Kirkton, but was closed soon after 1945. By 1951 the population of Fearn was only 450, though it was a post town, and some facilities served a hinterland of about 3250: there was an inn, and a 160-pupil secondary school. Once the latter had been closed the population declined further. Nigg station closed to passengers in 1960 and to freight in 1964. In 1978 potatoes were still sent south by rail from Fearn as far afield as Cambridge, but now only passengers use the station. With the advent of North Sea oil and the Invergordon smelter the previous population total was regained by 1981, and for a time about then the airfield found a new user; some growth continued. Shopping and post office facilities are still available, and the Anta pottery serves visitors to the area.

## FENWICK

**Map 1, C1**

***Ayrshire village,*** *pop. 1050* — OS 70: NS 4643

An ancient dun near Hareshaw stands near the head of the Craufurdland Water, which was paralleled by the winding Fenwick Water. From the 16th century the tower of Craufurdland Castle stood beside the former, 4 km north-east of Kilmarnock. Pont's map of Cunninghame around 1600 marked *'Finnick'* on the other stream with a tiny symbol; it lies 3 km north of the castle. Ancient *'Powkelly'* to the north was depicted as a chess castle. Fenwick parish started a school in 1638, and built a fine new church in 1643. Roy's map, made about 1754, again showed *'Finnick'*, indicating a small village lining the Kilmarnock road, which passed the kirk and *'Gandlum'* (Gardrum) mill, forking to Glasgow and Hamilton.

**The World's First Co-op?**: At one time the village was known for its cobblers, but the *Fenwick Weavers*, an association founded in 1769, has been claimed to be the world's first co-operative society. In 1799 Heron described both Fenwick and Kirkton of Fenwick as *"small villages"*. In the early 19th century a woollen mill was at work at Waterside near Hareshaw; the building survives. At that time the old Craufurdland Castle was being embedded in a Gothic mansion designed by its laird John Howieson, of Braehead in Cramond, in whose wife's family the barony had been since the 13th century. By 1895 Laigh Fenwick was at the meeting point of no fewer than seven radial roads, though some were no more than short lanes. Less than 1 km up the road was Fenwick proper, where fewer roads met but there were churches, an inn, smithy and a post and telegraph office. Gardrum was then a corn mill, and nearby was Pokelly Castle and Hall; but the castle vanished in the early 20th century.

**A Modern Air of Prosperity**: By the 1950s there was a primary school at Hareshaw near Waterside. Fenwick had a population of about 1000 and the facilities of a small village, including a garage. Fenwick school then had 30 secondary pupils, but by 1977 although the population was creeping upwards, both schools were only primary. By 1971 an A77 bypass had been built, and Fenwick and Laigh Fenwick were coalescing. By 1977 the *Fenwick Hotel* had been enlarged; by 1980 two other hotels were open. By 1987 a tourist office had been provided, and a new residential estate had been built east of the Fenwick Water. In 1991 about 1050 people lived in the conserved but suburbanised village; professional or managerial jobs. predominated, and a third of householders had two or more cars. By 1998 more houses had been built, but the tourist office had gone. In 2000 the extension of the M77 motorway from Malletsheugh (Newton Mearns) to Fenwick was begun. The enlarged *Fenwick Hotel* offers 32 rooms, whilst the Pear Tree company employs 25 building tree houses.

## FERN & Noranside

**Map 6, C2**

***Angus communities,*** *pop. 325 (area)* — OS 44: NO 4861

Standing stones and an embanked church at Fern, on the northern edge of Strathmore11 km west of Brechin, show very early significance, and Fern had a parish school by 1619. However the Roy map made about 1750 showed the kirk in a trackless area, which has remained largely agricultural ever since. By 1894 a mansion stood in extensive policies at Noranside, 1.5 km west of Fern, which had a post office and smithy; the parish had 322 residents in 1901. A primary school was open in 1958 but soon closed, as did the post office. By 1953 Noranside had become a tuberculosis hospital, and by 1967 a Borstal institution, with a population of 114 in 1971, when 355 people lived in the rest of the parish. In all only 313 residents were enumerated in 1991. By 1992 Noranside had recently been modernised as an open prison, which it remains. There are now no facilities at Fern apart from a telephone exchange.

## FETLAR, Isle of

**Map 14, C2**

***Small Shetland island**, pop. 100* OS 1 or 2: HU 6290

The hilly but fertile northern island of Fetlar lies east of larger Yell. It has many interesting natural features *(see Haswell-Smith)* and the remains of brochs; on its eastern tip at Strandburgh was an early monastery. For a long time it has specialised in pony breeding. The Nicolson laird cleared many of the people in the mid 19th century. A fortnightly steamer called at Houbie pier in the 1930s, but by 1951 only about 160 people lived on the island, whose basic facilities were as scattered as its settlement. From 1972 vehicle ferries operated from a new terminal at Oddsta at the north western tip of the island to Belmont and Gutcher, and an airstrip called Turra Field had been laid out above Houbie. But the population had again halved by 1991 to just 90, so the community council advertised for and gained about 20 new residents, although these were mainly Franciscan nuns running a retreat for people with problems. By 1994 a museum was open at Houbie, and nearby was a caravan site – how many visitors would they attract?

## FETTERANGUS

**Map 10, C2**

***Aberdeenshire hamlet**, pop. 350* OS 30: NJ 9850

A standing stone, ancient earthworks and an old church show the antiquity of the parish of Fetterangus, lying between the Forest of Deer and the North Ugie Water, 3 km north of Old Deer. It was a tiny place at the time of Robert Gordon's survey, made prior to 1642. The field sheet of the Roy survey, made about 1750, showed a track between Old Deer and Fraserburgh, with *'Hithie'* mill as the only local feature of note. In 1752 a new village was laid out, but it was off the turnpike road and later railway systems, and failed to grow beyond a simple crossing of two streets. Though located in the Buchan area, it was an exclave of Banffshire as late as 1795. From 1927 the firm of Grays of Fetterangus manufactured fertiliser spreaders and other farm machinery. Otherwise the village remained agricultural, and had minimal facilities, largely depending on Mintlaw and elsewhere; the rural school at Kininmonth 4 km to the east provided a junior secondary class until the 1960s. The 1951 population was almost 600, but this rapidly shrank over the next thirty years to only some 350 by 1981, and there has been little new development.

## FETTERCAIRN

**Map 10, B5**

***Mearns village**, pop. 250* OS 45: NO 6573

Fettercairn lies on the little Burn of Caulcoats in the Howe of the Mearns, about 15 km north of Brechin and only 2 km from the ancient site of Kincardine Castle. Fettercairn had an early thanage, and other castles existed nearby in the tenth century. The thanage of Balbegno 1 km to the west passed in 1488 to Andrew Wood of Belhelvie; early in the 16th century his son John built the large tower-house of Balbegno Castle with its fine vaulted roof. Fettercairn was chartered as a burgh of barony in 1504 and took over Kincardine's mercat cross when that place died out around 1600, with Stonehaven becoming the county town. Blaeu's 1654 atlas map of north-east Scotland gave Fettercairn some emphasis, but the place was burned by Montrose in 1645.

**Shelter Between the Bridges**: A new market cross was erected in 1670 and Fettercairn held fairs from 1730, but it was largely ignored by early travellers from the south. It lay on the track between Brechin and what was then the important centre of Kincardine O'Neil on Deeside, a route regarded by the Commissioners in 1810 as a long-established military road. Some 7 km to the south this track – now a minor road – crosses the early Northwater Bridge (called *Bridge of Inglismaldie* in the mid 18th century). To the north it climbs over the 450 m Cairn o' Mount with its 20% and steeper gradients and stupendous views over the Mearns, and leads down to the 13-metre span Bridge of Dye, which was built about 1680, possibly replacing a medieval structure and itself now superseded. At the time of Roy's survey about 1750 this was the only road serving compact Fettercairn. To the east stood a mansion, the House of Fettercairn, and to the north in its great park was the mansion of Fasque, its name derived from the Gaelic for *'Shelter'*.

**Highland Whisky**: Fettercairn was laid out as a new village about 1760. Two fairs were to take place there in 1797. The parish church was built in 1803, the spire added later. The hills 3 km to the north were famed for whisky moonlighting, but the Fettercairn distillery officially dates from the start of legal distilling in 1824. According to Chambers, at that time Fettercairn was *"a neat little village, deriving its name from a stupendous cairn in the neighbourhood"*; this was probably the fort known as Green Cairn, 2 km to the south-west. Fettercairn post office was a fairly late arrival, around 1825.

**Triumphal Arch and Local Worthies**: John Milne, born in Fettercairn in 1822, became a well known architect in St Andrews and the designer of the unique Fettercairn Arch, built in 1861 for no better reason than that Queen Victoria had stayed there. No doubt she was visiting Fasque, by then a vast mansion which was the home of the great 19th century premier William Ewart Gladstone. In 1886 the distillery was substantial, though still water-powered, and it produced 385,000 litres of Highland malt whisky annually. A public hall was built in 1890, and to Murray in 1894 Fettercairn was a *"picturesque village"*. The *Eagle* inn had recently become the *"good" Ramsay Arms Hotel*; but Clattering Brig on the Cairn o' Mount road was only a footbridge, and the road itself still *"exceedingly rough"*.

**Openings and Closures**: Fettercairn was never served by a railway, and only the coming of motor cars led to a vehicular bridge being built at Clattering Brig, and later a tourist restaurant. Fettercairn remained only a small but pleasant village, which gained a modern primary school but between 1951 and 1981 saw the closure of half its shops, and some loss of status by the hotel. Fasque stood empty in a time-warp from the mid 1960s, but was opened to the public by Peter Gladstone, its owner from 1977 – a fascinating though chilly place to visit. In 1991 Fettercairn held under 250 residents, but held an agricultural show as recently as 1993. The distillery was then owned by White & Mackay, most of its output going for blending. Still very well maintained, it is open to the public; *Old Fettercairn* single malt can be bought in its visitor centre. Fettercairn's branch bank had closed about 1998, leaving few facilities in the village but the small hotel, a post office, general store, a tearoom, and a garage.

## FINDHORN **Map 9, C3**

***Moray coastal village,*** *pop. 700* OS 27: NJ 0464

In 1532 a burgh of barony was founded on the east side of the sandy mouth of the River Findhorn, 4 km from Kinloss Abbey. Its formal name *Seatoun of Kinloss* did not stick, because the sheltered bay at the river mouth – protected by the sandspit known as the Bar of Findhorn – had long functioned as the port for Forres. Pont's map made about 1600 showed *'Findorn'* as microscopic, but although in 1621 it paid under 1.5% of Scottish customs dues, Findhorn was regarded as a town by 1636. In 1655 it was *"a small place"* exporting salmon and importing salt. In 1694 Findhorn was buried by the Culbin Sands, a vast expanse of some 30 square kilometres of drifting coastal dunes which spread eastwards from the mouth of the River Nairn, but usually stayed west of the River Findhorn. An immediate replacement was built which very soon became Moray's main port, but was also luckless, being destroyed in 1701 by what seems to have been a tidal surge or minor tsunami.

**Findhorn tries again**: A third and successful attempt was soon made to form a permanent port, and the *Crown Inn* dates from 1739, yet the tiny village was still roadless in Roy's time about 1750. Fishing then supplanted trade: in 1799 Heron found Findhorn *"a considerable fishing-town, having a commodious station for ships, and a tolerable harbour; considerable quantities of dried white-fish are annually exported"*. The harbour was again rebuilt in 1840 when Findhorn was known as a fishing village. The description still applied in 1894; some old icehouses survive. Meantime the Findhorn Railway which opened from Kinloss in 1860 soon proved hopelessly uneconomic, was closed to passengers in 1869 and to goods in 1880 – surely something of a record. After that, locally caught salmon were collected by Wordie's carts and taken to Nairn station.

**Forestry, Evacuation, Community and Yachting**: Many local people were evacuated in 1943–44 so that rehearsals of the Normandy landings could take place on the coast of Culbin Forest, a Forestry Commission plantation which had gradually stabilised the sands since 1918. The Findhorn Community, a colourful international residential grouping of artists, craftsmen and eccentrics of a gentle and *'green'* character, was started in 1962 by Peter and Eileen Caddy. It grew in thirty years to a strength numbered in the hundreds, but some locals remained highly suspicious of their informal lifestyle. Though the sandbar and silting remained a perennial problem, by 1981 Findhorn was a yachting resort, with two more hotels, two caravan sites and picnic areas. The Royal Yacht Club was established there in 1985. The local salmon-fishing industry, which sadly closed in the 1980s, is remembered in the Findhorn heritage centre, but the *Crown & Anchor Inn* offers accommodation.

## FINDOCHTY **Map 10, A1**

***Moray coastal village,*** *pop. 1100* OS 28: NJ 4668

Findochty (pronounced *Finnechtie*), which is known to have existed by 1440, stands on the rocky south coast of the Moray Firth, 5 km west of Cullen. A cove known as Crooked Haven served as Findochty harbour when the Ord family bought the estate in 1568, soon building a tower house to the west. The village was re-founded in 1716 when 17 fishermen moved in from Fraserburgh at the laird's instigation. Findochty seems to have been overlooked when the fair copy of the Roy map was made some time after 1754. There was no post office until after 1840, but Findochty reached a peak of activity with 140 fishing boats in 1855. When in 1857 Buckie gained a new harbour the Findochty fishing fleet rapidly declined, to only four boats in 1880, when the local harbour was improved in self-defence. But Buckie's new Cluny harbour again proved more of a draw, and Findochty had no local boats at all in 1884.

**Conserved in Moray**: In 1886 came the Great North of Scotland Railway's coastal line and Findochty's inland station, and the population rose to some 1700 by 1901; in 1915 Findochty became a police burgh. The population was still about 1600 in 1951 when some fishing had been resumed, for a fish merchant was in business; but although there was a small secondary school (which soon closed) the burgh office was in Cullen. Other facilities were only those of a small village, and as the population fell these subsequently declined further, with the closure of the railway in 1968. The area was transferred to Moray District in 1975, and by 1981 Findochty had become a conservation village. Despite the temporary lack of a pub, the harbour was busy with yachts in the mid 1980s, there was a caravan and camping site by 1987 and the population had stabilised at nearly 1100 in 1991, with an affluent retired character. Lobster pots now accompany the yachts, some new housing has been built, and services include a public library, bank, and post office. A pub, church and the Salvation Army vie for attention.

## FINLAGGAN & Ballygrant **Map 4, B4**

***Area of east Islay,*** *pop. 200* OS 60: NR 3968

Near Port Askaig in Islay, Mesolithic and Neolithic remains dating back to 6000 BC have been found beside Loch Finlaggan, which contains a crannog, as do neighbouring lochans. Two duns and the early chapel of Kilmeny stood nearby. The Norse seized and held Islay until 1156, when Somerled drove them out and made Finlaggan his capital. Meetings took place on an artificial islet in the loch, whose Gaelic name is Eilean na Comhairl, *'Islet of the Council'*. Underwater causeways linked the islets, and where their axis intersects the shore are standing stones. Excavations on the larger islet have found evidence of a church, a large hall built in dressed stone, medieval paved roads, 14th century harp pins and jugs of a type also found at Dundonald in Ayrshire. Guard houses nearby could hold several hundred men. Ancient silver mines south and east of the loch were linked with the east coast by early trackways (revealed in 1999 on images from the Space Shuttle), implying an export trade.

**Capital of the Lords of the Isles**: From 1493 Somerled's descendants the seafaring Macdonalds were known as the Lords of the Isles, confirming Finlaggan as their capital and renaming the council the *Islay Parliament*. In 1703 Martin mentioned *"a good lead mine, having a mixture of silver in it"*. The island capital was moved to Bowmore in 1718, but Chambers claimed that the Lords' coronation stone *"as well as the ruins of the palace and its offices"* were still to be seen in the 1820s. Little of these features remain above ground; OS maps label the ruins as a *'castle'*. Silver mining had ceased by the late 19th century, but much limestone was quarried at nearby Ballygrant, a clachan with a long-standing inn. By 1981 the slowly shrinking population of the area was under 200. However, by 1998 Finlaggan had a visitor centre, and afforestation had covered extensive areas to the north.

## FINSTOWN & Firth — Map 13, B2

***Small Orkney village,*** *pop. 425* — OS 6: HY 3614

The remains of brochs, cairns and other ancient settlements surround the sheltered head of the Bay of Firth, which bites deeply into the Orkney Mainland midway between Kirkwall and Stromness. In the early 19th century the low gap in the hills enabled the island's main road between Kirkwall and Stromness to keep near sea level throughout, and the Firth meal mill was built. The name Finstown came about when a Napoleonic war veteran, an Irishman named Phin, opened a bar at the point where the road from Kirkwall to the northern limb of Mainland diverged. A village grew around it, by 1872 there was a post office, and a stone pier was built, at one time used by cargo vessels and oyster boats; but overexploitation destroyed the oyster beds. However a small wood, almost unique in windswept Orkney, was able to establish itself in the valley to the west. Tom Kent, born at Firth in 1863, became the first professional photographer in the Orkneys in 1897 and made a unique historical record.

**Woodland attracts Discerning Residents**: The population of Finstown in 1951 was about 450, with a post office and a 29-line telephone exchange. Two of its little shops sold clothing in 1953, but the small Firth secondary school for 110 pupils was closed about 1960, and just a primary remained. The long-standing Liberal MP for the northern isles, Jo Grimond, was a notable resident. The population had declined to about 365 by 1971, but by 1980 there were three motor businesses and an inn. In 1999 the Firth mill stood fully equipped but derelict. However, housing development continued in the 1990s, and this remarkably bosky place has five modern self catering lodges, four shops, post office and inn, MoT garage, a builder and agricultural merchant, and even a camera business. Some lobster fishing continues.

## FINTRY — Map 5, C4

***W. Stirlingshire village,*** *pop. 550* — OS 57: NS 6186

Fintry is remotely located about 20km west of Stirling and 7km east of Balfron, towards the steep upper end of Strathendrick, named after the Endrick Water. Ancient hill forts occupy crags either side of the river, where a standing stone shows Pictish occupation. Later came a medieval motte, and the 14th century tower of Culcreuch, extended in the 16th century. At this time – when it was still part of the province of Lennox – came Fintry Castle; this later vanished, and Fintry never became a burgh of barony. Fintry Kirk stood in a thickly settled area at the time of Pont's mapping visit around 1600; there was already a mill at Culcreuch west of the church, and by then the Endrick had been bridged near Gartcarron, 4km to the east. Gonachan bridge was built in 1750 2 km to the east on the track to Stirling; the Roy map made about 1754 showed the Kirk of *'Fintray'* near its meeting with other tracks to Balfron, Killearn, Campsie and Kippen.

*Culcreuch Cotton Mill, built in 1795 at Fintry as the mainstay of a new village, was designed to employ 1000 workers, but seems to have operated for under a century.* *(RCAHMS / JRH)*

**Cotton and the New Village**: The water-powered Culcreuch Cotton Mill was founded just north of the kirk in 1794–95, when a new village was erected for the workers. Heron in 1799 noted with interest that the *"great cotton-work lately erected is calculated to give employment to a thousand persons"*. With such big expectations a bridge connecting it with the kirk on the south bank was erected in 1804; the mansion of Culcreuch then stood in its own park. In 1827 Fintry was noted by Chambers as *"a village where the Endrick keeps in motion a large cotton mill at Calcreach"*. A primary school was built in 1839, and Fintry post office was issued with a date stamp about 1840.

**After Textiles, Tourism**: The mill eventually failed (but was still shown on the 1895 revision of the OS map, when the village was labelled *Newtown*). The *Clachan Inn* was already open; it was later renamed as a hotel. In 1951, with a parish population of only 356, Fintry had the facilities of a small village. A youth hostel was open in 1954, though it had closed by 1986; but in 1977 there was a modern primary school, plus the hotel, an inn, catering, a camp site, craft shops, a leisure centre (in the school of 1839), plus a village hall and two garages.

**Late Twentieth Century Growth**: Despite its remote situation, which had led by 1977 to its sole public transport being a 4-seater estate-car postbus, commuting by car to Glasgow and elsewhere was possible. So the population grew, with new housing estates erected north of the river. By 1986 a caravan site was open at Overglinns. However, by 1991 no more than 549 people lived in the whole parish. In 1989 a huge golf-based development was planned; this had not materialised by 1993, although an additional hotel was open east of the village. In 1994 industry was represented by Victor James, fudge manufacturer. By 2000 Fintry was large enough to support an effective rugby team, named Strathendrick. The imposing *Culcreuch Castle* in its country park is now a hotel.

## FIONNPHORT & Erraid

**Map 4, B2**

***Location, w. coast of Mull,*** *pop. 100* OS 48: NM 3023

Erray (later miscalled Erraid), a small isle off the extremity of the lengthy Ross of Mull 4 km south of Iona, was noted by Monro in 1549 as *"fruitful of corn and pasturage, with abundance of fishing"*. On the Ross some 3 km north of Erray was Fionnphort (*'Holy Port'* in Gaelic), the long-standing ferry point for Iona, shown as *'Bay of Finfort'* on Blaeu's Pont-based atlas map of 1654. Iona and the whole Ross of Mull lies in the extensive parish of Kilfinichen & Kilvickeon.

**Lighthouses at Skerryvore and Dubh Artach**: In 1840–42 the interlocking blocks of granite used to build the tower of Skerryvore lighthouse *(see Scarinish)* were supplied by a quarry in the area, either at the Bull Hole *(see below)* or on Erraid. There a granite quarry, pier, 9 cottages and base camp were established – or re-established – in 1867 by the Northern Lighthouse Board, for the construction in 1868–72 of the 36 m tall Dubh Artach *(Black Stone)* lighthouse. This was built on a horribly exposed domed rock rising at best 10 m above high water, 27 km south-west of Fionnphort *(for factual accounts of these dramatic operations see Munro, 1979)*. Pink granite used in the construction of the Albert Memorial and other London landmarks was also quarried at the Bull Hole north of Fionnphort. Around 1890 the lighthouse keepers' families were moved from Tiree to Erraid.

**Catering and Granite**: Some granite quarrying continued until about 1920, but Fionnphort remained little more than a scattered crofting township. In 1945 there was still a school at Erraid, which was the base for both lighthouses until 1967. Skerryvore lighthouse suffered a major fire in 1954, but was restored as a manned station in 1958; Dubh Artach was converted for automatic operation in 1971. From 1973 the Iona ferry was able to carry vehicles when necessary, by removing its garden seats! By 1981 the population of Fionnphort was predominantly elderly, but by 1986 there was some tourist trade, mainly eating facilities for the growing numbers using the ferry to visit Iona. A new and larger ferry was built in 1991 *(see St Monans)*. A disused granite quarry at Tormore, between the village and the Bull Hole, was reopened for building stone about 1996 by Scottish Natural Stones Ltd.

## FISHNISH

**Map 4, C2**

***Location, N-E. coast of Mull*** OS 49: NM 6452

Fishnish on the Sound of Mull was the site of an ancient ferry to Lochaline in Morvern; it was shown as *'Finchiness'* on Pont's original map of the late 16th century. In 1838 nearby Ballineanoch was the *'Receiving House'* for all post to Lochaline, by boat and runner, but the ferry was discontinued soon after. In 1973 this by then deserted but afforested location was provided with an access road and slipway, and a new car ferry was instituted to Lochaline. In 1985 a small cafe was the only other sign of development, but by 1996 forest walks had been laid out and a caravan site provided near the main road 1 km to the south.

## FLANNAN ISLES

**Map 11, A1**

***Small islands, Outer Hebrides*** OS 13: NA 7246

On the largest of the tiny uninhabited Flannan Isles, a cluster of sheer Atlantic rocks over 50 km west of Lewis, there was an ancient chapel; in the mid 16th century Monro found many very lean wild sheep. In 1896–99 a 21 m tall lighthouse was built there with great difficulty; the shore station for its keepers was at Breasclete. The light had been lit for a year when its three duty keepers were swept away without trace in the major December storm of 1900, apparently when securing equipment at a height of 33 m above the sea! So in 1907 Marconi installed his invention of wireless telegraphy at the lighthouse for Lloyds. However, it was 1971 before this treacherous location was automatically lit.

## FLEMINGTON, Newton & Hallside

**Map 15, D6**

***Urban area e. of Cambuslang,*** *pop. 7000* OS 64: NS 6659

Drumsargad Castle, now simply a motte, was one of the earliest known features of this area south of the Clyde 5 km east of Rutherglen; Gilbertfield Castle, an L-plan tower south of Flemington, is a ruined 16th century structure. Pont's crowded sketch map made in 1596 showed Flemington and *'Newtoun'* as tiny places; the name *'Colsyd'* implies that coal was already being mined, and a bridge crossed the Rotten Calder Water on the way to Hamilton. Roy's map surveyed about 1754 showed this as a made road between Hamilton and Rutherglen, with the house or farm of Newton on a spur road. In 1799 Heron noted that *"a cotton-works at the village of Flemington employs a considerable number of hands; the coal-works also furnish employment to many"*. The Clydesdale Junction Railway, later the main line of the Caledonian Railway (CR), avoided Flemington but opened in 1849 with a station at Newton, which became the junction for Hamilton.

**Iron and Steel Works multiply**: Between Drumsargad motte and Newton station, where there was an inn, was the Hallside steelworks, built by the Steel Company of Scotland in 1871–73, and extended in the 1880s; three coal pits surrounded it. The Flemington steelworks were established in 1890. In 1895 Flemington was a lengthy hamlet with an inn; Newton was a triangle of short congested streets just downwind of the Hallside steelworks. In common with many other of the industrial areas which supported the country's economy, none of these places was considered of interest by Murray's Handbook in 1894. Two years later the CR opened a connecting line across the Clyde between Newton and Carmyle.

**Transient Trams, and Halfway to Nowhere**: In 1904 Newton became the junction for a fifth railway route (as well as its innumerable mineral lines) when the CR's offshoot, the Lanarkshire & Ayrshire Railway, was opened to Cathcart; it gained county primary and Catholic schools. From about that time until 1931, electric trams of the Lanarkshire Tramways Company connected Hamilton via Flemington to Cambuslang, there meeting those of the Glasgow system. In the 1920s Flemington grew westwards with the building of the Lightburn area, and by 1931 the Flemington & Newton district held 4176 people; Wellside followed rather later. By 1934 Colvilles had acquired various local steelworks. The area was still a hive of activity, with the Hallside and Westburn steelworks, Gateside Colliery, and the estates known as Halfway (between the two older settlements) and Westburn (between its steelworks and the station). Newton House had vanished by 1971. Colliery and industrial closures were in train, though in this area the population changes are hard to follow from the Census data.

**The Fate of Hallside**: In 1975 the role of the re-equipped and still profitable Hallside works was to supply the Craigneuk bar mill with alloy steel billets, the steel being melted in electric arc furnaces. Closed in 1982, by 1995 its site was a wasteland of jumbled concrete blocks, buried in 1996 under a 2 m thick layer of mixed sewage sludge and coal waste, to be planted with 250,000 trees by Scottish Greenbelt. Trafalgar House, owner of RDL which still had a major structural steel works at Westburn, closed it in 1990 in favour of a Teesside works; 320 jobs and the rail connection were lost. In 1991 Halfway briefly held the Scottish HQ of the grocery store group Shoprite; in 1994 this was moved to Crossgates, Fife. Flemington and Westburn still have post offices; there are three primary schools, and Newton still has the station and a pub.

## FLOTTA & Fara Isles — Map 13, B3

***Small Orkney islands,** pop. 126* — OS 7: ND 3693

In Scapa Flow are two relatively low-lying islands, Flotta (*'Flat Isle'* in Norse) and small, rather inaccessible but fertile Fara. Flotta was for long simply a scattered crofting community of over 400 people, and Fara had nearly 100 in the late 19th century. During the two world wars Flotta was garrisoned, for it commanded the southern access to the naval anchorage of Scapa Flow. Two piers and a total of five batteries were built on Flotta itself, and others were scattered less thickly around the other shores of the Flow. Unstable cordite was blamed when in 1917 the huge battleship *Vanguard* suddenly exploded while at anchor north of Flotta, sadly killing over 800 of her vast crew. In the 1939–45 war a naval garrison was based on Flotta, afterwards leaving behind many rotting installations. By 1951 about 175 people lived on Flotta, served by a pier, post office, primary school and – remarkably – a doctor. However Fara was soon abandoned, and Flotta's population halved over the next twenty years.

**Water and Oil**: In 1970 a water pipeline was laid from Hoy, by 1974 a passenger ferry linked Flotta to Longhope, Lyness and Scapa, and it was in 1977 that its 65 consumers were first connected to mains electricity. This was due to the construction of a large oil terminal, conceived in 1973 to serve the Piper oilfield of the US-owned company Occidental. A pier and eleven storage tanks were complete by 1979, drastically altering Flotta's character, even to the introduction of a sub-branch bank, a new primary school and an airstrip on the west coast. A car ferry from Houton near Orphir was introduced, also serving Lyness. Although in 1991 the isle's population was still only 126, in 1994 Elf Oil was Orkney's largest single employer, providing 450 jobs on Flotta. The Elf terminal was chosen in 1995 to receive oil by tanker from the new Foinaven field, 200 km to the north-west; it was sold to Talisman Energy in 2000.

## FOCHABERS & Mosstodloch — Map 10, A1

***Villages on R. Spey,** pop. 2600* — OS 28: NJ 3458

In the 12th or 13th century the hospital of St Nicholas was established near the mouth of the River Spey, presumably to serve the passengers who crossed a ferry there; Speymouth parish lies west of the river. A castle on the east – named Bog of Gight – dated back to the 15th century or earlier; it stood in the equally earthily named Bellie parish, where a *"sumptuous house"* was built in the 16th century for George, 2nd Earl of Huntly. This was shown on Timothy Pont's sketch map, made about 1600, as a complex tower, surrounded by a park. Belliehill some 1.5 km to the north had become a burgh of barony in 1499, but Pont showed only the *'Kirk of Bolly'*, plus a single row of houses at Fochabers, which was chartered as a burgh of barony in 1598–99. Mosstodloch on the west bank of the Spey was also shown with the tiniest of symbols, aptly since in 1621 the entire Spey collection paid under 1.5% of Scottish Customs dues. *'North Boitt'* – probably a regular ferry boat – was shown between Mosstodloch and Bog of Gight, which still bore its ancient name as late as 1618.

**Improvements, Timber and Apples**: In 1707 the heir to the dukedom of Gordon married the agricultural improver Lady Henrietta Mordaunt, who introduced to backward Moray the English plough, foreign grasses and the art of haymaking. A post office was open by 1715. The Roy map made about 1750 showed *'Fockabers'* as a large village immediately south-west of what was by then called Gordon Castle. There was only one road, which ran east to west. The Spey was unbridged; the ferry was not named on the map but was known as the *Boat of Bog*. About 1754 a sawmill was built to cut up the timber floated down the river, and continued in use well into the 19th century. But these various improvements were slow to affect the settlement, seen as a *"populous but beggarly village"* by Carlyle in 1765, though the tenants did have apple orchards.

**Great House, New Village and Lilting Tunes**: The ferry which still interrupted the main route between Aberdeen and Inverness was very busy in 1769, then requiring many boats. In 1769–82 the 4th Duke of Gordon had Gordon Castle vastly extended under the direction of John Baxter, a mason employed by William Adam. William Marshall, who was born locally in 1749, became an outstanding composer of the elegant Strathspey dance tunes and slow airs. The reports of village dereliction must have been the result of the Duke of Gordon's deliberate rundown to 1776, when he had John Baxter lay out a new settlement with a square almost 1 km from the castle, twice as far away as the old village; Adams reproduced detailed plans of both. The first plots were feued the same year, and very soon the whole population was moved to the pleasing new village, which was described in 1799 by Heron as a *"town near a thousand inhabitants"*; it was at first devoted to spinning linen thread for the Nottingham hosiers.

**Spey Bridge and Christie's Nurseries**: A bridge designed by Telford to replace the ferry across the turbulent Spey (which the Duke had already begun in Spynie sandstone at his own expense) was completed in 1809 with the aid of a special parliamentary grant. Christie's founded a long-lasting nursery garden in the 1820s. Chambers described Fochabers in 1827 as *"a neat modern village, the appendage of Gordon Castle, by far the most magnificent structure and finest house north of the Firth of Forth. The road crosses the Spey by a handsome modern bridge"*. This was partly swept away like so many others in the great floods of 1829, but soon repaired, first in wood, then in cast-iron.

**High School, Jam and Railways**: In 1846 the ornate stone building of Milne's High School was erected to designs by Thomas Mackenzie and endowed by Alex Milne, a local who had made his fortune in America. In 1868 W A Baxter began small-scale preserve manufacture at Mosstodloch; opposite his place was built Fochabers station, terminus of a 4 km branch of the Highland Railway, opened in 1893. This left the main line (opened in 1858) at the original Fochabers station, renamed Orbliston Junction, where by 1860 Wordie & Co operated a rail to road cartage depot. Remarkably, a siding was laid into the large steading of Cowfords Farm.

**Public Services and Private Vandalism**: Murray's Handbook for 1894 found the *Gordon Arms "good"* and described Fochabers as *"a neat little place"*. Although it did not become a police burgh, in 1906 Fochabers was provided with its own small power station, and at some time a gasworks was established. However the branch line passenger service was withdrawn in 1931. By the 1950s Fochabers and Mosstodloch had a population of 1850 and the facilities of a typical village, including two hotels and a golf course, which seems soon to have closed. With the growth of Baxter's from eleven employees in 1948 into a major cannery and jam factory, population growth followed, but most of the magnificent Gordon Castle was most regrettably demolished about 1955. Orbliston station was closed by Beeching in 1964, and the terminus building became a residential home. A new bridge was built beside the old in the early 1970s.

**Forestry, Food Processing and Nurseries**: By that time Fochabers had the local Forestry Commission HQ, the Riddoch sawmills, and Christie's, then Britain's largest tree nursery – where in 1976 twelve million young trees, mainly Sitka Spruce, were growing. Christie's also had a substantial general nursery – among the most northerly in Britain – a pleasant place for a summer stroll. In 1981 the facilities in Fochabers were those of a large village, with a museum and a caravan site by 1986. By 1983 GKN had opened a steel stockyard, probably to serve remote oil-related developments, and the combined population by 1991 was 2600. By then Baxters' visitor centre attracted 170,000 people a year, who could also enjoy riverside walks and picnics on the factory site, where 550 people worked in 1994; today its turnover is £60m, and 900 are employed on several sites. After some controversy in 1993 the Milne's High School building was restored, and reopened for use by primary age children in 1995. By 2000 a former church had become the Fochabers Folk Museum.

## FORD

**Map 5, A4**

***Argyllshire hamlet,*** *pop. under 100* — OS 55: NM 8703

At 35 km in length, the wooded Loch Awe which nearly bisects Argyll is one of Scotland's longest freshwater lochs. At its western end it is joined to the tiny Loch Ederline by the Burn of Ederline, near which is a standing stone. The burn appeared as *'Edderlin'* on Pont's sketch map of around 1600, apparently crossed by an early bridge, beside which he wrote *'A na Gra'*, perhaps meaning the (Bridge) of Love (*Gradh* in Gaelic), implying that it was a gift to the community. The Roy maps made about 1750 showed no bridge, but named the Ferry of *Ariagua* (field sheet) or *Aragon* (fair copy), a link in a droving route or track linking Inveraray with Craignish.

**Steamers and Fishermen**: In the 19th century a steamer pier was built on Loch Awe, and eventually a permanent bridge was built at the ford on the Kilmartin to Dalmally road. So, however the burn was crossed, the location was strategic. In 1864 when the area was still Gaelic-speaking the *Auchinellan Inn* was built; later this anglers' retreat was blandly renamed the *Ford Hotel*. By 1881 there was a post office named Ford, and by the 1890s the older village name had vanished from small-scale maps. Steamer services continued – except during wartime – until 1951 *(see Dalmally)*.

**Twentieth Century Trout**: Although the population was only about 75 in 1951, the one-teacher primary school had contained 17 pupils in 1948; by that time there were two buses a week to English-speaking Lochgilphead and Ardrishaig, on which the village came to depend, and Gaelic speech was failing in the area. In 1950 a road was built north of the loch to serve the Forestry Commission's new village at Dalavich *(q.v.)*. Electricity reached Ford in 1963, and although the population remained virtually static, a village hall was built in 1968. Soon afterwards a new grocery shop was built, and although the primary school was closed in the early 1970s the population began to increase once more. By 1977 Gateway West Argyll Ltd had established a trout farm producing 100 tonnes a year and was even exporting to Canada (see *'Ford' by Stephenson, 1984)*. Ford's hotel and post office remained open in 1996.

## FORDYCE

**Map 10, B1**

***Small village near Portsoy,*** *pop. 250* — OS 29: NJ 5563

A Pictish fort on Durn Hill overlooks the open valley of the Burn of Fordyce. There was a church by 1272, 3 km inland from the Moray Firth and 4 km from Portsoy. A weekly market was chartered in 1490 to sell linens and produce, and Fordyce became a burgh of barony in 1499. A substantial L-plan tower house known as Fordyce Castle was built in 1592 by Thomas Menzies, an Aberdeen burgess. A parish school was held by 1624 and Fordyce seemed a place of some importance to Pont, but his sketch was blurred, and Gordon's map of about 1640 indicated little but the kirk, which was replaced in 1661. The Roy map of about 1750 showed a one-street village away from any roads. The local linen industry prospered in the late 18th century, but soon died.

**The Quiet Village embraces its Castle**: From 1884 to about 1960 the nearest railway station, Glassaugh, was a tiresome 2 km from the village, where a post office was open by 1900. By 1953 there was an inn, and Fordyce became noted for its secondary school, which survived the rationalisations up to at least 1976. Although the population in 1951 was over 400 there were few other facilities. Though the castle remained in residential use in the centre of the village, the resident population declined, and the inn was closed; by 1981 only about 265 residents remained. The school is still open as a primary, but a joiners' workshop is almost the only other activity in this quiet and sheltered spot, the epitome of a medieval Scottish Castle Town.

## FORFAR

**Map 6, C2**

***Angus town,*** *pop. 13,500* — OS 54: NO 4550

Hill forts dominate the tiny parish of Rescobie in Strathmore, the ancient Pictish province of Circenn, which was renamed Angus in the tenth century. Some 3 km west is Restenneth Priory, *"founded by Boniface, at the beginning of the seventh century, on an island in the centre of a lake" (Chambers)*. The early church of Restenneth had an extensive parish; its tower includes Pictish stonework, probably of the eighth century and perhaps built by masons from Jarrow. Restenneth Priory was rebuilt in the 11th and 12th centuries; it later became a cell of Jedburgh Abbey. Over 2 km to the west is Forfar, on an irregular site near Forfar Loch, which was then a longer sheet of water. The name Forfar apparently derives from the Gaelic for *'Terraced Slope'*, perhaps referring to an earthen defence work. Aberlemno some 8 km north-east of Forfar had a thanage from about the 11th century.

**Malcolm Canmore, Sheriff Caput and Royal Burgh**: Forfar was possibly chartered in 1057 by Malcolm III, as witness Chambers who wrote in the 1820s that Forfar Castle was *"a royal residence in the time of Malcolm Canmore"*, where the king *"held the parliament at which titles and surnames were first conferred upon the Scottish nobility. His illustrious queen had a nunnery, upon a small artificial island"* in Forfar Loch. In the time of William the Lion, Forfar Castle was already described as being old and redundant, the site being subdivided into private plots. Forfar was made sheriff caput of Angus between 1162 and 1174; the county was often called *Forfarshire*. The Royal Burgh of Forfar was chartered (or re-chartered) in 1184; Restenneth being so near, Forfar had a chapel rather than a church. Parliaments were held intermittently in the late 12th and early 13th centuries. Forfar had much potential as a market, due to its central position in one of Scotland's largest fertile plains; a market cross had been set up by 1230. In 1295 Forfar was described as *"a good town"* which still had a royal castle, apparently on a new site. The castle was taken by Bruce's followers about 1308; Barbour wrote that Bruce *"had the wall broken down and the castle and all its towers well destroyed"*.

**Oblivion and Slow Recovery**: The area was again recaptured by Bruce from English invaders about 1313, but in the 14th century Restenneth rather than Forfar was chosen for the occasional signing of royal charters. Forfar settled an argument about trade with Montrose in 1372, sharing the rights, and a parliament met there for the last time in the late 14th century. Then for a century significant references to Forfar seem to vanish. Even though in 1535–56 Forfar's tax contribution was rising, it paid under 1.5% of the total of Scottish burgh taxes. However in 1560 it was sufficiently important to be represented in Parliament, and held a parish school by 1576. Pont, who mapped Angus about 1600, showed Forfar as a major settlement beside the loch, but did not detail nearby castles, mills or bridges. In 1618 Taylor referred to Forfar merely as a *"town"*; the 1639 returns placed it a modest 25th in rank among burgh tax yields.

**Early Golf – and Quiet Clogs?**: Chambers noted that Forfar was for centuries renowned for its ale-houses and clog manufacture: *"from time immemorial, the manufacture of 'brogues' engaged the principal part of the inhabitants"*. This was the case by 1648, when there was more than one inn, but all refused to accommodate the poet Drummond of Hawthornden, on religious grounds! Tradition asserts that golf was played by 1651 on the site of the later course. Clogs may have clattered on the cobbles, but in 1689 Morer wrote of Forfar as *"a place of no great noise, saving that it is a country town, a royal burgh, and anciently the seat of several parliaments, and had once the King's palace, though now we scarce see the ruins of it"*.

**Road Improvements and Loch Draining**: A post office was open by 1715. The road between Forfar and Dundee was improved in 1736, and in 1750 the Forfar to Glamis road was made up. Roy's map surveyed about that year indicated Forfar as a largish settlement; made roads extended to Brechin and also met the Dundee–Brechin road north of Letham. Apart from two mills and the vanished mansionhouse of Fothringham there was then – and is now – little of interest in the parish of Inverarity on the Dundee road. The track to Kirriemuir bridged the head of the loch, south of which a mill was marked – presumably the Lochmill – while farther west was the hamlet of Bindarg. Forfar Loch was drained about the 1760s *"for the sake of the marl"* (lime-rich deposits used as fertiliser), but then allowed to refill.

**Linen, Municipal Neglect and Forfar Bridies**: Only about 40 weavers worked in the town before osnaburg linen manufacture began about 1745–46, but by 1750 over 140 looms were at work. By 1792 around 450 weavers were busy; in 1799 Heron stated that the population was *"about 3400. Much of the flax grown locally is here manufactured into osnaburgs, and a variety of linen goods"*. The town council had fallen on evil days (*detailed by Adams*), and around 1800 the town was noted for decay and filth. More wholesome was the tradition of *'Forfar Bridies'*, short-crust pastry turnovers with chopped beef filling.

**Banking, Water, Weaving and Brewing**: Despite these problems Forfar was a post town by 1797, when there were to be six fairs. The Dundee Banking Company had a branch in the town between at least 1793 and 1810, but had closed it by the time that the Arbroath Banking Company opened a Forfar branch in 1825. By then the Dundee Union Banking Company had also lately opened a branch in Forfar. Water bottling from a spring in Forfar began in 1800. Although the town lacked a good head of water to power its mills, the springs may have fed the five small breweries at work in 1825. By 1812 yarn was carted from Dundee to be used in Forfar's extensive hand weaving industry; however, both a canal scheme mentioned by Heron, and the lighthouse-builder Robert Stevenson's 1819 proposal to connect Forfar by a horse-drawn railway with Perth, Brechin and Montrose came to nothing. By 1817 2.4 million metres of linen were stamped locally each year.

**Whence came Padanaram?**: In 1824 Bindarg was renamed *Padanaram*: whether biblical or oriental in origin, the laird's choice is certainly remarkable! Forfar had recovered when according to Chambers in 1827 it was *"a small inland burgh, subsisting chiefly by its political consequence; the town has been, within the last few years, ornamented by a handsome suite of County Buildings"*. By then a new road had been built to Brechin by way of Finavon (the old road lay by Aberlemno).

**Forfar on the Railways**: In 1836 an Act was obtained for a railway to Arbroath, enabling a Dundee connection, the line being of a broad 5'6" (168 cm) gauge when it opened to its Forfar terminus near the castle site in 1839. Such accessibility brought down the price of coal, enabling a gasworks to be started in 1841, and stimulated power-loom factory development based on local flax. However, the railways killed the local breweries. In 1849 the main line of the Scottish Central Railway from Perth and Stanley reached Forfar, and – with a sharp reverse curve through a new station – joined the local line, which was converted to standard gauge. The Scottish North Eastern Railway to Aberdeen, built at the same time, diverged from the Arbroath & Forfar at Guthrie, 10km farther east. Later these lines were combined under the Caledonian Railway (CR), which opened lines from Forfar to Broughty Ferry (in 1870) and to Brechin (in 1895).

**Cheap Coal stimulates the Linen Mills**: About 1844 some 3000 hand weavers were at work in and around Forfar, making sheetings, osnaburgs and dowlas, a number which grew to nearly 5000 before power-looms began to take over in the 1850s. By 1864 four weaving works containing 482 steam-powered looms employed 600 workers. The Lowson family's two mills was most important, while J & H Craik & Co was to prove a very durable concern. Laird & Co was the smallest, but in addition some 4500 hand loom weavers were still struggling to compete; few of their products were bleached. However, in 1864 Charles Norrie & Sons of Dundee owned a large public calender, yarn windery and bleachfield in Forfar, employing about 100 people. By 1867 there were six textile factories in the town, employing 1865 workers, still mainly weaving brown linens.

**Fothringham, Forfar Rock – and Slate Quarrying**: Some 7km to the south of Forfar was the emparked second mansion called Fothringham House, built in 1859 to designs by David Bryce, but it had been demolished by 1967. Meantime the profits from local confectioner Peter Reid's sugary *'Forfar Rock'* paid for the Reid Hall (begun in 1869) and, after his death, the Reid Park, opened in 1896. Even harder rock was won at the Balmashanar or Slatefield slate quarry south of the town, one of the oldest in Scotland. In the 1860s other local quarries included the Tolbooth and Carsegownie. The Tillywhandland and Myrestone quarries, 4km north-east of Forfar, worked heavy grey roofing slates, employing between them some 50 men.

**Nineteenth century service developments**: A public library was commenced in 1870. The mock baronial building of the Royal Bank of Scotland was erected in 1862, and the British Linen Bank about 1899. Forfar golf club was founded in 1871, Tom Morris laying out an 18-hole course. New County Buildings were erected in 1873; the old County Buildings and Sheriff Court were reopened in 1891 as the Municipal Buildings. The local newspaper, the *Forfar Dispatch*, was established in 1884, followed in 1885 by Forfar Athletic Football Club at Station Park. In that year the *Queen's Hotel* at the Cross was largely rebuilt. The Meffan Institute was built in 1896. Meantime in 1894 Murray's Handbook noted only two local hotels, the *County* and the *Union*, but wrote of Forfar *"bristling with chimneys, it is by no means an attractive town"*; by then eight or nine large mills made coarse linens.

**Forfar enters decline**: Gradually most of the mills appear to have moved from linen to jute manufacture, though some were closed. The population fell slightly, to 12,750 by 1891, but about 1900 there were still over 3000 workers in eight factories and two bleachworks. The 27 pubs were a large number even for a market town, but droving in the days before cattle floats would have been thirsty work! In 1899 a large locomotive depot was built to replace obsolete premises. The population continued to decline in the early 20th century, to only 10,650 in 1951, but the town became more diversified, with the Forfar Foundry, Lockwoods the canners and other farm-related industries such as making ladders – essential in the days of haystacks and corn ricks. Forfar Academy was open by 1958.

*A Forfar linen mill. The manufacture of 'Osnaburg' linens began in Forfar about 1745. Jute largely supplanted linen in the late 19th century. Textiles continue in the town today, including polypropylene.* (RCAHMS / JRH)

**The Decline and Fall of Strathmore Railways**: In 1946 Wordie & Co ran a small rail to road cartage depot. The secondary railways – to Broughty Ferry, and to Kingsmuir – closed by the mid 1960s; these services lost out to buses, lorries and farmers' cars. But due to Beeching, major change came when the erstwhile main line railway was closed to passengers in 1967 in favour of the Dundee route with its higher traffic potential, and cut down to a mere goods branch from Stanley. In 1978 potatoes were still shipped south by rail from Forfar, but even this traffic ceased when the line was closed in 1982.

**Tweeds and Polypropylene**: In 1975 Forfar lost its county headquarters to Dundee-based Tayside Region, but became the centre of Angus District Council, which converted a former flax mill as its HQ. The well-known Forfar firm of Ramsay Ladders was a large concern by 1978, with seven stock depots around the UK. So was Lockwoods, though they laid off 85 workers in 1978. Don Brothers, Buist & Co (DBB) had acquired the Strathmore (or Canmore) Woollen Mill in the 1940s; by 1979 it was producing high quality tweeds and tartans for women's clothing. At that time the local jute industry was flourishing, with DBB's three other mills (St James, Haugh and Strang Street), Boath's Academy Street works and Craik's Manor works, which was also in cotton. In 1978 a factory at Newfordpark formerly run by Thiokol Fibres of USA was converted by DBB to make extruded polypropylene tape. Reekie Engineering of Forfar had a branch at Laurencekirk.

**Bypass and Potatoes**: In 1980 Forfar remained an important local and agricultural centre; there were nine small hotels, including the *Queen's Hotel*. A major western bypass was built in 1986–87. By 1991 the town had regained its 1891 population level at 12,961, but had a rather elderly emphasis. In 1991 Hillsdown Holdings protected their Forfar cannery at a time of problems in the raspberry industry by closing a plant at Brechin. The potato market was active in 1992, when Angus Marts dealt in cattle, sheep and pigs at Forfar; it was still very busy in 1994 under the Montrose Auction Company. By 1996 Agricar Ltd still dealt in farm machinery locally and at

Laurenckirk. *'Spud specialisation'* led by 1991 to the Forfar Foundry making potato cultivation systems, in 1993 exported to Romania and elsewhere.

**Bottled Water beats Perrier – and Pies Galore**: In 1983 Dunn's of Parkhead bought the spring-water source sold under the name of *Strathmore Spring*; in 1989 the capacity of the plant was quadrupled from 15 to 60 million 1-litre bottles a year, providing 40 jobs. In 1992 it outgrew its well and was sold to Matthew Clark Gaymer, who opened a new source in 1993; a further 70 jobs were planned. In 1995 Strathmore Spring water – which had doubled its sales in a year – finally ousted Perrier from top place in the British bottled water market. Meantime by 1994 Strathmore Foods of Forfar had a staff of 200, making 500,000 Scotch pies a week!

**Back to Angus – and the Gaelic!**: By 1990 DBB had become Don & Low and was expanding; in 1996 they opened new HQ offices at Newfordpark, the firm then employing 656 people. The windy home of Forfar Athletic FC was still called Station Park – though the nearest station was 20km away! In the 1990s the club sampled the first, second and third divisions. Forfar regained importance when an extended Angus became an all-purpose local authority in 1996. By then there was a Tesco store. Sadly when the HL cannery, the last in Tayside, closed in 1999 some 80 hitherto permanent jobs were lost, and the related seasonal work ended. In 1997 Forfar Academy had a roll of 1152. It was a remarkable event when in 1999 a class at Kirkriggs primary school began to be taught entirely in Gaelic – a language which had vanished from all but the high glens of Angus at least 500 years earlier! Forfar's *Royal Hotel* offers accommodation; there is still a weekly cattle mart, and the Neffan Institute tells the local story and stages other exhibitions; also in the vicinity is the Scottish training centre of guide dogs for the blind.

## FORGANDENNY

**Map 6, A3**

***Perthshire village**, pop. 250*

OS 58: NO 0918

Forgandenny lies on the south side of Strathearn 6km south-west of Perth, though by road it is over 10km away. A cluster of hill forts in the vicinity, plus the *For-* element in the names of this place and nearby Forteviot, may connect the area with the Pictish province of Fothrif, which originally seems to have extended as far north as Dunkeld, but re-emerged in medieval Scotland as a deanery south of the Ochil Hills. A barony charter was granted in 1630 under the name of *Forgound*. By the mid 18th century *'Forgan'* – as the Roy map named it – consisted of a single short street on the track between Bridge of Earn and Dunning, with the mansion of Freeland House to the east. Two fairs were scheduled for 1797.

**Railway and Hilltop Distillery**: The River Earn had to be diverted just north-east of Forgandenny when the Scottish Central Railway was being built, the excavated rock going into two bridges. A station was provided when the line opened in 1848, and a post and telegraph office was open by 1895. The remote and nowadays almost forgotten *Stronachie* distillery was located 10km south of Forgandenny at a height of 275m, beside a headwater of the Water of May near the Kinross boundary, where a bleak minor road crosses the Ochil Hills. It was built about 1900 by Alexander & Macdonald; after many ownership changes, from about 1918 it had its own narrow-gauge railway system, perhaps to carry peats. The industry's troubles closed the distillery in 1928, and the buildings fell into ruin. By 1978 the accompanying hamlet was depopulated.

**Agriculture and tele-cottaging**: The mansion of Freeland House, which was rebuilt in the 19th century and had *"fine limes"* in the 1890s, was taken over in 1920 by *Strathallan School*, a growing independent boys' boarding school from Bridge of Allan. The station was closed about 1960, but by 1967 another Victorian mansion 2 km south-west of the village had become the *Ardargie House Hotel*. By 1978 there was a village hall, Pearson was a significant firm of agricultural engineers, and the new Ardargie sawmill was at work near the hotel. In 1980 Strathallan School (with 68 staff) at last admitted girls amongst its 500 boarders. Forgandenny remained in other respects little more than a hamlet, of under 300 people in 1981; by 1988 a gravel pit was open to the north. The sawmill closed in 1998, to be replaced from 2000 by 21 detached houses including offices for home workers, plus a public internet *'tele-cottage'*, claimed as Scotland's first scheme of this kind.

## FORRES

**Map 9, C3**

***Moray town**, pop. 8500*

OS 27: NJ 0358

Forres lies at the foot of a hill astride a small tributary of the River Findhorn, 3km from where it now enters the Moray Firth through the land-locked Findhorn Bay. It may well be *Varis*, the ancient centre of the Vacomagi, as indicated by Ptolemy in 140 AD. Varis probably stood on tidewater, accessible to small vessels, but its early history was obscured by repeated Viking raids and desertion. The tall and intricately carved ancient monolith called *Sueno's Stone* (now protected by a clear plastic shelter) commemorates a battle; Jackson (1984) concluded that it was Kenneth MacAlpin's victory statement to the north Picts, but maybe it tells of the destruction of Burghhead about 900; either way, its proximity to Forres confirms a place of much early importance. Dyke about 4km to the west had a thanage from about the 11th century.

**Royal Burgh and Surrounding Castles**: Forres was apparently one of the first centres in the North to become a Scottish Royal Burgh under David I, in 1130 (or 1150, depending on source); to the south were his royal hunting preserves, including the Forests of Darnaway and Drumine. Forres became the caput of a sheriffdom in 1226 and acquired a 13th century castle, still royal property about 1300. The lands of Brodie in Dyke parish about 6km to the west were owned by the Brodie family from the 12th century; 3km south-east was the ancient church of Rafford. The town was burnt by the notorious *'Wolf of Badenoch'* in 1390 and had to be rebuilt. About 6km to the south-west stands the 14th century Darnaway Castle, including Earl Randolph's Hall, whose extremely fine timber roof was built of trees now known to have been felled in 1387. It too was a royal castle in 1455.

**Late Medieval Forres**: The town and castle of Forres passed to the powerful Earls of Moray when the sheriffdom was merged into Moray in the late 15th century; Darnaway became their seat. The town was rechartered by James IV in 1496. By then its tax value was similar to Montrose and nearly a quarter of that of Aberdeen, with which burgh it conducted much trade through the port of Findhorn. Forres itself rarely if ever collected Customs dues, and in 1535–56 paid under 1.5% of the total of burgh taxes, though its contribution was rising.

**After the Reformation – the Reivers**: Brodie Castle's central tower was built about 1567–75, and by 1582 Forres had a parish school; it was the centre of a presbytery by 1593. Pont's map made about 1600 showed that the Mosset Burn had been bridged just west of the town, and there was a mill on the other side of the Findhorn at Moy. We may assume a long-established ferry, for by then this turbulent river had been bridged at Relugas near Randolph's Leap, 12 km upstream. Blervie Castle, a Z-plan tower 4 km south-east of Forres, was erected in the 17th century, as were the wings of Brodie Castle. In 1639 Forres ranked a pitiful 42nd among Scottish burghs in tax yield, with about 2% of Aberdeen's trade; it continued to suffer from repeated raids by Highland clansmen and by 1647 was *"a poor decayed town"*. The site of Forres castle at the west end of the town was re-used, the surviving ruin being a Civil War structure. By 1656 Forres was astride the through road (or track!) from Aberdeen to Inverness.

**Slow Recovery with Linen Yarn**: A post office was open by 1713, and by 1725 Forres had recovered as a market town. Roy's map made about 1750 showed a substantial linear town on the main Elgin to Inverness road, which passed the Kirk of Dyke. The Findhorn was still unbridged below Relugas, and so it remained for another half century. Alexander Carlyle observed in 1765 that it was *"a very formidable river not often to be forded"*. Another road up the east side of the Findhorn connected with the south. Meantime the classical mansion of Dalvey House had been built near an existing estate doocot 3 km west of the town. A linen bleachfield was built in Forres between 1746 and 1760, by which date yarn was being produced in lint mills from locally grown flax. By 1765 the British Linen Company had a local agent, but little linen was woven locally and in 1765 Carlyle found *"no manufactures"*.

**Rich Land, Poor People**: Forres was surrounded by rich farmlands in 1765, but Carlyle thought the peasants had a *"poor appearance"*, and even the horses were small. But the town was *"most happily situated, a single street of half a mile from east to west; the Erse language is spoken in the streets. Brodies Inn is spacious, the traveller is really well accommodated"*. There was little left of Forres castle by the 1770s, at which time Boswell also found an *"admirable"* inn; possibly *Brodies*, probably the *Crown*, which is known to have existed in 1771.

**Bridging the Dangerous River Findhorn**: In the 1780s the yarn output was switched from Glasgow merchants to those of Aberdeen and Inverness. Forres was spinning and weaving flax on a substantial scale by 1792 and was a post town by 1797, when five fairs were held. In 1782 an accident at the Findhorn ferry drowned 13 unfortunate people; local demands were eventually satisfied when the Findhorn was bridged, about 1800–1805. Meantime the timber bridge at Relugas had been replaced in 1794 by the Daltulich bridge. In 1799 Heron noted over 2000 inhabitants in Forres, *"a neat small town"*. The Aberdeen Banking Company had a branch there between at least 1793 and 1810. Darnaway Castle was rebuilt as a mansion in 1802 for the 9th Earl of Moray, but the original great hall happily survived. In 1806 the prominent Nelson Tower was built.

**Famous Sons and Growing Commerce**: Joseph Mitchell, the son of a mason, was born in Forres in 1804; he was trained by Telford, became the Chief Inspector of Highland Roads and Bridges at the age of 21, and later laid out much of the Highland Railway. Donald Alexander Smith, born in

*Dallas Dhu distillery, built in 1899. It closed in 1983 but was acquired by Historic Scotland as a museum of distilling.* (JRH)

Forres in 1820, earned the title of Lord Strathcona through his activities in unifying Canada and pioneering the Canadian Pacific Railway. Brodie Castle was extended in mansion style in 1820–24 to Jacobean designs by William Burn. A brewery was in operation by 1825 and the *Commercial Hotel*, built in the 1820s, became a stagecoach inn. The catastrophic flood of 1829 swept away the bridge, though this was soon replaced. The local newspaper, the *Forres Gazette*, and a gasworks were both founded in 1837 and an elaborate market cross was erected in 1844.

**Forty Years of Railway Importance**: The Inverness & Aberdeen Junction Railway (I&A) reached Forres from Nairn in 1857, and was extended to Elgin and Keith in 1858. By 1860 Wordie & Co owned a rail to road cartage depot. In 1863 Forres became a triangular junction when the hilly main line of the Inverness & Perth Junction Railway (originally intended to meet the I&A at Nairn) was opened from Perth, crossing the dreaded snowy Dava Moor at 320 m altitude and winding downhill through the huge and empty Edinkillie parish. Hence their successor the Highland Railway took over a very unusual layout, of which only a remnant survives. The Falconer Museum was founded in 1871, and the large *Cluny Hydro* was open by 1886. Forres golf club, founded in 1889, laid out an 18-hole parkland course. In 1894 the *Commercial, Royal Station* and *Victoria* hotels were also open in what Murray called the *"clean little town"*.

**Rail Relegation, Whisky Problems and Villas**: In 1898 the direct rail route from Aviemore to Inverness was opened, and the importance of Forres as a junction was greatly reduced. The *Royal Station Hotel* became simply the *Royal*, but Forres engine shed remained as an outpost of Inverness until steam ended in the 1960s. The Benromach malt whisky distillery originated in 1898, and Dallas Dhu distillery was built in 1898–99 2 km to the south; but the great whisky boom very soon ended, and though both survived, Dallas Dhu whisky was usually only used in blending. In 1907 a villa was built which by 1954 was the *Ramnee Hotel*, and about 1914 another, now the *Knockomie*.

**Forres Comes Adrift**: Many local people were evacuated in 1943–44 so that rehearsals of the Normandy landings could take place on the coast of Culbin Forest north-west of the town. The people soon returned, and in the late 1940s six lorry loads of whisky a week were carried from Forres to Fort William, probably for direct shipment to earn foreign currency. By the 1950s Forres had nearly 5000 people, its typical market town facilities including a small hospital, seven small hotels and Forres Academy, a senior secondary school supplemented by junior secondary classes at Dyke near Brodie. But Elgin was usurping its trade, and the direct rail link to the south was severed by Beeching in 1965. The 1970s saw rapid population growth – the reasons said to be an influx of American drifters, following oil developments, the Findhorn *(q.v.)* Community, and nearby air bases.

**Preserving Castle, Daffodils and Distillery**: In 1978 Brodie Castle was bought for preservation by the National Trust for Scotland, but it remained occupied by the Brodies as for eight centuries past; thanks to their efforts it is now the home of the national daffodil collection. By 1981 there was a *'college'* – the Moray Steiner School – at Drumduan, and fifteen hotels. In the 1980s the *Forres Gazette* was renamed the *Forres & Nairn Gazette*. But the town's economic base was shaky: both distilleries closed in 1983, Dallas Dhu permanently. Jobless people in the Forres area in 1988 exceeded 20% of the workforce, the worst rural unemployment in the then Grampian Region. In keeping with the generally burgeoning tourist trade, in 1987 the disused Dallas Dhu distillery was taken into state care for conversion to a museum; this was open by 1995 when Historic Scotland called it *"a completely preserved time capsule of the distiller's craft"*. As late as 1991 some of its pale malt whisky matured in plain oak was still available. By contrast, in 1995 the town's Falconer Museum was of particular interest to geologists and musicians.

**Food, Drink and Passenger Trains**: A small food park had been provided by 1991 in an effort to attract new industry: Moray Coast Growers, a farmers' co-operative, had opened, shortly to be followed by Moray Fine Foods, making seafood patés for export to Europe. Although White's removal depot remained and a modern store had been built by William Low in the late 1980s, the once important station was reduced to a single platform, and by 1990 all its freight facilities had gone. Some 8500 people still lived in Forres in 1991, and male unemployment in the town itself had greatly fallen. By 1994 there was a branch office of Moray Badenoch & Strathspey Enterprise. J & W Hardie's Benromach distillery had made a single malt with a high reputation, still to be found in 1991; bought in 1993 by Gordon & McPhail of Elgin and slowly re-equipped, it eventually reopened in 2000.

**Telecom Enterprise**: In 1993 Hoskyns built a Business Service Centre at Forres, offering technical and administrative services to firms anywhere in the UK by exploiting telecommunications; it was hoped to employ 200 people. By 2000 as *Cap Gemini* it had branches in Dingwall, Nairn and Inverness and was to provide 700 more jobs in a new customer call-centre on the hitherto untenanted Forres Business Park. In 1996 Sellars still dealt in combine harvesters and farm machinery locally (and in four other towns and villages), and Tesco owned the former William Low store. The reconstruction of the railway station is being considered. AES Ltd make solar heating systems; Logie's make guns. Small hotels include the *Knockomie*, the *Ramnee* and the *Park*.

## FORSINARD

**Map 13, A5**

***Caithness settlement,*** *pop. under 100* OS 10: NC 8942

When Roy surveyed the northern Highlands about 1750, a trackway from Helmsdale led north-west up the Strath of Kildonan and then north over the moorland watershed at 170 m above sea level to end at the tiny clachan of Forsinard at the head of Strath Halladale. When the Sutherland Railway was built in 1871–74 it followed almost the same route as far as a crossing station named Forsinard (known jokingly as *'Frozenhard'*). By then a narrow made-up road continued to Melvich, while the railway climbed east up a shallow side valley to cross the bleak, treeless and often snowy *'Northern County March'* at an altitude of over 215 m, before meandering across the boggy moors and down to Georgemas Junction. By the 1890s an inn at Forsinard served mainly anglers; nearby was a school, open in the 1920s but closed by 1958 in favour of Kinbrace. The inn had been enlarged into a substantial hotel by 1995, and a visitor centre catered for naturalists visiting the unique local environment. The railway snow fences had become ruinous due to 75 years of neglect, but because the crossing loop was essential for rail operation – the only place where trains might cross in a distance of over 73 km – the station and signal box had survived the Beeching cuts. Some afforestation has altered the landscape; Forsinard is still a request stop for the few passenger trains, petrol is available at the hotel, and there is also a shop and post office.

## FORSS

**Map 13, A4**

***Caithness small village,*** *pop. 100* OS 12: ND 0368

Ancient brochs stand on the Old Red Sandstone plateau near the storm-swept north coast of Caithness. Forss is Norse for *'Waterfall'*; the Forss Water enters the sea some 8 km west of Thurso, near the ancient chapel of Crosskirk. Brims Castle, a small coastal tower house, was built about 1600 for the Sinclairs of Dunbeath; by 1993 it was a ruin. The Roy map of around 1750 showed no road west of Thurso in this well-settled area, though a Milltown was named upstream from *'Portcrosh'* (Crosskirk). Later the main road between Thurso and Tongue crossed the Bridge of Forss. The large water-powered Forss Mill was built early in the 19th century, replacing the earlier Milltown. By the 1950s Forss had 150 people, a primary school, post office and telephone exchange, but the school had closed by 1976. By 1987 there was also a US Navy satellite communications base, and by 1993 Forss House was a small fishing hotel; but by then Forss post office had closed, and Forss Mill stood vacant and neglected in 1994. However, in 2000 it was converted to houses by the Highland Building Preservation Trust.

## FORT AUGUSTUS

**Map 9, A5**

***Inverness-shire village, L. Ness,*** *pop. 500* OS 34: NH 3809

A crannog lies offshore at the south end of Loch Ness. The church and township of Kilcummin stood in the centre of the Great Glen at Abertarff – the mouth of Glen Tarff – just south of where the River Oich enters the loch. The names Kilcummin, Borlum, Pitmean and Lundy also appeared on Blaeu's map, prepared between 1642 and 1654 from Gordon's material. Following the Jacobite rebellion of 1715 the *'Kilwhimin'* Barracks were built from 1717, and identified by

*Fort Augustus locks (pictured in the 1970s), at the south-west end of Loch Ness. The flight of 5 locks was built under Telford's guidance in 1818–21 as part of the Caledonian Canal.* *(RCAHMS / JRH)*

Roy about 1750 as the *'Old Barrack'*. In 1731–34 General Wade's troops built the steep military road from the south via the high Corrieyairack Pass, crossing the intriguingly named Smugburrow Bridge in Glen Tarff. Other military roads were built along or parallel to the Glen. A larger fort or defended barracks for 300 men named Fort Augustus was built in 1729–42, as the kingpin of the strategy for suppressing the Highlanders. This fort was badly damaged in 1746 when the Jacobite army scored a direct hit on the powder magazine, hence further rebuilding was necessary: Heron called the outcome a *"small fortress"*.

**Civilian Development**: The Bernera road (to Glenelg), built by Caulfeild's men, was nearing completion when Roy mapped the Highlands around 1750. A new village was established at Fort Augustus in 1754, and from 1756 a civilian post office handled mail on a Great Glen postal route. Pennant noted that Fort Augustus had become a crossroads by 1769, Caulfeild's troops having bridged the River Oich to complete the Bernera road; Heron later commended their *"handsome bridge of three arches"*. In 1773 Boswell found the military road from Inverness open, but the inn at Fort Augustus was *"wretched"*. The area lacks good farming potential, and no burgh charter was obtained for Fort Augustus, but by then the Highlands had been pacified. Two fairs were scheduled for 1797.

**The Caledonian Canal**: In 1783 the second John Knox suggested digging a ship canal through the Great Glen to avoid the need for sailing vessels to fight their way through the stormy Pentland Firth. Planned by Telford for the government, work was begun on the Caledonian Canal in 1803, and from 1820 a steamboat service was possible between Fort Augustus and Inverness, provided by Henry Bell's *Stirling Castle (see Helensburgh)*. To proceed westwards required boats to rise 12 metres; to achieve this, five locks were built with great difficulty in 1818–21. The canal was opened at a shallow depth in 1822, enabling the *Stirling Castle* to ply through to Glasgow by 1824. The canal also stimulated the building of a distillery, though this worked only from 1826 to 1858. The canal management established workshops at Fort Augustus, whose structure was seen by Chambers about 1827 as *"resembling a gentleman's seat rather than a fortress, and garrisoned by three veteran artillerymen. There is a small village attached, with an inn"*.

**Canal Upstaged by Steamer Heyday**: But by the 1820s steamships were growing larger, and venturing into the open sea; the canal was therefore reconstructed and deepened from 1839. When fully reopened in 1847 it again became a mail route between Inverness and Fort William, though the through service was not resumed, and the small Hutcheson steamers plied only as far as Banavie. This service was operated in 1858 by the *Mountaineer*, and from 1866 to 1939 by a single vessel, the 173-ton Glasgow-built PS *Gondolier*, whose long career ended ignominiously as a sunken blockship *(see Burray)*. As ships became larger, few vessels other than fishing boats and pleasure craft could use the canal.

**Monkish Electricity**: The fort was still thinly garrisoned in 1858, but was made redundant in 1867, and in 1876–93 a large Benedictine abbey and boarding school incorporating parts of the old building was created by Thomas and Simon, successive Lords Lovat. Remarkably in 1890 they and the monks installed the hydro-electric generator which provided Scotland's first public electricity supply (a long nine years after the first in England, at Godalming). Little other development resulted, but by 1894 walking sticks were made locally, and the two hotels at what Murray called the *"clean and attractive village"* of Fort Augustus included the *"good" Lovat Arms*, which had been built on the site of the original barracks.

**The Beery Railway**: The *Lovat Arms* was owned by the Invergarry and Fort Augustus Railway, at least between 1903 and 1906. This line was financed from beer money by Lord Burton, the ludicrously overoptimistic English laird of the area west of Fort Augustus, and opened in 1903. It failed to make the longed-for connection to Inverness, and after a brief but highly chequered history *(delightfully described by John Thomas)* was effectively closed in 1933 as a result of the development of bus services. Meantime the Glasgow to Inverness steamers were withdrawn in 1927, and the Fort Augustus/Inverness steamer service ceased in 1929. However, a golf club founded in 1930 laid out a 9-hole course. The main road to Inverness via Drumnadrochit was reconstructed in 1932, and a new Oich bridge was built in 1934.

**Forestry and Tourism**: From about 1950 onwards the Forestry Commission built a workers' village at Inchnacardoch near Fort Augustus, which in 1951 had a local population of over 750, and the facilities of a typical village, plus a small local authority secondary school. For a time around 1970 the boarding school run by the Benedictine monks was apparently closed, but reappeared by 1979 – as the Abbey School. Four hotels were still open in 1981, when caravan and camping sites were available, and the former canal workshops had become an exhibition centre. Fort Augustus remained a village and angling resort whose population gradually declined to 522 by 1991. However, it still provided basic services for a scattered population of some 3000. The abbey closed in 1998. The golf course now has 18 tees. Local hotels include the *Inchnacardoch*, the *Lovat Arms* and the *Caledonian*.

## FORTEVIOT, Aberdalgie, Dupplin & Invermay

**Map 6, A3**

***Perthshire hamlets,*** *pop. 320* OS 58: NO 0517

A hill fort sited above the Water of May in Strathearn is believed to have been a Pictish provincial capital in the eighth century; the famous Dupplin cross from the rural parish of Aberdalgie north of the River Earn is now in the new Museum of Scotland. Forteviot or Invermay, near the confluence of the May with the Earn, had a thanage from about the 11th century. There was also an early medieval mill, the miller's daughter remarkably becoming Queen of Scots and the mother of Malcolm Canmore. Dupplin Castle was first built in the 13th century, and by 1560 the castle of Invermay was new (or lately rebuilt) for Lord Stewart of Innermeath. If Forteviot existed in the late 16th century then Pont failed to show it.

**The Heyday of Dupplin**: In the 1720s Dupplin Castle, lately enlarged, was the seat of the Earl of Kinnoull, and labelled *'Duplin House'* on Roy's map of about 1750, which also showed the Kirk of Invermay. The Water of May was already bridged below Invermay castle, on a track from Auchterarder to Bridge of Earn; a *'boat house'* indicated a ferry to Dupplin. By the 19th century the name Milltown had also appeared. In 1828–32 the enlarged Dupplin Castle was replaced by a large mansion of the same name, built for the 10th Earl of Kinnoul to designs by William Burn. From 1848 a station on the main line of the Scottish Central Railway (later the Caledonian) was named Forteviot, and in the late 19th century the church was accompanied by an inn, post office and smithy.

**Bad Luck dogs the New Village**: In 1923–26 the little village was rebuilt on garden suburb lines by the then Baron Forteviot, and provided with a village hall, school (c.1926), pub and bowling green. Dupplin Castle was damaged by fire in the early 1930s; only part was restored. At that time Aberdalgie had a post office (closed in the 1950s) and a small hotel. The station was closed about 1960, and the cut-down Dupplin Castle was demolished in 1967 and again replaced by a new and smaller structure. Forteviot had once more become no more than a (pub-less) hamlet, in a parish of 321 people in 1991. The railway bridge across the Water of May was severely damaged by floods in 1993, blocking the main line for at least three months; through services between Glasgow and the North had to be diverted via Kirkcaldy.

## FORTH, Wilsontown & Braehead

**Map 16, B5**

***Lanarkshire village,*** *pop. 2500 / 3500* OS 72: NS 9453

Forth – whose name may derive from the Gaelic *Forthan*, a stud of horses – stands at a height of nearly 300 metres on rolling moors 12 km north-east of Lanark; the area's natural drainage is to the Clyde by way of the Mouse Water. Pont's map of 1596 showed Easter and Wester Forth; Wilsontown was named by its owners between then and 1712. The Roy map of about 1754 showed the Cleugh Mill in the valley east of Forth, and to the north *'Locklimny Coalheugh'*; but the only road was an isolated stretch to the east. Wilsontown's coke-based ironworks, the second such in Scotland, were established in 1779. A second coal mine was opened there about the same time; in 1799 Heron called it the Cleugh, *"the most considerable work of this kind in Lanarkshire. A village is here built, for the workmen"*. It had a post office from 1805, but there was none in Forth as late as 1838. Wilsontown Ironworks was ruined by the depression of 1842, before it could be connected to Fauldhouse, and so to Wishaw, by the new line of the Wilsontown, Morningside & Coltness Railway. This involved fearsome gradients over the hills and was soon abandoned, in favour of a branch from the new Caledonian line at Auchengray, to a station beside the main road at Wilsontown, served by trains to and from Carstairs.

**Coal Mining and the growth of Forth**: By 1895 the former ironworks had largely disappeared, though a cluster of what appear to have been bell pits was to be seen just to the north, and four larger rail-connected collieries had been sunk: nearby at Heathland, plus one at Climpy 2 km north-west of Forth. In 1891 the population of Wilsontown was 651. With a 1901 population of only 680, Forth itself was a one-street village with an inn and post office; later Climpy and Wilsontown shrank to mere hamlets. A large new rail-connected pit was sunk at Kingshill, 4 km north-west of Forth, whose population reached 2100 in 1931; many council houses were built in two schemes, west and north-east of the village. By 1947 the LMS-owned Wordie & Co operated a road haulage depot 3 km south of Forth at the hamlet of Braehead, whose population of 300 supported an inn, post office and primary school. Three large collieries (Heathland, Climpy and Kingshill), were still open in 1951 when Forth village had 3217 people; but Wilsontown passenger station was closed by 1953.

**The End of Mining saps the Purpose of Forth**: The last mine, Kingshill, must have closed by 1964 when the branch railway was closed for freight; by 1971 it had been lifted. Surprisingly the population fell by only some 200 to 1971. The last remnants of the ironworks were demolished in 1974, and Forth secondary school had been closed by 1977. In 1980 coal was being worked in the vicinity by opencast. Bleak and lacking in continuing purpose it appeared, but Forth remained a large village, with average village facilities; Braehead had inched up to 360 people. Extensive afforestation north of Forth since 1945 has softened the area's character, but in 1988–89 the old Wilsontown coal bing caught fire, causing major air pollution problems for a time. Little urban development had occurred by 1991, when only 2560 people lived in Forth; male unemployment was high, at 18%. Little change is now evident except for further afforestation to the south and west.

## FORTINGALL & Fearnan

**Map 5, C2**

***Perthshire hamlets,*** *pop. under 100* OS 52: NN 7447

Dun Geal (*White Fort*) stands on a hill crest overlooking Glen Lyon, which also has standing stones and was an alleged birthplace of Pontius Pilate! Fortingall has an ancient church with a famed yew, one of Britain's oldest trees; it had a thanage from about the 11th century, and the thanage of Crannach was possibly also in Glenlyon. The 14th century Garth Castle was built at Drumcharaig (Drumcharry), 1 km east of Dun Geal, and sketched by Pont about 1600 as a solitary tower house; but although Balnald of Fortingall had been created a burgh of barony in 1511, Pont showed no such settlement. In the early 18th century Drumcharaig had a famous piping school of the MacGregors. Roy's map of about 1750 showed a substantial hamlet at *'Glenlyon's House'* a little to the west of the *'New Kirk of Fortnagaul'*, where the famous and very aged yew tree was already huge. A track ran through wooded Glen Lyon *(q.v.)*

*These thatched cottages at Fortingall date only from the late 19th century, being designed for the laird Sir Donald Currie, founder of the Union Castle shipping line.* (JRH)

and across desolate Rannoch Muir to Lochaber – a challenging through route subsequently abandoned.

**Heyday and Decline**: An annual fair was scheduled for Fortingall in 1797. In the late 19[th] century J M MacLaren designed estate cottages, many of them thatched, for the laird Sir Donald Currie, founder of the Union Castle shipping line. Murray found the *Fortingall Hotel "good"* in 1894, when it stood in *"a neat little hamlet"*. In 1951 the population was under a hundred. By about 1972 a riding centre had been established at Fearnan, a hamlet on Loch Tay 3km south of Fortingall. Meantime by 1954 an early youth hostel had been opened at Garth, though by 1985 it had closed. The only shop in picturesque Fortingall had also closed by 1987, and little activity remained; in the words of a local *"the heart went out of the village"* (much of which is now holiday homes); but the small *Fortingall Hotel* survives.

## FORT WILLIAM & Inverlochy — Map 5, A1

***Lochaber town, L. Linnhe,** pop. 10,400* — OS 41: NN 1074

Also see: *Corpach*

At the west end of the Great Glen and at the foot of Scotland's highest mountain, the 1343m Ben Nevis, is Inverlochy *(Mouth of the Lochy)*. This stands at a critical focus of sea lochs in the enormous parish of Kilmallie, and was the site of an eighth century fort, re-used when Inverlochy Castle was built 500 years later. To the west on the shore of Loch Linnhe grew the coastal clachan of *'Achaintour'*, as it was labelled on Pont's map of around 1600. This place was still in the sheriffdom of Ross when chartered in 1618 as the barony burgh of Gordonsburgh. When forces of the Commonwealth set out to conquer the turbulent Highlanders with their cattle-thieving reputation, General Monck founded the earthen Inverlochy fort, built on the shore of Loch Linnhe south of the castle in 1654–55. It was one of the five citadels, including others at Perth and Inverness, built from 1654 to dominate Scotland; but little survived the Restoration.

**Rebuilding, Renaming and Military Roads**: After the unseating of James VII & II in 1688, the citadel was reconstructed in 1690 as a wooden palisade on a triangular plan, by troops under General Mackay. Christened *'Fort William'*, it was garrisoned with 1200 men, while the settlement beside it was relabelled *Maryburgh*. Around 1730 General Wade's men built a military road over the new Nevis and Spean bridges to Fort Augustus. Fort William was badly damaged by the Highlanders in the '45. By the time of Roy's survey of about 1750, Caulfeild had lately built another road to the south via the long-established clachan of Blarmachfoldach and over the high *Devil's Staircase* to Kinlochleven. No other roads served the small village at Fort William, insignificant beside the repaired fort.

**Primary Products and Civilian Development**: From 1764 Fort William had a post office, its mail travelling via Inverness, and at some time the sheriffdom of Inverness took over. At that time the local economy relied mainly on cattle and salmon, while the raising of rents was already leading to emigration in Pennant's day. In 1769 he called Fort William *"a small town"*; but the peasant houses were merely wattle and sod huts. About 1785 a much better road south was constructed via the Ballachulish ferry and Glencoe. In 1797 fairs were held twice a year at *"Gordonsburgh near Fort William"*, but Heron in 1799 still referred to *"the village of Maryburgh"*; eventually the fort name prevailed. Around 1800 Fort William was the base for George Dunoon, an unscrupulous shipper of emigrants.

**Canal, Road to the Isles, Steamers and Stagnation**: Some urban development, including a brewery, followed the construction from 1803 of the Caledonian Canal, built eastwards from nearby Banavie *(see also Fort Augustus)*. In the first quarter of the 19[th] century a road was built by the Commissioners for Highland Roads and Bridges, westwards over the Lochy bridge to Arisaig. This, the *'Road to the Isles'*, must have stimulated the tiny local textile trade, for a waulk mill was erected at Fort William in 1808. The long-lasting hardware retailing firm of Marshall & Pearson was established there about 1815. In 1819 the famous steamship *Comet* pioneered a weekly service from Glasgow via Oban to Fort William, which according to Chambers – who visited Lochaber in 1826 – was *"a larger fortification than Fort Augustus"*. It was still manned, though *"in consequence of the diminution of the garrison, the town of Fort William has gone greatly into decay; a miserable place destitute of a market; and, except by means of an insignificant herring-fishery and of the strangers who come to climb Ben Nevis, seems to have no channels whatever for the admission of wealth"*. From about 1820 Ben Nevis was owned by the Fairfax-Lucy family, but public access was not needlessly restricted.

**Long John and his Whisky**: In 1825 *'Long John'* Macdonald, born at Torgulbin near Spean Bridge about 1796, founded the Ben Nevis distillery at Lochy Bridge, making *'Dew of Ben Nevis'* whisky. A Bank of Scotland branch was opened in 1825–26. From 1843 a coach service was provided via Glencoe and over the moors to Glasgow, and by 1847 a June market had been reinstated. By 1851 Hutcheson steamers served Fort William, which had a sheriff-substitute by 1854. Fontane commented in 1858 on the *"tall quayside"* at which the steamer berthed, for the Macdonalds had also built a steamer pier at Fort William for use by their own ships, and erected maltings nearby. The garrison left in 1864.

**New Mansion, Old Attitudes & Distillery Duplication**: Lord Abinger, absentee laird of the vast Inverlochy estate, had the new castellated mansion of Inverlochy Castle built in 1863 about 2 km north-east of the old, enabling it to enjoy dramatic views of the mountains. But he did nothing to improve the rest of the estate; restrictions on development by Sir Duncan Cameron of Fassifern, aged laird of the adjoining estate, also held the town back. In 1878 Macdonald junior built the completely new Nevis (or Glen Nevis) distillery closer to the town, water-powered by a turbine and complete with maltings, joiners, wheelwrights, engineering shops and smithy. The old Ben Nevis distillery was itself greatly extended in 1878. Its 1884–85 output was nearly 700,000 litres, and thirty men were employed, though this included some who minded the 200 cattle that were fed on the draff. By 1886 Macdonald's 200 employees were housed in a *"whole street of workmen's cottages"*, and the annual output of Highland malt whisky from the new distillery was nearly 1.2 million litres. By 1886 – when Fort William was variously described by Barnard as a *"village"* or *"little town"* – the *West End Hotel* was open, and also a *"clean little inn"*.

**Rivalry with the West Highland Railway**: Fort William – which had only 1870 people in 1891 – was the objective of railway developers long before the West Highland Railway (WHR) was completed through to the town in 1894 *(see Thomas, 1965)*. The terminal station adjoined the steamer pier, making a focal point for much of the West Highlands. By that year there was an observatory atop Ben Nevis (it closed in 1904), the Belford hospital, and four hotels (the *Alexandra, Caledonian, Imperial, West End)* of which Murray commended three; but the fort which would have become a tourist attraction had been largely demolished to make space for the railway yard! The Glenlochy distillery was built in 1898, but the Nevis distillery of 1878 was closed about 1908, becoming a bonded warehouse and workshops. The Mallaig Extension Railway was opened in 1901 through extremely beautiful but rugged and depopulated country, requiring government aid to build its many viaducts and tunnels, but making Fort William into an unusual terminal junction. Despite the line from Spean Bridge to Fort Augustus *(q.v.)* that was funded by beer money, absurd inter-company rivalry prevented a rail connection to Inverness.

**Lochaber Aluminium: Tunnelling the Ben**: A smelter was built from 1924 by North British Aluminium and Lochaber Power (later two British Aluminium Company (BAC) subsidiaries), for the reduction of alumina powder to the pure metal, using water power as was done at Kinlochleven. This required a private Act, and involved the manipulation of resources on a very large scale. The main contractors Balfour Beatty first erected a temporary hydro power station in the Monessie Gorge below Roy Bridge, giving drilling power for 300 men to blast a

*The aluminium works' power station, Fort William. Water from L. Treig powers turbines for making aluminium by the Heroult process. Built in 1924, it is still active today under Alcan.* *(JRH)*

4.6 m diameter high-level tunnel for 24 km under the northern flanks of the Nevis range. Through this the water of Lochs Treig and Laggan was led on a very low gradient of 1 in 1100. Initially the works turbines derived power from the water of various streams, combined in a surge chamber at the head of two (from 1937 five) pressure pipes each nearly 2 m in diameter.

**Construction by Railway, helped by Free Whisky?**: The tunnel was driven from 23 working faces, accessed from 1925 by the *'Upper Works Line'* (UWL), some 38 km of 90 cm gauge single track with about 10 passing loops. Requiring fearsome gradients of up to 4% (1 in 25) and many trestle bridges, this line connected the workers' hutments and new factory site with all the high level tunnel adits – passing close to an illicit still set up by the contractor's men! – to end at the intake valve shafts near the later Loch Treig dam site. It used local timber, war surplus rails and 13 steam locomotives; later a rail ambulance was added. Spoil from the tunnels of this vast project was tipped near each adit, adding to the morainic nature of the land surface.

**Starting Production**: A new 300 m pier built in the deep water of Loch Linnhe and eventually equipped with an Arrol electric crane was connected by a 2.5 km long 90 cm gauge steam railway to the smelter, where tiny battery electric locomotives shunted the raw materials trains. Coasters brought in bagged cryolite, and bagged alumina from Larne; they also carried away the aluminium ingots first produced in 1929, initially for rolling at Warrington *(see Howat: the industrial process is as described under Kinlochleven)*. Finally a permanent village for the workers was built at Inverlochy between factory and pier.

**Damming the Lochs and Doubling Output**: In stage 2, starting in 1930, a further 5 km of temporary 90 cm railway line linked the UWL with sidings laid on the WHR at Fersit, where from 1931 a temporary station served a 650-man campsite. It continued to the site of a new concrete dam intended to raise Loch Laggan to 250 m, where there was until 1934 a 60 m span lattice bridge leading to another camp for 350 men. The UWL was often used to bring down mountain rescue casualties. Loch Treig was also raised by 11 m to the same level by a rock dam. The lochs were connected by a new level tunnel; they soon rose, and full electricity output was reached. War preparations were accelerating, hence – in order to raise aluminium production – work was done in 1936–37 to double the size of the power house, and to build a carbon factory (whose raw material, American petroleum coke, also came by sea).

**War diverts the Spey to Fort William**: The Ministry of Aircraft Production ran the aluminium complex from 1939; the output of ingots was switched from shipping to the WHR. So as to increase the output and so build more bombers, Canadian army engineers held back the upper River Spey by a 17 m high dam built 3 km west of Laggan Bridge, and diverted its water through a new 3 km tunnel into the already raised Loch Laggan, so increasing the total catchment area by about 40%. Meantime Lord Abinger's estate and the mansion of Inverlochy Castle were used for commando training.

**All Hands to Clearance**: When floods in 1952 filled some intakes and parts of the tunnel with rubble, the 800 factory workers were used for 15 days to clear it by hand to enable production to restart. By 1953 (when the author first visited Fort William) its 4500 people and typical urban facilities were crammed into a narrow linear site, its focus the busy rail-bus-steamer interchange between British Railways (BR) and MacBraynes, with its enchanting view across the loch. The West Highland Museum had opened in 1949, but the local newspaper was just an edition of the *Highland News* of Inverness. In 1955 the Ben Nevis distillery began to make grain whisky as well as malt, but by 1983 it was out of use. Fort William steam locomotive depot was a remarkably illogical outpost of Perth from early BR days until its closure in 1962.

**Alumina on Rail**: A new shed was built at the carbon factory in 1958 for BAC (the *'North'* prefix was dropped in 1960). In 1965 with closure of the Ballachulish *(q.v.)* branch, all Lochaber rail alumina and aluminium traffic was concentrated at Fort William; at first the alumina came from Burntisland. In 1968 the pier railway was abandoned but the pier was retained; by 1980 it was again in use, by Underwater Trials Ltd. Service road accesses to tunnel intakes were completed in 1977 and the whole Lochaber Railway was closed (except for a short length at the timber impregnation plant, built in 1969, which treated the BA forest output of fencing materials). By 1971, when the population was 4214, a youth hostel had been opened in Glen Nevis. Lochaber High School was built in the 1970s. In 1963–69 the new Inverlochy Castle became a very luxurious hotel, and by 1977 the 60-room *Mercury Hotel* was open.

**Capital of Lochaber**: From 1975 Fort William was the headquarters of the Lochaber District Council, including related areas formerly in Argyll. A golf club was founded in 1974; its 18-hole course was open by 1976, by which time Glenlochy distillery had seen two long periods of closure. The railway station was re-sited 500 metres farther east in 1975 to enable an internal road bypass to be built along the shore. So while the rail distance from Glasgow to Mallaig was reduced by 1 km, an attractive waterfront remained unattainable.

**Pulp Mill Closes; Smelter Enlarges**: Serious unemployment problems resulted from the closure in 1980 of the Corpach *(q.v.)* pulp mill. By 1981 the population of the town itself exceeded 5600. Over a dozen hotels with improving star gradings, and numerous caravan and camping sites in the vicinity, showed the growing importance of the area's tourist industry. After 50 years of increasingly efficient operation the British Aluminium smelter employed 337 people in 1979 to produce 27,000 tonnes of aluminium a year; rebuilding with a European Investment Fund grant brought annual capacity to 40,000 tonnes. In 1981 it was acquired by the Alcan group of Canada. In 1988 a government grant to British Alcan helped to provide new rail facilities to handle up to 2000 tonnes of alumina a week from Blyth, but the capacity of the smelter remained small by world standards, and in 1990 Alcan cut job numbers to 300 in an effort to remain competitive.

**Service and Tourism Developments**: The oft-troubled Glenlochy distillery was closed in 1983; part was saved, part became derelict and its site went for development in 1991. From 1984 the Mallaig railway became a tourist attraction in itself, BR operating regular steam-hauled trains. In 1986 Finlay and Lorna Finlayson started Crannog Ltd, a combined shellfishing and marketing operation which flourished, and in 1989 converted the former MacBraynes office on the pier into a seafood restaurant; the firm expanded into Glasgow in 1991. By 1988 a swimming pool and squash courts were open. In 1989 new skiing facilities were opened at 655 m on Aonach Mor in the Nevis range, where up to 130 days' skiing were possible from Christmas to early May. Access was made from the Spean Bridge road, 10km north-east of Fort William, to an aerial ropeway with 6-person gondolas serving a restaurant, ski school and 8 tows. In 1991 a major low-level development was proposed on the site of a former tip at An Aird, including a hotel, supermarket and housing. By 1993 Inverness College gave courses at the Lochaber Centre. However a 1992 scheme for a seaplane service to Glasgow came to nothing.

**Industrial Change and Town Centre Improvements**: By 1991 the Ben Nevis malt distillery had been acquired and reopened for malt only by the Japanese firm Nikka, so that its output could go for blending in Japan. By 1991 a Marine Harvest fish processing factory had been built on the Blar Mhor industrial estate. Although rail-freight had its ups and downs in the 1990s, aluminium ingots and timber were carried out, whilst alumina and fuel oil came in. But sadly the oil traffic by rail ceased in 1993, though the sleeping-car trains survived – narrowly – and timber traffic had resumed by 1999. In 1992 a substantial improvement scheme was proposed for the Parade area west of the *Alexandra Hotel*, and in 1993 the High Street was pedestrianised, granite and other natural materials being used; by 1996 there was a Tesco store.

**Local Government ends**: The *Fort William Star* newspaper was started in 1994 by a disaffected former editor of the *Oban Times*, but now only the *Lochaber News* is produced in Fort William. Most regrettably the Lochaber District Council disappeared in 1996 into an all-purpose Highland Region, ending the town's role as a centre of independent local government. Old Inverlochy Castle was being restored in 1997 by Historic Scotland. In 2000 the John Muir Trust acquired Ben Nevis and launched an appeal for funds to assure its future conservation. A new BT call centre opened in 2001 with 20 jobs, expecting 200 by the year's end. This will add to existing medium-sized firms Underwater Centre (training divers), the Smoked Salmon company, and Nevisprint. There are now 5 hotels with 80 or more rooms, plus many smaller hotels, guest houses, and B&Bs; the Glen Nevis youth hostel and two independent hostels for backpackers are also open all year.

## FOULA — Map 14, A4

***Small island w. of Shetland,** pop. 40* — OS 4: HT 9739

The name of Foula, lofty western outlier of Shetland, aptly means *'Isle of Birds'*. Lying 45km west of Scalloway, Foula boasts the highest sea cliff in the British Isles, at over 420m. Midway on the much lower and relatively sheltered eastern side, some 5km long, lies the tiny inlet of Ham Voe, beside whose inflowing stream is the only landing place. The isle was settled by Norsemen and entitled *'Fule or Thule'* on Pont's map, probably made in 1592. Six places were identified, including *'Hami'* and the Midfield and Houb mills. The isolated fishing and farming community spoke Norn, and about 1700 were easily robbed of the title to their lands by the unscrupulous Scotts of Melby. So by the 19th century they had learned to speak English. In 1901 the isle contained 222 people, but overfishing and the extreme remoteness began to tell, and people drifted away.

**Decline and Revival**: In 1937 as a result of the film *"The Edge of the World"* – made in Foula to dramatise the risks of diphtheria in remote places – radio telephony was installed to link the isle with medical facilities in case of illness. But as recently as 1951 there was no conventional telephone service. Only 51 residents remained, though Ham had a school and a post office served by a weekly mail boat from Walls. This, the only regular access from Shetland, took six hours to reach the pier with its fixed crane for lifting boats clear of the waves. So the population fell further, to only 33 in 1971, mainly elderly farming people. But by the mid seventies a telephone exchange had been installed and an airstrip built on the east coast; in the summer of 1981 Loganair flew in weekly from Tingwall. A slow recovery had begun, to 40 people in 1981 and 1991; meantime in 1989 a new pier was built – and the first recorded crime since 1908 occurred! By 1994 a new school had been built and a summer passenger ferry to Scalloway supplemented the year-round Walls service. But with no harbour safe from easterlies, the long-term future of the nesting isle of the *'bonxie'* (Great Skua) cannot be easy for its human population.

## FOULDEN & Mordington — Map 3, C3

***Berwickshire village,** pop. 400* — OS 67, 74 or 75: NT 9255

Foulden, pronounced *Foolden*, lies near the English border, midway between Chirnside and Berwick. *'Fouldountoun & Kirk'*, *'Bastle'*, and a mill where its tiny stream met the Whiteadder Water, all appeared on Pont's map of the Merse; the substantial church tithe barn did not. A parish school was founded in 1619, but Roy's survey of about 1754 showed Foulden on a mere track, which later became a main road. Two annual fairs were to be held in 1799 but the next century added little except a post office, open by 1901. Mordington House – by then a mansion in a park beside an ancient church on the English border 2 km to the east – stood empty from about 1950, and was demolished in 1973. The population of Foulden plus Mordington was 550 in 1951. In 1991 Foulden parish had only 399 residents. The primary school and post office, still open in 1980, have since closed; the ancient tithe barn is now a tourist attraction.

## FOYERS, Boleskine, Inverfarigaig & Whitebridge — Map 9, A5

***Inverness-shire hamlets,** pop. 400 (area)* — OS 26: NH 4920

The River Foyers tumbles steeply into the south-east side of Loch Ness; by Pont's day (about 1600) the river was noted for its *'Great Lyn'*, a spectacular waterfall. His sketch map showed the river bridged in two places, both above the falls, and also higher up above the confluence of a tributary, which was also bridged. General Wade's men built a waterside road from Inverness beside Loch Ness, then climbing beside the falls to Bridge of Loin and Six Mile Bridge (now White Bridge (OS 34)), built in 1732, and down to Fort Augustus. The Kirk of Boleskine was perched above the loch east of the falls; to the north-east was General Wade's headquarters, in a building at Inverfarigaig, marked on the Roy map of about 1750 as the *'General's Hut'*. A secluded spot between two lochs 10km south west of Foyers (grid NH 4413) was chosen in the 18th century as the site for Knockie Lodge, a hunting lodge built for the chief of Clan Fraser. The falls greatly impressed Pennant in his 1769 journey on Wade's road, though only *"a poor inn"* was on offer. This was probably the *General's Hut Inn* noted by Heron in 1799 together with the *"stupendous bridge"* built above the *"celebrated"* falls.

**Young Pioneer of Hydro-electricity and Aluminium**: Chambers found the General's Hut *"a little inn"* in 1827, describing the falls in loving detail; below them *"people land from the* *passing steam-boats"*. By 1894 the Hut had been replaced by the *Foyers Hotel* close beside the falls; the *Whitebridge Inn* was open upstream, 5km to the south. In 1895–96 the North British Aluminium Company, pioneered by 22-year-old Murray Morrison, developed the falls in order to generate hydro-electricity on a modest scale to reduce aluminium at a lochside works – happily keeping their scenic qualities. This was the first use of water power for industrial electricity generation in Britain and earned him a knighthood *(but see Fort Augustus)*. Production was aided by a light railway until the late 1950s, and a settlement for 600 people was planned, but this figure if attained was not maintained, and the company's centre of interest shifted to a larger scheme at Kinlochleven (*q.v.*).

**Fishing, Pumped Storage and Luxury**: In the 1950s Foyers had about 350 people and a small secondary school, closed by 1976. The aluminium works were closed in 1967, but remained in use for a time to build narrow-boats for English canals. It is now an industrial monument and a generating station for the grid; in 1973 new transformers were installed, brought by sea from Manchester via Inverness and Loch Ness. By 1979 the generating station, remote-controlled from Dingwall, had been refurbished as part of a 300mw pumped storage scheme utilising Loch Mhor in Stratherrick. There are two seasonal hotels among the hills to the south: *Knockie Lodge* and the anglers' *Whitebridge Hotel*. Only a hamlet remains beside the falls, with the quiet *Foyers Hotel*, guest houses and a tiny year-round hostel for backpackers at Foyers House.

## FRASERBURGH (The Broch) — Map 10, C1

***Buchan town,*** *pop. 12,800* — OS 30: NJ 9967

On the bleak north coast of Buchan was the 14th century Castle of Cairnbulg; nearby Fathlie, known by the locals as the Broch, was first chartered in the 15th century. It was re-chartered in 1546 as a burgh of barony by Sir Alexander Fraser, laird of the estate of Philorth, to provide a safe haven. He had already built a harbour, though a more detailed source gave the date of the first stone pier as 1576; beside it was a building still known as the *'wine tower'*. In 1570–74 Fraser's grandson, another Alexander, erected nearby what Pratt called *"the Tower of Kinnaird's Head, since called the Castle of Fraserburgh, and the next year (1571) he built a new church there"*.

**The Failed University**: According to Chambers, *"Lord Saltoun, the superior, and chief proprietor, attempted to make Fraserburgh the site of a university"*. It was founded in 1592 but failed about a decade later. The burgh's name was changed to Fraserburgh by royal charter in 1601, and it was already evidently a substantial town bearing the new name when sketched by Pont (probably on a visit in the first decade of the 17th century). Thomas Tucker was damning about the port in 1655: *"Something now and then is brought in from Norway, but their only trade is coasting"*. Four vessels each of 20 tons were locally owned; he did not mention fishing or brewing, but both had probably become established by that time. Philorth House, 4km south of Fraserburgh, was built in 1666 for Lord Saltoun. A post office was open by 1715, and the Roy survey of about 1750 showed a large rectilinear settlement. Its small harbour was enclosed by converging piers, and there were perhaps three radial tracks: south to *'Happyhillock'*, southwestwards following the modern A981 to Strichen, and also a short distance westwards along the coast. Little appears generally known of the town's development until late in the century.

**Scotland's First Nationally Provided Lighthouse**: In 1787 the castle tower was leased at extortionate rates to the Northern Lighthouse Board, who equipped this ready-made site as their Kinnaird Head light, visible from 22 km at sea: not the first lighthouse in Scotland, but the very first to be lit by this then-new body. By 1792 Fraserburgh was growing into a significant fishing port. Heron found in 1799 *"a small but pleasant town with about 1000 inhabitants and a tolerable harbour"*. A new church was built in 1802, and the north pier was built between 1807 and 1812 to designs by Thomas Telford. Fish processing started in 1810, and the south pier was built with aid from the Commissioners in 1814–18. By 1825 the brewery had failed but the Aberdeen Banking Company had a local branch, followed by the Bank of Scotland in 1835. A lifeboat station had opened in 1831. The Glenbughty distillery worked at Phingask, 2 km west of the town, for 30 or more years from 1825, but was disused by 1871. In 1827 Chambers found *"a considerable town having a small harbour, a thriving fishing-station. The town, however from its remote situation is somewhat dull in point of ordinary trade."* By then a hilly road had been built to Banff, though as late as 1858 Pratt found it *"scarcely passable for carriages"*.

***'The Scottish Samurai':*** **from Broch to Butterfly**: Thomas Blake Glover, born in Fraserburgh in 1838, settled in Japan where he founded trading interests in brewing, coal mining and shipbuilding, largely opening up that country, which honoured him highly. He co-founded the vast Mitsubishi industrial empire, and is said to have inspired Puccini's opera *'Madam Butterfly'*. In 1855, when the Town House was built, the Broch had *"several banking offices and some good shops"*. Its people read the *Fraserburgh Advertiser*, there was the *Saltoun Arms, "a large and well appointed inn"*, baths had been provided, a jail had been built, and the port had a middle pier. Grain and potatoes were shipped out in exchange for timber, bricks, coal, lime and general cargoes, while cattle were transported between Orkney and London. A boat-building yard employed about 50 men to build from 500 to 600 tons of vessels annually. At that time 34 vessels averaging 165 tons were registered with the letters FR, there were five whalers and sealers, and in the season 3000 people were employed to produce some 50,000 barrels of herrings. Broadsea, sited in a cove to the west, was also a fishing village.

**Harbour Expansion and the Railway**: More extensions to the harbour began in 1855, notably the long north breakwater, and from their completion about 1880 Fraserburgh became a major fishing port and an important local centre, also acquiring a gasworks. In 1865 a Great North of Scotland Railway branch reached Fraserburgh from Aberdeen via Maud, enabling fresh fish (mainly herrings) to be sent in bulk to the markets of the south; Fraserburgh was also among the top ten Scottish ports for white fish curing. Associated processing industries developed, with Maconochie Brothers' cannery, opened in 1883. Fraserburgh had almost 7000 residents in 1881; its golf club, founded in that year, laid out an 18-hole course on the spacious links south-east of the town, whose later local newspaper the *Fraserburgh Herald* was published from 1884.

**Scotland's Biggest Fishing Port and its Industry**: By 1894, when the only hotel mentioned by Murray was the *"fair" Saltoun Arms*, Fraserburgh was said to be Scotland's biggest fishing port, a huge fleet of 805 small boats being based in the harbour; they were served by lifeboat and coastguard stations. A library, with Carnegie aid, started in 1903. By then the population had grown to over 9000; by 1921 it reached a long plateau at 10,500. A branch railway was opened to Inverallochy *(q.v.)* and St Combs in 1903. An important engineering works was established in 1905 by the Consolidated Pneumatic Tool Company; in 1914 Scott & Yule of Fraserburgh built steam drifters. The historic Philorth House sadly burnt down in 1915, leaving a shelter-belted park. The lighthouse became famous as the site of Marconi's early transatlantic broadcasts, and in 1929 was equipped with Scotland's first radio beacon. In 1939 when Maconochie's fish cannery was open in Bath Street near the harbour, barrel staves for salt herring were imported direct from Scandinavia. At that time Wordie & Co's local railway cartage operations were still entirely horse-drawn *(for a very full account see Paget-Tomlinson).*

**Chilly Resort loses Passenger Trains**: In 1940 G A Sheves, a general trader of Fraserburgh, bought the elderly 246-ton coaster SS *Archmoor* and later added other such ships, the oldest and longest-lasting being the 602-ton SS *Archgrove* of 1894, scrapped in 1957. After half a century of quiet development, and weathering the effects of two world wars, bright but chilly Fraserburgh – a popular resort until overtaken by Mediterranean package holidays – had acquired covered and open swimming pools and an esplanade. In 1957 a Fraserburgh firm built a new ferry boat for Ballachulish; a new building for Fraserburgh Academy was opened in 1962, and a general hospital, public library and new slaughterhouse were also erected in the 1960s. But the railways were closed to passengers in 1965 (the St Combs line being abandoned), though some locomotive facilities remained for a time. The lifeboat station was closed in 1973, by which time a new boat was based at Peterhead.

**Lost Rail Freight and Local Government**: A technical college and school of navigation opened in the 1970s, and by then the former Castle Brewery had become R Cruikshank & Co's aerated water factory (but by 1980 the firm had moved to Buckie). In 1975 Fraserburgh ceased to be a centre of local government, despite being more central in the sprawling new Banff & Buchan District than either tiny Banff or important Peterhead. Following the turning away by British Railways of the valuable fish traffic, other rail freight also declined, although the line stayed open for goods until 1979, the once fine station being replaced by an industrial site. By then industry was growing: bodies for refrigerated vans and trailers to move fish by road were made locally by Gray & Adams, Macrae's employed 500, canning mackerel, and about 1980 there were also two other large fish processors, Noble Brothers and British Fish Canners. There may well have been some North Sea oil work too. By 1981 the population had grown quite rapidly, to about 12,500.

**The Growing Town's Last Train**: In 1979 the writer rode on a Scottish Railway Preservation Society special, the last passenger train to visit Fraserburgh, whose railway closed that year; the postmaster was aptly named Buchan. The centre was busy, and had a large modern British Legion club, although

*Fraserburgh harbour in the 1880s, at the height of the herring boom which followed the ready availability of cotton machine-made drift nets. The boats seen here are lug-sailed herring drifters, catching fish for curing, mainly for export.* *(GWW collection)*

the former *Playhouse Cinema* with its 1010 seats, still open in 1970, was derelict. The town's football ground boasted a stand, and Fraserburgh offered a wide range of shops and services (including 5 banks!) At the very busy harbour was an ice factory, marine oil depot, chandlers, a large net shed, and the large very new premises of Richard Irvine fish salesmen. Fraserburgh remained a minor resort with a sandy beach, caravan and camping sites and four hotels (though their star rating had fallen since the 1950s).

**Industry and Education**: The long-established Consolidated Pneumatic Tool Company had a branch in Aberdeen by the early 1980s, and – after acquisition by Power Jacks – went on to make diggers and tools for use in building the Channel Tunnel around 1990. The harbour was deepened and a new fishmarket built in 1987. In the late 1980s Fraserburgh firms – including James Noble and Buchan, Hall & Mitchell – still specialised in building ferries and fishing boats, and an extensive boat slip was in use around 1990. In 1989 a long-standing US Navy relay station still stood atop the prominent Mormond Hill, 10km to the south. By 1991 the population had reached 12,843. In 1994 the Tidy Britain Group found the condition of Fraserburgh's beaches *'very good'*. In 1995 vocational qualifications could be gained at the Banff & Buchan College of Further Education.

**Lighthouse Museum and Cannery Troubles**: In 1990 two canning factories – International Canners with some 130 workers, and British Fish Canners' Kinnaird Head works (formerly Christian Salvesen), with about 100 employees – came under one ownership as International Fish Canners. In the 1990s the loss of nearly 150 jobs was feared when Premier Brands moved to Arbroath. Macrae's food processing factory stayed in production but was sold twice in two years. In 1992 the Northern Lighthouse Board made over the historic Kinnaird Head lighthouse of 1787 – the first and almost the last manned light in Scotland – for conservation by Historic Scotland, and a local trust built beside it a museum – featuring, among other exhibits, the Flannan Islands tragedy. In 1997 fish landed at this major port included catfish, cod, haddock, ling, monkfish, plaice, prawns, lemon sole, whiting and witch, but the Atlantic Seafoods plant which employed 70 full time and 40 part time workers was to close. Despite these setbacks, a large wastewater treatment plant was built in 2000 near the huge cold stores and other fish related industries west of the growing town. The traditional *Saltoun Arms Hotel* still serves; but worries about North Sea fish stocks were high in 2001.

## FRESWICK & Skirza — Map 13, B4

***Caithness settlements,*** *pop. 100* — OS 12: ND 3767

On the east coast of Caithness 6km south of Duncansby Head is a bay with a sandy beach and the sites of three Pictish brochs. It was a large scale centre for line fishing in medieval times. Bucholly Castle, the early and undated but complex home of the Mowat family, stood on a cliff above Castle Geo, 1.5km to the south. It became a gaunt ruin after about 1760 when the Mowats built the tower of Freswick House on the site of an older house. The poor soil enabled only a scatter of small scale farms to develop, but eventually a stone pier and curing shed were built at Skirza on the rocky north side of the bay; by 1951 a primary school and post office served a population of some 200. Skirza pier survived in 1985 but only two old half-decked boats were based there, the school had already closed and the population had fallen to some 135 over the past thirty years. By 1993 even the post office had gone.

## FREUCHIE & Kirkforthar — Map 6, B4

***Howe of Fife village & hamlet,*** *pop. 1025* — OS 59: NO 2806

Freuchie, whose Gaelic name means *'heathery'*, lies on the southern slopes of the fertile Howe of Fife. Some 2 km south-east is the ancient chapel and house of Kirkforthar. Freuchie appeared as a tiny place on Pont's map made around 1600. By then the River Eden had been bridged at Shiells, on the old track from Kirkcaldy to Newburgh. The mid 18th century Roy map showed Freuchie as a small linear settlement with a mill, associated hamlets, and roads to Falkland, Cupar, Kennoway and Kirkcaldy. Heron mentioned Freuchie in 1799 as a *"village"* with 500 inhabitants. By 1800 the *New Inn* some 2 km to the south had become a coaching stop, where the road to Cupar (turnpiked from 1790) left the Kirkcaldy/Falkland road and a new arrow-straight road cut across the marshes towards Luthrie and Newport-on-Tay. In 1826–27 *'Fruchie'* with its mill was a rather scattered settlement. A new and imposing corn mill was built in 1840.

**Textiles, Trains, Linen and Bricks**: Freuchie became a substantial village, despite being poorly served from 1847 to 1958 by *'Falkland Road'* railway station, which was 1km to the south. The Eden Valley Jute Mill worked from the mid 19th century, and four linen factories with power-looms were in operation by 1862. In 1864 the largest manufacturers were William Lumsden & Son, annually making a million metres of linen sheeting and hucks. Their steam-powered weaving works built in 1860 contained 100 power-looms, while the firm still employed 320 hand loom weavers. The Lumsden Memorial Hall was built in 1883. Kirkforthar became the site of a works making sand-lime bricks, but Freuchie's population remained stable around the thousand level during most of the 20th century, despite the demolition of the *New Inn* in mid-century and the complete disappearance of the textile industry with most of its buildings.

**Mushrooms, Cricket and Tourists**: By 1976 the last industrial survivor, the Eden Valley Jute Mill, was merely a warehouse, converted by Dumbreck for mushroom growing by 1980. However, Freuchie won the all-Britain village cricket title in the 1980s. By 1990 there was no sign of industry except for the mushrooms and the brickworks (now closed). The *Lomond Hills Hotel* (parts dating from 1753) was extended around 1970, and in 1991 a swimming pool was added. Although Freuchie is not itself of tourist interest – and has only a couple of shops, post office and primary school – it does enjoy spacious views, while Falkland Palace and Ladybank with its well known golf course are nearby. The resident population is about 1025. By 1999 the 1840 corn mill had been restored for use as housing.

## FRIOCKHEIM — Map 6, C2

***Angus village,*** *pop. 900* — OS 54: NO 5949

Guthrie, which lies north of the Lunan Water some 11km east of Forfar, had a church by about 1150. Guthrie Castle was built from 1468 onwards; the church became collegiate about 1479, being shown on Pont's map made about 1600 as *'Colledge of*

*Guthrie'*. Pont also depicted the 16th century Gardyne Castle, 2 km to the south-east across the Lunan Water in Kirkden parish. The great Fraser L-plan tower house of Braikie Castle was built of red sandstone in 1582, 6 km east of Guthrie. In between at Friock *(derived from the Gaelic for heather)* there was a mill on the Lunan Water, and another at *Pitmouis*.

**Flax Spinning and New Village**: Both *'Pitmuie'* mill and the *'Wakesmill'* east of it were shown by Roy about 1750, when Friock was a hamlet (which he quaintly labelled *'Fright'*), lying between the kirks of *'Gurthrey'* and *'Kennel'*. About 3 km to the east was a mill beside the long forgotten *'Castle of Boisack'; 'Midleton'* was a mansion, but there were no roads nearby. The water-powered Friock Mill was built beside the Lunan in 1773, spinning flax and then jute, moving on to produce canvas and linen. Other spinning mills were built on the Gighty Burn in Kirkden parish in 1796, and worked for half a century. A mill which was built in 1807 at Hatton, 2 km to the east contained 450 spindles in 1838, and in later years two smaller mills were added. Early in the 19th century John Andson laid out a new village on a unique triangular plan close to Friock Mill. It was originally known as *Friock Feus*. Though Scottish, Andson had lived in Germany, and by 1830 he had renamed the place Friockheim, or *'Heather Home'* – the locals pronounce it *Freakum*.

**The Railway Triangle**: In 1838 the Arbroath & Forfar Railway (A&FR) was opened, with a station named Friockheim at Pitmuies Mill just west of the village. This local company's broad gauge track was poor, but its alignment was generously planned; where it crossed the drive to Guthrie Castle it was forced to pay the laird to build an elaborate mock Tudor bridge – which still stands. Later the promoters of the Aberdeen Railway, coming up from the south via Perth, concluded after much argument that the Lunan valley and the low plateau to the north offered the easiest route between Forfar and Montrose. The western half of a suitable alignment was already built, and also served Dundee via Arbroath. So they leased and then bought the A&FR; the tracks were altered to carry standard gauge trains. An imposing 190 m-long viaduct was built of local red sandstone to carry an inland double track linking Arbroath to Montrose, with new stations at Guthrie and Glasterlaw, serving the main line trains which ran through from 1848.

**Quarrying for Slabs**: From about 1820 the proprietor, Carnegie of Boysack, worked the Leysmill Quarries 2 km to the south-east of Friockheim, producing *'Arbroath Pavement'*. Other quarries north of Friockheim, at The Dub and Montreathmont, were probably opened in the late 1840s to supply the railway builders. Friockheim had a post office by 1866, and the large Leysmill quarries (connected to what had by 1869 become the Caledonian Railway) employed 60 men, *"belonging chiefly to the villages of Friockheim and Leysmill"*; the other two quarries had 70 to 80 men between them. The parish church was built in 1885 at the apex of the street plan, and with 943 people by 1891, Friockheim was a substantial village with its station, church, smithy, inn and post and telegraph office; a whole series of mills were to be seen downstream.

**Wasted Assets around Friockheim**: The east side of the railway triangle was abandoned as redundant in 1908, though the viaduct long remained. In the second world war a small temporary airfield was built north of Kinnell. The quarries too had been abandoned by the 1950s, when Friockheim had 1100 people and typical village facilities, but the station was closed in 1955 and the freight service was ended in 1965. The erstwhile main line was closed in 1967 in favour of the shorter coastal route via Inverkeilor, and soon the area's railway tracks had all gone. The fine 1848 railway viaduct was destroyed in 1976; by then the 220-pupil secondary school had also closed. At that time the old mill was used by Douglas Fraser & Sons, who made candlewick bedspreads and rope-soled canvas shoes, employing 150 people; then in 1974 a fire destroyed much of the premises.

**Sacks, Screens and Protective Clothing**: The firm of Fraser bounced back on a smaller scale: they now make *'Perfectos'* waterproof and protective clothing for offshore oil workers and general severe weather uses. With the closure of a hotel, Friockheim's facilities had declined to those of a small village, which by 1991 had a reduced population of 896. But in 1993 S G Baker Ltd made agricultural and industrial sacks in extensive modernised premises; Wishart operated coaches and buses from a local base, M Lingard was in business as a gunmaker, and a useful range of basic facilities was still available, including food shops, modern health centre and primary school, and a well-equipped sports field and playground. By 2000 the Screen Manufacturing Company made meshes and sieving screens for industry at the old station yard.

## FURNACE

**Map 5, A4**

***Small Argyllshire village,*** *pop. 300* — OS 55: NN 0200

Blaeu's atlas map based on Pont's work of about 1600 showed *'Innerlackan'* on the steep northern shores of Loch Fyne in Argyll. In the mid 18th century this was a heavily wooded location where the coastal track forked. In 1754–55 the Duddon Furnace Company of Furness in Cumbria (where the forests had already been largely burned) selected this as the site for a new iron smelting works, at first known as *Craleckan*, as illustrated by Hay & Stell. Materials and labour were brought in by sea; the village which grew up was later called Furnace. Heron in 1799 called it *"a considerable iron-work, now carried on by the Argyll Furnace Company. The ore is imported from the west of England, and the smelting performed by charcoal, made from the wood cut in the neighbourhood"*. The smelter, which

*Furnace iron-smelting works, set up in 1755 by the Duddon Furnace Company from Furness in Cumbria; they made use of local timber to make charcoal for the furnace. The works closed in 1812.* (RCAHMS / JRH)

also had a forge, was closed in 1812 when coke had begun to be more generally available on sites near the coalfields.

**Quarrying and Auchindrain**: There was no post office at Furnace until after 1838, but gunpowder mills were established about 1840, by which time quarrying must have begun. The rock known as porphyrite was especially suitable for making into paving setts, many of which were used in the streets of Glasgow. In the 20th century Furnace was little more than a hamlet of 250 people, though in the 1990s Tilcon's quarry still produced roadstone chips. During the 1970s the population of the Furnace area grew by 20%. Some of the former furnace buildings still existed. Poor and abandoned Auchindrain, 3 km inland, which had been the last surviving joint-tenant farming settlement in Scotland, became an evocative museum of crofting.

## FYVIE

**Map 10, B2**

***Buchan village**, pop. 500 (2000, area)* OS 29: NJ 7638

Fyvie lies in a remote location on the upper reaches of the River Ythan, 12 km south of Turriff in Buchan, and was probably the centre of the extensive thanage of Formartine which existed from about the 11th century. Fyvie church was founded in 1179, probably by the Earl of Buchan. William the Lion soon gave it to the Abbot of Aberbrothock (Arbroath), and about 1285 Fyvie acquired a cell of that great abbey; this was improved about 1470. Fyvie was an unsuccessful anomaly as a Royal Burgh: chartered by Alexander III in 1264, it acquired little permanent lay development besides its 13th century royal hunting castle in courtyard style, which was visited by the marauding Edward I in 1296. About 1380 Fyvie became Lindsay property; around 1390 the castle was rebuilt, and in 1397 went to the Prestons; it was enlarged about 1500. But Fyvie, being 25 km inland, seems to have been a failure in terms of trade and in practically all the crafts except milling; consequently it paid no tax in 1535–56, even the friars having left.

**Seton exalts the Castle**: In 1597 the barony was made into a free lordship under Alexander Seton, who was created Lord Fyvie in 1598. He had the castle heightened in the early 17th century to four to six storeys in a magnificent French style. Seton became Earl of Dunfermline in 1606, with the privilege of holding a weekly market and three annual fairs at Fyvie. By 1633 a parish school was open, and by 1642, when Gordon supplied Blaeu with information for his atlas, Fyvie was a more significant settlement, with an Ythan bridge.

**The Barony Burgh**: In 1672–73 Fyvie was re-chartered as a burgh of barony, but from 1689 to 1726 the estate was forfeited to the Crown and decline set in. William, Earl of Aberdeen took over in 1726, followed in 1746 by William Gordon, who further enlarged the castle, adding a fifth great tower. Roy's map of about 1750 identified the castle as *'Fyvie House'*; its policies remained modest. By that time *'Fyvie Kirk'* apparently stood almost alone, 3 km east of the nearest track linking Turriff with Old Meldrum via Chapel of Seggat. But there were three mills, named Fyvie, Petty and Creechy, the last accompanied by a hamlet. A post office was open by 1755, and an annual fair was still to be held at Fyvie in 1797. The church was rebuilt on the old site in 1808. The New Statistical Account noted that the weekly market had been *"long in desuetude"*, but two annual fairs were still *"well frequented"*. Fyvie's railway station, opened in 1857 an inconvenient 1.5 km from the village, was on the Great North of Scotland Railway's single-track branch to Turriff and Macduff. The huge castle was transformed into a rich mansion, work completed in 1900–01.

**Tourist Village**: By 1951 nearly 900 people lived in and around Fyvie, and up to 4500 people depended on its facilities, including a junior secondary school with 80 pupils; another 20 studied at St Katherine's, 4 km to the south. But both secondary schools had closed by 1976, for rural populations were falling; the railway was closed to passengers in 1951 and to freight in 1966. The small maternity hospital which existed in the early years of the NHS had also closed by 1981, when Fyvie had a single hotel among its average village facilities, serving a largely arable farming area containing some 2250 people. By 1987 the National Trust for Scotland managed the great castle, and although there had been little new development in the village (which had under 500 people by 1991), the church – with a Tiffany glass window – also remains a tourist draw. Fyvie has the small *Vale Hotel*, a bank, a modern primary school, health centre, food stores and a bus depot; in 2000 the castle's walled garden was being recreated.

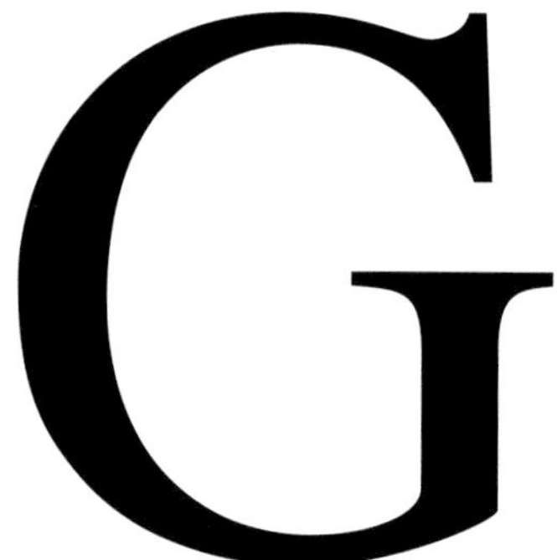

## GAIRLOCH & Flowerdale

**Map 8, B1**

***Wester Ross villages,*** *pop. 600*

OS 19: NG 8077

An ancient dun stood near the end of a sweep of fine sands bordering the Gair Loch of remote Wester Ross. This area was Macleod property until in 1488 James IV granted it to Hector Roy Mackenzie, sparking a bloody century of violence *(see Conon Bridge)*. In 1619, in more peaceful times, Gairloch – which was also known as Clive or Strath – was chartered as a burgh of barony. It was one of many settlements in the area that were shown on Gordon's maps. The old clay and wattle head house or *Tige Dige* of the Mackenzies was replaced in 1738 by a new mansionhouse near the parish kirk, shown on Roy's map of about 1750 standing in private policies. Central among a straggle of crofting townships to the north was the clachan of Ballygown, later translated as Smithstown. Roy's field sheet showed a track leading south-east towards the clachan of Talladale.

**Opening up by Road and Steamer**: In 1799 Heron noted the Gaelic-speaking area as roadless, while *"Gairloch is a large bay in which the fishing of cod and other white fish is very considerable"*. A road from Achnasheen and Kinlochewe was built into the area around 1843, passing alongside magnificent Loch Maree, where the River Talladale was bridged, and through wooded Kerrysdale where another bridge was built, with a by-road to Badachro. A steamer pier was constructed in a beautiful sheltered inlet aptly named Flowerdale some 2 km south of the main township, by that time simply called Gairloch. By 1850 a summer service of steamers from the pier plied to Portree, Tobermory, Oban and Glasgow. Queen Victoria stayed at the *Gairloch Hotel* in 1878, and by 1883 the *Loch Maree Hotel* had been built west of Talladale; until 1911 its steam launch *Mabel* sailed the loch in connection with seasonal road coaches to Achnasheen station, which had opened in 1870. From 1888 the weekly summer coastal steamer was extended to Lochinver, a service which ended in 1914.

**Electricity used and misused**: Gairloch golf club, founded in 1898, laid out its 9-hole course among the sand dunes. The mail coach plied to and from Achnasheen station until 1907 when it was joined – and soon replaced – by a *'public motor service'*. The lighthouse on Rubha Reidh, a headland 17 km north-west of Gairloch, was first lit in 1912. Most regrettably, about 1945 the beauties of wooded Kerrysdale on the approach road from the south were ruined by the crudely conceived Kerry Falls hydro-electric scheme, which brought the area's first electricity. By 1955 a seaside youth hostel was open at Carn Dearg 4 km to the west of the village. By then the resident population of Gairloch was about 450, a level approximately maintained to 1981. In 1954–80 the *Gairloch Hotel* had three stars and over 50 rooms; the small *Old Inn Hotel* was listed in 1974, and *Creag Mor* was open at Charlestown beside Flowerdale by 1977. Commercial fishing and sea angling from Flowerdale pier was expanding in 1975. By 1977 Gairloch Seafoods dealt in shell and white fish, and the main TV relay station for the north-west of Scotland had been sited on a high promontory beyond the township of Melvaig, 15 km to the north. By 1978 pottery was made locally.

**Gairloch for Tourists**: In 1981 Gairloch had the facilities of an average village plus a secondary school, serving in all some 2000 people around the loch and in the Poolewe area. Caravan and camping sites were available by 1984, the distant lighthouse was automated in 1986 and a new fire station was opened in 1990. The 1991 population of the villages was 613. By 1992 the Gairloch Heritage Museum was an added attraction, and the regional and local enterprise companies planned to open a training centre under their CELT programme for

*Prawn baskets, Flowerdale pier, Gairloch, in the 1960s.* *(RS)*

remote areas. Local boats were still landing prawns in 1995. In 1996 the sprawling village still boasted two post offices 3km apart, at Strath and Charlestown! Gairloch High School has around 200 pupils. Hotels include the *Creag Mor*, the newly extended *Myrtle Bank* and the *Old Inn*; there are also guest houses, a restaurant, and two hostels, plus another at Rubha Reidh lighthouse.

## GAIRLOCHY

**Map 5, A1**

***Lochaber hamlet,*** *pop. 100* — OS 41: NN 1784

Towards the west end of the Great Glen the River Lochy originally flowed south-westwards from Loch Lochy, to be joined by the River Spean a short way downstream. The Roy map of about 1750 showed *'Kilminevock'* (Kilmonivaig) on the north bank of the River Lochy, and tracks crossing both rivers, apparently by fording. When William Jessop and Thomas Telford planned the Caledonian Canal, of which the lengthy loch was to form a part, they decided to raise its level by 4m to avoid dredging a channel and, requiring a solid foundation for the regulating lock, found this in the bed of the River Lochy. Needing to keep the canal entrance free from the swift current of the river in spate, they had a new 500m-long channel cut from a lochside point some 250m to the south, through which Loch Lochy subsequently overflowed. Beside Mucomir Farm the diverted water plunged into the River Spean over artificial falls, spanned by a fine 3-arched bridge on a new single track road linking Spean Bridge with Achnacarry. The name Gairlochy *(Roar of the Lochy)* was adopted.

**Rebuilt Canal, Railway and Hydro Power**: A second lock was built in the 1840s as a safety measure against floods down the valley. Beside the locks a hamlet grew; it was given a station on the ill-fated Invergarry & Fort Augustus *(q.v.)* Railway; by the 1920s it had a post office and by 1951 a telephone exchange. The Mucomir hydro-electric power station beside the falls was built by the Hydro Board from 1960, affecting the water flow and requiring tree clearance to prevent obstruction of the sluices. The post office vanished about 1975, and of three caravan sites that had grown nearby by 1985, only that on the former railway station site survives. The *Glen Loy Lodge Hotel* is open 4km south-west, some Forestry Commission plantations offer access, and the Great Glen Cycle Route passes though Gairlochy. The canal locks are a well-kept attraction.

## GALASHIELS

**Map 3, B3**

***Borders town,*** *pop. 13,500* — OS 73: NT 4936

In the steep-sided valley of the swift-running Gala Water above its confluence with the River Tweed is the undateable ruined Peel of Galashiels, originally a hunting-tower within the extensive royal forest of Gala and Leader. Galashiels had a ferry across the Tweed at Boleside (or Boldside), 2 km south, by 1337, when invading English soldiers died after eating *'soor plums'*; the township took this phrase as its motto! In the 16th century the Hillslap and Buckholm Towers were built on the hill slopes to the east. By the 1580s there were already three fulling or *waulk* mills at Galashiels, later known as Bathgate's, Cochrane's (or Mid), and Waulkmillhead. Pont's map-work of about 1600 lacked detail in the area, merely indicating the emparked peel tower, *'Galasheels'* as a small settlement, and to the north a bridge across a tributary burn.

**Pringles and Scotts, Names to conjure With**: Galashiels was erected into a burgh of barony in 1599 by the Pringles, replaced as lairds in 1632 by the Scotts. Four kilometres north-east is Colmslie, where a parish school was opened in 1622, preceded in 1617 by one at Boleside. In 1622 when over 400 people lived in Galashiels the parish church was moved to it from Lindean and by 1630 a parish school was open in the burgh. There were already fair and market rights, the corn mill, and in 1655 still three waulk mills. Chambers noted that *"the thirlage of the corn-mill was exercised in Gala as well as all other feudal holdings"*. The Martinmas fair, first held in 1693, was *"principally a mart for black cattle"*; there was also a midsummer fair, and by 1699 a *'Weaver corporation'*. In 1723 eighteen people drowned in a ferry incident; with such hazards, Galashiels did not attract the attention of early travel writers from the south.

**Iron, Roads and Blankets**: Galashiels was known for woollens by 1733, when according to Bremner *"a few coarse kerseys, called Galashiels Greys"* were made. An ironworks was set up in 1744. Some ten years later, the Roy survey plotted only a medium-sized village confined to the right bank of the Gala Water, quaintly labelled *Gallow Shiels*. A side road connected it with the main north Tweedside road and so to Easter Langlee, from there continuing either to Melrose, or over the hills via Langshaw to Stow and Edinburgh. Westwards, there were no bridges nearby; the Boldside Boat still ferried people across the Tweed for Selkirk. In 1768 an Act created turnpikes, so enabling the roads to Edinburgh, Selkirk and Melrose to be made up. By 1774 blankets as well as its regular grey cloth were made in Galashiels, and in 1776, though there were only 600 people in the parish, David Loch regarded its people as *"very industrious"*: the energetic Gala folk of the day also played shinty and went curling in winter. There were 30 looms and still three waulk mills; wool consumption had more than doubled in two years.

**New Village, New Mills**: The village of Galashiels soon gained greater significance as a settlement, aided by its sympathetic lairds the Scotts. Chambers noted that about 1780 *"the old village of Galashiels which lay upon an eminence a little way to the south of the present town contained about four or five hundred inhabitants, the greater part of whom supported themselves by weaving. On the manufacture of cloth succeeding, and the people feeling a tendency to remove nearer to the river, the baron consented to feu out the necessary ground"* on which they built their own blue whin-stone houses. Wilderhaugh Burn Mill was built by Mercer in 1783, and in 1784 all four mills installed new scribbling machines for wool preparation. Pringle established Buckholmside Mill in 1788 to prepare wool for hand-spinning; the Cloth Hall was built in 1791, and in the same year a teazer was installed by its designer John Mercer at the new Wilderhaugh Mill, built in 1790–91; by that time 300 women spun wool for use in Galashiels. The rebuilding of the ancient Mid Mill as the nucleus of Cochrane's works took place in 1792–93, followed by the new Weirhaugh (or Botany) Mill in 1797–98.

**Galashiels becoming a Town**: Five fairs were held in Galashiels in 1797, when yarn was still taken over the hills to Hawick by pack horse. In 1799 Heron noted *"the village of Galashiels, in which a prosperous manufacture of woollen cloth is carried on by upwards of five hundred inhabitants"*. There was also a small tannery. These industries had grown *"notwithstanding their distance from a market-town"*. In 1803 Dorothy Wordsworth saw the *"village of Galashiels, pleasantly situated on the bank of the stream; a pretty place it once has been, but a manufactory is established there; and a townish bustle and ugly stone houses are fast taking the place of the brown-roofed thatched cottages, of which a great number yet remain"*. Waulkmillhead was rebuilt in 1802, followed in 1804–05 by the Nether weaving mill; in 1805 came the new Linburn Mill. The Rosebank Mill was built in 1803–05; it was there that wool spinning was mechanised when the mule frame was introduced by the Thomsons in 1814, one of many new processes innovated in the Galashiels mills. By 1810 the Leith Banking Company had opened a branch.

**Sir Walter Scott and Abbotsford**: Despite its very long established and by then important textile industry, there was no post office until 1803; in 1813 the post travelled via Melrose. Local sheriff and author Sir Walter Scott must have made great use of the posts. He bought Cartleyhole Farm, 3 km south-east of Galashiels, in 1812, gradually building there his eclectic baronial-style mansion of Abbotsford House, and adding enough land to create a park. The ironworks of 1744 adopted the name Waverley from his novels, and is still going as Aimers McLean. A *'wire bridge'* built across the Gala by Richard Lees in 1813 to an American concept was the first such in the old world, but Boldside ferry was still in use in 1827. Meantime the ancient Peel was pulled down in 1815. Bathgates of Galashiels had become known as millwrights by 1816. When the Huddersfield (1818) and Galabank (1818–19) Mills were followed in 1826 by the Wakefield Mill, Yorkshire names were perhaps adopted as sales gimmicks, yet only 175 looms were at work in 1826; by 1838 there were 265. By 1825 William Brown's brewery was in operation.

**Galashiels from 1827**: In 1827 Chambers noted that *"Galashiels, so remarkable for its woollen manufacture, contains two thousand inhabitants and nine thriving 'Factories' with all their appendages of waulking-mills, dyehouses etc; scarcely a vestige of the ancient village remains. It is remarkable that there are few shops of any consequence"* (though there was by then a bookseller). He added that *"in the present changed state of the country, the fairs have both fallen into complete desuetude"*, and although trade was still depressed in 1829, a gasworks was established in 1833 and by 1842 the *Bridge Inn* was open. No fewer than 16 water-powered mills had been built or rebuilt as integrated woollen plants in the long period from 1793 to 1853.

**Railways, Steam-driven Mills and Golf**: Galashiels interests were a driving force in the promotion of the Edinburgh & Hawick Railway, a subsidiary of the North British; this line which brought cheaper coal to the town was squeezed through the narrow valley and opened in 1849. This stimulated the building of yet more mills: Comelybank and the steam-driven Tweed Mill in 1852, the Victoria in 1853, the large Netherdale Mill in 1857, and in 1862 the Wilderbank Mill. About 1856 a shrinking-works and a skinworks were added. By the 1860s almost all the wool was imported; there were 76 sets of carding engines and nearly 70,000 spindles, supporting a population approaching 10,000, who had established co-operative provision stores. The privileged status of a Parliamentary Burgh was accorded in 1868, and during the 1870s very rapid population growth occurred in Selkirkshire, of which Galashiels was part. A library was opened in 1874. In 1884 the steep hillside at Ladhope became a municipal golf course, followed in 1895 by a 9-hole club course at Torwoodlee.

**The *'Woolly Tech'* – Training in Textiles**: A total of 21 mills existed by 1882, the year that a significant textiles training school was founded. Three more mills were extended: Buckholm in 1883, Wilderbank in 1890, and finally Netherdale in 1893. By 1894 Galashiels had *"drawn to itself all the trade of the district"*, there were two hotels, the *Abbotsford Arms* and *Commercial*, and the population crowded into its cramped site was over 17,000. The price of being *"celebrated for its woollen manufacture of tweeds and tartans"* was that the Gala Water was *"sadly polluted by the numerous factories"*. A local newspaper, the *Border Telegraph*, was founded in 1896. Then a slump in woollens caused by USA protectionist policies led to a major exodus which continued for years, and by 1901 a quarter of the 1891 population had been lost. However, a public electricity supply was provided in 1901, and a sewerage system was laid in 1908, by which time the first hire car in the Borders was available at Adam Purves & Sons. The Huddersfield Mill was renamed the Bridge Mill in 1907 by Peter Anderson. The large Auld corn mill was demolished in 1909. In that year the textile training school was expanded into a technical college, which became a Scottish Central Institution in 1922, irreverently known as the *'Woolly Tech'*!

**Silk, Stagnation, Takeovers and the Axe**: From 1932 silk weaving was introduced, and a Scottish Co-operative Wholesale Society creamery was built in 1935. The population stagnated with the woollen industry and was still around 12,500 in the 1950s. About 1960 the Academy moved into new buildings, a Technical College taking over its old ones. From 1964 the Scottish College of Textiles gained new buildings. Fine spinners included a branch of Munrospun of Restalrig, and Laidlaw & Fairgrieve, who were taken over in 1961 by Todd & Duncan of Kinross *(see also Selkirk)*. Galashiels was the main regional centre for the Borders and remained a busy place, but on the whole its facilities and tributary population were below the level expected of a Scottish regional centre. In 1969 the *'Waverley Route'* to Edinburgh and Carlisle was closed under Beeching's proposals, depriving both Galashiels and Hawick of their remaining rail service (the most remunerative stations in Scotland to be closed).

**Industrial Change and Tweedbank**: But then, against the odds, local matters began to improve, and several new industries were established. By 1970 Ballantyne Sportswear of Innerleithen was operating in the town. Industrial and commercial growth and the narrowness of the confining valley led in the early 1970s to the planned creation of a new settlement east of the town at Tweedbank. This was soon connected to Galashiels by a new bridge at the historic Abbot's Ford, and by 1977 a school had been built there – though in 1978 when Tweedbank contained 300 houses, no other basic facilities had been provided. By 1977 Galashiels was the headquarters of the Tweed River Purification Board. EMR Electrical, founded in an old textile mill by Stewart Gibson in 1970, employed 20 people in 1979, designing and making research devices for the Institute of Geological Sciences and US oil concerns. By 1979 Exacta Circuits of Selkirk had established a branch plant in Galashiels, and BEPI was making specialised printed circuits at Galabank Mill; by 1989 they employed 300 people. By 1981 a caravan site had been laid out at the top of the town. By 1987 an industrial estate and a new indoor bowling club had been erected at Tweedbank. A more marginal new firm was Sprague Electrical Engineering, which closed in 1987, as did the creamery.

**Textiles and a New *'Lang Toun'***: A large new supermarket was opened in 1987, and the town had various specialist shops. In 1988 the tweed industry was thriving and its suppliers Aimers MacLean made textile machinery. The Scottish College of Textiles – which had been further enlarged in 1973 and was already an exporter of talent worldwide – became in 1990 the Faculty of Textiles of Heriot-Watt University. The Galashiels Mill Museum contained the last of the town's working water turbines, and Peter Anderson's century-old mill was still weaving in 1992. By 1977 John Buchan Ltd operated the Waverley weaving mill; in 1994, as Lochcarron, it was still family-owned with 140 workers (and today is Scotland's biggest producer of tartan clothing). Nearby were Schofield Cloth Finishers. By then new housing estates had filled the gap between Galashiels, Tweedbank and Melrose, creating a *'Lang Toun'* beside Gala and Tweed some 9 km long but only 1 km wide.

**Software, Leather and Food Industries**: McQueen's of Nether Road were creating computer software by 1990; in 1993 they employed over 270 people, producing and fulfilling software packages throughout Europe. The regional LEC (Local Enterprise Company) *'Scottish Borders Enterprise'* established itself in the town in 1991. In 1993 Transatlantic Clothing, makers of leather clothing for the international and Far East market, moved from central London to a renovated building in Galashiels, and gained a Queen's Award for Export. Farne Salmon & Trout of Duns opened a branch factory nearby in 1993. By then this had the second lowest unemployment rate in Scotland, at 4.3%; by 1994 only 30% of the town's production jobs were in the volatile textile industries.

**Back on to the Rails?**: In 1994 a new company, Borders Transport Futures, was formed to try to recreate the rail link with Edinburgh. A recent arrival in the town is Strakan, a very ambitious medical research company run from Galashiels. Meantime the Douglas Bridge, completed in 1996, opened up another new area for development, and the town now has Tesco and Somerfield supermarkets. Galashiels Academy has over 950 pupils. Abbotsford is now owned by a trust and open in summer; the Torwoodlee golf course now has 18 holes. Hotels include the *Kingsknowes, Woodlands House, Abbotsford Arms, and King's.*

## GALSTON

**Map 1, C1**

***Small Ayrshire town,*** *pop. 5150* — OS 70: NS 5036

Galston stands at the meeting of the unusually named stream called Burn Anne with Ayrshire's River Irvine, and existed by 1307 when it was garrisoned by Robert Bruce. In the 15th century two castles were built nearby: Cessnock rose to the south and to the north the more important Loudoun Castle *(pronounced LOUD'on)*, once the home of the powerful hereditary sheriffs of Ayr. After being destroyed in 1527 it was soon rebuilt; Pont's map made about 1600 showed it standing within an extensive park. Two bridges existed across the burn near Galston Kirk, and the parish was known for woollen textiles, but there was no evidence of a village, and Galston never became a burgh of barony. A parish school was opened in 1627 and a grammar school was organised in 1639, but its classes were still held in a barn in 1671. An L-plan tower was built in 1660 at Sornhill, 3 km south of Galston, as a laird's mansion-house, and extended a century later.

**Market, Weaving, Shoes and Coal**: Dutch and Huguenots settled in the area in the 17th century, and moved from wool to flax and then to silk textiles; it appears that there was also a footwear industry, and a market was chartered in 1717. Roy's map showed that by the 1750s *'Gallstown'* was a small, squarish settlement with five radial roads; Loudoun Castle's policies were still very impressive. The Strath mill opened about 1770, making coarse papers, and about 1790 a local watermill dressed flax grown in the parish. Heron wrote in 1799 that *"the village of Galston contains near 600 inhabitants. Formerly the making of shoes was their chief object, now replaced by the weaving of lawns and gauze. There are near the village a valuable coal-work, and a rich vein of iron ore"*. The great pile of a new Loudoun Castle was built in 1804–11. By 1825 Galston was served by a penny post from Kilmarnock, and by that time cotton gowns were made. Chambers in 1827 noted that Galston was by then *"a town of considerable size and of very pleasant appearance"*. In 1832 the Marquis of Hastings was the laird of Loudoun Castle.

**Iron, Railway, Coal and Problems**: The Cessnock Ironworks, established in 1839, soon failed, but a branch railway, soon forming part of the Glasgow & South Western system, was opened from Kilmarnock to Galston in 1848, and extended to Newmilns in 1850. In 1862 Galston became a police burgh, and at some time acquired a gasworks. Cotton textiles were hit by the American civil war about 1865, and the local curtain trade – which made heavy chenilles – failed once they could be made more cheaply elsewhere on power looms. The Strath paper mill also closed in the late 19th century, but lace began to be made by machine in Galston in the 1870s as an outpost of Darvel and Newmilns. Galston had a population of 4300 in 1891; the village had an inn, a genuine secondary school, and was *"dependent principally on the coal trade"* (Murray, 1894) with three mines beside the river west of the town.

**Growth, Overcrowding and Decline**: A small spurt of growth in population caused the worst overcrowding in Ayrshire in 1901, with over a third of the families in single-apartment houses. In that year a large store was built by the local Co-operative Society. By then the varied local textile manufactures included blankets, hosiery, lace, and muslins produced using Jacquard cards on hand looms; bacon was cured and a creamery was in operation. The Loudoun golf club was formed in 1909, and in 1923 Galston FC joined the Scottish League, where they survived for just two seasons. Loudoun Castle was gutted by fire in 1941 and abandoned to ruin. By 1951 the population had grown to about 5600 and in 1958 Galston had a junior secondary school. But the last coal mine was disused by 1953, and the railway was closed by Beeching in 1964. In the 1970s Galston had William Sharp Ltd's small hosiery works, a small knitwear factory, and Grant Brothers were canning meat locally by 1979. About 40 mainly small shops provided little but daily needs; a fairly wide range of small basic services included a modern public library.

**Galston on Heat**: In 1981 Galston retained the facilities of a large village, plus the new Loudoun Academy; its population was down to 5154 in 1991. Grant Brothers remained a family firm, canning a range of speciality foods. At that time Norscot Engineering, a Norwegian subsidiary, was planning a small plant to manufacture unvented water heaters (newly legalised in Britain). KAD Detection Systems planned in 1993 to start manufacturing *'intelligent'* fire and gas systems. Sornhill, which had become a farmhouse, was vacated about 1985 and stood derelict in 1995, but the listed Co-op building was saved in 1997. Loudoun Castle Theme Park, opened in 1996, provided both white knuckle rides and what was claimed to be Britain's largest carousel. Loudoun Academy, now the largest school in East Ayrshire, has about 1100 pupils.

## GARDENSTOWN, Crovie, Gamrie & Troup

**Map 10, B1**

***Buchan villages,** pop. 800*

OS 29: NJ 8064

The Church of St John was founded as early as 1004 at the foot of 150m tall cliffs on the shore of the Moray Firth, 11km east of Banff. Its site was one of the few tiny sheltered sandy bays to be found on this rockbound shore, so giving rise to its name of *Gaineamhach* or Gamrie – pronounced *Gaym-ree* – deriving from the Gaelic for *'Sandy'*. A steep gully gave access to the plateau above. Troup, 4km to the east, was a chapel of Gamrie church as early as the 1190s. Gordon's mid 17th century mapwork showed Gamrie Kirk and *'Cruvie'* (Crovie) which lies between Gamrie and Troup.

**A Pioneer New Village**: In 1720 the laird, Alexander Garden of Troup House, selected a site on the extremely narrow raised beach at the foot of the steep cliffs between Crovie and Gamrie church to found a fishing village, which he named Gardenstown (pronounced *Gardenston). The Garden Arms Inn* was built in 1745. A small harbour consisting of two piers was constructed; a pier was also built at Crovie. When the Roy map was made about 1750, the piers and a regular line of buildings were sketched in, plus a hamlet round *'Gemry'* Kirk; but the area was entirely roadless. Although the Banff to Fraserburgh turnpike road was eventually built through the area, and according to Chambers by 1827 there was *"an excellent inn at Troup"*, the three settlements now known collectively as Gamrie did not get a post office until after 1838.

**Isolation Perpetuated**: Hugh Miller noted Gardenstown as a *"fishing village"*. A few years later, in the 1850s, Pratt found the ancient church a ruin, but Gardenstown was a *"village; at the Ironsides Inn we had comfortable accommodations and the harbour was crowded with boats"*. He also noted *"the little fishing village of Crovie"*. The area had no trains, nor was there a regular horse-drawn coach to a railhead, although by 1894 the population was about 1100. By the 1920s there were 250 fishermen and 48 boats. Access to the villages by large vehicles remained impossible due to steep hairpin bends; most of Crovie remained cradled in a 19th century timewarp, served only by a pathway. By 1951 over 1300 people lived in the area, with the facilities of a typical village including the *Garden Arms* inn, chemist, ironmonger and banks; but the population declined and the subsequent closure of the local secondary school reduced the local facilities to those of a small village.

**Sturdy Independence – and Holiday Homes**: However, although the larger Gamrie boats had to be based at more spacious ports such as Fraserburgh, the harbour was dredged in 1984; a dozen boats were based there and there was still a boatyard. In the 1980s the University of Virginia conducted a major survey of the Gamrie folk, who remained a sturdily independent fishing community of Plymouth Brethren – in a village with a parish Church of Scotland! Crovie, which was still an inshore fishing base, consisted largely of holiday homes. In 1991 Gardenstown had 810 residents. Gardenstown's public hall, post office, grocer, surgery, petrol station, and the primary school at nearby Bracoden are still open; many lobster pots adorn the quay and small pleasure boats use the harbour. There are recently built houses well above the village, and the 250-year-old *Garden Arms Hotel* is still on the go.

## GARELOCHHEAD

**Map 5, B4**

***Argyll village,** pop. 1300*

OS 56: NS 2491

North of the Firth of Clyde is the sheltered fiord of the Gare Loch, at whose head *'Kenlochgherr'* was noted by Pont about 1600. About 1750 as the Roy map showed, tracks from Balloch and Dumbarton joined to lead north over a 100m col to the ferry at Portincaple on Loch Long. These were later upgraded as roads, but the area was of little significance until the introduction of steamer cruising in the 1820s, when its beauty came to be appreciated. This had led by the 1890s to a pier, a post and telegraph office and an inn being provided at the small village at the head of the loch, its Gaelic name by then translated into English. From there a by-road already led to Rosneath; the Dumbarton to Arrochar road climbed steeply past the *Whistlefield Inn*, providing spectacular views. A similar route was followed by the West Highland Railway, which was opened in 1894 with high level stations above Garelochhead and at Whistlefield. A richer commuting element was soon added to the local population, and Garelochhead also became known as a resort and yachting centre.

**Defence and the Finnart Oil Terminal**: In the 1940s the military port of Faslane brought industry to the lochside. The population had risen to about 1100 by 1951, enjoying the facilities of a typical village, with two hotels. In 1951, nearly 15 years before North Sea oil, BP opened a deepwater terminal on a 25ha site at Finnart on Loch Long, 4km north of Garelochhead, to accept 100,000-ton tankers; from it a 90km crude-oil pipeline was laid to their new oil refinery at Grangemouth. Soon extended, by 1959 its six huge tanks held over 160 million litres of oil, but few permanent jobs were generated. The little-used Whistlefield station nearby was closed in 1964. Between 1985 and 1991 a 5km bypass of Garelochhead was built, linking Shandon with Whistlefield, whence a new road led to Coulport. To the east a new high-level military road was constructed, connecting to Loch Lomondside through the *'Major District Training Area'* of the Ministry of Defence in the hills east of Garelochhead, which was still active in 1994. By 1991 the population was 1298. The station and post office remained open.

## GARGUNNOCK

**Map 16, A1**

***Stirlingshire village,** pop. 725*

OS 57: NS 7094

An ancient broch stood on the slopes of the Gargunnock Hills 10km west of Stirling. In the 16th century the tower house of Old Leckie was built lower down the steep escarpment of the hills, and 2.5km to the east rose the L-plan tower of Gargunnock House, just above the flat floor of the Forth valley, locally called Blairdrummond Moss. This being one of the few areas apparently not mapped by the assiduous Pont, little is known until Gargunnock was chartered as a burgh of barony in 1677. By about 1754 it was a small settlement beside the straight thoroughfare named on Roy's map as the

*'Road from Dumbarton to Stirling'*. Heron noted it in 1799 as a *"village"* of about 400 inhabitants. The first industry seems to have been the tiny Glenfoyle distillery, built in 1826 by Chrystal & McNee; then in 1856 a station was provided on the cross-country Forth & Clyde Junction Railway. The distillery was enlarged in the early 1880s, but only to the modest annual capacity of about 135,000 litres of malt whisky. In 1895 Leckie House and its mill stood in a small park, there was an inn and also a tile works 1.5km east of Gargunnock House.

**Decline, Commuting and Antiques**: The tile works later vanished, and the distillery ceased production in 1923, becoming a warehouse; it finally closed about 1971. The station was closed to passengers in 1934 and in 1951 the population in and around the village was only 600. Gargunnock's facilities became little more than those of a hamlet, though by 1980 there was a sawmill beside the site of the station, and some quality housing had been built; the village population was 726 in 1991. The pub and post office were still open in 1993, by which time some more new housing had been added. Remarkably, although there was little for the tourist (save a waterfall on the Gargunnock Burn), by 1994 Mains Farm was the site of an antique furniture centre run by Ashworth & Christie, Auctioneers of Ladybank in Fife.

## GARLIESTON

**Map 1, C5**

***Galloway village,*** *pop. 500* — OS 83: NX 4746

About 7km north-east of Whithorn the Sorbie Burn enters Powtown Bay, the northern of a pair of sheltered coves which largely dry out at low tide. The area west of the broad expanse of Wigtown Bay was very thickly settled when Timothy Pont mapped it, perhaps as late as 1610; Powtown *('Pool Town')* and its mill already existed. A mansion built for the Earls of Galloway in 1740 was also named Powtown on Roy's map surveyed about 1754. This showed mills at the burn mouth beside a small settlement named *'Cashwhill'*, on whose site Lord Garlieston planned the small port of Garlieston. Building was begun in earnest in the 1780s on a geometric plan, and by 1786 a grain merchant was exporting barley for malting. Heron noted in 1799 *"the harbour and village of Garliestown, containing between four and five hundred inhabitants. It has a rope-walk, and employs ten coasting vessels"*.

**Industry, Post, Railways and Excursions**: Milling continued, sawmilling and boat building were carried on, and later for a time also chemical manufacture. Garlieston's first post office was opened about 1825; the harbour was rebuilt in 1838, and enlarged in 1855. The population in 1861 was 685. In 1875–77 the Wigtownshire Railway *(see Smith, 1969)* was extended from Wigtown to Whithorn via a junction at Millisle, 1km inland from Garlieston, where an engine shed was built; the 2km line to Garlieston harbour, opened in 1876, had regular passenger trains until 1903. Through running was permitted in 1907, enabling special trains to the harbour, connecting with steamer excursions to the Isle of Man. Both the *Queen's Arms* and *Galloway Arms* hotels were open in 1894, when Garlieston's population was still about 600.

**Motors kill the Railways**: The rail excursions ended about 1935, and the Whithorn railway passenger service ceased in 1950. By 1951 the population of Garlieston had risen to about 750. Despite much branch freight traffic, Beeching closed the harbour line in 1964, and the remainder in 1965. However the large mill was still in use in 1966, and by 1969 Galloway House had become a special school; under new owners Strathclyde Region it was closed about 1977, and has returned to private ownership. In the late 1970s Garlieston had a very active community council, and the quiet harbour was owned by a trust. By 1991 the resident population had fallen to under 500; Garlieston was a holiday boating and caravanning centre, with about four shops and its two long-established hotels. By 1995 the breakwater had succumbed to the weather, but fishing vessels still use the harbour, and a hotel and the post office remain open.

## GARLOGIE

**Map 10, B3**

***Aberdeenshire small village,*** *pop. 200* — OS 38: NJ 7805

16km west of Aberdeen is a low-lying area around the Loch of Skene, from which flows the Leuchar Burn; south of the burn is an ancient stone circle. By the late 16th century *'Caerlogy'* on the Dunecht Estate was a small settlement beside the burn, shown on Pont's map. However the area was still roadless when mapped by Roy about 1750. Roads had evidently been built by 1830, and in the 1830s Hadden & Green of Aberdeen established large 3-storey woollen mills *(well illustrated by Hay & Stell)* with a main floor area of over 1660m$^2$. The mills made carpets and tweeds, were lit by gas and powered by shafting driven by a waterwheel on the burn, and by a beam engine possibly made in Glasgow. In 1869 the firm's 1400 workforce was split between Don Mills and Garlogie, creating the Milton of Garlogie. By 1894 some ribbon development had occurred along the main road to the east at Roadside of Garlogie, and a primary school was built. The historic engine worked until the mills closed in 1904, and was preserved in situ beside the Dunecht estate hydro-electric power station, built for Viscount

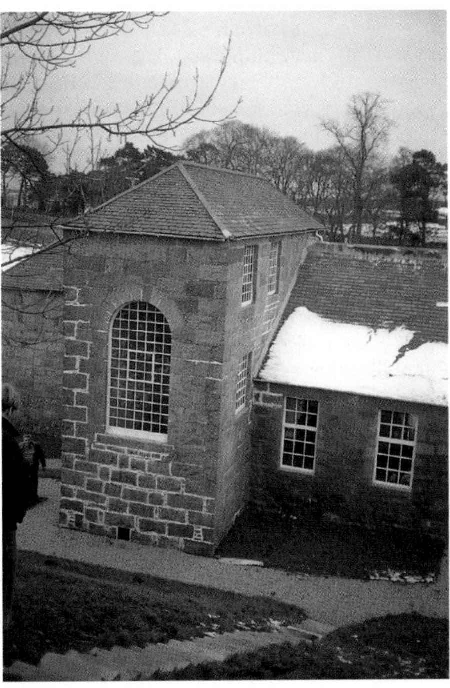

*Garlogie woollen mill, built in the 1830s by Hadden & Green of Aberdeen to use the water of the Leuchar Burn; carpets and tweeds were made. The beam-engine shed (pictured here) houses a significant engine, and is now open to the public.* (JRH)

Cowdray when the mills were demolished soon after 1910. By 1969 a pub was open, but the local focus of interest moved to Westhill, and the school was closed around 1970, leaving some 200 people in the Garlogie area. The beam engine and power station are open under the Aberdeenshire museum service.

## GARMOUTH, Kingston & Spey Bay — Map 10, A1

***Moray coastal villages,*** *pop. 1200* — OS 28: NJ 3464

A stone circle stood east of the mouth of the River Spey; Garmouth, to the west of the river's mouth, was established by the Innes family as a timber export port and fishing harbour, becoming a burgh of barony in 1587. In 1650 Garmouth was the landing point where Charles II made a first controversial return from exile. In 1655 Tucker noted for the Parliamentarians that only one boat was based in this *"small place"*, which exported salmon and imported mainly French salt. The Roy map surveyed about 1750 showed much the same substantial village form that existed two centuries later. The area was then roadless, though a ford was marked to *'Carsiemuir'*, the present Bogmoor near Upper Dallachy.

**The Kingston Shipyard**: In 1769 Garmouth still exported timber, floated down the Spey by raftsmen using coracles. This trade inspired the development of the shipyard which was set up by Yorkshire shipwrights in 1784 on an empty coastal site 1 km to the north, naming it Kingston after their home town (K. upon Hull). By 1788 it had houses for the workers, and two sawmills to cut up the timber floated down-river from the partnership's Glenmore estate. Heron wrote in 1799 of *"the village of Garmouth or Speymouth. There are here saw-mills, and docks for shipbuilding. The vessels are built of the fir from the woods of Glenmore. From this place immense quantities of salmon are sent to London"*. By 1815 one of Scotland's first circular saws had been installed at the yard, while the port was for a time significant for coal imports. In 1827 Chambers mentioned *"the town and harbour of Garmouth"*, but around that time changes in the course of the river left the harbour filled with shingle. The very large *Tugnet* icehouse was built in 1830 near Nether Dallachy on the opposite bank of the river; part of a salmon fishery station, it eventually became a fishery museum.

**Clipper Ships, Railway and Golf**: Garmouth's first post office was established in 1837. The yard turned to building clipper ships for the tea trade until the takeover by steel-hulled vessels later in the century. In 1886 the Great North of Scotland Railway opened a coastal line across a 290 m-long lattice girder viaduct, with a bowstring girder main span of nearly 107 m, built by Blaikie Brothers of Aberdeen; stations were placed on both sides of the constantly shifting river channel. Until 1918 the east bank crossing station was called *'Fochabers'*, though it lay 5 km from that place; it was then renamed Spey Bay. The 26-roomed *Gordon Richmond Hotel* and its privately operated 18-hole golf course were opened on the windy links in 1907. The Garmouth & Kingston club was founded in 1932, with another 18-hole course beside the river, producing between them a modestly favoured golfing resort.

**Spey Bay takes to the Air**: In the second world war a small airfield was opened between Upper and Nether Dallachy, but was soon abandoned after 1945; eventually it became the base of the Highland Gliding Club. By 1951 about 1250 people lived in the two settlements, served by the facilities of a small village. In 1968 the railway was closed completely. Following a serious fire about that time, the hotel was rebuilt with only 8 rooms as the *Spey Bay Hotel*. The total population had declined to 1000 by 1971, then stabilising. By 1985 holiday homes, caravan and camping sites were open at Spey Bay. In 1991 Garmouth (with Kingston) had 696 residents, and Spey Bay under 500. Minimal recent change has affected this minor – and economical – resort at the north end of the Speyside Way long distance path, now partly enveloped in Forestry Commission plantations. The Tugnet fishing station is now a wildlife centre emphasising the Moray Firth dolphins. Both the 18-hole golf courses and the hotel remain open, but the only direct ground connection between Garmouth and Spey Bay is on foot across the disused railway viaduct.

## GARRABOST, Bayble & Port nan Guiran — Map 11, C2

***Isle of Lewis townships,*** *pop. 875* — OS 8: NB 5132

The Eye Peninsula, about 10 km by 3 km, lies east of Stornoway; the 14th century St Columba's Church stands on the narrow isthmus. Crofting dominated, until a brickworks using local clay was opened at Garrabost in the 19th century, but it had closed by 1897. Tiumpan Head lighthouse on the tip of the peninsula was first lighted in 1900. By the 1950s the Eye's population of about 2500 was divided between half a dozen crofting townships, with as many post offices and three primary schools. The most central, Garrabost, was adjoined by the 190-pupil Bayble junior secondary school (still open today as a primary). There was a pier at Bayble, and Port nan Guiran was a small but active fishing port; by 1980 Garrabost had a guest house and the telephone exchange. The lighthouse was automated in 1987. In 1991 the combined population of Garrabost and Bayble was 832.

## GARTCOSH — Map 15, E4

***N. Lanarkshire village,*** *pop. 800* — OS 64: NS 6968

Gartcosh, on the Monklands plateau some 10 km east of Glasgow, appeared as *'Gartcaish'* on Pont's map of 1596. In Gaelic *Gart* means *'corn'*, and apart from its five small lochs this farming area was left largely featureless on Roy's map of about 1754. By the 19th century roads had been laid out. Gartcosh was served by the east–west Garnkirk & Glasgow Railway from 1831; by 1842 four daily trains linked it with Glasgow, Airdrie and Coatbridge. In 1848 Gartcosh became the junction where the Caledonian Railway's Glasgow to Stirling trains diverged north-eastwards from the Coatbridge line. By 1895 Smith & McLean had a small sheet-steel rolling-mill beside the station. The Mount Ellen golf club was founded in 1905. Meantime in 1896 the very large Gartloch Asylum had been opened beside Bishop Loch some 1.5 km to the west; enlarged in 1939, it was renamed as a mental hospital. By 1981 it had 811 beds and included geriatric patients. Half its beds were closed in 1991, and complete closure by 1995 left a *'building at risk'*, its centenary in 1996 just a wake.

**Steelworks, Strip Mill and Inaccessible Motorway**: By 1951 the population of Gartcosh had tripled in the half century to some 2400, with the expansion of the small steelworks. This was rebuilt by Colvilles between 1959 and 1962 as a cold reduction continuous strip mill using hot-rolled strip from Ravenscraig, expecting demands from the motor industry – which was required by the government of the day to place its new assembly plants in development areas – and from consumer-goods manufacturers such as Hoover of Cambuslang. A related primary substation was established to the south; five transmission lines converged there. The railway station was closed about 1960, and the junction lost importance with the closure of Glasgow's Buchanan Street station in 1966. The M73 motorway was built through the area in 1971, though no access was provided. It cut under the railway between the steelworks and Gartcosh village, which had by then been largely cleared and its population reduced to only about 1000, falling further by 1981.

**Gartcosh without the Steel Industry**: The Scottish motor industry failed *(see Linwood and Bathgate)*, so the Gartcosh mill was closed by British Steel (BSC) in 1986, putting Ravenscraig's future at grave risk. Part of the site was bought by the SDA (Scottish Development Agency) to build a road-to-rail terminal for the Channel Tunnel, but in 1991 a site at Mossend was chosen. Meantime John G Russell Transport of Gartcosh, Scotland's largest independent road hauliers – and keen users of rail for trunk hauls where possible since at least 1982 – kept their HQ at Gartcosh but also had a big depot at Deanside. In 1986 they installed container handling equipment, for *'dolofines'* (for Ravenscraig) and for coal.

**Problems with Paper Recycling and PowerGen**: In 1989 the strip mill site was agreed as the location of a large mill for North British Newsprint, producing some 200,000 tonnes a year, 11% of the total UK requirement; Stirling Recycling (SR), its owners, also planned a waste paper recycling plant nearby. But a slump in world demand caused their backers, Mirror Group newspapers and the Canadian newsprint giant Abitibi-Price, to withdraw in 1991; then 818 people lived in Gartcosh. SR shelved their plans, but despite extremely low prices for waste paper in 1993 due to German dumping, they still employed 30 people in the old BSC buildings to sort and bale it for export to Italy and Turkey. In 1994 Stirling Fibre again considered a 240-job recycling plant. As paper prices rose in 1995, so they expanded their intake of paper collected by local authorities, and were still busy in the Gartcosh Works in 2000. Meantime in 1996 English electricity generators PowerGen proposed a large gas-fired power station on the newly cleared strip mill site; seen as a threat to the Scottish coal-fired power stations and related pits (both deep and opencast), this was subject to a public inquiry in 1997. Should it go ahead, Norwegian company Pivco wanted part of the site for a factory to produce electric cars, bringing up to 525 jobs. In 1999 a new railway station was planned.

*Gartcosh. A small steelworks was replaced in 1959–62 by the continuous strip mill, using material from Ravenscraig. Intended for car bodies and white goods, it closed in 1986. (RCAHMS / JRH)*

## GARTMORE

**Map 5, B4**

***Small Stirlingshire village,*** *pop. 350* — OS 57: NS 5297

In Gaelic *Gart* means *'corn'*. The 16th century Z-plan tower of Gartartan Castle, which until 1975 was in Perthshire, stands between the River Forth and the Kelty Water, 3km south of Aberfoyle. Nearby Gartmore is a planned village, unusual for having a steep drop from end to end of its main street. It was associated with Gartmore House, the 18th century mansion of the Grahams: both were shown on the mid 18th century Roy map, when there were no roads, and a ford across the Forth connected with Aberfoyle. By about 1825 a penny post joined Gartmore with Kippen, 13km to the south-east, and by mid century a road system was complete, with a bridge to Aberfoyle. In 1882 the new Strathendrick & Aberfoyle Railway provided a station near the castle; a post office adjoined. By 1895 the village had another post office and an inn; a great park embraced both castle and mansion, then the home of R B Cunninghame Graham, radical politician and travel writer. Later it was bought by the Cayzer family, owners of the Clan Line.

**From Park to National Park – but Too Many Trees?**: In 1951 Gartmore had a primary school, inn and post office for a population of about 340. Passenger trains were withdrawn in 1951, followed by freight in 1959, and the track was lifted. St Ninians, a Catholic *'List D'* school, was open at Gartmore from 1960 to 1982, leaving allegations of abuse of the children to surface many years later. By 1993 the park had vanished, but two caravan sites and forest walks catered for tourists enjoying the vast new Loch Ard Forest to the west, and by 1999 Gartmore House was a conference centre. In 2000 the planting of 200ha of trees on what Stirling Council described as *"one of the most spectacular landscapes in the Loch Lomond & Trossachs National Park"* (so designated in 2001), was controversially approved by the Forestry Commission; however the same body rejected a Danish proposal to plant the last remaining open land near the village with Xmas trees.

## GARTOCHARN

**Map 5, B5**

***Dunbartonshire village,*** *pop. 700* — OS 56: NS 4286

In Gaelic *Gart* means *'corn'*, and Gartocharn – which was the main centre of Kilmaronock parish – indeed stands on rolling farmland south of Loch Lomond. When Roy mapped Lennox about 1754 it lay on a track between Balloch and Drymen, which was later made up as a turnpike road and eventually became the A811. From 1855 Caldarvan station on the cross-country Forth & Clyde Junction Railway, in a farming area some 3km to the south, gave an infrequent train service – until 1934. Meantime by 1895 there was an inn and a post and telegraph office at Gartocharn. By 1951 a telephone exchange and garage had been added, these basic facilities serving a farming population of about 450, though the nearest primary schools were at Balloch and Croftamie. By 1981 Gartocharn had the facilities of a small village, including a modern school and the 5-roomed hotel. By 1991, the Gartocharn area had 713 residents, many regarded as wealthy incomers. In 1997 a new village centre was planned.

## GARVALD & Morham — Map 3, B2

***E. Lothian hamlets,** pop. 200* — OS 67: NT 5870

An ancient fort stands above the Panana Water in the foothills of the Lammermuir Hills of East Lothian; all the burns in the vicinity are deeply incised. Some 3km to the north was a medieval convent, and 4km west of that the parish kirk and site of the medieval village of Morham. Garvald – which lies between the convent and the fort – derived its name from *Garbh Allt* (*'rough stream'* in Gaelic); its church dates from the 12th century, and in the 14th a *'hospital'* was founded at Bara, 3km to the south-west. A hundred years later Haddington nunnery built the keep of Nunraw, 1km east of Garvald, above the valley of the Thorter Burn. Nunraw was added to in the 16th century, becoming an impressive fortified mansion, shown emparked on Pont's map of about 1600. At Stonypath 500m east of Garvald was another early tower, which eventually fell into ruin.

**Roads but no Rails**: By the time of the Roy survey about 1754 there was a road from Gifford to the small village of *'Garval'*, and a *'Muir Road'* to Lauder; there was no marked connection to Dunbar. In 1825 there was a brewer and vintner at Garvald. By 1901 a school had been built at remote Kingside, near an ancient fort on the headwaters of the Whiteadder Water, a tributary of the River Tweed, 10km south-east of Garvald by a moorland road. Garvald itself was still a tiny place, though it had an inn and post and telegraph office among the facilities typical of a small village. The North British Railway's ambitious scheme for a Gifford & Garvald Light Railway reached only from Ormiston to Gifford.

**From Nuns to Monks, and Schools to Water**: In 1946 Nunraw Castle was taken over by a community of Cistercian monks from Roscrea in Ireland. A spacious new abbey was erected nearby in 1952–69, and the old building became a retreat house. By 1971 the Whiteadder Reservoir had covered the site of Kingside school. By 2000 the water treatment works at Castle Moffat 2km south-east of Garvald supplied 85,000 people in East Lothian. However, the local population had been shrinking steadily, from about 450 in 1951 to under 250 by 1981, and by 1976 the Garvald primary school had closed too; the post office has closed since 1995, but the *Garvald Hotel* remains open.

## GARVE — Map 9, A3

***Small Ross-shire village,** pop. 250 (area)* — OS 20: NH 3961

The Abhainn Killen or Black Water of Strathgarve flows south from the remote Strathvaich Forest through extremely rough (Gaelic *garbh*) country west of Ben Wyvis into what was once known as Loch Killen, and thence to join the River Conon near Contin, south of Strathpeffer. Pont's map made around 1600 showed the area well wooded but lacking in settlement, while the Roy map surveyed about 1750 showed no roads or tracks at all in the area around Loch Killen; later this came to be known as Loch Garve.

**Roads and Tracks**: In 1792–97 the British Fisheries Society built a road through Strathvaich with government aid, to link Ullapool with the east coast road system at Contin. About then the track through the western part of Strath Bran to Kinlochewe was extended past the head of Loch Luichart to the croft of Gorstan, 3km north of the west end of Loch Garve. Around 1800 Lady Seaforth's carriage was ruined by the state of the track past Loch Achanalt. Soon afterwards, in the years 1807–19, the *'Lochcarron Road'* to Achnasheen and Strome Ferry was very slowly built for the Commissioners of Highland Roads & Bridges. The labour force was housed in tents and huts at Garve, between Loch Garve and Gorstan. Postal services developed, and Garve post office was issued with a cancelling stamp in 1829. Strathgarve also acquired a primary school, and in the late 19th century a timber trestle bridge was built across the Black Water to serve Strathgarve Lodge.

**Garve on the Railway**: In 1870 the Dingwall & Skye Railway, a subsidiary of the Highland, opened a single line through Strath Bran with a crossing station at Garve and a wayside station at Lochluichart. In 1890 Garve might have become a railway junction, but the approved line to Ullapool – which would have provided the most direct route to Stornoway – was found to be too costly to build. By 1894 the *"good" Garve Hotel* was open near the station, and another hostelry called the *Hazel Brae*, which eventually vanished. By 1951 30 rooms were available in the two hotels, though the resident population was only 150.

**Power from the Rivers**: As part of the 1945–55 Fannich–Orrin scheme built by the North of Scotland Hydro-Electric Board, a tunnel from the artificial Loch Vaich 15km north of Garve feeds water into the artificial Loch Glascarnoch to the north-west, itself retained by a dam 30m tall across the river of that name, just above the long-established 22-roomed *Aultguish Inn* on the Ullapool road. From this point the 7.35km Glascarnoch tunnel feeds the Glascarnoch or Mossford power station on the north shore of Loch Luichart, with two 12,000kw machines and a head of 152m. Loch Fannich to the west was raised by a long dam 10m tall. From there a 6.5km tunnel feeds the almost identical Grudie Bridge power station at the head of Loch Luichart, with a head of 157m. By 1954 nearly 3km of the railway near the re-sited Lochluichart station had been raised to enable the level of Loch Luichart in turn to be raised by 12m, by the 20m tall Luichart Dam. From this a head of 50m of water passes through a short tunnel to the very similar Luichart power station at the Falls of Conon. In all the water from 1000 square kilometres, impounded by eight dams, is fed through nine tunnels into six power stations with a total capacity of 107,000kw. Despite all this development the completed power stations were remotely supervised, and the population of the Garve area shrank steadily.

**Still the Tourists Come**: However much the scenery might have been changed, more energetic tourists still found the area attractive: *Inchbae Lodge* some 10km to the north became a 13-roomed hotel in 1967, and by 1972 a country house hotel with another 20 or so rooms had been created east of the school, at *Strathgarve Lodge*. For some years around 1969 a mountain rescue post was located at Garve, which was also chosen as the centre for a group medical practice serving a wide area, yet in 1981 under 100 people lived locally. However, by then the

*Garve Hotel* had been enlarged to 33 rooms. For a time around 1985 there were caravan and camping sites at both Garve and Lochluichart, though these did not last. The Ullapool road had been heavily reconstructed by 1997, passing through forests which had been open moorland half a century earlier. The traditional lever frame (for point and signal operation) from Garve station is on display at the National Railway Museum in York, and can still be handled. Garve provides a hotel, station, shopping, schooling and a post office; Lochluichart still has a post office and station.

## GARVELLACHS (Isles of the Sea) — Map 4, C3

***Islands, Inner Hebrides*** — OS 55: NM 6611

In 1549 Dean Monro aptly described a small isle in the Firth of Lorne as a *'rocky knob'*. Nowadays called Garbh Eileach *(in Gaelic the 'Rough Islet')*, it lies some 10km north of Jura, of which parish it formed a part, and is 110m high and only 2km long. It was the site of one of the least favoured of all the Columban religious settlements. The adjoining islet of Dun Chonnuill took its name from its ancient *"round castle"*. Their collective history left little mark; Historic Scotland cares for the ruinous beehive huts of stone and a burial ground which remain on the Garvellachs, plus some remains of the undated castle.

## GATEHOUSE OF FLEET — Map 2, A5

***Galloway village,*** *pop. 900* — OS 83: NX 6056

Near the coast of hilly central Galloway is a vitrified hill fort bearing Pictish symbols; across the River Fleet on its east side was the most south-westerly known Roman fortlet in Scotland, created in the first century AD. Four km to the south is the ruined pre-Reformation church of Girthon. The Pictish fort later became known as *Trusty's Hill*; the name of the nearby church of Anwoth may derive from a Gaelic-Norse hybrid meaning *'the ford'*. Three medieval mottes in the area initiated three permanent strongholds: the original house of Cally was built 2km north of Girthon by the Murrays, the great tower of Cardoness Castle was erected by the McCullochs in the 15th century on a knoll beside the Fleet estuary, 1km from Anwoth church; and about 1494 Rusko Castle was constructed 5km to the north.

**The *'Gait'* to Ulster and its *'Gait-House'***: The plantation of Ulster in 1608–10 was furthered by improvement of the *'gait'* or hill track between Dumfries and Creetown via the Corse of Slakes as a military road linking Carlisle with Portpatrick. It crossed the Water of Fleet by a wooden bridge. The local improving lairds, the Murrays of Cally, whose home was already surrounded by a large park, erected a stone-built inn known as the *Gait-house* (i.e. Roadhouse) of Fleet; once *'gaits'* became known as roads its name became corrupted to Gatehouse. All these names were shown on Blaeu's atlas map of mid-Galloway (attributed to Timothy Pont c.1610). Without mentioning Gatehouse, William Lithgow observed in 1632 that he *"found in the road-way inns of Galloway good cheer, hospitality and serviceable attendance"*.

**Post, Tryst, Stone Bridge and new Cally House**: It was probably the Murrays who enabled the opening in 1642 (very likely in the inn) of an early post office on the new Carlisle–Ireland postal route: this was to remain for many years a highly unusual facility in such a remote location. By 1700 a cattle tryst was being held nearby. In 1721 the timber bridge was destroyed by a flood, and in 1729–30 the present Fleet Bridge was built in stone on a new site. Roy's survey of the 1750s showed the bridge, but at that time the main road crossed Glenquicken Moor to the west and Irelandton Moor to the east. Tracks led to Kirkcudbright and up the Fleet valley, but though there was scattered development around Anwoth, only one building of substance stood east of the river, the *'Gatehouse'*. About 1760 James Murray of Cally extended the old inn, renaming it the *Murray Arms*, and in 1763 Robert Mylne built for him a palatial residence, the new Cally House, a little south of the old one, which fell into ruin. Eventually in 1773 a post office was opened at Anwoth.

**New Village and Industrial Centre**: In 1765 Murray laid out a regularly and ambitiously planned village of three streets, to be known as Gatehouse of Fleet. In 1768 building began on a tannery supplied by bark mills. This was followed in 1784 by a water-powered brewery; it eventually failed. Kirkcudbright having spurned the cotton industry it had been offered, four water-powered cotton mills were instead constructed at Gatehouse, of which the first was started by Birtwhistle in 1785 and another in 1791, plus a soapworks and a brass foundry. The water was brought from Loch Whinyeon by a lade 5km long. A late burgh of barony charter was granted to James Murray in 1795. In 1797 Gatehouse had three postal services a week, and an annual fair was scheduled.

**Cotton and Boatbuilding**: By 1799 the four cotton-mills – which at their peak made over a million metres of cloth annually – employed over 500 hands from the total population of over 1100, and a branch of the Paisley Union Bank was open in what Heron called this *"rising village. Besides the parish school, there is an academy near the village, endowed by Mr Murray of Broughton. The weekly cattle-markets, held here in the beginning of winter, are of considerable advantage to the place. Small sloops come up the river, within a short distance of the town"* – to a wharf at Port McAdam on the canalised river. He also mentioned the *"Fine villas"* on the north side of Fleet Bay near the ruined Cardoness Castle. In 1817 Girthon church was abandoned for a new parish church near the Murray Arms. A yard building wooden boats operated at Anwoth Boatgreen during the first half of the 19th century; the *Anwoth Hotel* was originally the *Ship Inn*. Chambers who visited in 1826 noted *"the large modern village of Gatehouse"* and observed of Skyreburn, 3km to the west, that it was a *"little village, or rather mill-town, thoroughly old-fashioned"*.

**Industrial Decline and Remote Railway**: In this isolated location the various industries in Gatehouse had mostly failed by the mid 19th century, and were not replaced; the bank soon closed (eventually becoming the *Bank of Fleet Hotel*). After a fire in 1830 power looms were installed in the one remaining cotton mill – Birtwhistle's – but this too closed about 1857, becoming a bobbin mill. Tanning had also ceased by 1865. Gatehouse having lost its early importance, the Portpatrick Railway which was opened in 1865 passed far to the north. The nearest station, 10km away, was named Gatehouse of Fleet; not far to the east were two major granite viaducts across the Little and Big Waters of Fleet. The former was 109m in length and had 9 arches, the latter a problematical structure 274m long comprising 20 arches up to 21m tall, originally stone but later reinforced in brick. In 1894 just two scheduled horse-drawn coaches a day struggled up the winding hill road to meet the infrequent trains. Gatehouse had a population of about 1225 in 1891, though it was called a *"town"* by Murray, and in 1894 had two hotels, the *Murray Arms* and the *Commercial.*

**Golfing and Caravanning**: The golf club founded in 1922 laid out a 9-hole moorland course. By 1931 Gatehouse had a population of only 900, and the bobbin mill closed in 1938. By the 1950s Gatehouse had become a charming tourist village, a golfing and angling resort with a youth hostel and camping and caravan site. By then Cally House was the luxurious *Cally Hotel* (later immodestly renamed the *Cally Palace)*. Skyreburn primary school closed in the late 1950s when its local population fell below 250. The remote railway, which had for a century given tourists a spectacular ride, was sadly closed in 1965 by Beeching. By 1984 the youth hostel had been transferred to Minnigaff; however, the various hotels which already depended on car-borne tourism were being enlarged and going upmarket.

**Modern Gatehouse for the Tourist**: In 1981 Gatehouse had the facilities of a typical village; but its school's secondary department closed about 1982. A bypass was built in the late 1980s, relieving Gatehouse of through traffic, and in 1991, when the village had 919 residents, the former bobbin mill was restored by the Regional Council as a tourist centre, the *'Mill on the Fleet'*. The former brewery is now flats, and Cardoness Castle is open to the public. By 1996 the *Cream o' Galloway* Dairy at Rainton, 5 km south of Gatehouse, made fine dairy ice cream and was a tourist attraction. A caravan site and extensive facilities had been created beside Fleet Bay at Sandgreen, 2 km west of Rainton, and a visitor centre had been provided in the beautiful wilds of Dromore, north of the site of the long-vanished station. The *Cally Palace* now has 56 rooms and an 18-hole golf course; there is also the smaller *Murray Arms.*

## GAVINTON — Map 3, B3

***Berwickshire small village,*** *pop. 300* — OS 67 or 74: NT 7652

An ancient hill fort stands above the Langton Burn 4 km west of Duns. The Roy map made in the 1750s showed Langton astride a track linking Duns with Polwarth; it had an old castle and a parish church. In 1827 Chambers noted, *"Mr Gavin, the parvenu lord of the manor, has erected a neat and regular village named Gavinton to replace the old hamlet called Langton, the appendage of the castle of that name now entirely swept away"*. Gavin apparently also built the first Langton House; two mills turned nearby. In 1862 a new and ornate Langton House was built by David Bryce for the Marquis of Breadalbane; by about 1890 it stood in a large park, and Gavinton had a post office. In 1901 the parish population was 400. Langton House later fell on evil days and was demolished about 1950, to be replaced by a sawmill. In 1951 this was an agricultural parish, served by a primary school – soon closed, due to the population falling to only 278 in 1971. However, the post office survived and, with recovery to 310 residents by 1991, it is still open.

## GIFFORD & Yester — Map 3, B2

***E. Lothian village & hamlet,*** *pop. 700* — OS 66: NT 5368

Chesters, an ancient fort 5 km south of Haddington in East Lothian, was later part of Bolton parish, which has remained rural. Yester Castle, built in 1267 by Hugh Gifford, stands beside the Gifford Water 5 km to the south-east; its dungeon became known as *'Goblin Ha'*. A collegiate church known as Bothans was founded nearby in 1421. The protestant reformer John Knox was born at Yester about 1514. After the Reformation in which Knox played a leading role, and when Yester Castle was the seat of Lord Hay, Bothans became the parish church, and in 1606 gained a parish school. Yester was given great emphasis on Pont's map of around 1600, which showed a village as well as the emparked castle; the nearest mill shown was well downstream, at Colston near Haddington.

**Paper Mill, Gifford Village & Long Yester**: In 1694–95 the White Paper Company, based at Morningside (Edinburgh), also built a paper mill on the Gifford Water at Yester. Removal of the village from the vicinity of the castle began in 1708, to a new settlement 2 km nearer Haddington; it was provided with a new church in 1710, and given the family name of Gifford. The Adam mansion of Yester House was built in 1745–53 near the former collegiate church (between the new village and the old castle, which fell into ruin). The Roy map surveyed about 1754 showed most development at *'Long Yester'* on the east–west road 3 km south of the new Gifford Kirk; by then the area was well provided with a network of roads similar to the modern system. A bleachfield established in 1754 was still going in the 1830s; Gifford also gained a waulk mill. However, the paper mill was closed in the 1770s, being converted to a lint mill in 1781. Newton Hall, 3 km south-west of Gifford, was built in the late 18th century.

**From Yester to Princeton**: Gifford had two annual fairs in 1797, and was regarded as a *"pleasant village"* by Chambers in 1827. There was then no inn on the road to Duns beyond Danskine, which was east of the castle and *"of very old standing"*; he added that grain used to be brought from the Merse to Haddington market on horseback in single sacks. By about 1825 Gifford was served by a penny post from Haddington. The textile industry faded later in the century. However, John Witherspoon from Yester helped to draft the US Constitution and became the first president of Princeton College, which soon became one of America's premier universities. In 1894 Gifford was to Murray *"a picturesque village with an old market cross"*, a mill, an inn and a post and telegraph office; Long Yester had another mill and the parish school.

*A field of wheat near Gifford – a successful grain-growing area for centuries on account of its dry climate and light soils.*
*(SMPC / Niall Benvie)*

**Rustic Railway and Peripatetic Pottery**: In 1901 Gifford Mill became the terminus of a short-lived light railway from Ormiston, which closed to passengers in 1933 and to goods in 1948; a bungalow aptly called *Buffers* was built on the station site! However, the Gifford golf club founded in 1904 survived, and its 9-hole course prospered. By 1963 the mills too had vanished, and Long Yester school was closed soon afterwards. Newton Hall was demolished in 1966. Attractive Gifford was still served by the facilities of a typical small village, by 1972 including the daringly named *Goblin Ha' Hotel*. By 1991 Gifford's population was 688; new housing had arrived by 1996. The listed St Bothan's Chapel at Yester House was saved for posterity about 1997. A quarry which was opened 2 km south-west of Longyester around 1970 has worked intermittently, now producing aggregates. The local Chippendale company provides training in furniture restoration. Both the original golf course and a more recent one by the castle have 9 holes. Yester primary school, Gifford post office and the *Goblin Ha' Hotel* are still open.

## GIGHA, Isle of — Map 4, C5

***Small island, w. of Kintyre**, pop. 150* — OS 62: NR 6549

By the 13th century there was a church on the 9 km long Isle of Gigha (pronounced *Geea)* which lies about 4 km off the west coast of Kintyre. Despite a massacre in 1530, Pont's original map of about 1600 showed *'Gega'* well-settled. Martin, writing in 1703, noted Kilchattan church and an inn, serving a Protestant but still primarily Gaelic-speaking community. Cows, horses and sheep were bred and oats and barley grown, but there was *"no wood of any kind"* on the long, narrow island, which was owned by MacAlister of Lergy. By 1800 some 550 people lived there, and in the 19th century a regular ferry plied from Tayinloan to Gigha's tiny centre at Ardminish. This place made little mark, but was called a *"village"* in 1894, when about 400 people lived on Gigha, which was also served by steamers on the Tarbert to Port Ellen route.

**Achamore Gardens**: Sir James Horlick, who became the laird in 1944, lived in the mansion of Achamore House, where he established fine gardens with flowering shrubs amid sheltering trees. By 1951 the island had a population of only about 190, with the facilities of a small village. The steamers operated to Gigha on alternate days until at least 1969, both these and the passenger ferry then being replaced by a small car ferry. Ardminish remained the centre of activity in the dairying island, which had acquired a small cheese creamery by 1974; about then the inn was rebuilt and enlarged to 9 rooms. Around 1989 the transient owner, entrepreneur Malcolm Potier, enlarged the inn in the hope of holding conferences, and built a 730-metre airstrip. The 9-hole Isle of Gigha golf course was also laid out. By then the island's recently built fish farm, one of Scotland's largest, was producing 600 tonnes of fish a year. In 1991 the fish farm employed only nine people, the same number as there were pupils in the primary school, from a residential population down to 143; local secondary pupils were weekly boarders at Campbeltown. The island's versatile postman cum public figure bore the remarkable name of Seamus McSporran! Potier became bankrupt and was dispossessed early in 1992, leading to a hiatus in island affairs, resolved when Gigha was bought by Derek Holt *(see Inverkip)*.

## GILMERTON — Map 15, D2

***S-E. suburb of Edinburgh** Pop. 19,000* — OS 66: NT 2968

Gilmerton stands on rising ground 6 km south-east of Edinburgh. It may lie near the course of a first century Roman road connecting the upper Clyde Valley with Inveresk. Gilmerton was already a farming settlement dependent on Liberton 300 years before *'Long Gilmerton'* was named on Pont's map of Lothian of around 1600. This also showed the Edinburgh to Dalkeith road passing nearby. Just to the east was Lord Somerville's 17th century mansionhouse. This was added to in 1726–34 in the form of a classical mansion designed by William Adam and graced by fine interiors; it was later renamed The Drum.

**Mining Coal, Sand and Limestone – by Ladder**: Limestone was quarried in the Ferniehill area, and a unique underground smithy was created around 1720, followed by the sinking of a colliery in 1739. The seams being almost vertical, they were worked by ladders, up which women carried coal to the surface! Large limekilns were built at Burdiehouse; they are still prominent. By 1755 Roy's map showed that Gilmerton was a medium-sized village on a T-plan, with four radial roads. In 1787 a friendly society was founded to benefit local workpeople, and Heron wrote in 1799 *"the village of Gilmerton contains upwards of 750 inhabitants, chiefly employed in furnishing the city with coals, lime and a fine yellow sand"*. Gilmerton did not acquire status as a parish until 1838.

**Railway and new Facilities**: A branch of the North British Railway from Millerhill to Glencorse was opened in 1874, with a station at Gilmerton providing a roundabout passenger service to Edinburgh. In the same year 1874 a school was opened to serve the village, followed in 1878–88 by convalescent homes for working people. The mansion of Craigend Park was built near the road to Edinburgh in 1876–79; yet another mansion was Moredun. By 1894 Gilmerton had a post and telegraph office and an inn. At that time a coal pit was open 2 km to the south-west, near Burdiehouse, and apparently also the Brosie pit near the station. A bowling club was established in 1895, and two substantial new schools in 1903 and 1914, one of them a specialised *'industrial school'*. Gilmerton was included in Edinburgh City from 1920, but the city's tramways never reached it, and in 1933 the railway station was closed. The Moredun Research Institute, the Animal Diseases Research Laboratory for Scotland, was opened in 1926, and in 1929 the Murray Home was built for disabled veterans. The village also boasted a football ground.

**Suburban Growth – and Subsidence**: After 1945 extensive Edinburgh housing developments took place north and west of the village. Moredun was expanded in 1961, but by 1970 the Brosie coal pit beside the former station was disused. In 1981 when over 18,000 people lived in the area, Gilmerton's general facilities were only those of a village. In 1989 the remains of the old pit still marred the landscape, although it was soon cleared; British Coal closed its long-established Scottish area HQ at Green Park on Gilmerton Road. Craigend Park was used in the 1980s as the Kingston Clinic; it then became derelict, but its grounds were developed around 1990, and the house was restored in 1994. In 1993 Moredun Animal Health Ltd was an offshoot of the Moredun Research Institute. More new housing had been built by 1996 but Drum still stood in its park, accompanied in 2000 by a riding centre adjoining the steadily shrinking Green Belt. In 2000, subsidence compelled the demolition of 30 bungalows built in the 1960s over the old Ferniehill quarry workings, and 54 more homes were similarly threatened in 2001.

## GIRVAN

**Map 1, B3**

***S. Ayrshire coast town,*** *pop. 7450* OS 76: NX 1898

In the 16th century the tower of Ardmillan Castle was built on the Carrick coast, 4km south of the mouth of the Water of Girvan. Shalloch Mill just north of Ardmillan Castle was already turning when Timothy Pont mapped the developing area around 1600. North of Girvan Kirk the river had been bridged, and on its north bank were three water mills: the Bridgemill, and two upstream at Enoch. In 1636 Brereton found no *"good accommodation"* between Ayr and Stranraer, so if Girvan had an inn it did not suit. This route was soon followed by the Irish Mails, and a post office was opened at Girvan in 1642. However, Tucker's excise report made for the Commonwealth in 1655 still lumped Girvan together with other places having *"some five or six fisher boats, and not many more houses"*. Girvan became a burgh of barony in 1668, and at one time a form of Serpentine marble may have been quarried there; in the 1750s a salt pan was set up at Shalloch. The Roy map of about 1754 showed the bridge and a small one-street settlement with four radial roads, but no evident harbour works.

**Irish Weavers, Bootmaking and Herrings**: In 1799 Heron reported that *"the town of Girvan contains upwards of a thousand inhabitants. There are here some manufactures; particularly tanning, making shoes and boots, and a little in the weaving of cotton cloth"*. Girvan soon became well known for its hand loom weaving, with 500 muslin and other weavers by 1810. Chambers in 1827 found Girvan *"a large parvenu village"* based on home weaving for Glasgow manufacturers. *"Of the population, two thirds are of Irish extraction"*. By the 1840s as many as 2000 weavers were at work; the harbour was improved about 1847 in the interests of the herring fishery.

**The Railway and Harbour Works**: In 1860 the Maybole & Girvan Railway reached a terminal station in the town, bringing Glasgow folk and enabling its sandy beach to develop as a holiday resort. A short branch from the station led to the harbour, where a lifeboat station was opened in 1865 (rebuilt in 1869); more harbour works were carried out in 1881. Girvan's newspaper, the *Carrick Gazette*, was first published in 1870. In 1872 a new company started to build the winding and steeply graded Girvan & Portpatrick Junction Railway. This required a second station, and to the south a tunnel and two large viaducts in the valley of the treacherous River Stinchar. The line opened through to Dunragit for Stranraer in 1877; its years of building and early operation were full of problems *(see Smith, 1969)*.

**Hotels and Tourism**: Eventually in 1892 the Glasgow & South Western Railway (G&SWR) took over, and largely rebuilt the lightly-laid line for its through services between Glasgow and Stranraer. The *Kings Arms Hotel* was open by 1874 and *"good"* to Murray in 1894; the *Ailsa Hotel* was also open. The town became a police burgh in 1889, and at some time a gasworks was built. By 1894 when Girvan was described by Murray as a *"dull but neat town"* there was a secondary school, and some of the people worked in mines, as the placename *Coalpots* to the south-east suggests. Girvan's municipal golf course was laid out in 1900, and in 1904 another local newspaper, the *Carrick Herald*, was established, in what was by then a popular resort.

**Wasted Railway and Wartime Roles**: In 1906 the G&SWR opened a coastal railway from Ayr to Girvan via Turnberry; it never paid its way. In 1913, 16 steam locomotives were based at Girvan. Army officer David Henderson, born locally in 1862, learned to fly about the age of 50, and was one of three authors of the report which led to the formation of the Royal Flying Corps in 1912. He became Director General of Military Aeronautics, later headed the League of Red Cross Societies in Geneva, and was buried at Girvan. In the 1920s the South Ayrshire Collieries Ltd who owned pits around Dailly built an estate of good houses in Maxwell Street. Despite heavy railway traffic to and from Cairnryan *(q.v.)* in the 1939–45 war, the engine shed was closed in 1941. About then a major rail-connected munitions works was built 2 km to the north-east. Soon after the war Alexander Noble & Sons founded a boatyard to serve the Firth of Clyde fishing industry. By the 1950s Girvan was *"a well-known resort"* with 6200 residents, and the main centre of the Carrick area, with Girvan High School. By 1953 no passenger trains ran on the Turnberry line, which had gone by 1963.

**Whisky Galore – and Seaweed Processing**: In 1963 William Grant & Sons of Glasgow took over the redundant 26ha munitions works, immediately building the huge Girvan grain whisky distillery, able to produce 70 million litres of spirit a year. On the same site they added the Ladyburn Lowland Malt distillery in 1966, and by 1980 their whisky blending plant. Alginate Industries also opened a plant north of the town in the 1960s, processing 20 tonnes of seaweed (from Benbecula) to make one tonne of alginate for food products such as ice cream, and in 1978 expanded both there and at Barcaldine in Argyll. The town lost its role in local government to Ayr in 1975, an inconveniently remote 33km away. In spite of some decline in shopping and other facilities since the 1950s, its day-trip/resort role continued, with a dozen small hotels. About 1983 a coal mine employing around 75 men was opened at Girvan to supply the Roche vitamin C plant at Dalry.

**A Glitch in Girvan**: In 1987 Girvan was still also a small but busy fishing port, with Nobles' slipway for repairing fishing vessels, a coachbuilder, and an SDA industrial estate with a number of new small industries; however, the shopping centre had many vacant premises. In 1990 Grant's set up a management team in Girvan to cover all their Scottish locations; the firm also owned the leading pure malt, Glenfiddich. However, by then lowland malts were out of fashion, and the Ladyburn distillery was no longer in production in 1991. The population in 1991 was 7450. By 1992 Chilton Brothers were textile manufacturers.

**Chocolate, Caravans – and Virgin Vodka**: In 1994 Nestlé's chocolate crumb factory at Girvan drew most of its milk requirements from south of Scotland dairy farms. In 1994 William Grant agreed to distil Richard Branson's Virgin Vodka at their Girvan plant. A new yachting pontoon was available in 1995, the year that Kelco was bought by US giant Monsanto. Despite growing world demand (especially from textile printers who took 50% of world alginate output), in 1996 competition forced Kelco to concentrate development at Girvan (and San Diego). By 1996 Girvan Academy had 635 pupils, and the town had grown southwards with a new estate;

there were caravan sites both in the town and 3 km to the south near Ardmillan Castle. Girvan is still popular with holiday-makers; the *Westcliffe Hotel* plus smaller hotels and guest houses offer service.

## GLAMIS

**Map 6, B2**

***Small Angus village,*** *pop. 200* — OS 54: NO 3846

Denoon is an ancient fortress of great strength, perched on a knoll in a valley on the north-west flanks of the Sidlaw Hills of Angus. Glamis Castle, 4 km to the north-east, stands near the Dean Water in a remarkably level area, near the centre of fertile Strathmore. It apparently originated in a thanage, though according to Chambers the castle was *"anciently a royal residence"*, later owned by Macbeth. By the early 11th century a castle was certainly in existence, for Malcolm II is supposed to have been assassinated there in 1034, six years before the more renowned murder of his grandson Duncan at Cawdor. The name Glamis also appeared on the Gough map of about 1230. The church stood 1 km to the south of the castle, which became the seat of the Lyon family, Earls of Strathmore, in 1372; and so it has remained.

**Glamis as a Burgh**: Glamis was chartered as a burgh of barony in 1491, and a regular cattle market was soon held. In 1560 Glamis Castle was the seat of Lord Glamis, its great size sketched by Timothy Pont about 1600. To the north stood a windmill, and to the west the Dean Water had already been bridged long enough for the hamlet of Bridgend to develop. Beside the kirk was a bridge across the burn, and Glamis village, then apparently including 2-storey houses. Strathmore was already extensively developed with fermtouns and mills, including a mill north of Brigton of Kinnettles, 3 km to the east, of which more anon. The castle was extended by the architecturally inclined second earl soon after 1615, and again extended and remodelled before 1700. By the mid 18th century, when Roy mapped the area, a mansionhouse stood at Kinnettles adjoining the road from Forfar, which was made up in 1750. Glamis was only a hamlet of 17th century cottages where the road forked to either Eassie or by the *'upper road'* to Newtyle. The castle stood in extensively planted policies; late in the century houses were removed from its immediate vicinity by the Earl of Strathmore to enable landscaping.

**Machine Spinning creates Douglastown**: Lead was mined in the vicinity of Glamis for a short period from 1771. In 1778 James Ivory, a Dundee Academy teacher, used the old corn mill at Brigton, Kinnettles for successful experiments in spinning coarse linen yarns by machinery. In 1789–90, with assistance from the Board of Trustees, James Ivory & Co set up a large 5-storey flax spinning mill close by to produce yarn for osnaburg manufacture, and built the village of Douglastown, named after the laird. Jericho beside Douglastown was built to house hand-loom weavers. Two fairs were to be held at Glamis in 1797, and a post office was opened in 1802. In 1806 another mill was built beside the Glamis Burn to spin flax and tow into the yarn that was to be woven locally into osnaburgs and sheetings. The large Glamis mill had 600 spindles in 1822 when owned by William Baxter & Son, who then set up in Dundee *(q.v.)*, becoming an enormous concern. In 1822 the Douglastown mill, then owned by one James Watt, had 420 spindles.

**Show House and Horsedrawn Trains**: Chambers observed in 1827 that *"Glamis Castle, one of the principal show-houses in Scotland, is situated near the delightful little village"*. In 1820–30 steam engines were added to both mills, but the Brigton one failed about 1835; about 66 people were employed in the Glamis mill. The terminus of the horse-drawn Newtyle & Glamis Railway opened in 1837, but this was over 2 km north of the village, and the incorporation of this primitive and poorly maintained line into the main line to the north a decade later did not stimulate development. About then a dam was built in the Den of Glamis, and a 12 m diameter water wheel was installed at the Glamis mill, which spun yarn until about 1860, but was then dismantled. Alex Warden wrote in 1864 *"since the stoppage of the spinning-mill, the village has never been its former self"*; Brigton mill was also then derelict.

**Glamis and the Queen Mother**: Little further development was to occur for a century, though Glamis Castle came into the public eye in the 1920s when its youthful Lady Elizabeth Bowes Lyon married the future King George VI; though as Queen Mother half a century later she chose to buy the more secluded Castle of Mey. Buses abstracted the rail passengers, so the station and line disappeared in the 1950s, leaving a small village of some 300 people. By 1969 Glamis had been bypassed, but the National Trust for Scotland's fine Angus Folk museum was open; the Royally connected castle is also a notable tourist attraction. The tiny *Castleton House Hotel* serves the village.

## GLASGOW

**Map 15, C5**

***City (central area)*** — OS 64: NS 5965

Suburbs: *Anniesland, Baillieston, Bearsden, Bishopbriggs, Bridgeton, Busby, Cardonald, Castlemilk, Cathcart, Crookston, Drumchapel, Easterhouse, Gorbals, Govan, Maryhill, Millerston, Milngavie, Newton Mearns, Partick, Pollokshaws, Port Dundas, Possil, Queen's Park, Riddrie, Robroyston, Rutherglen, Shettleston, Springburn, Thornliebank, Tollcross, Whiteinch & Yoker*

A relatively straight and level line of Roman road followed the north bank of the River Clyde, from the North Calder Water to the end of the Antonine Wall at Old Kilpatrick. The ancient High Street of Glasgow, whose name means *green hollow* in Cumbric, paralleled the Molendinar *(Millers')* Burn to meet the Roman road, now called Argyle Street. The 12th century Bishop Jocelyn claimed that Glasgow's monastic church was founded on the hill in 543 AD by Saint Mungo or Kentigern, who became its first bishop in 560; but this fascinating tale *(see Traprain)* lacks contemporary backing.

**Diocese, King David and Cathedral**: There is then a long gap in local history, and the see may have lapsed for a time; but by 1114 Glasgow was a farming village straggling down beside the Molendinar from the monastic church to its confluence with the Clyde; it had by implication a water mill (the later town mill was north of the cathedral). Village maybe, but Glasgow's bishops already had an extensive sphere of influence which covered all of Cumbria. On their account Glasgow's church was elevated about the year 1114 to temporary cathedral status by the pious young King David of Strathclyde, then perhaps based in Partick, who was later to become a most energetic king of Scotland. A rather smaller but still extensive diocese was defined a few years later; in 1274 it included the Archdeaconry of Teviotdale, embracing

Dumfries. In 1123 the erection of the first phase of Glasgow's first permanent stone cathedral was begun over Mungo's grave on the eastwards sloping site of the Celtic monastery; the churches of St John and of the Holy Sepulchre existed by 1134 when the church of St James was dedicated, and the new cathedral was consecrated in 1136.

**Fair, Markets and Trades in the Bishop's Burgh**: The Clyde was then a shallow river, up which significant trading vessels could not usually venture, so Glasgow's external trade long remained unimportant relative to its more ancient rival Dumbarton. However, Glasgow fair was an 8-day event by about 1150. Between 1174 and 1178 William the Lion granted to the Bishop of Glasgow the right to erect an Episcopal Burgh (26th in order of burgh charter, so far as extant records can reveal), with the first recorded grant of a weekly market known in Scotland, plus confirmation of the annual fair, and all the rights and liberties of a royal burgh. By the 1220s the burgesses were definitely in business; among the earliest trades in Glasgow were fishermen, millers, bakers, cobblers, painters, and blacksmiths, while substantial timber merchant houses began to replace peasant huts.

**The Rebuilt Cathedral indebted to Florence**: The cathedral was badly damaged by fire in 1190, but its repair was sufficiently advanced for re-consecration in 1197 by Bishop Jocelyn, who by then also possessed a castle. In 1233 the diocesan authorities were still engaged in reconstructing the Cathedral, but by 1240 were deeply in debt to a banker from as far afield as Firenze (Florence), for around that year a fine 2-storey eastern extension was being added under Bishop Bondington, a low-level church over the grave of Kentigern being surmounted by the choir; the work was completed in 1258. Meantime by 1246 the Dominicans (Blackfriars) were building their own church; their priory precinct was walled.

**Bridge, Mines, Trades and Churches**: By 1286 Glasgow Bridge spanned the Clyde in timber. By 1293 the townspeople had another church, St Mary's; St Enoch's was recorded two years later, and by then a second water mill turned, on the Poldrait Burn beside the Gallowgate. In 1301 the conquering English king Edward I made a supposedly pious visit to Kentigern's tomb, but more significantly ordered the townspeople to fabricate a giant timber belfry or siege tower and to supply 30 waggons to carry the pieces so that his army could besiege Bothwell Castle, plus tools, iron, and coal – perhaps raised from nearby pits. Glasgow also developed a trade in cured salmon and herring from around that time. By 1320 St Thomas's church was also in existence, and in the 1320s the Dean was a Florentine – no doubt keeping an eye on debt repayments! Goldsmiths plied their trade and coins were minted, more especially in the 14th century. Enough finance must have been raised to complete the west end of the cathedral about 1330–50, about when Bishop Rae had the wooden bridge replaced by five stone spans, at the south end of modern Stockwell Street.

**University City**: For nearly a century during the aftermath of the Black Death of 1350, documentary evidence becomes rare – with one very intriguing exception. In 1415, according to Hume Brown, the English military spy John Hardyng described Glasgow as a *"goodly city and university in plentiful country, with corn and cattle in abundance"*, yet the University is generally stated to have been founded in 1450 or 1451 by Bishop Turnbull, a graduate of St Andrews, and established by Papal Bull beside the Blackfriars monastery. In 1453 the University was given a grant of privileges by John Stewart who was the first Provost of Glasgow, which had become a burgh of regality in 1450 – though it remained under the bishop, for whom a palace was built about 1438. By 1460 there was also a grammar school. William Elphinstone, born in Glasgow in 1431, obtained the Papal Bull for Aberdeen University in 1494, and introduced printing to Scotland in 1507.

*Provand's Lordship, the oldest house in Glasgow. The oldest parts date back to 1471, when it was constructed by Bishop Andrew Muirhead as part of a hospital. Extended and altered in the 17th/18th centuries, it is now a museum.* (JRH)

**Walled City and Archbishopric**: By 1460 fulling was carried on, and town walls were first mentioned about that time. St Nicholas Hospital was new in 1464, and their clergy house was built in 1471; its later name Provand's Lordship derives from its later use as the manse of Barlanark, a prebendary of the Cathedral; this survives as Glasgow's oldest house. St Ninian's Hospital was established in 1475, a Franciscan friary was founded in 1476, and by 1478 other stone houses were in existence, the material being quarried either at the Necropolis site or where Queen Street Station now stands. Glasgow became more important in contemporary terms in 1492 with the elevation of its see to become Scotland's second pre-reformation archbishopric (after St Andrews); the bishop's palace was therefore extended around 1510. In 1504 the plague again visited the city, leaving Glasgow only 11th among the Scottish burghs in terms of tax revenue. By 1520 the archdiocese had taken in the former diocese of Argyll, and in 1525 James Houston founded the very late Collegiate Tron Church. A fine extension to the college, begun in 1460, was far from finished when the University became more active from 1518, and actually took until 1660 to complete!

**Craft Guilds and Post-Reformation Revival**: The city's various craft guilds were incorporated between 1516 and 1559; Glasgow's hitherto negligible contribution to burgh taxes rose quickly, and in the period 1535–56 it paid between 1.5% and 3% of the Scottish total. By that period tanning was practised on the Molendinar Burn. During a depression around the siege of the castle in 1544 the city's population was said to have fallen as low as 3000, but had recovered to about 4500 by 1556, the year when the Tennent family took up commercial brewing at Wellpark. In 1560 the burgh was represented in Parliament, though the College of Glasgow had only one appropriated church at the time of the Reformation. Afterwards Andrew Melville rejuvenated the University from 1570, while Glasgow Grammar School was also re-founded in the 16th century. The Cathedral was fortunate to escape demolition in 1579, and by 1593 Glasgow was the centre of a presbytery of the new self-governing Church.

**Golf, Crafts and Exports**: The town council rebuilt its mill about 1576, Glasgow bakers owned a mill at Partick *(q.v.)* from 1578, and by 1608 four mills were at work on the Molendinar Burn. Golf was being played on Glasgow Green by 1589. In 1594 Glasgow reached fifth place among Scottish exporting burghs, with 4.5% of the export customs; by 1600 it had some 5000 people and was growing rapidly. By 1604 its 361 craftsmen worked in fourteen trades (including two surgeons), and there were 213 merchants recorded. In 1605 the *'Trades House'* and *'Merchant House'* were recognised as the bodies which would provide the members of the undemocratic town council.

**Royal Burgh and Benevolence**: Glasgow finally became a Royal Burgh in 1611, at last reflecting its growing importance; its population by then was some 7600. The Clyde in its natural state only gave access up to Glasgow bridge for tiny vessels of under 30 tons, but by 1621 Glasgow was paying between 3% and 10% of Scottish Customs duties. The first quay at the Broomielaw was constructed about 1625 and, with the ability to import grain in worthwhile quantities, Glasgow breweries soon became significant. The Tolbooth was erected in 1626, and by 1639 Glasgow was the third richest burgh in Scotland, but only a fifth as rich as Edinburgh. About 1640 there were two bridges across the Molendinar to the mills, and recognisable roads existed to Paisley and Kirkintilloch. The traveller Brereton who visited Glasgow in 1636 revealed a *"city"* – Glasgow still had an archbishop, though not a Catholic one – said to be of about 20,000 population (probably a gross overestimate), with 120 university students. Hutcheson's Hospital was founded in 1639 under the will of lawyer George Hutcheson; his younger brother Thomas endowed Hutcheson's Grammar School for orphan boys in the same way on his death in 1641 – buildings being erected in the Trongate in 1641–50. The fine neo-classical St Andrew's Church off Saltmarket, designed by Alan Dreghorn, was also begun before the civil war but could not be completed until after the Restoration.

**Fourth Centre under the Commonwealth**: In 1630 George Anderson established a printing business. He moved to Edinburgh about the year 1661 as the King's Printer, but the business continued under Saunders as Glasgow's sole printers until 1715. Meantime by 1649 Glasgow had displaced Perth as Scotland's fourth trading centre, paying 6.5% of its customs duties (Edinburgh through its port of Leith then paid 36%). Tucker in 1655 gave a very full account: *"a very neat burgh town, one of the most considerablest burghs of Scotland in structure and trade"*. Most inhabitants were *"traders and dealers: some for Ireland with small smiddy coals, in open boats, from four to ten tonnes; from whence they bring hoops, ronges, barrel staves, meal, oats, and butter; some to France with pladding, coals and herring for which they return salt, paper, rosin, and prunes; some to Norway for timber; and everyone with their neighbours the Highlanders, who come hither from the isles and western parts with pladding, dry hides, goat, kid and deerskins in return for commodities and provisions"*. The river was silting up again, and all trade in vessels above six tons involved ferrying goods to and from Newark (on the site of the later Port Glasgow), but the city headed the customs area from the Firth of Clyde to Irvine and Bute inclusive, and its traders owned twelve vessels of up to 150 tons, probably operating out of Greenock *(q.v.)*.

**Restoration Glasgow – Miles Better!**: In 1650 the town council set up a woollen cloth factory, though it did not really prosper. However, a great fire in 1652 which destroyed a third of the city led James Colquhoun of Edinburgh to supply an early fire engine for use by the city council; rebuilding was rapid, for Richard Franck in 1656 found Glasgow: *"a flourishing city, the nonsuch of Scotland"* and noted its *"strong stone wall"*. The city's population in 1660 was said to be nearing 15,000, although known facts suggest a rather smaller place, but it is hard to believe that the post office which opened in 1662 could have been the city's first. The old Merchants' House in Bridgegate was grandly rebuilt in 1659–65, containing a Guild Hall; its steeple still stands. A coal pit was reported in the Gorbals in 1660, and the next year de Rocheford wrote that *"in the environs of Glasgow are several pits, from whence they dig very good coal"*. He hailed Glasgow as *"the second town in Scotland; the streets are large and handsome, as if belonging to a new town; but the houses are only of wood, ornamented with carving"*. There were *"several rich shopkeepers"*, the *"hospital of the merchants"* and a twice-weekly market.

**Early Industry fails to blight the Orchards**: A *"good"* meat market existed by 1662, a *'soaperie'* was established in 1667, and in 1669 the Easter Sugar Work was founded, among Scotland's few substantial industrial operations of the day. In 1669 James Broom waxed lyrical about Glasgow, *"very eminent for its trade and merchandise; the city renowned for pleasantness of sight, sweetness of air, and delightfulness of its gardens and orchards, surpasses all other places in this tract"*.

**Port Expansion down-river makes the Second City**: Trade was still severely hampered by the shallowness of the river at the Broomielaw, until in 1668 the city fathers took the bold step of founding a new outport at Port Glasgow, nearly 30km downstream. This enabled the city's foreign trade to develop, and by 1670 it had displaced both Aberdeen and Dundee to become Scotland's second trading city, paying 12% of the customs. Another major fire occurred in 1677, after which there were few wooden buildings left in the city. In 1678 the first irregular stage coaches ran to Edinburgh, and in 1683 James Armour established a serge factory. By 1680 the population was said to be approaching 12,000, and there were in the burgh some 450 traders, of whom about 100 traded overseas. The Broomielaw Quay was reconstructed in 1688, following early attempts at dredging, and Scotland's first cordage works was started in 1690.

**The Finest Town in Scotland**: In 1689 Thomas Morer wrote of *"a place of great extent and good situation; and has the reputation of the finest town in Scotland, not excepting Edinburgh"*. The main streets were *"well paved and bounded with stately buildings, especially about the centre, where they are mostly new"*. Re-chartered as a Royal Burgh in 1690, Glasgow had one of the earliest Bank of Scotland branches, opened briefly in 1696. In 1702 the University had about 400 students. The 1707 Act of Union stimulated Clyde commerce, but by 1712 Glasgow owners possessed only 4% of the Scottish fleet, just 46 vessels; most of the recent increases had been farther down the river. Two careful estimates suggest a population of

13,000 about 1710 and as many as 15,000 a decade later, when over 200 shops were open; however, much of the city was liable to occasional flooding. Though woollen manufacture had failed, cotton printing appears to have begun by 1719. By 1720 a bark mill for a tannery was in operation and within a few years a sawmill had been set up on the Molendinar, only to close after a major dispute.

**New World Trade speeds Industry**: The first Glasgow vessel to sail to the New World is said to have left in 1718, yet in the 1720s Defoe wrote *"Glasgow is a city of business; they send near fifty sail of ships every year to Virginia, New England, and other English colonies in America, and are every year increasing"*. He noticed *"one or two very handsome sugar-baking houses, and a large distillery"*; this was using molasses to make *'Glasgow Brandy'*. Other manufactures included red and yellow *'pladding'*, fine striped muslins, and large quantities of linen for export to the plantations. Defoe urged the construction of a Forth & Clyde canal to speed the exports of Stirling serge, Musselburgh *'stuffs'*, Aberdeen stockings and Edinburgh shalloons and blankets.

**Newspapers and Textiles**: Meantime Glasgow's first newspaper, the *Courant*, had been established in 1715. Its presses worked for a few years, to be succeeded in 1729 by the *Glasgow Journal*. In 1740–41 the Foulis Brothers, Robert and Andrew, began high class printing; in 1743 they became printers to the University. John Smith from Strathblane set up his Glasgow bookshop in 1751, a firm which still exists. The linen trade noted by Defoe led by 1726 to some 2000 looms making linen cloth in the city, and by 1730 the Glasgow Linen Society had organised the merchants in the yarn market, effectively controlling hand spinning throughout the west of Scotland. Another cotton printing works was established in 1738, by which time Gray's Green was a well-established 20 ha bleachfield which trained bleachers from elsewhere. By 1740, when about 685,000 m of linen were stamped at Glasgow, a company was lapping and pressing linen cloth for the London market. About then the framework knitting of stockings was introduced to the city, perhaps from Edinburgh.

**The New Weaving Village of Anderston**: Anderston, a contraction of *'Andersontown'*, was built as a new village in 1721–35 by James Anderson some 1.5 km west of Glasgow Cross, outside the burgh boundary and hence free from its duties. The Anderston Weavers' Society was founded in 1738, and it is claimed that the new village had a significant effect in pulling the city westwards. An ironworking company was established in 1732 and from 1734 the Meikles were innovative millwrights. Glasgow shipowners possessed 67 ships by 1735. The first history of the city, by John McUre, was published in 1736, and in 1737–60 a new Town Hall was built west of the Tolbooth.

**Tobacco Trade aids Industrial Growth**: By 1741 the tobacco trade was well established, in retrospect an unfortunate outcome of the intercourse with the English colonies noted above; but in the absence of banks the income aided Glasgow's development very greatly. In 1741 three tobacco merchants set up a large weaving factory with 70 looms at Shuttlefield; with increasing production to monitor, the Trustees appointed a local yarn inspector about 1745. Drink and tobacco went together; Tennents opened a new brewery at their long established Wellpark site in 1745, based on a fine well 300 metres deep – it was a large industry by 1769.

**Pottery, Sugar and Linen**: Delft pottery was manufactured at the Broomielaw from 1748. (This was not the first pottery made in Scotland since Roman days, as claimed by Bremner, for there were medieval potteries in Perth.) By 1750 there were five sugar refineries in the city, processing unrefined cane sugar from the West Indies. The Bishop Street spinning mill was built in 1750, and a bleachfield was opened in 1753. The West Port was demolished in 1751; the burgeoning tobacco trade led to the name of Virginia Street, which was laid out in 1753. Although the British Linen Company's warehouse in the city lasted only from 1749 to 1755, Glasgow's linen stamping office checked over 2.2 million metres of cloth in 1757; at that time linens were also distributed through Glasgow fair. The redoubtable David Dale from Stewarton opened a draper's business in 1763; it prospered and stimulated his entrepreneurial flair.

**Turnpikes, Inns, Coaching and Dredging**: From 1749 two regular stage coaches ran to Edinburgh each week, but only during the summer months, due to poor roads. In 1753 an Act of Parliament provided for turnpiking of the main roads radiating from Glasgow; 40 years had passed since the Edinburgh (Midlothian) Act! In 1755 the city's population was carefully estimated by Webster to be about 23,500. The Roy map of that time showed the city as a very substantial but still quite compact X-shaped settlement, with Glasgow Cross at the centre of an extensive road system; at the bridgehead was a tiny settlement, the Gorbals. By then the former Archbishop's Palace had become a prison; part was demolished in 1755 and the stone used to build the city's first hotel, the *Saracen Head Inn* in Gallowgate, which opened the same year and soon became the coach terminus. The second hotel, the *Black Bull*, was erected in Argyle Street by the Highland Society in 1758–60. From 1763 regular stage coaches ran between Glasgow and Greenock, but the journey took all day. The first Act for deepening the river was obtained in 1759 by the town council on the recommendation of John Golborne, a Chester engineer whose own city's port had acute silting problems. The Clyde was confined by training walls or jetties from 1768–70, and a combination of tidal scour and dredging steadily deepened the river; by 1781 vessels of over 30 tons could at last reach the Broomielaw quay.

**The Triumph of the Technician James Watt**: Robert Foulis opened the Academy of Arts in 1754, though this survived for only 21 years. The Glasgow University medical school was started in the mid 18th century, and by 1760 there were 13 professors in the whole institution. But academics had failed to equal the mind of a University technician, James Watt of Greenock, who stumbled on the most significant idea of the century while he was walking across Glasgow Green in 1764: five years later he patented the separate condenser for the steam engine. But his partnership with Boulton meant that he hung on to his patents and also resisted the use of high pressure steam, so that very much of the coal raised was wasted for over 30 years, and technical progress was generally slow until the early 1800s.

**Markets, Carpets and Police**: By 1760 the city possessed four malt mills, Anderston brewery was built in 1763, and by 1764 the Broomielaw pottery had a bottle kiln for firing stoneware. Yet in 1764 Glasgow, which already had a population of about 28,000, was remarkably described as *"one of the most beautiful small towns in Europe"*. In 1769 Pennant commented on the existence in the city of the Exchange, with separate markets for meal, greens, fish and meat. The manufacture of nails had begun and an informal police force had been set up. He noted the traditional 400 university students, firms of booksellers and also printers, for up to 1778 Glasgow was the Scottish typefounding centre; but the leading role in this activity then moved to Edinburgh. By 1776 carpets were made in a single factory, said to be the only woollen industry in Glasgow.

**Bridges, Canals and Balloons**: In 1765 the closure to goods vehicles of the ancient and tottering Glasgow Bridge for reconstruction led to a new bridge being built at Rutherglen, completed in 1776 *(see Bridgeton)*. The new Glasgow Bridge at Jamaica Street was completed in 1772. The reconstruction and widening of the old Glasgow Bridge, completed in 1779, was repeated by Telford about 1820. Pavements were first laid in 1777 in Trongate and Argyle Street. Hamiltonhill *(see Possil)*, 2 km north of Glasgow, was connected with Grangemouth by the Forth & Clyde Canal (F&CC) in 1777, and the next year the separate Monkland Canal was opened from the Coatbridge area to Barlinnie, 3 km east of the Townhead. This brought more plentiful and cheaper coal to the vicinity. In 1785 bookseller John Knox reported that in 1782–83 the F&CC had saved the city from famine by enabling grain to be brought in from England, Germany and even Danzig. The fastest journey so far made from Glasgow took place in 1785 when the wind carried the Italian balloonist Vincenzo Lunardi to Hawick in only 150 minutes.

**The Apogee of Tobacco, and Famous Sons**: Finnieston, immediately west of Anderston, was founded as a village in 1768. In 1773 an Adam building replaced all of the Tron Church save its steeple. By then the city had shot to prominence through its growing sugar imports and the rum and tobacco trades: in 1771 54% of Britain's known tobacco imports nominally passed through Glasgow, amounting to 38% of all recorded Scottish imports! By the time that the trade peaked in 1775 (when Glasgow imported 63% of Britain's tobacco), Glaswegians owned 386 vessels, a six-fold growth in 40 years. However the trade (largely actually carried on at Port Glasgow and Greenock) was checked in 1776 by the American Declaration of Independence, and in 1799 Heron noted that the *"considerable trade in tobacco and rum of late has been on the decline"*. Meantime General Sir John Moore, who was to reform the British Army, was born in Glasgow in 1761, while Robert Stevenson, born in the city in 1772, became a famous civil engineer and designer of lighthouses.

**Glasgow becomes a Banking Centre**: The first Glasgow banks were set up in 1749 (the *Ship Bank*, which eventually became part of the Bank of Scotland) and in 1750 (the *Arms Bank*). From then on, many of the projects started in Glasgow and the West of Scotland were helped to raise capital by local bankers. The Thistle Bank opened its doors in 1761, and the long-lasting banking firm of J & R Watson started about 1763. The Merchant Banking Company of Glasgow traded from 1769 to its failure in 1798 (their Merchants' House in Bridgegate was demolished in 1817, its site used for a tenement and later for part of the fish market!). Meantime Thomsons were formed as bankers in 1785; none of these early banking firms had any branches until the Glasgow Bank, established in 1809, very soon opened a branch in Kirkcaldy – but this was its only venture outside the city.

*The Trades House, Glassford Street, built in 1791–94 to designs by Robert Adam, and re-fronted in 1927 by John Keppie. It was constructed as a meeting house for the incorporated trades of Glasgow, who still meet there.* *(JRH)*

**New Industries, George Square and Hotels**: A *'verreville'* crystal factory was built in 1777 by Provost Colquhoun. In 1780 when the city's population was some 43,000 the Gallowgate brewery was opened. About that time various warehouses were built in the Montrose Street area west of the High Street, and development was also spreading westwards along Argyle Street. The elegant George Square area, then at the west end of the city, was laid out in 1781–82, and with the growth of coaching its west side was soon taken up by a range of four hotels, the *Clarence, Crow, Globe* and *Waverley*, later joined by the *Queen's* on the north side. In 1781 the Tontine Society took over the Town Hall for conversion as their coffee house and as the *Tontine Hotel*, which opened in 1787; its fate was to become a warehouse in the 1850s, and to be burnt out and demolished in 1911.

**Heralding the *Herald* and Hospitals**: Meantime the year 1783 was among Glasgow's most remarkable. Not only did the weekly *Advertiser* newspaper make its debut (from 1803 it was called the *Glasgow Herald*), but the city founded Britain's first Chamber of Commerce, following New York's example. In 1780 David Dale had a mansionhouse built in Charlotte Street, perhaps designed by Robert Adam; later this became a convent and still later the city's Eye Infirmary. In the vintage year 1783, Dale became the first agent in the city for the Edinburgh-based Royal Bank, and was shortly to build New Lanark with Arkwright. The city's first hospital for physical illnesses, the Royal Infirmary, was founded in 1787, and the ruins of the Archbishop's castle and palace were cleared away in 1791 to make way for its new building, yet another designed by Robert Adam, which opened in 1794. In 1785 the city's residents possessed only 25 private carriages, but Walter Stirling endowed the first public library, opened in 1791 (which is now an art gallery).

**Improving Communications around 1790**: From 1781 a diligence ran to Carlisle and London in four days, and from 1783 the canal and coach passage between Glasgow, Falkirk and Edinburgh took twelve hours – a more sedate walking pace. But in 1788, the year the Glasgow City Police were formally established, mail coaches began to travel between Glasgow and London direct, taking 63 hours – twice walking speed, and very creditable in view of the many changes of horses involved. By 1799 the Edinburgh coach spent six hours en route, at much the same speed. In 1790 the Forth & Clyde Canal was extended from Hamiltonhill to a basin at Castle Street and Roystonhill *(see Port Dundas)* just north of the city, where it was linked with the Monkland Canal, itself extended from Barlinnie. Glasgow continued to develop rapidly; the Glasgow Cross bridge was begun in 1794, but was flood damaged in 1795 before completion (and replaced in 1829–33 by the Hutcheson Bridge, designed by the Glaswegian Robert Stevenson).

**Branch Banks, Fairs and Theatres**: Although three Glasgow banks failed in 1793 due to the war against France (the *Arms*, *Merchants*', and *Thomson's*), the city's progress hardly faltered; the Bank of Scotland finally opened a permanent Glasgow branch in 1802. Between 1788 and 1825 branches of banks from Paisley, Cupar, Falkirk, Greenock and Aberdeen were attempted in the city, many short-lived. The Glasgow Trades House in Glassford Street was completed in 1794 and the Assembly Rooms in Ingram Street, also designed by Robert Adam, were built in 1792–96. In 1797 fairs were held on about eleven days in the year (including the fair week). The city's first and second theatres, erected in 1752 and 1764, had both been burned by mobs in the name of religion; but the latter was rebuilt, and operated until 1780. The city's first really successful theatre, the *Caledonian* in Dunlop Street, was erected in 1795. It was again rebuilt in 1839–40 as the *Theatre Royal* (taking the name of the former *Theatre Royal* erected in Queen Street in 1804 for audiences of 1500, which was struggling in 1826 and burnt down in 1829).

**Steam, Dogs and Water drive Cotton Mills**: In 1780 there were nearly 3000 linen looms in the Barony parish alone, but in that year James Monteith started cotton muslin manufacture at Anderston; this had instant success. The Woodside cotton mill was built in 1784, and in 1786 local linen and cotton printers were active; cambric manufacture was noted in 1787, and by 1790 most weavers had changed to cotton and were making muslins. Cotton was first imported from America in 1792, the year when the first steam textile mill in Scotland was built in the city; a more sustainable approach the same year saw a city loom experimentally powered by a large dog! But it was on the basis of plentiful water power that Glasgow entrepreneurs then spread the textile industry around Scotland, aided by Robert Miller's power looms, developed in 1796–98; at the same time Gavin Lennox was making stocking frames in the city. Heron wrote in 1799 *"the cotton manufactures are daily increasing, and now rival those of Manchester in cheapness and elegance"*. Exports included *"cotton, linen and woollen stuffs, shoes, boots, saddles and harness"*. The pottery had been *"so much improved that it now emulates the beauty and elegance of the Staffordshire ware"*. Glass was also made in two works, for bottles and for crystal. Steam power was added to the 60m-long water-powered Clayslaps grain mill in 1801, the year that Glasgow Cross gained a post office. By then the burgeoning city's population had tripled in 37 years to about 84,000, compared to Edinburgh's 100,000.

**Glasgow in 1803**: Dorothy Wordsworth wrote in 1803 that her party found *"the first decent inn, quiet and tolerably cheap; a new building – the Saracen's Head"*; but its floors were dirty. *"The Trongate, an old street, is very picturesque. The New Town is built of fine stone, in the best style of the very best London streets. New houses are rising up in great numbers round Glasgow."* The shops were *"large, and like London shops, and we passed by the largest coffee-room you ever saw"* by the Exchange, where many men sat reading newspapers. Glasgow Green contained a large wash-house with *"two very large rooms, with each a cistern in the middle for hot water"*; at that time the Green was intensively used for *'bleaching'* (drying and whitening) the washing. In 1804 water was first piped to cisterns in Bath Street, and Buchanan Street was also built early in the 19th century.

**Houldsworth prospers at Anderston**: Despite another major cash crisis in the west of Scotland in 1802–03, Henry Houldsworth & Co's giant 8-storey *'fireproof'* (brick and cast iron) cotton mill in Cheapside at Anderston was built for its Manchester proprietor in 1804–06, designed – together with its steam engine – by Boulton & Watt *(for details see Hay & Stell)*. In 1823 Houldsworth established the Anderston Foundry, also in Cheapside Street, to make textile machinery; this too prospered for many decades *(see also Newmains & Waterside)*. Anderston was chartered as a burgh of barony in 1824, immediately constructing its own gasworks in 1826. Meantime in 1819 there were still over 12,000 handloom weavers in the city and in suburbs such as Calton; Glasgow was still being called *"a city of muslin-makers"*, for in 1825 two or three firms, including John Mair & Co, were still in the trade. About 1830 Cochrane & Browns of Donaghadee in Ulster moved their works to Glasgow, becoming the largest manufacturers of sewed muslins, and from 1837 they printed the designs by machine. Leather industries were still active in the city in 1826, and ropes were made there by 1827. About 1835 C S Cochran & Co erected a merino woollen spinning mill in St Vincent Street, and some 150 hand-frame knitters of worsted stockings were still at work in Glasgow in 1844, but wool then faded from the city.

**Grammar and Higher Education**: New buildings for the Grammar School had arisen in 1788; but in 1795 the original buildings of Hutcheson's Grammar School were demolished, and for many years its classes were held in temporary premises. A mansion named Shawfield, built in 1712, was also demolished in 1795 to allow the development of Glassford Street. The next year 1796 saw the foundation of John Anderson's *'University'* or Technical Institute, which led the way in higher education by accepting women as students. On the completion of yet another replacement Grammar School in 1828 it took over the former building and eventually became the nucleus of Strathclyde University. By 1825 Glasgow University, still in the High Street, had over 1200 students and about 30 professors; the Hunterian Museum stood to the rear of the court, in a building completed in 1805 under the will of William Hunter of East Kilbride.

**The First Public Park – and Publishing**: The city fire service was founded in 1809, and in 1814 Glasgow Green was laid out as Europe's first public park. A gas supply for Glasgow was commenced in 1818 by a private company, one year after Edinburgh. Meantime the large Glasgow Asylum for Lunatics was built in Dobbie's Loan in 1810–14 for 126 patients, their relatives paying. By 1813, five newspaper titles were published in Glasgow, though another eight had failed. Why? Perhaps because 57% of the sale price of the *Herald*, published twice weekly from 1815, was duty, so only 1100 copies were sold; in all only 1200 copies of all the newspapers combined were printed in Glasgow on an average weekday. Collins published their first book in the city in 1819, appropriately for the day titled *'The Christian and Civic Economy of Large Towns'* by the evangelist Dr Thomas Chalmers. Meantime early in the century Glasgow University Press had been set up in Stanhope Street; it was taken over by John Blackie about 1830, and his firm further developed the site as the Villafield Press, a well-known printing and book publishing business, up to 1890.

**Candle Wax, Canada, Coach and Postal Services**: Thomas Graham, born in the city in 1805, was to develop the science of colloid chemistry and became Master of the Mint. James Young, another Glasgow native born in 1811, also became a chemist; he invented a method of making paraffin wax for the candles that were so important before the general availability of gas light and electricity. He fathered the once enormous West Lothian industry of distilling oil from coal and shale, and became a major magnate better known as *'Paraffin'* Young *(see Bathgate)*. John Alexander Macdonald, born in Glasgow in 1815, emigrated to Canada, later becoming its first Prime Minister, the instigator of the Canadian Pacific Railway and a knight. By 1819 there were three daily coaches to Paisley and two to Greenock; others ran to Perth and Ayr. The frequency on the Edinburgh route doubled in six years, to ten coaches daily by 1825. Glasgow had been belatedly defined as a main postal route centre in 1808; by 1816 its penny post served Cathcart and Old Kilpatrick, and by 1825 its wide collection and delivery area extended to Balfron, Barrhead and Cumbernauld. With such fast-growing traffic, a new cast-iron bridge was built in 1826 to carry London Road over the Molendinar.

**Drinks and Tobacco Industries**: Glasgow worked hard and drank hard: mass production techniques were applied to barrel manufacture by the Scottish Patent Cooperage from 1816, and various other firms also made casks and barrels, serving the eighteen breweries in the city and suburbs which by 1820 vied to slake local thirsts. The development of legal whisky distilling from the mid 1820s led to the need to hold stocks in the city for distribution and export. For example, about 1844 P Robertson & Co built a bonded warehouse in Oswald Street. Tobacco importers had gone elsewhere, but in 1825 Mitchell's moved their tobacco business into the city from Linlithgow. The smoking addiction had spread to poorer people; In 1824, W White & Son began to manufacture clay tobacco pipes at Bain Street, expanding with new buildings in 1867–77.

**Napier, Marine Engineering and Ships**: Ironworking was well established by 1801 when John Napier was in the iron-founding business in Jamaica Street. This trade was essential for the marine engineering business which commenced in Glasgow – and effectively the world – in 1811 when John Napier & Sons, then of Howard Street, fabricated the boiler for Glasgow builder Henry Bell's pioneer steamship the *Comet*; John Robertson of Dempster Street constructed the engine *(see also Parkhead and Port Glasgow)*. By 1814 Archibald Maclachlan was building ships, while Barclay Curle & Co were established in 1818 as shipbuilders at Stobcross, between the Clyde and their engine works at Finnieston. The Clyde Shipping Company was founded in 1815, operating coasting and Irish services and providing towage; it was to survive into the 1980s as the oldest steamship company in the world. By 1820, 28 steamships offered Clyde estuary and West Coast services. Glasgow's importance as a shipping centre justified its single registration letter G (when most places had two-letter codes).

**Early Irish Influx fuels Expansion**: Textile development was hindered by labour disturbances from 1820, but following the Glasgow cotton strikes the leaders were transported, and the shameless exploitation of workers continued until after the Reform Act of 1832. Even so, Irish workers were flooding in, and in 1821 it was found that Glasgow was at last more populous than Edinburgh; only a quarter of the 147,000 people counted were native Glaswegians. People were crammed in at 5000 per acre in the old central area, with an average of 8 people per house – and most *'houses'* were one-apartment *'single ends'* without facilities. Further labour demands came from the Bishop Garden cotton mill of James Johnston and the Lancefield cotton spinning works in Hydepark Street. By 1839 102 cotton mills were jammed into the city and suburbs; in 1849 R F & J Alexander's Duke Street cotton thread mill was built. Meantime by 1831 the city's population exceeded 200,000, of whom a remarkable one in six were Irish (as against one in twenty for Scotland as a whole). Yet the richer people in the new West End had enough space for real furniture; cabinetmaking started on an industrial scale in 1828.

**Shipping and the deepening of the Clyde**: Glasgow's Allan shipping line was founded in 1820, followed in 1823 by James and George Burns, who in 1826 founded a Glasgow to Belfast steamer service, plying also to Liverpool from 1829. The City of Glasgow Steam Packet Company was started in 1831. By 1824 timber was being imported from Canada, and sawmills were in operation. By then steam dredgers were at work in the Clyde: by 1826 the river was navigable to the Broomielaw by vessels drawing about 7 feet (2.3 metres). By then the length of quays on the north bank of the Clyde exceeded 1 km. So successful were the three dredgers that from 1836 ships of 400 tons could reach the city, and Glasgow's foreign trade soon overtook that of its rival Greenock.

**Cobbett's Beautiful Glasgow**: William Cobbett visited Glasgow late in 1832, noting with pleasure the city's *"magnitude and opulence, commerce and manufactures, and splendid shops"*; the fine Argyll Arcade had opened in 1827. Glasgow was *"built of beautiful white stone; the manufacturing part, with the tall chimneys and the smoke, is at the east end of the city and somewhat separated from it* [he was evidently referring to Bridgeton] *so that there is very little smoke in Glasgow which is beautiful in all ways; the new Exchange is a most magnificent place"*. By then the *George Hotel* was also in use. Despite his enthusiasm, rapidly worsening congestion and pollution were soon to erode the city's former beauty and further injure the health of its people.

**Glasgow Green and Parliamentary Road**: The ancient Cathedral was still divided into two rather neglected churches. Meantime the Necropolis, established on the site of Fir Park east of the Cathedral in 1832–33 to inter the city's elite, defined the north-eastern limits of the city centre. As the west end of the city developed, the turnpiked Parliamentary Road was constructed from the head of Buchanan Street to improve its access to east and north: in 1835 nine coaches ran daily to Stirling. By 1842 the Glasgow Mechanics' Institute, founded in 1823, drew together over 600 sober artisans from the many new iron-founding and engineering enterprises that were established – such as Claud Girdwood & Co, textile machinery manufacturers, which in 1828 was building steam pumping engines for the ever deeper collieries and by 1832 had built a heavy crane capable of lifting 30 tonne loads for use on the local quays.

**Napier and Marine Engineering**: David Napier *(see also Dumbarton and Parkhead)* who had been trained in his father's works at Camlachie, had begun building marine engines at Lancefield between Stobcross and the Broomielaw in 1821. He engined the paddle steamer *United Kingdom* at 200 horsepower in 1826, and in 1827 built both an iron-hulled steam boat and a steam carriage. Some very significant marine engineers of the early days worked inland, but as engine sizes grew this soon proved inconvenient. In 1828 Robert Napier (David's cousin) moved his engine works from Camlachie to the Vulcan Foundry in Washington Street. By 1834 Napier was engining larger 400-ton steamers; his firm also built warships for foreign governments. Napier's made all four sets of engines for the fleet of Cunarders built by various firms about 1840; by 1847 some 1400 men worked for him.

**Glasgow Banks of the 1830s**: As schemes involving great capital outlay blossomed, so the small local banks found the going hard and either failed or merged. The Glasgow Savings Bank was established in 1836, eventually becoming the largest independent Trustee Savings Bank in Britain. The Glasgow Union Bank (GUB) was founded in 1830; It took over the 18th century Virginia Mansion in Ingram Street, later extending it with a beautiful telling room. The long-lasting Clydesdale Bank was founded in 1838, followed by several other Glasow ventures. About 1840 a major expansion in commerce led to new central branches being built for several of the major banks.

**Coal by Rail – and Steam Road Coaches**: Glasgow's industrial demands for coal grew daily. The first railway carrying coal from Garnkirk near Chryston, the Garnkirk & Glasgow (G&G), reached the Townhead in 1831; the *Black Bull Inn* hosted its opening festivities *(for its subsequent development see Springburn)*. In 1831 the coachbuilders Johnston & McNab built the first railway coach for the G&G, and in 1832 a locomotive. Murdoch & Aitken of the Hill Street Foundry also built locomotives; later they would make anything and everything mechanical. In 1834 steam road coaches (built in Edinburgh) were successfully operated between Glasgow and Paisley by the Steam Carriage Company of Scotland, until abandoned following what Bird called *"the first fatal motor accident in Great Britain"*. This was caused by piles of stones placed in its way by the unscrupulous turnpike trustees, who feared excessive damage to the road; the boiler burst, killing five people. This spelled the end to steam for road passenger transport, but not for trains or ships. Coal was big business by then; Ross & Co, founded as mineral surveyors in Glasgow in 1838, are still in business. With all the developments, space was at a premium: by 1839, well before the potato famine, Glasgow had the worst housing conditions in Britain. Many firms appeared like mushrooms, clustered in the growing suburbs, whose stories appear elsewhere in this volume under their various names.

**Ships of Iron and the Edinburgh Railway**: Hunter & Dow were building ships by 1834. So were Tod & McGregor, who built two pioneer iron-hulled steamers for the Glasgow–Liverpool run in 1838, followed by the third Clyde paddle steamer named *Inveraray Castle* in 1839; she sailed for 46 years. They also built the exceptionally durable iron-hulled paddler *Mary Jane* in 1846 for Matheson of Stornoway, before moving to Partick in 1847; this vessel (renamed *Glencoe)* when broken up in 1931 was the world's oldest steamer. Meanwhile the famous firm of J & G Thomson had started engine building at Finnieston in 1845, and shipbuilding at Govan in 1851. The Edinburgh & Glasgow Railway (E&G) which opened in 1842 was forced to burrow under the Monkland Canal and the G&G down a steep tunnel from Cowlairs, falling at 1 in 42 (nearly 2.4%) to a terminus at Queen Street. By 1848 *Carrick's Hotel* was also open. In 1848 the E&G took over for use as offices a fine neighbouring building in Renfield Street, built as a church in 1818; it was soon replaced nearby by a UP church attractively designed by James Brown.

**Neilson as Engineers to the Railways**: Walter M Neilson (son of James B Neilson who invented the hot blast iron furnace) became at the age of 17 a partner in a locomotive and marine engineering firm. In 1841 as Kerr, Neilson & Co they built the Cowlairs beam winding engine for the E&G, used to haul trains by rope up the gradient; it was designed in the style of a Greek temple! Meantime in 1840 R S Newall had patented untwisted wire rope, and set up a company to make such ropes to any length required; in 1847 they supplied the first wire rope, some 2.5 km in length, to work the Cowlairs incline. Neilson built crude tram locomotives for Cornwall's Redruth & Chacewater Railway In 1854, and a *Cornish* pattern pumping engine for the *Devon* Colliery near Alloa! In 1860–61 Neilson's and the Hyde Park name moved to Springburn.

**Squalor, Shopping, Public Buildings and Services**: Even after the Reform Act of 1832 there was still only one MP for Glasgow, Rutherglen, Renfrew and Dumbarton, and nothing was done to relieve the desperate overcrowding. In 1839 the city held 700 bars and a thousand shops. Some people drank tea; William Connal's *'Queen's Tea Store'* in York Street dated from 1839, and in 1837 the *Royal Polytechnic* department store began trading in Argyle Street. Public buildings then came apace: by 1840 a much-needed fever hospital was open at Albion Street. The Asylum for Lunatics was outmoded by 1841 and was replaced at Gartnavel; the old buildings became a poorhouse until demolition in 1908. A new Corn Exchange was built in Hope Street in 1841. A new City Hall and Merchants' House were also built between 1840 and 1843, but were also soon found inadequate. The Stock Exchange opened in Queen Street in 1845, as the Royal Exchange – converted from a tobacco merchant's mansion of 1770. A new sheriff court was built in Wilson Street in 1844. Anderston was absorbed into Glasgow in 1846. In 1849 the Cathedral's west towers were regrettably demolished, but the House of Fraser had its origins that year in city shopping. Jamieson & Co built oil works in Clydeferry Street, while R & J Jarvie's Anderston ropework was founded about 1849; rubber works were added to the ever-growing range of industry.

**Higher Education**: In 1837 the strangely named Normal School in Dundas Vale was opened to provide teacher training, and in 1840 the Glasgow Government School of Design was founded (later becoming Glasgow School of Art). In 1843 the even more oddly named *'Free Church Normal School'* in Cowcaddens was built for Glasgow silk merchant and liberal educationalist David Stow, whose name was perpetuated when it eventually became the nucleus of Stow College of Higher Education. The Commercial College was founded in 1845, the Glasgow Academy in 1846, and the Glasgow Athenaeum (later a constituent of the Royal Scottish Academy of Music & Drama) in 1847. Allan Glen was a shipwright who endowed the school named after him to provide technical education, which was erected in Cathedral Street in 1851–52; the buildings were greatly enlarged in the 1870s and 1880s.

**Printing and Publishing: Well-known Names**: By 1831 the *Glasgow Argus, Glasgow Chronicle* and *Glasgow Courier* were all published, but not daily. The first daily newspaper in Scotland was started in 1847, as the *North British Daily Mail*, later called the *Daily Record*; in 1854 the firm built printing works in Union Street, which were extended in 1898. By 1851 there were three other dailies in Glasgow alone. About 1851 William Collins & Co founded their Herriot Hill stationery and printing works in St James Road, extended repeatedly up to 1903. The second works of McCorquodale & Co, general printers, was built in 1854 and the third, in Maxwell Street, in 1868–70.

**The Port and Shipping Lines**: In 1840 a new Custom House was opened at Clyde Street, for overseas trade was growing. By 1844 some 75 steamers served the city, on routes extending to Inverness, Liverpool, Dublin and Sligo. The height of Irish immigration arrived on these boats in 1848 after the potato famine, bringing even cheaper labour. David Hutcheson & Co was founded in 1851 as steamship operators; in 1879 this firm became MacBraynes. The Anchor Line was founded in 1852 by Handyside and Henderson, and the Donaldson Line in 1854. Custom House Quay was added in 1852–57. By 1860 1.2 million tons of goods were being handled annually by the Port of Glasgow, including coal exports, and by 1870 Glasgow had overtaken Leith as Scotland's busiest foreign trading port. Much of the actual development was in nearby places *(see Gorbals, Govan and Partick)*.

**London Rail Services and New Bridges**: The somewhat indirect rail route to London from Glasgow's primitive Townhead station via Garnkirk, Coatbridge and the Caledonian Railway (CR) to Carlisle and the London & North Western was opened in 1848. Soon Buchanan Street station was the terminus. Old Glasgow Bridge at Stockwell was demolished in 1847, and replaced by the Victoria Bridge, built of sandstone and Dublin granite in 1851–54. The lightweight Portland Street suspension footbridge of 1851, erected by the Heritors of Gorbals, also linked the city with its growing southern suburbs.

**Grain Warehouses and Mills**: The demand for bread grew with the city; an elevator for imported grain was built following the repeal of the Corn Laws in 1846. Several warehouses were built around then. The Washington Street grain mills of J & R Snodgrass, built about 1849, twice extended. At the same time the Paisley milling firm of A & W Glen built the Cheapside Street flour mills; these closed about 1895. John Ure & Son built the Crown flour mills in Washington Street in 1862, later enlarged. In 1865 Harvie & McGavin had a cotton store converted into the Anderston Grain Mill. Around 1880 the North British Railway built yet another grain store, a tall 7-storey structure near Queen Street.

**Engineering in the 1850s**: In 1849 James White founded the instrument-making firm later known as Kelvin & Hughes. In 1854 the Cranstonhill Iron Foundry was set up by James Aitken & Co, engineers and millwrights; the Cranstonhill Engine Works in Port Street was built about 1858 for mechanical engineers and crane builders Alexander Chaplin & Co; in 1891 they moved to a new *'Cranstonhill'* works in Govan. Around 1856 Alexander Mathieson & Son founded the Saracen edge tool works at Bell Street, whilst Turnbull Grant & Jack were making steam engines.

**Screw Propulsion, Forgings – and Smoke**: In 1853 John Elder, a former millwright, patented the compound engine for screw steamships, giving his engineering firm an advantage for decades; in 1866 they built two iron floating docks measuring 91 x 23 metres. Meantime starting in 1854 the Lancefield Forge Company, already makers of engine shafts for warships and mail steamers, set out to make the giant crankshaft for Brunel's *Great Eastern*, by far the largest ship built to date and then on the stocks beside the Thames; they succeeded at the third attempt in 1857 in producing what was then the largest forging in the world. The German travel author Fontane noted in 1858 *"the chimney is the most characteristic thing in Glasgow"*.

**Shipyards move Downriver; Water from Loch Katrine**: The shipbuilders J & G Thomson had established their engine works in Finnieston Street in 1845, prophetically naming them the *'Clyde Bank Works'*. To facilitate the building of larger vessels the firm moved to Govan in 1851 and eventually to Clydebank itself. The shipbuilding firm of Barclay Curle also moved down-river, leaving for Whiteinch in 1855, not only because their yards were cramped but due to the shallowness of the Clyde at the Broomielaw, then little over 2m at low water. A large Sailors' Home was built at the Broomielaw in 1855. The city's bold scheme to supply water by a 55km pipeline from Loch Katrine was opened in 1859–60; later improvements gave by 1883 a storage capacity of 140 days' supply, in three lochs. In 1855 yet another inadequate City Hall was created by conversion, in 1857 the classical Queen's Rooms were built in Clifton Street, and the huge St Vincent Street Church designed by Alexander *'Greek'* Thomson arose in 1858–59. The Park area, the last buildable space within 2 km of the old centre, was covered with what were intended as high-class houses.

**Textiles and Banks hit by US Commercial Crisis**: The second largest muslin-sewing firm, M'Donalds, which like Cochrane & Browns retained many Irish needlewomen, failed in the American commercial crisis of 1857. Many of the 25,000 or so outworkers lost their jobs and the City of Glasgow Bank was temporarily closed. Less fortunate was the Edinburgh & Glasgow Bank which became bankrupt – taken over by the Clydesdale in 1858. Worst was the poorly run Western Bank; hit in the east by the Indian Mutiny, it collapsed totally in 1857. Perhaps as a reaction, the Glasgow Trades Council was formed in 1858, nine years after Edinburgh's. The City of Glasgow Bank eventually failed in 1878; by then a large organisation having 133 branches, and over-large headquarters recently built in Glassford Street, it dragged down many shareholders as its liability was not limited. But muslins were not dead; as late as 1861 over 7000 women still sewed muslins by hand.

**Mid-Victorian Horse Transport**: Although by the 1850s steam was triumphant in milling, shipping and railways, the horse still dominated the roads, so J Buchanan and J Henderson both built coach and harness works. In 1852 the railway carrier William Wordie of Stirling, moved his head office to Glasgow and built extensive stables at Paul Street in the 1860s. In the interim about 1868 the liveryman William Forbes had built the remarkably named Charing Cross Horse Bazaar at Berkeley Street. In 1869–70 the coachbuilder John E Walker built a factory at Buccleuch Street in the Garnethill area; when cars replaced coaches it became redundant, but still saw some horses, for it was converted into a veterinary college. About 1870 John Robertson built coachworks in St Vincent Street, James Gilligan hired out horses and carriages, and Alexander Grant, a cartwright, erected the St Rollox Spring Van and Lorry Works in Kennedy Street.

**Leather and Oil Merchants 1864–80**: Horse harness – like the travel goods and footwear of the day – was very largely of leather; J & W Stiell, leather merchants, extended an old warehouse in Montrose Street in 1864. In 1868–69 Schrader & Mitchell erected a leather warehouse in Fox Street, and John Inglis & Co, also leather factors, built premises at St Andrews Square in 1876–77; about 1880 the currier and leather merchant Thomas McBride built the St Catherine's Leather Works in Moir Lane.

**Medical and Service Developments**: In 1857 Robert Philip, later a pioneer in treating tuberculosis, was born in the city. Saint Aloysius' College, a Jesuit secondary school, was founded in 1859, with buildings at Garnethill designed by Elder & Cannon, and in 1861 came the Institute of the Fine Arts. The Royal Infirmary acquired a new surgical block about 1860: it was there in 1865–67 that the Englishman Joseph Lister first developed the antiseptic procedures that revolutionised surgery.

**Sugar, Sweets, Food and Drink**: About 1852 Hoyle, Martin & Co built a large 7-storey sugar refinery in Washington Street. With ample sugar and pure water available, the industrial manufacture of sweets in Glasgow began in 1857. By the mid 19th century Glasgow had store houses for virtually every commodity. In 1854–56 the general warehousemen Anderson & Co had built in Miller Street a finely designed three-storey warehouse in the style of a Venetian palazzo. William Anderson's huge spirit warehouses rose in Molendinar Street in 1873–74, and in 1877 John Baillie established a wine store in Goosedubs. Peter Paterson set up a fish wholesaling business in McFarlane Street about 1876.

**Ironfounding and Engineering**: About 1860 D McPherson & Co set up an iron foundry in Bishop Street. The small *'Saracen'* architectural iron foundry was built in Washington Street in 1862 for Walter Macfarlane & Co, founded in 1850, whose proprietor had a house built at Park Crescent, designed by James Boucher and incorporating many Saracen castings. Rapid expansion forced the firm to move to Anderston in 1862, then to Possil *(q.v.)* in 1869. In 1863 Law & Downie were building steam road locomotives, though English builders continued to dominate the traction engine market. About 1863 Neilson Brothers, engineers and toolmakers, built their Windlass Engine Works in Hydepark Street, and about 1865 Dugald Buchanan built the Anderston Galvanizing Works in Elliot Street. Crawhall & Campbell were making horizontal steam engines, shaping and planing machines and screwcutting lathes (some now on show at Summerlee). In 1865 Walker, Brown & Co built engineering works in Bishop Street, and by 1868 Napier's Lancefield engine works and Washington Street foundry employed about 1750 workers between them.

**Boilermaking**: As steamships became larger and more numerous the city's engineers specialised to serve their builders. About 1859 McLaren, Wright & Co built the Globe wrought-iron tube works in McAlpine Street. The ponderously named London & Glasgow Engineering & Iron Shipbuilding Company established their boiler works in Lancefield Street in 1864–65, frequently enlarged. The company's engine works were set up at Anderston Quay in 1888. In 1865 came the Lancefield Boiler Works in Houldsworth Street.

**Hydraulic and other Engineering Thriving**: Water turbines were invented in Glasgow in 1833 and were manufactured from 1839; Smith & Co built them in the 1870s. In 1865 A & P Steven, hydraulic engineers, built the Provanside engine works in St James Road. The Scotia Engine Works of Muir & Caldwell were built in Elliot Street in 1865–72; David Rowan, a marine engineer and boilermaker, erected works close by in Elliot Street – later greatly enlarged.

**Non-ferrous Fittings and the Gas Industry**: In 1869 J & W Young, ships' plumbers, built a foundry for brass fittings in Minerva Street, followed the next year by their competitors Steven & Struthers in Elliot Street; Miller & Pyle, coppersmiths, built premises in Robertson Lane. Such firms served the drinks trades as well as shipbuilding and the gas industry. 1867 saw the municipalisation of Glasgow's gas supplies. Sir Dugald Clerk, born in Glasgow in 1854, invented the Clerk Cycle (two-stroke) gas engine in 1877; he became Director of Engineering Research during the 1914–18 war. Coachbuilding was still active in the city in 1869, but it no longer made headlines. The Glasgow hide market was the largest in Scotland, handling nearly 55,000 hides in 1867; a city tannery then employed over 2000 workers. By 1869 Bell's Glasgow Pottery employed 800 people in making vases, table and toilet ware from Cornish stone, clay and flints. Meantime office blocks were rising in the city centre.

**Linens and the Decline of Cotton**: In 1868 about twelve Glasgow firms were still in the flax and jute industries, among which Alex Flather & Co, flax spinners, had about 2000 workers, the City of Glasgow Flax-spinning Company over a thousand, and the Glasgow Jute Company a similar number. William Graham & Co, cotton spinners, had about a thousand workers at their Lancefield mill, and many other firms producing muslins employed a large number of Irishwomen. The Anderston Parish Church, a remarkable galleried building, was erected in the 1860s and Houldsworth & Co's Anderston cotton mill was extended between 1854 and 1864. But when cotton supplies were cut off by the American Civil War in 1864 the industry temporarily slumped; its recovery was rapid, but not complete, and Glasgow's cotton industry steadily declined, Houldsworth's cotton mill being closed in 1878 and converted into a bonded warehouse.

**Engineers to the mid-Victorian Textile Trades**: R E Simpson & Co of Maxwell Street patented sewing machines in 1859; a decade later they were producing 350 machines a month. James Neilson & Son made weaving equipment at their Reed and Heddle factory in John Street, whilst the long-established Anderston Foundry made looms. Although the cotton industry had cut back, Duff & Towart (who engraved plates for calico printing) built works in Cathedral Street in 1883, and kindred firm James Gray & Co did likewise at McAslin Street about 1888.

**Specialist Engineers and Metal Merchants**: By about 1870 P & W MacLellan of the Gorbals *(q.v.)* had a vast city centre showroom for machinery made by themselves and others. The Sun Foundry in Kennedy Street which made fancy ironwork was built in 1870–71; the Vulcan Smith Works of P & R Fleming was founded in Houldsworth Street in 1871, and extended in 1877, probably by the mangle manufacturers J & A McFarlane. William Cook & Sons built their Glasgow Saw & File Works in 1870 at Elliot Street, and were still making machine knives over a century later in 1983. Dron & Lawson established the Cranstonhill Tool Works close by in 1872. John Bilsland & Co made bolts and rivets at Elliot Street,whilst Dempster Moore & Co made machine tools such as drilling machines and screwcutting lathes. In 1886 the steam instrumentation firm of Dobbie, McInnes was founded. Meantime, the quantities of metals in circulation having vastly increased, and various ironmongery stores developed.

**Evening and Morning Newspapers and Printers**: Meantime the excise duty on paper had been lifted in 1861, and with the abolition of the newspaper tax the city's first evening paper, the *Citizen*, was founded in 1864. In 1865 George Outram & Sons, publishers of the *Glasgow Herald*, built printing works in Buchanan Street, which were steadily added to. The *Glasgow Evening News* was founded in 1873 and in 1876 came the *Evening Times*, which within a few years claimed the largest circulation. In 1885–87 James Hedderwick & Sons, now almost forgotten publishers, built printing works in St Vincent Place for their *Evening Citizen* newspaper. Meantime about 1871 Gilmour & Dean, pioneers in colour printing, set up presses at North Hanover Street; they were still expanding in 1913.

**Theatres and the Fire Hazard**: Though some Glasgow people were so sober that they thought the theatre hateful, many Victorian Scots enjoyed their entertainments. In 1849, following two disastrous fires in largely wooden theatres (in the absence of electricity, lit by dangerous open flares), the *Queen's Theatre* was built of permanent brick. Even so, 65 lives were lost in a false fire alarm at the *Theatre Royal* in 1849, and in 1863 a real fire destroyed the building; again rebuilt, it was sold to the City of Glasgow Union Railway (see below) for their new station in 1866. The *Scotia Music Hall* in Stockwell Street was built in 1862 and later renamed the *Metropole Theatre*. The *Prince of Wales Theatre* in Cowcaddens which opened in 1867 was burnt out two years later; a huge replacement with 4000 seats opened soon afterwards, being renamed the *Grand* in 1881. The 2000-seat *Royalty Theatre* (later renamed the Lyric) was built in Sauchiehall Street in 1879–80.

**From Makeshift Music Halls to St Andrews Halls**: A warehouse built in the Trongate in 1857 was partly converted into the *Britannia Music Hall* in 1868–69; it was later renamed the *Panopticon – 'See it all'!* – and aptly became a cinema in 1904. St Andrew's Halls were begun at St George's Cross in 1873; their huge main hall, opened in 1877, became the venue for orchestral concerts. Meantime the small *Gaiety Theatre* was opened nearby in 1874; it was rebuilt in 1896–97 as the large *Empire Palace* with 2158 seats, and even more seats were added in 1931. Meantime in 1878 another warehouse in Watson Street was converted into two more music halls, a second *Britannia* and the *Shakespeare*. The latter, which opened in 1881 having 1800 seats, became the *Star* in 1884, but a panic caused 14 deaths and renaming as the *People's Palace of Varieties*. In 1897 it became the *Queen's Theatre*, but was used as a music hall and for a time as a cinema; it was destroyed by fire in 1952.

**Big Banks and Egyptian Halls**: The Bank of Scotland built a new principal branch in St Vincent Place in 1865–69; by 1896 it did ten times the lending business of any other of the firm's branches or of the Edinburgh head office itself! The Union Bank helped Thomsons the shipbuilders to move from Govan to Clydebank in 1874, but by 1885 had fallen from second to sixth place among Scottish banks. The Egyptian Halls was another large office building, erected in Union Street in 1871 to designs by Alexander *'Greek'* Thomson.

**Glasgow Rangers and Sundry Services**: In 1872 Glasgow Rangers began to play football on Glasgow Green, moving west to Partick in 1875. In 1875–78 an existing Robert Adam building in George Square was concealed within a large new 5-storey Head Post Office, designed by Matheson, Robertson & Oldrieve. This was followed in 1880 by the Commercial Buildings in Bell Street. There were soon many others of less distinction, but the head offices of some city firms are mentioned under other headings. Cowcaddens Church was built in 1872–73. In 1878–79 the pompous evangelical Christian Institute building that was to become the YMCA was erected in Bothwell Street and greatly enlarged in Scottish Baronial style in 1895–98 to contain a 190-bed hostel.

**Decentralisation and Suburbs, 1866–81**: Under the Glasgow Improvement Act of 1866 the Glasgow City Improvement Trust was founded to buy up and demolish slum property, clearing it and selling the sites for rebuilding. This was more of a success physically than socially or commercially, thirty new streets being formed and the once-sweet Molendinar – by then an open sewer – being covered in. But new space for streets spelled decongestion, and the people and firms that were displaced could not stay in the inner city. Suburbs both residential and industrial were by that time springing up in all directions and for a variety of purposes; to pick out but a few, upstream Calton produced textiles, the flat and grubby Gorbals and Hutchesontown attracted mechanics and mills, hilly Springburn built railway locomotives on the grand scale and down-river Whiteinch specialised in shipbuilding *(see the various articles)*. The Hutchesontown bridge was replaced in 1870–71 by the stone and iron Albert Bridge. By 1881 the city's population was 660,000. From 1885 to 1903 *'Cluthas'* (small steam-driven water buses named after the Gaelic word for the Clyde) moved many people across and along the river, eventually making eleven stops between Stockwell Street bridge and Whiteinch *(Riddell)*.

**The Uni Departs to Partick**: William Thomson, born in Ulster, was Professor of Natural Philosophy in the University of Glasgow from the age of 22 in 1846 until 1899; better known under his well-earned title of Lord Kelvin, he was one of the greatest physicists of all time and a major pioneer in the use of electricity. In 1868 the University began to move westwards, out of the cramped old city centre to what then seemed a spacious replacement site at Gilmorehill above the ancient centre of Partick *(q.v.)*.

**The Horse Tramways and The Manure Office**: The movement of workers around the fast-growing city was aided by the Glasgow Tramway & Omnibus Company (GTOC), operating

*The 'Benmore' leaving the Broomielaw, in the late Victorian era of steamer-trips down the Clyde. This vessel was built of iron by T B Seath at Rutherglen in 1876. It is seen here in the ownership of Williamson–Buchanan Steamers.* *(GWW collection)*

on lines aid down on main streets in 1869–72, and first used in 1872 on a north–south route between St George's Cross and Eglinton Toll by the horse-drawn cars of Andrew Menzies. The trams remained slow and horse-drawn until replaced by fast electric cars in 1898–1902. In 1873 headquarters for the city's cleansing services – then largely concerned with uplifting horse droppings from the streets – were established as the quaintly named City Manure Office in Parliamentary Road.

**Rail Services and Hotels**: From 1865 the E&G formed part of the North British (NBR), which joined with the Glasgow & South Western Railway (G&SWR) to promote the City of Glasgow Union Railway (CGUR). This contracted with Brassey & Co in 1864–67 to build the Union Bridge, the first rail bridge across the Clyde below Glasgow Green, to link the G&SWR's Paisley to Gorbals line with the NBR at Springburn, through the lower part of the ancient city centre. In 1865 the *Queen's Hotel* was renamed the *North British* when both it and the former E&G Queen Street station were taken over. The *Waverley* and *Crow* hotels were pulled down in the 1860s and replaced by a new head branch for the Bank of Scotland; the *Clarence* and *Globe* lasted longer. About 1870 the large *Cockburn Hotel* in Bath Street was created by enlarging houses. Railways then meant hotels: by then four hotels clustered in George Square beside Queen Street Station, where a new *North British Hotel* was built in 1878.

**All Change in Hotels – and enter Sleeping Cars**: In 1877 two hotels were replaced by the latest Merchants' House; a Bank of Scotland branch replaced a third. Richer travellers soon transferred to the truly *Grand Hotel* erected in 1875–78 at Charing Cross despite its relative remoteness from the city terminals which dominated Glasgow rail traffic. Hotels lost out when sleeping cars to and from London King's Cross were introduced in 1873 on the NBR via the east coast route; from 1874 the Caledonian (CR) ran cars to Euston via the west coast.

**St Enoch Station, 1870–85**: The burnt-out remains of the *Theatre Royal* and also MacLellans' showroom were obliterated by the large St Enoch Station, built by the CGUR in 1870–79; the great arched roof was not raised until 1877. The G&SWR's palatial 5-storey *St Enoch Hotel*, designed by architects Miles S Gibson of Glasgow and James Willson of Hampstead, opened in 1879; it had the earliest electric lighting in Glasgow.

**The Stations and the City Centre, 1876–90**: Queen Street station was lengthened northwards in the 1870s, and provided with an arched roof designed by NBR District Engineer James Carswell, built by P & W MacLellan in 1880. Meantime the CR had themselves promoted a Clyde bridge, built by William Arrol in 1876–78, and the first phase of Central Station, opened in 1879. The adjacent *Central Station Hotel*, designed with the station buildings by Sir Robert Rowand Anderson, was built in 1884–85 and enlarged in 1907; by 1886 the *Victoria Hotel* was also in operation. With the completion of the University's move in 1887, the fine old College building was sadly demolished. It is remarkable that by 1890 the city centre had actually shifted almost a kilometre westwards from its traditional site at Glasgow Cross to focus on Central Station, by then the city's prime terminus.

**Queen's Dock and the Clan Line**: The quantity of goods handled by the port had quadrupled in 30 years to nearly 5 million tons annually. Queen's Dock, Scotland's largest, was built in 1872–80 between Finnieston and Partick; founded on concrete piles and faced in Giffnock stone, it was connected to the NBR. The shipowners Cayzer, Irvine & Co, founded by Londoner Charles Cayzer in 1878 for the India run, made their base in Glasgow. They took the name Clan Line in 1881 and expanded into the South African service; their ships were mainly built by Alex Stephen of Govan and by 1890 the firm had 13 vessels. Cayzer lived in luxury at Ralston and was knighted in 1897; later the family bought Gartmore *(q.v.)*. There were many other shipowning firms. Excursions to Ayr by steamer were started in 1886, but lasted only one season. In 1888 the Glasgow to Campbeltown steamers called at Gourock, Greenock and various places in Arran, where they loaded barytes for delivery at Kingston Dock; from there it went to paint manufacturers.

**Lipton and Cooper, Fruit and Bread**: The grocery magnates-to-be Thomas Lipton from the Gorbals, and his arch-rival Cooper, both began their respective empires in 1871 selling groceries in Howard Street. In the same year David Minto opened coffee roasting and grinding works at Bell Street. As still more mouths had to be fed, a new wholesale fish market was built in the Bridgegate in 1873, and there was also a meat cannery in the city. Between 1872 and 1883, fruit merchants Benjamin Simons built several warehouses, and a fruit store at Blackfriars Street was built for Thomas Russell, who in 1904 developed what he called his *'Covent Garden Market'* for fruit in Blackfriars Street, close to the city's own fruit market. A City Cheese Market was built at Candleriggs in 1902–07. In 1877–78 B M & J Stevenson – pioneers of machine bread-baking – built a very large bakery at Cranston Street, twice extended later. In 1881 Bilsland Brothers built the large Hydepark Bakery with 38 ovens, further enlarged in 1912; by then the firm also stabled over 100 horses for its bread vans.

**Cloth and Clothing, Cabinetmaking and Shops**: The wholesale drapers Arthur & Co erected a shirt factory in William Street in 1866, T Macnee & Co built a clothing factory in Miller Street, and from 1887 J & J Walton made bedding and leather belting. About 1877 John Laird established a cabinet making works in the far west of Argyle Street. Wylie & Lochhead built cabinet works in Kent Road from 1879, extending them in 1900; this firm became the city's leading house furnishers, with a large shop in Buchanan Street. Bennett's also erected a furniture factory, at Ladywell Street. Copland & Lye's department store in Sauchiehall Street was built in 1877–78. By 1885 the Royal Polytechnic, a store founded in 1837, was profitable enough for its owner Alex Anderson to build himself a large mansion at Partick; by the end of its 99 years it was the largest store in Scotland. In 1896 came the Trerons' department store in Sauchiehall Street; in 1896–97 Pettigrew & Stephens' 6-storey department store called Manchester House was erected close by.

**Demolitions set a Bad Precedent**: Alfred Nobel's Explosives Company of Ardeer, which at that time had its HQ in Glasgow, operated a small fleet of coasting steamers from 1875. The philanthropic Nobel's products were probably not needed in 1885 when the remarkable 17th century buildings of Glasgow University in the High Street were demolished, together with the fine Hunterian Museum, but this thoughtless action set a most unfortunate precedent for the vandalism which was to become such a regrettable hallmark of the city for a century to come. The Assembly Rooms were demolished in 1890 to enable extension of the General Post Office. However, a fine building in Gordon Street, designed and built about 1862 by the architect Alexander *'Greek'* Thomson and his brother, was converted around 1900 into the magnificent Grosvenor restaurant complex. Eventually a fire led to its conversion into offices.

**Famous Contributors to the Arts**: Sir William Burrell, born in Glasgow in 1861, inherited a profitable *'puffer'* steamship line *(see Possil)*, became a major entrepreneurial shipowner, and used his wealth to amass the numerous works of fine art which he donated to the city, the basis of the Burrell Collection *(see Pollokshaws)*. William Reid Dick, born in the city in 1879, became a renowned sculptor of state subjects and was given a knighthood. The famous playwright *'James Bridie'* was born O H Mavor in Glasgow in 1888, and George Macleod, born in Glasgow in 1895, founded the Iona Community.

**Telephones, Education, Laundries, Books and Steamers**: Glasgow's first telephone exchange was opened in 1879. The independent Park Day School for Girls in Lynedoch Terrace was founded in 1879 by Georgina Kinnear, and Queen Margaret's, a pioneer women's college, opened in 1881. In 1886 the Mechanics' Institute amalgamated with Anderson's *'University'* and blossomed into the Glasgow & West of Scotland Technical College. In 1877 the first Mitchell Library had opened, the bequest of tobacco magnate Stephen Mitchell. As standards of living rose, James Ritchie built a laundry engineering works in North Frederick Street in 1886 to supply the growing number of laundries.

**Whisky Blending and the Brewing Industry**: William Teacher & Sons claim to have begun blending whisky in 1830, though probably not in Glasgow. Whisky was being blended at Dunlop Street by 1880, and in 1886 the annual throughput at Greenlees Brothers' Osborne Street blending and bottling plant was nearing 7 million litres. Other whisky blending firms included Wright & Greig of Waterloo Street. Tennents' Wellpark Brewery was enlarged in 1873, and from 1888 produced lager; the brewery was again greatly enlarged between 1890 and 1911.

**Distillery and Brewery Engineers**: Fleming Bennett & Co of Cranstonhill were long established as distillers' and brewers' coppersmiths and manufacturers of stills. John Miller & Co manufactured distillers' refrigeration equipment. In 1887 at least seven sizeable firms in greater Glasgow were competing to equip the continually growing distilling industry; brass-founding and allied trades employed about a thousand workers in Glasgow at that time, some 40% of the Scottish total *(see also Bridgeton, Gorbals and Port Dundas)*.

**Expansion of Local Government**: The City Chambers, designed by William Young, were built in 1883–89 seemingly regardless of expense, providing a fine centrepiece for the City of Glasgow, whose population grew – by actual increase and by the incorporation within its expanding boundaries of further suburbs like Maryhill, Hillhead and Pollokshields in 1891 – reaching 762,000 in 1901. Meantime the City Council was creating an ambitious series of parks, aiming to provide open-air recreation for both the teeming population of the city and its less congested new suburbs, and transport operators were facing up to its growing movement problems. But it took

4 attempts (votes) to persuade the city's rate-payers to agree to pay for a public library – agreed in 1899, and receiving Carnegie assistance.

**Going Underground**: In 1886 it was said that the main streets of Glasgow were *"traversed ceaselessly by tramcars"*; these were still horse-drawn and therefore slow. The NBR had lately promoted the Glasgow City & District Railway (GC&DR), a heavily engineered sub-surface line across the north side of the city centre. Completed in 1886, this allowed through running from Coatbridge, with stations at High Street, Queen Street Low Level, Charing Cross and Finnieston; it joined the company's harbour line at Stobcross, giving access to Milngavie, Clydebank, Balloch and Helensburgh. The great hammerhead crane at Stobcross Quay was installed with a view to handling indivisible export items such as locomotives from Springburn.

**The Caledonian's Low Level Route**: The CR's even more costly answer to this, the Glasgow Central Railway, was a lengthy sub-surface line closely paralleling the Clyde, connecting Dalmarnock with Stobcross. City centre stations were opened at Glasgow Cross, Central Low Level and Anderston Cross. Built in 1888–96, as many as 260 trains a day passed through the new Central Low Level station, filling it with choking smoke. It is hard to understand now why electric traction was not adopted from the start, for only two years later the first electric streetcars began to run in the city, quickly stealing riders from the grimy steam-worked lines.

**The Glasgow Subway**: This unique self-contained 4'0" (122 cm) gauge underground transit system was built from 1891 by the Glasgow District Subway Company, whose civil engineer was Alex Simpson. Its tiny two-car trains were hauled by endless cables on a circular route, offset to the west of the city centre to serve Hillhead, Partick, the busy port area, Gorbals and Govan. It opened in 1897, with city centre stations at St George's Cross, Cowcaddens, Queen Street – and St Enoch with its unique freestanding HQ office, a tiny pavilion in front of the main line station *(see Black, 1937 and Nock, 1973)*.

**Extending St Enoch and Central Stations**: St Enoch Station was extended in 1898–1902 with a second arched roof span; beneath the platforms was a bonded store. The City of Glasgow Union Railway bridge was reconstructed at the same time. The number of passengers at the CR's Central Station had grown to 15 million by 1897. It was therefore very expensively doubled in size between 1899 and 1908; its new Clyde bridge of 1899–1906, again built by William Arrol & Co, was no less than 33.5 m in width, carrying nine tracks. The CR also built a large HQ office block in Union Street in 1901 and extended their hotel in Hope Street in 1905–07, to designs by James Miller. Central Station handled almost 20 million passengers a year after the new scheme was completed.

**Stationery and Printing Works**: By 1892 the publishers Blackie and Collins occupied closely adjoining premises; in 1902 Collins & Co had a printing and stationery works erected in St James Road. Aird & Coghill, printers and publishers, had a six-storey printing works built at Cadogan Street in 1899. Another printing plant arose in 1899 at Hope Street for J M Smith Ltd, proprietors of the *Glasgow Evening News*.

**Paint Manufacturers**: The paint works were built in 1891 for the paint manufacturers J & J Dickson, and also for Gibson & Mathie, both in Brown Street. In 1897 Craig & Rose of Leith were also making paint and varnish in Glasgow, using a former church in Cadogan Street. In 1914 Smith & Rodger had the former Anderston brass foundry reconstructed as a paint works.

**Wire Ropes and Miscellaneous Industries**: In 1914 Frew Brothers, manufacturers of wire ropes, had a factory built in Dobbies Loan. A cold store and ice factory were erected in Osborne Street for William Milne in 1901–02. The cork workers Symington & Co built a substantial new warehouse in Clyde Street in 1914, and three tobacco firms survived into the 20th century.

**Market and Wholesale Developments in the early 1900s**: The St Rollox area had its own Co-op, which erected a warehouse in Lister Street in 1903. In 1905 William McGeoch & Co, wholesale architectural ironmongers, had an impressive 6-storey warehouse and office block of French Renaissance style erected at West Campbell Street. In the same year Liptons Ltd had a grocery warehouse built in Lancefield Street, and about 1913 their rivals Cooper & Co did the same in Bishop Street. In 1911 Isaac Levin founded the Clydesdale Supplies Company at the Barras Market; starting in hardware, his firm was to grew steadily to become for many years Scotland's prime white goods retailer.

**Circuses and Theatres 1885–1905**: The circus was a popular entertainment: the Danish Hengler family who had set up a permanent circus in West Nile Street moved it in 1885 to the assembly halls in Wellington Street known as the Waterloo Rooms, moving again in 1903–04 to the *Hippodrome* in Sauchiehall Street. About 1890 there arose a modest rival to St Andrew's Halls, the *Athenaeum Theatre*. The 2300-seat *Lyceum Theatre* was opened in 1899, briefly becoming the largest in Glasgow. In the same year the *Tivoli* music hall was opened at Anderston Cross. By 1902 there were already eleven theatres in the city centre. To these were added the unsuccessful *Hippodrome Variety Theatre* which opened in Sauchiehall Street in 1902, and in 1904 two more, the *King's* and the 1800-seat *Pavilion*. The City's umpteenth *Theatre Royal* was also open by 1905.

**Entertainment from Theatre to Cinema**: The first true cinema in Glasgow, the Sauchiehall Street hall – later known as the *MGM* – opened to silent movies in 1896; when licences became necessary in Scotland in 1909, the first cinema to be so authorised was the *Gaiety* (formerly the *Tivoli)*. In 1909 the cinema later best known as the *Gaumont* was opened, and at the same time came the actors' answer to falling variety audiences, repertory theatre. The Waterloo Rooms were replaced in 1910 by the new *Alhambra Theatre* with its 2400 seats, *"the best equipped theatre north of London" (Littlejohn)*. The *Savoy* music hall in Hope Street opened in 1911, though it became a cinema about 1916. Finally in 1913 the *Empress Theatre* was opened. By 1914 the city (including the suburbs) had six large music halls competing with *a hundred cinemas*, all the latter showing just silent films in black and white, typically with improvised piano accompaniments!

**International Culture, Special Education and Housing**: Glasgow held three successful international Expositions at Kelvingrove *(see Partick)* between 1888 and 1911. In 1894 Notre Dame teacher training college was established to provide what the Catholic Church saw as an acute need – segregated education for Irish immigrants. They also needed homes: it is noteworthy that by 1901 the city corporation had built over 1500 council houses; few enough, but apart from the Glasgow Workmen's Dwellings Company they were almost alone in Scotland. In 1901 the Glasgow & West of Scotland Technical College became a Central Institution, renamed as the Royal Technical College, and in 1903 built new premises on the site of the one-time Grammar School of 1788; eventually it became a constituent of Strathclyde University. Queen's College was formed in 1908, and in 1907–11 came new buildings for the Mitchell Library.

**Buildings by Mackintosh: a Designer Apart**: Charles Rennie Mackintosh, one of many children of a police superintendent, was born in Glasgow in 1868, and became the architect who designed a highly original series of tea rooms in 1903–04 for the redoubtable Miss Cranston; his larger works included the *Glasgow Herald* building of 1893–95 and the *Daily Record* printing works built in 1900 at St Vincent Lane. Best known are the externally attractive buildings for the Glasgow School of Art, erected in 1897–99. The congested site cramped, and consequently darkens, the idiosyncratic circulation spaces which link rooms that include design gems; the building was extended in 1907–09. Belatedly recognised at home for his bold originality of style, through German interest in his rather brief career Mackintosh made a unique contribution to the founding of the Modern Movement in architecture *(see also Gorbals, Govan, Maryhill and Helensburgh).*

**Distillers, Blenders and Bottlers**: The distillers Wright & Greig Ltd built a storage and office block in Waterloo Street, begun in 1898, but during the Boer War of 1899–1902 the market for whisky collapsed before the building was complete, and the bizarre detailing remained unfinished. About 1901, a major whisky firm, W P Lowrie & Co, built a cooperage at Hydepark Street in 1898 and another bonded warehouse in Washington Street in 1897–98. The firm was acquired in 1906 by James Buchanan & Co, whose *'Black & White'* blended whisky was heavily advertised by 1908; in 1907–11 their vat-building branch established a sizeable sawmill in Lancefield Street, and in 1910 the firm maintained three whisky blending and bottling plants in the city centre. Buchanans joined DCL in 1925.

**Kelvin Engines and Varied Engineering Products**: In 1904 the 23-year-old Walter Bergius founded the Bergius-Kelvin Company to manufacture cars, but they soon found it more profitable to concentrate on petrol-paraffin marine engines for fishing vessels; these were made from 1906 to 1945, mainly in their Kelvin Motor Works in Dobbies Loan at the top of the city centre, purpose built in 1909–14. About 1910 R G Ross & Son manufactured steam hammers, as they had for decades. The Lancefield Boiler Works were extended in 1909–10 by the shipbuilders Harland & Wolff, and in the 1930s to produce diesel engines. In 1908 Christie & Wilson were making binnacles for ships' wheelhouses *(for industrial buildings in Glasgow and suburbs to 1914 see Hume (1974), from which much information has been drawn).*

**The Port of Glasgow at its Peak**: The port reached its peak of importance in the early 20th century: in 1902–06 it was equal third (with Hull) among British export ports. In 1910 Glasgow was among Britain's top ten in coal exports and still among its top six for coastal trade. But the Anchor Line of Glasgow sold out to Cunard in 1912, and three years later the Allan Line merged into Canadian Pacific. Coastal shipping peaked in 1913, but the tonnage of foreign-going shipping using the port continued to grow until 1926–30.

**The Start of Glasgow's Decay: Edwardian Emigration**: But industrial development had to falter sometime, and in Glasgow the Edwardian years, when so many young people found more opportunities overseas, marked the end of an age of frantic growth and transient prosperity. The building boom had continued too long, so that the number of empty houses in the city as a whole quadrupled between 1902 and 1910, the 20,000 vacancies in the latter year demonstrating the massive emigration that had occurred. As a result of falling demand, fewer houses were built each year until in 1911 the supply almost ceased. In 1909 the former Alexander's cotton thread mill in Duke Street was converted into a hostel for workers unable to find other accommodation. Large families remained the norm, and in 1911 there were 785,000 people within the city boundary, further extended in 1912 with the inclusion of Govan, Partick and Pollokshaws. City centre redevelopment slowed but did not halt; the historic *Saracen Head Inn* was sadly demolished in 1905 and the Adam Royal Infirmary vanished about 1912, during a huge enlargement of the hospital.

**Trams versus Railways and Motor Vehicles**: Late railway developments included the NBR's High Street goods station, built in 1904–05, and in 1913 the St Enoch engine shed was home to 40 G&SWR steam locomotives. But the *caurs* competed all too effectively for passengers with the steam railways, whose suburban trains (except on the Cathcart circle) soon languished. Another early sign of things to come was the Western Motor Company's garage, built in Berkeley Street in 1906 and extended in 1911. By 1914 there were 850 tramcars, and routes reached out to Paisley, Renfrew, Dalmuir, Milngavie, Bishopbriggs, Cambuslang and Uddingston, there connecting to Motherwell, Newmains and Hamilton. After the 1914–18 war and an industrial crisis, Glasgow Corporation acquired the Airdrie tramways in 1922 and the Paisley tramways in 1923, bringing the Glasgow tramways to their apogee and spurring renewed suburban growth. By 1925 they reached about 200 track miles, with 1100 vehicles. But the arrival of go-anywhere petrol-engined buses built on innumerable war-surplus chassis had already caused problems for the tramways, which intensified when more powerful and economical diesel buses were introduced.

**Grouping hits Glasgow-based Railways and Banks**: In 1923, due to the government-imposed Grouping that followed its wartime control of the railways, both of the Glasgow-based railway companies became part of the enormous and at first unhappy London, Midland & Scottish (LMS) Railway, with headquarters in London, with the Glasgow offices becoming mere outposts. Locomotive and carriage design was moved south to Crewe, Derby and Wolverton. In 1926–27 the Union Bank of Scotland built a new head office in St Vincent Street, to a pompous and costly design by James Miller; it was unlucky that just at this time the United Alkali Company, owners of Tennant's of St Rollox, merged into the giant ICI, and its large volume of business fell to the latter's English bankers. The Union Bank, however, survived the loss, and some other significant head offices remained in the city: in 1927–31 an 8-storey office block was built for Scottish Legal Life Insurance.

**Railway Cartage under Grouping and Slump**: Wordie & Co, the major Scottish carriers of goods to and from railheads, including milk from farms in churns, had bought their first powered vehicle in 1905 – a steam tractor; but they were to stay with the horse for half a century. In 1929 the Wordie headquarters were in Glasgow's West Nile Street. But they were losing money, and in the slump of 1932 when motors were gradually superseding horses the firm's Scottish operations largely passed into LMS control. In 1936 the LMS-owned Wordie & Co Ltd took over Road Engines & Kerr, itself an amalgamation of two heavy haulage firms which moved export locomotives from Springburn to the docks. By 1938 Wordies had 272 motors and 1084 horses; by 1946 380 motors and 820 horses. In 1948 the firm and its subsidiaries passed into national ownership, and soon afterwards the horse-drawn carriers and Wordie name vanished *(see Paget-Tomlinson)*.

**Glasgow up to the Depression**: After the 1914–18 war, remarkable industrial developments in Glasgow were few. Beckett & Anderson were established to make mine haulage engines *(see also Bridgeton)*. In textiles McCallum & Craigie established a men's knitted outerwear factory in 1922, and Kidmar changed from knitting shawls to outerwear as Kid-Knit. The shoemakers Greenlees also began in the twenties. The King George V Bridge, erected in 1924–28, was built of reinforced concrete faced in Dalbeattie granite, followed by the confusingly named King's Bridge at Ballater Street, built in 1932–33. The Wall Street crash of 1929 and the ensuing Depression hit the city and its surrounding capital goods manufacturers very badly; when Stow College of Engineering opened in 1934 it was sadly just a century too late to serve the city's boom period.

**Glasgow's Later Coasting Fleets**: J & A Gardner – by the 1890s the Glasgow-based owners of the Ballachulish slate quarry – owned vessels which also carried granite from their Bonawe quarry, and although coastal trade generally continued to decline after 1918, Gardner bought five new vessels, carrying alumina to Kinlochleven and later Fort William, and aluminium ingots to other ports. The long-established Robertsons became known as the Gem Line, following their long-standing naming policy, and in the 1930s moved into motor vessels; they owned 36 small ships in 1938. Puffer proprietors John Hay & Sons survived as a company to be taken over by Everards in 1956 *(see Waine, 1976)*.

**The Port of Glasgow 1933–39**: The Clyde Shipping Company, noted above as originating in 1815, still operated steamers for passengers and cargo to Waterford, Cork and even London until 1939. In 1932 William Sloan & Co – who had run a cargo service to and from Bristol by sea for many years – gave up carrying passengers on this route. In 1933–37 Glasgow was still equal third among Britain's export ports. But the industrial disasters in the Glasgow hinterland in the great slump of the early thirties hit the city's trade very seriously, and the port rapidly declined from its former level. Yet within a framework of national decline in Britain, in 1937–38 Glasgow was still among the top ten ports for coastal trade, and helped by rearmament against Hitler's Germany, which gave a temporary respite to its heavy industries.

**Newspapers, Radio and Shopping between the Wars**: The *Sunday Post* newspaper, established in Glasgow in 1914, was re-founded in a couthy, reassuring mould in 1920. By then reassurance was much needed, and the paper flourished; it was later also printed in Dundee, to which the head office was transferred. In 1928 the London *Daily Express* started its Scottish subsidiary, and provided it with new offices and printing works at Albion Street in 1936. With unemployment in greater Glasgow running at some 30% in the early 1930s, the city still published seven daily and three Sunday papers – by then the dole allowed enough for the workless to buy them and search the small ads for jobs and bargains. In 1923 the new BBC established its first Scottish studio in Glasgow; this was briefly moved to Edinburgh about 1932 before returning west to Hillhead about 1935. Blackie's the publishers moved out to Bishopbriggs in 1931, their old premises being taken over by their rivals Collins. Marks & Spencer's first store in Scotland was opened in Argyle Street in 1919; their second Glasgow store was built in Sauchiehall Street in 1937. Meantime the nearby C & A store was built for the Dutch company in 1930. Anderson's 99-year-old store was acquired by Lewis's in 1936, demolished and replaced in 1937.

**More and Bigger Cinemas and Ballrooms**: The *Grand Theatre* burned out in 1918 but was reopened two years later as the *New Grand Picture House*. Hengler's Circus which closed in 1924 became the *Regal Cinema*, and in 1929 the huge *Coliseum* also became a picture theatre. In 1925–26 George Green built the *Playhouse* in Renfield Street, with 4400 seats the largest cinema in Europe, and with it a ballroom. Several other new dance halls were built in the 1920s and 1930s, including the *Plaza, Locarno* and *Albert*. In 1930–31 the *Empire Theatre* was fully reconstructed with 2100 seats. Despite growing unemployment, the new talking pictures offered escape from the street corner: the *Paramount Cinema* was built in 1934. By 1937 Glasgow had the highest provision of cinemas per head in the world. When the obsolete *Panopticon* closed in 1938 its shell remained in quiet decay, but in 1939 came the stylish *Cosmo Cinema*, opened in Rose Street by George Singleton. It showed many foreign-language films and was eventually sold by him in 1972 to become the successful Glasgow Film Theatre, still operating today.

**Glasgow Film Stars, Services and Housing**: Many would-be actors were finding roles in the cinema: the well-loved character Duncan Macrae was born in Glasgow in 1905, a star in the classic film *Whisky Galore*. Roddy McMillan, born in Glasgow in 1923, became an actor best remembered for his role as Para Handy in the BBC TV series as captain of the puffer *Vital Spark*. Mary Ure, later a well-known actress, was born in Glasgow in 1933. The National Academy of Music was formed in 1928, and the Glasgow Dental Hospital in Sauchiehall Street was built in 1932. Despite high unemployment, the lack of opportunities elsewhere kept people in the city, so that in 1936 Glasgow's overcrowding at 29% of all houses was the worst of the four cities (though a dozen large towns were even more congested). The city council boasted at the time that it allowed unplanned development.

**Transport Improvements of the 1930s hit by War Damage**: In the 1930s F A Macdonald & Partners of Glasgow, civil engineers, designed reinforced concrete bridges such as the Inverbervie viaduct. Movement around the city was aided by numerous fast bogie trams, built at Coplawhill up to 1940 and by growing numbers of buses; the circular Subway was converted to electric haulage in 1935. 1937 saw citywide automatic telephone dialling with the Director system. The Empire Exhibition at Bellahouston in 1938 *(see Govan)*, gave a resounding *Last Post* on the imperial trumpet; but the 8-storey *Beresford Hotel*, opened in that year, was to become in turn ICI offices, and eventually a Strathclyde University Hall of Residence. In 1939 came the war: the odd name HMS *Spartiate* was chosen for the Glasgow naval base, open until 1946. Although a bomb that hit Merkland Street station in 1940 caused closure of the Underground for four months, most of central Glasgow somehow escaped major air raid damage *(but see Clydebank).*

**Trams triumph, but Trolley Buses a Silent Menace**: In 1944 when there were four double-track tramways across the city centre from east to west and another four from north to south, some 14 million passengers were carried by the tramways; in 1952, on closure of the London system, Glasgow's became Britain's biggest tramway network, at 250 miles. Rubber-tyred trolley buses were introduced to the city in 1949, as a means of maintaining electrified services on the High Street, among other routes; but these were not popular with pedestrians – used to relying on hearing trams' gongs and screeching flanges – the trolleys' almost silent approach being known as *'whispering death'*; they ran until 1967.

**Extreme Congestion**: Edinburgh's 18th century congestion was as nothing by comparison with mid 20th century Glasgow: in 1945 despite its great range of fine civic and office buildings, Glasgow's housing conditions were truly appalling; the worst were in the industrial Gorbals *(q.v.)*. By 1951 about 225,000 people were crammed into the 10 square kilometres of the inner city, replete with shops, industries and facilities of all kinds. Dispersal from the city was inevitable, and together with its economic decline was to compound Glasgow's problems.

**Industries in Success and Decline 1945–60**: From 1946 Bergius-Kelvin built water cooled marine diesel engines; as a GEC subsidiary known as Kelvin Diesels the firm was still working at Dobbie's Loan in 1995. In the 1950s Beckett & Anderson still made mine haulage engines; but as coal declined in the 1970s they merged with Mavor & Coulson of Bridgeton *(q.v.)*. Around 1960 James Williamson & Partners of Glasgow were civil engineering consultants for the Cruachan pumped storage scheme. The Charing Cross Tower was built in the 1960s and at one time was the home of the Admiralty Research Department of Yarrow Shipbuilders *(see Whiteinch)*. But in the post-war period many of the remaining great industries of Clydeside collapsed one by one; by the end of the 1950s there was little or no textile work in the area, except for Templetons. In 1959 cigarette manufacturers Stephen Mitchell & Son became part of WD&HO Wills.

**Service Sector Struggles**: Progress in services was limited. In 1951 the comparatively old 4-star station hotels still dominated, led by the *Central (*258 rooms), *St Enoch* (155) and *North British* (85, later the *Copthorne)*. The Eye Infirmary was demolished in 1950, and in 1952–55 the weakened Union Bank of Scotland was absorbed by the Bank of Scotland, which took over the former's head office in Saint Vincent Street as its Glasgow Chief Office; this it remained in 1995, but by 1999 it had become a private club. The Royal Scottish Academy of Music and Drama was formed in 1951 by merger, and based in the former *Athenaeum Theatre* and neighbouring buildings.

**Live Entertainment in Ordeal**: Fire hit the *Queen's Theatre*, gutted in 1952; the *Metropole Theatre* was burned down in 1961, and in 1962 came the conflagration which destroyed the grand St Andrew's Halls, which sadly burnt out following an evening's use as a mere boxing arena. Fortunately the fine Ionic shell was eventually converted into an extension to the Mitchell Library, completed in 1980. Meantime TV had arrived in 1953 and cut down theatre and cinema-going; a spate of cinema closures resulted from massive audience desertion to television and then to nightclubs. About 1960 the *Theatre Royal* became the first headquarters of the new Scottish Television (STV); BBC Scotland remained at Hillhead. The *Britannia Music Hall* was closed and lay vacant for decades, neglected but intact in 1991. The *Empire Theatre*, the largest music hall outside London, closed in 1962 and sadly was demolished.

**Later Theatre Casualties**: The *Alhambra Theatre* which in 1957 had staged a season of grand opera, closed in 1969, was demolished in 1971 and became the site of an office block; the *Palace Theatre* which went over to Bingo in 1962 was demolished in 1977. Luckier for a time was the *Empress* at St George's Cross, originally designed as an opera house by Harry McElvie, variously thereafter a theatre or *'playhouse'*; it was saved from destruction in 1964 by Jimmy Logan, who renamed it the *New Metropole*; but this also closed in 1972. The *Savoy Cinema*, which had been converted into the Majestic Ballroom in 1958, was demolished in 1972. The *New Grand Cinema* also lasted into the 1970s. The *Lyceum Theatre*, which had gradually turned to films, declined still further to bingo in 1974.

**The Evisceration of the City from 1957**: About 1958 Lanarkshire County Council moved out from Ingram Street to a new and more conveniently located headquarters at Hamilton. Apart from the major movements of people already leaving for East Kilbride New Town, the demand for improved housing conditions led – in Glasgow's disastrous plan of 1957 – to the ruthless and unimaginative response of total clearance of the inner city, and the dispersal of a majority of its people to some of the largest (and soon the most problematical) housing estates in Europe. Ultimately some 140 flatted high rise blocks rose throughout the city and suburbs, the 650 blocks proposed in 1962 having thankfully been opposed by Sir Robert Grieve *(see Maryhill)*. Later movements were to Cumbernauld New Town and, by sundry agreements in the 1960s, to existing small burghs such as Haddington and Inverkeithing.

**Demolitions Good and Bad**: The miserable old Duke Street prison was demolished in 1960 and not missed, unlike the *Lyric Theatre*, pulled down in 1962 to make way for another crude office block. The Corn Exchange became redundant in 1963 and was soon cleared and replaced by an office block. Worship ended at the fine UP church in Renfield Street, demolished for redevelopment in 1965. In 1964 part of the former Houldsworth's Anderston cotton mill collapsed, and in 1967 the remainder was cleared. The Anderston Parish Church was also demolished in the vandal-ridden 1960s, and Anderson's fine Miller Street warehouse was demolished in 1969. In 1967 the large office block built by the former City of Glasgow Bank was pulled down, replaced by what was then Britain's biggest branch of Marks & Spencer, who at least had faith in the city. However, Radio Clyde moved from Anderston to Kilbowie Park at Clydebank.

**Newspapers shrink, Culture grows**: TV also cut reading time for the three evening papers in Glasgow; the *Glasgow Evening News* closed in 1957, and the *Evening Citizen*, then owned by the *Scottish Daily Express*, itself in publication by 1959, was closed in 1974, leaving the field to the *Evening Times* and its Albion Street building to the *Glasgow Herald*. In 1966 Howard & Wyndham sold the *King's Theatre* to the city council for use as a civic theatre. In the 1960s Scottish Opera found a permanent home at the *Theatre Royal*, and ballet too gained a base.

**Public Transport Degradation in the 1960s**: Glasgow's was the last of the original tramway systems to operate in a British city. The clean though noisy trams were regrettably abandoned in 1962, replaced by perhaps a thousand buses with their noxious stinking exhausts, a situation worsened when the clean 200-vehicle trolley bus system was abandoned in 1967. In 1964 what is now the Argyle Line through Central Low Level Station was closed and abandoned by Dr Beeching; the neo-classical Glasgow Cross station building was demolished. The original Central Station bridge was reduced to a disused skeleton in 1966, the year when two of the city's four terminal stations were closed: wretched Buchanan Street, which was immediately replaced by the *'Scotrail'* headquarters building, opened in 1967; and magnificent St Enoch, where the hotel was however retained for a time. Bridge Wharf saw its last daily summer steamers in 1969 and closed in 1970.

**The Decay of the Port of Glasgow**: The growing size of ships and the rapid development of containerisation had also made the port obsolescent. In 1965 the Clyde Port Authority took over the ailing system, and the Queen's Dock was closed to shipping in 1970; as a consequence the Sailors' Home at Broomielaw became redundant and was demolished in 1971, as were McGeoch's office and warehouse block. By 1972 Glasgow's remaining docks had little more than 2% of Britain's overseas trade; their final decline has been clearly described by Jackson (1983). When British Shipbuilders was formed in 1977, Fairfield's marine engineering subsidiary Fairfield-Rowan of Anderston was left to go to the wall, and by 1985 Glasgow was no longer a significant import port. Today, privatised Clydeport (formerly the Clyde dock authority), owns the rump of the port of Glasgow, plus Greenock, Ardrossan and Hunterston.

**The M8, Kingston Bridge and Demolitions**: In 1966 the Glasgow end of the Monkland Canal was obliterated to allow construction of the M8 motorway, and in 1969 the *Grand Hotel* at Charing Cross was demolished for the same reason. But the opening of the M8 and Kingston Bridge in 1970 removed much through traffic from the city centre, important parts of which in Argyle Street, Buchanan Street and Sauchiehall Street were then more or less attractively pedestrianised. Some sites remained vacant for a decade, until for example the *Holiday Inn* was built. In 1970 Allan Glen's School moved to new premises near its original site, and the much altered old buildings were pulled down. Stow College had also moved into new buildings in West Graham Street by 1973, when its original buildings were demolished. Both Copland & Lye's and Pettigrew & Stephens' fine department stores were demolished in 1973–74 to make way for the architecturally appalling *Sauchiehall Centre*.

**Departures and More Demolitions**: The AA's Scottish HQ was moved out to Erskine in 1974, and the wholesale fish market left Bridgegate for Blochairn Road in 1976. In order to escape closure, the High School of Glasgow became independent and moved to Anniesland in 1975, and about the same time Notre Dame Catholic teacher training college departed to Bearsden. The one-time *Garrick Temperance Hotel* in Stockwell Street, the last surviving tenement of 17th century Glasgow, was sadly demolished about 1975. In 1975 too the fine railway offices in West George Street, originally built as a church in 1818, were demolished and replaced by a miserably poor-looking substitute block, which nonetheless provided easier access and more facilities for station users. In the 1970s many warehouses and commercial users also left the Merchant City – the congested area between Glasgow Cross and the City Chambers – and by 1980 a third of the area's property was vacant. The vast YMCA lasted until demolition in 1980. But Wellpark Brewery continued in production, and was extensively rebuilt in the 1970s.

**A Queen Full of Saints, and Central Electric Trains**: St Enoch Station and the once great *St Enoch Hotel*, which had been closed in 1974 as it failed to meet new fire regulations, were demolished in 1977–78; the former station area was intended to be used for MOD offices and shopping. A quarter million m$^3$ of materials from the cleared site went towards infilling the Queen's Dock, the job being completed in 1979 with spoil from developments on the circular Glasgow Underground, extensively modernised in the late seventies. Electrification of Glasgow's remaining suburban railway lines and of the West Coast main line (completed in 1974) sustained Glasgow Central as the busiest station in Scotland. The Argyle Line through Central Low Level was reconstructed in 1977–79 and reopened with electric trains in 1979–80 with a new station at Finnieston to open up the area. By then the small Buchanan Bus Station at Parliamentary Road and Killermont Street had been rebuilt on a new site in its present spacious form, and a decade of comprehensive redevelopment had swept away almost the whole of the 1200 m-long Parliamentary Road and much of Dobbies Loan, introducing four more tower blocks of flats.

**Tall Blocks house New Services**: Heron House, a monstrous office block of 16,250 m$^2$, was built in the 1960s at Bothwell Street, towering over the fine Thomson church and St Vincent Street. The Mirror Group's multi-storey newspaper plant at Anderston Quay was opened in 1971, exploiting new technology to produce Scotland's most popular papers, the *Daily Record* and *Sunday Mail*, soon printing around three quarters of a million copies a day. Glasgow College of Technology was founded in 1971. The Scottish Development Agency (SDA), set up in 1976, had made their headquarters in Bothwell Street. The SDA employed 600 people up to 1991 when 200 headquarters jobs were cut, leaving just 400 in its successor Scottish Enterprise, with its 13 constituent LECs (Local Enterprise Companies).

**Capital of Strathclyde**: Glasgow and Clydeside were greatly stimulated when Strathclyde Region, created in 1975, sited its new headquarters in the city centre. But for decades closures had outnumbered new developments, and by 1981 male unemployment in the city as a whole was 21%. Newly built offices in West George Street intended for exchange control, which was abandoned, were sold by the Bank of England in 1981. A major new office complex of 40,000 m$^2$ at St Vincent Street included a unique French-designed roof garden and its own 25 m swimming pool. This became the 1986 headquarters of Britoil (part of BP from 1988); some other large blocks were created in suburbs. Such opportunities, and continuing emigration, had reduced unemployment to 13% by 1989, still twice the national average.

**Shopping Primacy**: Glasgow had nonetheless kept its role as the prime shopping centre for Strathclyde. Shopping developments included the 8-storey Sauchiehall Street Centre built in 1974–77, and the Savoy Centre, also of over 5000 $m^2$, which had appeared in the city centre by the mid eighties. In 1987 former offices reopened as the Princes' Square Centre with 54 shops around an atrium, and in 1989 the 72-unit St Enoch centre, financed by the Church of *England* Commissioners, replaced the former station with 26,000 $m^2$ of glass-roofed shopping (and a short-lived ice rink), adding some 10% to the city centre's shop floor area. Though a third of the units were still unlet its 750 parking spaces drew customers off public transport and increased the pressures for further motorways.

***'Miles Better'* and the SECC**: The essentially meaningless slogan *Glasgow's Miles Better* was invented by ad-man John Struthers in 1983, and had a remarkable success in raising confidence inside and outside the city. When the Queen's Dock infill had settled, its site was partly built over by the new Scottish Exhibition & Conference Centre (SECC), opened in 1985 and mainly served by car; a covered walkway made it accessible from Finnieston station, renamed Exhibition Centre. The SECC attracted 1.4 million visitors in 1988 when it was also linked across the Clyde by footbridge to the all too brief Glasgow Garden Festival; the next year it had to weather financial difficulties, but stayed open. By 1988 a helipad close to the SECC was used by Clyde Helicopters, who had four machines in 1995 when they sold out to Bond Helicopters, based at Aberdeen Airport.

**Entertainments and Town Houses**: Meantime in 1982 the former Tron church had reopened as the *Tron Theatre*. New buildings were erected in 1984–85 for the RSAMD, extended in 1997 for the Alexander Gibson School of Opera; the *Playhouse* which had become the *Apollo Theatre* was partly pulled down in 1987, and the remainder burned out in 1988 while being rebuilt into a huge 14-screen cinema. In 1988 the old *Metropole* theatre stood derelict, but in 1988–89 variety and traditional pantomime continued in the *Pavilion Theatre*. The *King's, Mitchell and Tron* theatres also staged pantos in 1994, and in 1996–97 Scottish Opera played at the *Theatre Royal*. In 1990 the *Hollywood Bowl*, the largest ten-pin bowling centre in Scotland, with 32 lanes, was opened in Anderston.

**Hotels grow, Their Names change**: Several large new hotels appeared in the 1970s, including the 14-storey 248-roomed *Albany* in Bothwell Street, built in 1970–71, and (by 1977) the *Glasgow Centre* in Argyle Street (125 rooms), the *Ingram* in Ingram Street (90) and *Lorne* in Sauchiehall Street (87), later enlarged to 100 rooms as the *Kelvin Park Lorne*. In the early 1980s the large *Holiday Inn* opened just north-east of the Kingston Bridge, and by 1984 the city as a whole held 42 hotels. The tall 300-room *Forum Hotel* opened in 1989 at Congress Road adjoining the SECC; it soon became the *Moat House International*. This was surpassed by the *Hospitality Inn & Convention Centre* which was Scotland's largest hotel in 1990, with 316 rooms; by 1994 it had become the *Glasgow Thistle Hotel*. Meanwhile the *Albany* had become the *Posthouse* and the historic *Central Station* was the *Quality Central*. The former Royal Academy of Music and Drama in West George Street had reopened in 1990 as the luxurious *Town House Hotel*. In 1991 the Swedish Scanda group planned a 234-room hotel in Cathedral Street. The tall 320-room five-star *Glasgow Hilton Hotel* was opened in 1992–93 beside the *Holiday Inn*. Charing Cross Tower, a former office block, was converted in 1994–95 into the *Charing Cross Tower Hotel* with 275 budget rooms, opened in 1995 for the YMCA.

**Brickworks Bosses, and Electronics bring More Office Jobs**: In 1980 the Scottish Brick Corporation (SBC) of Glasgow managed many brickworks, largely in the west of Scotland; in 1994 the firm was bought by Ibstock. In the 1980s the Merchant City became the site for 12,000 $m^2$ of new office floorspace. In 1989 BP moved 600 staff from London to Glasgow, helping to fill the many new speculative office buildings. Very significantly, Londoners' social benefit enquiries started to be remotely handled by over 400 Glasgow clerical workers at Cowcaddens from 1989, and in 1990 British Airways announced the creation of 450 jobs in a telephone booking centre to serve the whole of the UK. In 1994 Mercury Communications proposed 350 jobs at Waterloo Street merely to answer enquiries. As electronics annihilate space, these forms of displaced activity increasingly exploit pools of otherwise underused workers.

**European City of Culture 1990**: Glasgow's year as *'European City of Culture'* was opened in 1990 at the *King's Theatre*; the former *Athenaeum Theatre* was restored and reopened in 1990 as the Scottish Youth Theatre. The McLellan Galleries also reopened in 1990 for travelling exhibitions after a serious fire several years earlier. The 2500 seat *Glasgow International Concert Hall* was built at the top of Buchanan Street in 1988–90 for use by the famed Scottish National Orchestra, and the new City of Glasgow Philharmonic Orchestra, founded in 1988.

**City of Merchants, Architecture and Learning**: By 1992 some style-conscious shops were open in the Courthouse Centre and hundreds of upmarket houses had been created in the old Merchant City. By 1993 a new paved square had been created in front of the newly floodlit Cathedral, and new housing and a small hotel in the former Cathedral House were complete. In 1994 Walter Macfarlane's ornate house at Park

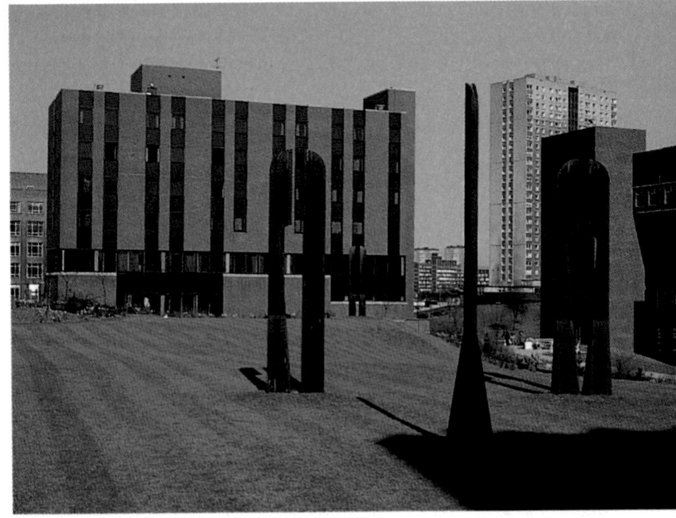

*Modern Strathclyde University buildings in the city centre. The institution derives from John Anderson's Technical Institute, founded in 1796.* *(JRH)*

Crescent was reopened as the *'Glasgow Palace of Weddings'*, and the former Cowcaddens Church was restored to use as a piping centre. The city won the Arts Council's 1994 UK City of Architecture award; the old *Glasgow Herald* building was to become the architecture centre. By 1993 Strathclyde University had converted the former Barony church into a multi-purpose hall, and was to teach pharmacy to 100 Malaysian students a year for ten years from 1995; in 2000 they launched the Hunter Centre for Entrepreneurship, a 1000-student course named for its benefactor Tom Hunter, founder of Sports Division.

**Travel, Consultancy – and Poor Health**: In 1990 the Glasgow civil engineering consultants Babtie Shaw & Morton still specialised in dam design, and consulting engineers Sir Alexander Gibb & Partners were expanding in 1991. The Royal Infirmary retained nearly 800 beds in 1993. In 1993 the Passport Office, located in Glasgow for many years, employed 260 people and a further 60 seasonal workers. Glasgow still possessed the headquarters of the Clydesdale Bank, but in 1991 about a third of the total 2100 jobs there were to be cut *(see also Clydebank)*.

**Whisky Headquarters Stay but Insurance Goes**: In 1977 William Teacher & Sons had their head office in St Enoch Square. In 1987 William Grant & Sons' Glasgow HQ celebrated their centenary as a family firm, five generations having produced malt whisky under the Glenfiddich label *(see Dufftown & Girvan)*. In 1994 Highland Distillers plc whose head office was in Glasgow owned the blenders Robertson & Baxter, but mainly depended on the *Famous Grouse* blend of their subsidiary blenders Gloag's of Perth, and Highland Park distillery at Kirkwall. In 1991 the Scottish Mutual Insurance Society of St Vincent Street with its 600 local workers was taken over by Abbey National, affecting the city's role adversely.

**Building on Tradition: Still More Shopping Centres**: By 1996 a Tesco Metro store was open. Nearby at Buchanan Street and Bath Street were two rundown hotels, the *Commercial* and *George*, both recently sold. Meantime in 1993 Marks & Spencer added a new sales floor to their Argyle Street store, and Frasers department store was still open in 1995, when John Smith the Glasgow booksellers founded in 1751 was also still trading, mainly in university centres, with ten Scottish stores under his name, second only in longevity among Glasgow traders to the tea merchants, James Finlay.

**Concentrated Educational Centre**: By 1990 in addition to Strathclyde University, which in 1993 boasted the largest engineering faculty in Scotland, the city centre contained no fewer than four colleges of further education, still operated at that time by Strathclyde Regional Council: (1) Building and Printing, (2) Central College of Commerce, (3) Food Technology, and (4) Stow College. Together with the College of Nautical Studies in the Gorbals, these comprised almost a quarter of all those in the far-flung region. Scotland's first Technology Academy was to be built on the site of an RC girls' secondary school in the city centre. In 1992 Glasgow Polytechnic and Queen's College were merged to become Glasgow Caledonian University, whose tower stands, just north of Buchanan Bus Station. The independent Roman Catholic school known as Saint Aloysius' College of Garnethill, had some 1000 pupils aged 8–18 in 1994, having lately absorbed St Francis School; a new junior school was soon built there. Park School for Girls which then had only some 255 pupils was closed in 1996, most staff and pupils merging into the larger Laurel Bank School at Hillhead as Laurel Park School; the premises went for sale. In 1997 the last secondary school in the city centre, Woodside, had 464 pupils. Mining (Scotland) Ltd, successful bidder in 1994 for the rump of the denationalised Scottish coalfield, made its HQ in Glasgow and expected to employ over 1000 people. By then Glasgow's Bothwell Street contained the base of the Tory government's controversial Student Loans Company.

**Atlantic Quay – and Empty Office Space**: *'Atlantic Quay'* was built on the historic Broomielaw in 1991 by Glasgow & Oriental, a London and Japanese combine; as Scotland's answer to London's vast Canary Wharf it provided no less than 26,000 m² of office space, claimed as Scotland's largest new office building. Some 250 jobs were brought there by the home loans division of the TSB, to be followed over 18 months by over 300 more in their mortgage division, and a major insurance company's northern office. In 1992 a second phase ten times the size covering six nearby sites was planned to provide major office, residential and public buildings. In 1994 the TSB announced the establishment at Atlantic Quay of a Phonebank Centre providing 250 jobs, with the possibility of growth to 900. Success there contrasted with the experience of Malcolm Potier *(see Gigha)* who promoted the 15,000 m² office block known as Tay House, a monstrous structure of seven storeys in pink and grey cladding, built in 1990–91 straddling the M8 opposite the Mitchell Library at Charing Cross; it was unlet when he went bankrupt in 1992 and still stood vacant in 1995. In 1992 BP Exploration decided to move all headquarters staff to Aberdeen. Though Abbey National Life soon found a use for some of the BP building, this move – plus vacancies and buildings still being completed – left the city centre with around 150,000 m² of empty modern floorspace.

**Central Glasgow's Remaining Industries**: Central Glasgow retained few important industries besides drinks; in 1992 Tennents were owned by Bass, Britain's biggest brewery combine. In 1990 Douglas Laing & Co gained a Queen's Award for the export of whisky, and in 1993 the surviving Clyde Cooperage of Robertson & Baxter, employer of some of the mere 250 coopers still at work in Britain, began the experimental production of whisky casks from new wood to meet a shortfall in the supply of used casks. Meantime in 1989 an *'Incubator'* for small hi-tech firms was opened at St James Road, and by 1991 Unicorn Fluid Injectors of Glasgow was an award-winning chemical engineering company. In 1993 despite the recession various small firms made garments in the Trongate area.

**Reinstating the Trams?**: In 1990 Strathclyde Region proposed a new LRT tram system, its first stage announced in 1994 aiming to link Maryhill with Easterhouse via Partick, George Square, Gallowgate, Riddrie, Ruchazie, Garthamlock and Provanhill. The planned new tram service was intended to use St Vincent Street in both directions, and extensions to Drumchapel, Tollcross and Balornock were being considered in 1995; but the abolition of Strathclyde in 1996 made the future cloudy. Meantime some further improvement of the

*The North Rotunda and the Stobcross crane. This rotunda and its southern partner were built to house the lifts and staircases which gave access to the Glasgow Harbour Tunnel, built between 1890 and 1896 to allow horse-drawn vehicles to travel under the Clyde. The crane was built in 1930–31 by Cowans, Sheldon & Co of Carlisle for shipping locomotives and for installing marine engines.*
*(SMPC / Angus Johnston)*

city centre's facilities for pedestrians and public transport was planned under the Millennium scheme.

**Railways Crossed, Flooded and Privatised**: In 1991 electric trains began to run between Glasgow Central and Edinburgh via Carstairs, extended to London down the East Coast route. The Argyle line was closed for many months from late 1994 due to floods some 3m in depth at Central Low Level Station, which submerged two standing trains. The Crossrail scheme, intended to link the passenger services on the three east–west railways by a central north–south service was under discussion in 1994, but rail privatisation intervened.

**Problems at the *Herald***: In 1992 the *Glasgow Herald* and the *Evening Times* were bought out from Outram's by the new Caledonian Publishing Company (CPC). Liam Kane, an arrival from Wapping who led the management buy-out, sadly dropped the name of Glasgow from the *Herald* masthead in the hope of raising its circulation to 150,000 covering a wider readership than Strathclyde, while cutting its staff in 1992–93 from 1077 to 883. But events proved otherwise; by 1994 its circulation was only about 115,000, the press hall in the black glass building in Albion Street used for nearly 50 years by the *Scottish Daily Express* became underused, and only 750 employees were left. CPC was to print a *Scottish Daily Mail* from 1995, 25 years after the paper gave up in Edinburgh and Scotland. CPC was itself taken over in 1996 by Scottish Television; however, the *Herald* is still a very effective newspaper. Meantime in 1994 the Mirror Group's *Daily Record* and *Sunday Mail* were moved from Anderston to a new plant at Cardonald. (The site is to be taken by US technology giant CISCO in 2002.)

**Redundant Sites and Public Buildings**: In 1994 a new business centre of 6500m$^2$ was proposed on the site of Wylie & Lochhead's former coachworks. The George Square post office building became redundant in the mid 1990s; in 1995 it was canvassed as the site for the proposed National Gallery in Glasgow. The intended closure of the Rottenrow Maternity Hospital was announced in 1995, when part of the Royal Infirmary in Castle Street was a *'building at risk'*. The former sheriff court in Ingram Street, derelict in 1996, was to become the HQ of a hotel chain. The awful Heron House in Bothwell Street was used by BT up to 1996, but was then declared unsafe, and proposed for redevelopment on lines providing a better setting for the fine Thomson church. The *Tron Theatre* in another important former church was upgraded in 1999. Glasgow Teledata, part of Scottish Telecom which was owned by Scottish Power, was to bring 500 jobs to Cadogan Square in 1997. St Andrew's Church near Saltmarket was finely renovated in 1998–2000.

**Paddler to cruise the World**: From 1993 the 3-masted steel barque *Glenlee*, built in Port Glasgow in 1896 and the last remaining Clyde-built sailing ship, was permanently berthed at Glasgow's Yorkhill Quay to undergo cosmetic restoration as a maritime exhibition centre. Capitalising on nearly two centuries of experience with powered vessels, the Paddle Steamer Cruise Line was set up in Glasgow in 1995, when an order was placed for its first vessel the *New Caledonia*, intended to cruise in the Mediterranean and the New World. There are also plans to bring back small pleasure craft to the once-vibrant Clyde. But industrial marine activity is not dead: Vships employ over 200 in ship management worldwide and Denholm's are in the same line, whilst Clyde Marine employ 600 manufacturing deck equipment for leisure vessels. Babtie is a long-established major construction company, with 3000 employees worldwide, and Aggreko supply generators and other industrial equipment around the globe (now Scotland's 7th-biggest firm). Glasgow also attracts call centres, Abbey National and Direct Line amongst them.

**Strathclyde's Sad End – and What Followed**: The abolition of the Strathclyde Regional Council in 1996 and the removal of Rutherglen and Cambuslang from Glasgow to a new unitary authority oddly entitled *'South Lanarkshire'* greatly reduced Glasgow's importance in this field, despite the City District itself gaining unitary powers. The loss of the wider West of Scotland perspective, following the established principle of the outgoing Tory government to weaken or eliminate all democratically elected opponents, was to be deeply regretted; what may the new Scottish Parliament decide when it eventually turns to local government reform? Meantime in 1996 Glasgow's new Labour-controlled City Council leased the Richmond Exchange, a very modern glass-clad office block of 4000m$^2$ at Cadogan Street; in 2001 the Council pulled out of COSLA, complaining of lack of support for their case as the Scottish council with the most deprivation in its area.

**Buchanan Galleries and Hotel Profusion**: Meantime another vast new shopping centre, first proposed in 1988, grew at the north end of Buchanan Street. Built in 1996–99, it opened as the *Buchanan Galleries*. Half the total floorspace is a vast new John Lewis store of nearly 28,000m$^2$; there are two more large stores, 80 smaller units and a huge car stack. Further hotels appeared: the *Carrick* (121 rooms), and *Malmaison* (72, converted from St Jude's church and extended), as well as several 'budget' establishments. The luxurious youth hostel is open all year round, and three other hostels in central Glasgow provide 140 beds for backpackers.

## GLASGOW AIRPORT & Abbotsinch **Map 15, B5**

***Airport area.*** OS 64: NS 4766

Walkinshaw House stood in almost flat country beside the Black Cart Water 3km north-west of Paisley; designed by Robert Adam, it was built in 1791 for D Macdowall. The straggling hamlet of Abbotsinch grew 2 km to the east, lining the road following the left bank of the White Cart Water from Paisley to the Black Cart bridge, and from 1885 was served by the horse-drawn cars of the Paisley District Tramways Company; the line was electrified in 1904. By 1903 the rail-connected Walkinshaw brickworks had been set up immediately south of Walkinshaw House, which was sadly to be demolished in 1920. The Abbotsinch to Paisley tram route was closed in the 1930s.

**From HMS *Sanderling* to Civil Airport**: In 1943 during World War II an airfield was laid out only 2 km north of the centre of Paisley, between the brickworks and Abbotsinch, as a Fleet Air Arm (FAA) maintenance base, called HMS *Sanderling*. In 1949 it was a Royal Naval Air Station, but in 1963 the FAA left Abbotsinch. The base was then taken over as Glasgow Airport, officially opened in 1966 to replace the small field at Renfrew; a proper terminal building was erected. This move provided a welcome growth point, particularly for the large, congested but industrially vulnerable town of Paisley. By 1972 the huge, 316-roomed *Excelsior Airport Hotel* was open.

**The Cost of Accessibility**: However, the area – once the site of gracious living – became assaulted by late 20th century noise and fumes. Access was arranged from the new M8 motorway, opened about 1970 round the south and west sides of the airport, which grew steadily, at first on a basis of charter flights and internal services, especially to the Highlands; the first Shuttle flew to London in 1975. By 1976 Loganair *(see Muir of Ord)* had a fleet of 14 aircraft; it was based at Glasgow Airport in 1979 when in spite of the impact on neighbouring communities of overflying on the built-up approaches, the extension of the runway from 1800m to 2658m was completed. The airport handled 3.6 million passengers in 1988, making it the busiest in Scotland, its traffic exceeded in Britain only by Heathrow, Gatwick and Manchester. In 1988–92 the improvement of the road access and a 70% expansion of the passenger terminal gave it the capacity for 6 million passengers a year.

**Scotland's New Gateway**: In 1990 the government reluctantly gave the airport gateway status for international services, which the airlines and business community had long wanted transferred from relatively remote Prestwick. Air Canada and North-West Airlines promptly made this move and began new services to Halifax, Toronto and Boston, while American Airlines opened a Chicago service in 1990. In 1992–93 4.7 million passengers passed through the privatised BAA airport. This traffic was growing at 12% a year, and by then British Airways (BA) flew to New York. In 1993 European services reached Amsterdam, Donegal, Dublin, Dusseldorf, Izmir, Larnaca, Paphos, Rhodes, Salzburg and Tenerife among other places. By then the 93 firms on the airport – which included 18 shops and catering outlets – generated 3500 jobs; a further 12,500 were believed to be airport related.

**Air Cargo moves by Road!**: In 1990 several freight concerns moved in from Prestwick, including the BA cargo handling trucking operation. In 1992–93 some 15,500 tonnes of air cargo was carried (more than through Prestwick) and daily cargo services operated to Frankfurt (Lufthansa), and Paris (DHL). However, rather more than half the region's air cargo still went long distances by road for carriage through Manchester and London airports; Lufthansa alone ran seven trucks to and from the south each day.

**Airport Museum, Business Parks and Access Problems**: By the 1990s a small museum near the airport commemorated the work of the 602 (City of Glasgow) Squadron of the RAF. In 1992 a new business park named *'Gateway International'* was created, backing on to the White Cart Water only 1 km from the airport terminal. In 1993 the Glasgow Airport Initiative was established, its aim to transform by major development over 7 years the shabby image of areas such as Inchinnan *(q.v.)*, and hoping to create some 15,000 jobs. A new major road flyover was opened in 1993 to connect the M8 and A870, so relieving the congestion of 60,000 vehicles per day at the St James roundabout; new links were provided on the congested landward side of the terminal. It was also proposed that a short electric railway link should be created from Paisley into the terminal area, where in 1993 competing buses and coaches milled in the unpleasant and dangerous confusion promoted by Thatcherite *'free for all'* transport legislation. An airport station near the Glasgow–Gourock line was still seen as a possibility in 1997 but has not yet been achieved due to rail privatisation.

**Loganair, and UK Passenger Services**: Loganair had become involved with British Midland Airways; from around 1991 it used Jetstream 31s, the first example of a Scottish airline using Scottish-built planes. In 1993 UK destinations of Glasgow flights included Aberdeen, Belfast, Birmingham, Bristol, Cardiff, East Midlands, Edinburgh, Humberside, Inverness, Kirkwall, London (Gatwick and Heathrow), Manchester, Newcastle, and Stornoway. By 1994 Loganair once again concentrated on services to the isles, and by 1997 it was again independently run, following a management buy-out.

**Transatlantic Business Retrenchment**: A further pier for international air traffic was built in 1993–95, with stands for 7 wide-bodied jets. But not until 1994 did NWA realise that golfers, and people tracing their Scottish roots, were the main sources of US travel to Scotland; it then axed its Glasgow to Boston flights due to a lack of premium business passengers. Similarly United Airlines (UA), a management buy-out which had started daily flights to Washington DC in summer 1993 and whose flights comprised 7% of all those at the airport, abandoned this service late in 1994, and AA withdrew its winter flights to Chicago in 1994, though they were to return to Glasgow in May 1995.

**Tourists make Air Canada and BAA Confident**: However in 1994 there were 22 charter flights a week to the USA alone. While maintaining its daily Toronto service, in 1994 AC whose trade was essentially in the leisure market successfully introduced a summer weekly Calgary and Vancouver service. In 1994–95 AC moved its services to the new international pier, and continued to provide at least three flights weekly to Toronto (daily in summer), plus twice weekly summer services to Calgary and Vancouver. BA was to fly 5 times a week to New York and Boston in 1995.

**The Busy Airport faces Competition**: In 1993–94 Glasgow had 102,000 aircraft movements (a quarter the number at Heathrow); over 90 companies handled nearly 27,000 tonnes of cargo and mail plus 5.33 million passengers (56% of them international). There were then 150 scheduled destinations, including places in Germany and Austria. Late in 1994 although BAA still showed confidence in the airport's future growth, phase 3 of the terminal expansion was delayed, because the 8 transatlantic flights a week in the summer of 1994 were not likely to be exceeded in the near future. However, by 1995 five more retail and catering outlets were open. In 1999 Scotairways *(see Dundee)* started successful scheduled air services between Glasgow, Dundee and London City Airport, but it seems that by then more passengers had begun to look east: by 2000 it was expected that Glasgow Airport would shortly be overtaken by the rapid growth of Edinburgh Airport at Turnhouse. By 1999 the *Excelsior Airport Hotel* had become the *Posthouse Glasgow Airport*, now with 298 rooms; there is also a new budget hotel, *Express by Holiday Inn. Days Inn* now plan another 230-bed hotel here.

## GLASS

**Map 10, A2**

***Buchan hamlet**, pop. 150 (area)* — OS 28: NJ 4239

Among the remote hills some 10 km west of Huntly, various tributaries join the River Deveron, so widening its valley to form a sheltered bowl, south of which is a stone circle. Beldorney Castle, a 16th century Z-plan tower, was built at its south end; near the kirk and the small village of Haugh of Glass 2.5 km to the north, some past significance is suggested by the name Markethill. By the 1750s Glass lay on a track between Huntly and Glenbuchat; later a road was built to Dufftown. In the 1950s when over 400 people lived around Glass there was an inn and even a junior secondary school, but the population was slowly falling, and both had gone by the 1970s, though an old corn mill remained. The post office had closed by 1986; afforestation continued in the surrounding hills. Meantime by 1977 Blairmore, 1.5 km east of Haugh of Glass, had become a preparatory school, still open in 1992 when it was favoured by service families, especially from the RAF.

## GLASSFORD

**Map 16, A5**

***Small S. Ayrshire village**, pop. 550* — OS 64: NS 7247

The site of a castle was marked on early OS maps of Glassford, whose ancient parish church stands high above the incised valley of the River Avon about 3 km north-east of Strathaven. This was a well-settled area where *'Glasfurd Mill'* turned when Pont sketch mapped Clydesdale in 1596; a parish school was started in 1620. Roads had been built by Roy's day in the 1750s, and in 1799 Heron named Glassford, which stands 500 m west of the church, as a *"village"*, though it never earned much distinction. A branch railway from Hamilton was opened in 1862–63, with a station 1.5 km west of the main settlement. This was named as *'West Quarter'* in the 1890s when it had a smithy, inn and post office. The mill still stood beside the Avon due south of the church, but was no longer on the map by 1953, when the population was nearly 700 and a primary school was also open. The station which then handled only freight had closed by 1971 and the line had been lifted; a new housing estate had recently been built north of the village. However, only 553 people lived in the closely defined village in 1991, and subsequently there has been little obvious change.

## GLENBARR, Bellochantuy & Muasdale

**Map 1, A1**

***S. Kintyre hamlets,*** *pop. 300* OS 68: NR 6636

Raised beaches, duns and standing stones are ancient features of the exposed west coast of south Kintyre, still a well-settled area when mapped by Pont around 1600; the Roy map of about 1750 showed a coastal track. The area made little mark on history. For centuries Glenbarr Abbey near the foot of the Barr Glen has been the home of the Macalisters of Glenbarr (by 1992 it was the Clan Macalister Museum and Visitor Centre). In 1951 the whole area held only some 330 scattered residents. Bellochantuy to the south had a primary school and post office, both of which soon closed, plus the *Argyll Arms Inn*; Muasdale to the north had a post office and the *Muasdale Inn*. Glenbarr had a primary school, post office and telephone exchange, and despite a 10% loss of population over 30 years, these facilities were still open about 1981. By 1977 the *Putechan Lodge Hotel* (now *Motel)* was also open at Bellochantuy. By 1985 Glenbarr and by 1997 Muasdale had caravan sites, and the post office at Muasdale has stayed open, though Glenbarr post office had closed; the hills to the east have been largely afforested.

## GLENBOIG

**Map 15, E4**

***Lanarkshire village,*** *pop. 2000* OS 64: NS 7268

Glenboig lies on a rolling plateau some 15km east of Glasgow, a formerly remote area unmapped by either Pont or Roy. It was opened up in 1826 by the primitive coal-carrying Monkland and Kirkintilloch Railway (M&K). In 1848 the Caledonian Railway (CR) made use of 1km of the M&K line to link its new main line from the south with the Scottish Central Railway to Stirling, by way of Glenboig and Castle Cary. To give access from the north to Glasgow (Townhead), a line was built westwards from just south of Glenboig station, crossing over the M&K to Gartcosh on the Glasgow & Garnkirk Railway of 1831.

**Fireclay and Coal**: Mark Hurll set up firebrick works just east of Glenboig station about 1861, aiming to meet the needs of the many furnaces and locomotive fireboxes of west central Scotland. A larger concern was James Dunnachie's Glenboig Union Fireclay Company, which gained a world reputation. Murray mentioned *"celebrated brick works"* in 1894, when Glenboig had a station, inn, and post and telegraph office. In 1901 the population of the village was 1670, and it grew further after the large Bedlay Colliery was sunk 2 km to the north about 1904. This was connected by rail to the old M&K and worked unusually thin seams, largely by hand, but successfully exploited coking coal in the Limestone Coal Group for a number of years. It gave rise to an adjacent settlement at Annathill and stimulated the hamlet of Mollinsburn to the north. From 1916 P & M Hurll used fireclay mined near Bo'ness, and Glenboig continued to grow steadily, with a sizeable new housing estate built at Marnock to the west: by 1951 its population was over 5100, but with only the facilities of a village.

**Rundown, Poverty and Neglect**: With the decline of steam the demand for firebricks fell and the works cut back production; Glenboig passenger station was closed about 1960. When the M73 was built in 1969, it passed west of Glenboig, whose population had shrunk to only 2500 by 1971, though with little physical clearance. However, several other facilities had been lost including the cinema, chemist, and hotel, and by 1973 most of Annathill had been demolished. In 1977 the colliery employed 740 men, but was soon closed. Hurlls apparently ceased production in 1980, probably due to the prevailing closure of open hearth steelworks, formerly large consumers of firebrick. By 1979 a gas storage installation had been constructed 2 km to the east; this would bring very little work; it was soon hidden by screen planting. By 1981 Glenboig's facilities were only those of a hamlet. By 1988 the Bedlay line had gone, and much derelict land remained, a mute reminder of past industrial importance. In 1991 Glenboig's population was 2038; transport work still employed a high proportion.

## GLENBRITTLE

**Map 8, A3**

***Glen, Isle of Skye,*** *pop. under 100* OS 32: NG 4121

This short and sheltered glen meets the sea at the foot of the jagged Cuillin Hills; the 992m peak of Sgurr Alasdair is only 3.5km from the shore of Loch Brittle, giving the glen tremendous potential as a starting point for climbers. Nineteenth century maps marked only a farm and Glenbrittle House, but by the 1950s over 100 people lived locally at the end of a steep 10km road from Carbost, served by a post office (which rated as a post town), and a 3-line telephone exchange! Facilities for climbers and tourists were appearing; already there was a youth hostel. Although by 1976 the postal address and phones were under Carbost, by the 1990s a car park, caravan and camping site, climbers' hut and a mountain rescue post clustered near the shore; the youth hostel is seasonal.

## GLENBUCK

**Map 2, A2**

***Former E. Ayrshire village,*** *pop. 0* OS 71: NS 7429

Glenbuck on the Ayrshire/Lanarkshire border stood at the high altitude of 275 metres, a col linking the heads of the Douglas and Muirkirk valleys. A reservoir was impounded to ensure an even flow of water via the River Ayr to power the Catrine cotton mills of 1787; later this was called Glenbuck Loch. A tiny ironworks was established in 1795–96, but this closed in 1813. Some coal and ironstone mining continued to feed the Muirkirk Ironworks, and a village resulted, whose football club was founded in 1872. In 1873 a Caledonian Railway (CR) branch reached Muirkirk from Douglas, completing a minor through route by utilising between Glenbuck and Muirkirk parts of an earlier line built by the Eglinton Iron Company. At one time there were five coal pits in the combined area, including the Viaduct Mine, and over 1200 people, with a church, inn, post office and railway station by the 1890s. The houses in the lengthy Grasshill Rows were particularly mean.

**Football Fame, Fun with Fuses – and Extinction**: Over 50 Glenbuck footballers became professionals; after the Boer War the team became famous and took the name *'Cherry Pickers'*. Footballer Bill Shankly, born in Glenbuck in the early 20th century, later became the famous manager of Liverpool FC, and his brother Bob managed Dundee FC. When Grasshill No.2, the last coal pit, was closed in 1931, drainage pumping ceased, the football ground at Burnside Park became a bog, and the famed football team was disbanded in 1932. There was still work for miners at nearby Muirkirk until well after World War II, during which the viaducts on the abortive Muirkirk & Lesmahagow Junction Railway were blown up as demolition practice. By the 1980s a large quarry had been established, and the small Viaduct Mine was privately exploiting a hitherto overlooked coal seam, generating between 25 and 50 jobs. In the early 1980s most of the village was compulsorily acquired for demolition, enabling a large opencast mine to be opened by 1992. The last house vanished in 1997, leaving a simple commemorative plaque on the site of the one-time football ground.

## GLENCAPLE, Bankend & Caerlaverock

**Map 2, B4**

***Dumfriesshire village & hamlets,*** *pop. 750* OS 84: NX 9968

An ancient hill fort and the Ward Law, a Roman site of the first century AD, overlook the shores of the Solway Firth south-east of Dumfries. Caerlaverock Castle, built nearby on tidewater and first recorded in 1220, gave its name to a parish. Largely built of pink sandstone, this moated Maxwell stronghold so untypical of Scotland was rebuilt on a unique triangular plan in the 15th century, improved in 1638, but spectacularly ruined after a siege in 1640. The Blaeu map showed that by then a tiny settlement named Glencaple stood near the east bank of the tidal River Nith, 4km from the castle and 8km south of Dumfries. In 1746–47 this site was chosen for a new village and port, but the Roy map made about 1754 showed no roads west of the inland hamlet of Bankend. Roads were subsequently built to serve Glencaple, its quay was rebuilt in 1836–40 to serve Dumfries traffic, and the village acquired basic facilities, but it was never industrialised; the 1901 population of Caerlaverock parish was 841. A village hall was built in 1939, and by 1951 the tiny *Nith Hotel* was open among the facilities of a small village, serving a parish population of 710. A National Nature Reserve was established on the Merse east of Caerlaverock. The harbour was little used by the 1970s, but in 1989 the village hall was still in active use, and Glencaple harbour was a sailing centre, with an inshore rescue boat; the 1991 population was 757. The adjacent post office stayed open, and the *Nith Hotel* has been enlarged.

## GLENCOE & Invercoe

**Map 5, A2**

***Lochaber village,*** *pop. 200* OS 41: NN 1058

The great defile of Glencoe, overshadowed by the 1070-metre mountain of Bidean nam Bian and formerly part of Argyll, reaches the sea in Loch Leven. On the right bank of the River Coe is Invercoe, the lowest of four tiny settlements in the glen when it was mapped by Pont about 1600. This was the site of the infamous massacre of 1692 when the clachans of the MacDonalds were burned down by troops led by Campbell of Glen Lyon, on the orders of the Lowlander Dalrymple, Master of Stair. Roy's map made about 1750 showed a ferry, later known as the *Dog Ferry*, from *'Invercoen'* to *'Calort'* in Lochaber, from which a steep track led over a 475-metre col to Fort William. Shortly after, Caulfeild's men built a road up the north bank of the River Coe to Kingshouse *(q.v.)* and the south. In 1769 Pennant thought that about 400 people lived in Glencoe. About 1780 the Bridge of Coe and the road to Ballachulish were built. On the latter grew Carnoch village, later called *Glencoe*; by 1782 the Glencoe road carried the Glasgow mails.

**Serving Tourists and Backpackers**: In 1803 the early tourist Dorothy Wordsworth found several stone houses near the foot of the depopulated glen and a *"carrier-merchant or shop-keeper"* who regularly journeyed *"to Glasgow with his horse and cart to fetch and carry goods and merchandise"*. By 1847 a pier at Glencoe was served by steamers. Glencoe village was bypassed in the early 1930s by building a carefully-sited new road on the left bank of the river. The *Glencoe Hotel* was open by 1939, a tiny hospital, and modern primary school have been built. For half a century much of the glen and its surrounding mountains have been owned and managed by the National Trust for Scotland. A youth hostel was open by 1982, and there are two caravan and camping sites and a controversial interpretation centre. About 3km and 5km up the glen are two bases for mountain rescue teams, one with a helicopter pad. Hotels are the *Glencoe* and the *Clachaig Inn* (3km south-east); there is also a guest house, plus the youth hostel and an independent bunkhouse for backpackers at Leacantuim.

## GLENCORSE, Auchendinny & Milton Bridge

**Map 15, C3**

***Midlothian villages,*** *pop. 2000* OS 66: NT 2463

Glencorse church stands beside the Glencorse Burn as it leaves the high Pentland Hills to form a tributary of the River North Esk. The riverside tower house of Woodhouselee Castle was built early in the 16th century for Oliver Sinclair 2 km south-east of the church, downstream from Penicuik. Pont's map of about 1600 showed roads linking Edinburgh to Peebles via Auchendinny on the North Esk, and to West Linton following the foothills of the Pentlands and bridging the Glencorse Burn. By 1746 the area's main roads had been made up under the 1713 Turnpike Act, and when Roy surveyed the area around 1754 its modern road pattern was established; Milton Bridge on the Edinburgh to Penicuik road spanned the Glencorse Burn between church and castle. In 1756 the water-powered Auchendinny paper mill was established by William Annandale, on the river 1 km west of the castle. Between the two was Auchendinny House.

**Banknote Paper and French Forgers**: Three prisoner of war camps were set up around Penicuik from 1803; after 1810 they held in all some 11,000 Frenchmen and their allies. In 1803 Alex Cowan had begun to make banknote paper at Penicuik; perhaps it was not coincidental that by 1811 forgers were busy drawing banknotes by hand in the confusingly titled Greenlaw Camp, later known as the Greenlaw barracks. Most proved to be incompetent! By 1832 Auchendinny mill was making writing and printing papers by machine. By about 1837 the Dalmore Mills of William Sommerville were open at Milton Bridge, and used steam to augment water power from 1843, when a papermaking machine was installed. In 1859 a second machine was added at Dalmore mills, which long continued under the Sommerville name. The valley-floor Penicuik Railway, which left the NBR at Rosewell, was opened in 1872 with a station at Auchendinny, where a post office and an inn soon appeared.

**Literacy and Golf**: With compulsory education, literacy gradually spread even among the soldiery, and some time after 1875 the Greenlaw Barracks were renamed Glencorse, maybe to prevent their families' letters going to Berwickshire! In 1877 a railway was opened to Glencorse itself. Glencorse golf club, founded in 1890, laid out an 18-hole course which passed under the railway. By then there was a post office at Milton Bridge and an emparked mansion at Bush, across the burn from the church. The barracks were the HQ of the Royal Scots when the Glencorse line was closed to passengers in 1933. By 1951 the other station had been closed to passengers, but Milton Bridge, also known as Loganlea, had nearly 1200 residents, the Glencorse primary school, five doctors, an inn and a garage. The local railways vanished between 1959 and 1967; the viaduct over the golf course lasted until 1985. In 1971 the barracks held 250 people. By 1981 the population of the entire area was around 2100. In 1989 Glencorse and Redford barracks were jointly the training depot of the Army's Scottish Division.

**Sludge and Science**: William Sommerville and their Dalmore mills were taken over in 1989 by the American James River paper company; but by 1992 the mill was owned by the Inveresk Group of Inverkeithing, and had gained a secondary effluent treatment plant, much more efficient than the old filters. The waste fibre, clay and chalk, formerly tipped, was now converted into a sludge suitable for agricultural soil conditioning. In 1995 160 people worked at the Dalmore mill. In the late 20th century research facilities were established on the Bush estate, plus the Centre for Rural Economy at Easter Bush. The already extensively developed Bush Estate was launched in 1994 by its owners Edinburgh University as the *'Technopole'* science park. By 1994 a 30-bay golf range adjoined Glencorse golf course. In 2000 the Midlothian Council applied for help to reopen the railway to passengers.

## GLENDARUEL — Map 5, A5

***Argyllshire glen,*** *pop. 200 (area)* — OS 55: NR 9984

Glen Daruel in Cowal has several ancient standing stones and a medieval motte. Deserted settlements abound on the braes above the glen, which equates with the parish of Kilmodan, whose early kirk was marked on the Roy map of about 1750. From there tracks followed the River Ruel to Loch Riddon and Strachur; another, now vanished, led over the hills to Kames. By the 1890s roads followed both sides of the glen, and beside the fine 18th century kirk at Clachan of Glendaruel was a hotel, a smithy and a post office. To the south was a waulkmill; a hill road crossed a nearby bridge and led west to Otter ferry. Near the motte some 3km north of the clachan stood Glendaruel House in its park; by the mid 20th century it had become the *Highland Hotel*, there was a telephone exchange, and the *Glendaruel Hotel* was open. The parish school was 3km to the south at Ormidale. By 1971 the Hydro Board had built the Striven power station at the head of Loch Striven, 10km east of Glendaruel, fed from tree-girt Loch Tarsan, raised by two dams (OS 56). By 1996 the former *Highland Hotel* had been replaced by a caravan park, and the post office had closed. Early in 2001 the 19th century Dunans Castle, 9km north-east (OS 56: operated as a hotel since 1999), was gutted by fire; but the *Glendaruel Hotel* and the kirk remain in the quiet glen.

## GLENDEVON — Map 6, A4

***S. Perthshire glen,*** *pop. 150 (area)* — OS 58: NN 9904

The River Devon which rises in the Ochil Hills flows south-east past a hill fort and the 15th century Glendevon Castle to Muckhart. The Roy map showed that by about 1750 a track from Auchterarder to Dunfermline followed this route, past the Kirk of Glendevon. After roads were made up, in the early 19th century a four in hand coach through the glen linked Rumbling Bridge with Auchterarder. Around 1880 a new reservoir was formed by damming Glen Sherup, a side valley of Glendevon; from there water was supplied to Dunfermline. By 1888 there was a *"very comfortable inn"* at the hamlet of Downhill; it claims droving origins, and became the *Tormaukin Hotel*. By 1895 a school was open near Glendevon Castle and Kirk. By 1940 two more reservoirs, the Lower Glendevon and Glenquey, also served Dunfermline. By 1951 the 30-room *Castle Hotel* stood opposite the small *Tormaukin*, and a youth hostel was open. By 1969 the Upper Glendevon reservoir had been added, and there was a caravan site; the old castle became a hostelry. In the late 1970s yet another reservoir, the Castlehill, was formed by damming the gorge 1.5km east of the village. But the *Castle Hotel* burned out in 1983 and was demolished in 1985, leaving only its tower, which was soon reinstated as a B&B. In 1991 the resident population of the parish was only 129. The *Tormaukin Hotel* and the youth hostel still serve, and the caravan park has been extended.

## GLENDRONACH & Forgue — Map 10, B2

***Small Aberdeenshire village,*** *pop. 625 (area)* — OS 29: NJ 6244

The small valley of Glen Dronach some 10km east of Huntly was for long the boundary between the county of Aberdeen and the detached part of Banffshire known as the Garioch (pronounced *Garie*, but *'Garviach'* on Blaeu's atlas). Forgue became a burgh of barony in 1599, and by 1628 held a parish school, but grew little, and this remote and hilly area appeared to be still roadless in the 1750s. The Glendronach distillery was built in 1826 by James Allardyce & Partners, taking its water and power from the Dronach Burn, a tributary of the River Deveron. About 1836 the finely designed mansion known as Haddo House – not to be confused with the National Trust for Scotland's property of that name near Tarves – was built at Inverkeithney, some 2.5km to the north. By 1886 the distillery was *"quaint and picturesque"*, its Highland Malt whisky *"held in high repute"* and at eight years old likened by the discerning Barnard to liqueur brandy; about 250,000 litres were produced annually. A farm and a tiny settlement adjoined.

**Grants, Teacher and Allied Distillers**: Glendronach distillery was acquired in 1920 by Charles Grant of the Glenfiddich family concern, who remodelled it; sold to William Teacher & Sons in 1960, it was extended from two to four stills in 1966–67. The small and shrinking village of Forgue, in the valley some 1.5km to the north-west, though of only 160 people by 1981, provided housing and a very limited range of facilities, including the modest 10-roomed *Bognie Arms Hotel* on the main Banff and Huntly road. By 1991 the distillery was going strong for Allied Distillers. However by then Haddo House had suffered from several changes of ownership and was a long-derelict shell, as it remained in 2000, when the distillery too was silent.

## GLENEAGLES — Map 6, A4

***Perthshire community*** — OS 58: NN 9111

Glen Eagles, a defile in the Ochil Hills through which passed a track linking Dunfermline with Crieff, may be named either from Eagles or *Eccles*, the early name for a church (Latin *ecclesia*). Its 15th century castle, on a property of the Haldanes ever since the 12th century, was abandoned in 1624 for the new mansionhouse of Gleneagles. Roy's map made about 1750 showed Glen Eagles house in its policies; well to the

*Gleneagles railway station, opened in 1856 as 'Crieff Junction' (named 'Gleneagles' from 1912). It was lavishly rebuilt in 1919 as a war memorial to employees of the Caledonian Railway Company, and to serve the Company's new hotel.* *(RCAHMS / JRH)*

north the track intersected another, linking Greenloaning in Strathallan with Auchterarder and Bridge of Earn. The area was still rural when the Scottish Central Railway's main line between Stirling and Perth, cheaply built through Strathallan and Strathearn, was opened in 1848. When the Crieff Junction Railway opened in 1856, a station named *Crieff Junction* was created 3 km south-west of Auchterarder, but no major development occurred.

**Gleneagles Hotel and Golf Courses**: In 1912 the station was renamed Gleneagles, to match the aspirations of the energetic civil engineer Donald Matheson, by then the General Manager of the Caledonian Railway (CR). He had realised the potential for a hotel offering a distant view of Gleneagles, accompanied by fine golf courses which could be laid out on the high-lying glacial outwash terrain known as kettle moraine, 3 km north of the castle. Due to the interruption of the 1914–18 war, the grand plan for a 200-room golfing hotel was only partly realised by the CR before the grouping of railway companies in 1923. The station was rebuilt on a lavish scale in 1919 as a war memorial to CR employees; from it a siding was laid to the hotel (which was partly built of stone from a collapsed railway viaduct at Motherwell). It was opened in 1924 by the CR's successor the LMS; two championship golf courses designed by James Braid were made available – the King's and Queen's. The complex soon became renowned, a frequent venue for the Scottish Open golf championship. An abortive experiment with unreliable railbuses failed to prevent closure of the little-used Crieff line in 1964.

**The Best Hotel?**: Gleneagles station was retained by Beeching on account of the five-star hotel, then open only seasonally and still associated with British Railways through British Transport Hotels (BTH). The 1971 census counted nearly 350 people in the hotel alone. In 1974 a third 18-hole course was opened, known as the Prince's. A fourth followed in 1980, named the Glendevon – another misnomer, for Glendevon is over the hills beyond Gleneagles! The sale of the complex was enforced on BTH by the Thatcher government in 1981; after some refurbishment the 5-star hotel was reopened on an all-year basis in 1982. A small upmarket holiday and residential settlement known as Muirton was then gradually developed around the hotel, including the Mark Phillips equestrian centre, opened in 1988. In 1990 while the AA rated Gleneagles as the best hotel in Scotland, the RAC preferred Turnberry on the Ayrshire coast. Jack Nicklaus designed the new 18-hole Monarch's golf course – now one of four. Even in depressed 1993 more housing was built at Queen's View. *Gleneagles Hotel* now has 222 rooms, whilst *Duchally House*, 3 km south-east, became a small hotel in the 1990s.

## GLENELG — Map 8, B4

***W. coast Highland village**, pop. 100* — OS 33: NG 8119

Two well-preserved ancient brochs stand on the narrow strait called *Kyle Rhea*, between Loch Alsh and the Sound of Sleat, longtime site of a ferry to Skye and once owned by the medieval king of the Isle of Man. Glenelg, 4 km from the ferry, is centred on the eastern shore between Glen More and Glen Beag. After the 1715 uprising this strategic location was guarded by troops based in a new barracks, built in 1717–22 at the clachan of Bernera at the foot of Glen More. By about 1750, when the Roy map was made, the military road from Fort Augustus had been completed to a point just east of the 350-metre Mam Ratagan pass, west of which not even a track was indicated. But the road must surely have been completed through Glen More to Glenelg by 1756, when the Trustees of Manufactures tried in vain to establish linen production there. Kylerhea was the usual drove crossing in the 18th and early 19th centuries, while Glenelg was the main contact point for trade between Skye and Inverness. By 1772 about 4000 cattle a year crossed the ferry, but in 1773 the *Glenelg Inn* was a highly marginal affair, as graphically reported by Boswell, who was then ferried to Armadale.

**From Destitution to Tourism**: The substantial barracks were abandoned some time after 1790. When visited by Robert Somers in 1847 Glenelg village had 148 families and much destitution, and Kylerhea was a mere huddle of poor huts; the people of Glenelg were cleared in 1849. By 1894 Glenelg had been rebuilt into what Murray called *"a pleasant neat village"* with the *"good" Glenelg Hotel*. A steamer to Oban called four or five times a week, and a market stance near the ferry was used until 1906. Later the steamers ceased to call, and the Bernera barracks, while still fairly complete, had become so ruinous that they were (temporarily) omitted from 1" OS maps. About 1978 a small lapidary business was established at Glenelg, now a small township with the small *Glenelg Inn*, a school, post office and under 100 people. By 1997 it also had a mountain rescue post. There is a fish farm just north at Ardintoul. Apart from the ferry which still plies in summer, Kylerhea's only facilities are a picnic area, though the Otter Haven 1 km north is an attraction.

## GLENESK — Map 6, C1

***Angus glen**, pop. 150* — OS 44: NO 4979

The most easterly of the Glens of Angus is Glenesk, containing a stone circle and many ancient cairns. At its forked head stands Invermark Castle, a 14th century keep, and the nearby Loch Lee with its ancient kirk; both forks of the glen are adorned by rocky outcrops and waterfalls. Gaelic was still spoken in this remote glen at least as late as 1618. At one time local iron ore was smelted at Bathangy or Tarfside, counterpart to a charcoal iron smelter that worked near Edzell around 1678 – apparently a short-lasting venture, for the Roy map of about 1750 showed an almost treeless glen, and little else except a track from Aboyne on Deeside, crossing Mount *Gannel* (Gannoch) and down beside the Water of Tarf to end at the *Bridge of Pausking* (Buskhead?) by present-day Tarfside: this track is now a footpath known as the Finmounth Road. Downstream were mills at *Kenny* (Keenie) and the Mill Den. Later a road was built up the glen, and Tarfside post office got its cancelling stamp in 1854. In 1951 this office, a school and a telephone exchange at Tarfside served some 250 people in the glen. By 1981 this number had dropped to about 180, but by 1985 the Retreat museum had been established east of Tarfside. By 1995 Loch Lee had been slightly raised and regulated by a weir for water supply; nearby is a filter station. The post office and school are still open in this pastoral glen.

## GLENETIVE — Map 5, A2

***Argyllshire glen*** — OS 50: NN 1246

The long mountain-girt defile of Glenetive links the head of Loch Etive with Kingshouse on Rannoch Moor. Roy found that about 1750 a track led along the south side of the loch from Taynuilt to end at Kinlochetive. Later the arrangement was reversed, when a road was built down the north side of the glen, passing Glenetive House to end at a lochside pier. This was served in 1847 by steamers from Oban, connecting with coaches plying to Kingshouse and Glencoe, and the lochside track became simply a footpath. A school was built 2 km east of Glenetive House, near which a post office was opened. But in the 20th century the steamer service was abandoned, and some time after 1953 the pier became derelict. Between 1979 and its closure in 1984 the school taught only one or two children, for by then only 13 people lived in the glen; the luckless pupils were then sent by car to the primary school in Glencoe, a daily round trip of 65 km, and to an even more distant secondary in Fort William. The inshore fishing was dead, leaving only declining deer stalking, cattle, sheep, and a little forestry. An unreliable water supply plagued the shopless post office, which was still marked on the 1993 OS map; there is hill walking, and occasional tenting campers.

## GLENFARG — Map 6, B4

***S. Perthshire village,*** *pop. 500* — OS 58: NO 1310

Glen Farg forms a winding defile connecting the west end of the Howe of Fife with lower Strathearn. Balvaird Castle, a 15th century L-plan tower, was built high on its eastern slopes, 3 km east of Arngask parish church (a chapel of Cambuskenneth until 1527). For three centuries or more the narrow glen north of these places was the route of the Great North Road between Queensferry and Perth, made up in 1808–10. By 1827 an inn was open, maybe the *Lomond Inn* that was a coaching stop in 1832; 2 km north of Arngask was a change point for the horses, the *"small but comfortable Beinn Inn"* noted by David Beveridge in 1888. On the main road near the church was a toll bar and the hamlet of Damhead. To Beveridge in 1888 this was a *"village with a little inn called the Damhead Hotel"*; this was just inside Fife until about 1890.

**Glenfarg Village created by the Railway**: When the North British Railway built its belated line between Kinross and Perth (opened with the Forth Bridge in 1890), Glenfarg station was placed at Damhead, and led to the building of the *Glenfarg Hotel* and a new settlement which took its name. By 1951 Glenfarg had 700 people and the facilities of a small village, including a new parish church and two other hotels. The closure of the railway in 1970 – soon followed by its obliteration for the M90 motorway which passes equally close by the village without having an access to it – hit Glenfarg hard. Although in 1978 it had a bowling green, tennis club and coach hirer, it became a pleasant backwater, which apart from its long-standing annual folk festival makes little news. Though under 500 in population by 1991, some new housing continued to be built close to the motorway into the 1990s, for people indifferent to noise and fumes. The castellated *Glenfarg Hotel* still serves, *and* a garage and primary school are still open.

## GLENFINNAN — Map 8, C5

***Lochaber small village,*** *pop. 150 (area)* — OS 40: NM 9081

Erosion along the geological grain of the West Highlands has given natural nodality to the mountainous head of Loch Shiel, a trackless but well wooded area when Roy's map was made about 1750. The only tiny settlement was *'Garbole'*, the spot where the pretender Prince Charles Edward had raised his standard in 1745. Work on the so-called Loch na Gaul road, the first of those to be built under Telford's control for the Commissioners of Highland Roads and Bridges, began in 1804 and was complete past Glenfinnan to Arisaig by 1812. This opened up the area and enabled Macdonald of Glenaladale, grandson of a Jacobite, to erect in 1815 a stone tower and statue as a monument to the luckless Prince; the Victorian family home is now a hotel.

**The Railway boosts Incipient Tourism**: By 1886 a hotel was open, and from 1896 a tiny passenger-carrying mail steamer plied daily the length of the delightful loch between Glenfinnan and Acharacle. The West Highland Extension Railway was opened in 1901 with a crossing station at Glenfinnan, where one of the most spectacular features of the scenic line was situated, *'Concrete Bob'* MacAlpine's 21-arched mass concrete viaduct. This photogenic structure 380 m in length was laid out on a 241 m radius curve, carrying trains 30 m above the valley of the River Finnan. With the withdrawal of the steamer in the late 1960s and Beeching cuts in the railway staff, the resident population had halved by 1981 to around 50.

**Facilities proliferate**: However, car tourism flourished, and in 1984 two hotels were open, the 13-room *Stage House Inn* and the 19-room *Glenfinnan House Hotel*; there was a shop, a primary school, a Catholic church, and the National Trust for Scotland's new visitor centre. Four council houses and about ten new bungalows were scattered wherever suitable sites could be found, but the almost disused pier was deteriorating. From the 1980s, occasional steam excursion trains have run to Mallaig. By 1995 the station buildings had become a railway museum and café, and by 1997 a substantial new jetty complex had been built; there is still a post office. The hotels are the *Glenfinnan House* and the modernised *Prince's House*; the *'Glenfinnan Sleeping Car'* forms a little year-round hostel for backpackers.

*The 21-arch mass concrete Glenfinnan viaduct, 30m high and 380m in length, built in 1901 by 'Concrete Bob' MacAlpine as part of the West Highland Extension Railway from Fort William to Mallaig.* *(RS)*

## GLENFOUDLAND & Bainshole — Map 10, B2

***Aberdeenshire settlements,*** *pop. 150* — OS 29: NJ 6135

About 10km south-east of Huntly is a defile called the Glens of Foudland; about 4km to the south east is the Kirkton of Culsalmond, said to be built over the site of a stone circle. When the area was mapped by Roy about 1750, a track linking Huntly and Old Rayne passed clusters of huts at Bainshole and Auchintender; later a road was made up, now the important A96. The flanks of the Hill of Foudland south of the road were soon heavily scarred by extensive slate quarries; some local slates were used to roof Balmoral Castle, but the quarries had ceased work by the 1950s. No village developed at Glenfoudland, but until about 1960 the small Glenfoudland Junior Secondary school served a scattered and fast-falling population. In the 1950s Bainshole School also had junior secondary classes. Bainshole post office was closed about 1968; by 1976 the schools too had vanished and the area's population had been halved in 35 years to perhaps 175. Now even the old quarries are being hidden by afforestation.

## GLENISLA — Map 6, B2

***Angus glen,*** *pop. 350* — OS 44: NO 2160

Early settlement in Glenisla, most westerly of the Glens of Angus, is attested by hut circles and field systems, but the 16th century L-plan Forter Castle of the Ogilvies was burnt out in 1640, and the Roy map of about 1750 showed a trackless area. The Kirk of Glenisla is 6km below Forter, and a further 6km downstream was a now vanished mansionhouse at *'Kilvey'* (Kilrie). In 1824 a suspension footbridge was built at the kirkton to enable children to walk to the parish school. Soon the river was spanned by a road at Bridge of Craigisla below Kilrie, and at Brewlands 2km above the kirk, and the beautiful glen was opened up by roads linking Kirriemuir with Glenshee. By 1951 the Kirkton served some 450 scattered people, having an inn, a post office, school, and a 44-line telephone exchange; by 1955 a youth hostel was open at Knockshannoch, 2km east. By 1977 although the population was under 350, *Kirkside House* was a small hotel. The youth hostel had closed by 1985, but the school, inn and post office still functioned in 1995, and ski trails are open in the nearby Glenisla Forest; the 5-storey Forter Castle has been re-roofed and renovated. The small 17th century *Glenisla Hotel* stands at the kirkton.

## GLENKINDIE, Towie & Glenbuchat — Map 10, A3

***Aberdeenshire village & hamlets,*** *pop. 300* — OS 37: NJ 4413

An ancient stone stands beside the River Don about 15km west of Alford; 2km to the east is a motte known as the Peel of Fichlie. The estate of Towie, on the opposite or south bank, was owned in 1309 by the Knights of St John and later became a parish. The Water of Buchat enters the River Don from the north as it winds through the hills 4km west of the standing stone; Glenbuchat Castle, a 16th century Z-plan tower, stands near its mouth, and beside Towie Kirk is the 17th century tower of Towie Castle. Roy's map of about 1750 showed a track along the north bank of the Don, which by the 1890s had been replaced by a main road which bridges over the Don near the standing stone, joining Towie with Glenkindie House, which had replaced the early castle of Glenkindie. The overshot water mill at Glenkindie was rebuilt in 1901–02.

**Rural Decline slowed**: By the 1950s the 275 or so local people enjoyed the facilities of a small village, with a garage, a pleasant old inn, two postmen and even a small junior secondary school. This had only primary status by 1976, when the post was sorted at Alford. By 1981 the population was down to about 150, but the remaining facilities including a shop and garage still catered to a further 325 or so people within 5 km. By 1986 there was a timber haulier, a caravan site served tourists, and the postmistress averred that the village hall was *"well used"*; the primary school had 24 pupils and two teachers. But the need then being expressed by locals was for sheltered housing. The mill had become derelict, but was restored as a house in the early 1990s. The post office has since closed, but the modest *Glenkindie Arms Hotel* is still open.

## GLENLIVET

**Map 10, A2**

***Moray / Speyside glen,*** *pop. 150* — OS 36: NJ 1929

Also see: *Ballindalloch, Tomintoul & Tomnavoulin*

The River Livet is a secondary tributary of the Spey, first joining the River Avon (pronounced *A'on*), in what was for centuries part of Banffshire. Glenlivet had a thanage from about the 11th century, though its exact site is doubtful. Blairfindy Castle, built in 1586, was only one of many local names shown on Robert Gordon's map, made about 1640. At some time a packhorse bridge of three spans was built at the sharp bend of the river about 1.5 km to the north of the castle, but it was after the Roy map was made about 1750 that a road was built through the glen; Glenlivet post office opened in 1804. About 1800 some 200 small illicit stills are believed to have worked in Glenlivet, whose whisky was in demand, while local people found the laws of the day too onerous to obey! After changes in the law, in 1823–24 George Smith (a tenant of the reluctant reformer the Duke of Gordon) *"a powerful robust young fellow"* who wished to expand legally, obtained a licence for his bothy distillery at Upper Drimin. Within a year the moonlighters' physical opposition and threats of arson had scared off the proprietors of three more small distilleries founded nearby in 1825–26, but the strong and persistent Smith faced down his lawless neighbours to establish Speyside's first legalised still.

**Minmore – the Classic Malt**: After a fire, Smith moved 1 km downhill to a more accessible site at Minmore in 1858–59. In the 1860s Glenlivet was regarded as the premier Highland malt, but was sold only through Andrew Usher of Edinburgh. Minmore became perhaps the most famous distillery of all, and in 1886 when operated by George Smith's son it was steam-driven and substantial, though it remained remote from railways; barley was fetched from Ballindalloch station in at least 16 horse-drawn carts, and local peat was used in producing 900,000 litres of best Highland Malt whisky a year. Including a cooperage, engineers, smithy and stables about 50 men were employed, and 120 cattle were fed on the draff and spent wash. By 1890 steam road tractors hauled some of the materials.

**Glenlivet in the Twentieth Century**: Glenlivet whisky's quality, supported by Bell's of Perth, enabled it to weather USA Prohibition, but the settlement remained small and scattered; about 1965 its small secondary school was downgraded to primary only. In 1975 the glen was placed in Moray district. *The Glenlivet*, as the famous distillery is known, was acquired by Seagram Distillers of Canada in 1977. Its product, always a renowned single malt, varies with the cask used to mature it. By 1980 a former shooting lodge had become the *Blairfindy Lodge Hotel*, whose guests could either stalk deer, or walk the Speyside Way or in nearby forests; the 40 farms in the glen were all owned by the Crown Estates. In 1992 Glenlivet whisky was sold at the exceptionally great ages of 31 and even 50 years, attracting a premium price; but by then the local post office had closed. In 1997 community action created a television relay station, at long last bringing the first clear pictures to the remote glen! The distillery has 8 gas-fired stills and a visitor centre; the *Minmore House Hotel* caters for the visitors.

## GLENLUCE, Auchenmalg & Stairhaven

**Map 1, B4**

***Galloway village & hamlets,*** *pop. 575* — OS 82: NX 1957

An ancient broch stands at Stairhaven on Luce Bay. In 1190–92 Roland, the new Lord of Galloway, founded the Cistercian Luce Abbey on a remote site beside the Water of Luce 5 km to the north. It became wealthy, as shown by its ownership of over 3000 sheep in the late 13th century. The lay brethren sold sorted wool around 1400, and a nearby settlement in Old Luce parish became a burgh of barony in 1496 under its Gaelic name of Ballinclach, *'Stone Village'*. In 1560 the abbey was unusual for a sizeable monastery in having no appropriated churches. In the 16th century the tower of Sinniness was built near Stairhaven, then known as *'Boatstone'*. Following the Reformation the Castle of Park was built in 1590 on the west bank of the Water of Luce, typically from the spoils of the abbey. Pont's map made around 1600–10 named both the abbey – secularised to Lawrence Gordon in 1602 – and a kirk at Glenluce. He did not show a bridge, nor the military road then apparently under construction between Carlisle, Dumfries and Ireland, predecessor of the A75.

**Village and Burgh**: In 1632 a parish school was founded, and in 1642 a very early postal service came to the place, which lay on the Irish route from Carlisle. Despite stone robbery, Heron noted that the abbey buildings were still *"almost entire in 1646"*. Though all coal had to be imported, there were salt pans by 1684, and by 1700 a cattle tryst. Ballinclach was officially re-chartered as Glenluce in 1705. In the 1750s the Roy map showed Glenluce as a nucleated settlement with four radial routes – comprising the main road east and west, with a bridge over the Water of Luce at Castle of Park; and a road from Whithorn, passing Luce Abbey and continuing over the Chirmorie towards Barrhill and Ayr.

**Posts, Harbour, Railway and Airships**: By 1797 Glenluce had a daily postal service, and qualified as a post town; Heron called it a *"small town"* in 1799. Chambers took an opposite view in 1826 when he described Glenluce as *"a small village of no great prosperity"*, merely a stage on the road from Dumfries to Portpatrick. A small harbour was constructed at Stairhaven in the early 19th century. The Portpatrick Railway which climbed over successive hills en route between Dumfries and

Stranraer came to Glenluce in 1861, crossing the Water of Luce on a whinstone viaduct of eight arches, but did not lead to significant development. However, in 1894 the Wigtownshire County golf club established a 9-hole course. An airship base operated briefly west of Glenluce during World War I. By 1953 Glenluce had a population of over 1000, two small hotels and a 220-pupil secondary school.

**Beeching and McGregor speed Decline**: The railway to Dumfries was closed completely by Beeching in 1965. A caravan and camping site was open by 1978 and the two small hotels of the 1950s had become five by 1981, but the secondary classes had gone, leaving Glenluce as a small agricultural village with basic shopping facilities. In 1989 the opening of a bypass removed the heavy through traffic, and Glenluce which had only 579 people in 1991 regained its peace. By 1991 a small motor museum had been opened, though there was little other work in the area outside of farming and tourism. The golf course now has 18 holes; the *Kelvin House Hotel* and a guest house offer accommodation.

## GLENLYON

***Perthshire glen,*** *pop. 200 (area)* — **Map 5, C2** — OS 51: NN 5344

Roy's map of about 1750 showed a track the length of beautiful Glen Lyon from Fortingall *(q.v.)*, passing mottes and ancient forts, the 16th century castles of Carnbane and Meggernie, and the sites of other castles, en route to Loch Lyon. It then went by way of Glen Meran and over a col 450 m in altitude to Loch Tulla, and so across Rannoch Moor to Lochaber – a severe through route. By the late 19th century a cross route from Dall on Loch Rannoch to Edramucky on Loch Tay crossed the River Lyon at Bridge of Balgie; nearby at Innerwick was an inn. The route to the west had been moved to a lower col, leading past an early chapel in the Auch Gleann and so to Tyndrum. By the 1930s a made road led up the north side of the glen to Invermearan, but both paths to the west had been totally abandoned above this point. The inn had been replaced by a school and post office.

**Hydro Schemes transform the Landscape**: Between 1953 and 1971 three dams, two of them 500 m long, were built in the upper reaches of the glen. Lubreoch dam incorporated a power station and extended Loch Lyon 4 km eastward, also raising its level by a few metres. A smaller dam downstream created the little Stronuich reservoir, below which was the Cashlie power station, largely fed by tunnel from Loch an Daimh. This now incorporates the former Loch Ciorra, its surface raised by 30 m by the major Loch an Daimh dam, built upstream of the waterfalls in the side glen of the Allt Conait. The school and post office among the woods at Bridge of Balgie have survived, to be accompanied by a gallery and picnic area.

## GLENMAVIS & Rochsoles

***N. Lanarkshire villages,*** *pop. 2350* — **Map 16, A3** — OS 64: NS 7567

Rochsoles House which stands on a hillside about 150 m above sea level 2 km north of Airdrie, was emphasised on Timothy Pont's 1592 map of Lower Clydesdale. By the mid 18th century (as the Roy map showed), roads were being laid out in this area. The adjacent hamlet became known as New Monkland from its parish church, and as Glenmavis from its steep wooded den where thrushes sang. Airdrie golf club, founded in 1877, laid out its course south of Rochsoles, which was emparked by 1899, when Glenmavis had an inn. However the idyll was somewhat marred by coal pits north of the church, served by a largely mineral railway which meandered across the moors from Kipps to Greengairs and Slamannan. Other pits and railways to the south were not so close, but some 600 people lived in Glenmavis.

**From Pits to Prosperity**: By 1955 the pits were closing, leaving bings to remember them by; Glenmavis had become a tightly knit village with a population of over 1100, a post office and New Monkland primary school. Though the mineral railways had gone by 1971 the village had grown westwards; a gas storage depot was built 1 km to the north-west in the 1970s, and development then looked eastwards. By 1981 although there was no longer an inn, garage services were available. Further expansion in the 1980s took over Rochsoles Park, and by 1991 2332 people lived in Glenmavis. The golf course, primary school, post office and a pub are open.

## GLENMORE

***Inverness-shire location*** — **Map 9, C5** — OS 36: NH 9709

From 1784 timber from the Glenmore estate near Loch Morlich, some 10 km east of Aviemore, was floated down the Spey to Garmouth *(q.v.)*. In the mid 19th century, the Duke of Richmond & Gordon cleared 15 farms from Glenmore, to create a deer forest embracing the high tops of the Cairngorms to the south. In the mid 20th century cross-country skiing was introduced to the area from Norway. By 1953 Glenmore Lodge was a mountaineering training centre with camping facilities. When the Aviemore Centre was developed from 1964 as a resort, much improved road access was created to Glenmore, where the Loch Morlich youth hostel was open and a mountain rescue centre had been established; farther up was the new White Lady Shieling, from which rose several ski tows and a ski lift, built by the Cairngorm Chairlift Company to exploit the snowy winter weather on the hills.

**Controversy delays Redevelopment**: By 1992 a watersports centre exploited Loch Morlich, the National Outdoor Training Centre had been erected near Glenmore Lodge, and the *Ptarmigan Restaurant* had been built some 1080 metres above sea level, at the head of the chair lifts and ski tows. In the early 1990s the company controversially planned five new ski lifts and intended to expand two others, including the original. The proposed additional means of access to the high tops of the area (which had been declared a National Nature Reserve), by either an aerial gondola system or a funicular railway, became a *cause celebre* for a strong lobby which adopted the argument *'do nothing, for the sake of wilderness'*. So when work on the chosen funicular began in 1999, it was heavily encumbered with conservation conditions. The youth hostel is open all year round.

## GLENMORISTON

***Inverness-shire glen,*** *pop. 360* — **Map 9, A5** — OS 34: NH 2912

The *'Road from Bernera to Fort Augustus'* through Glenmoriston was shown on the Roy map made about 1750. At *'Bun-do'* (later called Ceannacroc) where the River Doe joined the River Moriston there was a kingshouse named Aonach, still in use in 1773. There the road crossed from the south to the north bank, later by way of a Telford bridge. Some 8 km downstream was Torgyle, where in 1808 Telford built another bridge across the Moriston on the Commissioners' new *'Glen Shiel Road'* which replaced the older line; this bridge had to be rebuilt by Mitchell after the great floods of 1828. Between Aonach and Torgyle grew a hamlet, with Dalchreichart primary school, a post office and a minimal telephone exchange, which had just two connections in 1951! Between about 1954 and 1961 the Hydro-Electric Board built the new Ceannacroc power station *(see Cluanie)*. About 1970 they built the Dundreggan dam downstream from Torgyle to impound a small reservoir, supplying their new Glenmoriston power station 90 m below, and itself fed from the small Levishie underground power station to the north, built about 1950. Afforestation of this remote area continued through the latter half of the 20th century.

## GLENROTHES

**Map 6, B4**

***New Town, central Fife,*** *pop. 39,000* OS 59: NO 2701

The possible *Caer* element in the farm name Caskieberran, and the nearby intersection of ancient straight roads in cardinal directions, suggest Roman origins for settlement on the plateau 2 km south-east of Leslie in central Fife. By the 1890s there was an inn at the hamlet of Woodside, which stood at an ancient crossroads 2.5 km east of Caskieberran, some 2 km south-west of Markinch and 10 km north of Kirkcaldy on the Cupar road. The sinking half a century later of the Rothes colliery some 3 km farther south at Thornton *(q.v.)* was the prime reason for the designation in 1948 of Glenrothes, named for the Earls of Rothes, who had moved to Leslie *(q.v.)* from Rothes in Moray as long ago as 1700. As Britain's most northerly New Town, this entirely new settlement for a population of 70,000 was to have good facilities, and manufacturing industries to give it balance. Located mainly south of the incised River Leven, it was to infill the 4 km gap between the established small towns of Markinch and Leslie.

**Pigeons drop into the Precinct**: The existence of Woodside with its *'largely mining'* population of a thousand within the designated area of 2331 hectares led the New Town Development Corporation (DC) to make its first headquarters there. Building began in 1950 on the *'neighbourhood'* principle of distinct serviced housing areas, better described as *'townships'*. All were named after existing farms; South Parks, Caskieberran, Macedonia and Tanshall. By 1958 10,000 people lived in the New Town; in that year an 18-hole golf course was opened by the DC, west of the area for building development. By 1959 five incoming industries had brought 1500 employees and the associated services. The first phase of the town centre or *'Kingdom Centre'* was begun in 1960: a large store of the Markinch Co-op was accompanied by a sheltered shopping precinct beneath an open-ended greenhouse roof, soon sadly infested by pigeons! The large Glenwood Junior High School opened in 1962, then serving pupils up to 16.

**After the Rothes Debacle**: No sooner had a local newspaper, the *Glenrothes Gazette* (an offshoot from Kirkcaldy's *Fife Free Press*), been founded in 1962, than the Rothes pit failed due to flooding. Development of the New Town therefore slowed; it had no convenient railway station, and the East Fife Regional Road (A92), which was mentioned in the New Town Designation Order as conferring good access, was not built until the 1980s! However, work to develop infrastructure and to attract industry did not cease. By the end of 1965 Woodside had been bypassed, and a little grass airfield which could accept aircraft up to 6125 kilos fully loaded had been laid out near the golf course. By then 19 *'major industries'* on three industrial estates were at work, employing 4000 people. More than 5000 houses had been built, in which about 18,000 people lived. Of these, 56% were Fifers and only 10% came from outwith Scotland. By 1965 Auchmuty junior high school was also open, plus 5 primary schools.

**Industries at Queensway**: Queensway, north of the centre, held from 1959 a branch of Anderson Boyes, a Motherwell company, makers of mining equipment, plus three electronic component factories: Beckman, the US-owned instrumentation engineers, who came in 1958; Hughes International, a microelectronics firm which arrived in 1960, and Elliott Brothers (automation). Butchart & Sons made wire goods such as supermarket trolleys; by 1977 they were known as Buko Manufacturing. Minor firms were Formica (plastic extrusions and sports goods), London Knitwear (ladies' clothing), David Jonathan (shirts and pyjamas), an SMMB Creamery, and Charles Gray (building components).

**Viewfield and Eastfield Industrial Estates**: The large Viewfield estate south of the town contained a big AEI (later GEC) factory which opened in 1960, making telecommunications equipment; in 1972 GEC employed over 1200 people, two-thirds of them women. US-owned Sandusky, a specialised foundry and tube manufacturing company with international markets, arrived in 1964 to make rollers for paper-making, while Stowe-Woodward BTR Ltd made rubber coverings and Tay Spinners used man-made fibres. Robertson & Ferguson Ltd were steel fabricators. The Eastfield Estate just west of Coaltown of Balgonie took in Tokheim of USA, opened in 1964 to make petrol pumps, and Cessna Industrial Products, making hydraulic components expanded their factory to 17,000 m$^2$. Thomas Salter Toys was about to arrive in the town.

**Glenrothes becomes a Central Place**: Glenrothes gradually established itself as a central place. Glenrothes High School opened in 1966 and the Technical College in 1968. By 1970 there was a small Woolworth store; later they moved to larger premises and Boots took over the former shell. The early *Fraser Bowl* was one of the few ten-pin bowling centres to survive the demise of the 1960s craze; in 1990 its 10 lanes provided the only such facility north of the Forth. The Fife Institute of Physical Recreation, including a swimming pool, was opened in 1970–71; later a dry ski slope was added. By 1971 Glenrothes had a population of 27,000 and the facilities of an average town; a twin cinema later opened beside the successful Kingdom shopping centre, fully enclosed in the 1970s and further developed by stages.

**Smart Industrial Town becomes Regional Headquarters**: In 1974 the DC offered their own modern office block in a surprise bid to capture the headquarters of the new Fife Regional Council, which heard competing planning contributions (including a counter-submission by the present writer, then the Kirkcaldy planner) before making a decision; Kirkcaldy, the traditional Fife centre, lost out by a mere four votes. From that time Glenrothes really began to take off, and by 1981 its population was 32,500. Meantime Forth Tool & Valve, founded in 1973 by two engineers from Hamilton, grew steadily. Semtech of USA, opened in Glenrothes in 1973 to make power rectifiers. US-owned Brand-Rex, cable manufacturers, who also came in 1973, employed over 300 people in 1989, and were taken over by BICC.

**The Fate of Some Early Glenrothes Industries**: The 1980s saw the closure of some long-established firms which had helped the new town to get under way. The once-great GEC Telecommunications factory was closed in 1985. Elliott Automation's micro-electronics division, already in the town, started Scotland's first semiconductor plant in 1968; later taken over by General Instruments, it lasted only into the mid 1980s. A more spectacular failure was Burroughs, which opened a large branch factory about 1970; this was closed in the early 1980s and demolished. Salter Toys also prospered – and closed. Anderson Boyes became Anderson Strathclyde *(see Bridgeton)*. Their branch components factory employed over 250 in 1987, but the demand for mining machinery was vanishing, and the factory was sold.

**More Successful Firms from the Fifties and Sixties**: Castleblair, makers of women's and children's garments, expanded in 1989. The longest-established large firm in the town as at 1991 was Beckman, who employed nearly 500 by 1987; the shrunken Beckman workforce moved to the long-closed General Instruments factory. Hughes Aircraft, which employed over 750 in 1987, were then still expanding, while Sandusky had 150 employees. Cessna, taken over in 1989 by Eaton Hydraulics, then employed over 200 people.

**Silicon Glenrothes – Built on Sand?**: Many electrical and electronic developments made Glenrothes a leading centre of *'Silicon Glen'*. Rodime, makers of hard disc drives, opened in the town in 1980 and pioneered the 3.5" floppy disc *before* IBM adopted it as standard. By 1987 they employed nearly 500 people, but an ominous event in 1991 was the closure of their factory and transfer of production to Singapore in an effort to cut costs. However, the repair facility remained under new owners CRC to service hard disc drives, employing 56 people by 1994. By then Glendale Plastics, founded in 1980 by John Galloway, made vacuum-formed plastics for electronics, consumer durables and food industries at Southfield. Apricot Computers came to the town in 1983 and by 1987 employed over 200 people making networked systems; in 1989 the firm's distribution centre moved from the West Midlands to Glenrothes, bringing the total to 280. In 1990 they sold the operation to Mitsubishi, who found the workforce so good that they were soon making a complex video head formerly made in Japan (not just assembling PCBs), and aimed to employ 325 by 1995.

**Lots of Jobs – but Fife Airport makes a Forced Landing**: In the 1980s, despite the closures mentioned above, other development was continuous. By 1988 Glenrothes had the highest ratio of jobs to population of the five Scottish New Towns, some 17,520 jobs for 38,400 people, and was one of only two still growing in population. Its grass airstrip was optimistically renamed *Fife Airport* when a hard runway was laid about 1980; but traffic failed to develop, and its incautious sell-off to speculators a decade later resulted in complete closure for several years. Meantime the national dual carriageway road system finally reached Glenrothes along the new A92 East Fife Regional Road in 1990, and in 1991 the by then grossly inadequate bus station was greatly enlarged.

**Still More Silicon**: The first lettings in the town's small science park were made in 1987. By 1989 photomasks for semi-conductor manufacture were made by Compugraphics, a Laporte company. In 1989 Beckman and Hughes jointly spawned Rediffusion Simulation to design advanced training technology systems. By 1990 Kineticon designed and manufactured electronic equipment, soon acquired by Liquid Levers *(see Largoward)* to make their sunrise road safety product *Polar Eyes*; the small staff of 20 was expected to double. Soundtracs plc, a Surrey audio firm unable to recruit workers in the south, decided in 1990 to move to Glenrothes, bringing employment for 100 people. In 1994 Discovery Electronics, a subsidiary of BMM Weston of Faversham, moved its design and production facilities from small premises in Dundee to the Eastfield industrial estate, also hoping to expand. Tokheim employed 130 people in 1993, but had closed by 1999; in 2000 their former premises were taken over by US electronics firm Galgon, employing 50 people locally, and soon to double.

**Heather Tracks on Miniature Hard Discs?**: Calluna Technology was founded in 1991 by former Rodime executives, designing – and from 1993 being the only European manufacturer of – miniature removable 1.8 inch (46mm) hard disc drives for the laptop computer industry; in 1995 it was one of only four firms worldwide known to make this product and had 50 employees. A new 150-job factory at Westwood Park on the southern approaches to the town was built in 1992–93 for the Japanese copier manufacturers Canon, also of Livingston, for whose benefit a vast and wasteful road reconstruction scheme was carried out.

**Service Development and Covered Shopping**: A small hospital and the Crystals ice rink and bowling centre were opened in the mid 1980s, but the Crystals closed in 1988. The Regional Headquarters building at Fife House was greatly extended in 1988–89. In 1991 the Inland Revenue intended to bring an additional 300 jobs, and Fife Enterprise made its 90-worker base in Huntsman House. By 1991 Glenrothes College was a commercial languages centre. By the 1980s the Kingdom Centre claimed to be the largest undercover shopping centre in Scotland, rivalling Clydebank with over 100 shops including two grocery superstores on its 10ha, though it still lacked the

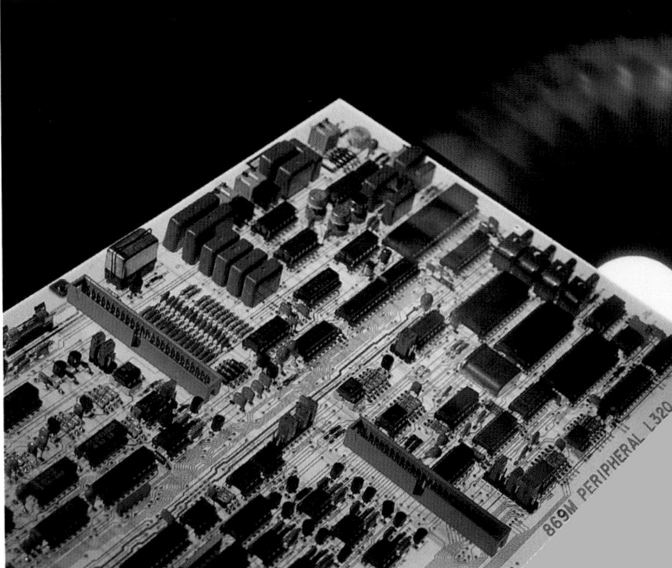


*• Printed circuit boards for computers – just one of the many high-tech manufactures of Glenrothes.* (SMPC / Bob West)

leading variety stores such as Marks & Spencer, Littlewoods and BHS. Its fourth and final phase of 22 shops opened in 1993, bringing the total to almost 150 shops. The Rothes Halls, opened by the DC in 1993, provided for a range of community uses with a 500-seat hall and other facilities; a 500-space multi-storey car park was to be built nearby.

**Engineering grows**: The 200-tonne steel girders for the A92 Cardenden viaduct were fabricated in 1989 by Robertson & Ferguson of Glenrothes. By that time Forth Tool & Valve employed 125 people machining Rolls-Royce engine castings and fan discs as well as undertaking oil-related work. By 1990 Prime Actuator Control Systems made gas and oil valves. Less happily, around 1990 Allivane apparently manufactured shells which found their way to the Iraqi dictator Saddam Hussein. Buko Manufacturing, where over 300 people made shopping trolleys, was bought out by its management in 1992. In 1993 G L Rexroth engineers, who made hydraulic equipment near Kirkcaldy, announced a move to larger premises at Viewfield, hoping to employ over 200 workers. Though Barr Thomson Engineering went into receivership in 1993, Technomarine of Aberdeen, for whom they made deepwater oil production tubing, saved 85 jobs by aiding a management buyout.

**Small Firms and Food**: In 1994 VZS made aluminium oxide products as small as the ceramic beads supporting cooker elements, and larger tubes for pumps and big vacuum switches serving textile, paper, power and nuclear industries. By 1995 US company Coors Ceramics Electronics produced hi-tech ceramic materials at Southfield. By 1988 Lowe's of Congleton employed 100 people in Glenrothes, manufacturing ties; Hilditch & Key, long-established makers of shirts for export, had 76 workers in the town in 1993. Alma Confectionery, originally in Kirkcaldy, took over Keiller of Dundee in 1989 and moved its HQ to a new factory in Glenrothes, bringing over 100 new jobs making sweets to the town in 1990; but the firm failed in 1992 and the factory closed. Nothing daunted, by 1993 the DC had lately created a Food Centre comprising specialist units for food manufacturers.

**Fife Council and Flying**: In 1995 the 23 ha Fife Airport with its 700 m hard runway was reopened under Tayside Aviation of Dundee, who established the Fife Flying Club; but little was to be seen there of real moment. The Development Corporation was wound up in 1995, having long ago proved its mettle; would the major artificially-induced growth of Glenrothes continue? The new town's status was confirmed in 1996 when Fife House, the modern HQ of the former Fife Region, became the main centre for the Fife Council, a new single-tier local authority for the whole of Fife. (However, the management of water and sewerage services was removed from its remit to Edinburgh.)

**Westwood Park for Electronics**: In 1995, when unemployment in Fife was the highest in mainland Britain, a large new speculative industrial development was begun at Westwood Park by Fife Enterprise. An early arrival was Marubeni of Japan, who in the guise of Birkby's intended to produce precision plastics for the electronics industry, creating 100 jobs in three years. Bermo of Minnesota decided in 1996 to build a factory at Westwood Park to produce electronic components, bringing up to 100 jobs in 1997; nearby Shin Ho Tech of Korea built a 300-job computer monitor factory. In 1996 Ductform Ventilation, makers of air-filtering equipment for electronics factories, announced an 80-job expansion, and Kodensha was also expanding by 87 workers to serve the Canon factory. By 1997 Canon had 140 workers at its photocopier re-manufacturing plant, but this work was moved to Germany; instead Canon aimed to employ 340 people making bubble ink jet printers. But by 2000 world printer prices had halved, the work was moved to Malaysia and the factory was closed, with 185 jobs lost. Raytheon now employ 600 in defence electronics.

**Moving to Glenrothes and Bankhead**: A new Central Fife ambulance station opened at Bankhead between Coaltown of Balgonie and Thornton in 1995. In 1995 new Fife Police headquarters on the former Burroughs site replaced the Dysart base, a further shift of activity from older towns to Glenrothes. In 1996 Haldanes of Gateside moved to a new factory at Bankhead; by then they made intricate woodcarvings by machine for customers as far afield as Windsor Castle, whose interlacing gothic panelling in St George's Hall was being restored. However, Aerpac UK, a subsidiary of a Dutch firm making glass-fibre blades for aero-generators, which set up in Glenrothes in 1997, moved to Mitchelston *(see Pathhead, Fife)* in 1999. By 2000 other jobs were being lost as well as gained: ABB Wylex, long established makers of circuit breakers, closed with the loss of over 90 jobs. A major development in 2000 brought the computer factory of the American home shopping telecoms company ADC to Bankhead, creating 1000 jobs with the promise of a further 500. Hotels include the brand-new *Express by Holiday Inn* (49 rooms).

## GLENSHEE — Map 6, B1

***Perthshire glen**, pop. 100* — OS 43: NJ 1070

The head of Glenshee some 50 km north of Perth, the remote site of a prehistoric stone circle and a standing stone, lies at an altitude of 340 metres. It was already well settled when Pont drew his map about 1600. Around the Chapel of *'Glenshy'* clustered several ferm touns such as *'Dalmungy'*, and a little to the north was the *'Spittel'* or hospice for travellers over the 670-metre Cairnwell Pass to Deeside. Early in the 18th century a military road was built through Glenshee, linking Blairgowrie with Braemar. Roy's map made about 1750 showed this as a trackway, joined at the hamlet of *'Spittle'* by another from Kirkmichael; but the steep zig-zag of the *'Devil's Elbow'* to the north became notorious for snow blockages. Dalnaglar Castle, 6 km south-east of Spittal, is a Victorian baronial mansion in a sporting estate of deer, salmon and grouse. By 1894 a *"comfortable"* hotel had been built at Spittal of Glenshee, and in 1948 this was joined by the isolated baronial *Dalmunzie House Hotel* and its 9-hole moorland golf course 2 km west of Spittal, remarkably linked with the remote Glenlochsie Lodge for some years by a 3 km long narrow-gauge railway.

**Skiing at the Cairnwell**: Skiing had taken place in the area for many years, but commercial development started in the early 1960s with the construction of the Cairnwell chairlift, 6 km north of Spittal, by the newly-formed Glenshee Chairlift Company. The *Spittal Hotel*, burnt down in 1957, was rebuilt in modern style, opening in 1959. As demand for skiing grew steadily, additional uplifts and facilities were continually added, both east and west of the A93 road summit. In the early 70s, the elbow was removed from the road. By 1990,

*Glenshee ski area, with the original 1962 chairlift in the centre. Two sculptured figures (left) admire the scene. When the snows come, there are economic benefits for the local communities of Blairgowrie and Braemar.* *(Roy Houston)*

about 20 uplifts existed, as well as ski-schools and other facilities (including a stylish new restaurant), and the very variable weather conditions prompted the introduction of snow-making equipment in 1991. Further lifts were soon created east of the pass, giving skiers access to the slopes up to just 50m below the 1068-metre summit of Glas Maol; by 2000 there were 26 uplifts in total, thereby rivalling Aviemore as the largest skiing centre in Britain. Below the slopes are the golfing, fishing and shooting *Dalmunzie House Hotel* and the *Spittal Hotel*, with a backpackers' hostel and other small hotels further down the glen.

## GLENSHIEL, Invershiel & Shiel Bridge — Map 8, C4

***W. Inverness-shire hamlets,** pop. 250 (area)* — OS 33: NG 9319

The military road built westwards from Fort Augustus in the mid 18th century followed Glenshiel through Kintail parish, between the steep mountains called the *Five Sisters of Kintail* and Glenshiel Forest, to meet seawater at Invershiel, a beautiful situation at the head of Loch Duich. From there it struck westwards over the hills to Glenelg: the fair copy of the Roy map showed it ending part way up the Ratagan pass, long noted for its views but enclosed by early 20th century afforestation. Shiel Bridge was built in the early 19th century as part of Telford's road improvements. The *Shiel Inn* was open by 1847, and in the early 20th century the mid 19th century shooting lodge nearby became the well-known *Kintail Lodge* hotel. The basic facilities of post office, school and telephone exchange were provided at Shiel Bridge; by 1967 the Five Sisters were in the care of the National Trust for Scotland. By 1977 *Ratagan House* was a hotel, with the nearby top grade Ratagan youth hostel, still open, as well as the *Kintail Lodge Hotel*.

## GLESPIN & Inches — Map 2, A2

***S. Lanarkshire small villages,** pop. 300* — OS 71: NS 8028

Glespin lies in a bowl of hills about 215m above sea level, 4km south-west of Douglas village, where the Douglas Water becomes a significant stream. By the time the Roy map was made in the 1750s the Douglas to Cumnock road was open and there were two mills, the Earls Mill and a now vanished Waukmill; a track (now non-existent), led across the hills to Nithsdale. Glespin was wholly rural until a branch of the Caledonian Railway was built between Douglas and Muirkirk in 1873–74; a station was opened at Inches, 3km to the west, and coal was sought. By the mid 20th century, when about 500 people lived in the Glespin/Inches area, mines were open at Kennox between Glespin and Inches, and near Earls Mill in the valley of the Glespin Burn; their output must have been low by the time the railway was abandoned in 1964. In 1980 a tiny mine at Glespin was still bagging coal, but in 1981 only some 350 people lived locally. By 1992 Ramages, hauliers of Rigside, had developed a large distribution depot for food, drink and electrical goods at Glespin; this employed 200 people by 1997. However a quarter of the houses in the village were empty, the post office had closed by 1992 and the school had only about 25 pupils. At that time Scottish Coal opened the vast Glentaggart opencast pit south of the village, a 22-year extraction scheme for 10 million tonnes of coal, which would be the second largest in Scotland.

## GOLSPIE & Dunrobin — Map 9, B2

***Sutherland small town,** pop. 1400* — OS 17/21: NC/NH 8300

Two Pictish brochs stand on the east coast of Sutherland, an area held by the Vikings until recovered for Scotland in 1228, when the Earldom of Sutherland was established; it remained in the patronage of the Earls. About 1275 Robert, the Second Earl, built or rebuilt his castle near the brochs, hence its Gaelic name Dunrobin; it was again rebuilt in the 15th century. Nearby Golspie (in Gaelic *Goillspidhe*, perhaps *'Wood Hospital'*) was shown on Blaeu's map in 1654 as Golspie Kirk, Golspiemoir and Golspietoun. The kirk was rebuilt in the 1730s. By the time of Roy's survey in the mid 18th century Golspie was a beach fishing centre, with a separate *Fisherton*, and there was a coastal road of sorts from the Little Ferry, 5 km to the south. In 1799 Heron referred to it as a *"village"*. So undisputed was the authority of the Earls (later made Dukes) that it was never made a formal barony burgh. Golspie had a post office from 1804, and an inn by 1813.

**Mansion, Statue, Fishing and Steamers**: Golspie remained disconnected from the national road network (except by ferries) until the Mound *(q.v.)* was built across Loch Fleet in 1815–18. In 1827 Chambers found *"One regular street. Improvements on an extensive scale are in progress all round the village"*. Telford believed by 1828 that the inn was *"equal to any to be found in England"*. Dunrobin was remodelled in 1835–50 to vast designs by Sir Charles Barry, who made it resemble a French chateau, faced with white freestone from the Dukes' own Brora quarry, and with superb gardens. In the 1840s a fine 30 m tall statue by the sculptor Chantrey of the controversial First or *'Black'* Duke, with an effusive inscription to this domineering English laird who had done so much to destroy the early communities of Sutherland, was placed on 394 m Ben a'Bhragaidh, 2 km west of Golspie. A pier supported a minor fishery in the 19th century, and by 1849 steamers plied from Inverness to Little Ferry; but much-cleared Sutherland's population began to decline after 1851.

**Duke's Railway, Golf, Drill and News**: The Sutherland Railway, largely financed by the Third Duke, reached Golspie from the south in 1868; a gasworks was built at once. The line was extended by stages to reach Wick in 1874. Golspie with 935 people in 1891 was already recognised as more populous and important than the tiny county town of Dornoch. Golspie golf club was founded in 1889 and provided a basic 18-hole course. The *Sutherland Arms Hotel* was described as *"very good"* in 1894, when Murray wrote that Golspie consisted of *"one long and cheerful street"*. In 1892 a large and decorative Territorial Army drill hall was lightly built of timber and corrugated iron. Meantime the local newspaper the *Northern Times* with its printing works was established in 1899. About the same time a harbour was built; though the latter was of little consequence, the ferry continued to ply into the 1930s. Population decline in Sutherland was fastest after 1911; Golspie continued to supersede Dornoch and Brora as its main centre. Wordie & Co worked from a small rail to road cartage depot in 1946. With a small hospital and four more hotels, Golspie was by 1951 a shopping village of around 1000 people.

**Private Education fails**: From 1965 to 1972 the castle was used as an independent school, but was too far from the homes of affluent parents to prosper. From 1975 Golspie's population rose, for it shared Sutherland District's administration with Dornoch. In 1978 the village was served by a score of shops, including specialists and tourist items such as stone cutting, and a restaurant. Two banks, a caravan site and some new housing were in evidence, but the 120 year old gasworks was on the point of closure, as spare parts were unobtainable! In 1989 the Swiss firm Hapimag planned a new hotel, sports complex and 150 timeshare cottages in the castle grounds, but this seems to have come to nothing. Some afforestation took place inland. In 1991 Golspie had 1434 residents, and by 1995 a new Golspie High School for some 600 pupils had been built in the village; there was a museum, a public swimming pool, and the Orcadian Stone Company welcomed visitors.

**No Press or Local Government, and a Statue too many?**: At New Year 1995, printing of the 6000 weekly copies of the *Northern Times* newspaper was moved from its press in Golspie to Wick, so putting the local team of paper-folding ladies out of work (but the newspaper office still employs 20 today). The imposition in 1996 of the all-purpose Highland Council nominally ended Golspie's role as a centre of local government; a tiny office of *Highland & Islands Enterprise* remained. This further downgrading of Golspie also led to calls to remove the Black Duke's huge and prominent statue. The disused TA hall which stood rotting in 1997 is still to be seen. The unstaffed station still serves passengers, but its attractive building of 1868 awaits a new user; in summer, trains also stop at Dunrobin, whose rustic station building was restored in the early 1990s. Golspie Mill still grinds cereals, and a garage is still open, but the shops seem slightly fewer. There is a police station and a bank, and the historic *Sutherland Arms Hotel*. New individual houses are still being added at both ends of the village.

## GORBALS, Kinning Park, Pollokshields & Tradeston

**Map 15, C5**

***S. parts of Glasgow***, *pop. 11,000* — OS 64: NS 5964

Gorbals – generally known as *'The Gorbals'* – lies south of the River Clyde opposite the ancient city centre of Glasgow, an exceptionally level and originally fertile area just as suitable for development as for farming. An ancient earthwork crowned the hill to the south, which eventually became Queen's Park *(q.v.)*. In medieval times the city's leper hospital was at Gorbals, and about the 12th or early 13th century a *'hospital'* was also established at Polmadie, 2 km south of the wooden bridge across the Clyde which existed by 1286, connecting to Glasgow's Bridgegate. About 1345–50 Bishop Rae had this replaced by a stone bridge of five arches. In 1633 a parish school was founded, and by about 1640 as the Blaeu atlas showed, a road existed from the bridgehead to Paisley. The Blaeu maps, based on the work of Timothy Pont in or about 1596, also showed Little Govan (near the later Caledonia Road), with a possible mansionhouse in a park; perhaps this was the tower house that some believe rose later. The maps were equivocal as to whether the area then owed allegiance to Renfrewshire or Lanarkshire.

**Coal, Cloth and Coaches**: By about 1650 there were also roads to Govan, Gushetfaulds and Rutherglen, but *'Gorbals and Brigend'* was still a tiny one-street village. A coal pit was first reported in the Gorbals in 1660, and in 1689 the traveller Thomas Morer referred to the Gorbals as *"a little town"*. The Roy map of the early 1750s showed a nuclear settlement at the bridgehead; at that time it comprised mostly weavers, but also developed a malting trade, being exempt from burgh duties. From 1763 regular stage coaches ran through the Gorbals en route between Glasgow and Greenock, but the journey took all day. In 1769 Pennant also noted the collieries in the Gorbals.

**Deepening, Controlling and Re-Crossing the Clyde**: The hitherto very shallow River Clyde was confined by training walls or jetties from 1768, and a combination of tidal scour and dredging steadily deepened it below Glasgow weir, which lay just above the ancient and tottering Glasgow Bridge at Stockwell Street and formed the tidal limit of the river. In 1765 the bridge was closed to goods vehicles; the new Glasgow Bridge 400 metres to the west at Jamaica Street was completed in 1772. For at least a decade this new bridge led almost due south to nowhere but Pollokshaws, by way of a deserted new boulevard named Eglinton Street. Old Glasgow Bridge was reconstructed and widened in 1771–79, and again by Telford about 1820. In 1775–78 William Dixon – who had mined coal in Meikle Govan since 1771 – built a wooden railway from there to Springfield Quay, at the foot of what is now West Street. By 1782 as James Barry's map showed, Gorbals had started to spread, and there was a scatter of development along Pollokshaws Road. The Glasgow Cross bridge which gave a direct connection between the ancient centre of Glasgow and Crown Street was built in 1794, but closed the next year due to flood damage.

**Carlton Place, Canal and Marine Engineering**: In 1806 the fine neo-classical Laurieston House was built as part of the terraced Carlton Place just east of the new Glasgow Bridge for merchant James Laurie, to designs by Peter Nicholson; it was described in 1998 as *"the most ornate Georgian town house in the UK"*. Unfortunately, except for some fine tenements in and south of Laurieston, its high standards were not to be followed by most development in the Gorbals. There was little industrial activity south of the river until between 1806 and 1813 when the Glasgow, Paisley & Ardrossan Canal (which never reached beyond Johnstone) was excavated from a terminus known as Port Eglinton, with a warehouse at Salkeld Street near the south end of Gorbals Street. In 1811 William Dixon Junior, of Calder, built (or rebuilt) a tramway to the basin from his family's Govan colliery. John Robertson, who was to construct the engine for Scotland's first practical steamship the *Comet*, was born in the Gorbals in 1782, and in 1814 James Cook of Tradeston – a westwards expansion of the Gorbals – built the engine for the paddle steamer *Margery*, the first steamboat to operate on the Thames and to cross to France. Cook also made sugar machinery, soon a Glasgow specialism.

**Gorbals Man becomes Top US Detective**: By 1819 three daily coaches ran through the Gorbals to Paisley and two to Greenock; others ran to Ayr. Gorbals man Allan Pinkerton, born in 1819, emigrated to the USA, became an investigator, and founded both its most famous private detective agency and the FBI. About 1822 Alexander Brown & Co founded a weaving factory at Rutherglen Road and Commercial Road, where by 1825 the Wellington cotton mills were also open. In 1825–26 C & D Gray set up the Adelphi Distillery at Inverkip Street. By 1832 quays on the south bank of the Clyde extended for 384 m, a third as much as on the Glasgow side.

**Hutcheson Bridge, Town and School**: In 1829–33 the site of the abortive Glasgow Cross Bridge was chosen for the Hutcheson Bridge, designed by the Glaswegian Robert Stevenson. Land was feued off in the 1830s by the trustees of Hutcheson's hospital for the suburb of Hutchesontown. New buildings for Hutcheson's Grammar School were built in Crown Street in 1839–41, originally for a mere 140 boys (previously taught in the city centre); major extensions took place from 1874.

**Steam Coaches, Gasworks and Piped Water**: Gorbals post office was issued with a cancelling stamp in 1830. Road coaches driven by steam briefly plied through Gorbals in 1834 *(see Paisley)*. In 1835–39 the Glasgow Gas Light Company built the Tradeston Gasworks south of the Gorbals at Kilbirnie Street, west of Eglinton Street. Rebuilt in 1869–74 and extended in 1886–89, it became very extensive, having four gasholders from 1897. Meantime from the 1840s the Gorbals had piped water, supplied by gravity from reservoirs near Barrhead, long before Glasgow's better-known scheme.

**The First Transatlantic Steamer, and Dixon's Blazes**: In 1823 Thomas Wingate & Co were established as engineers at Springfield Quay. In 1837 they made the 320 horsepower side-lever engines for the little 703-ton Leith-built brig *Sirius*, the first vessel to cross the Atlantic entirely by steam power (in 1838); but in 1848 the firm moved to Whiteinch. In 1839 the coalmaster William Dixon founded the so-called Govan Ironworks in Crown Street; within a decade it had five blast furnaces and was blighting Bridgeton with smoke, but because it lit up the night sky it became known as *Dixon's Blazes*. In 1840 Dixon extended his tramway to Rutherglen. The ironworks were expanded in 1888 and remained in operation into the mid 20th century.

**Enter the Railways**: In 1839–41 the Glasgow & Paisley Joint Railway (G&PJR) was built, paralleling the canal before turning north, west of Bridge Street, to its terminus at Bridge Street Station, which was given its own four storey hotel and was also the destination of Carlisle, Greenock and Ayr trains. The company had a tiny engine works at Cook Street by 1845. In 1848 the Glasgow, Barrhead & Neilston Direct Railway opened South Side station at the south end of Main Street; for a short time in 1849 this was the terminus for the new Caledonian Railway's London trains, but late that year they were transferred to Buchanan Street north of the city centre.

**Chemicals, Engineering and Cotton**: The new railway soon attracted various incoming industries: in 1841 Richard Smith founded the West Street Chemical Works in Tradeston; nearby were the Scotland Street Engine Works of P & W McOnie, founded about 1841 and greatly extended over at least six decades. From about 1840 G L Walker & Co created the Falfield Mills in Mauchline Street for cotton weaving by power looms, followed about 1844 by Robert Gilkinson Junior's comparable Cook Street Cotton Mill; Falfield Mill was expanded in 1861. The Albyn Cotton Mills in Waddell Street were built by McBride & Co about 1845, and expanded in 1868.

**General Terminus Quay and Lipton the Yachtsman Grocer**: In 1846–49 the General Terminus & Glasgow Harbour Railway – a freight branch – was opened from the G&PJR at Shields Road to fan out on a new Clyde quay built below the bridges; one siding ended at a hydraulic crane which could lift entire coal wagons and tip their contents into vessels. Known as General Terminus Quay, this played an important part in the industrial life of the city for well over a century. So in effect did Thomas Lipton, born in 1850 in Crown Street, who rapidly developed an early grocery chain; he became a keen yachtsman who repeatedly tried to recapture the America's Cup and was knighted in 1898. Meantime the Lauriston branch of the Bank of Scotland, opened in 1855 to promote the firm's interest in the West of Scotland, was a principal player by about 1880.

**Grain Milling: Massive Investment**: The Corn Laws were repealed in 1846, enabling grain imports: William Muir immediately built the Tradeston Grain Mills in Commerce Street; these became too dusty, and exploded in 1872, but were soon replaced. Following the introduction of roller-milling, and with rising imports of grain from North America, milling moved away from increasingly depressed rural grain-growing locations to the ports; the Gorbals got more than its share. The six-storey Kingston Grain Mills in West Street, the Plantation Starch Works in Mair Street, the Centre Street Grain Mills, William Primrose's 8-storey grain store in Centre Street, the Mavisbank Flour Mills in Mair Street, Buchanan's grain mill in Tradeston Street, the Victoria Grain Mill, built in West Street in 1879, and about 1884 the Gorbals Grain Mills were erected in Surrey Street. In 1910 the Riverside Milling Company converted stores at Shearer Street into the area's umpteenth grain mill, its tall silos being built in 1914. In addition to all the mills, various large grain stores were erected at this period.

**Industrial Baking in the Gorbals**: Bakery development followed the mills to the Gorbals. Around 1857 came the Parkholm biscuit bakery in Paisley Road. About 1870 the United Co-operative Baking Society built the Kingston Bakery, producing the distinctively soggy Glasgow white bread, and later premises rose in McNeil Street, originally styled the *'Garden Bakery'*. This baked biscuits as well as bread, and in 1912 136 tonnes of cakes emerged. In 1881 Milne's Clutha rusk bakery was erected in MacLellan Street, and McLintock's, makers of biscuits and jams, built a foodstuffs factory in Dunmore Lane. Then came Stevenson's Plantation bakery in Durham Street. And with all these firms in operation, it is not surprising that a specialist bakers' engineer, Andrew Gillespie, built a factory in Middlesex Street around 1882. Later, McNaught built a bakery in Eglinton Street, followed in 1903 by Reid's Victoria Road bakery.

**Victorian Road Bridges and Finnieston Crossings**: The Heritors (taxable landholders) of Gorbals erected the Portland Street suspension bridge in 1851, and the Victoria Bridge of sandstone and Dublin granite was built on the site of the original Glasgow Bridge in 1851–54, at once followed by the St Andrews Suspension Bridge, designed by Neil Robson, and erected in 1853–55 to link Calton and Bridgeton with new factories in Hutchesontown. Hutcheson Bridge was replaced in 1870–71 by the sandstone and cast-iron Albert Bridge. The Finnieston Ferry, authorised in 1878, carried vehicles from Marine Street in Kinning Park from 1890. The Harbour Tunnel, excavated in 1890–96, linked Plantation Place with Finnieston: hydraulic lifts powered from a pumping station east of Prince's Dock lowered and raised road vehicles.

**Pollokshields, Monumental Buildings and Varied Industries**: Pollokshields was laid out south-west of the Gorbals in 1849, and largely developed with villas in the 1850s. The imposing Caledonia Road Church was erected in 1856 and the long and rather magnificent Queen's Park Terrace in Eglinton Street was built in 1856–60, both to designs by Alexander *'Greek'* Thomson. Due to recent massive immigration from Ireland to the congested Gorbals, in 1859 the first school in the city to provide segregated education for Roman Catholic children opened in an attractive new building in Warwick Street. About 1855 Gourlie & Linn, upholsterers, set up a curled horsehair factory in Cavendish Street; oddly the firm later also entered and expanded in the foundry business. About 1858 Stewart & Brown founded the Glasgow Paper Mills in McNeil Street.

**Mid-Victorian Engineering Firms**: The Etna ironfoundry was built in 1854 in Milan Street by David Ritchie & Co. The Eglinton Engine Works in Tradeston Street were established about 1855 by the general engineers and ironfounders A & W Smith & Co; they made machinery for farms and later sugar refining, and ultimately became very large and a subsidiary of Tait & Lyle, using Mirrlees Watson as a brand name. A related firm under J B Mirrlees and William Tait established a second engineering works beside the railway in Scotland Street in 1860; later also known as Mirrlees Watson, it too specialised in sugar refining machinery. In 1858–60 the huge engineering works of Randolph, Elder & Co were built in Tradeston Street (later renamed Centre Street), where they built marine engines before moving to Govan in 1869 *(see Hay & Stell for building details)*. The Kingston Engine Works of the Smith Brothers was built in Milnpark Street between 1866 and 1873. About 1860 William Whitesmith erected a works in Florence Street where power looms were made until 1874, when the building became – a school! The first Clutha Ironworks were built at Florence Street in 1860 for P & W McLellan, structural engineers. In 1874 these became David Richmond's tube works, the McLellans having moved into new and much larger Clutha Works at McLellan Street; there they fabricated the arched roof for Queen Street Station in 1880.

**James Howden and other Engineers**: In 1862 James Howden & Co entered the marine engineering business at Scotland Street and had 3 plants in the vicinity of Scotland Street by the end of the century. Meantime W King & Co, shipbuilders and marine engineers, built the Dock Engine & Boiler Works in Weir Street in 1864, regularly expanded. By 1867 John Yule & Co were manufacturing steam hammers and horizontal engines at Hutchesontown. Kemp & Hume built another engine works about 1872, at Portman Street. John Thomson & Coy's Lilybank boiler works in Eglinton Street worked until the firm moved to Dalmarnock in the 1920s.

**Furniture, Shoes, and Co-operation**: Brown's furniture factory was in Surrey Street in 1862, Thomson's Port Eglinton Cabinet Works was in Ritchie Street, and later in Kilbirnie Street. Scott's opened their Oxford Street shoe factory around 1865. The establishment of the Scottish Co-operative Wholesale Society (SCWS) in 1867 created what was eventually probably the largest of the many wholesale concerns in the city. The Glasgow Storage Company had built a vast 6-storey warehouse in Wallace Street in 1871–72; in 1872 the SCWS began work on its adjoining four-storey warehouse complex, finely enlarged in 1888–92 and capped by their big head office in Morrison Street, built in 1893; by then their expansion was at Shieldhall *(see Govan)*, but the SCWS also built large workshops and warehouses in Laidlaw Street between 1889 and 1913, a ham and sausage factory at Milnpark Street in 1905, and a waterproof works at Middlesex Street in 1913.

**Kinning Park: Biscuits and Iron**: Kinning Place post office received a cancelling stamp in 1848, but industries in this area midway between Gorbals and Govan seem to have begun a decade later. In 1861 Gray, Dunn & Co opened a biscuit factory in Stanley Street off Paisley Road, which was greatly extended on various occasions, particularly about 1883 when it was known as the Kinning Park Bakery. In the 1860s came Bennie's Kinning Park Iron Foundry and the Paragon

Foundry of Duncan & Smith, followed by the Vulcan Tube Works in Cornwall Street which made malleable iron tubes for Cruikshanks, Low & Co, whilst the large Kinning Park Ironworks were established in 1875 by a blacksmith, Charles McNeil.

**Kingston Dock, new Railways and their Bridges**: The 2ha Kingston Dock, the first enclosed dock in the Port of Glasgow, was opened in 1867. Meantime Shields Road station at Kinning Park on the Paisley railway was opened in 1863; in 1885 it became the junction point for the G&SWR's Canal line, which replaced the former Paisley Canal. The City of Glasgow Union Railway bridge at Adelphi Street was built in 1864–67 and rebuilt in 1898–1902 to match the enlarged St Enoch station. In 1871 the Glasgow, Barrhead & Kilmarnock Joint Railway of the CR and G&SWR was opened southwards from a complex of junctions around Eglinton Street. In 1876–78 came the first CR bridge to their new Glasgow Central Station, built of granite and cast iron by William Arrol *(see Bridgeton)* – his first large contract – which with connecting lines and improvements brought London trains into the city through the Gorbals. The bridge was duplicated in 1899–1905, also by William Arrol. Bridge Street station was enlarged in 1890, but a change of mind by the CR Board had closed it by 1906, when all CR trains were extended to Glasgow Central.

**Confectionery, Clearance and Rivets by the Million**: About 1865 a large confectionery works was built in Admiral Street by Robert Wotherspoon & Co, followed 20 years later by Montgomery's in Kingston Street, and Hay Brothers' in Stanley Street. The original Gorbals village and the old tower house were swept away in 1870–75 by the City Improvement Trust, who laid out Gorbals Cross. The many and large iron and steel ships and bridges then being built needed millions of rivets: the Clyde Rivet Works were erected in Laidlaw Street in 1872, and Edward Crosher built his Rivet Works in Admiral Street about 1888.

**Engineering, Brass and Copper**: About 1873 Robertson & Thomson set up the Parkholm Iron Foundry in Middlesex Street, William Thomson & Co created the extensive Portman Street Engine Works, the boilermakers D Cockburn & Son established works in McNeil Street (but the firm later moved to Cardonald). Smith & McLean's extensive Clyde Galvanising Works in Marine Street was begun in 1875 and extended up to 1914. Clark's Victoria Brass Foundry made gasoliers in Gorbals Lane from 1876; allied trades were the Glasgow Copper Works of Miller & Pyle, and John Wilson & Son's brass works in Buchan Street.

**Timber, Sawmilling and Joinery**: In 1875 the Lillybank Sawmills were set up in Maxwell Road by Allan & Baxter, and Frost & Woyka built a sawmill in Ballater Street; A Bowie & Co and J Watt Torrance were later in the same business. The Glasgow Cabinet Works of William Hill were erected in Darnley Street. In 1892 Gilmour & Aitken, mahogany merchants, built sawmills and timber sheds, while Dick & Benzies built joinery works in Forth Street.

**Laundering and Dyeing**: Andrew Swan established an early laundry in Eglinton Street about 1877, the Lancefield Soap Works being built for Robert Burns & Co at Scotland Street almost simultaneously! Then about 1878 the Adelphi Dyeworks were built in Ballater Street, and further dyeworks were erected in West Street for James Mills about 1880. About 1895 Thomas Donald founded the Glasgow Laundry in Albert Drive; before the days of the vacuum cleaner, carpet beating was also carried out there. Then in 1896 a dyeworks and paint factory was built in West Street for Blacklock & McArthur.

**Recreation and Health Provision**: All the incoming industries had resulted in a wave of immigration, and the hasty erection – especially in Hutchesontown – of street upon street of closely packed rubble stone tenements surrounding tiny rear courts. Interestingly, in the 1880s over half the pupils in the Gorbals Primary School were of the Jewish faith, largely immigrants from central Europe. As the countryside receded, so indoor recreational provision blossomed. In 1878 *Her Majesty's Theatre* in Gorbals Street was opened by John Morrison (soon the *Royal Princess*). In 1885 swimming baths were constructed in the Gorbals by the Corporation. The Royal Samaritan Hospital for Women, founded in 1886, chose a site in half-developed Govanhill for its permanent buildings, erected from 1890. In the 1880s upmarket Pollokshields actually boasted a Philharmonic orchestra, and the fine Pollokshields Burgh Hall was built of Ballochmyle stone in 1889–91; but in the latter year the Burgh of Pollokshields was incorporated into the City of Glasgow!

**Steam Trams, Lorries and Boat Kits**: The Vale of Clyde steam tramway, the first such system in Britain, was laid in the streets via Paisley Road to Govan and opened in 1877; it was worked by steam until 1893. About 1879 the Caledonian Railway opened a major new engine shed at Polmadie Road, followed about 1880 by the nearby Sentinel Works of Alley & McLellan of Glasgow at Jessie Street. This was extended in 1893, and again using reinforced concrete – then a novel material – at various times between 1903 and 1914. The firm manufactured *'Sentinel'* steam lorries at Polmadie from 1906; the firm also made and exported ships and barges in kit form. Although in 1918 production was moved to Shrewsbury, and the works were taken over by British Electrical Repairs (BER), the firm stayed in business elsewhere in the area.

**Miscellany in Industry, Cleansing and Haulage**: In the late 19th century the Gorbals had the Thistle Rubber Works in Commerce Street, Currie's lithographers and printers in Centre Street, an extensive quilt factory in Ballater Street (Thomas Nicol), and the Standard Oil Works in Admiral Street. Glasgow Corporation Cleansing Department built a tall-chimneyed refuse destructor and extensive stables in Kilbirnie Street from 1882. In 1895 a large depot for Wordie & Co's railway haulage and delivery wagons, surmounted by two floors of stables for 180 horses, was built at West Street, Tradeston. In 1907–08 a warehouse was built in Durham Street for J & P Coats, the Paisley thread manufacturers. Many warehouses, stores and stables associated with shipping and industries were also provided.

**Drinks Industries of the 1880s and 90s**: There was an enormous and still growing demand for liquor to refresh the tens of thousands of workers. In 1883 the Clydesdale Brewery was erected in Victoria Road for M D Dawson & Co, but in 1896 at the height of the temperance movement it was taken over by the Tonbur Brewery Company to produce *'non-alcoholic beers'*, an enterprise whose name was derived from *'Burton'*, but unlike that English brewing centre did not last for long! In 1885 Barclay Brothers built an aerated water bottling works in Oxford Street, followed in 1897 by John Mackay & Co's factory in MacLellan Street, and in 1898 by G & P Barrie's similar plant in Maxwell Road. But not everyone drank beer, *'juice'* or whisky: in 1896–98 the Acme Tea Chest works were erected at Polmadie Road, and in 1906 the tea merchants Wight built a warehouse in Clyde Place.

**The Whisky Boom: from Adelphi to Loch Katrine**: A Walker of the Adelphi distillery was producing both grain and malt whiskies by 1886, also using malt from the firm's Port Dundas maltings. The distillery was acquired in 1907 by DCL who closed it; the buildings remained as bonds until demolition in 1968. In 1887 Blair, Campbell & McLean of Scotland Street in Kinning Park were brewery and distillery engineers, coppersmiths and brassfounders. During the 1890s whisky boom T Lindsay established a cooperage in Camden Street in 1896, and another for C S Whitelaw was built in Commerce Street in 1900. There were many bonded warehouses erected in this period, including for John Walker of Kilmarnock.

**Engineering, Gold Refining and Daylight Robbery**: In 1883 Watson, Laidlaw & Co built engineering works in Laidlaw Street, James Bennie & Co built the extensive Clyde Engine Works at Hamilton Street, and the adjoining Polmadie Iron Works were erected by pump manufacturers J H Carruthers & Co. The latter were twice extended, later incorporating Bennie's premises *(see Milngavie)*. About 1888 the Rosehill Works of the interestingly-named Scotch & Irish Oxygen Company were built at Aikenhead Road, producing oxygen for oxy-acetylene cutting and welding. Meantime John Stewart MacArthur, born in the city in 1856, had worked for Charles Tennant in the Gorbals. With William and Robert Forrest, he developed the MacArthur-Forrest Process, using potassium cyanide to refine gold; but though this work revolutionised the industry he was legally swindled out of his patents in South Africa in 1896 and turned to producing radium for X-ray use.

**The Final Phase of Railway Expansion**: In 1886 the CR's Cathcart District Railway was opened to Cathcart from Muirhouse North Junction on the Barrhead line, through a new station at Pollokshields East and other closely spaced stations around Queen's Park *(q.v.)*. In 1894 the line was extended as a return loop, rejoining the Barrhead line at Muirhouse South Junction with another new station, Pollokshields West, to complete the *'Cathcart Circle'* – Glasgow's most intensively used suburban line.

**Cable-drawn Tube Trains and Glasgow Bridge**: The unique circular and under-river tube railway of the Glasgow District Subway Company was built in 1891–97 *(see Govan)*; stations were provided at close intervals, there being four within the wider Gorbals area, at Bridge Street, West Street, Shields Road and Kinning Park. It was powered by endless cables driven from engines at Scotland Street. Glasgow Weir was regularly reconstructed, the third known occasion being in 1894–1901. Telford's Glasgow Bridge was replaced in 1894–99; the new structure designed by Blyth & Westland was faced in granite blocks saved from the old bridge. Eglinton Street station (later known as Cumberland Street) was opened in 1900 by the G&SWR.

**Electric Tramcars and Motor Vehicle Construction**: A Glasgow Corporation horse-tram depot was built in Admiral Street off Paisley Road about 1893. The car sheds and tram body works at Albert Drive, Coplawhill were first built in 1894, when they too served horse trams, and had belt-driven machinery. From 1899 up to 1912 they were extended into a huge complex, with a related depot at Barland Street *(see Twidale & Mack)*. In 1899–1900 Glasgow Corporation Electricity Department built the St Andrews generating station in Pollokshaws Road; this provided domestic and industrial supplies. In 1912 the former Etna ironfoundry became a Corporation gas depot. Meantime the automobile was lurking: in 1907 the Kennedy Motor Company built quite extensive motor works in Maxwell Road and in 1913 a motor car body works for William Park was built at Kilbirnie Street. The South West Motor Carriage Works, set up in 1914 at Scotland Street, was the area's first proper garage.

**Paint, Boots, Local Co-operation, Boilers and Biscuits**: The Strathclyde Paint & Varnish Works of Ferguson, Hamilton & Morrison was built about 1893 at Vermont Street, Hird, Hastie & Co erected their Kinning Park Colour Works, rivalled in this field by the Parkhouse Colour Works in Portman Street. In 1895 Melvin Brothers set up the St Crispin Works for boot and shoe making at Cornwall Street. The Kinning Park Co-operative Society built warehouses in Norfolk Street about 1896, a stables and garage in Stanley Street about 1899 and warehouses in Bridge Street and Coburg Street in 1902–09. In 1899–1900 the Tradeston Tube Works in Wallace Street were built for the Scottish Tube Company, but Cockburn's boiler works in McNeil Street was remarkably converted into a biscuit factory for W & J McLintock.

**Kinning Park Burgh: Sewage and *'Juice'***: Around 1900 Kinning Park was promoted to a police burgh, but had to wait ten years after Govan was supplied with electricity, for its own power station to be constructed in 1902. In 1901–03 the fine art publishers Miller & Lang built printing works at Darnley Street. The short-lived burgh's fate as a drainage authority was sealed when in 1909–10 Glasgow Corporation built a sewage pumping station at Seaward Street. With unconscious irony the SCWS built an aerated water factory at the same address in

*Housing, Gorbals, built in the mid 19th century as middle-class flatted tenements, but later 'made down' into single-roomed dwellings for working-class occupation. The generously wide street layout was typical of the area.* *(RCAHMS / JRH)*

1914–16! The engineers P & W MacLellan of the Clutha Ironworks operated at Vermont Street; they made planing machines around 1925. The Wellington Mills became Leon & Co's cabinet works about 1924, eventually demolished about 1970.

**Durable Bank, Theatres and Cinemas**: In 1900 a branch of the British Linen Bank was built in Gorbals Street, to designs by James Salmon which incorporated a 3-storey tenement; almost alone it was to survive for a century, as clearance went on all around. The *Palace Theatre* – a conversion – appeared in 1904, a good year for the city's theatres. In 1905 the bombastically named firm of Moss Empires opened their huge *Coliseum Theatre* at Gorbals Cross in Eglinton Street, with almost 2900 seats. This re-emerged as the giant 4000-seat *Colosseum Cinema*, among the first in Scotland to show talkies in 1929; it later became a vast bingo hall. Other early picture houses included the *Eglinton Electreum*, and the small *Gorbals Picturedrome* built in 1910–11.

**After WW I: Whisky, Aviation and New Bridges**: Despite the impact on the whisky trade of USA Prohibition from 1920, the Strathclyde grain whisky distillery was built in Moffat Street, Hutchesontown in 1927. Brave but reckless Jim Mollison, born in Pollokshields in 1905, his father a drunk, became a pioneer aviator among whose exploits was the first solo crossing of the Atlantic from east to west; for a time he was married to the more famous pilot Amy Johnson. In 1932 the *New Bedford Picture House* was built in Eglinton Street to art deco designs. The King George V Bridge was built in 1924–28 of reinforced concrete faced in Dalbeattie granite; it was confusingly followed by the King's Bridge from Ballater Street to Bridgeton Cross, built in 1932–33. But the slump almost killed the industrial Gorbals.

**Overcrowding, Drama, Nuts and Bolts**: In 1945 the tenement housing at Scotland Street averaged 528 per acre – the highest density in Britain. The *Glasgow Citizens' Theatre* was founded in 1943, and after the war in 1946 took over and renamed the *Royal Princess* with their own title; but the building lost its fine frontage in the clearances of the 1970s. The Polmadie tram route was withdrawn in 1949 and replaced by trolleybuses; about then Ogg Brothers still had a department store at Paisley Road Toll. The second Clutha Works remained prominent by the Paisley railway; by 1983 their owners P & W McLellan were down to making bolts, nuts and fasteners.

**Iron Ore leaves Dixon's Blazes – but other Fires Burn**: In 1957 General Terminus Quay was re-equipped to handle iron ore for Ravenscraig *(see Motherwell)*. Most once-famous Gorbals names slipped from view with the shrinkage of Scotland's mining and heavy industries. In 1958 *'Dixon's Blazes'* were taken over by Colvilles, and ceased production in 1960, making the city's air much cleaner; in 1966 its last remnants were demolished to make way for a new industrial estate on which Templeton Carpets of Bridgeton built a new works. In 1967 the Plantation Starch Works were destroyed by fire, and another blaze in 1968 burnt out the Riverside grain mills, powered until then by the last large steam engine in the city; only the silos were spared. Strathbungo Station was closed in 1962; about 1965 David Richmond's tube works was also knocked down. The Clydesdale Brewery was demolished in 1967.

**Lowland Malt, Freightliners and a Late College**: A few more jobs came with the Kinclaith Lowland Malt distillery, built in 1958 by Long John beside their Strathclyde grain distillery; the latter was completely rebuilt in 1973–78 to produce 45 million litres of grain whisky a year, which was blended and bottled across the Clyde at Parkhead, plus neutral spirit for gin and vodka. The Polmadie locomotive depot was one of the three top engine sheds in the west of Scotland until the end of steam in the 1960s; later it was rebuilt for diesels, and now houses electric locomotives. The former Caledonian Railway goods sidings at Gushetfaulds were remodelled into a parcels and Freightliner depot from which in 1965 was instituted Britain's first container train (between the Glasgow and London areas). In 1969 the 8-storey Glasgow College of Nautical Studies was belatedly opened in Crown Street.

**Transport Closures of the 1960s Commemorated**: The Harbour Tunnel was closed to vehicles when the new Clyde Tunnel was opened about 1964, 3 km farther from the city centre. The Cumberland Street, Eglinton Street and Shields Road stations were all closed by Beeching in 1965, and within five years their buildings were either burned out or pulled down. The original Central Station bridge was reduced to a disused skeleton in 1966, and the same year saw the end of vehicles on the Finnieston Ferry. The Coplawhill works built its last tramcars in 1954 and the trams vanished in 1962. But in 1964 the former works paint shop near Pollokshields East station became the first home of the famed Glasgow Museum of Transport.

**Redevelopment and the Kingston Bridge**: Housing redevelopment was in full swing in the old Gorbals in the 1960s, about 14 regrettably unsatisfactory multi-storey blocks of council flats and maisonettes designed by Sir Basil Spence and Sir Robert Matthew replacing the squalid crumbling tenements, which had so easily turned to dust during demolition. One such scheme of 19- and 21-storey slab blocks was Queen Elizabeth Square, designed by Spence and opened in 1965, which actually gained an award before its grave faults were recognised. Many other dwellings were cleared and the once crowded Kingston Dock was infilled to enable the construction of the M8 motorway and its Kingston Bridge, opened in 1970. Even the substantial tenements of the 1870s were themselves swept away a century later and replaced by yet more of the high-rise blocks that other cities were beginning to avoid.

**Sunset Falls on Gorbals Industries**: Meantime industrial closures continued: the Scotland Street works of Mirrlees Watson, who had lately made ejectors for Methil power station, were demolished in 1968, followed in 1968–69 by the Watson, Laidlaw works in Laidlaw Street; but in 1979 the former firm still made sugar machinery at Cook Street. In 1968–71 the Loch Katrine Distillery and its adjoining bonded stores bit the dust; and in 1969 the Scotland Street Engine Works and the Dock Engine & Boiler Works were pulled down. Randolph, Elder & Co's engineering works in Tradeston Street was also demolished in 1970, despite being a fine listed building; in that year gas production ceased at Tradeston.

**Deterioration and Clearance, Justified or Not**: The old buildings of Hutcheson's Grammar School *(see Glasgow & Pollokshaws)* were demolished in 1969–70 and replaced by housing, followed the next year by the original Catholic school. By that time the *Palace Theatre* had degenerated to bingo. In spite of housing improvements and redevelopment, decline was already in evidence by 1973 in such newer areas as late 19th century Strathbungo, and in that year the *New Bedford Picture House* also became a mere bingo hall. In 1980 the once magnificent Queen's Park Terrace was destroyed in a typically

*The Queen Elizabeth flats, Gorbals, designed by Sir Basil Spence, Glover and Ferguson, and built between 1960 and 1966 as part of the comprehensive redevelopment of the area. The deck access to houses led to problems, and the buildings were demolished in the mid 1990s.* *(JRH)*

Glaswegian act of vandalism – by Glasgow City District Council, its nominal guardians! The latter's Hutchesontown East housing estate, built in 1968 using a regrettable system called *'Tracoba'*, was soon so damp that it was cleared of residents in 1982 and demolished in 1987. The United Co-op Bakery was closed and demolished about 1977 and the former Kingston Grain Mills – which had become a bonded warehouse – followed in 1978. Iron ore imports through General Terminus Quay were transferred to Hunterston in 1978, and the massive equipment had been demolished by 1982. The unloved Kinclaith distillery was closed and demolished about 1982 when the demand for whisky slumped.

**What's New? Mainly Exhaust and other Gases**: In the 1970s most of Kinning Park disappeared under the M8 Motorway; by 1993 a short section of its complex at Kinning Park comprised no fewer than four three-lane roads! East of the shrunken Gorbals, BOC had by 1979 opened a large depot for industrial gases at Polmadie Road, still busy in 1992. Templeton Carpets still operated at Crown Street in 1983, though within a decade they were acquired for closure by Stoddards of Johnstone. Scottish Galvanisers Ltd, open at Mavisbank Works by 1983, remained at Kinning Park in 1994, as did Rupert Murdoch's News International, whose printing works were built in 1986 at the old Kingston Engineering Works to churn out the downmarket *Sun* and *News of the World* – and the upmarket *Times*.

**Tunnelling to Europe and Transient Garden Festival**: Engineering in the area went out with a flourish: all the English landward drives of the Channel Tunnel, and the English half of its undersea service tunnel, were bored by enormous 225m- and 250m-long machines built in 1987–88 at Scotland Street by Howden's; but the firm left the city for Renfrew in 1989. By 1993 a Local Development Company for the area was in being. Although the Port of Glasgow was already effectively dead, the Mavisbank works was demolished for the finely staged 1988 Garden Festival, which gave an all too temporary glow to the south bank. Why many of its amenities could not have been left intact to benefit greater Glasgow in perpetuity, only the short-term minds of the Thatcher government – who had set the principles for such festivals – could imagine.

**Drugs remain but Flats fall**: An acute problem in 1993 was drugs, for which the depressed Gorbals area had one of the worst records in greater Glasgow. Some linked this with the unpopularity of the 400 council flats in Spence's two last 21-storey blocks in Queen Elizabeth Square. Glasgow District Council found them too costly to convert to uses such as student accommodation, so in 1993 they were blown up in a single controlled series of explosions. Low rise housing would replace them, following a 1992 masterplan for the Crown Street area between Albert Bridge and Caledonia Road. This was designed by London architects under the acronym CZWG for the Glasgow Development Agency. It proposed to retain two existing tall slab blocks but return the rest of the area to 4-storey streetside tenement blocks and terraced houses; under prevailing government dogma, 75% would have to be owner-occupied.

**Museums Come – and Go**: Pollokshields Burgh Hall – which had suffered from neglect after amalgamation with Glasgow soon after its completion – was bought by a trust in 1986, becoming a community centre. It was to be restored from 1995 with help from the National Lottery. Meantime over thirty years a concentration of people of Asian origin had been developing in Pollokshields, whose primary school had become 80% Muslim by 1991. By 1994 the Edwardian Scotland Street School, designed by Charles Rennie Mackintosh, had become an interesting Museum of Education. Though the Museum of Transport was moved to Kelvinside in 1988, it had been replaced by 1994 by the *Tramway Theatre*, which was reconditioned in 2000 as a multi-purpose venue. The *Citizens' Theatre* is still active.

**Freightliners no More**: In 1990 the Freightliner terminal at Gushetfaulds handled some 50,000 boxes for English ports (also serving the J G Russell depot which handled vast quantities of containerised dogfood). But due to the recession and looming privatisation the terminal closed in 1993. Strathclyde PTE then proposed its Crossrail scheme, which would provide a station at Gorbals; this would be linked to the Airdrie to Partick line by a new curve to High Street; however local government reorganisation and impending rail privatisation sunk the plan.

**From Biscuits to Beefburgers**: Nestlé Rowntree decided in 1993 to phase out the 550 jobs in the ex-Gray's Dunn chocolate biscuit factory. However Gray's Dunn continued in production, only to call in the receivers in 2001 after 145 years, when an overseas contract was lost. Galloways – a butchery chain which had become Scotbeef, meat processors with factories in East Kilbride and Bridge of Allan – took over a disused bacon factory in the Gorbals to produce beefburgers, and in 1994 landed a contract to supply Marks & Spencer, resulting in up to 150 new jobs. At New Year 1994 the Glenlight Shipping Company, the last descendant of Clyde puffer operators and now a subsidiary of Clyde Shipping, gave up their island freighting business, but later in the year they introduced new barges to carry timber to Troon. In 1994 a German timber firm, Raab Karcher, was encouraged by the publicly funded Gorbals Initiative to set up a 2800m$^2$ factory in the area. By late 1996 half the Dixon's Blazes industrial estate had been let, and the Academy Business Park in Pollokshields was also regarded as a success story.

**Pacific Quay, IMAX and Science Centre**: In 1995 the 17ha Pacific Quay project on the garden festival site proposed to create some 2000 new jobs in business floorspace and tourist attractions – including refurbishing the listed Four Winds and South Rotunda buildings as offices. The first 4-storey office block, which was to become the Scottish Criminal Records office, was completed late in 2000, as was Scotland's first IMAX cinema. In June 2001 the *'Scottish National Science Centre'* opened, with a planetarium and interactive exhibits, plus the Glasgow Tower – the only tower in the world capable of rotating around 360° and Glasgow's tallest building. BBC Scotland also plan to move to Pacific Quay.

**Motorway Argument**: The restoration of the sadly fire-damaged *'A'* listed Caledonia Road church was begun in 2000. Transport issues remain contentious, in the form of the proposed south-eastern leg of the motorway system, to be built eastwards from the M8 Kingston Bridge approach at Cook Street to parallel the main railway past Rutherglen and join the M74 end-on. Opponents argue that this very non-green scheme, approved in 2000, would cost as much as rebuilding the whole of the lost railways of the Borders! The Gorbals now has a modern *Travelodge* with 100 rooms.

## GORDON — Map 3, B3

***Small Berwickshire village,*** *pop. 600* — OS 74: NT 6443

The little Eden Water in western Berwickshire winds around an upland area about midway between Lauder and Kelso, on which Greenknowe Tower was built to an L-plan in 1581. Close by was Wester Gordon, shown on Pont's map made about 1600, with two mills and an *'old mill'* in the valley nearby; *'Easter Gordoun'* appeared as a linear settlement. Some 4km farther south was another mill at Mellerstain, where a school was established in 1605. The two wings of Mellerstain House, built for George Baillie in 1725, were designed by William Adam; linked by his son Robert Adam from 1768, they still form a fine mansion complete with terraced gardens, a lake and extensive wooded policies. By the 1750s roads had linked East Gordon with Hume and Greenlaw, and Fans (2 km south-west of Greenholm) with Earlston, but between them around the mills lay a remarkable gap.

**Roads and Railway create Gordon**: Later Wester Gordon became the crossing point of the turnpike roads joining Edinburgh with Kelso and Earlston with Greenlaw. It grew into a village, still called West Gordon in the late 19th century when it had an inn, smithy and post and telegraph office. The Berwickshire Railway Company opened its rustic single-track line in 1863, linking Duns with Earlston through Gordon station (north of the village) and connecting with Newtown from 1865; later it became part of the North British system. In the early 20th century a small hospital was built 1km east of West Gordon, by now known simply as Gordon. In 1948 floods cut the railway line and only freight services were resumed; these ceased in the late 1960s.

**Agriculture and Archery**: Meantime a small local quarry had closed by the 1950s, when the population was 675, with the facilities of a small village, serving about 1200 people in all, including Mellerstain and Westruther; the hospital's 44 beds served chronic sick patients. By 1969 Lord Binning had opened Mellerstain to the public, and nearby by about 1980 was a pottery and the well-known Border Archery workshop, where some four people made longbows. By 1981 the hospital had been closed, but J Waldie ran an engineering firm at Gordon. The parish had 631 people in 1991. Greenknowe Tower is a tourist attraction, and Gordon still has its post office, primary school and the small *Gordon Arms Hotel*.

## GOREBRIDGE & Arniston — Map 15, D3

***Midlothian large village,*** *pop. 5900* — OS 66: NT 3461

In 1560 Byres Castle, 3km north-west of Borthwick Castle, was the seat of Lord Lindsay; later in the 16th century it was replaced by Newbyres Castle. Pont's map of around 1600 showed *'Kathuin'* (Catcune) Mill between the castles. The naming of Stobhill and to the north of it *'Colheuch'* showed that coal mining was already in progress north of Newbyres; very likely this fuelled the limekilns at Borthwick. The Palladian mansion of Arniston House, 2 km south-west of Newbyres Castle, was designed by William Adam about 1725 and became the home of the redoubtable Dundas family. The Roy map of about 1754 showed an extensive road system in the area around Newbyres, which fell into ruin. In 1794 a gunpowder mill was set up at Newbyres by an English firm; according to Heron this was the first in Scotland. He also mentioned *"the collieries of Arniston, Vogrie and Stobhill"* (Vogrie is 3km to the north-east). By 1838 a post office was opened at Gorebridge, which closely adjoined Newbyres. By the late 1830s the powder mills had become very extensive, though with only some 60 employees.

**The Railway: Emily's Deep Pit and Arniston Engine**: The steeply graded Edinburgh & Hawick Railway was opened through from Edinburgh to Gorebridge in 1847; the station provided a short level relief in the 1.4% (1 in 70) ruling gradient when the line was extended in 1849 to Galashiels and beyond, with a station named Fushiebridge beside Harvieston just south of Gorebridge. By 1869 Christie owned seven collieries in the area, employing 500 workers. His long-established Emily pit north-west of the village had three shafts, 32 km of roads and passages and raised 30 tonnes of coal an hour, by a combination of stoop and room with longwall working. It was then the deepest in eastern Scotland, its depth of 293m requiring a noteworthy steam engine, commemorated by 1895 in the name of the tiny settlement known as *Arniston Engine*.

**Late Victorian Activity**: The powder-mills and two collieries were all busy in 1894–95, when a rail connection had been laid from Catcune to limeworks near Esperston, south-east of Arniston. The OS 1" map showed none of the local settlements as more than a hamlet; yet by 1901 their combined populations exceeded 2500. Workpeople were crammed into small poor cottages, while richer folk erected mansions such as Kirkhill, enjoying a riverside site within a stone's throw. Gorebridge never became a burgh, but a gasworks was built in 1908 and it acquired a sawmill.

**Mines and Railways leave Problems**: By 1951 Kirkhill was a hotel, and Gorebridge with nearly 6000 people had the facilities of a very large village. The last local mine was closed between 1963 and 1970; the railway was closed completely in 1969 and had been lifted by 1973. Mining dereliction remained to the west of Gorebridge, where work was provided by the sawmill, the limeworks and the quarries. In 1991, when under 5900 residents remained, male unemployment was high. In 1993 a local farmer, Christopher Mann, started Scotland's first flock of ostriches. There had been little development by 1996; by then the surrounding dereliction had been swept away, but Newbyres Castle ruins had been demolished. Arniston (still in the Dundas family) is now open to the public in summer.

## GORGIE, Dalry, Craiglockhart, Roseburn & Slateford

**Map 15, C2**

***Western areas of Edinburgh,*** *pop. 40,000* — OS 66: NT 2271

Craiglockhart Castle was built in the 15th century some 3 km west of Edinburgh, near the Slate Ford by which users of the Lanark road crossed the Water of Leith. This drove the delightfully named *Jinkaboot* Mill at Slateford, which was grinding corn by 1506. Roseburn House was built 2 km to the north in 1562, but later much altered. Pont's map of about 1600 showed both *'Gorgy'* and *'Darry'* as mills, lying between the roads to Lanark and to Corstorphine; the latter road already crossed the *'New Bridge'* at Roseburn. Between the mills was *Sauchtoun*. By 1657 Redhall quarry was open south of Slateford.

**Scotland's First Paper Mill**: Early papermaking in the area is well documented. The West Mill on the Water of Leith at Dalry had the distinction of being the first paper mill in Scotland, opened in 1590 by the Russells, using German expertise. It made paper until a fire in 1679, after which it was restored as a grain mill. Boag's Mill was a waulk mill by 1598, and milled almost every common material in its time. About 1714 the Jinkaboot Mill was converted to beat rags for papermaking, but reverted to milling barley twenty years later; it was demolished about 1755. Another paper mill was in operation at Redhall before 1718, soon also becoming a grain mill.

**Textiles, Quarrying, Canal and Railway**: The *Cross Keys Inn* at Slateford (it's still going) originated in the 18th century; Hailes quarry was in production by mid-century, and James Reid's printfield was at work by 1755. Joseph Reid began bleaching and dyeing in 1773 at the Slateford bleachfield, beside which the Inglis Green Laundry was set up in 1820. By 1813 the Hailes quarry was already famous, cutting sixty tonnes of stone a day for city builders; Redhall quarries (there were two) employed 15 men in 1834 and remained open until at least 1886. In 1869 Hailes quarry was making indoor *'steps and plats'* from easily worked stone. Despite these varied small industries, the area remained rural in character until after the Union Canal, built from 1818, was opened across the 8-arched Slateford viaduct in 1822, passing east of Dalry. The Edinburgh & Glasgow Railway (E&G) which commenced services in 1842 skirted the northern edge of Dalry; the canal was soon financially ruined, and was taken over by the E&G in 1849. In the same year the Inglis Green bleachfield and laundry was taken over by A & J Macnab.

**Caledonian Railway and Distillery**: Development linking Slateford with Edinburgh really got going when the Caledonian Railway (CR) was opened through the area from Carstairs to Edinburgh in 1848. Their Dalry Road locomotive depot or *'shed'* stood beside the cemetery. The CR's Granton branch (which began at a junction at Slateford) opened in 1861, with stations at Dalry, and at Murrayfield just east of Roseburn. This crossed over the E&G – which was absorbed by the North British Railway (NBR) in 1865 – and some competition between these lines was to continue until 1947. The huge 5-storey Caledonian Distillery was built beside Haymarket station by Menzies, Bernard & Co in 1855. One of the two largest in Scotland in 1869, the annual output of its 150 employees was over 9 million litres of grain whisky, made in the largest Coffey still in Europe, using grain imported through Granton and brought by rail to sidings within the works. Much of the product was then despatched to London to be turned into gin. In 1884 it became part of DCL, and was the second largest grain whisky distillery in the UK; maize was part of the input, and in disregard of the views of the Water Trust it still used *canal water* for brewing!

**Silk, Rubber and Plastics**: The Castle Mills beside the Union Canal, originally a silk factory, were long vacant when replaced in 1855 by the North British Rubber Company works. By the 1860s it employed 600 workers, making nearly 2 million pairs of ladies' galoshes a year, plus waterproofs and solid rubber tyres. Nearby, the Scottish Vulcanite Company works was established in 1861 as a subsidiary, with about 500 workers making – among other moulded goods – 7.5 million combs a year from this early rubber-based plastic. By 1869 foundries were open in Gorgie – between Dalry and Slateford – and Cox's tanneries and leather works were active at Gorgie Mill.

**Brewing, Baking and Urbanisation**: Two breweries were also founded, John Jeffrey's Heriot Brewery at Roseburn in 1868 and the Caledonian Brewery of Lorimer & Clark on Slateford Road in 1869. McVitie's had a large bakery off Slateford Road. Many tenement streets were rapidly developed and children were numerous: by 1866 there was a school at Slateford; schools were built at both Gorgie and Dalry in 1876, and at Longstone in 1877. The huge but rather unsuccessful Craiglockhart Hydropathic was built beside the castle ruins in 1877–80.

**Football, Rugby and Suburban Trains**: The *'Heart of Midlothian'* football club, founded in 1873–74, leased ground in 1881 for a *'park'* at Tynecastle, opened in 1886. The Murrayfield golf club was formed in 1896 north of the growing suburbs, and the Murrayfield rugby ground at Roseburn was established around 1900; for those whose thuggery knew no such rules of play, Saughton Prison was thoughtfully provided, west of the Stenhouse or Saughton Mills. In 1884 the NBR opened their south side suburban line, Gorgie station being just north of Slateford Road; Craiglockhart station was added in 1887. The CR built its own large laundry at Slateford, and in 1889 Robert Peddie's Tynecastle Ironworks fabricated Edinburgh's Dean footbridge. In 1891 Slateford – still a distinct village – had a population of 521, for there was still little development west or south-west of Gorgie station. In 1897 Gorgie gained a branch library and hall in Dundee Street, with help from Thomas Nelson.

**North British Distillery, Markets, Bricks and Stone**: In 1885 the North British grain distillery was started by a blenders' co-operative whose prime mover and chairman was the blender Andrew Usher of Newington, who wanted to counter the emerging monopoly of DCL in grain whisky. It was completed in 1887 with a capacity of around 11 million litres (*'2 to 3 million gallons'*) a year, and some of Usher's share of the profits went towards building the city centre's Usher Hall. In 1890, Bernard's of the Edinburgh Canongate opened Slateford brewery beside the station, and maltings were built in Slateford Road in 1895. From 1902, extensive premises with railway sidings for Edinburgh's cattle market and slaughterhouses were built on a 10 ha site at Slateford; the move from Lauriston took place in 1907. A brickworks was built at

*The Caledonian brewery, Slateford Road, which began in 1869; it has been very successful since its management buy-out from Vaux in 1987.* *(JRH)*

Longstone Road about 1906 to use up quarry waste, of which there was plenty: by the time it closed – soon after 1913 – the Hailes quarry had produced red, blue and grey building stone, covered 12 ha, was over 35 m deep and even extended beneath the Union Canal! The Caledonian grain distillery suffered a major fire in 1911, but was soon repaired.

**Trams and Ferranti**: Cable trams reached Gorgie in 1899, and early in the 20th century electric trams ran to Slateford while the Edinburgh system was still cable-hauled. After the area was incorporated into the city of Edinburgh in 1920–21, the latter's services were electrified. The radial tram route bifurcated at Ardmillan Terrace and tramcars ran to both Slateford and to Stenhouse, the latter passing Robertson Avenue, where a car shed stood opposite the Ferranti factory (a branch of the electrical manufacturing firm which was founded at Hollinsworth in Lancashire before 1900). Many tramcars terminated at the Ferranti works; nearby was McVitie's large bakery.

**Between the Wars: Convent, Cinemas and Skating**: Craiglockhart Hydropathic was rather decayed when late in the 1914–18 war it was taken over for use as a military hospital; in 1920 its buildings became the Sacred Heart Convent and St Andrews College of Education. Hearts FC bought Tynecastle in 1926, but its restricted site limited improvement. Carrick Knowe municipal golf course was laid out in 1930. Meantime Boag's mill was destroyed by fire in 1924, and oil and cake mills were in operation at Dundee Street in 1932. The canal ceased to carry traffic in the 1930s, at the time when the Stenhouse local authority housing estate was being built. The *Lyceum Cinema* in Slateford Road was built in 1926, followed by *Poole's Roxy* in 1937 and the Murrayfield Ice Rink in 1938.

**Transport and other Changes from 1945**: With few exceptions the facilities of the area in the 1950s – when the population was approaching 70,000 – were only comparable to those of a country town, laid out along the tram routes of Dalry, Gorgie and Slateford Roads. The brickworks had closed by the time the Granton to Stenhouse trams were withdrawn in 1952, and the remaining trams ceased running to Slateford via Gorgie in 1953. The site of the tram shed was used for the city's large Longstone bus garage. In 1960 a railway curve was built across the University athletic field at Meggetland to connect the ex-CR line east of the foundry with the the ex-NB suburban route; a depot was created east of Slateford station, but in 1967 the cattle market lost its rail link. During the 1950s and 60s Hailes Quarry was infilled with rubbish and eventually laid out as Hailes Park.

**More Technology, Fewer People**: Westons Biscuits were baked beneath the *Locarno Ballroom* in Slateford Road until the firm relocated to Sighthill. T & J Bernard, brewers of Slateford, were absorbed by S&N in 1960. In the late 1960s the Bank of Scotland built its first Computer Centre at Robertson Avenue to house its new IBM mainframe. By 1977 Bertrams of Sciennes had an ironfoundry at Westfield Avenue, and the Edinburgh Telephone Area Headquarters was at Telephone House in Gorgie Road. In 1979 a large snooker and squash club was built at Slateford. Around 1980 the use of MacNab's site was switched from dry cleaning to cash and carry. The population had fallen by 40% in 30 years to only some 40,000 in 1981. However, there were by then 17 hotels, largely in the Murrayfield area, mostly small. From 1979 Murrayfield Ice Rink was adjoined by a new curling rink. Other facilities in general remained intact, and Slateford station was reopened in the mid 1980s. In 1986 Napier College (by 1993, University) took over the College of Education buildings at Craiglockhart.

**Drinks Industries and Refurbishment**: The once great Caledonian distillery closed in 1987. Luckier was the Caledonian Brewery, owned by Vaux but bought out by its management in 1987; it boiled the mash in its original open coppers, which they claimed were the last such in Britain. From 1991 it was the venue for Real Ale Festivals; it suffered fire damage in 1994 but was quickly rebuilt. The North British distillery was one of the largest in Scotland; by 1993 it contained the laboratory of Pentlands Scotch Whisky Research, working for a consortium of ten whisky companies. In that year the distillery was acquired by Grand Metropolitan and Highland Distillers. The century-old brewery maltings in Slateford Road were renovated for sale as flats in 1995.

**Fine Chemicals and Marketing**: Meantime two chemical firms, Macfarlan (founded in 1780) and Smith (1820) lately merged as Macfarlan Smith, had been bought by Glaxo in 1963. Based at Wheatfield Road by 1977, the firm became the world market leader in the supply of opiates for pain relief. Macfarlan Smith was bought out in 1990 by its management. A new abattoir had been built in 1981, and by 1989 Robertsons' meat products factory adjoined the 2ha site of two distinct livestock markets, Oliver & Sons – owned in 1994 by Lawrie & Symington of Lanark – and John Swan & Sons (who also traded at Newtown St Boswells). Both are still active in cattle, sheep and pigs. By 1994 the *Gorgie/Dalry Gazette* was in publication.

**Sports Stadiums Rebuilt and Flats Squeezed in**: By 1990 ten-pin bowling was available at the Murrayfield rugby football ground, which saw successive improvements in the 1980s. Enormous new covered stands, to seat 67,500 spectators, were built on all sides in 1992–94, including a conference centre and banqueting facilities for up to 700 delegates. In 1996 Murrayfield Royals were among the four Scottish ice hockey teams playing in the Northern Premier League. Hearts FC considered leaving inadequate Tynecastle for a greenbelt site; but, after examining 14 options over four years, decided instead to build three new stands at Tynecastle from 1994, cutting the ground's capacity from 25,000 to an all-seated 18,000. This improvement, and success on the field, has kept them in the Premier League. In 1997 Tynecastle High School had 830 pupils. The 3.5ha site of the former Caledonian Distillery south of Haymarket station was largely redeveloped in 1999–2001 with large numbers of ultra high density flats; the stone shell of the tallest original building was converted. Dalry Road remains a significant shopping centre, with some rare specialists such as retailers of electronic parts. The largish hotels in the Roseburn/Murrayfield area include the *Murrayfield* and the *Ellersly House*.

## GOURDON

**Map 10, B5**

***Mearns village,*** *pop. 950* — OS 45: NO 8270

This small cove which the locals call *'Gurden'* lies on the rocky shore of the Mearns 2km south of Inverbervie; it was mentioned as a farm and fisher town as early as 1315. By about 1750, as Roy's map showed, a coastal track passed through, linking Inverbervie with Johnshaven. By 1794 Gourdon's 42 houses held 188 people. In 1799 Heron implied that a harbour had already been constructed, when noting that *"the village of Gourdon employs a few small vessels in carrying coal and lime to Bervie and the neighbourhood"*. In 1827 Chambers wrote that *"on account of the inconvenience of Bervie harbour, the fishermen have now almost all removed to Gourdon, a more commodious place"*. Granaries were built about that time, and in 1830 came a herring station. In 1865 a branch of the North British Railway was opened from Montrose to Bervie, with a station at Gourdon. A lifeboat station was opened in 1878, by 1881 over 8000 barrels of salted herring were exported each year, and by 1891 there were 1100 people.

**Making the Best of Things**: The locally-built 6-oared surf-boat *Maggie Law* enabled the lives of 36 people to be saved up to 1930, and is still on display in the village. Meantime, when the herring failed about 1912, the locals turned to long line fishing from motor boats, and in the 1920s took up seine netting. Slow decline continued; in 1951, when over 900 people lived in Gourdon, the small but picturesque harbour was still packed with fishing vessels. However, the railway was closed to passengers in 1951 and to freight in 1966, and the Gourdon lifeboat station was soon closed; even so, there were still 651 people in Gourdon in 1991. In 1992 – when the long established Selbie Works of Sidlaw Yarns still provided about 60 jobs – twelve fishing boats were still based at Gourdon, catching cod in winter and shellfish at other times; occasional large catches would be auctioned. Gourdon harbour is still quite busy, with several small smokeries and at least three fish merchants – one both wholesale and retail. A primary school, general store and two pubs serve residents.

## GOUROCK

**Map 5, B5**

***Inverclyde town,*** *pop. 11,700* — OS 63: NS 2477

The imposing Levan Castle was built around 1400, overlooking the Firth of Clyde some 7km west of Greenock. Pont's map made around 1600 omitted Levan, but showed *'Gourok Castle'*, an undated structure of which little remains. On the bay to the west and midway between Greenock and Levan was *'Gourok Toun'*. From 1618 a road from Greenock led through Gourock and past Levan to Cloch Point, whence a ferry plied to Dunoon. Gourock became a burgh of barony in 1694, and its famous ropeworks was founded in 1711, supplying the needs of the Greenock and other shipowners with ropes and later sails. Roy's map of about 1754 showed Gourock as a one-street town lining the coast road. A lint mill was built late in the 18th century, and the Cloch lighthouse was first illuminated in 1797. In 1799 Heron noted that the *"rope walk"* manufactured over 160 tonnes of hemp a year, though Gourock was merely a *"village"* of about 400 people; it had a post office by 1813.

**Steamers and Yachts replace the Ropeworks**: In 1820 a pier was opened with a direct ferry to Dunoon, and in the mid 1820s Chambers found *"a considerable village and sea-port"*. Steamers on the Glasgow to Rothesay service called by 1845, and a gasworks was set up in 1849. By then Gourock and Helensburgh had become the Clyde's *"principal watering places"*. All the rope works eventually moved to Port Glasgow, and Gourock was not further industrialised, as for most of the 19th century it lay beyond the end of the railway. In 1873 a horse tramway was laid between Gourock and Greenock. St Ninian's Church was built in 1879, and in Glasgow fair week 1886, Barnard noted Gourock's *"little bay crowded with yachts"*.

**Longest Railway Tunnel serves Competing Steamers**: In 1889 the Caledonian Railway completed Scotland's longest railway tunnel at Newton Street, cut through seriously faulted rock and approached by cuttings with massive retaining walls, serving a new terminus and pier at Gourock. Peak hour express trains soon took only 35 minutes for the 40km or so from Glasgow to Gourock Pier, to serve which the firm created a subsidiary, the Caledonian Steam Packet Company (CSPC), an ancestor of Cal Mac. Steamboats sailed to all the favourite residential areas on the Firth in wasteful competition with the rival Glasgow & South Western – until a more rational pattern was worked out.

**Golf, Hotels, Trams and Buses**: By 1894 Murray's Handbook referred to Gourock as a *"town"* but noted that there was *"no good hotel"*. From 1894 trams ran from Ashton through Gourock to Greenock and Port Glasgow. Gourock golf club, founded in 1896, placed its hillside clubhouse to give a spectacular view. By about 1900 a steam laundry and the *Ashton Hotel* were open, and an electric power station was built in 1901. From 1929 the LMS Railway used Albion buses on a service between Greenock, Gourock and Largs. The Craigburn Pavilion was built in 1935–36 for live summer shows and dances, and the *Gourock Bay Hotel* followed in 1938. By 1951 Gourock's 9000 residents enjoyed normal urban facilities, with six hotels; steamers still plied to Dunoon and Craigendoran.

**Queen Mary II, Car Ferries and Electric Trains**: In 1970 Gourock pier became the base for the elderly 80m-long triple-screw turbine steamer *Queen Mary* – which for many years at King George V's and Cunard's insistence had carried the suffix *'II'*. She plied until 1977, but survived to become a Thames restaurant in 1988. By 1971 a passenger ferry plied to Kilcreggan. From 1972 two second-hand Scandinavian car ferries owned by Western Ferries plied from McInroy's Point, 2 km west of Gourock, to Hunter's Quay by Dunoon. The railway was electrified in 1967, but the town council (which owned only 27% of the town's houses in 1972) praised the bus services, calling their burgh a *"popular seaside resort"*; in 1975 it became part of the new Inverclyde District. Meantime by 1972 the 60-room *Gantock Hotel* had been built on Cloch Road just west of Levan Castle. Expanding Gourock had 7 other hotels in 1981, and a population of 11,743 residents in 1991. A big scheme approved in 1993 to infill part of Cardwell Bay adjoining Greenock, to create sites for a 300-berth marina, hotel and 150 houses, was not implemented. Newton Street railway tunnel was reconstructed in 1993–94, requiring a 6-month closure before double track operation could be restored.

**Mimtec brings a Jobs Bonanza**: A huge new 28,000m$^2$ factory at Faulds Park – cut into the hillside beyond existing housing development, which had already spread 3km west of the town centre – was opened in 1993 by electronic component manufacturers Mimtec of Livingston, part of Murray International. Rapidly expanded, it soon employed 250 people, and created more jobs in a new building opened in 1994, serving IBM at nearby Spango; by 1995 over 1200 workers were producing personal computers for export to Europe, Africa and the Middle East. Gourock remains the HQ of Cal Mac (ex CSPC and MacBrayne), which operates some 30 vessels serving 51 terminals; though there is pressure for the office to be moved to Oban. Car ferries still ply to Dunoon from Gourock and to Hunter's Quay from McInroy's Point; a passenger ferry still plies to Kilcreggan year-round, and in summer also to Helensburgh. Gourock High School has over 550 pupils. By 2000 the *Gantock Hotel* had been renamed the *Stakis Gourock* and enlarged to 100 rooms, with a swimming pool.

*The Cloch lighthouse, west of Gourock, first illuminated in 1797; it was built by the Clyde Lighthouse Trust to mark the entry to the upper Firth of Clyde.* (JRH)

## GOVAN & Ibrox — Map 15, C5

***Area of Glasgow**, pop. 28,000* — OS 64: NS 5565

In a very fertile area beside the River Clyde opposite the mouth of the River Kelvin, just 4km west of Glasgow Cross, was the ancient Columban monastery of Govan. By the eighth century it was an episcopal centre, and the community was vigorous around the year 975. But the bishopric passed back to Glasgow, and the monastery was succeeded by a church, east of which was a Norman motte, and a village. The renowned *Govan Ferry*, also a seasonal crossing for drovers, was operating to and from Partick by 1593 or earlier, and this north bank area was part of Govan parish. Pont's map of Renfrewshire – made about then – showed no ferry, but *'Mekle Gouan'* was already a large settlement for the day; a parish school was founded in 1614. Govan's early status and economic support remain in some doubt, but salmon fishing would have supplemented farming.

**Weaving, Mining and Co-operation**: Govan was known for handloom weaving before the Govan Weavers' Society was founded in 1756. Various early coal pits were dug in the areas of the later Broomloan Road, Cathcart Road and Helen Street. By the time of Roy's map of about 1754 *Meikle Govan* was a long village alongside the river, with three radial roads. In 1771 William Dixon started mining coal east of Meikle Govan. In 1777 the villagers formed an early quasi co-operative, the *Govan Victualling Society*. Heron observed in 1799 that *"the populous village of Govan contains upwards of 1100 inhabitants; there is a considerable bleachfield, and a cotton-mill (driven by a steam-engine) which gives employment to about a hundred hands"*. Mansions stood at Fairfield and Linthouse before their proprietors found more profitable uses for their estates: in 1824 Morris Pollok opened a 5-storey silk mill which later became part of the Fairfield shipyard. About 1839

MacArthur & Alexander set up a shipyard, later known as the Govan Old yard.

**The Dixons build a Tramway and Exploit Children in Deep Mines**: About 1811 Dixon's son, another William, built a tramway to carry coal from Govan colliery to the Gorbals terminus of the canal which served Paisley, but passed well south of Govan. The village expanded steadily; the first Govan post office opened around 1825, while Govan church was rebuilt in 1826 and again in 1888. Part of the tramway was converted to a railway, and extended to Rutherglen in 1840. Dixon's Govan colliery became notorious in 1842 when a nine year old Irish boy was found working twelve-hour shifts at the pit bottom in almost total darkness. Shamed into action, by the 1860s good houses had been provided for the miners at Dixon's Shawfield coal mine, said to be the most extensive in Scotland. The very fine corner tenement block at Walmer Crescent was designed by Alexander Thomson and built in 1857–62.

**Napier for Paddles, Screws, ... and Sails!**: Robert Napier of the Vulcan Foundry across the river at Anderston took over the MacArthur & Alexander yard in 1841 and moved his workforce from Lancefield. In 1849–50 they built the first train ferry, the PS *Leviathan*, conceived by Thomas Bouch for the Burntisland to Granton run. In 1850 Napier moved to the East or New yard, leaving the Old yard to build small liners and later trawlers under various owners. In 1856 Napiers built one of the first three iron ships for the Navy, followed by the novel ironclad battleship HMS *Black Prince* in 1861. By then the Clyde was building two-thirds of Britain's steamers. In 1862 Napiers made the engines for PS *Scotia*, last and finest of the Transatlantic paddlers, soon to be superseded by more seaworthy screw vessels. In 1868 the yard employed about 1750 workers, who built twin-screw ironclads of up to 3775 tons, for an Admiralty so conservative that they were still fully rigged! In 1874 Napiers built the iron paddle steamer *Pharos* for the Northern Lighthouse Board.

**Stephen of Linthouse**: Stephen's first shipyard at Burghhead on the Moray Firth started in 1750. In 1850 Alexander Stephen, then of Aberdeen (and later with yards at Arbroath and Dundee), opened his first small Linthouse yard at Holmfauld Road. Its speed and efficiency about 1863 – during the American civil war – enabled two small iron paddle steamers to be built as Confederate blockade runners in six weeks! The yard, by then called Alexander Stephen & Sons, was enlarged to 14 ha in 1864–69; a long-lasting engine works was added in 1869–72 *(see Hay & Stell)*. The mansionhouse of Linthouse became the yard offices until it was demolished in 1920. From 1878 the Glasgow shipowners Cayzer, Irvine (renamed the Clan Line in 1881) ordered most of their ships from Stephen. Tragedy struck Linthouse in 1883: nearly 150 men drowned when the ill-fated steamer *Daphne* of 500 tons capsized on launching.

**Smith & Roger, Thomson's, and McLean's**: Govan yards built very large and very small vessels, some very durable and others extremely curious. Smith and Rodger opened the Middleton shipbuilding yard at Govan in 1844, immediately building the iron PS *Glengarry*, which when scrapped in Inverness in 1927 was the oldest steamship in the world. In 1864 the yard was sold to the London & Glasgow Engineering and Iron Shipbuilding Company. J & G Thomson of the Finnieston engine works established a shipyard at Stag Street in Govan in 1851, at first building smallish paddle steamers. In 1872 their shipyard was transferred to a new site, at Clydebank *(q.v.)* to enable dry dock construction on its Govan site. Hugh McLean & Sons, established at Govan in 1880, built over 5000 small craft in their 63 years of existence – more than one and a half per week; many were lifeboats.

**Elder's Fairfield Shipyard from Tub to Titan**: The extensive Fairfield shipyard at Govan was opened in 1864 by John Elder (formerly of Randolph, Elder & Co, who had begun as marine engineers in Glasgow, owned works in Tradeston *(see Gorbals)* and also founded the Kingston yard at Port Glasgow). John followed this in 1869 by erecting nearby a great engine works 90 m square to replace the Tradeston premises *(for details and bird's eye view of the yard see Hay & Stell)*. Continued expansion of the order book led to improvement of Elder's yard in 1874, and it used steel from 1877. Among the smaller of many ships built was the uniquely tubby 4000-ton steam yacht *Livadia* for the Tsar of Russia in 1880; while only 72 m long, she had a beam of almost 47 m! After Elder's death the yard was extended again, and became the world's largest. Meantime Elder Park was gifted to the town by John Elder's widow, and opened in 1885.

**Govan Burgh: Pipers, Timber and Textiles**: Fast-growing Govan became a police burgh in 1864; the world's first pipe band was started in 1882 by the Govan police force. Govan had long attracted many Ulster Protestant workers to settle; their large Ibrox Methodist Church dated from 1867. By 1872 though the town was lit by gas, many thatched cottages still stood in Main Street. Broomloan Road school, built in 1875, was designed by Alexander Watt, and in 1894 was equally finely enlarged in red sandstone to designs by D Barclay into the largest council school in the burgh. Meantime in 1868 Hamilton Marr & Co founded the Govan Sawmills. Another fire hazard was the Clyde Match Works, opened in 1877 (but used as sawmills); in 1903 Milne & Co opened their Drumoyne sawmill. In 1877 John Wylie & Co built a power-loom weaving factory in Broomloan Road south of the town centre, and about 1886 another was built in Helen Street by the Govan Weaving Company. In 1883 James McIlwraith built tarpaulin works in Broomloan Road, and in 1890 the Govan Ropeworks was set up in Helen Street.

**Railways, Trams, Graving Docks and Beardmore**: In 1868 a short branch railway was opened to Govan from the Glasgow & Paisley joint line, providing a large goods facility – a very roundabout rail passenger service between Govan and Glasgow. Horse trams of the Glasgow Tramway & Omnibus Company first ran in 1872 between Govan Cross and the Fairfield shipyard. A more direct steam tramway operated from 1876 to 1880, and in the new century the shipyard freight line was electrified. In 1869 the excavation of a 168 m-long graving dock was begun at Stag Street by the Clyde Navigation Trust (CNT). In 1886 the CNT opened their second graving dock, 175 m in length, followed in 1898 by a 268 m dock able to take the largest vessel then afloat. In 1879 Napier's Govan East and Lancefield shipyards and marine engineering works were bought by William Beardmore of the Parkhead Forge.

**Boilermaking and Varied Engineering**: Steamship boilers needed many internal tubes, a special manufacturing problem. The Govan Tube Works in Helen Street were established in 1871, and the company built further premises in Broomloan Road about 1883. In 1878 Anderson & Lyall, engineers and boilermakers, built the Whitefield Works; the large Moorepark

Boiler Works of Lindsay Burnet & Co were founded about 1884. The Albion Works of G & A Harvey was built in 1880, and about 1899 J Bennie & Son built the Clyde Engine Works in Drumoyne Road; both made machine tools. The Colonial Ironworks of Aitken, McNeil & Co were built about 1882. The small Govan Steel Works and the Broomloan Foundry were also set up in the 1880s. The Caledonian Steel Foundry in Helen Street opened in 1893; nearby in 1893–98 arose the St Helens Engine Works of Hall-Brown, Buttery & Co, heavy marine and electrical engineers. David Cockburn built the Clydesdale Engineering Works about 1900 in Meiklewood Road, later expanded.

**Late Victorian Expansion and Edwardian Tragedy**: Govan had by then become a major local centre, with sub-post offices by 1884. In 1888 the publisher John Cossar set up the *Govan Press* as a local newspaper. Immigration was such that in 1896 a huge hostel for 536 homeless men was built in Govan Road for Thomas Paxton. Govan's own *Lyceum Theatre*, a music hall which opened in 1899, later became a cinema. 2 km to the west was a large new hospital, later known as the Southern General. From 1887 onwards the SCWS started to make varied *'own brand'* products at Shieldhall, west of the hospital; eventually the sprawling works had 17 departments. *'Glasgow Rangers'* FC which had started in 1872 on Glasgow Green, moved across the river in 1887 from Partick to another temporary site in open country between Govan and Kinning Park, beside which they built Ibrox stadium in 1899. Govan's Linthouse FC briefly played in the Scottish League (1895–1900). Rangers scooped the pool, but in 1902 an Ibrox timber grandstand collapsed under the weight and movement of the 68,000 crowd at a Scotland–England international, causing 25 deaths and 500 injuries. Rangers pressed on with piecemeal improvements, enclosing the pitch with oval earthen banks, and in 1928–29 erected a main stand to designs by engineer Archibald Leitch.

**The Glasgow Subway, Light and Power**: A busy industrial complex on the fringes of a city needed better links with the commercial and business centre, and in 1891 Govan was chosen as the site for the outermost station of the almost circular Glasgow Subway, the only cable-hauled underground railway ever built, and of the rare four foot gauge. (The heroic six-year struggle to complete its two shallow tunnels beneath the Clyde was graphically described by Black (1937).) Beside Govan station, opened in 1897, was the depot, accessed from the characteristically dank-smelling tunnels only by a vehicle lift. Other stations were opened south-east of Govan at Copland Road (later called Ibrox) and Cessnock; Partick station beyond the unseen river was less than 1 km to the north. A power station was built for Govan burgh in 1892, and a larger one in 1899, further enlarged in 1911. But not everyone could afford a supply of gas or electricity, even for lighting: about 1897 Shearer & Harvey built a new candle factory. A large church was built in 1902–04 at Craigton Road.

**Cranes, Copper, and Drummond's Locomotives**: In 1891 the crane builders Alexander Chaplin & Co moved from Cranstonhill to a new Cranstonhill Engine Works in Govan; about 1908 D Watson & Co also built crane works in Harmony Row. Robert Burley & Sons' Hammer Shaft factory and the adjacent Ibrox Ironworks were built in 1891 east of Govan – the latter plant was expanded by the pneumatic engineers J M Adam & Co in 1904. The burgeoning electricity industry – like distilling – needed copper, so the Phoenix Copperworks of D Brown & Co, built in 1897, was followed in 1903 by Blair, Campbell & McLean's copper works in Woodville Street, which made whisky and rum stills and sugar pans. About 1891 Dugald Drummond, in turn locomotive superintendent of the North British and Caledonian Railways and manager of the Australasian Locomotive Company, opened his Glasgow Railway Engineering Works in Helen Street. He left in 1895, but his sons ran the firm for 30 years.

**Bakeries, Brushes and Ventilation**: In 1892 Rowat & Co established the grandly named City of Glasgow Pickle & Sauce Works, and in 1903–04 two bakeries were erected in Copland Road, followed from 1911 by Galbraith's large bakery in Craigton Road. In 1897 William Morier opened a brush factory nearby, and about 1899 the Shieldhall Sawmills of John Woyka & Co moved from the Gorbals to Bogmoor Road. Then in 1907–08 the Thermotank Ventilating Company became established in Golspie Street.

**Fairfield at the Crest of the Wave**: Fairfield supplied a range of vessels, from modest-sized paddle and screw steamers to the outstanding 20,000-ton Cunard liner *Campania*, able to cruise at 22 knots. Built in 1892–93, she was so long at 600 feet that she had to be launched diagonally across the Clyde. Then came a plethora of warship orders, summarised below. In 1902 the 9000-ton Orient liner RMS *Orontes* came off the stocks for the Australian service *(see Aberdour)*, and the yard was yet again expanded in 1903 when Fairfields were building the Clyde steamer *Duchess of Fife* for the Caledonian Steam Packet Company. The Fairfield yard's boiler works were, remarkably, still adjoined by open country in 1902; the areas west and south of Elder Park and south of Crossloan Road were also undeveloped. Stephens' yard was also greatly enlarged, between 1905 and 1914.

**Prince's Dock and Edwardian Transport Developments**: Adjacent to the latest graving dock was the Cessnock (later Prince's) Dock, separating Govan from Kinning Park; it was dug out from 1893 and completed in 1897, with a huge 130-tonne steam crane which lasted for over 70 years. In 1894–98 Glasgow Corporation built their large Shieldhall Sewage Works north of the Southern General Hospital – later made an excuse for taking over Govan burgh. In 1900 two more passenger ferries were established, at Kelvinhaugh upstream of the ancient chain ferry – which now carried vehicles – and at Meadowside, only 300 m downstream, where Clyde steamers would also call; the Govan ferry itself was modernised in 1912. In that year the coachbuilders and cartwrights J & D Reid began to erect workshops in Elder Street, and in 1913–14 what was known as the Govan tram depot was built near Kinning Park.

**Warships – and an Aircraft – from Fairfield**: As the insane arms race with Kaiser Bill's Germany took its hold on the Admiralty, the Fairfield yard built five cruisers of steadily increasing size. In 1905 the First Sea Lord, *'Jackie'* Fisher of Rosyth fame, chose Alex Gracie of Fairfield's – whom he called *"the best Marine Engineer in the world"* – to join the Naval design committee; this resulted in the revolutionary battleship *Dreadnought*, built at Portsmouth in 1906. Fairfield built the 17,200-ton battle cruiser *Indomitable* in 1907–08, but there followed a yawning seven-year gap in the yard's work for the Navy. Meantime its manager had fathered the three Barnwell brothers, who in 1909–11 at the family's business at

Causewayhead built and tested Scotland's first modestly successful powered aircraft.

**Triumph, Disaster – and Empty Order Books**: The Fairfield yard was then building a succession of *Empress* liners for the Canadian Pacific Line; in 1910 Chatterton called the twin screw *Empress of Britain "one of the finest steamships on the Canadian route"*. But their 14,000-ton *Empress of Ireland*, launched by Fairfield in 1905, was struck in May 1914 by a large Norwegian collier in a fog off the coast of Canada, sinking quickly with the loss of 1012 lives – more passengers than had been lost from the *Titanic*. Meantime no large merchant ships seem to have been ordered from any local yard for several years from 1907. James Anderson's engine and boiler works in Fairley Street, built in 1901, failed and in 1908 was converted into a bakery, and the Govan Victualling Society ceased to trade in 1909; but somehow the yards kept going on smaller vessels.

**Govan Swallowed by Glasgow – and World War I Revival**: Govan burgh, by then the fifth largest in Scotland, thus became too poor to defend itself against incorporation into the City of Glasgow in 1912, under the very debatable premise that bigger meant better; the City Police took over the Pipe Band. In the same year Harland & Wolff (H&W) of Belfast bought the former Old, Middleton and East yards and rebuilt them into one huge operation. Then Britain lurched into war with Germany, bringing a frantic upsurge in naval orders. In 1914 Fairfields built the 32,700-ton battleship HMS *Valiant*, which served well in both world wars, and in 1915–16 they stripped out and refitted the hull of their best liner, which emerged as the 18,000-ton seaplane carrier, HMS *Campania*; later she sank in a collision in the Firth of Forth. Finally came the battle cruiser HMS *Renown* of 32,000 tons, built by Fairfield in 1916 but engined by Cammell Laird.

**Struggles after World War I**: In 1920 Harland and Wolff optimistically built the Clyde Foundry in Helen Street, the largest in the UK. It was contained within what was then probably the second biggest glass-clad structure in the world (after the Renfrew-built Crystal Palace). But engineering and shipbuilding sharply declined in the early 1920s, warships were no longer ordered; it appears that the supply of new private ventures in the area almost dried up. Remarkably, as late as 1924 the area between Langlands Road and the rural Cardonald station was largely undeveloped. Shieldhall Road was laid out by 1931 as a Govan bypass, becoming the A8. It served the large new King George V Dock west of Shieldhall, which was opened in 1931 by the Clyde Navigation Trust and also provided with rail access, but its traffic was slow to develop.

**The Depth of Depression**: Fairfields struggled on with small vessels, building at least two paddle steamers in 1930 for the Southern Railway's Isle of Wight service. They followed in 1931 with the 250-foot speedy pleasure vessel PS *Jeanie Deans* for the LNER's Craigendoran services; she turned out to be a favourite. In 1932 Harland & Wolff completed the luxurious TS *Duchess of Hamilton* for the LMS Ayr cruise service. But even Fairfields was at a low ebb by February 1933, with so little work that they had to sack their head craneman, William Lochtie, the driver for the previous 22 years of their giant 200-tonne electric crane. Happily, he was re-employed when two orders were landed, one late in 1933 for the PS *Mercury* for the LMS Railway, followed in the tentative start of rearmament by

*The Pearce Institute, Govan, endowed by Sir William Pearce, managing director of the Fairfield Shipbuilding and Engineering Co Ltd, as a community centre for the burgh. It was built between 1902 and 1906 to designs by Sir R Rowand Anderson.* *(JRH)*

the destroyer depot ship HMS *Woolwich* of 8750 tons, built in 1934.

**A Brief Industrial Revival**: In 1936 Fairfields built the last coal-burning Clyde steamer to remain in normal service, TS (turbine steamer) *Marchioness of Graham* for the Arran run; she was sold to Greece in 1958. In 1937–38 Fairfields built and engined the 11,100-ton Anchor Line motor vessels *Circassia* and *Cicilia*. In 1938 Stephens of Linthouse – which had somehow survived the slump – completed the 15,800-ton TS *Canton*, the last pre-war liner built for P&O. An industrial estate created at Shieldhall attracted soya meal works, a plasterboard manufacturer (Gyproc) and the Luma light factory, built in concrete in 1936 for the SCWS to designs by Cornelius Armour; but until the 1939–45 war no development occurred west of the King George V Dock

**Entertainment, Exhibition and the Greatest Crowd**: The huge *Vogue Cinema* with some 2500 seats was built about 1937 for George Singleton, and the *Lyceum Cinema* of 1937 replaced a burned-out music hall of that name. Despite poor weather the Empire Exhibition of 1938 drew 13.5 million visitors to the 70ha Bellahouston park south of Govan, where a 90m tower was built as a hilltop centrepiece, but only the Palace of Art was designed to be permanent; other buildings were re-erected at Monkton *(q.v.)* beside Prestwick Airport, and at Renfrew. In 1939 a crowd of 119,000 people watched a match at Ibrox, the British all-time record for league football.

**Govan-built Warships of World War II**: From 1939 came the hectic construction by Fairfields of 68 vessels in 9 years; meantime Stephens built 54 in 8 years. The battleship HMS *Howe* of 35,000 tons, originally named *Beatty*, was built by Fairfields in 1940, followed by the 26,000-ton aircraft carrier HMS *Implacable* in 1942. The famous sloop HMS *Amethyst* of 1350 tons was built by Stephens at Linthouse in 1943; in the same year they built the minelayer HMS *Ariadne* of 4000 tons. Then in 1944 there emerged sister aircraft carriers of 13,190 tons: HMS *Ocean*, built by Stephens, and HMS *Theseus* from the Fairfield yard. The cruiser HMS *Tiger* was laid down by Fairfield in 1946, but nuclear warfare fears led to redesign on the stocks; renamed HMS *Blake* and of 12,000 tons, the warship's final completion came in 1955. In the 1940s the large Clydesdale Engine Works of Bennie & Co were still prominent beside the Paisley railway.

**Postwar Boom in Shipbuilding**: Stephens' last passenger liners to be built were the 10,300-ton sisters TS *Kampala* and *Karanja* for the British India line, built in 1946–48. In 1947–48 Fairfields built and engined the *Caledonia*, half-sister of the two just-pre-war Anchor liners, followed in 1949 by the Bibby cargo liner *Leicestershire*. The St Francis geriatric nursing home at Merryland Street was opened in 1946, and later the 50-bed David Elder Infirmary or Hospital for specialist treatments was built at Shieldhall Road. In 1951 nearly 90,000 people lived in the area around Govan, which had extensive shopping facilities, Govan High School, a greyhound stadium and large bus garage; until its closure in 1958 Brand Street held the large 128-car Govan tram depot (then adapted as a bus garage).

**Clyde Tunnel and Freight Trains**: In 1957–64 Charles Brand & Co built the twin Linthouse road tunnels beneath the Clyde to link Whiteinch and Shieldhall; a flyover was built at Moss Road/Shieldhall Road (although some of the approaches were incomplete until 1969). Govan's vehicular ferry consequently ceased to operate in 1965, and the Meadowside ferry and the branch freight railway were closed in 1966. Fairfield goods trains were hauled by a steeple-cab electric locomotive right up to the late 1960s.

**Clearance and Shipbuilding Decline**: From 1957 Govan suffered severely from port decline and the City Council's manic policy of clearance – never in those days improvement – of old housing, and the resulting population dispersal. Shipbuilding orders also drifted away; the collapse of the industry began with Harland & Wolff's long underused yard, closed for some years in the early 1960s; it was soon largely dismantled, though the former H&W repair shed stood empty, to be used in 1994 by Bill Bryden to stage his World War I spectacular wryly named *'The Big Picnic'*. The huge Clyde Foundry in Helen Street was demolished in 1967, and the former crane works in Harmony Row were razed in 1968. The Govan Ropeworks, closed in 1967, was demolished in 1969.

**Up the Creek to Upper Clyde Shipbuilders**: Stephens' last major passenger ship job was a refit in 1961–62 of the ex-Cunarder *Parthia* for the New Zealand Shipping Company, and their last important naval vessel, the logistic landing ship HMS *Sir Geraint*, emerged in 1967. Meantime Fairfields, also in dire straits for orders, went bankrupt in 1964, then having 3400 Govan workers. With help from the Bank of Scotland, it joined the Connel, Yarrow, Stephens and John Brown yards as Upper Clyde Shipbuilders (UCS) in 1968. (In 1969 the Fairfield yard launched the largest dredger ever built in Britain.) But the combine was no more successful than its constituents, and was liquidated in 1971. Fairfields alone survived – with government help becoming Govan Shipbuilders, and incorporating the best of the two adjacent yards (Fairfield and Linthouse).

**The Despondent 1970s – Rescued by Drinks?**: By 1971, when the population of Govan was only 50,000, the once crowded Govan Road hostel which had become a warehouse was demolished. At the opposite end of the social scale, by 1972 the 3-star *Bellahouston Hotel* in Paisley Road West had 46 rooms. By 1973, when the author first walked around it, the historic central area of Govan resembled a bombed city, surrounded by cleared sites. Miserable, dirty and decayed, many shops and the *ABC* cinema were shuttered or derelict, and its remaining specialist shops were struggling to survive. The Shieldhall area, including the Luma building which had until lately been used for storage, lay mainly derelict and only the empty engine works remained at Linthouse. In 1973 the SCWS failed and was taken over by Manchester-based CWS; in 1978 the latter greatly modernised the Shieldhall complex, and created 80 new jobs there in 1980 in a new soft drinks plant. Meantime in 1975 DCL built a new whisky blending and bottling plant at Renfrew Road in Shieldhall for Walker of Kilmarnock – by 1990 as part of United Distillers it was bottling at least seven brands: *White Horse, Bell's, Johnnie Walker, Vat 69, Dewars, Black & White* and *Haig*!

**British Shipbuilders take over in a Social Desert**: In 1977 the Govan yard became part of British Shipbuilders (BS); but its marine engineering subsidiary Fairfield-Rowan had already closed. However, by then Simpson Lawrence Ltd of Ibrox was at work as yacht and boat fittings manufacturers; another successful firm was the sheet metal concern of George Gilmour Metals, at work by 1979 in Govan Road. The Subway, nowadays also called the Underground, was reconstructed in 1977–80. But the Kelvinhaugh ferry, last of the Clyde passenger ferries, ceased to operate in 1980. The situation for Govan's remaining 30,000 people in 1981 was grim. The crime rate in the early 1980s was the highest in Glasgow, in Scotland, and perhaps in Britain, largely it seems because a third of the area's young men were out of work; homes and factories were insecure, and job losses continued. However in 1985–87 the Govan yard built the ferry *Norsea* for the Hull-Rotterdam run; at 600 feet this was the longest passenger ship built in Britain since Clydebank's *Queen Elizabeth II*.

**Ibrox Disaster and Rebuilding**: Rangers FC had a huge following throughout central Scotland, and their matches drew great crowds to vast but makeshift Ibrox. At New Year 1971 a second major disaster occurred there when 80,000 people were leaving a Rangers–Celtic match: crowds pressing down stairway 13 crushed 66 people to death and injured 145. The phased job of rebuilding the stadium to a square plan designed by the Miller partnership was begun in 1978, and eventually completed in 1991 when Rangers were – as so often – at the top of the Scottish Premier League. The main stand of 1928–29 was boldly redesigned by Blyth & Blyth to hold 7000 seats, its new roof incorporating the world's largest clear-span stadium girder, 146m long and weighing over 500 tonnes, designed by Thorburn & Partners. The rebuilt stadium which provided around 46,000 seats also held the head office of the short-lived *Sunday Scot* newspaper, opened and closed in 1991.

**Thatcherism in Action and Mackintosh in Reality**: In 1986 the Govan Initiative, set up to attract new firms and the private housing (that alone was permitted by the Thatcher government), brought a fortress mentality and high security fencing. As a result Govan residents, whose fine town hall building still overlooked the unused Princes' Dock – temporarily transformed by the Glasgow Garden Festival's pleasant cosmetics – found this almost inaccessible. Nor did the Festival bring lasting benefit, its costly delights being deliberately abandoned. In 1987–88 the former Linthouse engine works were dismantled, for re-erection at the Scottish Maritime Museum in Irvine. However, by 1991 when the population was about 28,000 the Govan Initiative employed 50 people and had its effect in cutting crime; some improvements appeared. By 1990 a dry ski slope for the city had been laid out in Bellahouston Park, where Charles Rennie Mackintosh's 1901 design for a *House for an Art Lover* was at last built in 1989–90 for Graham Roxburgh, who hoped to use it as offices; completed by Glasgow City Council, it was opened to the public in 1996.

**Govan welcomes New Industries**: In 1989 the Scottish Milk Marketing Board's Govan creamery, known as Scottish Farm Dairy Foods, was claimed as Scotland's largest milk processor. From 1988 little Skylight International made reinforced skylights and self-luminous notices. In 1990 GEC's subsidiary Marconi also had a factory at Govan. In 1992 Pilkington subsidiary Barr & Stroud moved their 800 workers from Anniesland into a new but smaller factory at Linthouse, where despite few orders they continued to make periscopes and sights for military use; by 1995 the firm had cut their workforce to 700 but was back in profit. By 1993–94 Colourbond Coatings was using electrostatic coating techniques at Govan to colour-finish aluminium sheetings. But in 1992 Rank Xerox moved its Scottish head office and warehouse from Govan to Hillington, and in 1994 the Luma building stood long-derelict, though it was soon converted into flats. However, in 1994 Simpson Lawrence still made anchors and winches, and Howden Compressors and the oddly named Howden Buffalo were still open near the Clyde Tunnel. In 1992–93 the Underground acquired eight more trailer cars built at Kilmarnock, to enable three-car trains to be run as standard. At that time the huge century-old Southern General Hospital had 1132 beds.

**Kvaerner Govan for Gas & Chemicals Carriers**: About 1850 jobs still existed at the Govan shipyard shortly before its takeover in 1988 by the Norwegian company Kvaerner, but were then cut to 1350, for Govan's efficiency was only one third of that of their yards in Norway. Having sorted out many of their troubles, in 1990 they were able to claim that Kvaerner Govan (KG) was Britain's biggest merchant shipbuilder; they then recruited more workers, reaching a peak of 2140 early in 1991. Kvaerner had also acquired Kincaid of Greenock and Ferguson of Port Glasgow from BS (but planned to sell Kincaid in 1991). Govan became the firm's lead yard in developing the designs for LPG tankers and was building two of these vessels when late in 1991 – against intense competition from 70 other yards worldwide – Kvaerner gained a further order for six giant chemical tankers for Saudi and Norwegian interests. The KG yard was to build four of these, including a 35,500-ton deadweight bulk chemicals carrier for the Norwegian firm Odfjell. These involved a workforce of 1600 until 1993, though the firm did not expect to make a profit. The 37,500-ton *NCC-Riyadh* was completed in 1994 for Saudi National Chemical Carriers. Meantime in 1993 KG built the 36,800-ton chemical tanker *J O Selje* for J O Tankers of Norway; the yard was to build a sister ship in 1996–97.

**Record Productivity and Rocket Launchers**: In 1993 KG and VSEL of Barrow jointly won a contract to build a large helicopter carrier for the Royal Navy, creating 500 jobs on the Clyde, and KG built a further helicopter carrier in 1994–95. The yard – which by then specialised in ro-ro ferries and technical vessels – went into profit in 1994 for the first time in 30 years. Productivity had risen to two-thirds that of Kvaerner's Scandinavian yards, and by 1995 out-performed Japan and Korea. In mid 1995 the KG yard employed 1360 people. In 1996 KG completed the 23,000-ton international satellite rocket base ship *Sea Launcher*, with accommodation for 250 crew, scientific and technical staff. But their order book was almost empty, and in 1997 the jobs were down to 1200. KG then gained orders to build two platform supply vessels, but the yard was sold in 1999 to British Aerospace, who operated it in tandem with Yarrow's across the river. As BAe Systems Marine they launched an oil tanker for the Navy in February 2001, and two Type-45 destroyers are due in 2002. The King George V Dock is still in use.

**Enter ASDA but Exit *'Scottish Pride'***: Meantime, ASDA successfully opened a major new Govan store in 1995. The renowned Walmer Crescent tenement block was restored in the early 1990s, although the fine Broomloan schools had become vacant by 2000. In 1996 BBC Scotland planned to move from Partick's Queen Margaret Drive to new purpose-built premises at Govan; but the new Scottish Parliament in Edinburgh soon made this look a debatable choice. A small open-air Saturday market was still held in 1996. When the milk processors Scottish Pride lost supermarket contracts in 1997 it called in the receivers; when sold to Wiseman as a going concern the Govan plant was closed with 190 job losses. In 1997 Rangers FC – who by then employed more European mainland footballers than Scots – planned to build a hotel and leisure complex at Ibrox. In 1999 United Distillers & Vintners aimed to ship whisky from their Shieldhall warehouse through the Russell/Freightliner rail terminal at Hillingdon. In 2000 the recently established call centre of Response Handling at Ibrox planned to recruit a further 300 workers. Bellahouston Academy has around 740 pupils and Govan High School 525. The *Swallow Hotel* (ex-*Bellahouston)* has been twice enlarged, now having 117 rooms.

## GRAEMSAY, Isle of — Map 13, B2

***Small Orkney island,*** *pop. under 100* — OS 6 or 7: HY 2605

This small fertile sandstone island only 3 km in length lies between the Orkney Mainland and the tall island of Hoy. A tidal race or Roost mars the northern channel, and to improve navigational safety for the herring fleets a pair of lighthouses was built in 1851, Hoy High at the eastern tip of Graemsay and Hoy Low at the western. By 1881 there were 236 islanders, since when numbers have fallen by some 90%. The Low light was automated in 1966, and the High light (near the only pier) in 1978. The 1-pupil school was closed in 1996 but the post office/shop survives. Passenger ferries still ply to Stromness, and to Linksness on Hoy; the only work is crofting and lobster fishing.

## GRANGEMOUTH — Map 16, B2

***Firth of Forth town,*** *pop. 19,000* — OS 65: NS 9281

The Forth & Clyde Canal commences at the mouth of the River Carron, 1 km north of the ancient Abbots Grange, in one of the flattest parts of Scotland; its eastern end was built in 1768–73. Its success suggested to the laird, Sir Lawrence Dundas of Kerse House – who cut the first sod of the canal – what Chambers called *"the propriety of building this little seaport, which he accordingly commenced in 1777"*. An entirely new canal port and settlement was functional from 1779, soon replacing Bo'ness as the eastern port of Glasgow, importing Baltic timber, hemp and tallow via the canal. It grew rapidly, for there was already a post office when Heron writing in 1799 called it a *"populous village of upwards of 800 inhabitants"*.

***Charlotte Dundas(es)* and Robert Fulton**: In 1801 a boatyard was founded beside the River Carron by Alex Hart, son of a Bo'ness shipbuilder; in the same year the firm built the wooden hull of the first *Charlotte Dundas* for the Forth & Clyde Canal Company, whose Chairman or *'Governor'* was Lord Dundas. The boat, engined to designs by William Symington, was a failure. In 1803 John Allan built a new hull which, with an improved Symington engine having horizontal cylinders built by the Carron Company, and a stern paddle wheel, was successful (at the expense of wash damage to the canal banks), and reached Port Dundas in 6 hours for the 31 km. (The American Robert Fulton may have seen this vessel before his own pioneer steamboat *Clermont* of 1807 plied commercially on the Hudson River, using engine components made in England by Boulton and Watt, and five years before Henry Bell introduced his *Comet*.) In 1807 Grangemouth acquired a new post office, and the port's growing trade justified the transfer of the custom house from Bo'ness in 1810. In the same year Grangemouth became a Port of Registry, with the code letters GH. From 1819 steamers provided a direct service to Newhaven.

**The Port's Trade**: Chambers in 1826 commented that *"it is now a place of considerable importance; and, besides a commodious harbour, has a dry-dock, a rope-work, a custom-house, and spacious warehouses for goods. Vessels bring into this port timber and hemp, deals, flax, and iron, from the Baltic, Norway, and Sweden, besides grain from foreign parts and from the coasts of Scotland and England"*. Dues were lower than those at Leith, so Edinburgh goods were carried. Besides exporting iron goods, *"the numerous vessels belonging to the Carron Company usually bring home return-cargoes of grocery goods, dye stuffs, &c, for the supply of Glasgow, Stirling, and other towns in the West of Scotland"*.

**Grangemouth Docks**: Though a gasworks was set up in 1836 and the Grangemouth Dockyard Company's shipyard took over Hart's yard about 1839, the town's population in 1841 was still under 1500. Its first or *'Old'* dock was built by the canal company in 1838–43, and enlarged in 1859 when the Junction dock was added. In 1851 the Norwegian Salvesen brothers (Christian and Johann) started a shipping business in Grangemouth, later moving to Leith. From 1860 the canal company owned a rail connection from the docks to the North British Railway at Falkirk. From that time, due to legislative changes, timber imports from Scandinavia to Grangemouth greatly increased, two timber basins being added in 1864 and more sawmills were established. By then over 40 vessels were locally registered, and by 1866 Grangemouth was among the top six coal-exporting ports in Scotland.

**Docks expand under the Caledonian Railway**: In 1867 the Caledonian Railway (CR) acquired the canal and hence the rail connection; a passenger station was provided. But their real objective was the dock, where almost half a million tonnes of freight was handled annually. In 1872 Grangemouth was granted police burgh status and soon an attractive police station was built. Meanwhile the CR laid out elaborate facilities; traffic expanded so rapidly that they dredged the river and in 1876 obtained powers to build the 8 ha Carron Dock and a timber basin, which were completed in 1882–83; traffic continued to rise. By 1884 the town was large enough to require sub-post offices. Andrew Carnegie visited the town's temporary library in 1887 and gave £900, enabling the real thing to open 2 years later. In 1886 W Drake of Grangemouth built the little *Lord Erskine* for the steam ferry across the Forth at Alloa. The 1890s OS map shows Grangemouth as a small town, with an inn and a passenger ferry across the River Carron; Kerse House stood in an extensive park. Grangemouth's trade both inwards and outwards had passed 2.4 million tonnes a year by 1896. Further dock expansion by the CR was therefore authorised in 1897, comprising the Grange dock complex with its 25 ha of water in three basins, surrounded by reclaimed land and with a direct access from the Forth. It was opened for coal traffic in 1906, together with a new marshalling yard and locomotive shed at Fouldubs, by which time over 3 million tonnes a year was being handled.

**Short Sea Traders**: Though the total of locally-owned shipping had remained around the 10,000-ton mark since the 1850s, it had changed in 50 years from predominantly sail to 80% steam. Gillespie & Nicol of Grangemouth, founded in 1896, carried coal across the North Sea in little steamers. From 1911 Walker & Bain carried away coal, and brought back moulding sand for Falkirk foundries. From 1920 to 1954 Buchan & Hogg operated small colliers and later general freighters to London. J T Salvesen of Grangemouth was a Baltic shipowner (not to be confused with Christian Salvesen). Smaller concerns included the Kerse and Shield Steamship Companies.

**Soap, Ship Repair – and the First Oil Imports**: Soap was made locally by the Scottish Co-operative Wholesale Society from 1898. By 1901 the population exceeded 8000; Abbotsgrange Middle School was built in 1908, an electric power station was established in 1905 and a second rail access was completed in 1908. At that time Dundas Engineering and the Grangemouth Dockyard Company were in the ship repairing business. Around 1910 over 2.5 million tons of shipping were being handled in a year, and Grangemouth was among Britain's top ten coal export ports. Trade increased right up to World War I, soon enhanced by the import of oil by the Anglo-Persian Oil Company, which had been set up in the town by 1914.

**Naval Control, Ironworks and Oil Refining**: The port was taken over by the navy for the duration of the war, and to replace imports from Germany, a large new vat dyestuffs plant was built west of the town by a Carlisle concern known as *Scottish Dyes Ltd* (which later became part of ICI). In 1921 the Commissioners of the Forth Navigation were replaced by the Forth Conservancy Board, who made Grangemouth their HQ. From 1921 to 1936 Middle-East crude oil, brought by tankers to Grangemouth, went by pipeline to the Uphall *(q.v.)* refinery. By 1924 there were vast railway yards south of the Grange dock, and a large ironworks had been built north of Laurieston. In 1923–24 Scottish Oils – an Anglo-Persian Oil Company subsidiary set up in 1919 to take over the five remaining shale-oil companies – established a small refinery in Grangemouth to process gulf oil imports into motor spirit (petrol), kerosene and fuel oil; later the main firm became *'Anglo-Iranian'*. This refinery (and future developments) was a direct 'descendant' of the area's shale-oil industry, its technology, experience and personnel. Timber imports continued, and although general cargo languished the population was nearing 12,000 by 1931.

Six other oil depots, and Ross Creosote, had entered the area by 1939; between them the town's industries polluted the Forth with mercury and petrochemicals, which it was claimed destroyed the Bo'ness fisheries.

**Golf, Aviation, World War II and its Aftermath**: A golf course was laid out, and the *Station Hotel* was built in the 1930s. So was the Central Scotland Airport, opened south-east of the town for civil use on 1st July 1939; among its first users was KLM, but it operated for just two months, then being converted to an RAF fighter base. Had it reopened for civil use after the war, the whole transport story of the central belt of Scotland might have taken a different turn. During the 1939–45 war the ICI plant produced mepacrine, paludrine and other drugs, and the Grangemouth Dockyard Company launched a total of 53,000 tons of little ships of up to 3000 tons each. The docks could then accept tankers of up to 600 feet in length, carrying up to 18,000 tonnes of crude oil; some 2 million tonnes was imported annually. There were seven large sawmills by 1955, when with a population of 15,000 Grangemouth had the facilities of an average town; in 1952 there was still a steam locomotive shed, but by 1955 the one-time ironworks was just a depot, and the park of Kerse House had disappeared.

**Starting the Modern Petrochemical Industry**: Between 1949 and 1963 Anglo-Iranian – renamed British Petroleum (BP) in 1954 – built and extended Scotland's first major oil refinery, fed from 1951 by a 90km pipeline from a deepwater tanker terminal at Finnart on Loch Long. The pink bricks from which many of the buildings in the refinery are built were made from spent oil shale at Pumpherston *(q.v.)*. The refinery rapidly became a full-scale petrochemical complex: Grangemouth had the first ethylene plant in Europe, installed in 1951 and doubled in capacity in 1956, deriving ethylene from oil. Other industries were developed on the site of the former airfield during the same period. Among these were the Italian firm Enichem Elastomers, the US-owned Borg-Warner Chemicals, established in 1962 to produce thermoplastics, and British Hydrocarbon Chemicals, a joint venture between BP and distillers DCL.

**Pioneer Container Port – and Municipal Vandalism**: About 1965 Sea-Land introduced a container service to the port, which had lately commissioned the first container terminal in Britain. The fleche for St Michael's church at Linlithgow was fabricated in the 1960s by Muirheads of Grangemouth, from laminated timber covered in aluminium. In 1962 the canal – which had given birth to Grangemouth but had lately carried little but pleasure craft – was closed, and the section through the town was infilled in 1963 by a dull town council, which failed to note the emerging tourist boom, but did at least remember the pioneer boat by naming a new local shopping centre of dreary grey brick as *Charlotte Dundas Court*. Although a sports stadium was opened in 1966, the council also regrettably built over its only remaining lung, the golf course. (This was however replaced at Polmont.)

**Bottling, Pollution and Dock Development**: The railway passenger trains were withdrawn in 1968. Grangemouth's population had risen to 24,500 by 1971, by which time there were also a number of new facilities and a whisky blending and bottling complex; but the same town council which had destroyed the town's amenities boasted of the port's scrap metal imports! The polluting industries, the flat unrelieved man-made environment, and its proximity to the regional centre of Falkirk had ensured that it remained primarily an industrial port. In 1974 a new 29m-wide entrance lock was brought into use, and from 1978 was able to operate regardless of tidal conditions. In 1977 a new forest products terminal was opened and by 1978 there was a new liquefied petroleum gas (LPG) terminal for the export of this BP product; Carron Dock had been re-equipped with new mobile cranes. By 1978 half the 140ha Kinneil Kerse site had been reclaimed, and a new sea wall was enclosing further potential industrial land – at the expense of the dwindling wetlands and their natural fauna and flora.

**BP Grangemouth after North Sea Oil**: By 1974 oil for the BP refinery was brought in by a new pipeline from the Forties field in the North Sea. By then the refinery's capacity of 196,000 barrels of oil a day was considered modest; however in 1978 BP completed one of the world's largest benzene plants, to produce 250,000 tonnes a year. An ethylene pipeline to Teesside was completed in 1978, and BP – whose refinery by then had an annual capacity approaching 10 million tonnes – was adding plant to produce 54,000 tonnes a year of *'Rigidex'* high density polythene. The 1950s plant producing ethanol – a solvent with many uses, also deriving from ethylene – was replaced in 1982 by new plant with an annual capacity of 155,000 tonnes, employing 100 people. Later came oil from the Brae field, and also ethane and ethylene from the Mossmorran plant *(see Cowdenbeath)*.

**Carbon Black and Cyanide**: In 1970 Continex International opened a carbon black plant, creating 60 jobs making this ingredient of synthetic rubber from downstream refinery by-products; but the plant was closed in 1979. In 1975 ICI's two plants produced dyestuffs and Pyrimidine agricultural chemicals; Marbon made resins, and other chemicals firms were IS Rubber and British Xylonite. By 1975 the poisonous 'HCN' (Hydrocyanic acid, also called Hydrogen Cyanide) was being moved in block trainloads from Grangemouth to the ICI plant at Haverton Hill on Teesside. This rail traffic continued in 1989 when Grangemouth was Britain's main source of HCN, one of the most dangerous of all chemicals, but an essential input to making acrylic fibre. In 1978 Harris & Edgar Ltd operated a non-ferrous foundry and engineering works, making Admiralty and building products. The Grangemouth Dockyard closed its ship building and repair activities in 1980 after almost 180 years of operation.

**Poverty Amid Industrial Riches**: Although by then Grangemouth had a major local centre, it was one of the less pleasing of Scotland's major industrial location. However, by 1993 the pedestrianised town centre of the 1960s had been refurbished, and the former bus depot had been converted into the Newhouse Small Business Park. In 1987 BP suffered a serious fire in a petroleum cracker (plant which increases the yield of petrol from crude oil), which took two years to repair. About 1989 Grangemouth's BR locomotive shed was re-equipped to service the refinery locomotives, and in 1990 eight trains of petroleum products left Grangemouth daily en route to Bishopbriggs, and to Dalston in Cumbria.

**Containers by Sea and Road**: Grangemouth had been seen as a high-cost operation due to its narrow quays, the enclosed docks which tripled turnround times, and the requirement for constant dredging. However, the total of some 50,000 containers handled by the three firms concerned in 1990 represented an increase over 1988, when only one container

*The Grangemouth refinery and industrial complex. Its original siting here in the 1920s was a direct result of the technology and experience of the area's shale-oil industry. Major development began here in 1949; initially Middle East crude oil was processed, but today it's North Sea oil.* *(SMPC / Mika)*

ship had docked each week. But although in 1991 whisky was among Grangemouth's exports, and in 1992 the dock still provided daily container services to Hamburg, Bremerhaven, Rotterdam and Antwerp, far more containers went by rail through Coatbridge to and from English ports. In 1993 a new road link was planned to the docks, where simplified planning controls were in force, and the Taiwanese shipping line Evergreen began a Grangemouth to Thamesport service twice a week, specifically for *'Hi-Cube'* containers 2.9m in height, which British Rail could not carry. By 1995 Forth Ports' local container movements were at their highest ever, carried by 14 sailings a week, all moved on land by road. In 2001 containers dominate the port's traffic, largely with Felixstowe, Thamesport and Rotterdam.

**Petrochemicals Pollution Problems**: At the end of the 1980s the industrial complex including the BP oil refinery, BP Kinneil gas separation and ICI chemical plants were still stated to be illegally discharging into the Firth such pollutants as oil, alkalis, cyanide, phenols, nickel (and mercury from an ICI dye plant subsequently closed); ICI was having to invest heavily to overcome these problems. In 1991 the newly green-conscious firm set up the Jupiter Wildlife Trust to reclaim 77ha of derelict land adjoining its works for nature conservation, to be run jointly with the Scottish Wildlife Trust, including wetlands and involving the planting of 800 trees. To reduce its contribution to the problems, BP built an effluent treatment plant, opened in 1993.

**Perfume from Petroleum and Recycling Plastic**: In 1989 BP which already employed 1200 refinery workers announced a major development scheme at Kinneil which would require 3000 construction workers making the gas processing plant one of the world's largest ethylene plants; but it would require only 200 production workers. In 1991 they added a plant to make 15,000 tonnes a year of the perfume product *2,3 dimethylbutane*. In 1992 the BP plastics plant's 2050 workers were cut by 330 due to the continuing recession. But by late 1994 an experimental plant had been built there to recycle mixed plastics as a feedstock. In 1995 the BP refinery, one of the UK's largest oil and petrochemical complexes, stabilised and exported some 40% of offshore oil production and annually refined 9 million tonnes of crude oil.

**ICI to Zeneca**: The ICI plant had a workforce of a thousand in 1992 and still produced up to 10,000 tonnes of textile dyestuffs annually; its full list of products appeared on demerger from ICI in 1993, when Zeneca took over a 70ha site making *"colours, agricultural chemicals, pharmaceuticals and other fine organic chemicals"*. Meanwhile by 1990 ICS Scotland was established at the Abbotsinch estate; in 1991 Enichem Elastomers exported 80% of its output. In 1993 the bonded warehousemen William Muir Ltd of Leith employed about 200 people in their Grangemouth whisky blending and bottling plant. In 1995 the Baltic Quay industrial site of 38ha, adjacent to the docks, was opened up by Forth Ports.

**Railways Driven into Difficulties**: Grangemouth rail freight traffic other than petroleum ceased in 1991. Late in 1992 some 20 to 25 trainloads of petroleum products were still moved from the BP refinery each week. But *'economy'* measures imposed by the Tory government in preparation for rail privatisation had caused a decline in local rail petroleum traffic by 40% in two years. From 1993 oil traffic by rail to stations on the West Highland line ceased. The Blue Circle Cement depot was also to close, so cutting rail freight traffic still further.

**Rail Connection Secured**: Happily, rail freight was resumed to and from the Forth Ports docks in 1997, in 1999 a grant was made for rail freight facilities at the TDG Nexus plant in Grangemouth and in 2001 two more, one to BP for petroleum to the Dumfries area. The other was to W H Malcolm, whose Grangemouth warehouse had despatched 10 to 15 lorries to Northamptonshire daily, laden with pickle jars made by United Glass at Alloa for Campbell foods, but began in 2000 to carry the jars by rail; spirits traffic was to be added.

**Less Clothing, More Canal**: The solid Abbotsgrange Middle School was converted to 18 flats about 1994, leaving Grangemouth High School, with over 850 pupils. By then a Tesco store was open, and the town had a second museum by 1998. By 1998 a new link road had extended the A905 from Inchyra to Kinneil Kerse, and a new sewage treatment plant was built in 1997–2000. In 1999 the future of the local William Baird factory, which made clothing for Marks & Spencer, was threatened by the great retailer's troubles and soon 450 jobs were lost. The long-neglected 1870s police station building was demolished in 2000. To enable reopening of the Forth & Clyde Canal to the River Carron in 2001, two locks are being built and 550m of channel excavated.

## GRANTON, Pilton, Trinity & Warriston

**Map 15, C1**

***Northern parts of Edinburgh**, pop. 23,000* OS 66: NT 2376

By 1455 Granton – which lies about 3km to the west of Leith and a similar distance north of central Edinburgh – had a coastal castle, also known as Royston. This was rebuilt in 1544, perhaps using stone from a local quarry mentioned in 1531, and extended in 1619 into a bulky edifice. The surrounding area which formed part of the Buccleuch estate was already well settled with farms by 1600, as shown by Pont's map of about that date; *'Grantoun'* was marked just to the west of Royston. In 1683 Viscount Tarbat bought the Royston estate and in 1685 began to build a fine mansion nearby. On one of the local farms in 1716 was born George Cleghorn, who became a doctor and later pioneered the use of quinine in the treatment of malaria; he also founded the first school of anatomy in Ireland.

**Caroline Park, Quarrying, Botany and Harbour**: The mansion of Royston was renamed as Caroline Park by its Argyll purchaser in 1739; the old castle was left to fall into ruin. By the 1750s as the Roy map showed, roads connected Granton with the outside world through both Dean and Cramond. Granton Point quarry was open by 1831, but flooded in 1855; however two other sandstone quarries were soon open locally. Urban development on the southern fringes of the area began in the 1820s when the Royal Botanic Gardens moved from central Edinburgh to a spacious site at Inverleith; the Tropical Palm House was opened in 1834. To the west rose the mansions of Granton House and Drylaw. The tidal harbour of Granton was built by the Duke of Buccleuch in 1835–45 to overcome the difficulty of negotiating the Leith sandbar; facilities were provided for handling cattle, and berths for ten steamers were laid out alongside one of the two great piers of what was then described as *"the finest harbour in the Firth of Forth"*; a Custom House was established. Pleasure was not overlooked, for there was soon a hotel, and the Royal Eastern Yacht Club, the second in Scotland, was founded at Granton in 1836. Granton also became a Port of Registry, with the recognition letters GN.

**The Railway and the World's First Train Ferry**: The Edinburgh Leith & Granton Railway (ELGR) was opened between Scotland Street and Trinity in 1842. Urban development followed, and several post offices were soon opened; their dates of issue with a cancelling stamp were Granton Pier in 1842, Warriston in 1843 and Granton in 1854. The railway was extended to a station on the middle pier at Granton in 1846, and from 1847 a half-hourly passenger service from Granton was hauled by cable through Scotland Street tunnel to a terminus at Canal Street in Edinburgh (beneath Waverley Market). The ELGR almost immediately sold out to the Edinburgh & Northern Railway (E&N), which operated the line in connection with trains via the Fife ferry from Newhaven to Burntisland, which soon moved its southern landfall to Granton. From 1850 this, the world's first train ferry (with its terminals Thomas Bouch's most worthy creation) connected at Burntisland with the E&N and its successor the Edinburgh, Perth & Dundee Railway, giving a service to Kirkcaldy, Ladybank, Perth and Cupar, later extended to Tayport for Dundee and becoming part of the North British (NB).

**An Unlikely Excursion, Industries and More Railways**: A patent slipway was built in 1852 and was soon busy repairing – and building – steamers, which also plied from Granton to Kirkcaldy and Aberdeen. In 1855 the poor children of the aptly named Ragged School at Stirling enjoyed a rare treat – a free steamer outing to Granton; by 1858 the PS *Rob Roy* plied regularly to Stirling. The firm of Bruce Peebles, engineers, was founded at East Pilton in 1866. At that time grain was imported through Granton and transferred by rail to the Caledonian distillery. In 1879 a CR passenger service was introduced from a station at Granton Road to Leith North. The NB's train ferry operated until shortly after the opening of the Forth Bridge in 1890. Around that time the port exported coal, castings, machinery and whisky, and imported esparto grass and china clay for papermaking, as well as timber, iron and grain.

**Catching the Wind and maintaining the Lights**: The Royal Forth Yacht Club was founded in 1868, making its base at Granton, followed by a third club, the Forth Corinthian, in 1881; in that year the *Wardie Hotel* was built. By 1884 Granton had become the marine base of the Northern Lighthouse Board and home port of their main tender *Pharos*; the Board built their own gasworks in 1891. Trawler fishing was also based in Granton, reaching a peak before 1914. By 1895 the buildings of the Northern General Hospital had been erected at Ferry Road and there was a chemical works west of Caroline Park, whose policies were much abused by industry, the house being used as offices by an ink firm; but later it was sold back to the Duke of Buccleuch. Remarkably – despite all these activities – the population in 1891 was only 915, and there was still very little housing west of Stirling Road or near the harbour.

**Holding the Gas and subverting the Trains**: Some time after 1890 the Edinburgh & Leith Gasworks was relocated from Leith to Granton, its new and elephantine gasholders dominating the skyline of greater Edinburgh. The gasworks had its own 2'0" gauge internal rail system. Pennywell Parks quarry employed 19 people in 1902, but soon closed; Royston quarry, with 23 workers in 1922, closed in 1925. An oil depot was opened in 1909; on the outbreak of war in 1914 the Navy took over the harbour as a base. In 1909 Leith Corporation extended their electric tramways along Granton Road, with a very awkward jiggle at the Trinity railway bridge. Edinburgh cable trams ran to Goldenacre south-east of Granton before 1922; under early electrification the route was extended to Granton Square, where it met the earlier line and doubled back to Leith. Fishing resumed from 1918, and by the 1930s Granton was again an important trawler base. The harbour was reconstructed by the Duke's private company between 1919 and 1937, a new coal-loading plant being commissioned in the latter year.

**The Pilton Housing Scheme and Football**: Granton Castle was demolished in 1928, but its ancient gardens were retained and are still in use for commercial flower-growing. Meantime the large Pilton housing estate was built by Edinburgh city council in the 1920s. West Pilton was built to lower standards from 1939 onwards, and the Crematorium at Warriston was built about then. The short-lasting Edinburgh City FC, formed in 1928, played in the Scottish League in 1931–39, and from 1946 to 1949; their home, Edinburgh City Park, was at Ferry Road and Pilton Drive. A road vehicle ferry to Burntisland, which had replaced the train ferry, continued to operate until 1940.

**Ferranti, Toothill and Silicon Glen**: Early in the 1939–45 war Ferranti came to a new factory, built at Crewe Toll in 18 weeks to make the Gyro Gunsights developed by the firm's existing factory at Hollinwood, Lancs. In 1945 its manager, the cost accountant John Toothill, saved it from closure and ensured a hi-tech future for the factory and for Ferranti, whose HQ it was to become; in so doing he has been seen as the virtual founder of *'Silicon Glen'*. In the 1940s there were wireworks at Broompark Avenue, manufacturing endless wire-mesh belts for the paper-making industry; beside the oil and colour works at West Shore Road was an ironworks. Later the colour works was taken over by the Lothian Chemical Company, which in the 1970s operated it as a *'residual products'* works. By 1951 greater Granton had a population of over 25,000 and the facilities of a small town.

**Ferry fails but Yachts thrive**: The ferry service was reintroduced in 1951, using four former tank-landing craft, but was again withdrawn in 1953; the herrings also vanished from the Forth around that time. About 1955 some remaining fishing vessels, and ships carrying timber for the yard at West Harbour Road, still used the west harbour, where esparto was still unloaded at a special wharf on the west breakwater. Christie described Granton's east harbour with its three yacht clubs as then being *"the main yachting port on the east coast of Scotland"*. Bruce Peebles & Co had an internal electric rail system from about 1903 to 1961, and continued to make mine pumps and electrical equipment. In the early 1960s they made much of the auxiliary electrical equipment for the Cruachan power station. By 1977 Bruce Peebles had become Parsons Peebles, divided into companies making Motors & Generators, and Power Transformers. A third branch was at Broxburn.

**Electricity challenged, and Ferranti Football**: In 1949 Granton harbour was the terminus of no fewer than 7 electric tram services. But electricity gave way to diesel buses when Edinburgh's last trams, between Granton Road station and Braids, were withdrawn in November 1956. The passenger trains through Granton Road were withdrawn in 1962, leaving the field to buses and a growing number of cars. The Silverknowes laboratory was opened by Ferranti in 1961, and by 1968 the firm was one of Scotland's largest employers, with 6600 staff. Ferranti opened several other sites around Edinburgh *(see Dalkeith & Gorgie)*, for a time dominating the city's manufacturing sector. Their amateur football team Ferranti Thistle played at the nearby Edinburgh City Park – former home of the defunct team of that name – until moving to the Meadowbank stadium in 1974 and becoming more professional as Meadowbank Thistle FC.

**Sundry Changes and New Facilities**: By 1970 the former ironworks was a concrete works, later degenerating into builders' yards; but in the 1970s Croan's kippering facilities were still a large concern in Granton. Around 1980 Salvesens took over the timber yard as the site for a major cold store, and the western harbour was largely infilled to allow new development, much of it in the form of depots for Len Lothian oilfield services, BRS haulage and Leada Acrow scaffolding. Telford College – across the road from Ferranti – was built in the late 1960s, and a Ministry of Labour training centre was in use by the 1970s. Exhibition plant houses were built at the Royal Botanic Gardens in 1967, enhancing its tourist potential: by 1990 the gardens were the third most-visited free attraction in Scotland, after Glasgow's two great art museums. In 1984 the Scottish National Gallery of Modern Art was moved from Inverleith House to Belford Road.

**Granton keeps the Lights Burning**: By 1978 Ferranti had branch factories in Aberdeen, Bellshill, Dundee and Livingston and employed 7500 people in many defence applications, including radar, lasers and guidance systems. Granton's 1981 population was about 23,000. Despite the introduction of North Sea gas in the 1970s, gas production – latterly from light oil – continued at Granton until 1987, the last works to make town gas in Scotland. Most of the huge plant was then demolished, though the vast gasholders remain. The last of Granton's rail ways became a cycle path. By 1989 the Muirhouse shopping centre exceeded 5000 m$^2$. The Lothian Chemical Company, often in dispute with residents and pollution control agencies, planned in 1990 to incinerate up to 20 tonnes of chemical waste daily among their formaldehyde manufacturing and recycling operations.

**Ferranti falters, and falls to BAe**: In 1989 Ferranti, which had built a new plant at West Shore Road, announced 400 job cuts as a result of its unfortunate takeover of a US company – ISC, run by the crooked arms dealer James Guerlon, later jailed – and had to sell out to GEC in 1990. Some 2100 jobs remained, about half of them at the local plants, where the firm, briefly known as GEC-Ferranti, was developing the radar system for the European Fighter project, though this was somewhat cut back in 1992 by German economies. In 1993 GEC sadly extinguished the company's famous name in favour of *'GEC Marconi Avionics'*, and by 2000 the factory was just part of the giant BAe, with other plants at Silverknowes and South Gyle.

**A Revived Ferry fails**: The east harbour continued to be mainly used for yachting; in 1991 the rump of the west harbour became the terminus for a revived passenger ferry to Burntisland, operated in 1992 by the diesel catamaran *Spirit of Fife*. Intended for commuters, this succeeded only in carrying tourists, so in 1993 the north terminal of the summer ferry service was switched from Burntisland to serve the new Deep Sea World at North Queensferry. The harbour's poor and decidely neglected industrial environment was improved at Granton Square in 1992, when a new pilot station for the Forth Ports and a new sector base for HM Coastguard were both built on the middle pier.

**Parsons and Rolls, Computing and Superstore**: In 1988 Parsons Peebles gained a large contract to make turbines for use in Australia. By 1994 the Peebles companies were owned by Rolls-Royce, and the Power Transformer subsidiary (which had dropped the Parsons tag) gained a big order for the national grid. In 1995 Peebles was one of the three Scottish plants in the Rolls-Royce industrial power group, which together employed 1500 people. In 1994 the expanding WM Company in their new building at Crewe Toll claimed leadership in providing computerised investment information worldwide. The 3 ha site of the former Northern General Hospital was sold in 1995, and by 2000 had been redeveloped with a Safeway superstore and the government office called Ferryfield House, north of which was the new Ainslie Park Leisure Centre. Permission has been granted for Britain's second World Trade Centre; this and major re-planning elsewhere in the area, plus some land reclamation, is now in prospect to bring in new industry, offices, marina and leisure facilities. Croan's, seafood processers, are due to double their staff to 120, as exclusive supplier to Waitrose.

## GRANTOWN-ON-SPEY — Map 9, C4

***Speyside small town**, pop. 2400* — OS 36: NJ 0327

About the 11th century a thanage was established at Cromdale on the east bank of the River Spey, about 9 km downstream of the confluence of the Dulnain. Around 1500 the Comyns' tower house of Ballo Castle was built on the left bank of the Spey, 4 km north of the Kirkton of Inverallan and as far from Cromdale. For centuries a detached part of Inverness-shire, the area was still Gaelic-speaking when sketch-mapped by Pont about 1600, the castle town being shown as *'Ballachastel'*. One of Speyside's few mills turned below the castle, and across the river west of Cromdale was the Mill of Congash.

**A Still-born Barony Burgh**: Ballo Castle was described as *"a fair and stately house"* by Taylor in 1618. Ballo became Grant property in 1694, and following the custom of the day it was renamed *'Grant'*. *Castleton of Freuchie*, also later simply called *'Grant'* to avoid confusion with Freuchie in Fife, was a barony charter of 1694, possibly at Ballachastel; but apart from an inn which once stood at Ballieward, it appears to have got nowhere. Roy's map, here apparently dating to about 1753, showed a track from the north to Tomintoul, passing east of Grant Castle in its policies, and crossing the river at the Boat of Cromdale, where there was a hamlet. Between these points, 2 km east of Kirkton of Inverallan, was the brand new Spey Bridge completed for the military in 1754; but only tracks led to it.

**Planned Roads and Thoughtful Laird's Village**: Caulfeild's military road from Corgarff on the Don to Forres, built about 1754, crossed the new Spey bridge, and was joined 3 km south of the castle by another road, from Aviemore via Dulnain Bridge. In 1765 the castle was rebuilt into a mansion by John Adam for Sir Ludovic Grant. Seizing the opportunity presented by better communications, in the years 1765–66 the laird, Sir James Grant – also of Grant Castle – laid out *Grantown on Spey* on a virgin site around the new road junction. In this way – having enforced amalgamation of his farm holdings so that he could raise the rents – he avoided the need for his evicted tenants to leave the district.

**Industry and Astronomy**: Although very well laid out, the remoteness and high altitude of about 230 metres made for a slowish start to Grantown. About 1780 a short-lived brewery was built. A post office was opened in 1784, and by 1797 Grantown was a post town, and six fairs were scheduled for the year. Heron referred to it as a *"village"* in 1799, adding vaguely that *"some branches of manufacture have been introduced"*. By 1808 there was a woollen manufactory, and other industries included baking and candle-making. The *Grant Arms* inn was open by 1819 to serve coaches on a new road to Elgin, and its beautiful situation helped the little town to grow and prosper. The Balmenach distillery was established by James MacGregor in 1824 on the site of a bootlegger's still 1.5 km south of Cromdale; it was to be repeatedly enlarged. Robert Grant, born in Grantown in 1814, wrote the first history of astronomy, and catalogued over 8500 stars.

**Rival Railways and Royal Whisky**: From 1863 Grantown was served by a station on the new main line of the Inverness & Perth Junction Railway from Perth to Forres (very soon part of the Highland (HR) system). The Strathspey Railway, soon a Great North of Scotland Railway branch from Elgin and Keith to Nethy Bridge, opened simultaneously, to a station on the opposite side of the town. In 1886 a privately operated rail connection was laid to the water-powered Balmenach distillery, whose product – 410,000 litres of Highland malt whisky a year – was chosen by the Royal household, though all its plant was still *"of the most antiquated type"*. Some went for blending; 100 cattle were fed on the draff.

**Success beyond expectations**: Grantown golf club was founded in 1890 and laid out an attractive 18-hole parkland course adjoining the east end of the town, which had 1400 people in 1891. Alone of the villages that were planned from nothing to overcome enforced destitution, Grantown was becoming a really significant local service centre. It became a police burgh and was transferred to the county of Moray. In 1894 Grantown was described by Murray as *"a well-kept growing little town of granite cottages and villas"*; there were three banks and two hotels, the *Black Bull* and the *"very good" Grant Arms*. A local newspaper, the *Strathspey & Badenoch Herald*, was founded in 1907, setting the seal on Grantown, Scotland's highest altitude small town.

**The End of Railways and the Burgh**: A new Spey bridge was completed in 1931; in the 1940s Wordie & Co operated a small rail to road cartage depot. By the early 1950s Grantown, with an out of season population of a mere 1750, had no fewer than 15 hotels (totalling over 350 beds), and all the facilities of a well-equipped small town. These included such relative rareties as a head post office and trunk telephone exchange – also an abattoir; all to serve a total population of 10,500 in upper Speyside. In the 1950s Cromdale was a little village with a hotel. The railway passenger services were closed by Beeching in 1965, though freight lingered on the former GNSR line until 1968, and the HR station became an industrial site; but the last Balmenach distillery locomotive has been preserved. The head post office soon lost its status (like all such), but the cinema was still open in 1970 and appreciable population growth occurred after 1971. Burgh status too was lost in 1975, when Grantown became part of the Badenoch and Strathspey District, based in Kingussie.

**Grantown in 1978**: When visited in 1978 this small but attractive town was still as well endowed with facilities as it was lacking in industry. A very large modern telephone exchange was prominent and at least 40 good quality shops were open, including a number of specialist outlets, including sports equipment. The town also had the estate's HQ office, Crown post office, fire station, garages, and a branch library. Walker's bakery was a branch of the growing Aberlour firm. About 1980 Grantown was the location of the RAF School of Physical Training.

**Tourism Dominant in 1980**: No fewer than 18 hotels of all types and sizes were open in 1980, ranging downwards from the 60-room *Grant Arms* and *Craiglynne*, to smaller establishments and B&Bs. A caravan and camping site, golf, and other sports wee available. By 1981, an area with some 13,500 people was served. In 1990 among other enterprises on the small industrial estate, McKellar Engineering made the pontoons for Nairn harbour's marina development; they now employ 60. By 1991, new housing estates west of the town had raised its population to almost 2400, including an affluent retired element. By 1992 new buildings had been erected for the small local secondary, Grantown Grammar School.

**Drinks Problems and Castle Restoration**: By 1992 Cromdale had lost its post office but gained an inn. In 1991 Balmenach distillery was in full production under United Distillers, its single malt having a complex flavour; but problems in meeting effluent standards, and depression in the industry, caused its closure in 1993; it was sold to Inver House distillers in 1997. In 1994–95 the Grantown Auction Mart of Perth-based United Auctions held sheep and cattle sales, and there was a branch office of Moray Badenoch & Strathspey Enterprise. In 1995 the new Cairngorms Partnership, set up to protect both the natural heritage and socio-economic fabric of the Cairngorms area, established its HQ in Grantown. Castle Grant, abandoned in the 1950s, was restored to use in the 1990s. The many accommodation options in the town now include a backpackers hostel.

## GRANTSHOUSE

**Map 3, B2**

***Berwickshire small village,*** *pop. 175* — OS 67: NT 8065

When Pont's map was made around 1600, a mill turned at Butterden near the head of the Berwickshire Eye Water, but Grantshouse was not named. As late as the 1750s the original Great North Road followed the cliff tops past St Helens and Redheugh, at least 4 km seaward of Butterden, where the mill stood at a height of about 115 m at the head of a track following the Eye Water. Later a winding turnpike road was constructed up the steep valley of the Pease Burn from Cockburnspath to Butterden, and completed as a new through route, later labelled A1.

**Railway makes Grantshouse, but Eye Water ruins Railway**: The North British Railway, following almost the same alignment, was opened in 1846, steam engines struggling up the Cockburnspath Bank and passing at the summit through shaly rock in the short Penmanshiel Tunnel to a station beside the mill, but named Grantshouse. In 1901 these facilities were accompanied by a smithy, an inn and a post and telegraph office. The railway was closed for months following flash floods in the Eye valley in 1948, but was restored before Easter 1949 when the author rode the train into Scotland for his first visit. By 1951, Grantshouse with its main line station – but a mere 200 people – provided the facilities of a small village, some serving up to 1400 people in the extensive hilly rural area between Cockburnspath and Abbey St Bathans to the south-west.

**Beeching cuts, Tunnel falls and Floods recur**: The station, which had just three trains each way per day in 1963, was closed by Beeching about 1965. The local population and other facilities were badly hit; even the primary school had been closed by 1973. The Penmanshiel tunnel collapsed in 1979 while its invert was being lowered to enable trains carrying taller containers to pass through, sadly with the death of two workers; it was hurriedly blocked off and a short diversion speedily constructed. By the time that electrification of the East Coast Main Line was completed in 1991, two overtaking loops plus sidings for civil engineers occupied the site of Grantshouse station. There is now no post office, but *Haggerston House* is a small inn.

## GREENGAIRS, Riggend & Wattston **Map 16, A3**

***Lanarkshire small villages,*** *pop. 1140* OS 64: NS 7870

The early farm of Drumgray appeared on Pont's map of 1596; it stands at an altitude of 175 m at the edge of moorland, 6 km north-east of Airdrie. According to the Roy map of the 1750s the area was still largely featureless. Exploitation of the underlying coal was enabled after the little Slamannan Railway was opened in 1840. By 1899 at least six coal pits served by various mineral lines surrounded a village named Greengairs, with an inn and a post office, which had evolved 2 km north of the railway and 1 km east of Drumgray and its attendant hamlet of Wattston. By 1951 about 1800 people lived locally, mainly in Greengairs where there was a primary school, but there was also settlement around Riggend and Rigghead on the busy A73 trunk road 2 km to the west. There by 1953 stood an inn, a transport café and lorry drivers' dormitory, where the author stayed overnight as a penniless student.

**Quarrying, Opencast and Power from Garbage**: By 1955, although development extended to Wattston, the inn at Greengairs appeared to have closed, for there were no working pits left; although waste bings were prominent, the mineral railways were being lifted. By 1971 all railways had vanished, but two quarries were open south of the twin village, which had shrunk to under 1200 people. The quarries extended, and another had been opened west of Drumgray, but all were disused by 1979. A vast opencast mine was already open by 1988 south of Greengairs and Wattston, where by 1991 1140 residents remained, most living in local authority flats. By 1994 Shanks & McEwan were filling a 3 square kilometre landfill site with domestic waste. In 1995 they equipped it with methane collection piping, leading to a new gas-burning power station; the scheme was expected to produce worthwhile amounts of electricity for a century. By 1996 some new housing had been built at Wattston; Greengairs still had its post office, but now only the primary school remains.

## GREENLAW **Map 3, B3**

***Berwickshire village,*** *pop. 600* OS 74: NT 7146

Various ancient earthworks in the upper basin of the Blackadder Water, west of the Merse of Berwickshire, were shunned when Old Greenlaw was founded on a ridge south of the little river. It was marked with its present name on Pont's map, made about 1600. This also showed *'Grinnla Castle'* and an adjacent mill on the south bank of the Blackadder Water; the castle later vanished, leaving only the Castle Mill. Old Greenlaw became a burgh of barony in 1596 and in 1609 a mercat cross was set up; a parish school was established by 1633, but early travel writers ignored the place. About 1696 the mercat was moved to the present site at New Greenlaw, 1.5 km to the north and a similar distance west of the mill, enabling this upstart place to replace ancient Duns in a third change of county centre about 1700. The Roy map of around 1754 showed the Castle Mill and the new settlement, already a largish place on the north bank of the Blackadder Water; but the area's only road led from Gordon to Old Greenlaw, which later shrank to a mere farm.

**New Greenlaw on Roads and Railway**: In 1760 a Turnpike Act enabled a road to be made up from Coldstream through Greenlaw to Soutra Hill, and in 1788 a post office was opened at Greenlaw, which by 1796 had become the last Scottish staging point on the coach route from Edinburgh to the south via Wooler. There were two annual fairs, and Greenlaw was also a Post Town. Heron described Greenlaw in 1799 as a *"small town"* of only about 600 inhabitants, *"where the courts of justice are held"*. In 1826 Chambers found *"two bridges, a square market place and a handsome new jail"*. In 1829 a small but grandiose neo-classical county building was erected at Greenlaw, and the mansion of Charterhall, 5 km east, was built in 1851. However, from 1853 a further change of mind caused county administration to be shared with Duns. The Berwickshire Railway, a hopeful cross-country route between Reston and Newtown, served both Greenlaw and Duns from 1863; later it became an underused part of the North British system.

**From County Town to Quiet Village**: The county capital reverted fully to Duns some time after 1894, when Greenlaw – which had only 670 people in 1891 – was described by Murray as a *"small town"* with two hotels, the *Castle* and *Cross Keys*. Greenlaw was actually no more than a village when rail passenger services ceased in 1948; the line to Duns had been severed by 1963, and its freight services had ended by 1969. Charterhall House, demolished about 1960, was rather unusual in being replaced by an attractive modern house in traditional style. In 1980 James Renwick & Co of Hawick had a knitwear branch in Greenlaw. However, its slow decline continued: in 1973 the pleasing former County Building was converted to swimming baths, but these were soon closed, and by 1989 it was merely a second-hand dealer's store. By 1983 there was a caravan and camping site. Today, both the established hotels – *Blackadder* and *Cross Keys* – remain open in the quiet village of 589 people, along with a primary school and the post office stores.

## GREENOCK **Map 5, B5**

***Large Firth of Clyde town,*** *pop. 50,000* OS 63: NS 2776

Also see: *Gourock, Port Glasgow & Spango Valley*

Greenock Castle was built on the south shore of the inner Firth of Clyde in the 16th century, where the natural deep water channel is close inshore, and by 1591 when Greenock acquired its first church, it was known as a fishing village. Pont's map of about that date showed from west to east the castle, *'Grinock Toun'*, *'English Toun'* and *'Kar Burn'*. Chartered as a burgh of barony in 1635, Greenock soon acquired a market, and gained some of Glasgow's outport trade due to the shallowness of the Clyde above Dumbarton. Malt was very soon made, and a levy on its product was applied to build a mole and pier, seen by Tucker in 1655. Cartsdyke became an adjacent burgh of Barony in 1669; by the 1690s a high proportion of the manufacturing workforce in Greenock and Cartsdyke was engaged in shipbuilding and cooperage.

**Explosive Growth and Scotland's Most Significant Son**: Greenock's first full scale harbour was built in 1706–10, and Scott's, the first well-known local shipbuilding firm, opened their yard in 1711; it lasted for 277 years, the world's longest lasting major shipbuilders. Seven years later a vessel of 60 tons was built for Glasgow shipowners. Defoe writing in the 1720s commented on Greenock's recent growth, good *'road'* (anchorage) and skilled seamen, adding that *"It has a castle to command the road, and the town is well built, and has many rich trading families in it. It is the chief town on the west of Scotland for the herring fishing"*. In 1725–26 the Gourock Ropework Company built a hemp mill, ropeworks and a sailcloth factory. A grammar school was founded in 1727, and the epoch-making James Watt was born in the town in 1736. He became an instrument maker at Glasgow University and invented the centrifugal governor. His improvements to the Newcomen engine by adding a condenser led him into partnership with Matthew Boulton in Birmingham. He was probably the key figure in the Industrial Revolution.

**Library and Stagecoaches**: Meantime Roy's teams surveyed southern Scotland in 1752–55, recording Greenock harbour's three piers; the town itself was a large compact settlement, accompanied by a small linear village at Cartsdyke. A post office was opened in 1755, and about that time a library was pioneered in the town. Besides the coastal road, a winding lane climbed through the hills to the Spango Valley and down to Inverkip. From 1763 regular stage coaches plied between Glasgow and Greenock, but the journey took all day! Scott's built larger ships from 1765; several other shipyards were also established, Greenock being the main base for Glasgow's tobacco fleet.

**Fishing, Foreign Trade and Sugar**: Fishing nets were manufactured locally from 1772. The town was largely peopled by Highlanders, aided from the late 1770s by a ferry which plied to the new town of Helensburgh. John Wood started to build ships in 1780, moving to Port Glasgow in 1810. A graving dock was opened in 1786, and a quay was built in 1788. Steele & Carswell, long known as shipbuilders at Saltcoats, moved to Rue End in Greenock in 1796. By 1792 four coaches ran to and from Glasgow daily; at that time there appear to have been three breweries, two of which were large. In 1797 two annual fairs were scheduled, and in 1799 Heron referred to *"the town of Greenock, consisting of two burghs of barony and containing about 15,000 inhabitants"*. He emphasised the port's West Indian trade, sugar refining (see below), shipbuilding, rope and sail manufacture, fisheries and *"an excellent dry dock"*. By then Greenock had become a Port of Registry, with the code letters GK.

*Walker's sugar refinery, built originally in the 1830s, but later operated by Tate & Lyle. It closed in the 1970s, and has been demolished.* *(JRH)*

**Early Banking in Greenock**: Baillie Gammell who had built Garvel House on the promontory in 1777 founded the Greenock Banking Company in 1785; it later acquired various branches, but eventually merged with the Western in 1843. The Renfrewshire Banking Company, founded in Greenock in 1802, had branches in Glasgow and elsewhere, but failed in 1842. The joint-stock Greenock Union Bank had started only two years earlier; shaken by its neighbour's demise, this merged into the Clydesdale in 1843. Other players at times were the Bank of Scotland (a large lender) and the Paisley Union Bank. In 1816 James Watt gave £100 to found a scientific library in the town (the Watt Library).

**Industries and Communications**: Ironfounding commenced about 1800, the East India Harbour was built in 1805–09, and a second dry dock – later owned by James Lamont & Co, who overhauled Clyde steamers there a century later – was added in 1810–18. The coastal battery called Fort Matilda was built in 1813–15 to resist American privateers. About 1816 a flint-glass works and the Clyde Pottery Company opened to make bowls and jugs; another pottery started in 1820. The fine neo-classical Custom House – the largest in Scotland – was built in 1818 to designs by William Burn. The pioneer steamboat *Comet* (see Port Glasgow) plied between Greenock and Glasgow from 1812 to 1820; Greenock became the main base for Clyde steamboat operation, and by 1819 only two coaches a day plied to Glasgow. Greenock shipowners then operated nearly 300 of the small vessels of the day, averaging only about 130 tons. By about 1825 Greenock was the centre for a penny post serving Inverkip, near the quarries in Shielhill Glen about 5 km south-west of the town, from which in the early 19th century and up to about 1830 Greenock gained much of its building sandstone.

**Cane Sugar Refining: the Lyle Connection**: Sugar refining was begun by West Indian merchants in 1765 beside the West Burn; the original building was still in use a century later under Currie & Co, and a second successful refinery begun by local merchants also lasted a hundred years. Macfie & Sons built the third in 1802, but their Leith refinery was more successful and the Greenock one was out of use by 1869. Abram Lyle, born in Greenock in 1820, joined his father's cooperage and with John Kerr developed the Lyle shipping fleet, one of the town's largest. Among their cargoes was sugar, leading in 1865 to Lyle buying a share in the Glebe Sugar Refinery, which had opened in 1831. By 1869 it had 300 workers and was the largest of Greenock's 14 refineries, whose average employment was about 100; they jointly satisfied almost half of the rapidly growing British sugar market. Second in size was Walker's, also built in the 1830s; both produced about 700 tonnes a week. In 1868 about 400 vessels averaging 335 tons landed raw sugar at Greenock, mainly from Cuba; local refiners' demands had doubled twice in a decade, and Bremner noted that the Clyde to Ireland steamers drew *"the greater part of their freight from sugar"*.

**A Pompous Report of Poverty-led Emigration**: Chambers described Greenock in 1826 as *"the principal port for all transactions with America"*. It was also near the West Highlands, *"the overplus population of which has long been pouring itself through this channel into the unoccupied wilds of the western continent"*; hence Gaelic was often heard in the streets. Commerce brought much new building: *"the finest public building is an inn or Tontine"* just east of the square, built in the early 1820s. A gasworks was set up on a very cramped site in 1827. An *'ancient'* brewery had been converted into a distillery in 1824; there were still two breweries, but no water was available to power mills or for adequate domestic supply.

**Shaws Aqueduct powers Textile Industry**: In 1825–27 the 9km-long open aqueduct called Greenock Cut was built by the Shaws Water Company (to designs by Robert Thom of the Rothesay cotton mill) to supply water from the dammed Great Reservoir, also called Loch Thom, on the upper reaches of the Gryfe Water (now called the Black Cart). From there it meandered round Dunrod Hill to drive a power-loom factory. By 1832 the Overton paper mills turned on a feeder stream 2 km south-west of the town, from which point the aqueduct's steep lower section with a 500-foot fall also drove three other corn or flax mills. In 1832 William Cobbett much admired the *'Shaws Water'* when visiting this *"great commercial and fishing town, with a population of 30,000 and a custom-house like a palace; the streets are regular, conveniently wide; the houses built of stone, and everything wearing the appearance of ease, competence and great solidity"*.

**Clean Water and Big Wheel**: But despite his sentiments, the local people were sadly unhealthy, and welcomed the clean water newly available from the Cut for washing and cleaning as well as drinking. The chain of Scotch Wool and Hosiery Stores grew from its 1833 factory in Greenock. From about 1839 a 180-tonne iron water-wheel over 20m in diameter, then the world's largest, drove a cotton mill established partly to take unemployed youngsters off the streets. Shaw's Mill was opened in 1840 by Neill Fleming & Reid, and a large spinning works was built to make linen yarn for the Gourock Rope-Work Company's sailcloth factory. By 1864 this was regarded as the best in Britain, and the Greenock Spinning Company was also spinning and weaving jute. By the 1890s the mills, engine works and public drew water from four reservoirs covering 160ha and including the two Gryfe reservoirs.

**Shipbuilding up to the Crash of 1841**: So many shipbuilding firms worked in Greenock over the years that only leading and long-lasting firms can be mentioned here. Robert Duncan & Co, established in 1830, built the first Cunarder *Britannia*; what was probably their last ship was the paddle steamer PS *Clyde*, built in 1841 as the first Royal Mail liner *(see below)*. However, the demand for new timber ships collapsed and the yard then closed; by 1842 only two Greenock shipbuilders survived from the previous nine. From railway engines Scott, Sinclair & Co turned back to ships and in 1853 built the early steel clipper ship *Lord of the Isles*. In 1858 they constructed the iron PS *Carrier* as a Tay train ferry.

**Greenock Burgh enters the Railway Age**: In 1833 Greenock gained a new status as a Parliamentary Burgh. The Glasgow Paisley & Greenock Railway (GP&GR), promoted by William Dixon (coal and iron master of Govan and Gorbals), was opened in 1841, and added a steamer service to Clyde resorts. Its cramped engineering works opened at Greenock in 1844; in 1846 they built three engines to a London & North Western Railway design. This was also used in 1850 by engineers Scott, Sinclair & Co, who were already building ships in the 1830s; a nephew, Robert Sinclair, became a well-known locomotive engineer. Donaldson of Greenock supplied some early rolling stock to the Caledonian Railway and to the Scottish Central Railway of Perth. In 1849 a direct steamer service was begun between Greenock and Belfast; by 1851 Hutcheson steamers linked Greenock with various west coast destinations. By 1851 two *daily* newspapers were published, including the *Advertiser*; yet another, the *Greenock Telegraph*, founded in 1857, eventually became the only daily evening paper for the Firth of Clyde towns.

**Transport Competition**: In 1851 the Caledonian Railway (CR) took over the GP&GR, whose works had no space to build more than 7 to 8 locomotives per year; this function was moved to St Rollox in 1856. Meantime by 1853 Wordie & Co had a rail cartage depot. A branch line (opened in 1865) diverged at Port Glasgow, and climbed through the south side of Greenock. By 1903 a siding from the site of the present Whinhill Station served Overton Paper Mill; from there the line continued through the Spango Valley and so to Inverkip and Wemyss Bay. The last new line, the Greenock & Ayrshire Railway, was opened from Paisley via Kilmacolm in 1868–69, passing over the hills and down to the new Princes Pier; this line was soon absorbed by the Glasgow & South Western Railway (G&SWR). In the end Greenock had eight stations on the two competing systems, and the G&SWR offered hourly trains between Glasgow and Princes Pier, served by Hutcheson steamers from the start and in 1877 by the Lochgoil & Lochlong Steamboat Company. In addition, from 1873 horse-drawn trams plied to Gourock.

**Shipyards: Caird's and Steele's**: Meantime the Greenock foundry of Caird & Co which opened in 1825, had been building ships' engines and also ventured into locomotive construction; between 1835 and 1870 they erected extensive buildings in Arthur Street, and engined the PS *Clyde* in 1841. Subsequently becoming shipbuilders, in 1857–59 Caird's completed two fast 70m paddle steamers, the *Alice* and *Fannie*, which were soon used as blockade runners in the American Civil War; both later plied on the CR's Stranraer–Belfast service. Cairds expanded to Westburn in 1867, and in 1883 built the PS *Signal* for the Northern Lighthouse Board. (Caird's SS *Persia*, launched in 1900, was sunk in the Mediterranean during World War I; its maharajah's treasure of gold and jewels were being salvaged in 2001 by Alec and Moya Crawford from Fife.) The other enduring shipbuilding firm was Robert Steele & Co. In the 1860s they built the composite tea clipper ship *Sir Lancelot*, which made the fastest-ever passage under sail from Canton to London; but Steele's closed in 1883.

**Lengthy Docks and Sailing Ships**: The Victoria Harbour was built in 1846–50. The Albert Harbour, built from 1862 was later infilled, but its bonded warehouse survived into the 1980s. The Garvel Graving Dock was built in 1872–74, and the James Watt Dock in 1878–86; Garvel House was embraced by the latter. In all there were about 4km of docks and quays. In 1879 Russell & Co took over part of the Cartsdyke yard as an offshoot of their Port Glasgow business; in 1883, following a series of similar vessels, they built the fine iron-hulled sailing ship *Alcester*, and by 1892 were building four-masted steel barques; but they left the town in 1900. By about 1905 the Greenock & Grangemouth Dockyard Company was also building ships, and smaller firms built yachts and barges.

**Varied Industries**: Buchanans the sweet makers started in 1856, and from the 1870s the famed Drummond packaging works made decorated tins. Meantime by 1866 the CR was carrying enough coal to make Greenock seventh among Scottish coal export ports, and soon Greenock was among the top ten importing ports in Britain, by value. By 1872 the Greenock Sacking Company, which served the sugar industry, employed over 1000 workers. In a seminal development, in 1881–83 Abram Lyle & Sons of Greenock built a golden syrup factory on the Thames, but their lengthy range of raw-sugar warehouses in East Hamilton Street (Cartsdyke) was built about 1885 of red and yellow brick.

**Theatres, Famous Sons and Civic Buildings**: Kemble built Greenock's original theatre; the second, built in 1858, became in turn the *Theatre Royal, Palace, Pavilion* and *Hippodrome*! Hamish McCunn, born in Greenock in 1868 and the son of a shipowner, became a pianist, conductor and composer of the well-known orchestral piece *Land of the Mountain and the Flood*. Henry Bowers, born in 1883, accompanied Captain Scott in his tragic walk to the South Pole in 1912. Between their births came the McLean Museum and Art Gallery of 1876, designed by A Adamson, and the opulent Municipal Buildings, erected in 1879 to designs by H & D Barclay. Morton FC was formed at Cappielow Park in the same year. In 1886 Greenock was *"a busy manufacturing town, with closely packed streets and some fine buildings"* (Barnard); but the Greenock distillery was old-fashioned and employed 24 workers to make 590,000 litres of Lowland malt whisky a year. In 1886 the town's old Mansion House was demolished to make way for the CR's costly tunnelled extension to Gourock, completed in 1889.

**Golf, Trams and Aluminium**: Greenock had 63,000 people by 1891, and had really grown too large for its cramped site. The only inland lungs were the golf courses of the Greenock club, founded to the west in 1890, and to the south Greenock Whinhill of 1911. Only one hotel, the *Tontine*, was worth listing by Murray in 1894, but the town was described as *"a busy seaport, where all passengers for America, Ireland, etc. join their steamers. It is important likewise for its trade and industries, its sugar refineries, woollen spinning, iron-works, shipbuilding yards and docks"*. Although the Great Harbour begun in 1880 remained unfinished, in 1894 the reconstructed Princes' Pier was reopened, and from that year trams ran to Port Glasgow as well as Gourock on a unified system. The infant British Aluminium Company's foundry and rolling mill in Greenock worked from 1895 to 1903, and the firm's carbon plant lasted until 1909 *(see Falkirk, Foyers, Kinlochleven & Fort William)*.

**Ardgowan for Alcohol – and new Theatres**: A new distillery named *Ardgowan* (see Inverkip) was created at Greenock after 1886 and steadily expanded in the booming 1890s; it was acquired by DCL in 1902, and during the 1914–18 war it briefly distilled industrial alcohol from potatoes, and from

*Three Greenock tugs in the Victoria Harbour in 1981. The tugs were based there for handling vessels using the James Watt Dock and the Greenock Container Terminal.* (JRH)

1916 acetone for doping aircraft fabric; it continued to make industrial alcohol until the early 1950s (warehouse use followed, but it had vanished by 1976). In 1903 the *Empire Theatre* was opened, followed in 1905 by the 1900-seat *Alexandra Theatre*, later renamed the *King's*, which became the *Odeon Cinema* in 1928. Carnegie gave money for a public library in 1900.

**Turbines, Trade and Torpedoes**: From 1906 the world's first turbine-driven commercial passenger ship, the screw-propelled TS *King Edward* and her sister TS *Queen Alexandra*, sailed between Greenock and Campbeltown. Greenock's overseas trade was at its peak in the Edwardian years, inflated by the calls made by the Transatlantic liners. The Admiralty moved torpedo production from Woolwich to Battery Park in Greenock in 1909–11, but lack of space inhibited further industrial enterprises. At that time Fort Matilda was a barracks. Grasping at orders which might otherwise have gone to Govan yards, two battleships were built by Scott's of Greenock in 1910–12, HMS *Colossus* of 20,000 tons and the 23,000-ton *Ajax*. During World War I a short-lived firm made coasters and barges from concrete, cast at their West End yard; at that time some 30 steam locomotives were based in the G&SWR shed.

**Postwar Buses, Football and Congestion**: The liners left the Clyde after the 1914–18 war, and local shipping declined as motor transport grew. In 1921 Lyle's joined the cube sugar makers Tate, becoming Tate & Lyle. A new power station was built in 1923, but in that year the *Hippodrome Theatre* closed, and was demolished in 1930. In 1928 a new West Kirk replaced the 1591 building to allow what proved to be a futile shipyard expansion, and a disused church was converted into the *Argyle Theatre*, which struggled on for half a century in a variety of recreational uses. Greenock failed to absorb its neighbour burghs in 1926, and the Overton paper mill vanished, a victim of economic depression. From 1929 the LMS Railway, successor to the CR and G&SWR, used Albion buses on a coastal road service between Greenock and Largs. By 1929 J G Kincaid & Co, marine engineers, operated Caird's former engine works in Arthur Street; but Harland & Wolff who took over Caird's shipyards in 1916, saw their Westburn yard closed by the rationalisation body NSS in 1936. Despite local decline, in 1936 a third of the burgh's houses were statutorily overcrowded. A Marks & Spencer store was opened in that year, perhaps because rearmament had brought new warship orders to the town. A dairy was also built about that time.

**The Second World War**: From 1939 the port was once more extremely busy with Transatlantic shipping convoys. Besides being itself bombed in 1941, Greenock had to cater for wounded crewmen from arriving ships; so despite the wartime restrictions, a much-needed new hospital was built in 1943. Meantime Scott's Shipbuilding & Engineering Company had somehow kept going through the depression, and from 1936 to the end of the war built at least 4 military vessels, averaging 10,000 tons.

**Postwar Ships and their Engines**: In the late 1940s George Brown Marine of the Garvel shipyard built various small vessels. Rankine & Blackmore were still building ships' engines for paddle steamers – including for the *Maid of the Loch (see Balloch)*. Kincaid's engine works later became known as Clark Kincaid (CK). The various shipyards – including the Greenock Dockyard Company, which built large vessels – had replacement orders as late as 1958, and Brown & Co were still at Garvel. A new graving dock was built in 1959–64 for a consortium of Lithgow, Fairfield and John Brown. The 23,000-ton fleet replenishment ship HMS *Resource* built by Scott's was commissioned in 1967; but then orders fell away. Scott's became Scott Lithgow in 1969 when they merged with the famous Port Glasgow firm of Lithgows.

**Beeching Cuts**: The *Empire Theatre* was closed in 1957 and demolished in 1968, but general rebuilding of the town centre and the erection of a technical college was followed by the erection of an STD telephone exchange in 1960. Boat trains ran to Princes Pier station until the Beeching cuts in 1965; the Clydeport Container Terminal replaced it. In 1966 the entire route to Kilmacolm was closed and soon lifted. However, the original railway route of 1841 was electrified in 1967. In the early days of the National Coal Board, Joy-Sullivan of Greenock manufactured coal-cutting machinery; by 1979 they were making air compressors. Shaw's Mill still used Thom's conduit to power its turbines, when in 1971 a water supply tunnel some 2 km long short-circuited the open cut. Cornalees Visitor Centre opened near Loch Thom in 1973 as a centrepiece of the 142 square km Clyde-Muirshiel Regional Park.

**Failures and Successes**: Greenock found it difficult to keep its status as a regional centre, due to the decline in shipbuilding and many of its other industries, though major growth occurred in the Spango Valley *(q.v.)*. In 1973 the *Odeon Cinema* was closed, and Garvel House, lately used as flats, was abandoned by its owners Clydeport in the mid 1970s; it still stood derelict in 1998. Meantime in 1975 Greenock finally attained its ambition of heading a larger local authority, Inverclyde District; a hollow victory, as the town's industries faded away to closure; Walker's sugar refinery closed about then. Of the few success stories in 1978–80, Morton FC entered the Premier League, Thomas Auld had built up a diversified food and catering business, and Thomas Boag & Co of East Blackhall Street, once makers of tarpaulins and jute sacks, had successfully changed to making polythene sheeting.

**Job Losses**: In 1980 Patons' Merino Mill which had lately employed 460 people was closed. However Lithgow Electronics survived. Although by 1985 a reconstructed dual carriageway A8 connected Greenock with the national motorway system, this did not protect the once busy container terminal from closure in 1987. The 1800 shipbuilding jobs at Scott Lithgow in 1987 all vanished in 1988 when Trafalgar House, its owners since 1985, mothballed the yard, while converting part to build oil rigs and retaining its dry dock. The diesel engine works of CK were bought in 1988 by a management consortium, HLD. In 1989 its 450 other workers came under Kvaerner Govan, who demolished some of the plant, and cut jobs to 240 in 1991, making only engine parts. In 1989 CK took over the Ferguson shipyard at Port Glasgow, the last in Inverclyde.

**Bottom of Thatcher's Heap**: In the 1980s Greenock High School was relocated to Spango. In the late 1980s the Enterprise Zone concept was applied to the waterfront, in a Thatcher government attempt to stimulate growth by abandoning planning controls, which in a town like Greenock would have meant rubber-stamping *'approved'* on almost any scheme which meant jobs. Drummond Packaging still made decorated tins, and Buchanans still made confectionery at Fort Matilda. However, the two last and largest of the town's one-time seven cinemas, *ABC* and *Gaumont*, had closed by 1989 when 6500 jobless were recorded. More were actually out of work than the government's massaged statistics revealed, and an academic study of the economies of 280 British towns at that time ranked unfortunate Greenock in bottom place. The rather poor health of its people was confirmed in the 1991 census, when Greenock – including Spango – had 50,013 residents. It is perhaps significant that by then there was a Young Offenders' Institution, and that by 1994 this had *'matured'* into a prison.

**Climbing up the Ladder**: Meantime employment matters gradually improved; there was nowhere to go but up! In 1989 James Blair, makers of timber windows, took on 70 more workers, and about then Domain power entered the town, to make computer power packs. In 1989–90 US-owned Crusader Insurance built a 350-job HQ office on the Scotts site. By 1993 when Clydeport was privatised, locally important firms included Brands, Kinloch and Devol Engineering, plus electronics firms Minbea and HCS Global. A company known as Jess processed meat products, while Auld's Bakery was expanding into wider catering.

**Packing Everything**: Thomas Boag, by 1993 BPI (British Polythene Industries), had grown rapidly. They planned to open in China, actually becoming one of the world's top three packaging combines by 1994; in 1995 their 2500-plus workers made polybags for the main food supermarkets. By then – as Clairemont Electronics – the three former Lithgow plants employed over 5000 people, assembling equipment, monitors and cabling systems for IBM and Compaq. Meantime the Cartsburn Maritime Business Centre opened in 1994 on the site of the former Cartsdyke shipyard, and the Royal Bank opened a 400-job mortgage processing centre in a former Britannia Life building. By 1997 Mimtec *(see Gourock)* had 2000 workers in its plants in Inverclyde and Livingston, assembling computers, and One 2 One were making mobile phones.

**Services Improved**: In 1990 Whinhill station was opened south of the town centre on the Wemyss Bay line; by 1999 Drumfrochar station was also open only 1 km farther west. Meantime the town's McLean Museum already housed an industrial collection and a small but fine art gallery. The Custom House was restored about 1992 for continued use by Customs & Excise, and redevelopment of the disused Custom House Quay, East India and Victoria Docks was proposed. It was hoped to create a multi-screen cinema, hotel, marina and museum of shipbuilding; but local boat owners feared in 1994 for their use of the East India Dock, a public facility since 1772. The great hammerhead crane at the James Watt Dock, by then itself a *'listed building'*, was repaired in 1993.

**Education, Shopping and Sport**: By 1993 James Watt College was associated with the new Paisley University; as Scotland's most westerly higher education centre it also served Argyll, and completed a new waterfront campus in 1998; its new halls of residence opened in 1996. By 1994 the post-war pedestrian shopping centre had been roofed in and refurbished, and by 1995 Marks & Spencer, Littlewoods and Woolworth had joined it. Tesco had two stores in the town. From 1994 Morton FC had been Greenock Morton, an attempt to promote the town; throughout the 1990s they played at Cappielow Park as a First Division team. Meantime a new athletics track was opened in 1995, and a new ice and water leisure centre with 25 m pool and 4-lane curling rink opened in 1996.

**Sugar No More, but Local Government gains**: Tate & Lyle upgraded their Westburn works in 1992; these supplied liquid and granulated sugar and made chemicals for water treatment. The sugar warehouse on East Hamilton Street already stood rotting in 1995 when the struggling firm regretfully announced closure of the works with 170 job losses in 1997, consolidating on Thamesside. In 1996 Inverclyde became a unitary authority. In 2000 the coastguard station took over a share of the work of the lately closed Oban station, and as road congestion worsened, a new cargo service to the Mersey and Solent was begun from Greenock, mainly carrying whisky and electronic products; this is additional to the staples of paper, pulp and a revived container trade. The Garvel Dry Dock Company are still in business as ship repairers and engineers, and over 30 cruise liners still dock each year at the terminal. Greenock Academy has over 900 pupils, Notre Dame High School and St Columba's High over 800, and Wellington Academy 500. The historic *Tontine Hotel* is still an important hostelry. In 2001, plans were formed to revitalise the Greenock Cut waterway.

## GRETNA & Gretna Green

***Solway Firth villages,*** *pop. 3150* — **Map 2, C5** — OS 85: NY 3167

The *Clachmabenstane* at Old Gretna on the little River Sark is said to mark a Roman assembly point. An unusually straight road – which in the 1750s led north-westwards from Gretna Green to meet a proven Roman alignment at Kirkpatrick Fleming – probably also had a Roman origin. It is remarkable that only a few decades after the ending of centuries of border warfare there should have been so many local placenames on Pont's Annandale map, made around 1600. The *'Sarck'* Bridge already spanned the border, there was apparently a mill on the English side of the river, and both *'Graitna'* and its kirk were named. Sark Bridge was the starting point of the military road built across Galloway around 1610 to aid the Plantation of Ulster; it was along this road that the Irish Mails – an extension of the route established in 1642 from London to Carlisle – diverged towards Portpatrick.

***Woo'd an' Married an' a'***: When surveyed by Roy about 1754. *'Gratney House'*, a mansion built in 1710, stood in policies north of *'Gratney Green'*. Though only a small place, this was the main feature in the area north of *'Sarkbridge'*, and the point where the roads to Lockerbie and Dumfries parted. On the English side the only means of crossing the River Esk on the so-called road to Carlisle was the *'Green Ford'*, near the modern Metal Bridge. The strange romantic history of Gretna Green arose from 1754 due to Lord Hardwick's Marriage Act of that year, which required parental consent to marriages in England where either party was under 21. The smithy at Gretna Green was the nearest reasonably accessible point in Scotland, which then (as now) allowed marriages between consenting persons over 16 years of age, and at that time also lacked rules as to how they should be conducted.

**The Development of Springfield**: There was little of note but the church and the marriage smithy at the hamlet of Gretna Green until 1777, when a turnpike road reached the area, facilitating both elopement and parental pursuit! Springfield on the Roman road just to the east was feued off for building in 1791, and Heron in 1799 remarked on *"an elegant inn"*. This was the *Gretna Hall Hotel*, lately converted from Gretna House. He noted that *'Graitney'* was *"the resort of many young ladies and gentlemen from England, who have the misfortune to differ with their parents and guardians on the subject of marriage. A village has been erected by Sir William Maxwell of Springkell, and encouragement given to manufacturers to settle in it"*. Yet Dorothy Wordsworth wrote of Gretna Green in 1803 as *"a dreary place; the stone houses dirty and miserable, with broken windows"*.

**Eloping by Coach and Train**: From 1791 until 1818 Springfield was the first place over the border that English elopers came to. It soon acquired two inns, the *Maxwell Arms* and *Queens Head*, but never grew to more than a village. When the Bridge of Sark was replaced on a new road alignment in 1818, Gretna Green resumed its role as the first place encountered; from 1825 the hotel prospered. Chambers wrote in 1827 of *"the church and village of Graitney"* and described Springfield as a village *"of modern erection"*; about 300 of the pleasantly irregular marriages were performed there in a year by two *'practitioners'*. In 1847 the Caledonian Railway (CR) was opened between Carlisle and Beattock, with a *'first class'* station named Springfield. In 1848 the Glasgow Dumfries & Carlisle Railway – within two years a part of the Glasgow & South Western (G&SW) – provided a separate station with an engine shed at Gretna Green, near its junction with the CR just north of the border.

**Gretna Junction hit by Legal Changes**: Gretna Junction station was created in 1848 just within England. The *Gretna Chase Hotel* was built in 1856 for the punster John Murray, the keeper of the English tollbar, whose trade had been affected by the typical elopers' switch from road to rail. He was unlucky again, for in 1857 the English marriage law was changed, to require one or both parties to take a 3-week cooling-off period of residence in Scotland, if their vows made north of the border were to be legally accepted in England. This put a stop to most runaway marriages, and caused the closure of the hotel for many years; some time after 1857 the earlier hotel reverted to a house.

**Rail Triplication, and the Quintinshill Disaster**: In 1862 the North British Railway (NBR) opened a branch line from Longtown, with a junction south of the Sark rail bridge, in theory enabling through running from Edinburgh to Dumfries; surprisingly they built yet another station at Gretna. After a long quiet period the Smithy museum was opened in 1907;

the location was bogus, but the romance of old Gretna Green was recreated. In 1915, at Quintinshill just north of Gretna, a train full of troops bound for Flanders – lit by gas and speeding south – hit a stationary train head on; moments later a northbound express ploughed into the wreckage. An estimated 227 lives were lost and 245 people seriously injured in this, the worst-ever railway disaster in Britain *(see Rolt, 'Red for Danger').*

**Munitions and New Village**: At that time modern Gretna was being created, based on a national cordite explosives factory, deliberately sited far from German reach. There were more explosives works at Eastriggs *(q.v.)*. A military station named Gretna Township – the area's fourth passenger station! – opened in 1915 beside a hutted camp which was later developed into a dull but tidy village.

**Registry Office Weddings fail to Inspire Beeching**: With another war imminent, the *Gretna Hall Hotel* was reconverted in 1938, no doubt because the already extensive Gretna munitions factory was being expanded. From 1940 when *'irregular'* marriages were outlawed in Scotland, a set of registry offices was opened, sensibly including one at Gretna. By 1951 the area held some 2700 people, with the facilities of a large village, and seven hotels: besides serving the main roads to Scotland, runaway marriages were again popular! The ex-G&SW station – still called Gretna Green and the last one open in the area – survived into the 1960s to be closed by Beeching.

**Gretna Elopers in Limbo**: In 1970 the age of consent to marriage in England was cut to 18, once more reducing elopements, and when new bypass roads for the A74 and A75 opened in the mid 1970s, Gretna proper was left off the roads map too. The character of its 3000 residents in 1981 was quasi-military, quasi-civilian – a British no man's land, neither truly Scottish nor actually English. At the time Gretna was also unique by being the only place in Scotland bearing an English (Carlisle) postcode. There the story might have ended, but romantic notions still led young people to Gretna, where the registry office was used to capacity in the 1980s by around 1400 couples a year, enough marriages for a large town of 100,000 people *(see Sinclair, 1989)*. The registrar herself was married in 1990 – in Gretna church! That year the Old Blacksmith's Shop had over 300,000 paying visitors.

**Road and Rail serve a Three-Ring Marriage Circus**: In 1991 among Gretna's 3150 residents were few with higher qualifications, and a high proportion of plant and machine operatives. But almost 1900 young couples demanded urgent wedlock, so a smart new registry office was opened, with three wedding-rooms to cut delays. In 1993 the doomed British Rail at last tried to cash in on the act by reopening a station at Gretna Green on the Annan line, and with these new facilities available, a record 3530 couples were married at the register office in 1994. In 1994–95 the A74 in the area was converted into a motorway, major new sections being built and a service area and motel created north-west of Gretna. By 1995 *'Ancient Recipes'* foods were produced in Gretna, whose postcode had recently been changed from CA6.5 to DG16.5, reconfirming its Scottishness. Accommodation – for tourists, regular weddings and elopers – is available in at least 6 hotels, plus B&Bs and a caravan site.

## GRIMSAY (Isle), Cairinis & Ronay Isle (Uists) — Map 7, B3

***Small islands, Outer Hebrides,*** *pop. under 100* OS 22: NF 8457

From 1802 sailing packets carried the Uist mail between Dunvegan and a post office at the township of Carinish (in Gaelic *Cairinis)*, where an ancient church stood beside the sandy channel between the isles of Benbecula and North Uist. The passage was greatly obstructed by Grimsay, a small island of low hummocks and lochans, with the remains of a dun and an ancient chapel at Kallin at its east end. This adjoined Ronay, a small rugged island, which had 180 people in 1826 but was cleared in 1831, though a handful of people stayed on until the 1930s. About 1834 the Uist mail terminal was moved to more accessible Lochmaddy. In the 1950s Grimsay still had about 100 scattered crofters, a post office, and a 30-pupil secondary class in its school at Ballaglasa. This served children from the adjacent isles of Uist, then accessible only by the North Ford, which was replaced by a causeway in 1960. By 1976 the secondary class had gone. A small wooden boatbuilding business was still in operation in 1993. By 1996 the nearest primary school was at Cairinis, north of which a youth hostel had been opened near the causeway to the flat isle of Baleshare *(G. Baile Sear)*; however the hostel had closed by 2000. In the 1990s lobsters were fished from Kallin harbour, where there was a small fish processing plant.

## GUARDBRIDGE — Map 6, C3

***N-E. Fife village,*** *pop. 750* OS 59: NO 4519

The mouth of the River Eden in east Fife had to be forded at low tide until – between about 1420 and 1450 – the Guard Bridge of six stone arches was built, promoted by a bishop of nearby St Andrews. Probably by Pont's time about 1600, and certainly by 1654 as Blaeu's atlas showed, the small Motray Water had also been spanned by the *'Innerbridge'*. Between the two bridges was *'Brigend'*, where Roy's map of about 1750 showed no settlement, though four roads met at Guard Bridge, where later in the 18th century an inn was built. In 1810 William Haig, son in law of the inventive John Stein *(see Alloa)* set up the Seggie distillery north of the bridge. At first this was supplied with barley from his farms of Monksholm and Seggie, the product mainly going by sea to London to make gin, the boats returning with East Anglian grain and Tyneside coal. Haig also built a pantile and drainpipe works, but by 1833 his borrowings were half the trade of the St Andrews branch of the Bank of Scotland, which had to take over the business in 1835; Haig's son John managed the distillery for the bank until it closed in the 1860s. Meantime Brigend grew into the small village of Guardbridge to house the workers; there was a post office by 1838.

**From Spirits to Paper and transient Railway**: In 1852 the single-line St Andrews Railway was opened, crossing a new timber bridge north of the road bridge, and Guardbridge gained a station. In 1872 with the rapid growth of the newspaper industry its empty buildings were converted into a paper mill using wood pulp, and a wide newsprint machine was installed. By 1950 about 575 people worked at the mills, and Guardbridge had the facilities of a small village. The old Inner Bridge remained when a new road bridge was built in the mid 20th century. The station was closed to passengers by Beeching in 1965, and the whole railway closed in 1969; little remains but its bridge piers. The secondary school classes also ended about that time. The area had grown to 733 people by 1991, and Guardbridge still had the facilities of a small village. In 1989 GB Papers, as the mill was called, was owned by the American firm James River, who employed 350 people at Guardbridge by the mid-90s. The annual 2000 tonnes of waste fibre, clay and chalk (formerly just tipped) was converted in a new effluent plant into a sludge suitable for agricultural soil-conditioning. The firm – who today make uncoated writing, text and cover papers – also own the smaller Dalmore mill at Penicuik.

## GUILDTOWN & Wolfhill — Map 6, B3

***Small Perthshire village and hamlet,*** *pop. 300* — OS 53: 1332

Some 10 km north of Perth are two stone circles and a group of standing stones. Beside the River Tay 2 km farther north stand the 17th century buildings of Stobhall, whose name implies a hall predecessor built of timber studwork; by the time of Roy's survey made around 1750 it was a mansionhouse. To the east near some standing stones on an ancient north–south track is the intriguingly named hamlet of Wolfhill. The hamlet of Guildtown, lining the later road linking Perth and Blairgowrie, had a post office, inn and smithy by 1895. In the latter half of the 20th century Guildtown's population held steady at around 300; by 1977 the inn and a restaurant augmented its otherwise basic facilities. Remote Wolfhill also had a post office by 1971, and a small housing estate had been built there by 1993. Stobhall has fine riverside gardens, opened to the public at times in summer by its owner the Earl of Perth. Accommodation in Guildtown now includes the *Anglers Inn* and the Victorian mansion hotel of *Newmiln* (1.5 km south).

## GULLANE & Muirfield — Map 3, B2

***E. Lothian large village,*** *pop. 2230* — OS 66: NT 4882

Saltcoats Castle, 2 km from the sandy beaches of the low-lying north coast of East Lothian, dates from the 16th century, and with nearby *'Gulan'* appeared on Pont's map of about 1600. A parish school for Gullane began in 1598, and golf was being played on its seaside links by 1650. The name 'Muirfields' appeared on Roy's map of about 1754, near the intersection of two roads between Aberlady and North Berwick which bypassed Gullane, then a small village. A post office was opened about 1825, and although Gullane church was in ruins by 1827, Gullane Links was *"well known to sportsmen as a piece of excellent coursing-ground"*.

**Gullane for Golf and Greywalls**: A golf course was first laid out in 1880. In 1891 the Honourable Company of Edinburgh Golfers moved from Musselburgh to their fine new Muirfield course on Gullane Links; the later Gullane golf courses date from 1900 and 1910. In 1894 Murray described Gullane as a *"village"* with public golf links, and the *New Hotel, "good for golfers"*, had just two coaches a day to and from Longniddry station, so it was with undue optimism that a branch of the North British Railway was opened in 1898 from Lockhill east of Longniddry. By about 1901 when the local population was nearing 600 the famed London architect Edwin Lutyens designed the famed mansionhouse of Greywalls, built for sportsman Alfred Lyttleton beside the Muirfield course. Cars and buses soon prevented the new railway from thriving, and although the population grew to 1400 in 1931 the railway closed in 1932. In 1948 Greywalls became the *Greywalls Hotel*. By 1951 the population was nearing 1800, enjoying the facilities of a major village, with the 30-roomed *Bissets Hotel*, the smaller *Queens* and four minor hotels.

**Exclusive in More Ways than One**: In 1953 there was only one 18-hole and one 9-hole golf course in use, apart from Muirfield. There was also a convalescent hospital. The Scottish Fire Service Training School was based in Gullane by 1977. By 1981 the facilities had markedly declined. Garages, a dentist and chemist had gone; two hotels had closed, and those remaining had lower star ratings. Gullane was not so much a resort as an affluent residential area, described by Wright in 1985 as *"one of Scotland's most English-looking villages"*. A new public library had been provided by 1990. In that year the exclusive Muirfield Golf Club was vying with the Old Course at St Andrews for the coveted title of *'best golf course in Scotland'* – with prices to match! In 1994 as the Honourable Company celebrated its 250th anniversary and 100 years at Gullane, its 550 members remained all-male – a last bastion? Meantime in 1991 the population was about 2230, of affluent retired character; by 1996 the hospital had closed, and been replaced by some new housing. Gullane now has three 18-hole courses (Nos. 1, 2 & 3), as well as Muirfield – which is to host the 2002 Open Championship. This should be good news for the four hotels and other services.

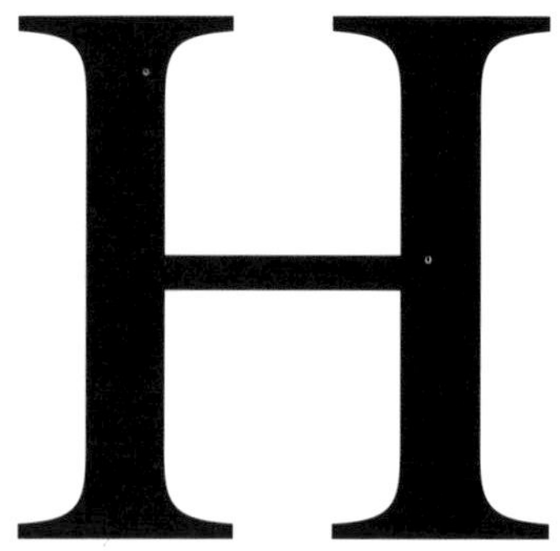

## HADDINGTON

**Map 3, B2**

***E. Lothian town,*** *pop. 8850* OS 66: NT 5173

An ancient hill fort known as *The Chesters* stands on the isolated Garleton Hills in East Lothian. Haddington, some 2 km to the south, lies beside Scotland's little-known River Tyne; it bears an Anglian name, and had a thanage from about the 11th century. In the 1130s under David I it became the caput of the sheriffdom of Haddingtonshire, now known as East Lothian. David made Haddington his demesne, and a palace was built, of which fragments survive. There was a church by about 1139, and a Royal Burgh charter was granted some time between 1124 and 1153. David's daughter-in-law Ada Warren, wife of Earl Henry, founded a Cistercian nunnery 2 km east of the town. By 1242 a Franciscan friary had been established. The town was burnt in 1244, and was eventually said to have been *"thrice burnt and thrice drowned"*. By about 1275 there was a grammar school, attended by the pundit *Duns (q.v.) Scotus*, and by the end of the 13th century a Royal castle. Later the burgh passed to a lord, and the sheriffdom was reduced to a constabulary of Edinburgh.

**Wars, Plague and Recovery**: During the wars of succession around 1300 Haddington was often ravaged by the English, and about the 14th century Lethington Tower, 2 km south of the town, was built in stone by the Giffords; it later passed to the Lauderdales and was incorporated into the mansion of Lennoxlove. Haddington seems to have missed the worst of the Black Death, and soon recovered from another English invasion in 1355–56 to become an important grain market centre. There was a bridge at the time of the worst flood in 1358; the first identifiable bridge was near the church and had three stone arches. In the 1360s – through its port of Aberlady – the town was among the chief sources of Scottish customs revenue, though its contribution shrank over the next two centuries to around 2% of the total. In the same period Haddington paid fairly consistently between 1.5% and 5% of burgh tax revenue; wool was exported by 1372.

**Repeated Floods, Milling and Textiles**: Another flood in 1421 swept away many houses, but a little cloth was being exported by 1434, and by 1444 Haddington merchants were trading as far afield as Danzig. Gimmers' Mills was founded in 1408. (It is still grinding malt flour today – possibly Scotland's oldest continuously operating industrial site.) After about 1450 Haddington's overseas trade tended to decrease, and a Dominican friary founded in 1471 did not thrive. However, St Mary's church was still being completed in 1462, and reached the great length of over 200 feet; it was described as *"sumptuous"* and *"the Lamp of Lothian"* by Fordoun. About 1540 it was briefly collegiate, but suffered when Haddington fell to the English under Protector Somerset in 1548 after yet another siege; they at once built strong artillery fortifications around the town, among the first in Britain on the bastion plan. Soon Scottish control was restored, and by 1560 the burgh had recovered to be represented in Parliament.

**After the Reformation**: The Reformation led to demolition of the friary in 1572, but despite the depredations of over-zealous followers of the reformer John Knox from nearby Yester, part of St Mary's choir survived to become the Protestant parish church, and by 1593 Haddington was the centre of a presbytery. Then the fifth most significant exporting centre in Scotland, it fell far short of the four major burghs. Pont's map of that period showed only a small place, named *'Hadyntoun'*, with its two bridges and friary, at the end of a spur road leading towards the Great North Road and Edinburgh. In 1598 the traveller Fynes Moryson described it as merely *"a pleasant village"*. As Pont's map indicated, Haddington lay on what was then the main overland route to England. This led to its selection as the site for one of Scotland's original three post offices on the inter-capitals mail service, newly established immediately following the Union of the Crowns in 1603. Remarkably, in 1639 Haddington's tax yield was nearly as high as Stirling's, making it 13th among Scottish centres. By then brewing was carried on commercially, but it was 1647 or later before Haddington's full sheriff status was restored.

**Textile Centre succeeds – and fails**: In the late 1640s weaving and fulling were established at Newmills by Edinburgh merchants, but developments were checked by General Monk in 1651. In 1681 a fresh start was made on the site by Colonel Sir James Stanfield who up to his death in 1687 was *"attempting a considerable manufactory"*, with workshops, fulling-mills and dyeing-houses; skilled tradesmen from England gave instruction. The enterprise was renamed Amisfield, but the manufacture of fine woollens ceased in 1713 and was transferred to Edinburgh. Defoe, writing in the 1720s, mentioned having seen very good broadcloth formerly being made there, and that there was *"still some business going on"* in Haddington which was, he wrote, *"an old half ruined town, formerly large, handsome, and well built, has some handsome streets and a good stone bridge over the Tyne"*. In 1729 the Rev. John Gray gave 1300 volumes to form a local library.

**Textiles, Mansion, Roads**: The town house of 1748 – though not its spire – was designed by William Adam. A further venture into textiles brought a bleachfield into operation by 1745, and the Tarred Wool Company's mill of 1750 was soon

*Gimmers' Mills on the River Tyne at Haddington, dating from 1408, and still grinding malt flour today.* *(JRH)*

making coarse woollens, particularly stockings; at one time silk stockings were knitted on frames. A malt mill, possibly Gimmers', was also in operation in mid-century. The Great North Road, turnpiked from Musselburgh to Dunbar by an Act of 1750, already passed through the town by the mid 18th century, when Roy's map showed ten radial roads; its present plan was already recognisable. The Palladian mansion of Amisfield House, designed by Isaac Ware, was built in 1756 1 km east of the town for Francis Charteris.

**Floods and Fairs**: Meantime a new post office was provided in 1764. Floods again damaged the town in 1775 when the river rose over 5 metres above normal. By then large-scale production had resumed at Amisfield, where there were about 800 workers, with an annual output of over 11,000 metres of woollen cloth. Two fairs a year were held by 1797, by which time Haddington was the first staging-point out of Edinburgh for the London coaches. In 1799 Heron noted that Haddington had about 2600 inhabitants, though of *"no considerable trade"*, but it did possess *"a good weekly market for grain, and manufacture some woollen cloth"*. Though the tarred Wool Company's mill closed around 1814, another mill (powered by a Boulton & Watt steam engine), a foundry and a skinnery were opened in the early 19th century.

**Drinks, Banking and Marketing**: Nungate brewery was established about 1801, and by 1825 three more were open. West Field distillery was established in 1813, with extensive 4-storey maltings beside the river at Distillery Park, and Nungate distillery opened in 1825. The East Lothian Banking Company of Dunbar had a branch in the town for a few years from 1810, the opening year of Haddington Academy, and by 1825 the town's penny post served Gifford and West Saltoun. The population of East Lothian reached a plateau in the 1820s. In 1827 Chambers found Haddington *"a much finer town in many respects than the world seems to be generally aware of"*, noted for *"its great weekly grain-market"*. From about 1835 town gas was available. More flour mills were founded in 1842 (turned to tweed manufacture in 1885).

**Rails and Drinks in Trouble; Travellers' Tales collated**: To avoid steep gradients the North British Railway main line bypassed Haddington, serving it from Longniddry in 1846 by a double track branch on which traffic failed to develop, leading to singling in 1856. The waulk mill closed around 1850, and Nungate distillery became a brewery in 1852, later changing to tanning. Meantime West Field distillery was converted to grain in 1846 and closed in the early 1860s, though the buildings remained. Peter Hume Brown, born in the town in 1850, became Professor of Scottish History in Edinburgh University, and prepared the fine compendium of reports by *'Early Travellers in Scotland'* from which many quotations appear in this book. Meantime the *East Lothian Courier* newspaper was founded in 1859 and the pioneer municipal golf course was laid out in 1865 on the Amisfield Estate.

**Grain, Knitwear and Hospitals**: Haddington burgh had 4043 residents in 1881, declining to 3770 in 1891. In 1894 the town seemingly had just one hotel, the *George*, serving *"one of the best grain-markets in Scotland"* (Murray). William Gillies, born in Haddington in 1898, became a famous landscape painter *(see Temple)*. The Victoria Bridge over the Tyne opened in 1900; by then a hospital and a *'lunatic asylum'* were open to the north. Population growth had resumed in the county and burgh, and a quarry had been opened close to an emparked mansion at Huntington, 3 km north-west; but this grew very little for half a century. Sidegate, the last brewery, appears to have closed in 1904, though in 1913 the Kilspindie Knitwear concern was founded in Haddington. Amisfield House was sadly demolished in 1928. The population reached 4405 in 1931, then stagnating. Through traffic on the A1 road was removed with the opening of a bypass in the 1930s, but it passed very close to three hospitals, including the former asylum, and its single carriageway had become somewhat ribbon developed before the start of effective planning controls. Haddington itself became very quiet, with five little hotels in 1951; by then the golf course had 18 holes.

**Glaswegians, Conservation, Shopping and Colour TVs**: By 1963 a sewage disposal works had been built near Abbeymill, enabling some housebuilding for *'overspill'* population from distant Glasgow in the mid 1960s, raising the burgh population to 6502 in 1971. However, the branch railway was closed in 1968. Meantime the imaginative and determined East Lothian planning officer Frank Tindall had happily ensured the town's conservation, at a time when clearance for redevelopment was more fashionable. By 1974 the 14-roomed *Maitlandfield House Hotel* was open. A small electronics factory west of the town, built in the 1970s, was sold to Mitsubishi and had become large by 1988, making colour TVs for home and overseas markets. The Distillery Park maltings closed down around 1980 and were derelict in 1994, but flour mills and merchants survived. In 1981 Haddington was a typical *'country town'*, with nine little hotels. About 1983 William Low built a 1400 m² supermarket behind a historic frontage in the town centre; in 1992 they replaced it with a new superstore at Newton Port, which soon passed to Tesco. 90 jobs vanished when the Kilspindie hosiery works closed in 1989.

**Quarry, Tourism and Local Government grow**: By 1996 the Huntington quarry – which had been reactivated around 1975 – was very large, perhaps connected with building the newly opened second A1 bypass, whose dual carriageways paralleled the first one. New housing estates had grown both east and west of the town, whose gardens had been a tourist attraction for some years, as had fascinating but chilly Lennoxlove – bought by the Duke of Hamilton in 1947 to replace his demolished palace. The population had grown to 8844 by 1991, but several derelict buildings on the Amisfield estate were still listed in 1997. In 1996 little East Lothian remarkably became a unitary authority, gaining major functions from the vanished Lothian Region; its headquarters are in Haddington, whose Knox Academy has a roll of almost 800. The Mitsubishi works closed in 1998; 550 people lost their jobs, though most soon found other work. Pure Malt Products continue at the old Gimmers' Mills by Victoria Bridge, with a staff of over 50; Lothian Electrical motor manufacturers have over 100, and the quarry continues. Half a dozen hotels cater for local and visiting needs.

## HALBEATH

**Map 6, B4**

***Hamlet e. of Dunfermline,*** *pop. 2000*

OS 65: NT1288

The Pont map of west Fife, made around 1600, did not name Halbeath, which stands some 4 km east of Dunfermline Abbey. The Roy map of about 1750 also showed little of interest between Dunfermline and the old north road from Inverkeithing to Perth, built in 1725. In 1756 work was begun to make up the ancient pathway between Dunfermline and Kirkcaldy as a road. A day-level coal mine at Halbeath 1 km north of this road had an engine by 1770 and a second by 1774; in 1781–83 it was connected to the coast by the horse-drawn Halbeath wagonway, originally using wooden rails, which passed west of Duloch Farm to Inverkeithing. But there was only scattered settlement in the area by the 1820s when one map marked *'Hallbeath Coal Pits'* west of *'Hallbeath'*.

**Railway and Trams**: The almost straight western branch of the Edinburgh & Northern Railway (E&NR) from Thornton to Dunfermline was opened in 1849, with a station at Halbeath, where a connection was made to the Halbeath wagonway, which the E&NR took over. Reconstructed to standard gauge, the wagonway was linked with quarries of freestone at Bonnyside and Rosebank (locations some 2 km to the south), and of limestone at Sunnybank north of Bellknowes. It operated until about 1867, ultimately using steam locomotives; wagon workshops were set up at Halbeath. In 1877 a branch of the North British Railway, successor to the E&NR, was extended down to North Queensferry via Dunfermline Lower station. Said to have closed by 1850, the Halbeath colliery was later reopened. By 1891 Halbeath was a small village of 800 people, with a post & telegraph office and an inn. From 1909 to 1937 the Dunfermline Tramways Company linked Dunfermline with Cowdenbeath via Halbeath; then buses took over.

**Motorway stimulates Development**: By 1946 Halbeath station had closed, but Halbeath held some 1800 people by 1951. The post-war mental hospital at Lynebank west of Halbeath was in use by 1967, but little save a primary school survived on the site of the old coal pits, and the population had shrunk to some 1300. The M90 motorway was part-opened about 1970, with a junction at Halbeath, giving better access to the Forth Road Bridge; the Lauder Technical College moved out from Dunfermline to new buildings at Halbeath around the same time. By 1976 Arthur Bell & Sons of Perth had built a whisky bond and bottling hall just east of the M90 junction. By 1980 the TK Valve works was open near Lynebank.

**Queen Margaret Hospital**: The first stage of a new general hospital for west Fife was completed north-west of Halbeath in 1984, a second phase was added in 1989–93 and it all opened that year as the Queen Margaret Hospital, then employing over 1400 people including 90 doctors, to staff its 25 wards and 541 beds. In the late 1980s an 8-unit retail warehouse park and 7400 m² ASDA hypermarket were built at Halbeath; the wagon works vanished about 1990. By 1989 – under United Distillers – the Halbeath bottling plant handled over 3 million cases of Bell's whisky each year, the top-selling brand in the UK, but it was closed in 1992, and 160 jobs vanished. In 1994 the empty premises briefly became the national headquarters of cut-price grocery chain Shoprite, a firm quickly swallowed by rivals Kwik-Save. Weatherguard Leisurewear adjoined. By 1991 the census treated Halbeath as part of Dunfermline.

**Hyundai left High and Dry, but Motorola to the Rescue**: In 1996–97 came the start of a vast development south of Halbeath for the Korean firm Hyundai, who intended to build two plants making semiconductors. A first phase to make silicon wafer microchips was intended to create 785 jobs within a year; the factory roofs were to cover an area equivalent to 13 football pitches. Vast changes in the M90 junction and a northern bypass for Halbeath were completed in 1997, and the new factory was already nearing completion, when a financial crisis in the Far East stopped all work. Eventually in 2000 Motorola took over the building and announced major expansion plans – but 2001 brought a company down-turn, and plans were put on hold. Meantime by 1999 the *Halfway House Hotel* had been opened at the hamlet of Kingseat, 1km north of Halbeath. The new *'Dunfermline Queen Margaret'* railway station was opened early in 2000 to serve the hospital, and later in the year came the *Odeon* 12-screen cinema beside the M90. The *Hideaway*, long a restaurant, is now also a small hotel.

## HALKIRK, Bower & Spittal — Map 13, A4

***Caithness village & hamlets,*** *pop. 975* — OS 11 or 12: ND 1359

Halkirk lies 10km south of Thurso beside the river of that name, and was an ancient Pictish settlement with a broch; it eventually became the site of a church. The early 13th century Bishop of Caithness having been murdered at Scrabster, his successor moved his residence or *Hall* to Halkirk, seeking greater security, but was himself murdered there in 1222. The next bishop found a less vulnerable site for a cathedral at Dornoch, and abandoned Halkirk (which was therefore *not* of sufficient interest to be shown on the ancient Gough map). The keep of Braal Castle was built around 1400, but *'Hackrig'* appeared without emphasis on Pont's map of around 1600.

**Replanned for Whisky and Flagstones**: The Roy map made about 1750 showed a roadless area, with clachans on both sides of the river just west of *Hallcraig Kirk*. At that time the parish had 14 distilleries! A post office was opened at Bridge of Halkirk in 1774. Halkirk was re-planned on rectangular lines about 1790, and by 1797 Bridge of Halkirk was a post town with mail three days a week; Gerston distillery *"enjoyed a reputation for the excellence of its whisky"* (Barnard). In 1869 flagstones were quarried to the south at both Banniskirk and especially Spittal, 5km to the south-east, where the workings became very extensive, aided from 1870 by customers from the former Harrow quarry at Mey.

**Stations Galore, and Big Mountain is Molehill**: When the Caithness (later Highland) Railway's main line from Inverness to Wick was completed in 1874, a station was provided at the roadside township of Scotscalder, at the edge of the bleak moors 4km south-west of Halkirk, which got its own station, while Hoy station on the Thurso branch was some 2 km to the east. The branch diverged from the main line to Wick in an isolated location some 4km distant from Halkirk; this became yet another station, spacious three-platform Georgemas, destined to remain the most northerly junction in Britain. A new Gerston distillery was about to open when visited by Barnard in 1886, close to the site of the old one; an annual output of about 365,000 litres was planned. Tautologically renamed in 1897 as the *'Ben Morven' (i.e. Mountain Big Mountain!)*, it failed in 1900, and no trace of its buildings seems to have survived by the 1930s.

**Peat and Sandstone**: By 1963 the 17-roomed *Ulbster Arms Hotel* was open, and there was a museum at Spittal. Halkirk secondary school was open in the 1950s, but by 1977 the pupils went to Thurso. Halkirk station was closed in 1960 and Hoy in 1965; a single windswept interchange platform for passengers remained at Georgemas. In 1991 Halkirk's population was 973. In 1993 the Highland Peat Company bagged peat lumps for domestic grates at Westerdale, 8km south. In the mid 1990s a quarry was opened at Achavrole, 3km west of Halkirk, by Scotstone, raising Devonian sandstone for building, and at that time both A & D Sutherland and Caithness Stone worked Devonian sandstone for building in separate quarries at Spittal.

**Freight Trains return**: In 1996 Georgemas became newly notable as a railhead; a daily service moved steel pipes and timber south, with Safeway groceries coming north. Remote Scotscalder station, whose station building and post office survive, is a request stop, south of which are extensive new forests. John Gunn & Sons still work the Bower quarry, 7km east of Halkirk, and A & D Sutherland raise flagstones from the Spittal quarry. JGC Welding is a sizeable mechanical engineering firm, and Halkirk also has the head office and factory of the window and conservatory maker HiGlaze. The Thurso river is still noted for its fishing, the *Ulbster Arms Hotel* provides service; cattle-rearing Halkirk is still growing, with many new bungalows.

## HAMILTON — Map 15, E6

***Lanarkshire large town,*** *pop. 50,000* — OS 64: NS 7255

Cadzow Castle – Chambers later spelled it phonetically as *Cadyow* – was built in the 12th century for King David I on a cliff-top promontory beside the River Avon, some 2.5km above its confluence with the middle Clyde. A century or so later, Cadzow was granted to the *de Bellemont* family, whose power in the land became legendary. A medieval motte stood beside the Clyde below the confluence at Hamilton, in whose parish church James, Lord Hamilton founded a college in 1451. Hamilton was chartered as a burgh of barony in either 1456 or 1475 (sources disagree) when the de Bellemont family decided to move from Cadzow Castle to a more pastoral site nearer the motte, where they erected the first Hamilton Palace. This enabled Hamilton the place – which Chambers noted as *"originally an appendage"* of the palace, i.e. a castle town – to become a significant centre. By 1560 the palace was the seat of the top Scottish noble, the Hamilton Earl of Arran, lately given the French Dukedom of Chatelherault. By 1568 it was the chief among several noble residences in the area.

**After the Reformation: Education, the Post and the Park**: Hamilton parish school was started in 1570, and nearby Earnock in 1619; by 1593 Hamilton was the centre of a presbytery. Pont's map dated 1596 showed Hamilton a bridge over the Avon not far above its confluence with the Clyde. The palace was gradually rebuilt between 1591 and 1627. One of the earliest post offices in Scotland was opened at Hamilton in 1642, on the new postal route between Edinburgh and Ireland via Blackburn, Bothwell Bridge and Newmilns. In 1643 a de Bellemont was created Duke of Hamilton. John Ray, who visited Hamilton in 1662, found a *"handsome little market-town"*, while James Broom seven years later wrote that Hamilton Palace already had *"a fair and spacious park"*.

**Palladian Dog-kennels**: Heron noted that *"in 1670 Hamilton was converted into a borough of regality, dependent on the Duke and his successors"*, who again started work on the palace in 1678; after redesign by James Smith for the 3rd Duke it was again rebuilt on a massive scale in 1693–1701. William Adam designed the *'great Palladian dog-kennels'* of Chatelherault, built nearby in the early 18th century; he also designed the fine parish church built in 1732 – apparently his only essay in ecclesiastical architecture – but the old collegiate church was demolished to enlarge the Low Parks. The Roy map of the 1750s showed four roads radiating from the town, the nearest crossing of the Clyde still being at Bothwell. Hamilton itself was only a medium-sized settlement with a T-shaped layout, adjoined by the extensive park.

**Turnpikes, Linen, Marketing, Racing and Banking**: An Act of 1753 turnpiked the roads to Edinburgh via Livingston, and to Strathaven. Linen was produced commercially in the town on hand looms by 1764, and Hamilton fair distributed linens, but Pennant in 1769 found *"a small town"* and did not mention seeing mines or industries on his route from Glasgow. In 1773 Boswell stayed at a *"good"* inn (later known as the *Hamilton Arms)*, and the turnpiking had been effective, for the road from Edinburgh was good too, as was its continuation to Galston. From 1781 a *'diligence'* or stage-coach ran between Glasgow, Hamilton, Carlisle and London in four days. Horse racing in the park was inaugurated in 1782, but abandoned about 1800. The Paisley Union Banking Company established a branch in the town around 1790.

**Hamilton in 1799**: By 1795 Hamilton had a distillery, but this was not mentioned by Heron in 1799 and had certainly gone by Barnard's day. In 1797 no fewer than seven annual fairs took place. In 1799 Heron described the Palace as *"a magnificent structure. The town is rather irregularly built, though it contains many handsome houses and about 3600 people. Cabinet-work, tanning and dressing of leather, saddlery, making of shoes and of candles, are carried on to a considerable extent: the other manufactures are the spinning of linen yarn, weaving linen and cotton cloth, making thread-lace, flowering muslin, and making stockings on the loom"*.

**Monstrously Noble**: A quarry was opened, and by 1819 there was a daily coach to Glasgow. By about 1825 Hamilton was the centre for a penny post serving Bellshill, Bothwell and Uddingston. The Palace was partly rebuilt yet again, and for the last time, being enlarged in 1822–27. In the latter year 700 weavers worked in this *"town of six thousand inhabitants"*. By then Lanarkshire's centre of population was rapidly moving down the Clyde, and to repress these unrepresented people if they asked for rights, the unreformed government made Hamilton a garrison town with substantial barracks; but in 1832 the people had the last laugh. Meantime in 1831 a gasworks was provided, kept well away from what Cobbett called the *"little borough"* and the *"monstrous yet fine and noble palace"* of his hated political rival the Duke of Hamilton, who in death was to be remembered in the vast Mausoleum designed by David Bryce and built in the Low Parks around 1850, probably the largest ever built except for the Pyramids of Giza!

**Into the Railway and Football Age**: Two breweries which had operated in the town in 1825 languished once the Caledonian Railway (CR) reached Hamilton West (from Glasgow via Newton) in 1849. A cloth factory was built in 1855, and the local newspaper, the *Hamilton Advertiser*, was established in 1856. A small iron-smelting works was built at Quarter, 4km south, where there were limekilns and coal pits which were also connected to the Strathaven branch of the CR from Blantyre. Hamilton Academical FC (known as the *'Accies'*) was formed in 1874. In 1876 a new CR line was opened from Hamilton West through a new station at Hamilton Central, winding across the Avon and tunnelling to Fernigair, so connecting with Motherwell. In 1878 the Glasgow, Hamilton & Coatbridge Railway, a North British Railway (NBR) protégé, opened a branch line to Hamilton from Shettleston, resulting in Hamilton – and Burnbank, its growing western satellite – possessing four stations. The 1881 population was 18,500.

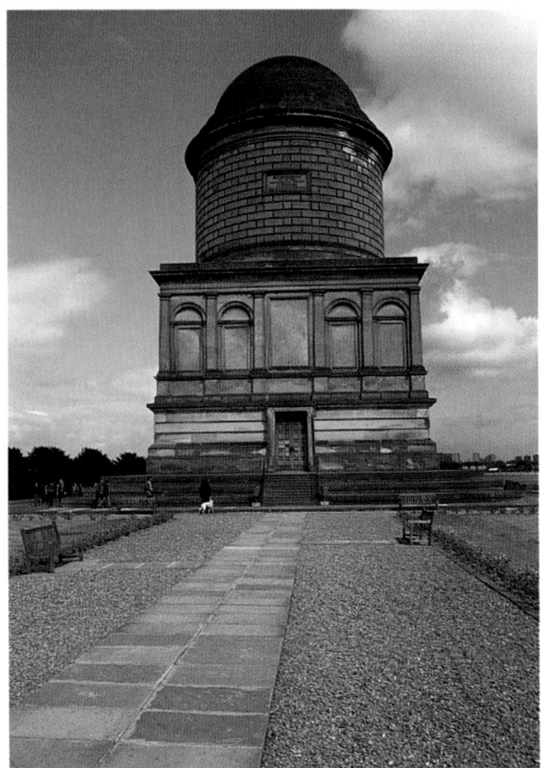

*The 10th Duke of Hamilton's Mausoleum in the Low Parks, designed by David Bryce and built in 1848; it is probably the largest ever built apart from the Pyramids at Giza.* *(JRH)*

**Palace Sale and Explosion in Booming Hamilton**: When the farm depression of the 1870s hit the Hamilton family, the resulting Palace auction was hailed as *"the greatest sale of French furniture since the Revolution"*. Though horse racing was revived with a new racecourse, opened in 1888 in the Duke's Low Park, this too failed, in 1907. But the Hamilton Estates survived on mining proceeds. In 1887 a disaster in Udston colliery 2 km west of Hamilton led to the use of limestone dust to prevent mine explosions. At that time Kesson & Campbell, pump manufacturers of Carntyne, owned the Greenfield foundry and engine works near Hamilton. The Victoria Halls opened in Quarry Street in 1887, later being known as the *Playhouse Theatre*, and in 1888 Hamilton Academical FC established Douglas Park. At that time a belt of woodlands still separated Hamilton from Low Blantyre. From 1892 the Riccarton golf course was constructed at Ferniegair, where there were collieries, a railway station, and post office. Murray mentioned two hotels in 1894, the *Commercial* and *Smith's Royal*, and while the town was *"cheerful and prosperous, surrounded at a distance by collieries and iron furnaces, which light up the horizon at night"*, it had an *"old and dirtier quarter below"*.

**Engineering, Electric Light, Trams and Baths**: At that time collieries also worked at Wellhill above Burnbank to the west, and at Low Waters, which was then a village with an inn, a post office, and a shop run since 1878 by the Labour pioneer Keir Hardie *(see Cumnock)*. By then the Hamilton Engineering Company was in a large way of business, and many of its machines have found their way into industrial museums. Fullwood Foundry operated in the 1890s, and Baird & Son made steel by the Tropenas process. The population reached almost 33,000 in 1901. Electric lighting added to the night brightness from 1898 when a power station was built, and Hamilton soon enjoyed the services of an electric tramway system, linking with Motherwell and Newmains; for a time Hamilton tramcars ran to Uddingston, there connecting with Glasgow trams. A public library got under way in 1901, with Carnegie assistance. A fine swimming pool and public baths complex was built by the town council in 1907–09.

**From the Palace to America – Revolutions in the Park**: Meantime the Hamilton Estates' desire for profit overcame their discretion, for they permitted coal mining to take place actually beneath the palace, which subsided. It took from 1922 to 1930 to dismantle it piecemeal, the drawing room panelling going to America – where it stayed in packing cases for some 70 years! Eventually the family took over Lennoxlove near Haddington. From 1920 a second golf course was laid out in the Low Parks, and a third racecourse was created on higher ground in 1926; both courses kept clear of the subsidence flashes which had taken over much of the park, whose close proximity made the town centre very congested. Overcrowding was severe, with 39% of all houses exceeding the statutory standard in 1936. By then Scottish Knitters was a large firm in the town; in that year British Bitumen Emulsions (Scotland) of the Imperial Works was incorporated to make road surfacings.

**Hamilton the New County Town**: Hamilton's role in the 1939–45 war evidently made few headlines, but Philips Electrical, part of the Dutch-owned group, established an appliance factory in the town in 1945. By the 1950s Hamilton had grown into a minor regional shopping centre, and had an Academy; Burnbank had extensive facilities for a village, including a secondary school, three chemists and a cinema. The largely wooden *Hippodrome Theatre* was destroyed by fire in 1946, appropriately on Burns Night! Eventually the *Playhouse Theatre* became the *Granada Cinema*, but closed in 1958, poignantly becoming a TV showroom. Meantime the Ferniegair colliery and railway station were closed; one Burnbank station became the site of a housing estate. By 1953 Bell College of Further Education was open in Almada Street. Being fairly central to the population of Lanarkshire, in 1959–64 a tall headquarters office block was built by the Lanarkshire County Council to designs by D G Bannerman, enabling Hamilton to take over the role of county town from Glasgow. Councillors and officials could enjoy a bird's eye view of the area from the top floor canteen.

**From Branch Railway to Electrical Centre**: Hamilton had a population of some 45,000 in the 1950s, when the great barracks appear to have closed, leaving the Cameronian regimental museum. Though a locomotive depot remained in Hamilton until the 1960s, in 1952 the former NBR branch railway which had carried 26 passenger trains a day in 1923 was closed to passengers. By 1971 it had vanished, together with the former Strathaven branch which passed Meikle Earnock, where there was a secondary school. By then the South of Scotland Electricity Board had built a primary substation and control room on which four (later five) major transmission lines converged, 3 km south-west of the town centre.

**The Motorway to outlast Teacher Training**: About 1965 – at the expense of what remained of the Palace Park – the M74 was constructed between the town and the Clyde as an effective bypass; meantime the built-up area was spreading steadily south-westwards. A college of education was opened in extensive premises at Bothwell Road in the Low Parks in 1966, but was regrettably closed by the Thatcher government in 1981, adding to the severe problems of education in Labour-controlled Strathclyde. Meantime, Marks & Spencer had opened a branch in Hamilton in the 1960s. The *Hamilton Advertiser* had a particularly large circulation by the 1970s, and by 1975 there was a covered shopping mall. Both the Hamilton and New Cross shopping centres exceeded 5000 m$^2$ in 1989.

**Industry and Rail Electrification**: In 1970 the Hamilton Estates operated the Deer Park sand quarry at Fernigair, and the plastics moulder Peter Tilling started business in the town in 1971. By 1973 the firm of Hamilton Tool & Gauge was also well established. British Bitumen Emulsions had been renamed Bitumuls by 1980. The electrification of the loop railway through Hamilton – as part of the Argyle Line works completed in 1979 – brought the town into closer touch with Motherwell, Glasgow and the lower Clyde. But in 1979 250 jobs were lost when a Hoover branch factory closed.

**Hamilton District and Cultural Conservation**: Hamilton ceased to be a county town in 1975 when it became the centre of a new District, but the tall office block became an important Divisional centre for the new Strathclyde Regional Council. By 1980 the Chatelherault hunting lodge had been lately acquired through the National Land Fund for restoration; a sandstone quarry at Deer Park was reopened to supply stone for its repair. By 1981 the Hamilton museum included both motor and industrial sections, and by 1988 a 200 ha country park had been established beside the ruined Cadzow Castle. In 1992 the Museum of Scotland acquired the palace drawing-room panelling and brought it back from the USA for re-assembly in Edinburgh.

**Racing and Education back to Form**: In 1992 the Hamilton Park Racecourse, improved in 1991 with the addition of a restaurant, attracted growing numbers of racegoers though it provided only flat races. Hamilton had a population of 50,000; there was 15% male unemployment, but among the varied qualifications offered by the renamed Bell College of Technology were degree and postgraduate courses in association with Strathclyde University. Meantime Hamilton College, an independent day-school, opened in 1983; a decade later it provided 775 places for pupils aged 4 to 18 in the former teacher-training college premises.

**Business Parks, Industrial Estates and Expansion**: By 1979 E G Steele & Co were manufacturing rail freight wagons, shunting equipment and plant; Steele's were still in the shrinking rail business in 1992. By then the Philips Lighting factory employed over 600 people, making lamps of various types for home and Scandinavian use. Peter Tilling Plastics was manufacturing cases for many types of electronic equipment, including car phones, cameras and computers; its premises and staff of 42 were expanding, hoping to reach about 130 in 1993.

A business park created on Bothwell Road was letting well by 1992, and was intended eventually to provide some 10,000 m$^2$ of office space. Another such park had been opened at Springhill beside the racecourse. The Hamilton Business Park and industrial estates at Hillhouse and Whistleberry had also been established by 1995. Although some housing and hospital development had continued, in 1994 a plan was approved for 700 new houses to be built over ten years on some 60 ha west of the town.

**No Joy for Peripatetic Footballers**: In the 1980s Hamilton FC played in the Scottish First Division (and for two seasons in the Premier League) at Douglas Park, which by 1990 was a hopelessly run-down ground with a capacity of 9000. This also provided a temporary home to peripatetic Clyde FC from 1992 until their move to Cumbernauld in 1994. In 1996 a new stadium was still intended to be built for the Accies on a 7 ha site adjoining condemned Douglas Park, which had been sold to retail developers; meantime up to 1999 the club played at Firhill. This did them no good, and in 2000–01 they were in the Third Division.

**Controlling Scotland's Power, making Aircraft and Improving the Centre**: In 1994 Scottish Power decided to close its other control rooms at Edinburgh and Kirkintilloch and concentrate computer control of the system at its Hamilton centre, using IBM equipment and a software control package by Ascada, a Lothian-based company only three years old. In 1994 Aviation Scotland of Burnbank launched their kit-built *'Highlander'* aircraft on the market. Decline in the town centre, which was bisected by a major one-way road, led to a major study and the establishment of the Hamilton Initiative, which in 1995 planned a better museum, a cinema and hotel, pedestrianisation and car parking. The Regent Way shopping mall was to be extended, and new retail park development plus a large food store was planned in the former Palace Park.

*The Tropenas Converter, at Archibald Baird's foundry, Hamilton (in the 1970s). This was the last of these small converters, which made steel from pig-iron, to be made into steel castings. (The converter vessel is now at Summerlee industrial heritage park.)* *(JRH)*

**Water Palace, New Local Authority – and a Dark Hole?**: In 1995 the Hamilton Water Palace was opened, including a 25 m swimming pool, leisure pool and flumes; the existing baths were then closed, and in 2000 a new use was sought for them. Up to 1996 the fine neo-Classical Town House was the headquarters of Hamilton District Council. With the abolition of Strathclyde Region in 1996 the new South Lanarkshire Council made its headquarters in Hamilton when East Kilbride, Clydesdale and the Cambuslang and Rutherglen areas were added to Hamilton District. Since 1996 *'Hamilton Ahead'*, a local authority/development agency partnership, has completed a new civic square, a retail park, and a sports centre north of the town centre; a private fitness and tennis entre has been opened. In 1997 the huge Holy Cross High School had 1645 pupils, John Ogilvie High 998, Hamilton Grammar School 1164 and Earnock High 1059. In 1997 an opencast mining application by LAW for 90,000 tonnes of coal and clay was very controversial. When in 2000 Philips Lighting closed their incandescent lamp factory and transferred production to Poland, not only the 225 jobs were lost, but the last plant of its kind in Western Europe. But major employers included Stiell (facilities management), Marubone (mining equipment), APW (precision engineering), Atlas Hydraulics, and SUN (newspaper printers). The long-lasting Stepek (domestic appliances) is still going. And the icing is provided by Lightbody Celebration Cakes!

## HAMNAVOE, West Burra & Trondra **Map 14, B4**

***Shetland communities***, *pop. 950* OS 4: HU 3735

About 5 km south-west of Scalloway as the gulls fly is the long narrow island of West Burra, with various prehistoric remains. Hamnavoe grew up as a fishing village between two small bays at the island's north end; its long-standing lighthouse at Fugla Ness is little publicised. When in 1951 the Shetland mainland was then only accessible by ferries, the population of West Burra plus the small farming island of Trondra was 518. By 1957 there was a pier and a junior secondary school, though this had closed by 1976; the new primary school was prefabricated in Aberdeen. Bridges to the mainland were opened about 1974, with a linking road across Trondra. In 1981 Tindall saw compact little Hamnavoe as a prosperous fishing *'town'*, and Maclean noted many fishing boats based in various creeks and inlets; but both isles provided new homes for Lerwick workers, and the village population had reached 629 in 1991, with 934 in the two isles together. The improved road from Scalloway had been reclassified *'B'* by 1994; more recently, Haswell-Smith described Hamnavoe as *"a busy fishing port"*.

## HAROLDSWICK (Unst) — Map 14, C1

***Island community, Shetland,** pop. 300* — OS 1: HP 6312

Some 3 km north of Baltasound is the inlet of Harold's Wick, an anchorage exposed only to the south-east, named after King Harald of Norway who landed there in 875 to annexe the Shetlands. At its head was an ancient chapel. By the time of Pont's visit about 1592 this was the nucleus of Scotland's most northerly village, though the hamlet of Norwick some 2 km farther north is its most remote significant settlement. The great outlying rock of Muckle Flugga, one of a group of skerries 1 km off Herma Ness, the north point of Unst, was first temporarily lit in 1854. A sheltered construction base at nearby Burrafirth, a sea inlet at the end of what was then a new road from Baltasound via Haroldswick, enabled the building of a permanent lighthouse by over 100 men in 1855–57, remarkably of brick, with a 1 m thickness. Its 20 m tower, first lit in 1858, became the most northerly habitation in Britain; although based 200 feet above average sea level it is reached by high North Atlantic storm waves. A school and pier were built at Haroldswick; both still existed in 1957 when the area's population was about 280, but the pier later vanished.

**Relying on the Cold War**: By 1969 the most northerly RAF installation in Britain, an early warning station, had been built on the 235m hill of Saxa Vord, 4 km to the north, its 78 minders in 1971 being housed in a camp midway between Haroldswick and Norwick. By 1981 the population in the Haroldswick area had reached 325; but in 1985 the main employer was RAF Saxa Vord, and the island's fishing tradition was dead. In 1987 a general merchant operated from a hut, and many new houses were being crammed into the RAF camp, which was still being extended. But with the ending of the Cold War, 30 jobs were lost from RAF Saxa Vord in 1992. However, by 1994 a heritage centre was open nearby, and a visitor centre at Hermaness. Some Muckle Flugga keepers' families were still based at Burrafirth until the light was automated in March 1995; later that year Haroldswick primary school faced possible closure, and what had been Britain's most northerly post office closed late in 1999. The planned reduction of RAF Saxa Vord to only 50 jobs in 2000 left the threat of its ultimate closure hanging over Unst. At least the remote isle would inherit an estate of 60 modern houses!

## HARTHILL, Eastfield & Greenrigg — Map 16, B4

***Lanarkshire / W. Lothian villages,** pop. 4000* — OS 65: NS 9064

Harthill stands beside the infant River Almond on the West Lothian and Lanarkshire county march at the high altitude of 200 metres; it has always been something of a Cinderella settlement. Pont's sketchy map made about 1600 showed a well-settled area. Harthill was a tiny place south of a road that ran west from Newbridge into Lanarkshire, but may have ended at the point now named Roadhead.

**Roads, Coal Mining and Co-operation – in Scotland**: The Edinburgh to Newhouse road via Livingston was turnpiked under an Act of 1753, but travellers passed hurriedly through Harthill without writing of their experiences. However, at some date serious coal mining began in the area. The post and telegraph office opened in the mid 19th century; its postmark originally identified it not by county but as *"Scotland"!* No public railway was built to serve Harthill, yet by 1895 it had grown to a village with an inn; at that time practically all its 1600 people lived in its Lanarkshire portion. To the west was a mineral line linking Shotts with the North British Railway's Glasgow branch at Blackridge, serving coal pits which had been sunk north-west of the village and around Benhar – a linear settlement of miners' rows that gave its name to a co-operative society. A miners' welfare institution was built at Harthill in 1924 (today it's a funeral parlour).

**East is West, and Quarry swallows Golf Course**: By 1931 the population was about 4000 and the Eastfield estate had been built (to the *west* of Harthill, but it was a traditional name!) Development had also begun to spill into West Lothian with the Greenrigg housing estate, which in 1951 held 20% of Harthill's population of about 5000; by then the postal address was *'Lanarkshire'*. The golf course which was open to the west of the village in 1955 had vanished into the Tam's Loup hard rock quarry by 1963; by then all mining had ceased and the mineral lines had been lifted.

**Motorway Services and the Split Community**: In the late 1960s the M8 was built to bypass Harthill to the north, with Scotland's first motorway service area adjoining the village; but the general access was over 3 km to the west. Local government reorganisation in 1975, generally thorough elsewhere, left the village split, the Strathclyde portion being in Motherwell district. Some population decline had occurred since 1951, to about 4650 in 1981. At that time Harthill's facilities remained those of a typical village. Tam's Loup quarry continued to grow enormously through the 1980s, and became a huge void, still active today. Meantime in 1990 British Coal proposed to opencast an area south of Harthill, creating 200 jobs. The 1991 locality population of 2900 was very disadvantaged; this figure excluded the Greenrigg estate, which remained as an anomaly within West Lothian even after the further reorganisation of 1996; rationalisation was desired, but bureaucrats seem not to care about anomalies at Harthill! Today, ACC (food distribution) and Davall (precision plastic parts) are sizeable employers.

## HATTON — Map 10, C2

***Buchan village,** pop. 950* — OS 30: NK 0537

Hatton stands on the Water of Cruden in Buchan, about 12 km south-west of Peterhead, and was already a kirkton by the late 16th century. Timothy Pont plotted it on his sketch map of Buchan, together with the Mill of Halkhillock. Roy's map made about 1750 indicated a large hamlet at *'Over Hatttown'* and another at Hillhead; to the east was Uppermill, which lies in a rocky gorge. A track set off from Ellon, although the track later became the Ellon to Peterhead turnpike road; there was no post office at Hatton until after 1838.

**The Disruption starts a Village**: In 1844 following the Disruption of the Church of Scotland, a Free Church was built near the Mill of Hatton, together with a school, so *"forming a nucleus of a rapidly-increasing village"*, as Pratt reported in 1858. In 1888 Forbes Simmers took over a bakery in the village; his firm was to prosper and flourish over a century later. In 1897 the Great North of Scotland Railway opened a branch line from Ellon to Boddam, and provided a station at Hatton. This proved uneconomic and was closed to passengers in 1932 and to goods in 1948. By that time there were three mills and an inn.

**The Simmers Bakery spreads its Wings**: In 1951 the Cruden Junior Secondary School was at Hatton, which otherwise possessed only the facilities of a small village for its population of 650. This fell away to under 500 by 1971, and the secondary classes had vanished by 1976. By then the Upper Mill had become the home of Simmers' quite substantial bakery, and there was another Simmers Forbes factory at Broxburn in West Lothian. Hatton – also known as Hatton of Cruden – had acquired residential development, raising its population to 957 by 1991. By then Simmers of Hatton also had a factory at Corstorphine near Edinburgh, and were developing a new biscuit factory at their Broxburn site; the firm made oatcakes, biscuits and shortbread, cakes and also jams, sold throughout Scotland. Simmers' Bakeries are still at work in Hatton, which keeps its post office and inn.

## HATTON OF FINTRAY & Cothall — Map 10, C3

***Aberdeenshire village & hamlet,** pop. 730* — OS 38: NJ 8416

Hatton of Fintray, which stands north of the River Don 5 km east of Kintore, was chartered as a barony burgh in 1625, but the ancient Fintray Kirk alone was shown on a map prepared by Robert Gordon before 1642. Little was made of the area when mapped by Roy about 1750. In 1805 John Crombie set up a woollen mill beside the Don at the hamlet of Cothal (now Cothall) 4 km east of Hatton, powered by what he claimed to be the world's largest water wheel, 7.6 m in diameter and 4.3 m wide. After 1830 the business moved to Grandhome near Woodside *(q.v.)*. Fintray House was built 1 km east of Hatton in 1829–31 for Sir John Forbes, and emparked. To the west was a mill, and to the south the Boat of Hatton. The Great North of Scotland Railway which opened in 1854 provided a station at Kinaldie south of the river; about then the Boat of Hatton was replaced by a bridge, itself rebuilt in concrete around 1930. Fintray parish had 866 people in 1901. By 1951 Hatton had basic facilities which complemented those at Blackburn *(q.v.)*, 4 km to the south. Fintray House was demolished in 1952, and Kinaldie station – which had three trains a day in 1963 – was closed by 1967. The population had dipped to only 496 by 1971, but with the rapid growth of Dyce, and the Aberdeen area in general, a little new development took place about 1990, and by 1991 the parish was back to 730 residents. Hatton has a pub but the nearest post office is at Cothall.

## HAWICK — Map 3, B4

***Borders town,** pop. 15,800* — OS 79: NT 5014

Hawick lies at the meeting of the River Teviot with the Slitrig Water. In the Norman period it had a large castle, probably wooden, for an ancient motte stood at the head of the town. The church dates from 1214, and Hawick was named on the Gough map of the mid 13th century. But most early travellers seem to have passed it by, the main routes to/from Scotland being by way of Berwick and Coldstream. Hawick became a burgh of barony in 1511, and the strong *'Black Tower of Drumlanrig'* was built by the Douglases at the west end of the town in the 16th century; it alone survived an arson attack on the town in 1570. Branxholme Tower, 4 km south-west of Hawick, was built about that time as the seat of the Scotts of Buccleuch. Hawick soon recovered, with a parish grammar school from 1592, and appeared as a substantial settlement on Pont's map made about 1600. This showed the Slitrig bridge, which Chambers noted over 200 years later as of *"peculiarly antique construction"*. Above it stood a mill by Hummelknowes, and on the west bank of the Teviot south of *'Wiltoun'* Kirk was the Den mill.

**Textile Town: Linen, Woollens and Carpets**: By 1640 *'websters'* were weaving linen and woollen plaidings, and there was an active market by 1669. In 1677 the Black Tower of Drumlanrig, whose walls were 1 m thick, was rebuilt as a hostelry, eventually becoming the *Tower Hotel*, which was central to Hawick's social and commercial life. The Roy map made in the 1750s showed a very small town south of the Teviot, where the Slitrig Burn appeared to be crossed by a combined bridge and mill; three other mills existed nearby, and a bridge across the Teviot was suggested at *Wiltoun Kirk*. There was a winding hilly road to Ashkirk and Selkirk, but only tracks to Jedburgh, Langholm and Ettrick. At that period linen checks were manufactured, and wool spun for use elsewhere, but about 1758 Robertson & Co established a carpet manufactory; this firm turned to making blankets about 1810.

**Hardy and the Stocking Trade**: In 1771 a Hawick merchant, Baillie John Hardy, began the framework knitting of stockings on a modest scale (some 200 years after its invention in Nottinghamshire) – in 1776 it involved only six of the total of 65 local looms on which linens and woollens were made. By 1780 wool was being sent to Galashiels for carding by Hardy's business successor John Nixon, the first local hosier to make non-bespoke goods; in 1782 a fulling mill was begun, and by 1791 twelve stocking frames engaged 65 workers making lambswool hose. In 1788 William Wilson began as a framework knitter of hosiery, using yarn brought from Galashiels by pack horse; in 1797 he built a small carding and spinning mill. An Englishman, William Beck, also started a hosiery concern about 1790.

**Better Roads, the Post and a Balloon Flight**: Turnpike Acts of 1764 (to Langholm) and 1768 (to Kelso, Selkirk and Carter Bar) greatly improved Hawick's accessibility, with carriers giving weekly services to Edinburgh, Glasgow, Carlisle, Newcastle and Berwick. Hawick's first post office was established in 1767, enabling contact with scattered customers. The fastest-yet journey to Hawick was made in 1785 by Italian balloonist Vincenzo Lunardi, the wind carrying him from Glasgow in only 150 minutes! A Town Hall had been built in 1781, a cattle tryst was established in 1785, and by 1797 two fairs were held each year. In 1799 Heron noted *"the town of Hawick where, notwithstanding many seeming disadvantages, manufactures flourish. Between two and three thousand inhabitants are employed in the manufacture of carpets, inkle* [a broad linen tape], *linen, woollen and hosiery goods"*.

**More Mills 1804–1830**: Dorothy Wordsworth noted in 1803 that *"Hawick is a small town; the inn is a large old house, formerly a gentleman's house"* (evidently the *Tower Hotel*). John Nixon developed the large Lynnwood yarn mills for carding and spinning in 1804; the 3-storey, centrally located Tower Mill and also a substantial corn mill were erected about 1805. Wilson's was the first Hawick firm to use steam power, and was joined by William Watson & Son; by 1812 the joint firm produced 20,000 kilos of yarn and about 50,000 pairs of hose a year, but in 1819 the partnership was dissolved. The Wilton Mills erected by Dicksons & Laings to spin yarn for coarse hosiery date from 1809–11; they were the first to install power looms in 1830, and stayed at work throughout the 19th century.

*The Dangerfield Mill, Hawick, erected in 1872–73 by Watson's as a carding and spinning mill. The firm went into liquidation in 1991, but an Australian entrepreneur took over, and it now makes hosiery. It still houses some of its original machinery.(JRH)*

**The Arrival of Pringle**: By 1812 the number of framework knitters had grown to about 500, a third of the Scottish total; they specialised in lambswool stockings, making a third of a million pairs a year, and threatening the hitherto dominant hand knitting industry of Aberdeen. John and Robert Pringle, having learned the craft from Beck, established their famous textile firm in 1815 *(see Gulvin's detailed account)*, and William Elliot & Sons was founded about 1820. Hand-frame knitting was thirsty work, and by 1825 there was a brewery. Dickson's Nurseries had been established for over a century by 1827, when Chambers thought that Hawick was *"a sort of Glasgow in miniature"*.

**'Tweel' into 'Tweed', and Long Hours**: The fabric name *'Tweed'* originated by accident about 1830 when James Locke of London, one of Watson's customers, misread the name *'Tweel'* (Twill) on an invoice; but it suited the case, and the name stuck. Long hours were worked in the mills, and gasworks for lighting were erected in the 1830s. In all some ten woollen spinning mills were in operation by 1838, plus a society of frame knitters and the millwright John Melrose, who in 1844 invented the *'piecing-machine'* which joined carded wool into continuous threads, work previously done by exploiting child labour. In 1851 almost all Hawick's 1100 hand-frame knitters were men, because the task was so arduous: their womenfolk and children worked longer hours in ancillary tasks because the pay was so low. Their small, overcrowded houses averaged over 7 persons each. Meantime Dicksons & Laings, who had added tweed and blanket manufacture, built extensions in 1841–43; the Hawick hand-frame knitting industry peaked about that time with some 1200 frames.

**The Railway Era**: The Edinburgh & Hawick Railway reached the town from Edinburgh in 1849; its only local newspaper, the *Hawick Advertiser*, was established in 1854. An archaeological society was founded in 1856. In 1862 the North British (NBR) extended the railway over the moors to Newcastleton and Carlisle, and a minor railway engine shed had been built at Hawick by 1869. The NBR also suggested that the town council should establish a rail-connected livestock market, since the former cattle fairs had apparently long ceased; the council acted on the idea, and the market prospered. But, as in other rural areas, the fresh horizons opened by the railways led to emigration, and the peak population of Roxburghshire passed in 1861. By the time of Bremner's survey in 1869 the woollen industry in Hawick was dominated by eight or nine firms, and the number of hand frames had fallen to about 900. Half a million kilos of wool were made into stockings, shirts and underwear, while hosiery yarn was also made for Leicester firms.

**Underwear, Fine Flannels and Fine Hosiery**: William Elliot & Sons acquired Stonefield mill and the ancient Waulk mill in 1850, demolishing the latter to build a large spinning mill on the site. By 1868 the firm was regarded as *"the leading firm in the Scotch Hosiery Trade"*; their spinning mill employed 332, and their new factory had 285 knitters making underwear on hand frames. William Laidlaw & Sons had built a very large mill at Teviot Crescent in 1834, to make tweeds; later they made hosiery, hand-frame knitwear, and bought the Lynnwood mill to spin stocking yarns. Walter Wilson, son of William, and his brothers inherited a tradition of making fine flannels from imported wool, and built large mills for frame knitting in the 1850s. John Laing, an offshoot of Dicksons & Laings, was himself a leading manufacturer by 1864, using merino yarn from Nottingham and Derbyshire to make fashioned hosiery on knitting frames powered by steam. Watson's, who made only their famous *'tweeds'*, enlarged their works, and in 1872–73 built the multi-storey Dangerfield carding and spinning mill.

**New Firms: Innes, Henderson and Scott**: Innes, Henderson & Co's Braemar Hosiery (Victoria) Works were founded in 1868. They made underwear on hand frames for, as fashions changed, production was shifting from hosiery towards underwear. Power knitting was generally slow to be adopted, being suited to cheaper lines than local firms had developed. A strike of the 770 stocking frame knitters in 1872 led to factory seaming on sewing machines and to John Wilson's turning to tweeds. In the same year local knitter Peter Scott began a hosiery business at Buccleuch Street using the trademark PESCO – not to be confused with Lyle & Scott who started in 1874 (borrowing from a local corn merchant to do so).

**Local Boom**: About 1875 the local economy took an upwards turn, and Melrose's, the local foundrymen and millwrights, expanded. In 1876 a town sewerage system was built; the golf club was founded in 1877. By 1881 the population had reached 16,000. By 1882 the *Buccleuch Temperance Hotel* was open, and a new Town Hall was built from 1884; the local Co-op built a substantial store in 1885–86. The Mansfield weaving mills came in 1880, the Eastfield weaving mills opened in 1882, and James Renwick began to make underwear in 1884. George Hogg's hosiery works rose at Millbank in 1887; the Glebe, Teviot and Weensland Spinning Mills were also built towards the end of the century. Henderson – having split from Innes – adopted steam power in a new works in 1888. Lyle & Scott, with over 200 hand frames, also began to use steam. There was a population of 19,000 in 1891; in 1894 Hawick was described by Murray as *"thriving but uninteresting"*; the *Crown* and *Tower* hotels were open, and in 1898 a new UP church was built.

**Slump – but Isobel aims High**: However, a slump in woollens hit the hand-frame knitting industry badly; by 1901 the burgh population had fallen to only 17,000, and the brewery seems to have closed by that time. In 1899 a new steam laundry employed at least 25 girls, but local girl Isobel Baillie, then aged 4, aimed higher and grew into a world famous soprano singer. By then Hawick fire brigade had a steam pump and at least 17 members. An electricity generating plant was also built in 1899; Henderson's soon used electric power. In 1902 Carnegie gave £10,000 for a grand new library building – so grand, in fact, that its costs almost prevented the buying of books to fill it!

**Power-Knitted Outerwear**: With declining demand for itchy woollen underwear, local firms turned to making the newly popular pullovers and cardigans, increasingly on power frames. James Henderson started on pullovers in 1905; Braemar Knitwear's Victoria works were greatly enlarged in 1908 and Turnbull's dyeworks were built in 1911. About 1910 John Laing & Co was making hosiery on hand and powered machines. Around that time Walker & Co of Leicester moved to Hawick to use its cheaper labour. By 1914 the largest firm was Peter Scott's who employed 800 and still made knitted underwear, but only 100 hand frames were still in use in Hawick as against 400 power frames. It was not quite exclusively a textile town: nearly 270,000 head of stock were dispatched by rail from Hawick's market in 1920; but then road transport began to step in.

**New Textile Firms and Products**: Remarkably, the new hosiery firm of Gladstone was founded in 1916 during World War I, followed in 1919 by Kenway. In 1920, when Peter Scott's employed 700 people, the firms of Innes and Henderson merged to become the town's largest firm, and they began to make *'Braemar'* cashmere knitwear. By 1923 a leading local hosier had established the Technical Institute, and 1927 was a boom year.

**Adventures after the Depression**: The early 1930s slump hit the luxury trade on which Hawick depended, and by 1932 unemployment at 1600 was eight times that of five years earlier. By 1937 Peter Scott's specialised in underwear, but Pringle's had done so less successfully and fell to a low in 1933; however, they blossomed with a new designer and had quadrupled their sales by the outbreak of war in 1939. The development of textiles in Hawick, with generally firm demand for its high quality woollen products, had created a substantial, independent but isolated and vulnerable industrial town with 23 textile firms in 1939. But there was little else apart from the market – which shipped 78,000 sheep by rail in 1935 – and an abiding passion for rugby. Lyle & Scott began to make American Y-fronts under licence in 1938 and then grew enormously, opening branches in Dunfermline, Gateshead and (unsuccessfully) in Lasswade. An overspill agreement with Glasgow in the 1950s was a failure. Braemar made woollen underwear for the successful Everest expedition of 1953. By 1962 a youth hostel was open near the rural post office of Borthwickbrae, 8 km west of Hawick.

**Independence Lost by Takeovers**: Lyle & Scott were taken over by Wolsey in 1964; the same year Jaeger acquired Renwick's, before themselves becoming part of Coats-Paton in 1965. Meantime Pringle's styled themselves *Pringle of Scotland* from 1959, and by 1964 were Britain's third largest knitwear concern. In 1967 they were taken over by the Dawson Group *(see Kinross)*. Though in 1969 they still employed over 2000 people, with a branch factory in Berwick, enforced reorganisation lay ahead, for in that year 1969 Glenmac Knitwear of Hawick also fell to the Dawson Group, while Braemar Knitwear (briefly owned by the Baird group from 1964), was taken over by Dawson in 1970. Hawick had already been set back by the total closure of its railway in 1969. In 1974 Dawson merged Braemar with Pringle as *Braeburn*; the unthinkable happened with the demolition of Pringle's modern factory, though their name survived, and Braemar production in Hawick was also run down and ceased by the mid 1970s. Although some compensatory industrial development occurred around 1970 the population of Hawick continued the slow fall experienced since 1951, and the Dawson name was not popular in the town.

**District Headquarters but no *Tower Hotel***: In 1975 Hawick became the headquarters of Roxburgh District, drawing together offices previously scattered throughout the former county. By 1977 Barrie Knitwear had a factory at Burnfoot, and Jon Spencer opened a factory at Heronhill in 1976; by 1980 it employed 150 people making middle market wool knitwear. But his workers were cut back by a third in 1980, and about the same time Dawsons closed what had become the Wilson & Glennie factory. Town centre redevelopment began in the Howegate area in 1979. In 1981 Hawick's facilities were still those of a major local centre, with its 10 hotels, but the historic 36-roomed *Tower Hotel* closed in 1981, and was semi-derelict by 1988. Despite the takeovers, local enterprise was not dead: McIan knitwear was established in 1982. By 1983 twelve knitwear concerns were operating in the town, including Peter Scott's (who were still using their own well water for scouring), and the Hawick Honeycomb Blanket Company of Trow Mills.

**Disaster for Woollens, Shrinkage for Hawick**: The later 1980s were unhappy for the textile industry and therefore for Hawick's service trades. Nearly 60 jobs were lost when the main Co-op store closed in 1987. Continuing general problems in the textile trade led to the loss of 120 jobs when Kintyre Knitwear of Glasgow closed its branch factory in 1989; altogether over a thousand Hawick textile workers were laid off in that year. In 1990–91 came the closure of George Hogg & Sons, hosiery manufacturers at Millbank since 1887, and in 1991 the 45 jobs at Marshall Lauder knitwear were threatened as the firm went into receivership. Courtaulds closed the Weensland spinning mill in 1991, and later in the year Jaeger closed the 5100 m² James Renwick factory. Watson's too went into liquidation in 1991 after 187 years and in 1994 the Dangerfield Mill stood disused, fully-equipped with largely traditional machinery and an uncertain future. By 1992 the number of workers in the Borders textile industry had been halved in twenty years to little over 5000. By 1991 the population was down to about 15,800, nearly half of whom lived in council flats, and the *Hawick Express* newspaper, formerly the *Advertiser*, had been absorbed by the *Southern Reporter* of Selkirk.

**The Continuing Importance of Textiles**: However, John Laing textiles were still a family business, expanding in high class knitwear in 1987–88, and the name of Pringle continued as one of Dawson's *'Premier Brands'*, its local headquarters being in the Victoria mills in 1989. Slumberdown International established a new factory in 1991, Barrie Knitwear was still busy, and another knitwear factory owned by Johnstons of Elgin made cashmere, lambswool and cotton goods; in 2000 they were still doing unexpectedly well in cashmere. The new knitwear firm of Stewart Noble opened in 1992, when despite recent redundancies Peter Scott's were still in business; they had new machinery and specialised in sweaters. By then the Dawson International subsidiary Pringle, aided by endorsement by golfer Nick Faldo, had expanded to a total of 1700 workers, making market-led designer sportswear on modern machinery in various Borders factories. In 1994 Dawson's United Brands had a modern knitwear factory on the Burnfoot Industrial Estate; at that time no less than 84% of the town's production jobs were in textiles.

**New Use for the Tower, but no Local Government**: By 1990 Oliver Homes was a substantial manufacturer and builder of timber kit houses, and a major town centre redevelopment was begun in 1991. Hawick was the centre of the Borders College, also providing business training at outposts in Galashiels, Duns and St Boswells. Lawrie & Symington of Gorgie sold the site of their former livestock auction mart in 1991: it was acquired by Safeway for a new superstore built in 1993, employing 250 people. The new Galalaw Business Park opened beside the A7 in 1993. The 16th century building formerly used as the *Tower Hotel* was fully restored and reopened in 1995 as a tourist information and visitor centre, museum and gallery for Tom Scott watercolours, with a knitwear gallery sponsored by Pringle. It reverted to the name *Drumlanrig's Tower*. This scheme had involved a partnership between Scottish Borders Enterprise, the Scottish Historic Buildings Trust, and the outgoing District and Regional councils. At that time Hawick High School had 1060 pupils. By 1995 Houstons of Hawick supplied *'Selkirk Bannocks'* to Safeway's Scottish stores, and by 1997 the town had a leisure centre.

**Mixed Fortunes in Textiles**: The restoration of remaining neglected buildings in the town centre, including the disused Tower Mill, was begun in 2000. At that time the cashmere producers *Clan Douglas* were working flat out and had bought another factory for expansion, whereas the 300-job Lyle & Scott factory was put up for sale by its then owners Courtaulds Textiles, and bought by investment company Harris Watson. In 2000 Dawsons sold fast-failing Pringle (down to 180 workers) to Fang Brothers Knitting of Hong Kong, who brought in designer Kim Winser to turn the firm around in 12 weeks – she did, and within months Pringle had 250 workers in its Glebe mill. And the old Dangerfield Mill is now back in production under new ownership, making hosiery. Hawick still has many small hotels, but the reopening of the railway to Edinburgh is still a long way off.

## HEITON & Sunlaws — Map 3, B4

***Borders village & hamlet**, pop. 200* — OS 74: NT 7130

The Blaeu map of Teviotdale based on Pont's sketches of around 1600 showed only *'Sanlaes'* on the east bank of the River Teviot opposite Roxburgh. By the 1750s a track connected *'Hightoun'*, 1 km north of Sunlaws, with Kelso 5 km to the north and Jedburgh to the south; turnpiking of this route followed under an Act of 1768. By 1895 the Dukes of Roxburghe had built Sunlaws House, an emparked Elizabethan-style mansion. Heiton was a hamlet with a smithy and a post office, but although a railway serving Roxburgh passed close by, its only direct connection to that place was a ford. By 1951 there was also a primary school at Heiton, but the population in the area shrank from 300 to 200 between then and 1981. After Roxburgh's railway was abandoned in 1969 its Teviot bridge was informally adapted to carry a minor road to Heiton. By 1983 the Dukes of Roxburghe had converted Sunlaws House into the *Roxburghe Hotel* in its own park. By 1996 it was adjoined by the tree-encircled Roxburghe golf course on the riverside, the only one of championship class in the Borders.

## HELENSBURGH, Ardencaple & Rhu — Map 5, B5

***Firth of Clyde town**, pop. 18,000* — OS 56: NS 2982

Ardencaple, a now vanished castle which appeared on Pont's map of Lennox, made about 1600, lay near the north shore of the Firth of Clyde 35 km west of Glasgow. Roy's survey about 1750 showed it adjoined by a hamlet on the coastal track, and the castle became incorporated in an emparked mansionhouse. A spa with baths was built there in 1776 by Sir Ian Colquhoun of Luss, adjoined to the east by an extensive rectilinearly planned settlement named after his wife as Helensburgh; a ferry from Greenock was immediately introduced. Helensburgh was chartered as a burgh of barony in 1802 and was to prove a centre of innovation. A post office was opened at Helensburgh in 1806.

**The Bathing Bells and their *Comet*** : Enter Henry Bell, who had trained as a millwright and shipwright *(see Torphichen and Bo'ness)* and worked as a builder in Glasgow; he also knew Alex Hart, who had worked with the steamship pioneer Symington. By 1810 Bell's wife ran a Helensburgh inn which later became the *Queen's Hotel*, and by 1811 the Bells also owned the *Helensburgh Baths*, a combined hotel and hydropathic establishment. In 1807 the American Robert Fulton had pioneered the steamboat *Clermont* in successful commercial use on the Hudson River, using English engine components made by Boulton and Watt *(see Grangemouth)*. But it was Henry Bell who fathered the world *seagoing* steamship industry when he had the famous pioneer paddle steamer *Comet* built to bring his wife's hotel and baths patrons from Glasgow down-river to Helensburgh. The boiler and castings were nominally made by John Napier, actually supervised by David Napier and finished by Glasgow engineer John Robertson. When *Comet* first entered service in January 1812 there was no pier at Helensburgh, so passengers were ferried across from Greenock; this proving a deterrent, a steamer pier was soon built.

**Yachts, Railways and Craigendoran Pier**: In 1832 Cobbett saw Helensburgh as still a *"little village"*, but subsequent rapid development ensured that by the 1850s it shared with Gourock the role of the Clyde's *"Principal watering place"*. The Gothic West Kirk, designed by James Hay, was built in 1853. The new town grew further with the opening of the Glasgow, Dumbarton & Helensburgh Railway (GDHR) to terminate by the shore in 1858; by 1860 Wordie & Co had a rail cartage depot. Helensburgh became a dormitory settlement and, due to its sheltered waters, a yachting resort. The town pier was rebuilt in 1861–72, and served from 1866 by the steamers of the GDHR's successor the North British Railway (NBR), supplemented in 1880 by the Lochlong & Lochlomond Steamboat Company. By 1881 Helensburgh was a burgh with a population of 7693, and continued to expand; the Victoria Halls were built in 1887 and improved in 1899. The major Craigendoran pier and station just east of the resort was built by the NBR for its steamer services in 1882–83, and was also served in 1885 by the Lochgoil & Lochlong Steamboat Company. By 1891 the population had reached 8400.

*'Cairndhu', Helensburgh, was built in 1871 (to designs by William Leiper) for John Ure, flour miller and merchant and Lord Provost of Glasgow. This is one of the grandest 'marine villas' which made Helensburgh a fashionable summer resort for Glasgow families. (JRH)*

**West Highland Railway and TV Pioneer**: In 1894 Craigendoran became the junction from which the West Highland Railway's lengthy line struck out, climbing behind the town towards Fort William. Helensburgh Upper and Row stations were opened on this line, the latter serving Rhu, a sprawling settlement of Victorian villas whose Gaelic name means *'Promontory'*, casually spelled *Row* until 1927. John Logie Baird, rightly famed as the inventor of television, was born in Helensburgh in 1888, but he researched elsewhere, and the system we now use was not his. The Helensburgh golf club, founded in 1893, laid out a moorland course, and the independent St Bride's School for Girls was opened in 1895.

**Mackintosh's Hill House**: By 1894 Murray noted the town comprised *"a row of shops and lodging-houses facing the sea, and a hill behind, covered with pleasant villas"*. The *Queen's Hotel* was *"very comfortable"*, and regular steamers plied to Greenock from the pier. Among the last opulent villas to be erected was Hill House, built in 1902–04 almost 100 metres above sea level on the northern outskirts for the yachting enthusiast Walter Blackie, third generation of the famed Glasgow publishing house. Designed by the brilliant Charles Rennie Mackintosh of Glasgow, it is internally highly original, while externally recalling the traditional L-plan harled and slated Scottish tower house.

**From Helensburgh to Hollywood and the Hills**: It seems out of character that Helensburgh FC actually played in the Scottish League in 1923–26, a time when the town made very little news. The 1940s film star Deborah Kerr was a native of Helensburgh, whose slowly growing population reached 10,000 in 1951, when it had 4 small to medium hotels, plus 3 more at Rhu. It had a secondary school, and approached the wide range of facilities expected of a minor regional centre and yachting resort, plus a recent public library. One Rhu villa, Ardenconnel, was then a holiday centre for young hill walkers; however, the historic mansion of Ardencaple House was pulled down in 1957. The railway was electrified in 1961 between Airdrie, Glasgow and Helensburgh, making the locomotive shed redundant, and Row station was closed in 1964. An inshore lifeboat station was opened in 1965. St Bride's School then had 375 pupils, still all girls; in 1971 the Edna Yarrow Children's Home had almost 100 inmates. Only one in five local houses was council-owned. Craigendoran pier was officially closed in 1972 when the car ferry to Gourock was withdrawn, and was last used about 1979.

**Independence Lost**: Of five hotels in 1980, the old *Queen's Hotel* with some 25 rooms was converted to flats in the 1990s; the largest, the *Commodore Hotel*, was badly damaged by fire in 1977 but soon back in business. Although still a major local centre, with development spreading both up the hillside north-eastwards, and around Rhu to the west, Helensburgh was absorbed into the new Dumbarton district in 1975. The large independent Lomond School which incorporated St Bride's was open by 1980. Various services including banks, doctors and dentists failed to keep pace with the rapid growth of the town's dormitory population. In 1991 Helensburgh had 15,850 generally fit and well-educated residents, and the adjacent affluent dormitory of *'Rhu and Shandon'* had some 2500 youngish people. Yachting was very popular, and Hill House with its pleasant gardens, lately taken over by the National Trust for Scotland, drew some 40,000 visitors a year.

**Helensburgh and its Yachts enter Argyll**: By 1992 the Royal Clyde Yacht Club of Hunter's Quay had merged with the Royal Northern Yacht Club of Rothesay and moved to a recent marina at Rhu, encouraging the developers of a water sports complex to buy the long-disused Craigendoran pier in 1994. By then the large Hermitage Academy had been built nearby; it had 1465 pupils in 1996. By then a Tesco store was open; in that year Helensburgh became part of the sprawling area of an extended Argyll & Bute Council, centred in faraway Lochgilphead. In 1995 a heavy storm ruined the glazing of the fine station canopies. In 1997 the St Bride's building of Lomond School suffered a serious fire. Today the US-owned data-processing company Crossaig employs 80 staff in Helensburgh. The larger of the hotels include the *Rosslea Hall* and the *Commodore*, and the *Ardencaple* at Rhu; a passenger ferry still sails to Gourock in summer.

## HELMSDALE

**Map 9, C1**

***Sutherland village,*** *pop. 825* — OS 17: ND 0215

A vast array of ancient remains – including brochs, souterrains and hut circles – line the River Helmsdale, which flows through the Strath of Kildonan to the east coast of Sutherland. In the 14th century a hospice was established, and about 1488 a castle was built at the river mouth; Blaeu's 17th century map used the name Helmsdale, so by then its old Gaelic name *Bunillidh ('Foot of the Mountain'* – the steep Ord of Caithness to the north) seems to have fallen out of use. When Roy mapped the area about 1750 there were two hamlets where the coastal track crossed the river by what Pennant in 1769 called a *"very dangerous"* ford. He saw mackerel and salmon fisheries, and *"a little village"* where he both *"dined"* and *"lay"*, so implying an inn. Heron in 1799 likewise found the water *"deep, rapid and dangerous to the traveller, there being no bridge over the river. At its mouth is a good salmon fishery"*.

**New Helmsdale's Shameful Origins**: Between 1806 and 1816 some 15,000 of the Duke of Sutherland's tenants were forced out of their homes and their cattle-herding livelihood in the Sutherland glens. The guilty parties were the estate's ruthless agents William Young and Patrick Sellars, never forgotten or forgiven. However, in 1811 Telford's contractors rebuilt the coastal track as a road – with proper bridges throughout – for the Commissioners for Highland Roads & Bridges. This enabled serious development to commence: fish-curing was started in 1813, and in 1814 a planned township was founded at Helmsdale by the Sutherland Estates, with a coaching inn and a harbour constructed in 1818 as a fishing base. The new settlement gave some prospect of survival to those of the destitute former tenants who had not fled the area altogether.

**Herrings, Inns and Whisky**: According to Chambers, a Lowlander who ignored the clearances but admired their results, *"Helmsdale deserves the appellation of town; for, while it is much more handsome and convenient, it possesses more inhabitants than many royal burghs. It has an excellent harbour, to which immense armadas of fishing-boats resort during the herring season (September). In the season of 1825, many thousands of barrels of herrings were prepared at Helmsdale; the town is increasing rapidly. Port Gower, the neatest of all possible fishing villages"* lay 3km south-west. What Telford called *"two very decent inns"* were open at Helmsdale in 1828. A distillery of 1825 worked only until 1840, and was dismantled; however, a post office was open by 1838.

**Railway, Coasting and Tourists**: The Duke of Sutherland's Railway eventually reached a temporary terminus at Helmsdale in 1870, soon being extended up the strath by the Highland Railway (HR) subsidiary the Sutherland & Caithness Railway, to reach Wick and Thurso in 1874. Murray called Helmsdale *"a busy fishing village"* in 1894, the year when a golf club was founded which laid out a 9-hole moorland course. Catches declined, but about a dozen boats continued to fish up to the 1920s. Between 1932 and 1947 George Couper & Co of Helmsdale operated three coasters – *Berriedale, Helmsdale, Navidale* – in the east coast coal trade. In 1946 Wordie & Co had a rail to road cartage depot, and steam locomotives were still based in Helmsdale's HR timber engine shed up to at least 1952; but by 1965 the shed had closed. A youth hostel had been opened by 1969, but Helmsdale's chemist, cinema, maternity unit and dental surgery had all closed by 1981, leaving only basic village and tourist facilities.

**Fish Processing**: A branch of a Thurso lobster merchant was open when the writer first visited Helmsdale in 1978, when Wick registered fishing boats used the harbour, and the station was tidily kept. Besides the old *Bridge Hotel* there were two pubs, a bank, post office, police station and a small range of shops and services. Golf and tennis clubs served the 875 local people; a couple of local boats still landed white fish and shellfish for the processing plant. By 1985 a caravan site and information office were open.

**Spanning Time and the Atlantic**: Creation of the Timespan Heritage Centre was begun in 1982 by local endeavour in a ruined cooperage. Opened in 1987, this historical exhibition was extended in 1989. In 1993 it employed 8 people, drew 18,000 visitors and planned to build a replica of an Iron Age broch. In 1991 Helmsdale had 828 residents. Meantime by 1989 the secondary school had closed. In 1992 Julia Wigan, wife of the Kildonan estate owner and author Michael Wigan, started Scotia Products to make tartan-covered hair accessories, soon employing 9 outworkers and supplying the Epcot Centre at Orlando! Three very controversial wind farms were refused on landscape grounds in 1996. There has been little new development; the station is still open for passengers, though its attractive building is disused; the youth hostel is seasonal. To the west Strath Ullie still bears the traditional sheep, birch woods and heather. Small boats still frequent the harbour, where 16 prawn-fishing boats were based in 2000. The *Navidale House Hotel* – a former shooting lodge – has 16 rooms, and the traditional *Belgrave Arms* is also open, but the inability to fill the local doctor's job in 2001 may mean having to share Brora's facilities.

## HERIOT

**Map 3, A3**

***Borders village,*** *pop. 300 (area)* OS 66 or 73: NT 4054

Ancient hill forts stand above the deep valley of the Heriot Water, the main headwater of the Gala Water, which rises over 400m above the sea on Heriot Moor. Timothy Pont's map of Lothian named a dozen or so farms which were to survive indefinitely; Heriot parish was in Midlothian until 1975. The Roy map of about 1754 showed a road from Edinburgh via Arniston surmounting the steep Wull Muir to cross the watershed west of Raeshaw, on the way to Innerleithen via Dewar Gill; later this route lost its importance to a new road via Falahill, passing the 16th century Crookston Tower. The Edinburgh & Hawick Railway was opened in 1849 via Falahill, later becoming a through route to Carlisle; Heriot station lay beside the new main road, 2 km south of the summit and nearly 260m above sea level. By 1901 it was adjoined by a post and telegraph office, and scattered activities included a mill; but no village of Heriot existed. By 1951 some development near the station had pulled together the facilities of a small village, the area's 400 people even enjoying such services as doctor, dentist and vet; but both the latter vanished, and the station – which until then had three trains each way per day – was closed with the whole of the Borders railway system in 1969. The population of Heriot parish shrank to only 222 in 1971, but was back to 304 by 1991; the primary school and post office are still open.

## HILLINGTON

**Map 15, B5**

***Renfrewshire industrial area*** OS 64: NS 5165

Hillington lies on low ground about 3km east of Paisley, a well-settled area on Pont's map of Renfrewshire, sketched about 1600; Gordon added to this map a winding though definite *'Way'* between Glasgow and Paisley, passing through Hillington. By the time of Roy's survey of about 1754 a straighter road rather than a track ran in this direction, and turnpiking this road in the late 18th century improved matters. From 1840 the dead straight Glasgow & Paisley Joint Railway traversed the area, but no station was opened, for in 1895 it was still open country. In 1903 the joint Caledonian and Glasgow & South Western Railways built a winding branch line between Cardonald, Deanside and Renfrew Porterfield, which was connected in 1916 to the Paisley & Renfrew line at Renfrew South; passenger trains on this line lasted only until the General Strike of 1926. Some housing was built from about 1919 in the areas of Gladsmuir Road, south of the main railway, and Earl Haig Road to the north.

**The Industrial Estate: Aero Engines dominate**: The large Hillington Industrial Estate was established west of Earl Haig Road in 1937 under the Special Areas Acts, primarily to relieve unemployment in the Govan shipyards and Paisley. By the end of 1938 it contained 75 businesses and provided over 1000 jobs, including those at Watson's whisky blenders and an industrial gases works. The Penilee council housing estate south of the railway dates from 1938–40. In 1939 a major shadow factory was opened at Hillington for Rolls-Royce (R-R) of Derby, aiming to employ 15,000 people to build 100 Merlin aero engines a week. Soon 26,000 people worked there, arriving at its own bus station or travelling through the new Hillington West station (there was also Hillington East, near Cardonald); but jobs had been cut back to 15,000 by 1945. A World War II development was the major rail-served transit depot at Deanside beside the branch railway, built by the Canadian Air Force.

**Rolls-Royce and Deanside Saved – but No Trams**: In 1945 only a change of R-R chairman, and the passionate pleadings of its general manager, Edinburgh man William Miller, prevented closure of the Hillington works – by enabling his plan to overhaul Merlin engines to be put into practice; by 1947 4200 jobs had been saved. Around 1950, R-R branch factories were opened at Blantyre, Cardonald, East Kilbride and Larkhall. Around 1960, trams ran to both Paisley and Glasgow. After the war Deanside became the property of the Clyde Navigation Trust, and later the Clyde Port Authority; but freight trains between there and Renfrew were withdrawn in 1964, and by the late 1970s it was little used. Hillington had acquired a training centre by 1971. Meantime the original railway was electrified in 1967, its stations all retained. Scottish Precision Castings made non-ferrous castings for various industries, employing some 60 to 70 people before closing about 1970. By 1977 foam packaging was made by the German firm Kay-Metzeler, and the R-R engine plant still had 6000 workers; but this number was falling. Prestcold had developed a large refrigerator plant, but this closed about 1980 with the loss of 900 jobs. Deanside depot was sold about 1982 to John G Russell Ltd of Gartcosh, who developed it as a rail-road interchange with some half million tonnes of rail traffic a year in the 1990s; much of this was whisky, plus some timber.

**Disposing of Hillington and Fouling up the Census**: In 1990 under the controversial Thatcher policy of selling off most national assets to the highest bidder, the Scottish Development Agency disposed of the huge Hillington estate and 60 other industrial sites to a new company known as Caledonian Land (CL) formed by the London & Edinburgh Trust, which thus became Scotland's largest industrial landlord; a majority share in CL was immediately acquired by the Scandinavian Trygg Hansa insurance group. By that time there were 280,000m$^2$ of floorspace on the Hillington estate, and some 8000 workers in countless firms. The 1991 Census data for the whole of Great Britain was collated and computer processed at Hillington; sadly its accuracy was compromised by the effects of public resistance to the Poll Tax.

**Golf Clubs and Remote Monitoring**: John Letters Ltd, founded in 1919 and long making golf clubs at Hillington, and long belonging to Dunlop, was bought out in 1991 which led to expansion downmarket; in 1994 it successfully exported to Japan. Malaysian-born Raj Samuels' electronic design firm Elm developed a device to monitor bacteria, adopted by Marks & Spencer for their freezer cabinets. The firm's Genus system now electronically monitors temperatures in freezing cabinets in over 200 supermarkets, and over 100 are employed. By 1994 the RAF's 602 Squadron Museum had been opened near Hillington West.

**Fan Blades, Copiers – but Toilets nearly Down the Pan**: In 1989 the R-R plant employed only some 2750 people, making blades and other components for turbofan aero engines; it was then hit by a protracted strike. About 1991 the combined employment generated by R-R at Hillington and East Kilbride was 5000, but 750 jobs were cut from the Hillington compressor fan blade factory in 1992–93, leaving just 1500 people in 1995; another 150 jobs were cut in 2000 (although a big new contract won in 2001 was good news). In 1992 Rank Xerox moved from Govan to open its newly-built Scottish HQ on the estate, whose firms were also hoping to gain a supermarket, hotel and other facilities. Barrhead Sanitaryware, formed by workers made redundant when Shanks of Barrhead was closed, opened a new factory at Hillington in 1993, employing 65 people; it was already in financial trouble in 1994 but was saved from closure by worker-owned Baxi, the gas-fire makers. IKEA's 1995 plan for a 300-worker furniture store at Hillington failed to win approval, on traffic grounds – but did get built in 2001. Major firms now are McAlpine (plumbing manufacturers), Wartsila (marine engineers), and family-run Reid's (furniture makers). And entrepreneur Chris Gorman is opening a 60-unit 'incubation' building for new enterprises.

## HILLSIDE

**Map 6, C2**

***N. Angus village**, pop. 1200*

OS 45: NO 7061

The River North Esk, forming the boundary between Angus and the Mearns, enters the North Sea about 4km north of Montrose. Morphie, on the north bank, has a standing stone, and both there, and at Kinnaber just across the river in Angus, there were thanages from about the 11th century. In 1591 there was a water mill at Kinnaber. The House of Dun, 5km to the west, was designed by William Adam and built in 1730 for David Erskine, Lord Dun. Nearby was the Mill of Dun, a corn mill. In the 1750s the coastal road depended on Kinnaber ferry, and the Roy map showed no other appreciable settlement in the area. In 1770–75 what Heron called *"a handsome bridge of seven arches"* was erected across the North Esk to designs by John Adam, John Smeaton and Andrew Barrie; John Hume describes this as *"one of the noblest bridges in Scotland"*.

**Charleton, Bricks and Bleaching**: Charleton House, some 1.5km south of the bridge, was built about 1810; the Dryleys brick and tile works was established in 1816, 1km farther west. From 1838 to 1856 pottery was also made there, and by 1860 it employed over 60 men. Hillside just north of Dryleys appeared in the record when its post office was opened in 1839, and by 1865 was a significant village. By 1864 Aberdein, Gordon & Co of Montrose had abandoned their Craigo *(q.v.)* bleachfield and built a steam-powered bleachworks west of the bridge at Sunnyside, employing 50 people and annually producing 800 tonnes of bleached yarn. In 1885 the brickworks was bought by the Seaton Brickworks of Aberdeen, who closed it about 1890. The Mill of Dun was last used in 1903.

**Dubton Junction: the End of the Line?**: Meantime in 1848 the Aberdeen Railway, extending north-eastwards from Guthrie, reached a junction station at Dubton south of Hillside, where it turned south-east to terminate at Montrose. From Dubton the main line was to swing round a hill spur to proceed northwards beside the River North Esk, but the opening to Aberdeen was delayed for a few months in 1848, during which time Dubton was the northernmost station of the British railway system. Another branch from the main line at Bridge of Dun, 4km west of Dubton, terminated at Brechin. In 1856 and 1866 all these lines became in turn part of the Scottish North Eastern and the Caledonian (CR). Meantime in 1865 a local railway linking Inverbervie with Montrose was opened, with a fine 10-arched stone viaduct across the North Esk, north of which was placed North Water Bridge station.

**Railway Races, Waterworks and Asylum**: In 1881 the North British Railway (NBR) completed a coastal line from Arbroath through Montrose, crossing over the CR branch near the brickworks to join the existing CR Aberdeen main line at Kinnaber Junction, north-east of a new Hillside station. After the opening of the Forth Bridge in 1890 this enabled Kinnaber to find a unique place in railway history, as the point where in 1895 the racing trains of the east and west coast routes converged; but good sense prevailed, and this hazardous rail racing soon ceased. Charleton House was remodelled in 1892 by the Carnegies. By then the Kinnaber Waterworks shared the old mill lade, and what was described in 1894 as *"the Sunnyside Lunatic Asylum, one of the largest and best in Scotland"* had been built on the hill spur beside Kinnaber Junction to replace the Montrose Lunatic Hospital. As a result Hillside village had developed considerably, with an inn by 1894. In 1901 the census population of the landward part of Montrose parish was 1600 – most would have been in Hillside.

**A Distillery – by Any Name?**: In 1897 the bleach works (Hume & Moss state a flax-spinning mill) was replaced by the *Highland Esk* malt whisky distillery, from 1899 known as the *North Esk*, but reduced to a mere maltings in 1919. It was reopened as the *Montrose* – a grain distillery – in 1938. When again converted back to Highland malt production in 1965 the distillery was renamed the *Hillside*, and in 1968–73 maltings were added. In 1980 it received its fifth name, *Glenesk*, only to close in 1985!

**Redundant Mansions re-used but Railways cut**: Meantime in 1923 Hillside station had just two daily trains to Montrose; it had closed by 1953. By 1954 the *House of Dun* was a 15-roomed hotel and by 1955 Charleton House had become the Angus Maternity Hospital. By then over 1800 people lived in the area, but in 1952 the passenger trains between Brechin, Dubton and Montrose were withdrawn, and Dubton station too was closed; in 1967 the original main line through Strathmore was closed completely, and all Aberdeen services were diverted through Montrose. Meanwhile the Inverbervie line was closed in 1966, though the viaduct remained.

**Hillside turns to Tourism**: By 1981 – despite the North Sea oil developments in Montrose – only 1400 people lived in the Hillside area, of whom some 400 were inmates of what was by that time called the *Royal Sunnyside Hospital*. The *House of Dun Hotel* was acquired by the National Trust for Scotland (NTS) in 1985; it was finely restored as a mansion, and opened to the public around 1990. The NTS also restored Dun Mill as a house in 1995. Meantime the Angus Maternity Hospital was fire damaged in 1986 while being converted into a hotel; in 1993 it stood derelict and ruinous. However, in 1992 Bridge of Dun station and the railway to Brechin *(q.v.)* were reopened for weekend tourists by a preservation society. By 1991 the hospital was being run down and had only 200 inmates; Hillside contained only some 835 private residents. US Navy communications facilities at Kinnaber which employed some 20 Scottish workers were closed in 1993. In 2000 it was intended to use the restored viaduct of the former Inverbervie railway to carry a cycle path; the great Adam road bridge is still in full use.

## HILLSWICK, Heylor & Urafirth

**Map 14, B2**

***Shetland village & hamlets**, pop. 500*

OS 3: HU 2877

Situated on a windy isthmus in the north-western lobe of the Shetland Mainland known as Northmavine, Hillswick has a fairly well-sheltered harbour known as Ura Firth. The ancient Kirk of St Ola, which has a circular graveyard, and a number of small settlements were shown on Pont's sketch-maps made about 1592. Hillswick was developed in the 18th century by Thomas Gifford, the laird of Busta, as a fishing centre; its post office was open by 1843. Steamers called at this *"pleasant village"* in the 1880s, before roads reached the area. The St Magnus Hotel, open by the late 19th century, was for many years owned by the North of Scotland Steamship Company, making Hillswick *"for long a leading tourist centre"* (Donaldson); package tours to Hillswick were pioneers of this type of holiday.

**Norse Whalers and Secondary Classes come and go**: Although there was no proper pier, Hillswick was still regarded in the early 20th century as a fishing centre. Heylor, 5 km to the north on the sheltered fjord of Ronas Voe, was a Norwegian whaling station from 1903 to 1928, with a stone pier at Skeo Head. Esha Ness lighthouse, 8 km west of Hillswick, was first lit as late as 1929, and automated early, in 1974. Hillswick itself had a tiny population, fluctuating around 100 people; yet in 1951 its small-village facilities served about 900 people scattered over a 10-km radius. The Heylor junior secondary school, 2 km east of the village at Urafirth, had 50 pupils; but although from 1962 Hillswick had been a rural planning *'holding point'*, the secondary classes had gone by 1976. A caravan site was open by 1973.

**Lighthouses, Fish and Oil**: An automatic lighthouse was first lit in 1979 on the Ve Skerries some 25 km south-west of Hillswick, to guide west-about tankers using the Sullom Voe oil terminal. By 1973 the Northmavine Fish Processing Company had built a new pier and factory at Heylor, where cod, haddock and whiting were frozen. In the 1980s one full-time trawler was based there, and others landed catches; but Heylor had a population of about a hundred, as elderly as its small croft houses, and when visited in 1987, rotting derelict vehicles gave an air of neglect. Hillswick too had evidently become a backwater, serving only 500 people and rather run down. However, it had striking coastal views, boasted Shetland's oldest pub, and the old timber-built hotel with its unexpected 33 rooms was being improved. The effects of the oil development at Sullom Voe – almost 30 km away by road – were pervasive, for a new telephone exchange and about 25 new houses had been built there, plus another 16 to 20 houses at Urafirth where there was a tiny knitwear shop. By 1994 a new primary school had been built between Hillswick and Urafirth, replacing smaller schools.

## HODDOM

**Map 2, C4**

***Dumfriesshire location,*** *pop. 100* — OS 85: NY 1573

Hoddom, near the River Annan, 4 km west of Ecclefechan, was the site of a stone chapel, built about 575 AD by St Mungo of Glasgow fame; by about 800 there was a large religious community covering about 8 ha. In the 14th century a *'hospital'* was founded at Trailtrow just to the south. Pont's map made around 1610 showed the Kirk of Hoddom and *'Hoddom Toun'*, upstream of which an emparked tower oddly styled *'Duke of Hoddoms'* faced the 16th century Hoddom Castle across the river. Its hilltop neighbour the Repentance Tower is of similar age. Hoddom Castle was extended in 1826 by William Burn for General Matthew Sharpe, and again in 1891. By 1958 a primary school at Trailtrow served the area, but soon closed. Part of the castle was demolished in the 1960s, but by 1978 its own 9-hole golf course had been laid out, and the ruined tower remained in the centre of a vast caravan park. A big scheme of the late 1980s to build a 254-room hotel and 600 houses at Hoddom Castle, dangling the carrot of 500 jobs, was bankrupt in 1991; then in 1993 the Dutch firm Sun-Parks planned a holiday complex to employ 250 people, but this too fell in the recession. A victim of the greedy modern world was the monastic site at Hoddom, *'dug'* by archaeologists in 1991 because commercial quarrying interests – which could have opted to win rock elsewhere in the largely empty spaces of south-west Scotland – were sadly allowed to destroy this historic site. Since the bigger schemes failed, the Hoddom caravan park has been reopened.

## HOLLYBUSH & Skeldon

**Map 1, C2**

***Ayrshire hamlets,*** *pop. 275* — OS 70: NS 3914

Skeldon lies on the north bank of the River Doon, 3 km east of Dalrymple and 10 km south-east of Ayr; it once had a castle. The area was already thickly settled when mapped by Pont around 1600; the Skeldon mills already existed. By the time that Roy surveyed Scotland in the 1750s, roads from Ayr and Dalrymple to Dalmellington joined at Hollybush, 1 km to the east, and close by was built Hollybush House. A Glasgow & South Western Railway branch reached a station at Hollybush from Ayr in 1856, also on its way to Dalmellington. In 1869 Skeldon Mill's 60 or so workers made blankets and plaidings, and they continued to make woollens, though no village as such appeared nearby. By 1951 the *Hollybush House Hotel* was open, its 28 rooms soon being cut to 10, though it gained three stars. By then some 270 people lived locally, served by a primary school, post office and garage. The rail passenger service was withdrawn in 1964, but the population grew to 300 by 1971 before falling back rapidly; the school and post office vanished before 1981. The hotel closed in the early 1980s, becoming a nursing home; however, Skeldon Mills and a nearby caravan site are still open.

## HOLM (St Mary's)

**Map 13, B3**

***Village, Orkney,*** *pop. 625 (area)* — OS 6: HY 4701

Ten kilometres south of Kirkwall in a very fertile part of the Orkney Mainland is the Bay of Ayre, where an ancient broch stands beside a pool; 2 km to the east is a prehistoric *'Burnt Mound'*. Pont's map (made about 1592) showed *'Cleat'* (Clett) in a well-settled parish, named as *'Hoom'*, reflecting its pronunciation. A fine 17th century *'rent house'* by the harbour shows that by then much grain was grown locally. Although most people lived on the closely spaced small farms, by 1895 St Mary's, which lies on the Bay of Ayre, was named in the Times Atlas. St Mary's post office was open by 1898, and a stone pier was built. The Scots patriot Florence Marian McNeill, born at Holm in 1885, collected traditional recipes in *'The Scots Kitchen'*, and folklore in *'The Silver Bough'*.

**Barriers and Italian Chapel**: The four Churchill Barriers, linking the Mainland near St Mary's with Burray and South Ronaldsay to keep German submarines out of Scapa Flow during the latter part of World War II, were largely constructed by 1200 Italian POWs. They lived in three camps, one being on the islet of Lamb Holm where a quarry was opened, linked with a concrete block casting yard by a 60 cm gauge railway system. In 1943–45 an artistic padre with help from other prisoners very finely decorated a pair of nissen huts as a Catholic chapel to serve the POWs; he returned to restore it in the 1960s.

**Yachting and Sea Angling**: By 1951 when the population of Holm parish was almost 700, including about 450 in the St Mary's area, there was a busy telephone exchange with 70 lines, and the Holm West primary school; but the parish population fell by 30% in 20 years, and Holm East school at Hurtiso soon closed. By about 1980 a doctor, a garage and a guest house were also available in St Mary's, a *"yachtsman's haven and attractive village"*. By then there was no commercial fishing, but St Mary's pier had become a sea angling centre and the population had stabilised. By 1997 the *Commodore Motel* had been built and a small maritime museum opened. There is also now a community centre and a builder; the famous Italian Chapel is still open, but little else remains at the site of the Lamb Holm complex save a fish farm base and a tiny airfield.

## HOLY ISLAND — Map 1, B2

***Small island off Arran*** — OS 69: NS 0630

The cave dwelling of the sixth century St Molas can still be seen on this mountainous and once wooded islet off the east coast of Arran. Monro noted in 1549 that one John, Lord of the Isles, had founded there a *"monastry of friars, which is decayit"*. Holy Island Inner lighthouse was lit from 1877, the outer or East light, a square tower on Pillar Rock, following in 1905. Both were eventually automated in 1977. The island was farmed until 1989. In 1991–92 a Buddhist community bought Holy Island as a retreat and nature reserve; they repaired the houses, built cells for 200 monks, and planted native trees, so completing the circle. By 1997 summer passenger ferries plied from Lamlash to the north end of the island's coastal footpath, and from Whiting Bay to the south end.

## HOLYTOWN & New Stevenston — Map 16, A4

***Lanarkshire urban area,** pop. 9000* — OS 64: NS 7659

By 1596 when a well-settled area some 6 km east of Bothwell was mapped by Timothy Pont, the South Calder Water had been bridged downstream of *'Caerfin'*. Nearby was *'Hole'*, probably literally a coal pit. Holytown, which by the 1750s was a tiny nuclear settlement on the main road between Glasgow and Edinburgh via Kirk of Shotts, may well have been so named for the innumerable tiny pits in its surroundings; there was already a *'coalhill'* well south of the village, which was still too small to be noticed by the assiduous Heron in 1799; however, its first post office opened in 1802. In 1834 the Wishaw & Coltness Railway – on the 4'6" (137 cm) *'Scotch'* gauge – was opened from Whifflet (Coatbridge) through the areas of shallow mining known as Carnbroe and Thankerton collieries (around Mossend) to New Stevenston colliery 1 km south-west of Holytown, to end at Carfin colliery. In 1842 Newarthill and Holytown merited a daily through coach to Glasgow. The line was later absorbed by the Caledonian and brought up to standard gauge.

**Railways, Mansion and Inns**: Local development had evidently proceeded quite far by the time a gasworks was established at Holytown in 1857. Holytown station at New Stevenston became the junction from which the Caledonian Railway branch to Shotts and Edinburgh was opened in 1869. In 1873 Wrangholm Hall near New Stevenston was built for A G Simpson, owner of a colliery and brickworks. In 1880, with the opening of the Wishaw loop to the south main line, the station was renamed *'Holytown Junction'*. Inns were open nearby, and at Holytown by 1895. By 1901 the population of the Holytown area, including Carfin, was nearing 6600.

**Prosperity and Facilities Elusive**: From 1935 Wrangholm Hall was used by the local education authority. Though the collieries had all closed by 1951, the population in the area was nearly 8000, for it was very accessible to Motherwell and Bellshill; but only the facilities of a typical village were available in Holytown, plus a Roman Catholic secondary school with 750 pupils, which – like the local cinema and hotel – later closed. Some housing development brought a slight increase in the population, and a new high school had been built by 1988. By 1991 Holytown's population was about 5800, plus 3115 in New Stevenston. The area was visually and functionally dominated by the nearby steelworks at Mossend and Ravenscraig until well after the latter closed in 1991–92. By 1996 the A723 had been diverted on to a bypass between Newarthill and Holytown. Wrangholm Hall, gutted by arson about the same time, was demolished. The local Taylor High School has around 850 pupils.

## HOLYWOOD, Newbridge & Terregles — Map 2, B4

***Dumfriesshire village & hamlets,** pop. 775* — OS 78 & 84: NX 9579

A stone circle stands beside the Cairn Water above its confluence with the River Nith, some 4 km north-west of Dumfries. The medieval church's aim of counteracting strong surviving pagan beliefs may have caused the circle to be given the name *'Twelve Apostles'*, and for the Premonstratensian abbey of Holywood to be founded nearby. Accounts of the abbey's beginnings vary; some give the founder as John Maxwell, Lord Kirkconnell and the date between 1121 and 1154; others credit the energetic and pious Lady Devorgilla Balliol and date it to the 13th century; Anthony New commented *"its history is thoroughly obscure"*! In the 14th century a *'hospital'* was also established. The abbey is now remembered in a farm name, and to the west and south of the river are medieval mottes, once lairds' strongholds.

**Bridge, Towers and Mills Aplenty**: Three tower houses were built in the 16th century: Cowhill beside the River Nith (4 km north of the *'Housbrigg'* which spanned the Cairn Water near *'Halywood Kirk'*), Isle Tower 1.5 km up-river, and Fourmerkland Tower 5 km to the west. In 1560 the Master of Terregles, another now vanished tower house 2 km south-west of the bridge, was a powerful noble. Pont's manuscript map made about 1610 showed *'Teregills'* as a kirk and an emparked tower. Near the bridge was another enclosure containing a towered building with an arch, probably the former abbey, which passed to Kirkpatrick of Closeburn in 1609, while the choir became the parish church. Cowhill Tower was given emphasis. West of the bridge was *'Holywood Mill'*, while opposite it along the south bank clustered the *'Mill of Cluden'* and possibly two other mills. The East Cluden mill in its final form before conversion to a house was illustrated by Hay & Stell (1986).

**Newbridge and the Railways**: Evidently a new bridge had replaced the old by about 1754, when Roy's map showed a road leading from Dumfries via Maxwelltown and Lincluden to *'New Bridge'* and Moniaive; from the bridge a track led north to Drumlanrig. A linen bleachfield was built at Terregles in the period 1746–60, and the mansion of Terregles House was built in 1788–89 near the old tower, itself demolished in 1830. The old parish church of Holywood had already been pulled down in 1778; its stone was re-used in building a new church. Holywood station some 2 km north of the bridge was provided on the main line of the Glasgow Dumfries & Carlisle Railway (soon Glasgow & South Western), opened in 1849, and surviving for 100 years, but the station was closed to passengers before 1953. Other scattered facilities provided in the area eventually amounted to those of a small village, but despite its accessibility and the continuance of milling into the 20th century, very little development followed. When the Cairn Valley Light Railway was laid in 1905 from a junction south of Holywood, only a goods station was provided; this remained open until 1952.

**Land Settlement, Vandalism and Urbanisation**: The government bought the Terregles estate in 1924 for division into smallholdings under their Land Settlement scheme, and a primary school was provided. The *Embassy Hotel* was open at Newbridge by 1954, but Terregles House was regrettably blown up in 1964. The area's scattered population of 450 in 1951 had gradually reduced over the years to about 350 in 1981, by which time it was well served by an additional hotel and three garages. However in recent years things have changed radically: small housing estates have been built, but these are tiny compared with the rapid advance of the urban area of Dumfries, right up to Newbridge Farm.

## HOPEMAN, Inverugie & Cummingstown

**Map 9, C3**

***Moray coast villages,*** *pop. 1460* — OS 28: NJ 1469

The ancient Camus's Stone stands on the rocky Moray coast east of Burghead. About 1 km inland are the scant undated remains of Inverugie Castle (not to be confused with that of the same name near Peterhead). Blaeu's map of 1654, based on Pont's and Gordon's work, lacked local placenames hereabouts other than *'Cammo'* and the farm of Burnside; a study of the Roy map implies that the area was still roadless about 1750. However, it seems that Inverugie Castle was soon rebuilt as a mansionhouse.

**Quarrying and New Villages**: The *Newtown of Hopeman* was neatly laid out on the coast in 1805–06 by Young of Inverugie, to house workers quarrying golden-coloured *'New Red'* Sandstone from Greenbrae pit, west of the village. From 1808 Cummingstown also came into existence, as a sprawl of cottages along the road between Hopeman and Burghead. In 1837 a harbour was built at Hopeman for Duff of Drummuir, to create a port for export of the stone and for use by fishermen from Ardersier east of Inverness, which had only an open beach. Hopeman had no post office until after 1838, and was never a burgh, but another quarry – Clashach – was opened on the coast 2 km east of the harbour. By 1855 there were 450 fishermen and five curing yards, and in the 1880s 120 fishing boats. In 1891 the population of Hopeman alone was 1464, but decline followed.

**Marginal Railway, Golf and Stone**: In 1892 the Highland Railway's Burghead branch was extended to terminate at Hopeman, which by 1894 – after two enlargements of the harbour – was regarded as primarily a fishing village. However, rail traffic was light; as early as 1904 the station built to serve the Cummingstown quarries was closed, and all passenger trains ended in 1931. In 1923 the Hopeman golf club was founded, and created a 9-hole cliff-top course (around 1960 this was extended to 18 holes). Though in 1951 about 1500 people lived in Hopeman and Cummingstown combined, local facilities were in general only those of a small village, with the *Station Hotel*. In 1946 Wordie & Co operated a small rail to road cartage depot. Rail freight lingered on until 1957, by which time the two quarries had produced stone used for facing Hydro Board power stations such as Fasnakyle on the River Beauly. Greenbrae quarry was still open in 1963.

**Absentee Fishermen**: Both quarries appear to have closed by 1980, together with the local authority secondary school; the population and other facilities remained much as in 1951. Eventually a caravan site was laid out beside the former station building, which survives. In 1983 Hopeman fishermen still owned over twenty boats, though they operated out of Lossiemouth. Hopeman harbour had partly silted up, and was largely used for pleasure boating (including by Gordonstoun school, which based its boats there); there was also a salmon-fishing station. The 1991 census showed 1460 residents. By 1994 an inn and a camping site were open. In the mid 1990s the Clashach quarry was reopened by Moray Stone Cutters to raise sandstone for building *(see also Elgin)*.

## HOUSTON, Hilpeter & Craigends

**Map 15, A5**

***Renfrewshire villages,*** *pop. 5500+* — OS 64: NS 4066

Hilpeter, located in a fertile lowland near the River and Castle of Gryfe some 8 km north-west of Paisley, was named after an early church dedicated to St Peter. Its modern name of Houston stems from a Norman knight, Hugo de Paduinan, who gained the barony from Malcolm IV; within 200 years Houston had acquired a market charter. A bridge spanned the burn through the village which appeared as a substantial settlement on Pont's map of about 1600. Nearby beside the Water of Gryfe were mills and a waulkmill, and to the east of the village stood the emparked 16th century mansionhouse of Houston, described as a *'palace'* in 1625. Houston became a burgh of barony in 1671, and the market cross was restored in 1713. By the time of the Roy map made about 1754, Houston was a linear village on a road linking the bridge of Johnstone with Port Glasgow.

**Banking, Weaving and Cotton Mills**: Robin Carrick, born in Houston in 1737, became the Manager of the important Ship Bank in Glasgow in 1775 and held the post till 1821. Meantime in 1781–82 Houston was enlarged by its eponymous proprietor, who encouraged the development of weaving. Soon afterwards a cotton mill was built on a tributary of the Gryfe, and Crosslee mill was established 1 km farther south on the river itself; both mills opened in 1793. By 1797 two annual fairs were scheduled, and Heron referred in 1799 to *"the villages of Houston and Hill-Peter"*. A post office opened at Houston around 1825. William Arrol the master bridge-builder *(see Bridgeton)* was born in Houston in 1839. A mansion called Craigends House was designed by David Bryce in baronial style for Alex Cunninghame, a noted iron- and coal-master, and built south of the village in 1857. By 1895 there was a bleachworks and an inn. Despite optimistic station names, no railway ever actually came nearer than 2 km to the villages of Houston and Crosslee, and they failed to grow beyond a hamlet's level of facilities.

**Fuse Factory Architecture better than Planning?**: The cotton mill was demolished and replaced in 1916 by a remarkable reinforced-concrete factory for spinning cordite fuses. New

Town proposals were made in the Clyde Valley Plan of the 1940s, but were not adopted, the population in 1971 remaining at only 650. Craigends House was partly demolished in 1967 by Taylor Woodrow, and dormitory growth then started in earnest. The new Gryffe High School opened in 1980 (and received a design award) but the fuse factory was demolished in 1986. The Craigends development, exploiting the former parkland setting of existing woodland belts south of the River Gryfe, was soon among the largest private housing estates in the west of Scotland, rather too close to the ever-spreading outer urban sprawl of the Clydeside conurbation, and quite distinct from Houston village. By 1991 almost 5500 people lived in this youthful and well-educated dormitory area; a high 82% of workers commuted by car. Some further housing development continued in the 1990s.

## HOWMORE & Grogarry

**Map 7, A3**

***South Uist townships,*** *pop. 300 (area)* OS 22: NF 7536

Midway along the sandy west coast of South Uist is a standing stone, near modern Stoneybridge *(in Gaelic Staoinebrig)*. About 4km to the north is Uist's most ancient medieval church, perhaps of seventh century origin. In Gaelic the adjoining clachan of Howmore is called *Tobha Mor*, meaning *'Big Rope'*, though *Tobar Mor ('Big Well')* would seem a more likely derivation. Its people turned Protestant at the Reformation, whereas the townships around Grogarry on the shore of Loch Druidibeag only 3km to the north remained Catholic, like most of South Uist. In 1879 a steamer pier was built on Loch Sgioport (Skipport), on the east coast about 6km from Grogarry on the island's new spine road; though linked by road, it completely failed to attract development, and became ruinous within a century.

**The Lady of the Isles**: By 1951 Grogarry had a 20-line telephone exchange; the erection on a nearby hillside in 1957 of a giant religious statue – carved in granite by Hew Lorimer – was all the more remarkable in a poor crofting community which was soon to lose its post office. The market stance marked on the 1956 OS map at Stoneybridge is little known. Grogarry had a guest house by 1981, and a caravan site was open for a few years around 1985; meantime the statue came to be overshadowed by Cold War installations. By 1996 Loch Druidibeag was a nature reserve. Tiny Howmore – which has one of Scotland's best groups of thatched houses – relies for schooling on Staoinebrig, but retains its post office; a newish youth hostel is open all year round.

## HOWWOOD

**Map 15, A5**

***Renfrewshire village,*** *pop. 1000* OS 63 (64): NS 3960

The 15th century keep of Elliston Castle was built beside the Black Cart Water about 9km west of Paisley. Pont's map made around 1600 showed the area thickly settled and the river bridged; but Howwood was not named. By about 1754 a road had been made between Paisley and Beith. The area was entirely rural until the Bowfield Bleachworks were founded in 1835 1km south of the castle. Howwood had a station on the Glasgow, Paisley Kilmarnock & Ayr Railway, opened in 1840 (later the Glasgow & South Western). The Bowfield and the Midtown (or Midtownfield) bleachworks, the latter a large enterprise 1km east of Howwood, were both at work in 1895, when Howwood had about 400 people, a post and telegraph office and an inn. By 1924 the castle was ruinous, but in 1951 Howwood had the facilities of a small village and a population of about 1250. The station was closed about 1960 and the Bowfield bleach works, were disused by the 1970s. In 1991 Howwood had 1035 people. At that time the major Johnstone bypass was being built, to take the heavy A737 traffic out of the village. New housing is being developed, and the belated opening of a new station with a car park in 2001 undid the damage of the 1960s. The *Bowfield Hotel and Country Club*, an extension of a converted textile mill, has 23 rooms and a range of leisure facilities.

## HOY & Linksness

**Map 13, B3**

***Island communities, Orkney,*** *pop. under 100* OS 7: HY 2403

The bleak and mountainous island of Hoy has stupendous sea cliffs which reach 340m at St John's Head; 2.5km to the south is the giant 450-foot tall sea stack known as the Old Man of Hoy, which seen from the north resembles an Easter Island statue. At the foot of a crag in what is now a vast nature reserve to the east is the prehistoric burial chamber known as the *Dwarfie Stane*, past which a road leads to the sandy bay beside depopulated Rackwick. Here the one-time school, closed by 1958, had by 1997 become a museum, adjoined by a Youth Hostel. Nearby is the home of the composer Peter Maxwell Davies. On the more sheltered shore of the small Bay of Quoys near Hoy's north tip stands an ancient broch; nearby is the small low-lying peninsula of Linksness, the long-standing location of Hoy post office and of a pier which for many years has been a terminal for passenger ferries to Stromness and Graemsay. By 1974 an outdoor centre was the other main feature near Linksness. By 1982 it had been replaced by another Youth Hostel, and by 1997 a pub had been opened nearby. *(For the main centres of the island see Longhope.)*

## HUMBIE

**Map 3, A2**

***Small E. Lothian village,*** *pop. 375* OS 66: NT 4562

Humbie's ancient church – centre of a wide parish – stood about 12 km south-west of Haddington, near the meeting of the Humbie and Keith Waters. In the 16th century the L-plan tower of Keith Marischal was built nearby. It figured largely on Pont's map of Lothian (1612), when the areas to south and east were well wooded and *'Humby'* was shown by a tiny symbol. Johnstounburn House was built in the 17th century. By about 1754 as the Roy map showed, Humbie Mill stood at the elbow of a road leading north-west and north-east. By 1901 the road system had been completed and a new church built; there was a Boys' Home at Highlee and a post and telegraph office at Upper Keith, which later became the village centre. Johnstounburn House stood in large grounds 1 km to the south. *'Humbie'* station on the light railway to Gifford was at Gilchriston (very remote, and open only from 1901 to 1933). The parish population in 1951 was 490, served by basic facilities, plus the 10-room *Johnstounburn House Hotel*. By 1963 the Boys' Home had been replaced by the Children's Village, a Christian foundation for youngsters with learning difficulties. This was still open in 1995, but had controversial management problems. The parish population in 1991 was 376. The post office closed in the late 1990s, but the *Johnstounburn House Hotel* has expanded. A sawmill and fencing operation at Windymains employs 25, and the small Pride of Lammermuir rug-makers have their own flock of Wensleydale sheep.

## HUME

**Map 3, B3**

***Borders hamlet***, *pop. 200*

OS 74: NT 7041

The rocky Sweethope Hill and nearby Hareheugh Craigs about 7km north of modern Kelso hold two Iron Age forts and a medieval settlement, while atop a prominent knoll 2 km north-east of Hareheugh was the 13th century Hume Castle. As described by Chambers, *"in 1560 Hume was the seat of the ancient and powerful family whose name it bears or rather conferred, the leading family of the Merse"*. Hume's castle-town nature led to its being a conspicuous feature on old maps of Berwickshire, including Pont's map of about 1600. This showed *'Hoome' Castle* and *Kirk, 'Hoometoune'* and also *'Hoomebyres'*. A parish school was founded in 1612. The castle was captured by Cromwell in 1651, and ruined. The Earls of Home retired to The Hirsel by Kelso, yet the Roy map – surveyed about 1754 – showed five roads radiating from the castle: one led to Kelso, another continued as a track to Duns but the others petered out within about 5km. Almost surrounding the castle was a sprawling cluster of the tiny red dots conventionally used throughout by Roy's artistic draughtsman Paul Sandby to represent the clachans and huts of the rural poor; a castle town that had fallen on evil days.

**Rural Backwater**: In 1826 Chambers confirmed this, noting *"The village of Hume was once much more extensive than now, inhabited by the numerous retainers of the Earl of Home"*. He added that in 1794 in a bogus restoration of the ancient castle enclosure *"the late Earl of Marchmont raised the walls from the ruins"*. The subsequent story of Hume was one of retrenchment. It was never served by rail, or industrialised apart from a small quarry; the parish school was closed around 1960, and by 1976 the post office and buses had gone. Only a one-sided hamlet remained by 1981 when the population in the area had shrunk to under 200 and, when last seen by the author, peaceful Hume looked a place interested only in agriculture. But the area's peace was threatened in 1992 by a farmer's controversial plans to work a third of Hareheugh Craigs for 150,000 tonnes of roadstone a year, hopefully while avoiding its historic features.

## HUNTLY & Strathbogie

**Map 10, B2**

***Aberdeenshire town***, *pop. 4200*

OS 29: NJ 5340

By the 12th century a tower near the confluence of the Aberdeenshire Rivers Bogie and Deveron was known as the Peel of Strathbogie. About 1452 Alexander Gordon, the first Earl of Huntly, built beside it his baronial seat, Strathbogie Castle. The small town of Huntley was chartered as a burgh of barony in 1488; it was long called *Milton of Strathbogie*, but was also known as *Tirrisoule*. The Earls became the heritable Sheriffs in 1509 and dominated much of the north of Scotland from Strathbogie, which was renamed *Huntly Castle* in 1544; in 1560 Lord Gordon had a seat in Parliament.

**From Castle to Mansion and Ruin**: Huntly Castle was blown up in 1594, but was rebuilt into a mansion by the fourth Earl in 1602; by 1613 there was a local school. When Blaeu's map was prepared about 1642, the baronial House of Lessendrum stood on a spur 5km north-east of Huntly; it showed the Deveron bridged at the castle, probably by the ancient stone arch still used by pedestrians today, and *'Strathbogie'* south of the bridge was a larger place than most. A post office was open by 1715. Repeated changes in the fortunes of the Catholic Gordon family led to Huntly being a focus of military road building around 1720, and once they became Dukes of Gordon in the 18th century *(see Fochabers)* they left the castle and had it quarried to build Huntly Lodge, leaving an impressive ruin.

**Early Linen Industries and Replanning**: Despite the troubles, textiles began in the 17,230s and 40s, with a linen works and two bleachfields, and the town had at least two yarn merchants by 1748. By the time of Roy's survey of about 1750 Strathbogie was a small nucleated settlement with a road or track from Inverurie via a bridge over the River Bogie, and tracks south to Alford, south-west to Glenbuchat and north-west to Keith. When pleasingly re-planned in 1769 for the laird the Duke of Gordon, the town name became Huntly; farming improvements made it an important market centre, and linen manufacture still prospered in 1792. Huntly was a post town with three posts a week by 1797, when three annual fairs were held. The Aberdeen Banking Company had a local branch around that time. In 1799 Heron noted *"the village or town of Huntly, which contains about 3000 inhabitants. This town has a weekly market, and some manufactures of linen and cotton"*. By then the River Bogie had also been bridged.

**Transport and Schooling improved, but Distilling fails**: By 1809 a coach ran to Aberdeen one day, returning the next. From 1811, due to turnpike road completions, it could return on the same day, and Huntly was also served by the new through coach between Aberdeen and Inverness, crossing the new Fochabers bridge. But a Bank of Scotland branch open by about 1820 was soon closed, and the linen industry failed; by 1864 it was long gone. A distillery founded in 1824 below the Bogie bridge was an early casualty, working only until 1860 (although the buildings survived as late as 1955). The Gordon secondary schools were founded in 1839, the building being completed in 1851. The Great North of Scotland Railway (GNSR) opened its main line from Aberdeen to Huntly in 1854, extending it to Keith in 1858 to link with Inverness via the Highland Railway. Huntly station became the railhead for a wide area in 1869 when Wordie & Co opened a rail to road cartage depot for the GNSR.

**Good Hotels, Golf, Gloves, Furrows and Flying**: A local newspaper, the *Huntly Express*, first appeared in 1863. By 1881 the population was 3500. In the 1890s a large clock tower was built overlooking the town square; at some date Huntly also acquired a gasworks. Murray noted two *"good"* hotels in 1894, the *Gordon Arms* and *Strathbogie*. Around that period the long-lasting Huntly firm of Sellar made fine horse-drawn ploughs from steel. Huntly golf club, founded in 1900, laid out a 9-hole parkland course. The population peaked at 4100 in 1901, then slowly falling. By 1903 William Spence & Co were making gloves and hosiery for the home market, and in 1910 Huntly people watched the flight of Scotland's first manned powered aeroplane.

**Centralisation and Shortbread**: After the carnage of 1914–18, Huntly's population bottomed out at 3750 in 1921. Lessendrum House, which had been enlarged in 1840, sadly burnt out in 1925 leaving another major ruin. By 1951 Huntly had the facilities of a good local centre; junior secondary classes were also held at Drumblade and Ythanwells, respectively 5km and 10km east of Huntly, but by 1976 these had been centralised in the Gordon Schools. Some time after 1953 the golf course was extended to 18 holes, but by 1971 the population had shrunk to under 3800. In 1975 Helen Dean started to sell home-baked shortbread in aid of Huntly Pipe Band; by 1991, as commercial bakers, Dean's of Huntly employed over 50 people and exported *"high quality shortbread"*. A bypass built in the late 1970s removed A96 through traffic from this most attractive town.

**Jobs Crises**: Huntly livestock market was active in 1980; but about then the cinema closed, and was derelict when the author first visited Huntly in 1986. It still had a reasonable range of small specialist shops, a hospital, covered swimming pool and other tourist amenities. By then R B Farquhar Ltd were the substantial manufacturers of portable buildings, there was a medium-sized Jaeger knitwear factory, and a number of depots. The distillery engineers Alexander Dey Ltd also made food processing plant, until they called in the receiver in 1990 and their 30 jobs were put at risk. A further jobs crisis hit Huntly in 1990 when long-established William Spence knitwear, its second largest employer, paid off 170 staff. To counter the industrial decline through tourism, a dry ski slope was built in 1991 when Huntly's population was 4183.

**Football Fame, Beer, Caravans and Timber Trains**: Remarkably, tiny Huntly FC were the 1993–94 champions of the Highland League, ahead of both Inverness Caledonian and Ross County: but it was those teams not Huntly who were then promoted to the enlarged Scottish League. In 1994 the Borve Brewhouse brewed Borve Ale at Huntly, and a new caravan park was laid out at Huntly Castle. In 1995 a single 5-doctor practice covered the area's health needs, the *Huntly Express* was still published, and Dean's still baked quantities of shortbread. In 1996 Huntly's prominent and very lovingly maintained old pendulum clock still kept time to an accuracy of nearly one in a million! The auction mart was busy with cattle and sheep, and Sellar's still dealt in combine harvesters and farm machinery locally (and in four other places). By then a daily timber train was run from Inverness to Shotton, calling to pick up more at Huntly, where a new station building was completed in 2000 with the aid of re-used materials. The *Gordon Arms Hotel* still provides service.

## HURLFORD

**Map 1, C1**

***Suburb, e. of Kilmarnock,*** *pop. 5400* — OS 70: NS 4536

Evidently taking its name from a ford across the River Irvine 3 km south-east of Kilmarnock, *'Whyrlfurd'* was a tiny place when Pont mapped Kyle about 1600, and the river was still unbridged. Roy's survey made about 1754 showed the Kilmarnock to Mauchline road passing that way, but Hurlford was still tiny. Its first post office had to await the penny post of 1840, and it was never a burgh; but when the river was at length bridged, the hamlet of Crookedholm on the north bank became effectively part of Hurlford. Growth seems to have begun with the Portland Iron Smelting Works, established in 1846. Hurlford station, on the new main line of the Glasgow & South Western Railway (G&SWR), which opened in 1848, became a junction in 1850 with the opening of the Galston branch. Various coal pits were sunk, and *Faience* (glazed coloured earthenware) was later made on a large scale from local fireclay. The Blair foundry opened in 1864 and the Vulcan foundry – large among many named after the Roman god of fire and metalworking, but casting such mundane items as manhole covers – was begun about 1890.

*An unfinished base for a propellor mould at the Blair foundry, Hurlford, which opened in 1864 and finally closed in the 1980s. The firm made cast-iron propellors, used on tugs and as spares for large merchant ships.* *(JRH)*

**Top Shed, Explosives and Whisky**: In 1877 the G&SWR closed Kilmarnock engine shed when it opened a new central locomotive depot at Hurlford, with facilities to service about a hundred steam locomotives. An inn was open by the 1890s, when four or more collieries were open nearby; one was the Portland Colliery Company's Kirkstyle pit, where five men died in an explosion in 1925. Meantime 92 locomotives were based at Hurlford in 1913, more than at any other of the company's depots. Under the LMS Railway a second station, known as Barleith, was provided south of the town on the Darvel branch; by 1953 this had replaced the original station for passengers. World War II saw the building of a munitions factory at Bowhouse near Haining Mains, 2 km south-east of the village. By 1951 the population of Hurlford exceeded 5000. Though in general having average village facilities, two hospitals were open in the area by 1953, and a Johnny Walker whisky blending and bottling plant had been built.

**Bowhouse from Bangs to Banging Up**: All the collieries had closed by 1954, and Hurlford ceased to be a railway junction when the Darvel branch and Barleith station closed in 1964. The engine shed was closed in 1966 with the end of steam in south-west Scotland. The secondary school had also closed by 1976. The Vulcan Foundry of R Simpson closed about 1981 and was soon demolished. The Blair Foundry, which specialised latterly in making cast-iron ships' propellors, also closed. Despite these various setbacks Hurlford was convenient to Kilmarnock; shirtmaking, fireclay products and ironfounding still largely dominated the local economy. Its 1991 population was 5400. Walker's premises are now a bottling plant. The Bowhouse munitions factory site (disused since 1972) was selected by the government in 1996 to accommodate the new privately financed and managed *'Kilmarnock'* prison, opened in 1999.

## INCHINNAN

**Map 15, B4**

***Renfrewshire village,*** *pop. 1800*

OS 64: NS 4769

The fifth century mother church of Strathgryffe *(see Bridge of Weir)* stood at Inchinnan, on the flat carselands 3 km north-west of Renfrew. By about 1163 it was held by the Knights Templars *(see Torphichen)*. There was once also a *'palace'* at Garnieland, shown as *'Inchinnan C(astle)'* on Pont's map of about 1600; this also showed the Bar mill, on the opposite bank of a tiny stream. A very early ferry plied to Dalmuir, and a parish school was opened in 1623, but the Roy map of about 1754 made nothing of Inchinnan. Two fine bridges were built across the Black and White Cart Waters in 1809–12 by Robertson Buchanan, but the palace had vanished by 1895 when – except for Inchinnan parish church and a Free Church – Inchinnan scarcely existed.

**Airships and Tyres come and go**: An airfield and aircraft factory was opened at Allans in 1916 by William Beardmore; the vast shed where the airships R24, R27, R34 and R36 were built from 1917 was illustrated by Hay & Stell. In 1919 the R34, whose design was based on a Zeppelin, made history by crossing the Atlantic both ways, but its home shed had been dismantled by 1923. In 1927 the other premises became the India motor tyre works, for which the striking art deco *'India of Inchinnan'* offices were built in 1929–30, just as the slump started. A village grew around the Free Church; by 1951 its minimal facilities served some 1500 people, but the factory was then extended and the population peaked at 2350 about 1971. An industrial estate was opened at Brownsfield about that time. By 1981 when the population was again below 2000 the tyre factory appears to have closed, being almost derelict by 1987 and soon largely demolished. By 1989 Inchinnan was on the edge of the new settlement of Erskine, its 1991 population of 1815 dominated by youngish well-educated people buying semi-detached houses. By 1996 the village itself had been expanded to reach the Clyde.

**Business Park Prostheses and Pies**: In 1990 the small firm of Vascutek of Inchinnan earned a Queen's Award for exporting implantable vascular prostheses. In 1992–93 Thomas Auld & Son of Greenock, bakers and makers of prepacked sandwiches, moved to a 270-job factory on the new Inchinnan Business Park, built next to Glasgow Airport by Renfrewshire Enterprise. By 1993 this held a new TSB data processing centre, the biomedical manufacturers Life Technologies (250 employees), a new factory for Apollo Blinds and Composite Panels, and 84 jobs in a newly opened 1600 m$^2$ factory making computer hardware connectors for US-owned Robinson Nugent. The Business Park was further expanded from 1995. Meantime work had begun early in 1994 on a major scheme, intended to create 16,000 jobs over 15 years, on a nearby area claimed to be as extensive as Glasgow city centre! The former tyre factory site was decontaminated in 1994, but its *'A'* listed office frontage building still stands derelict. Today, Inventec employ over 500 making and servicing laptop computers, and CTP Silleck employ 350 in plastic injection mouldings. Thomas Auld & Son are the champion makers of Scotch pies for 2001!

## INCHKEITH

**Map 6, B5**

***Small island, Firth of Forth***

OS 66: NT 2982

This originally fertile islet in the Firth of Forth shipping lanes, some 5 km south-east of Kinghorn, supported a seventh century religious community, and later a church infirmary. In 1010 King Malcolm II gave it to the Keiths, hence its present name; it became part of Fife. In the 1540s due to its strategic situation in the approaches to Leith, fortifications were erected in turn by the English attackers and the Scots' French allies. Later used as a prison and then as an isolation hospital, their domestic buildings were demolished to accommodate the lighthouse, first lit in 1804 when Britain was in conflict with the French! From 1825 Inchkeith was the venue for several Highland games, but was refortified in 1878–98 with three separate gun emplacements – this time the Germans were replacing the French as the foes! When not defensively manned the unbuilt portions of the isle have at times been farmed, but since the lighthouse was automated in 1986 it has been uninhabited, its extensive historical monuments being left inaccessible and neglected.

## INCHTURE

**Map 6, B3**

***Carse of Gowrie village,*** *pop. 800*

OS 53: NO 2828

Some 13 km west of Dundee in the fertile Carse of Gowrie is Inchture, which already had a parish school by 1613. Pont's map then showed three prominent 16th century towers: Moncur, near the Kirk of Inchture, Kinnaird, which stood emparked 4 km to the west, and some 2 km farther west Fingask. The farm shown as *'Mangillands'* by Pont, later unhappily known as *Maggotland*, eventually became Meggatland. Roy's map of about 1750 showed the track from Dundee to Perth looping round to the north of both the emparked Moncur Castle and the small linear village; when turnpiked, the road was rerouted through the village street. In the 1790s Inchture had a weekly corn-market, and although few linens were made locally there was an anomalous linen stamping office, which mainly served Lochee! A post office was opened in 1801. Heron noted in 1799 the *"neat village"* of Baledgarno *"lately erected by Lord Kinnaird"* some 1.5 km north of Inchture; little more than a hamlet, it was soon adjoined by Rossie Priory, a mansion built in 1807–15 by William Atkinson for the 8th Lord Kinnaird.

**Horsedrawn Tram and Sumptuous Mansion**: When the Dundee & Perth Railway came by in 1847 the station was placed 3 km from the village – too far! In an attempt to overcome this difficulty a 2 km long tramway was provided, opened in 1848 beside the road from the station, ending at Crossgates just west of the village. Horsedrawn trams plied on this line, and a siding received horse manure from Dundee streets. In the late 1850s Kinnaird Castle was rebuilt for the sixth Earl of Southesk to grandiose Scottish Baronial designs by Bryce, with thirty rooms and ten reception rooms. In Edwardian days it was still *"the most sumptuous mansion in Angus"*. The only other significant features of Edwardian Inchture were its post and telegraph office and school, though the *Inchture Hotel* was opened later. The tramway was closed in 1916; the rails were sent to the Western Front. Rossie Priory was demolished in 1949, except for the west wing.

**Speedy Growth of Commuters, Cars and Caravans**: The population of Inchture in 1951 was only 300, when it was known for strawberry growing. However, still smaller places around – including Kinnaird, and Abernyte, 3 km north-west, with its garage – brought the total dependent population to around 800. The little-used station was closed in 1956, and the village population was down to 250 by 1971. However, by 1969 Inchture was narrowly bypassed by the A85 trunk road; the erection of a new and attractive primary school and the building of a housing estate to the south brought a doubling of residents within a decade. By 1981 some 1200 people lived in the wider area, including Abernyte, where by 1978 Stout Brothers had developed their long-established garage into a major car dealership, particularly busy on Sundays; by 1982 there was a caravan site at Inchmartine, 2 km to the west. The 1991 population of the village was 774. There is a large potato warehouse and a joiner; the school, post office cum stationers and the pleasant *Inchture Hotel* are all open.

## INNELLAN & Toward

**Map 5, A5**

***Cowal (Argyll) village & hamlet,*** *pop. 1150* OS 63: NS 1570

The 15th century Toward Castle, a ruined courtyard structure, stands on a spur above the south coast of Cowal 2 km west of Toward Point; about 3 km north of the point are fragmentary remains of later but comparable Knockamillie Castle. Roy's map of about 1750 showed a coastal track, later a road, passing Knockamillie, which stands above modern Innellan. The lighthouse on Toward Point was first lit in 1811 by the Clyde Lighthouse Trust. Castle Toward was built in 1820–21 by David Hamilton as a bolt-hole for a rich Glaswegian, Kirman Finlay, who feared the current revolutionary mood. A pier was built at Innellan, served in 1864 by Hutcheson steamers, and in 1877 by the Lochgoil & Lochlong Steamboat Company. By 1886 Innellan was a *"pretty watering-place"*, with steamers to Wemyss Bay and Rothesay. Murray noted the *Royal Hotel* as *"good"* in 1894, and Innellan golf club, founded in 1895, laid out a scenic 9-hole course.

*A concrete platform (nearly complete) at the Ardyne construction yard near Innellan, pictured in May 1975. This yard, operated by McAlpine's, closed 2 years later as steel became preferred for oil platforms.* (RS)

**Loss of Steamers, Loss of Facilities**: Innellan was never the major attraction that Dunoon, only 6 km to the north, became in the late 19th century. Castle Toward was enlarged in 1920–24 for one of the Coats family *(see Paisley)*. By 1951 Innellan was a village of nearly 1000 people, with seven hotels, of which the long-established *Royal* was reputedly a *"posh establishment"*. With 32 rooms it was the largest of the four remaining by 1981, for the withdrawal of the Clyde steamers had hit the trade badly; Innellan had lost its dentist, lawyers and post town status. The area was by then heavily afforested. Castle Toward, an Outdoor School from 1947, was later run by Strathclyde Regional Council until the latter's demise in 1996, when a management buy-out from the closure-intent Glasgow City Council was intended.

**Concrete Platforms and Caravans**: The population rose marginally in the 1970s due to the 40 ha oil-platform fabrication yard opened by Sir Robert McAlpine & Sons about 1972 at Ardyne Point, some 7 km to the south-west. This also drew employees from Dunoon and Bute, and built three concrete platforms before steel became more popular, causing it to cease operations in 1977. The population of 1142 in 1991 had an affluent retired character. By 1994 the main road nearby had lost its *'A'* status, and a scheme to reopen the platform yard in 1994 came to nothing. By then a caravan site was open on the Dunoon road; by 2000 the future of Toward primary school was in doubt, but the tiny *Osborne Hotel* was still in business.

## INNERLEITHEN

**Map 3, A3**

***Large village e. of Peebles,*** *pop. 2500* OS 73: NT 3336

A British fort stood on a spur above *Inverleithen*, the confluence of the Leithen Water with the River Tweed. Its early corn and waulk mills were granted to the new Royal Burgh of Peebles in the reign of David I. Pont's map made around 1600 showed nothing save *'Innerlythe'* Kirk and *'Lythe'*. A bridge was built in 1701 across the Leithen Water on the main road from Peebles to Galashiels, but there was still no Tweed crossing when the Roy map was made about 1754. By then Innerleithen had developed in the area later known as Kirklands, becoming a substantial settlement lining a road which set off towards Edinburgh, but petered out near Whitehope, some 5 km north. The Tweedside road was turnpiked under an Act of

1771, and subsequently also became lined with development. The 5-storey Caerlee woollen weaving mill, promoted by Alexander Brodie, a Traquair blacksmith, was built in 1788–90. Heron noted this in 1799, adding that *"near the village is an excellent mineral spring rising in celebrity"*. In 1801 the parish population was little over 600, and the village grew very slowly; however, by about 1825 it was served by a penny post from Peebles.

**The Short-lived Spa and the Long-lived Printing Shop**: The spring known as *St Ronan's Well*, which gained fame through the writings of Sir Walter Scott, led to the creation of a spa, with a pumproom built in 1826. In 1827 Chambers emphasised the *"mineral spring which has of late years been resorted to by vast numbers of invalids, as well as others who only require the pleasure of a few weeks of summer rustication. The place has therefore undergone a recent change from a sequestered and unknown village, distinguished only by a woollen manufactory, into a fashionable watering-place."* However the spa failed, and instead the tweed industry grew from the 1830s with Rosebank mill; later came two wool spinning mills, the Leithen mill about 1845, and the St Ronans mill in 1846, steadily raising the population. In 1846 a gasworks was established, and by 1861 the population was over 1800. A water-powered printing works set up in 1848 was bought by Robert Smail in 1866.

**Railway, Hosiery, Golf and Cashmere**: In 1866 an extension of the Peebles Railway (later part of the North British system) was opened through the Tweed valley, connecting Peebles and Galashiels, with a station at Innerleithen. In 1869 two related firms named Dobson produced woollen shirtings, a spinning mill was operated by Roberts & Co of Selkirk, and the Caerlee tweed mill was by then owned by Walker, Gill & Co. At the same time Wilson made blankets and plaiding. In 1870 the Waverley woollen mills were established by the Walkerburn branch of the Ballantyne family. Innerleithen became a police burgh, with 2300 people in 1881, also manufacturing hosiery. It gained the facilities of a large village, including the 9-hole golf course founded in 1886; the *Traquair Arms Hotel* had been built by 1894, *"good"* according to Murray. The pumproom was rebuilt in 1896. Innerleithen was in effect a town, for Smail's published a local newspaper from 1893 to 1916, and

*The Caerlee Mill, Innerleithen, built in 1790 as a multi-storey woollen spinning mill, and subsequently extended. In recent years, as Ballantyne's, it has produced cashmere garments.* *(JRH)*

a Carnegie-aided library began in 1902. About 1930 the River Leithen was dammed for another mill which became known for complex cashmere knitting. The facilities of a large village were still available in 1951, when the burgh population was 2361.

**Closures and Takeovers**: The railway station was closed to passengers in 1962, and by 1971 the track had been lifted. In 1967 Dawsons (then essentially Todd & Duncan of Kinross) took over the Waverley mill, and in 1970 Ballantyne Cashmere of Innerleithen also fell into the Dawson group, who immediately closed the Ballantyne Spinning Company, putting 15% of the local people out of work. The population had declined little since 1951, at 2216 in 1971, but by 1976 St Ronans mill was disused and was later demolished, the secondary school, cinema, and post town status were no more, and many other facilities had been reduced. By 1981 Innerleithen had a caravan and camping site.

**Recovery and Growth**: Spinners were still at work in the Leithen mill in 1983, and the Waverley mill was again spinning by 1986; Murray Allan Textiles expanded in 1987–88, and in 1990 earned a Queen's Award for exporting cashmere and wool knitwear. By 1995 they had close links with Italian designers and yarn spinners. By 1989 Caerlee Mill had the head office of Ballantyne Sportswear, and in 1990–91 of the Ballantyne Cashmere Company, makers of knitwear and part of the Dawson group, which in 1991 itself earned a Queen's Award. The knitters, mainly men, could still take up to 17 hours to knit a complex cashmere garment by machine using the *'intasia'* technique. By 1989 the southern approaches to the village were dominated by the Tweedside Sawmill of the London firm Tropical Hardwoods Ltd. Smail's printing works had closed in 1985, but was reopened by the National Trust for Scotland in 1990 as a working industrial museum, complete with its Victorian presses. By 1991 the population had grown to 2515, and there has been little subsequent development. St Ronan's Well is still open to the public, as are the *Traquair Arms Hotel*, guest houses and the caravan and camping site.

## INNERWICK, Oxwellmains & Torness **Map 3, B2**

***E. Lothian village & hamlets**, pop. 275* OS 67: NT 7274

The keep of Innerwick Castle was built in the 15th century in a strong position above the Thornton Burn, 8 km south-east of Dunbar and 2 km from the coast. Parish schools were founded at East Barns in 1612 and at Innerwick in 1630. In 1636 James Maxwell of Innerwick (later the first Earl of Dirleton) was a promoter of the pioneering May Isle *(q.v.)* lighthouse. There was a mill on the Dryburn just to the north by the 1750s. The Great North Road passed between the castle and the rocky sea shore, ignored by the small village that grew 1.5 km west of the castle – which fell into ruin, replaced by the emparked mansion of Thurston, 1 km west of the village. The North British Railway opened between Edinburgh and Berwick in 1846, with a station named Innerwick 2 km east of the village, which by the 1890s had a church, smithy and post office, as well as its parish school. Barns Ness lighthouse, 3 km to the north, was first lit in 1901 when 780 people lived in the wide farming parish.

**Transformation**: By 1951 there was a 50-line telephone exchange serving 600 people in the parish; by then Innerwick station handled only goods, and was soon abandoned. But two major developments were to transform the area for ever. Only

2 km to the north was Oxwellmains, a farm overlying enormously thick strata of limestone, where in 1963 APCM built a huge rail-connected cement works. This, Scotland's only such works, provided relatively few jobs while seriously affecting the area with its lung-damaging dust, and remodelling the landscape with its vast quarries. Thurston park and mansion had vanished by 1965, soon followed by closure of the country primary school at East Barns. In 1966 Barns Ness was the first lighthouse to be converted to multiple sealed beam operation; it was fully automated in 1985. Meantime in 1979 Blue Circle Cement began expansion of the works to raise its output to 1.1 million tonnes a year, and to reduce its emissions; the A1 trunk road was replaced by a new road 1 km inland to enable ever larger quarries to be opened.

**Caravans and Nuclear Power**: By 1982 there was a coastal caravan site at Catcraig, only 1.5 km from the works, whose reconstruction was completed about 1985; dust suppression was now enforced. In the 1980s Torness nuclear power station was built beside another coastal caravan site, at Thorntonloch some 2.5 km east of shrinking Innerwick village; the construction workers largely lived in Dunbar. Torness was on load from 1988 but officially opened in 1989; by then a new rail siding had been laid to handle its flasks of spent nuclear fuel, carried by rail to Sellafield for reprocessing. By 1991 only 275 residents remained in the parish.

**Rubbish helps Rail and Cement**: By 1990 three-quarters of a million tonnes of cement was despatched annually by rail from Oxwellmains; at one time in 1990 there were at least five shunting locomotives on the site. On the east side of the main line – which was electrified in 1991 – was a wagon repair works, but in the mid 1990s this was replaced by a reception point for Edinburgh refuse, brought in by container trains from Powderhall and placed in the worked-out limestone quarries. In 2000 old tyres were being burnt in an approved experiment to cut the cement works' fuel costs. Another caravan and camping site, at Thurston, has been open for some years.

## INSCH

**Map 10, B2**

***Aberdeenshire village,*** *pop. 1550* — OS 37: NJ 6328

Above the headwaters of the River Urie, in the Garioch area about 15 km north-west of Inverurie, is a conical hill topped by a hill fort known as Dunnideer, meaning *'Oaken Fort'* in the Gaelic; a stone castle was built within this in the 14th century. *'Inche'* Kirk, some 2 km downstream and originally part of Banffshire, was shown on Blaeu's map (from Gordon's 1642 data). Insch was granted a charter as a burgh of barony in 1677. Licklyhead Castle was erected 4 km south of Insch in the 17th century; in the 1690s seven of the tiny town's fifteen tradesmen were building workers. Roy's survey made about 1750 showed a trackless area between the two roads linking Inverurie with Strathbogie, via Old Rayne and via Leslie. Insch village comprised a square north of the church, with the Mill of Insch to the south. The river also drove the *'Mill of Dunadiere'* and Gordonsmill. Later a bridge was built over the tiny River Urie, but for a century Insch developed very little. In 1824 a pious distiller built the Jericho distillery on the Jordan Burn near the Foudland road 5 km north of the village, but this too was a small affair. Insch had no post office before the penny post of 1840, and it lost burgh status in the 19th century reforms.

**Railway arrives but Distillery goes**: The Great North of Scotland Railway, authorised in 1846, was opened through Insch station in 1854. This seems to have stimulated development, including the water-powered Husk Mill built in the mid 19th century, and in 1880 a better station was constructed. By 1886 the tiny distillery had been renamed the *'Bennachie'* after the prominent 528 m hill south-east of the village; it then used local barley and peat to make only about 115,000 litres of malt whisky annually, but was in the process of being doubled in size. Murray's 1894 Handbook was strangely silent about the self-effacing village of Insch, the centre of an agricultural enclave rather lacking in tourist interest, for there remained little to see of the castle. The early 20th century problems of the whisky trade closed the distillery for good about 1910.

**Farm Machinery, Hospital and Golf**: A library was built in 1928, and by the 1950s Insch – with about 1000 people – had the facilities of a large village, providing agricultural and general services to about 4000 people in all; there were still two mills, plus a timber merchant and a weekly market. By 1971 there had been some decline in population, especially in the surrounding rural area; but Insch was the smallest place between Aberdeen and Inverness to have succeeded in retaining its railway station. In 1980 Big John Farm Equipment was a prominent feature, a cattle market was still held, and shops included fitted carpet specialists. Insch still possessed two small hotels and a secondary school, though this soon closed. In 1981 the 15-bed War Memorial Hospital provided maternity and GP care. Insch golf club was a latecomer: founded in 1982, it laid out a 9-hole parkland course.

**Small Retirement Town with big Tractors**: By 1991 the population was nearing 1550, and by 1995 several small housing estates had been built. Although the Husk Mill stood vacant in 1993, the large depot of HRN Tractors is conspicuous among other farm-related and hauliers' depots in the compact village. Thanks to local initiative, the station building had been restored by 1997 as a tourist information centre and museum, with 10 trains each way on weekdays and 5 on Sundays in 1999. Facilities now include the hospital, a health centre, primary school, library, community centre, golf and bowling clubs, post office, and a fair range of shops, including a kiltmakers. There are also police and fire stations, and an agricultural services firm. Deer are farmed in the vicinity, and there is a modest hotel and a pub.

## INVERALLOCHY & Cairnbulg

**Map 10, C1**

***Buchan coast villages,*** *pop. 1400* — OS 30: NK 0465

Two coastal seats of the Comyn Earls of Buchan were the 14th century castle of Cairnbulg and the bulky 16th castle of Inverallochy, respectively 4 km and 6 km south-east of Fraserburgh. Cairnbulg was enlarged about 1545 into *"a structure of imposing magnitude"*; Pont's sketch map of around 1600 showed both castles, and Cairnbulg appeared as a tiny place on Gordon's map made by 1642 and engraved by Blaeu, while Roy's map of about 1750 showed both Cairnbulg and *'Innerlochy'* as coastal hamlets, sited where rock and sand adjoined. In 1858 Pratt found Inverallochy castle ruined and Cairnbulg derelict; at that time a coble was the only means of crossing the Water of Philorth which separated the area from Fraserburgh. Both Inverallochy and Cairnbulg were *"fishing villages"*, consisting of little more than huts.

**Epidemic, Reconstruction and Golf**: After a cholera epidemic in the 1860s the huts were replaced by new cottages, all turned gable to sea to enable fishing boats to be drawn through between them across the intervening roads to those farthest from the beach. Between 1878 and 1905 a lifeboat was stationed at Whitelink Bay, between Inverallochy and St Combs; the little drying harbour of West Haven at Cairnbulg is nearly 1 km from the village centre. By 1891 about 600 people lived at Inverallochy, and an inn, post and telegraph offices were open. A coastguard station had been provided, and in 1899 an 18-hole public golf course was laid out on the links.

**Railway Interlude, Decline – and Farming**: In 1903 the Great North of Scotland Railway opened a light railway from Fraserburgh to St Combs, with a station at Inverallochy (almost immediately renamed Cairnbulg), so that local fishermen could crew Fraserburgh steam drifters. By the 1950s the population had risen to some 1750, with the facilities of a small village. But the railway was closed in 1965, the secondary classes had ceased by 1976, and by 1981 the two places had the facilities of a mere hamlet; at that time beach-based fishing still took place. In 1991 a higher proportion – over 30% – of the 1410 people in the twin villages worked in agriculture than in any other locality of over 1000 people in Scotland. A little development continued in the 1990s.

## INVERARAY

**Map 5, A4**

***Argyll village,*** *pop. 500* — OS 56: NN 0908

A standing stone, the hill fort of Dunchuach and the ancient church of Kilmalieu were finely situated east of the River Aray where it enters upper Loch Fyne. A little to the east once stood the tiny Castle of Eilean Dhu, on an islet in the Dubh Loch near the mouth of Glen Shira. A possibly 14th century castle was built just west of the church at Inveraray; what are now called *'Highland'* games were already being held there. The castle became the seat of the Campbell Earls of Argyll, a title conferred in 1457–58, and Inveraray was made a burgh of barony in 1474. In the 16th century the tower of Dundarave Castle was built 7 km east of Inveraray Castle. In desperation at the turbulence of the Lords of the Isles, in 1509 the ageing James IV made the Earls hereditary sheriffs of Argyll, and Inveraray became their caput. When Pont made his map about 1600, *'Inreyra'* castle was an imposing building, and by 1619 the burgh had a school.

**The Royal Burgh and New Inveraray**: The Earls' original main seat, Castle Campbell at Dollar, was slighted by Montrose in 1644, so they moved to Inveraray, which was promoted to a Royal Burgh by Charles I in 1648, its charter signed when he was in the Isle of Wight! By 1680 a ferry plied across Loch Fyne to St Catherine's, and Inveraray had a post office from about 1716, served on foot from Dumbarton. Starting in 1742, the third Duke gradually removed the town a few hundred metres away from the vicinity of the old castle to a low promontory a little to the south. Two years later an inn was open in the new town, and by that time the Islay packet boat gave Inveraray a more regular postal service. A new castle was slowly built as a mansion between 1745 and 1761, to designs by Roger Morris, but supervised by the architects William and John Adam and William Mylne, while Robert Mylne laid out the new town.

**Military Roads, Grandeur and Poverty**: The Garron bridge at the mouth of Glen Shira was built in 1748, completing the military road that had been built over the *Rest and be Thankful* pass from Arrochar; Roy's map made about that date showed the small square of new settlement, and its importance as a communications centre. Tracks led north through Glen Shira, north-east by way of Glen Aray, and beside Loch Fyne to the west; a ferry connected to St Catherines, and another between Craigan and Strachur gave access into Cowal. At that time the little-known Carnagaballoch lead mines were being worked in Glen Shira. The *'Great Inn'* was built about 1755. The Dubh Loch bridge, designed by Robert Mylne, was built above the Garron Bridge in 1757, and the attractive Garden Bridge by John Adam dates from 1761; but too much was being spent on the grand features. By 1769 when Pennant visited Inveraray he noted a huge herring fishery said to employ 2400 men, but commented on the continued existence of *"the old town, composed of the most wretched hovels that can be imagined"*, because the move to the new site had faltered after completion of the inn, the customs house and a few houses.

**Linen in the Bilingual Town**: From 1772 the post was carried on horseback, and Boswell described the inn as *"excellent"*. Linen manufacture was begun for the Duke around 1748, but in 1774 the woollen factory originally included in his plan was instead built 5 km to the west, at Clunary *(G. Claonairigh)*. The new Aray Bridge was designed by Robert Mylne and built in 1776, and linen weaving was prospering in 1792. When the new church was built in 1793–1802 it was in two parts for simultaneous services in two languages, for Gaelic was still generally spoken. By 1797 Inveraray was a post town with connections every day but Tuesday, so encouraging the increasing dominance of English. Heron in 1799 found *"a handsome town"* of over a thousand people, in which the Dukes had established a school. These events explain why in 1803 Dorothy Wordsworth heard local children at play chattering in what she loftily regarded as broken English.

**Lordly Bridges – and Dirty People?**: She noted *"two bridges of lordly architecture east of this small town, the inn being a large house with very large stables, and the county gaol. The houses are plastered or rough-cast, and washed yellow – well built, well sized, and sash-windowed."* They were two-storeyed, unlike Highland huts, but she considered them and the people equally dirty. However there was tea and sugar on sale, many boats on the loch, and landscaping of the castle policies had been carried out by *'Capability'* Brown. The woollen mill closed after many problems around 1805, but some woollen work continued. Around then the Renfrewshire Banking Company of Greenock opened a branch in Inveraray, and by 1809 there was a pier; this was served by occasional passenger steamers from 1815, and regularly from 1818. Inveraray had a combined brewery and bakery in 1825. Chambers in 1827 found *"the county-town, small and irregularly built, has some manufactures of woollens, &c, but chiefly depends for its subsistence upon the herring-fishery"*; the Castle was *"a modern square edifice"*.

**Inveraray Author parodies the Puffers**: A gasworks was built for the seventh Duke in 1841, but by 1864 the linen trade was extinct. Neil Munro, born in the town in 1864, became a Glasgow journalist, famous in middle age as the author of the Para Handy stories, portraying the colourful crews of the tiny Clyde puffers that provided an informal cargo shipping service.

He also wrote *'The New Road'*, regarded by John Buchan as the best historical novel since Scott. By 1886 there was a ferry to Strachur. Inveraray remained a renowned though typically erratic herring fishing station, the centre of the Duke's vast estate – in 1887 an enormous 700 square kilometres. In 1894 Murray noted a *"slow"* but year-round daily steamer service to Glasgow from this *"very small (pop. 743) sleepy and isolated county town"*. At that time the former *Great Inn* had become the *"good" Argyll Arms Hotel.*

**Hydro Power comes, Gas goes**: Dundarave Castle was restored in 1912. The herring fishery eventually failed, and the year-round steamer service died with the 1939–45 war. However, steamer excursions from Gourock continued into the 1960s. Around 1951 over 500 men were housed in a camp in Glen Shira, building a hydro-electric scheme, the carefully sited dam – in much the same place as the one-time lead mines – impounding Lochan Shira and feeding the Sron More power station. By 1953 a 9-hole golf course was open. The gasworks *(see Hay & Stell)* which had been updated in 1949 was closed in 1964, the ferry service ended in 1962, and by 1972 Lochgilphead had become the undisputed county town. Meantime Inveraray Castle was first opened to the public in 1954; it was severely damaged by fire in 1975, but restoration was completed in 1978 and the castle fully reopened.

**Inveraray from the 1970s**: Inveraray's basic facilities included a primary school, doctor, fire station, police station, and about 18 shops. By 1980 Sinclair were specialist canners at Upper Riochan. In 1981 Inveraray had a youth hostel, four hotels and the facilities of a large tourist village; pleasure and inshore fishing craft used its old pier.

**Parading the Prison**: A trout farm was started in the early 1980s. By then the old court house contained the district council's archives. Land disposals shrank the Argyll estates to only 300 square kilometres in 1994. By 1991 when the resident population was 512, further development had taken place at Newtown, and a wildfowl park and two caravan and camping sites were open on the coast to the west. Inveraray's lochside Jail had become a remarkable tourist draw, with over 100,000 visitors a year, earning a Europa Nostra award. In 2000 a steel-hulled schooner was moored at the pier as a maritime heritage centre. The golf course still has only 9 holes. A fierce debate rages over the detrimental effects of a planned car-park. Amongst the hotels are the *Argyll*, the Georgian *Fernpoint*, and the large *Loch Fyne* (80 rooms), and there's a seasonal youth hostel.

## INVERBERVIE (or Bervie) — Map 10, C5

***Large Mearns village,** pop. 1880* — OS 45: NO 8372

Bervie or Inverbervie lies beside the winding Bervie Water in the Mearns, near the rocky coast of the North Sea; 4 km upstream at Arbuthnott was an 11th century or earlier monastic site. Inverbervie was of some significance at an early date, being shown as *Enderburie* on the Gough map which is dateable to around 1250. In 1341 King David II was driven ashore nearby, and conferred Royal Burgh status on the place, because according to Chambers he was *"kindly treated by the inhabitants"*. No fewer than seven castles or mansions were built within 5 km, ranging from 14th century Hallgreen in the village, through the 16th century Arbuthnott House, to 17th century Allardice, imposingly built in a loop of the river 2 km upstream. The town of Bervie was so insignificant that it paid no tax in 1535–56. By 1614 Bervie parish had a school.

**Early Communications, Sailcloth and Fishing**: In 1696 a two-arched bridge was built where the main way to the north crossed the Bervie Water, and by 1715 Bervie had a post office. Roy's map of about 1750 showed Bervie as a compact settlement, with a coastal track southwards through Gourdon, and a track inland beside the river leading to Arbuthnott and on to Mondynes. Bervie was one of the more locally accessible of Scotland's small burghs; it was already centred on the Market Square. In 1750 a firm of Montrose merchants set up a sailcloth manufactory, and a small linen bleachfield was built in the 1750s. But Alexander Carlyle simply described Bervie in 1765 as *"a very insignificant fishing town of about 200 people"*. Completion of the River North Esk bridge near Hillside *(q.v.)* in 1775 made the coast road much more important.

**Scotland's First Powered Flax Mill**: About 1775 a thread works was established in Bervie, employing about 50 people making locally bleached high-quality thread. In 1787 – to the chagrin of local hand spinners – a 192-spindle water-powered flax spinning mill was erected on the Haughs of Bervie by Walter Sim & Walter Thom. Probably the first such enterprise in Scotland, its 90 workers used the latest machinery from Darlington. The sailcloth factory failed about 1790, and bleaching became extinct. By 1797 Bervie was a post town; in 1799 Heron noted that with the aid of a royal subsidy *"a handsome bridge has lately been built"*, replacing the old bridge. Bervie then contained about 600 people, *"a small town with a good salmon fishery"*.

**Harbour Improvements Scorned**: By 1811 Bervie was served by daily coaches between Montrose and Aberdeen, and for a time in the early 19th century there was again a sailcloth works employing 100 weavers. A pier to shelter four vessels was nearing completion for the Commissioners and the laird Mr Farquhar when inspected by its designer Thomas Telford in 1819. His companion on the trip, the poet Robert Southey, noted that coal and lime were imported from Sunderland and corn exported through this *"little, wild, dangerous but not unimportant port"*, whose basin had also been deepened. Yet in 1827 Chambers wrote that *"on account of the inconvenience of the harbour, the fishermen have now almost all removed to Gourdon, a more commodious place"*.

**Brewing, Milling, Spinning – and *Cutty Sark***: A brewery operated by Robert Miller was in use in 1825, and by 1838 there were five mills, all water-powered. Later steam power and new machinery were installed at Haugh of Bervie mill, and in 1864 it was very busy under James Gibb with 808 spindles; four other small mills contained 1024 spindles, but there was no other local industry. Bervie was the birthplace in 1837 of Hercules Linton, who became a Dumbarton shipbuilder and designer of the famous clipper ship *Cutty Sark*, completed in 1869. In 1865 a branch of the North British Railway was opened from Montrose to terminate on the shore at Bervie, where 1100 people lived in 1881; but as late as about 1910 a horse-drawn coach maintained the daily connection with Stonehaven. In 1931 the population was 1032; in 1935 an impressive curved 7-span concrete viaduct was built for the A92 coast road. The railway was closed to passengers in 1951, and freight traffic was ended in 1966. By

1971, although it apparently had gas supplies, Bervie was no more than a substantial village of 850 people, with a little beach fishing, though a quarry was open 2 km to the west.

**Industries Old and New spur Growth**: In 1975 a seafood factory was opened by Young's, who soon employed 120 people all year round, drawing supplies from all over Scotland, the shellfish including crabs and scampi, plus salmon for smoking; the waste went to an animal feed mill. A new housing estate was under construction at the south end of Bervie in 1976. There were then about 15 shops, two small hotels and a range of other services including a caravan site. Southwards expansion continued, and the village population in 1991 was 1880. However, in the slump of 1992, labour was shed by Inlak Seafoods, at that time shellfish processors in Inverbervie, where the long-established Craigview flax mill also made 36 people redundant; housing was soon built on its site. In 2000 Wire Rope Services had extensive yards around the old riverside sheds, and the old works of JPE Engineering had been recently much enlarged.

**Tourism and Services**: By 1995 Arbuthnott House with its steep 17th century terraced gardens was open daily to the public and by 1996 the Grassic Gibbon Centre was open nearby. In 1997 a new full-size replica of the Cutty Sark figurehead was prominently installed beside the A92 to commemorate Hercules Linton; the big modern fish restaurant was the *'UK chip shop of the year'* in 1997–98! The great bridge of 1799 still proudly stands close by, useable by pedestrians. Services include post office, inn and pubs, police and fire stations, and veterinary services. There are various sports facilities, but as yet no golf course.

## INVERGARRY

**Map 9, A5**

***Inverness-shire village,*** *pop. 160* OS 34: NH 3001

The possibly 16th century castle of the MacDonells of Glengarry stands where the River Garry enters Loch Oich, in the Great Glen about 10km south-west of Fort Augustus. A charcoal-burning iron furnace was established at Invergarry in 1727, by the laird John MacDonell and the ironmaster Thomas Rawlinson from Furness. Ore supply must have been very problematical, and the furnace closed after only a few years, in 1736. Glengarry had entertained the Pretender during the *'Forty-five'*, so the ancient castle was burned down in 1746 by the ruthless Hanoverian commander, the Duke of Cumberland. The Roy map made about 1750 showed little else in the area north-west of the loch except *'Castle Gary'*, near the end of a track from Fort Augustus.

**Drowned at the Ferry or Shipped out by the Laird**: Pennant passed through in 1769, noting only the ruined castle; he did not refer to the furnace, so it must have left little local impact. Nor however did he mention the ferry, where 18 people had drowned in an accident as recently as 1767. Tenants' welfare seemed of little value to cantankerous clan chiefs such as Alexander MacDonell of Glengarry, who in 1785 cleared 520 people from Glenquoich Forest, the area around Kingie east of Loch Quoich, leaving very few to mind the sheep roaming the bleak hills. By 1799 he had erected a sawmill near his family seat at Invergarry, described by Chambers as *"a handsome modern building"*. Many more of his tenants emigrated to Canada in 1803 (but their *'New Glengarry'*, like old Invergarry, did not grow into a significant centre).

**Transport, Deforestation, and the *'Tail'*** : The ferry was superseded when a road was built up Glengarry in the early 19th century, subsidised by the Commissioners for Highland Roads & Bridges, with the advice of Thomas Telford. The same agencies converted Loch Oich into part of the Caledonian Canal: in 1816–19 a 216-ton dredger named *Glengarry* was locally built to deepen the summit channel in the loch, and equipped with machinery by a Northumbrian, Bryan Donkin. This and the construction works at Laggan Locks had helped The Glengarry to denude his estate of timber by 1831 (though within a century it was again well wooded). In 1827 Chambers described Glengarry as *"the last of the northern lairds that keeps up the ancient system of 'a tail', that is, a body of personal attendants"*. A post office was open by 1835 and a school was built; the canal steamers could call at a pier, but no railway ever directly served Invergarry: the so-called Invergarry & Fort Augustus *(q.v.)* Railway actually kept to the opposite side of the loch; no wonder it failed!

**Angling, Tourism and Hydro Power**: By the 1890s the *Tomandoun Inn*, an angling hostelry later called the *Tomdoun Hotel*, was open some 15km up Glen Garry. What Murray called the *"very good" Invergarry Hotel* was open by 1894. The lochside road was improved in the 1930s with a large concrete arch spanning the river. By the mid 20th century Invergarry was a small village, though with an ambulance station in 1953. About 1960 the castle was converted into the *Glengarry Castle Hotel*, and by 1961 the *'Loch Lochy'* youth hostel was open at South Laggan, 4km south-west. In the 1960s a concrete gravity dam was built by the Hydro Board at the former Falls of Garry, greatly raising the level of Loch Garry to supply water through a tunnel to the Invergarry power station. Upstream, the largest rockfill dam in Britain – 38m tall and 320m long – was built 9km west of Tomdoun at Loch Quoich, supplying the Quoich power station 100m below. Such schemes create little permanent employment, and Invergarry's 1981 resident population was only about 160. About 1980 the Great Glen Water Park was opened at the north-east end of Loch Oich, and by 1984 there were caravan and camping sites. The *Glengarry Castle Hotel*, owned and run by the MacCallum family for over 40 years, now has 26 rooms; the youth hostel is seasonal.

## INVERGORDON

**Map 9, B3**

***Cromarty Firth small town,*** *pop. 3900* OS 21: NH 7068

Located on the sheltered deep water of the Cromarty Firth 1.5km east of the old parish centre of Rosskeen, Invergordon is on much the same site as the one-time 13th century Inverbreackie *(or Innerbrachie)* Castle. This was shown on Pont's map of the Tarbat peninsula made about 1600, and suggested that it was already a ferry point. Certainly a *"rugged"* ferry was operating to Balblair by 1656. Invergordon Mains was laid out by the laird Sir William Gordon early in the 18th century to a rectilinear plan as a farming estate with plantations, replacing the ancient castle. Only a tiny nucleus of settlement existed in the 1750s at the ferry landing, where the town centre later developed. Although by 1755 there was a post office, in 1769 Pennant noted only Sir John Gordon's *"handsome house amidst fine plantations"*. The ferry was connected with Tain

*An oil rig off Invergordon. Today it is common to see several rigs in the Cromarty Firth awaiting repairs at the yard, which was established during the North Sea oil boom of the 1970s .* *(SMPC / Tom Robertson)*

by a track (whose original line north-eastwards to Priesthill has been lost).

**The Planned Village of Invergordon**: Invergordon was marked on Heron's map, engraved in 1796, but its precise date of founding as a planned village seems uncertain. A grid layout (at an angle to the first) was adopted for village development, and by 1797 Invergordon was already a post town, served on alternate days. The new through road improved by the Commissioners was open via Conon Bridge from 1816; soon the *Commercial* coaching inn was built to serve the north mails. By 1817 the little-known Pollo distillery had been built on the shore 5km north-east of Invergordon; but it fell silent in 1826. Invergordon's first harbour work was a slip built in 1817, for the Balblair (Inverbreackie) ferry; a proper harbour was built in 1828. From 1834 this was served by a steamer from Glasgow via the Caledonian Canal and Cromarty. In 1847 grain was being shipped out despite the general famine caused by potato blight, locally exacerbated by an influx of people fleeing the inland clearances. Growing trade led to expansion of the harbour in 1857.

**Railway, a little Whisky and a Naval Base**: The Inverness & Ross-shire Railway reached Invergordon in 1863, was extended to Bonar Bridge in 1864, and from 1874 formed part of the Highland Railway's *'Farther North'* main line to Wick. By 1872 Wordie & Co operated a rail to road cartage depot; a long siding was laid to the harbour. In 1891, 1100 people lived in Invergordon, described by Murray in 1894 as *"a flourishing little port"* where the *"good" Commercial Hotel* was open. Pollo distillery was reopened in 1896 after 70 years of disuse – but when the industry hit problems in 1903 it closed for good. Early in the 1914–18 war a naval pier, oil tank farm, fuelling and victualling bases for light cruisers were established; floating docks handled hull maintenance, and nearly every day for four years saw a special supply train being dealt with. During the 1939–45 war, flying boats too were based at Invergordon; though the naval base was closed in 1956 it remained a fuelling station. By the 1950s Invergordon had the facilities of a small town, including banks, an ageing open-air swimming pool, one of the North's few builders' merchants, and two small hotels besides the 22-roomed *Royal Hotel*, which seems to have closed in the mid-70s.

**Golf, More Whisky and Oil Work**: Invergordon golf club, founded in 1954, soon laid out a 9-hole parkland course. The Invergordon distillery complex was planned in 1959 by local interests – led by Frank Thomson the Provost of Inverness – to offset the effects of the naval base closure; the grain distillery was opened in 1961, followed by the Ben Wyvis Highland malt distillery, opened in 1965 *(see also Dingwall).* From 1979 Invergordon Distillers began to use wheat as a cheaper alternative to maize as the basis for grain spirit. Meantime a pipe-coating plant started up in 1972, and around that time an oil rig servicing base was established beside the harbour, which from 1974 was under a Port Authority. Although the traditional boatbuilder gave up in 1975, by 1978 the Caledonian Towage Company had four tugs stationed at Invergordon, largely to handle oil rigs in for repair, and tankers using the Nigg *(q.v.)* tank farm. Invergordon Academy was built around 1980.

**The Smelter: Promise Unfulfilled**: The British Aluminium Company (BAC) smelter, built in 1968–71, comprised four cell rooms each over 450m in length, and a deep water jetty carrying a 2 km conveyor belt for the Jamaican bauxite that was its main raw material. The plant was also rail-connected, but was the one conspicuous and admitted failure in the otherwise fine career of Sir Robert Grieve; it was an absurdity that much of its huge demand for electricity was supplied from Hunterston by lengthy transmission lines, so adding voltage losses to already high costs. Even so, for a time the plant produced 100,000 tonnes of aluminium a year and employed over 1000 people at its peak. The Balblair ferry was reopened for a time in the 1970s to carry workers to Invergordon, but the Ben Wyvis malt distillery closed in 1977 and was dismantled. By 1981 the town's 1951 population had doubled to some 4000, and had overspilled to Alness. Then world demand for aluminium fell away, BAC was taken over by the Canadian giant Alcan, and the smelter was closed in 1981 as a high-cost producer. Though 96% of its prominent exhaust plume had been claimed to consist of steam, restoration of the crystal air of the Cromarty Firth on which so much tourism by now depended was as welcome as the problems of those thrown out of work were regrettable.

**After the Smelter the Enterprise Zone**: An Enterprise Zone (EZ) was introduced in an attempt to combat the unemployment caused by the departure of the smelter, and in 1987 a firm making magnetic tape, unable to find labour in Surrey, decided to move to the town, creating 50 jobs. In 1988 Scottish grain export records were broken with a single 34,000-tonne shipment, and for a short time in 1988 coal was imported through the Invergordon jetty and moved by rail to South of Scotland power stations. By 1989 BP had built a large factory to make food for farmed fish. In that year Mari of Gateshead opened a training centre in business and microelectronics, and Caledonian Textiles (Hong Kong owned) set up an overcoat factory, with HIDB support. In 1991 the resident population was holding up at 3900.

**Bilgewater or Gin?**: Invergordon Single Grain whisky was on the market by 1992, but in 1993–94 Scottish-owned Invergordon Distillers were acquired by their US-owned rivals White & Mackay. In 1996 the distillery's blending plant produced some 200 supermarket and private brands of whisky, vodka, and gin, one of the gins being madly marketed as *'Bilgewater 43'*, this being its proof strength! By the mid 90s Mupor, industrial materials handlers, had moved into the EZ, and MacGregor Engineering, which already employed 450 people, was to take on another 300 in all trades for three oil rig maintenance contracts. Briggs Environmental Services stands by to tackle any oil-spill incidents. In 1993 the new safety standards introduced following the *Piper Alpha* disaster led the Cromarty Firth Port Authority to build a new berth out into the Firth just west of the town for refitting oil rigs.

**Fixing Rigs**: In 1996 Sellar's still dealt in combine harvesters and farm machinery locally, and in four other towns and villages. Little remains of the smelter above foundation level, but other activities are very evident on the site, including a number of small/medium marine engineering firms. The smelter jetty, which was already used by the pipe-coating plant, continues in use as a cargo terminal, and an alumina storage tank has become a silo for 30,000 tonnes of surplus sugar. The barrels piled up in thousands beside the railway show the continuing local role of whisky. Despite soaring oil prices in autumn 2000, a parade of six oil rigs could be seen moored in the Firth; another was undergoing a refit at the yard. Rosskeen's interesting but long disused early 19th century church was in danger of dereliction by 2000. In summer cruise liners berth at Invergordon, coaches taking passengers to many Highland destinations. The golf course now has 18 holes. Since about 1995 *Kincraig House*, 3km inland, has been a 20-roomed hotel.

## INVERGOWRIE, Gray & Mylnefield **Map 6, B3**

***Village / W. suburb of Dundee,*** *pop. 3000* OS 54: NO 3430

The 16th century Invergowrie Castle stands 5km west of Dundee where the Gowrie Burn, a traditional boundary between Angus and Perthshire, enters the Firth of Tay; to the south are extensive tidal sands. Pont who mapped the area about 1600 also showed the Den mill to the north. The large House of Gray was built in 1715. Nearby Benvie was the birthplace in 1748 of the mathematician John Playfair, who also pioneered the study of fossils in geology. By about 1750 when surveyed by Roy, the Gowrie had been bridged at its mouth to carry the primitive track then joining Dundee and Perth; east of the bridge stood Invergowrie House in its policies. To the west was a hamlet later known as Mylnefield Feus, where the track split to offer two alternative ways to Perth. The Mylnefield or Kingoodie East Quarry supplied a core of sandstone for the famous Bell Rock lighthouse, built in 1807–10, and stone to build Perth prison.

**Bullionfield Mills and the Railway**: The small Bullionfield flax spinning mill was for sale in 1813; in 1822 it belonged to David Stephen and had 180 spindles. About 1845 Mylnefield acquired a post office. The Dundee & Perth Railway which opened from Perth to Barnhill in 1849 provided a station, named Invergowrie, west of the river. The line was carried on a 21m-high timber viaduct – later rebuilt in stone – spanning the Mylnefield Quarry. The coming of the railway may have persuaded Charles Cowan to establish the Bullionfield paper mill between Mylnefield and the burn in 1850, with a papermaking machine.

**Over the Hills to Newtyle**: In 1861 the little Dundee & Newtyle Railway opened a track from a junction east of Invergowrie, on a roundabout route climbing through a rural station named Liff, which actually lay on South Road opposite Myrekirk Road, some 3km from the small village of Liff. The quarry closed soon after 1870 and became flooded, hiding the viaduct piers. Meantime the opening of the Crombie Reservoir in 1866 enabled Dundee to supply pure water to the Invergowrie area, and by 1895 Mylnefield Feus was a substantial village with the mill, a post and telegraph office, an inn and a pier; Kingoodie was then just a hamlet. Over 2 km to the north, and just east of Liff, lay the asylum which was later called the Royal Liff Hospital. Little more development took place until the 1920s when the Dundee and Mylnefield bypass was constructed, here known as Kingsway West. After 1939 the House of Gray became derelict; it was to stand in a neglected state for half a century.

**Soft Fruit Research**: By 1951 Mylnefield had become known as Invergowrie, a significant village approaching 1500 people, with a small secondary school and average village facilities. However, Liff station was closed to passengers in 1955 and the Bullionfield paper mill ceased production in 1965. By then the foreshore to the east was being extended by municipal refuse tipping. By 1967 Mylnefield Farm had become the Scottish Horticultural Research Institute, engaged in the improvement of soft fruit, for which the Carse of Gowrie and Strathmore had long been famous. The enormous Ninewells Hospital with its medical school was built on the hill to the east in 1964–67. By 1967 a Victorian baronial villa close to Kingsway West had become the small *Greystone House Hotel*. The Newtyle railway was closed completely in 1967, but Invergowrie station on the Perth line remained open for passengers; in 1973 British Rail embedded the largely underwater viaduct in an embankment. In 1971 the population was around 1800, but in the 1975 reform of local government the whole area was sensibly placed in Dundee city district. By 1978 Invergowrie had a chemist, an inn, two grocers, a garage and a car dealer. By 1990 the horticultural establishment was known as the Scottish Crop Research Institute, its commercial arm being Mylnefield Research Services; it is now a large complex.

**Fine Hotels and a Foolish Boundary**: The suburbanised village area south of the A85, with a 1991 population of some 3000, was transferred in 1996 for local government purposes from adjacent Dundee to the vast Perth-based authority (an example of blatant gerrymandering which benefited their party not a whit!). The *Greystone House Hotel* had been renamed and enlarged by 1980 as the 69-roomed *Swallow Hotel (*now 107 rooms). Meantime the fine but long-derelict *House of Gray* was restored in 1991–94 as a hotel and conference centre. The primary school, post office, food shops and surgery are among local facilities in the village.

## INVERKEILOR, Lunan, Red Castle & Chance Inn

**Map 6, C2**

***Angus small villages,*** *pop. 900 (area)* OS 54: NO 6649

Inverkeilor stands above the Lunan Water 9km north of Arbroath, and had a thanage from about the 11th century. Its name *('Mouth of the Keilor')* is remarkable, for the place is 3km from the river's mouth at Lunan. By 1455 the royal Red Castle had been built on a bluff above the estuary, but it was largely destroyed in 1579. Meantime the tower of Ethie Castle 3km south-east of Inverkeilor had also been built in the 15th century. The Roy map made about 1750 showed the main coastal road between Ferryden and Arbroath passing seaward of the post-Reformation Lunan Kirk. Southwards it passed the *Chance Inn* at Cotton *(Cot Town)* of Inchock, which by 1715 acted as a post office. Roy also indicated Kirkton Mill, which in a remarkable reversal of the usual pattern came to bear the Gaelic name *Balmullie*, i.e. Milton, on 20th century maps! By 1797 the *Chance Inn* was formally a post town, with a daily mail service.

**Post, Road and Railway**: Eventually a new main road was built through Inverkeilor village, which acquired its own post office, whose post town became Arbroath; the old road remained in local use. From about 1863 a tile works was in operation 1.5km to the south of Inverkeilor, which in 1880 gave its name to a station on the North British Railway's new line from Arbroath to Montrose and Kinnaber. By 1894 Lunan House stood in wooded policies beside the beach, and a 6-roomed inn was open between the church and the station; the *Old Chance Inn* still existed, though without its post office. By 1954 Lunan House had become the *Lunan Bay Hotel*. Inverkeilor itself had only one inn, about 550 people, and a secondary school (which was soon closed). Passenger trains were withdrawn from Inverkeilor before 1953, and not restored in 1967 when the railway became the main line to Aberdeen. With the closure of the tile works in 1971, Inverkeilor became small indeed with some 300 people; Ethie Haven, 3km to the east and once a fishing village, is just a few holiday homes. A bypass was built about 1990 to eliminate poor alignment of the main road, and nowadays Inverkeilor has a quality restaurant.

## INVERKEITHING

**Map 6, B5**

***W. Fife town,*** *pop. 6000* OS 65: NT 1383

Inverkeithing on the Fife shore of the Firth of Forth lies at the mouth of the little Keithing Burn, on a bay well sheltered by the igneous Ferry Hills to the south. Many straight alignments in the former Great North Road imply a Roman road, and use of the harbour to connect the Roman forts at Cramond and Bertha (ner Perth); but much evidence is lacking. About 1120 Inverkeithing was listed as the only trading community in Fife, and one source gives 1124 as its charter date; by 1130 there was a *'ship and passage'* to the Lothian shore. In 1153 Inverkeithing certainly became a Royal Burgh and one of the ports for Dunfermline, 5km inland *(see also Limekilns)*, but it later passed to another lord and was unusual in not possessing a castle. It acquired a merchant guild during the period 1165–1214, and horn and hoof carving was among local medieval crafts, as proven by archaeology; but its fortunes fluctuated.

**Trading Rights and Early Buildings**: William the Lion who died in 1214 confirmed the lost charter, and gave trading rights to Inverkeithing against Stirling, Perth and Cupar as far as the River Devon, Milnathort and the River Leven. Inverkeithing was on occasion a royal residence, and also for a time according to Chambers *"the place where the Convention of Royal Burghs was appointed to meet, before that distinction was removed to Edinburgh"*. He added that *"numerous religious buildings were known to have existed in Inverkeithing before the Reformation"*. The chief of these was the Franciscan friary (Greyfriars), probably founded in 1268 by Philip de Mowbray; there was also a Dominican monastery. The church tower dates from the 14th century, as does the *Hospitium* of the Grey Friars, their best preserved building in Scotland and now the local museum. The medieval mercat cross is a rare survival, while the mansion called *'Rotmells Inns'* on the south side of the square was a royal lodging by 1403.

**Wool Trade Zenith and Decline**: In 1327–31 Inverkeithing ranked seventh among Scottish ports in terms of Customs receipts, and in 1332 was the main Scottish port for English trade. Its dealings were largely in wool, peaking about 1368, when as its Customs dues showed, the tidal port was of major importance for the time. In 1415 Hardyng reported that ships could be victualled at Inverkeithing, but after 1431 its overseas trade tended to fall away. Although its merchants were trading in Danzig in 1444 and their vessels appeared in the Baltic up to around 1500, government data of the day show that by then their amount of business was trivial. In 1535–56 Inverkeithing paid under 1.5% of the total of burgh taxes, but remained sufficiently important to be represented in Parliament in 1560. Pont's fragmentary map made about 1600 showed a bridge across the burn and three ships in the harbour.

**Revival from Fordell Coal**: Beveridge noted that *"the Hendersons of Fordell had great influence"* in the burgh, where they had a town house by the mid 15th century. In the late 16th century coal was discovered at Fordell *(see Crossgates)*. The coal was initially carried down to Inverkeithing harbour on horseback, but improvements were made from 1683 to enable increasing coal exports as well as fishing to be carried on. In the 1720s Defoe called Inverkeithing *"an ancient walled town, with a spacious harbour; but as there is not any great trade here, and consequently no use for shipping of burthen, the harbour has been much neglected: however, small vessels may come up to the quay"*.

**Linen Industry and Russian Admiral**: Defoe continued *"the town is large, and is still populous, but decayed, yet the market for linen not only remains, but is rather more considerable than formerly, by reason of the increase of that manufacture since the Union. The market for provisions is also very considerable here."* The pier was extended in 1738, and table linens were manufactured by 1744. In 1735 Inverkeithing was the birthplace of Samuel Greig, son of a local shipowner, who became a *"celebrated Russian admiral"* (Beveridge). In 1753 the salt pans used between 12,000 and 15,000 horse-loads of coal a year. A post office was open by 1755. Many thousands of cattle passed through on the great north road from Kinross, first made up via Jamestown in 1756, and rerouted in 1772. No doubt the tolls, also collected at Kinross and Tullibole, paid for Inverkeithing Town Hall, dated 1770.

**Halbeath Wagonway and Boreland Distillery**: The wooden Halbeath Wagonway connected the harbour with the coal mines at Halbeath from 1783, by way of a quarry and limeworks west of Prathouse; only 14 coal wagons were in use in 1795. In 1790 in order to give access to larger vessels, a channel was cut through a reef which obstructed the harbour. By 1797 Inverkeithing had five annual fairs and was a post town with a daily service; it was a key point in the mails network. Heron noted a population *"upwards of 1300"* in 1799, and wrote that the bay was *"beautiful"*. Iron rails were laid on the wagonway about 1810, further harbour improvements saw the East Ness pier built in the early 1820s, and up to 1835 there was a lazaretto or government quarantine at the West Ness. In 1836 Inverkeithing was the base for twenty vessels of between 20 and 100 tons, exporting coal from various pits and importing timber, bark and bones. The Boreland distillery was built just north of the town in 1827, and a large maltings was erected beside it in the mid 19th century; but it was closed in 1851.

**Shipyards, Railways and the Forth Bridge Effect**: The wagonway was connected to the Edinburgh & Northern Railway at Townhill Junction in 1848 and reconstructed to match. By 1858 J Scott was building small wooden steamships at Inverkeithing, and two *"considerable"* shipyards were in operation by 1869; but by 1886 Scott's had moved to Kinghorn *(q.v.)*. By 1888 shipbuilding and an ironfounding industry had also recently ceased. In 1877 the North British Railway (NBR) built a new branch line from Dunfermline, to enable the former wagonway's steep route from Halbeath to be abandoned. It passed immediately east of Inverkeithing to link with North Queensferry pier, providing rail access to the harbour and to a brickworks south of the inner bay. In 1888 Beveridge noted *"the only works in full operation are a ropework, a brickfield, a tannery, and a sawmill. The Borland distillery is a depressing-looking ruin."* The *Royal Hotel* was also open in 1888. Inverkeithing was still very compact when a tunnel was driven under its eastern side to enable the station to become a main line junction, with the opening in 1890 of the Forth Bridge and its connecting line to Burntisland for Kirkcaldy, Dundee and Aberdeen.

**Paper and Shipbreaking: *Dreadnought* cut down to Scrap**: Caldwell's paper mill was working by 1906; electricity became available in 1911 and the mill was greatly enlarged in 1914 (later being acquired by Inveresk). In 1921 large-scale shipbreaking was begun on the former brickworks site by Thomas W Ward; among the first of the big vessels to go was the battleship HMS *Magnificent* of 14,900 tons, built in 1894. Probably the most famous battleship ever built, HMS *Dreadnought* of 17,900 tons, which had made all other capital ships obsolete when it appeared in 1906, was itself obsolete within as little as 15 years and was also sold for scrapping at Inverkeithing in 1921. In 1929 the yard broke up the old 80-gun *'wooden wall' Mars*, built in 1848, long used as a training ship at Dundee. The battlecruiser HMS *Tiger* of 28,500 tons was scrapped there in 1932, followed by large liners including the former White Star Line's *Homeric* and *Olympic*; some of the former's fine flooring went into Balgeddie House *(see Leslie)*. Between the wars A F Henry & MacGregor's coasters of Leith carried stone from Inverkeithing to the Thames, for by then a hard rock quarry was open east of the breakers' yard.

**The Battleship Graveyard**: After the second world war Inverkeithing took a major part in disposing of the Royal Navy's outmoded capital ships – including battleships, cruisers, and even aircraft carriers. The largest were the huge battleship HMS *Howe* of 35,000 tons, in 1958, and (amongst merchant vessels) the second Cunard liner *Mauretania*, of over 35,000 tons, in 1965 – both dismantled by Wards.

*The ship-breaking yard at Inverkeithing, which began in 1921 as Thomas Ward's. Some breaking still continues at the yard.*
*(RCAHMS / JRH)*

**Overspill, M90 and other Activities**: Coal exports ceased, but esparto grass and clay were still imported at the paper mill quay in the early 1950s, when the local facilities were those of a large village. Some Glasgow overspill was accepted in the 1960s, when houses were piled up on the hill behind the town. Despite the collapse of a new flyover at Masterton in 1962, Inverkeithing's road accessibility improved from 1964 with the opening of the Forth Road Bridge and the first section of the M90, passing behind the hill. The large Inverkeithing High School was built on a new site east of the town in the 1970s. While the breakers' yard remained in business, fewer and smaller ships entered the silty bay to tie up for the last time, the 11,700 ton cruiser HMS *Lion*, scrapped in 1975, being among the last of the big vessels to go. The Bellknowes industrial estate created beside the M90 in the 1970s soon filled up with warehousing, contractors' and road haulage yards and plant hire. Local facilities generally remained those of a large village in 1981. A tall warehouse near the scrapyard retailed furniture under various names in the late 20th century.

**The Station keeps Busy and Electronics arrives**: The station is still the junction for Dunfermline, with a growing Edinburgh commuter traffic, and in the 1980s was among the busiest non-city passenger stations in Scotland, justifying its down-side rebuilding. New car parks were successively added in the 1980s and 90s. The large maltings which had stood vacant beside the station for decades were replaced in 1987 by new private flats, but fragments of the medieval harbour still exist beside the paper mill. Cairntech, set up in 1983 to make electronic security devices and police radio scramblers, struggled until 1993 when its seven staff headed by Timothy Laing innovated a cordless non-tape answering machine based on a microchip and obtained a major contract from BT as The Phone Box Ltd. Ortec started in existing modern premises at East Ness in 1989; in 1990 their 33 workers soon fabricated the new railway bridge for Inverness, and made special engineering equipment. In 1991 the population was 6000, many sadly suffering some disadvantage. United Carriers had a very large road haulage depot at Bellknowes. Close by, NCR (Dundee) set up a branch, which as AT&T Global Information Solutions employed 100 people before moving to the new St Davids Business Park at Dalgety Bay in 1994.

**Independence on Paper**: By 1989 the paper mill was producing high-quality plain and coloured printing and writing paper for the giant American Georgia Pacific Corporation. Recession in the USA ended plans to increase capacity by 60%, and in 1990 they sold the mill and their other three British mills at Westfield, Carrongrove and in Somerset to their largely Scottish management, who kept the name Inveresk and made Inverkeithing their HQ. In 1995 the mill employed over 200 people, and exported half of its output.

**Exit Rock, Enter Park and Ride**: Some shipbreaking and the giant quarry keep the bay busy; by 1993 the head office of the quarrymasters John Fyfe Ltd (*see Kemnay*) was at Inverkeithing. The removal of a further 2.5 million tonnes of rock for roadstone from Preston Hill quarry was approved in 1993 against the residents' opposition, and yet further expansion of the vast quarry south of the bay is to come for Fife coast protection. In 2000 a new company, Stone Manganese Services, promised 50 jobs in marine equipment. A major park and ride complex was completed at Jamestown in 2000, relying on buses to relieve the Forth Road Bridge of those car commuters to Edinburgh who do not use Inverkeithing railway station with its ever-growing car parks, accessed from 2000 by a new, disabled-friendly footbridge.

## INVERKIP

**Map 5, B5**

***Inverclyde coastal village,*** *pop. 1250* — OS 63: NS 2072

Inverkip, which may take its name from a tiny watercourse, stands on the lower Firth of Clyde in west Renfrewshire; its strong castle was held by the English during the Wars of Succession, but the nearby castle keep of Ardgowan *(Gaelic for 'Smith's Point')* is attributed to the 15th century. It was the centre of an emparked estate at the time of Pont's map of about 1600. Inverkip was only one of the many little places in the area. A tributary of the much larger stream which enters the Firth at Inverkip, marked by Pont as the Daf, was already bridged some way upstream at *'Brigend'* near the site of Dunrod Castle; above it stood a mill which survived into the mid 18th century – modern Bridgend is about 2 km downstream.

**Barony Burgh with Identity Problems**: Ardgowan was chartered as a burgh of barony in 1634, but the linear settlement on the road which by then joined Greenock with Skelmorlie was marked on Roy's map of about 1754 as Inverkip, while the Daf was named as the Dunrod Water: later it was called the Spango. In 1798 Ardgowan House was built beside the castle, and in 1799 Heron noted about 400 people in *"the village of Daff"*. This confusion ended about 1825, when Inverkip got a penny post from Greenock. In 1865 the Caledonian Railway opened a branch from Greenock, passing through the Spango valley, Inverkip station and tunnel, to Wemyss Bay. By 1895 Inverkip was a village with a post and telegraph office, hotel and coastguard station. In 1931 about 400 people lived there, but by 1951 the facilities of a small village and (allegedly) a 9-hole golf course – no longer in evidence – served a mere 300 residents.

**Prospering with Electrification**: The railway was electrified in 1967, and residential development began at once, exploiting the fine view over the Clyde to Cowal. Despite the overpowering presence of the giant 2000mW oil-fired power station completed in 1976 only 1.5km south-west of the village centre, Inverkip's population was nearing 1000 in 1981, still reliant on the facilities of a small village, plus the *Langhouse Hotel*, a converted mansion to the south, and the *Inverkip Hotel*. The power station was mothballed in 1987 with the opening of Torness (and remained so in the 1990s under Scottish Power). By 1989 Derek Holt had developed a marina at the mouth of the Spango by opening out an existing inlet. In 1991 Inverkip's 1250 people were mainly highly educated, buying their own houses in new estates; these now extend at least 1250m eastwards from the station, towards the industries of the Spango valley.

## INVERMORISTON

**Map 9, A5**

***Small Inverness-shire village,*** *pop. 170* — OS 34: NH 4117

Invermoriston on Loch Ness-side was shown by a tiny symbol on Pont's sketch-maps of about 1600; as early as 1643 a sawmill was in operation there. The Roy map surveyed about 1750 showed areas of estate woodland near the mansionhouse, but no roads or tracks. About 1753 the Forfeited Estates Commissioners set up a linen manufacture there with six looms, but it did not thrive. A primitive inn built of turf was open when Johnson and Boswell rode by in 1773. The lochside and Glenshiel roads were built for the Highland Road Commissioners in 1813, and Glenmoriston post office opened about 1839. By 1894 the Loch Ness steamers called at a pier and jetty over 1 km south of the site where what Murray called the *"good" Invermoriston Hotel* had been erected. A new church was built in 1913, but the steamers eventually ceased to ply. By 1954 the hotel had been renamed the *Glenmoriston Arms*, and by 1982 a youth hostel was open on the lochside 5 km to the north, at Alltsigh. Invermoriston declined over the post-war years to a tiny village of 170 people, and by 1994 the Church of Scotland building was disused. When the 37 square km sporting estate of Glenmoriston was sold in 1988 it included the hotel, four shops, 16 holiday chalets, caravan and camping sites, a salmon hatchery – and also the inn at *Cluanie (q.v.)*, 35 km to the west. The *Glenmoriston Arms Hotel* and the *'Loch Ness'* youth hostel serve the visitors.

## INVERNESS

**Map 9, B4**

***City on Moray Firth,*** *pop. 45,000* — OS 26: NH 6645

Suburbs: *Culloden, Dalcross, Milton of Leys & North Kessock*

Located on the east bank of the short River Ness as it flows from Loch Ness to the Moray Firth, Inverness – now Scotland's fifth city – has a highly strategic site for a centre of Highland communications. A timber fort perched 160 m above the flood plain west of the river was occupied from the fourth century BC, maybe by the *Caledonii* who held the area in Ptolemy's day around 140 AD. By about 565 it was known as Craig Phadrig *(Patrick's Rock)*. Somewhere near Inverness the Pictish High King Bridei I was visited by St Columba. Craig Phadrig was vitrified by fire in the eighth century and for 300 years the area disappeared from the record.

**Thanage, Sheriff, Royal Burgh and Bridge**: Essie, possibly marked by the Boar's Stone 4 km south of Inverness, had a thanage from about the 11th century. An early castle, supposed to have been at the east end of the town, was destroyed by Malcolm Canmore, who erected another on a more prominent site beside the Ness. Inverness became the caput of a sheriffdom in 1136. Sources differ as to when it became a Royal Burgh, most probably by 1153; it was granted the standard weekly market. The burghal charter was confirmed by William the Lion in 1196–97; by then the burgh had acquired a merchant guild. Tanning appears from archaeological evidence to have been a trade in medieval Inverness, as was horn and hoof carving, including red deer antlers. Although some farming tools were obtained from Perth there was also a medieval smithy in Inverness, a substantial furnace for leadworking, and a pottery worked near the town; barrels were re-used to line wells.

**Herrings, Priory, Whisky and Wool**: By 1249 the Ness had been bridged in timber, and boats were being built; in 1266 herrings were caught in great quantity and sold in the town. A Dominican priory was founded at Inverness in 1233, and the town's High Church was originally built in the late 13th century. For some time after 1306 the jurisdiction of the sheriff based in the royal castle included the fertile area of (Easter) Ross as well as the huge area of glens and wilderness later known as Inverness-shire. Whisky is reputed to have been distilled in Inverness by the 14th century, and after the Black Death some wool was traded to the Low Countries. In the 1360s Inverness ranked eighth among Scottish ports in terms of Customs receipts – and held at least that position for two centuries.

**Arson and Stagnation**: The town was burned in 1411 by a Lord of the Isles, and although there was still a Royal castle in 1455, the trade of Inverness became ever less significant as the 15th century rolled on. The 16th century was even quieter in terms of development; the contribution of Inverness in burgh taxes was very slight, and it was 1535–56 before it paid much over 1% of Scotland's burgh tax revenue. But in 1560, though its church was an appurtenance of Arbroath Abbey, the burgh was sufficiently important to be represented in Parliament. Abertarff House was built about 1592, and by 1593 Inverness was the centre of a presbytery. Pont's two maps made at about that time clearly showed a bridge across the River Ness, and on one map another bridge was indicated above the Ness Islands.

**The Language Barrier, and little trade**: Defoe noted that *"Oliver Cromwell thought it a place of such importance, that he built a strong citadel here"*. Known as Oliver's Fort, this was erected from 1652 under General Deane, one of five citadels created under the Commonwealth to control Scotland, as at Inverlochy and Perth. Tucker in 1655 noted that *"the town is a small one, though the chief of the whole north"*; for shipping purposes it headed the area from west of Banff to Orkney inclusive. He added that *"the inhabitants beyond Murray land (except in the Orkneys) speak generally Ober Garlikh, or Highlands, and the mixture of both in the town of Inverness is such that one half of the people understand not one another. The trade of this port is only a coast trade, there being no more than one single merchant in all the town, who brings home sometimes a little timber, salt, or wine"*; he had only one tiny 10-ton vessel. In 1656 Richard Franck found a *"weak"* bridge across the River Ness, apparently timber-built. Inverness, whose defences had formerly included ditches, ramparts and palisades, was then *"defended with a weather-beaten tottering wall"*.

**Perfect English, and a Stately Bridge**: In 1666 the Citadel of Inverness gained a barony charter as Kingsburgh – a strange turn beside an existing Royal Burgh, especially since Chambers reported that Cromwell's fort in Shore Street *"was destroyed immediately after the Restoration"*; only its clock tower survived. Defoe noted that *"three regiments of English soldiers"* were disbanded in the area; many settled, improving its agriculture and – was he was being serious? – bringing *"perfect English"* to the local speech! Certainly some energy was imported, for Dunbar's Hospital was built as almshouses in 1668, and a post office opened in 1669, when all mail went via Aberdeen. Inverness gradually became more prosperous, with a new hump-backed stone bridge from 1684, paid for by public subscription. Defoe called it *"a stately stone bridge of seven large arches"*, Chambers adding that even after another century it was the town's *"best public edifice, with an aspect of peculiar solidity and strength"*. Bunchrew House, a coastal mansion 5 km west, was also built in the 17th century.

**Maltsters, Merchants, School, Hostelry and Explosion**: Inverness built a new Town House in 1708, and became known as a malting centre in the early 18th century. However, it was 1715 before the Earl of Seaforth introduced *"the first coach ever seen in or about Inverness"* the town was not directly connected to the south by road until 1730, when Gen. George Wade's military road over Drumochter was completed. In the 1720s Defoe found *"a pleasant, clean, and well built town: there are some merchants in it, and some good share of trade; small vessels may come up to the town, but larger ships, when such come thither, as they often do for corn, lie at some distance east from the town"*. Bow Court was built in 1722–29, having many uses over the years. By 1745 a grammar school or Academy was functioning, at one time within Dunbar's Hospital, and Inverness was known as the *"Highland Capital"*. The *Horns Inn* was open by the time of the troubles of 1745 and was used as headquarters by the Hanoverian *'Butcher'* Cumberland. The tall old castle near the bridge, which had been rebuilt under General Mackay in the late 17th century, was blown up by Jacobite supporters in 1746; Chambers observed in 1827 *"the place where it stood is so smooth as to be used as a bowling-green"*.

**Textiles, Roads and Ferries**: Bailie Hossack owned a fine linen factory by 1732, and although the troubles of 1745–46 held the town back, by 1749 master linen spinners worked there for the British Linen Company; the local thread company then sent most of its output to London by sea. Baltic Flax was heckled locally, and about that time the town acquired a bleachfield. By then the population was around 6000 or 7000. Roy's map, made about 1750 for military use, showed Inverness as a large nucleated settlement with the Ness bridge, and four radial roads: one almost due south (the later B861), and two others following the coast east and west; beyond Clachnaharry this last road soon became a mere track. The fourth was the Great Glen military road, following the south-east bank of the river, meeting Loch Ness at the minor parish centre of Dores, and leading to Fort Augustus and Fort William. The Bona ferry across the River Ness where it flowed out of Loch Ness was at one time important. Another even more important ferry connected to North Kessock *(q.v.)*.

**Textiles, Deerskins, Poverty and Squalor**: In the 1750s a spinning school was successfully established by the Commissioners for the Forfeited Estates, who also opened a prison: a second bleachfield was recorded, and by 1765 the British Linen Company had a local agent. In 1765 a very large hemp factory was set up; for a time this employed a thousand people using Baltic hemp to make tarpaulins and sacking – much of the latter was exported to the West Indies to cover cotton bales. James Macintosh, born at Aldourie near Loch Ness in 1765, became the reforming MP for Nairn; he was among the promoters of the Reform Bill of 1832, and earned a knighthood. In 1769 Pennant noted that a ropery and sail maker were available, and saw Highlanders selling deerskins at a fair; at that time Inverness had four or five fairs annually, at which basic necessities were traded on a pitifully small scale. The High Church was rebuilt in 1769–72, but retained the 14th century tower. Muirtown brewery was established in 1771, and in 1775 it was said that Inverness had become the chief malting centre in Scotland. In 1773 Boswell stayed in a *"dirty and ill-furnished"* inn; even street cleaning was unknown in the town until the 1790s. There was at least a quay, for the river port was commercially active, though fishing except for salmon was always limited.

**Consolidation and Progress**: By 1774 there was a tannery and bark mill. Woollen manufacture was reported in 1776, and a woollen mill was set up in 1780, by which date the inn had been improved with aid from the Commissioners for the Forfeited Estates. By about 1780 linen thread was spun by up to 10,000 outworkers, supervised by 19 district agents (though this trade faded away early in the next century). The Bank of Scotland branch which was opened in 1775 was successfully established, among the first five to be so. The Aberdeen Banking Company also had a branch in the town in 1793, but it was soon closed. In 1797 five fairs were scheduled to be held and there was a daily postal connection, but the regularity of the Edinburgh carrier's service was *"uncertain"*; the only roads to the south were poorly constructed and still included the major ferry boat crossings at Dunkeld or if going east, at Fochabers. Heron's account in 1799 was of *"an ancient and flourishing town, being the chief market to a wide tract of country around. An Academy is here established on a very respectable footing."* He noted *"a considerable manufacture of ropes and canvas"* being carried on in *"several large buildings on the north side of the town"*, which had over 10,000 inhabitants, and boasted *"a safe and convenient harbour, and a good deal of shipping"*. The *"very considerable"* salmon fishery was *"let to London fishmongers"*.

**Improved Roads and Stage Coaches**: Highland roads were improved with government aid under Telford's guidance from 1803, and Inverness really began to benefit from its nodality. But Chambers noted that the first stage-coach that reached Inverness in 1806 *"did not pay, and was soon after abandoned"*. Regular stage coaches began to run over the Drumochter pass to Perth from 1808, and from 1811 two mail coaches ran daily to Aberdeen via Elgin. But in 1814 the *"narrow ill-paved streets"* of Inverness were noted with distaste by Elizabeth Grant. By the time the Thurso mail-coach began to run in 1819, the Highland main road system had been largely completed, and by 1828 there were four coachworks in Inverness.

**The Caledonian Canal and New Foundry**: William Jessop advised Telford in the design of the government's Caledonian Canal, whose eastern construction base was at Muirtown, where a staircase of locks was built *(see Cameron)*. This work greatly stimulated the town; for example, about 1805 two 50-ton sloops to carry stone from Redcastle quarry on the Black Isle were built at Inverness by Samuel Deadman and John Nicol. By 1809 the Inverness New Foundry had been opened by Jonathan Wells, supplying iron rails and castings to the contractors. The canal was partly opened in 1818, and carried a steamer to Fort Augustus from 1820. But this problematical construction turned out to have been under-engineered by Telford, and generated disappointingly little trade even after its completion at a shallow depth in 1822. Its early traffic largely comprised general cargo from east to west, including Danish flour, grain, herrings from Cromarty, linseed from Riga, Bremen oak and oak bark, salt, slates and Baltic timber. By contrast, its Muirtown Basin at Inverness effectively extended the port, and a steamer service to Glasgow which was started in 1824 became weekly the next year.

**Inverness Profits from the Clearances**: Inverness was quick to take advantage of the widespread clearances of people and cattle from the glens by the ruthless Highland lairds, who introduced more profitable sheep: the Holm Woollen Mills were already open when Millburn distillery was built in 1805–07. In 1808 the tarred timber Black Bridge was built at the Ness mouth, and the gasworks and Imray's (unsuccessful) brewery were opened. In 1809 came the first newspaper, the *Inverness Journal*, published until 1849. Between 1810 and 1825 the Perth Banking Company established a branch in Inverness. In 1817 an annual sheep and wool market was arranged and the *Inverness Courier* newspaper was started, becoming a firm supporter of the lairds (and still in publication).

**An Anglicised Town with a Gaelic Hinterland**: By 1827 Inverness was according to Chambers *"a thriving sea-port, the chief town of the county, and, in fact, the capital of the Highlands. The Academy of Inverness has long been distinguished, and is conducted upon a very liberal and splendid scale."* The town had *"two subscription reading-rooms"*, plus the recently established *"Northern Institution for Science and Literature"* which had already created a museum *"worthy of a visit"*. By then the site of the Cromwellian fort was *"chiefly occupied by the peaceful shops of a tribe of weavers"*. While the townspeople spoke good English, *"few of the neighbouring peasantry, when addressed, are found to speak anything but Erse"*. By 1834 the *Muirtown Hotel* was *"a tolerably respectable inn"*.

**Floods, Banking and County Hall**: Like many other Highland arches, some spans of the seven-arched stone bridge of 1684 fell in the floods of 1829; it was soon repaired, and at the same time footbridges were built to the Ness Islands. From 1836 the mail was sent via Perth, and about then, three coaches a week ran through to and from Edinburgh. The Caledonian Bank, founded in Inverness in 1838, created a 20-branch network around the Moray Firth, and in 1847 built a fine head office in the High Street, designed by Mackenzie & Matthews. A new County Hall and Sheriff Court was built of pink sandstone in 1834–46 on the site of the former castle. Glen Albyn distillery was set up in 1846 on the site of a former brewery, perhaps Imray's, but was soon out of use. In the 1840s a weir was built to raise and regulate the level of Loch Ness, and when improvements to the canal were completed, the quay was extended in 1847. By 1851 Hutcheson steamers reached Inverness from the west, but the improved canal remained a commercial flop, and with the effect of all the clearances, from 1841 the population of Inverness county entered a century of decline. In 1849 a great flood finally swept away the much-patched stone bridge, which was replaced about 1854 by a suspension bridge.

**The Highland Railway and Forward Thrust**: By 1849 there were three local newspapers, including the short-lived *Northern Ensign* and the new *Inverness Advertiser*, published until 1885. In 1854 Cluny Macpherson chaired a company promoted by the Earls of Grant and Seafield to build the Inverness & Nairn Railway. Engineered by Joseph Mitchell – one of three brothers from Forres whose road surveyor father had, like him, been trained by Telford and were all to be involved in railways – the easily-built line crossed flat land and opened in 1855, including a harbour branch. As the Inverness & Aberdeen Junction Railway it was extended with more difficulty by stages to Forres and Keith, where in 1858 it met the Great North of Scotland's line from Aberdeen; from that time there were only two coaches a week on the Inverness to Perth road. By then the *Union Hotel* adjoined Macdougall's Highland Store in what the German traveller Fontane called *"a forward-thrusting town"* of 15,000 people, which still had three local newspapers.

*The Town House of Inverness, designed by Matthews & Lawrie and erected in 1878–82. The baronial style was popular in the Highlands at that time.* *(JRH)*

**Rails to North and South, and Local Distribution**: The allied Ross-shire Railway to the north crossed a new stone-arched Ness rail bridge, and a swing bridge over the canal at Clachnaharry, where there was a station – and also one at Bunchrew – to reach Dingwall in 1862. These lines and that between Forres *(q.v.)* and Dunkeld, brilliantly engineered by Mitchell and completed in 1863, amalgamated in 1865 as the Inverness-based Highland Railway Company (HR). In 1867 over 97% of the HR's 400km of route was single line, and most remained so *(see Vallance, 1938 & Nock, 1965)*. By 1860 Wordie & Co had a busy rail to road cartage depot and district office at Inverness station; in 1903 95 horses were based there.

**Locomotive and Carriage Works and Expansion**: The modest Lochgorm works which serviced the HR's 55 locomotives were built in the 1860s. The carriage and wagon works nearby was known as Needlefield. Nearby was the HR's roundhouse engine shed. The Atlantic shores were reached by rail at Strome Ferry in 1870, and the *'farther north'* line was extended to reach Wick and Thurso in 1874. The HR's fine *Station Hotel* was open by 1886, and the *'direct'* railway line to Aviemore, with its great sweeping climb over Culloden Muir, was opened throughout as late as 1898.

**Coasters, Castings and Whisky**: Small wooden coasters were still built at Inverness in the 1860s, but the registration letters INS more often referred to fishing vessels based in Lossiemouth than in Inverness itself. Farm machinery was manufactured in Inverness from 1872 by the Northern Agricultural Implement & Foundry Company; in 1882 they also cast the iron chairs used to hold bullhead rails. Their Rose Street foundry, which moved into new premises in 1893 *(see Hay & Stell)*, also produced the HR's lattice footbridges, locomotive parts, and later marine engines. About 1865–66 the former Glen Albyn distillery became a flour mill, but reverted to malt whisky production when rebuilt by Gregory & Co in 1884, to produce about 35,000 litres a year. The Millburn distillery was rebuilt in 1876 and made 275,000 litres of Highland malt annually. Glen Albyn distillery was acquired in the 1890s by James Mackinlay of Leith and Birnie of Inverness; this firm, Mackinlay & Birnie, then built Glen Mhor distillery, opened in 1892.

**Late Nineteenth Century Textile Industries**: By 1864 thread manufacture was long gone, though the early hemp factory continued in reduced production, making coal sacks in 1869. Holm mills, then under Nicol & Co, employed about 100 workers, using water and steam power to spin and weave tweeds, plaiding and blankets from Highland and Colonial wool. A former meal mill at Culcabock was converted to a small woollen factory in the 1860s, with a carding machine and hand looms. King's Mills, Bute Mills and the enlarged Holm Woollen Mills were all at work in 1894.

***'A Modern City'***: Craig Dunain Hospital 3km to the west of Inverness was built in the 1860s as a *'Lunatic Asylum'*, and Hilton Hospital was the poorhouse. For the more fortunate, the retailing outlets of 1869 included the Royal Tartan Warehouse of Macdougall & Co, celebrated for its Highland homespuns. By 1878 the Caledonian Bank had 34 branches, including one as far away as Stornoway. It then suffered a crisis and declined, with the help of a too-large investment in the unfortunate Scottish India Coffee Company of Madras, and had to join the Bank of Scotland in 1907; its former head office building became the latter's Highland Regional Office. Meantime came new facilities, including an Episcopal Cathedral, built in 1866–71, and a striking new Gothic Town House designed by Matthews & Lawrie, erected in 1878–82 on the site of its predecessor. In 1877 a public library was begun (with Carnegie assistance). Inverness golf club, founded in 1883, laid out an 18-hole parkland course at Culcabock. The *Northern Chronicle* was published from 1881 to 1962; the *Highland News* has given an alternative information service from 1883 to the present. By 1886 Inverness was thought *"a lively and interesting place: a modern city, bright, clean and evidently prosperous"*. It was certainly active, boasting six football teams in 1893; both Caledonian and Thistle had formed in 1885.

**Entertainment and a Local Lad o' Pairts**: In 1886 the *New Theatre Royal* in Bank Street replaced very makeshift premises in Hamilton Street, and the town's first cinema seems to have opened in 1896. In 1887 David MacBrayne's steamer *Cavalier* offered two return services each week to Greenock and Glasgow, via the Caledonian Canal and the Mull of Kintyre. Murdoch MacDonald, son of a carter, born in Inverness in 1866, became the Civil Engineer for the Highland Railway, and laid out its Black Isle branch, opened in 1894. He then assisted in building Egypt's Aswan Dam, designed the Esna barrage, the rebuilt Delta barrage and the Jordan Valley irrigation project; he became President of the Institution of Civil Engineers, and finally the long-serving Liberal MP for Inverness.

**The Highland Capital Booms in the 1890s**: The Cameron Barracks, built beside the Mill Burn, were completed in 1890 as the base for the Queen's Own Cameron Highlanders. In 1891 the town's population passed 19,000, by 1894 there was an inn at South Kessock, and Culcabock was already a substantial village with an inn. Inverness had four hotels that Murray called *"good"* in 1894 – the *Caledonian, Palace, Royal* and *Station*, for expansion was particularly marked in tourism – but then as now this was chiefly for the riverside and surrounding scenery, rather than for the historic distinction of the burgh. The Waterloo Bridge was built in 1896, replacing the Black Bridge, while the Victoria Bridge opened in 1898; the Kessock ferry became steam-operated in 1907. In 1899 an electricity generating station was built, and about then James Ferries & Co made belt-driven threshing mills.

**Rail and Football Mergers**: World War I saw the station's odd layout altered to speed the handling of the vast naval traffic, and a new line was hastily laid to the quay. A proposal of 1906 to merge the Highland and Great North of Scotland railway companies under the latter's head office at Aberdeen had been supported by few HR shareholders, and quietly dropped, but in 1923 Inverness was hit by the enforced merger of the proud Highland Railway into the giant and remote LMS, losing its headquarters and the Lochgorm locomotive works (which were reduced to doing light overhauls). Though both the Haugh and Thornbush breweries were at work in 1906, they were soon closed. The author Neil Gunn from Dunbeath was an exciseman at Glen Mhor distillery from 1923 to 1937, in which year a move to unify the town's three surviving football clubs failed.

**Maritime Sadness and Uncertainty**: A marine steam engine constructed in 1914 by the Rose Street Foundry was fitted in 1921 to the SS *Torwood*, built by Jones of Buckie. Buses abstracted the canal's passenger traffic in the 1920s; MacBrayne's Glasgow–Inverness steamer service ended in 1927, since the ratio of summer to winter passengers could reach 100 to 1; the shuttle steamers between Inverness and Fort Augustus did not ply between 1929 and 1934, but in the 1930s there were still sparse summer services the length of the canal. In 1928 the Rose Street foundry, which had built boom defence equipment in 1914–18, broke up the oldest steamship then surviving in the world, the little paddler *Glengarry*, built in Govan in 1844; the ancient engine was lost too, despite its special interest for marine archaeologists.

**Airways, Road Haulage and Coasters challenge Rail**: By 1931 Inverness-shire had its lowest population since 1811, at 82,000, of whom 22,500 lived in the burgh. However, in 1933 Highland Airways of Inverness, an offshoot of local bus firm Macrae & Dick, began flights to Wick and Kirkwall from an airfield at Longman. This served as the local airport as late as 1945, but was soon superseded by the present airport at Dalcross. In 1938 J C Brooke & Co of Inverness – whose eight lorries made runs to Wick and Glasgow carrying steel, timber and merchandise – were absorbed by Wordies, by then owned by the LMS. Many sheep were already carried in lorries between farm and station, and even from Kyle to Inverness auction mart. In the 1930s and '40s cable drums were moved by road from Inverness station to build the new national electric grid, and after 1943 Wordies carried equipment to Hydro sites. In 1939 whisky in wooden hogsheads was taken by road direct from Millburn distillery to Glasgow docks. By then Coast Lines had their own fleet of motor vehicles, delivering sea-borne barley to distilleries, and flour to bakers via their warehouse at the harbour; J D Smith hauliers were based at Clachnaharry.

**Slow Progress Centres on Services**: The *Theatre Royal* burned down in 1931; as a result the *Central Hall Picture House* (which had been built in 1912) was converted into the *Empire Theatre*, and reopened in 1934. In that year Inverness Royal Academy, as it is now styled, gained new buildings. After World War II, the former HR works was still doing minor repairs to locomotives, and some machine-shop jobs for outlying depots, all newly under British Railways in 1948; but by about 1970 the unusual roundhouse engine shed had vanished. Meantime Inverness had become the main hospital centre for the Highlands, with the opening of the Royal Northern Infirmary, and by 1957 the later Raigmore Hospital; by then Craig Phadrig was remembered in the name of a second mental hospital. By 1955 the 19$^{th}$ century Culduthel House had become a hospital; extended to 100 beds, it was reserved in 1980 for infectious diseases. The long-established museum held important medieval material.

**Growth resumes, especially under the HIDB**: By 1951 population growth in the county of Inverness had resumed, adding 3000 people in 20 years since 1931. By 1953 there was a Woolworth store in the town, plus the long established indoor market; but larger chain stores were still noticeably absent when the author first visited Inverness in the mid 1960s. The numbers of pleasure vessels passing through the Caledonian Canal first exceeded cargo boats in 1956; fishing boats still traversed it. A new Ness Bridge of three prestressed concrete spans was opened in 1961, and in 1962 a fine 18-hole municipal golf course was opened beside the canal at Torvean; by then there was a youth hostel. The *Thistle Hotel* was built about then at Nairn Road, and the 19-room *Kingsmills Hotel* was open by 1963, doubled in size by 1980. Growth in and around the town spurted when in 1965 the new grant-making HIDB (Highlands & Islands Development Board) made its headquarters in Inverness. Moray Firth Maltings established a large new plant in 1968 (later expanding to Turriff and Arbroath), and in 1968–70 historic Bow Court was reconditioned as shops and flats.

**Cruising and Oil spur Expansion**: The first cruise vessel on the canal was offered for hire in 1970; by 1976 six firms were hiring 77 cruisers and yachts, and by 1992, 114. Day trips were also quite popular. An ice rink was opened about 1969, and the next major chain store to colonise Inverness was Littlewoods (around 1970); in 1980 Marks & Spencer's most northerly branch opened in Inverness as part of the highly successful Eastgate shopping centre. Though decline had become the exception in booming Inverness, the *Empire Theatre* was closed in 1970. By 1971 Loch Ness Marine built boats at Muirtown, and Caley Cruisers started to hire pleasure vessels in 1970, reaching 54 boats by 1981. The newly built 120-room *Caledonian Hotel* was open by 1972. In the 1970s North Sea Oil work made the port much busier, and new industries developed on estates to the east of the town. A cheese factory was opened in 1973. By 1979 James Pringle & Co operated the Holm Woollen Mills beside the River Ness 3 km south of the town centre, but the Rose Street Foundry, still so named in 1981, soon changed its name to A1 Welders.

**Distillery Closures of the 1980s**: Local prosperity fluctuated, because distilling in Inverness was failing: the Glen Albyn and Glen Mhor plants were closed in 1983, their sites sold for shopping development, and ancient Millburn was closed in 1985 – part became a restaurant, the rest being cleared. The large Millburn Academy had by then been built on a greenfield site; there is also an older and more central Inverness High School. In 1989 it was proposed to close the Craig Dunain Hospital, which specialised in treating alcoholism (but a new psychiatric hospital, New Craigs, has now replaced it).

**Heading Highland Region: as Big as Belgium!**: In 1975 Inverness lost county town and burgh status, but became the centre of a new District, and more importantly gained the HQ of the new Highland Regional Council, with its extreme length of almost 300 km the most extensive local authority in Britain, larger in area than Belgium! This encouraged centralisation in Inverness, which was still among the fastest-growing towns in Scotland in the late 1980s; by 1991 the population was over 41,000. Highland Fuels, formed in 1961 as a distribution subsidiary of Esso, has its head offices in Inverness, whose Crematorium, the first in the Highlands, opened at Kilvean in 1995.

**Entertainments Thrive**: 1976–78 saw the building of the *Eden Court Theatre*, which by 1988 drew its audiences for plays, films and one-night variety from as far afield as the Western Isles, and including visits by Scottish Opera; meantime the local *Scala* was still open in 1993 as the *CAC* 2-screen cinema. In 1995 there was no mainland cinema open north or west of Inverness; even here only one other cinema survived. A ten-pin bowling facility was proposed in 1993 to replace carpet bowls, the new 18-hole Loch Ness golf course was opened at Castle Heather, and new golf driving ranges at Culduthel were thriving. By 1994 a new public sports centre had been erected up-river of the town centre, and in 1995 a new aquadrome was to be built nearby.

**Communications – Ups and Downs**: The Kessock road bridge suffered foundation problems before being opened in 1982, bringing the north Highlands closer to the south, and bypassing the town to the east. All railway signalling for the Highlands was concentrated in Inverness in 1987, using radio links. The Ness railway bridge was washed away by floods in February 1989, cutting the northern rail link and killing its freight traffic; passenger services were kept going by bus to Dingwall until a new bridge was completed in 1990. In 1992 the former HR works were used as the BR Sprinter depot. The Scottish Bus Group's Inverness maintenance workshops survived when many others were closed in 1990 as a prelude to privatisation.

**Industry and Shopping Booms**: Though Inverness was not primarily an industrial centre, by 1979 Inverness Precast Concrete of Longman Road was making blocks and cladding materials; in 1993 they claimed to be among the leading Scottish manufacturers. By the 1990s a new boatbuilding yard was open at Burnfoot, and by 1992, despite a lack of local demand, White Electronics of Inverness made mine detectors! In 1994 timber from Estonia was landed at Inverness harbour for sawmilling by Brownlie's five BSW mills and by James Jones & Sons; nearby was an oil depot. By 1990 large stores had been built outwith the town centre for both Presto and Safeway, yet in the period 1991–94 Inverness outperformed all other of 250 British shopping centres except St Andrews in terms of growth in rents and property values, helped by a huge new 950-space car stack. In 1994 Arnott's Inverness department store

*A general view of Inverness, with the Greig Street Suspension Bridge over the R. Ness. The steeples and towers are (from the left): Free North Church, St Columba's Church of Scotland, the Town Steeple, and Inverness Castle – built as courthouse and jail.*
*(SMPC / Harvey Wood)*

was the most northerly in the House of Fraser chain of 56 stores. By 1996 there was a Tesco store, with a second about to open.

**Inverness Services Advance**: Meantime by 1988 Charleston Academy had been built at Kinmylies; the Cameron Barracks was still the base of the Queen's Own Highlanders. The HIDB, which then had 250 staff, was changed in 1991 into a more limited body, *'Highlands & Islands Enterprise'* – its imposing Gaelic title *Iomart na Gaidhealtacht*; ten tiny local enterprise companies (LECs) were set up under its wing. In 1993 the expanding Raigmore Hospital employed some 2000 people and was the major health institution serving the Highlands. In 1995 Inverness became the home of the marketing arm of the Scottish Tourist Board (till then in Edinburgh). Inverness Auction Mart had outposts at Dingwall and Thurso in 1993, and was still busy with cattle sales in 1995. US-owned Inverness Medical made diagnostic kits from about 1995 – by 2000 employed over 200. By then call centres were multiplying, Cap Gemini employing about 80 and Westminster Health Care about 50.

**University (?) and Footballing**: By 1993 Inverness College – with a staff of 440 on two sites in the town – was the region's largest further and higher education centre, serving over 5500 students up to degree level. As the new *'University'* of the Highlands and Islands (in name only) it went *'on line'* early in 1997, enabling remote teaching in twelve further or higher education institutions from Shetland to Skye. Despite some troubles in 2000, it became the 'Millennium Institute' in 2001. Meantime the three local Highland League football clubs *(Thistle, Caledonian*, and for a time privately owned *Clachnacuddin)*, vied to join the Scottish Football League (SFL). In 1993 the two first named reluctantly united as *'Caledonian Thistle' (CT)*, which was admitted to the newly enlarged SFL of 40 clubs in 1994, and in 1995 was allowed to build a new stadium at Longman East, completed by 2000 with a single lonely stand, part paid for by ill-fated Texas Homecare who bought the old Caley ground at Telford Street. By 1999 as *'Inverness CT'* the team had worked its way up to the First Division.

**Rail Freight Killed Off**: Restoration of rail services north of Inverness in 1990 excluded goods, and about 1991 coal ceased to be delivered by rail to the Inverness terminal of J G Russell. Prior to the BR sell-off, rail traffics to Inverness were shed: gas oil, cement, and trainloads of LPG from Grangemouth. But pulpwood trains from Inverness and other more easterly loading points to Shotton survived and prospered, as did the passenger business. The doomed BR still based some freight locomotives at Inverness, but by 1995 the once-busy yard was a sad sea of rust.

**Rail Revival Started**: The new Royal Mail sorting office was built near the station. The new rail freight operators EWS, resumed traffic on the Far North line. Now lime, coal, cement, and Safeway groceries are again being rail-hauled to Millburn Yard at Inverness – where Harbro Farm Sales have large new premises. A complex of car showrooms has been built at Harbour Road. The substantial and long-established *Queensgate Hotel* in the town centre was destroyed by fire in 1992; its burnt-out shell was rebuilt in 1996–97 into 21 housing association flats. Redevelopment of the site of the old Royal Northern Infirmary for housing is imminent.

**Local Government and Music Thrive**: From 1997 the second Tesco anchored the huge new out of town Inverness Retail & Business Park beside Nairn road, serving the fast-growing suburbs around Culloden *(q.v.)*. Meantime in 1996 Inverness gained further importance when the headquarters of all local government activities for the vast Highland Region were centralised in the town; but water and sewerage services were controversially removed. By 1997 the historic Balnain House, saved from dereliction by a local trust, had become a centre for Highland music, and was taken over by the National Trust for Scotland; but it closed late in 2000. Highlands & Islands Enterprise, based in Bridge House, is to move in 2002 into new purpose-built offices at Inverness Retail & Business Park on the eastern outskirts.

**Fast-growing Highland City of Hotels**: There are now at least 5 hotels with over 80 rooms, as well as a host of smaller establishments, including the fine youth hostel and four other hostels providing some 200 beds for backpackers. The famous *Station Hotel* was renamed the *Royal Highland* in 2000. Another central hotel is planned by Tulloch's, the Inverness-based construction company (which is the largest employer in the Highlands outside of the oil firms). Developments on all sides support the claim that Inverness is Britain's fastest-growing town – but from December 2000 it's a city!

## INVERSNAID — Map 5, B4

***L. Lomond locality,*** *pop. under 100* — OS 56: NN 3409

The Arklet Falls tumble into Loch Lomond near its north-east extremity from the pass of the Arklet Water, which forms a fairly easy way to Loch Katrine. In 1713–17 a *'garrison'* or defended barracks was built in the pass by the government to resist the outlaw – and local hero – Rob Roy MacGregor. Roy's survey of about 1750, which indicated no means of access, entitled it *'Inversnaid Barracks'*, and soldiers were stationed there until about 1790. Dorothy Wordsworth described it in 1803 as *"a very large stone building with a high wall round it"*; she saw squatters, *"some wretchedly poor families"*. Although there was an established ferry from beside the falls to the Inveruglas area, she found no inn, merely a ferry-hut in a *"miserable condition"*, which the occupants would not improve for fear of the laird raising their rent. The road east was *"a mountain horse-track"* which passed the little Loch Arklet to end at the bare shore of Loch Katrine.

**Tourism through Inversnaid**: Steamboats plied on Loch Lomond by 1826. The large and *"good" Inversnaid Hotel* had been built beside the falls by 1886, with a post and telegraph office. By 1893 the ferry had been regularised, a road had been built from Aberfoyle, and about 1900 a pier was constructed for the railway paddle steamers which had operated from 1883, timed in conjunction with trains and horse-drawn coaches to provide circular tours from Glasgow and Stirling via Balloch and Loch Katrine. Early in the 20th century Glasgow Corporation built a dam near the old garrison, in order to augment the capacity of their Loch Katrine reservoir system: Loch Arklet was doubled in length and its surface raised by a few metres. The tiny steamer *Sir Walter Scott*, built in 1900 for service on Loch Katrine, was in memorably spotless condition when it carried the author in 1974, and is still at work. In 1953 Calmac introduced the paddle steamer *Maid of the Loch* for Loch Lomond cruises from Balloch. In 1979 the immediate replacement of Inversnaid pier was approved to enable the *Maid*, the last steamer on Loch Lomond, to call there again; but this comfortable vessel, on which the writer and his family had spent some pleasant hours, was sadly withdrawn about 1984 and left to await restoration at Balloch in the 1990s. In 2000 the Scottish Executive proposed to establish the Trossachs and Loch Lomond as Scotland's first National Park.

## INVERURIE & Port Elphinstone — Map 10, B3

***Aberdeenshire town,*** *pop. 9500* — OS 38: NJ 7721

Inverurie lies in the one-time Earldom of Garioch (pronounced *Geerie)* where the River Urie meets the Don. Some 4 km to the west is a well-known small stone circle with a large recumbent block, at the seemingly unpronounceable East Aquhorthies. Inverurie itself was for long an important prehistoric settlement. It has Pictish stones, and the remains of several ancient fortified sites including the large hill fort now called Bruce's Camp; it bears a Gaelic placename. By the 11th century a monastery with a lay abbot and six chapels existed at Kinkell, 2 km south-east in the parish of Rothket, also known as Keithhall & Kinkell. In the 12th century a noble brought in by David I raised the large motte known as The Bass at the rivers' confluence.

**The Burgh of Inverurie**: Inverurie was chartered as a burgh in 1195. Sources disagree as to whether the charter was always Royal or at first only baronial, but it has a long and uneventful history as a market centre. By 1307 there was no *'stronghold'* where the sick Robert Bruce could safely remain, but Inverurie town was already lengthy, as Barbour's account shows. Inverurie paid no burgh tax in 1535–56, but was the centre of a presbytery by 1593, and by 1606 had a grammar school. Gordon's map-work of 1642 depicted *'Inner-ourie'* as the principal settlement in the Garioch (which was still a detached part of Banffshire), but there were no bridges; though lying on the main way from Aberdeen to Strathbogie and Inverness, travellers relied on fords and ferries. The Roy map of about 1750 showed a one-street town some 800 m long, on the area's only through road – roughly the line of the A96 before its late 20th century improvements, but without its bridges. A road led to Kemnay via a ferry some 2 km to the west, and the *'Boat of Keithhall'* linked to the east bank of the Urie.

**Improving Communications by Road and Canal**: Bridges were soon built on the main road, and a Don bridge was built in 1791 to carry Formartine traffic. However, as late as 1797 no fairs were to be held at Inverurie, whose post town was Old Meldrum. Port Elphinstone just south of Inverurie became the terminus of the Aberdeen Canal, opened in 1805, being named in honour of the support given to the project by Sir Robert Elphinstone, the laird of Westhall near Oyne: his kinsman Sir James was to become chairman of its successor railway. Thainstone, a Palladian mansion, was built in a small park 3 km south of the town. Inverurie itself gained a post office in 1811 and the fine *Kintore Arms* was built as a coaching inn; by 1825 there was a brewery. In 1839 Watsons founded an ironmongery business – which still thrives.

**Paper Mill and Railway bring Growth**: Thomas Tait & Sons established their paper mill at Port Elphinstone in 1852, and it was expanded about 1890 to use wood pulp with the aid of calcium bisulphate made on site *(see Hay & Stell)*. Meantime the Great North of Scotland Railway (GNSR) had bought the canal and infilled it, reaching the town in 1854 en route from Aberdeen to Inverness (a link completed at Keith in 1858). Eventually Wordie & Co operated a rail to road cartage depot in Inverurie, where at some time a gasworks was set up. A branch line to Oldmeldrum was opened in 1856, and another from Inveramsay, 5 km north-west of the town, opened to Turriff in 1857. Inverurie's importance soared, so a new Town Hall was built in 1862–63 (after 1902 a Carnegie library was added to it). In 1894 Inverurie was described by Murray as *"a neat small town"* with the *"good" Kintore Arms Hotel.*

**Railway Works and New Station**: Between 1898 and 1905 the GNSR built on a 6 ha site east of Harlaw Road its extensive, granite-walled and electrically-powered locomotive, carriage and wagon works, the last such built in Scotland. In 1901–05 four streets of substantial granite houses were provided for the employees, plus a park and other amenities such as electric light; the works had their own 14-strong fire brigade. In 1902 the GNSR also opened a new station 1 km north of the poky original, a spacious showpiece in granite, lavishly panelled internally. Locomotive building began in 1909; when GNSR No. 31 was completed in 1910 it was used on the Royal train from Aberdeen to Ballater. From 1914 some HR engines were repaired at Inverurie, but war and financial problems ended building work in 1921 when a mere 10 engines had been completed.

**Beef, Golf, Films and Railway Closures**: After the 1923 grouping into the London & North Eastern Railway (LNER), the GNSR works were demoted to repair shops. However, beef carted from the local abattoir by Wordies was still carried to Aberdeen and London by daily trains. Optimists founded the Inverurie golf club in 1923, with a 9-hole parkland course; one unusual job for Wordies was to shift the club house across the course (which was extended to 18 holes around 1960). Meantime the 460-seat *Victoria Cinema* was built in 1935 to attractive designs by T Scott Sutherland, and the stark buildings of Inverurie Academy were erected in mid-century. The Oldmeldrum branch railway had already been closed to passengers in 1931, and the Turriff branch followed in 1951, when Inverurie had small-town facilities and a population rather over 5000. In 1947 the former GNSR works buildings still covered 11,300 m², and their 240 staff repaired locomotives, carriages and (mainly) wagons. Freight services to Turriff and Oldmeldrum ended in 1966; Inverurie then ceased to be a junction, and lost its engine shed; falling workloads caused closure of the wagon works in 1969.

**Local Government and Marketing Grow**: In 1971 the population was 5500; by 1972 there was a local museum. In 1975 Inverurie became the centre of the new Gordon District, which built Gordon House for its needs, and grew substantially as a service centre. With local authority aid the wagon works premises were re-used by three engineering firms, and later also for a North Sea pipe-coating plant. By 1980 Mathers processed meat at Harlaw Road. New industrial and housing estates blossomed north-west of the town, whose population grew rapidly. In 1990 the District Council developed a *'Food Park'*, and a new sewage disposal works was built. A second local newspaper, the *Inverurie Herald*, was published by 1991 as an offshoot of the *Forfar Dispatch*. In 1989–90 Aberdeen & Northern Marts built the Thainstone auction mart complex, described as the largest in Europe; it sells cattle and sheep from as far afield as Shetland, though most come from a 25 km radius. By 1991 over 9500 people lived in Inverurie, served by a large 8-doctor practice based in its health centre, and the fine station building was refurbished.

**Paper, Pulpwood and Meat**: Tait's paper mill was taken over in 1989 by the American company Federal Paper & Board, which set about tripling its capacity, to 125,000 tonnes of uncoated paper a year. In 1994 Scotch Premier Meat described itself as a young company, operating modern slaughter and boning facilities in Inverurie, Edinburgh and Sheffield. In 1995 Reekie Davidson Ltd was still a big dealer in farm machinery, with a Turriff branch. Scotframe manufacture kit houses (80 staff by 2001, including at Cumbernauld). Some pulpwood still goes south by rail (now run by EW&S).

**Growth in Services and Administration**: The mansion of *Thainstone House* became a hotel in 1995, when the *Victoria Cinema* was still remarkably in use, its time evenly divided between films and bingo. The town museum features the former railway industry (which gave its name to the local football team). In 1996 Gordon district disappeared, joining Banff & Buchan and Kincardine & Deeside in a new unitary local authority, named Aberdeenshire; Inverurie became one of its centres. By 1999 Inverurie and Port Elphinstone had been bypassed by the A96; the town is still spreading up the valley of the Urie.

**Bustling Centre with much-needed Plans**: Besides Tesco and Gateway supermarkets, the town's shops include a wide range of specialists, and its services include a bus station, public library, swimming pool and fire station. At least half a dozen small/medium hotels serve the area. The Council plans extensive improvements to the traffic-dominated town centre – including pedestrian links, the extension of the old town hall to provide performance, gallery and meeting spaces, and a new library and museum.

## IONA, Isle of — Map 4, B2

***Island, Inner Hebrides,*** *pop. 130* — OS 48: NM 2824

In 563 AD Columba, a Christian Irish prince, landed in the Inner Hebrides, then under Pictish control, with other Dalriadans or Irish Scots. About 566 he founded a monastery on the small isle of Iona off the western tip or Ross of Mull, and there he based his missionary journeys until his death in 597, by which time much of Pictland or Pictavia (now Scotland) was Christian. Columba was made a saint, and the isle became the centre of a bishopric. In the seventh century the Culdees honoured him by building an important abbey, from which Oswald went to found famed Lindisfarne about 633. Cash may have been paid to his mother house, for a hoard mainly comprising Anglo-Saxon coins was found on what is commonly named Iona, deriving from *Ioua* (from the Irish for a yew tree), or *I-Una*, meaning the first isle to be converted to Christianity. It is also named *'Icolmkill'* (from Gaelic *'Isle of Columba's church')*. The abbey was plundered six times between 793 and 986 by Vikings from the north; the worst such visitation was in 806 when no fewer than 68 monks were massacred! Following the seizure of Pictland by the Scots, Columba's relics were taken from Iona to Dunkeld in 849, but despite these repeated depredations the island was apparently never entirely deserted.

**Before and after the Reformation**: The abbey was rebuilt from 1203 for Benedictines by Reginald of Islay, using red granite from Tormore on Mull, and by 1208 there was an

*The Iona Marble works. This quarry, operated in the early 20th century, extracted blocks of the greenish Iona Marble and cut it into thin slabs, using a frame-saw powered by this engine. (JRH)*

Augustinian nunnery. In 1549 Monro noted *'I-Colm-kill'* as *"fruitful of corn and pasturage, and good for fishing; formerly the most honourable and ancient place in Scotland"*. An alleged total of 48 Scottish kings were buried there until either Duncan (1040) or Macbeth (1057) – sources differ as to the last – plus eight kings of Norway and most of the Lords of the Isles. It still possessed an abbey with monks, which had become the cathedral church of the Bishops of the Isles since the latter were expelled by the English from the Isle of Man. The nunnery had a prioress, and there was a parish kirk and other chapels. In 1560 the Bishop from Icolmkill sat in Parliament. The abbey was ruined at the Reformation; its associated settlement called *Baile Mor* (*'big village'* in Gaelic) survived – just! Pont's original map of around 1600 named the isle as *'Iona or Cholumbkil'* and its settlement as *'Sodore'*, i.e. the head of what the Norse called the Sudereys or Southern Islands.

**Poverty and Ignorance Rules**: In the 18th century Icomkill was a poor and totally illiterate community; in 1772 Pennant found *"the remains of the old town still inhabited, with about 50 houses, mostly very mean"*. The abbey mill was out of use, and people ground with hand querns. In 1773 Boswell noted a *"village"* of drystone huts, self-sufficient except for iron, with no inn, no school, and only two English speakers. Iona was still called Icomkill up to the mid 1820s; from time to time a little coloured marble (ophicalcite) was quarried on the shore at the southern tip of the isle.

**Iona's Ruins draw Tourists**: From 1826 summer steamers linked Iona twice weekly with Oban via the islet of Staffa with its spectacular basalt-columned caves. Felix Mendelssohn visited Staffa in 1829, and his fine *Hebrides Overture* helped to popularise the area; for a time from 1846 the steamer service became thrice weekly. However, although 500 people lived on Iona in 1841, no post office seems to have existed until 1856, and in 1858 the German traveller Fontane found that Baile Mor was just *"possibly 40 wretched huts"*, occupied by families with undisciplined begging children. There were then two excursion steamers a week from Oban and Tobermory to view the *'cathedral'*, which he regarded as *"among the finest ruins in Scotland"*. Emigration then halved the population in 40 years.

**Return to Prosperity: Abbey and Community Rebuilt**: The ruins had such historic charisma that the 8th Duke of Argyll gave them to the Church of Scotland. With growing national prosperity came more tourists: one of them, named Thomas Cook, donated a library! By 1894 two hotels were open, the *Argyll* and *Saint Columba's*, served by a daily steamer from Oban. A little marble was again quarried from 1907 to 1914, shipped from a nearby quay, but by 1931 the population had halved again. The ruined Abbey was rebuilt from about 1900 to 1910 by the Church of Scotland, and the Iona Community was founded by Glasgow-born George Macleod in 1938, with financial aid from Sir James Lithgow, the Greenock industrialist. The tourist trade was steadily expanding, the Highland Folk Museum being founded on the island; but by 1953 it had been moved to more central Kingussie. When the author first visited Iona from Oban on the steamer *King George V* in 1953, an adventurous transfer to small boats landed passengers at a basic pier.

**In Trust after the Campbells**: These adventures were ended about 1964 in favour of a frequent passenger ferry from Fionnphort, capable of carrying a vehicle when necessary. Then in 1979 after 300 years of ownership the Campbells sold the isle to pay off death duties; the buyer Sir Hugh Fraser of Allander gave it to the National Trust for Scotland. By the late 1980s Iona supported a regular day-trip trade from Oban, involving two ferries and a coach line across Mull; the island has a quite substantial local store. In 1991 when the resident population of the isle was 130, a new ferry was built (at St Monans) for the Iona run, to carry 250 passengers (and also ten cars, though these are not normally carried). By 1997 the former manse – designed by Telford – had become a Heritage Centre. In 1999 Historic Scotland took over the abbey buildings. The two century-old hotels are the *Argyll* (15 rooms) and the *Columba* (26).

## IRVINE

**Map 1, C1**

***Ayrshire large town,*** *pop. 33,000*

OS 70: NS 3238

Irvine stands on a high bank above the river of that name; it may have been the site of the Roman *Vindogara*, but little is known of the area until a burgh was established around 1140 by David I's Great Constable of Scotland, Hugh de Morville. As the centre of justice for Cunninghame, its castle would probably have dated from that time, but was certainly in existence in 1297. Two kilometres north-east was Stane Castle, evidently dating back to a time when most castles were of wood, though the surviving tower is apparently of the 16th century. Although from 1205 Ayr took over as the centre of the wider sheriffdom, Irvine became a baronial burgh between 1214 and 1314 (being shown on the mid 13th century Gough map, probably nearer the former date).

**Royal Burgh**: Irvine was re-chartered as a Royal Burgh in 1371, and had a 14th century Carmelite friary. Despite its dangerous sandbar it became a river port, where contact with the south bank depended on a ferry. In 1432 Ayr tried to seize the trade in hides, but despite this, Irvine's Customs receipts – though very small and not including wool – tended to grow through the century and to contribute significantly to Scotland's Customs revenue, rising to around 2% in the mid 16th century. An English report of that time showed the harbour depth was 3m at high tide, though it warned of the narrow sandbarred entrance. Irvine's contribution to burgh taxes rose but little, and remained under 1% in 1535. However in 1560 the burgh was sufficiently important to be represented in Parliament, and greater success enabled Irvine Academy to be founded in 1572; a parish school was added in 1586. By 1593 the town was the centre of a presbytery, and Timothy Pont's map made about then showed *'Irrwin'* as a large town with a river bridge, and upstream three mills.

**Troubled by Mud**: By 1621 the port was again paying sizeable Scottish Customs duties, and by 1636 its shipowners traded with Bordeaux and Dublin; although there was less shipping than at Ayr, Irvine was described by Brereton as *"a town daintily situate"*. In 1639 it was the 14th burgh in Scotland in tax terms; in 1645–47 Glasgow University temporarily operated at Irvine to escape the city's plague. Tucker found in 1655 *"a small burgh town"*, its port so badly affected by silting that *"it wrestles for life to maintain a small trade to France, Norway and Ireland, with herring and other goods, brought on horseback from Glasgow, for the purchasing of timber, wine, and other commodities"*. However, by then a brewery was active.

**Recovery into Textiles, Quays and Roads**: By 1677 the town council was building a quay at the river mouth; in 1680 one of the earliest post offices in Scotland was opened. Fullarton, across the bridge from Irvine, was granted a barony charter in 1707. Defoe noted in the 1720s, *"Here are two handsome streets, a good quay, and not only room in the harbour for a great many ships, but a great many ships in it also." Irwin*, as he called it, had more trade than Ayr, especially in coal for export to Ireland; this may have come from pits at Dreghorn, 3 km to the east. A bleachfield was set up in 1738. By the mid 1750s *Irwin* (as the town was still named on Roy's survey), had seven radial roads – an unusually large number for the time, especially since the surrounding area was entirely rural. Uniquely, the road to Neilston – which then passed between Stewarton and Dunlop – was labelled *"Cart road from Irwin to Glasgow"*. By 1760 and for a short period after – silting problems apparently overcome – Irvine was said to be the third port in Scotland.

**Late Eighteenth Century Prosperity**: The new Turnpike Trust for Ayrshire, set up in 1767, made improvement of the Irvine–Kilmarnock road its first priority. Later, the Girdle Toll was set up near Stane Castle, where what Roy labelled as the *'Post Road to Glasgow'* already forked off to Stewarton. By the late 18th century some 400 people worked in three cotton spinning mills in Irvine, and boats were being built. In the 1790s three coaches a week served the town en route from Ayr to Glasgow, and there was an annual fair. Hunters & Co, bankers of Ayr, had a branch in Irvine by 1793, as did the Paisley Banking Company. Heron (1799) noted the banks, and the population of *"about 4500"*, including over 300 sailors, who *"export annually to Ireland about 24,000 tonnes of coals"*. It also exported the local novelist John Galt, born in 1779, who emigrated to Canada and founded the towns of Guelph and Galt. The ugly Fullarton House which existed by 1790 was rebuilt in 1845; it contained fine plasterwork.

**Lifeboat, Chemicals and Railways**: The brewery closed early in the 19th century, but more coal mines were sunk, and in 1807 over 50 little ships were Irvine-owned, taking coal as far as America; as a Port of Registry, its vessels carried the letters IE. In 1827 Chambers found Irvine *"a small but thriving royal burgh and seaport"* where *"a new academy has been erected"*; this had been an 1816 relocation. A gasworks was established in 1827, and a lifeboat station was opened at the river's mouth in 1834, the first in southern Scotland to be provided by the RNLI's predecessor, the Shipwreck Institution. The first section of the Glasgow Paisley Kilmarnock & Ayr Railway was opened from Ayr to Irvine in 1839, and extended to Glasgow the next year; at that time there were still 400 handloom weavers in the town. By 1847, the year that the harbour branch railway opened, racing was established at Bogside beside the Garnock estuary. The harbour was rebuilt, and with the completion in 1848 of the Glasgow & South Western Railway (G&SWR) *'Busby'* line from Kilmarnock to Irvine through the colliery-rich areas of Springside and Dreghorn, the port prospered still more from coal. Chemical industries and a large ironworks were also begun.

**Shipbuilding and Diversification**: Shipbuilding flourished under various names from about 1868, but the harbour again declined later in the century. Trawlers and coasters were built by the Irvine Shipbuilding & Engineering Company until 1912, then by Mackie and Thomson from Govan. Two local newspapers were founded in the 1870s, the *Irvine Herald* in 1871 and the *Irvine Times* in 1873. By 1876 the G&SWR had established workshops in the town, and the Lanarkshire & Ayrshire Railway – the Caledonian in disguise – opened a branch from Kilwinning in 1890. The Irvine golf club was founded in 1887; by 1894 its Bogside course was adjoined by a railway station, while collieries operated to the east and at Bartonholme north of Bogside, where the racecourse circuit actually surrounded a colliery! Two hotels were open in the town, whose population was nearing 10,000. A power station was built at Irvine in 1903, and the Ravenspark municipal golf course was laid out in 1907. The lifeboat station was closed in 1914.

**Hosiery and Hospitals**: From handloom weaving had grown a knitwear industry – but the shipyard closed in 1928, and was extinguished by the voluntary rationalisation body NSS in 1934. Coal exports dwindled, and the port then handled mainly chemicals. In the 1930s and 1940s John Campbell of Irvine owned a few coasting steamers; at least one carried bricks to Lerwick. The railway from Kilwinning closed in the 1930s. An arms factory was built in 1937, by which time the local Hosiery Manufacturing Company employed 700 workers and expanded into Troon; Cunningham of Stewarton opened a textile factory in Irvine. The building of the Ayrshire Central Hospital began north of the town in 1935. Across the golf course by 1963 was the sprawling Ravenspark mental hospital (by 1981 each had around 400 beds). Meantime by the 1950s Irvine's other facilities were those of a typical town, with seven tiny hotels or inns. The suburb which had rapidly developed by 1963 at Girdle Toll had gained some 3000 inhabitants by 1971.

**Irvine New Town – a Difficult Start**: Irvine was selected as a growth area in an SDD white paper of 1963, and was designated as a New Town with a Development Corporation (DC) in 1966, the year that Fullarton House was sadly demolished. Irvine refused a Glasgow overspill connection, and its industrial estates – though attracting some new knitwear firms and stimulating population inflow – were at first relatively unsuccessful for a new town. However, it developed fine public housing, notably at Bourtreehill, and replaced old chemical waste dumps with a river-mouth park. A major bypass built in the mid 1970s removed the A78 through traffic, and in 1975 Volvo Trucks of Sweden opened a new manufacturing plant,

*The Caledonian paper mill at Irvine, built by its Finnish owners in 1989, and the largest paper mill in Scotland. Over 400 workers produce glossy printing papers using Scottish softwood pulp and Cornish china clay.* (SMPC / Doug Corrance)

able to produce four new trucks a day. In 1975 Irvine was chosen as the headquarters of the large Cunninghame District; but they proceeded to erect a dismally basic office block beside the town centre. By 1980 Rockware Glass had established the Portland Factory.

**The Magnum Centre**: The Magnum Leisure Centre on the seafront, which opened in 1976, is a major sports complex, including by 1994 both an indoor and a heated outdoor swimming pool, as well as a 1200-seat concert hall, and a 323-seat film/ show theatre. The involuntary leisure time bestowed by unemployment helped it to become in the late 1980s Scotland's most popular single attraction, peaking at over a million entrants a year. In 1990–93 it held second place, having slipped to 800,000 annual entries; but unlike top-placed Edinburgh Castle, they were mainly drawn from the local area, and central Scotland.

**More Industry, but Britain's Highest Unemployment!**: Hyster Ltd, makers of mechanical handling equipment, had established a plant at Irvine by 1978, when further development was carried out. Scotboard (later known as Caberboard) was manufacturing chipboard in Irvine by 1979, smoke from the works blowing over the town centre. In 1979 Skefco – the ball-bearing manufacturers SKF(UK) – ran down their Irvine plant, with the loss of 750 jobs, and Hyster decided to expand in Northern Ireland instead. In August of that year the town had the highest rate of joblessness in Great Britain, at 15.5%, when the national average was only 5.1%; and worse was to come: further industrial closures caused unemployment to peak at over 22% in 1983.

**Regaining the Role of District Centre**: Even so, by 1981 Irvine had become a major local centre, serving nearly twice the population of 1951. Although the Bogside racecourse had closed by 1987, much had been done to improve the town's facilities. About then the large 127-roomed *Hospitality Inn* was built beside the Annick Water. The Bridgegate shopping centre exceeded 5000 m$^2$ by 1989, and an international telephone exchange was also provided. The old bridge was swept away to enable the building of the covered Rivergate shopping centre, bridging across the river. Although this was rather crude in design and execution, at least it effectively joined with the ancient town centre. In 1991 Rivergate was expanded to a floor area of over 31,000 m$^2$, including a new ASDA superstore and more parking space. By 1990 Blue Circle had a rail-served cement depot at Irvine, which remained a minor river port.

**Volvo Prospers in Irvine: it's an Ill Wind**: By 1988 Volvo was able to produce ten trucks a day, also celebrating their 20,000$^{th}$ truck. Further investment was to take the plant's capacity to 12 per day in 1989. However, with orders hit by the Thatcher government's deregulation of bus services in England, Volvo decided in 1991 to cease bus production, close their Whitehaven bus plant, and transfer the assembly of bus chassis to Irvine, which now had spare capacity. The firm was recruiting again at Irvine in 1995, planning a 60% rise in production to 5500 vehicles a year, including its new long-haul vehicle. In 1997 the plant had 550 workers, making bus chassis for Alexanders.

**The Caledonian Mill**: The very large but pleasingly designed *Caledonian* paper mill built by the Finnish company Kymmene at Meadowhead 3 km south of the town, was opened in 1989 to produce lightweight coated paper for glossy printing; in 1991, 432 workers, mainly men, produced 162,000 tonnes of paper. China clay (from St Austell, Cornwall) and Sitka spruce timber were brought in by rail – although timber arrived at only a fifth of the desired rate, due to British Rail's inability to provide the required service. Pulp was also used for input. In 1993 half of Caledonian's 200,000 tonnes of timber was bought from the Forestry Commission. By 1995 Caledonian Paper – which had been working flat out since early 1994 – was at last making profits.

**Electronics buck the Recession**: With a thousand new jobs a year in the town since 1985, unemployment had fallen to only 10% by 1990. By 1990 a new firm, Grayhill, was making electronic switchgear in the town. In 1990 Conner Peripherals of the USA, manufacturers of computer disc drives, located a new plant at Irvine; although they abandoned expansion plans for Irvine, by 1995 the operation employed almost 400 people. Electroconnect, set up early in 1991 to manufacture specialist circuit boards in a new 3000 m$^2$ factory, was soon snapped up for expansion by Prestwick Circuits, which were still expanding in PCBs at both Irvine and Ayr in 1995. In 1993 the German-owned computer firm Escom UK, lately established at Prestwick, set up a 3700 m$^2$ facility in Irvine as a distribution centre, providing 140 new jobs within two years and marketing through their own growing chain of shops throughout Britain. In 1996 computer manufacturers Digital *(see Ayr)* employed 450 people at Irvine. In 2000 Fullarton of Kilwinning announced a new 700-job factory at Irvine to make computer components.

**Services Expand, but Education Problematic**: There was already a museum at Irvine when in 1987–88 the Linthouse engine works building at Govan was dismantled and re-erected at Irvine's new Scottish Maritime Museum at Harbourside, which by 1991 showed several historic vessels. The hull of the world's oldest clipper ship, the 791-ton *Carrick* – built in Sunderland in 1864 as the *City of Adelaide* – which had sunk in Princes' Dock Govan about 1990, was raised in 1992 to become an extra exhibit. The tucked-away Riverway retail park with five retail warehouses was open by mid 1990. At that time the population was a youthful 33,000; a majority rented terraced houses from public authorities, and almost half of all households lacked a car. Higher qualifications were few, and Strathclyde Region wanted to close Irvine Royal Academy in 1992, to make economies; but, after 420 years, it survived and now has almost 1100 pupils.

**Takeovers, Slump and Failures**: A new leisure clothing factory set up in 1989 by Unitex of Hong Kong, which employed 120 people by mid 1990, failed in 1992 and 140 jobs were lost. In 1990 Itech employed 400 people assembling printed circuit boards, when they were taken over by the Korean firm Ankor Anam, who hoped to provide 1000 jobs making semiconductors; but in depressed 1992 the 200 remaining staff were shed and the firm moved out of the town. Meantime in 1991 the closure of the little-known Courtaulds Textiles plant led to the loss of 250 jobs. Irvine's beaches were among the most polluted in Britain in 1990–94.

**North Ayrshire as a Unitary Authority**: More happily, in 1994 Smith Kline Beecham had a 770-worker penicillin plant at Irvine; in 1995 the Turkish clothing firm MIC announced 450 new jobs at Meadowhead, making T-shirts and sweatshirts; and in 2001, Citiraya of Singapore planned a computer recycling plant (there's gold in them thar computers!). SCI provide 900 jobs in computer equipment. Irvine was the last Scottish New Town to remain active; the DC which had lately completed some striking and popular new housing at Harbourside, was wound up in 1996, when *'North Ayrshire'* became a unitary authority, with Irvine's Cunninghame House as its capital. By 1998 Girdle Toll had been entirely bypassed, enabling major housing developments to be added to the north. A new *'discovery centre'* has been opened as a millennium project on the north side of the harbour, accessed by a new opening footbridge, but sadly in 2000 the Scottish Maritime Museum was under threat of closure, and was even intending to demolish the *Carrick's* listed hull for lack of finance. The *Hospitality Inn* (127 rooms) is the largest hotel, but there's also the small *Annfield House* and the long-established *Redburn*.

## ISLE OF WHITHORN

**Map 1, C5**

***Galloway coastal village,*** *pop. 350* — OS 83: NX 4736

Traces of various ancient forts and carved rocks survive on the remote coast of the Galloway Machers, which culminates in the 50m promontory of Burrow Head. In 397 AD St Ninian is said to have founded a chapel on the rocky Isle of Whithorn, 3km north-east, which shelters a cove at the mouth of the Drummullin *('Millhill')* Burn. Some 900 years later a chapel was built, a centre of pilgrimage round which grew one of Scotland's two most southerly settlements. Castle Feather at Burrow Head is a 16th century tower; the 17th century L-plan Isle of Whithorn Castle stands in the village. A school was opened at nearby Bysbie (a Nordic name) in 1631. The Roy map shows that by the 1750s a road led to Whithorn, 5km inland, for which it was the port until Garlieston *(q.v.)* was developed in the 1770s.

**Harbour, Fishing and Yachting**: A safer though shallow harbour was created by a causeway built in 1790 to link the islet with the mainland, and an inn was built. Despite its low trade potential, in 1799 Heron found about 400 people in *"a neat small town with a harbour; eight or nine sloops belong to it"*. More than 450 people lived in and around the village in 1861, and a lifeboat station was open from 1869 to 1919. During the 1939–45 war there was an artillery training ground at Burrow Head. There were over 550 residents by 1951, with a small boatyard, though this had closed by 1976. By 1979 a caravan and camping site was open at Burrow Head. The population had fallen to only some 350 by the 1980s, but two inns were open in this mainly yachting resort, and there had been some new development in the village. The year 2000 opened with disaster when the scallop dredger *Solway Harvester* sank in a severe gale off the Isle of Man, its 7-man crew from the Isle, Whithorn village and Garlieston all sadly drowned. The *Queens Arms*, the *Steam Packet Hotel* and the post office serve the area.

## ISLE ORNSAY

**Map 8, B4**

***Skye village,*** *pop. 200* — OS 32: NG 7012

Southern Skye comprises the lengthy peninsula of Sleat *(q.v.)*. Monro noted in 1549 that Donald MacDonald Gorm owned both Trotternish in the north of Skye and Sleat in the south, including the castle of *Camns in Sleit*, identifiable with Dun Ban at Camas Croise on the east side of Sleat. About 5km to the north of this is the inlet of Loch na Dal, where Kinloch Lodge was built in 1680 by the Clan Donald. Between these places, the offshore islet Ornsay shelters a natural harbour where in later years a substantial stone pier was built, served from 1820 by steamers on a route from Glasgow via the Crinan Canal; by 1826 they also served Portree. An outstandingly beautiful prospect across the Sound of Sleat helped to create a minor fishing resort with an inn; 1.5km north was Duisdale House. From the mid 19th century, railways made other places more accessible, and development at Isle Ornsay ceased.

**Gaelic Tourism, Art and Oysters**: The so-called Ornsay lighthouse, first lighted in 1857, and automated in 1962, actually stands on Eilean Sionnach, an outlying rock. By 1953 Duisdale House had become the *Duisdale Hotel*. By then the resident population of the village was about 175. *Kinloch Lodge*, extended in 1972, became in 1973 both the residence of the clan chief, Lord Macdonald of Macdonald, and a hotel. In 1991, 188 people lived in the area, including crofting Drumfearn, 5km north. The facilities of a small village are available in what the locally strong Gaelic community calls *Eilean Iarmain* after an Ossianic character; by 1997 there was also a gallery. There's the *Duisdale Hotel*, the *Kinloch Lodge*, and the 19th century inn on Sir Iain Noble's estate, the *Hotel Eilean Iarmain*, with Gaelic-speaking staff – and its own oyster beds!

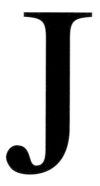

## JEDBURGH & Oxnam

**Map 3, B4**

***Borders town,*** *pop. 4100* OS 74 & 80: NT 6520

The many early earthworks in Jed Forest, south of the River Teviot, imply an area already well settled when in the first and second centuries the Romans built a small fort at Cappuck on the little Oxnam Water. This fort, 4km south of its confluence with the Teviot, guarded the key road from Corbridge to Inveresk, later called Dere Street, which crossed the Teviot at its confluence with the Jed Water. Roman roads gave marauders swift movement, so *Geddewrd*, also called *Jeddart*, the supposed capital of the post-Roman *Gadeni*, was tucked away among the hills 10km up the Jed Water, at the place now known as Old Jedward. Following the Anglian conquests, by 854 AD the Northumbrian see of Lindisfarne had established a monastery there; the church which existed by about 1080 is also believed to have been at Old Jedward, though a carved panel found at the later abbey is possibly of seventh century origin, and a silver hoard of about 1025 contained English coins. Another parish church was founded at Oxnam.

**The Abbey and Burgh**: An Augustinian priory for French monks from St Quentin in Picardy was founded by David I in 1138, below the red-rock gorge of the Jed, and about 6km north of the original settlement. In 1147 he elevated the priory to the status of an abbey for canons regular, and its great buildings were completed within a century. Although not a good site for a trading centre, the new Jedburgh became a Royal Burgh between 1124 and 1214 (sources disagree). A royal castle was built in the 12th century, and a *'hospital'* was established. However, as late as 1220 the Abbey chapel also functioned as the parish church. By 1296 the Abbot owned three properties in Berwick, where the community seems to have bought its wine.

**Border Burnings and the Bridge**: South of the town is an area that was a royal forest from the 13th century. Some 2 km south is Lintalee, where about 1320 Bruce's lieutenant Sir James Douglas built what Barbour, writing in 1375, called *"a fair manor in the meadow"*. It seems that this was soon ruined in a battle with the English, who found Jedburgh castle so useful that the Scots themselves destroyed it in 1409. However, Jedburgh did eventually become the caput of the shire of Roxburgh (whose own castle was abandoned in 1460). The late 15th century Ferniehirst Castle, across the river from Lintalee, was a seat of the Kerrs, later Marquises of Lothian. The little town became a minor local centre, whose contribution to burgh taxes rose but little, remaining under 1% in 1535. The Jed was bridged in the 16th century, but the fine Abbey buildings were burned in 1523. When also burning the town for Henry VIII, the Earl of Surrey reported *"there was two times more houses therein than Berwick, and well builded"*. Further havoc was wreaked in 1544–45, but the Abbey recovered enough to be represented in Parliament in 1560, as was the burgh.

**Problems After the Reformation**: An early parish school was founded in 1569, and later the abbey properties passed to Lord Home. The Teviot had been bridged at Bonjedward by the time that Pont visited the area around 1600, but his map did not show the Jed bridge; however the name of the tiny town that he indicated appeared as *'Iedd-brugh'*, and there was a mill above Ferniehurst. By 1593 Jedburgh was the centre of a presbytery, and in 1608 another parish school was opened, at Hundalee to the south. In 1639 Jedburgh ranked only 39th of Scottish burghs in tax rents, but three mills were turning in the town by 1670, and a post office was opened at the early date of 1689. By 1728 the Jedburgh magistrates – aided by the Trustees for the Improvement of Manufactures – had built the town's first woollen factory; but this was not very successful. Roy's map of the early 1750s showed the bridge, but only three radial trackways led from the very small cross-shaped town: to Kelso, to Hawick and over Carter Bar to England. In 1760 Pococke reported on Jedburgh's *"decayed"* woollen manufacture, and in 1776 James Loch commented that local political dissension had led to neglect of business and manufactures; the 56 local looms then did only jobbing work.

**Colourful Growth**: The way from England via Carter Bar and Jedburgh to Galashiels and Lauder was turnpiked by an Act of 1768, opening up the valley to the world. By 1780 John Hardy of Hawick had introduced framework knitting to the moribund little town, and Hilson & Sons (who acquired the woollen factory in 1786) made more of it over the years, specialising in tartan weaving. Sir David Brewster, born in Jedburgh in 1781, made a scientific study of light and invented the kaleidoscope. By 1790 Jedburgh enjoyed two coaches a week to Edinburgh, and the postal service operated daily by 1797, a year when four fairs were scheduled in Jedburgh. In 1799 Heron found about two thousand people in what had become *"a considerable town. It has a good market for corn and cattle and is the seat of the courts of justice for the county."*

**Pears, Brewing, Banking, Tanning and Slating**: Dorothy Wordsworth wrote in 1803 of the stone bridge across the Teviot north of the town, where Assizes were in progress, and the resulting fullness of what seemed to be the only inn, adding

*A general view of Jedburgh in the late 19th century, with the town dominated by the very complete ruin of the Romanesque Abbey Church – as it still is today.* (GWW collection)

*"The town looks exceedingly beautiful on its low eminence. Jedburgh is famous in Scotland for pears, which were first cultivated there in the gardens of the monks, where there are many remarkably old pear-trees."* Snuff mills and tanneries opened early in the 19th century, and by then there was a substantial brewery in the town; two others were also open by 1825. By 1807 wool was being carded commercially, and by 1817 a shearing mill was finishing the woollen fabrics; a woollen raising mill was proposed in the 1820s. The old jail, still in use in 1816, was replaced in 1823 by a new prison on the site of the one-time castle. By 1825 there was a British Linen Company branch bank, at which local sheriff and author Sir Walter Scott was a customer. According to Chambers in 1827, Jedburgh *"now contains about 5000 inhabitants. It has a considerable manufacture of stockings, flannels and narrow cloths, the seat of a circuit and of a presbytery."* Still the county town, it was in the process of changing from thatched to slated roofs.

**Into the Railway Age**: The knitting industry was in decline by 1825, but in 1844 there were 60 stocking frames in and around Jedburgh, whose *'Border Games'* became an annual event in 1853. Hartrigge House, designed by David Bryce, was built in 1854 on the hill just east of the town. In 1856 a local company opened a line from Roxburgh to Jedburgh; this soon joined the North British Railway and led to the opening of a town gasworks; four small woollen factories were built in the late 1860s. By 1869 over 200 workers were making textiles, mainly tweeds; Bongate mill made woollens from the late 19th century. The population in 1891 was 3400, enough to spawn a golf club the next year; this laid out a hillside course of 9 holes (as it still is). A public library began in 1892, aided by Carnegie. Despite what Murray called *"an air of antiquity"* there were two hotels by 1894, the *Royal* (which was to endure), and the merely *"fair" Spread Eagle*.

**A quiet Early Twentieth Century**: In 1899 county town status was lost to the more nodal Newtown St Boswells. An electric power station was built in 1901, an early development for such a small town; but the last brewery closed about 1906. A large rayon factory was built in 1928 but this too closed, in 1956. The rail passenger service was not reinstated after the disastrous floods of 1948, and by 1968 the goods service and rail tracks had vanished; little industry remained except agricultural engineering. Despite these setbacks Jedburgh remained a very pleasant place in which to live, so its population hovered round 4000 throughout the century, and its small-town facilities were relatively stable. By 1953 a 16th century bastel house where Queen Mary is reputed to have stayed in 1566 had been restored as a museum, and by 1963 a country house near Old Jedward had become the *Jedforest Hotel*. By 1961 Ferniehurst Castle was a youth hostel, though by 1995 it was no longer used as such.

**Mainetti make Millions of Coathangers**: Some new small industrial concerns started operating on the site of the former railway station around 1970, when leather, skin and fibreglass works were open. Covered municipal swimming baths and the library were available when burgh status was lost to (Hawick-based) Roxburgh District of Borders Region in 1975. By 1977 Orde of Jedburgh were manufacturing ladies' outerwear; by 1991 much of their production was exported. Mainetti UK, a subsidiary of the Dutch firm Mauna, were making plastic coathangers in the town by 1977; by 1990 300 people were employed by Mainetti, and 120 million of these light items were produced each year. The factory also made plastic pipes and ducts, some from recycled material; but in 1991 recession cut the jobs by 200.

**Saws and Tourist Sights**: Meantime about 1977 L S Starrett, makers of tools and saws, had built a large plant in hillside parkland east of the town, where Hartrigge House was already ruinous. About that time the historic town centre was saved from the through traffic on the A68 when a short internal bypass was built, and benefited when a substantial new tourist information centre was opened beside it in 1978. This forms an important gateway to Scotland for travellers arriving over Carter Bar; the spectacular abbey ruins remain a notable visual attraction, and a caravan site had been established north of the town by 1983.

**Skiers and Walkers**: By 1990 Jedburgh's one-time local newspaper the *Jedburgh Gazette* had been absorbed into the *Southern Reporter* of Selkirk. At that time Starretts employed 300 people at Jedburgh, producing bandsaws, saw blades, hand tools and engineers' precision measuring devices; internationally owned, they exported well over half their output. By then a dry ski slope, the only one in the Borders, had been laid out at Jedburgh Grammar School's Anna sports complex; this school had some 400 pupils. The 1991 population of Jedburgh was 4100; male unemployment was relatively low, and 42% of those in jobs walked to work. By 1998 a second museum was open in this remarkably busy little place. The *Jedforest Hotel* is 6km south; in the town are the little *Glenfriars House*, plus guest houses, restaurants, pubs and caravan sites, offering tourists a good choice of facilities.

## JOHN O'GROATS, Canisbay & Huna **Map 13, B4**

***Caithness settlements,*** *pop. 600 (area)* OS 12: ND 3872

Water mills are believed to have worked since Viking times at Huna in north-east Caithness, where a small stream enters the Pentland Firth. Soon after the Orkney Isles were annexed to Scotland in 1472 Jan de Ghroot, a Dutchman, began to operate the first regular ferry to Orkney across the treacherous waters of the Pentland Firth, from a mere crack in the rocks just east of Huna. His curious octagonal house built there in 1509 found lasting fame as Scotland's most extreme point (though not its most northerly). Pont's distorted original map of around 1600 showed a substantial village as *'Duncans bay'*. A bridge was built at Huna in 1651, and Martin noted in 1703 that the ferry plied from Duncansby to the south end of Burray in Orkney. The Roy map of about 1750 named *'Iohny Grotts house'* but showed no road or track (or ferry); nearby with its headland stood *'Dungsbay'!*

*The long-lasting Huna Mill at John o'Groats. The first mill on this site was built in 1750, but the watermill building seen here was constructed in 1901 – and is still in use.* *(RCAHMS / JRH)*

**Lifeboat, Tourists, Lighthouses, Desolation and Disaster**: Huna post office was opened in 1804. From 1856 the main Orkney ferry was a steamer between Scrabster and Stromness, but by that time the road system was complete. When the railway reached Thurso and Wick in 1874 more visitors came to John o' Groats, and the name Duncansby fell into disuse. Huna lifeboat station opened in 1877, and its water mill was rebuilt in 1860 and 1902. A new bridge was built there at the same time as the *John o' Groats Hotel*, erected in 1875; this was *"good"* to Murray in 1894. Duncansby Head lighthouse, first lit in 1924, was remarkably late, but enabled the Huna lifeboat station to be closed as redundant in 1930. However, in 1959 the Aberdeen trawler *George Robb* was driven on to the rocks of Duncansby, and 13 lives were lost. John o' Groats remained a tiny farming, fishing and tourist village and acquired two more small hotels, but the population shrank from nearly 400 in 1951 to only 250 by 1981, and primary schooling was moved 3km west to Canisbay.

**Ferries and Fishing**: By 1974 the 'John o' Groats' youth hostel was open at Canisbay, plus caravan and camping sites at Huna and near the tiny harbour. Pottery and jewellery were made on a small scale in the 1970s, and in 1978 John o' Groats had three hotels, a post office/stores, and four tourist shops. Only Wick boats could be seen in the harbour when the author visited that summer. By then a summer passenger ferry was again plying to Burwick in Orkney. The harbour was expanded into a basin about 1980, and eight lobster and trawling boats were based there in the early 1980s. By 1993 a museum was open near the harbour; the school was still active then (but no more).

**The Gills Bay Debacle**: In 1989 work was begun on a new private ferry terminal at Gills Bay 2km west of Canisbay, to enable a roll-on service to Burwick. Although professional advice was ignored and the scheme had been greatly undercosted, it was assisted by the Orkney Islands Council. However, since the piers were underdesigned for such an exposed site they suffered storm damage in 1990. Worse still, the ferry ran aground, and although by 1992 estimates of cost had already been exceeded by 133%, rectification would have cost more than the sum already spent! On a happier note, the intrusive Huna caravan site has been moved away from the coast, and a museum and craft centre were established at John o' Groats by 1997. Huna mill still works, though renamed as the *John o' Groats Mill*, and the post office survives. There's the *Seaview Hotel* at John O'Groats and a guest house; the youth hostel is seasonal, as is the Burwick passenger ferry.

## JOHNSHAVEN **Map 10, B5**

***Mearns coastal village,*** *pop. 650* OS 45: NO 7967

Johnshaven is located on the rocky coast of the Mearns some 5km south of Inverbervie. In the 15th century the keep of Benholm Castle was built 4km to the north-east. The Roy map made about 1750 showed a coastal track, and just inland from the undetailed *'Iohns Haven'* was the emparked house of Brotherton. About 1790 a Dundee firm set up a sailcloth factory at Johnshaven, employing 50 men and a number of women. In 1799 Heron referred to *"a considerable fishing-town, containing upwards of a thousand inhabitants"*. The harbour was built early in the 19th century, and a brewery was in operation in 1825, though this later closed. Chambers claimed in the 1820s that Johnshaven *"was formerly one of the greatest fishing villages on the East Coast, but now exhibits more of the character of a manufacturing town, being a sort of colony for the manufacturers of Dundee"*; in 1864 linen was still produced, but on a smaller scale.

**Railway and Mansions**: The Montrose & Bervie Railway was opened in 1865, with a station at Johnshaven, whose harbour was extended in 1884, and which had a population of some 1100 in 1891; by then the line had been a branch of the North British for a decade. In the 19th century a mansionhouse was built on to Benholm Castle. Brotherton House was also rebuilt as a mansion in the late Victorian period; a post and telegraph office, lifeboat and coastguard stations were open in 1894. Fishing was at its maximum locally in the Edwardian period, when there were 30 to 40 large drifters based in Johnshaven; but with the first world war the fishing declined rapidly, and by 1931 the population had shrunk to around 700. However by 1951 nearly 900 people were resident, and although the passenger trains were withdrawn in 1953 the local facilities then included a small hotel, and – remarkably – three *'clothiers'* and a chiropodist. Rail freight ceased in 1966 and the track was lifted.

**Lathallan School and Lobsters**: In 1948 the independent Lathallan School moved from Fife to Brotherton House. By 1974 there was a coastal caravan park, but Benholm Castle had become derelict by 1980. The resident population had again shrunk to under 700 by 1971, and though there were two hotels by the mid 1980s only a single local fishing boat remained, seeking shellfish. In 1991 the population was only 645. Lathallan, a mixed preparatory school, now has 160 pupils. Johnshaven is still the base of the large and long-established lobster dealer Murray McBay, and another shellfish merchant is active. Small boats are repaired, but the harbour is less busy than nearby Gourdon. Two small hotels, a garage, post office and newsagent are among the few local facilities, along with a caravan park.

## JOHNSTONE & Milliken Park

**Map 15, A5**

***Renfrewshire town,*** *pop. 18,600* — OS 64: NS 4263

In the 16th century Easter Cochrane Castle was built on the Black Cart Water 2 km west of Elderslie. By about 1600 a bridge already spanned the river nearby, being marked on Pont's map of Renfrewshire. The castle was enlarged in 1700. Milliken House was built in 1733, 2 km north-west of the castle, which in the same year was renamed Johnstone. Roy's map made about 1754 showed the road from Paisley to Kilbarchan, Houston and Greenock crossing *'Johnston Bridge'*. In 1782 the very large *'Old End'* cotton mill (the biggest in Scotland) was set up by Corse, Burns & Co. A new and very successful planned town was created to house the workers, between Johnstone Castle and Milliken House. Its rectangular site about 230m x 460m was feued by George Houston. The Old End was followed by the similar Laigh Mill of 1785 and the Cartside and Hag mills of 1794. Heron reported in 1799, *"At the bridge of Johnstone, there is building, on a neat plan, a new town, which already contains upward of 1400 inhabitants. It has two cotton-mills, and promises to be a very flourishing place."*

**Thick Coal, and Thick Canal Promoters?**: Heron also remarked on *"the village of Quarrelton, with its singular coal-work, consisting of five contiguous strata"*. Heron added that these were 15 m thick, confirming Bremner's claim that this colliery, at Johnstone Castle, exploited the thickest seam in Scotland. Johnstone Castle was redesigned in the early 19th century, probably by James Gillespie Graham, and no doubt paid for from the proceeds of the colliery. The first post office opened in 1802. The Glasgow Paisley & Ardrossan Canal, surveyed by Thomas Telford, was intended to take cargoes from overseas to those parts of south Glasgow that could be served by canal; dug from the Glasgow end, it opened as far as Johnstone in 1811 at a single level throughout. This rather barmy scheme was abandoned when – following an Act of 1809 – the Clyde was deepened by dredging. As the canal's *de facto* terminus until it closed in 1885, Johnstone steadily grew into a substantial town.

**Railways and Diversification**: In 1816 a foundry was opened at Johnstone, and in 1824 a gasworks. In 1832 Cobbett lectured in this *"nice little manufacturing town"*. By 1839 there were 16 cotton spinning mills, almost all steam-powered. A through station was opened on the new Glasgow, Paisley, Kilmarnock & Ayr Railway in 1840. A short branch line soon connected to Bridge of Weir; this was extended to Greenock in 1869. Meantime, despite the problems of the cotton industry, Johnstone adapted to changing times. One mill was converted to make linen thread in 1849, the Empress mill became an engineering works around 1850, and the Old End became Paton's bootlace factory (they're still going in 2001). In 1869 Finlayson, Bousfield & Co had over 1000 workers in their two flax mills.

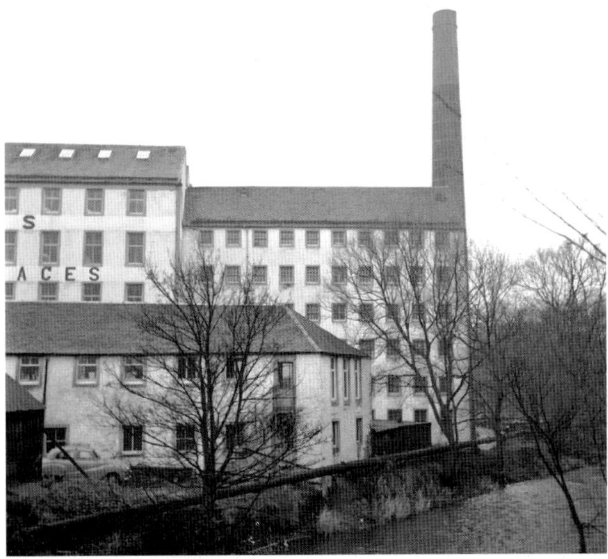

*Johnstone Old End cotton mill was the biggest in Scotland when it was built in 1782. The premises, which originally gave rise to the planned town of Johnstone, remain in business as Paton's bootlace works.* *(RCAHMS / JRH)*

About 1870 the Cartside Mill at the hamlet of Milliken Park was taken over by MacLaurin for coated paper manufacture.

**News, Machine Tools, Trams and League Football**: Johnstone grew into a major local service centre; in 1890 its local newspaper the *Johnstone Advertiser* was established, and in 1891 the population was almost 10,000. Murray's 1894 Handbook found *"a busy town, with a considerable reputation for its flax and cotton manufactories and engineering works"*. By 1896 there was also a station at Milliken Park, and Clifton & Baird made machine tools at Johnstone; other major firms in this field were Craig & Donald, Loudon Brothers, Thomas MacDowall & Sons and Thomas Shanks. By 1903 a short spur railway had been built from the Greenock line to a terminal station near the mills at Johnstone North; this spur was extended through Kilbarchan to Brownhill Junction and so to Dalry in 1905, in part competing with Paisley's new electric trams, which reached Johnstone in 1904 and ran through to Kilbarchan from 1906 to 1932. Johnstone FC played 8 seasons in the Scottish League (1912–15 and 1921–26).

**Golf, Trunk Calls, Paper and Chemicals**: Milliken House was demolished in 1921, some of its materials being used to extend the factor's house into a new mansion. Around this time Johnstone also acquired a trunk telephone exchange and the 18-hole Cochrane Castle golf course. Craigenfeoch quarry, 2 km south of the town, was open by 1920, and by 1945 another small quarry worked near it at Windyhill. By 1931 Johnstone had 12,800 people; but with the effects of the slump the town's growth slowed. The trams were withdrawn from Johnstone in the 1930s. The many additions to Johnstone Castle were demolished about 1958, but an impressive ruin remains. Finlayson, Bousfield & Co (by then part of the Linen Thread Company), closed in the late 1950s. As a result of the developments at nearby Linwood and Glasgow Airport, the population grew by over 7000 from 1951 to its census peak of 22,600 in 1971. By that time two-thirds of the houses in the burgh were let by public authorities. A new and much larger quarry was open west of Windyhill, and by 1980 the Strathclyde chemical works, formerly in the Gorbals, was producing solvents and thinners.

**Problems fuel Decline**: However, by 1981 the area's renewed economic problems *(see Linwood)* had cut back part of the population increase. Smith & McLaurin were taken over by the giant American paper firm James River in 1984, but their Cartside Mills continued in operation under the traditional name, still providing about 240 jobs making specialist papers at Milliken Park in 1989 (but in 2001 producing labels and tags). At that time growing suburban traffic to Glasgow justified the reopening of Milliken Park station. By 1991 the population had fallen to 18,635; few had purchased their homes from the council. It also appeared that by 1991 the *Johnstone Advertiser* had ceased publication. At that time the motorway-standard Johnstone Bypass (A737) was forced through the small gap between Kilbarchan and Millikenpark; part of the one-time Kilmacolm railway became a cycle route. A proposal for another large quarry at Windyhill was not surprisingly controversial in 1993; the High Craig quarry is now active. Johnstone High School has around 1150 pupils, and the *Lynnhurst Hotel* is one of several serving the town.

## JOHNSTONEBRIDGE

**Map 2, B4**

***Dumfriesshire hamlet,*** *pop. 700* — OS 78: NY 1091

The Roman road from Carlisle to the north through Upper Annandale paralleled the River Annan on the east. William Johnstone who died in 1721 was a Marquess of Annandale; in his time the area west of the river was Johnstone's Muir, an undeveloped expanse until Johnstone Kirk was built in 1733 just west of a river ford, some 10km north of Lockerbie. By about 1754 it stood at the end of the made road from Lochmaben to Millhousebridge (6km south), then the highest dryshod crossing of the Annan; northwards was just a track. East of the river was the main road – labelled *'Roman Way'* by Roy. The bridge at Johnstone seems to date from the major improvements to the Glasgow–Carlisle road carried out by Telford in the early 19th century.

**Rail and Road, Growth and Decline**: When the Caledonian Railway was opened in 1848, a station was provided at Dinwoodie, 1.5km south of the bridge. In 1895 Johnstone mills, a school and a post office stood near the bridge. By 1951 the name Johnstonebridge had been adopted for the small village whose facilities served a wider area containing about 925 people; by 1954 *Dinwoodie Lodge* was a small hotel. The station was closed about 1960, and by 1981 the fading facilities at Johnstonebridge served under 700 people. With little to draw the tourist, and both the railway and the A74 improved to carry only fast traffic, this declining rural area was seen by most passing travellers as simply a backcloth; not even a post office remained. By 1997 the A74 south of Johnstonebridge had been converted into a motorway, and work was starting on the section to the north – completing the final link in the motorway system between Glasgow and the English Channel; a motorway service station has since been built there, whilst the *Dinwoodie Lodge* hotel still serves.

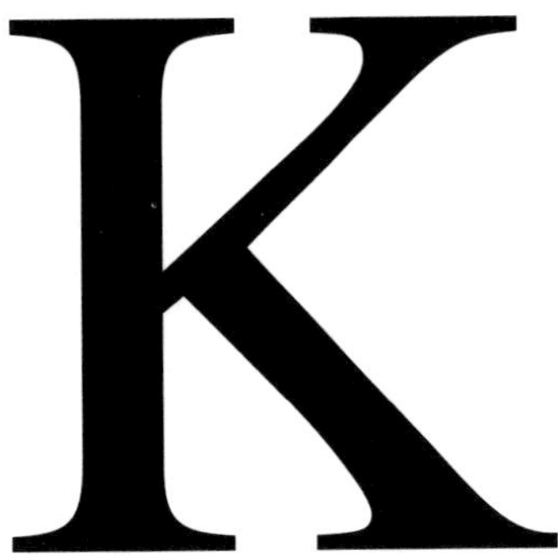

## KEISS

**Map 13, B4**

***Caithness small coastal village,*** *pop. 350* OS 12: ND 3461

The Sands (or Links) of Keiss on the low-lying east coast of Caithness are pierced by the outfall from the Loch of Wester; several ancient brochs stood on the shore and inland, with an Iron Age broch on Brough Head beside Auckengill, about 3km to the north. Pont noted of *'Keece'* on his map made about 1600: *"Here groweth gall abundantly"*. The late 16th century Keiss Castle was a 5-storey Z-plan coastal tower built for George Sinclair, 5th Earl of Caithness; it was his favourite home, but ruinous by 1700. About 1750 as the Roy map showed, roadless Keiss comprised Easter and Wester hamlets; the loch outfall obstructed access to the track which connected to Wick some 7km to the south.

**From Herrings to Crabs**: In 1820 a harbour with two basins, warehouse and ice house was built near the castle to exploit the herring shoals *(see Hay & Stell)*, and a bridge was built in 1835 to a design by Telford. By 1849 Keiss boasted 49 boats, 180 fishermen, 7 coopers, and over 300 netmakers, gutters, packers and curers. Keiss House, a 4-storey crenellated mansionhouse a little way inland, was built in the 19th century near the old castle, later adopting its title. The *"fair" Keiss Inn* of Murray's Handbook for 1894 was shown as a hotel on the OS map of the same date. Crabs later became the mainstay of the harbour to the extent that tiny Keiss was in 1928 the sixth most important crabbing port on the east coast; there was also a salmon bothy, used until 1940. In 1951 the population was about 450, served by the facilities of a small village.

**Golf, Crafts and Pipelines**: About 1970 Keiss Links became a formal golf course, for a few years only. The Lyth Arts Centre was set up by local man William Wilson in the mid 1970s in the old Lyth school, some 10km inland from Keiss; its achievements by 1979 were largely on the crafts side. In 1978 Keiss had a post office, butcher's shop, garage with buses and some new housing. Though by 1981 its population had fallen to under 400, in 1985 the harbour was still used by lobster and salmon fishermen. The hamlet of Auckengill supported some fishing, based at a concrete pier in a mere fissure in the rocks, and also had a Viking museum by 1993. By then a dead straight narrow gauge railway 6km long had been laid from the Moss of Kirk, west of Keiss, to a works on the coast at Westerloch, 3km south of the village, to fabricate long welded sections of under-water pipelines for the oil industry. Today, the school and post office are still open.

## KEITH, Newmill & Fife-Keith

**Map 10, A2**

***Moray small town,*** *pop. 4800* OS 28: NJ 4350

Keith in Strathisla, originally in Banffshire, was first mentioned as *Geth* in a charter of about 1177. Parishioners of Keith church are known to have brewed ale as early as 1208, and there must have been at least one early mill, for Milton Tower was built for the Ogilvies about 1480. The Milton brewery stood on the site of Keith's later Strathisla distillery as early as 1545. The first bridge across the River Isla was built in 1609 for Thomas Murray and Janet Lindsay. This, the Old Bridge of Keith (which still stands) can only have been used by pedestrians and pack animals. Blaeu's map showed both Milton and Newmill near the symbol for Keith Kirk. By 1620 a parish school was held, and by 1667 Keith had an annual fair. Although *'Newmill in Strathisla'* was *'erected'* in a legal sense as a burgh of barony in 1673, the present-day rectangularly planned Newmill was built after Roy's map was made about 1750. Keith's first post office had opened in 1742, and Keith was shown by Roy as the one small compact core in an area of scattered rural settlement, with a single road following the general line of the modern A96 Elgin–Huntly route.

**Formally Enlarged for Distilling and Textiles**: Keith's square was laid out in 1751, and in 1755 the town was enlarged southwards by the Earl of Findlater to a formal plan as *"New Keith"*; Pennant reported that nearly 2000 people took feus there in the late 1750s – surely an overestimate – but Keith does not seem to have become a chartered burgh prior to the 19th century reforms. In 1785 Milton brewery was converted to make whisky – one of the earliest legal distilleries in Scotland: as an alternative name to *'Milton distillery'* it was also known as *Milton Keith*. G & G Kynoch of the Isla Bank woollen mill started up in 1788, and Keith also became a prosperous linen manufacturing centre in the late 18th century, Milton bleachfield dating from 1789; but the linen trade then faded away due to the poor quality of local yarns. The Aberdeen Banking Company had a branch in Keith from at least 1793. By 1797 Keith was a post town with services three days a week, though according to Elder no fairs were scheduled for that year. In 1799 Heron described the place as a *"handsome village with over a thousand people who are chiefly manufacturers. Here is one of the best markets in the north for black cattle and horses."*

**Mills, Quarry and Lime**: In 1794 James Gordon Bennett, who was to found the *New York Herald*, was born in Newmill. From 1811 there was a coach serving Keith on the Inverness to Aberdeen route. In 1817 the Earl of Fife laid out *Fife-Keith* on the

*The Strathisla distillery, Keith, in the 1970s. This was founded in 1785 as the Milton distillery. It was extended by Chivas Brothers Ltd in 1965, when it took the form shown here.* (JRH)

west bank of the river, the Strathisla corn and flour mills were built in 1823, and a brewery still existed in Union Street. The small Hyde Park tannery was built early in the 19th century. In 1830 an elaborate Roman Catholic church was built. By the 1840s the quarry and limeworks at Blackhillock some 2 km south of Keith was using coal imported through Portgordon, which also exported some of the lime. The town also had a gasworks.

**Keith Junction**: The Great North of Scotland Railway, struggling westwards from Aberdeen, reached Keith in 1856; in 1858 Keith Junction station was constructed where the Highland Railway (HR), pushing eastwards from Inverness, met the earlier line end-on. By 1860 Wordie & Co operated a rail to road cartage depot. In 1862 Keith also became the junction for Dufftown, from which a connection to Grantown and the south was completed at Boat of Garten four years later. In 1884 a late branch of the HR opened to Portessie (for Buckie); by that time Keith was quite a significant railway centre, with six platform faces from 1885, two turntables and three small engine sheds.

**Tweeds and More and Larger Distilleries**: Tweeds were manufactured by Kynoch of Isla Bank from 1857, and there was a carding mill for blankets by 1882. By then Keith had a population of over 5500 and was an important agricultural centre, with a farm implement factory, grain mills and manure works; the brewery still functioned, and the town was still noted for great cattle and horse fairs. Barnard found the *Gordon Arms* a *"rare old-fashioned hostelry"* in 1886; the *Queen's Hotel* (very soon renamed the *Royal*) was also open by 1884, and to Murray in 1894 both were *"good"*. Keith had a sheriff court, and eventually became a police burgh; the local newspaper the *Banffshire Herald* was established in 1892. Milton distillery had been steadily enlarged and modernised, and employed twenty men in 1886 producing some 410,000 litres of Strathisla Highland malt whisky annually, using some Orkney peat and steam power. The Strathmill distillery, an 1891 conversion of the 1823 mills, was acquired in 1895 by W & A Gilbey of London. The old Crooksmill was rebuilt in 1895 as a meal mill, and worked until at least 1988, but is now derelict. Aultmore distillery, 4 km north-west, was built beside the Portessie railway in 1896–97; the tiny Forgie station was enlarged with sidings and renamed after it, and in 1897 Earlsmill station was renamed Keith Town.

**Struggling, Smuggling and Shrinking Railways**: By 1915 a regular livestock market had replaced the occasional fairs. The Portessie branch railway was closed beyond Aultmore in that wartime year, and it was 1926 before a bus service reconnected Keith with Buckie. Government decree closed all the distilleries during 1917–19; Aultmore was acquired by Dewar about 1923. Distilleries also suffered in the Prohibition period, during which the whisky smuggler Samuel Bronfman acquired Keith Maltings, Keith Bonds and Milton distillery (later renamed Strathisla-Glenlivet). All were placed under another of his acquisitions, Chivas Brothers, founded in 1801 in Aberdeen; the latter became a subsidiary of his Canadian acquisition Seagrams. The Isla Bank mills were extended in 1926 and 1930, but generally the second quarter of the 20th century was a period of some decline in Keith, whose population fell to 4500 by 1951, though it retained quite full urban facilities. A railway engine shed also remained in use, and Chivas Brothers' Glen Keith-Glenlivet Distillery was built in 1957–60 and incorporated a meal mill. Passenger services to Dufftown ended in 1968, and the use of rail-freight by distilleries declined.

**Golf and Chivas offset the Collapse of Kynoch**: Meantime Keith golf club was founded in 1963 and laid out an 18-hole parkland course. Part of the old GNSR engine sheds were incorporated into a new whisky vatting and blending complex opened by Chivas in 1976, which filled rail tankers, sent south to Dalmuir; bonded warehouses were extended alongside the railway for 900 m. But apart from the growth of its number of hotels to eight, Keith's importance as a service centre reduced over the years with the continuing growth of Elgin. Keith lost its status as a local government centre in 1975, and became part of the enlarged Moray District based in Elgin. In 1979 Anderson Engineering of Keith was associated with R Anderson & Son of Paisley. At that time G & G Kynoch's Isla Bank woollen mills made scarves and piece goods, and up to 1988 still employed 200 people and exported 90% of their output; but the heavy overcoat business collapsed in 1988, and bulk manufacturing at Keith stopped by 1990. The firm cut their remaining weaving workforce of 110 by a third, then being taken over by Kevin D'Silva of Berkshire who closed the mill, sacked all but ten design staff and by 1991 had contracted out the remaining manufacturing *(see Sandwick (Shetland))*. Later in 1991 the rump of the Kynoch business was sold on to Joshua Ellis, a Yorkshire firm.

**Rail, Pulpwood and Distillery Design**: The railway passenger station building was rebuilt in 1988, relying on a single platform. In 1990 a rail-connected freight depot at Keith was used by Macphersons Transport of Aberlour; pulpwood was forwarded by rail, and coal came in. Chivas Brothers, still part of the Seagram Distillers group in 1991, had production managers at Keith who also designed changes to plant and equipment for their nine distilleries and other facilities in the north of Scotland. Chivas still shipped 12-year-old *Chivas Regal* and *100 Pipers* whisky in their 13 rail tankers, until rail privatisation forced them to use MacPhersons and the road. In 1995 when Joshua Ellis employed just 8 people at Isla Bank on design, development and marketing, the firm sold Kynoch's Shetland subsidiary to its management. The Kynoch Group name then fell to its offshoot, a Hampshire company. Meantime its former boss, the MP George Kynoch, had become the industry and local government minister for Scotland in the Major government! By 1995 the Isla Bank Mill held Scotland's only school of kiltmaking, a success story which survived the traumas and was still supported by local government in 1997.

**Glenisla and Agriculture on Show**: Meantime by 1991 when the population was 4793, *'Glenlivet'* had been dropped from the titles of the Glen Keith and Strathisla distilleries. The attractive traditional buildings of Strathisla were renovated and reopened to visitors by Chivas in 1995. Meantime the former Hyde Park tannery stood vacant and neglected in 1993. By 1996 there was a Tesco store. Though Keith livestock market had closed in the 1980s, in 1996 the Central Banffshire Farmers' Club still ran an agricultural, craft and cultural show at Seafield Park; it drew most support from a 40 km radius, but some from as far afield as Torphins and even Mull. In 2000 the Keith & Dufftown Railway was reopened by a preservation group, with a diesel passenger service between Dufftown and a temporary terminus at Drummuir; reopening to Keith is planned for 2001. Keith Grammar School has about 525 pupils.

## KELSO

**Map 3, B4**

***Borders town,*** *pop. 6000*

OS 74: NT 7234

Kelso on the north bank of the lower River Tweed had a Dark Age church with an extensive parish; its Anglian name means *'Chalk Hill'*. In 1128 under David I a community of Tironensian (Benedictine) tradesmen monks moved there from Selkirk and soon transformed Kelso church into a great abbey, which briefly vied with St Andrews for primacy in Scotland, but later failed. The adjacent settlement was described as a *'villa'* (village) in a charter of 1159, and by around 1200 a *'hospital'* had been opened there; in the 1180s and 1190s churches at both Dumfries and Peebles were made subject to Kelso Abbey. By 1237 Kelso was an ecclesiastical burgh under the abbey, which by 1296 also owned nine properties in Berwick. From there coal, salt and corn were brought to Kelso by pack-horse.

**Through Siege and Fire to the Reformation**: After the war, in 1323 the name Westerkelso was applied to the Abbey's burgh, where an unusually large water mill was constructed for the abbey, with a great weir or *'Cauld'* across the Tweed. Little is known of the late 14th or 15th centuries in Kelso, for although it was more readily reinforced than Roxburgh had been, it was not exactly a secure place. The abbey still did duty as the parish church as late as 1517. Kelso paid no burgh tax in 1535–56, and the abbey buildings were almost totally destroyed in the sieges of 1542 and 1545, but an important religious community remained – possessing 23 appropriated churches and a very substantial outpost at Lesmahagow – until the suppression of the abbey in 1560. It is possible that an early parish school at Ednam, 3 km to the north, was founded in that very year; Kelso followed in 1585.

**Enter Floors Castle**: One of Pont's maps of about 1600 showed *'Brigend'* on the south bank of the River Teviot, at the landfall where the Teviot bridge was to arise much later, but nothing seems known of its medieval predecessor. Nenthorn Kirk stood some 6 km north-west. Permanent peace with England having been established, *'Cailso'* was by then quite a substantial town with a church, and nearby *'Fleures'* a castle within policies. In 1607 the ruined abbey buildings passed to the owner of Floors – Robert, Earl of Roxburghe – and in 1614 Kelso was again chartered, as a burgh of barony. In 1628 a parish school was opened at Maxwellheugh on the opposite bank of the Tweed. The town burnt down yet again in 1644, this time accidentally; 750 people were left homeless.

**Brewing before the Bridge**: The patient Kelso folk rebuilt once more, enabling an important market to develop in what was to be Scotland's largest market square, which also served as cattle market and St James' Fair stance. Brewing was on a commercial scale by about 1650, and by 1669 the Grammar School was a *"flourishing secondary school"*. The street names, such as Horse Market and Wood Market, reflected their specialised functions. When the town burnt down yet again in 1684, an appeal to all Scots raised the cash to rebuild; a post office was open from 1689. Floors Castle was totally rebuilt for the first Duke of Roxburghe in 1718–26 by William Adam, its single block possibly to designs by Vanbrugh. Defoe saw Kelso at that time as *"a handsome market-town; one of the great roads from Edinburgh to Newcastle lying through this town, and a nearer way by far than the road through Berwick. They only want a good bridge over the Tweed: at present they have a ferry just at the town, and a good ford through the river, a little below it."*

**Bleaching, Bridging and Coaching**: Bleachfields were at work in Kelso and at Ednam in 1745, and Kelso had a linen merchant by 1755. At the time of Roy's survey the Tweed had lately been bridged (with what Heron later described as *"a very handsome stone bridge of six arches")*, and a track led south via Heiton to Jedburgh. The town was then about a kilometre long; north of the river roads led to Stichill, to Ednam, and passed north of Floors towards Smailholm. Soon there was yet another serious fire. James Nisbet designed a church whose curious shape led it to become known as the Mustard Pot, and the *Cross Keys Inn* of 1761 – which became about 1766 a staging point on the newly turnpiked Edinburgh to Newcastle coach route; turnpiking of the Hawick road via Heiton followed under an Act of 1768.

**Bad Boy Builds Good House**: Local tearaway John Dixon became a pirate in the West Indies, returning to have the small but exquisitely detailed mansion now called Ednam House built in Bridge Street in 1761. Others had less cash: the Bank of Scotland had a Kelso agency from 1774, but no full branch for nearly 200 years. Some forty local weavers made blankets and flannels in 1776, and by 1780 John Hardy of Hawick had introduced framework knitting. The *Border Mail*, founded in Kelso in 1779, was among Scotland's first local newspapers.

**Beer and Bootmaking**: By 1794 two Kelso breweries were producing 2500 barrels of beer each year, and at some time the ancient Abbey Mill was converted into a distillery, later reverting to milling. A new Teviot bridge was built to designs by Alexander Stevens, for the second time linking to the site of Roxburgh Castle. Although the Tweed bridge fell in floods around 1795 – four fairs were to be held in 1797. Heron noted in 1799 *"Kelso is a neat and populous town; it contains between four and five thousand inhabitants, and has a good weekly market for corn; but the making of shoes is its principal manufacture"*; however, under 150 people were actually engaged in this craft. He also mentioned Ednam and Sprouston (3 km east) as *"villages"*, but while Ednam had a brewery from about 1795 to 1815, and an early 19th century flour mill, neither place developed into centres of much interest.

**Books, Bridges and the Brilliance of Brunlees**: In the early 19th century the Kelso mills were reconstructed, and Ballantyne of Kelso published Scotland's first really outstanding printed book, Scott's *Minstrelsy of the Scottish Border*. John Rennie's new Tweed bridge was planned in 1799, originally intended to consist of two cast-iron arches. It was however finely built in stone with five arches: opened in 1803, it was to outlast his more famous Waterloo Bridge across the Thames. A new town hall was built in 1816 (its arcaded ground floor was infilled in 1905). James Brunlees, a gardener's son born in Kelso in 1816, may have been inspired by these impressive structures to become a civil engineer, assisting in the early days of the Caledonian Railway. Later he designed the ill-fated Solway Viaduct of 1865–69, the successful Mersey Railway tunnel of 1880–86, Avonmouth Dock and the renowned Southend pier in Essex, earning a knighthood.

**A View of Kelso in 1827**: In 1827 Chambers opined that Kelso *"though not the county town, is the largest in the county; a thriving town, the resort of a great number of idle and affluent people, whose suburban villas give it an air of comfort and refinement. The town possesses a manufacture of stockings and of leather, but seems to subsist chiefly upon the money spent in it by its genteel inhabitants, and has well-attended races."* A more mundane examination shows that brewing continued until at least 1825, a gasworks was set up in 1831, and a second local newspaper, the *Kelso Chronicle*, was established in 1834. Around this period William Playfair vastly extended Floors Castle into a wedding-cake fantasy for the Duke.

**Kelso in the Railway Age**: In 1849 the York, Newcastle and Berwick Railway – soon part of the North Eastern Railway (NER) – opened a branch from Tweedmouth to Sprouston, extended to Kelso in 1851. From 1851 the North British Railway served Kelso by a branch from Newtown; the station was built at Maxwellheugh and also served the NER trains. A mill, an abattoir and a foundry were built at the station, and a woollen mill was open by 1859. However, although the population still exceeded 4000 in 1891, the burgh gained few other industries. Meantime in 1863 a Free Church was built to *'Saracen Gothic'* designs by Pilkington, the prominent Trinity church was built in 1885, and Sir Robert Rowand Anderson designed the Episcopal church. Kelso golf club, founded in 1887, provided an 18-hole course; in 1894 besides the racecourse there were racing stables. That year Murray noted Kelso as *"a busy town"*, with a monthly cattle fair and the small *Queens Head* – an old coaching inn; the larger *Cross Keys* hotel – to which a floor was added about that time and which could stable 50 horses – was *"good"*. Carnegie money assisted the start of a public library, around 1901.

**Buildings of Taste and Controversy**: The abbey cloisters were finely reconstructed in 1933 for May, the American widow of the 8th Duke of Roxburghe; she also had original rooms recreated in the castle. Kelso still had many fine buildings, but the Royal Bank used incongruous red and yellow brick in its 1934 building, and the Academy's new building of 1936 was a dull reinforced concrete version of *'art deco'*. The two local newspapers amalgamated in 1949, and by 1953 Kelso Rugby Football Club had its own ground. In 1957 the Bank of Scotland agency in Kelso finally became a proper branch bank, for despite its uneventful recent history the town remained the main centre for a wide rural area. About 1966 Kelso became noteworthy for the sport of curling, with the opening of the Borders Ice Rink, and a new medical centre was built in 1967. However, the railway was closed in 1968, and about 1975 the Corn Exchange and its grain market were also closed. A new hospital, planned in 1976, was later built in Inch Road.

**Industrial Growth**: Attracted by development area grants, seven new firms created over 300 jobs in the town between 1968 and 1973. Among them was Rupert Neve & Co, which opened a factory in 1970 to make electronic sound reproduction equipment. New food processors were open by 1975; by 1980 two firms of agricultural engineers, D M Wallace and Rutherford's of Coldstream, worked in Kelso. By 1977 Lyle & Scott had a knitwear factory at the Pinnaclehill industrial area, to which Middlemas & Son, aerated water makers in Distillery Lane beside the Abbey Mill, moved about 1980.

**Blooming in the Electronic Age**: Keltek Electronics, established about 1980, was assembling PCB components at Kelso in 1989; in 2000 Keltek built a new factory to enable a 150-job expansion (making 300 in total); it is now owned by the American group Plexus. Meantime in 1984 the town had won an award in the Britain in Bloom competition, and in 1987 unemployment in the area, as in the Borders in general, was the lowest in Scotland. By 1990 Neve Electronics, by then a Siemens subsidiary, employed 150 people and had earned a Queen's Award for Industry. Another new electronics concern was BHK Circuits, and Forbes Plastics and ICI Seeds were also represented at Pinnaclehill. In 2000 Plexus, a local electronics firm already employing 255 people, announced a further 117 jobs of which 25 would be highly-paid design and engineering staff.

**Traditional and Modern Kelso**: By 1991 the population was almost 6000; new housing had been built at Oakfield to the east, but the *Kelso Chronicle* had been absorbed by the *Southern Reporter* of Selkirk. In 1990 John Hogarth Ltd still milled animal feeds at the ancient Abbey Mill, and Pettigrew Preserves were active in 1995. The long-established 600-seat *Roxy Cinema* was still open in 1992, and the Duke of Roxburghe's small National Hunt racecourse was still flourishing. A plain new river bridge, and an internal bypass partly following the route of the former railway, were complete by 1998. By then there was a museum, and a mountain rescue post was open to serve the wild Cheviot Hills to the south-east. Though most shops in the town are still private traders, a small shopping centre has replaced the stables of the historic and imposing 4-storey *Cross Keys Hotel*. Another hotel is the long-established *Ednam House* (with fine plasterwork, woodwork and fireplaces). In 2000 the Millennium Parterre garden was laid out at Floors Castle as a tourist attraction. The Duke's 5-year-old golf course is now staging serious tournaments.

## KELTON HILL, Bridge of Dee & Gelston

**Map 2, A5**

***Galloway hamlets****, pop. 500* OS 84 (or 83): NX 7360

The ancient parish Kirk of Kelton stands in the Stewartry, about 12 km inland from Kirkcudbright, and south of Carlingwark Loch; 2 km north-west of it, on an island in the River Dee, stands the starkly ruined Threave Castle of the Black Douglases, its tower built by Archibald the Grim about 1370–80; the enveloping curtain walls 1.5 m thick were added about 1447. At that time the castle was said to have been kept by what

Chambers called *"a pompous retinue of more than a thousand armed men"*; there is evidence of a substantial castle town on the island. Threave was forfeited to the crown by the rebellious 8th Earl of Douglas in 1453, and after the castle was stormed in a siege in 1455 it became until 1716 a property of the Maxwell Lords of Nithsdale.

**Kelton Hill or Rhonehouse**: A military road was built across Galloway in about 1608–10 to aid the plantation of Ulster; but when Pont mapped the area about 1610 there was apparently no bridge across the River Dee, the name Boatcroft 2 km south of the castle showing the site of the ferry. The nearby hamlet of Kelton Hill grew up at the point where the Kirkcudbright road diverged; apparently a weary packman who rested there made good sales and settled down as a trader. He seems to have built a substantial shop, for the alternative village name Rhonehouse implies an early slated and guttered roof, then a thing of wonder in a primitive area of thatched huts. Kelton Hill became a burgh of barony in 1705 and had a regular fair by 1723. By 1749 the Bridge of Dee had been erected beside Boatcroft; the Roy map of about 1754 named it *'Graniford Bridge'*, on the *'Road from Portpatrick to Dumfries'*. By 1778 Kelton had a parish school, where in that year the precocious author Robert Heron (much quoted in this book) became its Master at the age of 14! In 1797 Kelton Hill still had two fairs, but was doomed by the greater success of the upstart planned village of Castle Douglas, which very soon became a town, leaving the Kelton area to farming. A new Dee bridge designed by John Rennie was built in 1825.

**Rail Fails – Gardening Success**: For a century from 1861 there was a station at Bridge of Dee on the Dumfries to Stranraer railway, but this had been reduced to goods only by 1953, and the line was closed completely by Beeching in 1965. Meantime by 1953 both the grim Threave Castle – accessed by a picturesque path and rowing ferry – and the 19th century mansion of Threave House with its glorious garden, were owned and opened to the public by the National Trust for Scotland (NTS). In 1960 the NTS added what soon became a well known Gardening School at Threave House to service their many properties. However, between 1951 and 1981 the scattered local population (including the hamlet of Gelston) fell from some 750 to 550. By 1996 Bridge of Dee lay at the end of the new Castle Douglas bypass and the Dildawn Kennels on the back road to Tongland had become a museum; Kelton Hill post office was recently still open – but no longer.

## KELTY

**Map 6, B4**

***Large village, Fife,*** *pop. 5450* OS 58: NT 1494

Possible Roman origins are suggested by the very straight though hilly north–south road alignment through Kelty and west Fife, and by the many straight sections of the east–west road from Saline past Kelty to Ballingry and Auchmuir, Leslie, Markinch and Scoonie. The name Kelty may mean *'Woods'*, or contain the *Caer* element implying a Roman fort. However, this is speculation, for Kelty was little noticed until Blaeu's map of west Fife (made from Pont's lost originals of about 1600) showed *'Bin Keltey'*. By 1627 *Keltiehaugh* had a mixed school, but the only settlements shown nearby were Lurr, Woodend and *'Blair of Krammey'* (Crambeth); no ways were marked, and no bridges crossed the various burns that flow east into the River Ore. The Drumnagoil Burn was bridged in 1696, and by 1722 repairs were required to the Cantsdam bridge which crossed the Lochfittie Burn on the Old North Road between Inverkeithing and Kinross (the possible Roman line). By about 1750, as Roy showed, Kelty was a tiny nucleated settlement, and the old North Road (now A909/B996) was a steep coach road, with another bridge 3 km to the north at *'Gairneystains'*.

**Blair Crambeth, the Adam Family and Blairadam**: In 1733 William Adam of Kirkcaldy, architect and Master Mason for Scotland, bought the Blair Crambeth estate immediately north of Kelty, and at once planted 400 ha of the grounds with native trees. He soon built a home there for his growing family, and laid out the tiny planned village of Maryburgh, named after his wife. A linen bleachfield was built at Maryburgh, probably around 1756 when the Kinross linen weavers founded a union to regulate their craft. Blair mansionhouse appeared on Roy's map made about 1750; it was renamed Blairadam by William's grandson, a well-known lawyer. The Old North Road was turnpiked from 1753; John Ainslie's map of 1775 showed Kelty Bridge. In 1765 Alexander Carlyle noted Kelty, where *"the inhabitants of the village are well lodged"*; he mentioned but did not describe an industry to the south.

**Gas, Coal and Coaching**: The first post office was opened in 1803 at Kelty Bridge, and coal mining evidently played an early part, for a gasworks was opened at Kelty in 1804, apparently the second or third in Scotland. From 1809 less hilly lanes were made up to take the main coaching traffic, winding past the Blair Adam Inn and southwards through the area where Cowdenbeath later grew. This route formed an eastern bypass for Kelty, south of which Lassodie Mill was the only industry marked on Sharp, Greenwood & Fowler's map of 1826–27.

**Railway brings Mines and Hamlets**: The North British Railway's branch line from Cowdenbeath to Kinross was opened in 1860, but Kelty station was over 1 km east of the village. At least three pits must have been open in the Kelty collieries, just south of the park, before the large Kelty Nos.4/5 shafts (later called the Lindsay colliery), were sunk just east of the station in 1873–74 to a depth of 128 m; one was deepened in 1886 to 240 m. Coal pits soon multiplied in all directions. From the station a mineral line connected south-west to Whitemyre, serving on the way the Rosewell Gas Coal Company's Lassodie Mill pit, west of Cantsdam. By 1893 Thomas Spowart & Co worked the Lassodie Collieries, a distinct complex some 2 km farther west, just north of Loch Fitty. Nearby were the miners' hamlets of Fairfield and Parley (formerly named Lassodie) – both doomed to obliteration in mid century.

**Mining on the Grand Scale**: In 1888 Beveridge saw Kelty as a *"village"*, as were Maryburgh, 1 km north, and Oakfield, at the main crossroads with the Saline road 1 km to the south. The deep Aitken pit, named after the chairman of the Fife Coal Company (FCC), and connected underground with the Lindsay, was sunk south of the Lochfitty Burn in 1893–95, its single 372 m shaft lined only with timber; its best seam sloped steeply, at 1 in 2. A power station with timber cooling towers was added, eventually supplying 13 FCC pits. In 1896 the FCC bought the Cowdenbeath Coal Company's new Lumphinnans No. XI pit, located south-east of Kelty (also known locally as the *Peesweep* or *Peewit* – *see Lochgelly*).

**Pubs owned by the Mining Public**: All this activity brought in a large new population, and Kelty steadily grew to coalesce with Maryburgh and Oakfield, with an inn by 1895 (although by then the *Blair Adam Inn* had vanished). Blairenbathie colliery, sunk 2 km west of the village passed to the FCC in 1901 but proved problematical, and closed with the 1926 miners' strike. In all by 1901 when 3800 people lived in Kelty, no fewer than six radiating railways and mineral lines converged on the station; a marshalling yard and engine shed were necessary to cope with their mineral traffic. Lassodie Mill pit was bought by the FCC in 1905. Four *'Gothenburg'* co-operative pubs *(also see Cardenden & Crossgates)* built after 1896 were followed by the Gothenburg Hall, built in the High Street in 1910.

**Electric Trams hit by Buses and Subsidence**: In 1910 the Dunfermline tramways were extended from Cowdenbeath to Kelty as a single track on a reserved route. The Lindsay headworks were rebuilt after a fire in 1919; the last mineshaft to be sunk was the 416m deep Lumphinnans No. XII of 1924 and in 1928 this pit gained a new washery. Meantime the tramlines were already seriously affected by colliery subsidence, and in the 1920s trams were hit by bus services, so the Kelty route was closed in 1931, a year after the passenger trains were withdrawn from its poorly sited station. In 1924 and 1939 two adits were added to the Lindsay complex, and in 1933 the Lumphinnans gained pit-head baths.

**Adit Mines, Snowblocks and Cinemas**: Three more adit mines, employing up to 250 men in all, were opened by the FCC in 1944–46 at Benarty, at Blairenbathie; and at Oakfield (which lasted only 3 years). In the severe winter of 1947–48 two locomotives and a snowplough were derailed and snowed in near Kelty, clearance requiring many days' work by numerous railmen and 300 ex-POWs. This long-remembered problem may perhaps have contributed to the line's later closure. In 1948 the Aitken power station was given new concrete cooling towers; it then had 1280 workers, while the deep Lumphinnans complex employed 790 and the Lindsay 780; an explosion occurred there in 1957, killing 9 men. Meantime by 1951 Kelty had a population of 7750, but with facilities typical of a large village. These included the large 1000-seat *Gothenburg Cinema* – installed in the co-operatively owned hall – and the smaller *Regal* next door.

**Goodbye Coal, Rail and Bricks: Hello M90!**: The railway marshalling yard was extended about 1950, but coal mine closure began with Benarty in 1959, followed by Blairenbathie in 1962, the Aitken in 1963, the Lindsay early in 1965 and the last, the Lumphinnans XI-XII, in 1965–66. In 1968–70 the remaining railways were all closed and lifted. The local section of the M90 motorway, which was built in 1969, served Kelty with a convenient junction, forming a second (western) bypass; but by then the population was only some 6700. About 1980 the modern works of the Fife Brick Company north of Lassodie – opened in 1963 – ceased production, the site later being sold as a tip. By 1981 the secondary school and hotel had closed. The *Regal Cinema*, still open in 1980, was derelict when demolished in 1993.

**Restaurant, Road Haulage – and Opencasting?**: By 1991 the population was down to 5450; almost 60% of homes were publicly rented. Resurgence was on the way, however: by 1992 some new private housing was appearing. Farm steadings beside the M90 junction were converted into the popular Butterchurn restaurant, and the *Gothenburg* became a factory, where for a time over 100 workers made *'Swallow'* raincoats. By 1994 Nelson Haulage (whose yard lay on the site of a former coal bing east of Oakfield) was a large concern shifting timber, livestock, bulk products and flatbed loads by road; they expanded further in 2000. A large new opencast mine proposed in 1994 at Greenbank by Loch Fitty, which is now a fishing loch, was perhaps the last fling of British Coal; it meant demolishing Lassodie Mains and Viewfield, the last remnants of the former hamlets. Following controversy, a smaller area (named St Ninians) to the west on the site of Lassodie is now being worked. By 2000 Marinades of Scotland processed seafoods on the small Kelty Industrial Estate.

## KEMNAY

**Map 10, B3**

***Aberdeenshire large village,*** *pop. 3150* — OS 38: NJ 7316

A Pictish standing stone, the *Lang Stane o' Craigearn*, was erected beside the River Don 7km south west of Inverurie. Fetternear, 2 km downstream on the opposite bank was recorded in 1157, becoming the site of the summer Palace of the Bishops of Aberdeen. About 2.5km south of the stone was the great 15th century Castle Fraser, originally called *Muchall in Mar*. At the Reformation, Fetternear passed to William Leslie, who built a new house after 1566, repeatedly enlarged. Kemnay, 1.5km north-east of the Lang Stane, had a parish school by 1628, and was shown on Gordon's map-work of around 1640. Kemnay House was built around that time; Roy's map made about 1750 showed it surrounded by shelter-belted policies. The nearby Kirk of Kemnay and a few other buildings stood beside a road leading from Castle Fraser, by way of a ferry at Haughton, to Inverurie. Boatleys opposite Kemnay commemorates another ferry site.

**John Fyfe's Granite Village**: Bremner stated that in 1799 Kemnay was a *"country hamlet"*. It remained so until John Fyfe established a granite quarry in 1858. Following the opening of the Alford Valley Railway in 1859, the quarry – which lay beside the line – rapidly became the largest in Aberdeenshire. Together with the young engineer Andrew Barclay of Kilmarnock, they produced the Scottish steam derrick, which greatly improved the ability to quarry downwards for better stone. The completion of Aberdeen Town House in granite was an early important success for Fyfe. The enterprising quarrymaster went on to gain the main contract to supply material for the Thames Embankment then under construction. He also built houses for his workmen, of whom 250 were employed in 1868, producing several thousand tonnes a month of near-white granite, used in Aberdeen's Marischal College, docks at Hull, Leith, Newcastle and Sunderland, and in the 1880s, the Forth Bridge piers and also the Tay Bridge. In 1868 he opened a second quarry at a higher level; his 1873 invention, the *'Blondin'* cableway, was adopted at quarries world-wide. In 1894 Murray noted Kemnay, formerly the Kirkton and close to the station, as *"a village built of granite"*, with the *"fair" Burnett Arms Hotel*; its population was about 700. The quarry was already 60m deep; the stone was then used in building, as paving setts, and especially for making the monuments so favoured at the time.

**Golf and *'Fyfestone'***: Kemnay golf club, founded in 1908, originally laid out a basic 9-hole parkland course. Fetternear House was gutted by fire in 1919 and became a derelict shell. In dark 1940 Fyfe's quarry – by then 122m deep – began to make *'Fyfestone'*, coloured facing blocks of reconstructed stone. This could be made by machine, and was therefore cheaper as well as much more easily laid than natural stone; the latter

*Kemnay granite quarry, established by John Fyfe in 1858, pictured here in 1939. It has provided stone for an impressive list of buildings over the years – now to include the facing stone for the new Scottish Parliament.* *(British Geological Survey)*

was very soon largely ousted for general use. The railway was closed to passengers in 1950, but by then the population had risen to nearly 1500 and Kemnay had the facilities of an average village. The rail freight service ended in 1966. Meantime Castle Fraser was restored from the 1950s onwards by Michael Smiley, passing to the National Trust for Scotland in 1976.

**Facing the Parliament Building**: By 1981 – with the growth of the whole Aberdeen area due to North Sea Oil, plus the attractive setting and local tourism – large housing estates had been built west of Kemnay, whose population had doubled in thirty years. About then a new Kemnay Academy was built – necessary because in 1991 Kemnay's 3150 residents, of strongly dormitory character, were found to include Scotland's highest known proportion of school-age children. Granite is still quarried within the immense and ever-growing void of John Fyfe's quarry, which in 1989 supplied large quantities to face the new Bon Accord Centre in Aberdeen. By 1990 the company HQ was at Westhill, and by 1993 at Inverkeithing, for the firm had more extensive interests; but Kemnay remained their main sales office and main building stone quarry; 34 are now employed at Westhill. The quarry was honoured in 2000 by the choice of Kemnay granite to face the Scottish Parliament building.

**Almost a Town?**: Further housing developments continued through the 1990s and are in full swing south of Kemnay. The recent upgrading of the golf course to 18 holes, the marble fireplace manufacturer and the major millennium facelift under way at the parish church show the emerging upmarket nature of Kemnay. As well as 15 or so shops, a fair range of local services include a primary school, public hall and police station. The modest *Burnett Arms Hotel* is still open.

## KENMORE **Map 5, C2**

***Small Perthshire village, L. Tay,*** *pop. 500* OS 52: NN 7745

A stone circle and other early remains stand beside the River Tay as it flows from Loch Tay, beneath which are the remains of an ancient crannog; an islet known as Inchadnie in the east end of the loch was the site of a medieval priory or castle. In 1480 the Crown sold Eddergoll mill, which already stood on the south shore opposite Inchadnie. In 1572 an inn was built of stone near the outlet of the loch at Kenmore *('Big Head'* in Gaelic). Balloch Castle a little to the east was built by Sir Colin Campbell in 1580. Pont's map made about 1600 showed this elaborate castle as *'Ballach'*, too common a name to last. A building which then stood beside the kirk at *'Keand-moir'* was probably the inn, for today the hotel on this site claims to be the oldest in Scotland. Kenmore became a burgh of barony in 1694. Taymouth Castle was created around the keep of Balloch Castle by William Adam in 1733, for the first Earl of Breadalbane; the Roy map made about 1750 showed it as a mansionhouse. By then tracks led west along the north side of Loch Tay to Killin, and eastwards across the River Lyon by a ferry to Weem. Another track from *'Port Kenachragan'* at Kenmore led over the hills to Amulree.

**Linen, Tay Bridges and New Village**: A linen bleachfield was built just prior to the River Tay being bridged at Kenmore in 1760. The current Lord Breadalbane had begun to rebuild the village, on condition that its people followed trades. In 1769 Pennant found a wooden bridge and *"a neat village"* with four fairs per year; locally-made thread was among the items sold. In 1774 the wooden bridge was replaced by what Heron called an *"elegant"* stone bridge of five arches, and by 1797 there were six fair days per year. Dorothy Wordsworth noted in 1803 that *"The village of Kenmore, with its neat church and cleanly houses, stands on a gentle eminence at the end of the water"*. This description holds good today, but oddly she did not mention the old *Breadalbane Hotel* (as it was called at that time) at which she must have stayed.

**The Second Taymouth Castle and Steamers**: She had eyes instead for the new building begun nearby in 1801; this *"large mansion"* then under construction close to Lord Breadalbane's old house (demolished soon afterwards) was to be the second Taymouth Castle, completed in 1806. By 1826 roads to Killin led along both shores of Loch Tay. Chambers then thought *"Taymouth Castle, the seat of the Earl of Breadalbane, whose estate, extending 70 miles (113 km) westward, is said to be the longest in Britain, is a magnificent dark-gray mansion"*. Further work on it was completed in 1835. By 1894 Murray saw Kenmore as *"a neat, picturesque village"* with a pier for loch steamers from the railway terminus at Killin Pier, and the hotel as *"very good"*. Taymouth Castle was sold in 1922; it became a hotel, and a golf course was laid out there, opened in 1923. Alas, the steamers ceased to ply in 1939.

**Caravans, Golf and Water Sports**: Taymouth Castle was a Polish hospital during the 1939–45 war, and later a civil defence school and an American school. About 1969 Eddergoll Mill was restored by Raymond Morris *(see Milton of Balgonie)*, and about 1972 the ancient *Breadalbane Hotel* was renamed the *Kenmore Hotel*, now 40 rooms; by then Kenmore had added a riverside caravan site to its facilities. In the 1970s an engineering business was active in the village, and a firm of agricultural engineers was based in the woods at the foot of the picturesque Acharn Falls. Sadly by 1993 Taymouth Castle stood vacant and deteriorating, but there was a new golf course north of the river by 1998. A timeshare development, another hotel, the Crannog Centre and a water sports centre had been added on the Acharn road, and walks and cycle routes had been formed in the forests on Drummond Hill.

## KENNETHMONT, Gartly, Clatt & Wardhouse — Map 10, B2

***Aberdeenshire village & hamlets,*** *pop. 500* — OS 37: NJ 5429

The Kirkhill of Kennethmont lies on the east side of Strathbogie, about 12 km south of Huntly Castle. The modest mansion of Leith Hall was erected in the 17th century in a small valley 800 m north of the Kirkhill. At the time of the Roy survey of about 1750, a road from Huntly via the Mill of Gartly (OS 29) and a *'Wakemill'* at Bogs of Noth, made its tortous and bridgeless way past the kirk and climbed over a low col en route to Clatt – which had been chartered as a burgh of barony in 1501 but never came to much – continuing to Leslie and Inverurie. Apart from ferm touns few other features were shown. The sprawling Palladian mansion of Wardhouse, 2.5 km north-east of the Kirkhill, was built in 1757 for one of the Gordons of Haddo.

**Stations Galore**: In 1854 the Great North of Scotland Railway's single-track main line was opened between Aberdeen and Huntly, following the valley known as The Shevock from the headwaters of the River Urie to an altitude of about 180 m, then passing beside Leith Hall and into Strathbogie. Though the area was deeply rural, Gartly station (which became a settlement focus) was placed 3 km south of the old mill, Kennethmont station was 1.5 km east of its Kirkhill, and Wardhouse station 2.5 km east of that.

**Distillery and Tenuous Rail Connections**: The Ardmore distillery was built beside Kennethmont station in 1898 by the family firm of Teachers, who provided a tidy estate of houses for the workers but kept its entire output for blending until at least the 1970s, when it was much enlarged. The Rannes Hall was built in 1909. By the 1950s the otherwise rambling village had acquired a population of over 350, a hotel, an agricultural engineer, and a secondary class in the local school. However, all these features soon vanished. Leith Hall with its sheltered gardens had become a property of the National Trust for Scotland; it was open to the public by 1969. Wardhouse station had closed and Kennethmont had become a halt by 1968, though from that year the distillery was one of only two on the former GNSR to retain its rail freight connection. The line from Keith to Kennethmont was singled in 1970 and the halt had been closed by 1971, at which time the local population had fallen to about 250.

**Distilling after Wardhouse**: However, Ardmore distillery still used rail transport in 1979; by 1983 it had become one of the largest and most modern malt distilleries, accompanied by bonded warehouses. In 1990 Ardmore was still in full production under Teachers (by then a subsidiary of Allied Distillers); nearby was a small animal feed factory. The prominent mansion of Wardhouse which had been abandoned about 1950 still stood in 1994, a gaunt and roofless ruin. By 1995 Kennethmont had a pub but no post office. The garage had closed by 2000, but licensed stores and the primary school remain open.

## KENNOWAY — Map 6, B4

***Large central Fife village,*** *pop. 4600* — OS 59: NO 3502

Kennoway 3 km north-west of Leven in Fife was founded in the sixth century by St Kenny (Cainneach), an Ulster contemporary of Columba. A medieval motte known as *Maiden Castle* is a striking feature of Kennoway; it was chosen by Timothy Pont (who mapped Scotland around 1600) as a landmark. Kennoway had a parish school by 1575, and was a substantial settlement clustered round the church long before it became a burgh of barony in 1663. By 1679 a coach road, later doomed to become congested by ribbon development, existed from Cameron Bridge through Kennoway to Ceres and St Andrews; by about 1750, as the Roy map showed, there was also a road from Kennoway to Falkland. Heron in 1799 noted Kennoway's 600 people, a *"village overlooking a beautiful and romantic den*; from 1800 it had a post office. The original hillcrest mansion of Montrave (*'Monthrive'* on Sharp's map) was built about 1820 at a height of 185 m, some 5 km north-east of the village. By 1827 there was an *'engine'*, no doubt in connection with coal mining, where the St Andrews road crossed the Scoonie

Burn, and 1.5km farther north was *'Colleston'*. Despite the mining, Kennoway was described by Barnard in 1886 as a *"delightful place situated at the head of a romantic glen"*.

**Montrave Rebuilt – and the ephemeral Rural Railway**: Montrave was rebuilt in 1890–93 for Sir John Gilmour to designs by Gillespie & Scott of St Andrews. Due to the growth of distilling at Cameron Bridge *(q.v.)*, by 1895 Kennoway was a substantial village with two inns, the second being at its top end in the hamlet of Bonnybank. In 1898 the winding and hilly East Fife Central Railway was opened from east of Cameron Bridge through stations at Kennoway and Montrave to terminate in the rural wilds 10km south of St Andrews at Lochty Farm *(see Largoward)*; its passenger trains lasted only until 1930. In 1931 a gasworks was established in the previously attractive glen between Windygates and Kennoway.

**Twentieth Century Growth misses Montrave**: By 1951 the area had a population of 3800 and the facilities of an average village, plus a large secondary school. New public authority housing was belatedly built at Kennoway for the Methil area miners. By the 1960s a quarry was open at Langside just to the north. By 1971, when all local jobs underground had vanished, the population was 4800. About 1976 a new trunk telephone exchange to serve the Levenmouth area was established at Kennoway, but the secondary school had closed by 1976, its pupils moved to Levenmouth, and by 1980 Montrave House had been demolished. The population was down to 4600 in 1991, when despite growing private estate development, over 60% of households still lived in public authority housing. An old beam engine house, relic of an abortive mine sinking, still exists at Kilmux 1.5km north of Kennoway.

## KERRERA, Isle of — Map 4, C2

***W. coast island, Argyll,** pop. under 100* — OS 49: NM 8228

Oban Bay is sheltered by this rocky, hummocky island with its caves and ancient remains. Near its southern tip is Gylen Castle, a 16th century tower of the MacDougalls, roofless since 1647. A school and church were built in 1872 at the central clachan of Balliemore, and a post office opened in 1879. By the mid 20th century Kerrera was supported by about eight small farms and famed for its lobsters, had a telephone exchange and a passenger ferry to Gallanach, 3km south-west of Oban. By 1980 a fish packing station was at work at Horseshoe Bay; it now packs lobsters from Cullipool, and a boatyard is open at Ardantrive at the north end of the island, whose total population was only 39 in 1991. Sadly the post office had vanished by 1996 and the school was closed in 1997; the essential ferry survives, and a tiny bothy now accommodates summer backpackers.

## KETTLE, Kingskettle & Kettlebridge — Map 6, B4

***Howe of Fife villages,** pop. 1000* — OS 59: NO 3108

The parish of Kettle in the Howe of Fife is apparently named from *Cautel*, meaning battle, though which battle is unclear – perhaps *Mons Graupius (see Stonehaven and Strathmiglo)*. However a possible greater Roman presence in the area than has so far been acknowledged is suggested to the author by the long straight road alignment which existed by about 1750 eastwards from Kirkforthar, passing Kettle and the Roman camp at Crawford *(Caer Ro*, later + *Ford?)* to Cupar, and on to Dairsie and St Andrews. Chapel of Kettle and *'Holkettle'*, both shown on Pont's sketch-maps of around 1600, lay just south of King's Kettle, whose prefix was added by charter in 1541. It became a small square settlement round the church and had an early parish school by 1571.

**Bridges, Bleaching, Coal, Lime and Railway**: By 1700 the River Eden had been bridged at Ramornie; by Roy's time this was named the Bridge of Kettle, nowadays Kettlebridge. A linen bleachfield was constructed around 1750. Heron wrote in 1799 that *"the village of Kettle has about 500 inhabitants"*. By about 1800 a coal pit on the hilltop was known as *Burnturk Engine*; limekilns nearby were linked by short canals with limestone quarries to the east. Quarrying continued after mining ended about 1830, leaving a hamlet called Coaltown of Burnturk. By 1825 Kettle and Balmalcolm were served by a penny post from Falkland, and by the time of the New Statistical Account linen weaving was well established, for in 1836 there were 378 hand looms in the parish; a co-operative society was founded in 1843. From 1847 Kingskettle had a station on the Burntisland to Ladybank section of the Edinburgh & Northern Railway (later the North British main line).

**From Weaving to Vegetables**: By 1864 most of the remaining weavers were working for Alex Lawson, making sheets and other bleached linens. In 1869 Bremner noted the *"recently erected"* power-loom linen weaving factory, and by 1895 there were two inns. The tiny Rameldry colliery was opened at Coaltown of Burnturk in the 1890s, giving work to perhaps 20 men until closing in the 1920s; the linen industry eventually failed too. The station was closed in 1967, but passing train travellers continued to look down into the roofless ruins of the weaving sheds, long derelict by 1977 and demolished in 1991; the site went for housing. Both the population and facilities of the Kettle area have fallen since the 1950s. In 1991 the village population was 975; industry included Barclay's small dairy. But the facilities were few for a place of that size; even the Co-op mini-market has since closed. Nowadays the intensive market garden business and packeries of Kettle Produce dominate the area.

## KILBARCHAN — Map 15, A5

***Large Renfrewshire village,** pop. 3800* — OS 64 & 63: NS 4063

Kilbarchan lies in a bowl in the hills 8km west of Paisley, and was a village by Pont's time around 1600; confirmed as such about 1660, it became a burgh of barony in 1704. Linen thread was made locally from 1739, and Heron observed *"the manufacture of lawns and cambric was introduced here as early as 1742"*. A bleachfield was built in mid-century. The Roy map made about 1754 showed a cross-shaped village, where the road from Paisley divided towards Lochwinnoch and Kilmacolm. Two annual fairs were scheduled for 1797, and Heron wrote in 1799 of *"the flourishing village of Kilbarchan, neatly built of free-stone, surrounded with thriving plantations and containing upwards of a thousand inhabitants. The manufacture of lawns and cambric still continues, though that of cotton seems of late to have become the chief object of attention. There are in this village three bleachfields, two candle-works, and a brewery."*

**Hand Looms, Steam Trains and Electric Trams**: At one time up to 1000 handloom weavers worked in Kilbarchan, a gasworks built in 1846 giving them light for long hours of toil. As

*Kilbarchan weaver's cottage; this one is owned by the NTS, and contains a working hand loom. There were up to 1000 handloom weavers in Kilbarchan in the mid 19th century.* *(JRH)*

late as 1869 Bremner noted about 800 handloom weavers on low and declining wages, *"entirely employed on woollen fabrics for Paisley manufacturers"*. The population had reached 2750 by 1891. By 1895 the small Locher printworks were in operation 1 km to the north of the village, and Kilbarchan had an inn. Kilbarchan was directly served by rail only from 1905, when a station was opened on the new Glasgow & South Western Railway's loop line between Elderslie and Dalry. From 1906 the village was also served by electric cars of the Paisley District Tramways Company, extended from Johnstone. After 1923 trams from Glasgow worked out as far as Kilbarchan, but were withdrawn in 1932.

**Modern Dormitory on Rubber Tyres**: During the early post-war period the large Tandlehill housing estate was built south-east of Kilbarchan, and by 1951 the population was over 3000, with the facilities of a small village, plus a bookseller. Tartan weaving on hand looms was still mentioned in 1953. By then the printworks had been enlarged, and by 1963 the National Trust for Scotland had restored an 18th century weaver's cottage as a museum. A quarry already open east of the village had become very large by 1988. Kilbarchan station was closed by Beeching about 1965, leaving only buses and fast-growing numbers of cars; by 1979 the railway had been lifted (and in the 1990s became a cycle route). By 1981 the facilities resembled an average village. In 1991 3800 people lived in Kilbarchan, a largely prosperous and well-educated community. At that time the motorway-standard Johnstone Bypass (A737) was being forced through the small gap between Kilbarchan and Millikenpark. The former primary school was demolished about 1997, when the St Cuthbert's High School had only 461 pupils.

## KILBERRY, Ormsary & Ardpatrick — Map 4, C4

***Argyllshire coastal villages**, pop. 200 (350)* — OS 62: NR 7164

Loch Caolisport cuts deeply into the west coast of Knapdale, but gives little shelter to ancient Dun Cragach or to the sculptured stones near the Point of Kilberry to the south, where once there was a monastery. Kilberry castle started as a late 16th century tower; Kilberry had a parish school by 1617, and Pont's map of around 1600 showed settlements all along the coast from Ormsary to Castle Sween; but they tended to fade away. The Roy map of about 1750 marked a substantial hamlet at Ormsary, served by both a coastal track and a direct way to Tarbert, but little at Kilberry. The castle was rebuilt in baronial style around the ancient tower in 1844–49. The adjoining stable clachan was the birthplace in 1877 of Archibald Campbell, who became a famous piper, a collector of pipe tunes and a historian of piping. Ardpatrick to the south had a primary school, a post office in 1913, and a telephone exchange in 1951, but all had gone by 1981, while Ormsary House and post office stood almost alone. In 1953 Bolton admired tiny Kilberry, then a clean hamlet with nearly 200 people, a school and *"rose-covered post office"*; these facilities served some 350 people, but the whole area's population was slowly falling. The nearby caravan site at Port Ban was in existence by 1981; the post office is open, as is the *Kilberry Inn*.

## KILBIRNIE & Glengarnock — Map 1, C1

***Ayrshire town**, pop. 8100* — OS 63: NS 3154

Pont's map of around 1600 showed *'Kilbirnan Kirk'*, standing beside the upper reaches of the River Garnock in Cunninghame; nearby are the ruins of a 14th century castle. Kilbirnie parish started a school in 1617 and a burgh of barony was chartered in 1642, but long remained unimportant; the Roy map of the mid 18th century showed many hamlets but no roads in the area. Near the present town centre was the name *'Bridgeend'* and a *'wake mill'*. Heron wrote in 1799 of a *"village with upwards of 300 inhabitants, employed chiefly in the silk manufacture"*. Early in the 19th century limestone quarries were in production south-west of Kilbirnie, and there was a limeworks at Hourat, 3 km west. The first Kilbirnie post office opened around 1825. A spinning mill was founded about 1830, the large Stoneyholm cotton mill began work in 1831, and the Garnock flax spinning mill started in 1834. Despite the mills, 140 handloom weavers were still at work in 1840. Knox's net works took over the Stoneyholm cotton mill in 1864, and soon there was also a ropeworks.

**Railway, Iron and Steel Works**: The main line of the Glasgow, Paisley, Kilmarnock & Ayr Railway – later Glasgow & South Western (G&SW) – which opened in 1840 served Kilbirnie indirectly, its nominal station being actually located at Glengarnock, 2 km to the south. The subsequent growth of Kilbirnie was largely related to Merry & Cunningham's Glengarnock ironworks which was first developed between station and village in 1840–43. The works which eventually had 8 blast furnaces were from the start very dependent on the railway; the firm also set up the Ardeer ironworks at Stevenston a few years later. About 1860 a small foundry was also opened at Auchengree near Glengarnock. Kilbirnie Station post office was renamed Glengarnock in 1874. Bessemer steel was made at Glengarnock from 1885; the works was soon also served by a new branch of the Lanarkshire & Ayrshire Railway – a Caledonian subsidiary – from Giffen (OS grid 3650) west of Barrmill, serving some collieries south of Glengarnock and terminating at a new station at Kilbirnie proper. The latter had 3528 residents in 1891, but was still called a *"village"* by Murray in 1894, when there was an inn; at Swinlees to the west

*The Stoneyholm mill, Kilbirnie, which started spinning cotton in 1831; it later made nets and produced linen thread.* (JRH)

were rail-connected quarries. The G&SW loop line between Elderslie and Dalry was opened in 1905, with yet another Kilbirnie station, just east of the village. Early in the 20th century Knox's made linen thread on a large scale in the Stoneyholm, Garnock and Dennyholm mills.

**Glengarnock's Heyday and Demise**: The iron and steelworks were rebuilt by Colvilles in 1916–18 to meet wartime demands, reaching a peak of some 3000 workers (though 1500 was more typical). Both the quarries and the various local collieries seem to have closed by the 1920s, and iron smelting ended in the 1930s. However, in 1922 came the Kilbirnie Place golf club. By 1950 Glengarnock had some 1350 people and a good range of village facilities; Kilbirnie had some 8000 residents and the facilities of a large village. By then the Giffen branch railway had no passenger trains, and by 1971 it had been largely lifted. Extensive housing estates had been built both north and south of Kilbirnie by 1963, but the loop railway station was closed about 1965; by then the original station had been renamed Glengarnock. In 1975 the open hearth furnaces at the steelworks were fed with iron from Clyde Ironworks; they supplied steel to the Dalzell bar mill – an uneconomic arrangement – as well as to the Glengarnock section mill, which made flat-bottomed rails. Its final product was flat plates for shipbuilding, but its last 800 jobs vanished when the still nationally-owned works were closed in 1979.

**Decline at Kilbirnie**: Redpath Engineering stayed on the site as steel fabricators, narrowly escaping closure in 1980 when 137 workers were employed. By the 1970s the Dennyholm spinning mill had become a sawmill and the limeworks were long disused. By 1981 Kilbirnie had the facilities of a large village, and fishing nets were still made. In the 1980s land reclamation improved the former steelworks site. In 1987 the railway was electrified, bringing good services to Glasgow, Ayr and Largs, and about then the new Garnock Academy was built. In 1991 the population was almost static at 8060. By 1992 AMS Boyswear had a local factory, but the last railfreight user, Young Transport at Glengarnock, had ceased by 1993; soon much of the former loop railway route had become a cycle path. Garnock Academy has almost 1200 pupils, and a hotel is still open.

## KILBRIDE *(Cille Bhrighde)* & Saltavik

***Townships, S. Uist,*** *pop. 150* — **Map 7, A4** — OS 31: NF 7514

At the south end of South Uist is the sheltered harbour of Saltavik Bay *(G. Bagh Shaltabhaig)*, long the terminus of passenger ferries to Eoligarry in Barra and to the Isle of Eriskay. By the mid 20th century some 360 people lived nearby in the scattered crofts of Boisdale *(Baghasdal)*, Garrynamonie with its primary school, and Kilbride with its post office. About 1.5km farther east is a tiny township, South Glen Dale *(G. Gleann Dail bho Deas)*, roadless until about 1973 when its school was closed. About then the Eriskay ferry was replaced by a roll-on vehicular ferry. Some 3km to the west at Pollachar is the long-established *Polochar Inn*; for a time around 1980 this was only a bar, but is now a 10-roomed hostelry. A lengthy causeway link to Eriskay was opened late in 2000.

## KILCHOAN

***Ardnamurchan village,*** *pop. 150* — **Map 4, B1** — OS 47: NM 4863

The ruined, 13th century curtain-walled castle of Mingary stands on the rocky south shore of the Ardnamurchan peninsula 1.5km east of Kilchoan *(pronounced Kilhone)*, the most westerly village in mainland Britain. The Roy map of about 1750 showed a small cluster of huts on a trackless peninsula, where clearances were still taking place as late as the 1850s. The lighthouse on Ardnamurchan Point was first illuminated in 1849. Eventually around 1900 a single-track road which circled round the modest but dramatic Ben Hiant reached Kilchoan, and a pier with a small crane was built at Mingary. Up to 1949 this was served by Oban to Lochboisdale steamers; then a passenger ferry to Tobermory was substituted. The population in 1951 was about 150, with minimal facilities including the *Kilchoan Hotel*. The population had fallen to around 120 by 1971.

**Resurgence despite Ferry Difficulties**: Growing appreciation of the remoteness, clean air and ever-changing sea views of Mull and the other islands around hilly Ardnamuchan led more people to live in the area and especially to visit it. By 1984 the primary school had been extended; there was a village hall, post office and general stores, a new guest house, two small craft shops, a district nurse and a modern telephone exchange. Even farther west was the *Sonachan Hotel*, 4km out of town, and the tiny townships of Achosnich and Portuaird. In 1984 the four ferry trips each day were under threat due to lack of usage, a problem thought to have been solved by 1991 with a new roll-on pier at Mingary and calls by the Oban to Castlebay, Coll and Tiree car ferry. However, by 1996 only a service to Tobermory was open, and this – which often had the wind abeam – did not run in the depths of winter. The Ardnamurchan lighthouse was automated in 1988, and by 1999 its keepers' houses had been converted as holiday lets.

## KILCHRENAN

***Small Argyll village, L. Awe,*** *pop. 100* — **Map 5, A3** — OS 50: NN 0322

Prehistoric crannogs in Loch Awe adjoined the peninsula that divides the main body of the loch from the defile of the Pass of Brander. A Columban monastery called *Cella Duini*, now vanished, was established on the south side of the peninsula, later replaced by a church called Kilchrenan, where for a time a cattle tryst was held. The Roy map showed tracks meeting there on the lines of the later roads to Taynuilt and Dalavich, and two ferries across northern Loch Awe: the long-vanished Ruachan Ferry from Ardanaiseig to Clashdrenich east of Cladich, and that from the North Port to South Port near Portsonachan *(q.v.)* which survived to carry passengers as recently as 1956. Meantime the woods of Glen Nant were coppiced to provide charcoal for the ironworks at Taynuilt. About the 1950s the Nant hydro-electric power station was built 3 km south-west of Kilchrenan, fed by aqueduct and tunnel from Loch Nant. The small *Taychreggan Hotel* beside Loch Awe was enlarged from a drovers' inn, reaching 22 rooms by 1980. Both this, and the 14-roomed country house *Ardanaiseig Hotel* in its fine gardens beside the loch 6 km to the east, have beautiful situations. There is also a pub near Kilchrenan Kirk; about 100 people live in the area, and Glen Nant has informative forest trails.

## KILCREGGAN & Cove

**Map 5, B5**

***Firth of Clyde village,*** *pop. 1600* — OS 63 & 56: NS 2480

Portkil at the south end of the Rosneath peninsula on the Firth of Clyde appeared as *'Porte'* on Pont's map of about 1600. Though chartered as a burgh of barony in 1667, Roy's 1750s map showed a trackless area, a church and a mansion at *'Camsale'* (Camsail). Early in the 19th century piers were built west of Portkil at both Cove and Kilcreggan, served by the frequent steamer services in the Gourock area; both soon grew into small residential resorts. The prominent mock baronial Knockderry House (or Castle) designed by Alexander Thomson was built in 1851–54, and ornately remodelled in 1896–97 by William Leiper for the owner of Templeton Carpets. Another such mansion, Craigrownie Castle, arose at Cove in 1850–55, and was later extended into a major edifice. A gasworks was built in 1871, and about then the combined area became a police burgh.

**Mansions and Villas**: Both places had post and telegraph offices by 1889, and in 1894 Murray noted a *"mansion and villa"* ambience; at Cove, villas lined the shore as far north as Knockderry House. Later an artillery fort named Portkil was built between Kilcreggan and Rosneath Point. Kilcreggan had a fire station by 1951, when the combined population was about 1000, with typical village services, which still functioned in 1989 as did the long-established passenger ferry to Gourock, augmented by 1995 with a summer ferry to Helensburgh. The population had grown to 1586 by 1991. Knockderry Castle stood vacant and deteriorating in 1997; *Craigrownie Castle*, at one time a home for the mentally handicapped and later abandoned, was fully restored in the 1990s; recently sold, it offers luxury accommodation.

## KILDONAN & Pladda Isle

**Map 1, B2**

***Small village, Arran,*** *pop. 100* — OS 69: NS 0321

A standing stone at the south-eastern tip of Arran was later joined by Kildonan church and the 14th century keep of Kildonan Castle. In 1790 the Northern Lighthouse Board built a pier and lit two lighthouses on the offshore islet of Pladda; later, one sufficed. A lifeboat station opened at Kildonan in 1870, but lasted only until 1902. By 1953, when about 130 people lived locally, a coastguard station, hotel and inn stood among the facilities of a small village, whose 9-hole golf course closed around 1960. By 1976 the population had fallen and the primary school had been closed; by 1979 the families of the Pladda lightkeepers lived in Lamlash, but the light was automated in 1989. By 1981 the population of this largely farming area with holiday cottages had recovered, and there was a garage. The 30-room *Kildonan Hotel* serves the area.

## KILLEARN

**Map 5, C5**

***W. Stirlingshire village,*** *pop. 1800* — OS 57: NS 5285

Dumgoyne in Strathblane, about 20 km north-west of Glasgow, was named after a prominent hill at the end of the Campsie Fells; it was also known as *Old Killearn*. However, Pont's map of about 1600 showed the name Killearn near the Blane Water, well north of Dumgoyne, and very probably represented the Kirk of Killearn, built on a hilltop 3 km from Dumgoyne. The school attended by George Buchanan – born locally in 1505, who became the severe tutor to James VI – could have been at either place. From 1630 there was a parish school, and the Roy map made about 1754 showed a nucleated settlement round the kirk, from which tracks led to Glasgow via the route later labelled A875, and to Drymen and Fintry. As recently as 1791 the Kirkton consisted of Highland-style earthen cottages, which were regularly razed and rebuilt every five to seven years. However, a woollen mill was established on the Endrick Water nearby in the 1790s, and in 1799 Heron merely described Killearn as a *"village"*; by about 1825 it was served by a penny post from Glasgow. The woollen mill worked until at least the 1830s.

**Distilling and Railways**: What was originally named the *Glenguin* distillery was built in 1833 south of Dumgoyne, a small operation. Later this was served by a station on the North British Railway's Blane Valley branch, opened in 1866. For some years the line ended at Killearn station near the confluence of the Blane Water with the Endrick Water, over 1 km from the village and 75 m below it. Then in 1882 the railway was extended northwards, joining at Gartness Junction 2 km north-west of Killearn with the Balloch to Aberfoyle line, opened in 1856. By 1886 the distillery was owned by Lang Brothers, whose nine workers made about 200,000 litres of Highland malt whisky annually, mainly sold in Glasgow and London. By 1902 its name had been amended to *Glengoyne*, so avoiding its being pronounced like *'Penguin'*! In 1891 the village population was 354; the *Killearn Inn* was open by 1894.

**The Hospital and its Disposal**: During World War II a large 400-bed emergency hospital was built adjoining Killearn station. By 1951 when the railway closed to passengers, about 1500 people lived in the area; Killearn had typical village facilities, including the small *Black Bull Hotel*. Rail freight ended in 1959. By 1971 the transformation into a dormitory village by large estate developments had begun: the population had risen to 1900. This included about 250 in the hospital, which was last used in 1972 and stood empty for over a decade. Its proposed sale for development as a leisure complex failed in 1979 and its final method of disposal by the government was highly controversial; by 1994 little was left on the site.

**Affluent Modern Killearn**: Carbeth House to the north, a Graham home, still stands in extensive parkland. The West Highland Way follows the old railway beside the Blane Water; it passes by Killearn, which by 1991 was a dormitory containing some 1800 people, mainly youngish and well-educated;

over 75% lived in detached houses. The Way passes close to the small traditional Glengoyne distillery, attractively rebuilt with 3 stills in 1966–67, and open to visitors by 1991. Still in the ownership of Lang Brothers of Glasgow – since 1965 part of the Robertson & Baxter group – it makes an unpeated Highland single malt. This sells at ten years old, and at 25 years old; it also goes into the blended *Langs' Supreme*. Production in 1992 was at a high rate, which led to some breaches of effluent quality. The *Black Bull Hotel* – extended about 1977 – serves the locality.

## KILLIECRANKIE

**Map 6, A2**

***Small Perthshire village,*** *pop. 200* — OS 43: NN 9162

The decisive battle of Killiecrankie was fought in 1689 during the first Jacobite rebellion, where Glen Garry opens out north of the narrow Pass of Killiecrankie, about 5km north of Pitlochry. The River Garry was followed by the later military road, by Telford's coach road, and by the Inverness & Perth Junction (later Highland) Railway, opened in 1863 with a station. Skilfully engineered by Joseph Mitchell, the railway traverses a curving 10-arched viaduct 16m tall and a short tunnel. By 1951 Killiecrankie House had become a hotel, and the village had about 250 residents. The station was closed in 1963–65, so the National Trust for Scotland's visitor centre – built about that time to introduce the forest trails which access the spectacular riverbed features in the gorge – can only be reached by road. By 1977 a former shooting lodge 5km west of the A9 near the east end of Loch Tummel had become the *Queen's View Hotel*, and a youth hostel was open nearby. A costly bypass, built with some difficulty on a viaduct along the steep east side of the pass, was opened in 1986 as the final section of the reconstruction of the A9 road between Perth and Inverness. The post office has stayed open. The *Killiecrankie Hotel* and *Queen's View Hotel* are open, but the adjacent youth hostel is no longer in use.

## KILLIN

**Map 5, C3**

***Village, w. end of L. Tay,*** *pop. 650* — OS 51: NN 5733

Near the spectacularly tumbling rapids of the Falls of Dochart at the head of Loch Tay is a stone circle. Adjacent Killin's Pictish name means *'Church by the Loch'*, and Glendochart had an early lay abbot. Killin was also known as *Kilfin*, from the alleged grave of St Fingal, for whom nearby Finlarig Castle at the foot of Glen Lochay was named. This appeared on Pont's sketch map of about 1600, which implied that the famous irregular bridge had already been built across the falls. A parish school was held by 1627. Killin became a burgh of barony in 1694 under Sir John Campbell of Glenorchy, first Earl of Breadalbane *(see Kenmore)*. The Earls rebuilt Finlarig in the 17th century; the Roy map showed that by 1750 it stood in formal policies, but the settlement at Killin was only one of several hamlets in the area. The Roy map also showed the *'Dochart Bridge'*, which was rebuilt in 1760, the *'Lochay*

*Mill on the River Dochart, Killin, pictured in the late 19th century. This mill, known as Millmore, was built by the Breadalbane estates around 1840 as a corn mill. It is now a visitor centre.* *(GWW collection)*

*Bridge'*, and four radial tracks which made regional connections west, south and also east on the north side of Loch Tay.

**Textiles and Tourism**: A lint mill was in use by 1761; about the same time an inn was built for the laird, Lord Breadalbane. Around 1790 locally-grown flax was spun, woven into linen by 36 weavers and sold at the six annual fairs. Killin's first post office opened in the village in 1800. Dorothy Wordsworth noted in 1803 that the road to Kenmore then lay south of the loch – evidently it was better than the older track on the north side. Corn was growing well at the mouth of the more placid River Lochay, beside which were the *"village of Killin"* with its kirk and a large inn. To the west at Luib was an inn which served her wine with a *"bad supper"*; a post office opened there in 1806. In the 1820s Chambers found Killin *"a straggling little village"* with mills. By 1850 coach tours were run from Aberfeldy via Killin and Crianlarich to connect with steamers at Inverarnan on Loch Lomond.

**The Killin Railway**: In 1870 the Callander & Oban Railway reached Ardchyle at the head of the glen, and was extended to Crianlarich in 1873, with a station at desolate Luib. Killin had a branch of the Bank of Scotland by 1882 when, with the keen backing of Lord Breadalbane, the villagers promoted their own railway. This opened in 1886 from Ardchyle, renamed Killin Junction, to a pier on Loch Tay, which had limited steamer services. In 1891 the village population was 589. In 1894 Murray noted *"a considerable village"*, the *"good" Killin Hotel*, and the *Bridge of Lochay Hotel, "plain but comfortable"*. Killin golf club was founded in 1913 and laid out a 9-hole parkland course on the hillside. The Caledonian Steam Packet Company bought the Loch Tay steamers in 1922 and they continued to serve Killin pier until the service ended in 1939.

**New Hydro Power and Railway Demise**: The Finlarig hydro-electricity generating station was built on the lochside in the 1950s, fed by aqueduct and tunnel from the Lochan na Lairige dam 5 km to the north. The smaller Lochay power station 3 km north-west of Killin was fed by tunnel and pressure pipes from the Cashlie power station in Glenlyon *(q.v.)*. The area's railways were abruptly closed by Beeching in 1965; Killin station site became a car park. The long-standing youth hostel had closed by 1982. The closure also killed off the *Luib Hotel*, but not long after it had been demolished, the small *Suie Lodge Hotel* replaced it. Killin's 760 or so residents retained a generous village level of facilities in 1981, when these served about 1400 people in all. The long-standing and best hotels were then the 32-roomed *Killin* and the 18-roomed *Bridge of Lochay*.

**Folklore, Riding and Accommodation**: Killin had 651 residents in 1991; its surroundings are beautiful but its immediate tourist role depends heavily on the views of the Falls of Dochart, especially well seen from the bridge when in spate. In 1994 the former St Fillans water mill close by was reopened as the Breadalbane Folklore Centre; the first Killin festival of traditional music and dance was held in 1995, sponsored by the Killin Traders Association. By 1998 a youth hostel was again open. The *Dall Lodge Hotel* has added to Killin's caravan sites, many guest houses and restaurants. About 4 km east is a former shooting lodge, now the *Morenish Lodge Hotel*, beyond which is an equestrian centre, and a caravan and camping site. By 1998 there was a caravan site also at Luib.

## KILMACOLM — Map 5, B5

***Large Renfrewshire village**, pop. 4350* — OS 63: NS 3569

Kilmacolm on the eastern slopes of the open valley of Strathgryfe some 12 km west of Paisley is an ancient settlement, whose Gaelic name is a corruption of *Kil na Colm* meaning *'Church of Columba'*. A medieval motte was raised some 1.5 km south of the church, and 2 km west of the motte was the 14th century keep of Duchal Castle. This was shown as a mansion or tower on Pont's rather confused original sketch map of about 1600, which also depicted a chapel, *'Brigend'*, *'Wakmil'* and Milton. Little now remains of Duchal Castle, which was abandoned in favour of a site across the River Gryfe from the motte, where Duchal House was built. A parish school was opened in 1623. The Roy map of about 1754 showed the Kirk and village on a north–south road system which also served the Bridgend and Glen mills, and linked with Port Glasgow and Paisley. However, Kilmacolm was never a burgh, and there was still no post office by 1838.

**The Railway stimulates Development**: Kilmacolm began to develop as an upmarket dormitory after the opening of the Greenock branch of the Glasgow & South Western Railway in 1869, its station also providing direct trains to Paisley and Glasgow. In the 1890s the compact village with its church and inn had Bridgend mill to the west, and a large hydropathic establishment to the east. The name Milton, probably the location of the Glen mill, was applied to the area south of the village. Kilmacolm golf club was founded in 1891 and laid out its course to the east; the mansion of Auchenbothie House, designed by William Leiper, was built on a virgin site 1 km north-west of the village in 1898. Both a gasworks and an electricity generating station were established in 1899–1900.

**Independent Education, Orphanage and Grouse Trains**: The independent St Columba's School for Girls was opened in 1897 in purpose-built premises. By the 1930s the Sailors' Orphan Homes (later known as Balrossie School), had also been built, 2 km south-west of the village. The very extensive Duchal Moor Railway 5 km to the west was built after 1918 to give access to grouse moors, using war-surplus track and locomotives and unemployed workers; remarkably, it still survived in 1994. By 1951 the population in the area was about 3000 and the facilities of a large village were available. The Bridgend mill still existed in 1963, but the 110-room *Kilmacolm Hydro* closed in the 1960s. In 1966, the Greenock rail connection was broken north of Kilmacolm; by 1971 the track had been lifted. The expanding village was placed rather uncomfortably in the new and heavily industrial Inverclyde district from 1975.

**After the Railway – Spacious Suburbia**: Kilmacolm's truncated rail passenger service to Paisley and Glasgow, made uneconomic by high levels of car commuting, was regrettably closed in 1983 after a bitter struggle, and the line was lifted. But housing development continued, with quite large estates and a new primary school built in the 1980s. By 1991 the resident population of 4343 was affluent, and one of the best-educated in Scotland; only one house in eight was publicly owned. Much of the abandoned railway is now a cycle route. Kamscot has become a medium-sized civil engineering firm in the area. The former mansion of Auchenbothie House was converted into flats in 1995, with new housing in the grounds. In 2001 *'Manor Kingdom'* of Fife were building a large speculative mansion-house in a half-hectare plot in a former stone quarry in Houston Road, and had reconditioned another called the Old Hall.

## KILMARNOCK

**Map 1, C1**
***Ayrshire large town,*** *pop. 44,300* OS 70: NS 4238
Suburbs: *Hurlford & Riccarton*

Kilmarnock in Cunninghame was *"so named after Saint Marnock, who is said to have died in 322"* wrote Heron nearly 1500 years later; Mackay cites St Ernan. The ancient Craufurdland tower beside the Craufurdland Water is reputed to have had an underground connection with the large Dean Castle, built by about 1300 by the Earls of Kilmarnock over 2 km to the south-west, where the Craufurdland and Fenwick Waters join to form the Kilmarnock Water. The very substantial tower of the Laigh Kirk, built in 1410 some 1.5 km downstream from Dean Castle, was the nucleus around which Kilmarnock town grew. Dean Castle was rebuilt in the 15th century when Kilmarnock was a property of the powerful Angus and Bothwell families, and in 1560 was the seat of Lord Boyd. Chambers noted that Kilmarnock, chartered to the Boyds as a burgh of barony in 1591 (the year that a parish school was opened), was *"at first an appendage"* to Dean Castle.

**Crowded Cutlers and Dirty Bonnetmakers**: The burgh rapidly became important, appearing as a compact place on Pont's map made around 1600; a bridge across the Kilmarnock Water was shown, but there was no bridge to Riccarton and the south until 1726. Richard Franck wrote of Kilmarnock in 1656 that it was *"heaped up and crowded with men and mechanics and brew-houses, with dirty streets cleaned only by rain, crazy tottering ports and ugly houses, little better than huts, with not one good structure to be found"* (he overlooked the solid church tower!). Its crafts included making good dirks, razors and knives, the *"knitting of bonnets, and spinning* (sic) *of Scottish cloth"*. Kilmarnock had a post office as early as 1662, for it lay on the Edinburgh–Ireland route. In 1672 the mansion of Treesbank in Ayr Road was built for the Campbell family; a stable block was added about 1770.

**Maria Gardiner leads Expansion in Woollens**: A grammar school was open by 1696, yet by the early 1700s the town's population was allegedly only about 1000, and Chambers claimed that it was then just *"a mean village"* noted only for making night-caps. Kilmarnock's fame as a textile centre grew from about 1728 through the remarkable initiative of one woman, Maria Gardiner, who brought spinners and carpet weavers from Dalkeith to begin carpet and blanket manufacture on hand looms. By 1733 Kilmarnock was regarded as one of the principal centres of Scottish woollens, making cheap serges and shawls; Chambers wrote that it had been transformed in *"an amazingly brief space of time"* – half a century – into *"a minor city"*, based on *"all the more important branches of the woollen manufacture"*. Dean Castle burned down in 1731 but was the Earls' nominal home until 1745.

**Seedsmen, Roads, Cheese, Bankers – and a Real Dick Whittington**: Dickie, Fowlds & Co set up as seed merchants in 1750; by then Kilmarnock was the largest town in Ayrshire. The mid 1750s Roy map showed a big higgledy-piggledy place with two bridges and five radial roads. The surrounding area showed greater indications of agricultural development than most parts of Scotland at the time; Kilmarnock's cheese fairs were famous *(see Dunlop)*. A linen bleachfield was built around then, as was a waulk mill. The first road to be improved by the new Ayrshire Turnpike Trust joined Kilmarnock and Irvine in 1767; in 1775 the Bank of Scotland opened a branch in Kilmarnock. James Shaw, born in Riccarton *(q.v.)* in 1764 and educated at Kilmarnock Grammar School, made his fortune, became Lord Mayor of London, and earned the statue long displayed at the Cross.

**Varied Industry and Culture**: Of 146 looms making woollens in the town in 1776, 66 made carpets, and this industry spurted in the following year. By 1785 a local bark mill served the tanning trade, which soon had over 400 leather workers. There was an agricultural improvement society, and the *Wheatsheaf Hotel* was open. John Wilson's printing press – which first gave Robert Burns' poems to the world – was in Kilmarnock; he published other books before moving operations to Ayr. Coal mining was locally important by the late 18th century, and a public library service was started in 1797, a year when four fairs were scheduled to be held in the town. Heron wrote in 1799 that Kilmarnock was a *"town of near 6000 inhabitants"*. Its manufactures were *"carpets, tanning and dressing leather, making shoes and gloves, cotton cloth, calico-printing, duffles, knitted caps, mits and other woollen goods"*.

**Coal, Iron and Passengers are all Freight**: By then Kilmarnock was also significant for cotton spinning and for malting, and had a brewery; daily mail coaches ran from Glasgow via Kilmarnock and Cumnock to Dumfries and Carlisle. Ironfounding began about 1800, and the Portland Colliery opened about 1807. Kilmarnock Academy was founded in that year; by then tobacco and snuff were processed. The Kilmarnock Banking Company, established in 1802, was taken over in 1821 by Hunters & Co, bankers of Ayr. The four-foot (122 cm) gauge Kilmarnock & Troon Railway, a plateway which opened in 1812 with horse haulage, was promoted by the local landed proprietor the Duke of Portland to facilitate coal export; it was engineered by William Jessop. Passengers were weighed and carried as freight – to overcome a lack of legal powers to carry them at all! In 1817 the line acquired a primitive Stephenson locomotive, but this damaged the track and its use was discontinued.

**Town Improvements and Johnnie Walker**: Early in the 19th century the main streets were re-planned, and gas-lit from 1822 from a coal-gas works established in 1810. By 1825 Kilmarnock was the centre for a penny post serving Galston, Kilmaurs and Newmilns. A second brewery opened about that time. John Walker set up in the licensed grocery business in 1820; the firm was expanded into whisky blending and exporting by his son and grandson, both named Alexander, and bonded warehouses were built. (As John Walker & Sons they were to adopt the well-known Johnnie Walker brand name in 1907).

**Textile Development and Philosophy**: By 1810 calico was printed in the large Bishopfield printworks, and by 1822 worsted combing had been mechanised at Crookholm mill. Bonnets were still produced, and printed worsted shawls were made from 1824, the industry soon employing 1400 printers and weavers – until fashions changed. In the early 1820s about twelve firms were making carpets, and by 1830 about 1000 carpet looms were in use, though the number of firms gradually reduced. A philosophical institute spread knowledge from 1823, and although the ancient burned-out castle had fallen into a state of ruin by 1827, Kilmarnock was then according to Chambers *"the largest and most elegant town in Ayrshire. The magnificent house which the baron of Dean Castle had for his residence in Kilmarnock is now a boarding-school for the young cotton lords of the west."*

**Carpets and Concerts**: After the Reform Act became law in 1832, William Cobbett, one of its progenitors, lectured and stayed overnight at the inn in what he called this *"very beautiful, solid and opulent place"* – which became a Parliamentary Burgh in 1833 as a result of the Act. A new Bank of Scotland branch office was opened in 1838. In the 1830s Gregory, Thomson & Co made the high-quality carpets then described as *'Scots-Persian'*. Another Kilmarnock carpet manufacturer, Thomas Morton, invented triple carpet fabric, and by 1839 employed some 1200 workers. Later his firm was to become known as Blackwood-Morton, and ultimately as BMK. By 1848 the local carpet industry had stabilised under five firms, with three associated spinning mills. About 150 stocking frames were also in use, and as industry broadened so did culture: a philharmonic society was established in 1845.

**Into the Railway Age**: In 1843 Kilmarnock was rather indirectly connected to Glasgow by the Glasgow, Paisley, Kilmarnock & Ayr Railway, through what began as a branch from Dalry; the company also established a local engine shed. The line was extended to Dumfries and Carlisle, opening in 1850, when companies combined to form the Glasgow & South Western (G&SWR). But in 1863 Scott's of Kilmarnock were the contractors who built the Peebles branch for the rival Caledonian Railway (CR). In 1873 the direct railway to Barrhead and Glasgow was opened by the CR and G&SWR – for once acting jointly. By the end of the railway-building epoch Kilmarnock was the focus for six radiating lines, the latest leading to Irvine and Strathaven.

**Railway Locomotives and Milk Churns**: Andrew Barclay of Kilmarnock began to build locomotives in 1840, and his Caledonia works and foundry was built in 1847. The Townholm engineering works also dated from this time, the Vulcan foundry was built about 1850, and in this pre-tanker epoch the manufacture of milk churns began, as Kilmarnock lay in a dairying area. The G&SWR's main locomotive and wagon works were built in 1853–58. In the 1870s Allen Andrews also built locomotives in Kilmarnock.

*The erecting shop at Andrew Barclay's Caledonia Works, Kilmarnock, in 1972, showing production for the National Coal Board (NCB) and for East African Railways (EAR).* (JRH)

**Textile Developments, Bonnets and Lace**: Brussels carpets were made from 1857 by Gregory Thomson using steam power; soon they were Scotland's largest carpet manufacturer. Carpet-weaving of Brussels and Wilton types was the *"principal manufacture"* of the town in 1869 (Bremner); there was also a large 500-loom wincey factory. However, as fashions changed, shawls were replaced by bonnets, manufactured in bulk in Kilmarnock by 1860; in 1869 six firms employed some 1500 workers in this trade, the largest being Douglas, Reyburn & Co. Worsteds were made by some 60 workers using steam power at Crookedholm Mill, and a lace factory was opened about 1880.

**Building Engines for Industries**: Andrew Barclay's 269th locomotive, built in 1883, still exists – as does the firm – which also built mining equipment until the 1950s, including pumping engines, colliery winding engines, and blowing engines for iron-smelting. Meantime Grant, Ritchie & Co were building locomotives between at least 1880–1907, and made large colliery winding engines for such pits as the Lady Victoria at Newtongrange, and Newcraighall. W B Dick & Co produced tramway equipment from the late 1870s, and also made railway equipment at their Britannia Works. By 1890 the name Dick, Kerr & Co had been adopted. In 1908 they built tiny tank engines for the Karachi Port's two-foot (60 cm) gauge line; in 1981 these durable little machines were still at work elsewhere in the Indian sub-continent.

**Water Meters and Hydraulic Signalling**: Water meter manufacture began in 1852, and the Kennedy water meter works commenced operations in 1871. In the late 19th century the ironfounders Glenfield & Co of Kilmarnock supplied many cast iron manhole covers to London's Metropolitan Water Board, still to be seen on some London streets; and about 1890 Glenfield collaborated with Stevens & Sons to produce a hydraulically operated signalling system for the CR. Then they joined with Kennedy to become the hydraulic engineers Glenfield & Kennedy – a firm which specialised in valve manufacture, and also made ornate compound steam pumping engines; one which they supplied in 1902 to Bristol Waterworks still survives. Other late 19th century enterprises included a tileworks, two printing works, and a nursery with seed dressing. The Corn Exchange was built in 1863, and St Marnock's Church was another fine Victorian structure. A local newspaper, the *Kilmarnock Standard* was established in 1863, and a large, tall fever hospital was built on Mount Pleasant in 1867–68 to designs by William Railton; it was later extended to form the Kilmarnock Infirmary. Many of the public buildings were constructed using red sandstone, from quarries such as Ballochmyle and Locharbriggs.

**Rugby, Football, Phones and Documentaries**: Kilmarnock FC, the second oldest football club in Scotland, was established in 1869 – to play Rugby! Hence the name of Rugby Park, their home locality from 1877. They soon changed to the round ball game, and from 1899 Rugby Park was a good stadium for the day. Meantime a so-called *Operetta House*, finely faced in pink sandstone, was built in 1874–75, but failed – and in 1885 remarkably became a church. Public parks were provided in 1879 and 1894. From 1886 the new telephone system linked Kilmarnock with Glasgow and Ayr. The population of the town was nearing 30,000, but only the *"fair" George Hotel* was mentioned by Murray, who described Kilmarnock in 1894 as a *"place of considerable importance in the manufacturing* *world"*. John Grierson, born in the town in 1898, became the first renowned maker of documentary films, including *Drifters* and *Night Mail*.

**Current, Culture, and Short-lived Tramways**: A new municipal electricity supply was provided from a generating station established in 1899. A pottery dated from about 1900, and the neo-classical Dick Institute with its library was opened in 1901. In 1903 the Corn Exchange was converted into the *Palace Theatre*, and in 1904 the *King's Theatre* was built to seat 2200 people. Though brewing seems to have ceased about 1906, Saxone began to manufacture boots around then. A new coal mine which opened at Kelk Place in 1908 was the last sinking in the area. In 1904 a short and simple T-shaped municipal electric tramway system was opened. Based on the Kirkcaldy system, but of standard gauge, it extended only the 3.75km from Beansburn in the north to Riccarton, where the power station and depot were located, with a branch of almost 3km from The Cross to Hurlford. It had only 14 cars and was slow – averaging a mere 7mph; the Hurlford branch succumbed to bus competition in 1924, and the General Strike of 1926 finished the remainder *(see Deans 1986)*.

**Falling Fortunes in Locomotive Building**: Meantime in 1904 Barclay's had built their thousandth locomotive, and kept up an average build of 45 a year until 1920 (No. 1719); then the output rate nearly halved. The G&SWR Kilmarnock works were very inadequate and outworn by 1913, but built about 425 steam locomotives over the 64 years to 1921. Heavy work was moved to St Rollox after the London Midland & Scottish Railway (LMS) took over in 1923, and most of the premises were demolished in 1929. Dick, Kerrs closed following amalgamation in 1919, but in 1928 the Kilmarnock Engineering Company built some bogies for Glasgow trams, carrying bodies built by R Y Pickering & Co of Wishaw and Hurst Nelson of Motherwell.

**Blackwood, Buses and Cinemas**: Blackwood & Morton prospered meantime, and in 1926 Gavin Morton had the Tudor-style mansion of Treesbank House built on the site of the earlier house, and surrounded by wooded policies. The generating station was enlarged in the 1920s and connected to the grid in 1932 as a base-load station; in 1931 the population was about 38,000. A bus station was built as early as 1923 and, having disposed of the tramways, in 1932 Kilmarnock became the HQ of the large Western Scottish Motor Traction (SMT) bus company. In 1934 the *King's Theatre* became a cinema, later known successively as the *Regal* and the *ABC*. Marks & Spencer opened a tiny store in 1936, and an indoor swimming pool was opened in 1940. During the war, army oil-tanks occupied Rugby Park.

**Railway Change and Decline**: About 1947 Barclays built three small steam locomotives for the Irish Peat Authority, and in 1954 supplied standard fireless locomotives. But to stay in business they had to build diesels, including 200hp shunters for British Railways in 1956. Meantime by 1948 the LMS works had been much reduced, doing just repair work and break-ups until closure in 1959. The Beeching cuts hit Kilmarnock hard: the Darvel and Barassie branches lost passenger trains in 1964 and 1969 respectively.

**Glenfield, Golf and Football Flourish**: Glenfield & Kennedy employed 2400 workers in 1948; in the mid 1960s they supplied a fish pass and other equipment for the Cruachan hydro power scheme. In 1957 a second municipal golf course was laid out at Annanhill; Kilmarnock FC built their main stand in 1961 and won the championship in 1965. The Technical College was opened in 1966, and about then a large modern branch of the Royal Bank was built. Chronic central congestion was relieved when the A77 bypass road was opened east of the town in 1973. Up to 1975 the town council operated many facilities including the *Palace Theatre*, and called Kilmarnock *"the commercial and industrial capital of Ayrshire"*.

**Expansion in Shopping and Facilities**: In 1973 Marks & Spencer quintupled the floorspace of their little store, followed by the Foregate pedestrian shopping area opened in 1974, the Burns shopping mall of 1976, a new and busy bus station, multi-storey car park and civic centre. About 1979 the Clydesdale Bank opened one of their largest branches at the charmingly named Square of Ales. A large modern police station was built, and in 1987 came five new Sheriff Courts in a fine pink sandstone building designed by David Gregory. At the same time the dual-carriageway bypass for the A71 was built to the south. By then the 50-roomed *Howard Park Hotel* had been built on Glasgow Road, supplementing 7 or 8 older small hostelries. Kilmarnock became the centre of the Kilmarnock and Loudoun District in 1975, but was badly hit when the tractor manufacturers Massey-Ferguson of Crosshouse failed in 1977 with the loss of some 2000 jobs. BMK also suffered serious contraction. In 1976 Treesbank House became a conference centre for the STUC. By 1979 Jaeger Tailoring had a factory in the town, providing 260 jobs.

**Entertainments and Shopping**: In 1976 the *ABC Cinema* was converted to accommodate three screens and bingo, and in the early 1980s the *Palace Theatre* was renovated to seat 500 people. Many major national chain stores including Woolworth, BHS, Presto and Tesco had lately invested heavily in the town, and in 1979 a group of 130 local Marks & Spencer customers asked for a still larger store to be provided. By 1990 Safeway had built a new store at West Shaw Street. Dean Castle, restored by Lord Howard de Walden, became a museum, and its policies a country park.

*A kiln carriage at Longpark Pottery, Kilmarnock, loaded with sanitary ware, in which this pottery specialised from its foundation in about 1888 until its closure in 1981.* (JRH)

**Industrial Decline and Railway Decay**: The original fever hospital later became a nurses' home; it fell vacant when the Infirmary was closed in 1982 *(see Crosshouse)*, was gutted by fire in 1994 and was demolished about 1997. Meantime further industrial decline had appeared when Glenfield & Kennedy failed, though a small part remained in American ownership; Saxone shoe production also ceased, with the loss of a thousand jobs, and Armitage Shanks *(see Barrhead)* which had a major plant in 1979, had pulled out by 1989. For a time the football club sank into the Second Division. To counter the many problems, the Kilmarnock Venture Enterprise Trust (KVET) was established in 1983, leading to the town being chosen in 1991 as the centre for *'Enterprise Ayrshire'*. Meantime in 1989 Kilmarnock was considered to be in a parlous state, having on national indicators one of the very weakest economies in Britain, 278th out of 280 towns studied. In 1991 the large six-platform station was a shadow of its former self, only four platforms remaining in use under rotting canopies; by 1997 the listed original Station House had been demolished.

**New and Established Industries**: By 1990 former employees of the failed Glenfield & Kennedy had given rise to small successors, including Bywater Valves, who employed 240 people in 1992, making new cooling-water condenser valves for Hinkley Point *'A'* nuclear power station. Proven Engineering, who made oil production control equipment, won an award about 1990 for their *Valveshield* valve-locking device. By 1992 Coldstore Packaging made aluminium foil containers. Spinning and tanning continued. In 1990 BMK had a growing workforce of about 400, specialising into contract carpeting; however in the 1992 recession they were acquired by Stoddard Sekers of Elderslie, who concentrated all tufted carpet production there in 1996. In 1990 Burlington Shoes employed nearly 600 workers, and the footwear plant opposite the station was advertising *'Hush Puppies'* (soft shoes) in 1992. Johnnie Walker was part of the United Distillers empire by 1989; their important Kilmarnock blending and bottling plant still exported whisky to the Continent of Europe by rail.

*A new railbus produced at Barclays, Kilmarnock (around 1985). Andrew Barclay's was founded in 1840, and became well-known for industrial locomotives. As Hunslet–Barclay it is now Scotland's only locomotive builder.* *(Hunslet–Barclay)*

**Service Activities from 1990**: In 1990 vacant areas and premises were awaiting re-use in an otherwise bustling town, for Irvine's recent successes challenged Kilmarnock's role. Treesbank House became disused about 1991, and stood decaying in 1995 as did its former stables. Telecommunications and postal roles remained important in 1990, the year when Kilmarnock's bus maintenance workshops escaped the closures which privatisation brought to several others in Scotland. By then James Borland & Sons' seed stores incorporated the 240-year old Dickie, Fowlds business. The livestock market was still actively dealing in cattle and sheep in 1992. The Western Scottish bus company of Kilmarnock was bought out in 1994 by Stagecoach of Perth.

**Recreational Facilities and Retail Development**: The town was proud of its Grand Hall and the new Galleon Leisure Centre, opened in 1987, comprising an ice rink, swimming pool, indoor bowling, sports halls and other facilities. The Dick Institute gallery and museum staged many exhibitions, and important collections of arms, armour and early musical instruments were open at Dean Castle by 1992. Although the former *Operetta House* was gutted by fire in 1989, leaving only the facade standing, the *Palace Theatre* was still active in 1994. Kilmarnock FC gained promotion to the Premier League in 1993; a prestigious new entertainment suite was completed, and new stands to convert Rugby Park into a stadium with 18,000 seats were built in 1994–95. The team still plays in the Premier League. Conversion of the Gateway supermarket into a discount *'Food Giant'* operation in 1991 more than doubled the number of customers to 25,000 a week, from as far afield as Ardrossan and even Sanquhar (45km). In 1990 the clearance of further areas of the town centre was intended to be followed by redevelopment at Portland Street, plus a retail park at Hood Street. The 10,000m$^2$ Glencairn Retail Park was built in 1994 and by 1996 two Tesco stores were open.

**Hunslet-Barclay Revived**: Barclay's survived in a small way of business building industrial locomotives, but joined Hunslet of Leeds in 1987. In 1990 their Hugh Smith division was expanding, making heavy-duty plateworking machine tools for export worldwide. A huge new rail-vehicle assembly shed of some 10,000m$^2$ was completed in 1991 on a site between their old works and the station. Their 160 jobs in 1990 rose to 200 when the firm built eight additional cars for the Glasgow subway in 1992–93. They had also landed the weed-killing contract for the entire British Rail system, but this was lost when Railtrack took over in 1994, and the hoped-for share in rolling stock construction for BR was stifled by privatisation. By then Hunslet-Barclay was owned by Jensbacher of Austria. They were still doing some railway work: centralised locking of doors for Inter-City 125 coaches, and (in 2000) reconditioning industrial locomotives.

**The Floods**: Kilmarnock (including Riccarton) had 44,307 residents in 1991. In 1994 a number of houses in the valley of the Kilmarnock Water were damaged by floods, which were repeated in 1995. In 1996 Kilmarnock and Cumnock & Doon Valley Districts were combined as the East Ayrshire unitary authority. In 2000 Coats Viyella had recently halved their Scottish workforce, now employing only 400 in Kilmarnock and Campbeltown, but 200 jobs arrived with a Travel Choice call centre. Kilmarnock has four secondary schools: Grange Academy with 1050 pupils, Kilmarnock Academy with 950, James Hamilton with 775 and St Joseph's with 675.

## KILMARTIN

**Map 4, C3**

***Argyllshire village,*** *pop. 500 (area)* OS 55: NR 8399

Kilmartin in Lorn lies in a sheltered valley 5 km north of ancient Dunadd, which it outdoes in ancient remains such as stone circles, chambered cairns and standing stones; a silver hoard of 1000 AD was discovered there. Three castles arose: the first, Duntrune, was built on the coast 5 km to the west in the 13th century. Some 300 years later came two more: the bulky Kilmartin Castle, and Carnassarie, an important tower built by Bishop Carswell of Argyll & the Isles, 2 km to the north but now a ruin. Pont's map of around 1600 showed that the Kilmartin Burn had already been bridged both above and below Kilmartin church, but there were no proper roads until after the 1750s. The name of the neighbouring hamlet of Slockavoulin means *'Mill Gorge'* in the Gaelic tongue, which was spoken here into the mid 20th century.

**Overcoming Problems with Tourism?**: The substantial Victoria Hall was built in 1897 by the Poltalloch Estate. In 1951 when the area's population was about 440 the telephone exchange already had 38 lines. Poltalloch House, built in 1849–53 for the Malcolm family, was abandoned in 1957; it survives as a ruin. In 1960 the villagers would not even accept the Victoria Hall as a gift, and as the population dipped it fell out of use. However, the post office stayed open, by 1974 there was a caravan site, and a garage and a doctor had been added. A new primary school was built in the 1980s. The 1991 parish population was 494, and Kilmartin Castle was restored as a house in the 1990s. By 1996 the Kilmartin House museum was open, and in 1997 Kilmartin manse became a *'Centre for Archaeology and Landscape'*. Tourists have long been served by the small *Kilmartin Hotel*.

## KILMAURS

**Map 1, C1**

***N. Ayrshire village,*** *pop. 2750* OS 70: NS 4141

Kilmaurs Place – which already existed in the 12th century as a noble residence – stands just east of the Carmel Water in north Ayrshire, some 4 km north-west of Kilmarnock. By 1413 it was a seat of William Cunningham, Earl of Glencairn *(see Moniaive & Langbank)*, who in that year made collegiate the church of Kilmaurs, which was originally built nearby in 1404. A later earl obtained a charter for Kilmaurs as a burgh of barony in 1527, but ensured that the village grew on the opposite side of the stream. Rowallan Castle, 3 km to the north-east of Kilmaurs, was strikingly rebuilt to an L-plan in 1560–62. Pont's map of about 1600 showed a bridge across the Carmel Water and a mill beside Kilmaurs Place, by then an emparked mansionhouse. Though a school was founded in 1614 and rebuilt in 1671, it closed for a time around 1696, and the Roy map made about 1754 implied that Kilmaurs, which remained just a village with a tiny tolbooth which still exists, was not yet served by a road.

**Cutlery, Bonnets and an Infamous Son**: This deficiency had presumably been remedied by 1799 when Heron called Kilmaurs a *"town with upwards of 500 inhabitants"*. He mentioned no activities, but by 1810 Kilmaurs had become known as a cutlery-making centre, a spin-off from Kilmarnock's early knife-making industry. Soon a large grain mill was built, and by about 1825 Kilmaurs was served by a penny post from Kilmarnock. Bonnet knitting on powered machines was established in the 1860s on a substantial scale, with 170 workers by 1869. Meantime Kilmaurs was the birthplace of the engineer James Reid, who about 1883 became by dubious means the sole proprietor of Europe's largest locomotive works *(see Springburn)*.

**Railway, Boots, Hosiery and Cream**: From 1873 Kilmaurs was served by the direct line linking Glasgow and Kilmarnock, jointly built by the Glasgow & South Western and Caledonian Railways. In 1888 Robert Ingram designed a rebuilt church, which incorporated part of the earlier one. The population in 1891 was 1700. In 1894 the village of Kilmaurs was described by Murray as *"an old burgh"*; at that time there was an inn. A boot factory was opened in the late 19th century, but this closed and was taken over in the 1930s by Cunningham of Stewarton as a hosiery works. With 2500 people in the Kilmaurs area in 1951, its local facilities at that time were those of a village, yet until 1952 it anachronistically remained officially a burgh of barony. By 1953 a large creamery was open. The railway station was closed by Beeching about 1965, and by 1976 the grain mill had become disused. However, by 1981 some housing had been built to the west. The creamery and knitwear factory were still in use, and by 1987 the station had happily been reopened. In 1991 the village population was about 2750. The most interesting features are the Old Place and the tolbooth; there is still an inn.

## KILMELFORD

**Map 4, C3**

***Small Argyllshire village,*** *pop. 200 (area)* OS 55: NM 8513

Ancient duns stand beside the sheltered sea inlet of Loch Melfort, among the tumbled and in places wooded hills 17 km south of Oban. By the time of Timothy Pont's visit around 1600 the short River Oude at its head had been bridged near the church of Kilmelfort, around which were several settlements. The Roy map showed that by about 1750 four tracks met in this vicinity; they later became roads, but even the main road between Oban and Lochgilphead was very winding and in places hilly. Extensive gunpowder works – using local charcoal as a raw material – were established well before 1871 by the proprietors of the Bonawe Ironworks, dispersed along the

*Melfort gunpowder works, Kilmelford, which were established before 1870 by the owners of the Bonawe Ironworks, and were out of use by the 1950s. This view shows a courtyard of workers' housing – now converted to time-share apartments.* (JRH)

river bank northwards from Melfort House *(see Hay & Stell, and article on Taynuilt)*; a short pier was built nearby to allow access to shipping.

**Fishing, Forestry and Holidays**: The gunpowder works had been long closed by the mid 20th century. By then basic village facilities were available, including the *Cuilfail Hotel*, a Victorian angling centre. The locality population was down to a mere 100 in 1951, and fell so far that the primary school was closed by 1976. By 1978 the Kilmelfort hydro power station – fed from weirs on the River Oude – had been built by the Hydro Board near Melfort House. Some of the powder works buildings were converted to timeshare apartments in the 1980s; others are ruins in the woodland. The resident population of the parish (including Kilninver) was only 186 in 1991. The area to the north has been extensively afforested. About 1990 new luxury homes and eight serviced holiday lodges of stone and timber were built at Melfort Pier; sailing boats and other activities were provided, and the *Cuilfail Hotel* continues to serve.

## KILMICHAEL GLASSARY & Bridgend

**Map 4, C3**

***Small Argyllshire village,*** *pop. 200* — OS 55: NR 8393

Amid the Moine Mhor, an extensive bog which divides Kintyre from Lorn, stands the 50m-tall isolated hill of Dunadd, beside the only feasible land route between Lorn and Kintyre. Rocks carved with *'cup and ring'* marks imply Bronze Age settlement. Dunadd was a small sixth century fort, the capital of King Gabhran of Dalriada and his descendant Aidan, ancestors of the Scottish royal house. The nearby Dun Mor was also fortified. Nearby Kilmichael Glassary was an early Christian centre; Glassary in Gaelic means *'Grey Shieling'*. Dunadd was besieged by the Picts in 683 and fell to them in the eighth century; standing stones were erected between the two duns, and Dunadd became a coronation site for Scottish kings. Pont's map of around 1600 showed a building still standing on the hilltop.

**Roads, Bridges and Development**: Glassary had a parish school by 1629, but the area was roadless until 1737, when the County of Argyll built a bridge across the River Add, and *'Kilmichel'* appeared on Roy's map of about 1750 as a substantial clachan on a track connecting the head of Loch Gilp with the vicinity of Ford on Loch Awe. In the 18th century a cattle tryst was held at Kilmichael Glassary, but its development was cut short by the appearance of the planned village of Lochgilphead *(q.v.)*. Glassary had a post office by 1888, and around 1900 there was again a cattle market, which later vanished. By 1977 the *Kilmichael Hotel* was open at what remained a typical kirkton, its small population slowly climbing towards 200. Although by 1996 a small housing estate and an inn had been developed at Bridgend, in 2000 the low number of primary age pupils made the village school's future uncertain.

## KILMORE

**Map 4, C2**

***Argyll hamlet,*** *pop. 250* — OS 49: NM 8825

Many ancient cairns and duns among the tumbled hills attest to ancient settlement in and around the little Glen Feochan and the larger Glen Lonan, whose waters unite to enter the sea at the sheltered head of Loch Feochan, 5 km south of Oban as the crow flies. Roy's map of about 1750 showed half a dozen tracks radiating from Kilmore (Gaelic *'Big Church'*), a kirkton and cattle tryst in Glen Feochan, a site which failed to develop when Oban grew. Eventually the coastal road was made up 1 km to the west, joined not far from a new church by a back road leading to Connel, passing Loch Nell with its ancient crannogs. By 1951 about 170 people lived in this scattered hill farming area, served by a primary school, post office and 30-line telephone exchange. Despite a slowly growing population – 265 by 1981 – the primary school was closed by 1976, while that at even smaller and more remote Kilninver 8 km to the south stayed open (and still does). By 1996 a rare breeds centre was open 4 km north on the Connel road, afforestation had clothed many of the surrounding hills, and a new housing estate at Barran had provided a new focus of development. Some 4 km to the west on the south shore of Loch Feochan is the new *Knipoch House Hotel*, with a *'Salmon visitor centre'* 2 km farther west towards Kilninver. Opposite on the north shore is the modern *Foxholes Hotel*.

## KILMORY & Lagg

**Map 1, B2**

***Small S. Arran village,*** *pop. 300 (area)* — OS 69: NR 9621

Ancient remains of barrows and stone circles surround one of the earliest parish centres of Arran, at Kilmory *('Big Church')* which stands above the major raised beach on the south coast of the island. Pont's crude map of Arran made about 1600 showed Kilmory, *'Clachack'* (Clauchog) East, and *'Torlean'*; at the mouth of the Kilmory Water was the Mill of Torrylin. Kilbride just to the east gained a baronial charter in 1668, but grew little. A school was built in 1704, and eventually a distillery known as Lagg was built near the Mill of Torrylin. Later a road was constructed round the island, with a bridge beside which the *Lagg Inn* was built in 1791; in Gaelic its name implies a place to rest, and it has claimed to have been a coaching inn. Soon there was also a flax mill at Lagg, and a carding mill at Burican on the Sliddery Water, 2 km to the west. In 1836 Lagg was the last of three legal distilleries on Arran to close, and the 1830s clearances seem also to have put paid to the mills. The tiny village, with a 20th century population hovering around 100, acquired a school, post office and even a sub-branch bank, serving surrounding farms and hamlets. The *Lagg Inn* became a hotel around 1951. By 1956 the Scottish Milk Marketing Board owned the Torrylinn Creamery; this produced cheese by 1980 and in 2001 makes *'Arran Cheddar'*. Now the *Lagg Hotel* in its woodland setting is augmenting by the local shop and restaurant.

## KILSYTH

**Map 16, A2**

***Strathkelvin town,*** *pop. 9900* — OS 64: NS 7177

Kilsyth north of the upper reaches of the River Kelvin is roughly equidistant from Glasgow and Stirling; rising steeply immediately to the north is the high range of hills to which it gives its name. The cattle-herding *Maeatae* tribe held the area in 143 AD when the Romans built the earthen Antonine Wall some 2 km to the south, with a fort at Croy Hill. By 208 the Maeatae fought with both horses and chariots, and the Romans abandoned the area. The Garrel Burn, a tributary of the river Kelvin, rises in the hills and in early Christian times separated the lost kirk of Monyabroch from Kilsyth, whose Gaelic name shows its Dark Age origin. In 1216 Maldoven,

Earl of Lennox, granted Kilsyth to Malcolm de Callander. Kilsyth parish (which was in Stirlingshire for centuries) held two baronies, each with three or four ferm touns and a motte with a timber castle. Balcastle at Kilsyth held an English garrison from 1304; their Callander supporters consequently lost their lands, given to the Livingstones. In 1402 Sir William Livingstone built a stone castle with 2 m thick walls at Allanfauld in the West Barony, just north of the modern town; this was destroyed in 1650. Another Livingstone held the East Barony, whose motte stood 2 km farther east, and in the early 16th century built nearby Colzium castle in stone, soon replaced 100 m farther south by Colzium House, which was greatly enlarged in 1575.

**Ministers, Mansions and Barony Burgh**: In 1560 when Monyabroch was a Linlithgow property, another Livingstone became its first Protestant Minister; a strong presbyterian tradition grew up, and soon a plain new Kilsyth parish kirk was built; a parish school was founded in 1590. The area was well settled when Timothy Pont made his maps about 1600. Both castles featured prominently on his map as emparked mansions, that at *'Killsayth'* comprising a complex of buildings. In 1620 Sir William Livingstone of Kilsyth bought Monyabroch with help from his wife, a German heiress, and gained a charter as a burgh of barony. The bloody Battle of Kilsyth was fought north-east of the town in the plague year of 1645. Linen weaving developed, and a post office was opened in 1662. In 1679 45 feus were granted in the town by the second Viscount Kilsyth, a title granted to the Livingstones by Charles II; their informal layout *(see Hutchison)* implies that this grant merely regularised existing holdings around the medieval meal market. Among the buildings then erected was the Orange Hall. The laird's Garrel water mill was built in 1700, on the Garrel Burn. The Kilsyth Curling Club was founded in 1711, one of the world's first.

**The York Building Company and Bible Thumpers**: In 1716 when the Livingstone estates were forfeited, their old mansionhouse at Newtown became the manse; the estate was sold to the York Buildings Company, who leased it to Campbell of Shawfield from 1728–82. Defoe noticed Kilsyth in the 1720s as *"a good plain country burgh, tolerably well built, but not large"*. In 1729 potatoes were first grown as a field crop in Scotland near Kilsyth. In 1742–43 under its eager minister James Robe, Kilsyth turned to the revivalist Christianity that was repeatedly to affect the town's development for over two centuries. A linen bleachfield was built in mid-century; by then lint mills had been built at Burngreen and Inns Bridge.

**Turnpikes, Quarrying and Independence**: A road from Glasgow and Kirkintilloch was shown on Roy's map made around 1755, turning sharply northwards at the mill by the bridge over the Garrel (labelled the *'Kilsyth Burn'*) to head over the hills to Carron Bridge – the steep and winding *'Takma-Doon Road'* to Stirling. Kilsyth was a large village on a north–south axis; three tracks radiated from the market square at its south end, one leading to Bonnybridge and Falkirk, the others petering out. The roads from Kilsyth to Kirkintilloch and to Falkirk were turnpiked under an Act of 1752, and by 1758 a turnpike trust was completing this as a toll road between Edinburgh and Glasgow. Robe's successor John Telfer started a school around 1760, but it did not last. A breakaway church built at Low Craigends in 1770 used white freestone, already quarried for decades in the Garrel Glen near Allanfauld. Robert Livingstone, a son of a former local minister, emigrated to America and was a signatory of the Declaration of Independence in 1776. The original Colzium House was replaced in 1783 by a new mansion for the Edmonstones, who retained the original icehouse.

**Early Coal Mining and the Canal**: In 1760 William Cadell of the Carron works bought the East Barony or Banton estates for their coalfields. In 1769 the Forth & Clyde (F&C) Canal was being cut past Auchinstarry 1.5 km south of Kilsyth, and later fed from Townhead Reservoir (the *'Big Dam'* or Banton Loch). It was opened throughout in 1790; whinstone was soon being quarried north of the canal bridge at Auchinstarry for use in paving Glasgow streets. Coal pits were open in the West Barony using an engine; there were also early mines at Barhill north of Auchinstarry, and soon also at Strone to the south.

**New Laird, new Inn, Posts, Weavers and Water**: In 1782 the York Buildings Company and Campbell sold on the Kilsyth estate to Edmonstone of Duntreath, hence the name of the new *Duntreath Arms Hotel*, a staging point for the coaches (though from 1794 a shorter route was available). Textiles dominated in 1796 when 400 male home weavers worked for Glasgow merchants, 280 females *'tamboured'* muslin, and there were about 250 other workers. By 1797 Kilsyth was a post town with daily collections; four fairs were scheduled for the year. Heron noted in 1799 *"the village of Kilsyth has some share of the cotton manufacture"*. By 1801, the year the harvest failed, the town held some 1800 people; its water came from many wells. By 1805 there were some small private schools, but the people remained largely illiterate. In 1809 passenger boats were started on the canal, an inn was built near the bridge at Auchinstarry, and stables at Craigmarloch to the east.

**Industrial Growth**: From the early 1800s Paterson of Upper Banton 3 km to the east, where there was then a coal mine, made farm implements including sickles or scythe hooks for harvesting and for trimming roadside banks by hand. About 1830 he began to make Bell reaping machines at the Garrel Mill in Kilsyth; later this mill ground coal to *'charcoal'* for Glasgow foundries. A new parish church was built beside the by then ruinous manse in 1816, using Garrel Glen stone (which later became worked out). By 1824 the former five fair days had been cut to two. Textile mills were established between 1815 and 1840 by White, Lennie, Laurie and Maxwell at Newtown, Banton and also at Queenzieburn *(q.v.)*. James Marshall mined coal at Neilston from 1825 and also at Balcastle, later worked by Robert Bow, both pits sending coal away by canal from Auchinstarry; and at Curriemire, from which a tramway ran to the canal near Craigmarloch. The Kilsyth Gas Company was formed in 1835, and soon various streets in the village were lit. In 1837 Banton acquired a chapel and in 1839 J & P Wilson built a small steam mill there; it was extended in 1848.

**Coaches, Coffins and Catholic Coal Miners**: When Croy *(q.v.)* station on the Edinburgh & Glasgow Railway was opened in 1846 a two-horse coach connected it with Kilsyth, a town so concerned for the hereafter that Murdoch & Co, coffin goods manufacturers, grew over a century from 1849, developing a large export trade and even a branch in South Africa. From 1846 the pits drew in many Irish miners; by 1851 the town's population was almost 4000, and a Roman Catholic church was opened in 1866. Congregationalists, active by the 1840s had a church by 1866, and the Salvation Army were busy locally from 1880; a larger Methodist church was built in 1885.

**Barhill, Baird and the Demise of the Barony**: The Barhill mines were further developed in the 1850s by James Wallace. By then Brown & Rennie's Highland Park pit was open at the foot of the hills; pits to the west sunk by this firm soon after the Crimean War were named Balaclava and Inkerman! In 1861 Colzium House was enlarged. In 1860 the old barony court-house and jail in the tiny sloping Market Square was demolished and replaced by the Market Chambers – a meeting room for the town council, a police station and lock-up. But in 1863 the Barony burgh was abolished, and town commissioners then managed Kilsyth, taking over the gas company in 1884: better street lighting followed. In 1860 Curriemire pit was leased to the William Baird Mining Company, an offshoot of William Baird & Co of Gartsherrie *(see Coatbridge)*, who then began to mine ironstone in the hills above Neilston, building four miners' rows in the town and a railway down past Balmalloch and the Haughs, which they leased in 1869 to sink a pit.

**Schooling, Disaster, Railways and more Coal and Coke**: By 1872 there were schools at Banton and Burngreen; but until the Act of that decade the town itself lacked a real school. By 1880 the new makeshift burgh school had 785 pupils, and by 1901 the new school at Craigends held 1422! The tiny new Kilsyth Academy of 1876 had to be replaced in 1901 by another building. In 1878 twelve miners died in an explosion in the Craigends pit lately sunk by Baird, with its rail incline to the valley where in that year the Kelvin Valley Railway (KVR) was opened, with passenger trains from Glasgow via Lenzie to Kirkintilloch and Kilsyth; from 1879 it also connected to Maryhill via Torrance. In the 1870s Muir & Woods made coke from Neilston coal at ovens on the Tak-Ma-Doon Road. The North British Railway took over the KVR in 1885 and in 1888 opened an extended line to Bonnybridge and Larbert, through a new station at Kilsyth and another serving emparked Colzium. The burgh's 1891 population was just over 6000.

**Quarries Galore**: In the 1880s various new quarries were opened, by the North British Granite & Whinstone Company at Colzium (still open in 1914), at Neilston and Easter Auchinstarry, where Alex Stark & Son crushed 100 tonnes of whinstone a day. They had a new quarry at Craigstanes, and Provost Wilson & Son had one at Belt Moss. Shaw & Thorn quarried at North Barrwood and also Queenzieburn. In all there were 230 quarrymen and some 4500 miners. Wilson's mill was damaged by a flood in 1856 but recovered to be again extended in 1896, when it employed 120 girls. By then the Craigmarloch paper mill was at work, and the Birkenburn Reservoir had been built on the headwaters of the Garrel Burn.

**Information, Recreation and Entertainment**: Cricket was played locally by the 1880s. The *Kilsyth Chronicle* was first published in 1891; by then the Victoria Hall held assemblies and by 1898 showed silent cinema films. From 1894 *Queen* steamers plied on the canal from Glasgow to a large tearoom at Craigmarloch, a service which increased and which survived until 1939. Kilsyth Wanderers FC played in the Scottish Midlands League by 1895, and in 1896 there was even a women's football team. The Dullatur golf course was opened in 1896; the 9-hole moorland course of the Kilsyth Lennox golf club was founded beside the hill road in the early 1900s. There were two hotels in Kilsyth by 1894, the *Crown* and *Duntreath Arms*, but Murray's Handbook noted little of interest, because late Victorian tourists preferred to avoid places with the coal pits whose workers brought them heat, light and prosperity. By 1898 the *Inns Park Hotel* was open and by 1900 the *Commercial Hotel*. The Kilsyth Co-op was founded in 1895; by then there were two banks and over a hundred shops.

**Town Council, Tote, Hosiery and Blackboards**: In 1901 when the population was almost 7300 a new town-elected council replaced the Commissioners, soon established a proper water supply from the Corrie Reservoir, and built an infectious diseases hospital. By 1904 William Clelland, a hosiery manufacturer in Cumbernauld, had moved his knitting machines to King Street in Kilsyth, where the firm became known as the Kilsyth Hosiery Company, building a new factory at Allanfaulds. By 1906 there was a town band, by 1910 the RC school had 375 pupils, and in 1911 Kilsyth was second only to Armadale in the poorness of its housing, many families living at four persons per room. In 1911 the *King's Theatre* showed films and variety turns, and for some time until 1916 there was an indoor skating rink. The Auchingeich Colliery was open by 1914, by which time Wilson & Garden were working for the building industry, moving on to make the racecourse totalisators (the *'Tote'*) invented by William Garden Senior, and later his patent revolving blackboards, for which a major export trade developed.

**War, Overcrowding, Coal Strikes and Drought**: Laird Edmonstone was killed on the Somme in 1916, many other breadwinners died and the 1914–18 war stopped housing development; by the time of the 1921 coal strike most of the 7600 people in Kilsyth lived in terrible conditions. The seven local pits were then owned by Baird and by Alex Nimmo & Sons. The town became *'dry'* from 1923 on a vote of 1396 to 904, becoming one of Scotland's few alcohol-free zones, so the *Cross Keys, Red Lion* and all the pubs had to close; the site of the *Duntreath Arms Hotel* became the bus station. By way of compensation the *Pavilion* cinema was built in 1924–25, but *'no alcohol'* meant *'no tourism'*, a loss that even rather dull Kilsyth could not afford. After the 1926 strikes, at which time the Kilsyth Co-op had about 3500 members, all coal owners held down wages to near starvation levels to keep going. In 1929 Labour took over the town council, who tackled the housing problem with zeal and in 1934–39 built nearly 600 council houses at Barrwood and the vast but dreary Balmulloch scheme on the steep hillside to the north; but almost a third of Kilsyth's houses were still overcrowded, an even worse state of affairs than pertained in Glasgow. In 1930 the Edmonstone lands were sold to Mackay Lennox, who in 1937 bequeathed most of his estate to the town council. From 1933 the hospital became a secondary school for the large local RC community.

**Transatlantic Billiard Tables but no Trains or Mines**: Passenger trains to Bonnybridge ceased to run in 1935, while the paper mill turned to board manufacture from 1936. About then a Kilsyth firm (no longer extant) made the billiard tables for RMS *Queen Mary* from Aberfoyle slate. Colzium House became a youth hostel in 1938. It had closed by 1955 and was later bought by the town council, who found dry rot and had to demolish its oldest portion. By 1951 Kilsyth was a place of over 9500 people with small-town facilities; but that year saw the end of its passenger trains, and all the local pits closed around 1960. However by then the Kilsyth Hosiery Company factory had been enlarged to some 3350 m$^2$. A new RC secondary school opened at Bogside Park in 1964; in 1965 came a dramatic new St Patrick's RC church – and a new Salvation

Army hall. In 1966 the *Kilsyth Chronicle* was absorbed by the upstart *Cumbernauld News*, which had so much more to report; but it continued in publication.

**After the Drought, Disadvantage**: In 1967 a further local vote narrowly reversed years of *'total abstention'* – i.e. *'bona fide'* travel out of town to buy drink! By 1978 the *Coachman Hotel* had appeared, and three pubs were open. Meantime by 1971 Kilsyth with over 81% of its houses council-owned was second only to Airdrie in this respect among all Scottish burghs; its facilities remained of small-town scale. In 1972 bricks, hosiery and blackboards were still made. A new police station was built in 1974, and about then new premises were built for the Royal Bank. In 1975 Kilsyth was swallowed by Strathclyde Region's Cumbernauld & Kilsyth district, based in Cumbernauld. About that time the brickworks closed, but the Kilsyth Co-op enlarged its premises to include a new supermarket. In the 1980s W Paterson (Safety) Ltd made foundry materials and compressors for charging firefighters' air cylinders. By then some of the large quarries north of the town were disused; Auchinstarry quarry to the south had become a pool with rock-climbing facilities and a picnic area. By 1986 the Kilsyth Hosiery factory had been sold to Courtaulds, and was soon closed.

**Flowers, Conservation, Contractors and Views**: In 1994 the town was well kept, with floral displays atop the bus shelters! The *Kilsyth Chronicle* still had an office in the market square and a new covered swimming pool was under construction. By 1996 an out of town Tesco store was open at Craigmarloch. Though many shops in the small recently pedestrianised town centre had closed, by 2000 an action programme to bring new uses was largely complete. In 1994 Wilson & Garden still manufactured blackboards, whiteboards and nursery furniture; foundry materials and some textiles were still made, and in 1996 Kilsyth was the Scottish base for Mowlem the contractors. In 1999 the remaining parts of Colzium House were used for community events. North of the town on the *Tak-ma-Doon* hill road to Carron Bridge is the active Risk End Quarry, above which a fine viewpoint at a height of 200m gives a prospect across the Lowlands from Glasgow to West Lomond, backed by North Berwick Law, Tinto Hill and the far distant Carsphairn Forest. Restoration of the canal throughout in 2001 should bring more visitors to the town, which the *Coachman Hotel* still serves.

## KILWINNING

**Map 1, C1**

***Ayrshire town, by Irvine,*** *pop. 15,500* OS 63 or 70: NS 3043

Kilwinning near the mouth of the River Garnock in Cunninghame was once known uninspiringly as *Segdoune*. According to tradition its church was founded by St Winning *(or Wynnyn)* in 715, and some 300 years later an early monastery was established. This was replaced in 1162 by a Tironensian abbey, an offshoot of Kelso, founded by Hugh de Moreville, Lord of Cunninghame and High Constable of Scotland. The abbey soon became the most important religious centre in the Cunninghame area; its name appeared on the early Gough map (around 1250). The abbey was partly rebuilt after damage in Edwardian invasions, and the Garnock was bridged about 1439. By the 15th century Kilwinning was a well-known archery centre with a market, though it seems never to have become a medieval burgh.

**After the Reformation, Decay**: Kilwinning Abbey was represented in Parliament up to 1560; most of it was ruined by over-zealous reformers in 1561, but part of the church was saved for parish use. William Melville obtained the decaying abbey ruins in 1592. The bridge was still in evidence and the town was substantial on Pont's map, made around 1600, but despite the opening of a parish school in 1605 Kilwinning languished, hastened by the decline of archery. Eglinton Castle, 2 km south-east, was a 16th century tower, round which Adam and others built a mansion beside the Lugton Water, a tributary of the Garnock; the Roy map surveyed about 1754 showed its large policies. Kilwinning was then a small town on the road between Stevenston and Beith.

**Old-fashioned Industrial Village**: In 1775 the parishioners built a new church. Ayrshire's main roads were turnpiked in the late 18th century, and by about 1800 three coaches a week ran through Kilwinning between Glasgow, Irvine and Ayr. Both a colliery and a large cotton mill for carding and spinning were open by 1790, and lawns and linen gauzes were woven for the Irish market. Heron in 1799 merely referred to a *"village of over 1200 inhabitants"*, where in 1797 a single fair was scheduled. By 1810 there were over 300 weavers, and milling was also important in the early 19th century; Kilwinning's first post office opened around 1825. But in 1827 Chambers wrote of the abbey's *"miserably dilapidated ruins, beside a curious old-fashioned town"*.

**Railways, Canning and the Start of the Baird Empire**: The primitive Ardrossan & Johnstone Railway connected Kilwinning with Ardrossan from 1831, though it seems to have got no further. The Glasgow, Paisley, Kilmarnock & Ayr Railway joined it just north of Kilwinning from 1840; the earlier line was regauged as a branch. In 1846 William Baird set up the Eglinton Ironworks 1 km south of the town, 2 km west of the castle; from this base his Eglinton Iron Company briefly dominated the Ayrshire iron industry. Robert Wilson opened a food cannery in 1849 – a smaller but much more long-lasting enterprise. By the 1880s insane competition between railway companies had brought in the *'Lanarkshire & Ayrshire'* line (L&A), creating two sub-parallel railway systems, both with junction stations at Kilwinning. This mere one-street town became a police burgh in 1889, and by 1894 had a secondary school, the *Eglinton Arms Hotel* and an inn. At one time Howie & Co of Kilwinning made cast-iron manhole covers. In the 1890s the Glasgow & South Western Railway's Doura mineral branch left the main line at Byre Hill Junction south of Kilwinning, swinging around the extensive Eglinton Deer Park to serve Fergushill colliery south west of Montgreenan, and then south-east to Perceton. An offshoot west of the park served another colliery 2 km north of Irvine.

**Declining – but with Clean Gloves**: North-east of the town the Redstone quarries near Lylestone School appear to have been opened around 1900 (also served by mineral lines). The Eglinton ironworks closed in the 1920s, and Eglinton Castle was unroofed in 1925, its walls left as a ruin and its park vanishing. The L&A railway line to Irvine was closed to passengers in 1930 and to all traffic in 1939. However, a clay mine was still open at High Monkcastle in the 1950s. Kilwinning had become a bottleneck before it was bypassed in 1961 by a new dual carriageway section of the A78 coastal trunk road. The aftermath of its industrial history led Hubert Fenwick in 1978 to call Kilwinning *"an ugly little town"*; the neglected abbey ruins made a *"dismal prospect"*. This sorry tale helps to explain why at a time of burgeoning tourism, in 1981 Kilwinning had only one hotel. But in the 1970s Italian-born Gio Benedetti had founded a small firm to clean soiled industrial gloves for the doomed Chrysler car plant at Linwood; by 1995 it employed 400 people in Kilwinning and served the entire UK motor industry.

**Irvine New Town, New Academies – and Fullarton**: The inclusion of Kilwinning within the designated area of Irvine New Town in 1966 led to a doubling of its population to over 16,000 between 1971 and 1981, with some massive developments to the west; but Kilwinning's facilities remained those of a small town. A new French-owned whisky blending and bottling plant was opened in 1979 by Pernod-Ricard under the House of Campbell name. Despite Beeching's closures, a triangle of railways including the original line had survived, to be electrified in 1986; as an important junction, Kilwinning station kept its four platforms and civil engineers' sidings. By 1987 St Michael's Academy and primary schools had been built on Stevenston Road, Kilwinning Academy had risen on Dalry Road, and there was a visitor centre at Eglinton. In 1987 Fullarton Fabrications, lately founded by six redundant local metal workers, soon expanded into plastics; by 1990, taken over by the Laird group, it had grown into the biggest employers in Kilwinning with over 1000 workers making plastics extrusions and electronic assemblies. By 1993, renamed Fullarton Computer Industries, the firm employed 1500 people, and was opening a large branch factory in North Carolina to make components for IBM and AST. In 2000 Fullarton was expanding into Irvine from its Kilwinning HQ.

**Downs and Ups in the 1990s**: Meantime Hugh King & Co's Hullerhill quarry had raised industrial sand throughout the 1980s; by 1990 Campbell whisky employed 250 people on six sites. The town's population in 1991 was almost 15,500. In 1993 Altamira Colouring opened a new textile dyeing and finishing works in Kilwinning, creating 50 jobs. But in 1995 the Dawson Group decided to close its Blackwoods Carpet Yarn plant, with the loss of 138 jobs, due to rising costs and slow demand for domestic carpets (this saved jobs at other Dawson plants in Cumnock and Kilmarnock). In 1996 after 147 years the Robert Wilson & Sons cannery was closed by its new owners Hillsdown Holdings, with the loss of 270 jobs. By 1989 Dalgarven Mill was a museum of country life, and by 1998 the Eglinton Country Park was open north of the Lugton Water; the abbey has a new visitor centre, the main street has been pedestrianised, and a cycle route now follows the River Garnock.

## KINBRACE & Kildonan

**Map 13, A5**

***Sutherland small villages,*** *pop. under 100* — OS 17: NC 8631

Brochs and many hut circles show early settlement in the Strath of Kildonan, upstream of Helmsdale, but Pont's map made around 1600 did not detail this part of Sutherland; the Roy map of about 1750 marked a kirk and many huts beside a track from Brora and Lothbeg to Forsinard, but little else of note. Between 1806 and 1816 many of the Duke of Sutherland's cattle-herding tenants were evicted from the strath in favour of sheep by the estate's ruthless agents Young and Sellars, creating Kildonan Farm. The alluvial gold found in the Kildonan Burn in 1868–69, which caused Britain's only gold rush, proved a literal flash in the pan, but left the name *Baile an Or ('Village of Gold')*. Eventually a road with attractive stone bridges was built through the strath, which by then was largely kept for shooting and angling, by the 1890s extending through Kinbrace, some 25 km from Helmsdale, and via Forsinard to Melvich.

**Railway and Schools in the Wilderness**: In 1871–74 the Sutherland & Caithness Railway – later Highland (HR) – was built from Helmsdale to Wick and Thurso, climbing up the Strath of Kildonan, with crossing stations at Kildonan and Kinbrace, also passing the delightfully named Salzcraggie and Borrobol platforms – the latter serving the large baronial Borrobol Lodge, near which are several good level fields. By the 1930s Kildonan had a post and telegraph office and Kinbrace was actually a *'post town'*; both had primary schools. In 1964–66 the little rail freight traffic to and from sidings in the strath was ended by Beeching, and the crossing loops and signalmens' jobs were removed, leaving just a single line with infrequent trains.

**Forestry, Rowans and Rowing Boats**: By 1981 Kildonan school and post office had closed, leaving little there save a request station stop serving Kildonan Lodge. From 1978 to its closure in 2000 a makeshift primary school served a very few children on the ultra-remote Loch Choire estate, well off the Bettyhill road some 21 km to the west. Kinbrace had gained a telephone exchange, but by 1996 its post office was no more. A shop and the extended primary school remain open, serving a group of four new bungalows plus the few hill farms and crofts amid the heather and sheep to the north. About 13 square km of the area has been afforested since 1956; birch trees, rowans and rowing boats feature largely at Kildonan. The improved train service carries newspapers for distribution from Kinbrace via the postbus; but in 2001 a passenger train became stuck in a snowdrift for 6 hours! On the platform beside the former station building, now a house, is a cast-iron weighing machine worthy of a museum.

## KINCARDINE (Mearns)

**Map 10, B4**

***Mearns ex-village*** — OS 45: NO 6775

The scant ruins of Kincardine Castle stand beside the insignificant Devilly Burn at the edge of the fertile lowland called the Howe of the Mearns, between two forests – hilly Drumtochty and low-lying Inglismaldie; its Gaelic name means *'Head of the Thicket'*. By 994 it was already a stronghold, according to Chambers *"the principal palace of King Kenneth III"*. Kincardine had an extensive thanage from about the 11th century, and was still a royal castle when Stirling Burgh was re-chartered there in 1226. When John Balliol lived there about 1295, Kincardine Castle was described as *"a fair manor"* by an English invader. It never spawned a Royal Burgh, its supporting settlement remaining stubbornly rural.

**The County Town that never was!**: Kincardine's thunder was stolen when Fettercairn *(q.v.)* was chartered in 1504 only 2 km away. Although Kincardine was itself chartered as a burgh of barony as late as 1531, and in 1562 gave its name to the county formerly called the Mearns, it gained no real importance; the burgh charter having proved worthless, the market cross was removed to Fettercairn in 1600. Stonehaven became the county town in 1607, and forsaken Kincardine was not shown by either Blaeu or Roy. The castle was largely destroyed by fire, and was demolished in 1646; the fair stance was relocated to Fettercairn in 1730. By 1827 only the castle's foundations remained beside Castleton, which Chambers called *"a small congregation of little tenements, like the out-houses of an old farm; the miserable remains of the former county-town. This hamlet contains only about 60 or 70 inhabitants."* By the 20th century Castleton primary school was open nearby, but this closed around 1970; little but the name King's Park remains.

## KINCARDINE O'NEIL

**Map 10, B3**

***Small Deeside village,*** *pop. 300* OS 37: NO 5999

Located 10km west of Banchory on the north bank of the River Dee, this Kincardine was the fifth century site of St Erchard's church, and the centre of the thanage of O'Neil from about the 11th century. Its early church was ruined in 1233; the first Dee crossing, a wooden footbridge built in the early 13th century by Thomas Durward, also did not last. About then a *'hospital'* was established. Kincardine formed part of the Mearns by 1295. A burgh of barony was chartered in 1511, and by 1593 it was the centre of an Aberdeenshire presbytery; a parish school was recorded in 1625, the year the ancient hospice was demolished. Roy's survey of about 1750 showed Kincardine as a substantial village on the area's only road, which followed the north side of the river; there was a mill at the mouth of the Dess. A *'boat'* across the Dee served a track to the *'Boat of Inchbare'* which plied farther downstream in the vicinity of the later Potarch Bridge; thence another track led south to Bridge of Whitestone, Bridge of Dye and the Cairn O'Mount.

**Facilities Develop to Coaches – but not Trains**: Kincardine was called *"a little village"* by Pennant who dined there in 1769, so presumably there was already an inn. From 1791 the occasional Bartle (Bartholomew?) fair and market was held, and thousands of cattle were sold annually. The first post office opened in 1793, and by 1797 Kincardine had become a post town, with connections three days a week. However, the fair was apparently not intended to be held in that year, and in 1799 Heron noted only a *"village"*. Kincardine O'Neil lost nodal significance when the Potarch bridge, designed by Telford, was built in 1811–13 across the Dee 3km down-river. However, the road to Huntly was constructed about 1815 and the *Gordon Arms* was built as a stagecoach inn about 1830. Likewise, the northward detour made by the Deeside Railway to serve Torphins and Lumphanan, prevented Kincardine gaining a direct service, though there was a station at Dess about 3km to the west. A *'female school'* was built in 1856, and a new parish church in 1862, followed in 1866 by the first Episcopal church on Deeside

**Character Outlasts Decline**: In 1895 a new parish school was built. The late Victorian mansionhouse of Anniesland, built 1km south-east of the village, was later renamed Tillydrine House. Kincardine remained a service village, with a timber merchant and a population of over 400 in 1956. But post-town status was lost in the early 1970s as the population fell steadily to a mere 300; by 1981 it had facilities to match. Tillydrine House was used as a hotel for a time, but in 1994 stood abandoned by its owner. The pleasant village now has an extended primary school; a post office and inn stand near the remains of the ancient church. A bowling green, tennis court and playing field serve the energetic, and a large hairdressing establishment the less so. Information can be found at the Old Smiddy; petrol, a village store and a joiner and builder are still active. A restaurant and a horse rescue centre stand beside the Aboyne road.

## KINCARDINE ON FORTH

**Map 16, B2**

***Large village, W. Fife,*** *pop. 3200* OS 65: NS 9387

Kincardine on Forth lies at the south-western corner of the upland of Devilla Forest; its Gaelic name means *'Head of the Thicket'*. Perhaps within the Pictish half-province of Fothrif, it later became a detached part of Perthshire. Tulliallan Castle of the Edmistons, 2km to the north, existed by 1304; it was acquired by the Blackadders in the 15th century and soon rebuilt. By 1606 at least two salt pans were in operation on the shore, the ashes being used to reclaim the marshland on which the village was built; there was a parish school by 1618. As early as 1655 Kincardine was described by Tucker as *"a small town"*, mining a little coal for its own use and exporting salt. Longannet quarry to the east is reputed to have then provided the stone for Amsterdam Town Hall.

**Burgh, Ships, Salt, and Paper – or Pepper?**: In 1663 Kincardine on Forth was created a burgh of barony and granted a market; a new church was built in 1675, and by 1700 several ships were locally owned. By 1735 there were 35 salt pans, and by 1740 the number of local vessels had risen to 60; a pier was built around that year. The Roy map of about 1750 showed Kincardine as a small nucleated settlement on a spur from the Clackmannan to Dunfermline road. By that time either a *paper* or more probably *a pepper* mill existed at Kilbagie (OS 58) near Tulliallan.

**Whisky and Shipbuilding, Shipping and Stone**: Later in the 18th century the mill was apparently converted into Kilbagie distillery, for a time the largest in Scotland. Kincardine's first post office opened in 1779. At various times small ships were built at Kincardine, and local ownership prospered mightily: in 1786 its 91 vessels averaged some 50 tons, exporting coal in exchange for wood, iron, flax, linseed and barley. The modest mansion of Kennet House was built in 1793–94, and by 1797 Kincardine was a post town with a daily service. The West Port brewery was built in 1798. In 1799 Heron described both Tulliallan and Kincardine as just *"villages"*; yet the latter owned more than five thousand tons of shipping. He noticed *"the extensive distilleries of Kilbagie and Kennetpans, which afforded, at one period, a greater revenue to government than all the land-tax of Scotland"*. He also noted that *"the quarries of Longannet furnished stone for the Royal Exchange, Infirmary and Register Office in Edinburgh"*. The high-level road across Culross Muir was laid out in the early 1800s, but Kennetpans distillery closed in the 1820s.

**Steam Ferryboats and Grain Whisky**: Kincardine became a ferry point connecting to the Falkirk area at Higgins Neuk near Airth, which justified two new piers between 1811 and 1827. John Gray built the small early wooden paddle steamer *Lady of the Lake* in 1815, and simultaneously Ralph Rae created the slightly larger *Morning Star*. A new Tulliallan Castle was built as a mansion about 1820 for Admiral Lord Keith; by 1826 the old castle was a ruin. The brewery was still in use in 1825, a sawmill was set up in 1825, and soon the local ferry was worked by the *Tulliallan Castle*, another wooden paddler built by Gray in 1828. Kilbagie distillery made grain whisky from the 1820s; it was connected with Kennet Pans by canal and tramway, but closed around 1860. In the 1820s Chambers described Kincardine as *"a thriving sea-port town, remarkable for ship-building"*. The Sands quarry worked between 1835 and 1899.

**Paper, Vacuum Flasks and Depression**: Sir James Dewar, born in Kincardine in 1842, was the prolific inventor – of the vacuum flask in 1872, of cordite explosive, and of the processes to liquefy oxygen and to solidify and liquefy hydrogen. Although the early railways missed out Kincardine, by 1860 the Stirling carriers Wordie & Co had a cartage depot. In 1872–74 the former Kilbagie distillery was replaced on the same site by the large Forth paper mill – so perhaps reverting to its original use. In 1888 coal was mined near Kennet, to Beveridge a *"clean and substantial looking village"* of the Bruces, who had lately become Balfours of Burleigh. The *Commercial Hotel* was then open, plus a rope-work, a woollen mill and the Kilbagie paper mill of J A Weir; but shipbuilding was extinct, and Beveridge noted that *"an air of depression"* hung over the little town.

**Kincardine in Fife**: Tulliallan parish remained in *'Perthshire on Forth'* until local government was reorganised in 1890, when it oddly became part of Fife rather than of Clackmannanshire. In 1894 Kincardine was described as *"a small port with a steam ferry across the Forth"*; this still plied to Higginsneuk. There were coal and ironstone pits west of Kilbagie, connected by tramway to Kennetpans. Tulliallan golf club, founded in 1902, laid out an 18-hole parkland course. Longannet quarry employed 155 men in 1910, but like local brewing and mining it then failed to prosper. Nor did passenger services thrive on the branch railway from Alloa, opened to Kincardine by the North British in 1893 and extended along the coast to Culross and Dunfermline in 1906 – they ended in 1930.

**Kincardine Bridge and early Twentieth Century mines**: In 1936 the ferry was replaced by a major road bridge, its steel centre span – then the longest swinging span in Europe – allowing ships to visit Alloa and Stirling; the new approach road required on the south shore led to the opening of the Silver Link roadhouse in 1938. By 1939 the Castlehill mine 5 km north-east of Kincardine was working both the Productive Coal Measures and the deeper Limestone Coal Group. Some 4 km to the north was the small Brucefield pit owned by the Fordel Mains (Midlothian) Colliery Company; around 1947 it produced about 70,000 tons annually from shallow measures. By the early 1950s Kincardine was a village of over 2000 people, known for its interesting 17th century mercat cross, and also the Scottish Police College at Tulliallan Castle.

*The driving installation for Kincardine swing bridge. It had the longest swinging span in Europe when built in 1936. The span was fixed in 1988 due to the closure of the port of Alloa. (JRH)*

**Power Station, Bogside Mine and Tower Blocks**: In 1952 the interim British Electricity Authority chose Kincardine as the site for a new power station to burn 6000 tonnes a day of pulverised low grade coal from nearby collieries. Some came from Bogside, a drift mine opened in 1959 only 1 km south of Castlehill, driven from 1957 to exploit the hitherto unsaleable Upper Hirst seam, which although high in ash and phosphorus was shallow and around 2m thick. In 1955 the new South of Scotland Electricity Board (SSEB) took over the project, which opened in 1960, soon producing a third of all Scotland's power. Uniquely for a village, three tower blocks of flats were built to house its workers. By 1962 Bogside was raising around 2000 tonnes a day, but work there had ceased by 1989.

**Longannet Power Station and its Mine**: The giant 2600 mW Longannet Generating Station east of Kincardine was begun by the SSEB in 1962; its foundations took 270,000m$^3$ of concrete, and at 183 m its chimney became Scotland's tallest concrete structure. Fully operational from 1973, it required 10,000 tonnes of coal daily. A circular rail system allowed trains of hopper wagons to arrive from either east or west, unload their coal automatically into the bunkers, and depart in either direction without stopping. The NCB Area Manager William Rowell devised an automated delivery system to bring a torrent of pulverised coal directly into the power station stockyard from far inland, by a cable belt rising through an inclined tunnel 9 km long from a new drift mine at Solsgirth, working the Upper Hirst seam at the point where Fife, Kinross and Clackmannan met. The laden belt emerged like a blackened escalator from the distant depths at around 3 metres a second, from 1970 also carrying the output from the similar new Castlehill drift mine south-east of Bogside. The Castlebridge mine, 2 km south-west of Forest Mill, a manriding and materials shaft sunk from 1978, was a late addition to the Longannet complex.

**Keeping Kincardine in Fife**: Meantime Kennet House was demolished in 1967. Kincardine narrowly escaped what would have seemed a logical transfer from proud and possessive Fife to the new Central Region by a Commons vote in 1973. By 1977 in addition to at least a thousand power station workers the mines employed nearly 2800 men. Although many travelled into the area to work, the village population had grown by half; however, its secondary school had been closed by 1978. With the decline of the ports of Stirling and Alloa, there was little need to open the swing bridge for shipping, and it became a fixed structure in 1988. In 1989 Kilbagie, owned by Weir Paper Products, made specialist papers for offices, printing and publishing; a major effluent improvement programme began in 1990. In 1991, 3184 people lived locally.

**The Last Deep Mine Breaks the Records**: Work at Castlehill had ceased by 1989, when the Longannet complex, then comprising Solsgirth and Castlebridge, was the only deep mine still at work in Scotland; in 1990 it raised more coal than any single Scottish colliery had achieved in any past year, and in 1992 the 1300 workers again broke all records for single-pit output in Scotland; productivity had doubled in 15 years to almost 6 tonnes per man/shift. Kincardine power station was out of use from about 1990. From 1992 Castlebridge mine cut coal

*Longannet power station, near Kincardine on Forth – the largest coal-fired power station ever built in Scotland. The 183m chimney is Scotland's tallest concrete structure. Longannet began operating in 1973, and is intended to keep working until the year 2020, using local and imported coal.* *(SMPC / Tom Robertson)*

with a new electric shearer made by Anderson Strathclyde of Motherwell. In 1993 the recently privatised Scottish Power and Scottish Hydro Electric agreed to take at least 2 million tonnes of coal a year from the Longannet complex till 1998; it then employed 1100 miners. The mine complex was sold in 1994 to Mining (Scotland), who expected it to produce coal until 2020, the lifetime of the adjoining power station, then running below capacity.

**Goodbye to a Major Landmark**: By 1992 the railway between Kincardine and Alloa was out of use. Private house-building north-east of the village began in 1993, and in 1994 the long-vacant *Silver Forth Hotel* was converted into a nursing home. It seems that in 1995 Longannet was adapted to burn imported coal of poorer quality, as well as the local product, but Ayrshire coal was still moved there by rail from Killoch in 1997. Weir Paper Products at Kilbagie – bought in 1995 by Inveresk *(see Inverkeithing)* – soon profited from new recycling plant. The disused Kincardine power station remained for some years, the twin towers being blown up in April 2001. The Longannet mine employs over 650 people, Scotland's last deep miners. An eastern bypass is to be built by 2004, and an additional river crossing is also planned.

## KINCRAIG, Alvie, Feshiebridge & Insh

**Map 9, B5**

***Inverness-shire village & hamlets,*** *pop. 525* OS 35: NH 8305

Midway between Kingussie and Aviemore the River Spey broadens into Loch Insh, below which it is joined from the south by the lengthy Glen Feshie, which emerges from the Grampian mountains. Dunachton west of the loch gained a baronial burgh charter in 1690, but saw no development. The Kirk of *'Inch'* on the peninsula between the loch and the River Feshie was shown on Roy's map of about 1750 as the terminus of a track from Ruthven. On the north bank of the Spey was Wade's *'King's Road from Stirling to Inverness'*. The two came to be connected by the Boat of Insh ferry, serving Insh House, though the small village of Insh grew up 4 km farther south-west. In the early 1800s Telford remade Wade's road. By 1842 a post office was open across the valley at Feshiebridge.

**Railway Nomenclature Problems**: When the Inverness & Perth Junction Railway opened its single-track main line in 1863, roughly parallel to the road (later the A9), a crossing station opposite the kirk was named Boat of Insh. In 1865 the Highland Railway took over, and renamed the station as Kincraig in 1871, perhaps the date that the Spey was bridged at that point. A post office, the 11-room *Suie Hotel*, a 9-hole golf course and a small village grew close by. Its *'Alvie'* primary school was named from Alvie Kirk, 4 km downstream. Despite these facilities, in 1951 the local population was only about 225. By then a small hospital was open 3 km south-west of Kincraig.

**Varied Leisure without Station or Golf**: Kincraig station was closed in 1964. However, later tourists came by road; by 1977 Inverfeshie House near the kirk was a hotel, and the *Ossian Hotel* was also open. However, it seems odd that around that time the golf course was closed. In 1978 the hamlet of Inshriach 4 km north-east of Feshiebridge had a forestry office, sawmill, Osprey Joiners, and a nursery for alpine plants. From the 1970s Feshiebridge also had an airstrip used for gliders, and the Lagganlia Outdoor Centre. Kincraig was bypassed in the early 1980s. The hospital had been closed by 1985, and replaced by the Royal Zoological Society of Scotland's Highland Wildlife Park, close to the new water sports centre at Loch Insh. In 1994 the Will Charitable Trust bought the huge 170 square km Glen Feshie estate, for woodland conservation. By 1997 the Alvie Trust had opened a quarry at Easter Delfour, 3 km to the north, to raise Monadhliath granite for use as building stone. Three tiny hostels for backpackers at Kincraig, Glenfeshie and Insh are open all year, as is the wildlife park, which features native Scottish and European animals.

## KINGAIRLOCH, Camasnacroise & Glensanda

**Map 4, C1**

***Argyllshire settlements,*** *pop. under 100* — OS 49: NM 8353

This remote and hilly area in Morvern centres round the sea inlet of Loch a'Choire, part of Loch Linnhe; 6 km south are the ruins of the 15th century Glensanda Castle. The Roy map showed woodlands and a tiny roadless settlement at the foot of Glen Galmadale, 3 km to the east. By the 1890s a single-track road had been made up, linking Lochaline with the Corran Ferry, and Kingairloch House had been built. At various times a church and school were built at Camasnacroise near Glengalmadale, and a mill, pier and post office were provided. The Kingairloch estate was bought for *'sport'* in 1902 by Derbyshire cotton tycoons, the Strutts, whose last survivor, bloodthirsty markswoman Patricia Strutt – who died at a great age in 1999 – slaughtered so many stags on the hills that she was known as the *'Killer Lady of Kingairloch'*. Meanwhile the human population had declined from some 85 people in 1951 to under 40 by 1981, though the church, school and post office were still open in 1977. In 1985 although the narrow and little-used road had a grassy centre, the estate still contained both conventional and fish farms.

**Glensanda Granite for Eurotunnel**: In 1986 John Foster Yeoman, a West of England quarrymaster, opened the Glensanda superquarry in the heart of a mountain called Meall na h-Easaiche, 4 km south-west of Kingairloch. A track zigzags up to the quarry, whose prime purpose was to supply a total of 1.3 million tonnes of particularly hard pink granite, crushed and carried by conveyor through a 2 km-long tunnel for shipment from a new jetty to the Isle of Grain in Kent in 30,000 ton bulk carriers, for use in the 465,000 reinforced concrete segments cast there in 1987–91 to line the British half of the Channel Tunnel. At the peak two vessels sailed daily; nearby an airstrip was laid out. Of some 170 men employed at the quarry in 1989, 80 lived in hutments on the site. In 1992 some 150 men including Lismore people still worked at the quarry, much of its hard rock then being shipped to Hamburg.

## KINGARTH & Kilchattan

**Map 1, B1**

***Small villages, S. Bute,*** *pop. 415 (area)* — OS 63: NS 1055

The south end of the Isle of Bute was anciently of importance, having a stone circle, standing stones and a 2000 year old vitrified fort at Dunagoil, the ruins of an early monastery, the seat of a bishop in 660 and into the 8th century. In the 12th century came St Blane's Church, whose ruins were saved from collapse by the laird in the late 19th century. Pont's map-work of about 1600 marked Kilchattan, on a sheltered sandy bay on the east coast, and Kilchattan Beg to the north. Kilchattan was just a fishing village until around 1880, when a pier was built, served by steamers from Fairlie and Millport. Kingarth (later Bute) golf club was founded in 1888, laying out a secluded 9-hole links course. In 1894 Murray described Kilchattan as *"a pleasant quiet watering-place"* with frequent horse-drawn coaches from Rothesay, and the *"very comfortable" St Blane's Hotel*. A hotel or inn had also appeared at Kingarth by 1953, but steamers had ceased to call at Kilchattan, whose pier became disused in 1955. The area's population tended to fall, stabilising at under 300 by 1971, and in 1973 the one-class primary school had 25 pupils. The facilities of a small village were available in 1981, and little development had occurred by 1991 when the parish had 415 residents. Haswell-Smith describes the area as *"a rambler's delight"*; the little-known 9-hole Bute golf course is still open.

## KING EDWARD

**Map 10, B1**

***Buchan settlement,*** *pop. under 100* — OS 29: NJ 7256

Before Moray became an effective part of Scotland in the 12th century the Castle of Kinedart *('Head of the Boundary'* in Gaelic) was built to defend Buchan, standing beside the Kinedar Burn in a rolling area 6 km north of Turriff. A century later it was rebuilt by the Comyn Earl of Buchan, and nearby an early bridge spanned the burn, beside which stand the ruins of the medieval parish church. As English speech spread north and west from Aberdeen, the name Kinedart became corrupted to *'King Edward'*; in the late 15th century it was still the seat of the powerful Buchan family. In the 1950s there were still junior secondary classes at King Edward school, but the area never developed so much as a village, and remains entirely rural.

## KINGENNIE, Murroes, Newbigging & Wellbank

**Map 6, C3**

***Hamlets, n-e. of Dundee,*** *pop. 1000+ (area)* — OS 54: NO 4737

This area of Angus is rich in ancient remains including a souterrain, a dun known as St Bride's Ring, and the 16th century tower of Murroes Castle beside the Fithie Burn, 4 km north of Broughty Ferry. *'Murraes'* church, beside the Sweet Burn 1.5 km east of the castle, appeared on Timothy Pont's late 16th century sketch map. The Roy map – made about 1750 – showed it as the *'Kirk of Muirhouses'*, but no village grew there. By then a road linked Dundee and Brechin via North Kingennie, 2 km farther north, west of which a quarry was opened at Wellbank farm. In 1822 W & P Craik owned two mills – probably on the Buddon Burn – at Omachie east of Wellbank, with 258 spindles between them. William Braid's large 396-spindle Duntrune flax mill stood on the Fithie Burn near the castle.

**Producing Arbroath Pavement**: By 1869 the Wellbank quarry and four others nearby had become famous for producing the slabs known as *'Arbroath Pavement'*. To the east of Wellbank quarry was the Pitairlie, Cunmont or Omachie quarry of Lord Dalhousie, which then employed about 50 men; to the west was another, near the old mansionhouse of Gagie, and near the castle the Duntrune quarry, which also produced *'thick rock'*, probably for walling. In 1870 the Caledonian Railway opened a circuitous branch line from Broughty Ferry to Forfar, with a station at the hamlet of South Kingennie east of the church. There was little more than a church and post office at Newbigging, 1 km south-east of the Omachie quarry.

**Wellbank, Newbigging and Quarries**: When around 1950 council housing was built to house the Omachie workers, it was concentrated at Newbigging, whose population has since hovered around the 400 mark. Although by 1969 the *Ballumbie Hotel* was open beside the castle, few other services existed in the 1950s except for the 220-pupil Murroes junior secondary school 2 km farther north, soon reduced to a primary. Passenger train services to Kingennie ended in 1955 and the line was lifted in 1967. In 1979 Keillers of Murroes were specialist builders of cattle floats and horseboxes. Kings worked the Cunmont quarry in 1980, by then a spreading excavation; it is now still larger. Two late 20th century quarries between Murroes and Monifieth are now extensive; the other quarries are long closed and the wet pits they left have been infilled. Both Wellbank and Newbigging have post offices, and stable populations of nearly 500.

## KINGHORN

**Map 6, B4**

***Fife coast village,*** *pop. 2950*

OS 66: NT 2787

Kinghorn's Gaelic name signifies either *'Head of the Corner'* or *'Blue Head' (Kingorm* in Gaelic*)*, relating to its high promontory site with panoramic views over the Firth of Forth. A part of ancient Fothrif, it was already known by 649 AD when St Fillan of Pittenweem died there, and had an early *'Apdaine'* – i.e. land held by an abbot. It was chartered in 1165 by Malcolm IV, his only Royal Burgh creation, and re-chartered in 1284; the church retains traces of work of about that time. In 1285 or 1286 King Alexander III's horse fatally slipped from a perilous cliff path near adjacent Pettycur Bay, then the way to Burntisland; his accidental death was a catastrophe, precipitating the disastrous wars of the succession, but this seminal event was not commemorated on the spot until 700 years later. Ferry rights for the crossing to the Lothians already existed in the 14th century from both Pettycur and Kinghorn. Ships could be victualled at Kinghorn in 1415, though the tiny harbour can have afforded little shelter from the east; between 1400 and 1460 Kinghorn exported small quantities of wool, but this commodity was absent from later Customs returns.

**Baltic Trade, School and Spa**: In the early 16th century Kinghorn vessels traded in the Baltic, and were in Bergen in 1525; yet in spite of its intrepid sailors, in 1535 it paid no burgh taxes, and in 1535–56 (and 1621) Kinghorn contributed under 1.5% of Scotland's Customs dues. However, in 1560 the burgh was represented in Parliament, and by 1575 had a school. In 1598 the traveller Fynes Moryson called Kinghorn a *"village"*, where a largely new church was built in 1609. Grain was exported in 1618, in which year a medicinal spring was discovered and named *'Kinghorn Spa'*; though promoted by Dr Patrick Anderson, it was a nine days' wonder. Kinghorn's trade died in 1623, when some of its ships were lost to the Turks and the harbour was destroyed by a storm. In 1639 Kinghorn ranked a pitiful 40th among Scottish burghs in tax yield, or about 1% of Edinburgh's trade. A primitive postal service to the north passed through Kinghorn by 1641, and by 1663 a coach road existed from Kinghorn to Kirkcaldy and Falkland.

**Porpoises, Kinghorn Inn and Pettycur Harbour**: Defoe noted in the 1720s that *"here is a thread manufacture, which they make very good, and bleach or whiten it themselves"*. There was also the grisly *'sport'* of shooting porpoises, *"of which very great numbers are seen almost constantly in the Firth"*. The carcasses were boiled down for oil, and as with whaling, this bloody activity was carried to such excess that the schools of porpoises vanished. Kinghorn had a post office by 1745, and by about 1750 as Roy's map showed, the coast road westwards was complete. There was an inn at Kinghorn by 1773 and the *'Sailor's Aisle'*, part of the earlier church, was incorporated in its 1774 rebuilding. Though not even the name Pettycur appeared on Roy's map, its tiny harbour was built about 1760 and rebuilt in 1792, when an inn was erected there for ferry passengers; nine boats of 50 to 60 tons worked the ferry service, despite problems of drifting sand.

**Kinghorn Loch Textiles**: One of Scotland's earliest flax-spinning mills was set up near Kinghorn about 1790, and in 1793–94 three more water mills were built for flax and cotton spinning at the outlet from Kinghorn Loch, James Aytoun's having 144 spindles. In 1797 two fairs were to be held in Kinghorn, where Heron in 1799 referred to a population of about 1800, noting *"some machinery has lately been here erected for spinning cotton and flax. The harbour of Pettycur is the ordinary landing place of the passage-boats from Leith"*, a ferry role badly hit in the early 19th century by Kirkcaldy competition. In 1826 a new Town Hall was built, followed in 1829 by a new primary school, both designed by Thomas Hamilton. Chambers wrote in 1827 that Kinghorn possessed *"a small share of trade, with some manufactures"*. The limited water supply from Kinghorn Loch led all three mills to install early steam engines, and by 1840 they jointly employed 467 people, and a bleachworks another 70.

**The Twisting Tunnel**: Building of the Edinburgh & Northern Railway began on the cliffs above Kinghorn in 1846, engineered by Grainger, who must be blamed for not correcting the severe kinks in the hard-rock tunnel, which delay every train to this day. The line was opened in 1848. The coming of the steam train ferry from Granton to Burntisland in 1850 caused the Pettycur ferry to be discontinued; only a little fishing and salt panning remained there. In 1864 Swan Brothers – who also owned Kirkcaldy mills and ships – ran the bleachworks and the St Leonards and Mid Mills, which together employed 400 people on 4624 spindles. They later ceased to prosper; the last, a spinning mill beside the loch, worked till about 1886, later becoming a large tannery.

**Shipbuilding under Difficulties**: About 1865 John Key, a well-known Kirkcaldy marine engineer, founded a shipbuilding yard on a cramped site beside Kinghorn church, so exposed to the waves that completed steamships had to be launched with their engines running! The yard had rail access, and started auspiciously by building a 2000-ton 85 m ship for P&O, followed by the 600-ton sailing barque *River Tay*, the first iron whaler, built in 1868 for Gilroy Brothers of Dundee. By 1869 Key's 350 workers were launching iron ships of over 2600 tons. In 1876–79 they built three ferries for the North British Railway – including the paddler *John Beaumont*, and the *William Muir*, an 800-passenger vessel which monopolised the Burntisland to Granton ferry service from 1890 to 1937.

**Making the Best of the Tay Bridge Disaster**: About 1880 a crane, built of girders salvaged from the fallen Tay Bridge, was installed at the shipyard, which had been sold to Scotts of Inverkeithing by 1886 and built the coaster SS *Abbotshall in* 1890. Scotts expanded the yard in 1894, and at times employed up to a thousand men, completing the steel passenger liner SS *Paringa* in 1908 for the Adelaide Steamship Company of Australia; but they closed the yard in 1909. An 18-hole municipal golf course was laid out on the hillside in 1887; its clubhouse was added on the other side of the main road, because the most obvious site was required for a reversing spur; this enabled a mineral railway built in 1886–87 to gain enough height to connect the station to the short-lived Binnend shale works *(see Burntisland)*. A related candle factory was set up at Kinghorn.

**Glass and the Final Ship**: In 1902 a glass whisky-bottle works was established in an old saltworks at Pettycur; a steep rail siding was laid down to serve it. Gun batteries at both Kinghorn and Pettycur were either strengthened or rebuilt around 1904 *(see Inchkeith)*. In the early 20th century the *Rockingham Hotel* was open near the golf clubhouse; it later became private housing. Electricity was supplied in the town from 1911. The shipyard was reopened in 1919, but only one ship was launched, appropriately the SS *Kinghorn*. The yard was closed for ever in 1921; within half a century its levelled terraces had become a caravan site.

**Tram Bodies, Caravans, Haggis and Sheepskins**: By 1939 a makeshift holiday camp of old tram bodies had set a woeful precedent in leisure development, but Kinghorn's cliff-top cinema had already closed by 1952. There were two hotels by 1953, but one of Scotland's largest and most prominent caravan sites was regrettably allowed to sprawl high on the steep hillsides above Pettycur's sandy beach; it has been much improved over the years. An inshore lifeboat station was opened in 1965. In 1972 the United Glass Containers works employed 120 people; it was rated as very efficient when it had to be closed in 1982 after the demand for bottled whisky fell; it was soon demolished, and the site was developed for housing in 1992. About 1980 a meat products factory was established beside the tannery by the Kirkcaldy butchers Stahly, making and canning such foods as haggis. In 1991 the tannery was owned by Highland Fleece Ltd; a covered sewage disposal works had been built at the harbour, struggling to cope with its strong effluents.

**Commuters and Community**: The population had remained near 3000 for many years, but Kinghorn had gradually changed from a compact place into a lower density residential village. In 1991 the 2931 people had a high percentage of well-qualified professional and technical people. For a short time there were four small hotels, but one soon became a retirement home, and the old *Kinghorn Hotel* burned down in 1988; derelict for six years, it was demolished in 1994 and replaced in 1999 by flats. About 1993 the one-time cinema was converted into a very spacious private house. After the completion of a new primary school, in 1996 the school building of 1829 was restored and attractively extended as a public library and community centre. In 1999 the Pettycur Bay caravan park added a large pyramidal facilities building containing a swimming pool. In 2000 while the former Town Hall stood derelict, awaiting restoration, Kinghorn's flowery railway station was judged the best-kept in Scotland – all the work of Linda Mullen.

## KINGLASSIE

**Map 6, B4**

***Central Fife village,*** *pop. 1425* — OS 58: NT 2398

A stone in the form of a cross which stands in rolling country at Dogton, 2 km north-east of Auchterderran, may date from the tenth century; by the early 13th century a church stood above the Lochty Burn 2 km to the north. The extensive parish of Kinglassie, whose name derives from St Glass or Finglassin, was in Fothrif until 1426, and briefly in the County of Kinross, then in Fife; a parish school existed by 1630. Mining seems to have begun early, for Pont's original map of about 1600, showed a *'Coltoune'* in roughly that location. The Roy map of about 1750 marked a track which linked the Kirkcaldy area by way of Strathore and the isolated Kinglassie Kirk to the Gullet bridge and Scotlandwell.

**Farming Community, Mansion and Mining**: The prominent folly of Blyth's Tower was built in 1812, and an annual agricultural show was founded in 1814; by 1836 about 40 farmers were members. Sharp, Greenwood & Fowler's map of 1826–27 showed the mansionhouse of Inchdairnie, 2 km to the east; this seat of the wealthy Aytouns was rebuilt in 1845. Meantime in 1836 the parish school had about 100 pupils; an adequate road system served the hamlet at the Kirkton. Spinning and weaving were home crafts, and a little coal was dug from pits at Clunybridge and The Squirrel. The *Burnside Inn* is long-established, and by 1851 the parish had a range of tradesmen. Later a colliery was sunk at Kininmonth 2 km to the west; by 1895 this stood at the end of a rail connection via another colliery at Crosshill, joining the North British system at Kelty. The village school was replaced in 1883. By 1895 *'Inchdairnie Park'* stood in vast policies and plantations, covering some two square kilometres, while Kinglassie was a small village with a post office and smithy. In 1896 the Mitchell Halls were built and in 1905 a substantial local Co-op shop.

**The great Kinglassie Colliery and its Culture**: The mineral railway was extended to the Fife Coal Company's very much larger Kinglassie Colliery, sunk from about 1906 south-east of the village and west of the park. By 1910 miners' rows had been built; a new 9-class village primary school was provided in 1913, and between 1901 and 1931 the population doubled. Though the pit had water problems in the early 1920s, more miners' homes were built by the company in 1926 just before the Coal Strike, and in 1931 when the parish population was 2400, a miners' welfare club was built, complete with bowling green. A *'surface mine'* or adit was driven from the east in 1933 to increase coal production, and in 1934 the mine's workshops alone employed 14 men; by then there was a newly formed pipe band. From 1934 the Mitchell Hall was a cinema operated by Williamson from Newburgh, and there was also an active dramatic society. By 1939 some 700 miners in all worked in the complex, using the longwall system. A prefab housing estate was built in the late 1940s, and pithead baths and a canteen were opened by the NCB in 1950. At some time before 1967 the big Inchdairnie house was destroyed by fire, and vanished with its park.

**Piping Success precedes Decline**: In 1951 when the highly successful pipe band held the World Grade 1 second prize, Kinglassie had a secondary school and some 2000 people; though there was no hotel it enjoyed the other facilities of a small village, but was surrounded by coal bings. About 1960 the mineral railway was extended eastwards to Thornton yard to serve the huge Westfield gas plant and its opencast mine, which swallowed up the Kininmonth pit *(see Lochore)*. Until 1962 (when the cinema closed) the school had over 300 children of all ages to 16, but from that year the secondary pupils were sent to the new Glenwood School in Glenrothes. The surface mine was closed in 1962, and the deep pit closed in 1966 due to geological problems; the pipe band was in abeyance until 1984, and the chemist's shop closed about 1977. The population drifted downwards, though a hotel was again open by 1981. A one-time mission hall was used by the 1980s for building glass-fibre boats *(see local booklets by Dan Imrie)*. In the 1980s the Kinglassie colliery bings were largely reclaimed to farmland, but only 1419 people lived locally in 1991, generally disadvantaged by lacking higher education, old age and poor health, and there has been little subsequent development.

## KINGSBARNS & Cambo — Map 6, C4

***Small E. Fife villages**, pop. 500 (area)* — OS 59: NO 5912

Cambo stands on the low plateau of the East Neuk of Fife, where the Kippo Burn runs down to the coast 5km north-west of Crail, on the way to St Andrews. Cambo was shown on Pont's map of about 1600; its mill existed by 1642 when James Gordon mapped Fife for Blaeu, and nearby was Kingsbarns with its kirk. Cambo House became the home of the Erskines in the 1670s. By the time of Roy's map of about 1750 there was a developed road system. The early Kingsbarns Golfing society was founded in 1815, using local links. A single-line railway was extended from Crail in 1883 through Kingsbarns station (some 1.5km west of the village) to reach St Andrews in 1887. By then the compact village had an inn and a post and telegraph office. Cambo House, destroyed in 1878, was soon rebuilt as a mansion. In the 1939–45 war a fighter airfield was laid out at Upper Kenley 3km west of the village; by 1953 it was disused. The farming parish then had over 500 residents, basic facilities and two small hotels, one of which later closed, as did the railway in 1965. For several years in the 1980s there was a peaceful country park at Cambo; this did not last, but the gardens are open. Kingsbarns parish had 497 people in 1991; this compact and attractive residential village keeps its post office, and its golf links – very expensive to play (and not on the OS map!).

## KINGSHOUSE & Altnafeadh — Map 5, B2

***Settlement, w. of Rannoch Moor*** — OS 41: NN 2654

Around 1750 Caulfeild's troops laid out a military road across the bleak Rannoch Moor, linking Dumbarton with Fort William; the fair copy of the Roy map showed this as a track, forking near Altnafeadh to strike north up the steep zigzags of the *'Devil's Staircase'*, over Mam Grianau and down to Kinlochleven. The more sheltered Glencoe route was built down Glencoe about 1780–82. By the latter date the Glencoe road carried the Glasgow mails, and the Devil's Staircase route was abandoned to the sheep. The *Kingshouse Inn* was built in a slight hollow 250m above sea level 4km east of Altnafeadh, to provide essential shelter at the head of Glencoe; in 1769 Pennant found it *"in a manner unfurnished"*. On tour in 1803 Dorothy Wordsworth found it large and busy but full of *"poverty and misery"*. She rated the road from Ballachulish as *"bad"*; it was still *'second class'* in the 1890s.

**West Highland Way and Glencoe Ski Centre**: In the early 1930s a new motor road was built across Rannoch Moor and down Glencoe. After 1945, skiing grew on nearby Meall a'Bhuiridh, with an early ski-lift in 1956, though only a three-month season could be expected. By 1963 the totally isolated inn (which had only recently acquired a telephone) had become a 14-room hotel; it was later extended, and also became a mountain rescue post. By 1983 the West Highland Way had been defined, following the military road, and a chairlift led up from White Corries, 2 km south of the hotel, where a further annexe was added by 1985 to provide cheap shelter for walkers and skiers. In 1987 a new plateau tow to nursery slopes was opened at the Glencoe ski centre; in 1993 there were six lifts, a new restaurant and *two* new museums. In the mid 1990s the local ski company became part of the Glenshee Chairlift Company. The ancient *King's House Hotel* still serves.

## KINGSWELLS — Map 10, C3

***Aberdeenshire village**, pop. 1120* — OS 38: NJ 8606

In 1894 Kingswells, a mansionhouse near the Alford road in an area of isolated farms some 8km west of Aberdeen, was accompanied by a scatter of facilities – a post office, a smithy, and a crossroads with a free church. By 1950 there was also an agricultural engineer and a small all-age school, by 1976 simply a primary, serving some 400 people. Meantime, as a result of pressures due to the oil industry, a residential caravan site was permitted within a loop of shelter belts 800m to the north; its replacement by the 100 houses of a new estate called Kingswood was approved in 1975 and a reality by 1982. By then the village that was slowly growing round the crossroads comprised the primary school, church, shops, hotel, filling station and 58 houses.

**Explosive growth of an Oil-Rich Suburb**: A further major planned development approved in 1984 was still in progress in 1991 when Kingswells was a youthful dormitory in character, with a total of 422 houses, two-thirds of them detached. These contained 1120 people, among them Scotland's highest proportion of adults with higher qualifications (over 50%), the lowest male unemployment (under 1%) and the highest ratio of households with two or more cars – over 60%! It also had the highest proportion in jobs related to energy – evidently oil and gas – at 25%. By 1999 Kingswells had a western bypass and had become a built-up area nearly 2 km in length; the A944 road linking it to Aberdeen and Westhills had been largely upgraded to a dual carriageway.

## KINGUSSIE, Ruthven & Pitmain — Map 9, B5

***Large Inverness-shire village,*** *pop. 1300* — OS 35: NH 7500

The murderous 14th century royal bastard known as the Wolf of Badenoch had his castle near the River Spey at Ruthven, in the Badenoch area of upper Strathspey. Kingussie – meaning *'Head of the Pinewood'* and pronounced with a long 'u' – lies on the Allt Mhor *(Big Stream)* where it enters the Spey opposite Ruthven. It became a burgh of barony as early as 1464, with a kirk and a minor Carmelite priory. The *'strong house'* of the Earl of Enzie at Ruthven was still occupied in 1618. Gordon's map-work of about 1645 showed *'Ruffen'* as a substantial settlement, plus Kingussie Kirk with *'Pitmean'* to the west and Kingussie Beg to the east, and many other nearby names. A barony charter of 1684 was made to Ruthven or *St George Burgh*.

**Ruthven Barracks and Wade Roads**: After the 1715 rebellion the Hanoverian government built Ruthven Barracks in 1716–19 on the site of the Wolf's castle as a show of strength. They were soon served by the new military road from the south, built by General Wade's troops between 1725 and 1736, which crossed the Spey by a ford and ferry near the Kirk of Kingussie, below the confluence of the Allt Mor. From 1727 Wade made the barracks the main base for his cavalry, with stables built by 1734. Ruthven fair was still the main local market in 1745, but when the ferry boat was destroyed in that troubled year it took two years to obtain a replacement. Soon after their final defeat at Culloden in 1746, clan survivors burned Ruthven barracks and then dispersed. Kingussie had a school by 1745. However, Roy's map made in the early 1750s showed only the *Kirk of Kingussie* and a few dots suggesting huts beside a winding road crossing a ford to Ruthven. This was a small nodal settlement on General Wade's military road south of the barracks, where three other tracks converged from the east and south-east.

**Pitmain and the New Village of Kingussie**: Once the Highlands were pacified Ruthven declined; a bleachfield was built at Pitmain in 1785 and a post office was opened there in 1788. The author of the 1792 Statistical Account observed that there was still *"no village"* in the parish of Kingussie & Insch, a problem for traders and public alike, though three fairs were still scheduled at Ruthven for 1797; by then Pitmain was a post town, but with only a Saturday service. Kingussie was laid out by its proprietor the Duke of Gordon in 1799, had a post office from 1802 and an annual tryst by 1804; a small woollen firm was working by 1805. The road from the south, built for the Commissioners, had reached Kingussie via a new Spey bridge at Newtonmore by 1808, when a through coach began to run between Perth and Inverness. Elizabeth Grant wrote that in 1812 she saw at Kingussie only *"the indications of a village, a few very untidy slated stone houses each side of a road"*.

**The Laggan Road brings Development**: In 1815 the River Laggan was bridged, enabling a regular coach to be run on the new road to Fort William. With this increased nodality, Kingussie soon became the main centre of upper Speyside – for example a footwear shop was established in 1827 by D McIntosh – and the names of Pitmain and Ruthven sank into obscurity. Robert Somers who visited in 1847 noted *"Kingussie, of which scarcely a nucleus existed sixty years ago, grew rapidly into a considerable village"* as a result of the clearances from remoter areas; to enable the displaced peasants to feed themselves, an *'overspill'* settlement had been started at Newtonmore *(q.v.)*, although the population of the whole parish (including Dalwhinnie and Insh) was little over 2000!

**Railway, Golf, Hotels – and Shinty Centre**: Fontane in 1858 found an inn at Kingussie, and a fair in progress at this *"old (sic) Highland village, a sort of capital of the MacPhersons"*. The Highland Railway's main line opened in 1863 with a crossing station at Kingussie, greatly stimulating the village, which became a burgh in 1867. A timber engine shed was built in 1889–90, and a much larger station building in 1895. Kingussie golf club, founded in 1890, laid out its 18-hole course among gravel, rocks and heather, and in 1893 Kingussie's Victoria Hall was the venue where the Camanachd Association was formed to regulate the game of Shinty. By 1894 Murray called Kingussie *"a large village annually growing in size and in favour with summer visitors"*: the *Star Hotel was "very fair"*, and two banks were open.

**A Flirtation with Whisky – and the Last Mail Coach**: The large *Speyside* or Kingussie distillery, built in 1895, was insolvent and for sale in 1912; it closed and was dismantled, leaving the name *'Old Distillery Road'*. In 1906 came a new post office and the imposing *Duke of Gordon Hotel*, which boasted 30 chaises for hire. The Kingussie to Fort William coach was cut back to Tulloch Station when the West Highland Railway opened in 1894. Having few through passengers, it ceased to run beyond the (Kinloch*) Laggan Hotel* in 1908. It was Britain's last horse-drawn mail coach when replaced by a motor bus in the summer of 1914.

**New Facilities and Industries – back to Whisky!**: In 1946 Wordie & Co still ran a small rail to road cartage depot. By the 1950s Kingussie had gained another five hotels, a youth hostel and a new High School for 360 pupils; the Highland Folk Museum had moved from Iona to Kingussie by 1953. The Speyside Distillery Company – originally blenders and bottlers in Rutherglen – built and equipped the new, small Speyside distillery at Invertromie, about 3 km to the east, opening in 1987, with a capacity of 600,000 litres a year. Meantime around 1970 Rotary Precision Products opened a small factory, still active in 1992 under the name *'Roller'*. By 1979 the peripatetic Castlewynd Pottery had moved from Aviemore into a modern factory next door, the only one in Scotland to make bone china. In 1975 Kingussie became the centre of the new Badenoch & Strathspey District; by 1992 much of the lengthy stone-built station building had been converted into new offices for the District Council. In 1981 Kingussie's facilities – though showing some decline since the 1950s – remained those of a large tourist village.

**Bypassed by the A9**: By 1984 there was a caravan site beside the golf course, and by 1985 the village had been bypassed by a new alignment of the A9. By 1991 Kingussie had 1298 people. The former Castlewynd Pottery factory was still active in 1992 as Highland China. By 1992 the Highland Folk Museum included many examples of farm equipment and machinery over the centuries. A tiny livestock market with minimal facilities, and an HRC roads depot, were still evident. The D McIntosh shop, established as early as 1827, was still open up to 1992 as footwear retailers, then being for sale.

**Shining at Shinty, but Goodbye Local Government**: In 1993 the local shinty team won the final of the National League of this ancient game – for the seventh successive year! In 1996 Kingussie lost some of its brief significance as a local government centre when the district council disappeared into an all-purpose Highland Council. Historic Scotland cares for the prominent old Ruthven barracks, now floodlit. There are some new houses, and the signal box still supervises the level crossing beside Kingussie High School, which has just under 400 pupils. In 1999 the *Duke of Gordon Hotel* was damaged by fire, but soon repaired. There are at least 5 others hotels, plus guest houses and B&Bs, and although the youth hostel has closed, it has been replaced by an independent year-round backpackers' hostel.

## KINKELL, Findo Gask & Millearn — Map 6, A3

***Perthshire localities**, pop. 125 (area)* — OS 58: NN 9316

Parallel to and north of the lower River Earn is the Gask ridge, along which ran a 1st century Roman road, serving a line of signal stations able to warn of attacks from the north. Nearby Findo Gask, 12 km west of Perth, is an ancient parish centre, always deeply rural. The old Kinkell Kirk on the south bank of the river near the confluence of the Machany Water, some 7 km farther west, appeared on Timothy Pont's map of Strathearn, made around 1600; Little Kinkell adjoined, and to the west was Colquhalzie, an imposing tower house whose spelling gave Pont much trouble! The *'Mil of Ern'* on the north bank already existed, adjoined to the east by Meikle Kinkell; but it appears from the Roy map that there was no bridge until after 1750. In 1821–38 Meikle Kinkell was replaced by the mansion of Millearn, built for J G H Drummond to designs by the Dicksons; the misnamed *Strathallan* Castle in its large park had also been built 2 km west of the church by 1895. By 1860 there was also a post office, which later vanished. Millearn was demolished and replaced by a new house in 1969, the year that landowner Sir William Roberts started the *'Strathallan'* historic aircraft collection, with its grass airfield. Air shows were held by 1976 and the museum drew up to 70,000 visitors a year, but it closed in 1981, five of its exhibits going to East Fortune; the tiny airfield remains in use by the Strathallan Flying Club.

## KINLOCHBERVIE — Map 12, A1

***W. Sutherland village**, pop. 500* — OS 9: NC 2256

The Roy map of about 1750 named Kinlochbervie, which stands between Loch Inchard, the most northerly sea loch on the west coast of Sutherland, and the head of the small freshwater loch which Roy labelled *'Insh Balwy'*, a corruption of the Gaelic name *Innis na Ba buidhe* ('Pasture of Yellow Cattle') shown on modern OS maps. This remote crofting township was among those where in the late 1820s the government subsidised the erection of a building for the Church of Scotland; the winding road from the south arrived only in the mid 19th century. In 1883 a much straighter road was completed from Rhiconich, 6 km east of Kinlochbervie, north-eastwards over the moors to Durness. The 1894 edition of Murray's Handbook mentioned nothing west of Rhiconich. However, the finely sited 15-roomed *Garbet Hotel* was open by 1939 at Kinlochbervie, whose name it later took. The *Rhiconich Hotel* appeared not long after.

*Fishing boats, Kinlochbervie, in 1976. This fishing port was developed after World War II as a fish-landing place for boats fishing in the North Atlantic. (RCAHMS / JRH)*

**Modern Fishing Port**: From the late 1940s under the Pulford Estates the construction of a new pier and improved road access led to growing landings of fish, making Kinlochbervie Britain's most north-westerly mainland fishing port, a harbour of refuge and an important township by 1953. However, although a local bus ran to the outlying clachan of Balchrick, whose 150 people enjoyed a post office and primary school, as late as 1958 the Kinlochbervie pupils attended either this or the Achriesgill school near Rhiconich. By 1978 the new facilities included a marine engine fuelling point and ice plant, fish-selling shed, chandlery, mission to seamen, Department of Agriculture & Fisheries office, garage, new primary school and some 30 new houses. By then Kinlochbervie was a real village, serving the area's growing population of over 500. In 1987 almost 20,000 tonnes of fish were landed, about 3% of the Scottish total. By 1991 though the village itself still had under 500 residents, the Kinlochbervie Bakery served about 3000 customers in total. In 1993 the old manse (built in 1829) stood vacant and ruinous near the recently opened fish factory. In 1995–97 large quantities of whitefish were landed from Scottish and Faroese boats; in 1997 a typical week yielded 5000 boxes. There's also mussel farming. E & M Engineering Services operate here and at Thurso. The converted *Old School Hotel* at Inshegra, 3 km east, has 6 rooms and the *Rhiconich Hotel* 12 rooms.

## KINLOCHEWE & Bord — Map 8, C2

***Small Wester Ross village**, pop. 100* — OS 19: NH 0262

The Roy map of Wester Ross made about 1750 showed long-distance tracks crossing at a remote and tiny place between Glen Docherty and the head of Loch Maree, which in earlier days was known as Loch Ewe. Its early name of *Bord* was soon abandoned in favour of the district name *'Kenlochew'*, to which Roy gave the capital letters usually reserved for the larger burghs. By 1803 there was a drovers' inn, and in the mid 19th century proper roads were made through the area to link Gairloch with Dingwall and serve Loch Torridonside. In 1894 Murray's Handbook noted the *"good" Kinlochewe Hotel*; a post office was open by 1913, and minimal village facilities developed, though the one-time golf course did not survive the 1939–45 war. By the 1960s energetic walkers could explore the nearby Beinn Eighe nature reserve, with its ancient pines and spectacular views across the loch to the shapely mountain called Slioch. By 1982 there was a Caravan Club site and by 1996 the Reserve had its own visitor centre; there was also a mountain rescue post. Although during the 20th century the resident population hovered around the hundred mark, the hotel and post office have happily survived.

## KINLOCH LAGGAN & Ardverikie **Map 5, C1**

***Central highland area,*** *pop. under 100* OS 42: NN 5489

Loch Laggan forms a natural routeway between Strathspey and Lochaber, marked on the Roy map of about 1750 by a track along its northern shore and woods on the south side; St Kenneth's church stood at its east end, and at one time the now long-abandoned village of Druiminard stood near Feagour. The track was made up into a road by the Commissioners in the early 19th century, and in 1869 the vast Ardverikie Estate was bought by the Pennington-Ramsden family; their new fairy-tale baronial *'castle'* matched it well. By the late 19th century the small *(Loch) Laggan Hotel* stood near the church, served by the coach linking Kingussie and Fort William. This was cut back to Tulloch Station when the West Highland Railway opened in 1894. Having few through passengers, it ceased to run beyond the hotel in 1908; it was Britain's last horse-drawn mail coach when replaced by a motor bus in 1914. Loch Laggan was later regulated by a weir at its western end as part of the Lochaber power scheme *(see Fort William)*. Decline has long affected the 175 square km Ardverikie estate, which once supported 120 workers, living in scattered houses. The hotel closed in the 1960s, and by 1984 the school had only 7 pupils. By 1990, under the care of Patrick Gordon-Duff-Pennington, the beautiful estate employed just twelve people in sheep farming, deer stalking and forestry. Ardverikie is now familiar to millions through the romantic TV comedy series *'Monarch of the Glen'*.

## KINLOCHLEVEN & Kinlochmore **Map 5, B2**

***Lochaber village,*** *pop. 1076* OS 41: NN 1862

Kinlochmore in Lochaber, which stands on the north side of the River Leven at the richly-wooded head of Loch Leven, was the only significant settlement shown on the best-finished of Pont's surviving maps, made about 1600. Kinlochbeg across the river lay in what was then Argyll. Caulfeild's adventurous and hilly military road, built in the 1740s to link Fort William with the south, appeared as a track on Roy's map made about 1750, passing both places, which were shown as hamlets. Kinlochleven was already a small village by 1769 when Pennant breakfasted there, so it presumably had an inn. The hill track was abandoned to walkers when the better-graded track down Glencoe was reconstructed as a coach road about 1780–82, leaving Kinlochleven effectively accessible only by boat, and consequently underdeveloped.

**Aluminium Smelting on the Grand Scale**: From 1900 bauxite mined on the Antrim plateau in Ulster had been moved by rail to Larne, where it was converted to alumina for shipment in small vessels through the Caledonian Canal to the Foyers *(q.v.)* works of the North British Aluminium Company. Seeking a more economic scale of production, in 1907–09 – with finance from the Bank of Scotland – the firm set up a large smelting works and carbon factory on the south bank of the river. There a pier had first to be built, and then the big 1km-long dam which created the Blackwater reservoir 6km to the east. This enabled hydro-electric power to be generated at the factory for the Hall-Heroult smelting process, also used at Foyers and later at Fort William. This process electrolyses alumina at 1000°C in a carbon-lined cathode bath or *'pot'* of molten cryolite with a carbon anode. About 17,000kWh of electricity applied to two

*The Aluminium Works, Kinlochleven, in 1976. It operated from 1909, using hydro-electric power generated on site to create temperatures of 1000°C for converting alumina powder to the metal. Production has now come to an end, but the hydro power station continues to supply the grid.* *(JRH)*

tonnes of alumina yields one tonne of aluminium ingots, but consumes half a tonne of carbon electrode.

**Company Village, Tramway, Shipping and Road**: A company village of 1200 people was built, known as Kinlochleven; for some years this lacked any road link. The smelter was extended in 1916, when aluminium was first used in military aircraft. The works were linked to the pier by a narrow-gauge electric freight tramway. Until 1927 at least, J & A Gardner of Glasgow used coasters such as the 362-ton *Saint Aidan* to carry alumina from Larne to Kinlochleven and aluminium ingots to other ports *(see Ballachulish)*. In 1927 a road was opened between Invercoe and Kinlochleven, after which the works received rail-borne alumina by lorry from Ballachulish. By 1947 the road had also reached Onich via the north bank of the loch. In 1951 the population was nearly 2000, with good village facilities, but in addition to its relative isolation this one-industry settlement suffered from being divided between the two counties of Argyll and Inverness.

**Run Down to Closure**: The pier tramway was abandoned in 1959, and from 1965 the alumina came by road from Fort William rail yard. In 1975 the whole of the Kinlochleven area was placed in the new Lochaber district of Highland Region. With improved production techniques and falling demand for aluminium, the number of jobs and the population fell. The village centre was run-down by 1984, and the cinema and hotel had closed. Though in a beautiful setting, Kinlochleven had little to offer the less energetic tourist except a relatively inaccessible waterfall. The carbon factory was largely demolished in 1989, leaving its distinctive silos, which still exist. By 1991 the village population was 1076; in 1992 Lochaber Ltd was trying to attract new enterprises. By 1997 the small Kinlochleven High School had only 126 pupils. In 2000 the aluminium plant still employed 50 people, but was shortly to close; 30 workers would move to the Fort William plant. However, the hydro power station will remain – supplying the national grid via Fort William – with a heritage centre for the tourists, now served by the 10-roomed *MacDonald Hotel* and an independent hostel for backpackers enjoying the surrounding mountains or walking the old deserted military road, now the West Highland Way.

## KINLOCH RANNOCH — Map 5, C2

***Central Perthshire village**, pop. 300* — OS 42 or 51: NN 6658

Loch Rannoch lies in a beautiful but remote part of Atholl; ancient remains cluster on the level area at its eastern end. Pont's unfinished sketch map of around 1600 outlined the loch but showed no settlements, though the name *'Keanloch'* on the River Tummel as it flowed from the loch was marked on Gordon's original map of about 1645. By 1661 this was the site of a multipurpose corn/saw/waulk mill. The Duke of Atholl disputed its builder's rights, and in 1676 sent his private army to destroy it! The Roy map of about 1750 showed *'Kinloch'* as a hamlet where a hill track from Loch Garry met the track from Tummel Bridge, along the north side of Loch Rannoch, to end at Loch *'Euch' (Eigheach)*. In the late 1750s the Commissioners for the Forfeited Estates aided the construction of an inn; they founded a more permanent settlement in 1763 and built a bridge in 1764, followed by roads. There was a school by about that time, and Pennant noted a sawmill in 1769, though by then as he remarked, trees were scarce; according to Heron (1799) the second sawmill was a government project. A limestone stamping mill also erected in 1766–67 was swept away by floods before 1806.

**Weighing Schiehallion, Tourism and Hydro Power**: In 1774 the isolated 1083 m peak of Schiehallion 7 km south-east of Kinloch Rannoch was used in the gravity-proving experiments of the Astronomer Royal Nevil Maskelyne, whose assistant at the time, Charles Hutton, invented contours. Dorothy and William Wordsworth entered the Tummel valley in 1803 but found the locals spoke no English, and turned back when the road became impassable to their horse and cart, so they never reached Loch Rannoch. The roads were later improved and a mansionhouse was built 5 km to the east, named Mount Alistair. By 1895 J C Bunten, the Caledonian Railway Chairman, had replaced it by his even grander mansion of Dunalastair. By then a post office was available. Tourism also grew, and in 1894 Murray saw Kinloch Rannoch as *"a neat little village"* with a coach from Struan and two *"large, and very good"* hotels – the *Dunalastair* and *Bunrannoch*. By 1927 there was also a golf course. A major hydro-electric scheme built by the Grampian Electricity Supply Company in the 1920s used as reservoirs Lochs Ericht and Rannoch, and created the shallow Dunalastair Water to the east *(see Tummel Bridge)*. It was on load from 1930, long before the Hydro Board was founded.

**Education and Outdoor Activities**: The golf course, still open in 1953, was just a memory by 1963. In the decades to 1981, with a population of around 300, the facilities at Kinloch Rannoch remained those of a small village, with useful basic shopping; but Dunalastair was long ruinous. Rannoch School, an independent boys' boarding establishment at Dall 7 km west of Kinloch, was opened in the 1960s, had 265 pupils in 1979 (and had been extended by 1998). In the 1970s table mats were locally made by Rollo. Caravan and camping sites were open by 1984, when neither of the old hotels exceeded 24 rooms; this was much the size of the more recent *Loch Rannoch Hotel and Highland Club* on the lochside, with a timeshare project where by 1991 an outdoor activity centre and a dry ski slope had been built. The prominent Allt Mhor cascade can still be admired when in spate. By 1998 a woodland caravan site had been laid out 5 km west of the village, and forest walks signposted between there and Kinloch Rannoch, whose school and post office remain open. along with the two old hotels.

## KINLOSS — Map 9, C3

***Moray village / RAF station**, pop. 2300* — OS 27: NJ 0661

About 1150 King David I founded the important Cistercian abbey of Kinloss beside the Kinloss Burn, as it entered Findhorn Bay 4 km north-east of Forres. Kinloss Abbey was settled by monks from Melrose, and itself set up an offshoot at Old Deer in 1219. It owned a house in Berwick in 1296 and, having survived the wars, was sometimes chosen in the next century for the signing of royal charters. Nearby grew a small settlement which became a burgh of barony under the abbot in 1497, but although additions were made to the abbey as late as the early 1500s, and in 1560 it was represented in Parliament, it had only two appropriated churches. In 1574 the central tower collapsed, but around 1600 Pont sketched a still-imposing abbey building, and also noted two mills near East Grange, 3 km to the east. The abbey was sold in 1601 to Edward Bruce, Lord Kinloss, and in 1650 Cromwell's troops took most of its stone to build the fort at Inverness; just two arches were left. Muirtown 1 km north-east of Kinloss gained a baronial burgh charter in 1674 but came to nothing, and Kinloss village barely survived; the Roy map of about 1750 merely showed a hamlet beside a house in small policies.

**Railways and Distilling**: In 1858 the Inverness & Aberdeen Junction Railway opened its line between Nairn and Keith, with a station at Kinloss. This became the junction for the hopelessly uneconomic Findhorn Railway which opened in 1860, was closed to passengers in 1869 and to goods in 1880. Meantime the Kilnflat (now Glenburgie) distillery was founded in 1810, farther up the burn south of the mills; in 1886 this was still tiny and according to Barnard *"about as old-fashioned as is possible to conceive"*, making only 110,000 litres of fine-quality Highland malt whisky annually. It was closed 1927–35, but in 1936 the distillers Hiram Walker of Canada acquired George Ballantine & Son, and with the firm came Glenburgie, which was doubled in size in 1958. Later renamed Glenburgie-Glenlivet and at one stage was under J & G Stodart Ltd; it is now under Allied Distillers, but silent in 2000.

**RAF Kinloss**: A flying training school established north of the tiny village about 1936 became a large permanent RAF station. In 1989 it was the base for Nimrod early warning aircraft and an Air-sea Rescue flight. Due to its many young service families, the 2281 residents in Kinloss contained the highest proportion of children under 5 in Scotland at the 1991 census. In 1994 its role was maritime patrol, the Nimrods flying to ocean emergencies to co-ordinate the work of ships and helicopters. There was also a gliding school. By 1996 a caravan site was open. In the late 1990s the headquarters of UK air-sea rescue was centralised at RAF Kinloss, moving from Pitreavie and Plymouth.

## KINROSS

**Map 6, B4**

***County town, by L. Leven,*** *pop. 4550*

OS 58: NO 1202

The Gaelic name Leven may derive from *Liomh-amhuinn*, meaning *'smooth (or shining) water'*. According to Chambers, the island stronghold later known as Loch Leven Castle *"belonged originally to Dongart, King of the Picts"*; it was apparently founded about 490, when Loch Leven was in their province of Fothrif. Kinross *('Head of the Point')*, named from its original church site jutting into the loch, was first mentioned in 1195 as a thanage, and certainly had a church by 1240. The island castle was already old when repaired in 1258, while by 1319 the loch was famed for fishing. The castle was used as a long-term prison by Robert Bruce around 1320, and passed to the Douglas Earls of Morton in 1390 *(see Aberdour)*; they soon had it rebuilt with a perimeter wall.

**Sheriffdom Confusion**: Kinross became the caput of a tiny sheriffdom, according to one source in 1252. By 1372 there was a mill and in 1385 Kinross was a *"town"*; by 1404 it definitely headed a *'shire'*, then including Kinglassie. But Beveridge noted, *"The parishes of Kinross, Orwell and Portmoak were disjoined from Fife and formed into a separate county in 1426."* By 1428 Kinross was the main settlement in the upper Leven basin, though about 1500 its population was only about 250. The sheriffdom appears to have lapsed after Kinross-shire was ravaged by plague in 1497. Kinross had to wait until 1540 for its erection as a burgh of barony of Robert Douglas, the Earl of Morton; in 1555, 1563 and as late as 1645 Kinross-shire was noted as part of the Fife sheriffdom. By 1567 Kinross had a Protestant minister.

**Prison, Posts and Plague**: Loch Leven Castle was again repaired in 1545, and used in 1567–68 as a less than secure prison for Queen Mary; although this made it a very early tourist attraction, it was falling into disrepair by 1587, and was abandoned around 1660. A *'New House'*, reputedly a castle, built by the Earls near the old church of Kinross was first mentioned in 1590. From 1595 Kinross was served by the Edinburgh to Aberdeen post, routed via the early Bridge of Earn and Perth. By then of the 300 Kinross inhabitants, 60 were weavers. In 1597 the shire was again severely afflicted by the plague – and yet again in 1645. However, there had been a school in the town since 1615. The map made by Richard Gordon in 1642 showed New House, with Kinross on its present site. Kinross curling club was active on the loch by 1667. In 1675 Sir William Bruce of Balcaskie, who was Scotland's most notable architect of the period, bought the estate from the Douglas Earls of Morton, with fines he collected from Covenanters as Clerk of the Bills! Bruce was the Royal architect, and perhaps by way of reward was made high sheriff of the tiny county, which had shrunk over the years but was redefined in 1685, when Cleish, Fossoway and part of Arngask were added. Kinross already had a mercat cross.

**New Mansion, New Cutlers**: Bruce designed the fine Kinross House – as Heron wrote *"the first house of regular architecture in Scotland"* – built between 1685 and 1693 for his own use, with a great walled garden. Any remnant of the early Kinross town, which was still stated to be *"on a beginning or head of a point of land"* in 1682, must shortly have been shifted by Bruce, who added to the extent of local farmland the *'Flow Moss'* immediately to the north, which was drained in 1684–97. Cutlery was first made in Kinross in 1680, very likely to meet the new laird's needs, for in 1706 Sibbald noted *"some tradesmen of several employments have been brought to it by Sir William Bruce"*; it appeared that an inn had been provided *"for the accommodation of passengers"*. In 1687 Bruce had a three-arched bridge built over the South Queich; from 1689 there was a post office as such, but ruinous Loch Leven castle appears to have lost its roof in 1698. Bruce, otherwise the epitome of the improving laird, died in 1710.

**New Inn, New Churches**: In 1700 Kinross had a population of 620, though in 1708 it contained a mere *"47 tofts or steadings"*: large families were then the norm. There were some 200 weavers, plus shoemakers and cutlers. The *Salutation Inn* was built in 1721. Defoe noted on his visit in 1722 that *"at the town is a very good market, and the street tolerably well built"*; admiring the *"noble palace"* he added that the current laird, still a Mr Bruce, was a great fir-tree planter; the next year he had the remains of New House demolished. In 1724 Kinross contained 320 weavers, 35 cutlers, 22 shoemakers and ten *"in the iron trade"*. Between 1741–51 *"the town having receded from the church"* of 1240, the latter was superseded by two new churches, and demolished.

**Communications Improvements**: By 1700 the Gairney Water had been bridged 3 km to the south of the little town. The Perth road, hitherto *"a corduroy one, very narrow, full of ruts"* was made up by General Wade's troops in 1726 and became the first route north of the Forth to be turnpiked, under an Act of 1753. The Roy map of about 1750 also showed an east–west route from Alloa, broadly via the 20th century A977, leading through Kinross to meet the Perth-Burntisland road at Balgedie, where it turned north-east to Strathmiglo, a link now lost. The old County House was improved by Robert Adam in 1771. A light coach or *'fly'* began running through between Perth and Edinburgh in 1776; in 1796 the North Road was improved for stage coaches, but the post was carried in a one-horse open mail-cart until covered mail coaches began to run in 1799.

**Cutlery, Street Lights and Kinross Pennies**: In 1760, 45 cutlers and 18 other craftsmen in iron were working in Kinross; this industry peaked between then and 1783 when the Kinross hammermen founded a Friendly Society. Alexander Carlyle in 1765 still regarded the area as part of Fife, and noted the *"village of Kinross, remarkable for cutlery ware"* and what he called *Kelton's Inn*. In 1769 Pennant found *"a small town"* with many trees and a good inn (by 1775 known as the *Red Lion*) about 1 km to the north. The number of hand looms at Kinross doubled between 1790 and 1796, to 400; they made narrow linens called *'Silesias'*. Street lighting by oil (probably whale oil) was introduced in 1793. Three schools with 208 scholars of both sexes were open in 1795; the population of the town was over 1400 in 1796. Four fairs were scheduled to be held in 1797, a year when a local merchant issued a penny coin.

**The Peak and Speedy End of Kinross Cutlery**: James Hall, who visited Kinross in 1803, found the town a *"thriving place; considerable manufactures of linen, leather, shoes, and above all, of hardware, particularly cutlery, scissors, razors and pen knives"*. The four fairs were *"well frequented, especially for cattle and horses"*. However, by then the cutlery trade was *"fast dying out"*, and in 1820 the last Kinross cutler, Michael Whyte, retired from work. Cotton weaving on hand looms was introduced to Kinross about 1805; 60 to 70 new houses had been added to the town in forty years. A mill was built near the South Queich in 1815, but Greenwood's map made in 1826–27 showed only a waulkmill 1 km west of the town. By 1825 there was a local brewery, and Kinross was the centre for a penny post also serving Milnathort.

**The Rise of the Coaching Inns**: A new South Queich Bridge of one arch was erected in 1811–12 and the Gairney was re-bridged in 1822–23. By 1825 Kinross was served by a mail coach and four stage coaches. In 1823 a building (demolished in 1969) was erected for Kinross High School, and the County Buildings and jail opposite its site date from 1826. The markets held in 1827 still paid tolls to Inverkeithing, the Royal Burgh within whose trade area Kinross lay. In 1827 Chambers while on a walking tour commented that Kinross, *"the chief town of the little county has no independent manufactories, but contains more than 400 weavers, who procure employment from Glasgow, and is enlivened by the transit of numerous coaches along the North Road"*. It had also become a major coaching crossroads; the *Green Inn* (later a hotel) was built in 1829, and the *Kirklands Inn* (from about 1845 also called a hotel) was also certainly a coaching stop by 1832, when the town's population was some 2200 and a new parish church was opened.

**Books, Banking and the End of Coaching**: In 1807 the sheriffdoms of Kinross and Clackmannan were combined, and a library was established in Kinross. Between 1810 and 1825 the Stirling Banking Company opened a branch in the town; the successful British Linen Bank office was built in 1829–30. The *'Kinross-shire Bank for Savings'* lasted only from 1815 to 1833, but by 1852 another such bank was open. By 1840 there was a branch of the Clydesdale Bank, and the City of Glasgow Bank opened a branch in the town in 1856. In 1828–31 the area of usable farmland round Loch Leven was enlarged by lowering the level of its outfall via the River Leven by a metre. In 1834 nearly 400 weavers were still at work for Dunfermline and Glasgow firms, but in 1838 a tanner's bark mill burned to the ground. The Kinross & Milnathort Gas Company was formed in 1835, supplying gas to both towns from a works midway between them from 1836. A market hall was built in 1841 and a corn market established in 1844. However, after 1831 the county's population entered a long decline. A scheme for an Edinburgh & Perth Railway on a direct route via Kinross failed in 1846, so from 1847 the North Mails bypassed Kinross by train through Ladybank, and in 1849 the famous *Defiance* coach line consequently ceased running.

**Woollens, Shawls – and Suits for Aussies**: Woollen weaving for Tillicoultry firms began in 1836. The history is convoluted, but it seems that in 1839 the Kinross *'Tartan Manufactory'* (apparently also known as Bellfield mill) was established by W & R Beveridge who made shawls, and the West Tillyochie loom mill became a wool carding and spinning mill. Then came the Lochleven woollen mills, erected south of the town by the Kinross Spinning Company in 1846–47 to spin shawl yarns; these mills grew to have great significance. Less happy was Thomson & Co's large new *'zinc-roofed'* weaving mill at Swan's Acre, built in 1847 to manufacture shawls and plaids – but in that year the woollen trade faltered, and in 1865 this mill was largely demolished; part was converted into a printing works. However by 1852 a local tailor was making suits for the new Australian market, and the Kinross Dyeing Company was in business. In 1857 over 600 people were weaving *"ginghams, pulicates and checks"* for Glasgow.

**The Local Press and New Facilities**: The recent textile changes and the railway mania stimulated the publication of a local newspaper, the *Kinross-shire Advertiser*, from 1847; at first monthly, it was fortnightly from 1855 and weekly from 1861. A circus visited the town in 1849 and by 1855 there was a cricket club, and doctors and a solicitor were in practice. In 1861 the first OS 1" map for the area was published. The island castle's roofless walls were re-pointed in 1861–63 by the new laird Sir Graham Montgomery, but at that time he did not occupy Kinross House. In 1864 a Co-operative society was founded, and by 1867 there was a bookseller; at that time over 1400 letters were delivered weekly in Kinross. A new Town Hall was opened in 1869 and a Loch Leven pleasure boat was launched in 1870, serving new piers and the ruined castle, already open as a tourist attraction.

**Kinross as a minor Railway Junction**: The Fife & Kinross Railway from Ladybank via Auchtermuchty, was opened through to Kinross on the very day in August 1858 that the keen German traveller Fontane rode the trains from Queensferry to Kinross – via Dunfermline and Ladybank! He found an *"unpretentious little town"*, where the *Salutation Inn* was the only hotel in the centre. A direct rail link from Cowdenbeath was opened in 1860, ending the area's last stagecoach service (from Burntisland). Yet another rural line, the Devon Valley Railway, was begun in 1860 at Kinross, opened to Rumbling Bridge in 1863 and through to Alloa in 1870; but traffic was never heavy on any of these rustic lines, all eventually owned by the North British.

*Kinross House, designed by Sir William Bruce and built between 1685 and 1693 for his own use. It was one of the most advanced houses of its period, much influenced by continental practice.* (RS)

**The Quiet Burgh**: By 1863 Kinross-shire had its own police force, and in 1865 Kinross became a police burgh; there were then some 130 school pupils. Another large mill was built by the Kinross Woollen Company on the south side of the South Queich in 1866–67, and although by then hand loom weaving was almost extinct, stocking yarns were made for Dumfries firms, and the growing demand for clan tartans was again stimulating the local woollen industry. But then the town almost ceased to develop, and eventually only the one large woollen complex remained in production. In 1888 David Beveridge found Kinross unattractive, but noted a tourist trade and observed that, *"Besides smaller inns, it contains two good hotels – Kirkland's and the Green Hotel, which in coaching days was one of the best-appointed inns in Scotland, and is specially to be commended; always good horses and carriages to be procured."*

**Kinross Sleeps beside its *'Main Line'***: From 1890 Kinross-shire was again administered jointly with Perthshire, aided by a rail link between Edinburgh and Perth by the most direct route, which was completed in that year by the opening of the Forth Bridge and of a new line from Mawcarse Junction north of Kinross via Glenfarg to Perth. This line never carried the hoped-for traffic, but did stimulate some population growth in the miniature county, from a nadir of only 6280 at the 1891 census, when only 1902 people lived in the burgh. By 1894 there were two stations, but Murray noted Kinross as *"a sleepy little town"* where coarse linens and woollens were manufactured; three hotels – the *Brigend, Kirklands* and *Harris's* – drew custom from the romantic story of the queen's imprisonment, and from angling on the loch. Forbes Brothers' small brewery closed in 1894 as a result of pressure from the temperance movement, and eventually the linen industry also folded.

**Todd & Duncan, Airfield, and Radio**: However, in a seminal move the textile concern Todd & Duncan transferred from Alva to the Lochleven mills at Kinross in 1895. The *Green Hotel* had its own attractive 18-hole golf course from 1900, and a full public library commenced around 1905, with Carnegie assistance. In 1907 a new building was erected for Kinross High School, but matters continued on the 1890s theme for half a century, while the outside world tore itself apart. During the second World war an airfield was established at Balado, 3 km west of Kinross. After the war this was adapted to various uses, including the site of a military radio station with masts and a prominent geodesic dome. Kinross had only 2700 people by 1951, though with many normal town facilities. Sand and gravel pits were opened west of the town, and about 1970 John Dye & Son established a pallet factory.

**Todd & Duncan Expands as Dawson Group**: Around that time the Lochleven woollen mill was enlarged; it used phosphates in the dyeing process, the effluent regrettably polluting Loch Leven. In 1960 Todd & Duncan took over their main supplier, Joseph Dawson of Bradford; in 1961 the Galashiels spinners Laidlaw & Fairgrieve were acquired, and in 1967 Barrie Knitwear and Pringle of Hawick. The name Dawson Group was then adopted – of which Todd & Duncan became a subsidiary – and under the energetic accountant Ronald Miller, proceeded to buy up the Borders knitwear industry: in 1968–70 McGeorge of Dumfries, Braemar and Glenmac of Hawick, and Ballantyne Cashmere of Innerleithen. In 1980 Dawson bought British Replin Weavers of Ayr, and in 1984 set out to expand in the USA.

**Railways to Motor Auctions and M90 Services**: All the Kinross railways were closed piecemeal: passenger trains to Ladybank ended in 1950, and freight in 1964 when the Dollar line too was closed completely by Beeching; even the Cowdenbeath and Perth line was abandoned in 1970, apparently to simplify the building of a motorway through Glenfarg; this led to Kinross becoming a stop on an express bus service between Perth and Edinburgh. Kinross-shire faded into history in 1975 when the county became part of the huge Perth & Kinross District of Tayside Region; the town council which latterly met above Wilson's solicitor's office was replaced by a powerless community council. Kinross was bypassed in the early 1970s when the second section of the M90 was opened, with a service area west of the town, also providing caravan and camp sites. By then Kinross had acquired large motor auctions, and a Sunday market which exploits the lack of laws restricting Sunday trading in Scotland. By 1985 a highways depot had been built.

**Kinross Hotels Flourish**: By 1970 there were eight hotels, and with the arrival of the M90 came the large new *Windlestrae Hotel*, open by 1977. By 1979 the *Green Hotel* had provided an important leisure centre, with an indoor heated swimming pool, curling rink and squash courts in addition to the golf course. By 1981 the local facilities were those of a small town, as they remain. In the 1980s Mozolowski & Murray began to prefabricate hardwood conservatories, soon opening a permanent show centre at Dalgety Bay, and Koronka Engineering & Tanks were becoming significant in agricultural engineering.

**Cashmere Dyeing and Spinning**: By the 1980s the Dawson group claimed Kinross as the world centre of Cashmere spinning, though this had declined by a third between 1967 and 1976. Again in 1989 the firm had to make 160 Kinross workers redundant. In 1991 Dawson International's Bradford branch sorted the hair from 11 million Inner Mongolian goats, brought it to Kinross to be dyed, blended to any of 10,000 shades by being blown to and fro between gigantic bins, and spun into enough yarn to make 3 million sweaters a year at the firm's Innerleithen and other mills. In 1992, despite the slump, Todd & Duncan was spinning at full capacity in single and two-ply, while China was eyeing the role of Kinross with envy. In 1991 Kinross had 4552 residents, generally well-educated, as in most rural areas. The Sandport caravan site was developed for housing in 1992–93, and in 1992 Presto opened a large new store in Station Road.

**Leisure Developments**: By 1993 the Scottish Centre for Falconry was open to the public at Turfhills. By 1993 the *Windlestrae Hotel* had recently added a leisure club with swimming pool, snooker and fitness suite, a 250-person conference and function suite and video theatre. Meantime Fergusknowe Farm, 1.5 km west of the town, had turned to glasshouses in the mid 20th century, and been deeply excavated for sand and gravel in the 1980s. By 1994 the resulting wet pits had become trout fishing lakes; the upstanding farmstead had been adapted by the Cairns family to form a restaurant and gallery, renamed as Heatheryford. The gardens of Kinross House, open by appointment only in 1986, are now a tourist attraction.

**Seconds First?**: Loch Leven Leisure, opened north of the town in 1992, provides public swimming and squash facilities; a new health centre was built alongside, amid a large Beazer housing estate, which threatens to unite Kinross with Milnathort. A scheme for a 27-unit *'factory shopping'* centre and other developments was submitted in 1994 for a site near the M90 Kinross access – but hasn't happened. In 1995 Kinross had one of the three centres of the big Scottish Motor Auction Group. Loch Leven is still Scotland's premier locale for fishing brown trout; Historic Scotland takes visitors to the castle by boat. The 15-room *Bridgend Hotel* sadly burnt down early in 2001, becoming a write-off, but the long-established hotels continue, and a new *Travelodge* is also open.

## KINTORE

**Map 10, B3**

***Aberdeenshire village,*** *pop. 2050* — OS 38: NJ 7916

The Roman legions briefly camped beside the south bank of the River Don 18 km north-west of its mouth. Nearby Kintore takes its Gaelic name *Ceann-Tor*, *'Head of the Bush'*, from the wild and wooded hills to the west, and evidently began as a hunting seat. It had a thanage from about the 11th century, and gave its name to an Earldom before its charter as a Royal Burgh in 1187. Reinforcing its earlier role, in the late 13th century the Earl of Mar built Hallforest Castle, one of the earliest tower houses, sited 1.5 km south-west of Kintore. Balbithan House, an L-plan tower, was built three centuries later 3 km north-east of Kintore, which was rechartered in 1506, but was among the most lethargic of burghs, its relation to Inverurie as subservient as that of Auldearn to Nairn; it paid no tax in 1535–56. Although by 1619 a parish school was held, Kintore was shown with no more emphasis than *'Hal of Forest'* on Gordon's map of around 1640. Kintore developed very little until a tolbooth was built in 1740, and the Roy map of about 1750 showed only a small nucleus of settlement, on a track connecting Old Aberdeen with Inverurie. The *'Boat of Kintore'* led to a roadless area east of the River Don. From 1762 Kintore lay on a new road from Aberdeen by Tyrebagger Hill to Inverurie; from 1776 it had a post office, and by 1797 it was a post town, connected with the outside world three days a week.

**Canal and Railway: Timber, Stone and Golf**: In 1805 a canal link opened to Aberdeen, but little or no industry followed; the canal was bought and infilled by the Great North of Scotland Railway (GNSR) which laid a track on its alignment, opened with Kintore station in 1854. In 1855 Mitchell & Japp, lessees of a sawmill and woodyard from the Earl of Kintore, lost part to the proposed Alford Valley Railway; for over a century from 1859 Kintore was the junction for this line, which soon became the GNSR's Alford branch. From its early days to at least 1894 an important quarry at Ratch-hill 3 km west of Kintore was served by a lengthy goods siding. But the railway brought little development, and in 1891 the population of Kintore was still under 700. A public hall was built in 1894; Kintore Golf Club was founded in 1911 and provided a basic 9-hole parkland course. In the 1930s George Gandar Dower *(see Dyce)* built a hangar on a grass airstrip at Kintore as an emergency refuge for the new Gandar Dower air services. The village population had risen to some 1150 by 1951, with a tiny secondary school and two hotels.

**Bypassed by Rail**: The branch line lost its passenger trains in 1950; the junction and Kintore station vanished in 1966, at which time the population was about 1100 and falling. By 1967 the former Ratch-hill quarry was full of water. Kintore remained a village throughout its 788 uneventful years as a Royal Burgh, which ended in 1975 along with all other such places, most of them more deserving of the title. However, in 1980 a 1-bay fire station and some new private housing were in evidence. Its proximity to Aberdeen's oil-based development resulted in population growth, and it had three hotels. In the 1980s John Fyfe began to work Tom's Forest Quarry, adjacent to the former Ratch-hill pit, with road access utilising the route of the former Alford railway, but there was little other growth to 1991 when 2028 residents were enumerated, mostly healthy and well-educated. In 1992 the Kintore bakers R Scott & Son ceased trading, with 20 jobs lost.

**Off Road, Into the Air – and Back to Rail?**: Another small housing estate appeared in the 1990s. The dual carriageway A96 bypass, built in 1995–96, gives access to a new small business park at Tavelty, which now includes the base of Grampian Helicopters, and dealers in tanks, pipes, garage doors and garden furniture. The local councils are interested in reopening a railway station at Kintore, which boasts a primary school, two garages, police station, pleasure park, and post office. The golf course now has 18 holes, and the *Torryburn* is the local hotel.

## KIPPEN & Arnprior

**Map 5, C4**

***W. Stirlingshire villages,*** *pop. 800* — OS 57: NS 6594

Between the Gargunnock Hills and the wastes of Flanders Moss 2 km south of the River Forth and 14 km west of Stirling, are an earthwork and an early motte, showing the early importance of the Kippen estate – in the 16th century the seat of the Buchanans of Arnprior. The emparked *'Wester Bruich'* was shown on Pont's map of Stirlingshire, made about 1600. By that time the parish was already extensively developed with farms, and the burn which flows from Kippen Muir was already bridged nearby; above the bridge on the east bank stood the *'Mil of Loch Laggan'*. The Boquhan Burn was also bridged, near the emparked *'Glentyrren'* (Glentirrenmuir), below which was another mill. Although no road was depicted, the bridges imply that there was already a significant routeway to Stirling. Kippen was chartered as a burgh of barony in 1643 under the name of *West Kerse*.

**The Military Road**: In the early 18th century a military road was built to connect Stirling with Dumbarton; this was still the only road when Roy's surveyors mapped the area about 1754, labelling the linear village *'Kippon'*; from there a track wandered across the hills to Fintry. To the north, Flanders Moss was still evidently impassable anywhere west of *'Midd Frew'*; the minor cross road to Doune which circumvented the moss was yet to be built. Attempts to establish a regular tryst failed and the Old Statistical Account simply described Kippen as a *"village"*, but there were five annual fairs in 1797. Heron writing in 1799 put the village population at a mere 300, but besides the fairs there were some weekly markets in December, and some muslin was manufactured. He pointed out that there were then no other villages between Buchlyvie and Gargunnock; certainly in the 1750s there had been little at Arnprior (4 km west).

**Postal Service and Failed Railway**: A post office opened in 1801, and by about 1825 Kippen was the centre for a penny post serving Gartmore. The grandly named Forth & Clyde Railway, opened from Stirling to Buchlyvie and Balloch in 1856, provided a station named Kippen over 1 km from the village. The line served a rural area and never prospered. Although by 1895 there was an inn, Kippen never acquired modern industries. The rail passenger services were ended by the LNER in 1934 and Kippen was only a small village of 700 people in 1951; the line was abandoned by British Railways in 1957.

**Quiet Modern Kippen**: In 1971 a new section of the A811 was built west of the village to speed the passing traffic, using a short section of the former railway alignment. In 1977 Kippen was clearly a satellite of Stirling but had its own facilities, including the *Cross Keys Hotel*, the *Crown* pub/restaurant, a primary school, post office, police office, half a dozen shops and two churches. Several small new housing areas allowed the 1991 population to reach 782. In 1996 a listed wheelwright's shop was saved from demolition, but little else of special note seems to have occurred.

## KIPPFORD

**Map 2, B5**

***Galloway village,*** *pop. 500* — OS 84: NX 8355

Also known as Scaur, this place stands at the tidal mouth of the Urr Water where it flows into the small Rough Firth, a branch of the Solway. The important earthwork of the Mote of Mark had been raised beneath the steep slopes of the 110 m Mark Hill by the seventh century. It was evidently at that time a key centre, by far the most important location in southern Scotland for finds of French pottery of that date, outdoing Whithorn; but it soon faded. Timothy Pont cannot have visited the immediate area, for the Rough Firth was omitted from his map made about 1600, but the names Kipp and Barbarraugh appeared opposite tiny symbols. Evidently the Urr could be forded, giving a name to the village, but the area was still roadless at the time of Roy's survey about 1754. Quarries were opened for a time, small ships were built at Kippford by the mid 19th century and an inn was erected. By the late 19th century a road had been constructed around the coast from Dalbeattie, with a spur to Kippford.

**Catering for Golfers, Barons, Sailors and Caravanners**: By 1951 Kippford's population of some 360 enjoyed the facilities of a small village, with three hotels and an adjacent 9-hole golf course; it was known as a yachting resort, and an inshore lifeboat station was opened in 1966. However a fifth of the 1951 population had been lost by 1971 and the Barnbarroch primary school was closed. By 1980 tourists were offered a caravan and camping site at Barnbarroch, two hotels, a guest house and much B&B accommodation. The original Kippford golf course was closed about the 1960s and overgrown by 1986, when Kippford was very much a yachting resort with a large yacht repair yard and significant retirement development which had brought the population near 400. A pleasant footpath led south through a National Trust for Scotland estate to the Mote of Mark and the seashore hamlet of Rockcliffe. This had 150 people, the area's telephone exchange, craft shops, another caravan site and the *Barons Craig* – a long-established country house hotel, now with 22 rooms. By 1997 a new golf course had been established at Kippford, and small new areas of housing were evident.

## KIRKBEAN & Carsethorn

**Map 2, B5**

***Solway Firth small villages,*** *pop. 300* — OS 84: NX 9759

About 7 km south of New Abbey is a strip of fertile soil between the hill massif of Criffell and the coast of the Solway Firth, on which are the remains of the ancient fort known as McCulloch's Castle. In the 16th century the Z-plan castle of Auchenskeoch was built on the Southwick Burn, and 6 km to the east the contemporary Wreaths Tower. When Pont mapped the Stewartry about 1610, this stood in a well-settled area south of the Kirk of Kirkbean. Nearby were two water mills; later another turned at Preston. Cavens, a small country house, was built in 1752. The Roy map (about 1754) showed Kirkbean as a cluster of huts on the track from New Abbey, which ended 5 km west, at Broadyards by Southwick; later this became a road.

**Gardens, Piracy and Emigrant Steamers**: John Paul Jones, son of a landscape gardener in the coastal gardens of Arbigland House, 2 km south-east of Kirkbean, was born locally in 1747; he soon tired of working in the gardens and went off to become an American, a pirate – and founder of the US Navy! In the mid 19th century a timber jetty at Carsethorn, 1.5 km east of Kirkbean, was served by steam packets to Liverpool, and there many thousands of emigrants embarked for Canada and the Antipodes. Despite this, in 1951 over 300 people still lived in the area, served by basic facilities; but some depopulation and the closure of the hotel and post office had by 1981 left a tiny place of 275 people. By the mid '80s the house and gardens of Arbigland were open to the public. The Kirkbean primary school and the Steamboat Inn at Carsethorn remain open, and for some years *Cavens* has been a small hotel.

## KIRKCALDY

**Map 6, B4**

***Large Fife town,*** *pop. 47,000* — OS 59 & 66: NT 2891

Suburbs: *Dysart, Pathhead & Templehall*

Kirkcaldy stands on a bay on the south coast of Fife. Its odd name which now rhymes with *'toddy'* was first recorded as *Kirkcaladunt*, perhaps *'Fort of the Caledonians'*. The *Caer* element usually signifies a Roman fort, whose most likely site is the cliff-top fort of Dunnikier at nearby Pathhead *(q.v.)*; Roman coins have been found near Kirkcaldy harbour, which lay on the line of a possibly Roman road linking Inverkeithing with Crail. But the name might also mean *'Church of the Culdees'*, the early Christians who are known to have practised there. In 1075 Malcolm III granted Kirkcaldy to Dunfermline church, and at Abbotshall, 1 km inland, was a priory connected with Dunfermline Abbey; perhaps so that Rome might more easily convert the local Culdees from their *'heresy'*. Coal outcropped, and mining was long carried out by the monks, who left many uncharted workings beneath the town.

**Castles, Church, Mills and Baltic Interests**: Balwearie Castle, 3km south-west, was the birthplace in 1214 of the scholar and translator Michael Scot. On a hilltop north of Balwearie is Raith, whose name may stem from the Irish word *Rath*, a fort; it heads a large estate. Kirkcaldy Old parish church was consecrated in 1244; according to Chambers the place was also *"a haven of some note so early as 1315, when David II made the town over to the Abbot of Dunfermline as a burgh of regality"*. The strong Balwearie Castle was built for William Scot in 1463 on the site of the earlier castle. Though the sandy shore was exposed to easterly gales, a farming hinterland encouraged port development, and by the early 16th century, when the Seafield tower was built on the shore 3km to the south (OS 66), Kirkcaldy vessels were trading as far afield as the Baltic; by 1535 the town was making a tiny contribution in burgh taxes. An ideal site for water mills was the steep Den Burn, where the East Bridge Mills turned by about 1560.

**The Royal Burgh's Angel – from the Priory?**: A coastal location and outcrop coal led to no fewer than 23 salt pans being at work by 1573. Kirkcaldy evidently gained a Royal Burgh charter very soon after the Reformation, for it joined the Convention of Royal Burghs in 1574, had a burgh school from 1582, and its landward trading area – wrested from Dunfermline and Inverkeithing – reached Kinglassie. Kirkcaldy presbytery was active by 1593. The good ship *Angel* of Kirkcaldy, specially hired in 1589 to carry James VI's bride Anne from her home in Denmark, is the likely subject of a mural painting that survived forgotten for four centuries in a contemporary merchant's house, then newly built at the Port Brae by the Law family. The ship's name and the ashlar frontage of the house could both originate from that victim of the Reformation, the vanished priory, whose great enclosing wall alone remains.

**Beer, and Battles Far away from the Lang Toun**: The Pont map of west Fife shows that the West Bridge already spanned the Tiel Burn by about 1600; Invertiel Mill and the West Mill also existed, and *'Kirk Caldey'* was already definitely a *lang toun – 'Long Town'* in English. Grain was exported by 1618; Kirkcaldy traders went far afield. By 1625 local merchants were importing Continental beer, finer than the Fife brew, and in 1632 the merchantman *Blessing* of Kirkcaldy was captured in the Mediterranean by Turkish pirates. Kirkcaldy was 16th in tax yield among Scottish burghs in 1639, and it had about 100 ships when re-chartered as a Royal Burgh in 1644.

**Cockly Kirkcaldy supports the Parliament**: In 1645 a Kirkcaldy unit was decimated in a battle at Kilsyth and 200 widows were left; from this, Kirkcaldy's population has been estimated at some 3000. *"In the time of Charles I it was a populous place, with about 100 vessels belonging to it. By its exertions in behalf of the Parliament during the Civil War its prosperity was much reduced"* (Chambers). Even so, in 1655 the Commonwealth Customs investigator Tucker noted that Kirkcaldy shipowners had twelve vessels of up to what was then the large size of 100 tons. He was apparently the first Sassenach traveller to write about the town – and not scathingly as he did of most Fife ports. In 1656 Richard Franck described *"pleasant cockly Carcawdy, a little pretty maritime town built all with stone, where the inhabitants live more upon fish than flesh"*.

**Flax, Fairs and Trouble with Finance and Ferries**: About the time of the Restoration the townspeople turned to flax manufacture, with growing success. By 1663 a coach road existed from the Kinghorn ferry through the lengthening town to Pathhead and Falkland. In that year the Linktown of Abbotshall on the coal outcrop only a kilometre to the south was chartered as a burgh of barony with two annual fairs; its Easter fair or *'Links Market'* became renowned, despite the narrowness of the street in which it was held. By 1684 Kirkcaldy was, briefly, Scotland's leading port for long-distance trade with England, Spain and America, and second only to Bo'ness in Netherlands trade; more than the permissible four ferry boats were in use to connect the town directly with the Lothians, but Kinghorn successfully challenged this abuse. Mismanagement compelled the town council *"to petition the Convention of Royal Burghs for relief"* in 1682; by 1687 its debts were horrendous.

**Port Prosperity draws Adam, and Enter Ceramics**: However, this did not hinder trade, for by 1692 Kirkcaldy was among Scotland's top five ports, and it must have been building work that drew an Angus stonemason to settle in Linktown about that time. His son William Adam was born in 1684, becoming the Royal mason for Scotland, creator of Fort George, a well-respected architect and entrepreneur who designed the original Royal Infirmary of Edinburgh, the House of Dun, and Duff House, eventually moving to Blair near Kelty *(q.v.)*. Meantime in 1694 Lord Raith of the Melville family built the hilltop mansion of Raith House, soon sold to Ferguson of Kirkcaldy. By 1715 there was a post office. The long-lasting Links Pottery, founded by William Adam and William Robertson, was opened in 1714; in the 19th century its products included elaborate earthenware kettles, now rare. The Den brickworks were in operation by 1728. A replacement burgh school was built in 1725 and Kirkcaldy had a new post office from 1729.

**Prosperity and Trade, Salt and Shipbuilding**: Defoe wrote in the 1720s that Kirkcaldy was *"a larger, more populous, and better built town than any on this coast. The streets clean and well paved. It has some considerable merchants in the true sense of the word. There are also several good ships belonging to the town. Great quantities of linen and corn were shipped to England and to Holland, and as these ships return freighted they bring all needful supplies of foreign goods; so that the traders in Kirkcaldy have really a very considerable traffick, both at home and abroad. There are several coal-pits here even close to the very sea, at the west end of the town, and where, one would think, the tide should make it impossible to work them. At the east end of the town is a convenient yard for building and repairing of ships, and several salt-pans."* At that time Kirkcaldy was a main centre for the much-troubled Customs service.

**Famous Sons in Economics and Architecture**: Adam Smith, born in the town in 1723, was later a Glasgow University professor, author of *The Wealth of Nations* and the internationally famous founder of market economics. Five years later in 1728 came the birth of William Adam's son Robert, the greatly renowned architect who designed Register House in Edinburgh, the Royal Society of Arts, and the huge Adelphi development in London, amongst many others. Robert Adam also made measured drawings of Diocletian's palace at Split, and created the delicate interiors of such famous buildings as Syon, Kedleston and Culzean, and dozens more.

**The Development of the Linen Industry**: By 1733 the district – including Dysart and Leslie – produced 160,000 metres of linens annually, mostly handkerchiefs, checks and ticks for export to the West Indies. In 1739 the town council set up an annual July market for linen cloth. Robert Whyte was appointed as a yarn sorter and stockist soon after 1740, and by 1743 a district output of about 300,000m of linen was being authenticated annually; Kirkcaldy had a main linen stamping office by 1760, and a dyehouse was soon built. Roy's map made about 1750 showed a substantial linear settlement with a pier and a coastal road system; several coal mines existed in the Gallatown to Balgonie areas to the north-east near the main road to Cupar *(see Pathhead).*

**A Home Market for Linen**: Local shipping interests had decayed by 1760 when only three tiny vessels were locally owned, but shipbuilding was resumed in 1770. John Fergus, born in Newburgh, moved to Kirkcaldy where he became a key linen manufacturer, his family name commemorated in local streets. Export trade fell after the American revolution of 1773, but James Fergus found a home market for improved ticking. Five radial roads were turnpiked in 1790; by that time Kirkcaldy had expanded greatly. By 1792, 566 looms were at work in the burgh and nearby Abbotshall, where there were two bleachworks. Up till then nearly all the yarn was hand spun by women, but soon they joined the ranks of the weavers, and suitable yarn had mostly to be imported from Germany. About 75% of the town's linen was exported to England, and St Brycedale House was built in the late 18th century on the proceeds by millowner George Heggie.

**Late Eighteenth Century Industries**: In the 18th century corn mills were founded on the Tiel Burn, and in 1795 Speirs' distillery was built on the north side of the Den Burn at East Bridge, then in Dysart parish. At that time, following a burgeoning of trade, 29 ships were locally owned, averaging over 125 tons, and a sawmill was also at work. Two annual fairs were scheduled to be held in 1797, but the Links Market was apparently in abeyance. In 1799 Heron wrote that *"the town consists chiefly of one very long street with linen, leather, cotton spinning, shipbuilding and salt-making industries"*; Abbotshall *"village"* had considerable cotton manufactures and two extensive bleachfields. Heron guessed the population of Kirkcaldy *"and its suburbs"* at nearly 5000. Precocious *'Pet Marjory'* Fleming, born in the town in 1803, became a quite well known child poet and diarist, but sadly died in 1811. She would have seen the body of the Old Kirk being rebuilt in 1806–08, to designs by James Elliott.

**How Not to Run a Bank**: For some reason the generally enterprising town did not develop its own banking firms, but the Dundee Banking Company had a short-lived branch around 1793. Between 1802 and 1810 the doomed Fife Banking Company of Cupar also opened a Kirkcaldy branch. The Glasgow Banking Company (GBC) did likewise in 1809, but with greater success. In 1816 the cantankerous David Morgan became the Bank of Scotland's Kirkcaldy agent in Kirk Wynd; in 1826 he challenged a local linen merchant, David Langdale, to the last duel in Scotland; they fought and Morgan lost. His bank's trade suffered too, especially after linen manufacturer and ex-Provost Walter Fergus persuaded the Union Bank to open a local branch in 1834. The National Bank had built a new branch near the Tolbooth in 1826; this eventually passed to the Royal Bank and remained in use as a bank till 1988.

**Windpower for Mills and More Illegal Ferries**: By 1800 up to a million metres of ticking and other linen was woven annually in the town; the water-powered West Bridge flax mills were built on the Tiel Burn in 1806. By then 1.5 million metres of linen was stamped each year, and ten years later nearly 2 million, including sailcloth. By 1817 some 5000 people worked in the local flax and linen industry; much Riga flax was imported, and most of the output was sold in England. On petition from Kinghorn Town Council the 17 ferry boats illegally operating out of Kirkcaldy were again suppressed by the Commissioners of Supply! Sailcloth had other uses: Thomas Carlyle who taught in Kirkcaldy in 1816–18 remembered *"its flax mill machinery was turned mainly by wind, and curious blue-painted wheels with oblique vanes rose from many roofs"*.

**Spinning and Weaving by Steam**: Meantime the first steam-powered flax spinning mill in Fife had opened in Kirkcaldy in 1807, and by 1818 a local coal mine was using a steam engine. In 1821 steam-powered weaving of white dowlas was introduced, in *"perhaps the first power-loom factory ever erected for linen"* (*Warden*). This cut the cost of the product by a third. Then in 1822 James Aytoun erected a mill to spin tow; another followed in 1826 and a third later. About 1832 he began to spin jute. By 1838 there were ten flax spinning mills, all steam-powered; most flax still came from eastern Europe. By then about 440 looms were at work in the town, whose linen manufacturers owned another 660 elsewhere. By 1842, 13,000 spindles were owned by local manufacturers.

**Whaling and other Industries of the 'Best Town in Fife'**: Locally, whaling began in 1816 with two ships, peaked in 1828 with nine vessels totalling over 3000 tons, then as quickly declined to five in 1834. This was due to town gas replacing whale oil in lighting, both nationally and locally, for a gas supply company built its works in Linktown in the mid 1830s. Kirkcaldy's whaling ended in 1865. By 1825 when the Chamber of Commerce was founded, Kirkcaldy's penny post also served Leslie and Markinch and there were four breweries, all in the Links/Bridgeton area. Alexander Dowie built coaches in Kirkcaldy in the early years of the 19th century, for by 1825 it was an important coaching centre, with routes running to Glasgow, Kinross, Anstruther, via Cupar to Tayport, and to Perth, as well as to the Pettycur ferry. In the town centre in the 1820s the buildings were, according to Chambers, *"tall and elegant, resembling Edinburgh; and the shops are equally well-furnished and brilliant with the better sort of the metropolis. A stranger is, altogether, apt to be surprised at the appearance of high respectability and opulence presented by this burgh, which is, beyond all dispute, the best town in Fife. The harbour is not very good. It has, however, a considerable trade. About 40 vessels belong to the port."*

**Canvas, Flint Grinding and Furniture**: Michael Nairn began canvas weaving south of Coal Wynd in 1828. The tidal harbour, placed under trustees in 1829, was improved from 1843 when the building of a small wet dock was begun; but only a narrow road divided buildings on the west side of the High Street from the harbour, hence its name *'Sailor's Walk'*. A new school was also built in 1843; another charity school, built in Charlotte Street by local philanthropist Philp in 1850, later became the Masonic Hall. The fortnightly *Fifeshire Advertiser* was founded in 1838 or 1845 (sources differ). By 1833 some of the mills on the Tiel Burn were calcining and grinding flint for the local potteries; Balwearie mill was so converted after 1855. A great waterwheel from one of these mills has been restored at New Lanark *(q.v.)*. Meantime from 1827 Samuel Barnet & Son had built up a cabinet-making business in Linktown; Alexander H McIntosh worked there for 15 years, founding his own firm in 1869; it made top quality furniture, equipped hotels and ships, won many awards and still survives. The Barnets also founded Barnet & Morton as engineers and retailers.

**Railway development and the Port**: In 1845 Kirkcaldy had a weekly corn market, and its Corn Exchange was built in 1859, but used as such for under 30 years, due to the impact of railways. At that time Methven & Son's pottery in the Links used clay brought from a pit west of Pratt Street by a tramway, hence the low narrow arch, built to maintain the connection when the Edinburgh & Northern Railway came to the town in 1847. The railway relied at first wholly on ferries to the Lothians via Burntisland *(q.v.)* but was joined by land with the national system the following year – very indirectly, via Perth – and soon renamed the Edinburgh Perth & Dundee. The Kirkcaldy Harbour branch was in use from 1848; it was graded at 5% (1 in 20) – so steep that in both 1901 and 1954 engines ran away and fell from the pier into the harbour! The town council used its own shunting locomotive at the harbour until the 1950s. No private sidings existed until after 1855; no linen mill had one. A small mansionhouse named Bennochy, built by 1824, adjoined the station and had become the *Railway Inn* by 1853.

**Floorcloth, Ropes and Fishing Nets**: In 1847 Michael Nairn built at the east end of the town an *"extensive establishment"* for making floorcloth (painted linen), and expanded this about 1860, dominating the trade by 1862. The processes – fully described by Bremner – were almost all manual even in 1869, when about 200 people were employed. About 1865 Nairn's one-time partner James Shepherd joined Beveridge in another floorcloth enterprise. Meanwhile the making of soft ropes was begun at Invertiel in 1850 by a local twine manufacturer, whose ropewalk was soon extended to 374m in length; in 1896 it became the Forth & Clyde Roperie and started making hard fibre ropes *(see Hay & Stell)*. N & L Lockhart began to make twine and nets in 1854, and about 1865 built a factory with 64 net-looms, becoming the second largest fishing-net manufacturers in Scotland, as befitted a port of registry, whose letters KY adorned most Fife fishing boats.

**Kirkcaldy Linen in 1864**: Linen grew little for two decades, but the Nicol Street flax spinning mills had been opened by 1853 under the name *'Abbotshall Mills'*. West Bridge mills were rebuilt on a grand scale as a steam-powered spinning mill in 1855–56. In 1864 nine linen firms used steam power, in all having some 1460 workers, 12,000 spindles, and 400 power looms. Spinning firms were Swan Brothers (also based in Kinghorn), J & W Hendry, R & A Aytoun, and A G Malcolm. Power weaving firms were John Jeffrey, and Robert Wemyss. Several bleaching and dyeing works, some large for the day, were pleased in 1867–68 when a piped water supply was provided, from the first of several reservoirs formed on the Lothrie Burn north-west of Leslie; sewers were soon laid in the town streets. Textiles continued to expand, some flax mills changing to jute spinning.

**The Peak of Kirkcaldy Linen, and its first Carpets**: The Abden linen works opened in 1864; in 1865 came the Bennochy flax spinning works by Abbotshall Church, known in 1896 as the Bennochy Net & Twine Works and still later as Abbotshall Mills, the earlier Nicol Street mills of that name becoming Halley's dyeworks. In 1867 the 18 flax, jute and hemp factories in the Kirkcaldy area had 3900 workers; Bremner noted *"Kirkcaldy is the chief seat of the trade in Fife, with some fine mills"*. The St Mary's canvas factory beside the harbour was added in 1869 by Michael Nairn & Co. The Abbotshall Factory, later hidden behind the Olympia Arcade, soon followed. Much later in its chequered career it became a tenpin bowling centre; it was demolished in 1994. But cotton hit the town's linen industry, which by 1880 had only some 2000 workers. However, by 1891 over 27,000 people lived in Kirkcaldy (including Pathhead). In the late 19th century Kirkcaldy also developed into a carpet-weaving centre, although in 1901 the Victoria Carpet Company moved from comparatively new premises in Victoria Road to Kidderminster. By 1896 Robert Wemyss & Co had lately built the Caledonian Linen Mills in the historically but oddly named Prime Gilt Box Street; later these became Meikles' carpet factory.

**Engineering Globe Champion?**: The Dunnikier Foundry of Robert Douglas was opened beside the railway line west of Den Road near Smeaton Street about 1855 to make munitions for the Crimean War, later specialising in rice, sugar, jute and colliery machinery, especially for export. In 1863 it built the first Corliss steam engine in Europe. It had been enlarged under Douglas & Grant by 1896, making horizontal steam engines, colliery winding gear and boilers, sent by rail to the harbour for export; the firm had their own shunting engine and about 1902 built the great winding engine for the country's deepest pit, the Mary at Lochgelly, and about 1907 two for the Wellesley at Buckhaven. Across the railway from 1865 was John Key's Whitebank Foundry, making marine engines and employing about 200 men by 1869; he also operated a shipyard at Kinghorn *(q.v.)*, but the foundry closed in 1884. James Brown was making small printing presses by 1869, and by 1885 the firm was building steam engines for use in distilleries. Another Victorian foundry was J W Mackie, making mangles bearing the immodest trademark *Globe Champion*! The Tiel engineering works began around 1870. A steel pipe works active in 1896 later became the site of the fire station.

**The Congested Harbour peaks – and declines**: In 1854 the 3-masted sailing ship *Windhover* was built by Brown of Kirkcaldy; but shipbuilding ended, just when Kirkcaldy's coal exports were growing with the development of the central Fife coalfield; by 1866 it was the fourth coal export port in Scotland, its tiny harbour highly congested. The fishing also declined as pollution of the Firth increased, and as prophesied by an early opponent of the railway, the locally owned merchant fleet also faded, from 95 vessels totalling over 10,000 tons in 1831 to only 18 ships in 1883.

**New Facilities and the Printing Industry**: A telegraph service was introduced in 1868–70, and a public telephone exchange was installed in 1882. A second local newspaper, the weekly *Fife Free Press and Kirkcaldy Times* was founded in 1871 (some time after 1918 the town name was dropped from the title). As the population rose, the West Primary School, designed by well-known architect Rowand Anderson, was built in 1874–80. The West Bridge Brewery existed in 1878–79, as shown on the fine large-scale maps of the burgh engraved for the town council in 1880 by Archibald Beveridge, a local lithographic printer since 1845, who had built a factory near the Old Kirk in 1877. On his death in 1892 the firm was bought by its manager Henry Allen with a partner, and despite a disastrous fire in 1900 Allen alone rebuilt the printing business. This soon became well known as *'Allen Litho'* and did printing work for Webb seeds and Rowntrees chocolates; they also printed and bound books. Meantime the very fine Gothic St Brycedale Church was built in 1880–81. The *Grand Theatre* was also in use in Kirk Wynd by 1889 when it burned down; then for fifteen years or more, drama and variety was presented in the Corn Exchange, later a silent cinema.

**Cabinets, Football and Linoleum**: In 1879 A H McIntosh – who already made and fitted reproduction furniture for hotels and ships – bought premises at Victoria Road, opening the Victoria Cabinet Works alongside; imported hardwood logs arrived by rail for lengthy seasoning. From 1888 Whitebank was included, enabling an extension. McIntosh's mansion-house, built beside the factory in 1892, eventually became the *Victoria Hotel* in 1946. Raith Rovers Football Club was formed in 1883, and after roving for some years settled in 1891–92 at Stark's Park, named after its owner, a local farmer and inn-keeper; in 1902 they became Fife's first Scottish League club, and Stark's Park main stand was built in 1922. From floorcloth manufacture came the linoleum industry, discussed in more detail under Pathhead, where its manufacture began in the 1870s. For 85 years the burgh – which by then embraced both places – was to enjoy the smelly distinction of being the linoleum producing capital of the world. The jute backing came from Dundee and cork was imported from Portugal; the filling was sawdust, milled near Bo'ness and in Edinburgh. Major changes were altering the town's character, for with all-round expansion, especially in mining, the population of Fife was growing rapidly; Kirkcaldy (including Pathhead) had 23,500 people in 1881 and 34,000 in 1901. The prominent Victoria Road (St Andrews) church opened in 1903, built of red sandstone from the West of Scotland. Growth continued up to the 1914 war, as the large areas of Victorian and Edwardian villas attest.

**Barry's Linoleum**: By 1890 Barry, Ostlere were in the linoleum business in Kirkcaldy, absorbing Shepherd's of Pathhead in 1899 to become Barry, Ostlere & Shepherd (BO&S). By 1896 their National Works, which made both floorcloth and linoleum, stood near Bennochy Bridge; the Walton works was named after the new product's inventor from Staines. The nearby Caledonia works were between the railway station and Forth Avenue North; in Forth Avenue South were the Forth and Abbotshall works. In 1900 BO&S extended the Walton factory into the big works illustrated by Hay & Stell, to make the dearer

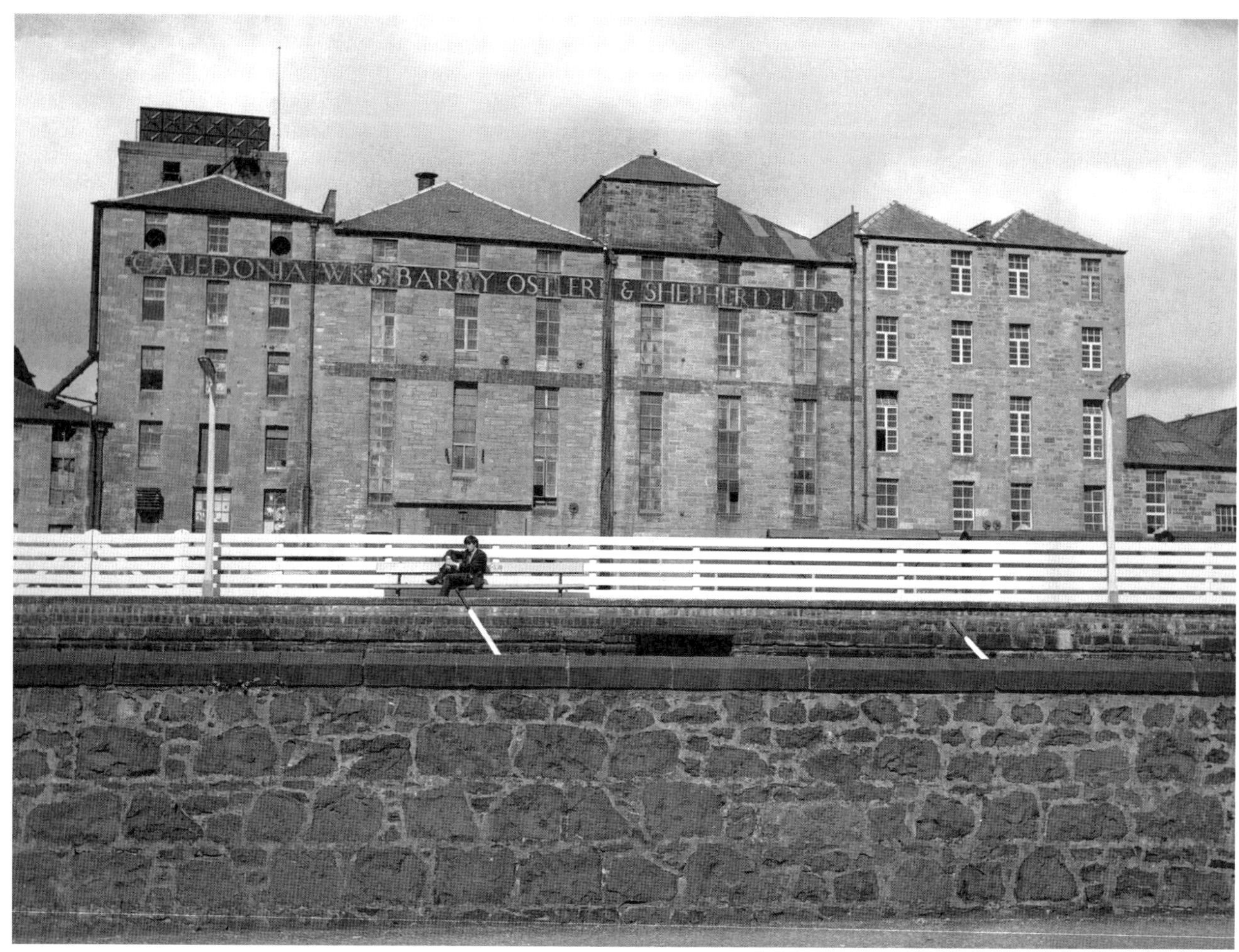


*The late 19th century Caledonian linoleum works of Barry, Ostlere & Shepherd; they were demolished in the 1960s.(RCAHMS / JRH)*

inlaid linoleum to meet an increasingly affluent market; the firm (later called Barry Staines) built a works power station in Forth Avenue South about 1930, and made much use of rail transport.

**Milling and Malting**: In 1896 the West Mills almost beneath the Tiel railway viaduct produced flour. By the 1880s railway sidings had been provided off the harbour branch for Spiers' East Bridge distillery, but by 1886 this had again become a flour mill and maltings for Robert Hutchison & Co, who built the Victoria maltings farther inland beside the railway about 1890. Meantime local brewing faded. James Hogarth Ltd, flour millers nearer the station, were busy by around 1900, their rail siding crossing Bennochy Road. About that time pitch was made and exported by Ravenscraig Chemicals.

**Seafield Harbour and a Railway to Cowdenbeath**: In 1894 Murray's Handbook noted Kirkcaldy's principal industries *as "cloth, floorcloth, and linoleum factories, iron works, engineering works, and pottery works; it now possesses a large shipping business in coals, etc."*. It was because of the smallness of Kirkcaldy's old harbour that the Seafield harbour, a crude early mass concrete structure intended for coal exports, was under construction south of Linktown in 1890... when it was bought out by opposing interests from Burntisland, and work stopped forever! However, from 1896 the NBR's freight-only Kirkcaldy & District Railway connected Invertiel via Auchtertool with the mines of Cowdenbeath. In 1903–06 the original harbour was improved for the last time with a second, outer dock bounded by public rail sidings. Imports then comprised mainly cork, linseed oil and whiting for linoleum production; exports included linoleum, coal, paper and potatoes. Coasting vessels were operated by three shipping lines serving London, Leith and Hull.

**The Civic Centre takes Shape**: An elaborate Sheriff Courthouse designed by James Gillespie was built in 1891–94, and a large new building for the High School was opened in St Brycedale Avenue in 1894, as was the fine red sandstone Swan Memorial YMCA. Two hotels, the *George* and *National*, were open in 1894. A green field became the site for the stone-built *Station Hotel* about 1899, the year that the adjoining Adam Smith Halls were completed, including Beveridge's public library bequest. A fine new Police Station, built of stone from Grange quarry at Burntisland, was opened in 1902, the same year that an attractive new Head Post Office was opened in Hunter Street; in 1913 a new TA HQ for Fife was built nearby. Meantime by 1896 the former *Railway Inn* had become Balsusney House, which was demolished after the 1914–18 war to become the site for the imposing War Memorial and its gardens, overlooked by the cultural facilities gifted to the town by Michael Nairn the younger: the Museum and Art Gallery designed by J S Mackay, which opened in 1925 and subsumed earlier collections, and the adjoining Central Library of 1928. From 1929 further education was available in the evenings at a Technical School, built beside the High School in St Brycedale Avenue.

**Recreational Developments**: Beveridge Park, a bequest of linen manufacturer Michael Beveridge, was begun in 1890; the Teuchit Mire was dug out to form the shapely lake round which the fine park was laid out, opening in 1892. Kirkcaldy golf club, founded in 1904, laid out an attractive 18-hole course at nearby Balwearie. The 2000-seat *King's Theatre* was built in 1904, ventilation being provided by a sliding roof! Later it was called the *Hippodrome* and by 1930 when talking film equipment was fitted, the *Opera House*; from 1937 it became in turn *Regal, ABC, Cannon* and *ABC*! By about 1908 the *Palace Cinema* was open beside the tramway terminus at Whytescauseway and Park Place. Other of the many cinemas for which Kirkcaldy became renowned were the *Gaumont (later Odeon)* in the High Street and the *Raith* in Link Street.

**Lang Toun Electricity and Narrow Trams**: Meantime the town council's coal-fired electric power station in Victoria Road was built in 1899–1903, its rail siding being in use for coal reception until the generators stopped turning in 1946, then for cable drums for a decade. The associated town council tramway system was linear; its gauge of 3'6" (107cm) and the double-decker trams were narrow, as was the *'lang toun'* itself. A single-line tramway from Linktown through the High Street to Gallatown via The Path was opened in 1903. The Victoria bridge across the Den to Sinclairtown was completed in 1902, enabling a double-track line to be laid on the near-parallel inland route of Victoria Road and Whytescauseway, with a branch to Beveridge Park.

**Industry in the early 20th Century**: In 1914 Nairn's St Mary's canvas factory was greatly expanded, and eventually held some 200 looms, making all the canvas for the Pathhead firm's floorcloth; Melville Brodie Engineering still built floorcloth printing machines in 1921. The US navy took over the harbour opposite in the 1914–18 war, when McIntosh made aircraft wings and Douglas & Grant's Dunnikier Foundry made capstans. In 1923 they built No.739 (now in the Museum of Scotland in Edinburgh), one of their last mill engines, for Glentana mill at Alva, but went into voluntary liquidation in 1926. Their former premises were taken over by Nairns as a mill to make roofing felt, using wood-pulp, rags and waste paper, and to serve their *'Congoleum'* works. The builders George Smith & Sons had their Victoria stone-dressing works nearby; the Invertiel quarry owners Alex Birrell & Sons were also farmers. Around 1920 the Bank of Scotland funded heavy investment by linoleum makers Barry, Ostlere & Shepherd.

**The Esplanade and the Links Market**: The sea wall with its spacious Esplanade was built in 1922–23 by the Town Council *"to relieve unemployment during the great trade depression"*, but was placed rather too far down the beach, which thereby lost its attraction. However, with a vast mining hinterland to draw on, the annual April *Links Market* was revived on the new Esplanade. It soon became the largest street funfair in Europe, the spring rendezvous of the Scottish Showmen's Guild.

**Inter-Urban Tramway – Beaten by Buses**: Interworking with the Wemyss tramway system from 1906 took Kirkcaldy trams to Leven and Wemyss trams to Kirkcaldy, and in 1911 a branch reached Dysart. At their peak the average local person was making a hundred tram journeys a year. From 1927 bus routes focused on the town in a pattern very similar to the coaching routes of the 1830s, a very meagre and exposed bus station being created on the Esplanade. As the buses began to cream off the passengers, the town council warned off the bus operators from competing with the trams – despite their lack of legal powers to do so! But from 1928 Walter Alexander bought out the many small local bus companies, and on closure of the tramways in 1931 officially took over their routes on behalf of the council. Alexander built large bus garages south of the Esplanade in 1930 and 1938, converting the adjacent Tiel engineering works for bus maintenance.

**Furnishing the Queens and Progress in Services**: Although the town was still important for linens, weaving gradually declined, and the Methven's Links pottery closed in 1928–30. The burgh had 44,000 people in 1921, declining slightly in the following decade. At this time, when most industries were in such deep depression that 1922 seemed like a picnic, a substantial public abattoir was erected in the short Oriel Road in 1932. McIntosh made domestic furniture, fitted out the liner *Empress of Japan*, weathered the slump, and recovered by making furniture for the cabins and public rooms in the great liners *Queen Mary*, 1934–36, and later *Queen Elizabeth* – but after fitting out the *Maid of the Loch* they abandoned ship fitting, just in time! A new fire station was built on the site of the steel pipe works. In 1935–36 St Brycedale House was enlarged and opened as the Hunter Hospital, endowed by a local builder. A failed chemical works south of Invertiel was replaced by a lido in 1936, though this lasted only until 1948. Marks & Spencer opened a modest store in 1938 (it had been enlarged twice by 1990). Work on the imposing Town House, begun in 1937 to designs by Carr & Howard, was stopped by the war in 1939, its basement being used as a static water tank. In 1946 the *Palace Cinema* in Whytescauseway burned down, its site later being used for a stone-clad insurance office built about 1970.

**Seafield, Sweeties – and Carpet Comeback**: The large Seafield Colliery was sunk south of Linktown between 1954 and 1957; its shafts were to be 558 m deep and its reserves in 1955 were said to be the greatest in Scotland, at 350 million tonnes. But difficulties soon caused work on the deep Limestone Coal Group to be abandoned, and the shallower but steeply inclined Productive Coal Measures were worked seaward at increasing depths beneath the Forth. For some years over 2000 miners were employed, and by 1970 7600 tonnes a day were being raised, but the profitability of the pit – which in its later years provided pulverised coal for power stations – was often questioned. As the demand for whisky returned, Hutchison's Harbour Maltings were expanded repeatedly through the post-war period, although the firm closed the small Victoria Maltings about 1965. Alma Confectionery was started about 1960 in the former lido by a Maciocia, one of the local Italian community. James Meikle & Co of Dysart bought the Caledonian Linen Mills in 1956, and moved their spool Axminster carpet and rug making plant from Dysart. Meikles bought in yarn until 1967 when they opened a new wool spinning and dyeing works at Dysart. In their heyday the firm exported to 34 countries and reached a total of some 650 employees, including a Tillicoultry branch.

**Developing as a Regional centre**: Between 1955 and 1975 most of Kirkcaldy's many cinemas closed one by one, but in many respects the town was developing as a service centre. In 1961 when the nationally owned Alexander bus empire (*see Camelon & Larbert*) was split into three, Kirkcaldy became the headquarters of Fife buses, and a new town bus station was laid out. New buildings for the railway passenger station were opened in 1965. In the 1960s too the first BHS store in Scotland was opened in Kirkcaldy High Street, and the town acquired central Fife's trunk telephone exchange at Wemyssfield and its telephone maintenance depot at Hayfield. However, in 1965 the two local newspapers were merged under the junior title of the *Fife Free Press*, whose printing works moved out to Mitchelston from Kirk Wynd, where new editorial offices were built.

**New Public Buildings**: The Town House was eventually completed in 1956, ending use of the villa called Stanley Park. A Technical College was opened in 1958 in the former Technical & High School buildings when the latter was moved out to Dunnikier Way; the 1894 building was demolished, and on its site was built a tall and ugly block, unusual for its paternoster lift. Balwearie Secondary School, opened on the old Links Pottery claypits site in 1964, then took over the role of High School for the original burgh area. Beside the little Victoria Hospital of about 1900 was built the first major acute hospital in Fife, opened around 1960 under the same name, and a largely new maternity hospital was built on to the mansion-house of Forth Park in the 1970s. The YMCA moved out to Templehall; in 1972 its Kirk Wynd premises became offices. In 1971 what was claimed to be the first general industrial museum in Scotland was opened by the town council at Forth House, but it was not well promoted and lasted only a few years. The Adam Smith Halls were converted into the fine Adam Smith Theatre in 1973.

**Linoleum Troubles create Industrial Estates**: The cartel operated by the Linoleum Manufacturers Association was forced into competition in 1961 by the Restrictive Practices Act of 1960, leading to price cuts; the situation was worsened by the advent of cheap tufted carpeting. Nairns survived at Pathhead *(q.v.)*, but Barry Staines – the Kirkcaldy half of the industry – collapsed in 1964. The steep decline of linoleum led the town council to create suburban industrial estates; Babygro (children's clothing manufacturers), grain warehouses and concrete product makers were soon established at Hayfield. The Victoria Cabinet Works were largely demolished soon after A H McIntosh, then Scotland's largest furniture manufacturers, moved in 1970 to large new works at Mitchelston, the site of most other major local developments (*see Pathhead*). About 1974 a government office building took its place at Victoria Road. The harbour public sidings closed in 1967, and after rail grain traffic at Kirkcaldy ceased, the steep harbour branch railway was closed in 1984.

**Shopping Develops**: Meantime most of Barry's various works were soon demolished, the power station becoming the site of Laidlaw's garage, others providing for the Forth Avenue gardens, a fine station car park, and later the College of Nursing. The Mercat covered shopping centre of 1972 with its Tesco store was adjoined by a new covered swimming pool, opened in 1973. A second covered mall – replacing the premises of lately defunct removal contractors Fifeshire Posting, hence *'The Postings'* – opened in 1979 with a new William Low store, overlying major underground extensions to the 1960s Littlewoods store. Two multi-storey car parks were built near the Mercat between 1972 and 1982. After 1975 Barry's imposing head office building, Forth House, was converted to District Council use. Attached weaving sheds were demolished, later becoming the site of another garage.

**Collapse of the Linen Industry, and Lost Hopes**: In 1972 A & N Lockhart employed 100 at their Abbotshall spinning mill, N Lockhart & Sons had 80 linen weavers at Links Street and the Robert Stocks Abden linen mill in Linktown employed 100. This soon closed and about 1974 became a minor retail complex under the Stocks name; within a year or so the linen industry had vanished from the old town. West Bridge mills made cordage until they too closed in 1974, becoming derelict, and the very lengthy but Dickensian Forth and Clyde Roperie

*The Kirkcaldy Ring, depicting the varied activities of the town. Its sculptor Doug Cocker (left) is pictured with Cllr. Ballantyne at its unveiling in 1991.* *(RS)*

at Seafield was closed and demolished in the same fateful year. In 1974 the author was present when the new Fife Regional Council narrowly chose Glenrothes for its headquarters despite the best efforts by local councillors and officials (including himself as Planning Officer), to attract them to Kirkcaldy. In 1978 Kirkcaldy Technical College was promoted in status, becoming Fife College of Technology. The shopping centre drifted southwards, with a Safeway supermarket built about 1974 beside a newly extended Nicol Street.

**Industrial Change, Rolls-Royce Expert – and Decline**: The printers Allen Litho entered electronic picture scanning in 1962, and remained family-owned until 1988 when Inglis Paul of Falkirk bought the firm, renaming it Inglis Allen. In the 1970s Stewart Miller from Kirkcaldy became the Rolls-Royce engineer responsible for fitting the RB211 jet engine into the Boeing 757 airliner, and by 1994 headed the firm's Aerospace Group. Around 1980 Paul's Malt of Ipswich took over and extended the large Holmes maltings of Robert Hutchison. This left Hutchison as independent flour millers across the road at East Bridge. In 1972 James Meikle & Co employed over 600 people on two sites, but ceased carpet weaving in 1980 when the pound was very high due to the over-hasty exploitation of North Sea oil – the site soon redeveloped for private housing.

**Economic Disaster**: The town's last small iron and brass foundry – John Leitch & Co, established in 1921, which had largely made manhole covers of *'Kirkcaldy Pattern'* – closed in the early 1980s. Beatties Bakery had employed 200 people in 1972 in Coal Wynd, but closed about 1984, almost the same time as Halley's dyeworks. Flax spinning ended when the large stone-built Bennochy mill was closed and demolished in 1985, soon replaced by the private flats of Abbots' Mill. The council-owned abattoir was also closed about then. Two of the three faces at Seafield colliery were lost following the miners' strike of 1984–85; the pit was closed in 1988 and its surface works demolished in 1989. Unemployment – which already stood above the high average for Scotland – reached crisis proportions, and academics calculated that between 1985 and 1990 the Kirkcaldy area had fallen in economic prosperity from 198th to 277th out of 280 British towns. Alma Confectionery took over Keiller of Dundee in 1989, and moved their HQ from Seafield to a new factory in Glenrothes in 1990; the firm failed in 1992 with the loss of its remaining 73 Kirkcaldy jobs. The Holmes Maltings ceased production. Although milling, concrete products, printing, clothing, and plastic goods manufacture continued, in the wider District 6000 people were unemployed, because only Glenrothes had *'sunrise'* industries.

**Services Struggle under Industrial Collapse**: The town's small department store, patched together over the years by Barnet & Morton, was taken over by the House of Fraser as Arnotts in the 1970s; but it was closed in 1988, joining a growing number of vacant shops due to overprovision of new floorspace and the rapid decline in local spending power. The *Station Hotel*, once the town's largest, was closed in the mid 1980s, but reopened as the Station Court nursing home in 1990 – indicative of the town's fast-ageing population. The bus maintenance workshops were closed with the loss of about 55 jobs in 1991, when Stagecoach of Perth took over the Fife buses. In 1992 the Co-op, until the 1970s an independent society, closed its modern and substantial town centre store; the old Hunter Hospital was also closed in 1992. However, at least education was growing: a new College of Nursing and Midwifery was opened in 1986 on the site of a Barry works (by 1996 it was the School of Nursing and Midwifery of Dundee University). The steadily expanding Fife College had over 6000 students in 1990–91; its building crafts were taught in Nairns' former canvas factory near the harbour where, commerce having died, a major dockside housing development by Morrisons began in 2000.

**Communications Revolutions and Seafront Improvements**: The railway station's main building burned out in 1988, an attractive though cramped replacement being opened in 1991 when the population (including Dysart, Pathhead and Templehall) was remarkably steady at a balanced 47,155. In a hectic weekend in 1997 Railtrack demolished the 150-year old stone arch across Nicol Street and replaced it by a precast concrete bridge on the original abutments. Kirkcaldy telephone exchange, which employed about 80 people in 1989, acquired 75 new jobs in 1990, its 125 operators using electronic techniques to deal with 9 million *London area* directory enquiries annually; Fife enquiries were transferred to Dundee! The central portion of the High Street was finally pedestrianised and repaved in 1990. In 1992–93 much European investment helped to create a scarcely needed dual carriageway along the

Esplanade, and thanks to Kirkcaldy Civic Society new public gardens were created at Volunteers' Green, a former drying green; the extensive but grotty surface car parks were greatly improved. Redevelopment of the Seafield Colliery site for housing began in 1993.

**Business, Shopping and Football Developments**: In 1989 the Kirkcaldy and Dunfermline Chambers of Commerce merged as *Fife Chamber of Commerce & Industry*, based in Kirkcaldy. In 1990 the well-run Museum and Art Gallery drew 46,500 visitors, and was twice improved by 1998 with an attractive shop and cafe. Limited shopping investments in 1990 concentrated on indoor markets, one successfully replacing the large but closed Woolworths; the second phase of the Mercat was slow to let. In 1994 the former Head Post Office counters were transferred to Low's superstore, which soon became a Tesco; the GPO building became the *Auld Post Hotel*, opened by Maciocia in 1997. First Division Raith Rovers won promotion to the Premier League against Dunfermline in 1993 in front of 6500 spectators. They fell back in 1994, but beat Celtic to win the League Cup at Ibrox in front of 45,000 people – including a fifth of the Kirkcaldy townsfolk – putting them into the UEFA Cup, performing credibly against mighty Bayern Munich! But Stark's Park was cramped, sloping and short of seating. In 1996 Barr Construction levelled the pitch and built large stands at either end; but luck ran out, Rovers gained no place in the enlarged Premier League of 2000 and are now struggling.

**Local Government, Shops and Offices on the Move**: In 1996 the District Council disappeared into the new Glenrothes-based Fife Council (only an area committee carried on in Kirkcaldy). Thomson Brothers, ironmongers since 1870, traded in the centre until 1994 when, having bought up similar businesses elsewhere in Scotland and with a total staff of 170, they moved to new premises at Gallatown. Until 1995 the National Trust for Scotland maintained a regional office in Kirkcaldy; then the work was transferred back to Edinburgh. In 1995 the ex-Safeway supermarket was closed by the Argyll Group, whose plans for a new store at Oriel Road had been sadly foiled by the planning system. When an attractive new Jobcentre was opened in Hunter Street in 1995 as many as 50 staff were moved in from other premises.

**Central Kirkcaldy's changing role**: In 1997 Tesco closed their original Kirkcaldy store, which after reconstruction emerged as a new Woolworths. In 1997 Inglis Allen printers – who employed 150 people in Kirkcaldy, Falkirk and Tillicoultry – printed Historic Scotland's *'Buildings at Risk'* bulletins, were expanding their exports, and installed a German-made Heidelberg Speedmaster colour press to print calendars and corporate in-house magazines. The *'B'* listed National Bank building of 1826 – long empty – was reconditioned in 1999, and new shops and flats replaced long-derelict buildings at High Street/Kirk Wynd; other empty shops were filling up, but the last commercial cinema, in the listed building originally the *King's Theatre*, closed late in 2000 due to competition from the new Halbeath multiplex. Kirkcaldy proper is no longer an industrial area but a compact centre for shopping, education and health, among its best features the Art Gallery/Museum and Beveridge Park. Central hotels include the 35-roomed *Parkway*, the *Abbotshall, Old Post* and *Victoria*.

## KIRKCOLM

**Map 1, B4**

***Small Galloway village****, pop. 350* — OS 82: NX 0268

About 9km north-west of Stranraer a sheltered valley and the delta of its small stream form a favourable site for settlement near the shores of Loch Ryan. Pont's map made around 1610 showed many ferm touns, and a mill up-stream of Kirkcolm kirk; 5km to the north-west stood the impressive 15th century Carsewall castle, then surrounded by trees; nowadays little remains of this structure. Two kilometres beyond was the sandy cove of *'Poirt of Garvellan'*, now spelt Gavillan, described by Tucker in 1655 as *"a creek, whither boats come and go to and from Ireland"*. The Roy map made in the 1750s showed the kirk in a trackless area of ferm touns, and no road nearer than Leswalt, 5km to the south. Sir John Ross, born in the parish in 1777, became famed as an Arctic explorer *(see Stranraer)*. The lack of roads had evidently been remedied by about 1790 when a planned village was built at Kirkcolm, having about 30 houses by 1792, when most contained *"tradesmen"* and public houses.

*Corsewall Point Lighthouse, near Kirkcolm – designed by Robert Stevenson and first lit in 1816. Automated in the 1990s, its keepers' houses have been turned into a small hotel.* *(JRH)*

**Lighthouse, Tourism and Depopulation**: Corsewall Point lighthouse, the first to mark the southern entrance to the Firth of Clyde, was built on the low cliffs 1.5km north-west of the castle ruins by the Northern Lighthouse Board and first illuminated in 1816. Railways and industry never came to Kirkcolm, but there was an inn and a population of almost 850, with a small secondary school and two tiny hotels serving some 1600 people in the north Rhinns. At Marian Port, 2 km to the south, was a pier which by 1978 had been replaced by a jetty 300m farther south, later described as a slipway. But rural depopulation had hit especially hard, and by 1971 only 440 people lived in Kirkcolm. The secondary school had been closed by 1976, but a caravan site was open on the coast 3km south of the village. By 1981 the resident population was down to 350, with the facilities of a small village remained, the modest *Corsewall Arms Hotel* having been lately enlarged. The lighthouse was automated about 1994, and its keepers' houses are now the STB 6-roomed *Corsewall Lighthouse Hotel*; the inn and post office are still active.

## KIRKCONNEL

**Map 2, A3**

***Dumfriesshire village,*** *pop. 2350* OS 71: NS 7312

The ancient church of St Connel stood on a hillside above the upper River Nith, and was marked as *'Kirkconnell'* on Timothy Pont's map made about 1600; there was then a mill where the Grain Burn met the Nith. By about 1754 the Roy map showed the new *'Kirk of Kirkconnell'* and a few scattered hamlets on what was then a notoriously inadequate road from Sanquhar to New Cumnock. A drove road led north over the hills past the *'Old Kirk'*. Kirkconnel began to grow due to coal mining at least as early as 1794, a woollen spinning mill was built around 1800, and the village gained its first post office about 1825. The Knockenjig pit was sunk around 1840, with water-powered drainage. The arrival of a station on the main line of the Glasgow & South Western Railway in 1850 achieved little, for despite the coalfield being leased in 1886 by young James McConnel, by 1891 there were only 500 people in the village.

**Coal Mining Prospers – and Fails**: The sinking of the major Fauldhead mine near the station in 1896 soon brought a fragile prosperity, and a Co-op society was established; in 1911 a second pair of shafts was sunk nearby and a gasworks was provided. Riverside Terrace of 1913 improved on earlier mean row houses, and Kirkconnel with its 1920s and later satellite Kelloholm grew into a large village, with 3300 people by 1931. Bairds, who had taken over the coalfield in 1925, built pithead baths for Fauldhead in 1933. The NCB's Rigg drift mine 3km to the west worked from 1949 to 1966. By 1951 Kirkconnel had 4500 people, and average village facilities plus a secondary school, though this was subsequently closed. The Fauldhead mine produced 1000 tonnes of high-sulphur coal a day until loss of its main market with the dieselisation of British Railways led to closure in 1968. The last coal mine, the cheaply developed Roger Colliery of 1953, still provided 260 jobs in 1977, ceasing operations in 1980.

**Kirkconnel in Collapse**: By 1981 Kirkconnel's population had slumped, and the facilities were only those of a small village. In 1986 the local economy and facilities were visibly in a state of collapse, though the railway station remained against all the odds. In 1990 the small electronics factory, a branch of Holden & Fisher of Possil, was sadly closed with the loss of 30 jobs. By 1991 Kirkconnel was the most disadvantaged locality in Dumfries & Galloway. The population, which had continued to shrink, was down to 2329; the male unemployment rate was 20%.

**An Unloved Outpost brings home Little Bacon**: In 1992 two bings still dominated the skyline to the east, huge opencast mines were turning over the hills to the west and even on a warm May day a miasma of coal smoke from a hundred domestic chimneys hung over the sad little town, an unloved outpost of the agricultural Dumfries and Galloway Region. In 1992 Kerr Little Meats moved into a costly new factory on the Kelloholm industrial estate, built to meet new EC regulations; they employed 24 people, making gammon and other products, when the firm sadly went into receivership just one year later. At least unfortunate Kirkconnel still has its inn, school and post office… and 70 jobs proposed in 2001 by Scottish Coal for extracting 2 million tons by opencasting just north at Glenmackloch.

## KIRKCOWAN

**Map 1, C4**

***Galloway village,*** *pop. 600 (area)* OS 82: NX 3260

The ancient Kirk Cowan stood on a spur above the Tarf Water 2km from its confluence with the River Bladnoch, 13km east of Glenluce. On the moors to the south was once the lost Castle of Mindork. The fine 15th century Drumwalt Castle was built in Mochrum parish some 8km south of Kirkcowan, still a remote area of moors and lochans. Pont's early 17th century map showed a mill nearby, and a bridge near Kirk Cowan; the original of the map probably dates from about 1610, soon after the military road was made from Dumfries to Stranraer. Roy's survey about 1754 showed this as a track labelled *'Road from Portpatrick to Minnigaff, Ferrytown of Cree &c'*. The *'Kirk of Kirkcoan'* (as Roy described it), stood beside a by-road on the line of the later B733 to Wigtown, which ran through the small accompanying hamlet; there were still no other roads. However, in 1799 Kirkcowan was described by Heron as a *"village"*.

**Textiles and the Railway**: A long-lasting Waulk Mill was established on the Tarf in 1814 by Robert Milroy; completed in 1821 and enlarged in 1835, it was driven by a 12-horsepower water wheel and about 40 people were employed in weaving woollen cloth. Although there was still no post office in the village in 1838, a station was provided when the Portpatrick Railway was opened through the area in 1861, linking Kirkcowan with Newton Stewart, Glenluce and Stranraer. By the late 19th century Drumwalt Castle was known as the *'Old Place of Mochrum'*. By the 1890s the population of Kirkcowan was about 700; the mill had been extended and used steam power. It gained tweed weaving sheds in 1910–17. Then came problems: the Waulk Mill closed about 1946, though it was not demolished.

**Local Service Centre survives Decline**: In 1951 the population of the Kirkcowan area was about 870, served by quite good village facilities including a small hotel; by then the Old Place of Mochrum had been restored. The station still had two trains each way on weekdays until the whole Galloway railway was brutally axed by Beeching in 1965, and with growing farm mechanisation the area's population had fallen to only 620 by 1971. However, the facilities remained remarkably intact, with an additional hotel by 1980. In 1991 Kirkcowan was a quiet parish of 576 people; the village had some new bungalows, a modest hotel, garages, coach hirer, three shops, a substantial modern village hall, and visits by a mobile bank. The Waulk Mill was vacant and becoming ruinous in 1995, but the inn and post office remain open, and Shennanton House, 3km to the north, is a tourist attraction.

## KIRKCUDBRIGHT

**Map 2, A5**

***Galloway coastal town,*** *pop. 4000* OS 83 or 84: NX 6851

*"Vestiges of ancient camps and fortresses in the vicinity of the town are innumerable"*, wrote Chambers of Kirkcudbright, which stands beside the shallow well-sheltered estuary of the River Dee in Galloway. The odd name (pronounced *KirKOObry)* means *'St Cuthbert's Church'*; by the 11th century there was a community of Christian clergy. Presumably there was a ferry across the Dee estuary to Kirkchrist, and during the early medieval period a Cistercian nunnery stood west of the river, hence the name Nunton. On St Mary's *'Isle'*, a peninsula

2 km south-west of the town, was the great walled precinct of an Augustinian priory, perhaps founded by Fergus Lord of Galloway about 1129. Medieval mottes also abound in the area, and about 1160 a stone castle appears to have been constructed as a Royal fortress. Some accounts credit Roger de Quincy, a later Lord of Galloway, with founding a Franciscan friary nearby in 1239. Kirkcudbright was exporting grain around 1300, and it was chartered – or more probably re-chartered – as a Royal Burgh in 1330.

**Cloth Exports, English King and Italian Merchant**: After the Black Death, the town was transferred about 1369 to the Douglas Lords of Galloway as a *burgh of regality*. Archibald the Grim, later the powerful Earl of Douglas, appointed a steward to collect his revenues – hence the alternative county name Stewartry. In 1434–35 when Kirkcudbright was still under the Douglas patronage it was second only to Edinburgh in the value of its cloth exports, dealing with over a quarter of the Scottish cloth trade; it is believed this was with Atlantic coast ports as far south as Spain. In the mid 15th century Henry VI of England was exiled to the castle, which according to Chambers was *"among the strongest and most important fortresses in Galloway"*. Kirkcudbright was re-chartered by King James II in 1455, when a Franciscan (Greyfriars) friary was established (or re-established); fragments of their church remain. Wool and other goods were still exported in the period 1455–60 when a Genoese merchant, by name Lazarino Grello, was acting as Customs officer, and in the late 15th century the port paid between 1.5% and 3% of Scottish Customs dues.

**Recovery from Disaster and Holding off Henry**: Kirkcudbright was largely destroyed in 1507 by Manx raiders, and the castle had been reduced to a site called *Castledykes*; only vestiges remain of this early structure. But Kirkcudbright burgh was soon rebuilt, for in 1526 Boece described it as *"ane rich town, and of good trade in merchandise"*. However, its contribution to Scotland's burgh taxes remained under 1% in 1535, and in 1535–56 it paid under 1.5% of the total of Customs duties. While Henry VIII was brutally throwing his vast weight about in Scotland the town council wisely looked to its own security, and had walled the town to a height of over 3 m by the year 1547, when it held off an English raid. In 1560 Kirkcudbright church was an appurtenance of Holyrood Abbey, but both St Mary's Isle and the burgh were represented in Parliament.

**After the Reformation: MacLellan's Castle**: Following the Reformation Sir Thomas MacLellan, the town's Provost – who was also the proprietor of the 13th century Bombie Castle 3 km to the east – obtained the friary site in 1569, and built himself a new baronial castle near the quay in 1577–84, using stone from the friary. St Mary's priory was converted into a mansion, the seat of Earl Dunbar and the Earl of Selkirk until 1608, when it passed to James Lidderdale. By 1577 a parish school had been opened and by 1593 Kirkcudbright was the centre of a presbytery. Pont's map made about 1610 showed a rectilinear settlement; there was a *'Newmil'* on the tiny stream flowing from the miniature Loch Fergus. By the mid 17th century commercial brewing had begun in the town, and in 1639 its tax yield was similar to Linlithgow or Dumbarton.

**Civil War brings Poverty**: The Civil War evidently hit Kirkcudbright badly, for Tucker in 1655 wrote of it rather pathetically as *"a pretty and one of the best ports on this side of Scotland, where there are a few, and those very poor, merchants, or pedlars rather, trading for Ireland"*. Then matters temporarily improved again, for Kirkcudbright had a harbour basin by 1684 and was one of the earliest small towns to acquire a post office, because from 1689 it lay on the postal route from Carlisle to Ireland. Defoe writing in the 1720s evidently regarded Kirkcudbright as a disaster area in *"a pleasant situation, and yet nothing pleasant to be seen. Here is a harbour without ships, a port without trade, a fishery without nets, a people without business; there is not a vessel, that deserves the name of a ship, belongs to it; the reason is poverty."* He blamed an overall lack of enterprise, the local people being *"contented with such things as they have"* – which was very little.

**Roads, Parterres and Piracy**: The Roy map surveyed about 1754 showed Kirkcudbright as a compact L-shaped town – essentially the present High Street – with just two connecting roads, the *'Low Road to Dumfries'* (the present-day B727) and the main road northwards past the contiguous hamlet of Millburn to the then new Tongland Bridge. From this, roads connected north to New Galloway and eastwards to Dumfries. A ferry still crossed the Dee at Kirkcudbright; from the *'Ferryhouse'* a track connected westwards via Kirkchrist, and through an area of many farms to Gatehouse. About 2 km south of the town was a *'Millhouse'* (the modern Mutehill). In the 1750s much of *'St Mary Isle'* consisted of parterres, which had been formally laid out for the Earl of Selkirk by the local landscape gardener John Jones. John's son became the infamous US privateer, John Paul Jones *(see Kirkbean)*. Chambers noted that *"in the 18th century the town was for a time a place of some foreign trade with our West India Colonies and America"*.

**Industries rise but Banks fail**: Shipbuilding took place in that period, and at some time a distillery was erected across the river at Stell. A corn merchant was trading by 1786, and a mill was grinding in the late 18th century. Around 1793 the Paisley Union Banking Company had a short-lived branch in the town, though in 1797 only one fair-day appeared on the year's calendar. The bank's closure can be explained by Heron's comment in 1799 that *"the county town possesses but an inconsiderable trade"*, though it contained over 1300 people; he added that *"some manufactures have lately been introduced to give them bread and employment"*. He also noted *"a fine salmon-fishing"* and waxed lyrical on the potential of the harbour. But the Galloway Banking Company of Castle Douglas, which opened a branch in Kirkcudbright between 1806 and 1810, also had to close it in 1821.

**Communal Housebuilding**: By 1825 a brewery operated beside the Mill Burn, and there was also a paper mill, but it soon closed. In 1827 Chambers was clearly referring to Kirkcudbright Academy's new building of 1815 when mentioning the town's *"good"* high school, but he noted little or no foreign trade and *"no manufactures except hosiery upon a small scale"*. However Kirkcudbright was *"well built, and contains about 2000 inhabitants; there is no town in Scotland which possesses such a proportion of new houses"*. In a remarkable display of public spirit – anticipating building societies – these were communally built and *"acquired by lot"* (as at Larkhall). The Little Ross lighthouse on an islet at the mouth of the bay was first lit in 1843, and a lifeboat station was opened in 1862. But the population of the Stewartry peaked about 1851, limiting opportunities for service development at Kirkcudbright.

**Iron Bridge, Iron Road and Artists**: An iron bowstring girder road-bridge across the Dee was built in the 1860s, replacing the ancient ferry and the detour via Tongland. The Glasgow & South Western Railway's branch from Dumfries – to the upstart but by then more important town of Castle Douglas – was extended to Kirkcudbright in 1864, and by about 1885 a minor engine shed had been built. Meantime Australian-born E A Hornel, who had been raised in the town, became a famous painter, and eventually returned there, bequeathing his house to the public; the illustrator Jessie M King also lived in the town. A gasworks was established in 1886, the Stewartry Museum was built in 1892–93, and by 1894 there were three hotels *(Commercial, Royal, Selkirk Arms)* in what was called by Murray *"a pleasant and clean little town"*. The golf club founded in 1895 laid out a steep 18-hole course.

**Milk Powder, Furniture and Oil**: About 1910 the old harbour was infilled and a quay built. A creamery to make milk powder was opened by the Stewartry Dairy Association in 1935 at Mersecroft, the western bridgehead. By 1938 Wordie & Co's rail to road cartage depot was also their southern district office; its drivers collected milk from farms in churns for delivery to the new creamery, and during the war also direct to Glasgow dairies. About 1950 James Jones of Larbert opened a furniture factory in a wartime sea rescue base, and in 1956 BP set up an oil depot to serve all the south-west, fed by tiny coastal tankers. By the 1950s there were six hotels, and in 1957 an 18th century cottage by the harbour became an art gallery.

**Lighthouse Tragedy and Peaceful Retrenchment**: The Little Ross lighthouse was hurriedly converted to automatic operation in 1960 after a lightkeeper murdered a colleague. The railway was closed by Beeching in 1965; Kirkcudbright thus became a still quieter though picturesque small town, still providing basic shopping facilities. It lost the county headquarters in 1975 when the Stewartry was trimmed in extent and reduced to Kirkcudbright District Council within Dumfries & Galloway Region. Kirkcudbright with its wide tree-shaded streets had long been a minor resort; by 1979 there were caravan and camping sites. About that time Robertsons of Dumfries established a knitwear factory, but this was closed in 1989 with the loss of 80 jobs.

**Foods, Fisheries and Retirement**: Castle MacLellan Foods, started in 1982 by Warden & Carswell to make meat paté, moved their 22 jobs to a new factory in 1988. In 1991 the decidedly elderly population was 3588. The creamery was among the four largest still under the Scottish Milk Marketing Board. Several substantial fishing boats were based at the quay; in 2000 one of them was sadly to be lost with all hands *(see Isle of Whithorn)*. In 1993 the Tolbooth Arts Centre opened in a converted mill adjoining the old tolbooth, and won an award for tourism as it catered so well for the disabled. By then a former rubbish tip had been reclaimed and put to use as a Wildlife Park. In 1996 the town lost its Stewartry into the sprawling Dumfries-based unitary council of Dumfries & Galloway; by then substantial new housing estates had grown north of the town and at Mersecroft. By 2000 Castle MacLellan Foods had 50 workers and handled products from Rannoch, Orkney, and Shetland. The Scottish Executive now plans a large wind-farm offshore from the Rockcliffe–Kirkcudbright area. Hornel's house is open to the public. Small hotels include the *Selkirk Arms*, the *Arden House*, and *Royal*.

## KIRKGUNZEON & Beeswing — Map 2, B5

***Galloway small villages,*** *pop. 700* — OS 84: NX 8666

An ancient lake dwelling has been found in the small Loch Arthur, which lies in a bowl among hills some 10km south-west of Dumfries; there are also some ancient earthworks. Kirkgunzeon, 4km farther south-west, gets its strange name from the Gaelic *Guinneain ('Finnian')*; the stream even more oddly called *'Kirkgunzeon Lane'* reaches tidewater at Dalbeattie. Pont's map of the thickly settled Stewartry made about 1610 showed the Kirk and Mill of *'Carguinnan'*, with an emparked castle, whose ruins are now slight. Not so the ruined 16th century L-plan tower of Drumcoltran, 2 km to the north, now a Historic Scotland property. Kirkgunzeon itself has a fine Georgian parish church. By the time of the Roy survey about 1754 the area was traversed by the *'Lower Road from Kirkcudbright to Dumfries'* via the Buthel and Cargen bridges. Later this became a turnpike, with a toll bar between Kirkgunzeon and the 19th century *Beeswing Inn* – named after a successful bet on a racehorse of that name! In turn a hamlet took its name from the inn (Mackay).

**On and Off the Railway**: In 1859 the Glasgow & South Western Railway opened a branch line from Dumfries to Castle Douglas, through stations at Tillywhan near Beeswing, Kirkgunzeon, and Dalbeattie, but it seems to have been 1891 before Kirkgunzeon had a post office. By 1951 its station had already closed, but there was a population of some 300, served by a post office, telephone exchange, primary school, garage and doctor; the latter also served Beeswing, otherwise similar but with 250 people. Beeching closed the railway in 1965, but the population of both settlements remained quite steady, at least up to 1981; a new school was built at Beeswing. By 1985 both places had caravan sites. The extensive Kirkgunzeon parish (which excludes Beeswing) had 447 people in 1991; the post offices have closed, but Kirkgunzeon still has a pub.

## KIRKHILL — Map 9, B4

***Village w. of Inverness,*** *pop. 550* — OS 26: NH 5545

Some 10km west of Inverness the Moniack Burn enters the south side of the gentle Beauly Firth, a sheltered area left remarkably blank on Blaeu's atlas maps. The tower house of Moniack Castle was built in the 17th century, apparently replacing the earlier Castle Spynie in the wooded hills to the south. In 1634 the Lovat Frasers built the Wardlaw Mausoleum on the site of an ancient church, repeating its form; an unusual belfry was added in 1722. The Roy map of about 1750 showed the *'Kirk of Kirkhill'* on a low ridge 2 km north of the castle; between these points passed a track from Inverness to Strathglass. Achnagairn House was built south of the kirk around 1800 and rebuilt in 1905–10; at some time the second kirk was replaced a little to the east. In 1862 the Ross-shire Railway opened its single-track main line, with a wayside station named Clunes north of the kirk, and by 1894 the *Bogroy Inn* (which claims 16th century origins) was open 1.5km to the east; there were a number of emparked villas such as Achnagairn in the area.

**Fish, Soap and Wine**: By 1951 the facilities of a small village served about 700 people in the tiny nuclear post town of Kirkhill and the scattered settlements around; two local primary schools were open, at Inchmore and Knockbain. But the population fell in the 1960s and as bus services and road hauliers took their toll, Clunes station was closed to passengers in 1960 and to freight in 1964. Although by 1976 Kirkhill was no longer a post town, by 1977 the HIDB had opened a fish hatchery at Moniack, and by 1978 Highland Aromatics made fine soaps in a former church at Drumchardine. By 1993 Achnagairn House stood vacant in its 16ha policies, but in 1998 a local Trust restored the mausoleum. By 1992 the proprietors of the modernised Moniack Castle were making 7000 bottles of wine a year from the sap of silver birch trees; their winery which now uses other local materials has become a tourist attraction. The *Bogroy Inn* continues in business.

## KIRKINNER & Whauphill — Map 1, C5

***Galloway small village,*** *pop. 750* — OS 83: NX 4251

The fertile area south of Wigtown contains many ancient remains, and was very thickly settled when mapped by Pont around 1600. A school had been established in 1581 at the kirk of Longcastle, a now vanished parish 3km south-west of Whauphill, on what became the main road from Wigtown to Port William. This and the road to Whithorn existed by about 1754 when Roy surveyed the area; Kirkinner was marked, but early travellers found little of interest. The mansion of Barnbarroch House was built 3km west of Kirkinner about 1770, and later extended. The Wigtownshire Railway was extended to Whithorn in 1877, with stations at both Kirkinner and at Whauphill crossroads. South of Kirkinner is Kilsture Forest.

**Fire and Closures**: A fire gutted Barnbarroch House in 1941, but its gaunt ruins still stood in 1995. In the 1940s the *Kirkinner Inn*, Milldriggan mill and sawmills stood near Kirkinner station, while Whauphill had the *Whaup Hotel* and a depot of Scottish Agricultural Industries; both places had post offices. Passenger trains were withdrawn in 1950. The 1951 population of the parish (including the outlying Longcastle area) was just over 1000; at that time Kirkinner still provided primary education and the telephone exchange for some 775 people in the more immediate area. To the consternation of the locals, Beeching closed the still busy freight railway in 1965, and by 1971 the parish population was down to 754. Soon a garage was open at Kirkinner, but the sawmill had gone by 1979, followed by the mill after 1980. However, by then Whauphill had a tractor depot, and the population held steady to 1991. Although a few houses had recently been built at Whauphill, its post office had closed by 1996; both inns and the Kirkinner post office survive.

## KIRKINTILLOCH — Map 15, D4

***Strathkelvin town,*** *pop. 20,800* — OS 64: NS 6573

The name Kirkintilloch has nothing to do with churches or lochs, Nicolaisen noting its origin in the tenth century as *Caerpentaloch*, in Gaelic *'Fort at end of ridge'*, referring to a Roman fort on the Antonine Wall, standing above the junction of the Luggie Water with the River Kelvin. At the end of the 12th century a church to the west was granted to Cambuskenneth Abbey by its lord, the Sheriff of Stirling. Heron wrote that Kirkintilloch became a burgh of barony as early as 1170 when granted to Lord Cumbernauld; Pryde gave the date as 1211. Its medieval motte and 13th century peel tower overlie the Roman fort in the modern town's Peel Park. Kirkintilloch also acquired a chapel but developed little, and paid no tax in 1535–56. Pont's manuscript map made in 1596 showed a bridge across the River Kelvin about 1km north of the burgh, near *'Inchbelly'*. By 1642 Kirkintilloch was connected to Glasgow by some sort of road, as shown on the map engraved by Blaeu.

**From Poverty to Roads, Textiles and Canal**: In 1636 Brereton thought the area around the *"town"* (which he called *Cuntullen)* had the *"poorest houses and people that I have seen"*. The houses had no windows; roofs were of *'clods'*, i.e. turf; however, one superior town house and St Mary's church, both dated 1644, still survive. About 1661 de Rocheford called the place *Cartelock*, but noted only *"a castle on a river"*. The Roy map of the 1750s showed a medium-sized nucleated settlement with a road following the line of the wall, and another southwards towards Stepps. The roads to Glasgow and to Kilsyth were turnpiked under an Act of 1752, and a linen bleachfield was built at Glorat around that time; by 1768 there was a printfield. Development was stimulated by the opening of the eastern part of the Forth & Clyde Canal in 1785, crossing the Luggie Water by aqueduct at Kirkintilloch, where a post office opened in that year. It was a post town by 1797, when an annual fair was scheduled. Heron wrote in 1799 *"Kirkintulloch is a thriving village, containing upwards of 1500 inhabitants; manufactures of linen and cotton are carried on to a considerable extent"*. Kirkintilloch suffered a cholera epidemic in 1832.

**Railway and Canal Integration**: Meantime the primitive Monkland & Kirkintilloch Railway (M&K) opened in 1826 with horse power to carry Monklands coal to the canal; locomotives took over five years later. Large lumps of coal were then highly prized, so to avoid breaking them before they reached Carron, Falkirk or Edinburgh, flat scows on the canal were adapted in 1833 to carry laden coal carts, and from 1835 railway coal wagons were also moved in this way. In 1835 nearly 50,000 tonnes of coal and over 3000 tonnes of Monklands pig iron were transhipped from the M&K railway to the canal. *'Puffers'*, many locally built, were steamers small enough to negotiate the canal locks. No *'passenger waggons'* were allowed on the M&K in 1839, but from 1848 there was a rail passenger service on a new branch line from Lenzie *(q.v.)* on the Edinburgh & Glasgow Railway, via Kirkintilloch to Lennoxtown; this was extended to Killearn in 1866 and in 1882 reached Aberfoyle.

**Cotton, Castings and Secretary of State**: By then the town specialised in cotton weaving; yet handloom weavers continued to work there up to the end of the century. Cameron & Robertson made small cast-iron goods such as valve covers, and the large Lion iron foundry was established about 1880. The 1881 population was 7700. A local newspaper, the *Lennox Herald* was started about 1880, and a gasworks was built in 1887. In 1894 Kirkintilloch was described by Murray as *"an ancient little town"*; there was still no hotel. Meantime Thomas Johnston had been born in the town in 1881; he was to become Secretary of State for Scotland during World War II, pushing through the Bill establishing the North of Scotland Hydro-Electricity Board, which he headed until 1959, and also instigating the Scottish Tourist Board.

**Saintly Coal Mining, Golf, and Soap in a Drought**: By the 1890s the nearest colliery appears to have been at Waterside, 3km to the east; the piously named St Flanan's Colliery was a large late 19th century sinking, and the large Meiklehill colliery was operating by 1920. An electric power station was built in 1903, and in 1914 a new and larger St Mary's church left the old one empty. Kirkintilloch golf club was founded in 1895, and the Hayston club in 1926; both built 18-hole courses. The local temperance movement was so strong that Kirkintilloch was a *'dry'* area from the 1920s to the 1970s *(compare Kilsyth)*. The Caurnie Soap Company was founded in 1922; its specialist glycerine-based toilet soaps still serve a niche market today.

**Railways Lost but Glasgow Overspill Found**: The railway to Aberfoyle was closed in 1951; Meiklehill colliery was no longer shown on the 1960s OS map, and thanks to Beeching the rail connection to Glasgow via Lenzie was ended in 1964. The Monkland railway survived until 1966 as a mineral line from Glenboig. By 1971 mining had ceased, leaving extensive ruins, and all the railway lines had been lifted, but the Lion Foundry kept busy casting GPO pillarboxes, pre-BT telephone boxes – and counterweights for fork-lift trucks. Glasgow overspill was accepted in the 1960s, and with rapid dormitory growth for Glasgow, the 1951 population of 11,000 had almost doubled by 1971, changing the town's character. A new sewage disposal works was therefore built near Glasgow Bridge. Meantime the Waterside and Rosebank area had rapidly grown from 560 in 1951 to 1600 in 1971 and almost 2000 by 1981, with two post offices and a garage.

**Strathkelvin HQ and Town Centre Redevelopment**: In 1975 Kirkintilloch became the main headquarters of what was soon pleasingly named *Strathkelvin* district, and by 1977 there was at last an inn, plus the big central plant and repair unit of the Scottish Special Housing Association (called *Scottish Homes* from 1989). The mining equipment manufacturers Anderson Strathclyde employed over 400 people at their Kelvinside Works in 1979, engaged in electrical engineering; but they then began cutting back jobs, and the works appear to have closed soon after 1980. Only local facilities were available; over the 1951–81 period some had grown rapidly while others languished or closed. Meantime housing development was moving eastwards through the Harestanes area. The local parliamentary constituency, including Lenzie and Bearsden, was quite exceptionally prosperous for the west of Scotland in terms of its low unemployment. Town centre redevelopment started in 1990; in 1991 when the population had reached 20,780, William Low opened a new superstore (later Tesco's), and the new shopping centre had proved quite successful to 1992. Up to 1994 Kirkintilloch was the location of Scottish Power's Glasgow Area Grid Control Centre; it was then moved to Hamilton.

**The McGavigan Saga**: Long ago in 1860, John McGavigan had founded a printing firm at Dumbarton. After 1946 his grandson Jack McGavigan moved it to Kirkintilloch, printing posters and showcards. It progressed to printing on plastic at the instigation of J & P Coats, then to self-adhesive plastic stickers, instruction plates and brand badges for domestic and office equipment. From about 1975 at Ford's invitation they made back-lit graphics for dashboard instrumentation, and by 1989 had moved into electronic graphics for the American automobile market, lauded by the Glasgow Business School as *"the most innovative firm in Scotland"*. In 1991 their 315 workers supplied information panels to many of the world's largest car manufacturers, claiming to make products for 10% of the world's cars. In 1994 the firm was sold to Pressac Holdings of Long Eaton, makers of moulded dashboards and heating, lighting and radio circuits.

**Other Modern Industries and *'East Dunbartonshire'***: By 1989 the Macfarlane group of Kirkintilloch were making injection mouldings. In 1990, Daniel Montgomery's (cork merchants) specialised in bottle closures; Archibald Young, brass founders by 1979, cast bronze sculptures for Kirkcaldy High Street in 1991–92. By 2000 *'Scot-nail'* made nails at Waterside. In a retrogressive move by the Major government in 1996, a new unitary local authority was created from Strathkelvin and Bearsden & Milngavie districts – rejecting the Strathclyde overview – and reviving the ancient name of the crazily split county as *'East Dunbartonshire'*. May the name Strathkelvin arise once more! By 1998 the new council had abandoned the fine late-Victorian Camphill House, which had been the William Patrick Memorial Library, but by 1999 had adopted the Auld Kirk as its museum HQ. Kirkintilloch High School and St Ninian's RC High both have between 700 and 800 pupils. The Forth & Clyde Canal was reopened between Bishopbriggs and Kirkintilloch in May 2000. This should benefit tourism, though the town lacks hotels of note – a legacy of the *'dry'* era.

## KIRKLISTON

**Map 15, A1**

***Village, w. of Edinburgh,*** *pop. 2700* — OS 65: NT 1274

From the 12th century there was a parish church at Temple Liston on the River Almond 4 km south of Queensferry; parts of its stonework survive in the present church. The Knights Templars *(see Temple)* held the lands until 1309 when they passed to the Knights Hospitallers as part of their barony of Torphichen *(q.v.)*. By 1539 a mill, shown on Pont's map of the Lothians made about 1600, turned at the mouth of the Niddry Burn, east of Over and Nether Newliston. The Edinburgh and Linlithgow road already passed just north of Kirkliston, but no bridge was shown. Kirkliston was created a burgh of barony in 1621. The Roy map made about 1754 showed a village on a fully-developed road system, with linen weaving works in use, but this had run down by 1770. An old laird's house south-west of the village was replaced for Thomas Hog (one of the Dalrymples of Stair) by the fine mansion of Newliston, built 1789–92, completed in the year its designer Robert Adam died.

**Drambuie, Distilling and Quarrying**: From the mid 18th century the liqueur whisky known as *Drambuie* was produced at Kirkliston by the MacKinnon family of Linlithgow, who reputedly obtained the recipe from Prince Charles Edward. (Only from 1906 was *Drambuie* on public sale, then being produced in Edinburgh by Malcolm MacKinnon.) A distillery was first officially recorded at Kirkliston in 1795, when worked by George Simpson & Co. This was a small affair, ignored by Heron in 1799 when he described Kirkliston as a *"village"*; its first post office opened in 1801. The distillery was much enlarged in 1825 by Buchan & Co; in 1828–29 Stein experimented there with a patent still, and part of the plant was converted to make grain liquor. Humbie quarry, 2 km north-west of Kirkliston, was worked for many years for building stone, though abandoned by 1869; by that time the Hopetoun Estate had opened the New Humbie quarry, which supplied stone for building many houses in Newington, Edinburgh.

**On the Railway**: In 1866 the North British Railway opened its South Queensferry branch from Ratho. This also served a station at Kirkliston; what was by then a large distillery acquired a rail connection, and soon its water power was being supplemented by steam. It was owned in 1876 by Stewart & Co, who had at some time moved their blending and bottling operation to new premises at South Queensferry, and in 1877 joined DCL as founder members of this new grain whisky combine. Up to 1878 all the wastes had simply spilled into the river, but by 1886 the liquid wastes were pumped through a pipe laid beside the railway to fall into the Forth at South Queensferry, while 450 pigs were fed on the draff. Barnard thought Kirkliston a *"pretty village"* in 1886, when both pot-still and grain whisky continued to be made; the total output of the distillery was some 3.2 million litres a year, for a 4 ha reservoir supplied ample water. By 1891 the population was 960; an inn stood at the crossroads. The quarry was still open in 1895, but later became flooded; the distillery eventually became a malt products factory, for which its maltings remained in use, but rail passenger services ended in 1930.

**Late Twentieth Century Growth**: By 1951 Kirkliston was a village of some 1400 people. The rail freight service was withdrawn in 1966, at about the time the first short sections of the M9 motorway were built west of the village. By 1971 new housing estates had been begun north and south of the village, and the population had risen to 2400. Between then and 1975 the former main road to Edinburgh was severed to allow a new main runway to be built at Edinburgh Airport. At the same time the MacKinnon family company erected a large building on Stirling Road, where *Drambuie* liqueur was blended from a secret mix of whiskies, honey, herbs and spices. The village population was 2700 in 1991, of youngish well-educated dormitory character. Some further development of industry continued: Brewing Products (UK) employed 50 making malt extract for food manufacturers, and home brewing kits for Eastern Europeans. In 2000 the MacKinnon family launched a new blend, *Drambuie Cream*, to compete with the Irish firm Bailey's delicious product, which dates only from 1974.

## KIRKMICHAEL (Ayrshire) — Map 1, C2

***Ayrshire village,** pop. 650* — OS 70 or 76: NS 3408

Beside the Water of Girvan 6 km east of Maybole is the ruined 16th century Cloncaird Castle. When Pont mapped Kyle about 1600, the sheltered valley of its tributary the Dyrock Burn 2 km west of the castle was thickly settled; beside a tiny loch were Kirkmichael kirk, tower and mill; to the east was Guiltree Mill. A parish school was started in 1630, and by the time the Roy map was made about 1754 a road led to Maybole. Guiltree Mill still existed in 1895, when the village with its inn was adjoined by the large baronial Kirkmichael House in its 44 ha policies; this became a miners' welfare home in the 1920s. In 1936 United Dairies opened a creamery (in the 1970s it made condensed milk). In the 1950s when nearly 600 people lived in the area, served by basic facilities, another convalescent home near Cloncaird Castle had 29 beds. The miners' home closed in 1956 and some decline in population followed, and also the closure of the hotel. However, around 1960 the Spallander Burn was dammed for water supply purposes 4 km east of Kirkmichael, enlarging the little Loch into the Spallander Reservoir. Kirkmichael House School was open by 1977. In 1986 Kirkmichael was an attractive village with a substantial modern primary school, the regional council's small Meadowbank School, a post office, two shops, two pubs, a public hall and a well-kept bowling green. The Co-op's Semi-Chem works was open at Aitkenhead. The primary school and pub survived in 2001.

## KIRKMICHAEL (Perthshire) — Map 6, A2

***Perthshire small village,** pop. 900 (area)* — OS 43/53: NO 0860

Many ancient settlement sites have been discovered in Strathardle. Kirkmichael, which lies astride the small River Ardle some 20 km upstream from Blairgowrie, had an early *'Apdaine'*, i.e. land held by an abbot, and Strathardle had a thanage from about the 11th century; to the west was the royal hunting forest of Clunie. The later development of Kirkmichael parish began with competing landowners establishing burghs of barony on adjacent sites. In 1510 and 1511 no fewer than three charters were granted to places in the immediate area: to Dalnagairn, to Balnald, and to Kirkmichael itself. In the 16th century Ashintully and Whitefield castles were built some 2 km north-east of Kirkmichael; Ashintully appeared on Pont's map made about 1600, but the other fell into ruin. Though Pont emphasised Kirkmichael as a settlement – almost opposite which was the *'Mill of Pitchartnick'* – no urban growth ensued.

**Comin' through the Rye**: The Roy map surveyed about 1750 showed Kirkmichael as no more than a hamlet, at the intersection of the Strathardle track with a hill track joining Spittal of Glenshee with Dowally in Strathtay. Robert Petrie, born in Kirkmichael in 1767, was a talented violinist who composed *Comin' through the Rye*. In 1797 a single fair was to be held at Kirkmichael, which was said to have a big market by 1811; there was a school by the early 19th century and an inn by 1818. But by the 1830s Kirkmichael market had succumbed to Blairgowrie's developing urban role, and its future lay in farming and the quieter forms of countryside leisure. Strathardle was never served by rail, access to what Murray described as a *"village"* in 1894 being by coach from Blairgowrie or mail-gig from Pitlochry; both the *Ardchlappie* and *Kirkmichael* hotels were open.

**Centre for Log Cabins and Field Studies**: By the 1950s Dalnagairn and Balnald were just farms; Kirkmichael with only some 125 residents provided the facilities of a small village to some 650 people in Strathardle. About 1975 a group of holiday homes was built around 300 m above sea level in Glen Derby beside Balnald, including the single-storey 12-room *Log Cabin Hotel*, built of Norwegian pine logs. The Kindrogan Field Study Centre 4 km upstream west of Enochdhu was well-established by 1977. By 1980 a total of four hotels emphasised Kirkmichael's resort function, and interestingly although its resident population was even smaller at under 100, its facilities remained, for the population served had risen to about 900. The area remains peaceful; although Kirkmichael still has a post office, the primary school is at Straloch, 5 km up the valley.

## KIRKMUIRHILL, Blackwood & Auchenheath — Map 2, A2

***S. Lanarkshire villages,** pop. 3800 (area)* — OS 71: NS 7943

A Roman road crossed the area west of Kirkmuirhill, which stands about 180 m above sea level, high above the valley of the River Nethan, 4 km north-west of Lesmahagow. Pont's detailed but rather confused map of 1596 showed Blackwood and Draffan (OS 64) among numerous placenames in a thickly settled area, but Kirkmuirhill was not named. By the time that the Roy map was made in the mid 18th century the area had a well-developed road system, but the main settlement was *'Drafen'*, 2 km north of the kirk. From 1856 the Caledonian Railway served the area through Auchenheath station on the Coalburn line, across the valley 2 km to the east. In 1860 a short mineral branch from the delightfully named Tillietudlem Junction (OS 72) east of Draffan served a coal pit at Southwood; it was extended a short way to another in 1862, and the first Blackwood station was opened as the terminus of the further-extended branch in 1866. In the late 19th century another mineral line served a coal pit north of the Auchenheath Brick & Tile Works and extended almost to Crossford; in 1891 the population in the area was about 500. By 1902 there was an inn north of Blackwood station and a post and telegraph office at Kirkmuirhill; a lengthy mineral line south from Blackwood served a large quarry at Dunduff.

**From Mining to Motorway and Hydraulic Loaders**: In 1905 a new railway was completed, linking Strathaven with Lesmahagow via a new Blackwood station, which then became a junction. By 1931 the local population was about 1800, and by 1951 it exceeded 2500, mainly centred at Kirkmuirhill, which lay just off the increasingly busy A74 trunk road; a tiny secondary school was open. Though only the general facilities of a small village were available, plus an agricultural engineer, there was (remarkably) a cinema, the tiny 250-seat *Orcadia*. All the collieries had vanished by 1955, when the quarry was a water-filled hole; only Blackwood station was still open for passengers. The brickworks and all the railways had been closed by 1971, and the villages had been bypassed by the A74. By 1976 the hotels, secondary school and cinema had also gone. However, by 1979 Atlas hydraulic loaders were manufactured at Blackwood, and a large new housing estate was built north of the town. By 1988 the A74 had been reconstructed into the M74, and by 1991 the area had a population of 3800, and very basic facilities. It holds little for the casual visitor, though it is on the simplest route to Craignethan Castle.

## KIRKNEWTON — Map 15, A2

***W. Lothian village**, pop. 1350* — OS 65: NT 1167

Kirknewton lies some 170 m above sea level, 2 km west of the ancient forts on Dalmahoy Hill and Kaimes Hill, outliers of the Pentland Hills. Pont's map showed *'Kirknewtoun'* north of the boldly engraved *'Kirkneutoun Moore'*, across which passed an early road from Edinburgh, 15 km to the north-east, to Causewayend some 6 km south-west. A parish school was founded in 1627. When Roy mapped the area about 1754, Kirknewton lay on another road, from Hermiston and Dalmahoy, turning south at the kirk to cross the earlier road and continue as a track across the Pentlands to West Linton. Shelter planting was transforming the moor up to an altitude of about 250 metres. Meadowbank House was already a mansion in its own policies; Ormiston Hill House was built soon afterwards. The main line of the Caledonian Railway was opened between Carstairs and Edinburgh in 1848; a station 1 km west of the tiny village of Kirknewton was named Midcalder, though that larger village was over 3 km away. By 1895 Kirknewton had a post and telegraph office, inn and smithy.

**Shale, Airfield, Quarry and Dormitory**: By 1902 a mineral railway left the main line 1 km east of the station, dipping to serve quarries at Camps and an oil shale mine between Kirknewton and East Calder, then linking to the Pumpherston *(q.v.)* shale oil works. In 1921 the parish (including East Calder and Wilkieston) held 3000 people, falling to 2910 in 1931. A small military airfield laid out at Whitemoss during the 1939–45 war found a use in general aviation. The shale quarry had vanished by the 1950s when the Kirknewton area alone had a population of some 1250 and there was a primary school and a group medical practice; Meadowbank House had been renamed Kirknewton House, but Ormiston Hill House became derelict from 1951. By 1963 a hard rock quarry had been opened in Kaimes Hill. The station, served by local trains on the Shotts line, survived to be renamed Kirknewton in the 1980s. By the mid 1970s a housing estate had been added north of the village, and by 1981 garage facilities were also available. By 1991 over 1350 people lived in the village and Camps area, many in close-packed terraced houses. In 1989 Econowaste began to accept domestic waste as landfill at Kaimes quarry, brought by rail in containers from Edinburgh; but by 1999 the available space was full, and controversy raged locally. Soon this traffic went to Oxwellmains instead. In 1994 the airfield was a gliding school. By 1998 a cycle route passed through the village, which still has its primary school and post office, as well as medium-sized companies in construction, asphalt work, haulage, and coachworks.

## KIRKOSWALD — Map 1, C3

***Ayrshire village**, pop. 450* — OS 70 or 76: NS 2407

A hill fort and the ancient church of St Oswald stood some 6 km west of Maybole, in a rather hilly area that was nevertheless well settled when Pont mapped Kyle around 1600; at Ballochniel 2 km to the west was a mill. When the Roy map was made about 1754, a road through Kirkoswald linked Maybole and Turnberry. Robert Adam designed the new parish church built in 1777; beside it are buried two of Robert Burns' immortalised characters, Souter Johnnie and Tam o' Shanter (a farm 2.5 km west of the kirk). By 1895 Kirkoswald had a post and telegraph office and an inn. Souter Johnnie's thatched cottage of 1786 was acquired by the National Trust for Scotland, and by 1956 was open as a museum. At that time there was also a 4-roomed inn and a timber merchant at Kirkoswald. In the latter half of the 20th century a population of around 475 was served by a good range of basic village facilities, but there was little new development; by 1998 the post office had closed and the inn was just a pub, but the parish church had been extensively repaired.

## KIRKPATRICK DURHAM & Springholm — Map 2, A4

***Galloway villages**, pop. 700 (area)* — OS 84: NX 7870

A medieval motte was thrown up in the valley of the Water of Urr some 20 km west of Dumfries. Nearby at the time of Pont's survey around 1610 stood the Kirk of Kirkpatrick, now known as Kirkpatrick Durham (KD), and a mill at Minnydow. Roy's survey of about 1754 showed tracks to Dumfries, Bridge of Urr and Parton radiating from the kirk. In 1785 David Lamont began to erect a model village and brought in various craftsmen, whose work certainly made them thirsty: by 1811 the 1150 local people could choose between seven inns, and there was even a racecourse! This later vanished, being well away from railways and industries.

**Prophet without Honour?**: Born in 1831, lawyer's son James Clerk Maxwell of Glenlair House, 4 km north-west of the village, learned to control electrical forces, stated the set of four equations on which our understanding of magnetism and electricity is based, and became the famous founder of the modern science of physics. He invented colour photography in 1861 and predicted the practicability of harnessing radio waves. Maxwell's birthplace, Glenlair House, was burnt out in 1929 and remained sadly derelict in 1997, its potential value as a shrine to the memory of this most outstanding scientist so far ignored. By 1951 KD had only around 335 of the 803 people in its parish, and the facilities of a small village, but the school, built in 1885, and the telephone exchange served a wider area of some 1150 people. This included the larger but less interesting village of Springholm with its post office, inn and woollen mill, 2 km to the east. Although Springholm held steady, by 1991 the pastoral parish had only 708 people, and the pupils had been moved to school in Springholm, leaving KD's attractive old school building still rotting in 1998. In 1994 Drew MacTaggart's long-established road haulage business ran twelve lorries carrying livestock throughout the UK and moving 2500 sheep a week to France. But by 1996 there was little new development; both the KD and Springholm post offices had closed, and the inns were just pubs.

## KIRKPATRICK FLEMING — Map 2, C4

***Small Dumfriesshire village,*** *pop. 750 (area)* — OS 85: NY 2770

About 6 km west of its crossing of the River Sark, the Roman road from Carlisle to the Clyde paralleled the Kirtle Water through the site of Kirkpatrick. The area became thickly studded with tower houses, mainly of the 16th century – Woodhouse to the west, Kirkpatrick near the church, and 1 km to the east Redhall; little remains of the latter two. When Pont mapped Annandale around 1610 the area was well settled; to the north was the extensive Dunskelly Wood, now vanished. The Roy map of about 1754 showed a road on and near the Roman line; in wilds to the east was the curiously named Half Morton kirk, only 1 km from the English border. Later this kirk lay beside a road from Annan to Canonbie, crossing the Roman road at Kirkpatrick, which then began to grow into a village. James Currie, born there in 1756, became in 1800 the first editor of the works of Robert Burns. The post office was opened with the arrival of the Caledonian Railway and Kirkpatrick station, in 1847–48. By 1895 there was an inn and a workhouse. By 1951 the parish held just over 1000 people, with the facilities of a small village. But the station was closed about 1960, and the pounding traffic of the A74 made life miserable until a bypass was built about 1970; the inn was also closed for a time, and the population shrank steadily. However by 1985 there was a caravan and camping site. The parish population in 1991 was 747; there are now two caravan and camping sites, the 27-roomed chalet-style *Mill*, a pub and a post office, all accessible from the A74(M).

## KIRKWALL — Map 13, B2

***Main town of Orkney,*** *pop. 6500* — OS 6: HY 4411

Roman coins from the first century AD were found beside a Pictish broch at Scapa, near the centre of the rolling, treeless but fertile Orkney Mainland. Kirkwall lies some 2 km to the north across an isthmus; it has a natural harbour, an inlet of the inland sea called Wide Firth, more sheltered from westerly gales than Scapa, and well placed for access by sea to several of the outer islands. In the early 11th century when the church of St Olaf was founded there by Earl Rognvald, Orkney was part of Norway. The *Orkneyinga Saga* of 1046 named *Kirkjuvagr* (*'Church Bay'* in Norse) as a market centre, though of *"only a few houses"*. Already Orkney was a livestock farming area, comprising 50% cattle, 30% sheep and many pigs. Earl Rognvald Kol's Son (Reginald, Count of Orkney), founded Kirkwall cathedral in memory of the murdered Earl Magnus. Erection of the impressively tall and lengthy Norman cathedral was begun in red sandstone beside St Olaf's church by Bishop William in 1137; he also built a palace in the form of a hall house. By 1274 Kirkwall – with its better farmland and more central site – had superseded ancient Birsay (*q.v.*) as the cathedral city of the Diocese, which included Shetland but remained under the control of Trondheim. Kirkwall became the main town in this wide area, and an entrepot for trade between Scotland and Norway.

**From Norway to Scotland**: From 1266 Orkney and Shetland were administered by Norway from Kirkwall as a single entity. The *'King's Castle'* was completed in 1383 but has not survived. This was the last area to be added to Scotland, ceded by Norway in 1468–69, and Kirkwall was chartered as a Scottish Royal Burgh in 1486 by James III, with two weekly markets. In 1540 Kirkwall became the caput of the late sheriffdom of Orkney and Shetland, but Norse *Odal* landholding law was not generally supplanted by feudal superiors, and gave the security of tenure which enabled the use of rubble stone for most buildings, recorded as early as 1577. Bishop Reid added a round tower to his palace in 1541–48, but the cathedral's triple-arcaded nave was not completed until the fateful year 1558. Tankerness House was perhaps originally the manse of the medieval chapter. Unlike most Scottish cathedrals, Kirkwall's was owned by the town council, not by the Catholic church, and continued in use for worship after the Reformation, enabling its fine wood carvings to survive. By this time the Earls employed blacksmiths, one moving north from Falkirk.

**Earl's Palace, Cromwellian Fort and Books**: By 1593 a presbytery had been established, centred on Kirkwall. The castle almost disappeared, but a new Palace was built in 1600–07

*St Magnus Cathedral, Kirkwall, first begun in 1137 when the Orkney Islands were part of Norway. Unusually, the Cathedral survived the Reformation with its roof intact.* *(JRH)*

by the oppressive Patrick Stewart, Earl of Orkney. Kirkwall gradually absorbed a growing proportion of the activity and population of the islands, which in the mid 17th century exported corn, fish, butter, tallow and hides and imported Norwegian timber, usually owning a fleet of about a dozen boats. In 1621 Kirkwall collected between 1.5% and 3% of Scottish Customs dues at its new town cross. Cromwell built a fort on the east shore in 1650; like the castle this did not last. The first public library in Scotland was opened in Kirkwall in 1683. Martin in 1703 found *"two fine Palaces in this the only town in Orkney"*, plus the St Magnus church, the seat of justice, sheriff and commissary, and *"a public school for teaching of grammar learning"* (founded 1544, it still stands).

**Linen, Posts and Trade**: By 1749 master linen spinners were importing flax directly from the Baltic, and around then Kirkwall acquired a bleachfield. A post office had also opened by 1746; the mails came weekly from John o' Groats via Burwick. Some people in the Orkneys still spoke Norn into the 18th century, and there were no roads at all in the islands until the 1760s, but their coming was followed by a doubling in the value of Orkney's exports between 1770 and 1790. By 1775 the population of Kirkwall was about 1500. The linen yarn trade was at its best round 1780, then declining. Kirkwall was one of the few ports of registry to boast a single letter identity code, K, for its fishing boats (introduced in the 1780s). By 1797 Kirkwall had an annual fair and was a post town, but although Heron in 1799 called it a *"town, the seat of the head courts"*, he added *"few of the modern improvements of agriculture have yet reached this remote part of the country"*.

**Beer and Whisky at the Fairs**: From 1804 Orkney had two posts a week. Kirkwall's first major harbour works were completed in 1811, followed by the West Pier. In 1814 Sir Walter Scott found *"a poor and dirty place, especially towards the harbour"*. Whaling, then based at an *'oily house'* on the site of Cromwell's fort, though very important, was not aesthetic. What is now the *West End Hotel* was built in 1824. Two breweries existed in 1825, but soon failed, whereas Scotland's most northerly distillery, known as Highland Park, was officially founded as early as 1798, on the site where Magnus Eunson had lately based his whisky smuggling operations. In the 1820s though the castle and both the palaces were deserted, Kirkwall was in Chambers' opinion *"a town of considerable size, containing above 2000 inhabitants. One of the greatest fairs, if not the very greatest, in the kingdom, is annually held at Kirkwall, in September; it continues for twenty days, and is resorted to by people from all parts, and even by foreigners; being, in fact, a brief period into which all the twelvemonth's commerce of these northern islands is concentrated."*

**News from the Niger, and more Whisky**: William Balfour Baikie, born in Kirkwall in 1824, became an explorer of the upper Niger and founded a city there. Nearer home, Thomas Clouston from Orkney, born in 1840, became a pioneer in Edinburgh in the treatment of mental illness. Meantime in 1839 Thomas Flett built the Ayre Mill as a tidal sawmill; later steam

*Fish-gutting, Kirkwall, in the late 19th century. Kirkwall is still a minor fishing port, but has a larger commercial cargo role, and is also a yachting base.* *(GWW collection)*

power was installed and it became a meal mill. Kirkwall's long-lasting weekly newspaper *The Orcadian* was established in 1854. However, the population of Orkney peaked at 32,400 about 1861, when the average occupancy per room in the island county was very high, between two and three persons. More harbour improvements were made in the 1860s and in 1884 a substantial town hall was built. In 1886 Barnard described both the Earl's and the Bishop's palaces as *"magnificent ruins"*. He noted that Highland Park distillery's raw material was local bere rather than barley, the malt being dried by a mixture of heather and peat; water and steam power were in use, the 15 workers producing about 225,000 litres of Highland malt whisky annually. James Grant took over the distillery in 1888; eventually the firm became a subsidiary of Highland Distillers. The Scapa distillery south of the town dates from 1885; built by a Glasgow firm, it was similarly powered but designed to make only 180,000 litres of whisky a year.

**Golf, Hotels, Lighthouses and Steamers**: Kirkwall (now Orkney) golf club was founded in 1889, and laid out an 18-hole course at Grainbank on the lower slopes of Wideford Hill. The large old tolbooth was demolished in 1890, and a new Carnegie-aided library began at that time. The *Castle Hotel* was open by 1886 – to Murray, it was *"comfortable, well managed"* in 1894 when the *"large and very comfortable" Kirkwall Hotel* (a four-storey building of 1890) and the *"comfortable, moderate" Ayre Temperance Hotel* (built a century before as the town house of a Westray laird) were also open. Kirkwall which had a chemist's shop was a *"little town"*. Maxwell's boatyard was active around that time, and the harbour approaches were safeguarded when the Helliar Holm lighthouse off Shapinsay was lighted in 1893. In 1894 the steamer *St Olaf* provided a connection from Scapa pier to Scrabster. Another steamer, the *St Rognvald*, called on a weekly service to Leith and Lerwick for half a century from 1901.

**Air, Sea and the *Royal Oak* Tragedy**: An airship base comprising two large timber and corrugated iron sheds each 67m long was built at Caldale some 3km to the west during World War I, but operated only briefly. Highland Airways of Inverness pioneered flights to Wick and Kirkwall in 1933 and carried air mails from 1934. In the 1930s the little ships of A F Henry & MacGregor of Leith carried cement to Kirkwall, dropping off half cargoes (typically of 300 tonnes) en route to Lerwick. In World War II Hatston immediately north-west of the town was the site of a large Royal Naval Air Station, opened in 1939 and named HMS *Sparrowhawk*. The field at Grimsetter to the east was also built for the RNAS, becoming Kirkwall Airport after the war. Meantime in 1939 the German submarine *U47* crept past the Scapa Flow blockships and torpedoed the battleship HMS *Royal Oak* 2 km south of Scapa pier; she capsized, sadly killing over 800 of her crew, just as had happened at Flotta *(q.v.)* 22 years earlier *(for the outcome see Burray)*.

**Dairying, Diesel Power and Decline**: Orkney developed a dairy industry in the 1940s to serve the numerous sailors and naval airmen, but its population had declined to some 21,250 in 1951, of whom about 4850 lived in Kirkwall, where a butter and cheese creamery was built. The attractively designed stone-faced electric power station (diesel-driven) was built in 1950, Boots the chemists were in the town by 1953 and – until fire supervened – entertainment was provided by the small 260-seat *Albert* Cinema, which soon reopened with 680 seats in 1958 as the *Phoenix*. At about that time a tiny Woolworth store was opened. In 1957 there were two small hospitals, the Balfour (in 1981 general and maternity) and Eastbank (chronic), both of 60–70 beds. Timber and building materials entered treeless Orkney via a Kirkwall merchant, and there was a coastguard station. But some other services departed, and in the decade 1951–61 the islands experienced the most rapid population decline in the seven crofting counties, almost 12%.

**Car Ferries, Lifeboats, Oatcakes and Jewellery**: However, renewal was beginning: by 1969 the new car ferry on the Scrabster to Stromness route enabled tourists seeking its many ancient sites to explore the Orkney mainland in their own cars. By 1975 there was an indoor heated swimming pool. The Helliar Holm light was automated in 1967, and a lifeboat station was opened in 1972, gaining a new building in 1990. In 1978 some 10,000 head of cattle passing through Kirkwall market were exported, by 1979 R Garden & Co baked oatcakes for wide distribution, and the town then had nine hotels. John Scarth Engineering operated a slipway at Great Western Road (and also the boatyard at Stromness). The disused airfield at Hatston was replaced by a covered auction mart and a new industrial estate, where the prominent *Ortak* jewellery factory was well established by 1982; there was already a youth hostel.

**Fishing, Whiskies and Ferries fuel Expansion**: By 1985 Kirkwall had a fishing fleet of some two dozen boats and a new fish processing factory; an older firm was Orkney Seafood. The cinema appears to have closed in 1991. By 1993 the former Custom House was appropriately the Norwegian Consulate. The Papdale primary school, built about 1980, was by 1996 the largest in Orkney, with over 600 pupils. In 1990 the outer isles ferry ship *Orcadia* was retired, replaced by the roll-on vessel *Earl Thorfinn*. In 1991 almost 6500 people lived in Kirkwall; here and throughout the Orkneys most people owned or were buying their homes, suggesting that the benefits of *Odal* tenure had continued. Highland Park distillery was then operated by Gloag's of Perth, producing a dark single malt matured in sherry casks, for sale at twelve years old. By 1994 (under Highland Distillers of Glasgow), Gloag's welcomed in the public. Scapa looks much less attractive, but its single malt was a rich whisky, said to be suited to drinking outdoors – perhaps with Garden's oatcakes? However, in 1994 Stockans took over Garden's business and transferred most production to their Stromness plant, becoming Tod's of Orkney, though this firm still has an old Kirkwall factory as its base. In 1994 a smart new stone-faced terminal was built for the ferries; the inner harbour (now mainly a yachting base) was still used by inshore potting boats in 1998, but a modern ice plant served the fisheries.

**Cattle for Invergordon, Oil for the Falklands**: By 1995 as many as 90,000 live animals left Orkney each year; by then a daily service by the Orkney Freight Services' ferry *Orcargo* shipped livestock in special open-sided rollable containers from Kirkwall to Invergordon, for onward movement by road to Aberdeen (but the cattle ferry was withdrawn in 2001). In 1995 the Kirkwall Creamery made a fine Cheddar cheese, each batch matured for a year. By 1996 the Islands Council ran not only Kirkwall Grammar School but also the modest Orkney College, which was to play a role in the new University of the Highlands and Islands. A new Shore Road was built in 1995, passing the HQ of S & J D Robertson who until 1997 were oil distributors for the islands, then incongruously focusing their business on the far distant Falkland Islands! Late in 2000 the

Pentlands coastguard station was closed, with 12 jobs lost, its work going to Lerwick and Aberdeen. Kirkwall still has a BP oil depot, and its recently extended pier – on which North Eastern Farmers have built silos – is an active general cargo port. A&E services are provided at the Balfour hospital, and there's a small fire station, police station and sheriff court.

**Leisure for the Long Dark Nights**: Kirkwall holds BBC Radio Orkney's tiny studio, and its old town hall is a community centre. It offers tourists a visitor centre and two museums – that in the historic Tankerness House being particularly fine. Several garages and taxi hire are significant businesses, and there is a wide range of banks and professional offices. A food warehouse and a large new Safeway store rival the sheltered shopping street – which sells virtually everything, including the local *Ortak* jewellery (who employ over 50). The Islands Council, aided by the Millennium Commission, have newly built the Pickaquoy Leisure Centre, including the 247-seat *New Phoenix Cinema*, a large sports hall, floodlit all weather pitch, athletics track and many other fine facilities. In summer the cathedral is the focus of an important cultural festival. There are at least half a dozen small/medium hotels, but most close in midwinter, and the youth hostel is also seasonal.

## KIRRIEMUIR

**Map 6, B2**

***Angus town**, pop. 5600*

OS 54: NO 3854

An ancient crannog at the Loch of Kinnordy in north Angus is 2 km west of this town, which – despite its early name implying a Celtic church, and its tight medieval street plan – escaped the notice of most early travellers. It became the centre of the powerful Angus family, who apparently had no fortified base here, but gained a burgh of barony charter in 1458. Some 10 km to the west was built the 15th century keep of Airlie Castle, by 1560 the seat of Lord Ogilvie, and subsequently of the Earls of Airlie. Ballinshoe Castle, a small 16th century tower house now in ruins, arose 3 km east of the town. Pont's map marked *'Kelliemoore'*, where a school was open by 1598. Kingoldrum parish to the west has made little mark. By 1715 there was a post office in *'Killymure'* as it was named on Roy's map made about 1750, a small nucleated settlement from which four radial tracks led to Blairgowrie, Glen Clova, Forfar, and – crossing the River South Esk by the Boat of Whitewall near Tannadyce – to Brechin.

**Taking the Strain of Tight Lacing**: By then flax and yarn were sold at two annual fairs, and cheap brown linen was being woven as a major cottage industry; Kirriemuir (as the town was now being called), was the smallest of the towns which had a main linen stamping office by 1760. Unnaturally slender fashions being the vogue, about then local weaver David Sands developed a way to make very strong double cloth to meet the needs of local staymakers. Tight-laced styles were to create a strong demand for 150 years, and as the number of women willing – and able to afford – to imprison themselves for life in fashionably trumpet-shaped and immensely rigid corsets rose, so Kirriemuir developed this linen fabric as its speciality. By 1792, 228 weavers were at work, and by 1806 the locally stamped output of linen was over two million metres a year, over half as much as in Dundee! By 1816 there were eighteen hundred hand looms in the district. The 1806 linen output had tripled by 1833, and later Kirriemuir (*Kirrie to the locals)* also acquired a jute industry, though in those days sacks contributed nothing to fashion.

**The Foundation of Geological Science**: Sir Charles Lyell, born in 1797, was the son of the laird of Kinnordy which stands 2 km north-west of Kirriemuir, practically on the Highland boundary fault. He learned much from James Hutton's obscure geological treatise of 1795 and expanded on it in his world-famous work *'Principles of Geology'*, first published in 1833. This introduced the modern science of evolutionary geology, and ran through twelve editions in his long lifetime. When he was born Kirriemuir was already a post town with an annual fair; Heron noted a weekly market in 1799 when it was a *"village or town of about 1600 people"*. In the early 1800s the Fife Banking Company of Cupar established a branch in Kirriemuir; Chambers in 1827 noted it as *"a thriving minor town"*. Balintore Castle, a large mock-baronial mansion designed by William Burn, was built for David Lyon some 12 km north-west of Kirriemuir in 1859–65.

**Weaving for Wasp Waists brings Prosperity**: In 1861 a short branch of the Caledonian Railway was opened to Kirriemuir, with a train service from Forfar; by 1870 Wordie & Co had a small depot for road to rail cartage. In 1864 some 1500 handloom weavers worked in the town and 500 in the country around, plus a similar number of ancillary workers; coarse linen *'osnaburgs'* and hessians were the main products. J & D Wilkie's textile works were founded in 1868. In 1869, around the maximum tightness of the Victorian wasp-waist fashion, Bremner wrote that Kirriemuir was *"in the singular position of doing a large and prosperous weaving trade by means of the hand-loom alone"*. There were then about 4000 workers in the town, over half of them weavers, producing 8.2 million metres of cloth annually – an average of about 13 metres per weaver per working day! Was this high productivity the origin of the phrase *'Get Weaving'*?

**Munros, Peter Pan, Sandstone and Golf**: The energetic Sir Hugh Munro, born in London in 1857, became the laird of Lindertis, 5 km south-west of Kirriemuir. He is better known as the hillclimber after whom all Scottish mountains over 3000 feet (914 m) came to be named. James Barrie, born in Kirriemuir in 1860, moved south and achieved fame as an author, playwright, and the creator of *Peter Pan*. A gasworks was established in 1881, at a time when over 4000 people lived locally, and the pink and yellow sandstone town hall was opened in 1885, later extended with a library. In 1891 only 1500 people were still engaged in linen, but tourist coaches served Glens Clova and Prosen. There was said to be a good variety of shops, and the weekly *Kirriemuir Advertiser* was then in publication. By 1894 Kirriemuir had two hotels, the *Airlie Arms* and the *Crown*. It was called *"a brisk little manufacturing town with a trade in brown linen"* and had a red sandstone quarry. The Kirriemuir Players golf club was founded in 1908; James Braid laid out their 18-hole hillside course beside Caddam Wood, which gave its name to one of the most lively of all traditional Scottish dance tunes.

**Easy Clothing Hard on Weavers**: Tight lacing went out of fashion with the 1914–18 war, and as wasp waists expanded, so Kirriemuir's trade in corset fabrics shrank: the discomfort was transferred from wearers to weavers, who rapidly became unemployed. During this dull period for the town David Niven, born in Kirriemuir in 1909, became a renowned film actor and autobiographer. The *Kirriemuir Herald*, an offshoot of Forfar's local newspaper, was established in 1949; about then the National Trust for Scotland opened Barrie's birthplace to the public. The branch passenger trains were replaced by buses

*The Garie Mill, Kirriemuir, built as a flax mill, and still in use. This 1968 picture shows narrow looms weaving jute fabric.* *(JRH)*

in 1952, at which time Kirriemuir had about 4000 people, but below-average urban facilities; most interesting was its camera obscura. The railway was closed to goods in 1965 and the station site was cleared. Some of Kirriemuir's other facilities also declined over the post-war period, though the motor trade did well due to the high car ownership in the rural hinterland; in 1976 there was a large garage and motor dealer, and three other garages. By 1980 Webster's High School was open. Meantime Balintore Castle, by then a shooting lodge, was abandoned in the 1960s; it still stood sadly derelict in 2000.

**Raspberries, Retirement and RAF**: The Kirriemuir area grew grain, raspberries and cattle, but except for Wilkie's two Gairie jute and polypropylene weaving factories and a miller, the little town seemed in 1976 to be primarily a shopping centre. Its 55 or so small shops – overwhelmingly private traders – included 14 supplying clothing and footwear; but few specialised in luxuries. Some ten small hotels plus B&Bs catered for tourists, with facilities for golf and other sports. Kirriemuir is reputed to have been a favoured retirement area for English people, and by 1981 its population had risen due to substantial housing development at Northmuir. In the early 1980s, former RAF man Richard Moss created at Bellies Brae an aviation museum emphasising World War II. By 1983 J & D Wilkie spun jute, polypropylene and cotton blends at the Gairie Works and had a branch at Buckhaven. In the 1980s the population stabilised, with 5571 residents in 1991, with a large quite affluent retired element; only small town facilities remained available.

**Damask, Shopping, and Jute**: In 1992 Scotland's last firm of commercial handloom damask weavers was still at work in the town, having to make its own Jacquard patterns. A facelift for Kirriemuir in 1994 included erecting a statue of Barrie's *Peter Pan*, and by 1996 there was a Tesco store. The narrow street called Roods has been pedestrianised. Services include three banks, post office, police station, garages and a library. Wilkie are still busy in the modernised Marywell Works, the only UK firm still making both woven and non-woven jute; they also produce a range of industrial materials, plus digitally printed flags. Webster's High School has 730 pupils. Despite the draw of Barrie's birthplace, catering is not a major line and the hotels and inns are small, including the *Airlie Arms, Hooks, Ogilvy Arms* and *Town*. The Loch of Kinnordy (2 km west) is an RSPB bird reserve,

## KISHORN

**Map 8, B3**

***Wester Ross locality,*** *pop. 250* — OS 24: NG 8339

Loch Kishorn is a short sea loch just north of Loch Carron in Wester Ross; Roy's map made about 1750 showed the remote and mountainous area around it as trackless waste. The Torridon road, with its western offshoot over the fearsome Bealach na Ba to its estate centre at Applecross, was built through the area in the early 19th century, and by the 1950s Kishorn had a crofting population of 150, a post office, youth hostel, and little else; by 1982 even the youth hostel had closed. As a result of controversy over their development proposals for Drumbuie near Plockton, the Howard Doris group – who had built three huge concrete oil production platforms in Scandinavia since 1973 – were permitted in 1975 to establish a wharf, dock and construction yard for deepwater oil platforms on the north shore of Loch Kishorn, near the foot of the Applecross road. The yard was located at the end of a 4 km access road built in 12 days; its 2000 workers (at the peak in 1977 some 3250) were accommodated in a rapidly-built hutted village for 1200 people, and in two old liners moored nearby, the *Odysseus* and *Rangatira*.

**Building the World's Largest Movable Structure**: A vast dry dock was excavated in the rock to build for the US-owned Chevron oil company the complex cylindrical structure that was to be the largest movable object ever made by man, the 600,000 tonne concrete *Ninian Central Platform*. Aggregate for the continuous concrete pour came by sea from a quarry at Kyleakin, and cement by rail to Strome Ferry. After completion off Raasay to its full height of 237 m, it required seven tugs to move it into position in the North Sea in 1978, where it stood in nearly 140 m of water. Though the local population of Kishorn had not even doubled, a garage and a new telephone exchange had been provided. But the days of such costly structures as the Ninian Platform were numbered, and in 1979 the yard diversified into steel. By 1984 only some 2000 jobs remained; the firm became bankrupt in 1986 and the yard closed in 1987. In 1989 the huts had gone but the site remained only roughly cleared, and for a time in 1990 it seemed that the yard might reopen. Though a bond for restoration was still held, the uneasy feeling remains that one of Scotland's finest wilderness areas was sullied forever by outside interests for short-term gain. Nearby, 'Kinloch Damph' employ 30 in fish-farming and sports holiday provision.

## KNOCK & Grange

**Map 10, B1**

***Small Moray village,*** *pop. 725 (area)* — OS 29: NJ 5452

Knock in Strathisla is located in a lowland basin about 12 km east of Keith, and 2 km south of the conspicuous isolated Knock Hill (absurdly named, since in Gaelic *cnoc* also means *'hill'*). Grange to the south had a parish school by 1631. Roy's map surveyed about 1750 showed a tiny settlement named *'Middton of Knock'* in a trackless area. The settlement of Gordonstown, founded about 4 km to the north in 1720 and re-founded in 1750, remained a farming hamlet. However, agricultural improvements and roads followed, opening up another wide farming area around the hamlet at Grange Crossroads, 6 km south-west of Knock Hill. The single-track Banff, Portsoy & Strathisla Railway – later a branch of the Great North of Scotland (GNS) – was opened to Portsoy in

1859, from a junction station at Grange on the GNS main line beside the River Isla (which here skirts another range of hills). Other stations were provided on the branch at Millegan (soon closed), at Knock, and at a passing loop named Glenbarry 2 km farther north. In 1886 the branch was extended via Buckie to form an alternative route to Elgin.

**Knockdhu Distillery and Depopulation**: In 1893–94 James Munro & Son (the Distillers' Company under another name) had built Knockdhu distillery beside the Shiel Burn near Knock station. Its malt whisky was at first used for blending by Haig of Markinch, later by DCL at South Queensferry. By 1951 it was accompanied by a village with a population of nearly 400, and there was a quarry (now a wet pit) and works near Grange, whose parish had 1035 people. Knock station was served by only two or three passenger trains a day by the time the coast railway was closed completely in 1968, when Grange and Cairnie also vanished from the railway map; a garage bought the Glenbarry station site. With farm labour cuts all around, the population of Knock fell rapidly to only 250 by 1971, and by 1976 the primary school had been abandoned. The distillery was mothballed by DCL in 1983, when Knock had only half its 1951 population; sold by their successors United Distillers, its was brought back into production in 1989 under Inver House, as the Knockdhu Distillery Co; in 1991 Grange parish held only 723 people. Knock post office and a short-lived hotel near the site of Grange Station have both gone since 1987, leaving only farms, hamlets and the distillery.

## KNOCKANDO (or Knockandhu) — Map 10, A2

***Speyside hamlet**, pop. 730 (area)* — OS 28: NJ 1842

Knockando – strictly *Knockandhu*, (*'Black Hill'* in Gaelic) – lies on the north side of Strath Spey, 10km west of Craigellachie. Pont's late 16th century map indicated the *'Kirk of KnockAndich'*, a hamlet and a *'Milton'*. The Roy map of about 1750 showed Knockando Kirk in a trackless wooded area, but no mill was indicated. Later a tiny woollen mill was established, and Knockando House was built nearby. Cardow distillery, high on the hillside east of the Kirkton, was an illicit operation until it was licensed in 1823–24 by the Cumming family. In 1863 the Great North of Scotland Railway opened a riverside line from Dufftown, winding up the deep valley; in 1869 a private platform named Knockando was provided. In 1886 the distillery, still under the control of the Cummings, was in Barnard's words *"very straggling and primitive"*. It made only 115,000 litres of malt whisky annually, sold mainly in Leith. It very soon closed, but the stills were re-used at Glenfiddich *(see Dufftown)*.

**Distilleries and Stations Multiply – until Beeching**: In 1886 a new water-powered Cardow distillery was built alongside for the proprietor, Mrs Cumming, using peat brought from a distance of 5km and able to produce 270,000 litres a year of the *"thickest and richest"* blending malt. In 1893 the Cardow complex was sold to John Walker & Sons of Kilmarnock. Knockando post office was open near Cardow by 1894. In 1897 the Tamdhu-Glenlivet distillery was established at the site of the ancient Milton at the mouth of the Knockando burn to produce a Highland malt; a year later it was joined by the adjoining Knockando distillery. A rail siding was provided, and a public railway station named after Dalbeallie farm was opened there in 1899. Knockando parish (including Archiestown) had 1750 residents in 1901. Knockando distillery was acquired in 1904 by the London wine merchants W & A Gilbey, who from 1905 used its product in blending, and also built workers' cottages, for which another rail halt was provided. Dalbeallie station was renamed Knockando, and the private platform became Knockando House Halt. Remarkably, although Tamdhu was closed for 20 years from 1927, all three distilleries survived the many problems of the early 20th century, though by 1951 Knockando parish had only 1206 residents. They enjoyed few local facilities, and the Beeching Report led to closure of the railway in 1965–68.

**Hikers and Single Malts still Walking**: Its curvaceous route among the increasingly afforested hills was soon converted into the Speyside Way long-distance path; the former station building was adapted as the visitor centre for Tamdhu-Glenlivet distillery, fully refitted by 1976. Knockando distillery was refitted in 1969 and in the 1970s specialised in making blending whisky, but by 1990 its product was sold as a single malt by Justerini & Brooks after 14 years of maturation. Cardow remained within the *'Johnnie Walker'* setup through DCL days, and in 1992 – its spelling lately re-Gaelicised under their successors United Distillers as *Cardhu* – it claimed to be the *'home'* of Johnnie Walker whisky; it had actually been so for 99 years. By 1989 it was also making a single malt, for sale at twelve years, and boasted a major new visitor centre. However, the riverside post office closed about 1990, and in 1991 when the parish held only 730 residents, Cardhu's high rate of production was causing effluent problems. Tamdhu (*'Glenlivet'* dropped from its title by 1991), was then licensed to Matthew Gloag & Son of Perth, producing a mellow single malt matured in sherry casks, sold at ten to twelve years old. Both Cardhu and Knockando are now owned by United Distillers & Vintners. The tiny woollen mill has survived, latterly making high-class woollen cloth; in 2000 a trust was set up to secure its future.

*The stills at the Tamdhu malt whisky distillery, Knockando, which was established in 1897 and is still in production today.* (JRH)

## KNOYDART **Map 8, B4**

***West highland peninsula,*** *pop. under 100* OS 33: NG/NM 7600

The mountainous Knoydart peninsula is separated from most of Lochaber by Loch Nevis. Pont's maps of about 1600 knew of its existence but ignored its geography, while 150 years later, Roy noted no settlement or trackways between now vanished clachans at Kinlochnevis (later known as Camusrory) and Scammadale on Loch Hourn. Inverie on the wooded south coast was promoted in the 1760s by the Commissioners for Forfeited Estates, and became the focus of what little development took place. The substantial Georgian Inverie House may have originated as an earlier tacksman's house of the Macdonells of Glengarry, who owned the Camusrory estate to the east. They cleared Camusrory of crofters within a decade from 1853; its woodlands succumbed to deer and sheep and it became utterly desolate.

**Absentee Landlords Galore**: From its frequent appearances in the media it is easy to overestimate the modern importance of Inverie, whose pier remains generally accessible only on foot or by sea, usually from Mallaig. A school and post office were available by the 1950s. Inverie has belonged to a confusing succession of absentee owners, some would-be developers and others sporting in approach. It changed hands in 1952 and 1972; deer ranching for venison was the main activity in 1977, and a fish farm was created about 1980. In 1982 ferries operated from Mallaig three days per week. When again for sale in 1983 the 61 residents of Inverie were served by the estate's own hydro-electric station. The John Muir Trust acquired 1500ha on the Loch Hourn side of the peninsula for conservation in 1987. Camusrory was sold again in 1988 to Roger Wadsworth of Kent, who culled the deer, built a pier and arranged a seaplane service to Glasgow. Knoydart was bought in 1993 by Reg Brearley of the Indian jute company Titaghur, and by 1997 the passenger ferry from Mallaig also extended to Tarbet in North Morar; the pub and post office were still open. However in 1997 Inverie House stood empty and at risk when the estate with its sawmill and hydro plant was for enforced sale due to Titaghur's financial problems. A tiny hostel for backpackers is open all year near Inverie.

## KYLEAKIN **Map 8, B3**

***Village, eastern Skye,*** *pop. 400* OS 33: NG 7526

The mountainous eastern part of the Isle of Skye, known as Strathaird, has at its tip the natural harbour of Kyleakin *('Kyle'* or *'Caol'* meaning a strait in Gaelic). The *Caisteal Maol* was built in the 15[th] century on a knoll overlooking the strait. Monro noted in 1549 that McKinnon owned Strathaird and had two castles, *'Dunringill'* (see Broadford), and *'Dunnakyne'*, probably Maol. Pont who mapped the mainland parish of Lochalsh across the Kyle about 1600 named the *'Ferry of Keulakyn'*, and Martin in 1703 mentioned *"the natives at Kyleakin"*. The Roy map of about 1750 showed a small settlement named *'Kyleachkine'* west of the castle, which eventually crumbled to complete ruin. Although the Kyle is about 600m across at its narrowest point, in 1799 Heron noted that *"cattle are sometimes made to swim across"*.

**New Village and Bright Water**: Kyleakin had a postal receiving office from 1805; a new village was laid out in 1811, and from 1826 there was a weekly steamer service from West Loch Tarbert via Tobermory, for a time extended to Portree. Two lighthouses were built by the Stevensons in 1857, one at the end of a causeway, the other on the islet of Eilean Ban. Kyleakin was described by Murray in 1894 as *"the neatest village in Skye"*, with the *"good" King's Arms Hotel*. In the 20[th] century Kyleakin became a minor fishing port and growing tourist village with whitewashed houses and a quaint harbour. The causeway lighthouse became an automatic light in 1960, while that on Eilean Ban had a keeper's cottage, the last home of the author Gavin Maxwell, who wrote of his otters in *'Ring of Bright Water'*, published in 1960 and soon the subject of a famous film; the islet became an NTS property.

**Publicising and Threatening Natural Beauty**: The campaigning *West Highland Free Press* was founded at Kyleakin in 1972, but later moved its base to Breakish *(see Broadford)*. Kyleakin was the location of the seashore quarry used in 1975–78 to supply the aggregate for the Kishorn concrete oil platform yard, but this was managed well enough to retain most of the natural amenities. By 1977 the *Dunringell* was one of several hotels; in 1980 the long-established *Marine Hotel* was another. Kyleakin village was so attractive as viewed from the air in its setting of mountains and sea lochs that in the early 1980s it featured on many an English billboard on behalf of the Scottish Tourist Board. Despite the dramatic unspoiled beauty of the Kyle and the special interest of a ferry crossing to tourists, Highland Regional Council in its quest for economic activity at almost any price, controversially proposed a bridge to the mainland. This scheme was pushed through by the Tory government in 1990 as a private project, against amenity and nature conservation opposition led by the Countryside Commission for Scotland (which unfortunately advocated a prohibitively costly seabed tunnel).

**Bulldozing Over the Sea to Skye**: In 1991 Miller Construction were selected to build the bridge, but early in 1992 an absurdly belated public inquiry allegedly heard objections! Despite an official rebuke to the Secretary of State by the World Conservation Union for his inadequate consideration of the impact of the scheme on key otter habitats, the objections were largely ignored by the Scottish Office, and building went ahead; in 1993 protesters on site failed to halt the work. Compulsorily acquired in 1992 to form a stepping stone in the highly controversial bridge scheme, from 1997 Eilean Ban was to be managed by a trust as a nature reserve accessible only by boat. With the loss of convenient free pedestrian access to the facilities in Kyle when the elegant private box-girder toll bridge replaced the ferryboats in 1995, it was inevitable that bypassed Kyleakin would experience a loss of tourists and economic decline, and protests continue – as does some inshore fishing. The 18-roomed *Dunringell Hotel* has been joined by the new youth hostel and two backpackers hostels.

## KYLE OF LOCHALSH **Map 8, B3**

***Wester Ross village,*** *pop. 850* OS 33: NG 7627

Kyle or *Kyle of Lochalsh* in Wester Ross was a ferry point by about 1600. The Roy map made about 1750 showed a few unnamed buildings on the south shore of the cramped rocky promontory opposite Kyleakin, but there were no roads or tracks. Kyle had been provided with its first post office by 1800; it became the slipway for a regular ferry to Skye when the road from Dingwall via Achnasheen and the Strome Ferry was completed in 1819, and was called *'Kyle Akin Ferry'* in Murray's 1894 Handbook. Alex Newlands, later the Civil Engineer of the Highland Railway (HR), supervised the extension of their Dingwall and Skye line from Strome Ferry through rock cuttings to a broad new pier built of stone for the Outer Isles mailboats, surmounted by a new station named Kyle of Lochalsh, opened in 1897. The railway very soon carried sheep, fish and cattle in quantity; an engine shed and railway hotel were built, and a village rapidly grew. Kyle was an important port in the two world wars and acquired the telephone group centre for Skye and a coastguard station.

**The Railway Port leads a Charmed Life**: In 1940 the quays and sidings were full of mines, and Kyle was very fortunate not to be obliterated when the loaded minelayer *Port Napier* – which might well have exploded – merely burnt out and sank at its moorings. In 1946 Wordie & Co operated a rail to road cartage depot at Kyle, which was a key village by the 1950s; outsiders including this writer found it a concentrated little place. By 1951 the *"palatial"* 37-room *Lochalsh Hotel* and the smaller *Norwest Hotel* were open. Two new and larger ferries, *Loch Fyne* and *Loch Dunvegan*, were introduced for the short Skye crossing in 1961. By 1964 the engine shed had gone due to dieselisation, but there were two youth hostels.

**After the Mailboats and Rail Freight**: Kyle's importance ebbed somewhat with the withdrawal of the last Stornoway mailboat in 1973 *(see Ullapool)*, but the railway was saved from closure by a subsidy to passenger trains only, on social grounds, and by 1975 an industrial site had been established. Kyle acquired a branch office of the Skye & Lochalsh District Council, whose creation in 1974–75 recognised that the ferry had brought together areas which had for long been in different sheriffdoms and counties. One youth hostel was still open in 1982 but was eventually closed, replaced across the water at Kyleakin. By the late 1980s many scenic rail excursions and the *Royal Highlander* touring train ran to Kyle, but by 1990 British Rail had removed the goods sidings, making the despatch of timber difficult, despite the existence of a demand. In 1991 Kyle had 862 residents and was one of Hydro Electric's distribution engineering bases.

**Private Road Bridge kills Public Ferry**: The road ferry was so busy that the huge government-sponsored but privately funded bridge – with tolls 13 times the charge made for trips across the Forth – was built in 1992–95 despite many protests *(see Kyleakin)*. The 44 crew members of the two ferries faced unemployment, because despite the faraway Tory government's lip service to competition, state-owned Caledonian MacBrayne was not allowed to continue the ferry operation, until then its most profitable route: a small private passenger ferry would try to keep a service going. After nearly 15 years without rail freight at Kyle, in 1997 EWS moved a 400-tonne train of timber from the south siding, relaid with Highland Council aid, but neither timber nor bulk food for farmed fish was a success, and by 2000 EWS seemed to have abandoned Kyle rail freight. But several fish-related companies provide significant employment, as does the military operation SERCO. The *Lochalsh Hotel* remains in business; the *Old Schoolhouse* at Erbusaig (3km north) is a restaurant with rooms, and a tiny hostel for backpackers is open also.

*Kyle of Lochalsh ferry, pictured in 1995, not long before it was replaced by the controversial new road bridge to Skye.* *(RS)*

## KYLESKU, Kylestrome & Unapool — Map 12, B2

***W. Sutherland locations**, pop. 100* — OS 15: NC 2334

Unapool and Kylestrome with its ancient broch lie on either side of the west Sutherland narrows called Kylesku, where the three mountain-girt sea lochs of Glencoul, Glendhu and a'Chairn Bhain dramatically converge. The Roy map of about 1750 showed Ardvar 6km to the west as the nearest settlement. The clachan of Unapool on Loch Glencoul, not named by Roy, was unkindly described by Macculloch in 1824 as *"half a dozen dunghills buried under the lee of a high bank"*. The road from Inchnadamph through this lovely, remote but desolate area was completed in 1831. Piers enabled a ferry link across the Kyle; Kylesku post office first appeared after 1838. The winding road was continued from Kylestrome to Scourie, but despite its wild beauty the area's population and traffic was minimal.

**20th Century Changes**: An inn later built on a small promontory had become by 1953 the tiny *Kylesku Hotel*; by then the ferry plied for free on seven days a week, though Bolton found the Scourie road *"execrable and full of pot-holes"*. Two-car diesel boats worked the ferry by 1954, and by 1978 a new timber-built school and a telephone exchange had been provided. The ferry was closed in 1984 with the opening of the elegantly curved Kylestrome bridge, designed by Ove Arup & Partners; the ferrymen had to leave or somehow find other work. However, the hotel, seasonal accommodation and the post office are still open, plus a tiny hostel for backpackers, open in spring and summer.

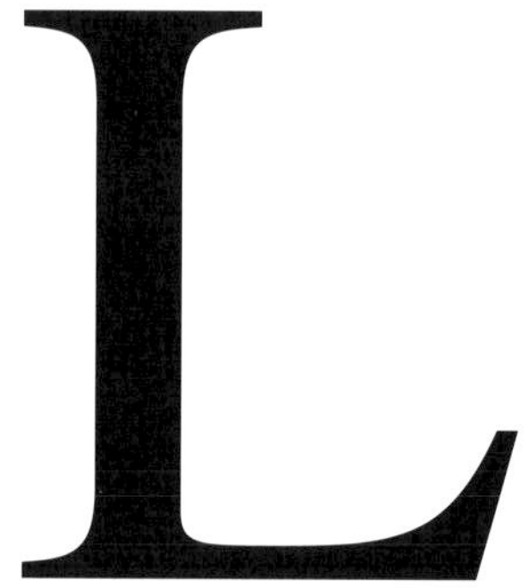

## LADYBANK

**Map 6, B4**

***Howe of Fife village,*** *pop. 1400* OS 59: NO 3009

Pont's maps of Fife made about 1600 named Loch Rossie, 4 km north-east of Falkland in the Howe of Fife. Shiells Bridge already spanned the River Eden, and farms existed at Bowhouse, Easter Kilwhiss, Pitlair and *'Drumgennand'*. But there was no settlement between the two last named, an area which James Gordon's map made in 1642 gave as *'Monks Muir'*. Loch Rossie was drained in 1741, but remained a boggy area. The Roy map made about 1750, in places a superficial sketch, implied that no road and little settlement existed west of the mansion of Rankeilour in the low-lying marshy area then called *Ladybog*, between the Eden and the Cupar–Auchtermuchty road.

*Bonthrone maltings, Ladybank, built in the late 19th century to make malt for brewing and distilling. It latterly belonged to DCL, who closed it in 1968. (It has since been demolished.)* *(JRH)*

**Roads and the Railway Village**: After 1790 a road was built from the *New Inn* on the hilltop south of Freuchie, northwards to Letham, with a new bridge over the River Eden; north of this by 1828 was the hamlet of Monkstown, on the edge of extensive plantations. In 1846–47 the builders of the Edinburgh & Northern Railway (E&NR) created Ladybank Junction just east of Monkstown, where a branch curving away to Cupar diverged from what was originally the double-track main line from Burntisland and Kirkcaldy to Perth. A station, a fine stone-built locomotive depot and an inn were established, and a new settlement was laid out on a grid plan; this took its name from the station. The Cupar line was soon extended to Leuchars (1848) and Tayport (1850) by the E&NR's successors the Edinburgh Perth & Dundee Railway (EP&D).

**Junction, Golf, Burgh and Hotel**: In 1857–58 the single-track Fife & Kinross Railway was opened from the south end of Ladybank station to Auchtermuchty and Kinross. In 1869 Bremner mentioned a *"recently erected"* power-loom factory at Ladybank, but unless he was referring to the mill at Kingskettle, this appears to have been a fairly short-lived industry. In 1879 the first Tay Bridge was opened to Dundee by the EP&D's new owners the North British Railway (NBR), when the Cupar fork became the main line. (After an intermission caused by the disastrous collapse of the Tay Bridge its main line status was restored in 1886.) Ladybank golf club was founded in 1879 and engaged Tom Morris to lay out a parkland course on sandy land; this was later extended to 18 holes. In 1891 the population was 1200, rising to 1340 in 1901, by which time Ladybank was a police burgh. By 1894 the *Royal Hotel* was open, and there was also a sawmill beside the railway.

**Various Set-backs, Golf Success**: Buses took their toll in the early 20th century, and rail passenger services to Kinross were withdrawn in 1950. By 1951 when the population was down to 1150, the hotel was no longer such, but village facilities were available, plus a Crown post office with post town status; there were also agricultural engineers. The Perth passenger trains were withdrawn in 1955, and in 1964 the Kinross line was closed completely by Beeching. Maltings, latterly owned by DCL, were closed in 1968. In 1975 Ladybank burgh vanished into North East Fife District. In 1978 potatoes were still despatched south by rail, and potato merchants Stokes Bomford still existed in 1981, when Ladybank retained average village facilities plus a large garage and an auction room. By then the Ladybank golf course was a qualifying course for the St Andrews Opens of 1978 and 1984.

**Passenger Trains Saved by a Whisker**: A forest trail had been opened by 1982, and by 1986 a caravan and camping site was open beside the golf course. The quiet village still had a primary school, post office, a large garage and car dealer, two banks, and medical facilities, plus about 8 shops. The population was 1373 in 1991. G S Brown have been precision engineers for some years. By 1994 the Ladybank auctioneers Ashworth & Christie had a branch at Gargunnock, and by 1995 the Fife Equestrian Centre had built its indoor arena north of the hamlet of Giffordstown. Few passengers use the trains to Dundee or to Perth which stop at Ladybank, but many of the original station buildings and railway workshops remain.

## LADYKIRK, Upsettlington & Horndean

**Map 3, C3**

***Berwickshire hamlets,*** *pop. 166 (area)* OS 74: NT 8846

Two early earthworks stand on the Scottish bank of the River Tweed, respectively some 12 and 17 km above Berwick. Between the two is Upsettlington, which was the site of two fords, regularly used for cross-border invasions before Berwick Bridge was built. By 1300 a *'hospital'* or inn for travellers existed at Horndean, 4 km to the north. Norham Castle on the south bank of the river was besieged by the Scots right up to the Treaty of Northampton in 1328, when it was conceded to be part of England; a large village developed beside it. The parish church was founded 1 km north of Upsettlington in 1500, and built all in stone; this remarkable structure became the site of a small kirkton. There was already a mansion on the site of Ladykirk House just south of Upsettlington by about 1754, when a riverside road had also been built to join Berwick and Coldstream; but the Dam Ford, named after a weir across the river, was still in use.

**The Emparked Village**: A grander Ladykirk House was built in 1797 for William Robertson, who laid out a huge riverside park over 2 km in length which nearly enveloped Upsettlington. In 1799 Heron wrote that Ladykirk was a *"village"*. Railways stayed away, but in 1901 316 people lived in the parish and a road bridge spanned the river north of Upsettlington, which had a post office. In the second world war a military airfield was laid out near Horndean, where there was still an inn; this had gone and the airfield was disused by 1963, but the runways stayed in being. In 1951 Ladykirk had a school and post office; the parish held 261 people and little else but farms. The Ladykirk House of 1797 was demolished in 1966, and replaced close by with a modern house of the same name, within the same extensive park. By 1981 the school had closed. The post office at Upsettlington also soon vanished, leaving the 166 people still living in rural Ladykirk parish in 1991, largely reliant for local facilities on Norham across the river in England. The 16th century church is still used.

## LAGAVULIN, Ardbeg, Kildalton & Laphroaig

**Map 4, B5**

***Isle of Islay localities,*** *pop. 140* OS 60: NR 4045

Standing stones adorn the indented south coast of Islay; beside an ancient ruined church 8 km east of Lagavulin stands the great Kildalton Cross, finely carved about the year 800. In between is Dunyveg Castle, a ruined round tower built in 1090

*An aerial view of Laphroaig distillery, Islay. It dates from the 1820s, and is still producing its very distinctive malt whisky, which is highly peated.* *(JRH)*

on a seaside crag. It was enlarged in 1207 by the Macdonald Lords of the Isles and was described by Monro in 1549 as a *"strength"*. Nearby is Lagavulin *('Valley of the Mill')*. Whisky smuggling from this area has been dated back to about 1742, making it the earliest known quantity producer of *'fire water'* on Islay. Ardbeg distillery (also known as Trobeg), 1 km to the east and of similarly uncertain origin, is known to have failed as early as 1794. Ardbeg was reopened in 1815, and officially joined by two others at Lagavulin in 1816 and 1817, of which only one survived. Laphroaig distillery 2 km to the west originated in the period 1815–26 and after 1848 incorporated a failed neighbour, Ardenistiel. The baronial Kildalton House or *'Castle'*, 3 km east of Ardbeg, was built in 1867 to designs by J Burnet for John Ramsay, a newly rich local lad who became an MP and at one time owned half the island; he enforced massive clearances before his early death. The lighthouse on McArthur's Head, overlooking the Sound of Islay some 15 km north-east of Lagavulin, was first lit in 1861.

**Islay Malts and Exotic Gardens**: Barnard attributed the distinctive flavour of Islay malt whiskies to the absence of sulphur in the local peat used to dry the malt. The uniqueness of each distillery's output undoubtedly secured their survival. He saw Lagavulin as a *"village"* in 1886, when Ardbeg was a big distillery, with an annual output of over 1.1 million litres. Smaller Lagavulin had been enlarged around 1850, but most of its 340,000 litres output went for blending; it was owned around 1900 by Mackie & Co, renamed by 1927 as White Horse Distillers. Tiny Laphroaig was of *"a very old-fashioned type"* in 1886, making only 105,000 litres of high-value whisky, all sold through Glasgow; it was much extended after 1886, probably before 1910. A giant plantsman, a Mr Clifton from Lytham St Annes, who was 2.1m (7 feet) tall, bought Kildalton House and imported tropical plants up to his death in 1928.

**Single Malts Triumph**: From 1908 to about 1960 a small distillery – the Malt Mill – worked within the Lagavulin premises, making a highly-peated malt whisky in the style perpetuated by Laphroaig. In the 1950s Ardbeg had a primary school, but a room at Laphroaig distillery doubled as the village hall for the three townships. The McArthur's Head light was manned until automated in 1969, but Kildalton Castle was vacant by 1977 and derelict by 2000. In the 1980s the three townships combined had only 140 people. Ardbeg – which has had several owners and twice been closed for a time – reopened under Allied Distillers in 1989 with a staff of ten to make a single malt, matured in sherry casks and much valued by connoisseurs; it was sold in 1997 to Glenmorangie. Allied Distillers, who still own Laphroaig, make a well-known single malt, a golden peated whisky. The output of Lagavulin, long associated with White Horse, is sold by its owners UDV as a 12- or 16-year old single malt. All three distilleries welcome visitors.

## LAGG, Inverlussa & Kinuachdrachd — Map 4, C4

***Townships, Isle of Jura,*** *pop. under 100* — OS 61: NR 5978

The large and hilly Isle of Jura is almost bisected by Loch Tarbert, a long and in part sheltered sea inlet, at whose east end are standing stones and an ancient chapel. About 5 km to the south is a dun, near the small bay of Lagg, named from the Gaelic for a hollow; by 1764 it was the terminus of a ferry route to Keills south of Tayvallich. Jura's only road – narrow, winding and in places steep – was constructed in 1804–10 from Feolin Ferry via Craighouse *(q.v.)*, Lagg and Inverlussa, to Kinuachdrachd Harbour at the north end of the isle, from which natural inlet a ferry plied to Craignish until at least 1903. Two new piers were built at Lagg in 1815 and by the 1830s it definitely had an inn, used by drovers; a post office was also opened there, and another at tiny Inverlussa, 10 km farther north, near the Ardlussa primary school. The *Lagg Inn* was still open in 1894, but by 1953 this and the Lagg ferry had closed, victims of the inexorable depopulation of the island. Lagg post office and Ardlussa school closed in the 1960s, and Inverlussa's post office had gone by 1997. Meantime a 1980s proposal to revive the Lagg ferry came to nothing; the present population is minuscule.

## LAGGAN — Map 9, B5

***Small Upper Speyside village,*** *pop. 150* — OS 35: NN 6194

Also see: *Kinloch Laggan*

In the 14th century Cluny Castle was built on the north side of Lochan Ruadh, a widening of the upper reaches of the River Spey, accessible to the south via a pass to Dalwhinnie. Wade's military roads from south and east met south of the river at *'Catalach'* (Catlodge), and in 1731 a kingshouse was built 12 km farther west at remote Garvamore, whence the perilous Corrieyairack road set off towards Fort Augustus. The Roy map of about 1750 emphasised *'Catalach'* and *'Cluny's House'*, the mansion that had replaced the castle but later took its name. Many houses clustered around Lochan Ruadh, by then reduced to an extensive upland basin. This was probably opened to farming by the time that a post office was opened in 1806. Laggan Bridge, 3 km west of Cluny Castle, was built across the River Spey to Telford's design in 1818 as part of the improved Laggan road to the west.

**After Corrieyairack and the Gaelic**: The Corrieyairack road was abandoned in 1827, but the Catlodge inn lasted into the late 19th century, when Laggan had a post office, a small inn and a smithy; horse-drawn coaches plied up to 1914. In the 20th century Glenshirra or Glenshiro Lodge, 6 km west of the bridge, was a centre for grouse and stag shoots. A primary school was built near the bridge, and a garage where one of the last coachmen in Scotland tended the petrol pump in his retirement. Around the year 1900 the area's population of about 1000 contained 660 Gaelic speakers, but a mere 200 residents remained by 1951.

**Tourism and Co-ops**: In the early 1970s the post office was closed, and tiny Laggan, screened by the mountains, was also denied a TV transmitter, so the 150 remaining locals jointly provided their own. By 1972 Gaskmore House had become a small hotel, and by 1984 the *Monadhliath Hotel* was also open, plus a pottery, but the nearest post office was at Newtonmore. By 1961 the original Spey Dam had been built 3 km west of the bridge; by 1989 it had been raised. In 1990 the locals again formed a co-operative to save their licensed grocery shop; they also saved the good village hall, and in 1994 Laggan Primary School still had 18 pupils. In 1997 when a small business used local timber, the villagers through their Laggan Community Trading company took over the management of the Forestry Commission's 1200 ha Strathmashie Forest, to develop recreation, locally-based timber work and sawmilling. The two hotels continue, and at the Caoldair Pottery is an independent backpackers bunkhouse.

## LAIDE, Gruinard, Sand & Mellon Udrigle

**Map 8, C1**

***Wester Ross communities,*** *pop. 150* OS 19: NG 9091

The ancient chapel at Laide in Wester Ross stood beside a slight recess in the coast of Gruinard Bay, whose rocks are now believed to be the oldest in Europe, at 3.3 billion years. Laide appeared on neither the Blaeu nor Roy maps, the area being trackless, with only two or three clachans sketched in by Roy. After the potato famine of 1846 which caused great distress in remote western areas, the *Destitution Road* was built westwards from Braemore, south of Ullapool, via Laide, which stood where this road cut inland to make for Aultbea; it was completed to Poolewe in 1851. By the late 19th century the inland clearances had led to several more coastal clachans appearing, and by the 1930s a jetty, a post office, and a primary school served Laide. There was also a school doomed to early closure at Mellon Udrigle, on a branch road 5km to the north. By 1951 Laide telephone exchange had 8 *'connexions'* as the authorities styled them. With only some 150 residents scattered along nearly 20km of coast, including a handful at Gruinard, it was unsurprising that the Laide school had also closed by the mid seventies. Despite the north-easterly aspect of the coast, the 10-roomed *Ocean View Hotel* was opened about 1970 at Sand, 1 km east of Laide and by 1985 there was also a caravan and camping site. The limited new development is concentrated in Sand and Laide, where there is a guest house.

## LAIRG

**Map 9, B1**

***Central Sutherland village,*** *pop. 600* OS 16: NC 5806

Many ancient hut circles and a broch surround the long narrow Loch Shin in the centre of Sutherland, from which an easy pass (*Lairig* in Gaelic) leads eastwards to Strath Fleet, past the later Kirk of Lairg. The Roy map of about 1750 showed clachans nearby, but no roads. In 1828 the Commissioners completed a road from Bonar Bridge on the Kyle of Sutherland up the steep valley of the foaming River Shin to the loch, and thence through depopulated country to Tongue on the north coast. Later in the century further new roads radiated east to Dornoch, westwards to Lochinver, and beside Loch Shin to Scourie. The communications centre of Lairg grew up where the five roads converged at the south-east end of Loch Shin. A post office was open by 1838, and later in the century the *Mulandarin Inn*, whose name suggests there was a water mill.

**Lairg's Railhead Role**: In 1868 the Sutherland & Caithness Railway was constructed from Bonar Bridge to Golspie, deliberately detouring to serve the Lairg area owned by the Duke of Sutherland. The station with its long passing loop was oddly sited nearly 3km south of the village, but performed a regional role for a scattered population. Limestone quarried beside Loch Shin was brought by barge to the village and carted to the station to be burned in kilns in the goods yard, using rail-borne coal. Livestock markets were also held close by. By 1886 Lairg was described variously as a hamlet or village, *"the headquarters of most tourists and sportsmen in Sutherlandshire" (sic)*; it was a *"breezy"* place *"not to be commended for a sojourn"!* By 1894 Murray saw it as a *"village"* whose *Sutherland Hotel* was *"good but dear, favourite angling quarters"*. By then the *Overscaig Inn* was open beside the loch, some 18km north-west. About then Andrew Carnegie built Aultnagar Lodge, a large mansion 5km south of the station; by 1954 it was a hotel.

**Oil Depot, Hydro-electricity, Milk and Trees**: Between the wars the river and the loch were regulated by a series of weirs, and two small petrol and oil depots in the station yard were opened by Anglo-American and Scottish Oils (Shell-Mex), supplied by rail tankers. By about 1956 a dam had been built 1km upstream of the village, raising the level of Loch Shin by about 12m to power hydroelectric turbines. The water was re-used by driving a tunnel to feed a second power station near sea level at Inveran, 10km south, using a head of some 80m; other smaller power stations were built near and south of the distant head of the loch. By then Lairg also had the Lochside Creamery and typical village services; Sutherland Transport & Trading ran buses and lorries. The village had some 600 people, but provided banking and some other services for about 4000 others around the north-west coast between Bettyhill and Gairloch, daily buses converging on the village and station; about 1978 the Cape Wrath lighthouse keepers' families actually lived at Lairg. However, growth at Thurso and Ullapool hit Lairg's service role and its secondary school was closed.

**Sheep by the Thousand, and Marble to Italy!**: The creamery ceased to be listed, but a restaurant was open by 1977 when there were two hotels, two pubs, cafe, bank, pharmacy, district nurse – and, remarkably, a launderette. Lairg's postcode sector was the most extensive in Scotland, reaching Cape Wrath; caravan and camping sites were open by 1984, and forest walks by 1997. In 1989 Robertson's received 12 rail tankers of oil a week for distribution throughout the far north, but the collapse of the Inverness rail bridge ended BR's goods trains. In 1996 United Auctions claimed that their August sheep sales at Lairg were the largest in Europe, selling some 36,750 head. In 1995 Transrail (now EWS) started carrying marble from a quarry near Elphin *(q.v.)* to Italy by rail, through Lairg and Mossend. The station building is now a cottage. Vast areas, particularly to the east, are undergoing afforestation, but crofting remains in the area. The remote *Overscaig Hotel* offers loch-fishing boats, and there is a choice of B&Bs.

## LAMINGTON & Wiston

**Map 2, B2**

***S. Lanarkshire hamlets,*** *pop. 300 (area)* OS 72: NS 9731

Ancient earthworks crown hills overlooking the River Clyde about 13km south-west of Biggar. Located beside the river on the course of a Roman road, Lamington's name may express its spring lambing function for early shepherds on the adjacent hills; it had a medieval motte, replaced by a 15th century keep known as Lamington Tower. The area was well settled when Timothy Pont mapped Clydesdale in 1596. About 2.5km to the west across the river is Wiston, where a parish school was started in 1612; by 1622 Lamington had one too. The Roy map made about 1754 showed a riverside road passing Lamington Kirk; across the unbridged river another road led past Wiston towards Crookboat. In 1799 Heron wrote that Lamington was a *"village"*.

**Postal and Railway Services**: Lamington is a fine estate village, whose post office was issued with a date stamp in 1842. The river was evidently crossed by a road bridge before Lamington station was provided on the Caledonian Railway, which opened in 1848, for it lay west of the river. Apart from Lamington House and the post office at Wiston there was little other development by the 1890s, or in the following century.

Lamington station had three daily trains each way until it was inevitably closed by Beeching about 1965; Wiston PO closed about 1968. For some years around 1971 Wiston had a youth hostel (closed by 1984), and by 1993 Wiston Lodge was a YWCA conference centre; but by then only some 300 people lived in the whole area, and Lamington post office closed around 1990. Wiston now has a caravan and camping site and a nature trail.

## LAMLASH & Margnaheglish — Map 1, B2

***E. Arran village,*** *pop. 900* — OS 69: NS 0231

The sandy shores of Lamlash Bay on the east coast of the Isle of Arran are sheltered by the small but mountainous Holy Island *(q.v.)*. The early chapel of Kilbride in the bayside township of Margnaheglish was noted by Pont on his map about 1600. In the 17th century a pier was built which took the name of the bay, noted by Martin in 1703 as Arran's only *"good harbour, with great fishing of cod and whiting"*. In the 1820s Chambers saw Lamlash as Arran's *"principal harbour"*. About then a waulk and dye mill turned at Monamore, 1 km south. In 1829–40 the greedy Dukes of Hamilton had their factor *'clear'* many small subsistence tenants from Gaelic-speaking Arran, i.e. expel them from their homes and lands so as to raise the rental values through farming for profit. As elsewhere in such areas, English was enforced in the two Lamlash schools that were open by 1845, and came to be generally spoken. There were still 23 local fishing boats in 1847.

**Resort and Potato Development**: The Victorians found the local beach suitable for sea bathing, its waters being among the least chilly in Scotland. By 1871 an inn was open, and a new school was built after 1872. Resort development largely took place in Margnaheglish, but the easier placename of Lamlash tended to stick. Keepers' houses were built there for the two Holy Island *(q.v.)* lighthouses of 1877 and 1905. A steamer pier was built from 1883; over the next 70 years many of the Clyde pleasure ships called there. Lamlash golf club was founded in 1889, and by 1892 a short 18-hole hillside course had been laid out. In that year the village hall was built and by 1894 there was a post and telegraph office and a coastguard station. Donald McKelvie of Lamlash developed the famous *'Arran'* strains of potato there: *'Banner, 'Chief'* and *'Pilot'*.

**From Steamers to Lifeboats and Helicopters**: McKelvie's trial plots were replaced by the Arran High School building, completed in 1941; this was used by the Navy during the war – when the bay was protected by booms to form a safe anchorage for convoy escort vessels – and became a junior secondary in 1946. The old school building became Bute County Council's administrative offices for Arran. By the 1950s a resident population of more than 900 enjoyed the facilities of a typical resort village, including four hotels and three doctors. Lamlash was a minor bus service centre, because its tiny general hospital served over 3000 people. There were also ambulance and fire stations, but the steamer pier was closed in 1954. Up to about 1960 the village hall was used as a cinema.

**Lamlash goes Upmarket**: A lifeboat station was opened in 1970. In 1979 the lighthouse keepers' houses at Lamlash held the families of Pladda keepers, whose light was by then serviced by helicopter from the Lamlash base. By 1981 there were seven hotels in Lamlash, plus a yachting centre with ships' chandlers and craft shops, but the growth of Brodick meant that fewer islanders would look to Lamlash for general services. By 1985 there was a caravan and camping site. The firm of Arran Provisions, founded by Iain Russell in 1973 to make upmarket delicatessen products, built a new factory at Lamlash in the late 1980s. This made them the island's largest employer, packing teas and making sweets and biscuits, by 1991 adding shortbread and jams, and now also mustards. In 1991 the resident population was 900. By 1997 new housing had appeared, much afforestation had clothed the surrounding hills, and in summer passenger ferries plied from Lamlash quay to Holy Island. The *Glenisle Hotel* and the smaller *Lilybank* supply accommodation, and there is a restaurant.

## LANARK — Map 2, B2

***S. Lanarkshire town,*** *pop. 8900* — OS 72 (or 71): NS 8843

Beside the middle reaches of the River Clyde is Castledykes Roman fort, which stood astride a Roman road linking Carlisle with the Antonine Wall. Lanark – whose name means *'The Glade'* in Cumbric – stands on a spur 5 km to the west, rising to almost 200 metres above sea level. It was a settled area long before Welsh-speaking Strathclyde became part of Scotland. According to Heron a parliament was held there as early as 978 under Kenneth II. The ancient Church of St Kentigern at Lanark seems to have been the centre of a large parish before it was granted to Dryburgh Abbey about 1150 by David I.

**The Royal Burgh weathers the Black Death**: Pryde believed that Lanark was promoted by David I to become one of the early Royal Burghs between 1124 and 1153, but Cowan placed the date between 1153 and 1159. Lanark certainly became the caput of a sheriffdom in 1161; it also had an earthen motte, but this was not developed into a stone castle. By the 12th or 13th century a *'hospital'* had been established; by then much of the area was reserved for Royal hunting and called Mauldslie Forest. In 1326–29 Robert I founded a Franciscan friary, and before 1350 kings signed three Royal charters in the town, which despite not being a seaport, was able to contribute some 6% of all burgh taxes in 1330. Lanark seems to have weathered the Black Death better than most; in the 1370s it was still remarkable for an inland burgh in being among the eight leading centres of the very modest Scottish Customs revenue, which may have derived from the wool trade; but it was simply described as a *"town"* by John Hardyng in 1415 and its tax payments then declined steadily.

**Improving Communications – and the Reformation**: In 1444 Lanark merchants were trading with Danzig, very likely through Leith, but trade again declined. By 1491 a ferry plied across the river at Clydesholm Ford by Kirkfield, giving access towards Hamilton. Lanark contributed only about 1% of burgh taxation by 1535, and the priory had been dissolved by 1566. By 1593 Lanark was the centre of a presbytery, and appeared as a substantial town on Pont's map of 1596; by then the Mouse Water (pronounced *'Moose')* had been bridged at its confluence with the Clyde; a mill adjoined, and another turned at *'Lokair'*, above which another bridge and a third mill were in use at Cleghorn on the way to Edinburgh. Douglas was connected to Lanark by a Clyde ferry at Crookboat, 5 km south-east of Lanark, where the river makes its dramatic 150-degree change of direction just above the confluence of the Douglas Water. In 1607 a burgh of barony charter was granted to Cartland, a hilltop location 3 km north-west, but little development ensued. In 1639 Lanark ranked only 35th of Scottish burghs in tax rents, and apart from being ravaged by bubonic plague in

1644–49, the 17th century largely passed it by. However, up to 1707 Lanark town council retained sole charge of the standard Scottish weights, and growth was stirring when a three-arched bridge was built across the Clyde at Kirkfieldbank in 1694–99.

**Markets, Mansion, Linens and New Lanark**: Defoe commented in the 1720s that apart from being the capital of the county, Lanark was *"but a very indifferent place"*. However, a post office was open by 1730, when Lanark was a main horse and yarn market. Lanark bleachfield processed 20,000 yards of cloth in 1744, and its fair distributed linens in the mid 18th century. By the 1750s, as the Roy map showed, Lanark was quite a large town, with seven radial roads; but the Biggar road still crossed the Clyde at *Carmichael Boat*. The ancient Crookboat ferry was replaced when the Hyndford Bridge of five arches of *"elegant simplicity"* was erected later in the century (Heron 1799). The mansion of Smyllum Park east of the town was built about then for Sir William Honeyman. By 1774 woollen manufacture was well established, and a new parish church was built in 1777; Lanark also had a school by the 18th century. The local textile trade was greatly expanded from 1785 by the foundation of New Lanark only 2 km away. By 1797 Lanark had ten fair days a year, ranking among the top seven stances in Scotland for frequency. It was also a post town, connected to the national mails via Douglas Mill in 1802.

**Stockings and Conservation**: Heron in 1799 found *"upwards of 2200 inhabitants. Agriculture, the cotton manufacture, and a considerable manufacture of stockings, furnish sufficient employment."* By that time a bowling-green had taken up the site of the former castle, but Lanark was still the county town. Dorothy Wordsworth was told in 1803 that *"the New Inn was the best; a handsome old stone building, formerly a gentleman's house"* , though it was not very clean. The *Black Bull* was another possibility. Lanark did not really impress, *"the doors and windows dirty, the shops dull; the houses are of grey stone, the streets not very narrow, and the market-place decent"*. Chambers in 1827 described Lanark as *"this ancient town, the very beau-ideal of a rotten burgh"*, and Cobbett in 1832 merely mentioned it as a *"town"*. The second Cartland Craigs bridge, its three arches of 15 m span soaring 37 m above the Mouse Water, was designed by Telford and opened in 1822. The ancient narrow bridge beneath was saved for posterity by Mr Linning, a local lawyer.

*Lanark livestock market, showing one of the two octagonal salerooms, characteristic of auction marts in the south-west.* (JRH)

**Trying to Catch the Train**: Two breweries were in operation in 1825. A gasworks was set up in 1833, but Lanark cannot have been regarded as an important centre because it was bypassed by a mere 3 km when the Caledonian Railway (CR) main line was built in the late 1840s; perhaps to avoid building a viaduct across the gorge of the Mouse Water. The near miss by the railway made the town look to its laurels, for Lanark Auction Mart began to trade in beasts around 1850, and in 1851 came the foundation of the Lanark golf club, which laid out an 18-hole course. A private company then built a branch railway, which opened to a terminus at Lanark in 1855. In 1864 this line was extended to serve Douglas from a triangular junction east of the station, crossing the Clyde at Crookboat; later it became part of the CR. The Caledonian Boxworks was established in 1860 to produce fancy wooden boxes akin to Mauchline Ware. The small but attractively baronial William Smellie Memorial Hospital, designed by David Bryce, was built in 1874. Lanark had 4900 residents in 1881, rising to 5500 by 1891.

**Glasgow's Miles Further**: Though by 1894 Lanark still supported two hotels, and a short racecourse had been laid out on Lanark Moor, late Victorian opinion as expressed by Murray found it *"an uninteresting town on a cold upland"*. The newly formed Lanarkshire County Council must have felt much the same, and decided to base their operations in Glasgow from about 1900. From 1896 Cloburn Quarry in Cairngryffe Hill, 7 km south-east of Lanark, produced red granite ballast (still used to surface roads in south Lanarkshire in the 1970s); but a flying school founded in 1911, which held Scotland's first air show that year, failed soon after. In a time when many parts of Scotland suffered torments, Lanark was more positive for jobs – though it may seem strange nowadays that in the 1930s children as young as 13 could still be indentured for a year as farm servants at hiring fairs such as Lanark's. By 1937 four firms were making hosiery or knitwear, the largest being McDougall, makers of outerwear. By the 1950s Lanark was a major local centre with 8000 people; the Winston barracks had been built near the racecourse 3 km south-east of the town at Hyndford Bridge, and a second hospital, a sanatorium and a bus station had been acquired.

**Lanark even bores its councillors!**: Lanark Grammar School was a senior secondary by 1958, serving the *'Upper Ward'* of Lanarkshire. The Douglas railway was closed completely in the 1960s, and passenger trains to Edinburgh via Carstairs ceased to run in 1966. Although the *Royal Oak Hotel* was one of at least three open in the 1960s, the town council had nothing to say about Lanark in the Municipal Yearbook for 1972:

shades of 1894! However from 1974 the remaining railway (which still carried goods services) became an electrified spur with passenger trains to Hamilton, Motherwell and Glasgow. In 1975 Lanark became the headquarters of the extensive but thinly peopled Clydesdale District.

**Lanark Grows by Clothing the Golfer**: In 1976 Lanark was visibly prosperous. It had the headquarters of the *Lanark Gazette*, which also published an edition for Carluke – where the title had started in 1906; other local papers from Hamilton and Wishaw were also competing. The town centre held many professional services, including architects and town planning consultants, *'Surgeon Dentists'* and Writers to the Signet; some chain stores and various specialised shops sold what were then relative exotica such as continental foods and tropical fish. Strathclyde Region had already established a local office. In 1980 there was a firm of agricultural engineers at Hyndford Bridge, near the by then disused Winston Barracks. Lanark remained a major local centre, with six small hotels, including the baronial grade *'A'* listed *Cartland Bridge* and the *Clydesdale*. By 1985 a caravan site was in use at Kirkfieldbank. Glenmuir of Lanark claimed to fill 30% of the British market for golfers' clothing when the manufacturing firm changed hands in 1990 (it still employed 100 in 2001). By 1991 the population had risen to 8877. There were still four tiny hospitals scattered around the town in 1992; the St Mary's and Lockhart hospitals are still open.

**Still Marketing, but Local Government Ends**: In 1992 Lawrie & Symington claimed their weekly sheep and cattle market at Lanark was Scotland's largest for Blackface sheep; they hosted Scotland's largest farm implement sales, had branches at Gorgie and Peebles, and also sold beasts electronically. Lanark mart was still busy in 1997, when Lawrie & Symington planned to sell its 9 ha site to Safeway and for development as a heritage centre, and to build a new market on the outskirts of the town. The new Mouse Valley Golf Course was opened in 1993. In 1995 Border Biscuits Ltd baked chocolate ginger biscuits in the town, and by 1996 a Tesco store was open. In 1996 ancient Lanark lost its role as a centre of independent local government after perhaps a thousand years; its name survives in the new *'South Lanarkshire'* Council. About 1997 the former William Smellie Memorial Hospital was converted to flats, and new housing was built around it. Cloburn Quarry, famous for *Lanark Red* granite chips, claims massive reserves – "enough to last another hundred years". There is now a town museum. Smyllum House, the imposing 18th century mansionhouse, has recently been converted to 5 apartments. The *Cartland Bridge Hotel* beside the Clyde now has 18 rooms.

## LANGBANK

**Map 5, B5**

***Renfrewshire village,*** *pop. 950* — OS 63: NS 3873

An emparked mansion beside the Clyde west of Bishopton featured on Pont's sketch map of Renfrewshire, made about 1600; it was named as Finlaystone, already being the home of the Earls of Glencairn *(see Moniaive)*. Roy's map, made about 1754, showed a road paralleling the south bank of the estuary, and at some time the West Ferry plied from Dumbarton to an inn of that name, nearly 3 km east of Finlaystone House. The name Langbank is said to derive from the long straight training wall built in the Clyde nearby in the late 18th century to encourage tidal scour, so keeping the channel open. Langbank station, sited between the inn and Finlaystone, was provided on the Glasgow, Paisley & Greenock Railway which opened in 1841, but – except for some large villas and a post and telegraph office – little development resulted until the early 20th century, when a small settlement grew west of the station. Finlaystone House, rebuilt in the 18th century, was again remodelled in 1898–1903 by V J Burnet.

**Electrification and Golf stimulate Hotel Growth**: Langbank's population in 1951 was 400, with the facilities of a small village, plus the 18-roomed *Eastbank Hotel*, formerly the Victorian Eastbank House; but this venture did not last. A caravan site had been developed by 1956, and by 1961 there was an RC holiday home for poor people. This was then converted into an RC junior seminary, which was extended in 1964; but this in turn was closed in 1978, and the building reverted to use as the St Vincent de Paul Centre for the poor. Meantime the railway was electrified in 1967; the population had risen to 500 by 1971. The Gleddoch golf club was founded in 1974, laying out an 18-hole course, and by 1977 the nearby mansionhouse had become the *Gleddoch House Hotel*. The A8 coast road had been dualled by 1978. The population then grew quite markedly, and by 1989 the village had doubled in extent due to low density dormitory development on the slopes south of the station; but it had only reached 934 people by 1991. Finlaystone, the home of the Earls of Glencairn for four centuries, was in 1994 both the seat of the chief of Clan MacMillan and a tourist attraction. The *Gleddoch House Hotel* has been enlarged to 39 rooms, and offers golf, riding and clay pigeon shooting.

## LANGHOLM

**Map 2, C4**

***Dumfriesshire small town,*** *pop. 2550* — OS 79: NY 3684

Tucked into the steep-sided valley of the Dumfriesshire River Esk was an isolated first century Roman fort, at modern Broomholm. Above Ewes or Kirkstile some 10 km to the north was a hill fort, and in the valley of the Ewes Water were ancient settlements. The early burgh of barony of Staplegorton, chartered in 1320, lay over a hill to the west, beside the winding Esk. In the early 16th century James V purged the area of its notorious border reivers, who had denied any importance to Staplegorton; only its kirk was named on Pont's map made around 1610. Midway between Broomhill and Staplegorton stood the *'Castle of Langhorme'*, in a wooded area north of the confluence of the Ewes Water, on which a mill turned a little way upstream. Opposite stood *'Wachopp'* kirk, north of the mouth of its burn; it was accompanied by another castle.

**Burgh, Bridges and Whisky**: Langholm was chartered as a burgh of barony in 1621, sited just south of the Ewes Water; by 1715 a post office was open. Roy's map made around 1754 showed Langholm as a substantial settlement confined to the east bank of the Esk. The river was already spanned 1 km below the town at Skipper's Bridge (then called Langholm Bridge); the Ewes Water had been bridged at Erkinholme. Staplegorton was unnamed – apparently little more existed than the ruined castle. Langholm lay on the old high road from Carlisle to Berwick via Mosspaul and Hawick, then a mere track, but later turnpiked under an Act of 1764; other tracks led up Eskdale to its kirk and to Waterhouse; another connected to Lockerbie. In 1765 the early Langholm distillery was founded.

**Telford and his Masonry, Textiles and Antimony**: Thomas Telford, born in the remote parish of Westerkirk in the upper Esk valley in 1757, and apprenticed as a mason at Langholm in 1770 (see under), later became the Shropshire County Surveyor, the first President of the Institution of Civil Engineers, did much to open up Scottish roads, canals and harbours, and in the 20th century was honoured in the name of Telford New Town in Shropshire. By 1780 framework knitting had been introduced to Langholm by John Hardy of Hawick. A tannery and paper mill were also established around 1780. In 1788 the Duke of Buccleuch laid out the grid plan of *'New Langholm'* west of the river, accessed by a new bridge. From 1788 antimony – used in alloys and for pigments – was worked at Westerhall 5 km north-west of Langholm; the only other such mine in Great Britain was near New Cumnock. The miners had their own library, but the mine appears to have ceased production fairly soon after 1799.

**Marriage Fairs, Textiles, Brewing, Banking and Bridges**: By 1797 Langholm was a post town with three services per week, and five fairs were held each year, including the August Handfasting Fair where trial marriages could be entered into for a year! Heron noted a *"town"* of some 1500 people; New Langholm opposite was *"a considerable village"*. Irvine & Co founded a woollen mill in 1799; for a time the Whiteshiels mill went over to cotton, developing an extensive trade with Glasgow and Carlisle. The Langholm Library was founded in 1800. By the time that Dorothy Wordsworth visited Langholm in 1803 the second bridge was open at the town, which she wrote *"looked very pretty, the houses being roofed with blue slates; the inn neat and comfortable – exceedingly clean"*. But she made a sad though salient comment on the prevailing poverty of much of what some called North Britain by adding *"I could hardly believe we were still in Scotland"*. A brewery was opened in 1810, by which time the Leith Banking Company had a branch in the town. The elegant cast-iron Duchess footbridge was built across the Esk in 1813 to connect the mansion of Holmhead with the west bank *(see Hay & Stell)*.

**Posts, Whisky, Yarn and Tweeds**: By 1825 Langholm was the centre for a penny post serving Newcastleton, and in 1827 was according to Chambers (who was used to the very small towns of the Borders) *"a large thriving manufacturing town"*. David Reid was making plaids for shepherds from about 1832, and Andrew Byers built the Buccleuch Square mill – at around the same time that a gas works was built in 1836. In 1839 Glentarras distillery was erected 4 km south of the town by J Kennedy, using river boulders in wall-building. James Bowman & Son began a woollen business about 1840, and by 1844 92 stocking frames were in use. The *Crown Inn* was open in 1845, and the local newspaper, the *Eskdale & Liddesdale Advertiser*, was founded in 1848. The Langholm and Whiteshiels mills, then under T & A Renwick, were engaged in yarn manufacture prior to 1851, when the latter was taken over by Reid & Taylor to manufacture tweeds; during the next fifteen years or so they were extended *"almost yearly"* (Bremner).

**The Railway Age – a missed opportunity**: As late as 1857 there seemed a good chance that the support of the powerful Duke of Buccleuch would secure Langholm a place on a new line of the North British (NB) or Caledonian Railways, proposed to link Hawick with Carlisle, crossing the hills via Mosspaul. But this steep though logical route, now followed by the A7, was rejected in favour of a much steeper and very costly route via Liddesdale, and from 1864 a dead-end branch of the NB connected the little town to Carlisle via Riddings Junction. In that year the National Bank of Scotland built substantial premises in the town centre. The apprentice piece archway of Thomas Telford, who endowed the Langholm Library, remains beside the new library buildings of 1877, the birthplace in 1892 of the poet Hugh MacDiarmid.

*Gas retorts at the Langholm Gas Works, established in 1836 and re-built in 1887; it was one of the last coal-gas works to operate in mainland Scotland.* *(JRH)*

**Distilling at its Peak, and the famous Sheep Fairs**: In 1881 the burgh population peaked at 4200. By 1886 the water-powered Glentarras distillery was served by a private siding and had cottages for its workmen; it produced about 345,000 litres of malt whisky a year, mainly sold in London. In 1886 all the malt for the smaller Langholm distillery came from Bernard & Co of East Lothian; entirely water-powered, it made about 200,000 litres of malt whisky annually, mainly for blending and sale in England. A larger gasworks was needed by 1887. Two more mills, at least one of which made woollens, were also built in the later 19th century, but meantime framework knitting had declined to nothing, and by 1891 the population had fallen to 3600. Langholm golf club was founded in 1892 and laid out its 9-hole course. In 1894 Murray noted Langholm as *"a thriving town, an industrious place, famous for its sheep fairs and woollen manufactures"*; there were two hotels, the *Crown* and *Eskdale Temperance*. In 1896 the Thomas Hope Hospital was erected, and in 1898 a bowling club was founded. The Glenesk Mills weaving sheds were built around that time, and so were parts of what later became the large complex of Neill Johnstone the sheepskin curers.

**From Whisky to Fellmongery**: The brewery eventually became a foundry, and both distilleries failed early in the 20th century; one was converted into a garage. However, a new Crown post office was built in stone in 1935, and Arthur Bell – apparently unconnected with the Perth distiller of that name – built a small tweed manufactory in the mid 20th century. By the 1950s Langholm's facilities were those of a small town, but the railway was closed in 1967; the station site became a housing estate. In 1970 the Glenesk mills were very large, operated by R G Neill & Son and making woollen piece goods; the *Eskdale Cinema* was still open, and Charles Paisley & Sons operated

Johnstone's growing fellmongery, cheek by jowl with houses. In 1981 Langholm remained a small textile town, solidly built in stone, but with a shrinking hinterland population in an enormous but by then otherwise almost empty postcode sector; by 1985 there was a caravan site.

**Enterprising Processors of Sheep Products**: In 1989 John Packer's whimsically named *'Woolly Mill'* produced the first 100% Scottish cashmere fabric ever woven, from the combings of no fewer than 5800 goats; the resulting 7 metres of cloth weighed 3.8 kg and were *"beyond price"*. In 1991 Langholm's 2538 people were fortunate to have the greatest percentage in Scotland who walked to work – over 60%! At that time fork lift trucks bustled around with Charles Paisley's sheepskins beside the water's meet, while the Edinburgh Woollen Mill operated huge mill premises and a modern transport depot lower down beside the Esk. In 1991 the Illingworth Morris combine moved Crombie's fine woollen manufacture from Bucksburn near Aberdeen into premises adjoining R G Neill's mill at Langholm, already part of their empire. Lightweight worsteds were to be made, for use in the firm's Leeds tailoring factory. Meantime the tiny local newspaper still struggled on with outworn presses to serve what remains in essentials a rare yet pleasing survival – the isolated, relatively self-sufficient industrial town. By 1997 a museum was open; four hotels serve the town.

## LARBERT & Stenhousemuir — Map 16, B2

***Towns n. of Falkirk,*** *pop. 16,700* — OS 65: NS 8682

Larbert lies 4 km north-west of Falkirk, where the River Carron reaches the plains beside the upper Firth of Forth. Stated on early Ordnance Survey maps to be the site of a Roman bridge across the Carron, it was certainly on the Roman road from Camelon to Stirling, which passed near a large prehistoric broch *(details of the Roman 'Stane House' appear under Carron)*. The L-plan Torwood Castle was built beside the Roman road in 1566 and later extended, but eventually fell into ruin. Kinnaird House was the home of one Robert Bruce, a founder of the Church of Scotland, and the turreted mansion of Stenhouse was built in the 17th century. Timothy Pont's map of about 1600 noted *Larbarr Kirk*, but no bridge was built until later in the 17th century, and Larbert was not mentioned by early travel writers. By the 1750s an early Larbert House stood west of a small compact settlement on the main road between Falkirk and Stirling (later the A9), which was turnpiked under an Act of 1752. It already had seven radiating routeways, and at least three mills. *'Stenhouse'* also already had a corn mill, but Stenhousemuir appeared on Roy's map as a single dot, apparently marking the site of the Stane House; later development under this name lay farther to the west.

**Carron Company, Falkirk Tryst and Paper Mills**: The Stenhouse mill lade was adopted by the Carron *(q.v.)* Ironworks from 1760; it had a pleasant walkway beside it. The Carron Company bought a mill west of Larbert church and used it to polish cast-iron grates. The success of the Carron ironworks led to a new dormitory settlement developing at Stenhousemuir, the 1 km square policies of Larbert House preventing westwards development. At that time beasts were driven to the annual cattle tryst near Falkirk *(q.v.)*, but when the Forth & Clyde Canal was built in the 1770s the animals balked at crossing the bridges, so the tryst was moved to the sandy Stenhouse Muir. From 1781 the Highland Society organised Highland games at the tryst. By 1792, 60,000 head of cattle passed through this great fair annually, and Heron observed in 1799 that they *"are for the most part sent into England, and fattened for the butcher"*. When the price of black cattle halved between 1818 and the mid 1820s the tryst shrank accordingly, but remained very significant. In 1820 came two buildings designed by David Hamilton, a new Larbert House and a parish church. A house named Broomage was enlarged about 1820 into the modest mansion of Carronvale, and post offices first opened in both villages around 1825, but the area never had burgh status.

**Railways Kill the Tryst**: Larbert station was opened in 1848 on the new Scottish Central Railway (SCR), an extension of the Caledonian Railway (CR) to Stirling. This crossed the stone-arched Carron (or Larbert) Viaduct, built in 1845–46; beside Rough Castle, 1.5 km to the south, it burrowed beneath the Forth & Clyde Canal through twin tunnels. The first triangular Carmuirs junction, located between tunnels and viaduct, was opened in 1850 by the Stirlingshire & Midland Junction Railway, connecting via Falkirk Grahamston to the Edinburgh & Glasgow Railway at Polmont, so linking Edinburgh with Stirling and the north. A second triangular junction was opened in 1858 westwards from Carmuirs to give the SCR access to Denny; all these lines soon came under the CR, for whom Wordie & Co had established a rail cartage depot by 1860. As the rail network spread, cattle were soon moved by rail from stations near the rearing areas to urban markets; by 1866 a third of a million cattle were carried by Scottish railways each year, and by 1885 the Tryst was extinct.

**Mental Hospitals, Golf and the Railway Apogee**: The large Scottish National Hospital (SNH) for mental patients of all ages was built north of the already large village of Stenhousemuir in 1862–64; the Stirling District Asylum opened in 1869. Larbert bowling club was founded in 1873, and the mock half-timbered *Station Hotel* was open by 1884. A Co-op founded in 1861 built fine shops in Stenhousemuir in 1889. Stenhousemuir FC *('The Warriors')* was founded in 1884 and laid out their Ochilview ground in 1890. Cricket has also long been a feature of Stenhousemuir, and in 1885 the Falkirk Tryst golf club was established, siting its course where the tryst had been held. The Larbert Central School was opened in 1886 and another in 1891; by then Larbert had 900 people and Stenhousemuir 3200. In 1888 a North British Railway route was opened from the Denny line to Kilsyth. In 1892 a new 4-tracked station was built at Larbert, then the solar plexus of the Scottish railway system; in 1894 Murray called it *"much-needed"* and an *"important junction"*. In 1897 a new mansion called Kinnaird House was built to replace the old; it was to have a mixed history.

**Ironworks, Timber Boatbuilding, and Bus Bodies**: In the 1870s Robert Dobbie, Forbes & Co established the Larbert Stove & Iron Works. Their cashier later joined James Jones, founder of sawmills at Larbert, to set up another ironfoundry – Jones & Campbell – in 1888; by 1895 their Torwood Foundry and the station dominated the crossroads village of Larbert, with the *Commercial* and *Station* hotels and the *Red Lion* inn. Jones named his new villa Torwood Hall, and later carried sawn timber to his shipyard – Jones of Buckie – in his home-built wooden-hulled coaster SS *Torwood*, probably from Carron wharf. Dobbie built the Dobbie Hall, opened for public use in 1901, and also Beechmount House, set in fine policies (now covered with houses). A public library started around then beside the Dobbie Hall, with Carnegie aid. From 1905 a circular route of the Falkirk & District Tramways Company passed through Larbert and Stenhousemuir, en route between Camelon and Carron. Walter Alexander who opened a local bicycle shop in 1902 became an early motor bus operator, and first made primitive bus bodies in 1906. Around 1930 he built the extensive Midland Bluebird depot and coachworks just south of the bridge, nominally in Camelon.

**More Asylums, Toffee and Golf**: In 1921 Stenhousemuir FC joined the Scottish League. By then the ironworks had been enlarged, and A McCowan & Sons of Stenhousemuir were making toffee trademarked *'Cow'*, and later *'Highland'*. The Glenbervie golf club, founded in 1932, established its course in the large park of the mansion of Glenbervie, 2 km north-west of Larbert. About then Larbert House became part of the SNH, then glorified with the prefix *'Royal'*, and in 1936 a third mental hospital, the Colonies, was added in its grounds. Still more traffic, this time on the roads, found its way through Larbert en route between Glasgow and Fife after the opening of the Kincardine Bridge in 1936, the year that the trams vanished; their car shed became a bus garage. Crownest Park was laid out just before the 1939–45 war *(see Hutton G, 1995)*.

**Aluminium Buses and Rail Retrenchment**: From 1928 secondary education was provided at Larbert Central school, which became Larbert High School in 1946. After 1945 Alexanders pioneered the first aluminium bus bodies, using techniques developed by Scottish Aviation *(see Monkton)*. By the 1950s Larbert with Stenhousemuir had a population of over 15,000 and the general facilities of a small town. From 1951 Ochilview – which had only a tiny stand, built in 1928 – was the first football ground in Scotland to be floodlit, after a fashion. The Denny passenger trains had gone by 1953, the Denny line was closed in 1965 and Larbert gradually lost most of its importance as a rail passenger interchange; only lines built in 1848–50 survived. The rail connection to Alloa was closed completely in 1968, though a goods line to Throsk remained until 1978. The Stenhouse mansion was sadly demolished in the 1960s. There was some subsequent decrease in urban facilities, though the mental hospitals – Stirling District Asylum, renamed Bellsdyke, and the even larger SNH – still had a combined population of 2350 in 1971. By then the Larbert Pottery was at work. Valeview School was open at Torwood at least from 1963 to 1973. The *Palace Cinema* at Stenhousemuir closed in the 1970s; the Cannon Shopping Centre opened there in 1980.

*The main road of the Carbrook clay mine, Torwood, near Larbert, pictured in 1982. This was one of the last fireclay mines in Scotland. One (not far away) at Birkhill near Bo'ness has been preserved and is open to the public.* *(Graham Douglas)*

**Big Buses, Ironfounding and Football Fame**: During the 1970s Alexander's coachworks employed some 700 people, rising to 830 in 1978, making bus and coach bodies for home and export use, with an assembly facility for double-deckers in Hong Kong. In the late 1970s through traffic was largely diverted from Larbert on to the newly built M9/M876 motorways. By 1979 Daniel Industries Ltd of Datchet had a factory at the Lochlands estate, manufacturing fluid flow metering equipment. In 1980 three ferrous foundries were at work, Jones & Campbell at Torwood, Macintyre at Muirhall, and Agaheat Appliances in association with Glynwed of Falkirk. In 1991 the area population was 16,711. In 1987 Carronvale became the Scottish HQ of the Boys' Brigade. Stenhousemuir FC built a new 700-seat stand at Ochilview Park in 1994–95, when they also achieved their first major success, with the Challenge Cup; but despite having an amazing fan club of overseas supporters, particularly in Norway, they remain in the second division.

**Forestry Machinery and Bus Bodies**: In 1990 a local management buyout created Outreach, claimed to be the UK's largest forestry machinery agency, and the HQ of the Taylor Group of engineering companies was at Larbert. Following the Thatcher government's controversial deregulation of bus services the local buses were acquired by GRT Holdings, the one-time Aberdeen Corporation Transport, who reintroduced the name Midland Bluebird. The Walter Alexander coachworks was sold in 1990 to Spotlaunch of London. In 1992 the works were building the bodies for a fleet of Leyland Olympians to be used by Fife Scottish Buses, lately acquired by the fast-growing Stagecoach Group of Perth. This led in 1993 to the largest British order for bus bodies for years – 380 vehicles, with an option for a further 240.

**Other Industries**: In 1988–89 the Tayforth Foundry and Daniel Industries collaborated to cast and machine the cylinder for the Falkirk Museum's replica of the pioneer steamboat *Charlotte Dundas*. Daniel Industries' success in designing and manufacturing systems for process flow measurement and analysis led to rapid expansion, and the opening of a factory extension in 1994. In 1990 Jones & Campbell specialised in making diesel engine oil sumps and took over a bankrupt Ayr foundry employing 100 men; but they closed it in 1992 and transferred workers to Larbert, where 40 more staff were recruited, bringing the total to 300 jobs. By 1992 Drysdale Brothers' foundry produced castings in aluminium and bronze. Larbert's ICI siding was still the destination in 1992 of a weekly train of soda ash (sodium carbonate) from Brunner Mond in Northwich; Marcroft Engineering also had a siding.

**From Asylums to Business Parks**: In 1992 the 19 ha east site of the RNSH became the Central Regional Council's Central Park, a technology park or campus for hi-tech firms, of which the US data storage Exabyte Corporation was the first in 1993, soon with 80 workers. By 1993 three other hi-tech buildings had been completed or were planned, bringing Central Park to 14,000 m$^2$ of floorspace, half occupied by Exabyte. The adjacent Glenbervie site of 28 ha was also to be developed for firms of various sizes. Only the best of the original asylum buildings remained in 1993 – unused – and by 1997 the SNH faced total closure and Larbert House itself stood vacant. In 1996 PM Support Services of Manchester opened a new service centre for electronics users at Central Park, with an initial 50 jobs, hopefully rising to 350 within three years. Torwood Castle was partly restored in the 1990s; work continues under a Trust.

**Alexanders Flowering – with some Help**: Again sold in 1995, and acquired by the Mayflower Group, Alexanders then obtained their chassis from the Volvo plant in Irvine and their aluminium sections from Multi Metals of Bellshill. Alexanders supplied 30% of the home market, their largest customer still being Stagecoach, which had bought 2500 buses in six years; yet in 1996 over half the plant's output went for export. Early in 1997 Stagecoach ordered a further 500 buses, to be completed in a year, keeping the 850 workers busy. A new range of bodies was launched later in 1997, some recruitment was hoped for and the firm had their eye on future developments in electrically powered vehicles. In 2000 Alexanders employed 950 people in Larbert and Falkirk, making bodies for DAF and Volvo vehicles, when owners Mayflower merged with rival coachbuilders Plaxton; a 340-bus Stagecoach order late in 2000 was to use chassis made in Surrey by Dennis. Meantime in 1999 Outreach made road/rail access and inspection vehicles based on Unimog equipment. Some 700 more call centre jobs on the business park were promised in 2000 by TSM. The new *Premier Lodge* at Bellsdyke has 60 rooms.

## LARGO & Lundin Links — Map 6, B4

***E. Fife coastal villages**, pop. 2375* — OS 59: NO 4103

The tall *'Standing Stanes o' Lundie'* are to be found near the south coast of east Fife, 3 km east of Leven. Only three remain of at least four that were erected in the Bronze Age around 1500 BC. They adjoin an ancient straight road, very possibly part of a Roman alignment from Crail to Pathhead *(see Cameron Bridge)*. The nearby Lundin Castle, and Pitcruvie Castle 2 km inland beside the Boghall Burn, were built as tower houses in the 16th century. Largo east of the burn became a burgh of barony in 1513, and Drummochy on the coast to the west in 1540, though the latter never seems to have blossomed. By 1623 there was a Largo parish school. Blaeu's atlas map, based on work by Robert Gordon's son James in 1642, showed the Kirkton (Upper Largo), and *'Lundy Mill'* on the Boghall Burn. At its mouth was *'Largow Burnemouth'*, now known as Lower Largo, not yet a port in 1655 (it was ignored by the thorough Cromwellian Customs official Thomas Tucker).

**The Real Robinson Crusoe, Linen and Milling**: Largo was the birthplace in 1676 of Alexander Selkirk, quarrelsome son of a fisherman. Educated at the local school, he later became a navigator, freebooter and voluntary castaway, his story romanticised by Defoe as *'Robinson Crusoe'*. Roy's map of about 1750 showed Lower Largo as a medium-sized linear settlement on the coast road which crossed the links from Leven; Upper Largo was a tiny place on the winding lane later labelled A917. In 1750 the classical Largo House was built on a nearby hilltop for James Durham – and later twice enlarged about 1815–31. Meantime in 1762 Pearson made linen for the British Linen Company, and in the 1790s many local hand weavers made linen and checks. In the 1770s a new road was built from the village to St Andrews. In 1799 Heron's comments implied that salt was still made locally; his *"village of Lundin"* must refer to the settlement at Lundin Mill, where the new coast road – turnpiked under the 1790 Act – crossed the Boghall Burn; the toll bar stood where the lane to Lower Largo diverged just south of Lundin Mill, and by 1794 a coaching inn had been opened there.

**Coaching and Fishing Nets, Coal and Fashion**: By 1813 the Kirkcaldy to Crail mail coach passed through, and by about 1825 Largo was served by a penny post from Leven. By the 1820s Lundin was a mansionhouse in an extensive park north of the turnpike, though the park did not last. *'Drumochy'* appeared on Sharp, Greenwood & Fowler's map, made about the time that Chambers noted in 1827 that *"Nether Largo is an extensive fishing village"*. Upper Largo was *"a remarkably agreeable little village much resorted to as summer quarters"*. For a time some coal was exported from the pier which had been built at Lower Largo by 1827. From this in 1838 a steam ferry plied twice daily to and from Newhaven near Edinburgh, in connection with coaches to the Dundee ferry and horse omnibuses to Anstruther. In 1855, 36 herring boats were based at Lower Largo, crewed by eighty men and boys. In 1867 David Gillies built the mechanised Cardy fishing net factory, employing at least 25 women and girls *(see Hay & Stell)*.

**Express Trains to Lundin Links for Golfing**: The East Fife Railway was built eastwards from Thornton Junction via Leven and opened as far as Kilconquhar in 1857, with stations at (Lower) Largo and at Lundin Links, only 1600 m to the west. In 1869 the Lundin Links golf club was founded, a fine 18-hole course being laid out near the standing stones. The Institute in Upper Largo was built in 1889. By 1894 Lundin Mill had become the largest of the local settlements; Largo was still *"a considerable fishing village"* which like Upper Largo (Kirkton of Largo to the OS) had an inn; while in Lundin Links, Murray noted *"houses let to summer visitors"*. After the Forth Bridge opened in 1890, the North British Railway began to run fast services via Kirkcaldy to Edinburgh (and Glasgow), aiding residential growth in Lundin Links and the attainment of the facilities of a large village. The prominent 20-room *Lundin Links Hotel*, designed by Edinburgh architect Peter Lyle Henderson, was built in 1899–1900 on the site of the coaching inn. The Lundin Ladies' Golf Club (which still exists!) was founded in 1891 and moved in 1908–10 to a new 9-hole course, sportily embracing the standing stanes in the second hole. A late gasworks was built in 1919.

**After Trains – Caravans, Yachts and Retirement**: Largo House housed Polish forces in World War II; later a boys' preparatory school, it was burnt out during the summer holidays about 1950. The roofless shell still stands, adjoined by a caravan park. The area's population was almost steady at around 2250 for many years in mid century. The Cardy net factory was closed about 1958; its buildings were converted into housing in 1999–2000. The railway closed in 1966, the Largo station site adjoining the attractive listed stone viaduct becoming a car park. By 1977 a mansionhouse overlooking the links had become the *Old Manor Hotel*, to which a new bedroom wing was added in 1985. In 1991 the population reached 2375 and showed an affluent retired character. By then serious fishing from Lower Largo was practically a thing of the past; in 1996 the Largo Bay Sailing Club was based there in cramped and exposed quarters. Lower Largo was still expanding in the 1990s, and in 1999 the

*Lundin Links Hotel* was improved ready for its centenary. The *Old Manor Hotel* has 24 rooms, the harbourside *Crusoe Hotel* 16.

## LARGOWARD

**Map 6, B4**

***E. Fife village,*** *pop. 350* OS 59: NO 4607

By the late 16th century there was a coal mine at Largoward on the hills of east Fife, and in 1653 loads of coal were sent overland from Largo parish to Falkland, implying a reasonable road. In the 1730s Cupar got its coal from pits near Greigston north of the township of Westfield of Radernie, in 1827 labelled *'Collierrow'* but later called *Peat Inn*. The Roy map surveyed about 1750 showed a road from Colinsburgh passing west of Balcarres House to a crossroads north of *'Lawthorns'* (Lathones), near which the punningly named *King of the Moors*, a late 17th century inn, stood in isolation. In 1775 there were several coal pits and a *'fire engine'* – probably for pumping - between New Gilston and Pitscottie; by 1787 a made road existed to Cupar, and coal was also worked at Drumcarrow to the north. In the Napoleonic wars the coal pits at Lochty were used as refuges from the press gangs. By 1827 the Radernie quarry and limeworks were open some 2 km to the north of Loans tollbar, where a turnpike road from Colinsburgh forked to Cupar and St Andrews; it was there that straggling Largoward with its inn and post office was to be built later in the century.

**Coal on the Central Line?**: The Drumcarrow coal pit lasted until at least 1895, as did one at North Callange near Pitscottie. The Largoward or Largobeath pits at West Cassingray just east of Largoward, where the Browns (father and son) had been coalmasters for half a century, worked until 1914. The scale was small: all coal had to be hauled by horse and cart, and all these places remained mere hamlets. Meantime in 1898 the East Fife Central Railway, essentially a freight line, was opened from Cameron Bridge through Largoward to a terminus at Lochty Farm. This revived the small Radernie Colliery, some of its coal going for export through Methil; it still employed 80 workers when its immediate closure was announced on the eve of nationalisation in 1946. The freight trains must have survived on potatoes until the line was abandoned in 1964, leaving a short preserved length at Lochty in the ownership of an enthusiastic farmer, John Cameron, who later chaired the board of Scotrail. His preserved railway at Lochty was closed in 1993 and soon lifted *(see Leven)*.

**Largoward shows Enterprise**: The one-time *Peat Inn* became a restaurant of the same name in 1973 under David & Patricia Wilson; it was soon well-known, and a wing of 10 bedrooms was added in 1987. By 1980 the small firm of Osprey Kitchens of Largoward (founded as Dobie's joinery in 1905, and still in the family) made built-in kitchens on an industrial basis, and the 350 or so local people enjoyed the facilities of a small village. From the mid 1980s Nigel Buchanan of New Gilston became renowned as an inventor. In 1987 he bought the disused Radernie school to house his firm Liquid Levers, winning awards for devising pumps for servicing *'Hydro-lastic'* suspensions. His brake fluid safety meters, made by Kineticon of Glenrothes, were voted the best product of 1992 by 16,500 UK garages. By 1991 the firm employed 24 people at Radernie, but being unable to meet the demand for *Polar Eyes* (a replacement for *'Cats Eyes'* road markers), had to contract out initial production – to Buxton (Derbyshire)! In 1992 rising orders enabled acquisition of the Kineticon factory, to which the workers from Radernie and another workshop at Arncroach were transferred. Local hotels are the *Peat Inn* and the *Inn at Lathones* (the *'King of the Moors'* in an extended form).

## LARGS

**Map 1, B1**

***Clyde Coast town,*** *pop. 11,000* OS 63: NS 2059

Largs Bay, a recess in the hills of the north Cunninghame coast, is somewhat sheltered from the west by the Isle of Great Cumbrae. Above the lower land at the mouth of the Gogo Water is an ancient hill fort. Largs was in existence by the time of David I, and there was a motte by 1263 at the time of the famous battle between Alexander III and the Norsemen; Kelsoland west of the Noddsdale Water, 2.5 km north of Largs, was also recorded about that time. However, little else is known of the development of the area until the towers of Knock and Kelburn Castles north and south of Largs were built in the 16th century. These were emphasised on Pont's map of Cunninghame, probably made between 1604 and 1608. On this *'Lairgs'* appeared full-blown as a major settlement; only the drawing of Irvine was larger, and Kilwinning much the same size. To the north of Largs was a mill on the *Noddle* (Noddsdale) Water.

**Burgh, Brisbanes and Intermittent Schooling**: Largs had a parish school from 1595 – with some intermissions such as around 1696 – and became a burgh of barony in 1629. The unusual gabled mansionhouse built at Kelsoland in 1636 was bought in 1671 by James Brisbane of Bishopton, who renamed it Brisbane House. James' descendant Sir Thomas Brisbane became a navigator, a noted astronomer and an early Governor-General of New South Wales; the Queensland city of Brisbane was named in his honour. By the 1750s as the Roy map demonstrated, Largs was a large sprawling village on the coast road; both the Gogo and Noddle Waters were bridged, and the mill on the latter still turned. A post office was open by 1793, its mails being handled via Greenock, and four fair days were scheduled for 1797; a new post office opened in 1798, but according to Heron in 1799, Largs was no more than a *"village"* of some 400 people. By 1813 a ferry to Kerrycroy in Bute was long-established, and in 1827 the place was described by Chambers as a *"beautifully picturesque town"*. By 1831 Clyde steamers were making regular offshore calls, and a steamer pier was built of stone in 1834, stimulating residential development on the west-facing slopes with their views of the Isles of Cumbrae, Bute and Arran.

**Yachting, Railway and Golf**: In 1876 Largs became a police burgh, with 3000 residents in 1881. The *Largs & Millport Weekly News* originated in 1877 and the Royal Largs Yacht Club in 1882. In 1885 the Glasgow & South Western Railway extended a branch to Largs via Ardrossan and West Kilbride, offering a circuitous connection with Glasgow. At some date a gasworks was provided. A coastguard station, secondary school and a hotel were open by 1894, when steamers plied to Wemyss Bay, providing a round trip from Glasgow by rail and sea. Largs, which still sprawled along the shore, was then described by Murray as *"a clean town containing numerous houses for summer visitors, and comfortable residential villas, an excellent place for boating; there is now a golf course"* – the club had been founded in 1891. The historic Brisbane House was sadly demolished about 1920, the year that Routenburn golf club was founded, providing Largs with a second, hillside course with fine views.

**Quality Resort Development**: The Barrfields Pavilion was gifted to the town by Robert Barr and opened in 1929 as a thousand-seat theatre and dance venue; in World War II it was used for the repair of seaplanes. From 1929 the LMS Railway used Albion buses on a coastal service between Largs and Greenock. Though the Kerrycroy ferry service ended in the 1930s, Largs remained mainly a residential and resort town, with significant growth in that decade. The Moorings and Nardini restaurants dated from 1935, and the *Viking Cinema* from 1939. The Combined Operations base of World War II which operated at Largs in 1942–46 was named HMS *Monck*. The *Moorings Ballroom* was added to the *Viking Cinema* in the 1950s, when in addition to the service to Wemyss Bay, steamers plied to Millport all the year round. The town's population had reached 8600 by 1951, when Largs already had the facilities of an average town, plus no fewer than 26 hotels, which between them had over 450 rooms. By 1963 the *Marine* and *Curlinghall* hotels had combined under their joint names, providing 90 rooms; there was a holiday camp at Millrig, 5 km to the north. An inshore lifeboat station was opened at Largs in 1964.

**Retirement Resort**: In 1972 over four-fifths of the housing at Largs was privately owned, a very high proportion for a Scottish burgh. By then the lower end of the summer trade had been badly hit by cheap Spanish package holidays, and the upper by car mobility; by 1979 a roll-on vehicle ferry plied to Cumbrae Slip, replacing a pleasure steamer to Millport, and the Wemyss Bay service was no more. In 1980 the Barrfields Pavilion became a leisure centre rather than a theatre, and around that time both the *Moorings Ballroom* and *Viking Cinema* were closed and sadly demolished; various hotels either suffered the same fate, or became homes for the elderly, for whom many flats were also built. By 1981 a quarter of the affluent population of 10,000 were over retirement age, but in respect of overall services there was little net change from 1951; Largs was also a dormitory and yachting centre. A large marina was built out into the Clyde south of the town in the 1980s, while residential development extended it to the north and east.

***'Sparks Effect'*, Flatted Pensioners and Country Park**: The electrification of the railway, completed early in 1987, led to a 40% increase in passenger usage and gave rise to renewed growth: in 1990 a further marina and 261 flats were approved and by 1995 a sailing school was in operation. By 1991 the residents numbered 10,925 and kept their affluent retired character; over 38% of Largs households consisted solely of pensioners. In 1992 Nardini's ice cream, made in Largs with 48% double cream, was a well-established luxury product. Largs Academy is a well-established school, now with almost 900 pupils in 1997. A new station building completed in 2000 has replaced the original, demolished by a runaway train in 1994. The Kelburn Country Park, created by 1994 around his home at Kelburn Castle by the 10th Earl of Glasgow, offers varied unsophisticated pleasures for families. In addition to the many small and medium-sized hotels, there are guest houses aplenty, and a tiny hostel for backpackers is open.

## LARKHALL & Millheugh — Map 16, A5

***Lanarkshire town**, pop. 15,500* — OS 64: NS 7651

In the 16th century the tower of Plotcock Castle was built in a well-settled area 5 km south-east of Hamilton. Pont's rough sketch map made in 1596 showed tiny symbols for Patrickholm, Millheugh, and *'Lakhouse'* – perhaps Larkhall. In the mid 18th century the Roy map showed *'Larrockhall'* as a farm on a dead-end road from the hamlet of Crossgates (later known as Canderside Toll), which lay near the Avon Water, astride the road between Stonehouse and Overtown. The Avonbank print works were built about 1796; in 1799 Heron noted that *"the rising village of Millheugh, built on a regular plan, in a narrow vale on the Avon, contains above 100 houses inhabited chiefly by manufacturers. Larkhall is another thriving village."* The Avonbank works were converted into a distillery in 1827; it closed in 1830 and was reconverted for bleaching about 1836. Avonbank workers set up a co-operative at Larkhall – before the more famous Rochdale Pioneers were founded in 1844. Many Irish Protestants settled in Larkhall in the hungry 1840s.

**Railways, Mining, Bricks and Textiles**: A mineral railway from Coalburn to Motherwell was opened in 1856, passing east of Larkhall, where the Caledonian Railway later provided a passenger station. A silk-weaving factory was opened in 1879, and brick and tile works operated beside the station in the 1890s, when the large and sprawling settlement of Larkhall was surrounded by fireclay mines and at least four coal pits; unusually for Scotland some miners already owned their own homes, having won them by lot through an early *'building*

*The Avonbank Works, Larkhall, originally built in about 1796. In its time it was a paper works, a distillery, a bleachworks, and (from 1898) a cotton-finishing plant. These beetling machines closed up the texture of cloth for the making of window-blinds. The works closed in 1981.* *(JRH)*

*society'*, as at Kirkcudbright. An inn and a post and telegraph office were open. Though it was already nearing a population of 12,000, Murray's famous tourist guide found nothing to mention in the Larkhall of 1894. But the Avon sanitary engineering works and foundry was started in 1895, and the Avonbank bleach works was enlarged in 1898 with beetling machines to convert Lancashire cotton cloth into roller blind material *(see Hay & Stell)*.

**Golf, Rolls and Motors**: Larkhall continued to grow slowly in the 20th century, with a municipal golf course of 9 holes from 1909, and a football team – Royal Albert FC – that played in the Scottish League for 3 seasons, 1923–26. Provided with serviced sites by the Scottish Industrial Estates Corporation in the late 1930s, Larkhall still grew slowly, to over 14,000 people by 1951, though with only small-town facilities. Around 1950 Rolls-Royce of Hillington set up a branch factory at Larkhall. Mining and brickmaking had ceased in the vicinity by 1954, but in the 1960s a trunk road haulage route between Glasgow and London was operated by Glasgow & District Motorways of Larkhall. The rail passenger service was closed about 1965, and all railways in the area had been lifted by 1971. However by then Larkhall was conveniently served by junction 7 of the new M74 motorway, from which a new link road had been built. Hareleeshill was then an expanding area.

**Clothing and Plastics**: From 1973 DAKS-Simpson had a big factory at Larkhall, making clothing for Marks & Spencer. The Avonbank works of D C Miller & Co closed in 1981 and the beetling machines were dismantled. In 1991 there were 15,493 residents. Peter Tilling Plastics opened a new factory in 1991 employing 40 people, hoping to reach 300 within three years. In 1993 nearly 300 extra jobs were created at DAKS-Simpson; in 1995 they employed 1700 at Larkhall. Meantime the District Council had built units at Larkhall Industrial Estate, and units were also available on the 1980s Strutherhill estate. By 1994 there was a full-scale modern swimming pool, but the golf course still has only 9 holes, though with hopes of 18. Larkhall Academy has around 1100 pupils. The relaying of the railway to Hamilton to give an electrified link with Glasgow was seriously mooted before the regrettable standstill due to privatisation, and is still being considered. In 2001, due to the problems of Marks & Spencer, DAKS cut 262 jobs, but Rosti (plastic component makers) were significant local employers.

## LASSWADE & Bonnyrigg — Map 15, D3

***Midlothian small towns,** pop. 13,700* — OS 66: NT 3066

Lasswade on the River North Esk 9 km south of Edinburgh may take its name from the Old English for *'Meadow Ford'*, or – according to Chambers – *"a lass, or peasant girl, who supplied the want of a bridge, by wading through the water with travellers upon her back"*. She must have been a strapping wench! Lasswade had a Norman church whose original parish embraced Dalkeith, and had a *'hospital'* from 1480. By the time that Timothy Pont mapped Lothian around 1600 a bridge had been built to replace the ford on the Edinburgh to Heriot road. By then *'Over Leswodd'* was a settlement on the north bank of the river; a parish school was opened in 1615.

**Paper, Linen and Coal**: Lasswade's first paper mill was built in 1742. Roy's map of 1752 showed a bridge linking two small places, and six radial roads; Bonnyrigg was a tiny hamlet at a crossroads south of Lasswade. A linen bleachfield was built in mid-century, and about 1781 the thatched Barony House was built; for a time it was the home of Sir Walter Scott. In 1786–91 a new gothic mansion designed by James Playfair was built for Henry Dundas, later Viscount Melville, replacing an earlier Melville Castle. By the 1790s four paper mills in the parish employed 260 people, and there was a colliery; Lasswade post office was established in 1796, with daily connections to and from Edinburgh. Heron noted in 1799 that *"Lasswade is a thriving village and has a substantial bridge"*. A paper mill engine was in use by 1803, but in 1827 Chambers merely described Lasswade as a *"village"* and by 1843 only three paper mills remained.

**Carpets, Railways, Coal and Coaches**: In 1834 Richard Whytock moved his firm out from Edinburgh to make *"tapestry and velvet-pile carpet"*. The Peebles Railway, which left the Edinburgh & Hawick at Eskbank, was opened in 1855 with a station at Bonnyrigg. A gasworks was set up in 1857. The 600 power looms then made about 9000 m of carpet a day. When a short branch railway from the Peebles line through Lasswade to Polton was opened in 1867 the carpet factory was even busier, and expanded later in the century. By 1891 Bonnyrigg had 2550 people and Lasswade 1300. By 1894 a rail-connected colliery had been sunk south of Bonnyrigg; both places had inns. Lasswade was *"a busy village surrounded by chimneys of carpet and other factories"*. Four horse-drawn road coaches plied each day to Edinburgh.

**Golf – and a Variety of Problems**: Bonnyrigg's Broomieknowe golf club was founded in 1906, and the public library's beginning was Carnegie-aided soon after. By 1929 both villages were police burghs, but were then united. Unlike Lasswade, Bonnyrigg became a planned settlement, dominated by large areas of public housing to replace the former miners' rows. A large laundry was built, but the colliery had long gone, and passenger trains were withdrawn in 1951. The large Lasswade High School was built at Bonnyrigg prior to 1963. Melville Castle was a hotel between at least 1954 and 1980, but by the latter date fell below AA standards, was closed and soon became derelict. The oldest paper mill ceased work about 1955 and the railways were all closed to freight by Beeching in the early 1960s; Lasswade station site became a housing estate. A branch knitwear factory opened by Lyle & Scott of Hawick soon closed due to the lack of a suitably skilled workforce. However, the area was just outside the Edinburgh green belt, and continued to increase both in population and the importance of its industries and facilities; the *'Hawthornden'* primary school was built around 1970, 1.5 km from the historic original.

**Catering Equipment and Sandwiches**: By 1981 Bonnyrigg was a town in terms of facilities. Kelly's were making catering equipment by 1977, and in 1979 carpets were still made at Bonnyrigg by Henry Widnell & Stewart, though by 1983 they had moved their HQ to Eskbank. By 1981 the head office and printing works of Scottish County Press – the *Dalkeith Advertiser* series – was on the Sherwood industrial estate at Bonnyrigg. In 1989 the large UB Chilled Foods factory at Bonnyrigg employed some 500 people, but in 1991 when the resident population was 13,700, about 200 jobs were shed from the firm's sandwich-making plant. By 1996 more new housing had been built in several areas and the former railway was a cycle route. The Melville and King's Acre golf courses are now open north of the area, making three courses in all, and the old *Laird & Dog Inn* offers hospitality and rooms. *Melville Castle Hotel*, long vacant, has now been restored as a hotel. Although many inhabitants of the two places now work in Edinburgh, both localities retain their character, Bonnyrigg remaining a real community centre.

## LATHERON & Latheronwheel — Map 13, B5

***Caithness small coastal villages,** pop. 200* — OS 11: ND 1933

Near the coast of Caithness about 30km south-west of Wick are ancient brochs, cairns, a stone circle, standing stones and a church founded in the fifth century. However, recorded history largely passed the area by, leaving undateable remnants of the Forse and Latheron castles. Pont's map of about 1600 showed both *'Lather'* and *'Lathern'* as tiny settlements: the name derives from the Gaelic for *'Mirey'*. About 1813 the coastal track shown on Roy's survey of about 1750 was made up as a coach road by the Commissioners for Highland Roads & Bridges. Meantime in the late 18th century the Latheron to Thurso road was laid out and (allegedly) actually built in a single day by Sir John Sinclair's tenants, organised on military lines. About that time Janetstown was laid out as a new village – 1.5km south-west of Latheron and 50m above the glen of the Latheronwheel Burn – where a fishing harbour was built in the 1860s.

**Ponies, Publishing and Lobsters**: The name Latheronwheel (the second element said by Mackay to derive from the Gaelic for 'Hole' or 'Pool', rather than from a mill), was also adopted for a mansionhouse, and nowadays is used for Janetstown, where the *"comfortable" Latheron Inn* was noted in 1894. A Poor Law institution was also built; part of this was used as a hospital by the 1950s, when a population of some 430 in Latheron and Forse was served by the facilities of a small village. Lidhay, run as a croft until 1957, became a museum of crofting in the mid 1970s. New housing was built by the local authority at Latheronwheel in the 1970s. Although by then the local population was down to little over 200, they supported a pony club. Five small fishing vessels registered at Wick were still trapping lobsters from Latheron in the 1980s. Whittles the technical publishers are based in Roseleigh House at Latheronwheel.

## LAUDER — Map 3, B3

***Borders village,** pop. 1050* — OS 73: NT 5347

The Roman road later known as Dere Street paralleled the Leader Water, a tributary of the Tweed. Some 4km to the east were an ancient fort and earthwork above the Boondreigh Water, and the original little tower of Thirlestane; there was also an ancient chapel. The extensive royal forests of Gala and Leader were recorded in the 12th century, but Lauder must have already been the main centre of thinly peopled Lauderdale when it was shown on the Gough map of around 1250; by 1300 there was a *'hospital'*. At the end of the 13th century a fort was built 500m east of the village for the invading English king Edward I, who wore the Scottish crown in 1298, the date for Lauder's charter as a Royal Burgh. After recovery by the Scots it was re-chartered in 1328, and again in 1502. The fort was rebuilt in stone in the 15th century and by 1482 a bridge crossed the Leader Water, probably a wooden structure that would facilitate the hanging from it of the unlucky Royal architect, Sir Thomas Cochrane. Lauder's minuscule burgh tax contribution rose, but remained slight in 1535.

**Peaceful Millers get Busy**: The fort was again rebuilt in 1548 by the English under Protector Somerset, becoming one of the first in Britain designed for artillery on the bastion plan. Pont's map made around 1600 showed a handful of buildings at Lauder, including *'The Fort'* heavily emphasised within a rectilinear enclosure; however the bridge had vanished. Just below the fort stood a watermill, and there was a waulk mill at the mouth of the Muircleugh Burn, plus two or three more mills on the Brunta Burn above *'Dods'*, where *'Spottswood'* was an emparked tower. A parish school was open by 1621 and the mills must have been busy in 1639, when little Lauder held 23rd place among Scottish burghs in tax yield, easily outdoing Lanark.

**Thirlestane moves to Lauder Fort**: In 1661 Thirlestane was granted a charter as a burgh of barony, but second thoughts led the Duke of Lauderdale to move his family to an enlarged Lauder Fort in 1672, renaming it Thirlestane; in 1673 he moved the adjoining church to a new site in the burgh. The Roy map made in the 1750s showed only three roads or tracks out of Lauder – leading to Edinburgh via Oxton, to Stow, and to Melrose via Darnick. The former fort was then labelled *'Lauder Castle'*; there was still no bridge, but the *'Wakemill'*, the now vanished Boon Mill and a third mill just below it still turned. By then the Kelso to Carfraemill road crossed the Boondreigh Water near its mouth on the line of the present footpath, and paralleled the east side of the Leader to Carfraemill.

**Fairs, Coaching and Barefoot Children**: The main road to Earlston and Jedburgh was turnpiked under an Act of 1768, and by 1776 Lauder had a post office. By the 1790s numerous flour mills lined the Leader Water, and by 1797 Lauder had five fairs per year; it was also a post town with a service on alternate days. Norton, on the Kelso road, was then a coach staging point on the Edinburgh to Greenlaw route. In 1799 Heron wrote that Lauder had over 1000 inhabitants and was a *"town (which) has of late been much improved"*. Chambers commented in 1827 that the old bridge where Cochrane was hanged *"has not existed for a century; the foundations alone are to be seen about 200 yards below the Castle, and the river is now crossed by a modern erection, a good way farther down"*. A Bank of Scotland branch opened in 1833, and at some time a gasworks was built. Only the *"very fair" Black Bull Hotel* was noted in 1894, but in 1896 the council laid out a 9-hole municipal golf course on Chester Hill. In 1901 the burgh population was only 724.

**Light Railway and Tourism**: From 1901 to 1932 (1958 for goods) Lauder was the terminus of a light railway from Fountainhall on the main Edinburgh to Galashiels route; on closure the station site became an industrial estate. By 1953 there were typical village facilities, but later Lauder declined as a centre; its gasworks was closed in 1965. By 1971 a mere 600 people lived in the burgh; however, agricultural engineering was carried on. Thirlestane Castle and its Border Country Life Museum were opened to the public in 1982 after major restoration; by 1985 there was a caravan site, and some new housing built north of the village had brought its 1991 population up to 1064. By then the Regional Council had established an industrial estate in an attempt to compensate for the decline in farm work in what had remained an exclusively agricultural area. In 1994 the A68 which still passed through Lauder was chosen for improvement. The Southern Upland Way long-distance route also passes through the village, which retains two small hotels – the *Lauderdale* and the long-lasting *Black Bull*.

## LAURENCEKIRK

**Map 10, B5**

***Mearns small town,*** *pop. 1600* OS 45: NO 7171

Located in the fertile Howe of the Mearns, the tower house of Thornton Castle was built in the 16th century. Halkerton 2 km to the east was chartered as a burgh of barony in 1612, but never thrived. By 1695 a little settlement nearby, named *Conveth*, already had a school where Ruddiman, a *"celebrated grammarian"*, was master (Heron). By the early 18th century it also possessed an inn. Roy's map showed that about 1750 adjacent Laurencekirk was a very small place on the Brechin to Stonehaven road (later the A94) where it was joined by the area's only other road, leading north to Auchenblae. The linen industry was already its principal support.

**Planned Expansion for Linen**: Around 1770 Lord Gardenston had *"formed the resolution of creating a town, here laid out a plan for buildings, and soon succeeded in attracting settlers"* (Chambers). This planned expansion of the village was for linen making, and was laid out southwards along the main road as far as the point where the new road to Montrose diverged. In 1773 Boswell found the *Gardenston Arms Inn* open; he and Johnson were critical of the small library which it contained! The village houses were built of clay, of brick and stone, or of stone, apparently all thatched. By 1778 framework knitters were at work. Chambers added, *"In 1779 Lord Gardenston procured for Laurencekirk a burgh of barony with the privilege of holding weekly markets, and an annual fair. Before he died, he had the satisfaction of seeing a thriving little town."* He had a bleachfield or printfield built about 1785, establishing lawn, cambric and linen manufactures; C Stiven & Son of Laurencekirk made fine snuff-boxes from 1780 for almost a hundred years.

**Consolidation, Farmers' Market and Railway**: The area's first post office opened in 1792; the annual fair was still held in Laurencekirk in 1797. Heron wrote in 1799 that *"the new village of Laurence-kirk, now a burgh of barony, and containing about 500 inhabitants, merits particular notice"*. A new post office opened in 1803. In 1825 a small brewery was also run in conjunction with a tavern. The firm of Winter's Linens used a French Jacquard hand loom made in 1829, and the *Gardenston Arms* soon became a coaching inn. Laurencekirk had become a significant agricultural market, and gained a station on the main line when the Aberdeen Railway (later part of the Caledonian) opened in 1849. The population had grown to 1400 by 1891.

**New Academy, but no Passenger Trains**: The population fluctuated but little for half a century, and peaked at 1485 in 1951. Although Laurencekirk then had only the facilities of a large village, a new Mearns Academy was built about 1960. But as local farm populations fell and the traffic on the dead straight road through Laurencekirk grew in volume and speed, its shopping role and consequently its own population seriously declined. The old *Gardenston Arms* ceased to be used as an inn some time after 1963, and thanks to Beeching, passenger trains no longer stopped at Laurencekirk from about 1965.

**Laurencekirk in the 1970s**: When visited by the author in 1976 Laurencekirk was a workaday place, a small town based in agriculture, with a large active livestock market, feed merchants, livestock haulier, blacksmith and no fewer than four farm machinery dealers, two of them large. Rail freight traffic was still present on a fair scale. But the place was an evident auxiliary to Montrose and had no real centre, its facilities loosely strung along a busy main road, its 25 or so shops mainly small and modest. Mearns Academy and a primary school, Crown post office, fire and police stations were the main services, and there were still four churches. Four or five small hotels and a tiny tea room offered basic facilities for the tourist.

**The Market Centre Happily Bypassed**: Laurencekirk was bypassed about 1984, and residents must have been mightily relieved that they could at last go about their business with ease and safety. As late as 1978 potatoes were still despatched south by rail, and the railway sidings were used in 1990 for deliveries of agricultural lime to Thompsons. Into the 1990s the market, operated by Aberdeen & Northern Marts, still dealt in cattle and sheep, serving a local area mainly north of the town, extending from Edzell and Inverbervie to Portlethen. In 1991 the population had recovered to about 1600, with an affluent retired element; Mearns Academy had 360 pupils. Agricar continue to deal in farm machinery, both locally and at Forfar. Rail freight has resumed under EW&S, with timber and other traffic on regular trains to Aberdeen; the reopening of a passenger station was again seen as possible.

## LAURIESTON

**Map 16, B2**

***Village / suburb e. of Falkirk,*** *pop. 3500+* OS 65: NS 9179

The Romans' insubstantial Antonine Wall crossed southern Stirlingshire on an east–west line en route to Bo'ness, with its largest fort, a 2.6ha enclosure, at low-lying Mumrills between modern Falkirk and the River Avon. The Pont map of around 1600 showed *'Woodend'*, *'Godsbrig'* and *'Mumrils'* just east of the heavily wooded Callendar Castle estate. The hamlet of Laurieston, 2 km east of Falkirk, emerged as the point where the early road from Falkirk, following the military way beside the wall – or perhaps built on its stone foundation – forked towards Kinneil for Bo'ness, and to Polmont en route to Linlithgow. Perhaps because its houses were built right over the wall it seems to have attracted no interest among early travel writers, until in 1799 Heron called it a *"populous village"*. The Stirlingshire Midland Junction Railway, opened in 1850 from Polmont to Larbert, divided Laurieston from the Callendar estate, but provided no station. By 1895 Laurieston had a post and telegraph office, inn and smithy. In the 20th century it expanded steadily as a suburb, reaching 3300 people in 1971 and having a remarkable four garages by 1980, but its 1991 *'locality'* population was subsumed in Polmont. In the 1990s a new A9 bypass was built to the north, to relieve the village street of traffic between Falkirk town centre and Edinburgh via the M9.

## LAURIESTON

**Map 2, A5**

***Galloway hamlet,*** *pop. 150* OS 83 or 84: NX 6864

Earthworks, including the Dinnance Motte, show early settlement beside a narrow loch 2 km in length, in this remote area 15km north of Kirkcudbright; it was named Loch Grenoch on Pont's map-work of around 1610. Thick woods lay to the west, and a water mill, later known as Blates Mill, turned near its south-eastern end, fed by a small burn. The village of Laurieston was founded 2 km south of the mill in the early

18th century, at a crossroads on the road between New Galloway and Kirkcudbright, completed by about 1754. The loch was then named Loch Gannoch, but later this was changed to Woodhall. Victorian philanthropist and novelist S R Crockett was born locally in 1859. The mansion of Laurieston Hall was a hospital by 1951, and Laurieston, though little more than a hamlet of 250 people, had a sawmill, related to the 4 square km Laurieston Forest to the west, which has since been enlarged fivefold. By 1981 the population had fallen below 200 and the hospital had reverted to domestic use; by 1996 the post office too had closed, but at least there is a pub.

## LAW

**Map 16, B5**

***Lanarkshire village,*** *pop. 2900* — OS 65 or 72: NS 8152

Law is a hilltop settlement above the Garrion Burn 3 km north-west of Carluke in Lanarkshire. Although near the Roman road, in the 1750s Roy noted nothing of substance between Carluke and Overtown. The large mansion of Mauldslie Castle was designed by Robert Adam for the 5th Earl of Hyndford and built beside the Clyde in 1792–96. The village of Law grew 2 km away, after coal mining began in 1792, but a post office was not opened until after 1838. From 1848 Law was served by a station on the main line of the Caledonian Railway (CR), and expanded substantially as a mining centre from 1877. From 1880 the station was renamed *Law Junction*, becoming the divergence of a new alternative CR route to the north via Wishaw. By the 1890s there were coal pits in all directions, and a large late 19th century tileworks between Law and Carluke made field drains and flowerpots. However, Law remained a series of hamlets and never became a burgh. During the 1939–45 war a large emergency general hospital was built to the east.

**Recovering from a Dip in Fortunes**: In 1951 about 2000 people enjoyed the facilities of a small village, plus a secondary school; mining had gone, leaving coal bings, and there was a jam factory which later disappeared. Mauldslie Castle was demolished in 1959, the station closed about 1965, the tileworks were disused by 1976 and by then the secondary school had also closed. The hospital was retained and enlarged, and some village facilities increased, but the many closures had hit Law hard. Matters had improved by 1991, when there were 2900 residents, many young and in services such as the hospital, distribution and catering. In 1995 it was announced that a new General Hospital in Netherton, Wishaw would replace Law Hospital; the Wishaw General opened in May 2001, and all patients were transferred. Meantime more housing development has continued in Law village.

## LAWERS

**Map 5, C3**

***Location on L. Tay,*** *pop. under 100* — OS 51: NN 6739

A crannog lies near the north shore of Loch Tay, where a stone circle and a ruined church stand at the foot of the bulky 1214 m Ben Lawers. The Roy map of the 1750s showed a substantial *"Milltown"* near the church, on a lochside track from Kenmore to Killin. By the late 19th century this was a metalled road and Lawers had a mill, pier and post office. By the 1930s there was a school, and a ferry plied across the loch to Ardtalnaig. By 1951 the tiny *Ben Lawers Hotel* was open but the ferry and mill had gone, and the school was out of use. Lawers post office closed about 1972; by then only about 65 residents remained. The visitor centre and mountain rescue post for Ben Lawers are some 10 km to the west. The *Ben Lawers Hotel* remains; apart from a few farms it now stands in isolation.

## LEADBURN

**Map 3, A3**

***Midlothian location,*** *pop. under 100* — OS 66 or 73: NT 2355

Located 4 km south of Penicuik at a height of over 260 m, east of the wastes of Auchencorth Moss, remote Leadburn had become a road junction by about 1754, but little growth followed except for the mansion of Whim House, built in the late 18th century 3 km to the south-west at the high altitude of 275 metres, and variously attributed to Adam and to David Henderson. Leadburn station on the Peebles Railway, which opened from Eskbank in 1855, became in 1864 one of Scotland's most unlikely railway junctions, with the completion of the highly optimistic line passing near the Whim, Lamancha and West Linton to reach Dolphinton; both lines became parts of the North British system. But little more than the *Leadburn Inn* and a post office appeared at bleak Leadburn, and the Dolphinton line was closed to passengers in 1933.

**Mineral Operations**: The population in the area was only about 250 by 1951, by which time Whim House was a 24-roomed hotel (later called the *White House Hotel*); the Peebles railway was closed in 1962. By 1963 the boarding establishment originally known as the Wellington Farm School had been built on the Penicuik road 1 km north of the crossroads; it was moved to new buildings across the road around 1990. The Nether Falla sand and gravel quarry 4 km south of Leadburn was already extensive by the 1960s and remains active, unlike a small quarry at Craigburn. Peat is also extracted locally. Meantime the post office had closed by 1970, and the hotel vanished after 1972, part of its outbuildings becoming five houses; but the long-established *Leadburn Inn* with its railway carriage diner is still open.

## LEADHILLS

**Map 2, B3**

***S. Lanarkshire village,*** *pop. 300* — OS 71 or 78: NS 8815

The aptly named village of Leadhills which stands about 395 metres above sea level in upper Clydesdale was among the earliest Scottish mining settlements, its people digging lead ore possibly from the 12th century and certainly as early as 1264. Around 1500 James IV opened a gold mine, where the largest nugget found apparently weighed about 60 grams. The Earl of Hopetoun operated lead mines from 1517; a larger lead mine was opened by Foulis in 1590, producing up to 400 tonnes of ore a year from veins which Heron described as being up to 12 metres in thickness. Pont's map of Clydesdale, sketched about 1596, was somewhat confused in this area, but the words *Auri* (gold) and *'Level'* were clear, and *'Leadmills'* was noted. Despite the lack of proper roads, exports were occurring by 1614, but only one of the two smelting mills was in use in 1638. The mines were then acquired by Sir John Hope (of the Hopetoun House family) and "developed to a degree of perfection unknown before".

**The Burgh and its Highway to Leith**: Leadhills was chartered as a burgh of barony in 1661; at the same time an Act empowered the proprietor to improve the highway to Leith to enable lead ore to be exported – all of 75 km via Biggar, and by no means all downhill – pity the horses! Much Dutch *'Delft'* ware was lead-glazed using Leadhills ore; some was smelted overseas. The Clyde Bridge north of Abington seems to have been one outcome. John Ray who visited the village in 1662 opined that it *"will in time, it is likely, increase to a good considerable town"*. A large lead cistern dated 1696, whether cast at Leadhills or Leith, still showed its excellent craftsmanship in the garden of a Scottish mansion visited by the author in 1989 – best left nameless. The poet Allan Ramsay was born in Leadhills in 1684, son of the then manager of the lead mines; in 1713 he became the father of a second Allan Ramsay, the famous portrait artist.

**Lead Miners' Library and Steamboat Pioneer**: There were about 50 mine workers at Leadhills when the unique *Lead Miners' Library* was founded in 1741 by the men themselves, led by James Wells and William Wright. Allan Ramsay senior gifted the building, erected in 1756. Also, the first post office was opened in 1755. Roy's map made about that time showed Leadhills as a very substantial though irregular settlement, its name appearing in the capitals usually reserved for Royal Burghs. There were roads to both Abington and Elvanfoot, but to the south the only connection was the perilous *Entriken Path* to Drumlanrig. As it was difficult to cut drainage levels through the hard rock, pumps were installed from 1763, in which year William Symington the steamship pioneer was born in Leadhills.

**Steam Pumps and Lead Poisoning**: Steam pumps were introduced to the mines in 1792; by that time about 1400 tonnes of lead were smelted annually. By 1797 Leadhills was a post town, connected with Elvanfoot and the outside world on alternate days. Lead poisoning was already a recognised local hazard when Heron called Leadhills a *"village"* in 1799, noting that of its population of about a thousand, most were miners, commended for their *"circulating library for the instruction and amusement of the little community"*. By then the Earl of Hopetoun was the proprietor, and *"the lead smelted at this place is all sent to Leith"*

**Bad Roads no bar to Enlightenment**: Surprisingly, the road north to Douglas Mill was *"very bad"* in 1803 – the worst section travelled by Dorothy Wordsworth in the south of Scotland; her lengthy description of Leadhills is evocative. At that time there were two shops open and also the *"decent-looking" Hopetoun Arms* Inn. A wash mill was in use by 1813, and according to Chambers in 1827 *"the little village of Leadhills flourishes; the inhabitants, though chiefly miners, are an enlightened set of people, having more than one public library"*. The Scots Mining Company paid a sixth of their takings to the proprietor, Hopetoun. Lead shot mills were opened in 1834, and new water-powered engines for haulage were employed from the mid 19th century. By the 1860s a large lead smelting complex was in use, but Bremner then called Leadhills and its neighbour Wanlockhead *"the dreariest inhabited places in the country"*. By 1894 the *'decent inn'* had become the *"good" Hopetoun Arms Hotel*.

**The Transient Railway and the End of Mining**: Leadhills' population was still about a thousand when a belated light railway was built from Elvanfoot in 1901, following legislation which permitted a much cheaper form of construction than normal lines; it reached Britain's highest standard gauge summit at almost 457 m before dropping to a terminus at Wanlockhead. Lead, silver and gold mining ended around 1928, and the population shrank inexorably; the railway could not then pay its way, and was closed in 1939. Despite its high altitude Leadhills was not abandoned, because almost uniquely for Scotland at that time the plots on which the houses stood were effectively freehold, not feus.

**Struggling to find a New Role**: By 1953 there was a 9-hole golf course – reputedly the highest in Britain – and the hotel survived as such until the mid 1970s. In the early 1980s Leadhills was a small village of 300 people in a remote narrow valley, an untidy huddle of small old cottages, some derelict; a library still existed, and it was also a very minor ski resort when the weather permitted. In 1991 the blockage of the 18th century Gripps drainage level below the village caused concern over possible sudden floods due to rising water backing up in the old lead workings. However in 1995 there was still a post office, a pub, the golf course, and 600 m of 60 cm-gauge tourist railway laid by the Lowthers Railway Society on the old alignment to the Hillhead summit, with the aim of eventually reaching Wanlockhead.

## LEITH & Newhaven — Map 15, C1

***Port and suburb of Edinburgh**, pop. 28,000* — OS 66: NT 2676

Leith at the mouth of the Water of Leith some 3 km from Edinburgh is known to have been a seaport since 1134, and its development in trading is very well documented; it also had a fishing role. Although in the 13th century Leith was scarcely involved in overseas trade, many opportunities for it to develop were opened by the sacking in 1296 of Scotland's former principal southern port of Berwick. Under Robert I's policy of providing landlocked burghs with their own ports, a charter of 1329 made over *"the port and mills of Leith"* to the Royal Burgh of Edinburgh, so it must already have been trading in grain; a medieval manse later incorporated into a granary still survives, as do wine vaults built for Newbattle Abbey about that time.

**Wool and Wine: Scotland's Premier Port**: Around 1330 Leith exported 170 tonnes of wool a year, making it the third wool port in Scotland after Berwick and Aberdeen. By 1360 Edinburgh was regarded as Scotland's capital; this benefited Leith, which by 1375 handled half Scotland's wool for export. Even good years would see no more than thirty foreign-going vessels cleared by the Leith Customs, though these ships were among the largest then in use, and physical improvements must have been made to the port so as to handle them; in 1415 John Hardyng wrote that at Leith the navy *"may rest safely"*. In the early 15th century wool exports first slumped, then soon recovered to nearly 300 tonnes a year around 1430. Leith had a shipyard by 1437, and by the mid 15th century although wool exports had halved in value, it had become the main entrepot for imports to Scotland such as wheat, French salt and wine, some of which was re-exported to Denmark in 1479. In return the northern Scottish ports sent to Leith hides and salmon for the court. Leith again benefited after 1482 by the final loss of Berwick to England.

**Newhaven, Horse Racing and Baltic Trade**: As trading and port congestion grew at Leith, so from 1488 the local fishermen moved their base to its suburb of Newhaven, from whose shores oysters too were harvested by the 16th century. In the 1490s Leith and Edinburgh had about 71% of the revived Scottish wool trade – including a monopoly of raw wool exports, and predominance in woollen cloth and hides. Horse racing began on the sands at Leith around 1500. In 1497 five Leith ships were among the 21 Scottish vessels passing through the

Sound to and from the Baltic; in 1512 a Leith vessel was trading in Hamburg, but the port's largest trade in wool and cloth was with the Netherlands through Veere, and in hides and fish with Normandy through Dieppe. By 1540 about 40% of ships on the Baltic route came from Leith.

**Newhaven Naval Dockyard and the *Great Michael***: Newhaven's royal dockyard was making ropes and cables by 1506; the great four-masted ship *Michael* was built there in 1507–11 in rivalry with Henry VIII of England, her construction supervised by Leith-born merchant and sea-captain Andrew Wood. She was 73 m in length with sides a metre thick, and Robert Lindsay of Pitscottie recorded that her construction *"wasted all the woods in Fife which was oakwood, save Falkland"*. In 1510 Edinburgh Corporation bought Newhaven harbour and village. In 1544 the brutish Henry's troops destroyed the town and seized another locally built ship, the *Unicorn*. Tall sea marks had been erected by 1553, and golf balls were being made in North Leith by 1554. Leith was then fortified, but a third of the town was again burned down in 1560, this time accidentally.

**After the Fire**: Rebuilding was rapid, for in 1561–63 over 350 Leith merchants exported hides and skins, though only 10% of them seem to have been physically involved in skinning carcases and treating the pelts. Edinburgh town council, pursuing their search for monopoly, bought the superiority of South Leith in 1567. With rising coal and salt trade after the siege of 1571–72, the port began to grow from *"a bare village"* (Fynes Moryson 1598). In James VI's reign a building was erected *"partly as an asylum for indigent old women, and partly for a grammar school"* (Heron); this would be in 1598, when South Leith also gained a parish school. The refining of silver for the Scots coinage began in 1592, and Leith definitely had golf links by 1593, but it was still a *"village"* to the French visitor de Rohan in 1600.

**Roads and Coaches to Edinburgh**: Edinburgh town council became the feudal superior of the remainder of Leith in the early 17th century, adding Bonnington mills to its properties in 1617. Pont's map of Lothian showed *'Lyth'* as two arcs of buildings lining the harbour, united into a semicircle by a bridge across the Water of Leith; east of the harbour was a breakwater. Newhaven was indicated by a tiny symbol, but a road was shown connecting the port of Leith with Edinburgh. This confirms the account that in 1610 the first public coaches in Scotland were brought from Pomerania by Henry Anderson, to provide a service from Leith to Edinburgh. Grain exports were again noted in 1618, and commercial brewing began two years later. Around that time Pilrig House was built for the Monypennys on a site between Leith and Edinburgh. After 1625 stone from the wharf of the lately defunct Culross coal mine was brought across the Forth for use in building Leith pier, for its trade with London was booming. By 1631 the Society of Free Fishermen of Newhaven was flourishing.

*Newhaven harbour, which was rebuilt in 1876–81 as Edinburgh's main fishing port. It was first 'new' in 1488 when Leith had become congested.* *(JRH)*

**Edinburgh Dominates Posts and Barony**: A post office was opened in Leith as early as 1632, but the port was never strictly a *'post town'* in its own right. Similarly when it was created a burgh of barony in 1636, its council of course included Edinburgh nominees. In that year the traveller Brereton found a town which despite being all built of stone, he considered a poor place with few ships; fewer than 200 merchants in Leith and Edinburgh were handling about two-thirds of Scotland's overseas trade with western Europe. However, by 1638 Leith had a high school (now an Academy) and was linked by road with Musselburgh. In 1639 South and North Leith together amounted to the fifth richest centre in Scotland, after Edinburgh, Aberdeen, Glasgow and Dundee.

**Prosperity under Cromwell**: A ropeworks started in 1638, and the making of woollens at Bonnington began in the 1640s. In 1650 Leith Walk was built beside the road as a defended link between Leith and Edinburgh. The Leith Citadel, built the same year, was remarkably granted a charter as a separate burgh of barony in 1662. A printing works was established at Leith during Cromwell's rule; from 1651 to 1655 it printed the first newspaper in Scotland, the *Mercurius Scoticus* (largely an edition of a London paper). When Tucker made his detailed Customs investigation for Cromwell in 1655 he found Leith owned only two or three North Sea trading vessels of 200 to 300 tons; it was *"a pretty small town"* with a single quay, which was still nonetheless *"the chief port of all Scotland"*. Maybe *"pretty"* was used in the visual sense, for Richard Franck in the following year was more impressed: *"The houses and structures are large and lofty; a substantial causeway leads to the bridge."* Cloth of various kinds seems to have been the chief export, but meat and fish were also traded.

**Beer, Wine, Lead and Glass**: A survey map of North Leith dated 1661 showed that it was part of the Regality of Canongate. East of the river mouth was a timber yard, and there were three tiny dry docks, a Custom House, and a drawbridge across the Water of Leith upstream from the main bridge. In that year, 1661, de Rocheford noted that *"the largest vessels can come up into the centre of the town, and lie loaded along the quay, sometimes to the number of more than fifty"*. Adjoining was the large maritime village of Newhaven. The small shipyard, at that time apparently the only one in eastern Scotland, was active, and frequent coaches rolled along a paved road to Edinburgh. Leith continued to prosper. About 1670 the Englishman Sir Charles Stansfield built the Yardhead brewery, then Scotland's largest. He was active in setting up the smelting of lead ore, carried overland from Leadhills and Wanlockhead, and had also built a bottle works by 1679; another glassworks was established in 1682 to make bottles and drinking glasses, for at that time Leith imported about two-thirds of all the wine drunk in Scotland.

**Leith as a Resort?**: Morer in 1689 thought Leith was emerging as a resort, *"a thriving mart-town having a fine pier stretching itself a great way into the sea, and serves for the safety of the vessels, and the pleasure of those who walk on it"*. Edinburgh people *"flock by foot or in coaches to divert themselves"*. By 1692 Leith possessed 29 ships, averaging 59 tons, and fine three- and four-storey buildings lined the harbour head. At that time a third of Leith's 733 manufacturing workers were in shipbuilding and other wood trades, plus the glass works, 14 small breweries, sugar refineries, a wind-powered sawmill, and the soapworks founded by Nathaniel Uddart. The smelter had been rebuilt to refine silver, lead and zinc, with a water-powered ore-crushing mill; it may have cast a uniquely decorated lead cistern dated 1696 for a mansion garden – best left unnamed here – where it could still be seen in the 1980s.

**After the Union of Parliaments**: Newhaven was a ferry port for Fife, and had a school by the early 18th century, while North Leith was long known for the import of tar, hemp and flax; a sailcloth factory was established in 1708. Ale and beer was exported by the time of the Union, when Leith's 35 ships represented 16% of the Scottish fleet. With growth elsewhere, notably at Greenock, this proportion had plummeted by 1712 to only 4%, though the number of locally-owned vessels actually rose. Dry docks were opened in 1720; Defoe writing a few years later called Leith *"a large and populous town with a good stone bridge, a very fine quay well wharfed up with stone and a very long and well built pier"*. A paved road and walkway – Leith Walk – linked with Edinburgh, many of whose merchants kept warehouses in the city. By then there was a regular – though too often stormy – ferry to Burntisland.

**Leith Golf Pioneers a World Industry**: By 1743 golf clubs, and the golf balls long made locally, were being exported from Leith to South Carolina. It was not (as commonly claimed) in St Andrews but in Leith in 1744 that the rules of the game were first formalised for the *Gentlemen Golfers* by their Captain, John Rattray; the Golf House built at Leith in 1767 was the world's first golf clubhouse. After three centuries of local horse-racing, a regular programme of races on the sands was well established by 1772. Meantime scutching mills were built at Bonnington in 1730 by James Spalding, who had been sent to Holland to learn this new trade. *Osnaburgs* were being made for the British Linen Company (BLC) in 1746, and from then until its closure in 1760, Leith had the BLC's yarn staplery; cordage was also made, and the port soon became paramount in the thread export trade to London. The linen weaving works noted in 1757 had run down by 1770, but framework knitting was an established trade in Leith by 1778.

**Ironwork, Ale and Dyeing**: In 1747 a large smithy was established in Leith, but this was moved to Cramond *(q.v.)* in 1752 to obtain more waterpower. In 1749 William Younger opened the first of his family's breweries in Leith. Hugo Pollock, author of the great *History of Edinburgh* under his adopted name of Arnot, was born in Leith in 1749. Roy's map of 1752–55 showed no fewer than eight roads converging on an already large settlement with a pier, but no harbour was indicated at Newhaven, though by 1759 the *Peacock Inn* was open there. The purple *Cudbeare* dye was made there from lichens from 1758 to 1777, when the activity was moved to Calton beside Glasgow. Paper mills were promoted elsewhere by Leith merchants, who traded in the rags then used as their raw material. In 1769 Pennant found Leith a large but *"dirty"* town. The wine vaults were rebuilt in 1785 by John Thompson.

**Whaling, Wool, Oysters and Pioneer Paddle Steamer**: Whaling from Leith began in 1750, and six ships were engaged by 1788. Although by the 1770s the predominance of general trade had switched to the west coast, Leith market still handled about 200 tonnes of wool, and one glassworks alone made over 800 tonnes of bottles. No fewer than 4800 barrels of oysters were exported in 1778. The fort – built between Leith and Newhaven in 1780–81 to protect the harbour – was soon masked from the sea by new dock works! In 1788 Allan & Stewart of Leith built the pioneering paddle steamer *Experiment*, designed by Patrick Millar of Dalswinton, but for a full generation nothing came of this *(see Helensburgh)*. However, by 1790 some owners of sailing ships specialised in trade with the north of Scotland, Orkney and Shetland. All this development more than doubled the population of Leith in the 18th century; Heron suggested over 12,000 people by 1799.

**Docks for Trade, Fishing and Shipbuilding**: In 1791 Leith became the headquarters of the Leith & Berwick Shipping Company which operated vessels to London, picking up Tweed salmon on the way; two more such firms were competing on this route by 1814. The Leith Banking Company was established in 1792, the same year that a new pier was built at Newhaven for the Burntisland ferry. Herring having been found in the Forth in 1793, the fishing industry developed further at Newhaven, which Heron in 1799 described as a *"fishing village off which there is an oyster bed"*. Leith also became a key export centre for salted herring and cod, and was by then a Port of Registry, with the identification letters LH. Two dry docks had been provided since 1777, and the opening of Leith's first wet docks took place in 1799. In 1793 five shipbuilders employing over 150 carpenters dominated North Leith, building vessels of 200 to 300 tons, and soon there were four or five daily mail services between Leith and Edinburgh.

**Leith's Trade in the 1790s**: The Quayside Mills were established late in the 18th century, just one of the 80 mills spread throughout the Water of Leith in 1799. The Bonnington distillery was started in 1798, but local brewing was declining fast: the last Leith brewery (Scott's) failed in 1821. In 1799 Heron quoted from Arnot's History of Edinburgh: *"the vessels employed in the London trade, called 'Berwick Smacks', have good accommodation for passengers. The largest ships at this port are those employed in the Greenland whale fishery, and in the trade to the West Indies. To Germany, Holland and the Baltic, are exported lead, glassware, linen and woollen stuffs, and a variety of other goods. From thence are imported immense quantities of timber, oak-bark, hides, linen rags, pearl-ashes, flax, hemp, tar and many other articles. From France, Spain and Portugal wines, brandy, oranges and lemons. From the West Indies and America rice, indigo, rum, sugar and logwood."*

**Leith at the end of the Eighteenth Century**: Heron added his own description of *"a populous town, containing many handsome modern houses, though the ancient buildings are for most part neither elegant nor commodious. 165 vessels belong to this port, navigated by upwards of a thousand seamen. In 1791 the registered tonnage at Leith was 130,000. Ships of* *considerable size are built at this port, and several extensive rope-works are here carried on. The flourishing manufacture of bottle-glass, window-glass and crystal has long employed three glass-houses, and three others have lately been erected. A carpet-manufacture, a soap-work, and some iron-forges, are also worthy of being mentioned."* Leith Walk was then *"a kind of terrace, for a foot-path, raised of dry gravel"* along the east side of the Edinburgh road.

**Rennie's Dock and Ginger Wine**: An Act of 1799 enabled big dock works designed by John Rennie to go ahead: the eastern wet dock was built in 1800–06, its entrance crossed by a swing bridge of about 1810; a Custom House was built in 1811, and the middle dock in 1810–17. Three graving docks were created, and a basin was built at Newhaven from 1812 onwards. During the Napoleonic wars trade stagnated, with only some 20,000 tons of shipping locally owned in 1808, and necessary improvements to the dock entrance were not made. However, the long-lasting John Crabbie & Co started to brew ginger wine at Great Junction Street in 1801, and a post office was opened at Duke Street in 1804. By 1810 the Leith Banking Company had established branches in Callander, Dalkeith, Galashiels and Langholm. Horse racing on the sands was no longer satisfactory, and in 1816 the events were moved to Musselburgh *(q.v.)*.

**Developments in Shipping**: The Trinity House of Leith, headquarters of a friendly society of master mariners, was built in 1816–18 and still survives. For a time in 1818 the pioneer steamboat *Comet* provided a service between Leith and Grangemouth, and in 1821 a chain pier was built at Newhaven for the new steam packets which were plying to Stirling via Queensferry and Alloa. In the early 1820s came general expansion, with four new shipping firms, including one for the Australian trade, and from 1821 steam packets of over 400 tons were making the passage to London in less than the four days previously required. In the 1820s William Lindsay and Alex Leckie of Leith built many of the East Fife fishing boats. Chambers observed in 1827, *"The Custom-House is the seat of the Board of Customs for Scotland."* Besides glass, Leith factories included sugar-works and maltings. Newhaven was *"an ancient fishing village"* where fishwives concentrated on oysters *(c.f. Fisherrow)*. Pilrig House was extended in 1828, and Leith Links were laid out in 1829. A Bank of Scotland branch had opened in 1825.

**Treacle, Sugar and Canned Meat**: John Macfie from Greenock first made treacle in Leith's Elbe Street in 1804. Flour mills were built in 1828, and grain imports and larger-scale milling developed after the repeal of the Corn Laws in 1846. John Gillon established a meat cannery in 1837 at Mitchell Street; by 1869 this made about 500 products, ranging from stock cubes to canned haggis. The North Leith sugar refinery was closed about 1860 after many years, but Macfie's remained active, and the Bonnington Sugar Refining Company built a new factory at Breadalbane Street in 1865–66; its 100 workers produced about 250 tonnes of sugar a week in 1869.

**Building Bigger Ships and Early Engines**: Menzies & Co of Leith built three wooden paddle steamships of increasing size: the *Queen Margaret* of 100 tons in 1821 for the Queensferry passage; the hull for the famous first transatlantic steamer *Sirius* of 703 tons, built in 1837 but with an engine made in Shettleston; and the *Forth* of 1940 tons, constructed in 1841 for the Royal Mail Steam Packet Company. In 1840 they built the world's two largest steamships to date, but after this *tour de force* the firm then declined into mainly repair work. Meantime Craig & Rose of Leith Walk, who had started up as paint manufacturers in 1829, were destined to become famous. In 1824 Timothy Burstall of Leith designed an early steam-driven road carriage, and later built one of the unsuccessful engines vanquished by Stephenson's *Rocket* at the Rainhill trials of 1829 on the Liverpool & Manchester Railway.

*The premises of the Leith Banking Company, established in 1792 when local banks played a vital role in mobilising capital for industrial investment. Seen here as the Royal Bank, the building has now been converted into offices.* *(JRH)*

**Financial Problems Inhibit Trade**: Henderson & Turnbull started up in 1820 as whisky merchants and blenders, as did William Muir in 1823; Lochend distillery was built in 1825. A major role in the whisky blending, bottling and shipping trade developed in the second quarter of the century, with a blending plant at Great Junction Street and many bonded warehouses. The Bonnington distillery was closed in 1853 and became a bonded store, but malting was expanding, and in 1856 Younger's ale, exported through Leith, actually reached Australia. In 1826–29 – under new Port Commissioners who replaced the failing Edinburgh City Council – the east and west piers were extended to confine the channel and induce natural scour. Dues were raised to pay for the improvements, deterring shippers, and by 1832 local ownership had fallen to little over the 1808 level. In that year Cobbett wrote of Leith simply as *"a pretty little sea-port"*. It did not help that the City Council finally went bankrupt in 1833, and although five whalers still operated from Leith in 1834, the Australian line went out of business. The Leith Banking Company also failed, in 1842.

**Gas Works, Steamship Lines and Railways**: A small gasworks had been built in 1806, eleven years before one was provided at Edinburgh. The larger joint Edinburgh & Leith Gasworks at Baltic Street was erected in 1840. The *Ben Line* of Leith began trading in 1839, and the General Steam Navigation Company about the same time. From 1845 the Edinburgh & Dundee Steam Packet Company's steamer *Britannia* also called regularly at East Fife ports. In 1838 a branch of the primitive horse-drawn Edinburgh & Dalkeith Railway (E&D) was built along the shore to a terminus at the mouth of the Water of Leith, beside the dock gates at Constitution Street, and coal export became possible. In its first year it also carried over 31,000 passengers; later the station was known as South Leith. The Edinburgh, Leith & Granton Railway (EL&G) opened in

1842 to Trinity station above the chain pier, creating a suburb. In 1846 the EL&G opened a Bonnington to Leith line, with the first of several direct rail passenger services between the centre of Edinburgh and a station at Citadel, later named North Leith under the North British Railway (NB) which had bought the E&D in 1845.

**Locomotive Engineering for Rail and Road**: R & W Hawthorn & Co of Newcastle established a branch works at Great Junction Street beside the Water of Leith in 1846, building engines for the new North British Railway and others. By about 1860 they had 700 workers, and by 1872 425 locomotives had been built there. Meantime the little-known T M Tennent & Co of Bowershall Works in Leith's Bonnington Road built steam road locomotives (traction engines) for a time from 1862, and L J Todd, well known as a wagon builder by 1860, did the same around 1870.

**Railway Developments, plus Horses**: The EL&G was absorbed by the Edinburgh & Northern Railway in 1847 and two years later became part of the Edinburgh Perth & Dundee (EP&D), whose services between Edinburgh and Dundee plied via Granton. In 1862 the EP&D was itself absorbed by the NB. By 1860 Wordie & Co had a rail cartage depot, and later also a district office, for in 1903 they based over 200 horses in Leith. The rival Caledonian Railway (CR) had opened a goods and passenger service to their own North Leith station by 1879.

**Early Victorian Trade, Industry and Dock Extensions**: About 1845 a deeper channel was dredged into the port. The east pier extension was completed in 1851 and the new rail-connected Victoria Dock in 1852. In the 1850s several ships plied daily to Burntisland, and others to Alloa and Stirling. Weekly or more often, vessels would leave for London, Kirkwall, Lerwick, and even Glasgow. Manufactures then included ships, sails, ropes, paint, barrels, glassware, sawn timber, sugar, preserved foods, soap, candles, leather, chemicals, flour and whisky, plus the products of four foundries and machine shops. A sixth graving dock was constructed in 1858, and Bremner noted that in the late 1860s all were generally occupied; the Prince of Wales graving dock could accept any merchant vessel of the day except the huge *Great Eastern*. In 1864 a breakwater designed by Robert Stevenson was built at Newhaven, through which the Fife and North mails passed for the Pettycur ferry (still ignoring the railway's ferries between Granton and Burntisland). The Albert Dock was built in 1863–69. In 1866 Leith was second only to Bo'ness among Scottish ports in the value of coal exported, and over 100 oyster boats worked out of Newhaven.

**Varied Industries**: Christmas card printing began in the 1840s, and from 1852 writing ink was manufactured; this industry was later moved to Granton. A grand golf tournament was held on the Links in 1867, perhaps the last to take place there. Although paper was not made locally, Cowans of Penicuik had a rag warehouse in Leith, while Campbell & Co were Scotland's largest lead and zinc roofing manufacturers, with 50 workers – by then using imported materials. Meantime the glassworks established in 1682 had acquired seven furnaces, though only two were in use in 1869. In 1861 the Leith foundry of the Shotts Iron Company was casting architectural ironwork. Clay pipes for smokers were still made at Leith in William Christie's factory, until at least 1908. A large tannery opened at Bonnington in 1879, and rubber was processed in the Leith area from the late 19th century.

**Late Victorian Shipbuilding & Engineering**: By the 1840s Mortons of Leith were prosperous shipbuilders. Between 1855 and 1887 this firm built a succession of paddle vessels for service on the Forth, including a train ferry; they used both wood and iron hulls and constructed patent slipways. In 1882 a total of seven shipyards in the area were building vessels ranging from wooden steam trawlers and yachts to 1200-ton iron steamships. Meantime James Bertram & Son, relatives of Bertrams of Sciennes *(see Newington)* had started engineering in Leith Walk in 1845; by 1909 they too made papermaking machinery, and the two companies eventually merged in the 1950s.

**Port Facilities Expanded**: Whaling was in abeyance by 1865, but general cargo trade flourished: despite large exports, imports were even greater. Although by 1870 Glasgow's burgeoning exports exceeded Leith's, by 1876 almost a million tons of shipping moved in and out each year. From 1873 the Leith, Hull & Hamburg Steam Packet Company of Leith owned numerous puffers. Newhaven harbour was rebuilt in 1876–81, while pressure on Leith docks was further relieved by land reclamation from 1874, enabling the completion of the Edinburgh Dock, intended for coal shipment and opened in 1881 together with a graving dock over 100 metres in length. A large Sailors' Home was built in 1883–85 at Tower Street by the Harbour Head. At that time the population was 60,000, rising to 77,500 by 1901.

**Late Victorian Seaborne Trade – and Whisky**: By 1885 esparto grass was being imported for paper making. Fishing still continued from Newhaven, where a new fish market was opened in 1896; but its chain pier, by then no longer a packet terminal, was destroyed by a storm in 1898. By that time cattle were being imported from Canada, and Leith ships went whaling again, especially in the 1890s; by 1904 the firm of Christian Salvesen from Grangemouth were well established in Leith, as shipowners in the Norway trade and with a large fleet of whalers *(see also Bonar Bridge)*. Exports through Leith Docks included principally coal and whisky, while grain, wine and timber were still imported. Steamers based in Leith plied locally throughout the Forth. Although distilling ended at Lochend in 1884, Leith distillery was still named on Johnston's map of 1902. By 1887 at least five firms of whisky blenders were at work in Leith: Ainslie, Buchanan, Mackie Scott, Robertson Sanderson, and Rose. The firm of J & G Stewart of Leith, whisky bondholders, was acquired by DCL in 1917, but continued to trade under their old name.

**Leith makes Forth Bridge Paint as the Port Expands**: Craig & Rose of Leith Walk made the first paint for the Forth Bridge in the 1880s, and were still the sole suppliers a century later. In 1891 Leith's population was nearing 70,000, making it the fifth largest centre in Scotland; the last green fields separating Leith from Edinburgh vanished about that time. Leith had three commercial hotels in 1894 – the *Old Ship, New Ship* and *Commercial*. The *Princess Theatre* (later the *Gaiety)* in Kirkgate was opened in 1889, and prospered up to 1914 when a second theatre – the *Alhambra* – was opened. The Edinburgh & Leith Gasworks was extended up to 1890, soon afterwards being relocated to Granton; an electric power station was built in 1897, by which time the *Marine Hotel* was open. The Eastern General Hospital was built east of Leith in the early 20th century. From 1893 yet another sea wall enclosed the 32 ha void in which the Imperial Dock was to be built; this opened in 1904, able to take vessels up to 165 m x 20 m with a draught of 8.5 m; meantime a second graving dock was available from 1896, and an early swing bridge at Bernard Street was replaced in 1898–99. A large grain silo was built at the Edinburgh Dock in 1903. In 1904 over 6000 vessels totalling nearly 2 million tons were handled, and approaching a million tons of coal were exported. In 1907 J Cran & Co of Leith was building tugs for Liverpool.

**Tramway Confusion 1898–1922**: The horse-drawn vehicles of the standard gauge Edinburgh Street Tramways Company (ESTC) appeared in 1871 on a Leith to Haymarket route, but in 1892 this was severed from the Edinburgh system at Pilrig. In 1898 the power station for Edinburgh's slow cable tramway system was built at Shrubhill, half way down Leith Walk. In 1903–05 Leith town council, by then democratically elected and not in thrall to Edinburgh, established its own more soundly conceived electric tramway, which from 1909 also served Newhaven and Granton. Trams of the two incompatible systems met at Pilrig. From 1920 management of the Leith tramways came under Edinburgh, and in 1922 through running was reinstated, this time under electric traction throughout.

**Late Rail Developments and Dock Expansion**: In 1903 the Caledonian Railway opened a costly winding high-level line linking Trinity with Seafield. Also in 1903 the North British opened its 4-platform Leith Central station just south of Duke Street, elaborately roofed in steel by Arrols of Dalmarnock, and providing trains reaching Waverley in 7 minutes; others ran to Morningside, and even to Glasgow. Coal exports from Lothian – mainly to Europe – quadrupled between 1904 and 1912 to 4 million tonnes. In 1922 NB stations were also open at Junction Road and Easter Road; others were at Powderhall and also at one time at Shrubhill. The CR's Bonnington and Leith Walk stations fell to the LMS in 1923, the NB lines and stations to the LNER; so this wasteful competition continued. In the last period of port expansion, 1912 saw another large new dry dock opened, while grain imports peaked at over 450,000 tons. By 1913 Leith had 1.7% of Britain's overseas trade, and about that time Seafield Road was built as a new eastern approach to the docks, which were taken over by the Admiralty in the 1914–18 war.

**Mixed fortunes Inter-war**: In 1920 Edinburgh finally swallowed Leith for local government purposes – not especially to the advantage of the latter, whose range of facilities was great enough for it to be a minor regional centre. In 1924 Ainslie's six-storey No.1 Bond and bottling plant, able to fill 4800 bottles a day, was acquired by Arthur Bell & Sons & Co of Perth; they extended it in 1938; another bond owned by Mackenzie & Sons was acquired in 1933. A new Leith Academy was built in 1928, and the East Pilton housing estate was laid out in the early thirties. Meantime from the 1890s both St Bernards FC (of Royal Gymnasium Park) and Leith Athletic FC (originally of Logie Green) played for various periods in the Scottish Football League; the former vanished after 1939, but during 1946–53 a briefly revived Athletic played at Portobello, and finally at Old Meadowbank. The *Alhambra* became a cinema in 1930 and the *State Cinema*, opened in 1939, was another of the few inter-war developments of note.

**Coasting Steamer Companies**: A F Henry & MacGregor of Leith had started as shipowners in 1907; they took delivery of three new ships in 1921 and became the main tramp shipping operator of the port, with twelve coasters by 1939, specialising in cargoes of cement from Thamesside to eastern Scottish ports as far as Lerwick, returning south with coal and also stone from Inverkeithing. From 1941 the firm was owned by the London & Edinburgh Shipping Company. W N Lindsay of Leith were grain merchants and stevedores before 1932 when they entered the shipping trade, carrying grain, and also coal to the Peterhead Co-op, until at least 1955. The cement trade declined with the opening of the rail-connected Oxwellmains works near Dunbar in 1963.

**Mixed Fortunes in Shipbuilding and Docks**: In 1929 Allan & Brown of Newhaven launched the last boat to be built there. Another local yard which built coasters was Ramage & Ferguson, later bought by Henry Robb for expansion; by 1936 the yard was launching a vessel a month. But with the general slump in orders the other Leith shipbuilding firms became largely repairers or closed down altogether. Leith's proportion of Britain's overseas trade had fallen to 1.3% by 1932, though in 1934 a new grain silo of 36,500 tonnes capacity replaced a warehouse which had burned out in 1930. Work on a major new western breakwater, begun in 1936 at Newhaven Pier, was suspended during the second world war but apparently completed by 1953, enclosing the new Western Harbour. By the 1960s Salvesens – who are said to have employed nearly 2000 men in whaling in 1955 – had abandoned this controversial activity.

**News and Flour**: In 1952 the *Leith Gazette* was belatedly founded as a local newspaper. George Gibson of Leith was a shipowner in the small freight liner trade, and in the 1950s also operated gas tankers. The Laverock Shipping Company started up in Leith in 1951 to carry chemicals, later called the *'Enid Line'*. In the early 1950s Rank's built the big Caledonia flour mill; later the firm amalgamated as Rank Hovis McDougall (RHM). The large Chancelot Mill was newly built by 1963; for many years it was rail-connected. By 1955 eight dry docks were available to the two firms of ship repairers. Robb's launched their largest vessel, the 94-metre 6000-ton general cargo ship *Cavallo*, in 1957 when their workforce exceeded a thousand. But then their apogee was past, and a general decline in Leith's fortunes was already under way.

**Comprehensive Rail and Tramway Closures 1947–70**: North Leith ex-NB station was closed to passengers by the LNER in 1947. Newhaven was served by trams until Leith depot was closed in 1956, a few months before the whole system was abandoned. Leith Central station had meantime lost ground from unification of the tram services in 1922, and its last passenger train called in 1952; minor roles continued until it was demolished in 1989 and its site sold to the City District Council. Leith's last passenger trains were to the ex-CR station at North Leith, which retained services to Princes Street until closure in 1962; its site became an industrial estate.

**Decline and Demolition**: The Bernard Street bridge was last swung in 1956, and by 1963 had been replaced by a fixed concrete structure. The *Gaiety Theatre* in Kirkgate was closed in 1956, and demolished in 1963; the *Alhambra Cinema* which closed in 1958 remained unused until demolition in 1974. In the 1960s Graham Tiso started to retail outdoor sports gear; the successful firm now has 10 shops in Scotland and Northern Ireland. The Leith Fort housing scheme of the 1960s contained two blocks of brutalist design – reprieved from demolition in later years after a remarkable public outcry. Pilrig House was burnt out in 1969; its shell, derelict in 1980 was later rebuilt. While whisky exports remained important, and Baltic container traffic was passing through the Albert Dock by 1971, the next year Leith handled only 0.5% of Britain's trade. Robb's built the large 81-metre motor tug *Lloydsman* in 1971 for United Towing of Hull, but then struggled to survive. Alexander Stephen of Govan and Leith were liquidated in 1976, but their Leith repair yard was taken over by the Edinburgh Dry Dock Company, which was repairing 300 ships a year in 1979.

**The Post-war Wine and Whisky Trade**: Around 1950 John Crabbie & Co installed new oak vats for making their ginger wine, but were taken over in 1964 by DCL, who continued the traditional processes; but demand gradually fell from the 120,000 cases sold in 1979. Meantime in 1956–57 efficiency changes cut the workforce of Bell's bottling plant from 60 to 35, but whisky sales were expanding and the firm moved the operation to a larger plant at Broxburn about 1965; by 1976 Bells had abandoned Leith. DCL subsidiary J & G Stewart of Maritime Street were advertising *'Usher's Green Stripe'* blend in 1959, and five years later Macdonald & Muir of Leith were advertising the *'Highland Queen'*. As Macdonald Martin, owners of Glenmorangie distillery and blenders of other whiskies, they modernised their Queens Dock bottling plant in 1979. By 1977 Bruce & Co were whisky exporters; in 1993 they were blenders of *'Northern Scot'* whisky.

**Scotch from Action to Control and Commemoration**: The medieval wine vaults in St Giles Street were still used as such by J & G Thomson & Co in 1981; in 1983 part became the Scottish National Whisky Museum. The site also became the headquarters of the Scotch Malt Whisky Society, an informal body selecting, describing and distributing unusual single malts to discerning customers *(see Hills)*; in 1993 the Society's bottling for its 15,000 members was done by Drambuie of Kirkliston. By 1990 Leith also held the head offices of Invergordon Distillers and of Macdonald Martin plc, at that time distillers and blenders in Elgin and Tain. But in 1991 a former maltings at Bonnington, by then bonded warehouses, were converted to offices, and early in 1993 United Distillers decided to close its Leith blending and bottling plant.

**The Basics – Pipe Coating and Sewage Disposal**: By 1984 Leith's variety of industries included the SAI fertiliser factory, and pipe-coating for North Sea oil – by 2000 Europe's largest such plant. Much decline over the previous 65 years meant that unemployment was a problem in the 1980s; Leith's poor areas received attention from the SDA. However, Leith was still a significant port and a major local centre, with some affluent areas. By 1988 Quarryhole Park had been created from former sawmills, and the old East and West Docks had been infilled. The City of Edinburgh had very recently gained an overdue sewage disposal plant, built on reclaimed land at Seafield, though some further industries had closed, including the large tannery at Bonnington by 1986. A covered market had been built by the end of the decade. The *Leith Gazette* seems to have ceased publication by 1991 when the population of Leith (EH6) was 28,227.

**Varied Industries, Varied Success**: Spider Systems of Bonnington were expanding in computers in the early 90s. Colour Response printers, established in 1989 by the Colorgraphic group, was growing at Newhaven Road, and in 1990 Scotsman Publications of Edinburgh opened new colour presses at Newhaven Road under the name of Caledonian Offset. The Powderhall Bronze Foundry was established in 1989 by the aptly named Brian Caster and Terry Hammond to produce fine art castings; in 1994 the tiny firm gained financial support to enable expansion. The family firm of Kinloch Anderson, tailors and kiltmakers, acquired new headquarters in Leith in 1990. By 1993 the historic paint firm of Craig & Rose was a plc with branches in Glasgow and Dartford, Kent. Chancelot Mill retained its own test bakery, but in 1991 the RHM company's Caledonia Mill was closed, with the loss of 158 jobs. J Smith & Sons' Hawkhill bakery, active in the 1950s, later became part of the Sunblest group. In 1990 Crawfords, one of Scotland's largest industrial bakery groups, were bought out by their managers, but losses ensued and the Crawford bakery was closed late in 1996 with the loss of some 200 jobs.

**Rubbish by Rail, and Rail Freight at the Docks**: The former South Leith goods station was closed, and by 1988 a postal sorting office had been built there; in 1989 the site of Powderhall station became a compaction and loading point for half the city's domestic waste. This was packed into containers for rail movement to disposal sites outwith the city; in 1992 it went to Kaimes near Balerno, but by 2000 was dumped at Oxwellmains near Dunbar. Rail-freight from the docks included grain, timber, cement and steel pipes, plus coal from Blindwells opencast pit near Tranent; but the scale of operation at Leith is but a vestige of what had once been. The ICI fertiliser factory was sold in 1990 to a Finnish company.

**Port, Commerce and Industry: Salvesens Leave**: Because enclosed docks double the turn-round time for shipping, and poor road access also inhibited Leith's role, the redundant south part of the Edinburgh Dock was infilled in the 1990s to create a development site. In 1994 Oceaneering-Multiflex of Victoria Dock manufactured hose bundles, and electro-hydraulic umbilicals for subsea oil and gas production. By late 1994 Blue Circle had built a new cement export terminal on the docks, and in 1994 Fertiliser Products of Nottingham selected Leith docks as the site for a new blending and bagging plant. By 1995 – after the major sale of Salvesen Bricks – only 8% of Christian Salvesens' business was in Scotland, its new emphasis being on European distribution, and its HQ staff had been reduced from 270 to just 90 people before moving to Northampton in 1997.

**Crabbie's Ginger Up**: DCL's successors United Distillers retained Crabbie's premises in 1993 when ginger wine production was only 40,000 cases a year; the Crabbies name and recipe was acquired by neighbours Macdonald Martin. Until late 1994 ginger wine was still brewed weekly from Cyprus raisins, the product being slowly flavoured with Zanzibar spices, Mediterranean oranges and lemons, with cowslips and elderflowers from Romania and Bulgaria, then fortified with ginger root in molasses spirit and matured for two and a half years; but in 1995 production was re-started on a modified basis at Macdonald Martins' Commercial Street bottling plant; this fine tipple now contains 13.5% alcohol, but is made at Broxburn.

**Maritime Recreation – and Government**: About 36 cruise liners were using the port each year around 1990. The site of Central station was redeveloped in 1992 for a large Scotmid supermarket and sports complex. The adjacent *'Leith Waterworld'* was opened by the city council in 1992. In 1993–95 *'Victoria Quay'*, a new office complex of 30,000 m$^2$ for a Scottish Office staff of 1400, was built on the south quay of Victoria Dock. Thanks to smart politicking by Forth Ports, the former Royal Yacht *Britannia* – built on the Clyde! – was

*The Malmaison Restaurant at the entrance to Leith Docks. The building was built as a sailors' home in the 1880s.* *(AL)*

moored as a permanent tourist attraction at Leith in the late 1990s. The adjacent new Ocean Terminal on the site of the former shipyard is to open in 2001, enabling cruise liners to berth rather than lying offshore; it will become Edinburgh's largest shopping centre. More mundanely, Forth ports have opened a new *'virtual quarry'* for the buffer storage of aggregates in transit. Other main cargoes are grain, forest products, steel, petroleum products and chemicals.

**Conservation and Catering, Flats and Offices**: The former seamen's mission at Tower Street was reconstructed internally, and relaunched in 1994 by Forth Ports plc and Ken McCulloch of Glasgow as the luxurious 25-room *Malmaison Hotel*. By late 1994 a dock shed had become the centre of a new radio station, Scot-FM, and in Commercial Street bonded warehouses were becoming offices and shops, wine bars and restaurants. The vast Donaldson's Warehouse was converted into flats in the 1990s, and architects Simpson & Brown saved the ancient and prominent St Ninian's manse, reconditioning it as their office by 1999. And Forth Ports (with Morrisons) have built many quality houses around the dock area. The old 364-bed Eastern General Hospital was to close by the end of the century. Today, both Leith Academy and Trinity Academy have about 900 pupils. Two budget hotels have recently arrived in the area; the ancient *Peacock Inn* is still open at Newhaven.

## LEITHOLM — Map 3, B3

***Small Berwickshire village,*** *pop. 500 (area)* — OS 74: NT 7944

Leithholm stands in the gentle Merse of Berwickshire, near the ancient earthwork known as Belchester and about 8 km north-west of Coldstream. Eccles (= church in Cumbric) is 4 km south-west. Little remains of the 15th century Mersington Tower, and little more of the 16th century Leitholm Peel. When Pont mapped the thickly settled Merse around 1600 there was already a mill at Mersington. A Cistercian nunnery, founded in 1156 by Derdere, Countess Gospatric, may have been the origin of the emparked building adjoining *'Ekkills Kirk'* shown on Pont's map. Roy's map of about 1754 showed a road from Coldstream to Fogo, east of which Leitholm appeared as a mere group of huts, with a partly completed road towards Swinton. In 1799 Heron noted Eccles as *"a village"*. By about 1825 Leitholm was served by a penny post from Coldstream, and in 1901 there was an inn and a post and telegraph office. Anton's Hill then had the largest policies of the several local mansion-houses. In 1951 with a population of some 330, Leitholm's basic facilities served in all some 750 people in the Eccles and Leitholm area. By 1976 when its own population was down to 200 and only 500 people in all were served, its primary school was seen as a marginal case for survival; still open in 1980, it had closed by 1994. Rural Leitholm has little to interest the tourist (and the convent ruins at Eccles are slight), but it still has its post office and pub. *Stainrigg* to the west is a mansion hotel.

## LENNOXTOWN — Map 5, C5

***Strathkelvin large village,*** *pop. 4500* — OS 64: NS 6277

Some 5 km north of Kirkintilloch, in the lee of the steep Campsie Fells and beyond the Glazert Water, is the medieval motte and bailey known as Maiden Castle. *'Lennocx'* 1.5 km to the west was just one of many tiny settlements shown on Blaeu's map in the early 17th century, at which time Bencloich tower was being built to the east. When Roy mapped the area around 1754 the *'Lenox Mills'* were in existence, and Lennoxtown became known for handmade nails, though there were no roads, merely tracks. Four small bleachfields existed in 1786 when Lennoxmill printfield was set up by Lindsay, Smith & Co, and this was soon followed by houses and shops.

**Cotton, Chemicals, Co-op and Lennox Castle**: Heron in 1799 referred to *"the lately erected village of Lennoxfield, containing above 300 inhabitants, employed chiefly in the cotton manufacture"*. It was also called Newton of Campsie, and later Lennoxtown. The Campsie Alum Works was established in 1808 by Charles Macintosh *(see also Nitshill)* and by 1835 was producing 2000 tonnes of alum a year; limekilns also existed from the early 19th century. A post office named Lennoxtown was open by 1838, and a co-operative existed there before the Rochdale Pioneers were founded in 1844. The large battlemented red sandstone mansion of Lennox Castle was built in 1837–41 on the ridge south of the Glazert Water.

**Railway Development and Calico Printing**: A branch of the Edinburgh & Glasgow Railway was opened to Lennoxtown in 1848; this had sidings for the Campsie Alum Works and the Underwood Chemical Works; a gasworks was established in 1852. When the railway was extended to Killearn in 1866–67, a new station was provided for Lennoxtown; the line reached Aberfoyle in 1882. In 1868 Dalglish, Falconer & Co's Campsie calico printing works employed about a thousand people, making it one of the *'big three'* of the day. In 1891 there were 2800 residents; Lennoxtown never became a burgh, being described in 1894 as *"a small town dependent on various print, bleaching and alum works"*. Coal and limestone were jointly mined to the west of the alum works, which by the 1890s also had its own coal mine at Barhill. The Campsie golf club was founded in 1895, laying out a steep course on the lower slopes of the Fells.

**Lennox Castle Hospital**: More jobs became available in the Lennox Castle mental hospital, which was first created in World War I, and took over the mansion in the 1920s; it became the nursing home of a new mental hospital built in its park, so large that it possessed its own railway siding until 1964. Meantime the calico printing works closed in 1930, and by the

1950s there was no textile work in the area. By 1945 the alum works too had gone; its waste bing remained until about 1970. In 1951 Lennoxtown had 5400 people and village facilities, but in that year the railway passenger service was withdrawn; the goods service ended in 1966 and by 1971 the rails had been lifted; eventually its route was laid out as an attractive footpath.

**Modern Lennoxtown Shuts up Shop**: Somerville Nails was still in production at the station works in 1980, but later closed. However, apart from the loss of secondary schooling, village facilities were still available. By 1987 a large area of housing had been developed east of the village, and the rundown mental hospital with its 800 beds was undergoing upgrading in the late 1980s. Another 1980s enterprise, again exploiting the area's main renewable resource, was the bottling of *Campsie Spring* water. In 1991 the population was about 4500, of whom some 765 were mental patients. Last used for staff accommodation about 1987, Lennox Castle stood vacant in 1993, though parts of the hospital *'village'* remained in use. By 1996 forest walks had been laid out west of the village.

## LENZIE & Auchinloch — Map 15, D4

***Village / dormitory by Kirkintilloch,*** *pop. 9500* OS 64: NS 6571

Auchinloch about 10 km north-east of Glasgow, where Lanarkshire met the detached portion of Lennox, was named on Pont's map of 1596, and Lenzie parish founded a school in 1625. Roy's map made about 1754 showed *'Acherloch'* as a small village at the apex of a vee of roads from Kirkintilloch and Cadder. The early Monkland & Kirkintilloch Railway which passed through the area north-east of the village created no significant development, and the present site of Lenzie about 1200 m north of Auchinloch long remained an empty peat moor about 60 m above sea level, near the small Gadloch.

**Railway Development**: Lenzie had a station from the opening of the Edinburgh & Glasgow Railway (E&GR) in 1842. At first named *'Kirkintilloch'*, it was sited 1 km west of a junction formed with the M&K, where the line crossed the Auchinloch to Kirkintilloch road and the county boundary. The company laid out a spacious net of residential roads to encourage the building of large houses, offering villa feus with Glasgow travel concessions – five years of free season tickets – for householders only! In 1848 the station was renamed *'Campsie Junction'*, being the starting point of the new Campsie branch to Kirkintilloch and Lennoxtown; it was soon again renamed as *'Lenzie Junction'*.

**Asylum, Colliery and Academy**: Development was slow and costly, for in the 1860s the remnants of Lenzie Moss, west of the village, could still swallow a horse! The finely designed *Barony Parochial Asylum* for 500 Glasgow mental patients was built in 1871–75, and by 1894 had been *"largely increased"* as the *Woodilee Lunatic Asylum*. There was also a convalescent home just north of Auchinloch, and nearby for a time was the Woodilee Colliery. Around 1880 the famous locomotive engineer Dugald Drummond lived at Lenzie, to Murray in 1894 *"a growing place of residential villas"*. By about 1895 Lenzie Academy was open.

**Golf Arrives, Hospital Grows**: Long-standing mineral lines converged 2 km west of the station at Cadder, where by 1945 a railway marshalling yard had been built. Meantime in 1935 Lenzie golf club was established and its course laid out at Auchinloch. Lenzie, the northern half of which was by then part of Kirkintilloch burgh, had a population approaching 7500 in 1951, but apart from its large Academy, only village facilities were available. The erstwhile Monkland & Kirkintilloch railway vanished in 1966, the year that – with the closure of the Kirkintilloch branch line – Lenzie ceased to be a junction; the trackbed and former colliery site were subsequently landscaped. The gradually expanding mental hospital at Woodilee had no fewer than 1169 beds by 1981.

**Care and the Community?**: Though Lenzie's general development had been hampered by the deep peat deposits, the population had risen to create a large suburban settlement, enjoying the facilities of a fairly large village by 1980. By then the small Lenzie Hospital, the former convalescent home, held geriatric patients. Meantime fashions for the mentally ill had changed to *'care in the community'*; the number of patients was soon cut drastically, and the original Woodilee asylum buildings were abandoned to decay and fire in 1987. By 1988 much further housing development had taken place around Lenzie at Boghead and Millersneuk, and Auchinloch was itself expanding. By 1991 when almost 9500 private residents lived in Lenzie, giving it a young and well-educated dormitory character, the closure of the last remaining 470 beds at Woodilee Hospital was proposed. This was a fact by 1995, when the empty hospital, a *'building at risk'*, was sadly largely demolished; the remains stood derelict in 2000.

## LERWICK — Map 14, B4

***Main town of Shetland,*** *pop. 7400* OS 4: HU 4741

On the east coast of the Shetlands is Bressay Sound, sheltered by the Isle of Bressay; in the nearby freshwater loch of Clickhimin stands an imposing broch which, like that at Sumburgh (*q.v.*), overlies farming settlements from the late Bronze Age onwards. This is within 1.5 km of the centre of modern Lerwick. However, the area of good agricultural land there was very limited, and there was no continuity of settlement near Lerwick into the Viking and early Scottish periods, when the Norse festival of Uphalliday held on 29$^{th}$ January came to be miscalled *Up-Helly-Aa*. Timothy Pont, who made a mineral survey of the island group about 1592, noted only a tiny settlement at *'Brawick'*, a bay just to the south.

**A Promiscuous Start**: However, by 1602 Dutch *'busses'* – large 2-masted fishing vessels – paid annual midsummer visits seeking herring, congregating off Shetland on June 24$^{th}$. The subsistence farming Shetlanders would briefly gather at Bressay Sound to trade and to enjoy what appears to have been an uninhibited social intercourse with the Dutch, who would then move off southwards. By 1614 some vessels were large, with crews of up to 24 men. So much went on to offend the newly Protestant element in the community that ordinances in 1602, 1615 and again in 1625 decreed that the booths erected along the shore for the fair should be burnt, together with any houses. Lerwick (the name means *Muddy creek*) is therefore a comparatively modern creation; only isolated houses existed beside the Sound until after 1625.

**Fort Charlotte**: The substantial naval Fort Charlotte was built on a knoll above the Sound in 1665, during the Dutch wars of 1651 to 1677. When Lerwick really got going beside the fort, the locals already knew just how to place their booths to shelter themselves from the piercing winds blowing down the sound, and soon enclosed a narrow, curving waterside street with practically continuous lines of buildings. By 1673 Lerwick was large enough for it to be reported that *"part of the town was burned"*. The Royal Dutch Hospital which was built in 1690 was really just an almshouse, and two centuries were to elapse before proper medical facilities appeared.

**The Shetlands in 1703: Lerwick peopled by Incomers**: Martin writing in 1703 noted the treelessness, poor land and poverty of the Shetland isles, then simply an appurtenance of the Orkneys. However, many Shetlanders could speak English, *'Norn'* (Norse) and also Dutch, *"acquired by their converse with the Hollanders, that fish yearly in those isles. As a result Shetland is much more populous now, than it was thirty years ago. The latest built town is Lerwick, on a hard rock between the sea and a moss. On the north is the citadel, built in 1665 but never completed; little remains but the walls. Lerwick then had but three or four families, now about 300 families"*, few of whom were Shetlanders, most being from the north and east coasts of Scotland. Proprietors would let their houses as shops to the *"Hamburgers, Bremeners and others who come in mid-May, set up shops and sell linen, muslin, beer, brandy and bread which they barter for fish, stockings, mutton and hens"* – or would sell for cash.

**Lerwick to Leith via the Elbe**: The locals ate largely Orkney corn, Shetland mutton, local sea fowl and their eggs, and the plentiful herring; however, even by 1703 overfishing was already affecting the nearer stocks of cod and ling, and for a time Lerwick – which had overtaken Scalloway around 1700 – seems to have shrunk; in 1733 only some 200 families lived in the little town. Until 1736, almost incredibly, the most reliable way to Leith was *via Hamburg*; but in 1736 Lerwick acquired an infrequent postal service, with mails via Leith. By about 1750 Shetland ponies were exported to England for use in coal pits.

**Monthly Sailings to Scotland!**: A proper post office was opened in 1763, and from 1766 the Morton family held the islands for the Crown. Lerwick was not really a fishing port, having only one *buss* by 1774, and so minor as a trading centre that a mere ten regular sailings annually linked Shetland with Scotland: poverty and the press gang ruled the island group. In the 1780s Lerwick became the port of registry for the Shetlands with the letters LK; by 1797 Lerwick was a post town, *"the chief town of Shetland"* in the words of Heron, when its population was about 900, but growing fast.

**Barony, Banking and General Merchants**: Lerwick became a late burgh of barony in 1818, from which in 1822 the main exports were fish, fish oil and barrelled beef. The Shetland Banking Company was formed by Hay and Ogilvy in 1821; it operated in a small way as an adjunct to their speculative trading business until its failure in 1842. Later the Union Bank provided a service. Chambers in 1827 noted *"Lerwick, the principal town in Shetland, contains about 2000 inhabitants. There is scarcely any thing like a mercantile community in Shetland. The shopkeepers of Lerwick, though styled merchants, are just like the omne-gatherum (i.e. general) dealers of little lowland towns. There is only one mile of road in all Shetland! This extends from Lerwick towards the west."*

**Shetlanders Fast at Sea but Slow on Shore**: Though backward in land transport, Shetlanders were daring and innovative at sea. One of them, John Anderson, became a London merchant, MP for Shetland, and in 1836 with Brodie Willox founded the Peninsula Steam Navigation Company, renowned from 1840 as the P&O *(Peninsula & Oriental)*. In 1854 another Shetlander, John Gray, became the well known captain for 18 years of Brunel's pioneer iron steamship *The Great Britain*. But as late as 1838, when an Aberdeen firm began a steamer service to Lerwick for the mails, there were still no other post offices in the Shetland Isles, nor roads beyond Tingwall. The herring fishery failed for 30 years from 1842, and when the potato crop also failed, a system of roads was built for famine relief in the late 1840s. Lerwick's first gasworks was built in 1856. In 1861 housing conditions in Shetland were the worst in Scotland in terms of overcrowding, with an *average* of over three persons per room. The subsistence population of the isles – which at that time still used oxen as draught animals – peaked at 18,600 at the 1861 census, then steadily declined for a century.

**Lerwick from Rags...**: Bressay lighthouse, guarding the south approach to Lerwick harbour, was first illuminated in 1858. The Zetland New Shipping Company, based in Lerwick, traded to Leith using sailing schooners until 1882. Smuggling was rife around the islands right up to 1885, and Elizabeth Balneaves mentioned eight known smugglers' caves beneath Commercial Street. The herrings came back in 1875, and the Shetland fishing fleet grew from nothing in 1876 to 344 boats within a decade, during which a fishing disaster in 1881 *(see Cullivoe)* sped the transition from open boats to sturdier and steam powered craft.

**... to Riches**: Meantime in 1862 John Anderson had built the Anderson Institute as a school – which still exists as the Anderson High School – and he founded the *Shetland Times* newspaper in 1872. Morrison's Pier was improved in 1865 as the Victoria Pier. The substantial Town Hall was built in 1882–84, in 1885 a telephone cable was laid to Sinclair Bay in Caithness, bringing instant communication with Scotland at last, and the Victoria Pier was further improved in 1886, enabling serious tourism to commence. In that year Lerwick was described as *"a busy thriving little metropolis"* with an important wool trade. By 1887 the Albert Wharf had been constructed. The burning of a longship was introduced at the traditional *Up Helly A'a* festival in 1889. The isles were virtually treeless, and until then the Shetlanders could not afford to build mock Viking boats, still less to burn them just for fun. But open air barrelling continued at a host of *'herring stations'* around the islands; in the peak herring year 1905 there were 36 of these seasonal centres in and around Lerwick, the Skibbadock being the most impressive.

**Going to Hospital – in Edinburgh!**: Lerwick naturally became the centre where county buildings were erected from 1884, so that in 1889 Shetland (under the name of *Zetland*) could become a County separate from Orkney. By 1891 the population of Lerwick was nearing 3800, and by 1894 there were two *"very good"* hotels in the town, the *Grand* and the newer *Queen's*. Fish auctions began in 1894, and in 1895 came the opening of Gilbertson Park, the gift of a local man who had made a fortune in Africa. Around 1900 most connections were with Aberdeen: but the two sailings a week from Leith via Aberdeen and Kirkwall by the paddle steamer *St Magnus* were the only way to get Shetland patients to hospital, for the Edinburgh Royal Infirmary provided all such treatment until the Gilbert Bain Hospital was built in Lerwick in 1901–02.

*Lerwick harbour, steamer pier, in 1976, when local trade was still carried by conventional ships. The port has been transformed since then by North Sea oil activity.* (JRH)

**Steamer Services**: The *St Rognvald* provided a weekly service to Leith via Kirkwall from 1901 into the 1920s, supplementing the two direct steamer services (four in summer) carried on from 1908 to 1967 by successive batches of steamers named after *Saints: Clair, Magnus, Sunniva*. Two successive eight-knot steamers named *Earl of Zetland* served the North Isles for 98 years, 1877–1946–1975, calling at many places including: Symbister (Whalsay); Skerries; Mossbank, Bardister, Ollaberry and North Roe (North Mainland); West Sandwick, Ulsta, Burravoe, and Mid Yell (Yell); Brough Lodge and Houbie (Fetlar); Uyeasound and Baltasound (Unst), the terminus. Flitboats were used at various places without piers. In the 1920s coasters would deliver herring barrels from a cooperage at Buckie; Hay & Co (Lerwick) Ltd, formerly owners of fishing schooners, then operated bunkering facilities which handled up to 1800 tonnes of coal a week from Fife.

**Slow Development**: A new fish market on its own quay called Alexandra Wharf was built in 1904–07, and by 1906 a co-operative store sold grocery and drapery. A new and larger gasworks was built in 1926, and a lifeboat station was opened in 1930. In the 1930s small ships of A F Henry & MacGregor of Leith carried cement to Hay & Co of Lerwick, whose trade in it rose from 100 tonnes a year in 1890 to 6000 tonnes in the 1960s. But as late as 1939 the only tarred road in Shetland linked Lerwick and Cunningsburgh, 15km to the south. The odd name HMS *Fox* was adopted in 1939 for a naval base at Lerwick, gone by 1986. In 1955 the small Isle of Noss immediately east of Bressay became a national nature reserve.

**Before North Sea Oil**: By 1951 Lerwick had some 5600 people; it was a significant fishing port, and a town of full urban status, though still with only two hotels. Remarkably, two local newspapers appeared weekly until the *Shetland News* ceased publication in 1963. However, new premises were built in 1966 for the Shetland Library and Museum, the latter a new facility, and by the 1970s the Hydro Board had built a diesel-driven power station. Up to the 1970s the main steamer route connected Lerwick, Kirkwall, Aberdeen and Leith, but from 1971 all cargo was handled via Aberdeen in ro-ro ferries; in 1977 former herring stations were replaced by P&O's new Holmsgarth ro-ro terminal. By 1973 a geophysical laboratory had been established at Uppersound (Gulberwick), 3km south-west of the town, an area soon sprinkled with new bungalows. By 1975, the year when Zetland County Council became the Shetland Islands Council, the mails travelled by air via Kirkwall. There was also a coastguard station.

**The Oil Boom Expands Lerwick**: The oil revolution *(see Sullom Voe)* resulted in the creation of a superb road system in Shetland for relatively little traffic. The new *Lerwick Hotel* was open by 1972, by the late 1970s Bressay was linked by a new vehicle ferry, and a youth hostel was open by 1982. The plastics firm Thulecraft was set up in the early 1970s and from 1986 supplied the growing Shetland salmon farming industry with polystyrene boxes. Oil-related development provided new port facilities along more than 3km of the coastline north of the town centre, created extensive housing estates at Sound and Holmsgarth, plus two more new hotels, raising the population to about 7200 in 1981. By 1980 Shetland Marts was based at Scalloway Road. When seen by the writer in the late 1980s the relatively modest scale and range of Lerwick's shopping facilities for a totally isolated town of its size suggested that much mail order purchasing was taking place. However, apart from all the necessities, oil revenues had enabled the provision of a new and first-rate public hall at Clickhimin, from which even symphony concerts were broadcast in 1987. By that time Lerwick was an extremely busy ferry port and a substantial commercial centre.

**Using Klondikers as Hired Hands**: In 1989 Williamsons, fish processors, employed 90 people, but the *Shetland Catch* fish processing plant made news by employing Russian and Polish sailors from offshore *'Klondiker'* factory ships to help in loading frozen fish into other refrigerated vessels. Malakoff & William operated a ship repair dock. The Bressay lighthouse was converted to automatic working; but about that time the *North Star* cinema closed down. The population in 1991 was 7336, with a fit and well-educated emphasis. By 1994 a second museum was open near the enlarged diesel-driven power station. Waterfront development in 1994 led Thulecraft to move its 14 workers to new premises on the Gremista Industrial Estate. By 1995 a boatyard in Shetland was owned by Lithgows *(see Port Glasgow)*; Malakoff & William Moore Ltd now operate boatyards at North Ness in Lerwick and at Scalloway. In 1994 Bressay isle retained its post office and school, and had gained some new housing, but lost its golf course, which had moved to a new site near Scalloway. By 1998 the number of Shetland-registered fishing boats had fallen since 1980 from 194 to 65.

**Replacing the Ferry?**: Late in 2000 the Shetland coastguard station took on a share of the workload of the former Pentland station. A controversial scheme for a major bridge to replace the Bressay ferry was shelved by the Islands Council in 1994, but decided upon in 2001. Lerwick has at least half a dozen hotels in the 20–60 rooms range, including the islands' oldest, the *Grand*. The youth hostel – the only one in Shetland – is open on a seasonal basis.

## LESLIE

**Map 6, B4**

***Small Fife town,*** *pop. 3100* OS 59 & 58: NO 2401

In the 13th century a church sited on a hilltop above the Leven valley in central Fife was called *'Fithkil'* (Fettykil). When a burgh of barony was chartered there in 1457 it was named Leslie or *Leslie Green*, after the powerful Leslie family, Earls (and later Dukes) of Rothes in Moray; by 1560 this was their seat. Strathendry (or Strathenry) Castle, 3km to the west (OS 58), was built in the 16th century. By 1623 a parish school was open, and the Leslie area also developed as a water-powered milling centre: James Gordon's map of about 1642 showed at least four mills on the Leven nearby – Millden, Prinlaws, Sparrsmill and another (unnamed), while some distance to the north was Conland Mill. Defoe noted in the 1720s that *"the palace of Rothes, built for the Duke of Rothes in the reign of King Charles II by Sir William Bruce, is the glory of the place, and indeed of the whole province of Fife. The town of Leslie has a good market, but otherwise it is not considerable."*

**Bull-baiting, Palace Fire and Textiles at Prinlaws**: Being in a backwater apparently devoid of any roads as late as 1750, matters got rather out of hand, and Leslie became notorious for bull-baiting. The palace of Rothes was destroyed by fire in 1763; the Earls of Rothes replaced it by Leslie House, a huge and rather plain mansion. They were noted agricultural improvers in the 18th century, and by the 1790s plain linen was being hand woven. Milldeans corn mill, just down-river from Strathendry, was owned by the Earl until in 1798 a flax spinning and bleaching complex known as Prinlaws was built alongside by John Melville of Dysart. Heron wrote in 1799 of *"Lesley (sic), the seat of the Earl of Rothes, and a neat village, containing about 800 inhabitants. These are chiefly employed in the manufacture of linen and cotton."* Only a single fair day was scheduled for 1797. The River Leven was canalised in the 1820s to reclaim land from Loch Leven and provide regulated water power, and additional mills were built: textiles were their main purpose. Leslie post office was a relatively late opener in 1824.

**Mills aplenty**: Sharp, Greenwood & Fowler's map of 1827 showed a mill north of the town, at Ballingall on the Lothrie Burn. But on the more powerful Leven were the following, working downstream from west to east: a mill and bleachfield at *'Auchmoor'* near Scotlandwell, two mills at Walkerton, and one at Strathendry just opposite two at Milldeans, one at Prinlaws, and no fewer than six clustered in the steep valley at Fettykil where the road swooped down from the village. These included Snuff, Lint and the Sparrow Mill on the south bank, which had been taken over about 1805 for snuff grinding by Robert Kirk, a Kirkcaldy tobacconist. He later also owned Leslie lint mill on the north bank and the south bank Rothes mill *(later of Tullis Russell – see Markinch)*, but in 1835 his business failed.

**The Fergus complex and Fettykil Paper Mill**: About 1830 John Fergus & Co of Kirkcaldy took over the original Milldeans site, adding a steam engine. By 1836 Leslie boasted six spinning mills, 260 weavers and three bleachfields; the early Leslie Co-operative Society was established in 1839. Fergus bought the West mill in 1836 and the North mills in 1853. By 1864 the firm owned three spinning mills (Prinlaws, East Prinlaws and Milldeans). They then sold their Kinghorn mills and developed Prinlaws to employ at maximum some 1500 people, for whom they erected houses and provided facilities. Cant's mill, owned by the Earl of Rothes, was used at one time by Andrew Cant, a flax spinner. The Leven Bank paper mill, which began work in 1848, failed in 1859. Meantime by 1856 there was also a paper mill at Prinlaws. About 1860 a firm founded by William Tullis, J T Smith and Charles Anderson (a Newburgh linen manufacturer) bought the failed Leven Bank Mill and renamed it Fettykil (later the firm became known as Smith Anderson). The adjacent mill started in 1807 by flax spinner Andrew Haggart was still at work in 1867, but was later also incorporated into Fettykil mill.

**Walkerton and the Railway**: The Walkerton Mills stood one on each bank with a connecting bridge; woollens were made, and from around 1855 flax was used. Robert Suttie produced woollen cloth there from 1857–68, and a village developed, of some 65 buildings, shop and post office. By 1891 the Livingstone family owned both the mills, as flax spinners, and in the north mill as bleachers. These various westerly developments led to urban growth called the New Town, which became the site of the terminus of an independent branch railway from Markinch, engineered by Thomas Bouch and opened in 1861. This evidently had to be kept as far as possible from the laird in Leslie House, entailing an indirect route and two substantial viaducts. The south bank mills were demolished about the time the Leslie viaduct was built.

**The Busy 1860s**: In 1864 D Dewar, Son & Sons (!) of London owned a power loom linen weaving works and bleach works, and Alex Gilchrist and James Haggart operated smaller lint mills. In 1865 came the Leslie gasworks. In 1869 Bremner noted that *"several extensive linen mills, beautifully situated on the banks of the Leven, give employment to a large number of persons"*. Fergus & Co still had over 1000 workers in flax, hemp and jute. Strathendry was a meal mill when taken over by Kilbagie paper makers James Weir & Co in 1869 to make high-grade papers from rags and wood pulp.

**Electricity, Golf and the Lino Laird**: In 1891 Leslie had 3400 residents. Soon Fettykil Mill was rail-connected and was supplied with electric light from its own steam-driven generator. Leslie was called by Murray *"a populous and busy place"*, still having flax-spinning and bleaching industries; there was also an inn. Leslie golf club, founded in 1898, laid out an *"interesting"* 9-hole parkland course in a sandy valley north of the town. From 1919 Leslie House was owned by the Spencer-Nairn linoleum family of Pathhead (Kirkcaldy), who built the small mansion of Balgeddie House in 1936–37 to designs by Alfred Scott of St Andrews; its floors came from the German-built liner *Homeric*, then lately broken up at Inverkeithing.

**Closures, Pens and Plastics**: The Walkerton flax mills were disused by 1914; the government took over and ran them during the war, but they finally closed in the early 1920s. Weirs closed the Strathendry mill in 1924 and moved some plant and workers to Kilbagie. In 1927 Thomas De la Rue took over the Strathendry buildings to make Onoto fountain pens, and from 1939 plastic seats for aircraft, as well as printing foreign currency; but this industry, the flax mill, bleachfields and the hamlet of Walkerton eventually vanished (leaving a single chimney stack).

**Post-war changes**: By 1951 Leslie had a secondary school with over 600 pupils, five doctors and a chiropodist. But after changes of ownership at Prinlaws, John Fergus & Co was liquidated in 1957. The Nairns gifted Leslie House to the Church of Scotland in 1954, and left Balgeddie House in 1966; by 1972 it had become a luxury hotel. By 1976 the secondary pupils attended schools in Glenrothes.

**Leslie on the Fringe of Glenrothes**: Sand extraction north of the town was a feature by 1977, and by 1980 Leslie House had become a Church of Scotland eventide home. But Leslie remained essentially a long narrow industrial village. By 1981 there were four hotels, probably more related to their dearth in adjacent Glenrothes than to tourism. Similarly by 1985 the large practice of the local doctors served 7000 people within a 10 km radius. In the 1980s it became more and more difficult to distinguish where Leslie ended and Glenrothes began, for private housing development was filling the space between them. A spacious villa built in 1929 for a Mrs Jobson on the hill above the station was promoted in 1987 from a guest house to the *Balcomie Hotel*.

**Smith Anderson of Leslie**: Leslie had 3062 people in 1991. It still called itself *"a paper-making town"*, for by 1990 Smith Anderson of Fettykil mills were the UK's largest producer of machine-glazed papers, also making supermarket bags and other products from recycled paper; their total output was some 55,000 tonnes a year and, including their Falkland plant, 800 people were employed. The buildings of the Cabbagehall bleachfield which once stood above the River Leven were eventually converted into flats, as was Christ's Church on the Green, redesigned by Robin Clunie. The Strathendry buildings were mainly used for farming purposes, but various small industries were still at work there in 1994, when the site of Prinlaws Mill was proposed for residential development. Today, the *Rescobie Hotel* adds to those already mentioned.

## LESMAHAGOW — Map 2, A2

***Lanarkshire village**, pop. 3250* — OS 71 (or 72): NS 8140

Lesmahagow, named after the obscure Culdee *St Mahego*, stands on the River Nethan 8 km south-west of Lanark. In 1140–44 an important Tironensian priory was founded there in his name by David I, as an adjunct of Kelso. The priory was burnt in 1335–36 by a delinquent sibling of the English King Edward III, who consequently gave the boastful lad a deadly blow. The monks rebuilt, and up to the time of the Reformation in 1560, the priory had 14 appropriated churches, in places as far away and important as Dumfries. The monks had pioneered fruit growing, and the village of Lesmahagow remained famous for its orchards. Pont's manuscript map of this part of Clydesdale, made in 1596, is largely illegible, but showed the area closely settled, with already a bridge across the Nethan at Craighead.

**After the Reformation**: In 1607 the priory buildings passed to Robert, Earl of Roxburghe, but except for the church which was in parish use, they were destroyed later in the century. In 1617 the way south to Drumlanrig was suitable only for horses, not carts, and although a parish school was established in 1623, it was 1668 before Lesmahagow became a burgh of barony. The Roy map made in the 1750s showed it as a substantial village from which roads led to Strathaven, Douglas, Hamilton and Lanark. The name Auchtyfardle was given to a Georgian mansionhouse north of the town; two fairs were to be held in 1797, and a mill was built around 1800. The ancient priory church was sadly destroyed in 1803 to provide a site for a large new church, required because (according to Chambers) *"the kirk-town of Lesmahagow, popularly called Abbey-Green is the capital of a parish of great extent, fertility, and population"*.

**Mining, Railway and Municipal Golf**: A post office was opened around 1825 and a gasworks in 1844; there was certainly coal mining in the area by 1846. A railway from Motherwell was financed by the coal owners, and opened through Lesmahagow to Coalburn. In the late 19th century there was an inn, and two mills near the bridge at Craighead; Hay & Stell (1986) illustrated one of these. The Hollandbush municipal golf course was laid out in 1889. Although in 1894 Lesmahagow was called a *"mining town"* by Murray there was no evidence on the 1" Ordnance Survey map of that date that this activity took place any nearer than 2 km to the south.

**Decline into the modern age**: By 1951, with a population approaching 4000, Lesmahagow had facilities typical of a large village, plus the Birkwood mental hospital. But the house of Auchtyfardle which had been enlarged in 1864 was demolished in 1957, the branch railway lost its passenger service in 1965, and the whole line had been lifted by 1971; a school was built on the station site. The priory ruins were being excavated in 1978. By 1981 Lesmahagow had lost both its cinemas, its only lawyer, and dentist, becoming little more than an ordinary village in terms of facilities. By 1985 it was in the process of being bypassed for the second time, the A74 being replaced by the M74 motorway. The small firm of Plato Scotland, founded in 1990, manufactured mobile children's playgrounds in 1992 with a staff of only six. In 1991 the population was down to 3266; male unemployment was high. The tourist office has closed, but Birkwood Hospital is still open, and Lesmahagow High School has over 700 pupils.

## LESWALT & Lochnaw — Map 1, B4

***Small Galloway villages**, pop. 300* — OS 82: NX 0163

The hilly but formerly heavily settled peninsula of the Rhinns of Galloway west of Stranraer has various ancient earthworks, an ancient church at Leswalt and the remains of at least three castles, the earliest being the ruined 14th century keep of the first Lochnaw Castle on its islet in the tiny loch. When Pont mapped Wigtownshire about 1610 he emphasised its replacement, the 16th century Lochnaw Castle on the south shore of the loch. From this flows the Galdenoch Burn, which then turned two mills in its short course westwards to the sea; it shares its name with a now ruined L-plan tower house 2 km to the west, built by Gilbert Agnew in 1547–70. Lochnaw appeared on the Roy map of about 1754 as an emparked mansion at the end of a road from Stranraer via the Kirk of Leswalt, surrounded by a trackless area of ferm touns. Eventually roads were made up, and although the mills vanished, Leswalt gained a post office and primary school, which in the 1950s served over 500 people. Then rural depopulation hit hard, a 1970s hotel appears to have failed, and although a caravan site was successfully established at Lochnaw, by 1981 only 300 residents remained in Leswalt, their journeys assured by two garages. By 1996 there had been some development in the village, which is only 1.5 km from Stranraer golf course, and a deer farm was an attraction. The post office is still open.

## LETHAM & Dunnichen — Map 6, C2

***Angus villages**, pop. 1200* — OS 54: NO 5348

The Pictish hill fort of Dunnichen *(Dun Nechtan)* about 5 km east of Forfar was probably a factor in the battle of Nechtansmere, fought nearby in 685; standing stones east and west of Rescobie Loch may commemorate the Picts' decisive defeat of the Anglians. But its role as the centre of fertile Strathmore was later usurped by Forfar, and only a hamlet developed near Dunnichen church. However, Idvies across the

Lunan Water some 3km south-east of Dunnichen had a thanage from about the 11th century, and also retained a church. Both names appeared on Pont's manuscript map made about 1600, while 3km north-east of Dunnichen was Balgavies (also known as Greenmyre), chartered as a barony burgh in 1587. The Roy map of about 1750 showed the kirk at Idvies, beside the main Dundee to Brechin road of the day. This crossed a bridge over the Lunan Water, just north of which was a tiny settlement named *'Latham'*.

**Dempster's New Village and Linens**: The hill fort was quarried away in the late 18th century, perhaps for building stone for the model village of Letham, established in 1788 by George Dempster, who began a fortnightly market for the sale of locally spun and woven linens. A road system was laid out, and in 1822 three small flax spinning mills at Idvies totalled 276 spindles. In 1839 a station was provided on the early Arbroath & Forfar Railway at Auldbar Road some 2 km to the north, but although in 1850 this became part of the main line to Aberdeen it attracted little local traffic, and Letham was almost unnoticed by the guide books because it lay off the main roads. However, a rather sprawling village steadily grew, and by 1864 had *"long been in repute for its linen fabrics"*. A post office was open by 1885, and by 1894 an inn, a smithy and two churches.

**Neeps to the Swedes; Consultations and Cash by Video**: By the mid 20th century Letham had the facilities of a small village plus a secondary school, and over 800 residents; a large village hall was built in 1955. The railway was closed completely in 1967, and the secondary school had gone by 1976. However by 1987 Letham was once more a significant centre, with a large agricultural engineer and farm machinery dealer, firms of game and poultry packers, and a specialist road haulier for refrigerated freight. Among half a dozen shops was the remarkably large Taurus Crafts, whose repute covered Fife as well as Tayside, while a Victorian mansion had become the attractive *Idvies House Hotel*. An estate under construction was adding to Letham's numerous modern bungalows, and by 1991 the resident population was over 1200, of established dormitory character. In 1993 Jim McGugan of Letham was exporting vegetables, including carrots to Finland, potatoes to Romania – and turnips to the Swedes! For many years Letham had relied on doctors based in Forfar and Friockheim, when in 1995 the Green Street medical practice in Forfar established an experimental video link with an unstaffed building in Letham; this was also to be used as an experimental video banking centre by the Bank of Scotland.

## LETHAM & Monimail — Map 6, B3

***Fife village & hamlet,*** *pop. 550* — OS 59: NO 3014

The 14th century courtyard castle of Collairnie stands in a bowl among dissected hills some 7km north-west of Cupar. About 3km south of this is Monimail, a retreat of the Archbishops of St Andrews from 1328, its sole surviving tower being a compact 16th century structure. Between these and somewhat to the east is Fernie Castle, a 16th century L-plan tower. From 1564 Monimail was a Balfour property, and from 1592 belonged to the Melvilles; there was a parish school from 1632. Letham, a hamlet on a sunny slope 1km east of Monimail, came to light when James Gordon mapped Fife about 1642. The very early neo-classical mansion of Melville House was built beside the church of Monimail for the Earls of Leven & Melville in 1689–92, probably designed by Sir William Bruce or perhaps by James Smith; Defoe called it *"a regular and beautiful building"*. Monimail was shown on Roy's map made around 1750 as *'Melvill Kirk'*. The Cupar to Letham road was the first in the area to be included in a Turnpike Act, and in 1802 a toll bar was installed south-east of Letham, which was marked on Sharp's map of 1826–27 as a one-street settlement named Nesbitfield. By this time the area's road system was complete, the road long numbered A914 (now A92) was also a turnpike, and both Melville House and *'Fernie House'* were emparked.

**Education and Tourism**: Letham primary school was rebuilt in 1890 after a fire. By the early 20th century Letham had gained a post office, inn, community *'orchestra'* and soon a telephone exchange. Melville House was used by Polish forces during 1939–45. In 1951 Letham's facilities served a mainly farming population of some 625, including Bow of Fife, but by 1981 (also including Collessie) this was down to about 550. However, by 1972 the ancient castle had become the *Fernie Castle Hotel*. Melville House has been various forms of residential school, but is now a private residence. The historic and impressive *Fernie Castle Hotel* in its parkland setting has been twice extended, with a function suite added by 1995, now having 20 rooms.

## LETHAM, Inveralmond — Map 6, A3

***Western part of Perth,*** *pop. 14,000* — OS 58: NO 0924

In the first century a Roman fort called *Bertha* was built at the confluence of the Rivers Almond and Tay, a site then abandoned, though medieval Perth eventually took its name. The burghers of Perth diverted water to drive their mills by digging the winding Town's Lade from the River Almond at Almondbank, 5km west of the town. The Roy map made about 1750 showed little else between Perth and Almondbank, but marked a break in the straight main road to the north where it crossed the River Almond, by ford or ferry. Heron in 1799 noted *"some remains of the wooden frame of a bridge"* which had crossed the Tay there, though improbably as long ago as Roman times. By 1794 a bleachfield at Tulloch, half way down the lade, processed about 300,000m of cheap linens a year, and there was a linen handkerchief printing works.

**Railway, Council Houses and Dewars**: The site of Bertha was cut through by the Perth & Dunkeld Railway, opened in 1848, later becoming part of the Caledonian Railway's Strathmore main line and used as far as Stanley by Highland Railway trains to Inverness. There was no station at Bertha or at North Muirton, the divergence of the Methven branch from 1858. John Sandeman's Tulloch bleachfield, still busy in 1864, had become a dyeworks by 1895. The area around Letham House was rural up to 1945, but about then the railways laid out the extensive Perth New Yard. Perth town council built most of its post-war public housing west of the Wellshill cemetery, rapidly creating Letham as a new community. By 1951 it held nearly 12,000 people, and by 1971 15,000, with village facilities. Around 1963 came Dewars' large new Inveralmond whisky blending and bottling plant on a 27ha site at Dunkeld Road, with a siding from Perth New Yard.

**Inveralmond and Caithness Glass**: In the mid 1970s the Inveralmond industrial estate was laid out beside the River Almond north of Tulloch. There in 1978–79 Caithness Glass built a new factory with five furnaces and a cafe, shop and viewing gallery overlooking the area where 30 employees made engraved glass items such as paperweights and goblets. By 1988 new buildings for Perth College of Higher Education had been erected south of the Crieff road. The 1980s also saw the transfer of the head office of the General Accident insurance group from central Perth to the Letham area, which was made much more accessible by the opening of the M90/A9 bypass road around its western side. The intervening area was largely filled up with more new housing within ten years.

**McDiarmid Park and other new Attractions**: In 1989 St Johnstone FC *(see Perth)* opened McDiarmid Park on farmland donated by a supporter of that name, within the bypass north of Crieff Road. Scotland's first all-seater stadium, this has an all-weather pitch, restaurant and conference facilities, 1000 parking spaces and a capacity of 10,100 spectators. A plastic training pitch was laid, also used for hockey. The club immediately won promotion to the Premier League.

**More Offices but Different Glass**: In 1993 the newly privatised Hydro Electric moved most of its 700 headquarters staff from Edinburgh to new buildings at Inveralmond. The adjacent United Distillers (Dewar) blending and bottling plant was closed in 1994, throwing 300 employees out of work and cutting employment in the Perth area by 2%. However by then Caithness Glass had also moved its headquarters to Inveralmond, retaining their other works at Wick and Oban. MacNaughton's Woollens (Pitlochry) also have their production here. General Accident are much diminished, now part of the huge CGNU. In 1996 Perth College expanded at Perth Aerodrome *(q.v.)*. The former Dewar's site was proposed by THI in 1996 for a 10-screen multiplex cinema (but didn't happen). By 1997 two visitor centres, *'Noah's Ark'* and the Cherrybank Gardens drew visitors to this formerly dull area. An *Express by Holiday Inn* has arrived.

## LETTEREWE

**Map 8, C2**
***Locality on L. Maree, Wester Ross*** OS 19: NG 9571

From 1605 the remnants of the Caledonian forest at Letterewe – *'The wood of Ewe'* – on the steep north-eastern shores of Loch Maree in Wester Ross were exploited to provide charcoal for Scotland's second iron smelter, built nearby by Sir George Hay *(see also Bettyhill)*. Skilled workers and iron ore from England were landed at Poolewe; piers were built to enable the ore to be taken across the loch by water. About 1750 Roy mapped a track linking Kinlochewe *(q.v.)* with woodland north of tiny *'Lettyr Ew'* and *'Furnace'*; but the area remained roadless and when later in the century work ceased, little was left but deserted buildings – still visible to walkers on the lengthy lochside footpath from Kinlochewe.

## LETTERFINLAY & Invergloy

**Map 5, B1**
***W. Highland locality,*** *pop. under 100* OS 34: NN 2591

General Wade's military road between Inverness and Fort William was built beside Loch Lochy around 1730. By 1826 there was a *"lonely little inn"* at Letterfinlay *(G. 'Finlay's Wood')*, 27km from Fort William; no village has ever developed there. In 1903 the Invergarry & Fort Augustus Railway was built alongside Loch Lochy for the beer tycoon Lord Burton, with a station serving Invergloy House, 5km south-west. The uneconomic line closed to passengers in 1933 and was abandoned in 1946 *(see Thomas, 1965)*. The steep lochside, partly clothed by the South Laggan Forest, is now followed by the A82 trunk road. The *Letterfinlay Inn* had vanished by 1961. By 1963 the 12-roomed *Letterfinlay Lodge Hotel* was open, and by 1974 also the nearby *Corriegour Lodge Hotel*.

## LEUCHARS

**Map 6, C3**
***N. Fife village,*** *pop. 5200 (area)* OS 59: NO 4521

Kinnear on the Motray Water in east Fife had a thanage from about the 11th century. Some 6km downstream where the Motray enters the Eden estuary is Leuchars, whose Gaelic name *Luachair* means 'Rushes'; its stone church, founded by St Athernase from County Kildare, was built in the 12th century at the edge of the Tentsmuir plain, and its castle a century later. Nearby Earlshall Castle was built in the 16th century. An early parish school opened in 1594; a century later, Leuchars was one of only four Fife parishes still able to fund a school. James Gordon's map of about 1642 showed Brackmont mill, where by 1700 a bridge had been built across the Motray Water. The Roy map of about 1750 showed Leuchars Kirk almost alone beside a road linking Guardbridge with Partan Craigs (Tayport); Leuchars Castle (of which little now remains) was the centre of a squarely planted estate.

**Leuchars Village and Junction**: Two fairs were held at Leuchars in 1797; in 1799 Heron called it *"a rising village, having a considerable number of inhabitants, mostly manufacturers"*. In 1794 – and as late as 1864 – handloom linen weaving for Cupar and Dundee merchants was their main work. There was still no post office in 1813, though by 1825 Leuchars was served by a penny post from Cupar. By then the *St Michael's Inn* stood at a road junction 2 km to the north. The Edinburgh Perth & Dundee Railway was opened from Cupar in 1848 to a temporary terminus near Leuchars church; the line was extended to Tayport in 1850. Leuchars Junction station was created in 1852 at the divergence of the St Andrews Railway, and became in 1878 the starting point of the new main line to the Tay bridge. In 1894 there was an inn near the church, and a mill and a sawmill on the Motray Water beside the new station, but little recent development. In 1891 Earlshall was attractively restored to designs by Robert Lorimer. St Michaels golf club was established in 1903 and laid out a sandy 9-hole course beside the railway 1.5km north of the village. About 1914 the present station buildings replaced fire-damaged predecessors.

**RAF Leuchars: More Facilities, Fewer Trains**: In 1908 the army bought flat land east of the junction to test man-lifting kites; from this and the area's lack of fog grew one of the world's longest-lasting air bases, in turn RFC and RAF, modernised in 1935. In the 1939–45 war BOAC flew a Leuchars to Stockholm air service, bringing in Skefco ball bearings, and a 2950m runway was laid for the heaviest bombers; tiny Leuchars was soon swamped by service housing, but gained the facilities of a typical village – though in 1951 the telephone exchange had 370 *'connexions'*. The railway to Tayport and the old station were closed in 1956. The new station ceased to be a junction when the St Andrews branch was abandoned in 1969, leaving passengers to make do with buses; but it continued to be served by Aberdeen to London trains. In 1971 there were 460 service personnel. By 1980 Leuchars was no longer a post town, but there was a 5-doctor practice.

**Fighter Base and More Golf**: By 1989 Leuchars had an Air-Sea Rescue unit and had become Britain's biggest fighter base, with Phantoms. Until 1992 aviation fuel came direct to Leuchars by rail from Grangemouth, and then to a new terminal at Linkswood near Wormit. When Pitreavie closed in 1996, the UK Rescue Co-ordination Centre was moved to RAF Leuchars. In 1999 the base employed 1627 service people and 294 civilians; it was to become one of Britain's three Eurofighter bases. Its annual air show is a great crowd-puller. A new station car park and an impressive ramped footbridge were built in 1995; in 1996 a new golf course, the Scottish National Golf Training Centre and new housing were built at Drumoig north of St Michaels. Earlshall with its fine topiary garden is a tourist attraction, and the choir and apse of the 12th century church still survive. Hotels include the new *Drumoig Golf* and the old *St Michael's Inn*.

## LEVEN & Scoonie

**Map 6, B4**

***Fife coastal town,*** *pop. 8300*

OS 59: NO 3800

The early Scoonie church stood near the mouth of a burn falling into the Firth of Forth where Fife met Fothrif. In the mid 11th century it was given to the Culdees of Loch Leven and by 1152 there was a kirkton. About 1km to the south the River Leven also entered the Firth, at a point where the narrow raised beaches to the east and west gave way to sandy links. A *'Keeper of the Harbour'* was appointed to Leven in 1556, and must have worked hard, for it is a remarkable fact that the next source of information readily to hand, Blaeu's atlas map of East Fife based on Pont's originals of about 1600, showed *'Leauins mouth'* as a higgledy-piggledy settlement already larger than Dysart.

**The Barony Burgh**: Leven became a burgh of barony in 1609; logically it could have been called *Inverleven*, but this name, corrupted to Innerleven, referred to that part of Methil across the river which was originally a detached part of Markinch parish. By 1626 Scoonie parish ran a school, by 1633 Leven had one too, and about 1642 when James Gordon surveyed Fife for Blaeu, the Burn Mill stood beside *'Levin'*. In 1655 Leven was lumped together with other Fife ports by the CromwellianTucker, with the disparaging comment that they were *"pitiful small towns inhabited by seamen, colliers, salt makers and such like people"*. So much for the dignity of labour! At that time Leven possessed two sailing vessels of about 20 tons. The *Caledonian Hotel* began as a hostelry in the late 17th century, and there was at one time a *mercat* (market).

**Coal and Linen, Cotton and the Post**: Inland of Scoonie was Durie, where by about 1700 a coal mine had a water-driven pump. Linen textiles also developed locally, for a bleachfield was in operation by 1745. The Roy map made about 1750 showed Leven as a large place of squarish layout on the coast road, which forded the River Leven, with a connecting road to meet the present-day A915; there was a tiny settlement at *'Skeenie'* Kirk. Leven had a post office by 1751. Leven's small industrial base grew when Kirkland Mill was built 1km upriver in 1788 to spin cotton, soon employing 300 people. In 1791 six trading vessels of up to 150 tons belonged to the town, and 140 looms were making brown linen in Scoonie parish, where there was a public bleachfield and a monthly fair for the sale of white linen. By 1797 Leven was a post town with a daily service, and five fairs were scheduled for the year. Heron described it in 1799 as *"a handsome village which may soon become a place of considerable trade, having already nearly 1200 inhabitants. A very considerable cotton-work, lately erected employs over 300 people."*

**Ironfounding, Golf, Shops and Shipping**: The Durie iron foundry, built in 1808–10 was bought by Henry Balfour in 1817; by 1837 he was in business as an engine maker. By 1825 Leven was the centre for a penny post serving Largo. Leven Golfing Society – and its first course on the links – were established in 1820. Chambers then noted that *"formerly it had a great trade with the Baltic, and a great many ships belonged to it. It now only boasts of six or seven."* To him it was *"a thriving village at the mouth of the River Leven, over which there is a new wire-bridge for foot-passengers. The shops are more elegant and respectable in appearance than those of any other town of similar size in Fife, and perhaps in Scotland."* A new quay was built between 1821 and 1833, and in 1838 Leven proprietors owned two 374-ton brigs trading to America, plus five coasting sloops; in 1844 43,000 tons of coal was shipped.

**Leven's Beer, Bricks and Bridge**: By 1806 Kirkland Mill was making linen yarn from Russian flax, and from 1810 was the first in Scotland to be lit by gas, apparently from its own plant. By 1838 nearly 700 people worked there, of whom 240 were hand weavers. By 1836 there were five other spinning mills, with 250 workers in all, and about 170 other weavers; but the Scoonie linen trade then declined. A brewery was working by 1825, as was a brick and tile works near the Scoonie mouth; Scoonie Kirk was a ruin. The town was then a compact place. An ochre mine, a sawmill and a flint-grinding mill for pottery were at work by 1830. In 1839 a town gasworks was built, and the notorious Sawmill Ford on the coast road was at last replaced by the Bawbee (halfpenny) bridge in 1840. Leven Golf Club was re-founded in 1846 and laid out a new 9-hole course, extended to 18 holes in 1868.

**Bouch's Railway, Engineering, Timber and Nets**: The cheaply constructed Leven Railway that opened in 1854 was laid out by the opportunist engineer Thomas Bouch, its remarkably winding line closely following the river from Thornton Junction to its mouth. The Leven extremity remained as a short goods branch when the railway was extended from a junction at Kirkland eastwards to Kilconquhar by another company in 1857, and ultimately round the East Neuk to St Andrews. James Donaldson & Sons' timber import and sawmilling business was founded in 1860. By 1864 sailcloth was also woven in Leven, but only Boswell & Co were spinning flax; they also made nets at Hawkslaw Mills from the 1860s to 1886 when the undertaking passed to the Boase Spinning Company. By then Kirkland mill's 500 workers processed flax, hemp and jute by water and steam power, also using hand looms. In 1867 there were nine flax, jute and hemp mills in the area, with nearly 3050 workers in total. About 1862 Henry Balfour's engineering output included vertical steam engines, and in the 1880s steel headgear and winding engines for collieries.

**Tiny Dock and Good Golf**: In 1867 Leven became a police burgh, but its port remained inadequate until a small wet dock was built east of the river in 1876–80; even this could only accept 800-ton vessels. The North British Railway bought the amalgamated Leven & East Fife Railway in 1877, and the population passed 3000 in 1881. The railway was extended from Leven quay to Methil docks, probably in 1889–94. The *Caledonian Hotel* was *'commercial'* in 1894, when Leven was *"a small seaport with good golfing links"*. By then a rail siding served the Durie Pit east of the town, and another the Silverburn Flax Mill, once owned by Tullis Russell of Markinch; the small mansionhouse of Silverburn had lately been built nearby. By 1901 John Balfour & Co operated oil-cake and bone mills in Leven, whose population had rapidly grown, to 5550 by 1901.

**Trams, Electricity, Coalowner's Mansion and Resort**: From 1904 to 1932 the Wemyss & District Tramway Company linked Durie Street in Leven by electric trams (powered from Aberhill) to Methil, East Wemyss, Coaltown and Gallatown (and so by a through service to central Kirkcaldy). Augustus Carlow, the chairman of the great Fife Coal Company, whose head office was in Leven, built Linnwood Hall in 1904, in policies covering 5ha. Although a public electricity supply was provided in 1911, James Donaldson & Sons bought a new steam engine for their Wemyss Sawmills in 1923 (this has been preserved by the National Museums of Scotland). The local pit was soon closed and its site added to a new 18-hole Scoonie municipal golf course, laid out north of the railway from 1909; later Silverburn too became a public asset, and its grounds were opened as a small park. By 1922 the *Leven Advertiser & Wemyss Gazette* was in publication and *Green's Picturedrome* was open; Letham Glen was laid out as a public park in 1925. The Beach Pavilion, built in 1929, offered summer shows until 1965, and the *Jubilee Theatre*, originally the Town Hall, also provided varied entertainment until its demolition in 1973.

**Balfour of Leven: Yanks and Tanks**: The long-established firm of Henry Balfour had added gasworks plant to their output by 1913; they merged with the American Pfaudler Company in 1933. Beside the existing foundry, engineering and boiler shops was soon built a new works to manufacture large glass-lined steel containers for the brewing, chemical and pharmaceutical industries. This was originally known as EPC (Enamelled Products Corporation), but later became part of Henry Balfour. The prominent and extensive Baroque style stone-built shop complex of the Leven Co-operative Society was erected in 1935, for Leven had become an important local centre, aided by the scattered nature of commercial development in Methil.

**Exit Dock and Passenger Trains – enter Pop Art**: But Leven's significance as a port without proper facilities became very marginal with the growth of the adjacent Methil Docks, as ships grew larger and Leven dock silted up; it was eventually infilled to extend the railway coal yard. In 1946 Linnwood Hall was gifted for use as a convalescent home for miners' wives. Jack Hoggan, born in the town in 1951, became a mining engineer, but is now generally known as the self-taught artist Jack Vettriano (his mother's maiden name). To the disgust of the snooty arts establishment he was a rich man by 2000, best known for his popular, colourful and erotic poster-style paintings. Meantime the fine new Bawbee road bridge spanning the river and railway was built for Fife County Council by Melville Dundas & Whitson and opened in 1957. By then Leven had a population of 9000. But thanks to Beeching, all rail services on the line to St Andrews ceased in 1965 and the passenger train services from Thornton were withdrawn in 1969. However, the riverside line remained open to Methil for freight.

**Whisky Blending, Bottling and Bonding**: The local newspaper, by then called the *Leven Mail*, had become associated with the *Fifeshire Advertiser* of Kirkcaldy, which ceased publication in 1965; the former was re-titled the *East Fife Mail* in 1966 by its new owners the Fife Free Press of Kirkcaldy. The Carlow Home closed about 1970, its functions transferred to a related centre at Culross. The population peaked in 1971 at around 9500, but Leven's local government status was lost to Kirkcaldy District in 1975. In the 1970s the giant DCL whisky blending and bottling plant and its many bonded stores were built at Banbeath 2 km to the west. In 1975 Donaldsons built a replacement for the fire-damaged Wemyss Sawmills on a new site, while staying near their traditional riverside location. They also established a roof truss assembly plant in 1980 *(see Buckhaven)*. In 1963–66 Balfours built the six giant digesters which cooked wood chips into pulp at ill-fated Corpach *(q.v.)*; they also made machinery for rice processing. The US-owned firm also supplied huge glass-lined tanks to major breweries such as Wellpark (Glasgow). About 1970 the process equipment division was closed, and the remainder – which continued to specialise in large glass-lined pressure vessels – was belatedly renamed Pfaudler-Balfour (PB).

**Pennsylvanian Paints and Pedestrians Prosper**: Silberline Inc of Tamaqua, Pennsylvania, established a small factory at Banbeath in 1974 making silvery pigments for metallic car paints; the operation grew fast, in 1981 adding buildings to make granules for printing inks and plastics, and won export awards in the 1980s. By contrast, in 1979 valve manufacturers Forrest Randall employed 50 people, but were cutting back. About then some local facilities were closed, but with a caravan site, two golf courses and a children's park, Leven continued to cater for simple holidays. Its fortune is tied to the adjacent one-time mining town and coal port of Methil, with its dominant power station and high unemployment. Against this rather dispiriting background, Leven succeeded in maintaining its modest commercial role, aided in the early 1980s by pedestrianisation of the High Street and the erection of a supermarket beside a new bus station.

**Hotel Problems, Success for Swimming and Industry**: The ancient *Caledonian Hotel* was burnt out in 1986 and had to be demolished. The 22-room *New Caledonian Hotel* opened in 1987; this employed 30 staff in 1995 when poor trading, said to stem from redundancies at the Methil fabrication yard, sadly forced closure. In 1988–89 a new swimming pool and leisure centre was built for Kirkcaldy District Council on the former railway coalyard – the original port site. In 1991 the independent firm James Donaldson & Sons was Scotland's largest maker of trussed rafters, soon with 280 employees on 8 sites from Inverness to northern England. In 1994 they installed computerised sawing equipment to meet soaring demand for timber frames, a type of construction by then used in over half of all new Scottish houses. Meantime in 1991 James Jones & Sons expanded their creosote works at Kirkland. Silberline Ltd expanded to 135 workers by 2000, including a research facility.

**More Bottling, More Tourism – and an unusual Drive-in**: From 1993, the recently extended Leven bottling plant employed some 800 people. By 1993 the US-owned Balfour works – which supplied 80% of the UK's needs for glassed steel equipment, until recently using plates supplied by British Steel from Motherwell – had a subsidiary factory, Stoline, making ancillary plant; they also owned Chemical Reactor Services of Bolton. In 1994 Praytis Farm, 5km north of Leven, opened as a deer park, with a golf driving range, a restaurant, shop and farming museum in its converted buildings. In 1994

Leven was unique in possessing the only drive-in bank in Scotland, a Royal Bank branch. The Co-op shops, abandoned by the CWS around 1990, were converted into flats about 1998, while Sainsburys were building a supermarket beside the Bawbee Bridge. The re-erection of a mercat cross on the traditional site was proposed in 1999. The *Caledonian Hotel* is now back in business.

## LEVERBURGH *(An't-Ob)*

**Map 11, B4**

***Township, Harris,*** *pop. 200* — OS 18: NG 0186

Also see: *Berneray & Rodel*

In 1894 the crofting township of An't-Ob or Obbe *(G.'The Creek')* in south Harris had a temperance inn and a pier with a weekly steamer to Glasgow. In 1918 the philanthropic Sunlight Soap magnate Lord Leverhulme bought Harris and Lewis; Obbe was renamed Leverburgh in 1921 and developed with a water supply from a circular hilltop reservoir, and a pier with fishing facilities, to serve the national chain of shops he named *MacFisheries*. His ambitious ideas met local opposition and he pulled out after a few years. Meantime the Bank of Scotland had opened a local sub-branch in a wooden hut in 1924; business never developed, and the same tiny premises were used until its closure in 1994! In 1951 the 350 local people and 800 more in associated townships were served by a post office, the 90-pupil Leverhulme junior secondary school, a doctor and ambulance. Glasgow steamers lasted into the 1960s, but the inn was no more. In 1974 a passenger ferry plied to Newtonferry in North Uist, uprated by 1984 to carry vehicles and to serve Berneray *(q.v.)*. By 1976 tiny Leverburgh had been uprated to a post town. Its 230 people founded a co-operative about 1980 and set up a craft and tourist centre. In 1991 the Western Islands council, which had recently lost its investments in the BCCI bank crash, closed the secondary school. In the 1990s Haswell-Smith regretfully described Leverburgh as *"a small, sad, rather down at heel port"*.

## LHANBRYDE

**Map 10, A1**

***Moray village,*** *pop. 2000* — OS 28: NJ 2761

A prehistoric stone circle was erected on the fertile plain of the Laigh of Moray, east of the River Lossie. At nearby Urquhart a Benedictine priory was founded in 1136 by David I, but the monks soon moved to Pluscarden, and the buildings vanished. Pont's map sketched about 1600 showed the Kirks of *'Vrwhart'*, accompanied by a mill (and by 1631 a parish school), and to the west on the Longhill Burn *'Lambry'*, named after St Bride or Bridget. The elaborate tower of *'Cokston Castle'*, then newly built west of the kirk for Sir William Innes, was added to until 1644. A motte 4km north of Lhanbryde had been replaced nearby with a plain tower, called Innes Castle, which was rebuilt in 1640–53 as a mansion style tower called Innes House, to designs by William Aytoun, an Edinburgh master mason.

**New Village and Railways**: The Roy map of about 1750 showed the *'Kirk of Longbride'*, standing south of the track between Elgin and the lower Spey. Urquhart new village was laid out 2 km north-east of Lhanbryde about 1783, and both Lhanbryde and Urquhart had post offices from 1839. When the Highland Railway opened its main line from Elgin to Keith in 1858, a station was provided at Lhanbryde, which being only 5km from the steadily developing business centre of Elgin, became a favoured growth centre at the expense of Urquhart. In 1884 the latter gained its own small station on the Great North of Scotland Railway's coast line linking Elgin with Garmouth and later Buckie; a passing station was built at rural Calcots, 4km to the west. None of these can ever have been busy places except when a military airfield was open north-west of Innes House; it was built during the 1939–45 war, after which it became disused, though remaining in existence.

**Dormitory Settlement**: The population of Lhanbryde in 1951 was approaching 1400, but with the facilities of only a small village, plus a 220-pupil junior secondary school. This related to another 1300 people in the wider area, but was solely primary by 1976. Although the main line remained open to passing trains, Lhanbryde station was closed in the mid 60s, and the less viable coast line was closed completely in 1968; Urquhart station became a caravan and camping park. As Elgin grew and farm work declined, housing estates were built east and north of Lhanbryde; by 1981 they were supported by two garages and two inns. In 1991 Lhanbryde's younger than average population touched 2000. Certain of its local facilities still serve smaller places including Urquhart, but overall they remain those of a small village. Innes House, which had been extended into a large mansion with extensive formal gardens, was still beautifully kept around 1990 but is not open to the public. The village was bypassed by the A96 trunk road in the early 1990s. The *St Andrews Hotel* serves the locality.

## LIBERTON

**Map 15, C2**

***S-E. suburb of Edinburgh,*** *pop. 20,000* — OS 66: NT 2768

By 1143 AD, and perhaps a century earlier, there was a church at Kirk Liberton about 5km south of Edinburgh, though within its parish. Liberton Tower was probably erected in the 15th century, one of many defensive dwellings built by the nobility in the environs of what had lately become the capital city; about a century later, perhaps in 1570, its owners the Littles built the mansion of Liberton House. A parish school was founded in 1598, and the Edinburgh to Lasswade road existed by the time that Blaeu engraved Pont's map of around 1600; it served the closely settled area around Nether Liberton some 4km from the city. By the 1750s, as the Roy map showed, this place was a medium-sized nuclear settlement, with a side road to Craigmillar Castle and another to Straiton. Liberton had a brewery by 1789; water from the Braid Burn was pumped up to the growing city. A school was open at Liberton by 1792 when a weekly market was held. There was a water mill on the Braid Burn in the 19th century; Liberton had a post office from 1804, and a library was opened in 1828; but it never became a burgh nor was it ever on a railway. Development south of the Braid Burn got under way when in 1875–79 the city's new waterworks were constructed at Alnwickhill. Whereas in 1873 there were only 48 school pupils in Liberton, Dr Guthrie's large *Industrial School*, later a boys' secondary, was opened there in 1888; by 1896 even the village school had 240 pupils, but the growing village was still separated from Newington by 1.5km of open country.

**Trams make a Suburb**: In 1900 Edinburgh's cable trams were extended from Newington to Nether Liberton, a route which required a single cable over 10km long. They were converted to electric traction in 1922 and by 1929 had been extended up Liberton Brae to a new terminus at Kirkgate; an extension to Kaimes was planned but never built. A sanatorium built in Lasswade Road in the early 20th century was later called the Southfield Hospital. Liberton golf club had already been founded in 1920, laying out an 18-hole course, and these facilities speeded the extensive development of the Liberton area as a sprawling suburb. The Southhouse estate had been built by 1939, and Liberton's total population passed 12,000 about 1951. The Liberton trams sadly vanished in 1956.

**Council Estates, Waterworks and Geriatric Care**: Between 1945 and 1971 large Edinburgh council housing estates – linked to the city by frequent bus services – were built at the Inch to the north and Gracemount to the south. Liberton High School was built in 1959 and Gracemount High School was open by 1970; the Alnwickhill water-works were also substantially expanded in the post-war period. The population peaked about 1971 at over 22,500. The Mortonhall crematorium was built in 1964, and by 1977 a caravan site and garden centre were open nearby. Despite riding stables and a golf driving range, the scattered local facilities (the equivalent of those typical of a large village) were still considered inadequate in the late 1980s for the population, which in 1991 was 19,740. In 1994 Associated Nursing Services developed a 120-bed private nursing home at Liberton, an unusually large-scale response to the typical problems of an ageing population; care was then being switched back to the private sector, and the geriatric section of the NHS 69-bed Southfield Hospital had closed by the end of the century. Today, Gracemount High has a roll of 540, and Liberton High 600.

## LILLIESLEAF — Map 3, B4

***Border village,** pop. 350 (area)* — OS 73: NT 5325

Lilliesleaf lies in the valley of the Ale Water 9 km south-west of St Boswells; it had a kirk by the 12th century, and a medieval motte stands at Riddell or Wester Lilliesleaf, 2 km to the west. The valley was thickly settled when Pont mapped the Borders around 1600. To the east was a mill near Chapel, while beyond Riddell, later a mansion in large policies, was *'Bowismiln'*. When Roy mapped the area about 1754, Lilliesleaf was not yet on the road system. The industrial revolution passed by, though from 1849 rural Belses, 4 km to the east, had a station on the Edinburgh & Hawick Railway. In 1951 Lilliesleaf's single substantial street still housed most of the parish population of 431, its facilities typical of a small village, serving in all some 750 people within about 5 km. Belses station enjoyed two trains a day till the whole Waverley Route was closed in 1968, but by 1980 an agricultural engineer had developed from Belses Smithy. Lilliesleaf services including a licensed grocer and two pubs held up well, with the addition of a pottery; although there was little else for tourists, for a time around 1980 the *Cross Keys Inn* provided accommodation; it now rates as a pub. The parish had 334 residents in 1991; the primary school and post office are still open.

## LIMEKILNS, Brucehaven & Charlestown — Map 16, C2

***W. Fife villages,** pop. 1620* — OS 65: NT 0783

The area south of Dunfermline was originally known as *(the)* Gellet, a farm name which survives. At some early date kilns were built on an adjoining site to produce lime for use in building with stone, rather than for farming; by the 15th century there was a road to Dunfermline, where extensive stone buildings had been erected. Meantime by 1362 Brucehaven – beside the early Rosyth church – was the port for the Scottish Court when in Dunfermline, hence the 14th century royal wine cellar there (now restored); but it seems that no actual overseas trade was handled in the medieval period. Pont's map of about 1600 showed *'Galletts'*, south of which on the coast was *'Lyme kylls'*. The massive beds of limestone dip westwards from the Gellet Rock, and exploitation naturally began at the nearby outcrop; sea shells were also collected for burning, and coal from inland pits was evidently exported. On the coast west of Limekilns was *'Tournirch'*, roughly where Charlestown was later built; the Lyne Burn had been bridged west of *'Medaw End'*, probably at Foodiesmiln, and its mouth some 2 km to the west of Limekilns was labelled *'Whale heaven'*.

**The Iron Mill and Bo'ness Ferry**: About 1630 George Hay established an Iron Mill or forge near the mouth of the Lyne Burn. This appears to have made the large pans in which salt was evaporated, including some installed west of Limekilns. In the 1640s Lord Elgin's mansion of Broomhall had been erected on the 45-metre hill behind the King's cellar, and on the burn the Judge Mill and the Wake (Waulk) Mill had also been built. In all at least five mills including the Midmill are known to have worked on the lower part of the burn. In 1655 Tucker reported Limekilns as *"a little town"* whose trade in small coal was already declining. Roy's map of about 1750 showed the iron mill and Limekilns pier, from which a ferry operated to Bo'ness for centuries; except for the (perhaps inadvertent) omission of the Dunfermline link, the area's system of roads or tracks had attained much of its 20th century lines.

**Village Plan Commemorates Charles Elgin**: About 1758 the new village of Charlestown was laid out east of the iron mill by Charles Bruce, fifth Earl of Elgin, hence its *'CE'* pattern to commemorate his titular name, *'Charles Elgin'*. This may well have been the first planned industrial settlement in Scotland. A new range of limekilns was built on the adjacent coast in 1761, and evidently also a harbour; the original kilns seem to have been abandoned. Burning was in full swing at Charlestown at the time of Pennant's visit (in 1769). In 1765 Elgin had also opened Crombie pier, to which a wagonway brought iron ore and coal from Berrylaw west of Dunfermline, for shipment to Carron.

**The Elgin Railway**: Charlestown was soon served by the *'Elgin Railway'*, a wooden-railed horse-drawn wagonway completed in 1774, which ended beside the inn at *'The Run'*, a short steep self-acting incline to the harbour, nowadays a footpath. A large granary was built, and extensive stables for the horses. From 1778 the sixth Earl further developed Charlestown as a coal exporting port. By 1792 some 85,000 tonnes of limestone were being excavated annually, by mining westwards underground rather than by further quarrying. Two fairs were to be held at Charlestown in 1797. Heron in 1799 noted that *"the lime-works begun by the Earl of Elgin are among the greatest in Britain; situated on the shore, they supply the whole eastern coast of Scotland. Two villages are built here, chiefly for the accommodation of the workmen."* Limekilns and Charlestown together contained about 1200 people.

**Broomhall and Brewing**: Iron rails were laid on the Elgin Railway in 1804, and by 1821 500 tonnes of coal a day were being exported from the loading bank at Charlestown, tipped down chutes into the holds of ships which also carried lime, returning with sand ballast (which was tipped west of the harbour). In the early 19th century a new Broomhall mansion was built for Lord Elgin, its policies filling the space behind the two villages. A thread mill was erected in 1815, and by 1825 there was a brewery. In 1828 as many as 75 ships belonged to the two ports, and soon steam locomotives were in use on the Elgin wagonway, despite its sharp corners; in 1834 it was improved into a properly aligned railway, which carried the first fare-paying rail passengers in Fife, meeting steamships for Leith and a steam ferry to Bo'ness.

**Lime at its Peak, and the North British Railway**: From around 1830 the limestone was carried from quarry to kiln by a rope-hauled tramway of two-foot (60 cm) gauge powered by a steam engine at the *'Gin Head'*, from which the bogies rolled to the harbour by gravity. Charlestown harbour was extended about 1840; by 1854 there were brick and tile works and a saw-mill north-west of Broomhall. In 1864 the steeply graded Elgin line was sold to the North British Railway, which soon created the present cliff when cutting stone to build the outer harbour, east of which was the terminal station. Around 1869 a shipyard was briefly in operation, but local prosperity was short-lived, and the thread mill was converted to grind corn in 1870. When in 1877 Dunfermline was joined to North Queensferry by a railway, the passengers evidently preferred this route to the Bo'ness ferry, which was closed.

**An 1888 Overview of Charlestown**: In 1888 Beveridge mentioned that there were still three daily coaches to Dunfermline. He enthused that *"the village is a model for neatness and general amenity; the port of Charlestown is both a large emporium of merchandise, and supports an extensive export traffic of coal, lime, and ironstone. Formerly, when the Stirling steamers touched at the pier, there used to be a tramway for passengers to Dunfermline, but this has long reverted into a mineral railway."* Coal shipments ceased after the Forth Bridge was opened in 1890, and in 1891 Hume Brown noted that Limekilns had *"long ceased to be a place of any commercial importance"*. By 1900 there was a *'Hygienic laundry'*. When the *Elgin Hotel* was built in 1912 the former inn became the estate office.

**Armaments arrive; Limekilns and Warships depart**: The RNAD (Royal Naval Armaments Depot) built into the cliffs at Crombie, with its attendant rail connection and village, were products of the first world war; but passenger trains continued to serve Charlestown only until 1926. Until about 1930 some 70 men worked at the Charlestown Foundry, which had taken over the iron mill; this was originally linked to the harbour by a miniature canal, and later rail-connected. In the 1920s W McCrone of Pitliver, who was concerned in raising the German warships from Scapa Flow, established the British Oxygen Company (BOC); some of the vessels were towed to Charlestown for breaking up by Metal Industries. Lime shipment ceased in 1937 at about the time the quarrying stopped, and for the ensuing twenty years of operation of the kilns all the limestone burned came from elsewhere. One kiln charge required 20 tonnes of coal to 160 tonnes of limestone. In 1951 the two villages had a combined population of about 830. Lime burning finally ceased in 1956, and about 1958 the Leith Salt Company's surviving depot was also closed. Naval vessels demolished post-war included the 1050-ton destroyers HMS *Teazer* in 1960 and *Talybont* in 1961; scrapping at Charlestown ended in 1964. The railway station was demolished about 1968, and in 1970 the laundry was closed; its site was used for housing, and other new homes were built on the former ballast banks.

**Recreating an industry**: Renovation of the Charlestown kilns began in 1989 and a museum was planned. In 1991 the great limestone quarry was overgrown and threatened with infilling, and the Iron Mill ruins still stood. A sewage disposal plant for Dunfermline was planned just north of the site. A new pier was built at the RNAD about 1990, when 250 people were employed. When in 1991 the residents numbered 1620, the twin villages tended to be of dormitory character. By 1994 the Scottish Lime Centre had built a tiny new kiln at Charlestown to burn limestone from the local quarry for building conservation work, followed in 2000 by a larger one. The harbour is now a yacht basin for vessels able to take the mud at low tide. The *Elgin Hotel* was extended to 12 rooms in 1989, and remains in business.

## LINLITHGOW — Map 16, C2

***W. Lothian town,*** *pop. 11,750* — OS 65: NT 0077

Linlithgow was for many centuries just called *Lithgow*. Its name is Welsh Gaelic, *Llaith Cau* meaning *'Moist Hollow'*. The prefix *Llyn-* or *Lin-* is redundant, meaning Loch or Lake. To the west is the incised valley of the Avon (Cumbric for *'River')*, on both sides of which the placenames and other evidence imply early Strathclyde territory. The Anglians of Lothian seized the area east of the Avon, but failing to conquer the Picts in Angus in 685 AD, had to be content with staying south of the Forth: for three centuries Linlithgow was theirs, being protected by a fort on a knoll beside the lake. About 960 King Indulf of Alba defied the water frontiers of the Forth and Avon, and by conquest incorporated West Lothian into his kingdom, soon known as Scotia or Scotland. No local detail was recorded for another century or more, until Scotland's most active king David I chartered Linlithgow as a Royal Burgh between 1124 and 1138.

**The Power of the Church**: By that date a church dedicated to St Michael existed; in 1139 the pious realist David I gave it to the Bishop of St Andrews. In 1161 the burgh was made the caput of a sheriffdom which took its name, the basis of modern West Lothian; but later the status of the local sheriffdom was reduced to a mere constabulary of Edinburgh. A new St Michael's Church was consecrated in 1242, and about 1274 Linlithgow's extensive Deanery reached from Stirling to as far east as Edinburgh, Restalrig, Lasswade and Penicuik. By about 1282 the Priory of St Andrews also owned various well-let mills in Linlithgow, where tanning was a smelly local trade, wisely carried on just outside the burgh. In 1290 a Carmelite or Whitefriar priory or convent was founded; its exact status and site are unknown. There was also a Blackfriars monastery, and the Knights Hospitallers had a tower house.

**Inflammable English Castle and Scots Town**: *'Sea Coal'* was already being taken from Blackness to Linlithgow by 1300, at the time when the English invader Edward I employed 80 ditchers and 107 carpenters to construct a timber castle on the knoll. Barbour called this *"a peel great and strong, well garrisoned with Englishmen, a refuge for those going from Edinburgh to Stirling and back with arms and food"*. In 1313 this was seized for Bruce with the aid of a local small farmer, the *"stubborn and bold"* William Bunnock or Binnie, who devised a famous hay cart stratagem akin to the Trojan horse.

*Linlithgow Palace, from the south-west, with the turreted porch added for James V. The private royal apartments, where Mary Queen of Scots was born, were in the range to the left. The palace was gutted by fire in 1746, and was never rebuilt.* *(JRH)*

Bruce rewarded him, but had the peel *"thrown down to the ground"*. By way of retaliation the town was torched by the English in 1337.

**It's an Ill Wind: the Royal Residence**: Linlithgow castle was repaired in 1350, just in time, for by virtue of being served by many springs of pure water from the hill to the south, the town seems to have avoided the worst impact of the Black Death. This good fortune and the loss of Berwick to the English worked to the advantage of Linlithgow's trade in the next few years. Between 1330 and 1360 the burgh rose from a poor sixth place to become one of the four largest sources of Scottish Customs revenue. By 1372–76 its port of Blackness had become Scotland's second most important wool exporting centre, and was visited by Prussian merchants in 1393. By then Scotland's centre of gravity had moved from Perth to Edinburgh. No doubt because of Linlithgow's geographically central location and its site's greater spaciousness than the cramped summit of Edinburgh Castle Rock, the fort was rebuilt into a readily defended palace. This replaced Dunfermline as the most favoured home for the royal family, and the town expanded as a service centre at its gate.

**Trade Prosperity, Fire and Recovery**: In 1389 Linlithgow was re-chartered by Robert II and with Edinburgh, Lanark and Stirling – another Royal stronghold – became one of the leading group of Four Burghs; by 1400 it ranked third in trade. It had eight trades guilds: baxters (bakers), cloth fullers, coopers, cordiners (or leather workers), hammermen (smiths), tailors, weavers, and wrights (carpenters). Twice more the town was set on fire by the English, in 1411 and 1424; on the latter occasion the church and the makeshift palace were also burnt. But recovery was rapid: the local contribution to burgh tax revenue was as much as 11% in 1425; goods for and from the west of Scotland were carried via Linlithgow and shipped through Blackness, and by 1435 these two places acted as Scotland's third port for cloth exports.

**Rebuilding Palace, Church and Mill**: The Royal Palace of Scotland was majestically rebuilt in stone under King James I, largely in 1424–28, and completed in 1430 with a bowling green and a real tennis court. The royal mint stood where the railway station was eventually sited. However, it was 1468 before Linlithgow's full status as a sheriff caput was restored; the town council then felt more confident, and about 1475 rebuilt the burgh mill. St Michael's Church had been steadily rebuilt since 1424 on a vast scale for so small a town. It was completed in 1490 to approximately its current form, the choir being the last addition. In the late 15th century the town's overseas trading importance rapidly faded, probably due to the growing success of Leith, its contributions to Customs revenue falling to under 1.5%. However, Linlithgow retained its inland trading role, and up to 1707 the town council had sole charge of the standard Scottish grain measure, the *Firlot*, some 53.5 litres in capacity; this vessel still exists.

**Royalty's Final Fling at the Palace**: The Palace chapel, used from 1490, was completed in 1507. James IV, father of James V who was born in the Palace in 1512, lived well and carried on numerous affairs – small wonder, if the character of his wife Margaret Tudor resembled that of her great bully of a brother, Henry VIII! By 1526 or earlier the River Avon had been spanned by Linlithgow Bridge, 2 km west of the Palace, which was repeatedly improved up to completion of the vast fireplace in the Great Hall in 1539 by James V. His Queen, Mary of Guise, said she had *"never seen such a princely palace"*. It was the birthplace in 1542 of their unfortunate daughter, the beautiful but unhappy Mary, who became Queen of Scots as a baby. By that time there was a grammar school, and the houses of Hamilton's Land were built in stone, in the ancient format of *'gable to street'*.

**Before and After the Reformation**: The town's tax contribution averaged only 3% in the period 1535–56; about that time the fleshers ousted the fullers from the Guildry, and the Loch Mill was a meal mill. In 1560 the burgh was represented in Parliament, and a parish school was established in 1575. In the plague years 1585/93/96 Linlithgow again escaped, and the Palace Hall was used as the Scottish Parliament House. By 1593 Linlithgow was the centre of a presbytery, and in 1600 when James Hamilton was completing his West Port House, the traveller de Rohan regarded the town as more important than Stirling. Pont's map engraved in 1612 showed *'Linlitquo'* as a compact town with some of Scotland's earliest roads, leading to Edinburgh and westwards across Linlithgow Bridge towards Falkirk. The Hole Mill and the Loch Mill were both in existence, and north of the loch was the clearly demarcated *'Palace Park'*.

**Linlithgow declines after the Royal Departure**: The Union of the Crowns removed the Court and ended Linlithgow's period of national significance; the once bustling town became very quiet. Much of the north range of the neglected Palace collapsed into the courtyard in 1607; after a decade's delay it was rebuilt in 1618–24 by master mason William Wallace, using stone from Kingscavill Quarry, 2.5 km east of the town. The suppressed Carmelite friary was sold in 1624 and eventually demolished. The Edinburgh road was mended in 1633 for use by the carts carrying Charles I's heavy baggage to the Palace; this was used for one night! Brereton in 1636 found Linlithgow *"a fair, ancient town, and well built, some part of it in stone"*. Remarkably, it still held 18th place in tax yield among the Scottish burghs, though only a sixth of Glasgow's wealth and a fortieth that of Edinburgh with Leith.

**Cromwell, Leather Trades and the Tawse**: In 1645–46, when there was an attack of the plague in Edinburgh, the Palace temporarily housed the courts of justice and the University, and in 1646 the Scottish Parliament met there again.

In 1647 the burgh carriers were incorporated, despite the minimal traffic even on the potentially busy way to Edinburgh, where only three horseloads a day were moved. Yet in 1648 Linlithgow was still regarded as one of the *"greater towns"* of Scotland. Lord Protector Cromwell stayed at the Palace, but had the Town House pulled down about 1650 for use as building material. The Cromwellian troops included leather workers who taught the locals improved tanning techniques, and Linlithgow then became a more noted centre for leather production. The Fraternity of Tanners was founded in 1722. At its peak the town had 12 skinners, 17 tanneries and 18 currying works, plus many *'snabs'*, as shoemakers were called. Among well-known local products were leather straps or *tawses*, then mercilessly used for whipping school children into submission, and high sea boots for whalers; tinkers made the nails for the common tackety boots.

**Beer, Linen, Latin and Needlework**: Beer was brewed commercially and cloth was manufactured in Linlithgow by 1661; a post office was open from 1662. A new Town House designed by John Mylne was built in 1668–70 by John Smith. The Palace was used again in 1681 when James VII & II stayed there. Weekly markets and four annual fairs were held in the late 17th century, when the Royal Scots Greys were raised by local General Tam Dalyell for use against the Covenanters. At that time timber was brought from Bo'ness *"over Flints"*, implying some sort of made road. Four staff then taught little but Latin in the boys-only grammar school; less academic but more useful boys monopolised craft apprenticeships, while girls were taught reading and needlework by women in dame schools.

**Bleaching, Dyeing and Ashes to Ashes**: Though the town council complained of the collapse of its trade in 1692, by about 1700 the dyers had also become incorporated, and the thread industry was well established in the town by the 1720s, when Defoe commented that *"there is a very great linen manufacture, a thousand women and children tending and managing the bleaching business. Lithgow is a pleasant, handsome, well built town."* He added that *"The noble palace though decaying with the rest, is yet less decayed, because much later repaired than others."* Meantime the town council had laid on an early public water supply from west of the town to further *'wells'*, actually more akin to fountains. Sadly the palace was carelessly burned by Hawley's dragoons in 1746. Its ruination by fire must have fascinated young William Hamilton, born at Riccarton south-east of the town in 1730, for he went on to become the distinguished antiquarian who led the massive task of excavating Italy's rediscovered Pompeii and Herculaneum from their blanket of Vesuvian ash. The 18th century Annet House was built as the town house of a merchant, and rebuilt early in the next century. Another linen bleachfield was laid out between 1746 and 1760; about then a printfield was built at Bonnytoun.

**Smokes, Snuff and Whisky**: Stephen Mitchell & Son were established in 1723 as tobacco curers; they also had a snuff mill by about 1750, but moved to Glasgow in 1825. Roy's map of about 1754 showed all eight of the town's early radial roads (which lasted to the present); the long-established main road from Edinburgh to Falkirk via Linlithgow Bridge was turnpiked under an Act of 1752. By that time some six mills clustered north of Linlithgow Bridge, including Justinhaugh and Washmilton; there was also a distillery at Bulzion, followed late in the century by Sebastian Henderson's St Magdalene distillery on an adjoining site. By 1766 an oil mill was at work by the bridge, and a bark mill for the tanning industry also worked from 1773 to 1789, when it was converted to flint-grinding. Cast-iron edge rails for carts were still in situ in 1996 at the High Street pend entrance to a former lochside tannery. Woollen manufacture was noted in 1776, and more new mills were built in 1785.

**Inns, Fairs, Glue, Paper, and more Drinks**: By about 1790 both the *Golden Lion* (later the *Red Lion*) and *Star & Garter* were coaching inns, and the *Bridge Inn* also appears to be of 17th or 18th century origin. The eight fair days scheduled for 1797 put Linlithgow into the top dozen stances in Scotland. Brewing was important by that time, when 180 head of cattle were fed on the draff from the brewery at West End; the Mains or Maines distillery was built about 1795 by William Glen. Heron wrote in 1799 that *"the town is ancient, pretty large, regular, and tolerably well built. It contains about 2300 inhabitants. Tanning of leather, and making of shoes, constitute two principal branches of their employment."* He also mentioned stocking making, *tambouring* (embroidery) and a cotton printfield – the old Loch Mill. Dorothy Wordsworth wrote in 1803 of breakfasting in *"Linlithgow, a small town"*. In 1806 Thomas Nimmo established a glue factory, by 1811 paper was being made by water power at the ancient Loch Mill, in 1814 part of Bonnington Farm was converted into Dawson's Distillery, and in 1819 an award was made by the Board of Trustees to John Spence of Linlithgow for improvements in the spinning wheel.

**Canal, Degradation and Decay**: The Union Canal was dug in 1817–22 to link Edinburgh with the Forth & Clyde Canal at Camelon, and so with Glasgow. It passed immediately south of the town, was stone-lined, and was free of locks except at its western end – at the cost of crossing the Avon by a 26m high 12-arched aqueduct. At 247m in length this was the second longest in Britain, designed by the canal's engineer Hugh Baird with advice from Thomas Telford. Passenger and freight barges plied on the canal, from which St Magdalene distillery, by then one of five in the town, subsequently drew its water supply! A quarry was opened at Kettleston Mains south-west of the town to supply stone via the canal for buildings in Edinburgh's New Town. Chambers in 1827 described Linlithgow as *"this delightful and most entire specimen of the old Scottish royal burgh. Many of the houses formerly belonged to the nobility attending the court."* But the canal had not stimulated the town, and he bemoaned its decline to a *"state of degradation and decay"*.

**Scientists, Railway and Industries**: A gasworks was erected in the 1830s; by 1843 the prison in the Town House was gas-lit, and another gas with local associations was chloroform, isolated by Linlithgow chemist David Waldie. In 1830 Sir Charles Wyville Thomson was born at Bonsyde; he became a famous biologist, pioneered deep-sea exploration and led the first scientific circumnavigation of the globe by HMS *Challenger*. Meantime in 1842 a station was provided on the new Edinburgh & Glasgow Railway, which to maintain a level route was squeezed through between canal and High Street, cutting through the long back rigs of many houses; to the west it too crossed a substantial viaduct. Soon afterwards the *St Michaels* and *Palace* hotels were built, while a pleasure paddle launch operated on the Loch. Hardy's Tannery, established at the lochside in 1845, worked till 1951. A poorhouse was also erected in 1845, but for some years little other development occurred. After 1855 the Mains distillery became a brewery maltings and the Loch Mill was enlarged to use esparto in making glazed paper, including for a time that for the *Illustrated London News*. The large castellated branch office of the Commercial (later the Royal) Bank was built in 1859, and a sheriff courthouse was erected in the 1860s.

**Ploughs, Drinks, Press and Paper**: Because the town was known for its smiths, Newlands Engineering moved from Aberdeenshire in 1874 to manufacture farm machinery. About 1880 they built the St Magdalen Engineering Works and became famous for their horse-drawn ploughs. Meantime the Mains maltings were enlarged by James Aitken, a brewer of Falkirk, in 1875. From 1878 a local newspaper, the *Linlithgowshire Advertiser* was published. The Avonmill, another printfield, was converted in the 1870s by the Lovells to manufacture writing paper. The burgh population was 3900 in 1881. Barnard who explored the town and its sole remaining distillery in 1886 considered it *"a dull, sleepy place"*. By that time Dawson's establishment had merged with the St Magdalene distillery and become a large operation, with a canal wharf and an internal tramway system. It used peat from the Slamannan area, its water now coming not from the canal but from an artesian well and a spring; the plant was driven by a beam engine, and its 40 workers produced about 9 million litres of Lowland malt whisky annually. In the 1890s an 88-inch-wide papermaking machine was installed at Loch Mill by Chalmers.

**Public Buildings and Activities**: The ornate Victoria Hall with 800 seats was built in 1886–89. A second local newspaper, the *Linlithgowshire Gazette*, was established in 1891 as an offshoot of the *Falkirk Herald*. The ancient grammar school became a mere board school – a primary – before burning down in 1902. Linlithgow Academy was opened as a tiny independent school in 1894, acquired new buildings for its 52 privileged pupils in 1900–02, and in 1929 was wisely opened to all. The much-abused St Michaels Kirk was restored in the 1890s, and in 1894 shoes were still being made in Linlithgow, but the town was according to Murray still *"not flourishing"* and its sole hotel, the little *Star & Garter*, was *"poor"*. The Springfield Chemical Company made soaps just east of the town, closing in 1914.

**Ice, Explosives and Candles**: In the very hard winter of 1895 a vast icicle reached from the aqueduct spillway to the river bed 26 m below! The Crown Post Office was built in 1904. In 1914 the Mains Distillery, apparently an almost brand new concern in the old buildings, was closed and they reverted to a maltings. Meantime the Regent Works, a Nobel safety fuse factory at Low Port, had been built in 1900–01; in World War I – and as part of ICI in 1939–45 – it made ammunition. At some time a candle factory was built beside the St Magdalene distillery, which was owned in 1909 by A & J Dawson Ltd, who had overproduced and went into liquidation; it was sold in 1912 to a combine including DCL and John Walker & Sons. Later bonded warehouses enclosed these fire hazards in the most dangerous location imaginable!

**Electricity and Golf, Water, Petrol and Buses**: But the days of the candle were nearly over: from 1912 electricity was available from a burgh power station. Linlithgow golf club was founded in 1913 and provided a 9-hole course. During World War I Beecraigs Reservoir, 3 km south of the town, was built by German POWs. The first petrol pump in Scotland was put in at Donaldson's garage in 1919, and by 1923 locally based buses were running; when a garage and bus station were built it could not have been on a more central site. Soon a greyhound track was established in what had been a football ground. New County Buildings for West Lothian were opened in 1940. After 1945 the poorhouse became St Michael's geriatric Hospital. By 1951 Linlithgow's population was about 5000, with the facilities of a small town; but the local papers amalgamated in 1952. A Polish army camp at Low Port was converted into the *Laetare* youth hostel (but had closed by 1971). In 1956 the Victoria Hall was robbed of the top of its baronial facade and converted into the *Ritz Cinema*, which later became a bingo hall and in the 1980s a gaming arcade, before closing altogether around 1990; it awaited a new use in 1999.

**Industrial Closures and the Regent Centre**: The long-established glue works in Preston Road – known as Thomas Nimmo or Gowan Stank *('Daisy Pond')* – worked at its smelly trade until 1958. In 1964 through traffic on the canal was ended, and in 1965 it was blocked at Preston Road; other sections of the canal were also regrettably blocked. In the late 1960s Spence's manufactured clothing, but the Mains maltings were closed in 1968 and in 1971 the Avon paper mill ceased work. After 1945 the Regent Works became an ICI pharmaceutical factory, until the work was moved to Macclesfield in the 1970s; the buildings were demolished, and the site redeveloped as the small Regent Shopping Centre, including a Tesco supermarket. Newlands Engineering ploughs could also be pulled by tractors; but the integral Ferguson system killed their market and the firm closed in 1983.

**Controversial Reawakening**: The highly prominent fleche on St Michael's church was erected in 1964 *(see Grangemouth)*. New buildings to accommodate the 650 pupils of Linlithgow Academy were opened in 1968; the Low Port primary school soon moved into the vacated buildings. In 1969 when the start of the M9 motorway brought continuous noise to the once peaceful loch, a quarry was opened for construction materials; it was later infilled with demolition materials when an over-zealous town council cleared many ancient buildings for *'modern'* redevelopment – some, such as the Spanish Ambassador's house, sadly missed. However, once the M9 motorway was opened linking Newbridge west of Edinburgh with Falkirk, Grangemouth and Stirling, in response the train service was repeatedly improved. This enhancement of east–west accessibility was complemented by major industrial developments to both north and south at Grangemouth and Livingston. As a result Linlithgow developed as a dormitory, the population growing rapidly, aided when the quarry became the site of the Avontoun housing estate. The Union Canal Society, formed in 1975, created in 1977 a small museum in the former canal stables; the golf course has been enlarged to 18 holes.

**Burgh, Co-Op & Paper Lost; Country Park Gained**: Meantime Burgh and County status had been lost in 1975; though the sheriff court survived, and the town retained some district offices, by 1981 the headquarters of West Lothian district had been moved to Bathgate. A supermarket built in 1969 by the Bo'ness Co-op failed in 1984, and was converted into a health centre in 1989. By 1989 the Loch Mill had been acquired by the Inveresk group and also closed down. In the early 1980s a country park with sailing, canoeing, archery, caravan site and other activities was developed at Beecraigs, 3 km to the south.

**From Whisky and Candles to Sunrise Industries**: The St Magdalene distillery – whose single malt was a traditional whisky – was closed in 1983, and was damaged by fire in

January 1988 (though not because of the candle factory!). By 1992 the east block had been newly converted into flats. The surviving bond on the site was owned in 1995 by Morrison Bowmore, while the listed remainder of the distillery building – the large 5-storey West Malt Barns – stood empty and for sale in 1995–2000, with permission for conversion into 28 flats. Meantime by 1983 Racal MESL had built a factory to make radar systems in the town. In the mid 1990s as Racal Radar Defence Systems it was still busy with military orders for missile guidance systems. Sun Microsystems of the USA – itself established as recently as 1982 – chose the site of the former Springfield Chemical Company as the location for their European HQ, and in 1989–90 built a pleasing new factory to produce computer workstations. In 1995 Sun was a leading firm in the production of workstations (a market then still growing at 10% a year), microprocessors and computer servers, and the works was to grow to 550 jobs by also making networking equipment. A further extension announced in 2000 was to add further jobs, making around 1000 in all.

**Another Museum, and the Canal Reactivated**: As a result of these developments, by 1991 the population exceeded 11,750, with a youngish well-educated dormitory character, and in 1992 the Academy had to squeeze in no fewer than 1060 pupils. Even more residential development continued in the 1990s. Although in 1989 the canal museum was the sole museum in Linlithgow *(for an illustrated general history of the town see Hendrie, 1989)*, in 1993 a very fine small town museum with A-V displays of local industries was opened in Annet House by a partnership of public and local interests. Meantime a new bridge built at Preston Road in 1990 enabled the local section of the canal to be reopened, and by 1996 with over 300 members the Canal Society ran local pleasure-boat trips. Not surprisingly, by 1997 the traditional town centre seemed skewed to craft shops and tourism, although small/medium firms operate in coachbuilding, haulage, civil engineering, and safety equipment. The historic *Star & Garter Hotel* is still open, as are some ancient pubs, Livingston's restaurant, and the 16-roomed *Champany Inn*, 3km north-east. The reopening of the whole canal system in 2001 must surely benefit the pleasure boating industry, in Linlithgow above all.

## LINTRATHEN

**Map 6, B2**

***Angus glen area,*** *pop. under 100* — OS 53: NO 2854

Lintrathen Loch in the valley of the Melgam Water – a tributary of the River Isla – bears a Brythonic name, *'Llyn'* meaning *'Lake'* as in Welsh. In 1870 the water supplied to Dundee from Monikie *(q.v.)* ran dry, hence a much larger scheme was promoted to bring hill water from Lintrathen Loch, nearly 30km north-west of the city. In 1871–75 a dam was built at the hamlet of Bridgend of Lintrathen, to raise the loch level by 6m; in 1911 it was raised by a further metre. Bridgend remained a hamlet of about 90 people, its remarkably large telephone exchange having 46 connections in 1951. The local post office closed about the time that an Act of 1964 enabled Dundee City Council to build the 30m-tall Backwater Dam 5km to the north-west, impounding the Melgam Water, the main tributary of Lintrathen Loch. Completed by 1971, its new reservoir augmented the loch and made the supply secure. A primary school is the other feature of this remote but attractive area.

## LINWOOD

**Map 15, A5**

***Renfrewshire urban area,*** *pop. 10,100* — OS 64: NS 4464

Linwood stands on gently sloping ground beside the Black Cart Water 4km west of Paisley; it was named on Pont's map of Refrewshire, made about 1600. It was still a tiny hamlet in the 1750s, with roads to Paisley and Houston. A large cotton mill was opened in 1792 with a small planned village adjacent to it, but Linwood did not have a post office until after the penny post of 1840. A soap works was later opened, and a paper mill took over the cotton mill for a time from about 1880, but none of the various 19th century railways and freight lines which passed close by the village provided a passenger station. Nor did anything about Linwood attract the attention of the authors of Murray's Handbook for 1894, it remaining quite a small village.

**Hardwoods and the Big Shadow of Pressed Steel**: Normans of Linwood began to import hardwoods in the 1930s. In 1941 during World War II a large new government-sponsored *'shadow'* factory, managed by Beardmores of Parkhead, was built to make gun barrels at Linwood, which had grown to 2500 people by the 1950s, but had only the facilities of a small village. By then the shadow factory had become the huge Pressed Steel works which manufactured electric trains, railway wagons, refrigerated containers, army trailers, cabs and car bodies. From 1959 it built Class 117 diesel trains for British Railways; some were in service for 40 years. From 1960 Pressed Steel also made bodies for Swedish Volvo cars, and took on 200 extra workers.

**The Imp creates a Disaster-prone Quasi Town**: In 1961 the Hillman car factory was *'guided'* to Linwood by a moderate Conservative government which wanted the motor industry to expand in *'development areas'* rather than in the jobs-rich English Midlands. Both terraced and flatted houses were built for the workers, and the plant which opened in 1963 was proclaimed as producing something special, the new but cramped little Hillman Imp with its aluminium cylinder block; Pressed Steel made the body panels. In 1964 many Imps, the plant's main product, were sent by train to Coventry for distribution. At its peak the plant employed 4800 people, and by 1971 almost 11,000 people lived in Linwood, though except for schooling – both Linwood and St Brendan's High Schools had been built in the early 1970s – the facilities were still those of a mere village. The new *Linwood Gazette* newspaper briefly prospered with the factory. In 1973 Hillman Hunters and Estate cars were also being produced; total output reached 55 cars an hour. The Chrysler takeover of Hillman and the subsequent debacle under Talbot led to the entire car factory being closed in 1981 by its third unhappy owners, Peugeot; all the workers lost their jobs. Linwood's 12,000 people therefore had a disadvantaged character in 1981.

**The Hard Road Back to Phoenix**: The 140ha former car plant site was sold in 1988; some 120ha became the Phoenix mixed development area, soon including the 19,000m² Phoenix retail park, built in 1989–91, with its 7000m² ASDA superstore; offices comprising the first phase of the Phoenix business park were completed in 1992, as was the A737 Johnstone bypass to the south. About 10,100 people still lived in Linwood in 1991; male unemployment was still high, and higher qualifications few. Normans were still importing hardwoods. The last major sheds on the car plant site were demolished in 1996 when the big Distribution Centre of Chivas of Paisley was opened with a staff of only 20; its computerised operations could load a lorry in 15 minutes and handle 7 million cases of drinks a year. By then Phoenix Honda, a very large main car dealership, was also on the site; Foam Plus Ltd employ over 100 making packaging. Today, both Linwood and St Brendan's High Schools have small rolls of around 400; a new 40-room *Travel Inn* has been built. The varied housing built for the car-workers has mainly stood up well; some private housing has recently been built, reinforcing Linwood's role as a dormitory for people working in Paisley and Glasgow.

## LISMORE, Isle of — Map 4, C2

***Argyll island,*** *pop. 150* — OS 49: NM 8441

A number of duns and a broch on this long, narrow, limestone-rich and therefore fertile island in the Firth of Lorne show that there was much early settlement; its Gaelic name means *'big garden'*. The church of Lismore was founded by St Moluag between 561 and 585 AD; it was also a Columban monastic site and the possible source of the famous Book of Kells. About 1200 Lismore gained the cathedral of the Diocese of Argyll, which was created because the English Bishop of Dunkeld could not understand the Gaelic. The new bishop lived at Achadun Castle, now ruined, as is the 13th century Coeffin Castle. The diocese then included Lochaber but not the Isles, which were still under Norse rule. The see was moved to Saddell in 1507 and the cathedral was ruinous by 1512 – but until at least 1560 the *'Bishop of Lismore'* sat in Parliament. In 1549 Monro noted a parish kirk, actually a repaired section of the cathedral choir; this was burnt at the Reformation, and its cut-down walls re-roofed in 1749 to form a little church.

**Lead, Lighthouse and Limestone**: Pont's map of around 1600 named two dozen places on the island, which remained agricultural, and never acquired a village centre. However, in 1703 Martin mentioned lead ores. By the time the Roy map was made about 1750 there was a regular ferry to Port Appin from the north tip of the island, an area later called Port Ramsay. A waulk mill was built in 1759 and in the early 19th century, limestone for the Caledonian Canal was quarried on Eilean nan Caorach (Sheep Island) off the northern tip of Lismore. The lighthouse on Eilean Musdile off the south-west point of Lismore was built for the Northern Lighthouse Board by John Smith of Inverness to designs by Robert Stevenson and first lit in 1833 (it was made automatic in 1965). By 1841 some 1400 people lived on Lismore; however this number was halved in 30 years and continued to decline.

**Remote Jobs, Remote Teaching**: Gaelic was still generally spoken in the 1930s by the remaining 280 people, when limestone was quarried midway along the west coast and burnt near Port Ramsay. The limeworkers' cottages eventually became holiday homes, aided by the car ferry from Achnacroish to Oban which started about 1975; cattle were the mainstay of Lismore until the advent of the Glensanda superquarry in 1986 *(see Kingairloch)*. Lismore was still linked to Port Appin, the start-point of the Glensanda workers' boat service, by the traditional passenger ferry. By 1994 only about 20 of the 150 people on the island were fluent in the Gaelic, and most services were obtained from Oban. In 1995 remote teaching was introduced to the primary school, which then had 11 pupils.

## LIVINGSTON — Map 16, C3

***W. Lothian New Town,*** *pop. 42,000* — OS 65: NT 0366

Suburbs: *Bellsquarry & Deans.* Also see: *Mid Calder*

When Timothy Pont surveyed the Lothians about 1600 *'Levistoun Peel'* (a now-vanished tower) and an accompanying kirk stood on the north side of the River Almond some 20km west of Edinburgh, beside the road to Blackburn. A burgh of barony was chartered at Livingston in 1604 and a parish school was founded in 1633, but the place did not grow. The Roy map made in the 1750s showed *'Long Livingston'* as a tiny linear settlement just west of the point where the Edinburgh road to Blackburn and Hamilton threw off a fork to Carluke; another road linked to West Calder and Bathgate. The main road through Livingston was turnpiked from 1763, and the now-restored water mill dates from about 1770. In 1797 two annual fairs were scheduled, but the place remained devoted to farming, and the railways provided no station within 2 km of the village *(see Deans)*. Raeburn's Grange shale oil works at Charlesfield just south of Livingston is stated to have been in operation by 1868. By 1895 Livingston had an inn, post office and smithy, but little obvious change to the tiny village occurred until 1962.

**New Town: Flawed Concepts**: Livingston New Town was treated as an entirely new settlement when designated in 1962 for Glasgow overspill, and to compensate for the declining extractive industries of West Lothian; but in the author's opinion as a retired town planner, a number of important and regrettable planning mistakes were made. Firstly, its choice of site and the imposed loose grid layout reminiscent of America destroyed the only pleasant countryside that survived in an area which had until then endured a century of abuse by mineral extractors. Secondly, the 1963 White Paper on Central Scotland was highly disingenuous in attempting to define a regional context *after* the New Town had been designated! – a classic case of the cart before the horse. Thirdly, being planned in the car-happy 1960s the M8 was to be the peg on which the town was to be hung, and the central feature of the plan was a monstrous and featureless high-level spinal dual carriageway, the A899. Fourthly, the planners ignored the significant existing centres of Mid Calder, 4km to the east, and West Calder a similar distance to the south-west, and even turned their back on Livingston village itself, so following the sad Cumbernauld model rather than East Kilbride *(q.v.)*. In keeping with this cloud cuckoo approach they set out instead to compete with the existing main centre of West Lothian at Bathgate, by building a brand new centre. Its concept was further marred by choosing a location as far as possible from the two railways, 5km apart, which passed either side of the new town, but which by then had lost their stations. In fact the potential of railways was deliberately ignored.

**Early stages of the New Town**: Industrially, at first Livingston enjoyed mixed success: in 1963 work began on the Houston Industrial estate with the Cameron Ironworks, to employ 2000 people producing forgings for aero engines, power generation, nuclear power, valves and oil tools. Craigshill (east of the spine road) and Howden and Ladywell (on the west) were the first residential areas to be started. A postal sorting office was opened in 1965, when the *'Village'* appellation was added to the original settlement. A local newspaper, the *Livingston Post* was first published as early as 1968, but was slow to build up a circulation because the town lacked a focus. A textile plant was also established in the early days, but was bought up and closed by the Dawson Group in 1969.

**The New Town Changes its Role**: It was found that Glasgow people preferred to stay in the West of Scotland rather than move east, forcing a rethink. Meantime new industries which would have been better distributed elsewhere – where they were needed to support the economies of fading centres in the Lothians and the Motherwell and Clydesdale areas – happily set up in Livingston, drawn by practised promotional staff, serviced greenfield sites and generous financial incentives. As a result by 1971 the area's population had risen by about 5000. Residential expansion was begun at Knightsridge to the north-west, and (as soon as the A899 extension already under construction had been completed to the Lanark road, A71) at Dedridge to the south. However, problems followed the Pye TMC electronics factory, open by 1974; this was operated by Philips and employed 475 people in 1979 when it was abruptly closed.

**Precision Engineering Dominates**: Livingston is strategically placed between Glasgow and Edinburgh, and – Pye's fate apart – the New Town began to attract a growing number of new industries. Many chose sites in Deans *(q.v.)* after the opening of the M8 motorway between Newbridge and Newhouse about 1970. Also taking advantage of and adjoining the M8 was Dundee grocer William Low's main distribution depot (taken over by Tesco in 1994). US-owned industries open by 1977 included Crown Cork, Scotland's largest manufacturer of drink cans. By 1978 a branch of Ferranti was open and soon Sonicaid of Sussex, makers of ultrasonic medical equipment, had a small plant in Livingston. By 1980 the firms in production included Abbey Chemicals, the protective clothing makers Hy-Co, and Lothian Electric Machines. The many precision engineers numbered such firms as Adroit Tools, Bowman, Deans, Glenesk, Haggart and Tulloch.

**The Almondvale Centre**: The bland new enclosed Almondvale Centre which opened between near-complete Dedridge and the river about 1979 was only moderately successful by contrast with industry. Just as in Cumbernauld, the major chain stores decided to *'wait and see'*. The Almondvale entertainment complex and the Deer Park country club and 18-hole golf course founded in 1978 were soon open. By 1981 Livingston's population had grown rapidly to reach 38,600. By then the *Livingston Courier* had been established as a localised edition of the *Lothian Courier* of Bathgate.

**Local Facilities Expand**: Eventually the need for railway passenger services was grudgingly accepted; Livingston South station on the Shotts line was opened in 1984 and the Livingston North station on the Bathgate line in 1986, serving the large Nether Dechmont housing area which had infilled the 2 km between Deans and Knightsridge. But it was far too late for either station to be related to the town centre. By 1988 housing had already spilled across the A71 to and beyond Murieston. The Scottish Office Computer Centre, the *Hilton National Hotel* at Almondvale and an ice rink were open. By 1989 Littlewoods had opened a huge mail-order centre near the M8 and Uphall Station, and an satellite of West Lothian College from Bathgate was in action; a new campus for the college was planned in 1994. The youthful population of the New Town (including Deans) had been edging steadily upwards, reaching 41,647 in 1991.

**Lockers, Textiles – and Burnt Bread**: In the 1980s Laidlaw Drew, combustion engineers, moved out from Sighthill (Edinburgh), and in 1990 gained a Queen's Award for the export of their burners. In 1991 Livingston Precision Engineering (from Larbert) manufactured electronic business machines. By then Raand Systems of Livingston made an innovative product – *'Loksafe'* electronically operated keyless luggage lockers – for British Rail and other customers, some overseas, and in 1992 obtained a large order for Netherlands Railways, securing or creating a hundred jobs. In 1993 Raand also gained a similar contract from Danish Railways but was facing stiff and allegedly unfair competition from Mors of France. The US-owned textile works of W L Gore & Associates (UK) was in operation by 1989 and the Russell Corporation UK, a branch of the US leisurewear manufacturer Russell, opened a textile factory at the Houston industrial estate in 1989–92. But the Houston land was sold off in 1994 at government diktat, being acquired by Highcross Properties. When the factory of Abel Eastern Foods at Houston which employed 280 people baking speciality breads – including Nan bread for Marks & Spencer – was burned down in mid 1995, the firm was put into liquidation.

**Sunrises and Sunsets in Silicon Glen II**: In 1980 Unisys of the USA opened a production facility, which had built up to 686 jobs by 1991 when its intended closure was announced. This gives a new meaning to industrial *'sunrise'* – remember that the winter's day in Scotland is short, and sunset can follow all too soon! Mitsubishi of Japan *(see also Haddington)* began to manufacture video cassette recorders at the Houston Industrial Estate in 1983 and employed 500 in two factories by 1989, aiming to rise to 700. Apollo Computer, founded in Massachusetts as recently as 1980 but which entered Livingston in 1984, began to make workstations in the town in 1988. The firm opened its European research and development centre in 1989 as the third stage of expansion in Livingston, but it was then taken over by Hewlett-Packard whose Scottish base was at Dalmeny.

**Software, still more Silicon and Cellphones**: In 1985 Shinetsu of Japan opened a silicon wafer factory, planned another 100 jobs in a 1989 expansion and yet another 100 in 1994; in 1996 they were again extending their factory at Eliburn. By 1989 Ian Bilsland's Graphic Information Systems of Blairgowrie had opened a development centre at Livingston, employing about 20 people in producing sophisticated software to control entire electricity networks, including that of London. Hardware industries included Seagate, making semiconductors by 1989, when Seiko Instruments of Japan also proposed a new plant (now with 110 jobs). In 1990–91 Motorola opened a start-up cellphone manufacturing facility at Livingston's Brucefield industrial park, preparatory to moving to Easter Inch beside Bathgate. In 1994 Eraba Ltd made sheet metal and other products for the electronics industry (today employing 150). *(For Silicon Glen attributes compare Livingston with Glenrothes; see also Deans).*

**Smart Kirkton Campus**: *'Smart Card'* manufacture began late in 1989 on the Kirkton Campus, laid out in the 1980s south of Livingston Village. By 1990 Surgikos, a subsidiary of Johnson & Johnson, was making infection control products at KC. Another such firm by 1991 was the pharmaceuticals manufacturer Bochringer Mannheim UK. Early in 1992 another newcomer to Kirkton, Bull HN Information Systems, was set up (now 500 jobs); while in the depths of the recession in 1992 the Cubix Corporation decided to bring 100 jobs in computer networking. The American electronics firm Jabil Circuits decided late in 1992 to establish a 400-job factory for PCB assemblies; by 1997 the firm had two plants in the town (and now has over 500 employees). Advanced Automation Systems of Korea – which took over Ferranti Metrology of Dalkeith in 1992 – were to move the operation to Livingston in 1993 and add 45 more skilled jobs.

**Medical Services**: Meantime the large new St Johns Hospital had opened at Howden in 1989, its name reflecting the old role of Torphichen *(q.v.)*; in 1992 it was planned to make it one of the three main hospitals for acute care in the Lothian Region. And the medical firm Ethicon were established in town, with over 400 jobs.

***'Town without a Heart'***: Livingston's exhibit at the Glasgow Garden Festival of 1988 was pathetically thin, and in 1989 it was described in *The Guardian* as *"the town with no heart"*: it had little locational rationale, no natural centre, no mellowness and almost everything in it except for a growing number of private houses was owned by outside interests. It also had little history of its own, though in 1990 the Scottish Shale Oil Museum was established at the Almond Valley Heritage Centre, which also gained a 500m miniature railway, and by 1995 had restored the 18th century watermill to working order. The *Livingston Post* seems to have ceased publication by 1991, but by 1994 the *West Lothian Evening News* had a local office.

***'Shoebox Town'* brings Jobs as Kirkton reaches for Sky**: In 1990 BSkyB Television established its subscriber management centre at Kirkton, dealing with customer enquiries and subscriptions throughout Britain; it rapidly expanded with the

*The Alba Centre, Livingston – a development location for cutting-edge software.* *(Alba Centre)*

growth of Pay-TV by satellite, becoming by mid 1994 the town's largest employer, with over 1500 people on three sites. In 1994 *Scotland on Sunday* described Livingston as a town of *"shoebox developments; its major auditorium is a converted stable. What passes for the town centre, its shopping mall, is a depressing place"* whose supermarket had become a Shoprite discount food store. But unlike the equally heartless Tin Man in *The Wizard of Oz*, Livingston was an evident technological success, with 24,500 jobs for 44,000 people. During the New Town's lifetime the West Lothian unemployment rate had been cut from some 25% to around 10%. In 1995 the *"prestigious"* Kirkton Campus had among its hi-tech firms Award plc, with 1200 making disposable contact lenses – a Scottish invention. By 1993 the Scottish branch of the government's Transport Research Laboratory of Crowthorne was based in Livingston.

**Football and Education**: In 1995 lowly Meadowbank Thistle FC moved for the second time, from Meadowbank *(see Restalrig)* to a new stadium built for them at Almondvale, becoming Livingston FC. They soon drew good crowds, prospered on the field, by early 1997 headed the Second Division and in 2000 were firmly in the First. In 1997 Inveralmond High School had 1010 pupils, the James Young High School 774, and St Margaret's Academy 906.

**Expanding – Away from Livingston**: In 1993 Mitsubishi announced their intention to open a further new factory to employ 200 people in Livingston, and in 1994 the computer supplies company Shin-Etsu Handotai decided to invest in a new 100-job plant. Canon Manufacturing (UK) of Livingston was expanding in Glenrothes in 1992, while in 1993 Mimtech of Livingston opened a new electronics plant at Greenock; but soon both sites were to share a jobs cut of 200. Meantime in 1993 due to falling demand the US-owned Cooper Oil Tool Company closed its Livingston factory, with the loss of 300 jobs; the work was moved to France. Mimtech was owned in 1994 by Murray International Metals and was involved in press metal fabrication; in 1997 the firm assembled computers for both IBM and Hewlett Packard, and had a sheet metal branch at Dundee; in all about 2000 people were employed. Then in 1994 BSkyB announced that due to lack of space in their three large factory-like office sheds (where 75% of the workforce was female), they were to develop a large subscriber management centre at Dunfermline; by then Gore's also had a Dunfermline offshoot. Prominent among 1996 developments was a vast 28,000m$^2$ distribution warehouse for Booker.

**After the New Town: Clocks and Big Shopping**: The Development Corporation was wound down in 1995–98, leaving the new town to dominate West Lothian – based in Linlithgow and Bathgate until the new West Lothian House was opened by the new unitary council at Almondvale Boulevard. On the withdrawal of the artificial stimuli to growth, what many saw as an ugly sprawling town would have to find its heart in new facilities, or be doomed to remain a boring collection of branch plants in a desert of motorways and cheap housing. Yet a remarkable and overtly independent study in 1996–97 claimed that Livingston's quality of life was among the highest in Britain: evidently it all depends on one's point of view. And job potential seems good: in addition to all the major companies mentioned, there are dozens of modern firms in the 50–200 jobs range. In the late 1990s Oakbank Business Park was developed to the south and J Ritchie & Son, clock manufacturers, moved to Livingston after 190 years in Edinburgh. A larger and important company is Kymata, employing

350 in optoelectronics. In 2000 the USA retail giant McArthur Glen opened their 28,000m² domed complex – their first in Scotland – in the centre of the town, including a multiplex cinema, food courts, and swimming pool; 1000 jobs would hopefully result. ASDA-Wal-Mart plan to build Scotland's biggest shop in Livingston. Hotels include the 120-room *Jarvis International* at Almondvale and the 52-room *Travel Inn* at Knightsridge.

## LOANHEAD

**Map 15, C3**

***Midlothian large village**, pop. 8000* OS 66: NT 2865

A first century Roman road connected the upper Clyde Valley with Inveresk; it paralleled the Pentland Hills, and its lost eastern section may well have passed by way of Straiton, between Loanhead and Edinburgh. When Pont mapped the Lothians about 1600, Loanhead – which stands above the North Esk valley – was a tiny place west of the Lasswade road. Coal was mined in the vicinity from 1685 for Sir John Clerk of Penicuik; his mine was soon making good profits, and in 1723–27 William Adam designed and built for him the elegant mansion of Mavisbank, in its 30ha policies between the village and the River North Esk. Loanhead's Springfield paper mill, located in the valley south of the village, started work in 1742, and a second paper mill (Polton) was opened in 1750; this had the then large total of five vats by 1767. Meantime, Roy's survey of about 1754 showed Loanhead as a medium-sized linear settlement, with three radial roads connecting to the already established main road system.

**The Limestone Industry**: From about 1760 limestone was quarried around Burdiehouse some 1.5km to the north-west, where lime-burning was established on a substantial scale; from about 1790 the stone was mined underground by *'stoop and room'* working, and by the late 1790s there was a steam pumping engine at work. About 1825 there were fifty limestone miners, but only 30 in 1845. Loanhead's first post office was opened and a gasworks were established, and Polton paper mill had become a large concern by 1851; eventually Loanhead became a police burgh.

**Railways, Coal and Oil Shale**: From 1874 the new but roundabout Edinburgh, Loanhead & Roslin Railway (EL&R) branching from Millerhill provided a station in the centre of Loanhead. The line, later part of the North British Railway (NBR), was extended in 1877 through a tunnel under the town to serve Glencorse Barracks, and a siding was laid to the new Burghlee Colliery, 1km south-west of Loanhead. By then the Straiton Oil Company mined oil shale in the area between the village and Burdiehouse. In 1880 the Clippens Oil Company of Paisley took over and built large new rail-connected oil extraction works, and 2-storey rows for their workers. By 1895 the oil works extended on both sides of the main road south of Straiton, and the population was 3250. In 1892 the NBR built a daring structure, a 192m span steel lattice-girder box viaduct across Bilston Glen 500m south of the village, as a replacement for the original EL&R viaduct designed by Thomas Bouch – either because his designs were now rightly mistrusted, or due to mining subsidence. The mining of oil shale was continued from a pit east of Burdiehouse Mains down to a depth exceeding 350m. Murray in 1894 described Loanhead as *"a large mining village"* which had four horse-drawn coaches daily to Edinburgh – much more direct than the railway. By then a roadside inn was open at Bilston, 2 km to the west.

**Developments in Lime and Transport**: Eventually incoming water from the Edinburgh waterworks aqueducts forced the shale workings and oilworks to close in 1909, but the colliery stayed open. The Burdiehouse limeworks were also abandoned in 1912, but by then the Clippens Lime Works were mining the limestone around Straiton; in 1930 the workings were acquired by the Shotts Iron Company. The horse-drawn coaches were replaced by buses, to which the passenger trains in turn succumbed in 1933, though coal traffic continued on the railway; at nationalisation in 1947 Burghlee pit was working the Limestone Coal Group. For a time limestone continued to be carried by rail to the Gartsherrie Ironworks, but limestone mining ended in 1960. Loanhead was already a large village in terms of facilities in the 1950s, with some 5350 people, a small early 20th century hospital, and the Polton paper mill, which continued in production until about 1955.

**Bilston Glen Colliery and Bilston Village**: The large Bilston Glen colliery was sunk only 1km west of the village centre between 1952 and 1961, with shafts 775m deep to work the Limestone Coal Group: it was in full production by 1964. About the same time a housing estate or village known as Bilston, complete with primary school and post office, was built beside the Bilston Inn. In 1971 a large static caravan site at Nivensknowe by Bilston had 400 residents. Although an underground connection was established between Bilston Glen and Monktonhall collieries, the former's scale of operation was much reduced in 1988 and it was closed, ending deep mining in the Lothians for a time *(see Millerhill)*. By 1996 its site had been cleared.

**Losing Mavisbank but finding Light Industries and Shops**: Meantime Mavisbank was regrettably bought in the 1950s by the oddball Archie Stevenson; sadly neglected and affected by subsidence, the once fine mansion was shamefully burnt out in 1973. In 1992 Historic Scotland proposed to acquire the ruined shell and gradually reconstruct the mansion to its former glory; but Stevenson had perversely dispersed ownership to four Americans so that after his death in 1993 even the Scottish Office has found itself unable to acquire it by compulsion. The Pentlands industrial estate had been established in the 1970s; by 1977 Liquid Gas Equipment Ltd was in operation, and by 1990 was part of the Weir Group of Cathcart, building gas process plants and terminals worldwide. Among other lighter

*Polton paper mill, which opened in 1750 and continued in production until the mid 20th century. It began making paper by hand, but was mechanised in the mid 19th century.* (JRH)

industries in the 1980s was printing, while by 1990 Dansco Dairy Products made Mozzarella cheese at their New Pentland Creamery. Carmichael Design & Engineering were developing a new range of packaging and labelling machinery in 1991. By then Loanhead's population was about 5650, while Bilston held some 1650 people, with high male unemployment at 17.5%.

**No Trains but Plenty Haggis**: In 1991 Scottish Power opened one of their first two superstores on the Pentland Retail Park at Straiton; in 1999 this was renamed the Straiton Retail Park, and by 2000 was home to IKEA's sole Scottish store. The Moredun Foundation for livestock research *(see Gilmerton)* was the basis for the Pentlands Science Park, whose final phase was planned in 1995 jointly with Lothian & Edinburgh Enterprise. In the mid 1990s MacSween of Bruntsfield (Edinburgh) moved out to larger premises at Loanhead in an attempt to meet rising demand for haggis. The small 42-bed Loanhead Hospital for geriatrics was to close by the end of the century.The magnificent Bilston Glen Viaduct was fully restored in 1998–99; all it needed then was track and trains.

## LOCHAILORT — Map 8, B5

***Small Lochaber village,** pop. c. 100* — OS 40: NM 7682

It is known that by 1650 an inn was open where the short River Ailort, flowing from the tumbled rocky hills 35 km west of Fort William, enters the sea in the winding Loch Ailort, and that there was an early school. Roy's map made about 1750 – probably the first survey of this area – identified it as *'Kinloch Holyort'*. The inn became a staging point on Telford's *'Road to the Isles'*, built from Fort William to Arisaig early in the 19th century, a school was opened nearby, and a jetty was built. Murray in 1894 noted the *"plain, comfortable Kinlochailort Hotel"*, which was not connected to mains electricity for another half century.

**Concrete Bob's Railway and Salmon Farming**: The old schoolhouse was used as an 8-bed hospital – the first on a British construction site – by the West Highland Extension Railway's contractor *'Concrete Bob'* McAlpine, whose son Malcolm was among its few serious patients *(see Thomas, 1965)*. The line was opened to Arisaig and Mallaig in 1901, with an adjacent station named Lochailort. An entirely new coastal road leading to Glenuig with its inn and lobster fishing, and continuing to quiet Kinlochmoidart, was opened about 1966, increasing the nodality of Lochailort. By 1973 Marine Harvest, a Unilever subsidiary, had established a salmon farm, then producing over 50 tonnes a year; by 1984 it included a sizeable processing plant. The population had long been in decline and by 1981 was as low as 75, the primary school having been closed; but by 1984 most of the fifteen or so houses near the cosy inn were under twenty years old. In 1984 the local children were still divided for primary schooling, going to either Arisaig or Acharacle, depending on religion! The station remains open as a request stop, while McDonald's Smoked Produce do rattlesnake as well as fish and meat!

## LOCHALINE (or Morvern) — Map 4, C1

***Ardnamurchan village,** pop. 350* — OS 49: NM 6744

It is said that in the sixth century two saints – Columba and Moluag – founded the church of Choluimchille at Lochaline (pronounced *Lochallen*), a sheltered sea loch on the south coast of Morvern. This district forms a lobe of Britain's most westerly mainland peninsula, Ardnamurchan, a name traditionally pronounced with rolled r's as *Arrudnamurrachan*. To the south are the grim ruins of the 14th century Ardtornish Castle, prominent on its point which projects into the Sound of Mull; modern Ardtornish is a mansion at the head of the loch. The sheltered Kinlochaline Castle is a 15th century keep, shown on Pont's late 16th century map of Mull as *'Castel Loch Alyn'*, while Huddart's chart of 1791 named the *'Kirkton of Kinlochalin'*. The manse of Fiunary, 6 km west, was built in 1779 and rebuilt about 1860; it became noted for producing six McLeods who became Moderators of the Church of Scotland, and inspiring the Victorian classic *Reminiscences of a Highland Parish*. A post office named Morvern opened in 1805, but because there was no road in 1838, Lochaline was still served with post by ferry boat from Salen or Fishnish in Mull. At one time lead was mined in Glen Dubh, well inland to the north. By 1894 Lochaline was connected by through roads; it was called a *"village"* by Murray at that time.

**Fine Sand from Underground**: Deposits of silica sand very suitable for the glass industry were discovered close by in 1940, and a deep mine was developed by 1953, with a light railway to the pier which was also served by a MacBrayne steamer from Oban to Tobermory. The pier was extended in 1963, so that when the steamer service ended in 1964 a new car ferry could be provided from Oban, also calling at Craignure. In 1973 a smaller vessel was provided instead, to operate a shuttle ferry to Fishnish; the terrible road to Strontian was being radically rebuilt around that time. A hotel was open by 1977, and by 1985 Lochaline also had a club and craft shops. The population in 1991 was 340. Lochaline still had its inn and post office in 1996, and the Ardtornish Garden was a tourist attraction; Fiunary had a caravan site, but the manse stood vacant and deteriorating in 1997. Sand is still mined deep underground; other accessible work includes fish farming and the Glensanda Superquarry *(see Kingairloch)*. Timber from maturing Forestry Commission plantations is soon to be despatched by sea through a refurbished pier at Lochaline.

## LOCHARBRIGGS — Map 2, B4

***Small town by Dumfries,** pop. 5350* — OS 78/84: NX 9980

A Roman fort lies between the River Nith and the Kirkton of Kirkmahoe, 6 km north of Dumfries, and on a hilltop 5 km to the north-east is an ancient fort. The Norse name of Tinwald – a location in the shallow valley of the Amisfield Burn between the fort and the Kirkton – shows that it began as a meeting-place. Nearby is an ancient motte, and 2 km to the north is the tall Amisfield Tower, built in the 16th century on lands already owned by the Charteris family for 400 years. A small place styled *'Amisfield Town'* grew in a wooded area between the tower and Tinwald. Nearer to Dumfries, where the Amisfield and Park Burns join to form the Lochar Water, was a mill, clearly shown on Pont's map of Annandale made about 1610. By then the Lochar Water had been bridged at or near its modern position, not far from the emparked *'Tyndell'*. A parish school was founded at Tinwald in 1627.

**Bank of England, Quarrying, Mansion and Railway**: William Paterson, born at Skipmyre near Tinwald in 1658, became a merchant in the West Indies, co-founded the Bank of England in 1694, and actively promoted the Union of the Parliaments. Locharbriggs' first sandstone quarry was opened around 1700. Tinwald House was designed by William Adam for Charles Erskine and built in 1738–40. The Roy map made about 1754 showed the name *'Locherbriggs'* on the Moffat road where it was crossed by a track from Kirkmahoe to *The Rosken* (Roucan) near Torthorwald. Carnsalloch House, 2 km west, was built in 1759. In 1799 Heron described Amisfield as a *"village"*. But as late as 1838 there was not even a post office at Locharbriggs – the site of a new quarry of Permian pink sandstone, opened in mid-century. A station on the new Lockerbie to Dumfries branch of the Caledonian Railway opened in 1863 beside the rail-linked quarry, which grew large, opened several pits, and also had a brickmaking plant. By 1899 there was a post office, a school and a tiny village; 267 quarrymen were employed. Opposite Heath Hall, 1 km south of Locharbriggs, was a wood called The Grove.

**Country Cars Fail but Locharbriggs Bounces Back**: In 1912–13 Arroll-Johnston Cars of Paisley moved their assembly plant to large new premises at Heathhall, giving space for expansion in a low-wage area. But the firm collapsed in the great depression after the Wall Street crash of 1929. In 1936 the defunct car works were adapted as a large rubber factory, apparently making motor tyres as part of North British Rubber of Edinburgh (NB). An airfield was built east of Heathhall in the 1939–45 war, used to receive and check aircraft from manufacturers, before their dispersal to squadrons.

**Golf Balls and Rubber Flooring**: Tinwald House, gutted by fire in 1946, was reconstructed in 1948. By 1951 some 3000 people lived locally, though the facilities remained minimal. Golf balls – another rubber product – were made from the 1940s, and by 1955 the NB rubber works was also making gym shoes and rubber flooring. The station was closed to passengers by 1953, and to freight in 1966. One of the various quarries was reopened in 1968 to supply stone for rebuilding Maxwelton House near Moniaive *(q.v.)*. By 1971 The Grove, no longer a wood but a housing estate, held 260 residents. A new community centre was built in 1970; a small trading estate and a garden centre were open by 1977. By 1979 the tyre factory was US-owned by Uniroyal, and employed about 1300 people. By 1981 the population was that of a small town at some 4750, but with fewer facilities than a typical village. Abernethy's still made golf balls, and by 1986 a College of Technology had been built on the former airfield.

*A Locharbriggs quarry. Sandstone has been worked in the vicinity since around 1700 – and still continues.* (British Geological Survey)

*The Arrol–Johnston car works at Heathhall, which started in 1913, but which changed to a rubber works in the mid 1930s, and is still making advanced rubber products today. This was a very advanced factory building of its kind, with a reinforced-concrete frame of American design.* (JRH)

**Flooring the Underground – and part of Dumfries?**: In 1991 a population of about 5350 lived in the sprawling settlement; Baird & Stevenson still quarried building stone, Penman Engineering was quite large, there was a British Telecom depot, and the considerable local motor trade included the vast yard of Curries Transport *'of Dumfries'*, who by 1997 had European depots at Paris, Frankfurt and Nijmegen. Meantime in 1990 the Gates Rubber Company of Denver, who then owned the Uniroyal works, opened a large new factory; in 1993 their 900 employees used Dupont ethylene/acrylic elastomers to make *'Floormaster Plus'* fire-safe industrial carpeting, fitted at Rosyth to refurbished London Underground vehicles, as well as for British Rail and the Glasgow Underground; other products were *'Tredaire'* and *'Grenadier'* carpet underlay, Hunter gumboots, and transmission and conveyor belts. Not surprisingly, by 1996 more new housing estates had been built, largely around the new college but also west of the quarry, which was still producing pink sandstone for building under Baird & Stevenson *(see also Newcastleton)*. By 1997 Carnsalloch House has become a Cheshire Home.

## LOCHBOISDALE & Daliburgh

**Map 7, A4**

***South Uist villages,*** *pop. 750 (area)* — OS 31: NF 7919

Some prehistoric cairns and wheel-houses survive near the south end of South Uist, but the isle's most ancient medieval church, perhaps of seventh century origin, was at more central Howmore. Monro reported in 1549 that the south end of South Uist belonged to McNeill of Barra and the north end to Clanranald of Clandonald; each part had a parish church. However he did not mention Loch Boisdale. The Reformation had passed the island by, when Pont's map of about 1600 showed *'Byisdaill'*, modern South Boisdale, near the west coast of South Uist; but no settlement on *'Loch Byisdal'* on the east coast. Martin, writing in 1703, did not mention these places. Near the west coast some 12 km north of Daliburgh is the ruined Ormiclate Castle, home of Ranald Macdonald, burnt down when almost new in 1715 *(see Balivanish)*. Flora Macdonald who took pity on the luckless Prince Charles Edward was born about 1720 at nearby Milton *(see Staffin (Skye))*.

**Cluny's Cruel Clearances – and Brainwashing**: Eventually townships grew at Lochboisdale and inland at Daliburgh, 4 km to the west, which acquired their first post office in 1834 under the laird, by then Clanranald. Postal deliveries were by runner from Lochmaddy, the hardy postie wading the fords both north and south of Benbecula. In 1838 the people of South Uist, Benbecula and Barra found themselves under the heel of a new proprietor, Colonel John Gordon of Cluny, one of the most notorious of absentee landlords, intent on profiting from sheep farming and oblivious to the well-being of inherited tenants. His brutal agent Fleming proceeded at once to clear them from the islands, and shipped them to Canada; this process took 13 years to complete, to 1851. Progress was impossible under the conditions of abasement that it created, and relief from feudal oppression for the tenants who remained had to await the Crofters Acts. Although the children got some education, until 1889 all teachers in Gaelic-speaking Catholic South Uist were required to be Protestant! Only English might be spoken in the schools, a brainwashing process which continued well into the 20th century when a new school was built at Lochboisdale in 1909.

**Tourists and Golfers Replace the Islanders**: The remote lighthouse of Ushenish, on the east coast of South Uist some 20 km north of Lochboisdale, was lighted in 1857, warning mariners to keep off. South Uist, by then dominated by sheep, was not opened up to the outside world until a steamer pier was constructed about 1880, followed by the *Lochboisdale Hotel* in 1882. The Askernish *(G. Aisgernis)* golf club was founded in 1891, 8 km north-west of Lochboisdale, where Tom Morris laid out a 9-hole course on the windy Machair. The hotel was *"good"* to Murray in 1894, when its *"excellent fishing"* was commended; there were already three steamers a week from Oban and two from Glasgow; but the latter service did not outlast two world wars.

**Cluny clears off**: The Cluny family had lived down the reputation of their repressive ancestor, but sold the island in 1942, no doubt to universal relief. During the 1939–45 war South Uist was linked with Benbecula by a new causeway. By 1951 Lochboisdale had grown to a small village with a population of about 425, its facilities including an ambulance station and veterinary surgeon. In 1953 MacBrayne's mailboats connected with Castlebay, Tobermory and Oban; with Mallaig; and with Lochmaddy, Tarbert and Kyle. The inland township of Daliburgh, which is more nodal for the island's road system, had about 305 people, a small secondary school and a hospital. It was also the site of the Isle's new diesel-powered electricity generating station.

**The Era of Car Ferries**: The pier was rebuilt in 1965–66, enabling the operation of a car ferry from Lochboisdale to Oban and Castlebay; in 1970 Ushenish light was converted to automatic operation. Despite a static population in both townships, both slightly improved their facilities, sharing the role of South Uist's main settlement, and providing by 1981 a small yachting, fishing, shooting and now 18-hole golfing resort with two hotels. Secondary pupils attended Lionaclett from 1988, and by 1999 the former school building at Lochboisdale had been vacant for some years. By 1996 a museum had been opened near Flora Macdonald's birthplace. The *Borrodale Hotel* at Daliburgh has 14 rooms, and the old *Lochboisdale Hotel* and a large guest house stand at Lochboisdale.

## LOCHBUIE

**Map 4, C2**

***Community, Isle of Mull,** pop. 68* — OS 49: NM 6125

A stone circle, standing stone and ruined chapel at the head of this broad sea loch on the south coast of Mull attest to ancient settlement. The 14th century Lochbuie Castle, at that time one of only three on Mull, belonged to Clan M'Gillayne *(MacLean)*; it is nowadays a ruin, called Moy. Monro noted in 1549 a *"great take of herring and other fishings"*. There were no roads at all on Mull as late as 1773, when the regular Mull ferry plied between Oban and the boulder-strewn beach at Lochbuie, which is open to south-westerly gales. Although a mansionhouse and a tiny village were developed, the ferry terminal moved to Auchnacraig around 1790. Lochbuie depends on farming and stands at the remote end of a minor road following the winding shores of two lochs, but with only 68 people in 1991 it still held post town status, and had its own postcode sector!

## LOCHCARRON, Dalchuirn & Slumbay

**Map 8, C3**

***Wester Ross village,** pop. 660* — OS 24/25: NG 9040

Hut circles on the hillsides above Loch Carron in Wester Ross tell of life long before the nearby coastal crofting and inshore fishing communities grew around the sheltered natural harbour of Slumbay. This had a kirk when noted by Pont in the late 16th century as *'Slumpa'*, perhaps derived from Gaelic *Slugag*, a small pool. Although a post office was open from at least 1750, Roy's map made at that time showed an entirely trackless area. Two townships occupied the area of Dalchuirn, later called Jeantown or Janetown, but always known to the Royal Mail as Lochcarron. In 1755 the Board of Trustees for Manufactures brought in an instructor to promote a linen industry – with only limited success, because of the area's extreme isolation; the first post office opened in 1756. There was still only a weekly postal service in 1797, when roadless Lochcarron was a post town; the letter-carrier was probably a runner, possibly a horseman. Despite its own tenuous service it provided the sole mail connection for Skye in 1797 – a weekly sailing packet (a mail and passenger vessel) to Sconser.

**Road and Rail Connections**: A road from Dingwall was built for the Commissioners in 1813–19, and a large inn was open by 1847. But the clearances had caused grave social problems, a pier had been only part built, and the socially concerned observer Robert Somers then wrote *"Janetown consists of a single row, fully a mile long, of mean-looking cottages"*. The fishing boats were tiny, the people poor and untutored. There were one or two shops but the recent potato famine and failure of the herring fishing had been disastrous, as elsewhere in the Highlands; it took decades to bring about a fragile equilibrium.

Strathcarron station was opened 5km to the east in 1870, with another station 10km up the narrow glen at Achnashellach. The inn – by that time called a hotel – was only *"fair"* in 1894, when Lochcarron's horse-drawn postal and public transport service operated from the station on alternate days. A new road bridge was built at Strathcarron in 1934; its station, post office and hotel saw out the century.

**Lochside Resort**: By the 1950s Lochcarron was still a small village of under 500 people, with two little hotels. A 9-hole golf course was laid out about 1960, but Achnashellach lost its crossing loop and signalmens' jobs in 1966. Lochcarron was soon stimulated by the oil-rig yard at Kishorn *(q.v.)*, leading to a new housing estate near the school, and a typical village level of facilities in 1981. But the prosperity was short-lived, for the Kishorn yard was closed in 1987. Lochcarron village, with 660 people in 1991, has shops, post office, primary school and golf course; a museum is open, and weavers provide a tourist attraction beside the road to Strome castle. The *Rockvilla* and the *Lochcarron Hotel* are open, and there is a caravan and camping site, plus a hostel for backpackers is open all year at Craig, 4km east of Achnashellach.

## LOCHDON & Auchnacraig — Map 4, C2

***Island community, E. Mull,*** *pop. under 100* — OS 49: NM 7333

A standing stone shows ancient occupation near the shallow Loch Don, an inlet on the east coast of Mull, 4km south of Craignure. The nearby farm of *'Achanacarig'* appeared on Blaeu's map, attributed to Pont who worked around 1600. In 1790 a road was built linking Salen with Grass Point near *'Achnacraggy'* (which was shown on Huddart's chart of 1791) enabling the Mull post – formerly carried via Lochbuie – to be ferried between Oban and Auchnacraig, which was already a designated post town by 1797. The ferry service had again been transferred by 1953, to Craignure, but a pier remained, which was the terminus of motor-boat excursions from Oban. The small settlement of Lochdon at the head of the loch was then the post town and, despite a mere 50 or so people, had a primary school and a garage, since closed. In 1981 it mainly comprised unimproved houses and elderly people, but by 1985 half a dozen new bungalows had been built and the primary school had been extended to serve other places in east Mull. In 1991 its tiny postcode sector held 83 residents; the post office is still open.

## LOCHEARNHEAD & Edinample — Map 5, C3

***Central highlands village,*** *pop. 500 (area)* — OS 51: NN 5823

The remains of an ancient crannog lie in the head of Loch Earn, near waterfalls where the Burn of Ample enters the loch. Nearby was built the 16$^{th}$ century castle of Edinample, which appeared on Pont's map of Strathearn made about 1600, as did the name Edinchip – the seat of The MacGregor. The modern village developed around *'Wester Achra'*, which the Roy map of around 1750 marked as the meeting point of a track along the north shore of the loch with a north–south track through Glen Ogle. This line was to be taken up by Caulfeild's military road from Stirling to Tyndrum and Fort William, already partly built, and completed by 1761. The road allowed a post office to open in 1800 and evidently encouraged early tourism in this beautiful area, for in 1803 Dorothy Wordsworth walked up it after dining *"at the head of the lake; the inn is in a small village – a decent house"*. Chambers concurred in 1826: *"a little village with a good inn"*.

**The Railway Epoch**: The Callander & Oban Railway followed the same general route; its first section opened in 1870 through Lochearnhead station, which stood high above the village – near Edinchip and the viaduct across the Kendrum Burn. Murray found the *Lochearnhead Hotel "good"* in 1894. In 1904 a station was provided nearer to the village, on a new lochside railway from St Fillans to Balquhidder. The *Mary Stuart Hotel*, built in the 1920s, was like its namesake ill-fated. By 1951 the local population of some 300 enjoyed the facilities of a small village and there were four hotels, with a hundred beds in all. The closure of the St Fillans railway in 1951 preceded the closure of the original line under the Beeching plan; a landslide accelerated its demise in 1965, and it was soon lifted.

**Scouting and Sailing**: In 1962 the Hertfordshire Scouts took over the former village station building as their Highland adventure base. Roadborne tourism prospered; a slipway for water-skiing and a sailing school was open by the 1970s, a short-lived caravan site was open in 1977, and by 1981 there was a population of 350, and five hotels, including the *Lochearnhead* and the *Clachan Cottage*. A new village hall was built in 1989. The *Mary Stuart Hotel*, closed in the late 1980s, was derelict by 1995, suffered a fire, and had been largely demolished by 1997. In 2000 the abandoned Kendrum railway viaduct gained a new role in a footpath and cycleway, with a new 30m steel span. The school and post office are both still open, the *Mansewood* has added to the hotels, and there are also B&Bs for the tourists.

## LOCHEE & Camperdown — Map 6, B3

***N-W. parts of Dundee,*** *pop. 33,000* — OS 54: NO 3731

The map of Angus made by Timothy Pont about 1600 showed a tiny unnamed loch on the headwaters of a burn flowing westwards past the Denmill to join the Gowrie Burn, which enters the Tay at Invergowrie. Warden noted that this *"small brook furnished the necessary supply of water for boiling and bleaching yarn and cloth"*. Dundee's market supplied yarn and distributed the finished products. The first member of the Cox family began in the linen trade in the area around 1707, and before his death in 1741 had established a bleachfield called *Lochee-field*. The feuing of small plots in Lochee began around 1735–40. An emparked house named *'Liogy'* was shown on Roy's map made about 1750, when the road from Dundee to Newtyle and Coupar Angus (later the A923) passed through an area west of Dundee Law and 3km from the town centre.

**The Cox Dynasty and Coarse Linens**: By 1791 Lochee was a village, with some 276 handloom weavers making coarse linens; some of their output was taken to Inchture for stamping. Of the five *'merchant manufacturers'* in Lochee, the largest was the Cox family, which by 1793 also owned a nearby bleachworks, which they gradually extended, first weaving broad hessian in 1815. In 1816 their weaving works and 10ha bleachfield passed to the fourth generation Cox, who after a major warehouse fire in 1819, moved the business about 1820 to *"the most populous part of Lochee"*, where he established a weaving factory. In 1822 two small steam flax spinning mills were at work at Lochee: Watt & Brown owned the East Mill and William Anderson the West. In 1831 some 700 people were employed locally in the linen industry.

*A view, from Balgay Hill, of Lochee and Cox's Camperdown textile works (with Cox's stack) in the late 19th century. At that time Lochee was entirely separate from Dundee. The works became the largest jute works in the world and burned 15,000 tonnes of coal a year. At one time Cox's employed 14,000 at their various factories.* (GWW collection)

**Horse-drawn Trains and Big Railroad Deals**: The primitive Dundee & Newtyle Railway which opened in 1831 served the area: Lochee High Street station became the largest on the line; there was also a station named Camperdown, 1 km to the west on South Road. Robert Fleming, born in Lochee in 1845, became a bookkeeper for Baxter of Dundee, founded the Scottish American Investment Trust and many others, invested in USA railroads, reorganised them and finally established Fleming's merchant bank in London.

**Camperdown Works and its Merchant Princes**: Cox Brothers, as the firm was known from 1841, built the steam-powered vertically integrated 5.5 ha Camperdown flax spinning and weaving works on level ground north of the village in 1845–50. In 1861 they enlarged it for jute processing and – because the works burned so much coal – laid in a railway connection. In 1862 the firm installed an electric telegraph, early precursor of the telephone. By 1864 the Coxes were *"merchant princes"* with 3200 employees who were spinning, bleaching and dyeing linen and jute yarns, weaving jute carpets, and calendering linen. By then the firm was also in the jute shipping business and was the mainstay of Lochee. By 1864 James Donald had erected the Pitalpine Works, employing 300 spinners and power loom weavers, and Edward Parker's West Mills had 170 workers; Lochee grew so fast that the population more than quadrupled in the decade, greatly aided by the water supplied to Lochee and other suburbs from Dundee's Crombie Reservoir, completed in 1866.

**World's Largest Jute Works Dwarfed by Cox's Lum**: Warden opined in 1864 that *"Lochee, formerly a small village, is now an important manufacturing place, and although municipally connected with Dundee, it is yet so distinct and so important, as to demand a separate notice"*. Cox's monumental chimney, 90 m tall and 11 m wide at the base, was built at the Camperdown works in 1865–66 to serve its 39 boilers, which by 1869 burned 50 tonnes of coal a day! It was the tallest by far of the scores of such smokestacks in the vicinity of the city (but nothing to Townsend's at Port Dundas). The jute industry did well by making sandbags for the American Civil War, and Cox's later changed to 100% jute manufacture, becoming the largest jute works in the world. In 1869 it was fully integrated in operation, containing 700 power looms making mainly sacking, and also 300 hand-looms making carpets *"so cheap as to be within the reach of the humblest householder"* (Bremner). As well as 4300 employees in the mill, 400 outworkers sewed sacks at home; in all nearly 20 million metres of textiles came out of this one factory annually. The firm already ran a school for 400 pupils.

**Textile Records and Quaint Trams**: Cox's had some 5000 workers by the 1880s and at one time employed no fewer than 14,000 people; probably only Singer of Clydebank among Scottish industries ever had more employees on a single site. Various improvements were made to the circuitous railway and completed in 1868. Cox's drew much labour from Dundee, with which Lochee was also connected by horse tramway in 1879, by steam trams from 1885, and by electric cars from 1900, when it gained a city tramway depot; by then there was already a cinema in Lochee. Camperdown House (of the Viscount of that name) stood some 3 km to the north-west, isolated in 150 hectares of heavily wooded policies. These later became the Camperdown Park, gifted to the city by the Earl around 1900.

**From Jute to Dentures at Kingsway**: The evolution of bulk cargo handling methods began to reduce the demand for jute sacks, and Cox's faltered. Meanwhile the Kingsway bypass road was built in the 1920s, and new jobs arrived in the late 1930s on the extensive Kingsway West industrial estate of the Scottish Industrial Estates Corporation (SIEC). Firms opening there included the large US-owned NCR (National Cash Register) Ltd in 1946–47. In 1948 Veeder Root of Connecticut, a long-established manufacturer of counting devices, opened a substantial factory at Kilspindie Road to make petrol pump equipment. The Wright Dental Group, makers of dentures in Dundee since 1898, and smaller battery and toy makers, also built there. By 1951 Lochee had some 42,500 people, but only the facilities of a large village.

**Dryburgh Industrial Estate – Clocks to Electronics**: In 1946 the Timex Corporation of USA *(see also Craigie)* opened their Camperdown clock factory at Harrison Road on the new Dryburgh industrial estate north of the Kingsway, using skills from a small Dundee industry, and built up to a maximum employment of about 4000. The much less well-known works of metal container manufacturers Van Leer Tay, with its extensive sports facilities, was built in 1946 as a pair with the Timex factory. By 1980 Torbrex Engineering made precision sheet metal products at Dunsinane Avenue. Meantime an electrical engineering plant close by, owned by Ferranti Components Division by 1978, was bought out in 1990 by its management to create the firm of Albacom, to manufacture electronic components (microwave devices). In 1995 the factory was shared between Albacom and Laser Ecosse (industrial carbon dioxide lasers).

**Goodbye to Trains and Trams – enter Tachographs**: Passenger trains ceased in 1955, and trams stopped running to the Lochee terminus in 1956, being replaced by buses. From 1960 Camperdown Park contained a fine 18-hole municipal golf course, *"a stiff test of golfing skill"* (Price). As Cox's gradually ran down production, rail freight services ceased in 1967 and Lochee station became a Burns club! Meantime Woolworths opened a branch at Lochee in the 1960s, and there was a swimming pool and a large transport depot by the 1970s. In 1979 Veeder Root who employed over 1000 people and had three other local factories were expanding one of these, opened at Wester Gourdie west of Lochee as recently as 1976, to create 300 additional jobs making tachographs. Although Lochee's population had risen to about 54,000 by 1981, its facilities were those of only a small town.

**Cox and Timex Collapse**: In 1981 the Camperdown mills closed, and lay derelict and partly demolished in 1987. The 13 ha works were sold in 1988 to an East Anglian development company (the chimney and the roofless mill still stood alongside new buildings about 1990). Caught out by the digital revolution, by 1990 Timex were down to 650 employees, and further cuts were soon made. By 1993, then owned by the Norwegian Fred Olsen, they employed only 100 staff and 343 hourly-paid workers: a bitter dispute over pay and conditions led to factory closure later in the year. The Van Leer Factory stood vacant in 1994.

**New Industries include Sweet Tourism**: From 1984 further areas at Wester Gourdie were laid out as industrial estates, part of the Dundee Enterprise Zone. In 1991 new firms at Gourdie included Amoco Fabrics, Bonar Carelle – also in textiles, and the continuous-casting firm Rautomead. By 1990 Highland Kit Homes of Lochee offered twenty different designs, and in 1994 W A Simpson Marine of Logie Avenue built 7 m *'Argyll'* motor yachts. Shaws Dundee Sweet Factory (originally founded in 1879) was re-started in 1989 in new premises at Fulton Road in Wester Gourdie as a small traditional manufacturing and tourist operation by Derek & Gloria Shaw, who had experience with Keillers *(see Dundee)*; in 1994 it made boiled sweets, toffees and fudges. In 1993 William Low built a large store nearby; it passed to Tesco in 1994. In 1996 the local sheet metal firm Torbrex was sold to Mimtec of Livingston and Greenock. In 1999 Levi Strauss employed over 500 people making jeans at Dunsinane.

**Filling the Holes in the World's Walls**: By 1989 NCR's successes in computers, and more recently as the world leader in the field of ATMs (Automatic Teller Machines), 500,000 of

*Cox's lum, of the Camperdown jute works – 280 feet high and built in 1865–66. It still stands, although the works have gone. (JRH)*

which had been delivered by 1988, had brought 1400 jobs to their new Gourdie factory, the HQ of the Self-service Systems Division – appropriately the only part of NCR whose administration was centred outside the USA. NCR was bought in 1991 by AT&T, also US-owned. In 1992, they claimed to design and manufacture 60% of the world's ATMs at their Kingsway West factory, exporting to over 90 countries, using 1600 employees.

**Saving the Lum – and Keeping Camperdown**: By 1991 when Lochee had only about 32,780 residents, a dry ski slope had been constructed at Ancrum Road, and a zoo was open at Camperdown Park; by 1994 part of the Camperdown Works had been replaced by a multi-screen cinema, bingo and shopping. By 1997 the huge High Mill had been converted to flats, watched over by Cox's magnificent lum. NCR's old factory at Camperdown was vacated, and with adjacent land was the subject in 1997 of rival schemes for major leisure developments, including an ice rink (now complete) and a hotel, multiplex cinema, tennis, bowls and ten-pin bowling. The proposed exclusion of Camperdown Park from the new all-purpose Dundee City by the gerrymandered boundary alterations of the Tories' 1994–96 rehash of local government was highly controversial and did not succeed. St John's High has over 800 pupils, Menzieshill High over 900. Two budget hotels have recently arrived by the Kingsway.

## LOCHFOOT (or Lochrutton) — Map 2, B4

***Small Galloway village,** pop. 300* — OS 84: NX 8973

An ancient stone circle stands on the hills about 6km west of modern Dumfries; 2 km farther west is an earthwork, near Lochrutton Loch with its prehistoric crannog. The Cargen Water flows from the loch past Cullochan's medieval motte some 3km to the east, which gave rise to a tower house, and at the time of Pont's map of about 1610 two mills, one of them marked *'Neu'* (sic). But like Auchenfranco Castle to the south, the tower and mills later almost disappeared, leaving standing only the substantial 16th century tower of Hill's Castle 1km east of the loch. In about 1608–10 a military road was built into Galloway, passing north of the loch, and it was there at the loch's outlet that the settlement of Lochfoot developed; in 1869 Paterson of Dumfries had a hosiery mill there. Though this later closed, by 1951 Lochfoot had some 350 people, but the compact village provided only the most basic facilities of the Lochfoot post office and telephone exchange, and Lochrutton primary school. By 1953 there was a modern water works. Though the area's population later fell slightly, by 1980 a garage was open, also serving the winding A75 which had ousted the role of the better aligned military road. Little recent change has been evident.

## LOCHGAIR — Map 5, A4

***Argyll small village,** pop. 100* — OS 55: NR 9290

The shores of this shallow sheltered bay on the west coast of Loch Fyne some 12 km east of Lochgilphead were the site of ancient cairns, a medieval church, and the mansionhouse of Kinlochgair, which was shown on Roy's map of the 1750s. The track which then followed the shore had been made up by the 1890s as the main road to Kintyre, and an inn, school and post office had appeared south of the mansion, all simply styled Lochgair. Later the mansion lost its policies, and its name was omitted from the map in favour of Asknish. By 1951 the school and post office had closed and the population was only about 75. However, there was a tiny 7-line telephone exchange, and the inn had been enlarged into the *Lochgair Hotel*. By 1963 Asknish Forest clothed the surrounding hills, and for some years from about 1965 there was again a post office. Around 1970 the Hydro Board built a long dam 2 km north of Lochgair to raise the level of the small Loch Glashan by some 10 metres, to supply a hydro power station on the shore; this incorporates stone from the medieval church, whose site was drowned. By 1966 a housing estate had been built beside the delectable bay; the Loch Glashan cycle trails meander through the surrounding woods.

## LOCHGELLY — Map 6, B4

***Central Fife town,** pop. 7050* — OS 58: NT 1893

By about 1600 two farms took their name from the small Loch Gelly, a broadening of a tributary of the River Ore in central Fife. Roy's map made about 1750 also showed Lochgelly House, which stood on a nearby hilltop, south of a track linking Bow Bridge with Kirk of Beath. A weaving hamlet developed close by, and by 1799 Heron was able to refer to Lochgelly as *"a considerable village"*, though he gave no indication as to why it had grown so much. The only nearby economic activity to be seen on Sharp, Greenwood & Fowler's map surveyed in 1826–27 was 3–4km east of the village, where a quarry and limeworks were working south of two mills, Powguild and Shaw's. By that time roads linked Lochgelly with Auchterderran, with Kirk of Beath, and to Kirkcaldy via Shawsmill; the Beath to Kirkcaldy road was turnpiked in 1829.

**Railway, Ironworks, Coal and Tawse**: Urban growth dates from the 1849 opening of the Edinburgh & Northern Railway's Dunfermline and Thornton branch, on which a station was provided at Lochgelly. Blast furnaces were set up 1.5km south-west of the village in 1847 by the Lochgelly Iron Company – later the Lochgelly Iron & Coal Company. The Earl of Zetland's Lumphinnans No.1 Colliery *(see Cowdenbeath & Kelty)* was sunk nearby from 1852; firebrick works were also at work by 1855. The tiny Jenny Gray pit was sunk in 1854, Lochgelly post office was issued with a cancelling stamp in 1857, and within twenty years the village had grown rapidly to a population of about 2500. The early Lochgelly colliery, west of the village, suffered from a great fire in 1870–71, but from 1872 the company sank their Mary pit in the valley near Glencraig to the north, also working this and the Nellie pit which was sunk in 1876–80, as part of the Lochgelly Colliery; for some of its chequered history see *Hutton (1999)*. However, in 1875 the early working out of the blackband ironstone led to the closure of the ironworks. The company provided a school; though there was apparently no tanning tradition, Lochgelly replaced Linlithgow as the place where the infamous tawses were made – the leather straps with which discipline was mercilessly enforced in many Scottish schools.

**Burgh and Urban Services**: Lochgelly was part of Auchterderran parish until it became a police burgh in 1876, but in 1888 it was still thought of by Beveridge as a *"village"*, then owned by Earl Minto. The Rosewell colliery was open by 1889, and by 1891 the population was 4100 and a range of local services had developed, including a vigorous co-operative society and a gasworks. The large Lumphinnans Public School was built by the Council in 1892, actually being nearer to Cowdenbeath. A local newspaper, the *Central Fife Times & Advertiser*, was also established in 1892. Although there was an inn by 1894, only Lochgelly station's name appeared in Murray's Handbook – probably because genteel readers would not wish to know that numerous small coal mines operated west, north and east of the town. Railway junctions to the west connected with Kelty and Kinross. In 1894 it was decided to extend Lochgelly school by 150 places.

**Trams, Golf, Football and big Co-op Shopping**: From 1909 the Dunfermline Tramways Company connected to Lochgelly via Cowdenbeath. The Lochgelly Co-op's large premises burned down in 1910, but were soon rebuilt on an even larger scale. Lochgelly golf club, founded in 1910, laid out a 9-hole course just west of the town, and a public electricity supply was available from that year. Lochgelly United FC played in the Scottish League in 1914–15 and 1921–26. The tramway was extended to Lochore in 1912, but the whole system closed in 1937. Meantime during a coal strike in 1921 local people found and exploited an outcrop seam on the hill north of the Loch (in the 1970s this area was opencasted). In 1936 overcrowding in Lochgelly was bad, at 36% of all houses – though Cowdenbeath was even worse. Meantime the Jenny Gray's third shaft was sunk in 1927.

**The Decline of Lochgelly Mining**: By 1951 Lochgelly had almost 12,000 people and the facilities of a small town, including a hotel, miners' welfare institute, bowling greens, the substantial co-operative shopping facilities and a bus garage. The tiny Jenny Gray pit worked until 1959; the Nellie Colliery was closed following a fire in 1965, its site being reclaimed from 1967 as part of the Lochore Meadows scheme *(see Lochore)*. Peak-hour train services to Dunfermline and Edinburgh continued, but in the period to about 1970 the rapid closure of all the area's major mineral activities occurred, leaving only occasional opencast working. By 1971 Lochgelly's population had slumped to 8700; as in most other such towns, their homes were mainly council-owned (78%).

**Telecoms, Theatre, more Golf but fewer Buses**: In a seminal move for the town, Andrew Antenna, an Illinois corporation making communications dishes, was persuaded to establish a Lochgelly factory in 1966. By 1967 there was also a clothing factory, and Lochgelly House had become the *Lochview Hotel*. The outgoing Fife County Council built a 400-seat theatre and successful leisure complex, opened about 1975; but in the same year Lochgelly lost its burgh status and became part of Dunfermline District. The Fife Omnibus garage, heir to the trams, was closed about 1980. By 1981, despite its many setbacks, Lochgelly had become an established town where four small hotels were open. During the 1980s the golf club extended its activities to the new municipal course at Lochore *(q.v.)*, but the Lochgelly course stayed open; water skiing on Loch Gelly had been popular for many years *(see Townhill)*.

**Back on the Map**: The large new Lochgelly High School was opened in 1987 north of the town to replace Auchterderran secondary and relieve Beath High. From almost the same time, the opening of the western section of the new A92 expressway connected Lochgelly with the M90 motorway; in 1990 it was extended to Gallatown. In 1989 the rail passenger service was also extended as the *'Fife Circle'*, providing all-day trains to Dunfermline, Edinburgh and Kirkcaldy. In 1991 when the population was under 7050, still very disadvantaged, Seamac Agricultural of Kinross and Lochgelly were manufacturers and distributors of fertilisers; Weathermac made protective clothing. Andrew Antenna then employed 230 people and were expanding in the European cellular telephone field, by also making coaxial cable and elliptical waveguide equipment.

**New Companies Climbing Stairs**: Profab Engineering, set up in Lochgelly High Street for repair work by Steve Harvey in 1985, soon built up a reputation for efficient structural and architectural steelwork; by 1994 their 40 workers did specialist design and construction work on staircases in Glasgow, and a record-breaking 670-tonne wellhead lifting beam for Spain. In 1994 the Regal Rubber Company of Cartmore industrial estate made roller coverings and other rubber products. In 1995 Strand Lighting *(see Pathhead, Fife)* expanded into Lochgelly for assembly, warehousing and distribution, 80% of the output going overseas. In 2000 the Scottish Co-op proposed redevelopment to create a new store and flats behind the existing imposing frontage of its Bank Street premises.

## LOCHGILPHEAD

**Map 4, C4**

***Argyll town**, pop. 2400*

OS 55: NR 8688

There are standing stones both north and south of Kilmore at the head of Loch Gilp, an inlet of Loch Fyne. Timothy Pont's map made about 1600 showed this as a tiny settlement, while Sanson's 1665 map prepared in Paris depicted Kilmore as one of the chief settlements in Argyll. However, the Roy survey of about 1750 showed *'Killmorvay'* (Kilmory) as just one of a cluster of hamlets, where a track from Inveraray along the north shore of Loch Fyne turned inland through Kilmichael Glassary to the Ferry of Arragon (Ford) and infant Oban, throwing off a branch to Bellanoch and so to Kintyre. Another hamlet's Gaelic placename *Polnacannaloch ('Pool at the Head of the Loch')* was translated as Lochgilphead.

**Road, Village, Canal and Steamers**: In 1780 a proper road was opened along the shores of Loch Fyne and Loch Gilp to link Inveraray with Campbeltown, and in the late 18th century Lochgilphead was laid out as a planned village. It had the area's first post office, opened in 1799, which became the centre for a penny post serving Crinan and Kintra (Barbreck). It was there that the Crinan Canal, opened in 1801, met the Campbeltown road, from which point a spur road was being constructed northwards to Oban. The canal's terminus lay to the south at Ardrishaig, which was connected with Glasgow by steamers from 1819, Lochgilphead being served by a trackboat on the canal because its foreshore dried out at low tide.

**Poverty, Nodality and Riches**: Lochgilphead was still too poor to provide a building for Church of Scotland worship until the government stepped in with aid in 1828, by which time the Oban road was complete; this made Lochgilphead much more nodal in position than either Inveraray or Ardrishaig. By 1831 the quay and landing stage must have been built, for Lochgilphead was served by regular steamers; in 1858 the Crinan Canal steamer interchanged passengers there with the Glasgow boat. A mansion called Kilmory Castle was built by stages from the 18th century to the 1870s, 1.5km to the south-east of Lochgilphead, accompanied from the 1830s by a remarkable Germanic gatehouse.

**Urban and Hospital Development**: Lochgilphead gradually grew into a small town and was made a police burgh; it was later said to have been an important centre for fishing as recently as 1900. Meantime in 1860 what Murray described as *"a large Poors' House"* was built. By 1894 this was adjoined by a *"Lunatic Asylum"*. Lochgilphead already had a hotel, and was described as *"a watering-place"*. A local newspaper – the *Argyllshire Advertiser* – was published for many years, and the *Empire Cinema* building is rumoured to have been originally located at Bellahouston as part of the 1938 Empire Exhibition (McKean).

**County Town, Golf Course and Hotels**: Lochgilphead became by degrees the *de facto* county town of the enormous, sparsely-peopled county of Argyll, and a centre for both road maintenance and trunk telephone communications. Lochgilphead High School, shopping and tourist services developed. Under the NHS the Victorian institutions became maternity, geriatric and psychiatric hospitals, with the headquarters of the Argyll & Bute Health District. The golf club was founded in 1963, its 9-hole homespun course designed and laid out by hospital staff and patients. About 1960 the centrally located *Stag Hotel* was extended; a modest boating and coaching inn 3km north-west of Lochgilphead was extended about 1970 into the 24-room *Cairnbaan Hotel*. In 1975 the sprawling Argyll & Bute District, the most extensive lower tier unit of local government in Britain, was created as part of the vast new Strathclyde Region. Kilmory Castle was adapted as its headquarters. The new system evidently generated many additional telephone calls to Glasgow, and in 1976 the trunk telephone exchange was extended.

*The Oakfield Bridge, built in 1871 by P & W MacLellan of Glasgow during an upgrading of the Crinan Canal (which first opened in 1801).* *(JRH)*

**Service and Industrial Centre**: In 1976 Lochgilphead was a tightly knit, bustling and remarkably specialised service town, with about 35 shops and a good range of practical services, plus three substantial hotels. The small modern Knapdale Woollen Mill was in production, Macleod Homes manufactured kit houses at Achnaba and two new housing estates had been built. But the local office of the *Argyllshire Advertiser* produced just a single sheet printed by the *Oban Times*, and the divisional HQ of the police was under threat. By 1977 a privately owned fish farming research station had been established at nearby Stronachullin, and afforestation was steadily covering nearly all the hills around. By the late 1980s Highbank Porcelain made ornaments.

**Local Government by Helicopter**: Lochgilphead's unique local government role was shown by the following remarkable comment in the Municipal Yearbook: *"Travelling time to the nearest Area Office from HQ is approximately one hour."* In 1991 just 2421 people lived in Lochgilphead, which is for its size a quite exceptionally important centre, whose varied urban facilities serve a hinterland which contained some 15,000 people in 1981. A regular helicopter service to Glasgow showed the importance of its role as a public service centre. By 1992 the industrial estate was full, and being extended. In 1996 Lochgilphead gained yet more significance when Argyll & Bute became a unitary local authority, also taking over the extensive Helensburgh and Arrochar area from Dumbarton. By 1996 further new housing had been erected and walks and cycle trails laid out through the forests; there is a woodland walk at Kilmory Castle. The Mid-Argyll Sports Centre is now open. Today, the long-established M & K Macleod employ almost 200 manufacturing their *'Argyll'* kit houses at the Kilmory industrial estate. There is a range of small/medium hotels, plus a lochside caravan site.

## LOCHGOILHEAD

**Map 5, B4**

***Argyll village,*** *pop. 825 (area)* — OS 56: NN 2001

Sheltered among the steep hills of Cowal lies Loch Goil, a short deep offshoot from Loch Long; at its head where the River Goil enters the loch is a medieval church with some interesting features. By about 1400 the impressive 3-storey tower of Carrick Castle had been built by the Campbell Earls of Argyll on a rock jutting from the shore of the loch 8 km to the south, commanding the approach to their cattle-rearing fiefdom by sea from the Clyde – until it was gutted by fire in 1685. Perhaps the first map to include details in this area was surveyed by William Roy about 1750: a bridge spanning the River Goil at the head of the loch carried a track, later a road, linking north and west to Inveraray across the St Catherines Ferry. This went by way of Gleann Beag or *'Hell's Glen'*, where clearances for sheep were about to start. Southwards a track – lost by 1895 – climbed through the Ardgoil estate over a 550 m col in the steep hills fancifully dubbed *'Argyll's Bowling Green'* to a now-vanished ferry called Chrigan opposite Portincaple, and so to Dumbarton.

**Steamers bring Villas and Tourists**: There was an early mill near Lochgoilhead, and the Campbell lairds of Ardkinglas, who had banished the herdsmen, introduced weavers to the area around 1800. By 1819, very soon after steamers were invented, they regularly puffed their way up the loch to a pier at Lochgoilhead, but there was still no post office in 1838. A string of villas was built along the eastern shore from the 1840s onwards, and a new pier was constructed in the 1860s. By 1895 an inn and a post and telegraph office were open. To the west was the mansion of Drimsynie House, and a lochside track to another post office and inn at Carrick Castle; this was later made up as a road. By then the Portincaple ferry plied to isolated Mark (Chrigan). Lochgoilhead was served by MacBrayne steamers in summer up to 1946, but developed little more, remaining a small village with a resident population of about 350. After the steamers ceased to call, the population fell back slightly, the most striking feature for so small a place being a 4-doctor group practice. By 1977 Drimsynie House had become a hotel, and by 1984 there was a caravan site.

**Enterprise and Vandalism**: In 1991 the population of the vast parish – including Cairndow – was 813. By 1992 Douglas Campbell, owner of the *Drimsynie House Hotel*, had greatly expanded it into a leisure centre and holiday village, with closely packed lodges, restaurants, swimming pool, skating and curling rink, and golf. Sadly *Campbell's Kingdom* as the locals called it had been despoiled by the unlicensed felling of 20 ha of ancient woodland. Carrick Castle was restored in 1996, although in 2000 Lochgoilhead's main street was becoming marred by an increasingly derelict church; but the small *Shorehouse Inn* still serves.

## LOCHINVER

**Map 12, A2**

***W. Sutherland coast village,*** *pop. 550* — OS 15: NC 0922

When Timothy Pont sketch-mapped northern Scotland about 1600 he marked Torbreck, near the coast of Assynt in west Sutherland. Only trackless wastes were shown on the Roy map made about 1750, the unique isolated 731 m-tall Suilven *(Pillar Mountain)* being dramatically sketched in colour on the fair copy by Paul Sandby. There was by then a small township at the head of the short Loch Inver some 2 km south of Torbreck; as late as 1786 it had no pier, boats being launched from the open beach. From the 1820s Lochinver was served by a branch off the Tongue road, built for the Parliamentary Commissioners. What later became the *Culag Hotel* was built on a small peninsula in the loch as a residence of the Duke of Sutherland, of whose notoriously oppressive estates Lochinver was still a part. A pier must also have been constructed, enabling steamers en route between Portree and Stornoway to serve Lochinver in alternate weeks from about 1846.

**Resort Development amid Decline**: By 1886 this *"beautiful rising watering-place"* where steamers called was served by the *Lochinver Hotel*. A horse-drawn mail cart across the moors provided the 75 km connection to the nearest railway at Lairg, giving views of Suilven and other peaks. A few years later a mail coach linked Lochinver and Drumbeg with Bonar Bridge, and by 1894 Lochinver visitors found the two hotels, *"both large and first class, under the same management; trout and salmon fishing"* (Murray). The area became famed for the brown trout to be found in its innumerable tiny lochs. During the summers from 1888 to 1914 a weekly steamer provided a service from Kyle and Gairloch, giving Oban connections. In 1901 the vast Assynt parish had 2400 people, but voluntary emigration had cut this by 1951 to only 900.

**Growing Fishing Port and Resort**: Lochinver's substantial primary school was uniquely sited on a low peninsula in a nearby lochan; although pupil numbers fell to 26 in the 1930s, its remoteness meant that it had to stay open. By 1951 Lochinver had little else besides the pier, the *Culag Hotel* and the facilities of a small village. By 1962 a coastal youth hostel was open at Achmelvich, 5 km to the west, and a caravan site was established nearby. Lochinver benefited from the post-war years of Minch fishing by boats from the east coast, the catch being sold on the pier, which was extended three times between 1945 and 1977; on the last occasion a fish-selling shed was added. The fishing boat *Golden Emblem*, which was built in Lochinver in 1956, sailed from the port until sold to Campbeltown in 1988. A lifeboat station was opened in 1967, and a new mission canteen was erected in 1969.

**Tourists and Salmon Farming**: New housing was erected, and by 1976 the school roll had risen to 70, requiring an extension to the building. A second though tiny hotel was open by 1977; in 1978 the tourist trade was evident in remote little Inverkirkaig to the south of Lochinver, with weavers and even a bookshop, while at Inverpolly were several new houses evidently related to a salmon farm which was already being extended. In 1978 there was little other new development away from the pier at Lochinver itself. Besides fishing vessels and a fish merchant and hauliers there were the post office, a garage, a handful of shops, buses twice a week to Ullapool and a postbus to Drumbeg.

**Pots, Pipe Band and Fish Processing**: The population of Lochinver was nearing 400 in 1981, but the local facilities remained in general those of a small village. Local man David Grant had bought a second-hand kiln on graduation in 1976, using china clay in his Highland Stoneware pottery; he built a larger factory around his kiln in 1982, and soon created about 10 steady jobs. Development continued, infilling the space between Lochinver and the clachan of Baddidarach, and in 1988 Lochinver boasted the only mainland pipe band north-west of Fort William. By 1991 a fish processing factory provided 35 jobs, while another was proposed. By then the population was 558. Business at Highland Stoneware took off around 1990, and by 1993 Grant employed 25 people at Lochinver and 8 at Ullapool.

**New Pier and South Europeans**: By 1992 it was claimed not only that there was no unemployment, but that a major new pier built in 1991–92 would give Lochinver the best mainland harbour north of Oban. However, it became used by French and Spanish boats licensed to fish in Scottish waters, to the chagrin of local crews. In 1995–96 French and Spanish trawlers landed deepwater fish; white fish and prawns were also landed from Scottish boats. In a typical week in 1997, Lochinver was Scotland's busiest port for fish landings, at 5600 boxes of white fish, deepwater species and prawns.

**The Crofters' Famous Victory**: Early in 1993 the *Culag Hotel* hosted the celebrations for the acquisition by the Assynt Crofters Trust of 85 square kilometres of crofts and semi-wilderness, including Stoer and the Drumbeg *(q.v.)* fishing school, for the price of three suburban detached houses in Fife! Bill Ritchie and Allan MacRae were leading Trust members among the 120 tenants of the North Assynt estate, bought from a short-term speculative owner. Its prior owners the Vestey family, with their Liverpool connections, had retained a home and inland sporting estates in the area. There are now several small hotels, and there is also the Achmelvich youth hostel.

## LOCHMABEN

**Map 2, B4**

***Large Dumfriesshire village**, pop. 2000*

OS 78: NY 0882

About 12 km north-east of Dumfries and 2 km west of the River Annan stands Lochmaben, sited between the Kirk Loch, the Castle Loch and the Mill Loch; it has an ancient earthwork and a Norman motte. An excellent defensive site, a low promontory at the south end of the Castle Loch, was chosen for a later castle, probably begun in 1298 by Edward I; it was the home of Robert the Bruce when Lord of Annandale. Lochmaben became a baronial burgh between 1214 and 1314, and was shown on the mid 13th century Gough map. The castle was rebuilt in stone in the mid 14th century, with twin towers spanning its short moat or *'canal'*. Lochmaben became a Royal Burgh in 1440; the castle became royal property in 1455 and a banqueting hall was added in the 1490s. Later most of its ashlar stone was robbed for domestic building.

**Sound Schooling, and Famous Sons**: Lochmaben paid no tax in the years 1535–56, having failed to develop beyond a country village. In the 16th century the town mill was swapped by the dunderheaded town council for a stone market cross supplied by the astute laird of Elsieshields, who was then building himself an L-plan tower house 3 km north-west of the town. The area was among those few parts of Scotland not mapped by Pont, but Lochmaben evidently had a good school in the 17th century, when William Paterson from Tinwald, co-founder of the Bank of England, was educated there. By 1715 Lochmaben had a post office. William Jardine, locally born in 1784 and also locally taught, became the co-founder of the vast East Asia trading firm of Jardine Mathieson, and later owned Lanrick Castle in Perthshire. James Mounsey of Rammerscales near Hightae, 5 km south of Lochmaben, became in the mid 18th century the first physician to the Tsar of Russia.

**Lime and Linen**: The Roy map made about 1754 showed three tracks radiating from Lochmaben, by then a substantial village on a north–south axis; to the south were *'Lime Kills'*. Around 1770 there were two lint mills, and some 60,000 m of coarse linen was hand-woven annually for the English market. Lochmaben was a post town by 1797, with a service on alternate weekdays; three fairs were held in the year. Heron opined in 1799 that *"though ancient, and pleasantly situated, it has never risen to great eminence. The number of its inhabitants* *may amount to about 700, who manufacture coarse linen, follow mechanic employments, and cultivate the adjacent fields."*

**Poorest Royal Burgh in the South of Scotland?**: In 1827 Chambers noted that the castle was a ruin, still being robbed for building stone, and *"the town, at this day the poorest royal burgh in the south of Scotland, so decayed that houses have lain in ruins for a century even at its market-cross"*. Yet it had a modern church and a new school. From 1863 Lochmaben had a station on a new Caledonian Railway branch line which meandered between Dumfries and Lockerbie. Framework knitting grew and prospered in the mid 19th century but withered away, replaced by 1913 with a branch textile factory opened by McGeorge of Dumfries. In 1891 Lochmaben held just 1038 residents, and had two small hotels by 1894, the *Crown* and *King's Arms*.

**Chest Infections, Bread and Golf**: Lochmaben Hospital was opened in 1908 as the infectious diseases centre for the county of Dumfries; by the 1950s it was a 146-bed chest sanatorium. Lochmaben golf club was founded in 1925 and laid out a 9-hole course beside the Kirk Loch. The little burgh, which had 1100 people in 1951, also gained a quite large bakery, and the facilities of a village. The railway was closed to passengers before 1953, and to freight in 1966. In the 1960s a modest mansion-house near the church became the small *Balcastle Hotel*, its garden sadly replaced by a sea of tarmac parking. In 1981 two other small hotels were still open, plus another at Hightae, which had grown to 500 people and also had a school and post office.

**Cheese by the Tonne**: By 1980 Express Dairy Foods of Middlesex had built a substantial local plant near the river and the Lockerbie road, in 1991 described as the *'Scottish Pride'* dairy. In the mid 90s, its 200-worker *'Lockerbie'* creamery processed 150 million litres of milk annually to produce 15,000 tonnes of cheese, plus other products. In 1997 this large enterprise dominated the area between the two small towns.

**Driving Away to Work – and No Hole in the Wall**: In 1991, the population was just over 2000, but many worked elsewhere. In 1993 Fortex, a New Zealand meat processor, proposed a plant to deal with up to 7000 sheep a day beside the creamery at Priestdykes, 2 km south-east of Lochmaben, promising 576 jobs. Substantial extensions to the former sanatorium in the mid 1990s turned it into a Community Hospital. By then there was the small *Balcastle Hotel*, two caravan sites, and the golf course (extended to 18 holes in 1996); the Castle Loch supported a sailing club in 1997, and Lochmaben Bowling Club was still active. It was absurd that no cashpoint machine could be placed in this town of the pioneer banker, because the bank was a listed building!

## LOCHMADDY

**Map 7, B2**

***Main village of N. Uist,*** *pop. 1600 (area)* OS 18: NF 9168

A sea loch on the east coast of North Uist takes its name from two or three rocks at the entrance, supposedly shaped like the heads of dogs (in Gaelic *Madadh)*; some say wolves. Monro noted in 1549 that the isle, which the locals called *Kentnache*, belonged to Donald MacDonald Gorm of Sleat. Despite many rebels hiding in heather-covered holes in the ground it was *"more of profit"* than Benbecula or South Uist, perhaps because *'Loch Ebi' (Loch Eport?)* had been ingeniously dammed by *"a thick dyke of rough stones"* among which the tidal ebb and flow left sticking *"flukes, podloches, skates and herrings"*. The Reformation made North Uist a Presbyterian island. The wealth of herrings in Loch Maddy led to a *'magazine'* for casks and salt being built at Vacksay Isle by the English after the Restoration. Martin, writing in 1703, did not mention the fish dam, but noted a quay, adding that the three rocks at the loch entrance were covered in big mussels; he thought they too were known as *'Maddies'*.

**Developing a Village**: Lochmaddy exported a few cattle by 1799, when Heron referred to *"the harbour of Lochmaddie, where it is hoped a village will soon be erected"*. He added that the inhabitants of the Uists lived *"chiefly by fishing, and by a pitiful kind of agriculture"*. A fishing village was actually developed in 1802, and by 1804 – as James Hogg noted – Lochmaddy had *"a good slated inn of two stories"*, where Lord Macdonald's tenants had to attend to pay their rents. Lochmaddy soon exported kelp, on which a fragile prosperity was based. At that time sailing packets carried the Uist mail between Dunvegan in Skye and Carinish. About 1834 the Uist terminal was moved to Lochmaddy, which acquired a steamer pier and a post office handling all mail for the Uists and Barra (and, temporarily, for Harris).

**Law, Fishing Resort and Seaweed**: Lochmaddy consisted of few but significant buildings in 1894: the post office, a pier house, the *"good" Lochmaddy Hotel* (which once had 29 boats on its fishing lochs), the imposing court house and the Inverness-shire county buildings for the Uists, a sheriff-substitute whose mansion of 1804 was known as Sponish House, a bank, school, poorhouse, general merchant and the estate factor's house. By 1951 Lochmaddy had about 450 people, a 43-bed general and maternity hospital, and the Head Post Office; the school held junior secondary classes. In 1956 Alginate Industries built a seaweed grinding mill beside neglected Sponish House. In 1960 a causeway was opened, linking the Uists via Benbecula, and in 1964 Lochmaddy became a terminal of the triangular Tarbert (Harris) and Uig (Skye) car ferry route. Centralisation ended the Head Post Office role by 1970, and the secondary classes by 1976, and the hospital treated only the chronic sick.

**Sunday Ferries change local Character**: By 1981 Lochmaddy's population was only 360, its remaining facilities serving some 1650 people in the area. The courthouse still functioned, loch fishing continued, and by 1982 tourists were served by an information office and a youth hostel, though the latter had closed by 2000, in favour of Berneray. Sadly in 1986 the alginate factory was closed. Sunday ferries, introduced in 1989 after a century of Free Presbyterian opposition, stimulated tourism: a former inn was restored in 1994 as a museum, cafe and arts centre by the Southern Isles Amenity Trust. But by then Sponish House had been gutted by fire, and the MacEacherns' small mid-Victorian mansionhouse beside the harbour stood derelict in 1997. However the bank and a garage remained. The *Lochmaddy Hotel* with 15 rooms aims at anglers; the Uist Outdoor Centre at Lochmaddy provides a year-round hostel for backpackers. *Langass Lodge*, near a stone circle and chambered cairn on the shores of Locheport, 13km south-west, is now a small hotel.

## LOCHORE, Ballingry, Crosshill & Glencraig

**Map 6, B4**

***Central Fife town / villages,*** *pop. 7000 (area)* OS 58: NT 1897

Ballingry on the southern slopes of Ben Arty in central Fife has a Gaelic name *('Village of the Cave')* and had an ancient church; at one time the parishes of Auchterderran and Ballingry comprised the obscure administrative unit of *'Lochoreshire'*. Beveridge believed that the castle of the Vallances which stood on the islet of Inchgall in the shallow Loch Ore, 1 km south of Ballingry, went back to Malcolm Canmore. Certainly by 1395 Lochore was already a barony, later owned by the Wardlaws. In 1511 nearby *Corshill* (now Crosshill) became a burgh of barony, but only a milltown appeared on James Gordon's map of 1642. About 1658 John Malcolm of Balbedie built a mansionhouse named Inchgall, 500 m south-west of the tiny Kirkton of Ballingry. Inchgall became the House of Orr, which stood in modest policies when shown on the Roy map of about 1750, but there were no roads; later used for illicit distilling, it was again renamed Lochore House.

**After the Loch: Stills, Mills and Mines**: The loch was drained around 1800, but by 1826 Lochore Castle stood in ruins, and apart from Lochore House and its farms there were just the two water mills of Inchgall and Glencraig on the *'Orr Water'*, served by winding lanes; as late as 1850 no turnpike road or railway closely approached the area. By 1888 the Lochore estate was owned by the Lochore Mining Company; by 1895 an inn and smithy stood at Shank, just east of Ballingry, and a *'second class metalled road'* had been made up between Ballingry Kirk and Lochgelly. A chain of four or more coal pits lined a mineral railway linking Kinglassie with Kelty, and the Glencraig pit was sunk from 1895 by a subsidiary of Coltness Iron, but in 1901 there were still only some 1300 people in the scattered hamlets and miners' rows. Over the next 40 years several more pits were sunk, including from 1902 the Fife Coal Company's Mary pit 500 m south of Lochore House, then the country's deepest at 603 m, with a chimney 54 m tall. A second shaft, with a concrete headframe which still survives, was sunk for this Mary colliery in the 1920s, aiming to employ 1000 men *(Hutton, 1999)*.

**Trams and Flashes**: From 1912 to 1937 electric trams ran to Lochgelly, Cowdenbeath and Dunfermline – on which towns the soon huge mining village, which sprawled along the route, came to rely for most services. Ballingry parish contained about 10,350 people in both 1921 and 1931, and had an early miners' institute, but was never a burgh. Subsidence gradually recreated Loch Ore, which became seamed with various railway embankments, burning bings, and a sinking sewage disposal plant. By 1951 the facilities of a small village and a 470-pupil junior secondary school served a population which had fallen towards 8000; over the next decade or so, Fife County Council steadily moved the people out of squalid miners' rows into a vast new estate of houses at Ballingry.

**Opencasting, Lurgi Gas and Lochore Meadows**: The Westfield opencast coal scheme 2 km east of Ballingry was begun in 1960 to feed a major gasworks, using the German Lurgi process to gasify low-grade coal, to supply a fifth of Scotland's gas requirements; Westfield gradually became enormous, one of the deepest man-made holes in Europe. The Mary Colliery was still working in 1958, but the deep mines around Loch Ore were then rapidly abandoned, the last – Glencraig – being closed in 1966, leaving a ravaged wasteland and many seriously deprived people. By 1967 three electricity transmission lines converged opposite the Lurgi plant, at a major substation (which was to be repeatedly enlarged). From that time the dereliction and burning bings in an area of some 3 square km west and south of the village were rapidly removed by intrepid contractors in a dramatic operation, led and well publicised by Fife County Council's larger-than-life Planning Officer, Maurice Taylor. This enabled their successor, Fife Region, to create the Lochore Meadows Country Park, which

*Lochore Meadows, now a country park, which was created in the 1970s from a huge coal-waste area – an enormous environmental engineering project. The winding-gear of the 1902 Mary Pit (on the left) was an early use of reinforced concrete. (RS)*

was opened in 1977, including a large interpretation centre and such activities as sailing and horse-riding, while preserving the Mary pit's reinforced concrete winding tower.

**From Gas Production to Research, Golf and Baking**: North Sea gas exploitation led to the closure of the Westfield gas plant in the mid 1970s; but it became a major coal gasification research centre. In 1979 the Westfield opencast pit was the deepest ever worked by the NCB, at 150m nearly twice the average maximum depth; when closed about 1985 it had reached a yawning 270 metres. Lochore's population fell from 8200 in 1971 to 7000 by 1981. The Lochgelly golf club expanded to use the new golf course opened by 1982 at Lochore Meadows – which had been newly designated as part of Scotland's first Regional Park – and was in 1990 the leading attraction in Fife, with 400,000 visitors. A dispensing chemist had opened in Lochore, where by 1977 S M Bayne & Co were bakers and butchers with a string of nearly 20 shops in central Fife; by 1994 they had a payroll of 250.

**Ballingry in a Sad Time-warp**: The secondary school was downgraded to primary in 1987 when Lochgelly High School opened, and in 1991 the ancient Lochore House was derelict. In the autumn of 1990 Ballingry seemed stuck in a 1950s time-warp beneath its blanket of free-coal smog. By 1990 Community Business Fife had opened a store for members, which by 1993 had proved a success in this very deprived area, where there were no public eating facilities and even a proposed cafe aroused favourable comment. In 1991 only 6400 people remained, with over 20% out of work. Occasional new private houses were appearing, but as late as 1996 Willie Clarke was again returned to sit on the new Fife Council as Scotland's last remaining Communist councillor.

**New Coal Hole Fills with Rubbish**: The British Gas Westfield plant with its 27mW gas turbine was last used in 1991. In the mid 1990s the Westfield rail link, recently only used for slurry trains to Methil power station, sent large quantities of opencast coal to power stations in the north and midlands of England; the track was moved south to serve a new opencasting site, the Westfield Link, where 50 men excavated 4 million tonnes of coal over five years; about 1998 the filling of the resulting hole with domestic waste from central Fife was begun.

**Power from Sludge and Chicken Litter!**: Between 1994 and 1999, Fife Energy (a subsidiary of Global Energy Europe) converted the Westfield gas centre into an *'integrated gasification combined cycle power plant'* of 75mW, creating 70 permanent jobs. Briquetted coal and dried sewage sludge brought in by rail are burned in the closed system. In 1997–99 another subsidiary, EPR Scotland, built an additional, 10mW power station with a 34m chimney, fired by 12 lorry loads a day of Fife poultry litter! (A mere 13 staff are needed.) A further similar scheme on the south frontage for Fibrowatt is possible (if enough chicken litter, straw and wood waste can be found) and possibly also using landfill gas from the new domestic waste tip nearby.

## LOCHRANZA

**Map 1, B1**

***Small village, N. Arran,*** *pop. 200* — OS 69: NR 9350

The sea inlet of Loch Ranza (*Rowan Tree River* in Norse) is little more than a deep bay at the northern tip of the hilly Isle of Arran, overlooked by a hill fort. A castle probably existed before 1452; Monro noted in 1549 that at the head of Lochranza was *"an old house called the castle"*. This tall double tower house, today a roofless ruin, was shown on Pont's map of around 1600, when it was accompanied by several small settlements. Arran long remained essentially a crofting island, although the name Loch a'Muillin shows there was an early mill at Lochranza, and in the early 18th century coal was worked on the remote coast 1km east of the Cock of Arran. Salt was extracted there from seawater between 1710 and 1735 *(see Hay & Stell)*. Pirnmill, at the mouth of the Allt Gobhlach *('Forked Stream')* 10km to the south-west, took its name from a 19th century bobbin factory.

**Resort, Herring Port and Geologists' Hunting Ground**: A school was open at Lochranza by 1845, when twelve local fishing boats were busy. In 1885 a road was built from Brodick via North Glen Sannox, and tourist development followed the authorisation in 1886 of a steamer pier. In 1888 the Glasgow to Campbeltown steamers called at Greenock, Gourock, Lochranza, Pirnmill, Carradale and Saddell. The hotel at Lochranza was considered only *"tolerable"* by Murray's 1894 Handbook; by then a post & telegraph office was available, and a school had been built at Pirnmill. Herring fishing still continued in 1914 from both Lochranza and Pirnmill. North Arran proved fascinating for geological study as well as for leisure pursuits, and by 1953 a youth hostel was open. There was also a twelve-hole golf course (later reduced to nine, but now 18). Lochranza remained only a small village and yachting resort, with an out-of-season population of about 250. The pier was still a calling point for the turbine steamer *Duchess of Hamilton* as late as 1967.

**Kintyre Ferry and New Distillery**: The steamers were things of the past when a new slipway was built in 1972 for a roll-on summer ferry to another new slip at Claonaig in Kintyre. By 1980 a public slip was available, a second hotel was open, and it was commented that all the large houses were boarding houses. By 1985 the few local children attended Pirnmill school. In 1992 a new ferry built at St Monans (Fife) was introduced, able to carry 18 cars and 150 passengers. In 1994–95 Isle of Arran Distillers Ltd, led by Harold Currie (formerly of Chivas Regal) built the first legal malt whisky distillery on the island for 150 years. Designed by his co-director and local architect David Hutchison, it draws its water from the Easan Biorach south of Lochranza, a stream fed from peat and red granite. Though deliberately small, it includes a visitor centre. When its first whisky was distilled in 1995 it employed 12 to 15 people, intended to rise to 60 when a whisky- and water-bottling plant is added. *Butt Lodge*, a former hunting lodge is now a small hotel, there is a guest house, and also the youth hostel.

## LOCHWINNOCH

**Map 1, C1**

***Renfrewshire small town,*** *pop. 2350* — OS 63: NS 3558

Lochwinnoch commands a broad gap in the hills 9km west of Johnstone. In Timothy Pont's day around 1600 *'Milbanck'* stood beside a burn that flowed into the shallow Barr Loch, overlooked by the square 16th century tower of Barr Castle. The steep River Calder which flowed into the adjacent Castle Semple Loch had been bridged at both *'Brigend'* and beside Lochwinnoch Kirk. A peel tower built about 1555 stands on an island in this loch, north of which is the Semple collegiate church, built in 1501–05 by John, first Lord Sempill or Semphill (and now cared for by Historic Scotland). His own Castle

Semple was large and important, eventually having fishponds, an icehouse, and 18th century landscaping. Meantime a parish school had opened in 1622.

**The Textile Industry**: The Roy map of about 1754 showed Lochwinnoch as a village with roads to Beith, Kilbarchan and Kilmacolm. About then a linen bleachworks was set up on the River Calder 1 km north of the village; a limeworks also existed by 1782. The Old or Calderhaugh cotton mill was established on the Calder in 1788 by the laird, William McDowall, and two partners. The New Mill followed in 1790, and two coal mines were open by 1796, enabling the Old Mill to add steam power. Heron wrote in 1799 of the *"village of Loch Winnoch, with upwards of 500 people"*. Boghead Mill had been built by 1813, and Lochwinnoch's first post office opened between then and 1838.

**On the Railway: Bleaching, Cabinets and Golf**: The Glasgow, Paisley, Kilmarnock & Ayr Railway was completed in 1840, passing east of the loch, where Lochwinnoch station long stood alone. However, by 1857 barytes was being mined in the vicinity, and crushed at Muirshields Mill. Three cabinet-making works were set up in the 1880s, and by 1891 the population was 1400. Murray noted in 1894 that, having abandoned cotton, Lochwinnoch was *"a large village, engaged in the bleaching of linen for the Paisley manufactories"*. Barr Loch had been drained by then, but it later reflooded. Lochwinnoch golf club was founded in 1897 and laid out an 18-hole parkland course.

**The Silk Industry and a Tale of two Stations**: Lochwinnoch station was renamed Lochside by its later owners the Glasgow & South Western Railway, who built a new loop line west of the lochs, opened as late as 1905 with a more convenient station for Lochwinnoch. Castle Semple, by then long rebuilt into a classical mansion, was gutted by fire in 1935, and largely demolished in the 1960s. By 1951 Lochwinnoch was a village of 2600 people, still with two industrial cabinet makers, but Calderhaugh Mill had by that time changed fibres once more, to silk weaving and printing. At some time McKinlay of Burnfoot were also textile printers, and a missionary college was open by 1963. Lochwinnoch station was closed to passengers in 1966, the less conveniently placed Lochside being reopened at the same time.

**Back to Water and the Hills**: In 1976 the Calderhaugh Mill was still engaged in silk weaving and printing. Lochwinnoch had maintained average village facilities since the 1950s, and grown little in population. In 1978 the RSPB opened a visitor centre beside Castle Semple Loch, north of which a country park was established; by 1979 another country park was open in the upper Calder valley at Muirshiel, 7 km north-west. Little expansion took place during the 1980s except close beside the River Calder, but a hotel was opened near the station. In 1991 Lochwinnoch's population was 2347. By 1994 Castle Semple Loch was a water park for rowing, sailing, surfing and water skiing; its country park includes a bird reserve. Barr Loch is also a nature reserve, and a visitor centre has been built at Muirshiel. By 1996 a consortium of three of the new local authorities managed a new watersports and interpretive centre with a prominent tower, though the ancient castle is still an inaccessible ruin. Meantime by 1999 the old-established firm of Struthers bottled natural mineral water at the Krystal Klear Works, Lochwinnoch.

## LOCKERBIE

**Map 2, B4**

***Dumfriesshire town,*** *pop. 4000* — OS 78: NY 1381

Lockerbie in Annandale lies near the point of convergence of Roman roads; 1.5 km to the west is the site of a Roman camp. The name Lockerbie, first recorded in 1306, derives from a Norse personal name, and about 3 km north-west is tiny Applegarth, on an 8th to 11th century monastic site. By the 15th century the original Castle Milk (OS 85) stood in St Mungo parish 4 km south of the site of Lockerbie, which had a 16th century tower house. It seems that no burgh of barony charter is recorded, nor did Lockerbie appear on Mercator's map of 1595, while Pont's map of the area was lost. In intervals of peace a tryst was held and much business was done with English sheep dealers; the start of the famed Lamb Fair certainly preceded the 18th century. The *King's Arms* claims 17th century origin and a coaching pedigree; the *Blue Bell* is also ancient. Castle Milk was later replaced by a mansion with notable gardens, built for one of the Jardines (of Jardine Mathieson of Hong Kong); through a family removal this gave its name to the vast Glasgow housing scheme of Castlemilk *(q.v.)*. By 1715 there was a post office in Lockerbie.

**Market Tracks and Through Coach**: The Roy map of the 1750s showed Lockerbie as a substantial settlement on the main Carlisle–Glasgow road, on which the Bridge of Milk was already in use. But the road eastwards to Langholm through the rural parish of Tundergarth with its mill was no more than a track, north of which the moorland parish of Hutton & Corrie had no detail. The ways west and north appeared to rely on fording the River Annan or the Dryfe Water; the latter gave its name to Lockerbie's Dryfesdale Parish. From 1781 a diligence ran from London to Glasgow via Carlisle and Lockerbie, and the *Blue Bell Hotel* was established in 1789. By 1797 Lockerbie was a post town and fairs were held as frequently as nine days in the year. In 1799 Heron noted *"the thriving town of Lockerby, containing upwards of 700 inhabitants, and having excellent cattle-markets"*. The emparked Lockerbie House was built 2 km north of the town about 1814.

**Proper Roads and a First Class Station**: The Glasgow–Carlisle road had become impassable by 1814; so under an Act of 1816 it was reconstructed to Telford's specifications, with a width of 5.5 m. In 1827 Chambers remarked that *"for several centuries past Lockerbie has been a lamb and wool market, though not upon the same scale as at present. Lockerbie is a neat cleanly little town, with perhaps 800 inhabitants."* The main line of the Caledonian Railway (CR), which opened from Carlisle to Beattock in 1847 and through to Glasgow in 1848, provided what it called a *'first class station'* close to the town centre, its buildings designed by Andrew Heiton of Perth (most other stations were merely *'second class'*). The railway brought down the price of coal, enabling a gasworks to be established in 1855. A local newspaper, the *Annandale Herald and Record*, was first published in 1862. The next year saw Lockerbie become a minor junction, with the opening of a CR branch line to Dumfries via Lochmaben.

**Industries and Facilities**: In the mid 19th century Hawick and Dumfries could not meet the demand for framework knitting, which briefly flourished in Lockerbie. A tweed factory worked at Sandbed in 1869, and at some time a bobbin mill turned 2 km north on the Dryfe Water. Lockerbie became a police burgh, and its golf club – formed in 1889 – laid out a 9-hole course. By 1894 Murray noted *"a handsome town library"* (later aided by Carnegie) and two hotels, the *King's Arms* and the *Blue Bell*; the August lamb fair was *"the largest in Scotland"*. Lockerbie creamery was opened in 1899 by the Annandale Dairy Company. The Mid-Annandale FC played in the Scottish League for just 3 years, 1923–26. A fairly large Co-op shop was built in 1933; about then the *Rex Cinema* was opened. In the 1930s the LMS-owned hauliers Wordies bought the 18-vehicle Lockerbie business of South Western Transports. Although the importance of the A74 trunk road steadily rose as motor vehicles took over, most development at Lockerbie was slow during the troubled first half of the 20th century.

**Hotel Development – and Bypassed but Busy**: By 1951 the facilities of a typical market town were provided for a population of over 3000, but by 1953 passenger trains on the Lochmaben branch railway had succumbed to buses and cars, and it was closed completely in 1966. Applegarth had little but a primary school, and lost half its population in 30 years. Meantime by 1954 Lockerbie House was a 40-room hotel, and the Dryfesdale manse had become the tiny *Dryfesdale Hotel*, gradually enlarged. By 1963 the small *Queens Hotel* was in business, later being twice extended, and the converted villa of *Somerton House* was a small hotel by 1972, when Lockerbie also sported a small ice rink for curling. The branch railway closure facilitated the building by 1973 of a short western bypass for the growing A74 traffic. The main-line railway was electrified in 1974; the passenger station became the only stop between Carstairs and Carlisle. By 1981 Lockerbie's hotels had grown both in quality and in number from six in the 1950s to ten; the population then and in 1991 was nearly 4000, maintained by dint of quite extensive new housing areas and an influx of retired people. A large Safeway store was built in the 1980s.

**Disasters strike Peaceful Annandale**: It is a remarkable though grisly fact that the two worst transport disasters to have occurred on British soil to date took place in Annandale, within a few kilometres of each other: the Quintinshill troop train crash of 1915 near Gretna, when 227 soldiers died and 246 were injured due to signalmen's carelessness, and the crash at Christmas 1988 of the fuel-laden wings and people-laden fuselage of the sabotaged Pan-American jumbo jet which fell on two streets in Lockerbie; 270 civilian lives were lost, including 11 local residents. Into the 1990s, the fortnightly cattle and sheep market of Harrison & Hetherington was still active; in 1994, due to uncertainty over government plans for the Scottish examination system, Lockerbie Academy decided to become the first school in Scotland to offer pupils the international Baccalaureat. In 1994–95 the A74 between Gretna and Johnstonebridge was converted into a motorway, with major new sections.

**More Golf, Hotels and Boring Buildings, Fewer Shops**: The golf course was enlarged to 18 holes in the 1990s, but the Co-op fell on evil days, becoming a Kwik Save cut-price store before closing in 1997; many other smaller specialist shops had closed and were on the market, making the town look depressed. Nearby were extensive but unattractive Royal Mail facilities, and an ugly modern police station built in the dullest of dark bricks. In 2000 the timber company James Jones proposed a sawmill beside the main line, and Forest Fencing of Stevens Croft aimed to create 100 new jobs over 3 years. Lockerbie Meat Packers' abattoir stands beside (but not using) the railway. There are at least half a dozen small/medium hotels in the town, and the *Rex Cinema/Bingo* continues in business.

## LOGIEALMOND, Harrietfield & Glenalmond — Map 6, A3

***Perthshire localities,*** *pop. 200* — OS 52 or 58: NN 9829

Pont's map made about 1600 showed *'Logie Almont'* as a mansionhouse in wooded policies near Chapelhill, north of the River Almond about 15 km north-west of Perth. Well upstream were mills on the Allt Moulin, and Kerny Mill. Between there and Logie was Millhaugh, whose arch bridge, of a daring 19 m span, was built in 1619; the Roy map of about 1750 showed a track north of the river, linking Buchanty and Redgorton via a mansion at Logiealmond. About then the Earl of Mansfield opened a slate quarry at Craig Lea, at an altitude of about 475 m, above the Milton Burn 6 km north-west of Millhaugh. An independent boys' boarding school called *Trinity College* (generally known as Glenalmond) was founded by Sir William Gladstone in 1841 in a 117 ha estate south of the river. The quarry operation was enlarged in 1865, and by 1869 it was the third largest source of slate in Scotland. Harrietfield, a hamlet with an inn and Logiealmond post office, was developed to house quarry workers on a more sheltered site, 1.5 km west of Millhaugh; but the quarry had closed by 1933. By 1954 a golf course had been created south of the school, which went fully co-educational in 1995. Its 300 pupils aged 12–18 mostly board; it has a 400-seat theatre, indoor swimming pool and dry ski slope. Harrietfield with its pub and post office is connected to the school by a footbridge.

## LOGIERAIT & Ballinluig — Map 6, A2

***Perthshire village,*** *pop. 400* — OS 52 or 53; NN 9752

A stone circle stands beside the River Tummel, 2.5 km above its confluence with the River Tay; there are standing stones and other ancient remains in the area. Two early ferries joined the three adjacent land areas, under the protection of a castle built by King Robert III in the 14th century. The name Logierait derives from the Gaelic *Lag-an-Raith*, *'the hollow of the castle'*, which appeared on Pont's manuscript map of about 1600. The area was Gaelic-speaking until after 1730 when a road from the south was built by General Wade's troops. Roy's 1750s map showed little else of note, though about then a flax heckling centre was set up at Logierait by the Trustees for Manufactures. The Dukes of Atholl held a Court of Regality in the castle until 1748; associated with this was a jail. Both buildings were becoming ruinous in 1803 when Dorothy Wordsworth noted *"Logierait, the village where we dined at a little public house. We had to cross the Tummel by a ferry."* In 1799 Heron too had mentioned Logierait as a *"village"*, and a post office opened there in 1803.

**The North Road, Distilleries, Railways and far-fetched Peat**: The north road was rebuilt under Telford's supervision in the early 19th century, about the time that various small distilleries were built in the area: the two best known are the Ballechin of 1810 some 4 km west of Logierait, which was to use local barley, and the Auchnagie or Tullimet of 1812, 3 km to the east. What soon became the Highland Railway's main line was opened in 1863. The station named Ballinluig *(Balla-na-Luig, G. 'Village of the Hollow')* beside Logierait became a junction when the decorative girder bridges of the Aberfeldy branch railway were completed across the two rivers in 1865. By 1886 both distilleries produced about 85,000 litres of whisky annually and used peat from remote areas, incurring high transport costs: the *"quaint old-fashioned"* Ballechin, though steam-powered, found its peat in Inverness-shire and from the Orkneys; the Duke of Atholl's Auchnagie somehow fetched peat from distant Loch Broom; in 1890 its lease was acquired by John Dewar & Sons of Perth but it was closed in 1911, at a time of shrinking demand for whisky, and little remains. A poorhouse for a *'Union'* of parishes had been built by 1895. The Tummel was bridged by road in 1889, but the Tay was crossed by a chain ferry for many years until eventually a road bridge was built. Ballechin distillery was closed in 1927, but remains as a farm.

**Decline beside the Speedway**: In 1953 Ballinluig had an oil depot, each place had an inn, and there was still a mill. The former poorhouse at Logierait had become an *'institution'* for geriatric patients. The station was closed to passengers by Beeching in 1965 when the Aberfeldy branch was abandoned, and the Tummel railway bridge was then adapted to carry road traffic. A remarkable facility at Ballinluig in 1978 was a Registrar's office. Despite a severe fall in population from nearly 800 in 1951 to under 400 in 1981 – aided by the demolitions needed to squeeze in the rebuilding of the A9 as a fast dual carriageway road – the facilities of a small village persist at Ballinluig; wooden chalets now adjoin the inn at Logierait. Increasing quantities of timber are grown locally. The Edwardian riverside mansion of the 3600 ha Kinnaird estate 2 km south of Logierait is now the small *Kinnaird Hotel.*

## LONGFORGAN — Map 6, B3

***Village, w. of Dundee,** pop. 650* — OS 53: NO 3130

Longforgan in the fertile Carse of Gowrie about 10 km west of Dundee had a thanage from about the 11th century, and became an appendage of the very large 15th century tower originally known as Castle Lyon. This had evidently been renamed Castle Huntly by the time that Pont made his map about 1600, when Longforgan was indicated as a lengthy row of buildings in a thickly settled area. Castle Huntly gave its name to a burgh of barony erected in 1672. Presumably this was sited at the Market Knowe, 500 m north of Longforgan village, for on the Roy map surveyed about 1750 the area's only track *'The Brae Road'* between Dundee and Perth, passed a little to the north of Longforgan. The castle had resumed its early name of Lyon.

**Road and Rail**: Longforgan had an annual fair in 1797, and was given greater accessibility by the construction of the Dundee to Perth turnpike road, and by 1799 had a population of over 600 *(Heron)*. In the early 19th century the mansion of Balruddery House was built 2 km north of the village. In 1845 Longforgan post office was issued with a cancelling stamp, and in 1849 a station was provided 1.5 km south of the village by the Perth & Dundee Railway. Some linen was still woven locally on handlooms as late as 1864, and by 1895 there was an inn. The area remained as part of Perthshire despite its nearness to Dundee.

**Raspberries for Boundary Changes?**: The station was closed to passengers in 1956, and Balruddery House was demolished in 1965. By 1971 the village had been bypassed by a fast dual carriageway (the A85), and Castle Huntly had become the site of a *'Borstal'* establishment, later a *'Young Offenders Institution'*. The Wheatley reforms sensibly placed Longforgan under Dundee from 1975, a change reversed in 1996 by the Major government, though this did not achieve a Tory authority for Perth & Kinross! Meantime the population of the Longforgan area, characterised by intensive raspberry cultivation, rose slowly from 800 in 1951 to 950 in 1981. By 1986 the inn had reopened as a hotel. By 1991 the village population alone was 627. In 1998 major roadworks created an underpass of the A85, a much-needed aid to safety. The impending closure of Castle Huntly – by then a prison – was announced in 2000. There is a bowling green, primary school, post office, and village store; two new housing estates are under construction. The fertile area to the south-west is under the major agribusiness of Broomhall.

## LONGFORMACUS — Map 3, B3

***Small Berwickshire village,** pop. 250* — OS 67: NT 6957

Longformacus, whose name seems to be Brythonic in origin, stands at a height of about 205 m in the upland valley of the Dye Water, a tributary of the Whiteadder, some 10 km north-west of Duns. Pont's map of Berwickshire made around 1600 showed *'Lochyrmacus'* Kirk. The area was well settled; mills turned nearby, and also at Raburne on the Watch Water to the west, near which was the tower of Scarlaw Peel. Five kilometres to the north was another 16th century tower, Cranshaws, with its attendant church and no fewer than three mills. Roy's map made about 1754 gave Longformacus its modern spelling and marked a mill, but only tracks served the area, plus the moorland road which tops 420 m on its way to Gifford, at 20 km the nearest village in Lothian. By 1901 Longformacus had a post and telegraph office; Cranshaws, no longer linked to Longformacus by a direct public road, had a school and post office. Besides its own Longformacus House, the mansion-house of Rathburne stood 1 km west of the village; this later became a hotel. By 1965 the Watchwater Reservoir had been created on the burn 2 km to the west. In 1951 some 320 people lived in and around Longformacus, served by basic facilities, including a primary school which survived a near halving of population to about 180 by 1981; but meantime the *Rathburne Hotel* was enlarged to 19 rooms. Not surprisingly, buses had ceased to serve the area by 1976, when with a mere 250 people in all, both primary schools were marginal operations; only Cranshaws school now survives. By 1998 the Southern Upland Way passed through Longformacus, which still has the use of its post office. A 2001 proposal by Renewable Energy Systems is to erect a 22-turbine wind farm on Black Hill, 4 km east of Longformacus.

## LONGHOPE, Walls & Lyness — Map 13, B3

***Communities, Island of Hoy, Orkney,** pop. 500* — OS 7: ND 3090

The Brims Ness peninsula of the mountainous island of Hoy shelters the waters known as Long Hope and Aith Hope, which almost meet around the west side of the small low-lying farming peninsula of South Walls, with its brochs and standing stone. Pont's map, made about 1592, showed South Walls well settled, with St Colm's Kirk, Snelster, Ayth, Wards and Kirbuster. A pier and the village of Longhope developed on the north shore of South Walls, and to the west was Melsetter House. Martello towers were built in 1812–15 on the eastern ends of both isles to defend the Long Hope anchorage (an offtshoot of the inland sea known as Scapa Flow) against French and American privateers; there was also a battery. Scarcely an essential project here, but militarism drives good sense out of the window!

**Lighthouse and Lifeboat guard the Sunken Fleet**: The lighthouse on Cantick Head, the most south-easterly point of South Walls, was first lit in 1858. In 1874 the Longhope lifeboat station was established on the eastern shore of Brims Ness, well placed on the sheltered Aith Hope to aid vessels in danger in the stormy waters of the Pentland Firth. In 1898 Melsetter House was substantially enlarged in Arts & Crafts style by W R Lethaby, and gained fine gardens. In the 1914–18 war sheltered Scapa Flow became a naval base; the area around the islet of Cava east of Hoy was chosen in 1918 as the anchorage for the captive German High Seas Fleet – which was scuttled there in 1919. The salvage firm Cox & Danks and their successors Metal Industries were based between the wars at the naval wharf at Lyness, 3 km north of the Long Hope, and raised many German wrecks *(see Limekilns & Inverkeithing)*.

**The Navy on Land**: The naval facilities at Lyness and elsewhere, sold off soon after 1919, were hurriedly reinstated in 1938–39 as HMS *Proserpine*: *'Prosser-pyne'* to untutored sailors! They included a naval dockyard, ammunition dumps and 16 oil fuel tanks at Lyness, which was given a cinema of corrugated iron, complete with an art deco brick front! A short causeway called The Ayre was built to connect the two islands, and other camps and fortifications were built around Scapa Flow. In 1951 Longhope had around 280 people and the facilities of a small village, serving over a thousand people by means of passenger ferries which plied to Lyness, Flotta and Graemsay as late as 1974, also linking to Scapa and Stromness. The navy left in 1957; most of their facilities at Lyness were demolished or abandoned, except for oil pumping and storage facilities, a wharf, two piers and a naval cemetery. However, a post office remained nearby, and 2 km to the south was an isolated primary school.

**Disaster strikes Longhope**: Based more on farming than on fishing, the Isle of Hoy suffered extreme depopulation in the second half of the 20th century, aggravated by tragedy in 1969 when the Longhope lifeboat was lost at sea with all eight hands. By 1971 58% of the 1951 population had vanished, but later years saw the stabilisation of Hoy at around 500, half the former population level. By 1976 only the Lyness primary school was open to serve the whole area, but Longhope with its inn (formerly the *Royal Hotel*) offered the other facilities of a small village. In 1977–80 the redundant naval sites were bought by the Orkney Islands Council, which in 1984 began to clear the dereliction, and created a permanent exhibition at the steam-powered oil-pumping station at Lyness. By 1985 a car ferry connected Longhope with the oil terminal island of Flotta and with Stromness. Cantick Head lighthouse was automated in 1991. By 1997 Lyness was the ferry landing point, with a hotel and a passenger ferry to Longhope, whose inn is still open.

*Oil-pumping machinery at Lyness, Hoy, installed in 1938 when Lyness was revived as a naval base. These steam pumps pumped oil from a jetty to storage tanks – working until the 1970s. (JRH)*

## LONGMORN

**Moray small village,** *pop. 250*

**Map 10, A1**
OS 28: NJ 2357

Birnie near the River Lossie, 4 km south of modern Elgin, was a settlement in the 3rd century AD, when a hoard of Roman coins was buried there. A standing stone about 5 km south-east of Birnie church marks the entrance to Rothes Glen. Pont's map made about 1600 showed a *'Miltoun'* in the flattish area around Longmorn, midway between the stone and Elgin, and 3 km east of Birnie Kirk. The latter was emphasised on the Roy map of about 1750, which showed a trackless area. Soon roads were constructed, and in 1861 the Morayshire Railway, later part of the Great North of Scotland, opened a single-track line from Elgin to Rothes, with a station at Longmorn. In 1876 the large Glenlossie distillery was established at Thomshill, 2 km west of Longmorn, by Duff & Co of Elgin. In 1886 this was entirely water-powered, employed twenty workers, and produced 410,000 litres of Highland malt whisky annually; fifty cattle were fed on the draff and spent wash.

**Distilleries Galore see Decline**: By 1901 the Birnie parish school stood south of Thomshill, and there was a post office 1 km south of Longmorn. About 1 km farther south was the Coleburn woollen mill, and near the standing stone was the Coleburn distillery, established in 1896 by John Robertson & Sons of Dundee. The rail-served Longmorn-Glenlivet distillery was set up at Longmorn in 1897; its neighbour the Benriach-Glenlivet also started in 1897, but had scarcely become known when the hard times came, and it was closed from 1903 to 1965! Finally in 1900 the Glen Elgin distillery was established at the hamlet of Fywatt or Fogwatt between Coleburn and Longmorn. Coleburn distillery was sold in 1915, two-thirds to DCL and a third to Walker; it was subsequently managed with Clynelish. By the 1950s Longmorn had a garage and a telephone exchange, but the railway was closed completely in 1968 and soon lifted, the station building being added to the Longmorn distillery. The post office had closed by 1971 and Birnie school closed about the same time; by 1994 it had become a pub!

**Resurgence**: The old Benriach-Glenlivet distillery, which had at last reopened in 1965 under Glenlivet, was doubled in size in 1972–74; the Longmorn-Glenlivet was greatly enlarged at the same time to 8 stills. Yet another distillery, the Mannochmore beside the Glenlossie at Thomshill, was established by DCL in 1971. Although closed for a time from 1983, it was reopened in 1989 by their successors United Distillers (now UDV), who also own Glenlossie, whose malt is dark and sweet. Around

1980 two quarries were opened near Coleburn, that at Gedloch growing rapidly. By 1986 the Millbuies Country Park was open at Fogwatt, which had developed considerably. Coleburn still made a dark strong single malt, matured for 9 years in sherry casks, until the distillery was closed by DCL in 1985. Since 1977 Seagram has owned the Benriach distillery (which almost uniquely retains its own floors for malting), and Longmorn, whose whisky is sold as a single malt; its disused water-wheel still exists.

## LONGNIDDRY

**Map 3, A2**

***E. Lothian village**, pop. 2900* — OS 66: NT 4476

The 16th century courtyard castle known as Redhouse in East Lothian is now ruinous. Pont's map of 1612 showed Longniddry right on the coast, but in fact it is a short way inland. Little seems to have been published about the place prior to the Roy survey of about 1754, by which time there was a complete road system in the area and Longniddry was already a village. In 1827 it was described by Chambers as *"a curious little old-fashioned village, formerly much larger, and the appendage of a baronial mansion-house"*, i.e. a castle town. In 1846 the Haddington branch of the new North British Railway left the main line at Longniddry station; an engine shed was erected there, and in 1894 horse-drawn road coaches connected the station with Aberlady and Gullane. By 1901 a small quarry adjoined the junction, but there had been little other development apart from a post office.

**From Railway Junction to Golfing Suburb**: The well-known 18-hole seaside and parkland golf course on the Wemyss estate seaward of the village was established in 1921–22, and could eventually demand premium fees. By 1951 Longniddry had a population of over 1000 and village facilities, including primary school, garages, bank, an 8-roomed inn, 8 doctors, chemist and a remarkably large telephone exchange with 232 *'connexions'*. The quarry was disused by 1963 and the Haddington branch railway was closed in 1968, while leaving Longniddry station open for local trains. A large dormitory estate was built west of the station in the 1960s and early 1970s. More doctors and dentists practised locally, but little further change was evident to 1991, when the population was about 2900, of well-educated dormitory character; the railway was newly electrified. A further housing estate had been added by 1996, and a cycle route to Haddington had been created along the route of the former branch railway. The Wemyss Estate employs a few dozen locally.

## LONGRIDGE

**Map 16, B4**

***W. Lothian village**, pop. 600* — OS 65: NS 9562

Longridge in West Lothian, which stands at the relatively high altitude of 250m some 2.5km south of Whitburn, and a similar distance from Fauldhouse, has little of historic interest. It escaped the impact of the collieries which affected most of the surrounding area in the 19th and early 20th centuries. By 1899 it had a church, an inn and a post office, and probably also a primary school. These comprised most of the basic facilities still there in the mid 20th century, when the village had a fairly steady population of about 700. This had dropped to 530 by 1991, but by 1998 a small new housing estate had been built, and the post office and primary school survive.

## LONGRIGGEND

**Map 16, B3**

***Lanarkshire village**, pop. 200* — OS 65: NS 8270

Longriggend stands 220m above sea level on a bleak moorland plateau in the east of New Monkland parish, 8km north-east of Airdrie. Isolated *'Langrodge'* was shown by a tiny symbol on Pont's map of 1596. Although the area was rich in coal seams it was apparently still almost deserted when mapped by Roy about 1754, and very little development took place there for another century. The hilly Slamannan Railway was built in 1840, connecting Airdrie with the Union Canal via Longriggend; the line linked with the Monklands system, but due to its gauge of 4'6" (137 cm) did not connect with the standard gauge Edinburgh & Glasgow Railway. It adopted the standard gauge in 1847. Numerous coal pits were opened throughout the area, connected to the railway by a web of mineral lines and adjoined by miners' rows. By 1895 there was a station at Longriggend, which by 1901 had a population of over 1500, a post and telegraph office, and an inn at Avonhead to the west.

**Decline and Fall on Remand Radio**: The passenger trains were withdrawn in 1930, but the local miners' welfare institution also operated as a cinema up to about 1950. Eventually the coal seams became exhausted, and by 1954 all the pits and associated mineral railways had gone, leaving only scattered bings. Avonhead's rows and inn had vanished too, but a tuberculosis sanatorium had been built in a small valley 2km north-west of Longriggend; by 1971 this had become the Uppertown Remand Institution (URI). Peat was extracted south of the hamlet from the 1950s to around 1980, served by two short narrow-gauge tramways. The primary school and post office were closed in the early 1970s, and by 1981 the total population was under 600, of whom most were inmates of the URI, which was expanded for a time, and gained the only AM radio station in a Scottish prison, but even the telephone call box in the one-time village vanished in the 1980s, and with the planned closure of the remand centre in April 2000, only a small hamlet would be left.

## LONGSIDE

**Map 10, C2**

***Buchan village**, pop. 700* — OS 30: NK 0347

Timothy Pont's map of Buchan made about 1601 included *'Langsyid'*, the *'Mill of Keirnga'* and *'Tifry Mill'*, which stood on the Burn of Ludquharn (or Cairngall) in the low-lying area beside the South Ugie Water, about 10km west of Peterhead. Longside became a parish in 1620, and ran a village school by 1626, but when Roy mapped the area in the 1750s, Longside Kirk and Cairngall apparently stood almost alone, with the *'Mill of Taffery'* to the south. About 2km to the north on the North Ugie Water were the Mill and Bridge of Rora, probably the same that Pratt a century later called *"the old crooked bridge of Auchlee"*. The area was apparently trackless.

**Granite, Cloth and Whisky**: When a road was built past the church, it linked Peterhead and Old Deer. Longside had three fairs in 1797, and the Cairngall granite quarry was open 1km to the east by 1799, but the new village proposed at Longside in 1801 by James Ferguson of Pitfour was no more than a pleasant rebuild. In the early 19th century Kilgours had a large water-powered *"cloth manufactory"* at Auchlee, below what was probably an earlier lint mill, its wheels fed from an artificial

*The peat railway at Longriggend, which worked from the 1950s until about 1980. This was one of a number of such operations in central Scotland producing peat litter from raised bogs.* *(RCAHMS / JRH)*

loch. Kilgours closed in 1828 and the machinery was sold. About 1 km west of the kirk Pratt noted in 1858 *"Glenugie, where there was formerly a distillery of some note, now gone to decay"* (but see Boddam).

**Granite for Engineering, Grand Buildings and Memorials**: Cairngall's rock being closer-grained and harder than Aberdeen granite, the quarry was opened out in 1808 to provide the huge blocks for the foundations of Stevenson's Bell Rock lighthouse. Worked for many years by Hutchison of Monyruy, it also provided stone for the foundations of the early 19th century London Bridge, and columns in Covent Garden Market and St George's Hall Liverpool. Between 1840 and 1860 the quarry supplied stone for pier-walls in the Palace of Westminster. By 1858 it was worked by Macdonald & Leslie. Of the three old corn mills, only Cairngall still worked at that time. Despite losing its other industries, prosperity had come to Longside, and due to the growing population a new parish church was built in 1835; the first Longside post office appeared between 1838 and 1858. In the latter year Pratt wrote of *"the thriving village of Longside"*, which had two inns and *"several good shops"*. In 1862 Longside acquired a station on the new Peterhead branch of the Great North of Scotland Railway (GNSR). In 1869 Cairngall quarry was leased by Alex Macdonald, Field & Co, continuing to produce a fine-grained granite for polishing and ornamental work, including Prince Albert's sarcophagus. By 1894 there was an episcopal church.

**Pigs Lumber into the Air**: The short-lived Royal Naval Airship station *(illustrated by Hay & Stell)*, sited in a sheltered hollow at Lenabo some 5 km south of Longside, was built in 1915–16 for rigid and non-rigid airships, with three great sheds of which the largest was 213 m long. A lengthy siding was laid from the GNSR, which during its five years of existence to 1920 brought in some 32,000 tonnes of materials – hardly lighter than air, but then the locals called the airships *'Lenabo Pigs'*! In the 1939–45 war an airfield was built near Thunderton, 4 km east of the village, but like Lenabo had only a short life. Longside had over 700 people by the 1950s, but the railway station was closed by Beeching in 1965, the line was closed completely in 1970, and the population had declined to only 600 in 1971. Many other facilities had been lost by 1981 including the secondary school, chemist, a bank and post town status, but those of an average village remained. Since 1971 there had been some compensatory population growth, no doubt due to Peterhead's oil-based expansion. By 1986 the quarry was disused, but an 18-hole golf course had been laid out. The village population was 702 in 1991; there has been little recent change of significance.

## LONMAY

**Map 10, C1**

***Buchan hamlet**, pop. 1130 (area)*

OS 30: NK 0158

About 10 km south of Fraserburgh is the isolated Mormond Hill, east of which are stone circles and the low-lying parish of Lonmay, which had a school by 1613. Robert Gordon's map of about 1640 showed a lack of settlement in the area south of Rathen, as did Roy's map of about 1750, which did mark a track joining Fraserburgh and Old Deer. However, by then several mills stood beside the burns flowing into what was to become the Loch of Strathbeg: from north to south the Mills of *Elich, Saach*, and *Logy*, with a mansionhouse; to the east was the hamlet of Millhill. Later the area was improved for farming, opened up by a network of roads, and the neo-classical mansion of Crimonmogate was built in 1825 to designs by Archibald Simpson of Aberdeen. A post office was open by 1858 at Cortes, where the turnpike road south from Fraserburgh forked to Peterhead and Mintlaw.

**Railway Interlude, Decline and Closures**: The Great North of Scotland Railway's Fraserburgh branch was opened in 1865; Lonmay station was sited near Spillarsford where the line crossed the Rathen–Peterhead turnpike road, and the post and telegraph office was moved there. But most development in 1894 was 3 km farther east around Lonmay Kirk (now marked by cemeteries), the Crofts of Savoch, and Crimonmogate in its large policies. By 1951, with 1716 people in the parish, there was an inn near the station, and Lonmay post office had become a post town, with a service hamlet at the focus of a rural area some 10km in diameter, including Crimond and New Leeds. Secondary classes were still held in the 1950s in the schools at Lonmay Kirkton and Rathen, but were soon closed. The station was closed to passengers by Beeching in 1965 and the line, by then freight-only, was abandoned in 1979. Post town status had already been withdrawn, and North Sea oil developments around Buchan did not aid Lonmay. The inn (now a hotel) at the station site was optimistically named the *'Ban-Car'*! The growth of Crimond into a significant village ended Lonmay's central role, the very scattered population of the parish was down to only 1130 in 1991, and the formerly significant post office has vanished.

## LOSSIEMOUTH

**Map 10, A1**

***Moray town,*** *pop. 7200*

OS 28: NJ 2370

The Kirk of Kinnedar or Drainie and the hamlet of Stotfold pre-dated the port of Lossiemouth, whose site was blank on Pont's map of central Moray, made about 1600. In 1698 the inland Royal Burgh of Elgin superseded old Covesea *(q.v.)* by building a quay, sheltered by a promontory on the outside of a sharp bend in the River Lossie where it entered the Moray Firth. The Roy map of about 1750 sketched only 8 buildings at roadless *Lossie Mouth*, which became known as Seatown. By 1780 grain was shipped to brewers in central Scotland, and a breakwater was needed; but silting remained a problem, and any fishing was from tiny boats. Heron wrote in 1799 only that *"the village of Lossiemouth possesses some coasting trade"*.

**Branderburgh and the Railway**: Herring fishing became worthwhile from 1819 when local fish-curing was started. To further it, in 1830–39 Colonel Brander of Pitgaveny House near Spynie Palace built a large new harbour and planned village (called *Branderburgh*, after its promoter) on the promontory within a few hundred metres of Seatown; by 1840, 45 fishing boats were based there. A post office was open by 1838, and the straight and level line to Elgin, built by the Morayshire Railway (at first isolated, but later part of the Great North of Scotland) opened in 1852, together with the *Steamboat & Railway Hotel*. For a time Wordie & Co operated a rail to road cartage depot. A lifeboat station was opened in 1859, and by 1879 an innovative boatyard was in operation.

**Fishing Port, Premier's Home and Resort**: The Moray golf club was founded in 1889, Tom Morris laying out an 18-hole links course. By then the various settlements had merged to become a substantial fishing port, with a population of 3500 in 1891. Lossiemouth was made a police burgh in 1892; the harbour was deepened in 1893–94, by which time the little-known Spynie Canal had been dug from Seatown to drain Spynie Loch. But in 1894 Murray frankly noted the only inn, the *Station Hotel*, as *"poor"*. James Ramsay Macdonald, a labourer's son born in Lossiemouth in 1866, became an instigator of the Labour Party in 1900, and was later their first and controversial prime minister. Library facilities began after 1901, with Carnegie assistance. A small electric power station was built in 1913, and there was also a coastguard station, though the lifeboat station was closed in 1923. In time tennis and bowling were catered for, and Lossiemouth was described by the AA in their 1938 Road Book as *"a well-known resort, with good sands and bathing"*.

**Airbases and more Golf**: An airfield was built 3km west of the town in 1936 as an RAF flying training school; it passed to the Fleet Air Arm in 1946, and was developed by them and later by the RAF into a major base from which Shackleton aircraft operated on search, rescue and early warning roles from 1951 (until their replacement in 1991). There was also an airfield at Milltown, 6km to the south-east, but it was disused by the 1980s. By 1953 Lossiemouth with a population of some 5750 had four small hotels. By then an additional 9-hole golf course was open, enlarged to 18 holes in 1979 to plans by Henry Cotton. The railway closed to passengers in 1964 and to freight in 1966. The small-town facilities in the 1970s included a cinema and a fisheries museum; Campbell's boatyard – where the first modern seine netter was built – still worked, and a housing estate and the new Lossiemouth High School were built south of the town.

**Fishing, Tourism and Pilot Training**: Lossiemouth joined Moray District in 1975. Its population was nearing 7000 by 1981, with seven hotels and two caravan and camping sites; the dry, sunny micro-climate and the sandy beaches retain a holiday trade for the area. In the mid 1980s about 15 boats were still fishing for prawns and white fish, and there was a daily fish market. The Moray Golf Club was the centre for the Northern Open Championship in 1989 and 1991. Nearly 7200 people lived in Lossiemouth in 1991. *'Tornado'* pilot training was soon moved from Suffolk to RAF Lossiemouth, where *'Buccaneers'* were based in 1992. In 1993 RAF Lossiemouth existed to strike a potential enemy; its training role also embraced Jaguars, and Sea King Search and Rescue helicopters were based there. From 2000 its total workforce was about 2500, due to transfers from closed bases in Germany. By 1994 the caravan site at Seatown had closed. The local voluntary museum in its former net loft focuses on fishing, which has declined further in recent years. The railway station site has become an ultra-tidy seafront park, and the *Stotfield Hotel* has 45 rooms. The spacious planned layouts and neat two-storey houses give these places a clean freshness.

## LUGTON, Giffen & Waterland

**Map 1, C1**

***Ayrshire hamlets,*** *pop. 420*

OS 64: NS 4152

Pont's map of Cunninghame, probably made around 1604–08, showed Waterland and its mill near the head of the Lugton Water, 4km north of Dunlop. This forms a natural routeway between Kilmarnock and Glasgow, rising near *'Hall'* on map 15 in this volume. Roy's map made about 1754 showed a road from Beith to Neilston, but little settlement. In the early 19th century a small limestone quarry and limekilns were developed. Lugton station on the Glasgow, Barrhead & Kilmarnock Joint Railway was located 1km north-east of the mill where five roads met. Opened in 1871, in 1873 it became the junction for the Beith branch. By 1895 a church and an inn had appeared there, but little else. The Lanarkshire & Ayrshire Railway (a Caledonian protégé) was built westwards from Barrmill (OS 63) on the Beith branch to Ardrossan and opened in 1888; a further section of this railway between Lugton and Cathcart via Neilston High opened in 1903. However, a post office was open by 1951, when the hamlet of Lugton and scattered farms had a population of 340.

**Retrenchment**: The railways between Lugton and Neilston High, and Barrmill and Beith, were abandoned in 1964, and Lugton lost its passenger trains at the same time; by 1971 all that remained was a freight branch to Giffen RNAD at Whitespot, 3 km beyond Barrmill. The first quarry was inactive by 1963, though another had been opened 2 km west of the junction; the limekilns were derelict by 1976, and by 1985 the second quarry was inactive. The *Paraffin Lamp Roadhouse* was open as a hotel by 1980; in 1981 the local population was about 420. Although a new hotel was open at Burnhouse (OS 63), 4 km south-west, Lugton post office had closed by 1987. In 1992 William Clegg had a contractors' siding, and palletised fertilisers still arrived at Lugton by rail from England. The impending closure of the Royal Naval Armaments Depot (RNAD) at Giffen was announced in 1994, with the loss of 128 jobs. There has been little other recent significant change.

## LUING, Isle of — Map 4, C3

***Island, west coast of Argyll,*** *pop. 175* — OS 55: NM 7408

Iron Age forts adorn the relatively low but hard-rock Isle of Luing, which belonged to the Earl of Argyll in 1549, when Monro found it *"good for store and corn, with a haven sufficient for Highland galleys"* and a parish church, probably that at Kilchattan near Toberonochy, now a ruin bearing a carving of a galley. Slate was formerly quarried there, but in greater quantities at Port Mary north of Cullipool, where at one time 170 men hewed and split 700,000 slates a year: in 1891 there were 632 islanders, but decline was imminent. Fladda lighthouse on an islet in the Sound of Luing 2 km west of Cullipool was first lit in 1860 (it was among the earliest to be automated, in 1956). By the 1950s most of Luing's remaining 170 people lived on the coast in the two former quarrymen's villages, Cullipool and Toberonochy, both with marginal post offices. A free County Council passenger ferry (by 1956 vehicular) linked Luing to the mainland across Cuan Sound. Cullipool slate quarries closed in 1965, and the North Luing school at Cullipool was no longer open by 1976, though due to some local development its post office stayed open after that at Toberonochy closed, pre-1996. In 1991 the isle had 179 residents. The ferry boat, 25 years old in 1999, was unusual in that it carried the island's water supplies, sourced from Oban. Achafolla watermill, complete with its machinery, stands ruinous near the remaining primary school at the centre of the island. Many lobsters are farmed near Cullipool; otherwise Luing remains dedicated to agriculture.

## LUMPHANAN — Map 10, B3

***Small Aberdeenshire village,*** *pop. 500* — OS 37: NJ 5804

Lumphanan, among the Deeside hills some 16 km north-west of Banchory, was first noted in 1057 when King Macbeth, the last Scoto-Pictish monarch, was slain nearby. The huge earthen ring-work known as the Peel of Lumphanan was possibly raised in the 12th century, though the site plaque attributes it to 1228 under the Durwards of Coull Castle. The stronghold was still in use when Edward I of England visited it in 1296, but was soon abandoned. In the 16th century two stone castles were erected: Auchinhove, which stood near a mill some 2 km west of the peel but soon fell into ruin, and the tower of Corse, 4 km to the north-west, near which was built a mansionhouse. Lumphanan was apparently never a burgh of barony, being shown as a tiny place on Gordon's map of about 1640. Roy's map, made about 1750, showed only the Kirk and a north–south track from the Mill of Dess past the mansionhouse of Auchlossan to Alford; a later road connected south-east to Torphins.

**The Deeside Railway creates a Village**: In 1859 the Deeside Railway was extended on a circuitous route from Banchory to Aboyne to serve stations at Torphins and Lumphanan, with steep climbs over the hills. By 1891 a post and telegraph office, inn and smithy were open close to the station, round which a village was developing; a parish hall was built in 1897. In 1951 with a parish population of 831, Lumphanan rather surprisingly possessed a cinema, a 9-hole golf course and an oil depot. Secondary school classes were held locally and at O'Neil Corse, 6 km to the north-west, by which time the *House of Corse* was an inn. Freight trains were withdrawn in 1964 and the railway was closed in 1966. Both the secondary schools, the golf course and the cinema were also lost as the parish population shrank to only 600 in 1971; quiet Lumphanan continued to depend for several services on Torphins. In 1991, after 20 years of minor developments related to oil and the growth of Aberdeen, 1052 people lived in the parish; but the village still had fewer than 500 residents. However, by 1995 small housing estates had been built across and north of the station site. Lumphanan now has a modern primary school, two shops, post office and the modest *Macbeth Arms Hotel*; a tiny hostel for backpackers is open at Tornaveen, 3 km east, and sheepskins are tanned at O'Neil Corse, 5 km north.

## LUMSDEN — Map 10, A3

***Aberdeenshire village,*** *pop. 700 (area)* — OS 37: NJ 4722

The great stone castle of Kildrummy – which stands beside a gorge on a small tributary of the River Don 12 km west of Alford – was perhaps begun in the early 13th century by the Bishop of Caithness. It was certainly completed by the Earl of Mar, whose main centre it became. Kildrummy was the refuge for Robert Bruce's queen in 1306–07, being strengthened before resisting a siege by Edward I's forces. But Barbour wrote that once its thick timber floor was set alight by a traitor *"the flame spread all over the castle so that no power of man could master it"*. Following its capture, a quarter of the building was destroyed and the garrison slaughtered by the dying Edward. The castle was repaired, and featured on the contemporary Gough map. Kildrummy Kirk stands 1 km to the north and retains many original fittings.

**An Informal Burgh**: Lumsden, a previously little developed but scenically attractive area in Auchindoir parish 4 km north of Kildrummy Kirk, was a nominal burgh of barony from 1509, but did not appear on the Gordon map around 1642. The Earl of Mar organised the 1715 rebellion, so his great Kildrummy castle was slighted and became an impressive ruin. The Roy map made about 1750 showed its water mill, in the area now called Milltown of Kildrummy; the mill was rebuilt in 1762. A nearby track linked Aberdeen and Corgarff, and another from Alford Kirk to Kildrummy crossed the River Don to Invermossat, the probable site of a ferry known as Boat of Forbes, where a post office was open by 1838. In 1825 Lumsden was re-founded as a new village. Building continued until at least 1840, although there was no post office until after 1838. Lumsden remained remote from railways, and Murray found nothing remarkable there in 1894. In 1901 Auchindoir parish had 1200 residents, but only 770 by 1951.

**Scottish Sculptors Congregate**: By 1951 Lumsden had typical small-village facilities, plus a chemist and a tiny secondary school. An early youth hostel was still in use in 1967. All three of these facilities subsequently closed, with steady depopulation to only 500 in 1971. Kildrummy mill was abandoned about 1970, but by 1977 the country house that had replaced the adjacent castle had been converted into the *Kildrummy Castle Hotel*. Lumsden survived as a small village, with an inn, a haulier's business and minuscule tourist trade. Unusually for so remote a place, in 1986 a group of 17 flats was built by a housing association, and by 1991 Auchindoir parish had recovered to 697 residents. By 1992 the Scottish Sculpture Workshop at the pleasant village of Lumsden was a mecca for working sculptors, and a Sculpture Walk near the primary school now features as a tourist attraction. Hotels include the *Lumsden Arms* and the *Kildrummy Castle*.

## LUNCARTY

**Map 6, A3**

***Perthshire village,*** *pop. 1200 (area)* — OS 53: NO 0929

Standing stones adjoin the confluence of the Shochie Burn with the River Tay some 7km north of Perth; 3km west is the kirk of rural Moneydie parish. Roy's map surveyed about 1750 showed only one house at nearby Luncarty on the main road to the north, where an enormous and long-lasting linen bleachfield was founded in 1752 by William Sandeman. The works was enlarged in stages, becoming the largest in Scotland by 1760, when 330,000 metres of cloth were processed. By the 1790s over 300 people were regularly employed, and in 1794 the great bleachworks treated about 600,000m of linens. By 1811 there was a ferry across the Tay to Stormontfield, confirming that Luncarty bleachfield drew its labour from miles around, for no substantial village appeared, and there was no post office until after 1838.

**The Railway Comes – and the Trains Pass By**: A station was provided when the main line of the Scottish Midland Junction Railway was opened from Perth to Forfar in 1848. In 1864 under Marshall, Sandeman & Co, the bleachfield was still *"very large and prosperous"*. By 1895 a school and post office were open at Redgorton a little to the south; nearby was the mansionhouse of Battleby. Strathord Station near the Ordie Mill 1.5km north of Luncarty was already open by 1895 and became the junction for the Bankfoot branch, opened in 1906. At that time the mill made shuttles, and the dyeing business continued. But from 1931 the branch had no passenger trains, by 1953 the stations had been closed, and the branch was abandoned in 1964; in that year the ferry also ceased to ply.

**Caring for the Countryside**: About 1970 the new Countryside Commission for Scotland (CCS) made their headquarters at Battleby House. Luncarty was then considerably expanded with bungalow estates. In the early 1980s the winding A9 was replaced piecemeal by a new road, the section south of Luncarty being dual carriageway. Although by 1981 the local population had risen to some 875, its facilities remained those of a mere hamlet. In 1983 James Burt-Marshall Ltd were still in the dyeing trade; extensive sand workings had been opened north-east of the village. By 1991 the population of this youngish well-educated dormitory was nearing 1200. In 1992 Scottish Natural Heritage, the government's new watchdog body for the outdoor environment, was formed by the merger of the CCS with the Nature Conservancy Council for Scotland; the HQ initially remained split between Battleby and Edinburgh. The bleachworks owners, by then Whitecroft, announced its closure in 1996; 97 jobs were lost and the buildings – the last remnants of central Perthshire's once-great bleaching industry – were speedily demolished.

## LUSS

**Map 5, B4**

***Village, w. of L. Lomond,*** *pop. 250* — OS 56: NS 3693

Inchtavannach *('Isle of Monks')* in Loch Lomond contains a Dark Age monastic site connected with St Kessog, who lived in the area around 500 AD. By 1315 there was a church dedicated to Kessog at Luss, on the west side of the loch 20km north of Dumbarton; its Gaelic name can simply mean *'plant'*, but it is supposed to relate here to the wild iris, as in *Fleur de Lys*. In the 16th century the tower of Inchgalbraith was built on a tiny islet near Inchtavannach, and a tower house known as Rossdhu Castle was built on a promontory 4km south of Luss for the local lairds, already Colquhouns (pronounced *Cahoon*). Luss was for long a tiny place, as indicated by Timothy Pont's map of about 1600, but it became a burgh of barony in 1642 and was shown on the Roy map of about 1750 as a group of houses on the new military road to Inveraray, which had been built by Caulfeild's troops in 1746–50. From about 1750 Luss had a post office, and Pennant in 1769 found *"a little village with a tolerable inn"*. Some local people already spoke English by 1612, as shown by a local inscription, but Gaelic was still the common tongue in 1769.

**Slate – and Thatched Houses**: About 1775 Rossdhu castle was rebuilt as Rossdhu House. Two fairs were scheduled to be held in 1797, and two years later Heron wrote *"above the village of Luss, noted more for the longevity than for the number of its inhabitants, there are two slate-quarries; in it there is a cotton-work, on a small scale"*. A new post office opened in 1801. The impressionable Dorothy Wordsworth admired the beauty of the surroundings, and noted that the people wore Highland dress. She was offered thread to buy, noted boats on the loch but found slow service and was ill-fed at *"a nice-looking white house, clean for a Scotch inn; the village a cluster of thatched houses without windows, the smoke coming out of the open window-places":* the slate was strictly for export, and slovenliness and dirt were general. No doubt the people were too overworked and underpaid to pull themselves up to the standards of the leisured Miss Wordsworth!

**Rebuilding and Tourism**: Many visitors followed in her footsteps, and the Colquhouns invested in better tenant housing, for in 1826 Chambers found Luss *"a delightful little village much resorted to in summer"*. By then a ferry plied between Rowardennan and Inverbeg, 5km north of Luss. In 1869 a wharf was built to ship the slates which were still being quarried on a large scale above Camstradden House. The Colquhouns built a new church in 1875, and Luss was called a *"pretty village"* in 1886, when its steamer pier was served by Loch Lomond paddlers. The *"plain" Colquhoun Arms Hotel* was noted by Murray in 1894. The slate quarries were in decline at that time, and employed only five men; they later closed, but another quarry was open at Auchengavin by 1954. By then a small hotel and a youth hostel were open at Inverbeg; later it gained a caravan site, but its youth hostel closed in the 1990s. The pier, closed to steamers about then, was reopened in 1980. The ferry was still running in 1954, but by 1991 plied in summer only.

**Television, Championship Golf – and a move to Argyll**: The A82 trunk road traffic was removed about a hundred metres to the west when Luss was bypassed about 1990. It remains a small attractive village of under 250 people, adopted as the pleasing backdrop to the Scottish Television (STV) soap opera *'(Take the) High Road'*. The Loch Lomond Golf Course at Rossdhu, of championship standard, was planned by Stirling Investments – of Middlesex! Designed by Tom Weiskopf, the 1973 Open champion – *"my finest work"* – it was begun in 1990 and after a change of ownership was bought in 1994 by American Lyn Anderson, who converted Rossdhu House and its outbuildings into the clubhouse and planned to add a second course. In 1996 Luss – which has a post office, visitor centre and campsite – was removed from industrial Dunbartonshire and became part of the vast rural Argyll & Bute authority. Hotels include the modern waterside *Lodge on Loch Lomond*, the old *Inverbeg Inn*, and the long-established *Colquhoun Arms*.

## LYBSTER — Map 13, B5

***Caithness E. coast village,** pop. 700* — OS 11: ND 2436

Many vestiges of ancient settlement surround Lybster on the coast of Caithness 20 km south-west of Wick; it was possibly the settlement of the Lugi tribe noted by Ptolemy in the second century, though the present form of its name is Norse. It long remained insignificant according to Pont's map of around 1600. Lybster House was marked on the Roy map of about 1750, when it stood inland of the coastal track, along which sprawled numerous crofts. In 1790 a flight of 300 stone steps was built down a steep cliff face 9 km north-east of Lybster to give access to the natural harbour of Whaligoe; a fishing hamlet grew on the cliff top. In 1793 fishing from Lybster Bay was promoted by Sir John Sinclair, author of the *First Statistical Account of Scotland*. In 1797 the oddly named *Poakmast*, at or near Occumster, was a coaching stage on the inadequate road.

**Herring and Lobsters from Lybster**: Lybster's village street was laid out in 1802 on a spur high above the shore, evidently with husbandry also in mind; a wooden pier was constructed in 1810. The road from the south was being made up for coaches when the first bridge over the Reisgill Burn was built for the Commissioners in 1815. A coaching inn was erected, and a post office opened around 1825. The first stone harbour, built at the mouth of the burn about 1830–33, was enlarged and altered in 1849–57 (and again in 1882) *(see Hay & Stell)*; herring and lobsters proved good catches. In the mid 19th century over 200 fishermen lived in Lybster, which became a centre for local services but was never a burgh. The overfished shoals of herring vanished from the area in 1882, and the number of boats began to shrink. The coaching inn – which became the *Portland Arms Hotel* – was still functioning in 1894, when Lybster had 50 boats and was still regarded as a herring-fishing village; but only 3 boats remained by 1913.

**Light Railway, Light House, and Golf Problems**: A light railway was opened in 1903, built from Wick to Lybster with War Office aid as a coast defence measure, the last and most marginal expansion by the Highland Railway. It also had stations at Occumster and Ulbster, but lasted only until closure in 1944, though in 1946 Wordie & Co still used their small ex-rail cartage depot. The lighthouse on Clyth Ness, 5 km east of Lybster, was first lit in 1916 to aid naval vessels on passage between Invergordon and Scapa; it was automated in 1964. Lybster golf club was founded in 1926 and laid out a 9-hole moorland course, which later adopted the abandoned station building as its clubhouse. In 1951 Lybster had nearly 900 people. With a subsequent fall in the local population, the golf course was closed for a time. Lybster also lost its secondary school, and gaps appeared in its one street. Lybster still boasted a dozen shops in 1978, and a small pottery had opened in the former school. In 1984 a new quay was built, and the fishing then revived to around a dozen boats; three hotels and some local craftspeople catered for the tourist, and by then the golf course was open again. In 1991 there were 677 people and an average village level of facilities. The Whaligoe steps were rebuilt in 1992 by the Wick Civic Society with aid from Shell. By 1996 only a few lobsters were caught from Lybster, where a museum collection is now being built up. D Gow and Sons are steel and pipework fabricators, and tasty Lybster cheese is made locally. The fine old *Portland Arms Hotel* has 22 rooms, and offers free access to the 9-hole golf course.

## LYNE — Map 2, C2

***Hamlet w. of Peebles,** pop. under 50* — OS 72/73: NT 2040

Several ancient hill forts surround a group of standing stones at the confluence of the Lyne Water with the River Tweed, some 5 km west of Peebles. These strong points may explain why the Roman invaders built their own 1st century fort farther up the Tweed at Easter Happrew, in turn replaced in the 2nd century by one at Lyne. This lay on a new road, built to link the fort near Melrose with Castledykes. Since the Romans left, the area has remained pastoral. A parish school was opened in 1600, and from 1614 there was another at Brig of Lyne. Lyne's tiny 17th century parish church has notable interior features. The Roy map of about 1754 marked a road from Peebles leading up the Lyne valley, and a track to Stobo (now B712). In 1864 the Caledonian Railway's branch line from Symington opened to Peebles, with a station named Lyne; but apart from a mill there was little near it in 1901, when the parish held only 98 people. Passenger trains had gone by 1953 and the whole line had vanished by 1963; about then the school also closed. The 1971 population of Lyne parish was 40, and so little development has occurred since that it no longer appears in the census volume *'Index of Populated Areas'*!

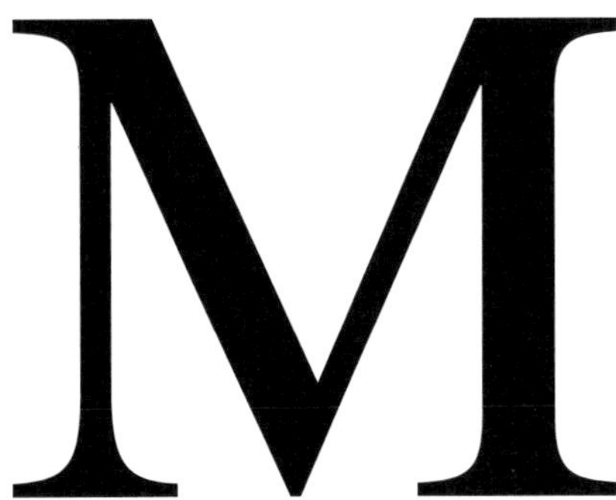

## MACDUFF

**Map 10, B1**

***Banff* coastal town,** *pop. 3900*

OS 29: NJ 7064

A standing stone – the remains of a *'cairn circle'* beside the River Deveron 1.5 km south-east of Banff, may mark the centre of the thanage of Glendowachy, which was established about the 11th century and became a corn-growing estate. Kirkside, 1 km west of the circle, was presumably the location of the first church. In 1528 a small fishing village about 2 km seaward of the circle was chartered to the Earl of Buchan as a burgh of barony under the name of Down (pronounced *Doon*). Pont's map made about 1600 named *'Doun'* in capitals and indicated a substantial settlement on the site of today's Macduff. The barony changed hands in 1733. The fair copy of Roy's survey of about 1750 showed a trackless area east of the Deveron *'Boat'* at Kirkside. There were at that time 400 people and seven boats at Down, then a single row of buildings; at Tarlair cove to the east were a few more.

**Harbour, Name Change and Spa potential**: The construction of a harbour was begun in the 1760s, and the services of a ship's carpenter were soon available. A mineral spring was found at Tarlair in 1770; when eventually roads were built this helped to make the village a minor spa resort, despite its northerly aspect. A new settlement laid out in the late 18th century at Longmanhill, 4 km to the south-east, remained just a hamlet. In 1783 it was rechartered with a market as *Macduff*, its owner Lord Fife's family name being Duff. Heron in 1799 described it as *"a farming and fishing town belonging wholly to Earl Fife, who was also at the expense of forming a harbour and building a pier"*. Macduff became a herring fishing port, with a fish curing enterprise from 1815; by 1819 Lord Fife had begun work on a new pier.

**Roads and Baltic Trade**: In 1821 the town council contributed to the cost of building the coastal turnpike road to Fraserburgh. Chambers wrote of Macduff in the 1820s as a *"modern village and sea-port; the harbour being better than that of Banff, has much more trade, possessing upwards of a dozen vessels which trade with London and the Baltic, besides innumerable fishing-boats. The town contains about 1400 inhabitants."* Trade being so important and the welfare state undreamed of in 1847, meal was being shipped out of Macduff by schooner to the south, rather than westwards to feed the many Highlanders who were starving. The market had been abandoned before 1850, yet Pratt described Macduff in 1858 as *"a thriving seaport town, rapidly increasing in extent and commercial enterprise, much frequented by sea-bathers during the summer"*. About 4 km east of the town was the Melrose slate quarry, but this enterprise was evidently not as durable as the material, and seems to have failed.

**The Railway Period**: In 1860 the Banff, Macduff & Turriff Junction Railway reached a temporary station (named Banff & Macduff) at Gellyhill, high above the town, and was extended round the hillside to Banff Bridge and Macduff proper in 1872; for a time Wordie & Co ran a small rail to road cartage depot. Macduff harbour was enlarged from 1877 and effectively replaced Banff as the local fishing port, with 109 boats by 1881. The Town Hall was built in 1884, and by 1894 Murray noted the *Fife Arms* as a *"good"* hotel. The 1901 population was 3400. Unlike many herring ports Macduff continued as such after the 1914–18 war, and developed further as a resort. The Tarlair golf club's 18-hole course on the cliff-tops east of the town opened in 1926, later being patronised by royalty and renamed Royal Tarlair. The sea-level open-air swimming pool in a niche below the cliffs at Tarlair was opened in 1931. By 1951 Macduff had 3300 people and the facilities of a large village, and three small hotels. Passenger trains were withdrawn in 1951 and railway goods traffic ended in 1961.

**Enter Whisky: Fishing Thrives**: Macduff Highland malt distillery was built in 1962–63 by William Lawson; by 1968 it had been extended twice. In 1990 its Glendeveron Single Malt was said to vary in flavour with the cask. Meantime the harbour was rebuilt in 1965, when there were 36 fishing vessels. Macduff was growing, with eight hotels in 1980, all quite small, and by 1985 a caravan site. In 1988 it had Customs facilities, a modern fish market, and a covered boatyard still constructing wooden fishing vessels; the Seaway Net Company still made fishing nets by hand in the old railway station. In 1990 it was claimed that, due to the general lack of orders, the Macduff boatyard was one of only three still building fishing vessels in Scotland. In 1991 the population was 3900.

**Was *Beryl* to be the Last Wooden Fishing Boat?**: Despite a chronic dearth of orders due to denial of EU aid by the Tory government, in 1995 Macduff Shipyard built the wooden fishing vessel *Beryl* for John Mitchell, to fish for cod, haddock and monkfish in the North Sea. Traditional oak and larch timbers were selected by its director Bill Farquhar, who was then the Chairman of the British Boatbuilding Association. The boatyard is still busy with repairs and there are ships' chandlers, an ice factory, several fish and shellfish merchants, marine and general engineers and *Cummins* diesel services. A score of medium-sized fishing vessels can be seen in port on a Sunday.

New features created in the 1990s are the Macduff Marine Aquarium and the adjacent base for an inshore rescue boat. A good range of shops and services is available, with bus depot, plus the *Highland Haven Hotel* with 30 rooms. East of Tarlair is a quarry.

## MACHRIHANISH & Drumlemble — Map 1, A2

***Kintyre small villages,*** *pop. 600* — OS 68: NR 6320

Near the exposed west coast of Kintyre lies the isolated Machrihanish coalfield, whose main seam in the Limestone Coal Group was nearly 4m thick. A mine was open from 1498, the coal being used for salt panning – hence the alternative name *Mary Pans*, which appeared as a small settlement on Roy's map of about 1750, when a *'coalhill'* was indicated south of another settlement at Drumlemble, 3km farther east. A mill turned at the mouth of the Lossit Burn, and tracks connected with Campbeltown and Tarbert. Shallow mining continued until the early 18th century; after a break, a deeper mine was opened. In 1785 a coal-carrying canal was dug to the sheltered port of Campbeltown, greatly benefiting exports from the mine, which raised up to 14,000 tons of coal a year and had an engine in the 1790s. There was once a bleachfield north of Drumlemble. Despite the lack of a safe harbour, fishing was carried on from the beach. William McTaggart, born locally in 1835, became an outstanding landscape painter. A new coal pit was opened in 1837, but when mining ceased in 1855 the canal was very soon infilled *(for details see Macmillan, 1970)*.

**Deep Mining, Golf and Trains**: After spasmodic coal hewing, a new shaft was sunk in 1876, when a 2'3" (68 cm) gauge mineral railway was laid from Campbeltown. A second shaft was completed 5 years later. Machrihanish golf club was founded in 1876 and an 18-hole course was laid out (described by Price in 1989 as *"one of the finest links courses in Scotland")*. In 1894 Murray noted the nearby *Pans Hotel* as *"good, large; crowded with golfers in summer"*. By 1903 a peak output of about 25,000 tonnes of coal was being raised annually, and sandstone was also mined. In 1906 the railway was extended and made fit to carry passengers; by that time seaside villas had appeared and the hotel was called the *Ugadale Arms*. The area remained generally rural, and a lifeboat station which was opened in 1911 lasted only until 1930. The mine closed in 1929, actually before the date of the Wall Street crash, and the railway followed in 1932.

**Flying, Drift Mining, and Marine Biology**: In 1933–34 Midland & Scottish Air Ferries briefly plied between Renfrew, a field at *'Campbeltown'* (probably Machrihanish) and Belfast. By 1939 Northern & Scottish Airways made *'Campbeltown'* the base for an air ambulance. About 1940 a Royal Naval Air station was built 3km from the village, and curiously named HMS *Landrail*; it remained in use post-war, and also formally became the civil airport for Campbeltown. In 1946 a new drift mine was opened (at least the fourth attempt to exploit the coal reserves). In 1951 when the population was around 240 this produced 100,000 tonnes of a poor quality coal suitable for boilers, and employed some 260 men by 1954; but it too was closed in 1967. By 1979 Sanda lighthouse *(see Southend)* was being serviced by helicopter from Machrihanish. In 1981 this was still a small holiday place of some 300 people, with the hotel, golf course and caravan and camping site; Drumlemble then had a similar population. Stirling University Institute of Aquaculture opened their Marine Biological Centre at Machrihanish in 1992. The airfield, which in 1989 was a US Navy reserve base for anti-submarine warfare, reverted in 1996 to wholly civilian use. Drumlemble school has fewer than 16 primary-age pupils, its future now uncertain. Seasonal accommodation, the caravan and camping site, and a pub and post office are still available. And Vestas Wind Systems of Denmark are to start making wind turbine equipment at the old RAF station.

## MACMERRY & Gladsmuir — Map 3, A2

***E. Lothian villages,*** *pop. 1200* — OS 66: NT 4372

Gladsmuir, on the Great North Road 6km west of Haddington, was the 16th century birthplace of George Heriot, founder of Heriot's School *(see Edinburgh)*; in 1799 Robert Heron called it a *"village"*, but it was doomed to decline. In 1867 a mineral branch of the North British Railway from Monktonhall near Musselburgh was opened through Ormiston to end at the Great North Road midway between Gladsmuir and Tranent, where a coal pit was sunk at the delightfully named hamlet of Macmerry. This line enjoyed a passenger service from 1872. By 1901 Macmerry had several miners' rows and a post and telegraph office; shafts as far afield as Greendykes showed the extent of hidden coal workings. At one time Scotland's most easterly iron smelting works operated at Macmerry. Withdrawal of passenger trains due to the spread of bus routes took place in 1925.

**More Merry than Erudite?**: By 1951 Macmerry had a school and a population of nearly 1000, most living in council houses; but its rail goods service ended in 1960, leaving a bing to mark the former pit head. Gladsmuir was just a hamlet with a garage and post office, when the site of an 1890s shaft at Penston 1km to the east became an industrial estate, the aim being to compensate for lost mining jobs. Several small firms accepted incentives and moved out from Edinburgh to this estate. In 1991 Macmerry – which still comprised 60% council houses – had a population of about 1175 and (if the 10% sample is to be believed) Scotland's lowest proportion of residents with higher educational qualifications – a mere 1%! Large local enterprises now include Weber (who make marking labels), Optima (who make telecoms equipment), and Hart Construction. In 1996 tiny Gladsmuir was relieved of through traffic by the completion of a new dual carriageway alignment of the A1 road; it also got a karting track nearby. Macmerry primary school, post office and general store are still open.

## MAIDENS — Map 1, B3

***Ayrshire village,*** *pop. 575* — OS 70 or 76: NS 2107

The Maidens of Turnberry, a series of partly submerged coastal rocks, form a natural harbour on the coast of Carrick some 20km south-west of Ayr; close by is a standing stone. The 13th century Turnberry Castle on Turnberry Head, a rocky promontory nearby, was first recorded in 1307 when held by the English under Henry Percy for Edward I. Its adjacent village was seized by Robert Bruce, whose *"property and residence"* it became (Chambers). The early Culzean Castle (pronounced *Killane)* 2 km north-east of the Maidens was owned by the Earls of Carrick and later by the Kennedys; its cliff-top site enjoys a dramatic view across the Firth of Clyde to Arran and Ailsa Craig. Thomaston Castle 1 km inland from Culzean was a

16th century L-plan tower house, emphasised as *'Thomastoun'* on Pont's map made around 1600; on the coast nearby stood the imposing *'Koif Castle'*, evidently Culzean. South of this at Ardlochan a mill turned on the stream which emerges from a natural lochan. The area was well settled, including the *'Clachan of Turnberry'*; but the latter's castle must have been ruinous and was not marked, and the nearest settlement to the Maidens rocks was *'Riddelstoun'*.

**The Castle Mansion and Fishing Pier**: Turnberry had salt pans for many years from about 1710. The Roy map made about 1754 showed a coastal road, and another from Turnberry to Maybole. Extensive wooded policies already enveloped *'Collen'* (Culzean) castle. The castle was further enlarged between 1776 and 1790 by Robert Adam for the Earl of Cassilis, creating a fine mansion for his Montgomerie family, Ayshire's largest landowners. The Turnberry Point lighthouse was first lit in 1873. Maidens was known as Douglaston in the 19th century, and must have been a fishing centre, for vestiges of an earlier stone structure were incorporated in the new pier built in mass concrete in 1880. By the 1890s the hamlet was served by a post and telegraph office.

**Railway, Turnberry Golf Hotel – and Air Bases**: In 1906 the Glasgow & South Western Railway opened a coastal line from Ayr to Girvan, with a station beside their large luxury golfing hotel designed by James Miller and newly completed at Turnberry. Its two fine courses date from 1903 (Ailsa) and 1912 (Arran). Two other stations were also provided, named Maidens and Glenside, the latter serving Culzean. The hotel thrived, but soon its necessarily rich patrons came by car and the railway was a failure: the section north of Turnberry was closed to passengers in 1933. Turnberry was used as an air training base in World War I, the hotel becoming the Officers' Mess. Maidens grew into a quiet little residential resort. In the 1939–45 war an RAF Coastal Command airfield with hard runways was built between Maidens and Turnberry, taking over parts of the golf courses. From 1942 there were no passenger trains.

**Telephones galore at posh Turnberry**: From 1948 under Frank Hole, Chairman of British Transport Hotels, the hotel was refurbished and the Ailsa course reopened in 1951. Maidens then had a population of about 700, with another 300 at Turnberry, and the combined facilities of a small village. Turnberry's public telephone exchange had an amazing 317 *'connexions'* – was there no private branch exchange in the 5-star, 156-room *Turnberry Hotel*? The whole railway had vanished by 1963; Turnberry station roof was moved to Dumbarton's football ground, while Maidens and Glenside stations became caravan sites. By then the remainder of the airfield was disused as such, but for a time was used for motor racing.

**Modern Maidens – Old Folks in Disguise?**: By 1953 Culzean Castle had been opened to the public by the National Trust for Scotland, its fine forested grounds being used as a country park. However, the resident population of the two small villages fell slightly over the next thirty years. The Open championship first came to Turnberry in 1977. By 1979 Turnberry was the land base for the helicopter which relieved the Ailsa Craig lighthouse, until it was automated in 1987. Maidens had three holiday caravan sites and a bowling green. Two new hotels were built there after 1963, the seaside *Bruce Hotel*, open by 1977, and the hilltop *Malin Court*, open by 1980, which at that time most unusually overtly combined its hotel function with that of a luxurious home for the elderly. Too bad for the author, then a would-be visitor!

**The Japanese pile Luxury on Luxury**: The *Turnberry Hotel* complex was bought in 1987 by the Japanese golf company Nitto Kogyo, which built a new spa, a second restaurant and 17 more rooms, and converted its swimming pool to house a conference suite. A new golf clubhouse was built in 1992–93. In 1990 Culzean country park with its Adam mansion drew nearly 400,000 visitors – the west of Scotland's prime outdoor paid attraction. At that time some lobster fishing continued from Maidens harbour. By 1996 no fewer than six caravan sites were open along this section of the coast. Turnberry has retained its post office. The 5-star *Turnberry Hotel* (132 rooms, golf courses, indoor swimming and many sports), long rated by the RAC as the best in Scotland, now has the brand new Colin Montgomerie Golf Academy and some new lodges.

## MALLAIG — **Map 8, B4**

***Lochaber port town**, pop. 950* — OS 40: NM 6797

Up to 1892 Mallaig was nothing but *"a pretty wee bay"* with only a few thatched croft houses, to which the road from Fort William to Arisaig had been extended by way of Morar. In 1892 an exposed promontory just west of Mallaig was selected as a suitable site for a fishing port, at the seaward end of what was to become a subsidised extension of the West Highland Railway from Fort William. Mallaig was more remote than, and definitely the second best site to, a farm known as *Roshven* on Loch Ailort which had been chosen about 1890, but whose development was successfully opposed by its powerful proprietor.

**The Steamer Terminal**: The Mallaig rail terminus and adjacent pier opened in 1901, creating Scotland's last significant new settlement of the steam age. The Oban to Gairloch steamers immediately transferred their Arisaig call to Mallaig, which grew to become a congested village and herring fishing base with fish curers, and a busy ferry terminal with steamers and ferries to Armadale *(see Sleat)* and to the various Small Isles. In 1931 there was also a mail steamer to Kyle and Portree in Skye. A lifeboat station was opened in 1948. In 1951 Mallaig had 950 people, a junior secondary school and average village facilities, plus a minor steam engine shed; motor boats served Soay. By 1954 the prominent *Station Hotel* had been renamed the *West Highland Hotel*; it then had 30 rooms. The *Marine Hotel* was open by the 1960s. The steam engine shed was closed about 1962 when tall oil tanks for refuelling diesel trains were built at the station.

**British Rail Rejects Fish Traffic**: The fish traffic for which the line was built was abandoned by BR without advance warning about 1965. Local herring landings almost ceased, to be replaced by prawns. A new fish pier and market was built about 1971, and there were quick-freezing and cold storage facilities by 1977. Kippering continued until 1978 when the herring fishing ban was imposed; it was lifted in 1981. Meantime in 1977 the exposed station's canopy roof was demolished. In 1981 Mallaig had the facilities of a large village, all crammed into a tiny urbanised area among the rocks, with land being reclaimed from the sea to provide expansion sites. By 1982 there were

*Mallaig harbour in 1984. The port and village were created by the West Highland Extension Railway, built from 1892 to 1901 with government aid. Mallaig has continued to grow as a fishing harbour and ferry port.* (RS)

about ten shops, plus two banks; pottery was made. To serve the fisheries there was a marine engine dealer, a large ship's chandler and an ice factory, and two large wooden fishing vessels were being refitted on Henderson's two slips.

**Prawns and Tourist Steam Trains**: The summer season steam-hauled tourist trains between Fort William and Mallaig were started in 1984 by British Rail. Fishing boats from ports as far afield as the Tyne and Belfast could then be seen at Mallaig, served by such further features as a rail-served oil depot and seamen's mission; a new trunk telephone exchange served a wide area. Despite pressures for closure, Mallaig remained the home base for 13 train drivers and guards, but the former railway dormitory was sold that year to house a heritage museum, which was slow to materialise. A new breakwater was built in 1984–85, and by 1987 Mallaig was Britain's busiest prawn port. In 1988 a new 3km-long southern access road was opened, squeezed in between the railway and the sea and across the site of the former engine shed.

**Six-Year Schooling – but Rail Freight Ends**: A new extension to create Mallaig High School – of six-year status for 170 pupils – was built in 1988, the excavated rock providing reclamation infill for industrial sites. Up to 1993 petroleum products were still carried by rail to Mallaig from the Esso storage terminal at Bowling, but this traffic then ceased. Meantime Andy Race had begun a specialist fish-dealing business in the 1980s, and by 1991 supplied 200 hotels within a 100-km radius. Despite some new housing, the population of Mallaig was still only 944. In 1993 Caledonian MacBrayne with the support of the Regional Council and Highlands & Islands Enterprise planned a new linkspan terminal to speed the loading of vehicles on the Armadale ferries, which still relied on the slow side-loading method and could only make five crossings per day.

**Prawn Fishing – and Falling Quotas**: White fish, prawns and scallops were still the main seafoods landed at the improved harbour in 1995–97, and also some herrings. The huge fish lorries vied with tourists' cars on the last sections of single-track road, for plans to complete improved road access throughout by 1995 were still incomplete by some 8km in 1997. By 1998 the number of Mallaig-registered fishing boats had fallen since 1980 from 132 to 64, but Mallaig was said to have Scotland's largest prawning fleet.

**Tourist Attractions, Trains and Boats**: By 1993 the *'Sea Life Centre'* was open beside the harbour; by 1995 visitors also found a covered swimming pool and a small museum of local history beside the 2-platform station, which contains a gift shop. In 2000 a new community hall was built on the site of the old engine shed, and an oil depot was established at the new outer harbour, freeing space for the re-installation of a turntable for the steam locomotives hauling tourist and charter trains. Tourists can ride the summer car ferries to Armadale, Castlebay, Coll or Tiree (all passenger-only in winter), year-round ferries to the Small Isles, most of which are now able to receive cars, and in summer cruises to Loch Scavaig and passenger ferries to Kyle of Lochalsh. Hotels include the *Marine* and the *West Highland*, and there is a tiny hostel for backpackers.

## MANNOFIELD, Rubislaw & Ruthrieston

**Map 10, C3**

***S-W. parts of Aberdeen**, pop. 40,000* — OS 38: NJ 9105

Around 1350 the Town Council of Aberdeen bought the Rubislaw estate, 3km west of the city centre and north of the River Dee, for use as common grazings. The Bridge of Dee was promoted by the Bishop of Aberdeen and built 3km south west of Aberdeen in 1527–29; two centuries later, Defoe admired its seven *"very stately fine arches"*. Pont's map made about 1600 showed the Mill of Kincorth near the bridge; interestingly for a map which showed scarcely any roads, a *'causeway'* was indicated running south from Broadgreens, 2 km south-west of the bridge. This ancient road, the *'Causey Mounth'*, conceivably Roman in origin, and which had already been built by the 14th century, was shown as a made road on the Roy map of about 1750, when it joined the coastal track near *'Mains of Kingchusey'* west of Portlethen. It can still be readily traced on modern OS maps for some 10km, almost as far as Muchalls. The Nellie Mill stood west of the bridge below the Kirk of Banchory Devenick.

**Granite Quarrying**: The Rubislaw quarry was opened in 1741 to exploit the dark blue-grey granite of the locality. By 1800 some 600 quarrymen (at more than one quarry in the Aberdeen area) were making granite setts for the London market alone. Aberdeen was itself being rebuilt and extended using granite, especially the building stone from Rubislaw, which also provided the facings for the Bell Rock lighthouse, built in 1807–10. The Rubislaw quarry was operated by Gibb in 1869; the stone was used in building the docks at Portsmouth, Sheerness and Southampton, and in 1892–95 Rubislaw supplied the many dressed blocks for the unique Rattray Head lighthouse.

**Communications Developments**: Water was piped to the city from near Bridge of Dee from 1829, and the ancient bridge was widened in 1841–42. When the Deeside Railway was opened in 1853, closely-spaced stations were provided at Holburn Street and Ruthrieston. The area between the quarry and the stations grew with the city, as a suburb; by 1894 three ribbons of development had pushed out: along Holburn Street, along Queen's Road towards the quarry, and especially beside the Great Western Road to Mannofield, where a post office was open by 1902. Some very attractive granite-faced houses and bungalows date from the late 19th and early 20th centuries, when the area was also served by Aberdeen electric trams; between 1904 and 1927 these were extended to Bieldside by the Aberdeen Suburban Tramways Company. Anderson Drive was laid out in the 1920s as a city bypass, but development overflowed its line.

**From Stone to Suburbs and Education**: Operations at the Rubislaw quarry were electrified in 1920 and further modernised in 1928 when it employed 130 quarrymen; but demand fell, and only 60 workers remained in 1939, when the pit was 122m deep. The quarry became surrounded by suburban and educational development, including the Macaulay Institute for Soil Research, established at Craigiebuckler in 1930, and a school of domestic science at Kepplestone. By 1953 buses had replaced the trams; the area held some 30,000 people, but had the facilities of a mere village. New council housing was built in the 1950s south of the Bridge of Dee; Kincorth Academy was open by 1978. By 1955 the Aberdeen youth hostel was open, and by 1967 Gray's School of Art and the Scott Sutherland School of Architecture had been built at Garthdee. With new large private housing developments such as Braeside to the west, and attractions including the Gordon Highlanders Museum – open at Viewfield Road by 1969 – the population in the area peaked around 1971 at nearly 35,000.

**From Granite to Oil in a Single Day**: Over 230 years a volume of some 3 million $m^3$ of granite had been extracted from the pit of Rubislaw, ultimately 142m in depth, and at one time the deepest open quarry in Britain. Quarrying ceased on the 28th April 1970 – by coincidence the day that the momentous discovery of oil in the North Sea was announced – and the deep pit filled with water. Though oil brought a boom, further housing growth in the vicinity was constrained, and the population was down to under 30,000 by 1981. Meantime the area's facilities, including a successful local shopping area, had somewhat increased. The hotel trade prospered as a result of North Sea oil development and the availability of large mansionhouses suitable for conversion; some 15 hotels were open in the area by 1981, the largest the 103-room *Treetops*.

**Offices and Hotels for Oil and Management People**: By 1992 the offices of Shell, Marathon and Conoco ringed the great void of Rubislaw quarry, and by then a dry ski slope had been laid out at Kaimhill. In 1996 Sainsburys opened a large new store at Garthdee, its sixth in Scotland, to employ 400 people. Later in 1996 Britannia Oil, a joint venture between

*Rubislaw granite quarry (Mannofield), first opened in 1741; over its 230 years of operation, 3 million cubic metres of granite were extracted. At one time it was the deepest open quarry in Britain, at over 140m.* *(British Geological Survey)*

Chevron and Conoco, moved its 70-job HQ from London to Royfold House near the Marathon offices. In 1998 the arched Faculty of Management of Robert Gordon's University, designed by Foster & Partners, was opened on the steep slopes at Garthdee. An even greater challenge to architects and structural engineers was faced when in 1999 a scheme was approved to develop 86 houses and a 7-storey office block at the Rubislaw Quarry. In 2000 Robert Gordon's University planned to move its faculty of health and food to Garthdee, financed by selling the 5-storey building and its Kepplestone campus to Safeway for redevelopment as a supermarket. Kincorth Academy has around 825 pupils. A large number of hotels are sited here, in what they claim as the city's West End.

## MANOR (or Kirkton Manor) — Map 3, A3

***Locality s-w. of Peebles,** pop. 150* — OS 73: NT 2135

Many ancient hill forts and settlements lined the hill-enclosed valley of the Manor Water, a substantial southern tributary of the River Tweed west of Peebles. The courtyard castle of Castlehill was built in the 16th century 4km up the Manor Water, as were the Posso and Kirkhope Towers farther upstream, and about the same time Barns Tower was built beside the Tweed. The area was roadless as late as the mid 18th century, according to the Roy map, and the valley has remained an agricultural cul de sac. A water mill was built around 1800; a century later 257 people lived in Manor parish, centred on its kirkton and post office 2.5km north of Castlehill. By 1951 there was a telephone exchange. With only 171 people by 1971 – a level since approximately maintained – the isolated primary school, 1km north of Castlehill Tower, had become marginal, and was soon closed. In 1962 a youth hostel was open beside Barns Tower, but had vanished by 1985. The post office had closed by 1993 and by then the water mill was long disused, but still retained its old machinery in 1994. Castlehill Tower is the best preserved of the local fortified houses.

## MARKINCH — Map 6, B4

***Central Fife large village,** pop. 2200* — OS 59: NO 2901

The church of St Drostan at Markinch was given to the Culdees of Loch Leven in 1050. It stands on a sheltered site north of the River Leven, which up to that time probably formed the boundary between the ex-Pictish half provinces of *Fib* (East Fife) and *Fothrif* (West Fife plus). Markinch is reputed to have been a former capital of Fife, presumably at the time of merger around 1200, because Crail and possibly Fordell were the two earlier centres, and in 1212 Cupar assumed the combined role. A cairn which stands on a hilltop near the river may point the way to a *'Boundary Island' (Mark+Inch)*, a suitably neutral meeting ground for negotiations. When visited by Edward I of England in 1295 there was nothing beside the church except three houses, but the oddly conical graveyard looks remarkably like an abandoned motte.

**Barony Burgh, Mining and Inns**: By 1378 Markinch had passed from the Balfour family to the Beatons. Chambers noted that there was a school at Markinch as early as the time of James V, but the placename appeared without emphasis on the Blaeu maps of Fife published in 1654. Markinch was created a burgh of barony in 1673. Coal mining at Cadham 1km to the west, near the area's only road (which later became the A92) must have been started for the Earls of Rothes well before 1710, in which year a water-operated engine was set up to drain the mines, and by 1717 the River Leven had been bridged 2km west of Markinch. By 1725 there were two hostelries on this part of the road, the *Plasterers Inn* just south of the Leven being well known. Another mine at Cadham was begun about 1740. The Roy map showed that about 1750 Markinch village was still of minimal importance, lying away from all roads and still comprising a single crescent of buildings round the west side of the church.

**The Textile Industry and Balbirnie House**: The Russell Brothers of Kirkcaldy set up the Rothes linen bleachfield on the river almost 2km west of Markinch between 1746 and 1760, and the great classical Balbirnie House and its fine estate buildings were developed in a large park to the north-west of the village in the period 1760–1820. Local roads were laid out, and in 1780 a second water engine was installed, this one being to drain the Balbirnie coal workings (it gave way to steam in 1840). In 1790 the main road became a turnpike, and Haugh spinning mill was erected in 1794; it worked until about 1860, and restarted in 1864. Heron in 1799 saw Markinch as a *"village with an excellent bleachfield, and some manufactures"*; while in 1800 Balbirnie too was a *"small village"*.

**Tullis Paper and the Wool Mill**: Robert Tullis & Co of Cupar bought the Auchmuty meal mill on the River Leven south of Cadham soon afterwards, and in 1810 converted it into a paper mill. The Rothes paper mill was then set up beside the bleachfield by William Keith of Dalkeith; Tullis bought this mill in 1836, and steam power was soon added to the Tullis mills. The Balbirnie Paper Mills, 1km west of the village, were started in 1816 by Alexander Grieve of Balerno, who had lately been Tullis's mill manager. A papermaking machine was installed there in 1834 to produce wrapping paper, thick for grocers and thin for drapers. Bought in 1866 by P Dixon and W Grosset, from 1880 it was known as Dixon's Mill. Balbirnie Wool Mill, originally a meal mill, was bought in 1835 by John Drysdale of Alloa, who turned it into a weaving mill for plaids, blankets and shawls. Later it was owned by William Mitchell, who installed steam to give additional power.

**Water Engine, Water Mills and Railways**: The first Markinch post office opened in 1824. Greenwood's map (surveyed in 1826–27) showed the village considerably enlarged. An *'engine'* stood 1km west of Balbirnie and a *'water engine'* at Cadham, while no fewer than twelve mills and bleachfields of various types stood beside the 2.2km of the river from Auchmuty to Sythrum due south of Markinch, between which points there is a total fall of some 20m. Markinch had a station on the main line of the Edinburgh & Northern Railway from its opening in 1847; a tall stone viaduct of five arches crosses the river. A winding freight spur from the station yard served the growing paper mills; a longer, lower viaduct was built for the branch line to Leslie, opened in 1861. In 1864 the Balgonie works of J G Stuart & Co had 3000 spindles and 32 power looms; there were still several large bleachfields. Markinch became a police burgh, and N & N Lockhart of Kirkcaldy converted the Sythrum meal mill to spin twine by water and steam power; in 1864 it made hemp twine on 820 spindles. By 1867 Sythrum was bleaching yarn and calendering cloth and in 1869 was the area's sole works using flax, jute or hemp.

**Tullis Russell and Haig**: In 1874 Tullis was joined by David and Arthur Russell, owners of the Rothes bleachfield; in 1896 the firm, still called R Tullis & Co, was compelled by the new Fife County Council to instal an effluent purification plant for their various works. In 1906 the firm was renamed Tullis Russell (TR). Meantime in 1877 the distillers Haig of Cameron Bridge sold the production side of their business to DCL, and moved their blending and bottling operations to a site near Markinch station, later building vast new red brick premises. However, they had become thirled to DCL, who in 1919 acquired their prominent hilltop bottling hall and bonded warehouses; Earl Haig joined the DCL board and the trade name Haig was kept, using the slogan *'Don't be Vague, ask for Haig'*.

**Co-op, Closures – and Paper Galore**: Markinch which had 1400 people in 1891 grew further – electricity was available from 1911 – and it set up a Co-operative society. The Leslie branch railway was closed to passengers by the LNER in 1932, but Markinch had gained the facilities of a small town, plus the agricultural engineer Bowen. In the 1920s a tiny coal mine at Star, a hamlet 2 km north-east, was worked by half a dozen men. Sythrum mill closed in 1936 (and had been obliterated by the 1990s); the Balbirnie Wool Mill closed about the same time that TR's original Rothes bleachfield was abandoned, in 1957. But by 1969 TR employed 1500 people in the Auchmuty mills and had one of the world's largest paper-making machines.

**Markinch, Glenrothes and Balbirnie relate**: In the late 1950s Markinch Co-op took the largest unit in the centre of the New Town of Glenrothes, sited less than 3 km from Markinch, many of whose facilities consequently closed over the years, including its secondary school; in 1979 some young Markinch children were to be seen travelling by local trains to independent schools in Dundee! Though claiming to serve the New Town, Markinch station was never provided with an Inter-City train service. For a time from 1972 Balbirnie House became the HQ of Glenrothes New Town Development Corporation; in 1972–74 they established a craft centre in its fine stable block and laid out the 9-hole Balbirnie golf course in the rolling wooded park. Some population decline occurred in Markinch, which became no more than a mature industrial village on the edge of the new town.

**Exit Whisky – enter a Top Hotel**: The whisky blending plant was closed in the mid 1980s, and *its* offices then became the HQ of the Development Corporation. This enabled the renovated Balbirnie House to be opened in 1989 as a luxury hotel. Employment at the TR paper mill gradually fell, to just over 1000 in 1989; but it remained a family firm with a Europe-wide export base. By 1990 the mill was producing 80,000 tonnes of high-quality paper a year, and claimed to be Europe's leading independent paper-makers. Until 1992 the rail connection into the works brought a daily train of Cornish china clay, which crept under the main road through a tiny bridge having less than 3 cm clearance!

**Tullis into Employee Ownership**: In depressed 1992, more jobs were shed by TR, who in 1993 operated three mills – Auchmuty, Rothes and Crocker. In 1994 ownership of the firm was transferred from the Erdal family to its 850 or so workers, becoming the second largest employee-owned business in the UK. In 1994–95 TR broke all its output records by exceeding the 100,000 tonne mark, a 26% growth compared with the previous year. The smaller 'Fife' paper mill continued under the DRG Transcript name, making carbonless copy paper in 1989, with a growing workforce of some 250 people; it then became part of the Sappi Europe group as the *'Sappi Graphics Transcript Mill'*; it was partly re-equipped in 1991 and fully computerised in 1994. By the 1990s the Balbirnie paper mills were owned by Dickinson Paper & Board.

**Media, Barley and Building on to Balbirnie**: By 1991, when the population was an elderly 2176, the *Markinch News* had been established by Kirkcaldy's *Fife Free Press Group*. In the mid 90s the studios of the new *Kingdom FM* radio were established in the Haig Business Park at Markinch, joined in 1994 by Lothian Barley, an Auchtermuchty crop and fertiliser trading subsidiary of S&N. New private housing estates have been steadily filling the gap between Markinch and Glenrothes. Balbirnie Park golf course now has 18 holes and a smart new club-house. The *'A'* listed *Balbirnie House Hotel* (30 rooms) was enlarged in 2000 with a function suite and orangery dining room in classical style; it retains its fine parkland setting.

## MARYHILL

**Map 15, C4**

***N.-W. part of Glasgow,*** *pop. 37,000* — OS 64: NS 5668

Pont's map of Lennox made about 1600 showed Garscube Mill, which turned near Killermont on the River Kelvin, 7 km north-west of Glasgow. By the time that the Roy survey was made about 1754, a road linked Glasgow with the New Kirk of Kilpatrick (Bearsden) via Garscube, but Maryhill seems not to have existed as a settlement, and the Killermont Bridge was apparently built later in the century. In 1746 a little water-powered paper mill was established at Balgray, midway between Garscube and Partick, by Edward Collins, whose son found the water supply inadequate and moved away to Dalmuir in 1747, leaving the Balgray paper mill to others. In 1790 James Duncan was operating it; later Balgray became a snuff mill.

**Hankies, Paper and the Forth & Clyde Canal**: In 1746 a paper mill was built by Edward Collins at Balgray, on a tiny burn with a limited water supply; although mentioned again in 1790 it was extinct by 1825. In 1750 William Stirling established a handkerchief printworks which also exploited the power of the River Kelvin, at Dalsholm or Dawsholm between Balgray and Garscube; but he too moved west, going to the Vale of Leven in 1770. The small Dalsholm paper mills were set up about 1783 by William McArthur. Meantime the middle section of the Forth & Clyde Canal, which roughly paralleled the River Kelvin westwards from Kirkintilloch, was opened in 1775, doubling back at Wyndford Ferry to serve Glasgow's Port Dundas. In 1787–90 the canal was provided with a timber basin at Firhill and extended westwards from Wyndford, since then known as Stockingfield junction, over a road arch, past a dry dock, slipway (and later puffer boatyard) and down five locks, to cross the Kelvin on a four-arched viaduct over 120 m long and 20 m tall *(see Hay & Stell)* and eventually to reach the Clyde at Bowling.

**Industries and Maryhill Village**: Industries soon lined the canal: Ferguson first made confectionery nearby in 1794. About 1790 the Dalsholm Road bridge was erected across the River Kelvin, and Maryhill – originally called Kelvin Dock – grew into a village along the road from Wyndford to Killermont Bridge. By about 1825 Maryhill was served by a penny post from Glasgow. A new Garscube House was built in 1826 for Sir Archibald Campbell, designed by William Burn. About 1830 John Barr established the Maryhill Printworks at Bantaskin Street. Then about 1840 Edward Collins & Son returned to re-acquire and greatly expand the Balgray snuff mill into the Kelvindale Paper Mills, where they installed a papermaking machine in 1845. In 1846 the pottery manufacturers Kidston, Cochran & Co erected their North Woodside flint mill downstream of Collins' mill in Garriochmill Road, again using a waterwheel as the power source. Around 1849 William Galbraith established a marble-cutting works in Balnain Street; the works was rebuilt in 1908. Grovepark Mills in North Woodside Road were erected in 1857 for the power-loom weavers Mitchell & Whytlaw, and enlarged five times up to 1900. In 1874 the Violet Grove power-loom weaving mills of Aitken, Wilson & Co were built at Grovepark Street.

**Railways Serving Maryhill**: The Glasgow, Dumbarton & Helensburgh Railway was opened westwards from Cowlairs in 1858, keeping north of the canal. A station named Maryhill was provided north of the village centre, and a viaduct was built across the Kelvin; the Milngavie branch of 1863 forked from a junction at Westerton, 2 km west. Two later lines diverging near Maryhill station were the Stobcross branch of the North British (NB) built southwards in 1870–73 to the industrial bank of the Clyde, and the bucolic single-track Kelvin Valley Railway, which connected north-eastwards with Kirkintilloch, and opened in 1879 (becoming part of the NB in 1885).

**Soldiers and Ironworks**: In 1870 the River Kelvin was spanned by the Belmont bridge and the first Queen Margaret bridge. From about 1877 the Maryhill Barracks was the Glasgow depot of the HLI (Highland Light Infantry). McDowall & Co established their Milton Ironworks in North Woodside Road about 1856. Shaw & McInnes' Firhill Ironworks were set up about 1866, to produce architectural castings. In 1867 Thomas Allan & Sons established their North Woodside Ironworks; these were extended from 1893–94 by J & A Macfarlane, who made mangles around 1900. Thomson & Co made railway springs at the Crown Ironworks in North Woodside Road from about 1869; these were rebuilt in 1908. The Maryhill Ironworks at Stockingfield was among the largest and longest lasting.

**Gas and Chemicals Taint the Air**: Dawsholm gasworks were built in 1871–72 for Glasgow Corporation and subsequently greatly expanded; Alexander, Fergusson & Co's Glasgow Lead & Colour Works were erected about 1874 beside the canal at Ruchill Street. About 1875 the Maryhill Printworks were converted into Cumming's blacking factory, extended in 1900 with a 7-storey block. The Glasgow Rubber Works in Shuna Street were established by George McLellan & Co about 1876, and the Craighall Chemical Works were built about 1879. Meantime came the Ruchill Oil Works of John Sandeman, a rosin distiller, around 1883; the Kent Works of Blacklock, Goudie & Co, makers of waterproofs, built about 1885; and the Phoenix Chemical Works, built from 1886 and repeatedly enlarged. Finally about 1892 the Eglinton Chrome Tannery was erected at Firhill Road. Between them these sundry bad-neighbour industries added a most unhealthy flavour to the air, capped when the Craighall Works were expanded between 1895 and 1914 to add asbestos manufacture.

**Glass, Stained Glass and Horses**: The Glasgow Glass Works were built about 1874 for rolling plate glass, and were accompanied from 1892 by Scott & Co's Caledonian Glass Bottle Works, with a canal wharf; having borrowed two characteristics from Venice, a third was thought appropriate, for the address became Murano Street. The plate glass works were extended by Chance Brothers between 1893 and 1911. Meantime in 1871–74 the Episcopal Cathedral for Glasgow had been built within the Maryhill postal area, though fronting Great Western Road. In 1883 a local newspaper was established for Maryhill, which was by that time a police burgh, and in the same year a tram depot was built near the station, from which horse trams connected with the city. About 1885 Ruchill sawmills were opened by D McFarlane & Son, later becoming part of Bryant & May's match factory.

**Bread and Jam**: Although still a distinct settlement, Maryhill was incorporated into the City of Glasgow in 1891. The delightfully named Friendly Bread Association opened their bakery in Clarendon Street about 1887; this eventually passed to City Bakers, who rebuilt the premises in 1926. The Kelvinside Bakery was built in Arden Street for John Currie about 1893, and in 1898 John Neil & Son established a bread and biscuit bakery at St George's Road. About 1888 the Glasgow Sausage Works of R D Waddell were erected at North Woodside Road, rebuilt in 1897. Thomas Bishop's jam and confectionery works, also in Herbert Street, was destroyed by fire in 1907, but rebuilt.

**Trains vs Trams (and Motors)**: Between 1894 and 1896 the Glasgow Central and Lanarkshire & Dunbartonshire Railways – both Caledonian (CR) subsidiaries – were built through the southern area of Maryhill with many twists and turns, a tight triangle of lines south of the barracks, a tunnel under the canal, the ambitiously laid out Maryhill Central, Dawsholm and Kirklee stations, and yet another viaduct across the river, south of the canal viaduct. By 1899 the CR had opened an engine shed at Dawsholm. But their success was short lived, for Glasgow's electric trams reached as far as Garbraid by 1901; Maryhill Road consequently developed further, with linear shopping and tenement housing. From 1884 Alexander Frew built and hired carriages from premises in Cromwell Street, which became a garage in 1910 under the Apex Motor Engineering Company; another garage was built for John Foster in Hopehill Road in 1913, and Maryhill was the surprising location from 1906 of the *'Glasgow and Paris'* Motor Garage!

**More Industries and Services**: The Kelvinbridge Artistic Stationery Works in Herbert Street were built in the 1890s for Alexander Baird & Son. The Firhill Sawmills of Graham & Roxburgh also dated from that period, and about 1906 a factory for making bedroom furniture was built in Grovepark Street for Fred M Walker Ltd. Four laundries were built in Maryhill between 1873 and 1910; these were handy to serve the West End residences. Glasgow Corporation built a refuse destructor in 1901; later it too passed to Bryant & May.

**Worshipping God, Football and Golf**: Charles Rennie Mackintosh designed the notable Queen's Cross church east of Maryhill Road; this was not the last in the area, for churches continued to be built in Maryhill until the 1930s and later. It was adjoined from 1909 by Firhill Park, opened as a league football ground by the hitherto peripatetic team *'The Jags'* formed in 1876 and formally called *Partick Thistle* – now rather anomalously, for Firhill is 3 km from Partick. The main stand at Firhill was built in 1927, and in 1928 almost 55,000 people watched a Scotland–Ireland match there. The trams were extended to Bearsden in 1924 through 2 km of open country. Perhaps they caused Killermont Bridge to be replaced by a new structure in 1925–29. The second Queen Margaret Bridge was built in 1926–29, also in reinforced concrete but faced with sandstone, with parapets of Peterhead granite. A 9-hole municipal golf course was laid out at Ruchill in 1928, and by 1931 the crematorium had been built at the Western Necropolis. About 1935 Dalsholm paper mills were re-equipped with a 2.5 m-wide machine.

**Maryhill's Peak Planner of Scotland's Places**: Maryhill's most famous native was modest Robert Grieve, the son of a shipyard boilermaker, who was born in the Maryhill tenements in 1910. He became a civil engineer, local government officer, visionary town planner and civil servant, and the acknowledged brains behind the Clyde Valley Regional Plan of the 1940s with its proposals for new towns. He was promoted to chief planner at the Scottish Office, became Professor of Planning at Glasgow University, and the first Chairman of the Highlands & Islands Development Board; he was an early advocate of a University of the Highlands. He was an accomplished climber, President of the Scottish Mountaineering Council and Club. Justly knighted in 1969, he earned other honours for public service in his 85 years, and near the end of his life was prominently involved in the Scottish self-government movement.

**Maryhill in Decline**: After the 1939–45 war the Maryhill area with its population of some 50,000 ran down in economic activity and acquired a rough reputation. Garscube House was demolished in 1955, regrettably by Glasgow University. The 93-car tram depot at Celtic Street lasted into the latter years of the tramways, which still served Maryhill up to almost the end of the system in 1961–62. Maryhill Central station was closed to passengers in 1959 and to freight in 1964, and its line – together with that through Kirklee – was soon lifted. The engine shed, trams and barracks had all gone by the 1970s, the latter being replaced by barrack-like housing, the station site becoming a supermarket. Firhill sawmills were demolished in 1968, the Grovepark mills in 1969, Dalsholm paper mills ceased production in 1970, and about 1971 the Eglinton tannery and the original Queen Margaret Bridge were demolished.

**The Thirty-odd Tower Blocks and Summerston**: Drastic redevelopment created two monstrous clusters of the tower blocks so characteristic of Glasgow Corporation's attempt to keep its population chained to its administrative area whatever the cost. Although Maryhill's congested population had nevertheless declined by a third since the 1940s, in 1980 the CWS built a new superstore. South Caddercuilt Farm north of Maryhill was replaced from about 1975 by the Summerston estate; this was phased over some 20 years. Meantime Glasgow's small Science Park was opened in 1983 east of Maryhill Road; by 1992 this included the Kelvin Conference Centre. The population had fallen to around 37,000 by 1991, when although small-town urban facilities remained, Maryhill was in difficulty, and by 1993 there were serious drugs problems. The formerly imposing *Roxy* cinema, once one of many in the area, had been killed by television and was demolished by 1995.

**Football Fall and Return to the Rails**: In 1991 Partick Thistle FC, then a First Division club, began to improve its mediocre ground at Firhill. (Clyde FC which had shared the ground since having to leave Rutherglen in 1986, moved to Hamilton in 1992.) While in the Premier League in 1992–93, Thistle reconstructed the main stand at Firhill and soon built another to seat 6500 more spectators, bringing the total seating to 9400. Sadly the spectator improvements did not extend to the team, which fell rapidly from grace and now languishes in the Second Division. Meantime in 1993 passenger train services were reintroduced on the circuitous route from Maryhill, via a new station at Summerston, to Possilpark and Glasgow Queen Street. In 2000 it was suggested that Dawsholm deserved to regain a railway station, for Maryhill had shed its industrial past and depended on jobs elsewhere in the city. The John Paul Academy has over 800 pupils and North Kelvinside Secondary about 460. The Forth & Clyde Canal is fully reopening in 2001.

## MASTRICK — Map 10, C3

*N-W. part of Aberdeen, pop. 41,000* — OS 38: NJ 9007

In the 19th century the farms of Mastrick and Northfield were among those standing in a somewhat exposed position over 100 m above sea level, 4 km north-west of central Aberdeen. The surrounding area between the city's Den Burn and the Bux Burn was almost entirely rural in 1894, its most evident features being the Oldmill Reformatory (beside the Den Burn), the grid layout north of the long straight road called the Lang Stracht, and the mansionhouses of Sheddocksley, Springhill, Woodhill, and Buxburn (later spelled Bucksburn).

**Golf, Maze, Parks and Housing**: The city tramways were extended in 1924 to the new Hazlehead Park at Skene Road, just south of the Reformatory, where in 1927 Aberdeen City Council established a parkland golf course and in 1935 laid out Scotland's largest maze. North Anderson Drive was built inter-war as a city bypass, upgrading the line of an existing road. The Royal Hospital for Sick Children rose west of Kittybrewster, and the Forresterhill Hospital erected in 1936 was later renamed as the Royal Infirmary. The rest of the area remained largely rural until after 1945 when Aberdeen City Council built very large housing estates at Mastrick and Northfield. A new centre erected on the site of Mastrick Farm soon had facilities at least equivalent to those of a large village; to the west was the small Springhill Park. By 1953 there were two golf courses at Hazlehead, of 18 and 9 holes. By 1955 the Reformatory had been renamed Woodend Hospital.

**Shops, Recreation, Development**: A Woolworth store was among the central facilities opened in the 1960s, and by 1967 both Summerhill Academy and the Oakbank Approved School had appeared. In 1971 almost 50,000 people lived in the Mastrick area. By 1974 camping and caravanning were provided for, and in 1975 the city council laid out a 9-hole golf course at Auchmill, between the Northfield estate and Bucksburn. By 1978 the Sheddocksley Estate had been begun to the west and the Jessiefield Crematorium had been built off Skene Road. However, the two shopping schemes were not well let, although Mastrick's population was over 46,000 in 1981, and the North Sea oil boom was then near its height.

**New Activities with Regional Importance**: By 1978 Hazlehead Academy was a large new secondary school, and by 1983 Sheddocksley had doubled in size. By 1981 Mastrick had the unusual distinction for a council *'scheme'* of possessing the editorial offices of the regional daily newspapers, the *Press and Journal* and *Evening Express*, relocated from the city centre.

Woodhill House, built in the late 1970s on the site of the former mansion, became the HQ of Grampian Regional Council, a body which vanished in the 1996 reorganisation; the building is now the anomalous HQ of the unitary Aberdeenshire Council, but not within it! Meantime by 1989 a third golf course, of 18 holes, had been laid out at Hazlehead, where over 250,000 rounds of golf were played each year. In 1991 about 41,000 people lived in the area, Hazlehead Academy now having 1050 pupils and Northfield Academy 930. Hotels include the *Atholl* (35 rooms) and a modern *Premier Lodge* (60).

## MAUCHLINE

**Map 1, C2**

***Ayrshire small town,*** *pop. 3900* — OS 70: NS 4927

Mauchline lies in the area originally known as Kyle, north of the River Ayr and 16km east of Ayr itself. A *"colony of religious belonging to Melrose"* (Chambers) was established in the 12th century by Walter Fitzalan, King David I's Steward of Scotland, and Mauchline soon became the ecclesiastical centre of a wide area, administered from its 12th to 15th century castle known as Abbot Hunter's Tower. Mauchline was chartered as a burgh of barony in 1510. Pont's map made about 1600 showed a church, a tower and a bridged stream; 1600m south was the 16th century L-plan tower of Kingencleuch Castle. West of this castle the River Ayr was already spanned at Bridgend, below its confluence with the Lugar Water, on which was a mill. Some 6km to the north the Cessnock Water had also been bridged near Carnell Mill and Craig Mill. A parish school founded in 1622 was reopened about 1671, and a fair was recorded in 1702.

**Sandstone and Coal support Mansion-Building**: Red sandstone was quarried from early times at Barskimming – 2 km south-west of Mauchline – and at Failford, 4km west. By the 1750s as the Roy map showed, Mauchline enjoyed high nodality – seven radial roads met at what was still quite a small cross-shaped settlement, leading *inter alia* to Galston and Glasgow; to Irvine, and to Dumfries. The Mauchline to Cumnock road crossed the River Ayr in the Ballochmyle gorge by the Bowford Bridge. Mauchline had a post office from 1788, and an inn by the late 18th century. A colliery with an engine had been sunk by 1791, the year when Ballochmyle House, designed by John Adam for the Whiteford family, was completed; the laird then banked in Ayr. In 1799 Heron mentioned *"the town of Machline, containing about a thousand inhabitants"* but did not discuss its livelihood, merely its connections with Robert Burns, *"a poet of distinguished merit"*, whose work there first appeared in the Kilmarnock Edition. Poosie Nansie's inn in Mauchline was one of his haunts. Heron also noted *"a beautiful bridge of one lofty arch over the united streams of Luggar and Ayr"*. In 1797 seven fair days were scheduled, rising by 1811 to no fewer than twelve.

**Woollens and Snuffboxes**: A woollen mill was built early in the 19th century; in 1827 Chambers wrote of *"a small parish town"*. The main industry from the late 18th century was snuff-box and cigar box manufacture, led by William Smith who developed a large export trade, and in 1832 greatly impressed William Cobbett, who briefly described the work after his visit to this *"little town"* on the stagecoach route to Cumnock and the south. The finely painted boxes of polished sycamore wood, later sometimes tartan-covered, became well known as *'Mauchline Ware'*.

**Ballochmyle Viaduct and Quarries**: The Glasgow & South Western Railway's unique *Ballochmyle* viaduct was erected across the River Ayr south-east of Mauchline in 1848. Its spectacular 55m central span was the greatest masonry arch ever built to carry rail traffic, rising 50m above the river *(see Hay & Stell)*. Designed by John Miller, it was constructed in local Permian sandstone, hewn from the banks of the gorge itself, not from the famous Ballochmyle Quarry which was opened beside the line, some 1200m nearer the village. Mauchline station became a junction in 1870 when a connecting railway was opened, enabling through running from the south to Ayr via Annbank Junction (now Mossblown). Ballochmyle House was remodelled in 1886–90 for Sir Claud Alexander by H M Wardrop, becoming a huge mansion of 1400m$^2$. Mauchline did not become a post-reform burgh, and had only 1450 residents in 1891. In 1893 a mill was rebuilt as an engine works; by 1894 the *Loudoun Arms Hotel* and a secondary school were open, and Mauchline was described by Murray as *"a town"*.

**Butter and Ballochmyle Hospital**: About 1km west of the main quarry – which was still open in 1921 and reached a depth of some 65 m – was a second pit, where the massive and strikingly red *'Ballochmyle'* sandstone was also raised for building; but by 1921 this west pit was abandoned and

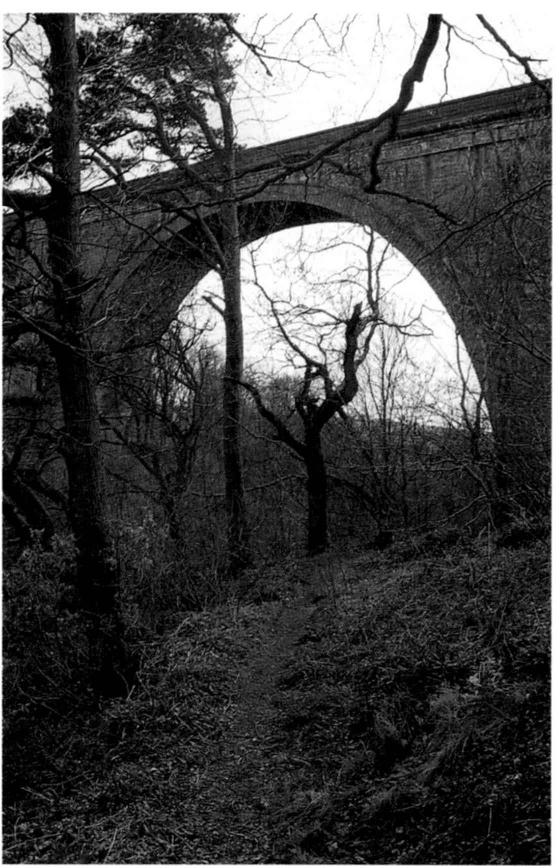

*Ballochmyle viaduct across the R. Ayr near Mauchline, built in 1846–48 to designs by John Miller. Its 55m central span is the greatest masonry arch ever built to carry rail traffic (which it still does, on the Glasgow–Dumfries route). (JRH)*

water-filled. In 1925 the rail-connected Mauchline colliery was sunk by Caprington & Auchlochan Collieries at Knowehead to the north of the village; by 1947 its later owners – Baird's & Dalmellington – employed over 800 men there. The Ballochmyle Creamery – at first noted for butter and milk powder manufacture, for margarine, and later for cheese making – was opened in the 1930s, but the manufacture of Mauchline Ware ceased when a fire destroyed Smith's factory in 1933. Ballochmyle golf club was founded in 1937 and soon laid out an 18-hole course. From 1940 until 1968, Ballochmyle House was used as staff accommodation for the sprawling wartime emergency Ballochmyle Hospital, established in its grounds in 1940 using prefabricated buildings. However, the rail passenger services between Ayr and Mauchline were withdrawn in 1951.

**New Industries, new Bridge and Curling Stones**: By 1953 the local population of 3800 was served in most respects by the facilities of a large village, though there were two hotels. By then Mauchline's industries included a plastics factory and an adjunct to Kilmarnock's Johnny Walker whisky concern, and for a time miners' houses were built by Ayr County Council, for quarrying continued until at least 1962. A new high-level Bowford Bridge with a concrete span of 91 m was built in 1962 to improve the A76 road, but the railway station was closed about 1965, the colliery closed in 1966, and from 1968 Ballochmyle House was no longer used by the hospital. In 1975 Mauchline was placed in Cumnock & Doon Valley district. In 1976 Andrew Kay's long-established curling-stone factory, the only one in the world, had just 8 workers: the stones last indefinitely, being made from granite – the bulk apart from the running surface no longer being obtained from Ailsa Craig but from North Wales. By 1980 Mauchline had three hotels; but some other local facilities had tended to decline over the previous thirty years, and there was no longer a secondary school. The railside quarry, which had reached a depth of some 65 metres, was infilled about that time.

**Crystal and Cream**: However, by 1987 a museum was open, and in 1988 the railway to Annbank Junction, mothballed in 1985, was reopened for the coal traffic from Knockshinnoch (New Cumnock) to Ayr. The Burns Crystal works was open by 1989, and in 1990 the Ballochmyle Creamery was one of the four principal plants of the Scottish Milk Marketing Board, which then adopted the name *'Scottish Pride'*. In 1991 the population was 3931. The reintroduction of the passenger trains on the Ayr–Mauchline line was considered in 1992, but hasn't yet happened. In 1993 it was decided to build a new small hospital to replace the old makeshift buildings; the long-empty Ballochmyle House was proposed for demolition in 1991, but in 1995 it was for sale, a derelict *'building at risk'*, as it still is. By 1998 two of the six hospital blocks had been demolished. Ten crystal engravers are still at work.

## MAUD

**Map 10, C2**

***Buchan village,*** *pop. 770*

OS 30: NJ 9248

Fedderate Castle was built in the 13[th] century on a knoll above the Water of Fedderate, a tributary of the South Ugie Water 7 km west of Old Deer. Timothy Pont's map of Buchan made about 1600 showed it as a lofty tower house; little now remains. Atherb on the north, and Clackriach (*'Grey Stone'* in Gaelic) to the south, were settlements on either side of the valley, in which turned the *'Mill of Kraig'*, which was an undated castle of the Keiths. *'Aldmad'* (nowadays Oldmaud) lay between them, its name perhaps deriving from the Gaelic for *'Stream of the Wolf'*. In the 17[th] century Brucklay Castle was built 1 km east of Fedderate. At the time of the Roy survey about 1750, the area was trackless; the castles were accompanied by the farms of Hennynook and Aulmaud. Brucklay Castle was remodelled in 1849, but in 1858 Pratt found little else, Clackriach being *"the old manor-house"*, inhabited until the early 19[th] century but *"fast falling to decay"*.

**Maud Junction – a Railway Village**: The Great North of Scotland Railway's Peterhead branch, built northwards from Dyce in 1858–61, descended through the valley. Apparently deriving its name from Aulmaud, Maud Junction station was opened in 1865 where the new line to Fraserburgh diverged from the main stem of the Buchan lines. Wordie & Co soon operated a rail to road cartage depot, which also served New Deer; in the winter a horse-drawn sledge replaced the usual *'lorry'*, a wheeled flatbed. About 1870 a poorhouse was built, by 1873 there was a post office and a school; streets were laid out, and *'New Maud'* grew into a village, with an inn and smithy by 1894. By 1900 a livestock market had been opened, and by 1902 the Victoria Hall. Later the placename became simply *'Maud'*. The poorhouse had become a small general hospital by 1951 when there were also veterinary surgeons, an oil depot and a mill; the population was about 1000, and other more typical village facilities were available. But Brucklay Castle was unroofed in 1953, and a ruin by 1964.

**Maud loses the Railway**: Livestock traffic by rail ceased in 1963, buses helped Maud to lose its passenger trains in 1965, and the Peterhead branch was closed completely in 1970. By 1971 Maud's population was only 634. In the early days of North Sea oil, Maud goods yard handled concrete-coated pipes from Invergordon, and also oxygen for welding. The line to Fraserburgh lingered on for freight until 1979 when one last special passenger train was run, on which the author rode; by that time the once busy junction station was in a deplorable state of neglect. Though by 1981 the population had stabilised, the local secondary school, chemist, dentist and vets had been lost, and the hospital was converted to geriatric use. However, some new housing had been built west of the village, and in 1991, 771 people lived in Maud.

**Farmers Still Well Served**: By 1995 the long-overgrown railway platforms had been transformed into an attractive picnic area; a small railway museum is open for limited hours in the former station building. In 1996 Sellar's still dealt in combine harvesters and farm machinery in Maud and in four other localities. The small but well-kept livestock market continued to sell sheep and cattle under Aberdeen & Northern Marts of Inverurie – until closure in 2001 due to the foot and mouth outbreak. Maud retains a bank, fire station, doctor, primary school, post office, and a small range of shops and services. Farmers are served by Grampian Tractors, New Holland Farm Services, and CSC Crop Protection among others, and a tiny factory makes power cleaning equipment. The modest *Station Hotel* still reminds us of the origins of the village.

## MAY ISLE (or Isle of May) — Map 6, C4

***Island in Firth of Forth*** — OS 59: NT 6599

An early monastery on the small cliffy flat-topped Isle of May, in the outer Firth of Forth 8 km off the coast of Fife, had the Irish monk Ethernan or Adrian as Abbot *(see Cellardyke)*. All the May Isle monks were killed when the monastery was destroyed by Viking raiders in 875; a mound was raised over their burial place, and Adrian was canonised. In the early 12th century a Cluniac priory was briefly established on the May, relying on revenues earned by the fishermen of Pittenweem, to whose new Priory the monks transferred in 1141. In 1145 David I gave May Isle to Reading Abbey in Berkshire; they built a new small monastery, but still suffered from raiders. By 1170 the May marked a renowned fishing ground among Scots, English, Flemish and French fishermen. Being a remote and outlying problem for Reading Abbey, the isle was donated to the Bishop of St Andrews in 1288, only to be ruined in the Wars of Independence. A new chapel was built in the 14th century at the monastery, which became a centre for pilgrims, who slowly piled some 1.5 million beach cobbles atop the burial mound until the Reformation ended pilgrimages.

**Pioneer Lighthouse, Tragedy and Conservation**: Between Crail and the May is the Hirst, once a famed herring spawning area. In 1625 the laird of the May was Sir James Learmonth of Balcomie, who set up a beacon for mariners on the isle. The first proper lighthouse in Scotland, a 12 m-tall tower bearing a coal-fired brazier, was built on the May in 1636 by its laird, Alexander Cunningham of West Barns and James Maxwell of Innerwick (both of East Lothian). The light was financed by dues collected from shipping entering the Forth and remained coal-lit till 1816, when replaced on a new tower by the Northern Lighthouse Board. In the winter of 1833 bad weather marooned 500 people on the May. In summer it was a very popular destination for pleasure trips – until in 1837 the exposed nature of its rocky landing place caused a tragedy which drowned 13 of the 65 passengers on the boat *Johns*. (Present-day pleasure boat operators keep its dangers well in mind). An elaborate experiment in electric lighting was installed in 1886 *(see Munro, 1979)*; the light reverted to oil in 1924 and was eventually automated in 1989. By 1994 the Isle of May was a national nature reserve owned by Scottish Natural Heritage, and excavations of the monastic communities continued throughout the 1990s.

## MAYBOLE — Map 1, C2

***Ayrshire small town,*** *pop. 4800* — OS 70: NS 3010

Maybole in the Carrick area some 12 km south of Ayr occupies what is for Scotland an unusual site, a fairly steep south-easterly hillside far from significant waterways, but above a marshy hollow. Its early name was *Miniboll*, which probably derived from the Brythonic Welsh, *Mynydd y Pwll* ('mount of the pool') or perhaps from Gaelic *Minis na Poll* ('portion of the hollow'). It was first mentioned in 1189, when the area was certainly Gaelic-speaking, and there was a parish church from about that date. Some 3 km to the west was Crossraguel Abbey, whose name may derive from an existing Cross of Riaghail, whose origination is debatable. Raised to the status of an abbey in 1286, it became important and dominated religious affairs in Carrick.

**Lairds Proliferate after the Black Death**: Until heritable jurisdictions were abolished, Maybole was the seat of the *"court of the Bailiery of Carrick"*, the effective capital of that area. The little settlement had a *Spital* or monastic hospital; about 5 km north-east of Maybole was the 14th century Cassilis Castle. The abbey suffered greatly in 1306 during the Wars of Independence, but was repaired. After the Black Death, Maybole's parish church was augmented by a collegiate establishment by John and Gilbert Kennedy of Dunure, in three stages from 1371 to 1441. The surrounding area bristled with 16th century castles, including Crossraguel keep, and the Baltersan and Brockloch towers. In 1516 Maybole was granted a charter as a burgh of barony. It once contained no fewer than 28 lairds' winter residences, of which the chief was another 16th century tower house, the *'castle'* of the Kennedy Earls of Cassilis.

**From Reformation Destruction to Education**: It was said of Carrick in the 1560s that *"the people for the most part speak Irish"*, i.e. Gaelic. The collegiate church was desecrated in 1561 at the Reformation. The abbey too was brutally ravished in 1570, but monks remained until 1592 and the abbey was shown on Pont's map made around 1600, together with Deans Mill. *'Minnyboll'* was shown as a sprawling place, east of which was the *'Loch of Mackrymoir'* (which later silted up) and the mill *Machar Mor* (Gaelic for *'big plain')*; it was later renamed Myremill. Though a school existed from 1602, and a post office was opened in 1689, Maybole was ignored by early travel writers.

**Wool, Leather and Cotton**: By the time of the Roy survey about 1754, Maybole was a substantial place where the winding road from Ayr to Girvan was crossed by a road linking Turnberry with Straiton. A woollen manufactory was established in the mid 18th century, and around 1793 both Hunters & Co (bankers of Ayr) and the Paisley Union Banking Company had short-lived branches in the town. Maybole, which was long known as a leatherworking centre, was also a post town by 1797. Heron noted in 1799 that *"the town of Maybole, situated on a ridge, with a southern exposure, and an amphitheatre of hills behind it, contains about 1200 inhabitants, many of them remarkable for their longevity; about 300 are employed in the manufacture of coarse woollens. The cotton manufacture has also been lately introduced."*

**Irish Protestants move to Maybole**: It appears that many of the weavers were Irish Protestant immigrants, who founded the first Orange Lodge in Scotland at Maybole around 1800. A new parish church was built in 1808, and by 1811 four fairs were held each year. In 1827 Chambers found *"Maybole, the capital of Carrick, is a good-looking town whose principal business is cotton-weaving, a considerable trade in shoes, and a large manufactory of blankets. Such is the general prosperity, that at present there are several whole streets rising at once in the suburbs. The population is greatly tinged with Irish."* The one-time provost's house of the ruined collegiate church had become an inn.

**Reapers, Rakes and Railway**: Alexander Jack began to make reaping machines in the town in the 1850s, and his firm later manufactured a variety of farm implements from wood and iron, including horse-drawn hayrakes. Police burgh status was granted in 1857. The Ayr & Maybole Railway (a Glasgow & South Western subsidiary) opened in 1856. It was extended to

*St Cuthberts boot & shoe factory, Maybole, pictured in 1968. Maybole was a centre for boot and shoe manufacture in the late 19th and 20th centuries.* *(JRH)*

Girvan in 1860 and to Stranraer in 1870. Maybole grew into a substantial town which had the largest school in Ayrshire by 1882, with over 600 pupils; this became a secondary school in 1894 and is now Carrick Academy.

**Footwear Prospers – then given the Boot**: By 1886 five factories in Maybole were producing 200,000 pairs of shoes a year. At least fifty traders existed by then, a gas works and the *King's Arms Hotel* were open by 1894, and Maybole had ten footwear manufacturers by about 1900, when the population reached some 5000. A public library got under way in 1903, with Carnegie assistance. In the early 20th century most new development was council housing, and Maybole was hit by the growing preference for lighter footwear; only two boot factories with 300 jobs remained by 1948. There were three hotels by the 1950s, and the population remained around 5000. A 9-hole municipal golf course was provided in 1970. The Maybole boot industry was extinct by 1976, and although McQuater Brothers remained in business as agricultural merchants, there had been an appreciable decline in Maybole's small-town facilities, including the loss of a hotel and both cinemas by 1981. The town was then dominated by council housing.

**Fine Packaging – but not for Maybole**: Further decline in shopping occurred in the 1980s due to heavy through traffic and the narrowness of the pavements. In 1991 the population was 4737; for a country town Maybole gave a depressing and workaday impression, and showed more than its share of vandalism. For some reason Maybole had specialised into packaging, with the Ripley Group's Clyde Gravure works, Clark Stephen in the print, packaging and display business, and a substantial and shiny new extension had been built to the small modern factory of International Packaging UK; there was also a road haulier. Today Carrick Academy has a roll just over 600, Maybole still enjoys a passenger train service, and there has been a little more housing development.

## MEIGLE

**Map 6, B2**

***Small Angus village**, pop. 675 (area)* OS 53: NO 2844

In the first century a Roman fort was built on the banks of the Dean Water, in a once marshy area of Strathmore; its later name Cardean means *'Valley Fort'*. One of many ancient carved stones in the area depicted a chariot, perhaps as used by the Picts at the battle of *Mons Graupius*. Later there may have been a 9th century monastery at Meigle, 1.5 km south of Cardean, which was (according to Chambers) a former seat of the Bishops of Dunkeld. Belmont Castle dated from the 15th or 16th century, and by 1593 Meigle had become the centre of a presbytery. About 1600 Timothy Pont made several rather confused sketch maps: the name Drumkilbo can be recognised, and an inset showed buildings beside the *'Kirk of Meigill'*. Another Pont map indicated a bridge across the Dean Water – which still stood, though roadless, about 1750. Meigle was chartered as a burgh of Barony in 1608. Its growth was slow for 150 years despite its situation on the Coupar Angus to Forfar road, shown on the Roy map of the 1750s. Much of the area was still marshy, with a small loch east of *'Drumkelby'*, whose mansionhouse stood on a ridge.

**Farms, Roads and Services**: The area was drained during the prevailing agricultural improvements, and a new land use pattern was created. Meigle House was built by 1785. A water mill was built at Cardean, the turnpike road to Dundee was completed in the 1790s, and a crossroads was formed north of Belmont Castle, then the seat of the Mackenzies although little now remains of the original. Round the crossroads grew permanent buildings. Two fairs were scheduled at Meigle in 1797, and in 1799 Heron wrote of Meigle as a *"village"*; a post office opened there in 1802. The stone Bridge of Crathies across the Isla on the Alyth road was built in 1819, and Chambers described Meigle in 1827 as *"a little parish town"*. By about 1830 John Alexander kept an inn.

**Railway Confusion**: In 1837 the primitive Dundee & Newtyle Railway (DNR) was extended east to Glamis and west to Coupar Angus from a junction near Belmont, 2 km south of the crossroads. The Scottish Midland Junction Railway which opened in 1848 linked Perth with Forfar by using much of the DNR's new Strathmore alignment. An inn was built near its Meigle station, which became a 4-way junction when the Alyth branch was opened in 1861, with direct access from Dundee to Alyth. A new station was opened on the branch close to Meigle village, named Fullarton until 1876 when it was renamed Meigle; the main line station became *Alyth Junction*. As road traffic grew, the Bridge of Crathies was reconstructed in 1935. By 1951 the facilities of a typical small village, including a primary school, served a population of about 750, having two inns, a famed museum of Pictish sculptured stones, a haulier and also a cottage hospital.

**Going off the Tracks**: The Alyth branch railway was closed to passengers in 1951 and to goods in 1965, but Alyth Junction remained open as a station until the whole Strathmore line lost its passenger services in 1967; rail freight ended in 1982. By 1971 the seasonal Belmont outdoor centre added a changing youthful population; in 1993 it could accommodate 250 residential students. In 1974 Meigle was a small but busy service village with six shops, three motor businesses including a new car showroom, and a cattle transport depot. By 1977 the mansionhouse of Kinloch 2 km west of Meigle had become the

*Kings of Kinloch Hotel*. By 1980 there were four small hotels in or near the village, whose tiny population had tended to rise somewhat over the years. However, some village businesses closed, including the Royal Bank in 1996. The remarkable steading to Meigle House was restored in 1999; the museum, garage, central hotel, a grocery, antiques and coffee shop are still open, and the restored Cardean mill forms self-catering accommodation.

## MEIKLE FERRY

**Map 9, B2**

***E. Ross location***

OS 21: NH 7386

By 1560 the Meikle Ferry across the Dornoch Firth 6 km north-west of Tain was an important link in the overland route to the far north. *'Ferrytoun'* was shown on the north bank in Blaeu's 17th century atlas, and the Roy map of about 1750 also named the ferry; from the *'Ferryhouse'* on the north bank a track led to Dornoch, while on the south side, tracks connected to Tain and the Kyle of Sutherland. In 1809 a disaster on the Meikle Ferry killed 99 people attending the Lammas Fair in Tain. In 1819 a pathetic gathering of evicted Sutherland tenants met at the *Meikle Ferry Inn* on the north shore. After the Bonar Bridge was opened way upstream in 1812 the ferry remained *"for pedestrians and small vehicles"* (Chambers), for whom it saved some 25 km. It was also used by the mails, and early in the 19th century the Postmaster General paid for an inn to be built to serve the ferry. The Inverness & Ross-shire Railway made Meikle Ferry its temporary terminus in 1864, but after the circuitous Sutherland Railway reached Golspie from the south in 1868, ferry usage declined, and the station was closed within 9 months. The inn was not shown on the 1894 OS map, and the ferry was confined to foot passengers from the early 20th century until its demise about 1948. About 1970 an inn bearing the traditional name was built on the approach to the south terminal of the former ferry, and by 1978 a caravan and camping site had been established nearby. A new road bridge was built in 1988–91 somewhat east of the ferry site to shorten the A9, controversially omitting the rail link which had also been planned but which the anti-rail Thatcher government would not fund. In 2001 this question was reopened.

## MEIKLEOUR

**Map 6, B3**

***Small Perthshire village,*** *pop. 800 (area)*

OS 53: NO 1639

In the 11th century, Kinclaven Castle was built by its thane in the sharp elbow of the River Tay at its confluence with the River Isla, confronting a medieval motte east of the river at Cargill. Lethendy is a tiny rural parish to the north. Kinclaven, where a parish school was held by 1609, was for centuries connected by a ferry with Meikleour, north of the two rivers, which was chartered as a burgh of barony in 1665. The famous 600 m-long beech hedge at Meikleour was planted in 1746 beside the track between Perth and Blairgowrie; the Isla was not yet bridged and may have been forded. A linen bleachfield was built at Lawton near Cargill in the period 1746–60. Meikleour was shown as a mere hamlet on Roy's map of about 1750. The Bridge of Isla was opened in 1796, and three annual fairs were held at Meikleour in 1797.

**World's Best Salmon Beat?**: Cargill bridge on the Scottish Midland Junction Railway had piers built of stone from Keithick quarry near Burrelton, and five cast-iron arches; the line opened in 1848, Cargill station lying 2 km to the south of Meikleour across the (road) Bridge of Isla. A railway goods siding near Kinclaven school was at first named Innernytie, and later renamed after the Victorian baronial mansion of Ballathie House, which was built west of the river. By 1895 Meikleour had a post office and an inn. Kinclaven Bridge was opened for road traffic in 1905, replacing the Tay ferry; by that time the beech hedge was 26 m tall. In 1951 the village population was only 300, and with the closure of Cargill station about 1960, had declined to only 200 by 1981. *Ballathie House* became a hotel about 1972, and Meikleour still retained a minimum of facilities to serve the wider area's 800 people. Little change was evident by 2000 when the Tay Salmon Fisheries Company, who employed 3 ghillies on the 1 km Islamouth beat (claimed as the world's best), put it up for sale.

## MELROSE

**Map 3, B4**

***Borders small town,*** *pop. 3000*

OS 73: NT 5434

Near the centre of the wide basin of the River Tweed are the triple-peaked Eildon Hills, which bore the major Iron Age fort of the Votadini tribe. The Roman fort of Trimontium, named after the hills and intended to help subdue the natives, was first built on the river bank about 80 AD. It was repeatedly strengthened, becoming in the Antonine period a major base covering 4.4 ha. At one time 800 cavalry were stationed there, and a dig in 1905–08 found the remains of much Roman equipment (*Johnson*). In 1993 the site of what was probably the most northerly amphitheatre in the Roman Empire was discovered close by. The fort was occupied until about 180 AD, then being forgotten.

**Monastic Development on the Grand Scale**: The much later Anglian village of Newstead was built more or less over the Roman fort. Meantime during the Dark Ages a monastery was set up at Old Melrose *(q.v.)* 2 km to the east. When a Cistercian abbey was founded by David I at Melrose in 1136 as a major offshoot of Rievaulx Abbey in Yorkshire, a new site 2 km west of the Roman fort was chosen, where a huge church was built, 87 m long and 48 m at its greatest breadth; it also acted as the parish church. The abbey held property in Glasgow from the foundation of that burgh. In 1225 it sent wool and other merchandise to Flanders, the monks regularly communicating with Berwick by cart – demonstrating the existence of a viable road for the monastery's valuable wool exports. By 1240 the abbey also held some property as distant as Boston in Lincolnshire, and in 1296 owned ten properties in Berwick, one of them a *'large house'*.

**Wool and Wars, Pestilence and Fire**: Among other activities the monks bred horses, and owned some 12,500 sheep in the late 13th century, probably the largest flock in Scotland. Despite the Cistercians' charter requirement of remoteness, a settlement grew up beside the abbey, and Melrose town was walled and gated by 1322. The abbey was twice wrecked by the English, in 1322 and 1385, and twice rebuilt. The lay brothers still sold sorted wool around 1400, although by the late 15th century there were only 17 monks. Darnick Tower 1 km west of Melrose was built in the 16th century, and a bridge existed near Darnick by 1545 when the village and abbey of Melrose were yet again burned by the English; the bridge was evidently torn down too. Even so in 1560 the abbey possessed seven appropriated churches; in 1569 its Commendator, James Douglas of Loch Leven Castle, took over. By 1593 the lay settlement had been rebuilt and become the centre of a presbytery, but was shown as a small place on Pont's map of Lauderdale. There was no Tweed bridge at that time between Peebles and Berwick, though the name *'Briggend'* west of Darnick showed where one had formerly stood.

**Burgh, Linen and Woollens**: Melrose was made a burgh of barony in 1605, a parish school was founded in 1608 and in 1609 the abbey became the property of Viscount Haddington. A market was held from at least 1642, but Melrose remained off the map so far as early travel writers were concerned. In 1668 the Earl of Haddington as laird incorporated the burgh's weavers, who had long made linen, but the trade had declined locally by 1744. The Roy map surveyed around 1754 showed *'Mulross'* as a small crossroads village, with roads to Edinburgh via Darnick's reinstated bridge, and to Selkirk and Kelso. A new linen bleachfield had been built by 1760, and for a time cloth was exported to London and the continent. In all 140 looms were in use in 1776 – most were manufacturing woollen cloth.

**Post and Industry in "A Curious Antique Place"**: There was a post office in Melrose from 1768, which in 1813 was a key junction for the mails (a function later transferred to Galashiels). By 1778 flour mills had been constructed for the Earl of Melrose, and Vanhegen's brewery was quite large by the 1790s. Four fairs were to be held in 1797. In 1799 Heron mentioned Newstead as a *"village"*, while *"the town of Melrose"* had some manufactures of linen, woollens and cotton; he noted the *"fine bridges"* that had been built not only at Darnick but also at Drygrange (Leaderfoot), 3 km to the east. In 1803 Dorothy Wordsworth found Melrose was a *"town"* with an inn, but remarked on the *"insignificant houses"* crowding the abbey ruins and the *"ugliest church"* within the abbey walls. However, a new parish church was erected in 1810. In the early 19th century a second mill was built, but the bleachfield was closed by the late 1820s. Chambers in 1827 found *"the celebrated abbey of Melrose, surrounded by the little village of the same name, an extremely curious and antique little place, in a great measure built out of the ruins of the abbey"*.

*Melrose Abbey church from the south-east, as rebuilt in the 15th century by French masons. This is the finest church architecture of the later Middle Ages in Scotland.* *(JRH)*

A chain suspension bridge had recently been built across the Tweed to the hamlet of Gattonside.

**Melrose on the Railway**: The North British Railway's protégé which opened between Edinburgh and Hawick in 1849 provided a very attractive wayside station at Melrose, enabling a tourist trade to develop, based on the abbey ruins and local associations with Sir Walter Scott. The German travel writer Fontane complained in 1858 that tolls were still payable to use the turnpike to Abbotsford; he noted the *Railway Hotel* open in the *"little town"*. Melrose golf club was founded in 1880, laying out its 9-hole course on the lower slopes of the Eildon Hills. The large *Waverley Hydropathic Establishment* was built between Melrose and Darnick in 1869–71, later being renamed the *Waverley Castle Hotel*. By about 1890 there was a local fire brigade, and Gattonside had a post office. In 1894 Melrose was dismissed by Murray as *"unattractive"*, and the *Abbey Hotel* which still stood on the site of the abbey narthex was only *"fair"*. The *Station Hotel* was mentioned in 1905. Electricity was supplied from a burgh power station built in 1901, and a gasworks was built (or rebuilt) in 1908.

**From Railway to Motor Museum**: A youth hostel was opened in the 1930s, and by 1951 there were five hotels offering almost 100 rooms between them. Melrose retained its station until the closure of the whole Waverley Route in 1969, but the textile industry, still functioning into the 1970s, seems to have closed by 1980. However, the opening of a motor museum, the laying out of a garden by the National Trust for Scotland, and the general growth of tourism, ensured that Melrose kept its status as a large village, on the margin of being a town. (The dividing line is of course a matter of opinion! Maybe the existence by 1977 of so specialised a retailer as Clinkscale's musical instrument shop confirmed its urbanity.) In 1981 Newstead still had a post office, but its population had fallen below 300. Melrose remained a fairly prosperous inland tourist resort, where the *Waverley Castle Hotel* – the erstwhile hydro – was merely the largest of seven hotels; though the station building had been conserved, the route of the old railway was used in 1987 to create a bypass road.

**Borders Hospital and Teddy Bear Museum**: Melrose assumed new importance when the Borders District General Hospital at Huntlyburn was completed in 1987, replacing Peel Hospital near Clovenfords. By 1991 the 2270 residents in Melrose showed an affluent retired character. Despite some new housing, Gattonside still had under 500 people; its post office, and that at Newstead, had closed in the 1980s. In 1992 Felix Sear opened a new tourist attraction in Melrose, his Teddy Bear Museum, claiming the world's third largest collection of these soft toys. The Abbey ruins are still an important draw. Some more housing has been built near the hospital, and a new road approach from the east has been constructed. There are several hotels for visitors (the King's Arms Inn claims 300 years of service), and a youth hostel.

## MELVICH, Portskerra & Strathy — **Map 13, A4**

***Small N. Sutherland villages,*** *pop. 420* — OS 10: NC 8765

The exposed north coast of Sutherland has some ancient remains, and all three of the above places were named on Blaeu's mid 17th century atlas map; but the area was still roadless in the 1750s except for an isolated stretch along the coast of Farr, between Strathy at the mouth of the River Strathy and Tongue. Roy then noted some settlement at Melvich and Tore, either side of the mouth of the River Halladale about 5km east of Strathy. Melvich post office was issued with a cancelling stamp in 1832, and Portskerra to the north became a fishing village, with 330 people in 1891. By the late 19th century the coastal road was complete, and joined to Forsinard station and the south by a road up Strath Halladale. By the time of World War II the 20-room *Melvich Hotel* was open and there was a pier. By the 1950s the primary school, garage and other basic local facilities served about 850 people, 550 of them living locally. The elaborate but squat and squarely built lighthouse on Strathy Point came into use as late as 1958; though the first in Scotland to be all-electric, it was the last to be built for manned operation. Although the population was falling, by 1978 there was a tourist office and pony trekking. In 1991 the local population was around 420. By 1996 lighthouse automation ruled, even at Strathy Point.

## MENSTRIE

**Map 16, B1**

***Clackmannanshire small town,*** *pop. 2300* — OS 58: NS 8596

In the 16th century a castle was built at Menstrie, a hillfoot site 5km north-west of Alloa; it had an early mill. There was also a castle beside the Forth at Manor (OS 57), 3km south-west of Menstrie, but the Roy map of about 1750 showed little settlement and no roads. The very early Glenochil malt whisky distillery had been founded in 1746; in 1845–46 it was greatly enlarged and converted to produce grain whisky. By 1800 the Archibalds had opened the Elmbank wool scribbling mill, which was extended in 1810–13 to make blankets; by 1841 its 50 workers made shawls. Menstrie post office opened around 1825. From 1863 the Alva Railway Company (later part of the North British) provided passenger and freight services, including a siding to the distillery. Elmbank Mill was enlarged about 1860 by Drummond & Johnstone, with an attractive two-storey extension of 1100 m² for woollen spinning and weaving; in 1869 this was a large factory with eight sets of very recent steam-driven carding engines. In the mid 1880s Menstrie was described by Beveridge as *"a thriving village manufacturing tartans and woollen goods"*, one of the three main Hillfoot woollen centres.

**Enter DCL and Manor Powis Colliery**: Glenochil distillery was owned in 1876 by McNab Brothers, who produced yeast commercially from the 1870s; in 1877 they joined DCL as founder members of this new grain whisky combine. By 1886 steam power had been introduced; Coffey stills made about 4.5 million litres of grain whisky annually, and over 100 DCL workers included those in a large cooperage. Furniture manufacture also developed, though Menstrie remained small, with only 900 people in 1901. By that time the castle at Manor was a ruin (and within 50 years it had disappeared). The small Manor Powis colliery was sunk in 1912 on the north bank of the Forth, its output at first including anthracite; a third shaft was sunk in 1923. By 1945 production was down to 128,000 tonnes, mainly of the poor quality Upper Hirst coal. In 1955 the deepening of No.3 shaft to 410m was begun by the new Alloa Area of the NCB, hoping to raise 1500 tonnes of anthracite a day until the year 2040; but geological advice was sought too late and work was done in vain up to 1959. The pit was still open in 1966, but only the waste bing now remains.

**Modern Menstrie**: At some time after 1924 whisky distilling ceased, but yeast production continued. Menstrie Castle was gutted by fire in 1950 and fell into ruin. By 1951 there were 1400 people in Menstrie, plus a furniture factory, but still only the facilities of a small village. The passenger trains were withdrawn in 1954 and freight services beyond the yeast factory ended in 1964. By 1976 the woollen mill had become water board offices, and a vast complex of bonded warehouses had been erected 3km south of the village. In the 1980s the Regional Council bought Elmbank mill for use as a store, but it stood vacant in 1993. The Glenochil yeast factory, which in 1976 had the DCL research laboratory, had become by 1989 the Unilever subsidiary Quest International, Britain's only manufacturer of yeast powder, much used to add flavour to snack foods. By 1991 the population was 2274. In the late 1990s Quest still made flavours and food ingredients from yeast. Menstrie still has its ruined castle, post office and inn.

## METHIL & Methilhill

**Map 6, B4**

***Fife coast town,*** *pop. 8000* — OS 59: NT 3799

Also see: *Buckhaven & Leven*

Methil on the south coast of Fife existed by 1212: its church and fulling mills stood beside the River Leven some 2 km from its mouth at Innerleven. Pont's map – made perhaps as early as 1585 – showed Cameron Bridge 1km farther upstream, but not Methil, where coal mining began at an early date. There were already five saltpans on the coast west of Leven by 1592, and *'Cold-cotts'* was shown on James Gordon's map of about 1642. This was perhaps the location of the wooden jetty for coal and salt export which existed before David, the second Earl of Wemyss, obtained full mining powers in 1661 and a burgh of barony charter in 1662. Earl David built Methil's first small tidal harbour, and coal was first shipped from it in 1664. The harbour's two breakwaters were shown on John May's chart of about 1680. Meantime two more saltpans were added, and an annual fair was held from 1666. Some time after 1711 the original riverside settlement was abandoned.

**Methil moves to the Coast**: Defoe noted in the 1720s that Methil was *"a little town, but a very safe and good harbour, firmly built of stone. Here my Lord Wemyss brings his coal, which he digs two miles off, on the banks of the River Leven"* (where water was causing problems in the coal workings) *"and here it is sold or shipped off; as also what salt he can make, which is not a great deal."* This was probably produced at *'Methill Pans'* on the coast road, which appeared on the Roy map of about 1750, though the mine was evidently at Coaltown of Methil in the Crossroads area, some way inland. Kirkland Spinning Mills and nearby housing were established in the 1780s on the river about 1km east of the ancient church. A wagonway was completed in 1789 for the seventh Earl, to carry coal from his nearby pit at Kirkland to Methil harbour. In 1799 Heron noted *"shipbuilding, a good harbour, and abundance of coal. The village contains about 300 inhabitants."*

**Storm brings Quietude**: The harbour was destroyed in a storm in 1803 and not reinstated until 1838, and the nine saltpans open in the 1790s ceased to operate after the Salt Tax was imposed in 1825. However, in 1826 there were colliery pumping engines at Kirkland, and north of the river was the extensive Durie Haugh bleachfield. A new parish church was built in 1837, but the Leven Railway, which opened in 1854, kept north of the river. In 1866 Peter & Co's Kirkland spinning

*Methil was developed in the late 19th century as a coal mining and shipment centre, by the Wemyss family; they built housing and community facilities of quality, like these 2-storey cottages.* (JRH)

mill and linen factory dominated the local economy; there was also a paraffin oil works and about a dozen shops.

**The Expansion of Mining**: Methil looked under its feet and found more coal: its stunted growth resumed when the Fife Coal Company – formed in 1872 – sank the two Leven pits west of Innerleven in 1877–78. This understandably very wet colliery worked the Chemiss seam from 270m and eventually had three shafts. It was connected by mineral railways with the North British (NBR) line at Cameron Bridge, and by a tunnel with Methil harbour. In 1875 the first school was built at Methil. At the instigation of Lady Wemyss, a dedicated coal dock was built in 1872–75 by a Wemyss estate subsidiary; in 1876 some 35,000 tonnes of coal were shipped. Methil station was opened in 1881, with passenger trains to Buckhaven, Wemyss and Thornton. A second dock was constructed in 1883–87 by Randolph Wemyss, and rail-connected to the NBR at Leven. In 1887 the dock's single wagon tippler exported some 200,000 tonnes of coal. In that year a telegraph pole creosoting plant was opened; this gradually expanded until after World War II.

**Coal and Fish Exports Peak**: Only 1662 people lived in the burgh in 1891. Methil then comprised four parts: Kirkland was a hamlet; inland of the linear coastal settlement at Innerleven were three collieries, served by a mineral railway parallel to the river. From east to west these were the Leven Nos.1 & 2 and the Pirnie – (worked from about 1860 to 1920) at Methilhill, where by 1895 a tiny mining village with an inn had been built. Methil proper (now Lower Methil) was a small seaport town on the narrow coastal plain; a port of registry, its code letters were *'ML'*. What became its No.1 dock was reconstructed from the two earlier docks by the NBR and reopened in 1897; No.2 dock was added in 1894–1900. The coal docks were notable for their gloomy road tunnel access under the linking railway. By then four coal hoists were tipping well over 1.5 million tonnes into vessels each year, and large amounts of fish were rail-hauled from Anstruther to Methil docks for export, particularly to Germany, which took so much of Methil's trade that in 1900 a German seamen's mission was opened.

**Football, Wemyss Private Railway and Tramways**: In 1901 the new combined police burgh of Buckhaven & Methil was created; remarkably its offices were located in the smaller town of Buckhaven. The football club formed in 1903 at the tiny Bayview Park took the much snappier name of *'East Fife'*. The Wemyss Private Railway was begun by the estate in 1898. Not a passenger line, it was intended to link collieries around East and West Wemyss via the rather later Wemyss brickworks to the central washery, and to Methil docks. In 1904 the Wemyss & District Tramways were opened, with a depot at Aberhill. They operated electric cars from Scoonie and Leven to East Wemyss and Gallatown along Wellesley Road, which was built by the Company to allow closure of the coast road to accommodate the colliery.

**Coal, Coasting, and *'Liners'* to Leith**: In 1906 Matthew Taylor of Methil started a coastwise coal business with the old 300-ton coaster *Wans Fell*. In 1907 Methil shipped some 2.8 million tonnes, a third of Fife's peak mining production; it was then among Britain's top ten coal exporting ports. In 1907 work began on No.3 dock, built by the NBR on land reclaimed from the Forth; when opened with its six coal hoists in 1913 it completed Scotland's largest coal port. Its associated new railway yard, named Kirkland, on the Leven bank of the river, had almost 20km of tracks for coal trucks. In that year Methil's foreign shipping movements alone approached a million tons. By around 1910 passenger steamships of the Galloway Line plied between Methil and Leith. Later with more ships Taylor also carried such cargoes as oats to London, goods from the Continent, coal for the Admiralty, china clay, and empty fish barrels from Buckie to Lerwick. In 1921 he added Mediterranean cargo trading; although this was killed by the 1939–45 war, coasting continued.

**New Industries, Housing and Services**: The prominent *White Swan Hotel* was built in 1906 and the *Gaiety Theatre* in 1907; by about 1914 the larger 1000-seater *Palace Picture House* was open, and in the 1920s the former also turned to films as the *Western Cinema*. Aberhill brickworks was opened by Messrs Rose in 1908. In 1910 the Kirkland Steel Foundry was established; in 1914 it became the National Steel Foundry, and was extended in 1938. Large-scale urban development began on the plateau at Upper Methil from the time that electricity was available in the town from 1911, and after the war the 230 houses in the Methilhill estate were built by the WCC in 1924–25. Meantime in 1923 Central Farmers commenced their trading business in fertilisers and animal feedstuffs. In that year some 3 million tonnes of coal were exported, but the Leven colliery was failing, and closed in 1931.

**Wonder in the Shops and on the Park**: The Wonder Store began to trade about 1925, its various departments gradually coming to dominate retailing in the town, and in 1935 a new public library was built. After the abandonment of the tramway in 1932, the depot building passed to Alexander's bus company. Methil's coal exports held up well until stopped by the 1939–45 war; they resumed after 1945, and six pilots were still employed about 1955. Methil's housing was largely rebuilt with extensive council estates during the inter-war and early post-war period, becoming a single urban entity with Buckhaven. Its football heyday was between 1938, when East Fife won the Scottish Cup, and 1953 when they last won the

League Cup; 21,000 spectators squeezed into Bayview Park. By then Methil had a population of 13,000 and the facilities of a small town, though these were rather unfocused.

**The End of the Coal Trade**: By the 1950s the railway engine shed had closed. Passenger trains to Thornton were withdrawn in 1955, leaving the town heavily dependent on Leven's services. Then in 1957 the locally based Taylor coasting fleet ceased to trade, and Aberhill brickworks was closed around 1960. Following the Michael colliery fire *(see East Wemyss)* the Wemyss Private Railway was closed in 1970, and swiftly almost every trace was removed. Coal exports from Methil, the last coal port in Fife, ceased entirely in 1976–77, leaving feedstuffs, pulp and timber trade. In the 1960s the *Western Cinema* turned to bingo; by the 1990s it was a night club. For years the increasingly sad, drab town centre had been enlivened by the opportunistic shopping developments of the Wonder Store. Their main premises were destroyed by fire in 1974, but they struggled on. In 1975 the burgh was merged into the new Kirkcaldy District. In 1978 the bus depot was closed, but was soon converted into the East Fife indoor bowling rink.

**The Slurry Power Station and other Developments**: A new 60mW power station of two units, unique in Britain in being designed to burn slurry from Coal Board washeries, was built at Innerleven in 1962–66, with boilers by Babcock of Renfrew, their furnaces fed by gantry grabs made at Carnoustie by Anderson-Grice. Kirkland High School was opened in 1963, and much redevelopment further improved the town's housing. As mining declined, so Central Farmers took over the site of the Leven colliery, and gradually came to dominate the much-reduced trade of the port, where the SDA undertook massive clearance operations. The gloomy arches at the dock entrance vanished in 1979, and in the early 1980s Number 3 dock was largely infilled to create an industrial estate, though this attracted few new concerns.

**Offshore Fabrication and other Industry**: In 1972 the site of the Wellesley colliery *(see Buckhaven)* was taken over by Redpath Dorman Long (RDL) to form a construction yard for gigantic steel-built oil platform jackets; however a sizeable bing remained. The yard was later acquired and more successfully operated by Redpath de Groot Caledonian (RGC). A contract for an 8500-tonne platform for the Gannet field kept most of the 730 workers going in 1989–92, and then work began on the 9500-tonne Total Dunbar jacket. In 1981 Methil had only the facilities of a large village. Local industries included mechanical engineering, knitwear, and a Babygro (Kirkcaldy) branch clothing factory. The National Steel Foundry, known as Glencast from 1983, had 660 workers in 1987, making about 100 tonnes of castings a week, and in 1990 gained a technology award for the *'Replicast'* process of high quality casting. In 1990 the Wemyss brickworks, which had improved its efficiency by computer control of kiln firing, was making a million bricks a week. The works now draws its fireclay from Cults *(see Pitlessie)*. The 1991 population of Methil (including Buckhaven) was 11,824, still somewhat disadvantaged.

**Slurry from Russia and Boatbuilding from St Monans**: In 1990 120 outdated rail wagons were in use to bring in local coal slurry for the base load power station; Russian slurry was also expected to help to keep the station open for 10–15 more years. A timber industry was still active in 1990. By then Miller of St Monans also used a covered wet dock at Methil as a fitting-out yard; in 1992 its last owners closed the ancient firm, but its former production director Bill Syvret established Miller Methil from the ruins, and it was said in 1994–95 to have a healthy order book, with 15–20 employees working there, still mainly serving the fishing industry. A little trade in paper pulp and grain still continued through Methil docks. In 1992 the Babygro factory was bought by local drapers and outfitters Cumming (Leven) Ltd.

**Languishing in the 1990s**: Many shops had closed as trade gradually shifted to Leven, Glenrothes and Kirkcaldy. The Wonder Store closed most departments in 1984, but was still trading in 1994, the year when the former Lower Methil Crown post office was reopened as a Heritage Centre. Though 300 workers were made redundant, in 1993–94 Trafalgar House Offshore Fabricators, by then owners of the yard, built the 3600-tonne Phillips Judy compression module; in all some 300,000 tonnes of offshore steelwork had been fabricated there. By 1996 it was owned by Kvaerner Oil & Gas, who on completing the deck for the British Gas Armada project in 1997 shed 200 jobs at Methil, while retaining a permanent workforce of some 500. East Fife FC sold rundown Bayview Park for a supermarket, enabling a move about 1998 to a new site near the power station, where a single stand suffices for the supporters of a third division team.

## METHLICK

**Map 10, C2**

***Aberdeenshire village,*** *pop. 900* — OS 30: NJ 8537

Hut circles and an ancient field system have survived on Bellmuir beside the middle reaches of the River Ythan, some 12 km north-west of Ellon. Methlick on the south bank of the river gained a parish school by 1614, but was shown as a tiny place on Gordon's map (made about 1640). The only really significant feature on the Roy map of the area, made about 1750, was Methlick Kirk. At that time the nearest track crossed the river 3 km downstream at Tanglandford. Roads were soon built into the area, and in 1858 Pratt noted Methlick as a *"village"* with a bridge of stone and iron. The name Milltown 1.5 km upstream must be significant, and the Mill at Cessnie, 3 km north-east, also appeared on the 1890s OS map. Methlick became a local centre at the end of a horse-drawn coach route to Udny Station, on which motor buses first plied in 1904. By 1951 Methlick had good facilities, serving its own 900 people plus 1300 more within a 5 km radius. But its senior secondary school was downgraded to junior status about 1955, and by 1976 had no secondary classes; those at Barthol Chapel school, some 5 km south-west of Methlick, had also closed.

**Depopulation and famous Daughter**: As one of the largest essentially agricultural villages, Methlick suffered the full force of depopulation, and between 1951 and 1971 the number of residents fell to under 650, with the facilities of a small village. Oil-based prosperity brought some new housing by 1981, when the area's population was back to 900, but facilities remained at a modest level with three shops, a general store, baker and butcher. Meantime Methlick farmer's daughter Evelyn Glennie, born in 1966, had become profoundly deaf, yet by her mid-twenties had almost single-handedly revolutionised the world role of the percussionist as a soloist of the concert platform. By 1995 a hotel was open in addition to the village inn.

## METHVEN
**Map 6, A3**

***Perthshire village,** pop. 1150* OS 53 or 58: NO 0226

The name of Methven, 9km west of Perth, may refer to a Pictish boundary stone; nearby Culdeesland marks an early religious community. Inchaffray, 8km farther west beside the Pow Water was another, whose Augustinian priory, established by the Earl of Strathearn in 1200 for Canons Regular from Scone, was raised to an abbey in 1220–21; close by was Madderty parish church. The abbot was still active in 1314, but the priory may have been a casualty of the Black Death, for little more seems known of it. However, Methven Park existed by 1306 when a battle was fought there, and in 1433 the Earl of Athole founded a college in the existing Methven parish church. Methven Castle, built 1.5km to the east, was besieged in 1444; it was rebuilt in the 16th century, and was neatly sketched by Pont about 1600. He also labelled *'Meffen Kirkton'*, probably the location of the parish school of 1632.

**Hand Weaving, Brewing and the Heat Engine**: Roy's map made about 1750 showed no roads in the area, but added what may have been the policies of Woodhead mansionhouse north of Methven. A new church was built in 1783, and linen manufacture grew rapidly around 1790, to 160 hand weavers making over 100,000m of cloth a year. Methven was called a *"village"* by Heron in 1799, when there were about 400 people. He also noted Almondbank *(q.v.)*, part of which was in Methven parish. By 1813 there was a post office at the *Pack Horse Inn*, and in 1825 a brewery. Robert Stirling, born at Methven in 1790, lacked engineering training but invented the hot air *'heat'* engine in 1816. From this very efficient and *'green'* principle, still not widely adopted, Lord Kelvin was later to develop the laws of thermodynamics. Stirling's sons Patrick and James became notable locomotive engineers.

**The Railways Come and Go**: In 1858 the tiny but grandly named Perth, Almond Valley & Methven Railway was opened from a junction north of Perth to a terminus in the village. In 1866 a junction station was created 1.5km south of Methven, and a line built from there to Crieff by another short-lived company; later both were absorbed by the Caledonian Railway. In 1891 Methven had a population of 650, the two stations, a post and telegraph office, school, and inn. As the population shrank in later years the passenger trains to the terminus were withdrawn in 1937, and from Methven Junction in 1951; freight services lingered until the mid 1960s.

**Growing Village**: By then many detached houses were being built, the population had recovered to about 850, a sawmill and a secondary school were open. The population rose past the 1000 mark about 1976 and a second small hotel was opened, but by then the secondary school had closed, and the local facilities were rather below those of a typical village. In the 1980s some new housing estates further consolidated Methven to 1140 people in 1991. There has been little more new development; the tiny *Methven Arms* provides accommodation.

## MEY, Barrogill & Harrow
**Map 13, B4**

***Caithness hamlets,** pop. 200 (area)* OS 12: ND 2872

In the 16th century the Castle of Barrogill or Mey was built in a gently sloping farming area near the north coast of Caithness, 9km west of John o' Groats. The Roy map showed a clachan at East Mey, but no roads or tracks. These were later laid out; Mey had a post office by about 1839, and in the 19th century the castle was expanded into a 5-storey baronial pile for the Earls of Caithness. In 1856 the 14th Earl opened the Harrow pavement works to quarry and dress the local flagstone, exported via a tramway to a pier completed in 1861 at Harrow, 1km to the west beside the tiny sheltered Wester Haven. However in 1870 a severe storm ruined the pier and the works closed; Spittal quarry took their thwarted customers. The pier was later repaired, and used to import estate needs in coal, lime and drainage tiles. By 1894 there was a school at West Mey, near the small and confusingly named coaching inn, the *Berriedale Arms*. By 1953 the Castle of Mey had become a private home of Elizabeth, the Queen Mother. By 1999 the *Berriedale Arms* had been renamed the *Castle Arms Hotel*, and had a gallery of royal photographs. The post office is still open.

## MID CALDER & East Calder
**Map 16, C3**

***W. Lothian large villages,** pop. 8700* OS 65: NT 0767

Mid Calder stands on a peninsula in the angle between the River Almond and its tributaries, the combined Linhouse and Murieston Waters, some 18km west of Edinburgh; the *Cunnigar* is an ancient earthwork. Calder House became the seat of the Sandilands in the mid 14th century, and the church was already old by 1541. Pont's map, made around 1600, showed the area already thickly settled; Calder House was depicted as substantial and emparked. Pont also showed that both rivers had already been bridged. Mid Calder, which had a parish school from 1611, grew as a village between the bridges. Although not a burgh of barony, it lay on the winding road which came into being between Edinburgh and Livingston, and acquired a market charter. A school was also opened at East Calder, on the hillside 1km to the east.

**Lime, Paper, Post and Canal Water**: The Roy map of the early 1750s showed Mid Calder as a medium-sized nucleated settlement whose two bridges were the focus of five radial roads (a pattern which persists). Limekilns worked at East Calder from around 1770. In 1761 a paper mill was founded at Mid Calder, which had a post office from 1786 and was a post town by 1797, with a service three days a week; it also had an annual fair. In 1799 Heron noted Mid Calder as a *"neat village"* of about 560 people. Early in the 19th century corn mills were built and by 1825 it also possessed a brewery. Calder Hall was built near East Calder in 1810 for Dr James Hare, but was unroofed in 1870. The Bog Burn, remote headwaters of the Murieston Water, was dammed around 1820 to form Cobbinshaw Reservoir, to ensure water supply to the Union Canal; weirs below Mid Calder diverted it into a lade beside the river through Almondell to the canal west of Ratho.

**Oil from Shale**: The Oakbank shale oil works *(see Hay & Stell)* was erected 1km to the south about 1863, and by 1872 employed 350 men, making a full range of refined products; the company built almost 200 houses for its workers. In 1894 Murray remarked that *"Pits and oil works now dot the country all round Mid- and West-Calder, contributing sadly to mar the scenery and pollute the rivers"*. East Calder had a mine, quarries and an inn; there were mineral railways, but no passenger station was handy (the so-called Mid Calder station was at Kirknewton, 3km east). By 1901 the area held over 1000 people. The Oakbank mine was closed in 1908 in favour of a mine at Dedridge, 2km west, which was worked in 1909–19, but the Oakbank refinery worked until 1931. By 1951 some 3000 people lived in the area, with three post offices including Oakbank. Although East Calder was larger in population, Mid Calder with its ancient Cunnigar and emparked Calder House had the facilities of a large village; but the immediate area was once more rural except at Oakbank.

**The Impact of Livingston New Town**: Livingston New Town *(q.v.)*, whose new Almondvale Centre was built only 2 km away, brought many jobs, but built over the rural area to the west, leaving historic Mid Calder largely undisturbed. By 1975 Almondell and Calder Wood had become a linear country park, and between then and 1981 a 5 km bypass on the A71 was built to the south to remove through traffic from the village centres. The ruins of Calder Hall still stood in 1981; Calder House was occupied by Lord Torphichen. The modernised corn mills were still in production, and during the 1980s the dereliction at Oakbank was cleared and afforested. Meantime East Calder was rapidly spreading up the hillside with private housing; by 1991 East and Mid Calder together held 8700 people, of young dormitory character; three-quarters were buying their own homes. In 1995 a further business park related to Livingston was planned for Oakbank by Lothian & Edinburgh Enterprise. Resident there are Jabil (PCB assemby) and Irish construction firm Farrans. East Calder is the base of a large security firm. Much of the one-time park of Calder House has been developed with housing, but a cycleway threads the Almond valley past the Cunnigar, now almost surrounded by development.

## MID CLYTH

**Map 13, B5**

***Caithness settlement,** pop. 100* — OS 11: ND 2937

Around 1750 a coastal track served this scattered Caithness township, some 15 km south of Wick. By 1800, flights of steps led down the 60 m-high cliffs to a tiny fishing harbour. This was crammed in 1855 with 121 boats, but as fisheries dwindled, so they moved to more conventional ports. Mid Clyth had a station on the Wick & Lybster Light Railway, which ran from 1903 to 1944. Barytes was mined nearby during the 1914–18 war, but as the rural population fell below 140 after 1951, post town status was lost; the local primary school closed about 1957, and by 1978 had become a small confectionery works. This left the few people in the area very dependent on Lybster.

## MIDMAR

**Map 10, B3**

***Aberdeenshire small village,** pop. 400* — OS 38: NJ 7005

This area north of the Hill of Fare 24 km west of Aberdeen has much evidence of significant occupation since the prehistoric period, including stone circles. The name of the areas now known as Mar and Moray may derive from the local tribe, known to the Romans as the *Vacomagi*.The first element of the tribal name may arise from the cattle which dominated the economy of the area. Midmar had an ancient church and was perhaps the one-time centre of the extensive Pictish province (later earldom) of Mar. A motte was raised there before the Earls of Mar moved to Kildrummy in the 13th century, leaving a *'manor house'*' (a rare title in Scotland) as the centre of a one-time hunting barony. The sizeable castle was built in the late 16th century by the mason George Bell; but according to Roy it was still trackless around 1750. Later came a proper road system and modern farming. From 1905 motor buses of the Great North of Scotland Railway linked Midmar with Echt and Aberdeen, but despite its 650 people in 1951 the large parish failed to acquire a village centre and stayed firmly agricultural; the secondary class in the parish school was closed around 1960, and by 1991 the population had fallen to 424. By 1999 Midmar Forest was access land, but the castle is privately owned.

## MID YELL, Shetland

**Map 14, B2**

***Main village, Isle of Yell,** pop. 1075* — OS 1 or 2: HU 5190

On the eastern coast of the peaty Shetland island of Yell was the Kirk of *'Refurd'*, shown on Pont's sketch-maps, made on his visit about 1592; it stood on the shores of the sheltered inlet of Reafirth. By the late 19th century the scattered settlement in that area was more mundanely known as Mid Yell; Reafirth had become Mid Yell Voe, though the original name survived, oddly applied to the nearby hills. A herring fishing station with a wooden pier was for many years a calling-point for the North Isles steamers; a permanent pier was belatedly built in 1953, by which time over 300 people lived locally.

**Fishing, Education and Leisure**: From 1962 Mid Yell became a rural planning *'holding point'*; the local junior high school (still S1-S4) and the doctor were conveniently located to serve a total population of about 1650, scattered around the by then reasonably accessible island in eight or ten other hamlets. The policy succeeded, and by 1980 there was also a dental clinic and a fish factory. By 1985 there were two fish factories, because Mid Yell was by then an active fishing port where six trawlers were based. By 1987 there was also a boating club, a large brand new leisure centre – paid for by the oil industry, as evident throughout Shetland! – three shops and a highways and cleansing depot. Scottish country dancing is sometimes broadcast from the *'village hall'* by Radio Scotland. In 1991 the population of the Isle of Yell was 1075, a decrease from pre-oil numbers. Mid Yell Junior High School (S1-S4) is still open.

## MILLERHILL, Edmonston, Woolmet, Danderhall & Monktonhall Colliery

**Map 15, D2**

***Midlothian villages,** pop. 2500* — OS 66: NT 3269

The L-plan tower of Monkton House was built in the 16th century in the plain of the Midlothian coalfield at Old Craighall, 2.5 km south-west of Musselburgh. A similar distance west of Monkton was Edmonston, shown on Pont's map made about 1600. Nearby Woolmet had an ancient church, and the fine mansion of Woolmet House was built in 1686 for Sir Hew Wallace. The first known mine in the area was the long-lasting Woolmet Colliery, which was open nearby by 1703; Edmonston Colliery had an engine by 1725. The Roy map made about 1754 showed a road linking Duddingston and Dalkeith by way of Niddry Mills, 1 km north of *'Edmiston'* beside Woolmet Kirk, which was then a village, but later declined to a small hamlet.

**Horsedrawn Railways turned to Steam**: In 1818 the Edmonston Railway began to move coal from Newton colliery to local users; it was later connected to the almost equally primitive Edinburgh & Dalkeith Railway (E&DR) which opened in 1831 with horses as its motive power. Near the hamlet of Millerhill, 2 km east of Edmonston, appeared a complex of miners' rows such as Red Row, Adams Row and Square

Town. The rustic E&DR was taken over by the up-to-date Edinburgh & Hawick Railway in 1845–49, and the line was realigned, with a station provided at Millerhill. This became a minor junction in 1874, with the opening by its later owner the North British Railway of their Loanhead & Roslin branch. By 1895 Millerhill had a post office but Danderhall was a single house; later a few cottages were added. Woolmet House was derelict by 1915; it was demolished in 1953.

**Danderhall, Monktonhall Colliery and Millerhill Rail Yard**: Danderhall came into its own between 1931 and 1951; by the latter date over 1100 people lived there. The post office was transferred from Millerhill, whose passenger station was closed in 1955. Danderhall's greatest fillip to growth came with the sinking by the National Coal Board (NCB) of the great Monktonhall Colliery in 1953–64. Its shafts, 914 m deep – probably the deepest ever sunk in Scotland – successfully reached the Limestone Coal Group where it lay level at the bottom of the geological basin, only to find the seams were thinner than expected, especially northwards; intended work undersea was therefore abandoned. Meantime an associated railway marshalling yard at Millerhill was completed in 1962–63, also serving the Waverley Route; but its 35 or so tracks were never used to capacity, because by then rail freight was falling. Woolmet colliery which was still open in 1963 was disused by the seventies.

**Monktonhall from Peak to Closure**: At its peak under the NCB, Monktonhall had over 2000 miners, raising a million tons of low-sulphur-content coal a year. Danderhall's population peaked at about 3800 in 1971; but the facilities in the area were still only those of a hamlet in 1981. An 80 m deep mineshaft of the 18th century was found and infilled in 1987. Monktonhall colliery – linked underground with Bilston Glen, and which still employed 1800 men in 1981 – was closed in 1989 by British Coal, then under Tory Governmental pressure to produce coal profitably so as to enable privatisation. Millerhill rail freight yard declined, to become an engineers' yard and a diesel locomotive depot which closed soon after 1993. In 1991 Danderhall's reduced population of 2600 contained Scotland's highest percentage of people travelling to work by bus – nearly half; Danderhall leisure centre was built around that time.

**Miners' Colliery Flooded out**: Monktonhall Colliery was retained on a care and maintenance basis until in 1991 a 10-year reopening agreement was reached with over 100 miners, led by Jackie Aitchison and Jim Palmer and including some from Ayrshire. They put up the cash for Monktonhall Mineworkers, a co-operative set up to lease and reopen the pit, on a small scale and using obsolete equipment. Late in 1992 longwall production resumed with a trial order for Scottish Power and a contract was signed for 175,000 tonnes – for British Coal! A second face brought a total output of 0.5 million tonnes a year, and up to April 1997 the colliery supplied Cockenzie power station; then serious water inflow problems caused work to end and the operating company went into liquidation, eliminating deep mining in Scotland south of the Forth. Meanwhile a bizarre attempt by Hearts FC *(see Gorgie)* to gain approval for a new stadium and supporting development at Millerhill – in the Edinburgh Green Belt – came to nothing in 1992. However, in 1994 land for 5500 houses and 20 ha of industry was earmarked for development north and west of Danderhall, which retains its miners' welfare club. There is a modern 45-roomed *Travelodge* at Old Craighall.

## MILLPORT

**Map 1, B1**

***Main village of Isles of Cumbrae,** pop. 1340* OS 63: NS 1654

The keep of Little Cumbrae Castle was built in the 15th century on an islet beside this small island in the Firth of Clyde. Pont's map made about 1600 showed nine settlements on the adjacent Great Cumbrae, extending from Kirkton in the south-west – where St Colm's kirk had earned a mention by Dean Monro in 1549 – through Kames to *'Portroy'* in the north. Great Cumbrae was usually reached by sea from Fairlie, though sometimes by a ferry from Portrye (Downcraig) to Largs. Around 1690 Montgomery of Skelmorlie owned both the Cumbraes; the former kirk was then just a chapel. A small barracks built in 1745 to designs by James Crawford became known through the local Gaelic speakers as *'The Garrison'*, yet Great Cumbrae had only about 250 people in 1755.

**Marine Developments**: Kirkton and Kames became the most substantial of its little fishing and weaving places; Millport emerged in the late 18th century as an amalgamation of these two. A lighthouse, the first to be erected in Scotland, was built on Little Cumbrae in 1757 by the Clyde Lighthouse Trust – representing Glasgow, Greenock and Port Glasgow; this was replaced in 1793 by the Northern Lighthouse Board. Around 1800 Millport was the base for a revenue cutter, a small vessel commanding the approaches to Glasgow; its captain rebuilt *'The Garrison'* as a mansion in the 19th century. By 1831 Millport was served by regular steamers and in 1865 Little Cumbrae was provided with the first foghorn in Scotland.

**Resort and Cathedral *'City'***: Steamships made Millport more accessible, a pier being built in 1833 by Lord Glasgow, and resort activities began. A post office was open by 1838, and a gasworks was set up in 1840. In 1849 Millport was the strange choice of site for the Episcopal Cathedral of Argyll and the Isles, built of stone quarried on site; it opened in 1876. The fine West church was built in 1878 to designs by Daniel Cottier. Meantime Millport had become a police burgh in 1864. Its golf club dating from 1888 built an 18-hole course and there was a hotel by 1894, when Millport was strung out around the bay and called *"a small town"* by Murray. Keppel pier, opened in 1888, was by 1901 the terminus of a ferry to Fairlie. In 1901 the population was some 1750; *'The Garrison'* was rebuilt and enlarged in 1908.

*Millport gas-works, set up in the 1840s; it was the last in Scotland to use solid fuel, and closed in 1981.* *(JRH)*

**Apogee and Decline of the Tourist Trade**: By 1951 Millport burgh had become a large village of 2000 people; it was a small port and popular resort, with Glasgow University's marine biological station, an aquarium and the Clyde Sea Museum, four hotels and a small secondary school. Up to the 1970s a passenger ferry plied from Millport pier to Largs, but vehicles already came by Cumbrae Slip, just north of Downcraig. A serious fall in resident population between 1951 and 1971 – when it was 1250 – was caused by cheap overseas package holidays; in 1972 came the ending of direct steamer services to the island, leaving the vehicle ferry as the sole everyday public access. Its distant rural views across the water were replaced by the bleakness of the Hunterston nuclear power stations, oil rig construction yards and ore terminals *(see Fairlie)*. By 1979 the National Water Sports Training Centre was open at the former Downcraig Ferry terminus. Millport's 1840s gasworks, the last in Scotland to use solid fuel, was finally closed in 1981. The pier was closed for a time, but later rebuilt to receive cruises by the PS *Waverley*. A few more houses were built at Millport in the 1980s.

**Lairds Galore and Anneka's Challenge**: By 1991 when its population was 1340, Millport was an affluent retirement centre, with some of Scotland's highest proportions of self-employed men and of outright house ownership: 52% of household heads were lairds! Old 1940s military buildings at Greycraigs, long used as an outdoor centre for deprived children from Easterhouse, were converted to modern standards in 1992, the BBC's Challenge team led by the ebullient Anneka Rice creating a permanent sports centre in three days! By 1994 a caravan site had been laid out at Kirkton. In 1993 The Garrison was partly in use as local government offices, and in 1997 as a public library and museum; but the remainder was deteriorating, and the *'A'* listed West church stood disused. Up to 1996 the Marine Biological Station, by then a joint venture by the Universities of Glasgow and London, suffered repeated cuts in government support. In 1999 the Isle of Little Cumbrae was sold to its inhabitants, and in 2000 a new tourist use was planned for the long-neglected Garrison. Hotel accommodation is still available.

## MILNATHORT

**Map 6, B4**

***Kinross-shire village,*** *pop. 1350* — OS 58: NO 1204

Milnathort just north of Kinross lies on the early Great North Road between Queensferry and Roman Bertha (near Perth); its long straight sections suggest a Roman origin. Beside the north end of Loch Leven are Pictish standing stones, leading some to suggest that the strange name is a corruption of *Maol na Coirthe, 'Hill of the Standing Stones'*: unlikely, since these are 3km away at Orwell, which was a chapel of Kinross by 1315 and had given its name to the parish by about 1580. A charter of 1411 defined the northern limit of Inverkeithing's trading area by a stone near *'Elnathorte'*; in the light of this and other evidence a more likely derivation of the name of the village and its Fochy Burn is from the Gaelic *Muileann na Foiriomal*, meaning *'Mill on the (County) Boundary'*. Burleigh Castle was founded near this point in 1434, passed to John Balfour in 1445 and was rebuilt in 1582. In 1621 an existing bridge over the North Queich was rebuilt; the Balfours had been elevated to the peerage in 1606, and Lord Balfour still occupied the castle in 1650.

**Mills of Forth?**: The Pont-derived map of west Fife (which then included Kinross), made around 1600, showed Burleigh and the nearby *'Mills of Forth'* beside the Forth Burn. James Gordon's map showed *'Thuart Mills'*. In 1729 Orwell parish kirk was rebuilt near the Mills of Forth; there was also at that time a mill four or five kilometres to the west, near Touchie on the North Queich. By then Milnathort was already a compact medium-sized settlement on the *'coach road'* between Kinross and Perth via Bridge of Queich, Middleton and Bridge of Earn, soon turnpiked under an Act of 1753. From Middleton a hill track led by Path of Condie to Invermay.

**Famous Engineering Son of Serious People**: In 1765 Alexander Carlyle, himself a minister, found three churches and grim-faced people at *'Mills of Forth'*, a name also used on John Ainslie's map made in 1775, which labelled Blairnathort farm to the north *'Blair of Forth'*; the Pew Mill was on the Greens Burn at old Orwell. Street lighting by oil – probably whale oil – was introduced in 1793. In 1796 a waulk mill turned 1km below the village, which never became a burgh. David Elder, born at Little Seggie west of Milnathort in 1785, became manager of Robert Napier's Glasgow *(q.v.)* works and as father of John Elder (leading proprietor of Randolph, Elder & Co) was hailed as *"the father of marine engineering in Scotland"*.

**Distilling and Brewing**: By 1806 a distillery was at work. Forsyth, who recorded this, added that the placename *"is vulgarly pronounced Mills of Forth, from a rivulet upon which are several mills; many of the houses in this village are built of a white coloured freestone"*. By 1811 the *"town"* had almost 1200 people. Milnathort also acquired an inn, which became a coach route junction around 1816. Appropriately for a milling centre, the village sported a brewery by 1825. Greenwood's accurately surveyed map of 1826–27 which used the name Milnathort, showed the distillery, 1km north-east of the cross, but only one mill in the town – plus a waulk mill 2km to the west. Burleigh Castle was in ruins, but a turnpike connected to Alloa via Carnbo. By 1825 Milnathort was served by a penny post from Kinross, but the lower road past Cuthill to Glenfarg and Perth dates only from 1832, when it became the main road.

**Gas, Woollens, Steam Trains – but no Whisky**: The Kinross & Milnathort Gas Company supplied both towns from a works midway between them, opened in 1836. By 1849 there were two hotels or inns and by 1850 a woollen industry. A town hall was built in 1854–55, and the City of Glasgow Bank built a branch in 1854–56; eventually this passed to the Clydesdale. By 1857 there was a mission school, and another school opened in 1862. A station was provided on the Fife & Kinross Railway, whose single track reached Milnathort from Ladybank early in 1858 and was extended to Kinross later in the year; excursions to Edinburgh by this rather roundabout route began in 1859. Perhaps a steam engine's spark ignited John Ewing's meal and flour mill, which was burnt out in 1861. The first edition OS map completed in 1863 showed that the distillery had been demolished; the population was under 1500, but the *Thistle Inn* was open; by 1866 it had been styled a hotel, along with the *Royal*.

**Steam-Driven Mills and Short-lived Main Line**: In 1860 the first steam-powered linen factory in the tiny county of Kinross was opened at Milnathort, being extended in 1866 to employ 100 people. A new 40-loom factory was completed in 1864 *'at the foot of Milnathort'* and a spinning mill was built in 1865–66. A woollen mill larger than any then open at Kinross was built in 1867, and a large new church followed in 1867–69. In 1888 Milnathort was *"a large village, or rather small town, containing several woollen factories – a thriving manufacturing place"*; the 1891 population was 1133. In 1890 the North British Railway's direct line from the new Forth Bridge to Perth was completed by a new link from Mawcarse Junction, 2 km north-east of Milnathort, through Glenfarg to Bridge of Earn. A golf club was founded in 1910 and laid out a 9-hole parkland course. In the early 20th century a livestock market boosted typical village facilities, and 4 km away in the hills was the large newly-built Ochil Hills tuberculosis hospital. A bacon curing factory was another local activity by 1953, when there were over 1400 people; traffic on the two trunk roads conflicted at the central crossroads.

**Trains Depart; Motorway makes a Quiet Start**: The passenger trains to Ladybank were withdrawn in 1950, and that line was closed east of Mawcarse in 1964. The Perth railway was closed in 1970, facilitating completion of the M90 motorway, which had bypassed the village by 1974. The bacon factory was still open as Cunningham's in 1977, together with the big sheds of Harley & Son, seedsmen, and Hatrick Bruce, engineers. Robertsons supplied farmers, and there was an industrial painting contractor. Four small hotels now included the *Commercial* and *Cross Keys* as well as those already named; a restaurant, two garages and a branch bank were available. By 1981 the Ochil Hills Hospital was a convalescent centre for the Stirling area, which closed around 1990; Milnathort's former industries did not flourish, and its 1981 population was only some 1275.

**Farm Services and Computing**: In 1987 Milnathort's continuing importance as an agricultural service village was shown by grain and potato merchants, substantial agricultural engineers, a farm trailer builder and veterinary surgeons. Forth Wines had built a large new wine and spirits warehouse. The golf course was extended to 18 holes about 1990. Some new development enabled about 1350 people to live in Milnathort in 1991, including a fit, retired element; the large church building was converted to flats in 1994. By 1989 the former railway station was the base of Kinross Computer Systems, who had become by 1996 leading suppliers of commodity trading software in the UK, and expanding into export markets. The Central Farmers sheds were still then prominent. The recently built health and leisure centres north of Kinross, and new housing both there and in Milnathort, threaten to close the small gap between these places. The ruined Burleigh Castle is cared for by Historic Scotland; the small *Royal* and *Thistle* hotels are still open.

## MILNGAVIE

**Map 15, C4**

***Town, Strathkelvin,*** *pop. 13,000* — OS 64: NS 5574

The large 14th century Mugdock Castle stands high above the valley of the Allander Water 13 km north-west of Glasgow. Two centuries later two towers were built east and south-east of Mugdock, Bardowie beside its small loch near the Allander's confluence with the River Kelvin, and Craigmaddie, marked *'Kragin'* on Pont's sketchy map of Lennox made about 1600. This showed a thickly settled area between the three castles; *'Milgay'* was then a mill and a bridge on the Allander Water, with another mill at *'Dugalstoun'* 1.5 km to the east. The Roy map made in the 1750s showed Milngavie (pronounced *Millguy*) as a tiny village and bridge from which roads ran east, west and north.

**Watt and a Daughter, Whisky and Water**: By 1766 James MacGregor had a bleachfield near Milngavie; James Watt experimented with chlorine bleaching there in the 1780s, and subsequently married MacGregor's daughter. The works probably stood 1 km south of the village, where a post office was opened in 1793. Tambowie distillery, about 3 km to the north-west, dated from the smuggling days pre-1824, and Gavin's mill was built early in the 19th century; by 1825 there was a penny post from Glasgow. In the 1850s Glasgow Corporation built a great aqueduct from Loch Katrine to bring the city's new water supply to the 2500 million litre capacity Mugdock balancing reservoir above the village; it was later duplicated at Craigmaddie, *'Wolf Rock'*, near the site of the demolished castle.

**Railway and Paper, Commuters and Golf**: Milngavie was still a textile village in 1863 when the North British Railway opened a branch line from Glasgow via Maryhill; by 1871 the population was over 2000. Milngavie became a police burgh in 1875, and at some time a gasworks was established. The rail-connected Ellangowan paper mill began about 1880. By 1894 a dyeworks 1 km to the south had replaced the bleachfield and the *Douglas Arms Hotel* was open. Being as Milngavie was one of the few places near Glasgow to be unaffected by coal mining, from the 1880s onwards villas were built by well-to-do commuters. The Milngavie golf club was founded in 1895, followed by a local newspaper, the *Milngavie and Bearsden Herald*, first published in 1901. The Tambowie distillery, still open in 1902, closed about 1910.

**Trams Trundle but Bennie's Railplane fails to Take Off**: Trams arrived via Bearsden in 1924, boosting suburban growth; one Milngavie route ran via Glasgow city centre right through to Renfrew. The Allander and Hilton Park golf courses date from 1928. In 1930 the Bank of Scotland partly funded the erection of a length of about 1.5 km of complex overhead girder track officially known as Hamilton's Aerial Railway, above and beside the branch railway line between Milngavie and Bearsden: this carried an experimental propellor-driven railcar, named the Bennie Railplane after its slightly dotty designer George Bennie (apparently the owner of a Bridgeton engineering firm), but being inherently both very costly and unsightly, it lacked potential as a serious transport system. The unsaleable structure stayed rusting away after his death until it was scrapped to enable the railway to be electrified in 1961 – on the by then conventional overhead system. There were some light industries, but in 1964 the paper mill was closed.

**Golf Courses – a Bewildering Choice?**: By 1951 the population was nearing 8000 and Milngavie had the facilities of a small town; trams ceased to run to Milngavie in 1956, but the *Black Bull*, then an inn with 6 rooms, expanded steadily to 27 rooms by 1980. Milngavie's golf courses were still further augmented with the Clober of 1951 and the Dougalston in 1978; by the 1970s the Lillie Art Gallery was open, and the large new Douglas Academy was built in the 1970s.

**Affluence, Quarrying – and Music**: Milngavie was merged with Bearsden in 1975 in a small gerrymandered district, intended to keep the rates paid by its growing dormitory population out of Glasgow corporation's clutches. In the 1980s the Douglas Muir quarry was opened west of the A809, and rapidly expanded. Some housebuilding continued, and by 1988

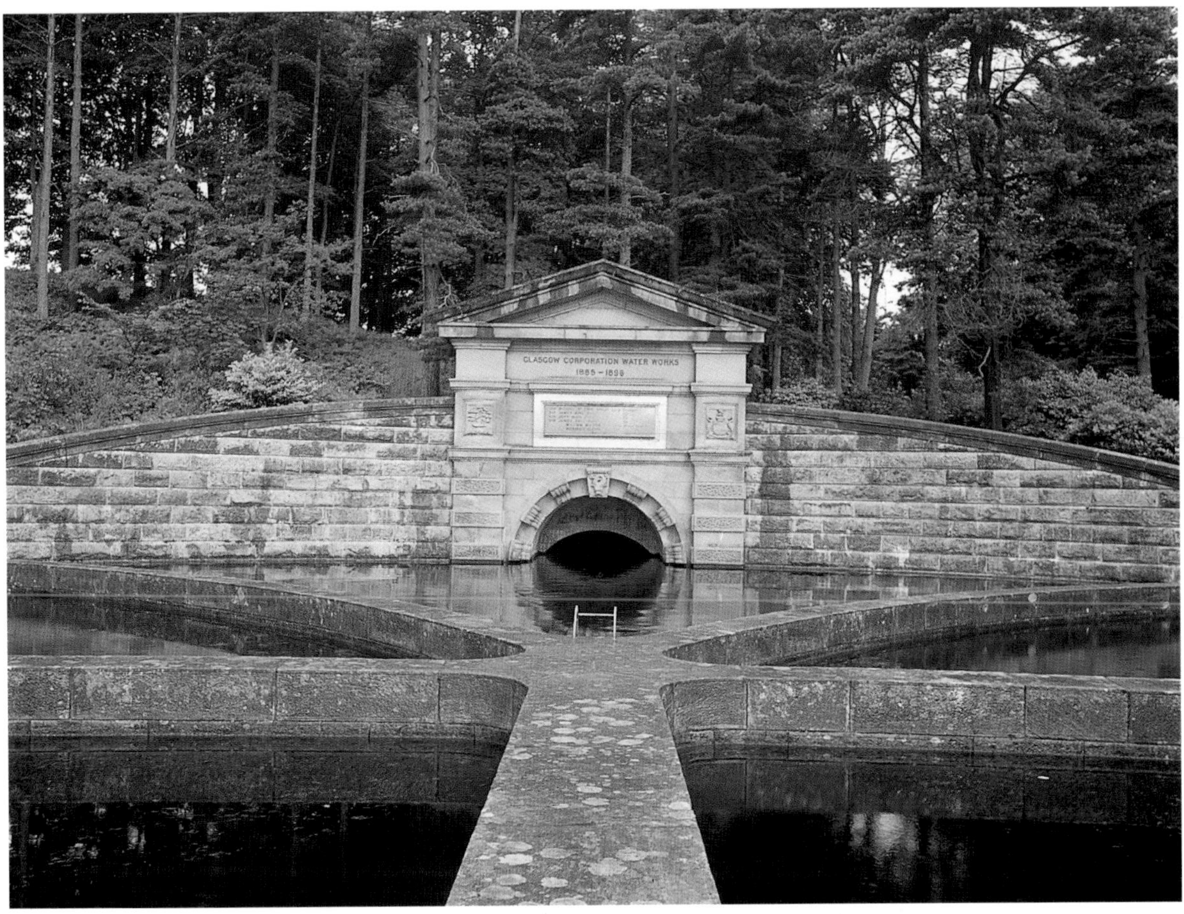


*Craigmaddie Reservoir, Milngavie, constructed in the 1880s, when the capacity of Glasgow's Loch Katrine water supply scheme (built in the 1850s) was doubled. This is the gauge basin where water from Loch Katrine enters a holding reservoir.* *(JRH)*

there was a new sports centre, and the Mugdock Country Park (3km north). The population in 1991 was 12,592, a well-educated dormitory with major managerial and professional elements. By 1992 Douglas Academy (with about 900 pupils) held Strathclyde Region's specialist music school. Residential development continued north-westwards and a Tesco store was open by 1996, the year when Milngavie was merged into a unitary authority, East Dunbartonshire. Including a second 18-hole course at Hilton Park, there is now a choice of five golf courses. The old Black Bull Inn has become a Marks & Spencer foodstore.

## MILTON

**Map 9, B3**

***Easter Ross village,*** *pop. 850* OS 21: NH 7674

About 8km south of Tain the Balnagown River follows the defile of Strathrory to enter the Cromarty Firth at Nigg Bay, passing an ancient hill fort, the medieval Kirk of Logie Easter parish and the 15th century Balnagown Castle, which Pont's neat manuscript map of the area, made around 1600, depicted as a twin tower of three storeys. Upstream a knoll above a watermill was called Knockmoulin – *Mill Hill* – and at least two more mills turned down-river beside the 16th century tower-house of Milton. On the shore of the Firth 1.5km to the south-west was Kilmuir Kirk. Parkhill nearby had a post office from 1717. The Roy map made about 1750 showed the mansion of New Tarbat, built about 1690 for Sir George McKenzie beside the river's mouth, and a track linking Invergordon with Tain – the route shown on later maps as the King's Causeway. Tarbat House was gradually rebuilt for the Earls of Cromarty in 1787–1802 into a classical mansion to designs by James McLeran.

**Improved Transport**: Later roads focused on a bridge built between Milton and Balnagown, probably around 1810. The Ross-shire Railway opened in 1864, with a minor station at Delny, 3km south-west near the large hamlet of Barbaraville on the Invergordon road, and a crossing station named Parkhill just south of the road bridge. In 1868 the latter station was renamed Kildary after a nearby house, the same name being given to the post and telegraph office at the hamlet of Ballchraggan east of the river; later this place too came to be called Kildary. By 1894 there was an inn at the hamlet of Milton, and the *Shandwick Inn* east of Ballchraggan; the well-wooded area held many churches, both ruined and recent. A parish school was built at Kilmuir. The parkland around Balnagown and Tarbat did not survive into the 1950s, but there were still two mills, and 400 people lived in the area, a number which was down to some 300 by 1971.

**Dormitory, Jackdaw and Harrods Tycoon**: Both stations were closed to passengers in 1960 and to goods in 1965. About 1970 a gravel pit was opened near the *Shandwick Inn*.

By 1976 a primary school to augment Kilmuir had been built at Milton, where a compact housing estate was laid out to serve the aluminium and oil-related developments around the Firth. The 20-roomed *Jackdaw Hotel* at Barbaraville was brand new in 1972. Around 1971 Mohammad Al-Fayed, the wealthy Egyptian of Harrods fame, bought Balnagown Castle from the Ross family, extensively refurbishing it for his use in 1995, by which time he had amassed a vast surrounding estate of 16,000 hectares. Far less lucky was Tarbat House, abandoned by the Earls of Cromarty in 1967; damaged by fire in 1987, it became derelict and in 2000 its ruinous shell awaited restoration. The 1991 population was 849; about that time the A9 – which until then had passed through the village – was rebuilt on a new bypass alignment. Kildary has a large Peugeot dealer, there is a small industrial estate at Delny, and the *Shandwick Inn* is still open.

## MILTON OF BALGONIE

**Map 6, B4**

***Small central Fife village,** pop. 450* — OS 59: NO 3200

Balgonie on the River Leven east of Markinch in Fife existed by around 1100, as shown by the Gaelic prefix *Baile* – a settlement. The tall tower of Balgonie Castle was built of fine ashlar, probably in the late 14th century for Sir John Sibbald; beside it is a strongly walled barmkin. Milton of Balgonie stands between the castle and the ancient mansionhouse of Balfour; it appeared on Pont's map made about 1600 as *'Miltoun'*. James Gordon's map of about 1642 showed *'Balgowny mill'* and *'Colton mill'* south of the river, and an unnamed mill on the north bank opposite and between the castles. About 1655 Balgonie Castle was much enlarged into a primitive mansion for Sir Alexander Leslie, first Earl of Leven. By 1700 the Leven was bridged nearby, but the Roy map of about 1750 showed no roads.

**Milton of Balgonie Grows – and Shrinks**: Balgonie Flax & Spinning Mill, built in 1807 by William Drummond at the west end of the village, was later worked by Joseph Stuart who installed condensing steam engines around 1850; but the mill closed about 1885. Balgonie Castle was abandoned by the eighth Earl about 1824, but a new church was opened in 1836. Balfour Mill was still there in 1895; Balfour, then an important residence in its own park, later became a ruin. By 1951 Milton was a small village with a school and post office and a population of about 600, shrinking to 425 by 1981. Restoration of the spectacular castle was begun in the 1970s by Raymond Morris *(see Kenmore)*. Now occupied, used for weddings and full of interest for the visiting public, it deserves to be better known. By 1996 a small new housing estate had been built at Milton, still with its post office and school. The small *Fife Arms Hotel* has offered accommodation since the 1970s.

## MILTON OF CAMPSIE

**Map 5, C5**

***Strathkelvin village,** pop. 4000+* — OS 64: NS 6576

Milton of Campsie lies on the Glazert Water at the foot of the Campsie Fells some 2 km north of Kirkintilloch. To the north is the motte and bailey called Maiden Castle. The *'Frechmill'* (Heather Mill) shown on Pont's map of Lennox, made around 1600, was already accompanied by a bridge; another mill turned at the outlet of the Antermony Loch. The *'Freachmills'* also appeared on the Roy map made about 1754, when the area was served by tracks connecting with the main road system at Kirkintilloch. Houses were built for the workers in the large Kincaid or Milton Printworks which was erected downstream of the bridge in 1786, for in 1799 Heron referred to *"the lately erected village of Kincaid"* with over 300 inhabitants *"employed chiefly in the cotton manufacture"*. What was claimed to be the first power loom in Scotland was installed in the cotton mill (long vanished). The new village became absorbed into Milton of Campsie.

**Railway, Dams and Hospital**: In 1848 the Edinburgh & Glasgow Railway built a branch from Lenzie to Lennoxtown, with a station at Milton of Campsie. By the 1890s two small dams had been constructed, impounding the Woodburn reservoir, 2 km north-east, and the Alloch to serve the Glorat Mill and Newmill which were open above the village. Milton had an inn and a post and telegraph office; the population in 1901 was about 700. By 1953 an Infectious Diseases hospital with 60 beds had been built, and Milton Printworks had become the UPC *'Safansound'* pulp container works. The population of Milton grew steadily to about 1350 by 1951, and by 1954 *Kincaid House* had become a hotel.

**After the Railway the Car Commuters**: The ending of the railway passenger service in 1954, and of the goods service soon after, did not inhibit growth. The population exceeded 1600 by 1971, and then, aided by being only 13km from central Glasgow, and with estate development south of the village, rocketed upwards; by 1981 the very basic local facilities had grown to those of a small village. Watches were assembled there for Timex until about 1983. In the 1980s rapid housing development continued, principally south of the village, which by 1991 had a young well-educated dormitory population of 4056.

## MILTON OF LEYS

**Map 9, B4**

***Location near Inverness*** — OS 26/27: NH 7042

Located about 175m above sea level 5km south-east of Inverness, between the earliest and latest roads south from the Highland capital, this new development of 223ha in a hitherto rural area was started by Arab interests in 1989. It was planned to include 1250 houses, holiday homes, a 200-bed luxury hotel, two golf courses (one of championship standard), plus a spring water bottling plant. Despite elaborate road and sewer works, including a new junction on the A9 dual carriageway, only twelve houses had been built by 1991, little more being done by 1993 when the site was repossessed by Lloyds Bank. Local builders Tulloch's took over about 1997, and significant housebuilding has taken place since.

## MINARD & Crarae

**Map 5, A4**

***Argyll small village & hamlet,** pop. 160* — OS 55: NR 9796

A chambered cairn and an early church stood on the north shore of Loch Fyne, which when Roy mapped this area in the 1750s was followed by a trackway south to Kintyre. By the 1890s this ran through extensive woodlands and had been made up to what the OS called a *"first class metalled road"*, alongside which were scattered a Free Church, smithy and post office. In wooded policies on a promontory to the south stood Minard House, later renamed Minard Castle. A granite quarry producing setts for Glasgow streets had been opened to the north-east. The Free Church became the focus of a hamlet (also called Crarae). By then despite a population of under 100 it also had a telephone exchange and a primary school. By 1969 the *"notable gardens"* of Crarae Lodge were open to the public. The quarry then produced road chippings, but soon closed, and closure of the primary school was proposed in 1986. However by 1996 a number of new developments had appreciably enlarged Minard village, which retains its post office, and a fish farm had been formed near the quarry.

## MINGULAY

**Map 7, A5**

***Small island, s. of Barra*** OS 31: NL 5683

Monro in 1549 noted that the steep little isles of Mingulay, Berneray, Pabbay, Sandray and *"pretty little"* Flodday nearly 20km south of Barra all belonged to the Bishop of the Isles. Mingulay with its remarkable 215m-high sea cliffs was *"inhabited and well manured, good for fishing and corn"*. At that time all these isles (and some even smaller) had a chapel. Later the property of the MacNeils of Barra, a school was built around 1880 when, despite the lack of a safe harbour, 150 people lived on Mingulay. But emigration accelerated between 1908 and 1912, when the island was abandoned to sheep. From 1955 it has been owned by a group of Barra crofters, who visit Mingulay to tend the sheep only once a year.

## MINISHANT

**Map 1, C2**

***Ayrshire small village,*** *pop. 400* OS 70: NS 3214

Two ancient duns and an old tower still stand west of a loop of the River Doon, some 6km north-east of Maybole; but only the site remains of the former Auchendrane Castle. The area was well settled when mapped by Pont around 1600, but the Roy map of about 1754 showed little beside the winding main road *'from Portpatrick to Air'*; nor did early travellers leave memorable comments. The Ayr & Maybole Railway, a Glasgow & South Western subsidiary, opened a line through the area in 1856, providing a station at Cassillis, where it crossed the road now labelled B7045. About 1km to the north is Minishant, a hamlet with an 18th century waulk mill (now the village hall), round which two inns, a smithy and a post office clustered by 1895. In 1951 a garage was open and some 425 people lived in this farming area, but numbers slowly declined. The station was closed to passengers about 1954, and to goods by 1972. The one inn still open in 1951 was a pub by 1981, though by then there were two garages; Minishant primary school, pub and post office have stayed open.

## MINTLAW

**Map 10, C2**

***Buchan village,*** *pop. 2500+* OS 30: NK 0048

Timothy Pont's map of Buchan made about 1600 showed both *'Mintla'* and Aden Mill in the valley of the South Ugie Water, 3km east of the Abbey of Old Deer and 14km west of Peterhead. The Roy map made about 1750 showed a roadless area, containing only the hamlet of Nether Aden and a number of farms. When later in that century turnpike roads were built linking Aberdeen to Fraserburgh and Banff to Peterhead, they crossed at Mintlaw. This was an obvious site for a new village, founded around 1810 by James Ferguson of Pitfour. By 1825 Mintlaw was the centre for a penny post to Pitsligo, and was a post town by 1845; in 1858 Pratt noted that *"the village of Mintlaw has also two inns"*, while 3km to the south at Millbreck was *"a woollen-manufactory for blankets, winseys and other kinds of cloth"*.

**Mintlaw's Railway Era**: The Formartine & Buchan Railway (later the Great North of Scotland's Peterhead branch) was opened in 1861 as far as Mintlaw station; being sited 1km west of Mintlaw crossroads, this also served Old Deer. A year later the line was opened through to Peterhead. The 1891 population was 400; by then an inn was open in the village, and a post office at the station. Mintlaw did not interest Murray in 1894, but it later gained a tiny hotel, an oil depot near the station and also an agricultural engineer, becoming a substantial village of some 800 people in 1951, its telephone exchange having 123 *'connexions'*. Thanks to lorries, buses, cars and Beeching, passenger train services ended in 1965 and the line was closed completely between Maud and Peterhead in 1970.

**The Oil Boom Dormitory**: By 1971 the population had fallen to 650. Then the area joined the oil boom; Mintlaw grew rapidly to about 2400 people in 1981, large estates of mainly semi-detached houses being built to the south and west, where the new 1000-pupil Mintlaw Academy was also open by 1987. Mintlaw thus became one of the few old planned villages providing secondary education, and soon also had four garages, five doctors and a chemist's shop; in 1991 the population was about 2500. In 1996 major aid from the National Lottery was to help build a community swimming pool. By then new housing was extending farther westwards towards Old Deer. The Abacus fish-processing company of Mintlaw went into liquidation in 2000.

## MINTO

**Map 3, B4**

***Borders hamlet,*** *pop. 150* OS 73 & 80: NT 5720

On a crag nearly 150m above the north bank of the River Teviot, 3km downstream from Denholm, is the intriguingly named 16th century tower of Fatlips Castle. The twin Minto Hills also shelter Minto parish, which opened a school in 1616. Minto House, in a dell near Fatlips, was designed by William Adam for Lord Minto, and built in 1738–43. The railway station on the Waverley route at Hassendean, 2 km west of Minto, gave little impetus, though in 1926 a golf club was founded which laid out its course in Minto Park. Minto House became a hospital in the 1939–45 war, and from the mid 1950s held the independent Craigmount School, but like the primary school and the station this was abandoned in the 1960s. Minto with 325 people in 1951 was already no more than a hamlet. Despite the old mansion's fine interior it was derelict by 1981, when only 150 people lived locally; the mansion was demolished in the early 1990s and Fatlips Castle is decaying, but the 18-hole golf course is still open.

## MOFFAT

**Map 2, B3**

***Dumfriesshire small town,*** *pop. 2350* OS 78: NT 0805

The line of the Roman road from Carlisle to the Clyde is well marked where it strides across the hills west of upper Annandale. Hill forts and mottes are also evident in the area around the sheltered Auldton of Moffat, where there was a church by 1177, transferred to the see of Glasgow by the newly imposed Bruce laird. Of the eight castles later built in the area, the 16th century L-plan tower of Frenchland Castle 1km south of the Auldton and 1.5km east of modern Moffat is the most striking relic. Moffat must have been of some importance to be shown on Mercator's atlas published in 1595, and gained a parish school in 1612, but if the assiduous Pont did map upper Annandale his work has been lost. In 1618 Taylor the waterman-poet found Moffat was already a *"town"* with an *"indifferent"* inn. To reach Moffat from Carlisle involved wading both the Esk and the Annan – and this on the only direct land route then available to Glasgow!

**Scotland's earliest Spa**: A sulphurous mineral spring was found 1 km north of the Auldton by a Miss Whiteford in 1633, and in 1648 Moffat was definitely chartered as a burgh of barony (an earlier charter may have existed). The *Black Bull Inn* on the present town site was in use by 1683, when it became the headquarters of the stern Graham of Claverhouse, sent in to crush religious dissent. An early bridge enabled the old Carlisle Road to cross the Mill Burn to the east, but the River Annan south of the town was bridged later. A traveller of 1704 noted Moffat as *"a small straggling town"*; however, by 1715 there was a post office. In 1748 a second mineral spring of chalybeate was discovered high on Hartfell some 8 km to the north. The Roy map of about 1754 showed the characteristically shaped core area of the town, from which through roads led north to Crawford and Tweedsmuir, south-east over the *'Moffatwaterbrig'* to Lockerbie, and east to Selkirk; that to the west petered out beyond *'Evonbrig'* into a track to Dumfries.

**Hotels, Mail Coaches and Textiles**: Both the *Annandale Arms Hotel* and the rival *Buccleuch Arms Hotel* were built in 1760. In 1769 Pennant while on tour called at Moffat, *"a small neat town, famous for its spas"*, both of which were open at that time. In 1776 about 50 looms were in use making *'shalloons'*, blankets, serges etc. From 1781 a diligence ran from Glasgow via Moffat to Carlisle and London in four days. A large new parish church was built in 1790; at one time at the centre of the town was a bowling green enclosed by a yew hedge. A new woollen mill was established in 1796, and four fairs a year were then scheduled. Heron noted in 1799 *"the town of Moffat has a manufacture of coarse woollen stuffs: but it is chiefly supported by its mineral springs, which attract much genteel company"*. With over 800 residents, it had *"many good houses"* built for the users of the two spas. Of these the waters of the Hartfell were *"of a very bracing quality, and are accounted the strongest in Britain"*.

**Mail Coach Crossroads**: The building of the new Carlisle road beside the Elvan Water to the west enabled Moffat to become an important mails crossroads by 1813. A new spa was built in 1827, which later became the town hall; nearby was the early site of Moffat Academy. The Caledonian Railway provided a station at nearby Beattock in 1848, lowering the price of coal sufficiently to make a gasworks at Moffat an economic proposition, but it took 30 years before development really took off when the large *Moffat Hydropathic Hotel* was built in 1878.

**Moffat Grows – and Commands the Fighters**: In 1879 a former Fettes schoolmaster founded the Saint Ninians Preparatory School for boys at Moffat; his son Hugh Dowding, born locally in 1882, joined the RFC in 1914, and in 1936 became commander-in-chief of RAF Fighter Command and the mastermind in the Battle of Britain. Meantime a short branch of the Caledonian Railway was opened from Beattock in 1883. The largest church in south-west Scotland, the very ornate St Andrews Church of Scotland – designed by John Starforth of Edinburgh and built of sandstone from Corncockle quarry near Templand – was opened in 1887. Moffat golf club was founded in 1884 and provided a steep 18-hole moorland course. For strolling by the less energetic, the park was laid out in the 1890s, when the population was almost 2300.

**Green Heart becomes Car Park**: By 1894 – although the bowling green had gone from the centre – there were three banks and three *"good"* hotels in what Murray called this *"clean thriving little town"* – the *Annandale Arms, Buccleuch Arms* and *Hydro*. By 1913 (if not before) the *Hydro* had its own golf course, and up to 1914 an evening residential express train from Glasgow terminated at Moffat! However, when the *Hydro* building burned down in 1921 it was not replaced, and Moffat slept until touring charabancs and cars became commonplace. Inevitably the town's once green central space sadly became just another car park, but very convenient in view of the function of Moffat as a stopping point just off the busy A74; meantime the branch line passenger traffic withered.

**Tourist Gateway: strictly by Road Only**: By the 1950s though Moffat's population was under 2500 it had all the usual facilities of a small town, plus no fewer than eleven small hotels offering 100 rooms in all. From 1954 when the branch railway lost its passenger trains, all the tourists had to complete their journeys by road; the main-line Beattock station was closed in 1972. Perfumes were made locally in 1978, while Moffat Weavers ran a mill and a large shop for tourists. Besides cafes and gift boutiques there was a full range of shops, including a garden centre; the air of prosperity and bustle was added to by a scatter of new houses. In 1980 the Economic Forestry Group still had its HQ in the little town, where the hotels had been augmented by the quite large new *Mercury Motor Inn*.

**Upgrading Hotels and Pleading for Trains**: The hotels on average were larger and of higher star class in 1981 than in 1950, and St Ninian's School was still open until around 1990. Knitwear was sold from the old mill; Moffat was for many visitors their first experience of Scotland when their car or coach turned off the A74. The cottage hospital (which had only 13 beds in 1981) remarkably provided emergency services for some of the Lockerbie people injured in the air disaster of 1988. By 1991 the population was 2342, decidedly elderly and quite well-off. By 1995 there was a mountain rescue post. Highly prosperous Moffat with its many eating places, tourist shops, caravan site and museum is popular with visitors; the 'A' listed Moffat House Hotel dates from 1751. In 2000 the locals asked for the reopening of Beattock station.

## MONACH ISLES

**Map 7, A2**

***Islets w. of N. Uist***

OS 22: NF 5962

The low-lying Heisker or Monach Isles lie some 20 km west of Benbecula, to which they were said to have been linked by drying sands before a 16th century tsunami changed matters for ever. The exposed Monach lighthouse, built on the tiny outlying islet of Shillay, was first lit in 1864. In 1891, 140 crofting people served by a school and post office lived on the Monachs, mostly on the largest, Ceann Ear. The lighthouse was one of the first to be equipped with radio, but the last islanders left for North Uist in 1933, and in 1942 wartime conditions caused the light to be extinguished. The lighthouse was permanently abandoned in 1947, perhaps to prevent its keepers being struck by errant rockets from South Uist. Otherwise its closure was unfathomable, leaving as it did an enormous gap of some 170km between the powerful lights on Barra Head and the Flannan Isles. The lighthouse still stood deteriorating in 1997 with its original equipment, but at least by then it had an automatic solar-powered replacement.

## MONIAIVE

**Map 2, A4**

***Dumfriesshire village,*** *pop. 500* OS 78: NX 7790

The Dark Age hill fort of Tynron Doon stands 5km west of the River Nith about 25km upstream of Dumfries. Two medieval mottes lie either side of the Cairn Water, 4km to the south of the Doon near the Kirk of Glencairn (Kirkton on modern maps). In 1370 Robert II gave the barony of Glencairn to Robert Danielston, who had the tower house of Glencairn Castle built on the braes 1.5km south-east of the Kirk. In 1488 his great-grandson William Cunningham of Kilmaurs became the first Earl of Glencairn. When English superseded Gaelic speech the glen came to be called the Cairn Valley or Cairndale. Timothy Pont who mapped south-west Scotland, perhaps about 1610, sketched the very imposing castle, and found a bridge across the Dalwhat Water 3km west of the Kirk, just above the confluence of the Cairn Water; two nearby mills were also shown. There were various other settlements and tower houses in the vicinity.

**From Glencairn to Maxwelton – and Annie Laurie**: In 1611 the earls sold the estate to Stephen Laurie, who enlarged the castle. Moniaive, sited beside the Dalwhat bridge, gained its charter as a burgh of barony in 1636. In 1641 the Lauries renamed the castle as Maxwelton House; the famed Anna (Annie) Laurie was born there in 1682. By 1715 a post office was open, at first named *'Minnhyve'* – nowadays the place-name is pronounced *Monnie-eyve*. The Fergusson mansion of Craigdarroch, designed by William Adam, was built in 1729 on the site of an older house 4km west of Moniaive; Annie later lived there. About 1753 Roy's surveyors found *'Monyhive'* a small compact place little larger than the tiny settlement around the Kirk of Glencairn, through which a road connected Moniaive with Dumfries. Another road linked with New Galloway, and a track led to Penpont and Drumlanrig. Moniaive was a post town by 1797, but with a service on only two days a week; it remained a village of one-storey cottages. Heron wrote in 1799 of Tynron (another Kirkland!) as a *"village"*, and of *"the little town of Monyhive which contains about 400 inhabitants"*.

**Light Railway, Light Traffic**: Victorian owners enlarged Maxwelton House, and an ornate chapel was built nearby for Isabella Laurie in 1868. Moniaive became a minor summer resort and artists' colony, so the Glasgow & South Western optimistically promoted the Cairn Valley Light Railway, climbing up the valley from Dumfries to end at Moniaive and opened in 1905. But buses were cheaper and cars more convenient; the passenger service lasted only until 1943, and with little freight, the line was disused by 1953 and was soon lifted. By 1951 Moniaive had average village facilities and a population of 750; another 250 people at Tynron also had a school and post office, but these and a quarter of the people had gone by 1971, leaving a mere hamlet.

**Private Education and Private Restoration**: The Laurie family had died out and the long-neglected Maxwelton House was at risk. From 1968 the new owners, financier Hugh Stenhouse and his family, had Maxwelton House cut back to expose the earlier castle, and fully restored it in 17th century style with extensive rebuilding, completed in 1972 without grant aid. The population of Moniaive had declined to about 600 by 1971; the economic bases of Moniaive were said to be retirement and tourism. However, by 1976 the emparked Crawfordton House between Moniaive and Kirkton had become an independent mixed preparatory school. By 1991 Moniaive had fewer than 500 residents. Pleasant Maxwelton House with its restored chapel and small museum of rural life is open to the public, its owners proud to conduct tours. For many years *Woodlea* has been a 12-roomed hotel, now with leisure facilities.

## MONIFIETH

**Map 6, C3**

***Small town / suburb e. of Dundee,*** *pop. 9500* OS 54: NO 4932

Monifieth lies east of the mouth of the Dighty Water on the coast of Angus, 9km east of Dundee and 3km east of Broughty Castle. It was the site of a Culdee monastery with a shrine of Pictish date, and had a thanage from about the 11th century. Pont's map made about 1600 showed Monifieth as a village, with a bridge near the mouth of the Dighty Water, the Mill of Balmossy and the house of Grange. Monifieth parish boasted a school from 1599, and remarkably for a non-burghal place, already had a post office by 1715. The Roy map made about 1750 showed it as a small nucleated settlement on the road from Dundee to Arbroath; to the west was a snuff mill below the Dighty crossing. A linseed oil mill was busy in 1790, when the parish contained a thread mill and about 38 hand weavers; two fairs were held each year. In 1799 Heron noted that on the banks of the Dighty Water *"near Broughty Castle are a lint mill, an oil mill, and a mill for spinning coarse yarn"*. These were probably in the area of Milton of Monifieth, for in 1822 the Monifieth spinning mill of Banks & Fairweather had 264 spindles, and the Grange mill of P Kinmond & Co 114.

**The Railway and Golf**: Monifieth acquired a station when the Dundee & Arbroath Railway was opened in 1838. In 1845 Allan Robertson and Alex Pirie from St Andrews designed an early 9-hole golf course on the links, which encouraged Monifieth to develop into a small outer suburb of Dundee with *'jute-baron mansions'*; further growth after 1850 led to its becoming a police burgh. In 1858 came the founding of the area's first formal golf club. By 1864 Daniel Drimmie & Co's large Panmure bleachfield had been bleaching yarn for many years and remained busy, but the spinning mill at Milton of Monifieth had long been ruinous. In 1880 the first golf course was extended to 18 holes. The 1891 population was over 1800, and an inn was open. In 1899 one local golf club left Monifieth, to reappear 2 km farther east (as 'Barry') at Buddon Links near Carnoustie (q.v.). However, the Broughty course remained, and around 1900 there was a local clubmaker.

**Tuberculosis, Trams and Textile Machinery**: The large Ashludie Hospital, built 1km inland early in the 20th century to isolate tuberculosis cases, later became a geriatric unit with over 200 beds. From 1905 to 1931 Monifieth was served by electric trams to Dundee. In 1935 Charles Dick & Son of Monifieth built the great concrete viaduct at Inverbervie. In the mid 20th century the long-established foundry of J F Low & Co of Monifieth made carding engines and other textile machinery, much going for export. Other industries included carpet weaving and confectionery machinery manufacture. By 1951 the population had doubled to 3700, enjoying the facilities of a large village.

**Suburbs and Holidays**: By 1974 a caravan and camping site was open, and by 1987 two. In the 1975 reorganisation of local government, Monifieth's dormitory role took it into Dundee City District; about then a quarry was opened at Ardownie, 2 km to the north. The population had again doubled to 7100 by 1981, with small-town facilities including Monifieth High School, recent shopping parades, a William Low store (now Tesco) and a suburban character. Further residential development continued north of the town during the 1980s. In 1991 the resident population had risen further, to some 9400.

**Gerrymandering and Bad Planning?**: By 1999 a new western approach road had enabled further housing development. In 1996 the Tory government removed Monifieth from Dundee City and placed it in the Angus all-purpose local authority, but this did not achieve their aim of regaining control of Angus! In the 1990s the former quarry was reopened and much rock removed, and by 1999 a major new commercial development had been built near it, comprising a hotel, a Dobbies' garden centre, Macdonald's and farm restaurants, accessed from a new roundabout on the A92. This planning decision merely worsened the heavy overloading of this road, which by 2000 had been limited to 50mph (80kmph) all the way to Arbroath. The two busy golf courses, the Ashludie and Medal, share the links. Small hotels include the *Panmure Hotel* and the *Monifieth House*. Monifieth High School has a roll of about 875.

## MONIKIE, Craigton & Kirkbuddo — Map 6, C3

***Angus small villages**, pop. 1100* — OS 54: NO 5038

The Kirkton of Monikie stands on the Angus hills some 7km inland from the mouth of the Firth of Tay. In the 15th century the keep of Affleck Castle was built 2 km to the west. Pont's crude sketch map of Angus made around 1600 showed a thickly settled countryside with many ferm touns around the kirk; however the Roy map of around 1750 implied that there were still no roads in the area. But these had been provided by the 19th century, when there were two mills; most people evidently lived south-west of the Kirkton in the straggling hamlet of Craigton, with its post office. The Dundee (Monikie) Water Act of 1845 enabled the engineer James Leslie to take water from the Crombie Burn to a large hilltop settling reservoir at Monikie, and thence by aqueduct and pipeline to another reservoir beside Dundee Law to serve the growing city. The adjacent Crombie Reservoir of 1866 enlarged the city's area of supply to embrace its suburbs.

**On and Off the Lines – and on the Water**: In 1870 the Caledonian Railway opened a branch line from Forfar to Broughty Ferry, with a station named Monikie between Affleck and Craigton. There was also a passing loop at Kirkbuddo station, 5km north of Monikie, with the hamlet of Whigstreet and a sawmill nearby. Houses and a post office soon clustered around Monikie station, and a new mill was built. In 1951 Monikie had nearly 550 people and the facilities of a small village, the Craigton primary school and also a medical practice. Closure of the railway to passengers in 1955, and the end of goods traffic and lifting of the line in 1967, were followed by a dip in the parish population to only 827 in 1971. Then two dormitory estates were built near the station site, raising the village population to about 600 by 1981; there has been little further development. The Lintrathen *(q.v.)* schemes developed larger sources, enabling Monikie to cease to supply water in 1981, when its tree-girt reservoirs were converted to a water-based Country Park by Tayside Regional Council, then the water supply authority; Crombie followed suit in 1983. In 1991, 1105 people lived in the parish. Affleck Castle is in private ownership; the twin villages still have a primary school, post office and two pubs.

## MONKTON — Map 1, C2

***Ayrshire village**, pop. 850* — OS 70: NS 3527

Monkton in Kyle, 6km north of Ayr, was evidently religious in origin. It lies near the mouth of the small Pow Burn, south of which is Prestwick. Pont's sketch-mapping work about 1600 showed *'Muncktoun'* with its Kirk, a now forgotten emparked Castle, and a mill. When Roy mapped southern Scotland about 1754, *'Monktown'* was a village; in 1799 Heron wrote of it as a *"small village"*. The tower of a 17th century windmill survives. The Paisley, Kilmarnock & Ayr Railway was opened in 1839 with a station west of Monkton. A new freight railway was opened in 1892 to link Annbank to the east with Monkton, which by then had an inn, smithy, and post office; Adamton House stood emparked 2 km to the east.

**Airfield Developments and Atlantic Role**: In 1935 David McIntyre *(see Troon)* and the Marquess of Clydesdale & Douglas jointly laid out *'Prestwick'* airport at Monkton as a grass field, established Scottish Aviation (SA) to build aircraft beside it, and in 1936 founded the Prestwick Flying Training School near the *Orangefield Hotel*. In 1939 the large *Palace of Engineering* from the Glasgow Empire Exhibition of 1938 at Bellahouston was re-erected by SA at Monkton, originally simply to repair aircraft. A large new roadhouse, the *Dutch House*, was built at about the same time. By 1940 the field was an RAF fighter station, an air training base – which by 1941 had trained over half the RAF's pilots – and a military transport airport, soon selected for its fog-free character as the landing place of American-built aircraft flown across the Atlantic for the British war effort. Some 37,000 transatlantic flights had used Prestwick by 1945; it was still under David McIntyre, by then a Group Captain, and by then was Britain's best airport, with the transatlantic air control centre and a 2 km runway 91m wide. In 1947 SA's *STOL 'Prestwick Pioneer'* became the first aircraft to be both designed (by the unrelated Robert McIntyre) and built entirely in Scotland.

**National and International**: Prestwick airport was soon nationalised along with the SA premises, and officially became an international airport in 1946, though a military presence remained – the Fleet Air Arm's HMS *Gannet*. Its enlargement and subsequent history is continued under Prestwick *(q.v.)*, while SA's story goes on below. By then Monkton had a school, post office, garage and inn, and nearly 1700 people. In the early 1950s, BEA (British European Airways) had a fleet of Douglas DC3s which was modernised by SA, becoming the 32-seat *'Pionair'* class; in 1955 came the 16-passenger Twin Pioneer. Monkton station had lost its passenger trains by 1953; soon afterwards a new airport passenger terminal was to be built just across the road! By 1972 Monkton and Prestwick had been bypassed with a major dual carriageway of the A77.

**The Jetstream – Success under whatever name**: From 1965 SA built parts of Hercules aircraft for Lockheed, and wings for the Handley Page turbo-prop feeder airliner later called the *Jetstream*. In 1966 SA became part of Cammell Laird of Birkenhead and in 1971 took over the manufacture of the Jetstream and the Bulldog trainer from the failed Handley Page and Beagle concerns. In 1978 SA was bought by BAC, later known as British Aerospace (BAe), who at once added aero-engine overhaul equipment at the plant. By 1989 over 300 *Jetstream* aircraft had been built, mainly for North American airlines; BAe gained an order for 100 improved planes, the *'31'*, from Eagle Airlines of Dallas as well as other substantial orders, bringing the workforce of 2100 to 2300 by 1992 and a peak of 2500 in 1994. By 1987 caravan sites were available north and west of Monkton, but the resident population had fallen to 866 by 1991.

**Flying Training Resumed and Engine Overhauls Intensified**: In 1987–88 BAe founded the British Aerospace Flying College, by 1994 operating 52 training aircraft and training 200 airline pilots a year; they converted the former hotel Adamton House and its annexe into a 257-room hostel for cadets from British Airways, Cathay Pacific and Gulf Air. The overhaul section of the plant, *Caledonian Airmotive*, was sold to Ryder International in 1987; in 1990 the firm gained a Queen's Award for export for the overhaul and refurbishment of jet engines.

**Manchester and Brazil Lose: Scottish Aviation hangs on**: By 1993 the *'Jetstream ATP'* was emerging in 64–68 seat versions and a *'stretched'* machine was planned. In 1993 BAe decided to move advanced turboprop production from Manchester to Monkton, installing new plant. Then harsh cuts began in the 2500 workforce because the *'J61'*, launched in 1994, gained just one contract, but strong orders for the 30-seat *'J41'* model kept the 2100 remaining workers busy.

**Overproduction, Overseas Partners and Job Cuts**: Excess world capacity in the regional aircraft market led to Jetstream seeking a partner in the turbo-prop field, and to a 1995 agreement with their main competitors Aerospatiale of France and Alenia of Italy. The production of the Jetstream 61 was phased out in 1995, and more jobs went. Some 1200 workers at Monkton continued to build the successful 29-seat *'J41'*. Further job cuts in 1996 were held to 200 due to newly placed defence contracts; but in 1997 aircraft production in Scotland seemed doomed. However, it appeared that from 2000 Bae would make *'Airbus'* parts at Monkton.

## MONTGREENAN — Map 1, C1

***Ayrshire area,*** *pop. 175* — OS 63 or 70: NS 3343

The 15th century keep of Auchenharvie Castle stands midway between Stewarton and Kilwinning; near waterfalls on the Lugton Water 2 km to the west was Montgreenan Castle, which featured equally clearly on Pont's map of around 1600, and the 16th century tower of Clonbeith Castle. By about 1754 the *'Cart Road from Irvine to Glasgow'* passed Auchenharvie Castle *(see also Stevenston)*. In 1817 the emparked mansion of Montgreenan replaced the castle of that name. A railway was completed in 1843 between Dalry and Kilmarnock, but the station named after the mansion was first opened on this line as late as 1878 by the Glasgow & South Western Railway (G&SWR). By 1895 Auchenharvie Castle was in ruins, but had given rise to an inn. The Fergushill Colliery was open west of the station, accompanied by something of a village, and Doura Smithy, 1.5 km to the south, lay at the end of a G&SWR goods branch from Kilwinning.

**Wiping the Slate**: Fergushill village, the colliery and the goods line had all gone by 1951; but there was a primary school at Doura, the station and post office at Montgreenan and 2 km to the east the *Torranyard Inn* and telephone exchange. In 1951 some 1250 residents in the surrounding area enjoyed these varied facilities, but there was nothing resembling a village. The station was closed in 1955, the post office had gone by 1970 and the school had closed by 1976. The railway had been lifted by 1985, and by then, apart from a sawmill beside the Lugton Water, the area seemed entirely rural. Montgreenan House of 1817 remained in private use until 1980; by 1996 it had become the 21-room *Montgreenan Mansion House*.

## MONTROSE, Craig & Ferryden — Map 6, C2

***Angus coast town,*** *pop. 11,500* — OS 54: NO 7157

A church dedicated to St Brioc in Pictish times gave its name to the islet on which it stood, Inchbraoch (or Rossie Isle) at the mouth of the South Esk in Angus; finely carved Pictish stones were found there. It seems that by about 900 the mainland locality to the north was named Sallork, or more probably *Saloch*, presumably meaning *'Salt Lake'* and referring to the large tidal lake later known as Montrose Basin; but a Danish attack in 980 seems to have been disastrous. The name Montrose, first recorded in that year, probably referred to *Old Montrose*, which lay on the western shore of the Basin 4 km west of Inchbraoch; it had an early *'Apdaine'* – i.e. land held by an abbot – and may well therefore have been the original port for ancient Brechin. Hume Brown believed the name derived from *Allt-moine-ros*, *'the burn of the mossy point'*, which fits Old Montrose but not the sandy peninsula which forms the site of the later town.

**The Royal Burgh**: The Royal Burgh of Montrose was chartered by David I between 1124 and 1153, and relocated from Old Montrose to the point opposite Inchbraoch where deep water was found, scoured as the tidal South Esk ebbed and flowed between the Basin and the North Sea. Though Montrose did not head a sheriffdom, its trading area included the Mearns to the north. By about 1150 Montrose had salt pans, presumably fired by wood or peat, and a mill, probably on the site of the windmill which stood near the harbour for centuries. By 1178 there was a royal castle, of which little is known except that its site was called the Castlested. In 1178 William the Lion granted the rights for the ferry across the South Esk between *'Munros'* and Ferryden to the new Abbey of Arbroath, which also had a salt pan at Montrose. A well-endowed leper hospital existed by about that time, and up to at least 1370.

**Early success as a Port cut short**: By the early 13th century Montrose had a church and the town houses of the Earls of Menteith and other notables. By 1275 there was a Dominican or Black Friary, founded by Sir Alan Durward. The Malherbes, French lairds of Rossie, lived atop a motte at Maryton Law 4 km south-west of Montrose until late in the 13th century, when Rossie Manor, also called Craig House, was finely built for them in stone as the centre of Craig parish, just south-west of Inchbraoch. By the later 13th century the new Montrose had become one of Scotland's four principal wool export centres; coins were minted at Montrose Castle under Alexander III. In

1287–89 the town was in dispute with Aberdeen and Banff regarding trading rights at fairs in north-east Scotland. By 1295 Montrose was being described as *"a good town"*, but its royal castle was destroyed by Wallace in 1297. The Bruces who owned Old Montrose with its castle and church of St Mary, swapped properties in 1325 with the Grahams, who moved from Cardross to Old Montrose. By 1330 Dundee had abstracted most of the local wool trade; Montrose made only small and irregular Customs payments in 1327–31.

**Montrose after the Black Death**: Montrose was able to recover relatively quickly from the Black Death calamity of 1350. The Black Friars built a new church in 1359, but their friary was burned in a war around 1400 and not rebuilt. Customs dues from Montrose climbed to ninth place by the 1360s, and in 1372 it was among the top eight exporting centres of Scotland. In that year the town council agreed to co-operate in trading with Forfar, to the exclusion of their intervening rival Brechin! The burgh had been re-chartered in 1370; in 1380 it was importing wine for the king's use, and in the late 14th century Montrose was chosen for the signing of a dozen royal charters. A school was first recorded there in the 14th century.

**Fishing and the Decline of the Wool Trade**: No doubt the local fisheries were long established before 1400, when Montrose was named as one of the three leading salmon fishing centres of Scotland. In the 15th century large numbers of dried white fish and crabs were despatched from Montrose, and by the late 1470s it was exporting much herring and cod. From 1492 to 1513 the rights to the mussel beds of the Basin were disputed with the Erskine lairds of the House of Dun. Meantime the Montrose wool trade, which had recovered after the Black Death, had fallen into terminal decline. After 1431 its wool exports almost ceased, though in 1434–35 trivial quantities of cloth were exported. There may well have been a shift from sheep to cattle in the hinterland, for hides were exported in the 15th century, when Montrose paid about 5% of Scottish Customs dues.

**Hospital and Mansion House**: Records of the burgh court remain from the 1450s, and it is possible that the hospital was converted into a Dominican friary in 1471, for a new hospital – really an almshouse – had been built at Newhame near the town by 1473. A new tolbooth was built in 1478. Around that time the fine town house called Castlested was built on the castle site, probably by Sir David Wood, but it was acquired in 1488 by the Earl of Montrose; it was the birthplace about 1612 of the Royalist James Graham, the *'Great Marquis'*, and it lasted 300 years. Meantime by 1485 the importance of Montrose as a trading centre was only a fifth of that of Aberdeen, and by the early 16th century Aberdeen merchants were calling in to supply Montrose with wheat, salt and wine imported through Leith. Development in the hinterland continued, and by 1505 there was a Milltown of Rossie just west of Craig. The hospital, in ruins by 1507 because its endowments had been misappropriated, was then reinstated by Patrick Paniter, the king's secretary. The parish church was also well rebuilt with aid from Paniter in 1510–12, with some fine wood carvings.

**Traffic Noise and Golf in the Beautiful Town**: By that time the town had begun a strong recovery, and in 1519 the Blackfriars who had taken over the hospital in 1516 were complaining at the rumble of carts and other traffic past their new home. About 1530 Rossie Manor was greatly enlarged by Sir David Wood, Chancellor to James V, who renamed it *'Craigtoun of Inchebriock'*. By 1535 the local contributions of burgh tax had grown to fifth or sixth place in Scotland, and by 1540 Montrose vessels were trading into the Baltic. Andrew Melville, who revived the Universities of Glasgow, Aberdeen and St Andrews and headed the Church of Scotland, was born at Baldovy near Montrose in 1545. In 1548 Jean de Beauge considered it *"a beautiful town"*, and favourable comments by travellers were general over the next three centuries. In 1549 the burgh was large enough to muster a thousand fighting men to defend it against the English, and it was represented in Parliament in 1560. Very soon after the Reformation, in 1566, an early parish school was opened, and the game of *'goff'* was being taught by the minister who ran a boarding school at Logie on the Dun estate. In the newly peaceful conditions Montrose flourished, and by the 1590s it was again among the top eight Scottish ports.

**Trading Prosperity and the Multilingual Bishop**: By 1612 a traveller noted *"this toune is all builded with stone"*; at that time a quarry near St Cyrus supplied dressed stone for rebuilding in Montrose. By the 1620s the Mid Links was a regular golf course, and Provost Patrick Lychtoun was a grain merchant who also traded through a large commercial wine cellar. Robert Leighton who was born near Montrose in 1611 – and may have been a relative – learned to speak twelve languages, became Principal of Edinburgh University and the reluctant Episcopal Bishop of Dunblane, to which town *(q.v.)* he donated his famous library. By 1621 the Scott family of Montrose was providing a form of banking service with borrowers as far afield as Aberdeen; soon they specialised as salmon exporters, for salmon fishing was booming until the Civil War. In 1628 the tower house of Old Montrose was restored. In 1639 Montrose was the tenth richest burgh in Scotland, with nearly half the tax yield of Dundee.

**Trade dips through Civil War and Plague**: After a raid by Royalist Highlanders in 1644 the town was walled in a makeshift fashion by requiring the householders to heighten all their *'back dykes'*. In 1648–49 Montrose was ravaged by plague for the last time, and all trade was suspended for a year. Yet in 1655 Tucker found *"a pretty town, with a safe harbour"*. Its shipowners then had twelve vessels, importing salt and exporting salmon, *'pladding'* and corn. In 1656 Richard Franck found Montrose *"adorned with excellent buildings, whose foundations are laid with polished stone"*; presumably he meant ashlar; there were *"merchants and manufacture"*. Trade resumed little changed, for salmon, grain and sheepskins were exported, with salt the main import.

**Trade Flourishes but Coutts moves south to Success**: In the 1670s and 80s the weekly market with its sales of such items as shoes, fish and flesh was well managed, but full-time shops were appearing: this required more floorspace, regulated by bringing forward the building line. By 1693 there was a proper slaughterhouse on the outskirts, and exports included corn, linen, woollen cloth, stockings, salmon and white fish. Two more windmills, one of them new, stood north of the town, erected by local millwrights who worked as far afield as Banff. However, though there had for long been commercial and family ties with Norway and especially Sweden – from which iron gates were imported in exchange for grain plus increasing quantities of locally-made malt – the port had just one short pier. John Coutts, a Montrose maltster and grain merchant, was exporting to Norway by 1668; though his Jacobite son sadly entered the slave trade, the family moved into Edinburgh banking. Thomas Coutts, who entered an existing London bank in 1755, made it so famous that it took his name – which it still retains. Montrose itself had one of the earliest branches of the Bank of Scotland, opened in 1696 but soon closed like all the others due to the troubled times.

**Town Council Improvements**: In the 1670s the council set out to reclaim half the Basin by building an east–west rubble embankment, the *Dronners' Dyke*; but it was heavily damaged by a storm in 1679 and never completed, though its line can still be detected. In 1682–83 the Grammar School was in a bad way, but about 1685–86 the town council founded a public library, which famously acquired books dating back to 1475. *(See Fraser's interesting illustrated local history of Montrose to 1700.)* The first Montrose post office was opened in 1707, and in 1715 a row of buildings which stood in the centre of the wide High Street was demolished, leaving what is now claimed as the widest main street in Scotland. Defoe was dismissive in the 1720s, simply writing that Montrose *"is a sea-port, and, in proportion to its number of inhabitants, has a considerable trade, and is tolerably well built"*.

**Linen Sailcloth**: The town already exported linens by the 1720s, and was famous for its annual market for linen yarn from *"all parts of Angus and Mearns"* and even farther afield; some yarn went to London. A partnership was set up about 1745 to manufacture sailcloth and coarse linens in a 30-loom factory, with its own bleachfield by 1754. The town's largely seaborne trade financed further fine buildings, among them the Town Hall of 1763. In 1765 Alexander Carlyle commented approvingly that there was *"a great manufacture of sailduck as well as of osnaburgh"* in Montrose, *"as happily situated as any town in Britain"*, surrounded by improved farmland and gentlemen's seats. He enjoyed a meal of local salmon in an *"agreeable inn"* run by a *"South Brittain"* – an Englishman? In 1773 Boswell noted that Montrose had an apothecary's shop.

**Poor Land Transport – Seaborne Success**: As late as 1750 the Roy map showed the sole defined land access to the quite large town of Montrose to be a track inland towards Brechin. In that year the road from Ferryden to Arbroath was made up, but the coast road from Dundee to Aberdeen still relied on ferries across both the River South Esk at Montrose and the North Esk at Kinnaber, 5 km to the north. In 1765 Carlyle noted that the South Esk ferry lacked piers for the embarkation of horses, and the boats were *"not convenient"*; the current was still thought too strong for the erection of a bridge. But one was soon built across the narrower channel linking Inchbraoch with Ferryden, and in 1775 a bridge was opened across the North Esk *(see Hillside)*. Montrose was among Britain's top ten ports for coastwise coal imports in 1780–85; its exports included river salmon, barley and malt. A marine insurance agency was started, for in 1789 as many as 53 small merchant vessels averaging 67 tons were locally owned.

**Knitting, Thread, Bridge and *'Lunatics'***: Seventy hands worked in a woollen factory in 1776, and framework knitting had begun by 1778. The end of the American War of Independence in 1783 cut the demand for sailcloth, so two firms moved into thread manufacture for the London and Manchester markets; Osnaburgs and yarns went to Glasgow. By 1789 there was a very substantial linen merchant, and during the century the harbour was improved to accommodate peaks of flax imports. A timber toll bridge with a lifting span, begun in 1792, finally replaced the South Esk ferry in 1795. In the late 18th century Montrose continued to specialise in manufacturing coarse linens, especially sailcloth. The Chapel linen and rope works in Eastern Road was established in 1795 and repeatedly extended. Paton's were also founded in textiles and built their major premises in 1828. *'Montrose Lunatic Hospital'*, the first proper provision in Scotland for the mentally handicapped, was built in 1781. In 1785 a library "free to teachers of the young, and university students" was available.

**Churches, Brewing and Bawbees**: In 1789 the old parish church was demolished; the new 2500-seat Parish Church built in 1791 acquired its landmark steeple in 1832–34. The Gothic Craig Kirk was finely built in 1799. Several small breweries were built in the late 18th century – that opened north of the town by Deuchars taking over the site of a windmill. Though permanent shops were appearing, no annual fair was listed for Montrose in 1797; if none was held, it was unusual for such a sizeable commercial centre, where two local traders issued their own bawbees (half old penny coins). Heron noted in 1799 *"a well built town"*, where *"a great quantity of malt, coarse linens, coloured and white thread are made"*.

**The Port and Fisheries Various**: He noted Montrose harbour as *"a fine semicircular basin, defended by a stone pier. At the harbour is a wet dock where ships are built and repaired."* The 5000 inhabitants owned *"a great number of trading vessels, of which several are employed in the whale fishing"*. However, the *"formerly considerable"* pearl fishery on the South Esk contrasted with the *"very valuable"* salmon fishings on both the rivers. The Fishtown of Usan to the south (its name a contraction of Ullishaven) had a remarkable lobster fishery supplying the London market. A lifeboat station was opened in 1800, sharing with St Andrews the honour of being the first in Scotland. As late as 1819 Montrose Basin, rich in mussel beds, was known as the *'Lands of Sands'*. Meantime in 1809 Alexander Allan had been born in Montrose; he was to become a famous locomotive engineer.

**Early 19th Century Developments**: In 1798 William Ford was a local sailcloth manufacturer; his may have been the first local flax spinning factory, built in 1805, but in 1817 his firm failed and their 1820-spindle four-storey steam-powered flax

*Montrose Academy, built in 1815. It still flourishes, the buildings having been repeatedly extended from 1841 onwards.* (RS)

mill was sold. A lace school was established in 1815, and by 1817 some 425,000m of linen was being stamped annually. By 1811 there was a daily coach to Aberdeen, and an early golf club that was founded in 1810 was later renamed the *'Royal Albert'* – perhaps the Prince Consort had played it while holidaying at Balmoral. In 1822 there was also a well-defined racecourse on the nearby links. The local newspaper, the *Montrose Review*, was established in 1811, and about then the Standard Press was founded. The impressive central block of Montrose Academy was built in 1815 and extended in 1841. Maryton, 3km west of Ferryden, was unsuccessfully promoted as the site of a new settlement in 1824. By 1825 five breweries were at work, including William Ross's at Lochside.

**Banks Galore**: The Montrose Banking Company was established in 1814, and by 1825 this had opened branches in Arbroath and Brechin; but in 1829 it merged with the National Bank. Early 19th century branches included the Dundee Union Banking Company, the Aberdeen bankers John Maberly, and the Bank of Scotland. Chambers writing about 1827 said *"it contains 7000 inhabitants, is a royal burgh, a thriving sea-port, a town of great activity in the manufacture of sail-cloth, &c; a seat of wealth and amusement, as much as that of industry and commerce"*.

**New Bridge kills off Old Montrose**: The lifting bridge across the South Esk actually lasted only until 1828, being replaced in 1829 by an iron suspension bridge which denied access by masted vessels to Old Montrose, which consequently ceased to trade. The salmon and some sea fisheries continued, especially from Ferryden, and in 1834 three whaling vessels were based in Montrose. The town's 108 vessels then totalled 11,000 tons; 2500 tonnes of flax was imported annually, serving four large steam-powered linen works producing very varied products. Montrose firms owned three other works powered by the waters of the North Esk *(see Hillside and Craigo)*. Farina (potato starch) was manufactured from about that time.

**The early Victorian Era**: In 1837 the harbour was taken over by trustees, including Brechin people and landward interests, and a small new wet dock was complete by 1840; though mainly used by coasting vessels, three times the tonnage of the 1790s was soon being handled. A gasworks was set up in 1838, and in 1845 five flax spinning mills were open, mainly steam driven; milling, brewing and tanning industries were all in operation. The Eastern Road ropeworks, reconstructed in 1825, was extended in 1846; it later became George Morton's bottling plant. The interesting Montrose museum was founded in 1837; its fine building was opened in 1842 and extended in 1890. The Infirmary was founded in 1839.

**Roundabout Rail, Busy Shipyard, Regularised Golf**: From 1848 branches of the Aberdeen Railway, coming up from the south via Friockheim *(q.v.)*, linked Montrose to Dundee and Perth, and also to Brechin. Remarkably, the company's line entered Montrose from the north at Dubton, and crossed the links east of the town to terminate at a station beside Railway Place; the nearby harbour was served by sidings which extended along the quayside to the bridge. Montrose passengers had to take a 5km ride on a branch train to change at Dubton, from which the main line, later part of the Caledonian, swerved away up the valley of the North Esk to end near Stonehaven; the connection from there to Aberdeen was completed in 1850. In 1865 a separate company, the Montrose & Bervie, opened a line from Broomfield (east of the Brechin turn) up the coast to Inverbervie. Meantime Birnie's shipyard was busy by around 1850, and in 1863 the odd 17-hole links golf course – later known as the Medal course – was brought into line with the 18-hole standard, becoming popular and lengthy.

**Over 2000 work in Montrose Mills in 1864**: In 1864 Warden found the district's linen trade *"very prosperous; all classes are satisfied, and happy contentment reigns"*. The four main works continued, all powered by steam and then employing 2100 people. The largest was J & G Paton, whose huge flax mill contained 12,000 spindles driven by a 120hp steam engine and employed 800 operatives. Other spinning companies were Richards & Co (who also had power-looms for weaving), Aberdein, Gordon & Co, and G & A Gordon. James Mudie still employed about 135 hand-loom weavers producing both floorcloth and broad sheetings, but he too was erecting a power-loom works. By 1867 six local factories used flax, jute and hemp; most were flax spinning mills, absorbing some 50,000 tonnes of flax annually, and employing almost 2500 workers.

**Timber Imports and Shipbuilding**: Montrose with the registration letters *'ME'* was then among the top ten Scottish ports in white-fish curing, and by 1869 three shipyards were at work building wooden vessels – Birnie, Petrie, and Strachan. In the 1860–80 period Montrose also became second only to Greenock as Scotland's main importers of Scandinavian raw lumber, the firms of Millar and Birnie re-exporting sawn and planed wood to London. Then Sweden built its own sawmills and damaged the Montrose timber trade, but Robert Millar & Sons continued for over a century as major timber importers. The town's population, 15,250 in 1851, actually fell to 13,100 by 1891. The Scurdie Ness lighthouse overlooking the harbour was first lighted in 1870, and Montrose Football Club was formed in 1879.

**On a Through Line at Last**: By 1870 Wordie & Co had a substantial depot for road to rail cartage. Many cattle were carried between farm, station and auction mart, and grain for export was moved from farm and granary to harbour. Sand collected from the beach went into locomotive sandboxes until evident erosion called a halt. In 1881 the direct railway line from Arbroath was opened by the North British Railway (NBR), with a new through station at Montrose. Trains ran directly to Aberdeen from 1883, and completion of the Forth Bridge in 1890 put Montrose on a main line, over which the East Coast companies briefly raced to Aberdeen. As rail communications improved, Montrose became a minor holiday resort; the Melville and Mid-Links Gardens were laid out in the late 19th century, with facilities for tennis, croquet and bowling.

**Fishery, Brewery and Resort Facilities**: The South Esk ferry had been resuscitated for passengers by 1881, when fishing continued on a large scale from Ferryden, which was the chief fishing port of Angus at its peak around 1890, with 150 boats; the ferry plied until at least 1894. In spite of all its industries Montrose was called *"a handsome town"* in 1886, and in 1887 Links Park was opened to serve the new local football club. The Lochside brewery was rebuilt in 1889 to designs by Elgin architect C C Doig. The 1891 population was 13,000; by then Paton's employed about 1000 people. Three hotels were open by 1894 – the newly-built *Central*, the *Star*, and *Commercial*. In 1897 the 18-hole Victoria golf course – later known as the Broomfield course – was added, and by 1900 there was also a

*Fishing boats at Ferryden in the late 19th century, with herring drifters on the right. In the background is Inchbrayock Viaduct, built by the North British Railway in 1879–80. Ferryden was the chief fishing port of Angus at its peak around 1890. In 1974 a servicing base for North Sea oil was created here, with a new 6-berth quay.* (GWW collection)

shorter 18-hole course for ladies. A power station was established in 1898, a Savings Bank was built in 1900, and a fine red sandstone public library arose opposite in 1905 – opened by the benefactor himself, Andrew Carnegie.

**Coasting Steamers and Pioneer Aerodrome**: About 1905 the London & Montrose Shipbuilding Company built the collier SS *Penshurst*, whose remarkable story was told by Waine (1980); but the yard closed soon after. In 1913 a Royal Flying Corps airfield was established north of the town at Broomfield, the first operational air base in Britain *(see Hay & Stell)*; but this closed in 1919. About that time James Deuchars used the coasters *Lochside* of 1905, and later the *Lochside II* of 1925, to carry beer from the Lochside Brewery to Newcastle, and general cargo back. J M Piggins set up in the coasting business in Montrose in 1923; his various vessels soon carried coal, manure, potatoes, timber, salt and soda, and in the 1930s shipped barreled herrings from Lerwick, but he abandoned coasting about 1945. Four of the five breweries faded away and flax imports fell as the textile industry shrank by the 1900s; only the tidal scour caused by the Basin kept the harbour open, and a tug was no longer required. However, the HQ of the East Coast salmon fisheries remained.

**Concrete and Canning**: In 1925 a food preparation plant was opened, later operated by Premier Brands, and a cannery opened in 1930. An ugly new concrete road bridge across the South Esk was built in 1928–31, replacing the suspension bridge, and as buses abstracted branch line traffic, the original Caledonian Railway station was closed in 1934. The *Playhouse Cinema* was built in 1933. The airfield was reopened in 1936, becoming a fighter base in 1940, and also a principal training base; after World War II it became a depot. By 1950 Montrose was a major local centre for shopping and business, with ten hotels. The Inverbervie branch railway was closed to passengers in 1951.

**Enter Glaxo and the Aberdeen Main Line**: In 1952 Glaxochem was established to manufacture medical chemicals in Montrose, taking advantage of the tidal scour to sweep its effluents well out to sea. In 1957 Deuchars' brewery was converted to form the Lochside grain and malt distillery. A large plain extension to Montrose Academy was opened in 1960, and another in the late 1980s. In 1962 a new indoor swimming pool was opened, followed in 1963 by the Town Hall, mainly intended for functions but simply equipped as a theatre. A primitive engine shed lasted until the end of steam; at that time freight trains were propelled, i.e. pushed, up to Kinnaber! From 1967, with the closure of the Strathmore route, the railway through Montrose became the only line between Aberdeen and the south. Because of the high cost of widening rock cuttings and the basin bridge, this still retains a 2 km single line section across the South Esk from Usan, the only such permanent bottleneck between London and Aberdeen. In 1971 the burgh population was just under 10,000.

**Oil Development at Ferryden**: Sea Oil Services, part of the P&O Group, had begun the reclamation of land for oil development in the estuary by 1973, due to the suitability of the channel between Ferryden and Inchbraoch for the development of a North Sea oil servicing base. By 1974 they had created 15 ha of reclaimed land with its own 6-berth quay, having a minimum water depth of 5.5 m. In 1976 an active engineering works was prominent, and an industrial estate had mushroomed north of the town; there in 1978 the Petroleum Industry Training Board opened a unique training centre teaching drilling and fire-fighting techniques.

**Montrose loses Local Government**: In 1975 historic Montrose was sadly deprived of its local government status, to the ultimate advantage of Forfar. However, in 1976 ships from as far afield as Singapore used the harbour, and Montrose remained well known as the chief potato exporting port in Scotland, shipping up to 30,000 tonnes a year; potatoes were also still despatched south by rail. Montrose was still a flourishing place with many substantial buildings, including a new Co-op department store. Despite the bleak dune coastline, and visible pollution from the Glaxo works, the caravan sites were extensive. Montrose had a Cadbury-Schweppes factory and a small airstrip by about 1979.

**Food and Drink Decline but Glaxo Gains**: At some time the historic Chapel works became a whisky bottling plant for George Morton of Dundee, part of Chivas; but by 1989 it was vacant and stood awaiting a user in 1993. Premier Brands closed its food preparation plant, on moving the work to Arbroath in 1990, with the loss of 220 full-time and as many part-time jobs. Macnab Distilleries' Lochside grain whisky plant with its prominent tower and gloomy array of bonds was out of use in 1983, and though busy again by 1991, in 1992 it was closed permanently. By 1991 the population had risen to 11,440. In 1989 the largest employer was Glaxochem, its 700 workers making fine medical chemicals, and a new pharmaceuticals plant opened in 1992; the firm forecast at least another 40 years at Montrose. By 1993 the Glaxochem plant was huge and largely ultra-modern, said to manufacture a quarter of the firm's products.

**Transport Developments**: Scurdie Ness lighthouse was automated in 1987. In 1989, after improvements to the handling capacity of the port, small timber was actually being *exported* through Montrose to Scandinavia for pulping! Rail-freight included pulpwood, grain, and agricultural lime. The NBR station building had recently been replaced by a small modern structure. The ugly concrete road bridge suffered from alkali and chloride deterioration and required strengthening in 1994. In the late 1990s an internal bypass road was constructed, part following a disused railway alignment, so relieving the crowded High Street of through traffic; nowadays large car dealerships are prominent.

**Industrial Successes include Oil Work**: By 1990 a Gateway store had been built near the station, and in 1992–93 the former auction mart was replaced by a new William Low superstore (later Tesco). By 1993 CAM Shipping of Aberdeen, responding to growing congestion in Aberdeen harbour, had moved its base for 36 North Sea standby vessels to Montrose. In 1993 Rix were important petroleum distributors, and the tall silo of the flour mill bore the name Ian Glen; by 1993 a new 10,000-tonne grain store had led to growth in the grain trade through the port, which also claimed to handle most of the pulp imported for Scottish paper mills. *'Plasboard'* boxes and trays were manufactured in Montrose, and oil-related firms included Pipeline Cleaning Services, and the much enlarged ABB Velco Gray Brown Boveri. Private traders still operate many of the shops lining the congested High Street, traversed by multiple controlled pedestrian crossings.

**Leisure and Problems**: Scottish Second Division football had been played at Links Park, a pleasant spot where a new 1400-seater stand and entertainment suite built by new owner Bryan Keith opened in 1992; but in 1994 Montrose FC joined the new lowly Third Division, where it has stayed. In 1994 the Tidy Britain group found the state of the Montrose beaches *'disappointing'*. In 1992 a part of the former RAF station dating from 1913 was acquired by a trust, which by 1999 had opened the Montrose Aerodrome Museum there to commemorate its long history. By 1997 Craig Kirk stood empty. The former Lochside distillery was expected to be replaced from 1996 by housing, shops, a nursing home and garden centre; the dominant tower, allegedly structurally unsound, was to vanish – yet it still stood in 2000, by then being earmarked for retail development. In that year the lifeboat station celebrated its bicentenary; by then the Scottish Wildlife Trust had built a viewing centre on the south shore of the Basin. The Mercantile golf course is now open, and the hotels include the *Carlton*, the *Links*, and the larger, golf-oriented *Montrose Park*. Glaxo decided to sell their plant in 2001, threatening many of the 700 jobs.

## MONYMUSK — Map 10, B3

***Aberdeenshire village,*** *pop. 750* — OS 38: NJ 6815

Monymusk lies beside the River Don 11 km south-west of Inverurie, among remains of standing stones and a seventh century Culdee priory church. Its remarkable name could well derive from the Gaelic *Moine Musgan*, *'Bog of Rotten Trees'*. An Augustinian priory was set up in 1170, and Monymusk was mentioned as a significant trading centre by 1499. The towers of Pitfichie Castle, 1.5 km upstream, the Place of Tillyfoury beside the river 5 km to the north-west and Tillycairn Castle, 4 km to the south-west, were all originally built in the 16th century. The castle keep called Monymusk House dates from 1587, and Monymusk became a tiny burgh of barony in 1588, but it was still insignificant on Gordon's map of about 1640.

**Green Proprietor's Paradise Village**: Although there was an early ferry and an inn, Monymusk's development really dates from 1717 when its proprietor, a Grant, began afforestation. Over two million trees were planted, as shown on the Roy map made about 1750, when plantations extended from west of the riverside House of Monymusk to the confluence of the Ton Burn with the Don. Monymusk village was sketched with about ten buildings. Tracks linked with Cluny parish (and its later mansion *'castle')* to the south, and also east and west between Inverurie and Alford Kirkton via the Don's wooded glen, part happily named *'Paradise'*. The Grants – among Scotland's most celebrated farm improvers – also founded a flax dressing mill about 1750, and had the village rebuilt very pleasingly about 1767, focused on a square. Ord mill was converted from grain to sawmilling in 1768, and one Grant also tried to set up a lapidary, a venture which failed. Two fairs were scheduled to take place in 1797; by then Pitfichie Castle was roofless. In 1808 the water-powered sawmill was rebuilt on a large scale with 42 saws in four frames, but Monymusk was slow to obtain a post office, opened around 1825. Estate houses were enlarged and rebuilt in the late 19th century.

**Railway and Quarrying**: From 1859 Monymusk was indirectly served by a station and siding 1 km south of the village on the Alford Valley Railway (later the Great North of Scotland

Railway's Alford branch), which climbed through a col where the granite hills converged at the little-used Tillyfourie Station (OS 37), 5 km south-west of Monymusk. Nearby, two important quarries were opened – one in Tillyfourie Hill, probably in use by 1867, and the somewhat later Corrennie quarry to the south, whose granitic gneiss with pink feldspar was originally exploited for decorative uses, as in Glasgow City Chambers. In 1894 Monymusk had a post and telegraph office and an inn; the parish held 1100 people in 1901.

**After the Trains, School Buses**: Both quarries long remained open – Corrennie, by then producing diorite, was 76 m deep by 1939 – but apparently both had closed by 1980. The railway was closed to passengers in 1950, and goods services on the line were abandoned in 1966. The parish population was down to 515 by 1971. Pitfichie Castle was finely restored in 1978. The secondary classes held in Sauchen school 4 km to the south had ceased by 1976, but a fleet of school buses is still based at Sauchen, now a hamlet. To the west are many areas of Forestry Commission access land. House-building brought Monymusk's parish population to 723 in 1991; another cluster of houses has since been added, but it remains an attractive estate village with a post office. The *Grant Arms Hotel* has been enlarged to 17 rooms.

## MOODIESBURN & Gartferry

**Map 15, E4**

***N. Lanarkshire small town,*** *pop. 6000* — OS 64: NS 6970

In 1895 and well into the 20th century, Moodiesburn was only a few houses at a crossroads on the Glasgow to Falkirk road, 12 km north-east of Glasgow; 500 m north-west was Gartferry House. By the 1920s a large colliery was open 1.5 km north-west of Moodiesburn at Auchengeich, and 1 km north of Gartferry was the Stoneyetts Institution (later a psychiatric hospital). By 1953 the grounds of Gartferry House had been developed with a large new housing estate. By 1971 Moodiesburn had a post office, and the main A80 road had been given a second carriageway, but the coal mine had closed. Meantime in the 1960s spin-off from research by the US-owned Johnson & Johnson led to the setting up of the firm of Devro east of Moodiesburn, making synthetic sausage casings using collagen protein, a cowhide-derived tannery by-product. So busy was the A80 by 1979 that a footbridge had been built across it. By 1991 the youthful population of Moodiesburn was almost 6000.

**Sausage Casings Stretch to the Sun**: In 1991 a management buy-out separated Devro from Johnson & Johnson; at that time Devro employed some 600 people in Scotland, and the profitable modern Moodiesburn plant was said to be making a third of the World's sausage casings. Meantime, it was proposed to close the 180-bed Stoneyetts Hospital. In 1993 Devro went public, Moodiesburn becoming the group HQ of an international company employing nearly 1000 people there and at Bellshill, and in Australia and the USA. It claimed by then to make over half the world's small diameter sausage skins at a rate of about 500 metres a second, totalling 1.5 billion metres a year – far enough to reach the sun! The use of collagen film for wrapping other meat products was also rapidly growing. In 1995 Devro bought their USA rival Teepak, becoming Devro Teepak and raising their world-wide labour force to over 3000, including plants in Belgium and Eastern Europe. In 1996 Scottish Power decided to move their local facilities from Moodiesburn to Eurocentral at Mossend. Semple & Cochrane, building services, are large local employers, as are Johnson Control Systems; NCR, Modus Media, and Tenma are in high-tech sectors.The once small *Moodiesburn House Hotel* now has 60 rooms.

*Annathill housing, Moodiesburn, built to house miners working in Bedlay Colliery. The external stairs leading to the upper flats was typical of Lanarkshire.* (RCAHMS / JRH)

## MORAR

**Map 8, B5**

***Small Lochaber village,*** *pop. 225* — OS 40: NM 6793

The Roy map made about 1750 was the first to survey the huge trackless parish of Arisaig. It showed *'Beorig'* as a hamlet on the north side of the abbreviated gorge in which were the falls which enabled the fresh waters of Loch Morar, the deepest natural lake in Britain, to overflow almost directly into the sea. The shores of the loch were still heavily wooded, and the whole area completely trackless; so remote that after the Reformation a Roman Catholic college was able to operate clandestinely on an island in the loch despite the proscription of services. In 1847 there was no school nearer than Arisaig, and as late as 1896 there was no road of any kind north of the river, where stood the township then known in English as *'Poris'* (Beoraid).

**Railway opens up Tourism**: The West Highland Extension Railway was opened in 1901, spanning the gorge to a station at Beoraid, which it called Morar, the last before the new Mallaig terminus. A hotel was soon built there, and in the early 20th century Morar was a post town. Eventually a road was carried through to Mallaig too, and in 1948 the falls were tamed by a weir to generate hydro-electricity. A council housing estate was built, and the population of Morar in 1951–81 was very stable at about 225. The hotel was enlarged about 1969; a caravan site and a youth hostel were already open at Garramor to the south. In 1981 the local facilities remained those of a small village. By 1984 there were also two cruiser bases operating at the lochside, and a boatbuilder by the sea. The youth hostel closed around 1990, and by 1997 the village and level crossing had been bypassed. The *Morar Hotel* has 27 rooms and offers fishing.

## MOREBATTLE

**Map 3, B4**

***Borders village,*** *pop. 575 (area)* OS 74: NT 7724

Ancient hill forts stand on a spur of the Cheviot Hills overlooking a crook of the Kale Water, which joins the River Tweed at Kalemouth above Kelso. In the Iron Age hundreds of huts huddled within the fort on Hownam Law, nearly 450m above sea level, 4km south-east of aptly named Morebattle on the Kale Water. Being so near the later English border (and raids), defensive works abounded: two from the 15th century are the L-plan Cessford Castle 3km west of the village, and the greatly decayed Moss Tower near Kalemouth. Defenders based in the 16th century Corbet tower 1km to the south, the 17th century Whitton Tower 2.5km south-west, and the enigmatic Chesterhouse near the hamlet of Hownam to the south, may have collectively deterred border raiders, for when Pont studied the Merse around 1600 the area was thickly settled, with no fewer than five mills on the stream above the village, and Caverton Mill 2 km to the west.

**Country Schools and Mills**: Only 1.5km north is the kirk of Linton parish. Parish schools were founded in 1608 at Eckford near Kalemouth, at Hownam in 1609, at Caverton to the north-west in 1617, at Samieston south of Cessford by 1619 and at Morebattle itself in 1628; all save the last seemed doomed to close. Four mills were shown on Roy's map, made about 1754, when the only track to Morebattle led south via Hownam Kirk to the Roman Way at Blackhall Hill – and so to England! Heron wrote in 1799 that Morebattle was a *"rising village"*, the Kale Water then supporting a sawmill, a fulling-mill, and *"several others"*. In 1901 it had a smithy, an inn and a post and telegraph office, but the oddly named Grubbit Mill was the sole survivor of the five above the village.

**Over the Hill?**: By 1951 a 200-pupil junior secondary school augmented the facilities of a small village, serving a population of some 1250 in an area reaching to the head of the valley at remote Tow Ford; Hownam had an inn, which soon closed. Rural depopulation had led to closure of the secondary classes by 1976, and by 1981 under 800 people lived in the wider area. In 1990 the quiet place still boasted a village hall, post office cum newsagent, a general store, a garage, a haulier (based in an old church), B&Bs and the *Templehall Hotel*. The parish population was 575 in 1991. By 1998 the *St Cuthbert's Way* long-distance route passed through Morebattle, whose substantial primary school is among the few facilities still open.

## MORNINGSIDE, Marchmont, Merchiston & Braid

**Map 15, C2**

***S. & S-W. areas of Edinburgh*** OS 66: NT 2471

One of the earliest features of this area of undulating ground south of Edinburgh's former South Loch was Merchiston Tower, of 14th or 15th century construction; its eighth laird John Napier, the celebrated mathematician who invented logarithms and the decimal point, was born there about 1550. The 15th century Bruntsfield House and its farm were bought in 1695 by the Warrender family. Quarrying in the very extensive Burgh Muir south of the loch – especially what is now Bruntsfield Links and Warrender Park Terrace – was active by 1554; in 1586 much of the Muir was feued off, and Pont's map made around 1600 showed a road to the south passing through the area. In 1694 a paper mill was opened on the Braid Burn some 3km out of the city, to make banknote paper for the Bank of Scotland, which it did until 1735; the mill remained in some use until 1774, but the area was a stranger to later industry. From 1722 the South Loch was drained to become the Meadows, and golf was officially played in the area from 1735. Roy's map of about 1754 showed both Merchiston and Morningside as two small linear settlements on the Biggar road, the clear origins of the later commercial ribbon.

**Suburban Development and Schools**: About 1780 came the Canaan Estate, and Lord Gardenstone commissioned Morningside House. The Hermitage of Braid, a late 18th century baronial style villa, was designed for Charles Gordon of Cluny by Robert Burn; its policies beside the Braid Burn later became a public park. James Gillespie's School opened in Bruntsfield Place in 1803, and a post office was opened at Boroughmuirhead in 1804, serving new housing for the city's growing workforce. In 1813 an asylum was built off Morningside Park, a parish school opened in 1823, and the independent Merchiston Castle Academy for boys was founded in 1833. St Margaret's Convent was founded in 1834 in the Whitehouse, an old mansionhouse; Gillespie Graham designed its fine chapel of 1835.

**Holy Corner and Marchmont**: In 1838 the parish church was dedicated, giving its name to Church Hill, and the tall-spired Barclay Bruntsfield church, designed by Edinburgh architect Fred Pilkington, was built in 1862–64. Melville Drive, laid out in 1858, provided both access to Marchmont and a definite northern limit to development of the Sciennes area to the east. Sir George Warrender feued off Marchmont farm from 1869, to a layout plan by David Bryce. Facings had to be from Redhall quarries nearby, or from distant Dunmore. The main development of Marchmont with fine four- and five-storey tenements followed, from 1876 to 1916; 150 small shops were also provided. There was an inn in Morningside by 1871, the year when the prominent spired (Marchmont) St Giles church opened; the City Quarry in Burgh Muir was last active in 1880. Warrender Park school was built in 1882, and Warrender Baths in 1887 (public only since 1908); meantime in 1883 the main Morningside road became free of the expensive toll just south of Tollcross. A pious new residential area to the south soon filled with rival churches, built in 1865 (United Presbyterian), 1875–78 (Episcopal), and 1879–81 (Church of Scotland); the nickname *'Holy Corner'* was bestowed on the junction with Colinton Road *(see Cant, 1987).*

**Golf, Schools, Health Services and Railway**: Suburban growth was stimulated when Morningside station on the new Edinburgh Suburban & South Side Junction Railway, a subsidiary of the North British, was opened in 1884 in a cutting 2 km south of Tollcross. A major International Exhibition was staged in the West Meadows in 1886; its extensive buildings were promptly removed. By 1892 when South Morningside School was opened, with a roll of nearly 600 pupils, the spearhead of roadside development had reached the Braid Burn, with growing estates to either side. The two steep 18-hole municipal golf courses at Braid Hills date from 1893–94; a fire station was built in 1893. Murray in 1894 wrote lyrically of *"the pleasant suburb of Morningside, with numerous fine villas in grounds"*. He ignored the new poorhouse, tucked away in the still open country at Greenbank, and the old asylum, later tactfully renamed as the Royal Edinburgh Hospital. A veil was also drawn over the failure of both the hydropathic at Morningside Drive, apparently built in the 1870s, and of its later user the short-lived Morningside College of the 1880s. In the 1890s an ancient building called Craig House gave its name to an asylum of which it became part, later restyled as a mental hospital. The first Boroughmuir School opened in 1904; proving too small, it was re-sited at Viewforth in 1914.

**Tramways, Hotel and Health Developments**: From 1899 the area was served by Edinburgh cable trams, running from Pilrig via Princes Street and Tollcross, Bruntsfield Place and Morningside Road past the station, up to the foot of the Braid Hills, and also east–west via Strathearn Road; the *Braid Hills Hotel* also dated from the late 19th century. In 1904 a public library was opened, and from about the same time there was a cinema in Springvalley Gardens. The Merchants of Edinburgh golf club was founded in 1907 and laid out its own hilly 18-hole course. The Bruntsfield Hospital for Women and Children, founded in 1898, was largely built at Whitehouse Loan in 1910–11. The Astley Ainslie Institute was started in 1923 (on a site used long ago for nursing plague victims), pioneering rehabilitative medicine in Britain, and a large fever hospital was also built, south of the poorhouse. In 1922 the tramway was electrified, and extended to Fairmilehead in 1936; from 1924 some trams plied right along Princes Street to Churchhill, thence to Newington on the *'Marchmont Circle'* route and so back via the Bridges – and the reverse.

**Education, Entertainment – but no Trams or Trains**: The original Boroughmuir and Warrender Park council schools became James Gillespie's about 1923, taking only girls from 1929. In 1926 the *Plaza* ballroom was opened; the large *Dominion Cinema* was privately built in 1937–38 and the *Springvalley Cinema* was soon converted into a ballroom. Merchiston Castle School moved from its original cramped site to Colinton in 1930, and in 1932 George Watson's College moved out of the city centre to new buildings off Morningside's Colinton Road. The first mansion flats in Edinburgh were built in 1935 at Napier Road, and speculative housing was being built in the Morningside Drive area at about the same time. After 1945 the fever hospital became the City Hospital, Bruntsfield House was taken over by James Gillespie's School,

*archmont's high-quality, high-density tenements, built from around 370 to 1905 for middle-class occupation. Today, many provide accom- odation for students.* *(AL)*

and the great Napier Technical College aptly replaced Merchiston Castle, though the original tower house was retained. In 1949 a former hotel at Bruntsfield became a youth hostel for less privileged young travellers. By 1951, 26,000 people lived in the area, but Edinburgh's last electric trams, linking Braids with Granton Station, ran through Morningside in November 1956. In 1962 the suburban railway passenger service was also withdrawn, though the line remains open for freight traffic. In 1963 Bruntsfield House became the centrepiece of a new James Gillespie's school, opened in 1966 and soon co-educational.

**Entertainment and Education**: The *Bruntsfield Hotel* was open by 1963, and in 1965 a redundant church was converted into the *Church Hill Theatre*. The German church, a rare feature, was built in Marchmont in 1966. In 1972 the *Dominion* became a twin cinema, and a third screen was added in 1980; however, the *Plaza* ballroom was closed in 1975, and replaced in 1981 by a large Safeway supermarket with rooftop parking. By 1977 St Denis School at Ettrick Road was an established independent school, as was Cranley School for Girls. By 1979 the old Morningside station building had become the site of a branch of the Bank of Scotland. The Bruntsfield Hospital for Women and Children had become a 72-bed general hospital by 1980; later closed, it was converted to flats about 1997. In 1981 the Morningside area was affluent, with most of the facilities of a free-standing town plus no fewer than 18 small to medium-sized hotels; the largest were the long established *Braid Hills* and the *Bruntsfield*, each with about 50 rooms. But there has always been a large student element among the residents.

**Affluent Morningside's Comfy Cinema**: In 1987 the *Dominion Cinema* received Britain's top award for comfort and décor; it now has 4 screens. In 1991 the original parish church became redundant. By 1988 Craig House included the Thomas Clouston Clinic, but by 1997 it had been taken over as the Craighouse Campus of Napier University. The rundown of the old City Hospital of 546 beds began in 1992; parts are now being converted to housing. In the mid 1990s the long-established haggis-makers MacSween of Bruntsfield moved out to larger premises at Loanhead, in an attempt to meet rising demand. By 1992 George Watson's College, essentially a huge independent mixed day school, had 2100 pupils aged from 3 to 18. By 1994 the merged St Denis and Cranley School was an independent school for girls of ages 3 to 18. The council-run James Gillespie's High School now has a roll of 1100, and Boroughmuir High 1080. Half a dozen small hotels across the area augment the larger *Bruntsfield* and *Braid Hills*, and the youth hostel is busy all year round. In 2001, the famous Morningside Clock was moved! – but only 10 metres, to improve the road layout.

## MOSSBANK

**Map 14, B2**

***Small community, Shetland,*** *pop. 500*

OS 2: HU 4575

In 1951 a County Council pier was built at the hamlet of Toft on a northern peninsula of the Shetland mainland, as the terminus for a new vehicular ferry to Ulsta in the Isle of Yell. During the late 1970s Mossbank overlooking Yell Sound was developed from a crofting and fishing township by building several large self-contained dormitory blocks for the construction workers of the new Sullom Voe oil terminal, to which a new road was constructed. The blocks stood empty by 1987, but by then housing estates for permanent workers had totally urbanised Mossbank, raising its population from perhaps 130 in 1971 to over a thousand by 1981. A large social centre and new primary school had been built by 1987, as well as other basic facilities. However, by 1991 fewer than 500 people were resident in Mossbank, but there was a diving survey company and Burgess & Garrick employing 30 in oil-waste management.

## MOTHERWELL & Craigneuk **Map 16, A4**

***Lanarkshire large town,*** *pop. 31,000* OS 64: NS 7557

The Roman road from Carlisle to Old Kilpatrick traversed the north side of the middle Clyde valley, with a fort and bath house beside the South Calder Water. In the 12th to 15th centuries a castle was built, perched above a deep glen at Dalzell *(pronounced Diyell)*. It was shown emparked on Pont's map of Clydesdale dated 1596; in the 17th century Dalzell House embraced the ancient keep. The name *'Moderwele'* was one of many in this already well-settled area, but it is uncertain whether this was a holy well or a ferm toun. But the winding South Calder Water was already bridged near the 16th century tower of Jerviston on the way to Carfin. The name *Windmillhill* already appeared on Roy's map made about 1754, when the ancient Roman and modern Edinburgh roads intersected nearby, about 1 km south-west of Jerviston; from there a ferry crossed the River Clyde to Hamilton. The modest policies of Jerviston tower became the site of Robert Adam's gem Jerviston House, built in 1782 for James Cannison. In 1785 a water-powered grain mill named *Motherwell* was built on the South Calder Water near the Edinburgh–Hamilton road. William Cobbett, who stayed with Hamilton of Dalzell in 1832, found its rural surroundings beautiful; but radical change was at hand.

**The Railway triggers Settlement**: The Wishaw & Coltness Railway (W&CR) reached the area on the 4'6" *'Scotch'* gauge (137 cm) about 1833, en route from Whifflet by Coatbridge, and a hamlet called Motherwell began to develop around the crossroads. There was no post office until some time after 1838, and the population only passed the 750 mark in 1841. The W&CR was acquired by the infant Caledonian Railway (CR) about 1845 so that part of its route could form a link in the new chain of lines northward from Carstairs to Larbert, Stirling, Perth and Aberdeen; it first had to be converted to the standard gauge.

**Branching into Iron, Steel and Engineering**: Motherwell station became the junction in 1849 of the Clydesdale Junction Railway, part of the CR's new trunk route to Rutherglen and Glasgow, and its strategic role developed as various mineral lines serving coal pits branched from the original W&CR line. Another station was provided near Craigneuk, 2 km east of Motherwell, but confusingly named Flemington, despite the existence of Flemington near Cambuslang. Gasworks were established in 1850, and a Caledonian engine shed was open by 1869 (if not earlier). In 1876 Motherwell became the junction for a winding new CR line crossing the Clyde to Hamilton. A Motherwell branch of the Glasgow Iron Company was in the malleable iron business by 1869 and probably earlier, for Alex Findlay & Co (later the Motherwell Bridge & Engineering Company) made iron and steel bridges at Parkneuk Works from the mid 19th century – for example in 1893 a main footbridge for Perth General station, and in 1901 the Banavie railway swing bridge across the Caledonian Canal. In 1905 the Brandon Bridge Building Company was also active.

**MacAlpine Empire and Colville's Dalzell Works**: MacAlpine's famous company was started in Motherwell in 1868, and soon became (as a Wimpey man once remarked to the writer) *'an expanding contracting firm'*! In 1869 Bremner noted that in Motherwell *"a large number of houses of an improved kind have recently been built"* – for miners. The great Dalzell malleable ironworks was established in 1871–72 by David Colville of Glasgow, equipped with a steam hammer made by the Airdrie Engine Works; from 1880–81 steel was also made there in four open-hearth furnaces, using pig-iron imported from the Tees via Grangemouth at great cost. By 1878 a sandstone quarry was open at Auchinlea; by 1895 two quarries there employed over 300 people, but both were closed after 1914.

**New Town – not without Trauma**: In the 1870s Motherwell passed the 10,000 population mark and was well established as a town, for Pugin & Pugin, sons of the well-known architect, were called in to design a Catholic church in 1882, and a local newspaper – the *Motherwell Times* – was established in 1883. There was plenty to report: for instance, Motherwell FC was formed in 1885–86, and moved to Fir Park in 1895. A strike in 1890 against excessive working hours on the railways led to evictions from houses the CR had built for its workers, and to the destruction of the passenger station by an enraged mob. The former Wishaw & Coltness Railway viaduct (spanning the South Calder just west of Jerviston House) was doubtless affected by coal-mining subsidence, as there were two pits in the North Motherwell area. It also stood in ruins when the OS map was revised in the 1890s; later the stonework from its piers was used in building the *Gleneagles Hotel*. By about that time (and as late as the 1940s) Marshall Fleming & Co manufactured rail-mounted steam cranes. The Clason Memorial Church was built about 1892; by then Craigneuk lined the Wishaw road as a straggling village with a post office, station, and rail-connected works.

**Electricity, Structural Steelwork, Schools and Theatres**: An early power station provided electricity from 1895, and by then it was claimed that the Motherwell works of the Glasgow Malleable Iron & Steel Company was the largest in Scotland; local engineering products also included boilers, bolts and shovels. Yet more industrial development came with the establishment of the Lanarkshire steelworks at Flemington in 1899. Between 1899 and 1905 the Motherwell Bridge & Engineering Company supplied and erected the steelwork for the large extensions to Glasgow Central Station. In 1903 Dalzell was Scotland's largest iron and steel works, employing over 2000 men. One of the first RC secondary schools in Scotland, Our Lady's High (despite its name, all-boys!), was founded in 1895. Carnegie gave money for the library, started in 1902. The *New Century Theatre* was built in Windmill Street in 1903, followed in 1911 by the *Electric Theatre* and picture house. In 1905 Motherwell FC joined the Scottish League. Meantime by 1901 the population was about 30,000, and in 1911 40,000; housing development was concentrated south of Windmillhill and in North Motherwell, where coal pits were superseded.

**Trams and Coal-cutters**: From around 1900 the town was served by the Lanarkshire Tramways Company, which for a time connected to Newmains, to Cambuslang via Hamilton, and – from 1907 to 1931 – to Uddingston, connecting with Glasgow cars at both the latter places. Hurst Nelson built wagons and trams by 1910, produced petrol-electric trams for

Dublin in 1915, and in 1928 built 30 tram bodies for Glasgow, carried on bogies from Kilmarnock. By 1910 Anderson Boyes of Motherwell made coal-cutting machinery; one item supplied to Auchlochan colliery survives at Prestongrange museum.

**Wars and Recession 1914–1945**: Colvilles did well making munitions in World War I, and one result was the Colville Park golf club of 1922; by 1936 the firm owned almost all the Scottish steel industry. In 1920 the burgh absorbed Wishaw, but a decade later came slump and population fallback – yet in 1932 Motherwell FC won the League championship. Overcrowding remained extreme, affecting 40% of the houses in the enlarged burgh in 1936. The *New Century Theatre* closed in 1934, but growth resumed with rearmament from about 1935 and the *Odeon Cinema* was built in 1938. A flour mill was still at work in the 1930s, and the steelworks – like all British industry – worked flat out until 1945. From at least 1947 Murdoch Mackenzie Ltd of Motherwell were civil engineering contractors; by 1970 they employed over 750 people.

**Colvilles, Cranes and Anderson Strathclyde**: By 1951 Motherwell was a major local centre with a substantial hospital to the south, a trunk telephone exchange and some 37,500 people; from about then the firm of Arthur Low were patternmakers. An early change of government made the 1951 nationalisation of steel a dead letter, so Colvilles remained functionally intact; but the coming of television cut Motherwell's five cinemas of 1952 to two by 1970. Craigneuk's *Rio* cinema and its railway station were closed about 1960; yet within a few years there were three garages in the place, which kept its pair of primary schools. Robert Adam's Jerviston House, by then known as Colville Park, was most regrettably demolished in 1965, the Year of the Vandal. In 1963 the long-established engineers Marshall Fleming & Co built the gantry crane for the underground powerhouse of the Cruachan generating station in Argyll. From 1959 Anderson Boyes had a components plant in Glenrothes. Merged with Mavor & Coulson of Bridgeton in the 1970s, they became briefly known as Anderson Mavor. About 1979 they adopted the name Anderson Strathclyde, with headquarters at Bridgeton, but Motherwell was their main production plant.

**Ravenscraig Steelworks**: In 1958 premier Harold Macmillan persuaded Colvilles to build a hot strip steel mill at Motherwell, able to roll out half a million tonnes a year to supply their ill-fated cold reduction plant at Gartcosh, anticipating demands from the motor industry in Bathgate and Linwood. So the huge Ravenscraig project 2 km east of the town was begun by Colvilles in 1959. Two new blast furnaces were completed there in 1961, bringing iron capacity to over 1.2 million tonnes a year – more than the entire output of the Victorian iron industry in Scotland. The basic oxygen plant provided steel for the new continuous casting plant, slabbing mill, strip mill and universal beam mill which were added in stages up to about 1963. The hot strip mill opened in 1962, but only a quarter of its output found a Scottish market. Renationalisation in 1967 revealed the complex web of linkages in the Scottish steel industry, but destroyed them by pairing works throughout Britain by function. Ravenscraig iron was also supplied to open-hearth furnaces feeding the Dalzell Plate Mill.

**Civic Centre, Motorway and Electric Trains**: The BR steam locomotive depot, though secondary in importance, was still open into the 1960s, at which time the town council built a fine Civic Centre, including a combined concert hall/theatre, followed by a Technical College with residential accommodation at Dalzell Drive, which became the centre of a new schools campus. By 1972 the *Garrion Hotel* in Merry Street had 57 rooms. In 1972 as a result of major building programmes, almost 75% of the houses in the burgh were publicly owned. By 1971 the M74 motorway had been built beside the Clyde, with a junction on the Hamilton road. The main line railway was electrified by British Rail, completed in 1974, with a major signalling centre at Motherwell, whose four-platform station was extensively rebuilt.

**Scotland's Biggest School and Steel Industry Linkages**: Our Lady's High School – which had also taught girls since 1945 – moved to new buildings at Dalzell Drive in 1974, briefly becoming Scotland's largest school, with 2325 pupils in 1975! In 1975 Motherwell became the centre of an important District within Strathclyde Region. From 1972 the British Steel Corporation (BSC) enlarged output at Ravenscraig to over 3 million ingot tonnes a year from three blast furnaces; this huge project, including a continuous casting machine, raised employment in the Motherwell steel complex to 13,000 people around 1975, and was completed in 1977. Meantime in 1975 the old Clyde ironworks at Carmyle fed two of the Motherwell steel production units – the Lanarkshire steelworks and the Dalzell open-hearth furnaces. The former, comprising open-hearth furnaces, supplied a section mill which made RSJs (Rolled Steel Joists), used for instance in the Markinch Station footbridge; it also supplied the bar mill at Dalzell, whose plate and section rolling mills, about to be expanded in 1976, were supplied from the Dalzell open hearths. Craigneuk works was then a bar mill and steel foundry using alloy steel billets from Hallside; a new, quieter and less dusty steel foundry opened there in 1978, replacing the Tollcross foundry and creating about 300 new jobs; these brought the total workforce on the Craigneuk site to about 850.

**Strathclyde Park and Motherwell's Apogee**: The SDA (Scottish Development Agency) established a Special Area project to improve the environment and industrial infrastructure, especially an area of mining flashes west of the town *(see Bothwellhaugh)*. This became the 800 ha Strathclyde Country Park, created in 1973–75, aided by Lanark County and the burghs of Motherwell and Hamilton. An oxbow in the River Clyde was diverted to reduce flooding, and to create an extensive lake in a landscaped setting; Roman remains were found. By 1981 Motherwell's facilities had improved to those of a minor regional centre.

**Strikingly Counter-Productive**: After the three-month steel strike of 1980 which cost BSC some 10% of its market, and the closure of the Linwood car plant in 1981, rationalisation by British Steel soon swept away the old open-hearth Lanarkshire Steelworks, the Dalzell melting shop and bar mill, and the Craigneuk rolling mill, leaving just Ravenscraig and the Dalzell plate mills which had a capacity of 370,000 tonnes a year. Matters worsened when vehicle production ended at Bathgate in 1986, and by 1989 Ravenscraig employed just 3200 people. Limestone for fluxing the iron ore was brought by rail from Shap and from Frislington in Durham; slag was dumped 2 km north of the works. Its hot strip output (some 60% of its total production) was sent by rail to Shotton in North Wales for finishing; at that time five daily trains carried the products south.

**Cutbacks at Privatised Ravenscraig**: BSC was again privatised by the Thatcher regime in 1988, losing its social remit. Due also to falling demand worldwide, the firm closed one of the two remaining blast furnaces, and the strip mill with its 770 workers was abandoned early in 1991, when the town's population was already down to 30,700; very many suffered from ill health and and 18.5% of men were out of work. By mid-year only the curtailed steelmaking plant and slabbing mill with a mere 1200 jobs were left – to drift along until closure, which was then intended in 1994.

**Decline and Prosperity in Engineering**: A further blow to employment in 1990 was the closure of the Scottish Bus Group maintenance workshops, with the loss of nearly 100 jobs. Kelvin Central, one of the replacement companies, made Motherwell its HQ until it was bought out in 1994 by employee-owned Strathclyde Buses. The Motherwell Bridge works remained beside the station, and in 1992 the firm was helping the Lanarkshire Development Agency with product development for small businesses. In 1993 its overseas and offshore oil contracts were going well, and between 1996 and 1999 Motherwell Bridge Air Systems was to supply and install the complete compressed air system for the Chunghwa plant at Newhouse.

**Anderson going to the Wall?**: In 1990 due to falling demand for British coal and many colliery closures, the mining equipment manufacturers – then making coal cutters and known as Anderson Longwall – began to run down their workforce of 1100, to 700 by early 1992 when the firm's Bridgeton factory was closed. Late in 1992 when British Coal was in extreme crisis due to the privatisation of electricity generation and the switch to gas, Anderson still employed about 600 people at Motherwell producing coal shearers and tunnelling equipment, exported to such countries as China, France and Poland. The Anderson Group still made mining equipment when bought out in 1995 by USA firm Marmion, which promised to invest in the struggling company.

**The End of Scottish Steel Production**: The world price of hot rolled steel coil fell by a third in 18 months to the end of 1991, and in 1992 BSC twice accelerated the closure of the Ravenscraig plant. The Tory government then asked the European Community to permit Ravenscraig to become an Enterprise Zone; many wondered why this had not been done long before, since the area already had 12.3% unemployment against a high Scottish average of 9.5%. Scottish iron and steel production ceased on 24th June 1992 and the works was closed two days later. This ended some 400 years of Scottish ironmaking and gravely affected 52 firms in the Motherwell area, including slag processors Colville Clugston Shanks; the loss of no less than 40% of Scottish rail-freight revenue was expected after the stockpiled ore, sinter and coke was moved away by rail to Llanwern.

**Services Compensate – to an Extent**: But meantime some development of services was still taking place: a new station was opened in 1989 at Airbles on the Hamilton line, by which time the Brandon shopping centre of over 5000 m$^2$ was open. In 1990 the *Aquatec* was opened as a year-round recreation centre based on ice and water, attracting nearly half a million visitors in its first year. Despite the employment losses in the town, successful Motherwell FC (*'The Well'*) had managed to win the Cup in 1991 and to improve Fir Park in 1992–94 to an all-seater stadium for 14,500 spectators; they have kept their place in the Premier League. By 1996 a former mansionhouse of the Colvilles had become the 14-roomed *Moorings Hotel*; from 1998 Motherwell College was to use the new hotel at New Lanark to train catering students on the job.

**Hope at Dalzell and Country Park Success**: BSC had previously intended to close the Dalzell plant within five years in favour of a million-tonne capacity hot-rolling plant being planned on Tesside, and had run down its workforce to 600 by depressed 1992. It then decided that the big Teesside scheme could not be justified, and deferred the closure of Dalzell until the end of the century, with consequent limited investment, and promised job security for seven years. By late 1992 Dalzell employed nearly 900 workers, rolling slabs and ingots brought in daily by rail in 2200-tonne trains from Teesside to a brand-new works siding. In 1993 Motherwell became the only rail freight locomotive depot in Scotland; in the dying days of British Rail in 1994, the Trainload Freight business still based a fleet of 43 locomotives there. By 1995 the Strathclyde Country Park included Olympic-standard rowing courses, a nine-hole golf course, tennis, playing fields, a nature reserve with a heronry, and much woodland, bridle paths and footpaths. Its many free attractions, including an amusement park about to be doubled in size, drew in 1994 an amazing 6.75 million visitors. Dalzell House, converted to flats, was by then accompanied by its own small country park and a nature reserve. But the Clason Memorial Church stood derelict in 1995, as did the former *Rex Cinema* alongside, both intended as the site for a supermarket.

**Reclamation after Ravenscraig**: Some 1.5 million m$^3$ of the Ravenscraig site was contaminated with the heavy metals cadmium, nickel and arsenic, and unsaleable plant remained *in situ*. Site reclamation work began late in 1994 by burying coke-oven pollution beneath 30 m of cover, as phase 1 of a major redevelopment scheme by the Lanarkshire Development Agency. Simultaneous controlled explosions on a Sunday in July 1996 demolished the landmark gasholders and cooling towers of Ravenscraig and marked the end of an era.

**All Power to the Civic Centre and Corus**: In 1996 Motherwell District vanished into the major new unitary authority of North Lanarkshire. Though its most central town was Coatbridge, less controversial Motherwell became the HQ; as a result, in 1996 a new train service was instituted between the two towns and also Cumbernauld, the third main centre in this so-called *'local'* authority. In 1997 the by then doomed Anderson works employed some 360 people – since closed and demolished. The site of Ravenscraig is being developed as a new community. The Dalzell plate mills employed 390 people early in 2001 under Corus, British Steel's successors, and escaped the major job cuts being made elsewhere. Motherwell Bridge now employ about 1000 in various divisions, and Scomagg Ltd employ 150 making industrial control systems; Bank of Scotland have a 200-person call centre, and Strathclyde Hospital specialises in geriatric care. Local schools are Braidhurst High School (about 450 pupils), Dalziel High (940), and Our Lady's RC High (770). The *Moorings Hotel* has been enlarged to 30 rooms.

## MOUND (The) & Littleferry

**Map 9, B2**

***E. Sutherland location,*** *pop. under 100* — OS 21: NH 7798

The tidal Loch Fleet, around which were many ancient settlements and a stone circle, was a natural obstacle between Dornoch and Golspie, 5 km to the north; for centuries a ferry across its mouth connected most of Sutherland with its southerly county town. In 1621 the *'Ferry Innes'* collection (later known as Little Ferry) paid under 1.5% of Scottish Customs dues. The 1750 Roy map labelled Loch Fleet the *'Little Kyle'*; a track followed its south shore upstream to Rogart, and from the north shore *'Ferryhouse'* another track led to Golspie and the north. In 1814–18 Telford's embanked road known as The Mound, and its associated bridge with its cunning sluice flaps, was built across Loch Fleet in the shadow of the 208 m-tall Mound Rock, about 4 km inland from the passenger ferry. This also enabled some land reclamation inland of the Mound, both sides of which are now nature reserves.

**Mound Junction and Cambusavie Hospital**: The circuitous Sutherland Railway (SR) was opened in 1868 along the north shore of Loch Fleet; road coaches plied to Dornoch from a station at the Mound's end, until in 1902 a light railway to Dornoch was laid across the Mound by the SR's successor the Highland Railway. By 1940 a 37-bed infectious diseases hospital had been built at Cambusavie, 2 km to the south. The passenger ferry continued to ply into the 1950s. Although there was a post office which actually rated as a post town until about 1961, no village appeared at the Mound; the total population in the area was around 100. The station was closed to passengers in 1960 and ceased to exist as a junction when freight was withdrawn and the Dornoch branch was lifted in 1964, though many traces remain. By 1981 the hospital was used for the chronic sick; by 1998 it was no longer a hospital. In 1988 a new bridge was built, carrying a new shortened section of the A9 road across Telford's famous structure and over the railway line. A landslide at the point of land just to the east briefly disrupted the train service in 2000.

## MOUNTSTUART

**Map 1, B1**

***Large mansion, Isle of Bute*** — OS 63: NS 1059

Around 1600 only tiny settlements lined the east coast of the Isle of Bute south of Rothesay. The original early 18th century mansion of the Bute family, known as Mountstuart, was built in very extensive policies overlooking the Clyde 5 km south of the burgh. By 1818 a ferry sailed to Largs from Kerrycroy just north of Mountstuart. Chambers wrote in 1827 *"Mountstuart, residence of the Marquis of Bute, is a splendid mansion"*. The young third Marquess of Bute became Britain's richest man, his family's wealth largely derived from deep-mined coal won in South Wales at enormous human cost, and exported through their extensive Bute Docks at Cardiff. A polymath, religious zealot, nature lover and yachtsman, he had already built a small yacht harbour when Mountstuart was largely destroyed by fire in 1877.

**Richest Man's Monster Mansion Visible at Last**: The new mansion was to be a vast and eclectic five-storey Gothic pile designed by Sir Robert Rowand Anderson on the scale of a

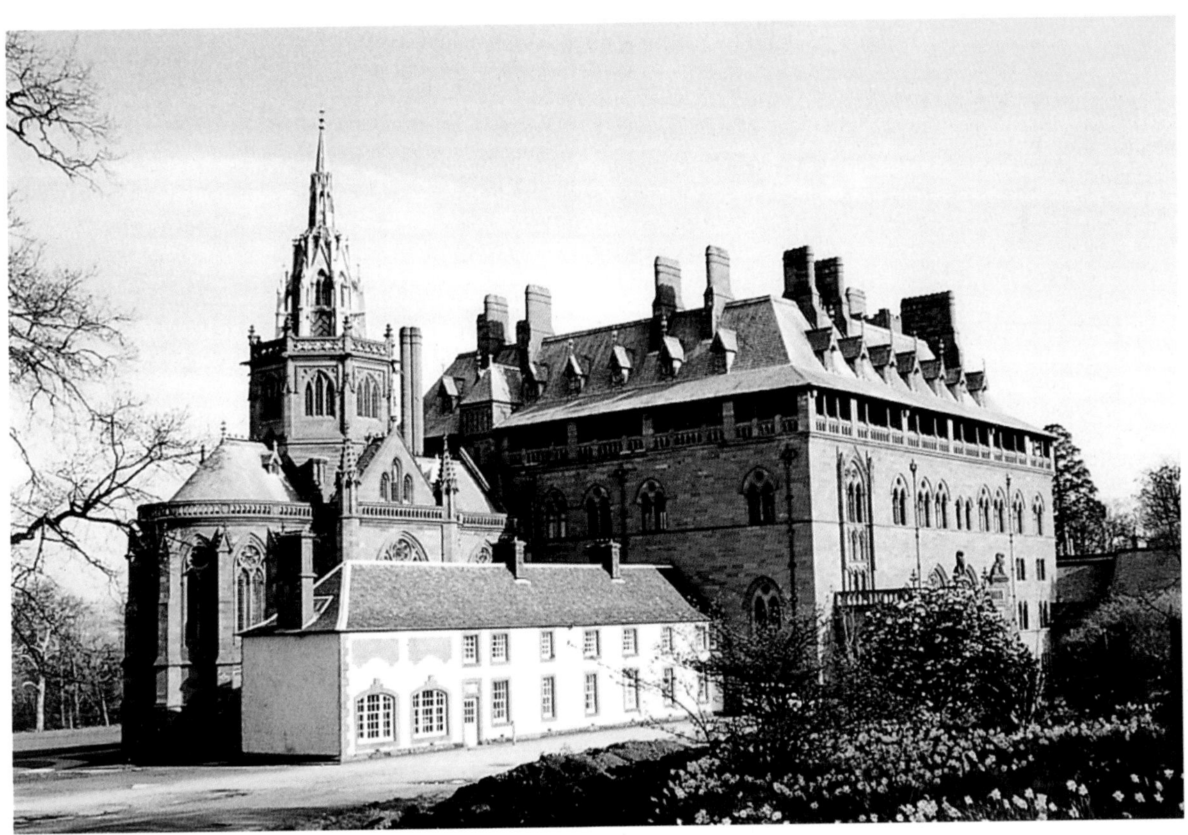

*Mountstuart, Bute, is 5 miles south of Rothesay; it was built of pink sandstone in the late 19th century to designs by Robert Rowand Anderson for the 3rd Marquis of Bute, one of the richest landowners in Britain.* (JRH)

cathedral, and as highly decorated. Built of pink sandstone in 1879–1900 by sixty skilled craftsmen, it had a 24m-high marble hall spanned by fantastic star-studded vaults, much stained glass, many marble columns, and a big indoor swimming pool in Gothic style. The great extravaganza was all but complete when Bute's early death in 1900 stopped the work abruptly. The ferry service ended in the 1930s. The 4th and 5th Marquesses – who had inherited other mansions elsewhere, and been heavily taxed to finance Britain's wars and later social improvements – were content to leave matters in Bute much as they were. The completion of Mountstuart, and the creation of an international conifer arboretum in its policies, was resumed in 1988 under a charitable trust founded by the 6th Marquess; but he too died young, and it was 1995 before his successor could open the huge pile to the public for the first time.

## MOY **Map 9, B4**

***Inverness-shire location,*** *pop. under 100* OS 27: NH 7635

Loch Moy lies in Strathdearn, a valley linking the basins of the Rivers Nairn and Findhorn,15km south-east of Inverness; on an islet stood a 14th century castle, of which little remains. Moy Hall, an early tower house and the seat of The Mackintosh, was built later overlooking the loch. A road was first built through the area between 1725 and 1736 by General Wade's troops; by 1745 there was a blacksmith, and by 1805 a post office. Moy Hall was enlarged in 1872 and again about 1895. A station was provided on the Highland Railway's new main line, opened in 1897–98, which crossed a unique timber trestle bridge near Moy *(see Hay & Stell)*. Moy Hall was replaced in 1955 by a new house, the ancient tower being regrettably demolished in 1957. Only a hamlet of under 100 people remained, though remarkably having a medical practice. The station was closed by Beeching in 1964–65 and by 1981 Moy had been bypassed by a new section of the A9, leaving a caravan site – now vanished – overlooking the loch and castle ruin. There is still a primary school.

## MUCK, Isle of **Map 8, A5**

***Small island, Inner Hebrides,*** *pop. under 100* OS 39: NM 4279

Between Ardnamurchan and Rum lies the small 4km-long isle of Muck (in Gaelic meaning *'Pig')*, on which a rocky outcrop was sculpted by Bronze Age people into a drum-shaped fort now called Dun Ban. Monro in 1549 rapturously described this possession of the Bishop of the Isles (see Iona) as *'Swynes Ile... very fertile and fruitful of corn and grassing for all store (cattle), inhabited and manured, with a good Highland haven very good for fishing"*. Muck also had an old castle, but made little mark on history. In Napoleonic times kelp gathering gave some economic support to 280 people, but the isle was cleared in 1826 when 150 people were evicted.

**To the Brink and Back**: In 1896 Muck was bought by the more benevolent MacEwen family, and in due course a pier, a post office and makeshift school were provided at Port Mor. But being off the scheduled steamer services, Muck with its 1951 population of about 30 was remote indeed. The school soon closed, for by 1971 the population was down to 24. However, by 1980 the school had reopened and the farming and crofting island was said to be in reasonable shape, with a pony stud, lobster fishing, cattle rearing, wood turning and an 8-roomed guest house built by the owners. The population had risen to about 30, but was back to 24 in 1991; in 1992, when a new school was built to serve just three children, a passenger ferry sailed three days a week between Muck and Mallaig; in 1997 it also served Eigg, Rum and Canna. Two aerogenerators brought a secure electricity supply in 2000; a new pier to be completed in 2001 will bring a vehicular ferry; the residents of Muck have advertised in the hope of attracting incomers, as the isle's population has recently fallen.

## MUCKHART, Pool & Yetts **Map 6, A4**

***Small Clack'shire village,*** *pop. 700 (area)* OS 58: NO 0000

The River Devon flows south-east from the Ochil Hills, passes east of Muckhart, which means *'Pig height'* (in Gaelic *Mhic-ard)*, then turns sharply west at the Crook of Devon, tumbling into an incised valley before heading for Stirling. If the later Roy map is any guide, the route that joined Falkland and Stirling by 1415 crossed the Devon at the Crook, passing south of Muckhart Kirk to recross the river at the site of the Vicar's Bridge some 5km west of the Crook. By about 1750 the Roy map showed another early track from Dunfermline and Saline intersecting the east–west road south of Yetts *(Gates)* of Muckhart and continuing via Glen Devon to Auchterarder. Muckhart Mill and a *'wakemill'* just below it turned some 2 km downstream of Rumbling Bridge, where the River Devon falls 27m in two leaps at Cauldron Linn. A school was held from the 1790s and in 1806 an inn was built at Pool of Muckhart, 1km south-west of the Yetts.

**Roads, Traffic and Golf**: Around 1820 a turnpike road from Dunfermline reached the Yetts, and was continued northwards to Crieff via a toll-house which still stands at the Dunning turn, 1km north of the former Yetts toll gates. The church was rebuilt on its traditional site in 1838, and a primary school was built 1km south-west of the Pool in 1845. Up to the mid 19th century a four-in-hand coach used to link Rumbling Bridge with Auchterarder via what Beveridge called a *"large and important inn"* at Yetts of Muckhart, past which *"an immense number of carts used to pass, going to Strathearn with coal and lime from Blairingone and Fife"*. Muckhart village held some 200 people in 1891. In 1895 the *New Inn*, which did not last, stood at the Dunning turn, and there was a post office at Pool of Muckhart. The Muckhart golf club, founded in 1908, laid out a 9-hole moorland course; in 1970 this was extended to 18 holes, and in 1990 to 27. Mains electricity arrived in 1935. By 1951 when the parish population was 493, Pool of Muckhart had the facilities of a small village and a population of some 350, which fell away until the 1970s and 80s, when a number of new houses was built. By 1991 Muckhart parish had 705 people; the golf course, village inn and post office shop are in good shape.

## MUIRHEAD, Chryston & Garnkirk **Map 15, E4**

***Large villages n-e. of Glasgow,*** *pop. 4000* OS 64: NS 6869

Ten kilometres north-east of Glasgow stands the 16th century Bedlay House or Castle, near the Kirkton of Chryston. Pont's map dated 1596 named tiny settlements at *'Christoun'*, *'Gartick'* and *'Gartintoun'*. Garnkirk House was built in the mid 17th century for one John Dunlop, a merchant. When Roy surveyed the area about 1752, several other hamlets existed between Chryston and the Colm Loch at Stepps. These included Garnkirk, 2 km south of Bedlay; to the south of

Garnkirk was an extensive *Coleheughhill* or colliery. The few fragments of road previously existing in the area had been connected by the late 18th century, when the Glasgow to Stirling road, the future A80, was turnpiked. Garnkirk House was altered in 1780 and again in 1820, for development of the area was stimulated by a coal mine sunk at Garnkirk in the early 19th century.

**Garnkirk Fireclay and the Railways**: The primitive Monkland & Kirkintilloch Railway (M&KR) was opened in 1826, its steam-hauled coal wagons on the *'Scotch'* or 4'6" (137 cm) gauge, passing under the turnpike at Bedlay through an arch only 2.7 m high.The Garnkirk colliers discovered a 2 m-thick fireclay seam at a depth of about 50 m; the Garnkirk fireclay works which resulted was well-established and already boasted a dozen chimneys by the opening day of the Garnkirk & Glasgow Railway (G&GR) in 1831. Besides bricks, this line carried Monklands coal and passengers between Gartsherrie on the M&KR and Glasgow's Townhead. Operated by steam, it provided four daily trains serving its Garnkirk station, linking it with Glasgow, Airdrie and emergent Coatbridge. The G&GR was re-gauged in 1847 to become functionally a part of the new Caledonian Railway.

**Scotland's Biggest Brickworks – and Whisky**: About 1861 the Garnkirk Fire-Clay Company fathered the nowadays better known Glenboig *(q.v.)* fireclay works. By 1869 it operated at Garnkirk the *"most extensive"* of the 122 brickworks in Scotland, with 300 men and boys making hand-moulded bricks, daily consuming 200 tonnes of clay and a similar amount of coal. The firm also made glazed fireclay pipes for water and sewerage, and terra cotta products such as chimney pots. By 1895 the population in the area was over 1100, with an inn at Chryston, by then a substantial village. A second fireclay works was in operation near Garnkirk station, and a mill turned 1 km north of Chryston. Post offices were open at Chryston and at Muirhead, a hamlet on the main road between Chryston and Garnkirk. The ill-fated Gartloch grain distillery was built in 1897 by the Alloa brewer and Bo'ness distiller James Calder, sited east of Cardowan House; it was sold to DCL in 1921 for closure; its warehouses lasted until the 1980s.

**Golf and Tourism**: The Crow Wood golf club dates from 1925. In 1931 some 3600 people lived in the area – including emergent Moodiesburn *(q.v.)*, rising to 7600 by the 1950s; by then Muirhead enjoyed typical village facilities, including two post offices. However, the station had been closed by 1953 and about 1960 the original M&KR line was also closed. A dual carriageway realignment of the A80 was built about 1960. The last coal mine in the area had been closed by 1971, and the fireclay works were not listed by 1979. Despite other local workplace closures, jobs were available for commuters at Moodiesburn and Cumbernauld as well as Glasgow. But although Crow Wood House (now the *Crow Wood Hotel)* was extended in the early 1970s, the facilities in this group of settlements were still only at village level by 1981. By 1991 the population of Chryston was 3057, while Muirhead proper was only just over 1000. The local Chryston High School has around 750 pupils. There is a public library, and Bedlay Castle is still inhabited. A *Premier Lodge* with 38 rooms has recently arrived.

## MUIRHEAD — Map 6, B3

***Village n-w. of Dundee,*** *pop. 2000+* — OS 53/54: NO 3434

Fowlis Easter which lies among the Sidlaw Hills some 10 km north-west of Dundee had a chapel by 1142; in 1453 Andrew Lord Gray made this a collegiate church. In the 15th century a castle keep was built at Auchterhouse, 4 km to the north. Pont's sketch map of Angus made about 1600 showed the large 16th century tower house known as Fowlis Castle, which in 1560 was the seat of Lord Gray, while nearby was the old village of Liff, whose parish school was open by 1626. Some 2 km north-east of this was an unnamed settlement which can be identified as Muirhead of Liff, which stands on the Dundee to Coupar Angus road. Except for the Kirk of Lundie up in the Sidlaw Hills to the west, this area was largely blank on Roy's map made about 1750, but the Fowlis Grain Mill was developed in the 18th and 19th centuries beside the waterfall in Fowlis Den.

**Railway, Asylum and Sanatorium**: Dronley station on the early Dundee & Newtyle Railway was sited about 1.5 km north of Muirhead; the line which opened in 1831 was later reconstructed as part of the Caledonian. There was also a station 2.5 km farther north, serving Auchterhouse with its castle and tiny Kirkton. Muirhead School was built for the Free Church in 1846 and enlarged in 1912. By 1895 an *'Asylum'* had been built east of Liff; there were inns at Liff, Birkhill Feus (later just known as Birkhill) and also at Muirhead, but the latter had the post office and other facilities. In the early 20th century the Sidlaw Sanatorium was built at the high altitude of 260 m on the hills above Auchterhouse. Proximity to Dundee and especially to the golf courses in Camperdown Park evidently speeded housebuilding. In 1951 the population of Muirhead and Birkhill was about 1900; the local facilities were those of a small village, but also included a 200-pupil junior secondary school, and so served a rather wider area.

**Mortgaged Suburban Development**: Under the NHS the asylum was renamed the Royal Dundee Liff Hospital, its 600 beds catering for mentally ill patients, while Sidlaw Sanatorium became a convalescent hospital of 44 beds. The by then little-used railway was closed to passengers in 1955, and to goods in 1958. Although the secondary school was soon closed, the ancient Fowlis Easter church survives. New estates north of Birkhill have led to a slowly rising population. In 1991 there were some 1840 generally well-educated residents in the village proper; few men were unemployed, and over 55% of its heads of households were mortgagees, the highest proportion in any Tayside locality. Fowlis Mill stood derelict in 1995, but Liff Hospital is still open. By 1993 a new fishing loch had been formed at Piperdam, 4 km to the west (OS 53), and a golf course was also open there by 1999. The area's local government was returned to Angus from Dundee in 1996. Muirhead's school building of 1846 has recently become an activity centre, the historic *Old Mansion House Hotel* continues at Auchterhouse, and the *Birkhill Inn* has been expanded.

## MUIRKIRK & Smallburn — Map 2, A2

***Ayrshire village,*** *pop. 1860* — OS 71: NS 6927

The new parish of Muirkirk on the headwaters of the River Ayr 20 km east of Mauchline was founded in 1631, and in 1650 the moorland church from which the village takes its name was built above the Ponesk Burn at the high altitude of about 220m. Though a market was established, Muirkirk did not obtain a barony charter, and as late as 1735 there was no school. However, local iron ores were briefly exploited in the 1740s and iron was smelted nearby at Terreoch. The Roy map showed that by about 1754 the new village was served by a road linking Cumnock with Douglas (today the A70).

**Tarmac *not* invented by McAdam the Tarman**: Then a coal seam nearly 3m thick was discovered, and besides the ironworks discussed below, works for coal and tar distilling were established by Lord Dundonald in 1786. On the opening of the British Tar Company's works in 1789, John Loudoun McAdam of Ayr became the manager, and bought the concern in 1790. It seems quite amazing that he failed to note the binding effect of tar on the broken stone that he so strongly advocated for road construction, and which acquired the name *'macadam'* after he moved to England in 1798 and then became a noted turnpike road improver. Others who followed invented tarmacadam, and it is faintly absurd that this so-useful substance was indirectly named after him, and also that his gravestone at Moffat does not mention roads! Meantime, Heron noted in 1799 that limestone and freestone were quarried near Muirkirk, and lamp-black was also made at the tar works.

**The Muirkirk Ironworks**: In 1786–88 Thomas Edington of Cleland and others set up an important early water-powered iron smelting works, to make pig-iron and roll bar iron; it used coal from the Auldhouseburn area south-east of the village, where a pit was sunk in 1808; a short canal was dug to bring water to the furnaces and to facilitate local mineral carriage. Meanwhile a post office opened in 1789. Although no fairs appear to have been scheduled in 1797, Muirkirk was then a post town with a service on three days a week; in 1813 the mails were carried via Douglas. The ironworks became bankrupt as early as 1803, but was soon reopened. In 1827 Chambers found Muirkirk *"not a village of the most attractive possible character, surrounded by coal-pits and iron-works; the land either black heath or blacker clay, destitute of trees; the air perpetually clouded with smoke. The large works give employment to about 500 men."* By then a public road linked to Cumnock. From about 1828 Neilson's hot blast process was used in the ironworks, which as the Eglinton Iron Company eventually became part of the Baird Iron & Coal empire in 1856.

**Railways, Coal and Iron at the Apogee**: Two coal pits were open in 1848 when the Glasgow & South Western Railway (G&SWR) opened a branch from Auchinleck; from 1859 there was a municipal gasworks, and soon two groups of cottages were built at Bankhead near Auldhouseburn, and two more by Bairds at South Muirkirk. In 1873 a Caledonian Railway (CR) branch reached Muirkirk from the Douglas area to the east. By 1884 the G&SWR had a locomotive depot at Muirkirk, whose population exceeded 5500; a total of eight coal pits large and small were open about that time, one remarkably named *'Royal George'*, plus scattered ironstone mines. By 1894 the emparked mansion of Wellwood, a name also borne by the estate's 14 coal pits, stood 4km west of Muirkirk, which was still called a *"town"* by Murray, although its inn was not mentioned. With impending exhaustion of the ironstone reserves, by 1901 its population had fallen below 4000.

**Decline, Decay and Disaster**: The Auldhouseburn pit closed in 1911. In 1916, 13 G&SWR steam locomotives were still based in Muirkirk, handling mainly freight traffic, including ironstone imported from Spain. After the war came a brief boom, then a depression and in 1921 a long coal strike; the ironworks were closed by Baird's about 1922. Only one coal pit was active in the area from 1931, the Kaimes (or Kames) mine. In 1951 the passenger trains to Auchinleck were withdrawn, leaving four a day to Lanark. By then the population was down to around 3200 and Muirkirk's facilities were only those of an average village; by 1954 Wellwood and its park had vanished. The Lanark railway was closed completely in 1964, the very wet Kaimes Colliery (where 17 men were killed in an underground explosion in 1957) was closed in 1968, and the whole railway had disappeared by 1969.

**Down and Down**: Not surprisingly, by 1976 Muirkirk gave a gloomy impression; its secondary school had also been closed; the shops were at one end of the shrinking village, the remaining houses concentrated in the large Smallburn estate at the other. Although by 1980 Kinloch Anderson of Restalrig in Edinburgh had set up a branch clothing factory, the population of Muirkirk was down to 2400 by 1981; after such a long period of decline it was then of disadvantaged character. Its general facilities had declined further and were only those of a small village, emphasising its disadvantaged state. By 1991 only 1860 residents remained, male unemployment was high and female unemployment worse. However, the school, post office, and inn survive, a new 18-hole golf course is now open, and recently some new houses have been built.

## MUIR OF ORD — Map 9, B3

***Large Easter Ross village***, *pop. 2000* — OS 26: NH 5250

At Urray on the River Orrin at the base of the Black Isle peninsula of Easter Ross is a stone circle. The area lies on glacial moraine and is rich in ancient earthworks, standing stones and chambered cairns. In the late 16th century the Mackenzies erected Fairburn Tower, later ruined. But early maps were blanks, as late as Roy's of about 1750. Sir Roderick Murchison of Tarradale, an estate on the Firth between the castles, was born in 1792; he became a leading geologist and founded the Chair of Geology at Edinburgh University. In the droving period up to and around 1800, major cattle fairs were held on the Muir, linked to the Kessock Ferry by a track from Strathconon.

**Hamlet, Whisky and Railway Junction**: A hamlet first known as Tarradale grew where Telford's road, built about 1813 to link the new Conon and Lovat bridges, crossed the older track; but the River Orrin remained unbridged at Urray for some years. By then the water-powered Mill of Ord also distilled hooch whisky, until licensed in 1838 as the Ord distillery. The Inverness & Ross-shire Railway was opened in 1862, with a station called Muir of Ord at Tarradale. The Muir of Ord golf club, founded in 1875, laid out an 18-hole parkland course, sprawling across the track! In 1886 the distillery made about 365,000 litres of Highland malt whisky annually, wholly by water power. Large sheep and cattle fairs were still held in 1894, when two hamlets clustered round the station and the distillery respectively; of the three local inns, Murray rated the *Station* as *"good"*. In that year Muir of Ord became the junction for the Fortrose branch railway, as a three-platform station with extensive sidings. In 1923 James Watson & Co of Dundee sold Ord distillery to John Dewar & Sons, who soon joined the DCL combine.

**Willie Logan Builds Dams, Bridges and Airline**: By 1951 Muir of Ord had grown into a typical village of 1500 people, but the branch passenger trains stopped running then and the station was closed completely in 1960, though sidings remained. Duncan Logan's stone-cutting business was built up by his son William in the 1950s into a major contracting firm which built roads, dams and the Corpach pulp mill. Logan also built the Tay Road Bridge, and in 1962 founded the Scottish airline Loganair *(see Renfrew, & Glasgow Airport)*. Muir of Ord continued its slow growth, but Willie Logan died in an accident in 1966, and his construction company failed about 1970, after building Glasgow's Kingston Bridge. The HIDB took over its extensive yard as an industrial estate, rapidly developed due to North Sea oil. In 1972 Haig's – another part of DCL – still brought in grain by rail. By 1977 the local shops included an oatcake specialist and in 1978 a cycle dealer. There were then a timber yard, metals fabrication, plant hire and maltings, but the secondary school had closed.

**Modern Muir of Ord**: The passenger station was reopened about 1979, when Muir of Ord's population had stabilised at around 2000, its facilities those of a large village. Main road traffic through the village was eased with the opening of the Kessock bridge in 1982. By 1985 a caravan site was open at Old Urray, 3 km north-west. The population was 2033 in 1991. By 1992 the distillery, which made a single malt, was naming itself after a mythical *'Glen Ord'*, and later opened a visitor centre. RK Carbon Fibres, makers of aircraft brake blocks, had moved to Muir of Ord from Cheshire by 1992, but fire damaged the factory. RK recovered to employ a steady 100 workers; it was taken over by a German firm in 1997, and now employs 150 as SGL Technic Ltd. There are medium-sized firms in construction and metal fabrication, and expansion of the industrial estate continues. Meantime rail freight had ceased to be handled locally by 1995, but peak-hour passengers use the station in some numbers. Shopping, banking, postal facilities and petrol are available. Small hotels include the *Ord House*, and (since about 1988) the cottage-style *Dower House* – built in the late 18th century by the Mackenzie-Gillanders family.

## MULBEN

**Map 10, A2**

***Speyside hamlet,*** *pop. 400*

OS 28: NJ 3550

Mulben may derive its name from milling, or from the ancient thanage of Munbrie. It stands on the Burn of Mulben, whose valley provided an easy routeway to the east from the lower River Spey, which was crossed by a very early wooden bridge. This had been replaced as early as 1303 by a ferry, consequently called *Boat o' Brig*. Pont's sketch map made about 1600 showed *'Malben'* among other small places in the parish of Boharm. Beside the Spey was the word *'Bridge'*, but no actual bridge was marked either by Pont or on the Roy map of about 1750, on which *'Millben'* was a hamlet in a trackless area. The Boat o' Brig ferry, which by then formed a link in the turnpike road from Rothes to Keith, was replaced in 1831 by a suspension bridge built at Orton, for which the Burn of Mulben provided an easy route.

**Railway in a Box, and Glentauchers in Black & White**: The Inverness & Aberdeen Junction Railway opened in 1858 through Joseph Mitchell's Spey Viaduct – a 70 m-span box-girder built beside the suspension bridge. Wide enough for two tracks, it was replaced in 1905–06 by the Highland Railway, using a single-line steel Whipple truss. Mulben station was sited at Blackhillock, 4 km east of Boat o' Brig. Glentauchers distillery, 2 km east of Mulben, was built in 1897–98 by James Buchanan & Co; equipped with two rail sidings and extensive bonds, its malt later contributed to the *'Black & White'* blend. The rural Boharm parish had a remarkable 1128 people in 1901. The suspension bridge was replaced in 1939 by a new road bridge. By 1951 only 665 people lived in the parish, with the facilities of a small village. About 1955 Tauchers Halt was opened to serve the enlarged distillery: trains only stopped when required, and ceased to call when Mulben station itself was closed by Beeching in 1964; the population continued to fall.

**Whisky all the Way**: In 1972–74 the waters of Dorie's Well, some 2 km west of Mulben, were harnessed to feed the large but highly automated Auchroisk distillery, built for IDV (International Distillers & Vintners) of Dumbarton, its annual capacity of 5 million litres of blending malt going into *'J&B Rare'*. It could be operated around the clock by only nine workers, though it was claimed about 1980 that some 50 people in all worked there. By 1986 a vast complex of bonded warehouses had been built near the site of Mulben station. Auchroisk's product was so fine that from 1987 it was also sold unblended as *The Singleton*, soon winning awards. Glentauchers distillery was closed for a time from 1983 by DCL, but was reopened in 1989 by new owners, Allied Distillers, making malt whisky for their Ballantyne's brand. Only 399 people remained in the parish by 1991, and distilleries, bonds and trees are its main features.

## MUNLOCHY

**Map 9, B3**

***Easter Ross village,*** *pop. 450*

OS 26: NH 6453

Munlochy Bay is a shallow inlet on the east coast of the Black Isle. In the 1750s a track joining the Kessock and Innerbreakie ferries passed a small settlement at the head of the bay. In the 1760s stone for Fort George was quarried at the mouth of the bay. Any early travel authors who passed that way made no comments, but roads were made up, Munlochy post office was opened in 1806, and in 1894 a simple station was opened on the new Fortrose branch of the Highland Railway. By 1940 there were also a mill and a rifle range. In the 1950s a small hotel, a branch bank, garage, ironmonger and two doctors contributed to facilities typical of a small farming and forestry village, serving 400 locals, plus 450 in the Knockbain and Tore areas. The station was closed to passengers in 1951 and to goods in 1960. The Kessock bridge allowed Munlochy to attract enough new housing to continue an unruffled existence throughout the 20th century. It retains its post office and now has a hotel; there is much access land owned by the Forestry Commission, and Munlochy Bay is now a nature reserve.

## MURTHLY

**Map 6, B3**

***Small Perthshire village,*** *pop. 225 (area)*

OS 53: NO 1038

A standing stone and an ancient chapel adjoin the 16th century keep of Murthly Castle, which stands on low ground in a loop of the River Tay about 5 km below Dunkeld. Pont sketched it on two maps made around 1600, as both a plain and a grandly turreted structure, adjoined by the Wood of Murthly; perhaps it was glorified between Pont's visits. Well downstream and close to an ancient stone circle was a small settlement, apparently named Burnben. The Roy map made about 1750 showed *'Muthlea'* as an emparked mansionhouse. An imposing new

Murthly Castle, designed by James Gillespie Graham for Sir John Drummond Stewart, was built on to it in 1829–32.

**Station and Asylum Come and Go**: In 1856 the Perth & Dunkeld Railway was opened, with a station named Murthly sited 3km east of the castle, though the scatter of houses nearby was then known as Gellyburn. By 1895 the Tay ferry to Caputh had been replaced by a bridge, and an inn and a rail-connected *'Lunatic Asylum'* had been built near the station; the name Murthly became attached to a nearby post office. Murthly Castle was long empty before being demolished about 1950. By 1951 about 800 people lived in the area (including the asylum), and enjoyed the facilities of a small village. The station was closed in the late 60s. By 1971 the population was down to about 660; but by 1978 the local garage sold both cars and farm machinery. Under the NHS the enlarged asylum had been renamed Murthly Hospital; in 1981 this had 310 beds and specialised in mental illness. But by then the Murthly telephone exchange had been closed, and the one-time Gellyburn was known as Broompark. Murthly Hospital was run down, and had closed by 1993; by 1995 it was a *'building at risk'*. However, new housing is now rising, with this building and the nearby garage as a nucleus.

## MUSSELBURGH, Inveresk & Fisherrow

**Map 15, D2**

***E. Lothian town,*** *pop. 20,600*

OS 66: NT 3472

A Roman fort of the 1st and 2nd centuries was located where their road from Corbridge on the Northumbrian River Tyne reached the Forth at the mouth of the River Esk, 9km east of modern Edinburgh. It was sited on a bluff over 1km inland from the present-day mouth of the river. In 1827 Chambers summarised its Roman role: a *"station upon the top of Inveresk Hill, and a municipium or town upon the site of Fisherrow, several of the modern houses of which are founded upon the lower stones of the Roman buildings. The harbour of Fisherrow was most important."* Another first century Roman road connected with the upper Clyde valley, though its route hereabouts is lost.

**Re-using Roman Bricks**: *"Mussleborrow was a borrow when Edenborough was none"*. This antique saying, quoted by the traveller Sir William Brereton in 1636, may stem from an early church on the site of the Roman praetorium, built with what Chambers called *"many old stones and Roman bricks"*. About the 11th century its people adopted the Gaelic name Inveresk, later vying with Whithorn as the oldest town in Scotland. Musselburgh was chartered in 1315 as an Ecclesiastical Burgh of Dunfermline Abbey, which held the Chapel of Loretto east of the town and a nearby tower of 1390. By 1496 its port was trading extensively with the Dutch. An earlier charter may be lost, for arson by the English destroyed the burgh records in 1547, when Inveresk consisted of two shepherds' huts and a stone bridge (which may rest upon Roman foundations). Halkerston Lodge was also an ancient building.

**Burgh, Fish, and Education**: Musselburgh was rechartered in 1562 as a burgh of barony. A grammar school began in 1580, and the building of a large tolbooth occurred in about 1591; Fynes Moryson in 1598 called both Musselburgh and Fisherrow *"villages"*. Pont's map made around 1600 showed the bridge connecting defined roads to Edinburgh and Dunbar, and emphasised *'Muscle Brug'* as compared with *'Innervysk'* and *'Fisheraw'*, although both of them had schools by 1615. In 1613 Chancellor Alexander Seton, Lord Fyvie and Earl of Dunfermline, incorporated the old abbot's tower into the fine new mansion of Pinkie House. As Musselburgh, Inveresk and Fisherrow expanded, Thomas Tucker of the English Customs service wrote in 1655 of *"three or four small towns joining together, the inhabitants fishermen or husbandmen"*.

**Mining, Manufacturing, Woollens and Country Houses**: From the 1660s the burgh grew with the backing of the rich and powerful Earl of Lauderdale. The mansion of Whitehall west of Fisherrow, designed by architect and coalowner James Smith, was built for him in 1686; after purchase by the lawyer Sir David Dalrymple, it was extended in 1707 as Newhailes, the birthplace in 1737 of Alexander Dalrymple, a founder of the science of oceanography. By the 1690s Musselburgh's pollable population of 1800 exceeded that of Leith; nearly half were in manufacturing. Hides were brought from Dalkeith fleshers to be tanned in Musselburgh. Coal had been mined in the area for some time before 1707 when a *"drowned colliery near Musselburgh"* was reported. Large woollen manufactures also existed well before 1703, financed by Edinburgh merchants; the main road to Edinburgh was turnpiked under an Act of 1713. Defoe's rambling account written in the 1720s named *'Musclebro'* as one of a *"cluster of towns"*, including Fisherrow where the mussel-fishing had declined. Woollen cloth was made *"for poor people's wearing"*; an account of 1733 confirmed *"a considerable manufacture of low-priced narrow goods"*. Besides the emparked residence of the Marquess of Tweeddale at Pinkie, Defoe noted *"some handsome country houses with gardens"*.

**Going in for Golf**: The Royal Musselburgh Golfing Society of 1774 – an offshoot of Edinburgh's Royal Burgess Society – created a course on the Links, part of which became Scotland's oldest municipal course to survive to the present day. Woollen manufacture struggled to maintain its importance through the century; in 1776 only ten tonnes of worsted yarn spun at Peebles and Selkirk was made up in Musselburgh. Mining was again being carried on at Inveresk by 1778. Musselburgh's first post office was established in 1774, but a new office opened in 1793 and soon there were two mails a day to Edinburgh and Prestonpans, and an annual fair was scheduled for Musselburgh.

**Towns, Village and Villas**: Writing in 1799, Heron described Musselburgh and Fisherrow as *"towns"*, while upmarket Inveresk with its fine church was a *"village. These contain many handsome houses, and several elegant villas are seen in the vicinity. The inhabitants amount to about 4000; but have scarce any share in manufactures. A flourishing grammar-school, and some other boarding-schools, are worthy of notice. Salt and fish are sent in considerable quantity to the Edinburgh market."* The new Esk bridge was built in 1806 to designs by John Rennie; by then a brewery operated at Fisherrow, one of three in operation by 1825. Fisherrow's pier was rebuilt in 1806, and in 1814 a wagonway was opened to connect it with Pinkie Hill colliery.

**Netmaking, Horse Racing and Top Golf**: James Paterson, who was born locally about 1770 and became a cooper at one of the local breweries, perfected a net-making machine between 1815 and 1820; about the latter year he set up a net factory in Bridge Street. A rival works set up by Robertson about

1832 was closed for infringing the patents! By 1839 Paterson's net works had 18 looms and over 50 workers. In 1816–17 Musselburgh Links, whose sandy turf suited horse racing, had been railed in for the *'Edinburgh'* Races (formerly held at Leith Sands), leaving the golfers – who by then embraced many clubs – crowded in the centre of the narrow oval racecourse. The golf hole size was first standardised there in 1829, the Royal Burgess Society moved in from Bruntsfield in 1836, and both golf clubs and balls were made locally in the mid 19th century. Despite the shortcomings of the course, which seems to have been of only 9 holes, Musselburgh rather than St Andrews was then the golfing Mecca; the Open Golf championships were held there until 1891, when the *'Honourable'* golfers moved to Muirfield.

**Sea Bathing and Fish Baskets**: Chambers, a recent visitor, wrote in 1827 *"the town is now well built, though, within the remembrance of people still alive almost all the houses were mere hovels of one storey covered with thatch. This improvement is attributable to the demand for summer and sea-bathing quarters, which, till the rise of Portobello, prevailed in this town. Musselburgh is divided from Fisherrow by the Esk, over which there are two stone and one wooden bridge."* Inveresk was a *"pleasant village, or suburb; the whole hill is now thickly covered over by villas"*. At that time Fisherrow was still chiefly the home of fishermen and fishwives; the latter's *"employment is the transportation of fish to the capital and to Leith. They usually carry loads of fish in creels or willow-baskets upon their backs"*; after this labour they would have to haggle with potential purchasers. By then the site of the ancient chapel had been used for the *"modern villa of Loretto"*, which by 1841 had become an independent Episcopal boarding school.

**Town – or Village – gets Gas and Railways**: Musselburgh gasworks was set up about 1831, also serving Portobello *(see Hay & Stell)*. Fisherrow was served from 1838 by a branch from Niddrie on the primitive horse-drawn Edinburgh & Dalkeith Railway (E&DR), also connecting with Leith. The station was like a farmyard! The North British Railway (NBR) having embraced and modernised the E&DR, opened the new east coast main line to Berwick in 1847, built a station at Inveresk, and diverted the Fisherrow line into a new station nearer the centre of Musselburgh.

**Mechanised Netmaking**: Fisherrow harbour was again improved in 1850. Paterson's net works was taken over by J & W Stuart in 1849; about 1854 this firm opened a new factory with 3500 spindles and 100 net looms near Musselburgh station. From 1857 longer-lasting cotton nets replaced their original hemp, and in 1867 the size of the works was more than doubled to 20,000 spindles and 300 looms akin to large knitting frames. With 800 employees, mostly female, it was the largest of its kind in Scotland. Although there was an early works canteen in 1869, Bremner then considered that the technology was already *"primitive"*. In 1870 the firm bought a net factory in Buckhaven, where they soon expanded.

**Esparto Preparation and Ropes**: Meantime the town's ancient tanning industry continued under Miller. In the 1860s Cowans of Penicuik built an esparto grass preparation plant beside the net works at Inveresk. Bruntons the rope makers were founded in 1876, and their works beside the station, which had their own rail siding, produced wire colliery winding ropes between at least 1890 and 1970. The gasworks was modernised in 1887, and large maltings and chemical works were built west of Fisherrow in the late 19th century; but in 1894 Musselburgh was described as *"old-world"*. In 1895 the Royal Burgess Golfing Society moved to a larger site at Cramond.

*The Eskbank net mills, Musselburgh, built from 1867 for W & S Stuart, who had developed a mechanical loom for making fishing nets. This works was the largest net factory in Scotland, with 800 workers at that time. It closed in the 1970s.* (JRH)

**Electric Trams and Paper**: From 1899 a small local power station provided a public electricity supply, and a second station extended the supply to Inveresk from 1906. By the 1920s the Musselburgh Tramways Company ran between Port Seton, past its depot in the High Street to the Edinburgh boundary; taken over by Edinburgh in 1932, the line was abandoned east of Levenhall. Meantime in 1922 came the large Inveresk paper mill, developed from the esparto factory. In 1925 Midlothian opened one of the first county library branches: it's said that the queues were out into the street! In 1926 the famous Royal Musselburgh golf club moved to a new 18-hole parkland course at Prestonpans, but when in 1938 the Monktonhall golf course was laid out in parkland, 18 holes at last became available to the more modest Musselburgh club. By 1951 the population of Musselburgh with its satellites was about 17,600, with the facilities of an average town. The tram services were abandoned in 1954. By 1955 a small fishing fleet and a few cargo vessels used Fisherrow's shallow tidal harbour.

**Downs and Ups from 1960**: Beeching closed both the Musselburgh branch and Inveresk main line station to passengers in 1964, and the freight connection to the paper mill was cut soon afterwards. In the vandal-ridden 1960s Musselburgh Sands were enclosed by a new sea wall and devoted to the accumulation of fly ash from Cockenzie power station. The gasworks was closed by 1966, but Ladywell brewery at Fisherrow survived to be taken over for closure by Whitbread in 1968, its site later being used for SSHA housing, completed in 1981. The *Brunton Theatre*, funded by John D Brunton, son of the founder of the Brunton wireworks, was opened in 1971 and – besides theatrical works – an annual folk festival was established there. In 1975 Musselburgh was transferred from Midlothian county to the new East Lothian district (a unitary authority from 1996). By 1981 its general facilities were those of a typical town, though by then the local paper, the *Musselburgh News*, was based at Bonnyrigg. About then a new link road was built over much of the route of the branch railway.

**From Paper to Printing**: Stuarts net works closed about 1980; by then Fisherrow served mainly as a yacht harbour, its remaining fishermen working out of other ports. The owners of Inveresk paper collapsed in 1982 as a result of general difficulties in the industry, but the Inveresk mill was the only one of the firm's plants to be closed. The paper mill had been replaced by 1990 by an industrial park, on which Scotprint was an innovative firm of book printers, whose 30 staff produced a remarkable 9 million volumes a year under 600 titles. The main block of the net works was converted to offices. The major A1 bypass was opened in 1987, relieving the town of the through road traffic between Edinburgh and East Lothian. By 1989 a new railway station had also been opened, on the main line. In 1987 the flat racecourse was adapted to add National Hunt racing, but by 1992 it was in crisis. Then regarded as the poorest of Scotland's five courses, and jointly owned by Edinburgh Racecourse Ltd and the East Lothian District Council; the latter took over financial management, and improvements to the grandstand and new hospitality suites were completed in 1995.

**Modern Musselburgh Exploding**: Ben Dawson Furniture, established in 1986, employed twenty craftsmen in 1990, fitting out executive suites. By that time large private housing estates were under construction at Stoneybank south-west of the town; the 1991 census found a population of 20,630. In the 1990s a Gateway store was built in the High Street, and the extensive premises of the former Brunton rope works were partly replaced by a Tesco supermarket. As well as many small/medium firms, there is Zot Engineering at Inveresk Mills Industrial Park, employing over 100 in PCB and sheet-metal manufacture. Pollock's haulage firm is also sizeable. The *Brunton Theatre* was extensively refurbished in 1997, and about then the listed Drumhor House was saved for posterity. Pinkie House had long been part of the independent Loretto School, Scotland's longest lasting boarding school for boys; the closure of Oxenfoord Castle School led to Loretto going fully co-educational in 1995. Musselburgh Grammar School has around 1000 pupils. Upmarket housing was built around Inveresk House in 1999. There are many small hotels and guest houses on the eastern approaches to the town, and a 40-room *Travel Inn* has recently arrived near Inveresk. Hailes House is being restored by the National Trust for Scotland.

## MUTHILL

**Map 6, A3**

***Perthshire village,*** *pop. 650*

OS 58: NN 8717

Strageath, a 1st century Roman fort in Strathearn, stood north of the River Isla on their road and line of fortlets between Ardoch and Bertha near Perth; it was also used as an outpost in the Antonine period. Muthil (pronounced *Mewthil)*, a hillside location 2 km to the south-west, was an episcopal centre by the eighth century; its name is the Gaelic *Maothail*, *'Emollient'* – a downy spot for soft monks! Its Culdee community stayed into the 12th century, gave their name to Culdees Castle and probably erected the ancient tower on to which a 15th century church was built (now a ruin). The tower house of Drummond Castle which stands on a lengthy igneous dyke, a remarkable geological feature 2 km to the north-west, was built in 1490–91. In 1501 three of its daughters were poisoned there; the eldest, Margaret Drummond, reputedly already the spouse of James IV, was apparently the victim of the successful plot to marry off the Scottish monarch to Margaret Tudor, daughter of the usurper Henry VII of England, which later secured the Union of the Crowns. The castle was shown as a triple tower and named in capitals on Pont's manuscript map of about 1600; nearby was little *'Ochtermuthil'*, where an early parish school was opened in 1583.

**From Mill Girl to Moroccan Empress**: Old soldiers were resettled at Muthill by the Commissioners for Forfeited Estates, because the Earl of Perth, owner of Drummond Castle, had been exiled after the 1715. In 1745 the castle was partly demolished, but later a mansion was built beside the old tower. The mid 18th century Roy map showed Muthill as a very small place, its main street forming a zig-zag in the otherwise almost straight section of the King's Road from Stirling to Dalnacardoch. Beside this road where it crossed the Machany Water south of Muthill was the *'Miln of Steps'*: in the 18th century a girl born there became by chance the Empress of Morocco *(Chambers – see also Forteviot)*. Lower down was the Bishop's Bridge, not connected to a road; the Roy map showed no other roads in the area. Four fairs were to be held in 1797, but in 1799 Heron noted more than 400 residents in a *"village"* (which was never a burgh). A new Culdees Castle designed for a General Drummond by James Gillespie Graham was built in 1810; the old Culdees Castle vanished. Chambers called Muthill *"a delightful little village"* where a new church was built in the 1820s; but there was no post office until after 1838.

**The Ineffectual Railway**: A Caledonian Railway branch line from Gleneagles to Crieff was opened in 1856. Though passing within 1.5 km of the village, the station was sited 2.5 km from Muthill, and had little effect. The 1891 population was 800, and there was a village inn by 1895. Culdees Castle was altered in 1910 by Lorimer, but stood empty in 1980. Muthill golf club, founded in 1935, provided its members with a parkland course; it still has 9 holes. Nearly 1250 people lived in the area in 1951, but with only the facilities of a small village, including two little hotels, ironmonger and doctor. The station was closed completely in 1964, and the line lifted. The population fell steadily, though remarkably the doctor had gained a partner by 1980. In 1991 the village population was 679; Muthill remained in outward appearance little changed in decades. Drummond Castle's large and exotic Italianate garden is open to the public, and Historic Scotland care for the remains of the old 15th century church.

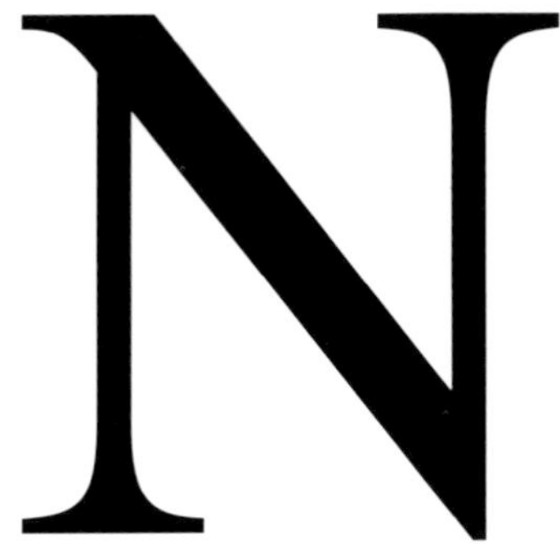

## NAIRN

**Map 9, C3**

***Moray Firth town,*** *pop. 7900*

OS 27: NH 8856

Norsemen founded a settlement on the south coast of the Moray Firth, where a river tumbled into the sea from a rocky gorge, forming a natural harbour; its Norse name is lost. There was however an early chapel at inland Auldearn *(q.v.)*, 3 km to the east, which became the parish church when the castle and Royal Burgh of *Invernaren* (Mouth of the River Aren or Arun) were created together in 1189. In 1204 this burgh replaced Auldearn as the caput of a tiny sheriffdom, whose jurisdiction included exclaves in adjoining shires.

**No Cause for Joy**: There was still a royal castle about 1300. From 1304 for a time the sheriffdom was combined with that of Forres, but was again distinct by the late 15th century. The hall house of Rait Castle, 4 km south of Nairn, was the early 14th century home of Sir Andrew de Rait, at that time the surveyor of the royal domain of Scotland. Highland incursions caused repeated destruction in Nairn, and not until 1535–56 was the struggling town able to contribute tiny sums in burgh taxes. The royal castle was shown as being in ruins on Pont's map made about 1600, when there were many mills around the town. Already both Gaelic and English were spoken. Geddes 4 km south of Nairn was granted a baronial burgh charter in 1600, but failed to grow, as did Lochloy, 4 km to the east, a similar charter of 1608. In 1639 Nairn ranked a lowly 47th of Scottish burghs in tax rents, last but two of those which rendered returns.

**Bridges and the Divided Town**: Nairn's first bridge was apparently built between Pont's visit and 1654, when the bridge and a little town were shown on Gordon's map of about 1642. Nairn had a post office by 1715, and Roy's map made about 1750 showed Nairn bridge leading to a little one-street town with four or five radial roads. In 1755 Caulfeild's troops built Dulsie Bridge across the River Findhorn at Glenferness, on the military road about 15 km south of Nairn. In 1769 Pennant confirmed Nairn as a *"small town"*, then split by a recognisable boundary between Gaelic and English speech, while in 1773 Boswell called it *"a very poor place to be a county town and a Royal Burgh"*. As Scotland rapidly developed, even Nairn had to catch up; by 1797 as many as seven fair days were scheduled for the year, and with the completion of the road system across Moray, Nairn bridge became for a decade the best road access to the north from south and east Scotland – via Aberdeen! However, the area's agriculture remained backward, for in 1799 Heron found plough-oxen still being used rather than horses, *"the soil being rocky"*. The town had *"little trade. Its exports are some fish, corn, cattle, yarn, and a few other articles."* Its population was about 2000.

**Gaelic and Fish, Gas and News**: A new bridge erected in 1803 had to be partly rebuilt after the great flood of 1829. Meantime a new sheriff court-house was built in 1818, though Chambers found in the 1820s *"a small town, with narrow streets and no public buildings of any importance; the ear of the stranger coming from the east is there first startled by the deep gutturals of the Gaelic tongue. The river Nairn, over which there is a good bridge, here forms a small harbour."* Under Telford's guidance in 1820–29 the river mouth was trained between two short piers. This enabled Nairn to become a significant fishing port, with over 400 fishermen and 60 boats in 1850, leading to early enlargement of the harbour; meantime a gasworks was set up in 1839 and a local newspaper, the *Nairnshire Telegraph*, was established in 1841. The Romanesque UP church was built in 1852.

**Nairn's Home-Grown Railway**: The town prospered from the opening of the Inverness & Nairn Railway in 1855. This locally-promoted concern was extended eastwards across the river by the Inverness & Aberdeen Junction Railway in 1857, and to Forres and Keith in 1858. By 1860 Wordie & Co operated a rail to road cartage depot, from which carts would go to Findhorn to collect netted salmon, for despatch from Nairn station. From 1863 the line formed part of the original dog-leg route between Inverness and the south via Forres, the whole being part of the Highland Railway (HR) from 1865. By 1869 a poorhouse had been built south-west of the station, while to its south-east was a brewery and corn and flour mills beside the River Nairn. A lifeboat station was opened in 1878. In 1881, 91 boats were based at Nairn, then a flourishing herring port with a population of over 4000. But the population of Nairnshire peaked about then.

**Golfing Resort and Local Centre**: Having good accessibility, a relatively sheltered position, a dry and sunny climate and a good beach, Nairn was described by Barnard in 1886 as *"most charming – the Brighton of Scotland"*! Nairn's first 18-hole links golf course was laid out in 1887; by 1894 Nairn was a very successful golfing resort, with two hotels noted by Murray – the *"good" Marine* and the *"very good" Shaw's* – plus a remarkably early covered swimming pool. A second 18-hole golf course was laid out in 1899, and the very substantial *Station Hotel* was built in the late 19th century. But Nairn became less accessible in 1898 when the through trains from the south were diverted to the HR's new main line direct from Inverness to Aviemore.

**From Ale to Cheese via Whisky**: In 1898 the mills were rebuilt into the Glen Cawdor Distillery, which was taken over by John Haig & Co in 1903; but by 1905 the brewery had gone, and in 1927 the distillery was among the many casualties of USA Prohibition. Meantime a power station was built in 1902; by 1905 an auction mart had been opened near the station, and there was also a slaughterhouse. Later came a butter and cheese creamery. The lifeboat station was closed in 1911, and although the harbour was rebuilt in 1932 it soon became largely recreational, for the fishing had greatly declined. Meantime the road bridge was widened in 1936. A school built west of the town around 1900 had become the *Alton Burn Hotel* by the 1960s.

**The End of Nairnshire**: In the 1950s Nairn had 5000 people, a dozen hotels and two cinemas; by then the *Station Hotel* had become the *Highland*. Wartime cutbacks meant that as late as 1953 only the Dunbar golf course was open, but by 1969 Nairn Golf Club offered both 18- and 9-hole courses. A cinema was still open in 1970, later used as a bingo hall. At that time Nairnshire was administered from Elgin by a joint County Council for Moray and Nairn. In compensation for the loss of burgh status and its transfer to Highland Region in 1975, Nairn became the centre of a small local government district – the old Nairn county area. The small Literary Institute Museum was open by 1980, and by 1985 the Fishertown Museum emphasised the former herring industry. A new industrial estate had been laid out by 1981, when the number of hotels had doubled to 18, the largest being the tall and long-established *Golf View Hotel* with 57 rooms. Completely new buildings for Nairn Academy were erected in the 1980s. However, the UP church had fallen on evil days in 1979 and was nearly derelict by 1997.

**Running a Railway by Pushbike**: Although by 1990 Presto had built a supermarket, most shops were still occupied by private traders. In the 1990s the railway yard was still in some use, but the primitive signalling arrangements still involved the duty railman in a frantic cycle ride between listed signal boxes at either end of the lengthy platform to enable the signals to be cleared! Nairn Sailing Club stood beside the harbour, where yachting was popular but little else continued; a small new marina was built in the early 1990s. There were 7892 residents in 1991. The Nairn Leisure Park was open, and three caravan and camping sites adjoined the town, which still offered a choice of three golf courses, and had been styled *"the premier seaside resort of the Highland Region"*, its beach *'very good'*. This did not prevent the *Highland Hotel* becoming disused in 1992, but it had been converted to flats by 2000.

**Efficiency Ends Quaint Anomalies**: A 1994 local government initiative led to grant-improved shopfronts in the centre of Nairn; a coastal nature reserve had been declared, and other proposals in train included a shopping mall, visitor centre, sports facility and motor museum. But in 1996 Nairn District Council disappeared into the vast all-purpose Highland authority, ending eight centuries of independent local government debate in Nairn. Electronic signalling installed in 1999–2000 made the signaller's push-bike redundant! By then the Claymore creamery employed over 100 workers, and a Safeway store had arrived. A large range of hotels exist – the largish *Golf View* and *Newton* sharing a leisure club – and there are many smaller hotels and guest houses.

## NEILSTON

**Map 15, B6**

***Renfrewshire small town,*** *pop. 5300* — OS 64: NS 4857

When Timothy Pont mapped Renfrewshire around 1600, Neilston Kirk stood high up on a spur in a thickly settled area, 50m above the little Levern Water some 7km south of Paisley. To the east was another burn, and north of the Levern there was a bridge across the Killoch Burn. A small nucleated settlement existed at Neilston by the time that Roy's survey was made about 1754, with roads to Glasgow, Irvine and Paisley.

*The Crofthead cotton mill, Neilston, which was built in 1792 and extended in 1858. It closed in 1993, but now it is partly used for engineering research.* *(JRH)*

John Robertson, born in Neilston in 1782, built the engine for the steamship *Comet* in 1811 *(see Glasgow)*. Neilston had a post office from 1783 and a coal mine with an engine by 1791. Manufacturing developed with two water-powered cotton mills – the Broadlie Mill built in 1790 and the Crofthead Mill, established beside the old Hall in 1792 by Stewart, Orr & Co to spin cotton and twist thread. By 1797 Neilston was a post town with a service on three days a week; in 1799 Heron found what he called a *"village"* of over 400 people, and noted one or more printfields. The mine was a fairly short-lived enterprise, but Crofthead Mill was extended in 1858. Neilston never became a burgh, becoming mainly known for its cotton thread and for textile printing.

**Railways and Bleachworks**: The Glasgow, Barrhead & Kilmarnock Railway, a joint enterprise of the Glasgow & South Western (G&SW) and Caledonian companies, was opened from Barrhead in 1871–73 along the narrow valley floor, with a station near Crofthead mill. This mill was again extended in 1880 and 1928 into a vast complex. By 1895 there was an inn; Kirkton Bleachworks on the Kirkton Burn to the east were supplied by a complex of reservoirs on the moors above, of which the largest was the Harelaw Dam. A second such works stood just downstream and a third, short-lived bleachworks and lint mill worked for a time on the Levern south-west of the village.

**Rail Duplication, Electrification and Closures**: A second through railway, the Caledonian's *'Lanarkshire & Ayrshire'* offshoot, was opened in 1903 from Cathcart via Giffnock to Kilwinning and the Ayrshire coast, with a high-level station at Kirkton. A gasworks was built about 1907. By the third quarter of the 20th century only one bleachworks remained open, the Kirkton. Meantime a little suburban development for Glasgow was taking place; by 1951 Neilston had 4000 people and a full range of village facilities. Electric trains on the line to Glasgow encouraged some population increase, and Neilston was by 1981 a large urbanised village. In the 1980s residential development continued west of the centre, and by 1991 the youngish population was 5260.

**Leather, and Research after the Thread Snaps**: Meantime the Broadlie Mill had been rebuilt in 1970 into works for the Clyde Leather Company. By then huge Crofthead, one of Scotland's longest-lasting cotton factories, was making thread, boldly though very misleadingly labelled high up on the building as *"English Sewing"*, this being a subsidiary of Coats Viyella; but the mill was closed in 1993, leaving a vacant area of no less than 24,000m² on six floors. By 1994 the Crofthead Mill had been acquired for use as an automotive engineering research centre, plus some production. Another small residential estate had been built by 1996. Elcomatic are a firm employing over 100 making valves for the oil industry.

## NESS, Cros, Swainbost, & Europie

***Townships, Isle of Lewis,*** *pop. 1400 (area)* — **Map 11, C1** OS 8: NB 5263

At Ballantrushal, one of a sprawling complex of crofting townships on the remote and rocky north-west coast of the Isle of Lewis is the tallest standing stone in Scotland. At Shader, 17km south-west of Ness *(in Gaelic 'Nis')*, are other early remains. The restored *Teampull Mholuidh* stands at Europie *(Eoropaidh)*; the far islet of Rona, 71km north of the Butt of Lewis, had an ancient chapel, and scant remains of other churches date from the 12th century. The soil is relatively fertile and free of both rocks and the peat which covered the land farther south; it was divided into crofts of 1ha to 4ha. Roads first reached Ness in the mid 19th century; a major lighthouse was then built at Butt of Lewis, first lit in 1862.

**Fishing, Boats – and Enforced English**: A generation later, despite Gaelic being the local tongue of the area, teaching in the new local primary schools was imposed in English. The 1891 population of a central township, Swainbost *(Suainebost)* was around 1500. At that time the kirk, and the free church and manse, were remarkably identified even on small scale atlas maps of Lewis, for in this most underdeveloped part of Scotland there was little else of note other than the lighthouse and the tiny fishing pier at Port of Ness *(Port Nis)*, greatly enlarged at government expense in the late 1890s. The nearest larger centre, Stornoway, is 43km away by road. In 1907 the lighthouse became an early wireless telegraphy station. At that time there were some 300 fishermen in Ness, and a distinctive boatbuilding tradition which continued even though the industry shrank inter-war, with fewer fish and smaller boats.

**Ness Works Away**: After World War II, Ness men began to take up contracting work on mainland hydro-electric schemes. By 1951 there were several primary schools, three post offices, and a junior secondary school with 230 pupils at Lionel, but few other facilities were available to serve the area's 2000 people. The manually operated Port of Ness telephone exchange with a mere 14 lines had been converted to automatic operation before 1974, but a sub-branch bank which opened in the 1960s was soon closed. In the early 1970s some Ness men seized the chance to work four weeks out of five at Sullom Voe or Kishorn. In 1984 an automatic lighthouse was placed on Rona; even now some men *'fish'* for gannets on Sula Sgeir, a 70m-tall rocky islet 20km west of Rona.

**Content in Isolation?**: Visitors in the 1970s found little to attract them, but the tiny *Cross Inn* and a small restaurant were open; other facilities were those of a small village. The secondary school at Lionel was still in operation in 1980, and some classes were at last taught in Gaelic. Boats were still built at Port of Ness in the 1980s, but there was no other industry. In 1991 when the rather elderly population had fallen to 1400, Ness held the highest proportion of Gaelic

*Port of Ness, Lewis, built in 1893–94 in mass concrete, with government aid, to improve conditions for local fishermen – but virtually disused when seen here in 1976.* *(JRH)*

speakers in Scotland – over 90%. Outright home ownership of the mainly detached houses was equally high, but sheer remoteness remains a great economic disadvantage. A coastal *'heritage trail'* some 20 km in length now encourages hardy walkers to link Ness with North Tolsta, and a tiny bunkhouse for backpackers is open at Galson, 7 km west of Cros.

## NETHY BRIDGE

**Map 9, C5**

***Speyside village,*** *pop. 500* OS 36: NJ 0020

Standing stones beside the River Spey near the Boat of Balliefurth suggest that a regular ferry may have existed in Pictish times. *'Balefont or Ferry Town'* appeared on Timothy Pont's map of middle Speyside, made around 1600. By then Abernethy church stood 3 km to the south at Coulnakyle, near the 13th century Castle Roy; west of this the tributary River Nethy was already bridged. The Dorback Burn, a substantial tributary of the Nethy, had also been bridged in two places. Milton stood beside the *'Alltamoulin'* (mill stream), later simply known as the Allt Mor *(big stream)*. In 1630 the local forests were leased to the Earl of Tullibardine, and a water-powered sawmill was established at Coulnakyle. Despite the lack of roads in the area, a second sawmill was set up in 1728 by the highly speculative York Buildings Company; about 1730 they also opened iron furnaces, using local charcoal to smelt ore from Tomintoul. But these *"great ironworks"* (Heron) lasted only a few years, and were not even identified on Roy's map of about 1750.

**Military Road and Timber Products**: The Roy map showed a trackless area containing no development beside the Abernethy Kirk – except for the castle (which eventually became a ruin), and the tiny settlement most optimistically called Ballimore (*Big Village*). Of Pont's bridge there was no sign. Caulfeild's military road down middle Speyside was built during the next decade, with a new Nethy Bridge about 1 km upstream of the original site; eventually the Spey too was bridged nearby. By 1770 tree trunks were being bored out at the sawmill and floated downstream to be shipped to London as water pipes. In 1799 Heron found four sawmills at *"the village of Abernethy"*; but there was no post office until after 1838.

**Railway Competition and Connection**: Within three weeks in 1863 two railways were opened on opposite sides of the Spey: the original main line of the Inverness & Perth Junction Railway, with a station at Broomhill – from 1865 part of the Highland (HR); and the terminating Strathspey Railway from Dufftown – soon a branch of the Great North of Scotland Railway (GNSR), which extended the line westwards across the Spey in 1866 to connect with the HR at Boat of Garten. In 1894 Murray described the village as *"a pleasant summer retreat"*, with the *Nethy Bridge Hotel "very fair"*. In that year a timber trestle road bridge was built across the Spey to Broomhill. Abernethy golf club was founded in 1895, laying out a 9-hole course. After 1923 Broomhill station was renamed Nethy Bridge by the HR's successor the LMS.

**Golf and Fishing Rods outlast Trains and Films**: By the 1950s the *Nethy Bridge Hotel* had 70 rooms and four stars; the 675 local residents had a 130-pupil secondary school and even a cinema, though this was soon closed. Both railways closed in the late 60s, but a new secondary school was built at Nethy Bridge – a policy blunder followed by its closure in the 1970s so that more pupils could be mustered at Grantown! By 1977 the Abernethy Outdoor Centre was open. In 1981 Nethy Bridge was a small tourist village with four hotels. By 1991 when under 500 people lived in Nethy Bridge proper, it was famous for the workshop of Harry Jamieson, the maker of 500 high-quality fishing rods annually for over 30 years. Said to be the last traditional rod maker in Scotland, he then licensed production to the Japanese makers Daiwa *(see Wishaw)*. The post office and primary school remain open, and the *Nethy Bridge* is the largest of the local hotels; the golf course is still only 9 holes.

## NEW ABBEY

**Map 2, B5**

***Village s. of Dumfries,*** *pop. 800 (area)* OS 84: NX 9666

A crannog in Loch Kindar 12 km south of Dumfries shows early settlement west of the Nith estuary. A medieval motte was raised on a spur near the mouth of a stream later known as New Abbey Pow, in a fertile area north of the loch. In 1273–75 Lady Devorgilla, daughter of Alan, the last Lord of Galloway and widow of John Balliol, chose a site 2 km upstream for her New Abbey, founded for the Cistercian order. Balliol's embalmed heart was buried with her, hence the Latin name *Abbacia Dulcis Cordis, 'Sweetheart Abbey'*. Its magnificent church was complete by the mid 14th century. In the turbulent 16th century the precinct was enclosed by a great wall, and the

*New Abbey mill, probably built on the site of a monastic meal mill in the 18th century, and restored by the Stewarts of Shambellie in the 1970s. It is now a tourist attraction (Historic Scotland). (JRH)*

defensive Abbot's Tower was built on a spur beyond the New Abbey Pow. Until 1560 Sweetheart was still a very significant abbey, represented in Parliament and having five appropriated churches. The estate of Kirkconnell 2 km north of the Pow had been granted to the Maxwells in 1235; their L-plan tower was built on the shore in the 16th century.

**Scotland's Second Brick House?**: Despite the Order's vows of remoteness, Pont's map which dated from about 1610 showed this was a well-settled area; the tiny settlement beside the motte was by then known as *'Englishtoun'*. New Abbey had no centrality and was never chartered as a burgh. The map also showed to seaward a water mill on the New Abbey Pow. A little inland was the intriguingly inelegant name *Schanbilby*, later known as a mansionhouse spelled Shambellie. A parish school was founded at New Abbey in 1628. In 1750 one James Maxwell, having narrowly escaped estate forfeiture for supporting the Jacobites, returned from France with bricklayers who built on to Kirkconnell Tower a modest mansionhouse, perhaps the second-earliest brick house in Scotland; his son added a walled garden. Roy's map made about 1754 showed the rectangular enclosures of the ruined abbey, within which was a scatter of buildings; it lay on a track from Dumfries to Kirkbean and *'Prestonsmill'*.

**Textile Manufacture and Sawmilling**: In the late 18th century a new mill and a water-powered woollen mill were built on the Pow. In 1799 when there were over 200 people, Heron called New Abbey a *"small village"*. Its harbour or pow, used in the 1790s, was in a bad state by 1844, perhaps because by 1827 roads had been built to Dumfries and Dalbeattie; a post office was open by 1838. The abbey's spectacular ruins – saved from quarrying by local gentlemen – were becoming a popular tourist haunt, though it was never thought worthwhile to build a railway into the area. A new Shambellie House was built for William Stewart in the 1850s to designs by David Bryce. Robert Laing operated the woollen mill as a tweed factory in 1868, but about 1900 it became a sawmill. New Abbey possessed an inn by 1894, when it was called a *"village"* by Murray. A modern day Charles Stewart of Shambellie House soon began to collect fashionable costumes. New Abbey corn mill closed in 1945, but the sawmill survived until at least 1951, when some 550 people lived in the vicinity. There were two small hotels, and the school had secondary classes, but by 1976 these had been moved elsewhere.

**Forestry and Fashion for Tourists**: The afforestation of the hills to the west has largely taken place since the 1950s. In 1981 the slowly growing population was nearing 600, served by the facilities of a small village. By then the abbey's tourist draw was augmented by craft and coffee shops, and the 18th century water-driven oatmeal mill was reconditioned and re-opened as a visitor attraction in 1983 by Historic Scotland's predecessors. In 1991 the parish held 820 people. About then the National Museums of Scotland took over Shambellie House, with Stewart's small exhibition of costumes, which was doubled in size in 1993 and opens to the public in summer. By 1996 a small housing estate had been built south of the village. The water mill was still in full working order in 1995, but by 1997 its worn-out equipment prevented regular demonstrations. In 2000 Kirkconnell House and its ancient tower was put on the market for the very first time by its unlucky laird, Francis Maxwell.

## NEW ABERDOUR

**Map 10, C1**

***Small Buchan village,*** *pop. 500* — OS 30: NJ 8863

A Dark Age monastery once existed on the bleak cliffs of the north coast of Buchan 11 km west of modern Fraserburgh. In the 13th century the coastal Castle of Dundarg rose on the cliffs to the east, but the early church of Aberdour, built at the same period, was sited in a sheltered valley beside the mouth of the Dour Burn (*Dour* means *'Otter'* in Gaelic). Pont's map of around 1600 showed *'Dundairgh'*; other tiny settlements included *'Ardlahill'* (Aldyhill!), 3 km to the south. Some agricultural improvements were made, and the fine mansion of Aberdour House was built in 1740, 2.5 km east of the Kirk. But persistence yielded relatively little reward in this harsh and isolated area, for Aberdour parish remained roadless when about 1750 Roy's surveyors sketched a mere five buildings beside Aberdour Kirk, though a mill turned at the mouth of the burn for at least another century.

**The New Village**: The creation of the planned village of New Aberdour took place in 1798. The chosen site was a bleak 100 m above the sea near the long-established hill farm of Aldyhill, but beside the turnpike road that had been laid out between Banff and Fraserburgh. By 1838 there was a postal receiving house nearby named Crathes Brae; later the postal service moved to a New Aberdour office. By 1858, when New Aberdour was mentioned by Pratt as a *"village"*, the ancient church was a ruin, and a new parish church had been built at the end of its single main street.

**Remote and Windswept**: The 1891 population was 620. New Aberdour remained a little windswept one-street settlement and was never approached by a railway, though by 1912 Simpson operated motor buses between New Aberdour, Rosehearty and Fraserburgh. Up to the 1950s secondary classes were held at New Aberdour and at the crossroads school at Tyrie, 3 km to the south-east, but by 1976 secondary pupils had to travel farther afield. New Aberdour had no industries or significant tourist interests; it is a small and very bare village with a post office and two small hotels, and by 1991 had under 500 residents. However, there is now a modern primary school and a golf driving range.

## NEWARTHILL, Carfin & Yett

**Map 16, A4**

***Villages n-e. of Motherwell,*** *pop. 7800* — OS 64: NS 7859

By 1596 when a well-settled area some 8 km east of Bothwell was mapped by Timothy Pont, the South Calder Water had been bridged both up- and down-stream of *'Caerfin'*, which seems an ancient Brythonic name; it had a school by 1627. By the time of Roy's map, made about 1750, there was a road from Hamilton to Kirk of Shotts, on which Newarthill was to develop. In 1834 the *'Scotch'* gauge Wishaw & Coltness Railway (W&CR) was opened from Whifflet (Coatbridge) through Mossend and New Stevenston to a terminus at Carfin colliery south-west of Newarthill, whose workforce was reputedly largely Irish in origin. By 1842 a daily W&CR through coach to Glasgow, serving Newarthill and Holytown, was attached to Glasgow & Garnkirk Railway trains at Gartsherrie. In 1844 the line was extended to the Coltness ironworks at Newmains, an enterprise of the Houldsworth cotton magnates *(see also Glasgow & Waterside)*.

**The Railway and Yett**: The Caledonian Railway branch from Holytown Junction to Shotts and Edinburgh was opened in 1869, but although around Carfin the line forked south-eastwards into five various routes, for many years there was no station nearer than Holytown Junction. Carfin already had an inn, a post office and a population of over 1500 in 1891, when Newarthill had an inn, post office and smithy. Newarthill primary school was built in 1897, soon serving Yett, a large new settlement laid out on the site of the recently abandoned Stevenston Colliery between Newarthill and Carfin. A new station was apparently open by about 1910, named Newarthill; seemingly it failed to attract traffic, and had closed by 1913.

**Carfin Grotto and Industrial Estate**: In the 1920s some unemployed Catholic miners built a grotto which drew pilgrims, leading to reopening of the closed station as Carfin Halt. This was also used by workers in the Scottish Industrial Estates Corporation development, laid out in the late 1930s on the site of the by then closed Carfin colliery. By 1951 1800 people lived in Carfin and the total with Newarthill and Yett was about 8500. Soon more facilities were established at Newarthill, which had attained typical village facilities by 1979.

**Heavy Metal Industries?**: By then the large Fullwood Foundry and Clyde Crane Works were prominent, as was the huge Ravenscraig steelworks *(see Motherwell)* which loomed only 1 km to the south. In 1981 though the total population was similar, a higher proportion lived in Newarthill. About then the Brannock High School was built in Newarthill. By 1991 the combined populations of youngish Newarthill and elderly Carfin totalled about 7800, and the male unemployment rate was very high, concentrated in Carfin where it was almost 30%. Carfin still had a greyhound racing track in 1993. In 1994 due to prolonged heavy rainfall an electricity pylon near Newarthill fell into a deep opencast pit, disrupting power supplies over a wide area. By 1996 the A723 had been diverted onto a bypass between Newarthill and Holytown.

## NEWBRIDGE & Ratho Station — Map 15, A2

***W. Lothian villages**, pop. 1200* — OS 65: NT 1372

A Bronze Age tumulus now known as Huley Hill was raised in the River Almond floodplain 13 km west of Edinburgh Castle rock. (Early in 2001 an Iron Age chariot from about 250 BC was discovered buried nearby; this unique find is being conserved by the Museums of Scotland.) Local placenames imply that a mill and a bridge had once existed and been replaced by about 1600, when Timothy Pont mapped the area. By then the New Bridge had been built to carry a road from the city to West Lothian across the River Almond. West of the bridge the road forked to Bathgate and Blackburn, while to the south stood the New Mill. A tiny symbol named *'Halyards'* to the east was probably the predecessor of the 17th century tower of Hallyards Castle. The *Newbridge Inn* bears the date 1683, but Roy's map implied little further development by 1754.

**The Railway and Ratho Station**: The engineers of the Edinburgh & Glasgow Railway, constructed in 1838–42, chose a high-level route, crossing the Almond on Scotland's longest masonry railway viaduct; Ratho Station (so called) was opened on this line just east of Newbridge (nearly 2 km from Ratho village). From 1842 William Wordie operated a rail to road cartage depot at Ratho Station, where a tiny settlement grew. In 1849 the station was made the junction for the Bathgate branch (which eventually became a secondary route to Glasgow), and was also the starting point of the Queensferry line which opened to Kirkliston and Dalmeny in 1866. Clifton Hall stood 2 km south-west of Newbridge by 1895, when emparked Norton still lacked buildings; otherwise the area remained wholly rural. The hamlet of Ratho Station expanded in the early 20th century between the railway and the main road; a quarry was opened in the hill nearby (and by the 1980s was very large). However, passenger trains to Queensferry succumbed in 1930, and Ratho station had already been closed to passengers by 1953. Meanwhile further development had grown between it and the *Newbridge Inn*. In the 1950s though the population of the three settlements (including Ratho proper) totalled over 2500, their combined facilities were those of a small village, plus the *Norton House Hotel* south of the railway.

**A Planning Disaster Area**: The M8 and M9 motorways were built in the 1960s with the intention of linking Edinburgh with Glasgow and Stirling, meeting head-on in a fast wide roundabout at the A8. It divided the two settlements, whose unfortunate local residents were tenuously connected by a windy footbridge. Industrial development was promoted around Newbridge (with incentives available in West Lothian but not in Edinburgh). By then the new industries included the head office and poultry packing station of the major chicken farmers D B Marshall, who owned farms across Fife and West Lothian. Another 1970s arrival was Fleming Howden, wholesale food distributors. A new whisky blending and bottling plant was also built in the 1970s by Hill Thomson of Edinburgh, which by 1991 had become part of Chivas of Paisley. Miscellaneous developments continued. The Newbridge area, with all its newly created problems, was transferred to Edinburgh district in 1975. By 1977 Clifton Hall was an independent preparatory school (as it remains).

**Tyres and Plastics Come and Go**: The large, originally US-owned Uniroyal tyre factory was built between 1970 and 1975, apparently replacing that at Locharbriggs. Not in principle a very good neighbour, it certainly helped employment, for about 1000 people worked there by 1979, when it was adjoined by the firm's plastics factory, employing 300 people. By 1990 the tyre factory was named Uniroyal Engelbert Tyres. It was soon sold to the German giant Continental, which operated 12 other factories and profitably provided 900 jobs in mid 1995, making 12,600 tyres a day at Newbridge, of a possible 140 varieties. But the high pound meant that the 5 million tyres made annually were losing money for Continental, who then closed the plant.

**Overflying**: By 1981 the local facilities had risen, but were divided between the communities. In the late 1980s Racal-MESL moved into the area to make microwave ovens; in 1995 some 200 people worked there, producing microwave components and sub-systems; by 1991 MTS Healthcare operated one of their national chain of testing laboratories. In 1991 some 1150 people lived in the settlement defined as Ratho Station. In 1993 the recently expanded Scotcem roof tile plant was at work beside the Bathgate railway line south of Newbridge. In 1994 James Fleming & Co, fondant manufacturers, were active at Newbridge.

**Cutting Chicken Packers in Cacotopia**: The M8 Edinburgh extension, first proposed in the mid-eighties and built in 1994–96, included a 36 m-span bridge whose enormous 68-tonne concrete beams were precast at Coltness, and relieved the infamous roundabout with an underpass. In 1995 Booker Foodservice of the Clifton trading estate ran a fleet of 29 vehicles distributing foods to the catering industry. The Marshall Food Group were still busy at Newbridge where they employed 600 workers in 1997, but in 2000 new owners Grampian Country Foods cut 540 of what were by then 1200 jobs in the Newbridge chicken packery, while expanding in Tayside. The *'Edinburgh Interchange Development'* will soon stand on the site where the ancient chariot was unearthed; nearby the *Norton House Hotel* has grown to 47 rooms.

## NEWBURGH

**Map 10, C3**
***Buchan village,*** *pop. 1500* — OS 38: NJ 9925

This very early burgh of barony stands beside the Foveran Burn as it enters the tidal estuary of the River Ythan 20km north of Aberdeen; it was chartered in 1261 by Lord Sinclair. In the 12th or 13th century Deer Abbey established an outpost there, a *'hospital'* of the Holy Rood. Newburgh became a salmon fishing centre, and in the 16th century Knockhall Castle was built 1.5km to the north. A school was opened in 1605, and Newburgh appeared as a town on Robert Gordon's 1650s mapwork; on the opposite bank of the Ythan was the meaningful name *'Ferrie'*. In 1655 Tucker recorded a minimal timber import trade. Roy's map of about 1750 showed the coastal track from Aberdeen turning inland at Blairtown, 3km south of Newburgh, making for Ellon via the *'Kirk of Favron'* and adjoining Newmill. Nearby it intersected another track from Old Meldrum and Udny which ended at Newburgh, a cross-shaped nucleus of settlement beside the burn. Just west of this was *'Bridgend'* and a bridge, but no road. In 1769 Pennant found that travellers on the main coast road to Peterhead crossed a ford at Newburgh – then a *"small village"*.

**Scotland's First RNLI Lifeboat; Grain, Golf and Manure**: A lifeboat station was opened in 1828, the first in Scotland to be provided by the *'Shipwreck Institution'* (later the RNLI). Newburgh post office was open by 1845, but burgh status was withdrawn in an early reorganisation of local government. By 1858 Newburgh had a proper quay with *"lighters and punts actively plying with corn, coal, lime, and bone-dust"* to merchants upstream at Waterton by Ellon. En route they passed a *'boat'* to the sheep farm of Waterside, 2 km to the north, one of many owned by the rapacious Colonel Gordon of Cluny. Rails never approached Newburgh, whose grain and general merchants Mitchell & Rae owned sailing vessels up to 1878, when the SS *Gem* was built for them, followed in 1882 by the 234-ton *Ruby*. Newburgh had eleven fishing boats in the 1880s; in 1888 a golf club was founded, a 9-hole golf course being laid out on Udny Links. The 1891 population was 650; Newburgh was described by Murray as *"a little seaport town"* in 1894. Mussel-pearls were still collected from the river, timber imports continued, grain was exported and a large *'manure works'* gave rise to a brisk trade, possibly grinding animal bones to meal for superphosphate. The *Udny Arms Hotel* is Victorian in origin.

**Decline and Recovery**: From 1907 motor buses of the Great North of Scotland Railway linked Newburgh with Aberdeen; the estuary was bridged, apparently in the 1920s, putting Newburgh on a through road. Mitchell & Rae continued at work, but owned no ships from about 1914 to 1952, when they had a motor vessel built. In the 1950s Newburgh was still a substantial village of nearly 900 people, with two hotels, two doctors and a mill. The lifeboat station was closed in 1965, being moved to more strategically located Peterhead. The hotels remained but other facilities declined to those of a small village. By 1971 the population was below 700; the doctors were not replaced. By 1981 the mill seems to have been abandoned, the estuary had become primarily a nature reserve, and the fishing was minimal. However, the oil boom had led to new housing estates, and a caravan and camping site was open by 1985; by then the Newburgh-on-Ythan golf club was in action, extending the course to 18 holes in the early 1990s. The 1991 population of 1401 was young and well-educated, and still more new housing has since been built west of the village centre. The modernised *Udny Arms Hotel* offers 26 rooms.

## NEWBURGH

**Map 6, B3**
***Large N. Fife village,*** *pop. 2000* — OS 58/59: NO 2418

Where the Ochil Hills meet the upper Tay estuary is Abdie parish, with the tenth century Mugdrum Cross; a silver hoard buried about 1025 contained English coins. Abdie's old kirk and a medieval motte stood on opposite sides of the freshwater Lindores Loch, a name probably deriving from the Brythonic *Llyn (Lake)*. This loch gives rise to a burn, beside whose mouth David, Earl of Huntingdon, founded the important Tironensian Abbey of Lindores in the late 12th century. This had property in Dundee from the inception of that burgh, and also in Berwick by 1296. Royal charters were sometimes signed at the abbey. In 1302 the monks used wagons on a well-defined *'way'* to fetch peats from Monagrey south of Collessie. Lindores Castle, built in the 13th century, stood near the present Lindores House but later completely vanished; in the 14th century the great courtyard Castle of Ballinbreich was built on the shore 3km to the east.

**The Abbot's Burgh destroys the Abbey**: Beside the abbey grew the Ecclesiastical Burgh of Newburgh, chartered by the abbot as early as 1266, and rechartered in 1457 as a burgh of regality, whose court book of 1459 still exists; beside it is Parkhill, whose mill wheel still exists. By 1473 Abdie was almost uninhabited, and a new church was built in Newburgh where most of the parishioners lived, and a school was open by 1526. The abbey buildings were largely destroyed by a rabble of Knox's over-zealous followers in 1559, but the monks were still represented in Parliament in 1560. By 1597 the parish ran the school. Pont's map made about 1600 showed a mill at the mouth of the burn and another at Denmill, 1.5km upstream; the adjacent large 16th century tower of Denmylne Castle later became ruinous, as did Ballinbreich.

**Burghs, Gardens and Riots**: Sir Andrew Balfour who co-founded Edinburgh's famous Physic Garden was born in Newburgh in 1630. In 1631, to support the little town's privileges despite the demise of the abbey, Newburgh became a Royal Burgh. In 1687 a baronial burgh charter was granted to Dunbog, 4km east of the abbey ruins, but apart from Dunbog House – home in the 18th century of the Earls of Zetland – little development ensued. The only land route to the town at that time was a track leading over the hills to Cupar. In 1736 a proper road was planned on a similar line, and Roy's map surveyed about 1750 indicated it as a made road; Den mill still

*Newburgh linoleum works, which was started up in 1891 by the Tayside Linoleum Company. This outpost of the Fife linoleum industry closed in 1980 and has been demolished.* (JRH)

existed. In 1773 Newburgh was large enough for mobs to riot again; this time the problem was meal.

**Revival of the Port as Linen Flourishes**: Before 1780 Newburgh was described as *"a poor country village"*, its main industry being the handloom weaving of linen; John Fergus, born in Newburgh, became a key linen manufacturer in Kirkcaldy. Though there was no dock, in the 18th century flax from Dundee was landed for local use and for dispatch to Auchtermuchty. By the 1790s Newburgh quay was also used as an outport by Perth traders, whose own port had silted up. Lime, potatoes and pit props were shipped, and coal imported from as far as Sunderland. The crews of the little vessels caroused in nearly 30 alehouses! A post office opened in 1793 and a fair was scheduled for 1797, the year when a turnpike road to the south was established. Heron noted in 1799 a *"village of nearly 1600 inhabitants with some share of trade and manufactures"*. But Newburgh remained essentially a one-street town; it had a draper around 1800, and by then Abdie too had a school.

**Railway, Ships & Textiles**: Inchrye *'Abbey'*, a fine emparked house beside the loch, was built in 1827–28 for George Ramsay. Thomas Brown who died in 1882 was for 57 years the blacksmith at Grange of Lindores. Meantime by 1833, 564 looms were making linens for 13 small firms, largely from homespun yarn. About then a gasworks was set up. The Ladybank to Perth section of the Edinburgh & Northern Railway opened in 1848, climbing to surmount the hills south of Lindores Loch. Newburgh station was therefore too high up to enable a rail link to the quay, whose trade slumped; its boatyard, which built small wooden vessels of up to 260 tons, failed under Scrimgeour around 1869. In 1862 good quality sheetings were made on a similar scale to the 1830s, many pieces being bleached by John Hendry at the *'prosperous'* Clunie bleachfield. Robert Watson of the 1859 oilskin, net and buoy factory at Cellardyke later opened a branch at Newburgh; around 1870, of a population of some 3000, most were still handloom weavers, a trade in rapid decline.

**Linoleum and Rock: Newburgh in Decline**: The 1891 population was under 1700. From that year linoleum was made in Newburgh by the Tayside Linoleum Company, emulating its success at Kirkcaldy, and replacing weaving as the main industry. The Laing library was built in 1894. Up to 1914 a ferry plied across the Tay to Port Allen, for Errol, and until the 1930s pleasure steamers sailing between Perth and Dundee served a pier. The railway's passenger service was withdrawn in 1955, and the station building was left to decay; a new rail-served hard-rock quarry at Clatchard Craig above the town – replacing an earlier quarry at Mount Pleasant, 1 km to the west – helped to keep the line open for freight. Inchrye was sadly demolished in 1960, and much-altered Dunbog had largely vanished by 1980. The linoleum works closed in 1980; only the facilities of a large village remained, but the Laing library contained a local museum, while the quarry and the well-established Watsons' Fabrics continued at work. By 1988 the quay had become practically disused.

**Trains rush past the Declining Village**: In 1991 when the population barely exceeded 2000 it had an affluent retired element but twenty jobs were lost with the closure of the former Fife bus garage by its new owners, Stagecoach of Perth. The quarry was operated by Tarmac Roadstone by 1992. By 1995 though Watsons were extinct, a new factory had been built for Newburgh Clothing & Textiles Ltd. In 1998 the Tay Salmon Fishing Company, which had its office and coble-building yard in Newburgh, finally abandoned its work. There is less to be seen of the abbey than of the striking ruins of the great Castle of Ballinbreich, which stand inaccessible on the shore to the east, well seen from the scenic Tayside road to Balmerino. The village still has a primary school, bank, chemist, garages, doctors, vets, and several shops. Local campaigners want the station reopened, to catch trains to Edinburgh, Kirkcaldy, Perth and Inverness. The loch remains popular with boating anglers, and the small *George Hotel* and B&Bs offer service.

## NEW BYTH

**Map 10, B1**

***Small Buchan village,*** *pop. 400*

OS 30: NJ 8254

Gordon's map pre-1642 marked Byth, a name pronounced with a very long vowel. It stands in the eastern part of the sprawling parish of King Edward in west Aberdeenshire, shown on the Roy map of about 1750 as a roadless area of farms and watermills; *'Bieth'* House already stood among shelter-belted parkland on the headwaters of the Burn of Monquhitter *(see Cuminestown)*. New Byth was founded on a steep spur some 2.5 km to the south in 1763–64 to promote home industries, chiefly handloom weaving. It was laid out on an 'L' plan, focusing on a hilltop church, and built of red sandstone, apparently from the local quarry which had yielded the dressings for Deer Abbey. The Mill of Byth lay on the burn nearby, and it seems that windmills also turned in the area at one time.

**Rural Dominance**: Roads were built, and in 1799 Heron described New Byth as a *"rising village"*. But it rose no farther, for handloom weaving faded away and no railway came. Its people relied on local peat for fuel in 1858, when Pratt simply referred to New Byth as a *"village"*. A pub was built in 1906, and the essentially farming population was nearly 550 in 1951, but although there was a secondary class in the village school, other local facilities were minimal and much reliance was placed on Cuminestown, 4km to the south. As the resident population fell so the secondary pupils were transferred elsewhere, but garages opened; by 1981 under 400 people lived locally. By 1995 there was a small museum, and by 2000 a little new development; New Byth now has a primary school, post office, pub, coach hirer and two garages.

## NEWCASTLETON

**Map 3, B5**

***Borders village,*** *pop. 800*

OS 79: NY 4487

The 12th century Liddel Castle or *'Liddel Strength'* (now marked as *'Castle Earthworks')* was built beside the Liddel (or Liddle) Water in southern Roxburghshire, near the English border; at its gate grew a small place called Castleton, with the parish church. Early in the 13th century the massive and unusually designed stone tower of Hermitage Castle was erected on a knoll beside the Hermitage Water, a tributary 6km to the north. A variety of peel towers were built in the area, mainly in the 16th century; little remains of most of them. The ground beside the river 4km south of Liddel Castle was lower, flatter and well wooded; when Pont mapped the area around 1600, a mill turned there at Whithaugh, and several small settlements or fermtouns named *Copyhaugh* were shown on the west bank of the river, opposite Whithaugh and Greens.

**Watergate and New Village**: The Roy map made in the early 1750s showed that the woodlands had been cleared, water mills built and the Copyhaughs consolidated into the farm of Park – past which the *gait* marked *'Road to Jedburgh'* criss-crossed the Liddel Water from England to the *'Kirk of Castletown'*. No made roads existed in Liddesdale until 1792; the only bridge was a natural arch on the Black Burn above Park. A generation later, Chambers confirmed Roy's map by noting that travellers *"had to cross the Liddel twenty-four times in the course of 16 miles. The road lay rather in the river than upon its banks, or indeed simply consisted of what is called the Watergate."* A new church was built near Park Farm in 1777 and altered in 1808. Meantime in 1793 the laird – the Duke of Buccleuch – chose Park as the site for a geometrically planned weaving village on the new road and mail route between Carlisle and Jedburgh. Chambers wrote in 1827 *"the large modern village called New-Castleton consists in two long streets of neat new houses, and owes its rise to Henry Duke of Buccleuch; but it is not very prosperous"*. By about 1825 Newcastleton was served by a penny post from Langholm.

**A Love Affair with the Railway**: From 1862 Newcastleton, and the hamlet of Hermitage (where the station was named Steele Road) lay on the Border Union Railway (BU) linking Hawick to Carlisle. After the Midland Railway's Settle & Carlisle line was opened, the BU (whose new owner was the North British Railway) was named the *'Waverley Route'* as a promotional gimmick. But in 1894 Murray echoed Chambers: a *"town of two streets"*, for there had been little growth. By the mid 20th century, afforestation of huge areas to the east was in full swing, but even in 1951 Newcastleton was no more than a substantial village of under 1250 people, though there was a secondary school. The church of 1777 was closed in 1952; in 1997 it still stood, awaiting a new use. The influence of railways was waning, as was Newcastleton's limited draw as a service centre; although a livestock market still operated. Despite strong local protests, all train services were withdrawn in 1969, an aftermath of Beeching's draconian policies. (Attempts to arrange a private reopening failed and the track was soon lifted.)

**Still in the Borders – as Copshaw Holm?**: By 1981 over 25% of Newcastleton's 1951 population, its secondary school, lawyer, and cinema had gone. Local government reorganisation in 1975 left the area still uncomfortably attached to Roxburgh District in the new Borders region. By 1984 it had at least acquired a 9-hole golf course. By 1991 the shrinking village had only 813 people; it looked to Langholm (15km away) and to Carlisle for many facilities. By 1997 a quarry called Newcastleton Forest had been open for some years in Carby Hill, 3km to the south, hewing Carboniferous sandstone for building under Baird & Stevenson. A visitor centre and cycle trails exploited the forests to the east of the village, which had acquired a museum, re-using a former Congregational church. Newcastleton was by then also known as Copshaw Holm – a name seemingly corrupted from Copyhaugh. By 1999 the possible reopening of the railway as a timber carrier serving the vast forests to the east was being considered.

## NEWCRAIGHALL & Niddrie

**Map 15, D2**

***S-E. parts of Edinburgh,*** *pop. 300 (N'hall)*

OS 66: NT 3171

Niddrie Marischal, which lay near the variously named Burdiehouse, Niddrie or Brunstane Burn in the low-lying coal basin midway between Edinburgh and Musselburgh, had a quarry by 1529 and was a tiny settlement when Pont mapped the Lothians about 1600. The Niddrie Collieries were open by 1739, and Niddrie Mills – which lay where the Leith to Dalkeith road crossed the burn – were shown on the Roy map, made about 1754. Niddrie had become a recognised mining village by 1792. Newcraighall, some 1.5km to the east, was also to grow from practically nothing in the early 19th century; in 1828 its first recognised colliery acquired a steam pumping engine.

**Horse Trains and Handpumps**: The early coal-carrying Edinburgh & Dalkeith Railway (E&D) was opened through Niddrie to Craighall in 1831 using horse traction, and rapidly extended to Dalkeith; a branch line was built from Niddrie to Leith by stages between 1835 and 1838, and another to Fisherrow opened in the latter year. In 1842 another small coal pit at Newcraighall used stoop and room working, drained by a hand pump worked by an unfortunate boy aged ten! In 1846 the North British Railway (NBR) main line was opened between Edinburgh and Berwick, with a station east of Newcraighall named New Hailes (after the mansion between there and Musselburgh); in 1849 much of the former E&D disappeared under the NBR's line to Hawick, which passed just west of Newcraighall.

**Gold and Jewels in the Klondyke?**: A church was eventually built at Newcraighall in 1878. By then the Niddrie & Benhar Colliery Company was in the area; their adit mine, opened in 1897, was topically nicknamed *'The Klondyke'*. Adjoining Niddrie colliery's pit head was Niddrie Quarry (open from the 1850s), the probable source of masonry used in building the Edinburgh Dock at Leith in 1874–81. In 1895 the square of miners' rows at what is now Newcraighall Drive possessed a school, football ground and bowling green. By 1895 Jewel

Cottages adjoined Niddrie Road, and Steele Brothers & Sons made white sanitary stoneware at Niddrie in the late 19th and early 20th century, but there was little else at Niddrie except a school, and no passenger station was provided at either place. By 1902 the area was alive with steam locomotives hauling coal trucks on a spider's web of lines.

**Deep Mining at Niddrie**: In 1909 Grant Ritchie & Co of Kilmarnock made the steam winding engine for the new vertical shaft some 300m deep then being sunk at Niddrie colliery. By the 1920s this great pit employed over a thousand men producing over 250,000 tonnes a year from workings which extended 1 km out to sea. In 1925 a library, public hall and social facilities were provided. About the mid 20th century a brickworks was opened at Newcraighall (and lasted about 50 years), but New Hailes station had been closed by 1953. The Niddrie & Benhar pit was renamed Newcraighall in 1947 by the new National Coal Board; it worked until 1968. In 1981 Newcraighall had the facilities of a hamlet.

**From Mines to Multiscreen and Mega Bowl**: The A1 Musselburgh bypass was built about 1985 as a major road flying over the railway triangle between Newcraighall and Niddrie. A new road named The Jewel was soon laid out to join it with the Jewel cottages and a new park. Meanwhile ASDA had opened their first Edinburgh area store just north of Niddrie; however, this succeeded too well for its small site, and by 1988 had been moved east to a larger site where the A1 met The Jewel. By 1989 the Mega Bowl had been opened at Kinnaird Park, a new retail park north of Newcraighall Road, and by 1990 there was a twelve-screen cinema – all these facilities relying on the so-called bypass, now turned development road, to bring patrons from a wide area. The development of Brunstane Farm for new housing was started in the 1990s. By 2000 a large complex of retail stores – for some reason named Edinburgh Fort – had been opened south of Newcraighall Road. A third shopping area was built in 2001, next to Kinnaird, including a *Premier Lodge*.

## NEW CUMNOCK

**Map 2, A3**

***Large S. Ayrshire village,*** *pop. 3800* — OS 71: NS 6113

The undateable ruins of Blackcraig Castle stand where the remote Afton Water meets the headwaters of the River Nith. This may be the castle named *'Kumnock'*, marked on Timothy Pont's map of Kyle made about 1600, when there were two water mills. Though at an altitude of nearly 200 metres, the area was then well settled, and the valley south of the castle was wooded. New Cumnock formed a separate parish from 1650, but it never became a burgh of barony and had no school as late as 1735. By about that time the Bank estate (now known as Bankglen), south-west of the village, was the home of the Hyslop family.

**Mining starts with Lead and Lime**: The Roy map made about 1754 showed a hamlet, an old mill, a church, and a bridge across the Nith on what others noted as a poor road linking Cumnock with Sanquhar. A lead mine was open on the slopes of Ewe Hill above the Connel Burn. Heron noted New Cumnock in 1799 as a *"village near which are some lead-mines"*. By then the large Guelt limeworks was open on the moors 5km to the north-east. Later an antimony mine was worked, bleakly located on the hill known as The Knipe, 5km south-east of the village *(see also Langholm)*. In 1827

*The pit-head gear of the Knockshinnoch Castle Colliery, N[e]w Cumnock; the pit was sunk in 1938–42 and suffered a serious accid[ent] in 1950. Today, it is opencast operations that are used to win coal in t[he] area.* (JR

Chambers dismissed New Cumnock as *"a little village totally destitute of interest"*. By 1838 there was a post office, which survived, but the Afton ironworks of the Nithsdale Iron Company – which opened near Bank in 1845 and implied both coal and ironstone mining – soon failed.

**The Railway and Coal**: The Glasgow & South Western Railway main line served New Cumnock from 1850. Very soon a colliery had been sunk near Pathhead by Archibald Grey & Co, and the Bank of Scotland built a new branch office in New Cumnock around 1870. Meantime in the 1860s John Hyslop of Bank House built a mineral railway to open up the south side of the valley for his Bank Coal Company. This took over the failed iron company's mines, which were to last for another century; from 1871 the line served the small Afton Colliery near Straid, and also Dalleagles, 5km south-west of the village. In the 1870s the Lanemark Coal Company – set up by Hyslop's son William – built 250 prosaic houses in 8 rows at Connel Park some 2 km south-west of New Cumnock; better cottages appeared at Bank Glen and Craigbank, while 2 km farther out were Burnside and the awful Burnfoot Rows. By 1901 New Cumnock had some 2000 people, and a golf club founded in that year laid out a 9-hole course. Mergers enabled Lanemark to dominate the area's mining from 1908 as the New Cumnock Collieries Company, which also set up the Afton terra cotta brick and tile works.

**Carelessness, Tragedy, Precision and Heroic Speed**: Although the Pathhead Colliery closed in 1926, by 1931 the population had more than doubled to 4500; several pits and mineral railways were open in the area in 1933, and a large council housing estate was built around that time to enable the Rows to be cleared. The elderly Afton colliery, which raised cannel coal, had an experimental oil distillation plant around 1939, but was closed a decade later on takeover by the NCB. Meantime Knockshinnoch Castle Colliery was sunk in 1938–42 on a long-abandoned site near Connel Park. In 1950 an upwards heading in this shallow mine was incautiously extended into an area of soft peat; when this slumped into the heading 129 miners were trapped, of whom 13 died. However, a very accurate survey existed of a lately abandoned part of Bank Colliery to the west; it was found that cutting through just 7 m of rock separating passages in the two mines would quickly release the remaining 116 miners.

**The Deep Mines decline**: Meantime the Seaforth mine, sunk at South Boig during the 1939–45 war, worked only until 1953. By then the Guelt limeworks and antimony mine had closed, though a 100-bed tuberculosis hospital had been built 4 km south of the village. The *Afton Cinema* was still open up to about 1952 at Connel Park. New Cumnock was still a large village of 4500 people, with three coal pits, including a small private one at Bridgend, two hotels and a small secondary school. Bank Colliery's settlement, Bankglen, held 600 people and also offered junior secondary education, but the last Bank pit closed in 1969; by 1971 under 200 people were left there and the school closed. The area's last water mill also closed in the 1960s *(see Hay & Stell)*. Some time before the 1971 census the population of New Cumnock itself had peaked at over 5300, but all the remaining mines were then rapidly closed. By 1981 its character was disadvantaged and its population had fallen below 4700, with the facilities of a typical village.

**Coal goes opencast**: The new Knockshinnoch coal treatment plant was opened in 1983 (on the site of the former Connel Park colliery), and a new rail loading point for coal was opened in 1985 on the site of the ill-fated Castle Pit's washery. By 1986 large-scale opencasting, particularly south of the B741 Dalmellington road, had replaced the deep mines. The opencast activities, though horrendous in their impact on the local environment, provided some jobs and eliminated some earlier mining dereliction. By 1986 a pleasant-looking hotel was among the good social facilities available in the village, essential if people were to continue to live in this bleak and isolated area. The old Dalleagles school had found a use under the opencasting contractor Derek Crouch, and the nearby *Heather Restaurant* catered more for the workers than for the few remaining residents in the Burnside cottages and at Bankglen. By 1986 the industrial estate had attracted only one firm – an agricultural merchant. By 1991 the population was just under 4000. An inn and two post offices were still open in the village and there was even a tourist office, since at Lochside, 2 km to the west, was another hotel, and near it a caravan site.

**Coal, Trains, Tourists and Wind Power**: Coal was still moved by rail via Ayr to Northern Ireland's power stations, but government-induced competition turned them to imported coal and by late 1992 the coal loading point was disused. In 1996 the new private rail freight operators EWS recommenced coal haulage from Knockshinnoch, supplying Longannet power station with three to four daily trainloads. The rail passenger station which was experimentally reopened in 1991 still enjoys eight or nine weekday trains each way, to and from Kilmarnock and Carlisle. In 1999 a government grant was given to LAW Mining of Hamilton to construct a coal loading terminal and sidings at New Cumnock; the coal might originate at Knockshinnoch. Late in 2000 Scottish Power erected 20 aerogenerators on Hare Hill, 5 km south-east of New Cumnock, to produce 13 mW, forming the UK's first unsubsidised wind farm.

## NEW DEER & Auchreddie

**Map 10, C2**

***Buchan village**, pop. 630*

OS 30: NJ 8847

In the remote uplands 10 km west of the parish centre of Old Deer was a stone circle. One of many in Buchan, it stood at Culsh above the South Ugie Water; 4 km to the south there were other standing stones. By about 1600 as Pont's map of Buchan showed, *'Mekle Achredy'* and *'Achredy'* already lay in the small valley between these mysterious monuments. In 1620 a church was built close by, and a new parish created, by the Earl Marischal and other proprietors. In 1720 it was referred to as *"Auchreddy, <u>alias</u> New Deer"*. The latter name appeared on the Roy survey of about 1750, when it was the terminus of a track (now an unclassified road) extending northwards from Tanglandford on the River Ythan. From a point just south of New Deer a branch track led towards Fyvie, but reached only to Millbrex some 7 km to the west, passing Cairnbanno where illicit whisky was distilled; otherwise the area was trackless. By 1797 three annual fairs were scheduled at New Deer, and two years later, Heron referred to it as a *"village"*; it had been laid out by James Ferguson of Pitfour. Metalled roads were constructed and a bridge was built at Cairnbanno about 1800. New Deer was expanded in 1805, its main street on the crest of a spur; a mill was established, and its first post office opened around 1825.

**Consolidation and Slow Decline**: In 1858 Pratt described New Deer as *"a long straggling place with about 100 houses, a school, several inns, and a few tolerably good shops and houses"*. It was never raised to burgh status, had only 750 inhabitants in 1891 and was connected with the railways in the early 20th century by horse-drawn coaches running between Maud and Turriff. It had grown into a substantial village of nearly 1000 people by 1951, when secondary education, ironmongery and veterinary services were among those available. Despite some population decline, its village facilities still served about 3000 people in a wider area in 1981. Only 633 village residents were counted in 1991, but an agricultural show was still being staged in 1995. Two churches are now redundant; active facilities include a primary school, garage, bank, post office, health centre, and veterinary practice – plus a handful of shops and two pubs.

## NEW GALLOWAY & Balmaclellan

**Map 2, A4**

***Galloway villages**, pop. 700 (area)*

OS 77: NX 6377

The Water of Ken gives its name to the hilly Glenkens area of the Stewartry; east of the river is Balmaclellan, with a standing stone and a medieval motte. Some 3 km to the south-west, at the head of the Loch of Kenmure, is the 16th century moated tower of Kenmure Castle, a property of the Gordons from 1297. Timothy Pont's map made about 1610 showed this as a major emparked feature. Some 2 km to the north stood the Kirk of Kells parish, and *'North Fintilloch'* (Fintloch Farm); across the river was Balmaclellan Kirk. The Glenkens, where Gaelic was spoken into the mid 18th century, were sparsely settled. New Galloway, sited between Kenmure Castle and Kells Kirk, became a Royal Burgh in 1629–30; it was chartered as a market centre to serve the Glenkens, despite opposition from Kirkcudbright some 27 km to the south. The L-plan tower of Barscobe Castle was built about 2 km north-east of Balmaclellan in 1648 for William Maclellan of Bombie. New Galloway had a post office from 1705.

**Young Teacher Heron and the Statistical Account**: Roy's survey – made about 1754 – showed a compact place with roads south to Kirkcudbright, and west to Newton Stewart across the Bridge of Dee at Clatteringshaws. Eastwards the Water of Ken was not yet bridged, merely a *'boathouse'* being shown – implying a ferry – on the road to Moniaive via the hamlet of Balmaclellan. Only a track led northwards to Carsphairn. Robert Heron, a weaver's son born in New Galloway in 1764, was so bright that he became the parish schoolmaster in 1773 at the age of 14. He later attended Edinburgh University and aided Sir John Sinclair in producing the famous *First Statistical Account* of Scotland. Though luckless, his prolific writings included *Scotland Delineated*, from which many comments in this volume are drawn. By 1780 a bark mill for tanning was at work at New Galloway, which had a new post office from 1792; in 1797 it had three deliveries a week through Castle Douglas. There were also to be three fair days that year, and the Ken had been spanned by what Heron called in 1799 a *"fine bridge"*, but he wrote *"New Galloway is a small inland town, entirely destitute of trade"*.

**Stagnation, Golf and Hydro Electricity**: A new Ken bridge was built in 1820–21 to designs by John Rennie. In 1821 the population was only some 500, and Chambers wrote in 1827 *"the little burgh of New Galloway is the most deplorable of all Scottish Burghs, except perhaps Dornoch"*. Kenmure Castle was fully remodelled as a mansion about 1880. No railway ever approached nearer than 8 km. The population declined to about 400 people by 1891, when the Royal Burgh was described as *"a village"*. New Galloway golf club, founded in 1902, laid out a 9-hole course. The Glenlee generating station was built from 1933 4 km north-west of the village as part of the pioneering Galloway hydro-electric scheme. Although most of the modernised Kenmure Castle was demolished in 1950, a square ruin was left. By then New Galloway possessed the facilities of a typical village, for a mere 300 people. The village population then stabilised, a new primary school was built, and by 1972 there were four little hotels.

**Struggling to Survive**: Like all historic local government units the tiny town council, which had built just 16 houses, was abolished in 1975. Continuing rural depopulation in the surrounding area, where afforestation continued to encroach on hill farming, had seriously affected New Galloway's role as a village shopping and service centre. Kells parish had 713 people in 1991. The regional council's microscopic industrial estate may have helped these small remote communities to stay above the margin for survival: both New Galloway and Balmaclellan post offices are still open, golf continues with 9 holes, and there's the 12-roomed *Kenmure Arms Hotel*.

## NEWHOUSE & Legbranock

**Map 16, A4**

***Lanarkshire ind. estate***

OS 64: NS 7961

Pont's map of 1596 named many tiny settlements in the far east of Bothwell parish, among them *'Lekbranok'*, but there was no evidence of mills or bridges nearby. Roy's map made about 1754 also showed little of note in the area save a hamlet at Legbranock, and the intersection (just to the east) of the road from Glasgow and Hamilton to Edinburgh via Kirk of Shotts, with the Airdrie to Carluke road. Under an Act of 1753, the main roads were turnpiked, and Newhouse was built at their junction – perhaps originating as an inn. By the 1790s the Legbranock colliery was certainly active; this was literally a coalfield, apparently a number of shallow pits south of the Glasgow road. Legbranock remained no more than a hamlet, notable as the birthplace in 1856 of James Keir Hardie, a mineworker from the age of ten, who became the founder of the Independent Labour Party and a leading Socialist MP *(see Cumnock)*. Little development occurred until in 1888 a sinuous branch of the Caledonian Railway was opened from Cleland to Airdrie via Calderbank. This enabled several other small pits linked by mineral lines to come into production in the area by 1895, when Newhouse had a passenger station, a smithy and an inn.

**The Newhouse Industrial Estate**: The new A8 trunk road direct from Newhouse to Glasgow was constructed in the 1920s, and was a factor in locating the large SIEC industrial estate 2 km west of Newhouse, established in the late 1930s under the Special Areas Acts, to offset unemployment in the mining and metals industries in the several major urban areas in the vicinity. A hotel was built in 1938 at what had become a six-way road junction; but with ample surrounding labour to draw upon, Newhouse never needed to develop into a village. The estate gained such branch factories as Viyella, Miller cycle accessories, and most importantly the US firm of Honeywell Control Systems, which by 1972 employed 4600 people. The station was closed before 1953, mining in the area was extinct by the mid 1950s, and the railway vanished in the 1960s.

**Chemicals, Motorway, Earth Movers, and Electronics**: From about 1960 Organon Laboratories made fine chemicals, and from about 1970 the area was served by an interchange at the point where the A8 made an end-on junction with the new M8 motorway to Edinburgh. By 1979 Terex Engineering (started at Newhouse in 1950) was owned by General Motors, and made earth-moving machinery and trucks. In 1979 Honeywell took over an SDA factory, to enlarge their local capacity to make electronic process-control instruments, providing a further 125 jobs (750 in total in 2001). The medium-sized NUB Engineering, which made earth boring augers, was established about 1980.

**Shopping Schemes and Pharmaceutical Research**: Terex reached a peak in 1990, employing 1000 people, but as recession bit early in 1991 the firm put its remaining 700 workers on short time, cutting 64 more jobs in depressed 1992, when NUB also made many of its workers redundant. A planning application to build a giant shopping centre at Newhouse was rejected in 1989 for its *'overkill'* intentions, and again refused in 1993. Yet another big scheme proposed in 1994 would include shops, cinemas, ten-pin bowling and restaurants. In 1994 Akzo Pharma of Holland owned the prominent Organon Research Laboratories, whose 250 workers included a remarkable 80 researchers; its prime product, locally researched, was *Pavulon*, a muscle relaxant for surgery. Organon is to recruit another 100 or more workers from 2000. By then the large warehouses of W H Malcolm stood opposite.

**Taiwan brings more Work**: An adjacent 80 ha greenfield site beside the A8 at Newhouse West/Mossend *(nominally in Bellshill)* became part of the Lanarkshire Enterprise Zone, where in the mid 1990s the Lanarkshire Development Agency and others secured the building of the Chunghwa Picture Tubes factory. This huge Taiwanese venture aimed to employ 3000 people; site work was begun in 1996, including providing a new overpass junction on the A8, and the vast building with its striking triple sculpture, the *'Big Heids'* by Scotsman David Mach, was complete by 2000. Another Taiwanese firm, Lite-On, was building alongside, wishing to employ 1000 people making TV monitors (but the lights soon went out); and a third, Allied Precision, hoped to offer 200 jobs making components for Chunghwa (who now employ 900). Terex now employ 600, and make 1200 heavy vehicles a year.

## NEWINGTON, Sciennes & Cameron Toll

**Map 15, C2**

***S-E. parts of Edinburgh,*** *pop. 27,500*

OS 66: NT 2671

Priestfield, east of Edinburgh and south of Holyrood Park, was a monastic establishment in the 14th century. Nearer the city, part of the one-time Sciennes brewery beside the convent of Sciennes was possibly built as early as 1430. Both Sciennes and Priestfield were among many names shown on Pont's map of the Lothians around 1600; Sciennes was spelt as it was said, *'Shean'*. Causewayside already led south from Edinburgh to Dalkeith and Lasswade, passing the emparked mansionhouse of Grange, and crossing the Braid Burn; the name Blackford was placed well north of the burn. In 1681 Priestfield was burnt down, but rebuilt in 1687 for the Dick family as the small mansion of Prestonfield House. By the time of the Roy survey about 1754, the Dalkeith Road had also appeared, and turnpiking created Cameron Toll.

**Industry at Sciennes and the Dalkeith Railway**: Bertrams – two brothers – started in engineering at Sciennes in 1821 and began to make papermaking machinery in 1862; James Bertram & Son *(see Leith)* were engineering relatives. By 1825 James Kerr was brewing at East Sciennes; feuing for villas in the area began in earnest in 1827. The Edinburgh & Dalkeith (E&D) Railway which was opened in 1831 to a terminus at St Leonards was approached through a 523 m-long tunnel on a steep gradient of 1 in 30. Coal trains carrying 300 tonnes a day were drawn by horses to the foot of the incline and hauled up to St Leonards by a stationary engine built by Carmichaels of Dundee. The E&D also served limestone quarries, and carried passengers until 1847. Urban growth soon moved south of the narrow neck of developable land where Holyrood Park most closely approached The Meadows. Newington post office was open by 1839; in 1844 John Millar set up a confectionery business (still going today).

**Usher the Brewer, Distiller and Pioneer Blender**: In 1849 the Sciennes brewery passed to the firm of Andrew Usher, who was born in 1826. In 1860 he bought the so-called *'Glen Sciennes'*(!) pot distillery of Duncanson & Co and renamed it the Edinburgh Lowland Malt distillery. He is supposed to have founded the modern blending industry, by adding grain whisky to make the premium product go further; this was done in a large bonded warehouse beside Holyrood Park. By 1867 the St Leonards Brewery was at work and by 1886 nearby maltings

*Nelsons' printworks at Parkside, Newington, built in the 1880s; they disappeared in the 1970s to be replaced by Scottish Widows' brown glass building. The Nelson family of printers and publishers were significant public benefactors, providing branch libraries in several parts of Edinburgh.* *(RCAHMS / JRH)*

served Usher's distillery, which then used water from the Pentland Hills. Its 25 workers produced about 600,000 litres of Lowland malt whisky annually. The Longmore Hospital for Incurables off Causewayside was built in 1878–80 to designs by M Dick Peddie. From the 1880s Thomas Nelson had printing works at Parkside.

**Railway, Cable Trams and Golf**: In 1884 a station named *'Newington'* was opened on the circuitous Edinburgh Suburban & South Side Junction Railway; it was west of the street named Craigmillar Park, and drew development south of Grange Loan. Rails laid on Nicolson Street by 1886 carried a slow cable tram service. In 1900 this was extended to Nether Liberton, requiring a single cable over 10km long! Meantime St Margaret's School for girls was established in 1890, and by 1894 the Royal Observatory had also been built on Blackford Hill; the move from Calton Hill in central Edinburgh was completed in 1896. 1896 also saw the founding of the Craigmillar Park golf club – at Blackford, nearly 3km west of the ancient castle – followed in 1920 by the Prestonfield club. Ushers' Edinburgh Lowland Malt distillery was acquired in 1919 by Scottish Malt Distillers.

**Electric Tramways, Maps – and the Real St Trinians**: Newington grew quickly after electrification was installed along the main tramway route via Minto Street to Liberton in 1922, with the development of a school for the blind. The independent yet free and easy St Trinneans School for girls at Park Road really DID exist, from 1922 to 1946; it was cartoonist Ronald Searle – who met and drew inspiration from some of its uninhibited pupils – who spelt it St Trinians. Another development (in Duncan Street) was Bartholomew's Edinburgh Geographical Institute – the famed cartographers and publishers of maps and books, including from the 1920s the prestigious *Times Atlas*.

**University Buildings**: By 1930 development had reached south-west to Blackford. The St Leonards brewery was still working in 1933 when owned by Mackay's. Edinburgh University's southwards expansion made a large impact in Newington, particularly the great new 1930s science campus at King's Buildings. In 1951 about 21,000 people lived in the area, which had acquired the facilities of a town, and also one of Scotland's very few synagogues. Buses replaced the trams about 1956, and the suburban circle passenger trains were withdrawn in 1962. The one-time E&D railway was dismantled about 1970; it soon became a walkway to Duddingston Loch, with the tunnel section reopened in the 1990s.

**Swimming, Insurance, Geology and Farm Research**: The Royal Commonwealth Pool was opened in the early 1960s for the 1964 Commonwealth Games, and around 1970 Edinburgh University's Pollok Halls of Residence replaced St Trinneans School; soon came the erection of the remarkable headquarters of Scottish Widows insurance, faced in dark brown glass. In the early 1970s Murchison House, the office of the British Geological Survey, was erected beside King's Buildings. Next door at West Mains Road was built the Scottish Agricultural College, which claimed in 1993 to be the HQ of the UK's largest educational centre for food, land and environment.

**Hotels and Cameron Toll Shopping**: By 1977 *Prestonfield House* was a 5-roomed hotel, later much extended. By 1981 the resident population of the area had fallen to about 18,000, partly through such conversions of large houses to hotels, of which no fewer than 37 were then open in Newington. Bertrams absorbed James Bertram & Son of Leith in the 1950s; the firm also had an iron foundry in Gorgie. Their Sciennes works, by then out of place in the area, was closed in the 1980s, soon replaced by flats. Around 1980 Newington parish church was converted into the Queen's Hall, for concerts. The large Cameron Toll shopping centre of some 12,000m² which opened at the south end of Newington in 1984 greatly added to car traffic in the area, the drivers mainly seeking its *Savacentre* complex, which dominated the food trade throughout southern Edinburgh. Until then Newington had for many years been demarcated from Edinburgh by long-neglected ruins at St Patrick Square – extraordinary neglect in a tourist-oriented city! But in 1988 flats and shops were built there.

**The National Library, Health and History**: The first stage of the National Library of Scotland's new (interestingly designed) annexe at Causewayside was built in 1987–88 and the second in 1991–92. By 1990 the Royal Observatory drew between 15,000 and 20,000 visitors a year. In 1993 the Lothian College of Nursing and Midwifery was based at Chalmers Crescent near the long-standing Royal Hospital for Sick Children in Sciennes. The Longmore Hospital was closed in 1991 and had been converted by 1995 into headquarters offices for Historic Scotland. St Margaret's was an independent all-age girls' day and boarding school with 720 pupils in 1994.

**Bartholomew's falls prey to Murdoch**: Bartholomew's famous map-making establishment, until the late 1970s a family business, had been acquired by 1990 by Harper Collins of Bishopbriggs. As their Cartographic Division it operated from Duncan Street until 1995, when its highly skilled staff were moved to Bishopbriggs *(q.v.)*. Dozens of small hotels and guest houses dominate the main road south; the University provides 180 rooms during vacations at its Pollock Halls.

## NEW LANARK

**Map 2, B2**

***Village s. of Lanark**, pop. 250* — OS 71 or 72: NS 8842

In the 18th century the multiple linns or waterfalls in the gorge of the River Clyde 1km south of the town of Lanark were on the Grand Tour; the Bonnington and Corra Linns were described a century later as *"the finest south of Foyers"*. In 1784 Richard Arkwright, badly affronted by Lancashire mill owners over the patent rights to his spinning machine, joined David Dale to promote a rival cotton industry in Scotland. Influenced by the views of many cultured visitors to the falls, they decided to locate their new mill on the narrow floor of the steep-sided valley to exploit the water power of Dundaff Linn. Building began in 1785 and spinning apparently started in 1786; the Number Two mill was built upstream of the first in 1788–89. A weir across the river diverted water into a lade massively built in stone; Bremner noted that it was in 1790 that the little-known engineer, Kelly of Lanark Mills *"applied water power to work the mill"*, using possibly the world's first bevel gearing (Shaw). About then 300 emigrating Highlanders, stormbound aboard the ship *Fortune*, were persuaded by Dale to come instead to work at the New Lanark cotton mills; for them he had the Caithness Row houses built, and also provided a school of sorts. By 1799 two more numbered mills had been built just upstream; all had six storeys. New Lanark then

*Mills and housing at New Lanark, established on the R. Clyde by Dale and Arkwright in 1785. It became renowned for its experiments in benign social conditions. Today it is nominated as a World Heritage site.* *(JRH)*

comprised the largest complex of cotton mills in Scotland and according to Heron had *"upwards of 1500 inhabitants"*.

**Robert Owen's Enlightenment**: In 1800 Dale's son-in-law Robert Owen took over the complex, where over 1300 people were then employed, 500 of whom were children taken from poor-houses – some as young as five years – working a 13-hour day. He saw how this injured them and took highly enlightened steps to improve matters, establishing proper schools for all the children between 3 and 10 years of age. The usually acute Dorothy Wordsworth ignored such matters, writing in 1803 that New Lanark mills were *"the largest and loftiest"* she had ever seen. *"The Falls of Clyde were shut up in a gentleman's grounds, and to be viewed only by means of lock and key"*. Owen soon extended the famous model village and built his educational institutions on the slopes above the mills; the village store was erected in 1813. In 1816 Robert Owen employed about 1650 of the 2300 people living in New Lanark, including children from the age of ten upwards, actually working 10 hours 45 minutes of the 12 hour working day. He wished to raise the entry age for full-time work to twelve, giving half-time schooling to those of 10–12, but he admitted that to pay for the schooling, their wages had to be much lower.

**Chambers finds Contentment**: Number Three mill burned down in 1819 *(see Hay & Stell)*. In 1820 the population of the new village was 2400, of whom 1700 were employed in the remaining mills; by 1826 these had their own foundry and gasworks. In 1827 Chambers found about 2000 workers, still under the direction of Robert Owen – *"so remarkable for his fantastic projects in regard to the domestic polity of mankind"*. Cloth was sold to the workers, who seemed a contented bunch, the profits being used to educate their children. Having earned at New Lanark the title of *"the visionary socialist"* (Murray 1894), Owen left for a socio-political career in the USA.

**Four Mills and 2000 Workers fascinate Cobbett**: By the time that the social reformer Cobbett visited New Lanark in 1832 the water-powered mills were managed by Walkers, and the falls were again accessible. He described New Lanark as *"the most interesting spot that I ever set my foot upon in the course of my long and rambling life; the people all bespoke cleanliness and well being; all savoured of the Quaker"*. At that time about 1400 people lived there, and the school was still open, though with segregated classes. The workforce peaked at about 2500, and New Lanark was still thriving in 1869. In 1881 a 650hp steam engine by Petrie of Rochdale was installed at New Lanark. Activities then and later included net- and canvas-making, as well as spinning and weaving from raw cotton to finished product; nets were also made there during the 1914–18 war.

**Hydro-Electricity and the New Lanark Association**: Two hydro-electric stations were built on the Clyde nearby in 1926–27, cutting the flow over the various falls (nowadays Corra Linn is permitted to flow in full spate only twice a year, as a tourist spectacle). In 1945 two storeys were removed from No.1 mill for safety; the steam engine was scrapped in the

1950s. The New Lanark Association was formed in 1963 to restore the housing, but only 350 workers remained when the decision was made to close the mills in 1968. By 1974 the population was down to about 45, and about then parts of the mills were used by Metal Extractions, recoverers of scrap aluminium. From 1974 unassuming Harry Smith, the last Provost of Lanark, chaired the New Lanark Conservation Trust which set out to reclaim this World Heritage site, ably assisted over the next quarter century by the energetic and forward-looking political historian Jim Arnold.

**The Prizewinning Conservation of New Lanark**: Conservation of the whole historic mill village was begun in 1974. By the late 1980s the foundry and dyeworks were used as an award-winning interpretation centre, the Edinburgh Woollen Mill had opened their largest Scottish store, and some small industries used other parts of the old mills. A large woollen spinning mule was rescued from the Ettrick & Yarrow Mill in Selkirk and installed in No.3 mill about 1989; it was still in commercial use in 1997. A replacement antique steam engine – a 250 horsepower compound by the same makers – was rescued from a mill at Philiphaugh, Selkirk, and around 1990 was installed in the engine house atop a new electricity substation; though it still lacked a boiler in 1997. By 1991, when awarded top prize by the British Tourist Authority, 260,000 visitors came annually to see the best-preserved early cotton spinning village in Britain.

**Youth Hostel and Passing Attractions**: During 1992–94 a comfortable 60-bed youth hostel was created from a block of cottages. By 1995 the former Number 4 Mill's Great Wheel had also been replaced for display by a wheel from a Kirkcaldy flint-grinding mill. New attractions included knitwear and tourist shops, a collection of 40 *'classic'* cars, and an extensive model railway representing the range of Scottish scenery. But by 1997 the classic car museum in No.2 mill had closed, its exhibits moved to Alexandria *(q.v.)*, and the model railway had also been removed, sold profitably to a millionaire for his own enjoyment. By then about 225 people lived in the village, both housing association tenants and owner-occupiers.

**The New Lanark Mill Hotel**: From 1991 the Conservation Trust created a new hotel, half funded by ERDF grants, within the shell of Number 1 Mill, which was reconstructed to its original height of six floors, and powered by a 380kW generator designed by Edinburgh Hydro Systems, driven by a Boving turbine in the basement of Mill Three. Opened in 1998 as the 20-room *New Lanark Mill Hotel*, it is run by a Trust subsidiary and associated for training purposes with Motherwell College. The youth hostel is open for 10 months of the year. Further leisure and educational plans are in hand.

## NEW LEEDS — **Map 10, C1**

***Aberdeenshire hamlet,*** *pop. 150* — OS 30: NJ 9954

In the 17th century the moorland area 13km south of Fraserburgh held little settlement except a few farms, shown on Robert Gordon's map. Roy's map of about 1750 simply indicated a track linking Old Deer with Rathen and Fraserburgh. New Leeds, which was founded in 1798 beside the lately turnpiked road, never came to much. The industries that were started at New Leeds failed, the post office was late in coming, and in 1858 Pratt passed by the *"straggling and miserable-looking village"*. The railways found it of no interest, and Murray's comprehensive Guide for 1894 ignored the place. Its primary school was closed around 1960, and continuing agricultural job losses cut the population of 300 by 40% between 1951 and 1981. There has been little new development for a century, and by 1995 even the post office had closed.

## NEW LUCE & Glenwhilly — **Map 1, B4**

***Galloway hamlets,*** *pop. 200* — OS 82: NX 1764

Ancient hut circles and cairns surround the meeting of the Cross and Main Waters of Luce on the moors of the Galloway Rhinns, some 6km north of Luce (or Glenluce) Abbey. Timothy Pont's map of about 1610 showed Knockibae, Mill of Larg – whose weir alone survives – and Galdenoch; New Luce which lies near the confluence seems to have been founded a few years later; it had a minister by 1659. The Roy map made about 1754 showed the *'New Kirk of Luce'* on a road linking Glenluce with Barr in Carrick, and tracks to Castle Kennedy and to App from the Main Water bridge. Heron writing in 1799 described New Luce as a *"village"*, but did not mention the little-known Knockiebae Lead Mines, which were active at some period in the hills 2 km north-east of the village; late 19th century maps showed a *'Minehouse'*.

**Decline On and Beside the Rails**: The hilly single-track Girvan & Portpatrick Junction Railway passed down the valley, crossing the Main Water of Luce by a 12-arched stone viaduct and opening in 1877 with passing stations at New Luce and remote Glenwhilly, 8km farther north; the local children found the few trains a great attraction as late as 1950, when the author rode that way as a young conscript. By 1951 lead mining had ceased but New Luce had a school, post office and inn to serve a scattered population of about 300, and Glenwhilly had a post office for 125 people. In 1965 the station was closed, and New Luce primary school had closed by 1977. About then the population stabilised at around 200, and despite New Luce being 2 km off the Southern Upland Way, a camp site had been provided. The inn remains open, but the post office has recently closed.

## NEWMACHAR (or Summerhill) — **Map 10, C3**

***Aberdeenshire village,*** *pop. 1500+* — OS 38: NJ 8819

The long narrow parish of New Machar lies north-west of Old Aberdeen (Old Machar); New Machar Kirk, some 12 km from the cathedral, was named on Gordon's map of about 1640. The Roy map made about 1750 showed a hamlet around the *'New Kirk'*, which stood beside a track linking Old Aberdeen with Old Meldrum. Two mills turned north-west of the kirk, and beyond them was the mansion of Straloch in its park. New Machar station on the Formartine & Buchan Railway, later the Buchan branch of the Great North of Scotland, was opened in 1861 just north of the kirkton. This was known as Summerhill in 1894, when it had a post office, inn and smithy. Later known as Newmachar, it grew appreciably as a result of the opening in 1904 of the extensive Kingseat Hospital for mental illness, 2 km to the east. The hospital had 760 patients in the 1950s when Newmachar had a population of about 800 and the facilities of a small village, plus a vet and a small secondary school. It thus formed a significant though rather weak local focus for some 3000 people. But Beeching closed the station to passengers in 1965, secondary school classes were abandoned, and a 10% dip in population took place to 1971. The railway was closed altogether in 1979; Kingseat Hospital then still had 750 beds.

**Golf blossoms, Windpower rejected and Kingseat closed**: By then the rapid building of housing estates was in progress east and west of the village, to serve the exploding industrial complex around Aberdeen Airport some 7 km to the south *(see Dyce)*. By 1991, 1504 people lived in Newmachar, giving it a dormitory character. The Newmachar Golf Club appointed its first professional in 1991 and formed a difficult 18-hole course in the pine and birch forest at Hawkshill, 3 km south of the village; a 12-bay driving range was added in 1995 and there is now a second 18-hole course. In 1993 Grampian Windpower proposed to erect a wind farm at Wardhill, 4 km east of Newmachar; this scheme was rejected by Gordon District Council. On the closure of Kingseat in 1995 all psycho-geriatric services and its last 120 patients were transferred to the Royal Cornhill Hospital at Kittybrewster. In 1997 Grampian Health Care Trust proposed to build there 500 houses, a school and business development. The former railway route is now a footpath, the *'Formartine & Buchan Way'*.

## NEWMAINS — Map 16, B4

***Lanarkshire small town,*** *pop. 5800* — OS 65 or 72: NS 8256

Pont's map of Lanarkshire dated 1596 marked a bridge across the South Calder Water just below the confluence of the Auchter Water, and near two symbols for Crindledykes. The Auchter was bridged nearby at *'Bridgend'* (nowadays called Bonkle), and to the south was *'Moruinsyid'* (Morningside) and *'Watstoun Chappell'*. By the mid 18th century there were already roads in the Coltness estate beside the Auchter Water: at Hainshaw the Carluke to Airdrie road met another leading past the then new Cambusnethan Kirk to the ferry for Hamilton. By about 1833 the local lairds the Houldsworths, who had recently bought the Coltness estate, had sunk the Chapel Colliery beside the Auchter Water. In that year the Wishaw & Coltness Railway was opened, connecting the colliery with the Monklands system near Coatbridge, and so with Glasgow.

**Iron, and Ribbon Development**: The Coltness Iron Company's works was opened near the colliery in 1836; the substantial village of Newmains grew around Hainshaw, which by then had become a crossroads. A passenger station was soon established there, becoming surrounded by a web of mineral lines serving other collieries. Newmains was soon joined with Cambusnethan by a ribbon of roadside development, and the latter was similarly linked with Wishaw. In 1864 Morningside and Chapel Colliery were linked by rail with Bathgate by the Wilsontown, Morningside & Coltness Railway, later part of the North British. By 1891 perhaps 3000 people lived at Newmains, still enmeshed by mineral railways; besides its railway station there was a post and telegraph office, while Morningside was a hamlet with another station and post office. Murdostoun Castle 1 km north, was an emparked mansion.

**Change Trams for Glasgow**: The Lanarkshire Tramways Company's electric trams terminated at Newmains in the early 20th century, connecting to Motherwell, Hamilton and – by changing at Uddingston – to Glasgow. In the same period extensive housing estates were built north and east of the crossroads. Although in 1911 the Coltness Iron Company sank the Blairhall Colliery in Fife *(see Oakley)*, and remained its proprietors in 1946, iron making ceased in the 1920s, and the Coltness works were reduced to steel founding until closure in 1953. By then Newmains was a grim industrial settlement of over 7600 people, but with only the general facilities of a small village, plus a secondary school. The site of the ironworks became Costain's Coltness concrete products factory, making concrete railway sleepers.

**Cars and Coal**: By 1963 the Chapel Colliery was derelict, the trams had vanished and by 1971 the railway eastwards from Morningside had been severed beyond Allanton. In the early 1970s the A71 was largely diverted onto a new bypass. The secondary school had gone by 1976, although in some respects the facilities of the village had improved as its population had slowly declined, and woodlands had taken over some of the surrounding dereliction. By 1987 a new wasteland of opencast mine workings had largely replaced the woodlands between Newmains and Waterloo; by 1991 the population was 5878. By then Newmains had the extensive motor auction premises of the big ADT Group – in 1995 one of their three Scottish centres. Costain Dow-Mac Concrete shed 70 jobs in 1992, but in 1994 the works pre-cast the 68-tonne 36 m-long concrete beams to form a bridge on the M8 Edinburgh extension. About 400,000 tonnes of coal for Longannet power station are being raised from a new rail-connected opencast site, opened in 2000 at Watsonhead south-east of Morningside.

## NEWMILNS & Greenholm — Map 1, C1

***Large Ayrshire village,*** *pop: 3400* — OS 70: NS 5337

In 1491 the Campbell Earl of Loudoun, who was also Sheriff of Ayr, founded Newmilns beside the River Irvine 3 km east of Loudoun castle as a burgh of barony, probably to promote corn milling using the power of its steep headwaters. The success of milling enabled a later Earl to build Newmilns Tower about 1586, and when Pont mapped the area around 1600 there was also a bridge to Greenholm. From 1601 there was a parish school. Newmilns gained a post office in 1642 on the Edinburgh–Portpatrick–Ireland route. In the 1750s the Roy map showed Newmilns as a medium-sized linear settlement following the only road down the valley. Muslin weaving grew rapidly from the late 18th century; in 1799 Heron noted Newmilns as a *"manufacturing village"* with 260 weavers. The Loudon mill harnessed the power of the river to textile production, soon followed by Pate's (or in Ramsay's song *Patie's*) mill a short way downstream. In the early 19th century J Hood made Jacquard hand looms in Newmilns. Five fairs were held annually in the period 1797–1811.

**Curtain Weavers, Railway and Lace**: By about 1825 Newmilns was served by a penny post from Kilmarnock. Chambers wrote in 1827 of a *"considerable"* town, containing 700 weavers, who later specialised in making curtain fabrics. There was an inn by 1832, when Cobbett visited Newmilns, which he found a *"little and most beautifully situated manufacturing town"*. In 1850 Newmilns became the terminus of a Glasgow & South Western Railway branch line from Kilmarnock. Police burgh status was attained in 1872 as *'Newmilns & Greenholm'*. Specialisation in curtains led to lace making, which emerged in 1877 with Alexander Morton's two factories; three more were built in the next decade, as it was found possible to undercut the Nottingham lace industry. The population in 1891 was 3700. In 1894 Murray called Newmilns *"a small manufacturing town, noted for its fine muslins"*. In 1896 the railway was extended east to Darvel, and further factories for lace and muslins were built in 1897, 1898, 1904–5 (two), 1908, and finally at the outbreak of the 1914 war. The

*Lace-making machinery at Newmilns, an industry which started up in the area in the 1870s. There are still at least 4 firms operating in the trade today.* *(RCAHMS / JRH)*

prominent Co-op department store was built in 1900, and a library service started soon after.

**Lace starts to Decline**: By 1948 there were thirteen lace-making factories in Newmilns, mainly very small. McLelland Jamieson made lace up to 137 cm wide in the 1950s. Some made a fancy muslin called *'Madras'*. By then although there were 4300 people, Newmilns was still just a large village in terms of facilities. The railway was closed to passengers by Beeching in 1964 and had vanished by 1972. Newmilns' local newspaper, secondary school and employment office had also closed by 1976, with the loss of some 20% of the population in 30 years. By then one mill was used by the delightfully named *Vesuvius Crucible Company* to manufacture crucibles and refractories. In 1976 Newmilns was reasonably well kept and had a new junior school. It had a local office of the Lace & Textile Workers' Union; there was also a dairy. The wee *Rex Cinema* gave four showings a week; there were three small hotels, including the traditional *Loudoun Arms Inn*, two pubs, a library, three clubs, and a bowling club. Some 33 shops catered mainly for basic needs, but clothing, footwear, sports goods and furniture could be bought, and some 20 services were open, including banks. Three garages allowed for a degree of mobility unknown when the railway provided the main access to the valley.

**Lace Survives and Skiing Thrives**: Around 1981 the Greenholm Factory of Haddow Aird & Crerar (HA&C) still made traditionally designed lace, curtains and bedspreads using modern yarns. Seven other lace and Madras manufacturers were also still active: the large factory of Hood Morton, Jamieson Anderson, Johnston Shields' Vale Lace Mills, Morton Young & Borland, A J Muir, J Muir, and J & J Wilson's Greenhead Mills. Light engineering had recently been established. By 1985 a dry ski slope had been laid out; this was one of only two in depressed Strathclyde in 1990, at a time when eleven were available elsewhere in Scotland. In 1991, when the population was still about 3400, M W Wilson of Newmilns was one of only six firms still making cotton lace in Ayrshire, with about 600 workers between them. The *Loudoun Arms Inn* stood derelict in 1994, but was restored in 1995 as a pub and flats; an Institute and an inn had also become housing. Newmilns Tower, long derelict, was restored in 1995 by the Strathclyde Building Preservation Trust, and was to become holiday accommodation, but the former Co-op store stood vacant in 1997 and there has been little new development in the 90s. A Townscape Heritage Initiative improvement scheme was begun in 2000; at least 4 firms are still involved in the lace business.

## NEW PITSLIGO

**Map 10, C1**

***Buchan village,*** *pop. 1100* — OS 30: NJ 8856

In a roadless and remote upland area of Buchan some 12 km north-west of Old Deer was Tyrie parish, where about 1700 a bridge was built across the Gonar Burn at Tillinamolt. Beyond the Red Bog some 3 km south of the bridge was the fermtoun called *Benemean* (Balnamoon), while Cairnywhing lay to the west of the Hill of Turlundie. Both farm names appeared on Robert Gordon's map completed before 1642, and again on the Roy map of about 1750. The latter also very intriguingly named the *'Coll. of Cairnywhing'*. Cavoch Farm was soon created between the earlier places, sited on the eastern slopes of the boggy hill at the rather high altitude of 150 m. In 1785 Sir William Forbes of Monymusk chose a site on this farm to set up a small bleachfield on a headwater of the North Ugie Water, which became the less than ideal location of a new village which he founded in 1787. He named it New Pitsligo, having inherited the title of Lord Pitsligo in an indirect way from the last owner of the castle of Pitsligo near Rosehearty, who was the husband of his maternal aunt!

**Road, Coaches and Granite**: The Peterhead to Banff turnpike road (here later labelled A950) soon opened up the area, making a substantial detour to serve New Pitsligo, whose first post office was served by 1825 with a penny post from Mintlaw. When feuing ceased around 1841 the population exceeded 1250. In 1858 Pratt described a *"populous village – the houses and gardens well sheltered and interspersed with clumps of trees"*. Sir William Forbes had built the *Pitsligo Arms, "the principal inn fitted up in sufficient style and comfort as to be made the headquarters of the family when in the neighbourhood"*. By 1894 there was also a telegraph office, and at Tillinamolt a mill. The 1891 population was almost 1700, a number maintained through the early 20$^{th}$ century. Though never approached by railways, as late as 1909 horse-drawn coaches linked New Pitsligo with Banff, Strichen and Brucklay station on the line to Aberdeen; at some time it had granite quarries.

**Biscuits support declining Pitsligo**: By the 1950s New Pitsligo had a wide range of services, and also commercial peat-cutting on the abandoned Red Moss farm. A significant biscuit bakery, operated in 1963 by John Smith & Sons, had branches in Aberdeen and Fraserburgh by 1980. Then the local economy began to collapse, and despite coastal growth in employment, new residents from warmer climes were evidently deterred by the north-easterly aspect of the village – though this at least protects it from south-westerly gales. New Pitsligo fell into serious decline, losing 400 of its population between 1951 and 1981, together with two primary schools, its cinema, lawyers and post town status, but two hotels survived in 1980. Commercial peat-cutting apparently ceased for a time in the 1980s; New Pitsligo had 1100 people at the 1991 census. In 1997 locally owned Lovie Ltd made a large variety of concrete products near a quarry at Cowbog, 3 km west of the village, and by 2000 large-scale peat stripping had resumed beside the Strichen road; two Pitsligo companies are involved in the trade. The medium-sized bakery and biscuit factory is still open, as is the old *Pitsligo Arms Hotel*; one of the two pubs occupies an old church! There are also a police station, library, primary school, bank, post office and medical centre, plus various shops in this far from unattractive village.

## NEWPORT ON TAY, Woodhaven & Wormit — Map 6, B3

***N. Fife villages,** pop. 4400* — OS 59: NO 4228

By the 12th century there was a ferry to Dundee from the parish of Forgan or Forganby on the steep shores of north Fife. By 1526 tide mills or *Sea Myles* turned at Inverdivot *('Mouth of the Divot')*, a placename also strangely applied to a farm some way inland! By 1599 a school was open. By 1710 a ferry plied from Woodhaven to Dundee. A harbour and pier, built 1 km west of Inverdivot in 1713 by the Dundee guildry, appeared on the Roy map, surveyed about 1750, as a jetty labelled *'East Ferry'*; a few dots farther west showed the hamlet of Woodhaven. The sole road from East Ferry then led to Cupar; it was made up around 1750–70, and turnpiked from 1797 although its harbour was *"very inconsiderable"*. In 1799 Heron mentioned *"Woodhaven, a small sea-port, where the passage boats ply between Dundee and the coast of Fife"*. A slow coach connected with Pettycur from 1803, and the small *Newport Hotel* was built in 1806. As the northern focus of the Fife turnpike roads, an inn was provided at Woodhaven in 1816.

**Steam Ferries, Suburbs and the Tay Bridge Disaster**: The Newport ferry terminal and a new pier were built in 1816–22; from 1821 this ferry was operated by steamboats, whose reliability killed the Woodhaven ferry in 1824, but enabled villa building for Dundee's richer elements to begin. Newport's first post office was open by 1838. In 1845 the Scottish Central Railway acquired the ferry, in a move typical of the spoiling tactics of early railway promoters; it was over 30 years before the first and ill-fated Tay Rail Bridge – the brainchild of the over-enthusiastic but inattentive Thomas Bouch – was opened in 1878 by the North British Railway from Newport's neighbour Wormit to Dundee. Very lengthy at over 3 km it was an audacious project, and earned Bouch a knighthood from Queen Victoria. For a short time Newport enjoyed a local railway service, opened in 1879 along the coast to join the original train ferry line at Tayport *(q.v.)*. But the central section of the inadequately designed and carelessly constructed bridge was blown down in December that year as a train crossed the high girders, with the loss of all its 75 passengers and crew *(see Prebble's striking account)*.

**The New Bridge and New Suburb of Wormit**: The second rail bridge of 85 spans, designed by W H and Crawford Barlow, was opened in 1887, re-using the best of the old girders, and through trains again began to run to Dundee; simultaneously Newport became a police burgh. The 1891 population was 2500. In 1894 it was oddly described by Murray as a *"watering-place"*, with a steam ferry, hotel and mill. Wormit, till then a cliff-top hamlet between Woodhaven and the bridge, was laid out as a suburb by A S Stewart, who installed the first electric street lighting. From 1900 a gasworks and electric power station gave public supplies, aided until 1930 by an early wind generator. A secondary school was built in 1933, but although there was by the 1950s a 17-bed maternity unit, Newport with Wormit was still only a large village. In 1953 a Dundee Harbour Trust vehicle ferry plied between Newport and Dundee, giving a half-hourly service from 0700 to 2200 on weekdays, and hourly and for shorter periods on Sundays; a complex scale of charges was applied. By 1953 sandpits near *'St Fort'* station at Sandford south-east of Wormit were rail-served, but the station was soon closed, and by 1968 all the output from the growing complex of sand workings in the area went by road.

**Road Bridge, Hotel and Bees**: In 1966 the ferry was replaced by the 2.5 km-long Tay Road Bridge, which like the earlier Tay rail bridges is really a viaduct over the sea. Connecting a point just east of Newport with central Dundee, it gave car commuters a bonanza despite the tolls. In 1969 the local trains to Dundee were withdrawn, and despite local pressure BR declined to open a station on the main line at Wormit; about 1980 the station building was removed to Bo'ness (q.v.). By 1972 a small mansionhouse had become the *Sandford Hills Hotel*. In 1979 Wormit had little more than a post office, three grocery stores, a new primary school and Steele & Brodie's Beehive Works. Newport had two tiny hotels; its secondary school had closed by 1981, but it had retained the facilities of a large village.

**Underseas Concerns of an Affluent Dormitory**: In 1990 Remuscraft of Newport built unmanned submersibles, and in 1991 the nearby firm of Deep Water Recovery & Exploration was raising heavy cargo from depths of 1200 and potentially 1800 metres; they had a new ship for undersea mineral exploration on order from a Scottish yard. In 1991 Newport – including Wormit – had 4343 residents, an affluent dormitory with Scotland's highest proportion in professional and technical occupations. Some new infill housing is still being built, including in 1996 a group on the site of the former Wormit station. The former Newport ferry terminal is now the University of Dundee's Tay Estuary Research Centre, and Steele & Brodie are still in business. However, the central facilities in Newport are now very limited, with a useful handful of village shops, a bank and post office; the old *Newport Hotel* is a pub. The 16-room *Sandford Hills Hotel* has been recently refurbished.

## NEW SCONE — Map 6, B3

***Village / suburb of Perth,** pop. 4500* — OS 53 or 58: NO 1326

Pont's map of about 1600 showed the Park Mills in the Den of Scone *(pronounced Scoon)*, over 2 km east of Old Scone *(q.v.)*. The Roy map of about 1750 marked only the Balgary Mill, where the road from Perth to Coupar Angus crossed the den. Between 1805 and 1807 the laird, the Earl of Mansfield, compelled the people of Old Scone to remove to a new site north of the Balgary bridge. By 1831 New Scone had a post office, and its location within 3 km of the centre of Perth made it an attractive place to live. Horse buses began to ply to Perth in the 1860s. The 1891 population was around 1300, and by then New Scone was a substantial low-density village with a school and inn; a new parish church was built of red sandstone. The buses were replaced in 1895 by the horse-drawn trams of the Perth & District Tramways Company, which had its stables and depot at Scone until electrification by Perth Corporation in 1905. In 1916 and 1918 serious flooding from the Annaty Burn damaged unwisely sited houses which had replaced others destroyed by earlier floods. The tramway was closed in 1928.

**Growing Suburb and Golfing Hotel**: By 1951 New Scone had nearly 2500 residents, with facilities typical of a village, and a secondary school. Its affluent social character was evident from the 335 connections already made to its telephone exchange. By 1978 there was a coachworks. About 1980 the 19th century mansion of Murrayshall, 2 km east, became a country house hotel, with an 18-hole golf course. By then several large private housing estates had been added, one of which was eating into Scone Wood. New Scone had become a very sizeable suburb of Perth, increasingly afflicted by through traffic on the A94; by 1991 the population had reached 4500, with an affluent retired emphasis. The tram depot was still in use as a council recycling centre in 1995. More of Scone Wood had fallen to housing by 1997. Scotsire, a Scone-based cattle genetics branch of Perth's United Auctions, was closed in 1999. Housebuilding continues on the outskirts; a large new furniture shop has been built in the centre, where a bank, chemist and the *Scone Arms* are prominent; an eastern bypass was built in 2000–01. The *Murrayshall Hotel* has recovered from a 1995 fire, and now has a second 18-hole golf course.

## NEWTONGRANGE & Mayfield — Map 15, D3

***Midlothian small towns***, *pop. 12,000* — OS 66: NT 3364

Dalhousie Castle on the west bank of the River South Esk 4 km south of Dalkeith goes back to between 1200 and 1500 – sources wildly disagree; when Pont mapped Lothian around 1600 it stood emparked beside the Lasswade to Heriot road. Small-scale mining took place in the area in medieval days. From 1602 the adjacent parish centre of Cockpen had a school. By 1799 the river had been spanned near the castle by a *"stately bridge"*, and Heron noted Cockpen as a *"village"*. In 1795 the Newbattle paper mill was opened at Lothianbridge. Lingerwood colliery 1 km east of the bridge was sunk in 1798, and about 1831 the Marquis of Lothian, proprietor of Dalhousie (by then a mansion incorporating the earlier castle) had rails laid and a cast-iron viaduct built to connect it to the Edinburgh & Dalkeith Railway (E&DR) at South Esk near Lothianbridge. The Lord Dalhousie who became the Governor General of India worked to get the construction of the Indian railway system under way, and was also in name the Governor of the Bank of Scotland from 1851.

**Mining Village, Bricks and Railway; Exit Paper**: Newton Grange (as it was first recorded) developed east of the river between Lingerwood pit and the mill, starting around 1835 as a few miners' rows on either side of a mineral railway. A brick and tile works was established in 1840. The Edinburgh & Hawick Railway took over the E&DR's alignment, extended it southwards over Glenesk viaduct, and opened a station at Dalhousie Mains immediately west of the river in 1849; they replaced the cast-iron viaduct spans. At that time the paper mill had over 300 workers. By 1870 the Marquis owned 260 miners' houses, built of stone from his Masterton quarry. A gasworks was established in 1873, and at some time an oil-from-coal works operated south of the village. Following disagreement over the lease of Newbattle paper mill, in 1890 Robert Craig transferred his operations from Newtongrange to his family's Caldercruix mill. By then Cockpen had shrunk to a farm.

**Enter Lady Victoria and the Dean**: The population of Newtongrange in 1891 was 950. The 500 m-deep shaft of the Lady Victoria colliery was sunk in 1890–95 by the Lothian Coal Company, exploiting the Limestone Coal Group and incorporating Lingerwood on an immediately adjacent site to create a model pit which innovated the use of steel pit-props; Grant, Ritchie & Co of Kilmarnock built its very large winding engine in 1894. The pit incorporated the brickworks, whose products enabled the tiny mining village and the old hamlet of Easthouses to expand rapidly, to 2400 people in 1901; some basic houses were built by an early form of housing association, others were speculative. In 1899 the coal company established the *Dean Tavern* to control the miners' drinking habits. The profits from this *'Goth'* over the years provided Institutes, sports grounds, a public park and support for local societies; it has been community-run for a long time now.

**Films, Electricity and Mayfield**: Dalhousie station was closed as early as 1908, replaced by another 1 km south at Newtongrange, where the *Picture House* opened in 1915. The population had again tripled by 1931; the colliery and two neighbours employed 3000 men in the 1930s, and was among the first to generate electricity, also used in the village; but the brickworks closed in 1950. As more housing was demanded, the Mayfield *'scheme'* was built on the hillside south of Easthouses as a high-altitude extension to the area's council

*The winding engine at the Lady Victoria colliery, Newtongrange. pit was sunk in 1890, becoming one of the most innovative in the co try. This was the largest steam winding engine in Scotland, buil Kilmarnock by Grant, Ritchie & Co; it worked until 1981. Today colliery is the Scottish Mining Museum.* (J

housing. Though attaining a population of 2700 by 1951, it had few facilities except two (later four) primary schools; at that time Newtongrange itself had over 6000 people, but only average village facilities. Mayfield continued to expand up to a bleak 210m above sea level, and by 1971 had nearly 10,000 people – and also the range of facilities of a typical village.

**The Decline of Newtongrange and Mayfield**: Dalhousie Castle was vacated by the Earls in the mid 20th century in favour of Brechin Castle; it became a preparatory school for some years, but by 1977 was a hotel. After 1951 Newtongrange lost its secondary school, the cinema (closed 1960) and dentist; Lingerwood colliery closed in 1967, and the former main line railway was unforgivably closed in 1969. By 1975 a Mines Rescue Centre was open. Lady Victoria colliery had 850 miners in 1977 *(see Hay & Stell)* and still relied on the Grant Ritchie winding engine until closure in 1981; by then it had raised 40 million tonnes of coal. At that time the Coal Board owned nearly all the houses in Newtongrange. By 1977 Tullis Neil were paper converters at Peggy's Mill on the industrial estate at Mayfield, so recreating the area's first industry. In 1981 the population of Newtongrange was down to 4700; the two places combined held only some 12,000 people, fairly young but with few having higher qualifications.

**A Monument to Mining**: By 1986 the colliery site had become the Scottish Mining Museum, with a staff of 18 to 20; despite its 31,000 visitors in 1989 it consistently lost money. Sadly, despite the public funds invested in building a new restaurant in 1998–99, the museum was temporarily closed in 2000 due to the loss of the running costs deficit previously made up by the former Lothian Region, which had been abolished by the government in the 1996 changes. More positively, in 1994 a new junior league ground for Newtongrange Star FC was opened on the site of a former bing, and by 1996 new housing had replaced the former Mines Rescue Centre. The Glenesk railway viaduct – restored in 1992 by the Edinburgh Green Belt Trust – was reopened as a walkway, eventually to be a cycle track. The *Dalhousie Castle Hotel* continues, now with 34 rooms.

## NEWTONHILL & Muchalls — Map 10, C4

***Aberdeenshire villages,*** *pop. 2150* — OS 45: NO 9193

When Pont made his sketch map about 1600, Muchalls Castle already stood about 1km inland from the Mearns coast, some 6km north of Stonehaven. Coastal places north of the Burn of Muchalls included *'Stranachro'*, later called Muchalls, and *'Skaterow'*, which became Newtonhill. By about 1750 the Roy map showed that the coast road had been made up and a mill turned at the mouth of the Burn of Muchalls. In 1849 the Aberdeen Railway, later part of the Caledonian, opened its line along the cliff-tops, with stations at each village. By then Newtonhill had a tiny harbour, important for white fishing. Muchalls Castle was rebuilt about 1865.

**Decline, and Regrowth**: Muchalls station had been closed by 1953, when the combined population of the twin villages was about 1170; their basic facilities were largely duplicated, though agricultural engineers were based at Bridge of Muchalls. In 1955 a small golf course was in play at Newtonhill, but later closed. Despite the further loss of Newtonhill station by 1963, the population slowly rose to 1275 in 1971. Newtonhill pier had become ruinous by the mid 80s, but its other facilities remained those of of a small village. As a result of oil developments south of Aberdeen, extensive new housing estates were built at Newtonhill. The youthful dormitory population was nearing 2150 by 1991. By 1985 Muchalls too had become a commuter settlement, but by 1999 its hotel and post office no longer featured. In 1992 a new station had been proposed at Newtonhill, with a suburban rail service to and through Aberdeen; then came rail privatisation. By 1999 money had gone instead to build a flyover on the A90 to serve the housing estates still growing north of the village.

## NEWTON MEARNS — Map 15, C6

***Renfrewshire town / Glasgow suburb,*** *pop. 20,000*

OS 64: NS 5355

The 15th century Mearns Tower or Castle some 10km south-west of Glasgow was emparked by the time that Timothy Pont mapped Renfrewshire around 1600. Although some 125m in altitude, the area was quite closely settled. Mearns Kirk gained a parish school in 1605. In 1621 a burgh of barony was chartered, either at Mearns Kirk or more probably at Newton Mearns – distinct settlements about 1km west of the castle. Newton, *'Renfrew'* had a post office from 1733. Roads had been defined by about 1754 when Roy's map showed that the Kirk stood beside the main road from Glasgow and Cathcart to Kilmarnock. In the 18th century Netherplace bleachworks was built 1.5km to the west of what Heron in 1799 mentioned as *"the village of Newton"*.

**Gas, Upmarket Golf & Belated Railway**: A new Mearns Kirk was built in 1813 and a post office was open by 1838, but the area was not served by the early railway systems. The population in 1891 was only 900. The Eastwood golf club was founded on the hills 3km south-west of Newton Mearns in 1893; in 1895 this was still a small village with a post and telegraph office and two inns on the main road – but there was also a gasworks in the valley to the west, anticipating the suburban development that the area was to experience after 1924. In 1903 the Caledonian Railway opened a new line from Glasgow to the Ayrshire coast, with stations some 2 km north-east and north of Newton Mearns, respectively named Whitecraigs and Patterton. A parkland golf course was soon created by the Whitecraigs club, founded in 1905, encouraging this area to develop before Patterton. The area's third good 18-hole course was laid out at Pilmuir near the Eastwood course by the East Renfrewshire club of 1922. However, by then a quarry was open near Mearns Kirk.

**Suburban Newton Mearns**: From the mid 1920s Newton Mearns was also well served by bus services; but the speculative housing – the Broom estate – that was being built along the Glasgow road opposite the fashionable Whitecraigs golf course was of upmarket types, bringing the money which enabled Mearns Kirk to be renovated in 1931–32. By 1939 this ribbon of development was several streets deep. The large Mearnskirk General Hospital of 732 beds was created about the time of the second world war. By the 1950s Newton Mearns had 6000 residents and all the facilities of a large village. In 1962 the railway was electrified, and Patterton station started to draw new building towards it; Eastwood High School was built nearby in the 1970s. The bleachworks was still in use in 1976.

**Quarries Open and Closed?**: By 1981 continuing suburban development had brought Mearns Kirk into greater Newton Mearns, whose population of 11,000 enjoyed the facilities of

*The 15th century Mearns Castle with the Maxwell-Mearns Church, built in the 1970s when the surrounding area was being developed for private housing.* *(JRH)*

a small town. A second hard-rock quarry was open at Pilmuir by 1963 and had become deep, with an area of 12ha before its closure in the mid 1980s; planning permission was granted for infilling the wet pit by tipping in 1987, but had not been taken up by 1992, when its legality was being questioned. In the 1980s residential growth continued eastwards and particularly north-westwards at Crookfur towards Patterton Station, and in 1990 a sports centre opened in Crookfur Park.

**Rich Suburbs attract Marks & Spencer**: A major retail warehouse and leisure complex scheme at Greenlaw Farm was refused in 1989, but an indoor shopping mall was opened. In 1991 the population of this well-educated Glasgow suburb was approaching 19,500, rich in youngish managers and professionals. In 1991 Marks & Spencer opened what they termed a *'neighbourhood store'*, their first such in Scotland, costing only a seventh of the investment in their new top of the range Gyle store *(see Corstorphine)*. In 1995–96 the controversial M77 motorway was built, bypassing Newton Mearns on the west; by then the area had one of Scotland's few synagogues. Part of Mearnskirk Hospital was converted to 24 flats in 1999, and in 2000 the extension of the M77 motorway from Malletsheugh (Newton Mearns) to Fenwick was proposed. A Coats thread factory employs over 200 locally. Both Mearns Castle and Eastwood High Schools have about 1000 pupils, and Mearns Castle now forms part of the Maxwell-Mearns church.

## NEWTONMORE — Map 9, B5

***Speyside village,** pop. 1050* — OS 35: NN 7199

By about 1645 Banchor *('White Corrie')* Farm was already tucked into the lower reaches of the upper Speyside glen of that name, though it appeared as *'Bandachar'* on Blaeu's map. A bridge across the Falls of Truim near the hamlet of Crubenbeg 7km south was built by General Wade's troops in 1730, carrying the *'King's Road to Inverness'* on its way from Drumochter to Ruthven Barracks. In the 1750s Roy's map showed Banchor as the nearest settlement west of the Kirk of Kingussie, and there were no roads north of the River Spey. Immediately to the east of Banchor was the site where Newtonmore *('The big new town')* began to grow. By 1770 it had a shoemaker, from whom the local tacksman made extensive purchases.

**Overspill Village and Through Traffic**: The main development of the village, which although at the high altitude of 250 metres was well sited on a gentle south-easterly slope, occurred in the early 19th century as an overspill settlement for poor families displaced by the clearances and for whom there was no room to raise subsistence crops in the compactly planned new village of Kingussie. By 1817 Newtonmore stood on the Laggan road, newly built for the Parliamentary commissioners as a link between Kingussie and Lochaber, while at the same time the new Spey Bridge enabled the main road north (later the A9) to be diverted through Newtonmore – at that time to have through traffic was advantageous.

**Railway and Resort Development**: The main line of the Inverness & Perth Junction (later Highland) Railway, which opened in 1863, served Newtonmore with a crossing station. When in 1890 the Newtonmore golf club laid out an 18 hole course, it was remarkably bisected by the railway line. Newtonmore did not become a police burgh – the 1891 population was only 360 – and in 1894 although the *"good" Newtonmore Hotel* was open, only sheep pastures drew Murray's attention. A new A9 bridge was built in 1926. Newtonmore reached a population of 1000 about 1951, when it had the facilities of a typical village, plus six hotels. The Clan Macpherson Museum was opened in the early post-war years. Newtonmore was freed of through traffic when a bypass opened in 1979. About 1980 the *Balavil Arms Hotel* provided pony trekking holidays and the village had a doctors' group practice. In 1980 there were eleven small hotels, and by 1985 caravan and camping sites. Up to 1991 the population remained stable at almost 1050 residents, including a high proportion of affluent retired people.

**Stag's Breath, Smart Ropes and Waltzing Waters**: By 1992 the whisky and honeycomb liqueur called *'Stag's Breath'* was being blended locally by Meikles, while the Cairngorm Climbing Rope Company occupied several of the dozen or so nursery factory units built near the station. In 1993 they had a new factory of 650 m$^2$, a full order book, and were about to produce a *'smart rope'* which would change colour when damaged. For the less daring, local shopkeeper Alex Donald had created by 1992 a colourful indoor spectacle known as *Waltzing Waters*, described as a *'water, light and music spectacular'* using computer technology and pumps delivering 8000 litres a minute. By 1995 the new Highland Folk Park was open, rivalling Kingussie with a Museum of Highland Sport – featuring shinty. The Russwood sawmill is prominent, and there are some new houses. Despite the removal of all station facilities except one platform, this is still served by a few trains. Long-established hotels include the fair-sized *Balavil Sport* and the *Mains*, and the smaller *Glen*; a small hostel for backpackers is also open.

## NEWTON STEWART & Minnigaff — Map 1, C4

***Galloway town,** pop. 3675* — OS 83: NX 4165

Near the mouth of the River Cree in Galloway were ancient cairns. In the Gaelic *Muillin an Ath* means *'Mill at the Ford'* so there was evidently an early mill at Minnigaff; later came a church; and by around 1200 also a *'hospital'*. Some 3km to the north among a cluster of five castles was the 14th century Garlies Castle, the original home of the Earls of Galloway who later moved to Creebridge House. Early in the 17th century a military road was built, crossing the *'Black Ford of Cree'* en route from Dumfries to Portpatrick, to aid in the fateful Plantation of Ulster. Despite the lack of a bridge the area was already well developed for the period: Pont's map of the Stewartry made at that time showed two mills and a *'wakmil'* on the Penkin Burn above Minnigaff Kirk; on the west bank of the river, which was thickly studded with tiny settlements, was the *'Threethrid Mill'*. Five kilometres up-river was the ancient Castle Stewart, near which lead was at one time mined; nearby was the emparked Penninghame House with its mill. Minnigaff was chartered in 1619 as a burgh of barony and had a parish school from 1622.

**Enter Newton Stewart: puzzle find Heron**: Newton Stewart was created on the west bank of the Cree by a barony charter of 1677, granted to William Stewart of Castle Stewart. As early as 1684 Newton Stewart had acquired a *"very considerable"* weekly market for meal and malt, and a cattle market was also regularly held by 1700. A barony burgh charter to *'Heron'* granted in 1698 appears to relate to Minnigaff (whose first post office was opened in 1715), because it was the Heron family who built the elegant Kirroughtree House at Minnigaff in 1719. What the later writer Robert Heron called the *"handsome"* Cree bridge was erected in 1745 (and shown on Roy's map made in the 1750s), when both Newton Stewart and Minnigaff were quite substantial places. The latter's waulkmill still existed, and a total of six radial routes was shown, most of those to the north and east being depicted as tracks.

**Industrial Growth and an abortive Change of Name**: Newton Stewart post office first opened in 1765. Lead was worked for many years in the late 18th century on the Kirroughtree and Mochramore estates east of the river. In 1792 William Douglas of Penninghame, a self-made man who had risen from toting a pedlar's pack to buying the Stewart estate, set up a mill in Newton Stewart to card and spin cotton. By the next year he had added to this *"thriving village"*; the total population was then about a thousand, and the Paisley Union Banking Company had a short-lived branch there. In 1797, when mails came on alternate days, the post town was named as Newton Stewart, but Heron in 1799 wrote of *"the village formerly called Newton Stewart, now Newton-Douglas, having changed its name with its proprietor. It is a regular well built town with about 1200 inhabitants. Several manufactures are here begun very successfully; of these the cotton is the principal."* There was also a *"valuable salmon fishing"*, while Minnigaff was an *"ancient village"*.

**Brewing and Bridging, Leather and Slate**: In 1799 Archibald Richardson established what was to be a very long-lasting country brewery. The first Cree bridge was washed away in 1806; its replacement of 1813 was designed by John Rennie and erected by Mathison of Stranraer. Douglas's tannery was a success, but the cotton mills relapsed on his death, the carpet factory also failed – and the name reverted to Newton Stewart by 1813. The substantial stone-built four-storey Mealmill on the Penkiln Brook at Minnigaff was built in 1823. According to Chambers in 1827 Newton Stewart was *"a large modern village fast rising into importance. About fifty years ago, all the houses consisted of one story and were covered in thatch; but more than half of them are now two stories in height and slated; Newton-Stewart is a stage on the road from Dumfries to Portpatrick."*

**Newton Stewart on the Railway**: The *Galloway Arms, Crown Hotel* and *Grapes Inn* were in use by 1861 when a station was opened on completion of the Portpatrick Railway (later the Portpatrick & Wigtownshire Joint), connecting Castle Douglas to Stranraer. This crossed the river about 4 km south of the town by the Cree Viaduct, near a tileworks and quay at Carty Port. The local newspaper, the *Galloway Gazette* was established in 1870, and from 1875 the station was the 3-platform junction for the Wigtownshire Railway (to Wigtown and Whithorn); there were quite extensive goods facilities, and from 1895 a minor locomotive depot. Newton Stewart proved a much more nodal location than the older Wigtown, which it gradually largely superseded as a shopping centre. In 1884 a large public hall was built, a gift of local merchants the McMillans. The population in 1891 was 2750. In 1894 the two main hotels at Newton Stewart were the *"comfortable" Crown* and the *"fair" Galloway Arms*; the town was well over 1 km long, and the cattle market was described as *"important"*.

**A Quiet Early 20th Century**: Later the Douglas Ewart High School was opened; a gasworks was built in 1911, but the brewery was bought up and closed in 1925, becoming a mere depot. The Newton Stewart golf club founded in 1930 laid out a 9-hole parkland course at Minnigaff. In 1946 Wordie & Co operated a small rail to road cartage depot. In the 1950s the old Cumloden Mills were unused, the only industries of note being the Cree Woollen Mills, then making scarves, and a modern sawmill at Minnigaff. With rural depopulation over the following three decades, Newton Stewart lost some of the full range of urban facilities that its 2750 people enjoyed in the 1950s, but its auction mart survived.

**Railway Axed but Great Houses find New Uses**: The locomotive depot was closed in 1959. Beeching withdrew what the locals believed to be the profitable freight services from the Wigtown branch in 1964, and ensured that the entire Galloway main line through Newton Stewart was closed in 1965. By 1971 Penninghame House had become a small open prison with 62 inmates. On the brighter side, a town bypass opened in 1978, and roadborne tourist trade flourished. By 1977 Kirroughtree House had become a hotel with 18 rooms, and by 1979 there were also a youth hostel, caravan and camping sites at Minnigaff. By 1980 the seven hotels of the 1950s, now also including the *Creebridge House Hotel* with 20 rooms, had grown to ten, of generally higher star rating.

**Growing Population, Growing Unemployment!**: The mid 1980s saw community support for the struggling cinema, and the erection of a substantial new garage at Minnigaff. Although in 1986 Newton Stewart appeared a less vigorous centre than comparable Castle Douglas, the former's livestock market was active with sheep in 1989. By 1991 the rather elderly population was 3675, although with new housing estates both sides of the river. Minnigaff mill was converted into sheltered accommodation, but the woollen mills remained an active concern as Creebridge Mohair, manufacturing and exporting mohair scarves, stoles, and rugs worldwide. Yet in the recession of 1992 local unemployment reached 20%. But development resumed: the golf course was enlarged to 18 holes, by 1996 the Cree Viaduct had been dismantled, a large new school built and a museum opened. Due to public demand and local fund-raising, the cinema was restored and reopened in 1997. Hotels now include the *Kirroughtree House*, the *Bruce*, the *Creebridge House* and the long-established *Crown*, and the youth hostel is also open.

## NEWTOWN ST BOSWELLS

**Map 3, B4**

***Borders small town,*** *pop. 1100* OS 73 or 74: NT 5731

Bowden lies 4km south of Melrose, near the Eildon Hills; it had a 12th century church, and to the west was built the 16th century Holydean Castle, adjacent to an ancient chapel; by the 18th century Bowden was a little village known for cottage linen weaving. Between Bowden and St Boswells, roads turnpiked under an Act of 1768 converged from Galashiels, Jedburgh and Earlston. Newtown St Boswells which grew at the crossroads had a mill by 1849. In 1849 the new Edinburgh & Hawick Railway opened its St Boswells station at Newtown; later the line became part of the North British (NB) *'Waverley Route'* to Carlisle. From 1851 Newtown was the junction for Kelso, and in 1865 a single-track line built by the Berwickshire Railway Company was completed across the 19-arched Leaderfoot Viaduct from the main line at Ravenswood Junction 2.5 km north of Newtown, to Earlston and Duns; later it too became part of the NB. Both these branch lines ran through the fertile Merse to reach the east coast main line; to deal with the resulting grain traffic a substantial railway granary was built.

**A New Administrative Centre is Born**: The Langlands spinning mill was established in 1889, and by 1894 the *Railway Inn* was open. The auction mart and the *'County Rooms'* for little Roxburghshire had also been established by 1899, the latter a seminal decision resulting from the nodality the place had gained from the railways. By then Holydean Castle was surrounded by a deer park, but this and the Holydean chapel were casualties of the early 20th century. By the second world war agricultural engineers were based at Newtown, whose population was about 1150, with village services. Major floods in 1948 cut the Earlston line and only freight services were resumed; the other railways which had given birth to Newtown were also closed, the last being the main line in 1969. But new offices for a staff of 160 had lately been built there by the County Council.

**Regional Capital**: From 1975 these modern offices became the headquarters of the new Borders Regional Council (BRC); although Roxburghshire continued as the title of a new district, the Newtown area was transferred to the new Ettrick and Lauderdale district, centred in Galashiels! St Columba's College, a Roman Catholic seminary, was open by 1977. Despite the loss of such services as the secondary school and post town status, spinning continued locally. In 1981 Bowden had only some basic facilities and 300 people; in 1991, when Newtown had a quite healthy and well-educated population of 1108, an extension to the BRC offices was completed, but another phase was to come, to provide proper space for a staff of 320.

**Bypass, Education and SustainableTechnology**: By 1993 an eastern bypass had been built, matching the 1994 decision to select the A68 for future improvement as the key route between Edinburgh and the south. At that time John Swan *(also at Gorgie)* ran the very successful cattle and livestock market at Newtown. By 1995 the fairly recently established Monksford School provided independent boarding education for girls aged 8–16. About 1994 under Scottish Borders Enterprise the former Dryburgh monastery with its 10 ha gardens had become the Tweed Horizons Centre for Sustainable Technology, whose ten companies embraced a wide range of expertise in fields such as transport, power, heating, recycling, farming and water treatment. Its own combined heat and power plant was to burn coppiced willows. In 1996 the Scottish Borders unitary authority replaced the Borders Region and its four thinly populated Districts, conferring on Newtown (as also Lochgilphead) a remarkable importance for its size. By 1998 a college had been built south of the little town.

## NEWTYLE

**Map 6, B2**

***Angus village,*** *pop. 700* OS 53: NO 2941

Newtyle in Strathmore, 7 km east of Coupar Angus, lies at the outlet of the Glack of Newtyle, a valley which offers a fairly easy route across the Sidlaw Hills to Dundee. Kinpurney Hill to the east was surmounted by an ancient fort, later replaced by Kinpurnie Castle, now vanished. Hatton Castle which was built in the 16th century also later became a ruin. Between these castles was erected the early mansion of Bannatyne House, the little-known birthplace in 1545 of George Bannatyne, who became an eminent Edinburgh burgess and collected ancient Scots poetry. This may have been the tower named *'Newtyll'* that was clearly depicted on one of Pont's maps made about 1600. From 1622 Newtyle parish ran a school, and a burgh of barony was chartered in 1682, which apparently lay on the original postal route between Perth and Forfar. It was a mere hamlet about 1750 when Roy's surveyors noted the *'Old House of Newtyle'*, a mill and the Kirkton. These stood where an east–west track labelled the *'Upper road'* intersected the road between Coupar Angus and Dundee via the Mill of Dronley. It was the 1790s before the latter road was made up, and very little further growth occurred until about 1830.

**The Railway Village**: Little Newtyle became the unlikely objective of the locally promoted Dundee & Newtyle Railway (D&N), built in 1826–31 to the very odd gauge of 138 cm, which scrambled over the hills by means of inclined planes, stationary engines, and (where less steep) horse traction. The aim was to link fertile Strathmore with the growing food and flax demands of Dundee, and its protagonist Lord Wharncliff feued off plots at Newtyle in 1832–33 *"for the railway"*. The line also served Pithappie quarry, 1.5 km south-east of the village, above the Hatton incline. The line was extended on a T-plan in 1837 (as the Newtyle & Glamis Railway), forking 1.5 km north of Newtyle to both Glamis and Coupar Angus. The D&N was altered to standard gauge in 1846–47, and connected to Perth and the Strathmore main line.

**No Trains, and Little Else**: Total reconstruction of the D&N as a conventional railway in 1861–68 looped the line around the west of the village to ease the gradient. The 1891 population was just over 400; though by then mills had been built, virtually no more development took place. Newtyle's trains services to Dundee were withdrawn in the 1950s. Newtyle had 684 people in 1991, with the facilities of a small village; even its inn had closed. Although a new primary school had been built by 1993, the former A927 Dundee to Meigle road has been downgraded to become the mere B954.

## NIGG FERRY & Balnapaling

**Map 9, B3**

***Easter Ross location,*** *pop. under 100* OS 21: NH 7969

In the 12th century Dunskeath Castle was built on the bold headland called the *'North Sutor'* to command the mouth of the Cromarty Firth. A *'King's Ferry'* plied to Cromarty by the 15th century, though it was not marked on Pont's map made about 1600, only *'Nig'*. In the 1750s a *"ferryhouse"* at the north terminus of the *'Ferry of Cromarty'* was shown on the Roy map, but the track from this place – also called Balnapaling – to the north ended after 5 km at Ankerville. Eventually the local road system was completed and by 1906 a steam ferryboat was in use. Coastal defence batteries were built at the North Sutor in both world wars to protect the Invergordon naval base. By 1939 there was a golf course on the North Sutor at Castlecraig, also serving Cromarty; by 1953 it was of 18 holes. With the continuing decline of Cromarty, the ferry had failed by 1965 and the golf course was closed – rare indeed in Scotland! It left behind a tiny settlement nucleus with a pier and an inn.

**Oil Resurrection, Ferry Regained but Jobs Seesaw**: Nigg was dominated from 1972 by the huge oil platform yard and graving dock of Highland Fabricators (HF), where 3000 workers were briefly employed. In 1977 HF floated out a 20,000-tonne steel platform, the first of two for the Ninian oilfield. In 1976 Cromarty Petroleum obtained planning permission for an oil refinery, but made a slow start. From 1978 the output from the new Beatrice oilfield in the Moray Firth was piped to a terminal, storage tanks and pier at Nigg. HF employed 4000 workers for a short time in 1983, but within a year only 1000. Another spurt in 1987 reinvigorated the ferry, but in 1988 the HF yard was put on *'care and maintenance'* with employment at under 40. Then a new contract was won and by early 1990 there were 3000 workers. Under a further large contract won in 1990, jackets were built for the Everest and Lomond fields. In 1992 the ferryboat could carry two cars and 100 passengers, plying at HF shift-change times, plus a frequent summer tourist service. In 1993–95 between 350 and 600 jobs were provided as the 6000-tonne Elf Froy jacket was built for the Norwegian oil industry, then four platforms for gas extraction in Liverpool Bay, and a 2500-tonne structure for the BP Cleeton field off the Humber.

**The Stop Start Ferry, and the Start Stop Yard**: In 1995 the yard's owners merged with those at Ardersier *(q.v.)*. In 1996 the privately run ferry, MV *Cromarty Rose*, carried over 20,000 passengers and 5500 vehicles, its most successful year ever; only to lose its 37% subsidy and close early in 1997, due to cuts in local government funding. This absurd decision left a 50 km road journey as the only alternative for the rig yard workers and tourists wishing to cross the Firth, so the ferry was soon re-opened. In 1999 under US-owned Barmac, the jobs (combined with Ardesier) peaked at 4700, but closure came again when the last rig floated out in mid 2000, although some jobs would stay for a time on care and maintenance work in the hope of new orders.

## NITSHILL, Hurlet, Priesthill & Darnley

**Map 15, B6**

***S-W. suburbs of Glasgow,*** *pop. 20,000+* — OS 64: NS 5260

When Timothy Pont mapped Renfrewshire about 1600 there were already bridges across the Levern Water and its tributary the Brock Burn in the vicinity of *'Prasthil'* and *'N Darly'*, two of many small settlements in the area. Glasgow radial roads traversed the area by the time of Roy's survey, made in the early 1750s. In the year 1753 a Liverpool firm built Scotland's first *'Copperas'* plant at Hurlet on the Levern, 4 km west of Pollokshaws and some 9 km south-west of Glasgow. This used local shales in the production of ferrous sulphate, employed to fix textile dyes. The firm flourished into the 19th century as Lightbody's, and had a branch in Bo'ness from about 1808. In 1807 a second works was built at Househill by Charles Macintosh, partner to the great Charles Tennant; this became Britain's biggest alum and copperas works until production ceased about 1880.

**Railways, Mine Disaster, Lime and Phosphates**: The small Crossmill print works was built at the adjoining village of Nitshill (an unfortunate corruption of *'Nuts-Hill")* which from 1848 had a station on the Caledonian Railway's Barrhead line; from this sidings soon diverged eastwards to various mineral industries. In 1851, 63 men and boys died in an underground explosion in the Victoria colliery, at Nitshill Road/Peat Road, destroying the hopes of their many dependants. But recovery at Nitshill by 1869 created Scotland's deepest coal pit at 320 m; the Hurlet coal was a pyritous seam containing much iron. The Arden Limeworks at Corselet Road, founded about 1874 by Allan Kirkwood, used limestone brought by rail from Darnley quarries to the south. The population in 1891 was just over 1000. By 1895 the coal pit was accompanied by Perry & Hope's works, making phosphoric acid and phosphates; Nitshill had an inn, and a mill on the Brock Burn.

**Trams and Glasgow Housing Schemes**: The Levern Water was spanned about 1910 by a bridge for the Paisley District Tramways Company, serving the still small but growing village with electric trams on tracks between Giffnock, Thornliebank and Barrhead; this concern later became part of the Glasgow tramways. Fireclay works and the small Darnley hospital were in existence by 1920. In 1929 Nitshill was absorbed by Glasgow, whose overspill estate at Househillwood was begun shortly before the second war, with the areas at Carnock Road and between Barrhead Road and Glenlora Drive rising first. By 1951 Nitshill had typical village facilities – but nearly 20,000 people lived there! The railway to the quarry was abandoned in 1954 and the limeworks were demolished in 1965. The trams stopped running in 1957, around the time that the fireclay works vanished and the Priesthill estate was added.

**Industrial and Other Newcomers face the M77**: By 1979 both Reinholds, long-established knitwear manufacturers from Glasgow, and Philips Arc Welding Ltd, makers of this trade's equipment, were busy on the Nitshill industrial estate. Later housing development in South Nitshill brought the total population by 1981 to some 24,000, with several schools and a remarkable number of garages, but otherwise village facilities. In the 1980s the last remaining fields between Nitshill and Thornliebank became the Darnley estate, and in 1990 an additional railway station was opened named *'Priesthill & Darnley'*. By 1991 the population was down to about 20,300. In 1992 Sainsbury's opened a superstore across the road from Darnley, an unexpected element which was nevertheless a success; by 1994 *'Southpark Village'* had been added close by, west of Darnley Mains. In 1996 B&Q added a vast new DIY and trade warehouse nearby, served by the newly opened but winding M77 motorway which had been controversially squeezed through the erstwhile green lung to the east.

## NORTHBAY & Eoligarry

**Map 7, A4**

***Isle of Barra communities,*** *pop. 270* OS 31: NF 7003

Monro in 1549 enthused over the *"great cockles"* in the sands of the Traigh Mhor, a very shallow bay on the north-east coast of the Isle of Barra, and the good fishing around the nearby *"fruitful"* islets. In 1703 Martin noted sheltered Northbay *(G. Bagh Shiarabhagh)* as a *"safe harbour where there is plenty of fish"*; the cod and ling even attracted Orkney boats. Crofting dominated until Barra's famous inter-tidal airfield was opened in 1935 on the Traigh Mhor sands; scheduled flights began in 1936. In 1951 some 380 people lived in the nearby crofts. By 1974 a passenger ferry plied to Saltavik Bay at Ludag in South Uist, and to Eriskay, from a new pier at the traditional boat harbour at the scattered township of Eoligarry on Barra's northmost tip, 3 km north of the informal airfield. By then solitary *Suidheachan*, Compton Mackenzie's former home near the airfield, had become a small factory where cockleshells were ground in the one-time billiard room for use as harling grit *(see Castlebay)*. An inn and a new deepwater fishing station had been established at Northbay, a larger township. In 1978 the American Vincent Company of Tampa, Florida, built a fish meal factory at Ardveenish east of Northbay, providing 36 welcome jobs for these two small and shrinking communities, by then containing between them only some 270 people. In 1994 an air service linked Northbay with Stornoway via Benbecula. There is now a heritage trail at Eoligarry; its school and Northbay post office and pub are open.

## NORTH BERWICK

**Map 3, B2**

***E. Lothian coast town,*** *pop. 5800* OS 66 & 67: NT 5585

Offshore rocks shelter North Berwick – a name associated with corn – sited where the Firth of Forth meets the stormy North Sea, 30 km east of Edinburgh. In the mid 12th century David, Earl of Fife, instituted a ferry between this point and Earlsferry in Fife, and had a hospice built for pilgrims to St Andrews. A *'Black'* or Cistercian nunnery was founded about 1150 by Duncan, Earl of Fife, but North Berwick did not appear on the mid 13th century Gough map. The cliff-top castle of Tantallon 4 km to the east was built by the Douglas earls around 1370, its defensive earthworks and towered curtain wall 15 m tall cutting off a promontory. North Berwick had a tiny export trade in wool by the time its barony charter was granted in 1381. Although an all-stone quay was built, the Earls then moved away to Threave, and little more was being shipped by the time the town was upgraded to a Royal Burgh in 1425; even at its peak around 1429 a mere ten tonnes of wool a year were exported!

**John Major teaches John Knox**: One John Major born in North Berwick in 1469 became the first modern historian at St Andrews University, and taught the young reformer John Knox. North Berwick made useful contributions to Customs revenue before the port's trade shrank to almost nothing by 1500, and the burgh tax revenues remained negligible as late as 1535. Fenton Tower was built in the 16th century 2 km southwest of the Law; it later fell into ruin. Sixteen nuns lived at the priory until its destruction in 1565; in 1588 Alexander Home acquired the site. Meantime in 1581 a parish school had been established. Pont's map of Lothian made about 1600 showed a line of buildings hugging the shore at North Berwick; to the west was the *'Ferry Gate'*, and offshore *'Rodes'* showed an anchorage. The place revived as a beach fishing station, with a herring *'works'* set up in 1642 by the rich William Dick of Edinburgh. About then the aptly named mansion of Seacliff was built 1 km east of Tantallon, which remained strong until slighted in 1651 by General Monk.

**Slow Recovery**: The ferry to Fife was extinct by the late 17th century, and all the early travel authors who visited Scotland seem to have passed by regardless. Even Tucker's account of Scottish ports in 1655 seems to have omitted North Berwick. The vast volcanic plug called the Bass Rock, 2 km offshore from Tantallon, became a prison for Covenanters in 1671. In the 18th century a breakwater was built, and later a tidal basin; grain was exported, and a waulk mill was added to an existing mill in 1739. In 1769 Pennant found just *"a small town"*. In the 1790s there were two fair days per year and 700 people, but Heron in 1799 dismissed North Berwick as *"an inconsiderable town"*. A post office was opened in 1801, two breweries were at work in 1825, and Chambers wrote in 1827 that *"North Berwick is a snug little royal burgh and sea-port, undistinguished by any trade or manufacture"*. But he saw it as a *"town"*, with a daily coach to Edinburgh.

**Railway and Golfing**: Golf was already played in the area before the early North Berwick golf club was established in 1832. By 1841, the year when Seacliff was enlarged by David Bryce for George Sligo, the harbour exported potatoes and imported coal; at some time a gasworks was established. The North Berwick branch of the North British Railway was opened in 1850 and for a decade struggled to survive, but traffic grew with the town's development as an Edinburgh dormitory, and two more golf courses were in use by 1874. A lifeboat station was opened in 1860, and in 1885 a lighthouse was completed on the offshore islet of Fidra, 5 km west of North Berwick; by 1894 there was also a coastguard station.

**North Berwick for Toffs?**: In 1891 the winter population had risen to almost 2400; in 1894 North Berwick was described as *"the most favourite watering-place for the Edinburgh upper classes"*. The three hotels ranged from the *"excellent" Marine* and the *"good" Royal* to *Bradbury's Private*, and *"numerous lodgings and villas for summer (very high rents)"*; but it was still a minor herring fishing port, its boats marked *'LH'* – registered in Leith. Soon electricity was provided from a local power station, and in 1906 the New or Glen golf club was established on the East Links; an 18-hole course was built. The remarkably late lighthouse on the Bass Rock was completed in 1902, its keepers' families then living at Granton. The Fife ferry was revived early in the 20th century but closed in 1914. Seacliff House was gutted by fire in 1907, remaining as a ruin. The two world wars ended the use of the harbour for cargoes of guano, potatoes and grain, for it dried out at low tide, so limiting its development; the lifeboat station was closed in 1925 and the few remaining fishing boats switched to white fish and then to shellfish.

**Yachting and Sewage**: However, by 1951 the resident population had reached 4500, for whom typical town facilities were available, including North Berwick High School and two 18-hole and one 9-hole golf courses. By 1955 the East Lothian Yacht Club (ELYC) was based in an old granary beside the harbour, catering for the users of about 50 boats. By then the town council had provided various amenities including a fine heated open-air swimming pool adjoining the harbour, but failed to construct a sewage treatment plant, and all local sewage poured

Scottish Seabird Centre at North Berwick, opened in 2000 – a visitor attraction linked to cameras on the Bass Rock. (AL)

straight into the sea – too close to the town for comfort or health. A Woolworth store, then a considerable draw in a small town, was opened about 1955. An inshore lifeboat station was opened in 1967, replacing a long-lost facility; Fidra lighthouse was automated in 1970, but the Bass light was still manned until 1988.

**Retirement beside the Dirty Sea**: A caravan site was open by 1975, the year that the town council was abolished in favour of the double act of East Lothian District and Lothian Region, but the latter had more serious pollution problems to handle elsewhere, and despite new housing schemes completed to south and west, nothing was done about the sewage. In 1980 the 85-room *Marine* and the 49-room *Royal* were still the largest among a dozen or so hotels. By then another caravan site had been established, east of the town. Only a handful of small lobster and crab boats were based locally by the mid 1980s, but the harbour was still the base of the ELYC. Even in 1990 the beaches remained polluted because no sewage disposal plant yet existed, but despite this some building continued; by 1991 the population had crept up to some 5700, of affluent retired character plus a dormitory element.

**Rail Electrification and Seabird Centre**: The branch railway had narrowly escaped Dr Beeching's axe, but improvement began in the mid 1980s when its few rattling diesel commuter trains began to serve Edinburgh's Haymarket station as well as Waverley. The railway was electrified in 1991, with improved frequency, though with second-hand slam-door trains. In 1994 Presto opened a new store, and residential development has now speeded up. The Scottish Seabird Centre, built beside the former open-air swimming pool in 1999–2000, exploits the proximity of the Bass Rock, the world's largest gannetry. There are half a dozen hotels (together providing considerable employment), plus other smaller establishments for visitors. The company Caledonian Golf makes and supplies golf equipment.

## NORTH KESSOCK & Charlestown — Map 9, B4

***Easter Ross villages**, pop. 900* — OS 26: NH 6548

The name Kessock – applied to the former ferry across the firth between Inverness and the Black Isle – probably derives from the sixth century St Kessog. Ferry rights were granted as early as 1437 to the Dominican monastery in Inverness, and the ferry continued to operate after the Reformation – Pont's map of Moray made about 1600 faintly shows the word *'fyirr'*. By the 1750s North Kessock was a small village at the ferry terminal, from which a track led north to the Inverbreackie Ferry *(see Invergordon)*. Piers and an inn were constructed at North Kessock early in the 19th century. The sailing ferry was belatedly converted to steam in 1907, and later became a diesel car ferry, but the village remained small until the late 20th century; its population was about 570 in 1971. Much new housing has since grown at Charlestown, and new development along the waterside; but apart from a coastal caravan site 4 km to the west there were still only half a dozen basic facilities in 1980. The ferry was superseded in 1982 by the high-level Kessock Bridge, the first cable-stayed structure in Britain. Its devious approaches brought the A9, but took North Kessock to a considerable 7 km from Inverness, not 3 km as before! In 1991 the population was 883. By 1997 there was a new school at Charlestown. Continuing development is to be seen from the bridge approach; a hotel and the Dolphin Centre stand on the shore, and there is an orienteering course in Forestry Commission plantations to the north.

## NORTH QUEENSFERRY — Map 6, B5

***W. Fife village**, pop. 1050* — OS 65: NT 1380

Originally called *Ardchinnechenan* in the tongue-twisting 11th century Gaelic, North Queensferry in Fife lies on a promontory of hard rock extending into the Firth of Forth, later known as the Cruicks. It took its English name from Queen Margaret, the pious but energetic wife of Malcolm Canmore, who travelled this way across the Firth between Dunfermline and Edinburgh. The Fife shore became the base for the ferrymen and for shell fisheries; a *'hospital'* for travellers was established in the 12th century, and as early as 1415 North Ferry was a port at which ships could be victualled. At the Reformation the ferry rights passed from the abbey to the first joint-stock company in Scotland, in which eighteen people each bought a one-16th share – how they shared out the proceeds is a mystery! North Queensferry was still the base for the boats in 1750; the several routes radiating from the ferry were simply marked as tracks on the Roy survey of about 1750. However, the road to Kinross, which had already been improved north of Beath Kirk, was turnpiked in the 1750s, the first such scheme north of the Forth.

**Quarrying, Quarantine and Coaching**: Pennant noted what he called *"great granite quarries"* in 1769, actually cutting whinstone setts for paving London streets, and early in the 19th century the Earl of Hopetoun's quarry was cutting stone blocks to build docks at Leith. A post office opened in 1777, and by 1797 the ferry carried a daily postal service; both the terminals were post towns, though in 1799 Heron regarded North Queensferry as a *"village"*. The ferry piers were rebuilt about 1812, and the ferry was steam-operated from 1821; but it still paid duties to Inverkeithing in 1827, when Chambers named North Queensferry as a *"little village"*, distinguished by having the *"Lazaretto, where all goods to be landed on this part of the coast of Scotland from tropical countries, have to pass quarantine"*; but this feature was closed around 1830. By 1832 when William Cobbett landed at *"a little place called North Ferry"* en route to Dunfermline by post chaise, the *Ship Inn* was a key coaching point; it remained so up to 1845.

**Early Railways**: In 1847 the importance of the Queen's Ferry was diminished due to the new combined railway and ferry service from Edinburgh via Granton and Burntisland to Perth and Dundee. In 1867 the Queensferry rights were acquired by the North British Railway, which made North Ferry the base for three steamers and built a short low-level goods branch line from Inverkeithing, the main whinstone quarry at that time being on the Dunfermline road. A local coach for Dunfermline continued until a rail passenger service was provided in 1877. The *Albert Hotel* was open by 1888, and the 1891 population was 410.

**The Forth Railway Bridge**: In 1878–79 a start was made on building a flimsy rail suspension bridge designed by Thomas Bouch, who was discredited by the Tay Bridge disaster late in 1879. One pier was completed west of Inchgarvie (it now carries a navigation light) before all work was stopped, and a sturdy cantilever design by Fowler and Baker was adopted instead. The famous contractor William Arrol *(see Bridgeton)* took eight years to build the Forth Rail Bridge. This enormous steel cantilever structure, 110 m tall and 2.5 km in length (including approach viaducts), was financed by a consortium of railways, 65% of the capital coming from English companies. Opened in 1890, its 520-metre spans carry trains across the Firth at a height of 45 m; a high-level through station at North Queensferry replaced the low level terminus at the ferry. Although this still plied, the village lost much of its importance.

**Defences Over the Firth...**: A battery for two 152 mm guns was built on the cliffs at Carlingnose between 1894 and 1901, together with the smaller Coastguard Battery, to protect the Forth Bridge from a possible attack by sea. In the 1914–18 war a seaplane base was briefly established at Port Laing on the exposed east side of the peninsula, but its hangars were, it seems, very soon moved to Stannergate, Dundee. In 1953 the elderly little 20 m puffer *Arran Rose* was bought from Arran shipowners by J A White of North Queensferry. The ferry ceased to ply on the opening in 1964 of the 2.5 km long Forth Road Bridge, a fine government-financed suspension structure of conventional design by Freeman Fox & Partners, tolls being charged, originally in each direction. In the mid to late 20th century the village developed as a pleasure-sailing centre; in 1991 it had 1051 residents. A visitor centre, the *Queensferry Lodge* hotel and conference centre were built in 1988–89 high on the Ferry Hills beside the approach to the road bridge.

**...and Under Water**: While old quarries remain as dramatic cliffs in the Ferry Hills, a good use was found for the huge wet pit at Battery Quay beside and beneath the Forth Rail Bridge, where Phil Crane's *'Deep Sea World'* was built in 1992–93, creating a 5 million litre salt water *'walk through'* aquarium, spanning a deep level transparent passageway below sea level. In 1993 the catamaran *Spirit of Fife*, for a short time used on the abortively revived Burntisland to Granton run, was transferred to link Granton with North Queensferry to serve Deep Sea World. Locals feared the traffic and parking implications of what was claimed to be the largest *'indoor'* fish display in the world, which immediately became Fife's leading tourist attraction, with 300,000 customers within four months of opening.

**Floating a Second Road Bridge to Sink the Railways?**: In 1993 highly controversial plans for a second suspension bridge for road traffic, privately financed and to be built west of the 1960s bridge, were put forward by the Major government, supported by Fife Regional Council – but opposed in Edinburgh, which is quite unable to cater for any increase in car traffic. Meantime British Rail was even denied sufficient cash to continue a full painting programme on the vast extent of rusting steelwork of the magnificent but century-old bridge. Its 1994 successor Railtrack, once privatised, did however make a good start on treating the bridge, using modern paint systems; but progress was too slow and the work has sadly been suspended. Park and ride schemes have now been introduced, and the second road bridge scheme is on the back burner. Hard rock quarrying is remorselessly approaching North Queensferry from the Inverkeithing side.

## NORTH ROE — Map 14, B2

***Township, N. Shetland,*** *pop. 100* — OS 1 or 2: HU 3689

The most northerly settlement on the Shetland Mainland, the crofting centre of North Roe, lies on a low isthmus between two sheltered arms of the sea, known as voes. The area was already well-settled and had a church when Pont roughly mapped the northern isles about 1592. Later a herring station of no great significance, in 1951 its 133 or so people were served by an old village hall, a school, post office, and 7-line telephone exchange. A major unmanned lighthouse was first illuminated in 1977 on the Point of Fethaland, 5 km north of North Roe, to aid navigation on the approaches to the Sullom Voe oil terminal. The scattered population continued to decline for a quarter century and some crofts fell vacant; but 16 new houses arose around 1980, including six built by Hjaltland, Britain's most northerly housing association. In 1987 sheepskin rugs were produced at this bleak spot, which had a shop and 1-pump petrol filling station; the post office has closed since 1993, but the primary school is still open.

## NORTH RONALDSAY — Map 13, C1

***Small island, N. Orkney,*** *pop. 100* — OS 5: HY 7553

This, the most north-easterly of the Orkney Isles, is low, flat, agricultural and noted for an ancient settlement site, the Broch of Burrian, a Pictish standing stone and ornithology. At least ten settlements including St Ola Kirk were shown on Pont's tiny map dating from about 1592. But the island lacks good harbours and attracted little notice until the first true lighthouse in northern Scottish waters was built at Dennis Head by the Northern Lighthouse Board; this 21 m-tall tower was first lit in 1789, but discontinued in 1809 when the Sanday lighthouse came into service. It was reinstated in 1854 on a taller structure built on a slightly different site, leaving the original tower as a seamark. Airmail services were inaugurated to a small airfield in 1939. By 1951 the scattered population was about 225, but had fallen to 134 by 1971. By 1974 a passenger ferry to Kirkwall had opened up the remote island, where in 1981 two ornithologically minded doctors were among its few residents. Its famous seaweed-eating sheep, confined to the foreshore by a circumferential wall, then outnumbered people by fifteen to one! The sheep wall, badly damaged by gales in 1993, was rebuilt with naval help. In 1991 there were just 92 islanders and in 1994 the primary school had only 7 pupils (now 'Community School'); by 1999 the church built in 1812 was becoming derelict.

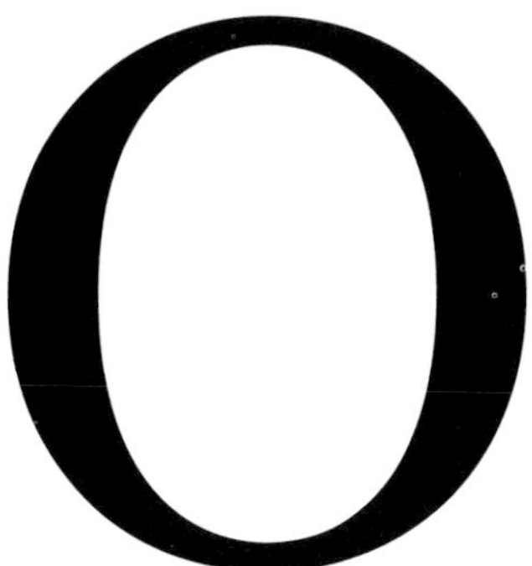

## OAKLEY, Carnock & Comrie — Map 16, C1

***W. Fife villages**, pop. 4200* — OS 65: NT 0389

Shiresmill, a hamlet on the Bluther Burn 9 km west of Dunfermline, was the 16th century birthplace of Robert Pont, but does not appear on any surviving maps made by his son, the geographer Timothy. As late as 1750 the Roy map showed the area around the ancient church of Carnock, 5 km west of Dunfermline, as trackless. The Dunfermline to Alloa road was turnpiked in 1810. The emparked Luscar House was finely built around 1840 near the hamlet of Balclune, 1 km north-east of Carnock, to designs by David Bryce. Some time after 1825 a deposit of blackband ironstone was discovered beside the Comrie Burn, 2 km west of Carnock, and the Forth Ironworks Company was established close by in 1845. The Stirling & Dunfermline Railway was opened in 1849 from Dunfermline to Oakley station beside the ironworks; it was extended to Alloa and Stirling soon after, completing a direct rail connection between Fife, the west of Scotland and the south. Later this line became part of the North British system, but passenger traffic did not build up. The ironstone was soon worked out, and in 1869 the ironworks was closed. By 1888 only its coke ovens remained, and eventually a school was built on the ironworks site.

**Iron and Coal from Blairhall**: In 1888 Beveridge described Comrie as a *"village, in great measure created by the Forth Ironworks. Several mining villages erected in connection with them, are now either wholly obliterated, or unroofed and dismantled"*. In the 1870s the Carron Iron Company developed the Blairhall pit, originally an ironstone mine but later also a colliery, 2 km west of the miners' rows at Oakley. Comrie had a post office by 1895. By 1901 the Oakley Collieries' Kinneddar pit lay near Blairsgreen to the north. However, in the 1890s production at Blairhall faltered, and in 1901 the population was still only about 400. The Coltness Iron Company took over Blairhall Colliery, and in 1906–11 sank two deep shafts close by to a depth of 612 m, to win coal from five seams. In 1924 a miners' welfare institute was opened at Blairhall. By then Balclune had been renamed Gowkhall, implying the presence of cuckoos!

**Comrie Colliery and Prefabs**: In 1935–40 the large Comrie Colliery was sunk west of Blairsgreen by the Fife Coal Company, to a depth of 385 m, linked to the siding of the by then defunct Kinneddar pit, and a small railway marshalling yard was built. However, the local coke ovens took their coal from Bannockburn Colliery. By then much basic council housing – including *'prefab'* bungalows – had been provided, and the population of Oakley was over 3750, with a timber merchant but little more than the facilities of a hamlet. Luscar House had lost its park during World War II, the railway station was closed in 1968, and by 1977 Comrie had also lost its secondary school. Meanwhile Blairhall colliery, which in 1947 had employed 1015 miners, was closed in 1969 (and demolished between 1975 and 1988). However the Comrie pit raised up to 3200 tonnes of coal a day in 1969 by the longwall method, and still employed 1150 men in 1977. There was also a *Rexco* smokeless fuel plant, presumably deriving from the former coke ovens.

**No Coal, More Forests, but Ill-health**: By 1981 Oakley had acquired a hotel, garages, doctors and a chemist. Comrie Colliery closed in 1986, and by 1988 the railway had been closed and lifted, soon becoming a footpath. This left only the abandoned pithead buildings and a scatter of bings to explain the existence of the rather grim-looking council estates of Oakley in this otherwise rural area. Though parts of Blairhall had been demolished, several private housing estates had recently been added to Comrie, Carnock and Gowkhall. In 1991 the quite youthful population of 4181 had 14% of the male workers jobless. But the environment was improving: by 1997 Comrie Colliery had been demolished and most of the bings had been cleared and afforested. It was therefore sad that in 1998 Luscar House was gutted by fire.

## OBAN & Dunollie — Map 4, C2

***Main town of Argyll**, pop. 8200* — OS 49: NM 8630

The Dalriadan centre of Dunollie was built in the sixth century on a defensible headland overlooking the Firth of Lorne, and was occupied into the eighth century. In the 12th or 13th centuries a simple stone castle of the MacDougalls was built atop Dunollie. Under 2 km to the south was Oban bay, an excellent anchorage, sheltered from the west by the Isle of Kerrera. The bay, whose name means *White* or *Empty* in Gaelic, was used as a fleet rendezvous by King Haco of Norway in 1263. Though its extremely hilly shores were blank on Pont's map of the Firth of Lorne about 1600, a water mill had turned just to the south at one time, for Pont named the *'Loch en na Oullin' (Lochan na muileann)* – Mill Pond in English.

**Trading Port and Custom House**: According to Chambers, the port of Oban was *"founded in the year 1713, by a trading company belonging to Renfrew"*. The first house was built about 1715; all its communication was then by sea, on foot or on horseback. In 1746 the MacDougalls abandoned the wind-swept Dunollie castle for a fine new house in a sheltered glen close by. Roy's map of about 1750 showed four tracks radiating from the small and still informal settlement of Oban, where a custom house was opened in 1765, and a post office in 1767. Although Boswell in 1773 described Oban as a *"small village, if a very few houses should be so called"*, it had already acquired two *"tolerable"* inns. An attempt was made in 1776 to establish Oban as a fishing station, but it lacked an adequate road. The harbour was at first used by only a few herring busses; but soon it became a port of registry, with the identification letters OB.

**Stevensons' Commerce and Industry create a Town**: *"About 1778 the spirit of building arose in this village"*, noted the Old Statistical Account in the 1790s; a tannery and a brewery existed by then, and a coasting trade had developed. In 1780 a new mansionhouse was built south-west of the growing village on what was to become Gallanach Road, as the centre of the Oban estate of the Duke of Argyll. By 1790 the Duke had also built a school, and in that year came both a new *Oban Inn* and the Oban branch of a Paisley bank. By 1797 Oban was a post town with a service on alternate days. The tiny Oban distillery – one of the earliest to become legal – dates from 1794, *"built by the family of Stevenson, the founders of the town of Oban, which previous to their advent was only a small fishing village"* (Barnard). The distillery buildings became closely enveloped by the town centre. About 1804–05 John Stevenson built the sloop *Caledonia* at Oban to carry stone for building the Caledonian Canal.

**Recognising the Potential and building the Roads**: Heron wrote prophetically in 1799 of a *"rising village; an excellent fishing-station which contains about 600 inhabitants, has a capacious harbour with good anchoring ground, and is likely to become, in a short time, a place of considerable importance"*. Oban was chartered as a very late burgh of barony in 1811, and in 1812 a continuous road was opened to Lochgilphead. Not until 1821 was Oban connected by a properly metalled road to the military road system (which had stopped short at Taynuilt), and so linked with the rest of Scotland; but from that year stage coaches ran regularly between Oban and Inveraray.

*The railway pier, Oban. Opened in 1880, it was not the town's first pier but became its busiest. The station was rebuilt in 1985.* *(JRH)*

**Centre for Steamship Lines**: From 1819 the earliest steamers, among them the *Comet*, connected Oban with Fort William, and with Glasgow via the Crinan Canal. From the building of the South Pier about 1820, Oban rapidly became a major ferry terminal for the Hebrides; regular steamers were extended to Tobermory by 1822, and to Portree and Iona by 1826. In 1827 Chambers described Oban as *"a flourishing village; the place of general rendezvous for the herring busses on the west coast, and admirably situated for trade. Oban is called at by the steam-boats which ply between Inverness and Glasgow through the Caledonian Canal"*. From 1828 the steamers regularly ventured across the open Minch to Stornoway. By 1829 the summer steamers to Iona landed tourist passengers at Fingal's Cave on Staffa, among them Felix Mendelssohn. The population of Argyll peaked about 1831, when it was still predominantly a subsistence economy, therefore limiting the scope for the development of non-tourist services and particularly industries at Oban.

**Famine, Tourism and Hutcheson's Steamers**: In the potato famine of 1846–47, Oban was one of two places chosen as the site for a grain depot as a temporary relief measure. By then tourist steamer services operated to the foot of Glenetive, with coach connections to Glencoe; they called at Loch Coruisk (Skye) from 1855. In 1851 David Hutcheson & Co of Glasgow (which became MacBraynes in 1879) started a steamer service between the Clyde and Stornoway, calling at Oban where it evidently made a great impact. When in the height of the tourist season of 1858 the observant German Fontana visited Oban – a *"little town graced with villas, the Charing Cross of the Highlands"* – he found the *Caledonian Hotel "packed to the roof"*, and also a makeshift dirty inn. In 1861 the well-known *Oban Times* newspaper was founded; the less successful *Oban Telegraph* was in publication in 1877. Meantime the *Great Western Hotel* and a gasworks had arrived in 1863, and about 1870 the Bank of Scotland built a new branch office.

**Railhead and Resort**: After sixteen years of effort the final section of the Callander & Oban Railway was opened from Dalmally to Oban in 1880, and the *Station Hotel* was built in 1881, when the population was just over 4000. Oban also grew as a yachting resort and a boatbuilding and shopping centre. The *Oban Times* flourished accordingly, acquiring a new office from 1883 and exporting large numbers of copies to expatriates from Argyll. Gaelic was still spoken by large numbers of people in the town in 1886 when the *"lately enlarged"* distillery was still small, producing only 160,000 litres of Highland malt annually.

**Tourism Rampant**: In 1886 Barnard found the *Craigard Hotel "decidedly well-appointed in every respect; pitched on top of a rock with a signally fine view"*. A *"mammoth hydropathic"* was finished only to the first storey, and later fell into ruin. The 1891 population was almost 5000; Oban High School was founded in 1892. In addition to those named above, six hotels were open by 1894, including the *Alexandra*, to Murray *"first class but expensive"*. McCaig, an Oban builder, erected McCaig's Tower, a large circular hilltop folly built as a job creation project. In 1895 he also built a fine home, which by 1953 had become the *Barriemore Hotel*. The tall *Royal Hotel* was built of pink sandstone in 1895, and Oban Town Hall was begun in 1897. Argyll Mansions and the *Marine* (later *Regent*)

*Hotel* were built about 1900. The station was expanded in 1903, and in 1905 Oban golf club established at Glencruitten a rocky 18-hole course designed by James Braid.

**Base for Lighthouses and the Navy**: Oban became the shore station for the keepers of the lighthouse on the remote Hyskeir or Oigh-sgeir, an islet 20 km west of Rhum, first lighted in 1904; from 1907 the Northern Lighthouse Board's tender *Hesperus* was based at Oban. Oban distillery was among those still busy about 1914. The small Roman Catholic cathedral was built on the waterfront in the 1930s. A Naval shore establishment called HMS *Caledonia* was based at Oban from 1943 to 1946. An inshore lifeboat station was opened in 1972, and by 1979 Oban had the base from which a helicopter serviced remote Hebridean lighthouses.

**Continuous Growth Post-war**: Meantime by 1953 a 9-hole municipal golf course had been laid out at Ganavan, where a large seaside pavilion was built. A youth hostel was open by the 1950s and the central Corran Restaurant dates from the 1960s. As a Transatlantic cable terminal, Oban was an early telephone group centre; by 1972 its trunk telephone exchange was large. A railway engine shed remained until the closure in 1965 of the line between Callander and Crianlarich; from that date Oban's train service connected (much more conveniently) directly to Glasgow via Crianlarich and Dumbarton, although the Ballachulish line from Connel was closed. Despite its mediocre road access, Oban's resident population has grown, from over 6000 in 1951, to 6900 in 1971 and 8203 in 1991; about then Oban High School had 1000 pupils. Glassware was made at Lochavullin from 1969 by Oban Glass; owned by Caithness Glass of Wick by 1983, the factory later made items such as paperweights – popular tourist buys.

**Fire Tragedy hits Hoteliers**: Meantime the 24-room *Esplanade Hotel* burnt down in 1973 with the tragic loss of 9 lives, leading to much tighter fire prevention measures for all British hotels and major alterations to many. But Oban grew in importance as a resort, with a slowly rising complement of nearly 50 hotels by 1980, perhaps aided by partial afforestation of the formerly bare hills to the north-east, and particularly to the south. The tiny *'World in Miniature'* museum was opened in 1984, and by 1992 contained over 60 exquisite displays by British craftsmen. A new small railway station building was opened in 1985. In 1989 the luxurious *Hebridean Princess*, converted from the Calmac ferry *Columba*, reinstated cruises from Oban to the islands.

**Overall Growth, but Rail Freight ends**: Space was freed for a new central hotel, ice rink, tourist centre, shops, fish hall and offices when in 1988–90 Low's built a new supermarket on the Lochavullin industrial estate; from 1994 this was a Tesco store, and another was to open in 1996. Highland cattle sales resumed after an interval of three years when a new livestock market was opened in 1994 a further 1 km to the south. The *Oban Star* newspaper was started in 1994 by a disaffected former editor of the *Oban Times*. The goods yard was released for other development when outwards timber traffic by rail ended in 1991; oil and gas freight soon ended also. By 1996 a striking growth of housing estates had occurred on all sides of the town, including Ganavan where a caravan site was laid out, and had created a virtually new settlement 2 km to the south at Soroba; close by was a new hospital.

**Fishing and Tourism**: The reduced station freed land at the South Pier for Stewart Allan's knitwear, and for Oban Glass, who left Lochavullin for a new town centre factory and shop, built in 1991–92. In the early 1990s Oban whisky was sold as a 14 year old single malt; the distillery is now owned by United Distillers & Vintners. By 1992 over 100 jobs were provided by fishing vessels using the new quay; whitefish, prawns and scallops are landed. In 1994 Weldfab of Lochavullin built a steel raft for Seawork of Dunstaffnage. A leisure centre project of 1995 was to have National Lottery aid. In 2000 the long-established Oban coastguard station was controversially closed, with 21 jobs lost; the work was transferred to electronic overviews from Stornoway and Greenock. By 1993 the Duke's mansion of 1780 had become the anglicised *Manor House Hotel*, joining the huge list of hotels, guest houses, and B&Bs; the youth hostel is still open, as are two backpackers' hostels.

## OCHILTREE

**Map 1, C2**

***Ayrshire village**, pop. 1000*

OS 70: NS 5021

The name *Ucheldref* in the Welsh language of ancient Strathclyde means *'High Settlement'*, implying an early date and a site on the top of the spur which separates the Burnock Water and the Lugar Water, 8 km west of Cumnock. But the 12th century motte and the later village of Ochiltree stand beside the Lugar Water 2 km farther east, at a moderate 100 m above sea level. A later castle keep, the seat of Lord Stewart in 1560 and the place where John Knox was married in 1564, appeared as *'Uchiltre'* Castle on Pont's map made around 1600; it later fell into ruin. Nearby was a bridge across the lade to a mill on the peninsula between the motte and the Kirk. A market was chartered in 1669. By the 1750s the Roy map showed Ochiltree as a linear settlement, partly on the Ayr–Cumnock road – later a turnpike – which doubled back in the centre of the village to cross over a bridge spanning the Burnock Water; a road also led northwards to Tarbolton.

**Railway, Mining and *'Green Shutters'***: Ochiltree was a *"village"* to Heron in 1799, but remained small. A sawmill was erected in the mid 19th century. When the Glasgow & South Western Railway opened its Ayr to Cumnock branch in 1872, Ochiltree station was placed 2 km south of the village. The population in 1891 was 500. A substantial drainage tile works was working by 1895, when Ochiltree also had a post office and a hotel, though it was scarcely the small town reflected in the famous novel *The House with the Green Shutters* by George Douglas Brown, who had been born in Ochiltree in 1869. The very large Barony colliery was sunk 2 km to the east of the village from 1906 *(see Auchinleck)*. But by 1951 Ochiltree was only a small village in terms of facilities, though with about 1250 people; the station had already closed, and the ancient mill, still apparently working in 1953, soon ceased to grind.

**Killoch Colliery**: The sinking of the large Killoch colliery was started in 1952 by the National Coal Board 3 km to the west. Its shafts which were surmounted by 54 m tall concrete winding towers were 700 m deep, tapping the reserves of the Mauchline basin, stated at 170 million tonnes in 1955, then the second greatest in Scotland. The mine was in full production by 1964 and for some time raised about a million tonnes a year from 8 seams, using modern methods including conveyors. Most of the housing for the miners was located elsewhere *(see Drongan)*, because they were no longer compelled as serfs to

*The tile works at Ochiltree, which operated from the late 19th century until the 1980s. This works made clay field-drain tiles, which were used in large numbers until plastic drainage pipes were introduced in the 1970s.* (RCAHMS / JRH)

live beside the pit, or to suffer at home the environmental degradation caused by large scale mineral working. So Ochiltree gradually shrank to a small village of just under 900 people in 1971. By 1972 the railway had vanished east of Killoch Colliery, then the largest in the west of Scotland, employing 2165 men in 1977. The sawmill and the tile works still worked until about 1981.

**Goodbye to Deep-Mined Coal**: Serious blows fell on Ochiltree when Killoch Colliery was closed in 1986, followed by the closure of the long-lasting Barony pit in 1989, ending an activity in which 13,000 Ayrshire men had worked a century earlier. The village population in 1991 was 983. However, the modern washery and blending plant at Killoch was retained, and in 1991–92 was treating opencast coal from Chalmerston near Dalmellington, rail-hauled via Ayr and Annbank Junction. It despatched by rail both washed coal to the Roche Products plant at Dalry, and slurry to Methil power station until that was mothballed. In 1997 coal was still moved by rail from Killoch to Longannet, and two trains a week carried coal to the Ketton cement works near Peterborough. Ochiltree still has its pub and post office.

## OLD ABERDEEN — Map 10, C3

***North-central part of Aberdeen,*** *pop. 16,700* — OS 38: NJ 9408

In the sixth century St Mochricha or Machar gave his name to the parish of Old Machar at the mouth *(aber)* of the River Don, and so founded Old Aberdeen, originally called *Aberdon*, hence the term *Aberdonian*. Aberdon had a thanage from about the 11th century, and was named about 1120 as the most northerly trading community in Scotland. It was already sufficiently important for David I to decide to transfer the episcopal see from Mortlach (*see Dufftown*), around 1125. Work on a grander cathedral was begun in sandstone in 1164 by Bishop Cheyne, who also founded St Peter's Hospice for aged priests about 1168.

**Competition from New Aberdeen**: The name Aberdeen originated when a 12th century trading burgh was founded at the mouth of the Dee only 3km to the south, a shift to a much better harbour, despite the old saw *"Ae mile o' Don's worth twa o' Dee, except for salmon, stane and tree"* – i.e. the Don generally passed through more fertile areas. Bishop Cheyne is credited with building the Bridge of Balgownie across the Don narrows. It is hard to believe that its single gothic arch was not completed until 1329; probably this was a rebuilding date after the Wars of the Succession, by which time New Aberdeen had become the main commercial centre. In the building season of 1330 the masons began to create a Bishop's Palace, but Old Aberdeen was burned by Edward III of England in 1336. After the Black Death of 1350, some work was resumed on the cathedral, but went slowly for 75 years.

**15th Century University and Burgh**: The bulk of the cathedral was built in granite by a local mason in the years 1425–40, and the Bishop's palace was rebuilt about 1459. Until 1489 Old Aberdeen was regarded as a township; the bishop then obtained a barony charter, with a market and two annual fairs. The contemporary traveller John Hardyng mentioned a university at Aberdeen as early as 1415, long before the normally quoted date. Such are the uncertainties of history! On the evidence of a papal bull of 1495, what is usually regarded as the oldest part of the University, King's College, was founded in Old Aberdeen in 1494 by Bishop Elphinstone. The cathedral served as the sole parish church until 1498, when the expansion of Old Aberdeen resulted in Elphinstone creating an additional parish named Snow *(St Mary ad Nives)*, where he also arranged the building of a church.

**Golf on the Links and Lead in the Sea**: Medicine of a kind was taught at the University from 1505; the erection of its oldest surviving building, King's College Chapel, was completed in 1506. In 1560 King's College had seven appropriated churches. Meantime by 1538 golf was being played on the King's Links between the Aulton and the sea. The cathedral's famous ceiling, dating from 1520, most fortunately survived the stripping of the lead from the roof by Regent Murray in 1567; the stolen lead, and that seized from Elgin cathedral, was lost when the ship carrying it struck the Girdlestone rock 2 km east of New Aberdeen harbour; more was obtained and the roof repaired.

**After the Reformation**: Water was channelled to the Aulton from the Don at Gordon's Mills and Kettock's Mills, 1 km or so to the west; these together with a *'Miltoun'* were shown on Robert Gordon's map of Aberdeenshire, made by 1642. About 1650 the bishop's palace was largely destroyed by troops under the inappropriately named General Monk. By that time the names *Kirktown of Seaton* or *The Aulton* were used for Old Aberdeen, called *"mother city of New Aberdeen"* by the traveller Richard Franck in 1656. The cathedral tower above the crossing, weakened by neglect and Monk's depredations, collapsed in 1688, taking the choir and transepts with it.

**Paper and Poverty**: In 1690 Gordon's Mills brought the fledgling paper industry to the area, and Balgownie was chartered as a burgh of barony in 1707. Roy's map made about 1750 showed radial tracks to Aberdeen, Kintore, Old Meldrum, Udny and Ellon, but no mills close by. Leys, Still & Co refounded Gordon's Mill in 1758 and soon had become large manufacturers of thread. The Gordon's Mills Farming Club, founded in 1758, helped to improve the moors to the west for agriculture. In 1765 when Alexander Carlyle visited Old Aberdeen he called it *"a village by no means magnificent"*. The College then had nine professors, but like Marischal College was *"ill-endowed and ruinous, attended by so small a number of students"* that he suggested amalgamation (this came about 95 years later). Pennant too called Old Aberdeen *"a poor town"* in 1769; its population was around 4000, with about 100 students in the College, living mainly on oatmeal.

**One Dull Miserable Street**: Despite cash problems, the attractive granite Town House was built in 1788. By 1797 there was only one annual fair, and Heron noted in 1799 that *"this town consists of one street, the buildings of which are for the most part ancient"*; but the College library held *"a good collection of modern books"*. From that time most new developments took place in the Woodside and Kittybrewster areas, though the Aulton and Seaton breweries were in use by 1825; the former lasted until at least 1906. In 1827 Chambers found the Aulton *"subsisting chiefly by its college and a few trifling manufactures"*. The college had *"about 500 students, mainly of theology."* The mail coach then went by way of Inverurie and Huntly to Fochabers.

**Post Office, Plants and Pittodrie Park**: Telford's new Don Bridge *(see Bridge of Don)* was built in 1830–31, bypassing Old Aberdeen and the Brig o' Balgownie. Old Aberdeen post office was in business by 1845, and at some time a militia depot was built south of the Aulton. The burgh of Old Aberdeen was merged with New Aberdeen in 1891. In 1898 the University laid out its small botanic garden beside the Aulton. Pittodrie, a former rubbish tip beside a gasworks just east of the Aulton, became the home of Aberdeen FC in 1899, 18 years after the club's foundation. A new King's College building was erected in 1913, and in 1925 the King's Links 18-hole municipal golf course was laid out. At that time Aberdeen FC began to improve Pittodrie.

**Submerged in the City**: Though the bulk of the rather bleak 1960s buildings of the enlarged University were located in the Old Aberdeen area, its lovingly conserved core had by then been largely submerged in Aberdeen's council housing estates. The School of Agriculture was also at King Street by 1978; new development had moved on beyond Balgownie and to the north of Bridge of Don. In 1978 Pittodrie became Britain's first all-seater football ground, and in 1983 Aberdeen FC won the European Cup-Winners' Cup by beating Real Madrid in Gothenberg. The last gasholder beside Pittodrie was cleared in 1995. The King's Links golf courses are now called Bon Accord, Caledonian, and Northern; Linksfield Academy now has about 400 pupils. Old Aberdeen is conserved with care, and changes slowly despite the swirling activities of the many surrounding places that comprise the Oil City *(see head of Aberdeen article)*.

## OLD DAILLY

**Map 1, C3**

***Ayrshire hamlet**, pop. 200* — OS 76: NX 2299

By about 1600 Dailly Kirk stood some 4 km east of Girvan, at a place nowadays known as Old Dailly, west of which was the undateable Camregan Castle. To the south-east was the 16th century tower of Penkill Castle; north of the Water of Girvan stood the L-plan tower of Killochan Castle, of similar age. Pont's map showed castles emparked, while downstream stood three water mills, for the area was well settled. There was a parish school from 1630, but over the centuries the other features largely vanished. The Roy map of about 1754 showed a road paralleling each bank of the river, that to the south passing both the *'Old Kirk of Dailly'* (from which another road led south to Barr) and 5 km upstream the early 18th century Dailly *(q.v.)* Kirk. John Thomson, born in Dailly parish in 1718, became a well known painter of Scottish landscapes; long afterwards Penkill Castle became a haunt of the pre-Raphaelites, and the emparked mansion of Bargany was built 2 km east of the old church. Unlike New Dailly 5 km upstream, the area remained entirely rural; in 1951 some 450 people lived around Old Dailly, and a quarry was open north-east of Killochan. The Penwhapple reservoir, 4 km to the south-east, had been lately impounded by 1963. By 1981 there were probably under 200 residents, though the parish primary school had remained in use (but no longer). Barr now operate the Tormitchell quarry. Old Dailly Kirk is a ruin and, like the Bargany Gardens, now a tourist attraction.

## OLD DEER

**Map 10, C2**

***Small Buchan village**, pop. 250* — OS 30: NJ 9747

This little place in the centre of Buchan has a long, chequered but fascinating history. A prehistoric stone circle, one of several nearby, stood on Parkhouse Hill above the South Ugie Water. The early St Drostan established a church in the valley about 500 AD; his brother Yochoch, a Pictish king, is said to have given his name to the nearby Aikey Brae and hence to the later fair; the name Deer comes from the Gaelic word *Doire*, meaning a grove or hollow. The Abbey of Deer was founded later in the sixth century, allegedly by St Columba, and sited on a sunward slope 1 km north-east of the stone circle. All that remains of the original Abbey of Deer is the famous ninth to twelfth century *Book of Deer*, including the earliest Gaelic writing to have survived.

**The New Abbey**: In 1218 the abbey was re-founded for three Cistercian monks from Kinloss Abbey by a Norman knight, William Comyn, who by marriage became Earl of Buchan. A rectangular precinct wall was erected, and the new buildings were trimmed with red sandstone mouldings from a quarry at Byth. The area was devastated in the early 14th century wars of independence, but the abbey – whose mill turned within the precinct – was able to recover. There were 14 brethren in 1544, and before the Reformation the abbey owned three other mills, plus the *"fishertown of Peterhead"*, and wide estates mainly in Aberdeenshire; but it had only four appropriated churches.

**Deer in Lay Hands**: In 1560 the abbey was *'represented'* in Parliament by its egregious Commendator Robert Keith, who with his brother George secured its temporal lordship from James VI in 1587 and renamed the abbey the *'Manor Place of Deer'*; but sadly this did not prevent the abbey from becoming a ruin like its predecessor. By 1593 the village of Deer a kilometre east of the abbey, though not apparently a burgh of barony, had become the centre of a presbytery. Pont's manuscript map made about 1600 showed a substantial settlement with a smithy, a waulkmill and a bridge. By 1720 there was also development at New Deer *(q.v.)*.

**Mansions, and Fairs Galore**: In 1750 according to the Roy map four tracks converged on Old Deer, connecting Udny and Ellon to the south with Strichen and Fraserburgh to the north, by way of three bridges over the South Ugie Water. The most northerly was at Bridgend, where for many years the famous three-day *Aikey Fair* was held each July; beside the southernmost bridge of Pitlarg was the Mill of Aden – pronounced *Adden*. In the early 18th century Pitfour House was built north of the old village for the Ferguson family; James Ferguson, born in 1734, laid out the villages of Longside, Mintlaw and New Deer. Saplinbrae was built as a dower house for Pitfour in 1756, Aden House was built for James Russell from 1781, and a new parish church was built in 1788, adjoining the ruins of its predecessor. In 1797 Old Deer or Aikey had the distinction of the largest number of fair days scheduled for any stance in Scotland, fourteen no less. In 1799 Heron described Old Deer as a *"village noted for a great annual fair of cattle"*.

**Post, Brewing, Distilling and Rebuilding**: A post office opened in 1802. From 1809 one Ferguson of Pitfour sensibly preserved the abbey ruins; Pitfour House was much enlarged for him about 1816, and in 1820–35 was given fine outbuildings designed by John Smith, surrounded by a major park with a lake. In 1832 a new manse was built on the site of the sixth century abbey. But Old Deer in the 1820s was still *"a mean unsightly place, consisting of one street"*; another village of primitive huts also stood near the Aikey Brae. Strange to say nothing more permanent came of the frequent fairs except for Biffie brewery, which may have originated in the 1830s; in 1845 its proprietors Milne & Co erected the tiny Glenadon (or Glenaden) distillery nearby. The village of Old Deer was largely rebuilt in the second quarter of the 19th century, and in 1850 an Episcopal church was added.

**The Abbey desecrated**: Sadly another Ferguson laird, an Admiral, mindlessly destroyed much of the abbey ruins in 1854. Pratt noted in 1858 that Aden House was *"an elegant and commodious mansion"*, also mentioning the *"new mill of Bruxie"*, 1 km north-west of the abbey; by then the Aikey Fair was just a one-day event. From 1861 a railway line passed between the abbey site and the fair stance, but the nearest station – Mintlaw – was nearly 2 km east of the village. About 1880 Saplinbrae was enlarged into a modest mansion. In 1886 Wilson & Co owned both the brewery and the distillery, which used homegrown barley to make a mere 55,000 litres of Highland malt whisky per year. In 1894 Old Deer had an inn, smithy and post office; Biffie survived as a farm. The distillery closed about 1910 and the brewery also soon closed. Pitfour House was demolished in 1926–27; its unique conservatory was moved to Kinloch House at St Fergus. In 1937 a church hall was gifted by a well-heeled minister. The Aikey Fair stance was marked on OS maps as late as 1955.

**Using the Rural Heritage**: By 1951 Old Deer was a small village with a tiny secondary school, and some 400 people. The secondary classes were abandoned before primary classes were moved to a new school at Stuartfield in 1979; the old building later became Maidstone House, an extraordinarily spacious luxury home, its kitchen the former science lab! Aden House had fallen on evil days, but by 1980 its shell had been preserved by the then District Council as the centre for a country park. In the early 1980s Saplinbrae House became a hotel, and by 1992 other tourist facilities included a 5-star caravan site, camping ground and the North-East Scotland Agricultural Heritage Centre. By 1995 the railway formation had become the Buchan Line Walkway, since renamed the *'Formartine and Buchan Way'*. The neo-classical stable block and mock Doric temple of Pitfour House survived benign neglect to be sold for restoration in 2000. Thistle Marine has modest premises, and a few modern houses can be seen. *Saplinbrae* remains a small hotel, while the *Aden Arms* and the imposing *Old Bank House* provide B&B in the mellow stone village.

## OLD KILPATRICK — Map 15, B4

***N. Clyde small town,*** *pop. 2400* — OS 64: NS 4673

Around 140 AD the Romans built a large fort on the north bank of the tidal River Clyde some 7 km east of Dumbarton Rock, where the hills approach the river and a stream provided ample fresh water. Under Antoninus they decided in 142 to wall off the northern unconquerable part of Caledonia; the western end of their short-lived wall sprang from this fort. By about 170 the Romans had abandoned the wall and the area entered the dark ages, but settlement may have lingered on. The site may have been the birthplace of St Patrick, which would explain its Gaelic name *'the Church of Patrick'* and the dedication of an ancient well. The ancient Erskine Ferry crossed the Clyde from Old Kilpatrick, where a *'hospital'* was set up around 1200. When mapped by Timothy Pont around 1600, Kilpatrick Kirk and a mill stood on either side of the stream in a thickly settled area; a parish school was started in 1622.

**Textiles, Transport and a Fine Old Lady**: By the time of Roy's survey about 1754, roads from Glasgow and Bearsden via Duntocher converged at a recognisable village, en route to Dumbarton. Then came the Forth & Clyde Canal, constructed along the riverside to its junction with the Firth at Bowling, and opened in 1790. A post office opened in 1793, served by a penny post from Glasgow. In 1799 the area also contained two or more bleachfields and two printfields. In 1858 the Glasgow, Dumbarton & Helensburgh Railway (later a North British branch) was opened between Bowling and the national rail system at Cowlairs on the Edinburgh & Glasgow Railway, passing north of the village and crossing the Lusset Glen on a four-arched viaduct. A station was sited at Old Kilpatrick, whose population in 1891 was 1300; it remained a rural village with an inn. Jane Cross, born locally in 1887, became a war nurse, medical missionary and the revered founder of a school in Malawi; she was Scotland's oldest woman on her death in 1996 at 109.

**Rail Competition, Ships, Buses and Oil**: In 1896 a second railway was opened, the nominally independent Lanarkshire & Dunbartonshire – backed by the Caledonian Railway (CR). It followed a route between the canal and the river, with a second station. This encouraged development, and in 1906 Napier & Miller moved their shipyard to Old Kilpatrick from the site of Clydebank's Rothesay Dock. For a time in the 1920s the Atlantic Engine Company also built small vessels at a yard in the village, and Aurora Lamps made street lighting bulbs until the 1960s. Housing was unfortunately built over part of the Roman fort site about 1925, and a bus garage, the base for Glasgow to Balloch services, covered the remainder. The main shipyard was closed in 1930, but was reactivated from 1941 to 1945 so that Alex Findlay & Co could erect vessels that were prefabricated at Motherwell; a government food store was also built. By 1941 a large Admiralty oil depot and wharves occupied the river frontage between the village and Dalmuir, extending 1 km inland; of about 75 oil tanks, eleven burned in the 1941 air raids. After the war Esso took over the depot. By 1945 the village had been bypassed by the A82 (later a dual carriageway), and the Erskine Ferry carried motor vehicles.

**Erskine Bridge dominates**: In 1951 Old Kilpatrick had a population of over 3200, which remained quite steady for decades; but most of its facilities were only those of a small village. The original railway was electrified in 1961, giving Kilpatrick station the benefit of the famous *'Blue Trains'*. In 1964 the ex-CR route was closed west of the ferry approach; that to the east remained open for freight, but was not in regular use by 1993. The car ferry ceased to ply in 1972 as soon as the Erskine Bridge opened; its complex approaches sterilised much of the village surroundings. At least in the 1980s the inland extensions of the oil depot were cleared of tanks. In 1991 the quite elderly population was down to 2408, half of whom lived in flats. The station, school and library remain open.

## OLDMELDRUM

**Map 10, B2**

***Aberdeenshire small town,*** *pop. 2000* — OS 38: NJ 8027

About 5 km north-east of Inverurie in the rural parish of Bourtie is the hill fort of Barra. This stands guard above Oldmeldrum or Old Meldrum, sited on a windy col over 100 m above sea level in Meldrum parish, part of the rolling agricultural district of Garioch *(pronounced Geerie)*. The name Meldrum may derive from a windmill on a *drum* or knoll, and the settlement is certainly old, for the Earl of Buchan's army was quartered in Old Meldrum at Christmas 1307 before fleeing from Bruce. The use of the prefix *'Old'* can perhaps be explained if the Duff family's 13th century Meldrum Castle, 2 km north of the village, replaced an earlier fortification and was therefore originally named *'New Meldrum'*. Pont and Gordon's maps of the 1640s showed *'Auld Meldrum'* as a tiny place; at that time the Garioch was a detached part of Banffshire.

**Burgh, Inns, Mansions and Post**: In the 17th century the tower of Mounie Castle was built 4 km west of Old Meldrum, and the defensible mansion of Barra Castle was erected 2 km south-west of the village. This became a burgh of barony in 1671, and the small *Morris's Hotel* was built in 1673; the *Meldrum Arms* inn was also of this period and a church was built in 1684. About the same time Meldrum Castle was converted into the mansion of Meldrum House by descendants of its original owners. Roy's map of about 1749 showed Old Meldrum as a large village, served by three radial tracks, the way east to Udny being boldly marked; the others followed the line of the modern A947, leading to Turriff and *'New Kirk'*, i.e. Newmachar. A post office existed, but no road to Inverurie.

**Linen, Distilling, Knitting – and Malaria?**: Linen was produced commercially by 1764 at Old Meldrum, called by Alexander Carlyle in 1765 *"a pretty little thriving village, very populous"*; it is clear that there was already a surprisingly good inn. In 1797 Old Meldrum was a post town with a daily service, and also an annual fair. The Glengarioch (pronounced *Glengeerie)* distillery was built in 1791–97 by Ingram, Lamb & Co; there was also at one time a brewery. In 1799 Heron referred to Old Meldrum as a *"town of almost 800 inhabitants, its chief manufacture stockings"*; as in other parts of the county these were evidently knitted for sale through Aberdeen. In 1844 Old Meldrum was the birthplace of Patrick Manson, a pioneer in tropical medicine and discoverer of the role of the mosquito in transmitting malaria; he was later knighted.

**Golf and Whisky outlast the Railway**: In 1856 Old Meldrum became the terminus of a branch of the Great North of Scotland Railway from Inverurie, and a new Town Hall was built in 1857. Barnard in 1886 described Old Meldrum as *"a market town very irregularly built"*; the distillery was then steam powered, using local barley and peat and employing twelve men to produce 225,000 litres of malt whisky annually. About 1887 it was sold to William Sanderson, a Leith blender. The golf club was founded in 1885 and laid out a 9-hole moorland course. The 1890s population was over 1300, and the village inn was the *Meldrum Arms*. The railway was closed to passengers in 1931, the first service in north-east Scotland to be withdrawn. In the 1930s Meldrum House was reduced in size, and by 1954 had been converted by Robin Duff into one of the area's three hotels. Old Meldrum had a population of under 1700 in the 1950s, with average village facilities. The railway was closed

*The Glengarioch distillery, Old Meldrum – one of the oldest malt whisky distilleries, founded in the 1790s. It is now owned by the Japanese company Suntory.* *(JRH)*

to freight in 1966 and was lifted, the station site becoming an industrial estate.

**Whisky, Tomatoes and Pigs**: Other facilities generally survived, and the place retained a compact urban appearance. An internal bypass, opened in 1968, took through traffic out of the main square. Temporary closure of the distillery was announced in 1968, on the day of the author's first visit to Old Meldrum! The burgh vanished into Gordon district in 1975, but three hotels remained. By 1976 the distillery had reopened under Stanley P Morrison Ltd, making a peaty single malt; visitors were welcomed, and tomatoes and peppers were grown, using the waste heat and $CO_2$. By 1990 the Pig Improvement Company had its Scottish base on the Meadows industrial site, agriculture being by then just another industry. The population was stable at almost 2000 in 1991, when the *Meldrum House Hotel* was on the market for the first time in 700 years! In 1996 Sellar's still dealt in combine harvesters and farm machinery locally (and in four other towns and villages).

**Industries, Shops and Golf**: The distillery now works under Morrison Bowmore, and a quite substantial modern industrial estate south of the village includes the works of Monyana Engineering, D & R Engineers (winch and lifting services), Filpumps (waste water pumps), and CSC Crop Protection. A primary school, bank and post office are open, as are medical and other services, including fire and police stations, and there's a remarkably wide range of shops. The local club's course has been extended to 18 holes. The *Meldrum House Hotel* opened its new golf course in 2000; a listed statue of a sailor stands outside the pleasant *Meldrum Arms Hotel* in the centre of this tiny town.

## OLD MELROSE

**Map 3, B4**

***Borders location,*** *pop. under 100* — OS 73 or 74: NT 5834

The Roman road later called *Dere Street* crossed the River Tweed 4 km east of the site of the ancient fort on the triple Eildon Hills, which they aptly named *Trimontium*. By about 630 St Aidan of Lindisfarne had founded an abbey in the vicinity, a meadowland location in a loop of the River Tweed. Its name may derive from St Maolruabh, founder of Applecross, or perhaps from Mailros, meaning *bare point* in Gaelic, for Dorothy Wordsworth wrote in 1803 of the *"green promontory, a small hill skirted by the river"* where Walter Scott told her the monks had *"first fixed their abode and raised a temporary building of wood"*. Old Melrose had a bishop for a time, and was said by Bede to be surrounded in the seventh century by towns and villages where St Cuthbert preached. It also had a thanage by about the year 1000, but its Columban monastic community had been deserted by 1074, half a century before the foundation of the present Melrose. A tiny farming settlement survived to be shown as *'Old Melross'* on Pont's maps made about 1600, and into the present day.

## OLD RATTRAY

**Map 10, C1**

***Buchan settlement,*** *pop. under 100* — OS 30: NK 0858

In the 13th century Old Rattray had a church and a castle of the Comyn Earls of Buchan. It lay beside a large inlet of the sea on the coast about 12 km north of Peterhead; but its port was too remote and too subject to shifting sandbars to be successful. Its trivial trade and turf-walled houses were the subject of a legal tug-of-war between the Earls Marischal and Errol, which was resolved in 1564 by that ill-fated monarch, Mary. She created there the least successful of all Royal Burghs – perhaps fortunately, her only such act! Pont's map of about 1600 named the inlet as Strathbeg, and sketched a row of buildings at *'Rattra'*. Out at sea he noted *'Rattra bridges'*; Rattray Briggs is an unofficial name for some offshore rocks. Cod fishing and trade with the Dutch developed, and in 1675 the burgh still functioned; but in 1696 only 17 adults lived at Rattray.

**The Great Storm**: About 1720 a great storm blocked the inlet, turning it into a brackish loch, which then rose appreciably in level. In 1732 there were nine or ten houses, but the harbour was still choked by sand, and the burgh was functionally long extinct: it was noted that *"there is no custom paid at its markets"*. However Roy's map, surveyed about 1750, showed the sea inlet was again open and about fourteen scattered buildings still existed in the area of Rattray Chapel, including Lochbank, Watertown and to the west the house of Haddo in its garden. A track – of which remnants survived two centuries later – led southwards to pass east of St Fergus Kirk. It is possible that there was a ferry to the tip of the large sandspit which depended from the north, for another track was indicated along it to Fraserburgh. The harbour was soon finally choked by sand to form the landlocked Loch of Strathbeg, which became a prime crossroads for wild geese.

**Lighthouse and Birds**: Better known than the old burgh is the low-lying coastal feature of Rattray Head, 2 km to the east. Rattray Head lighthouse, whose tower stands on a solid drum of Rubislaw granite nearly 17 m in diameter, was built on the Ron Rock, an offshore tidal reef, in 1892–94 and first lit in 1895; its keepers' houses were among the dunes. During the second world war an airfield was laid out south of the loch, but then fell into disuse. By 1980 the pub in the hamlet of Blackhill on the main road had become the *Keyhead Hotel*, but in the 1980s Old Rattray proper consisted of a country lane giving access to a dozen scattered buildings, the castle earthworks and remains of the chapel. The lighthouse was automated in 1982. By 1991 the RSPB had created a visitor centre for the Loch of Strathbeg nature reserve.

## OLD RAYNE

**Map 10, B2**

***Aberdeenshire small village,*** *pop. 750 (area)* — OS 38: NJ 6728

An ancient stone circle stands on a knoll near the headwaters of the River Urie, 12 km north-west of Inverurie in the Garioch area, originally part of Banffshire. (Old) Rayne was chartered nearby in 1492–93 as a burgh of barony. Rayne parish supported a school from 1602, perhaps at the Kirkton at New Rayne 1.5 km to the north, which never flourished. Blaeu's map based on Pont's and Gordon's pre-1642 data showed the Kirkton as a separate place and gave *'Auld Rayn'* no emphasis. However, Old Rayne market was chartered in 1628, an inn was opened and it had a post office by 1745. Roy's map of about 1750 showed a track between Inverurie and Strathbogie following the east bank of the river, passing *'Old Rain'*, a small village with a church; *'Pitmachy'*, west of the unbridged Urie, was six buildings. Old Rayne was a post town by 1797, with a mail service on alternate days; five or six fair days were scheduled, of which the St Lawrence fair was perhaps the most important. But industry shunned Old Rayne and it was never closely approached by a railway. Its market had vanished by

*The mercat cross at Old Rayne, which was chartered as a burgh in 1492 and as a market in 1628. The market had ceased by 1875 and little but a hamlet remains around the cross.* *(JRH)*

about 1875, and Murray ignored the village in 1894. Old Rayne became little more than a declining hamlet, though its inn remained open and its mercat cross still stands. Around 1980 a joinery business at Pitmachie specialised in farm buildings. By 1999 some development had resumed, and the inn had become the *Lodge Hotel.*

## OLD SCONE

**Map 6, B3**

***Hamlet n. of Perth,*** *pop. under 100* — OS 53 or 58: NO 1126

Scone – pronounced *Scoon* – lies on the east bank of the Tay, Scotland's longest river, beside a ford and near the convergence of several tributaries. An ancient stone circle to the east was later perhaps a meeting point for the Caledonians; two Roman fort sites not far away imply that the legions intended to overawe their meetings at a site later marked by the *Mote* (or *'Boot') Hill.* Scone was central to four of the seven Pictish provinces, and had a Culdee monastery from the sixth century; it was first recorded as the Pictish capital in 710. When the Scottish usurper Kenneth MacAlpin treacherously assassinated the Pictish nobility at Scone in 843, and greatly enlarged the state of Alba by adding their lands to his, Scone became its capital. Their symbolic Coronation Stone or *'Stone of Destiny'* was either brought to Scone from Dunstaffnage (*q.v.*) via Dunkeld, as legend tells, or – as others claim and MacAlpin's devious character suggests was more likely – merely quarried locally to bamboozle the credulous!

**From Coronation Centre to Perth's Second Fiddle**: Scotland's kings were crowned at Scone, which had a thanage from about the 11th century, and a large Augustinian abbey was founded on a 5ha site in 1114. According to Heron, the abbot owned a ship to carry its goods. In 1128 Scone became the caput of a sheriffdom – a temporary measure, for that most perspicacious of Scottish kings, David I, had already selected a greenfield location with more trading potential, at the head of tidewater 3km to the south on the opposite bank of the river; there about 1125 he founded the Royal Burgh of Perth. Though Scone had a market, and in the 12th or 13th century a *'hospital'* was provided, it appears never to have been made a burgh, and by 1228 had lost its sheriffdom to Perth. The Stone of Scone was stolen by the English in 1296 to symbolise the Speaker's power in their parliament, where it remained, except for one colourful episode in 1950, until 1996. However, during the 14th century Scone was still the place third most often chosen for the signing of the Scottish royal charters.

**The Impact of the Reformation**: Around 1500 Robert Carver, an Augustinian canon at Scone Abbey, was composing complex and beautiful sacred music in up to 19 parts. But in 1559 the abbey was destroyed by a mob from Perth, and was later replaced by the Earl of Gowrie's palace, built in 1580. A church was built on the Boot Hill, and coronations were continued at Scone up to the crowning of Charles II in 1651. But Scone's people became weavers and bleachers, and the ancient capital was only *"the bulk of a country village"* in 1689. Defoe noted that in the 1720s the palace was in good repair, and *"very large, the front 65 yards in breadth"*.

**Famous Sons, Bleaching – and Obliteration**: William Murray, Lord Mansfield, born in Scone in 1705, did much to codify England's muddled laws of commerce. In the late 18th century a large bleachfield was built at Stormontfield 3km to the north, which in 1794 was bleaching about 450,000m of linens a year. In 1799 Heron saw Old Scone as a *"village of nearly 500 inhabitants"*, but soon afterwards their rights were bought out by the feudal landlord, the Earl of Mansfield, who in an act of single-minded vandalism demolished the village, leaving standing only the town gate, the mercat cross and the Boot Hill. David Douglas, born in Old Scone in 1798, was said to have been its last baby; he became the naturalist who collected specimens in North America and brought to Europe the first Douglas fir, a species named in his honour. The first tree that Douglas planted was still standing in 1995.

**Old Scone replaced for Private Pleasure**: In 1802–12 Mansfield had parts of the Gowrie palace rebuilt into the private mansion called Scone Palace, and in 1805 he founded New Scone *(q.v.)*. Chambers wrote that by 1827 *"the Earl of Mansfield, who represents the old family of Stormont"* had replaced the old village by *"a wilderness of pleasure-grounds"*. Stormontfield too fell silent in 1861, and in 1894 when the Palace Park monopolised 4km of Tay frontage, Murray stated *"no admittance is granted except by special order"*. In 1895 a tile works was open 1.5km north of Old Scone. By 1939 the Stormontfield bleach works had been reactivated and the Perth National Hunt Racecourse adjoined the Moot Hill; in 1992 it was the only permanent course open north of the Forth, but hosted Scotland's top jump event, the Perth Festival. Meantime around 1960 a successor Earl of Mansfield made amends for his ancestors' misdeeds by opening the stately home and its vast pinetum to the public. In 1972 Stormontfield Mill burnt down, its site soon going for housing. In November 1996 thanks to Michael Forsyth, then Secretary of State for Scotland, the Stone of Destiny was finally returned to Scotland on the 700th anniversary of its removal – only to rest in the security of Edinburgh Castle rather than in the ancient capital.

## OLLABERRY

**Map 14, B2**

***Small Shetland village,*** *pop. 100* — OS 2 or 3: HU 3680

Ollaberry, a sheltered bay on Yell Sound, has some of the better farmland in the Northmavine extremity of the Shetland mainland. When Pont sketch-mapped Shetland about 1592 it was a well settled area, with St Ola Kirk. Despite its rocky shore, Ollaberry became known as a fishing village, and had a post office by 1843. Collafirth some 5 km to the north was a Norwegian whaling station from 1903 to 1928. In 1951 Ollaberry's scattered population was perhaps 130, served by a primary school. By 1985 four or five fishing boat crews lived there, but their vessels – including the very large purse seine-netter *Altaire* – all worked out of better harbours. In 1987 there were 18 newish timber houses, a large new village hall, post office, school, pub and a sizeable modern Toyota car dealer. The pier at Collafirth has been extended to serve the big fishing vessels of the 1990s.

*Collafirth pier, Ollaberry, built in the late 20th century to accommodate some of the larger Shetland fishing vessels. The largest, the 'Altaire', is seen in this view.* *(JRH)*

## ONICH

**Map 5, A2**

***Small Lochaber village,*** *pop. 100* — OS 41: NN 0361

Pont's finest surviving sketch map shows Loch Leven as it was about 1600, with *'Onen'* – 3 km west of the Ballachulish ferry – depicted as a double building. The mid 18th century Roy map showed Onich as a clachan on the coastal track. There was an early inn, and by 1840 a penny post. As roads and steamers developed, its well wooded south-facing slope and glorious views across Loch Leven to the mountains of Glencoe made it a popular location to build mansionhouses and shooting lodges. The tiny inn was extended to 5 rooms in 1880. By the 1950s there were two primary schools, a shop, post office and pier. One Onich mansion was Creag Mhor, which when the author first stayed there in 1953 was a hostel for the Co-operative Holidays Association; nearby was a similar base for its then rival the Holiday Fellowship. There were three mansion-style hotels in 1954: the 30-room *Creagdhu* (now the *Lodge on the Loch)*, the *Allt-nan-Rhos*, and the *Onich Hotel*. By 1980 the pier was disused, and the two schools had been merged. In 1984 two shops and a tree nursery supplemented the main industry of tourism. The traditional *Nether Lochaber* has joined the other hotels and guest houses, and there's also a backpackers' bunkhouse.

## ORMISTON

**Map 15, E2**

***E. Lothian village,*** *pop. 2075* — OS 66: NT 4169

Ormiston lies in a natural basin on the headwaters of the River Tyne in East Lothian, midway between Haddington and Dalkeith. It had an ancient church, and by 1545 a castle, shown emparked on the map made by Pont about 1600. *'Ormestoun'* was emphasised, but the adjacent row of buildings was equally close to the name *'Penkethland'*, giving no clue as to their relative importance at that time. Ormiston Castle, later known as Ormiston Hall, was owned by the Cockburns, who became early agricultural improvers in the 1690s. McGibbon & Ross admired the House o' Muir, 3 km to the south. One of the ten original Scottish spinning schools was established at Ormiston about 1730. A bleachfield developed by the Christies from 1731 dealt in coarse linens; it was expanded in 1734 and 1768.

**Planned Village, Geology and Flint Grinding**: The well-known planned village was laid out about 1740 by John Cockburn, and a coal mine was opened nearby in 1743. A new Ormiston House was designed by John Baxter and built in 1745–49 for Cockburn, who had soon to sell the estate – but immediately afterwards in 1750 started a brewery, which lasted into the early 19th century. Ormiston, as shown on Roy's map of about 1754, had a road linking westwards to Cousland. Charles MacLaren, born locally in 1782, became a leading geologist, and Robert Moffat, another native (b.1795), first took the Scots form of civilisation to tribal Bechuanaland (and now has a statue in Ormiston). Two fairs were to take place in 1797, and in 1799 Heron noted *"the village of Ormiston is pretty regular and neatly built, has an ancient (15th century) market-cross, and contains near 600 inhabitants"*. A flint mill was in operation by 1831 to serve coastal potteries, and a post office was open by 1838.

**Railways and Coal Mines**: In 1867 a mineral branch of the North British Railway was opened from Monktonhall through Ormiston and by way of Penston Colliery to Macmerry, 4 km north-east. Both Ormiston and Macmerry enjoyed a passenger service from 1872. Two small collieries were sunk north of Ormiston station, which served various industrial concerns. The population in 1891 was 555. By 1894 several pits were also open just west of the village between Cousland and Tranent: Bellyford, at the junction of a mineral line northwards to a colliery near Elphinstone; Limeylands, west of the junction, and another at Cousland Park, 2 km west of the village, which by then had an inn. Oxenford Collieries were sunk farther south early in the 20th century by the Ormiston Coal Company, and connected to the station by a narrow-gauge railway. The Meadow pit was opened just east of the village about 1900 and the next year its mineral line – on which the company operated a colourful fleet of coal wagons – became the starting point of a light railway to Pencaitland and Gifford.

**From Mining to Cycling**: However, with the spread of bus routes, the Macmerry passenger service lasted only to 1925, and the remaining passenger trains came off in 1933. Most of Ormiston House was demolished in 1940, but part of the medieval house was retained. In the 1950s Ormiston had a population of 2000, with the facilities of a small village. The Macmerry rail goods service ended in 1960. The last coal mines, at Bellyford and near Fleets Farm, were disused by 1965, when the railway was cut back to Smeaton near Cousland, leaving bings, some of which had been made into picnic sites by the 1980s. There was little new development to 1986, and by 1991 the population had fallen to some 2075; few owned their homes outright. It is a tribute to Cockburn's planning that Ormiston remains an attractive place. By 1996 some new housing had been built; the route of the former railway is a cycleway, with a picnic site where the station once stood. Campbell & Smith (over 50 employees), are building contractors specialising in the restoration of historic buildings.

## ORPHIR (or Swanbister) — Map 13, B2

***Communities, S. Orkney,*** *pop. 200* — OS 6: HY 3406

Orphir which lies on the agricultural south coast of the Orkney mainland some 10km west of Kirkwall has the remains of a broch. At Clestran about 5km farther north-west there was until recent years a Pictish standing stone. Orphir had a corn mill by around 1000, there was some working of iron and bronze, and in 1017 the seat of Earl Haakon Paulsson, who, having murdered Earl Magnus of Egilsay, visited Jerusalem as a penance and later built a circular church at Orphir, where by 1135 there was also a *"great drinking-hall"*. Then for centuries Orphir made little news, but the Hall of Clestrain, built for Patrick Honeyman in 1768, became the home of the explorer John Rae, one-time head of the Hudson's Bay Company *(see Stromness)*. A Victorian laird's villa at Grindally overlooked a stone pier in the Bay of Houton, 3km to the west of Swanbister.

**Modern Developments**: In the 1950s when the local population was under 300 the school at Crya – which served a wide area – still boasted 70 secondary pupils, but these classes had closed by 1976. By 1981 Orphir was a small scattered village of only some 220 people, on the secondary main road between Kirkwall and Stromness; 3km to the east, near the Loch of Kirbister with its important waterworks, was a youth hostel (which later closed) and a nature reserve on the moors to the east. By 1985 a car ferry plied to Flotta and Lyness from a new pier and extensive car park at Houton, and by 1997 there was also a new hotel nearby. Other recent developments – including a new community school replacing the Crya school – cluster at Swanbister with its post office and church; Crya has a pub, and between Swanbister and Houton a heritage centre has opened beside the ancient church. Sadly the old Hall of Clestrain stood derelict in 1999.

## OTTER FERRY, Ballimore & Largiemore — Map 5, A5

***Cowal (Argyll) area,*** *pop. 100* — OS 55: NR 9384

A medieval motte was raised at Ballimore *('Big Village')* on the east shore of Loch Fyne, part of Cowal. About 1600 Timothy Pont noted on his manuscript map of Argyll *"I think I came over Loch Fyne from Otter to Silvercraigs"*. So most probably by then, and certainly by 1747, a minor ferry plied between the sandy shore at Otter Ferry, 1km north of Ballimore, and Port Ann or West Otter Ferry in Knapdale, just north of Silvercraigs. The name derives from *Oitir*, the Gaelic for a sandspit – nothing to do with aquatic mammals! The Roy map of about 1750, which showed a clachan and coastal track in this location, made no reference to the ferry, but later a pier was built north of the Oitir, and the ferry plied again until 1894. After 1900 when a new steamer pier was built, slow steamers on local runs still called, including in 1904 occasional services to Ardrishaig. A pedestrian ferry was reinstated for a time but closed about 1948, leaving Otter Ferry as a little hamlet. The hills to the east have been largely afforested over the past half century. At Kilfinan, 5km to the south, is the *Kilfinan Hotel* (opened by the 1950s). A coastal fish farm and housing estate has been created at Largiemore, 2km north of Otter Ferry, which now has a post office, serving a substantial coastal development near Ballimore.

## OUT SKERRIES — Map 14, C3

***Small islands, N-E. Shetland,*** *pop. 100* — OS 2: HU 6871

About 10km north-east of Whalsay the three islets of Housay, Bruray and Grunay surround the small natural harbour that Donaldson called a *"wonderful lagoon"*. They were settled in prehistoric times and were a fishing base by the time that Pont mapped Shetland about 1592. The lighthouse on the outlying rock of Bound Skerry was begun in 1852 and lit in 1854 (until 1950 the lightkeepers' families lived on Grunay, but later at Lerwick). These remote islands also gained a pier, primary school and post office, and 165 people lived there by 1891. In 1899 Housay and Bruray were joined by a bridge, replaced in 1957. But the population was shrinking and there was no telephone exchange as late as 1951. A new school was built in 1965 and the lighthouse was automated in 1972, when there were about 100 residents.

**Modernisation**: In 1974 a tiny airstrip occasionally served by Loganair was opened on Bruray. In 1975 the 25 households were served by two shops, and the school's 18 pupils were aged 5 to 15; the recently built fish-freezing plant exported to the USA. A new community hall was built with oil money in 1981, and by 1983 all the 27 households had a telephone. In 1983 the Skerries had four seine and lobster boats, with another on order. The one teacher had 10 primary and three secondary pupils. A dozen people worked in the fish processing plant; another was a silversmith, and almost everyone else was a knitter. Mains electricity was laid on in 1983 via an undersea cable from Whalsay. Until 1986, when a new pier was built, a passenger ferry plied to Lerwick in three hours in normal conditions. Subsequently roll-on ferries sailed to Vidlin in two hours and also to Lerwick. In 1995 the Out Skerries were put up for sale by the absentee lairds the Cussons soap family, to the surprise of the 85 inhabitants. Sadly by the late 1990s the fish factory was no longer in use.

## OVERTOWN

**Map 16, A5**

***Village, s. of Wishaw,*** *pop. 2000* OS 64/65 or 64/72: NS 8052

The main Roman road paralleling the middle River Clyde kept to the high ground on its north side. The 'Overtoun of Cambusnethan' which stands about 140m above sea level could be seen on Pont's map dated 1596; it is some 2 km east of the riverside site of Cambusnethan House. By the time of Roy's survey of about 1754, Overtoun was a small village 1km on the river side of the Roman road, by then a main highway; three roads converged from the north, but the river and the steep defile of Garriongill kept Overtown isolated. An early 19th century hamlet named Waterloo developed where the Overtown to Newmains road crossed the Roman road. In the mid 19th century two main lines of railway were built through the area by the Caledonian Railway, diverging at Law Junction 2 km to the east; a station named Overtown was opened on the Wishaw Central line close to Waterloo. The population in 1891 was 1385. By 1895 the Clyde had been bridged at Dalserf and a mineral railway served several collieries to the west of *'Overton'*, which appeared to consist largely of miners' rows and had an inn, smithy, and a post and telegraph office. In 1901 Overtown's population was 1400. By 1931 some 1800 people lived in the village and in 1951 about 3750; by then there was a post office at Waterloo.

**After the Coal was Cut**: By 1953 the station and collieries had closed and only bings remained; after 1955 the inn became just a pub. Severe decline cut the population to about 2150 by 1971, but then it stabilised. Overtown had never enjoyed more than the most basic facilities, including a post office and primary school, but the large new Clyde Valley High School was built west of the village about 1972, and by 1980 a garage was open. In 1991 Overtown still held 1975 people (excluding Waterloo). By 1998 another housing estate had been added to the north; tiny Waterloo has lost both its pub and post office.

## OXTON

**Map 3, B3**

***Border village,*** *pop. 330 (area)* OS 66 or 73: NT 4953

Several ancient hill forts and a Roman camp overlook upper Lauderdale, traversed by the Roman road later called Dere Street. The 16th century tower or bastel of Carfrae Peel stood in a well settled area when Pont mapped the area around 1600; nearby was a mill, presumably Carfraemill, and to the west Oxton and the Kirk of *'Chingilkirk'*. Roy named it *'Chingle Kirk'*, but by the time of his map (about 1754) the modern road pattern was evident; near the later *Carfraemill Inn* was Boghall, and there was more development at Oxton, probably Heron's *"village of Channelkirk"* of 1799. In 1901 Channelkirk parish held 570 people; Oxton had a post office, and a station on the brand new Lauder Light Railway. An inn was open at Carfraemill (where there was no longer a mill), and another inn (which later vanished) near Mountmill, 1km to the north. The little railway was closed to passengers in 1932 and to freight in 1958. In 1951, 400 people still lived in the parish, with basic services plus the small *Tower Hotel* in the main street and also the isolated inn, upgraded as the *Carfraemill Hotel*. But the quarry open in the hills to the west by 1963 had closed by 1975. Despite only 327 people in the parish in 1991, Oxton post office, inn and store still function, and *Carfraemill Hotel* is now *'The Lodge at Carfraemill'*.

## OYNE

**Map 10, B3**

***Aberdeenshire small village,*** *pop. 375 (area)* OS 38: NJ 6725

Stone circles and Pictish carved stones abound near Oyne, which lies between the River Urie and Bennachie 10km north-west of Inverurie. The 16th century tower of Westhall and the 17th century double tower of Harthill Castle appeared in a well settled area on Robert Gordon's map, made about 1640. The Roy map of about 1750 showed Oyne Kirk on a track linking Inverurie and Clatt; over 2 km to the east was Craig Mill, later replaced closer to Oyne by the Mill of Carden. Roads were made up and Sir Robert Elphinstone, the laird of the ancient house and estate of Westhall, promoted the Aberdeenshire Canal, begun in 1796 to link Inverurie with Aberdeen. Sir Robert's kinsman Sir James Elphinstone became chairman of the canal's successor the Great North of Scotland Railway, built from 1852; Oyne's conveniently sited station opened in 1854, but attracted no industry.

**Decline – and an Attempt at Resurgence**: The population of the farming parish – 770 in 1901 – was down to 680 by 1951 and only 400 by 1971. The railway station closed about 1968, and the Longcroft Dairy near Westhall vanished around 1975. Eight new houses were built at Oyne in the early 1970s, its school roll rose to 30, and in 1981 there was still a village hall; but the parish population was only 364 in 1991, and the shop and post office closed in 1992. In 1994–96, the last years of Gordon District Council, it used ERDF help to build *'Archaeolink'*, an elaborate 16ha visitor centre reconstructing settlements from Iron Age and Roman times – strangely sited where Roman legionaries had never settled, merely marching, fighting off the Caledonians and briefly camping (at Durno near Pitcaple). Archaeolink was open for summer seasons by 2000, but having already met financial problems, found that it attracted too few visitors; its future seemed in doubt at the time of writing.

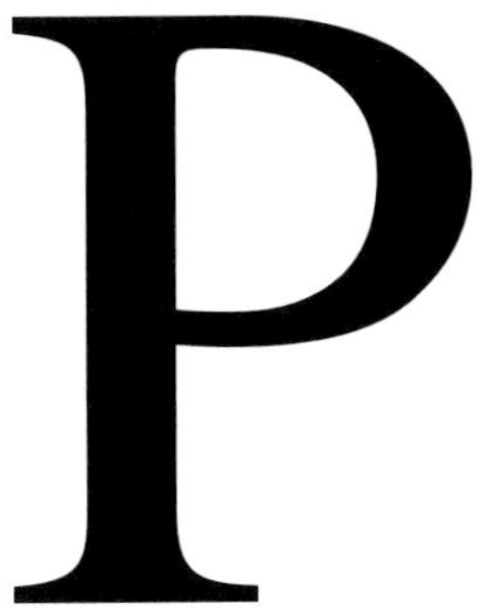

## PAISLEY

**Map 15, B5**

***Renfrewshire large town,*** *pop. 75,000* OS 64: NS 4864

Saint Mirin or Mirren, who came from Bangor in Ulster, sited his early Celtic church and monastery on the White Cart Water 5 km south of the tidal River Clyde, near a low but steep hill; he became the patron saint of Paisley. A Cluniac priory at Renfrew soon failed, but in 1163–64 Walter, the High Steward of Scotland, selected a new site beside the river at Paisley, and success brought abbey status in 1219. The Cluniacs held property in Glasgow from an early date, and purchased more in the 13th century. The name of Paisley was important enough to be shown on the Gough map of about 1250. The abbey had 25 monks in 1300, but was burned by the English in 1307 and remained in ruins for about a hundred years.

**Stone Buildings and the Burgh of Paisley**: By the mid 15th century the monks had again become rich and powerful, oddly having 20% of *Ayrshire* parishes under their control, so Abbot Jarvas encouraged the community to rebuild the abbey buildings in stone and slate. The low-lying precinct was then drained by a stone-arched tunnel 90 m in length, which was abandoned at the Reformation and remained undiscovered until 1991. About 1484 Abbot George of Shaw had a stone wall 6 km in length built round the abbey park; by then the hill bore the name Oakshaw. Paisley also had a castle beside the river. Chambers opined that the town was *"originally only the hamlet gathered around the abbey":* in 1488 the king allowed the abbot to charter this place as a burgh of barony, and the first tolbooth was built in 1491. Although the abbey was again burned in 1498, very soon Paisley was in a trade dispute with Glasgow (noted in surviving burgh records which begin in the early 16th century). Yet Paisley Abbey was once more very important in 1560, with no fewer than 28 appropriated churches dominating its local area and also some parts of the Borders.

**After the Reformation: Textile Industries**: Paisley was no doubt badly hit by the Act of 1561 which proscribed all monastic institutions. From 1587 the parishioners worshipped in the Abbey church, while the estate passed to Lord Claud Hamilton, later Lord Paisley, who reconstructed some of its secular buildings into the mansion known as the Place of Paisley. In the 16th century the Maxwells built the L-plan Stanely Castle 3 km south-west of the town. By 1593 Paisley was the centre of a presbytery, and there were booths in the market. Pont's manuscript map of the Barony of Renfrew, made around 1600, showed *PASLAY* in capitals as its largest settlement, with a bridge and a double enclosure around the large abbey buildings. Prosperity enabled the tolbooth to be rebuilt in 1601, 1751 and again in 1821. Paisley's pollable male population of almost 1150 in 1634 was mainly engaged in manufacturing. By 1661 de Rocheford noted that the White Cart Water was *"forded by a large bridge abutting to the castle, where there is a very spacious garden enclosed by thick walls of hewn stone"*. By the 1690s Paisley had taken over the role of Renfrew as the centre of its sheriffdom, and Hawkhead House was built 3 km south-east of the town about 1700. Paisley had already become specialised in textiles; Chambers later suggested that its success in the 18th century was owed to entrepreneurial *"pedlers, otherwise called packmen"*, whose capital was insufficient for them to start up manufacturing textiles in affluent Glasgow.

**Thanks, Miss Christian Shaw!**: Chambers added: *"At first, Paisley was celebrated for coarse chequered linen cloth, afterwards for chequered linen handkerchiefs, succeeded by fabrics of a lighter and more fanciful kind"*. This was thanks to Miss Christian Shaw of Bargarran near Erskine, who around 1700 brought to Paisley methods of spinning finer linen thread; improved techniques enabled lawn manufacture to begin. The Paisley concerns also developed their own patterns, which outdid those of both Paris and London's Spittalfields. A hundred hand looms were in use in 1707, and Paisley linens were soon twice as valuable per yard as Angus stuff. Paisley had a post office by 1715. Scotland's first mechanised flax mill, drawing its expertise from Holland, was recorded in Paisley in 1726, and hand-operated thread twisting machines were pioneered there in the same decade. Paisley muslins were well known by 1730, several linen bleachfields were built between 1746 and 1760, and by the latter year Paisley had a main linen stamping office. Whereas in 1738 Paisley's population was about 4000, by 1755 it had reached 6800. Roy's map shows that in the 1750s it was for the period a large sprawling town lying mainly west of the bridge, with seven radial roads.

**Distilling and Gauze, Bird Painter and Abercorns**: During the second half of the 18th century Paisley's rise was meteoric. Distilling began to be carried on commercially, and in 1759 *"the manufacture of silk gauze was introduced into Paisley by Mr M'Kerral, of Hillhouse, in Ayrshire"*. Chambers later noted that the gauze industry soon *"filled the country round to a distance of 20 miles"*. The number of looms grew to over 850 by 1766, and 1360 by 1776, making muslins above all. By the time of Pennant's tour in 1769 Paisley had *"the greatest cambric manufactury"*. The peak year for flax was 1778; by then there were eight bleachfields in and around the town, that at Foxbar being nearly 4 km away below the Gleniffer Braes. Alex Wilson, born in Paisley in 1766, emigrated to the USA, where he scientifically studied and finely painted birds, stimulating the more famous Audubon. In 1780 the former abbey estate passed to the Earls of Abercorn; in 1781 the new owner threw open the abbey site for development, selling the stone enclosing wall as building material. But Heron, who saw the Abbey in the 1790s, wrote that it was *"still pretty entire, and has been a very superb building"*. Underhill Mill was built in the 1780s; the hand weaving of the shawls for which Paisley became renowned was also of 18th century origin, and by 1785 the population had exploded to about 24,000. Hawkhead House was improved in 1788 by Playfair.

**From Flax to Cotton and Paisley Patterns**: In the late 18th century Paisley's flax industry was gradually replaced by cotton, especially for fancy fabrics. By 1795 there were eleven firms in cotton, and four fairs were scheduled annually. In 1799 Heron wrote *"Paisley is truly a manufacturing town. The names which many of the streets have obtained, are descriptive of the people's employment: Silk Street, Gauze Street, Lawn Street, Inkle Street, and Cotton Street. All these are wide and regular, and contain many good houses. The manufacture carried on is chiefly in silk and thread gauze"*, adding that it was of a quality acceptable to royalty. *"Multitudes of women, and of very young girls, are employed in the extensive cotton-works in this place. Many of the principal manufacturers in Paisley, having made considerable fortunes, have built elegant houses, in which they live in a style suitable to their easy circumstances"*. There were also *"ten bleachfields for muslins and lawns, and an equal number for thread. It also has two soap-works"*. He further noted that a *"great printfield"* was at work near Hawkhead; his population of *"about 20,000"* seems to have been a gross underestimate. By 1800 Seedhill tannery was also in operation. The swirling designs that became known as Paisley patterns were of Kashmiri origin, introduced to the shawl industry in 1805 in emulation of Empress Josephine.

**Early Banking – then Mergers**: The Paisley Banking Company, established in 1783, was expanding by 1790 as industry grew; by 1793 it had opened branches in Glasgow and Dundee. By 1795 there was also a Bank of Scotland branch, short-lived it seems. Meantime the Paisley Union Banking Company, set up in 1788, rapidly expanded with 13 branches; by 1800 the two local banks issued notes, making Paisley about fifth in importance among Scottish banking centres. The Paisley Bank was declining in 1837 when it merged with the British Linen Bank. A permanent Bank of Scotland branch opened in 1836. In 1838 the Glasgow Union Bank took over the Paisley Union Bank, and the joint-stock Paisley Commercial Bank, founded in 1839, merged into the Western Bank of Scotland in 1844.

**Aquaplaning by Horse on the Curtailed Canal**: In 1802 the Robert Barr school was built, later part of Paisley Grammar School. By 1796 Paisley was a post town; with rapid expansion, by 1823 the Paisley post office was of considerable importance. The Saucel brewery and the large Saucel distillery on its 3ha site were in use from about the 1790s; Dobie's tobacco works opened in 1809. Ralston House was built 3km east of Paisley in 1810 for William Orr. The Glasgow Paisley & Ardrossan Canal, surveyed by Telford, was intended to take cargoes from overseas to Glasgow via Ayrshire – a barmy idea, exposed when instead the Clyde was deepened by dredging following an Act of 1809. Meantime part of the canal had actually been dug, and was opened in 1813 from Glasgow via Paisley to Johnstone at a single level throughout, stimulating further industrial growth. On it from the 1820s aquaplaning *'fly boats'* drawing only 14 cm of water when laden were pulled by fast horses, halving the passenger journey time to Glasgow to 45 minutes. Meantime from 1816 Reid & Hanna built iron boats at the Cartvale yard.

**Clark's, Coats' – and Management under Fire**: Brown, Sharp & Co made sewed muslins early in the 19th century; most production was by outworkers in Ayrshire, and later in Ulster. Meantime factory work was taking over: in 1812 William and James Carlile opened the town's first steam-powered thread mill, and Clark's built their Anchor Mill. From 1819 three daily horse-drawn coaches ran between Paisley and Glasgow. By 1820 the Underwood cotton mill had become notorious for its tense labour relations, descending to the use of firearms! The population of Paisley had risen to 38,000 by 1821. In the 1820s many steam-powered cotton mills were built, including to the west of the town the large Ferguslie thread mills of James Coats, erected in 1826 *(see Hay & Stell)*. The great Blacklandmill bleach works, over 2 km south of the town, was opened in 1830. Alexander Gardiner, born in the town in that year, became famous as the photographer who recorded the American Civil War of 1861–65. A gas undertaking opened its works in 1827, and a second brewery was in operation by 1825.

**Silk, Rags and Sabotaged Steam Buses**: In 1832 the polemical reformer Cobbett saw shawls and waistcoat material being woven in Bissett's works; he noted that a barracks had been built (in 1820) which he claimed was to keep the people *"in a state of obedience, for the weavers of Paisley are covered in rags and are half starved"*. However he interspersed admiration for Fulton & Son's silk manufacture, where although the machines were powered by three men endlessly turning a wheel, he noted *"a great number of young women and girls employed at the work, all very neatly and nicely dressed"*. Until 1834 all the famous Paisley shawls were hand woven. The Blackhall silk factory (named after an ancient house) dated from 1848. Meantime for seven months in 1834, John Scott Russell's Steam Carriage Company of Scotland operated a successful service of steam buses between Paisley and Glasgow. But they were sabotaged by the unscrupulous turnpike trustees, who feared damage to the roads: their minions heaped up stones which overturned a bus, causing its boiler to explode with the death of five passengers, the service, and the idea of the steam bus.

**Parliamentary Burgh – but Shawls out of Fashion**: Its large population caused Paisley to be given enhanced status as a *'Parliamentary Burgh'* under the 1833 Act (passed when Cobbett was an MP). In 1836–38 a dam was built to impound a reservoir for water supply at Stanely, surrounding the castle. A quay was constructed in 1836–40, and the important Vulcan Foundry and engineering works of what became Fullarton, Hodgart & Barclay began in 1838; they made large steam engines, and later chemical plant. Also in 1838 a large complex of shawl warehouses was opened in Forbes Place by James Forbes, shawl merchant. By 1839 there were 14 cotton mills, all steam-powered, and the population had reached 48,000. However, a serious setback in 1841–42 was the near collapse of the hand craft shawl industry as fashions changed and industrial methods took over, and in that year a quarter of the population was living on charity, bankrupting the parish. The shawl industry later recovered somewhat, until about 1870.

**Early Railways and Locomotive Builders**: The *'Scotch'* 4'6" gauge Paisley & Renfrew Railway (P&R) opened in 1837 from Hamilton Street; from 1842–52 it was worked by horses! In 1838 the shipbuilders Barr & McNab opened the Abercorn yard, and built the iron paddle steamer *Royal Victoria* for the Clyde and West Highland service; in 1840 the firm's foundry built their first locomotives, possibly for the Glasgow Paisley Kilmarnock & Ayr Railway (GPKA), constructed in 1836–39, which connected the town with Glasgow and the Ayrshire coast (and absorbed the P&R). In 1846 the GPKA Secretary said that the area was *"in a needy and disaffected state"*, yet his line soon carried nearly seven times the forecast number of passengers! In 1847 it advertised as the *'Glasgow & Ayrshire Railway'*. In 1841 the associated Glasgow Paisley & Greenock line opened, sharing the route from Glasgow. In 1852 they became part of the Glasgow & South Western (G&SWR) which regauged the P&R line in 1866, connecting it to the main line at Gallowhill Junction 1 km east of Gilmour Street; Hamilton Street station was closed, replaced by a new station at Renfrew Road. R Grierson & Co of Glasgow did the rail cartage in Paisley until they were absorbed by Wordies in 1903.

**Sago, Soap, Snodgrass and Public Buildings**: Brown & Polson began sago and starch manufacture in 1842, later adding cornflour at their new Royal starch works of 1856; by 1870 they employed 200 people. Soap manufacture began at the St Mirren works about 1865, and Robertsons began to make marmalade in Paisley in 1866. At the 1878 Paris Exhibition a medal was awarded to the Saucel Mills for their *'Snodgrass celebrated brose meal or Scotch pea flour'*! Meantime workaday Paisley was acquiring some fine public buildings, especially the prominent John Neilson Institution, built as a school by a Paisley grocer in 1849–52, its dome being irreverently referred to by locals as *'The Porridge Pot'*. Ralston House was enlarged in 1864, but the ancient tolbooth had to be demolished as unsafe in 1870, its site being redeveloped with shops; its function was replaced by the palatial Town Hall, largely paid for by Clarks of the Anchor thread mill. The Ionic Paisley Museum and Art Gallery, intended as a museum and library, was gifted to the town in 1871 by Clarks' rival Sir Peter Coats; it built up an industrial collection, featuring Paisley shawls. Wheelchair-bound astronomer Thomas Coats insisted on good access for the disabled to his Coats observatory, built in 1883; he was evidently an optimist, for in 1887 Paisley was called *"one of the smokiest towns in Scotland"*. The population in 1891 was over 66,000; a power station was established in that year, only one year after Glasgow's first.

**Woollens, Carpets, Ropes and Clothing**: Well before shawls failed, other textiles were sought: other woollens were made from the 1840s, and the St James Street wool dyeworks started in an old mill in 1868. Even though at that time 42% of Paisley families lived in one room, population growth resumed in the 1870s and soon reached 1000 extra persons per year. There was already a carpet industry by 1869, although about 900 people were still hand weaving woollens. Jacks' carpet factory, built in 1870, was enlarged in 1912; meantime in 1884 the Abercorn ropeworks had been established, and the SCWS Colinslee clothing works was also built in the late 19th century.

**Engineering – and Transport Exploitation**: In 1857 Barr & McNab, and in 1860 Alexander Craig McKechnie, were still building steam engines. The Saucel ironworks opened in the mid 19th century, while in 1868 A F Craig & Co built the Caledonia Engineering works and foundry; in 1883 under J Craig they produced plant and retorts for the new oil industry *(see Pumpherston)*, and about 1900 manufactured carpet cropping machinery and brasswork. Coachbuilding started about 1875, and the Soho engine works and a brassworks a few years later. In the early 1880s the Vulcan Foundry and engineering works made the important hydraulic press which formed the curved plates for the main compression tubes of the Forth bridge. Meantime the Paisley Canal was bought by the G&SWR in 1869 and closed in 1881, being replaced on the same route by a sinuous but level railway opened in 1885, the Canal Line. This provided the town with its second principal station and also pushed a branch serving bleach and scouring works up to Potterhill in 1886, extending to Barrhead in 1902. The Paisley District Tramways Company, opened in 1885, had 3 km of horse tramway; its drivers worked a *100-hour week* for a pittance.

**Little Ships from Paisley Yards**: In 1870 the Merksworth shipyard of John Fullarton & Co (founded 1866) built the iron paddle steamer *Carrick Castle* for the Loch Goil service. They later built coasters and colliers, some engined by Ross & Duncan of Glasgow. Fullarton's was second only to Ailsa among British yards in terms of the number of its coasters in service when the yard closed in 1928. The Thistle shipyard was started in 1880 by Campbell & Co; in 1888 their successors J MacArthur & Co built the 62 m iron and steel paddler *Fusilier* for MacBrayne's West Highland services, followed by various coasters for J G Frew of Glasgow; in 1900 engineering firm Bow, McLachlan & Co acquired the yard. Meantime in 1877 H McIntyre & Co of Paisley had opened the Phoenix shipyard; in 1885 Fleming & Ferguson took over the Phoenix yard and built dredgers and specialist shallow draught craft for over 80 years. But the old Abercorn shipyard vanished after 1901.

**Coats Thread – King among Paisley's Textiles**: Coats' Ferguslie mills defied the slump to expand in 1858, and in 1870 the family – having made their pile – built a baronial mansion called Ferguslie Park 1 km west of the town centre. Their mills were again extended in 1887, when an ornate *'Halftime School'* was added, designed by Woodhouse & Morley. Meanwhile Clarks' Anchor mill complex beside the White Cart weir was expanded in 1871–83 with the huge 162 m-long Atlantic and Pacific mills, largely built of red brick, and each powered by shafting driven by a compound steam engine *(see Hay & Stell)*. The major thread firms of Clarks and Coats – both of which had drawn huge profits from thread made overseas behind protectionist tariff barriers – amalgamated in the mid 1890s. The huge Thomas Coats Memorial Baptist Church, designed by the curiously named Edinburgh architect Hippolyte J Blanc, was built in 1894 and its cathedral-like bulk at once dominated the High Street. The Coats name also became synonymous with Paisley – then the virtual centre of the World thread industry, and with a 1901 population of almost 80,000. More building in 1899–1900 brought the rapid growth in textiles to a close, due to rising overseas competition.

**Services and Chemicals grow, Distilling fails**: A local newspaper was first published in 1864, and the *Paisley Daily Express* – sole daily evening paper in Scotland outside the four cities – started in 1874. St Mirren FC was formed in 1876–77 by local cricket and rugby players, soon playing at Westmarch; in 1890 they became founder members of the Scottish League (along with Abercorn FC – named from the estate's proprietor –

*The Town Hall, Paisley. It was largely paid for by the Clarks of the Anchor thread mills, and built in 1879–82 to designs by W G Lynn, a Belfast architect.* *(JRH)*

who then played at nearby Underwood Park, and whose 25 years in the League ended in 1915). In 1890 the *Paisley Theatre*, later renamed the *Victory*, was opened in Smithills Street. The Greenhill oil refinery had begun in 1880. In 1886 the Cartvale Chemical Company made acetates from distilled wood, and the Saucel distillery was making both malt and grain whisky; it was dismantled before Robert Menzies sold it in 1915 to DCL, who continued to use its maltings and bonds. The 1890s also saw a small harbour built, and the foundation of Paisley Technical College.

**Riches and Poverty**: Extreme congestion and dirt dominated in 1894, when all of the town's three hotels – *Commercial, County, Globe* – were condemned by Murray as *"not good"*; the *Bull Inn* was rebuilt in 1901 in Art Nouveau style. A great Victorian mansion at Ralston was leased and later bought by Sir Charles Cayzer, founder of the Glasgow-based Clan Line. He was one of a lucky few, for the 1895 OS map showed Paisley as a heavily built-up area only 2 km in diameter. A small outlier among ironstone pits and mineral lines at Inkerman 2 km to the west also comprised close-packed row houses. In 1895 the Paisley golf club was founded, and laid out an 18-hole moorland course at Braehead, 4 km south-west of the town centre; the area's second golf club, at Ralston, was founded in 1904. The start of the Galbraith chain of multiple shops dated from the same period. Paisley town council must have had an eye on tourism, growing civic pride, or at least a sense of shame, for in 1897 it set about a major (and in Scotland at least, unique) scheme of restoration of the abbey ruins and improvement of their setting, where the medieval secular buildings (the Old Palace) were used as a pub!

**Electric Trams, Villas, Yachts and Motor Cars**: Electric trams, introduced in 1902–04, eventually extended to Kilbarchan, Barrhead, Renfrew, and Abbotsinch, with through running to Glasgow. For most people poverty still ruled, for when St Mirren FC bought land at Love Street in 1905 they had to ask patrons to bring *'rubbish'* (probably mainly ash from domestic fires) to form banking! At the other end of the social scale, a villa estate was built at Thornly Park in the early 20th century, and in 1910 the Coats (or Glen-Coats) family of Ferguslie House owned no fewer than 12 yachts, the largest being of 500 tons! The imposing Methodist Central Hall was erected in 1908. Renfrewshire's population peaked at the 1911 census, but Paisley continued to grow. Arrol-Johnston cars *(see Springburn)* were made at the Caledonia Works for only two years from 1910; in 1912 the firm made a very strange move, to Locharbriggs near Dumfries. This left the premises to become Beardmore's Underwood Works. A racecourse, also used as a showground, was open in 1913; the next year a railway halt was opened at Sandyford, 2 km north of the town, to serve Ogston & Tennant's confusingly titled St Rollox soap works.

**Hospitals and their Inmates in Confusion**: The Royal Alexandra Infirmary was built in 1896–1900. South-east of the town was Dykebar Mental Hospital, with three wards built of sandstone in 1909 as separate mansion style houses to designs by T G Abercrombie. The modernist Infectious Diseases Hospital of 1932–33 designed by local architect Thomas S Tait was built at Hawkhead Road, taking its name – although Glasgow had already used the name for Hawkhead Mental Hospital at Pollok only 1.5 km to the east! Ralston House became a hospital for some years before its demolition in 1934; its stables became the golf clubhouse.

**Pumps and Aero Engines, Taxis and Tragedy**: Hodgart & Barclay's Vulcan Engine Works made heavy machine tools such as shell presses during World War I, plus electrically driven hydraulic pumps. Meantime William Beardmore & Co had been building aero engines at Paisley *(see also Inchinnan)*. At the end of the war the demand for aircraft fell like a stone, and Beardmores built taxicabs at Paisley from 1919; an improved model for the London market was made for a time from 1923. The Paisley & District Tramways Company was absorbed into the Glasgow system in 1923; the Abbotsinch route was closed in the 1930s. The Art Deco style Russell Institute was built as a mother and baby clinic in 1924–26 (it still remains in this use). In 1927 a municipal golf course was laid out at Barshaw, its fees kept low. In 1929 a crowd of 70 children sadly died in a ghastly smoke panic at the *Glen Cinema*.

**Shrinking Industry, New Facilities, Old Overcrowding**: Wool dyeing ceased around 1930 in the midst of decades of industrial depression in the west of Scotland. However, Marks & Spencer came to the town in 1931 with their second Scottish branch, and what was later to become Arnott's Paisley department store was built around the same time. Bow, McLachlan & Co were still building paddle tugs at the Thistle yard in 1931. In 1935 Fleming & Ferguson of the Phoenix yard built a steam ferry for the Renfrew passage; she was saved, and is moored at Renfrew. The Abbey Bridge was rebuilt in 1933. An ice rink was open by the start of the war in 1939, but even in 1936 after much emigration, 32% of Paisley housing was overcrowded. By then housing estates had been built at Charleston, Gateside, South Candren (replacing the Inkerman rows) and Williamsburgh. Paisley's role in the 1939–45 war is little publicised; the Thistle yard built landing craft, then falling out of use, and the barracks were disused by about 1947.

**Education, Cup Success and Transport Revolutions**: By 1951 Paisley's population was over 93,000; it had a large general hospital, and in 1950 Paisley College of Technology was promoted to a Scottish Central Institution, which moved into new buildings in 1963. Hawkhead House was pulled down about 1952, and the ice rink closed. However, St Mirren FC (known locally as *The Buddies*) had a good year in 1959 when they erected floodlights at their ground, won their first floodlit match 10–0 and went on to win the Cup. Even so, the *Victory Theatre* had to admit defeat in 1959; it was demolished in 1967. The tramways which still ran through to Elderslie were abandoned in 1957. The Renfrew passenger trains were withdrawn in 1967, and the harbour, the Phoenix shipyard and the Saucel ironworks all closed in 1969. Meantime the M8 motorway was built in the late 1960s, relieving Paisley of through traffic between Glasgow and Greenock. Housing estates to relieve inner congestion and enable redevelopment had continued to sprout around the town, and by 1971 – when Paisley's population was at its peak, 95,344 – were largely complete at Ferguslie Park (extending South Candren), at Foxbar 4 km south-west, at Gallowhill (extending Gateside), at Glenburn and at Shortroods. The Foxbar estate continued to grow during the 1970s and gained garages, post office, a chemist and doctors, though mainly notable for its plethora of primary and secondary schools both secular and Catholic.

**Covering the River with Grot**: Although housing redevelopment was carried out by the town council to better concepts than in Glasgow, meanwhile in the town centre some fine 19th

*Part of the Anchor Mills, Paisley, founded by J & J Clark around 1812 to make cotton thread. This is the Domestic Finishing Mill, built in 1886, where thread for domestic use was wound onto wooden bobbins.* *(JRH)*

century buildings were replaced by the awful late 1960s Piazza shopping centre, which also covered over the river north of Gauze Street. In the 1970s the cattle market left its old site west of the town centre, moving to Glenfield. From 1975 the huge 1960s buildings of the County Council near the abbey became a Strathclyde Region branch office, but what had been Paisley Burgh headed the new Renfrew District.

**Bottling booms but Canning ceases**: The ropeworks still functioned in 1972, but the soapworks closed and by 1976 the Saucel Brewery had long been a bonded store. By 1977 the former Saucel corn mill at Lonend had become the 30-room *Watermill Hotel*. Blacklandmill bleach works had become the Glenburn whisky bottling plant by 1976, where by 1979 William Grant's whiskies were bottled; and Chivas Brothers, distillery owners and whisky blenders, were based at Renfrew Road where they too had a large bottling plant, complete with what John Hume calls *"an extraordinary 17th century revival office block"*. In 1978 revamping of what had become the awful council estate which had taken its name from the doomed mansion of Ferguslie Park was promoted – unsuccessfully. At that time the *Paisley Daily Express* was still published at New Street, Paisley – a morning paper with a tiny 11,000 circulation.

**Shrinking Thread, but Brown & Polson in the Soup**: Thread production was hit by the general decline of hand embroidery in the 1960s, and Coats Paton (as they had become) diversified by acquiring Jaeger; in 1970 they employed about 8000 people in Paisley, but soon cut back. The Atlantic and Pacific mills were demolished in 1972 and part of the Anchor Mill had gone by 1977; by 1980 Coats' employment locally was down to a mere 800. In 1978 CIBA-Geigy employed 1000 people in their CIBA Pigments plant at Hawkhead, which was soon partly modernised to make Azo pigments. The Brown & Polson works was much reduced, although with nearly 1400 workers in 1979 it was still Scotland's largest food factory, making instant custard, mayonnnaise and soups. In 1979 R Anderson & Son provided pipework, pressure vessels and steel fabrication services to the distilling and oil process industries; they had an associate company at Keith. But the famed engineers Fullarton, Hodgart & Barclay closed in 1977, and A F Craig in 1981.

**Facilities and Transport Downs and Ups**: Paisley possessed a covered swimming pool by 1972, and in the 1980s the Gleniffer Braes became a country park. By then the Abbey church from which it all began had been rebuilt seven times in all! In 1983 the Canal station and railway was closed; equally unhappy was the abolition of the Paisley headquarters of *'Clydeside Scottish'* buses in 1989, the routes then falling to Kilmarnock. The Canal railway route was reopened in 1990 with six stations, using Sprinter trains; frequencies on the Canal line were doubled late in 1992, leading to a 63% rise in passenger numbers.

**Weaving remembered, but No More Ferguslie Thread**: In 1983 the Old Paisley Society began to convert the Sma' Shot weavers' cottages at Shuttle Street, built about 1759, into a museum of local crafts. In 1986 Coats Paton merged into the Viyella group, becoming Coats Viyella, the biggest pure textile company in Europe – but no longer Scottish. Ferguslie Thread Works lay long-empty and much vandalised in 1990; a threat came in 1991 to its derelict though historically important No.1 Spinning Mill, in the form of a proposal of demolition for housing, and by 1994 little still stood on its largely vacant site but the great classical Counting House – built in 1890 – derelict and awaiting a user. The site was redeveloped for housing in the mid 1990s; the fine Bridge Lane gatehouse became flats, and the stables were restored by 1999, but the small and striking north gatehouse still stands unused.

**Problems in the Park, and Prospects for Patterns**: A new district general hospital was built in the 1980s, but the industrial decline had taken its toll, and in 1987 – the year St Mirren FC won the Cup! – the government set up a partnership scheme (one of four in Scotland's poorest council estates), once more with the aim of improving housing conditions at Ferguslie Park. There by 1990 no fewer than 46% of its *'economically active'* population were out of work, and late in 1994 both this estate and parts of the south of the town suffered severe flooding. Meantime, however, in 1990 the magnificent though empty remainder of the 5-storey Anchor Mill had been proposed for conversion into the Paisley Pattern Centre, for crafts and tourism, shops, offices and flats. In 1991 the remaining population was only 75,526, a loss of almost 20,000 in 20 years, but Paisley remained an important and compact subregional centre. Continuing industries included GIBCO in biotechnology research, and a branch of Dalgety Bay shopfitters Havelock Europa.

**New University – and Aid from an Unlikely Quarter**: By 1985 Paisley College was a major centre of higher education, with 2700 full-time students; renamed the University of Paisley in 1992 and absorbing Ayr's Craigie teacher training College in 1993, it passed 6000 students. In 1994 its associated Reid Kerr College of Further Education – which by 1988 had an extensive campus at Renfrew Road – offered its 10,000 full- and part-time students over 100 courses. In 1993 its Technology and Business Centre, set up in 1985 with support from 50 companies in the west of Scotland, expanded hopefully into Yaroslavl in northern Russia. Meantime Paisley's ancient Grammar School was saved from closure in 1988 by a remarkable personal intervention by Tory Prime Minister Margaret Thatcher, who probably assumed it was a selective school; but rather than opting out as she hoped, in 1993 its parents decided to stay with local authority control. The Grammar School building of 1802 was abandoned, and awaiting restoration in 2000.

**Colourful once more in Food and Drink**: In 1990 a Queen's Award for the export of whisky, gin and rum was won by Paisley-based Chivas Brothers (by then a subsidiary of Seagram International). In 1992 Paisley Welding & Fabrication was working for the highway construction industry. Meantime CIBA Pigments had nearly failed; but heavy investment and a 100-strong research and development branch overcame the problems, and by 1993 they were supplying blue dyes, plastics colourings for electric cables, and inks for colour printing; over three-quarters of their output was exported. Paisley was the HQ of the Scottish Milk Marketing Board until its dissolution in 1994.

**Shopping Successes – and Failures**: In 1990 the former Coats Memorial Home in New Street vanished when work was started on the highly central 32,000 m² 50-unit Paisley Centre, on three floors between Causeyside Street and New Street. It was anchored by a 4830 m² Co-operative department store, and its High Street access was taken through the restored frontage of the former *Picture House*. In 1993 the District Council claimed this had *"completely revitalised"* local retailing; it was certainly fully let – at the expense of large numbers of vacancies elsewhere in the centre, particularly on the west. The grubby non-pedestrian town centre with its problem of alcoholism became notorious in 1993 for street violence and murder. By 1994 major upgrading of the Piazza Centre could no longer be delayed, and was undertaken with vigour; there is now also a substantial pedestrian area. The Arnotts department store stayed open as part of the House of Fraser chain.

**The Uncertain Future of the Past**: In 1991 the large nurses' home at the Infirmary stood vacant, as did parts of Hawkhead Hospital in 2000. In 1994 the former cattle market site in the town centre was derelict and awaiting University development, while the possible conversion of Mile End Mill into a budget hotel for the YMCA was being examined. Dykebar Hospital's characterful wards 20, 22 and 23 were vacated in 1995, becoming *'buildings at risk'*. Although 14 houses were provided about 1997 in the former stable block of Ferguslie Park, and the listed Blackland Lodge was also saved, sadly the exotic *'Halftime School'* was gutted by fire in 1997 and it was left a ruin. In 1992 Renfrewshire Enterprise moved its offices from Hillington to a former Co-op building in the centre of Paisley, where by then the new Lagoon Leisure Centre was open, with ice-hockey and swimming facilities; in 1996 the Paisley Pirates were among the four Scottish ice hockey teams playing in the Northern Premier League. In 1994–95 the new 3000-seat Caledonia stand containing several sports halls was built for St Mirren FC by Barr's of Ayr at Love Street, completing an all-seated stadium worthy of the Premier League status that the club retained in 2000. The great Town Hall is, among its other uses, still a venue for Scottish Dancing.

**Local Authority Independence, but Losses leave Problems**: In 1993 William Grant & Sons moved their headquarters and whisky blending activities to a new site at Bellshill, and CPC's Paisley plant – the former Brown & Polson works – then making Knorr products, was closed with the loss of its 300 jobs; production was transferred to France. In 1995 six new office buildings were planned beside the River Cart as the Gateway International Office Park. In 1996 Renfrew District, less Barrhead, became a unitary authority: Paisley's gain. The Glenfield fatstock market of A & J Wilson continues in use, and the John Neilson Institution has recently been converted into flats. The Grammar School, Castlehead, and Gleniffer High Schools all have around 1100 pupils; St Andrew's Academy has 875 and St Mirin's High School 360. The family-run *Brabloch Hotel* has 30 rooms, but Paisley does not have a large number of hotels.

## PARKHEAD, Camlachie & Westmuir **Map 15, D5**

***Eastern parts of Glasgow,*** *pop. 8500* OS 64: NS 6263

Glasgow's ancient Gallowgate, possibly deriving from a Roman road linking Bothwellhaugh with Old Kilpatrick, crossed the Camlachie Burn some 2 km east of Glasgow Cross. Timothy Pont's map made in 1596 showed no such road, but indicated that the burn was bridged; the Gallowgate bridge was rebuilt in 1665. The hamlet of Camlachie stood nearby on the way to Airdrie; however the area east of Glasgow was still only sparsely settled. In 1737 a coal mine was sunk at Westmuir, 3 km east of Glasgow Cross; this was possibly later called the Old School pit, for that was on Westmuir Street. By 1741 Alex Wilson was type-founding at Camlachie, and the Napier family made vinegar and chemicals at Vinegarhill in Camlachie from an early date (until the 1880s). By about 1754 when the Roy map was made there were two roads through the area, focusing on Glasgow. The first pub, the *Black Bull*, was founded in 1760, but the first known mention of the name *Parkhead* came in 1794 when it was an inn at the fork where Tollcross Road – the road to Bothwell Bridge – diverged from the Airdrie road at the end of Gallowgate. At that time the combined population of Parkhead and Westmuir was under 700, but Camlachie had grown into a weaving settlement with nearly 1000 people. A post office was opened in 1800 at Parkhead Cross, also known as Sheddens, with a penny post from Glasgow.

**Collieries, Marine Engines – and David Napier**: In 1812 Robert Gray of Carntyne owned the Wester Pit and also the Black Engine pit on East Wellington Street. The main shaft with its pumps was at the Caroline Pit (named after Queen Caroline), east of Quarrybrae Street. The Camlachie foundry and forge was begun by Duncan McArthur in 1812; it made major components for colliery beam engines, and by 1815 built ships' engines, including three for McLauchlan of Dumbarton and two for John Wood of Port Glasgow. Duncan McArthur employed David Napier, who had been trained in his father's works at Camlachie and about 1816 established his own foundry beside the Camlachie Burn, immediately engining the shallow draught Clyde padddle steamer *Marion* which carried passengers between Glasgow and Rutherglen; in 1821 he sold the works to his cousin Robert Napier, and moved to Lancefield.

**Dyestuffs, Brewing and Distilling**: About 1813 the linen dyestuffs manufacturers Turnbull & Ramsay founded works in Camlachie Street. By 1821 the many developments in the Monklands had made the main road very busy, and new trading opportunities emerged: a local Co-operative was formed in 1831 and a scientific association was started in 1838. By 1825 a Camlachie brewery was in production; this may have become a distillery later. The Home brewery was established by George Dalrymple on Burn Street in 1860 and rebuilt in 1865–66 on Invernairn Street; it was again rebuilt in 1897.

**Parkhead Forge – Serving the Shipyards**: The famous Parkhead Forge was founded west of Duke Street about 1837 by the brothers John and Andrew Reoch of Cramond, who used only scrap iron; but in 1841 it was sold to David Napier. By 1861 the forge had installed rolling mills to make ships' armour plating, and also made propellors. In 1863 it was taken over by William Rigby and William Beardmore, bringing a name to conjure with, and by 1869 this partnership employed 700 workers, using 15,000 tonnes of iron a year in its 22 puddling furnaces. It boasted 50-tonne cranes, fifteen steam hammers, a 25 cm boring machine and what was then the world's largest turning-lathe, to make crankshafts and propellor shafts of up to 32 tonnes and 60 cm diameter, both for liners and for Napier's warships. Ships' plates and armour plating were a speciality; for the latter a new rolling mill of 5000m$^2$ was built in 1869. The firm made the armour for HMS *Black Prince*, one of the world's first all-metal battleships. But some contracts were lost because the forge was then too far (1500m) from a railway which could transport heavy items economically.

**Other Industries and Competing Railways**: The Netherfield Chemical Works, the Westmuir sandstone quarry and the Crown fireclay works at Millerston Street were important in the 1850s and early 60s. In 1865 Clark & Struthers founded their Parkhead weaving factory to make gingham and the fine handkerchief check known as pullicate; the factory was extended in 1897. But in 1870 Parkhead consisted of little more than three main streets. The Belvidere Fever Hospital was built in 1870 beside the Clyde to the south. Commercial recreation came to this workaday area when the Glasgow showmen moved out from the Saltmarket to Vinegarhill in 1870. In 1871 the North British opened the area's first railway; this formed part of a secondary route from Edinburgh via Bathgate to Glasgow High Street, and cut through the sprawling chemical works, a station and engine sheds being provided north of Parkhead. A goods and mineral station was opened at Camlachie about 1875 when the line was connected to Springburn *(see Bridgeton)*. From 1875 a minor Caledonian Railway (CR) line passed through Camlachie on a north–south route connecting Dalmarnock with St Rollox; from 1885 a further CR line with a station immediately south of Parkhead linked the area with Glasgow London Road.

**Parkhead fabricates London's Tower Bridge**: Proper rail access having been provided, Beardmore took sole control of the Parkhead Forge in 1879. He immediately laid down open hearth steel plant, and the works were repeatedly extended over the lengthy period of 30 years from 1884; for example, the *Samson* 100-tonne drop hammer of 1881 was superseded by the 600-tonne *Goliath*. Between 1890 and 1894 the Parkhead Forge supplied about 12,000 tonnes of steel for London's Tower Bridge, fabricated and erected by Sir William Arrol's Dalmarnock workers: all the parts were transported to the Thames in Clyde Shipping Company coasters. By 1900 it covered 18 hectares of steelworks, forge and armour plate manufactory. Meantime in 1875 came Joseph Jack's North British Oil & Grease Works at Vinegarhill Street, and more heavy industries: Kesson & Campbell started the Carntyne Foundry and Engineering Works, while Park & Paterson built the Parkhead Metal Refining Works. The Macrae family built the long-lasting Hartshead bedding factory in 1877–83, while in 1883 McArthur, Scott & Co established the Carntyne Dyewood Mills, twice later enlarged.

**'Juice' and Wire, Ropes and Wringers**: In 1887 R F Barr moved his cork-cutting business from Falkirk to Parkhead, taking over the *Black Bull's* tiny mineral water factory. Barr's own lemonade works in Gallowgate was built in 1889 on the site of the early Belvidere. In 1901 Barr's launched a soft drink at first called *Iron-Brew*; flavoured with iron salt and fruit extracts, it was immediately popular. Andrew G Barr renamed the firm A G Barr & Co in 1904 and expanded the works in 1907–14. Meantime, about 1888, development of the Springfield Road wireworks was begun by W Riddell & Co. In 1890 H Winning & Co erected the Carntyne Rope & Twine Works in Caroline Street, and D & J Tullis was founded in Parkhead as laundry machinery makers, but moved to Clydebank about 1900.

**Celtic Park, Horses, Cars and Vans**: Celtic Football Club, which originated at Bridgeton *(q.v.)* in 1887, moved to the first Celtic Park in 1888, and then in 1892 to fresh turf laid on a nearby brickfield riddled with old mineworkings – the present site! In 1898 the new Celtic Park hosted the Scotland–England International with 50,000 spectators; it was also used for athletics and cycling, and in 1928 for speedway. Though *Murray's Handbook* could find nothing to say about Parkhead in 1894, it was rapidly growing towards both Glasgow and Shettleston. In 1896 Sir William Arrol and others – including Johnston, a locomotive engineer from Springburn's Hyde Park works – founded a motor factory at Camlachie, soon known as the Arrol-Johnston car company; but the works burned down in 1901 and production was then re-established at Paisley *(see also Bathgate and Locharbriggs)*. In 1904 J H Kelly built a van and lorry factory – in Van Street!

*Parkhead forge, founded by the brothers John and Andrew Reoch of Cramond about 1837; it was taken over by Beardmore in 1879. This view shows a hydraulic forging press, latterly used to make rolling-mill rolls. The works closed in 1983.* *(JRH)*

**Making Silks – and Burning Rubbish**: In 1895 the City Council built a large refuse destructor at Haghill Road, and not far away in 1899 came the incongruous development of Vanduara's Parkhead Silk Factory. The cheek by jowl mixture of varied industries continued to accrete: about 1896 Crichton & Mooney built their Phoenix Cabinet Works in Salamanca Street, and the Parkhead Grain Mills in Gallowgate were erected in 1897–1900 for John Kent. In 1903–04 the Glasgow Electric Crane & Hoist Company built an engineering works in Rigby Street. New workers' tenements filled every available remaining space in the area, which was served by Glasgow's electric trams from about 1898; soon after 1900 they ran on a Shettleston–Parkhead–Paisley route. The local Co-op amalgamated with the Eastern in 1901. Two bank buildings, a library and swimming baths were built in the Edwardian period, when Parkhead Cross became a minor civic centre.

**Beardmores employ 100,000 people!**: In 1900 Beardmore joined the Vickers group, and after acquiring the Mossend steelworks and building a shipyard at Dalmuir, William Beardmore & Co became the largest employer in Scotland. A wheel and axle depot was built in 1903, and as the arms race with Germany intensified, a gun quenching shop over 33 m in height was built at the Parkhead Forge in 1905. The works was still being extended on a large scale up to 1915, and played a major role in supplying *'materiel'* for waging the war of 1914–18; at the peak the firm's many works employed about 100,000 people. Meantime in 1906 Rennie's Steel Casting Company had established a foundry in Cuthelton Street. Different types of ventures then were a gut factory at Vinegarhill Street, an oil and tallow works in Westmuir Street, and the Govancroft Pottery – set up to make stoneware at London Road. In 1921 the 80-car Parkhead tram depot in Tollcross Road was built by Glasgow Corporation on part of the departmental recreation ground. Various facilities for physical recreation were established beside the Clyde, and a greyhound track was built beside the engine sheds at Carntyne, but there few other local developments found space.

**Decline begins**: From 1919, demand for the Forge's capital goods slumped. Beardmore's immediately responded by taking over Kelly's works in Van Street to build coaches and lorries; but the firm was in difficulties by 1927, and vehicle production was soon stopped. Meantime in 1920 – the year that Prohibition was imposed in America and the whisky trade collapsed – DCL had bought the Camlachie malt whisky distillery; they closed it about 1927, while retaining the bonded stores in the hope that their maturing stocks would become more saleable.

**Redefining *'Juice'***: During the depression of the early 1930s unemployment became rife, and with no spending money to spare, the Vinegarhill showground was closed in 1931. But the Forge was again deeply involved in armaments for the second war, and a large biscuit factory was built at Clydeford Drive by MacFarlane Lang. Somehow Barrs weathered a wartime ban on their soft drinks production, and in 1947 the misleading name of *Iron-Brew* – not actually brewed – was cleverly changed to *Irn-Bru*; many still call it *'ginger'* or *'juice'*, even though its mysterious ingredients probably do not include much fruit juice! By that time the congested population in the area had reached some 85,000; the Forge, engine sheds, Celtic Park and Belvidere Hospital still gave the place its character. But Parkhead North station was shut by 1960; the engine shed was closed with the opening of electrification to Airdrie in that year.

**The Destruction of Parkhead**: The trams saw their last day in September 1962; the Tollcross Road tram depot became a bus garage (still used as such). Celtic FC prospered, winning the European Cup in 1967, but football crowds cannot have favoured the train in sufficient numbers, because Parkhead Stadium station was closed by Beeching in 1964 and all the area's former Caledonian lines were immediately lifted. The closed Cuthelton Street foundry was demolished about 1967, and in 1969 the Forge pulled down its gun quenching shop, once claimed as Scotland's tallest building. As shipbuilding on Clydeside declined catastrophically, Beardmore's ceased trading in 1975; the famous Parkhead Forge lingered on under Firth Brown, latterly making rolls for rolling-mills, until closure in 1983, bringing an era to an end.

**Old and New Industries but shrinking Population**: About 1970 the Netherfield Chemical Works still produced fertilisers north of the railway, and sulphuric acid in a modern plant south of it. By then Long John Whisky's new Westhorn blending and bottling plant had been built beside the Clyde; in 1979 it covered 40 ha, and also contained a bond of some 90 million litres of maturing whisky. Meantime the ruthless clearance of tenement housing both good and bad, which was started in 1957, plus the catastrophic loss of jobs, cut the population of Parkhead by 75% over the 30 years to 1981, although the local facilities were still those of a small town.

**Irn Bru Fizzing Again – but Not from Girders**: Confidence looked up when in 1975 A G Barr & Co bought the *Tizer* soft drink brand, and in 1975 built a new HQ at Parkhead. From 1987 the firm was hailed as Britain's largest manufacturer of soft drinks, their biggest seller still *Irn-Bru*, its clever (and later banned) slogan *"Brewed in Scotland – from Girrrders!"* reminding us of the industrial history of Parkhead – although by 1992 the cans were all aluminium! Meantime the Camlachie bonded stores had been closed and demolished about 1980, but the Westhorn plant of United Distillers was to share the company's work with Kilmarnock and Leven plants. The bakery was still active in 1990 as part of United Biscuits. By 1993 a Local Development Company for the East End of Glasgow was in being.

**Celtic Park – to Move or Not to Move**: In 1988 a new facade was built at Celtic Park, at that time a grubby old ground for Premier Division matches, providing seating for only 16% of its capacity crowds of 53,000, and with structures subject to mining subsidence; so in 1992–93 Celtic FC sought finance to enable a move to a new stadium at Cambuslang. But cash was not forthcoming, the scheme did not meet the 70 conditions for planning permission, and boardroom rows unseated its autocratic proposers the Kelly family. In 1994 Celtic FC's new and realistic management set out to reconstruct their existing stadium to 52,000 seats, despite a setback when lowly Raith Rovers beat them in the Coca-Cola Cup Final! They followed this by further expansion in 1997 to 61,000 seats.

**From Ashes to ASDA, and Barr goes Global**: The demise of the Forge left a void, filled by an enormous retail development of over 32,000 m$^2$ which took its name on completion in 1988, a third of the area being a huge Gateway supermarket; there was also a 7-screen Cannon cinema. Despite a slow start to trading, the centre's impact soon went far beyond the disadvantaged areas of eastern Glasgow. In 1991 The Forge had 60 shops, over 1800 car parking spaces, and the largest ASDA hypermarket in Scotland. In 1993 it was bought by GUS (Great Universal Stores). By 1995 family-owned Barrs had a staff of 1200, but while their HQ stayed in Parkhead to manage their growing international operations, their Scottish production facilities were centralised at Cumbernauld. In 2000 under the guidance of A G Barr's great nephew Robin Barr, *Irn-Bru* equalled the consumption of *Coca-Cola* in Scotland. What is now Parkhead was stitched together from a series of small textile and coal-mining hamlets, and it still shows. However, despite the loss of its characteristic industries, it retains a degree of community identity.

## PARTICK, Hillhead & Kelvingrove — Map 15, C5

***Western parts of Glasgow,*** *pop. 40,000* — OS 64: NS 5667

In the 2nd century AD the Romans appear to have built a Clydeside road, joining their fort at Bothwellhaugh with the western end of the Antonine Wall at Old Kilpatrick. Old maps imply that its route is probably followed by Glasgow's Argyle Street, crossing the River Kelvin near its mouth to show the way for the later Dumbarton Road. The name Partick may be corrupted from Patrick (or vice versa), for there is a tradition that this saint was born in the area, perhaps at Old Kilpatrick. The early Kingdom of Strathclyde, whose defensive base was Dumbarton, apparently had its royal palace at Partick, on the right bank of the Kelvin; remarkably, this was part of the ancient Govan parish across the Clyde.

**Bishop's Retreat, Watermills, a Bridge and a Ferry**: Strathclyde was united with Scotland in the early 12th century, and Partick became a part of the Earldom of Lennox. By 1290 its former royal castle or palace had been rebuilt as a country retreat for the bishops of Glasgow; this role appears to have stultified development at Partick, and most subsequent activity up to the Reformation was centred on Glasgow itself. However the river provided much greater water power potential than Glasgow's Molendinar Burn, and two mills stood in its east bank by the time that Timothy Pont mapped Lennox about 1600: the Bishop's, and the Old or Meal Mill (leased by the City council in 1608). The Glasgow Incorporation of Bakers owned a mill at Partick from 1578 and later two, Clayslaps a little way up-river, and farther down the well-named Bunhouse! Eventually the Slit mills stood at the mouth of the River Kelvin. In 1577 a four-arched stone bridge was built across the Kelvin close to its mouth; Pont showed the bridge beside *'Water Inch'*, and *'Hydland'* also existed by that time. By 1593 a ferry to Govan operated from the spit of land at the river's mouth on which stood the *'Point House'*. Partick castle was rebuilt in 1611 by the mason William Myllar.

**Mines, Mills and Villas**: After a quiet century, in 1737 a colliery was sunk at Kelvinhaugh, and Partick's growth began in earnest. The Roy map of about 1754 showed a medium-sized settlement with mills, its bridge forming part of the Glasgow–Dumbarton road; from Partick another road led north by Garscube to New Kilpatrick. In the 1760s a logwood dye mill was built. Pennant in 1769 described Partick as a *"village"*, with *"villas belonging to the citizens of Glasgow on the gentle risings to the west"*, foreshadowing later suburban growth. Robert Adam designed Kelvingrove House, built in 1782–83 for a Glasgow merchant, Patrick Colquhoun. The water-powered South Woodside cotton spinning mill, the first large cotton mill in the Glasgow area, was built about 1784 for William Gillespie, near where a new four-arched Kelvin bridge was to be built in 1800.

**Early Victorian Shipbuilding and Milling**: There was a post office at Partick by 1838, and the upper level Kelvin Bridge, of three arches like its low-level precursor, was opened in 1840. Hunter & Dow, the first of several Partick shipyards, began work at Kelvinhaugh Slip in the 1830s. Tod & McGregor, founded in Glasgow by two of Napier's managers, moved their shipyard to Partick's Meadowside (west of the Kelvin's mouth) in 1847; they pioneered ocean-going screw vessels such as the famous SS *City of Glasgow*, in 1857 built the double-hulled PS *Alliance* for the Arrochar service, and at the same time had a 144 m dry dock built alongside. The original water-powered Scotstoun flour mills, alone on the west bank, were in being by 1847. In keeping with the milling tradition, in 1849 the *Wheatsheaf* inn was noted as long-established. About 1848 Black & Wingate built their Kelvinhaugh cotton spinning and weaving mills in Sandyford Street, which were later enlarged to accommodate 30,000 spindles in the 1870s.

**North from Partick: the early development of Hillhead**: The arrow-straight Great Western Road was built as the first stage of a Glasgow to Dumbarton turnpike in 1838–39, passing through Hillhead, about 1 km inland from Partick, to terminate at Anniesland. Over the years it helped various large space users from Glasgow to move out, giving the wider area around Partick a special character among Glasgow's inner suburbs. The Botanic Gardens were established at Hillhead in 1841, keeping upwind of the increasingly smoky city, and connected with Partick by Byres Road; in 1873 they acquired the great conservatory of Kibble Palace. From 1847 horse buses connected Cleveden Road with the city centre, 4 km away. Large terraced villas were built along Great Western Road from 1845, notably Great Western Terrace, finely designed by Alexander *'Greek'* Thomson and built in 1867. Meantime an impressive police station had opened in 1853, as had Kelvingrove Park, between Partick and the growing city. Hillhead became a burgh in 1869, and had a fine Burgh Hall built in Byres Road in 1871–72.

**Pointhouse Shipyard and Partick Foundry**: The Pointhouse yard opened in 1862 when A & J Inglis moved out from Glasgow, providing a huge slip dock and tall sheer legs; just inland they erected a boiler works in 1873–78. In 1880 they built the British India liner *Camorta* of only 2119 tons, lost with all 740 people on board when she sank in a typhoon in 1902 off the Burma coast. Partick Foundry was built on the site of the Bishop's Palace in Castlebank Street for Kelt & Duncan about 1864, and subsequently extended. The Scotstoun flour mills were rebuilt in 1877 and twice greatly enlarged.

**The University of Glasgow and Western Infirmary**: Partick became a burgh in the mid 19th century, and built its town hall off Dumbarton Road, now Burgh Hall Street. Including its adjuncts of Hillhead, and fashionable Dowanhill with its Notre Dame RC High School for girls, it grew into a major suburb of Glasgow. Apparently its early gasworks was at Keith Street. Kelvingrove Museum was founded in 1871 as *'The Public Industrial Museum'*; this took over Kelvingrove House, which was extended in 1874. Pressures on space and from railway promoters induced the ancient University to move out of central Glasgow to new buildings north of the new park at Gilmorehill, where work was begun in 1868. The first building for the Western Infirmary was erected nearby in 1871–74.

*Meadowside Quay, Partick, seen from Govan (in 1979) – with the granary on the left and a small general cargo motor-ship at the quay.* *(JRH)*

**Football: Famous Pioneers**: Partick Thistle FC was founded in 1868, and in 1872 the world's first international football match was played before a crowd of over 5000, the outcome a 0–0 draw between England and Queen's Park, which had provided the Scottish team! The venue was probably the West of Scotland Cricket Ground (which still survives behind Partick Town Hall) – or possibly Queen's Park, for sources disagree. For a few years from 1872 the fledgling Glasgow Rangers FC played at Great Western Road, along which the horse trams of the Glasgow Tramway & Omnibus Company then slowly plied to and from Glasgow. Recognising where most of their supporters lived, in 1887 Rangers moved across the Clyde to Ibrox; Thistle moved to Maryhill in 1909.

**Docks, Rail Access and Shipbuilding**: The 13.5 ha Queen's Dock at Stobcross, proposed in 1846 to replace a great cotton mill, was eventually built by the Clyde Navigation Trust in 1872–77; hydraulic-powered cranes were added in 1880. In 1873 a North British Railway (NBR) goods branch opened to Stobcross goods depot on the north side of the new dock, with a steep link to the quayside. In 1874 Hutson & Corbett founded the Kelvinhaugh engine works, extended four times by 1900; nearby were the Kelvinhaugh boiler works of J & G Thomson, built in 1880–81. In 1877–78 a new Partick Bridge at Dumbarton Road was built to carry a double tramline; about 1883 a horse tram depot was built at Thurso Street, later becoming a grain store. In 1871–72 Tod & McGregor built the slow 64 m PS *Princess Louise* for the new Larne & Stranraer Steamboat Company.

**Upmarket Schools, Facilities and Homes**: Two independent schools were the Westbourne School for Girls, opened in 1877, and the Kelvinside Academy of 1878, its buildings designed by James Sellars. Laurel Bank School for Girls at Hillhead was founded in 1903. Meantime in 1878 came the Western Baths Club, a private swimming pool complex. A small music hall was built, but burned down in 1884. In 1885 Alex Anderson, owner of Glasgow's Royal Polytechnic, had the large mansion of Red Hall built on Great Western Road. Murray's 1894 Handbook called Partick *"an important suburb"*.

**New Industries from the 1880s**: In 1880–81 William Smith & Sons set up the Partick Engine Works, making boilers, sugar mills and weighing machines; they were soon taken over by the doyens of the latter industry, W & T Avery. The ancient weir survived when Bunhouse mill burnt down in 1886, replaced by the much larger Regent Flour Mills, built in 1887–90 for John Ure and enlarged about 1903 by their new owners the Scottish Co-operative Wholesale Society. Two professors of Glasgow University, Barr and Stroud, founded optical instrument works at Ashton Lane, Hillhead in 1888 to make War Office artillery rangefinders, later moving out to Anniesland *(q.v.)*. A new gasworks for Partick was established at Temple in 1891, when the population of the police burgh was 36,500. About 1892 large sawmills were built at Kelvinhaugh Street for a timber merchant, John Scott, and cabinets and upholstery were made locally; in 1897 Steven & Struthers established a brass and bell foundry.

**Railways compete to link Partick with Glasgow**: The grandly titled Glasgow City & District Railway (GCD), a NBR subsidiary, was opened in 1886, linking Partick station at Dumbarton Road/Norval Street with Charing Cross, Queen Street and the east of Glasgow; a now-vanished spur led to Hyndland Road. Botanic Gardens and Kelvinbridge stations were built about 1894 for the Glasgow Central Railway (promoted by the rival Caledonian Railway (CR)) removing the South Woodside mill. In 1896 the CR opened the Clydeside duplicating line named the Lanarkshire & Dunbartonshire (L&D), crossing the Kelvin at Bishop Mills weir. It involved replacing the bridge of 1577, and provided Partick with two local stations: Central (later renamed Kelvin Hall) and Partick West, at Meadow Road, plus a branch line tunnelled northwards to Maryhill past two new stations, Crow Road (at Clarence Drive), and Kelvinside (at Lismore Road). Passenger traffic was badly hit by the arrival of electric trams in 1901, and these lines were eventually to vanish west of Partick Central.

**International Expositions, Bridges and Transport**: In 1888 Glasgow used Kelvingrove Park to stage an International Exposition, which drew 5.75 million visitors; its Moorish style buildings were designed to be temporary, and vanished within the year. A new Kelvin Bridge on Great Western Road was replaced by a grander structure in 1891 (probably the last cast-iron bridge built in Scotland), and the ancient bridge almost beneath it was sadly demolished as redundant in 1895 after the Prince of Wales Bridge had been built in the park in 1894–95. The Eldon Street bridge was also opened in 1895. Two new depots were built in 1893–95 for horse-drawn Glasgow Corporation tramcars – at Kelvinhaugh Street, and the Partick depot in Hayburn Street. The 1888 show was surpassed by the Glasgow Exhibition of 1901, held on the same site with its then brand-new Kelvingrove Museum and Art Gallery at Clayslaps. Robert Adam's Kelvingrove House was demolished in 1900 to clear the 30 ha site for vast Spanish style buildings, again soon demolished. Twice as many people visited this second extravaganza, justifying – for a time – the city's claim to be the Second City of the Empire. A third exhibition was held in 1911 *(for the fourth such spree in 1938, and the 1980s Garden Festival, see Govan)*.

**The Henderson and Shearer Shipyards**: Tod & McGregor's successors at Meadowside, D & W Henderson, built the fine PS *Lord of the Isles* in 1891 for the Glasgow & Inveraray Steamboat Company; better known for Far East merchant ships, they also built the Anchor liner *Columbia* of 8500 tons in 1902 for their Glasgow to New York service. Meantime in 1896 John Shearer & Son of the small Kelvinhaugh Slip built their Yard No.19, the 678-ton coaster SS *Pearl* for William Robertson of Glasgow, an auxiliary sailing vessel engined by Muir & Houston of Glasgow. In 1904 the Yorkhill Quay and Basin of the Clyde Navigation Trust was authorised, on the site of Shearer's coaster-building yard, which vanished.

**Glasgow City Utilities Developments**: In 1889–90 Glasgow Corporation had built the Kelvinhaugh refuse disposal works with a tall chimney, and also workers' tenements at Gilbert Street. Hillhead joined the City of Glasgow in 1891, followed by the building of the Kelvinside electricity generating station in Hughenden Lane in 1892–93, and the Partick power station and integral refuse destructor, built in 1905 for the Partick Electric Company. In 1904 a steam-driven sewage pumping station was built for Glasgow Corporation near the trunk sewer's crossing of the Kelvin.

**Cable Subway, Electric Trams and Motor Cars**: Another spurt in terrace building occurred from 1897 when the unique circular cable-hauled Glasgow Subway was opened, with stations at Partick and Hillhead, linking them with the city centre and under the Clyde to Govan. The Kelvinhaugh passenger ferry to Govan was established about 1900, upstream of the ancient chain ferry. Many of the visitors to the 1901 Exhibition were brought by the electric trams, new to Partick that year. More ominously, about 1906 A K Kennedy founded the Botanic Gardens Motor Garage in Vinicombe Street, rebuilt in 1911 to serve the area's richer citizens, perhaps including the University's first Professor of Scottish History, appointed in 1913 (a post paid for by the 1911 exhibition proceeds). In 1905–06 Walter Hubbard's bakery was built in Otago Street Hillhead. The first part of the huge 13-storey Meadowside Granary was built in 1911–13 for the Clyde Navigation Trust, to hold 31,500 tonnes of grain imported across the adjacent quay, and later extended to a length of some 620m. The tramway electricity supply needed reinforcement in 1910, but in 1912 a car ferry replaced the chain ferry from Partick to Govan.

**Entertainments, Kelvin Hall, Sick Kids and BBC**: In 1912 the City of Glasgow was allowed to take over Partick burgh, without its consent! The Kelvin Way bridge was opened in 1914. The famed 400-seat *Hillhead Picture House* in Vinicombe Street opened in 1913; it was later called the *Salon Cinema*. The Kelvin Hall exhibition and Museum complex was built some time after 1905; the Hall burned down in 1925 and was replaced in 1927. The Royal Hospital for Sick Children (the *'Sick Kids'*) was built at Old Dumbarton Road in the 1920s, which otherwise seem to have been rather uneventful; but at some time part of the former Avery's works became a dance hall, and a music hall still existed at Partick until after 1945. In 1935 the erratic cable-driven subway was cheaply electrified, adapting the original trains. About then the headquarters of BBC Scotland was moved from Edinburgh to Hillhead's Queen Margaret Drive; this helped to set the seal on the westwards move of city centre activities which had been under way for a century. Hillhead High School was built during the 1930s, when University development continued, including construction of the great Reading Room.

**Whisky, Cargo Ships and Air Raids**: Hepburn & Ross, cabinet makers of Otago Street since 1887, diversified in 1919 as blenders of *'Red Hackle'* whisky, the name deriving from the regimental cap ornament of the Black Watch. The firm and brand prospered until the 1940s; the firm sold out in 1959 to Robertson & Baxter. From 1929 D & W Henderson built four cargo ships for Richard Hughes of Liverpool; but their yard was closed by the shipbuilding industry's rationalisation body NSS in 1934, though it was revived to build landing craft in World War II, when the Kelvin Hall was used as a barrage balloon factory. Meantime Botanic Gardens station was closed in 1939. The Partick, Hillhead and Hyndland areas were damaged in air raids in 1941.

**Inglis Paddlers include two *'Waverleys'***: Among a succession of paddle steamers built by A & J Inglis of Pointhouse were two named *Waverley*. The first, built in 1899 for the NBSP, was sunk at Dunkirk in 1940; its replacement of 1947, 73m in length, was the London & North Eastern Railway vessel that eventually became famous as the world's last seagoing paddle steamer. Meantime the cargo steamer *Cygnet* was built in 1904 for David MacBrayne and used on the Inveraray service. MacBrayne's abandoned paddlers much sooner: their last, the little *Mountaineer*, was launched by Inglis in 1910 for the Oban and Sound of Mull services. Another Inglis steamer was the 300-ton PS *Prince Edward* for Loch Lomond in 1910–11.

**The *'Maids'* bring the end of Partick Shipbuilding**: The 58m-long *Maid of the Loch* for Loch Lomond services was fabricated by Inglis at Pointhouse in 1952, and re-erected at Balloch; then came the sister ships *Maid of Argyll* and *Maid of Skelmorlie* for service between Craigendoran, Rothesay and Arrochar, plus cruising. But the Inglis yard, the last shipbuilder in Partick, was closed in 1962, its boiler works were demolished in 1964 and after a fire in 1965 the yard was completely cleared of buildings. Another earlier blaze in 1960 destroyed a store at Yorkhill Quay containing 46,000 cases of whisky!

**Electrifying the Mill and Abandoning Trams**: By 1951 the area had 46,000 residents; there were shops throughout Byres Road from Partick Cross to Hillhead, and along Dumbarton Road to Whiteinch, offering with other services to take a significant share in Glasgow's role as a major regional centre. Meantime the ancient Bishop Mills, which had been powered in turn by water wheels and water turbines, had been electrified in the early 1950s. In 1962 the 124-car Partick tram depot in Hayburn Street and its last route to Dalmuir West and Auchenshuggle vanished when the pollution-free Glasgow tramways were regrettably abandoned, the depot soon being replaced by a new garage for the air-polluting diesel buses.

**Blue Trains and Expressway, Goodbye Old Routes**: Kelvinbridge station was closed in 1952. Other duplicate lines and stations including Hyndland had been closed by 1960–61 when the area's main (ex-GCD) railway was electrified, serving Partick and a new Hyndland through station 500m west of the former terminus, with the multiple-unit *'Blue Trains'*. The opening of the Clyde Tunnel at Whiteinch in 1964 caused closure of the vehicle ferry to Govan. Also in 1964 Kelvin Hall station and the L&D's Maryhill branch through Crow Road station were abandoned, some of the lines later going under the new Clydeside Expressway, built in the 1970s, which also crossed the head of the former Tod & MacGregor dry dock, infilled when the Queen's Dock was closed in 1969.

**Developments in Public and Private Services**: By 1967 Westbourne School for Girls had 600 pupils, but the equally independent Laurel Bank School for Girls at Hillhead was smaller. Hillhead Burgh Hall, which had been used as a bank since about 1950, was demolished in 1972 and a new public library built on the site in 1973. The architecturally important *Grosvenor Hotel* in Great Western Road, built as terraced houses in 1855 and lately doubled in size to 100 rooms, was destroyed by fire in 1978, but reconstructed in 1979. The former CR line through Central Low Level was reconstructed and reopened as the Argyle Line in 1979–80 with electric trains. Decongestion and industrial decline cut the population of the Partick area to about 41,000 by 1981. The University and hospitals were among many specialised services: the Hunterian Art Gallery – including a reproduction of the Charles Rennie Mackintosh House – was built in 1981, and the Western Baths Club was refurbished for its well-off subscribers in the 1980s.

**Hospitals and Maternity Units**: By 1941 the Western Infirmary was a teaching hospital, and Redlands in Lancaster Crescent had become a makeshift maternity home; it was demolished in 1968, because of the opening in 1964 of the Queen Mother's Hospital for maternity cases beside the Royal Hospital for Sick Children, which was rebuilt in 1968–71. In 1992 the former was delivering an average of ten babies a day, while the 305 beds in the *'Sick Kids'* were serviced by a staff of 1400 people. The Western Infirmary had grown to 600 beds by 1993, but its proposed closure was announced in 1995, its work to be eventually transferred to Gartnavel Hospital at Anniesland. Meantime the private 32-bed Nuffield McAlpin Clinic, open in Beaconsfield Road by 1981, was developed in the 1980s into a BUPA acute hospital, the 48-bed Glasgow Nuffield.

**Scotland's Premier Tourist Draw**: Part of the Kelvin Hall, made redundant by the opening in 1985 of Glasgow's SECC, was then converted into a much-needed indoor athletics stadium, and reopened in 1988; the remainder became the Glasgow Museum of Transport, moved from Pollokshields in the same year. In 1989, when the Garden Festival was no more, the Kelvingrove Museum and Art Gallery was Scotland's busiest free tourist attraction, its 1 million visitors actually exceeding the number visiting Edinburgh Castle; the Botanic Garden was eighth. When in 1993 Kelvingrove Park was selected as the site for a new National Gallery of Scotland, many opponents appeared, heartened by a lack of cash for the project. The *'A'* listed Kelvingrove Parish Church was saved for posterity in the mid 1990s. The *Salon Cinema* closed in 1992 and the Victorian police station in 1993, but the unseated cinema interior remained otherwise almost unaltered in 1997, when the police station was being restored; in 2000 the cinema was restored and converted into a restaurant.

**Hotel, Schools and University Developments**: In 1985 the energetic Glaswegian caterers Ken McCulloch and Amanda Rosa opened a small, traditional terraced hotel in Kelvinside, using its address as its name – *One Devonshire Gardens* – and catering for the luxury end of the market. Soon well known, by 1990 it had 27 well-filled rooms, and – along with other leading Scottish luxury hoteliers – advertised as *'Connoisseurs Scotland'*. By 1993 Laurel Bank School and the Kelvinside Academy for boys were among the few remaining single-sex schools in Scotland, for by then the recently expanded Glasgow Academy had absorbed the Westbourne School and served 1000 co-ed pupils. The new 6-storey Robertson building, a research laboratory complex, opened in 1992 at the University, which in 1994 had some 14,000 full-time students. In 1996 Laurel Bank School with 335 pupils absorbed Glasgow's Park School with some 255; the enlarged school at Hillhead, still for girls only, was renamed Laurel Park – but in 2001 it was to merge with Hutcheson's Grammar. City Council schools are the Clevedon Secondary with 850 pupils, Hillhead High School with 750 and Hyndland Secondary with 840.

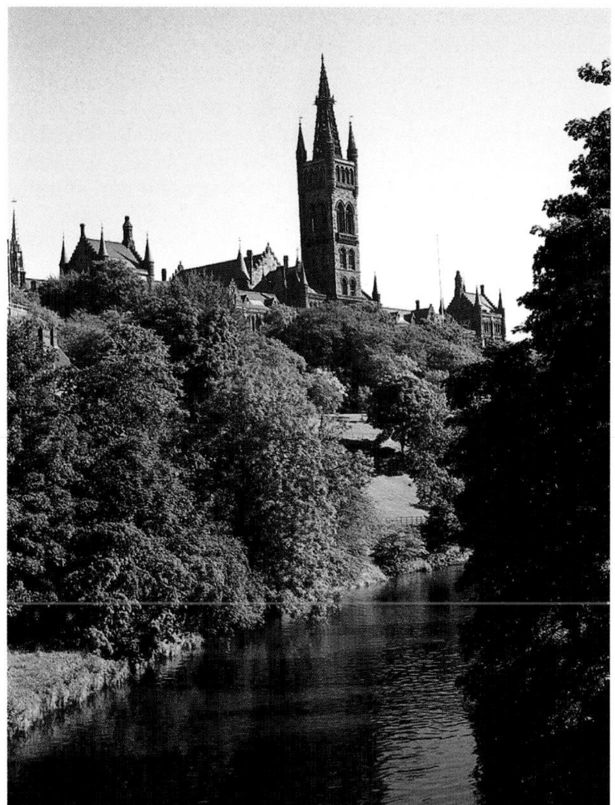

*Glasgow University made the move from the city centre in the late 1860s to this building, designed by Sir George Gilbert Scott. The tower was built to provide ventilation. Its open-work spire was added by Scott's son, J Oldrid Scott.* *(JRH)*

**BBC and Clydeport Schemes – and Hotels**: In 1996 BBC Scotland announced plans to move from Queen Margaret Drive to new purpose-built premises at Govan; the new Parliament in prospect in Edinburgh from 1997 made this seem a strange choice of location. Clydeport has ambitious plans for Yorkhill Quay and basin – a major leisure complex and the development of housing and hotels. These presently cluster along Great Western Road, and now include the large *Hilton Grosvenor* (ex-*Stakis*), and half a dozen smaller establishments.

**The 3 areas – character and change**: Though linked for convenience in organising this book, Partick, Hillhead and Kelvinside remain distinct places.

*Partick*'s history as a riparian settlement and shops is still reflected in its layout: the long spine of tenements and shops that runs, with little interruption, from the river Kelvin to the Clyde Tunnel approaches, with a band of tenements to the north and a much-reduced strip of houses to the south – now separated from riverside commerce by the Clyde Expressway.

With its churches, schools and (reducing number of) public buildings, it retains a strong sense of community.

*Hillhead* never had the core of shared industrial experience of Partick and was, rather, an enclave of tenements and terraces serving Glasgow. Its primacy as a middle-class West End suburb was relatively brief, and it is now largely a student quarter, with a fairly large ethnic minority. Its proximity to the University, the Western Infirmary and the BBC gives it a cosmopolitan character.

*Kelvinside* was deliberately laid out as a high-class residential suburb, and though the very wealthy moved out long ago, it still has much of its original character. Its spine is Great Western Road, providing an arrow-straight route to the north edge of Glasgow's city centre. With its related suburbs of Kirkleee, Dowanhill and Hughenden, it still provides a leafy environment for middle-class living.

## PARTON & Mossdale **Map 2, A4**

***Galloway village,*** *pop. 360 (area)* OS 84: NX 6970

Parton's medieval Boreland motte stood in mediocre farmland on the east shore of Loch Ken in the Stewartry of Kirkcudbright. A long-vanished castle on Burned Island, 4 km north-west in Loch Ken, was the 14th century base of Edward Balliol. A fine 17th century pulpit from Parton parish church is in Edinburgh's Museum of Scotland. By the mid 18th century the ferry known as the *Boat of Rhone* crossed the ribbon loch at its narrowest point near Parton House, and road builders were following the lochsides. When the Portpatrick Railway was approved in 1858 the ferry was not replaced by a joint rail and road crossing as the road trustees wished; instead a rail-only viaduct of three 42 m lattice girder spans was built on stone piers. Stations were opened at highly rural Parton, a tiny estate village, and at the hamlet of Mossdale in Kells parish west of the loch; the latter station was named New Galloway, though 8 km from that place. The line opened in 1861 and the ferry faded from view. The famous Scottish scientist James Clerk Maxwell *(see Kirkpatrick Durham)* is buried and commemorated at Parton. Parton parish held 600 people in 1901.

**Loch Skerrow and the End of the Line**: At one time there was a substantial quarry at Parton, out of use by 1951. West of Mossdale, where Wordie & Co still had a rail cartage depot in 1946, the trains toiled uphill and across another viaduct for some 6 km to a height of about 130 m at roadless Loch Skerrow, where there was a crossing loop and a water tank to replenish steam locomotives, both vital features. Fishermen arrived by train and some railway families lived nearby. By 1951 Cairn Edward forest had replaced much of the moorland west of the loch and about 425 people lived in the whole Parton and Mossdale area; there were two primary schools and two post offices. The whole railway was destroyed by Beeching in 1965, both the schools had been closed by 1976, and by 1981 only 200 people were left. By 1985 there was a caravan site beside the loch at Parton, but virtually no other recent development except forestry on the hills to the north. Though Parton parish had only 364 people in 1991, both the local post offices and the viaduct remarkably survive. The Galloway Sailing Centre on Loch Ken opposite Burned Island also provides a hostel for backpackers.

## PATHHEAD **Map 15, E3**

***Midlothian village,*** *pop. 925 (area)* OS 66: NT 3964

The Roman road from Inveresk to Corbridge in Northumberland strode over hill and dale, crossing the steep valley of the Tyne Water 8 km south-east of Dalkeith, in an area which was part of the Lordship of Newbattle. During the 15th century a collegiate church was founded near Preston Hall in Cranston parish, 1 km north of the ford; beside the original church was a *'hospitium'* or inn for pilgrims, and in 1631 a parish school was founded. Pont's map of Lothian made about 1600 showed Turniedykes, *'Furd'* (Ford) Mill where the Roman road crossed the Tyne, and the L-plan tower of *'Southsyit'* Castle, rebuilt for Patrick Eleis in 1640–44. Preston was chartered as a burgh of barony in 1663, but this came to nothing except Preston Hall; Ford House was built in 1680.

**Oxenfoord and early Pathhead**: Pathhead grew up unrecorded by Pont, Roy and most early travellers, at the head of the steep path up from the ford. It seems to have arisen from a linen factory with over 50 looms, established at Cranston in 1738 by Sir William Dalrymple, and a small linen bleachfield built at Ford in the early 1750s. The mansion known as Oxenfoord Castle, designed by Robert Adam, was also built at that time; in emulation, Preston Hall was rebuilt about 1794. In 1799 Heron mentioned collieries at Vogrie, 2 km southwest, and said that at Upper Cranston there were *"works for extracting tar from pit-coal. The villages of Crichton and Pathhead contain upwards of 450 inhabitants"*.

**Pathhead or Ford?**: Ford post office first opened in 1805 – so far as can be ascertained actually located at Pathhead, though for over a century its address was Pathhead Ford, to distinguish it from the larger Pathhead in Fife. In 1831 the main road was diverted from its Roman route to a less hilly line over the tall Lothian Bridge, built across the Tyne Water north of the ford to designs by Telford, as part of a plan for a new Great North Road. This scheme had been aborted by 1850 due to the advent of railways, but none came close to Pathhead. Southsyde Castle was heavily rebuilt around 1850. The population of the village of Pathhead in 1891 was 545. By 1895 it had a telegraph office and two inns including the *Stair Arms*. A sawmill was at work north of Ford, and limeworks were active near Hope, 2 km south-east of Pathhead village; these later closed.

**The Brief Career of Oxenfoord Castle School**: By 1951 the population of 900 in the Pathhead area had the facilities of an average village, a situation since broadly maintained; for many years the *Stair Arms* was a small hotel. By 1977 Oxenfoord Castle had become an independent girls' boarding school, by 1986 a country park had been opened near Vogrie to the west, and in 1990 Baxter of Pathhead was a timber haulier. Oxenfoord Castle School was closed in 1993 *(see Musselburgh)*, but its fine building soon reverted to domestic use. A golf course has been developed at Vogrie; Pathhead primary school and post office remain open.

## PATHHEAD, Gallatown & Sinclairtown **Map 6, B4**

***E. parts of Kirkcaldy,*** *pop. 12,200* OS 59: NT 2992

An ancient fort on the coastal cliffs 1 km east of Kirkcaldy was originally known in the Gaelic as Dunnikier (*in Gaelic 'Castle of the Fort'*). The *Caer* element in the name and the rectilinear layout of Pathhead both suggest Roman origins, as do three generally straight ancient road lines. One runs north via Carlton (another Caer where an ancient east–west alignment crosses) to Kirkforthar – which contains the Forth element of ancient Pictish Fothrif. A second, sub-parallel route from Pathhead towards Leslie passed Carberry, another *Caer* name: multiple Roman camps of different date are quite often found in a small area. But the most obvious ancient straight alignment is the Standing Stanes road to Cameron Bridge *(q.v.)*.

**Medieval Ravenscraig and Pathhead**: Dunnikier was in the parish of Dysart, and a *'fair ready way'* already led from Dysart to Falkland by 1415; it probably also had a link to Kirkcaldy. Ravenscraig Castle was built on the cliffs for James II in 1460–61, a very early example of an artillery fort, but soon passed to the Sinclair Earls of Orkney. Pont's sketch maps of about 1600 showed a settlement curiously labelled *Pichltillhim* in this location (there is also a Pickletillem near Leuchars); the original steep path (later a road) led up from the mouth of the Den Burn, and gave Pathhead its better-known name. It developed independently of both the adjacent Royal Burghs of Kirkcaldy and Dysart, and apparently became a burgh of barony. At some time Pathhead had a market, its site still marked today by a circle of pavings. But it was to become Kirkcaldy's largely industrial partner.

**Smuggling, Linens, Coal and the shift of Dunnikier**: By 1642 when James Gordon visited Fife to prepare his map, the distinct village of Pathhead had grown up beside the castle, then labelled *'Ravensheugh'*. In 1692–95 John or James Watson built a substantial town house on the Path, which later became the Oswald family's Dunnikier House, and then a manse. By the early 18th century the Path continued as a road, possibly on the Roman line, via Gallatown to Woodhaven and the Dundee ferry. Andrew Wilson, a Pathhead baker, was a notorious smuggler whose hanging in Edinburgh in 1736 helped to precipitate the Porteous riots. Arnots made linens at Pathhead by 1748, including shirting, sheeting and towelling on a commercial scale; by 1750 the *Path Tavern* was already a hostelry. Roy's map of that date showed quite a large settlement at Pathhead, a coastal road to Dysart, and *'coal hills'* where the thick Dysart Main seam outcropped on the hilltop 1.5 km inland, east of the small village of Gallatown. There was plenty of accessible coal elsewhere in the area too, notably in the valley of the Den Burn. A fine new Dunnikier House was built west of Gallatown about 1780 as a mansion of Lord St Oswald and surrounded by parkland.

**Nails and the Wealth of Nations**: Meantime Defoe told of nails being made *'in Dysart'* in 1724. Chambers noted that Adam Smith of Kirkcaldy who wrote the pioneer text on economics, *The Wealth of Nations*, published in 1776, "*is said to have first conceived his notions about the division of labour from observing the process of nail-making at a large manufactory in Pathhead*". Its site is unknown. Heron in 1799 noted Pathhead as a *"considerable village"* of over 2000 people, *"most of whom are employed in the linen manufacture"*. About 100 nailmakers were at work in Dysart parish in 1800, but this trade had practically ceased by 1836. In 1807 Alex Robertson of Pathhead invented a spring-loaded flax heckling device.

**Gallatown and Pottery, Maltings and Whale Oil**: Heron noted that Gallatown, a weaving village with its old *Royal Oak* inn, had over 400 people soon after the famous Fife Pottery was opened there in 1790; later a linen works was added. By 1794 over 200 $m^3$ of barley were malted annually at Pathhead, and 2500 barrels of ale were brewed: *"Pathhead for Meal and Malt"* wrote a local poet, for milling had been carried on beside the Den Burn for at least two centuries *(see Kirkcaldy)*. Tongue in cheek, Chambers in 1827 mentioned *"an extensive and most savoury oil-manufactory"* – the whale oil works on the foreshore, near the Holmes Maltings. Much later the Dunnikier maltings were established farther up the hill by Robert Kilgour.

**Bleaching, the Railway and Floorcloth**: The Denburn bleachfield was open well inland by 1827 and remained in use for about 70 years. By 1838 both Pathhead and Gallatown had post offices. The Edinburgh & Northern Railway was opened through the area in 1847, with a station in a cutting at Sinclairtown, on the road between Pathhead and Gallatown. In the same year the floorcloth (painted linen) manufacturer Michael Nairn of Kirkcaldy erected a four storey building nearly 50 metres long, seaward of Nether Street; it was at first derisively labelled *Nairn's Folly*, because floorcloth had to be aged for ten months before sale. In 1854 there was practically no development inland of the railway and west of St Clair Street except the Denburn bleachfield; in 1864 under David Lumsden (who also owned Pitcairnfield bleachworks at Almondbank near Perth) it employed about 30 people.

**Teapots and Ceramic Cats**: The Sinclairtown pottery was founded at the hilltop in Rosslyn Street in 1869 by George MacLauchlan, and soon employed 30 men. Under the Kirks and later the Buists its one or two kilns fired large numbers of teapots, bowls and dishes made from both local and imported clays until 1899, when the firm moved to Oswald Road at Gallatown, working there until about 1930. The original site was sold to McLaren's who made linens in an adjoining factory. Meantime in 1879 Morrison & Crawford had opened the Rosslyn pottery nearby, and around that time the Fife Pottery made the flamboyant *Wemyss Ware* from Devon clay imported through Dysart; its most spectacular products were large, whimsical, decorated pottery cats *(see Ceres)*.

**Propellor Shafts, More Linen, Coal, and Bricks**: Fife Forge, established in 1873 at the foot of Overton Road, later moved to the Ingleside Foundry beside the railway; its rail siding received ingots from William Beardmore of the Parkhead Forge, and despatched finished products such as propellor shafting. The Victoria Linen Works were built at Sinclairtown between 1854 and 1879. The Hawklymuir Linen Factory also existed by 1879, developed by the Blyth family; but the founder's son John Blyth spent his fortune on works of art, many of which found their way to the Kirkcaldy art gallery, while the factory was neglected. By 1896 the Denburn power-loom linen works and Denburn rope works were also open between Pathhead and Kirkcaldy. The rail-connected Dunnikier Colliery (the *'Pannie Pit')*, was opened west of Smeaton Road in the early 1880s by Walter Herd & Sons. It was later sold to the Fife Coal Company who used a shunting engine there and owned 400 coal wagons by 1948. By 1896 the Den brickworks were also open close by.

**Linoleum: Source of the Queer-like Smell**: Much more important to the locality in the long-term than coal was linoleum, whose local manufacture is actually connected more with Pathhead than with Kirkcaldy proper. This durable product – made from finely ground cork, wood flour and boiled linseed oil on a hessian base – had been invented by Frederick Walton of Staines in 1860. When his patent expired in 1876, two local manufacturers of floorcloth moved into linoleum.

Michael Nairn's son Michael Barker Nairn first made linoleum in 1877; in 1879 he erected the world's first linoleum factory, in Victoria Road; it still stands, listed but derelict. From 1881 Nairns made linoleum twelve feet in width. The firm – which also made all its own paint – was soon to become the area's largest industry, and among its most lasting.

**Rival Floorcoverings Manufacturers**: By 1880 the North British floorcloth (later also linoleum) works stood west of Factory Road, north of the Denburn Works. From 1865 local linen manufacturer Michael Beveridge, with James Shepherd, had operated the *'Kirkcaldy Floorcloth Works'*, also west of Factory Road but south of the railway; they built the Kirkcaldy Linoleum (later Rosslyn) Works between Junction Road and the railway by 1880, and were soon equally successful. Beveridge died in 1890, bequeathing important facilities to Kirkcaldy (where he lived), and the firm of his survivor Shepherd merged with Barry Ostlere of Kirkcaldy in 1899, their factories remaining in production as Barry, Ostlere and Shepherd.

**The Development of Facilities and Tramways**: In 1876 the Barony Burgh of Pathhead joined with Kirkcaldy; hence the reason why the name Kirkcaldy was given to the area's first small but much-needed cliff-top hospital, its unique circular ward built in stone at Ravenscraig in 1889 – a gift to the town by Michael Barker Nairn. Meantime the Pathhead Hall was erected by public subscription in 1883. Pathhead school opened in 1894, built of red sandstone from the West of Scotland; not far away in upmarket Loughborough Road appeared the so-called Dysart telephone exchange, and the Viewforth junior secondary school. Pathhead also spawned its own substantial Co-operative society. Gallatown was the north terminus of the Kirkcaldy municipal electric tramways of 3'6" gauge, whose depot was built at Oswald Road in 1903, and in 1906 became the end-on junction with the Wemyss Tramways, connecting to Leven. In 1911 a line was laid to Dysart.

**Cork, Clay & Congoleum**: By 1900 Michael Nairn & Co had a German factory and an American branch at Kearney, New Jersey, which acquired the Congoleum Company, USA makers of a cheap bitumen-impregnated paper-backed printed floor covering, soon also produced in Kirkcaldy. A coal siding with wagon tippler was installed for their first power station, built in 1911; a post-1921 power plant also received coal supplies by rail. Nairn's also had a siding for their linseed oil tank wagons, though most came by sea from Hull crushers; the annual supply of waste cork (from which bottle corks had been cut) was brought from Portugal by sea to the harbour. China clay also came by sea, from Cornwall. For a century the firm's finished products, 90-foot (27 m) rolls of linoleum both printed and inlaid, were despatched as rail parcels traffic through nearby stations. Other significant industries were Alex Fraser's (builders) who owned the Nydie quarry near St Andrews, Melville Brodie Engineering, and Robert Kilgour Ltd, maltsters.

**Ravenscraig Park, Sawmills, Steam and Ice**: The fine coastal policies of Dysart House, given to the town by Sir Michael Nairn about 1928, became Ravenscraig Park. The Pannie pit worked down to about 425 m by the time it was closed in 1929, its site becoming the Dunnikier Sawmills and municipal yards. The Fife pottery had four bottle kilns before it closed about 1930, as did the Rosslyn concern. The Kirkcaldy trams stopped running in 1931, their sheds becoming a bus garage and eventually a haulage depot; some tram bodies went to form *'chalets'* in a Kinghorn holiday camp! About that time two steam laundries were built to serve the hotel trade. The *'Kirkcaldy'* ice rink, built at Gallatown in 1937, soon became the home of the *Fife Flyers* ice hockey team.

**Braehead House and Bouncing Bombs**: By 1938 about 3000 people were employed by Nairn, who began work on an imposing head office building; delayed by the 1939–45 war, it was completed in the mid 1950s as Braehead House. During World War II Nairn's recruited a largely female workforce, who used linseed oil to proof over 140 million metres of cambric fabric against gas, using a process researched by Nairns. They also made jute fabric used in bunks for air raid shelterers in London tube stations, roofing felt for blitz repairs, some 200 million metres of garnishing for camouflage netting, and 214,000 shipping containers. Turning to engineering, Nairns also produced 627,000 shell casings and 9500 bomb tails, fabricated over 7000 light alloy fuel tanks for Halifax bombers, machined 43 casings for 5-tonne and 10-tonne bombs, pierced 3 m-long forgings with 280 mm holes to make 77 large armour piercing bombs, and made many specialised naval gun mountings, torpedo parts, anti-submarine missiles, and crankshafts for Hercules engines. In 1943 Nairns made the casings for Barnes Wallis' *'Bouncing Bombs'*. Alumina was also stored in vast quantities. No doubt other firms' records would reveal similar heroic efforts.

**Lino Tiles and Propellor Shafts**: Jute backing for linoleum being unobtainable in 1945, Nairn's tried paper, but the product tore on laying and was unsaleable until the idea of cutting it into squares produced the popular lino tile – just as DIY became general! By 1951 the population in the area, including Dysart, was nearly 20,000, with urban facilities; St Andrew's RC High School was built around that time. The Fife Forge then exported shafting to shipbuilders throughout western Europe. The Hawklymuir Linen Factory employed only 40 people using ancient steam-driven non-automatic looms until John Blyth's death at the age of 92 in 1960 caused its closure, the substantial building later becoming a local authority store. Meantime S&N built a brewery depot in McKenzie Street. Kilgour's maltings were gradually extended, by the early 1970s producing malt for Ballantine's whisky.

**Linoleum struggles but Golf Trolleys roll**: In the 1960s the linoleum industry hit grave difficulties *(see Kirkcaldy)*, and Nairn's – who admitted to *"weak and indecisive"* management – merged with Williamson's of Lancaster in 1962, becoming Nairn Williamson (NW). In 1964 came the failure of Barry Staines (successor to Barry Ostlere & Shepherd); their various factories were abandoned. Most were demolished, though the local family of Meiklejohn soon established their small *'Kingslaw'* golf trolley factory and electroplating plant in the Rosslyn works (which closed in 1999). The NW felt mill closed around 1970.

**Telephone Equipment and Theatre Lighting**: In the 1960s Kirkcaldy Town Council laid out the Mitchelston and Randolph industrial estates, respectively west and east of Gallatown, to counter the loss of Barrys and the contraction of NW. Soon GEC made telephone equipment in a large factory, opened at Mitchelston about 1965; in 1972 GEC employed 1440 people there, of whom only 200 were male; at one time the workforce exceeded 2000. Other newcomers were Rank Strand Electric, who in 1972 had 300 workers making theatre and studio lighting; the Canadian firm Butler making steel buildings, Carron Hydraulics manufacturing pumps, and the *Fife Free Press* group's printing works.

**Furniture at Mitchelston**: In 1970 A H McIntosh, then Scotland's largest furniture manufacturers, moved from inner Kirkcaldy to large new works at Mitchelston – the first factory in Britain built to metric dimensions – continued making high quality furniture with 470 employees. Soon McIntosh could not meet demand, and took over Beithcraft (of Beith) in 1976; finding two-site working a problem, the Beith works was run down and an extension opened at Mitchelston in 1981 – at a time of world trade depression! McIntosh had only 230 workers when they became insolvent in 1984; they were taken over by ESA of Stevenage to make school furniture. In 1986–7 they became that firm's sole plant, with 280 workers by 1988, when a management buy-out enabled a partial return to good quality domestic furniture.

**Golf, Caravans, Scrap Cars and Butter!**: From 1963 the Town Council laid out an 18-hole public golf course at Dunnikier Park, where the former mansion became a hotel, and a touring caravan site was laid out about 1972. About 1970 a prominent group of car scrapyards was unwisely allowed to develop on the undermined ground of the Randolph industrial estate, helping to explain why northbound traffic on the Forth Road Bridge always exceeded southbound! Other old cars went to Muir Metals' car crusher at Denburn. Despite the rusty wrecks nearby, the Fife Creamery moved their butter factory from the Leven area to Randolph about 1973.

**Closures and *Cushionflor***: *'Nairn's Folly'* was demolished in 1969, and replaced by terraced gardens in the early 1970s. Sinclairtown station was closed in 1969, and the old hospital ceased to function about 1970. By 1972 only one local linen factory still worked; the one-time Denfield linen works became a grain warehouse about 1973. In 1972 Fife Forge had 135 workers, but the ending of much of the European shipbuilding industry caused its closure in 1984. In 1967 NW's New Jersey factory invented Cushionflor, from 1968 made in Pathhead of printed vinyl on a fibreglass web, covered with a *'wear layer'* and backed by foam. Around 1970 they built the first phase of extensive single-storey floorspace to the north-west, enabling the tall, old unadaptable premises to be pulled down one by one. NW, which employed about 2000 people in 1972, was bought by Unilever in 1976. An extension to the modern factory opened in 1979 to make *Cushionflor* in a 4 m width, but by then the workforce had shrunk greatly. A subsidiary, Nairn Travel, reached a staff of 500 before being sold to A T Mays of Saltcoats in 1983; its offices at Braehead House were converted to flats around 1990.

**Large Stores and Sewage Treatment**: By 1981 the area had a greatly reduced population of only 11,000 and the facilities of a small town. The Hutt family developed a small department store in the 1970s; closed for several years, it was reopened in 1987 by local firm Rejects, and was extended to become one of Fife's largest durable goods stores, later with a Dunfermline branch. An ASDA hypermarket, resisted for 20 years by the town and district councils, was permitted by Fife Regional Council, and opened in 1988 on the Mitchelston estate; it soon dominated the grocery trade in Pathhead. A primary sewage treatment plant for Pathhead, Kirkcaldy, Dysart and Templehall was opened in 1989 beside the Harbour Maltings, replacing direct sea outfall; secondary treatment plant is now being added.

**Forbo Nairn: Linoleum Renascent**: In 1985 Unilever sold Nairn Floors to the Swiss Forbo group, owners *inter alia* of the Dutch lino industry, who built new offices for the plant and publicised lino as a *'green'* product, emphasising its jute backing and linseed oil binder. A computerised system now controls the process which soon employed 120 out of Forbo Nairn's 500 workers. One of only four such in the world, its annual output of three million $m^2$ sold worldwide; a new range was launched in 1991. About 1989 the 75-year-old Co-operative bakery closed; the premises were later converted into flats. When the Fife Coast Laundry in Cairns Street burned down in 1990 the firm moved to Cowdenbeath. In 1990 the new A92 expressway was opened through from the M90 to Redhouse north of Gallatown. The 1991 population of the area was 12,231. The site of the former Sinclairtown pottery was studied by archaeologists before vanishing under the Royal Bank of Scotland's new Central Branch for Fife; this opened in 1991 and employed nearly 100 people, becoming one of their largest operations. In 1992 the Bank of Scotland also opened a new branch at Mitchelston.

**Arson and the End of the Telephone Line**: By 1991 the former Carron factory was owned by the hydraulic equipment manufacturers G L Rexroth; it employed 115 people at Mitchelston, but to expand production it moved to much larger premises at Glenrothes. Nearby was the new Kingdom Bakery of Fife Bakers and Confectioners, opened in 1985 and employing 60 people as Fife's largest bakery. Suspiciously burnt out on New Year's Day 1992, it was again destroyed by a flagrant arson attack at Christmas 1994. From 1989 the GEC factory was known as GPT, mostly making Amstrad computer parts; a total of 1000 people were employed at the end of 1990, but the consortium sold out in 1991 to Hutchison Telecoms of Hong Kong, and Amstrad cancelled their order; the great factory was closed completely later in the year.

**Lighting up the Olympics**: In 1990–93 Strand Theatre Lighting, owned by the Rank Corporation, employed some 200 people; soon sold to its managers, in 1995 it raised its workforce at Mitchelston to 280 and expanded into Lochgelly; in 2000 it supplied the computerised control system for the 3.2 million watts of lighting for the Olympic Stadium in Sydney. Peter Greig & Co's Victoria linen works is still active, the last of many in the immediate area of Kirkcaldy. In 1993 Robert Kilgour & Co was a subsidiary of Allied Distillers of Dumbarton, producing all the malt for their 14 malt whisky and 2 grain distilleries, including for Laphroaig and for various blends. In 1996 the firm with its 40 or more workers was sold to Munton plc of Suffolk, who set out to expand production by heavy investment in new plant.

**Computers cut Linoleum with Water**: From about 1990 the Forbo Nairn Aquajet process has cut linoleum to finely detailed one-off patterns using a computer controlled water jet. The inlaid product was supplied to London's Great Ormond Street Hospital, and soon exported worldwide. In 1994 Forbo Nairn introduced a new range of lino called Marmoleum; by then the 4 m-wide glass fibre basis for *Cushionflor* came from Germany and the plant employed 480 people. Meantime in 1993–94 the south half of St Clair Street, the spine road linking Pathhead with Gallatown, was torn apart and rebuilt with four lanes, part becoming a dual carriageway. The Rejects department store was enlarged still further in 1994–95.

**Recreation – and Industrial Change**: In 1995 Kirkcaldy Ice Rink, which can seat about 3000 spectators, was reconditioned with help from the Foundation for Sport & the Arts; Fife Flyers now play ice hockey in the Northern Premier League. Also in 1995 the renovated Pathhead Hall of 1883 was reopened as the Arts & Leisure Centre of Fife College. Most of the giant complex of outmoded Nairn factories was demolished, and ground down to hardcore on site, leaving only the original building standing south-east of the railway; Forbo Nairn built a factory close by to make lino tiles and are still developing the works. Aerpac UK, subsidiary of a Dutch firm making glass-fibre blades up to 29 m long for its parent's aero-generators, moved from Glenrothes to Mitchelston in 1999. It grew rapidly and employed some 145 people in 2001 when its parent went into administration, putting its future at risk.

**Successful Incomers**: In 1994 Fife Indmar, owners of Thomson Brothers, ironmongers of Kirkcaldy which then operated in six other principal centres in Scotland, with a total staff of over 170, moved to new HQ premises at Randolph Place, claiming to be *"Scotland's largest group of ironmongers and industrial suppliers"*. In 2000 the *Fife Free Press* group moved their printing work to Camelon and sold the Mitchelston premises. In 1996 Lewis C Grant of Dysart moved much of their production to a new works at Mitchelston to develop their sheet metal and assemblies manufacture; by 2000 they had a workforce of 340, producing mainframe computer cabinets for firms including Motorola. They were then taken over by Swedish company Segerstrom & Svensson, but they shed 50 jobs in 2001. St Andrews High School have around 800 pupils and Viewforth 420. The *Dunnikier House Hotel* stands between the golf course and the park; a larger new hotel is to be built at Gallatown to replace the *Top of the Town* pub.

## PATNA

**Map 1, C2**

***S. Ayrshire village,*** *pop. 2300* — OS 70: NS 4110

Pont's map made around 1600 marked *'Preestoun'* in the Doon Valley some 15 km south-east of Ayr; there was a Milton nearby, and a road existed up the valley by the time the Roy map was made in the mid 18th century; Polnessan was the site of a ford. The name of nearby Patna was only introduced in the early 19th century, by the laird, William Fullarton of Skeldon *(see Hollybush)* who had been born in that Indian city. The river was bridged and coal must soon have been found, for a miners' row and accompanying church were built, but there was no post office in 1838. A railway with a station named Patna was opened by the Ayr & Dalmellington Railway in 1856 to serve the Houldsworths' Dalmellington Iron Company *(see Waterside)*, and slowly-growing Patna eventually got its post office later in the century. The population in 1891 was 450.

**Houldsworth and Smithton Pits**: Houldsworth colliery high above Polnessan, sunk in 1904–05 and served by a 5 km long mineral railway sloping down to Waterside, was for a time Scotland's deepest pit, at 371 metres. However, Patna's village population was still only about 500 in 1931, despite the building there of superior housing for miners; council housing was added in the mid 20th century to accept people from the cleared hamlet of Lethanhill above Waterside, where there were other mines. The population in 1951 was over 2500 and rising, with the facilities of a small village, but already including the 9-hole Doon Valley golf course. Houldsworth colliery closed about 1965, but Smithton mine (some 2 km to the north) remained in operation. The rail passenger service was withdrawn in 1964, but freight services continued. Almost 3000 people lived in Patna in 1971.

**Forests mask the Declining Valley**: Then came massive afforestation of the hillsides to the south-west of the village, radically changing the hitherto bleak landscape. By 1976 Patna had lost its small secondary school, and as employment opportunities in the mines rapidly disappeared the population speedily declined; the facilities of a small village remained available in 1981. Love's Smithton mine was apparently still open in 1987, by which time a caravan site was available on the edge of the forest at Carskeoch. By 1991 the population had slipped below 2400, and demolitions had fragmented the village centre; by 1998 the Smithton mine was disused. Afforestation continues to spread across the hills; much of the land has Forestry Commission access rights.

## PAXTON

**Map 3, C3**

***Berwickshire small village,*** *pop. 250* — OS 67 or 74: NT 9353

Located just north of the River Tweed and 6 km west of Berwick, the originally Anglian settlement of Paxton *('Sheep-town')* stands above the incised valley of the Whiteadder Water, opposite the 14th century Smithfield Castle; both places only narrowly remained in Scotland after the boundary was fixed in the 16th century. Smithfield must have become a ruin by the time, for Pont's map, made around 1600, showed no castle nearer than the 15th century keep of Edrington, itself now a slight ruin. However, a water mill turned on the Whiteadder, and a parish school was started in 1619. The Roy map of the early 1750s named the Dow Mills some way downstream, and by then a road passing the village linked Berwick with Coldstream.

**Paxton House, Union Bridge, Philanthropy and Art**: The Tweedside mansion of Paxton House which looks across the river to Northumberland was possibly designed by John and James Adam, and built in 1758 for the unhappy Patrick Home; its interiors of about 1773 were designed by Robert Adam. Heron in 1799 wrote of Paxton as a *"village by no means large or populous"*. The Union suspension bridge of 133 m span – a vast distance for its day – was designed by Captain Sir Samuel Brown and John Rennie, and built in 1819–20 to cross the Tweed south of Paxton House and complete a minor road to the English village of Horncliffe; it was the first suspension bridge in Great Britain stiff enough to take carriages *(see Hay & Stell)*. By the 1890s agricultural Paxton had a post and telegraph office and an inn. By 1951 the local population of over 350 was also served by a school, but this had closed by 1981 when only some 250 residents remained. Paxton House in its much reduced park was presented to the nation by Labour MP John Home Robertson, and opened to the public in 1993 as the first outpost of the National Galleries of Scotland. Paxton village still has a pub and post office.

## PEEBLES

**Map 3, A3**

***Tweedside town,*** *pop. 7100+* — OS 73: NT 2540

Several of the high hills around Peebles are crowned by ancient forts. It lies in an area of only limited agricultural potential, at an altitude of about 160 metres, in the angle formed by the Eddleston Water at its confluence with the upper River Tweed. Though this is the latter's nearest point to Edinburgh, Peebles was part of ancient Strathclyde, as shown by the inclusion of its church of St Mary (first recorded in about 1114) in an early list prepared in Glasgow, and by the derivation of its name from the Cumbric word for *'Tent'*, perhaps referring to early market stalls or (as Mackay suggests), shielings. After Strathclyde became part of Scotland, David I made Peebles a Royal Burgh in 1152. The town arms included three salmon; trout were also heavily fished from the upper Tweed, and Peebles was the occasional residence of kings while hunting in Ettrick Forest. The easy route to Edinburgh by the Eddleston Water gave it strategic significance to expanding Scotland, and it was made the caput of a sheriffdom known as *Tweed-dale* in a charter of 1184. By about 1193 the royal castle contained a chapel, and two years later the church of St Andrew was consecrated; there was once also a nunnery.

**Bridges, School, Castle and Troubles**: A wooden bridge was built across the Tweed, and by the 13th century there was a monastery and a hospital; Peebles appeared on the ancient Gough map, probably made in the mid 13th century. The Cross Kirk *"with cloisters for 70 Red Friars"* was built there for King Alexander III in 1261. The early Neidpath Castle, built above a crook of the river 1 km west of the town, was owned by the Frasers till 1303; its rebuilding in the 15th century as an L-plan tower was instigated by the Hays of Yester, Peebles having been burned by the English in 1403. However, by 1444 Peebles was trading with Danzig, very likely through the port of Leith. The burgh records begin in the 1450s, a school was in existence as early as 1464, and the fine – though then very narrow – stone bridge dates from 1467, the first such bridge across the Tweed. The Trinitarian (Red) friary was re-founded at the Cross Kirk in 1474. Peebles' contribution to burgh taxes remained almost negligible in 1535, and although a college was established in the parish church in 1543 the town was again burnt down by troops of the English tyrant Henry VIII in 1548; only the Cross Kirk and the parish church tower survived.

**From Reformation to Stagnation**: Following this a more defensible site was sought, hence the shift to the New Town to the east of the Eddleston Water; it was at first walled. By 1560 the burgh was again in being and represented in Parliament; the Cross church became the public school (until about 1700). Though looted by some lawless Scots in 1583, by 1593 Peebles had become the centre of a presbytery, and Pont's map made around 1600 showed bridges across the Eddleston Water, the Lyne Water north-west of the town, and the Manor Water to the south-west; two mills stood downstream of the town. In 1639 Peebles ranked only 36th of Scottish burghs in tax rents and was unlucky to be visited by the plague in 1644. However, it retained its significance as a market, and the ancient market cross survived. After the Restoration, Neidpath Castle was sold to the Earls of March (who abandoned it to ruin in the late 18th century). Defoe wrote in the 1720s that *"the town is small, and but indifferently built or inhabited, yet the High Street has some good houses in it; there is a handsome stone-bridge over the Tweed"*.

**Post and Turnpikes, Textiles and Marketing**: Roy's map made in the 1750s showed bridges spanning both the Tweed and the Eddleston Water, and six radial roads. Peebles' first post office opened in 1765, and the roads to Edinburgh and Selkirk were turnpiked under an Act of 1771. By 1776 Peebles spun worsted yarn for weaving in factories at Musselburgh, also supplying forty local weavers of coarse woollens; a local woollen factory was established in the late 1790s. Meantime the small baronial *'Castle'* Venlaw was built on a hill in 1782, and a new parish church arose in 1784. By 1797 Peebles was a post town with a daily service (by 1825 the centre for a penny post serving Innerleithen); there were seven fair days a year. Two years later Heron wrote *"Though Peebles cannot boast of much trade, yet it has some manufacture of carpets and serges, and a weekly market for corn and cattle. Its inhabitants may amount to 1500"*. In fact the industrial revolution nearly overlooked Peebles, though its cloth was sheared by water power from 1812.

**Old-fashioned Pub and Peripatetic Publisher**: In 1803, a generation before local hotel development began, Dorothy Wordsworth stayed in *"a comfortable old-fashioned public-house in Peebles, an old town, built of grey stone where well-dressed people were going to church"*. But it was not lacking in enterprise: the King's Meadows footbridge – built in 1817 – was the first cable cantilever bridge in Britain, with a span of nearly 34 metres; its replacement, Priorsford Bridge of 1905, still stands. Robert Chambers, who was born in Peebles in 1802, made a walking tour of Scotland as a young man in the 1820s, written up in a two-volume work from which many quotations in this book are drawn. With his brother William (who became Lord Provost of Edinburgh) he founded the Edinburgh publishing firm of Chambers, also becoming a glacial geologist and an early proponent of devolution. William presented the town with Chambers' Institution (1859), now a library and gallery containing a reproduction of the Parthenon frieze.

**Brewing, Boarding Schools and Railways**: Two breweries existed in the mid 1820s when, according to Chambers the town had over 2000 residents, being known for *"woollen, linen and cotton weaving; various mills; retail merchandise, a weekly market and seven annual fairs"*. It had a recently provided free school for girls, and two boys' boarding schools; though of *"celebrated excellence"* these did not last! The old town to the west of the Eddleston Water was of single storey cottages and still unpaved in 1827. A gasworks was established in 1829, and the ancient Tweed bridge was widened in 1830. In 1855 the Peebles Railway opened its line from Edinburgh, later extending to Galashiels, and later still becoming part of the North British Railway (NBR); in 1864 the Caledonian provided a connection westwards to Broughton and beyond. In 1869 Laing & Irvine of Hawick operated a woollen mill in Peebles; stocking yarns were made for Dumfries firms.

**The Peebles Hydro**: In 1881 – when the resident population was 3500 – a big luxury hotel with special baths was opened, called the *Peebles Hydropathic Establishment*. This helped to put Peebles on the map as an inland touring and fishing resort (and eventually as a conference centre). The March Street woollen mill was built in 1883 by Ballantynes from Walkerburn, and extended in 1910. The *Peeblesshire News* was established in 1887, and by 1891 the population was 4700. A municipal golf course was laid out in 1892 and the Tweed bridge was again widened in 1900.

**Fire before the Fire Service**: Peeblesshire's population reached a plateau about 1901. The great *'Hydro'* burned out in 1905, having to be completely rebuilt; yet it was 1911 before so much as a horse-drawn fire engine was provided in the town!

The Hydro had its own golf course by 1913 (now just pitch and putt), and a municipal swimming pool was constructed. Peebles Rovers FC remarkably played in the Scottish League, for just 3 years, 1923–26. But otherwise Peebles' early 20th century history was somewhat uneventful: it had grown to be a major local shopping and business centre by 1951, despite its small population, then only 6500. By 1954 *Castle Venlaw* was one of at least seven local hotels, and a touring caravan site was opened. By 1957 the High School was open. However, by 1953 there were no longer trains to Biggar, and the railway connecting Peebles with Edinburgh and Galashiels was more regrettably closed to passengers by Beeching in 1962; by 1970 all the local lines had been lifted. Peebles West station became the site of a new health centre, and hotels grew in number, but there was some decline in other urban facilities. In 1972 only 15% of houses were council-owned, the second lowest proportion among Scottish burghs.

**After Peebles-shire, it's Tweeddale**: In 1975 the erstwhile Peebles-shire was downgraded to become Tweeddale District, within the Borders Region, but Peebles remained the centre for this newly limited role. It also became the HQ for the Forestry Commission's Lothian & Tweed District; the afforestation of Glentress and adjoining hills to the east of Peebles was carried out from the 1940s to 1980s, and much is now made officially accessible for walkers and mountain bikers. A small hospital was built around 1980, and a new swimming pool was provided beside the river. By 1977 Holland & Sherry were making woollens, and by 1981 Peebles had acquired some new small industries, including Litsters' colour film processors – and 500 more people.

**Edinburgh Commuting grows as the Market shrinks**: In the 1980s Peebles' housing was in great demand by Edinburgh car commuters, and spread considerably in the King's Muir area south of the river. The town centre, where a substantial supermarket was built, was evidently prosperous in 1989; the March Street mills still made woollen cloth. By 1991 the population was steady at around 7065 – with a quite affluent retirement emphasis; however, Borders Regional Council had provided an industrial estate in Peebles, and Cameo Fine Arts were printing greetings cards. Lawrie & Symington of Lanark still held cattle and sheep auctions until 1997, but due to falling sales the firm closed their livestock mart and sold the site. Shopping was by contrast prospering, and by then Holland & Sherry's large mill claimed to make the *"finest cloths in the world"!* More substantial areas of housing were developed south of the river in the 1990s. In 2000 Powergen gained permission to build a wind farm near Peebles. The High School today has almost 1000 pupils, whilst the *Hydro* (133 rooms) remains by far the largest of the hotels and guest-houses which serve the town.

## PENCAITLAND & the Saltouns — Map 3, A2

*E. Lothian villages, pop. 1500* — OS 66: NT 4468

Saltoun Castle was built in the 12th century beside the Birns Water above its confluence with the East Lothian River Tyne, 8 km south-west of Haddington; there is an ancient church. Part of a 13th century church in Pencaitland, the adjacent parish 2 km to the west, also still survives in use, including the tower built in 1601. In 1505 Pencaitland was chartered as a burgh of barony, becoming a small market centre; in 1510 a bridge was built there across the Tyne Water. Saltoun Castle, the seat of Lord Saltoun in 1560, appeared emparked on Pont's map made around 1600. So did the 16th century Wintoun Castle, 500 m north of Pencaitland, which had been ravaged by the aggressive tyrant Henry VIII of England in the *'Rough Wooing'* and was eventually rebuilt in 1620 for George Seton, third Earl of Wintoun. Miltoun (later known as Spindleton) stood at the confluence of the Birns Water with the Tyne. A parish school for Saltoun, begun in 1589, seems soon to have closed. *'Penkethland'* where a parish school followed in 1613, was given emphasis on Pont's map. Fountainhall, 2 km south-west, was built in the 16th century as an L-plan tower house, and extended in the 17th century, with noted panelling; Pilmuir House near East Saltoun was built in 1624 for the Cairns family.

**Industrial Pioneers: Fletcher and Meikle**: In the late 17th century a school was reopened at Saltoun, whose proprietors were the Fletchers. In the early 18th century Andrew Fletcher, a native of the parish and strong opponent of the 1707 Union, brought back from Holland what were to be described by Chambers as *"models of a barley-mill, fanners for cleaning corn, and the art of weaving and bleaching Holland cloth"*. James Meikle, born locally in 1690, became a millwright, and was credited as the inventor of the winnowing machine (part of the threshing machine); but perhaps his actual role was simply to make a full-size machine on Dutch lines. The Fletchers set up a weaving mill in 1710 to make fine *'hollands'*, the first to be woven in Britain. In 1720 the Fletchers established Scotland's first pearl barley mill on the Birns Water south of West Saltoun, near its confluence with the Kinchie Burn. Chambers added, *"Strange to tell, the barley-mill was the only one in Britain for forty years, and the fanners for nearly the same period"*. James Meikle's son Andrew, born in 1719, designed the threshing drum about 1786, and the Fletchers also established a factory to make moveable threshing machines, which were to be used for nearly two centuries before being absorbed into workings of the combine harvester.

**The British Linen Company's Bleachfield**: With textiles well established locally, the British Linen Company laid out a huge bleachfield in 1747–48 on the west bank of the Birns Water north of West Saltoun. This became a training ground for bleachers, and processed 263,000 linear metres of cloth in 1761, having more than doubled its throughput in a decade; half a tonne of local coal was used each day, probably from the Fletchers' Huntlaw pit 1 km south of Wester Pencaitland. Roy's map of the 1750s showed a substantial and complex village at Pencaitland, with roads east, south and south-east past Spindleton Mill to East Saltoun, which was already a substantial village with its present day road pattern clearly established. The bleachfield was also emphasised by Roy, but as the centre of gravity of the textile industry shifted west and north it was sold in 1772 – according to one source, for conversion to a pleasure ground.

**Paper, Distilling and Mining**: A paper mill was first recorded at Saltoun in 1773; it seems that the bleachfield property was divided and part of the buildings put to that use, for Heron noted in 1799 that *"there are here a starch-work, a paper-mill, and a bleachfield"*. He added that in the *"villages"* of Pencaitland, Winton and Nisbet (2 km east of Pencaitland) there were over 500 people, and in those of East and West Saltoun over 400. Early in the 19th century the paper mill was owned by the Cadells of Penicuik, and by 1825 West Saltoun was served by a penny post from Haddington. Chambers, writing in 1827, noted that Saltoun was *"a little village"*. He implied that the weaving mill and threshing machine factory had closed. About 1837 the Glenkinchie lowland malt distillery was founded on the Kinchie Water 2 km west of West Saltoun and not far from the Huntlaw coal pit; in 1852 another pit, the Woodhall colliery, was sunk west of Pencaitland. In 1886 when visited by Barnard (who found Pencaitland *"a pretty little village")*, the distillery used local barley to produce 350,000 litres of Lowland malt whisky annually; the spent wash was used for field irrigation. The distillery was rebuilt from 1890 under James Gray, who took the lead in founding Scottish Malt Distillers Ltd in 1914.

**The Light Railway**: In 1901 a light railway was opened by the North British Railway from Ormiston to Gifford *(q.v.)*. A station was provided at Pencaitland, which was then a double hamlet with a post and telegraph office and a smithy. West Saltoun also had a station and post office, while East Saltoun had an inn. The railway served the distillery through a siding at Lempock Wells and encouraged the enlargement of Woodhall colliery, which lasted until 1944; but meantime the passenger service had been withdrawn in 1933. Limeworks were opened by the Scottish Co-operative Wholesale Society near East Saltoun in 1943, but these were disused by 1973. By 1951 Pencaitland had grown into a village of nearly 1200 people; its *Old Smiddy Inn* was open by 1963. The freight railway ended in the 1960s.

**Dormitory Development**: Two sawmills worked near East Saltoun in 1973, about which time the Baird maltings were built at Pencaitland; only small-village facilities were available, but the ancient Barley Mill survived on the Humbie Water. A nature trail and picnic area was provided by 1986. In 1991, the population of Pencaitland was 1287. Glenkinchie whisky was sold as a ten-year-old single malt; a museum and visitor centre have been created in an old malt barn. By 1996 several small new housing estates had begun to transform Pencaitland into a dormitory, still having its post office, garage, shop, inn and pub; rural traffic lights are required at the narrow bridge! Both Pencaitland and rural East Saltoun still have primary schools. Malt products, the distillery, and timber operations make local employment. The route of the former railway is now a cycleway to the distillery and beyond.

## PENICUIK & Howgate

**Map 15, C3**

***Midlothian town,*** *pop. 15,000*

OS 66: NT 2359

Ancient forts and settlements in the Pentland Hills and the Cumbric name Penicuik (which probably means *Cuckoo Hill)* reveal very early origins; the remains of the 12th century church of St Kentigern stand high above the deeply incised River North Esk, 14km south of Edinburgh. Ravensneuk Castle 1.5km upstream of Penicuik, and the tower of Brunston Castle 3km to the west, were both built in the 16th century and shown on Pont's map of about 1600. By then roads linked Edinburgh to Peebles via Howgate, and to West Linton following the foothills of the Pentlands. *'Pennycook'* is known to have possessed corn and waulk mills, but did not become a pre-reform burgh. Valleyfield paper mill was built on the river in 1708–09 by Agnes Campbell the King's Printer; the Low Mill was converted from a waulk mill to papermaking in 1746. By that time the area's main roads had been made up under the 1713 Turnpike Act. The *Howgate Inn*, 2 km to the south-east, was built about 1743. The Roy map made about 1754 showed *'Pinnikuick'* as a substantial village with roads to Roslin, to Howgate and two northwards.

**The Short-lived Cotton industry**: In 1761 Penicuik House, which had been built for Sir James Clerk across the valley from Ravensneuk, had become the centre of a large park; in the same century the nearby Woodhouselee Castle was forsaken for a new mansionhouse; this was extended in 1843 for James Tytler. A second industry was introduced when in 1779 Scotland's first or second cotton mill was opened below the remaining waulk mill. The large Esk cotton mill 1 km downstream of the village began operations about 1790. Heron noted in 1799 that besides two paper mills *"the village of Penicuik has a great cotton-work where about 500 hands are employed"*; the entire population was about a thousand. A post office which opened at Howgate in 1788 was still the post town for Penicuik until its own post office opened in 1802. Three POW camps were set up around Penicuik from 1803; after 1810 they held in all some 11,000 Frenchmen and their allies. In 1803 Alex Cowan, a Leith merchant, converted the corn mill by the bridge on the Peebles road to make banknote paper; hence its name, the Bank Mill. By 1805 the Esk cotton mill had also apparently been converted to a paper mill; by 1813 a post office was open in Penicuik itself, and Haughhead brewery was quite large by 1814, run by John White, who also made cotton and paper; but it soon closed.

**Coal, Cowan contributions, Cricket and Trains**: Coal mining was recorded by 1815. In that year Cowan acquired the Low paper mill from Nimmo of Edinburgh, and in 1823 the firm provided a school for their workers' children; by the 1860s it had 120 pupils. The enlightened Cowans employed Edinburgh architect F T Pilkington to design housing for single women employees, and also the South Church of 1862–63; they also donated an Institute to the town. A cricket club was founded in 1844 by an English paper mill manager, Charles Green – and is still active! By 1851 the Valleyfield paper mill was the largest in Scotland, having 500 workers by 1866. The Peebles Railway which opened in 1855 provided a station named Pomathorn on the hillside 1 km south-east of Penicuik.

*Houses built by Cowan's, the paper-mill owners, for their single female employees in 1860. The buildings were designed by the Edinburgh architect F T Pilkington.* *(JRH)*

This enabled the Esk mills to use esparto grass, imported through Granton, as its main raw material.

**Esparto Pollution and More Railways**: The resulting pollution caused litigation in 1866, forcing the early removal of this operation to new mills at Inveresk, while filters and settling ponds had to be installed at Penicuik – partly because chloride of lime was still used to bleach rags, then the raw material for finer papers. In 1869 Cowan & Sons ran three Penicuik area paper mills as one, 600 workers making about 2500 tonnes of their fine papers a year on five machines driven by waterwheels and steam engines. The valley floor Penicuik Railway (PR) which left the NBR at Rosewell was opened in 1872, providing a station at the Esk mills and a more central terminus beside the Valleyfield mills. New gasworks were set up in 1877, and the Edinburgh Loanhead & Roslin Railway was extended through Glencorse to serve a new coal mine east of Mauricewood (not named on the 1895 one-inch OS map), making three sub-parallel lines.

**The Burgh of Penicuik**: Eventually Penicuik became a police burgh. The Episcopal church was built in 1882 and a blocky tower added in 1899. The extended Penicuik House was gutted by fire in 1890; today it still stands in ruins. The Low and Bank mills were cleared of machinery in 1889, but Valleyfield Mill acquired a papermaking machine of the great width of 2.33 metres, and soon employed about 750 people. The population in 1891 was 3600. In 1894 Cowan's paper mill was reputedly the largest in Scotland, and the *Royal Hotel* was open in what Murray called this *"pleasantly situated little town"*, still a compact place; but tiny Howgate had lost its post office.

**Industrial Dormitory**: The Esk Mills were still expanding in 1931. By 1951 Penicuik had a population of 6500, but had only the facilities of a large village, and lost its passenger trains that year. Much Edinburgh-related dormitory development subsequently occurred, all to the north of the original centre, mainly in the Cuiken area. Penicuik Junior Secondary School graduated into Penicuik High, but Woodhouselee Castle was regrettably demolished in 1965, the peak year for mansion vandalism. The erstwhile PR line was closed to freight in 1967, and its station incorporated in the Valleyfield paper mill; but the mill stopped in 1975, when the Spicer Cowan operation was transferred to Livingston, and the station site was later cleared. But the huge Cornbank area was developed with housing in the 1963–73 period, and by 1981 Penicuik had small-town facilities, which continued to grow in the 1980s with the building of the large Beeslack High School.

**Edinburgh Crystal Rolled though a Cloudy Patch**: The long-established Edinburgh Crystal (EC) glass company, which had moved out of the city and was known as the *"Rolls-Royce of the crystal trade"*, had works on the Eastfield industrial estate in Penicuik by 1977. In 1988 the greedy and predatory Coloroll group took over, pushed the product downmarket, cut employment from 300 to 200, including many key workers, and moved essential functions to Stourbridge. Luckily for the survival of EC, Coloroll's bankruptcy in 1990 enabled Caledonia Investments to take over and reverse the decline; by 1994 EC's sales outlet served over 100,000 visitors a year, a third of whom inspected the factory too. In 1994 the nearby firm of Fraser Creations produced tiny but exquisitely detailed ceramic models of traditional Scottish buildings. The heavily advertised Penicuik Conservatories were also made adjacent to the EC works from around 1990.

**Baking Pans and Computing**: By 1989 the NERC's Institute of Terrestrial Ecology had a base in Penicuik. *'Pullman Pans'*, founded in 1942, weathered a crisis in 1990, and in 1992 its 50 or so workers made baking pans. By 1991 United Distillers' computing facilities were concentrated at Penicuik, whose population in that year *(including the Glencorse area, q.v.)* was about 17,000, with a young well-educated dormitory character, including high proportions in government service and banking. Today both Penicuik High and Beeslack High have over 900 pupils. The historic *Howgate Inn* to the west closed as a restaurant about 1990.

## PENNAN — Map 10, C1

***Buchan coastal village,*** *pop. 125* — OS 30: NJ 8465

Pennan Bay forms a slight recess in the cliff-bound north coast of Buchan, 15km west of Fraserburgh. It is adjoined to the west by the precipitous valley known as the Tore of Troup. On the adjacent headland – with its cliff features of Hell's Lum and the Lion's Head – is an ancient fort. Both Pennan and Auchmedden existed in some form when Robert Gordon mapped the area about 1640. The Roy map made about 1750 showed a roadless area and little settlement; this is confirmed by the Old Statistical Account. Pennan was laid out in 1798 as a fishing village, built of red sandstone and accessed by a steep lane down from the coast road. By 1894 it was served by Auchmedden school, an inn, post and telegraph office, a mill and coastguard station; piers were later built to form a small enclosed harbour. By 1951 there was a falling population of under 250, though remarkably there was a clothier. By 1955 the coastguard station had gone, and the primary school was closed, probably during the 1960s; however by 1980 the *Pennan Inn* again offered accommodation. The cult film *Local Hero* was shot on location in tiny but characterful Pennan in the 1980s. It was soon noted that professional people had moved in, but locals in small boats still used hand lines for white fish and also trapped lobsters and crabs. The inn is still open.

## PENNYGHAEL & Carsaig — Map 4, B2

***Communities, S-W. Mull,*** *pop. 200 (area)* — OS 48: NM 5126

In the year 1500, sandstone for dressing Iona Abbey was quarried from the 200m-tall cliffs of the Sron nam Boc on the south coast of the Ross of Mull, and shipped from a tiny natural harbour called Carsaig. There was a pier and a herring station there in the 19th century. The Pennyghael estate lies on the thinly settled south shore of Loch Scridain. Pennyghael House was built in 1819 for the new laird John MacGillivray, and was extended about 1920. About 3km to the east was an inn, later the *Kinloch Hotel*. In 1951 tiny Pennyghael was a post town and had a school, serving a declining population of some 200, scattered between Tiroran and Carsaig, the area being agricultural. Pennyghael House was disused from 1957 to 1971, then being reoccupied. By 1985 the post office and shop formerly near the big house had moved into part of the *Kinloch Hotel* building; there were several modern bungalows, a pub, petrol station, sawmill and oyster farm. About then Pennyghael House again fell empty, and was in a sad state by 1997. The *Pennyghael Hotel* offers 6 rooms and holiday cottages.

## PENPONT

**Map 2, B3**

***Small Dumfriesshire village,*** *pop. 625 (area)* OS 78: NX 8494

About 25 km above Dumfries is an ancient earthwork between the River Nith and its tributary the Scar Water. Nearby is Penpont, whose church stands literally at the *'Head of the Bridge'*, a literal translation of the name if it is seen as Brythonic in origin. A rival theory claims it is named after the *'Penny Pont'*, a wooden toll bridge which crossed the Scar by about 1400. Some 5 km to the south-east stands the 16th century L-plan tower of Barjarg, beside which Boatcroft ferry crossed the River Nith. By about 1610 when the area was mapped by Timothy Pont, himself presumably descended from a bridgebuilder, the bridge had vanished in a flood; on the bank of the Nith was *'Waterfyrd'* and 2 km farther south *'Keyr Myll'*. In the 1750s Roy noted only three tracks converging on the Kirk of Penpont; to Chambers in 1827 it was *"a much smaller village than Thornhill, and only remarkable as the seat of a presbytery"*. Eventually the bridge was replaced and roads were made up around the area.

**Blacksmith's Bicycle and Limestone Mine**: In 1813 Kirkpatrick Macmillan was born in the area; in 1839 when working as a blacksmith at Keir Mill he invented a rod-driven pedal bicycle, which he rode for years – potentially one of the world's most valuable ideas, but not commercially exploited at the time. Joseph Thomson, born at Penpont in 1856, became a geologist and explorer of central Africa. An extensive limestone mine at Barjarg, drained by a waterwheel-driven pump (now in the Museum of Scotland in Edinburgh) was open in the second half of the 19th century. By 1951 when 1000 people lived in the area, both Penpont and Keir Mill had post offices and primary schools; Penpont also had an inn, and by 1980 a garage. But the population fell to about 800 by 1971 and Keir lost its facilities. By 1985 Penpont had gained a caravan site, and keeps its pub and post office, but development hereabouts is slow.

## PERTH

**Map 6, B3**

***Large town on R. Tay,*** *pop. 40,000* OS 53 or 58: NO 1123

Suburbs: *Letham & New Scone*

Modern Perth lies 3 km downstream of the one-time Roman fort of *Bertha*, but on the same (west) bank of the broad and swift River Tay. The name Bertha/Perth meant *'wood'* in Cumbric and apparently also in Pictish Gaelic. Sea-going boats could at one time reach Bertha and Old Scone, the historic centre of Pictland, but silting steadily moved the head of tidewater downstream. East of the river is wooded Moncrieffe Hill, on which a Pictish fort once stood. This overlooked the level and flood-prone site on which modern Perth grew, first being mentioned as a trading community about 1120.

**St John's Town as a Burgh**: About 1125 David I decided that a tidewater site was needed for a new Royal Burgh and sheriff caput to serve the Tay basin, choosing Perth, whose earliest charter may have been lost. The first part of the town to develop was Watergate, where boats could tie up at the foot of the line of the later High Street. Opposite this lay the fords and the site for the medieval bridge, Scotland's second earliest known post-Roman bridge. For over 600 years (except for a century when the bridge was down) Perth was the lowest bridgepoint on the Tay. The church of St John the Baptist was founded west of Watergate in 1126, and until well after the Reformation Perth was normally called *Saint John's Toun*. In 1128 the church was granted to Dunfermline Abbey. Although the town adopted a fairly rectilinear layout it was not rigidly planned, but developed in stages *(as demonstrated in Lynch et al)*; it was originally built of timber and wattle. Perth became the caput of a sheriffdom around 1150 and was certainly a Royal Burgh by 1153.

**Crafts and Castle**: Perth soon attracted craftsmen: cattle hides were tanned, shoes were made, and cattle, goat and deer bones and horns were skilfully worked into combs and other necessities. By 1153 Perth was rich enough in customs duties to subsidise three abbeys; those of Coupar Angus and Arbroath later acquired properties in the town. By about 1160 the new castle on its earthen motte north of the High Street was connected to Kirkgate by Skinnergate, crossing the parallel mill lade (*see Letham*) and Mill Street, where grain was dried before being ground for local bakeries. Barrels were made, smithies were soon at work and copper alloys were cast into jewellery; pottery was also made near the town. Development on South Street was begun in 1178, and by 1214 was well established. By 1189 a merchant guild was active.

**A Good Town expands its Role**: By 1207 Perth contained shipowners, and dyers of woollen cloth woven on vertical looms were important; Perth was then a regular exporter of wool. Some flax was made into linen, but only a third of the stuffs were dyed, and even this low proportion was not maintained, for apparently Perth's dyers then disappeared from the record for four centuries. The great flood of 1209 swept away or severely damaged both the first bridge and the castle motte, which was abandoned; of the second Tay bridge we know little or nothing. But castle or no, by 1228 the sheriffdom from Scone had been merged under Perth, whose trade and burghal privileges ensured the decline of Scone. In the 12th or 13th century a *'hospital'* was established, and a Dominican friary was founded in Kinnoul Street in 1231 by Alexander II. In the 13th century there was also an Augustinian nunnery, and at some time a Carmelite friary at Tullylumb just west of the burgh. Perth was soon second only to Edinburgh as the place where royal charters were signed. In 1291 there were 70 burgesses and a population of perhaps 500. Perth was called "*a metely good town*" by an English traveller who accompanied Edward I in his perambulation in 1295.

**Defences Stormed and Destroyed**: By 1306 Perth was held on behalf of the English and according to Barbour *"walled all about, with many high embattled towers to defend it against assault"*. If not by then, certainly by 1312 the walls were all of stone and surrounded by a deep moat. A second lade or ditch leaving the first about 600 m west of the Tay formed a moat outside the walls on the west and south sides of the town, giving rise to Canal Street. But its shallowest point could be waded by night, and the brave and cunning Bruce soon seized Perth. Barbour added *"He left no stone tower or wall standing about that town, but wholly destroyed them all"*. After the wars, a third bridge was built by John Mylne about 1326 (which lasted into the mid 16th century). By 1348 Perth was among the four *'great towns'* of Scotland, as recognised from Bruges; by then expert woodworking was among its crafts. In the 14th to 16th centuries Perth generally ranked around fourth among Scottish towns in terms of burgh taxes, and fifth in Customs dues. By then it had taken over most of Scone's importance;

but Perth never quite attained to Scone's role of capital, that being already challenged by Edinburgh.

**After the Black Death: Recovery from Reduced Circumstances**: After the inhabitants were decimated by the Black Death in the 1350s, the extent of the burgh was ample to contain its reduced population; by the 1370s there were still only some 370 properties or *'burgage plots'* within the renewed defences. Customs records show that after Perth's bumper wool export years in 1372–76 the port entered a long decline. However in 1382, although its small ships did not apparently venture far, a Perth merchant visited Prussia on royal business, and the Tay was still navigable by ships carrying 40 tonnes of wine. About 1390 Perth was chosen to stage the pitched battle between the rival Mackay and Macpherson clans. By 1415 the town was again strongly walled, with a 5 m-deep ditch. In 1429 a Carthusian priory was founded in New Row, outside the canal; farther east the Franciscans did likewise in 1460. By 1428 Perth merchants were buying flax in Danzig, but in 1427–31 Perth was down to sixth place in terms of customs receipts, largely from wool, and the town's cloth exports were then minimal – but the City Mills were at work.

**Capital Hopes Dashed**: Perth had great potential as a communications focus, and had an early Royal residence. But in 1437 King James I was assassinated by Sir Robert Graham in Perth's Blackfriars (Dominican) convent. Succeeding monarchs never returned to Perth as their home. The official recognition of Edinburgh as capital in 1452 meant that the Scottish Parliament also ceased to meet in Perth – though from 1458 the town was one of the three centres for the Supreme Court of Scotland, and the Bishops of Dunkeld lived in Perth.

**Consolidation on Trade, Crafts and Lairds' Houses**: The guild records begin in 1452, informing us that that Burghers were required to give one day's work per year to maintain the mill lade. By that time skins and hides were being acquired from Aberdeen, and furriers worked in Perth amongst over a hundred other craftsmen. But by then Perth was only half as important as Dundee in both customs and tax terms. De Ayala in 1498 called Perth *"a very considerable town and well armed"*; its main craft was metalworking, and there were as many merchants as craftsmen. In 1520 the Grays of Pitfauns, Earls of Gowrie, built a great mansion (Gowrie House) in Tay Street; Pitheavlis Castle, a 16th century tower, was built 1 km west of the town by the Oliphants, its owners for over 300 years. From 1536 a ferry plied across the Tay at Kincarrathie just north of the town. Perth's 9 craft guilds were represented on the town council. The total number of guild members was little over fifty, but they were in constant argument with each other and with the merchants.

**At the Reformation: Illiterate, Poor and Sick**: In the troubled period 1535–56 Perth paid between 3% and 10% of burgh tax revenue; by 1550 it still ranked fourth among Scottish burghs, with a population of some 3000, and had a seat in Parliament. The Friary was sacked in 1559, and by 1560 silting in the river was so severe that Perth no longer regarded itself as a port, but as a craft centre, proved by its thriving hammermen – goldsmiths and other metal workers – and also craftsmen in leather goods, sold in Edinburgh. But in 1561 only 31 out of 259 Perth burgesses could so much as sign their name, and by 1579 the burgh's tax assessment had been cut. Plague attacked again in 1584–85 when 1427 Perth people died, though enough survived for the Grammar School to contain 300 pupils afterwards.

**A Prosperous Interlude and a New Bridge**: By 1593 Perth had become the centre of a presbytery, but to meet Protestant needs St John's Church was divided into three; three suburbs of Perth were accepted into the kirk session. Although there were three-storeyed buildings of stone and timber framing, Perth was still a farming centre, with an influx of migrant workers at harvest time. In the 1590s arguments raged about the proper location of the fishmarket, a smelly neighbour! From 1595 Perth lay on Scotland's first postal route, linking Edinburgh and Aberdeen. Pont's sketch map suggests that the recently built bridge had four spans, and stood a little north of the High Street.

**Plagues, Decay, Floods – and the Bridge falls again!**: Flemish workers brought over about the year 1600 to improve local textiles soon gave up, for some 200 people succumbed when plague came yet again in 1608–09. Taylor wrote in 1618 *"a fine town it is, but much decayed"* – though there was still a good inn. Craigie, south-west of the town, was the birthplace in 1600 of Sir Robert Murray, who moved south and became the first President of the Royal Society of London. In 1621 Perth suffered from floods – during which the new bridge partly collapsed – although it had been patched up by 1636. Silversmithing of high quality was being carried on by 1630, but by 1639 Perth had slipped to eighth place among Scottish burghs in terms of tax rents. In 1644–49 the town again suffered severely from bubonic plague, and about then the bridge was finally swept away and replaced by a ferry to the suburb of Bridgend. In 1652 Cromwell's forces demolished the medieval Grammar School building, at the north east corner of the riverside meadow known as South Inch, in 1654–55 erecting in its place a citadel, one of five built to subdue Scotland.

**Cricket, Inns, Posts and Paving**: Though little of the citadel survived the Restoration, the school did recover. The corresponding North Inch was reputedly the site of Scotland's first cricket match. The *Old Ship Inn* was established in 1665, a time of rising prosperity, for the linen industry had taken hold and in 1670 Perth paid as much as 4% of struggling Scotland's diminished customs dues. Bridgend obtained a charter for a *'free port'* in 1688, and Perth's first proper post office was opened in 1689. Thomas Morer wrote *"the second city in Scotland is Perth, or St John's town; the two long spacious streets being well paved, are at all times tolerably clean; the trade of the town depends chiefly on linen"*. This was already renowned for its fine quality, and Perth also specialised in glovemaking. It was then among the larger and richer towns, with nearly 1700 pollable males, of whom well over a thousand were in manufacturing, a very high proportion for the time. However, metalworking had almost vanished as a local craft and the town council was complaining that no fewer than 24 other market centres had been permitted to develop around it, to the detriment of its trade. Brewing was on a commercial scale by the time the famous *Salutation Inn* was established in 1699 in a converted town house.

**Linen, Ships and Yarn**: In 1706 when the ferry was still essential, Bridgend (also known as Kinnoull) obtained a barony charter. In 1712 Perth itself contained just 404 households, but the Highland troubles of 1715 had actually boosted trade due to Gowrie House being used to quarter the armies; it became a permanent barracks. Subsequent changes in the laws affecting calicos benefited linen manufacture, enabling the erection of a

Guildhall in 1722, plus a new Tolbooth and much investment in housing. Defoe noted that in the 1720s *"the chief business of this town is the linen manufacture which is considerable here, all the neighbouring country being employed in it. The Tay is navigable up to the town for ships of good burthen; and they ship off here so great a quantity of linen (all for England) that all the rest of Scotland is said not to ship off so much more"*. A bleachfield was set up in 1735, and by the early 1740s Perth – which already had a large yarn market of low quality – was made a yarn sorting centre.

**Poor Roads and No Bridge**: Alex Clunie established the South Inch brewery in 1741. Then came another setback, the 1745 rebellion. William Roy's great military sketch map made about 1750 showed the existence of what passed as good roads from Perth south over the Bridge of Earn, and north up the west bank of the Tay, though there was no bridge over the Almond on the latter road until the early 1760s. Westwards to Crieff there was only a track, and there was still no replacement Tay bridge, nor a road to Scone. *'Bridge End'* which stood on the east bank was the focus of a fan of tracks leading to Dundee, and to Coupar Angus and Blairgowrie; only that to Coupar Angus was indicated as a coach road on Roy's map. By 1751 there was a millwright, and – to the chagrin of the town council – another brewery was built outwith the wall to the west of the square medieval burgh. The population had then reached about 9000, and a further linen bleachfield was built; by the 1760s Perth had a main linen stamping office and a beetling mill, and there was a British Linen Company manufacturer, Sanderson.

**Perth Banking leads the Way**: No fewer than six local banking services began in 1763 when the town gates and Mercat Cross, deemed obstructions to traffic, were all swept away. Alexander Carlyle noted in 1765 that the linen trade was *"in a very flourishing state in the shire and town of Perth"*; the weekly market was prosperous, and *Hickson's* was *"reckoned a very good inn"* but he found *"the houses not handsome nor the streets clean"*. There was still no Tay bridge in August 1765, but the river was so low that Carlyle forded it on horseback. Around then, two coaches a week began to run between Perth and North Queensferry. All the local banks amalgamated in 1766 into the Perth United Banking Company, which had branches in Crieff, Dunkeld and Auchtermuchty. It was relaunched in 1787 as the Perth Banking Company (PBC), which was important enough to issue notes. Meantime the General Bank of Perth, founded in 1767, retired in 1772.

**Schooling, New Bridge, Wagons and Salmon**: Perth Academy, founded in 1761, was said to be the first of its kind in Scotland, offering a wider education than the old Grammar School, which was rebuilt in 1773. Meantime Thomas Pennant noted some wooden houses still existing in 1769, when Perth exported linen, salmon, wheat, barley and Tay pearls. By 1769 a temporary bridge had been erected while Smeaton's new bridge was under construction; this was described later by Heron as *"an elegant stone bridge of nine arches"*. It was opened to road traffic in 1771, and the Kincarrathie ferry gave up. A local bookseller developed into a printer from 1770, and Morrisons were publishers by 1796. From 1780 a regular wagon service was in operation between Aberdeen and Glasgow; such services were aided when the Post Road to Dundee was built in the 1790s. About then Cornhill House was built west of the town. With nine fair days per year, Perth was among the ten most frequent fair stances in Scotland in 1797. Two years later Heron estimated the population of this *"very flourishing town as about twenty thousand. The salmon-fishings in the Tay form a great object of commerce"*.

**Grain, Drinks, Flax, Cotton and other Industries**: The burgh mills for malt, corn and flour were enlarged about 1787 and an oatmeal mill was erected in the early 1800s. In 1790 George Sandeman of Perth founded the drinks dealership Sandemans of Oporto. Matthew Gloag & Son began in business as wine shippers, hence Bordeaux House as the name of their headquarters; they entered the spirit trade in 1800. J & T Currie became whisky merchants in 1824. By 1794 Ramsay's Craigie brewery was substantial and by 1825 five breweries were at work in Perth (two of which lasted into the 20th century). By 1790 nearly 80 tonnes of flax was imported annually; though apparently spun into yarn elsewhere, over 1500 looms in the town and its suburbs made linen and cotton goods of many kinds, and Irish cloth was being bleached. Other industries then included the making of linseed oil, boots and shoes. In 1796 linen was still the staple manufacture, but two cotton mills were built in the 1790s, the making of cotton stockings began, and cotton soon ousted linen (*see Warden*).

**Foundry, Academy and Prison, Press and Post Office**: A foundry erected in 1802 was extended in 1820, later casting such items as manhole covers, and a town gasworks was established in 1811. In 1807 new buildings were again provided for Perth Academy, which absorbed the Grammar School; the latter's old building became a theatre. (However the name was eventually revived, and Perth Grammar School still exists.) The Gowrie barracks which fronted Tay Street were pulled down in 1806–07 so as *"to afford room for a splendid suite of county buildings"* (Chambers). Though work began at once, it was interrupted during the Napoleonic wars – when the Prison was built of stone from Invergowrie, initially to hold POWs. The Sheriff Court was completed in 1816, but the County Buildings were not finished until 1820. By this time there was a daily coach to Glasgow. By 1812 the *Perthshire Courier* newspaper was in existence (it was still published in 1865). Meantime 1829 saw the first issue of the weekly *Perthshire Advertiser*; its rival the *Perthshire Constitutional and Journal* dated from 1835.

**Banks, Pullar of Perth and Public Buildings**: A new Perth Union Banking Company was established in 1810; by 1825 this had branches in Alloa, Coupar Angus and Dunkeld, but in 1836 it merged with the National Bank. Meantime in 1821 John Pullar built a dyeworks above its water supply, the Town Lade. In 1848 Pullars branched out as silk dyers, building large works in Mill Street. The classical rotunda originally known as the Marshall Monument in George Street was erected in 1822–23 in memory of Lord Provost Thomas Hay Marshall, after whom Marshall Place was also named. The makeshift theatre burned down in 1823, but its replacement, the *Theatre Royal* of the later 1820s lasted little more than twenty years. The Perth Banking Co remained independent until 1848 when, although it was in good order and had 11 branches, it was absorbed by the Glasgow-based Union Bank. Finally the joint-stock Central Bank of Scotland, founded in St John Street in 1834, had seven branches when bought by the Bank of Scotland in 1868.

**At the Peak of Perthshire Population**: Chambers wrote in 1827 of Perth as *"An ancient royal burgh, a thriving manufacturing town, a sea-port, the metropolis of a large portion of*

*Perth Waterworks 'Round House', built in 1832 and housing a steam pumping engine; it took its supply from the river near by, and stored it in the cast-iron tank which forms the upper part of the building. It is now the J D Fergusson art gallery.* *(JRH)*

*the kingdom, noted for the excellence of its schools"*; there was an antiquarian society, hospitals and *"several good inns"*. The *Salutation* was the best of these in 1831, when the town was served by 38 coaches a day and, as that year's census showed, the county's population peaked. The Perth Waterworks *'Round House'* was built in 1832 as a steam pumping house and water tower; the supply came from the river. The County & City Infirmary in York Place was designed by W M Mackenzie; it stood on land owned by the Glover Incorporation of Perth and was opened in 1836. By then agricultural shows were being held.

**Harbour and Shipbuilding improved by Dredging**: In the 1790s more than one ship entered Perth harbour on an average day; these were however very small (due to the shifting sandbanks in the estuary), as were the vessels of some 60–70 tons that were built in local yards. The largest vessel that could be handled was of some 144 tons burthen, and although Perth was made a port of registry with the code letters PEH, Newburgh was used as an outport. Dredging soon improved access so that in 1821 Brown's boatyard could build both the 257-ton wooden paddle steamer *Tourist* for the Leith and Aberdeen service, and also the double hull for the first Tay steam ferry, *Union*. A Harbour Commission was set up in 1830, which began to build a short quay and approach road (though this took ten years to complete). In 1836 Macfarlane's yard built Tayside's first iron-hulled vessel, and by 1848 further dredging had enabled Perth shipowners to purchase three vessels of over 400 tons. The immediate outcome was closure of the Perth–Dundee lighter service.

**Famous Sons, Prison and Golf**: David Octavius Hill, born in Perth in 1802, was a renowned artist who also became one of Scotland's earliest photographers; James Croll, born in 1821, became a pioneer climatologist. Sir Henry Littlejohn, born locally in 1828, was Edinburgh's first Medical Officer of Health and a pioneer in slum clearance and forensic medicine. Three flax spinning mills were founded in the 1830s, and in 1844 there were 108 stocking frames in use in the town. Silver-smithing peaked locally about 1836. Perthshire's population was entering a slow decline as farm machinery improved and the repeal of the Corn Laws was felt, but a farina mill was in operation by about 1850. In 1841 the old military prison was converted for use as a civilian jail. The Perth Royal Golf Club was founded in 1842, and laid out a regular 18-hole course on the municipally-owned North Inch, long the site of informal golfing. By 1845 the *George Hotel* (now the *Royal George*) overlooked the Tay and the *Star Hotel* was also open by 1848.

**Railways revolutionise Perth**: From 1845 the 1080m-long Moncrieff tunnel of the locally promoted Scottish Central Railway (SCR) was painfully drilled beneath Craigend *(Marshall has a detailed if confusing account)*. There was already a bone mill at Friarton on Sir Thomas Moncrieff's estate, and Buick's ropeworks stood near the prison; indeed for a time the much loved South Inch, already partly used as a cattle market, seemed likely to vanish under railways. The overall route via Stirling was surveyed by the Mitchell brothers of Inverness (whose assessment of traffic potential is fascinating); at times up to 4250 men and 380 horses were engaged in its construction, and Patrick Wallace of Perth built some of its carriages. The SCR opened in August 1848, with a London connection. The General Station – approved in 1846 – was sited on the wide natural river terrace just above the south-west corner of the still compact town. Its fine building, soon shared by all the local companies, was designed by Sir William Tite. The SCR also built a locomotive works; this also served neighbouring systems, and engines were built there from 1856 to 1866.

**Railways to East Coast Destinations**: The Scottish Midland Junction Railway (SMJR), a direct extension of the SCR through Strathmore, was opened late in 1848 to Forfar, there making connections to Dundee, Montrose and later Aberdeen. By then the original main line of the Edinburgh & Northern Railway was also open, diverging at Hilton Junction (at the south end of Moncrieff tunnel) to Abernethy, Ladybank and Burntisland. The almost level Dundee & Perth Railway (D&PR) had opened in 1847 from Dundee to a temporary terminus on the east bank of the Tay; in 1849 the line was raised to cross both branches of the river, Moncrieffe Island and Tay Street by a shaky timber bridge with a swing span for shipping, to end at Princes Street station. The costly high-level line then crossed over six or seven streets to the General station.

**Perth anglicised by Rail**: In 1858 the King James VI golf club, whose low-lying 18-hole course was uniquely placed on Moncrieff Island, used the new railway bridge to provide pedestrian access. In 1862–64 this bridge was replaced by a 400m-long stone and iron plate-girder structure of 22 spans, then the most easterly bridge across the Tay and one of the first large plate-girder bridges in Scotland. The harbour branch was opened from Friarton in 1852, but the railways bankrupted the port in 1854, and it reverted to the town council. Sunday working on the SCR was originally barred on a 3:2 vote of shareholders, but the company's consulting engineers Locke and Errington were English (due to the lack of rail experience in Scotland) as were the SCR senior staff, strengthening the English influence on Perth. In 1858 the German traveller Fontane stayed in *Poples English Hotel*; already Saturday trains from England were arriving in Perth on Sunday, ignoring the SCR's original policy and breaking Sabbatarian traditions. An Episcopal cathedral was erected in 1849–50, the first built in Britain since London's St Paul's.

**Highland Railway, Station Hotel, and Cartage**: In 1856 Perth was linked by rail with Dunkeld. In 1863 the Inverness & Perth Junction (later Highland) Railway opened from Dunkeld to Aviemore and Forres, so serving Inverness, to which two road coaches a week had previously plied. Perth thus became a key junction, where in 1865 the erection of the large *Station Hotel* actually justified its own Act of Parliament; David Smart of Perth designed it. Wordie & Co had a rail to road cartage depot, later making Perth a district HQ. By the 1880s they were also taking whisky by horse and cart from a source at Inveralmond to the Dundee, Perth & London Shipping Company's wharf; in 1903 the firm's Perth cartage operation required 49 horses.

**More Famous People from Perth**: Patrick Geddes, born in Perth in 1854, became a noted biologist, educator and pioneer sociologist, and the founder of Edinburgh's Outlook Tower; he inspired the town planning profession and certainly earned his knighthood. Viscount Haldane, a Perthshire native of 1856, founded the National Physical Laboratory and the Royal Aircraft Establishment. John Buchan, born in Perth in 1875, became an adventure writer best known for such novels as *The Thirty-Nine Steps, Greenmantle* and *John MacNab*, and was also a statesman, becoming governor-general of Canada and earning the title of Lord Tweedsmuir. His sister Anna became the popular novelist O Douglas *(see Broughton)*.

**Frenzy at the General Station**: Perth General Station was extended in the 1866 and thoroughly rebuilt and enlarged in the 1880s to designs by the engineers Blyth & Cunningham of Edinburgh, making it enormous for the size of the town, with four signal boxes. By then Perth station handled a frenzied traffic for the August grouse shooting season, when it was according to Murray *"one of the finest in Scotland, with excellent dining and refreshment rooms, a great social rendezvous"*. Over 200 men worked there in 1905, their hectic work graphically outlined by Peter Marshall.

**Bell, Dewar – and Isla Whisky**: Arthur Bell had joined the tiny Sandeman drinks business in 1851 and began to blend whisky in the shop basement, using only Edradour and Lowland sources. In 1865 Bell became sole owner, adopting a policy of *'only the best, and no advertising'*; he was exporting to several countries by 1889. Meantime in 1846 his rival John Dewar (born in 1806) had set up a wholesale wine and spirit business in Perth. In 1886 John Forbes operated the small steam powered *'Isla'* distillery at Bridgend, using Tay river water for brewing, and distilling only some 135,000 litres of malt whisky a year. Eventually in troubled 1926 – and after the importance of using only pure water sources was realised – this enterprise vanished, but not the Perth blending trade.

**Glass, Textiles, and Coasters**: Gauge glasses for steam boilers were made by Tomey's Tay Glassworks, established about 1850. John Moncrieff, born in Cherrybank in 1835, took over Todd's Ink and Bottle works in 1865, and in 1881 also established his own glassworks to make commercial and industrial glass at St Catherine's Road. By 1864 John Shields & Co had built a steam powered weaving works with 230 looms making damasks and other fabrics, and had a smaller works at Cromwell Park; their large Wallace Works was built in Dunkeld Road in 1868 with 300 looms. In 1869 three factories in the flax, jute and hemp trades employed over 900 workers in the area. Despite growing railway ascendancy, as late as 1869 a road coach builder was still at work in Perth and four small yards were building small wooden coasters.

**Religion, Societies and General Accident Insurance**: St Mary's Catholic monastery was built at Bridgend in 1868–70, to designs by Perth architect Andrew Heiton. In 1883 the City of Perth Co-operative Society built a row of shops, and the long-established Natural History society opened their Perth Museum in a new building in Tay Street. In 1883–85 came the imposing St Leonard's Free Church in Marshall Place; while it was slowly rising, St Johnstone FC was formed in 1884, playing on a field beside the prison until 1924. The General Accident Insurance Company (GA) was established in 1885 by a group of local businessmen in the then recently erected Victoria Buildings on Tay Street. Innovative in approach under its general manager Francis Norie-Miller (later knighted), it soon became a highly significant concern and developed a large business in the USA. In 1901 GA opened a fine new HQ building at High Street and Tay Street.

**Shops, Hotels and Another Bridge**: By 1891 the population of Perth had reached 30,000; by 1894 some of the more unfortunate lived in the *Lunatic Asylum* (later called the Murray Royal Hospital) which like the prison was clearly outwith the ancient tightly built-up area, still under 1 km square. Five booksellers and three chemists shops met more general needs. Of the five hotels and inns, the still relatively new *Station Hotel* (which had been enlarged in 1890) enjoyed two stars in Murray's Handbook for its special excellence, but the ancient *Salutation* was *'commercial'*. The *Queen's Hotel* was open by 1900. Friarton Gasworks was opened in 1897, and the Sandeman public library, dated 1898, was built of pink sandstone, the fruit of a bequest by Professor Archibald Sandeman. The 500-seat *Perth Theatre* was built in 1899–1900. At the same time came the new steel Victoria Bridge which crossed the River Tay opposite South Street, which thus became a main artery for road traffic.

**Famous Grouse, White Label and other Blends**: By 1897 Matthew Gloag & Son blended the *'Famous Grouse'*, and from about 1900 R B Smith & Son produced the less well-known *'Moorland'* whisky. By 1902 the *'White Label'* blend, lately granted a royal warrant by the ageing playboy who had just become king, was being extensively promoted by John Dewar & Co, who built their 6-storey North Bond at Glover Street in 1903, boasting its own railway siding; in 1911 they erected an enormous electric advertising sign on a Thames wharf, facing the City of London. Arthur Bell's son 'A. K.' was active in his family business by 1892 and the leading partner from 1895. From 1904 the Arthur Bell concern sold whisky under its own label, and in 1908 moved their whisky business to new premises in Victoria Street. In 1908 Peter Thomson also established a wines and spirits business in Perth, making his name with *'Beneagles'* blended whisky and eventually giving rise to Waverley Vintners.

**Livestock Markets, Tramways and Tunnel Trouble**: Perth's annual bull sales had begun in 1885. By 1900 three separate livestock auction marts were in use: the largest, where there was a large wool store, stood west of the railway at Glasgow Road; the Northern Central lay west of the station at Abbot Street; another smaller mart was in Caledonian Road. In 1895 a horse tramway was opened by the Perth & District Tramways Company, with stables and depot at its Scone terminus; its main route ran through Bridgend, the High Street and South Methven Street to Cherrybank – a hamlet which had gained a school in 1865, and which was soon connected to Perth by ribbon development; a branch through King Street and Priory Place served Craigie. Moncrieffe Tunnel had to be heavily rebuilt in 1901–03 – with great difficulty, as steam-hauled rail traffic was continuous: imagine the hot, choking smoke! A power station built at the turn of the century enabled the Town Council to take over the tramways in 1903 and electrify the line in 1905, adding another branch which terminated at Dunkeld Road/Crieff Road.

**Pullar's expands; So does Glass**: John Shields & Co's Wallace textile works had been extended by 1900 to 900 looms. In 1901 Pullars built a great 3-storey stone building in Mill Street, larger than their existing cleaning and dyeing works; Pullars grew so large that at one time it had its own 14-man fire brigade, which averted a major fire in 1903. The Moncrieff glass concern erected three new buildings in 1906–13, and in the 1914–18 war turned to making laboratory glassware, previously imported from central Europe.

*Pullar's dyeworks. The firm began in 1821, erecting new buildings in 1901. They employed over 2000 in the 1920s, claiming to be the largest dyeworks in the world.* *(JRH)*

**Pleasure Steamers, Football and Hospitals**: In 1908 the Clyde steamer *Marchioness of Bute* was brought to the Tay and provided popular pleasure trips from Perth and Dundee until 1914; smaller steamers plied into the 1930s. Meantime a third 18-hole golf course, the rugged home of the Craigie Hill club, had been laid out in 1911. Perth Guildhall of 1722 was rebuilt in 1907 and the City Halls were opened in 1911, replacing a building of 1845. In 1911 too, St Johnstone FC joined the Scottish Football League. By 1913 the *Grand (Temperance) Hotel* stood on the tram route *'opposite New General Post Office'*. In 1914 the Perth Royal Infirmary was opened at Rose Crescent off the Glasgow Road, largely superseding the County & City Infirmary. In 1917 R F McAuley & Co was producing fringe making machines, whose relation to the then desperate war effort seems obscure – were they for making epaulettes for top brass dress uniforms?

**After World War I: Muirton Park and Skating**: In 1919 John Moncrieff's glassworks absorbed Tomey's, and in 1921 took on the talented Spanish glass blower Salvador Ysart and his sons to make decorative ware. A fine model of Pullar's works was made in 1923 when the firm was prospering; by 1924 they had over 2000 workers, and were not only the town's largest employer but claimed to be the world's largest dyeworks. In 1924 St Johnstone opened Muirton Park, a stadium on Dunkeld Road; in 1936 an ice rink was built beside it. Water supply was still taken from the Tay in 1924, when a scheme to bring supplies from Loch Ordie north of Dunkeld was proposed. Regrettably the historic structure of St John's Church was radically remodelled in the 1920s to designs by Sir Robert Lorimer. A Woolworth store, noted for cheap goods, first came to Perth in 1925. The tramway system was closed in 1928; in that year the site of Cromwell's Citadel became that of the *Pavilion Theatre* (itself pulled down within 60 years).

**Activity continues in the 1930s**: The Royal Infirmary was extended about 1931, the fine old County & City Infirmary later becoming the County Council headquarters. In 1932 Perth Academy moved out from Rose Terrace to Viewlands. The main part of Perth Museum & Art Gallery, which replaced the Natural History Museum, was built on to the Marshall Monument in 1932–35, a bequest of local grocer Robert Hay Robertson, who died in 1926. The crudely ugly *Playhouse Cinema* with 1700 seats was erected in the very short time of 9 weeks in 1933 – and showed it (by the 1980s it had been divided into three). Despite the impact of Prohibition – which in theory closed the American market – in 1925–32 Arthur Bell & Sons built 150 artisan houses for their employees at Gannochy north of Bridgend, and by 1935 the firm was exporting to 20 countries. However, the great depression also affected Perth, and by 1933 the port was moribund. About 1936 the town's last linen firm, John Shields & Co of the Wallace Works, was acquired by Arthur Bell & Sons to avert closure; the Wallace Works made linens under Bells until at least 1960. A creamery was established in 1938. In 1938 locomotive maintenance was concentrated by the LMS into an improved shed, its ugly but necessary coaling plant vying with the prison as visual blots on the city's southern approach; over 100 locomotives were based there.

**Glass blooms and fades**: Although whisky was not distilled locally, after 1945 the Perth area developed an even more important whisky blending and bottling role (*see Letham*). In the 1940s Dewars (who had joined DCL in 1925) sold whisky in the USA; Bell's went public in 1949, and were soon exporting to 84 countries. But John Wright's, the last brewery, closed in 1961 when taken over by Vaux. Meantime in 1946 Salvador Ysart and family established their own decorative glassworks at The Shore as Ysart Brothers; in 1956 the firm combined with a Potters Bar company and became Vasart Glass, moving to Crieff in 1964. John Moncrieff's glassworks finally lost its independence in 1952. The *Perthshire Constitutional & Journal* ceased publication in 1948, but a Repertory company was based in the theatre by 1952. About that time a quarry was opened at Friarton (later significant). The Victoria Bridge was replaced by the Queen's Bridge – an early prestressed concrete structure, opened in 1960 on the 750th anniversary of William the Lion's charter of the Royal Burgh. About then the National Trust for Scotland opened the hillside Branklyn Garden to visitors.

**Perth's Railway Role reduced**: The long-unopened movable span of the railway viaduct over the river was fixed in 1955. The last steam locomotives were withdrawn in 1967 and at the same time Perth's junction role was greatly reduced when the Strathmore route was severed east of Forfar and the Dundee link was given main line status. A new travel centre opened in 1970, quite out of keeping with the historic station around it, whose roof had been cut back the previous year.

**Headquarters and Hotels on the Move**: By 1972 Perth High School and St Columba's RC High School were located side by side at Muirton, and there was a youth hostel. By 1977 the ancient Upper City Mills formed part of a new Stakis hotel which took their name; the restored waterwheel in it was among the largest still turning in Scotland. The *Isle of Skye Hotel* then had 50 rooms. In 1975 Perth lost its Royal Burgh and County Town status, becoming the centre of the sparsely peopled Perth & Kinross District within Tayside Region; by 1980 Perth was also the HQ of the Tay River Purification Board. In 1983 GA, then Britain's fourth largest insurance company, moved their 1100 headquarters staff to a fine new 23,000 $m^2$ building at Pitheavlis on the Glasgow road, the District Council taking over their older offices in the town centre; by 1990 GA employed 30,000 people in 45 countries.

**Shopping Facilities expand**: Woolworths redeveloped their store in 1966, Marks & Spencer (M&S) had opened a Perth branch south of the High Street in the 1960s but soon found it too small; a new and larger M&S was opened opposite in 1979. BHS took over the old M&S building. Tesco had 2 stores by 1987. In 1983 the site of the former central fire station was used for a small new House of Fraser department store. St John's Square was replaced in 1987–88 by the attractive covered St John's Centre of 42 shops (with a basic 450-space multi-storey car park). A William Low superstore was erected nearby, and by 1992 a Safeway superstore had also been built near the station. Part of the High Street east of Scott Street was pedestrianised in 1990, though by 1994 the Co-op shops were derelict.

**Other Developments in the 1980s**: Pullar's who were still active in 1980 – but could now dry-clean customers' clothes at their many shops – were bought out by Johnson's from Merseyside. In 1994 their older building was sold, and by then the 1901 building had become government offices. Cloister flats were built on the site of the ancient friary in 1985. In 1988 a large 4-storey block of sheltered flats was erected by a housing association beside the courts, which were still based in their early 19th century buildings in Tay Street. After a series of takeovers, in 1992 the John Moncrieff glassworks was renamed Monax, then specialising in making coloured glasses for airport runway lights.

**Whisky Headquarters bought out**: By 1976 Arthur Bell & Sons had built a new HQ office at Cherrybank and set up the Gannochy Trust, which built a sports complex at the North Inch, including the domed Bell's Sports Centre; they began the Cherrybank Gardens five years later. These were repeatedly extended, adding the Bell's National Heather Collection. Bell's were taken over by Guinness in 1985; the latter seized DCL in 1986, and by 1990 Bell's were merely the marketing branch of United Distillers. By 1990 the firm of Peter Thomson had become Waverley Vintners. Spirit merchants Matthew Gloag & Son kept their head office in Perth; as proprietors of *Famous Grouse* whisky, they claimed in 1990 that this was Scotland's top selling brand, at a half million cases per year. In 1994 Highland Distillers of Glasgow owned Gloag's, who bottled their whisky across the road from their head office.

**Motorway makes Fairer City**: The town had longed been cursed by heavy congestion caused by Scotland's interregional road traffic, but the situation was relieved when the tall new Friarton bridge across the Tay and a system of bypass motorways to south and west of Perth were completed in the early 1980s. In supplying the road materials the Friarton quarry had assumed enormous proportions by 1985. By 1988 one of the four Mechanised Letter Offices in Scotland – the key sorting centres for the Post Office – had been built on the site of the former South engine shed, and in 1992 a substantial Parcel Force depot was also active at Feus Road. By 1991 Perth's population, including the Letham area, was nearing 41,500, its occupations skewed towards services. The Royal Infirmary was extended in the 1990s, but adjacent Cornhill House became derelict.

**Stagecoaches travel Farther and Faster**: The last remaining rail freight services rapidly withered in the early 1990s, and many of the remaining staff left Perth in 1994. Despite its tiny and primitive bus station Perth had become an important bus centre, where *'Citylink'* buses on routes to Aberdeen, Glasgow, Edinburgh and Inverness exchange passengers. The local firm of *'Stagecoach'*, begun in 1980 by Brian Souter and his sister Ann Gloag, became a vigorously expanding concern. In 1989 they took over National Coaches of Birmingham. In 1990 their 70 Scottish vehicles were based at Kinnoull, and on privatisation of the Scottish Bus Group in 1991 they acquired the Fife buses. In 1993 Stagecoach was floated as a public company, by then owning 3300 buses and coaches and employing 11,000 people in Scotland, England, Hong Kong, Kenya, Malawi and New Zealand. In 1994 they acquired Western Scottish of Kilmarnock and Busways of Tyneside, so raising their fleet to 5000 vehicles, and then also purchased the Cleveland services, most of the Hull buses and an Australian firm. Rail privatisation enabled further expansion for Stagecoach, which now owns South West Trains, a stake in Virgin Trains – and (from 2000) also owns the huge Coach USA. Stagecoach now claims to own 20,000 vehicles worldwide.

**Busy Harbour, Leisure and Prison Variety**: Thanks to exclusion from the ill-fated national dock labour scheme, by the mid 1980s Perth harbour had regained a minor but regular narrow seas trade, largely in agricultural goods. By 1988 there was a fortnightly small-ship service to Finland, and many vessels able to navigate the Rhine used the harbour, where a new berth was planned. In 1983 St Johnstone FC was briefly promoted to the Premier League and, having had Muirton's capacity cut for safety reasons, accepted ASDA's offer to buy the Muirton ground (and the ice rink) for yet another supermarket. This enabled them to build a fine new stadium at Letham *(q.v.)*, to which they moved in 1989. Perth's fine leisure pool, which opened in 1988 opposite Dewars' substantial whisky bond, was the third most popular paid attraction in Scotland by 1990, with over 700,000 users. The Dewars Rinks which replaced the old ice rink were opened in 1990, and in 1993 hosted the European Curling Championships. At that time the old high security prison housed 440 inmates: both the non-violent (who by the 1980s bred tropical fish), and a riotous group who had caused repeated damage to the jail up to 1992.

**Cultural Centres, and Ghosts of Trains Past**: By 1990 the regimental museum of the Black Watch occupied the 16th century Balhousie Castle. By then Perth Museum & Art Gallery had a large collection of equipment from the by then virtually defunct dyeing and cleaning industry. The Round House – the original water pumping station – later used as a tourist office, was converted into an art gallery for the works of John Duncan Fergusson, and adjudged *'Museum of the Year'* in 1992. The former County Council offices in York Place (originally the County & City Infirmary), had been long vacant before its frontage was incorporated in the fine new public library which opened in 1995 – named in memory of benefactor A K Bell, and replacing the Sandeman and Shore Road premises. In 1997 Perth High School had the largest roll in the new Perth & Kinross Council area – almost 1500; St Columba's had only 442. Today, Perth station's extensive 7-platform station with its fine large sandstone buildings is an echoing covered space, through which Scotrail's occasional short diesel trains and a daily GNER Inter-City 125 between London and Inverness carry modest but growing numbers of passengers over intricate traditional trackwork.

**Premier Market Centre hit by Floods and BSE**: Early in 1993 the city's flood defences failed under pressure. More than a metre of Tay water submerged the North Muirton estate, Rose Terrace and other parts of the town, and hundreds had to flee their homes. The city centre was largely unaffected, but in 2000 the South Inch was being transformed by a major flood protection scheme. In 1994 Tay Salmon Produce packed fine smoked salmon near the harbour, and the Perth Business Park, a development of small offices, was completed in 1995, but local flour milling company Veda was not prospering. In 1994 the United Auctions (UA), market was still very busy with cattle and sheep, and Perth had the offices of the Aberdeen-Angus Cattle Society and the Shetland Pony Stud book. In the BSE-CJD crisis of 1996–97, Perth Fresh Meat failed, but the 300 workers hoped to be saved when a Bathgate firm purchased their packaging plant. By 2000 the annual Aberdeen Angus bull sales were back to 1979 levels at 228 animals. With these and two substantial livestock auction marts, Perth is probably the premier market town in Scotland.

**Conservation, Retailing and Local Government**: The gothic Middle Church of 1887, designed by Hippolyte Blanc, was converted to flats in the early 1990s, and Annat Lodge, a classical villa of the early 19th century, was restored in 1995. By 1996 a new retail park at St Catherine's Road adjoined the not long closed Monax glassworks. The *Perth Theatre* keeps busy, and St Johnstone FC plays in the Premier League. The North Inch golf course now has only 9 holes. There were by now four Tesco stores, but the monthly outdoor Farmers' Market – started in 1999 as an antidote to supermarket dominance – was soon adjudged a success. In 1996 an enlarged Perth & Kinross District became a unitary local authority, the Tory government adding eastward-looking areas which had since 1975 been within Dundee city district.

**Hotels and Accommodation**: The town has quite a number of largish hotels, some of long standing like the *Stakis*, the *Station* (now *'Quality'*), the *Queen's* (51), the *George*, and the *Isle of Skye* – and the ancient *Salutation*, a favourite venue for fiddlers' rallies and Scottish dancing. There are many smaller establishments. The youth hostel is still open, and the road to Coupar Angus is lined with a parade of guest houses.

## PERTH AERODROME — Map 6, B3

*Aero facility near Perth* — OS 53: NO 1528

About 3km north-east of New Scone is a level farming area, overlooked by prehistoric stone circles on a knoll. In the 1930s David Kay of Scone designed a Gyroplane, built by Shields Garage of Perth, whose town council bought land in 1935 to create a municipal airfield; this opened as Perth Aerodrome in 1936. At once Airwork began to train pilots there, and until 1939 North Eastern Airways flew from Perth to Newcastle, Leeds, London, Aberdeen, Inverness and Renfrew; an early British Airways service flew from Perth via Dyce to Stavanger. Grangemouth was served for two months in 1939. The aerodrome became an operational base in dark 1940, when a new hangar was hastily erected – in error – and as hurriedly dismantled! The training airfield, also known as Scone, was taken over by Airwork in 1946 and although its air routes were not revived it hosted the Scottish Flying Club (later renamed the Scottish Aero Club) while they were excluded from Renfrew in 1946–52. In 1960 Airwork bought the Hamble Engineering College and moved it from Hampshire to Perth Aerodrome, where 250 service personnel were also based in 1971. By 1972 the English language was also taught, due to the high proportion of overseas pupils. The large Stormont Hall was built, and the Air Service Training College tutored commercial pilots and engineers for worldwide service, and trained the British Army's helicopter pilots; but severe competition, particularly from Prestwick, caused its closure in 1996. Perth College bought the Engineering Training School, whilst the airfield – with three runways, hangars, control tower and living accommodation – was for sale; parts were still for let in 2000.

## PETERCULTER (or Culter) & Milltimber — Map 10, B3

***Villages / suburbs of Aberdeen,** pop. 8000+* — OS 38: NJ 8400

A large Roman marching camp of the first century AD was placed on the north bank of the River Dee, 13km south-west of its mouth at modern Aberdeen, and above the confluence of the fast-flowing Leuchar Burn. Many centuries later this site fell within Peterculter parish, owned by Kelso Abbey in the 13th century, whereas in 1309 Maryculter which lies on the south bank was owned by the Knights of St John *(see Temple)*. Pont's map of about 1600 showed the Leuchar Burn already bridged, and a mill and a *'wakmil'* stood on its tributary the Gormack Burn. East of the bridge was the Kirk of

*'Petercouter'*, and east of that *'Koutyir'*; Roy's map of about 1750 showed *'Hallmill'*, and farther up another tributary was the mill of *'Ordd'*. *'Couter'* was then a mansionhouse, which stood above the North Deeside Road. In 1750–51 the Englishman Bartholomew Smith rented some of the several waulk mills on the Leuchar Burn west of the Kirkton of Culter, and *"set them going"* as the Culter Paper Mills. These slowly expanded, the first papermaking machine in Scotland being installed by 1811, and another about 1820. In 1837 a very large 2.1 metre wide papermaking machine was introduced. In the early 19th century a small snuff mill also operated. Culter became a tiny village, but there was no post office until after 1838.

**The Railway Era**: The single-track Deeside Railway (later part of the Great North of Scotland) was opened through Culter station to Banchory in 1853, crossing the burn on a 5-span bridge originally built of timber. Double track from Aberdeen reached Culter in 1892, enabling suburban trains to be introduced between Culter and the city in 1894. Though Culter was tiny on the OS map of 1894 – with a post office, but not even an inn – the better train service must have stimulated growth, for by 1901 the village population was over 1000. By 1920 the Culter Paper Works were rail-connected, and they had their own shunting engine. Thanks to buses, dormitory growth continued, doubling the population by 1931, but this did not save the suburban trains, which were withdrawn by the LNER in 1937. By 1951 3800 people lived in a place by then generally called Peterculter, and the local facilities were those of a large village. The Deeside line was reduced to single track in 1951, and despite timber traffic was completely closed in 1965–67 by Beeching; all track had gone by 1974. Meantime by 1967 the independent St Margaret's School for Girls in Aberdeen had its boarding house at the former mansion of Culter House.

**Suburbia replaces the Paper Mill**: The village was placed in Aberdeen City district in 1975. Its one-time senior secondary school was also closed by 1977, but by that time the Camphill-Rudolf Steiner school had been established at Milltimber to the east, an area rapidly suburbanised in the 1970s as Aberdeen burgeoned with oil-related development. In 1981 Peterculter was suburban, its population nearly 6500. The paper mills were still in operation in 1979, though they were closed soon afterwards and demolished about 1986. By 1985 considerable development had taken place at the Holemill, and housing estates were continuing to expand. At the 1991 census Peterculter had 7312 people and Maryculter 385. Peterculter's 18-hole golf course is a 1990s development. Housing has now covered the paper mill site, a theme park *('Storybook Glen')* is open at Maryculter (which is now outwith from the city), and there is access to Forestry Commission land nearby. The 23-room *Maryculter House Hotel* claims 13th century origins, and there's also the *Old Mill Inn*.

## PETERHEAD, Keithinch, Invernettie & Inverugie

**Map 10, C2**

***Buchan coastal town,*** *pop. 18,700* — OS 30: NK 1346

Also see: *Boddam*

Around the year 1250 a church dedicated to Saint Peter was built on the shores of a south-east facing bay on the east coast of Buchan. A medieval motte was raised beside the River Ugie about 3 km above its mouth, which lay 1.5 km north of the church. Later came the building by the Cheyne family of two strongpoints close by, the 13th to 15th century Ravenscraig Castle and Inverugie Castle, which passed to Sir John de Keith about 1380. He or his descendants founded *Keithinch*, on an islet adjoining the point of land east of the church. Later called *"the fishertown of Peterhead"*, this was owned by Deer Abbey in 1560 when Robert Keith was its Commendator. The Keiths also built a new Inverugie tower in the 16th century.

**Burgh, Fishhouse and Harbour**: After the Reformation, Robert Keith obtained a barony and harbour charter for Peterhead in 1587; at the same time his brother George Keith the Earl Marischal obtained a charter for white fishing. In 1593 when Peterhead had a population of only about 56, a proper harbour was completed, named Port Henry after its builder Henry Middleton, and by 1597 a parish school had been opened. Pont's sketch map of Buchan made about 1601 showed a *'fishhouse'* at Buchanhaven beside the river's mouth, probably the one built in 1585. Some 2 km south-east, just offshore of the church of Peterhead, was an island where Keith had lately built another castle, *'Mekle Kathyl'*, doomed within a century to *"degenerate into a fish-house"*. Pont indicated both the older castles, Inverugie being sketched as an imposing structure; he showed a substantial settlement named *'Innernety'*, and its mill.

**Fish Processing Town**: Peterhead grew and prospered, the harbour being much used by the Dutch; by 1621 it was already referred to as a *"town"* and was known for its ale. However, in 1655 Tucker noted only *"a small town"* with just one trading vessel of 20 tons. About 1686 the Ugie was spanned by a 2-arched bridge, probably near Inverugie. In the early 18th century a fishing village known as Roanheads grew between the church and the Ugie. Peterhead had a post office by 1715, the year that the contemporary Keith supported the Pretender in the rising, so the estate was forfeited; it was sold to the speculative York Buildings Company. The harbour was too small in 1720 to offer refuge to all the vessels needing shelter, but in 1721 Hepburn praised Peterhead for its primacy in *"drying, salting and curing fish for export"*. A year or two later Defoe called Peterhead *"a good market-town, and a port with a small harbour for fishing vessels, but no considerable trade, Aberdeen being so near"*. (In fact as the crow flies it is at least 45 km!) The harbour was *"all dry at low-water"*, but it could accommodate six to eight 100-ton ships. There were then about 230 families in the town.

**Roy's Map Problems, Spa and Textile Industries**: In 1728 Peterhead passed to the strangely named Merchant Maiden Hospital of Edinburgh. The Roy map made about 1750 showed a quite large and for those days sprawling town, with Inch Keith Castle and a clearly enclosed harbour; Keith Inch was developed by Dutch herring fishers. Already the locals liked their comforts: when in 1759 the Keith Mason-Lodge was built it had both a pump-room and a billiard room. Meantime Warden noted that in 1764 *"two young ladies"* (not named) introduced linen thread manufacture; by 1765 the British Linen Company had a local agent, by about 1775 thread mills operated in the town, and a linen bleachfield was established in 1780. The South Harbour was built under Smeaton's direction in 1773–75, and a town house was erected in 1778. Two woollen factories were soon in production; the firm of Rennie began wool spinning in 1789, and in 1794 about 1150 people were employed in the town making thread from homespun yarn. In

1798 Thomas Arbuthnot & Co established a sailcloth manufactory.

**White Fishing Port and Resort**: Two fairs were to be held in 1797. In 1799 Heron wrote of *"a neat and regular town, having about 2000 inhabitants, its excellent harbour secured by a handsome new pier. Great quantities of white fish are caught on the neighbouring coast; and several large sloops are annually sent from this place to different fishing stations. The traders in this town have frequently obtained the highest premiums allowed by the government for curing white fish. A trade is also carried on directly to the Baltic for deals, iron, hemp, tar and other articles. Here is a manufacture of sewing-thread, which employs many young girls. In the summer season, Peterhead is a place of polite resort, on account of its mineral spring; many good houses have been built for the accommodation of strangers. There is also a ballroom, under which are two salt-water baths"*. In 1800 James Arbuthnot built a swimming pool 27 m x 9 m, followed in 1802 by a suite of warm baths.

**Early Nineteenth Century activities**: By 1811 there was a daily coach to Aberdeen via Ellon. A police force was founded in 1820, not perhaps unconnected with the two breweries still in operation in 1825. In 1821 Peterhead builder John Reid erected the lighthouse at Sumburgh Head in Shetland. The Aberdeen Banking company had a branch in the town between at least 1810 and 1825, and in 1814 Arbuthnot, Scott & Co was making fine woollens, but the firm seems to have failed; their premises became a corn mill and then a distillery until about 1850.

**Britain's Top Whaling Port**: From a start in 1788, four whaling vessels were soon based in Peterhead; with a peak of 16 whalers in 1821, it was Scotland's premier whaling port, and second in the UK (after Hull). Although other centres had declined, this activity continued to flourish locally for many years. In 1852 the sail and steam whaler *Active* was built at Peterhead for Dundee owners, and in 1857 Peterhead had the largest whaling fleet in Britain, with 32 whalers and sealers. The swift reduction in whale stocks and the introduction of mineral oil brought about a rapid decline, which reduced the Peterhead whaling fleet to only 12 vessels in 1868, and local men returned increasingly to white fishing. The last Peterhead owner to give up seems to have been Captain D Gray, for whom Alex Hall & Co of Aberdeen built the sail and steam whaler *Eclipse* in 1867. Hall kept her until 1892; she ultimately became a USSR survey ship and was in use until at least the age of 69.

**Peterhead's Herring Fishery and Life**: Meantime, aided by the Commissioners, the additional North Harbour was built in 1818–22 to Telford's plans, and herring fishing began in 1823. By then Peterhead – whose registration letters were PD – was (according to Chambers) *"the fifth sea-port in Scotland and by far the most flourishing little town in this part of the country, with several tolerable streets of recent erection"*. Butter, a great product of Buchan, *"is here salted and exported in vast quantities."* By that time Adam Arbuthnot had collected a natural history museum; however, both Inverugie and Ravenscraig castles had become ruinous. In 1832 an influx of fisherfolk arrived from cholera-stricken Wick and helped the town's development. A gasworks was established in 1833, and about then work commenced on the slow construction of a new dock to Stevenson's plans; this was finally completed in 1855. By 1850 there were no fewer than 400 herring boats based in Peterhead; Methuen had lately built new curing yards, though these were damaged by a great storm in 1859 when 15 local people died.

**Peterhead in the 1850s**: A golf club was founded in 1841 but its 18-hole links course was apparently slow to be developed. In 1857 twenty-one merchant ships were based at Peterhead. By then there was a jail in Queen Street – predecessor of the later prison. In 1854 Smith & Co revived woollen weaving in the early 19th century premises once used by Arbuthnot & Scott. In 1858 Pratt noted south of the town Yule & Milne's brick and tile works and Hutchison's ropework, *"both prosperous establishments"*. Bricks and tiles were also made at Downiehills, 5 km west. Burnhaven was also a *"fishing village"*, and the mills at Invernettie had a number of wheels of various sizes. At that time the principal inns were four in number: the *Royal Hotel, New Inn, Laing's Temperance Hotel* and *The Inn*.

**Railway, Boatbuilding, Canning and Whisky**: The *Buchan Observer* newspaper was first published in 1862, the year the Great North of Scotland Railway reached the town's terminus at Balmoor Terrace from Aberdeen via Maud; a 1 km extension to the harbour was opened in 1865. However by 1864 thread making was said to be *'long extinct'*. In the late 1860s wooden coasters were among the boats built locally. By 1869 nearly 500 men and boys were fishing herring and haddock from Invernettie, and Ritchies were early fish canners. Meat too was canned in Peterhead by 1869. Taking its name from a failed enterprise at Longside, the Glenugie distillery, which was built in 1875 beside the old mills at Invernettie, used steam power in processing locally grown barley, and was very well equipped; it produced over 400,000 litres of Highland Malt whisky annually in the 1880s. In 1886 Barnard called Peterhead *"a thriving little town, the chief town of Buchan"*.

**Prison Labour builds Harbour of Refuge**: Herring fishing peaked in the 1880s. In 1884 the Admiralty belatedly decided to form an extensive National Harbour of Refuge for sailing vessels in Peterhead Bay, mainly by building a gigantic 900 m breakwater from Salthouse Head (another shorter one extends south from Keith Inch). A mineral railway was constructed to convey blocks of granite from Stirling Hill south of Boddam *(q.v.)*, down to the base at Burnhaven. The new Peterhead prison, opened at Invernettie in 1888, supplied convict labour, used on the breakwater construction; a giant hammerhead crane placed the huge granite blocks. Convict involvement meant that it took 70 years to complete! The 1891 population of Peterhead was over 12,000, after which it declined, for about that time the herring fishing peaked. The 577 fishing vessels at that time were mainly small sailing boats, but is it any wonder the overfished herring declined so quickly? By 1890 when Peterhead FC was founded, Raemoss Park was open, and the team played there. Public library provision started in 1890, aided by Carnegie money. Murray commended three hotels in 1894: the *North Eastern, Royal* and *Laing's Temperance*.

**Peterhead in the Early Twentieth Century**: Brewing seems to have ceased early in the 20th century, but fishing remained prosperous; from 1918 seven trainloads of fish were often despatched each working day. In 1919 Crosse & Blackwell (C&B) took over and greatly expanded Ritchies' cannery, despatching their products by rail. But the harbour line was largely disused by 1938. The Drifter Coal Company's stock came by coaster, as did the tinplate for fish canning. The Admiralty railway was

*Peterhead harbour in the 1970s. First used as a fishing harbour in 1593, its South Harbour was added in the 1779s by Smeaton, the North Harbour by Telford in 1818–22, and the Harbour of Refuge from 1884, built by convict labour.* (JRH)

closed in 1950. By then Peterhead had very good urban facilities, including an art gallery and swimming baths. Thomas Murison founded his Peterhead ironmongery business in 1904 (by 1994 the firm had branches in Ellon and Fraserburgh). A lifeboat station was opened in 1965, replacing the venerable Newburgh station in a more strategic location.

**Rail Closure, Real Oil, and Bureaucratic Nonsense**: Peterhead station kept some locomotive facilities until 1965 when Beeching closed the railway to passengers; rail freight ended in 1970. To be fair, Beeching could not then have predicted that Peterhead would become a major North Sea oil base! A tanker terminal for vessels of up to 40,000 tonnes was soon constructed. From 1975, *local* government (district) services for important Peterhead were for 20 years administered from tiny Banff, a remarkable *50km* away – even more remote than the new Grampian Regional offices in Mastrick!

**Oil Boom fails to save Cinema and Distillery**: In 1981 Peterhead had the facilities of an average town. Although workaday-looking, it had a caravan and camping site and ten hotels, double the number of the 1950s; the new *Waterside Inn* at Inverugie had 40 rooms. A school and community centre were built on the railway station site. The Glenugie distillery, part of the Long John empire in the 1970s, was closed in 1983 by Whitbread, and soon demolished. By 1987 a bypass had been built round the newly swollen town with its many new housing estates for workers related to the oil and gas industry, linking Invernettie and its new industrial estate to Inverugie with its new hotel. Rennies the woollen spinners still worked in 1987 as one of Scotland's oldest established concerns. But in that year the *Playhouse*, last cinema in Banff and Buchan, closed its doors.

**Europe's Biggest Fish Market, and a New Hospital**: Peterhead's main claim to fame was as Europe's premier white fishing port, landing 117,000 tonnes in 1987, 20% of the Scottish total. The town boasted Europe's largest fish market, 380m in length, and a striking feature when seen either on the ground or from the air. Though still more harbour improvement was under way in 1988, the slashed haddock quotas held back the local economy, and new developments were slower to appear. By 1998 the number of Peterhead-registered fishing boats had fallen since 1980 from 148 to 116. However, they were on average larger, and actually landing more fish. Peterhead's cottage hospital was being developed into a general hospital by the addition of new units; the first, a new 36-bed hospital, was opened in 1993.

**Closures, Changes and Promotion**: Peterhead's coastguard station was closed in 1989, seeming an absurb decision. In 1991 the population was 18,674. By then the Nestlé group owned the C&B cannery (which shed jobs in 1994) and the C&B pickle factory, which was to close in 1997 with 170 jobs to go. About then Macrae Foods of Peterhead packed cockles, mussels, and rollmops. Crawfords the Edinburgh bakers also had a Peterhead bakery, supplying ten shops when the firm went bankrupt in 1996. In that year Peterhead returned to a unified Aberdeenshire Council, now administered from Mastrick. The dilapidated Queen Street football ground of Peterhead FC was developed with a new Safeway store, in return for a new ground, Balmoor Stadium, constructed north of the town in 1995–97. This move was so successful that in 2000 Peterhead was admitted (with Elgin) to the Scottish Football League, starting in the third division.

**Maritime Dominance continues**: The harbour of refuge is mainly used by the oil industry rather than by fishing boats: in 1990 ASCO employed 145 dockers at South Bay. In 1994 a new quay was under construction next to the ASCO base, while a new marina with berths for 92 yachts and a new caravan site were being completed. Soon afterwards a maritime heritage centre for visitors was built at the Lido south of the town. In 1997 the fish species landed included cod, coley, dogfish, haddock, ling, megrim, monkfish, plaice, lemon sole, whiting and witch. In 1999 it was proposed to build a new fish market – Europe's largest – with refrigerated storage enabling catches to be landed at any time or state of tide; but will shrinking fish stocks stand it? Today Peterhead Academy has almost 1600 pupils. The larger of the hotels include the *Waterside Inn* (over 100 rooms) and the central *Palace* (66); there are also smaller hotels and guest houses.

## PHILPSTOUN, Kingscavil & Bridgend

**Map 16, C2**

***W. Lothian small villages,*** *pop. 800* — OS 65: NT 0477

Pont's map of Lothian engraved in 1612 showed the then new House of The Binns on its prominent hill 5km east of Linlithgow; it was already held by an early Tam Dalyell. The early Edinburgh road was also marked; another modest mansion, Philpstoun House – distinguished by its six sundials – was built 1.5km east of The Binns about 1676 by John Dundas. Philpstoun was a small roadside settlement when Roy's map was made about 1754. From 1822 local transport was improved by the Union Canal, built to link Edinburgh with the Forth & Clyde Canal at Camelon, and so with Glasgow. The Edinburgh & Glasgow Railway was opened through the area in 1842; Philpstoun station was convenient to both mansions. Stone from Kingscavil quarry, much nearer to Linlithgow, was widely used in the mid 19$^{th}$ century for foundations and interior work. Craigton sandstone quarries to the east worked between 1890 and 1933.

**Oil and Petrol from Shale**: In 1883 James Ross & Co of Falkirk built an oil-works just west of Philpstoun station, between the railway and the canal, connected by a mineral line with a shale pit 1.5km to the south. The works manager,

*Philpstoun Crude Oil Works – a very large operation in the 1920s, but it closed in 1931. In this view the retorts are to the right of the chimney. Improved retorts for crude oil distillation were developed here by Archibald Crichton.* (Scottish Oils/BP)

Archibald Crichton, developed improved retorts for crude oil distillation. Two mines produced 200 tonnes of shale a day, at one time employing 400 men – for whom the firm built houses and recreational facilities, creating a model village near Pardovan church. Just west of this was another oil works and shale pit. Ross & Co's pits and oil works employed 300 men in 1920, processing 850 tonnes of shale a day and refining 'Ross petrol'; but it closed in the 1930s.

**Back to the Canal**: By 1953 a new settlement had been built at Bridgend, between the shale mines; together with Philpstoun they had the basic facilities of a small village, and held some 1700 people. Philpstoun station had been closed, but a rail link to Winchburgh still served a shale mine; this had closed by 1962, and the population shrank. The opening of the M9, with an access point near Old Philpstoun, actually accelerated the decline of the area, still scarred by former mineral workings. Apart from a bowling green, only the most basic facilities were available. The bings have still not been restored, but Philpstoun and Bridgend – neither of which had as many as 500 people in 1991 – still have their post office, pub and primary school, and the reopening of the canal as a through route in 2001 may add something to the area.

## PIEROWALL, Westray & Papa Westray — Map 13, B1

***Village & small islands, N. Orkney,*** *pop. 800* — OS 5: HY 4348

The best harbour on the 17 km-long sandstone jigsaw puzzle piece that is the northern Orkney isle of Westray was once known as Hofn, now the Bay of Pierowall (Norse *Piril Vagr, 'Little Bay')*. Sheltered by Papa Westray Isle, it forms a welcome haven for north Atlantic mariners. It has the remains of a prehistoric village, had an ancient church with Viking burials by about 800, and has been used as a regular harbour since at least 1136. In the late 16th century the domineering Gilbert Balfour leased the bishop's estates and built the fine double tower of Noltland Castle with its 2 m-thick walls, 1 km inland from the head of the bay. Noltland was sketched but unnamed on Pont's map, made about 1592; it also showed a vessel sheltering in the bay, and the island thickly settled with some 25 tiny places. However Noltland became a ruin in 1746.

**Steamers, Post and Hotels**: Orkney was really opened up by steamers which overcame the lengthy delays caused to sailing vessels by the severe storms and tide rips in the Pentland Firth. By 1839 a post office known as Westray was open at Pierowall, where the island's piers were built. Another post office was opened at Valdigarth (Skelwick). Both islands contain good arable land, and prosperous farms developed. Westray's population peaked at 2200 about 1881, when another 345 lived on Papa Westray. In 1894 three hotels were listed by Murray: the *Trenabie "(very comfortable, close to pier); Pierowall, (very comfortable 1 mile from pier)"*, and a temperance establishment. Noup Head lighthouse, 5 km west of Pierowall on the north-westerly tip of the Orkneys, was first lighted in 1898.

**The World's Shortest Scheduled Air Service**: In the 1950s, when the combined population of the two islands was down to 1275, Pierowall contained some 400 residents and had typical village facilities, including the 7-room *Pierowall Hotel*, plus a small secondary school, mill, and 9-hole golf course. By then Aikerness, a peninsula 4 km to the north, held the island's tiny airstrip, separated by a mere 2.5 km from its partner on Papa Westray and offering the shortest commercial flights in the world – scheduled at two minutes. Of four piers in existence by 1957 only that at Gill had sufficiently deep water to support the passenger ferries which still connected the islands with each other and with Kirkwall. Noup Head lighthouse was converted to automatic operation in 1964. By 1971 Pierowall had sunk to about 275 people. However, Westray people formed a Knitters Society, based at Valdigarth.

**Tourism, Fish and Knitting**: Mains electricity came to Westray by undersea cable in 1980, when several trawlers and lobster boats worked out of Pierowall. They supplied a co-owned processing factory at a new pier, built at Gill in 1980 so that vehicle ferries could be introduced, for the combined population of the two isles was slowly falling. By 1982 a local co-operative had recently built a guest house and youth hostel on Papa Westray, and in 1985 there were six local seine netters and a recently improved harbour; there is another modern pier at Huro near the south tip of the isle, though population decline continued, to 85 by 1991, when there were 704 people on Westray. The golf course is still open, as is the textile company Hume Sweet Hume. A costly recent proposal – opposed by most people of Papa Westray (which has a 5-pupil primary school, the guest house, and a youth hostel) – would see a 2 km-long causeway being built to join it with Westray.

## PINMORE

**Map 1, B3**

***S. Ayrshire hamlet,*** *pop. 100* — OS 76: NX 2092

The Dinvin motte stands on a col 5 km south of Girvan – eventually beside the winding and hilly road between Girvan and Pinwherry by the time of the Roy survey in the 1750s. The name of Pinmore, which lies on this road beside the Water of Assel a little to the south, suggests that in the days of Gaelic speech, then fading in Kyle, it was the most significant *(Mor)* of the various *Pin-* places in the area. But it was of no greater account until 1877, when it gained a station on the Girvan & Portpatrick Junction Railway, which tunnelled under the col for 500 m and repeatedly criss-crossed the road. By 1951 a post office and the Assel primary school were open, serving about 250 scattered people, but except for a large quarry up the valley at Tormitchell (still going) there was little save farm work. The railway halt and post office were closed in successive decades; by 1981 the population had been halved, and nowadays only a tiny hamlet remains beside the road and railway.

## PINWHERRY

**Map 1, B3**

***S. Ayrshire hamlet,*** *pop. 175* — OS 76: NX 1986

In the deep valley formed by the meeting of the waters of the Rivers Stinchar and Duisk about 12 km south of Girvan is a medieval motte. Nearby stands the 16th century L-plan tower of Pinwherry Castle, which may take its name from the nature of the ferry boat of the day. Never much more than a grouping of tiny hamlets, Pinwherry lay on a road by Roy's day in the mid 18th century, and later became a road junction. The brand new Daljarrock viaduct on the winding and hilly Girvan & Portpatrick Junction Railway was destroyed in a great flood in 1875, and had to be rebuilt before the line could be opened through to Dunragit for Stranraer in 1877. A conveniently sited station served Pinwherry. By 1951 about 270 people lived in the area, also served by a primary school, post office and 48-line telephone exchange. There were three trains a day in the 60s, but by 1967 Beeching had shut the station. In 1986 despite the loss of over a quarter of the population, a garage, shop and post office formed a single business. The 5-roomed *Daljarrock Hotel*, open by 1977, is still in business, although by 1996 there was no post office.

## PITCAPLE, Chapel of Garioch & Daviot

**Map 10, B3**

***Ab'shire village & hamlets,*** *pop. 700 (area)* — OS 38: NJ 7225

A prehistoric stone circle was created near the River Urie about 5 km upstream of modern Inverurie, 4 km east of the ancient fort now known as Maiden Castle; another circle stands on a hill at Daviot, 5 km north-east. A Roman legion once briefly camped nearby at Durno. The 15th century keep of Balquhain Castle was built near the riverside circle, and the House of Pittodrie was erected near Maiden Castle in 1490 by the Erskines. Then in the 16th century the twin-towered Pitcaple Castle was built beside the River Urie 2.5 km north of Balquhain. In 1628 a tryst was authorised at Chapel of Garioch, central to the three castles, but later faded. By 1642 the Blaeu map showed the area thickly settled, and the river had been bridged at Whiteford, just west of Pitcaple Castle. Pittodrie House, burnt by Montrose, was rebuilt and extended in 1675. Logie Elphinstone House near the old Kirk of Durno some 1.5 km west of the bridge was built in 1680 for its laird, Elphinstone of Resseviot.

**Roy, Roads, Railways and Postal Services**: Roy's map of about 1750 showed the emparked House of Pitcaple, though by then the bridge seems to have fallen, for there was a gap in the track from Inverurie to Old Rayne at the Urie crossing at Whiteford just to the west. Subsequently a rather winding road network was built, and the Great North of Scotland Railway's main line and Pitcaple station were opened in 1854. In 1857 a branch line to Turriff and eventually Macduff was opened from a station at the Milton of Inveramsay, on the main line 1 km south-east of Pitcaple Castle (which was greatly extended in the 19th century). By 1894 Logie Elphinstone stood in an extensive park; Pitcaple, though not itself a village, had a post and telegraph office. In 1898 the Pittodrie estate passed to the Smith family, and later a post office was opened at Chapel of Garioch.

**Daviot Hospital, Decline, Tourism – and Dereliction**: By 1951 the Pitcaple area including the hamlet of Whiteford had about 580 people, and some local facilities served about twice that number. In 1955 a large quarry was open north of Pitcaple Castle, and in the 1950s to 1970s there were primary schools at both Whiteford (Logie Durno) and Chapel of Garioch. But the branch railway was closed to passengers in 1951 and for freight in 1966; Inveramsay station vanished. By 1955 the House of Daviot near the stone circle and small village of Daviot, had become a hospital which had 145 inmates in 1971; in 1981 it treated mental illness. The Mill of Durno had closed by 1967, and Pitcaple station was closed about 1968. The Smith family converted their big house to the *Pittodrie Hotel* in 1977; it doubled in size to 24 rooms in 1989–90. Meantime Logie House, a hotel until it was gutted by fire in 1974, was still ruinous 25 years later. By 1981 the area's population had fallen by a third since 1951 and, apart from the growing quarry and hotel, it remained essentially agricultural. By 1999 neither Pitcaple nor Daviot had post offices, though the latter place was starting to develop.

## PITLOCHRY & Moulin

**Map 6, A2**

***Highland Perthshire town,*** *pop. 2500* OS 52: NN 9458

Standing stones adorn the steep northern braes of the Tummel valley in Atholl. Pitlochry near the river bears a Pictish name *(Pit* meaning portion of land), while uphill Moulin's name implies milling. In 1180 Malcolm Earl of Atholl granted Moulin church to Dunfermline Abbey. There the *Caisteal Dubh* or Black Castle was built in the 13th or 14th century, preceding the chartering in 1511 of a burgh of barony with the Gaelic name of *Balnakeilly*. Moulin kirk was rebuilt in 1613, a parish school was started in 1649 and the *Moulin Arms* inn dates from 1695. In 1727 General Wade's soldiers constructed a military road on the northern side of the valley, ultimately leading to Inverness. The Roy map also showed that in the 1750s another road of sorts led eastwards into Strathardle. Pitlochry and Moulin were tiny clachans, north of which near the confluence of the River Garry was the mansion of *'Fasklie'*.

**Linen and Drinks Industry – Rather Over the Top**: In the late 18th century the main local activity was flax growing and spinning, serviced in 1790 by seven lint mills. Both Pitlochry and Moulin had annual fairs in 1797; until around that period the yarn was mainly sold at the Moulin February fair. By 1793 there were 30 licensed victuallers and two licensed stills in Moulin parish; the *Blair Atholl* distillery at Pitlochry was officially founded in 1798, though parts date back to the early 18th century; its water was drawn from the Allt Dour (Otter Burn). In 1799 Heron mentioned Moulin as a *"village"*. The area had seven licensed distilleries (mostly short-lived) in the early 1800s!

**Roads, Coaches, Mails and Gas**: In 1803 Dorothy Wordsworth crossed the Bridge of Garry but was unable to obtain accommodation at what appeared to be the only inn at *'Fascally'*, the landlady having been *"sitting up the whole of one or two nights before on account of a fair"*; this was evidently the drunken September fair at Blair. Her experience showed that the roads north of Dunkeld were not properly maintained. During the next few years under Telford's direction the Commissioners greatly improved the roads, and in 1808 it was possible to start a stage coach route from Perth to Inverness via Pitlochry, which had a post office by 1821; however, it was 1830 before the North mails went that way. Posts encouraged literacy: separate schools for boys and girls were started in the 1820s. There must have been a gasworks by 1830, for in that year the *Star Inn* (later *Scotland's Hotel)* was connected.

**Whisky, Woollens, Tourism and Games**: The tiny Edradour distillery with its dam was created on the Duke of Atholl's estate at Moulin in the years 1825–37 by a farmers' co-operative, trading as John McGlashan & Co. In 1835 A & J Macnaughton set up water-powered mills, embracing all processes from raw wool to finished tweeds. *Fisher's Hotel* was opened as a coaching establishment in 1839, the year that a brewery was started; this lasted only until about 1870. In 1852 Highland games were established, one of the first following the lifting of the Hanoverian ban on Highland culture in 1831.

**Royalty and Robbery on the Railway**: From 1863 Pitlochry was served by a station on the new main line of the Inverness & Perth Junction (soon Highland). This not only enabled Queen Victoria to travel to Blair Castle in its first week of service, but also allowed the Blair Atholl distillery's owner in 1873 – one Connacher – to flee by train after evading excise duty! Wordie & Co operated a small rail to road cartage depot (still open in 1946). The great Atholl Palace Hydropathic establishment was opened in 1878, but when Barnard visited Pitlochry in 1886 he thought of it as a *"village"*; *Fisher's Hotel* was *"splendid"*, though its 150 beds were *"in summer crowded to overflowing"*. The Blair Atholl distillery – under new management! – had recently been enlarged, and used Orkney peat in the annual production of 275,000 litres of Highland malt whisky. The tiny Edradour distillery produced a mere 30,000 litres of the same genre; at that time apparently all went for blending, but it must have been good stuff to survive the traumas to come.

**Mass Tourism, and Stillborn Pioneer in Hydro Power**: The large *Pitlochry Hydro* opened in 1890; Murray rated it *"very fair"* in 1894, as were *Scotland's Hotel* and *Craigower*, but *Fisher's* was *"excellent"*, the *Atholl Hydro "good"* and the *Moulin Hotel "very comfortable"*. Almost 1150 people were resident in the area in 1891, but according to Murray Pitlochry had *"long been a favourite summer resort"*. Although it had grown considerably in the recent past, with its six hotels, three banks and *"numerous lodgings"*, it was still called a *"village"*. By 1895 Faskally, rebuilt as a Victorian mansionhouse, stood in extensive policies beside the Tummel/Garry confluence, below which was the Port na Craig ferry, replaced by a suspension bridge in 1913. In 1896 the Pitlochry Gas Company commissioned a feasibility study for hydro-electric power from the Falls of Tummel, but did not act on the favourable report. However, Pitlochry continued to grow: its golf club, founded in 1909, laid out a rocky 18-hole hillside course, and in 1912 the first telephones were connected. Eventually in 1930 a public electricity supply arrived, and the *Regal Cinema* opened in 1935.

**Power Stations, Lochs and More Tourists**: As part of the North of Scotland Hydro-Electric Board's Tummel/Garry project of 1945–52, the level of Loch Tummel was raised 3.5 m by the 20 m tall Clunie Dam, 3 km upstream from Faskally. From there a head of 53 m of water fell through a 3 km tunnel to feed the three 20,000 kw machines of the Clunie Power Station. This stood at the head of the artificial Loch Faskally, which was itself impounded by the 16.5 m tall Pitlochry dam, built close to the town in 1947–50. There all the water from 1800 square kilometres is fed through two 7500 kw machines, with a head of 15 m *(see Olivier)*. It is accompanied by a highly visible salmon ladder, and originally had a control room and the Board's central freshwater fisheries laboratory. Pitlochry became a burgh in 1947, and in 1952 had 22 hotels, including the Victorian mansion which had become the *Pine Trees*; all greatly benefited from the scenic effect of the new loch, the forest walks around it, and the salmon ladder and displays in the power station. By 1980 these latter drew 350,000 visitors a year; however the cinema closed about that time, being converted into the Atholl Leisure Centre.

**Pitlochry Festival Theatre**: The original Festival Theatre promoted by John Stewart was opened in a tent in 1951; this blew down in 1953 and was replaced by a *"glorified shed"* in the town in 1953–54. Erection of the new 530-seat *Festival Theatre* on the west bank of the river in 1978–81 was aided by a large EEC Regional Development Fund grant, its first made to a theatre.

*Macnaughton's woollens shop on Pitlochry's main street. The firm started in the town with water-powered mills in 1832, producing quality tweed clothing. The shop continues to sell the same kinds of merchandise, but production is now at the Inveralmond industrial estate, on the outskirts of Perth.* *(Macnaughton's)*

**Distilleries Old and Reinstated**: The Blair Atholl distillery, owned by Mackenzie & Sons of Edinburgh, had been long closed when Arthur Bell & Sons of Perth bought it in 1933. It stayed shut until modernisation enabled a restart in 1949, a dark grains plant being added to convert its waste into cattle food. In 1990 it was in full production under United Distillers. Meantime Edradour still used a water-wheel until about 1950 *(see Hay & Stell)*; from about 1980 it supplied a ten-year-old single malt whisky. By 1989 its malt was milled at Aberlour and it had the last working refrigerator by Morton. It claimed to be the world's smallest distillery, with only three workers; but in 1990 two more were taken on to staff its new visitor centre by its new owners, the House of Campbell. Faskally House in its 27ha grounds was taken over as an outdoor centre by Glasgow City Council prior to 1975, and then used by Strathclyde Regional Council. Macnaughton's ceased to produce woollens in Pitlochry in 1980, in favour of a mill in Aberdeenshire, while retaining their original retail shop. In 1981 there were about 30 hotels in Pitlochry, and two large touring caravan sites.

**Benefits of the Bypass; Hotels Aplenty**: Chaotic summer conditions in the narrow main street were greatly improved by the opening of the A9 bypass south-west of the town in the early 1980s. In 1991 there were 2541 residents, with an affluent retired emphasis. Heartland FM, opened in Pitlochry in 1992, claimed to be Britain's smallest independent local radio station. In 1993 Hydro-Electric – whose operations HQ was previously in Fonab House beside the dam – opened a new centre at Clunie power station, controlling all their 25 southern area power stations. The well-used railway station keeps its crossing loop; a supermarket is now open. By 1993 Bonskeid House was a YMCA conference centre, one of two in Scotland and able to house 115 participants. The Faskally Outdoor Centre was closed in that year, but sold in 1996 to the Christian Youth Centre Trust for reopening. Pitlochry's (junior, S1-S4) High School has only about 160 pupils.

**Accommodation Aplenty**: At Moulin the mansion called *Baledmund Castle* may be rented, and the historic *Moulin Arms* has a brewery attached. Pitlochry itself has dozens of hotels, of all sizes, many of them of long standing; in all over 7000 beds are available for tourists. The youth hostel is open all year round, and pottery features large on the tourist signs.

## PITMEDDEN & Udny — Map 10, C2

***Aberdeenshire village & hamlet,*** *pop. 1100+* — OS 38: NJ 8827

Some 9km west of Ellon on the rolling plateau of Formartine stood the old parish church of Udny. The tall keep of the 15th century Udny Castle stood nearby; 1km north of that was the estate of Pitmedden with its Pictish placename, and 1km farther north-west was the granite tower of Tolquhon Castle, built for the Forbes family in the early 15th century. Tolquhon was enlarged in 1584–89 to form a big courtyard mansion with a highly decorated gatehouse; it was emphasised on the map made by Robert Gordon about 1640, but eventually fell into ruin. Tiny symbols represented Udny, where a parish school was founded in 1614, and Pitmedden, where from 1675 a great formal garden was created round Pitmedden House by Sir Alexander Seton.

**Tracks, Roads, Railway and Facilities**: The Roy map made about 1750 showed tracks crossing in the vicinity of the hamlets around Udny, leading to Ellon, Newburgh, Old Meldrum, Old Aberdeen and northwards by Tanglandford; proper roads were built during the next century. The Formartine & Buchan Railway, later part of the Great North of Scotland, was opened in 1861 with a station named Udny some 3km south-east of the Kirkton; a hamlet had grown there by 1894. Udny, later called Udny Green, then comprised the old castle, church, an inn (later the *Udny Arms Hotel*) and little else. Pitmedden House had given rise to a hamlet, a church, an inn and (at some distance) a post office. By 1955 there was also the *Station Hotel* and a post office at Udny Station. In 1951 nearly 1300 people lived in the area, most of them in Pitmedden, which had the facilities of a small village. Both the schools at Udny Green and Pitmedden then had secondary classes; these were all removed to Ellon by 1976.

**Garden made Public, and North Sea Commuters**: In 1952 Pitmedden House, its garden and the 40ha Pitmedden estate were presented to the National Trust for Scotland (NTS), the garden being remade to become a substantial tourist attraction, best in late summer. Beeching closed the railway to passengers in 1965, but for a few years around 1967 a quarry was open between Pitmedden and its post office. The decline in farm labour needs had reduced the area's population to a thousand by 1971. Then came North Sea oil developments; new housing estates were built between the garden and Pitmedden, which though retaining only the facilities of a small village, had 1082 people in 1991, a youthful dormitory in character. The railway vanished in 1979; its small erstwhile settlement is still called Udny Station, but the actual station site has been taken for more housing. By 1985 the NTS had created a Museum of Farming Life, and Tolquhon Castle was an ancient monument; both are open to the public. Still more housing has been built at each of the three settlements, all of which have pubs, and the railway formation has become a long distance footpath, the Formartine & Buchan Way.

## PITTENWEEM & Kellie

**Map 6, C4**

***Fife coastal village,*** *pop. 1650*

OS 59: NO 5502

In the early seventh century, St Fillan lived in a cave in the cliffs in the *East Neuk* (corner) of Fife, becoming the abbot of a Christian community. Chambers wrote that he *"afterwards retired, for the sake of more perfect seclusion, to the wild vale near Tyndrum which still bears his name"*. The original name *Pitnaweem* means *'Place of the Cave'* in Gaelic; St Fillan's cave can still be seen. Pittenweem Priory was founded on the cliff top over the cave in 1141 as an offshoot from St Andrews; the Cluniac monks of May Isle soon transferred to this establishment. Kellie in the rural parish of Carnbee some 4km inland had a thanage from about the 11th century, and Kellie Castle (which dates back to 1360) was mainly built around 1600. The estate of Balcaskie, 3km north-west of the town, was owned by the Strangs in 1362.

**Burgh built on Fish Galore**: One mile offshore was the rich fishing ground of the Traith or Fluke Hole. In 1526 Pittenweem became a burgh of barony promoted by the abbot. This justified the building of a church in 1532, and chartering as a Royal Burgh in 1541 led to the construction of a harbour which for many years did Scotland's largest trade in cod and its second largest in herrings. Pittenweem, which had not previously figured as a port, appeared in the 1542 returns with a yield of some 5% of Scottish Customs (a figure probably including Anstruther and other minor ports); but it made little or no tax contribution as a burgh. Harbour works have been carried out intermittently ever since. The Reformation destroyed the priory church, but much of the priory escaped, since at that time it was in the care of a Royal bastard. The church was rebuilt in 1588. No trade figures are available for Pittenweem as such until 1579, but its trade was then rising, and by 1590 the East Neuk ports in general were doing relatively well; a parish school was founded in 1592.

**War Losses leave Boats Rotting**: James Gordon's detailed map made about 1642 named *'Pitnaweem'* as a substantial place between Anstruther and St Monans. In 1639 it ranked a pitiful 44th among Scottish burghs in tax yield, or about 1% of Edinburgh's trade. Chambers noted that *"between the years 1639 and 1645, it lost no fewer than thirteen sail of large vessels, which were either wrecked or taken by the enemy"*. Over 100 local men were killed at the Battle of Kilsyth in 1645, with the result that 17 of the remaining boats rotted at their moorings. However in 1655 two large vessels of 80 and 100 tons were still locally owned.

**Architecture, Post, Malting and Brewing**: Balcaskie was the birthplace in 1630 of Sir William Bruce, who became the Royal architect and designed the present Balcaskie House, built about 1675, plus Kinross House and part of Hopetoun House. John May's chart of about 1680 showed two breakwaters at Pittenweem. Defoe mentioned the Pittenweem of the 1720s as a *"small town"*. In 1736 there was an inn in Marygate, a post office was open by 1740, and the harbour's main outer pier had been constructed by 1745. By that time mills had been erected to grind malt, implying a brewing industry (the old granary still standing at the harbour could be of 17th or early 18th century date). Roy's map made about 1750 indicated a nucleated settlement, the harbour, and the coast road with its characteristic inland fork to Colinsburgh.

**Coal and Clever Clocks**: Roy did not show evidence of mining; however, coal was mined at Coal Farm on the cliffs to the west, at least during the period 1764–1794; further harbour works were undertaken in 1771 to facilitate coal exports, though the industry cannot have been on a large scale and is little known *(but see Largoward)*. The clockmaking genius John Smith was in business in Pittenweem from 1770 to 1814, producing high-class clocks with multiple functions – a remarkable skill for so small a place. But it was not actually remote: by 1797 Pittenweem was a post town with a daily service, and also readily accessible by sea to the packets sailing between Leith and London. Heron in 1799 thought there were *"upwards of 1100 inhabitants"*. After Smith's death his apprentice George Lumsden and his son of the same name carried on the business into mid century, making conventional long-case clocks.

**New Harbour and Railway**: Chambers concluded in 1827 that the town had formerly been more important: *"it was a great fishing station before the failure of that branch of employment on this coast. The present harbour is a modern and extensive work"*. Map comparisons certainly show great changes to the harbour around 1830, when a further pier and wharf were completed, and the western dock was added in 1855. In 1847–50 there was actually a local newspaper, the *Pittenweem Register*. From 1863 a station 500m inland on the meandering Leven & East of Fife Railway served Pittenweem on the way to Anstruther; but the railway made little difference to the village and did not reach the harbour. Most of the fishing was then based on Anstruther. Sir Robert Lorimer, born at Kellie Castle in 1864, became a famous architect and restorer – including his own castle – and designed the Scottish National War Memorial in Edinburgh Castle and also the spectacular gates for Dunfermline's Pittencrieff Park. The 1891 population of Pittenweem was just under 2000, but in 1894 Murray

*Pittenweem harbour and houses (in 1980). Dating originally from the 16th century, this has for many years been Fife's main fishing port, successively re-equipped whilst still retaining its picturesque character.* (RS)

described it as *"a poor place"*. At that time the tiny Kellie Colliery was open between the castle and Newton. In 1895 boat-builders Fulton of Pittenweem built a steam line-fishing vessel.

**West Coast Fishermen ring the Changes**: Little development except for housing occurred early in the 20th century. However, in the 1920s Pittenweem played host to West Coast boats using ring nets and then adopted the technique. After the second war Pittenweem's snug though tricky harbour recovered to become Fife's premier fishing port. Most of the Anstruther fishing fleet moved to Pittenweem, where a new fish-selling shed had been erected by 1955, plus ice-making and fuelling facilities. In most respects it remained a village, with about 1650 people in 1951 and apparently no hotels, though there was a swimming pool and until about 1970 the 300-seat *Picture House*; the priory formed a minor focus of attraction.

**No Trains, but Fishing Harbour Rejuvenated**: In 1965–66 Beeching closed the railway; the tiny station became a riding school. In 1972 the town council claimed Pittenweem as *"a popular summer resort"*, and two small hotels and an inland caravan and camping site were open by 1977. In 1991, 1561 people lived locally; many owned their homes outright as in most fishing ports, but there was a large elderly element. Further harbour development was carried out in 1993–95 when the east breakwater was lengthened by some 90m, using concrete sections cast at Leith and moved across the Firth by barge. The ancient Granary was altered to contain a new Norwegian ice plant and the harbour offices. The fish-selling shed was replaced on the same site by a new fish market, including chilled storage. Catches still include prawns, scallops, haddock, cod, whiting and lemon sole, and the Fishermen's Mutual Association and a chandlery remain active. Near Kellie Castle, a National Trust for Scotland property with a fine garden, is the hamlet of Arncroach, which still has a post office.

## PLAINS & Ballochney

**Map 16, A3**

***E. Lanarkshire villages,*** *pop. 2500* — OS 64: NS 7966

The Ballochney Railway was opened in 1828, to carry coal from Ballochney colliery some 4km east of Airdrie, through the area north of the North Calder Water, to Kipps on the early Monkland & Kirkintilloch Railway. In 1862 the Glasgow extension of the Edinburgh & Bathgate Railway was opened, linking the head of the valley with Airdrie and Coatbridge; on this line near Ballochney was a station named Plains. By 1899 Plains – which had a population of about 900 – had an inn, smithy and mill, and also the emparked mansionhouse of Easter Moffat; at Drumshangie 2 km to the north was another inn. By 1951 Plains had been greatly expanded with council housing to about 2400 people, served by two primary schools, a hotel and post office. The station was closed about 1954, by which time the mines had vanished. Barbleus Forge, the last water-powered shovel-mill in Scotland, closed in the early 1960s. However, by 1988 opencast coal mining was in full swing east of Drumshangie, 2 km to the north. In 1991 Plains still contained 2581 people, male unemployment was 30%. In 1992 the extraction of a further 3 million tonnes of opencast coal was proposed at Drumshangie; this work continued through the 90s.

## PLEAN & Cowie

**Map 16, B2**

***Stirlingshire villages,*** *pop. 3600* — OS 65: NS 8387

The Romans laid out a road to the north through the undulating open country between Larbert and Stirling, but the actual roadway was evidently not well built, for it was not shown on Pont's map made about 1600. There the 14th century keep of Plean Castle appeared as *'Plaine'*, while *'Achinbowy'* – an estate with a mill on its eponymous burn about 6km south-east of Stirling burgh – was Auchenbowie, known in medieval times for its coal mine; for centuries this supplied fuel to the town. Easter and Wester *'Cowy'* also stood in this rather sparsely settled area. Roy's map, made about 1754, showed a winding road linking Stirling with Larbert. In 1842 three separate coal undertakings worked around West Plean: the Auchenbowie mine had 56 workers including young children, as did the so-called Bannockburn pit which employed 300 people. The Plean Muir pit had 93 workers, 35 of them under 18, working in wet conditions underground for over twelve hours a day.

**Railways and Quarrying**: The Scottish Central Railway (later Caledonian – CR) opened in 1848. The Plean Mills quarry immediately requested a siding, becoming a major source of coarse but durable building stone, used as far afield as London by 1867; it may have been the source of the *'Bannockburn'* stone used in the late 1870s to build Dundee's Tay Bridge station. Dunmore quarry raised sandstone by 1855; it employed 55 men in 1895 but closed about 1912. Meantime in 1850 the South Alloa Harbour branch-line was opened; near the adjacent ferry – which the CR opened in 1865 – was a tileworks. In 1885 a CR branch line from Dunmore Junction on the South Alloa line to Alloa was opened across the Forth and the ferry was closed. In the 1890s the only settlement of note was the hamlet of Plean with its church, post office and smithy, east of the policies of Plean House.

**Deep Mining and Population Growth**: The second *'Bannockburn'* Colliery, almost 300m deep, was sunk at the appropriately named *Sink* at Cowie by the Carron Company. Opened in 1894, its *'Bannockburn Steam'* became a well-known coal, and there were other minor pits in the area. Plean passenger station was opened about 1900. By 1901 Plean had over 600 people, and Cowie – which was merely two miners' rows in 1895 – almost 850. The big Cowie pit sunk at Hillhead 2 km east of Cowie employed some 1200 men in 1913, but in the slump of 1934 less than 300 were still at work there. By 1924 a post office had been provided at Cowie, whose population was rising, to nearly 2700 in 1931 and 3000 in 1951. Meantime a settlement at East Plean – just north of old Plean – had over 1400 people in 1931, rising by 1951 to nearly 1900. Bannockburn Colliery was working at a loss in 1951 (as part of the NCB Alloa Area) sending coal by rail to Carnock coke ovens; it was therefore closed, replaced from 1954 by a small drift mine. Plean colliery was still at work in 1955, but Plean station and the Hillhead mine vanished around 1960, and by 1971 all the mines had closed and their railway links had been lifted.

**Timber Products, Motorway and Quarrying**: Plean's population peaked at over 2000 in 1971, then falling, while Cowie reduced slowly, due to the opening on the colliery site of Scottish Timber Products' factory around 1972. It became bankrupt and was closed in 1977 with the loss of 400 jobs, though 150 were restored by the purchasers, Bison Werke of Germany who had installed the original machinery. A new road bridge spanned the railway nearby, and by 1981 the M9 motorway passed close to Plean. By 1981 Cowie had attained the facilities of a small village. A new Dunmore quarry was opened in 1985 at Castleton (3km to the east) by Scottish Natural Stones, to raise Carboniferous sandstone for building; this provided a number of local jobs. Plean's population was 1670 in 1991, and Cowie's was down to 2050. By 1993 the grounds of Plean House had become a country park.

**Fibreboard and Formaldehyde**: By 1985 the Cowie factory had re-emerged as Caber Fibreboard, still in German ownership; the firm also had a branch in Irvine. In 1990 it was alleged that toxic formaldehyde resins had been dumped on an unfenced part of the site; but the expanding firm had lately invested in a new drying plant and aimed to cut its emissions. In 1994 the internationally owned Blagden Chemicals of Haverhill, makers of chemicals and resins, also had a plant at Cowie – producing amino formaldehyde resins! The mooted reopening of a rail passenger station at Cowie has not yet happened. Both villages still have primary schools, post offices and libraries; West Plean House farm now offers accommodation.

## PLOCKTON

**Map 8, B3**

***Wester Ross village**, pop. 360* — OS 24: NG 8033

On the south shore of Loch Carron in Wester Ross, a beautiful mountain-girt sea inlet, is a natural harbour sheltered by a low peninsula in the form of a round mass (in Gaelic *ploc*). Roy's survey of about 1750 showed little in the area save woods. The village of Plockton was founded in the late 18th century as a crofting and fishing community, with a baronial burgh charter from 1808. A lighthouse (now disused) was built on the offshore rock of Eilean a'Chait. The mansion known as Duncraig Castle was built in 1866 for Sir Alexander Matheson to designs by Alexander Ross. Plockton lacked land access until about 1897, when the Highland Railway extended its line from Strome Ferry to Kyle. A public station was provided at Plockton, and a private station 2 km to the east served Duncraig Castle. The castle was bequeathed to the education authority by the Hamiltons about 1946, used as a secondary school and later as a college; from 1949 Duncraig station became public. The population of Plockton in 1951 was about 375, with very nearly the facilities of a typical village.

**Television boosts Tourism**: By 1953 the Balmacara Estate, including open land around attractive Plockton, had been acquired by the National Trust for Scotland. Plockton Aerodrome was opened west of the village about 1970, but other new development was restricted. In 1980, although a second hotel was open – helping to exploit sea angling – the facilities were those of a small village. The resident population in 1991 was 364. In 1988 the college was closed and the *'castle'* was left empty. In 1994 an air ambulance was based at Plockton, and by 1997 the new Plockton High School for some 300 pupils had been built beside the station; a centre for excellence in traditional music has now been attached to the school. The making of the popular television series *Hamish Macbeth* in Plockton in the mid to late 1990s injected some much needed money into the local economy during filming, and led to a dramatic increase in tourism. Facilities include the *Highland Farm* (a tourist draw), shops, post, and petrol; 3 or 4 trains call daily each way. Small hotels include the *Haven* and the *Plockton Inn*, and there is a backpackers' hostel.

## PLUSCARDEN

**Map 9, C3**

***Moray location / abbey**, pop. 100* — OS 28: NJ 1457

In 1230 King Alexander II chose a site for a Valliscaulian Priory in the remote valley of the Black Burn 10km south-west of Elgin, within Pluscarden Forest, a royal hunting preserve. The priory became a Benedictine community in 1454, but was ruined as a result of the Reformation. Pont's late 16th century map showed a mill and small adjoining places, but even Roy's map made about 1750 indicated a trackless area. Roads were later built, and a church, primary school and post office opened near the ruins, part of which had been adapted as a village dance hall before five energetic Benedictine monks from Prinknash Abbey in Gloucestershire reactivated the priory in 1945–48. The population was then around 375 and falling. Abbey status was granted in 1974, and by 1994 there were 24 monks and a new visitors' wing for retreats. The quiet farming valley is now surrounded by coniferous forests.

## POLLOKSHAWS & Pollok

**Map 15, C5**

***S-W. suburbs of Glasgow*** — OS 64: NS 5661

The north bank of the White Cart Water, some 6km south-west of Glasgow Cross, was the site of the first Pollok House, built around 1500. Timothy Pont surveyed the area around 1600, noting both *'Pookshawes'*, with its river bridge, and also the nearby Auldhouse Bridge across its eponymous burn. Some 1.5km north of Pollokshaws bridge stood the emparked *'Hags'*

Castle, which had been built in 1585 for Sir John Maxwell of Pollok. A replacement Pollok House (perhaps designed by William Adam) was built for the Maxwells of Haggs in 1747–52, much of the area between the river and Barrhead Road being within its vast policies. In 1742 Alex Ingram & Co set up a large bleachfield and calico printworks, around which a substantial village had grown by about 1754; by then Pollokshaws bridge carried the *'Cart Road to Irvine'*, from which the Stewarton road forked.

**Printfield, Leather and Cotton**: Haggs Castle was abandoned after the building of Pollok House, and became ruinous in the late 18th century, about the time that Robert Dunmore of Ballindalloch built the Pollokshaws printfield *(see also Balfron)*. Leather was being *"shamoyed"* in a Pollokshaws mill by 1782. A cotton mill was opened in 1792; in 1799 Heron mentioned *"the town of Pollockshaws, of considerable extent, and chiefly possessed by manufacturers. Here are two cotton-mills, a printfield, and several bleachfields"*. Another new cotton factory, built in 1810 with 200 improved power-looms, was slow to thrive. The extensive Newlandsfield print and bleach works worked from about 1812, and Pollokshaws became a burgh of barony in 1813; by about 1825 it was served by a penny post from Glasgow, and Langside also had a post office from 1845.

**Railways, Industry and Education**: From 1848 the Glasgow, Barrhead & Neilston Railway served the area with a station at Pollokshaws (later named Pollokshaws West by the Caledonian Railway (CR)); in 1866 this became the junction for the new Busby Railway. About 1851 R Cogan founded the Auldfield Weaving Mills, which were still making cotton goods on power looms half a century later under Lowndes, Macdonald & Co. About 1858 the Coustonholm Weaving Company also built a large factory. In the 1850s a large bakery opened at nearby Crossmyloof, an old name meaning *'Cross my palm'*; in 1888 a station was provided nearby. Pollok Academy opened in Pollokshaws Road in 1856 and was extended in 1874–75.

**Hydro-Electricity, Engineering, Paper and Cloth**: As the trees matured, the Pollok estate built a dam on the White Cart to retain a head of water for its own sawmill, powered at first by a water wheel and from 1888 by a Holyoake turbine; an estate hydro-electricity station was soon constructed alongside by Carrick & Ritchie of Edinburgh. About 1874 John Dalglish founded the Avenue Ironworks, specialising in textile finishing machinery, and in 1898–99 A & W Dalglish erected the West of Scotland Boiler Works nearby. About 1889 Haythorn & Stuart built the Eastwood Engine Works and Brassfoundry, and the Riverbank Works for bleaching and finishing soon followed. A paper mill operated for some ten years around 1885; reopened about 1900, it only made wrapping paper, and closed about 1930. David Barbour & Co built the Renfield Weaving Works from about 1891 when the population was 10,400, including Mansewood. In 1889 William Yuill started one of the earliest wholesale electrical goods dealerships, but one source states it was not until 1905 that a public electricity supply was available in the area! There was also a beetling works, destroyed by a German air raid in the early 1940s when making blackout cloth.

**Cathcart Circle, Suburbs, Golf and Trams**: The CR's Cathcart Circle suburban railway was completed in 1894, with stations at Langside, Shawlands and Maxwell Park, where Craigholme School for Girls was founded in 1894. Robert Miller designed a large YMCA at 320–328 Pollokshaws Road, built in 1894–96, and Sherbrooke Castle, now a hotel, was built in 1896 – both of red sandstone. By 1894 the area north of Newlands Road was full of villas; Newlands south of Pollokshaws became more affluent than Langside to the east, which lay downwind of the local factories. Haggs Castle was rebuilt as flats in the late 19th century. Three golf clubs laid out 18-hole courses in the parkland to the west: Pollok (1892), Cowglen (1906) and Haggs Castle (1910). By then the railways faced severe competition from the city's frequent electric trams, whose carefully detailed depot for 200 cars, the largest on the system, was built in 1909 at Newlands.

**Pollokshaws in Glasgow: enter Hutchesons**: About 1907 an old mill beside Shaw Bridge was reconstructed as the Bridge Turbine Works of John Macdonald & Co (founded 1882), and about 1914 came the Viking Thread Mills of George Melville Ltd, which worked until 1969. Pollokshaws was absorbed by Glasgow in 1912; further suburban housing was built between the wars. Private and later local authority estates at Auldhouse, Mansewood and Eastwood had brought a vast combined population of some 100,000 by 1951. In the 1950s Shawlands' *Elephant Cinema* and *Cameo Ballroom* were under the same management. The independent Hutchesons Grammar School, founded in Glasgow in 1641, moved from Hutchesontown to Crossmyloof in the late 1950s. Various local centres had been built, while Crossmyloof had acquired an ice skating and

*Pollokshaws Burgh Hall, built in 1895–98, largely with money provided by local landowner Sir John Stirling Maxwell of Pollok. The architect, R Rowand Anderson, took its inspiration from the 17th century Old College of Glasgow building. Pollokshaws was a burgh from 1813 to 1912, when it was incorporated into Glasgow.* (JRH)

curling rink. John Macdonald & Co moved to East Kilbride in the 1950s.

**Electric Trains and Shopping Precinct**: The Cathcart Circle railway was electrified in 1962, the year that the tramways were abandoned; Newlands depot became a bus garage in 1961. In 1967 Pollok House was donated to the city council by Mrs Maxwell MacDonald. Pollok Academy, like most of the old village, was demolished in 1968 and replaced by flats, including tower blocks. By 1972 the new *Tinto Firs Hotel* was in business, and there were many others. A sub-regional shopping centre had emerged around Shawlands, where by 1973 there was a modern precinct of over 5000 m² with a Co-op department store, a large Woolworths and the 20-room *Shawlands Hotel*. The Shawbridge arcade was itself a sizeable shopping centre. Haggs Castle was converted from flats into a museum, open by 1980, but by 1981 the area's population had sunk to under 85,000. By 1979 Arcol Thermoplastics, (a John Waddington subsidiary by 1989) was producing packaging, and Eclipse made window blinds; in 1990 they gained a Queen's Award for export.

**The Burrell Collection**: In 1983 the City Council's striking building housing the Burrell Collection – a gallery cum museum of the finest works of international art, gifted by Glaswegian Sir William Burrell – was opened in the parkland of the Pollok estate to the west. By 1990 it drew nearly 900,000 people a year (Scotland's second most popular free attraction), helping to improve greater Glasgow's image. By 1988 the Crossmyloof Ice Rink at Newlands was derelict, but was replaced in 1992 by a new Safeway superstore. In 1989 Yuill's celebrated a century in the electrical business. The former YMCA closed about 1990 and stood derelict in 1995, but about then the *'A'* listed Camphill House was saved for posterity. Claremont Garments, a branch of Courtaulds Textiles, until then a major supplier to Marks & Spencer, employed 700 people before closure in 1996.

**Schools and Hotels; the Arcade Improved**: Hutchesons Grammar School has about 1870 co-ed day pupils, the independent Craigholme School at Maxwell Park has 470 (all the 280 senior pupils being girls), Hillpark Secondary has 750 pupils, Shawlands Academy 1420, and Notre Dame RC High School 830 (girls only). The Shawlands Arcade shopping centre was radically improved with a glass canopy added in 1996; its hotel was demolished, enabling 9000 m² of shopping space to be added. Hotels include the long-established *Sherbrooke Castle* and the modern *Tinto Firs*.

## POLMAISE & Fallin — Map 16, B1

***Villages s-e. of Stirling,*** *pop. 2500* — OS 57: NS 8391

Polmaise was a long-established but historically little-known estate on the flat carselands some 5 km east of Stirling, south of the tidal River Forth. The word *poll*, derived from the Gaelic for mud or mire, means a creek or landing place. At some time an unauthorised market or fair was held at Polmaise in defiance of the privileges of Stirling. Pont's map made about 1600 showed Wester and Easter *'Powmais'* on either side of the tidal mouth of the winding course of the Bannock Burn; some way upstream there stood a mill. Easter Powmais was already emparked, the mansionhouse standing close to a great meander in the Forth, on the promontory east of which was *'Benteith'*, later strangely corrupted to Bandeath (pronounced *'Bandeeth'*). A new mansion of (Easter) Polmaise, built in 1697 for John Murray, stood on a spur from the 1750s road linking St Ninians to Throsk, later linked to Airth. A sandstone quarry on the estate was the likely source of stone for the new Polmaise Castle, built in 1865–66 for another John Murray; the quarry employed 38 in 1897, slowly fading to close in the 1930s.

**New Colliery, Fallin Village and Naval Ordnance**: A new colliery was sunk at Fallin from 1894; until then the area was wholly rural and the road from Broadleys to Stirling was quite extraordinarily winding. In 1904 major new shafts were sunk for coal at Bandeath and Polmaise No.1 collieries, linked by a mineral railway to the Larbert–Stirling line north of Bannockburn station. Initially no houses were built for the numerous miners, many of whom had to commute from the overcrowded tenements of Stirling. However, by 1924 a new village named Fallin had been built along the roadside near the pit; this already had a school, post and telegraph office, and the road to Stirling had been improved. Soon after 1924 Polmaise No.2 pit was developed at Broadleys, 2.5 km west of Fallin, whose 1931 population was about 1300. The various mines were a large operation, and by 1951 Fallin had nearly 3000 people – but the facilities of a tiny village; despite the population growth, it remained excessively dependent on Bannockburn and Stirling. By then the Royal Naval Armaments Depot (RNAD) – sited at Bandeath Farm – occupied a site of some 280 ha with a pier on the Forth to the east, its regularly spaced sheds probably built during the 1939–45 war. A security veil was drawn over it until 1978 when it was closed and the 150 remaining jobs were lost.

**Mining Peak, Closure and Aftermath**: Polmaise No.3/4 colliery was working in 1953, and the National Coal Board then hoped to supply Kincardine power station. The combined pits' deep Limestone Coal Group seams failed after 1955 but production continued in the Upper Hirst. Meantime the parklands of Polmaise House became mere farmland. By 1971 the population of Fallin was nearing 3300, but with the closure of Bandeath and the rundown of the colliery to only about 200 jobs by 1978 a decline set in. However, the former RNAD became the Bandeath Industrial Estate. Polmaise Colliery was closed following the disastrous miners' strike of 1984, but reclamation work continued until 1987. By 1991 only 2479 people lived in Fallin; 82% of the households still occupied public housing, over half had no car. Fallin still has a post office, primary school, library and pub.

## POLMONT, Redding & Shieldhill — Map 16, B2

***Central town / villages,*** *pop. 20,000* — OS 65: NS 9277

Mumrills, a turf-walled Roman fort, was built on a knoll above the Westquarter Burn around 140 AD. At 2.6 ha it was the most extensive on the Antonine Wall which was built soon afterwards; this did not consistently follow the high ground overlooking the inner Firth of Forth east of Falkirk. The fort commander's timber *praetorium* was among the principal buildings which were reconstructed in stone; a complex bath-house was added before the legions left. Timothy Pont's map of Stirlingshire made about 1600 showed *'Poumont'*, which became an abortive burgh of barony in 1611, and also Redding and West Quarter; it also indicated the incipient Linlithgow road – which had been firmed up by the mid 18th century. By then side roads served a sizeable hamlet at Tackreddings (later known as Redding) to the west, near the site of the Falkirk Tryst at Shieldhill; the interestingly named Ginkabout Mill stood on the carse near the crook of the River Avon.

**Coal, Canal, Brightons and the Railway**: In 1761 the Carron Company employed 34 people in coal mining – at Brightons (a hamlet 1 km south of Polmont), at Shieldhill and Croftandy. The Union Canal opened past Brightons in 1822 and seems to have stimulated growth; a post office was opened in 1824, and Redding colliery was at work in 1845. Meantime in 1842 the new Edinburgh & Glasgow Railway opened a station called Polmont at Brightons. This became the junction for the Stirlingshire & Midland Junction Railway, opened in 1850 through Falkirk Grahamston to Larbert and Stirling; engine sheds were built at Polmont. In 1877 Nobel Explosives built a detonator factory at Westquarter; this soon used mercury fulminate, made at Redding Moor from 1880, which polluted the Union Canal.

**Correction, Golf, Disaster and Decline**: In 1894 both Polmont and Brightons possessed post and telegraph offices; Redding and Redding Muirhead had post offices, and all except the last-named had inns. There was also what Murray described as an *"excellent Boys' Boarding School"*, which eventually became a Young Offenders Institution. Polmont golf club, formed in 1901, laid out a 9-hole course 1.5 km east of the station. By then and into the inter-war period various coal mines worked on the hillsides to the west in the areas of Maddiston, Redding Muir, and to within 3 km of Slamannan, with sporadic development at such places as Wallacestone and the hopefully named California, and with zig-zag mineral railways down to the main line. In 1916 a new depot for 40 engines replaced one at Bo'ness. The Redding Colliery was flooded in 1923 in a disaster which sadly cost 40 lives. A gasworks was provided in 1928, and Westquarter nearby was built as a planned village for miners in 1934. But by 1954 the detonator factory, all the pits and mineral lines had been closed, and about that time the locomotive shed also ceased to be used.

**Polmont's String of Dormitory Villages**: In the 1950s there was still a Saturday market at Polmont; though the straggle of development then centering on Brightons had a population nearing 3500, and there were four small hotels, it was in most respects only a cluster of villages. By 1965 it was growing together and being called a *"town"* by outsiders. Industries such as bacon curing were started, and there was a large haulier's depot at Maddiston, which had a school, post office and inn serving around 3000 people; Shieldhill had similar facilities to Maddiston. Grangemouth town council built a new municipal golf course just north of Polmont in 1973, and much new private housing was built in the 1970s as nearby Grangemouth's petrochemical industry grew. By 1980 the *Inchyra Grange Hotel* had been extended. Local residents then claimed that they lived in 'villages', not a 'town'; the combined local facilities were those of a large village.

**Greater Polmont's Skiing and Health Spa**: In 1991 the youngish population of the *'greater Polmont'* of the Census (including Lauriston, Maddiston and expanding Shieldhill) totalled about 20,100. By 1991 the Polmonthill Ski Centre had a dry ski slope, still a rare facility; also unusual in 1992 was the office of the Central Scotland Chamber of Commerce. By 1996 the Scottish Prison Service College was open at Newlands Road, Brightons, and in 1998 Polmont still had its Young Offenders Institution. A settlement for travelling folk has been built at Redding. The greatly extended *Inchyra Grange Hotel* now has over 100 rooms, indoor swimming and a health spa.

## POLWARTH & Marchmont — Map 3, B3

***Berwickshire hamlets,*** *pop. under 100 (area)* — OS 74: NT 7450

When Pont mapped Berwickshire around 1600, *'Polwoart'* Kirk – which stands in a hilly area some 5 km south-west of Duns – was accompanied by a mill and a parish school (founded in 1586); it was never a burgh of Barony. The kirk was rebuilt in 1703, and in 1750–54 William Adam probably built the nearby mansion of Marchmont House in its great park for the 3rd Earl of Marchmont. The Roy map of the 1750s showed *'Polwart'* as a scattered settlement on a track linking Duns with Hume Castle. Heron named it as a *"village"* in 1799, when the song *'Polwarth on the Green'* was already known. Chambers wrote in 1827 that Polwarth, *"rather a field powdered with cottages than a village, was once much more extensive – a place of some trade, especially in shoemaking, there having been at one time no fewer than fourteen, each of whom tanned his own leather. There is now scarcely a tradesman of any kind, the people all living by agriculture or by weaving"*. From 1863 to 1948 Marchmont had a station, originally provided by the Berwickshire Railway. The parish held 200 people in 1901, and in 1913–16 Marchmont House was much enlarged by Sir Robert Lorimer. Later the main road through Polwarth was given an 'A' classification. But by the 1950s, when the parish population was 115, the only facility recorded was a primary school. This had closed by 1976, and by 1991 the parish held just 92 people. By 1998 Marchmont House was a Sue Ryder home for people with disabilities.

## POOLEWE — Map 8, C1

***Small Wester Ross village,*** *pop. 150* — OS 19: NG 8580

Poolewe in Wester Ross stands at the sheltered head of Loch Ewe, where the short River Ewe drains Loch Maree to the sea. In the early 17th century Sir George Hay briefly had a charcoal-fuelled blast furnace here, the *'Red Smiddy'*. Roy's survey of about 1750 showed a trackless area, containing a cluster of clachans and a church. In 1756 Poolewe became the first organised terminal of a mail ferry service to Stornoway; but it was not classed as a post town. The mail was carried via Dingwall by a weekly foot runner, who was the sole regular link as late as 1797. Poolewe was also distinguished from most crofting townships by its seasonal cattle trade, which by 1803 was flourishing both by sea and along a network of drove roads *(see Haldane, 1952)*.

**From Heather Tracks to Steamers and Roads**: Steamers could operate longer mail routes to a reliable timetable, so Strome Ferry – which had a road by 1819 – was soon adopted as the steamer terminal. In 1827 the Parliamentary Commissioners of Highland Roads and Bridges therefore gave up their attempt to promote a road to Poolewe, which was left accessible only by pathways through the heather. After the potato famine of 1846 which caused great distress in remote western areas, the *'Destitution Road'* was built westwards from Braemore south of Ullapool via Little Loch Broom, and completed to Poolewe in 1851. This and a steamer service to Stornoway which commenced in 1849, at last enabled permanent development.

*Tuyere Arch, Red Smiddy Furnace, Poolewe (in 1980). This was a charcoal-fired blast furnace of the early 17th century, constructed by Sir George Hay under licence from James VI.* *(JRH)*

**Corsican Pines and Rhododendrons put in Trust**: From 1862 onwards the exotic Inverewe Gardens were gradually created on a rocky promontory for his own pleasure by Osgood Mackenzie. Pines were planted to give shelter, and soil was brought in using baskets. Wisely, the railways never ventured into such a sparsely peopled area, but by the 1890s there was a weekly steamer from Glasgow, and Poolewe's inn was rated *"comfortable"*. By the 1930s it was a hotel in a quiet, sheltered little village with a post office; in 1951 it had 130 residents, a primary school, 23-line telephone exchange and even a *'clothier'*. The National Trust for Scotland took over the Inverewe Gardens in 1952 and opened them to the public, providing catering facilities and attracting many tourists to the area, whose beauties made Poolewe widely known. By 1981 a caravan and camping site was available, but although the basic facilities remain open there has been relatively little new development. Hospitality is provided by the *Poolewe Hotel*, the *Pool House*, and B&Bs.

## PORT ASKAIG & Keills

**Map 4, B4**

***Village, Isle of Islay,*** *pop. 240*

OS 60: NR 4369

An ancient chapel was built on an 80m knoll at Keills, 2km inland from the Sound of Islay; by about 1600 an inn was open nearby. Port Askaig, perhaps named from Gaelic *Asgaidh*, a Gift, is a mere nick in the steep coastline nearby. Islay was Protestant by 1703, when Martin mentioned *St Columbus'* (sic) church at Port *'Escock'*. From 1767 there was a post office at Port Askaig. By 1786 this place was the terminus of two ferries, one – which still carried many cattle – crossing the 900m-wide Sound of Islay to Feolin in increasingly desolate Jura, and another making the lengthy open sea crossing to West Loch Tarbert. Steamers plied from Port Askaig to Glasgow, starting about 1821, with a weekly service to West Loch Tarbert from 1826.

**Caol Ila Distillery**: The Caol Ila *('Islay Narrows')* distillery was built a few hundred metres to the north in 1846 by Bulloch, Lade & Co of Glasgow. By 1886 the distillery had been much extended, and produced nearly 670,000 litres of Islay malt annually, not enough to meet demand for this *"favourite whisky"*. Barnard noted *"comfortable dwellings have been provided for the employees, forming quite a little village in themselves"*. The pier was served twice a week by MacBrayne steamers shipping whisky, and chartered vessels brought in barley. In 1896 a new Excise Officer's house was added, and around 1900 a large 3-storey bonded warehouse was built on the shore beside Caol Ila.

**Tourism, Life Saving and Ferry Competition**: Although by 1894 the main access to the island was at Port Ellen, tiny Port Askaig was grandly called a *"town"* by Murray, its hotel *"small, comfortable"*. The Islay lifeboat station was opened in 1934. The distillery was mothballed between 1930 and 1937, and by the 1950s Port Askaig was only a tiny village whose basic facilities served rather over 200 residents, the lifeboat station, and a passenger ferry to Feolin. From 1960 a MacBrayne's car ferry plied to West Loch Tarbert, and from about 1970 the Feolin ferry also carried cars. By 1972 two competing companies provided car ferries to Kennacraig or Tarbert West (both piers on West Loch Tarbert) as the main access to Islay; but the latter route had closed by 1980.

**Whisky by Pushbutton**: Though the Caol Ila distillery was completely rebuilt on a larger scale in 1972–74, slow population decline continued. By 1978, under DCL's subsidiary Bulloch, Lade & Co, it was a modernised push-button plant, using 18,000 tonnes of barley a year and supplying whisky for some 40 blends by way of container lorries and the ro-ro ferries. By then lobsters were being landed at Port Askaig, which (even including Bunnahabhain and Keills) had only 243 residents in 1991. Caol Ila distillery then produced a very dry single malt; it is now owned by UDV. The Port Askaig–Kennacraig vehicle ferries are the year-round access to the twin islands, also serving Colonsay in summer. The long-established *Port Askaig Hotel* serves the community, and the post office is still open.

## PORTAVADIE & Polphail

**Map 5, A5**

***Argyll village***

OS 62: NR 9269

In the first heady days of Scottish oil development in the 1970s, the deep water off the eastern shore of hitherto unspoiled Loch Fyne attracted the government to Portavadie *('Port of the Boat')*, across the Cowal peninsula west of Tighnabruaich. The construction of nearby Polphail was a panic response by the Scottish Office to a faulty scenario which postulated that still more concrete platform yards would be needed. A huge basin was dug out when a Dutch firm briefly promised 500 jobs, and workers' barracks were built with fine facilities convertible to self-catering. By 1978 the yard was complete but already redundant, for concrete oil production platforms had fallen out of favour, and neither the yard nor the village was ever used. Worse still, in their haste the Scottish Office had failed to buy the land, so presenting the development to the landowner, who breached the basin to insert a tidal fish farm. Boarded up, Polphail (Polphailure?) was sold covertly by an embarrassed government in 1988, and was the barely concealed subject of an episode of the BBC TV series *'Yes Minister'*. In the early 1990s Calmac started a summer-only car ferry between Portavadie and Tarbert, which by 1997 plied all-year; but in 1996 the 45ha fish farm was closed and for sale.

## PORT BANNATYNE & Ardbeg

**Map 5, A5**

***Village, Isle of Bute,*** *pop. 1400*

OS 63: NS 0767

Many ancient remains are to be found in the valley of the St Colmac Burn, which flows into Ettrick Bay, almost bisecting the Isle of Bute. The 14th century Kames Castle takes its name from the Gaelic *Camas*, a bay on the east coast 3 km north of Rothesay. Pont's map of about 1600 named only Wester Kames, a 16th century tower in the parish of North Bute. In the mid 19th century a steamer pier named Port Bannatyne was built east of the castle, and from 1879 horse-drawn trams linked it with Rothesay. The 1891 population was 750. A hydropathic was open by 1895, by which time many villas had been built, and in 1902 the tramway was electrified and extended alongside the road to Ettrick Bay.

**Golf, Yachts and Boat-building**: By the 1920s there was a moorland golf course, and the Bute Slipdock boatyard was at work at Ardmaleish Point, 2 km north. The trams to Ettrick Bay were withdrawn in 1936; some say they still ran to Rothesay until 1949. The steamer pier had closed by 1940 and the Hydro vanished, but the resident population was over 2300 in 1951, though with few facilities, relying on Rothesay. By that time the golf course comprised the unusual number of 13 holes. McIntyre's boatyard, which formerly built yachts, was long-established by 1973 when over 40 people were employed in repairs; at that time the Bute Slipdock employed 20 people, building fibreglass yachts. In 1973 the three-class primary school served 70 pupils. By 1981 three hotels were open; in 1991 Port Bannatyne's reduced but well-educated population of 1385 contained many affluent retired people. There has been little new development; the quiet road to Ettrick Bay had lost its *'A'* rating. Sterling Yacht Services still run a boat repair yard; the golf course now has 18 holes, and the small *Ardmory House Hotel* offers service.

## PORT CHARLOTTE

**Map 4, B5**

***Small village, Isle of Islay,*** *pop. 350*

OS 60: NR 2558

By the late 16th century numerous clachans lined the west shore of Loch Indaal. In order to house the workers in the Lochindaal distillery, then under construction, the local minister, a Rev Maclaurin, laid out a small, well-planned village named Port Charlotte in 1828, on the sites of two clachans at the mouth of a burn. The Loch Indaal lighthouse just north of the village dates from 1869. The distillery was *"old fashioned"* by 1886, when Barnard described Port Charlotte as *"a village of little importance and interest except for the large distillery"*. This produced about 580,000 litres of Islay malt whisky in 1884–85. Some was shipped through Bruaichladdich pier, the rest being floated out to the ships in casks! The 1891 population was 570. The distillery was closed in 1929 by its new owners DCL; the malt barns became the Islay Creamery, making cheese, but the warehouses were retained. By 1951 Port Charlotte had two hotels, a population of some 440 and the facilities of a small village. Having been little altered over the years it was designated as an outstanding conservation area. Local facilities remain significant, by 1981 including the Museum of Islay Life in a redundant church; in the 1980s a former bond became a community centre. The resident population (including nearby farms) had declined to 336 by 1991. By 1998 a Field Centre and a camp site were open, but the creamery closed in 2000. Local pastimes include diving, fishing and sea-angling. The 10-roomed *Port Charlotte Hotel* and the recently-opened *'Islay'* youth hostel offer accommodation.

## PORT DUNDAS & Broomhill

**Map 15, C5**

***North-central parts of Glasgow***

OS 64: NS 5966

A small chapel dedicated to the 14th century St Roche or Rollox once stood at the Townhead near Glasgow Cathedral, nowadays Castle Street. The area to the north-west stands high above the centre of Glasgow, but was originally bisected by the little Pinkston Burn. It seems to have remained entirely rural until about 1770, when the Dundashill distillery was set up, perhaps by Harvey; this was extended by Daniel McFarlane about 1811. The Glasgow branch of the Forth & Clyde Canal was dug south-eastwards, reaching a terminal basin beside Applecross Street in 1777. The canal company established its workshops there. In 1790 the canal was extended eastwards from this *'Old Basin'* to meet the Monkland Canal at Castle Street, enabling the construction between these points of the inland Port Dundas, which Heron writing in 1799 called *"a fine bason"* (sic). A Collector's house was built by the canal company in 1790 at North Speirs Wharf, which actually lies on the east side of the winding canal.

**Two Charlies, Bleaching Powder and Raincoats**: Charles Macintosh, born in Glasgow in 1766, pioneered the use of bleaching powder (chloride of lime) for the textile industry; he also set up a white lead factory in the city, and patented *'waterproof'* fabric in 1824. The St Rollox chemical works was founded in 1798 by Charles Tennant, Knox & Co to make bleaching powder; from 1803 the firm made soap, soda, etc, using the by-product sodium sulphate – especially from 1825 when the excise duty on salt was lifted. Tennant's made about 9000 tonnes of bleaching powder in 1825, becoming the world's largest chemical producer in the 1830s and 40s when James 'Paraffin' Young *(see Bathgate)* worked there. They used 30,000 tons of coal a year; in 1842 they built a great chimney *'stalk'* about 135 m tall, a city landmark for 80 years. Charles Tennant built himself a Borders mansion, The Glen *(see Traquair)*.

**Industries Galore**: In the 1820s half a dozen works around Port Dundas produced vitriol (sulphuric acid). There were two Port Dundas Distilleries, both built in North Canal Bank Street: Daniel McFarlane's Dundashill and in 1817–20 J Gourlay & Co. After merging as MacFarlane's, from 1845 each plant had one of the first patent Coffey stills in Scotland and the combine became huge *(see below)*. By 1842 Hugh Baird & Co had built a maltings and malt store beside the canal in Dawson Road. The Eagle Foundry at North Speirs Wharf, founded about 1820 by James Edington, worked for about half a century. By about then John Neilson & Co had established their Garscube Road foundry, where in 1831 the first small iron *ship* – as distinct from tiny canal boats – was constructed, remarkably named the *Faerie Queen* (*see Coatbridge*). They also made beam engines, and from 1836 were marine engineers, gradually shifting to railways.

**Railway, Locomotives, and Pipes**: In 1831 the coal-carrying Garnkirk & Glasgow Railway bisected the huge St Rollox chemical works to terminate at Glebe Street station, beside the canal east of Port Dundas. That year also saw the opening of the Port Dundas or St Rollox Pottery; the St Rollox Flint Glass Works in Kennedy Street was established by

Cochran & Couper about 1838. Thomas Edington & Sons of the Phoenix Ironworks built locomotives below the canal at Port Dundas in 1840–41, and trained apprentice locomotive engineers. G B Edington built the Victoria Foundry beside the Old Basin about 1845, and the Port Dundas Engine Works of millwrights William Forrest & Co was begun around 1849; this firm also developed the *'Scotch'* derrick crane, much used in quarries. The Glasgow Pipe Foundry in Charles Street, served by a branch of the Monkland Canal, was set up about 1852 by D Y Stewart & Co, and became a large business exporting water pipes worldwide, later moving to the Monklands, becoming welded tube manufacturers and eventually merging into Stewarts & Lloyds.

**Cotton and Linen, Woven by Women**: About 1838 Alexander Brown & Co built the South Sawmillfield Mill, a cotton spinning and weaving factory, at Burns Street; its name suggests previous occupancy of the site. Then around 1845 James Clark erected large steam-powered cotton spinning mills at Royston Road, St Rollox; well before 1864 these had become the flax mills of Alex Fletcher & Co, who employed about 850 *'hands'* making linens, almost the sole Glasgow user of this material. In 1868 Galbraith's owned both the Oakbank and St Rollox cotton factories, each of them already enlarged over many years, with a total of 1700 workers – of whom only a hundred were male. In one year their 95,000 spindles and 1532 power looms made over 15 million metres of plain cloth for printing and dyeing.

**Digging under Port Dundas**: When the Edinburgh & Glasgow Railway (E&G) was built in 1838–42 it had to fall steeply from Cowlairs so as to pass under the existing canal and the Garnkirk & Glasgow line, using a rope-worked incline down to Queen Street station; most of it was in tunnel. The Buchanan Street Tunnel, which was threaded under the canal but over the Queen Street tunnel, was opened in 1849 to give access to Buchanan Street station. This new passenger terminal nearer the city centre was originally intended for the expanded Garnkirk system, and was built very cheaply; but by the time of opening it was part of the Caledonian Railway (CR) system, and came to fulfil a major role somewhat inadequately.

**Grain Mills, Bakeries and Everything**: By 1849 the many works in the area were producing an amazing variety of goods, including bread, flour, castings, machinery, glass, mirrors, pottery, whisky, textiles, soap, chemicals, colours and dyes from logwood. Grain establishments included the Port Dundas Grain Mills with their beam engine at North Speirs Wharf, followed by the adjacent City of Glasgow grain mills (extended in 1869–70 to a total of 53 bays); there was also the Caledonian Grain Mills at Tayport Street, and the Scottish Grain Company in Vintner Street. Several bakeries also appeared in the area. Meantime James Brownlee had established the City Sawmills, later absorbing the Rock Villa Sawmill; Cumming & Smith opened upholstered furniture works (after a fire in 1897 rebuilt as the City Cabinet Works), and by 1897 R & J Irving were making packing cases at Port Dundas Road.

**Townsend's Chemical Works: Scotland's Tallest Lum**: In 1857 Brown & Co built a factory for making metal casks beside the canal at Wigton Street, and by 1869 the Glasgow Iron Company had malleable ironworks at St Rollox *(see also Motherwell)*. Meantime in 1856 Joseph Townsend set about rivalling Tennant, engaging John Dingwall of Helensburgh as his architect, to design his own chemical works in Townsend Street to make arsenic compounds and saltpetre, among other products. Together with a team of unnamed but intrepid bricklayers they created the immense *Townsend's Stalk*, the tallest chimney in greater Glasgow, at 142.6m surpassing even Tennant's great *'Stalk'*.

**Soap, Sugar and Sweets**: From 1864 onwards several firms became involved in oil refining and asphalt, including in 1889 the large London & Glasgow Colour Works in Dobbies Loan. Around then Dick & Parker established soap works in Milton Street. Meantime the 7-storey Port Dundas sugar refinery, the third in the city, was built at North Speirs Wharf in 1865–66 for Murdoch & Dodrell. By 1865 Buchanan Brothers were manufacturing sweets; their works at Stewart Street were greatly expanded between 1897 and 1907.

**Foundries flourish**: Many firms flourished in iron-work from 1870 onwards, including The Pinkston iron foundry, the Keppoch Ironworks at Keppochhill Road, the Tower Buildings iron foundry at Possil Road, plus Melvin's St Rollox Ironworks. In 1873–74 the quite new but later well-known firm of Smith & Wellstood of Bonnybridge built their oddly named but attractively designed Victoress Stove Works in Renton Street. Thirty years later the Coxhill Ironworks of James Robertson & Co were built to make railings, gates, cauldrons and smithwork; they were extended in 1913.

**Coal Canal, Protective Clothing and Clay Pipes**: About 1875 a canal branch was cut into a hillside at Hamiltonhill, to carry coal raised from an adjacent pit of the Strone Colliery Company; after this closed, puddle clay for stopping canal leaks was obtained there. In 1870 P W Hall erected an oilskin manufacturing business, and the Wellington Mills of Edward Macbean & Co were built in Mary Street to produce tarpaulins, oilskins and kindred products. About 1889 D McDougall & Co built works in Charles Street to make clay tobacco pipes, which they made for nearly 80 years; in use these too-popular pre-cigarette products became impregnated with carcinogens.

**Education, Refuse Disposal and Giant Grain Distillery**: Education having become compulsory, the large Milton School for 1150 pupils was opened in 1878. In 1880 Glasgow Corporation built a refuse destructor in Charles Street. There were also numerous warehouses for various goods in the area, and haulage contractors' stables and depots, including the large 98-stall Calgary Street depot of Wordie & Co, built in 1899–1904 just before practical motor lorries started to make the horses redundant. Port Dundas distillery was owned in 1876 by M MacFarlane & Co, who in 1877 joined DCL as founder members of this new grain whisky combine; by 1886 it had grown into the largest in Scotland and covered nearly 4ha, employing 250 workers and 21 excise staff. Barley and American maize, brought in by rail and canal, were processed with Loch Katrine water from the City's public supply to produce nearly 12 million litres of grain whisky annually; over 400 resident pigs and many privately-reared dairy cows lived on the draff *(a full description was given by Barnard)*. About 1890 when Port Dundas distillery was equipped for yeast-making, the canal was still so busy that a Boatmen's Institute was built.

**Biggest Malt Distillery becomes Cooperage**: In 1886 Harvey's Dundashill distillery produced only 13% as much whisky as Port Dundas – yet it was the largest Malt distillery in Scotland, and 400 dairy cows were fed on the draff. However, its continued use of the by then polluted canal water for cooling seems questionable. Though a patent still was added in the 1890s this distillery did not survive long, being taken over for closure by DCL in 1907; part became their central cooperage. Meantime the Clyde Cooperage Company was open at Port Dundas in 1887, and about 1906 R Williamson & Sons built another cooperage at Coxhill Street. Hugh Baird & Sons erected the Great Canal Maltings at Garscube Road in 1888; their 7-storey Vulcan Maltings were built from 1893 at Vintner Street. Bonded warehouses were added to the Port Dundas distillery in 1889 and 1899, and at Borron Street in 1897–1911 for Peter Mackie & Co, the blenders of the much advertised *'White Horse'* whisky. About 1911 this firm opened new bonded warehouses in Port Dundas, changing their name to White Horse Distillers Ltd until in 1927 they sold out to DCL. Engineers of distillery equipment were the Canal Basin Foundry, and the Pulteney Street Engine Works at Dobbies Loan who also made grinding and sugar refinery machines.

**Exit Tennants – enter Trams and Electricity**: The Tennant complex was sold to the United Alkali Company (UAC) in 1892 and soda manufacture soon ceased. Port Dundas Power Station was opened in 1898 for the Corporation Electricity Department, and from that year electric trams first began to run to Springburn; the tiny power station was enlarged in 1909, when it filled the whole site between Spiers Wharf and Sawmillfield Road. The Corporation trams were soon supplied from their own Pinkston Power Station, built in 1900–01 between Port Dundas East and the Edinburgh railway. Both power stations used the canal for cooling water and to supply coal.

**Housing Men and Horses; Brass and Drinks**: In 1892 the closed South Sawmillfield cotton mill was converted into a model lodging house. In 1899 a nearby site became the stables and cart sheds of the Glasgow Corporation cleansing depot. In 1896–1902 the engineers Murdoch & Cameron, and brassfounders J W Russell & Co, erected buildings in the Charles Street area which later became part of the St Rollox Ironworks. Aerated water was produced in the area from the 1890s; English brewers Whitbread's built a bottling works, Vaux built a large store in Garscube Road.

**Flammable Edwardian Activities**: Between 1906 and 1911 D C Thomson & Co, the newspaper publishers of Dundee, erected offices and printing works at Port Dundas Road. About 1907 T D Cowieson & Co began to produce portable buildings at Charles Street, a concern which expanded after 1918 to make bus bodies. A fire in 1913 caused major rebuilding of the huge Port Dundas distillery by DCL. In 1922 the UAC demolished Tennant's giant chimney *'stalk'*, long a symbol of the city's virility; but sulphuric acid was still made there. In 1931 part of the Port Dundas sugar refinery was converted into the Wheatsheaf Mills for John M White. Generally the inter-war period saw a gradual rundown of most of the area's long-established industries.

**Closures, Abandonments, and the Motorway**: In 1952–54 a large cooling tower, claimed as the largest in Europe at that time, was built at Pinkston Power Station. The canal was closed in 1962; so the Canal Boatmen's Institute became redundant, and was also demolished in 1967 to enable the M8 motorway to be driven through the area. The original Port Dundas Basin was drained and partly incorporated into the M8 site. Another seminal event was the closure and demolition in 1964–65 of what remained of the former Tennant's works; the St Rollox Flint Glass Works were also demolished. The Buchanan Street Tunnel was abandoned in 1967 with the closure of its station; Glebe Street station was demolished in the same year, as was the Glasgow Pipe Foundry and the large confectionery works in Stewart Street. 1967–68 saw the Port Dundas Engine Works pulled down; the Keppoch Ironworks with its small cupola furnace remained in operation until 1968. The Milton Street Glassworks, Victoress Stove Works and Royston Road cotton mill were demolished in 1968, followed in 1969 by the City Cabinet Works; the great Canal Maltings were felled in 1972, by which time the motorway was open west of Wishart Street.

**Diesels and CHP, but no more White Horses**: Of the canal only some basins at Port Dundas East remained, and east of them the new Sighthill Park was created south of Pinkston Power Station, which still stood in 1974. The fine buildings of Milton School survived – until 1978. By then the Scottish Adhesives Company had its factory in Farnell Street, but after such wholesale clearance few other firms remained. Port Dundas grain distillery was accompanied by the *'White Horse'* whisky blending and bottling plant until the latter was closed by DCL in 1984–85 and the work transferred to Shieldhall. By 1990 a large CHP (Combined Heat & Power) plant had been installed there by DCL's successors, United Malt & Grain Distillers.

**The Canal returns and Printing prospers**: In 1987 the restoration of 19 km of the canal to a navigable state (from North Spiers Wharf northwards) was begun with EC help, steadily creating a tourist industry with sailing, cruises, and a floating museum and restaurants. In 1991 Victorian grain mills and a sugar refinery of 5 and 6 storeys at North Speirs Wharf were converted into 150 luxury flats. The Craighall rail yard had vanished by 1992 but a business park was open. D C Thomson of Dundee had recently installed a new colour printing plant at Port Dundas, where it was to print the *Sunday Post, Weekly News*, some local newspapers and, under contract from 1995, the *Daily Star* and the *Daily Express* Scottish edition. A 5 ha food park was proposed in 1995. The millennium project which aims to reopen the entire Forth & Clyde Canal in 2001 was nearing completion at the time of writing; further development is planned for Speirs Wharf.

## PORT ELLEN

**Map 4, B5**

***Village, Isle of Islay**, pop. 900*

OS 60: NR 3645

At the southern extremity of Islay is the semicircular Kilnaughton Bay with its ancient chapel. On the eastern side of the bay is the tiny sheltered inlet of Loch Leodamais, round whose curving sandy shore the planned village of Port Ellen was laid out in 1821 by W F Campbell, and named after his wife Elinor. A distillery was opened in 1825 by A K Mackay, but as late as 1838 there was no post office. From 1845 steamers called on a weekly service from Ardrossan and Campbeltown to Oban, Tobermory and Portree. From 1846 two steamers per week connected with West Loch Tarbert, and there was a weekly return service to Glasgow. From 1867 to 1876 a further steamer plied to Glasgow, via Portrush in Ulster. In 1886 Barnard found that the distillery had been extended several times *(see Hay & Stell)* and produced some 635,000 litres of Islay malt whisky annually. He wrote of Port Ellen as a *"town"* with *"excellent"* accommodation at the *White Hart Inn*, though *"lodging-houses"* were lacking. The 18-hole Machrie (links) golf course 6 km north-west of the harbour was laid out in 1891, when the population was 900. By 1894 Port Ellen had a twice-weekly steamer from Glasgow and had ousted Port Askaig as the Islay landfall. Murray's Handbook for 1894 opined that *"Islay is seldom visited by tourists"*, but again referred to the *"very good" White Hart Hotel*. Port Ellen distillery was acquired about 1920 by Buchanan. It was closed down in 1929, apart from the maltings.

**Distillery returns in Style**: The Islay lifeboat station was opened in 1934; for a few years this was located at Port Ellen. In 1942 an RAF base was built 7 km to the north at Glenegedale; after 1945 this became the island's airport, and by the 1950s the 30-room *Machrie Hotel* stood nearby. The distillery was revived by Scottish Malt Distillers in 1966; a new drum maltings was built there in 1973 to supply malt to all their Islay distilleries. By 1972 a car ferry operated to Tarbert West. The ferry destination had changed to Kennacraig by 1980, at which time Gigha was also served; but the Islay end of the service remained tied to Port Ellen, the island's only deep harbour. The population of Port Ellen was 932 in 1951, with average village facilities, which it retained in 1981.

**Closing a Treasured Distillery**: Although its single malt was highly regarded by the Scotch Malt Whisky Society, the distillery was closed in 1983 and soon dismantled: doubtless there were good boardroom reasons, but to an outsider the closure seems plain daft! By 1984 Port Ellen's car ferry operated in summer only, to Kennacraig, and the main access to Islay was by way of Port Askaig. Port Ellen which had 917 people in 1991 was said by the local authority planner to be very depressed. But there had been some new development by 1998, when it retained a school, post office, tourist information office and the Kennacraig car ferry. The *Machrie Hotel* has 17 rooms and its related 18-hole Islay Club golf course; there are guest-houses in the village and a backpackers' hostel is open in summer at Kintra Farm, 6 km north-west on Laggan Bay, where there is also a caravan and camping site.

## PORT GLASGOW

**Map 5, B5**

***Inverclyde town,*** *pop. 19,700*

OS 63: NS 3274

Newark Castle on the Firth of Clyde a short way up-river from Greenock was built in the 15th century by George Maxwell, and attractively enlarged a century later by his descendant Patrick Maxwell to accommodate his vast family. The area was thickly wooded about 1600. In 1655 Tucker found there only the *"laird's house"* – i.e. the castle, still owned by the Maxwells – and four or five others, *"but before them a pretty good road"* (i.e. anchorage), *"where all vessels unload, and send their goods up the river to Glasgow in small boats"*. In 1668, being well aware of the deficiencies of their own shallow river port, Glasgow Corporation promoted an outport by acquiring the Newark estate and obtaining a charter for a burgh of barony to be named Port Glasgow. Aided by legislation – which from 1672 permitted such places to trade overseas – this soon became Scotland's chief west coast port, and an early ferry connected with Cardross. The castle fell out of use and the trade privileges were curtailed in 1690, but by then Port Glasgow already had shipyards.

**Head Custom House and Scotland's Premier Port**: Trade was freed by the Union in 1707, and Port Glasgow acquired the Clyde's head custom house in 1710, retaining this key role for a century. In 1725 two steel grain mills were commissioned, and a post office was open by 1730. In 1735, 47 different square-rigged ships sailed from Port Glasgow, some as far afield as the West Indies. The Port Glasgow Rope & Duck Company, known as Birkmyre's, was founded in 1736; *'duck'* is a light canvas. In the 1750s Roy's survey showed a medium-sized town for the period, and a harbour with two piers – but the only road followed the coast. By 1760 Port Glasgow had ousted Leith as Scotland's principal port, although overtaken a few years later by Greenock. Port Glasgow's first graving dock dated from 1763–68, and in 1774 a prominent new church was built for Newark parish. Local customs revenues, largely based on tobacco, fell by three-quarters between 1772 and 1785 due to the War of American independence. However, Port Glasgow did become a Port of Registry, probably from the start of the system in 1786, with the recognition letters PGW. Birkmyre's hemp mill and ropeworks became the major site of the Gourock Ropeworks Company (GRC) when the firms merged in 1797, and they greatly extended it *(see Hay & Stell)*.

**Sugar and Sailcloth**: Sugar refining was being carried on close by at the end of the century, the brewery at Devil's Glen opened in 1794, and Port Glasgow was a post town by 1797. In 1799 Heron enthused over *"the excellent harbour, with a noble pier. Here many vessels, belonging to Glasgow, take in and unload their cargoes."* He also praised the Clyde herring fisheries under his note on Port Glasgow. Sailcloth was made by the GRC from the early 19th century, and a gasworks established in 1803 may well have been Scotland's first. Between 1810 and 1825 both the Greenock Banking Company and the Renfrewshire Banking Company (also based in Greenock) opened branches in Port Glasgow, whose fine Town Buildings were erected in 1815.

**Pioneer Steamship Building**: In 1811–12 John Wood & Sons of the East yard built the hull of the world's first practical seagoing steamship, Henry Bell's *Comet*. This vessel was engined either by John Robertson of Glasgow or by Anderson, Campbell & Co – sources disagree – but its boiler was made by David Napier, *"then a workman"* (Bremner). It entered service in January 1812, initially apparently as a ferry plying from Port Glasgow to Helensburgh, but soon advertised on the Glasgow to Greenock run. The early 18 m steamboat *Elizabeth* was also built by Wood's for John Thomson, a friend of Henry Bell's, and given more power than *Comet*; she went to the Mersey in 1814. In 1815 the firm built the *Thames*, engined at 14 horsepower by one James Cook, which undertook the first long sea voyage under steam (1500 miles – to the Thames!). That year John Hunter of Port Glasgow built the topically named *Waterloo*, another paddle steamer for use on Clyde, West Highland and Irish services. Other firms building early steamships included Wood & Barclay by 1816, and Ritchie & Wood by 1826. In 1834 Charles Randolph and Richard Cunliffe founded the Kingston yard.

**The First Cunarder, the Railway and Birkmyre's Mansion**: Port Glasgow's shipbuilding industry then grew mightily, and not all the firms and yards can be considered here, though the first Cunarder, the *Britannia* of 1840, built by Duncan and engined by Napier, was outstanding. By that time the outport trade was affected by the deepening of the River Clyde, but the opening of the Glasgow & Greenock Railway through Port Glasgow in 1841 restored some of the advantage that the port had lost to Glasgow. The old sugar refinery in Bay Street was rebuilt as a massive 8-storey building by new owners about 1866 (by 1910 it had been converted by the GRC to produce waterproofed canvas and sailcloth). In 1869–70 the vast baronial mansion of Broadfield, designed by David Bryce, was built in sandstone on the hillside 1.5 km east of the town for the Birkmyres, by then monied owners of the huge Gourock Ropework Company, which employed over 1000 workers. The prominent West church was built in 1885 to designs by J J Burnet.

**Shipbuilding Maturity and Variety**: The small Castle shipyard opened about 1858, being run from 1860 to 1900 by Blackwood & Gordon from Paisley, who by 1891 were also marine engineers. The two Glen yards dated from 1863–69; William Hamilton & Co was established at the Glen in 1871. Meantime the Kingston yard, later the biggest on the lower Clyde, was taken over by Henry Murray in 1867. Russell & Co's Bay shipyard existed by 1874, and when Murray moved to Dumbarton in 1882 Russell's took over the Kingston yard to build large cargo sailing ships, and later ocean tramp steamers. The distinct firm of Murdoch & Murray Ltd, founded in 1875, were still building small paddle steamers in 1912. The tug *Scot* was built in 1876 by Cunliffe & Dunlop of Port Glasgow for the Caledonian Canal, where it worked until 1931. In 1891 Rodger & Co took over the Bay yard, building the 3-masted barque *Glenlee* for Archibald Stirling in 1896; as the last surviving Clyde-built sailing ship, her steel hull, for years beached near Seville, was saved for posterity in 1993 *(see Glasgow)*.

**The Peak of Prosperity?**: The population in 1891 was 14,700. Although 1300 more than in 1881, Murray's Handbook for 1894 noted of the port that *"it has declined in importance, and ships that do not stop at Greenock go right up to Glasgow"*. However, the *Star Hotel* was open, and from that year trams ran through to Greenock and Gourock on a single system. Port Glasgow Athletic FC played in the Scottish League for 18 years, 1893–1911. The Port Glasgow golf club was founded in the boom year 1895, laying out its 18-hole course on a moorland hilltop south of the town. A famous name appeared when Ferguson Brothers established the Newark yard just west of the castle in 1902–03; in 1911 they built a new type of vessel for the Garston (Liverpool) docks, a combined suction and grab dredger. Meantime in 1909 Russell & Co had built the 64 m-long steel screw coaster *Orkney Coast*. This great shipbuilding firm which had dominated the town for decades took over Rodgers' Bay yard for the second time in 1912, and in 1914 completed the 8300-ton Spanish liner *Principe de Asturias*, which was to be sadly lost with 425 lives on rocks off the coast of Brazil in 1916. From 1913 a public electricity supply was available from a new power station. In 1916 W Hamilton & Co built HMS *Melton*, a paddle minesweeper.

**Jobs Disaster breaks British Records**: Russell's – long owned by Lithgow's – took that name in 1918, but in common with most other shipbuilding towns, Port Glasgow fell on evil days from 1921 (see Reid's *James Lithgow, Master of Work*). With the collapse in demand for ropes for rigging, much of Broadfield's park was sold off and it eventually became a nursing home, renamed as Broadstone. In 1927 the former Murdoch & Murray yard was closed and dismantled, and no building took place at the Castle yard from 1929 to 1938. In the depths of the 1931 slump, when even the pushy Sir James Lithgow had to close his yard for a time, there was 92% male

*The Gourock Ropeworks building at Port Glasgow. The firm moved here from Gourock in 1797, and at one time employed over 1000 workers. This building was built in the 1860s as a sugar refinery. It still stands empty, awaiting re-use.* *(JRH)*

unemployment in the town, believed to be the highest figure ever recorded in Britain. Many left for jobs in the new light industries around London.

**Shipbreaking before and after World War II**: The situation was eased somewhat in 1936 by the major shipbreaking work of Smith & Houston, whose yard at the east end of the waterfront adjoining Lamont's Castle shipyard broke up the burnt-out wreck of the great 42,000-ton French liner *L'Atlantique*. Very soon rearmament too brought work, and people returned. In 1936 Port Glasgow was second to Coatbridge among Scottish burghs in the proportion of its houses that were overcrowded (42%). No doubt even worse conditions prevailed during the feverish building activity of World War II, when the harbour was also intensively used. Afterwards the aircraft maintenance carrier HMS *Perseus* of 13,350 tons was scrapped at Port Glasgow in 1958, when Hamiltons' yard still separated Lithgow's two yards; these were reconstructed about 1961, their 225-ton Goliath crane being built by Arrol. In 1962 a full-sized working replica of Henry Bell's *Comet* steamship of 1812 was built for its 150th anniversary; local firms equipped a Buckie-built hull in Lithgow's yard. It was later put on permanent display at Shore Street.

**New Industries – and into Inverclyde**: In the 1940s Sangamo Controls opened a timeswitch factory, and by the 1950s Port Glasgow was a largish town with normal urban facilities. Its newspaper, the *Port Glasgow Express & Observer*, was published from Johnstone, but later vanished. The firm of AMP, established in 1956, was in electronics by 1979 and in 1995 as makers of connectors for electronic equipment employed some

*Scott Lithgow's Glen Yard, Port Glasgow. This yard was created in the 1960s to build very large vessels. The 225-ton Goliath crane seen here was built by Arrol of Kilmarnock to hoist large pieces of ship into place, but it was demolished in 1997.* *(RS)*

300 people, a number expected to double within three years. By 1953 Woodhall Halt had been opened 2 km east of the main station to serve a new council housing estate; at nearby Boglestone the 10-roomed *Clune Brae Hotel* was open by 1974. But by the 1960s only yachts and coasters used the old harbour. By 1972 over 70% of the housing was owned by the town council, who had also provided a covered swimming pool, but in 1975 Port Glasgow became part of the Greenock-led Inverclyde District. The former sugar-refinery turned ropeworks and sailcloth works in Bay Street was closed in 1976 and partly demolished; the rest stood ruinous and unsaleable in 1993. Though a large increase in the number of garages had occurred over the postwar period, and there were two hotels by 1979, Port Glasgow was of disadvantaged character in 1981.

**Lingerie expands Wonderfully**: From 1955 women's underclothing was made in the town by Playtex; over the years the firm expanded to work on a substantial scale making brassieres, and by 1992 had stretched its employment to 700. The European head office of Playtex was in Rome in 1994, and its design studio in Paris, but its main European production centre was still at Port Glasgow. In 1994 the firm successfully produced emerald green bras for supporters of the Irish team in the World Cup, and the Playtex *'Wonderbra'* was selling 20,000 a week in 1994, requiring 250 workers. In 1994 the less exotic Puffer Protective Clothing was also made at Port Glasgow. In 1993 Anaplast, a subsidiary of BPI of Greenock *(see also Stevenston)*, invested in new plant to make plastic pallets.

**Shipbuilding Nationalised and Privatised**: In the 1970s Lamont's Castle shipyard built a series of *'Island'* class ferries for Calmac (Caledonian MacBrayne), before closing in 1979. Meantime the Ferguson yard was nationalised in 1977; then merged with Ailsa of Troon and Appledore of Devon, it had become Ailsa Ferguson by 1981. Privatised in 1988, it completed a Calmac ferry early in 1989. Though most of the workforce became redundant for a time, in that year the orderless yard was purchased by HLD, the managers who had lately taken over Clark Kincaid of Greenock. In turn HLD was bought in 1990 by Norwegian-owned Kvaerner of Govan, the main customer for Clark Kincaid, becoming a subsidiary of Kvaerner Kincaid. Some 50 staff were still employed at Newark when the luckless yard was sold off in 1991, its new owners – led by Sir Ross Belch, former Scott Lithgow Managing Director – reverting to the name Ferguson Marine. By then the town's population was 19,700. In 1992 Scott Lithgow (then part of Trafalgar House) was still recruiting key personnel at the Kingston yard.

**All Change, for Better or Worse**: In 1995 the *'A'* listed former Town Buildings were restored as a library (and with the aim of creating a maritime museum), and about then the listed Jean Street school was also saved. Permission was sadly granted to demolish the important Gourock Ropeworks in Bay Street, but this had not been done by mid 2000. Lithgow's landmark Goliath crane was demolished in 1997, and in 1998 the former Clune Park church stood derelict; the Newark church, vacated for repairs, was burnt out early in 2000. Rather luckier was tall *'A'* listed Broadfield with its wooded grounds; no longer a nursing home, it was sold to a housebuilder in 2000. The West church – which had been a carpet store – was converted into 12 flats in 1999–2000. Port Glasgow High School now has 680 pupils and St Stephen's High 820.

**Recovery under Ferguson Marine**: Ferguson had soon resumed production: in 1992 its workforce was back to 200, speedily building two ferries for Calmac's Ullapool, Skye and Stornoway services, the tender *Pharos* for the Northern Lighthouse Board, and the 3000-ton offshore supply vessel *Star Pegasus*. Two ferries for the Red Funnel Line's Southampton and Cowes service followed in 1992–93. The workforce rose to 300 to build the car ferry *Isle of Lewis*, the largest in the Calmac fleet, for service between Ullapool and Stornoway. In 1994 when building two new tugs for Shetland Towage they intended to recommission another slip and an outfitting quay to reduce their dependence on suppliers. In 1995–96 Ferguson built a Shell North Sea rig supply vessel, adding 60 jobs, in 1996 delivered two tugs for use at the Sullom Voe oil terminal, and were still busy in mid 2000 when they launched the 90-car ferry MV *Hebrides*. Clydeport now has permission to develop a new roll-on terminal, while Solectron are significant employers in electronics.

## PORTGORDON — Map 10, A1

***Moray coast village**, pop. 775* — OS 28: NJ 3964

Portgordon was created in 1797 by the Duke of Gordon on a hitherto undeveloped section of the Banffshire coast, 3 km west of Buckie. It was once renowned for salmon, but the harbour was also used for general bulk cargoes. As a very small place, there was no post office until after 1838, though a corn dealer operated by 1847. By then a limeworks at Blackhillock near Keith was using coal imported through Portgordon, over 16 km distant; lime exports formed lighter return cartloads. A new harbour built by a later Duke was completed in 1874. Although by 1884 the 15 Portgordon boats had deserted it for Buckie's new Cluny harbour, the Great North of Scotland Railway which opened its coastal line through the village in 1886 provided a station and sidings. The 1891 population was 1254. The 1894 OS map marked the *'Old Mill of Gollachy (woollen)'*.

**Destruction, Decline – and Malting**: In 1951 Portgordon had 1200 people and the facilities of a small village, but the harbour was badly damaged in a gale in 1953, and the population then declined rapidly. The railway was closed in 1968. In the 1975 reorganisation of local government Portgordon was transferred from Banffshire to Moray. It also saw the loss of its secondary school, bank, chemist and garage, becoming a small outpost of

Buckie. In the 1980s the repaired harbour was mainly used by pleasure craft, and the former station site offered bowls and a playground. About 1990 the Crisp malting group built a large maltings south of the village, whose 1991 population was down to 775. There has been little new development since, but lobsters are still caught; facilities include a church, pub, library, grocery, post office and newsagent. At Tynet, 3 km south-west, is the 15-roomed *Mill House Hotel*, a former mill.

## PORTKNOCKIE — Map 10, A1

***Moray coast village,** pop. 1300* — OS 28: NJ 4868

A Pictish fort known to us as Green Castle once dominated the natural harbour of Portknockie, on the west side of a rocky promontory 3 km west of Cullen in Banffshire. In 1677 a group of Cullen fishermen chose it as a new base. Named *'Port Knochies'* on the Roy map of about 1750, it was roadless and a mere eight buildings were sketched around the cove – not necessarily an accurate count, but certainly Portknockie was very slow to develop. It was after 1838 before it had a post office, in 1880 there was only one fishing boat, and none at all by 1884. In 1886 the Great North of Scotland Railway's coast line was opened with a station 45 m above the sea. A new deep harbour had been completed by 1890, when despite its steep and angular approach road, over 140 boats were based there. The 1891 population was 1300. This resurgence led to Portknockie being made a late police burgh in 1912, and in 1921 it was a small town with a population of 1664. In 1929 its fleet of steam drifters was crewed by 555 fishermen.

**Fishing Decline**: Economic decline then set in, and was continuous from about 1930 through the 1950s, when though some 1500 people remained, the services were those of a village. An agreement to take overspill from Glasgow came to nothing, and the railway was closed in 1968. From 25 vessels in 1957 the harbour became almost deserted, and the secondary school had closed by 1970. By 1972 the very small burgh had a tiny open-air swimming pool for the hardy, but was actually administered from offices in Macduff; this connection was severed when Portknockie became part of Moray district in 1975. Some cod, crabs and lobsters were still landed by 8 small boats at this now quiet port in the 1980s; there was some pleasure boating, and by 1986 a caravan and camping site, but only the facilities of a small village to serve its 1296 people in 1991. Very many owned their homes outright. Some new housing has since appeared, the harbour serves pleasure boats and lobster potters, and the rocky coast at Scar Nose just to the east still well displays its great natural arch, the *Bow-fiddle*. Facilities include a small hotel, pub, primary school, post office, garage anda few shops – and the open-air pool!

## PORTLETHEN & Findon — Map 10, C4

***Mearns villages / Ab. dormitories,** pop. 6500* — OS 45: NO 9296

The Mearns fishing villages of *'Portletthyn'* (10 km south of Aberdeen) and nearby Findon, both existed as small settlements by the late 16th century, when shown by Pont on his sketch map. He added *"renowned for dryed..."* but the next word is illegible; the later speciality of Findon or Finnan was smoked haddock. Roy's map made about 1750 showed *'Port Letham'* with a *'Millton'* – probably the Mill of Findon – on a track from the south, leading to Ferryhill for Aberdeen; the main road or *'causeway'* lay some way inland. In 1827 Chambers mentioned *"the fishing village of Finnan, remarkable for its dried fish called 'speldings'"*. At that time the proprietor was energetically promoting settlement in the surrounding barren area. When the Aberdeen Railway was opened in 1850 about 1 km inland, a station was provided to serve Portlethen, spawning a new settlement. The 1891 population of Portlethen was 350. Half a century later the combined population of the two places was only about 850, and the station was closed by 1963.

**Meat, Salmon, Golf – and Oilfield Services**: During the oil boom from 1971 much hastily planned building took place between the railway and the main road. By 1979 William Donald & Sons ran a large abattoir or *'meat factory'* serving their extensive range of farms. The rapid growth led to a population of over 3300 by 1981, and the creation of a new primary school, garages, shopping facilities and an 18-hole golf course, whose club was in 1990 the first to appoint a woman professional, Muriel Thomson. A new (unstaffed) railway station was opened in 1985; meantime salmon were still fished from the steep beach. In 1990 McIntosh Donald Ltd claimed to be the largest meat wholesaler in north-east Scotland. In 1990 53 ha of farmland 2 km to the north-west became the isolated Badentoy Industrial Park, and soon attracted branches of both the Cameron Ironworks of Livingston and Canada's Nowsco Well Services. By 1991, when a new 50 m outdoor heated swimming pool was opened, the only such pool in Scotland, the population had risen to a young and healthy 6225. Today the new Portlethen Academy has 800 pupils. Findon and *'Portlethen Village'* remain quiet, but the abattoir still exists, and a 40-room *Travel Inn* has arrived.

## PORT LOGAN — Map 1, B5

***Galloway small village,** pop. 200* — OS 82: NX 0940

This small bay on the west coast of the Rhinns of Galloway long remained undeveloped; 3 km to the east on the east coast at Terally was a standing stone and a motte. Pont's map of Galloway made around 1600 showed a few tiny settlements in the area, perhaps ferm touns, among which was Logan, 3 km to the north of the bay. In 1682 the McDouall lairds established a pier and small village at Port Nessock, shown on the Roy survey made about 1754; by then farms had been enclosed and an early Georgian mansionhouse had been built at Logan, but the nearest road followed the east coast. A remarkable tidal fishpond was built on the bay in 1788–1800, and the pier was rebuilt with a lighthouse to a design by Rennie in 1818–20 for Colonel Andrew McDouall, who traded in Irish cattle *(see Hay & Stell)*. The Terally tileworks was established near the east coast about 1840, later becoming a brickworks.

**Logan Gardens**: The fine Logan Gardens with their sub-tropical vegetation were created around the mansion by Agnes Buchan-Hepburn in the mid 19th century. A lifeboat station was opened at Port Logan in 1866, but closed in 1932. In 1951 the Port Logan area had a population of over 250, with an inn, post office and primary school. The Terally brickworks was still active in 1951 but had become derelict by 1976; rural depopulation had reduced the residents to about 180 by 1971, at which level stability was reached, though the primary school had closed. By 1966 the gardens of Logan House were open to the public; in 1969 they were gifted to the nation and put under the Royal Botanic Garden, Edinburgh. By 1978 a caravan and camping site was open at New England Bay north of Terally. By 1981 conversion of the mansionhouse had created a hotel, the *Port Logan Lodge*; but this was no longer a hotel by 1994, when it was divided into flats. The post office and a pub remain in business.

## PORTMAHOMACK

**Map 9, C2**

***Easter Ross village,*** *pop. 450* OS 21: NH 9184

The early Christian St Colmac built a chapel or monastery around 975 AD on a sandy bay on the western, relatively sheltered side of the remote Tarbat peninsula of Easter Ross. A Pictish slab, and late 1990s excavations on the site of Colmac's monastery, show that an important settlement existed by the 12th century, when Tarbat Old Kirk was built on or near the chapel site. Of five castles built nearby, only the 16th century cliff-top tower of Ballone can be dated. Pont's map of about 1600 showed the area well-settled; near *'Terbart'* castle was a mill on a now vanished stream, perhaps the site of the later Rockfield Mills. Portmahomack, known after its founder rather than by its charter name of Castlehaven, was chartered as a burgh of barony in 1678 and a pier with a warehouse or granary was built.

**Education, Fishing and Golf**: Roy's survey made about 1750 showed little besides the *'Castle of Balinloan'* and the *'Kirk of Tarbatt'* in a still trackless area. A new church was built on the old site in the 18th century, with the first school in the parish nearby. Telford designed extensions to the pier, built in 1810. The exceptionally tall tower of Tarbat Ness lighthouse (40 m), built by John Smith of Inverness to designs by Robert Stevenson, was first lighted in 1830. By then 100 boats fished from Portmahomack, served by six curing yards. Roads soon linked to the outside world, and from 1839 there was a post office. Later in the century the railway carriers Wordie & Co operated a road cartage depot, linking with Fearn station and also carrying some passengers in pre-1914 days. While the fishing slowly declined, a 9-hole links golf course was laid out by the Tarbat club, founded in 1908.

**Modern Portmahomack**: A road haulage depot was still active in 1953, implying that fish still left the port in some quantity. There were two hotels. Although the population was only 500, some of the local facilities also served Geanies and Inver, 5 km west. The population had declined to only 360 by 1971, but then began to rise with the development around the Cromarty Firth. The facilities by 1981 were those of a small village, but with three hotels, and by 1983 there was a caravan site. In 1985 when the lighthouse was automated, Portmahomack was a small but popular resort and *"thriving village"* with two full-time lobster boats and summer pleasure craft, but the 1991 population was under 500. The old parish church has become a visitor centre, *'Tarbat Discovery'*; the Tarbat golf course is still open nearby, and the 15-room *Caledonian Hotel* stands beside the sandy beach.

## PORTNAHAVEN & Orsay

**Map 4, A5**

***Island communities, Islay,*** *pop. 150* OS 60: NR 1652

The islet of Orsay off the western tip of Islay had a parish kirk when it was noted by Monro in 1549 as *"very good for fishing, inhabited and manured"*; but the tidal stream of Corrie Garrache was dangerous. The Rhinns of Islay lighthouse on Orsay, designed by Robert Stevenson, was first lit in 1825. The twin fishing villages of Portnahaven and harbourless Port Wemyss were founded on mainland Islay in the shelter of Orsay at the time of the Clearances. Later a post office and school were provided, and by the 1870s the population was some 700. The local boats, registered at Campbeltown, sold their fish at Ballycastle in Ireland. Overfishing caused decline, and by 1951 there were only some 200 people, a tiny inn and a riding centre. By 1977 the local waters were said to be fished out, except for scollops; the Easter Ellister wildfowl reserve meant the seabirds were increasing in numbers. Most fishermen's homes had become holiday cottages and only about 90 residents remained in the village, as there was no work for the young people. In 1977 the one-class school had 16 pupils. The resident population including local farms was 183 in 1991. Following experimental installations at Shorline Gully near Portnahaven, a wave-powered Wells turbine was installed in 1989; a 300 mw output was expected, to be fed into the island mains. As Wavegen Islay, truly commercial output started in 2000 with an air-powered generator, using the same principle of airflow created by wave action in a concrete chamber. There may be no fish, but wave power should last for ever. The lighthouse was automated in the 1990s; the school, pier, post office and pub are still in use.

## PORTOBELLO & Joppa

**Map 15, D1**

***E. suburbs of Edinburgh,*** *pop. 19,700* OS 66: NT 3073

The burn variously named Braid, Fisher, Frigate or Figgate, which reaches the coast of the Firth of Forth about 5 km east of Edinburgh, was crossed by the early road from Edinburgh to Musselburgh, shown on Pont's map of about 1600, though no bridge was marked. Farther east the Magdalen Bridge already spanned the larger Burdiehouse Burn. In 1749 a sailor – who had been present at the taking of the town of Portobello in Panama ten years earlier – built a hut as a home on the Figgate Muir, the hitherto undeveloped section of coast between these points, whimsically naming it after the scene of his exploits: this more mellifluous name stuck. The Roy map made about five years later showed a road from Duddingston meeting the coast road at approximately that point. About 1770 William Jamieson founded a pottery at Portobello to make white stoneware, later known as the Waverley Pottery. In 1778 one Rathbone founded his Midlothian Pottery and its dedicated harbour; a flint mill was built to grind material for glazes in 1775, and a second was in use by the 1790s, when about 300 people lived in the area. From 1785 Prussian blue dye was also made, and in 1799 Heron described Portobello as a *"rising village manufacturing brick, tiles, brown pottery, and white stone-ware"*; it seems that the brickworks was at Westbank. In the early 19th century decorative pottery was also made.

**Resort Facilities and Railways**: Portobello had a post office from 1802, and a suite of warm baths was built in 1807. Chambers saw in 1827 *"a considerable village formed of villas, manufactories and shops, greatly resorted to during the summer months for sea-bathing. The village is yearly increasing"*. By 1838 a station was open about 700 m inland, on the newly completed Leith branch of the horse-drawn Edinburgh & Dalkeith Railway; and about that time a paper mill was also established. When the North British Railway (NBR) opened its main line from Edinburgh to Berwick in 1846, Joppa station was sited east of Brunstane Road, while Portobello station was on an upgraded portion of the old line, so becoming a junction; Portobello's public park and golf course were established beside the station as early as 1853, and a pier with a concert party pavilion was opened on the shore in 1871.

**Trams, More Industries and Downmarket Resort**: The horse-drawn vehicles of the Edinburgh Street Tramways Company (ESTC) appeared at Portobello in the 1870s, and in 1881 a steam-hauled car was tried on this route. The Waverley Pottery in Harbour Road was acquired by the Buchan family in 1867 and renamed the Thistle Pottery; they rebuilt the works about 1879, and added three new bottle kilns in 1903–09 *(see Hay & Stell)*. Portobello was also the location of the long-established Westbank brickworks, the United Glass bottle works, and the NBR laundry. The population in 1891 was 8700. A gasworks was set up in 1896, and a 3-storey chocolate factory was built in Portobello Road in 1906, of sandstone and reinforced concrete. In 1894 the growing town of Portobello was still separated from the city's edge by 2 km of open country. By then it had become a popular resort or, to use the frank words of Murray's 1894 Handbook, *"a second-rate watering-place crowded in summer with bathing-machines, donkeys, and trippers"*.

**Keeping Coal Trains clear of Expresses**: Portobello was absorbed by Edinburgh in 1901, the year the stylish red sandstone swimming baths opened on the waterfront. The tramway was converted to cable operation in 1902, and the prominent St John's RC Church was built in 1903. In 1907 the *Tower Pavilion* opened on the promenade, but its concert parties lasted only until 1916, when the full grimness of the world war was recognised; the pier was demolished in 1917, possibly for safety reasons. Meantime Portobello town hall was built in 1912–14. From 1913 Portobello, through which growing NBR trainloads of coal passed to Leith docks for export, had the first train control centre in Scotland. In 1915 the NBR opened their Lothian Lines, linking the Waverley route and Suburban lines at Niddrie North to Seafield and Leith docks without interfering with the main line, by passing over it west of Joppa station and around the north side of the extensive Portobello goods yard.

**Electric Trams, Villas and Power Station**: The prominent new red-brick coal-fired power station on the sea front was built in 1919–23, and on its completion the cable trams were replaced by speedier electric cars, with further services added to Leith and to Musselburgh. Then suburbanisation took over vast areas of bungalows were built in the 1930s southwest of Portobello. From 1936 cooling water from the power station heated the outdoor swimming pool. The *George Cinema*, later known as the *County*, was built in 1937, and by 1939 Portobello had a short-lived ice rink. By 1949 the former chocolate factory was the Ramsay Technical School (and later became an annexe to Stevenson College). By the 1950s Portobello – minus its pier – had the other facilities of a typical seaside town, though its proximity to the Edinburgh sewage outfalls cannot have helped its resort role; the population was about 28,500. Meantime after 1946 Leith Athletic FC played briefly at Portobello, moving on to Old Meadowbank before vanishing in 1953, after 39 discontinuous years in the Scottish League.

**Buses, Beer and Freightliners**: The trams were replaced by buses in 1954, and the United Glass bottle works was still open in 1959. The railway station was sadly closed in 1964 by Beeching, whose plan established there a freightliner terminal for Edinburgh soon afterwards. Meantime as the incoming

*Pottery – including tableware and sanitary ware – was made in Portobello from 1770. Buchan's pottery kilns, seen here, were saved by Edinburgh Corporation, repaired, and are preserved as monuments. (Buchan's moved to Crieff in 1972.)* *(JRH)*

population of the 1930s grew older so total numbers fell, to 22,000 by 1971. The Thistle sanitary pottery works – which used clays from south-west England and had turned to making stone tableware – was again modernised in 1956 by A W Buchan & Co, but was closed in 1972; the firm moved to Crieff *(q.v.)*, leaving little industry in the Portobello area, which still had eleven hotels in 1981. In 1982 the freightliner terminal seemed to handle mainly beer – from the city's most bulk-producing industry – but was closed as unprofitable in 1987.

**Bypass Built but Old Landmarks fall**: Built about 1980, the Portobello bypass – called Sir Harry Lauder Road after the early 20th century popular entertainer and song composer, born in Portobello in 1870 – took over the route of the former Lothian Lines railway. The power station was closed and demolished as obsolete in 1979–80, with the resulting closure of its once-famed outdoor swimming pool, described by McKean in 1987 as *"magnificent in its dereliction"*; by 1989 its demolition had removed another local landmark. In 1990 the Scottish Bus Group's maintenance workshops at Seafield were closed, with the loss of another 86 jobs – a deliberate casualty, arranged in advance of privatisation. By 1995 the Jewel & Esk Valley College, built about 1987 on a site at Milton Road East and with an offshoot at Newbattle, was one of Scotland's largest Further Education colleges, offering many vocational subjects. In 1995 the former chocolate factory, redundant as the W M Ramsay Technical Institute, was converted into 36 flats.

**Retailing, Beach Cleaning and Railway Pointwork**: In the mid-eighties large ASDA and Comet stores were built south-east of Portobello, near the starting point of the major A1 bypass of Musselburgh. Sea bathing, inevitably cold, was still hazardous in 1994 when the beach was still infected with the *E.Coli* bacterium. Consequently a major treatment project was begun by East of Scotland Water, a large sewage pumping station being opened on the shore in the late 90s. In 2000 the Scottish Parliament approved a scheme to reopen a freight branch railway to passengers, with a service to Waverley from a terminal station at Kinnaird Park via a new station at Brunstane south-east of Portobello. In 2000–01 the Baileyfield depot was busy making up new pointwork for Railtrack following the Hatfield derailment. The *Kings Manor* on Milton Road has 70 rooms, but nowdays most of Portobello's hotels and guest houses are small. Portobello High School has 1400 pupils, the largest roll now in the city's care.

## PORT OF MENTEITH — Map 5, C4

***Perthshire hamlet**, pop. 150* — OS 57: NN 5801

In a low-lying area some 15 km west of Doune lies the small shallow Loch of Menteith, south of which was a Roman fort. Inchmahome Priory was founded on the largest island in the loch in 1238 by Walter Comyn. The nearby island castle of Inchtalla was the seat of the powerful Earls of Menteith, who sat in Parliament in 1560, as did the Augustinian Commendator of the priory. The priory fell into ruin after the Reformation, as did the castle of Inchtalla after the last earl died in the late 17th century, and also Rednock Castle 1.5 km to the east. Only Cardross Castle, a 16th century tower on the edge of Flanders Moss 4 km to the south-east was to survive. The area was still roadless about 1750, when Roy's map showed hamlets clustered around the *'Kirk of Port'* beside the landing place for the island ferry. Later in the 18th century the Port had a *"little inn"*. Rednock House, an emparked neo-classical mansion designed by Robert Brown of Edinburgh, was built early in the 19th century; its 1840s extensions seem unfortunate.

**Tourism renames the Loch**: About 1810 the loch was renamed the *'Lake'* of Menteith for the benefit of the growing trickle of English tourists arriving by coach along the new road from Stirling to the Trossachs. For many years a railway station was hopefully labelled *'Port of Menteith'*, but it was actually a winding 6 km distant to the south, at the hamlet of Arnprior – a name implying some relationship to the priory. By 1894 there was a *"fair"* hotel at the Port itself; this was a base for pike fishing in the loch, and it had gradually grown to 14 rooms by 1980. The last traditional curling *'Bonspiel'* or grand tournament on the icy loch was held in 1979, since when the winter ice has been too thin. By 1981 the local resident population had inched up to about 150 in all. The *Lake Hotel* has a view of the picturesque ruined priory and castle in the charming setting of the loch; these are still accessible by ferry.

## PORTPATRICK — Map 1, B5

***Galloway village**, pop. 550* — OS 82: NX 0054

Dunskey Castle was built in the 16th century on the rocky west coast of the Rhinns peninsula in Galloway. It was emphasised on Pont's map made about 1610, together with a mill, *'Chapel Patrick'*, and *'Poirtpatrick'*, the small steep-sided bay nearby. This was the probable objective of the military road lately laid out across Galloway to aid in the misconceived Plantation of Ulster, that was to bring so much grief in succeeding centuries. Portpatrick was chartered as a burgh of barony in 1620, under the now forgotten name of *Montgomerie*. Despite its exposure to westerly gales, by 1627 this had become the ferry port for Belfast via Donaghadee, and had a livestock trade – of sorts: Brereton, an intrepid traveller about 1636, noted *"a most craggy, filthy passage, and very dangerous for horses to go in and out. When any horses land here, they are thrown into the sea, and swim out"*.

**Posts and Harbour Improvements**: When Scotland's second and third postal routes were opened in 1642 – linking Edinburgh to Ireland via Ayr, and also Carlisle/Dumfries to Ireland – this perilous spot was the chosen embarkation point and was given a post office. The harbour works were rebuilt in 1716, and Defoe commented a few years later that *"it has a tolerable good harbour, and a safe road; but there is very little use for it, for the packet boat, and a few fishing vessels are the sum of the navigation"*. As the Roy map showed, there was still only one road to Portpatrick in the 1750s – from Stranraer. As trade burgeoned later in the century, a pier promoted by Sir James Hunter Blair and designed by Smeaton was added in 1774–78. From 1790 a mail coach ran through from Bridge of Sark (Gretna) to Portpatrick. Heron wrote in 1799 of a *"small town"* of about 500 people, *"chiefly noted for its ferry to Donaghadee. Shipbuilding is the only manufacture hitherto attempted here"*. About 11,000 cattle and 2000 horses were annually imported from Ireland.

**Paddle Steamers and Problems**: From 1819 paddle steamers called en route from Greenock to Douglas and Liverpool. Portpatrick was by 1827 (according to Chambers) *"a town of considerable size and thriving character, the chief point of communication between Scotland and Ireland; four packets sailing constantly. It possesses an excellent harbour with a reflecting light-house"*. However, all was not well. John Rennie re-designed the ambitious stone pier to improve the difficult harbour entrance, but by 1847 it was realised that the heavy investment had provided inadequate shelter from storm, so in the interests of safety and reliability the first GPO packet steamer service to Donaghadee ended in 1849.

**The Portpatrick Railway**: The Portpatrick Railway opened from Stranraer in 1862, with an intermediate station at Colfin; there were two trains a day. A siding, dropping down at 3% (1 in 35) from the terminus, was the sole rail access to the harbour, ending beside a basin 9 m deep and 63 m square, built at public expense in 1861–65. Meantime Stranraer took most of the traffic, although from 1868 Portpatrick again had various short-lived steamer services to Donaghadee. Public maintenance of the harbour ended in 1873; the steamers were immediately transferred to Stranraer. In 1874 the new piers were ruined by a gale, and Portpatrick was finally recognised as being too exposed; in 1875 the harbour line was lifted by the railway company (the rails being re-used at Newton Stewart).

**Electricity in Various Guises – and Golf**: Infrequent trains still ran to Portpatrick, but the population in 1891 was only 520 and in his 1894 Handbook Murray stated that *"the town is a poor little place"*. There were then two hotels, the *Crown* and *Downshire*; besides the latter name, all that remained evident of the Irish connection was the landfall of the undersea telegraph cable. In 1900 due to the illumination of a new light 3 km to the north-west at Killantringan, the harbour lighthouse was ignominiously dismantled, and shipped to Colombo! The Dunskey golf club's two cliff-top courses of 18 and 9 holes were founded in 1903, and from 1904 a public electricity supply was available from a small power station. The 65-room *Portpatrick Hotel* dates from the Edwardian period, and coastguard, lifeboat and radio stations were established during an otherwise uneventful half century. A creamery was built beside the railway at Colfin Croft, 4km east of Portpatrick, which remained a sleepy fishing port and minor resort village of 1000 people; the railway was closed completely in 1950, and the station became a caravan site. Colfin station was taken into the creamery, whose milk traffic kept the section of line to Stranraer open until 1959; the creamery later became a fish processing plant.

**Carpets, Caravans and Walkers**: By 1972 the modest *Fernhill Hotel* was open in Portpatrick, and by 1977 *Knockinaam Lodge*, on the coast 5km to the south, was a small hotel. By 1980 there were nine hotels and inns, and three caravan sites. Portpatrick harbour, seemingly uncared for by any authority, briefly regained its original role during ferry strikes: during one in 1966 the author photographed carpets made at Donaghadee being unloaded there from fishing boats; this activity recurred in 1970 and 1988. Killantringan lighthouse was automated in 1984. In 1991 the village population was 539. By 1996 Portpatrick was the western terminus of the Southern Upland Way long-distance path, and there has been some new development. Hotels now include the *Fernhill*, the long-established *Downshire Arms*, and *Knockinaam Lodge* (5km from the village). There are plenty small hotels (some now 100 years old or more), plus guest houses, restaurants and two caravan sites.

## PORTREE

**Map 8, A3**

***Main town, Isle of Skye,*** *pop. 2100* — OS 23: NG 4843

Monro noted in 1549 the *"rough and hard land"* of the Isle of Skye (whose name means *'Winged'* in Gaelic, from its many peninsulas). But he added that its twelve parish kirks were supported by *"manured and inhabited fertile land, namely for oats, pastures abounding in store cattle, many woods, many forests, many deer and good take of salmon and herrings"*. He mentioned its six districts, owned by four lairds – but didn't say that not long before, James V had visited a church and settlement on a fine natural harbour on the east coast, which was then renamed in his honour from Kiltaraglen to *Portrigh* (*King's Port* in Gaelic), anglicised as Portree. Nearby were ancient duns. Neither James nor any other monarch appears to have signed a burgh charter, but by the early 17th century Portree had acquired a cattle market which had become important; drovers' bills (cheques) were then acceptable as rent. Martin writing in 1703 noted *"there are two fairs of late held yearly at Portree; the convenience of the harbour made this the fittest place"*. Held in June and September, these traded in *"horses, cows, sheep, goats, hides, skins, butter, cheese, fish, wool &c."*

**Poverty and a Rare Proprietor spur Development**: In 1771 large groups of people were emigrating from Skye, fleeing from the poverty of overpopulation and underdevelopment – there was still hardly any cash in the whole of the isle, no wheeled vehicles, and not one shop. The local proprietor Sir James Macdonald – more enlightened than most of the island lairds – decided to try to stem the outflow by fostering Portree as a fishing village, and putting in hand other improvements such as a school. In 1773 Boswell stayed in *"a very good half-finished inn"* (later the *Royal Hotel*). Heron described Portree in 1799 as *"the only town or village on this island, its trade chiefly in black cattle, of which several thousands are annually exported"*.

**Roads, Steamers, Overpopulation and Poverty**: Portree saw the opening of its first post office in 1823, but still relied on Sconser and Dunvegan for its mails. Evidently a pier was also built, enabling steamers from West Loch Tarbert to ply to Portree via Tobermory, Isle Ornsay and Kyleakin. These arrived weekly from 1826, and roads were laid out by Telford from Kyleakin to Portree, Uig and Waternish, but the steamer service was cut back to monthly in 1828 and apparently discontinued between 1831 and 1838. By 1841 the population of Skye reached its highest count – over 23,000. In 1846–47 Portree was one of two places chosen for a central grain depot as a temporary measure during the potato famine, which encouraged the clearances, already in progress to expand sheep grazing. The majority were evicted from their crofts over the next 45 years and, finding little or no work in Portree, most emigrated.

**Development, but "Hard Living"**: From 1851 a call was made by a steamer on the weekly through service between Glasgow and Stornoway, and there was a branch bank, perhaps that of the Caledonian Bank of Inverness, which definitely had a Portree branch by about 1878. The opening of the railway to Strome Ferry in 1870 made the north-east coast of Skye the most accessible, helping Portree to develop, albeit slowly, rather than ancient Dunvegan. The Gathering Hall was built by local lairds after their first Skye Gathering in 1878, and in 1886 Barnard noted the *Portree Hotel* as *"recommended"*; but Portree was described by the same source as *"capital of Skye, island of poverty and hard living"*. The 1891 population was 1003.

**Steamer Service Heyday**: The Crofters Act then gave a measure of stability, and by 1894 Portree pier hosted many steamer services, daily to Strome Ferry and less often to Stornoway, Tarbert, Lochmaddy, Dunvegan, Oban, Gairloch, Ullapool, and Lochinver. Portree was then described by Murray as a *"town"* with a sizeable tweed mill, banks, a sheriff court and the *"good" Marine* and *Royal* hotels. Other industries did not develop, although by 1914 steamer cruises from Portree served a rollcall of tourist delights: Arisaig, Armadale, Balmacara, Broadford, Craignure, Eigg, Glenelg, Kyleakin, Kyle, Lochaline, Oronsay, Raasay, Salen, Staffin, Stein and Tobermory! By the 1920s there was a secondary school in Portree, but the population of all Skye was only 10,000. From the 1920s afforestation began to make parts of Skye less bleak and more attractive to tourists. In 1931 a mail steamer still plied between Mallaig, Kyle and Portree, and the traditional shipping services were reinstated after 1945.

**Decline in Skye holds back Portree**: The underdevelopment of the Isle remained notorious: there was no public electricity supply until 1949, when the Storr Lochs hydro power scheme on the coast 10km north of Portree was brought into operation by the Hydro Board. By 1953 the facilities of a small town were available in Portree, including banks, shops, garages and five hotels; the secondary school (now Portree High School) had a hostel for children from remote areas. Roll-on ferries on short routes *(see Uig)* ended most of the steamer calls, and road transport developed *(see Kyle)*. Although hand looms were still plentiful, there was just one textile factory in Skye, Pringle's spinning and weaving works at Portree, using wool dyed in Inverness and employing only about 25 people to make knitting wool, blankets and tweed. By that time Skye's population was nearing its 1971 minimum of 7200, of whom 40 worked in forestry.

**The Tide turns**: The Portree golf club was founded in 1964, and by 1969 a 9-hole course had been laid out west of the town. By 1972 a hotel named *Coolin Hills* was open; it had been extended to 30 rooms by 1977 (and its name was later amended to *Cuillin Hills*). In 1975 Portree became the centre of the new Skye & Lochalsh District; the telephone exchange – the last manual public exchange in the UK – was replaced by an automatic one in 1976. Then Portree had fish merchants, and its boats were fishing for white and shell fish including scallops, winkles and lobsters. By 1981 a tiny 12-bed general hospital was open; the number of hotels had doubled in 30 years, and their star ratings improved. Though by then its out of season population was only some 1500, Portree had become the most accessible quasi-urban centre for a vast area extending from Lochalsh to the Uists and Barra, containing some 20,000 people. By 1988 Portree was developing into a balanced town; recent additions included a little industrial estate, and a caravan and camping site, and a swimming pool; in 1990 Portree became the base for Skye's first lifeboat.

**Back to Gaelic and Remote *'Local'* Government**: In 1991 Portree's 2126 people had 43% Gaelic speakers. As a result of growing local demand, and a policy change by the Highland Regional Council, from 1992 more primary children in Portree were taught in Gaelic than English, and for the first time some High School subjects were also being taught through the medium of Gaelic. In the 1990s the Gathering Hall was still the venue for a successful Skye Gathering – a ball for a select few. In 1996 the district council was merged into an all-purpose Highland Region, sadly ending Portree's 21-year period as a true centre of local government. Sheep are still locally significant: in 1996 the August sales dealt in 2000 lambs. There's a large selection of hotels, and guest houses, and two backpackers' hostels provide 86 beds.

## PORTSONACHAN & Cladich — Map 5, A3

***Argyll locations, L. Awe,*** *pop. under 100* — OS 50 or 56: NN 0420

By the time of Roy's survey about 1750, a ferry plied across the narrows of Loch Awe from the North Port to South Port near Portsonachan, where there are some ancient remains. In 1779 Pennant dined at Cladich, a *"little village"* on Caulfeild's road where it met the south shore of Loch Awe between Portsonachan and Dalmally, but in 1803 Dorothy Wordsworth found there merely *"a hut where they kept a dram"*, and eventually the small hamlet of Cladich faded to practically nothing. The ferry and Ardchonnel primary school survived as recently as 1956, when the *Portsonachan Hotel* boasted 3 stars and a sublime view. At that time *Ardbrecknish House* 2 km to the east was also open as a hotel, though this closed about 1970. Tiny Portsonachan still has its hotel and post office, plus a country club.

## PORTSOY — Map 10, B1

***Buchan coastal village,*** *pop. 1800* — OS 29: NJ 5966

The Burn of Boyne enters the Moray Firth about 8 km west of Banff. Boyne had a thanage from about the 11th century, with a coastal castle. The present (but long ruinous) Boyne Castle overlooking the burn was built by the Ogilvies of Boyne around 1580. Portsoy, a small bay at the mouth of the Burn of Durn 2 km farther west, was chartered by them as a burgh of barony in 1550; they also built its harbour. Ordens parish, 5 km south-east, had a school by 1633. Portsoy was shown as a tiny place on Gordon's map of about 1640. An inner harbour was built for Patrick Ogilvie, Lord Boyne in 1692, using the old but effective technique of placing stones on end, and Portsoy then became known as a trading port renowned for shipping marble, more correctly described as Serpentine. The quarry west of the harbour yielded some of the fine dark green stone used to make chimney pieces in the Palace of Versailles. The *Old Star Inn* was built in 1727, and at some time a meal mill was powered by a lade from the small artificial Loch Soy. When Roy mapped the area about 1750 he found a G-shaped harbour and a substantial town, largely comprising one main street parallel to the burn, which was not bridged. The area's only routeway was a track on the general line of the later coast road.

**A Handsome Seaport Town**: Portsoy post office was opened in 1763, and a bleachfield was set up in 1767 for the local thread industry. When Pennant visited Portsoy in 1769 he found *"a small town"* of 600 people who made snuff and who owned 18 ships and fishing boats. Then development forged ahead: by 1797 Portsoy was a post town with a daily service. In 1799 Heron wrote *"Portsoy is a handsome seaport town. It contains nearly 2000 inhabitants, many of whom are employed in the fisheries, or in coasting or foreign trade. Here are manufactures of snuff, of thread, and incombustible cloth"*, made from asbestos fibres found within the local marble. Fish-curing began in 1815 and Portsoy acquired a new stone-built harbour about 1830, but as ships grew larger its general cargo trade shrank.

**The Railway and the Herring Peak**: From 1859 Portsoy had a covered station, the terminus of the Banff, Portsoy & Strathisla Railway, later part of the Great North of Scotland (GNSR), which left the Banff line at Tillynaught 4 km to the south. A steep siding – on which engines might handle only four wagons at a time – was laid down to the harbour. A peak of 50 herring boats and over 2000 people was reached in 1881, but a storm seriously damaged the harbour; it was rebuilt in 1884. In the same year the GNSR extended the line west to Tochieneal, and in 1886 it reached Buckie and Elgin. The old Portsoy terminus became a goods shed, and for a time Wordie & Co had a rail cartage depot.

**Charming Town declines with the Fishing**: Around that time MacDonald Brothers of Portsoy ran a foundry manufacturing reapers and specialised fishing equipment such as steam-powered line haulers. But the opening of the spacious Cluny Harbour at Buckie led to Portsoy's fishing role declining. The 1891 population was 2060. Described by Barnard in 1886 as *"a charming little seaport town"*, in 1894 Murray merely referred to *"a small port with marble and pink granite quarries"*; no hotel was named. The harbour branch, lifted in 1910, became a footpath, and by 1929 Portsoy was said to be very derelict. In the second world war an airfield was built 3 km to the south-east, but was disused by 1955. Though by then three hotels were open, fishing from Portsoy had ceased; its general facilities were still those of a large village. These declined further over the next thirty years, with closure of the railway in 1968. The secondary school and cinema closed and the little hospital was downgraded, becoming a geriatric unit. By 1971 the population had fallen below 1700.

**Recovery with Tourism**: Portsoy was then becoming a minor tourist centre, with a rejuvenated marble craft and a large caravan and camping site. The conservation of its characterful old buildings began in the 1960s, earning a Saltire Society award in 1967. Even so, in 1970 the shore immediately west of the empty harbour was marred by a council rubbish tip! This was soon removed, the station site of 1884 became a park, and the one-time station building a base for Scouts and Guides. The three hotels of the 1950s had increased to five by 1981. Though the harbour was just as deserted in the mid 1980s, and the salmon station was last used in 1989, by 1990 a new swimming pool had been built and by 1991 the population was 1825, with 40% of households still renting in the public sector but also an affluent retired element. Little lobster boats still use the harbour, where A & J Sutherland, seafood specialists (established in 1908) are still in business, and Barclays Transport nearby runs a fleet of 15 lorries. There are some recently built houses and a wide range of shops and services, including two banks, post office, police station, library, hotel, garage and pub. Some derelict buildings which remain have been acquired for conservation; an annual festival of wooden boats is well known.

## PORT WILLIAM — Map 1, C5

***Galloway village,*** *pop. 750 (area)* — OS 82: NX 3343

Important prehistoric earthworks and standing stones have survived south of and beside the White Loch of Myrton, about 9 km north-west of Whithorn in the Machars of Galloway. They stand in the large parish of Mochrum, which had a chapel by about 1000 AD, and also a medieval motte, 3 km north of the loch. Beside the loch was built the 16th century L-plan tower of Myrton (or Merton) Castle, with its failed barony burgh of 1504; it was later replaced by the mansion of Monreith House. Timothy Pont, who mapped Galloway around 1610, noted Killantrae (an ancient Gaelic placename meaning *'Church on the Sands')*, an exposed coastal site beside the mouth of the little Killantrae Burn, about 2 km west of the White Loch.

**New Harbour and Village**: In the 1750s Roy's surveyors found many roads in the area, but no significant man-made features were shown on the raised beach at Killantrae, which Sir William Maxwell of Monreith was to select as the site for the entirely new settlement of Port William, which his workers built between 1770 and 1776. Heron found in 1799 *"a neat little village with a good harbour"*. A grain mill was built about 1800, and the harbour was extended early in the 19th century; Port William post office was issued with a date stamp in 1829. The population in the late 19th century was 700 to 800, and Port William was too small and remote to be courted by the railways: in 1894 its public transport comprised two coaches a week to Glenluce, serving the *Monreith Arms Hotel* in this *"thriving little harbour"*. This was still a trading port until about 1918 – witness the *Commercial Hotel*.

**Golf, Caravanning, Yachting and Fishing**: From 1905 the 9-hole St Medan golf course was available at Monreith, 5 km to the south-east (OS 83). By 1953 Mochrum parish had 1284 residents, and Port William was regarded as a holiday resort. The SMMB's Airlour dairy factory was in production by then, 1 km south; it was still in use in 1966 though closed by 1979. The old mill was still turning in 1976. Knock primary school near Monreith closed in the 1960s, but Monreith had a post office until about 1971. By 1978 there were caravan sites on the coast north of Port William, and the hamlet of Kirk of Mochrum still had the small *Greenmantle Hotel*, its post office, and a youth hostel (though the latter closed around 1990). By 1985 coastal caravan sites were also open at Monreith, but the resident population of Mochrum parish has fallen steadily, to only 729 in 1991. Port William harbour was protected in the 1980s by forming a breakwater of tipped stone; still used for yachting and boating, it is the base for an inshore rescue boat. The long-standing *Commercial Hotel* is amongst those at Port William; Mochrum still has its post office and *Greenmantle Hotel*. The Victorian *Corsemalzie House* (10 km north on B7005) is now a 14-room fishing hotel.

## POSSIL & Possilpark — Map 15, C4

***Northern parts of Glasgow,*** *pop. 24,000* — OS 64: NS 5968

Possil, which stands high 2 km to the north of central Glasgow, appeared (in two places!) on Pont's map made about 1600. A mansionhouse built there around 1700 was extended in 1809 by West India merchant Alex Campbell. Coal mining had begun by 1733 at nearby Wester Common, which was linked to Glasgow by a road – shown on the Roy map made about 1754. From about 1777 the pits lay beside the Forth & Clyde Canal; the mining community of Lambhill, which possessed numerous coal pits, gained the canal stables, a post office and inn. The canal was extended in 1777 from Maryhill to Hamiltonhill basin, and in 1790 to Port Dundas. From about 1880 the Forth & Clyde Canal crossed Possil Road by an unusual bridge, its main arch being at two levels; north of the canal at Lambhill were two marshes called Possil Loch and West Possil Loch, so shallow that they dried out in summer

**The Saracen Foundries**: About 1867 the 40 ha Possil estate was acquired by Walter Macfarlane & Co of the Saracen Foundry in Anderston, who demolished the fine house to build a new and larger Saracen Foundry. This opened about 1869, to make ornamental cast ironwork such as bandstands and fountains – and signs for Guardbridge station in Fife. The foundry also cast roof parts for the Great Western Railway on a large scale, gave its name to the main street, and further expanded from 1897 to 1902. An ornate monumental horse-trough cast there in 1901 still stands prominent at Stromness, as does a Saracen drinking fountain at Pitlochry station. Fine canopied fountains can be seen at Fraserburgh, Rutherglen and Tayport, and in museums at Summerlee and in Edinburgh.

**Railway, Engineering, Boatbuilding and Burrell**: On the opening of the railway (later part of the North British – NB) from Cowlairs to Maryhill in 1858 no station was provided, but coal working was encouraged; however the pits generally seem to have closed in the late 19th century. In 1859 John Norman & Co, engineers, millwrights and boilermakers, opened the Keppochhill Engine Works. From 1875 to 1903 William Burrell & Son built their own puffers at Hamiltonhill to work on the Forth & Clyde Canal. The younger Burrell also made money by buying ships cheaply in slumps and selling them dearly in booms; his share went into amassing the famed Burrell Collection *(see Pollokshaws)*. In the last quarter of the century, many iron companies set up, including the long-lasting Possil Engine Works (making hydraulic flanging presses), the Clydesdale Iron Works (iron fences and gates), the Lambhill Iron Works (built for the gas and water engineers R Laidlaw & Son), the Possil Iron Works, the Keppoch Iron Works, and the North Woodside ironworks.

**Possil Park, Pottery, Trams & Industries**: A small area of housing round Bardowie Street was the first to develop after Lambhill. By 1879 a grid of streets had been laid out at Possil Park, a name later more generally adopted for a wider area; but despite the opening about 1881 of the Saracen Pottery Company's works in Denmark Street, most other streets were largely still awaiting the builders as late as 1895. There was little other development north of Keppochhill Road until the turn of the century; Possil Park was still a completely distinct settlement. A second railway, the Lanarkshire & Dunbartonshire (L&D), a protégé of the Caledonian, was opened in 1896 to tap the Clydebank market, and provided Possil with a station at Balmore Road. In 1900 Glasgow trams reached Hawthorn Street, where a 133-car depot was built, and about then the NB opened a more conveniently connected station named Possilpark a stone's throw from the L&D's; by 1925 both were closed. In 1902 the paint manufacturer A H Hamilton erected the Possil Park Paint Works.

**Hospital, Cemeteries and Council Houses**: The huge Ruchill Hospital was also built early in the 20th century. At that time the civil engineering contractors Balfour Beatty – who built the Lochaber Aluminium project – had their main depot at Possil Park. The remaining areas south of the foundry nucleus were filled around 1922 by the tenement blocks of Hamiltonhill housing estate, Glasgow Corporation's first slum clearance rehousing scheme, served by municipal trams and later buses. Vast cemeteries were laid out by 1925 at Lambhill, and after 1925 arose the Parkhouse estate to the north, completely surrounded by the competing railway lines. Possil station was reopened in 1934. After 1945 the High Possil and Balmore industrial estates were laid out, and West Possil Loch vanished into a *'site reserved for industry'* which never came. Glasgow Corporation's socially disastrous Milton housing scheme was completed in 1948; it centred on the Glasgow School for the Deaf, but also gained St Augustine's RC Secondary School, now a primary. While being far from most other facilities, its tenants could see prosperous Bishopbriggs across a narrow space. In 1958 the *Vogue Cinema* at Ruchill was still showing films; later it turned to bingo.

**Decline, Deprivation and Football**: Rail services were again withdrawn from Possil in 1964–66, the ex-Caledonian line being lifted. The once-great Saracen Foundry closed in 1966, soon demolished; its business was bought by Heritage Engineering of Carmyle, but it left its Saracen name to a pub football team, which was to win the Scottish Amateur Cup in 1990. The Clydesdale Iron Works also closed, in 1968, and the paint works was destroyed by fire. However, by 1979 Holden & Fisher made electronic devices at Glentanar Road; Hugh Smith & Sons' Possil Works still made machine tools in 1983. By 1980 Ashfield football ground had become the Ashfield Stadium, but in 1981 the area was far from prosperous. Possilpark and Hamiltonhill then had the lowest levels of car ownership in Britain, only about one household in ten having a car. Industrial employment was shrinking, and social problems including drugs burgeoned.

**Fighting Back Against the Odds**: Local people – who claimed with some justice that Possil was the most deprived area in Glasgow – formed a housing co-operative in 1984; by 1988 this had bought its first street for improvement, but the area's image remained disastrous. In 1992, due to falling rolls and the need for retrenchment, the Regional Council closed Possilpark Secondary School, which like most schools in deprived areas was decidedly non-academic, but at least provided a community focus for an area which ran its own little festival. At that time during the recession the official unemployment rate in Possil was 35.5%, even higher than in the most deprived ex-mining area of Scotland (Sanquhar), and by 1993 there were really serious drugs problems. In 1993 passenger train services were reintroduced on the east–west route from Maryhill via well-sited stations at Lambhill, Possilpark and Ashfield, extending to Queen Street via Cowlairs. A new commercial centre had been built by 1995, but by then Ruchill Hospital was a disused *'building at risk'*. By 1988 the marshy Possil Loch had been cleared out, and by 1996 was a nature reserve.

## POTTERTON & Belhelvie — Map 10, C3

***Aberdeenshire villages**, pop. 1200* — OS 38: NJ 9415

Belhelvie, in the rolling countryside about 12 km north of Aberdeen, had a thanage from about the 11th century. Robert Gordon's map of about 1640 showed *'Pottertown'* some 1.5 km south of Belhelvie Kirk. By 1894 Potterton House and the adjacent Milton of Potterton had developed on the Potterton Burn; at nearby Denhead was a Free Church, but otherwise only scattered farms. A quarry near Belhelvie was well established by 1967, but had closed by the mid 1980s. Meantime some houses had been built near the Aberdeen to Pitmedden road. By 1980, after a decade of North Sea oil development, garage services were available at the Potterton Shop, and growth had begun in earnest: by 1983 two large housing estates and a public house had been built around the Free Church, and a sandpit was open. By 1991 nearly 1150 people lived in this loosely defined youthful dormitory settlement, mostly buying detached houses. Although there has been little further development, there is now a post office.

## PRESTON, Bunkle & Cumledge — Map 3, B3

***Berwickshire hamlets**, pop. 200 (area)* — OS 67 or 74: NT 7957

Some 5 km north of Duns in Berwickshire is a hill fort, east of which are the scant remains of Bunkle Castle and the ancient church of Bunkle. When Pont mapped the area around 1600, the ancient *'Kirk of Prestoun'* stood beside the Whiteadder Water between Bunkle and Duns, with *'Brunnhouse'* mill 2 km downstream. Preston became a burgh of barony in 1602, but remained in obscurity – it was certainly off the roads until after Roy's survey, made about 1754. The Broomhouse paper mill was established on the Whiteadder Water around 1780, perhaps by conversion of the existing mill; in 1832 an early newsprint machine was installed, but paper manufacture later ceased. In 1901 Bunkle & Preston parish had 630 residents. Cumledge Mill near Preston church was making blankets and tweeds when its weaving sheds were ravaged by the floods of 1948. The steam-driven mill gave its name to a telephone exchange, which had 57 lines by 1951, but the nearby hamlet of Preston seems never to have possessed a post office. The mill closed about 1970, and was demolished. With ensuing population decline the parish school was closed in the mid 1970s. In 1991 Bunkle & Preston parish had only 237 people, its main distinction now being its antiquities.

## PRESTONPANS **Map 15, E1**

***E. Lothian large coastal village,*** *pop. 7000* OS 66: NT 3874

This coastal settlement about 13 km east of Edinburgh was founded in the 12th century by monks from Newbattle Abbey (the modern A6094 follows their route to the shore). Prestonpans was the *'Priest-town'* where seawater was evaporated from iron *pans* by burning small coal of very local origin, leaving unrefined dry salt. Eight tonnes of coal were needed to produce a tonne of salt, much of which went overland for use in the Borders. By about 1500 the tall L-plan Preston Tower had been built by the Hamiltons. In 1526 the abbot built a harbour at Prestonpans, and tide mills for meal grinding were permitted inside this in 1541. The *'Newhaven of Preston'* appeared in 1542 Customs returns. Prestonpans was made a burgh of barony in 1552, and a parish grammar school for *'three tongues'* was opened in 1591. Pont's map made around 1600 showed a curved pier named *'Achesons Haven'* as the principal feature of tiny *'Prestoun pans'*; at neighbouring Preston, just inland, the tall tower (to which two more storeys had been added shortly before 1600), was emphasised.

**Mansions, Mills and Glass**: The mansion of Northfield House was built in 1611, and about the same time Lord Magdalen, the Hamilton laird, erected his house opposite. By the 17th century local mills were driven by the drainage water from mine adits, and brewing was also carried on commercially. However in 1621 the harbour was still contributing under 1.5% of Scottish customs duties. Tucker in 1655 called Prestonpans *"a small place where there are many salt-pans; many small vessels come to fetch salt"*. After 1707 finer quality salt could be imported from brine fields in Cheshire, and for a time the local salt-making tended to decline. However, Bankton House, 1 km south-east, was built in 1717. Defoe noted that a glassworks had been set up at Prestonpans *"for making flint-glass, and other glass ware: but discontinued for want of skilful hands"*, but another brewery was founded in 1720. Timber was being imported by 1747, and boats were being built.

**Sulphuric Acid starts Scotland's Industrial Revolution**: Building on the cheapness of the local coal, in 1749 the Birmingham partners – the chemist John Roebuck and Samuel Garbett, pioneers of the industrial revolution in Scotland – opened the Prestonpans Vitriol Company's works, the world's first use of their *'lead-chamber'* process. Their dangerous product (sulphuric acid) was for use in linen bleaching, and in English and Dutch industries. In 1751 they also founded a pottery, perhaps at first making carboys. William Cadell managed local mines for the Commissioners for the Forfeited Estates. The Roy map of about 1754 showed Prestonpans as a long narrow village on the coast road, with three other radial roads; nearby Preston was a smaller place. In 1759 Roebuck and Garbett took Cadell into partnership, sold their various interests and moved away with their entrepreneurial skills to found the famed Carron *(q.v.)* Company in 1759. By 1784 under their successors the Prestonpans plant was Britain's largest acid works, much of the product being exported.

**Posts and Potteries**: About 1790 only six of the ten salt pans were in use, but the trade soon revived, for more were still being built around 1800. There was a postal service by 1775, and a new post office opened at Prestonpans in 1793, with two posts a day to and from Edinburgh, via Musselburgh. Further tide mills were built in the 1790s for grinding flint for the potteries, which then employed some 250 people. Twelve tonnes of coal were needed to fire a tonne of clay, most of which was imported from Devon and Cornwall; at one time a Prestonpans china factory used cobalt produced at Alva. In 1799 Heron wrote of *"about 1500 people in the town of Prestonpans, noted for its several salt-works, a brick and tile work, vitriol, manganese, and Glauber-salts manufactures, and two potteries. The fishing here is mainly for oysters, of which immense quantities were formerly caught and exported"*. The harbour was *"small but safe"*, with a custom-house. He added *"immense quantities of coal are dug from the inexhaustible mines"* in the area. Under the will of James Schaws, his mansion of Preston House had become a school *"for the education of boys whose parents are in poor circumstances"*. The repeal of the Salt Tax in 1823 nearly killed the salt industry in Scotland, but it struggled on at Prestonpans, which Chambers in 1827 described as an *"ancient seat of the salt manufacture, a considerable village which has a thriving manufactory of stone-ware"*. He fully described the salt panning process; women still carried the salt to Edinburgh for sale.

*The Cornish beam engine, installed at the Prestongrange colliery in 1874, when it was already 21 years old; it drained the mine-workings (which extended under the River Forth) until 1954. It is still preserved on site as part of a local museum.* *(JRH)*

**Railway, Broon Coos, and Deep Mining**: The North British Railway's main line opened in 1846, with a station (originally named *Tranent*) near Bankton House, which was made more imposing in 1852. A gasworks was built about the same time. In 1874 a huge, 21-year-old Cornish mine engine with a cylinder 178 cm in diameter was installed at the 244 m-deep Prestongrange colliery *(see Hay & Stell)*. The straggling village of Cuthill developed along the coast road between the colliery and Prestonpans, where there was an inn. In the late 19th century *'Broon Coo'* teapots were made locally in huge numbers. Bricks and tiles were locally made from fireclay from 1838. Prestongrange Brickworks at Morrison's Haven also made pottery such as urns; they drew clay from the coal mines, and their 100 or so workers used the Hoffman continuous kiln process, working into the 20th century. The population in 1891 was over 2200. By then John Fowler's brewery was large, but Prestonpans was a *"dingy place"* to Murray in 1894, when two mineral railways from mines near Tranent converged on the station. The local colliery was expanded in 1905 when pumps by Andrew Barclay of Kilmarnock were installed. And a public library (with Carnegie aid) started up around this time.

**Golf arrives; Trams, Salt and Brewing pass**: In 1926 the famous Royal Musselburgh golf club moved to a new 18-hole parkland course at Preston Grange; Preston Links colliery was at work around this time. From the 1920s the Musselburgh Tramways Company ran trams from the Edinburgh boundary through Prestonpans to Port Seton, but in 1932 the route was taken over by the Edinburgh tramways and the 5 km section east of Levenhall abandoned. Prestonpans remained a coal port until the 1920s, and both pits worked coal under the sea. Around 1935 sailing vessels from northern Europe ceased to trade in salt and the harbour became derelict, though Prestonpans had the last salt pan in Scotland when it closed in 1959. Soap was also made by 1953. Fowler's brewery succumbed to the giant United Breweries in 1960.

**From Deep Mining to Textiles and Power**: The Cornish mine engine worked at Prestongrange until 1954 and was preserved *in situ* when the colliery was closed in 1962, becoming the prime exhibit of the mining museum (now under East Lothian Council); Preston Links colliery closed in 1964. The Thorn Tree Golf Course vanished under the coal-fired Cockenzie power station, built in the 1960s; Prestonpans was dominated by its 500 or so steady jobs, and the population peaked at over 8500 around 1971. By 1979 Don Brothers of Dundee had a factory making PVC and polyurethane material for tarpaulins and protective clothing, Prestonpans then having the facilities of a large village. By 1988 a new Presto store and an active Co-op were local features. In 1991 the population was 7014. Bankton House, fire damaged in 1966, was restored as four flats in the early 1990s. Small/medium firms now include coppersmithing engineers, traffic systems experts, and suppliers of industrial knives. Preston Lodge High School has a roll of about 850. The tourist attractions, both 17th century, are the market cross (HS) and Hamilton House (NTS).

## PRESTWICK

**Map 1, C2**

***Ayrshire town,*** *pop. 13,700* — OS 70: NS 3526

Prestwick lies south of the mouth of the small Pow Burn on a flat and featureless coastal site in Kyle. Though its oldest record of a church dates from 1163, the name suggests an early Anglian religious origin. Walter Fitzalan, Steward of Scotland under David I, promoted Prestwick as the first Scottish burgh of barony around 1170. Though Fitzalan's castle was at Dundonald, some 9 km to the north, the whole area became known as *Kyle Stewart*. A leprosy hospital was founded by King Robert Bruce early in the 14th century, and a school by 1381. But by that time Ayr, 4 km to the south, had stolen Prestwick's thunder, and references to developments appear lacking for two centuries; it paid no tax in 1535–56. The area was however well settled by the time of Pont's sketch-mapping work about 1600, and the *'Sandmil'* stood on the Pow just north of *'Prestinck Kirk'*. When Roy mapped southern Scotland about 1754, Prestwick was a one-street village on the road between Ayr and Irvine, and another lane led inland. The Maryburgh Salt Works was built about 1760. In 1799 Heron did no more than mention *"the ancient borough of Prestic"*. Prestwick's importance remained minimal, with not so much as a post office until after the coming of the Glasgow Paisley Kilmarnock & Ayr Railway in 1839, when the new station initially served a mere 200 inhabitants.

**Enter Tom Morris and the Open**: The first Prestwick golf course *('Old Prestwick')* was laid out in 1851. When the clever clubmaker Tom Morris moved from St Andrews as greenkeeper and brought in the new gutta percha rubber ball, the place immediately began to thrive as a golfing resort and residential town. The very first Open championship was staged there in 1860, and a second course – the St Nicholas – had been laid out by 1875 around the Salt Works. The population in 1891 was almost 1500. In 1894 Murray noted *"one of the finest courses in Scotland"*. A third 18-hole course, the St Cuthbert, was added in 1899, and the population was nearing 3000 when Prestwick became a police burgh in 1903.

**Mining Quarrels, Quarrying, Swimming and Flying**: A new freight railway was opened in 1892 to link Monkton with Annbank to the east; beside this line the major Auchincruive No.4/5 colliery, usually called Glenburn, was sunk in 1912 some 2 km inland (though its workings extended under the sea). Despite being given its own housing, it developed a bad reputation for unofficial strikes. In the early 20th century two 20 m-deep quarries were excavated on the coast near the boundary between Prestwick and Ayr (by 1954 they had become water hazards on one of the golf courses). Coastal residential development continued, and a swimming pool was built in the 1930s. Aviation arrived in 1933 when pleasure flights took off from the beach.

**Prestwick International Airport and the End of Coal**: The early development of Prestwick's airfield is detailed under Monkton *(q.v.)*; south-east of Prestwick is Heathfield, where a fighter airfield was in use in wartime 1941. Prestwick officially became an international airport in 1946, though a military presence remained – the Fleet Air Arm's HMS *Gannet*. When in 1951 the USAF set up a base it had two relatively short runways on a Saltire plan. Its story is continued in this article, due to the extension of the main east–west runway to 2200 m in length by 1954 and the creation of a new third runway on a north–south alignment east of the town (crossing the line of the lately closed Annbank railway). Later, by diverting the Prestwick–Monkton road westwards, it grew to almost 3000 m – the longest civil runway in Scotland; Air Canada planes flew from it continuously for 44 years. The large new terminal building was opened in 1964. Meantime Glenburn Colliery had the area HQ and workshops of the NCB until the mid 1960s; it closed in 1973.

**Resort and Software Suburb**: In the 1950s Prestwick town had about 20 hotels totalling 250 rooms; the largest for some years was the 30-roomed *Queen's* on the Esplanade, succeeded by 1976 by the 39-roomed *Carlton* at Prestwick Toll and the short-lived *Towans Hotel*, which had 57 rooms in 1977 (but had been demolished by 1997 following a fire). In 1963 the software firm of GB Techniques was founded at Prestwick; Prestwick Circuits was founded by Bill and Eric Miller, sons of Rolls-Royce manager William Miller *(see Hillington)*. By 1971 Prestwick had a more sizeable town centre, serving a specialised settlement which had grown to over 13,000 people in its own right and also as a suburb of Ayr; under 30% of the houses were owned by the town council. By 1972 a major dual carriageway eastern bypass of Monkton and Prestwick had been built as the A77. In 1975 Prestwick burgh vanished into the Ayr-based Kyle & Carrick District.

**Glasgow Airport beats Prestwick**: North-West Airlines flights came to Prestwick in 1979, but in 1988 the echoing void of the 1964 terminal was still very much underused, with a mere 300,000 passengers a year, and in order to stimulate development the airport was made a freeport by the government, with a Scottish Development Agency area project; but for four years there were no takers. The railway was electrified in 1977, but trains passed by the terminal building without stopping; the provision of an airport passenger station was not seriously considered until 1989! The airport's status as Scotland's only long-haul gateway was very unpopular with the airlines and the business community; both wanted the flights transferred to Glasgow Airport. The government reluctantly conceded the points; Air Canada and US all-cargo airline Federal Express immediately transferred their operations to Glasgow Airport. A large airfreight depot announced by TNT in 1989 was cancelled, and British Airways' freight operation was also removed to Abbotsinch in 1990. However although passenger numbers fell by three quarters, the lately privatised owners BAA promised to keep the runway open, even though it required improvement.

**Hi-Tech Industry, Flying Training and Airspace Control**: Meantime Prestwick town was not only interested in aviation and golf: by 1989 GB Techniques were leaders in computerised newspaper production, and by 1991 the population was 13,700, including many affluent retired who owned their homes outright. The freeport's first firm, Escom Computer AG of Germany, began manufacturing there as *'European Monitors'* in 1992 and planned a factory with 500 workers making 50,000 computer monitors a month *(see Irvine)*. The airport remained very active except for passengers: since the BAe Flying College (see Monkton) opened in 1988, 700 daily aircraft movements frequently occurred. By 1991 Prestwick had the Scottish Oceanic Air Traffic Control Centre (SOATCC); this governed all civil airline movements from Iceland to France and as far east as the English crossroads over Daventry, the busiest controlled airspace in the world. SOATCC employed 600 when it was decided in 1996 that it should remain and be rebuilt; from 2000 some 700 construction jobs would be needed, safeguarding 530 permanent jobs from 2006. HMS *Gannet* was still operational, and in 1989 the US Air Force retained a staging facility. In 1993 Prestwick was the sole Royal Naval Air Service base in Scotland, the base for Sea King Search and Rescue helicopters. In 1994 the Canadian Air Force also used Prestwick as a staging point; the old Salt Works buildings still stood derelict.

**PIK Busy under New Ownership: Freight returns**: In 1992 BAe and others formed a new consortium including local authorities, named PIK – the airport's call sign – which bought the airport from BAA. There was an unexpected rise in all-cargo movements when Federal Express returned in 1993, launching a new daily air-freight service from Prestwick via Paris to America using wide-bodied DC10s, aiming to intercept some of the 78% of Scottish air freight exports that were moved by road to Heathrow for air shipment. Also in 1993 Polar Air Cargo of Columbus, Ohio planned to serve Prestwick on a round the world air cargo service. Then in April 1995 UPS launched a weekly Boeing 747 cargo service to New England for Scottish electronic exports, competing with the daily FE service.

**Better Facilities and Ground Links**: In 1993 almost 100 staff were still employed by PIK, and its own air traffic control system was to open; PIK was also planning a freight terminus able to serve at least ten wide-bodied aircraft. The second runway was to be fully reopened, and road access improved. In 1993–94 occasional loads of aviation fuel from Grangemouth still arrived by rail at Prestwick. A coach service was provided between the airport and the town railway station until the *'International Airport'* station was at last opened in 1994, from when Ryanair flew daily to Dublin. In 1998 the airport changed hands again, being bought by Stagecoach of Perth. In 1999 a new direct air freight service was begun to Singapore. In 2000 HMS *Gannet* with its search and rescue helicopter role was to be trimmed down from 450 jobs. There are several small-to-medium hotels in Prestwick, plus guest houses.

## PUMPHERSTON & Uphall Station — Map 16, C3

***W. Lothian villages**, pop. 1500* — OS 65: NT 0669

The hilltop settlement of *'Pomferston'* south of Uphall in West Lothian was probably named after early landowners named Pomfray; it was somewhat misplaced on Pont's map of around 1600. The mid 18th century Roy map showed that by then it lay on the Midcalder to Linlithgow road. The Edinburgh & Bathgate Railway, later part of the North British (NB) which opened in 1849 provided Uphall Station, midway between Pumpherston and Uphall. Neither place had any special significance until the Pumpherston oil shale works was opened in

*Pumpherston brickworks, built in 1934, worked for some 60 years, making the distinctive pink 'SOL' bricks from lime and spent shale – extensively used for internal and external work. (JRH)*

*The Pumpherston Oil Works – one of the most important and long-lasting sites of the shale-oil industry (beginning in 1883). By the 1950s it was refining oil made in other works. On the left in this view are coke stills, which were used for 'cracking' heavy oils to make motor fuel. The refinery closed in 1964, but a sulphonation plant continued here into the 1990s.* (Scottish Oils / BP)

1883 by William Fraser from the Uphall oil works and J Craig, whose Paisley engineering firm A F Craig & Co produced plant and retorts for the industry; the *'Pumpherston Retort'*, developed here, soon halved production costs. By 1894 the Pumpherston works employed 700 men processing 600 tons of ammonia-rich shale a day; their efficiency made for vast profits, peaking at 50% in 1901. The population of Pumpherston was then approaching 1500. The company also operated at Deans, and at Tarbrax from 1904.

**Housing, Facilities and Rundown**: By 1902 the firm had built 220 houses for its workers, including the new settlement of *'Station Rows'* where another 500 or so people lived. The works – which also treated oil brought from wells in England – was connected by a mineral railway with the NB and with further oil works east of Uphall Station; the line brought shale from a mine at East Calder and a quarry at Camps north of Kirknewton, where it connected with the Caledonian Railway. By then Pumpherston had acquired a post and telegraph office, primary schools and a substantial Institute built in 1891. The Pumpherston golf club, founded in 1910, laid out its 9-hole course in a small corner as enormous red bings gradually mounted into the sky on all sides. The oil works eventually became part of Scottish Oils and of BP. Shale distillation at Pumpherston ended in 1926–27, but the refinery continued at work, using crude oil from the Nottinghamshire/Lincolnshire field. In 1934 Scottish Oils built a plant nearby to make pink 'SOL' bricks from spent shale; these were sold, and also used for company buildings *(see Grangemouth)*.

**Diversifying the Oil Works beside Livingston**: In 1948 Young's Paraffin Light & Mineral Oil Company (part of BP) built a sulphonation plant at Pumpherston, where 1200 people lived in 1951. Uphall Station had only peak-hour trains, and in 1956 was closed completely; but the settlement and its name survived. In 1962 Pumpherston acquired a potentially huge new industrial neighbour, Livingston New Town. The refinery produced a third of the UK's paraffin wax until closure in 1964, but BP ran Young's sulphonation plant until 1993; Young's Detergents works, which made 100 different types of industrial and consumer products, stayed at work. Pumpherston continued to grow, but in 1981 was still served only by the facilities of a small village. Uphall Station was reopened to passengers with the rest of the Bathgate line in 1986. The erection of a new industrial laundry was proposed in 1993, and the Kirkforthar Brick Company from Fife still made bricks at Drumshoreland Road. Although the population in the 1991 census was subsumed in Livingston, both small settlements retain their identities and have several miners' rows; the Institute contains a small library. Young's Detergents are still going.

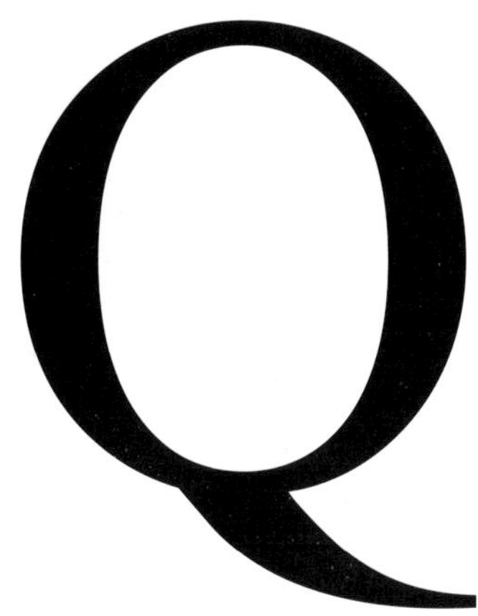

## QUARRIERS VILLAGE

**Map 5, B5**

***Small Renfrewshire village,*** *pop. 500* — OS 63: NS 3666

In 1878 William Quarrier of Glasgow opened his eponymous Orphan Homes for destitute boys beside the River Gryfe, 2 km to the west of Bridge of Weir. This institution, which housed the children in small groups in villas, grew and became famous: its *'Ardgour House'* of 1897, named after a mansion beside Loch Linnhe, was very fine. By 1953 Quarrier's Homes had 750 inmates, and to the south stood a 200-bed TB hospital staffed by 15 doctors; although by 1971 this had only 110 residents it remains open as Bridge of Weir Hospital. Quarrier's Homes had its own *'Orphan Homes'* primary school; this was soon renamed the William Quarrier Secondary and Primary School, and was accompanied in the 1970s by Carsemeadow school, which alone survives. About 1990 the settlement was renamed Quarriers Village; it had under 500 residents in 1991. In 1994 the locally based Alliance Wine Company were wine importers and distributors. The listed Ardgour House was restored in the mid 1990s; across the River Gryfe is a trout farm.

## QUEEN'S PARK

**Map 15, C5**

***Southern part of Glasgow,*** *pop. 15,000* — OS 64: NS 5862

This formerly rural tract south of the Gorbals, between the roads to Cathcart and Pollokshaws, started to urbanise once Strathbungo parish (named after St Mungo) acquired a church in 1839. This stood north of the new Queen's Park, whose eastern half was laid out by Paxton in 1862. As the vast swathe of industry south of Glasgow grew, housing rapidly developed in the area. Alexander *'Greek'* Thomson's Queen's Park church, a massive structure dominating Langside Road, rose in 1868–69. In 1864 Henry Dübs established the Queen's Park Locomotive Works well to the east at Polmadie or Little Govan, another green-field site south of the London railway line at Aikenhead Road; it was built of bricks burned on site from clay dug for the foundations. Dübs invented the crane engine, a small locomotive bearing a steam crane jib. During the 1890s Dübs & Co employed on average some 1850 people. American competition led to the amalgamation in 1903 of Dübs with two other firms, Neilson Reid and Sharp Stewart of Springburn, becoming the North British Locomotive Company (NBL) – to the locals *The Combine*; the works was reconstructed in the Edwardian period. *(For Dübs' antecedents and NBL later history see Springburn.)*

**Football Pioneers, First International and Hampden**: Meantime the Recreation Ground east of Langside Road was open by 1867, when Queen's Park, Scotland's first football club, was founded there, four years after the Football Association was formed in England. In 1868 a second football club, known as Third Lanark after the *'Third Lanark Rifle Volunteer Reserves'*, was founded nearby, their permanent ground being established later at Cathkin Park, east of the Recreation Ground. The first Football International, drawn 0–0, was played in 1872 – possibly at Partick – between the Queen's Park team, representing Scotland, and an all-England team! The Scottish Football Association (SFA) was formed in 1873 by eight clubs, including Queen's Park and Third Lanark. The Queen's Park secondary school was also opened in 1873. About then local builder George Eadie named Hampden Terrace after the renowned 17th century *English* parliamentarian John Hampden, so giving rise in 1873 to the first Hampden Park close by, which was vacated for railway work in 1878 for another not far away (now New Cathkin Park).

**Railway, Infirmary, Football League and Alu Foil**: Meantime in 1886 a subsidiary of the Caledonian (CR), known as the Cathcart District Railway, was opened from Pollokshields East to Cathcart, giving a service to central Glasgow. Closely-spaced stations were provided at Queen's Park, Crosshill and Mount Florida, these areas being taken into Glasgow in 1891. Strathbungo church was finely rebuilt in 1886, and the Victoria Infirmary pavilions at Langside were opened in 1889. The Scottish Football League was formed in 1890. Third Lanark prospered exceedingly, and in 1895 New Cathkin was the venue for the Scottish Cup Final. From 1884 to 1903 amateur and gentlemanly Queen's Park FC also played there on leased ground; they won the Scottish Cup in 1893. By 1895 Mount Florida, an emerging suburb of Glasgow, had its own post and telegraph office. The Acme Tea Chest Company built rolling mills for tea-chest linings beside the Queen's Park Locomotive Works in 1896–98.

**Trams, New Hampden Park – and Vast Crowds**: Glasgow's electric trams passed through Queen's Park and Mount Florida from 1900, when the large Langside car depot which held 130 cars was built at Battlefield Road. Queen's Park FC had

*A recent aerial view of Hampden Park, as redeveloped in the 1990s. Hampden on this site dates from 1903.* *(Hampden Park)*

remained outwith the League until 1900. Then their energetic secretary C B Miller led the club's purchase of 5ha of ground east of Mount Florida, on which their great stadium of Hampden Park was completed in 1903. With space for 65,000 spectators, better conditions for major matches than Cathkin Park, and no sectarian commitment, Hampden became effectively the Scottish national ground. But in 1909 an indecisive Scottish Cup Final at Hampden between Celtic and Rangers was followed by a riot: Victoria Infirmary staff treated the victims. Queen's Park itself was extended to Pollokshaws Road before 1925, and the triangle north of Titwood Road was infilled with houses around the 1930s. Langside College had been built by 1931. By 1935–36 Third Lanark played in the Scottish First Division and faced Rangers in the 1936 Cup Final, shortly after which Hampden was enlarged to hold a maximum crush crowd of 150,000 people, the largest capacity in Britain, almost reached when Scotland beat England in 1937; with such heavy usage, a stand built there in that year lasted only until 1972.

**Alcan Foil rolls on**: Third Lanark still had players in the scratch wartime Scotland team of 1942, but Queen's Park church was destroyed in an air raid in 1943. The private 60-bed Bon Secours Hospital was opened at Langside in 1961. Meantime around 1950 Acme had become a British Aluminium (Bacofoil Ltd) factory. After the loco works was closed in 1963, Bacofoil took over a portion (built in 1906); at one time it employed 350 workers and had an annual rolling capacity of 8000 tonnes of foil, but after British Aluminium was taken over by Alcan in 1981, it was in a poor state by 1986, and the workforce fell below 200. Then management and workforce pulled together to avert the closures which hit the firm's two Rolled Products division foil plants in England; new mills were installed to raise capacity to 14,000 tonnes. By 1993–94 its 230 workers made 13,500 tonnes of foil a year, ranging from thin sheet of 200 microns for pie cases, milk bottle tops, wallboards and telecommunications wire protection, down to even thinner products of a mere 6.5 microns; it earned a *'Best Factory in Scotland'* award.

**After Third Lanark: Hospitals and Education**: Third Lanark FC fell on evil days, and failed in 1967 after 70 years in the league; New Cathkin Park remained. By the 1980s the Victoria Infirmary had 450 beds. Queen's Park secondary school – which by then had moved to King's Park! – was closed in 1994 after 121 years, but in 1995 Langside College offered many vocational courses. In 1997 Holyrood Secondary School was the largest in Glasgow, with 2077 pupils, but Strathbungo church was derelict by 1998.

**Reconstructing Hampden – Superb Stadium, Tiny Team**: Meantime Hampden Park provided the main income of Second Division Queen's Park FC, but after 1979's improvement plans had foundered, by around 1990 it could seat only a sixth of its permitted crowd of 64,000. Seeking a better home for the Scotland team, its replacement elsewhere was canvassed, but eventually the improvement of Hampden Park was decided upon. The north and east sides were re-roofed and seated, using a quarter million red bricks and 1800 tonnes of steel; Hampden was reopened as an all-seater stadium in 1994. This left only the south side to be rebuilt as a double-deck 17,000-seat stand to complete a modern 52,000-seat stadium. But in 1994 historic Queen's Park FC joined the new and very lowly Third Division. By 2000 the club was in financial collapse; eventually the SFA took over the running of the stadium. In 1999 the name *Third Lanark* was revived for a new women's football team.

## QUEENZIEBURN

**Map 16, A2**

***Strathkelvin small village,*** *pop. 500* — OS 64: NS 6977

Queenzieburn or *Quinzie*, on the north side of the upper Kelvin valley 3km west of Kilsyth, existed by 1700, when it had a blacksmith. The Roy map made about 1754 showed a road linking Kilsyth with Kirkintilloch through a hamlet at Queenzieburn. Textile mills were established between 1815 and 1840. By 1872 the William Baird Mining Company had sunk the Dumbreck pit on the Kilsyth side of the hamlet, and built chemical works and workers' housing in the form of miners' rows; by 1872 Queenzieburn also had a school. The complex was linked to Kilsyth by a mineral railway which continued to and beyond Twechar – another recently developed Baird company village. The Kelvin Valley Railway, opened south of Queenzieburn in 1878, became a branch of the North British Railway (NBR) in 1885. The NBR opened Gavell station (named after a local villa) from which Muir & Woods of Kilsyth despatched their locally made coke.

**Mineral Exploitation Peak, Disaster and Loss**: In the 1890s Shaw & Thorn quarried at Queenzieburn, and at North Barrwood (Kilsyth); by then freestone quarrying had also commenced nearby under J & J Baxter, and Gray & Son, though none of the quarries became large or long-lasting. By the 1920s another coal pit was open just east of Queenzieburn, and a larger one at Auchinreoch 2 km to the west was connected to the adjacent railway. The LNER renamed the station Twechar after it took over in 1923. In 1938 nine miners died in a disaster at the Dumbreck coal pit. New coke ovens of German design had recently been installed nearby, and played an unwitting part in the 1939–45 war against Nazi Germany. The passenger train service was withdrawn by British Railways in 1951 when the population of a recently enlarged Queenzieburn was about 1125; it had gained a post office and in 1977 had a community centre. The Dumbreck mine was still open in 1955, but by 1971 the Auchenreoch pit had vanished, all the local railways including the connection to Dumbreck had been lifted, and the population was falling. By 1991 only 519 people remained in Queenzieburn. There has been little evident change; Chapelgreen primary school, the post office and a pub are still open.

## QUOYLOO & Skaill

**Map 13, B2**

***Island communities, Orkney,*** *pop. 200* — OS 6: HY 2420

Skara Brae, on the Bay of Skaill in the western lobe of the Orkney Mainland, is the oldest known Neolithic village in Europe, and the best-preserved because it lay buried by sand for five millennia. Its round stone houses date back to 3100 BC, antedating both Stonehenge and the Pyramids of Giza. Their outlines and details including stone drains, hearths and furniture, were uncovered by a storm in 1824. By then the imposing Skaill House had been built nearby for the local laird. The nearest hamlet is Quoyloo, 2 km north of Skaill; some 275 people lived in this part of the hilly farming parish of Sandwick in 1951. The Cruaday quarry 1 km to the north of Quoyloo was opened in Devonian sandstone by Orkney Builders around 1980; by 1997 it was closed, but despite some population decline Quoyloo retained a post office. In 1988 the former Sandwick North School was converted by Roger White into the Orkney Brewery, Britain's most northerly; its *'Dark Island'* beer is distributed nationally. Skaill House was opened to the public in 1997. A fine visitor centre and café – built with traditional stone walling and serving both Skaill and Skara Brae – was opened in 1998. Some 3km to the south (twice that by road) is exposed Yesnaby, where visitors can admire some of Britain's most impressive coastal scenery, with undercut cliff, *geos* (collapsed sea caves), seemingly boiling seas and distant views of the giant cliffs of Hoy.

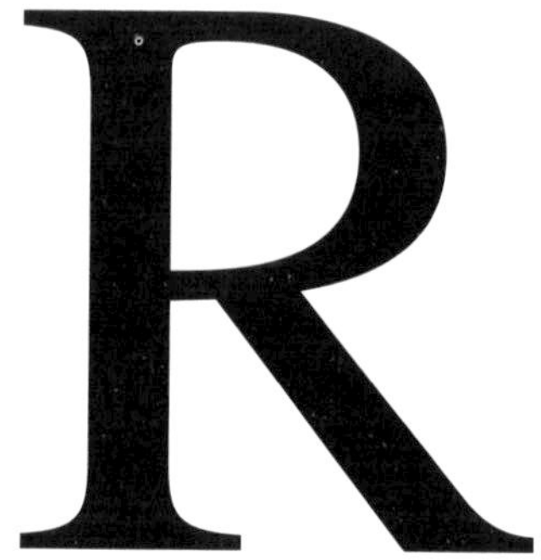

## RAASAY & Rona, Isles of

***Islands off E. Skye**, pop. 160* — **Map 8, B3** — OS 24: NG 5536

The 20 km-long, narrow but hilly Isle of Raasay lies off the east coast of Skye. Monro noted in 1549 that Raasay had *"excellent fishing; a rough country, but full of freestone and good quarries, partly birch woods with many deer and part profitable land, inhabited and manured, with two castles"*: Kilmaluag in the south, near the parish kirk, and Brochel in the north, each castle having *"a fair orchard"*. The Isle belonged to Monro's employer the Bishop of the Isles by heritage, but *"to M'Gyllachan of Raasay by the sword"*. This usurper had also seized Rona, Raasay's northern neighbour, whose *"haven for Highland galleys in the midst of it is good for fostering thieves, 'ruggairs' and rievers"*. Pont's map of about 1600 showed *'Castell Kilmabrock'* as Raasay's main settlement.

**After the Burning the Clearances**: All the houses were burnt after the Forty-Five for giving asylum to Prince Charles Edward. Consequently little remains of Raasay's two early castles, which had been replaced by 1773 with Raasay House, located in its more sheltered and relatively fertile south-west corner. By 1800 about 900 people lived on Raasay. In 1843 George Rainy of Edinburgh bought Raasay but, after failing to make any money, ruthlessly cleared much of the isle in 1846; 120 families were deported in favour of sheep. This brutality was followed by the expulsion of the tenants of the southern crofts at Suisnish in 1853 by Macdonald of Sleat. The lighthouse on the depopulated isle of Rona was illuminated from 1857. By 1891 under 500 people remained on Raasay, mainly in clachans near Raasay House; the facilities of a small village had developed near the pier served by the Kyle and Portree steamers.

**Iron in the Rocks**: Limestone of 30% iron content was found in the valley of the Inverarish Burn, leading Baird & Co to buy Raasay in 1912. The low grade ore was mined for use as a self-fluxing ironstone, conveyed by a steep mineral railway to a small calcining plant and a pier at the south end of the island; a pair of miners' rows was built for the workers. After World War I the industry soon ceased and in 1922 Bairds sold the isle to the government. In 1934 a great landslip occurred on its east side, where the spectacular 5 km long 300 m high fault escarpment of Druim an Aonaich includes rocks suitable for exploitation as oil shale; but these remained unworked. In 1937 the rambling Georgian mansion of Raasay House became a 20-room hotel, and the Alan Evans Memorial youth hostel was open by 1955.

**Recovering from Doctor No**: In 1960 the Isle and its two hundred or so mainly Sabbatarian people, now mostly living in the former miners' rows, again fell to an indifferent absentee landlord, the very South of England Dr John Green (known as *'Dr No'* for his total opposition to any economic projects); he closed the hotel and left it to rot. In 1975 the Rona light was converted to automatic operation, and once more that 10 square kilometre island became empty of people. In 1976 the HIDB succeeded in buying the run-down lodge known as Borrodale House from Dr Green for conversion to a hotel, and started a passenger ferry. The HIDB acquired the rest of Raasay in 1979, including the abandoned Raasay House, and opened a car ferry – between a new jetty at Suisnish, beside the former iron mine pier, and Sconser *(q.v.)* on Skye; but in 1979 sad Raasay's population was only 127. By 1981 the HIDB had reopened the lodge as the 15-room *Borrodale Hotel*, by 1991 the population of the island was up to 163, and by 1994 Raasay House had been reconditioned as the residential Raasay Outdoor Centre. A school, post office and forest walks make for an attractive little centre in the otherwise almost empty island. The hotel, now named the *Isle of Raasay*, has 12 rooms; the youth hostel is seasonal.

## RANKINSTON, Littlemill & Sinclairston

***Ayrshire village & hamlets**, pop. 500* — **Map 1, C2** — OS 70: NS 4514

When Timothy Pont mapped Kyle about 1590, Little Mill and Waterton stood beside the upper Water of Coyle some 13 km south-east of Ayr. The surrounding upland basin was already well settled, but it remained deeply rural at the time of Roy's military survey in the 1750s. The construction in 1872 of a branch line from Holehouse Junction on the Ayr & Dalmellington Railway, uphill at about 1% to a passenger terminus named Rankinston south of Littlemill, seems to have had as its objective the Littlemill colliery, sunk by the Coylton Coal Company on the bleak slopes of Ewe Hill. The siding connection zigzagged up the hillside with several reversals. This started the (ill-recorded) growth of a linear village at the high altitude of about 250 m above sea level. At the same time the Glasgow & South Western Railway opened a connecting mineral line from Rankinston, through Sinclairston (3 km to the north-east), to Belston junction on their Annbank and Cumnock branch. Sinclairston school also served Drongan.

**Coal and Ironstone**: The population in 1891 was 500; Rankinston consisted of miners' rows, a post office and a smithy. A little farther west near the top of Bow Hill was the Kerse ironstone mine, rail-connected to Waterside, and served until the 1920s by 40 miners' houses at Tongue Bridge Rows, and by another 20 with a school and store at Kerse. Between 1923 and 1940 another station, named Cairntable, was provided north of Tongue Bridge on the Holehouse line, where another colliery was sunk. By 1940 the Rankinston pit had closed, but the rail-served Polquhairn colliery *(see Hutton, 1996)* had been opened by the Polquhairn Coal Company beside the Drumbowie Burn south of Sinclairston; 1400m south-east of this was the Greenhill drift mine, sending anthracite to Polquhairn by aerial ropeway. The NCB invested heavily in this complex until faulting led to Polquhairn closing in 1958; Greenhill followed in 1962.

**Scattered Settlement and Vanishing Pits**: By 1951 some 1275 people lived in the Rankinston area, served by the facilities of a mere hamlet plus a 60-pupil junior secondary school at Littlemill and another for 80 pupils at Sinclairston. But all trains to Holehouse were withdrawn in 1950. Littlemill No.5 colliery, just west of Rankinston, started by the NCB in 1952 and with shafts ultimately 338m deep, aimed to raise 1000 tons a day, but worked only until 1974. Around 1960 there were also two quarries near Southcraig, 2 km to the west; but these had both closed by 1985. Meantime the population had fallen rapidly to some 750 by 1971; the last pit at Sinclairston closed about 1974, its railway link to Belston closed in 1975 and the secondary school classes had vanished by 1976. By 1984 only spoil heaps remained around shrunken Rankinston, which had under 500 people by 1991 but somehow kept its pub and post office as late as 1998; by then recent afforestation had covered the northern slopes of Bow Hill. Meantime a huge opencast mine had been worked during the 1990s east of Sinclairston; it awaited restoration in 1998.

## RANNOCH STATION & Bridge of Gaur

**Map 5, B2**

***Highland Perthshire hamlets,*** *pop. 150* — OS 51: NN 4257

Loch Laidon, Loch Eigheach and Roch Rannoch are linked by the River Gaur, flowing east from the Moor of Rannoch. Roads had entered the area from the east by the time of the Roy survey about 1750, and the Bridge of Gaur and the little-known Rannoch Barracks were built at Tighnalinn *('House of the Waterfall')* at the head of Loch Rannoch. When the West Highland Railway was opened in 1894 a crossing station named Rannoch was provided at an altitude of some 300m in a most desolate location east of Loch Laidon. Just to the south is the nine-span Rannoch Viaduct, 208m in length, the longest on the line. Soon a primary school and post office stood nearby. As part of the Hydro-Electric Board's Tummel/Garry scheme begun in 1945, Loch Eigheach was dammed to feed the small Gaur power station 4km east of Rannoch Station. Farther east, a tunnel from a major dam built at the south end of Loch Ericht *(see Dalwhinnie)* carried the latter's water with a head of 156m to the Rannoch power station on the shore of Loch Rannoch, having 3 generators of 16,000kw. By the 1950s about 80 people lived in the area, with a post office, primary school, and a 5-roomed hotel at the station. The Cloan trout hatchery near Bridge of Gaur, started in 1972, was by 1989 the largest specialist hatchery in the UK, producing 6.7 million fish a year. By the 1990s vast areas to the south had been afforested. The primary school is still open, and the listed station survives with its tea room, shop and post office; it has four Scotrail trains each way daily and two on summer Sundays.

## RATHO & Dalmahoy

**Map 15, A2**

***Village w. of Edinburgh,*** *pop. 1600* — OS 65: NT 1370

Ratho, whose early Gaelic name means *'Fortress'*, stands on a ridge of hard igneous rock above the plain of the River Almond, 12 km west of Edinburgh. Its church, built in a small valley to the north, was dedicated in the 12th century. A parish school was founded in 1599. *'Rathow'* appeared on Pont's map of around 1600, when *'Adestoun'* to the east, Dalmahoy 2 km to the south and the massive 15th century keep of *'Haltoun'* (Hatton) 2 km to the south-west, were all emparked. In 1664–75 Hatton Castle was rebuilt into the mansion of Hatton House for Charles Maitland, later Earl of Lauderdale. A road had been built through Ratho, linking Newbridge and Dalmahoy, by the time of Roy's survey about 1754. It remained a farming village, with a fair in 1797; Ratho post office was first opened in 1807. The Union Canal, built in 1818–22, passed between the church and the village through a gap in the ridge. An inn was built beside the canal bridge, and the Ratho whinstone quarry was opened north of the canal. The railways kept to lower ground 1.5km north of the village.

**Golf for the Well-off – and Boat Trips for All**: William Grant Stevenson, born in Ratho in 1849, became interested in stone carving and was the sculptor of the well-known statues of Robert Burns in Kilmarnock, and William Wallace in Aberdeen. The population in 1891 was 820. In 1926 the farm estate of Dalmahoy became the site of a golf club, whose first 18-hole course was built in 1927; no women were admitted as members for half a century. In 1928 the Ratho Park golf club was established just east of the village, and also built an 18-hole course. Hatton House had been much altered by the time it was burnt out in 1952, and soon demolished. From about that time Ratho's population grew with suburban (typically semi-detached) estate development. By 1973 Dalmahoy was a prestigious golf and country club; it was taken over by the Earl of Morton in 1978 and both sexes were at last given equal rights on its two 18-hole courses. By 1981 canal boat trips were being run from the *Bridge Inn*.

**The Impact of Quarries and Motorways**: By 1980 John Fyfe of Kemnay had opened a concrete products plant to the north. Quarrying for whinstone aggregate at Craigpark, south of the

*The Bridge Inn at Ratho, on the Union Canal, both dating from 1822. Today, it's pleasure barges rather than freight.* (AL)

canal, continued into the late 20th century with exclusively road haulage, despite the narrowness of the local roads; so when the *Craigpark Hotel* burned down about 1980 it was not rebuilt, for its site adjoined the active and dusty quarry. Even so, by 1988 another housing estate had been built, between Craigpark and the village, and in 1991 over 1600 people lived in Ratho. In 1995–96 the M8 motorway was extended at great cost through the hard rocks north of Ratho, which were also rapidly disappearing by quarrying. Meantime during the 1990s Whitbread's invested heavily in the self-contained golfing complex, and added 64 rooms to the large and luxurious *Dalmahoy Hotel*, which now has 215. The *Bridge Inn* encorporates the Union Canal Centre, the base for restaurant boats and *Seagull Trust* cruises for the disabled. The Union Canal was reopened between Broxburn and Ratho in May 2000, passing beneath the M8. A nearby quarry is being developed as an Adventure Centre, to contain the largest rock-climbing hall in the world.

## REAY

**Map 13, A4**

***Small Caithness village,*** *pop. 500* — OS 11: ND 9664

Beside Sandside Bay on the Caithness coast, some 15km west of Thurso, stands an ancient broch, now called Cnoc Stanger; inland are other brochs and cairns. The Roy map of around 1750 showed no road west of Thurso; later the main coast road between Thurso and Tongue passed by way of the small village of Reay. A tiny harbour was built in 1830 at Fresgo, 1.5km to the north. The links provided a ready-made course for Reay Golf Club, founded in 1893; by the early 20th century it also had a post and telegraph office. By 1951 when the population was about 300 a telephone exchange, sub-branch bank and inn were open. After the Experimental Reactor Establishment was founded in the mid 1950s at Dounreay *(q.v.)*, only 4km to the east, no substantial new residential development was permitted. However although the inn closed, by 1978 Reay had a garage, a pottery, two shops and a caravan and camping site. In 1991 Reay parish had 495 residents. In the mid 1990s G H Minter opened a quarry at Braxside, 1km south-west of Reay, to raise the igneous rock Diorite for use as building stone. Reay retains its harbour, golf course and post office.

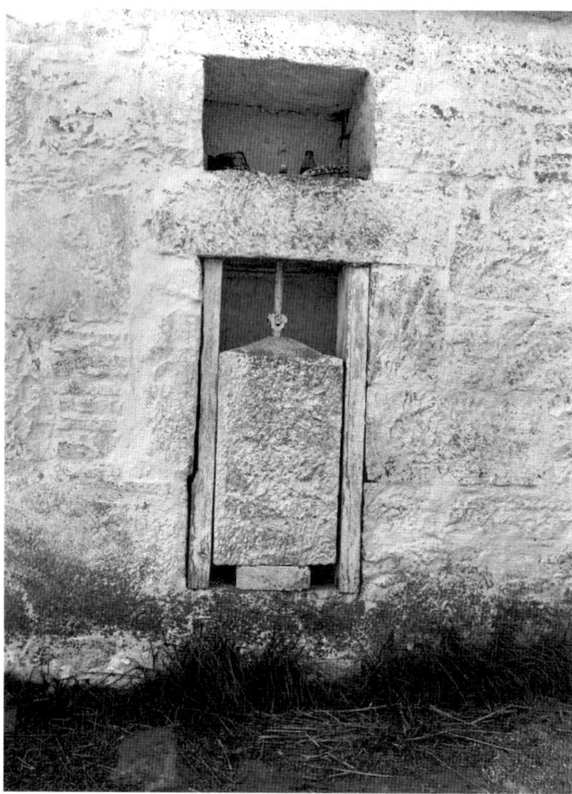

*Cheese presses of this type were common – using a weight raised by a screw to squeeze whey out of the curd in cheese-making. This one at Reay is unique in being built into the wall of a steading.* *(RCAHMS / JRH)*

## RENFREW

**Map 15, B5**

***Clydeside town,*** *pop. 20,800* — OS 64: NS 5067

The Cumbric name Renfrew means *Point of Current*, evidently referring to the meeting of the White and Black Cart Waters with the tidal River Clyde. From its early days a ferry plied to Yoker at the Marlin ford above the confluence, and nearby grew a settlement, at the natural head of navigation by small medieval ships. Salmon and herring fisheries were already at work at Renfrew when Strathclyde joined Scotland early in the 12th century, and by then there was probably a church. David I created the Royal Burgh of Renfrew as an outlet to the Irish Sea between 1124 and 1141. However, despite its flat and fertile site, its embryonic Cluniac abbey (an offshoot of Wenlock in Shropshire), failed and was transferred to Paisley in 1163. An evidently Royal castle stood on the King's Inch, then an extensive island in the Clyde. Later in the 12th century the burgh passed to Walter FitzAlan the Steward of Scotland; but in the late 13th century Kelso abbey still owned property in Renfrew.

**Silt and the Shire of Renfrew**: Renfrew was re-chartered as a Royal Burgh in 1396 and in 1414 became the caput of a sheriffdom, which according to Heron was created from part of Lanarkshire, which had it seems formerly included Strathgryfe *(see Bridge of Weir)*. In the 15th century Renfrew lost a trade dispute with Glasgow, and never seems to have attained commercial significance. Its contribution to Scottish burgh taxes rose but little, and was under 1% in 1535. A parish school opened in 1595, and Pont's manuscript map of Renfrewshire made around 1600 showed a well-settled area, naming Renfrew in capitals, but it was much smaller than Paisley. The castle still stood on the King's Inch, which remained an island. In 1639 Renfrew ranked only 34th of Scottish burghs in tax rents, but a handsome tolbooth was built in the 17th century, during which the King's Inch channel completely silted up to leave Renfrew about 1km inland from the Clyde: this explains why of all the early burghs it came nearest to total extinction. Comments made by the Excise chief Thomas Tucker – who surveyed the Scottish ports in 1655 for the Commonwealth – suggest that the process was far advanced, for Renfrew had only three or four tiny vessels of a mere 5 to 6 tons. Perhaps he was referring to kippering when noting that it was *"inhabited with fishermen, that catch herring and trade with Ireland with open boats"*. By 1690 Renfrew had also lost its status as the *de facto* County town to Paisley; by the 1750s as Roy's map showed it was a substantial farming village, at an elbow where the road from Govan turned inland to Paisley.

**Thread, Soap, Silk and Dredging**: Thread was manufactured locally from 1783, and Renfrew had a post office from 1786. The *Ferry Inn* was built about 1786 and extended in 1829, but the starting dates of the other industries which Heron was soon to mention are not well recorded. By 1797 Renfrew was a post town with a daily service, and there were five annual fairs. Heron noted a population of about a thousand in 1799, adding that *"it has but little trade. Its only manufactures are a soap and candle work, upon a pretty large scale; a branch of the thread manufacture, and some little work in silk and gauze, with a small bleachfield"*. A double bridge of ten arches – which still exists – had been built over the confluence of the White Cart Water with the Black Cart (then called the Gryfe), giving road access to Greenock. A third bridge soon spanned the short channel which was dug as a cutoff to enable masted vessels to reach Paisley, and a Clyde dredger depot was in use at Renfrew by the early 19th century.

**Coaching, Railways, Shipbuilding and Crystal Palace**: Blythswood House, designed by James Gillespie Graham for Archibald Campbell, was built on the point of land beside the Clyde 1.5 km north-west of the village in 1821. From 1824 the three daily coaches between Paisley and Glasgow were routed through Renfrew. The 4'6" *'Scotch'* gauge Paisley & Renfrew Railway was opened in 1836, terminating at Renfrew Wharf by the ferry, and with another station at the village; it began with horse traction and was not connected up with other lines until re-gauged by the Glasgow & South Western Railway in 1866, when a direct service was instituted to Glasgow via Gallowhill. In 1842 a gasworks was set up. Barr, later joined by MacNab, operated the (West) shipyard in the 1840s; from 1847 it became Henderson's. By 1850 the little-known firm of Fox, Henderson & Co of Renfrew had become expert in large-scale ironfounding, amply demonstrated when they cast the standardised frame sections for London's Crystal Palace of 1851 in record time: it proceeded from design to opening in eight months!

**Glorious Mud?**: The East shipyard was established in 1850 by J W Hoby, and taken over in 1860 by Simons, formerly of Greenock. Simons aptly specialised in dredgers and hopper barges, for by that time the Clyde had the largest dredging operation in Britain. In 1875 Simons built the iron PS *Dundee* for use in Dundee docks, and also three paddlers for the Great Western Railway. As deepening of the Clyde continued, from 1874 Lobnitz Coulborn & Co took over Henderson's yard, also specialising in building dredgers. Mudlarking evidently made money for Renfrew: the old tolbooth was pulled down to allow the Town Hall with its remarkable 50 m-tall turreted clock tower to be built in 1877, and the Lobnitz family built a mansion at Crookston *(see Cardonald)*.

**Trams tie in the Country Town**: The little town was served by the Paisley District Tramways Company, first opened in 1885 with horses, but electrified in 1904. Meantime the population in 1891 was 6800. In 1894 Renfrew proper was still a compact little place, extending little more than 1 km inland from the Clyde and only 700 m along the shore, separated from Paisley by 3 km of open country and the tiny hamlet of Newton. Renfrew itself boasted a smithy, shipyards, the *'London Works'* (Simons' shipyard) and an inn at the ferry, flanked by the extensive policies of Blythswood House to the west and Elderslie House just to the east – in whose park the Renfrew golf club, founded in 1894, laid out an 18-hole course.

**Babcock's, Soap, Candles and Electricity**: In 1894 Simons built the Woolwich ferry PS *Hutton*. Its boilers were made by Babcock & Wilcox (B&W) at Clydebank, where in 1891 this American firm of boilermakers and engineers had formed their British offshoot, actually within the great Singer works. Simons must have impressed them, for in 1895 B&W bought a 13 ha site at Renfrew, where they built a boilerworks; the site was later extended to a vast 210 ha. Building on local skills, the large St Rollox soapworks were established beside the White Cart in 1898 by the United Alkali Company, which had bought Tennant's Glasgow works of that name; candles were also made there. In 1903 Renfrew was connected to Cardonald by rail, opening up the south bank of the Clyde to further industrial development: a small power station was established in 1905, followed two years later by the arrival of the workshops of the Clyde Navigation Trust (later the Clydeport Authority) at Pudzeoch, replacing premises at Dalmuir. A small harbour was dug just east of the ferry terminal.

**Renfrew Aerodrome and Long-distance Trams**: An airfield was brought into use south of the town during the 1914–18 war. In 1920 it became the terminus of the Beardmore company's airline to London (Croydon), but this was soon abandoned, though the firm continued to run a flying school. In 1927 the field became the HQ of the Scottish Flying Club, who ran it for the town council from 1933. In 1933–34 Midland & Scottish Air Ferries made Renfrew Aerodrome the base for two air ambulances, and the firm also briefly plied between Renfrew, Campbeltown and Belfast. Soon *'Railway Air Services'* – formed by the four grouped railways – was carrying express mails to London. Meantime in 1918 Lobnitz built the sloop *Saxifrage*, which later became well known to Londoners as the RNR Thames drill ship *President*. From 1923 Renfrew's chain ferry was the terminus of the Glasgow electric tramcars, some connecting to Milngavie via Glasgow city centre, a 35-km run. Queues of tramcars would move the vast workforce of Babcock & Wilcox. By 1926 the passenger trains via Braehead had succumbed to tramcar competition, though both the Renfrew lines remained open for freight.

**Mansions crumble and Braehead turns to Industry**: Elderslie House had become ruinous before it was demolished in 1926, its site being used for the substantial rail-connected base-load Braehead Power Station and the Braehead repair berth. By 1931 a new direct road had been built to Glasgow, enabling Govan's King George V Dock to be excavated. In 1933 Hugh MacLean & Sons of Govan took over part of the East yard just east of Renfrew harbour to build small craft; Blythswood House was demolished in 1935. In 1934 a small oil-refining business began, which was to develop into Cleveland Fuels' incinerator and waste-oil recovery business; some recycling began there about 1945. In the 1930s blue trams ran between the Renfrew Ferry, Paisley and Barrhead, and beside the tracks grew housing estates at Knock and Moorpark. The population was 15,000 in 1931; in 1936 Renfrew's overcrowding, at 31% of all houses, was worse than that of Glasgow. In 1937–38 Simons built the powerful bucket hopper dredger SS *Carrick* for use in Ayr harbour by the LMS Railway.

**Assembling Aircraft – and Sludge Cruising!**: The aerodrome was requisitioned in 1939, and during the 1939–45 war Lockheed assembled aircraft there from parts brought by sea from the USA. In the late forties the field was renamed *'Glasgow Airport'*, and by 1950 a Renfrew–London–Paris service had been opened by British European Airways. In 1955 Lobnitz built for Glasgow Corporation the triple-expansion sewage sludge dumping vessel the SS *Shieldhall*;

this smelly vessel amazingly incorporated an 80-seat dining room, enabling use for old people's cruise treats! The tramways were abandoned in 1957; remarkably the Renfrew Wharf passenger trains lasted another decade. Simons and Lobnitz amalgamated their adjacent yards in 1957, and subsequently built three paddle tugs for the Royal Navy; but their combined shipyard closed in 1963. In 1958 H McLean & Sons were still building boats and tugs; they survived as the *Argyll* boatyard, in operation into the 1970s. By 1980 only GRP (glass-reinforced plastic) boats of under 8m were built in Renfrew. By 1958 a branch of Silcock's produced animal feedstuffs in Renfrew; by about 1970 it was part of BOCM (British Oil & Cake Mills). Loganair, set up as an air taxi business in 1962 *(see Muir of Ord)*, soon grew into an internal airline serving many island destinations from Renfrew. By 1963 the *Airport Hotel* had been built.

**Goodbye to Airport and Railway – Hello M8**: Success in airline development meant expansion – to enable which all flying was transferred to Abbotsinch in 1966 *(see Glasgow Airport)* and the tiny airport at Renfrew was closed. The golf course was later moved to south of the *Airport Hotel*, its site being developed into the Braehead Depot and an industrial estate. The former Paisley & Renfrew railway was closed to passengers in 1967 and the last fragment to freight in 1978. Meantime by 1971 the M8 motorway to Greenock had been opened south of the town. A big whisky storage and blending complex associated with Dumbarton was built around 1969 at Renfrew Road (strictly in Govan).

**After the Burgh and Power Station**: The burgh – whose development had coalesced with Paisley – was extinguished in the local government reorganisation of 1975, though giving its name to the new Renfrew District, and 450 jobs were lost when Scottish Cables closed their factory in 1977. However, the small *Glynhill Hotel* was open by 1977; by then the former *Airport Hotel* was the *Dean Park Hotel* and had 130 rooms. In the 1970s the park and outbuildings of the former Blythswood House became the new golf course and clubhouse of the Renfrew club; the large Afton Drive housing estate had covered the former Deanside golf course by 1979, later expanding westward beside the M8. Braehead Power Station survived in 1979 but was soon closed. Van Leer UK, who had built a works in Dundee in 1946, made metal drums at the Moorpark works by 1979.

**Babcock in the 1980s**: In 1978 Babcock & Wilcox employed 1300 workers. By that time the firm (which also had a tube works in Dumbarton) had for long built power station equipment, including overhead gantry cranes. Power stations wholly or partly boilered by B&W have included Cockenzie, Methil, Hunterston and Torness; also Zimbabwe. They then built a 700mw coal-fired power station for Hong Kong, and as Babcock Energy they prospered and grew; yet they were taken over by FKI during 1987 in a *"piranha swallows whale"* operation *(Bowen, 1990)*. The firm employed some 2000 at Renfrew in 1989, when making *inter alia* the experimental flue gas desulphurisation (FGD) plant for Drax power station in Yorkshire.

**Big Pieces for Power Stations, but Jobs go**: In 1990–91 Babcock Energy, whose plant included a 500-tonne gantry crane, built the European Transonic Windtunnel for installation near Cologne, plant for a Turkish oil refinery, alumina handling plant for Bahrain, and the Ash and Dust plant for Kilroot Power Station in Northern Ireland. The huge FGD ducts

*Renfrew Airport, pictured in 1955, with the then newly-completed terminal buildings. Renfrew, established as a flying field during the First World War, was Glasgow's airport until the present airport was developed in the mid 1960s. This site has since been developed with housing.*
*(T & R Annan)*

*The Renfrew ferry in the 1980s. This 1952 diesel vessel, built by Fleming & Ferguson of Paisley, is now moored in the centre of Glasgow as an entertainment venue. An earlier 1935 steam ferry is now moored at Renfrew. A passenger ferry still operates here.* (JRH)

for Drax – each a single load 11 x 11 x 15 metres – were then being shipped entire through the King George V Dock; and also (after nearly four years' work) BE were completing the four steam generators for Sizewell PWR power station. Despite other power-station contracts, falling demand for their products cut jobs to 1000 during 1993, when cost overruns on the Drax contract led to losses.

**Town Centre to Megacentre**: Renfrew High School was built in the early 1980s. The ancient vehicular ferry to Yoker was closed in 1984, though a Paisley-built steam ferry boat of 1935 was preserved, and is moored in the Pudzeoch at Renfrew; a diesel one became a Glasgow nightclub. By 1989 development of the Dean estate had left only such names as *Viscount Way* to remind people of the area's former airport role. Renfrew was just a local service centre when the controversial Braehead Megacentre, a leisure and shopping complex, was proposed about 1990 for the 45 ha site of the former power station on the riverside to the east. It was approved with the disregard for environmental impacts typical of the government of the day, but was on hold in 1993 when Sainsbury and Marks & Spencer acquired the site from Clydeport.

**Hello and Goodbye to James Howden**: James Howden of Glasgow moved out to Renfrew in 1989, continuing their specialisation on tunnelling machines with four such for the Danish Store Baelt rail tunnel, which ran into difficulties. They had already abandoned their work on wind turbines due to a regrettable lack of enthusiasm in the long years of Thatcher government. So when late in 1990 UN sanctions stopped the fabrication of a power station for Iraq, all 500 hourly paid workers were dismissed and manufacturing in their works ceased, leaving only the company HQ (with plants in Belfast and Canada).

**Environmentally Unfriendly Incinerator?**: By 1992 inventor Bernard Frutin of local firm Rocep Pressure Packs was making Lever packs for dispensing sealant. He was also to produce a revolutionary propellant system using Polygas as a truly environment friendly aerosol. The proposed installation of new incineration plant by the Caird Group firm Cleveland Fuels proved controversial in 1992: against the continuing protests of 14,000 residents, up to 10,000 tonnes of toxic and clinical waste was to be burned annually at Renfrew; protests still continued in 1993 and the proposed incinerator was rejected on appeal in 1997 following 1400 letters of objection to the Scottish Office. Meantime, by 1993 the David Lloyd Tennis Centre and recreation complex had created 100 jobs beside the M8, and by 1996 a Tesco store was open in Renfrew. The long neglected *Ferry Inn* was restored in 1999. Today, Mitsui Babcock employ about 600, and Balfour Kilpatrick are large employers in electrical control gear.

**Braehead: a New Centre for Renfrew**: In 1994 Sainsbury and M&S applied to build a shopping centre of 58,000 m² at Braehead, only half the size of the 1990 scheme, but to include a hotel and maritime museum; access would be from a new junction on the M8. In 1995 the doomed Strathclyde Region rejected the plans, so the two firms pressed ahead with their monster scheme as originally approved! This opened in September 1999 with business units, three multi-storey car parks and 58,000 m² of two-level shopping, 18,000 m² of leisure facilities, 39,000 m² of retail warehousing, and the maritime heritage museum *(compare Irvine and Anstruther)*. Both the Renfrew and Trinity High Schools have about 950 pupils. Renfrew hotels with over 100 rooms are the *Dean Park* and the *Glynhill*.

## RENTON & Dalquhurn

**Map 5, B5**

***Vale of Leven small town,*** *pop. 2100* OS 63: NS 3878

Over and Nether Dalquhurn were two among many small settlements on the west side of the Vale of Leven in Dunbartonshire when Timothy Pont mapped the area about 1600. Dalquhurn was owned by the Smollett family in the early 18th century; Tobias Smollett, born in 1721, became a well-known novelist. In 1715 three Glasgow merchants, impressed by the softness of the Loch Lomond water, began to build the large Dalquhurn linen bleaching works beside the River Leven. Fine linens were treated there from 1727, financially aided by the Trustees. As late as the mid 18th century there was no road on the west bank of the Leven below Bonhill Boat. As soon as twist mills became available the Dalquhurn's proprietors built a large 7-mill thread factory in 1763.

**Planned Village and Textiles**: Dumbarton Bridge was completed in 1765, making the area much more accessible, and the village of Renton was founded north of the Dalquhurn works in 1782 by Mrs Smollett of Bonhill. In 1791 the Dalquhurn works were acquired by William Stirling & Sons of Glasgow, and used to bleach cloth for printing at the small new Cordale printworks; by then over a thousand local people worked in textiles. In 1827 Chambers saw Renton as *"a large village chiefly occupied by persons engaged in bleaching, which flourishes to a greater extent in this district than anywhere else in Scotland, on account of the limpid purity of the Leven"*. The Dalquhurn works were extended in 1828 and Turkey-Red dyeing began; Renton prospered, the elaborate Gothic Millburn Church being built in 1845. The Caledonian & Dunbartonshire Railway (later a joint Caledonian and North British concern) and its Renton station were opened in 1850; a siding led into the Dalquhurn complex.

**Dyeing and Bleaching for Export**: In 1869 the Stirlings owned and ran both the Cordale print works (500 workers) and the Dalquhurn bleachfield (950 workers in 4 ha of buildings) as a major integrated unit, treating cloth woven in Glasgow and Manchester (Bremner gave a full account). Many Irish people were employed, and two-thirds of the hands were women. Raw materials were caustic soda, sulphuric acid, madder, alum, olive oil, chloride of lime – and nearly 600,000 litres of bullocks' blood a year; where the beasts were slaughtered was not stated! Two waterwheels drove machinery, and over 25,000 tonnes of coal were burned a year. All the yarn and over half the cloth dyed was exported, especially to India. The once pristine river was so badly polluted by that time that its poor condition was acknowledged in Murray's 1894 tourist guide, in which Renton was described as *"a flourishing town occupied by print and bleaching works and by the colossal Dye Works of Stirling and Buchanan"*. The Carman Reservoir had been impounded beside the Cardross road by 1895, and was enlarged early in the 20th century for Dumbarton County Council.

**Scottish League Pioneer – and Textile Decline**: Meantime Renton had formed an early football team which won the Scottish Cup in 1888, and in 1890 took the vital first step towards founding the Scottish Football League; but the going was soon too tough for a place with only 5250 people in 1891, and in 1898 the club was expelled from the league, never to return. Little seems to have happened to change Renton until India's own textile industries rapidly developed in the third quarter of the 20th century. Textile exports fell, and Renton – which still had over 5000 people in 1951 – declined greatly in industrial employment and population; its secondary school was closed around 1965. However, an efficient electric train service to Glasgow began in 1961. Any further development of Renton became severely constrained when the A82 bypass was built in the 1970s beside the railway; though inadequately connected to serve local needs, it at least removed some of the through traffic. The population had fallen to only half the 1951 total by 1981, when Renton's facilities were those of a village. Although Dalquhurn then retained a modest cotton industry, dyeing and bleaching there appeared dead, and by 1985 much of the Dalquhurn works had vanished. Renton's 1991 population was 2072, and there was little significant development in the 1990s; a station, primary school, post office and library are still open.

## RESTALRIG & Craigentinny

**Map 15, C1**

***Eastern parts of Edinburgh,*** *pop. 22,000* OS 66: NT 2874

Restalrig, which lies north of Holyrood Park and 3 km east of central Edinburgh, was originally called *Lestalric* in the sixth century account of its St Triduana, after whom a so-called *'healing well'* was named about 1438. A nearby church, begun in 1165, was made collegiate in 1487 by James III, but was ruined at the Reformation in 1560. Lochend Castle was built in the 14th century by the Logans, baronial overlords of Leith. *'Restalrigh'*, a tiny symbol on Pont's map of about 1600, was called a *"village"* in 1661, and became a burgh of barony in 1673 under Lord Balmerino. A paper and board mill, at work from about 1681, long held the Scottish monopoly in playing-card manufacture. Roy's map made about 1754 showed a small compact settlement with as many as six radial roads; Jock's Lodge was close by. In 1771 a fine gatehouse was added to St Margaret's church, and in 1793 the British Army built its chief cavalry barracks for Scotland at Piershill. This was described by Heron as *"an elegant addition to the village of Restalrig (pronounced 'Lesterrick')"* which then had some 400 people. In 1836 the ruins of the collegiate church were restored for parish use, and Jock's Lodge post office was open by 1839.

**Railway Development and Peripatetic Hibernians**: The North British Railway (NBR), constructed through the area in 1844–46, named the station Piershill, so avoiding the pronunciation difficulty, while its chief locomotive works, located at Restalrig, was named St Margaret's, its original locomotive shed a 16-sided *'roundhouse'*. Carriage and wagon shops were also open there in 1852, when the *'Queen's Station'* stood just west of London Road bridge. The NBR built 33 locomotives at St Margaret's between 1856 and 1869, when the main works was moved to Cowlairs. The St Margaret's engine sheds and a foundry remained, and in 1871 a North Eastern Railway shed was added. The Hibernian football club was founded by local Irishmen in 1875; their first (1880) ground at Easter Road was located on the fringes of Restalrig and Leith, but they disbanded when Bothwell Street was built over it in 1891, the year when the municipal golf course opened at Craigentinny. In 1893 Hibernian FC re-formed at the present Easter Road ground, only 200m from the first, but in 1902 wondered about moving to Aberdeen! In 1909, but for a legal problem connected with the railways which intersected the area, they would have completed a move to a partly completed ground at Piershill.

**Edinburgh Suburb and Maternity Pioneer**: In 1895 Restalrig village was still distinct from Edinburgh, but it then grew rapidly into a high density suburb. The Holyrood laundry and a brewery at Murray Park north of Marionville Road came in the late 19th century, and in 1899 the firm of Munro began to make woollens. Craigentinny carriage sidings were laid out to the east in the early 20th century, when St Margaret's depot employed about 1500 men, who provided their own library and repaired engines until 1925. But from about that time six electric tram services used the route between Abbeyhill and Portobello, taking traffic from the local trains. Hibernian leased and improved Easter Road stadium in 1922–24, and sports grounds were laid out between London Road and Marionville Road. *Capital Oatcake* baking was begun in the 1920s by J M & M Henderson, later allied with Simmers of Hatton. The Elsie Inglis Memorial maternity hospital, built beside Holyrood Park in 1923–25, commemorated a local suffragette and health pioneer who had opened her own maternity hospital in the city in 1901 staffed entirely by women.

**Council Building, Crowds and Closures**: The barracks went out of use in 1934 with the demise of cavalry. The Piershill council estate built in 1937–38 rocketed the population to some 54,000 by 1950, the year when over 65,000 spectators crammed Easter Road for a match against Hearts; but the local facilities generally developed only to those of a large village. Meantime Leith Athletic FC played briefly at Old Meadowbank, before expulsion from the Scottish League in 1953. The population then declined, to 42,000 by 1971. In 1952 St Margaret's was still the top locomotive depot for south-east Scotland, but gradually lost out to Haymarket, and latterly housed only local and freight engines. Piershill station was closed about 1964, and the locomotive sheds were closed at the end of steam in 1967, being replaced by St Margaret's House, a large dreary office block for the Scottish Home & Health Department.

**Meadowbank, Football Teams and Stadiums**: About 1960 the sports grounds next to the old locomotive works were developed by the city council into the 7000-seat Meadowbank Athletics Stadium, to host the Commonwealth Games. From 1974 it was rented to formerly non-league Ferranti Thistle FC, who became *'Meadowbank Thistle'*, and played in the First Division of the Scottish League by 1990. Meantime in 1991 Hibernian's Easter Road stadium was a decaying ground which could seat only a third of a maximum Premier Division crowd of 22,250; after nearly being closed down, and studying many options for relocation, its troubled holding company succeeded in carrying out major reconstruction, with new north and south stands built in 1995. By 1970 the Sunblest bakery had been built at Lochend, and by 1972 Kinloch Anderson had taken over Munro's large factory as their HQ. However, the brewery's extensive site was then used only for S&N maltings, and Miller & Co's London Road Foundry, which made rolling-mill rolls, closed around 1990.

**Servicing Express Trains – and Goodbye Thistle!**: From 1978 Craigentinny became the servicing point for HSTs – *'Inter-City 125s'* to the general public – and from 1991 for the new *'Inter-City 225'* electric trains too. Meantime the population declined steadily, to only 22,000 in 1991. The Elsie Inglis Hospital was closed in 1988, but its main block was restored to use as a nursing home in 1995. The redevelopment of the maltings site as a non-food retail park took place in the mid 1990s. In 1995, after an average gate of only 290, the lowest in Scotland, Meadowbank Thistle FC abandoned attempts to draw home crowds, and took the opportunity of moving out to Livingston *(q.v.)*, while non-league Edinburgh City moved in. Hibernian FC was once more in the Premier League in 2000; the original west stand is being replaced in 2001. Accommodation for visitors is very limited in this area of Edinburgh, though there are a few guest houses.

## RESTON

**Map 3, C3**

***Small Berwickshire village**, pop. 400* — OS 67: NT 8862

Although not generally known as a historic place, the then hamlets of East and West Reston – which lie on the Eye Water 4km from Coldingham – were already the location of no fewer than four water mills by the time that Timothy Pont mapped Berwickshire about 1600. A single linear settlement with four radial roads had developed by the time of the Roy map of the 1750s. In 1832 Cobbett found *" the Houndwood Inn, a place for changing horses, convenient and clean"*; this isolated hostelry stood on the A1 road midway between Reston and Grantshouse. Reston was too small to justify a post office before the North British Railway opened its main line and station in 1846. The station became a country railway junction in 1849 when the Duns branch was opened, replacing a daily horse-drawn road coach; its rail traffic was correspondingly light! – but the line was extended westwards, reaching St Boswells in 1865.

**Reston as a Market Centre**: The population in 1891 was 321. Reston had an inn by 1894 and, presumably because of its main line situation, early in the 20th century the village took over the role of livestock market centre from Duns; but it remained a village and no more. Its population was over 500 in 1951, but the branch railway was closed to passengers that year, and abandoned in 1966, when Reston station was closed. The *Houndwood Inn* was open until about 1980. Reston's population had declined to under 400 by 1981, but it retained the facilities of a small village, including a post office, with both the *Wheatsheaf* and *Red Lion* inns offering accommodation. Jeffrey & Son were agricultural engineers up to at least 1980. Reston livestock market, owned by the Berwick Auction Mart Company in 1992, was still very busy with cattle and sheep, and is still active. Nichol & Sons are agricultural contractors; the primary school is open, the *Wheatsheaf* is still a modest hotel, and the *Red Lion* is a pub.

## RHYNIE

**Map 10, A2**

***W. Aberdeenshire village**, pop. 450 (area)* — OS 37: NJ 4927

The Rhynie area in upper Strathbogie some 12km south of Huntly is full of Pictish remains, including a major vitrified fort on the 563m summit of the hill known as the Tap o' Noth, surrounded by the site of an ancient village *(see Traprain)*. Little medieval development occurred until the tower of Druminnor

Castle was built in 1440 for Lord Forbes; it was later extended into a mansion. In the 16th century the tower house known as Craig Castle was built 3km south-west of Rhynie, which had a parish school from 1626 but was shown as a tiny place on Robert Gordon's map, prepared before 1642. A burgh of barony known as *Muir of Rhynie* was set up in 1684; its site was 180m above sea level, in the words of the bothy ballad *"a cauld clay hole, a hungry place that disna suit a lowlan' loon"*, and at first the settlement came to little. A mansion was built on to Craig Castle in 1726. When the Roy map was made about 1750 it showed the *'Kirk of Reny'* with six accompanying buildings, on a track from Bogs of Noth to the Kirk of *'Achindore'*. *'Muir of Reny'* was a mere four buildings, remote from this track, seemingly a typical fermtoun.

**Some Success at the Second Attempt**: The old tower of Druminnor Castle was demolished in the early 19th century, but Rhynie was re-founded as an intended manufacturing centre in 1805, when its first post office also opened. It became a village, but was more successful in local commerce than in industry. A convenient point of refuge at the start of the notoriously snowbound hill road constructed to Dufftown (now A941), it was 6km from the nearest railway station, provided at Gartly in 1854. The 1891 population was 445, and Rhynie attracted no mention in Murray's Handbook for 1894. Craig Castle was unfortunately burnt in 1942. In the 1950s Rhynie parish had almost 700 residents, but some 3500 people in all were served by its little secondary school and 6-bed maternity hospital. The mansion of Druminnor Castle was restored in 1965.

**Decline of a Remote Service Village**: By 1981 Rhynie had lost nearly a third of its population, the hospital and secondary school. Although a useful range of village shops were still available in the 1980s, it was by then a very quiet place of under 400 people, with two hotels, a garage, a few new houses and a community minibus. Its bucolic remoteness made it a byword, fostered at that time by *'Scotland the What'* – Aberdeen's musical humorists. By 1991 the whole parish had only 480 residents. Rhynie retains a bank, post office, primary school, pub, petrol station, veterinary centre and a handful of shops; the Sinclair bakery and Reid's coaches are local small businesses.

## RICCARTON

**Map 1, C1**

***Southern suburb of Kilmarnock,*** *pop. 15,000* OS 70: NS 4336

The 15th century keep of Caprington Castle adjoins the River Irvine in Kyle; Pont's map of around 1600 showed *'Caprintoune'* emparked and emphasised, and also on the south bank of the Irvine was *'Rickartoun'* kirk, 2km to the east, which served an extensive parish. Although only 2km south of Kilmarnock, there was no bridge. In 1717 Riccarton obtained a market charter, and the Irvine was bridged in 1726. The mid 1750s Roy map showed Riccarton as a fairly large village, with roads to Ayr and also southwards, though only as far as Fail. Farmer's son James Shaw, born in Riccarton in 1764 and educated at Kilmarnock Grammar School, made his fortune and became Lord Mayor of London. Heron wrote in 1799 that *"the village of Riccarton, deriving its name from Sir Richard Wallace, uncle of the patriot hero Sir William, contains upwards of 500 inhabitants, mostly shoemakers and weavers"*.

**Railway, Trams and Power**: In 1827 Chambers noted Riccarton as *"a considerable village"*. It had a smithy, mill and post office by 1891 and an inn by 1894; by 1985 there was a coal pit at Caprington, rail-connected to Gatehead. In 1902 a freight railway was opened, bridging over the centre of Riccarton to link the Troon and Darvel lines and serve the gasworks at Greenholm Street. Alongside this the new 470kw power station and depot for Kilmarnock's small electric tramway system were built, opening in 1904 to a terminus at Riccarton. Kilmarnock Burgh took over Riccarton in 1909 and laid out the municipal golf course at Caprington, leaving the engine house of the early colliery as a feature. The General Strike of 1926 finished the rather feeble tramways, and the railway to the Troon line was abandoned, but the Craigie power station remained open until 1971.

**Housing, Industry and Roads**: By the 1950s Riccarton had some 9500 people, four primary schools and three banks; the huge Shortlees estate to the south had a junior secondary school. The Bellfield housing estate was added around 1960. Over the 20 years to 1971 another 10,000 residents and basic shopping facilities were added, and by 1972 the built-up area was defined by a new A77 trunk road bypass to the east. In 1987 came a second new dual carriageway road, the re-routed A71, which largely followed the route of the former railway and separated most of Riccarton from Kilmarnock. In the 1980s Treesbank House south-west of Riccarton was a Trades Union centre. An important new industry of the 1980s which located at Riccarton was Glacier Vandervell Metals from Hillington, specialist makers of automotive bearings; by 1990 they employed about 1000. By 1991 the area contained about 15,000 people. Trainloads of petroleum products from Grangemouth still arrive by rail down the siding to Scottish Oil's Riccarton depot, north of the new A71, beside which are a *Travel Inn* and a *Travelodge*, both of 40 rooms. Riccarton has a fire station, post offices and primary schools.

## RICCARTON JUNCTION

**Map 3, B5**

***ex Railway community, Borders*** OS 79: NY 5397

About 1600 when Pont mapped the head of Liddesdale, Over and Nether Riccarton were among several ferm touns in what was, despite its proximity to the English border, already a comparatively well settled area with some woodlands. Over 250 years later, in 1862, the Border Union Railway was opened. Built for the North British (NB) Railway to link Hawick with Carlisle, this double-tracked main line crossed the Tweed–Solway watershed at Whitrope Summit, some 307m above sea level. It was heavily engineered: Whitrope Tunnel 4km to the north of the junction was 1105m in length, and the Shankend viaduct, midway to Hawick, had 15 arches and a length of 182m. Riccarton Junction was created because this line was joined by the NB's ultra-rural Border Counties line, which followed the valley of the North Tyne down to Kielder and Hexham. To serve the needs of this struggling branch railway a whole new settlement was built, at an altitude of 260m on the bleak hillside 3km north of Riccarton Farm, by tipping a huge volume of furnace slag to create a level formation. On this were built the station, an engine shed, and 19 houses.

**The Waverley Route and its Fate**: After the Midland Railway's Settle & Carlisle line was opened in 1876 the main line grew in importance and was promoted as the *'Waverley'* route by the two companies. The village was extended to 33 houses, but apart from a school, a post office by 1882, a shop and a club it remained exclusively a railway settlement for the locomotive and permanent way depot staff. It had no road access until a Forestry Commission road link was opened to the public in 1963. Meantime the Hexham line had lost its passenger trains in 1956, and following the cost-cutting Beeching Report, rather than singling the track as an economy measure, the whole system was closed and abandoned in 1969. The consequently redundant settlement at Riccarton was almost totally demolished, leaving only three houses and the school embedded in the recently planted forests. In 1984 the removal of the slag was begun, for use in blockmaking.

## RIDDRIE & Provanmill — Map 15, D5

***Eastern areas of Glasgow,*** *pop. 39,000* — OS 64: NS 6265

In 1728 Provan Mill was established as a bleachfield on a tributary of the Molendinar Burn west of Hogganfield Loch; some 3 km east of Glasgow, a similar distance from the ancient Provan Hall and some 75 m above sea level, it operated for 20 years. In 1773 the high level Monkland Canal (MC), dug from coal pits at Calderbank, reached the area south of the mill at Barlinnie, and a basin was formed where coal was transhipped from barges into wagons for distribution in Glasgow. In 1778 the MC was extended westwards to Blackhill, where a new inclined plane was built to connect with a basin 29 m lower in level, at the end of a branch canal from Port Dundas *(q.v.)* on the Forth & Clyde Canal (F&CC); the coal was let down in boxes. In 1790 the MC was bought by William Stirling & Sons of Glasgow and a connecting flight of four locks was constructed by 1793, giving access down to the F&CC basin. By 1816 iron from Calder and Cleland was also being carried, with lime and manure as return cargoes. Haghill brewery at Birkenshaw Street was probably built about 1803, being converted to a distillery about 1837 by J & W Stewart; meantime distilleries had been founded about 1815 at Provanmill and in 1827 at Kennyhill; this became a large grain distillery in 1847. From 1850 to 1887 an improved canal incline paralleled the Blackhill locks, saving water and speeding passage.

**Railways, Brickworks, Prison, Pollution**: The Garnkirk & Glasgow Railway passed through the area from 1831, and eventually a complex of junctions was laid out west of the Provanmill distillery, where there was an inn. In 1870 the new Alexandra Park on the Cumbernauld road was opened with a municipal golf course; its west side covers the site of the Kennyhill distillery. But the area lay downwind of the huge St Rollox chemical works, and a still more downbeat character was set in 1882 when Barlinnie Prison – to hold 850 inmates – was built between the canal and a hamlet which had grown along Lethamhill Road. Otherwise the area east of the park was still largely rural in 1895; Riddrie was then a farm. The Anchor Chemical Works were built near the distillery in 1901 for Alexander Hope & Co; the nearby Provan Gas Works were built in a valley north of Alexandra Park by Glasgow Corporation in 1900–04, becoming enormous in the 1920s. St Rollox engine sheds were built by the Caledonian Railway in 1916, but USA Prohibition dried up the distillery company's funds and it was liquidated in 1929.

**Riddrie and The Black Mark of Blackhill**: The large Riddrie housing estate replaced the farm in the 1920s, and at the same time the straight Edinburgh Road was built across country as an eastwards continuation of Alexandra Parade, becoming the A8. To the north of the by then practically disused canal was Blackhill Farm, where 832 low-cost flatted dwellings were built in the 1930s as a slum clearance measure; many poor Catholic tenants were rehoused there. Among Scotland's many grim local authority housing developments of the period this was one of the very worst, surrounded by smoky railways, downwind of both the chemical works and the gasworks, and sited between the closed distillery's whisky bonds and the prison. This extremely poor environment gave Blackhill a depressing image, and it became a close but gang-ridden community.

**Drought in a wet Climate**: Bulk liquid returned when a huge milk depot was opened at Hogganfield in 1936 by the Scottish Milk Marketing Board. A third large Glasgow Corporation housing scheme was begun south of the prison at Carntyne in 1938–39, but hotels and bars were excluded from such estates by well-meaning but naive councillors, deliberately creating a major gap in community facilities. As a beacon of light in an area of imposed uniformity, the *ABC* and *Vogue* cinemas were built at Riddrie at about the same time, to show the carefully censored films of the day. After the standstill of World War II the Provanmill to Polmadie tram route was withdrawn in 1949 and replaced by trolleybuses. With these exceptions, by 1951 the 12,000 people in the area were simply served by the facilities of a large village, to which the 18-hole Lethamhill municipal golf course was added in 1954 between Barlinnie and Hogganfield Loch, which became the centre of a small park.

**Decline at Work and Expansion in Housing**: With rail dieselisation, the St Rollox engine sheds were closed in the 1960s and the clean trams were replaced by polluting diesel buses; the Anchor Chemical Works was closed in 1968, and soon cleared. With further massive housing schemes built since 1945 east of Riddrie at Ruchazie and Cranhill, the population was still rapidly growing, to over 60,000 by 1971. The seemingly redundant canal was drained in 1972.

**Degradation and Despair**: By that time the cinemas had closed, and in the words of a contemporary Glaswegian *"even bingo didn't last!"*; their premises had become derelict by 1973 when the writer first visited Blackhill, aptly called *"Glasgow's disgrace"*. A small windowless police station cowered among heavily shuttered units in its pitiful little shopping parade. In the 1970s the city's wholesale food markets were moved out to a site beside the gasworks, and the unusual circular Smithycroft secondary school was built beside Barlinnie. In the late 1970s the noisy M8 motorway was cut through the area, following and obliterating the alignment of the quiet canal, so resulting in the ferocious 400 m radius curve around the school. When the population had somewhat receded to 52,500 in 1981, the great majority were living at the poorest end of the socio-economic scale. In 1987 the Provan parliamentary constituency (including Easterhouse) had the highest unemployment rate in Scotland, with almost 6000 men out of work. In 1991 the area held only some 39,000 people.

**More Motorway, Prison Inmates**: A massive new girder bridge at Provanmill now carries the largely freight railway over the Stepps bypass, opened in 1992 as the M80, which swoops downhill to the M8 east and south of the gasworks, leaving Blackhill in the fork of two major highways. In 1994 giant gasholders remained, but 24 redundant hectares of the gasworks site was for sale. By 1994 much of Blackhill had been cleared and its social work office, clinic and police station closed. In 1995 the rest was derelict and was soon demolished; a little new housing was promised. The grim 110-year-old

Barlinnie prison held 1100 inmates in 1993, when it was still the largest jail in Scotland. In 1994 Strathclyde Region proposed a new tram system to link Easterhouse with Maryhill via Riddrie and the city centre, but nothing happened due to local government reorganisation. In 1995 Provanmill had one of the three Scottish motor auction centres of the big ADT Group.

## RIGSIDE & Douglas Water — Map 2, B2

***Small S. Lanarkshire villages,*** *pop. 900* OS 71 or 72: NS 8736

This locality beside the Douglas Water 8 km south of Lanark and 6 km north-east of Douglas Castle is poorly documented in terms of both olden-day and modern descriptive works on Scotland. But Timothy Pont's distorted map of Upper Clydesdale dated 1596 showed many features of the area: *'Broke croce Moore'* (Broken Cross Muir), *'Woodforuks'* (Wolfcrooks), *'Tour'* and *'The park'*, a cluster of places around the confluence of the Coal Burn; a little to the west was a mill and *'Udinghtou'* (Uddington), with *'Ponfich'* (Ponfeigh Burn) to the east. Pont's *'Tour'* appeared on the Roy map made around 1754 as *'Tower of Fochedejon'*, suggesting the Gaelic/French *Fochaid donjon* or *'Scoffing Tower'*; nowadays prosaically called Tower Farm.

**Road, Coal Mining and Railway**: By the 1750s a road had been made down the valley from Douglas Mill, passing Craigburn and Newtonhead to a hamlet labelled *'Newton'*, which implies some purpose, probably mining. This place was called Collierhall by the time that the Caledonian Railway branch line was opened in 1864 between Lanark and Douglas; close by was Rigside, perhaps a farm, and just west of Collierhall was Newtonfoot. A station named Ponfeigh was provided 2 km to the north. By 1902 rail-connected coal pits were open south of the station, with the intriguing name Burnengine; there was also a pit at Rigside, but these shafts were later closed in favour of a larger mine on the site of Newtonfoot. The village which later grew round the station came to be called Douglas Water after the golf club founded in 1922, which laid out a basic 9-hole course.

**Opencasting Wins**: By the 1950s the two distinct settlements had a combined population of about 2125 and jointly possessed the facilities of a small village, including a small secondary school and the 400-seat *Welfare Cinema*. This still contained a cafe in 1958; but both of these facilities soon closed, though the golf course stayed open. The railway was totally closed in 1964 and the track lifted by 1969, the year that the large mine was closed. With little work left, by 1971 Rigside's population had fallen to 1200, and by 1991 to 951. Much of the village of Douglas Water, and parts of Rigside, had vanished by 1988, but in 1992 the pub and school at Douglas Water were still in use. By 1992 Ramages, hauliers of Rigside had developed a large distribution depot at Glespin *(q.v.)*. By 1997 the locals had lost a protracted 7-year battle against opencast mining at Townhead between the two villages by a firm known as LAW, involving three public inquiries, and work was in full swing; local residents in this area of high unemployment held only 11 of the jobs. Broken Cross Muir is to be opencasted after Dalquhandy *(see Coalburn)*. The golf course is still open.

*Folkerton Mill at Rigside. This early 19th century mill still survives with waterwheel and machinery intact.* *(RCAHMS / JRH)*

## ROBERTON — Map 2, B2

***Clydesdale location,*** *pop. 400 (area)* OS 71 or 72: NS 9428

North of modern Abington the Roman road down Clydesdale followed the east bank of the River Clyde; part of the modern A702 overlies it. A medieval motte was raised on the west bank where Harten Hill nears the riverside at Moat, and another earthwork adjoined Roberton kirk, 2 km to the north. The undated tower known as the *'Bower of Wandel'* is a ruin on the east bank of the river. A burgh of barony charter was obtained for Roberton in 1631, but the Roy map made in the mid 1750s showed no roads and little detail in the area north of the Clyde Bridge, which had been built near the motte. When the roads came to be metalled, a turnpike was built along the west bank of the Clyde to link Abington with Symington via the hamlet of Roberton; no link was made to the Caledonian Railway's main line on the east bank. For the last century the parish of Wiston & Roberton has fluctuated in population around 400. Roberton primary school was closed in the 1960s; the post office lasted until about 1990.

## ROBROYSTON & Millerston — Map 15, D4

***N-E. suburbs of Glasgow*** OS 64: NS 6368

About 6 km north-east of Glasgow Cross was the old Robroyston House, which stood on or near the early track to Kirkintilloch shown on Pont's map of 1596. The mansion-house was shown emparked on Roy's map of about 1754, but its surroundings remained rural. The hamlet called Millerston grew up east of the point where the lately built Cumbernauld and Royston Roads converged on the shore of Hogganfield Loch, nearly 2 km south of Robroyston House. The Garnkirk & Glasgow Railway passed through the area from 1831, its Robroyston Station serving Millerston, where an inn and a post office were open by 1895; a smaller hamlet grew close by at Hogganfield. By 1899 a coal pit near Lumloch 1 km north-east of Robroyston was linked by a mineral railway to the North British at Cadder, and 500 m in the opposite direction was a quarry and brickworks, connected by rail to the Caledonian line near Stepps.

**Hospital and Suburban Growth**: In the early 20th century the huge Robroyston Hospital complex was erected 500 m south of the old house, and the Mossbank Industrial School was opened between Millerston and the station. The city's electric trams reached a terminus at Millerston by 1911, encouraging the erection of an estate of private housing just outside the city boundary in the 1920s, so as to avoid the city's high rates. By 1945 the colliery had gone, the tramways and Robroyston station were closed about 1960. The hospital had been extended by 1971, but the old Robroyston House had been demolished, and the brickworks and its siding were no more. The hospital itself was closed in the late 1970s, and by 1987 had been replaced by a housing estate; housing started to be added to Hogganfield in the 1980s. A motorway bypass of Stepps and Millerston (M80) was built in 1989–92, cutting between the railway and Robroyston, where in 1995 Glasgow City Council still owned a vacant 28 ha industrial site. Housing has since infilled much of the space between Robroyston and the fast-spreading city; Millerston remains divided by the city boundary and one can only guess at the area's population.

## RODEL *(Roghadel)*

**Map 11, B4**

***Settlement, S. Harris,*** *pop. 50*

OS 18: NG 0483

Rodel's tiny but perfectly sheltered anchorage near the south tip of rugged Harris was known in Gaelic as *Poll an Tighmail* or *'Pool of the Armoury'*, because Rodel (*'Path Dale'*) – from which an easy land route followed the south-west and west coasts – was a laird's residence from medieval times. The church dates from 1428 or earlier; a gravestone carved there in 1528 uniquely well depicts a *Birlinn* or Western Isles Galley. Dean Monro noted in 1549 *"a monastery with a steeple"*, adding perhaps naively that *'Harrey'* (Harris) was *"very fertile and fruitful for corn, store (sheep) and fishing, an abundance of deer"*. From 1780 Alexander Macleod of Berneray, a former captain of an East Indiaman and the new owner of Harris, improved the harbour. In 1786 the itinerant bookseller John Knox approvingly noted that Macleod, a genuine improving laird, had made *"an excellent graving bank, and formed two quays, built a store house for salt, casks, meal etc. and a manufacturing house for spinning woollen and linen thread, and twine for herring nets, and a boat-house"* to hold nine boats. He had installed a press, corn and fulling watermill, and was building *"good cart roads throughout the country"*. This vigorous entrepreneur had also brought in skilled East Coast fishermen to teach the locals, repaired the ancient church, built a school and an inn in the village where in 1804 James Hogg found *"plenty of everything"*.

**Superquarry Saga**: But development soon ceased, though in the 1890s steamers between Dunvegan and Tarbert served Rodel pier. That service ended before 1950, and by the 1980s Rodel was in a National Scenic Area; almost encased in a time capsule, it was still a popular harbour for hardy yachtspeople and wilderness lovers. However, the new *South Harris Motel* was competing with the older *Rodel Hotel* owned by Donnie MacDonald, who sought to benefit from ownership of the 460 m mountain of Roineabhal by promoting a superquarry there. Though this scheme was refused in the late 1970s, in 1992 Lafarge Redland Aggregates proposed to extract 600 million tonnes of anorthosite rock over 60 years, to use as armourstone for sea defences and to crush for road construction. This would create a corrie-like hole worked below sea level; ultimately the wall would be breached, forming a new sea loch. The rock would have been exported through a terminal at Lingarabay *(G.Lingreabhagh)*, 2 km east of Rodel. This highly controversial proposal was fought over for 8 years, becoming a *cause célèbre* worth a book in itself, before an apparently final refusal in 2000.

## ROGART & Pittentrail

**Map 9, B1**

***Sutherland village,*** *pop. 425 (area)*

OS 16: NC 7202

Rogart stands in lengthy Strath Fleet some 14 km inland from Golspie, at a location also known as Pittentrail. It made little mark in history, though its kirk which stands to the north, in the side valley of the Garbhallt *('Rough Stream')*, was shown on the Blaeu map based on Pont's and Gordon's work of the early 17th century. By 1845 a road led up the main valley to Lairg and a post office was open. The Sutherland Railway opened beside it in 1868, providing a crossing station. Both a meal mill and a woollen mill worked at Rogart, and an inn was open near the station by the 1920s, with a school at Kinnauld to the east. A garage and 33-line telephone exchange were also open by the 1950s, when some 570 people lived in the two valleys, mainly crofting and working small farms. Soon some council housing was built near the station, and by 1980 there were also two doctors in the area. In 1996 Dingwall Auction Mart's outpost at Rogart dealt in 9000 lambs. There is a primary school, post-office/shop, hotel, and two old railway sleeping cars serving as a small backpackers' hostel beside the station; the garage/filling station boasts a recovery vehicle.

## ROSEHALL, Altassmore & Invercassley

**Map 9, A2**

***Sutherland settlements,*** *pop. 150*

OS 16: NC 4702

Strath Oykel provides a sheltered route westwards from the Kyle of Sutherland and contains brochs and the ancient Caisteall nan Cor. Though it was trackless at the time of the Roy survey about 1750, he did show Glencassley Castle, 8 km farther up the River Cassley to the north, now a mansion. Another mansion, Rosehall House, was built in 1818–19 for the Baillie family on the site of an earlier house beside the Kyle. When the Assynt road was built up Strath Oykel in 1823 the Cassley was bridged at Invercassley, between Rosehall and the Achness waterfall; nearby were unspecified mines. By the 1890s an inn was open near the bridge, and about then the *Oykel Bridge Hotel* was built some 10 km to the west. Although the inn soon closed, by the 1930s there were post offices at Invercassley and near Rosehall primary school in the township of Altassmore; the area, which supported some 400 people, was well wooded. Two small hotels *(Achness House* and *Inveroykel Lodge)* opened in the 1970s, the area around Oykel Bridge was afforested, and forest walks were sign-posted. Rosehall House was vacant in 1993; now the school remains open, but the Altass post office is no more.

## ROSEHEARTY

**Map 10, C1**

***Buchan coastal village,*** *pop. 1200*

OS 30: NJ 9367

Near the Buchan coast about 8 km west of Fraserburgh are early names containing the Pictish element *Pit* (portion). Pitsligo Castle, rebuilt by Sir William Forbes of Druminnor in 1424 and altered up to 1663, was named for a muddy site, and the tower of Pittulie in the valley farther east, rebuilt by the Saltouns in the 17th century, for a misty one. Meantime in the 14th century some Danish fishermen had settled at Rosehearty, named not for roses or hearts, but from *'Pebble Point'*, in the Gaelic *Ros+Airtein*. Stone houses were built from about 1573 onwards at the site labelled *'Rasard'* on Timothy Pont's sketch map made about 1601; *'Rassarty'* was shown on the map made by Robert Gordon before 1642. This also confirmed that there was considerable settlement before a burgh of barony was chartered in 1681. Pitsligo church with its remarkable carved loft was built in 1632 by Sir Alex Forbes, later the first Lord Pitsligo, whose family forfeited the Castle of Pitsligo due to the last Lord's role in the 1715 rebellion; a successor to the title established New Pitsligo *(q.v.)* 12 km inland. The Roy map surveyed about 1750 showed *'Rossarty'* as a substantial village, with a street to the west and a cluster of buildings east of a deep cove; presumably its livelihood was still based on fishing. The area farther west was still trackless.

**Fishing and Curing**: By 1813 a post office was open at Rosehearty, but both the castles were in ruins by 1858. By then there were about 700 inhabitants, and Rosehearty had 88 boats and a dozen fish curers, but its harbour was still very narrow. Pratt noted in 1858 *"a weekly market, a regular post-office, and a comfortable inn; three vessels belong to this port, and about 60 boats are engaged in the herring-fishing"*; other boats caught white fish. Later in the century another pier was built a little farther south, and a new church built about 1890 incorporated the *'Forbes Loft'*, leaving the 1632 church roof-less. In 1891 the population was almost 1200, and there was a coastguard station. In 1894 Murray mentioned a coach from Rosehearty to Fraserburgh; about 1909, horse-drawn coaches were still running to the Broch, and to New Aberdour and Strichen. Simpson operated motor buses between Fraserburgh, Rosehearty and New Aberdour for a year or two until 1912 when the Great North of Scotland Railway took over the service. By 1951 the population had fallen to just over 1000, but Rosehearty's otherwise average village facilities were boosted by its own bus service, a small secondary school, hotel, optician and (according to one source) a 9-hole golf course.

**Golfing Resolved; Personal Needs Problematic**: By 1965 no golf course could be traced, but a remarkable 450 council houses had been built by 1971, and soon there was a caravan site. In the 1980s salmon cobles still worked from the harbour, there was a museum of fishing, three hotels and a small outdoor swimming pool in what was regarded as a pretty village, which then attracted some bungalow development. In 1991 some 1200 people lived in the village proper. By 1995 a new 9-hole golf course and clubhouse had been provided, the MoD had built a tall observation tower for their offshore firing range, and the North East Scotland Preservation Trust of Ellon was starting to restore the ruined Pitsligo Castle. The facilities now include a primary school, post office, and a handful of shops; a timber system builder, slater and coach hirer are small businesses. Pitsligo Castle with its 18th century gardens and a doocot are now tourist attractions.

## ROSEMARKIE & Fortrose

**Map 9, B3**

***Easter Ross villages,*** *pop. 1600+*

OS 27: NH 7357

Rosemarkie, on the south-east coast of the Black Isle, is said to have been established by monks in the sixth century. The name means *'Horse Head'*, while the county name Ross – of which it seems to have been the earliest main centre – merely means *'Headland'*. At least 15 Pictish sculptured stones have been discovered there. From 1124 Rosemarkie was the seat of the bishop of Ross (whose diocese included Cromarty), and it became an ecclesiastical burgh at some time. The see was later transferred to the twin village of Fortrose nearby, but Rosemarkie retained a unique law school. By the 14th century a ferry plied from the nearby Chanonry Point to Ardersier. Fortrose cathedral was completed in 1485. Rosemarkie paid no tax in 1535–56, and it was well after the Reformation, in 1590, that both places became Royal Burghs. Though their only commercial function of note seems to have been Rosemarkie's salmon station, by 1593 Chanonry was the title of a presbytery, presumably meeting in Fortrose.

**Vandalism makes Fortrose Inconsiderable**: Sadly, in the mid 17th century Cromwell's troops ruined the cathedral – already out of use – so as to use some of the stone in building a fort at Inverness, leaving just one aisle and the chapter house (now under Historic Scotland). A post office was open at Fortrose by 1715, and a new post office was opened in 1750 for what was then the key ferry carrying the north mails from Ardersier, mentioned by Pennant in 1769. Fortrose had three fairs scheduled for 1797; two years later, Heron wrote that *"this town, which comprehends Fortrose, Rosemarkie and Chanonry, contains nearly 800 inhabitants"*. At some time a little fishing and trading harbour was built there. Fortrose was morosely described by Chambers in 1827 as *"the inconsiderable remains of a once considerable episcopal city"*; its grammar-school was *"very inconsiderable"*, while Rosemarkie was a *"miserable"* village on the exciting road to Dornoch. The lighthouse on Chanonry Point, almost identical to one at Cromarty, was illuminated from 1846.

**Golf and the Railway**: The Fortrose & Rosemarkie golf club, founded in 1888, laid out an 18-hole course on the exposed Chanonry Links. In 1891 Fortrose alone had 870 residents. In 1894 – the year when a branch of the Highland Railway was opened from Muir of Ord to Fortrose – Murray noted the *"good" Fortrose Hotel*, and there were regular steamer services from Inverness, though Fortrose was *"a somewhat lifeless seaport"*. At that time the ferry operated from Chanonry to Fort George, and was still in use for passengers as recently as 1953. In 1946 Wordie & Co still operated a small rail to road cartage depot at Fortrose. The railway was closed to passengers in 1951 and to freight in 1960.

**No Rails – but Fortrose grows**: The ancient ferry had also closed by 1967, and by the 1980s Fortrose harbour's only function was to serve a yacht club. The lighthouse was automated in 1985. Meantime, Fortrose Academy had been extended about 1980 to accommodate 400 pupils. The two villages, by 1981 separated by a caravan site, made a pleasant quiet golfing resort; by 1991 they contained 1515 residents, including a substantial affluent retired element. In 1992 the regional and local enterprise companies planned to open a training centre at Fortrose under their CELT programme for remote areas. Salmon fishing from the beach at Rosemarkie continued until the early 1990s, at which time extensive housing development both east and west of Fortrose was causing severe overcrowding at the Academy, with 680 pupils by 1995! By 1996 the Pictish sculptured stones were displayed in the Groam House Museum at Rosemarkie; now the Highland Language Centre offers training in english and foreign languages.

## ROSEWELL

**Map 15, C3**

***Midlothian village,*** *pop. 1050*

OS 66: NT 2862

Hawthornden Castle stands in a fine situation on the banks of the River North Esk, 6 km south-west of Dalkeith. Chambers noted that it comprised a system of underground rooms in the rock, traditionally used by the Bruce, surmounted by an ancient structure of obscure history on the lip of the gorge; in the shell of this *"fortress-like edifice"*, nowadays dated to the 15th century, a new house was built in 1638 by William Drummond the poet. Rosewell was not shown on Pont's map made around 1600. By the time of Roy's survey of the mid 18th century a road linked Dalkeith with Howgate.

**Railways and Coal Mining**: The Peebles Railway opened in 1855 with a station at Hawthornden, which became a minor junction in 1862 with the opening of the Penicuik Railway; later the North British took over both lines. Mining must have been in full swing for a number of years by 1891 when the new village of Rosewell, about 1 km south of Hawthornden, stood astride the Dalkeith to Howgate road, on a plateau above the deep valley. Rosewell already had a post office and 1075 people housed in miners' rows, working either in the coal mine served by Whitehill Engine to the east, or in another colliery 1 km south of the station. By 1895 the mine owner had built himself the mansion of Whitehill beside the Dalhousie Burn. By then the Rosslynlee *'Asylum'* (later a Hospital) had been built some 3 km to the south-west. Some time after 1923 the station was renamed Rosewell & Hawthornden, and by 1951 2500 people lived in the vicinity, with the facilities of a small village.

**Nurses and Footballers outlast Miners**: The station was closed in 1962 and the railways had been lifted by 1970, but the mine which was disused by 1963 had become the site of a brickworks by 1975. Although by 1971 Whitehill mansion had become St Joseph's Hospital, a Catholic home for the mentally handicapped, a general population decline had set in, falling to under 1500 by 1981; the chemist and dentist had followed the station into obscurity. A new small coal mine had been opened 2 km south of the village by 1975. In 1982 there were 250 staff and 210 inmates at St Joseph's, and 288 beds at Rosslynlee Hospital. Little new building was evident by 1986, and by 1991 only about 1050 people lived locally. In 1992 the School of Nursing at St Joseph's joined with two others as Lothian College of Nursing and Midwifery. In the 1990s the local football team, Whitehill Welfare, gained a reputation as Cup giant-killers. By 1996 the brickworks had closed but a bypass was nearing completion; Rosslynlee Hospital narrowly survived at the end of the century.

## ROSLIN

**Map 15, C3**

***Midlothian village***, *pop. 1750*

OS 66: NT 2763

Roslin or Rosslyn Castle crowns a steep promontory above the incised meanders of the River North Esk in Midlothian, 10 km south of Edinburgh; its Gaelic name means *Point of the Waterfall*. It was the site of a famous Scottish victory over the English in 1302. The St Clair family built a tower house there about 1304; Chambers observed that it was *"separated from the neighbouring ground by a deep cut in the solid rock"*, later spanned in stone. The castle town of Roslin later moved by stages uphill to a more spacious site, where skilled masons from Iberia built the choir of a small but elaborate collegiate church in 1446–85 for Sir William de St Clair. It most fortunately survived the Reformation, for it contains some of the greatest masterpieces of stone carving in Scotland.

**Burgh, Textiles, Bridge and Housing**: Roslin became a burgh of barony in 1456, appeared on Mercator's small scale map of 1595, and was shown emparked on Pont's map made about 1600. James Gillespie, born in Roslin in 1726, became a snuff-miller at Colinton and founded the Edinburgh hospital (later school) that bears his name. In 1738 a bleachfield was started near Roslin, and expanded steadily with government grants throughout the century. Roy's survey of about 1754 shows that the river had been bridged, and the road system had assumed much of its modern form; an inn was open by 1773. In 1799 Heron wrote that Roslin Castle was *"accessible by a bridge of considerable height"*. Dorothy Wordsworth stayed at the inn in Roslin in 1803; she found the famous chapel structurally neglected but locked up.

**Industrial and Mining Centre**: A gunpowder mill – serving Napoleonic war needs and the mining and quarrying in the area – was founded before 1805, and Reid's bleachfield was further improved in 1808. Chambers observed smugly in 1827 that *"Amidst the castle ruins a modern mansion has been reared; yet in every direction around, the scenery is invested with all the disgusting attributes of a coal-country, overhung by the stifling smoke arising from the innumerable steam engines of the neighbourhood"*. Roslin was late in acquiring a post office – around 1825. A carpet factory was built in the mid 19th century, and the Rosslyn Gunpowder Company's works grew into the largest in Scotland; it employed 60 workers by the 1840s and exported the product, which was taken by cart to Newhaven.

**Railways and Deep Mining come – and go**: Tourism was boosted when the *Royal Hotel* (now the *Roslin Glen Hotel*) was built in 1868. The North British Railway opened to Roslin in 1874, crossing the Bilston Glen on a great iron viaduct some 40 m tall, replaced in the 1890s by a giant single span of steel; the line was extended to Glencorse in 1877. From that time rail transport took over the gunpowder traffic, which continued well into the 20th century. The population in 1891 was 730; by then an emparked mansion stood at Bush, 3 km west of Roslin, which was then dominated by two large coal and ironstone mines belonging to the Shotts Iron Company. But the Glencorse branch railway lost its passenger trains as early as 1933. In the 1950s came the National Coal Board's giant Bilston Glen colliery *(detailed in the Loanhead article)*. The mine just west of Roslin was closed about 1967; the railway track was lifted, but the viaduct survived and a brickworks stayed at work on the site. Roslin's facilities remained those of a village, with two hotels and about 1350 people from 1951 to 1971. About then a country park was established in Roslin Glen, including the remains of the gunpowder works.

**More Dollies, More Dollars?**: In 1987 Pharmacetical Proteins Ltd (PPL) was set up on a site east of Roslin, combining research with animal husbandry. By 1991 the growing dormitory village held over 1750 people, mainly well-educated, living in a wide range of housing. In 1993 PPL claimed to be a rapidly growing company using novel technology, the world leader in the esoteric field of therapeutic proteins: the *'production of recombinant proteins in the milk of transgenic livestock'*, including cows and sheep. In 1996 the world's first successful cloning was made of a sheep named *'Dolly'* by the Roslin Institute and PPL Therapeutics; resulting speculation on its implications greatly increased the value of the firm's shares. By 1996 the brickworks had vanished, its site being landscaped. In 1999 Roslin Chapel – while open, and with a new visitor centre – was drying out under a protective canopy roof in readiness for major conservation treatment. Roslin Castle, and the restored Bilston Glen viaduct, are also attractions.

## ROSNEATH (Rosebank) & Clynder

**Map 5, B5**

***Firth of Clyde villages,*** *pop. 1400* OS 56: NS 2583

When sketch mapping north of the Firth of Clyde about 1600, Timothy Pont noted various small settlements on the west shore of the Gare Loch, south of the Kirk of Rosneath. Though Rosneath Castle was built in the 16th century, the locality was of little note until John Anderson, born there in 1726, became a professor in Glasgow University and by his will established Glasgow's Anderson Institute, progenitor of Strathclyde University. By 1799 a ferry plied across the loch between Rosneath and Ardincaple (Rhu). Rosneath Castle burned down in 1802 and was replaced by a fine neo-classical house designed by Joseph Bonomi, built in 1803–06 for the 5th Duke of Argyll. Much later it was occupied by Princess Louise, who had Lutyens design a ferry house. By 1895 a pier and adjacent hotel had been built at Rosneath, and the ferry was steam driven. A villa settlement to the north was called Rosebank, and already had a post office.

**Boatbuilding and Caravanning**: Peter McLean opened a yacht-building yard at Clynder in the early 1900s; it was taken over in 1911 by McGruer & Co, who moved down the Clyde from Rutherglen. Rosneath boatyard was operated by Silvers, for many years builders of motor yachts. Rosneath Castle was used as a hospital during the 1914–18 war, but was regrettably gutted about 1947 and blown up in 1961, the decade of the vandal. The passenger ferry, still at work in 1931, seems to have closed with the 1939–45 war. By 1951 Rosebank had been renamed Clynder, had acquired an inn and was a small village of some 800 people; there was little change in facilities to 1980, but substantial development brought the quite young dormitory population up to 1393 by 1991. Caravan and camping sites at Rosneath Bay to the south became very extensive in the 1990s. McGruer's are still in business as boatbuilders.

*Boat-building at Rosneath, in Silver's boatyard. This yard specialised in building motor yachts, and this shows one of the last such vessels to be built, in 1973.* *(JRH)*

## ROSYTH & Pitreavie

**Map 6, B5**

***West Fife town,*** *pop. 13,400* OS 65: NT 1182

The bay called *St Margaret's Hope* west of North Queensferry, where that influential lady first set foot on Scottish soil in 1067, was long noted as a safe anchorage in easterly gales. Pitreavie, 3 km inland, bears a Pictish name and was an estate by the 14th century. The coastal Rosyth Castle of the Stewarts, southwest of the prominent Castleland Hill, was of 15th century construction, and soon after 1600 the Wardlaws built a new mansionhouse of advanced design at Pitreavie. Rosyth Kirk appeared on James Gordon's map, but its small parish was united with Inverkeithing in 1636. Under an Act of 1790 a turnpike road was built through the area to link North Queensferry and Torry, 10 km west. In 1827 Chambers described the ruined Rosyth Castle as *"a huge square tower, situated close by the sea, the waves of which encompass it at high water"*. Round it were a few farms, said by a mid Victorian writer to be *"a dreary treeless waste"*.

**Royal Naval Dockyard and Garden Village**: Rosyth Dockyard, promoted by *'Jackie'* Fisher, the revolutionary First Sea Lord, was built on this site from 1903 and hurriedly opened in 1905 with the strategic aim of counteracting the formerly friendly German navy. At first aptly called *'Tin Town'*, more permanent naval installations were built in 1909–16 on the reclaimed foreshore, when the base was home to Beatty's fast but frail battle cruisers. The main road was diverted inland north of Castleland Hill. Rosyth had a post office by 1913, for a naval garden village was being built, begun in 1909 and completed in 1921, centred on the crossroads of the new road with that from Queensferry to Dunfermline (fully discussed by Adams, 1978). Rosyth Halt was opened on the Inverkeithing and Dunfermline branch railway some time between 1913 and 1923, and from 1918 a branch of the Dunfermline Tramways Company also served Rosyth – until the whole system was closed in 1937.

**Graveyard for Battleship and Liner**: Between 1926 and the late 1930s the naval base was mothballed and used only for shipbreaking. The early battleships HMS *King George V* of 23,000 tons and *Colossus* of 20,000 tons were scrapped there in 1926–28 by the Alloa Shipbreaking Company. In 1931–32 Metal Industries broke up two more battleships, HMS *Benbow* and *Marlborough*, both of 25,000 tons. Later several of the world's largest liners were dismantled, including the huge four-funnelled *Mauretania* in 1935, the *Leviathan* in 1938, and in 1943 *Caledonia* (the former *Majestic)*, which had been the world's largest ship from 1914 to 1935. Meantime people with time to spare founded the Pitreavie golf club in 1932, and an 18-hole parkland course was laid out.

**The Pitreavie Bunker, and Mobile *'Caledonia'***: In 1938 Pitreavie Castle was bought by the RAF for command purposes, and the naval station and dockyard were greatly expanded between 1939 and 1945. After 1945 Pitreavie Castle was classified as a category *'A'* listed building, though a command bunker was excavated 25 m beneath its tennis court. The name HMS *Caledonia* was adopted in 1946 for the Naval marine engineering school at Rosyth. The elderly battleship HMS *Iron Duke* of 25,000 tons, Jellicoe's flagship at the indecisive battle of Jutland in 1916, was broken up in 1946.

The huge wartime workforce on the base was cut to 7500 by 1948, though it remained among Scotland's largest single-site employers. By the 1950s Rosyth had some 12,000 residents, but only village facilities, both Inverkeithing and Dunfermline being within 4km.

**Nuclear Deterrence – and Credit Cards**: Due to the Cold War, the development of naval facilities was resumed, including two docks for refitting Polaris and Hunter-killer nuclear submarines; the specialised equipment installed enabled the nuclear-powered submarine supply ship HMS *Maidstone* of 13,000 tons to be broken up at Rosyth in 1978 after a chequered career of 41 years. Pitreavie had become an athletics centre in addition to its military role. In 1985–87 the Bank of Scotland built its new credit card processing centre at Pitreavie, and the punning *Gladyer Inn* was built.

**Nuclear Pollution and a Futile Hole**: In the 1980s there were already rumours of radioactivity, though the former nuclear submarine HMS *Dreadnought* which had been stored at the yard since 1982 was minus its reactor. The work the nuclear ships brought in was nonetheless welcome in so populous an area, where the former mining industry had been largely closed. But a high price was paid, for it was authoritatively claimed in 1993 that over three million tonnes of dock dredgings polluted by radioactive cobalt-60 from nuclear submarines had for seven years been dumped at various sites in the Firth as far afield as Kinghorn, and that this was being swept by currents as far as Culross and Anstruther. This danger was later proved on the beach at Dalgety Bay, but the government in far-off Whitehall was regrettably unrepentant. Meantime from 1984 the Thatcher government poured public money into making Rosyth suitable to refit the new Trident nuclear submarine fleet. To build RD57 – a reinforced concrete dock some 30m deep, 165m long and 150m wide – more than 450,000 tonnes of rubble had to be removed – but even before the Cold War ended, Tory government thinking changed, causing abandonment of the project – an apparently total waste. In 1989 RN Rosyth was primarily a base for destroyers, minesweepers and fishery protection vessels, able in 1993 to dry-dock four ships at once.

**Rosyth moves Privately from Undersea to Underground**: The management of the RN Dockyard, then Scotland's largest industrial complex, was sold in 1987 to FKI Babcock (by 1989 Babcock Thorn), who began to build and repair small civilian vessels, but the 5500 jobs of 1989 were cut to 4000 by 1991. In 1992 Babcock joined OGL of Aberdeen to seek secondary offshore contracts, and in 1993 built accommodation modules for oil workers. In 1992 new rails were laid to bring in coaches to be refurbished for London suburban services. A new firm, Babcock Rail, was formed at Rosyth in 1993 and refurbished over 750 Tube vehicles, as well as painting coaches for GNER and building wagons for *Blue Circle* Cement.

**Pitreavie Business Park**: Courtauld's little-known clothing factory closed in 1989 with the loss of 180 jobs, but in 1991 Sidlaw Textiles were still weaving bed and table linens at Pitreavie. In 1992 the Dunfermline Building Society moved out of town to a new 150-job head office on the new Pitreavie Business Park, where by 1993 Inveresk Paper also had its new head office. In 1993 Chicago-based FMC added a large extension to its Pitreavie plant, making wellhead equipment for the oil and gas industry, raising its workforce to 390, whilst T K Valve made ball valves for the oil, gas and petrochemical industries. Solectron made PCBs at Pitreavie. The 14ha Fleet playing fields south of Admiralty Road were sold in 1994 to Fife Enterprise and the local councils, and were developed as an industrial park, where in 1996 Lexmark International opened a new 200 (hopefully 500) worker factory to make cartridges for ink-jet printers; meantime McGregor's Engineering and Design, a local firm, employed about 50 people for a time, and Woodrows made soft drinks.

**The Demotion of the Dockyard**: In 1993 with typical illogicality the Major government decided to shift the Trident work to Devonport, which lacked both the expertise and facilities! Rosyth dockyard lost 550 more jobs, but was promised work refitting half the surface fleet of conventional warships! By then only 3000 of Babcock Thorn's dockyard workers undertook defence work, with another 1000 on civilian contracts. In 1994 Thorn EMI was bought out to create Babcock Rosyth Defence (BRD), who increased naval refitting workers to 3600 and also won a New Zealand contract to run their antipodeal *Devonport* dockyard. By 1996 a Tesco store was open near the station.

**RN Rosyth and Pitreavie HQ Closed**: Early in 1994 the naval base employed some 1600 civilians, but was then cut to a support role. Its two flotillas of minehunters left for Faslane and Portsmouth in a striking procession one day late in 1995, and the fishery protection vessels too were lost. Some 1500 naval personnel left, and civilian jobs were cut to 900. In 1995 the MoD cut local jobs by up to 870 people and offered the 144ha naval base for sale (keeping part for naval stores use). The National Maritime HQ at Pitreavie also closed in 1996; the naval HQ for northern Britain were moved to Faslane, and the air-sea Search & Rescue HQ went to RAF Kinloss.

**Enter the University of Michigan!**: In 1996 the dockyard was sold to Babcock International; their 3200 workers refurbishing naval vessels were down to 3000 in 1999 and were to be cut to 2750. A further 400 Babcock Engineering jobs were to go in 2000 when the refitting of the submarine HMS *Sceptre* was complete. However, a new offshore equipment manufacturer, Oceaneering Multiflex, was established locally in 2000, and in 1999–2000 a partnership was forged between *'Rosyth Europark'* and the University of Michigan, to build an advanced engineering training centre on the dockyard site. Attempts to establish a direct ferry link with Europe are advancing with the help of Greek-owned Superfast Ferries. For those who need to pause overnight, the *Gladyer Inn* has 21 rooms.

## ROTHES

**Map 10, A2**

***Speyside village**, pop. 1350*

OS 28: NJ 2749

On the west side of the River Spey some 15km from Elgin was the 13th century castle of the Leslies, described as a *"manor"* by a companion of the English King Edward I who ravaged the area in 1295. So Rothes probably originated as a castle town, but although the Leslies were ennobled as Earls of Rothes in 1457 it appears not to have been chartered as a burgh. The earls sold the Rothes estate to the Seafields about 1700 and moved to Fife. (It was on their Fife lands that the 20th century New Town of Glenrothes was to be built.) The Roy map surveyed about 1750 showed only a few buildings beside Rothes Kirk and Castle, in an entirely roadless area. Rothes was laid out on a low-lying riverside site as a planned village for the Seafield family in 1763, when the square was built; the castle almost vanished, perhaps robbed for building stone. Rothes was not famed for industry when the village was severely flooded in 1829, but it had a post office by 1839.

**Whisky, Railways and Glen Grant Garden**: The site of Rothes is crossed by two burns which rise in an area providing exceptionally good quality water, turned to productive use in 1840 when the Glen Grant Distillery was opened by John & James Grant; this was gradually extended. From 1858 Rothes was linked to the expanding railway system at Orton, between Elgin and Keith, by the Morayshire Railway, which became a subsidiary of the Great North of Scotland. A direct line to Elgin was opened in 1861, resulting in the severance of the Orton connection in 1866; at some date a gasworks was built. Major James Grant who travelled widely in Africa and India inherited the Glen Grant whisky business in 1872, and with the aid of 11 gardeners established 11 ha of woodland gardens beside the distillery and imported many exotic species. In 1878 the large water-powered *'Glenrothes-Glenlivet'* distillery *('Glenrothes')* was founded by William Grant & Co, but actually located at Rothes; the *'Glenlivet'* suffix derived from the Excise District of that name. A third distillery, misleadingly named as *Glen Spey*, was established by James Stuart & Co in 1885; its first year's output was 275,000 litres of Highland Malt. It was acquired in 1887 by the London wine and spirit merchants W & A Gilbey.

**Glen Grant lights up**: In 1886 the even larger Glen Grant distillery used Moray barley and a combination of water and steam power. As a *'state of the art'* plant with a capacity of over a million litres of Highland malt, it was already lit by electricity – the first such installation in northern Scotland – and had its own cooperage, smithy, engineers' and carpenters' shops, and a farmstead where cattle were fed on the draff and spent wash. In 1886 Barnard found Rothes *"a village of considerable size with good hotels and shops"*. To meet the growing demand for new copper stills in the north-east, by 1887 Willisons of Alloa had opened a branch at Rothes, the Morayshire Copper Works. Both Glen Grant and Glenrothes sold their products as single malts and also for blending, but demand was falling; Glenrothes, with an annual capacity of 600,000 litres, was working far below this. Its owners therefore joined with the owners of Bunnahabhain *(q.v.)* in 1887 to found the Highland Distilleries Company. The demand for whisky soon revived – for a decade.

**Rothes Burgh and Whisky at the Peak – and beyond**: The 1891 population was 1550; Rothes had become a police burgh, described by Murray as a *"little town"*, with the *"good" Seafield Arms Hotel*; a large Free Church was built in 1900. The opening of two more distilleries took place in 1897: Speyburn which was attractively designed by C C Doig *(see Hay & Stell)* was a success, but the Boer War slump hit the almost new Glen Grant No.2 which closed in 1902 (though it was not demolished). Lloyd George's heavy taxes notwithstanding, Glen Grant distillery was still working in 1914, but for various reasons – especially American Prohibition – no more were built. Despite the long recession in whisky up to about 1950, and Rothes' almost total dependence on this trade, the town had a good range of local services in 1951, when the burgh population was down to 1200.

**Another Boom in Whisky feeds More Cows**: Copper stills were made in the village when the Glenrothes distillery was enlarged in 1963, drawing its brewing water from springs on its own 1200ha farm; it was again expanded in 1980. Meantime the sleeping Glen Grant No.2 distillery was reactivated in 1965, renamed Caperdonich and doubled in size by Glenlivet Distillers in 1967, with a whisky pipe which crossed above the main street! The already very large Glen Grant distillery was greatly expanded yet again by the same firm in 1973–77, and was also made into a tourist attraction. Meantime Gilbeys' Glen Spey distillery had also been doubled in 1970. To handle the by-products (and effluents) from all these projects the *'Combination of Rothes Distillers'* built a large dark-grains plant in the 1960s, producing a cattle-feed supplement.

**Declining Facilities**: It might be thought that all was well, but not so: since 1951 Rothes had lost its secondary school, employment office, cinema, one branch bank, a lawyer, and one doctor; its passenger and goods station had closed in 1968. It consisted by 1972 almost entirely of council houses, over which local control was lost when the burgh was submerged in the enlarged Moray district in 1975. Though a second hotel had opened, Rothes in the 1980s had only the facilities of a small village.

**Pollution Problems – and a Garden Renewed**: In 1990 the malt whisky boom kept busy those distilleries operated by the Combination of Rothes, but overproduction spoilt the condition of the Rothes Burn. In 1991 the resident population was nearly 1350. Seagram, based in Paisley, operated Caperdonich and Glen Grant, the latter's single malt described as for *'after dinner'*. Highland Distillers, blenders of the popular *'Famous Grouse'*, owned Glenrothes (and also Bunnahabhain and Glenglassaugh). By 1994 the Rothes Golf Club had laid out a 9-hole course; it now has two. The Glen Grant garden which had become overgrown and neglected was restored in 1993–96 under the Chivas & Glenlivet Group and reopened in 1997; the related distillery was also open in 2000. The 'Combination' now employs a couple of dozen in the animal feed business.

## ROTHESAY

**Map 5, A5**

***Main town, Isle of Bute,*** *pop. 5260* — OS 63: NS 0864

Rothesay, beautifully situated on a sheltered bay in the Isle of Bute, has ancient forts and standing stones in its vicinity. It also had an early *'Apdaine'* – i.e. land held by an abbot – and a quay was built in the 11th century. The large moated shell keep of Rothesay Castle was erected around 1150, its stone walls 6 m tall and 3 m thick (even so they were breached by the Norsemen in 1230); it was such an unusual feature for Scotland that it was actually sketched on the contemporary Gough map. Chambers noted that the castle was *"the favourite residence of Robert III"*, who chartered Rothesay as a Royal Burgh in 1401, so bringing Bute and its larger satellite Arran into the effective area of Scotland. In 1455 the castle was still in Royal hands, and by the end of the 15th century Rothesay had acquired a corn mill.

**Almost off the Map**: In the second quarter of the 16th century, when James V used the castle to base his challenge to the Lords of the Isles, an entrance tower and hall were added. By 1535 Rothesay was making a tiny contribution in burgh taxes. Monro noted in 1549 that the Isle of Bute was noted for growing oats. He described Rothesay as a *"burghs town called Bute; before it a bay, a good haven for ships"*. Pont's map of the Isle made about 1600 showed Rothesay as a very small place indeed, standing on an islet apparently created by a moat and therefore perhaps little more than the castle itself.

However, there was a school from 1619, and the 1639 tax returns placed Rothesay 24th among the burghs in terms of tax revenues, similar to Forfar and Tain; the streets were first paved in 1665. Chambers added that the castle, later *"the seat of the family of Bute, was burnt down in 1685 by the insurgent Earl of Argyle"*.

**Fish and Textiles**: Martin writing in 1703 noted the importance of fisheries in Bute, *"especially for herring, for which they use about 80 large boats"*. He mentioned *"a quarry of red stone near the town of which the fort there, and the chapel on its north side, have been built; this town is thinly peopled, there not being above a hundred families in it, and they have no foreign trade"*. It seems that the locals were bilingual in English and Gaelic; there was still the seat of the hereditary sheriff. A weaver already worked in the little town – precursor of an important industry. Some urban development had taken place by 1755 when Webster's informant carefully estimated Rothesay's population as 2222. The first public road in Bute was built before 1764. Apparently textiles were already the mainstay, for a lint mill was in use before Rothesay acquired one of the two first small water-powered cotton mills in Scotland *(see also Penicuik)*. This, the Broadcroft Mill, was opened in 1778 by Kenyon of Sheffield, illicitly using machinery patented by Richard Arkwright but financed by Robert Carrick, a Glasgow banker; steam power had been installed there by 1800.

**Heron on Herring; Whisky and Banking**: By 1797 Rothesay was a post town with mails on alternate days, and three annual fair days. In 1799 Robert Heron quoted the population as about 2600, with *"an excellent pier and harbour. Many are employed in the herring fishery"*. It was the *"chief town"* of Bute, where Gaelic speech still prevailed, though *"English also is pretty generally understood, even by the common people"*. A distillery built in 1798 quickly failed, but between 1802 and 1810 the Renfrewshire Banking Company of Greenock established a branch in the town.

**Steamers and Yachts**: The introduction of steamships in the early 19th century enabled Rothesay's main growth: as early as 1816 the elderly James Watt was a notable passenger on a primitive steamer plying between Greenock and Rothesay. A still better harbour was opened in 1822, and the Royal Northern Yacht Club of Rothesay was founded in 1824: this catered exclusively for the rich owners of large yachts. Chambers wrote in 1827 of Rothesay, *"the county-town, and a royal burgh, the chief point of resort"* in Bute. By 1831 Rothesay was served by regular steamers, and Robert Thom, a cotton spinner of Rothesay, was a founding partner of the Castle Steam Packet Company, set up in 1832 to provide better services from Rothesay to Glasgow and Loch Fyne. He also cut catchment canals to improve the mill water supplies.

**Rothesay Urbanised to serve Glaswegians**: Rothesay was already a port of registry with the code letters RO, and grew and prospered as a fishing port until its herring fisheries peaked around 1865. Meantime a gasworks was established in 1840, the large *Glenburn Hydropathic* dated from 1843, the prominent West Church was built in 1846, and by 1851 Hutcheson steamers were calling. *The Buteman* newspaper was established in 1854. For a short time around 1866 North British Railway steamers, and in 1877 those of the Lochgoil & Lochlong Steamboat Company, were among those visiting. A 3 km horse tramway to Port Bannatyne was laid on the 4'0" gauge in 1879–82. The cotton mill continued working until about 1882, jointly powered by steam and by water supplied from the Kirk Dam. The 1891 resident population was 9100.

**Late Victorian Day Tripping and the Glasgow Fair**: By 1894, day tripping made Rothesay pier second only to Greenock's in steamer traffic, for at that time people could travel from Glasgow to Rothesay in an hour by rail and steamer. This led to Murray ungraciously calling Rothesay *'the Margate of the Clyde'*; but although it had a *"squalid"* High Street the tourist trade also provided for longer stays, embodied in the song *Going doon the Watter for the Fair* – the Glasgow Fair Week. Consequently there was a plethora of boarding-houses and four hotels: the *Bute Arms, Queen's, Royal* and *M'Kinlay's Temperance*, all *"very fair"*, plus the *"good" Glenburn Hydro*. Other features were the yacht club, a coastguard station and the cotton mill. A hospital was built in 1897, and a power station provided a public electric supply from 1898.

**The Peak: Ten-minute Steamers and Electric Trams**: The resident population of the burgh (including Port Bannatyne) was 9400 in 1901, a peak census year for Bute. In 1901–02 the tramway was re-gauged to a narrower 3'6" and electrified. It was extended in 1905 as the Rothesay & Ettrick Bay Light Railway, comprising 8 km of double track, and going as the destination boards showed *"right across the island to the sands of Ettrick Bay"*. A second small hospital was built, a golf course was created, and by 1913 in the peak season over 100 steamers would call in a single day! Even in wartime 1916 the Caledonian Steam Packet Company still gave a service. Rothsay recovered well from the effects of the first world war and depression. In 1924 the concrete-floored *Winter Gardens* was built as a 1200-seat music hall; the *Pavilion* was built in 1936 as a restaurant, ballroom and conference centre, and at the same time indoor heated seawater swimming baths were provided. By then there were four cinemas, but in 1936 the trams ceased to run (either beyond Port Bannatyne or totally – experts disagree!). The corn mill closed about 1940, and the truncated tramway was apparently abandoned in 1949.

**Weaving, Cream and Cruising**: The resident population was over 10,000 in 1951. The handloom weaving concern of Bute Looms which was founded in 1947 by the then Marquess of Bute was a success, and a creamery and cheese factory was opened in 1954. In that year the car ferry MV *Cowal* was introduced, its turntable hoist for vehicles being halfway between derrick slings and modern ro-ro ferries. For Rothesay the peak tourist year was 1955, when there were nearly 40 hotels with 750 beds. But the popular taste for day pleasure cruising on smut-laden open decks in the doubtful Scottish weather was falling off, despite a liking for the scenery, the pipers and accordion bands playing in the lee of the funnels, and the fish and chips below.

**Speedy Decline**: With the sudden switch of demand to packaged holidays by air in sunny Spain, Rothesay's tourist trade rapidly diminished. White fisheries had been important for a time, but by the 1950s only ten boats were at work. The submarine depot ships finally left the bay around 1957. Rothesay Academy was rebuilt in 1958, but by then only two cinemas were still open. The few remaining steamers made under 40 calls a day by 1960, and were soon completely replaced by a full ro-ro car ferry from Wemyss Bay. Although Bute Pottery was started in 1960, Rothesay's general facilities speedily declined in the 1960s from those of a major local centre to an ordinary town, fronted by a characterless ferry terminal building thrown up in 1968. By 1971 the resident population had fallen to only 6600. At that time the rural areas of the isle were almost all owned by the Marquess of Bute; the shrinking number of dairy and early potato farms employed about 150 workers, and 30 foresters were also busy, as were Listers the dahlia specialists. Some 650 people still worked in tourism, but the *Winter Gardens* were closed in 1971 and left vacant. The building was saved from demolition and converted into a day-care centre in 1979. Main street decay became evident, for by 1972 the *Ritz Cinema* had been derelict for at least fourteen years.

**Kippers, Duffel Coats – and No County**: Some new economic activity appeared: Langan's clothing factory, which opened in 1969, made duffel coats, and Bute Looms turned to power looms in 1970. By then only about 40 fishermen remained, but Rothesay Seafoods, established about 1965, employed 70 people in 1973, when the long-established Ritchie Brothers were still kipperers; the sheriff court was still active. A new public library was built about 1972, at which time Rothesay's gasworks still produced coal gas. In 1973 Rothesay Academy had 535 pupils, of whom 40 from Arran and Cumbrae (then in the County of Bute) were boarders in lodgings. Following the report of the Wheatley Commission, the ancient County of Bute and Rothesay burgh were both abolished in 1975. At a stroke Rothesay's local government functions were split, and conferred either on distant Glasgow (Strathclyde Region) or distant, upstart and inaccessible Lochgilphead (Argyll & Bute District). Worse still, Arran went to Cunninghame District (for reasons of access). Why did this once popular resort get such rude treatment when Nairn received excessive consideration?

**A Struggling Minor Resort**: There were still 30 hotels in the town about 1980, though with only half the total beds and AA stars of 1956, while only the *Palace* cinema cum bingo hall remained in use. Although by 1992 an attractive new pier building had replaced the previous eyesore, by then the Royal Northern Yacht Club had merged with the Royal Clyde Yacht Club of Hunter's Quay and moved to Rhu *(see Helensburgh)*. This must have reinforced the poor trading which in the 1980s led to continued deterioration of the fabric of the town's shopping centre, and by 1991 the resident population of this elderly retirement centre was down again to 5264. By then a new swimming pool had proved more popular – though in this case less architecturally distinguished – than its predecessor. The Winter Gardens conference centre was still used, though threatened with closure in 1992; in 1993 a quarter of the island's 47 hotels were up for sale, and in 1994 the former West Church stood derelict.

**Bendy Boards and Crumbly Cheese**: Peter Timms, who worked with IBM in Spango Valley, founded the firm of Flexible Technology (FT) which started production in Bute in 1981, making flexible printed circuit boards, a novel product soon in demand. In 1986 FT was sold to Cambridge Electronic Industries and by 1988 had 140 staff. Problems and redundancies led Timms to buy it out again in 1992 when with over 80 staff FT was the island's largest private employer, exporting half its output. A new creamery, opened in 1992 by Scottish Pride, aimed to produce 1600 tonnes of crumbly Drumleish cheese a year and to oust FT as the island's largest employer. Telecom Service Centres now has its HQ in Rothesay, controlling a number of call centres in the Highlands and the West of Scotland.

## ROTHIEMAY (Milltown of R'may) — Map 10, B2

***Village, n. of Huntly,*** *pop. 400 (area)* — OS 29: NJ 5448

Some 8km north of Huntly the River Deveron turns east through a lowland basin where it is joined by the Isla, before cutting through a range of hills topped by the ancient Cairns of Geith. There are carved stones and a stone circle. The *'Fort of the Plain'*, in Gaelic *Rath a'Maigh*, was Rothiemay Castle, which stood near modern Avochie. Pont mentioned the name in a note on a particularly scruffy sketch map made about 1600. Woodland west of *'Rothymay'* was marked on Robert Gordon's pre-1642 map. Apparently the castle did not give rise to a burgh of barony, but only to a milltown. This appeared on Roy's map, surveyed about 1750, as an unnamed hamlet in a trackless area, close to the *'House of Rothiemay'* with its accompanying buildings. Later in the 18th century the Deveron was bridged at Milltown, and Rothiemay post office was opened in 1838.

**Communications Improvements – and Decline**: Rothiemay Station on the Great North of Scotland Railway's main line, opened in 1856, attracted little traffic, as it lay in ultra-rural Cairnie parish, across the river from the castle and 3km south-west of Milltown, the area's main settlement. The railway to Keith was doubled in 1898–1900, with a new Deveron bridge; but when traffic fell away it was singled again. By 1951 Milltown was a village of 750 people with an important timber merchant – Riddoch – a small hotel, secondary school, doctors and chemist. However, Rothiemay Castle was demolished about 1949, and agricultural depopulation hit hard. The station was closed completely about 1965. In the early 1970s Riddoch opened a branch sawmill at Corpach, claimed to be the largest in the EEC; but by 1979 they were Elgin-based, though still known as Riddoch of Rothiemay. By 1981 the secondary school and medical facilities had vanished and fewer than 400 people lived in the Milltown area, since when there has been little development. The former mill's weir, a post office and a pub remain.

## ROTHIENORMAN — Map 10, B2

***Buchan village,*** *pop. 450* — OS 29: NJ 7235

Rothienorman, *'Norman Fort'* (from Gaelic *Rath)*, lies in a bowl of hills on the Fordoun Burn, a tributary of the River Ythan, 5km south-west of the historic parish centre of Fyvie. There are no ancient features of note. Only the ferm touns of Kinbroon and Blackford appeared on Robert Gordon's map, made about 1640. By about 1750 the Roy map showed a mill at Blackford, and the hamlet of *'Meikle Rothy'* beside a track from Turriff to Inverurie; it appeared that the burn still had to be forded. Eventually a bridge was built, a waulk mill appeared on a nearby hill stream, and there was a smithy. From 1857 a station named Rothienorman was open on the Great North of Scotland's branch railway from Inveramsay to Turriff, later extended to Macduff. In 1946 an agricultural engineer replaced the smithy. In 1951 Rothienorman had a population of over 700 but near-average facilities for a village, serving up to 3000 people scattered within a radius of some 5km; but the station was closed to passengers in that year, freight services on the line ceased in 1966 and the track was soon lifted.

**Massive Helping of Ice Cream relieves Decline**: Junior secondary classes in deeply rural schools south of Rothienorman at Meikle Wartle and Rayne North did not survive cuts in farm jobs, which led to the loss of 200 Rothienorman residents by 1971; the loss of facilities and influence halved its overall importance as a service centre. However, the population soon stabilised, because by 1980 Westertown, 2 km south-west of Rothienorman, was the centre of a major dairy farming enterprise. By 1989 (as Mackie's Farmfoods) this combined a herd of 850 dairy cows with a dairy, ice cream factory and packing plant; business was expanding, dairy ice cream being marketed as far south as Bristol by 1992. In 1993 Mackie's opened a new factory; by then their herd had reached 1000 cows, but the firm sold out in 1994 to Wiseman Dairies of East Kilbride. Meantime Rothienorman remains a compact village with the tiny traditional *Rothie Inn* and a post office.

## ROUSAY, Eynhallow & Wyre — Map 13, B1

***Small islands, N. Orkney,*** *pop. 300* — OS 6: HY 4327

The islet of Eynhallow off the north coast of Orkney Mainland had an early monastery, hence its name meaning *'Holy Isle'*. The adjacent hilly sandstone isle of Rousay is full of prehistoric remains. Ancient brochs, of which the most notable is Midhowe where Iron Age blacksmiths worked, flank Rousay's later Viking centre of Westness, whose cemetery on Moa Ness yielded fine ninth century jewellery. Nearby was a palatial 12th century farmhouse 35 m in length, home of the great Earl Sigurd. At that time Kolbein Hruga, known as *'Cubbie Roo'* or *'Cobbie Row'* built his now ruined castle with its rectangular keep beside the church on the small island of Wyre south of Rousay, surrounded by an oval plan wall and ditch. Rousay's 17th century Traill lairds were Jacobites who lived at Westness House, which had to be rebuilt after the '45. In the 19th century nearly 1000 people lived on Rousay. The mansion of Trumland House overlooking Wyre was designed by David Bryce and built in 1870–73 for the incomer and detested local laird, General Traill Burroughs. However, he also built the nearby pier and houses at Brinyan on Wyre Sound, which became the focus of the ferries and early postal services. Eynhallow's last residents left in the 1920s; Historic Scotland cares for its ruined chapel and for Cubbie Roo's Castle.

**Shellfish and Organic Backpackers**: In the 1950s secondary classes were held at Sourin school on the east of the island; but by 1976 the older pupils were taught in Kirkwall. Rousay's population was down to about 180 by 1971; by then electricity arrived from Kirkwall by submarine cables. By 1974 vehicle ferries linked Brinyan and Wyre with Kirkwall, and passenger ferries plied to Tingwall on the Orkney Mainland. By 1981 Brinyan had the facilities of a small village, and a fishing cooperative was processing scallops, crabs and lobsters at the pier. In 1984 Rousay primary school had 36 pupils, but 33 older children from Rousay, Wyre and Egilsay boarded at Kirkwall Grammar School. Between then and 1989 new piers were built at Brinyan, Tingwall, Wyre and Egilsay, enabling a multiple link ro-ro ferry. Trumland House was gutted by fire in 1985 and stood vacant in 1993. By 1991 the population of Rousay had grown to 217, with 46 on Egilsay and 28 on Wyre. Now the only post office is at Sourin, the inn is at Frotoft, and a small hostel for backpackers is open all year on an organic farm at Trumland.

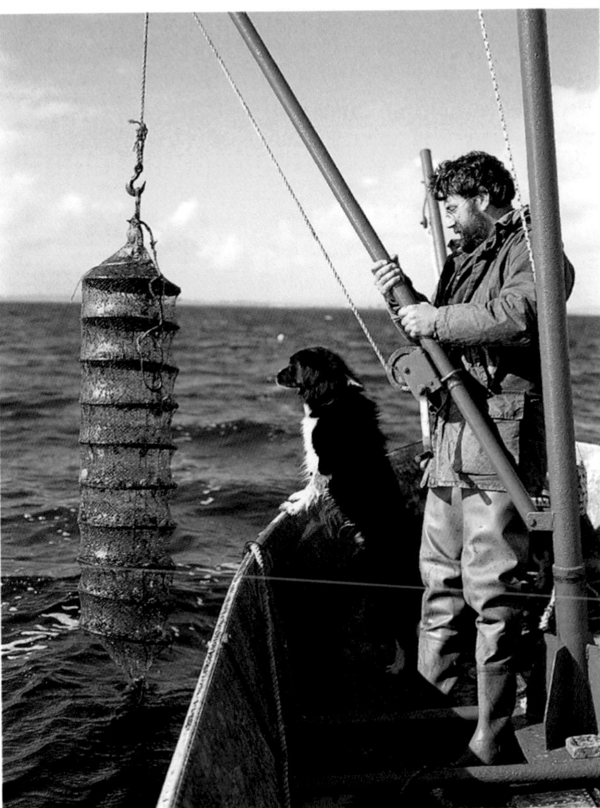

*Princess scallops, Rousay, showing one of the nets used for scallop farming being inspected for progress.* *(SMPC / Richard Welsby)*

## ROXBURGH — Map 3, B4

***Borders hamlet,*** *pop. 450 (area)* — OS 74: NT 6930

Ancient forts in Roxburgh parish lie on either side of the River Tweed 6 km upstream of Kelso. Roxburgh which stands on the west bank of the River Teviot 3 km to the east, was chartered as a Royal Burgh about 1120, by Earl David, the heir apparent to the Scottish throne (later David I). Roxburgh (or perhaps Berwick) was the first place in Scotland to be made the caput of a sheriffdom, established in the 1120s; its name was also given to a Dukedom. Roxburgh thus became one of the original group of *'Four Burghs'*, forerunner of the Convention of Royal Burghs (and ultimately of COSLA). Two churches and three *'hospitals'* were consecrated there, and by 1153 there was also an early Royal mint. Rutherford, beyond the forts 5 km west of Roxburgh, also had an early *'hospital'*.

**New Roxburgh Castle and Friary: Repeatedly Untenable**: To strengthen Scotland's defences in the Tweed valley, the narrow neck of a relatively high peninsula – where the River Teviot met the Tweed 3 km downstream of the burgh – was made defensible by cutting two wet ditches across it to form two islands. A new Royal Castle was built on the small westerly island, and on the larger eastern one (the rounded tip of the peninsula) an early Franciscan friary was founded in 1232; at some time a bridge linked it with the existing Kelso Abbey. A church was also built, probably before 1293 when the castle was a pawn in Edward I's humiliation of John Balliol. In 1313 (as fully described by Barbour) the castle was recaptured from the English by Douglas. Being exposed to attack from the south, the burgh was in English hands for half the time from the late 12th to the mid 15th centuries. In 1460 the foolhardy James II was killed there when a siege gun exploded.

**From Burnt Burgh to Farming Village**: Roxburgh re-emerged as a small farming village on the Teviot bank midway to *'Ormistoun'*. It was named as *'Old Roxburgh'* on Pont's map of about 1600; the 16th century Wallace's Tower stood there among a small group of buildings. The Royal castle of New Roxburgh was shown as if it were still walled; little now remains of it except steep earthen banks. The adjacent friary appeared as a building within an enclosure, labelled *'Freeres'*; across the Teviot at Maxwellheugh was *'Brigend'*, showing the site of a former bridge. *'Newtoun'*, now called Roxburgh Newtown, appeared near the ancient forts. Roxburgh parish school was opened in 1631; Rutherford became a burgh of barony in 1666 but stayed rural.

**From Burgh and Junction to Hamlet**: Roy's map made about 1754 showed Roxburgh Castle at the end of a road from Melrose, but little of the ancient burgh. From 1851 (Old) Roxburgh and Rutherford were served by stations on a North British Railway branch from Newtown to Kelso, later connected to Tweedmouth. In 1856 Roxburgh became the junction for the Jedburgh Railway's line. Roxburgh's water mill was in business in 1895; the parish population in 1901 was 835. As recently as 1951 Roxburgh itself had a population of some 300, with the facilities of a small village. But the Jedburgh railway was closed to passengers after disastrous floods in 1948, and later lifted; in 1968 rural depopulation ensured that Roxburgh and Rutherford stations were closed, and the original railway was abandoned, its Teviot viaduct being adapted to carry a minor road to Heiton. By 1981 the ancient burgh had only some 200 people. The primary school soon closed, the parish population in 1991 was only 463, and the post office – open in 1998 – has since closed. So historic Roxburgh is now little more than a hamlet.

## ROYBRIDGE

**Map 5, B1**

***Lochaber village,*** *pop. 300* — OS 41: NN 2781

Glen Roy joins Glen Spean 5km east of modern Spean Bridge. Roy's map of about 1750 showed settlements and tracks up both glens, but left an unbridged gap between Keppoch with its medieval motte and mansionhouse, and Achaderry to the east of the River Roy. In 1799 Heron noted a *"modern road"* ascending Glen Roy, though the relics of successive shorelines of a glacial lake, at that time misnamed the *"parallel roads"*, understandably baffled him. Telford's Laggan Road was completed through Glen Spean in 1818, with a bridge across the River Roy. When the West Highland Railway was opened in 1894 a crossing station named Roy Bridge was provided nearby. In the 1920s a substantial estate of local authority houses was built, relating to the vast Lochaber Aluminium Project *(see Fort William)*.

**Holiday Centres**: By 1947 there was a small hotel and a post and telegraph office. By the 1950s about 220 people lived in the area, also served by a primary school. By 1980 there were several caravan and camping sites, three local hotels had 38 rooms between them, and the *Glenspean Lodge Hotel* was open at Achluachrach; the resident population had risen to about 300. In 1984 the village had three small shops, a primary school and – rare in rural Scotland – a large Catholic church. The station now enjoys four weekday passenger trains to Fort William and Glasgow, and two or three on summer Sundays. Glen Roy is now a national nature reserve. Roybridge has a school, post office and the *Stronlossit Hotel*, while the *Glenspean Lodge Hotel* is 3km to the east. An independent hostel for back-packers is open all year, with another at Achluachrach and a third at the remote Tulloch Station some 9km to the east.

## RUM, Isle of

**Map 8, A4**

***Inner Hebridean island,*** *pop. under 100* — OS 39: NM 4099

Monro noted in 1549 that the Isle of *'Ronin'* – evidently geologically unusual Rum, 30km west of Mallaig Bay – was a *"forest of high mountains with abundance of little deer and solan geese"*. It already belonged to the MacLean lairds of Coll and appeared to have few inhabitants. However these increased greatly in numbers until in 1826–28 the island was cleared of two-thirds of its 400 poverty-stricken people to create a sheep farm, and the MacLean had Kinloch House built. Finding no more profit than before, in 1845 he sold out to the Marquis of Salisbury, who turned the by then treeless island into a deer forest.

**The Queen's Automatic Orchestra**: In 1888 John Bullough, a rich Lancashire manufacturer of cotton machinery, bought Rum for its sport. His even richer son Sir George Bullough renamed it *'Rhum'* and engaged London architects to design Kinloch Castle, a luxurious mansion built in 1900–02 in the most sheltered area above the sea inlet of Loch Scresort. A pier was built to which all the red sandstone and soil to be used in landscaping was brought from Ayrshire (some sources suggest Arran). The mansion's fittings included a remarkable mechanical automatic orchestra originally intended for the aged Queen Victoria, who died before its delivery by the makers. The self-important family also built a mock Greek temple on the far west coast of the isle as a mausoleum!

**Conservation combined with Tourism**: The island became publicly owned by the Nature Conservancy Council (NCC) in 1957; the last Bullough died in Kinloch Castle in 1967, aged 98. The NCC then turned the magnificent but deteriorating mansion over to hotel and hostel use and admitted walkers and naturalists, sea anglers and deer stalkers. In 1971 just 40 people were enumerated. By 1978 the NCC had reduced overgrazing and reintroduced lost species such as sea eagles. Rum had only 26 hardy residents by 1991; the school and a combined post office and shop in the only remaining part of Kinloch House provided the wild, wet island's basic needs, and a mountain rescue post was established. Accessible only by the infrequent and indirect Small Isles passenger ferries from Mallaig (and in summer from Arisaig), it was little changed in 2000 under the NCC's successors, Scottish Natural Heritage, for whom Cambridge University are studying the deer in detail. However, a new slipway to be completed in 2001 will enable vehicles to join or leave the new ferry already in service.

## RUMBLING BRIDGE & Powmill

**Map 16, C1**

***Kinross-shire hamlets,*** *pop. 225* — OS 58: NT 0199

The River Devon leaves the Ochil Hills, turns sharply west at the Crook of Devon into an incised valley and heads for Stirling, for long forming the Kinross/Clackmannan boundary. Remotely sited some 3km south-east of the Crook is Aldie Castle, a major 16th century tower. An early track from

Inverkeithing to Auchterarder via Glen Devon crossed the river 2 km downstream of the Crook at a very narrow gorge, where by 1643 a timber span known as the Rumbling Bridge had been thrown across, almost over a waterfall. In superstitious 1662 this was the shameful site of the burning to death of eleven *'witches and warlocks'*. The wooden bridge was superseded in 1713 by a stone arch built by William Gray, a mason from Saline.

**Mills, Hostelry and Railway**: By the 1750s Muchards Mill and a *'Wakemil'* turned downstream. The later Pow Mill, 1.5 km south of Rumbling Bridge, was built on the Gairney Burn, which eventually joins the Devon at another waterfall. The Rumbling Bridge was rebuilt in 1773, the roads were turnpiked in 1810, and a wider upper arch was built in 1816 to ease the gradients. By then Rumbling Bridge was well known to tourists, and by 1827 had given its name to an inn beside the fall, long linked with Auchterarder by a four in hand coach. In 1863 the Devon Valley Railway was opened from Kinross to Rumbling Bridge, which became the temporary terminus; by 1869 the inn had become the *Rumbling Bridge Hotel*. The line was linked through to Alloa in 1871, becoming part of the North British system. In 1894 the hotel was *"very fair"* to Murray, and nearby was a post and telegraph office.

**Powmill Blossoms with Fitted Kitchens**: By 1954 a quarry was open 1.5 km south-west of the hamlet of Powmill. There was little other change to 1964 when the under-used railway up the pleasant valley was closed. However a grocery store and the *Gartwhinzean Hotel* were open at Powmill by 1969; it also gained a roadside cafe. The hotel's restaurant was greatly enlarged in the 1980s. The old *Rumbling Bridge Hotel*, still open in 1980, could not compete and became a nursing home in the 1990s. By 1988 the recently enlarged quarry west of the hamlet of Powmill had closed, as had Rumbling Bridge post office. However, in the 1990s Powmill was steadily growing with new housing, and the local authority boundary was changed in 1996 to include the whole of both places in Perth & Kinross. By 1992 Crannog Kitchens fabricated fitted kitchens from solid wood at workshops in Rumbling Bridge; but in 1999 they moved to Lathalmond by Townhill.

## RUTHERGLEN — Map 15, D5

***Town / S-E. suburb of Glasgow**, pop. 35,000* — OS 64: NS 6161

Rutherglen (for centuries locally called *Ru'glen)* lies on the south bank of the River Clyde only 4 km east of Glasgow; in the 12th century it was the head of navigation. Chartered as a Royal Burgh in 1124, its church was substantially built around 1200, and its stone castle or peel tower dated from the 13th century. By 1286 Glasgow had spanned the Clyde, preventing masted vessels reaching Rutherglen, where an emergency Scottish Parliament was held in 1300. The town soon fell to the English, but in 1313 or 1314 its castle was recovered by Bruce's Scots. About 1330 the town contributed some 5% of Scotland's burgh taxes. In the 15th century the keep of Farme Castle was erected between the town and the river. However, by then Rutherglen was in the shadow of Glasgow, and its payments declined rapidly to under 1% of the Scottish total in the 16th century, when trade disputes continued between the two burghs. By 1560 the church was an appurtenance of Paisley Abbey.

**After the Reformation, the Horse Fairs**: Rutherglen castle was burnt in 1568, but a parish school was founded in 1590. Pont's maps, made in 1596, showed an emparked *'Castletoun'* south of the small town which was labelled *'Ruglan'*; *'Farm'* was also emparked, while to the west *'Sheafield'* and *'Pomadi'* nestled in a small wooded valley whose floor was known as *'Mauld's Mire'*. In 1639 Rutherglen ranked only 37th of Scottish burghs in tax rents, but it was known for its horse fairs, probably held in the wide main street, and some development continued in the 17th century. Then the pace evidently quickened, for by the time of Roy's survey of the 1750s Rutherglen was a large linear settlement, with no fewer than eight radial roads – a very extensive network for the period, but confined to the south bank of the river, for there was still no Clyde bridge between Glasgow and Bothwell.

**Mining, Bridge and Industry**: A coal mine was open locally by 1776, the year when the first Rutherglen bridge – a *"beautiful"* structure according to Heron – was built by its town council in order to overcome a ban on carts using Glasgow's ancient crumbling bridge. By 1778 edge tools were being made in Rutherglen by Bryce, apparently the only such manufacturer in all of Scotland at the time; they were ground sharp by water power. In 1787 a dyeworks was set up; by 1797 Rutherglen was one of the four most-used fair stances in Scotland, with twelve fair days in the year. Heron noted in 1799 that *"the fairs were famous for draught-horses. The Rutherglen and Shawfield printworks employ about 200 persons"*, but Rutherglen was *"inhabited chiefly by coal-hewers and manufacturers"*. By 1802 a Rutherglen coal mine had reached deep enough to make pumping engines necessary. In 1810 a locally-built Newcomen-type beam pumping and winding engine, said by some to be the last of its type ever installed, was set up at nearby Farme Colliery, working until 1915, and then being dismantled; it survived to be re-erected at Summerlee (Coatbridge) in 1990.

**Chromates: the Blackness of the Whites**: From 1808 John and James White ran a business at Shawfield which became a highly toxic chrome and chromates plant, run with the insouciance of the worst of early entrepreneurs. They became the world's largest chromium processors, regardless of the ill-health of their workforce, who developed nose and throat cancers and leukaemia. (It is now recognised that Chromium 3 in particular is highly carcinogenic.) It was not until around 1825 that Rutherglen acquired a post office. In 1860–63 the accumulated profits of half a century of ruthless exploitation enabled James White to build himself a mansion near Dumbarton *(q.v.)*, about as far away from Rutherglen as he could get without losing touch with Glasgow. Even his successors never informed their workers of the grave risks to health; extremely dangerous wastes were still carelessly tipped by hand almost to the end of the industry a century later.

**Railway, Lakes and Sea**: The Clydesdale Junction Railway – a subsidiary of the Caledonian Railway (CR) and later to become its main line – was opened through the town in 1849 to connect Motherwell with South Side station in Glasgow. About 1859 a freight-only branch was opened to Bridgeton, and in 1865 Rutherglen station also became the junction for the CR line to Carmyle and Coatbridge. A local newspaper, the *Rutherglen Reformer*, was established in 1874. In 1877 T B Seath of Rutherglen built the iron-hulled steamer *Lady of the Lake* for Ullswater and in 1889 her sister the *Raven*, both remarkably still in service in the 1990s under diesel power. Despite the limitations of the river, in 1878 they also built the 178-ton coaster SS *Agate*, engined by W King for William

Robertson of Glasgow, and the famous little paddle steamer *Lucy Ashton* in 1888; she worked until 1951. Clyde Football Club was founded in 1878 at Barrowfield Park, moving in 1898 to Shawfield, then a trotting track.

**Sundry Industries, and Trains versus Trams**: Rutherglen grew into a major industrial centre with a gasworks, a factory making brattice cloth – tarred for use to control ventilation in mines – a ropery, forge, and soap and soda works. The large Eastfield paper mills opened about 1880; the great Clydebridge Steel Works between Rutherglen and Carmyle *(q.v.)* was commenced in 1887–88. The population in 1891 was over 13,000. In 1895 power looms were made in Rutherglen, which had two coal pits to the east, but was still separated from Glasgow by a 1 km strip of farmland. The road bridge was rebuilt in 1896, in which year Rutherglen became the terminus of an intensive Caledonian Railway suburban service to and across Glasgow via Central Low Level to Partick and Maryhill; however, this was soon hit by electric tramway competition. since Rutherglen and Burnside (via Stonelaw Road) were served by Glasgow tramcars. In 1903 the Caledonian's Lanarkshire & Ayrshire Railway was opened, with a sparse passenger service from Glasgow Central to a station at Burnside south of Rutherglen, terminating at Kirkhill in Cambuslang. A power station was established in 1905, and early in the century a small public park was provided in Stonelaw Road, partly at least over a former toxic waste tip – of which more anon.

**Golf and Diversification of Industry**: Provision of a public library got under way in 1901, with Carnegie aid. The Blairbeth golf club was founded in 1910 and laid out an 18-hole course. However as engines – both steam and internal combustion – in turn took hold on the road, the horse fairs and markets faded. British Ropes Ltd built a fine new office block at their Farme Cross works in 1912. After 1925, Main Street Rutherglen was extended eastwards from Farmeloan Road to join Cambuslang Road. In 1921 the knitwear manufacturers McClure & McIntosh were established within a stone's throw of the town, in Rutherglen Road, Glasgow, and by 1937 were perhaps the largest firm of knitted outerwear makers in Britain. Oatcake baking on a commercial scale also began in the 1920s, and the Phoenix tubeworks adjoined the Clyde. The 1931 population was 25,000. The Cathkin laundry, east of the town, was one of the largest in the West of Scotland. In 1932 Shawfield became a greyhound stadium and Clyde FC, locally called the *'Bully Wee'*, were soon its tenants. By 1939 E K Cole had a factory in the town producing *'EKCO'* radios.

*Rutherglen town hall, designed by Charles Wilson, one of Glasgow's leading architects, and built in 1861–62. The distinctive profile of its tower is a symbol of the ancient burgh of Rutherglen (one of Scotland's earliest).* *(JRH)*

**Overcrowding and Suburbanisation adjoin**: By 1936 overcrowding in Rutherglen's tenements was even worse than in Glasgow, at 31% of all houses, but at the same time the 1930s saw Wardlawhill built up, plus large private housing developments at Burnside to the south of Rutherglen, and to the west where new stations were built at Croftfoot and King's Park. These areas were already within Glasgow for local government purposes; the *State Cinema* at King's Park was built about 1937. Molly Urquhart of Glasgow founded a repertory theatre in Rutherglen which successfully staged over a hundred plays; it was still active in 1952. Rutherglen Academy was open by 1958. By then Rutherglen was a major local centre, which it remained despite subsequent population decline.

**Trams to Electric Trains – and Chromate Closure**: The Glasgow tramcars were withdrawn in 1961 and the southern stations acquired electric trains in 1962 (though the main line Rutherglen station had to wait until 1974). In the interim the passenger trains to Carmyle and Coatbridge were withdrawn in 1966. After several changes of ownership that apparently did little to improve conditions at White's chromium refinery, Albright & Wilson bought this toxic disgrace in 1965; soon finding it impossible to operate safely and profitably, it was closed in 1968. The site was cleared, but apparently without full realisation of the hazards, and redeveloped with new shops and housing. The 1971 population of Rutherglen Large Burgh was just under 25,000, but its boundary was very tightly drawn and there was much adjacent housing development, especially to the south. The Mitchell shopping arcade was built in the heart of the town in the 1970s.

**Not Taking Care of Public Health**: In the 1970s a long-disused toxic waste tip, later part of the Rutherglen Public Park, became the site of the new 108-bed Rutherglen Maternity Hospital and health centre; this disgraceful oversight having been discovered, its intended closure was announced in 1995. Meantime in 1990 a 300-bed private nursing home had been planned beside it by an English firm with the remarkable name of *Takare*. It was to be hoped that they would take more care in developing the site than the NHS had next door! But unseen hazards were everywhere in the lower parts of the town: it was reckoned in 1991 that up to 275 million litres of toxic liquids including phenols and cyanides used to be pumped underground each year from the chemical and steel works in the area, with untold deleterious effects on underground water throughout the lower Clyde valley, where artesian pressure could bring it to the surface.

**Clydebridge winds Down**: In 1975 Clydebridge Steelworks, its open-hearth furnaces earmarked for closure under a British Steel plan of 1972, was still supplied with iron from the Clyde Ironworks just across the river in Carmyle. These furnaces and Hallside fed a slabbing mill, which itself supplied a plate mill. But Clydebridge's open-hearth plant was closed in 1978, and the works was cut down in the early 1980s to a shadow of its former self, though in 1992 some production continued on the site. Meantime from 1979 an electric rail service restored Rutherglen's links across the city centre and down as well as up the Clyde valley.

**Rutherglen within Glasgow**: The ancient burgh was incorporated into Glasgow City District from 1975. By 1980 the independent Catholic Fernhill School had been established at Burnside, where the *Burnside Hotel* existed, and there was also the central *Mill Hotel*. Rutherglen's population was falling, but although one of the paper mills had closed and another had been converted into a whisky blending plant, by that time there were numerous industrial estates. However, by 1994 the vacant office block was all that remained on the former British Ropes site. In 1986 Shawfield was sold for a failed redevelopment scheme by its owners, so the then local football team (Clyde FC) was forced to abandon the town, for a time uneasily sharing the Firhill ground at Maryhill with Partick Thistle. However there was by then an industrial collection in Rutherglen Museum, and the Rutherglen shopping centre of over 5000 m$^2$ had been built. By 1990 Scotrail had established its staff training centre in Rutherglen, where it also retained the Bridgeton yard as a major permanent way and civil engineering depot. In 1991 the population of *'greater Rutherglen'* was about 35,000.

**White Goods meet Darkness**: In 1993 the reopening to passenger trains of the line to Coatbridge occurred (but with diesel trains, not electric). Meantime Southcroft Road, Rutherglen became in 1962 the HQ and warehouse of Clydesdale Electrical, a retailer founded in Bridgeton in 1911, recently sold for a penny! Later the subject of a management buy-out, it was bought by a Dutch firm in 1985 as Scotland's leading retail electrical chain. Unwise expansion led to receivership in 1994. The 1300 jobs at its 120 stores were badly hit because Scottish Power bought only 50, of which only 14 were in Scotland, and the others had to close.

**Counting the Cost of Pollution in Children's Cancers**: Terrible statistics which showed that Rutherglen and Cambuslang had between them a quarter of all Scottish cases of childhood leukaemia, and a concentration of a rare children's kidney tumour, were revealed in 1992 on Channel 4 television. By then it was recognised that scattered around the area were at least 27 extremely dangerous former tipping sites with several times the permissible pollution, and some emergency work was undertaken to cover over the most dangerous. Little could be done with the worst of all, the Glencairn FC *'park'*, where the terracing was entirely composed of waste material containing some 26 times the allowable limits of toxins. Even worse in some ways was the chrome-impregnated ground adjoining Mall's Mire, where chromate pollution in the water entering the River Clyde reached 825 times the permissible limit. Other possible sources of carcinogens were being studied – including phenols, cyanogens and benzene from the area's former coke ovens.

**Rutherglen in *'South'* Lanarkshire!**: In 1996 Rutherglen and Cambuslang, Cinderallas both, were detached from closely related Glasgow and placed in a sprawling new unitary local authority, weirdly described as *'South Lanarkshire'*, a strange move indeed! In 1997 Robert Wiseman Dairies bought Rutherglen's Scottish Pride milk bottling plant. Other significant employers are Polywarm (duvets and sleeping-bags), Westcrowns (glass and ceramics), Samnex (household products), Campbell's construction, and the Speyside Distillery Company. The contentious south-eastern leg of the M74 motorway eastwards from Gorbals, paralleling the main railway past Polmadie to Cambuslang Road and through the site of the former Clydebridge Steelworks, crossing the River Clyde to meet the existing M74 end-on at Fullarton Road, was argued over for years but approved in 2000. The former *Mill Hotel* has been refurbished as the 26-room *Kings Park Hotel*. The independent Fernhill School offers mixed primary classes and girls' secondary education; Stonelaw High School has 1200 pupils and Trinity High 1120.

## RUTHWELL & Clarencefield — Map 2, B5

***Solway Firth small villages***, *pop. 400 (area)* — OS 85: NY 1068

Ruthwell, locally pronounced *'Rivvie'*, lies on the Solway coast 10 km west of Annan at the mouth of the tiny Thwaite Burn. It was the site of a monastery in the Dark Ages; a famous 5.5 m tall Northumbrian carved stone cross survives from the eighth century. In the 15th century the keep of Comlongon Castle was built 2 km west of Ruthwell, which became a burgh of barony in 1507–08. Comlongon appeared on Pont's map of Annandale, made around 1610, plus the names *'Rifwell'* and *'Riffel'*. The countryside was then thickly settled, with a mill on the Raffles Burn, an unusual feature being the extensive wooded *'Koigpool park'* (Cockpool) to the west. *'Saltcotts'* on the shore showed where Ruthwell folk made refined salt by washing encrusted salt from beach sand in sea water and boiling the brine, as was recorded in 1617. The Roy map surveyed around 1754 showed Brow just west of Ruthwell as the junction point of the coast road with the long straight road inland to Mouswald. In the late 18th century a limestone quarry was open at Comlongon. Heron referred to Ruthwell as a *"village"* in 1799.

**Pioneer Savings Bank and Castle Weddings**: It is a remarkable fact that Scotland's (and possibly Britain's) first Savings Bank was established in remote little Ruthwell in 1810, by the local minister, Henry Duncan. Chambers in 1827 noted that *"the shore is here graced by the little sea-bathing village of Brow"*, which had been a haunt of the ailing Robert Burns. The Glasgow & South Western Railway served Ruthwell from 1848, its station lying north of the hamlet of Clarencefield – which appears to be a 19th century development which eventually acquired a post office. In 1901 770 people lived in Ruthwell parish; soon afterwards a mansion was built beside the ancient keep and took its name of Comlongon Castle. In 1951, when the parish still had 680 people, there were agricultural engineers and a timber merchant in addition to the general facilities of a small village, but farmwork losses were accelerating. The railway station was down to one passenger train a day by 1963, and was closed completely soon after. By 1988 a very pleasant small hotel adjoined Ruthwell church. By 1991 only 400 people lived in the parish, but Clarencefield still has its pub and post office. The mansion, which has for a few years been the *Comlongon Castle Hotel*, has 12 bedrooms and offers wedding services in the restored Great Hall of the adjacent castle.

## ST ANDREWS

**Map 6, C3**

***E. Fife coastal town,*** *pop. 14,600* OS 59: NO 5116

Rocky cliffs on the coast of the East *Neuk* (Corner) of Fife formed a defensible area adjacent to a tiny natural harbour at the mouth of the Kinness Burn. About 6 km south-west on Drumcarrow Craig is the prehistoric stone broch or hill fort of Denork, probably a corruption of *Dunork*, the *'Fort of the young boar'*, while the promontory of St Andrews was called Muckross *('swine headland' in Gaelic)*. In the Dark Ages it was claimed that a ship carrying the Greek monk St Regulus or Rule, allegedly bringing with him the bones of the early Greek martyr Saint Andrew, came to shore there in the year 370. This legend made the site important to the early Columban or *Culdee* Christians, who sanctified it as Kilrule *('Rule's Church')*. St Kenny (*Cainneach*), an Ulster contemporary of Columba, had a cell at Kilrule, and founded the priory of Kirkheugh in Andrew's memory, perhaps in 550 AD. According to Chambers the place *"was probably the seat of a church, as well as a town, in the 6$^{th}$ century"*; certainly the remains of a Pictish shrine have been found. A bishopric followed in 736. Between 732 and 747 Angus I, the King of Picts, granted the monastery the *'Boar's Run'* extending to Boarhills, the River Eden and Kemback, and by 746 the religious establishment also boasted an abbot.

**Religious Capital of Scotland**: In 843 AD the lands of Dalriada and Pictland were forcibly merged into the new state of Alba by Kenneth MacAlpin. Kilrule became known as *Kinrimund*, probably meaning *'The High King's Hill'*; though many different versions of early names for the locality have been found such as *Cendrigmonaid* and *Kilrimont*. In 875 Bishop Adrian of Kilrimont was killed by Norsemen on the Isle of May; he was later made a saint. By 906 Dunkeld had ceded its role as the seat of the *'Bishop of Alban'* and hence of Scotland, to Kilrimont. Scotland adopted Andrew as its patron saint, and a flag whose X-shaped motif or *'Saltire'* reflected the shape of the wooden cross on which it was said the hapless Andrew had met his end. Chambers stated that the place was renamed St Andrews by Kenneth III about the year 1000. By about 1100 two long wooden piers enclosed the harbour, and in 1114 there were still thirteen Culdees attendant at St Leonard's parish church and *'hospital'*. The erection of a new St Regulus' or Rule's church above the harbour was begun in 1112, and by 1124 this was not only used as the parish church but also as the proto-cathedral; five of its married clergy ran a sort of hotel for pilgrims and travellers. Under King David I, Bishop Robert rebuilt the church between 1126 and 1144 to fill its more exalted role, but it must soon have been found inadequate.

**Burgh, Cathedral, Castle and Prosperity**: By about 1139 an Augustinian priory had also been founded by Bishop Robert; this took over St Rule's church in 1144, by which time the first Holy Trinity had become the parish church. St Andrews was an ecclesiastical burgh, and its first Provost, Mainard, was a Fleming. A large extension was laid out on the plateau west of the ancient tiny nucleus to a regular but highly subtle V-plan, focusing on the site for a huge new cathedral, almost 120 metres long, *"founded by Bishop Arnold in 1162, and finished by Bishop Lamberton in 1318"* (Chambers). Meantime the merchant guild of St Andrews was established, around 1200; fishing is known to have been based in the harbour in 1222. A new parish church (St Mary's on the Rock) was erected in the first half of the 13$^{th}$ century on the cliff-top near the east end of the cathedral, and the Culdees then moved there. The bishop's pentagonal castle on a cliff-top promontory to the west was begun about 1200 (and extended in 1401 by Bishop Trail). In 1274 St Andrews was the cathedral city of Scotland's largest diocese, which included Lothian, Gowrie (the area between Dundee and Perth) and the Mearns.

**Good Town but Little Trade**: By 1282 the priory owned several mills in Linlithgow and properties in Berwick. In 1295 St Andrews was described as *"a good town"*, its trade secured by charter; the castle was in royal hands about 1300. Despite the wars of the Succession, in 1312 St Andrews merchants were trading in Norway, but little more was recorded of the town before 1350 brought the terrible pestilence of the Black Death. After these major setbacks St Andrews did a minor export trade in wool, in the 1360s ranking seventh among Scottish ports in terms of Customs receipts; but perhaps due to trade disputes with the nearby burgh of Cupar in 1369, its later accounts are small and variable. By 1400 St Mary on the Rock was a collegiate church.

**University, More Churches and a Friary**: About 1411 Bishop Wardlaw founded the University, the first in Scotland. Though only having *"the title of a school"* (Chambers) this was a decisive move. The new parish church of the Holy Trinity was built near the centre of the burgh from 1412 onwards. In 1434/35 St Andrews exported small amounts of cloth, and during that period received salmon and skins from Aberdeen. St Andrews was again hit by pestilence in 1442, but copper alloys were cast into jewellery in late medieval St Andrews. Bishop Kennedy founded the secular St Salvator's College in 1450. Some stone-built town houses erected in the

15th century are regarded as the oldest in Scotland which still survive.

**Archbishopric and Prosperity**: In 1472 the see of St Andrews was elevated by Pope Sixtus VI to become Scotland's first Archbishopric, and so for a time its great church became a metropolitan cathedral. In 1497 four St Andrews ships entered the Baltic, nearly 20% of the Scottish total, some in that period going as far as Danzig. Despite this prosperity, in the late 15th and early 16th centuries the town council, sheltered by the powerful archbishop, typically paid between 1% and 3% of burgh tax revenue, a modest contribution to the Scots exchequer. Trade disputes with Cupar were renewed in 1498, but St Andrews was at the height of its prosperity. According to Chambers *"the city could boast of sixty ships; and at the Great Fair, which lasted fifteen days, no fewer than 300 vessels, many of them foreign, used to cast anchor in the bay"*.

**Education, Plague and Failing Trade**: In 1511 St Leonard's School was started, and St Leonard's College was founded as an Augustinian secular college in the existing hospital in 1512 by Archbishop Stewart. By 1514 there were two hospitals, St Mary's College was founded in 1538, and there are other early 16th century foundations in the city. Chambers listed *"a convent of Observantines, a convent of Dominicans, a collegiate church and a priory"* plus *"three colleges, then in a flourishing condition"*. Before the Reformation a printer was active in the town, but its trade was slipping. In 1529, due to a major attack of pestilence in St Andrews, goods shipped from there to Aberdeen were denied admission, and by 1540 the contribution of St Andrews to the Baltic trade had halved.

**The Downfall of the Roman Church in Scotland**: In 1546 the tyrannical Cardinal David Beaton burnt the Protestant visionary George Wishart to death in the castle, and was suitably rewarded by his own speedy assassination. When the castle was besieged in 1546 a mine and a counter-mine were dug; these rare survivals can still be explored by visitors. Estienne Perlin, a French traveller of 1551, thought St Andrews was the largest town in Scotland, and its new archbishop *"the richest man"*. This continuing abuse of power made the authoritarian Roman church an obvious target of the growing body of reformers. The sad result was that in 1559 the magnificent cathedral was *"to the everlasting disgrace of the Reformers, destroyed in a single afternoon by an idiot mob"* (Chambers).

**Decay After the Reformation**: In 1560 the Bishop of St Andrews – no longer accepted as an archbishop – sat in Parliament. The important St Andrews Priory was also represented there by the Commendator; its 25 appropriated churches were mainly in Fife, but included Linlithgow. St Salvator's College possessed nine churches, St Mary's College five (including Tyninghame in East Lothian), and St Leonard's College one. About 1571 during the Scottish civil war the oddly named Robert Lekpreuik, printer to the General Assembly of the new Church of Scotland, moved his work from Edinburgh to St Andrews, where the University carried on. The cartographer Timothy Pont was a student there about 1580–84, and by 1593 St Andrews was the centre of a Protestant presbytery. But the wrecked cathedral, one of Scotland's finest buildings, was effectively destroyed by quarrying to rebuild the harbour and town in stone, including the West Port in 1589; the process was aided by neglect, for the local economy decayed, having lost its main source of income.

**Royal Burgh, Trade Resurgence and Roads**: Grain export was reported in 1618, and the town was re-chartered as a Royal Burgh in 1620. Although in 1621 it paid under 1.5% of Scottish Customs dues, its traders still imported a little wine. St Andrews was the sixth largest centre in Scotland in 1639 in rent terms, and was still cited as one of the *"greater towns"* of Scotland in 1648, but its trading importance was reduced by the confusion of the English civil war and by storm damage to the harbour, and dwindled until the Restoration. Brewing was carried on commercially from at least the mid 17th century, and the harbour was repaired in 1662. By 1679 a coach road had been made from Kennoway to St Andrews, by 1700 the Kinaldy Burn had been bridged at Peekie near Boarhills, and St Andrews' first post office was opened in 1701. Defoe commented in the 1720s that *"the colleges are well supplied with men of learning in all sciences; the students are very numerous"*. Printing was resumed about 1740, but in 1747 St Leonard's College was alienated from the University and united with St Salvator. The Roy map made about 1750 showed the burn mouth already confined by piers and bridged. Of the six radial roads, that to the south passed *'Dunniny'* (Dunino) parish kirk and its bridge across the little Kinaldie Burn, east of which turned three mills (Dunino has since faded away). In the 1770s a new road was built south-westwards to join existing lanes to Largo and Elie.

**The World's First 18-hole Golf Course**: The rules of golf had been formalised in Leith in 1744, ten years before the St Andrews Golfing Society (forerunner of the Royal & Ancient) was founded in 1754. At first the Society played on part of the natural links, but in 1764 the club took a bold step and adopted the world's first 18-hole course *(see Price for details)*. The Denbrae Mill was built west of the town from 1764. John Gardner designed a new library for the University, built in 1764–67, but Boswell wrote of his visit in 1773, when he and Dr Johnson stayed at *Glass's Inn*, *"it was somewhat dispiriting to see this ancient archiepiscopal city so sadly deserted"*; perhaps it was out of term. More activity spurted when the pier was yet again rebuilt in 1783, and around the same time a woollen mill was opened and a new waulk mill was built alongside existing flour mills; by 1793 a sawmill was for let. In 1792 Edward Jenner, who was to be the pioneer of smallpox vaccination, graduated in medicine from the University. Five fair days were scheduled for 1797. Heron's comments implied a small and select University; he guessed the population in 1799 at about 2500, and noted *"the harbour is rather incommodious and admits only small vessels"*. John Rennie was very soon engaged in harbour works, and a lifeboat station was opened in 1800, sharing with Montrose the honour of being the first in Scotland; yet in 1803 only three or four small yawls fished from St Andrews.

**Sleepy St Andrews in the 1820s**: The Argyle Brewery was built in 1805 and soon the *Cross Keys* was a coaching inn. From 1806 a greenkeeper was employed on the Old Course, and the St Andrews Thistle golf club was founded in 1817. In 1827 Chambers was unimpressed by the thud of wooden clubs on feather-stuffed leather balls, dismissing St Andrews as merely a *"highly genteel town, the ghost of a fine city now only remarkable as the seat of the least prosperous University in Scotland; the number of students seldom exceeds 140 and its harbour boasts of little trade. There still pervades an almost monastic quiet"*.The old road across Magus Muir was *"now* *scarcely to be traced"*, and *"few post-chaises and coal-carts"* passed into the city under the arched West Port.

**University Growth, Madras College & Golf Advances**: In 1828 the United College of St Andrews made a start on new buildings designed by Robert Reid, who also added a Senate Room to the library in 1830. Building work stopped after the east wing was completed in 1831, and the quadrangle was eventually completed in 1849 to designs altered by William Nixon. Edinburgh architect William Burn designed the imposing and successful Madras College for Dr Andrew Bell of Cheltenham, set back from South Street and built in 1832–34 (by 1886 it had a mixed roll of some 900 pupils). A Bank of Scotland branch was open by 1833, but nearly half its business was for Haig of the Seggie distillery at Guardbridge *(q.v.)*. A St Andrews native of great energy was Allan Robertson, born in the town in 1815, who became the most renowned early golf professional and local clubmaker. Due to the patronage of William IV, in 1834 the St Andrews Golfing Society was pompously re-styled as the *'Royal & Ancient'* Club (R&A). A third golf club, the St Andrews Mechanics, was founded in 1843, the year that Robert Paterson is reputed to have made the first *'rubber'* golf ball, from gutta percha.

**Rae's Town Expansions, Hotels and a Certain Club**: George Rae, born in 1811 of a family of wheelwrights, was the first native of the town to become an architect, advising Provost Playfair – for whom North Bell Street was laid out in 1834–36 and South Bell Street in 1848–58. He designed Playfair Terrace, built for the town council in 1846–52; these works it seems nearly bankrupted them, and in 1848 the debt-ridden council tried to sell off the links. Rae masterminded the rebuilding of the *Cross Keys Hotel* in 1851–64 and designed the *Royal Hotel*, built in South Street in 1857–65, which eventually became the Southgait Hall of Residence. Rae also designed the Union Club, built in 1853–54 *(see below)*. In the 1860s he laid out Queen's Gardens and designed several baronial extravaganzas including Edgecliffe on The Scores and finally a huge villa in Gibson Place. Meantime John Chesser designed the large speculative development built from 1849 onwards at Hope Park and Abbotsford Crescent.

**The Railway remakes St Andrews**: It seems that it was the accessibility resulting from the opening of the cheaply built St Andrews railway from Leuchars Junction in 1852 that saved the town and helped to popularise golf. Though it split the Balgove Links from the Pilmuir Links, it must be seen in retrospect as one of the more successful projects of the incautious Thomas Bouch. In 1850 William Nixon's former architectural assistant Jesse Hall became manager of a new gasworks, soon using rail-borne coal. He designed Clifton Bank on The Scores in 1856, became superintendent of the University buildings, and designed the Volunteer Hall built in City Road in 1884, with its iron trussed arched roof similar to the large railway stations of the time. With the golfing talent and organisation available in the town by that time, and a suitable climate, St Andrews was ready for rapid development into the world's first and most famous golfing resort. The famous Tom Morris, born locally in 1821, was greenkeeper of the R&A for forty years from the mid 1860s, and laid out many other courses. Women also took up golf – though being hampered by stifling conventions and crippling corsets they could scarcely compete with men; so two clubs for ladies were founded in 1867 and 1873.

**Architects, Builders, Masons and Girls' School**: University House, built on The Scores in 1864–66 was designed by John Starforth, a pupil of William Burn's one-time assistant David Bryce, who himself designed the 1869 mansion of Castlecliffe on The Scores. This was built by local builder and quarry-master John McIntosh, who in 1871 employed 58 workers, 32 of them masons. The Bank of Scotland built a new branch office around 1870, when the town held under 800 houses, a number that doubled by 1904; most were built of stone from quarries at Strathkinness and Blebo Craigs. St Leonard's Hall, erected in 1867–68 to designs by J M Wardrop of Edinburgh, later became the Bishops Hall of the independent St Leonard's School for Girls, founded in 1877. Its junior school was started in 1894; in the 1890s the governors added the big St Rule Boarding House and Sanatorium, designed by the leading local architects James Gillespie from Dunfermline & James Scott from Kinnesswood. After Gillespie's death, Scott added the music wing in 1930.

**Town Hall, Newspapers and Fishing**: Anderson Hamilton of Edinburgh won a competition to design the new Town Hall, built in South Street in 1868–71. Meantime by 1869 the *St Andrews Gazette* was in publication, and a second local newspaper, the *St Andrews Citizen*, was established in 1870. A well-known St Andrews citizen, William Auchterlonie, born in 1873, eventually became the curator of the R&A's Museum of Golf. The population in 1881 was about 6500. Fishing activity had grown, to some 50 boats by 1882, seeking herring and crabs, with some 200 men involved. This degree of activity did not last, though minor timber imports continued in the late 19$^{th}$ century. A late railway connection with Anstruther was completed in 1887, cutting through the urban fabric at low level but spanning the burn on a short viaduct. For many years a slow through train went to Glasgow each day; even in the heyday of railways in 1913 this took 3 hours 46 minutes for the 95 miles – 25 mph!

**Eccentric Architect, and University for Men Only**: John Milne, born in Fettercairn in 1822, became an architect in St Andrews, known for unorthodox churches and mansionhouses such as the top-heavy Westerlee of 1865–67, which became the Wardlaw Hall of Residence. He may have designed the *Scores Hotel* of 1880; the villas of 1896–97 which later became the *Russell Hotel* and *Hazelbank Hotel* were certainly his work. In 1880–82 John Milne remodelled Rae's Union Clubhouse into the clubhouse of the Royal & Ancient, which soon became the effective headquarters of world golf. In 1886 the English traveller Dr Green noted that the game of golf was still little known in England; regarding the University he found it remarkable that *"in Scotland the honour and reward of learning are accessible to all, irrespective of their social rank"*. But not their sex – it was 1892 before women could matriculate at St Andrews!

**Botanics, Hospitals and Hotels**: A botanic garden was established at St Mary's College in 1889. Late in life David Henry from Carnoustie became a well-known architect in St Andrews, designing many houses and shops, the prominent Gibson Hospital in Argyle Street (an eventide home gifted by William Gibson, 1880–82), extensions to the Cottage Hospital in 1887–94, the *Imperial Temperance (Argyle) Hotel* of 1879–88, and the large hotel built for William Rusack in 1886–93. With the popularisation of golf and seaside holidays, by 1894 four hotels were open, those already mentioned plus the *Alexandra*. A fifth hotel, the *Grand*, designed by James Monro, was built in 1894–95 of red sandstone from Locharbriggs; it was to become the Hamilton Hall of Residence. Gillespie & Scott designed numerous villas – one of 1888 later became the *Kinburn Hotel* – and the Gatty Marine Laboratory of 1894–95 at East Sands. In 1894 the New golf course was opened, seaward of the Old; a third course, the Jubilee, following the eastern edge of the links, opened in 1899. All the town's courses were in municipal ownership. The 1901 population was 7600.

**The Rebirth of St Andrews University**: The University had begun to reawaken in the late 1870s, and its reorganisation from 1886 soon bore fruit: its growth required an extension to the then Students' Union in 1891. John Milne designed the Atholl Hotel (much later the John Burnet Hall of Residence) built in the 1890s, and various terraces; but perhaps his most valuable contribution was to cause trees to be planted in many local streets. Gillespie & Scott designed University Hall in St Leonard's Road in 1895, the Chemistry Building in North Street in 1903, an extension to United College in 1904, the Museum in Queen's Terrace in 1909 and in 1913 what later became the Hepburn Hall of Residence. In 1910 the partnership employed a staff of 13 and served much of the east of Scotland, particularly designing massive industrial buildings for Nairn's of Pathhead from a branch office in Kirkcaldy. However the University's Carnegie Library of 1906 was designed by Robert Lorimer of Kellie, and its book stacks were made of Carnegie's US steel!

**Churches, Current, Byre Theatre and Conservation**: In 1902–04 the massive St Leonard's Church designed by Peter Chalmers of Glasgow was built in Hepburn Gardens. The medieval style Catholic church on The Scores, dedicated in 1910, was designed by Reginald Fairlie *(see Frew, 1984)*. Electricity was provided from a generating station built in 1902, but the Argyle brewery closed in 1906. St Andrews continued to develop as a prime golfing resort: the 18-hole Eden course, squeezed in on either side of the railway, was opened in 1913. Rufflets House with its formal gardens 3 km west of the town was built in 1924 as a private residence. In 1930 James Scott designed the *New Picture House* in North Street, and in 1933 an improvised repertory theatre was created in a byre. For the really hardy the town council built a large open-air swimming pool. The St Andrews Preservation Society, formed in the 1930s, championed the conservation of minor historic buildings, and local conservation-oriented architect William Jack pioneered their protective listing. The town had also become a more significant local shopping centre and local focus, acquiring Alexander's small bus station and depot beside the railway station; but the lifeboat station was closed in 1938.

**After 1945**: Soon after 1951 the town's slowly expanding population passed 10,000, and as the University was extended to the west so did the town to the south and south-west. Rufflets House was sold in 1951, soon becoming the pleasant *Rufflets Hotel*. In 1963 the Botanic Garden was moved to a new and extensive site south-west of the town centre. Despite the cowshed locale, drama flourished so as to justify building the tiny modern *Byre Theatre*, which opened in 1970.

**British Railways Off Course**: The understandably uneconomic East Neuk railway was closed by Dr Beeching in 1964, the viaduct across the burn becoming a footway and cycle track. In what must have seemed a compensatory gesture, British Transport Hotels erected the 68-room *Old Course Hotel* beside the Leuchars line on the site of former railway sheds. It opened in 1968 when St Andrews had four golf courses, and might have been thought to ensure the survival of the rail link: but almost unbelievably, though sited beside the Old Course, the hotel had no golfing rights to offer to guests! The Leuchars rail link was closed in 1969; the station site and most of the infilled route of the line through the town became car parks. A golfing opportunity for beginners, the 9-hole municipal Balgove course, was opened by the town council in 1971, but burgh status was lost in 1975 when St Andrews was placed in the rural North-East Fife District centred on Cupar; the golf courses passed to this body. By 1980 about 20 hotels served the golfing fraternity, and two caravan sites (one regrettably most conspicuously sited) provided for cheaper seaside holidays. Tidy housing estates were growing inland, but Denbrae Mill was long abandoned.

*Golf-club making, St Andrews – a long-standing craft in 'the home of golf'.* *(SMPC / Doug Corrance)*

**Shopping and Leisure Development**: In the 1980s the shopping centre too expanded with the growth of tourism; by 1989 the economy of the St Andrews area was ranked 161st out of 280 British towns, putting it among the most prosperous in Scotland, in great contrast to much of Fife. A central William Low store built in the 1980s had been restyled by 1996 as a Tesco 'Metro'. Though the harbour was only used for small boats, the East Sands Leisure Centre, new in 1989, provided a new swimming pool and water slide; provision for an all-weather running track nearby was agreed in 1994. By 1989 the *Old Course Hotel & Country Club* was being upgraded for the second time by its predominantly Japanese owners, with another leisure complex, and the golf club manufacturer Swilken provided over 50 jobs. A major new clubhouse and restaurant to serve visitors to all six golf courses, including the oddly-named 18-hole Strathtyrum course, was built in 1994–95.

**Tourism and Car-parks**: By 1990 an interesting aquarium or *'Sea Life Centre'* was open at The Scores; in that year it drew 123,000 visitors, the castle over 65,000 and the cathedral ruins over 60,000; while Craigtoun *(q.v.)* Country Park outside the town attracted 140,000. More car spaces were laid out in 1994, when the Tidy Britain group found the condition of the St Andrews beaches *'very good'*.

**University Expansion**: The 1991 census found 3500 non-residents, most of them University students, in an affluent total population of 14,600, higher qualifications abounded, and there was a large retired element. Central congestion has worsened as new buildings and car ownership continue to rise, with a major hostel for 500 students opened in 1993. By 1999 the Denbrae and Dewars Mills had been restored for housing use. Madras College is now one of Fife Council's largest secondary schools, with over 1750 pupils; St Leonard's School for Girls has 400.

**For the Tourist**: St Andrews offers a fine stone-built ambience, few chain stores but a wealth of private traders (with a woolly emphasis), plus everything a golfer could possibly want, including the very modern British Golf Museum; there is an excellent town museum, and a cinema. In 2000–01 the successful *Byre Theatre* underwent major reconstruction. Fife Council runs the very well-stocked Botanic Garden with its extensive greenhouses. Access by rail is via Leuchars plus taxi, or by using the good bus/coach links. Hotels within pitching distance of the famous links include the 5-star *Old Course* (over 100 rooms), *Rusacks*, the *Golf*, and the *Scores*; there are many smaller establishments, and also University campus accommodation. The much-disputed Kingask development, about 3 km south-east of the town, opened in June 2001 – with two new golf courses, a hotel, and many other high-quality facilities.

## ST BOSWELLS & Maxton

**Map 3, B4**

***Borders villages,*** *pop. 1200* — OS 73 or 74: NT 5931

St Boswells on the south bank of the River Tweed opposite Dryburgh Abbey lacks early history, yet according to Chambers, when the village was burnt by the English in 1544, *"it contained no fewer than sixteen bastel-houses or towers"*. Maxton 2 km to the east was chartered as a burgh of barony in 1587–88, and had a parish school from 1611, but remained a scattered hamlet. Longnewton, 4 km to the south, which was similarly chartered in 1634 also grew very little. Pont's maps of the Borders made about 1600 did not name St Boswells, but south of the river showed the then new mansion of *'Lessiddinn'* (Lessudden) where a parish school was founded in 1631. By 1755 St Boswells had developed around it into a largish village, with roads to Melrose and east to Maxton. Later a road from St Boswells Green to Jedburgh was turnpiked under an Act of 1768.

**Markets at the Green**: As late as 1797 a traditional annual cattle and wool market was held on the extensive green at St Boswells, where later there was also a sheep market and a coaching inn. In 1817 John and Thomas Smith designed an 80 m-span chain suspension bridge, the first in Britain, built across the river near Mertoun for the laird of Dryburgh, the Earl of Buchan. Chambers wrote in 1827 that *"St Boswells, noted for a great annual cattle-fair, held in July, is now a small and unimportant village"*. Bremner later noted that the market also *"did great business in linens"* until the trade died out around 1850. Hiltonshill 1 km to the south was the birthplace in 1844 of Thomas Brunton, who became a famous physician, the author of the first comprehensive text on pharmacology, and justly earned a knighthood. When railways were opened In 1849–51, the station was placed at nearby Newtown *(q.v.)*; Maxton station on the Kelso line was east of its village. St Boswells' population in 1891 was 560.

**Golf and Retirement**: By 1899 the livestock market had been moved to Newtown. In that year St Boswells golf club was founded, and laid out a 9-hole parkland course north of the one-street village. By 1951 the population of St Boswells had risen to about 1200, but only village services were available, apart from the inn at the Green which had become the *Buccleuch Arms Hotel*. Maxton lost its skeleton train service, post office and telephone exchange in the 1960s and its population shrank to about 70. St Boswells lost post town status but developed to the south, plus a new trading estate 1.5 km to the south-west at Charlesfield. Marshall engineering continued at St Boswells, which in 1991 still had a population of 1128. In 1993 the three-day July Horse Fair on the Green was still a remarkably popular event. Today there is a primary school, a post office, the *Buccleuch Arms Hotel*, and the long-distance route of *'St Cuthbert's Way'* which follows the riverside.

## ST CATHERINES

**Map 5, A4**

***Argyll location, L. Fyne,*** *pop. 160* — OS 56: NN 1207

St Catherines on the east shore of Loch Fyne was named *'Kill-Catruin'* on Timothy Pont's late 16th century map; by 1680 a ferry plied to Inveraray. The Roy map surveyed about 1750 showed this ferry, and a track south through Hell's Glen leading to another ferry for Portincaple. By 1894 there was a lochside road, the Inveraray ferry was operated by steam and the *St Catherines Hotel* was *"good"* to Murray, but the locality never became more than a hamlet with a post office. The steamers to Glasgow which served many Loch Fyne piers vanished, and the passenger ferry service ceased about 1964; St Catherines became a residential retirement base for the well-off. By 1981 some 160 people lived locally. Today there are still some tiny hostelries in this wooded location, plus the old St Catherine's Hotel, all with their loch and hill views.

## ST COMBS

**Map 10, C1**

***Small Buchan village,*** *pop. 800* — OS 30: NK 0563

On the coast of Buchan 7 km south-east of Fraserburgh was the ancient church of Saint Columba or Colm. Pont's sketch map (probably made around 1601) showed a lake adjoining Inverallochy Castle; a mill stood on the outflowing stream, and other buildings stood at *'Ortnabidy'* inland of St Colm's Kirk. Robert Gordon's map of the 1640s showed only a tiny sheet of water, which later disappeared, as did the mill. St Combs was re-founded in 1771. The great neo-classical mansion of Cairness House, designed by James Playfair of Edinburgh, was built 2.5 km inland in 1791–97 for the Georgia sugar planter Charles Gordon of Buthlaw. In 1858 Pratt wrote simply of *"the fishing village of St Colm"*. The village was again rebuilt as parallel rows of houses in the 1860s; but although a post office was opened, there was no harbour, and fishing continued from the beach. The 1891 population was 560. St Combs was connected to Fraserburgh in 1903 by a light railway built by the Great North of Scotland, apparently to carry local men to work on steam drifters based in the latter port. By 1951 St Combs had a population of some 1175 but few local facilities, reduced still further when the rural railway was closed in 1965. A new hotel, the *Tufted Duck*, was built on the cliffs south of the village around 1975; there was some more new development by 1991 but only 799 people lived in St Combs, which is predominantly a Fraserburgh dormitory. Cairness House stood empty and deteriorating in 1994 but has since been sold for restoration. A little more development has continued.

## ST CYRUS

**Map 10, B5**

***Mearns coastal village,*** *pop. 850* OS 45: NO 7464

A very early Christian community called Ecclescraig *(Church on the Rock)* was founded on the cliffs of the Mearns, 2–3 km north of the sandy estuary of the North Esk; it may have been dedicated to St Cyr. There was a thanage from about the 11th century, a castle of Ecclescraig some 2 km inland, and a village of the same name on the nearby shore. The 13th century keep of Lauriston Castle was built on the lip of a gorge to the east. In 1421 the local laird Barclay murdered a sheriff, then hastily built the coastal tower known as the Kaim of Mathers as a refuge from royal vengeance; to the north where a stream entered the sea was the Milton of Mathers. By 1620 *'Ecclesgreig'* had a parish school, and in the 17th century a local quarry supplied stone for building work in Montrose. Miltonhaven was chartered as a burgh of barony in 1695. By the 1750s St Cyrus Kirk stood solitary on the coastal road, 4 km north of Kinnaber ferry across the North Esk; inland tracks led to the rural kirk of hilly Garvock parish. Lauriston Castle was greatly extended about 1780. Disasters then struck successively when Milton was obliterated by a landslip in 1792, and three years later a storm swept away Ecclescraig village. In 1844–49 Ecclescraig Castle was rebuilt into a baronial mansion, originally known as Mount Cyrus but later renamed Ecclesgreig.

*St Cyrus salmon fishing store.* *(JRH)*

**Rural Railway**: In 1865 the little Montrose & Bervie Railway was opened, with stations near St Cyrus church and Lauriston; in 1881 it became a North British branch. By 1894 inns were open near both stations, and St Cyrus had a post office. By 1951 almost 1200 people lived in the parish, with the facilities of a small village. The bucolic little railway was closed to passengers in 1951 and for freight in 1966. By 1969 a 92 ha nature reserve had been established on the shore. The village had only 340 residents in 1971, but oil-based developments at Montrose may explain why by 1974 four caravan parks surrounded St Cyrus. Lauriston Castle was largely derelict by 1980, and Ecclesgreig House had been gutted to contain a grain dryer, but its formal garden was retained. Local salmon fishing continued, and by 1988 there was an inn at Bush near Lauriston, and some new development in the village, where 851 residents were found in 1991. Around that time Ecclesgreig was acquired for a hotel and golfing development, but no work had been begun by 1995. Local facilities include a post office, shops, garage and modest hotel.

## ST DAVIDS

**Map 6, B5**

***S. Fife harbour / development*** OS 65: NT 1482

St Davids Harbour east of Letham Hill near Inverkeithing was opened in 1752 by Henderson of Fordell *(q.v.)* for the export of coal from his pits, via a horse-drawn wagonway. The harbour could take 600-ton vessels, or seven to eight small ships. Heron in 1799 noted *"salt-works, a spacious and excellent harbour, a wharf for the exportation of coals, and a foundry, all the property of Sir John Henderson"*. There were also some houses and the *Fordell Arms Inn (see Bruce, 1980)*. The harbour was enlarged and deepened in 1826–32 and the wagonway was upgraded in 1834 with inclined planes to carry some 50,000–70,000 tonnes of coal a year. Steam was used from 1868 but the line retained its non-standard gauge of 4'4" and made no junction with the new main line railway to the Forth Bridge, which crossed under its route from 1890. By then a smithy and inn stood beside the harbour.

**After the Wagonway the Houses**: St Davids harbour lost its primitive railway and coal export role in 1946 and became used for shipbreaking. About 1954 when several partly dismantled hulks were to be seen, a 37 m tall steel tower with living module was erected there by the Cleveland Bridge & Engineering Company, for use in boring for coal off Seafield colliery at Kirkcaldy. St Davids was near-derelict by 1980. In 1990 the unused piers remained, but the surrounding area was radically changed from 1992 when the tiny place was enveloped by a 60 ha development of quality housing by Tay Homes, to exploit the harbour and provide shopping, community and sports facilities – thereby adding St Davids to the already sprawling Dalgety Bay. This scheme was largely complete by 1999.

## ST FERGUS

**Map 10, C2**

***Small Buchan village,*** *pop. 500* OS 30: NK 0952

An ancient church stood on the low-lying sandy east coast of Buchan, some 50 km north of Aberdeen. In 1616, when still a detached parish of Banffshire, a new village and church was founded 1.5 km inland, but St Fergus was not noted by 17thh century mappers. The Mills of Essie on the burn which drains St Fergus Moss were the main feature. Roy's 1750s map showed a coastal track, crossing the burn by the *'Bridge of Auchy'* (Annachy). A new section of the village – probably Kirktown – was founded in 1806, and a new turnpike linking Peterhead with Fraserburgh was laid out passing near the kirk, but in 1858 Pratt glumly noted the *"new village, a rambling hamlet of no particular note"*.

**Twentieth-century Gas**: In 1951 the farming parish contained 952 people, but St Fergus had only the facilities of a large hamlet, plus a secondary school class. This soon vanished, for by 1971 the population was under 500. In the mid 1970s the extensive St Fergus natural gas terminal was constructed on the shore 2 km north of the village, to accept and reform for the gas grid the methane found in the North Sea. A few houses were built, and by 1991 the parish population was 519. In 1991–94, 700 construction workers greatly extended the terminal to handle up to 20% of the UK's daily gas supply, as the key point in the Far North Liquids and Associated Gas System of pipelines (FLAGS) which took the output from the Alwyn, Brent, Frigg, Ivanhoe, Rob Roy, Tartan and smaller fields, and fed Mossmorran; but the plant needed few operators. In 1996

International Offshore Chemicals proposed to build a 100-job methanol plant fed from the gas terminal, bringing 500 construction jobs. The primary school and pub continue, but the post office has gone.

## ST FILLANS

**Map 5, C3**

***Perthshire village, L. Earn,*** *pop. 300* OS 51: NN 6924

Dundurn at the head of Strathearn was a fifth to ninth century Pictish fort, originally oaken but later stone-built; it was besieged in 683. Nearby was an ancient Culdee chapel dedicated to St Fillan. By about 1600 (as Pont's map showed) buildings were scattered along the shore at *'Ken Loch Erin'*, and there was a mill on the River Earn near the clearly drawn conical structure of the Dun. Chambers wrote in the mid 1820s that St Fillans had until lately been *"a wretched hamlet denominated Port-more, but it is now one of the sweetest spots in Scotland, a little modern village reared and encouraged by Lord and Lady Gwydir, upon whose ground it is situated, and provided with an excellent inn"*. By then Highland games were held each year. St Fillans was described in 1894 as a *"pretty village"* with an *"excellent"* hotel, accessed by a coach from Comrie

**Failed Rails, Hidden Power, Golf and Seasonal Hotels**: In 1901 St Fillans became the terminus of a branch of a Caledonian Railway subsidiary from Crieff via Comrie, further extended in 1903, rising alongside Loch Earn to Lochearnhead (and joining the Callander & Oban Railway at Balquhidder). In the same year a golf club was founded, which laid out an attractive 9-hole course on the valley floor; St Fillans soon gained another hotel. The railway had little traffic potential, failed to withstand road competition and was closed in 1951. By then the *Drummond Arms Hotel* had 35 rooms; the smaller *Four Seasons Hotel* was open by 1977. Meantime a sailing school had been opened. In the late 20th century the residents numbered only some 300, but St Fillans is a favoured summer resort, with hotels, a primary school and post office. Few visitors realise that for nearly half a century there has been a Hydro Electric generating station hidden under the hills north of the village, powered by water impounded in the artificial Loch Lednock high above Comrie *(q.v.)*.

## ST KILDA (Isles)

**Map 7, A1**

***Atlantic islands*** OS 18: NA 1099

Some 70 km north-west of North Uist is remote St Kilda, three lofty Atlantic islets of granite and gabbro, remnants of one sunken circular island. Boreray has 384 m-tall sea cliffs, and Soay *(Sheep Island)* is famed for rare wild horned sheep which resemble goats. Monro noted in 1549 that Hirta, the main island, was visited annually for rent collection in kind on behalf of the long-time owner MacLeod of Harris. His steward would also take a vat to enable a brew up, causing a drunken orgy among the *"simple poor people"* who normally lived on meal, mutton and wild fowl. Whether this was a kindness or further exploitation is a moot point! A very full account of a visit by Martin in 1697 observed that 180 or so inhabitants *"live together in a little village, which carries all the signs of extreme poverty"*. The first tourists came in 1834 and found a tragically ignorant and exploitable community *(a story well told in the Keays' Encyclopaedia of Scotland)*. From 1899 there was a post office, but calling ships seem to have made little difference to the primitive lifestyle seen by Monro and Martin, while leading to bouts of emigration; in 1930 the remaining 36 aged inhabitants were evacuated from Hirta at their own request. In 1957 the National Trust for Scotland acquired the isles – the world's largest gannetry – but by 1971 Cold War defence installations had brought troops, a pub and shop to Hirta. Notwithstanding – or perhaps because of – this desecration, UNESCO has declared St Kilda a World Heritage Site.

## ST MADOES, Glencarse & Kinfauns

**Map 6, B3**

***Carse of Gowrie villages,*** *pop. 1200* OS 58 (or 53): NO 1921

Some 8 km east of Perth, where the hills of Kinfauns Forest recede from the riverside to form a highly fertile alluvial plain, is a Pictish stone at the ancient parish centre of St Madoes; nearby Pitfour has a Pictish name. Kilspindie, about 5 km to the north, had an early lay abbot but remained tiny. Balthayock Castle, built as a tower house at Kinfauns in sheltered Glen Carse 3 km to the west around 1400, may once have been owned by the Knights Templars. At Elcho, across the Tay from Kinfauns, was the 16th century tower of Elcho Castle and a little-known Cistercian nunnery, the only one north of the Forth, which was burned in 1548. Parish schools opened at St Madoes in 1595, at Kinfauns by 1613 and Kilspindie by 1614; Pont's sketch-map showed a twin tower at Elcho, plus the *'Kirk of Mado'* with *'Kerny'* Mill to the west; a plain building named *'Pitfower'* was also drawn by Pont. The ancient Cairniepier ferry was already operating in the 17th century to provide a connection with Carpow for Abernethy. An emparked *'Pitfour Castle'* was shown on Roy's incomplete map of about 1750, which indicated gaps in the *'Carse Road to Dundee'*, a muddy track from Perth via Inchyra and Errol. Cottown school was built of rammed earth and thatch in 1766; it still exists.

**Mansions, Railway, Brickworks and Ferries**: The mansion of Inchyra House 1 km inland from Pitfour was of late 18th century date, as was Seggieden, built beside the Tay at Kinfauns about 1792. Kinfauns Castle, a solid stone-built mansion, was designed in 1822 by Robert Smirk(e). A fine small mansionhouse at Glendoick to the north-east had a 19th century water mill. Eventually the notoriously muddy road was properly made up as a turnpike, and in 1849 the Dundee &

*Kinfauns Castle, built on a very large scale in the 1820s to designs by Sir Robert Smirke; it is now a hotel.* (JRH)

Perth Railwaywas opened; this was originally also intended to become the Edinburgh & Northern Railway's access to Perth via Newburgh and Mugdrum Island, but in the event simply provided stations at Kinfauns and Glencarse. The latter was 1 km north of Pitfour Castle, which like Inchyra remained emparked. Balthayock House was built near Balthayock Castle's ruins in 1870 for a railway contractor to designs by James Maclaren, who also reconstructed the ancient castle; later the house became a school. In 1895 Cottown was much the largest settlement in the area. About 500 m to the south was the Pitfour brick and tile works, which had its own narrow gauge railway system and was connected by a lengthy rail siding with the main line at the station. This with the inn, post and telegraph office all clustered at Newton of Glencarse; later the *'Newton of'* prefix was abandoned. Cairniepier ferry, and another from Inchyra to Rhynd, were both in operation, but the ferries and brickworks closed early in the 20th century. The mansion of Kinfauns Castle became a ramblers' hostel, and its station was closed in 1950.

**Azaleas, Rhododendrons, Hotels and Horses**: By 1951 the two parishes had 780 people, a figure which held steady for 20 years. Glencarse station was closed in 1956; the building became a private house. Seggieden was demolished about 1970, but the Glendoick Garden Centre beside its mansion-house was already busy by 1970, in those days sending its azaleas, rhododendrons and raspberry canes worldwide by rail through Errol station. About 1973–74 the locality was split when the A85 trunk road was rebuilt as a dual carriageway, with access from the local road which bridges it. By 1977 there were two hotels; some development continued in the 1980s, and in 1991 St Madoes parish had 753 residents and Kinfauns 460. Cottown's clay walled school and schoolhouse were restored in 1995 after a decade of dereliction. By 1997 the Heavy Horse Centre and another housing estate had been developed; there is a post office, community centre, garden centre and builder. Though both Balthayock House and its ancient castle stood derelict in 2000 and under threat of demolition, family-run Glendoick is still an attraction. In 1995 Fife-born James Smith, lately manager of the Hong Kong *Hilton Hotel*, took over the run-down hostel, and by 1999 had converted it into the *Kinfauns Castle Hotel*, with 16 rooms. Also available are the *Newton House* and the *Glencarse Hotel*.

## ST MARGARET'S HOPE — Map 13, B3

***Village, S. Ronaldsay, Orkney,*** *pop. 950 (area)* — OS 7: ND 4493

This sheltered bay, on the north coast of the Isle of South Ronaldsay, was named for Malcolm Canmore's wife, St. Margaret, to whom a chapel was dedicated. It was there that the Maid of Norway, heir to the Scottish throne, died in 1290, triggering decades of wasteful warfare with England. The Hope appeared full of vessels on Pont's map, made about 1592, and South Ronaldsay had a parish school from 1627. Burwick, 10 km south of St Margaret's Hope, had a post office from 1800 – this implies a mailboat from John o' Groats. In the 18th century a pier was built at St Margaret's Hope by a London firm of lobster fishers, and large herring fisheries grew in the early 19th century; a waterside granary was built. A school was erected in 1875 and a public hall in 1878. In the late 19th century there was a busy boatyard and tiny slipways, and by the 1890s the close-knit village which had grown beside the bay was important enough to appear on tiny atlas maps as Orkney's third settlement; it had a purpose-built shop.

**Wartime Work and Postwar Decline**: The veteran battleship HMS *Royal Oak* of 29,150 tons was sunk by a German submarine in Scapa Flow in 1939; this loss led to the urgent construction of the Churchill causeways *(see Holm)*, linking the islands of South Ronaldsay and Burray with the Orkney Mainland, to keep German vessels out of the naval anchorage. The civilian payoff was ultimately more important. In 1951 St Margaret's Hope had a population of over 500, with the facilities of a small village, plus a secondary school, taking some 120 pupils from South Ronaldsay and Burray. A former herring fishery at Herston on Widewall Bay south-west of St Margarets Hope became a base for lobster boats, but the local population was falling rapidly with the decline in farm labour needs, the secondary school closed, and the remaining local facilities chiefly served only South Ronaldsay. By the 1970s electricity arrived from Kirkwall via Burray by submarine cables. The population had stabilised by 1971 at around 350 and by the 1980s there were two tiny hotels. By then, supply vessels for the island oil terminal of Flotta *(q.v.)* were based at the short pier near this attractive village, but there was only one full-time fishing vessel. South Ronaldsay had 943 residents in 1991.

**A Service Village with Character**: By 1997 a new primary school had been built west of the sheltered village with its trees – rare in pastoral Orkney – but an experimental wind turbine faced demolition. In 2000 an optimist held his roll-on ferry vessel moored at the pier, hoping to reopen the Gill's Bay service; the former granary on the old quay stood vacant. Burwick has a summer passenger ferry to John o' Groats, and 3 km east of the terminal is a museum. St Margaret's Hope now has three stores, post office, telephone exchange, coach hirer, joiner, heating engineers, and the base for a mobile shop, plus a shellfish company. For tourists there is the small *Murray Arms Hotel*, a guest house, pub, eateries, a gallery and a *'blacksmith museum'*. A small backpackers' hostel is open at Eastside, 3 km south-east.

## ST MONANS — Map 6, B3

***E. Fife coastal village,*** *pop. 1400* — OS 59: NO 5201

Saint Moinan was perhaps a mid 6th century bishop of Clonfert in Ireland, whose remains were reinterred in the 9th century at Inverie in the East Neuk of Fife, whereby it was renamed St Monans. But Chambers wrote differently, of *"this saint of Scottish extraction"* killed there by Danes about 875. The place was known as a fishing base by 1265, and its fine seaside church can be dated to a rebuilding in 1265–67; it was again rebuilt in 1362–70. In 1471–77 James III added to it a minor Dominican friary. Newark Castle just to the west was also built in the 15th century, when it seems that a village already existed near the church (formerly spelt *'Monance')*. This was burned in 1544 by the fleet of Henry VIII, and its fishing boats seized. Pont's map made about 1600 showed St Monans as a tiny place, but it evidently grew after being chartered as a burgh of barony in 1596, and iron ore was being shipped out in 1620. However the ore body was small, and the port never had much commercial significance, although James Gordon's map made about 1642 showed St Monans as large as its neighbours Pittenweem and Elie, with the castle to the west. Two breakwaters were shown on John May's chart of about 1680.

*A Galway fishing-boat being lengthened on the St Monans slipway in 1996.* *(RS)*

**Boatyard, Coal, Salt and Self-Help**: St Monans had an active market in 1714 and was served by road by 1747, the year that Millers' famous boatyard was founded; this was to remain in the ownership of the same family for 230 years. Nine *'salt houses'* containing salt evaporating pans were built in 1772 on the raised beach east of the village by Sir Ralph Anstruther. They worked until about 1825, using coal brought from a pit just inland by a wagonway, which also connected to the two harbours of Pittenweem and St Monans. The pans were filled with seawater pumped by a cliff-top windmill (recently restored). In 1799 Heron noted St Monans as a *"town"* of about 800 people, but in the 1820s Chambers called it an *"ancient fishing village"*. A modest brewery was recorded in 1825, but it was after 1838 that St Monans had a post office. The harbour was rebuilt from 1861 onwards to accommodate a hundred fishing boats, the work financed by the fishermen themselves.

**Busy Boatyard, Drought and Doldrums**: The local section of the East Neuk's circuitous railway was opened in 1863, but the station was behind the town and as in the other East Neuk fishing ports it never served the harbour directly. However, at some time a gasworks was set up. In 1875 a great gale killed 21 local seamen, but recovery was swift and in 1891, around the peak of local prosperity, the population was over 1800. About that time J B Easton's foundry made cast iron wringers. Millers built many fishing vessels, pilot boats, launches, w-inches, capstans and even yachts. Being dominated at that time by religious fundamentalists such as the Brethren, St Monans burgh went *'dry'* in 1920. Consequently no tourist trade developed, although a huge open air swimming pool was cut into the rocks of the foreshore. In 1939 about 36 boats fished out of St Monans, but after the war in 1945 only a quarter of the fleet resumed work. Walter Reekie was also building boats around 1951, when the parish population was 1600, and there were still three fish merchants; but the small and ageing fleet tended to fish for herrings out of northern ports such as Fraserburgh.

**Wooden Boats and Plastic Models**: The railway was closed in 1964; by the 1970s there was little fishing from St Monans harbour, and both population and facilities had been falling. James Miller & Sons' boatyard with its antique timber shed failed in 1977, and was taken over by the McTay Group of Merseyside. Though half its 40 craftsmen were made redundant, the historic name was retained, and a new fabrication shed and boat repair slipway were soon built; boatbuilding was soon resumed. Millers were again taken over about 1982 – by the John Mowlem group; as late as 1985 the yard built a wooden fishing vessel. The population of St Monans in 1981 was around 1300, and the local facilities were those of a typical village. A caravan site was open by 1984 and in the early 1980s a small factory making plastic model railway kits was established by local man Ian Kirk, appropriately located on the site of the former station. In 1991 the resident population of the village was 1373; many owned their homes outright as in most fishing ports, but there was a large elderly element.

**Ferries as Millers' Final Fling**: Millers acquired fitting-out facilities at Methil, and in 1990–92 – when their combined workforce varied from 65 to 95 people – completed their largest-ever boat and first car ferry, a 35m vessel for the Shetlands Islands Council; followed by a 24m fishing vessel for Peterhead, and lastly two ferries for Calmac's Iona and Claonaig services. But despite being Britain's oldest boatyard, Millers was closed in the slump of 1992 due to a total lack of orders. In the summer of 1996 a tubby Irish fishing vessel from Galway was cut in half and greatly lengthened on the St Monans slipway by workers from Miller's of Methil. Sadly, by 1996 the outgoing district council no longer maintained the outdoor swimming pool. However, the excavated salt pans and windmill tower are of interest. There is a licensed restaurant with terrace overlooking the harbour; many cottages are holiday homes.

## ST NINIANS — Map 16, A1

***Village / suburb of Stirling,*** *pop. 8000* — OS 57: NS 7991

About 2 km south of Stirling castle, the line of the Roman road to Camelon was paralleled by a medieval trackway beside which stood the church of St Ninians (also called *St Ringans*), of Northumbrian origin before the 10th century. To the west was Royal forest, and nearby was the site where the crucial battle of Bannockburn *(q.v.)* was fought in 1314. The Scottish victory was aided by strewing the ways with a plentiful supply of four-spiked iron *'caltrops'*, a cruel device for laming passing horses, and very probably locally made – for the skills of the St Ninians nailmakers became proverbial. *'Ninians Kirk'* and several other small settlements appeared on Pont's map of about 1600. Williamsfield House was built in 1682 for the local lairds the Wordie family *(see Stirling)*. The old church was in use as a Jacobite powder store in 1746 when it was destroyed by an explosion. About 1750 St Ninians was still a leading Scottish centre for nail-making, and had quietly grown into a large settlement with at least six radial routes. Pennant described it as *"a small town"* in 1769, but it never became a burgh.

**Nails, Lime, Beer and Leather**: By 1794 four nail factories at Whins of Milton and Chartershall just to the south employed over 100 people, producing in total up to 40 million nails a year. Another 33 workers were busy at two limeworks, that at Craigend burning 2000 chalders (7000 $m^3$) of lime a year; there were also remarkably six distilleries. Writing in 1799, Heron noted *"the populous village of St Ninians, where there is a considerable manufacture of linen and woollen goods"*; together with Bannockburn its population rivalled or exceeded that of Stirling burgh. St Ninians' first post office opened around 1825; by then a brewery was open, and according to Chambers, St Ninians was *"a considerable village deriving subsistence from its manufactories of nails and of leather"*. *'Milltown'* (presumably Whins of Milton) was a *"considerable village remarkable for its manufactories of nails"*. A toll bar operated in 1837. In 1842, 182 hand nailmakers were busy (in much better conditions than the disgraceful nail factory described under Camelon), but nailmaking machines were introduced in the 1850s.

**Horse Trams, Health, Education and Ice**: From 1848 the Scottish Central (later Caledonian) Railway passed by, but provided no station, so a horse tramway which opened in 1874 between Bridge of Allan and Stirling was soon extended to St Ninians, which by the 1890s was a large village with an inn, post and telegraph office. Flat wrought iron nails were still made by hand, but in later years the trade contracted into a single powered workshop making cheap wire nails by machine. The horse tramway, the last of its kind in Scotland, was closed and lifted in 1920. Stirling Royal Infirmary was built at St Ninians in 1928, and St Modan's High School rose about the same time.

With suburban growth from the 1970s, St Ninians and Bannockburn soon coalesced with Stirling. The M9 – whose first section was opened in 1973 – bypassed fast-growing St Ninians, which kept its village facilities, plus a large *Pik'n Save* store open by 1978. By then the population was around 8000. Today St Modan's High School has around 830 pupils; there is now an ice rink at Torbrex.

## SALEN (L. Sunart) & Glenborrodale — Map 4, C1

***Ardnamurchan communities,*** *pop. under 100* — OS 40: NM 6864

Roy's map of about 1750 named only a single dot at *'Tarbert'* on beautiful wooded Loch Sunart in Ardnamurchan. Salen (*'Willow'* in Gaelic) was founded there in the late 18th century at the head of a tiny bay. In 1847 Somers found a scattered Gaelic-speaking hamlet with a small inn, and a factory employing 30 or more men and boys to make 75,000 pirns daily, using 1400 tonnes of wood a year. A weekly packet sailed to Tobermory, and later a pier was built at which regular steamers called on a cargo service from the Clyde via the Crinan Canal – until even coasting vessels grew too large to call and the pirn factory closed. The inn at Salen was noted by Murray in 1894 and continued busy through the 20th century, having become a fishing resort. It remained a tiny place of around 100 people with a post office, shop, and in more recent years a two-doctor practice. A cruiser base cum boat chandler was open at Salen in 1984. Some 8 km to the west, beyond the salmon pens of Laga, the baronial mansion of *Glenborrodale Castle* had become a luxury hotel by the mid 1970s; a decade earlier the less pretentious *Clan Morrison Hotel* had opened nearby, specialising in catering for the disabled. Glenborrodale primary school is still in business, as are the inn and post office, and a golf course and caravan site have been laid out 4 km to the east, at Resipole; at Glenmore, 4 km west of Glenborrodale, is a Natural History Centre.

## SALEN — Map 4, B1

***Central Mull village,*** *pop. 500* — OS 47 or 48: NM 5743

Gruline in central Mull between freshwater Loch Ba and the sea at Loch na Keal, has standing stones. On the opposite coast a dun was built on a ridge, 2 km east of which is Salen (*'Willow'* in Gaelic); Saint Columba is said to have preached there in the sixth century and to have commented on the scantiness of the congregation. This oral tradition implies that it was already a sizeable and Christian settlement, since continuously occupied. Monro noted in 1549 that Mull was *"a great rough Isle but fertile and fruitful with woods, many deer, two good fresh waters full of salmon (Ba and Glenforsa), sea lochs with good take of herrings, seven parish kirks (and) three castles"* (Aros, Duart and Lochbuie). The 14th century Aros Castle, built by the Lords of the Isles on the north side of Salen Bay, was owned in 1549 by MacLean of Duart, then the greatest of the four lairds on the isle. Aros means *'The Point'*; it was the place round which Mull's medieval history revolved.

**After Aros Castle, Australia**: Pont's map of Mull, made about 1600, showed what must have been early religious sites, at *'Kalchaille'* (modern Callachally) to the east, and to the west

*'Killenaillan' (the Church on the Islet)* beside the River Aros. This was already bridged near the castle, which fell into ruin by about 1690. In 1703 Martin noted that most Mull folk spoke the *'Irish'* Gaelic *"but those of the best rank speak English"*. Gruline was the birthplace in 1761 of Lachlan Macquarie, who was to become Governor of New South Wales and transform the penal colony of Botany Bay into civilised Sydney. In 1785, an early date for an island community, a post office was opened, named Aros after the castle; it was later relocated at Salen, where a regular market was held in the 18th century. As in other impoverished areas the government paid for the Church of Scotland edifice, built there in 1829.

**Sea and Air Transport bring Hotels and Hospital**: Killiechronan House near Gruline was built about 1840. By 1858 a steamer pier was in use at Salen; by 1894 this had given rise to what Murray called a *"good"* hotel. The pier was still served by Tobermory to Oban steamers in 1953, but became disused when Craignure pier was made the main access to Mull. However, Salen's centrality in the island's road system led to an airstrip being built by Sappers beside Glenforsa House, just east of the village; it was opened in 1966. Although in 1981 under 400 people lived in Salen, the road to Craignure had been rebuilt by 1982. Another unusual facility for a small village was the conversion in the 1980s of a 1960s old people's home into an accident hospital. In 1985 local provision also included a dentist, three hotels, a new primary school with 55 pupils and the Forestry Commission's Mull office, with a fish farm at Gruline. By 1996 *Glenforsa House* had become a hotel, as is *Killiechronan House* near Gruline; *Gruline Home Farm* also welcomes guests.

## SALINE & Steelend

***W. Fife village & hamlet,*** *pop. 1300 / 2000* — **Map 16, C1** — OS 58: NT 0292

A standing stone on a hilltop in west Fife overlooks Saline, whose name means *'Willow'* in Gaelic; across the valley to the north stand the ruins of the 16th century Killernie Castle. This featured on James Gordon's map of Fife made about 1642, which also showed *'Salin Kirk'* (which existed by 1567), and *'Salins Hall'*. The Roy map of about 1750 showed a hamlet at *'Salin'*, at the meeting point of tracks from Crossford and Dunfermline to Rumbling Bridge. The bridge which here crosses the Saline Burn bears the date 1785, and Saline – which lies some 115 m above sea level – had an annual fair in 1797. Heron referred to Saline as *"a rising village"* in 1799, and mentioned its situation at the west end of the Fife coalfield with its *"numerous collieries"*. Iron ore was also worked there up to the mid 19th century, and may have given rise to the farm name Steelend. However, in 1888 Beveridge thought Saline was *"a very clean and prettily situated village"*. By 1895 an inn was open, and the Saline Valley collieries 2 km to the east were served by a mineral railway from Townhill. The parish population in 1901 was about 1000. The rails were soon extended up a side valley and round the north side of Knock Hill to serve the Lethans No.1 & 2 collieries in the Black Devon valley, almost on the Kinross border. South of Steelend were a quarry and a large isolated primary school; these were all evidently in operation in the 1920s.

**Racy but Well-Educated**: Saline received electricity supplies from 1911; a golf club founded in 1912 developed a 9-hole parkland course. After 1918 a council housing estate called Steelend was built near the castle, and by 1953 a 32-bed hospital for convalescent children was in use. By 1967 the mines had closed and the mineral railway had been lifted, but in 1989 a private colliery was working on the Rhynd estate, 2 km south-east, and producing smokeless fuel as a new venture. Dormitory development has gradually grown, and by 1991 Saline parish held 1942 people, of whom 1235 lived in the village. Except for the Knock Hill motor circuit which had been created about 1970 some 4 km to the east, its facilities remain much as in 1951, those of a small village. Some more new housing was added in the 1990s; the golf course still has 9 holes.

## SALSBURGH & Kirk of Shotts

***Lanarkshire village,*** *pop. 1400* — **Map 16, B4** — OS 65: NS 8262

The prehistoric centre of the sprawling parish of Shotts may have been at Duntilland, a hard rock outcrop on the moorland plateau east of the Clyde valley; 1.5 km to the south-east was the Kirk of Shotts, shown as *'Schots'* on Pont's map of 1596; a parish school was founded in 1629. Near the isolated kirk passed the Edinburgh–Newhouse turnpike road of 1753. Heron wrote in 1799 of *"a wild and barren country. This dreary waste is covered with heath; it is chiefly employed as sheep-walks. Notwithstanding the vicinity of coal and lime, it seems scarce capable of cultivation"*. It was probably near the Kirk that five fairs were to be held in 1797, perhaps at the hamlet of Salsburgh. Shotts *(q.v.)* is now the name for a place founded in 1801 some 4 km to the south of the present prominent Kirk of Shotts, which was designed by James Gillespie Graham and James Brash, and dates from 1821.

**Coal, Quarrying and Television Masts**: In 1895, coal mines – linked by mineral lines with the Caledonian Railway near Cleland – were at work east of Kirk of Shotts and round the Roughrigg reservoir, on the Clattering Burn 2 km north-west of Salsburgh, which by then had an inn and a post office. By 1951 although the mines had stopped, the important rail-connected Duntilland Quarry had been opened north of the kirk, and the area had a population of 2000; but apart from a tiny secondary school (which was soon closed) its main centre, Salsburgh, had only the facilities of a small village. The main TV transmitters for central Scotland were sited east of Kirk of Shotts, opened in 1952, and at Blackhill 3 km to the north-west. The mineral railways were closed in 1964, and had been lifted by 1971, by which time the M8 motorway passed through the area (but without a convenient junction).

**Dogged by Ill Health – and Racing Motors?**: The population fell over the years to 1400 by 1991, leaving Salsburgh very disadvantaged, its residents having Scotland's highest incidence of long-term illnesses. The Edinburgh firm of McGlashen's was supplying sandstone facings from this area to the international building market by 1989; the huge Duntilland Quarry was operated by John Fyfe in 1995 and by Bardon Aggregates in 2000. Plans for an international-standard motor racing circuit at Forrestburn Reservoir were approved by the district council in 1995 despite local objections to the noise; the project was shelved due to local government reorganisation in 1966 in favour of a minor *'Race Track'*, now built. The Kirk of Shotts is now in urgent need of repair; Salsburgh still has a post office.

## SALTCOATS

**Map 1, C1**

***Ayrshire coast town,*** *pop. 12,000*

OS 70: NS 2441

Saltcoats on the Cunninghame coast must have had some of Scotland's first coal workings, for it was evaporating sea water to make salt for Kilwinning Abbey as early as the 13th century, its name arising from its function. Although chartered as a burgh of barony in 1528 and again in 1576, Pont's map of around 1600 gave Saltcoats only the smallest significance. Thomas Tucker, a Cromwellian exciseman more interested in sea trade, noted Saltcoats in 1655 as *"shores only of the road* [i.e. an open beach beside an anchorage] *with a few houses, the inhabitants fishermen, who carry fish and cattle for Ireland; bringing home corn and butter for their own use"*.

**Harbour, Deep Mining and Shipbuilding**: In 1684 Robert Cunningham of Auchenharvie by Montgreenan began work on a harbour, and in 1686 set up a new salt works; coal was still being raised locally, and the harbour was completed in 1700. He then sank deeper coal pits, where a Newcomen pumping engine was in use from about 1719 *(see also Stevenston)*. The Roy map made about 1754 showed Saltcoats as a large and complex town for the period, on the coast road and with a link inland from the extensive harbour; Ardrossan was then just a farm and a castle. By that time a shipyard had been opened by James Steele; from 1765 this was run by Robert Steele, and the locally built 80-ton brig, the *Saltcoats*, was launched in 1774. Soon some 10,000 tons of coal a year – arriving at the harbour from local pits to the east via Reid Cunninghame's short canal – was being exported, mainly to Ireland. By the 1790s many vessels were being built at Saltcoats, where William Ritchie also had a shipyard, but in 1791 he moved to Belfast, and Robert Steele moved to Greenock in 1796 to join Carswell.

**Rapid Growth: Bathing, Boats and Brewing**: Meanwhile by 1793 a change of emphasis had occurred, for Saltcoats was called *"the principal watering-place in Ayrshire"*, with 300 to 500 intrepid summer visitors bathing in the chilly sea, coming especially from Glasgow, Paisley and Hamilton. By then the Paisley Union Banking Company had a branch in the town, but this was short-lived. However, in 1798 over 200 men were still employed in coal mining and there was a timber merchant, probably dealing in pit props and boatbuilding timber. Robert Heron in 1799 described Saltcoats as a *"rising town"* of over 2300 people, *"favourable to manufactures in general"* and with *"upwards of forty vessels"*, some for fishing but *"most of them employed in the coal trade to Ireland"*. Salt making continued and since 1755 shipyards had *"done much. They have a rope-work, and three ship-carpenters yards employing a number of hands"*. Magnesia was being made in 1802, and Hugh Watt founded a brewery and corn business in 1805. In 1807 the thirty locally-owned vessels averaged 100 tons; 3000 people lived in the town in 1811. By 1827 Saltcoats had become (according to Chambers) *"a decent-looking town, with a handsome town-house"*.

**Railways Galore, but No Coal or Salt**: A post office was open by 1838 and from 1840, when the population was some 4000, a railway linked to Glasgow via Kilwinning. But local coal became exhausted, and Ardrossan's new harbour only 2 km to the west diverted the trade in the 1850s. Saltcoats nevertheless continued to grow, becoming a police burgh in 1885. A second railway (the Caledonian's daft baby, the needlessly duplicating Lanarkshire & Ayrshire) was opened through a station behind the town in 1888, on its way to Ardrossan harbour. Salt-making ceased in 1890 but the population in 1891 was 5895. By 1894 Murray called Saltcoats *"a dirty, straggling port and sea-bathing place"*, seemingly lacking a hotel worth mention. A power station was built in 1903, but a new harbour – constructed in 1914 – soon silted up and lost its nascent trade. Saltcoats continued to grow – it must be seen in relation to the major developments at Stevenston *(q.v.)* only 2 km to the east. A new gasworks was required in 1925 and the population passed 10,000 about 1930. However, the former Lanarkshire & Ayrshire railway's traffic began to decline from 1932, and by 1963 it had vanished. A swimming pool was built in the 1930s, and around that time a miners' convalescent home was in use.

**The Arrival of A T Mays**: By 1951 Saltcoats had acquired average urban facilities and by 1953 there were three hotels, and a golf course which soon vanished. In 1956 James Moffat, a Saltcoats bank clerk, established the tiny travel agency which was later to grow into the national firm of A T Mays after *'All Travel'* combined with *'Mays'*. The population of the town peaked around 1971 at over 15,000, and before the burgh lost its status in 1975 the town council described it as *"a holiday resort, residential and shopping area"*; it was popular for day trips and Glasgow Fair visitors. By 1979 the small firm of Glenhusky Knitwear was in production. The 1981 census showed that the population had fallen sharply to under 13,000. It still had average urban facilities, with a museum and half a dozen small hotels.

**The Travel Boom – and Bust?**: However, by 1983 Mays employed 300 people countrywide, and their Saltcoats head office became more important in that year when the numerous offices and 500 employees of Scotland's other main agency Nairn Travel *(see Pathhead, Fife)* were absorbed. The firm then expanded rapidly, though in 1987 it became a subsidiary of the Royal Bank. In that year the railway to Glasgow was electrified. By 1989 the North Ayrshire Museum had an industrial collection, and ATM was the fourth largest travel agency in Britain (employing 300 people in their Saltcoats head office alone), and Glenhusky was still in operation. By 1990 tenpin bowling was available at the Pavilion Bowl. Early in 1991 severe sea floods badly affected Saltcoats town centre; by then the population was down to 11,865, with craft and operative jobs predominating. By 1996 a Tesco store was open and some further development had taken place inland. After several different owners, Mays ended up under Thomas Cook in 1998–99, with a serious threat to the area's jobs. St Andrew's Academy has around 750 pupils.

## SANDAY

**Map 13, C1**

***Small island, N. Orkney,*** *pop. 550*

OS 5: HY 6538

The sprawling and largely low-lying sandstone island of Sanday lies some 35 km north-east of Kirkwall; its land is readily cultivable and there are many Neolithic and other ancient remains, including the site of a Viking ship burial. Sanday was thickly settled by 1592, the probable date of Pont's map, on which about 40 places were named; but despite the 18th century growth of the kelp industry, none developed into a significant village. The large plain mansionhouse of Scar on the Burness peninsula was built for the Traills early in the 19th century. The first lighthouse with revolving lenses in Scotland was built in

1806–09 on Start Point, the eastern tip of Sanday, replacing the light on North Ronaldsay. From 1839 there was a post office at Kettletoft pier on the south coast bay of that name; in the 1860s Stove Farm installed steam threshing equipment. In 1894 Murray found the *"very comfortable" Kettletoft Inn* and the nearby *Castlehill Inn*.

**Sanday rolls on, and takes to the Air**: By 1951 the basic facilities of Kettletoft, including a 9-room hotel and two sub-branch banks, served some 1250 people in Sanday, Eday and North Ronaldsay, and the island's junior secondary school at more central Broughtown or Quivals had 120 pupils; but in the ensuing twenty years the population fell by about 30%. Start Point lighthouse was automated in 1962; by the 1970s electricity arrived from Kirkwall by submarine cables, via Shapinsay and Stronsay. By 1974 passenger ferries connected Kettletoft with adjacent islands, and a small airfield was open near the hamlet of Overbister or Lady, with its post office. By 1984 ro-ro ferries served Kettletoft, and in 1988 the airfield had two daily flights. This quiet farming island then had two shops, and a golf course at Rusness. By 1991 the island's population was 533; Scar House stood empty in 1997 and Stove Farm steading was ruinous. Today Sanday Junior High School (S1-S4) has only about 30 pupils, the *Belsair Hotel* offers 6 rooms, and William and Elizabeth Sichel breed angora rabbits and make thermal clothing from their fur.

## SANDBANK

**Map 5, A5**

***Cowal (Argyll) village,*** *pop. 1500+*

OS 63: NS 1680

The sandy head of the short Holy Loch, an inlet of the Firth of Clyde opposite Gourock, was apparently devoid of development in the mid 18th century, when Roy's map showed little but the coastline. In the early 19th century a steamer pier made the area attractive to visitors, and enabled many villas to be built along a road around the head of the loch. About 1840 the extensive Clyde Powder Mills were opened at Clachaig in Glen Lean to the west, using local charcoal. The 1891 population was 720. The powder mills were still at work in 1895 when Sandbank had a hotel, a post and telegraph office – and a ferry to Kilmun. This later closed, and the powder mills became ruinous. By 1951 over 1200 people lived in Sandbank, which had an Esso oil depot and three small hotels, plus the facilities of a small village and two yachtbuilders; in 1958 one, Alex Robertson, built *Sceptre*, the unsuccessful British contender for the Americas Cup.

**Yanks yield to Frost, Glass and Growth**: By 1971 the population had fallen to little over a thousand, but was liable to sudden changes because Sandbank was the landfall for the US service personnel from the Holy Loch submarine base ships, who also dominated the Dunoon area. The Slip Dock was run by Morris & Lorimer in 1980. About then a new urban development known as Sandhaven was begun 2 km inland on the Strachur Road, and by 1995 more housing had arisen near Ardnadam to the east. Light industrial development had been promoted by 1989 when the Argyll Frosted Foods factory was in operation, and by 1992 Dr Sandy Spowart's SES Technology was making specialist glass. The population of this young well-educated dormitory settlement was 1543 in 1991. Closure of the US base in 1992 had been expected to create a large vacuum in the area, but with the removal of the eyesore ships and the implied nuclear war target threat, private house sales immediately picked up. In 1995 the speculative office block of Caledonia House was for let at the new Sandbank Business Park promoted by Highlands & Islands Enterprise. The small *Anchorage Hotel* offers service at Ardnadam.

## SANDEND & Glassaugh

**Map 10, B1**

***Moray coast communities,*** *pop. 500*

OS 29: NJ 5566

About 3 km west of Portsoy on the Moray Firth coast is a bay of white sand at the mouth of the Burn of Fordyce, near which a windmill was built on a knoll in 1761. A little to the west is Sandend, known to the locals as *'Sanyne'*, where a tiny 19th century pier formed a small and rather exposed fishing harbour, and a village grew. The water-powered Glenglassaugh distillery was established on the burn near the windmill in 1875; in 1886 its barley was grown on the distillery's own farm, peat came from Crombie Moss by Glenbarry, and 365,000 litres of Highland malt whisky was distilled annually. In 1884 the Great North of Scotland Railway's coast line was opened, Glassaugh's passing station and goods yard being conveniently near the distillery.

*Glassaugh windmill tower, Sandend, built in the 18th century for grinding corn. It is known locally as 'the cup and saucer'. (JRH)*

**Whisky's Ups & Downs**: Although in 1951 nearly 600 people lived in the area there were only basic facilities, and the station was closed in 1953. The distillery was disused by 1955 but was rebuilt in 1959. In 1976 it was busy under Highland Distillers of Glasgow but the local population shrank and the village school had closed, though the post office stayed on. By 1985 just two small boats fished for lobsters, though other men manned boats fishing out of Buckie. The white beaches attracted holidaymakers, and by then there was a caravan and camping park. The windmill was restored about 1989. In 1991 Glenglassaugh (closed in 1986) was still owned by Highland Distillers; its whisky was normally used only in blending, but when available as a single malt was highly liked. The population was then under 500, but some new housing had been built by 2000. The little harbour now holds only tiny boats, but a fish merchant is still in business; the beach is popular with surfers.

## SANDHAVEN & Pittulie

**Map 10, C1**

***Buchan coast village,*** *pop. 875* — OS 30: NJ 9667

Pont's sketch map of Buchan, made about 1601, showed ships sheltering in a harbour having the characteristic shape of Sandhaven, 3 km to the west of Fraserburgh. Both Pittendrum, an inland farm, and Pittulie which lies just west of Sandhaven, were named on Gordon's map around 1640; the 17th century tower of Pittulie Castle lies 1.5 km west of Pittulie. Sandhaven appeared on Roy's map (made about 1750) only as a natural feature, apparently devoid of settlement. The harbour was built in 1830, seeming to reinforce the existing features, and Sandhaven was founded as a new village in 1838; Pratt noted it in 1858 as a *"fishing village with a good and safe harbour, a pier having been erected by the proprietor, Sir John S Forbes, and the Fishing Board"*. Pittulie, a short way to the west, was then *"another fishing village but with nothing particularly worthy of notice"*. Sandhaven harbour was enlarged in 1873, in an early use of concrete, and by 1894 a post and telegraph office and an inn were open.

**Clouds over Boatyard and Comfort Station**: From 1918 Forbes' boatyard at Sandhaven built wooden steam drifters, and from 1920 wooden motor fishing vessels of 34 tons. In the latter half of the 20th century the picturesque twin villages had a stable population of around a thousand, but had only basic facilities. In the mid 1980s six lobster boats were based at Sandhaven – which is a strong bastion of the remarkable Buchan dialect. J & G Forbes was still a family business building good-looking and substantial wooden fishing vessels, but was soon forced to close. In the 1990s the rather shoddily constructed breakwaters suffered severe storm damage. About 1998 some work was resumed at the boatyard, whose two elderly sheds still tower over the little harbour, where lobster pots are still in evidence. A modern primary school, pub, post office, and a few shops are open; a marina is planned.

## SANDHEAD

**Map 1, B5**

***Small Galloway village,*** *pop. 325 (area)* — OS 82: NX 0949

Near the centre of the Rhinns of Galloway are ancient stones, beside which the early Christian centre of Kirkmadrine was founded. A Norman motte was thrown up above the sandy shore near Balgreggan, 3 km north-east of Kirkmadrine. The area was thickly settled when Timothy Pont sketch-mapped Wigtownshire around 1610; *'Sand Mill'* already existed by the shore, giving its name to the Sandmill Burn. Balgreggan House, 1 km to the west, was designed by William Adam for John McDowall and built in 1730. By the time of Roy's survey of about 1754 a road from Stranraer to Drummore met the shoreline near the mill; a *'Waakmill'* stood 2 km to the south near the mouth of the Cairnweil Burn, and between these and Balgreggan grew the coastal village of Sandhead. To the north was marked *'Castle McDougal'*, apparently Balgreggan House. No railway ever reached the area, but Sandhead, which had a post office by 1900, later became the site of a creamery. By 1951 it had a small inn and secondary school, and a population of over 700, providing the services of a small village to another 1300 people within a 6 km radius, including 600 around Stoneykirk. Balgreggan House was regrettably demolished in 1966. The secondary school and the Scottish Milk Marketing Board's Sandhead Creamery both closed between 1960 and 1979. By 1974 a caravan and camping site was open to the north, and by 1996 another; a picnic area had been laid out on the shore. The inn and post office are still open.

## SANDWICK

**Map 14, B4**

***S. Shetland village,*** *pop. 730* — OS 4: HU 4224

About 17 km south of Lerwick is Mousa, a small offshore island on which stands the best preserved of all Pictish brochs, still 13 m tall. Pont's map of about 1592 showed *"the ancient brugh of Mousa"*. Flagstones quarried nearby paved the streets of old Lerwick, but the 11 Mousa families recorded in 1774 had fallen to nil by 1861. Pont showed a cluster of hamlets on the mainland opposite, around the natural harbour sheltered by the promontory of No Ness: Sandwick, Cumlewick, Hoswick, Chanawick and Levenwick, all still recognisable. In the late 1840s Sandwick was the initial southern terminus of the island's newly developing road system; a post office was open by 1881. Cumlewick jetty was the centre of a major fishery in the early 20th century; however this faded as fish stocks were exhausted.

**Holding on to Knitting and Oil Services**: A 125-pupil secondary school serving the southern part of Mainland was open in 1951, when the local facilities in the hamlets combined to equal those of a small village and the population in the area was under 500. From 1962 Sandwick became a rural planning *'holding point'*, but by 1971 the population had fallen to under 400, though the junior high school stayed open. By 1969 a weaving and knitwear factory was at work at Hoswick (under Laurence J Smith in 1979). By then Hudsons Offshore had set up a plant-hire base. By 1981, with the general development of Shetland as a base for North Sea oil and gas activities, new housing had been built in each of the various hamlets. The population had grown, and two hotels were open; but fishing was by small boats only. By 1987 the new building of Sandwick Junior High School (S1-S4, some 150 pupils) and a social club were in evidence. In 1991 when the population of the village was 728, some 350 outworkers of Smiths' were knitting fashion sweaters for the rump of the Kynoch concern of Keith. A post office and hotel are still in business; the notable Broch of Mousa is accessible from Sandwick by a seasonal ferry.

## SANQUHAR

**Map 2, A3**

***Dumfriesshire small town,*** *pop. 2100* — OS 71 or 78: NS 7809

Sanquhar (pronounced *Sanker*) stands beside the upper reaches of the River Nith in north Dumfriesshire. Its name derives from an ancient earthwork, the *Sean Caer (G.'Old Fort')*, and it is surrounded by other ancient remains. Ryehill Castle dates back to the 12th century, but Sanquhar Castle nearby is of 15th century origin. Sanquhar was created a burgh of barony in 1484; the manuscript map by Timothy Pont who surveyed the area about 1600 showed *'Ryhill'* within its enclosing wall, the *'Castel of Sanchare'*, and beside it the smaller *'Sanchare town'*. It appeared that the Crawick Water had already been bridged, as had the Barr Burn on the opposite bank of the Nith, where there was a mill. Another mill lay to the south near Eliock, which was then a castle, the home of the Crichtons, and the probable birthplace in 1560 of the poet and scholar James, the *'Admirable'* Crichton. A rectory of 1540 later became known as Blackaddie House.

**Sanquhar Royal Burgh – a Sorry Tale**: Sanquhar parish school was founded in the year that Royal Burgh status was granted in 1598, but burgh rights and privileges were not exploited. Richard Franck who visited the burgh in 1656 and called it *'Zanker'* found a ruinous and decayed town in a poorly cultivated area, with a market place *"no man would know it to be such, were he not told so"*. Sanquhar still had a market cross in 1680, and the castle was still occupied by the 1st Duke of Queensberry *(see Drumlanrig)*. William Adam designed a tolbooth, built in 1735. However, the Lords of Justiciary complained in 1748 of the awful state of its only road, which formed the connection between their courts at Dumfries and Ayr. The Roy map made about 1753 showed Sanquhar as a substantial linear settlement; a side road connected *'To Crawford'*, but the nearest crossing of the River Nith was at Eliock.

**Post Office, Textiles and Coal**: Sanquhar began to look up after its ultimately famous post office was opened in 1763. A minor water-powered textile industry grew up, with *"a considerable trade in stocking-making"* in 1776; the geometrical style of knitting known as Sanquhar Pattern originated here. *Glance* coal was being mined by 1770, and the pit required an engine by 1790. Two fair days were scheduled for 1797, and two years later when Heron stated a population of nearly a thousand, Sanquhar was *"remarkable chiefly for its coal-trade, and a manufactory of worsted mittens and stockings. The manufacture of carpets has lately been introduced"*. Two breweries were at work by 1825, but these did not last.

**Once a Place of Importance?**: It was said that coal was not *"properly developed"* in the area until after the Dumfries to Kilmarnock section of the Glasgow & South Western Railway opened in 1850; a brickworks followed. Sanquhar Academy was built in the 1870s and enlarged about 1890. The population stagnated at about 1325 between 1881 and 1891, when worsted was stated as the local industry and the main interest was the castle ruins. In 1894 there were two hotels, the *Commercial* and the *Queensberry Arms*, but Sanquhar was described by Murray in less than glowing terms as *"once a place of importance, in a dreary situation"*. However, Sanquhar golf club was founded in 1894, though it provided only a 9-hole course, the Euchan. By 1906 McGeorge of Dumfries had opened a fancy hose factory employing 60 workers. Nithsdale Wanderers FC briefly played in the Scottish League (1923–37). A milk processing plant was built about 1938, but closed soon after 1960. Sanquhar suffered a spate of other closures and barely maintained the status of a large village, with 2240 people in 1961. The brickworks had closed by 1962, and the railway station was closed by Beeching about 1965, though passenger trains still served nearby Kirkconnel; the mines also ceased to raise coal some time before 1978.

**Prosperity Elusive: the Damp Squib**: However, around 1970 Blackaddie House became a hotel. By 1977 there were three hotels and a modern Academy building; the extensive buildings of its predecessor were abandoned, and still rotting in 1998. Shand Mills' carpet factory was still quite new when it failed in 1978, and the town had 18% unemployment before the factory was occupied by the Canadian firm Kingston Yarn Spinners, who moved their 50 employees from Dumfries in 1979, with the intention of expanding and creating 300 more jobs. By 1985 the tolbooth housed a museum, and a caravan site was open; however, there was still much dereliction on the site of the former coalmine. In 1986 a substantial industrial estate included Kingston's and a firm of plastics moulders, and near the town was the HQ and factory of Brocks' fireworks. Sadly, this was taken over by Standard Fireworks and closed in 1988 with the loss of over fifty jobs; in 1989 it was sold to makers of military pyrotechnics. Much more stability was shown by Sanquhar's post office, still in the building where it was established in 1763, and Britain's oldest.

**Cats Repelled, but Unemployment High**: Pet & Garden Manufacturing, established in 1988 by Chris Murley, took over the former creamery buildings; by 1993 they employed 12 people making cat and dog repellents, and were exporting to a dozen countries. But male unemployment in Sanquhar in 1991 was nearly 50% above the national average. The village population was 2095, with high proportions in manufacturing industry and construction. Sanquhar was a minor incident on the signposted Southern Upland Way; walkers were able to use the new railway station which was opened in 1994. In 1997 eight or nine daily trains each way served Dumfries, Kilmarnock and destinations beyond. A branch factory of Century Aluminium cut its staff from 160 to 110 during 1997, further damaging this isolated and rather neglected but still proud place, where unemployment still stood high at 16%. The golf course still has 9 holes; the *Blackaddie House* has 10 rooms.

## SAUCHIE, New Sauchie & Fishcross **Map 16, B1**

***N. parts of Alloa***, *pop. 8700+* OS 58: NS 8994

Sauchie Tower, a fine 15th century keep, was built near the River Devon 3km north of Alloa. West of it was Collyland Farm, linked to Alloa by road by about 1750 when Roy mapped the area. Collyland Colliery was sunk about 1764 and had an engine by 1776. About then Schawpark House was built for Lord Cathcart, 1.5km south-east of the tower. A paper mill was opened in 1787, and from about that time red sandstone was worked at the Devon quarry. In the early 19th century a water engine was installed to drain a colliery at New Sauchie, between Schawpark and Alloa. In 1851 a railway between Alloa and Kinross reached a station named Sauchie, located at Fishcross (near the tower or *'Old Sauchie'*), also serving the Devon Colliery, which was sunk nearby from 1854: Neilson & Co of Glasgow supplied its pumping engine. Alloa golf club, founded in 1891, laid out an 18-hole parkland course at Schawpark, and New Sauchie had an inn by 1895. By then a mineral line reached the small Meta or Sheriffyards colliery at the head of Gartmorn Dam *(see Alloa)*; it was still at work in 1950, but passenger trains no longer served Sauchie.

**Council Houses outlast Industry**: The Devon quarry was still worked as late as 1926. A large local authority estate was built at New Sauchie in the 1920s and 30s, and mining was still carried on in the area in 1954 if not later; Sauchie's 4500 people had the facilities of a tiny village. Schawpark House was in ruins before its demolition in 1961, but by 1967 a second 18-hole golf course was open at Schawpark. By then all trace of the Meta pit had gone; rail freight ended in 1973. The council housing was radically improved around 1970 and the remains of the Devon colliery engine were preserved as a monument. Sauchie is really a suburb of Alloa, with minimal facilities, though the population had reached about 8695 by 1991. By then Gartmorn Dam had become a country park, with a visitor centre by 1997. Meantime new private housing had been built at Fairfield west of New Sauchie, and Fishcross has once more begun to grow. The restoration of Sauchie Tower was begun in 2000.

## SCALLOWAY

**Map 14, B4**

***Shetland village,*** *pop. 1050* OS 4: HU 4039

Pont's map-work of about 1592 named this sheltered inlet on the west coast of Shetland as *'Scola Voe'*, meaning *Huts on the Bay* in Norse – a name now corrupted to Scalloway. The bay was depicted full of shipping, and surrounded by a cluster of tiny settlements. In 1600–02 the despotic Earl Patrick Stewart, son of the half-brother of Mary Queen of Scots, built the strong Scalloway Castle so that he could control the islands' Parliament, which had continued to meet at Tingwall *(q.v.)*. The Earls forsook Sumburgh *(q.v.)*, which must have been very relieved, as would the Scalloway folk when these Stewart tyrants were eventually executed for treason in 1615. Scalloway had a parish school from 1612, but the settlement tended to develop at the castle gate; however, Martin writing in 1703 noted the *"little town has no trade, and but few inhabitants – about 90 in number"*. The castle had been used by Cromwell's garrison but was by then almost ruinous. Chambers in the 1820s described Scalloway as *"a little old town"*, but it was never chartered as a burgh.

**The Road speeds Development**: Blacksness pier was built in the 1830s, but as late as 1838 there was not even a post office, and no road until 1846–49. Scalloway then developed very considerably; the 1891 population was 730. In 1894 it was regarded by Murray as a *"town"*, with the *"fair" Royal Hotel* and weekly steamers from Leith via Aberdeen and Stromness, which continued in the 1930s. The *Scalloway Hotel* also existed by about 1900. In 1906 cod fishing was important, and the kippering kilns supported its claim to be one of the three main Shetland herring stations. In 1911 Hay & Co of Scalloway built a 10m line fishing vessel for Goodland of Hamnavoe, unusually fitted with an auxiliary steam engine. Scalloway golf club was founded in 1907, and laid out a 9-hole moorland course, but the overfished herring soon vanished. For half a century little happened to strengthen Scalloway's claim to urban status, though in the 1940s the Norwegian resistance had a base there, from where the 'Shetland Bus' boat service kept open links to Norway. Shetland steamer services ended in the 1960s, and all public access became by road, via Lerwick or Sumburgh Airport, or later via Tingwall airport.

**Oil and Fish, Air Power and Golf**: Scalloway Junior High School (S1-S4) was enlarged after oil development hit Shetland in the 1970s, and Scalloway had Britain's most northerly public outdoor swimming pool – the Shetland children were hardy! Scalloway's role was still as a fishing port, with about 20 trawlers and seine netters, a large modern fish market and three fish processing factories. The dock area was extensively rebuilt in 1980–83 by the Islands Council, and the 3-slip boatyard was the largest in Shetland. In 1987 a large wind-driven generator stood above the village, which had a museum, a large knitwear shop and a generous range of smaller shops. There was also an ugly quarry, very large by 1994. The population in 1991 was 1056; many owned their homes outright, typical of Shetland in general. In 1988 recent local and international decisions were expected to damage the local fishing community; but it was the *Braer* tanker accident that actually did, in January 1993 *(see Sumburgh)* because the farmed salmon of south-west Shetland waters had to be destroyed. This fortuitously provided a ready-made research focus for the North Atlantic Fisheries College, opened at the Ness of Westshore in 1992 to study aquaculture, fish processing and marine engineering. By 1994 the new Dale golf course of 18 holes, 3km north of Scalloway, had replaced the Shetland Golf Club's old course on Bressay. The harbour moves about 50,000 tons of cargo a year. Today Malakoff & William Moore Ltd operate boatyards at West Shore Scalloway, and at Lerwick. The 24-roomed *Scalloway Hotel* offers service.

*Scalloway boat-repairing. The little fishing town now has large modern quays and a 3-slip boatyard.* *(RCAHMS / JRH)*

## SCALPAY, Isle of

**Map 11, B3**

***Small island, Isle of Harris,*** *pop. 380* OS 14: NG 2196

Monro noted in 1549 that this small island at the mouth of the East Loch Tarbert of Harris was *"a profitable isle in corn, grass and fishing"*, owned by McLeod of Harris. Pont's map made about 1600 showed just one settlement on Scalpay *(G.Scalpaigh)*, which has two small but very sheltered harbours: the main village developed on the narrow isthmus between them. The area's early importance for navigation is shown by the erection in 1787–89 of the low lighthouse tower on Eilean Glas, the eastern point of the island. One of the first on the west coast of Scotland, it was built for the Northern Lighthouse Board by one Campbell, tacksman to the beneficent laird, Captain Macleod of Harris *(see Rodel)*. A new tower was built in 1824. Many herring boats – seeking better weather protection than Tarbert – would shelter at Scalpay, whose Presbyterian community began to turn from potato farming to fishing.

**United with Harris – and Salmon by the Million**: Scalpay, which contained about 685 people in 1951, was until 1965 a calling point for the Kyle of Lochalsh to Tarbert mailboats, and provided junior secondary education, also serving the adjacent mainland crofting settlement of Kyles Scalpay. In 1965 the mailboat calls were replaced by a turntable car ferry across the narrow Kyle to Harris. Depopulation was rapid until 1971, but with concentration on fishing in the 1970s it had settled down by 1991 with 382 people, still served by typical facilities for a small village, including bed and breakfast houses. Scalpay's prawn fishing and knitting thrived, and in 1997–98 an elegant road bridge was built to mainland Harris. The original Eilean Glas lighthouse of 1789 stands largely disused, the 1824 lighthouse having been automated in 1980, but the granite cottages formerly used by the lightkeepers are holiday homes. In 2001 a desalination plant by Weir of Cathcart was installed to purify water for ice-making at Scalpay's new Norwegian-owned Stolt salmon farm, which plans to produce the vast total of 10,000 tonnes of salmon a year.

## SCARBA, Isle of

***Small island, n. of Jura, Inner Hebrides*** — **Map 4, C3** — OS 55: NM 7004

Named *'Sharp Island'* in Norse, this 450m-high almost circular peak of an island lacks a safe harbour, and is suitable for little but grazing. It separates wild Jura from softer Luing, and is itself isolated from these by dangerous straits; the notorious Gulf of Corrievreckan with its tidal whirlpool, where the film *I Know Where I'm Going* was partly filmed, was finely described by Martin, by Bolton and most recently by Haswell Smith. Scarba supported 50 people in 1794, but numbers tailed off to culminate in seasonal occupation only from the 1960s. The owners, the Duncan Sandys family, maintain a jetty, the main house of Kilmory Lodge, and a cottage used as an adventure school.

## SCARP, Isle of

***Small island off Harris*** — **Map 11, A3** — OS 13: NA 9813

In 1549 the ever-optimistic Dean Monro noted of this exposed round isle of gneiss and granite off the west coast of Harris that it was *"fertile and fruitful, good for corn, store and fish"*. Settled in 1823 by tragic refugees from the clearances, by 1881 213 poor people scraped a living from its rocks and fished from its exposed landing place. A zany experiment with rocket mail exploded in 1934. Better opportunities opened up, people drifted away and by 1951 fewer than 20 crofting people lived on Scarp. The one telephone of 1947 had become three, but there was no mains electricity, and the once very successful primary school closed about 1960, followed by the post office in 1969. The last two families left in 1971 and by 1981 Tindall observed *"holiday homes only"*. The island was repeatedly sold during the BCCI affair; a Harris crofter from the last Scarp family still grazes sheep there.

## SCONSER & Sligachan

***Locations, Isle of Skye,*** *pop. under 100* — **Map 8, B3** — OS 32: NG 5232

By 1773 *Sconser Lodge* was an inn at a clachan nestling beside the Sound of Raasay, at the foot of the peaks of Lord Macdonald's Forest at the entrance to Loch Sligachan. By 1773 this was a staging point in the weekly mail service to Dunvegan, and as late as 1823 Portree still relied on Sconser for its mails. The post office soon adjoined Skye's main road between Broadford and Portree. By 1886 the *Sligachan Inn* had been built beside the bridge where this met the Carbost road, and became the natural base for exploring the wild Cuillin Hills to the south. By 1953 what was now the *Sligachan Hotel* was in Bolton's opinion *"one of the best known hotels in Britain"*. Meantime about 1954 the much smaller Sconser Lodge also reverted to hotel use. In 1976 the HIDB started a passenger ferry to Raasay, replaced about 1980 by a car ferry, now Raasay's lifeline. A road-chippings quarry had been opened to the east. By 1992 the 9-hole Isle of Skye golf course had been laid out on the seaside near the *Sconser Lodge Hotel*; nearby is a post office. There is now a mountain rescue post and a caravan and camping site beside the *Sligachan Hotel*, and nearby a salmon fish-farm – and a coal-merchant.

*Sligachan hotel and bridge, Skye. Today the hotel has a mountain rescue post.* *(RS)*

## SCORAIG

***Wester Ross settlement,*** *pop. under 100* — **Map 8, C1** — OS 19: NH 0096

In the 1950s Scoraig in Wester Ross was a dying crofting settlement on the tip of the peninsula between Loch Broom and Little Loch Broom, accessible only by boat or by a lengthy trek on a footpath from Altnaharrie. It was repopulated in the 1960s by a group of well-qualified people dropping out of the *'rat race'* and electing to become modern-day crofters. They clubbed together to open a school with official help; when a new self-build school was opened in 1989, 60% of the parents of its 12 pupils had university degrees. But children grow up, and in 1994 the school was closed for a time as only one pupil was left. However, by 2000 there were ten pupils in the little school, with more expected, and rectangular patches of woodland planted on the hillside have proved that the north-west Highlands do not have to remain as bleak moorland.

## SCOTLANDWELL, Auchmuirbridge, Portmoak & Kinnesswood

***Kinross-shire villages / hamlets,*** *pop. 1100* — **Map 6, B4** — OS 58: NO 1801

About 600 AD an early Christian called Moak built his monastic cell on an islet in Loch Leven; but about 843 the last Pictish King Brude gave it to the Culdees, who dedicated it to St Serf. Their religious community became a priory about 980, and lasted until 1146 when David I gave it to the Augustinians, who rebuilt it in stone and also established it as a *'hospital'*. The early church of Kilmagad, which stood at the foot of the steep escarpment overlooking Loch Leven, was a part of Pictish Fothrif. A charter of 1152 mentioned *"the mills at the bridge"* in connection with Portmoak, the embarkation point for St Serf's Priory. This, the earliest known reference to a bridge in Scotland, evidently related to the Auchmuirbridge across the River Leven which was, if not unique, then sufficiently rare to be shown as the *Pons Aghmore* – the only bridge shown on the Scottish portion of the crude Gough map, of about 1230–50.

**The Holy Well and its Hospice**: An early track linking Edinburgh and Perth via Kinghorn and Cluny crossed the bridge, some 3km to the west of which was a spring or *'holy well'*, the *Scotlandwell*. In 1220 William Malvoisine the bishop of St Andrews founded a ministry there, hence the alternative area name Bishopshire, and in 1242–43 a church was built nearby, beside the loch at Portmoak. The area was in the sheriffdom of Fife by 1250 when the Red Friars founded a hospice beside the well; later Robert the Bruce claimed he had been cured of leprosy by its waters. Prior Andrew Wyntoun of St Serf's wrote his Chronicle of Scotland there in 1420–24. In 1426 Portmoak became part of Kinross sheriffdom. The Prior of St Serf's still sat in Parliament in 1560, but the priory was dissolved in 1570.

**Parchment Manufacture, Arnot Tower and Gullet Bridge**: For 300 years, including the period 1530–1760, local limekilns made the material used in workshops at Kinnesswood for treating calfskin to make parchment, also producing vellum for the chancery – both essential for legal documents. The estate of Arnot existed by 1481; in the 16th century, Arnot Tower was built on the hillside above the bridge, both being shown on Pont's map made about 1600. A new Auchmuir Bridge of three arches was built in 1612. *'Achmuir'*, and opposite it Arnot Mill, were among a cluster of names on the Leven, shown on James Gordon's map of Fife made about 1642. However, the Auchmuir bridge was not shown and had perhaps fallen by then – the nearest bridge across the meandering Leven being one built since 1617 to replace a ford at the Gullet, over 3km to the west near Kirkness. A new church of Portmoak was built in 1661, and in 1685 Portmoak parish again became part of the reinstated sheriffdom of Kinross. The Gullet bridge was rebuilt in 1697 with three arches; it lay on the track southwards from Perth via Scotlandwell to Auchtertool Kirk and Newbiggin, marked on the Roy map surveyed about 1750. Auchmuir Bridge was apparently repaired or rebuilt in 1709, and more repairs were requested in 1740.

**Turnpikes and Tanworks**: A re-sited school was built at Scotlandwell in 1777 (and a larger one followed in 1834). In 1810 the roads between Scotlandwell and Leslie, and between Ballingry and Auchmuirbridge, were turnpiked. Greenwood's map of 1826–27 showed Arnot and Auchmuir water mills, and a water-powered bleachfield stood just within Fife, some 350m east of Auchmuir Bridge; it was owned about then by Gavin Inglis, a textile manufacturer of Markinch. A tanworks operated at Kinniston, and two pumping windmills to the south were connected with land drainage of the marshy lochside. In the 1820s Kinnesswood, some 1.5km north-west of Scotlandwell, was *"a little sequestered village"* (Chambers).

**The Lowered Loch**: Auchmuir Bridge was rebuilt yet again in 1828 so that the Leven's course could be straightened and deepened in 1828–31 to lower the loch surface by a metre; 443ha of rather poor farmland was gained, mainly along the east shore. Many thatched houses in the area were re-roofed in slate in 1860. James Scott, born in Kinnesswood in 1861, was to become a leading architect around 1900 *(see St Andrews)*. To Beveridge in 1888 Scotlandwell, which never saw a railway, was *"a simple, rather ancient, and tumble-down looking village"* with a small inn. Nearby was the *"picturesque village of Kinnesswood, popularly pronounced 'Kinnaskit'"*. By 1895 Scotlandwell had a post office, and there was also an inn at Kinnesswood; both inns were long-lasting, unlike the mills and bleachfield.

**Golfing, Gliding and a Farm for the Birds**: From 1903 Kinnesswood had the Bishopshire golf club, which laid out a steep 9-hole course. Also in the early 20th century came the Glenlomond Hospital for tuberculosis cases, built 2 km north of Kinnesswood, which gradually became larger than Scotlandwell. The Scottish Gliding Union – which created the Scottish gliding centre of Portmoak on the carseland south of Scotlandwell – was founded in 1934 by Andrew Thorburn of Kirkcaldy. One member, fighter pilot George Lee, won the World Gliding Championship on three successive occasions. By 1951 the population of the parish was 1000. The Royal Society for the Protection of Birds later acquired Vane Farm south of their Loch Leven waterfowl reserve, and have developed it as a popular interpretation centre. There was a caravan site at Scotlandwell by 1974, and in the 1970s a private housing estate was built at Kinnesswood. However, although the combined settlements retain the facilities of a small village, the parish population was only 1086 in 1991. Glenlomond Hospital – which closed around 1990 – was soon converted into a nursing home and housing. The small *Well Country Inn* is prominent in the interesting old village of Scotlandwell, as is the *Lomond Country Inn* at Kinnesswood.

## SCOURIE — Map 12, A2

***Small W. Sutherland village,*** *pop. 300 (area)* — OS 9: NC 1544

The coast of west Sutherland is one of the most remote and inhospitable areas on the Scottish mainland, an ice-scoured wilderness of rocky hummocks and freshwater lochans offering fishing to the hardy. But some shelter from the north-westerly gales which can scream down from Iceland comes from the offshore isle of Handa, enabling Scourie in the vast parish of Eddrachilis to support the world's most northerly palm trees. Hut circles and chambered cairns show ancient settlement at *'Skowrie'*, which appeared on Pont's map, made around 1600, as two places, *More* and *Beg* (Great and Little). Roy's map of about 1750 showed the same two tiny hamlets isolated in a trackless waste, and Scourie remained off the road system even after the Highland Road and Bridge Commissioners ceased work in 1828. However, about 1834 a road reached the site where Laxford Bridge was to be built, some 10km to the east, and by 1838 a post office was open at Scourie. Handa was deserted after the 1840s potato famine and is now a bird sanctuary. The road system had been developed to its full extent by 1894, when Murray mentioned the *"small but comfortable and well managed" Scourie Inn*, a fishing hostelry at Scourie Beg.

**Cheap Holidays – and Good Accommodation**: In the mid 20th century Scourie and its environs remained a poor crofting area which was also able to offer the cheapest of self-catering holidays, and the local roadsides became littered with tiny weatherbeaten static caravans sheltering in nooks and crannies. The resident population remained fairly steady at around 100, with another 200 people scattered around the area who depended on Scourie's facilities, typical of a small village. To obtain more choice, the locals had to travel to east coast centres, especially Dingwall, 80km or more away. A second hotel and a proper caravan and camping site were open by 1975, but by then the tiny secondary school had been downgraded to primary and the older pupils were sent to distant Ullapool, where other facilities were increasingly available. These became more accessible with the opening of the Kylescu bridge in 1984; but Scourie makes little news. The *Scourie Hotel* and the *Scourie Lodge* offer accommodation, as does the *Eddrachiles* at Badcall Bay, 3km south.

## SCRABSTER

*N. Caithness village / port* — **Map 13, A4** — OS 12: ND 1070

Scrabster lies under the cliffs of Thurso Bay 3km west of the town, sheltered by Holburn Head. First mentioned in the 12th century as *Skarabolstathar*, Norse for *'Cliff Edge Homestead'*, it came to prominence with the early 13th century castle of the Bishops of Caithness. An early bishop having been murdered at Scrabster by Norsemen, his hopeful but also doomed successor stayed at less exposed Halkirk (*q.v.*). Scrabster was chartered as a burgh of barony in 1526, and Pont's map made around 1600 showed *'Scrabster Road'* (bay) full of shipping. About 1750 Scrabster was tiny, meriting only a few dots on Roy's map; there was then no jetty, and apparently no road of any sort west of Thurso. By 1828 a short pier and road link had been built by Telford and the Commissioners for Highland Roads.

**Ferry Port and Flagstones**: The Scrabster Harbour Trust was established in 1841, and by 1854 occasional steamers linked Scrabster with Oban; from 1856 Scrabster was the regular ferry port for the Orkney mail steamers, which plied across the Pentland Firth to Stromness and for some years also to Scapa (for Kirkwall). Holburn Head lighthouse, a domestic-looking building on the cliff above the harbour, was first lit in 1862, and flagstone quarries at Holburn Head and Scrabster itelf worked as late as 1910. The Highland Railway had reached Thurso in 1874, but was oddly not extended to Scrabster, which was linked with Thurso station by horse buses. For a time from about 1885 a steamer sailed to Stornoway; by 1894 there was also a hotel and a coastguard station. By the 1920s land reclamation had begun within a southern jetty. In the 1930s coaster owners A F Henry & MacGregor of Leith carried cement to Scrabster, dropping off half cargoes, typically of 300 tonnes en route to Lerwick.

**Ferro-cement, Faroese Ferries and Fishing**: Around 1950, 15-tonne loads of whale meat were carried from Scrabster to Melton Mowbray by lorry, there to become dogfood. By then Scrabster had become the official northern terminus of the trunk road that left London's Charing Cross as the A1 and ended as the A882. A fishermen's mission building was erected in 1956, and in 1960 the lifeboat station was transferred from Thurso to Scrabster, where the harbour was greatly enlarged with a second southern jetty and a northern pier. By 1975 a Scrabster boatbuilder had become the first in Scotland since World War I to try fabricating hulls from ferro-cement; not a great success! A large BP oil depot was in use by 1978, and by 1979 a summer-only ferry service sailed to the Faroes. Despite so much maritime activity and the erection of a few more houses, Scrabster remained in 1979 a small village of under 400 people. By the 1980s Scrabster was the terminus of the P&O ro-ro car ferry to Stromness, which also had an Iceland ferry link. The lighthouse was automated in 1987. By 1990 boats from Iceland and the Faroes were landing fish, and over the next 3 years the Harbour Trust built smart new headquarters as part of another major harbour expansion, forming a new basin south of the old to enable larger ocean-going vessels to land fish direct to a new fish market.

*The Holborn flagstone quarry, at Scrabster, pictured around 1910. The flags were shipped out for use as paving-stones in many cities all around Britain.* *(British Geological Survey)*

**Fish Records and Call Centre**: In the four years 1990–94 the amount of fish landed quadrupled, doubling again by 1995. All the area's petroleum fuel was delivered by sea in 1994, when the BP depot had a dozen tanks. In 1995–96 the port set new records for fish landings at over 14,000 boxes in a week, including white fish, haddock and prawns plus some scallops and a few crabs. These were landed by vessels from Orkney, other Scottish ports, Hull, Belgium, the Faroes, France, Norway and Spain. In 1997 white fish was still landed in large quantities from Scottish and Faroese boats; a typical week yielded 4000 boxes plus some crabs and prawns. Shark fishing also drew sea anglers to the port, which had a Customs office and was the base for a pilot cutter and fisheries protection vessel. An ice factory and a *'seafood park'* now adjoin. The sturdy but twice-renamed *St Ola* has been the Orkney ferry since 1992. Meantime the *New Weigh Inn* had been built at the Thurso turn by 1993, and now an adjacent *Lidl* store and nursing home stand amid much new housing which is making the cliff-top into a Thurso suburb. A call centre and a hi-tech battery factory have been built in a new business park to the west.

## SELKIRK

**Map 3, B4**

***Borders town***, *pop. 5900* OS 73: NT 4728

At Oakwood in the Ettrick Valley was a first century Roman fort. The name Selkirk for a place 6km downstream may well mark the site of the first Christian church of the *Selgovae*, the Iron Age tribe whose stronghold was on the Eildon Hills 8km to the east. Certainly the site of the later town beside the Ettrick Water was a hilly one, on which a church stood before 1113 when David I founded a Tironensian monastery. But in 1128 the monks departed for Kelso, leaving behind a second church, both coming under Kelso's control. By 1258 there was definitely a sheriff of Selkirk. There was also some early medieval trade by pack-horses between Selkirk and Berwick, but little seems to be known of developments in the Ettrick valley until a Royal castle called Selkirk Peel was erected in 1301–02. The first definite proof of a Royal Burgh of Selkirk appears in 1328; it had 110 burghal tenures in 1426, a substantial number, and by 1444 Selkirk merchants were trading with Danzig, probably through Leith.

**Castles, Sutters and the Tragedy of Flodden**: Selkirkshire was for long under natural woodland as a Royal hunting forest. In the late 15th century Selkirk Peel was a property of the powerful Angus family; Oakwood Tower was built beside the river near the Roman fort in the 16th century. Selkirk town was at one time surrounded by a palisade, and according to Chambers was already famous by 1513 for its *Sutters* (shoemakers) making *"thin or single-soled shoes"*. At the battle of Flodden in that year the town sadly lost most of its 100 fighting men, and was afterwards burned by the English; hence its almost negligible contribution to burgh taxes in 1535–56. James V encouraged sheep rearing and hence deforestation (though Blaeu's atlas showed that much woodland still survived in Selkirkshire at the end of the century). Selkirk was rebuilt, and in 1560 the burgh was represented in Parliament. The ready availability of hides from hill cattle was again exploited, Selkirk once more becoming famous for shoemaking.

**The Importance of Strong Footwear**: The town looked substantial on Timothy Pont's map of Tweeddale, made around 1600, and although there was no Ettrick bridge there had evidently formerly been one, for just below the town was *'Brigheuch'*; *'Aikwood'* mill already stood 3km above the town. Selkirk's weavers were incorporated in 1608, and in the same year a parish school was started. Although in 1639 Selkirk ranked a lowly 45th of Scottish burghs in tax rents, by 1645 there was a finely built 3-storeyed inn. Over 40% of all tradesmen in the town in the 1690s were engaged in leather working; good strong footwear was essential, for with the steepness of Selkirk's streets went a total absence of wheeled transport – until 1725 there was not so much as a cart in the town! However, the Ettrick was again bridged in the second quarter of the century. In 1745 Selkirk had a flesh market and was able to make over 2000 pairs of shoes for the army at short notice. The mansion of Philipburn House was built in 1745–51.

**Roads, Yarn Spinning and Stocking Weaving**: However, developments were starting, and by about 1754 when Roy's surveyors mapped the town the modern street pattern was substantially built up. There were six radial routes, including a *"New road from Selkirk to Edinburgh"* which was evidently in the course of construction northwards from the new Selkirk bridge to Fairnilee by the Tweed, where no bridge had yet been built. It was being continued on the north side of the Tweed to intersect the *'Road from Peebles to Lauder'* at Craighalls (Clovenfords, *q.v.*). The roads leading to Peebles, Galashiels and Hawick were turnpiked under an Act of 1768. In 1767 a woollen manufactory was established; by 1776 this spun worsted yarn for weaving in Musselburgh factories, for there were by then only a few jobbing weavers in Selkirk. By 1780 John Hardy of Hawick had introduced the framework knitting of stockings. Meantime the Ettrick bridge had been swept away by a flood; it was replaced in 1778 about 200m upstream of the former site.

**Postal Services, Bootmaking and Brewing**: Selkirk's first post office was opened about 1780, when it still took a fortnight for the carrier's cart to perform the round trip to Edinburgh! Even in 1797, when six fair days were scheduled for the year and Selkirk was a post town, mails came only on alternate days. Heron noted in 1799 *"this town, though not of considerable extent, contains some good houses, and about a thousand inhabitants; boots and shoes are still its chief manufacture"*. A bark mill for tanning was in existence in 1837 but probably

*The 1911 Petrie engine at Roberts' Philiphaugh Mill, Selkirk, pictured in 1967. It was a standby to the two water turbines which drove the woollen mill machinery. It was removed to New Lanark in the late 1970s, and has been re-erected there.* *(JRH)*

origginated centuries earlier. Agnes Haldane was the proprietress of a Selkirk brewery by 1825.

**Sheriff Author, Banks and Mansions**: In 1803 Walter Scott (later Sir) was the Sheriff of Selkirk, where for a few years from 1810 the East Lothian Banking Company had a far-flung branch; though by 1829 he had an account with the British Linen Company at its Selkirk branch. In 1816 Lord Napier had a 17th century farmhouse converted into an idiosyncratic mansion, which he confusingly named Thirlestane Castle. Chambers wrote that in 1827 Selkirk was *"a town of neat appearance; the jail is new, neat and commodious; many handsome houses have been recently erected"*. Souters still outnumbered all other trades, and Bowhill 4 km to the west was a Buccleuch hunting seat *"embowered amidst its beautiful new woods"*. In the 1830s Lord Murray's seat, Philiphaugh, was open to the public.

**Expansion in Selkirk Tweeds 1830–60**: Shearing machinery for cloth was introduced in 1813; the Bridgehaugh weaving mill of Dobie & Richardson may have arisen about that time, and was soon followed by several others. The Ettrick spinning mill of J H Brown & Co was erected in 1836. Dunsdale mill was also built in the 1830s, and from 1863 was run by Waddel & Turnbull; it was then enlarged to make both tweeds and tartans. The Forrest mill of George Roberts & Co, started

*Modern spinning technology at a Selkirk mill.*

*(SMPC / Doug Corrance)*

in 1838, was extended in 1868, when it made superior tweeds using yarn from the firm's Innerleithen spinning mill. Finally the large Linglie weaving mill also dated from the mid 19th century. In 1844 the historian and author Andrew Lang was born at Viewfields. By that year 128 stocking frames were in use locally, and in 1851 Watsons of Hawick who supplied the yarn had about 50 hosiery workers in Selkirk; in the 1860s this business was bought by their foreman George Hogg. From 1859 Robbie Douglas made the Selkirk Bannock, a round sultana loaf which acquired a world market.

**Selkirk Mills in late Victorian times**: Expansion continued, and in 1869 seven textile mills were at work, with over 1000 employees, using about 30,000 spindles, 181 power looms and 97 hand looms. Five made tweeds and two were in carding and spinning alone: Philiphaugh mill, beside the river 2 km west of the town and then still wholly water-powered, was enlarged in 1876. The newest, the Yarrow mill of Brydone & Brown, founded in 1867, was enlarged in 1892. Two more followed: the Bannerfield weaving mill about 1880 and the large St Mary's weaving mill of Gibson & Lumgair in 1894. Philiphaugh mill was again extended with water turbine power in 1922.

**Gas, Golf and Reporters**: Selkirk gasworks was established in 1835. William Young, son of its manager, became manager of the Clippens Oil Company works at Loanhead in the 1880s, and developed the Young–Beilby retort which gave improved ammonia yield from oil shale and was adopted across the industry. The *Southern Reporter* newspaper was first published about 1855. Although an engineering works and another tannery were also built at about that time, Selkirk had become better known for the manufacture of tweeds than for shoes. A branch railway from Galashiels was opened to the town in 1856, and by 1859 there was a brick and tile works at Haining. Selkirk golf club was founded in 1883 and laid out an 18-hole course. By 1880 the *County Hotel* was open, and by 1894 there were two other small hotels, the *Fleece* and *Station*. A public library was begun around 1888. The population in 1891 was 6400. By 1895 a hilltop racecourse had been laid out beside the Kelso road 3 km east. The Victoria Hall, begun in 1895, has stayed in use. The *Selkirk Saturday Advertiser* entered the newspaper business in 1897, and a sawmill was also opened late in the 19th century.

**Stagnation, Vandalism and Exacta Circuits**: Though new county offices were located at Galashiels, Selkirk – which had small-town facilities, including two more hotels – maintained a generally static population until the railway was closed to passengers in 1951 and to freight in 1964. Brown, Allen spinners were taken over by Todd & Duncan of Kinross in 1961. The local Thirlestane Castle was demolished in 1965 and Philiphaugh in 1967, victims of the architecturally deplorable sixties. The racecourse fell out of use around 1970. Exacta Circuits were established in the town in 1962 making printed circuit boards, and moved into a custom-built factory in 1972, where they employed over 200 people. Taken over by STC in 1974, expansion continued and by 1979 with 440 employees and a branch plant in Galashiels they had become Britain's biggest makers of circuit boards and one of the top three in Europe; a 3600 m$^2$ extension to the factory was under construction. By 1988 they employed 550 people, supplying major computer companies; however, in 1991 recession led to wage cuts, accepted to ensure continuity of employment.

**Textile Dominance**: In 1975 the town was absorbed into Ettrick and Lauderdale District, based largely in Galashiels. By 1976 there was a new clinic, and by 1977 *Philipburn House* had become a 15-roomed hotel. In 1979, although there was a shortage of labour in the Borders textile industry, the disused St Mary's textile mill was converted into small factory units. In 1981 Selkirk's facilities were still those of a small town; it had Selkirk High School, nine hotels, and at least as many mills, among them the Ettrickvale, Forrest and Linglie, still making woollen or other textiles. Only a single footwear wholesaler then remained to represent the one-time principal industry. By 1981 4 km of the former railway alignment had become a new A7 road. For some reason a Mountain Rescue post was open in Selkirk, but in the 1990s this was removed to Kelso, nearer the Cheviot Hills. Selkirk's industrial expansion in the late 1980s included another electronics concern and a disinfectant works, and by 1989 the valley below the town was crowded with modern industries. Its lately rather forlorn appearance had been transformed to that of a bustling centre, and a use had been found for the empty Yarrow Mill – mushroom-growing.

**Great News? Textiles totter but Philipburn Saved**: By 1981 the *Southern Reporter* had become part of the *Tweeddale Press* Group of Berwick; by 1991 it had absorbed the *Jedburgh Gazette, Hawick Express* and *Kelso Chronicle*. At that time the town's population was about 5900, with low male unemployment and a very high proportion in manufacturing. In 1995 Exacta Circuits of Selkirk was bought out by a Tamworth-based company named Forward; but they soon went into reverse and with little warning sadly closed down this remarkable firm. (Today, there is Signum Circuits, with 300 jobs.) By 1989 Forrest Mills was the base for Claridge's textile consultancy, and the small but award-winning exporters, Claridge textile mills, were weaving fashion fabrics in a new factory, plus by 1992 an increasing number of *'throw blankets'* for the American market. By 1990 Laidlaw & Fairgrieve of Riverside Mills (a Dawson subsidiary) employed 600 people at three sites in the Borders, making knitting yarns; but demand fell away, no purchasers appeared though the firm was marketed for two years, and in 2000 Dawson closed the operation with its last 290 jobs. Meantime the historic *Philipburn House Hotel*, fire-damaged in 1996, was reinstated in luxurious style in 1998.

## SHAWBOST

**Map 11, B1**

***Village, Isle of Lewis,*** *pop. 500* — OS 8: NB 2546

About 10 km to the west of Barvas on the bleak north-western coast of Lewis is a group of crofting townships comprising North, South and New Shawbost *(G.Siabost)*, each lining a road perpendicular to the coast and linked by the main road A858. The 1891 population of Shawbost was 600. A Harris Tweed mill was opened in 1915 to spin thread and finish the home-woven cloth. In 1951 a junior secondary school with 150 pupils was the most striking feature of this large crofting community, then having a population of 700, which fell rapidly to under 550 by 1971 but had recovered somewhat by 1981. Another element of interest was a large whalebone arch erected at Bragar township, 3 km to the east on the Barvas road. By 1975 a caravan and camping site was open at Dalbeg, 3 km to the west, and by 1977 one Shawbost school had become a crofting museum. By 1980 a thatched *'black house'* at the township of Arnol between Bragar and Barvas had been restored as a permanent exhibit of the medieval way of life that in Lewis lasted into the 20th century. The secondary school was reduced to primary by the new Western Islands Council some time after 1977, but a caravan site was open by 1985. The tweed mill employed some 40 people in 1986, and in 1992 the MacLeod Tweed Company of Shawbost acquired the Stornoway mill of Kenneth Mackenzie. Both these spinning and finishing mills stayed open, although the total number of weavers of Harris Tweed had fallen to only 400. In 1996 both mills were owned by the Murray family and still working, locally trading as Kenneth MacLeod (Shawbost) Ltd. The post office remains open.

## SHETTLESTON & Carntyne **Map 15, D5**

***E. suburbs of Glasgow,*** *pop. 29,000* OS 64: NS 6464

As early as the 1220s Shettleston Cross, which stood 5 km east of Glasgow and just within the latter's parish, was already a traditional point for the collection of tolls for Rutherglen, which burgh was only 4 km away. Shettleston was not named on Pont's map of 1596, though this did show Carntyne, where mining was already taking place under its lairds the Gray family. Shettleston's first coal mine was sunk some time before 1737, when coal was being dug there as well as some 500 m east of Carntyne House, where a hamlet grew up, also named Carntyne. By the 1750s (as the Roy map showed) both these places were linear settlements on the Glasgow–Airdrie road (later the A89), with two other radial roads. By about then a windmill was used to drain the local pits; the one at Shettleston was deep enough to require an engine by 1764. In 1768 a steam engine was installed at Carntyne; this worked for a century. A second engine was in use at Shettleston from 1791, and the profits from mining enabled Carntyne House to be rebuilt in 1802 by its owner Robert Gray (who also owned pits in Parkhead). James Beaumont Neilson, born in Shettleston in 1792, became manager of the Glasgow gasworks and invented the hot blast process which revolutionised iron production *(see Carmyle)*. Shettleston's first post office opened around 1825.

**Railways, Ropes, Iron and Dyes**: From 1871 Shettleston and Carntyne stations lay on the secondary line of the North British Railway (NBR) linking Glasgow and Edinburgh via Bathgate. But Gray's mines appear to have become worked out by 1875 when mining in their area ceased. However, about 1874 J & T Boyd, makers of textile machinery, set up the Shettleston Ironworks at Old Shettleston Road, and about 1877 Archibald Thomson & Co built the Glasgow Rope Works in Annick Street. In 1877 Shettleston became the junction for an NBR branch to Hamilton, on which a station was opened at Mount Vernon. About 1883–86 McArthur, Scott & Co (at some time known as the British Dyewood Company) first made dyes and inks at Carntyne.

**Bricks, Bottles and Golf, Laundry and Cream**: The population in 1891 was 5400; Shettleston already had an inn. At that time Carntyne and Shettleston were still distinct villages; north of Shettleston was the Lightburn Hospital, soon adjoined by the Greenfield Colliery. The Frankfield brickworks, north-west of the station, opened about 1899. To the south was Sandyhills House; Sandyhills golf club, founded in 1905, laid out an 18-hole course opposite. The North British Bottle Manufacturing Company's works in Old Shettleston Road was built about 1904; it was bought in 1907 by James Buchanan & Co, who brought new production techniques from America and enlarged the plant in 1912–13. The Wellshot Laundry was built about 1904 following a spate of tenement building. A power station was built in 1906, and the Shettleston Co-operative creamery about 1910–12.

**Sausages, Housing and Bleach**: In the 1920s the straight Edinburgh Road was built across country north of Shettleston, becoming the A8 and relieving Shettleston Road of through traffic; between 1925 and 1939 the building of a vast housing estate in the Killin Street/Ardgay Street area unified the settlements. By 1925 the Greenfield and Foxley collieries were open respectively north and south of Shettleston, where the Stanley sausage casings works in Westerburn Street was rebuilt in 1926. Carntyne House was demolished in the 1920s and its site was soon surrounded by the South Carntyne housing scheme, nearer to Parkhead than to Shettleston. The huge high-density Springboig housing estate between Shettleston station and Edinburgh Road dates mainly from the 1930s. The *State Cinema* was built about 1938; by that time a railway permanent way depot was in use, and the Parozone bleach works at Carntyne already used road hauliers for long distance traffic. The Foxley colliery was apparently the first to close.

**Decline sets in and Towers are raised**: By 1951 Shettleston with a population of 37,000 had the facilities of an average town, though it was by then almost bisected by the poorly drawn boundary of Glasgow city, whose electric trams had for many years served the area. Electric trains on the Airdrie to Glasgow and Helensburgh route served Shettleston and Carntyne from 1961, but the Mount Vernon station and railway were closed at the same time. By 1963 the collieries had disappeared, and as in the rest of the Glasgow area, industry had declined; the brickworks closed about 1970. The established Eastbank Senior Secondary school was central to the town; by 1971 when the population was about 32,000 the large St Andrew's Secondary had been built next to Lightburn Hospital, and shortly afterwards four tower blocks were built on the site of the demolished Sandyhills House, one of the few parts of the area not undermined. By 1974 J & T Boyd of Shettleston were the last makers of textile machinery in greater Glasgow, making ring spinning and preparation equipment; bottlemaking also continued.

**New Industries, College, Drugs and Ill-health**: By 1979 Gordon Graham & Co had a whisky business at London Road; later they blended Black Bottle whisky. Over 100 jobs were lost when Scofisco closed its seafood processing plant in 1978. By 1981 Shettleston's population had fallen; however, a good range of facilities was still available. Lightburn hospital for geriatrics had 120 beds. The GEAR (Glasgow Eastern Area Renewal) project created many jobs in the area around 1980; by 1986 the extended Fullarton housing estate covered much of the tubeworks site, and the bings south of Hamilton Road had been cleared. The John Wheatley College of Further Education was open at Shettleston Road by 1990, adjacent to the 1000-pupil Eastbank Academy (as it was by then styled). In 1991 the population was about 29,000. By 1994 a sports centre had been built in Shettleston town centre. By 1992–93 drugs dominated Carntyne's severe social problems and in 1999 Shettleston made news for the worst of reasons, gaining the dismal distinction of being statistically the unhealthiest area in the UK. Tesco decided in 2000 to site a new store in Shettleston.

## SHIELDAIG

**Map 8, B2**

***Wester Ross settlement,*** *pop. under 100* OS 24: NG 8153

Loch Shieldaig is a sheltered Wester Ross sea loch between Loch Torridon and Upper Loch Torridon, a particularly beautiful area which in the mid 18th century was well wooded but trackless. The coastal township of Shieldaig with its small inn, school and piers eventually became the terminus of a long single track road from Lochcarron; in 1953 when there was a post office and one or two shops only about 100 people lived in the area, known mainly for crofting and fishing. About 1965 a road was completed eastwards from Shieldaig, following the line of a footpath to Annat at the head of Upper Loch Torridon, giving fine views across the loch. A road was also built westwards from Shieldaig between 1965 and 1971 to Arinacrinachd (which until then also had a tiny school) and extended past various crofts around the north side of the Applecross peninsula, to reach Applecross in 1976. By 1997 there was a caravan site at Shieldaig, which had lost its post office but kept its primary school. The tiny Shieldaig Island is owned by the National Trust for Scotland; the loch contains a fish farm. The long-standing *Tigh an Eilean* (Island House) inn is now a hotel, and other accommodation is also available.

## SHOTTS, Stane & Dykehead

**Map 16, B4**

***Lanarkshire town,*** *pop. 8750* OS 65: NS 8759

Stane lies in the ancient and extensive parish of Cambusnethan, about 200m above sea level in the shallow valley of the South Calder Water, the boundary with the sprawling parish of Shotts. Stane appeared on Pont's map of Clydesdale, made in 1596, as an isolated and insignificant place labelled *'The Stoun'*. Little happened for two centuries other than the construction by the 1750s of a road between Carluke and Livingston, passing just south of Stane. In 1801–02, with the aid of John Baird, an ironworks was set up just north of Stane, but in the extreme south of Shotts parish, from which it took its name. Though it became well established and overlay a rich coalfield, the early collieries seem to have gone largely unrecorded, and the area remained otherwise unimportant for decades. Mail was delivered to the iron company across the moors from Whitburn in West Lothian until the first post office named *'Shotts'* opened in 1834, seemingly about 4km from the original parish centre at Kirk of Shotts. In 1861 the Shotts Iron Company also had a branch foundry in Leith Walk, Edinburgh (which made architectural ironwork), and at one time owned pits near Roslin *(q.v.)*.

**Railways**: In 1864 the North British Railway opened a line from Morningside (Newmains) to Bathgate, passing Blackhall Junction 2 km south of Stane, from which point a lengthy mineral line was laid to serve the ironworks. The Glasgow to Edinburgh line of the Caledonian Railway, which opened in 1869, followed the South Calder Water; Shotts station on this line was sited beside Stane, which had become the area's main village, and soon acquired a post and telegraph office and an inn. The nearby rapidly growing hamlet of Dykehead north of the railway also had an inn. In 1891 a settlement then known as *'Shotts & Torbothie'* had 1140 people, and *'Stane & Burnbrae'* had 1020. This emergent urban centre with its busy ironworks was surrounded by mineral lines and coal pits. Although it acquired a gasworks and eventually became known simply as Shotts, the town never became a burgh.

**Steel-founding, Golf and Football**: Steel-founding began at Shotts around 1900, when the population had reached 5500. Shotts golf club was founded in 1895, and laid out an 18-hole parkland course beside the railway at Blairhead. Dykehead FC played in the Scottish League for just three seasons, 1923–26. Many more people flooded in to mine coal in six or more pits in a crescent north and east of the town, and to work in the iron and steel works. The population in 1931 was over 10,000. The iron and steel works ceased production in 1947, and the railway to Blackhall Junction was closed in 1950, but the population held up; housing was concentrated in Dykehead, plus estates at Springhill and Torbothie. Four coal mines were still in operation and there were two cinemas, *Empire* and *Regal*, but only the general facilities of a large village were available.

**Diesel Engines thrive, Coal and Woollens fail**: By 1953 Hill Hospital and a rail-connected mill were in evidence, and Cummins of Shotts were making diesel engines in a new factory; by 1968 this exported combined diesel engines and generator sets to Switzerland. The mines had all closed by 1963, though a Coal Board training centre and workshops lingered into the 1970s. By 1971 the population had fallen below 10,000, and the cinemas both closed. Heather Valley Woollens – who then employed 105 people using old machinery – closed their factory about 1976; it was taken over by Thistle Knitwear, who provided 70 jobs with SDA backing

*The engine house and chimney of Shotts iron works, pictured in 1971. The house contained the steam-driven blowing engine which provided blast air for the row of furnaces, which stood to the right.* *(JRH)*

but failed in 1979. By 1981 a health centre was open among facilities typical of a small town.

**Prison, Puff Pastry and Privatisation Problems**: A new prison which opened north-west of the town in 1987 was welcomed for the jobs it brought, though if one was to believe the blank shown on the OS map, the inmates were kept in the open air! In 1988–90 the USA-owned Cummins works made engines for British Rail's Class 150 *Sprinter* and Class 158 *Express* trains, but job cuts came in 1991 as train building was stopped by the appalling doctrinaire muddle of rail privatisation. By 1991 only 8750 people remained in Shotts, many suffering from poor health and other disadvantages. Cummins also had a Daventry works by 1992, and of the Shotts factory workforce of 700 in 1995, only 270 were left by November 1996; the works had closed by 2000. Meantime the new Hawthorn Bakery was opened in 1993 by Bell Bakers Ltd, producing readymade puff pastry and other edibles. In 1995 the Central Scotland Forest project, combining public and private bodies, was based at the Hillhousebridge; but afforestation around Shotts was growing only slowly. By 1998 opencasting was active on a vast scale to the south and a smaller pit to the north; Stane primary school was burnt out in 1999. Today, Bells employ 280, and Balfour Beatty Construction about 240.

## SHUNA, Isle of — Map 4, C3

***Small island, Argyll*** — OS 55: NM 7709

Separated from Luing by the 1km wide Shuna Sound, this small knobbly island only 4km long effectively faces towards the mainland of Lorne at Arduaine, 3km to the east. It had many antiquities, and Shuna House was a mansion (ruinous by the 1990s). Shuna was once the site of limestone quarries, and supported nearly 70 people in 1841. This number steadily shrank to 1991 when a fish farm manager was the only resident on an isle otherwise devoted to woodland and sheep grazing.

## SIGHTHILL, Kingsknowe & Wester Hailes — Map 15, B2

***Western parts of Edinburgh,*** *pop. 33,000* — OS 66: NT 2070

When Timothy Pont mapped the Lothians about 1600, *'Balbertoun'* and Easter and Wester *'Hales'* stood beside the Edinburgh to Carnwath road about 6km south-west of the city; Hailes parish school was founded in 1599. The Hailes sandstone quarry – which opened in the early 1600s – long provided slabs for steps, and rubble for building, in colours ranging from white, grey, and blue to pink. Not much housing was built locally for over two centuries, despite successive improvements in the area's transport and job opportunities. By the 1750s a mansion had been built at Saughton Hall, a little to the north, where the Water of Leith turned the Saughton or Stenhouse mills. The Union Canal was opened in 1822 and the Caledonian Railway in 1848. By 1894 a station was open at Kingsknowe. The quarry was very large by 1908, having tunneled beneath the canal and extended northwards to the Hailes brickworks near Longstone Street, which used mudstones from beneath the sandstone, still very actively quarried at Hailes in 1899 by 225 men. The Kingsknowe golf club was founded in 1908, and laid out an 18-hole course.

**Industry and Government Offices**: Sighthill as a settlement was really commenced between the two world wars; Hailes quarry switched from sandstone to mudstone in 1920 but closed in 1943; the brick works was still in production in the 1940s. In 1938 a printing works and the Securex die-casting factory were built at Gylemuir. Around 1950 British Insulated Callendar's Cables (BICC) manufactured electric cables at a works in Calder Road. By then an area south of this road had been developed as a housing estate, and the Broomhouse estate was begun in 1946; by 1951 there were nearly 20,000 people in these drab, boxy developments. The electric tramways had been proposed to be extended to Sighthill, but never actually got beyond their 1950 Stenhouse terminus at Saughton Road South. The first health centre was pioneered in the area in 1953. By 1957 over 18,500m² of government offices of the most basic design had been erected at Saughton. By 1966 the Sighthill laboratory of EMI subsidiary Nuclear Enterprises was well established and winning awards for developments in medical instrumentation. Stevenson College of Further Education was built between 1963 and 1973.

**Canal Blocked to build Horrible Housing**: The soullessly congested and basic Wester Hailes estate was erected astride the railway south of Sighthill for Edinburgh City Council about 1965–75, to accommodate 18,000 unfortunate people; the author stayed in pleasanter barrack blocks in the 1940s. Another blunder was to pipe in the Union Canal at great cost, so nullifying its whole purpose. At least the attempt was made to provide a real central facility, including a large supermarket, and Wester Hailes community school opened in 1978. By 1977 Sighthill had the Burton's biscuit and *Edinburgh Shortbread* factories, William Thyne was making folding cartons, and the national computer centre of the National Coal Board (NCB) was open. About 1979 the Bank of Scotland also opened a new Information Technology centre to cope with the rapid growth in their autotellers, which reached 150 in 1981, and by the 1980s the Scottish Office also had a computer centre. But by 1981 the general range of facilities in the whole area, including Sighthill, was no more than a large village could expect. In 1987 an aqueduct was built to carry the remaining tail end of the canal across the new City Bypass.

**Housing Improvement, Departures and Successes**: A railway station was opened at Wester Hailes in 1987, at which time the government selected the estate for one of four partnership schemes intended to improve Scotland's worst public housing, this area being exceptionally prone to drug abuse and eventually AIDS. But so rapidly had the buildings deteriorated that by 1989 some 250 unlettable flats in the worst multi-storey blocks were of negative value and considered suitable only for clearance. In 1990 the Wester Hailes Community Housing Association made a substantial start on improving the area's appalling housing. But the combustion engineers Laidlaw, Drew left Sighthill for Livingston in the 1980s and Munro & Miller Fittings, in production at Sighthill in 1983, had moved to Broxburn by 1992. However, by 1990 Burton's Biscuits were expanding and Ethicon, a Johnson & Johnson company, was manufacturing surgical products with an expanding workforce of 1500 people, taking in adjoining buildings and planning a large new warehouse; by 1993 they specialised in making wound closure products for an international market.

**Access by Road, Canal – and a Second Station?**: By 1993 there was a newspaper entitled the *Wester Hailes Sentinel*, and by 1996 a Tesco store was open there. By 1994 the Parcel Force depot for Edinburgh West and Fife had been built on the west edge of the Sighthill industrial estate. The Hermiston Gait

Retail Park, an anti-environmental way of shopping primarily accessed from the City Bypass, opened in 1995. In 1995 one of the three centres of the big Scottish Motor Auction Group was at Murrayburn Road. In the late 1990s the M8 was extended through deep hard rock cuttings from Newbridge to terminate in a vast interchange on the city bypass at Hermiston Gait. There's now an *ABC Multiplex* cinema at Wester Hailes – where major engineering in 2000–01 was preparing the canal for full re-opening, hopefully late in 2001.

## SKEABOST — Map 8, A2

***Townships, Isle of Skye,*** *pop. 275 (area)* — OS 23: NG 4148

The fine broch of Dun Suladale overlooks Loch Snizort Beag, at whose head was an ancient chapel with associations with St Columba and the possible site of an ancient bishopric. Nearby crofting townships include Bernisdale, Glen Bernisdale, Preabost, Skeabost and Tote. The 19th century road from Dunvegan to Portree, now replaced by a new stretch of road, crossed the River Snizort at Skeabost Bridge. In 1950, when some 700 people lived in the area, served by the MacDiarmid primary school, a large Victorian shooting lodge was converted into the *Skeabost House Hotel*. This 26-roomed seasonal establishment replaced an earlier inn, which by 1988 was the post office and shop, also dealing in fine tweeds for fashion houses. Although the population had fallen somewhat, there is modern private and council housing. The hotel also now boasts a 9-hole golf course and 13km of salmon fishing; there is access to Forestry Commission woodlands.

## SKELD, Easter & Wester — Map 14, B4

***Shetland communities,*** *pop. 200* — OS 4: HU 3144

Among many natural harbours around the western limb of the Shetland Mainland is Skelda Voe, with natural arches, a standing stone and chambered cairns in the vicinity. At its head is Easter Skeld, where a pier and a school were built in the 19th century; it became a base for cod fishing. By 1953 there was a post office and also a golf course, which remarkably fell into disuse. By 1985 a large new seine netter, small creel boats and sea angling vessels were based at Skelda Voe. Skeld primary school and Reawick post office continue to serve the area.

## SKELLISTER & Garth — Map 14, B3

***Shetland communities,*** *pop. 200* — OS 3: HU 4654

A broch, burnt mound and standing stone show the ancient significance of this isthmus, part of the huge Nesting parish, which includes Whalsay *(q.v.)*; the parish church was evidently at Kirkabister, some 5km north-east. The Skellister and Garth area – accessed from the B9075 – has remained rural, more recently gaining the South Nesting primary school, a post office and telephone exchange. Some 150 to 200 people live in scattered hamlets and crofts, but the post office has closed since the 1970s.

## SKIPNESS & Claonaig — Map 1, B1

***Kintyre (Argyll) hamlets,*** *pop. 100* — OS 62: NR 9057

An ancient dun and chapel, and the 13th century Skipness Castle, were built on a promontory on the east coast of Kintyre. The castle and a mill were shown on Roy's map surveyed about 1750, when they stood at the end of a track from Tarbert via Whitehouse and Glen Bedale. In 1802 it was noted that Skipness was the terminus of an ancient ferry to Kilmichael in Bute, and although this no longer plied by the late 19th century there was still an inn on the coast north of the castle. By 1951 the inn had vanished, and only some 140 people lived in the area, with the minimal facilities of school and post office; the population continued to fall. By about 1972 a new slipway at Claonaig 3km west of Skipness had been provided as the terminus of a summer-only Calmac ferry to Lochranza, using small roll-on vessels. By 1984 there was a caravan and camping site, and in 1992 a larger vessel built in St Monans entered the ferry service, able to carry 18 cars.

## SKIRLING — Map 2, B2

***Tweeddale village,*** *pop. 150* — OS 72: NT 0739

Skirling lies some 4km east of Biggar, tucked away in the Peeblesshire hills at an altitude of 225 metres; 2 km north-east is an ancient hill fort and settlement, and there are fragmentary remains of a medieval castle, demolished in 1568. Skirling became a burgh of barony in 1592, but was shown as a very small place on Pont's map of Tweeddale made about 1600. A parish school opened in 1632. The Roy survey of about 1754 showed Skirling as a considerable hamlet quite well served with a road system; four fair days were scheduled there for 1797. However, apart from Skirling Mill it remained agricultural, was considered too insignificant to be served even by the optimistic builders of the area's railway, and its population steadily declined to under 200 by 1981. There is a village green and some 20th century wrought ironwork; the post office – still open in 1988 – had closed by 1996.

## SLAMANNAN — Map 16, B3

***Village s-w. of Falkirk,*** *pop. 1600* — OS 65: NS 8573

Slamannan stands at an altitude of 155 metres in the upper valley of the River Avon, in the southernmost part of Stirlingshire. It has a medieval motte, and was mentioned in 1275, its Gaelic name being interpreted by some as meaning the *Hill (or Moor) of Manu* or *Mannan (c.f. Clackmannan)*. Although it never became a barony burgh, the name *'Bochastell'* on Pont's map of Stirlingshire, made about 1600, implies a continuing castle on the site of the later mansionhouse. Alongside was a watermill, and *'Balquhatstone'* Kirk appeared close by Slamannan; *'Balmiller'* just downstream speaks for itself. A parish school was opened in 1632. The Roy map made around 1754 showed a hamlet at Slamannan Kirk, which stood beside a winding road linking Airdrie and Falkirk, passing the Black Loch 3km south of the Avon bridge.

**Railway, Coal, Coke and Peat**: The area was rich in coal seams, but there was very little other development until the hilly Slamannan Railway was built in 1840, connecting Slamannan with Airdrie and with Causewayend on the Union Canal. It offered for two years – until the present main line via Falkirk opened in 1842 – the fastest means of travel between Edinburgh and Glasgow. The Slamannan Railway was isolated by its slightly narrow gauge of 4'6" (137 cm) until changed to standard gauge in 1847; eventually it was owned by the North British Railway. In Victorian times many coal pits were opened all over the parish, linked to the railway by a web of mineral lines and served by miners' rows. Coke ovens were built at Jawcraig, 1 km north of the village. The population in 1891 was 1800. In 1895 Slamannan had a station, inn and post and telegraph office, and another post office was open near the Black Loch at Lochside, a mining centre which – combined with Limerigg – held 1400 people in 1891.

**After the Mining – Poverty and Afforestation**: Passenger trains were withdrawn in 1930. The line had been closed by 1953 and lifted by 1955, by which time the coke ovens, all the coal pits and associated mineral railways had disappeared, leaving only scattered bings. By then peat was dug commercially from Darnrig Moss near Jawcraig. In 1951 the approximate populations were: Slamannan 1900 and Limerigg 250. Extensive afforestation under the Central Scotland Woodlands Project began around Limerigg about 1960. Slamannan's secondary school closed, and its population fell, but it retained average village facilities in 1981, with a garage at Jawcraig. In 1991 Slamannan had 1430 people; meantime Limerigg grew slightly. In the late 1980s part of Darnrig Moss became an opencast mine – restored with a lochan and woodlands by 1998. Both Slamannan and Limerigg have post offices and pubs; Limerigg school is still open beside the Black Loch.

## SLEAT

**Map 8, B4**

***Locality, S. Skye,*** *pop. 450 (area)*

OS 32: NG 6303

Sleat (pronounced *Slate*), the southern peninsula of the Isle of Skye, has a relatively sheltered south-east coast which enjoys an exceptionally beautiful view across the Sound of Sleat to the mountains of Knoydart. Kilmore church (4 km north-east) is an ancient building, but little remains to date either the coastal Dun Ela or the tower house of Knock Castle, 2 km beyond Kilmore. In 1549 Donald MacDonald Gorm owned both Sleat and Trotternish, in the north of Skye. *'Armadall'*, both *'Moir' and 'Beg'*, appeared on Pont's distorted map of Skye made about 1600. From the mid 18th century the laird of Sleat, Sir Alexander MacDonald, showed *"supercilious indifference to his clansmen"* (Bray). He had been educated at Eton and tutored by the market economist Adam Smith and by Henry Scott, the third Duke of Buccleuch, owner of much vaster and more fertile areas, and he adopted an extreme policy. His family's mansion of 1815, a rebuilt Armadale Castle, was to be paid for by levying extortionate rents. His tenants and subtenants, goaded beyond endurance, soon upped and left in a body, leaving him to re-people the estate with fewer but more compliant mainlanders. Later Ostaig House was built nearby and an arboretum was created around the castle: trees could not answer back!

**Schools and Steamers**: Eventually schools were established in the tiny townships of Ardvasar and Teangue, and both became post towns; Armadale near Ardvasar became the site of the 19th century steamer pier. In the 1950s one could take ship to Glenelg and Kyle or join the outer isles mail steamer, or join the ferry to Mallaig; all of these carried the occasional car, slung on board by derrick. In 1951 the population in the area was under 300, but although two doctors were then in practice, the other facilities were those of a small village, mostly located at Ardvasar where there was an inn, later known as the *Ardvasar Hotel*. With the withdrawal of the steamers the population declined to under 200 by 1971 and Ardvasar primary school was closed. However, Teangue *(in Gaelic An Teanga)* remained a centre for postal distribution; a side-loading roll-on car ferry to Mallaig was introduced in 1964.

**The Gaelic College repopulates Sleat**: Development recommenced in the 1970s when Iain Noble, laird of the nearby estate of Eilean Iarmain (Isleornsay), established a unique independent Gaelic business college housed in former farm buildings at Ostaig, known as *'Sabhal Mor Ostaig' (Sabhal = 'barn')*. The population in the Ardvasar and Teangue area had risen to over 300 by 1981, but by then Armadale Castle – though still owned by the clan trust – was a roofless ruin, one outbuilding having become the Clan Donald Centre. A youth hostel was open at Armadale by 1982. By 1990 the college offered Gaelic-medium education in Business Studies, to HNC and HND levels; it was extended in 1992–93 with government aid to provide a proper library building and to raise its intake of students to 50 in 1993, with 40 staff. Meantime by 1988, when many new bungalows had been erected, a new primary school for Sleat had been built at Kilmore, and Armadale was the base of the Skye Yacht Club. The car ferry to Mallaig now plies in summer only, replaced in winter by a passenger ferry which also serves Eigg. Accommodation is provided by the traditional *Ardvasar Hotel*, the youth hostel, and the delightfully named *'Hairy Coo'* backpackers' hostel at the *Toravaig House Hotel* by Knock Castle; there is another hostel at Kilmore, plus other accommodation at Ord on the remote west coast of Sleat.

## SMAILHOLM

**Map 3, B3**

***Borders hamlet,*** *pop. 100*

OS 74: NT 6436

A line of remote hills 5 km north-east of Dryburgh shows much evidence of ancient settlement, including hill forts and standing stones; to the south beside the River Tweed is the ancient parish centre of Makerstoun. In the 16th century the stark Smailholm Tower was built to dominate a field which seems otherwise ideal for reivers to herd stolen cattle in privacy, being encircled by a jumble of crags. A parish school, opened in 1622, developed in equal obscurity. The Roy map of about 1754 showed the road from Kelso, 8 km south-east, dividing at *'Smeylem'* for Edinburgh, Earlston and Leaderfoot. Smailholm village stands on high ground 2 km from the tower, having a church, smithy and post office by 1895, and its parish held 340 people in 1901. By 1951 there was a primary school, 39-line telephone exchange and 200 people, but the school and post office had gone by 1976, and by 1991 only 107 people remained. However by 1999 a post office had been resuscitated, for besides its evocative tower (under Historic Scotland), Smailholm lies central to other greater tourist attractions at Dryburgh, Floors and Mellerstain.

## SOAY, Isle of

**Map 8, A4**

***Small island south of Skye,*** *pop. 14*

OS 32: NG 4513

The small infertile dumbell-shaped Isle of Soay *('Sheep Island')* lies south of Skye, dominated by the spiky Cuillin Hills. In the early 19th century, crofters pressured by clearances elsewhere established 25 holdings, and by 1851 there were 150 people. A century later, motor boats from Mallaig served Soay, which was sold in 1946 by its traditional owners the MacLeods to author Gavin Maxwell. For three years he promoted the commercial fishing of basking sharks with the aid of Tex Geddes, to the detriment of the species. Despite its sheltered harbour, communications are poor, and most Soay residents were assisted to leave for Craignure in 1953; the primary school was closed in 1963 when only the Geddes family remained. By 1978, when the population had risen to 13 and two boats fished for lobsters and other shellfish, a fortnightly mail boat to Mallaig was the only regular link with the mainland. In June that year Soay gained the world's first solar-powered telephone exchange, with just three lines. As there were four children the school was reopened, although there was no mains electricity on the isle, no road and no vehicles. Recently there were nine telephones and 14 people including two schoolchildren, but only a monthly mail service was provided.

## SOLLAS & Udal

**Map 7, A2**

***Township, N. Uist,*** *pop. 100* — OS 18: NF 8074

The settlement at Udal on a remote peninsula some 7km west of Newtonferry was occupied continuously from Neolithic times until about 1690, when as a tacksman's township it was finally covered by drifting sand. Sollas *(G.Solas)* is one of a cluster of crofting townships on a more favoured site 3km to the south. It had an early school, already open in 1849 when the hitherto reasonable laird, Lord MacDonald of Sleat, became insolvent, and being hounded by creditors decided to clear his tenants in favour of sheep: no fewer than 600 people were expelled, in what is remembered as one of the ugliest clearances. In the mid 20th century only 150 crofting people were left, falling to 115 by 1981. Udal was excavated by Iain Crawford over a 33-year period in the late 20th century. Dunskellor *(Dun Sgealair)* primary school and a post office remained open as far as 1995.

## SORBIE

**Map 1, C5**

***Small Galloway village,*** *pop. 250* — OS 83: NX 4346

A motte stands beside the Sorbie Burn 6km north of ancient Whithorn; near an even more ancient crannog about 4km to the south-west stands the 15th century tower of Ravenstone Castle. Near the motte is the 16th century L-plan Sorbie Tower, and 1km to the west the ancient roofless ruin of Sorbie church. Roy's map surveyed about 1754 showed mills at Sorbie Kirk, near the road between Powtown and the main Wigtown to Whithorn road; Sorbie's two mills were later known as the Waulk and Creech mills. In 1875 the Wigtownshire Railway *(see Smith, 1969)* was extended from Wigtown through a station at Sorbie to Millisle 1.5km east of Sorbie Tower, and later to both Garlieston and Whithorn; but passenger trains were withdrawn in 1950. Meantime Sorbie creamery was open by about 1900. By 1951 Sorbie also had a post office, telephone exchange, primary school and two inns, serving some 600 people in a wide rural area, but although the railway was closed in 1964 and the population was falling at 1% a year, most of these facilities stayed open to at least 1981. By 1975 an enlarged cheese creamery at Sorbie had replaced four smaller operations, including those at Bladnoch and Port William, but it too was closed about 1990. Forest walks were open nearby by 1996, and the ruin of Ravenstone Castle was for sale in 2000. Sorbie's post office has recently gone, but a pub and guest house are still open.

## SORN

**Map 1, C2**

***Ayrshire small village,*** *pop. 400* — OS 70/71: NS 5526

Sorn is an ancient parish centre on the upper reaches of the River Ayr, 5km east of Mauchline. The keep of Sorn Castle was originally built in 1409. Pont's map of about 1600 emphasisd *'Soirn Castle'*, which stood in a large wooded park opposite to *'Smythy Schaw'; 'wakmills'* lay beside the river both upstream opposite Dalgain and downstream at the site later called Catrine *(q.v.)*. A new church was built in the 17th century. The Roy map showed many ferm touns in the area, which lay at the end of a road from Mauchline. In the 18th century a bridge was built over the River Ayr, and Heron noted in 1799 that the village of Sorn was also known as Dalgain. The Farquharsons built the small mansion of Gilmilnscroft House in the early 19th century: two tongue-twisting names together!

**Coal Pits and Meadowside**: Sorn remained rural throughout the 19th century, so small that quoits was the only team game played locally! Coal was mined on a very small scale at Dalgain, and by Gilmour, Wood & Anderson of Auchinleck at a series of pits 2km south-east of the village near Gilmilnscroft. This enterprise, later worked by Baird's of Lugar, and its workers' cottages at Meadowside near South Logan, had vanished by 1954, leaving various bings extending over Airds Moss towards Lugar. In the 1950s Sorn had a population of about 525, and minimal services apart from the *Sorn Inn*. The NCB's small Sorn drift mine was established at Montgarswood west of Sorn Castle soon after 1947, and operated until 1983; by then the population was only about 400. The *Greyhound Inn* was saved from dereliction in 1997 and the post office is still open.

## SOUTHEND & Dunaverty

**Map 1, A2**

***S. Kintyre village,*** *pop. 450 (area)* — OS 68: NR 6908

The Mull of Kintyre thrusts out from Argyll towards Ulster, ending in 400m high cliffs only 20km from the Emerald Isle. These offer some shelter to a shallow bay with lowland margins, through which run the waters from various small glens. Several early churches left *Kil-* names, and defensive duns abounded. Dunaverty *('Good Fort')* on a promontory within the bay, 10km east of the Mull, was from the sixth century a centre of the *Cinel Gabhran*, a sector of the Scots–Irish kingdom of Dalriada *(see also Dunadd)*. Dunaverty was a seat of the Head King of Dalriada up to about 768, and therefore in the direct line leading to Scotland's capitals at Old Scone and Edinburgh. There is a medieval motte 4km east; the later Castle of Dunaverty was a refuge for Robert Bruce in 1306. Pont's map of about 1600 showed the area thickly settled, but the castle fell into ruin.

**Lighthouses, Lifeboat and Mill**: The local population seems to have dropped by the time of Roy's survey made about 1750, when the sole land access was a track up Conie Glen to Campbeltown about 12 km to the north. A crofter regularly displayed a warning light on the steep cliffs of the Mull until the Northern Lighthouse Board built the second of its lighthouses there, first lit in 1788. However the uniquely designed lighthouse on the steep islet of Sanda, about 6km south-east of Dunaverty, was not completed until 1850. Meantime in 1839 a new water mill had been built at Machrimore on the Conie Water. A lifeboat station was opened near Dunaverty in 1869, and by the 1890s the parish name Southend had been applied to a township between the mill and Dunaverty. In 1895 the Lighthouse Board's own tender *Signal* was wrecked on the Mull in fog.

**Golf, Keil School and Holidays**: Local farmers founded a golf club at Southend in 1889 and gave it the traditional name Dunaverty; an 18-hole links course was laid out. In 1900 the parish population was 730. The unusual Keil Technical School on the coast west of Dunaverty was destroyed by fire in 1924; its proprietors then re-established the school in Dumbarton. The lifeboat station was eventually closed in 1930, but a coastguard station was open by the 1950s near the tiny village of Southend. This village served a scattered and slowly declining parish population (501 in 1971) and also possessed two hotels, doctors, the mill and a pier. By 1974 three caravan sites and a camping site were available. The Mull light was automated in 1988 and Sanda in 1992. In 1991 the parish had only 455 residents. The school, an inn and one caravan and camping site remain open near the coastal golf course.

## SOUTHERNESS — Map 2, B5

***Solway coast village,*** *pop. 250* — OS 84: NX 9754

On the Solway coastal lowlands about 20km south of Dumfries was the one-time village of (East) Preston with its cross; Wreaths Tower was built 1.5km to the west in the 16th century. About 2 km to the south is Southerness Point, which projects far into the Solway Firth. A crude early beacon tower was built there in 1748 for the Burgh of Dumfries *(see Hay & Stell)*; it was described on the Roy map of about 1754 as a lighthouse, and later raised and improved with an oil lamp, but long remained isolated. In the late 18th century Richard Oswald of Auchincruive laid out feus for a model village, hoping in vain to mine coal. In the 20th century the rocky shore set in wide sands attracted car-borne visitors, and an exposed 18-hole golf course was established in 1947. The 34-room *Paul Jones Hotel*, named after a Kirkbean pirate, was open by 1954. A large holiday village and caravan park had been laid out by 1977; by 1994 this had an amusement centre and other developments, claimed by some to have ruined the area's environment and wildlife. However, by 1996 the RSPB ran Mersehead Farm, 5km to the west, as a coastal nature reserve. By 1997 there were two caravan parks at Southerness, a second golf course had been laid out farther inland at East Preston, the *19th Hole* pub was in business, and substantial new housing areas had been built.

## SOUTH QUEENSFERRY & Dalmeny — Map 15, A1

***Small town & village, F. of Forth,*** *pop. 9300* — OS 65: NT 1278

The largely overland route between Dunfermline and Edinburgh was much used by Queen Margaret from 1069, but was interrupted by the choppy waters of the Firth of Forth. In the second quarter of the 12th century her son King David I arranged for the monks of Dunfermline Abbey to provide a regular ferry service. Dalmeny's ancient church on the hilltop above the ferry dates from about 1150, and became the centre of a parish in the county of Linlithgow (West Lothian). The settlement now known as South Queensferry – in 1164 called the *'Queen's Port of Ferry'* – was built on the shore, being referred to by its modern name of Queensferry from 1184. On the shore to the east is Barnbougle Castle, originally built for the Moubrays in Norman times but repeatedly altered. In 1315 Queensferry became one of Dunfermline Abbey's Ecclesiastical Burghs, and a Carmelite friary with its tiny fortified private church was founded there about 1330 by Sir George Dundas. His castle already stood on the hills 2 km south-west of the friary; it was perhaps of timber, for the present-day Z-plan tower of Old Dundas Castle is now dated to around 1500.

**Forts, Communications, Burghs and Trading**: After the Black Death catastrophe of 1350, Queensferry was re-chartered in 1364 (though whether as a regality or Royal burgh seems uncertain). Nearly a century of evidently slow recovery enabled a fine church to be built from 1441 onwards. Ships from South Queensferry traded into the Baltic around the time (the 1490s) that Sir George's successor John Dundas fortified Inchgarvie, the *'rough island'* in mid-channel. The Reformation extinguished the friary. However, Pont's map of Lothian made around 1600 showed a heavily settled area, and although *'South Queenes Ferry'* was only small, it was already linked with Edinburgh by a road across a causeway, evidently that which still carries the B924 before it rises over the hill towards Cramond Brig. Dalmeny was chartered as a burgh of barony in 1616. By 1621 the tiny harbour at Queensferry was importing a little wine, but contributing under 1.5% of other customs duties; Queensferry was confirmed as a Royal Burgh in 1636. In 1655 Tucker noted it as *"a small town, where formerly goods have been landed"* – but this was now being prevented by the Cromwellian authorities. Queensferry acquired a post office as early as 1689 because of its strategic location between Edinburgh, Perth and the North.

**Herrings, Coaches, Walled Garden and Slippery Soap**: Defoe described Queensferry as being *"a very good town"* at the time of his visit about 1715, when the herring fishery was superabundant. At that time the brick-walled garden to Dalmeny House was being built by the Marquess of Annandale, who had the bricks made on the spot. The road to Edinburgh was turnpiked in the 1750s, and from 1765 a coach ran twice daily from Edinburgh carrying mainly ferry passengers to the *Hawes Inn* (also known as Newhalls). Soap was manufactured locally until about 1789, the ferry surviving as almost the sole other basis for the village. In 1797 it carried a daily postal service, and both South and North Queensferry were post towns. Heron noted in 1799 a population of 800 at most; *"it had formerly a good deal of shipping, but has now almost none. A soap-work flourished here for some time, but is also fallen off"*.

**A Distillery in a Mansion**: A remarkable change of use for Dundas Castle took place about 1800, when for a time it was *"fitted up as a distillery"* (*see MacGibbon & Ross*). In 1814–17 the Earl of Rosebery replaced Dalmeny House with a new mansion, Scotland's first in the Gothic Revival style, designed by William Wilkins. The harbour was rebuilt in 1809–18, and from 1820 steam vessels worked the ferry; by 1824 Port Edgar, a short way to the west, was also a small harbour. Storrie's brewery was in use by 1825, but according to Chambers in 1827 South Queensferry was *"a decayed town; there is no shipping belonging to it, except a few fishing-boats"*. However in 1832 Cobbett travelled from Edinburgh on *"the very finest turnpike-road that I ever saw"*, and crossed the Firth in about ten minutes in a large sailing-boat. A branch line from Ratho via Kirkliston was opened to Dalmeny by the North British Railway (NBR) in 1866; it was extended down to Queensferry

*The Forth Rail Bridge – the eighth wonder of the world when it was built between 1883 and 1890. The Road Bridge beyond was opened in 1964, replacing the ancient ferry.* (SMPC / Jim Dunn)

shore in 1868, and to a greatly enlarged Port Edgar ten years later, in connection with a ferry for the new Dunfermline railway. Shale was mined on the Dalmeny estate, and a shale oil works was built just south of Dalmeny village in 1871, with workers' housing in Dalmeny Rows. About 170 men were employed, processing 30,000 tonnes of shale a year to produce about 4.5 million litres of crude oil. A sandstone quarry, open at Dalmeny by 1874, was *"practically worked out"* by 1892.

**Whisky Developments**: Meantime in 1877 Stewart & Co of Kirkliston joined DCL as founder members of this new grain whisky combine. In the 1880s they built tall new red-brick blending premises at South Queensferry, where in 1886 DCL owned over a hectare of rail-connected bonded stores and bottling plant, continuing to operate in connection with Kirkliston distillery. Barnbougle Castle was rebuilt as a mansion in 1881 for the 5th Earl of Rosebery. In 1888 Beveridge found the *Hawes Inn "a very comfortable and well patronised hostelry"*. In 1887 J Arthur was building wooden steam launches; at some time a gasworks was set up.

**The Forth Rail Bridge and its Defences**: Fortunately for posterity, work on the foundations intended to carry Sir Thomas Bouch's frail-looking Forth rail bridge had been abandoned in 1880 after the fall of his Tay Bridge *(see Ellis, 1955)*. The current Forth Bridge, funded by a consortium of railway companies and designed by Fowler and Baker, mainly comprises three immense riveted steel cantilevers each weighing some 15,000 tonnes, erected on new foundations – including the islet of Inchgarvie on which the central cantilever was founded. Each pair of cantilevers is linked by suspended spans. The bridge was built between 1883 and 1890 by Tancred, Arrol & Co, headed by William Arroll, who used the then novel electric light to facilitate the work (*see Murray, 1988)*. The hilltop fabrication site at Dalmeny has continued in use as the Forth Bridge Workshops. The connecting lines which completed the NBR main line from Saughton Junction to Inverkeithing and Burntisland, and the link to Winchburgh Junction, were also opened in 1890, making Dalmeny's new station a significant junction point. A battery for two 120mm guns was built at Dalmeny between 1894 and 1901, plus a smaller battery on Inchgarvie, to protect the bridge from attack by sea. A steam ferry continued to ply across the Forth, though much less frequently than before.

**Living with the Rail Bridge and the Navy**: Murray called South Queensferry *"a small quaint place"* in 1894. The Dalmeny parish population (including the burgh) was around 4000 in 1901. Port Edgar was rebuilt about 1910–12 as a base for *'torpedo boat destroyers'*, and ugly naval installations associated with Rosyth included the *'Kirkliston'* RN Food Supply Depot on the hilltop. The Oakbank Oil Company of Bathgate absorbed the Dalmeny Oil Company in 1915; the mines and oil-works closed in the 1920s. In 1924 the DCL plant was blending whisky for export, in the guise of William Sanderson, for whose *'Vat 69'* blend a prominent bonded warehouse was built in the 1930s. In 1934 the NBR's successor the LNER (London & North Eastern Railway) sold the ferry rights to Denny's of Dumbarton, who built and operated roll-on diesel-electric ferries. Two were built in 1934 *(Queen Margaret* and *Robert the Bruce)*; as traffic built up the *Mary Queen of Scots* was added in 1949, and finally in 1956 came *Sir William Wallace*. In 1951 the parish population was 3700, and the facilities of a large village were available. Three more hotels were open, but there appeared to be no seaborne trade or fishing extant by the 1950s.

**Electronics and the Forth Road Bridge**: In 1962 the Californian electronics firm Hewlett-Packard set up a major factory beside Dalmeny station; by 1979 they made computers, and this – their leading UK plant – employed over 600 people. As road traffic grew so did ferry queues, but ferries continued to ply from piers at the *Hawes Inn* until 1964, the opening year of the 1000m-span Forth Road Bridge, designed by Freeman Fox and Mott Hay & Anderson. This suspension structure strides across the edge of the town on its way to Fife; it contains 30,000 tonnes of welded steel and also carries a footpath and cycleway. A new 100-room hotel, *Forth Bridges Lodge*, was built beside its toll plaza at the same time. As yachting built up from Queensferry harbour and later from Port Edgar, an inshore lifeboat station was opened in 1967, the year the blending and bottling plant lost its rail connection when the branch railway down to Queensferry was closed.

**Suburbanisation and Storing Oil and Water**: The twin villages, already steadily developing as dormitories, were placed in Edinburgh City District in 1975. Their combined population had passed the 6000 mark by 1971. Further estate developments continued, and the new 9-hole Dundas Parks golf course was opened in the parkland at Dundas Castle about 1980. In the mid 1970s the huge derelict oil shale bing near Dalmeny was hollowed out to contain a large but hidden tank farm, for the North Sea oil export terminal built for the Forth Ports Authority at Hound Point. This stores oil which arrives by pipeline from the north via Grangemouth, and also holds ships' tank-washing water. Forth Ports was privatised in 1992, when its former *'Authority'* tag was dropped; its successful terminal was expanded in 1992–93 and expected to ship 36 million tonnes of crude oil in 1995.

**Dormitory and Yachting Centre**: The DCL *'Vat 69'* blending and bottling plant was closed in 1984–85 and soon demolished. The rail bridge was floodlit by Scottish Power from the time of its centenary celebrations in 1990. By 1991 the parish population was 9313, with a young and quite well-educated dormitory character. By 1994 Port Edgar Marina was no longer a naval facility, but a yacht harbour and sailing school which sold boats. The RN Food Supply Depot closed in 1996, and the Royal Elizabeth Dockyard with considerable accommodation was sold to Highcross in 1996. Dormitory development has continued.

**Silicon to High Speed Chip – Digital to Motorola**: In 1989 a large new semiconductor factory west of South Queensferry was opened by the Digital Equipment Corporation – alone in Britain at the time able to design and manufacture direct from raw silicon to end product. In mid 1993 its 650 workers made AXP microchips, operating at double the speed then prevailing, for their *'Alpha AXP'* personal computer assembled at Ayr. But early in 1995, when employment was down to about 525, Digital sold the plant to Motorola of East Kilbride, who planned to recruit 100 more staff at Queensferry (but Motorola had problems globally in 2001). The Hewlett Packard factory, a leader among the 65 plants worldwide that had been established during the founders' lifetimes, was by then exporting all over the world. In 1992 a remarkable 40% of its output of telecommunications and medical testing equipment went to the USA. From 1992 it also accommodated the Scottish Software Partner Centre; by mid 1993 over twenty firms were involved, including Cray Systems. Agilent (telecoms testing equipment) are now significant employers also.

**Bridge Problems**: In 1993 the Major government – whose priorities were so strange that for a time they actually denied British Rail the cash to continue painting the rusting steelwork of the magnificent rail bridge – announced plans for a second suspension bridge for road traffic, to be built west of the 1960s bridge. Fife Regional Council backed this, Edinburgh District opposed it – the city being quite unable to cater for any further increase in car traffic. In 1995 the government conceded a public inquiry into their scheme, but by 2000 new and wiser counsels had prevailed and *'park and ride'* facilities were laid out at Inverkeithing instead. Although repainting of the Forth Bridge was resumed for Railtrack in the late 1990s, it had to be broken off in 2000 because of various problems. A *Travel Inn* has appeared (opposite the old motel); in S. Queensferry, the historic waterside *Hawes Inn* is one of several hostelries. Queensferry High School now has over 800 pupils, and a cycleway connects with Edinburgh.

**The Past Conserved**: Despite significant suburban growth and some industrial development, Queensferry (as locals simply call it) retains its historic core, now a Conservation Area; this contains buildings of quality from the late medieval period onwards, its Friary Church being a uniquely complete survival, and its Tolbooth a fine one. The narrow, winding main street strongly evokes the character of a small Scottish sea-port of the pre-industrial period.

## SOUTRA, Fala & Blackshiels — Map 3, A3

***Midlothian hamlets,*** *pop. 100* — OS 66: NT 4558

The Roman road from the south via Lauderdale crossed the bleak Soutra Hill, and was evidently still the main land route into Scotland in the 12th century, when Augustinian monks selected its summit to build the highest monastery in Britain, at 370m above sea level. The extensive red sandstone buildings of their Soutra Hospital appear to have formed the main primitive medical centre in Scotland. In its heyday it is believed to have contained about 300 people, patients and carers, but seems to have ceased work in the 15th century. *'Soltra'* was still emphasised on Pont's map of about 1600, but later it vanished, leaving visible only the scant remains of the Soutra Aisle. Roy's map of about 1754 showed Fala, also called Blackshiels, as a tiny village on the road some 3km north of Soutra, with a watermill at Fala Dam and a nearby mansionhouse. By 1773 an inn had been built at a height of 250m between Fala and Soutra, as a staging point for the Edinburgh to Wooler coaches, and Blackshiels post office first opened in 1796. By 1901 Fala & Soutra parish held 320 people, a church and a post and telegraph office. By 1951 the 200 people in the area also had a school, and two doctors – no longer evident by 1981. However, as late as 1978 the now-closed Fala primary school had 22 pupils, and the post office stayed open until about 1991, when the population was only 100. The *Juniper Lea Hotel* has now become *Juniperlea* restaurant. A large wind farm with some 24 aerogenerators was erected on Soutra Hill in 2000 by Renewable Energy Systems for Scottish Power.

## SPANGO VALLEY — Map 5, B5

***Urban extension of Greenock,*** *pop. 14,200* — OS 63: NS 2475

Timothy Pont's map of Renfrewshire, dating from about 1600, showed *'Alla mill'* south of Gourock on the headwaters of the *'Spango River'*, a hill burn that rises 3km south-west of Greenock and flows west to Inverkip. This strange name derives from the Gaelic *Spang*, meaning a thin sheet of metal. It probably relates to the output of the Drumshantie copper mine which was an early feature in the area, though it had been abandoned by 1799. By the 1750s a hill road linked Greenock with Inverkip, passing Spango Farm. From 1865 the newly opened Wemyss Bay Railway had a station named Ravenscraig, where the Gourock road met the main road. The Greenock poorhouse and asylum (later renamed Ravenscraig Hospital) was built high on the hillside 1km east of the station and was described by Murray as *"imposing"* in 1894. Gateside Hospital a little farther north-east had also been built by the 1920s, but Ravenscraig station failed to attract nearby development, and was closed in the 1930s. In the 1946 Regional Plan it was reckoned that half Greenock's population required rehousing; Spango was the obvious location. By 1951 Greenock Prison (east of Ravenscraig), the 81-bed Rankin Memorial Maternity Hospital in Munro Street, the Larkfield Hospital near its Gateside predecessor and the first town council estates gave the area a fast-growing population of 7000.

**Spango and IBM**: The first 11,000m$^2$ branch factory of the huge USA firm IBM was built in 1951–52, steered to the area to relieve chronic decline in the local shipbuilding industries.

Initially it made typewriters and punch card equipment, the early method of input to the then novel computers. By 1971 the enlarged works employed some 2000 people and made a variety of computer terminals and interfacing equipment. In the fifties and sixties several more housing estates – eventually including Ravenscraig, Larkfield and Braeside – were added to house IBM workers and to relieve the extreme congestion in Greenock proper, leading to the opening of the new Branchton station a little to the east of the former station site at about the time the line was electrified in 1967. A total population of 31,000 had been reached by 1971; hotels and public houses were excluded as a matter of council policy, and the facilities in the area were scarcely even at village level. Scarcely surprising, then, that half the population left the area over the next 20 years.

**National Semiconductor Phoenix**: National Semiconductor UK (NS), another American-owned electronics firm which had spent several unhappy years trying to make good in Cumbernauld, moved to Larkfield in 1970. They employed 450 people making sound reproduction equipment and semiconductor devices, when the factory burned down in 1977. However, 125 members of the enthusiastic workforce then moved to America for several months to learn new techniques while the plant was rebuilt and re-equipped. It was back in production within eight months, making 10 cm wafers from each of which up to 1780 micro-circuits could be cut; it was intended to employ 800 people by 1980 and to export 75% of NS Scotland's output.

**Electronics, Hospitals and Poverty Hand in Hand?**: By 1981 the Larkfield Hospital had been transformed into a 426-bed district general hospital called the Inverclyde Royal, and the 419-bed Ravenscraig Hospital coped with psychiatric and geriatric patients. Despite the sunrise industries, the total population in the Spango area had fallen. A smaller works built for Lee Jeans was handed over to IBM, who employed some 2300 people in 1979, a substantial increase in two years; they planned further expansion and by 1984 had their own railway halt, less than 2 km from Branchton station. But whereas NS had planned major expansion in 1984, 1985 saw instead a 450-job layoff. Two branch factories, however large and resilient, cannot alone be relied on to sustain a big town, particularly in a recession, and by 1987 the Greenock & Port Glasgow parliamentary constituency, including Spango, was the fifth highest in Scotland in terms of unemployment. However, by 1989 Greenock High School had been relocated beside the railway at Spango. The 1991 population was about 14,200.

**Clouds pass across the Copper Sun**: At the peak IBM employed some 2500 people at the plant in 1989–91, largely making personal computers (PCs). But then the company made its first losses for decades, and 60 redundancies at Spango were announced in 1992; however in 1993 an IBM workforce of 2300 made over a million PCs there. By 1994 IBM had 120,000 $m^2$ of floorspace in the Spango valley; the plant was the centre of development for all IBM monitors, and for the design and manufacture of PCs for the European and adjacent markets. In 1995 IBM, Apple and Motorola were developing the Power PC, a joint project for which East Kilbride would make chips and Spango some of the hardware.

**National Semiconductor and Lithgow Electronics**: Meantime in 1991 NS had recruited electronic design engineers for telecom integrated circuits, and 250 jobs were added at Larkfield in 1992, bringing their total to 1500. Though much smaller than IBM, this was the most extensive plant of multinational NS – some 28,000 $m^2$ in 1994. By mid 1996 NS employed 1800 at Spango, but announced that 200 jobs would be cut later in the year due to a newly arisen world oversupply of computer chips. Lithgow Electronics, an offshoot from the Greenock shipbuilders, made monitors and cable harnesses on the Larkfield Industrial Estate, by 1994 trading as Clairemont Electronics. By then new housing had practically linked Spango with Gourock. In 1995 the local Health Trust put the site of the recently-closed Rankin Memorial Hospital on the market for housing. Today IBM employs around 5000, having added software development and a call centre to their production. Greenock High School has a roll of almost 700, and there are primary schools, post offices and a library.

## SPEAN BRIDGE — Map 5, B1

***Lochaber village**, pop. 525* — OS 41: NN 2281

Before entering the Great Glen the River Spean flows through a 30 m deep gorge, where the High Bridge on General Wade's military road between Inverness and Fort William was built in 1723 or 1736 (authorities differ!); Heron thought it *"magnificent"* in 1799. It was superseded by a new arch, erected in 1819 by the Parliamentary Commissioners to Telford's design on a less spectacular site 2 km upstream, to which the rebuilt road was diverted. From that point the Laggan road, completed in 1821, diverged due east up Glen Spean. A tiny settlement grew at the new bridge, which had become the strategic point in the vast Kilmonivaig parish, and by 1838 had a post office; it slowly developed into a village. The Spean Bridge Hotel was *"good"* to Murray in 1894. The famous High Bridge was left to decay after 1893, and began a slow collapse in 1913, but although no longer on the map it has left spectacular remains.

**Beer Trains, Commandos, Golf and Trees**: In 1894 the West Highland Railway was opened, with a station and crossing point at Spean Bridge. In 1903 this became the substantial but little-used junction for the highly uneconomic and ill-starred Invergarry & Fort Augustus Railway (I&FA), built through the gorge and alongside Loch Lochy for the beer tycoon Lord Burton. After a highly chequered career the I&FA closed to passengers in 1933 – the year that widening of the Telford road bridge was completed – and it was abandoned in 1946, though its booking office still survives! *(See Thomas, 1965, for a classic account of these two lines.)* During the 1939–45 war, commandos trained in the wild country around Spean Bridge; a striking monument designed by Scott Sutherland was erected in 1952, 2 km west of Spean Bridge. This was then still a small village of fewer than 250 people, but with the *Spean Bridge Hotel*, and 80 secondary pupils in the school. A golf club founded in 1954 laid out a 9-hole parkland course south of the village, in use by 1969; it had been extended to 18 holes by 1989. Meantime the vast Leanachan Forest had been planted to the south.

**Tourism and Timber**: Though the school had been reduced to primary status by 1976, the local tourist industry had burgeoned since the 1950s, especially with the expansion of coach tours, for which Spean Bridge became a regular stop. In 1981 Spean Bridge had a typical range of village facilities, including the calling point for two mobile banks. A number of new activities had been established, including a substantial

*Spean Bridge station building, dating from 1894. Once the junction for Fort Augustus, it has been converted into the 'Old Station' restaurant. The station is still in use on the Glasgow–Fort William line. (JRH)*

Pitlochry Knitwear shop and cafe, new self-service grocery and half a dozen guest houses, and also holiday homes; two new garages and a restaurant opened, plus a modern joinery factory making roof trusses. At that time the post office was actually part of the railway station; the nearest doctor was based 16km away at Fort William. In 1991 thanks to British Rail's remarkable reluctance to handle the timber traffic, Ferguson of Spean Bridge was a substantial long-distance timber haulier. Passenger trains continued to call, and in the 1990s the attractive station building was converted into the *Old Station Restaurant*. Local hotels and other accommodation have been boosted following the skiing developments at nearby Aonach Mor on the Fort William road.

## SPINNINGDALE (or Invervehin) — Map 9, B2

**E. Sutherland hamlet,** *pop. under 100* — OS 21: NH 6789

The map of Sutherland prepared for Blaeu by Gordon about 1650 showed *'Spainidail'*, where a burn flowing from Loch Migdale entered the Dornoch Firth. Roy's survey of about 1750 showed a roadless clachan in that location with the name *'Invervehin'*. In the late 18th century a 4-storeyed water-powered cotton spinning mill was built there – aimed at counteracting the effects of the Highland clearances – by the textile entrepreneurs David Dale and George Mackintosh, plus George Dempster and Robert Dunmore. The burn came to be called the Migdale Burn and the older name, which anglicised as Spinningdale and was perhaps taken as a good omen, took over from Invervehin. But when the mill was ruined by fire in 1808 it must have been thought to be too remote from sources of raw materials and markets to be worth rebuilding, and was left standing in decay. Spinningdale remains as a hamlet; a caravan and camping site was open for a time around 1974 but there is now little more than an inn and post office.

## SPOTT — Map 3, B2

**E. Lothian hamlet,** *pop. 200* — OS 67: NT 6775

The hilly parish of Spott, some 4km south of Dunbar, is notable for a standing stone and for the hill fort known as *The Chesters*. Several local placenames appeared on the Pont map of around 1600. The Roy map of about 1754 showed a roadless area beside the *'Brox Burn'*, now called the Spott Burn, south of which was a mansion named Spott. Perhaps this represented the old Hall; this had vanished by 1901, when the OS map showed the new Spott House emparked, and a basic road system. Two widely spaced mills stood beside the burn, but beside Spott church and its parish school – open as late as 1958, now closed – was just a small hamlet. One mill has since vanished, Spott House appears to have lost its park, and the farming parish which had 280 residents in 1951, held only 150 in 1971 – but it had recovered to 208 people by 1991; there are still two old dovecotes.

## SPRINGBURN — Map 15, D4

**N. part of Glasgow,** *pop. 33,000* — OS 64: NS 6067

St Rollox or Roche was the dedicatee of a medieval church in the upland area of Barony parish about 3km north of Glasgow, whose High Street was eventually extended northwards as Springburn Road to Bishopbriggs and Kirkintilloch. The area comprised only farms and private mansions such as Cowlairs, which existed by 1841, perhaps named after a farm where Highland beasts were held ready for Glasgow market. Real growth started in 1831, when the coal-carrying Garnkirk & Glasgow Railway (G&GR) opened its east–west route to Glebe Street terminus at the Townhead, about 1km north of Glasgow cathedral, and built its workshops there; G&GR trains reached 20mph. In 1838–42 the Edinburgh & Glasgow Railway (E&G) built their line through the area on a north–south alignment west of Springburn Road, placing Cowlairs station at the end of Cowlairs Road. From there the almost level line from Edinburgh plunged down to the city on an incline at 1 in 41 and through a tunnel to the Queen Street terminus. An engine house with a 27m-tall chimney contained a stationary steam engine, built by Kerr, Neilson & Co of Stobcross to draw E&G trains up the hill, by means of a continuous hemp rope some 5km in length, weighing 15 tonnes.

**Sunday Trains, Big Church, Tiny Houses**: When the line opened in 1842 an interval service of 8 weekday trains was provided, plus some Sunday trains, resulting in a parish church being urgently built for the evidently sinful new settlement of Springburn! Such priorities now seem peculiar, for the early dwellings in Cowlairs Road were the poorest type of tenement, comprising *'single ends'* or one-room houses, some largely underground (see John Thomas's classic book *The Springburn Story*). In 1841–43 the E&G erected its Cowlairs Works at Springvale Farm, between Hawthorn Street and Gourlay Street and immediately west of the station. In 1842 a 5-tonne battery electric locomotive, the brainchild of Aberdonian Robert Davidson and probably the first of its kind in the world, was tried out on the level stretch of the new line above the incline at Eastfield, but the technology was half a century ahead of its time and was unfortunately not developed further at Springburn.

**Ropes and Locomotives**: In 1844 rope haulage on the incline was replaced by the relatively sophisticated steam banking engines *Hercules* and *Sampson*, designed by the E&G's locomotive engineer William Paton and built in the company's Cowlairs Works, the first works in Scotland to combine locomotive, carriage/wagon construction, and repairs. These locomotives worked the incline for three years, cutting the movement costs by two-thirds; but their fierce blast damaged the tunnel roof, so from 1847 an improved method of rope haulage was devised instead, using a wire rope. In 1849 the Townhead passenger terminus of the original G&GR line became redundant when its new owners the Caledonian Railway (CR) opened a diversion line 300 m farther north, crossing over the E&G tunnel and under the canal to terminate at Buchanan Street. But the 6 ha of ground east of Springburn Road, between this and the old line, found a new role in 1853–57 as the site for the CR's compactly laid out St Rollox locomotive and carriage works, which catered for the major needs of what soon became Scotland's largest railway company.

**Springburn Station, Model Village and Cowlairs Works**: The E&G Sighthill branch was approved in 1853, with Springburn passenger station and the Sighthill goods station, where by 1855 the rail carters Wordie & Co had a base. By 1870 some 40 locomotives a year were built at the NBR Cowlairs works, which were rebuilt under Dugald Drummond around 1880. He changed employers to the CR in 1882, and soon had the St Rollox carriage works rebuilt in 1882–84, bringing the iron foundry and paint shops south of the line, though separated by the Corporation refuse destructor of 1880–95 and the Tharsis Sulphur & Copper Company premises. From 1858 a triangular junction on the E&G just north of Hawthorn Street was the starting point of their ally the Glasgow, Dumbarton & Helensburgh Railway. Growing pressure on the minimal local housing resources led the E&G in 1863 to promote a competition for the layout of a model village at Cowlairs. This was won by Andrew Heiton of Perth, but only six blocks were built to his interesting designs, for in 1865 the North British Railway (NBR) absorbed the E&G. In 1866 the new owners chose the Cowlairs works as its locomotive and carriage building centre, soon employing some 1250 people. (Its activities were fully described by Bremner.)

**Hyde Park for Engines Hot and Cold**: Springburn's rapid rise to importance in the second half of the 19th century was also due to locomotive building for sale, which local entrepreneurs – exploiting established local skills – rapidly developed on a massive scale to meet world needs. The largest establishment was Walter Neilson's Hyde Park Locomotive Works, established in 1860 on a site west of the Sighthill branch railway to replace his foundry at Hyde Park Street in Stobcross. Walter Neilson imported Henry Dübs as works manager, but found him *"a most pig-headed German"*; in 1864 Dübs went off to found his own works *(see Queen's Park)*. Neilson – whose judgment of men was suspect – later adopted as partner the clever but unscrupulous James Reid, who came from Kilmaurs. Meantime in 1861 Hyde Park built a unique ski-equipped spiked-wheel *'ice locomotive'* for Russia, and in 1862 sold their first locomotive to Egypt; in the 1870s Neilson produced large 0–8–0 tank engines for use on steep gradients in India.

**Church, Beer, Cream, Exploitation and Trickery**: The town rapidly grew, the prominent spired Townhead Blochairn Church on Royston Hill being built in 1865–66. In 1866 Peter Wordie of Edinburgh built a brewery in Petershill Road. The Blochairn Ironworks was founded by 1880, and then the Barony Poorhouse served the ancient parish; later it was more sympathetically called the Foresthall Hospital. Cowlairs FC played three seasons in the Scottish League between 1890 and 1895. Meantime the Cowlairs Co-operative Society was founded in 1881, soon becoming the area's largest trader and building a creamery by stages between 1895 and 1911. In 1875 the City of Glasgow Union Railway was opened for freight only between Bellgrove and Springburn, where a new four-platform station was provided in 1887 for a new NBR passenger service through Barnhill. In the late 1880s the NBR shamelessly exploited their staff including engine drivers, to the point of extreme damage to health; serious strikes resulted in 1890. Springburn entrepreneurs also preyed on each other: about 1883 James Reid regrettably tricked Walter Neilson out of his share of the Hyde Park Works.

**Five Locomotive Works corner the British Market**: Stung but undismayed, Neilson alone immediately founded the Clyde Locomotive Company, which erected the smaller Clyde Locomotive Works east of the Sighthill branch railway in 1884–85; this brought the Springburn total to five locomotive building concerns. It was claimed in 1889 (by an admittedly biased source!) that 85% of the locomotives built in Britain came from Glasgow – all of them steam. Meantime the Clyde company had supplied two locomotives to the Ayrshire & Wigtownshire Railway in 1887, but was not a commercial success, and was sold in 1888 to Sharp, Stewart of the Atlas Works in Manchester – who then transferred their activities and the Atlas Works name to Springburn. In 1890 Sharp, Stewart built engines for Holland, soon followed by others for Belgium, and in 1894 the first 4–6–0 locomotives in Britain, for the Highland Railway. During the 1890s the firm – which also made machine tools – employed on average some 1400 people. About 1880 the Eclipse Works of Frederick Braby & Co was erected, apparently to produce the galvanised corrugated iron sheets then used as cladding for industrial buildings, for Dutch barns and bothies, and to replace thatch on croft houses. The Germiston Ironworks of Arrol's Bridge & Roof Company was established about 1883 – later extended and sold to A J Main & Co.

**Hyde Park and the Reids dominate the Town**: By the time of his death in 1893 James Reid had built Belmont, the largest private mansion in Glasgow, 1 km north-east of Springburn; his four sons then took over the business, whose employment averaged 2300 during the decade. In 1894 their Hyde Park Works built 12 locomotives for Japan in 84 days from the date of contract. (Interestingly, from 1898 to 1903 the firm was known as Neilson, Reid & Co.) In the 1890s congested Springburn was less than 1 km across, excluding the NB works. The tiny town's tenements somehow contained an amazing 27,000 people, supporting among other facilities a chemist's shop and a local newspaper, the *St Rollox and Springburn Express* (which later failed). Springburn Park with its bandstand was laid out south of Belmont between 1892 and 1904. Perhaps a pang of conscience led the Reid family to donate a great glasshouse, built in the park in 1900 as the Winter Gardens; bands played there too.

**Facilities and Electric Trams**: Public baths were opened in 1897 and a public hall was built in Springburn in 1905; police and fire stations were added. Sheds were built in 1893–94 for horse-drawn trams, behind which was placed the tiny power station for Glasgow Corporation's first electrified route, opened in 1899 between the foot of Balgrayhill Road and Mitchell Street in the city centre, via Springburn Road. In 1898 the city built a depot for its electric trams at Keppochhill Road, but in 1904 the redundant horse tram sheds became the large Springburn Steam Laundry.

**US Competition and the North British Locomotive Company**: Meantime American locomotive building competition was becoming intense; by the early 1900s Baldwins of USA produced one serviceable engine in under 5 man-years of work, as against 12.5 man-years required for Neilson Reid's more refined product. To combat this competition came the amalgamation in 1903 of Neilson Reid, Sharp Stewart and Dübs of the Gorbals as the North British Locomotive Company (NBL) – to locals *'The Combine'*. The new firm built a fine head office, designed by James Miller, and commissioned consulting engineers to produce standard steam locomotive designs for India's metre-gauge railways. About 1903 George Johnstone, practical son of the Springburn church minister, failed to interest the steam-thirled Reid brothers in building the motor car he had designed. Instead he teamed up with Sir William Arrol, and by 1910 they had founded the famed Arrol–Johnstone Car Company *(see Paisley)*. Experiments with a Ramsay electric locomotive driven by steam turbines began in 1909 at the Hyde Park Works, but these were unsuccessful.

**Others answer Competition**: In 1914 the Reids of NBL, still failing to see the writing on the wall, made a disastrous decision, rejecting a scheme to develop diesel locomotives put forward by C R H Bonn; they pressed blithely ahead, building ever bigger steam engines. The G&SWR who had operated a cross-city service left Springburn in 1902, and in 1903 tramcar competition closed most of the local suburban steam railway services except the NB's to Springburn and Cowlairs. By then the small but growing number of private motor cars were abstracting lucrative first class passengers from the Aberdeen main line services of both the CR and NB. So in 1905 the CR St Rollox Works – and in response in 1906 the NBR at Cowlairs – built trains of hitherto unknown luxury to compete more effectively with cars. The NBR's important Eastfield running sheds for 100 locomotives were built north-east of the triangle in 1902–04, Cowlairs shed being closed, and in 1908 the company finally abandoned rope haulage on the Cowlairs incline in favour of locomotives. By 1914 David Bennie of Hobden Street was manufacturing nails in vast quantities; one source quoted 0.5 million tonnes a year.

**Armageddon ends Fool's Paradise and Zany Scheme Fails**: During the awful conflict of 1914–18 the vast NBL works built not only 1412 steam locomotives, many for export, but also gun carriages, torpedo tubes, half a million shells and mines, the new fangled tanks, even aircraft – and wooden legs for maimed soldiers. In 1919 the Eastfield engine shed caught fire, badly damaging 19 locomotives; but it was rebuilt. After the war the financially embarrassed railway companies' demands for steam locomotives collapsed, and rail electrification began to close NBL's markets. Instead of turning to develop modern motive power, the ageing directors of struggling NBL revived steam turbine ideas, and a complex condensing turbine locomotive designed by James McLeod was shown at the Wembley Exhibition in 1924. It offered theoretical advantages but was too costly to produce for the newly impoverished world, and by then practical diesel locomotives and multiple unit electric trains were being built elsewhere.

**Grouping Economies, and Europe's Largest Hospital**: By 1923 when grouping caused the disappearance of all Scottish railway companies, a total of some 850 locomotives had been built at Cowlairs Works; but it was downgraded by the London-based LNER, and the construction of new engines ceased there in 1924. Within five years both St Rollox and Cowlairs were reduced to mere repair shops. Meantime under the London, Midland & Scottish Railway (LMS) which absorbed the CR, the St Rollox works soon took over the heavy jobs from Kilmarnock *(q.v.)*, while wagon work was moved to Barassie in 1927. The 74 years of new locomotive construction at St Rollox ceased in 1928. Meantime between 1910 and 1925 Stobhill Hospital was built east of Belmont, and was at one time claimed to be the largest general hospital in Europe. After 1925 much new housing was built at the Balornock estate east of Springburn. In the late 1920s home orders for steam locomotives revived, and NBL continued to build for the grouped railway companies, including in 1929 the LMS experimental high pressure locomotive *Fury* that sadly exploded on a test run at Carstairs. Orders plunged once more with the great Depression from 1929; but they recovered again. Some of the locomotives then built for export by NBL were so large that they would not fit the British loading or track gauges and had to be taken to the docks by road, hauled by traction engines from Springburn and Queen Street to the giant crane at Stobcross Quay. In 1936 LMS-owned Wordies took over the lately amalgamated haulage firm concerned, Road Engines & Kerr.

**Wartime Construction and the Works at Nationalisation**: During the 1939–45 war sections of Horsa gliders were built at the LNER Cowlairs Works by men and women skilled in repairing wooden carriages, and in 1947 the LNER still employed 2475 people at Cowlairs. By then its buildings covered some 28,750 m², nearly half the site, and locomotive, carriage and wagon repairs were done, new boilers built and all castings made for the entire LNER system in a well-designed mechanised foundry. The St Rollox site was 60% built over by the time of nationalisation in 1948 when 3382 people were employed in the 36,500 m² works, the most extensive railway workshops in Scotland, repairing locomotives and building new boilers for the remaining pre-1923 design Scottish locomotives; the 5000 LMS carriages in Scotland continued to be repaired there. Trolleybuses took over the Springburn–Mount Florida tram service in 1949.

**The Spring goes out of Springburn**: From 1948 – under British Railways – half the work lately done at Cowlairs was moved south to Horwich in Lancashire, and the staff was down to 1260 in 1949. However Eastfield was retained as one of the three principal steam locomotive sheds in the West of Scotland, with an outpost at St Rollox and seven minor sheds in its charge. Other local employment was still high, as were priorities for housing and health. Glasgow Corporation built the large Milton and Barmulloch housing schemes north and east of Springburn at medium to high densities, and by 1951 Springburn had the facilities of a large town. The war had stopped NBL development, and the 1940s had seen efficient diesel locomotives rapidly adopted by almost all USA railroads. Sadly NBL continued to ignore the portents, rejecting a chance to build US-designed diesel-electric locomotives under licence, and pressing on with steam to make good wartime losses. In 1951 they were still building steam locomotives for Australia, India, South Africa and New Zealand, and in 1953 were still optimistically completing the combine's 28,000th locomotive; but the price to NBL of ignoring alternatives to steam locomotives was heavy.

*The Hyde Park Locomotive Works, Springburn, in the 1950s, fulfilling an order for South African Railways – regular customers for Glasgow's private locomotive builders until the 1950s. Springburn was once the world's largest locomotive building centre.* (JRH)

**Experiments end NBL**: Foreign railways could no longer afford to buy these wasteful leviathans, and from the Railway Modernisation Plan of 1955, steam on Britain's railways was doomed too. From 1957 to 1959 NBL built 31 diesel locomotives of four types for British Railways' pilot scheme. None were much good, and one type was found to be the worst that BR had to endure; soon all were scrapped. NBL's overdue and hurriedly developed designs incorporating the German-made Voith diesel-hydraulic transmission system were not a success either, and a third experimental coal-burning gas turbine locomotive developed with Parsons was also a failure. Ten straight electric locomotives built jointly with GEC, and the engines of MAN design for the five Blue Pullman trains of 1960 (precursors of the Inter-City 125) were the company's swansong. All locomotive construction at Springburn had ceased by October 1962, when the once-famous NBL was ignominiously liquidated, with devastating effects on the local economy; the impact on adjacent Possil and Riddrie *(q.v.)* was even worse.

**Plunging to the Depths while Heading for the Clouds**: In that fateful year 1962 the St Rollox locomotive and carriage works were amalgamated, and in 1964 the carriage works was re-equipped. By then most locomotive repair work was on diesels and electrics. This enabled the transfer to St Rollox in 1968 of Cowlairs' remaining duties, and the station and works were closed, the latter becoming the Cowlairs Industrial Estate. Meantime in 1966 the former L&D Railway was closed and soon lifted. In 1968 the Cowlairs, Germiston and Eclipse Works were themselves eclipsed and demolished within twelve months. However the Springvale Mills were somewhat extended about that time. The soon to be notorious Red Road housing scheme of 31-storey blocks of flats, Britain's tallest, was designed by Sam Bunton. Often literally having their heads in the clouds, these skyscrapers 1.5 km east of Springburn were built for Glasgow Corporation and completed in 1966, fortunately with a sound structural framework. Regrettably, the railway housing of 1863 built on more sensible low-rise lines was demolished in 1967. In the 1970s the Sighthill flats were built on the site of the notorious *'Stinky Ocean'*, a chemical waste heap and pond from the St Rollox chemical works, and given the long-established but sadly inappropriate local name of Fountainwell.

**St Rollox Works Reorganised and Twice Renamed**: Following the Beeching cuts and the end of steam traction, the Eastfield sheds were rebuilt for diesel locomotive maintenance about 1970. In 1968–72 British Rail – which had closed the Inverurie and Barassie works – again reorganised St Rollox as its main Scottish workshops, under BREL (British Rail Engineering Ltd) from 1970, soon retitled the *'Glasgow Works'*, but it was again renamed in 1987 when it passed to British Rail Maintenance Ltd as *'Springburn Depot'*, subsequently doing all heavy repairs for Scotrail. Meantime by 1977 the Metal Box Company had replaced some of the lost locomotive building jobs with generally lower grade work; in 1979 the Tharsis Sulphur & Copper Company still dealt in pyrites, but not for local use.

**Seeking the Road to Recovery**: By 1977 the belated Springburn College of Engineering had opened, poignantly situated in the former NBL head office opposite the site of the Hyde Park Works at Flemington Street; by 1986 it was called Springburn College of Further Education. By 1980 Barmulloch College of Further Education had been built at Rye Road, a remote and inaccessible location for a facility serving a widespread young clientele, and by 1994 both institutions had merged as North Glasgow College. Meantime some new industries that had been built on cleared sites could not prevent Springburn's disadvantaged nature in 1981. However, in the 1980s a new dual carriageway bypass for the A803 was built west of the most congested part of Springburn Road, diving under Hawthorn Street; east of it was built the Springburn shopping centre of over 5000 m$^2$, in use by 1989. By 1996 the dual carriageways extended to the M8.

**Plenty Problems**: In 1990 the Springburn parliamentary constituency held over 6000 unemployed people, the worst in Scotland. At that time about 20,000 m$^2$ of the huge but largely disused former St Rollox works (Springburn Depot) were briefly utilised to stage a sad spectacle on past industry, as part of Glasgow's year as European City of Culture. With the continuing decline of Springburn, the gaunt vandalised frame of the Winter Gardens stood glassless by 1991, when Springburn's population was 32,852. Stanley Morrison's Springburn Bond was still dealing with the output of the firm's Bowmore distillery on Islay; but in 1994 this family firm sold out to the Japanese firm of Suntory. Although in 1990 the Lilley Construction Group which soon employed 1800 workers were expanding their base at Charles Street, sadly the overextended firm failed – but continued to trade there under Sunley Turriff Holdings. At that time Stobhill Hospital had almost 900 beds; by then a Local Development Company for the Glasgow North area was in being, but by 1994 the area had serious drugs problems.

**Rail Days not quite over**: The Eastfield diesel locomotive depot closed in 1992, its 120 jobs lost due to falling freight traffic and the triumph of more easily maintained push-pull and multiple-unit diesel and electric trains. In 1993 passenger train services were reintroduced on the roundabout east–west route between Maryhill, Possilpark and Queen Street via Cowlairs; a new station was provided at Ashfield on the way to Possil. In 1994 the Springburn depot (adjoined by the MC Metals scrapyard) rebuilt 80 parcel-vans for Rail Express Systems, and in 1995 the former British Rail works was bought by Babcock & Siemens Railcare – so Springburn's railway town days were not yet quite over.

**New Shopping Facilities**: In 1994 approval was given on a 5 ha industrial site at St Rollox, already permitted on appeal for shopping in 1991, to build a 13,000 m$^2$ *'warehouse shopping club'* for Price Costco. This US firm then operated only at Thurrock and Watford in south-east England, selling a wide variety of goods to members, allegedly at 20% below retail prices. Six years later Tesco also decided to site a new store at St Rollox. In 2000 the future of Springburn's small museum was under threat. However, by then the postal sorting centre at Turner Road handled 5 million items of mail a day. Nowdays the local secondary schools are All Saints (660 pupils), St Roch's Secondary (570), and Springburn Academy (570). When the derelict Townhead Blochairn church was recently demolished, the spire was saved to become the centrepiece of a public garden.

## SPRINGFIELD — Map 6, B4

***Central Fife village**, pop. 850* — OS 59: NO 3412

In the 12th or 13th century a *'hospital'* was built at oddly named Uthrogle, 4 km south-west of Cupar in the level lowland of the Howe of Fife, midway for travellers between similar foundations at Perth and St Andrews, and Portmoak and Tayport. Pitlessie beside the River Eden 4 km south of Uthrogle became a burgh of barony in 1540; its mill was shown on Pont's map of about 1600. The area was thickly settled: a bridge crossed the Eden just downstream near Rankeillour, and farther down were Cults mill by Cults Kirk, and the *'Spittell mill'*, serving Uthrogle. Roy's map made about 1750 showed at least four mills on this stretch of the Eden, and perhaps another at Uthrogle. *'Rankeeler'* was an emparked mansion, and Pitlessie a hamlet on the road from Cupar to Freuchie; in 1790 this road was turnpiked.

**Painting, Mansion and Racing**: Pitlessie had an annual fair by 1797; a painting of this event was the first success of Sir David Wilkie, born at Cults in 1785, who became a well known painter of Scottish rural life. Pitlessie also acquired maltings. Heron noted that much locally-grown flax was to be spun at Tarvit, where a spinning mill was erected in 1799; there were also limestone quarries. A house named Crawford Lodge just south of Springfield was replaced in 1809 by the Gothic pile of Crawford Priory, designed by David Hamilton and extended in 1811 into a large emparked mansion by James Gillespie Graham for an eccentric proprietress, Lady Mary Lindsay Crawford. In 1826–27 Sharp, Greenwood & Fowler's map showed limeworks open in the hills above Bunzean; the five mills on the Eden were named Pitlessie, Cults, Hospital (opposite Crawford Priory), and downstream Russell and Tarvit. Two bridges crossed the Eden, and Springfield was a hamlet on the road between the Hospital Mill and Uthrogle on the Cupar and Auchtermuchty turnpike, where there was a race course.

**Railways, Spinning and Stratheden Hospital**: From 1847 the low ground was traversed by the Edinburgh & Northern Railway, which later became the North British main line to Aberdeen. Springfield station building was of early design, but the station itself may not have been continuously open, until1906. Meantime in 1856 a steep mineral railway was built to connect the main line beside the Hospital mill with the Pitlessie maltings and the Cults and Bunzion lime works. Flax spinning at Russell Mill began in the mid 19th century, Crawford Priory was again enlarged in 1869, and Springfield had a post office by the 1880s. Its 1891 population was 750 (this figure probably included inmates in Stratheden Mental Hospital). This was certainly open as an Asylum by 1895, when both Springfield and Pitlessie had inns and post offices, and there were still at least four mills; but the racecourse had vanished. The mineral line closed with the Bunzion lime works in 1948; those at Cults became a brickworks.

**Potatoes, Concrete, and Oat Cuisine**: By 1951 A & R Scott's Uthrogle Mills, built on the site of the former racecourse, were producing Scott's Porage Oats. Some 2500 people lived locally, including about 750 hospital inmates. Rankeillour House, long owned by the Nairns *(see Pathhead, Fife)*, was demolished about 1956 and Crawford Priory was vacated in 1968; it fell into ruin. The population was in decline, especially at Pitlessie where the ancient maltings were closed in 1968, and the area remained heavily dependent on Cupar for services. Although the Cults brickworks and Stratheden linen works were still in being in the 1980s, the one-time Russell flax mill had become the concrete block works of Brand & Rae, while from a yard close by, Alex Lawson ran a fleet of potato lorries. Scott's was bought by Quaker Oats of Chicago in the early 1980s and in 1990 Uthrogle Mill was doubled in size to become the largest oat mill in western Europe. About 1990 a milk processing plant was built east of Uthrogle; it was owned in 1996 by Robert Wiseman Dairies. In 1996 Uthrogle's 100 workers processed 55,000 tonnes of oats annually into 30 million packets of porage oats, and Quaker was to make Uthrogle its sole European centre for oat milling, also filling some 14 million cans of rolled oats a year for export to Africa and the Middle East.

**Deer, Dereliction, Conversion and Golf**: In 1990 the Scottish Deer Centre, established a decade earlier in Rankeillour Park at Bow of Fife, drew 80,000 visitors. Springfield had 818 residents in 1991; in 1994–96 more new housing was built beside the station, but Stratheden Hospital was to close within 10 years. In the 1980s the fine interiors of Crawford Priory were spoiled, and since a fire in 1995 it has stood ruinous; however, the construction of a golf course in its grounds was approved in 1995. A new 18-hole golf course at Elmwood opened in 1997, part of the facilities of Elmwood College in Cupar which *inter alia* teaches greenkeeping. In 1996 the former Pitlessie maltings was converted to housing and more small dwellings were built at the rear. Cults lime works still produces lime and limebricks, and also fireclay for the Wemyss brickworks at Methil. Springfield's shop, post office and pub, the *Pitlessie Inn* and a nearby shop are all still open; the station lingers on as an unmanned halt with peak-hour trains only.

## SPRINGSIDE & Bankhead — Map 1, C1

***Ayrshire village,*** *pop. 1375* — OS 70: NS 3638

The gently undulating farming area between Kilmarnock and Irvine was well settled when Pont mapped it around 1600; Cunninghamhead was emphasised as a castle, but Springside, 3 km to the south, was not shown. A made road between the two towns was marked on the Roy map of about 1754. From 1848 it was roughly paralleled to the north by the Glasgow & South Western Railway's *'Busby Branch'*, which was closed for a while from 1850, but later reopened. Two local stations were provided, one being on this branch at Springside, 2 km east of Dreghorn. The other, on the diverging Kilmarnock and Dalry line, was at first misleadingly named Stewarton, but renamed Cunninghamhead in 1873.

**Transient Collieries and Traffic**: In the 1890s Cunninghamhead was the junction for Merry & Cunningham's Warwickhill and Warwickdale collieries, which lay 1.5 km north of Springside station; by then this and adjacent Bankhead (modern Springside) formed a scattered multi-colliery settlement with miners' rows, a post office, an inn and a population of about 1400. A primary school was built and slow development continued, to about 2150 people in the area by 1951, with 1700 of them in the increasingly compact village, through which ran the busy A71 road. Although the collieries and the *'Busby Branch'* railway had vanished by 1972, Springside had a garage by 1981; by 1987 a new A71 dual carriageway had been built to the south, removing the through traffic. In 1991, 1364 people lived in Springside. There has since been little new development, but the primary school and post office are still open.

## STAFFIN, Flodigarry & Culnacnoc — Map 8, A2

***Townships, N. Skye,*** *pop. 420 (area)* — OS 23: NG 4867

One of Scotland's most striking rock formations is the Quiraing, a series of weird towers which cluster below the eastern cliffs of the mountainous spine of the Trotternish peninsula of north Skye, and enclose an area formerly used to harbour stolen cattle. Below on the east coast are some ancient remains and the various crofting townships of Staffin, which line the coast road for about 12 km. Flora Macdonald *(see Lochboisdale, & Uig (Skye))* who famously aided the ineffectual Prince Charles Edward in 1746, was brought up in the early 18th century at the northern township, Flodigarry. In the early 20th century diatomite was mined near the tiny Loch Cuithir, 8 km south of Staffin; the course of a mineral railway to the coast road can still be traced.

**Tourism triumphs over Bad Roads**: By 1953, when about 750 crofting people lived in the area, there was a pier or slipway in the tiny bay called Ob nan Ron, and two clothiers in Staffin. The Portree road was then so bad that Bolton was jestingly told *"sheep could be lost in the potholes, and the local buses were dying a hideous death"*! By 1954 a Victorian mansion beside the Macdonald home had become the 38-room *Flodigarry Hotel*. A secondary school at Staffin had 90 pupils in the 1950s and still functioned in 1976, when the road was being improved; but the population had fallen by a quarter. By 1988 a large new community hall combined with a shop had been built at Staffin, which had some 420 residents by 1991 and was still reputedly Gaelic-speaking. By 1997 it had a new primary school, and a marine fossil museum stood beside a coastal waterfall at Ellishadder; and the small *Glenview Inn* was open in the southern township of Culnacnoc. The post office is still open, as is the *Flodigarry Hotel*; a large hostel at Dun Flodigarry serves backpackers.

## STAIR, Dalmore & Trabboch — Map 1, C2

***Ayrshire hamlets,*** *pop. 425 (area)* — OS 70: NS 4323

Pont's map of Kyle made around 1600 showed tiny lochs at Stair, south of the River Ayr 10 km from Ayr burgh, and near Trabboch, and emphasised the 14th century keep of Trabboch Castle (of which little now remains). About 2 km north-west is the 16th century tower of Stair House, opposite which, and north of the then unbridged river, a mill and Milton were marked. The Roy map (1754) showed this as Clune Mill, but there was still no bridge and still no road south of the river. The Stair Whetstone Works was started at Dalmore about 1821. The Annbank to Cronberry line of the Glasgow & South Western Railway (also called the Ayr & Cumnock branch) was opened in 1872, crossing the river by the 280 m-long Enterkine Viaduct; Trabboch station was sited near what appear to have been miners' rows. Mineral lines existing in 1902 implied mining –

probably the early Enterkine pits – in the area of Dalmore, where there was an inn, but no village *(see Annbank)*. By 1951 the parish had 550 people, and Stair school had junior secondary classes; but the population had fallen to 300 by 1971, and the school was soon completely closed. Gatefoot, which had been renamed Trabboch House, was briefly used as a hotel around 1972. The station was closed about 1960, though the line remains open for coal traffic to and from Killoch. The whetstone works closed in the 1980s; the former inn is a pub, and the parish which had 413 people in 1991 is now entirely rural.

## STANLEY

**Map 6, B3**

***Perthshire village,*** *pop. 1300*

OS 53: NO 1133

In a loop of the River Tay some 10km north of Perth and 1 km below the Tay's only waterfall, known as Campsie Linn, is a steep-sided spur on which a tower was built about 1400. Pont's sketch maps made about 1600 named it both *'Inchtyreuy'* and *'Inch-tor-uny'*; now called Inchbervie Castle, its remains can still be seen. The most conspicuous feature in the area on the Roy map surveyed about 1750 was a mansionhouse west of the castle, which took its name Stanley from a link between the local lairds the Atholls and the English Earls of Derby, whose family name is Stanley. The large and elegant Bell cotton mill was built beside the river in 1784–85 by the benevolent entrepreneur George Dempster of Dunnichen, who also laid out for the workers the 100-family village of Stanley on the plateau above the mill. Heron in 1799 noted the *"handsome village, built on a regular plan, and containing about 400 inhabitants"*. In 1802–13 the East mills were built beside the original mill and the Mid mill was added in the 1820s; ultimately there were seven giant water-wheels *(Hay & Stell show air view and plans)*. By 1828 a school, church and shops had been built, and in 1833 the whole place pleased the Factories Inquiry Commission which visited these *"magnificent"* mills, still in the cotton business but owned by Dennistoun, Buchanan & Co of Glasgow. The 2000 or so local people appeared to like the conditions, which were much better than in most smaller mills.

**Stanley Junction and Cotton Tape**: Stanley post office had a date stamp from 1845, anticipating the station opened in 1849 on the new main line of the Scottish Midland Junction Railway from Perth to Forfar and beyond; but no rail access was made to the mills, which were largely rebuilt in 1848–55 after a serious fire; at some time flax was introduced. In 1856 Stanley became the very oddly designed junction *(see Nock, 1965)* for the Perth & Dunkeld Railway, a puny concern that was soon to be extended to form what became the Highland Railway main line. The 1891 population was 1050. By 1895 a chain ferry crossed the river, leading to a viewpoint overlooking the falls, and nascent tourism was shown by an inn. The mills changed back to cotton early in the 20th century, and kept going in the slump of the 1930s by making tapes for cigarette production. By the 1950s they were run by Sidlaw Industries. Stanley had nearly 1500 people and two small hotels, but remained an ordinary village in terms of its facilities.

**Stanley retires as its Mills Stop Turning**: The railway station was closed in 1956, and the Strathmore main line was slighted in 1967 under the Beeching plan, becoming a mere goods branch to Forfar; the Inverness line remains very much in use. The secondary classes and a hotel had gone by 1980. The huge spinning mills were temporarily saved from closure in 1979, when they employed only 80 people spinning synthetic yarns for knitting and weaving, but finally closed in 1989. The goods branch to Forfar was lifted in 1982 but in 1992 the large signal box still bore the name *'Stanley Junction'*, its signalman merely controlling the end of the double track section from Perth. By 1991, 1275 people lived in Stanley. A large sand quarry was open to the south. In 1999 work was largely completed to restore the Bell Mill as a visitor centre and the Mid and East mills for housing. The *Tayside Hotel* serves the local area.

*Stanley, by the R. Tay, had mills for cotton from 1784. The Mills finally closed in 1989; part were successfully converted into housing in the late 1990s. The Bell Mill (the oldest block) is owned by Historic Scotland; its final use is yet to be determined.* *(RCAHMS / JRH)*

## STENNESS

**Map 13, B2**

***Locality, Orkney mainland,*** *pop. 265 (area)* OS 6: HY 3011

We do not know the original purpose of the Neolithic but extraordinarily thin Standing Stones of Stenness and the somewhat later and more complete 100m diameter stone circle of the Ring of Brodgar, which stand on the Wasbuster promontory in the western limb of the Orkney mainland, between the shallow Lochs of Harray and Stenness. Maes Howe on the opposite shore of the Loch of Harray is a Neolithic structure built before 2700 BC, its entrance passage aligned with the winter solstice, its chambers beautifully built of shaped flagstones with a corbelled roofing still relatively complete, and the whole covered by a large artificial mound; it is unique in western Europe.

**Stenness and the Tourist**: Farming developed on the fertile soils, and eventually the large Tormiston water mill was built in 1882. A causeway and bridge were built to link the Wasbuster promontory with the Maes Howe area and the Stromness to Kirkwall road. Around 1900 John Mackay *(see Stromness)* built a hotel at Stenness, apparently replaced by the 25-room *Standing Stones Hotel* which had been built near the junction by 1954. At that time the parish held 440 people; the scattered village of Stenness had a Monday market, primary school, post office and doctor, serving about another thousand people in the Finstown and Orphir areas. By 1968 there was a garage, but the mill closed in 1962 (though its equipment remained). The doctor's practice had also ceased by 1978, rural depopulation having reduced the local catchment. However, despite the parish population having fallen to only 265 by 1991, a new primary school was opened in 1994. The hotel, a post office stores cum filling station, an agricultural engineer and the preserved mill with its shop and café, service the local farmers and visitors to the two stone circles and Maes Howe. Together these form a famous tourist attraction, aided by excellent angling in both lochs and accessibility to the many other ancient remains on the Orkney Mainland. See them while you can – in 1980 a lightning strike split a Brodgar stone apart, felling half. The *Standing Stones Hotel* stands, and at Ireland, 3km south, is accommodation in a former water mill.

## STENTON & Whittinghame

**Map 3, B2**

***E. Lothian hamlets,*** *pop. 500 (area)* OS 67: NT 6274

About 4km south of East Linton was the 15th century keep of Whittinghame Castle, which appeared emparked on Pont's map of Lothian around 1600. South of tiny Stenton, which once had a regular fair, was a lost place intriguingly named *Fattlipps*, which shared an enclosure with the steep Presmennen Wood. A parish school for Whittinghame was started in 1620. The artificial Presmennan Lake dates only from 1819. The mansion of Whittinghame House was built in 1817, across the river from the ancient castle; it had a large park, and was the birthplace in 1848 of Arthur (Earl) Balfour, later a controversial Tory premier. By 1953 Whittinghame Tower contained a museum, and there was an agricultural engineer nearby; the basic facilities of Stenton and Whittinghame served in all some 750 people, but by 1971 only 560. The Holt School at Whittinghame House then had 85 residents; but rural depopulation was far advanced, and by 1981 the garage had gone; the Holt School appears to have closed by the 1990s. By 1991 only 479 people lived in the two parishes, but a post office is still in business at Stenton, where there is remarkably a commercial art gallery. More prosaically, nearby Ruchlaw Mains employs over 20 in pig-breeding.

## STEPPS

**Map 15, D4**

***Village / suburb n-e. of Glasgow,*** *pop. 4350* OS 64: NS 6568

One looks in vain on Pont's map for the name Stepps, which lies 7km north-east of Glasgow; the nearest road was at Cadder Kirk. William Roy's survey about 1754 showed no road in the area between Auchinloch and Provanmill, the most prominent feature being the shallow Colm Loch, later known as Frankfield Loch. But a turnpike road was soon built, passing north of the loch to link Stirling with Glasgow (replacing the detour via Cadder Kirk and Kilsyth); it became Cumbernauld Road. In 1831 the Garnkirk & Glasgow Railway was opened, crossing the new turnpike at *'Steps Road'* station, around which a hamlet developed. In 1842 four daily G&G trains served Stepps, linking it with Glasgow, Airdrie and Coatbridge. By 1899 a railway siding extended 2 km south from Steps Road to a small colliery that was in process of being sunk at Cardowan, a hamlet just north of Provan Hall. About 1900 Ferguson, Munro & Parker were brassfounders at Stepps, which was in 1901 only a small village with a post and telegraph office.

**Cardowan Colliery**: The main Cardowan Colliery was sunk north of the hamlet of Craigendmuir, 1km east of Steps Road station, in 1924–28 to the great depth of 622m; the pair of steam winding engines built for Cardowan in 1924 by Murray & Paterson of Coatbridge were used throughout its long life. The population of Stepps grew rapidly in the 1930s, peaking about 1951 at some 4500, when the facilities of a large village were available locally. By then Craigendmuir had a sizeable estate of better houses. Cardowan No.3 colliery successfully exploited coking coal in the Limestone Coal Group for a number of years; perhaps to facilitate its working, Frankfield Loch was drained about 1950. The railway stations were closed between 1953 and 1963, and some of the other facilities also disappeared.

*One of the two steam winding engines at Cardowan Colliery, Stepps, manufactured by Murray & Paterson of Coatbridge in 1924. The colliery finished in 1984, but one of its main winding engines is now at Summerlee industrial museum at Coatbridge.* (JRH)

**Whisky Blending, and Strathclyde's Last Deep Mine**: James Buchanan & Co, who had blended *'Black & White'* whisky in Glasgow since at least 1905, built a large blending and bottling plant on a new site at Cumbernauld Road just east of Stepps in 1969. By 1972 the 16-roomed *Garfield House Hotel* had been created from a large villa. Cardowan colliery, the last deep mine working in the Clyde basin, employed 1200 men as late as 1977, but was closed in 1983–84; one of its main winding engines was appropriately put on display at Summerlee in Coatbridge. The whisky bottling plant was no longer in operation by the mid 1980s, its site becoming the Buchanan Business Park in the 90s.

**New Station, New Motorway**: In 1989 a new railway station was opened at Stepps for trains between Glasgow, Springburn and Cumbernauld, near the colliery site. The quite young population was 4336 in 1991 (including Millerston). An 8 km motorway bypass (M80) was built to the north in 1989–92 between the M8 at Provan and the A80, which it joined just east of the long-established major bus garage; this remained in operation in 1994 under new operators, Kelvin Central of Motherwell. By 1996 there was a caravan site at Craigendmuir, and the extended *Garfield House Hotel* now has 46 rooms.

## STEVENSTON

**Map 1, C1**

*W. Ayrshire town, pop. 10,200* — OS 70: NS 2642

Stevenston near the Cunninghame coast only 2 km east of Saltcoats takes its name from a 12th century lordling, Stephen Loccart. Although Kerelaw Castle to the north dates from the 14th century, and the area was closely settled by about 1600, neither name seems to have featured on Pont's crowded map of Cunninghame at that time. At some time a market was chartered. About 1674 coal was discovered nearby, and a harbour was built between 1684 and 1700 from which coal was shipped to Dublin. Saltworks were integrated with the mines, which had engines from 1719. The Roy map made about 1754 showed Stevenston as a large village with roads to Saltcoats, Kilwinning, and via the mansion of Ardeer to Irvine. The short Coal Canal begun in the 1760s was opened from Stevenston to Saltcoats in 1772, and the mines were large by 1784. In 1799 Heron found Stevenston a *"populous village with upwards of a thousand inhabitants"*. Pottery was also being made by 1810, but in 1827 Stevenston was (according to Chambers) simply a *"large coal-village"*.

**Railways, Ardeer Ironworks, Dynamite and Golf**: From its authorisation in 1827 the non-standard *'Scotch'* gauge Ardrossan & Johnstone Railway (AJR) gradually connected up various places in the area, but it had little effect on development, and Stevenston did not even have a post office in 1838. Later, under the Glasgow & South Western Railway, Stevenston had a locomotive shed. The large Ardeer ironworks were established at Stevenston about 1849 by Merry & Cunningham of Glengarnock, and opened in 1852. By 1888 the substantial Ayrshire Foundry Company was also in operation. The Swedish chemist Alfred Nobel also chose the Ardeer site beside the River Garnock for his nitro-glycerine and dynamite factory in 1873; by 1911 it employed 2000 workers, and no doubt far more during the 1914–18 and 1939–45 wars. The Ardeer golf club was founded in 1880 and laid out an 18-hole parkland course. In 1888, the Caledonian-backed Lanarkshire & Ayrshire Railway was opened through Stevenston, providing a second station. In 1891 the population was 4250.

**Disaster, Explosives and Plastics**: In 1895 nine men died in a flooding accident in Auchenharvie No.4 coal pit; the last of the five associated collieries which had been united as the inaptly named Daylight Mine closed in 1915. Meantime a new gasworks was set up in 1900, but in the 1920s the ironworks were closed by new owners, Baird's of Coatbridge. In 1926 Nobel's became part of the new giant ICI. Stevenston was a very short-lived police burgh, incorporated as recently as 1952 when the population was nearing 9500, and served by small-town facilities. In 1972 68% of the houses were owned by the local authority; in 1975 Stevenston was merged into Cunninghame District, centred in Irvine. Ardeer remained a main centre for making explosives; in the 1970s the huge works still employed over 5000 people on the Ardeer site. By no means all worked in explosives: for instance, up to 1980 ICI made polyesters, there were silicon and nylon plants, and in 1974 Cameron McLatchie founded Anaplast to recycle plastics. In 1978–79 a new pipe was laid for ICI to carry its effluents 2 km out to sea, so cleaning up the River Garnock.

**Skating on Thin Ice in the Shadow of the Works**: Stevenston's facilities were still those of a small town in 1981. Although the new Ardeer 18-hole golf course had been laid out north of the town in the 1970s, and by 1987 the 9-hole Moorpark golf course was open at Auchenharvie, the polluting industrial ambience led those who could afford to travel in to Ardeer from a distance to do so. A remarkable leisure facility opened by the Cunninghame District Council in 1988 was a two-tier ice rink. Anaplast was acquired by Scott & Robertson of Greenock in 1983, and in 1990 passed to British Polythene, making heavy duty sacks and pallet covers as one of the firm's three Scottish plants *(see Port Glasgow)*. In 1990 ICI opened

*The huge Ardeer industrial site at Stevenston. The works was founded in 1873 by the British Dynamite Co Ltd to use Alfred Nobel's patent for dynamite manufacture. In the 1970s over 5000 worked here, making explosives, textiles and plastics.* (RCAHMS)

a plastic sheet recycling plant at Ardeer, to which caustic soda was still delivered by rail. By then Stevenston was also the centre for ASSET, the Ardrossan Saltcoats Stevenston Enterprise Trust. The population in 1991 was 10,153; male unemployment was 21%.

**Cuts in Jobs and Products – and The Big Idea**: The ICI explosives factory was said to be still discharging excessive quantities of copper, nickel, methyl phenol and acids into the sea. Meantime in 1988 the French state chemicals group Rhone-Poulenc had acquired ICI's silicone production plant at Ardeer; but they decided to cease production by 1992 with the loss of 180 jobs. About 1200 ICI workers then remained on the site, falling to little over 750 in 1994, but further job cuts were anticipated, and the town's future looked grim, as Auchenharvie Academy with 600 or so pupils was decidedly unacademic. The vast extent of the Ardeer works now loosely fills the entire peninsula between the Garnock estuary and the sea, plus an area south of Kilwinning – some 5 square km in all. The railway station still offers electric trains to Glasgow and Largs, and in 2000 *'The Big Idea'* – a millennium visitor attraction celebrating Scottish and other inventions – was opened at the south end of the Ardeer peninsula.

## STEWARTON — Map 1, C1

***N. Ayrshire town,** pop. 6500* — OS 64: NS 4245

Stewarton, on the Annick Water 9 km north of Kilmarnock, existed in the 12th century, but was not an early burgh. Little remains by which to date Corsehill Castle, but its name and that of *'Sivertoun Castle'*, plus a substantial settlement, and a bridge across the Annick Water, all featured on Pont's map made about 1600. A parish school was open by 1620, a market was chartered in 1707, and a post office was open by 1715. Roy's survey of about 1754 showed *Stewartown* as a linear settlement on a road from Glasgow to Gallowayford, where the little Glazert Burn was crossed by the *'cart road'* between Glasgow and Irvine. Another road between Beith, Dunlop and Kilmarnock intersected the first in the village. Stewarton grocer's son David Dale, born in 1739, became an apprentice weaver, and from 1763 a famed entrepreneur in Glasgow and joint creator of New Lanark and many other mills.

**Building on Wool: Bonnets for All**: Woollen mills were in fact built at Stewarton during the 18th century. By 1797 five fairs were pitched annually, and it was a post town. Two years later Heron noted this *"considerable post town, neatly built, contains upwards of 1000 inhabitants. Its principal manufacture is bonnets and Quebec caps"*. The market still functioned in 1802 and by 1810 there was a brewery, but temperance pressures gained the upper hand and it was short-lived. Chambers who visited in 1827 thought Stewarton *"a large thriving town"*. A gasworks was set up in 1832, providing light to enable cotton and silk to be woven on 300 hand looms by the 1840s. From about 1860 power knitting machines were used to make the increasingly popular Stewarton bonnets; by 1869 this burgeoning industry employed about 2500 workers, and hand weaving was in decline.

**Trains for the Teetotal Town**: Stewarton became a police burgh in 1868. The rather belated Glasgow Barrhead & Kilmarnock Joint Railway was opened in 1871–73, with a station at Stewarton. In 1891 the population was 2700; yet Stewarton was no more than a sizeable village, noticeable for the absence of an inn. Chapeltoun House some 3 km to the south-west was built by a rich merchant in 1900. Knitwear manufacture grew, and in the inter-war period the Stewarton firm of Cunningham expanded with branches in Irvine and Kilmaurs. The little burgh was remarkable for still being a *'dry'* area after the 1929 licensing poll. By the 1950s Stewarton still celebrated *'Bonnet Day'* and lacked a hotel, despite having grown to a large village of 3500 people enjoying a good range of other facilities, and it kept its railway station.

**From Abstinence to Growth – and a Breath of Whisky**: Local attitudes to alcohol evidently became more relaxed, for by 1981 three small hotels were open, including the converted Chapeltoun House, and whisky casks were being repaired! Two precision engineering firms and – more recently – egg packers and frozen food processors had been established; the hosiery industry and the spinning and dyeing of yarns for the carpet trade continued. Several estate developments took in the influx of people, and house building continued in the 1980s; Stewarton Academy was built in 1986 for 700 pupils, replacing a junior secondary school. In 1991 the population was 6481. By then the Riverside Bakery was a large concern, and in 1994 the *Chapeltoun House Hotel* was still giving good service. Today Stewarton Academy has over 900 pupils.

## STICHILL & Newton Don — Map 3, B3

***Border hamlet & estate,** pop. 170 (area)* — OS 74: NT 7138

Hill forts and ancient settlements crown the rather exposed site of Stichill, 5 km north of Kelso beyond the deep valley of the Eden Water. Pont's map of the Merse made about 1600 showed from north to south *'Old Stittchell'*, *'N Stittchell'*, *'Stittchell Kirk'* – which stands about 125 metres above sea level – while beside the Eden were *'Stittchell mill'*, and *'Newtoun'* with its own mill. The Roy map of about 1754 marked Newton Don on the Eden Water, 1 km to the south of *'Stitchill town'*, on roads linking Kelso with Hume; two mills including a *'Wak Mill'* still turned on the Eden. The railways kept away, but a gothic UP church was built in 1877. In 1895 the church, post office and smithy of a tiny village stood between two emparked mansions, Stichill House to the north and Newton Don to the south. The parish population was 300 in 1901. In 1951 Stichill had a post office, primary school and a telephone exchange with 58 lines serving a wide rural area, but the population was falling rapidly with the general decline in farm jobs, and the parish held only 239 people. By 1969 only stables stood near the site of the lately vanished Stichill House. By 1976 the village school had closed and there was no bus service. Only 169 people remained in 1991. Stichill finally lost its post office about 1996, but the self-effacing mansion of Newton Don, owned by the Balgonie Estate, still enjoys its landscaped park. The rather fine UP church – for a time used as a stonemason's yard – is now disused, but the parish church remains in use; its kirkton is correspondingly tiny.

## STIRLING & Causewayhead — Map 16, A1

***Large central town on R. Forth,** pop. 31,000* — OS 57: NS 7993

Suburbs: *Bannockburn, Bridge of Allan, Cambusbarron & St Ninians*

At the head of the Firth of Forth stands a spectacular 100 m tall rock, the ice-carved end of a volcanic sill, towering above the right bank of the meandering River Forth as it winds its sluggish way to tidewater. From the earliest times this dominated the best land route to the north of Scotland, for the long-impassable wastes of Flanders Moss barred north–south travel to the west, and to the east the tidal Forth became wider and was bordered by treacherous muddy flats. About 80 AD the Romans built a road which crossed the Forth north-west of the rock, then pushed north into Caledonia via Strathallan. Six hundred years later the Picts retreated northwards from the Forth as the Anglians followed the Roman line of advance – until a Pictish victory at the Battle of Nechtansmere near Forfar in 685 enabled them to push the Anglians back to Stirling. This was an Anglian stronghold for nearly 300 years, and probably the northernmost permanent Anglian settlement, anchoring the north-western extremity of greater Lothian. Its name seems to come from *'Striveling'*, Anglian for *Place of Strife*. About the year 960 the fortress of Stirling succumbed to the forces of the combined kingdom of the Picts and Scots, by then known as Alba, and was appropriated by them together with the rest of West Lothian.

**Scottish Burgh, Sheriffdom and Cambuskenneth Abbey**: By the 11th century a tiny settlement had grown on the lower slopes of the *'tail'* left by the ice sheets south of the castle crag. King Alexander I may have chartered this as a burgh in the early 12th century; he certainly granted a house at Stirling to Scone monks, and on his deathbed in the castle in 1124 he endowed its new chapel; there was also a town church by about that time. King David I re-chartered Stirling as a Royal Burgh about 1125, and it soon became the caput of a sheriffdom split off from Lothian, and also a member of the Court of the Four Burghs. Ships traded, and salt-pits were in use at Stirling by the time that the Augustinian Abbey of St Mary at Cambuskenneth was founded under David's aegis around 1140; its stone buildings on the north bank of the winding river were linked to the town by a ferry. By 1153 there were two churches and a school in Stirling. There was an important timber-built royal castle on the rock by 1171, and to south-west and north-east were royal hunting forests. King William the Lion enclosed the King's Park as a hunting ground; the Town Burn which flowed from the Park Loch powered the Town Mill.

**Charter, Wooden Bridge, Hospices and Fire**: Stirling was re-chartered in 1226 with a Saturday market and merchant guild; as in some other burghs this excluded weavers. Later there were two weekly markets. Well before 1259 a wooden bridge crossed the Forth at Kildean, probably on the line of the Roman road; it was shown on a map made by Matthew Paris, who died in that year. A Dominican friary was founded by Alexander II in 1233. By 1243 the leper *'spittal'* was outside the burgh at Causewayhead – the north end of the made-up road from the later bridge to firm ground; near the bridge there was also the St James's hospice for other travellers. In 1244 the timber-built town was accidentally destroyed by fire, but in 1257 Stirling castle was chosen as a safe haven for the juvenile king Alexander III, and strengthened in 1263. Although wolves were still being hunted in Stirlingshire as late as 1288, by 1276 Stirling's Horse Fair was so well known that the English court bought some mounts there.

**Wars of Succession, Destruction and Repairs**: A stone castle was in course of construction at Stirling in 1287. The Roman road was still usable when the very narrow timber bridge, probably of seven spans, either partly collapsed or was pulled down during Wallace's successful battle in 1297, and for a time ferries were relied on. The castle was slighted and the town was burned by the retreating Wallace in 1298, but the castle was repaired when recaptured by the Scots in 1299. Battered again in the siege of 1304, it fell to the English, who mended the bridge and held the castle, only to find it besieged by the Scots under Robert Bruce. When it was yielded after the battle of Bannockburn in 1314, Barbour wrote that Bruce *"caused the castle and towers to be mined and thrown down"*. In 1326 another parliament was held at Cambuskenneth. The English re-occupied the castle in 1336 and again strengthened it, but it was recovered by the Scots in 1342.

**Stirling slips but recovers as *de facto* Capital**: The abbey was damaged in various disturbances between 1350, year of the Black Death, and 1378. Stirling was re-chartered in 1360, and in 1365 had 31 burgesses; but the bridge again fell into ruin and was replaced by a ferry between 1361 and 1391. Stirling then slipped from 7th to 11th place in the table of Customs dues paid, and in 1372–76 only 10 tonnes of wool was exported per year; by 1378 more hides than wool featured in its export trade. The town was burnt down yet again in 1385 by Richard III of England. The castle became the favourite royal residence late in the 14th century, and often the signing place of royal charters; there was for long a royal mint in the castle, which was strengthened in 1380–81 and 1390 (its earliest remaining part, built in stone, dates from that period). A further major fire in 1406 destroyed the town church and tron; the bridge was repaired from 1408. Stirling was the principal Royal castle under James I, who gained power in 1425; James II was born there in 1430.

**Trade and Trading Standards, but Not the Capital**: In 1434/35 tiny quantities of cloth were exported from Stirling, but the wool trade was then unimportant and shrinking. In 1437 Edinburgh became the official capital of Scotland, but an additional Stirling fair was chartered in 1447, and a sketch of the town made at that time showed a mixture of one and two-storeyed buildings. In 1452–55 the town and its wooden church were twice burned down by the revengeful Earl of Douglas. Recovery was swift: from about 1457 the burgh had sole charge of the country's standard liquid measure, the old Scottish pint (some 1.5 litres) until English measures took over in 1707. The parish church (later known as the Holy Rude) was rebuilt in stone from Ballengeich quarry in 1456–70 and was extended in the early 16th century; its tower rose over 25 metres. The merchant guild had become very important by 1460, and by 1464 there was a leper hospital at Allanpark. In 1473 a site was feued for a tolbooth, in use by 1476, and by the next year there was a *'port'* or gate, implying a town wall. Stirling castle remained the favourite Royal residence and was improved in the mid 1460s; as a result some sixteen noble families had houses in the town, which had a gunsmith from medieval times; by 1477 there were 120 burgesses.

**Parliament Hall, Luxuries and Stone Bridge**: The Great or Parliament Hall was built at the castle for James III from around 1470; in 1475 cannon were cast by James Nory in a foundry within the castle. James IV established the King's Knot garden in the 1490s on the low ground west of the castle, and about 1500 the Chapel Royal became a collegiate church. The Great Hall was still incomplete in 1503, while the gateway and other work was new-built in 1500–11. At that time the merchant John Cowan imported such luxuries as saffron and prunes for the court. By 1503 the king was playing golf, and by 1508 strawberries were grown in the royal garden; James V was born in the castle in 1512. At some time around 1500 the bridge was massively rebuilt in stone, wide enough for single vehicles but with two gateways for burgh tolls and defence. (Described by Heron in 1799 as *"a stately ancient bridge of four arches"* it still proudly stands, though forbidden to vehicles *(see Hay & Stell)*.

**Baltic Trade, Building, Silting – and Decayed Tradesmen**: In 1488 Danish merchants were trading in Stirling, the wool trade perked up in 1500–05, and by then Stirling specialised in cloth for export to the Baltic. In the later 15th and 16th centuries Stirling generally paid between 2% and 5% of Scottish burgh tax revenue. The Greyfriars or Franciscan friary and its church were built around 1500 and the parish church was enlarged in 1507–20, using stone from a quarry at Raploch. By 1519 the tolbooth tower sported a clock, and in 1520 pig-keeping within the town was outlawed, further improving the image of what by 1525 was among the six leading merchant towns of Scotland, though it consisted of little more than a single street connecting the Kirk and the Town Mill; Broad Street was the original market place. But Stirling's importance as a port was already in decline: the river was silting, and by 1510 Airth had been chosen as the site for a royal dockyard. A further severe setback occurred in 1529 when an abbey ferry capsized with the loss of over fifty lives. In 1530 it was noted that the town's hospital was *"for relief of decayed tradesmen"*; the Royal tailor Robert Spittal established a hospital at Irvine Place in 1530–40.

**Crafts, Palace Building, Trades, Tax and Education**: By 1540 there were seven crafts in the guild, and six markets for various commodities in the burgh. The Royal Palace was built within the castle for James V in 1540–42 by masons transferred from Falkland Palace. In troubled 1547–48, by which time there was a mercat cross, the town's defensive walls were *"strengthened and builded"* in stone by the master mason John Coutts under Mary of Guise, the resident Regent. A windmill was built in 1548, perhaps in case the town was besieged and the water mills inaccessible. At that time 440 mainly male adults were counted, including a wide range of craftsmen within the seven incorporated trades, so the population was perhaps 1500. In 1550 Stirling with 385 householders was ranked 8th of the Royal Burghs in tax terms, nearly a fifth of its taxpayers being women. By 1557 Stirling Grammar School had two masters, but little was taught there except Latin. However, around that time there was already a printer in the town, and in 1559 over half of a group of guild members could sign their names, a much more literate showing than in contemporary Perth.

**Reformation Destruction and New Ownership**: Cambuskenneth Abbey was pillaged in 1559 and except for the bell-tower its buildings were sacked. In 1560 the burgh was represented in Parliament, as was the doomed abbey by its Commendator, the Erskine Earl of Mar, who acquired its lands. The Franciscan friary too was destroyed in 1559–60 and it became a slaughterhouse; after the Reformation the properties of both the friaries were transferred to the town council. In 1565 Queen Mary nursed and loved her cousin Henry Stewart (Lord Darnley) in Stirling Castle, and from their union came James VI and I, who was brought up there. The abbey's stone was being largely robbed for lay building purposes. The town walls were strengthened in 1574, and in 1594 the Chapel Royal was demolished and rebuilt for the baptism of James VI's son Prince Henry, the last heir to the throne to be reared at Stirling; he did not live to reign.

**Early Seventeenth Century Trade**: Around the year 1600 Stirling was sketched in some detail by Pont; the castle was clearly emparked, and the Brig Mill turned immediately below the bridge, where a burn adapted as a lade met the river. At this time the manufacture of the light woollen cloth called *'shalloon'* was introduced to the town, which had permanent shops as well as a twice-weekly market and two annual fairs. In 1603 exports included cloth, hides and skins; imports were wine, tallow, bark, lime, and from Scandinavia timber and wool. In 1603–07 improvement of the quay which lay downstream of the Abbey was carried out, but in 1606 over 600 people died from an outbreak of plague. By 1613 golf was played in the King's Park. A new burgh grain mill was built in 1616, but by 1621 Stirling paid under 1.5% of Scottish Customs dues.

**Private Houses and a Fine Almshouse**: About 1630 Stirling town council's tax levy was cut, to half that of Glasgow, enabling more fine houses to be created – despite being in fact only a quarter as rich as Glasgow in 1639, when it was down to 12th place in Scottish burgh tax yield. William Alexander of Menstrie and Tullibody (later Earl of Stirling) rebuilt an existing house in 1630–32 into a fine mansion, known from 1666 under its new owner's name as Argyll's Lodging; added to by the 9th Earl of Argyll until 1674, by 1691 it contained 16 fireplaces. In 1638 Stirling was the central point where the Convention of Royal Burghs met to approve the Covenant. In 1637–49 an almshouse (the *'Over Hospital'* for decayed guild brethren) was built under the will of John Cowan(e); by 1724 it was known as the Guildhall.

**Plagued, Robbed and Restored**: Besides civil strife, the years 1644–49 saw Stirling, like so many burghs, repeatedy hit by yet more attacks of plague; but it largely avoided destruction, though the national records were seized from the castle and regrettably lost at sea. There were just two coaches in the town by 1651. In 1655 the Cromwellian Tucker wrote of Stirling: *"a pretty burgh; here live some merchants"*, whose goods were carried up-river from Bo'ness in small boats. The following year's report by Richard Franck was of *"a walled city (but not a great one) that's built all with stone"* and had Lowland merchants at its south end, the river being navigable up to the bridge, though only by vessels of up to 70 tons burthen. In 1669 – over 200 years after the last of six major fires – a fire service was at last established, with buckets and ladders. About that time brewing was first conducted on a commercial scale, and in 1672 the Kerse Mill was built.

**Corrupt and Superstitious at the Union**: Stirling acquired its first post office as early as 1689. However, the town council was corrupt, and progress was minimal, though by the late 17th century Stirling was relatively sophisticated, banishing women superstitiously believed to be *'witches'*, rather than burning them as at benighted Dumfries! In 1691 the 275 properties within the burgh contained 639 households; one could guess at a total population of 3000. By 1692 the town council was complaining of the collapse of its inland trade. The loss of much local capital in the ill-fated Darien scheme, plus famine in the countryside, lowered Stirling by 1699 to 13th place in the Scottish tax returns. But one miller still had a staff of five, and matters soon improved, for a new Tolbooth was built west of Broad Street in 1701–03, and in 1705 two more annual fairs were granted, remarkably for winter dates, bringing the total to six. Though not generally Jacobite, many townspeople were unhappy about the Union of 1707, and Stirling was soon

*The Tolbooth, Broad Street, Stirling, designed by William Bruce and built between 1703 and 1705. The steeple and rubble section in this view down Gaol Wynd are of Bruce's design – the leaded steeple (of Dutch inspiration) being a rare survival. The section with round-headed windows is later.* *(JRH)*

heavily garrisoned; Queen Anne had the castle strengthened with outer defences against artillery in 1708–14. At the time of the 1715 rising the bridge was breached, but soon repaired. After the decisive battle of Sheriffmuir in 1716, Stirling town council returned to torpor.

**Defoe's Stirling, Serges and Schools**: Defoe writing in the 1720s described a strong castle and a small town, where *"the street is large and well built, but ancient. The palace and royal apartments are very magnificent, but all in decay. There is a very considerable manufacture of serges; they both make them and dye them there very well"*. The disputatious town council improved, providing new schools to teach the *'three Rs'* in 1740–47. The road to Crieff was rebuilt by Caulfeild's troops in 1741–42; about that time the mansion of Annfield was erected south of the town. Stirling was again heavily garrisoned and stayed loyal to the Hanoverians in 1745, when the Jacobites avoided it; but one arch of the bridge was demolished as a precaution. In 1746 the town council – though not the castle – submitted to the investing rebels, but the latter soon fled from *'Butcher'* Cumberland's troops, who patched up the bridge, which was properly repaired in 1748. A local jeweller named Ker made a fine box for the egregious Hanoverian.

**Communications mapped and Coaches run**: Meantime Thomas Wordie from St Ninians was in cartage in Stirling by 1745, establishing a family business that was to endure 200 years. By 1749 John Wilson & Co were brewing within Mar's Wark, selling the spent grain or *draff* as animal feed. In 1755 the population was almost 4000. Roy's maps showed that as late as the 1750s the only bridge across the Forth was at Stirling, access to Callander and the north west still being by the ferry at Drip, 4km upstream. However, the north road to Crieff and thence to Perth had bridges throughout, and a road led westwards to Dumbarton via Gargunnock and Drymen. In 1752 the post road to Falkirk was turnpiked, and from 1765 two coaches per week plied to and from Edinburgh. Argyll's Lodging was sold off in 1764 and became a military hospital in 1800. According to Mair, corruption dominated council affairs and stagnation ruled until exposure in 1773; then improvements began. The narrow Barras Yett was removed to improve the access from the south, where superior new development began to spread.

**Textile Industries, Water Supply and Schooling**: Stirling remained primarily a communications, market and business centre rather than an industrial town. Carpets were apparently being made there by the time of Pennant's visit in 1769, though it is easy to confuse the Stirling concerns with nearby enterprises in St Ninians and Bannockburn. In 1776 there were 17 carpet frames, 160 looms weaving the light woollen fabric known as shalloons, serges and plaids, and also 38 framework knitters. Drip Bridge was built between 1769 and 1782, replacing the ferry, and a piped water supply was laid on to Stirling from the Touch Hills to the west in 1774 *(see Cambusbarron)*. In 1783 new Grammar School buildings were erected near the castle, whose great hall was roofless when seen in 1787 by Robert Burns.

**Banking, Communications and Hotels**: The Bank of Scotland branch that was opened in the town in 1776 was only the sixth to be successfully established. This no doubt pushed the locals into the formation in 1777 of the Stirling Banking Company, which by 1793 had a branch in Alloa; it had also colonised Kinross by the time it failed in 1826. The Merchant Banking Company had been formed in Stirling in 1784; it set up no branches. Campbell, Thomson & Co, who set up as bankers in the town in 1787, lasted only ten years. By 1800 both the Stirling banks were important enough to be issuing notes, but the Merchant Bank failed in 1805 due to criminal mismanagement. Meantime from 1780 a regular wagon service was in operation through Stirling, linking Aberdeen, Perth and Glasgow; the vital causeway north of the bridge was maintained by statute labour until at least 1785. *Wingate's Inn* was opened in 1786; this later became in turn the *Red Lion* and the *Golden Lion Hotel*. From 1792 a light coach ran on three days a week between Stirling and Edinburgh, evidently returning the next day, and the Dumbarton road was turnpiked in 1794. In that year the cattle market was re-sited near the bridge; seven fairs were scheduled to take place in 1797.

**Industry in the 1790s**: In 1791 a spinning mill was equipped with jennies and in 1792 had 50 looms and nearly 100 workers; by 1792 over 250 weavers made coarse muslins for Glasgow firms. There was also a woollen spinning mill with over 100 workers producing and dyeing yarn, much of which was woven at Bannockburn, and 68 weavers worked in the town, largely making coarse shalloon, plus some 35 carpet looms, an industry which was to last for over a century at Forthbank. Heron thought Stirling's industries in the famine year of 1799 were much as they had been twenty to thirty years earlier. There was little foreign trade; he added that *"small vessels only can come* *up to the town"*. Heron noted three hospitals in Stirling, whose burgh population in 1801 was over 5250.

**Houses, Turnpikes and Barracks**: Georgian houses began to be built outwith the town walls, and the feuing of a ribbon of cottage development at Raploch was begun in 1799; by 1818 a school was in operation there. In 1802 the road from Causewayhead to Alloa was turnpiked, in 1810 the Dollar road, and in 1812 the Doune radial; finally in 1814 toll gates were placed across the main road north via Bridge of Allan, and its improvement was made possible. Meantime a new prison was erected in 1806–07. John Wordie of the haulage family ran an illegal mail service between Stirling and Glasgow from 1807 to 1825! During the French wars the Great Hall of the ancient castle was radically converted – to its great detriment – into what Chambers called a *'barrack'*, used as such for well over a century. In 1807 a parade ground was laid out between castle and town (in the 20th century it became a car park!)

**Racing, Dirt and Tyranny**: Dorothy Wordsworth wrote in 1803 that Stirling was *"an old irregular place, the town quite full; not a vacant room in the inn, it being the time of the assizes"*; she left the impression that there was no alternative hostelry. A horse racing track was demarcated at the King's Park in 1805. Industrial development continued, for a cotton mill was established about 1800, and a steam-powered woollen mill about 1811. By 1814 two coaches ran daily to Glasgow and to Edinburgh, and one to Perth. Besides Wingate's there were by then three other coaching inns, among them the long-lasting *Golden Grapes*. About 1814 a new corn exchange and the Athenaeum public library and hall replaced the meal market, its site being renamed King Street, and the Town Burn was culverted in 1816. By 1819 John Callander & Co were weaving fine cloth, but Stirling was still undrained and unswept; blood still ran down the gutters from the slaughterhouse in St John Street, and in that year Robert Southey found *"a general want of cleanliness"*. Governmental reform was needed, but in 1820 men were still being tried and executed in the town for demanding this from the oppressive Tories. The *Stirling Journal* (later the *Journal & Advertiser*) began publication in that year.

**Improvements, Exports and Racing Down the River**: The small classical mansion of Forthside House was built of ashlar stone in 1821. By 1825 eight breweries were in action, though none was particularly large or enduring. A gasworks was set up in 1825, and gas lighting was introduced to the town's streets. Enlightenment of another kind increased in 1825 when a School of Arts was established as a night school. But so ineffectual was the Grammar School that in 1826 a rival Academy was opened at the Guildhall. The Stirling Banking Company also failed in 1826 (but somehow its creditors were paid in full). In that year, according to Chambers, Stirling was *"a town of about 9000 inhabitants"*. Chambers added that *"the Forth produces vast quantities of excellent salmon, the greater part of which is exported"*. In that decade the Stevensons freed the river channel of rock ledges, enabling 300-ton vessels to reach Stirling wharf, just below the Abbey Ford; by 1833 passenger steamers plied to Newhaven and Granton. In 1835 two paddle steamers – the *Ben Lomond* and the feebler *Victoria* – used to race each other through the winding channel!

**Coaches, Disease and Child Labour**: A new granite bridge wide enough for two-way traffic was built just south of the ancient bridge in 1826–33 to designs by Allan (or Robert) Stevenson (sources differ!); this was followed by Murray Place – a new through road which bypassed the hilly and congested town centre. In 1835 nine coaches ran daily to Glasgow, four to Perth, two to Alloa and one to Callander. But coaches were for the richer elements. A public dispensary was opened in 1831 by the energetic Dr William Forrest – sorely tested in the next year's cholera epidemic. In 1832 half the fifty workers at Smith's woollen mills were under 16 years old and none had been to school. By 1841 the cotton and carpet industries were declining, but 140 workers in three mills spun wool for a 64-hour week; 280 looms made tartans and shawls, employing about 650 workers in a merciless 84-hour week.

**Reform, Paving, Water and Drains**: The first relatively democratically elected town council following the Reform Act of 1832 enabled the proper repaving and draining of streets to begin in 1834. The *Stirling Observer* newspaper was founded in 1836, and in 1838 a new Corn Exchange was begun. In 1840 the port of Stirling owned 22 vessels, but the Commissioners of the Forth Navigation, established in 1843, decided against improving the river above Alloa. Up to 1841 its filthy state held the burgh population below 9000, despite the many poor Highlanders, who had been drawn by the availability of local charities; conditions worsened still more following the famine of 1846–47. The little Tolbooth had 24 prisoners to a cell in 1844, hence the new 51-cell prison built opposite to it, opened in 1847. Then the urban tide turned: in 1848 a Stirling Waterworks Act enabled an improved supply to be arranged, and sewers were laid in the main streets in the 1850s.

**Railway Centre and Wordie's the Railway Carters**: Construction of the Scottish Central Railway (SCR) serving the Glasgow–Perth axis began in 1845, and in 1848 Stirling and Perth were linked to the national railway system. The station was probably designed by Andrew Heiton of Perth. The SCR (later Caledonian) was the only unbroken main line to and from the northern half of Scotland until the Forth Bridge was opened in 1890. Some of its rolling stock was built in Stirling by Thomson. In 1852 the Stirling & Dunfermline Railway opened a quite separate line to Alloa, providing a second station and bridge and eventually a link to Fife. In 1856 a cross-country line was opened westwards to Buchlyvie and Balloch. John Wordie's son William reinforced the Stirling to Glasgow cartage service via a Bannockburn depot, and launched onto the railway scene in 1842 in partnership with the Edinburgh & Glasgow Railway. In 1852 the firm moved its head office to Glasgow, but by 1854 had built a new Stirling district office and a substantial depot near the station at Thistle Street (this later had 156 horses); the Wordie name and its district operations centre remained there till 1950.

**Steamers and the Impact of Trains**: James Johnstone of Stirling built clipper sailing ships of 500 to 1000 tons in the 1850s, the largest being the *William Mitchell* of 1856, but then the yard faded. In 1858 Fontane travelled up the Forth from Granton on the steamer *Rob Roy*, but shallows prevented it from reaching Stirling, and passengers were transferred to a flat-bottomed boat. By that date the *Royal Hotel* was open, coach excursions ran to the Trossachs, and a late Saturday train from England provided a Sunday morning service to Perth; Sabbatarianism began to crumble. By 1869 both the Caledonian and North British had engine sheds at Stirling, and such was the impact of railways that in that year Bremner found it a matter for comment that road coaches were still built in Stirling, whereas *"cartwrights are to be found in nearly all the* *towns and villages of the country"*. As the rail carriage of cattle replaced droving, Stirling became one of Scotland's chief cattle market centres.

**Religious Publishing, Education – and Sport**: A religious tract publishing house founded by local seedsman Peter Drummond in 1848 lasted over a century, printing something like a thousand million booklets. A large new Free Church was finely built in stone in Murray Place in 1851–53, its spire becoming a local landmark. In 1854 Drummond's spoilsport pressure stopped local horse racing, and the grandstand became derelict. A new building for Stirling High School was erected in 1854–56 on the site of the Greyfriars slaughterhouse, soon having over 350 pupils; its old premises became the *Castle Hotel*. In 1856 new premises were built for the poor pupils of the Ragged School, previously taught above a pub. In 1857 a burgh police force was formed, and a Poorhouse to accommodate 200 people was built. By 1861 the population was about 11,500. By the 1870s there were clubs for most sports, including rugby in King's Park, whose football club of that name was formed in 1875. The golf club was founded in 1869, but continued to use much of the undulating terrain of King's Park as its informal course.

**Industry in the 1860s**: By 1865 two coachworks included William Kinross, whose hundred workers made the Queen's coaches and also railway rolling stock. Two firms were making farm machinery, including Kemp & Nicholson who made hand-operated hay presses; and small brick and tile works, rope works, brassfounding, chemicals, brewing, vinegar, aerated water and cattle food manufacturers all worked around that time. By 1868 all the local mills were steam powered, including the Forthvale Mills lately opened by John Todd & Sons for woollen yarn-spinning at Causewayhead, an area which eventually formed part of the burgh; these works had 65 workers and over 6000 spindles; the firm continued until about 1900.

**Tourism and Services**: Erection of the huge Wallace Monument, 67 metres tall, was begun in 1861 above Causewayhead, providing fine views from a gallery overlooking this pivotal area of Scotland. By 1868 nine hotels were open, named *Castle, Commercial, Corn Exchange, Eagle, Golden Lion, Queen's, Railway, Royal* and *Star*, plus two temperance hotels which had opened in the 1840s, and an amazing sixty lodging houses. Henry Campbell, MP for Stirling from 1868, became the Liberal premier in 1906 (as Campbell-Bannerman). In 1872 the town council's High School was classified as one of only 13 in the top grade of public authority schools in Scotland; it was then put under a School Board, which erected large new High School buildings in the town centre in 1888; by then there were many other smaller schools, public and private. A remarkably early fish farm, founded at Howietoun near Stirling in 1874, prospered and eventually became the basis for the University's involvement in this field.

**Builders' Bonanza, Trams, and Highland Soldiers**: In busy 1874 came the peripheral Sheriff Court, which was extended in 1912, the Royal Infirmary – appropriately sited in Spittal Street – and the Smith Art Gallery & Museum, funded by a bequest. In that remarkable year 1874 a horse tramway was also laid down, connecting the town with Causewayhead and Bridge of Allan, and soon after with St Ninians; but this was never electrified. Robert Smith of Cambusbarron *(q.v.)* built the mansion of Brentham Park in 1875. New County Buildings erected at Viewforth in 1874 were repeatedly extended (in 1927, 1937 and 1962). In 1881 the Gordon Highlanders replaced local soldiers at Stirling Castle, which with equal illogic became the Lowland HQ of a newly merged regiment, the Argyll & Sutherland Highlanders! Six fair days were still held in the town, which had become a varied shopping centre: in 1881 the attractive covered shopping arcade was opened, and about then came the department store of Graham & Morton. The Albert Halls were opened for concerts and dances in 1883, and in 1885 the new saloon steamer *Stirling Castle* provided day excursions to Leith. The village of Causewayhead had greatly grown since the railway came, and had an inn by 1888. Cambuskenneth was reached by ferry.

**Phones, Electricity, Rubber, Carpets – and Death**: The telephone arrived in Stirling in 1889. In 1891 the population was 16,750. In 1894 Murray noted only two hotels, the *"good" Golden Lion* and *Royal*, advising coyly that Bridge of Allan was *"a pleasanter place to stay"*. By then the ancient annual Strawberry Fair held at the Abbey site was fading, and in 1895 the erection of a power station was authorised – though it took until 1900 for the public electricity supply to be switched on. The first motor car arrived in 1896 (but the horse-drawn tramway system, last of its kind in Scotland, lingered on until closure and lifting in 1920.) About 1900 Forthvale Mills became a rubber factory and by 1914 the Caledonian Carpet Company was at work. In 1904 new coal mines were opened at Polmaise *(q.v.)*; no houses were built for the miners, who had to commute from overcrowded Stirling, which by 1908 enjoyed the unenviable distinction of having an even worse death rate than notoriously overcrowded Glasgow. But many people benefited from the new Carnegie Library, opened in 1904, and by 1908 they could read the *Stirling Sentinel*.

**Early Aircraft and Service Developments**: In 1908–11 the three Barnwell brothers, Harold, Frank and Archibald, built and tested Scotland's first modestly successful powered aircraft at the family's business at Causewayhead, the Grampian Motor & Engineeering Company *(see also Balfron)*, and the King's Park was the northern turning point in the famous Round Britain Air Race of 1911. A Royal Flying Corps Squadron (No.43) was founded at Stirling in 1916, and pilots were trained for a time up to 1918, flying from Falleninch Farm, and although no permanent airfield resulted because the area was too hilly, air shows were still held up to 1933. Meantime a roller-skating rink was opened; the first silent-film cinema was the *Arcade*, but the first of the town's eventual six true cinemas, the *Electric Theatre*, was opened in 1912, the year when a proper 18-hole golf course was opened in the King's Park. By then harbour freight was minimal, and in 1914 the pleasure steamer services were ended by the war. Fine new municipal offices had just been begun, and most remarkably were completed by 1918.

**New Station and Interwar Modernisation**: Pressure on the railway station had become so severe that in 1913–15 it was rebuilt with three signal boxes, nine platforms, and buildings designed by James Miller of Glasgow (who also designed Wemyss Bay station); even after the 1914–18 war a staff of 80 was employed. The long-established King's Park football club played in the Scottish League from 1921–39, playing at Forthbank. In the 1920s a ropeworks and a cooperage were established at Cambuskenneth. The main streets, still paved with setts, were covered with asphalt in 1921. Five garages were active in the town when Woolworths opened in Stirling in

*Fine glass and ironwork in the roof of Stirling railway station, as rebuilt in the early 20th century.* (RCAHMS / JRH)

1924; ten years later Marks & Spencer opened their first store in the town, which remained among Scotland's more important regional centres. The Raploch council housing estate was begun in 1927 to ease overcrowding in the warren of slums in the old town, where the rate of demolition soon became frenetic.

**Bombs upset Stirling Football**: In 1930 the Stirling Bonding Company was acquired by the Canadian distillers Hiram Walker. In the same year the poorhouse was renamed as Orchard House Hospital (which still survives), but the former prison was abandoned by the army in 1935 and left derelict. Argyll's Lodging was luckier, becoming an early youth hostel in the 1930s. The ancient Cambuskenneth abbey passenger ferry was replaced by a concrete footbridge in 1935. The *Allan Park Cinema* opened in 1938, proving the longest-lasting in the town; however, the *Alhambra*, its sole variety theatre (cum cinema) was closed in 1939, the buildings eventually becoming part of the Arcade shopping centre. During World War II the Scottish headquarters depot of the Royal Electrical & Mechanical Engineers (REME) was established at Forthside. In 1940 or 1941 (sources differ) the stands of King's Park FC were the sole local victims of bombing, causing disbandment. The team re-emerged in 1945 as Stirling Albion, with its base at Annfield Park and changing facilities in Annfield House. The *Stirling Journal* (later the *Journal & Advertiser*) was still published in 1945.

**Development and Clearance from 1945**: By 1952 there were four cinemas, including the large *Regal* with over 2200 seats and a cafe, but television closed the *Queen's* in the 1950s, and by 1970 only the *Allanpark* was open. The seven hotels were all small except the *Golden Lion*, which with the aid of an annexe had half the town's 175 hotel rooms. During the 1950s, despite protests by the burgh architect Walter Gillespie, the benighted town council continued unsympathetically to destroy most of the characterful and improvable buildings of the old town in their zeal to secure better housing. New High School buildings at Torbrex were opened in 1962. In the 1960s the Central Cattle Market was also moved out, from Wallace Street to Kildean. The Castle ceased to be used as a barracks in 1963, and its restoration into a major tourist attraction began the next year.

**Communications Change, and More Education**: By 1952 Stirling had only one steam engine shed, an outpost of Perth which lasted into the mid 1960s, when British Rail developed Stirling as the main Scottish terminal for Motorail services from London, a comfortable but expensive type of travel which was to wither as the road network was improved. In 1970 an eastern inner relief road was opened in Stirling, diving under the station approach, near which a bus station was provided. A section of the M9 motorway between Keir and Pirnhall was built from 1971; opened in 1973, this formed a western bypass. An industrial estate had already grown east of the town, and by 1980 Kirkpatricks had a bacon factory at Cornton Road. Stirling University opened in 1967 at Bridge of Allan *(q.v.)*. The new Wallace High School was opened at Causewayhead in 1972, but the town council, slow as ever with amenities, opened their first swimming pool in their last year 1974. *(For a history of the Royal Burgh, see Mair, 1990.)*

**County HQ to Regional Capital**: The fine new County buildings at Viewforth were erected in 1971–72, enabling removal of the old hotch-potch and influencing the selection of Stirling as HQ of the new Central Region (perhaps even being the justification for its existence). Stirlingshire re-emerged in the 1975 changes, with greatly altered boundaries, as Stirling District, hence retaining two local government centres in the town. In 1975 Kinross's coachworks was demolished, and work began on the large, covered Thistle Shopping Centre, but a sizeable part of the old town wall was retained in the basement of this very successful development, whose shopping draw extends to Dollar and beyond. In 1977 the ailing Smith Art Gallery & Museum was reopened and became a significant attraction, including an industrial collection. The town's last surviving cinema, the *Allanpark*, burned out in 1978 but was later reopened.

**Political Knife-Edge and Positive Changes**: Stirling's balanced overall socio-economic character in 1981 concealed considerable social extremes, as the long-standing but weird political contrast between its parliamentary and local government representatives demonstrated. In the mid 1980s Scottish Amicable Insurance moved all work except their head office from Glasgow city centre to Craigforth at Stirling, and in 1989 planned expansion from 1000 jobs to 1400. Major private housing developments took place at Causewayhead and also both south-east and south-west of the town, and an eastern bypass utilising a third river bridge was partly opened by 1986. By then Stirling Castle was one of Scotland's prime draws for tourists, the careful reconstruction of its Great Hall largely complete by 1994 except for the hammer-beam roof; it was completed and reopened in 1999.

**Rail Cuts and Rapid Industrial Change**: In the 1980s, British Rail (under pressure from the Thatcher regime) abandoned its Motorail services from the West of England and London. In 1990 Superglas glass fibre insulation continued to be made at Kerse Road. In 1991 the population was 30,515, the most typical households occupying public authority flats; a fortunate 16% could still walk to work. Meantime by 1992 the small quilted clothing manufacturer Duncan Honeyman had doubled its workforce in four years, to 80 people, and in 1993 North Cape of Stirling manufactured thermal and mountaineering garments. Although the Gates Rubber factory had closed *(see Locharbriggs)*, its site being redeveloped with student residences, in 1993 unemployment in the area was still below the British average at 9%.

**Facilities Flourishing**: In 1990 a Blackpool concern opened the private 24-bed King's Park Hospital at King's Park. The listed former High School building in Spittal Street was reopened in 1991 as the 76-roomed *Stirling Highland Hotel*, and the Stirling Business Centre was opened in the town centre in 1991. In 1992 the town's *'grand and spacious'* Albert Hall was still highly popular for many uses, including Scottish country dancing. Stirling Castle then drew around a quarter of a million visitors each year, benefiting from the restoration of the Great Hall and the Royal Chapel and apartments; the Smith Art Gallery and Museum was still growing as an attraction. But Scotland's first community radio station, *'Centresound'*, soon failed and had to be rescued in 1990 by Edinburgh's Radio Forth, becoming *'Central FM'*. By then the mansion of Annfield had become derelict, but was restored as a nursing home in the mid 1990s. Although only 700 people would watch a typical Second Division match when Stirling Albion FC played at adjacent Annfield Park (by then in council ownership) in 1992–93 a new stadium and other facilities taking the old name Forthbank was built at Springkerse, 1.5km east of the town centre; part of the money was found by selling the Annfield ground for housing.

**Shopping and Civic Improvements but Rail Regression**: A Safeway store was also built at Springkerse in 1993–94, to provide 250 jobs, and the Walker Group's adjoining 13-unit retail park opened fully let in 1994. A second phase was to be added to the prosperous Thistle Centre, which in 1995 contained both a large Marks & Spencer branch and a major Debenhams store; by contrast the off-centre Tesco store was a huge shed in olive drab cladding. A new civic square was proposed in 1995 to integrate the town centre with Stirling railway station, which still had ten roofed platforms (though with fewer trains only two of these were much used); in 1995 train movements were still controlled from a huge manual signal box, the largest remaining in Scotland. By 1999 EWS were despatching timber from Stirling by rail. In a typical winter's week in 1994 over 10,000 sheep and 325 cattle were sold by the United Auctions (formerly Live Stock Marts) and Caledonian Marts; both were still busy in 2000.

**Modern Roles for Some Historic Buildings**: Broad Street was remodelled with pedestrian areas in 1995; other pedestrian priority areas, road improvements, and a community sports complex were also proposed. The 19th century Erskine Mary Kirk had suffered fire damage after abandonment; its frontage was retained to give character to a major new youth hostel. This opened in 1994 near its former home in Argyll's Lodging, which was being restored in 1995, though its intended use as a University School of Scottish Studies did not materialise. Meanwhile by then Stirling Enterprise had converted a former John Player tobacco factory into a centre for 60 small businesses. By 1995 the old Tolbooth with its Courthouse had become a tartan museum, and its Jail a restaurant. The long disused prison was restored in 1995, partly as a *'Prison Experience'* for morbidly inclined visitors! But the closure of the army depot and engineer parks was announced in 1994, and after a chequered history Forthside House stood derelict in 1997 and was soon dismantled.

**Industry and Business**: The Springkerse Industrial Estate of 80ha was promoted with privately developed nursery factories, and the 24ha Broadleys Industrial Park was begun by the Regional Council. In 1995 another 5300m² of office space was added to recent schemes. The Scottish Amicable building at Craigforth was joined in 1995 by the Castle Business Park, beside junction 10 of the M9. Its first tenants were the medical and production departments of Scotia Pharmaceuticals, a biotechnology company transferring from Guildford; eventually the park was hoped to contain some 23,000m² of offices, a landscaped conference centre and the *Crannog* restaurant. However, Scotia – which employed 100 people and had a branch at Callanish *(see Breasclete)* – was in liquidation in 2001. But glass-makers Superglass now employ 140.

**Local Government and Hotels**: In 1996 Central Region was abolished; Stirling District became an all-purpose local authority, gerrymandered to exclude closely-related Clackmannan in a vain attempt to ensure Tory control. Having reduced the need for local government offices in the town, the then Scottish Office was to site its new Environmental Protection Agency in Stirling. In 2000 a business park replaced the former Motorail siding. After a chequered career, Cowane's Hospital is still in use – for weddings! Despite its modern stadium, Stirling Albion FC seems stuck in the Second Division. Hotels include the largish *Highland* and the historic *Golden Lion*, as well as a number of smaller establishments, plus the youth hostel.

## STOBO & Dawyck

**Map 3, A3**

***Tweedside hamlet,*** *pop. 100*

OS 72: NT 1736

A dark age Culdee community built an early church at Stobo, a sheltered area north-west of the upper Tweed. This had an extensive parish, and in the eighth century Stobo was actually an episcopal centre. However, it lacked natural centrality, and relapsed to a farming role: even the pious King David I seems not to have re-founded a religious community, but a Norman church was built. The valley was well settled when Stobo Kirk and Wester Stobo appeared on Pont's map of about 1600. Stobo parish school was opened in 1604. From 1650 onwards the policies of the early mansion of Dawyck House, across the Tweed 3km south of Stobo, were planted with specimen trees, especially in the 18th century when owned by Sir James Nasmyth. However the Roy map of about 1753 showed little else but the isolated Stobo Kirk, accessed by a track linking roads at Lyne and Drumelzier.

**Slate, Sleepy Station and Botanical Garden**: Eventually a road was made up, and in 1799 Heron mentioned a slate quarry; this long forgotten enterprise, once the most significant producer of slate in southern Scotland, created a major gash in the wooded Quarry Hill to the west. No doubt the profits went to build Stobo Castle, mentioned by Chambers in 1827 as *"the handsome modern mansion of Sir James Montgomery"*. There was from 1864 a very quiet station named Stobo on the Caledonian Railway's branch line from Symington to Peebles, by which time Stobo had a post office. The 1901 population of the parish was 400. But this fell to 240 by 1951, the station had lost its passenger trains by 1953 and the whole line had vanished completely by 1963. By 1969 the woodland gardens of Dawyck were regularly opened to the public, and by 1986 were administered as a fine public facility by the Royal Botanic Garden of Edinburgh; about 1997 the fine 1900s stable block was converted into housing. Stobo post office, near Dawyck Mill, was open in 1988, but has since closed. Only 98 residents remained in 1991; Stobo Castle is now a health clinic.

## STOER

**Map 12, A2**

***Small W. Sutherland village,*** *pop. 100* — OS 15: NC 0328

Pictish brochs stood beside the bays of Clashnessie and Stoer (pronounced *Store)*, on either side of the base of the Rubha Stoer, a remote knobbly peninsula in west Sutherland. The Roy map made about 1750 showed the clachan of Culkein as the only notable feature in this trackless area, whose many lochans became noted for angling. The lighthouse called Stoer Head – which stands 3 km south-west of the Point of Stoer – was first lit in 1870. By the end of the 19th century the various clachans in the area were served by a road from Lochinver, ending near Drumbeg. Stoer's *'Parliamentary'* church and post office stood near the broch, 2 km farther north was Stoer school, and another post office served Clashnessie. By 1951 there was yet another post office, at Culkein, but the total population was only 220, boasting just four telephone lines connected to Stoer exchange; the crofters who had to make a living from such marginal land were evidently very careful, for amazingly there was a sub-branch bank nearby! Clashnessie post office closed about 1968. The Stoer Head light was converted to automatic operation in 1978, its keepers' cottages becoming holiday homes for Northern Lighthouse Board personnel. In 1993 when the crofters happily bought their land, Stoer had a library. The post office has since gone, but there is still a school and a caravan and camping site, while beside the road to the lighthouse there now stands a small wood, almost the first trees to be seen on the bleak peninsula for centuries.

## STONEHAVEN & Cowie

**Map 10, C4**

***Mearns coastal town,*** *pop. 9500* — OS 45: NO 8785

Some 20 km south of Aberdeen the adjacent mouths of the Waters of Cowie and Carron interrupt the cliff-girt coast of the Mearns. Between them stands Cheyne Hill, the 170 m high end of Fetteresso Forest, where the central massif of Scotland, the *'Mounth'* – which in early days divided the Northern from the Southern Picts – most closely approaches the east coast. About 3 km north of the Cowie Water are Pictish standing stones; William Roy, the 18th century mapmaker, speculated that this was the site of the elusive battle of Mons Graupius; but there are other contenders, e.g. Strathmiglo. (If we could be sure, should we correct the spelling to Graupian TV?)

**Cowie – Briefly Important**: In historic times the area south of the Carron Water was for long a part of Dunnottar parish, while to the north were Fetteresso and Ury parishes; remains of the latter's church survive on the cliffs. Cowie on the coast of Ury parish was the first place to develop significance, having a castle and an extensive thanage from about the 11th century. In the 15th century the keep of Fetteresso Castle was built above the Carron Water 3 km west of Cowie, which was mentioned by Hardying about 1415, and chartered as a burgh of barony in 1542. By 1593 Cowie was the centre of a presbytery, and by the time that Pont sketch-mapped the area around 1600, *'Kowy'* was a major settlement for the period, with a bridge over the Cowie Water. Fetteresso Castle then stood in an extensive wooded park; below it was the Mill of Forest.

**Burgh and Fishy County Town**: Stonehaven – south of the Carron's mouth, about 1 km across the bay from Cowie – was chartered as a barony burgh in 1587, and a breakwater had already been built when Pont referred to it as *'Stonay or Duhiness'*. Stonehaven harbour was very soon extended, by 1600 a tolbooth stood on the quay, and in 1607 Stonehaven became the county town of problematical Kincardineshire. Ury held a parish school by 1618 and Fetteresso did so by 1628. Tucker noted Stonehaven in 1655 as *"a little fisher town, where formerly goods have been brought in, but not of late, hindered from doing so by the neighbourhood and privileges of the burgh of Montrose"*. The very next year, Richard Franck called *Steenhive*, as it was known, *"stinking hive, because it's so unsavoury"* (rotting fish?) – though the road south was better than the awful way to Aberdeen. A post office was opened in 1669. The so-called *'Bulwark'* pier was replaced in 1688, and the north harbour was built in 1700. The offending section of road was made up for military use early in the 18th century.

**Fishing and Imprisonment, Sailcloth and Sheeting**: Besides speculations about the battle, Roy's map made about 1750 showed Stonehaven as a nucleated settlement with a harbour, standing on the road from Montrose to Aberdeen and having two tracks inland. The town did not extend north of the Carron Water, and neither that nor the Cowie Water appeared to be bridged. By then Cowie was insignificant. Alexander Carlyle who traversed the area in 1765 wrote of *"Stonehive, a little fishing town, remarkable for nothing but its harbour, which is the only one on that coast that can be entered with a strong north-east wind, and is on that account of very great consequence"*. Between 1755 and 1784 a prison was built by the Commissioners for the Forfeited Estates. Development accelerated towards the end of the century: the *Ship Inn* was built on the Shore Head in 1771, and flax spinning became a local trade. About 1780 a 75-loom sailcloth works was set up by an Aberdeen merchant; it died with him, to be replaced in 1793 by a smaller works. Meantime in 1792 Arbroath merchants had set up the manufacture of Osnaburgs, sheetings and linen checks. Stonehaven built its Town House in 1790 and was a post town by 1797; two annual fairs were scheduled. In 1799 Heron described it as a *"fishing-town of over a thousand inhabitants, with a manufacture of canvas, and some trade in dried fish and oil"*, most of which came from dogfish.

**Tanning, Brewing and Distilling**: In 1809 John Paterson extended Fetteresso Castle into a vast mansion for the Duff family. Stonehaven was well served in the coaching era, by which time the Carron had also been bridged: by 1811 it lay on the route of a daily coach between Montrose and Aberdeen. A bark mill for tanneries was at work by 1823, and there were breweries at Carronside and Bridge of Cowie in 1825; and a Bank of Scotland branch opened. Chambers then called it *"a* *large town; the oldest part is irregularly and not very well built; but on the north bank of the rivulet, there is a New Town, composed of neat and regular streets. The harbour is at present undergoing a course of improvements, principally by the erection of a pier on the south side"*. Captain Barclay, a famed long-distance walker or runner who in 1809 covered 1000 miles in 1000 hours, established the water-powered Glenury-Royal distillery with a McDonald in 1825. It must have been about then that the neo-classical sheriff court and police station was built, using a white stone untypical of the area.

**Aberdeen Railway and Japanese Lighthouses**: From 1848 the Aberdeen Railway (later part of the Caledonian system) strode across the Ury valley on the originally timber-arched Glenury Viaduct at a height of nearly 50m. When completed to Aberdeen in 1850, it opened new horizons: Richard Brunton, born at Fetteresso in 1841, became a civil engineer under the Stevensons in Edinburgh. Through them he was appointed by the Japanese government in 1868 to design and supervise the construction of almost 50 lighthouses and the Yokohama harbour works; later he managed *'Paraffin'* Young's Scottish oil refineries. By 1860 Wordie & Co had a rail cartage depot. The population of the Mearns as a whole reached a plateau about 1850, when Stonehaven had some 30 fishing boats. A lifeboat station was opened in 1867, and as Stonehaven became an important herring fishing port, the number of local boats soon grew to a hundred; the fish jetty was extended in 1877. The *Marine Hotel* was built on the Shore Head in 1884. In 1886 the distillery had its own engineers and cooperage, and used local barley to make 600,000 litres of Highland malt whisky a year; Barnard found *"a cosy little inn near the station"*.

**Scenic Golf, Dodgy Hotels and Salt-water Bathing**: Stonehaven golf club, founded in 1888, laid out a spectacular 18-hole course on the cliffs north of the town, and the very substantial Dunnottar Public School (the parish primary) was built near the harbour in 1889; both are still used. The 1891 population was 4500. Murray's Handbook for 1894 called Stonehaven a *"flourishing little port"* and (surprisingly) *"considerably in repute as a bathing place"*. Its bleak sea wall and shingle beach, to say nothing of the water's low temperature, would nowadays discourage sea bathing! Repeating the doubts of most previous commentators, Murray remarked of each of three Stonehaven hotels – the *Commercial, Station* and *Urie Arms* – *"not good"*. A spire was added to the Town House in 1896; more importantly, a new breakwater was built in 1908. Stonehaven's local newspaper the *Mearns Leader* first appeared in 1912, but fishing fell away during the 20th century, and the lifeboat station was closed in 1934. However, an open-air heated salt water swimming pool 50m long was opened the same year. By 1951 there was a population of over 5000 and typical town facilities, with a prominent central store advertising *'millinery, costumes and outfitting'*. Fetteresso Castle was unroofed in 1954, and after a local mill closed about 1960 Stonehaven became very quiet.

**Local Government and Oil grow, but No Whisky!**: The old quayside Tolbooth was restored in 1963, becoming a museum. An inshore lifeboat station was opened in 1967, a century after the original but long-lost facility, and a new building was provided for Mackie Academy in the late 1960s. From 1975 Stonehaven became the administrative HQ of the large but very rural Kincardine and Deeside District (which incorporated the old county and part of Aberdeenshire). In the 1970s much expansion took place in the form of overspill from oil-pressurised Aberdeen, making Stonehaven more an Aberdeen dormitory than a fishing port; but both Fetteresso and the Victorian Ury House were derelict shells by 1980. In the 1980s some 20 fishing boats were still based in Stonehaven harbour, while Robert Gordon's Institute of Technology had opened a deep sea rescue research establishment; a pleasure sailing club (see below) also related it to Aberdeen. Carronhall Engineering made modular cabin units for oilfield use by 1983, and in 1990 Albyn Plastics was producing combs and hairbrushes for the European market. The Glenury-Royal distillery was extended in 1966, but closed in 1985 and in 1992 the site was sold for housing.

**Bypass, Better Pool – and the Last Home of the SOS**: Stonehaven was relieved of through traffic by the opening of a bypass in 1986, helping it to maintain its role as a significant local service centre for one of Scotland's least developed areas. Fast-growing itself, with 9445 residents by 1991, Stonehaven had developed a dormitory character. The roofless Fetteresso Castle was restored as flats in the early 1990s, and the former Cowie Mills were also converted to flats about 1993. The Tidy Britain Group found the condition of the beach at Stonehaven *'disappointing'* in 1994. So the reconditioning of the swimming pool – the last of its kind in Scotland – in 1997 was very welcome. Meantime by 1995 Morse was a slowly dying means of marine distress signalling, so in that year the BT radio station at Stonehaven with its staff of eleven became the sole translation point for Morse code messages received from within a 1000km radius by relay stations around Britain. A new 49-bed hospital to replace the NHS facilities was built in Stonehaven for the Grampian Health Board from 1996. Stonehaven ceased to head a local authority in that year when Kincardine & Deeside was merged into a new single-tier council for Aberdeenshire.

**Specialised Services**: Today, Mackie Academy has a roll of almost 1200 pupils. There is still a Stagecoach bus depot, at least two banks, a modern Somerfield store and various specialist shops and services. The ground floor of the former drapery store is an Alldays grocery, but the historic upper floor signs remain. A popular new beachhead boardwalk links the centre to the harbour with its ancient *Ship Inn*, the Tolbooth restaurant and the newer *Marine Hotel*, which has lately been enlarged by incorporating an old 4-storey granary. The inner basin is full of the yachts of the Aberdeen & Stonehaven Yacht Club, whose HQ is beside it; close by are boats of Maritime Rescue International. There is no longer a fish market, and only a few scallops go for processing. There are several small hotels and guest houses.

## STONEHOUSE

**Map 16, A5**

***Lanarkshire large village,*** *pop. 5400*

OS 64: NS 7546

Sited beside the Avon Water 9km south-east of Hamilton, Stonehouse was by the late 15th century a property of the powerful Arran family. Pont who mapped the area about 1600 showed a thickly-settled area, with a bridge across the Avon west of the undated Cots Castle. Humbie was 2.5km west of *'Stonhous'*, which was shown as a row of buildings, one at least presumably already constructed of stone, at a time when most Scottish peasantry still occupied huts. A parish school was started in 1630, and a burgh of barony charter was granted in

1667. The mid 18th century Roy map showed *'Stenhouse'* as a small village already served by three rather devious roads, the extremely indirect route to Strathaven via Glassford crossing the bridge which by then had been built north of the village at Linthaugh. When the Hamilton to Lesmahagow road was turnpiked it crossed the Dalserf to Stonehouse road at Canderside Toll near Swinhill, later a mining area. Stonehouse became known for handloom weaving; in 1799 Heron wrote of *"about 600 inhabitants"*. About then the silk industry took over for half a century; some handloom weaving continued into the late 19th century. Cots Castle had early 19th century limekilns, and Cander Mill to the east is also of that period. Stonehouse acquired its first post office around 1825, after the completion of Telford's east–west road through the town. A branch of the Caledonian Railway connecting Cots Castle with Larkhall was opened for minerals in 1864 and for passengers to Stonehouse in 1866; it reached Strathaven in 1905. In 1891 the population was 2800.

**Colliery, Hospital and Abortive New Town**: By 1895 a colliery had been sunk south-east of the village at Dovesdale, and a small hospital existed by 1903. By 1951 this had become a large general hospital and over 4000 people lived locally, but the other facilities of Stonehouse were those of a large village. The railway was closed to passengers in 1965, and had been lifted by 1971. Stonehouse was designated as a New Town in 1973, intended to take overspill from greater Glasgow and to promote economic development in Clydesdale. But as a result of an overdue policy shift towards urban renewal in the older settlements of Strathclyde, the project was cancelled in 1977 just as the first small group of New Town houses was nearing completion. The general hospital was said to be marginal by 1978, with 369 beds. By then, despite an appreciable rise in population, the other local facilities had fallen to those of an ordinary village, with the loss of its secondary school, post town status, and cinema. Local developments of substance were few up to 1991, when the population was 5328. However, the hospital stayed open. In the early 1990s some housing development resumed and an A71 bypass of the main part of the village was completed, following the route of the former railway.

## STONEYBURN & Bents

**Map 16, C4**

***W. Lothian village,*** *pop. 2000* — OS 65: NS 9762

Stoneyburn in West Lothian lies about 200m above sea level in a farming area, through which runs the Breich Water. A road linked Livingston with Carluke by the 1750s. Bents station was opened in 1864 on the new Morningside & Coltness Branch of the North British Railway, which linked Bathgate with the Motherwell area. By 1895 *'Stonyburn'* Farm – north of the Breich, 1km east of the station – adjoined the tiny Stonyburn Colliery, which was not connected to any of the various mineral lines in the area. The 1901 population of Stoneyburn was 600, rising to 2500 by 1931 and then falling back slightly; by then the colliery was a much larger rail-connected operation, with pitheads on both sides of the Breich Water. Stoneyburn had grown along the Fauldhouse to Livingston road, with housing estates at either end by 1951, and the facilities of a typical small village lining the main road. There were also two doctors and a 100-pupil secondary school; but Bents station had already closed. By 1971 the mine too had closed, the railway lines had all vanished and the population had fallen to 1000, plus 1400 in Bents. Slow decline continued; but apart from the closure of secondary classes, in 1981 the facilities remained much as before. Even by 1987 – when extensive landscaping had replaced the dereliction – almost no new development was evident except for a caravan site at Cuthill. By 1991 the combined population had fallen to 2003. The primary school and the Bentswood pub are still open, but the post office has gone.

## STONEYKIRK

**Map 1, B5**

***Galloway village,*** *pop. 300* — OS 82: NX 0953

The huge rural parish of Stoneykirk, 8km south-east of Stranraer, replaced that of Kirkmadrine, 5km farther south; Stony Kirk was marked in a well-settled area on Pont's map of around 1600. By the 1750s it stood beside the road from Stranraer to Drummore. In 1792 the Old Statistical Account noted four flax mills and a bleachfield in the parish, but these all faded to nothing, and no railway ever reached the area. Stoneykirk had a post office by 1901, when the parish population (including Sandhead) was 2420. The second world war airbase of West Freugh, 2 km to the east, later found another role as a part of the Royal Aircraft Establishment. The population declined rapidly from the 1950s, although a garage and post office long remained. Only 1062 residents were left in the whole parish in 1991, about 300 in Stoneykirk. The old parish church has closed, and the post office closed in the late 1990s; there is still a pub.

## STORNOWAY

**Map 11, C2**

***Main town of Isle of Lewis,*** *pop. 7200* — OS 8: NB 4232

The finest natural harbour in the huge and peaty Hebridean island of Lewis was named Stornoway – *Steering Bay* in Old Norse, meaning THE place to make for. By 1506 it was dominated by Lews Castle, home of the powerful MacLeods of Lewis. Monro noted in 1549 that the Isle of Lewis was *"fair and well inhabited at the coast, fertile and fruitful for bere, with many sheep, four parish kirks, and a castle called Stornoway"*. About 2 km to the north the River Laxdale (*'Salmon Valley'* in Norse) enters the sea at Loch a Tuath. Herrings, whiting, haddock and whales were also caught. The castle appeared surrounded by half a dozen tiny settlements on Pont's crude map of around 1600. From 1598 the *Fife Adventurers*, a group of east coast lairds, tried to take over the island and *'pacify'* the turbulent local clans; the Adventurers built stone houses at Stornoway, but these had already been ruined by several bombardments before the place was made a burgh of barony in 1607, and by 1610 the intended *'colony'* had failed. Lewis was granted to Lord Seaforth in 1628, but taken back by the capricious Charles I a few years later as part of the Lordship of the Isles.

**Stornoway in Ross-shire – and Dutch Settlers**: In the mid 17th century Stornoway was refortified by the Commonwealth, and with a view to enforcing order on the clansmen, Lewis was transferred from the Lordship of the Isles to the sheriffdom of Ross-shire in 1661. (Local administration from Dingwall across 200km of trackless moorland and storm-swept sea was not the most convenient or rational arrangement they could have devised, but because the mandarins in Edinburgh and Whitehall were even more remote it persisted until 1975!)

Martin, writing in 1703, noted that Loch Stornoway was still *"a harbour well known by seamen, with a village which consists of about sixty families with some houses of entertainment, a church and a school, in which Latin and English are taught. The Steward of the Lewis has his residence in this village"* which also held a *'magazine'* for storing casks and salt. Stornoway castle had been *"destroyed by the English garrison, kept there by Oliver Cromwell; however a few Dutch families settled in Stornoway after the Restoration and taught the islanders something of the art of fishing. Although cunning merchants conspired to remove the Dutch settlers, the people of the little village of Stornoway excel all those of the neighbouring isles in the fishing trade ever since that time"*.

**Urban Development to 1789**: Later a cattle tryst was established, from which beasts could be shipped to the mainland, and Stornoway – which also traded overseas in defiance of the Royal Burghs – acquired a post office in 1757. About 1763 the Commissioners for the Forfeited Estates founded a spinning school for girls, the first of eight in Lewis. Sir Alexander Mackenzie, after whom Canada's great Mackenzie River is named, was born in Stornoway in 1764. In 1786 John Knox II visited Stornoway, finding 13 ships at anchor, including one of 600 tons – then a very large size. *"The town of Stornoway being rebuilt with houses of stone, lime, and slate, makes a handsome appearance."* But he was surprised to find the lately built quay *"so much out of repair that the vessels load and unload upon the beach, or in the bay, by means of boats"*. Though there was an inn, the Earl of Seaforth – by then back in possession – entertained him at Seaforth Lodge which stood impressively at the head of the bay. By 1789 Stornoway comprised about fifty *"sash and slated"* houses.

**Fast Growth in Stornoway**: Classed as a post town in 1797, the mails came but once a week, via Poolewe. Later a more frequent mail service was arranged, roughly on alternate days, for the town was growing fast. Heron remarked of Stornoway in 1799 that *"by the attention of the noble proprietor Lord Seaforth, it is become a flourishing town, the only town in Lewis"*. It had a custom-house, and a trade *"chiefly in fish, kelp, oil, feathers and skins"*. The large Sail Loft was erected on the quayside in the early 19th century, and a small woollen mill was built about 1820. Chambers remarked of Lewis in 1827 that *"the chief town is Stornoway, which is rapidly acquiring the luxuries and elegancies of life"*. (But his claim of *"nearly 5000 inhabitants"* seems excessive.) By 1828 steamers were providing a fortnightly service between Stornoway and Glasgow's Broomielaw, leading to the building of the *Lewis Hotel* in 1829.

*Stornoway harbour in 1976, showing seine-netting boats built for local fishermen with government subsidy.* (JRH)

**The Mathesons develop Stornoway and Lewis**: Despite Heron's fulsome praise for Lord Seaforth, when Sir James Matheson bought the island in 1844 with the proceeds of his Hong Kong business there was only one wheeled vehicle on it! Over 2000 head of cattle were sold at the tryst in 1845, but gradually sheep replaced cattle in Lewis and Harris; a more substantial woollen mill was built of brick in James Street in the late 19th century. Meantime a sheriff court-house was built in the 1840s, and in 1845–75 Matheson carried through a road-building programme for Lewis. All the roads from Stornoway to north, south and west had to traverse the Laxdale area, which began to change from scattered crofts into a ribbon-developed for the town. He also arranged for a daily postal service using his ship *Mary Jane*, built for the purpose in 1846; this then linked with Portree and Lochinver. Gas lighting was made available from about the same time. Lady Matheson established a *'Female industrial school'* (domestic and academic) in 1848. Wooden clipper ships were built for a time, although every plank had to be imported; Stornoway was by then a port of registry, with the letters SY. From 1851 Hutcheson's weekly steamers linked Stornoway with Glasgow via Portree; from 1853 there was also an Oban service. The iron lighthouse at Arnish came into service in 1852.

**Herrings make a Small Town Cheerful?**: Herring fishing, which became the town's mainstay in the 19th century, saw over 6000 fishermen present at the port on peak days. Stornoway was the busiest herring port in Scotland in the 1867 season, and also at that time among the top ten in curing white fish. The herring fishery later died out from over-exploitation. The Caledonian Bank of Inverness had a branch in Stornoway by about 1878; David MacBrayne took over the steamers in 1879 and arranged a service of two steamers a week to Glasgow from 1881. A lifeboat station was opened in 1887, the first in the Outer Hebrides. The 1891 population was 3400. By 1894 there were also regular steamers to Stromness and to Liverpool; the daily steamer from the railhead at Strome Ferry arrived at *"a cheerful small town"* with three banks. The three hotels, the *Lewis, Imperial* and *Royal*, were all *"good"* according to Murray's Handbook, whose scout must have visited the sabbatarian island on a weekday. A sheriff-substitute and prison were necessary because Gaelic-speaking Lewis remained in the Ross Sheriffdom and County. This remote community was nominally administered from English-speaking Dingwall via the Highland Railway and MacBrayne's mail steamers *Clansman* and *Claymore*. A start was soon made on a Carnegie assisted public library.

**Optimism and Tragedy**: A carding and spinning mill for Harris Tweed was built at Stornoway in 1903–06, and the head office of the newly established Harris Tweed Association was opened at Stornoway in 1910. In 1914–15 a weekly freight steamer service was operated to Stornoway by John Hay of Glasgow. The local newspaper, the *Stornoway Gazette & West Coast Advertiser* was started in 1917, an optimistic venture in the third year of the war; yet it succeeded, being for many years the only bilingual newspaper in Scotland, and had its own printing business. In the *Iolaire* disaster of New Year's Day in 1919, 200 Lewismen returning from the war were drowned within sight of the town. Optimism returned when woollen spinning on a truly commercial scale began about 1920, and the herring reappeared in economic numbers in 1924.

**Into the Air Age**: In 1934 an air service was started to Inverness, and to Renfrew from 1935, flying from an airstrip which was combined with a golf course. Both were taken over in the second world war by RAF Coastal Command and made into a permanent base – which subsequently doubled as Stornoway Airport. The name HMS *Mentor* was adopted in 1939 for the Naval shore base at Stornoway, active until 1944. Stornoway golf club, founded in 1947, laid out a replacement 18-hole course in the policies of the derelict Lews Castle, which was converted to a technical college in 1951. The town's population was then about 5350, while Laxdale had about 950 people, a post office and a junior secondary school. About then a new Seamen's Institute was built, and Stornoway had a full range of urban facilities, including hospitals, plus the Hydro Board's new diesel-driven power station. In 1958 there was an isolated 2 km tramway leading up to Loch Mor an Stairr, and a group of radio masts. Arnish became an automatic light in 1963.

**Capital of the Western Isles**: Loganair first flew to Stornoway in the mid 1960s. Improved access from the mainland by a car ferry from Ullapool was introduced in 1973, the 40-room *Cabarfeidh Hotel* was built about that time, and by 1975 caravan and camping facilities were available at Laxdale. In the 1975 reorganisation the Western Islands Council *(Comhairle nan Eilean)* took over local government for the whole island chain – including Harris, the Uists and Barra (which had been under Inverness till then). The new council soon brought some 50 secondary pupils aged 16+ from Uist and Barra to board in hostels at Stornoway's Nicholson Institute. An attractive new council HQ building was brought into use in 1979. In 1978 the Royal Bank's mobile bank based in the town made a 2-week circuit of the whole of Lewis and Harris.

**Oil-Related Industry at Arnish**: The town also grew with oil-related industry, the Arnish Point yard at the harbour entrance being created in 1973–75 by Fred Olsen of Norway. It was operated by Lewis Offshore to build oil tanks and barges, providing up to 350 jobs, a third going to 'returners' from the mainland. In 1979 it converted a drilling rig for production; this required 400 temporary workers living in a moored liner. The Arnish yard passed to the Dutch firm Heerema in 1982. By 1989 it had closed, but reopened with a hundred jobs in 1990 following a buyout by former workers, under the reactivated title of Lewis Offshore. In 1992 it employed 170 people, but only about 130 in 1994; a new contract kept the yard open into 1995. Stornoway remained a fairly important fishing port, where two fish markets were held each week. Up to 200 tonnes of fish a day was processed into meal by the Rolf Olsen factory in 1979, when the Stornoway Pier & Harbour Commission decided to build a new fish market.

**Alginate, Boatbuilding, US Navy and BCCI**: Only primary classes remained at Laxdale by 1980, but a garage had opened. A 1960s alginate factory at the remote township of Keose on Loch Erisort south of Stornoway was taken over by a co-operative in 1981. In the late 1970s Fleming Engineering provided repair and slipway facilities for small ships of up to 750 tons, and by 1995 a Stornoway boatyard was owned by Lithgow's *(see Port Glasgow)*. By 1989 the military side of the airfield was a US Navy reserve base for anti-submarine warfare. Huge losses were caused by the unwise investment of much of the Island Council's funds in the fraud-ridden Bank of Credit & Commerce International, which was closed down in 1991; besides cuts in services, the immediate result was a huge rise in the demand for tourist information!

**Harris Tweed Troubles**: In 1979 the Harris Tweed group, Clansman Holdings, included Newall & Son, Smiths of Stornoway, and Stephen Burns Ltd. Gillies & Sons were manufacturers and merchants of woollens and worsteds at Sandwick, 2 km east of the town, but by 1983 appeared simply as merchants. Up to 1989 a hundred workers spun yarn and finished Harris Tweed at the Clansman mill in Bell's Road, but USA demand fell away and the factory closed. In 1990 Bruce Burns bought looms from bankrupt Coloroll and set up a factory to process gossamer weight Harris Tweed; by 1994 he employed 20 people and up to 50 of the more progressive home weavers. In 1992 tweedmaking was still taught at Lews Castle College, though the number of weavers of Harris Tweed had fallen to only 400. In 1992 Macleod of Shawbost *(q.v.)* acquired the Stornoway mill of Kenneth Mackenzie in Sandwick Road, installing machines to finish 150 cm wide cloth woven on the new type of hand loom. In 1996 both mills remained in production in the ownership of the Murray family. A new mill, independently owned by Harris Tweed Weavers, began production in 1996.

**Gaelic Twilight or Cultural Revival?**: Acair, a Gaelic publishing house established in Stornoway in 1977, now claims 370 titles in print. The BBC's *Radio nan Eilean* (Radio of the Isles) was established at Stornoway in 1979, both this and the Western Islands Council in some degree counteracting the effect of Stornoway as a powerful English-speaking enclave in the last bastion of Gaelic speech. This was spoken by fewer people in 1991 than ever before – barely half the town's (rather elderly) population of 7233 (including more youthful Laxdale). In 1985 an art gallery, *An Lanntair* (The Lantern) was opened in Stornoway. The cinema was still functioning as the *Twilight* in 1992, combined with a night club. The vacant Clansman mill in Bell's Road was taken over in 1992 as studios for STV's *Machair*, a Gaelic-language soap opera which, suitably subtitled, was seen as a way of re-popularising Gaelic speech. Some 66 jobs were created, but the audience for *Machair*, which started at 0.5 million, was down to 0.3 million by the end of 1993 and it eventually ceased production, leaving news, documentary and children's programmes to carry the torch.

**Gaelic and Galloway?**: In 1991 the *Stornoway Gazette* had remarkably been acquired by the *Galloway Gazette* of Newton Stewart; but in 1991 the LEC *'Iomart nan Eilean Siar'* (Western Isles Enterprise) set up its base in Stornoway – which still retained its sheriff court. By 1995 Safeway had two small Presto supermarkets in the town centre, at risk from a proposed Co-op superstore. Haddock, prawns, crabs, scallops and white fish were still landed in 1997, the August livestock sales dealt in ewes and lambs, and Tavay Organics still processed seaweed into alginates. Several marine engineering firms are locally in business.

**Uist Pupils spared Lewis School; University beckons**: Stornoway monopolised senior secondary education in the Western Isles until the opening of Lionacleit School in 1988,

*Quality Harris Tweed, as produced in Stornoway. Harris itself has no tweed factories, for this originated as a cottage industry.* *(SMPC / Ken Paterson)*

when Uist pupils were pleased to return south. With the provision of senior secondary education in Harris too, the boarding hostels in Stornoway were closed one by one – the last in 1995. Lews Castle School has secondary classes S3-S5 (about 150 pupils). In 1999 the good air services facilitated the integration of the College into the new virtual University of the Highlands and Islands. In 2000 the latest in telecoms also enabled the modern coastguard station to take over a share of the work formerly undertaken at Oban. The new 212-bed Western Isles Hospital opened at Laxdale in 1992, replacing two old local hospitals and also enabling some patients previously treated on the mainland to be cared for nearer home.

**Interest, Access and Accommodation**: Although by 1992 there was an interesting museum and a leisure and fitness centre, the characterful Sail Loft became disused in 1999. However, since 1998 new premises (opposite the ferry terminal) for the arts centre *An Lanntair* have been designed – and redesigned! Grampian TV have a 12-person staff in the town. The car ferry *Isle of Lewis*, built by Fergusons of Port Glasgow, became the largest in the Calmac fleet, entering service between Ullapool and Stornoway in 1995. Air services link Stornoway with Glasgow, Inverness, Benbecula, and Northbay on Barra. Medium-sized hotels now include the *Cabarfeidh* the *Royal* and the *Seaforth*; a small hostel for backpackers is open, plus another at Laxdale Holiday Park.

## STOW & Stagehall — Map 3, A3

***N. Borders village,*** *pop. 530 / 940 (area)* — OS 73: NT 4544

Stow, which bears a name typical of early Anglian settlement and therefore said with a long 'O' (though some now rhyme it with *'Cow')*, stands in the upper valley of the winding Gala Water, which long bore the Anglian name of *'Wedale'*. Stow's early church was of Northumbrian origin, i.e. pre-12th century. After the area was incorporated into Scotland it was placed in the sheriffdom of Edinburgh. By then the valley was administratively known as the Regality of Stow, as shown on Pont's maps of about 1600, though these provided no details except Stow Kirk. There are fragmentary remains of four undated castles in the vicinity, and there was a mill at Stow. A parish school was opened in 1628 and a packhorse bridge was built across the Gala Water in 1655, linking Stow with the hamlet of Stagehall on the west bank, which lay on the original road from Edinburgh to Galashiels and Melrose; its coaching function is implied by its name. However, the Roy map made about 1754 showed that north of Stow the so-called *'road'* to Edinburgh still criss-crossed the Gala Water about six times!

**Roads, Coaching, Trains and Woollens**: Turnpiking of the road was carried out under an Act of 1768. Stagehall had gained a post office by 1775 and was a post town, with a mail service on alternate weekdays by 1797. Heron mentioned Stow as a *"small village"* in 1799; by 1827 Chambers found *"the Stow a delightfully irregular and old-fashioned village, mostly inhabited by weavers"*. Nearby Torsonce, 1km to the south, had *"a first-rate inn"*. The Edinburgh & Hawick Railway opened in 1849, its Stow station being at Stagehall, but little development arose. In 1891 the population of Stow was 420. The parish population in 1951 was 1150 (including tiny Fountainhall), with the facilities of a small village, including the *Royal Hotel*, and agricultural engineers. The station stayed open until the railway was closed completely in 1969, while the population steadily shrank to 975 in 1971. Stow was transferred from Midlothian to the Borders Region (Ettrick & Lauderdale District) in 1975. Woollen goods were still made at Stow Mill in 1980 by Walter Mercer & Son, though this activity seems to have ceased by 1988. The 1991 parish population was 938 including 528 in Stow village, whose *Royal Hotel*, primary school and post office are still active.

## STRACATHRO, Inchbare & Northwater Bridge

**Map 6, C2**

***Angus localities,*** *pop. 400* — OS 45: NO 6265

The most northerly of all known Roman forts (as distinct from marching camps) was built about the year 85 on a peninsula between the Cruik Water and the West Water in Strathmore. After the Romans had gone the locals named the area *Strath Caer Ro*, meaning *'Wide Valley of the Roman Castle'*, and the Christian church of Stracathro parish was sited over the pagan fort. In 1296 John Balliol submitted to Edward I at Stracathro. In the 16th century the tower of Inglismaldie Castle was built north of the River North Esk 3km farther east. The important Northwater Bridge already spanned the North Esk when Pont noted it on a manuscript map around 1600. Roy's survey of about 1750 showed little around the kirk except the road from Brechin to Northwater Bridge (the later A94). Soon the Westwater Bridge was built across its eponymous stream 1km to the west of the kirk, and around it developed a nucleus which Heron in 1799 described as *"the village of Strickathrow"*, also known as Inchbare.

**Mansion and Hospital**: In 1827–30 Alexander Cruikshanks chose a site near the fort for his emparked classical mansion of Stracathro House, which was bought by the government in 1939 and became in 1940 the doctors' residence for a large Emergency Medical Service General Hospital of hutments built in the park, considered a *'safe'* rural site for use in the event of the destruction of Aberdeen or Dundee hospitals by bombing. Soon brought into full wartime use for service and civilian patients, it was gradually run down after 1945. Refitted for permanent use about 1971, it then provided 750 jobs, with laboratories, a school of nursing, and orthopaedic and skin-grafting specialisms. Inchbare lost its post office around 1973, but by 1986 had the small factory of Edzell Engineering, a timber yard and village hall. In 1993 it was controversially proposed that accident and emergency services should be transferred to Stracathro from Arbroath, but it was instead decided in 1999 that the whole hospital should be closed and replaced by a new community hospital, at either Stracathro or Arbroath.

## STRACHUR

**Map 5, A4**

***Argyll village, L. Fyne,*** *pop. 650 (area)* — OS 56: NN 0901

An ancient dun and a medieval motte stand near the south-east shore of Loch Fyne, where an easy routeway leads via Loch Eck to the Holy Loch. The ruined 15th century keep of Castle Lachlan stands on a small peninsula in Strathlachlan parish, 10km to the south-west (OS 55). By 1563 a ferry plied across the loch between Inverleachan (now called Furnace, OS 55) and Creggans on the south-east shore, a site identified as *'Port Chreigan'* by Pont about thirty years later. The Roy map surveyed around 1750 showed the *'Craigan'* Ferry, from which tracks led via the *'Kirk of Strachurr'* to Loch Eck, and south west via Kilmodan to the Kyles of Bute. From 1755 till about 1820 the ferry carried cattle eastwards, and charcoal for the smelter at Furnace westwards. Strachur House was built in the 1780s. Around 1810 Creggans was connected by road through its neighbouring township of Strachur by way of Loch Eckside with Ardentinny on Loch Long. A new Castle Lachlan was built on a more sheltered site by the Clan MacLachlan.

**Hostelry, Forestry and Sawmilling**: The *Creggans Inn* was established in 1863. A post office and the *Strachur Hotel* were open by 1894, and Strachur and Creggans had become a small resort village where the steamer *Lord of the Isles* on the service from Greenock called at Creggans pier. The 1901 population of Strachur parish was 500. The steamer in effect provided a ferry to its destination at Inveraray; but this service did not outlast the 1939–45 war, after which the Forestry Commission built houses at Strachur, and created the hamlet of Glenbranter, 4km south. A sawmill for timber brought from Inverleiver Forest beside Loch Awe was open at Strachur by 1959, making pit props. About 1962 Sir Fitzroy Maclean, who lived in Strachur House, upgraded the *Creggans Inn* to a substantial hotel, which claims one of the finest views in Scotland. The pier was derelict by 1991, when the parish had 628 residents. The post office, school and timber merchants BSW Harvesting are still open. The historic *Creggans Inn* has a new restaurant and 17 rooms, with access to sports in Strachur Park; *Castle Lachlan* may be hired.

## STRAITON

**Map 1, C3**

***Small Ayrshire village,*** *pop. 300* — OS 77: NS 3804

Little now remains of the 16th century castles of Cloncaird and Blairquhan, which stood either side of the Water of Girvan 6–8km south-east of Maybole. When Timothy Pont mapped Carrick about 1600 the area was thickly settled and both castles seem to have been emparked, Blairquhan later becoming a mansion. Pont's map showed the ancient kirk of *'Stratun'*, Kirkland, the Milton and a bridge across the Water of Girvan. By the middle of the 18th century the Kirk of Straiton was at the centre of a local road system towards the four cardinal points, much as shown on later maps. The *Black Bull Inn* dates from 1766, part of a contemporary and very attractively planned estate village, remarked on by Heron in 1799 as *"a small but beautiful village"*. By 1895 it also had a post and telegraph office; a smithy and mill were marked. An estate sawmill was in action throughout the later 20th century. The level of tiny Loch Bradan, 8km south-east, was raised by a dam constructed around 1972, by which time the planting of Carrick Forest was far advanced. The population of Straiton was about 300 in 1981. In 1984 the Forestry Commission's Ayrshire District Office was built there; afforestation of the moors between Straiton and Patna followed. At the same time a long terrace of modern houses was added to the village, which boasted a stud farm as well as good basic small-village facilities. Despite these additions, Heron's description still held good in 1991. The *Black Bull Inn* and the post office served through the 1990s; forest walks have been laid out nearby, and Blairquhan is opened to the public in summer.

## STRANRAER

**Map 1, B4**

***Galloway town / port,*** *pop. 11,500*

OS 82: NX 0660

Stranraer Castle, a tower house beside an extensive beach on sheltered Loch Ryan, was built about 1500 for the Adairs of Kinhilt. The eastern part of the town – originally called *Chapel* after the Chapel of St John – was an adjunct of the extensive Inch parish, within which a variety of mottes and castles had failed to give rise to a significant centre *(see Castle Kennedy)*; the western part was in Leswalt parish, whose church was 5 km to the north-west. Heron referred to the place as *'Stranrawer'*, reflecting the local *'Galloway Irish'* pronunciation of a name probably derived from *Strand-Ryan*. With its central position on the isthmus between the farming areas of the Rhinns and the Machars, Stranraer soon developed as a market centre, becoming the principal trading point in west Galloway. Its complex and irregular street pattern shows no sign of early planning, and perhaps property disputes explain why the place had notaries as early as 1588, seven years before it was made a burgh of barony in 1595. Pont's map of Galloway, made about 1610, showed both the names *'Stranrawer'* and Chapel as important. By then a military road had been or was being formed across Galloway to aid in the plantation of Ulster; although aiming for Portpatrick, it appears to have passed by way of Stranraer.

**Royal Burgh: Unrealised Potential**: Such rapid progress was being made that Stranraer – which only gained a parish school in 1614 – was raised to Royal Burgh status in 1617. Brereton found there in 1636 *"a town with good accommodation"*, but it was still not a port, and in 1639 it ranked a pitiful 46th among Scottish burghs in tax yield, less than 15% of Ayr's trade. Tucker's comments in 1655 are illuminating: *"Stranraer, otherwise called the Chapel, a small mercat town which would prove a pretty harbour for shelter of vessels in time of storm; but there is not now nor ever was any trade to be heard of here"*. Settled conditions appeared in Galloway by the end of the 17th century, and although the original chapel was demolished around 1700, Stranraer's first post office was opened in 1717. Stranraer was a natural stopping point when a droving route for Irish cattle became established between Portpatrick and Dumfries. The Roy map in the 1750s showed a large compact settlement; to the west was a mill, almost on the shore, while the town was well provided with four radial roads – though only a track appeared to lead towards Cairnryan and its coach road to Ayrshire. At that period much *'Galloway Plaiding'* was made for the Virginia market.

**Port and Industry**: A small harbour and two local vessels existed by 1764, and with the reconstruction of the military road in the 1760s a new post office was opened in 1765; a transient herring fishery developed. By 1770 linen had supplanted wool, the woven goods being bought by Glasgow and Kilmarnock merchants; by 1790 about 25,000 m of linen was made annually. The Town House was built in 1771, and after 1786 Stranraer became a Port of Registry, with the recognition letters SR. With surging demand from Glasgow brewers, by the late 1780s some 1750 m$^3$ of barley were being exported annually, and a market house was added to the Town House in 1802. Three fairs were scheduled for 1797, but Heron was not sanguine in 1799, opining that Stranraer was *"admirably well situated for commerce, yet almost without trade. The town is pretty large and populous, containing many handsome houses, and above two thousand inhabitants. It had once an extensive herring fishery; but the shoals which used to crowd into Loch Ryan have now almost quite forsaken it. Its vicinity to Ireland has introduced the manufacture of linen; and its markets are chiefly attended for this article. Tanning of leather is also a considerable branch of business here"*.

**Early Nineteenth Century Development**: Despite Heron's views, the Paisley Banking Company opened a branch in the town in the early years of the 19th century. The population of Wigtownshire almost doubled in the first half of the century, growing considerably faster than Scotland as a whole; by 1825 Stranraer had two breweries, and a gasworks was established in 1826. The West pier was also built in the 1820s. Stranraer in 1827 was according to Chambers *"a thriving and handsome sea-port town containing at least two thousand inhabitants"*. The castle was then being used as the jail. Another pseudo-castle became the home of Sir John Ross who explored the North-West Passage; it was consequently named the *'North West Castle'*. By 1831 Stranraer was served by regular steamers. In 1840 a corn exchange was added to the already enlarged Town House, and the local newspaper, the *Wigtown Free Press* was first published in 1843.

**The Railway Port**: In 1858 Stranraer became the site of the headquarters (and main locomotive and maintenance depots) of the decidedly hilly single-track Portpatrick Railway (PR), whose main line opened in 1861, connecting Stranraer with Dumfries via Castle Douglas. About 3 km south of Stranraer the Portpatrick extension – which opened in 1862 – crossed the huge 13-arched whinstone and brick Piltanton Viaduct, 170 m in length and 22 m tall (it was demolished in the 1980s). Steamers began to ply to Larne in Ulster from 1862; later in 1862 tracks were laid to enable trains to stand on the town council's new East pier, which became the Harbour station, rather than using the approved West Pier site. Boat trains then ran to and from Castle Douglas. By 1866 Wordie & Co had a rail cartage depot (which later required 11 horses).

**New Rail Routes, and the Dairy Industry**: Though for decades direct steamers from the Clyde to Belfast creamed off much of the traffic, from 1877 when the PR bought the pier, Stranraer also enjoyed a tenuous rail link to Girvan, Ayr and Glasgow via Challoch Junction, 10 km to the east. In 1885 the original line became the *Portpatrick & Wigtownshire Joint Railway*, owned by four major companies. One of these, the Glasgow & South Western Railway (G&SWR) took over and upgraded the Girvan line in 1892; soon the locomotive shed at Stranraer housed a dozen G&SWR engines. The harbour station was enlarged in 1893–98. Meantime the first cross-channel steamer to be named *Princess Victoria* was a Denny-built paddler of 1890. Although after the 1851 census the population of Wigtownshire had begun to decline, so limiting the potential for Stranraer as a centre, the dairy trade was burgeoning, and soon vast quantities of milk were being shipped in churns by special trains eastwards and even to England. About 1870 local ironmonger James McHarrie established the largest dairy utensils factory in Scotland. He co-founded the Wigtownshire Creamery Company in the 1880s, having sold the utensil factory to James Gray in 1882. Gray later expanded to Castle Douglas, and although by 1905 Gray was competing locally with the Castle Dairy Works of Thomas Macavoy, his *'Prize Dairy Works'* flourished until the 1920s.

**Stranraer as the County Town**: The characterful *George Hotel* was built in 1876 and was considered *"very good"* by Murray in 1894, when Stranraer was called *"an important seaport"*, from which daily steamers plied to Larne (two per day in summer); in 1891 the population was 6200. In 1904 Stranraer was referred to as *"the chief town of Galloway"*; early in the 20th century it became the county town of Wigtownshire, to whose council the Earl of Stair donated a public park (named in his honour), with a football ground opened for a local club in 1907. Stranraer golf club was founded in 1906 and laid out an attractive 18-hole parkland course beside Loch Ryan, 3 km north-west of town. Minesweepers and patrol vessels were based at Stranraer during the 1914–18 war, and troops involved in the Irish troubles made the harbour station busy in the early 1920s. In 1938 the steamers carried 75,000 head of livestock and over 200,000 passengers; 20,000 tonnes of freight and 5450 cars were slung aboard by derrick. When in 1938–39 a movable gangway was installed at the Harbour station, enabling cars to drive on board ship, the public was not told they were actually made sufficiently strong to carry tanks.

**Tragedy in the North Channel**: The 1939–45 war brought greater upheaval, with a seaplane base on the west shore of Loch Ryan and the huge Cairnryan *(q.v.)* military port *(see also Dunragit)*. The little-used Portpatrick branch railway was closed completely beyond Colfin creamery in 1950. By then Stranraer was a major local centre, with health services in the Dalrymple Hospital. Its various small industries were added to by the Rhinns Bacon Company of 1953; it also had an early youth hostel. Stranraer FC joined the Scottish League in 1955. The Stranraer–Larne ferry services continued on a year-round basis, and were among the earliest to be fully converted to roll-on, roll-off motor vessels; hence the weak stern doors and too-small car-deck scuppers of the 1947 MV *Princess Victoria*, like her predecessor built in Dumbarton. These led to the tragic loss of 133 lives when she foundered in the particularly severe January storm of 1953; all women and children on board perished, and only 43 men were saved *(see the graphic description in Smith D L, 1969)*. The Larne service was subsequently maintained by other much more adequately designed vessels.

**Better Ships, More Cars but Fewer Trains**: By 1960 18,000 road vehicles were being carried annually on the ferries, a figure which grew rapidly to 70,000 by 1966, with 400,000 passengers. In that year a fourth daily sailing to Larne was introduced from the harbour station (three in winter). By 1963 the *North West Castle* had become a hotel, and large new buildings for Stranraer Academy were built in 1965. The scenic railway to Dumfries – which should have been modernised to cut staff costs – was instead regrettably abandoned by Beeching in 1965. With rail no longer available, the Dumfries road, so quiet before vehicle ferries were introduced, soon became exceptionally busy with Irish traffic; in spite of the troubles in Northern Ireland which decimated the tourist trade, the ferries continued to develop, and the town acquired road haulage depots. In 1972 a rail-connected depot was opened for steel traffic to Ireland, and expanded with government aid in 1976. In 1978–79 Sealink constructed a new ro-ro terminal jetty and reclaimed 2.5 ha as a parking area, and also introduced the biggest ferry so far used on the route, the 7000-ton *Galloway Princess*.

**Service and Industrial Development**: In 1975 Stranraer became the HQ of Wigtownshire District within the sprawling Dumfries & Galloway Region; it also had an ice rink, and by 1978 a bus station and a health centre. Though the youth hostel had closed, a caravan and camping site was open and by 1980 there were ten hotels; the largest, the *North West Castle*, was extended to 82 rooms about 1975. As the sub-regional centre for Galloway, Stranraer had gained an extensive new schools campus; but until 1981 Stair Park was the last league football ground in Britain not floodlit. However, Stranraer livestock market was busy, especially with sheep; James Wyllie & Sons, grain merchants, had a large modern building near the harbour, and there were also agricultural engineers. The Baby Deer shoe factory was open by 1979. The vast Galloway creamery – already Scotland's largest by 1975 – was still run by the monopolistic Scottish Milk Marketing Board (SMMB) until becoming the Galloway Cheese Company (GCC) in 1991. Major modernisation was undertaken, and it became capable of processing over half a million litres of milk a day and annually producing 18,000 tonnes of cheese, about half mainland Scotland's output. By 1983 Top Tek had also become established, and was the next largest concern on the town's industrial estate in 1991, by which time Malden Timber also had a factory there. By 1991 the *Wigtown Free Press* had sensibly added *'& Stranraer Advertiser'* to its title.

**Problems and Rail Rundown**: In 1990 British Rail still carried steel and cars to Stranraer for shipment to Ireland, but withdrew the long-standing Stranraer–London sleeping car train. Civil engineering workshops and a freight depot with a container crane survived in 1991. The cattle and sheep market was busy in 1992, but unemployment was growing. Central Stranraer then boasted three supermarkets, an extensive range of specialised shops and business services, a substantial police station, a sheriff court, and a small museum focusing on the local dairy industry. In 1993 70 jobs were lost with the closure of the Baby Deer shoe factory. Worse, in 1994 the GCC failed – due to sharply rising milk prices following the Government's abolition of the SMMB – and its 130 employees lost their jobs. All rail-freight ended in 1994, after steel loads from Scunthorpe switched to road.

**Ferry Developments Falter**: Sealink, by then a subsidiary of the Swedish Stena Group, cut 180 ferry jobs due to recession in 1990. By 1991 the population of Stranraer was 11,348. Then in 1992 the firm of Sea Containers started a hovercraft service to Belfast using the *SeaCat*, a fast Tasmanian-built craft cruising at 35 knots with 100 cars and 450 passengers, performing four return trips daily and bringing about 130 new jobs to Stranraer. A second such vessel, the *Hoverspeed Great Britain*, capable of 42 knots, was introduced by *SeaCat Scotland* in 1993 to enable nine daily crossings instead of four, raising employment to 200. But this was not a great success, and in 2000 (when only 65 people were employed) the *SeaCat* services were transferred to Troon without warning.

**Town Growth, Local Government Decline**: A new stand was completed in 1995 at recently upgraded Stair Park, the council-owned home of Second Division Stranraer FC. By 1996 the town had grown very considerably, with a new access road acting as a southern bypass leading to a large new estate to the south, with others both east and west; a Tesco store was open, but the caravan site had closed. By then the Southern Upland Way long-distance route had been waymarked through

Stranraer. In what seemed a travesty of local democracy, the District Council was abolished in 1996 by the Tory government – all remaining *'local'* government functions to be managed from Dumfries, 110km away. Stranraer Academy has a roll of about 1100. The *North West Castle Hotel* remains the largest hotel, and there's a large variety of smaller hostelries and B&Bs; a tiny hostel for backpackers is open 3km east on the Cairnryan road.

## STRATHAVEN — Map 16, A5

***S. Lanarkshire small town,*** *pop. 6400* — OS 71 & 64: NS 7044

On the Avon Water some 11km south of Hamilton lies Strathaven (pronounced *Strayven*), the Gaelic name for the Avon's wide valley, whose Anglicised post-Reformation parish is called Avondale. Chambers noted that Strathaven was *"indebted for its origin to Avondale castle, an early seat of the Hamilton family"*, a baronial fortress probably completed in the early 15th century. Strathaven became a burgh of barony in 1450 and has a tight medieval street plan; an ancient bridge spans the little Powmillon Burn. The castle was slighted in 1455; the Pont map of about 1600 emphasised its striking remains, not tiny *'Strath Avon'*, whose parish school was founded in 1626; the *Tower Inn* was open by 1679. The Roy map of about 1754 showed a substantial spidery place where six roads met, of which the chief linked Ayr with Hamilton and Edinburgh; a Turnpike Act of that year enabled this to be made up. There was an early silk industry and a water-powered textile mill, but Strathaven was important for handloom weaving. An 18th century Duke of Hamilton bred Clydesdale horses at Strathaven, and five fairs were to be held there in 1797. In 1799 Heron noted a weekly market in a *"town of upwards of 1600 inhabitants. Some cotton-works have lately been erected"*.

**Post, Grain, Gas, Golf, Academy and the Railways**: Strathaven's first post office was opened in 1806, and a brewery was working by 1825. In 1827 Chambers found *"an irregular old town, full of long lanes and short streets"*. A grain mill and a gasworks were built in 1831, followed by an engineering works; a Bank of Scotland branch opened in 1838. On the evidence of its antique steam engine, the mill of Elder & Watson probably dated back to the 1850s. A locally-promoted branch railway from Hamilton was opened in 1863 with Caledonian Railway aid. A silk mill dating from about 1860 later became a weaving factory, and a second silk factory also originated in the 1880s. A hosiery factory was built in 1887. In 1891 the population was 3500. In 1894 Strathaven was simply described by Murray as *"a small town"*, with no inn worth a mention.

*Strathaven had an early silk industry, later turning to cotton and hosiery. These cottages, built in the 1820s to house hand-loom weavers, are typical of many in west of Scotland villages.* (JRH)

**Academy, Air and Sundry Rails**: In 1904 the hosiery works was taken over by The Hosiery Manufacturing Company and later moved to Irvine. Strathaven Academy was formed in 1905 from the Crosshill and Ballgreen primaries. In 1905 too, the railway was connected with Stonehouse, and rashly extended over the moors to Darvel (but the latter section was closed in 1939). Strathaven golf club, founded in 1908, laid out an 18-hole parkland course north of the town. In the 1930s the Scottish Flying Club of Renfrew bought Couplaw Farm, from which the Clydesdale Flying Club flew for a time. By 1951 Strathaven was a small town with 4500 people and three small hotels, boosted by the absurd law then restricting Sunday alcohol sales to *'bona fide travellers'* – it stimulated travel from large, thirsty towns no end! In 1949 the Strathaven Model Society laid out a miniature railway in the George Allan Park; it is still going strong and carrying 17,000 passengers a year. The last of the full-scale local railways was closed to passengers by Beeching in 1965, and all the tracks had gone by 1971, leaving an empty cutting through the town; by 1976 the engineering works and grain mill were both disused; the latter is now an arts centre.

**Professional Dormitory Development**: Accessibility to East Kilbride helped Strathaven to grow, reaching 6000 people about 1975; the mansion – which was by then the *Strathaven Hotel* – claims to have been designed by Robert Adam. Despite its small-town character, by 1980 the three hotels had become six. In 1981 Avon Glen Textiles still worked, but Elder & Watson's mill was demolished in the 1980s; the steam engine was saved and moved to New Lanark. By 1985 a caravan site had been laid out, by 1987 a one-time cinema had been remarkably converted into flats, and in 1991 the tiny town centre was again busy, with some retail expansion in progress. The town's very well-educated population was then 6384, with high proportions in professional and technical occupations and travelling to work by car. The John Hastie local museum was open by 1992, and L S Smellie & Sons' cattle and sheep auction market remained active. Smellie's are now active in a variety of fields, employing 120. The Williams Brothers' *Fraoch* Heather Ale *(see Taynuilt and Alloa)* is now based in Strathaven.

## STRATHBLANE & Blanefield — Map 5, C5

***W. Stirlingshire village,*** *pop. 2000* — OS 64: NS 5579

The deep valley of the northward-flowing Blane Water cuts through the gap between the Campsie Fells and the Kilpatrick Hills. Standing stones and the 15th century keep of Duntreath Castle rose near the bottom of the valley, an area which was thickly settled by the time that Lennox was mapped by Timothy Pont around 1600. By then the Kirk of Strathblane had been built 3km south-east of the castle. Roy's survey of about 1754 showed this church served only by a track to the Kirks of Campsie and Killearn; but roads were approaching from

Milngavie. Eventually the area was transferred from Lennox to Stirlingshire. Early in the 19th century the mansion called Craigend Castle was built for James Smith on the site of an earlier house 2 km south-west of Strathblane. By 1825 Strathblane was served by a penny post from Glasgow, and by the mid 19th century four roads met at the kirk. Though Duntreath Castle was a ruin, the long-lasting Blanefield calico printworks was in operation between the castle and kirk.

**Railway arrives and departs; the Retired stay**: When the single-line Blane Valley Railway was opened in 1867, Strathblane and Blanefield were both provided with stations (less than 1.5 km apart). By 1901 the parish had 880 residents. Although post and telegraph offices appeared in both places, and Strathblane had an inn by 1895, the stations generated only a little development, and lost their passenger trains in 1951; by 1969 the rails had vanished. The calico printing works was still in operation in 1953 but had been demolished by 1976. The 40-bed Strathblane Home Hospital used by Glasgow Children's Hospital was open by 1953. By then a population of 1250 was served by the facilities of a small village; these included the improving *Kirkhouse Inn*. By 1971 this had been joined by the *Country Club Hotel*, in the former mansion of Ardunan beside Milngavie Road. The mansion at Craigend Castle had been less lucky and was demolished in 1968. By 1981 the facilities had risen to typical village level, with daily banking services. Some housing development continued in the 1980s, and by 1991 with a total of 1981 residents, Strathblane was an affluent retirement area. However, a large quarry has been excavated since 1987 south of the *Country Club Hotel*; there is also an inn.

## STRATHCARRON — Map 9, A2

***Easter Ross valley,** pop. 150* — OS 20: NH 4791

Near the foot of Glencalvie with its waterfall, the remains of an ancient broch and cairn stand beside the River Carron. This flows into the Kyle of Sutherland near Ardgay, from which – at the time of the Roy survey about 1750 – a track following the south riverside passed near the House of Langwell, north of the river, to end at another mansion, Amat or *The Craigs*. Later roads were built on both sides of the river, combining above a bridge to end 2 km farther west at Croich or Cronach church. This was built in Strath Cuileannach to a Telford design before local clearances began in the Glencalvie area in 1845. Shooting lodges were built in the glens, a school was erected on the southern side of the river, and until about 1970 there was a post office at The Craigs. In 1965 *Braelangwell Lodge* to the east was in use as a hotel, but although set among steadily expanding woodlands it was apparently too remote to survive. By then only some 150 people lived in the 15 km long valley. The school was closed for some years, but had reopened by 1998.

## STRATHDON, Bellabeg & Colquhonnie — Map 10, A3

***Aberdeenshire village,** pop. 400* — OS 37: NJ 3512

The principal centre of feudal Strathdon, then part of Mar, was the massive Norman earthwork or motte known as the Doune of Invernochty, which stands at an altitude of 280 metres by the confluence of the Water of Nochty with the River Don. It later bore a stone curtain wall atop its 18 m tall mound, and was surrounded by a moat floodable at will. The incomplete Colquhonnie Castle to the east dates from the 16th century, and the nearby Castle Newe was built for Sir John Forbes in 1604; hence nearby Forbestown. The area though hilly was thickly settled by 1642, as shown on Robert Gordon's map; there were however apparently no bridges. Strathdon became a burgh of barony in 1677. In 1715 Poldullie Bridge was built by John Forbes, crossing the upper Don just west of the motte. The Roy map surveyed about 1750 showed no roads and only one track, which mainly followed the north side of the river, connecting Corgarff across Poldullie Bridge with the *'Kirk of Strathdon'* and then somehow recrossing near Colquhonnie en route to Glenbuchat. The *'Mill of Balbegg'* (Bellabeg) turned beside the motte. Around 1780 stocking knitting was replaced as the local women's work by flax spinning for Aberdeen businesses, which supplied the raw material and marketed the yarn. A post office was open at Strathdon from 1793.

**Two Quiet Centuries end in Decline**: Castle Newe was extended in 1831, a road system was created and several more bridges built, but no railway ever approached closer than Alford, 30 km to the east by winding roads, and the area remained agricultural. Murray's 1894 Handbook did not index Strathdon, but a search revealed the *"plain, clean Colquhonnie Inn"* and the *"large shop, bank and PO"* at Bellabeg. In 1901 the parish held 1100 people. Two horse-drawn coaches a day linked Strathdon with the outside world at Alford until 1906, when motor buses of the Great North of Scotland Railway first plied between Bellabeg and Alford. A mill was built near Castle Newe, which was itself demolished in 1929. By 1951 the population was down to 750 and, with growing afforestation of the surrounding hills, had collapsed to 450 by 1971, but remote Strathdon maintained the facilities of a typical fairly small village and angling resort. Growing traffic on the B973 through Strathdon led to its reclassification about 1990 as the A944. Although by 1991 the parish had only 381 residents, the school, the post office at Bellabeg and the small *Colquhonnie Hotel* are still open.

## STRATHGLASS (Cannich) & Tomich — Map 9, A4

***Inverness-shire valley,** pop. 530 (area)* — OS 26 & 25: NH 4040

An ancient dun stands above the L-plan tower of Erchless Castle, built in the 16th century where the River Farrar joins the River Glass about 15 km west of Beauly, for the head of Clan Chisholm. Strathglass was already well settled, but its upper reaches (OS 25) were still wooded when Robert Gordon mapped the area in the 1640s. Roy's survey of about 1750 showed a mill near the emparked mansion of Erchless Castle. A track leading westwards from Inverness via Kirkhill and Dounie (Beaufort) Castle then accompanied the River Glass, by way of a mill near Inchully, to the clachans of Invercannich (Cannich) – where Comar Lodge had been built for the Chisholms in 1740 – to Tomich 5 km to the south-west, where it turned up the foaming River Affric, passing the Dog Falls to end far up this lovely glen. Long known for its illicit whisky, Strathglass was cleared of its people by successive Chisholm lairds in stages between 1801 and 1831. The Struy bridge across the River Farrar near Erchless Castle was built to a Telford design between 1809 and 1817, and the small village of Tomich was re-planned in the 19th century.

**Tourists and Hydro Power**: By 1895 roads had been built to Invercannich from Drumnadrochit and Beauly, and both the *Glen Affric Hotel* at Cannich and the *Struy Inn* near Erchless Castle were open. By 1950 there were some 1400 people in upper Strathglass, of whom Cannich had about 680, served by basic facilities. These included a large 167-line telephone exchange, because it was the centre of a vast North of Scotland Hydro Electric Board scheme. Since 1945 Loch Mullardoch on the River Cannich (OS 25) had been greatly raised by a dam with an inbuilt power station, built 1 km above Mullardoch House, a shooting lodge. It was linked by a tunnel with Loch Benavean *(Beinn a'Mheadhoin)* in wooded Glen Affric. This had itself been raised and extended by a dam which supplied water to Fasnakyle 2 km south-west of Cannich, where a substantial power station was built, faced with golden sandstone from Burghead and opened in 1952. The Aigas Ferry 5 km east of Erchless Castle was still carrying passengers in 1957.

**Still More Hydro Power and More Tourism**: In 1957 the Strathfarrar scheme was begun, which greatly enlarged Loch Monar (OS 25) and created another power station in a nearby glen. By 1956 Fasnakyle was accompanied by Cannich youth hostel, to which a family wing had been added by 1977; another hostel was created at ultra-remote Alltbeithe, 30 km to the west in Glen Affric. By 1980 the *Glen Affric Hotel* had 23 rooms; in the glen were riverside and forest walks. But by 1971 the residents of Cannich numbered only 203 of the 530 or so people then living in Strathglass. In the mid 1980s a caravan and camping site was opened at Cannich, and the 9-hole Aigas golf course was added downstream in the 1990s. By 1997 Guisachan House, below the Plodda Falls south-west of Tomich, had become a ruin in a park. Vast areas of Forestry Commission access land, parts still unplanted, surround Strathglass. Hotels now include the *Mullardoch House* and the *Tomich*; the historic *Comar Lodge* is now a guest house. There is a large hostel for backpackers at Cannich, plus a tiny one at Tomich.

## STRATHMIGLO

**Map 6, B4**

***N. Fife village,*** *pop. 900*

OS 58: NO 2110

A hill fort stood 2 km to the north-west of Strathmiglo, which lies in the fertile western Howe of Fife astride the Miglo Burn, headwater of the River Eden. Some 3 km south-west is Gateside, in the shadow of the steep cone of the 522 m West Lomond. Local tradition claims that this was the *Mons Graupius* where the battle between the Roman legions and the Caledonians was fought in 83 AD, citing as proof the many skulls found buried in nearby pits. The broad valley (*Strath* in Gaelic) could well be what Tacitus called the *"flat space between the two armies"* where chariots manoeuvred. While there are other claimants *(see Stonehaven, and also Keppie's book)*, Gateside is consistent with the known positions of Roman marching camps in the area, and with Fifers strongly resisting the Romans and later becoming a client state, the *'kingdom'*. Over a millennium later, Strathmiglo had a castle, and became a burgh of barony in 1509. Pont's map of about 1600 showed a mill at Bannaty, 4 km upstream of Strathmiglo, and the Newmill beside the village.

**Roads and Textiles**: By 1734 the little burgh had a tolbooth incorporating a lock-up. The road to Falkland was made up between 1748 and 1753, a bridge being shown on Roy's map of about that date, which also showed the hill road to Abergie and Perth. A bleachfield was built at Strathmiglo in 1756, at which linen thread was being made by 1762, when Walker was a British Linen Company manufacturer; in 1763 a textile beetling mill was added, and cotton was also being spun locally by then. The main road (now A91) was turnpiked under an Act of 1790. Two fairs were scheduled in 1797, but Heron merely referred to Strathmiglo as a *"village"* in 1799. By 1825 it was served by a penny post from Auchtermuchty. No fewer than ten water mills, including a lint mill, were shown on Sharp's map of 1826 on the 6 km between Burnside and Strathmiglo, which was already a large village with its two parallel main streets. In 1839 about 500 linen weavers were working, many for Dysart businesses. From 1857 *'Strath'* had a station on the minor branch railway newly laid between Ladybank and Kinross. George Walker's bleachfield was still busy in 1864, and Alexander Troup had recently built a steam-driven works with nearly 100 power looms.

**Shoes, Cinema and Woodturning come and go**: A T Hogg founded a small footwear factory in the village centre in 1888, when the population was 1100, but half the water mills had disappeared from the map by 1895; by then Gateside had an inn and post office. Strathmiglo's tiny 256-seat *Royal Cinema* was claimed to have the first *'talkies'* in Scotland, and to have got its name as a result of royal patronage, probably on the opening day in 1929. In 1945 or earlier Haldane & Co began wood turning at Gateside, making bobbins. The railway was closed in 1950; then there were two little hotels and Strathmiglo's population was nearly 1200. The cinema lasted into the 1970s, its shell becoming a wood window factory by 1989. Strathmiglo remained a very pleasant village with a surprisingly full range of facilities including a small hotel (since closed), two pubs, a restaurant and a bowling club; by 1987 the telephone exchange had been doubled. In 1990 the Irvine Thread Company still maintained the textile activity, although the population was down to 890. By 1989 A T Hogg no longer made footwear, but now keep a warehouse for their small chain of shops, run from their Cupar head office. In 1996 Haldane & Co, who by then made intricate woodcarvings by machine, moved to Glenrothes. Local facilities still include a primary school, post office, food stores, garage and light engineering.

*Strathmiglo tolbooth, dating from 1734, when it was added to an existing building. The tower is slightly tapered, which increases its apparent height.* (JRH)

## STRATHPEFFER — Map 9, A3

***Easter Ross village,** pop. 1000* — OS 26: NH 4858

A crannog stands in the tiny Loch Kinellan about 8 km west of Dingwall in a hilly part of Easter Ross. Some 2 km north-east is Castle Leod, built in the 17th century near the tiny River Peffery. The Roy map made around 1750 showed the castle, and downstream Fodderty Kirk, as the main features of what was still a trackless area. In later years, sulphuretted hydrogen springs were found 1 km south of the castle, and a pump room was built in 1829; a post office named Strathpeffer originated at around that date. These facilities formed the basis for a small but spaciously laid out spa village; but despite the beauty of the location, growth was long restricted by its remoteness and by the cantankerous local laird Sir William MacKenzie, who led the opposition to a railway entering Strathpeffer, delaying the building of the Dingwall & Skye Railway (D&S) and forcing it to adopt the spectacular but steep route passing beside Raven Rock. The line was opened in 1870, with a station at Achterneed 2 km to the north of Strathpeffer.

**Railway and Further Spa Development**: The reclusive MacKenzie's demise made possible a 4 km branch to the town from Fodderty Junction, opened in 1885 by the Highland Railway, successors to the D&S. Meantime the sprawling stone-built *Ben Wyvis Hotel* was open by 1880, public rooms were built in 1881, and the Spa Pavilion in 1882. The Strathpeffer Spa golf club, founded in 1888, laid out an 18-hole course in hilly moorland. The 1891 resident population of this snooty refuge in the wilds was 350. In 1894 Murray noted four hotels: the *Ben Wyvis* and *Spa "first class"* and the *Strathpeffer* and *Macgregor's "good"*; two doctors were in attendance. Strathpeffer was *"a watering-place of increasing repute"* at which travellers should *"engage rooms beforehand"*, tactfully omitting to state that the waters smelt of bad eggs. The railway company built its own large *Highland Hotel* in 1911, and even ran an express service direct from Aviemore.

**Rock – and Passengers – on and off the Line**: Sidings were laid at Raven Rock in 1923 to serve a new County Council road metal quarry employing 21 men at its peak, when it produced 120 tonnes of stone a day, hauled away by a daily train until work ceased in 1939. Wordie & Co ran a small rail to road cartage depot at Strathpeffer, but road transport and two world wars took traffic from the branch line, which was closed to passengers by the LMS in 1946, and entirely by BR in 1951; Achterneed station was closed by Beeching in 1964. By 1951 the population had slowly risen to 870; there were eight hotels, and full village facilities plus a youth hostel.

**Limited Growth Resumed**: The industrial development of the Moray Firth caused a spurt of growth after 1971; by 1978 a new private housing estate had appeared, with its own grocery store. Strathpeffer was then unashamedly a resort, with 12 hotels, Scottish shows in the evenings, golf and crazy golf, plus a number of specialist tourist shops as well as basics. A post

*The late 19th century pump room at Strathpeffer (which replaced the original 1829 one). It is currently being redeveloped by the Highland Building Preservation Trust. The pump room contained facilities for taking water from the various mineral springs of the locality. A new such facility has recently been opened in the village.* (JRH)

office, police station and community council were active, and buses plied to Contin, Dornoch, Dingwall and Inverness. The fine canopied station building was eventually restored around 1980 as a shopping and tourist facility, including the Highland Museum of Childhood. The 1991 resident population was 966. A new pump room was opened in 1989, still dispensing dilute hydrogen sulphide; restoration of the old Spa Pavilion was under way in 2001. Kenneth Stewart's is a sizeable civil engineering company in the village. There are many hotels large and small, plus the youth hostel.

## STRATHTAY & Grandtully — Map 6, A2

***Small Perthshire villages,** pop. 300* — OS 52: NN 9153

Among the closely enclosing wooded hills about 8 km above the confluence of the River Tay with the River Tummel was an ancient church. The nearby Garntullich Castle, whose name probably means *'Grove of the Torrent'* in Gaelic, was built in 1560 beside a hillside stream. About 1600 Timothy Pont sketched the castle as an imposing structure, but omitted all detail of the area to the east, which contains much evidence of ancient occupation. Robert Gordon's map around 1642 showed half a dozen tiny settlements on each side of this short stretch of winding river with its rapids; the Roy map of about 1750 implied that it still remained trackless. Eventually roads were built beside both banks of the Tay, connected from 1870 by a bridge 3 km east of the castle, and by a passenger ferry further east at Pitnacree, which still plied in 1927.

**What's in a Name?**: The castle name had been poshly anglicised to *'Grandtully'* by the time that the Highland Railway opened its Aberfeldy branch through Strathtay in 1865. A station placed near the bridge at Little Ballinluig was named Grandtully to avoid confusion with Ballinluig Junction on the main line, but the adjacent post office was named Strathtay! By 1895 there was also a mill, the little *Grandtully Hotel*, and Pitnacree House, which had been emparked by 1927. In 1909 the Strathtay golf club was founded, creating a 9-hole parkland course. However, by 1951 Strathtay had only the general facilities of a small village. The expensively engineered railway was totally closed by Beeching in 1965. Meantime the population of Strathtay proper fell steadily, from 700 in 1951 to a mere 330 in 1981; Pitnacree House is no longer emparked, but the hills around have seen vast areas afforested since the 1950s. White-water enthusiasts enjoy the rapids; basic facilities remain, plus the 9-hole golf course and the hotel.

## STRATHYRE — Map 5, C3

***Small N. Stirlingshire village,** pop. 200* — OS 57: NN 5617

The River Balvag flows south through beautiful Strathyre into Loch Lubnaig and so to Callander. In the mid 18th century Caulfeild's men built a military road up the east side of Strathyre; Roy labelled it the *'King's Road from Stirling to Fort William'*. The Callander & Oban Railway opened its first section in 1870, with a crossing station at Strathyre; by 1894 there was a temperance hotel. By 1950 there were three hotels, and Strathyre had been largely afforested. In 1965 the railway closed, but a post office remained for a few more years. The facilities for the 225 or so residents now include a primary school, pubs, and basic shops, whilst several hotels serve the visitors.

## STRICHEN — Map 10, C1

***Buchan village,** pop. 1100* — OS 30: NJ 9455

A stone circle on a knoll near the headwaters of the North Ugie Water in Buchan indicates early settlement. The origin of the name Strichen is lost in the mists of time, but may derive from *Strath Ugin*. Pont's map of Buchan made about 1601 showed *'Strychin'* as a tower house, accompanied by the mills of *'Strichin'* and *'Adiel'*. The area was part of the vast Rathen parish *(see Lonmay)* until Strichen parish was formed in 1627, the first church in Strichen having been erected about 1620 for the laird, Thomas Fraser. In the 17th century the quarrying of limestone and its burning for fertiliser began on the flanks of the nearby Mormond Hill, and in 1700 the unique white horse was cut into the hillside. The Roy map made about 1750 showed the *'Kirk of Strichen'* on the area's only track, which connected with Old Deer by way of *'Achreny'* (Auchrynie), and north to Fraserburgh by the route later numbered A981. Round the church were hamlets or fermtouns, while to the west were large but nameless wooded policies in the area later occupied by Strichen House.

**The New Village: Short-lived Textiles**: A linen bleachfield was built on the west bank of the North Ugie Water between 1746 and 1760, and a rectilinearly planned village extension was laid out on the east bank in 1763–64. Locally-grown flax was spun here in the late 18th century, and sold at two annual yarn markets. By about 1775 thread mills worked in the village, a post office opened in 1788, and by 1797 Strichen was a post town with mails three times a week. As many as six fairs were scheduled for the year, and a new parish church was built in 1799 in a lumpish classical style; later an Episcopal church was added.

**Was Strichen a Burgh?**: The town-house was built in 1816, at a time when a few late burghs of barony were being chartered elsewhere; yet apparently Strichen never became a burgh. In 1818–21 the *"noble mansion"* of Strichen House was erected by the then lairds, the Frasers (Lord Lovat). However, the textile industry failed, and about 1850 the estate was sold to William Baird of the Gartsherrie ironworks at Coatbridge. Pratt wrote in 1858 that *"Strichen, or Mormond Village has several inns; the Town-house is the most prominent object"*. From 1865 Strichen had a station on the Great North of Scotland Railway's branch from Maud to Fraserburgh. The 1891 population was over 1100. In 1894 there was a mill and a post and telegraph office; Strichen House stood in large policies. Strichen slowly grew, becoming by the 1950s a large village with a long-standing tuberculosis sanatorium, secondary school, cinema, chemists and banks, but no industry apart from the quarry.

**Decline and Recovery**: Strichen House was gutted about 1954, and its ruins had vanished by 1974. With rapidly falling farm labour requirements, village decline set in and by 1971 the population was down to 960: the passenger station was closed in 1965 and, despite its use in some North Sea oil developments, the freight railway was abandoned in 1979 (its route has recently been restored as a long-distance path, the Formartine & Buchan Way). By 1981 the sanatorium was no longer a hospital, and by then the local services were typical of a village. In 1991 Strichen had recovered to a population of 1112 with an affluent retired element. There has since been a little development; the large and grim old school is blocked up, but there is a bank, two pubs, a handful of shops, a garage, and an important highways depot.

## STROMA, Isle of — Map 13, B4

***Small island off N. Caithness coast*** — OS 7: ND 3577

The small but fertile and low-lying sandstone island of Stroma – *Stream Isle* in Norse – stands in the tidal stream of the stormy Pentland Firth, about 5km offshore from John o' Groats. It has scanty remains of the undateable Castle Mestag. In 1769 Pennant noted about 30 families on Stroma, all digging the ground, not ploughing it! Despite its lack of a sheltered harbour, Stroma supported over 300 people in the 19th and early 20th centuries and had a church, a primary school and at one time four shops. Strange to say, the building of a pier at the Geo of Nethertown in 1955, using local labour, put so much cash in the crofters' pockets that most of the 80 remaining islanders decamped to the mainland. The school was closed in 1958, leaving only lighthouse keepers, whose families stayed in Thurso in 1979; the light was automated in 1996, and Stroma became deserted but for seals, sheep, birds – and summer excursionists from John O'Groats.

## STROMEFERRY — Map 8, C3

***Wester Ross location,*** *pop. under 100* — OS 24: NG 8635

In the 15th century Strome Castle was built on a small promontory on the north shore of the sea inlet of Loch Carron in Wester Ross; its Norse name refers to the tidal stream through the narrows. The castle was noted as an isolated feature by Pont about 1600, and so it remained, eventually becoming a fragmentary ruin; the area was still trackless in Roy's time around 1750. The Dingwall to Kintail road, constructed under Telford's guidance for the Commissioners for Highland Roads and Bridges from 1809 onwards, was complete when the Strome Ferry was established across the loch to a slip beside the castle in 1819. The location became much more important when the scenic Dingwall & Skye Railway was opened in 1870, to terminate on a new pier beside the ferry slip on the south shore. Steamers at first plied on weekdays to Portree and on alternate weekdays to Stornoway; later the Stornoway steamers also sailed each weekday, and in 1877 the line became part of the Highland Railway. A nearby shooting lodge built about 1840 had become by 1894 what Murray called a *"good"* hotel. The station complex burned down in 1891, but was rebuilt.

**Falling Importance**: When the railway was extended to Kyle in 1897 the short-lived importance of Strome Ferry station ended. By 1955 a youth hostel was open beside Strome Castle, now a National Trust for Scotland property. As car traffic grew the ferry became busier (though closed on Sundays); a new 6-car boat was brought into use in 1959. Stromeferry (south shore) survived as a mere hamlet with a station. The need for a ferry was eliminated on the opening by 1973 of a link road round the head of the sea loch from Strathcarron. In 1975–78 Strome Ferry was the railhead for cement supplies to the Kishorn *(q.v.)* oil platform yard across the loch. But the youth hostel on the north shore was closed in 1983, followed in 1990 by the 18-room *Strome Ferry Hotel*, which proved unsaleable and is still closed, leaving only the railway halt.

## STROMNESS — Map 13, B2

***Small town, Orkney,*** *pop. 1900* — OS 6 (or 7): HY 2509

The Picts had a complex settlement at Howe, 2.5km north-east of Hamnavoe, the only sheltered harbour on the west coast of the Orkney Mainland. Stromness bears a Norse name; *Straumr-* is the tidal race through the narrows of Hoy sound, and *-nes* is the point of land which protects it from Atlantic gales. The port of *'Strumnay'* was mentioned in the reign of Robert I, and again in 1445 when two ships exported wool, fleeces and hides. A charter of 1544, including a Stromness parish church, was reported by Martin, and an inn was opened about 1590. Stromness was named on Blaeu's map of Orkney, attributed to Pont, who probably first visited the islands in 1592. Although the bishops of Orkney *feued* (leased out) sites at Hamnavoe from the 1620s, and a parish school was opened in 1630.

**Port for Canada fights off Taxes**: Stromness village remained tiny, with only 13 houses in 1670, when it was chosen as the last port of call for ships of the Hudson's Bay Company. In 1680 came the first *'white house'*, built with lime mortar not clay. The name *'Cairston Roads'* – still used for the nearby anchorage – shows that Martin's 1703 reference to a *"good harbour at the bay of Kerston village, near the west end of the Isle, well secured against wind and weather"* was to the Kirkton and harbour of Stromness, where the oldest clearly dated house (that of a merchant named Miller), goes back to 1716. Such people had to pay a tax known as *'Cess'* to Kirkwall and other Royal Burghs, until in 1743–58 local merchant Alex Graham fought a costly but successful legal battle, by which – as his prominent local monument states – the smaller towns throughout Scotland were *"delivered from the thraldom of the Royal Burghs"*.

**Credulous Sailors, Straw Hats and Pumpkin Whisky**: Gordon of Cairston built a wharf in 1764, and Stromness became a major late 18th century whaling centre; it obtained a post office in 1788. Double lighthouses were built on the Pentland Skerries as Robert Stevenson's first job for the Northern Lighthouse Board; they were first lit in 1794. Although 40km distant, Stromness became the shore station for their lightkeepers. In 1794 the population was about 1350. Some sailors were so naive that they would *'buy fair winds'* from smart local girl Bessie Millie! Stromness was already noted as a *"town"* by Heron in 1799, and in 1814 built a new parish church (nowadays a community centre). It belatedly became a burgh of barony in 1817; as it happened, a boom in herring fishing followed, and by 1821 there were eleven local vessels, all of under 80 tons, while the parish held almost 3000 people, a remarkable 271 of whom made straw hats! The quaint little Stromness or *'Old Orkney'* distillery, allegedly built on a smugglers' site, was first licensed to John Crookshanks in 1817; one of its pot stills was shaped like a pumpkin, and said to come from a noted law evader.

**Museum, Banks and Mailboats**: The Stromness Museum was founded in 1837 by the Orkney Natural History Society, moving to its present site near the distillery in 1862. Meantime by 1841 three banks were open. In 1836 the Ness boatyard built the first mail packet for the Scrabster service and in 1856, under John Stanger, launched the first regular mailboat, PS *Royal Mail*. Another pair of lighthouses, Hoy Sound High and Low on the island of Graemsay, were designed by Alan

Stevenson and commissioned in 1851. Stromness became a police burgh in 1857, and the Royal Bank built a new branch office in 1864. A lifeboat station was opened in 1867; the herring fishery peaked in the 1880s. In 1886 when Barnard found the distillery powered by steam as well as water, its total annual output of Highland malt was only 32,000 litres. He wrote of Stromness as the second most important settlement in Orkney, *"unlike any other, the little town consists of one paved street so narrow and crooked that two vehicles cannot pass each other"*. Houses had jetties and quays of their own; a good pier was used by the Scrabster mail boats, and by the Arctic vessels calling for provisions.

**Enterprise and Beneficence**: Although the Hudson's Bay Company left Stromness in 1891, when the village population was 1698, further timber jetties were erected at Point of Ness in 1893 for the herring industry. Murray referred to the *"many jetties of its fine and important harbour"*. Shipping, shipbuilding and fisheries were all significant. There were two hotels, the *"very comfortable, moderate" Mason's Arms* and the *Commercial*. A daily steamer plied to Scrabster and two coaches a day to Kirkwall. Stromness Academy was open by about 1895. The very substantial *Stromness Hotel* with its remarkably sheltered garden was completed in 1901 by John Mackay *(see Durness)* who also started the local telephone, electricity and bus services. In 1901 the parish population peaked at 3200 and a public library was gifted at that time. However, herrings vanished from 1898 to 1908, a foretaste of the future.

**Lighthouse Base but No Whisky**: The most remote of all British lighthouses, on Sule Skerry, a tiny low-lying Atlantic islet over 60 km west of Stromness, was built with some difficulty in 1892–93 and illuminated in 1895 with the largest lantern of any lighthouse (almost 5 m in diameter). Houses were built in Stromness in 1892 for its keepers' families, and more rose later for the lighthouses lit in 1915 on Copinsay, an islet 20 km south-east of Kirkwall. In 1903–04 a pier and gasworks were completed in Stromness for the Northern Lighthouse Board, which based its northern tender *Pole Star* there. In 1902 the distillery was quaintly styled as the *Man o' Hoy*, after the rock climbers' favourite cliff stack, the Old Man of Hoy, on the west coast of that mountainous island. Though the distillery closed in 1928, probably a victim of USA Prohibition, surviving bottles of its *'Old Orkney'* malt became collectors' items. In the two world wars when Scapa Flow was a naval base, barracks were opened on the hill above Stromness, which retained its regular steamer service to Scrabster, and even in the depressed 1930s there was also a weekly steamer to Scalloway, Aberdeen and Leith.

**Stromness loses as Lighthouses are Automated**: By 1951 an 18-hole golf course had been laid out, but Stromness parish had lost over 1000 people in 50 years and only the main hotel offered accommodation; so the youth hostel which opened about 1970 was very welcome. By 1978 the locally based fishing was mainly for lobsters and crabs, there was a fish merchant, and John Scarth Engineering of Kirkwall operated the long-established Ness Boatyard. By then a helicopter based in Stromness serviced the remote Orkney lights. Lightkeepers from the Pentland Skerries and Fair Isle North still lived in Stromness in 1979; but the Hoy Sound lights were automated in 1966 (Low) and 1978 (High), followed by Sule Skerry in 1983, Copinsay in 1990, and finally Pentland Skerries in 1994, with computer control from the Northern Lighthouse Board's Edinburgh headquarters.

**Tourists, Fudge and Oatcakes**: By 1974 a caravan and camping site was available, an arts centre was opened in 1979, and by 1980 James P Robertson made *'Orkney Fudge'* at Cairston. Stockans' oatcake factory was working by 1982. By then an indoor swimming pool was open, and four hotels; Stromness facilities served some 6400 residents in the west of Orkney. In the mid 1980s Stromness was still a minor fishing port, with six full-time boats and sea angling, but no fish market. However, fish was processed by 1985. By 1991, 1890 people lived in the quaint but purposeful little port; a high proportion owned their homes outright, as did Orcadians in general, but there were more retired people than in the islands in general. Fortunately for Stromness, a 1989 scheme for a new car ferry from Gill's Bay to Burwick foundered, while by 1994 a vehicle ferry plied between Stromness and Lerwick. In 1994 Stockans took over Garden's oatcakes business; as Stockan & Garden their base is now in Kirkwall.

**Everything for Everybody**: Much recent development can now be seen, including the up to date Northern Lights wharf with its numerous buoys, a small industrial estate, substantial new buildings for Stromness Academy and a modern surgery; there are many small specialist retailers. Besides its major Scrabster ferry role (ro-ros several times a day), the harbour is busy – as a diving base, for fisheries, and for the small ferries to Graemsay and Hoy; a small boatbuilder and chandlery is open, and a better ice factory is being sought. In the Old Academy building are a sizeable environmental consultancy, and the Heriot-Watt Centre for Island Technology. Hotels include the central *Stromness* (42 rooms; "fuschias flourish in its sheltered garden"), and there are also smaller hostelries, plus the youth hostel.

## STRONE, Kilmun & Blairmore — Map 5, B5

***Cowal (Argyll) villages,** pop. 850* — OS 56 & 63: NS 1980

A coastal site at Kilmun in Cowal was occupied by a Christian church in the sixth century: hence the name *Holy Loch*, applied to a short offshoot of the Firth of Clyde. A collegiate church was established there by Sir Duncan Campbell in 1442; its refoundation was remarkable because Argyll was still nominally under the Lords of the Isles, but it would seem that the fortunes of the Campbells were already in the ascendant *(see Inveraray)*. Kilmun became a burgh of barony in 1490, but there was no space to expand, as the hills rise almost sheer from the later coastal road. Strone is 2 km to the east, sited on the point *(An t'Sron in Gaelic)* between Loch Long and the Holy Loch. It appeared on Pont's manuscript map of Cowal, made about 1600, as a tiny symbol named *'Stroin'*. However, the area was a blank on the Roy map made about 1750.

**Resort Development**: A Kilmun post office was opened, perhaps about 1828 when the engineer and steamship pioneer David Napier of Glasgow built a pier there. By 1831 this enjoyed regular steamer services, which in 1842 plied to Dunoon and Glasgow. A steamer pier was built at Strone in 1847, from which horse-drawn coaches ran to Loch Eck, on which a small steamer gave cruises, popular for many years. Later in the 19th century both Strone, and Blairmore on the east shore just 1 km to the north, acquired post and telegraph offices and inns, growing into small residential resorts in the period of intense competition between rival steamers. By 1880

Blairmore had a pier served by boats of the Lochlong & Lochlomond Steamboat Company, while Kilmun was served by Bob Campbell's steamers. In 1886 Kilmun was a *"pretty watering-place"*, with ferries to Ardnadam. By then all three settlements had a hotel or inn, but in 1894 Murray noted only the *"plain" Kilmun Hotel*. In 1895 Strone had steamer connections to Gourock, and a ferry to Hunter's Quay for Dunoon.

**Golf, Gardens and Caravanning**: The Blairmore & Strone golf club was founded in 1896 and laid out a steep 9-hole moorland course. In 1928 G H Younger bequeathed to the Forestry Commission his Benmore estate in Glen Eachaig (OS 56), 5 km north-west of Kilmun; the Younger Botanic Garden subsequently became the main tourist attraction in this hilly and wooded area. Meanwhile Kilmun gained an arboretum. The Strone ferry had ceased to ply by 1951, when the combined places had nearly 1100 people and the facilities of a small village. By 1953 the 30-bed Finnartmore geriatric hospital was open, and by 1971 also a convalescent home, but the ferries were no more. Despite its name the Holy Loch was known during the Cold War as the haunt of the US Navy's monstrous nuclear submarines *(see Dunoon)*. The Gourock steamers were withdrawn in the 1960s, but Strone and Blairmore saw more residential development and the facilities were maintained with little change. About 1990 a caravan and camping site was opened at Gairletter, 4 km north of Strone. In the 1991 census, Strone (apparently including Kilmun) had 865 residents; its ferry pier and buildings, unused for over 20 years, still stood in 1994. There are now no ferries, but Kilmun's hotel is still open, and post offices both there and Strone.

## STRONSAY

**Map 13, C2**

***Small island, Orkney,*** *pop. 380* — OS 5: HY 6528

Shaped like one of the more tricky pieces in a jigsaw, the rather flat farming island of Stronsay was known as a fishing base as early as the 14th century. Pont's map made about 1592 showed a vessel sheltering in Papa Sound. The later village of Whitehall took its name from a house built in the 1670s by a privateer, Patrick Fea. Whitehall was a key fishing centre from the 17th century through the herring boom of the early 19th century and until 1914, hence its substantial buildings. There was a kelp industry in the 18th century, and a post office at Widowell by 1838. Auskerry lighthouse, on an islet 5 km south of the southern tip of Stronsay on the approach to Kirkwall from Aberdeen, was first lighted in 1867 (the families lived on the islet until the light was automated in 1961). But the population steadily fell from about 1275 in 1891. A lifeboat station was established in 1909; this eventually closed in 1972 when the base was transferred to Kirkwall. As late as 1953 there was a fish merchant and two fish curers at Whitehall, and a fish processor was still at work in the 1990s. By the 1970s electricity arrived from Kirkwall by submarine cables. In 1974 passenger ferries from Whitehall to Sanday and Eday provided the only surface link with the outside world; there was however already a basic airfield, now with scheduled services. By 1977 the tiny *Stronsay Hotel* was open at Whitehall, which had the facilities of a small village; Aith school still had junior secondary classes. By 1985 the ubiquitous daily car ferries had taken over and by 1991 the island's population was 382. Whitehall village still has an inn, a post office and a heritage centre, while more central Aith still has the primary school and a post office.

## STRONTIAN

**Map 4, C1**

***Ardnamurchan village*** *pop. 200* — OS 40: NM 8161

The beautiful and sheltered Loch Sunart in the Morvern area of north Argyll was a blank on Pont's late 16th century sketch-maps. In 1724 Sir Alexander Murray of Stanhope opened mines for galena ore, the principal ore of lead, at an altitude of around 300 m on the slopes of Beinn Ruighe, some 5 km inland from the crofting township of Strontian, whose Gaelic name is supposed to mean *Nose of the Beacon*. Lodgings for workmen were erected at *"the grooves"*, at *"New York"* and at Strontian itself, and some 600 men were briefly employed by the York Buildings Company about 1730; the company threw a wooden bridge across the small River Strontian. The mines, together with a smelter, long remained in intermittent operation. Although closed in 1740, they were named on Roy's survey of about 1750 together with hamlets at Drumdoran and the delightfully named Tingouvalligan; could this have been named by a Cornish tin miner?

**Prefab Pub, Floating Church and Sinking Lead**: A post office was opened in 1775, and the mines were definitely open again in 1790, for the natural element strontium which was discovered in that year takes its name from the place (whilst the highly radioactive strontium-90 is a product of nuclear fission). Heron mentioned a *"smelting house"* in 1799, and – the Auld Alliance notwithstanding – many bullets for the Napoleonic wars were cast there. A regular cattle tryst was also held around 1800. The *London Inn* was so named because it had been prefabricated in the south of England. Strontian was a post town by 1797, served by mail three times a week, and early in the 19th century the *'Moydart Road'* was built under Telford's direction to connect with Corran. Steamers called at Strontian pier from the 1820s onwards; in 1828 there was a weekly service to Tobermory, and from 1833 Strontian had a daily post via Corran Ferry. Due to the Disruption of the Church of Scotland and the landowner's orthodoxy, the Free Church ordered a church-boat to hold a congregation of 700; this was built at Port Glasgow and moored offshore for 30 years! In 1847 the reopened mines employed 40–50 men out of a total population of some 920, only to close for a third time in 1872. By 1894 Strontian had a hotel and was the terminus for Oban excursion steamers. The lead mines once more reopened in 1901, but closed again in 1904; briefly reactivated in the 1920s, they were then abandoned, leaving eight old shafts.

**Integrated Rural Development**: In the mid 1960s the quiet crofting township of Strontian became the site of a Scottish Office experiment in integrated rural development. The single-track road from the Corran Ferry was rebuilt into a fast main road, and government agencies, local authorities and the Forestry Commission made Strontian the local base for various services; it even acquired a new Telephone Group Centre. A relatively ambitious new village centre was opened in 1969, tourist crafts were encouraged to set up, and holiday chalets and a caravan site were provided; the beautiful but in places steep side road to Polloch on Loch Shiel passed the site of the old mines. By 1972 the Georgian *Kilcamb Lodge* was a hotel.

**Morvern in Lochaber**: In 1975 the outlying Ardgour and Morvern areas around Strontian were sensibly transferred from sprawling Argyll to the Lochaber District of Highland Region, based in Fort William. About 1978 the former lead mines were owned by the Department of Agriculture and Fisheries for

Scotland (DAFS), and a quarry had been opened as a source of barytes for use in drilling muds for North Sea oil wells. In 1978 a new Forestry Commission administrative office was opened, which – as afforestation spread over the hills – became the HQ of a new forest district in 1985; there are forest walks. In 1979 the *Ben View Hotel* was also a sailing school. By then the erstwhile crofting township was a complex multi-purpose village, with three other hotels and an ambulance station, yet in 1981 its resident population was little over 200; by 1984 the pier was disused. The Linnhe Plant quarry, the post office and primary school are open, plus the long-established *Strontian Hotel*, and the *Kilcamb Lodge*.

## STRUAN & Bracadale — Map 8, A3

***Small villages, Isle of Skye,*** *pop. 250* — OS 23: NG 3438

Ancient brochs and duns line the north shore of Loch Harport, in Bracadale parish on the west coast of Skye. In the 18th century a sheriff lived at Ullinish Lodge, built by 1773 on a promontory, east of which grew the crofting township of Struan. By the 1950s this had some 200 people and very basic services, including a corrugated iron garage, and a shop which was remarkable for the monthly newspaper which it published from 1951 to 1957. By 1955 *Ullinish Lodge* had become a hotel, and there was also a restaurant in the village by 1988; the school had been extended, because the population had grown to some 250. The 8-roomed hotel now offers shooting and fishing.

## STUARTFIELD (or Crichie) — Map 10, C2

***Buchan village,*** *pop. 700* — OS 30: NJ 9745

The low-lying estate named '*Creeky*' on Blaeu's map, some 2 km south of Old Deer in Buchan, was free of development when selected by Burnett of Deans in 1774 as the site for the planned village of Stuartfield (named after Burnett's grandfather, Captain John Stuart). This was laid out on a gridiron pattern around a central square and nicely built, with a large triangular pond for wildfowl. Its success encouraged Burnett's relative, James Ferguson of Pitlour, to build anew at Longside, Mintlaw and New Deer. Stuartfield lay away from main roads and attracted piety not industry, for in 1858 it was to Pratt a *"quiet village full of churches"*. By 1894 Stuartfield had a post office, smithy, mill and inn. By 1951 its population had grown to about 670, with the facilities typical of a small village. As farms became fully mechanised it then shrank steadily, to a mere 400 or so people by 1981, about which time the last church vanished. The new primary school, opened at Stuartfield in 1979, also serves Old Deer, and has encouraged new housing developments; by 1991 as many as 693 residents were counted. Stuartfield has been for six years the *'best-kept village'* in the area. Besides the school it has a pub, the Crichie garage, post office and grocery. Its busy garden machinery dealer ensures its central green is well mown; the pond is frequented by swans and adorned with flower baskets.

## SULLOM VOE, Graven & Scatsta — Map 14, B3

***Location / oil facility, Shetland*** — OS 2: HU 4073

The sheltered haven of Sullom Voe in the north of the Shetland mainland took its name from a tiny settlement on its west side. In 1940 the military airfield called Scatsta was built near the little crofting township of Graven on its bleak eastern shore to defend a flying boat base, so becoming Britain's most northerly bastion in World War II; some 4 m of peat had to be speedily removed from the runway site! By 1957 the small *Sullom Voe Hotel* was open at Graven. In 1975 the airfield was reopened for use in connection with the first stage of the four-berth Sullom Voe oil terminal, built on the Vats Houllands peninsula north of Graven, to receive oil by pipeline from the Brent and Ninian fields for shipment by supertanker. Each berth allows for a vessel up to some 400 m in length. Over 5000 workers (1000 of them Shetlanders) worked from 1975 to 1982 to create the facility for BP and the Zetland County Council – and their successors the Shetland Islands Council. The inlet of Orka Voe was infilled with spoil to enlarge the site of some 450 ha. The hotel was extended, but explosion risks debarred residential and other development, which was diverted to Brae and Mossbank.

**Europe's Largest Oil Port, with Profit-sharing**: By 1979 a 25 mw power station had been built, not only the largest building on the islands but with an output higher than their mains station at Lerwick. On completion the Sullom Voe complex became the largest oil port in Europe, including 16 giant storage tanks each some 75 m in diameter, and a large new telephone exchange. Although only some 250 permanent jobs were provided, the Shetland Islands Council, which was also the harbour operator, had wisely negotiated a profit-sharing agreement with the oil companies, to expire in 2000; this paid for new social facilities throughout the islands. By the late 1980s unexpectedly heavy maintenance was required on the terminal due to the severity of the climate. The Advanced Oil Recovery Scheme – to be carried out in 2001 with a labour force of 1200, housed afloat – should secure the future of the terminal for 15 years.

## SUMBURGH, Dunrossness & Toab — Map 14, B5

***S. Shetland villages & airport,*** *pop. 700* — OS 4: HU 3811

The complex area of headlands, inlets and sandy isthmuses forming the parish of Dunrossness at the south end of the mainland of the Shetland Islands has a fascinating history. The excavated remains of the first known significant settlement in the northernmost island group, and one of the most complex and interesting places for its size in Europe, lie on a west facing shore, but slightly sheltered from Atlantic breakers by the Scat Ness (Norse *Nes*, peninsula). Bronze and Iron Age settlements going back to around 2000 BC underlie a Pictish broch dating from around the birth of Christ. This was already defunct by around 800 AD, when Norsemen built on an adjacent site a farm and fishing settlement; saithe fishing from there is recorded in the Sagas. All traces of settlement were later covered by drifting sand, and the name *Jarlshof* was coined by Sir Walter Scott. Another Iron Age house at Scatness was discovered in 1997.

**Oppression, House and Lighthouse**: After Scotland acquired the Shetlands in 1472 the Scots-Norse Sinclair oppressors made Sumburgh their base, and built yet another house or castle on the site in 1494. From this they imposed a greedy feudalism on the luckless islanders, who had previously been freeholders under Udal law. About 1600 Pont noted both *'Swenbrugh'* and *'The ancient fort of Swenbrugh'* (presumably the broch) on his map; the area round Toab and Dunrossness Kirk to the north was well settled. The house was occupied until 1608 *(see Scalloway)*. The lighthouse on the 100m high Sumburgh Head was designed by Robert Stevenson, built by John Reid of Peterhead and first lit in 1821; it gives a superb view of the tide race called the *Roost*. Troswick, 7km north of Sumburgh, has a tiny preserved horizontal mill, one of two chains of mills; the other was at Scousburgh on the west coast near the *Spiggie Hotel*, which was built of timber in 1896. In the 1890s the islands' principal proprietor, a Mr Bruce, lived in a new mansionhouse at Sumburgh; around 1930 it became a hotel.

**Air, Oil and Sprawl**: Air mail services from Thurso to Shetland began in 1937, and by 1938 regular flights from a newly laid-out airfield – sited between Toab and Sumburgh – connected Shetland with Orkney, Wick, Thurso, Inverness, Aberdeen, Perth and Glasgow. This became an RAF fighter base in 1940, reverting by 1953 to the Shetlands' main airport. Because the aircraft were based at less exposed airports, the local population stayed under 300. From 1962 Toab and Virkie became a rural planning *'holding point'*, but by 1971 only some 235 people lived in the area. North Sea oil service development brought helicopter operators British International to Sumburgh in 1971; the Bristow helicopter base arrived in 1978. An amazingly circuitous access route was provided to the new, optimistically overlarge and echoing airport terminal building erected in 1978: of its nine desks only three were used in 1987. By 1981 the area's population was over 600. By 1987 many modern bungalows, two hotels, a taxi, car hire and coach garage, boating and social clubs and a public hall were scattered in a typically inconsequential Shetland manner on the isthmus around the airport: Shetland planners denied that any such place could be called a village! By 1987 Sumburgh also had the Grutness pier from which the passenger ferry boat *Good Shepherd* served Fair Isle *(q.v.)*. The lighthouse was automated in 1991, when Sumburgh had 686 residents. By 1994 Quendale Mill, 3km from Dunrossness, was a tourist destination.

**Sumburgh's Pair of Disasters**: Sadly in 1986 45 men died when a Boeing helicopter crashed into the sea just offshore while attempting to land at Sumburgh. In January 1993 hurricane (force 12) winds and a series of errors of judgement drove the 17-year-old disabled Panamanian tanker *Braer* on to the rocks of Garths Ness, 3km west of Sumburgh. Though no lives were lost, the remarkably sturdy vessel broke up under a week of severe pounding, releasing her cargo of 86,000 tonnes of Norwegian light crude oil into the sea and sending polluted spray over the land. In retrospect it was fortunate that the 27 houses of Garth, which once stood in the col east of Fitful Head, had been razed in 1874 for sheep. Only the extreme severity of the weather, which rapidly dispersed the oil, prevented total catastrophe to Shetland's wildlife and fisheries – though farmed salmon in the south-west waters were destroyed in case of oil tainting *(see Scalloway)*. Even the 185-pupil Dunrossness primary and nursery schools escaped a general evacuation. In 1999 helicopter flights to the oilfields were abandoned, and 70 jobs lost. *'Jarlshof'* is opened to the public by Historic Scotland. The *Sumburgh Hotel* and *Spiggie Hotel* continue to serve.

## SWINTON — Map 3, C3

***Small Berwickshire village,*** *pop. 500 (area)* — OS 74: NT 8347

Swinton, 8km south-east of Duns in the fertile Merse of Berwickshire, was first owned by the Swinton family about 1060. Pont's map of about 1600 as engraved by Blaeu showed a kirk and mill. Roy's map made about 1754 showed an isolated road between the parish centre of Whitsome, 5km north-east, and Swinton, which had a *'mercat'* in 1769. By 1791 a quarry was open 2 km east of Swinton, which Heron noted in 1799 as a *"village"* of about 400 people, under its 22[nd] proprietor of that name. By 1825 it had a penny post from Duns, and a brewer cum baker. Chambers found in 1827 a *"considerable village"*, but in 1891 the population was still only 371. By 1902 Swinton had an inn, post and telegraph office, school and smithy. At that time sandstone blocks were carried by horse and cart from Swinton quarry, which employed 11 men, to Edrom Station near Chirnside, over 5km away; the quarry closed in 1920. By 1951 about 575 people enjoyed similar facilities to fifty years previous, plus a garage. In 1981 there was still a post office, inn, garage, primary school and telephone exchange, while Stair Brown were agricultural engineers, also based at Haddington. The parish population was 472 in 1991. By 1999 the engineering firm was larger and known as Thomas Sherriff, but there has been little other evident change.

## SYMBISTER, Isle of Whalsay — Map 14, C3

***Village / island, Shetland,*** *pop. 800 / 1050* — OS 2: HU 5462

Symbister at the south end of the outer Shetland island of Whalsay has the scanty remains of one of the earliest Iron Age brochs. As a little port it dates back beyond 1472, when the Norwegian crown ruled Shetland and the Bergen connection was particularly strong. The crude map made by Pont about 1600 included *'Sonebuster'* and *'Icebuster'* (Isbister!), the names transposed among about ten tiny places scattered seemingly at random. In the 17[th] century a Hanseatic trading post – *Bremen Bod* – was built at Symbister harbour, followed in 1823 by Symbister House, a home of the Bruce laird. At that time Whalsay was becoming a great herring fishing centre, making sad headlines for disasters in 1832 and 1840, but the population grew throughout the century to over 900 by 1891. Symbister never became a burgh, but the island was still *"a famous fishing station"* in 1894 (Murray).

**White Fish and Knitwear**: In the 1950s Whalsay school (which included secondary classes) was at Brough in the centre of the isle, but was transferred about 1970 to utilise the former mansion of the Bruces, one reason being that in 1962 Symbister had been selected as a rural planning *'holding point'*. By the 1970s electricity arrived from Kirkwall by submarine cables. Sadly in 1965–75 Norwegian vessels stripped the surrounding seas of herrings, and Whalsay fishermen, noted for purse-net fishing, had to find other prey. From 1974 a vehicular ferry plied to Laxo Voe on the Shetland mainland. By 1979 Whalsay Knitwear Ltd made hand-framed garments, and by 1983 an airstrip had been built at the north-eastern point of the island. By 1985 Symbister with its two piers was once more noted as a prosperous fishing village, with a sizeable white fish processing plant based on haddock and whiting for the USA market, plus its knitwear industry. In 1991 797 people lived in Symbister and 244 in the remainder of the island. High fish prices in 1996 made Symbister once more a wealthy place, its fisherfolk investing heavily in new boats and gear. At that time most pupils in the island school wanted to maintain the tradition.

## SYMINGTON

**Map 1, C2**

***Ayrshire village,*** *pop. 1150*

OS 70: NS 3831

An ancient motte stands in gently rolling country about 10km north of Ayr. The nearby Norman church of Symington stood apparently alone at the time that Timothy Pont mapped Kyle around 1600. Roy's map of about 1754 showed the straight road from Ayr to Kilmarnock (the later A77), crossed at Dyke some 1.5km east of the kirk by a winding road from Dundonald to Mauchline. Dyke was later called Bogend and gained a smithy. Heron in 1799 called Symington a *"small village"*. The neo-classical Coodham House was built north of Bogend in 1831, with substantial policies and a lake. In 1895 Symington was still a small kirkton with a post and telegraph office, a smithy, and on the main road an inn at Helentongate.

**The Impact of the Late Twentieth Century**: By 1951 the population was about 675 and there was a primary school. From 1949 to about 1987 Coodham House was used for monastic purposes by the Passionist Fathers. For a time around 1954 a youth hostel was open at Corraith, 2 km west of the village, where the start of a small housing estate heralded big changes to come. The estate was much larger by 1971, the parish population doubling since 1951. The A77 had become a dual carriageway by 1972; a new inn and a Wireless Telegraphy Station had been built. By 1987 the housing estate had grown, the inn was a hotel, and a caravan and camping site was in use 1.5km north of the village at Dankeith. A new quarry had been opened at Helenton Mains, but had been restored by 1998. In 1991, Symington's population had risen to 1145. Meantime, proposals of 1988 to convert the newly vacated Coodham House into a hotel with golf course did not materialise; by 1995 the vacant building was becoming dangerous and is still derelict. However Symington's Norman church remains in use.

## SYMINGTON

**Map 2, B2**

***S. Lanarkshire village,*** *pop. 500*

OS 72: NS 9935

Beside the River Clyde in the shadow of the prominent Tinto Hill is the earthwork of Castle Hill, while 2 km to the west are the ruins of Fatlips Castle, a 16th century tower. Pont's 1596 map of Clydesdale showed Symington's St John's Kirks, old and new, within a well settled area. Roy's map of about 1754 added a mill to the east, but no roads; these came later. The Caledonian Railway (CR) opened its main line in 1848, sweeping round Tinto Hill to Symington station, which in 1860 became the junction for the CR's little protégé the Symington, Biggar & Broughton Railway. By the 1890s Symington was a straggling village with an inn by the station, a post office and two mills. In 1950 the 3-star *Tinto Hotel* had 30 rooms; the facilities of a small village served both Symington's own 600 people and in some cases up to 1400 others, widely spread from Wiston to Thankerton and Carmichael. The branch railway was closed in 1966; by 1969 its track had been lifted, and even Symington station was no more. By 1972 *Wyndales House*, 3km south-west of the village, had become a 12-roomed hotel. By 1981 Symington's immediate population was under 500, but its small-village facilities still served some 1500 people in all. In 1991 the parish had 732 residents. Trains pass close by on the busy electrified main line; Carstairs station is 10km away.

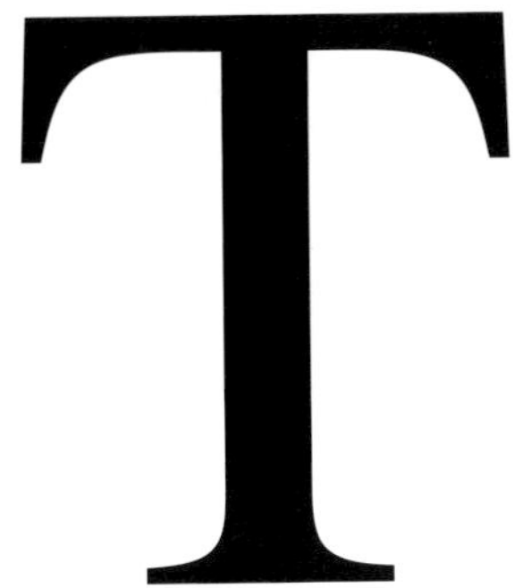

## TAIN

**Map 9, B2**

***Easter Ross small town,*** *pop. 3715* — OS 21: NH 7882

The offshore shoal named *'Mussel Scalps'* may show one good reason for early settlement on the south shore of the Dornoch Firth. St Duthac was born beside the River Tain about 1000 AD; a chapel called the *Girth of Tain* was built in his memory. Whereas Tain's Gaelic name is *Baile Dhubhthaich* or Duthac's Village, its usual name derives from the Norse *Thing* meaning *'court'*; although uncertainty surrounds its civil and religious history, its sheriff court is ancient. Tain town council claimed to have been chartered by Malcolm Canmore in 1066, though the records had long ago been destroyed by fire; but against them was the omission of the name from the 13th century Gough map. Another source suggests that Tain became a burgh *'of barony'* some time after 1314. Tain's present collegiate church was established between 1360 and 1481 *(four authorities give four different dates!)*, but the town definitely received a Royal Burgh charter in 1439. In 1535–56 Tain paid under 1.5% of the total of burgh taxes, and little remains of a castle built in the 16th century.

**Education, Ale and Tranquil Whisky**: A school was open by 1595, and Pont's map of about 1600 showed an enclosure round a substantial settlement; to the west was a mill at *'Tarlochy'*. By 1593 Tain was the centre of a presbytery, but in 1639 it ranked a modest 26th of the Scottish burghs in tax yield. Tucker in 1655 found it *"a small town"* with minimal trade of *"maybe a small barque once in a year from Leith, to fetch deals* (i.e. pine boards), *which are brought down from the hills"*. The sturdy tolbooth tower was built in the 17th century, and a post office was open on the Inverness–Thurso route by 1715. Writing in the 1720s, Defoe simply mentioned Tain as a *"town"*, apparently the most northerly he noted, without description. A brewery of importance was built at Morangie 2 km west of Tain about 1738, perhaps on the site of the 16th century mill. Morangie is said to mean *Tranquillity:* was this because whisky could be distilled on this remote coastal site from much the same materials as ale, and shipped out without interference by the Exciseman?

**Linen and Mills in Accessible – and Legal – Tain**: By 1749 master linen spinners were at work in Tain, which the Roy map of about 1750 showed as a relatively large town for those days, its grid plan evident. The town lay on the old north road or *'king's causeway'* between the Meikle and Inverbreackie Ferries, today in part an unclassified road and part lost; but at that time there were no other rural roads nearby. It had a frontage to the River Tain, which later changed its course by about 400 m. By 1768 Baillie John Reid of Tain was a skilled millwright. Though Pennant called Tain *"a small town distinguished for nothing but its large square tower"*, a fair was in full swing when he visited in 1769. In 1797 no fewer than seven fair days were scheduled at Tain; Heron in 1799 thought the population exceeded a thousand. The roads were greatly improved and extended northwards over the Bonar Bridge under Telford's guidance about 1810. A Bank of Scotland branch, open by about 1820, was soon closed; yet in 1827 Chambers saw Tain as *"the chief town in the county, a prosperous and pleasant little town, though somewhat confined and ill-paved, containing above 2000 inhabitants; though not a sea-port, Tain possesses a good jail, a good inn, and a good academy"*. In 1843 William Matheson adapted the Morangie brewery into the *Glenmorangie* Highland malt whisky distillery (no such glen appears to exist, and it was recognised that illicit whisky had been made there for over a century!).

**Tain on Rail designs its new Distillery**: The Inverness & Ross-shire Railway and its successors served Tain with a crossing station from 1864; by 1875 Wordie & Co operated a rail to road cartage depot. A new town hall was built in 1874–76 and for a time there was a woollen mill. In 1886 Tain was an *"antique, prettily-situated little town"*; it had an *"elegant"* court house and a *"very comfortable hotel"* (*Barnard*). Maitland & Sons of Tain were already specialist distillery architects. The old water-powered Glenmorangie distillery with its pot stills which produced 90,000 litres annually was *"almost in ruins"*, and replacement was imminent; this was to double its productive capacity. Tain golf club, founded in 1890, laid out an 18-hole links course. In 1891 Tain had a population of over 1600, and in 1894 Murray wrote of *"a picturesque old-fashioned place gradually decreasing in importance"*; but its *Royal Hotel* was *"good"*. Public library provision got under way about 1900, with Carnegie aid.

**Bombing the Life out of the Morrich More**: By the 1920s there was a poorhouse, later known as Arthurville, and quarries 3 km to the west, while rifle ranges lay to the east. In the 1930s RAF firing and bombing ranges were established farther east on the desolate dunes of the Morrich More, and an associated airfield was built 5 km east of the town. The village of Inver on the sandy coast 8 km east of Tain was temporarily cleared in 1943 for training for the Normandy landings. The airfield did not long outlast the war, but the ranges remained and became littered with ruined debris. By the 1950s Tain town hall was in use as a cinema, there were four hotels and small-town facilities, and the population had crept up to 1775. The *Picture-house* cinema closed in the 1960s.

*Stills at Glenmorangie distillery; it was converted from a brewery in 1843, but was completely rebuilt in 1887. The tall, narrow necks of the stills are said to be derived from London gin stills.* (JRH)

**Dormitory, Local Centre and Favourite Tipple**: In the 1970s considerable numbers of oil-related houses were built at Tain, which lost its burgh status to Ross & Cromarty District in 1975. By 1977 the *Morangie House Hotel*, converted from a Victorian villa, stood near the distillery. Tain then had a good range of services (including medical) and specialist shops. Morrison's Joinery factory showed recent extension; a scampi processor, salmon smokery and creamery were in operation. Glenmorangie distillery was again modernised in 1979, but its eight copper pot stills retained the tallest necks in Scotland. In 1987 when owned by Macdonald & Muir of Leith, it employed 16 men. In 1991–94 all production was matured in charred casks from the USA which had been used for maturing bourbon, as usual in the Scotch whisky trade, or in port barrels; it was sold as a single malt, between 10 and 18 years old. In 1996 Glenmorangie was said to be the most popular malt whisky in this country and the third such in the world; its owners then bought the mothballed Ardbeg distillery in Islay for reopening in 1997.

**Cheesy, Bypassed, Busy – and Taught in Gaelic!**: Meantime Highland Fine Cheeses, founded about 1960 to make *'Caboc'*, an ultra-rich cream cheese rolled in oatmeal, employed 12 people in 1994 and then landed a contract to supply Tesco. Six hotels were open shortly before the A9 bypassed Tain about 1981, when Tain's facilities served nearly 8000 people, including the Tarbat peninsula, as well as being a quiet resort. The population in 1991 was 3715. Remarkably by 1994 a primary school in English-speaking Tain taught in Gaelic!

**Facilities and Tourism**: By 1997 a substantial industrial unit had been built near Northwilds, 4 km east of Tain. Glasshouses stand on the outskirts of Tain. The ancient sheriff court is still active, supported by a police station. Small-town facilities remain, including a gun & angling shop, a gallery, and builders' merchants and agricultural engineers. Central Tain still has a timeless aura, with rooks roosting in the trees above the ancient church; a modern visitor centre concentrates on the town's religious history. In summer 3 weekday and 2 Sunday trains serve the once proudly-kept station, its building now sadly unstaffed and blocked up. Tain Royal Academy has 720 pupils, and a strong reputation in sport. Medium-sized hotels include the baronial *Mansfield House* and the extended *Morangie House*, and there are other smaller hostelries.

## TANNADICE, Finavon, Glencoull & Oathlaw

**Map 6, C2**

***Angus village & hamlets**, pop. 540 (area)* OS 54: NO 4758

The 11th century thanage of Tannadice may have been based at the ancient castle hill of Quiech, near Inshewan on the north bank of the South Esk, 7 km north of Forfar. In Gaelic *Uisge*, anglicised as *Esk*, means *'water'*, hence *'River South Esk'* is tautological. Oathlaw parish kirk stands on the south bank; 2 km to the east is the late 15th century Finavon Castle, seat of the powerful Crawford family. Near Tannadice Kirk, some 3 km to the east of Quiech, is Barnyards, where there was a 16th century castle. In Roy's time about 1750 the Boat of Shielhill crossed the river some 1.5 km west of Quiech, and the track from Brechin via Marcus Mill to Kirriemuir crossed by the ford and Boat of Whitewall or Whitewell, 1 km downstream of the church. When the roads were made up, this ferry was replaced by the bridges at Finavon, 1.5 km farther east, and at Justinhaugh between the kirk and castle hill. An attractive Gothic church was built in 1815.

**Railway, Distillery and Mills**: In 1895 the Caledonian Railway opened a branch line from Forfar to Brechin, through Justinhaugh station, sited south of the river. Tannadice parish had around 1100 residents at that time. In 1897 Murthill Mills, 1.5 km above Tannadice, were converted into the Glen Coull or Glencoull Distillery. This development on the Coull estate may have resulted from the railway; but the distillery was closed in 1929, its premises being reconverted into the Glencoull Mills. A large bowstring girder bridge was built to carry the road across the South Esk, and the tiny *Justinhaugh Hotel* was built nearby. The rural railway was a casualty of the bus and lorry era, closing to passengers in 1952. Goods traffic continued between Forfar and Justinhaugh until 1967; the latter's station site became used for agricultural engineering. A small secondary school was open at Tannadice in the 1950s but had become solely primary by 1976, and the village inn had closed, leaving Tannadice as a very rural parish, with 540 people in 1991. By 1996 the Glencoull Mills had been abandoned for some years, and by 1999 the church was redundant. However the primary school is still open, and *Finavon Castle* offers accommodation.

## TARANSAY, Isle of

**Map 11, B3**

***Small island off Harris*** OS 18: NB 0001

In 1549 Dean Monro wrote of rocky, hilly Taransay off the west coast of Harris that it was *"delved with spades"*, had *"certain touns, well inhabited and manured"*, and yielded bere, corn and fish. As late as 1841 88 people lived there, and until 1935 there was a school, but abandonment came in 1942. More recently a few hardy souls have stayed briefly on the treeless island to tend sheep, cattle and deer. The latest short-term group of 36 *'castaways'*, chosen and filmed by BBC Scotland, faced 100 mph gales at the start of the year 2000; though their so-called ordeal was wholly artificial, the 31 who stayed the whole year learned much to their advantage.

## TARBERT (Harris) — Map 11, B3

***Main village, Harris,*** *pop. 800 (1700 area)* — OS 14: NB 1500

Harris is a mountainous, rocky and lochan-strewn peninsula forming the south end of the large island mainly called Lewis, and was for centuries in Inverness-shire whilst Lewis was in Ross. At its centre a *tairbeart* (draw-boat) or isthmus almost cuts the peninsula in two, and its sheltered eastern anchorage forms a natural focal point. Blaeu's distorted map of 1654 showed (West) Loch Tarbert but there was no indication of settlement, and Martin writing of Harris in 1703 made no mention of Tarbert. When the national penny post started in 1840 a pier was built at Tarbert (East), to which mail steamers began that year, with a weekly sailing from Uig (twice a week in summer). This served a new post office, named Harris to distinguish it from Tarbert on Loch Fyne *(q.v.)*. In 1868 the mansion of Amhuinnsuidhe Castle was built about 15 km west of Tarbert for the Earl of Dunmore.

**Tourism, Whaling and Hydro Power**: In 1894 Murray noted Tarbert as *"the principal village"* of Harris, with the *"excellent" Tarbert Hotel*; steamers sailed three times a week to Dunvegan and Portree, and weekly to Glasgow. A carding mill for Harris Tweed was built in 1900. By 1914 Ardhasaig, a township 4 km north-west of Tarbert was a whaling station; but this closed in 1930. Though the largely Gaelic-speaking population of Harris and Tarbert had been sharply falling, Tarbert had some 700 people in 1951, with a junior secondary school and the facilities of a small village, plus an ambulance depot and a fish merchant. By 1956 the former school at Kyles Stockinish, some 10 km south of Tarbert, had become a youth hostel (still busy with overseas summer visitors 40 years later, but closed about 1995 in favour of Rainigadale). Meantime the village population had stabilised around 500, aided by electricity supplied from the Chliostair hydro-power station near Amhuinnsuidhe, supplied from a dam across the Abhainn Eabhal some 120 m above.

**Car Ferries bring Tourists**: A car ferry from Uig was started in 1964, replacing the mailboats; Tarbert's facilities grew, including a motel and by 1977 a restaurant. In 1981 the entire resident population served by Tarbert was only some 1700. In the 1980s Tarbert was a fishing and sea angling centre with the 24-room *Harris Hotel* and 12-room *Macleods Motel*; there were two seaside caravan sites on the winding roads south. The village population was 795 in 1991. In 1992 the High School at Tarbert was upgraded to sixth year status, ending boarding at Stornoway for senior pupils. Until 1989, when a road was opened from Maraig to Rainigadale (in Gaelic *Reinigeadal*) at the mouth of Loch Seaforth, Rainigadale had 11 people, a 1-pupil primary school, and access only by boat or footpath; by 1997 it had a youth hostel. By then there was a mountain rescue post at Tarbert, still the main ferry port of Harris, with daily services from Uig (Skye); the Post Office now uses 'HS' as the postcode for Harris and Lewis (formerly 'PA'). Shops, a tourist office and B&Bs are open in Tarbert; *Amhuinnsuidhe Castle* on the vast Amhuinnsuidhe estate – owned by the Bulmer cider family – offers accommodation, cookery and painting courses. Rainigadale youth hostel is open all year round, as are independent hostels for backpackers in Tarbert, and at Drinishader some 8 km south.

*Whaling station, Bunaveneader, Harris (in the 1970s). This was the last shore-based whaling station in Scotland, with whale-catching ships bringing in the carcasses for processing here.* *(JRH)*

## TARBERT (Loch Fyne) — Map 4, C4

***Small town, Kintyre (Argyll),*** *pop. 1350* — OS 62: NR 8668

Tarbert in Kintyre bears a Gaelic name – strictly *tairbeart* (draw-boat) – meaning *Isthmus*, for two sea voyages can there be linked by a short land crossing. As *'Tairpert Boitter'* it was a seat of the Head King of Dalriada up to about 768 AD. A boat carrying the Norse King Magnus Barefoot was actually dragged across the isthmus there in 1093 to establish a claim to Kintyre. Tarbert was chartered in 1329 as a Scottish Royal Burgh, and a castle was built for the sheriff of Argyll, held only until his office was moved to Inveraray some time after 1509. Pont's maps of Kintyre to the south and Knapdale to the north, made around 1600, showed only the castle, still emparked, at this north end of the parish of Kilcalmonell. Until the late 18th century all its significant communication was by sea. Tucker noted in 1655 that in winter the local Highlanders usually drew their small boats over the *"small neck of sandy land"*. The Roy map of about 1750 showed a small village west of the castle, and a track across the isthmus, then forking north to Castle Sween, Bellanoch and Kilmichael, and south to Campbeltown.

**Posts, Fishing Port and Steamer Centre**: Tarbert had a postal service from 1734, a proper post office from 1765, and was a post town by 1797, with mails on alternate weekdays. In the Town & Country Almanac for 1797, four fair days were scheduled for *'Tarbet'*, (probably this place). In the 19th century Tarbert became a major herring fishing centre and port of registry, with the identification letters TT. By 1827 steamers were operating on Loch Fyne, providing a weekly service to the village from Glasgow, Greenock and Rothesay, and from West Loch Tarbert weekly to Oban, Tobermory and Portree; boats also paddled across to Islay. By 1838 the Loch Fyne service had been extended to Ardrishaig, and from 1842 operated twice weekly. But in 1864 passengers from Hutcheson steamers still had to be ferried ashore. The 1891 population was 1775. In 1894, when Murray's Handbook called Tarbert *"a busy and important village"* with two steamers a day to Glasgow, there were three hotels: the *"good" Columba* and the *"very fair" Tarbert* and *Commercial*, though he noted that the castle was crumbling. Stonefield, 3 km north of Tarbert, was by then a mansion in a large park. West Loch Tarbert piers then provided steamer services to Islay, Jura and Gigha. In 1904 Ardrishaig and Tarbert steamers plied to Wemyss Bay, and Dickies were building small vessels in timber.

**Golf, Tourism and Transport Revolution**: Tarbert golf club was founded in 1910, laying out a basic 9-hole parkland course. By 1953 under 1500 people lived in Tarbert, where Bolton found *"a tangle of small fishing boats"*, but eight hotels were open, and its facilities were almost those of a small town. By then the mansion was the *Stonefield Castle Hotel*, with 24 rooms; ferries plied from the West Loch to Gigha, Colonsay, Islay and Jura. The mail steamers still sailed until the Ardrishaig to Glasgow service was withdrawn in 1970 as a result of the rapid growth in car ownership; two car ferries took over the island services from various West Loch piers *(see island centres for details)*.

**Crumbling Castle but New Ferry**: The reduced range of services seen in 1976 compared with the 1950s – for example the former *Regal Cinema* was derelict – strongly suggested a loss of role as a centre. Tarbert was certainly subordinate to Lochgilphead and Campbeltown, but remained a major village with about 24 shops including a gallery and bookseller, sports goods, clothing and footwear. A small cattle market was still held and there were banks and accountants. It was still a fairly active little fishing and yachting port, with a 1-slipway boatbuilder, chandler, oil fuel, a small ice plant, fish salesmen and Unkles' seafood depot (Scofisco from 1978); two hotels and modest tourist facilities served visitors. By the 1980s the herring fishery was dead, but a fish farm had been established by 1988, when locals were still complaining that the historic castle was crumbling. In 1991 the village population was an elderly 1347. A new tourist attraction, *'An Tairbeart'*, based on the rural heritage of the area, opened in 1994 at Baravalla, 4 km to the west. In the early 1990s Calmac started a summer-only ferry between Tarbert and Portavadie, which by 1997 plied all-year. The tiny Tarbert Academy remains open, and there are small hotels in addition to the baronial *Stonefield Castle* (33 rooms).

## TARBOLTON

***Ayrshire village**, pop. 1850* — **Map 1, C2** — OS 70: NS 4327

Tarbolton in Kyle stands on a hilltop above the Water of Fail 11 km north-east of Ayr; it has a medieval motte and bailey. About 2 km north-west at Fail was a Trinitarian (Red) friary, founded about 1252, which had a dubious history; damaged in 1561, its buildings passed to the Wallace family. Pont's map of about 1600 showed the emparked *'Feil Abbey'*; repaired, it became known as Fail Castle. *'Torboutoun'* and the *'Old toun'* just to the east lay in a thickly settled area. Coal had been dug near Tarbolton from the 15th century; a parochially-funded school was founded in 1601 and by 1643 there were private schools in the parish; Tarbolton became a burgh of barony in 1671. But the coal reserves soon ran out: no mines appeared on the Roy map made about 1754. *Tarboutting* was a large hamlet at the end of a spur from the Ayr to Mauchline road; mills turned at Park and Burnhouse. In 1780 Robert Burns founded Tarbolton's Bachelors Club. Paterson's Montgomerie House was built in 1798 1 km to the south-east. Heron in 1799 found what he called a *"village"* of perhaps 450 people; though it had an apothecary, urban development did not follow, but 140 hand loom weavers were working in cotton and silk by the 1840s.

**The Railway fails to impress**: Tarbolton station was open from 1870, but over 2 km south of the village, whose population was 900 in 1891. By 1902 Tarbolton had a mill, smithy, post office and inn; the *Failford Inn* was also open, beside the Mauchline road 4 km from Tarbolton. This inn became well established, but the station did little trade and had been closed by 1953. In 1938 the National Trust for Scotland acquired the Bachelors Club, now open as a tourist attraction for Burns aficionados. With a population of over 2000 in 1951, Tarbolton had average village facilities. But its small secondary school was later closed, and Montgomerie House was pulled down in 1970. Tarbolton remained a nominal burgh of barony until 1975. By 1985 a caravan and camping site had been opened 1 km south-east. In 1991, only 1850 people lived in Tarbolton, with a pub and post office, but with little recent development.

## TARLAND

***Deeside village**, pop. 550* — **Map 10, A3** — OS 37: NJ 4804

Among the granite hills north of the River Dee some 50 km west of Aberdeen is an extensive basin-like hollow with a diameter of about 10 km, known as the *Cromar*, meaning *'Circle of Mar'* in the Gaelic. It gives the strong impression of being an ancient impact crater, being still largely surrounded by a circular 300 m high rim, the central feature typical of such craters being called the Hill of Corrachree. Rather east of this hill is Tarland, some 8 km north-west of Aboyne; other smaller apparent craters nearby embrace Lumphanan and Torphins. However these unusual landforms were caused, the area is fertile and must have been important in later prehistoric times, for there are various stone circles and standing stones; but little remains of the 13th century castles of Migvie and Coull, the latter being the centre of an extensive rural parish east of Tarland.

**Living on the Highland Line**: The name Tarland may well derive from the Gaelic *tarbh*, a bull. It existed by 1642, being shown by a tiny symbol on Robert Gordon's map. When chartered as a burgh of barony in 1683, this was in order to remedy the situation where there was *"no burgh or mercat toun in the parish"* (*Adams*). The market was not a great success, and there were still no roads in the area about 1750, when Roy's surveyors found only the kirk and the tiny hamlet that remains close beside it to the west. The first post office at Tarland was opened in 1793 and replaced in 1802. At the end of the 18th century Heron noted *"the inhabitants of Cromar have for ages used the English language, although the Gaelic is still spoken around Ballater"*. The Deeside railway never approached closer than 6 km.

**Triumph, Tragedy and Benevolence**: The Tarland golf club, founded in 1908, laid out a 9-hole course in the policies of Douneside, an estate just north of Tarland that was bought by Alexander MacRobert. The son of a labourer at the Stoneywood paper works, he had taken over a failing Indian woollen mill, created the British India Corporation, made a fortune in textiles and been knighted, but suffered a tragic first marriage. His American second wife was later widowed and lost her three sons, who all died in air accidents or in action within the three years to 1941. Lady MacRobert responded by donating generously to buy planes for the RAF, and by giving the House of Cromar at Douneside to the RAF as a home – now renamed Alastrean after her sons. The MacRobert Memorial Hall in Tarland was built in 1951, and finally she established a trust which gave the MacRobert Centre for the Arts to Stirling University *(see Bridge of Allan)*, and also funded children's charities.

**Busy Service Village**: By the 1950s the village population was under 700, served by a typical shopping centre for its size, a combined primary and secondary school, and a mill; a market was still held on alternate Mondays. Another junior secondary school was at Logie Coldstone, 5 km farther west. By 1976 all the secondary classes had ended, reinforcing Tarland's archetypal village nature: its population had remained quite stable, but the village proper was down to 523 by 1991. An agricultural show was still staged in 1996, with classes for cattle, sheep, goats, horses and ponies. By then some housing development had resumed. Tarland has a primary school, garages, bank, post office, pharmacy, and a small range of shops. The Memorial Hall, a stonemason's yard, and the offices of AV Digital Productions and the Upper Deeside Access Trust complete the interesting village centre, where the *Aberdeen Arms* is a 5-roomed inn.

## TARVES — Map 10, C2

***Buchan village,*** *pop. 850* — OS 30: NJ 8631

A stone circle stands on the rolling plateau of Formartine, 7 km west of Ellon, an area long renowned for its cattle. Some 1.5 km to the west is Tarves – pronounced *Tarviss* – whose name derives appropriately from the Gaelic *tarbh*, meaning *'bull'*. As early as 966 its church came under Bishop Englat (later a Saint), whose name was applied to the river crossing of Tanglandford, 5 km north on the River Ythan. The House of Schivas, a 16th century L-plan tower, rose 1 km farther north; the late 16th century tower of Tillyhilt stood 1 km north-west of Tarves Kirk, where there was a parish school from 1621. Tarves was shown on Robert Gordon's map, produced by 1642, as if it was the most important place in the area; it was made a burgh of barony in 1673. The fine emparked mansion of Haddo House – designed by William Adam and built in 1731 for the area's traditional lairds the Gordons of Haddo – was prominent on the Roy map of about 1750. Tarves itself was still tiny. A single lonely track which forded the various burns linked to the south via Udny Green; northwards it passed east of Haddo House in its huge walled park to Tanglandford, and ended at New Deer.

**Coaches, Bulls and Books**: Tarves was later laid out on formal lines and had three fairs in 1797, but was late in acquiring a post office; by 1858 a wooden bridge bypassed the Tangland ford. The Melvin Hall was built in 1875. The area was never served by a railway, so in the early 20th century Tarves lay on a horse-drawn coach route between Methlick and Udny Station. It remained very much tied to agriculture, especially beef cattle breeding. Nonetheless literacy was highly prized in remote little Tarves – the first rural area to implement the Libraries Act and set up (with Carnegie aid) a public library, with the commendably large stock of six thousand books. Tarves had also gained a new school by 1911.

**Tarves for Meat and Haddo for the Public**: In the 1950s Tarves had a farm machinery supplier and a seed merchant, plus a tiny secondary school. Despite a fall in population to 700 by 1971, Tarves still retained typical village facilities; unlike many villages, it still provided secondary education in 1976. Some population growth occurred to 1981 as a result of North Sea oil activities on the coast, and by 1991 880 people lived in the village. Meantime, by 1980 the Haddo estate had lately been acquired through the National Land Fund for conservation and opening to the public; by 1986 it contained a country park, and Haddo House was in the care of the National Trust for Scotland. By 1980 John C Bain & Son was a substantial firm of butchers, game dealers and suppliers to the catering trade over much of Scotland. Hit by BSE and the strong pound, sadly in 2000 they called in the receivers. Meantime some housing development has continued. There is a remarkable late medieval monument in the churchyard. A modest hotel, an inn, bowling green, grocer and post office are among the village facilities.

## TAYINLOAN, Killean & Clachan — Map 4, C5

***Kintyre (Argyll) small village,*** *pop. 350* — OS 62: NR 6946

Between two prehistoric duns on Kintyre's west coast stands the ancient church of Killean. About 2 km to the north near a prehistoric cairn is Tayinloan *(The House on the Lane)*. Although its landing place is exposed to westerly gales, the tiny clachan shown on the Roy map of about 1750 became the starting point of the long-standing passenger ferry serving the interesting Isle of Gigha *(q.v.)*. By 1824 Clachan, near the ancient fort of Dunskeig 12 km to the north, had a post office; Tayinloan's first post office also opened about that time. Killean House, near the ancient church, was built in the 19th century. The *"village"* of Tayinloan had what Murray called a *"fair"* inn by 1894, the *Macdonald Arms*, that continued to function through the 20th century; but a 22-roomed hotel at Clachan closed about 1960. The undated Old Largie Castle, incorporated in a baronial pile just north of Tayinloan, was demolished in 1953. By 1981 there were caravan and camping sites near the school, some 2 km north of the inn. From about then the Gigha ferries have provided a frequent service carrying vehicles. Tayinloan remains little more than a scattered area of farms housing under 200 people, with a further 150 at Clachan, which retains basic facilities.

## TAYNUILT & Bonawe — Map 5, A3

***N. Argyll village,*** *pop. 615* — OS 50: NN 0031

Loch Etive is a lengthy arm of the sea in Lorn (north Argyll). On its south shore two rivers debouch within 1 km, each having an ancient dun or fort nearby. Dun Mhuirageul stood above the River Nant, 2 km south of the loch, while on the shore was Dun More, east of the mouth of the River Awe, and a key site at the Bonawe narrows in the centre of the loch. Some 3 km south-east in the strategic Pass of Brander is the Old Bridge of Awe, which existed as early as 1312 when Bruce fought nearby. On the north shore 3 km to the west was the Valliscaulian priory of Ardchattan, founded in 1230–31, and the location in 1308 of the last Scots Parliament to be held in the Gaelic language. Extended around 1500, it was secularised in 1602, becoming a mansionhouse. The former priory featured on Timothy Pont's map of Lorne made about 1600; south of the loch was *'Inner-aw'*, while west of the *'Avon Naint'* stood the church of *'Kilespik Kerrill'* – modern Taynuilt. By 1692 a ferry had been established across the loch, and an inn built.

**Kinglas Iron *'Forge'* and Bonawe Smelter**: Roy's map made about 1750 showed the ferry, Inverawe House, and also a little-known *'iron forge'* – actually a smelting works – at the foot of Glen Kinglas some 10km to the north-east, a place known as Ardmaddy *(Wolf Point)*. This quite large Irish venture – using local charcoal obtained from the woods of Campbell of Lochnell – had worked from 1722 to about 1738. Tracks or roads then radiated from the ferry in seven other directions, including the Pass of Brander, but the ancient bridge did not feature. Taynuilt was then the *'Kirk Town of Moncarn'*. The Bonawe iron smelting works on the Earl of Breadalbane's estate on the south shore of Loch Etive, west of Inverawe, was built in 1752–53 by the *'Lorn Company'* headed by Richard Ford of Newland near Ulverston, and Michael Knott; the firm also produced gunpowder at Kilmelford *(detailed in Hay & Stell, 1986)*. Ore from England was brought by sloops to Kelly's pier, a stone structure from which the whole annual output of some 700 tonnes of pig iron and shot was shipped south. The bellows were worked by a 4m diameter water wheel fed by a lade 1km in length from the River Awe; the workers were housed in new stone cottages nearby.

**The Military Road**: The furnace was the objective of the military road built from Dalmally by Caulfeild's troops, a second Bridge of Awe being completed in 1756 but having to be again replaced in 1779. Meantime Pennant had noted a large salmon fishery in 1769, but the sight of the big charcoal-fired blast furnace led him to remark rather sadly that it *"will soon devour the beautiful woods of the country"*. In later years coppicing was adopted so as to maintain a supply, up to 600 people within a 65km radius being engaged during the summer in making charcoal from oak, plus some birch, alder and hazel; oak bark was shipped south for use in tanning.

**The Rise of Taynuilt**: About 1777 the road on the south side of the loch was extended towards Connel; a post office (originally named *'Bonawe'*) had opened in 1775. From 1791 a post office was open at Taynuilt, a Gaelic name meaning *The House by the Burn*. Heron noted that by 1799 cobalt, talc, asbestos and *"a beautiful jasper"* had been found *"in small quantities near the village of Bunawe"*. Dorothy Wordsworth in 1803 described Taynuilt as *"a village of huts, with a chapel and one stone house, which was the inn"*; this she praised highly. *"The town of Bunawe"* was *"a small village or port"* with an *"iron foundry"*; the loch was crossed by a ferry and, unlike many Highland places, English was widely understood – no doubt brought in by the furnace management. The ironworks which cast shot in the Napoleonic wars survived the industrial revolution, only to close in 1874–76 when its woodland leases expired.

*The Bonawe iron-furnace building near Taynuilt, built in 1753 by Lake District ironmasters to use charcoal made from the local woodlands; it worked until 1876. The site has been restored by Historic Scotland and is open to the public.* *(RCAHMS / JRH)*

**Railway, Awe Barrage and Power Stations**: The belated arrival of the Callander & Oban Railway in 1880 had failed to save the smelter, but a centrally sited crossing station helped Taynuilt to grow into a substantial village. In 1894 it was called *"a growing little place"* with *"favourite angling quarters"* in its hotel; Loch Etive steamers called at the pier, from which there was a ferry to the already large Bonawe granite quarries on the north shore. About then the Bonawe quarry was bought by John Gardner, Glasgow shipowner and proprietor of the Ballachulish slate quarries. Its output of squared setts for tramway verges, and general roadstone, were wheeled to his coasting steamers in barrows to be loaded for Glasgow, Ireland and Liverpool. The Bonawe ferry carried cars from 1914 to about 1939 only, and the steamers also seem to have ceased with the 1939–45 war. The Bridge of Awe was again replaced in 1938. The ferry appears to have closed in 1966 when the Connel bridge was fully opened to motor traffic, but the railway station and the quarry (which in 1953 Bolton called a *"hideous gash"*) both remain in use. In the early 1960s the level of Loch Awe was regulated by the Awe Barrage, containing a fish pass and two 443kw hydro generating sets, but its main purpose was to supply water through a 7.4m diameter tunnel 5.2km in length to a new 25mw hydro power station at Inverawe. By 1972 the *Polfearn Hotel* was open. An increase in local population helped Taynuilt to reach the facilities of an average village, with four hotels in 1980.

**Varied Activities**: Inverawe Smokehouses were established about 1979, and in 1999 were smoking locally produced salmon and meat, mainly sold by mail order. Remarkably, the soundly-built buildings of the ironworks had survived, to be conserved and opened to the public by Historic Scotland. By 1985 caravan and camping sites were available, and about that time the Williams Brothers' West Highland Brewers set up a small brewery in the station building; but their *Fraoch 'Heather Ale'* is now brewed in Strathaven. A 9-hole golf course was laid out about 1990. The village had 615 residents in 1991; the obtrusive Bonawe granite quarries and a primary school were still active on the opposite shore. Up to 1990 Taynuilt was a railhead for the collection of timber for despatch to the south, but BR could not operate it profitably and the traffic was lost; but this trade revived under EWS, which in 2000 ran four freight trains a week between Taynuilt and Mossend. Arson sadly destroyed the vacated station building in 2000 before it could become a heritage centre. A garden and glasshouse is open at Barguillean 5km to the west; the *Polfearn Hotel* offers 16 rooms.

## TAYPORT

**Map 6, C3**

*N. Fife village, pop. 3350* OS 59: NO 4528

Near the mouth of the Firth of Tay was an early ferry, known from 1050 as the *'Ferry of the Loaf'*, Macduff's alleged payment to the ferryman as he fled south from Macbeth at Dunsinnan. In 1120 its landfall near the north-east tip of Fife was part of the barony of Leuchars. Late in the 12th century the Earl of Angus gave land and fishings to the new Arbroath Abbey, to set up a hospice or guest house on the south shore of the Tay as a refuge for stormbound pilgrims. This was evidently an adjunct to the ferry, which connected Arbroath with St Andrews. The Gaelic name *Partan Craig*, meaning Crab Rock, was applied to the nearby site where a chapel was built in the early 13th century; but as the use of English spread, so the name became more and more corrupted. From 1240 the estate belonged to the Scotts of Balwearie, and became known as Scotscraig. The estate was greatly expanded by later owners and a mansionhouse was built. When John Hardyng wrote his military guide to Scotland about 1415, the victualling of ships was possible at *Portincragge*, where the ferry was still working in 1425. A Royal castle built about 1455 just to the west was referred to in an Act of 1474 as *Port-in-Craige*, but was sold off to Sir Robert Melville in 1588. *(This castle was fully described by Scott, 1927.)*

**From Crab Rocks to Ferry Port**: The clumsily Anglicised name of *Ferryport on Craig* was adopted when the new owner chartered the place as a burgh of barony in 1598. But the map made by St Andrews graduate Timothy Pont around 1600 simply showed a place named *'East Ferry'*, west of the mouth of the Lundin Burn. In 1606–07 a church was built at Partan Craigs, while Scotscraig and *'Ferry-Port on Craig'* were set up as a separate parish. Gordon's map made in the 1640s labelled the latter *'Forgund Ferry'*, perhaps from the Gaelic *Foir-eiginn* meaning force or violence, because it was so exposed to storms whipped up by westerly gales. On the shore to the west was *'The Castell'*, and many of the modern farm names were shown. Roy's map of about 1750 showed only *'Partan Craigs'*; this small linear settlement lined the later main road, and was connected southwards by a track joining the road system at Brackmont Mill. But Roy did not show either a harbour or the ferry. Partan Craigs remained the name for the stance where a fair was to be held in 1797. To reassure the fainthearted in 1799, Heron wrote that *"the passage here, though much less frequented since the bridge at Perth was built, is reckoned remarkably safe; the village of Ferry-Port-on-Craigs has upwards of 700 inhabitants"*.

**Golf, Racing and Boatyard**: The 1801 census revealed an actual population of over 900; numerous shipmasters, some engaged in trade with Europe, were natives of the place, which for a time had a market. Scotscraig House was built in 1807, and from 1817 hosted the Scotscraig golf club. A golf course was laid out on the Garpit Links, but was twice ploughed up by the farmer, in 1843 and about 1870. A new course on the same site was opened in 1888, and by 1890 had nine holes; a clubhouse was built in 1896. Meantime in the late 1820s, as Sharp Greenwood & Fowler's map showed, there was also a racecourse which lay just south of the substantial village with its three piers; the road to Newport was laid out between then and 1845, and by then Calman's shipyard had opened.

**Ferryport becomes Tayport**: In the 19th century 60–70 men were engaged in mussel gathering to bait fishing lines. The coaching ferries between Newport and Dundee then dominated Tay traffic, but the local ferry rights still existed, and eventually a passenger ferry resumed. This was being operated by the steamboat *Mercury* when bought out in 1845 by the Edinburgh & Northern Railway (E&N), which though it did not yet reach the place, renamed it *'Tayport'*; being brief and apposite, this name stuck When in 1850 it became the northern terminus of the E&N's successor the Edinburgh Perth & Dundee Railway, a harbour was built to serve one of the world's first train ferries, from 1851 providing a direct route to Aberdeen via Broughty Ferry. Sliding tracks and lifting link-spans enabled wagons to be winched aboard the ferries, ingeniously designed by Thomas Bouch.

**Shipbuilding, Schooling, Timber and Varied Industries**: About 1855 the small remnant of the castle was demolished by being blown up, and Tayport expanded to absorb its site, for the growing population soon reached 2250. The railway cut off Calman's shipyard from the river, so he moved to Dundee; but James Moyes subsequently built ships at Tayport until moving to Broughty Ferry in 1870. By 1869 another shipyard (Dickie's) was in operation, though he failed in that year; the yard was bought by the Patent Slip Company, which built larger fishing vessels under cover until the premises were destroyed by fire in 1879. Four small schools served the town until one new school was built in 1876, after the Education Act. Meantime in 1850 David Spence had founded a woodyard and sawmill powered by water and steam. This was bought in 1860 by James Donaldson, who established a substantial joinery business there. This was expanded with help from his sons in 1888 and a railway siding laid; premises were also built at Leven (where the firm still prospers). In 1900 a watermill was still working at Tayport under a Mr Welsh. In 1901 the remarkably named Cynicus Publishing Company set up a picture postcard factory, but this had closed by the 1920s. By that time esparto was imported for paper making, presumably at Guardbridge.

**Textile Industries and the Ingenious James Scott**: A steam-powered jute spinning mill had been founded in 1864 by Matthew Blackie; railway sidings were laid to serve it, and the firm prospered into the 1920s as the Tayport Spinning Company. A smaller 600-spindle tow mill was also built in 1864 by Walker & Cleghorn. In 1867, 200 people worked in three flax, jute and hemp factories. The spinning mills served Scott & Fyfe's Scotscraig weaving mill, also built about 1864; in the 1920s its 140 looms were weaving mainly jute cloth, using female labour. Another spinning mill, operated by James Young, closed down in 1900. Walker & Cleghorn had closed about 1871, but reopened in 1875 to use hydraulic pressure to produce paper bobbins; but these failed in use, so wooden bobbins were then made until at least 1927. In 1865 Isaac Gray had built a small foundry; W & J Ferguson enlarged it, and it still worked in the 1920s. The Tayport Engine Works were built in 1875 by James Scott, who earned himself a knighthood by exporting most of the works' extraordinarily varied output of land and marine engines, and machinery for mining, pumping, ore separation, and for processing sugar, tea, coffee, rubber and coal, not to mention electrical plant! The works were closed in 1919 when the new owners moved to Dundee, but D & R B Scott continued as mechanical and electrical engineers in a smaller works at Shanwell Road.

**Ferries go – and return**: On the opening of the first Tay Rail Bridge in 1878, Tayport's role as a ferry port was doomed. By way of compensation, a local railway was opened in 1879 to Newport, Wormit and Dundee via the spidery bridge, which was blown down that December. So the train ferry was reprieved for six years, after which rich local residents ensured that a steam ferry continued to ply to Broughty Ferry several times a day until 1920. Tayport became a police burgh in 1887, and in 1888 a town council was elected, its first improvements being to bring in a supply of Dundee water (from a main laid across the new Tay Bridge and extended from Newport), and a sewerage system, also in use from 1890. The 1891 population was about 2875. A quarry was open by 1901. The golf course was extended to 18 holes in 1904 by James Braid; the club bought the course in 1923 and by 1927 had 600 members, a third of them ladies. An Infectious Diseases Hospital was opened in 1909, and in that year the gasworks was bought by the Town Council. By 1927 two garages were open in the town.

**Trees, Tank Traps and Decline**: Starting in 1928, the Forestry Commission planted up the barren sands of Tentsmuir to the east, creating the 1300 ha Tentsmuir Forest, a job completed by 1953. However, the sandspit was still naturally extending seawards at about 8 m a year. During World War II, anti-tank defences were built on the remaining open areas, to obstruct any German landing – so substantial that they are still there! Tayport's population peaked at 3300 about 1951, when there were sawmills, engineering, linen and jute works, but its facilities were only those of a large village. In later years the secondary school, employment office, cinema and dentist all closed, and the railway was abandoned in 1966 when the Tay Road Bridge was opened; small imports of timber and paper-making materials continued.

**Waiting for Gravity**: Tayport's facilities were only those of an average village, but Scott & Fyfe were early movers from jute to polypropylene weaving. Glasgow University's scheme of 1987 for a large experimental gravity laboratory in Tentsmuir Forest could have changed Tayport quite appreciably. The site of the former gasworks and a timber yard were converted into ten starter factories; this and the growth of the Universities in Dundee and St Andrews perhaps stimulated the growth in population by 1991 to 3346, with a generally well-educated character. The substantial Scott & Fyfe premises now make advanced industrial textiles, with a wide range of uses and large customers. There is now a computer dealer, and a very new estate of good quality houses beside the harbour; Tayport appears never to have possessed a hotel, but the *Bell Rock* pub is a focal point.

## TAYVALLICH

**Map 4, C4**

***Knapdale (Argyll) small village,*** *pop. 100* — OS 55: NR 7487

Loch Sween, an arm of the sea which bites deeply into north Knapdale to leave a long peninsula of lumpy hills, has on its west side Loch a'Bhealaich, a perfectly sheltered cove. This is linked to almost circular Carsaig Bay on the Sound of Jura by a level area a mere 1 km in length, which nearly cuts the peninsula in two; the surrounding area was the site of ancient duns and nearby standing stones. Beside the cove is Tayvallich *(G.Tigh a'Bhealaich)*, meaning House in the Valley. This was named on the Roy map of about 1750, when a track ran through the woods the length of Loch Sween to Keills at the end of the peninsula; from there an early ferry plied to Lagg *(q.v.)* in Jura. Telford had jetties built at both Carsaig and Tayvallich in the early 19th century. The latter place became a tiny fishing village, with an inn and basic facilities. In the 1950s a medical practice existed. Afforestation was extensive by 1960, and a prominent caravan and camping site had appeared at Carsaig by 1974; by 1981 there were only some 90 residents. Then came a change for the better: cycle trails, picnic sites and nature reserves were established in the area, the caravans were moved to a more suitable site, more housing was built around the village, and the pub and post office are still open.

## TEMPLAND

**Map 2, B4**

***Dumfriesshire village,*** *pop. 350* — OS 78: NY 0886

The Roman road from Carlisle to the north through Upper Annandale paralleled the River Annan on the east. The place-name Cumrue to the west suggests the long survival locally of a Welsh-speaking population. Spedlins Tower, a Norman to 15th century structure with red sandstone walls 3 m thick, was built on the west bank of the river 5 km north of Lochmaben; its stone may have come from Corncockle Quarry, 1 km west of the tower, which from an early date raised fine-grained Permian sandstone for building. Three more storeys were added to the tower in the 17th century, but it later fell into ruin. By the 1750s Millhousebridge spanned the River Annan, 2 km south of Spedlins and north of the ancient Applegarth Kirk. A road linked Lochmaben with Johnstone Kirk to the north on the River Annan, bridging its tributary the Kinnel Water – upstream on whose west bank near ancient mottes the farm of Ross Mains was later to be finely built.

**Short-lived Mansion, Long-lived Quarry**: Jardine Hall, erected in 1818 beside the Roman road opposite Spedlins Tower, was extended in 1893 into a great mansion in large policies. Meantime the Caledonian Railway, whose main line was opened in 1848, provided a station at Nethercleuch, 1.5 km east of Millhousebridge, where by the 1890s there was a post office. From the main line a lengthy siding skirted north of the park, crossing the Annan to serve Corncockle Quarry, which employed 124 quarrymen in 1898, worked until 1956 and seems to have been the mainstay of the nearby crossroads hamlet of Templand, to which the post office had transferred by 1951. At that time the 450 or so people in the area relied on the Applegarth parish primary school. The station had closed by 1963, replaced by a garage, and Jardine Hall was demolished in 1964; however, Spedlins Tower was restored in the 1980s. By 1991 only some 350 people remained. Although Templand post office had closed by 1994, Corncockle quarry was reopened in 1986 by Dunhouse Quarry and Onyx Contractors *(see also Annan)*. The 'A' listed Ross Mains was saved about 1997.

## TEMPLE & Carrington

**Map 15, D3**

***Midlothian villages,*** *pop. 600* — OS 66: NT 3158

An early earthwork lies beside the incised River South Esk 9 km south of Dalkeith; the Gaelic name *Balantrodach, 'village of starlings'*, must date from about the 11th century. Hugh de Paiens, who greatly influenced King David I, brought the crusading order of Knights Templars of St John of Jerusalem to Scotland in 1128. By the late 12th century Balantrodoch was

*The 1832 church at Temple village, which was converted in the mid 1970s into a private residence and the folk music recording studios of Temple Records. Close by are the ruins of the earlier church, built in the mid 14th century.* *(AL)*

their main Scottish preceptory; later it became known simply as Temple. The Templars in Scotland, abolished in 1312, lost their properties to the Knights Hospitallers *(see Torphichen)*, and their preceptory became the parish church; Pont's map made about 1600 also showed *'Clerkingtoun'* to the south-west as a church. Emparked *'Arnistoun'* – which was marked to the north-east – was later rebuilt into a Palladian mansion for the Dundas family. In 1664 Carrington, 2 km north of Temple, was chartered as a burgh of barony, to little avail. By about 1754 Arniston was served by road. A new church was built in 1832, and at that time Carrington Mill turned beside the river, while Arniston had an estate sawmill.

**Water Supply, Landscapes and Records**: By 1895 water from the Moorfoot Hills was impounded in the large Gladhouse and small Rosebery and Edgelaw reservoirs, south and south-west of Temple, which then boasted little else but a post office and to the east a sawmill, later moved to its west side. William Gillies from Haddington, who lived most of his life in Temple, became famous in the mid 20th century as a painter of the village and the surrounding landscape, also teaching in Edinburgh College of Art and being knighted. By 1951 Carrington with only 160 people had a primary school and post office; it was to grow very appreciably to 1981. Water treatment works were built west of Rosebery reservoir in the late 1940s, extended in 1965 – and again in 1989 to accept water from the huge and distant Megget reservoir. They could treat up to 34 mega litres of water per day for distribution in Edinburgh, Mid and East Lothian and the Borders. Carrington church has become a design studio, and in the mid 1970s Temple church became the recording studio of Temple Records. Temple village lost its post office after 1977, and in the late 20th century its population fell below 300. A gravel pit is now planned, 1 km south of Temple. Arniston House and estate, still in Dundas hands, is open to the public in summer.

## TEMPLEHALL, Chapel & Cluny — Map 6, B4

***N-W. parts of Kirkcaldy**, pop. 19,000* — OS 59: NT 2693

Cluny, 5 km north-west of Kirkcaldy, lies on an old road to Kinglassie and Auchmuirbridge. The River Ore was bridged by about 1600 when Fife was mapped by Pont; to the south were *'Ninians Chappell'* and *'Touch'*, later spelled Tough. From about 1720 coal was mined at Coalden west of Cluny for the Earls of Rothes; the road to Kirkcaldy was repaired in 1740 to aid the movement of coal from Cluny, and from the shallow coal workings in the Chapel valley. Cluny had mills by about 1750 when the sketchy Roy map was made. Sharp, Greenwood & Fowler's 1820s map showed *'Coalier houses'* and a school at Cluny; a limestone quarry with limeworks was open just north of the hamlet of Chapel, and collier cottages stood at nearby Tough Row. By 1896 the little Begg Colliery was open 1 km east of Dothan, and the farmstead of Wester Tough had been emparked; it was renamed Chapel House. An inn was available at Chapel, and later a second deep quarry was opened up, while in the early 20th century the short-lived Lena Colliery worked north of Chapel Level.

**Housing, Industries, High School and Crematorium**: In 1951 probably about 250 people lived in the area, but Kirkcaldy town council and the Scottish Special Housing Association (SSHA) were very soon to develop the Templehall area to the east of Chapel as a single large suburb of public authority housing. This was rapidly provided with primary N-W.schools and the Templehall secondary school, a significant group of shops and an industrial estate at Hayfield, where an American company built the Babygro clothing factory about 1962 *(see also Methil)*. A concrete products works, grain warehouses and the central Fife telephone depot were also built at Hayfield. About 1960 Kirkcaldy High School was moved from the town centre to a new building at Dunnikier Way, near a new town council crematorium, and Wimpey Homes began to develop the huge private *'Dunnikier'* housing estate, some 15 years in the building. About 1970 the Kirkcaldy YMCA left the town centre for new premises at Templehall. By 1971 the Chapel limeworks had closed and the deep quarries were being filled in, but in the past 20 years the population of the area had risen to 17,000. Soon the High School and Templehall School were merged into one of Scotland's largest schools, its 2000 or so pupils steadily moving to the former's site.

**New Facilities**: About 1977 Chapel House became the *Dean Park Hotel*. Further SSHA and private estates built in the 1970s engulfed Chapel. About 1990 it was bypassed to the west by Wester Bogie Road, the new main access to central Kirkcaldy from the new A92 East Fife Regional Road. Some housing development continued, but apart from education and the hotel only the facilities of a large village were available at Templehall by that time, when 19,000 people lived in the area. Meantime Cluny was still a hamlet, where by 1986 Stokes Bomford had huge potato warehouses. Cluny Clays, begun about that time, soon developed from clay pigeon shooting to archery, and now have ambitious expansion plans, including a 9-hole golf course.

**From Babies to Giants**: Babygro changed ownership twice in 5 years, but by 1993 provided 265 jobs in Templehall (and 185 in Cowdenbeath) under Delta Textiles. In 1992 a second function suite was added to the 20-room *Dean Park Hotel*, already catering for 150 wedding receptions a year; there were also

12 chalets. The much-vandalised buildings of Templehall secondary school were demolished in 1995 and have since been largely replaced by private housing. The major Central Fife Retail Park and its Sainsbury store, both much opposed by local interests, were opened north of Chapel Level in 1997. Nearby is a new restaurant and the speculative John Smith Business Park, where MGt, founded in 1998, had created 450 jobs by 2000 in its subscription TV call centre; an additional 500, including research and development staff, are to be recruited by 2002.

## TEVIOTHEAD

**Map 3, A5**

***Small Borders village (Teviotdale),*** *pop. 200* OS 79: NT 4206

The upper River Teviot drains the Southern Uplands and is overlooked by ancient hill forts. The Roy map of about 1750 showed a track beside it, later improved into a turnpike; Stew Mill (Newmill) was marked, 7km south-west of Hawick. From the kirk of Teviothead, 13km south-west of Hawick, the Frostlie Burn provides an easy pass into Eskdale via the lonely *Mosspaul Hotel*, some 205m above sea level, on the county march midway between Hawick and Langholm. (When the Wordsworths passed by in 1803 this was already a stone-built inn.) In 1901, 400 people lived in the scattered farms and hamlets of Teviothead parish. By 1951 the 300 who remained beside what had become the A7 trunk road were served by a primary school, post offices at Teviothead and Newmill, and a telephone exchange. As the surrounding hills were transformed by late 20th century afforestation, population decline continued, to only 203 in 1991, and both the post offices closed; but the Teviothead primary school, the historic *Mosspaul Hotel* and the *Newmill Country Inn* are still open.

## THANKERTON, Covington & Quothquan

**Map 2, B2**

***S. Lanarkshire hamlets,*** *pop. 600* OS 72: NS 9738

The middle course of the River Clyde sweeps round prominent Tinto Hill and past the lower Quothquan Law with its hill fort. Anglo-Norman settlement in the 11th and 12th centuries explains the Anglian names of the ancient mansionhouse of Shieldhill, which can be dated back to 1199, of Thankerton, which had a mill by 1539, and Covington, with its church and an old ruined tower. Pont marked the tower of *'Scheelhil'* on his 1599 map. Covington had a parish school from 1620, and Quothquan from a few years later. Roy's map of about 1754 showed three roads to Thankerton, 2.5km west of which stood the early 18th century villa oddly named East End; later a turnpike passed by, linking Lanark with Symington and the south. The Caledonian Railway opened its main line in 1848, sweeping round through Thankerton station. In 1851 East End House was rather peculiarly enlarged, to designs by David Bryce, and by the 1890s tiny Thankerton had a post office and two mills.

**Contrasting Fortunes**: Until 1914 evening *'residential'* trains from Glasgow and from Edinburgh, each known as the *'Tinto Express'*, ran non-stop to Thankerton's wayside station (the first south of Carstairs) there to be combined – destination Moffat! By 1951 the area had some 475 rather scattered people, the Covington primary school and a telephone exchange, but by 1969 this, the mills and the station were no more. However, around 1960 *Shieldhill* had become a country house hotel. By 1981 the population was down to about 420, and although there was still a post office as recently as 1988, by 1998 East End House was vacant and rotting. Trains speed through on the busy electrified main line; Carstairs station is 5 miles away. The *Shieldhill Castle Hotel* now has 16 rooms.

## THORNHILL (Dumfriesshire)

**Map 2, B3**

***Nithsdale village,*** *pop. 1633* OS 78: NX 8795

The area north of Dumfries was served by a Roman road which looped off their main route from Carlisle to Old Kilpatrick; the legions placed a fort some 25km up the River Nith *(see Carronbridge)*. By the 12th century this was within the parish of Morton. In 1369 *'The Thornhill'*, a settlement a little to the south of the fort, passed from the Earl of March to James Douglas. By about 1400 a wooden toll bridge crossed the Nith to Penpont; nearby Dalgarnock was the site of a 15th century ford and ferry across the Nith. By 1608 there was a castle at Thornhill, and also a mill; Timothy Pont's map recorded the *'Kirk of Dalgairnock'* and to the east *'Thorne-hill'*, plus *'Templan Mill'* and *'Mills of Cample'*. By then the bridge had vanished in a flood; on the opposite bank of the Nith were *'Waterfyrd'* and 2 km south of Thornhill *'Keyr Myll'*. Dalgarnock became a burgh of barony in 1636; this was re-chartered in 1664 by the Queensberry Estate *(see Drumlanrig)* as a burgh of regality called *New Delgarno*, and a tolbooth existed by 1700. Quarries were open at Gatelawbridge, some 2.5km to the east, as early as the 17th century.

**Planned Thornhill**: In turn a planned village was created on the Thornhill, which lay on the new road between Dumfries and Glasgow built in 1714–15. Thornhill's monumental column and an inn with the novelty of glass windows were erected in 1714, and by 1747 were the centre of a *"little village"* whose church had been built in 1741. The Roy map, made about 1754, showed Thornhill as a tiny settlement on the Dumfries to Sanquhar road, which passed south by way of Shawsmuir; there was as much or more development at *'Kirk Morton'* and a mill at Morton. New Delgarno was apparently then the nominal weekly market centre, with four annual fairs, but no settlement of that name was marked, and the bridge was still down. In 1773 six people drowned in a ferry accident, resulting in a new stone bridge, built in 1777.

**Coaching, the First Bicycle and Slaking Thirsts**: New Dalgarno, owned by the Duke of Queensberry, became known as the *'Auld Toon'* because by 1779 the fairs had been moved to Thornhill; a post office was opened there in 1782. In 1790 when the population was 430 the First Statistical Account stated that there was no industry at all in Thornhill. By 1796 it was however a post town with three mails a week, and three fairs were scheduled for the year. In 1799 Heron noted over 500 people in *"a neat little town. There are four markets or fairs held here, principally for woollen yarn and coarse woollen stuffs; at Barjarg there is a lime-work"*. Two coaching inns were open in the early 19th century – the *Thornhill Inn*, and by 1813 the quite new *Buccleuch Inn*. According to Chambers, Thornhill in 1827 was *"a large modern village, of a cruciform shape"*. A brewery was at work beside the bridge, and a pumped water supply was organised in 1834 by the Buccleuch Estates.

**Railway, Tweeds, Quarrying, Africa and Golf**: A committee of management was organised in 1835, a bowling green was laid out in 1838, a new church built in 1841 and a gas works and street lighting were provided by 1845; by then a doctor practised. By 1850 there were 13 pubs in Thornhill, but its brewery did not survive the century. After the Glasgow & South Western Railway main line was opened in 1850, the livestock auction market was moved to the new Thornhill station, some 1.5 km from the centre. Meantime the population of Thornhill peaked in 1861 at 1450. In 1867 the Buccleuch Estates arranged for an improved water supply and drainage scheme to be installed; Arrol & Peace operated a tweed mill at Cample, 2 km south-east of the town. In 1891 the population was 1125; Thornhill golf club, founded in 1892, laid out an attractive parkland course.

**Good Hotels, but a Poor Fair**: In 1894 Murray found a *"neat and well built town"* with the *"good" Buccleuch Arms Hotel*, the *George Hotel* and a museum. Not being a burgh, a parish hall to seat 650 people was built in 1894, and in 1896 an elected parish council replaced the Committee of Management. By 1913, after decades of farming depression, the Thornhill fairs had lost their jollification and survived only for hiring. Whereas in 1868 the Gatelawbridge quarries were busy, and still employed 108 men in 1905, Waugh noted in his fascinating local text of 1923 that *"the extensive quarries of Gatelawbridge and Closeburn are now unimportant"*. At that time 60 people were employed in Kirkpatrick's bacon, sausage and pie factory, which worked until about 1960. In 1951 Thornhill had the Morton Academy and the facilities of a large village, whose wide rural hinterland contained some 11,500 people; the *Elmarglen Hotel* was also open.

**Beeching axes the Station**: Thornhill railway station was closed in 1965. Even so, the population served by Thornhill remained remarkably stable, enabling the Academy (renamed Wallace Hall by 1990) to stay open. In 1980 there were three small hotels including the *Elmarglen*, a pub, guest house and two restaurants, a new 1-bay fire station, a long-established garage and coach hirer, plus 30 or so shops; health was covered by six doctors and a dentist, a small geriatric hospital, clinic and ambulance station. In 1991 the population was 1633.

**Stone and Livestock**: Gatelawbridge (Newton) quarry was reopened in 1986 and still raised sandstone for building in the 1990s, under Scottish Natural Stones. In 2000 Dumfries auctioneers Thomson, Roddick & Laurie sold their seasonal sheep mart in Thornhill to Cumberland & Dumfriesshire Farmers' Mart of Longtown – little knowing the role the latter was about to play in accidentally propagating the 2001 foot and mouth epidemic. Thornhill station – its former building lately converted into 5 flats – seems a likely candidate for reopening to passengers. With its road traffic calmed, Thornhill still looks attractive and prosperous, with a squash club; the *Buccleuch & Queensberry* and the *George* are both long-established hotels.

## THORNHILL (Menteith) — Map 5, C4

***Small village, w. of Doune**, pop. 550* — OS 57: NS 6699

Kincardine parish in Menteith, near the Goodie Water 6 km west of Doune, was trackless and only sketchily mapped by Roy about 1750; apparently the village of Thornhill was built soon afterwards to resettle Highlanders displaced in the 1745 rebellion. Heron commented in 1799 that *"the united villages of Thornhill and Norristown contain about 600 inhabitants. Here is a tannery and some other manufactures"*. Thornhill's first post office was opened around 1825, but it never became a burgh, nor was it served by railways. By 1895 a mill and inn were the salient features. By the 1950s Thornhill was a small village of under 800 people, with two small hotels and agricultural engineers. Menteith was transferred from Perthshire to Stirling district in 1975; by then Thornhill's agricultural engineer had become quite large. A small hotel, two pubs, post office, primary school and a small garage summed up the other village facilities. A caravan and camping site was open by 1986. The 1991 population was 550, and there has been little further change by 1993.

## THORNLIEBANK, Eastwood & Giffnock — Map 15, C6

***Renfrewshire suburbs of Glasgow**, pop. 16,200* OS 64: NS 5559

Pont's map of 1596 showed bridges across the White Cart Water and other nearby streams, implying that a significant east–west route to Paisley already existed through the thickly settled area around Eastwood church in Renfrewshire. Blaeu's version of the map showed Spiersbridge, still the name of the crossing of the Auldhouse Burn about 8 km out of the city of Glasgow. By the 1750s, as the Roy map showed, the bridge was traversed by the Glasgow to Irvine road (later B769); Giffnock was one of several farms off any made road. Thornliebank mill on the Auldhouse Burn began as a printfield, set up in 1778 by John Crum. This was extended as a cotton mill in 1792 and again in 1806–09, growing into a gigantic calico-printing concern. About that time the Wellwalls and Braidbar quarries were opened up to supply burgeoning Glasgow with building stone; one was important for white readily sculpted sandstone, the other for natural slabs known as *'Eastwood Pavement'*.

**The Railways**: In 1848 Kennishead station 1 km north-west of Thornliebank was opened by the Glasgow, Barrhead & Neilston Direct Railway. Thornliebank post office was issued with a date stamp in 1854. From 1866 the quarries were served by the Busby Railway, which left the Barrhead line at Busby Junction; stations were opened at both Thornliebank and Giffnock, and from 1868 the line also served East Kilbride. Later both railways formed part of the Caledonian system. Giffnock stone was used throughout the city, and to face Glasgow's Queen's Dock, built in 1872–80. In 1891 the population was 2100. By 1895 Giffnock had become a small village with a post office, and to the south a brick and tile works, while Thornliebank had an inn. By then Crum's Thornliebank mill had become one of the three largest centres of calico printing and bleaching in Scotland, and dominated the area; it had its own branch railway. By then Deaconsbank stood beside the Capelrig Burn, in the area which soon became Rouken Glen Park.

**Electricity, Two Tramways and Golf**: Thornliebank never became a burgh, though electricity was first made available from a local power station built in 1906. In the early 20th century the Glasgow tramways were extended to Eastwood Toll and then to Thornliebank Station. The lines of this and the Paisley & District Tramways later extended along Rouken Glen Road, where the Park was opened early in the 20th century, and from Thornliebank via Spiersbridge and beside Nitshill Road to Arden. This lay at the south end of the inter-war Carnwadric estate, which extended north to Kennishead station. A colliery was open at Wellwalls by the 1920s, but the sprawling quarries had already closed due to the depression and the advent of cheaper bricks. Crum's works eventually closed in 1930. The 18-hole Deaconsbank municipal golf course dates from 1922; Deaconsbank became its club house.

**Suburban Eastwood Gerrymandered**: With improved transport and the removal of industrial constraints, in the 1930s private housing estates were built for Glasgow professionals in the Giffnock, Merrylee and Whitecraigs areas; some of the west of Scotland's best council housing was also erected. From 1949 some Thornliebank trams were extended to turn back at the end of a new branch to Carnwadric, the last conventional first generation tramway line opened in Britain. By the 1950s there were about 13,500 people in the area, with average urban facilities. Woodfarm High School was built around 1960. The erection of private housing continued, and the population peaked at over 15,000 about 1971. By 1972 the 57-roomed *Macdonald Hotel* had been built at Eastwood Toll, and the sprawling but long-closed Braidbar quarries had been infilled by 1973, but a limestone quarry opened at Arden Head. Eastwood District was to remain outwith the enlarged Glasgow City of 1975's reorganisation, and its offices were sited between Giffnock and Thornliebank. By the late 1970s the site of Crum's works had lately been laid out as an industrial park and attracted a substantial foodstuffs processor, *Loyal Scot*; foods such as honey were packed.

**Keeping Thornliebank out of Glasgow**: The large 1000-pupil St Ninian's RC High School at Eastwood Park, approved in 1979, was built soon afterwards. Otherwise in 1980 the area kept much the same level of facilities as in the 1950s, plus 5 hotels. Housing development continued west of Rouken Glen, and in the 1991 census the area (identified as Giffnock) held 16,190 residents, of affluent suburban character. Thornliebank bus depot, formerly owned by the troubled Clydeside 2000 bus company, was acquired in 1994 by Stagecoach of Perth. In 1995 one of the three centres of the big Scottish Motor Auction Group was at Burnfield Road, Giffnock. The controversial M77 motorway, built in 1995–96, bypassed Thornliebank on the west. In 1996 the suburban Eastwood District, plus industrial Barrhead, became the all-purpose authority of *'East Renfrewshire'* (based in Eastwood Park, Giffnock). Significant firms in the area include Rawlplug, SIMPAC (packaging manufacturers), Turner Aviation components, and Star (refrigeration engineers). St Ninian's RC High School has over 1300 pupils and Woodfarm High School about 975; the railway is among the few Glasgow radial routes still worked by diesel trains.

## THORNTON

**Map 6, B4**

***Central Fife village, pop. 1900***

OS 59: NT 2897

In 1415 John Hardyng reported that there was already a *"fair ready way"* between Dysart and Falkland in central Fife. Timothy Pont's map of Fife, prepared about 1600, showed the River Ore bridged west of the south bank Mill of Ore. North of that stood a *'Spittell'*, a religious hospice. By 1663 the road between Falkland and Kirkcaldy was suitable for coaches, and by 1700 the Ore, the Lochty Burn and the Leven had all been bridged. But Thornton was not even a placename on early maps, up to and including Roy's of about 1750. Coal was mined in Strathore for the Earls of Rothes from about 1720. Boulton & Watt's first engine in Fife was erected very early, probably around 1776. The Thornton beam engine was certainly in use by about 1800, and it may have been this which was labelled as *'Old Engine'* on Sharp, Greenwood & Fowler's 1820s map; the engine house survives near the modern bypass. By 1826 there was also the extensive Lochty bleachfield, a waulk mill, the Ore mill and Mackie's mill; Thornton then lay mainly east of the road between the Ore and Lochty, but also lined its west side.

**Thornton Junction as a Railway Centre**: The Edinburgh & Northern Railway which passed between Ore Mills and Thornton was opened in 1847. The next year the triangular Thornton Junction with its main line station was created at the commencement of the western coalfield branch to Crossgates; this was soon extended to Dunfermline, and later reached Stirling. Though the first colliery had closed by 1854 – when the Leven Railway was opened from another junction at Thornton – the area acquired other small pits. Thornton grew into a mining, milling and railway village with an engine shed (built in 1880) and a complex of connecting lines. The 1891 population was 600; in 1895 the bleachfield was still in existence. For a time a cattle market was held at Station Road. Robert Hutchison & Co of Kirkcaldy owned the Lochty Maltings, which had a private siding in 1921.

**Turbines, Pitfalls, Golf, Greyhounds**: Early in the 20th century a mineral branch railway was built from Redford Junction west of Thornton to a colliery at Kinglassie; this later served the vast Westfield opencast pit *(see Lochore)*. The Thornton golf club, founded in 1921, laid out a 9-hole parkland course. In 1921–22 the Balgonie Colliery Company built a turbine house at Balgonie to power pumps at their Balgonie Colliery near Thornton. For decades the pitfalls around Thornton were the cause of seemingly endless speed restrictions on what became in 1923 the LNER main line to the north. In 1933 the LNER replaced the old locomotive depot, building a new shed with a tall locomotive coaling plant; at its peak 98 steam engines were stabled there. About 1945 the Fife Coal Company (FCC) opened their small Thornton drift mine, but it worked only until 1953. By 1951 Thornton's population was 2600, a village affected by mining subsidence, but for its size having a wide range of facilities, including a greyhound racing track. Its engine shed was one of Scotland's eight principal steam locomotive depots, and it was the base for the Fife *'P-Way'* gang

*Only this engine house now survives from an early 19th century colliery at Thornton; in recent times the building has been used as a farm steading.* *(JRH)*

responsible for track upkeep between the great rail bridges, and during World War II for manning an armoured train.

**The Rothes Colliery and Thornton Rail Yard**: Rothes Colliery was planned by the FCC as the largest pit in Scotland, against the advice of local miners who anticipated excessive water inflow. Taken over and continued by the National Coal Board (NCB), shafts were sunk from 1948 adjoining the locomotive shed. It was the prime reason for the creation of the New Town of Glenrothes *(q.v.)* just north of Thornton and became a showpiece (see *Hutton, 1999*). The NCB believed there were between 150 and 183 million tonnes of reserves; the intended annual output was around 2 million tonnes, requiring huge surface installations. In 1953–57 a large marshalling yard with over 40km of sidings for coal traffic was built at Strathore, west of Thornton. The Balgonie pumps worked until 1959, after which the power was used by the Rothes Colliery.

**A Herd of White Elephants**: From the start the contractors, Cementation, found endless problems with shattered waterbearing rock, causing No.1 shaft to take seven and a half years in the sinking to reach 765m. The horizon mining technique that was adopted did not suit the geological problems which were uncovered, and led to dissent and delay. When production began in 1957 at the 486m horizon, waterbearing whin and faulting in the seams caused many fresh starts, but work pressed ahead because in 1958 a Royal visit was planned. But, as feared, the still prestigious pit all too easily flooded, and raised little coal at huge cost, becoming a *"monumental failure" (Halliday)*. Soon after the Royals left, work on No.2 shaft was stopped to save money on reaching 644m. This prevented the proven lower, flatter and better reserves from being exploited, and the maximum annual output from the shallower level attained only 200,000 tonnes in 1960. As the demand for coal fell away, the ill-conceived and grossly uneconomic pit had to be closed in 1962, with apologies to the men who had worked so hard underground against the odds.

**After the Colliery – Decorland**: With so much less coal to be handled, the railway yard never reached its intended importance, but kept a limited freight role and locomotive running function. Thornton Junction station was closed to passengers in 1969 and was obliterated, followed by the engine shed in 1970. In 1971 the village population was 1900. Fife County Council took over the former Rothes Colliery buildings as its fire service headquarters, using one tower for hose drying; in the 1970s one of the flooded shafts was used for pressure-testing North Sea oil equipment. In 1981 council depots and Thomas Mitchell's post-war timber kit house factory were active, and by then the golf course had been extended to 18 holes. Thornton was bypassed by the very busy A92 about 1982. Decorland, founded about 1965 as a DIY shop, had become kitchen design and installation specialists, with showrooms in every Scottish city by 1990.

**Fife Circle and Glenrothes (?) Station**: In 1989 the *'Fife Circle'* of passenger trains from Edinburgh was introduced on the loop line via Dunfermline and Cardenden, passing Thornton without serving it, returning to the capital via Kirkcaldy, and *vice versa*. Thornton Yard, the meeting point of freight lines to Methil and Westfield, provided 60 jobs among its wastes of rusting sidings until the locomotive facilities were closed in 1991, when the local population was a rather elderly 1900. Some freight facilities remained. The Rothes Colliery's twin towers, whose tall skeletonic concrete boxes for so long dominated Strathore, were demolished with explosives in a single day in 1993; the rubble went into one of the shafts, so ending the dream. In 1992 a new passenger station misleadingly named *'Glenrothes with Thornton'* was opened on the Circle line at the south end of the village, but this has no main line trains, nor is it in Glenrothes! In 1996 opencast coal extraction began on 1 square kilometre of farmland south of the River Ore, opposite the site of the Rothes pit. Thomas Mitchell Homes are still very busy, and Thornton still has a range of facilities.

## THORNTONHALL & Philipshill — Map 15, C6

***Lanarkshire hamlets**, pop. 400* — OS 64: NS 5955

The Busby Railway's East Kilbride extension opened in 1868 through this farming area 1.5km south-east of Busby; it was worked by the Caledonian Railway, but there was no station until about 1900. By 1945 a post and telegraph office adjoined the station, and the Philipshill Hospital had been built some 1250m to the east, but in 1951 – apart from its patients – only about 150 people lived in this area. By 1971 dormitory development just east of the station had raised the population to about 230. There was also a branch of the Building Research Establishment at Thorntonhall. With more housebuilding it became a favourite choice of home for doctors; then green belting stopped much further development, and there were fewer than 500 residents in 1991. By 1981 Philipshill Hospital had 150 orthopaedic beds, but it was later closed and had been demolished by 1996. By then the post office had apparently closed too, but an outer ring road for East Kilbride had been built, passing about 1km east of Thorntonhall.

## THRUMSTER — Map 13, B5

***Caithness small village**, pop. 225* — OS 12: ND 3345

About 7km south of Wick are many ancient brochs and standing stones. By the 1750s Thrumster kirk stood on a track linking Wick and Helmsdale; Sarclet on the coast to the south-east was once a fishing centre, its tiny $19^{th}$ century harbour being destroyed by the sea early in the $20^{th}$ century. Between these points was the crofting township of Thrumster, served by a primary school and post office; it also had a station on the Wick & Lybster Light Railway, which ran from 1903 to 1944. Many humble thatched croft houses were occupied until the mid $20^{th}$ century; the 1951 population of some 250 has since slowly declined. Lying as it does astride the main A9 road, a garage and filling station was opened, while by 1978 a quarry at Borrowston served a block works. Thrumster's primary school and caravan site had closed by 1993, leaving just a small village.

## THURSO — Map 13, A4

***Caithness town**, pop. 8500* — OS 12: ND 1168

Thurso on the north coast of Caithness has a Norse placename, meaning *Thor's River*; the river which enters the Pentland Firth there bears the same name. Thurso was trading with Scandinavia and mentioned as being a populous place as far back as the $11^{th}$ century. The original Thurso castle, built by the Norse Earls, was destroyed in the $12^{th}$ century, when King William the Lion was seeking to assert Scottish power over Caithness; this was finally accomplished in 1228. A local church dated from the $14^{th}$ century, and following the

Reformation, by 1593 Thurso had become the centre of a presbytery. Pont's map made about that time showed a substantial town; the river was bridged a little upstream, and an array of shipping was depicted in the bay. In 1621 *'Strathnaver'*, which may have included Thurso, paid under 1.5% of Scottish Customs dues.

**Thurso as a Burgh**: Thurso had a parish school from 1628 and became a burgh of barony in 1633. Another new 5-storey castle was built after 1643 by George, 6th Earl of Caithness, but later destroyed. By 1711 there was a post office, probably the earliest in the far north, and a weekly market. The river port continued to trade with the continent at least until the early 18th century. The Roy survey of about 1750 showed what for those days was a large town, huddled irregularly on the point of land between the west bank of the river and Thurso Bay. A track from Wick led not to a bridge, for that must have fallen, but to a ferry across the River Thurso to the town; west of the river no rural tracks were shown. About that time Caithness flagstones were worked on the Crown lands of Scrabster and carried on men's backs to the harbour for export to Leith. In 1769 Thurso's large salmon fishery was noted. The Earls of Caithness built two warehouses for grain export.

**Statistics, Brewing, Weaving and Tanning**: The energetic Sir John Sinclair, born in the mid 18th century in the new Thurso East Castle, proposed and led the preparation of the First Statistical Account of Scotland, and had bridges and roads laid out in northern Scotland. It was no doubt at his instigation that the town acquired a large rectilinearly planned extension. A bleachfield was built in 1789; many people were soon engaged in spinning imported dressed flax for *"south-country merchants"*, and some was locally hand woven into linen. A brewery was built in 1798; however, the revised description published by Heron in 1799 did not mention this, while noting Thurso as a *"town greatly promoted"* by Sinclair, for whom Heron had worked on the editing of the Account. Woollen and linen cloth was made, with a bleachfield and *"a considerable tannery"*. Salmon, cod and ling fishing employed many hands.

**Thurso to London in 4 days**: In 1797 the post served Thurso on three days per week. In 1800 the ferry was replaced by a new bridge, but the Inverness to Thurso mail-coach first ran in 1819, initially taking a dog-leg route via Wick. However, Chambers noted in 1826 that *"a direct and modern road leads south to Berriedale Inn"*, and there was also a post-road eastwards to John o' Groats. He continued *"Thurso is a burgh of barony, holding of Sir John Sinclair of Ulbster whose residence is called Thurso East. It is about the same size as Wick, but not so prosperous or increasing so rapidly"*. In the 1840s stage coaches took 89 hours to reach London from Thurso's *Royal Hotel*, averaging about 7.5 mph.

**Flagstones Galore, and the Boys' Brigade**: In 1824 a tramway was laid from a flagstone quarry at Weydale some 5 km south-east of Thurso to a dressing yard on the riverside. At its peak this industry employed 1000 men, with various extensive quarries. The largest in 1869 were James Sinclair's, 3 km south-west at Hill of Forss, and Traill's at Castletown *(q.v.)*; nearby and at Olrig, John Swanson worked several smaller quarries. Those at White Moss, and at Youkil near Weydale, which was still substantial in 1910, are hard to identify on modern maps. In all – including production from the Halkirk area – about 45,000 m² of Caithness pavement flags were shipped annually. Meantime William Smith who founded the Boys' Brigade was born in Thurso in 1854. Although from mid-century serious port activity transferred to Scrabster, fishing and slab export continued, and a lifeboat station was opened in 1860. A fine Doric public library and art gallery was built as the Miller Institution in 1862, and in 1866 the local newspaper the *Caithness Courier* was founded.

**Farthest North Railway – but Slabs beat Flagstones**: A branch of the Caithness (later Highland) Railway from Georgemas Junction finally reached Britain's most northerly station at Thurso in 1874, and by 1875 Wordie & Co had a rail to road cartage depot. The town had a chemist's shop by 1876; kippering was also carried on around that time. In 1886 Thurso was a *"town of size and substantial appearance"* with piles of paving stones on its wharf. The river bridge was replaced yet again in 1887; the 1891 population was almost 4000. In 1894 Thurso's main activity was still flagstone dressing, but some fishing continued; the *Royal Hotel* was *"good"*. By that time there was a mill, a foundry making water wheels and a lifeboat station. A harbour was built in the 1890s, and for a time even larger quantities of flagstones were exported, many of which went to pave the streets of Paris; but concrete slabs were to prove cheaper and easier to lay, and almost killed the industry. However, Stonegunn quarry was open in 1910 (and again in 1996).

**Coaches and Buses, Lorries and Aircraft**: Horsedrawn coaches ran to Tongue until well into the 20th century, when they were replaced by buses; a stone-built post office apparently dates from 1916. A new (or more likely a re-equipped) gasworks was provided in 1933, when the bleachfield still existed; about that time Miller Academy (now Thurso High School) was built beside the station, and by then a small hospital and the golf course were open on the Halkirk road. By the 1930s a long-distance road motor freight service had started between the far north, Inverness and Glasgow, competing with the railways, whose Thurso and Wick sundries traffic – mostly shop deliveries – began to wither. In the mid thirties, air routes from Dyce began to serve Wick, Thurso and Orkney. Air mail services from Thurso to Shetland began in 1937, but were short-lived because the 1939–45 war ended Thurso's civil aviation; by 1950 the air service flew from Wick.

**Tourism, Nuclear Research and Markets**: Despite a population of under 3400, Thurso already enjoyed a full range of urban facilities, serving the north coast of Caithness and north-east Sutherland. In 1953 the long-established *Royal Hotel* boasted 3 stars, 90 rooms and an annexe; the *Pentland Hotel* (41 rooms) and the smaller *St Clair Hotel* were also open. The population more than doubled in the 1960s due to the prevention of residential settlement on any scale close to rapidly expanding Dounreay *(q.v.)*; its Experimental Reactor Establishment, opened in 1954 on a wartime airfield 13 km west of the town, led to a station siding being reserved for nuclear use. Thurso Technical College was added to the local facilities in 1959; new buildings for Thurso High School arose nearby. In the 1960s parts of the old town were quite pleasantly redeveloped and a small Woolworth store was opened. The firm of Caithness Livestock Breeders – engaged in agricultural contracting and sheep marketing – was also established in 1964, and an extensive cattle market was laid out beside the station, but by that time the Thurso railway locomotive depot had been closed, becoming used for car body repairs. In 1964 the town council laid out a 9-hole municipal golf course to the south-west, replacing the earlier course close by; it had been extended to 18 holes by 1989. By 1974 flagstone quarrying and Thurso retail market were practically extinct, but two caravan and camping sites were open.

**Atoms shrink**: The burgh was abolished in 1975, the offices of the new Caithness District being located in Wick. This left Thurso still more dependent on Dounreay, although by 1979 there were two agricultural markets, and the town was well known for lamb sales. In 1980 Thurso's small modern industries included a bakery, a dairy and a concrete block works; nine hotels were open. The town centre contained several specialist shops, but its general level of facilities had not risen appreciably, for some purposes still relying on Wick. Though there was by then a minor Rolls-Royce factory, the heavy staffing cutbacks under way at Dounreay in the late 1980s greatly damaged the local economy of Thurso, which had become its dormitory. Houses were unsaleable, and the Technical College, with 88 staff in 1988, was particularly threatened. In 1991, Thurso was largely a young, healthy and well-educated community of 8488.

**Stone expands**: However, by 1992 a new business park had been laid out. In 1993 despite its rail and sea links, Thurso received its LNG (Liquefied Natural Gas) in the most risky way possible, in bulk by road. Northscot Joinery was still manufacturing kit houses, and Ashley Ann Kitchens also served a wide market. In the mid 1990s Caithness Stone Ltd raised Devonian sandstone from the Stonegunn quarry, 5km south-east of the town, for use in building, and Caithness Flagstones worked the Weydale quarry nearby. In 2000 Granit Union worked the Cairnfield quarry at Weydale. Hamilton's Auction Mart, very busy with cattle and lamb sales in 1995–96, is still active; some cereals are also farmed in the vicinity of Thurso. In 1995 the future of the Scotrail depot which still employed 11 people was under threat due to rail privatisation economies.

**Modern Thurso**: The 3 daily passenger trains, which formerly divided at Georgemas, now serve Thurso by a detour en route between Inverness and Wick; buses connect them with the Scrabster–Stromness ferries. New houses are still appearing to the south of the town, whose good range of shops includes jewellers and furnishers; a new Co-op supermarket stands beside the river, which is still famed for its salmon, and Safeway also have a store. Nearby is a large modern *Ford* garage and the works of E & M Engineering Services (who also operate at Kinlochbervie), and AEA employ 80 making lithium batteries. There is a local museum and a modern police station. Hotels include the long-established *Royal* (102 rooms) and the much-extended *Pentland*; there are also smaller hotels and three hostels for backpackers.

## TIGHNABRUAICH & Kames

**Map 5, A5**

***Cowal (Argyll) villages,*** *pop. 900*

OS 62: NR 9772

When Roy surveyed Argyll about 1750, the steep site on the west side of the narrow Kyles of Bute where Tighnabruaich was later to grow was covered in woodland; its Gaelic name means *House on the Hillside*. Some 3km south is Blair's Ferry, from which a service must once have plied to Kilmichael in Bute. From Blair's Ferry a track led north, passing *'The Kaim'* (Kames) and Auchenlochan en route to Kilmodan and Strachur. Inland of Kames, which formerly held a small market, gunpowder mills were founded about 1840. From the 1820s excursion steamer services were developed from smoky Clydeside to the breezy Firth of Clyde and through the picturesque Kyles; the pleasures of a fine-weather trip on the open decks were complemented by calls at sheltered Tighnabruaich, where a pier was built in the mid 19th century, enabling its development as a day trip resort. In 1864 Tighnabruaich was served by Hutcheson steamers, and in 1877 by the Lochgoil & Lochlong Steamboat Company.

**A Crowded Resort in Days of Steam**: In 1886 Tighnabruaich was said to be *"rapidly becoming a crowded watering-place"*. The 1891 resident population was 515, and it was described by Murray as *"a small colony of marine villas"* – by then they sprawled along the braes for 4km. There were already two hotels, the *"good" Royal* which adjoined a second steamer

*Tighnabruaich pier, as rebuilt in 1885 – a typical Clyde steamer pier, with the waiting rooms at the landward end. This pier is still used in the summer months.* *(JRH)*

pier, and the *Tighnabruaich*. Kames also had two piers by 1895, one serving an adjacent saltpetre works, while at the powder works was a post and telegraph office. In 1902 steamers from Glasgow to the Kyles would first call in at Rothesay. In 1901, over 1900 people lived in the vast Kilfinan parish (which also includes Otter Ferry and Portavadie); but after the dislocation of two world wars, by 1951 only 1250. By 1953 the Kyles of Bute golf club had laid out a 9-hole moorland course and the small *Kames Hotel* was open, but the powder mills closed about 1959. The author visited picturesque Tighnabruaich by steamer from Glasgow in that year when its resident population was about 300, under half that of its larger satellite Kames, but found the typical facilities of a Scottish resort and residential village, with 8 hotels, as many as 18 shops including clothes, shoes and hardware, tea bars, tennis courts and putting greens.

**Yachting, Yachtbuilding and Liquor**: A lifeboat station was opened in 1967, for the area was much favoured by yachtspeople; by 1980 a local boatyard specialised in yachts, and there was a youth hostel. By 1981 Tighnabruaich's secondary school, dispensing chemist, dentist and its pre-NHS superfluity of doctors catering to well-to-do hypochondriacs had gone; the population was down to only 220, plus another 520 at Kames. The regular services by cruising ships were fading; until their withdrawal at the end of the 1992 season, some Calmac cruises still served Tighnabruaich pier; the preserved PS *Waverley* still calls in summer. Although the whole parish had only 906 residents in 1991, the *Kames Hotel* was still in business in 1993; however by 2000 the youth hostel had closed. The Meldalloch Liqueur Company of Tighnabruaich, founded in 1993 by Neil Jack and Sandy MacMillan (owner of the *Kyles of Bute Hotel*) soon marketed a single malt whisky liqueur, *'Scottish Island Malt'*; they did not state which island was its actual source. Within a year they employed 20 people, producing specialist foods laced with their liqueur. Little Tighnabruaich is still a busy yachting resort, with several hotels.

## TILLICOULTRY

**Map 16, B1**

***Clackmannanshire town,*** *pop. 5300* — OS 58: NS 9297

Tillicoultry, which lies at the foot of the steep Ochil Hills in Clackmannanshire, has a Gaelic name, probably *Tulach-cul-Treb*, *'Knoll behind House'*, referring to The Law which divides the valley behind the village. It first became known for the handloom weaving of woollen serges in the mid 16th century, gained a parish school in 1627 and was chartered as a burgh of barony in 1634. Tillicoultry House, which existed by about 1750, was rebuilt early in the 19th century. The later mansionhouse of Harvieston, 2 km east of Tillicoultry, was remodelled in 1804. However, in the mid 18th century the population was under 800, and the nearest road was at Coalsnaughton, 2 km to the south, where the poor-quality Coalsnaughton Main seam was being mined. There was a bridge by 1785, and in 1790 a waulk mill was set up in the Mill Glen. In the early 1790s there were still only 21 weavers, but a fulling mill was soon built; in 1799 Heron noted that *'Tillicoultry Serge'* had *"long been famous"*.

**Woollen Mills expand – Childhood shrinks**: The integrated Castle Mills were built in 1798–1800; then came the Midtown Mill of 1805–07, all of the above being promoted by the local woollen producer John Christie to produce good-quality serges. Craigfoot mill was established in 1806, Balfour's mill about 1812 and Dawson's in 1821. R Archibald & Sons, founded in 1817, at first made blankets and plaidings but soon became *"famous for the excellence of their tweeds"*. Paton's fine stone-built Clock Mill, making tartans and woollen shawls, dated from 1824. At that time Chambers wrote of a *"village of extreme pleasantness"*. By 1830 eight sizeable mills were open in Tillicoultry, employing 560 people, of whom 140 were young children. Craigfoot mill was rebuilt in 1838; by then a post office was open. The Devonvale tweed, tartan, shawl and shirting mill was built by J & R Archibald in 1846–51; from 1858 Robert Archibald of this mill patented and produced piecing machines – to join rolls *(G.'ruileag')* of carded wool into lengths for spinning – until at least 1883 (one survived in 1979 at Bridgend, Islay). Middleton mill was also built in the mid 19th century. Paton's mill was enlarged, powered by water and steam and at its peak in the 1860s had about 950 workers making tartans. A branch of the Stirling & Dunfermline Railway was opened from Alloa in 1851; it was extended to Dollar in 1869, with a Kinross link from 1871. By 1860 Wordie & Co had a rail cartage depot, and by 1861 the population was over 5000.

**Bremner finds Wool at its Maximum**: In 1869 Bremner counted twelve woollen factories employing over 2000 people, with 230 power looms and 340 hand looms. Australian and Cape wools were used, and about 180 hand loom weavers made shawls and napkins. Tillicoultry was made a police burgh in 1871, about the time that the last mill was established – Devonpark spinning mill. About 1880 the route for a mountain railway was surveyed to the summit of Ben Cleuch, but – unlike the *'Jacob's Ladder'* of wooden steps up the glen – it was never built. In 1888 Tillicoultry was one of the three main Hillfoot worsted and woollen towns (with Alva and Dollar), making blankets, shawls and tartans; the mill owners by then included William Gibson. James Wardlaw & Sons were long-established engineers and millwrights, and the *Crown Hotel* was open. The 1891 population was almost 4000. In 1894 Murray called Tillicoultry *"an important seat of woollen manufactures"*; Coalsnaughton had an inn and post office.

**Wool shrinks; Paper comes and goes**: Tillicoultry golf club, founded in 1899, laid out a 9-hole parkland course west of the town. In the 1930s the Devonvale Mills were owned by the paper converters Samuel Jones & Co, who also made paper for filter-tip cigarettes elsewhere in the town, and by whom the fine Devonvale Hall was gifted to the public in 1938; it is still a popular venue, e.g. for Scottish country dancing. The population of Tillicoultry was about 5500 in 1951, enjoying the facilities of a large village, even including a local newspaper; but this did not last, for with the decline of the woollen industry in the face of growth in synthetic fibres the mills were closing one by one. Harvieston was blown up in 1965, the peak year for such vandalism; its extensive outbuildings survived in 1980, but Tillicoultry House had long been in ruins. The rail passenger service was ended by Beeching in 1964, and with the closure of the paper mill about 1970, the line was closed to freight in 1976.

**Sterling not at Stirling, nor Strathallan in Strathallan!**: The Sterling furniture warehouse, established in 1974, took over the buildings of the Devonvale paper mills, one of the little town's largest and most historic mills. James Meikle &

*The Clock Mill, Tillicoultry, which began making tartans and woollen shawls in 1824. Converted to house craft workshops in the 1980s, it is now offices.* *(JRH)*

Co, carpet manufacturers of Kirkcaldy, had an offshoot in Tillicoultry for a time around 1970, and by 1976 Devonpark had become a knitwear factory. A quarry which had been worked in the Mill Glen for half a century had by then become a vast eyesore on the hillside, especially as seen from south of the river. In 1981 the facilities were still those of a large village. Woollen piece goods continued to be made by Paton's in Lower Mill Street until the factory was closed and sold in the 1980s. By 1989 the remarkably named Strathallan Dairy Foods were producing processed milk packs for the catering industry. By 1988 the old Clock Mill contained the tourist office and craft workshops, and by 1990 a local authority dry ski slope had been laid out at Firpark. In 1991 the population was 5269.

**Tourism and Furniture grow as Knitwear struggles**: By 1992 the *Harviestoun Inn* was open, providing conference facilities in a rural setting; by 1994 the Harvieston Brewery was brewing ale, using Bavarian hop pellets and Scottish malt. From 1992 the historic buildings of the former Paton's Mill in Lower Mill Street were converted into flats, adjoined by 80 new houses and a new industrial estate. Two small single-storey mills of 19th century origin still stood south of the town in 1994, the Devonside (which had given its name to the whole area south of the river) lately occupied by Bryant, and the active Callant knitwear factory and mill shop, catering particularly to golfers; beside them was the yard of Glen Transport, international van hauliers. Opposite the vast Sterling Furniture operation is a large Queensway Furniture store plus a recent 'Designer Outlet Village'.

## TINGWALL, Gott & Veensgarth — Map 14, B4

***Hamlets, Shetland,*** *pop. 400* — OS 4: HU 4244

Shetland's principal Norse church and steeple stood beside the Loch of Tingwall, in a valley some 3km north of Scalloway. The area had little farming potential but was central to the Shetland Isles, whose Parliament met there in the open air, for instance in 1307. The meeting point was known as the Law Ting Holm; Martin noted *"the ancient court of justice in these islands was held in the parish of Tingwall on Holm, an island in a freshwater lake"*. By 1593 Tingwall had been made the centre of the new Shetland Presbytery, but little else changed. By the 1950s most of the area's 200 or so people lived in nearby Veensgarth township, served by Gott, 3km to the north, which was little but a post office and primary school. By 1974 an airstrip had been laid out at Tingwall, with flights to Foula, to some extent compensating for the remoteness of Sumburgh Airport from Lerwick and Scalloway. By 1980 most new development too was in the Veensgarth area, and the local population was approaching 400; there was an agricultural museum. A quite extensive new council housing estate and the large new Tingwall Public Hall had been added by 1987; a quarry served a substantial concrete products works. Fish were farmed in Wadbister Voe, and Loganair operated the tiny airport, which had a hard runway by 1994, while Veensgarth has acquired an inn.

## TIREE, Isle of — Map 4, A1

***Island, inner Hebrides,*** *pop. 730* — OS 46: NM 0444

The remote and generally low-lying Isle of Tiree is windy but sunny and fertile; it has many ancient remains including crannogs, duns, standing stones and stone circles. Beside Gott Bay on its eastern side is Kirkapol, once the site of medieval chapels and monasteries; it was one of only three places on the island of *'Tyrryf'* marked on Pont's tiny map of the Hebrides, made about 1600. A sheltered harbour was built in 1771 at Scarinish on the south-east coast. By 1800 some 13,000 litres of whisky from Tiree's scattered stills was exported annually. The low Balephetrish Hill on the north coast had a marble quarry, open in 1791–94 (and again in 1910). Early travel writers shunned Tiree, but an inn was open there by 1801; eventually this became the *Scarinish Hotel*. A post office named Tiree was opened in 1803.

**Building the Skerryvore Lighthouse**: The Skerryvore reefs 27km south-west of Scarinish formed a major hazard to Atlantic mariners until a lighthouse was built. It was designed and supervised by the Northern Lighthouse Board's engineer Alan Stevenson, from a construction base at Hynish on the south tip of Tiree. Stone for a plinth of gneiss was hewn there, a job for 14 men in 1836–37. To make a safe barracks for the workmen on the reef took two years; then a 12m diameter pit was sunk into the rock in 1839–40. Within this a 42m tall tower was erected in 1840–42, its gneiss base solid for 8m. The upper walls 3m thick were built of interlocking blocks of granite from Earraid near Fionnphort. It was finally lit up in 1844. For 50 years the keepers' families were based in granite houses at Hynish, later being moved to Earraid.

**Clearances, Emigration – and Air Link**: By 1831 some 4500 people lived on Tiree, but very many of its small tenants were evicted by the laird, the Duke of Argyll, until clearances were banned in 1886. The remainder (2500 people in 1891)

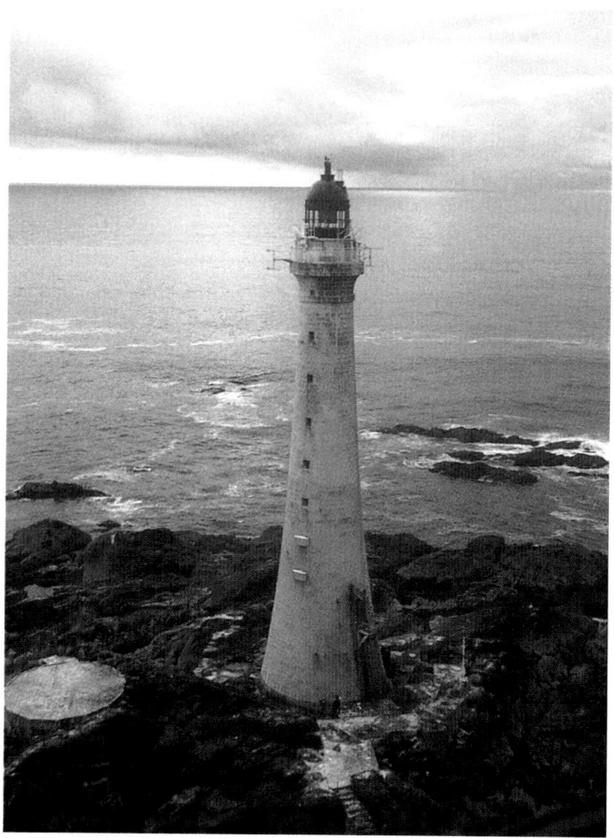

*Skerryvore lighthouse, a masterpiece in gneiss and granite, was built in 1836–44 from a construction base at Hynish in Tiree. The designer was Alan Stevenson, the uncle of Robert Louis Stevenson.* *(JRH)*

continued in crofting and lobster fishing, or drifted away during the ensuing 90 years. The steamer berth, postal centre, bank, police, doctor, dentist, ambulance and vets for Tiree were all eventually based in Scarinish, but its harbour was tiny. The Tiree golf club, founded in 1920, established a 9-hole course on the links at Vaul, 4km north of Scarinish; by 1953 this had been extended to 18 holes. A large military airfield was constructed in 1941 at The Reef, about 4km west of the village, later becoming the civil field, with a direct air link with Glasgow. By 1962 a new concrete pier, built into deeper water at Gott Bay 1km north of Scarinish, gave ships more room to manoeuvre, but in 1969 cars were still loaded and unloaded by crane. Tiree had a resident population of 875 in 1971; that of Scarinish – which had the island's diesel driven power station – was probably under a hundred!

**Modern Tiree: Surfing and Shrinkage**: The resident population served from Tiree – including some services provided to the Isle of Coll via Arinagour – shrank over the post-war period. However, the coming of the ubiquitous car ferry to Gott pier about 1971 stimulated tourism. A second golf course was soon laid out, 2 km west of Scarinish, and a second hotel, the *Lodge*, was built at Kirkapoll. Secondary, and by then also primary schooling was concentrated in the north-west of the island, at bilingual Cornaigmore. In 1986 the Tiree car ferry from Oban also served Coll, Tobermory, and Lochaline; by then Hynish had a museum. Five scattered post offices served a dispersed resident population of 768 in 1991, mainly crofters. Skerryvore, the last of Scotland's pillar rock lighthouses to be manned, was automated on Boxing Day 1991. In the 1990s Tiree's population declined to about 730 residents, including 120 pupils in the combined primary and junior secondary school. The Vaul golf course has now reverted to 9 holes. The 10-roomed *Tiree Lodge Hotel* at Gott Bay is near the venue for international wind surfing championships.

## TOBERMORY

**Map 4, B1**

***Main village, Isle of Mull,*** *pop. 825* — OS 47: NM 5055

Tobermory – which means *St Mary's Well* in Gaelic – refers to an early Christian chapel which stood beside a sheltered harbour near the northern corner of Mull; to the south are standing stones. Tobermory bay was the site for a battle in 1480 which resolved a family quarrel among the Lords of the Isles. A large ship, blown up with great loss of life in 1588 while at anchor in the bay, was part of the Spanish Armada. Whether it was the galleon *Florida* or the hired supply ship *San Juan de Sicilia* is not agreed. Martin in 1703 referred to the *"capacious and excellent bay"*, noting that local people *"were living at the harbour when this ship was blown up"*, implying that Tobermory already existed in the 16th century. The chapel was shown on Pont's map as *'Tobber moire'*, but was in ruins by the early 18th century. Island feuding was ended when a Hanoverian form of peace was imposed from 1746.

**Creating a Village**: Tobermory's inn was open by 1773, but there were apparently still no wheeled vehicles on Mull when in that year Dr Johnson described Tobermory as *"a busy place"*. His companion Boswell noted *"only two or three trees near the tolerable inn"*; the nearest post office was at Inveraray! A village extension was laid out in 1788, and in 1789 the British Fisheries Society under the governorship of the benevolent 5th Duke of Argyll set up a fish selling agency. Although neither this nor boatbuilding was very successful – every plank having to be imported – a pier was built under Telford's direction, and from 1791 there was a custom house. There was a post office in the village by the time that Ledaig distillery was started in 1795 by John Sinclair.

**Huts for Homes round a Modern Village**: In 1805 a new post office was opened, the mail then going via Aros, although the road from there was not completed until 1807. By 1821 steamers linked Tobermory with Glasgow via the Crinan Canal. Not long before Chambers visited in 1827, a traveller, Dr Clarke, had reported that apart from a few lairds' houses all the people on Mull lived in huts. Chambers found Tobermory *"a modern fishing and trading village, the seat of a custom-house, and the principal collection of houses in the island"*. By 1828 a weekly steamer service called at Oban and took tourists to Staffa; another served West Loch Tarbert. But Tobermory remained poor, being among the Highland settlements where the government erected a building for the Church of Scotland (1828). Although from 1834 the Glen Albyn Steamboat Company of Tobermory operated four paddle steamers, these carried involuntary emigrants as well as tourists and whisky, for Mull's population was in the process of being cut by two-thirds in 70 years by grasping landlords, from a peak of over 10,600 in 1821. In 1847 Somers, following in the wake of the potato famine, found Tobermory a village in deep poverty, many of its 1400 people being evictees. There was a Gaelic school, and the steamer *Tartar* called weekly on the Portree to Greenock route.

**Whisky Produced – and Denied**: But soon a modicum of investment returned, and by 1850 Tobermory had a bank. The lighthouse on Rubha nan Gall, 2 km north of the harbour, was first lighted in 1857. Fontane in 1858 described Tobermory as *"a little market-town"*; in summer at least, two tourist steamers a week called in on their Oban to Iona trips. In 1862 a courthouse was built, and also a poorhouse to offset the continuing destitution. The village contained 1850 people in the year 1871, and from 1875 Tobermory was a tiny police burgh. In 1886 Barnard found a *"little picturesque town"*; the distillery then employed twenty men and was powered by water and steam, using barley brought from Ross and Inverness-shire by MacBrayne's steamers to produce 280,000 litres of Highland malt whisky a year. The draff was fed to cattle on the distillery farm. A daily steamer plied to Oban, and in summer also to Portree. On the promontory above the town stood the *"fine" Western Isles Hotel*, described by Murray in 1894 as *"very good and well situated"*. By then Tobermory was *"a town rapidly increasing in popularity as a summer resort"*; the *Mishnish Hotel* and the *Royal* (temperance!) were also open, and *"thick woods"* also reveal a big change during the previous century. But opportunities overseas had increased and the island population had fallen, to 1154 by 1891, a quarter of Mull's earlier total.

**Golf but No Whisky, No Work, No Telephones**: The Tobermory golf club's unusual 9-hole moorland course was opened in 1896. Up to 1914 a mail steamer from Tobermory sailed to Coll, Tiree, Bunessan and Oban, taking two days for the round trip. In 1916 DCL bought the distillery from John Hopkins & Co, but it was closed in 1930 due to the crucial problems of the whisky industry, and Tobermory lost its year-round employment in a period of wars and economic stagnation. The village was too peripheral in its almost deserted island to grow into a real town, and its own population declined rapidly. It was 1930 before Mull's first telephone exchange was opened in Tobermory. A yacht club was formed in the 1930s, and a lifeboat station was opened in 1938 (but this service lasted only until 1947). In 1951 Tobermory remained an important service village of 700 people, whose other function was as a summer resort with a youth hostel. There was also a tiny hydro-electric station. The lighthouse was automated in 1960. Though Tobermory post office was the main centre for Mull, Iona, Tiree and Coll until 1964, it then lost this position to Oban. Other facilities including the chemist closed, making Tobermory little more than an average village in service terms; in 1971 its population bottomed out at 640.

**Recovery begins – and falters**: The Ledaig distillery was reopened in 1972 with 15 jobs, and a fish farm and a folk museum were established. A chemist was back in business by 1985. Mull was served by a mobile bank based in Tobermory, which remained a distribution centre for Caledonian MacBrayne. Ledaig was sold as a strong Single Malt, but in 1984 production again ceased. The Kilchoan passenger ferry was then very marginal at four trips a day. In 1985 there was a library. The secondary school taught its 112 pupils to *'O'* grade only, and all senior secondary pupils had to become weekly boarders in Oban; but the school's age range was soon extended, as Tobermory High School (today with about 170 pupils). An information centre, out of town caravan site and pony trekking served the tourist.

**A Modest Resurgence**: The lifeboat station was reopened in 1990, due to increased use of pleasure vessels in the seas around Mull; the population was 825 in 1991. From 1990 the Ledaig distillery was again active under Tobermory Distillers; in 1993 it was bought by Burn Stewart of Barrhead and now sells as a single malt. Tobermory Chocolate, founded in 1991 by Keith and Rhoda Drake, makes luxury chocolates. In the mid 90s, car ferries called in on the route from Oban to Coll and Tiree, and except in the depths of winter another served Kilchoan. Hotels (at least 4) include the long-established *Western Isles*; there are also several guest houses, plus the youth hostel.

## TOLLCROSS & Fullarton — Map 15, D5

***Eastern parts of Glasgow,*** *pop. 5700* — OS 64: NS 6363

Pont's map of 1596 showed *'Foulartoun'*, 5 km east of Glasgow, its name implying early textile work. Roy's map made about 1754 showed the London road via Uddingston separating Fullarton from Carmyle to the south. A coal pit was sunk at Fullarton in 1792, with an engine soon installed. In 1836 a local gasworks was started at the handloom-weaving village of Tollcross, just west of Fullarton. Tollcross House was built in 1848 by the Dunlops of the Clyde Iron Works at Carmyle. From 1871 a new secondary line of the North British Railway (NBR) linking Glasgow and Edinburgh via Bathgate, served a coal pit east of Tollcross. The population of Tollcross in 1891 was 3850; it already had a post office and an inn, and the policies of Tollcross House became a public park after its purchase by Glasgow City Council in 1896. In 1897 Tollcross – still a distinct village – was given a station on a new Caledonian Railway line linking Bridgeton Cross with Carmyle; this also served Fullarton. In the early 20th century the Dalbeth convent was established in a mansion beside the Clyde; extensive sand quarrying took place to the north.

**Tubes, Biscuits and Olympic Swimming**: The Tollcross Tube Works of the Clydeside Tube Company was built just east of Fullarton in 1913; it was connected to the Caledonian Railway. The works later formed part of Stewarts & Lloyds, but was closed about 1980. Between the wars Macfarlane, Lang & Co moved their biscuit factory from Bridgeton to large new works at Tollcross. By the 1950s Fullarton had a home for heavily handicapped children, and Tollcross House became the Tollcross Museum of Childhood. The London Road tram terminus at Auchenshuggle saw their last day in September 1962. Tollcross station was closed in 1964 and its line was lifted west of the tube works; this in turn closed about 1980, and by 1986 had been replaced by the extended Fullarton housing estate. The inclusion of Tollcross in the hoped-for reinstatement of a Glasgow tram service, considered in 1995, was stymied by local government reorganisation. The Tollcross Leisure Park, holding Scotland's first Olympic standard swimming pool (whose *'floating floor'* enables the depth to be altered), was opened in 1996.

## TOMATIN — Map 9, B4

***Inverness-shire village,*** *pop. 500 (area)* — OS 35: NH 8029

Some 22 km south-east of Inverness in the upper Findhorn valley, here known as Strathdearn, lies Tomatin, where whisky is said to have been distilled in the 15th century. Its Gaelic name *Tom-acfhuinn* means *'Hillock of the Distillery'*, and Pont's map made about 1600 named it *'Tomm-Ackenn'*. A road was

*The 400m-long railway viaduct near Tomatin, built as part of the Highland Railway's direct line from Aviemore to Inverness, and opened in 1897. It was designed under the supervision of Murdoch Paterson, the company's engineer.* *(RCAHMS / JRH)*

first built through the area between 1725 and 1736 by General Wade's troops; the Roy map surveyed about 1750 showed a gap where this crossed the River Findhorn at *'Currybrough'* (Corryburgh). The river had been bridged there by 1808, when the road was relocated and rebuilt to sound standards under Telford's guidance. The structure was swept away in the great floods of 1829, so a new Bridge of Findhorn was built, completed in 1833. Dalmagarrie 4km north of Tomatin (OS 27) was once a coaching inn.

**Main-line Railway, and Legal Whisky**: When the railway from Perth to Forres was opened in 1863 this left Tomatin far away, and abstracted most of the through road traffic; by 1894 Murray thought Tomatin's *Freeburn Inn* was *"poor"*. Matters looked up in 1897, when a crossing station was provided at Tomatin on the Highland Railway's new main line, with its great curving steel viaduct 400m long, and the same year the Tomatin distillery was established. After 1918 road traffic began to build up, and a new Findhorn bridge was constructed in 1926, adopting an aggressive concrete design. By 1951 the *Freeburn* had become an 8-roomed hotel, and 300 people lived in the Tomatin area; in those days there was a golf course. The distillery was doubled to four stills in 1956 and increased to ten in 1958–61, but in 1965 the station was closed by Beeching.

**The World's Largest Malt Distillery**: The world's largest malt distillery was created in 1974–75, by again doubling capacity to 14 million litres a year. But in 1982, due to improvements in distillery technology, there were only about 30 jobs, and the population of the village did not rise. The huge distillery, seen by connoisseurs as making an underrated single malt, was temporarily closed in 1985, but its large bonds remained. The Tomatin Distillery Company, which retained its name, was sold to the Japanese consortium of Takara & Okura in 1986. By 1989 Tomatin village had been expensively bypassed by the dual carriageway of the A9, crossing a 300m viaduct and obliterating the little golf course. The distillery was returned to full production by 1990, but the plant – which itself enjoyed very pure water supplies – was sadly still a frequent polluter of the river at that time. In 1991 just 445 people lived in Tomatin, Moy and rural Strath Dearn. The post office and primary school are still open, serving a small village which by now includes modern housing. The distillery, with its Visitor Centre, now employs 40.

## TOMINTOUL

**Map 10, A3**

***Moray village**, pop. 400 (area)*

OS 36: NJ 1618

Tomintoul in Strath Avon (pronounced *Strathann*) was not shown on Pont's map made about 1600, nor on Robert Gordon's map of the central Highlands made about 1645, but this did mark Kirkmichael (NJ 143,238). Tomintoul, formerly in Banffshire, stands 6km upstream of Kirkmichael church, on a col between the River Avon and the Conglass Water. First known as the location of an iron deposit, its Gaelic name which means *The Mound on the Hillside* probably originated from excavations begun about 1730. Small quantities of the ore were mined for smelting at Nethy Bridge nearly 20km to the west, carried over the hills by packhorse. The Bridge of Brown, 5km west, was built by the military under Caulfeild, who also constructed the Lecht road, opened to Corgarff in 1754. From this date Tomintoul appears to have existed as a clachan, as shown on the Roy map surveyed shortly before that date. The road was frequently blocked by winter snows where it crossed a 637m high pass south-east of Tomintoul.

**Planned Village snubbed by the Queen**: Tomintoul was expanded by the 4th Duke of Gordon in 1776–79, when the square was laid out by the surveyor George Milne. The new village was all built in stone, and slated from the Knockfergan quarry close to Kirkmichael church. In 1799 Heron wrote of

Tomintoul as a *"village"*, as was Kirkmichael, whose Kirkton later faded to almost nothing. Tomintoul's post office opened in 1800. The village was among the very poor Highland settlements where the government erected a building for the Church of Scotland in 1827. The stone-built *Gordon Arms Hotel* was open by 1838, but Tomintoul – which stands over 340 m above sea level – remains very marginal, being known as *"the highest village in the Highlands"* – though actually lower than Dalwhinnie! Queen Victoria wrote in 1860 that it was *"the most tumble-down, poor-looking place I ever saw"*. The 1891 population of the village was 500. In 1894 Murray called Tomintoul *"bare and uninteresting"* and rated both the *Richmond Arms* and the *Gordon Arms* as *"poor"* hotels; but they became well known to generations of anglers. The 1901 population of Kirkmichael parish was just over 1000. Up to 1910 a horse-drawn coach provided public transport to Ballindalloch station, but during peacetime summers from 1910 to 1925, railway company motor buses also provided a service over the Lecht to Corgarff and Alford.

**Skiers on the Tops, Distillers in the Valleys**: Growing appreciation of its panoramic views, and the start of winter sports in the Lecht area 8 km to the south-east, contributed to two more hotels being available in Tomintoul by 1951, and by 1953 a youth hostel was open. But rural depopulation was remorseless; the last conventional bus service to Tomintoul apparently ended in 1968, and an early golf course had closed by 1969. The Tomintoul-Glenlivet distillery was built in 1965 at Ballantruan, beyond Kirkmichael 7 km to the north; by 1982 a third of Tomintoul's male workforce was employed in distilleries, there being about 25 within 30 km. In 1975 Tomintoul was placed in Moray District. In 1978 there were 4 hotels, some tourist facilities (including pony trekking), a handful of shops, a police station, secondary school, and part-time library. By 1980 the Tomintoul Museum was open in the Square; a weekly cattle market was still held in 1982.

**Struggling despite Skiers – and Away-day Schooling**: By 1991 Whyte & Mackay owned the Tomintoul distillery and *'Glenlivet'* had been dropped from its title; only 387 people lived in the entire parish. The *Richmond Arms Hotel* was closed in 1992, not having benefited from walkers on the Speyside Way long distance footpath or the Lecht pistes. Most suited to novice skiers, by 1993 the Lecht had 11 lifts, a cafe, ski school and creche; in 1996 snow-making machinery was installed. The *Clock House Restaurant* was bought and improved in 1990 by the chancer Anthony Williams, who also bought and improved the rundown *Gordon Arms Hotel*, reopening it in 1994 with 30 rooms, and 24 staff. But he was then found to have defrauded Scotland Yard; by late 1994 the hotel was run for the receiver by a hard-pressed staff of nine. In 1996–2000 the new Moray Council transferred the 27 pupils from Tomintoul's 4-year secondary school to Speyside Academy in Aberlour, against fierce local opposition: small wonder, a winding 34 km of road separates them! Hotels still include the *Gordon*; the youth hostel and museum are seasonal. The mothballed Tomintoul distillery is now under the Speyside Distillery Company; its early reopening seems possible.

## TOMNAVOULIN — Map 10, A2

***Moray hamlet**, pop. 140* — OS 36: NJ 2126

The Gaelic name for this place on the River Livet some 2 km south of a standing stone means *'Millhill'*. During its proscription the Roman Catholic church operated a tiny seminary, the College of Scalan, at the remote Braes of Glenlivet, some 8 km south-east; the building still exists. There were still no roads in the 1750s, but the area was later opened up. The alternative spelling Tamnavoulin was applied to the post office, which was issued with a cancelling stamp in 1838. A new mill was built about 1870; by 1927 there was a primary school. The Tamnavoulin-Glenlivet distillery was built in 1965–66 by a subsidiary of Invergordon Distillers. In 1973 the Braes of Glenlivet Distillery was built for Chivas of Paisley on the Crombie Water, 4 km above the hamlet of Auchnarrow which lies 2.5 km south of Tomnavoulin. Several of the few workers needed by this modern plant travelled from Tomintoul, and between 1951 and 1981 the population of Tomnavoulin shrank from over 200 to a mere 140, the school being closed, though the post office remained open in 1992. The Tamnavoulin distillery – which made a highly recommended single malt – was in full production in 1990. *'Glenlivet'* had been dropped from its title by 1991, and by then the mill had been converted into its visitor centre; in 1992 some Tamnavoulin whisky was sold at 25 years old, over twice the normal age.

**The Wrong Sort of Bottles**: In 1992 the new Caledonia Glenlivet Water Company obtained rights to a supply of up to 6 million litres of high quality water per year from the Crown Estates' Clash and Slochd springs, 450 m up in the Ladder Hills. But their bottling factory built in 1993 was a failure: the undercapitalised firm had bought second-hand bottling equipment and the wrong sized bottles; it briefly employed nine people, but failed to sell its *'Braes of Glenlivet'* water. In 1994 the disused buildings reverted to Grampian Regional Council (GRC), one of several public bodies to lose money on the enterprise; late in 1994 GRC leased the plant to new operators. The Braes of Glenlivet (later Braeval) distillery produced some 225,000 litres of whisky a week in 1994 under Chivas, a subsidiary of Seagram, but was so automated that it could be operated by one person! In 1995 White & Mackay mothballed the Tamnavoulin distillery, with the loss of some 8 jobs; now under the Speyside Distillery Company, its early reopening seems possible.

## TONGLAND — Map 2, A5

***Galloway hamlet**, pop. 300 (area)* — OS 83 or 84: NX 6953

Ancient earthworks and a cluster of medieval mottes adjoin the site of Tongland, which lies at the head of tidewater on the River Dee 2 km above Kirkcudbright. According to Chambers, an abbey or priory *"was founded for Premonstratensian Monks, by Fergus Lord of Galloway in the reign of David I"*. It was not a great success, and was *"ruinous"* by 1509, though still occupied by an eccentric abbot! Cumstoun Castle was built west of the estuary in the 16th century. An ancient wooden bridge existed across the Dee about 2 km upstream, until it was crossed by Queen Mary in her flight from Loch Leven to England in 1568, and immediately pulled down by her attendants to hinder pursuit.

**Mills, Bridges, Paper and Church**: The Pont map made about 1610 showed Tongland Kirk apparently emparked, presumably indicating the former abbey precinct, and on the

*Tongland hydro-electric power station, which was completed in 1935. This is the largest power station in the Galloway hydro-electric scheme.* *(RCAHMS / JRH)*

opposite bank of the Dee a mill. A more permanent Tongland Bridge was built in 1737. The Roy map surveyed about 1754 showed a hamlet at Tongland Kirk; the bridge connected the south bank road between Kirkcudbright and Dumfries with a road northwards to New Galloway. A paper mill with glazing equipment was established at Tongland in 1766; it was repaired after fire damage in 1772 and was still listed in 1825, but had vanished by 1851. A new Tongland bridge with a single arch having the wide span of 34m was erected to a bold design by Alexander Nasmyth and Thomas Telford in 1804–06, using stone from Annan and Arran. Chambers noted this *"magnificent new bridge over the Dee is built of vast blocks of free-stone brought from the Isle of Arran"*. A new church was built on the abbey site in 1813.

**Railway, Dam and Power Station**: When the branch railway to Kirkcudbright was built in the mid 19th century, although it passed within 1km of the village the station was at Tarff, 3km north of the bridge but within Tongland parish – which (including Ringford) held 700 people in 1901. About 1916 Galloway Engineering built a small aero-engine factory, later making *'Galloway'* cars (but for many years used for storage). From about 1930 the Tongland dam was constructed across the Dee immediately above the village to regulate the supply of water for hydro-electricity generation; when completed in 1932 it was the largest single-arch dam yet built in Britain. The Tongland power station was completed in 1935, its associated earthworks not to be confused with ancient features. In the 1940s there was a creamery at Tarff, associated with the Colfin creamery. The former car factory was extended around 1990. With a steadily falling parish population – only 313 in 1991 – Tongland became a mere hamlet; by 1996 the post office had closed, and by 1997 the church had been disused for many years. However the scar of a quarry just to the north – worked from around 1960 – is still growing under Barr of Ayr.

## TONGUE & Kirkiboll — Map 12, C1

***Small N. Sutherland village,*** *pop. 550 (area)* — OS 10: NC 5956

The name Kirkiboll means *'Church Farm'* in Norse, guaranteeing that it was already an ancient settlement by about 1600, when north Sutherland was first sketchily mapped by Pont. Kirkiboll Kirk then stood high above the shallow sea loch called the Kyle of Tongue; the Norse word *Tongue* refers to the shape of the peninsula which juts into the Kyle, and later came to refer to the church. The 16th century tower of Varrich Castle (now a roofless ruin) stood on a rocky knoll above the shore, and there was already a mill at the mouth of the burn which flows from Loch Craisg, which Pont labelled *'Loch Tung'*. The Roy map showed that by about 1750 a track linked the Kirk of Tongue, its few small attendant clachans and the policy-girt Tongue House with Strathy some 16km to the east – but no farther. Another track led southwards, keeping to the west of Loch Loyal; though somewhat vague, the map confirmed that it petered out, giving no road connection to the south either.

**Hungry Tongue linked to Scotland**: Self-contained Tongue had a post office by 1755 and was a post town by 1797, with mails ferried to and from Thurso, more than 50km away, on alternate weekdays – either by boat or on foot. In those days the offshore Eilean nan Ron was inhabited. Heron described Tongue as a *"village"* in 1799, but it was 1828 before a Telford-engineered road was completed from Lairg over 40km of barren moorland to pick up the route of the Loch Loyal track into Tongue. It was later continued westwards to Durness – though interrupted for a century by a passenger ferry across the Kyle of Tongue. By 1836 a road connected with Thurso, with a daily coach from the *"very good" Tongue Inn*, and three coaches a week ran from Tongue to Lairg. Tongue was badly hit by the famine of 1836, when the local churchmen joined the landowners in pious inaction.

**Motor Age: Residents leave, Tourists come**: Horsedrawn coaches continued to run into the early Edwardian years, but by about 1909 a primitive bus on a *'motor road route'* linked Lairg, Tongue and Thurso. The parish population was over 1750 in 1901, but had halved to 830 by 1951. In the early 20th century a road was built around the head of the Kyle. By 1954 the *Bungalow Hotel* (later called the *Ben Loyal*) was open, and a youth hostel existed by 1956. The pedestrian ferry with its piers was replaced in 1971 by a causeway and road bridge. By 1978 Tongue had grown into a small though significant village with a caravan and camping site, pony trekking centre, the two hotels, a score of new homes, a population of over 200 and, in Peter Burr's emporium, the largest retail business in north Sutherland. The parish population was 552 in 1991. The 2 hotels and the youth hostel serve the area.

## TORE, Killearnan, Kilcoy & Redcastle — Map 9, B3

***Easter Ross communities,*** *pop. 450 (area)* — OS 26: NH 6052

Clusters of chambered cairns show the antiquity of settlement in this area of the whalebacked Black Isle, some 7km north-west of North Kessock and overlooking the Beauly Firth. There was a *'hospital'* by 1300. Redcastle on the coast to the south was originally a motte (anciently known as Edradour), thrown up for William the Lion about 1179; it was rebuilt in stone in the 16th century and was expanded as a mansion in 1790. Meantime in 1614 the Mackenzies of Fairburn built the large Kilcoy Castle 2 km inland, and by the time the Roy map was made about 1750, *'Torr Castle'* was a mansionhouse in an apparently still trackless moorland. West of Redcastle, which had a track to the Kessock ferry, was the Kirk of Redcastle at modern Milton; however the parish name is Killearnan. About

1804 the freestone quarry near Redcastle was reopened to supply facing stone for the locks on the Caledonian Canal, shipped via a 400 metre pier built out across the tidal flats; the important quarry was again busy in 1843–44 when the canal locks were being rebuilt.

**From Road to Rail and Back**: The area was improved with plantations and, despite the loss of its castle, Tore became an important road junction; Kilcoy Castle was rebuilt from a ruin in 1880. Kilcoy acquired a mill and post office, and by 1901 Killearnan parish had over 900 people; the school was located 2 km to the east, near Tore smithy. Redcastle station on the Black Isle branch of the Highland Railway which opened in 1894 was actually at Kilcoy; like the equally simple Allangrange station near the growing hamlet of Tore it was open for passengers only until 1951, and for goods until 1960. By 1951 Tore had a 4-roomed inn, clothier, garage and post office. Though only 500 people remained in 1971, most facilities were still available in the 1980s. When the Cromarty Firth and Kessock bridges and their lengthy approaches opened in 1979 and 1982 respectively, Tore became a successively more important road junction. Redcastle (unroofed after 1945) was derelict by 1980, but Sutherland's large silos and the Kilcoy grain mill were still important in the 1980s. The parish population was down to 438 by 1991. Redcastle station building was restored as a post office in 1997, and by 2000 the Black Isle Brewery was open at nearby Allangrange. Tore still has a pub, post office and primary school.

## TORPHICHEN

**Map 16, C3**

***W. Lothian small village,*** *pop. 600* — OS 65: NS 9672

An ancient fort on curiously named Torphichen Hill, 6 km south-west of Linlithgow, overlooked the site of a fifth century wooden church. This already ancient place was chosen by David I in the second quarter of the 12th century for the sole Scottish Preceptory or *'Hospital'* of the Knights of St John of Jerusalem, a religious and military order; they built a stone chapel, completed by 1172, which doubled as parish church *(see Cowan et al)*. The Hospital was developed further in the 13th century, and Torphichen was the site of Wallace's Parliament in 1298. Although added to in the 15th century, the Preceptory drew little attention from early travel writers. After the Reformation the community buildings became a property of Sir James Sandilands as Lord Torphichen, and soon little but the much-altered church remained.

**Hilderstone Silver Mine, Henry Bell and Distillery**: In 1606 Sandy Maund, a coal miner out for a Sunday stroll, discovered the Hilderstone silver deposit 1 km south of Torphichen; this was assayed at Leadhills. Skilled silver miners were imported from Saxony, smelting and stamping mills were in operation from 1609, and for a short time there were 60 employees; eventually seven mines were open under Sir Thomas Hamilton, who quickly became rich. But from 200 tonnes in the first year the output fell away, and about 1619 mining ceased, though the mines were marked on Blaeu's Pont-derived atlas dated 1642 *(see Hendrie's description)*. About 1725 a bridge was built across the River Avon on the Bathgate–Falkirk road some 1500 metres north-west of the church, whose nave was demolished in 1756 and replaced by a plain galleried parish church. Henry Bell, born at Torphichen Mill in 1767 and later apprenticed to a millwright, became the father of the seagoing steamship *(see Bo'ness and Helensburgh)*. In 1799 Heron noted *"the village of Torphichen has in it a considerable distillery"*; this would have been the 1795 plant of Simpson & Kay, which then dropped from view. In 1826 Chambers found *"a little straggling village remote from all public roads"*. It was soon connected to the main road system, though it remained off the railways. However by 1895 a post office and an inn were open at Torphichen.

**Nickel and Tourists**: Nickel was mined in the Bathgate Hills in 1870–73 when a 60 m shaft was sunk 2 km east of Torphichen, but again the ore body was small and the *'Silvermine'* of the OS maps was abandoned in 1898. In 1951 about 600 people lived in the area, also served by a primary school; by the 1960s there was a childrens' home (but this was closed in 1987). The crossing and transepts of the ancient and imposing medieval Preceptory chapel, long in state care, were renovated as a minor tourist attraction in 1975–77, a connection with the re-created lay order of the Knights of St John being retained. By 1988 a small housing estate had been added to this unusually attractive village, and in 1991 it had 559 residents; a little more development by 1998 has helped to maintain its character, its pub and its post office.

## TORPHINS

**Map 10, B3**

***Aberdeenshire village,*** *pop. 1000* — OS 37: NJ 6201

Situated in a bowl in the Deeside hills some 10 km north-west of Banchory, Torphins is adjoined by ancient stone circles and standing or symbol stones, but may take its present name from Thorfinn, an 11th century ally of Macbeth. This area 4 km from the centre of the anciently important parish of Kincardine O'Neil was well settled when Pont sketched it about 1600, but the name Torphins did not appear, nor was it named on Gordon's map of about 1640. The Roy map made about 1750 showed *'Turfins'* as one of many hamlets in a roadless area, and at one time or another there were three mills close by, including a waulkmill. Later a main road was built between Banchory and Lumphanan. When in 1859 the Deeside Railway was extended on much the same route, to turn south at Lumphanan to Aboyne and requiring quite steep climbs over the hills, a crossing station was built at Torphins.

**The Railway concentrates Development**: This evidently proved the catalyst for more concentrated development, for a village grew around the station, and in 1891 Torphins golf club was founded; it laid out a 9-hole moorland course. In 1951 with a resident population of under 850, Torphins had better services than a typical village, including two hotels, secondary school classes, an architect, clothier, a 10-bed maternity hospital and a fortnightly market; it served some 3500 people within a radius of about 6 km. The railway was closed by Beeching in 1966, and by 1971 the population had fallen by 20%, with similar losses of services including secondary schooling and the dispensing chemist. Then oil developments in the Aberdeen area stimulated some recovery. In 1981 Torphins still boasted two hotels, but was less significant as a rural service centre and relied more on Banchory. The village population in 1991 was 862, and several small housing estates had been added by 1995. A *Daihatsu* garage with its array of 4-tracks is prominent, and there is a road haulier. The services include the primary school, the modest *Learney Arms Hotel*, Kincardine O'Neil Hospital, a health centre, chemist, bank, a few shops, and a veterinary group.

## TORRANCE, Bardowie & Balmore — Map 15, D4

***Strathkelvin village & hamlets**, pop. 2500* — OS 64: NS 6274

In the 16th century the tower of Bardowie Castle was built beside the little Bardowie Loch in the hummocky Lennox parish of Baldernock, north of the River Kelvin, west of Kirkintilloch and 8km north of Glasgow. The castle was given much emphasis on Robert Gordon's map around 1640; at that time *'Balmoir'* 2 km east of the castle was one of many tiny places and the *'Calder'* (Cadder) bridge had been built across the Kelvin, but Torrance was not named. The bridge also featured on Roy's map of about 1754, when it formed a link in a road from west of Balmore, then a small village, to Kirkintilloch; but Torrance was still too small for Roy's surveyors to emphasise. Early travel writers ignored both places; in the mid 19th century both were still tiny, but a new Kelvin bridge close to Torrance gave it an advantage over Balmore, and it began to grow. The Kelvin Valley Railway, promoted in 1873 and opened in 1879, provided stations at both places, but ran perpendicular to desire lines, was a financial failure on its own, and in 1885 became part of the North British Railway.

**Golf, Quarrying and Commuters**: In 1891 the population was 466. By 1895 Torrance was in south Stirlingshire, a sprawling hamlet with an inn and post office; Balmore had nothing of note until the Balmore golf club, founded in 1906, laid out an 18-hole course among the drumlins west of the hamlet. By 1951, the year when the passenger trains were withdrawn, Torrance had a thousand people and Balmore 425, but few facilities apart from a large 218-line telephone exchange; Balmore's population then drifted downwards. A quarry was open at Blairskaith 2 km north of Balmore by 1963 and grew to a large size, but was disused by 1988. The railway had vanished by 1971 but Torrance had grown slightly; it then doubled in population in a decade, by 1981 it had the facilities of a typical small village, and by 1988 new housing estates had sprung up to east, north and west. By 1991 the population of Torrance was 2387, of a young well-educated dormitory character. Torrance retains its pub and post office; Balmore – where East of Scotland Water has a major water-treatment works supplying 400,000 people – is a hamlet with its golf course, plus footpath access to two more just across the river at Cadder.

## TORRIDON (Fasagh) & Inveralligin — Map 8, C2

***Small Wester Ross village**, pop. 400 (area)* — OS 24: NG 8956

Fasagh lies at the head of Loch Torridon, beneath the vast bulk of 1055m-high Liathach, the Grey Mountain of Wester Ross. It had an *'ironworks'* in the early 17th century, believed to have been a forge working up pig-iron made at Letterewe or Poolewe into wrought iron. Although the area was trackless when Roy surveyed the area about 1750, in the 1890s Fasagh was still the main settlement; its inn lay at the end of a road from Kinlochewe. By 1951 Fasagh had become generally known as Torridon, with a pier, post office, school, doctor, occasional bank – and a 2-line telephone exchange! By then the *Loch Torridon Hotel* was open in a former Victorian shooting lodge near the south shore at nearby Annat, from where there are stupendous views of Liathach and the other mountains of Torridon Forest. West from Fasagh the little road rises steeply above the shore, passing waterfalls and winding over the hills from Inver Alligin with its youth hostel to end at the pier at Diabaig, where there was a school and post office; 5km beyond that by 1965 was another youth hostel at Craig, accessible only on foot. A new road had recently been opened to beautiful Shieldaig.

**Tourism concentrates**: Gaelic was still spoken by *"a few old folk"* in 1979, when farming, fishing, forestry, toymaking, tourism, hillwalking and climbing kept the community alive. By then a mountain rescue team was based at the main youth hostel, which had been moved from Inver Alligin to Torridon, whose one-teacher school also served Kinlochewe; later Diabaig was added to its catchment. By 1981 the total population of these various tiny places was about 400. The National Trust for Scotland now owns Torridon Forest, including Liathach. There is a salmon farm at Diabaig, but no facilities. Torridon had gained a campsite, museum and countryside centre by 1997, but only the Inveralligin post office is still open. The much-praised *Loch Torridon Hotel* has 20 rooms, plus cheaper rooms in its *Ben Damph Inn* alongside; both youth hostels are seasonal.

## TORRIN, Elgol & Strathaird — Map 8, B3

***Hamlets, Isle of Skye**, pop. 225 (area)* — OS 32: NG 5720

Caves, a stone circle and ancient duns adorn the south facing coast of the Skye estate of Strathaird, east of the Cuillin Hills. Monro noted in 1549 that its owner was a McKinnon; one of his two castles was Dunringill on the shores of Loch Slapin, now ruinous. On its eastern shore is the Suisnish area, where in 1703 Martin noted *"large quarries of freestone"*; this may have included the coloured *'Skye Marble'*. Between Suisnish and the castle grew the township of Torrin. Some 10km to the south-west is the clachan of Elgol, which overlooks the Cuillin Hills and straggles steeply down to the dramatic west coast of Loch Skavaig, an area well described by Bolton. A narrow, winding road was open between Elgol, Torrin and Portree by the time that Strathaird was cleared of its people in 1851–52 by Macalister of Torrisdale.

**Tourists and Quarrying versus Conservation**: However, others moved in when the law gave crofters security, and by the 1950s both Elgol and Torrin had post offices and primary schools. Later Elgol grew somewhat, with a new telephone exchange named after Loch Skavaig, famed for its savage beauty, and by 1997 a jetty had been built. Although white marble for chippings was quarried east of Loch Slapin by 1980, and a slipway had been constructed by 1997, in the meantime Torrin school and later its post office were closed. In 1991 the John Muir Trust bought the 2000ha Torrin estate, including Elgol and the rocky 928m peak of Bla Bheinn (Blaven), to ensure its conservation. Elgol has a primary school, post office and jetty. *Strathaird House* at sheltered Kirkibost, midway between Elgol and Torrin, has 7 guest rooms.

## TORRYBURN & Valleyfield — Map 16, C2

***W. Fife coastal villages**, pop. 3000* — OS 65: NT 0286

In early medieval times the north coast of the inner Firth of Forth was split between Fothrif (east of the Bluther Burn and later part of Fife) and *'Perthshire on Forth'* to the west. By 1296 a great standing stone 2 km east of the burn's mouth, which may have marked the boundary, was adjoined by Torryburn church. The Newmill, also known as Torry Mills, existed by 1540 and was replaced in 1596. By 1610 the *'Brig of*

*Urquhart'* crossed a burn 2 km east of Torryburn, where a new church was erected in 1616 and a parish school was founded in 1620. By then salt pans were in operation, implying locally mined coal. Mining was very probably soon being carried out on a significant scale, for the symbol for *'Torry Burn'* on James Gordon's map of Fife (1645) was as large as that for Culross; between them were *'Torry pans'* and Newmill.

**Torryburn's Heyday**: Although apparently never chartered, Torryburn was reported by Tucker in 1655 as being *"a town, the chief place for shipping out small coals"*, owning three vessels of around 100 tons. Valleyfield west of the burn had a coal-mine for local use by 1655, and gained a burgh of barony charter in 1663, but unlike Torryburn – where another bridge was built around 1675 – it developed very little as a centre. Roy's map of about 1750 showed a bridge at Torry Mills on a coast road from Culross to Inverkeithing. Following the turnpiking of the road from Dunfermline under an Act of 1753, Torryburn people operated a ferry to Bo'ness by 1769. By the 1790s Torryburn – which owned 13 vessels, averaging over 75 tons and each crewed by at least 5 men – exported coal and Dunfermline linens. Torryburn also had an annual fair, and in 1800 another new church was built, followed in 1803 by the opening of a post office.

**Preston Island's Whisky Mines**: By then tiny Preston Island, 1 km offshore from Valleyfield, had been developed by Sir Robert Preston with workers' houses for salt pans, which were surrounded by three coal pits as deep as 50 metres. In 1811 a fire down below caused their closure, later followed by the salt-works, which were replaced by illicit stills. About then the extensive grounds around Valleyfield House, lately built 1 km inland, were being landscaped by Humphrey Repton. The Newmill was rebuilt in 1820; by 1825 Torryburn was served by a penny post from Dunfermline. In 1827 Torryburn and Newmill were still separate villages about 1 km apart; Torry pier just east of the mill was some 400 m long, and a similar distance inland was Torry House, its policies embracing almost all the land around the tight-packed village.

**Decline and Dereliction**: William Cobbett passed through in 1832, noting *"a long village, the houses in general having no upstairs; all the buildings extremely ugly and mean, many of the houses being empty, and many of them tumbling down"*. Preston Island's disused buildings still stood in 1888, when Torryburn was still shrunken. Newmills was then a *"village"* where the Newmill had been *"recently converted into a bleachworks"* by one Marshall, and Low Valleyfield was *"a succession of detached cottages"* formerly known for fruit-growing. The ferry had vanished, and all local coal mining seems to have remained in abeyance until after Valleyfield was transferred to Fife in 1889. At that time Valleyfield House stood in parkland. The 1891 population of Torryburn was 600 and an inn was open; Newmill – which had the main post and telegraph office – was named Torry on the 1890s OS map. The grounds of Torry House were for a time used as a golf course, apparently very early in the 20th century. A parish library was aided by Carnegie money around 1911.

**Railway, Coal, Gas and Disaster**: In 1906 a coastal branch of the North British Railway was opened from Kincardine to Dunfermline, with a station at Torryburn, enabling a new Valleyfield colliery to be sunk from 1906 by the Fife Coal Company. Gas and electricity were supplied from 1911 when the gas-troubled pit opened, producing coal which fired RN

*Salt pans on Preston Island, offshore site of much industrial activity over the years. The island was an artificial one, created in the early 19th century to form a platform for coal mining. The salt pans are the best surviving Scottish examples.* *(JRH)*

ships from Rosyth; but the railway was closed to passengers as early as 1930. A pit explosion in 1939 sadly killed 35 men, but war had just begun and the colliery was rapidly reopened. In 1941 some 450 men were employed and output was maintained at a high level; coal waste was tipped into the Forth. By 1945 High Valleyfield had been created as a council housing scheme to house the increased number of miners. Valleyfield House was demolished, but part of its Repton landscape remained in 1980.

**Mistakes and Successes after Nationalisation**: High Valleyfield was greatly extended in the mid 1950s for two reasons. Firstly the Torry drift mine was sunk to the north; it lasted only to 1965, the waste still being tipped in the estuary. Secondly, the sinking of the 722 m Valleyfield No.3 shaft was begun in 1954. Intended to exploit the Limestone Coal Group, it was completed but never used, because of a very costly change of mind: from 1964 Valleyfield's output was brought to the surface at Kinneil colliery near Bo'ness, which was linked under the Forth by a new tunnel 5.5 km long. A bypass road with a high bridge over the Bluther Burn was constructed to the north of the villages about 1960, and much of old Torryburn was rebuilt with stone-faced cottages – both schemes by Fife County Council, which also excavated and consolidated the industrial remains on Preston Island. From 1960 Valleyfield was cut off from the sea by extensive lagoons which were to be filled with fly ash from the Kincardine and Longannet generating stations. By 1971 4000 people lived in the Torryburn and Valleyfield area.

**After Mining**: Torry House was roofless by 1967, but had been saved and reconstructed by 1980. Valleyfield colliery was closed in 1978 with the loss of 600 jobs. The secondary school had been closed by 1981, for the population had fallen sharply, and only the facilities of a small village remained. By 1988 landscaping had obliterated the remains of the Valleyfield pithead. The 1991 population was 3162. In 1993 Scottish Power proposed to deposit a further 10 million tonnes of fly ash from Longannet in the area around Preston Island up to the year 2020; the resulting mounds would rise to 19 m above sea level. The Fife Regional Council also proposed a large reed-bed sewage treatment plant in the area. There is a pleasant walk up the valley.

## TOWNHILL

**Map 6, B4**

***Village / N. part of Dunfermline,*** *pop. 2000* OS 65 & 58: NT 1089

About 2 km north-east of Dunfermline is the Town Loch, but the area was of little interest to mapmaker Roy in the 1750s. To the east of the loch is Townhill, where by 1781 a coal mine had been sunk. By then there were limeworks both in the Valley of Balmule 1.5 km farther north, and up in the hills beyond at Roscobie. By the 1820s Townhill was a distinct village, which grew considerably during the ensuing century. The 1891 population was 1800; by then a church and a post and telegraph office had been added. Mineral railways from both west and east of Dunfermline converged at Lilliehill Junction, just north of Townhill. From there a line ran to Kelty via numerous coal pits around Loch Fitty, including the Muircockhall pit of Henry Ness & Co, in production by 1893. Another line diverged north-westwards past Bowershall with its mill to Gask Junction near Dunduff (from which a minor branch ran east to Gask limeworks), to Dunduff colliery, the Saline Valley Collieries and Steelend. By 1901 Balmule Colliery and limeworks lay on another spur from this line, and soon there was a primary school near Gask Junction. A Balfour Beatty electricity generating station was opened between the junction and the loch in 1906, using loch water for cooling; it supplied the Dunfermline Tramways (a Balfour Beatty subsidiary) which opened as a single line from Townhill to the High Street in 1909.

**Bricks, Water-Skiing and Vintage Buses**: The tramways closed in 1937, but there was by then a brickworks at the Town Loch, and soon a rail-linked naval stores depot at Lathalmond north of Balmule. Muircockhall ceased to raise coal in 1943 but was retained as a training pit for some years; by 1951 some 1600 people lived in the Townhill area. Though all the collieries, the Saline railway and the line to Kelty had closed by 1967, the population had grown to 1800 by 1971. When the power station was closed, the railway was abandoned, and lifted in the 1980s. Land restoration of the former brickworks site by the SDA created a country park, enabling the opening at the Town Loch in 1991 of the Scottish National Water Ski Centre, developed by the District Council and Scottish Sports Council *(see also Lochgelly)*. The 1991 census included Townhill in Dunfermline. The hopefully named M90 Commerce Park had taken over the Balmule or Lathallan naval depot when in 1995 the trustees of the Scottish Vintage Bus Museum bought some 20 ha of land and buildings there to develop as a tourist attraction, including some 160 vehicles by the year 2000; until recently remains of the Roscobie limeworks could still be seen, but the kilns have now been demolished. By 2001 Crannog Kitchens from Rumbling Bridge had moved to the M90 Commerce Park.

## TRANENT

**Map 15, E2**

***E. Lothian town,*** *pop. 8300* OS 66: NT 4072

Tranent stands on an 85 m hill about 3 km inland from Prestonpans in East Lothian. Chambers wrote that it was *"mentioned in a charter of the 12th century under the name of Travernent"*. Its church may go back to the 14th century, and in the 15th century came the tall keep of nearby Falside Castle, enlarged into a mansion in the early 16th century but ruined in the Battle of Pinkie in 1547. Tranent had become a burgh of barony in 1541; the town council used to claim it was the oldest mining community in Scotland, and a parish school was started in 1594. The mines could explain the emphasis given to Tranent on Pont's map of 1600; Tranent Tower was then quite new. By 1661 coal for shipment was certainly being mined at Tranent; an early steam pump, presumably of the Newcomen type, was employed from 1719, and by 1728 the disused coal workings even extended under the church.

**Pioneer Wagonway, Woollens and Shoes**: In 1722 what was probably the first wagonway in Scotland was laid to carry coal from Tranent pits to Cockenzie harbour; following Continental and Tyneside examples it consisted of wooden rails on stone blocks. From 1746 to 1750 stone was also quarried locally for the construction of the Saltoun bleachfield *(see Pencaitland)*. Roy's map of the 1750s showed Tranent as a large straggling place, with no fewer than seven radial roads, tracks or possibly wagonways, including the Great North Road; to the west was a *coalhill*. Woollen manufacture was recorded in 1776, and a post office opened in Tranent in 1795, with a daily post from Edinburgh. Heron ignored mining when he wrote in 1799 *"the village of Tranent is pleasantly situated in a rich country, and contains about 1400 inhabitants, among whom are many industrious weavers and shoemakers"*. Cobbett in 1832 noted otherwise, describing Tranent as *"a sort of colliery town; here are collieries and rail-roads; and the county, as well as the town of Haddington, are supplied with coals from this source"*.

**Coal dominates the Scene**: A gasworks was set up in 1872; in 1891 the population was 2400 and by then there was an inn and an industrial school. In 1894 Murray patronisingly described Tranent as *"a dingy place dependent on collieries"*. These lay on all sides of the town and were connected by mineral railways to Prestonpans station on the North British main line. In the early 20th century banks, chemists, a cinema, lawyers and a dentist joined those who found a living in Tranent. By 1951 the population was nearing 6500, with the facilities of a large village, plus a telephone exchange with 337 lines. By 1958 Ross High School was open. Glasshouses were established nearby, but the mines had all vanished by 1963. In the late 1970s major opencast workings were started north-east of the town at Blindwells, a farm name applied to the rail loading point constructed beside the east coast main line about 1980. Tranent had continued to grow in population, and by then had acquired a second small hotel. The removal of the A1 through traffic with the opening of the bypass in 1986 must have helped Tranent considerably; Falside Castle was fully restored in the 1980s. By 1991, 8313 people lived locally, and southwards housing development was continuing. In the 1990s coal from the vast Blindwells site was moved by rail to power stations at Cockenzie and in the north and midlands of England; some went to Leith for export to Denmark and Finland. It remains active, with over 50 employees. Inveresk Research (product testing) moved to Tranent some years ago, and DMI are precision engineers in the town. Ross High School now has almost 800 pupils.

## TRAPRAIN

**Map 3, B2**

***Hill, E. Lothian*** OS 67: NT 5874

In the Iron Age a hill fort and settlement of some 15 ha stood on the 220 m high whale-backed summit of a unique hard-rock structure – known as a *laccolith* – 7 km east of later Haddington. This superb defensive site, with space for up to 500 huts, was held by the *Votadini* through the Roman period until at least 518, So far from relating to trapping rain, as hill dwellers undoubtedly had to, the name Traprain is a corruption of the British (Welsh) description *Tref yr Bryn* meaning Hill Village. A legend more apposite than most to the story of urban development relates that about 500 – when it was apparently the capital of Lothian – its pagan King Loth ordered his daughter Thenaw, raped by Prince Ewan whom she spurned, to be rolled down the steep side of the hill in a chariot and cast adrift in a coracle – to fetch up at Culross, whose christian community educated her son Mungo or Kentigern, who became the founder of Glasgow. Traprain is in an area of low rainfall, nearly 1 km from running water and – unlike igneous crags such as Stirling and Edinburgh castle rocks – it lacked a tail of permeable rock in which wells could be sunk. So although the Picts erected a standing stone at its foot, the conquering Anglians spurned it, adding to the name Traprain the word *Law* which to them simply meant Hill. Their preferred settlement was at East Linton, and no more than a later hamlet grew near Traprain. In the mid-20th century part of this unique historic site was quarried away by East Lothian County Council for road metal; but in the mid 1970s this public vandalism was at last stopped, and extraction transferred to another less sensitive site 2 km west of East Linton.

## TRAQUAIR & The Glen — Map 3, A4

***Small communities, Tweeddale,*** *pop. 380* — OS 73: NT 3334

The name Traquair is clearly of very early date, deriving from the Cumbric *Tref-Quair*, meaning the village on the Quair Water; this stream joins the River Tweed some 10km east of Peebles. Traquair, near the stream's confluence, was already in existence as a royal residence, probably as a tower house, when King Alexander I stayed there in 1107: it therefore claims to be the oldest inhabited house in Scotland. From 1184 to 1259 Traquair was a sheriff caput; then Peebles took over this role. The castle was gifted by James III in 1479 to his musician William Rogers, who sold it in 1488 to the king's uncle, another James Stuart or Stewart, the Earl of Buchan. It appeared as *'Troquair'* on Pont's map made around 1600; this showed the parish kirk on its modern site 2 km up the well-wooded Quair valley. A parish school was opened in 1617. The castle was substantially extended in the mid 17th century by Sir John Stewart, the first Earl of Traquair, becoming known as Traquair House; the mid 18th century Roy map showed it in formal policies. Family impoverishment caused by the Earl's Jacobite sympathies left the great house fortunately little altered. By then hamlets clustered around the kirk which stood beside the road south, and on the droving *"Road from Peebles to Selkirk"*, which led eastwards over Minch Moor; it is now a footpath, part of the Southern Upland Way.

**Traquair Ale and Glen House**: Traquair was not made a burgh of barony, though a little ale was brewed on the estate. Dorothy Wordsworth wrote in 1803 of passing the *"gloomy residence of Lord Traquair, a Roman Catholic nobleman, of a decayed family"*. The imposing mansion of Glen House, 4km south-west, together with its estate houses and fine gardens, was built in the 19th century for Charles Tennant of the St Rollox chemical works (*see Port Dundas*), and is still owned by the Tennant family. The extensive parish, including Cardrona (*q.v.*), held 618 people in 1901 but only 380 in 1991. In the mid 20th century the ancient Traquair House with its tiny brewery and pleasant gardens (all remaining in a branch of the Stuart family) was opened as a considerable tourist attraction. The nearest village facilities are at Innerleithen.

## TROON & Loans — Map 1, C2

***Ayrshire town,*** *pop. 15,250* — OS 70: NS 3231

Suburb: *Barassie*

Pont's map of about 1600 showed *'The Truyn'* as the name of the prominent peninsula on the coast of Kyle, 6km north of Prestwick. The name derives from the Gaelic *An t-Sron* meaning *'The Nose'*. The 17th century L-plan Crosbie Castle (or House) is 2 km inland. Roy's survey of the 1750s showed only a *'temple'* on the point; to north and south were extensive sands. Heron noted in 1799 *"a fine natural harbour, called Troon Bay"*, to which a canal had been proposed from Glasgow via Kilmarnock *(see Johnstone)*. In Napoleonic times a smugglers' inn is said to have existed there. In 1808 the 4th Duke of Portland began to build a harbour on the north side of the headland, equipped with wet and graving docks. It was connected in 1812 with his coal pits near Kilmarnock by the Kilmarnock & Troon Railway (K&T), a horse-drawn wagonway or flanged plateway laid on stone blocks, engineered by William Jessop; coal exports to Ireland began at once.

**Passengers as Freight**: Lacking legal powers to carry passengers, the line's managers had the imagination to weigh people and carry them as freight! In 1817 they tried a primitive Stephenson engine, the first steam locomotive to run in Scotland; but this damaged the track, so the line was still entirely horse-operated in the late 1830s, when it carried coal seawards from the Duke of Portland's colliery and brought in timber, grain, slates and lime. Troon was soon Ayrshire's main coal port, although there was no post office locally until after 1838. In 1839–40 the Glasgow, Paisley, Kilmarnock & Ayr Railway opened by stages, with Troon station being near Willockston, inland of the emerging town. Resort growth began with Glasgow day trippers. The fine Portland Villa was built about that time in classical style. In 1846 the K&T was converted to the national standard and connected where the two railways crossed at Barassie 2 km to the north. A small locomotive depot was very soon built at the harbour by the two companies' successor the Glasgow & South Western Railway (GSWR), and at some date a gasworks was established.

**Ailsa Shipbuilding supersedes Coal Exports**: A lifeboat station was opened in 1871. Meantime the *'Portland'* – later Troon – shipyard was established in the 1860s, at first building wooden sailing vessels; in 1885 this became the Ailsa Shipbuilding Company, which in 1898 built the 284-ton coaster SS *Sarah Brough* for W A Savage. As late as 1885 Troon was among Britain's top ten ports for coastal coal shipment, but as the seams became worked out so Troon's share fell away to nothing. Meantime Loans on the Ayr to Irvine road 3km inland was a hamlet with a post office, inn and smithy. But thanks to the railway, Troon had also acquired another character, as a favoured commuter residence for wealthy professional and business people.

**Golf for Millionaires – and the Millions**: The Royal Troon golf club's Old Course on the links, adjoining the early Prestwick (*q.v.*) course, was founded in 1878 with 5 holes; it reached 18 holes in 1886 (and first hosted the Open championship in 1923). The club added the similar Portland course in 1894.

All became much-liked 18-hole courses and correspondingly expensive. In 1891 the population was 3300. In 1892 the present Troon station was opened on a loop line created by linking the original K&T harbour branch with the Ayr line at Lochgreen Junction, also forming a triangle of railways cutting through the town. By 1894 Troon had two hotels – the *Portland Arms* and *Commercial* – and was called *"a favourite sea-side resort"*. The imposing *Marine Hotel* was soon added, built of red sandstone. Troon became a police burgh in 1896, and in 1907 – to popularise the resort – the town council laid out its own three 18-hole courses, the Darley, Fullarton and Lochgreen. At that time (and into the 1950s) pleasure steamers from Ayr would make calls at Troon.

**Ailsa, Knitwear and Philanthropy**: In 1902 the the railway company bought Troon harbour for improvement; but the Troon engine shed was closed about 1915. In 1916 the shipyard built the Navy's first paddle minesweeper of the *Ailsa* class. The yard built and engined many small vessels such as the long-lasting paddle steamer, the *Medway Queen* in 1924. In the 1930s several coasters followed for John Hay of Glasgow; but Ailsa also had to undertake shipbreaking to survive. About 1928 the Hosiery Manufacturing Company of Irvine started a knitwear factory at Troon. Housing development spread inland to the original railway, and an open-air heated swimming pool was built in the 1930s. Portland Villa was acquired as a miners' families welfare home in 1924, and extended in 1936. A major local benefactor set up a higher educational trust which provided scholarships and funded Marr College, built east of the railway and opened as a secondary school in 1935.

**Flying over Everest – and Royal Tennis**: David McIntyre, son of the manager of the Ailsa shipyard, was born in Troon in 1905, learned to fly at Renfrew and became an RAF pilot. He joined another intrepid pilot, MP the Marquess of Clydesdale & Douglas, in three significant feats: in 1933 they overflew Everest, in 1935 jointly established Scottish Aviation to build aircraft at Prestwick, and in 1936 founded the Prestwick Flying Training School. By the 1950s Troon was a major local centre and 16-hotel resort, with a winter population of some 8500, three cinemas, and surrounded by numerous golf courses, both of its own and its neighbours. The principal hotel was the 71-room *Marine*, while the *Sun Court Hotel*, open by 1954, had one of the only two *'Real Tennis'* courts in Scotland *(see Falkland)*.

**Car Ferries triumph but Naval Ships scrapped**: In 1954 Ailsa built the small (34-vehicle) car-lift ferries MV *Bute* and *Cowal* for those respective services, and in 1957 the slightly larger MV *Glen Sannox* for Arran runs. In 1960 they launched the sturdy and attractive 3300-ton MV *St Clair* for the North of Scotland, Orkney & Shetland Shipping Company, the last non-car ferry vessel of any size for Scottish service. Many ships' hulls were scrapped at Troon in 1948–67 by the West of Scotland Shipbreaking Company: these included aircraft carriers, battleships, cruisers and destroyers; the firm also cut up BR steam locomotives in the 1960s.

**Two Decades of Decline**: By 1971 the population had fallen to little over 6000, and in 1975 Troon burgh was absorbed into Kyle & Carrick District. By 1980 the local facilities had declined to those of an average town, with only ten hotels, no cinema, and an urban caravan site. The half-timbered Edwardian Piersland Lodge, built for Alexander Walker (grandson of whisky blending baron Johnny Walker of Kilmarnock) and later called *Piersland House*, had become a hotel. By 1982 many parts of the outer harbour's quays were derelict, and the harbour rail connection had been removed by 1985; meanwhile the inner harbour had become a congested marina, the base for a cruising club.

**No Golden Age for Ailsa Yard as Troon Expands**: The Ailsa shipyard became known as Ferguson-Ailsa in 1981, but ceased to produce vessels for a time and changed hands, becoming *'Ailsa Perth'*. Ailsa then built motor yachts and cabin cruisers, but met difficulties when completing an Orkney ferry. The yard was twice taken over, bought in 1996 by the Cathelco Marine Engineering Group to carry out a 3-year MOD refurbishment contract, still then with 100 employees. Much new housing rose in the eighties in the Barassie and Loans areas. The *Sun Court Hotel* had been closed by 1990, but a demolition proposal was thwarted in 1991. By then the town's well-educated and still growing population was 15,231 (including Barassie and Loans); the local weekly newspaper was an edition of the *Ayr Advertiser*, not of the *Ardrossan & Saltcoats Herald* as formerly.

**Trees and Tourists come by Sea**: Troon was by then doing reasonably well as a resort: in 1994 West Coast Yachts claimed always to have 100 yachts for sale at Troon Marina, and in 1994 the Tidy Britain Group found Troon beach *'very good'* (unlike adjoining beaches at Ayr and Irvine). Troon boats were still fishing in 1994, and still hauling in war surplus explosives which had been dumped in their trawling grounds! From late 1994 some 30 lorryloads of timber a day from forests in the remoter Highlands and from isles such as Raasay were carried to Troon in new barges owned by Glenlight of Ardrossan, and then road-hauled to Caledonian Paper at Irvine. The British Open was again held at Royal Troon in 1997. Although by 1998 a new leisure centre had been built at Muirhead, Portland Villa – no longer needed for miners – stood in a poor state. Cathelco's Ailsa yard was acrimoniously closed in 2000 for lack of work, with the loss of its last 16 jobs. In 2000, Seacontainers abandoned their Stranraer to Belfast *'Sea-Cat'* high speed passenger service in favour of a route from Troon; this may have brought 65 jobs. Marr College is now a local authority secondary school with 1460 pupils. Many of Troon's hotels have half a century or more behind them, the *Marine* still being the largest.

## TROSSACHS (The) — Map 5, B4

***W. Stirlingshire area,*** *pop. under 100* — OS 57: NN 5007

The Roy map of west Menteith made about 1750 showed no tracks in the hilly wooded area known as the Trossachs, which lies around *'Loch Ketterin'* in west Perthshire; this old spelling supports Sir Walter Scott's claim that the real name of Loch Katrine derived from *Cateran*, meaning *'Thief'*. The River Achray which flows from the loch was bridged by the Commissioners for the Forfeited Estates, probably in 1763. In 1790 the minister of Callander produced the pamphlet which first publicised the beauty of the Trossachs and its loch, but in 1803 the nearest accommodation for tourists was at Callander. Tourism in the area quintupled on the publication of Scott's novel *The Lady of the Lake* in 1810. Roads to the Trossachs were therefore improved around 1820, and in summer coaches plied from Stirling via Callander. In 1826 Chambers found an *"excellent inn"* catering specially for tourists, described as being just east of the Trossachs. By 1844 the steamer *Rob Roy* was cruising on Loch Katrine, and in 1846 Thomas Cook's first tourists arrived there.

**Glasgow's Water Supply and Veteran Steamers**: The water level was raised by over a metre in the 1850s to supply water to Glasgow *(see also Callander)*, but the beauty of the loch was unimpaired, even after a further raising in the 1880s. The 60-room *Trossachs Hotel* with its triple ultra-tall conical turrets was erected about 1870 overlooking the little Loch Achray. In 1875 an ancient steamer, probably still the *Rob Roy*, plied from a rustic pier on Loch Katrine to another at Stronachlachar at its west end, for Inversnaid. By 1894 two daily coaches connected to Aberfoyle. A classic little pleasure vessel, the 33m 115-ton single-screw steamer *Sir Walter Scott*, was fabricated by Denny at Dumbarton in 1900 and erected at Loch Katrine. By 1954 the Lendrick Lodge Youth Hostel was open at Brig o' Turk. The Glen Finglas dam was built 1km north of Brig o' Turk about 1970, impounding the Glen Finglas reservoir, which drives a hydro-electric station. In the 1970s the *Loch Achray Hotel* had 44 rooms and the *Trossachs Hotel* 76, but by 1993 the latter had been taken over by the timeshare organisation HPB and renamed in the Gaelic as *Tigh Mor Trossachs*. By 1993 the youth hostel had closed, but there are forest drives and the *Sir Walter Scott* still sails, powered by her gleaming original engine. Brig o' Turk still has a primary school and post office. The Scottish Executive proposes to establish the Trossachs and Loch Lomond as Scotland's first National Park.

## TUMMEL BRIDGE, Foss & Strathtummel — Map 5, C2

***Perthshire localities**, pop. 100* — OS 42: NN 7659

Foss lies south-west of the original small Loch Tummel, in a comparatively level area among high hills where north–south routeways intersect the east–west Strath Tummel. It has a standing stone, and was the location of two ancient forts. Nearby is the Kirkton of Foss. Wade's road between Crieff and Dalnacardoch was constructed about 1730, the year that the bridge across the River Tummel 3km west of Foss was erected by John Stewart. This became the site for a kingshouse; the composer Mendelssohn stayed there in 1829, by which time a road from Killiecrankie led up the valley, where some areas of ancient woodland survived. The Tummel Bridge inn and another at White Bridge 5km south of Foss were still marked on late 19th century maps but had vanished by 1938. By then Foss had gained a post office, and at some time limekilns were built near the White Bridge.

**Hydro-Electricity**: By 1930 an electricity switching station had been established west of Tummel Bridge by the Grampian Electricity Supply Company. Close by was their new Tummel Bridge power station, with two 17,000kw generators and a head of 53m, fed by a 4km aqueduct from a weir retaining the Dunalastair Reservoir to the west. (This seems to have led to the post office being moved from dying Foss to the more strategically sited bridge.) By 1954 the small *Loch Tummel Hotel* was open at Tressait in Strathtummel, 6km east of Tummel Bridge. As part of the Hydro-Electric Board's vast Tummel/Garry project of 1945–52, the level of Loch Tummel was raised 3.5m by the 20m-tall Clunie Dam. This extended the loch westwards by 4km. Another dam 39m tall was built above the hamlet of Trinafour in Glen Errochty, some 8km north-west of Tummel Bridge, remarkably in a different watershed. This impounded Loch Errochty, a new reservoir which also accepts water taken from the River Bruar and upper River Garry far to the north-east, led across the A9 road through tunnels. Another short tunnel takes the Errochty compensation water through a small power station in Glen Errochty. From the Errochty reservoir yet another tunnel some 9km long enables the bulk of the water to discharge into Loch Tummel through the three 25,000kw generators of the Errochty power station, with a head of 186m. By 1962 the very prominent major substation and control centre for the scheme had been created east of Tummel Bridge, its area of control then including the Pitlochry power station. Seven main transmission lines led in all directions from the new and old switching stations, causing still more visual damage in the interests of otherwise non-polluting power.

**Barytes versus Conservation**: In 1986 American-owned MIGB began to mine barytes 7km south-east of Tummel Bridge, in the hills above Foss, and in 1990 opencasting for barytes began on a small scale near Beinn Eagach, in the National Scenic Area a few kilometres farther east. Demand for the powdered ore for use as a drill lubricant in offshore oil projects was high, but the mine faced exhaustion by 1997. Consequently in 1991 MIGB applied to mine 200,000 tonnes of barytes a year for 30 years through a new adit and accompanying yard at Duntanlich, 600m above sea level (clearly visible from the Queen's View at the east end of Loch Tummel) with access through Fonab Forest to Strathtay. Though up to 90 jobs would be provided for 30 years, this scheme was highly controversial and opposed by Scottish Natural Heritage. Refusal was followed by an Inquiry in 1993. By 1998 walks and cycle routes had been created in the forests and screen planting had so reduced the visual impact of the switchgear that a large hotel (the 100-room *Loch Tummel*) had recently been built, facing down the loch; despite the low population of around 100, a post office is still open.

## TURNHOUSE, Gogar, Ingliston & Edinburgh Airport — Map 15, B2

***Urbanised areas w. of Edinburgh.*** — OS 65: NT 1574

Gogar, 9km west of Edinburgh, had an ancient church, and both Gogar and Nether Gogar appeared as tiny settlements on Pont's map of around 1600. By then the line of the adjoining Glasgow road had been defined, and in 1625 came Gogar House or Castle and the later mansionhouse of Gogarburn. The Edinburgh & Glasgow Railway, opened in 1842, built a station at Gogar. When the southern approach line to the Forth Rail Bridge was opened in 1890 another station was provided, though traffic potential was little but for Turnhouse Farm, whose name it took. By 1895 a pit had been sunk beside the River Almond, near the end of a long, straight mineral line from Newbridge; later this enigmatic operation closed. In 1909 the Turnhouse golf club laid out its hilly 18-hole course near its eponymous station; but soon golfers came by car or bus, and sadly (in view of what was to follow) the station was closed to passengers around 1930. By 1939 Gogarburn had become a sanatorium, and a mental hospital had been built in its grounds.

**RAF Station, Airport and Highland Showground**: An airfield named RAF Turnhouse was opened between the railways in 1925; from 1935 it was expanded as a fighter station, with permanent buildings of RAF standard design. The first main hard runway of the airfield was laid in 1939 in an undesirably crosswind orientation. After 1945 the field combined RAF use with a civil role as *'Edinburgh (Turnhouse) Aerodrome'*, later renamed Edinburgh Airport. By 1951 British European Airways had resumed a London service; a new civilian terminal was built. In 1960 the Royal Highland & Agricultural Society, previously peripatetic, established its permanent showground south of the airport at Ingliston, hence its *Highland* name, incongruous for this Lowland location! Being unconnected by rail, the showground ensured acute congestion on the main A8 Edinburgh–Glasgow road whenever the site was in use. In 1978–79 a large, new single-span exhibition hall was built there. For obscure reasons the society was also permitted to hold a Sunday market alongside, and by 1988 the Scottish Agricultural Museum had been established close by; but in 2001 this is moving to Kittochside near East Kilbride *(q.v.)*. Meantime by 1970 Gogarburn had been greatly expanded as a mental deficiency hospital of nearly 650 beds. About 1970 the National Trust for Scotland opened its *'Suntrap'* garden at Gogarbank.

*A 'Lightning' aircraft which long stood at the entrance to the RAF's facility at Turnhouse airport, but which is now outside the premises of 'BAe Systems' at the South Gyle industrial estate.* *(AL)*

**Problem Runway, Misplaced Terminal, Costly Motorway**: RAF operations from Turnhouse ceased in 1970, but another runway 2560 m long was completed about 1975; while sensibly aligned into the prevailing winds, this nevertheless brought noise nuisance and potential risk to Newbridge and Cramond, and also conflicted with the Fife railway, which crossed the runway approach at a high level, requiring special signalling measures. The second new airport terminal was built in the 1980s, crassly sited on the Ingliston side of the airport near the showground and as far as possible from both the Fife and Glasgow railways, so preventing the ideal city centre rail connection already normal elsewhere in Europe. The author despairs at these gross inadequacies in planning, which also made more urgent the provision of a particularly costly and winding extension of the M8 motorway, approved in 1992 and built in 1995–96, further damaging the local environment, still nominally part of the Edinburgh Green Belt.

**Airport Success but Fertiliser Failure**: Due to the *'Open Skies'* policy the airport doubled its transatlantic passengers in 1990–91, and in 1992–93 2.6 million passengers passed through, especially drawn by new services to Stansted. In 1990 Scottish Agricultural Industries (SAI), fertiliser manufacturers and distributors, moved their group HQ from Edinburgh to new premises at Ingliston, but the firm ceased trading in 1991 and its assets were dispersed due to the economic problems of the farming industry. In 1992 the proprietors of the showground tried to attract a new football stadium for the Lothian clubs; but mercifully for the environment, rivals Hearts and Hibs could not agree to share. In 1995 Ingliston had one of the three Scottish centres of the big ADT Motor Auction Group. The RAF finally left Turnhouse in 1996, by which time the new 95-room *Airport Hotel* was open.

**Direct Flights Grow – Scotland's Busiest Airport?**: The 1996 Scottish flight destinations included Aberdeen, Kirkwall, and Sumburgh via Wick. Most of the main English cities were also served, and in the EU Holland, Belgium, Denmark, France and Germany. The airlines involved included Air UK, British Airways, British Midland, Easyjet and Sabena. Major modernisation and expansion of the airport terminal in 1996–2000 brought a new food court and departure lounge. In 1999 new scheduled services were introduced to European destinations, bringing a 43% rise in scheduled flights; both business and tourist passenger numbers were growing rapidly and expected to overtake Glasgow during the year. Plans for a railway station and for a segregated bus-route to the city centre have not yet happened, but in 2001 the Gogarburn hospital site was sold to the Royal Bank for its corporate headquarters.

## TURRIFF

**Map 10, B2**

***Aberdeenshire small town,*** *pop. 4000* OS 29: NJ 7250

Turriff is sited near the confluence of the Idoch Water or Burn of Turriff with the River Deveron; it has a name of uncertain meaning, but achieved early importance with the ancient church of St Congan or Cowan; by the 11th century the Columbans had a monastery, with an abbot by 1131 and also a monastic school. At one time there was a *'Castle Rainy'* and a sheriff court. However, so little remains of Turriff castle that it is undateable. By the 13th century Turriff church had Knights Templar connections, and in 1273 a *'hospital'* or block of almshouses was built there by Alexander Comyn, lasting into the 16th century. Turriff was chartered as a burgh of barony in 1511, and with its two annual fairs and weekly Sunday market, became a centre for collecting wool for despatch to Aberdeen. By 1546 there was a grammar school and from 1586 a parish school. Carnousie Castle was built in the 16th century near a stone circle 5 km west of the town, while Delgatie Castle, (built in Norman style, according to Pratt), is 3 km to the east of Turriff: its barnyards are famed in folksong. It was modernised in 1579 by the Hay family, Earls of Errol, who also had a *'lodging'* in the town, which was gradually reconstructed using red sandstone from a quarry near the castle. The tower of Craigston Castle, 6 km north-east near the hamlet of Fintry, was built in 1604–07 for John Urquhart of Craigfintrie.

**Textiles and Quarrying**: Pont's incomplete map of Buchan made about 1601 named *'Turra'*, while Gordon's later map gave *'Turreff'* some emphasis; Turriff fair was still active in 1662. The Roy map of about 1750 showed a smallish settlement whose only tracks led due north by Luncarty and Kinedart (King Edward) to rejoin the line of the later turnpike to Banff (A947); and south over the Idoch bridge at Bridgend, by what later became a back road via Seggat, passing by Fyvie towards Aberdeen. By 1752 there was a post office. A planned extension to the town was laid out from 1763, and a bleachfield for the locally-made linen and thread was erected in 1767 close to the Aberdeen to Banff road; but it worked only intermittently. By 1792 Turriff had a corn mill; another thread factory began in 1793, by which time there was a local office where some 6000m of linen were stamped annually. A new church was built in 1794, and no fewer than seven fair days were to be held in 1797. Heron thought the population of *"the town of Turreff about 700"* in 1799. By 1803 the Aberdeen turnpike had been improved; the adjoining bleachfield was upgraded in 1808. Andrews of Turriff were experienced millwrights by 1807, and the planned expansion was completed in 1819; a clock was placed on the ancient church tower in 1828. Delgaty quarries were still open in the mid 19th century.

**Railway, Threshing Mills, Coaches and Golf**: By 1857 Pratt noted *"two inns, several banking offices, and good shops"*, and from that year Turriff was the temporary terminal station of a meandering branch of the Great North of Scotland Railway (GNSR), from Inveramsay on the main line near Inverurie. This was extended to the Macduff area in 1860. As GNSR contractors, Wordie & Co ran a rail to road cartage depot; this also handled traffic for remote Gamrie, Gardenstown and Pennan on the north coast. The 1891 population was 2350. In 1894 Murray described Turriff as *"a thriving town"* with two *"good"* hotels, the *Fife Arms* and the *Commercial*. For many years Crichtons of Turriff built grain-handling equipment, including large portable threshing drums to be hauled from farm to farm by traction engines; Shearer Brothers manufactured pedal-driven threshing mills for poor but energetic crofters. An Episcopal church was built, and Turriff golf club, founded in the boom year of 1895, laid out a 9-hole parkland course. In the early 20th century a horse-drawn coach service plied from the station to Maud Junction via Cuminestown and New Deer.

**News but No Trains from the Traders' Town**: A local newspaper, the *Turriff and District Advertiser*, was first published in 1936. In the 1930s a daily train carried beef from the local abattoir to Aberdeen and London. Local flax scutching mills worked in World War II, but apart from agricultural engineering there was no other industry of note. The livestock market was busy in 1952, and there were three hotels by then. The railway lost its passenger service in 1951, a closure reflecting locally high car ownership, confirmed by the several motor parts wholesalers and other specialist vehicle services to be found in the compact little town in 1968. Freight trains ended in 1966, and later the station site at Bridgend was obliterated when a crossroads on the A947 was replaced by a new junction.

**Education, Grain, Marketing and Abattoir Anguish**: In 1975 Turriff burgh lost its local government role to the sprawling Banff and Buchan District in Grampian Region; this actually helped Turriff by enabling school centralisation at the modern Academy, and the closure of the rural junior secondary school at Forglen, 3km west of the town. In 1976 the *Advertiser* published editions for several surrounding towns, and about then the golf course was extended to 18 holes. By 1979 Moray Firth Maltings of Inverness had a granary in Turriff, still a farmers' market *par excellence*. In 1981 Turriff still had small-town facilities, including a 19-bed cottage hospital, six small hotels, and its livestock auction mart; there was also a knitwear factory. The 1991 census showed a town population of 3948, including an affluent retired element. In 1995 Reekie Davidson was still a major dealer in farm machinery at both Turriff and Inverurie. However, the withdrawal of land from agricultural use, very evident in Buchan in the late 1980s, was to have a negative effect on Turriff. This had been the location for some years of the HQ, abattoir and meat packery of the co-operative Buchan Meat Producers, prime suppliers of Scottish beef – until BSE caused its failure early in 1996 with the loss of 250 jobs. But Kepak Buchan were still processing beef and lamb at the Markethill Abattoir in 1996.

**Country Metropolis**: Bustling Turriff – its complicated centre threaded by far too many cars – has many banks, building societies, and professions. There are several supermarkets, and many smaller specialist shops. There is a fire station and the small hospital, plenty garages, and an industrial estate. *'Mr McKenzie's Biscuits'* of Turriff also make oatcakes for wide distribution. New houses are expanding the town to the north. Leisure facilities include the Auld Post Office Museum, a swimming pool and sports centre, a hotel, caravan and camping site, and angling on the River Deveron.

## TWATT

**Map 13, B2**

***Hamlet, Orkney,*** *pop. 275*

OS 6: HY 2623

The hamlet of Twatt lies among the hills and lochans of north Mainland, some 4km north-west of Dounby. There are ancient remains and a nature reserve. Twatt's military airfield was laid out in 1940 beside the small Loch of Isbister for the Royal Naval Air Service and labelled HMS *Tern*. Originally a satellite of Hatston *(see Kirkwall)*, it became the first British site for RN helicopter operations. Hard runways and sizeable hangars were built before major expansion was aborted in 1944. After a period in reserve it was mothballed in 1949 and sold off in 1959. Twatt's long-established garage and post office continued in use, and in 1997 there were still quite extensive remains of the airfield on the ground *(see Lamb G)*.

## TWECHAR

**Map 16, A3**

***Strathkelvin village,*** *pop. 1500*

OS 64: NS 6975

The very well built and well-known Roman fort on the Antonine Wall at Bar Hill overlooks the site of Twechar, beside the low-lying headwaters of the River Kelvin; it was accompanied – for a decade or so – by a civilian population. A millennium later, Kilsyth grew only 2 km to the north-east. The Twechar area seems to have remained completely rural, even after the local section of the Forth & Clyde Canal was dug in 1769. By 1872 an offshoot of the William Baird empire had recently developed Twechar as a village of close-packed rows of houses whose occupants served coal pits and workshops beside the canal. Twechar was connected with Kilsyth by a mineral railway via Queenzieburn; the line crossed the canal by a swing bridge, continuing to more pits and coke ovens south of Bar Hill, and joining the main line to Edinburgh west of Croy. An engine shed and workshops served this system. Although the population in 1901 was to reach about 1150, the only public facility recorded at Twechar was a letter box!

**Apogee and Decline**: By the 1920s another coal pit was open at St Flanan beside the canal to the west, and the Twechar pit was still at work in 1929; the population continued to grow, to nearly 2200 in 1951. By then they had been largely rehoused in flats and terraces by the local authority, between the wars or shortly after 1945, creating an unusual dumbell-shaped ground plan, probably due to avoiding potential subsidence problems.

There was also a secondary school for 280 pupils. However, the coke ovens had vanished by 1955 and in the mid 1960s the engine shed was closed and all the local railways lifted. The population was falling, to 2050 in 1971, and the secondary school had closed by 1976, leaving few facilities at Twechar but a primary school and post office. By 1991 Twechar had a mere 1499 residents, quite elderly. The post office has recently closed; but a change for the better should follow the complete reopening of the canal in 2001.

## TWEEDSMUIR

**Map 2, B2**

***Settlement, Upper Tweeddale,*** *pop. 100 (area)* OS 72: NT 1025

Standing stones and hill forts flank the upper River Tweed. The name *'Cruick'* appeared as one of many tiny symbols on Pont's map, made around 1600, suggesting the sheep farming nature of the steep surrounding hills. By 1797 the *Crook Inn* was open, 10km south of Broughton. By about 1754 Tweedsmuir Kirk stood 2 km farther south at an altitude of about 245m beside a road linking Broughton and Moffat; it became the focus for a minimum of non-farm development, including a school. In 1901 the parish had 435 residents. By 1940 the Talla Reservoir had been built for Edinburgh water supply, construction of the dam 2 km south of the kirk being aided by laying a temporary railway from Broughton. In 1951, 240 people lived locally, served by a post office, doctor, primary school and telephone exchange. Extensive afforestation – replacing hill farms – was blamed for more than halving the number of residents to a mere 100 in 1971; in 1978 only 28 of the 52 houses in the area were in year-round use. In that year the recently 6-pupil primary school was closed; by then the doctor too had gone. The parish population had stabilised, at 116 in 1991, enabling the post office to survive until recently. The *Crook Inn* (said to be 400 years old) still stands in splendid isolation, and now contains the local post office.

## TWYNHOLM

**Map 2, A5**

***Galloway village,*** *pop. 500 / 1075 (area)* OS 83: NX 6654

Several ancient earthworks – forts or mottes, of which the most notable is Twynholm Doon – and the ruined 16th century tower of Cumstoun Castle on the banks of the Dee estuary, give interest to this undulating farming area, centred some 4km north-west of Kirkcudbright. Pont's map of about 1610 showed two mills, the *'Old'* and *'New'*, beside the burn which passes through Twynholm, the kirkton of a large parish which has made little mark over the years. The 1901 parish population of 720 has gradually grown, largely by development at Mersecroft, on the west bank of the tidal River Dee at the Kirkcudbright bridgehead. In the 1950s over 500 people lived in and around the small village of Twynholm with its inn, post office, primary school and 67-line telephone exchange; there was also a timber merchant. Its main street, long bedevilled by heavy traffic negotiating the winding lane labelled A75 which carried the trunk road traffic to and from Stranraer, found relief by 1973 in the form of a new road alignment forming a bypass, though still uncomfortably close. With the expansion of Kempleton Mill – on the Tarff Water 2 km to the east – from a tiny facility in the 1950s, the village gained some new housing, a garage and a second hostelry. The parish population in 1991 was 1068. Although under 500 people lived in the village, its post office, inn and guest house are open.

## TYNDRUM

**Map 5, B3**

***Small W. Stirlingshire village,*** *pop. 100* OS 50: NN 3230

Bleak Tyndrum stands about 230m above sea level at the head of Strathfillan, which takes its name from the ancient chapel or priory of St Fillan, 3km south-east. Sir Robert Clifton of Nottinghamshire, who had spent a decade searching for lead, discovered an ore vein on the slopes of Meall Odhar west of Strathfillan in 1741. He immediately set about its extraction: the Roy map made about 1750 showed *'Clifton'* as a larger hamlet than Tyndrum (Gaelic *'House on the Knoll')*. There were already bridgeless tracks up Strathfillan, down Glen Lochy and over the pass to Loch Tulla. The military roads then being built by Caulfeild from Stirling and Dumbarton joined at Crianlarich, and followed the routes of the tracks when they diverged at Tyndrum, west to Taynuilt and north to Fort William; they were complete by 1761. In 1769 Pennant found Tyndrum a small village with an inn; lead ore was being worked by a *'level'* (adit). A lead smelter was at work by 1783, and Tyndrum's first post office opened in 1793.

**Tourist Hamlet with Two Stations**: Dorothy Wordsworth patronisingly observed in 1803 that *"the house was clean for a Scotch inn, with white table-cloth, glasses, English dishes etc; the people about the doors were well dressed"*. In 1818 the inn was again reported as *"good"*. About 1840 an ore crushing mill was built. Organised tourism began to affect Tyndrum in 1846; from that time a regular summer coach running from Glasgow and Dumbarton passed through Tyndrum en route to Oban. In 1873 Tyndrum became the temporary terminus of the very impecunious Callander & Oban Railway (a hopeful protégé of the Caledonian) and the railhead for a vast area of moors, from which sheep were soon being despatched to southern markets. Scenic horse-drawn coach tours were organised from the inn. In 1877 the railway was extended to Dalmally and reached Oban in 1880. By 1894 the local hostelry was the *"good" Royal Hotel*, but the lead mines were no longer worked. The West Highland Railway which opened in 1894 climbed much higher than the Oban line so as to cross the watershed to the north, hence Tyndrum's second (Upper) station. Tyndrum became an angling, climbing and winter sports resort; in 1951 there were about 85 residents and a primary school.

**Irish Gold in the Hills**: The school had closed by 1981, though the hamlet had gained a tourist information centre, garage, an additional hotel, caravan and camping site and the definition of the West Highland Way. Another large new hotel was built in 1992. At that time angling was said to be the main economic basis of Tyndrum, whose formerly bleak surroundings have been transformed by half a century of afforestation. In 1988 Fynegold Exploration, part of Dublin-based Ennex International, formed an access road to old lead mine adits in Glen Cononish 4km west of Tyndrum, and dug a 1000m tunnel to seek gold, which was found in 1990. With keen local support a full-scale mine was approved in 1993 on a well-hidden site 400m above sea level, to win 125,000 tonnes of ore a year, crushing it to powder for flotation in a solution of sodium xanthate to yield about 1 tonne of gold and silver a year for seven years. In 1997 Caledonian Mining began a full-scale gold mining operation, generating 80 jobs. A tailings dam is required, but site restoration will follow. Tyndrum has a variety of visitor accommodation, and a handful of shops, including for outdoor equipment. The stations are both still open.

## TYNINGHAME

**Map 3, B2**

***E. Lothian hamlet**, pop. 200*

OS 67: NT 6179

Tyninghame, at the mouth of the East Lothian River Tyne, 4 km down-river from East Linton, was reputed to have been on the site of a Roman settlement. By 756 there was an early monastic community, but in 941 this was destroyed by Norsemen. By the 12th century it had been replaced by St Baldred's, a church of Northumbrian origin. Tyninghame acquired the noble residence of the Earls of Haddington, who chartered a burgh of barony in 1591; a parish school was started in 1600. Tyninghame appeared with a larger than average symbol on Pont's map of about 1600, but remained a small village. Meantime the house and gardens were repeatedly improved. The surrounding woodlands were planted in the early 18th century by Thomas Hamilton, the 6th Earl, when the ancient Tyninghame House was greatly enlarged into a mansion.

**A Burgh Rooted Out**: About 1761 the aspiring laird of Tyninghame House, another Earl of Haddington, cleared away the village and its people with feudal ruthlessness, taking over the remains of its ancient church as a private chapel; a few indispensable tenants were rehoused a kilometre westwards. Chambers observed of the house in 1827 that *"all the ten successive Earls of Haddington have made a point of adding a piece"*. They continued in 1829, also extending and rebuilding the re-sited Tyninghame village in the 1830s. In 1901 it was still a small place, with a smithy and post office. In 1951 nearly 350 people lived in the area and there was a mill. The village lost its school about 1960 and had shrunk to only about 200 people by 1981. The fine gardens are opened to the public from time to time; the house has now been converted into several dwellings. Tyninghame post office, still open in 1995, has since closed.

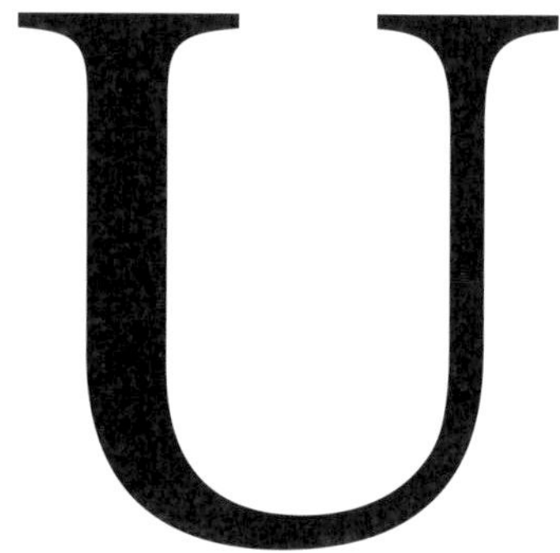

## UDDINGSTON

**Map 15, E5**

***Lanarkshire small town,*** *pop. 5400* OS 64: NS 6960

*'Udinstoun'* appeared as a tiny symbol on Pont's map dated 1596; it stands on the right bank of the Clyde 12 km east of Glasgow and 1.5km north of Bothwell Castle. Though it was never accorded burgh status, a monthly market appeared there, possibly in the 17th century. The Roy map showed that by the 1750s Uddingston was a small- to medium-sized settlement, with a very nodal situation on the emerging road system, having five radial roads effectively connecting every way save northwards; the Clyde could either be forded close by, or crossed at Bothwell Bridge. Around 1800 a new Bothwell Castle was built 250m east of the ancient building, a sprawling mansion surrounded by an enormous park, spreading from the Uddingston and Bothwell road to the river. Fashionably following the new mansion, Uddingston soon developed a primarily residential role, and by about 1825 it was served by a penny post from Hamilton. The Haughhead or *'Red'* bridge was built across the Clyde in 1840, replacing the earlier ford.

*Tunnock's Bakery, Uddingston, home of the teacake and caramel wafer. This family firm was founded in 1890, and expanded dramatically after the Second World War, when this factory was built.* (JRH)

**Railways, Commuters, Golf, Tunnock and Trams**: In 1849 came the Clydesdale Junction Railway, a section of the new main line of the Caledonian Railway, linking Motherwell to Newton and Glasgow; in 1869 Uddingston station became the junction for the Shotts line. Meantime a gas works had been set up in 1858. In 1877 the North British Railway opened a new line between Shettleston and Bothwell, passing east of the village, with a second station; both railways offered frequent passenger trains to Glasgow, leading to Kylepark being built north of the village in 1885 as a speculative dormitory housing estate for Glasgow workers. Thomas Tunnock opened a tiny bakery in 1890, when the population was already 5100. In 1894 Uddingston was a rare settlement for the area in being highly accessible, free of polluting industry and, as Murray wrote, *"composed almost entirely of villas"*. By 1901 its population was almost 7500. A power station was established in 1906, and from 1907 Uddingston Cross was a terminus for Glasgow's electric trams, connecting until 1931 with those of the Lanarkshire Tramways Company serving Bothwell, Blantyre and Motherwell (and, briefly, some more distant places).

**Coal, Caramel Wafers and Motorway**: The mansion called Bothwell Castle was demolished in 1926, for – after all – Uddingston was becoming largely industrial. Early in the century a colliery was sunk west of the river; disused by 1963, its site later held brick and aluminium alloy ingot works. By 1951 Uddingston had only 6500 people, but was a small town in terms of facilities. The Tunnock family opened a second bakery in 1949 and expanded production rapidly in the 1950s as sweet rationing ended, making marshmallow, chocolate and coconut delicacies from 1951 to an Italian recipe, and caramel wafers from 1952. The firm began to export their products in 1957, and opened another large new bakery at Uddingston in 1962. The Shettleston to Bothwell section of railway was closed by Beeching in 1961. Its abandoned route was roughly followed by the M74 motorway which was soon driven through the area, the noise impact deterring more affluent residents. The electrification of the railway service to Glasgow in 1974 added to the area's excellent accessibility to the city centre, but there was little space for infill development. In 1981 Uddingston retained small-town facilities.

**Building over the Park**: However in the early 1980s housing estates began to erode the former parkland, so that by 1991 the population reached 5367, still having high proportions of well-qualified professional and technical people. However by then the numbers of terraced houses and flats equalled the surviving villas, and although over 10% used trains to get to work, cars carried nearly six times that number. In 1990 the third and fourth generation of Tunnocks managed a factory of some 37,500m$^2$, and employed 700 people in Uddingston. However in 1994 growing competition from supermarket bakeries caused the closure of Tunnocks' bakery division with the loss of 108 jobs. Compensation soon appeared when British Gas announced a 100-job expansion of its Uddingston service centre. In 1997 Alexandra Workwear of Bristol intended to keep open their Bothwell Park factory, despite closing another at Coatbridge. Tunnocks are still busy, turning out caramel wafers, chocolate logs and chocolate mallows by the million, with 475 staff. Guilbert (office equipment) and Speedlink (deliveries) each employ over 100. Uddingston Grammar School now has well over 1200 pupils; and the *Redstones Hotel* has been joined by a 64-roomed *Travel Inn*, 3km north-west.

## UIG & Timsgarry

**Map 11, B2**

***Townships, Isle of Lewis,*** *pop. 450* — OS 13: NB 0534

The remote western extremity of the Isle of Lewis is the west part of the former vast parish of Uig, an area about 15km across, full of rocky hills and lochs, almost cut off by the long narrow sea inlet of Little Loch Roag. The ancient Dun Borranish stands by the silver sands in Camas Uig (Uig Bay). In the nearby dunes three almost complete sets of chessmen, finely carved in walrus ivory about the year 1150 and believed to be of Icelandic origin, were found hidden underground in 1831. A large medieval Benedictine convent stood at Mealista near the crofting township of Brenish on the remotest south-west coast, but little remains to be seen. There are the remains of many small horizontal corn mills in this area. Mealista also has a modern but bleakly sited mansionhouse, part of the vast Uig & Hamnavay estate now owned by the Bulmer family. An army camp of the 1939–45 war was built at northernmost Aird Uig, powered by 1969 with electricity from the small Gisla *(Giosla)* hydro power station, built below the dammed outlet of Loch Rog Beag, beside the single-track road into the area.

**Tiny Townships**: In 1971 Timsgarry *(G. Timsgearraidh),* not far from Dun Borranish, with perhaps 100 people, was the local metropolis for a scattered crofting population of about 575. It had the Uig or Crowlista *(Cradhlastadh)* primary school, a post office, telephone exchange, and by 1980 the *Scaliscro Lodge Hotel*. Brenish was once the terminus of one of Britain's remotest post-bus routes, which by 1982 linked Timsgarry post office with Stornoway. Tiny townships which at some recent time provided minimal services include Enaclete *(Einacleit)*, Miavaig *(Miabhaig)*, Mangersta *(Mangurstadh)* with a radio station, Islivig *(Islibhig)* with a post office, and particularly Valtos *(Bhaltos)*, which has a fishing pier, post office, primary school and caravan and camping site beside a sandy bay. By 1991 the area's total population was only around 450. The *Scaliscro Lodge Hotel* is still open at Timsgarry.

## UIG

**Map 8, A2**

***Village, N-W. Skye,*** *pop. 250* — OS 23: NG 3963

On the west coast of the Trotternish peninsula of north Skye is the prehistoric Dun Skudiburgh, probably the feature named *'Brugh Vyg'* on Pont's crude late 16th century map of Skye. The relatively sheltered Uig Bay to the south is overlooked by a standing stone and entered by two burns with many waterfalls. Martin in 1703 reported Uig as a parish. Its scattered townships surround the bay, which was the prime objective of a road from Portree, built for the Commissioners for Highland Roads and Bridges about 1812. Evidently the outer isles were the real target, and from 1840 there was a pier with regular shipping services, including a weekly mail steamer to Tarbert (Harris). As late as 1859 some of Uig's poverty-stricken residents still occupied windowless stone beehive huts. However, by 1894 the resident laird, Captain Fraser, owned what Murray styled a *"well-managed estate"* with *"neat houses and well to do cottages"*; there was *"a comfortable inn"* and a post and telegraph office.

**The Harris and North Uist Car Ferry**: A lone doctor's practice became established, and by 1951, when the population was under 300, the inn had become a hotel. A youth hostel and 9-bed maternity hospital were also open; however by 1973 the latter had become the youth hostel. The cargo steamers were withdrawn in 1961, but shortly afterwards a stark though spacious new pier was built at Uig, from which a triangular car ferry service to Lochmaddy and Tarbert was started in 1964. Uig kept its post office and primary school; into the 1970s secondary schooling was given at Gaelic-speaking Staffin *(q.v.)* on the east coast, about 10km away over a winding hill road. But despite the addition of a second hotel and a garage, the population of Uig itself in 1981 was only some 250. By 1985 there was a caravan and camping site, and in 1988 the principal public transport route to the Uists was via the Portree/Uig bus plus the Uig/Lochmaddy ferry. The post office is still open. However in 1999 it was feared that the terminal might be moved to Dunvegan. The *Uig Hotel* has 17 rooms and offers riding; as well as the youth hostel, there's a bunkhouse for backpackers at Glen Hinnisdal, 6km to the south.

## ULLAPOOL

**Map 12, A4**

***Wester Ross large village,*** *pop. 1231* — OS 19: NH 1394

Ullapool in Wester Ross stands on a level promontory on the otherwise hilly shores of Loch Broom; it was probably founded by a Norseman named Olaf, but quaintly labelled *'Ullabill'* on the Blaeu atlas map of the mid 17th century and *'Ulla Bill'* on the Roy Map made about 1750. The latter showed four hamlets, from which tracks led north to the head of Loch Kanaird (OS 15), south east to Inverlael (OS 20) and also up *'Strath'* Achall (OS 20). In 1753–55 the Board of Trustees for Manufactures set up a *'manufacturing station'* on Loch Broom, though with very little success, perhaps because of its extreme remoteness. At the same time Lochbroom was being tried as the site of a linen promotion by the Commissioners for the Forfeited Estates; about 1765 they built a waulk mill, apparently near Ullapool. But the local linen industry did not grow, and despite the Commissioners' building of a road to the north into Coigach (OS 15) in the 1770s, poverty and emigration continued. Perhaps in the hope of stimulating linen exports, the only customs house on the west coast north of Oban was

*Ullapool (seen in the 1960s) was founded as a fishing settlement in 1788 by the British Fisheries Society. Much of the waterfront building dates from the 19th century. Ullapool has become a busy centre since the start of the car ferry to Stornoway in 1973.* *(RS)*

established in 1776. For a time it was sited on Isle Martin, 6km seaward of Ullapool; but the Lochbroom linen industry had completely failed by 1789.

**New Fishing Village, Clearances and Tourism**: On a more positive note, Loch Broom had been *"long noted for herrings of peculiar excellence"* (*Heron*), which led to Ullapool being successfully re-founded by the British Fisheries Society (BFS) in 1788. It became a port of registry with the letters UL. In 1799 Heron described it as a *"newly erected village"*, which had been laid out to a grid plan by Thomas Telford. Ullapool was soon connected to Contin and Dingwall by a moorland road, built in 1792–97 by the BFS with government aid, and gained its first post office in 1802, served by a foot post twice a week. The BFS was still working at Ullapool in 1829, when the parish was still so poor that the government paid for a Church of Scotland building erected in that year. In 1852 the hated Sutherland estates began to clear Strathkanaird, a crofting area about 9km north of Ullapool, but met resistance. The herring fisheries were recovering, and in 1867 Ullapool was Scotland's third busiest herring station, crowded in the peak days by over 900 boats, most of them sailed and rowed by four men. It was also at that time one of the top ten places for white-fish curing. Tourism was boosted by the erection in 1867 by Sir John Fowler, the engineer of Forth Bridge fame, of a suspension footbridge across the deep wooded gorge at the 70m high Falls of Measach in his Corrieshalloch estate (OS 20), inland from the head of Loch Broom.

**Rails fail to reach the Scenic Beauty**: By 1886 a regular weekly steamer made calls on its Glasgow and Stornoway route. The Garve & Ullapool Railway Act was passed in 1890, but – as well explained by Thomas – the line was never built. The 1891 population was 870, and in 1894 though Ullapool was just *"a large dreary fishing village"* to Murray, he named two hotels, the *Royal* and the *Caledonian*, the latter having *"an obliging landlord"*. These exploited the glorious view up Loch Broom to the often snowy peaks of Braemore Forest. In 1894 there was just one daily horse-drawn coach from Garve station; by about 1910 this was competing with a *'road motor service'* which soon became undisputed on this hilly and at that time sparsely patronised route. Ullapool's fisheries then declined; it remained a very minor port with some fish curing, and a quiet resort. By the 1920s a passenger ferry plied across the loch to a small isolated hostelry at Altnaharrie.

**Hydro Power, Stornoway Ferry and Klondykers**: As part of the 1945 Fannich/Orrin scheme by the Hydro-Electric Board, water was diverted from the Allt a'Mhadaidh, a natural feeder of the Corrieshalloch Falls, by a weir and canal in the Dirrie More pass (OS 20), leading into a dammed Loch Droma, whose outlet was reversed to flow into the artificial Loch Glascarnoch. A smaller scheme in Strathkanaird (OS 15) dammed Loch Dubh and several lochans for hydro power. In the 1950s Ullapool had over 800 people and five hotels, plus average village facilities; a bus-rail link via Garve provided public transport, and by 1961 a large youth hostel was open. In 1973 a new car ferry to Stornoway enabled Ullapool – with its enlarged pier – to oust Kyle as the ferry port for Lewis. From that time with the growth of tourism and the new oil-related yard at Stornoway, the growing traffic through Ullapool rapidly raised the importance of the village. In 1977 many large fishing vessels were to be seen at the pier, transferring vast quantities of mackerel to road vehicles including French and Dutch lorries; a quasi-permanent East European settlement of *'Klondykers'* – fish factory ships – was moored offshore.

**New Hotels, Trunk Calls, Campers and Ceramics**: Besides the *Argyll Hotel* and the youth hostel, much recent investment was evident by 1978, including the *Mercury* and *Morefield* motor inns, the very new *Harbour Lights Hotel* and a quite substantial restaurant. The Royal Bank branch and the telephone exchange had been extended; a supermarket, large new woollens shop, an ironmonger with fishing tackle, and a Hydro-Electric showroom were also open. Many bungalows had been built at Braes to the east of the growing centre. Some 500 people had settled in eight years, including Fred and Gunn Brown, who in 1980 enlarged the little old *Altnaharrie Inn* into an 8-roomed hotel. With no fewer than eleven hotels and the general facilities of a large village, Ullapool then served a wide area to the north with a population of over 3000. From 1984 a new trunk telephone exchange or *'group centre'* added Skye, previously accessed via Kyle, to its already vast service area. By 1985 there was also a caravan and camping site, and by 1992 the regional and district councils had jointly built a sports centre. In 1991 the resident population was 1231, including an affluent retired element. The regional and local enterprise companies opened in Ullapool in 1992 the first training centre under their CELT programme for remote areas. By then Highland Stoneware of Lochinver had expanded into Ullapool, employing 8 people by 1993.

**Big Ferry, Remotest Soap and Hostels**: The car ferry *Isle of Lewis*, built by Fergusons of Port Glasgow in 1995 for the Ullapool and Stornoway service, became the largest in the Calmac fleet. The former church of 1829 was restored in 1995 as Ullapool Museum. A local radio station entitled Lochbroom FM was started by volunteers in 1995, even producing its own *'soap opera'!* By 1996 the new Ullapool High School had been built, a golf course had been squeezed in beside the river, housing development had spread beyond it, and a considerable area of urban development had climbed the Braes of Ullapool. At Rhue and Ardmair 5km to the north is more scattered new development, the latter including a caravan and camping site. White fish, prawns, crabs, scallops and mackerel are still landed, but the Klondykers are few. Employment comes from haulage, construction, engineering, the Summer Isles fish smokehouse, and the *Ullapool News* (weekly) paper. Hotels in and near Ullapool include the famed *Altnaharrie Inn* (across the loch), the modern *Four Seasons* and the *Ardvreck*, plus many guest houses; there's the youth hostel and a backpackers hostel.

## ULSTA

**Map 14, B2**

***Township, Yell, Shetland,*** *pop. under 100* OS 2 or 3: HU 4680

At the south end of the peaty island of Yell is the bleak crofting township of Ulsta, which by the 1930s had a shop, a post office and a passenger ferry from Toft. By the 1970s electricity arrived here from Lerwick by submarine cables. The vehicle ferry slip which opened in 1973 became the operating headquarters for the new North Isles vehicle ferries, sturdy boats built in the Faroes. In the mid 1980s Ulsta's facilities were basic, but with a post office, general merchant and community hall the new terminal had brought renewed purpose to a formerly shrinking settlement.

## ULVA & Gometra, Isles of

**Map 4, B2**

***Small islands off Mull,*** *pop. under 100* OS 48: NM 4439

This pair of hilly islands beside Mull was long owned by the benevolent MacQuaries; General Lachlan MacQuarie who was born on Ulva in 1761 earned great respect in Australia for his liberal reforms as Governor of New South Wales. His clever family entertained Johnson and Boswell in 1773 in what Boswell called their *"mean"* house, and their tenants benefited from their frugality: by 1800 every family had a boat, and potatoes were exported. In 1841, 570 people lived on Ulva, with a further 78 on Gometra. Then came hell: potato famine was followed in 1846–51 by instant clearances by fire under a frightful new owner named Clark, who even stole his tenants' livestock, and by 1871 had cut the total population to under 100. Remarkably, desolated Ulva gained its first post office in 1856–57. Meantime Clark had built a fine mansion, which itself succumbed to fire – one suspects retaliation. The Clark family built Ulva House as a replacement home, and occupied the sad islands until 1945. By 1954 Gometra had been linked to Ulva by a short causeway; the post office and primary school stood on the mainland at Lagganulva beside the ferry slip. In 1981 the public was still not welcome to the islands. This policy had been relaxed by 1985 when the private ferry plied twice a day. In 1986 the primary school had 8 pupils, but by 1991 the population of Ulva (apparently including Gometra) was only 30. Deer and oyster farming kept the few islanders in being, and by the late 1990s there were nature trails, a visitor centre, post office and a small seafood restaurant, served by a passenger ferry on request. The future of the little school is being reviewed in 2001.

## UPHALL & Ecclesmachan

**Map 16, C3**

***W. Lothian village & hamlet,*** *pop. 3300* OS 65: NT 0671

Ecclesmachan's Brythonic name *(Eglwys = church)* shows early Christian settlement in this undulating area of West Lothian, then part of Dark Age Strathclyde. The name was rendered as *'Inchmachan'* on Pont's map made around 1600. About 1.5 km south of the ancient church was a road between Newbridge and Bathgate, beside which were *'Uphal'* and just to the west the newly built 5-storey tower of Houston House, baronial seat of the Shairpes. The mansion of Middleton House was built in 1707. In the 1750s *Kirk of Uphall* (later known as Old or Upper Uphall) was one of a cluster of three hamlets on or near what had become a main road from Edinburgh to Glasgow. North of the kirk was a *'coal syke'*, evidently working the outcrop in the form of an open ditch.

**Quarry, Railway and Shale Oil**: The Binnie quarry which was open at Ecclesmachan by 1794 provided a brown sandstone speckled with bitumen, which added durability. The quarry was busiest about 1835, its stone being used in such important Edinburgh buildings as the National Gallery, Scott Monument, Donaldson's Hospital, and the Bank of Scotland headquarters; by 1858 three quarries were open and 22 quarrymen were employed in 1895, but by 1899 the stone was only used for monuments. Uphall expanded, and a post office opened between 1813 and 1838; Uphall Station on the Edinburgh & Bathgate Railway, later part of the North British (NBR), was opened in 1849. In the 1850s oil-shale quarries and mines were opened by McLagan, the Linlithgowshire MP. He then joined Meldrum (a former associate of the famed *'Paraffin' Young*), and Simpson (a coalmaster and oil-works owner), to form the Uphall Mineral Oil Company, whose mines and paraffin-oil works at Uphall Station were connected by mineral railway to their Hopetoun Oil Works near Winchburgh.

**Consolidation, Change and Closure**: The company owned other mines and works elsewhere in West Lothian; their Uphall works was extended in the mid 1860s into the second largest in Scotland. William Fraser left it to found the Pumpherston *(q.v.)* oil shale works of 1883. Young's company absorbed the local firm in 1884 and further expanded its works as their main centre. The settlement of Uphall – astride the main road – had a population of 922 in 1891, and was called a *"mining village"* by Murray in 1894, when there was a mill, an inn and

*The Houston House Hotel, Uphall. The historic core of this house was built in about 1600 for Sir Thomas Shairp, advocate. It was extended in 1737. More recently, it was converted to a hotel in 1970 by Wheeler and Sproson.* (JRH)

a post and telegraph office. Uphall was supplied with electricity from a local power station from 1905. In 1919 Middleton House became the headquarters of Scottish Oils, a firm which absorbed all the other shale-oil companies. From 1921 to its closure in 1936 the Uphall refinery processed Middle-East crude oil, brought by pipeline from the port of Grangemouth. The A8 trunk road diversion bypassed Uphall from the 1920s. The quarries, mines and oil works had all closed by 1955.

**Golf, Agricultural Education, Pigs and Plastics**: Over 1900 people lived in Uphall in 1951, when it had typical village facilities. By 1953 a 9-hole golf course had been laid out in the grounds of Houston (or Houstoun) House, which had become a fine 20-roomed hotel by 1974; meantime by 1969 the course had grown to 18 holes. Oatridge Agricultural College was opened at Ecclesmachan about 1970; a large new training unit for pig farmers opened there in 1995. Wimpey Homes had a transport depot and laboratory in the town by 1977, but Motherwell Bridge Thermal cut 40 jobs in 1978. Scottish Oils was still based at Middleton Avenue in 1977, but Middleton House is now a retirement home. Despite prominent dereliction to the south, Uphall's growth has continued. Among the concerns encouraged into the area by 1990 to compensate for job losses were Scotplas (plastics recyclers) and Tarmac's Neslo (partitions). Motherwell Bridge employ 125, and Wimtec are environmental site surveyors with 50 staff. In 1991 the population was around 3300. The greatly extended *Houstoun House Hotel* now has 74 rooms.

## UPLAWMOOR

**Map 15, A6**

***Renfrewshire village,*** *pop. 600* — OS 64: NS 4355

Some 5km south-west of Neilston is a steep-sided gap in the hills forming a natural routeway between Glasgow and Cunninghame and containing the little Loch Libo; the ruined Auchenbathie Tower, 1km west, dates from the 14th century. Pont's sketch map of Renfrewshire made around 1600 showed *'Coldwell'*, 1km south-west of Auchenbathie. Roy's map surveyed about 1754 showed a road from Beith to Neilston, which was later turnpiked and connected to Kilmarnock; but focused settlement in the area was of little account. A new Caldwell House, the castellated mansion of William Baron Mure, designed by Robert Adam, was built in 1772–73, and a coaching inn was in existence. In the 19th century a hamlet named *'Ouplaymoor'* grew up south of the loch, with a church. The Glasgow, Barrhead & Kilmarnock Joint Railway opened in 1871, naming the station Uplawmoor. The rival Lanarkshire & Ayrshire Railway joining Lugton and Cathcart via Neilston High was opened in 1903, paralleling the earlier line and giving tiny Uplawmoor a second station; the original one was then renamed Caldwell.

**Golf, Children's Hospital and Affluence**: In 1903 the Caldwell golf club was formed and laid out a 9-hole course in the Caldwell parkland, with its clubhouse near Uplawmoor; it was later extended to 18 holes. This and the railways stimulated some residential development, and by 1951 Uplawmoor had a population of 525 and the facilities of a small village. By 1963 Caldwell House had become a *'mental deficiency'* hospital for handicapped children, and lost its fine interiors, but the inn developed into a small hotel. The railway between Lugton and Neilston High was closed completely by Beeching in 1964, and Uplawmoor lost both its stations at the same time. Caldwell House Hospital held 134 staff and patients in 1971, but it was closed about 1985 and Caldwell House stood near-derelict in 1997. Uplawmoor's largely dormitory population had reached 619 by 1991. The post office and golf course are still open, and the very long-standing *Uplawmoor Hotel* continues to serve.

## URR (or Haugh of Urr)

**Map 2, A5**

***Small Galloway village,*** *pop. 550* — OS 84: NX 8066

The huge earthwork called the *'Mote'* or Motte of Urr stands beside a ford across the Urr Water, some 20km south-west of Dumfries. Sources disagree as to its date of origin, citing either the 6th century or Norman. Other large earthworks stand on both banks of the river. Urr was chartered as an early burgh of barony in 1262, but developed little apart from milling, and it paid no tax in 1535–56. Pont's map of the Stewartry, perhaps made as early as 1583, showed an emparked tower labelled *'Balgred Linn'* adjoining the motte. The *'Kirk of Orr'* stood 1km to the north, and beside the Spottes Burn just north of the kirk was the *'Hall of Spotts'*, with the Oldmill and Newmill. Farther upstream was the (Old) Bridge of Urr, and above that a *'wackmill'*. The military road to Portpatrick, laid out in the early 17th century, crossed the Urr near the motte, 3km east of the old bridge. In 1642 a very early post office was opened on the Carlisle–Ireland route, known as *'Steps of Urr'*. By Roy's time about 1754 a bridge *"usually called the Haugh-bridge" (Heron)* had been built there, giving rise to the village of Haugh of Urr between the kirk and Spottes Hall; Bridge of Urr gained a post office in 1765. The later main road passed between the old and new villages, and the ultimately ill-fated railway to Castle Douglas which passed only 500m from the motte provided no station. Despite remoteness and falling farm jobs, in the later 20th century Old Bridge of Urr had over 100 people and retained a post office as late as 1977. Haugh of Urr had a remarkably stable population of about 450; its post office was still active up to 1996 and an inn is still open.

## UYEASOUND

**Map 14, C1**

***Island community, Unst, Shetland,*** *pop. 200* — OS 1: HP 5901

An inlet on the south coast of Unst, sheltered by the small Isle of Uyea, forms a natural shelter for small vessels. Standing stones and the ancient Gletna Kirk show its early significance. This was reinforced in 1598 when the unpleasant Lawrence Bruce built the Z-plan tower of Muness Castle on a peninsula 4km east of the church. But this, Scotland's most northerly castle, soon suffered a mysterious fire and thereafter fell into ruin. This area of small farms and crofts changed slowly; by the 1950s there were 210 people and basic facilities, with a pier for fishing boats. By 1974 a youth hostel was open, and access by car ferries and North Sea oil activity had brought the 8-roomed *Maundeville Hotel* and more jetties; sea angling was introduced, and a post office cum shop was still open in 1987. However the impetus for development was lost, and the post office soon closed; the youth hostel, still open in 1994, had closed by 2000. The closure of the primary school was considered in 1995 – but it's still open.

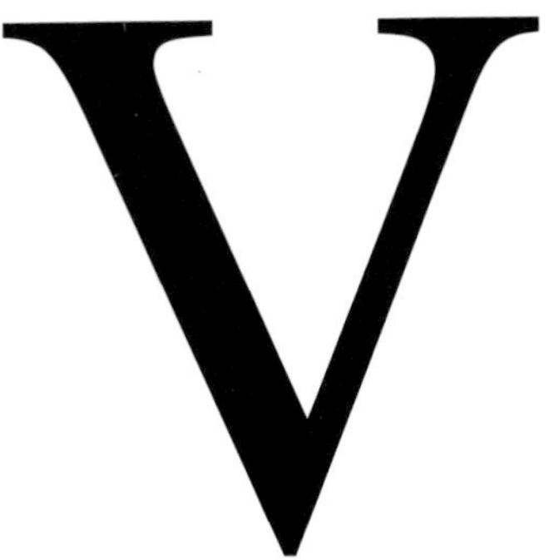

## VIDLIN & Lunna

**Map 14, B3**

***N. Shetland communities,*** *pop. 100* OS 3: HU 4765

When Pont sketch-mapped Shetland about 1592, settlement in the hilly Lunnasting peninsula in the north of the Mainland was mainly at the head of the sea inlet of Vidlin Voe. The remote Lunna House was built in 1660 near an ancient church 4km to the north, beside the sheltered inlet of West Lunna Voe. In World War II the house became the HQ of the Norwegian Resistance movement, and the starting point of its risky boat trips to the fjords. In 1951 Vidlin had under 100 people, with a post office and primary school. By 1974 a vehicular ferry plied to Whalsay from Flugarth, 4km south of Vidlin. In the 1970s *Lunna House* was a quiet 7-roomed seasonal hotel. Maclean noted a thriving little fishing village in 1985, lobster potting having been replaced by small scallop boats, and at the south end of the bay was the largest salmon farm in Shetland, where about 100,000 locally farmed salmon were processed annually. In 1986 Vidlin became the car ferry terminal for the Out Skerries *(q.v.)*, and by 1994 had two more new piers. There are a number of recently-built houses, the post office and Lunnasting School.

## VIEWPARK, Tannochside & Birkenshaw

**Map 15, E5**

***Lanarkshire communities,*** *pop. 15,000* OS 64: NS 7160

Some 3km north-east of Bothwell is the south-facing escarpment of a plateau which slopes northwards to the North Calder Water, as it flows westwards into the River Clyde. Pont's map of about 1600 showed a patch of woodland in the area. The original Glasgow–Newhouse–Edinburgh turnpike of 1753 followed a dead straight (possibly Roman) line along the crest to link the Calderpark bridges with Bellshill, but the later main road ran below the escarpment. The wayside station of Fallside was opened in 1849 on the Caledonian Railway's (CR) new low-level main line between Motherwell and Glasgow, soon becoming the junction for a short (and short-lived) branch to Bothwell. In 1869 a CR branch line was completed through the area between this and the escarpment, connecting Uddingston to Bellshill, Shotts and Midcalder. By the late 19th century the nearby mansion named Viewpark overlooked Uddingston and the park of Bothwell Castle from the escarpment, below which a large quarry of red sandstone lay beside the Bellshill line.

**Housing Schemes, Earth Moving – and Doctor Finlay?**: The rail-connected Aitkenhead Colliery was active in the 1890s west of Tannochside House, and several other coal pits served by mineral lines were open north of Viewpark, where miners' rows had developed at Ashley above Fallside, and in the area now called Tannochside – perhaps the inspiration for A J Cronin's fictional name *'Tannochbrae'?* By the 1920s these places were coalescing into a linear settlement along the Old Edinburgh Road (by then labelled B7001) as far as Birkenshaw; Tannochside had a post office. Aitkenhead Colliery seems to have closed about 1950. By 1951 Viewpark and its neighbours had almost 10,000 people, but the facilities of small villages. Fallside station was closed about 1954, when the former collieries were derelict, but large housing schemes had been begun north of Viewpark. In 1959 the large American-owned *Caterpillar* branch factory was opened at Tannochside to the south of the former colliery site, manufacturing earth-moving machinery. Around 1960 the site of a former tip beside the A721 was developed as an APCM cement depot, receiving supplies by rail. A hotel had opened at Viewpark by 1977, but local facilities remained those of small villages, relying on Uddingston and Bellshill.

**The Caterpillar that Crawled Away**: By 1986 the Caterpillar plant employed some 1200 workers but, after prophesying expansion, the plant's owners suddenly and cynically closed it in 1987 against bitter protests by the workforce. Production was moved to a factory at Grenoble in France. In 1991, when 14,872 people still lived in the area, 20% of the men were unemployed. The 32ha site of the former Caterpillar factory was redeveloped in 1992–93 for housing, commerce and the Tannochside Industrial Park, part of the Lanarkshire Enterprise Zone. The adjacent Aitkenhead Colliery bing, a partly re-worked eyesore, was to be reclaimed. In 1994 Centurion Brick of Tannochside was bought by Ibstock. In 1995 Watson & Philip (Alldays) of Dundee proposed a 100-job food distribution centre at the Industrial Park, where over 23,000m² of floorspace had already been built. Cement trains still arrive at Viewpark Sidings; Kwik-Fit Insurance now employ 800 at their Tannochside call centre.

## VOE, Delting & Olnafirth

**Map 14, B3**

***N. Shetland communities,*** *pop. 1200 (area)* OS 3: HU 4063

A small valley leading north from the head of the sheltered Olna Firth some 30km north of Lerwick provides a pocket of reasonable farmland among the windswept hills, where the ancient church of Delting parish stood near the shore. Voe post office was issued with a cancelling stamp in 1843, about the time that the road was built between Lerwick, Voe and Brae. Voe pier was a herring station in 1907, and from 1903 to 1928 Olnafirth was a whaling centre. Delting parish, including Brae,

*This wooden pier at Voe, Shetland, was built in the early 20th century. Herring fishing and whaling have been succeeded by scallop dredging; here a shellfish boat is unloading its catch.* *(JRH)*

Graven and Mossbank, held 1400 people in 1901 but only 675 in 1971. However, a primary school named Olnafirth was built, and by the 1950s, although remote Voe had only some 165 residents, there was also a doctor and a market stance. The market was soon abandoned, and the hotel noted in 1974 became a pub. By about 1980 there was a village store and tweed weaving workshop, and by 1985 a small boatyard. At that time two full-time scallop boats were based at the jetty, also popular for pleasure sailing, Voe being regarded as a picturesque spot. Sullom Voe's oil terminal brought several new housing developments and caused the road to Brae to be reconstructed; besides the jetty and primary school there are now two pubs.

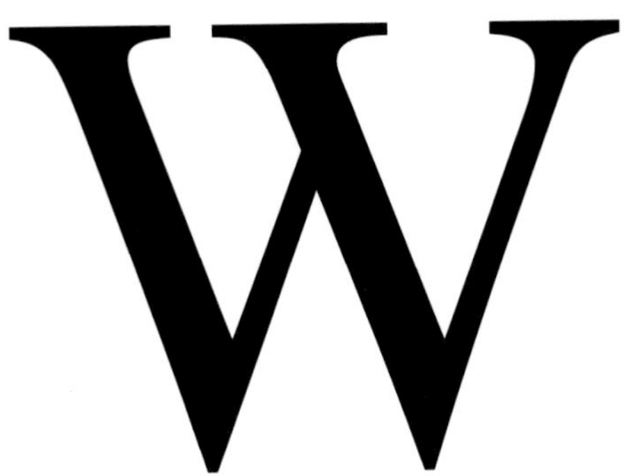

## WALKERBURN

**Map 3, A3**

***Tweeddale village,*** *pop. 650*

OS 73: NT 3637

The Priesthope Burn flowed into the River Tweed about 3 km east of Innerleithen. Roy's map surveyed about 1754 showed no development of any kind where the north Tweedside road crossed this stream – which was later renamed the Walker Burn, possibly because it was used to drive a mill for *'waulking'* cloth. The settlement of Walkerburn still *"had no existence"* in 1850 (Bremner), but in 1854–55 the large water-powered Tweedvale woollen mill was built at the burn mouth by Henry Ballantyne from Galashiels. Tweedholm mill followed in 1860; although burnt down in 1865, it was immediately rebuilt by James Dalziel & Co to employ about 130 workers. From 1866 Walkerburn was served by the Peebles & Galashiels branch of the North British Railway, and by a post office. By 1869 Ballantyne's mill was regarded by Bremner as *"the largest factory on the banks of the Tweed"*, employing 270 workers on 7260 spindles and 80 looms. By then the population of what he called a *"village"* had already exceeded 700, and peaked in 1891 at almost 1300.

**Apogee and Decline to a Museum Village**: In 1894 Walkerburn was described by Murray as *"a busy seat of woollen manufactures"*, but it never actually grew beyond the scale of a village, and in the 20th century declined slowly. In the 1920s a more sophisticated method of exploiting waterpower was developed for Tweedvale mill, using pumped storage and

*Walkerburn woollen mill, part of a large complex founded in 1855 by the Ballantyne family to manufacture tweeds and other woollens. This mill closed and was demolished in the 1980s.* (JRH)

a Pelton wheel. Although by 1963 the 15-room *Tweed Valley Hotel* was in business, the railway was closed by Beeching in 1962. The mill was reduced to the limited role of woollen yarn spinning in 1968, and the waterwheel had been abandoned by 1970. In 1971 the population was 840. Rathburn Chemicals, laboratory solvent manufacturers, established a plant in 1973 and hoped to expand it in 1979 when they exported to 25 countries. Although the small Scottish Museum of Woollen Textiles was opened in part of the mill about 1977, only the facilities of a small village were available. The yarn spinning mill changed hands to Laidlaw & Fairgrieve, who employed 170 people before it was finally closed by the Dawson group in 1988, leaving little but the mill shop and museum in an inactive village. But by 1991 when the population was only 658 the remaining part of the mill was being converted into small industrial units, and the primary school, post office and pub remain open, as does the *Tweed Valley Hotel*.

## WALLS, Vaila, Sandness & Sandsting

**Map 14, B3**

***W. Shetland village & hamlets,*** *pop. 550*

OS 3: HU 2449

Walls, on the western limb of the Shetland Mainland, lies at the head of Vaila Sound, a sea inlet around which are many ancient remains. It is protected from the severe north Atlantic weather by the islet of Linga and the larger island of Vaila (OS 4), once a smuggling centre, shown as *'Valu'* on Pont's crude map made around 1600. Walls seems then to have been unimportant. In 1696 James Mitchell, a Scalloway merchant, built the *'Old Haa'* on Vaila, and in 1759 Burrastow House was built on a peninsula 3 km west of Walls. A stone pier was constructed at Walls in the 18th century, and from 1838 the Shetland Fishery Company cured fish there, led by Arthur Anderson who later co-founded the P&O shipping company *(see Lerwick)*. Walls was later reached by a road, crossing the Bridge of Walls in rural Sandsting parish 2 km to the east, and Vaila Hall was greatly extended in the 1890s by Yorkshire millowner Herbert Anderton.

**Bridge, Harbour, Ferries – and Happyhansel**: Walls became the base for the mailboat serving the remote island of Foula, providing a deep water quay and harbour of refuge, and basic medical and commercial facilities. In the 1950s there was also a small primary and secondary school, delightfully named *Happyhansel*. From 1962 Walls on its single-track road became a rural planning *'holding point'*. However, by 1976 the secondary classes had been abandoned, for only about 400 people looked to Walls for services. In the 1980s *Burrastow*

*House* became a tiny luxury hotel and restaurant, and from 1993 long-neglected Vaila Hall was restored to full use by new owners. By 1994 Walls was the terminus of a year-round passenger ferry to Foula, and water-mills had become a tourist attraction in the remote crofting area of Sandness, some 15 km to the north-west, which like Walls has a pier, a primary school and post office.

## WALLYFORD

**Map 15, E2**

***E. Lothian village,*** *pop. 2800* OS 66: NT 3672

Wallyford is about 2 km east of Musselburgh, and 1 km inland, on the fertile lower slopes of Falside Hill. By about 1600 (as Pont's map showed) the Great North Road was in existence, but Wallyford, probably originally a farm beside the Dalkeith to Prestonpans road, was not marked. In 1786 the important St Clement's Wells distillery was opened; this closed in 1833. Margaret Oliphant, born at Wallyford in 1828, became a prolific novelist. The main line of the North British Railway, opened in 1846, passed just north of the hamlet of Wallyford but provided no station. In the late 19th century a rail-connected colliery was sunk beside the track to St Clement's Wells. This led to the growth of Wallyford's population to 675 in 1901 and to 1850 in 1951, with a primary school, post office, garage and inn. Miners' rows were replaced by council houses, but the colliery was soon closed. By 1970 the 47-room *Drummore Motor Inn* had been built at North Berwick Road, near the roundabout where the original A1 was joined by the Dalkeith road. By 1971 there were 2475 residents. By 1986 a new dual-carriageway A1 bypassed Wallyford, whose new railway station was opened in 1994, with trains to Edinburgh and North Berwick. This and the Wallyford sewage disposal works, built around the same time, stimulated the building from 1999 of a private housing estate nearby. The *Motor Inn* has demised, but there is now a garden centre, car showrooms, and the firm Allan & Co who make belts and pulleys on the industrial estate.

## WAMPHRAY & Newton

**Map 2, B3**

***Dumfriesshire small villages,*** *pop. 127* OS 78: NY 1194

The Roman road from Carlisle to the north through Upper Annandale paralleled the River Annan on the east; a standing stone was erected, and later a medieval motte and bailey were formed beside the Wamphray Water. By about 1754 this was crossed by the main road – labelled *'Roman Way'* by Roy – but there was apparently still no bridge until Telford's new road was built in the early 19th century. The Caledonian Railway, which opened in 1848, provided a station at Newton – named Wamphraygate, later shortened to Wamphray – and the Wamphray parish school was erected about 1880 for 138 pupils. A Free Church and post office followed, and in 1901 the parish population was 400. Rural depopulation followed, and the station was closed about 1960. Although by 1963 the little *Red House Hotel* had been recently opened near the A74 at Newton, only 127 residents remained by 1991. With the A74 improved to carry only fast traffic, and recently converted to the A74(M) motorway, this pleasant rural area at the foot of the sheltering hills is seen by most passing travellers as a mere backcloth. The hotel, post office and primary school remain open.

## WANLOCKHEAD

**Map 2, B3**

***N. Dumfriesshire village,*** *pop. 160* OS 71 or 78: NS 8713

Standing about 410m above sea level at the head of the Wanlock Water, a distant tributary of the River Nith, this remote place just over a col from Leadhills became Scotland's highest significant settlement. Its mineral wealth was probably known to the Romans, and lead and silver mines had been reopened by 1264. In the 16th century a little gold was found by lead miners, and Blaeu's mid 17th century engraving of Pont's distorted map of upper Clydesdale included the name *'Waundlokhead'*, but no settlement symbol. The again-deserted lead mines were reopened by the Duke of Buccleuch about 1680 and provided with a smelting mill and workers' houses. Fom 1710 the Loch Nell adit mine, originally a day level, was painfully cut in the hard rock, but by 1730 a water-powered drainage engine was necessary; by 1743 there were five, and also a stamping engine. Roy's map surveyed about 1754 showed a sprawling village. To the east – where its only road led to Leadhills – were the *'Smelting House'*, the *'Whimsy Shaft'* and *'Cove Vein Level'*, and to the west was the *'Great Level'*. Southwards the only connection was the narrow and hair-raising *'Entriken Path'* down to Nithsdale, which Defoe had earlier described in detail as traversing *"a precipice horrible and terrifying"*.

**Library, Lead Smelting and Steam Power**: In 1756 the miners formed a subscription library, following Leadhills' example. A smelt mill began work at Pates Knowes in 1764; a view from about 1775, reproduced by Hay & Stell, showed several beam drainage engines still at work, evidently water-powered. A Watt steam drainage engine was erected at the Bay mine at Wanlockhead by George Symington, the mine engineer, and his son William in 1778–79, with a second in use from 1787. Meantime in 1786 William Symington had designed an improved atmospheric engine, which he patented the next year and successfully used in the pioneer 24-foot Dalswinton Loch steamboat in 1788, and for pumping water from the Bay mine in the 1790s. Heron noted in 1799 *"the village of Wanlockhead, containing about eight hundred inhabitants, where there are considerable smelting-houses for the lead-ore"*. Dorothy Wordsworth reached Wanlockhead in 1803 by way of the new road from Sanquhar which had replaced the Enterkin Pass route. The village then consisted of *"a great number of huts, all alike, and all thatched, with a few larger slated houses among them, and a single modern-built one of a considerable size"*. (Her vivid though technically naive description of what seems to have been one of the Watt mine pumping engines is worth a look.) The mines then belonged to the Duke of Queensberry.

**Last Days of Lead Mining, and a Railway Record**: By 1827 there were five more steam engines, but when the price of lead plummeted from about 1830, the use of steam (which required coal to be carried uphill) was replaced by cheaper water power, such as the Straitsteps Mine engine (also illustrated by Hay & Stell); the Pates Knowes smelt mill was closed in 1842. Wanlockhead was the birthplace in 1850 of poet Robert Reid. The Loch Nell adit mine was closed in 1860; the remaining mines were said to be more productive than those of Leadhills, and in 1891 Wanlockhead had 750 people. The Caledonian branch railway which opened from Elvanfoot in 1902 reached – between Leadhills and Wanlockhead – the highest summit in Britain on the standard gauge, at 457m.

*Lead and silver were mined near Wanlockhead from the 13th century, continuing for 700 years. This little water balance engine was used to drain water from one of the lead veins in the area; it is now in the care of Historic Scotland.* (JRH)

The unprofitable line was an early casualty, closing in 1939. Lead mining continued at Wanlockhead, where a smelting mill was open 2 km downstream, until it was abandoned in the 1930s. Some sources imply a reopening around the time of the 1939–45 war and final closure of the Glencrieff mine in the 1950s; but the Straitsteps water engine remained in place. Wanlockhead survived, though its population was falling.

**Winter Sports and Museum**: A small tourist trade developed, with the Dumfries Skiing club by 1955 and a youth hostel by 1962. The closures had led to the formation of a village council, which set up a trust to run a Museum of Scottish Lead Mining, open by 1974; but the population continued to shrink, and the primary school was closed about 1976, becoming an outdoor centre. By 1986 the Southern Upland Way had been signposted and the shop, post office and bowling green were still maintained. By 1990 the museum – which included the beam engine, Pates Knowes smelt mill and the Loch Nell mine – drew about 30,000 tourists a year, but serious visitors should note that its distinction between Wanlockhead and Leadhills was then vague. At that time the local *'hotel'* (in 1986 comprising huts at the old station) had been taken over by a religious temperance group. The 1991 population was 160. The village council was still active in 1994, though in confrontation with a new community council! The post office and youth hostel remain open, but even before the 2001 foot and mouth scare, falling visitor numbers threatened the museum's future.

## WATERFOOT — Map 15, C6

***Renfrewshire dormitory,*** *pop. 1300* — OS 64: NS 5655

Waterfoot lies 3km north of Eaglesham, where the White Cart Water formed the traditional Renfrew/Lanark county boundary. It existed by about 1600, but in 1895 it was still just a hamlet with a mill, smithy and letter box. It also had the mansion of Brackenrig in its small park; by 1924 this had been renamed Eaglesham House and its park had been doubled in size, though it was to vanish in World War II. No other significant development had occurred by 1924. By 1951 there were over 500 residents, and by 1963 three distinct private housing estates had been built, though there were few or no facilities. The name of Eaglesham House disappeared from the map in the 1980s. The green belt held the main developed areas to a total of 1300 people in 1991 (with two distinctions among Scottish Census *'localities'* of over 1000 people – in having no public authority housing, and the greatest percentage of car commuters, at almost 85% of workers). Clearly among the most affluent young dormitories in the whole country, it still lacks so much as a post office; but the mill still stands.

## WATERNISH, Lochbay, Lusta & Stein — Map 8, A2

***N-W. Skye townships,*** *pop. 100* — OS 23: NG 2656

In the dark ages there was a monastic site at Annait in the remote Vaternish or Waternish peninsula of north-west Skye. Monro noted in 1549 that Waternish was owned by McLeod of Lewis, who alone of the Skye lairds had, it seems, no castle in the area. In 1578 the ancient Trumpan church at its western corner was ruined by clan warfare, and was never rebuilt. Waternish House was built for the Macleods in 1760 on Loch Bay 4km to the north of Annait, and twice remodelled in the 19th century. In 1786 nearby Stein became the first of the three stations of the British Fisheries Society, and by 1802 a tiny pier and Skye's second inn had been built. Stein was connected to Portree by road early in the 19th century, but it was after 1838 that a post office called Waternish was opened in the nearby township of Lusta. Nowhere in Waternish ever grew beyond township status. The Lochbay primary school was closed around the 1960s; in 1978 the Dutch owner of Lochbay sold the crofts to their occupiers. By 1988 about 8 new bungalows had been built above Stein, which was struggling to survive as a sub-aqua resort with a small seafood restaurant, its big house decaying; the area's total resident population was well under 100. The Forestry Commission offers access to a large area of recent afforestation to the east. Waternish House still stood unused and deteriorating in 1995. About 1990 the ancient and neglected inn had been bought by an English speculator; closed when his big plans failed, it had reopened as a pub by 1997. By then the post office had closed, and the only other significant facility in Waternish is the long-established primary school at Knockbreck.

## WATERSIDE — Map 1, C2

***S. Ayrshire community,*** *pop. 100 (area)* — OS 70 or 77: NS 4308

The ruins of a 13th century castle at Keirs, and the undated tower of Laight Castle beside the Dunaskin Burn, overlook the Doon valley 5km below Dalmellington. Between them lies Waterside, which was a ferm toun when Timothy Pont mapped Kyle about 1600. A road had been built up the valley by the time of Roy's survey about 1754. With the (unfulfilled)

*Dunaskin brickworks, Waterside, built in 1936 on the site of the Dalmellington Ironworks. The brickworks closed in 1976; the remains have been preserved by a local Trust.* (JRH)

prospect of service from the Ayrshire & Galloway Railway, the Dalmellington Iron Company – part of the Houldsworth empire *(see Newmains)* – built its works at Waterside in 1845–48; they had to rely on carts for transport. The company erected several ironworkers' rows beside the works, one of the longest containing 30 tiny cottages. About 1850 the Waterside Stores, a large shop to sell necessities to the workers, was added by the proprietors, who soon secured the construction of a branch of the Glasgow & South Western Railway (G&SWR) from Ayr. This opened in 1856 through a station at Waterside to end at Dalmellington village.

**Little Boxes on the Hillside – and Brass Bands**: In 1869 the Dalmellington Ironworks (brass) Band was formed; it still exists as the Dunaskin Doon Silver Band. From about 1870 various high-level mineral railways were laid out by the iron company on the bleak hillside to the east and extending northwards around Bow Hill *(see Rankinston)*, serving small coal and ironstone mines whose workers lived nearby in groups of lengthy miners' rows. The firm built primary schools in two larger hamlets: Lethanhill with its church and satellite of Burnfoothill, 2 km north of the works and 290m above sea level; and Benquhat *(Benwhat)* 3 km to the east, which served the three Corbie Craigs ironstone mines and stood about 30 metres higher still – it too had a brass band by 1871, and also a company store. In 1891 the population of Waterside was over 1200, while its forlorn satellites had a combined population of over 1700. They were soon admitted to be *"without the basic conveniences of life"*, and bleak Benquhat was abandoned as a settlement in the 1920s.

**Ironmaking replaced by Bricks**: The operations of the iron company were well described by Turnock (1982) and illustrated by Hutton (1996); the main incline bringing ore and coal to the furnaces led down at 17% (1 in 6) from Lethanhill to Drumgrange. The works had grown to five furnaces and 42 ha by 1894, when the extensive system of mineral railways spread eastwards over the watershed into the headwaters of the Nith, 10 km from the works. About 1600 people were crowded into Waterside, where the company built a primary school and later an institute; others of the workforce evidently lived in Dalmellington and Patna. The ironworks closed in 1921, and the company was combined with Baird's in 1930, becoming Baird's & Dalmellington Ltd; but many of the local collieries stayed open until at least 1933, when the Drumgrange incline was abandoned. In 1936 the Dunaskin brickworks were built on the site of the former blast furnaces. Waterside's housing was largely cleared in favour of council estates at Patna and Dalmellington. Windswept Lethanhill was obliterated between 1954 and 1962, leaving only memorials on the hillside.

**Closures, Opencast, Restoration and Museum**: Rail passenger services between Dalmellington and Ayr ceased in 1964 thanks to Beeching; about then the former company store became the *Waterside Inn*. What was still widely known as the Dalmellington Iron Company (since 1947 in fact the National Coal Board) retained the lower level sections of its antique private railway system. For some time after 1962 this still linked collieries above Patna, and until 1979 at Pennyvenie near Dalmellington, with British Railways east of the Waterside coal washery. The line was then closed beyond Waterside, where a loading point was built for transferring opencast coal to rail wagons. The brickworks closed in 1976 and became just a depot. In 1988 the railway was reinstated for 3 km to a new opencast coal loading point at Chalmerston, 1 km north of Dalmellington, still active for freight in 1992 when the tiny hamlet of Waterside lost its historic pub. By 1993 the Dalmellington & District Conservation Trust was restoring the ironworks buildings and relics, including the scant remains of the former beam blowing engine, to create a heritage centre at Waterside; this was open by 1998 as an industrial museum.

## WATTEN

**Map 13, B4**

***Small Caithness village**, pop. 640*

OS 2: ND 2454

Numerous ancient brochs stand around the shores of Loch Watten about 15 km west of Wick, and at Bilbster 4 km to the east is a standing stone. This area of gentle terrain was well-settled when mapped by Pont and/or Gordon around 1600; a bridge had been built at the loch's outfall into the Wick River. Roy's map of about 1750 showed Watten Kirk, Bridgend beside the track joining Wick and Thurso, and in the surrounding area many dots indicating scattered settlement. The road was improved by the Commissioners in the early 19th century, and Watten was eventually the focus of nine radial roads. The

*Achingale Mill, Watten, a large oatmeal mill of the early/mid 19th century, built of and roofed with locally-quarried flagstone. Disused since the 1960s, it is still reasonably intact.* (JRH)

Sutherland & Caithness Railway (later part of the Highland system) was opened in 1874, but the station, some 1.5 km north of Watten crossroads, made little impact. The parish population was 1230 in 1901. By the 1930s there was a garage at the crossroads, and east of it a hotel; Watten had a post and telegraph office, and a water mill, still evident in 1956. In 1951 Watten itself had a population of nearly 500, and provided the facilities of a small village to a further 800 or so people within a radius of 5–10 km. The station was closed to passengers in 1960 and to freight in 1964. The hotel – and by 1974 a caravan and camping site 4 km to the west – continued to cater for guests fishing for trout in Loch Watten. Though the 1991 population of the parish was only 641, these facilities and the post office were still open in 1993. A & W Sinclair now work the Stonehouse quarry at Ruther, 4 km north, near which is a covered livestock market built in the 1980s.

## WEISDALE, Hellister & Whiteness — Map 14, B3

***Shetland communities,*** *Pop. 600 (area)* — OS 3: HU 3949

The sea loch known as Weisdale Voe runs deep into the Shetland mainland about 15 km north of Lerwick, and continues northwards beyond Setter as the Valley of Kergord, some 500 m wide but 10 km long. At its south end in the lee of 250 m hills is Weisdale, probably the most sheltered area of the Shetland Isles, with most of their few large trees and the attractive southern style farm of Kergord. Traditionally an area of small farms and crofts, with about 350 people in all, it was transformed in the 1970s by oil wealth. A practically new settlement named Hellister was developed near the head of Weisdale Voe. A small new factory was built there for Shetland Silvercraft, accompanied by a re-sited Weisdale post office cum general merchant, a motor service station, a Scottish Women's Rural Institute and many new houses both public and private. The *Westings Hotel* had been built by 1974 about 4 km to the south (OS 4), at a fine viewpoint overlooking a panorama of cliff-girt islands and peninsulas. Nearby is scattered Whiteness, with its post office shop, jewellery workshops, new public hall and a new primary school opened in 1978, serving a population that had roughly doubled in 10 years due to oil-related housing development. Weisdale mill had become a tourist attraction by 1994.

## WEMYSS BAY & Skelmorlie — Map 5, B5

***Clyde Coast villages,*** *pop. 3400* — OS 63: NS 1968

Skelmorlie Castle, on the west-facing coast of the lower Firth of Clyde in north Cunninghame, dates back to 1502; in 1560 it was the seat of the powerful Earl of Eglinton. Pont's map of Cunninghame made about 1600 showed an area both well wooded and thickly scattered with tiny settlements, some linked by a coastal trackway. By contrast, north of the adjoining Kelly Burn – which formed the boundary with Renfrewshire – there was very little settlement. By about 1754, when the Roy survey was made, a road followed the coast throughout. At that time there was a mill near Skelmorlie castle, but Wemyss Bay north of the burn was still not named (the name Wemyss is derived from the Gaelic for *'Caves'*). In 1865 the Wemyss Bay Railway (WBR), a Caledonian Railway (CR) protégé, opened from Port Glasgow to a terminal station and pier at Wemyss Bay, to serve steamer services to Rothesay and Arran.

**Golf, Hydro, Rich Residents and Palatial Station**: In 1890 a golf club was established at Skelmorlie, laying out an unusual moorland course of 13 holes. The population of Skelmorlie was 950 in 1891; by then the measured *'Skelmorlie Mile'* was in use offshore for steamer speed tests. By 1894 Skelmorlie also had what Murray called a *"good, well-situated"* hydropathic establishment and an inn; it was *"a quiet but fashionable watering-place with handsome villas"*. The *"small, good" Wemyss Bay Hotel* was adjoined by *"large villas"* occupied by such affluent personages as the Chairman of Cunard and the veteran *'Paraffin'* Young of Bathgate and Uphall fame. The Kelly Dam had been built and there was also at one time a quarry, perhaps the source of stone for villa construction. In 1893 the WBR was absorbed by the CR. In 1903 the station was very attractively rebuilt to designs by James Miller and Donald Mathieson, its buildings curving onto the pier, from which steamers served many Clyde resorts; in 1904 steamers also plied twice a day to Ardrishaig via the Kyles of Bute and Tarbert. Electricity was first supplied to Skelmorlie from a local power station built in 1910. From 1929 the CR's successor the LMS Railway used Albion buses on a service filling the rail gaps between Greenock, Gourock, Wemyss Bay and Largs.

**Electric Trains, Roll-on Ferries – and *'Vanish'***: By 1951 there were at least four AA-standard hotels, including the *Manor Park*. The otherwise typical village facilities served a population of nearly 1800 in the two merging settlements; there were year-round car-carrying ferry sailings to Rothesay and Largs, plus various summer services. By 1963 the ancient Skelmorlie Castle had been restored. The railway was electrified in 1967, essentially only for passenger services, and about then a roll-on, roll-off ferry was introduced to Rothesay. Despite the rather overpowering presence of the giant chimney of the Inverkip power station (completed in 1976 only 2 km north of the pier), Wemyss Bay and Skelmorlie were still of dormitory character in 1981, served by village facilities. In the early 1980s a small Skelmorlie firm pioneered a new type of cleaning soap, *Vanish*; but by 1993 products of this brand came instead from Swindon. In 1991 the combined settlements shared 3371 people almost equally. There were also two caravan and camping sites, although by 1994 the Wemyss Bay site

*Wemyss Bay station. The railway arrived from Glasgow in 1865, and the station was rebuilt in 1903 to cope with the very large numbers of people transferring from trains to the steamers berthing at the adjacent pier.* (JRH)

had closed. More housing has been built immediately south of the now disused power station. For local government purposes, Wemyss Bay is in Inverclyde and Skelmorlie is in N. Ayrshire. Though the largest and finest of the marine villas have gone, there are still some splendid houses, both on the shore line and on the cliff tops above. Small-villa building in recent years has not affected this core character, and the Glasgow and Greenock men who built the Victorian villas would still recognise the places.

## WEST BURRAFIRTH & Papa Stour (Isle of)

**Map 14, B3**

***N. Shetland communities,*** *pop. under 100* — OS 3: HU 2556

A prehistoric broch and other ancient remains are found in the sheltered inlet of West Burrafirth, some 10km north of Walls. Until a generation ago this was an area of a few scattered crofts. However, around 1980 a new pier was built, which became the base for half a dozen creel boats. It was enlarged about 1985 as the terminus of a new passenger ferry to the small island of Papa Stour, which has many prehistoric remains and had 33 residents in 1991; it now has an airstrip, a post office and primary school, lately with 3 pupils.

## WEST CALDER & Polbeth

**Map 16, C4**

***W. Lothian town & village,*** *pop. 5300* — OS 65: NT 0163

West Calder stands about 180 metres above sea level south of the convergence of the various headwaters of the River Almond, an area of upland farms and mosses. Pont's map of Lothian made about 1600 showed West Calder as *'The Cappel'*, probably a chapel of the original kirk of (East) Calder; the area was then roadless. When Roy's map was surveyed about 1754, West Calder was a hamlet on the Edinburgh to Lanark road. It was described by Heron in 1799 as *"an inconsiderable place"*; even as late as 1838 there was no post office. However, in 1804 the fine villa of Limefield House was built at Polbeth, 2 km east of the hamlet. In 1865 the house and estate were bought by James *'Paraffin'* Young *(see Bathgate)*.

**Railways, and Oil from Shale**: The oil shale works of the West Calder Oil Company (of Fell and others) opened in 1863 at Gavieside, north-east of the emergent village. Taking advantage of the North British Railway's branch line which was opened through Whitburn in 1864, mineral railways were laid from West Foulshiels south of Whitburn to Addiewell, and extended to connect with the West Calder installations. By 1872 200 men were employed in its nearby shale and coal pits, while another 200 or more in the works refined 4.5 million litres of oil a year. This process polluted the river, leading local landowners to obtaining an injunction against the firm, which collapsed in 1878, its assets being bought by *'Paraffin'* Young's company. Other such companies active locally in the 1860s included Westwood, and the Hermand Company on the estate of that name. Meantime in 1869 the Caledonian Railway's Cleland and Midcalder branch had brought a station to West Calder, where many houses were built by Young, also serving his Addiewell works. The West Calder Co-operative Society was founded in 1875, creating the main shopping centre for a whole cluster of small shale-mining and processing places. The Hermand quarry worked between at least 1883 and 1896, when 14 were employed.

*The Westwood shale-oil works, West Calder, in the 1940s. They were built in 1938–41 as a large and efficient works. The huge shale-heating retorts are at the back middle of the picture, with the conveyor gantry leading to them. This works closed in 1962.* *(Scottish Oils)*

**Gas, Golf, and Lorries**: In 1894 Murray stated *"the small town has grown rapidly in consequence of Young's large paraffin works"*. Although West Calder streets had been lit by gas from Young's Addiewell works since the 1860s, a town gasworks was rather remarkably established in 1891. In 1901 the population was 2650, and a public library was commenced, with Carnegie aid, from 1902. By then the area was littered with old shafts and shale mines linked by mineral railways. In 1913 the successful West Calder Co-op, which gradually absorbed most other such societies in the area, built a new store in the main street; it still stands. Harburn golf club, founded in 1921, laid out and planted an 18-hole course on the moors 3 km from West Calder, near the very rural Harburn station on the Caledonian line to Carstairs; there was also at one time a Harburn primary school. In the early 1930s the Caledonian's successors the LMS bought the road hauliers Wordie *(see Stirling)*, who in turn bought the 17-lorry West Calder transport business of John Russell & Son.

**More Oil, Explosive Shale, and Polbeth Village**: In 1938–41 another large and efficient oil works was built beside an existing shale-mine at Westwood, 1 km north-west of West Calder; it processed 1200 tonnes of shale a day. The waste was tipped to form the unusual group of conical bings known as the Five Sisters, the last shale bings to be created in Scotland. In 1947 an explosion wrecked the Burn Grange oil shale mine, sadly killing 15 men in the shale industry's worst disaster. By the 1950s there was also a limestone quarry, and Midlothian County Council had built a substantial new settlement with a post office at Polbeth, 1 km to the east. Limefield House was donated to the public by James Young's grand-daughter, and from 1954 was an old folk's home. In 1962 all the surviving oil works and shale pits were closed by then owners BP, leaving horrendous landscape dereliction to north and west of the village; much remained as recently as 1988.

**Making a Virtue of Necessity?**: By 1971 West Calder High School had been relocated at Polbeth, where by 1977 Daks-Simpson of Larkhall were making clothing in an advance factory. In 1978 a new telephone exchange was opened at West Calder for 1300 subscribers in the area, which by then had small-town facilities and a total population of 6500. By 1988 some more residential development had taken place at West Calder. However, from 1990 Limefield House stood vacant. In 1991 West Calder itself held 2888 people, while there were 2352 residents in Polbeth. Though some people thought the Five Sisters bing was an eyesore, the District Council intended in 1992 to preserve it, and introduce tourist facilities there; it is now an ancient monument. In 1996 Freeport Leisure was to open a retail centre or *'village'* at Westwood, and hoping to expand it greatly into the leisure field. By 1998 little other new development was evident, other than the ever expanding tentacles of Livingston, but the largest bing west of the village had been reclaimed. Sadly in 2000 Daks-Simpson closed their Polbeth operation with the loss of 260 jobs, but Mulholland (civil engineers) and Watson (construction) are large local concerns.

## WESTFIELD

**Map 16, B3**

***W. Lothian hamlet**, pop. 500*

OS 65: NS 9372

The large 14th century Bridge Castle lies in the valley of the little Logie Water about 4 km north-west of Bathgate. Pont's map of Lothian made about 1600 showed *'Straith'* mill on the Avon just west of the confluence. By the time that Roy surveyed the area about 1754 it had a fairly comprehensive road system either side of the Avon. The Westfield paper mill was established on the Logie Water 1 km to the north of the castle, possibly as early as 1834. In 1855 the Slamannan Railway opened a branch from Blackstone near Avonbridge, following the valley and crossing the river by a viaduct north of Westfield station, en route to a junction with the North British Railway at Bathgate. This passed beside the mill, which by 1860 was under Daniel Ferguson and had two papermaking machines. The area was still rural in 1895.

**Labels in Fifty-seven Varieties?**: The paper mill was later enlarged and connected to the railway, but in the 1920s only three trains a day called at Westfield station. By 1953 the line had been closed to passengers; in 1955 Westfield was just a small village with a post office and primary school. In later years Westfield held a steady population of some 700, though with only basic facilities. The railway was later closed to freight and the track had been lifted by 1971, leaving only the viaduct. By 1973 Bridge Castle was a hotel, but this use lasted only a decade or so. By 1980 the paper mill was owned by Inveresk; it survived the group's failure, purchase and management buy-out. In 1991, when Westfield's population was below 500, the mill was improved; its 200 or so workers made labels and wrapping-paper for the food industries of 57 countries, exporting 55% of its output. The Finnish-owned firm Ewos produces fish feed with a workforce of 70. There has been little other new development, but the post office and the *Logievale Inn* are still open.

## WESTHILL, Skene & Elrick

**Map 10, B3**

***Aberdeenshire 'new town'**, pop. 8500+*

OS 38: NJ 8307

Neither Pont's map made about 1600 nor the later Roy map showed anything of significance between Brimmond Hill and the Kirkton of Skene, which is 12 km west of Aberdeen and then stood beside a track to Castle Fraser and Alford. By 1805 there was a post office at Tulloch on the slopes of Brimmond Hill. Later a new sub-parallel road was built a little to the south, on which the hamlet of Elrick, some 2 km east of the Kirkton, developed very slowly. It had a post office by the 1890s, an 80-pupil secondary school by the 1950s and although the secondary classes had gone by 1976, an inn and caravan site had been added by 1971. Westhill, 1.5 km east of Elrick on the original road, was then little more than a tiny crossroads with a primary school in an area of scattered development; the total population in the Skene area was about 1000.

**New Village, Oil, and Major Companies**: In the mid 1970s extreme pressure on the Aberdeen housing market from North Sea oil work led to a plan for the rapid development of Westhill (which from 1975 was in the new Gordon District) into a new dormitory village based on car commuting. Westhill golf club, founded in 1977, provided an 18-hole course of parkland and moorland. The new settlement had over 5000 people by 1981, with new facilities including the Westhill Academy, the 48-roomed *Westhill Hotel*, a garage and post office. By 1985 the Elrick caravan site had closed, but Westhill had embraced Elrick in some 3 square kilometres of development. Oil-related subsea contractor Stena Offshore moved its 100 staff to Westhill in 1988; by 1994, 400 of its worldwide total of 1100 employees were based there, and a single new building was proposed. The Stewart Milne group, largest private construction firm in the Grampian Region, also chose Westhill. In 1993 Wellgrove Timber Systems of Westhill rivalled Donaldson of Leven with claims to lead Scotland in timber engineering.

**Quarry Headquarters and New Facilities**: John Fyfe Construction, originally of Kemnay, moved its headquarters to Fyfe House on the Westhill industrial estate in the 1980s; by 1995 the firm had some 75 production locations and depots throughout Scotland. In 1991 Westhill was a youthful and well-educated dormitory, its 8450 residents enjoying a new swimming pool, and a shopping centre with a Norco superstore (sold to Safeway in 1992), a community centre, police station, bank, and a veterinary practice. By 1995 tennis courts, bowling green, park and library were open at Westhill, which has continued to grow into a virtual new town. The original school is now used by a pre-school playgroup, since at least two new primary schools have been built. Tiny Kirkton of Skene has little more than its inn, primary school, and a licensed grocer. A recent *Premier Lodge* has added to the existing *Westhill Hotel*. Milne's factory now produces 6000 timber housing-frames a year.

## WEST KILBRIDE & Seamill

**Map 1, B1**

***N. Ayrshire coastal small town,*** *pop. 4500* OS 63: NS 2048

An ancient fort, a dun and the large 14th century keep of Portencross Castle stand on the Firth of Clyde promontory of Farland Head. Law Castle, another keep 4 km inland, and the vestigial Tarbet Castle nearby both date from the 15th century and appeared with some emphasis on Pont's map of Cunninghame, made about 1600; nearby the little Crosbie Burn enters the sea. The parish centre of *'Kilbryd'* 1.5 km inland and nearby *'Seamil'* on the coast were both then tiny places among many others in the area. West Kilbride started a parish school in 1603, but this was in abeyance in 1696. By about 1754, when the Roy map was surveyed, a coastal road had been made; there was a mill at Seamill, but *'Killbride'* was just a hamlet. In the late 18th century much local flax was spun and woven by hand, and sold at an annual market; most was then exported to the West Indies. The settlement which had grown up near Law Castle and the church was described as a *"village"* by Heron in 1799. Millstones were made by 1810, and a post office was open by 1838; in the 1840s there were about a hundred handloom weavers.

**Railway and Dormitory Development**: The Glasgow & South Western Railway reached West Kilbride in 1878 en route to Largs. In 1891 the population was 1600, and a gasworks was set up the following year. West Kilbride golf club, founded in 1893, laid out an 18-hole course on the links north of nearby Seamill, still a distinct hamlet with a mill; Murray noted it in 1894 as *"somewhat of a summer resort"*. At that time both places had post and telegraph offices, and West Kilbride – by then a select dormitory – had an inn. By 1951 there was a population of 3800, enjoying the facilities of a major village or small town with six hotels, notably the 55-room *Seamill Hydro*. By 1981 there were nine hotels. Some development continued in the 1980s, anticipating the electrification of the railway in 1987. In 1991, 4488 people lived in West Kilbride village, with an affluent retired character. Portencross Castle stands awaiting a user, as it has for many years.

## WEST LINTON

**Map 2, B1**

***Village, s-w. of Penicuik,*** *pop. 1500* OS 72 (or 65): NT 1552

Many ancient hill forts stand above the Lyne Water, a northern tributary of the River Tweed, which was crossed by a first century Roman road paralleling the Pentland Hills, connecting the upper Clyde Valley with Inveresk. West Linton is 1 km north of this road, where the Lyne Water emerges from the Pentland Hills – a Royal forest in the 12th century. Once known as *Lintoun Roderick*, it was the birthplace about 1270 of Bernard of Lintoun, who drafted Scotland's famed Declaration of Arbroath in fine style. Linton was chartered as a burgh of barony in 1306. One of the oldest places in Scotland essentially set up as a market, there seems to be no record of a castle; instead it acquired an intricate medieval street pattern. Pont's Tweeddale map of around 1600 showed a watermill upstream of the village of *'Lintoun'*, and Romanno Mill on the Lyne near the Kirk of Newland. The road by then linking Edinburgh with West Linton may already have continued as far as Dolphinton, but there were apparently no bridges. In 1602 the Linton parish school was founded.

**Monuments, Turnpikes, Droving and Weaving**: From 1666 Linton was well known for its laird, a tombstone carver named Gifford; his art became an important local craft. The Roy survey made about 1754 showed *'Lintoun'* as a compact settlement on a north–south axis, already having six radial routes. The name *'Brigghouse'* shows that by then a bridge spanned the Lyne on the *'Road from Moffat, Bigger, and Lintoun to Edinburgh'*. There was also a bridge 4 km north of Lintoun at *'Carlops Turnpike'*. It was there that Carlops was established as a weaving village in 1784, but though in 1792 it acquired the *Allan Ramsay* inn, the settlement remained tiny. From about the time that West Linton post office was opened in 1765 it also lay on the droving route across the Pentland Hills between the Falkirk Tryst and the Tweed valley. By 1797 West Linton had an annual fair, and was a minor post town with a service only two days a week. Heron in 1799 mentioned *"the village of Linton, near which are found fullers' earth, both red and white free-stone, limestone, and a mineral spring"*. According to Chambers, in 1827 there were *"always great quantities of sheep for sale at the annual markets"* in June and July at West Linton, which was *"inhabited chiefly by weavers, shoemakers, and other mechanics"* – a term for artisans in general.

**Railway Interlude and Hotel**: 1864 saw the opening of a rambling branch railway between Leadburn and Dolphinton, serving West Linton through a station 1 km to the south, later called Broomlee. West Linton was never industrialised; its golf club, founded in 1890, provided an 18-hole moorland course. In 1894, when the population was about 400, according to Murray there were two hotels, the *"clean" Mowbray's* and the unqualified *Linton*, leaving the distinct impression that maybe the latter's hygiene was in doubt! The railway did not survive the growth in bus services and the great depression, losing passenger trains in 1933 and being lifted by 1953. However, by 1953 the Baddinsgill Reservoir had been impounded in the Pentland Hills 4 km to the north, soon followed by the West Water Reservoir 3 km to the west. When confidence returned, a substantial new roadhouse hotel was built on the main road in the late 1930s, when the population passed the thousand mark. By the 1950s West Linton had the facilities of a large village, with a 150-pupil junior secondary school – although that had been closed by 1976.

**Handicapped Children and Professional Dormitory**: The Broomlee Residential School, 1.5 km south of the village, had 220 pupils in 1971; by 1987 it had become the Broomlee Centre. The remote hamlet of Blyth Bridge was by 1976 the site of a residential school for physically handicapped children; its own Kirkurd primary school was however closed in 1985. West Linton had become something of a dormitory in the 1970s, particularly for long-distance car commuters to Edinburgh, and had declined in facilities to average village status by 1981. The 1930s hotel, by then known as the *Linton Roderick*, was demolished in the 1980s and its site used for upmarket housing. In 1991 Linton's 1157 residents contained three times the national figure with higher qualifications; it was very much an affluent dormitory, clearly related to the Edinburgh universities and the intervening research parks. In the late 1990s still more select housing was built north-east of the village, which has a primary school, post office and bookshop, plus 3 small hotels. The old inn at Carlops, and Newlands primary school at Romanno Bridge, both remain open.

## WESTRUTHER

**Map 3, B3**

***Small Borders village,*** *pop. 225* — OS 74: NT 6350

The tower houses of Wedderlie and Evelaw were built in the 16th century at the high altitude of 245 m, near the head of the Blackadder Water, about 12 km east of Lauder. About 4 km west of Wedderly at a similar height was the ancient House of Spottiswood, shown emparked when Pont mapped Lauderdale around 1600. His Berwickshire map showed tiny *'Oustruther'*, which stands on rather marginal farmland at an altitude of some 215 m between Wedderly and Spottiswood. As late as the 1750s the Roy map showed Spottiswood as a mansionhouse in a trackless area. In the early 19th century its old tower was incorporated into a new mansion designed by William Burn. The parish held 500 people in 1901, when Westruther was a small village with a post and telegraph office, an inn and a smithy. Spottiswood was sadly demolished about 1928. In 1951 Westruther's 400 people were served by basic facilities, but severe decline continued; by 1976 there were no buses, and the primary school was marginal. It is still open, even though by 1991 the parish held only 221 people, and this, the pub and the church ruins distinguish Westruther from other remote hamlets.

## WEST WEMYSS

**Map 6, B4**

***Fife coastal village,*** *pop. 300* — OS 59: NT 3294

Wemyss Castle stands boldly between two ravines on a cliff-top site on the Fife coast, 3 km north-east of Dysart. Pronounced *'Weems'*, its name derives from the Gaelic for *Cave*, several of which are found in the local cliffs and show evidence of ancient occupation. The castle existed by the 12th century, was shown on the early Gough map, and was rebuilt in stone from 1250 and again in the 15th century. Coal mining was recorded on the Wemyss estate by 1428. West Wemyss, a coastal site just west of the castle, became a burgh of barony in 1511 and acquired a tolbooth with a prominent tower. By 1557 a nearby coal working reached 4 m below sea level. Pont's map made about 1600 showed only tiny symbols for *'West Weemis'* and on the coast to the west the *'Chapel of Weems'*, where ancient towers survive. Around 1600 George Hay built Scotland's first glassworks – in a cave, probably just east of the castle – but the works later became ruinous. James Gordon's map of about 1642 noted *'Weemistoun'* between the earlier settlements. Large extensions designed by Mylne were added to the castle about 1670, when it was also modernised; an extensive series of gardens were enclosed by one of the longest systems of tall brick walls in Scotland.

**Coal Exports and Shipbuilding**: A breakwater was shown on John May's chart of about 1680; soon Earl David Wemyss commissioned a proper harbour basin. By 1692 a stone tower on the cliff just west of the castle served a windpump draining an adit mine, and West Wemyss exported coal and locally-produced salt; local craftsmen carved *cannel coal* into ornaments. The high-walled churchyard and probably the church appear to date from 1703. In the 1720s Defoe described West Wemyss as a *"small town"* where the cliff-top coast road linking Dysart with Leven passed close beside the north side of the castle; the Roy map surveyed about 1750 showed a substantial settlement at the foot of the cliffs. By 1795 a local coal mine had an engine, and 6000 tons of coal a year was being exported across the North Sea; an annual fair was scheduled for 1797. Two years later Heron called West Wemyss a *"village of over 700 people"*, where shipbuilding was carried on.

**Coal, Salt and Squalor, and *Cutty Sark***: The *Wemyss Arms* inn was built in 1802, and a new coast road (on the current alignment) was defined in a turnpike Act of 1807; although not yet gated by 1827, this road passed through the hamlet of Coaltown, 1 km inland. A small and squalid coal pit was sunk early in the century on the shore 850 m north-west of the castle; it was renamed Victoria in 1837 and a number of local men met their end there in various sad accidents. Chambers found West Wemyss in 1827 *"the most ruinous town in Fife, a long street of dingy houses, overspread with smoke, and paved with dark oily mud"*. But it had *"many salt-pans, and a harbour much resorted to for the shipping of coal"*, while the emparked Wemyss Castle had become *"a splendid modern mansion"*. The maritime tradition of West Wemyss bred Captain Moodie – first master of the clipper ship *Cutty Sark*, famous from 1869 – and many other 19th century shipmasters.

**Railway, Sumptuous Mansion and School of Needlework**: The Wemyss family coal company remained highly profitable, and Wemyss Castle was again rebuilt in 1876 as a *"sumptuous mansion"*. Around that time the headgear of the two shafts of the Victoria pit stood on the raised beach beside and west of the harbour. The Wemyss School of Needlework operated from 1877 until the 1940s, sewing many a fine seam and embroidering to perfection, but then became more of an informal museum. In 1879 the Earl of Wemyss opened a railway between Thornton and Buckhaven; ten years later it became part of the North British (NBR). It served the inland Lady Lilian (later Lochhead) colliery, sunk in the early 1890s east of West Wemyss station on Standing Stanes Road (now A915) to work the 7 m thick Dysart Main seam, and linked to the Victoria pit. The 1891 population of West Wemyss was 1300; it had a gas works, a coastguard station and a post and telegraph office. Coaltown also had a post office, and both places gained primary schools.

**Model Village, Private Railway and Drift Mine**: Coaltown was being pleasantly rebuilt as an model estate mining village, to designs by Alexander Tod, whose descendants are still keenly involved in these villages in this and other roles. The Lochhead pit was itself modernised around 1900 when a new

*The tolbooth of West Wemyss.* *(JRH)*

mineral line, the Wemyss Private Railway, linked the twin pits with the Hugo depot at Coaltown, the NBR, and also to the harbour through a tunnel. From 1904 the unusual Earlseat Mine was created north of the Standing Stanes Road, with five adits to the Dysart Main seam; abandoned in 1926, it was recreated by the National Coal Board (NCB) and worked from 1951 to 1958.

**Tramways, Boatbuilding and Decline**: From 1906 until 1932 the single-deck electric cars of the Wemyss & District Tramway Company connected Coaltown with East Wemyss and Leven, and until 1931 with Kirkcaldy via a cross-country line to Gallatown. The *Earl David* inn at Coaltown was opened in 1911 and its miners' institute in 1925; another was built at West Wemyss. As late as 1919 the term *'barony burgh'* was still in use locally to describe West Wemyss, where Willie Burns built a series of yawls in the 1930s. The Victoria pit ceased work some time after 1935, and some of the Castle's Victorian additions were cut down from 1953. West Wemyss station was closed to passengers in 1955 and to goods in 1963. During the 1960s the silted-up dock basin was largely infilled by Coal Board tipping, and while parts of the ancient village were gradually conserved, many other estate houses were sadly blocked up. Lochhead Colliery still worked, and the Wemyss Private Railway used steam locomotives, until both were closed by the NCB in 1970; most surface evidence of both was quickly removed. West Wemyss school was closed and later demolished, while the village shops closed one by one.

**A French Start to Tourism – and Bathrooms Galore**: In the late 1970s the estate pleasingly converted the former Miners' Welfare Institute at West Wemyss, with its fine coastal view and panorama of the Forth, into the small *Belvedere Hotel*, for a time offering French cuisine based in the family's lands in France. Wemyss Castle has been in the same family since the 12th century, its chatelaine for many years the redoubtable motoring centenarian Lady Victoria Wemyss, who died in 1994. In 1995 Michael Wemyss and family could still choose from 17 rooms and 15 bathrooms. The *Earl David Hotel* at Coaltown was modernised in 1995. The tiny harbour was brought back to life for inshore fishing in the mid 1990s by the West Wemyss Boat Club, and a new section of sea wall was built on the site of the gas works. The radical restoration of the derelict houses on the shore (by Fife Historic Buildings Trust and the estate) is practically complete, and more new sea walls are under construction.

## WHITBURN

**Map 16, B4**

***W. Lothian town,*** *pop. 11,500* OS 65: NS 9465

*'Whytburns'* appeared as a small place on Timothy Pont's map dating from about 1600. It stands 5 km south-west of Bathgate in West Lothian at an altitude of over 170 m, and was then well away from the area's early east–west roads. Roy's survey made about 1754 showed Whitburn as a small crossroads settlement on the Edinburgh–Glasgow road via Kirk of Shotts, which was turnpiked under an Act of 1753. The first post office in Whitburn opened in 1786; by 1797 it was a post town with mails three days a week, soon handling the post for the Shotts ironworks. In 1799 Heron referred to Whitburn as a *"village"* of about 500 people, with a cotton manufactory; several people were *"employed in flowering muslins"*. From 1864 East Whitburn was served by a branch of the North British Railway connecting Bathgate and Wishaw, but the station was inconveniently remote from Whitburn village, which long remained quite rural, although by 1891 the population was almost 1200 and it did possess an inn; eventually it became a police burgh.

**Miners take home the Grime**: The large Polkemmet Colliery was sunk in the years 1913–22, connected by mineral railway with an earlier mine south of Harthill and so to the Fauldhouse area; like fifty or so other mines in Scotland it did not have pithead baths until about 1930. In the 1920s the A8 trunk road traffic was diverted from the village onto a new main road via Broxburn. By 1931 the population of Whitburn had risen to 2440. Whitburn continued to grow to over 6000 people by 1951, when another small mine was open to the north. The Whitrigg Colliery near East Whitburn was still working as a fireclay mine in 1966. The general facilities of a village were available, plus two cinemas, though TV closed them by 1970. By 1953 East Whitburn station had closed to passengers, and by 1971 the whole line had been lifted. Polkemmet Colliery was rebuilt in the 1950s to produce coal for South of Scotland Electricity Board (SSEB) power stations, and by 1977 employed 1440 men. The M8 motorway built in the late 1960s had bypassed the town by 1971. By 1979 Levi Strauss had an overall factory, and in 1980 Whitburn Coachbuilders were busy at the Croftmalloch Works. By then the 76-bed Tippethill Hospital provided for geriatric cases.

**Whitburn from Apogee to Nadir**: By 1981 though the fireclay mine was disused, the small mine near the hospital was still open, and Whitburn had grown to well over 12,000 people, mainly living in council houses. Despite the closures, its general facilities had been greatly enhanced over the previous 30 years, to those of a small town. Polkemmet Colliery then employed some 2000 men and was the last deep mine in West Lothian, working coking coal in the Limestone Coal Group; for many years this was used at the Ravenscraig steelworks. During the bitter miners' strike of 1984–85, the Polkemmet colliery became flooded, worsening unemployment in an area already reeling from the Bathgate *(q.v.)* closure. Some local people even claimed that its managers had done this deliberately to ensure its immediate closure.

**Golf, Fire and Diagnosis**: By 1988 the Polkemmet country park with its 9-hole golf course had been created 2 km west of the village centre. However the huge bing had caught fire in 1985; it burned again for over six months in 1988–89, with resulting ill-health in Whitburn, and was still unrestored in 1998. In 1991 the population was 11,511, leaving 14% male unemployment. By then Diagnostic Instruments of Whitburn made portable instrumentation systems. By 1998 a caravan site was open at East Whitburn, where there was also some new housing. The Levi Strauss factory employed 630 workers in 1996, but in 1999, due to the undercutting of its carefully cultivated brand image by the supermarkets, the factory was rapidly run down and closed. Industrial cleaners Able, a chicken packery, HBM construction and two vehicle hire firms still provide work; Tippethill Hospital, despite concerns, remains open. Remarkably for a small industrial town with problems, the 31-roomed *Hilcroft*, a business hotel in East Main Street, employs over 50 people. The local Whitburn Academy school has over 1000 pupils.

## WHITECROSS, Manuel & Causewayend

**Map 16, C3**

***Village w. of Linlithgow**, pop. 875*

OS 65: NS 9676

The Bernardine Convent of Emmanuel was founded on the banks of the River Avon 4 km west of Linlithgow by Malcolm IV in 1156, hence the name Manuel. Nearby was built the 15th century keep of Almond Castle, or *'Hanings Castell'* as it was labelled on Pont's map of Stirlingshire, made about 1600. The nunnery, which was still functioning as late as 1552, was labelled as *'Abbey of Manwall'*: an unnamed mill adjoined, and *'Kenilstoun'* (Kettlestone) mill stood on the opposite bank. The Roy map made about 1754 named *Inmarril Abbey*, by then in ruins adjoining the Linlithgow to Airdrie road; erosion by the river subsequently swept away most of the remains, and the wide area to the west became Muiravonside parish. Tod's Mill, on the River Almond to the east, ground flints in the late 18th century. Rather unusually, though far from unique in Scotland, there was also an ancient windmill nearby, though by 1899 it had no sails.

**Canal, Railways and Varied Industry**: The Union Canal was cut through the area in 1817–22, crossing the Avon by the fine stone aqueduct of twelve arches illustrated by Hay & Stell, and from 1840 coal was transhipped into canal barges at Causewayend Basin near Almond from the then new 4'6" gauge Slamannan Railway. The Edinburgh & Glasgow Railway (E&G) passed through the area from 1842, crossing another viaduct. In 1849–51 the Slamannan line (recently converted to standard gauge) was extended from Causewayend, passing beneath the E&G to Bo'ness, and also directly connecting with the main line at Manuel Junction. Firebricks were made at Birkhill beside this line between about 1855 and 1910; by 1899 the small Almond Ironworks at Causewayend were connected to further mineral lines from various coal pits south of Polmont. Around that time Tod's mill ground sawdust from Bo'ness sawmills into wood flour for Fife linoleum manufacture. However, there was no village in the area as recently as 1895, and although a post office was open by 1924 the ironworks had disappeared. The Birkhill fireclay mines were developed further in 1910–16 by P & M Hurll of Glenboig *(q.v.)*, to which place the clay was taken by rail.

**Firebricks**: John G Stein & Co's large rail-connected Manuel firebrick works were built beside the castle ruins in 1928–30. Despite firing up in a slump, G & R Stein (as they were later known) grew into a leading maker of refractories. The village of Whitecross with a population of over 1000 had been built immediately south of Manuel station by 1931. By the 1950s it held nearly 1400 people but had minimal facilities; the station ceased to be a passenger junction in 1956 and was closed about 1965. By 1971 the original Slamannan railway had been lifted, and Whitecross was declining in population.

**Tourism Underground – and back on the Canal?**: The Birkhill fireclay mine closed in 1980 but was reopened to tourists in 1989 when the railway from Bo'ness was reinstated to that point by the Scottish Railway Preservation Society, which also soon completed a reconnection with British Rail. By 1989 Stein's had installed the World's longest tunnel kilns (over 200 m) and exported to more than 140 countries: 610 workers were then employed, but by 1991 only 873 people lived in Whitecross. In 1990 the Manuel works made refractory products for the iron and steel and other heat process industries; they are now *'Premier Refractories'*. There has been little new development, but the primary school, pub and post office are still open; the canal is to reopen fully as a through route in 2001.

## WHITEHILLS

**Map 10, B1**

***Banff village**, pop. 1000*

OS 29: NJ 6565

The ancient Boyndie church stood near the mouth of the Burn of Boyndie 2 km west of Banff, but was superseded by another at Nether Dallachy, 2 km farther west. On the low but rocky coast between these churches was a small bay, a virgin site sheltered from the east by the modest Knock Head. Whitehills was founded there in 1681 as a fishing village. It began slowly, for at the time of Roy's survey made about 1750 there was just a tiny village and fishing harbour, and only a coastal track; but at least four watermills already turned on the burn. From about 1780 a small brick and tile works promoted by a Doctor Saunders was in business at Blackpots north of the village; its own tiny harbour to the east of Knock Head was used to import coal and export its products, which from about 1840 included drainage tiles *(see Hay & Stell)*. Inverboyndie distillery was set up in 1824 at the Mill of Banff, one of those on the Burn of Boyndie. No post office was opened at Whitehills until after 1838, and the small Ladysbridge railway station which opened on the new Banff branch in 1859 was 2 km inland.

**New Distillery, Fishing Peak, and no more Bricks**: In 1863 the distillery was rebuilt on a larger scale on a new site adjacent to the railway, and renamed *'Banff'* although having its own *'Boyndie siding'*. It was burned down in 1877, but again rebuilt to use steam and water power to produce 900,000 litres of Highland malt whisky annually. It was accompanied from 1866 by the *Ladysbridge Asylum*. Fishing development at Whitehills proceeded apace; a lifeboat station was opened in 1860, and by 1880 no fewer than 158 boats filled the tiny harbour. This seems to have been the peak, for in 1890 Whitehills owned under 100 boats, although it was still almost as important for fishing as Macduff. The 1891 population was 1100. A new harbour completed in 1900 was still the base for 65 boats in 1929. Banff distillery suffered from German bombs in the 1940s, but later resumed production.

**No Whisky, but Fish come to the Door**: By 1951 there was a small secondary school and the population total was unchanged, though the general facilities were only those of a small village. The brick and tile works was modernised in 1953, but remained small, employing only 11 men in 1971, and was closed about 1975. The school's secondary classes ceased in the 1960s and the lifeboat station was closed in 1969. By 1981 Ladysbridge Asylum had been redesignated as a 568-bed Mental Deficiency Hospital. The unlucky distillery was disused in 1976, closed in 1983 and finally demolished in 1988; by then Whitehills still had around two dozen fishing boats, mostly over 10m, a regular fish market, five fish merchants and a 60-year tradition of delivering white fish throughout the Grampian Region. The former brick works site became a caravan park about 1987. The village population had scarcely fallen, and in 1991 was 971. Little more housing has been built. Whitehills harbour combines pleasure sailing and fishing, aided by a fish seller, a substantial fish packer, savoury foods producer and a chandlery. General services include a primary school, library, post office, a few shops, and a coach operator and builder – and there's the *Banff Links Hotel* near Inverboyndie.

## WHITEINCH & Scotstoun

**Map 15, C5**

*W. parts of Glasgow, pop. 13,000*

OS 64: NS 5367

Scotstoun stands on the north bank of the Clyde 8km west of Glasgow; it was shown on Pont's map of Lennox made about 1600. Whiteinch, a little to the east and also now on the north side of the river, was an actual island in 1654. Early in the 18th century Scotstoun House was built beside the Clyde; it was enlarged in 1825. By about 1754 there was a road from Glasgow to Dumbarton. Urban development at Whiteinch began as late as 1826, when William Simons of Greenock opened the Jordanvale shipyard, building ferries, dredgers and hopper barges. The firm moved to Renfrew *(q.v.)* in 1860, after which the Jordanvale yard had a chequered career. In 1848 Thomas Wingate & Co moved their shipbuilding and engineering work from the Gorbals to found the Whiteinch East yard, where they built the world's first triple expansion steam engine in 1872; but the firm closed in 1878. The Park shipyard was set up in 1854 by J G Lawrie.

**Barclay, Curle: Peebles to Punta Arenas**: In 1855 Barclay, Curle & Co moved their yard from Stobcross in Glasgow to the new Clydeholme yard at Whiteinch, and in 1861 Charles Connell & Co established the long-lasting Scotstoun East shipyard. The substantial Scotstoun Ironworks were started immediately to the west by Mechan & Sons in 1862, and rebuilt around 1900 to prepare ships' platework and build lifeboats From 1875 Barclay, Curle built six identical 110m four-masted clippers, the first of which, the *County of Peebles*, was beached at Punta Arenas in Chile in 1911. Still intact in 1993, she remains there awaiting a benefactor to salvage her, and hopefully return her to the Clyde. In 1884 Barclay, Curle built two Clyde steamers for the North British Railway, the poor *Meg Merrilees* and then the good *Jeanie Deans*.

**80,000 Rolls of Wallpaper a Week**: Repeal of the paper duty in 1861 led Wylie & Lochhead of Glasgow to build a very large wallpaper factory at Whiteinch. Two buildings 100m in length contained 8 cylinder printing machines, some of which could apply 20 colours at a time. In 1868 bought-in paper was converted by about 300 workers into 80,000 11-metre *'pieces'* of up to 240 varieties each week. They also block-printed embossed and flocked special papers, and exported to Australia and France *(Bremner)*. About 1870 a sawmill was opened in Whiteinch; McDougall's Bellfield Sawmills were built in Byron Street in 1899–1903, and a third mill in 1905 at South Street, for the Scottish Wood *Haskinizing* Co.

**Trams, Railways, and Water Buses**: Horse trams of the Glasgow Tramway & Omnibus Company first ran to Whiteinch in 1872. The Whiteinch Tramway which ran along South Street to serve the riverside industries was originally a horse-drawn extension of a North British Railway (NB) goods branch from Jordanhill; both opened in 1874. In 1882 the Glasgow, Yoker & Clydebank Railway was opened well inland of the shipyards by its sponsor the NB; a station on this line was opened at Scotstounhill in 1887. The completion of deepening by dredging in 1886 gave the Clyde six metres' clear depth at low water. From 1885 to 1903 *'Cluthas'* (small steam-driven water buses named after the Gaelic word for the Clyde) moved many people across and along the river, eventually making eleven stops between Whiteinch and the city centre. (Some unconfirmed sources suggest later and more extensive operations up to the 1940s.)

**Victoria Park, Fossil Trees and Ironworks**: Victoria Park was being laid out in 1887 at the then western limit of urban development, when a fossilised grove of the extinct Scale Tree was uncovered; this was preserved under cover for posterity to visit. By 1895 Whiteinch, including works named Scotstoun, extended no farther inland than the park, and no farther west than Mechans' ironworks. However, in 1897 the NB opened a station named Victoria Park at its western end, and converted their goods branch to carry passenger trains. In 1895 Ritchie Graham & Milne from Govan took over the East shipyard; perhaps it incorporated the earlier Park yard, for they soon renamed it as Park. McEwan, Law & Lindsay built the Cyclops iron foundry in 1898, and almost simultaneously came the Clyde Structural Iron Company's Clydeside Ironworks (where roof structures and bridges were fabricated), plus the Whiteinch Galvanising Works in Harmsworth Street, and the Roxburgh Works of Macfarlane Brothers, enamellers.

**Shipyard Railway, Ferries and Washing**: The Lanarkshire & Dunbartonshire Railway, a subsidiary of the Caledonian, opened in 1896 alongside the north bank, with stations at Whiteinch (Riverside) and Scotstoun East and West; but useful as it proved for shipyard traffic, the trains soon lost most of their suburban passengers to the electric trams which plied on the routes parallel to the Clyde from 1903… one terminated at Balmoral Street in Scotstoun. A ferry linked Clydeholm with Linthouse from 1891, and a vehicular ferry plied from 1900 between Ferryden Street and Holmfauld Road in Shieldhall. The West End Laundry in Byron Street was erected for A B Boyd & Co in 1898–99, followed in 1899 by the Royal Laundry in Curle Street, built for G Laing. James Ritchie established the Glenavon Engineering Works in Byron Street in 1899 to manufacture specialised laundry machinery, and the Victoria Park Laundry was built in 1901.

**Armaments spur Yarrow's Move to Whiteinch**: A remarkable move took place when Alfred Yarrow & Co uprooted their shipyard, boiler and engine shops from the Thames to reopen at their new Scotstoun shipyard in 1904–06; they built naval vessels from the start. The Coventry Ordnance Works, opened in Scotstoun before World War I to make gun mountings, later built the newly invented tanks, and doubtless most local manufacturing firms helped the war effort. In 1916 Yarrow built the destroyer HMS *Surprise* of 885 tons, and in 1926 made the boilers for Denny's TS *King George V*. In 1919 the Blythswood Shipbuilding Company (BSC) laid out large new yards near Scotstoun West, but as Admiralty orders were cancelled these and other yards rapidly proved to have excessive capacity.

**Scotstoun House yields to Albion Lorries**: Meantime a new Scotstoun House was built inland of the old, which vanished under South Street and the Albion Motors commercial vehicle works – opened in 1904 when the firm moved across from Bathgate. Albion expanded in 1912, having become renowned for simple, rugged designs, but lacked innovation. Their early range was dominated by the 3-tonne A10 which was made from 1910 to 1926, 6000 of this type being built for the forces in World War I; Albion also made motor cars for a time, and in 1929 supplied bus chassis to the LMS Railway. In the 1920s more housing was built inland from Scotstoun to serve the new industries, but it was stopped at Danes Drive, north of which a showground site was left open.

**Barclay, Curle and Albion to 1945**: In 1909 Barclay, Curle – for long the area's greatest firm – took over the often-sold Park shipyard, but became a subsidiary of Swan Hunter in 1912. Their North British diesel engine works were established next door to the Park yard in 1913–14 and absorbed its site in 1922. In 1927–28 Barclay, Curle built what was then a large cargo liner for Canadian Pacific, the 10,000-ton TS *Beaverhill*. Despite the slump which cut vast numbers of Clydeside jobs, this firm managed not only to build a second dry dock in 1933 but to launch four or five new vessels a year up to the second world war, including the 11,000-ton Ellerman liner *City of Benares*, launched in 1936 but torpedoed in 1940. By then the whole area was almost completely built up. In the 1920s Harland & Wolff (of Belfast) acquired the Coventry Ordnance works. Later this became part of the Albion works, which then made light and medium vans and lorries (with forward control cabs and of capacities up to 15 tonnes), and Albion-engined chassis were built for buses and Merryweather fire appliances. In the 1930s more jobs returned with rearmament; 3-tonne Army trucks and tractors for tank transporters were built by Albion at Scotstoun in the 1939–45 war.

**Boilers for the Queens, and Welded Naval Ships**: In 1929 Yarrow & Co built the experimental high pressure boiler for designer Nigel Gresley's LNER locomotive number 10,000, followed in the 1930s by the huge boilers for the Queen liners. In 1943 a hammerhead crane was installed on tracks at the Scotstoun shipyard of Charles Connell & Co to handle prefabricated sections of welded ships, then a new technique. After the war in 1953 Yarrow's yard – which as always specialised in building warships, such as corvettes – built their first Clyde passenger vessel, the *Maid of Ashton*, for the Loch Long service from Hunter's Quay. In 1958 Mechans were still busy on ships' platework. In the early 1960s two of the 100mw generators for the North of Scotland Hydro-Electric Board Cruachan scheme were built by Harland & Wolff.

**Boom, Bang and Barclay Curle's Demise**: In a short post-war shipbuilding boom the large Blythswood yard at Scotstoun became tanker specialists, but the last ship built there was the 1342-ton tender *Fingal*, completed for the Northern Lighthouse Board in 1963. Barclay, Curle built four liners for the British India Line; one of these, the *Dara*, was blown up by a terrorist bomb in 1961 en route from Bombay to Dubai with the loss of 238 lives. Their great yard was extensively modernised in the early 1950s with new covered slips, and their separate graving docks near Yoker were expanded with a third dry dock in 1965; but further orders were lacking, and the famous yard closed in 1967, becoming the site of the Jordan Vale industrial estate.

**Roads replace Trams, Trains and Parkland**: By the 1950s the area contained some 25,000 people and extensive urban facilities. The popular trams ran to Scotstoun until the system sadly vanished altogether in 1962, and Whiteinch (Riverside) station was closed by Beeching in 1964; at much the same time the riverside freight tramway closed. As motor traffic grew, the Clyde Road Tunnel was built beneath the river just upstream of Whiteinch in 1957–64, its cleverly designed *'loopy'* junction sadly cutting into Victoria Park. The West End Laundry and adjoining Glenavon Engineering Works were demolished in 1971 to enable the construction of the dual carriageway A814 Clydeside Expressway, which further damaged Victoria Park.

**Albion submerged – and More Closures**: Meantime from 1947 Albion made a range of commercial vehicles from 1.5 to 14.5 tonnes capacity, but in 1951 the firm was bought by the Lancashire firm of Leyland Motors, and gradually its own characteristic features vanished. Cab standardisation came in 1968, and the name Albion was dropped from vehicles in 1972, though production of the smaller Leyland Redline series continued at Whiteinch up to at least 1983. The North British Engine Works closed in 1977, and Connells' Scotstoun East yard – which in 1968 had passed to the abortive Upper Clyde Shipbuilders (UCS) – became a subsidiary of Govan

*Shipbuilding at Whiteinch – an industry begun here in 1826. The firm of Barclay, Curle was one of Clydeside's finest.* (RCAHMS / JRH)

Shipbuilders before closing in 1980. After over half a century of industrial decline the lower Clyde was mainly lined with ghostly industrial areas.

**Cold War saves Yarrow; DAFS wilt but Albion lives**: In 1970 Yarrow escaped just in time from UCS, and alone of the Whiteinch yards continued at work, becoming fully dedicated to defence contracts and building ten Type 22 frigates for the Royal Navy. The population of the area had more than halved since 1951, and by 1981 the local facilities had shrunk to those of a small town. The Whiteinch area in 1991 had only some 13,000 people. In 1988 the Albion plant was still making truck transmissions for its owners, by then the Dutch-owned Leyland DAF. Following DAF's collapse in the Europe-wide recession of the early 1990s, Albion had to sack 220 of its 550 staff; the plant was relaunched on an independent basis late in 1993 under Dan Wright's management buy-out team as Albion Automotive, with 330 workers at Whiteinch and a branch in Lancashire. By 1995 Albion Automotive had 11 customers as against just 4 in 1993, employed some 440 people in the former Coventry Ordnance works making axles, crankshafts and chassis parts, and were to invest heavily in new equipment.

**Yarrow Almost Struck Off**: In 1990 Yarrow, by then a GEC subsidiary, still employed up to 3400 workers and had built a new module assembly hall where six Royal Navy Type 23 frigates were being completed. In 1992 GEC Naval Systems (based within the GEC Yarrow works) acted as the prime contractor for warship building and equipping by GEC Marconi. Despite the ending of the Cold War, an order for three more frigates was gained in 1992, plus two for Malaysia; but the workforce, already down to 2800, had to be cut by 500 workers in fitting-out trades. The construction of these vessels was stopped early in 1993 when the 1300 remaining manual workers struck over pay and conditions, a foolish action in the trough of a long depression; their 1000 staff colleagues stayed at their posts. The strike was only settled at the cost of 150 redundancies, followed by a further 210 job cuts, including 70 staff posts.

**Sport and Struggle**: In 1993 the development of a new sports and leisure complex was begun at the former Scotstoun Showground. In 1997 St Thomas Aquinas Secondary School had 644 pupils and Victoria Drive Secondary 435. Yarrow recovered, and late in 1994 had work until 1997 building Type 23 frigates for the Royal Navy. It still employed some 2000 people in 1995. The Acronym YARD stood for Yarrow Admiralty Research Department, owned in 1995 by the Franco-British conglomerate BAeSema; this designed a survey ship for the Royal Navy, but it was built at Appledore. In 2000, after amalgamation with the Govan yard, the BAe complex fought successfully to gain a contract to avoid early closure.

## WHITEKIRK

**Map 3, B2**

***E. Lothian hamlet***, *pop. 450 (area)* OS 67: NT 5981

Whitekirk is an ancient settlement dating back at least to 1294, with a 15th century church and a later tithe barn, of two storeys. Binning Wood to the south dates from 1707. The Roy map of about 1754 showed that Whitekirk lay on the road between East Linton and North Berwick. A mansion with walled gardens was built at Newbyth, 2 km south-west. This stood in extensive parkland in the late 19th century, but despite a parish population of 835 in 1901, including Tyninghame, Whitekirk itself was only a tiny kirkton with a post office; after suffragettes torched the church in 1914 it was soon restored. By 1951 the farming parish held 642 people; Whitekirk had a primary school and a telephone exchange. But by 1965 the population was falling fast; by 1982 the post office had closed, followed by the school, and in 1991 only 449 people remained in the parish. In 1993–94 the Whitekirk Golf Company laid out a new 18-hole course north of the hamlet; the old mansionhouse and dovecote of Newbyth still stand.

## WHITHORN

**Map 1, C5**

***Galloway village***, *pop. 950* OS 83: NX 4440

The ancient trading settlement of Whithorn stands about 60 metres above sea level in a fairly fertile area of Galloway, not far from the coast. With the probable exception of Forres – and possibly Crail – it is probably the oldest town in Scotland in terms of continuity of occupancy. Ptolemy's map of about 140 AD showed *Lucafibia*, translatable as *'Bright Port'*; according to local archaeologist Peter Hill it may well have been a seamark. Ample evidence now exists that Whithorn was a trading centre in the fourth to sixth centuries. Though north of Hadrian's Wall, its inhabitants of the *Novantae* tribe had become Romanised; the Christians among them petitioned for a bishopric in the late fourth century. Chambers averred that Whithorn was *"the seat of the oldest bishopric in Scotland, that of Galloway"*. The legend has it that in 397 AD St Ninian or Nynia, probably a local Novanta, built the monastery of Candida Casa; meaning much the same as the earlier name, i.e. *'Shining Warehouse'*; archaeological excavations in 1987–91 certainly revealed the crude stone foundations of a very large early timber church, the first known in northern Britain.

**Whithorn in Rheged, Northumbria and Galloway**: About 525 a Pictish princess called Drustice was educated there, for Whithorn was probably part of the Romano–Pictish kingdom of Rheged which was described by the author of the Anglo–Saxon Chronicle for 565 as the *'South Picts'*. Rheged was fortunate that a relatively peaceful Anglian (Northumbrian) takeover by marriage took place about the year 645, and the area was renamed Galloway; Whithorn remained the centre of its see, and the name of Candida Casa was directly translated into Anglo-Saxon as *Hvitaern*, hence the name Whithorn. A clay chapel with stained glass windows was built, whitewashed to keep out the rain. Bede recorded bishops of Whithorn in the archdiocese of York from 731 to 791 AD; there was also an abbot and therefore a monastery until at least the year 800. Despite a lack of historical evidence, the excavations at Whithorn demonstrated that in the period 1000–1128 Irish, Viking and Scandinavian influence was considerable, and a continuing high standard of living for some at least was evidenced by French wine glasses.

**Priory and Burgh**: Strong action by David I made later influences more easterly. Whithorn's large Premonstratensian priory was founded on the monastery site in the mid 12th century by Fergus, Lord of Galloway, as an offshoot of Soulseat Abbey. The cathedral which served as its church was soon finely rebuilt on a larger scale, but about 1274 the diocese still covered only Galloway. The graveyard excavations which continued in 1991 had revealed enough to be able to estimate a local population of about 500 in the 13th to 15th centuries. Once the area had become effectively a part of Scotland, about 1327

Whithorn was granted the rights of an Ecclesiastical Burgh by King Robert I, an inveterate pilgrim to St Ninian's shrine.

**Royal Burgh, Roads and Windmill**: Whithorn was elevated to Royal Burgh status in 1511, though its contribution to burgh taxes remained under 1% in 1535. The Bishop sat in Parliament in 1560, but Whithorn was especially badly hit when pilgrimages were banned in 1581, and eventually lost its ecclesiastical significance. Even so, Pont's map made about 1610 showed it on a par with or slightly larger than Wigtown and Kirkcudbright. In 1628 a parish school was founded, and about 1635 the cathedral was repaired, later serving as the parish church. A new school was built in 1730. In the 1750s Roy's surveyors found five roads already radiating from a quite substantial linear settlement; only the Garlieston road is more recent. One of Scotland's relatively rare windmills turned at Whithorn, where a post office opened in 1769, a corn merchant was trading by 1786, and a small brewery existed in the 18th and 19th centuries.

**Mansion, Commerce, Railway and Creamery**: Glasserton House, 4km south-west of Whithorn, was designed by Robert Adam and built in 1787 for Admiral Keith Stewart. Whithorn was a post town by 1797. Heron estimated the population in 1799 at around 750, noting that *"the very ancient royal borough is an inconsiderable town, without either trade or manufacture, its cathedral completely in ruins"*. Rather than repair it, a new church was built in 1822. A Bank of Scotland branch was opened in 1838, and the burgh population in 1861 was a little over 1600. In 1877 the Wigtownshire Railway from Newton Stewart and Wigtown reached and terminated at Whithorn, the southernmost station in Scotland, but no industry followed and by 1891 the population had fallen to 1400. The *Grapes Hotel* was open by 1894, and around that period a small creamery was established.

**After the Railway – Digging into the Past**: Regrettably, Glasserton House was gutted in 1934 and left roofless. About then Whithorn acquired a small bus garage, and bus competition led to the railway being closed to passengers in 1950, when some 1350 people lived in Whithorn and vicinity. By 1963 the small *Castlewigg Hotel* was open near Castlewigg, 2 km north of the village. Despite considerable freight traffic the railway was closed completely by Beeching in 1964 and soon lifted; the station site was used for a fire station. The creamery too had been closed by 1979. Meantime an old school had become a museum, open by 1957 and by the 1990s containing many early Christian stones and a visitor centre. In 1991 Whithorn remained a very quiet village, itself housing 952 residents and conveying a timeless air. Behind the modest stone facades of the village street the tiny archaeological team of the Whithorn Dig was painstakingly revealing more of the reality underlying the obscure history of one of Scotland's oldest and most fascinating settlements. The primary school has about 130 pupils, and a caravan site has been established at Castlewigg.

## WHITING BAY

**Map 1, B2**

***Village, Isle of Arran,*** *pop. 500*

OS 69: NS 0426

The south-east corner of the hilly Isle of Arran contains the Glenashdale Falls of 12m and 30m, the highest in the island, and there are various ancient remains. From 1790 a ferry plied to Saltcoats from the shallow, rather rocky foreshore of Whiting Bay; in 1829 it was replaced by steamers to Glasgow, from which passengers were disembarked in small boats. The clearance of many poor crofting tenants of the Duke of Hamilton blighted the area in the 1830s. However, by the 1840s there was a church school, and the bay harboured 9 local fishing boats in 1847. Arran was little visited until the mid 19th century, but the area around Whiting Bay began to attract holidaymakers and geologists, and from 1860 a new ferry plied to and from Ardrossan. Whiting Bay golf club was founded in 1895 and laid out a short 18-hole parkland course, and a steamer pier completed in 1901 stimulated growth, but this was checked by two world wars.

**Quiet Holidays – in Season**: A new school was built after 1945. By 1951 Whiting Bay had the facilities of a typical village; under 600 people lived there out of season. Tourists found the 20-room *Whiting Bay Hotel* and ten smaller hotels, a small cinema and a youth hostel. In 1953 the British Rail ferryboat from Ardrossan called first at Brodick, terminating at Whiting Bay (where cars could still be disembarked); summer steamers from Gourock, Dunoon, Wemyss Bay and Rothesay also called. Some visitors would take houses for a month or more. In 1954 a roll-on ferry was introduced to serve Brodick alone, and the Whiting Bay steamer pier was closed in 1957. The cinema also soon closed, and the resident population fell to little over 400 by 1971. Even so, in the 1980 season ten hotels and many craft shops were open; pony trekking and cycle hire were available. The 1991 resident population was still under 500. Whiting Bay continues its quiet existence; by 1997 a summer passenger ferry sailed to Holy Island *(q.v.)*.

## WICK & Pulteneytown

**Map 13, B5**

***Caithness coastal town,*** *pop. 7700*

OS 12: ND 3650

The ruined dark age keep of the Castle of Old Wick (or Oliphant), near which copper was once worked, stands on the bleak east coast cliffs of Caithness. The town of Wick, which lies in much gentler country at the mouth of the Wick River 2 km to the north, was first mentioned in 1140. The name means *Bay* in Norse, for the area was under Norwegian control until 1231, and although Wick was shown on the 13th century Gough map, Danish incursions continued until about 1266. Wick became a burgh of barony around 1393, and about then the Castle of Old Wick was rebuilt for Sir Reginald Duchesne. In the next century the square keep of Ackergill Tower arose on the shore 4km to the north-west, and Girnigoe Castle was built on the cliffs 2 km to the east of Ackergill. From 1503 Wick was the caput of the new sheriffdom of Caithness. In 1560 Girnigoe Castle was the large and complex seat of the Earl of Caithness and Master Sinclair, both of whom sat in Parliament. Pont noted on his sketch map made about 1600 *"now called Castle Sincleer"*. (Some authorities distinguish two castles here, Sinclair and Girnigoe; both were abandoned in 1690.)

**Royal Burgh, Clan Battles and Linen**: In 1589 Wick was promoted to Royal Burgh status, and Pont's map showed *'Old Wick'* as a substantial town, with a bridge to a *'New town'* on the south bank; to the north there were ships in *'Papingho'*, and tiny settlements both there and at *'Staxigho'*. In 1617 a parish school was opened. However, in 1621 Wick paid under 1.5% of Scotland's Customs dues, and Tucker reported in 1655 that it had no ships of its own, despite being already a *"small port from whence good store of beef, hides and tallow are sent"*. A new bridge was built in 1665. Clan battles marred Wick and its attendant castles for half a century, during which the second bridge vanished. However, by 1715 there was a post office, and by 1749 master linen spinners were at work. Roy's survey made about 1750 showed no bridge, nor was reference made to a ferry. The one track from the south, much later labelled A9, at that time terminated on the south side of the Wick River opposite the little linear town on the north bank; from there another track (now the B874) led westwards to end at Thurso. In those days the only herring fishery was from Staxigoe, 2 km north-east.

**Sinclair and the British Fisheries Society**: In 1768 the laird Sir John Sinclair had a quay built at Wick to designs by John Rennie, so as to promote herring fishing, and also brought in Dutch expertise. Pennant in 1769 found Wick *"a small burgh town"*, noting that many salmon were caught; but success with the herring was slight as late as 1782 when the season's salted catch was only 363 barrels. Wick was heavily promoted from 1787 by the British Fisheries Society, and harbour improvements planned by Telford were put in hand. Though it remained rather exposed there were soon about 200 boats, and in 1790 over 13,000 barrels of fish were salted. In 1799 Heron guessed the population at a thousand, and observed *"the chief trade of this town depends on the cod and herring fishery"*, adding, probably in respect of coal rather than peat, that *"the inhabitants suffer great inconvenience from the scarcity of fuel"*. The suburb of Pulteneytown on the south side of the river was laid out in 1808, the harbour works were completed in 1810, and the river was again bridged about that time, by Telford.

**Wick invents the Fax but consolidates into Whisky**: Ingenious Alexander Bain, born in 1810 at the vanished Leanmore croft, was apprenticed to a Wick clockmaker, invented the electric clock, and in 1843 patented a forerunner of the fax machine. The equally little-known Caithness Banking Company was formed in the town in 1812, but amalgamated into the Commercial Bank of Scotland in 1825. Mail coaches served Wick from 1819. By 1825 Alex Miller's brewery was open in Pulteneytown, and in 1826 Pulteney Distillery was built by James Henderson – lately the proprietor of a small inland distillery – to meet the rising demand for whisky. In 1827 Chambers found the road to John o' Groats *"execrable"*, but Wick was *"bustling and thriving. In the suburb called Pulteneytown building proceeds rapidly. The population does not much exceed 2000, but the increasing importance of the herring fishery promises to produce a rapid increase. Hitherto the maritime trade of Wick has been chiefly carried on through Staxigo, a small village with a convenient harbour. But a new pier proposed at Wick will greatly improve the inconvenient harbour"*; this was completed in 1831.

**Epidemic, Starvation – and the Northernmost Private Park**: A quarry at Holm Head was worked until an accident about 1830; then in 1832 a cholera epidemic caused many Wick fisherfolk to move to Peterhead. A gasworks was set up in 1840. The Northern Lighthouse Board wanted to build a light on Sarclet Head, but were overruled by the Board of Trade. The resulting lighthouse on Noss Head, 5 km north of the harbour and 1 km to the east of Girnigoe, was first lit in 1849. In 1847, despite the widespread potato famine in the North, grain was still being exported. While many starved, Ackergill Tower was being massively rebuilt for the Dunbars of Hempriggs to plans by David Bryce; he also designed the baronial mansion of Stirkoke House, built in 1858 for the Hornes some 5 km west of Wick, and surrounded by perhaps the most northerly shelterbelted parkland in Britain.

**Caithness Overcrowding**: Meantime the local newspaper, the *John o' Groat Journal*, had begun publication in 1836; in 1851 its owner Peter Reid built a mill for flax dressing. This had ceased operations before 1864, due to agricultural depression and a lack of interest by local farmers; linen manufacture had also ceased. The 1861 census marked the peak of population in Caithness, a largely rural area where the housing was greatly overcrowded, with between two and three persons per room. The Wick herring fisheries increased each year to a maximum of over 1100 sailing boats in 1862, when not surprisingly it was a port of registry, with the code letters WK. Fish curing, including kippering, was a major industry; a *'great waterwheel'* drove a quayside sawmill cutting barrel staves. Salt and sawdust caused dry throats: 45 pubs were open in Wick to serve the 3800 fishermen and 4000 ancilliary workers!

**Overfished Herring and Broken Breakwater**: George Manson introduced netmaking machinery to Wick about 1866. In 1867 18,000 tons of shipping, with 1300 crew, brought in wood and salt for herring curing, and exported barrelled fish. At the peak, over 5800 men sailed in 970 small vessels, making Wick Scotland's second busiest herring port that season, and among the top ten centres for curing white fish. The 293 coopers were the largest number in any Scottish port; a skilled man could make five barrels a day! But as early as 1869 questions were being asked by Bremner about the wisdom of the herring industry's total lack of conservation measures; unlike salmon, there was no close season. About then Bremner noted *"a large proportion of Wick Bay is being enclosed by a gigantic breakwater"* to form a harbour of refuge. This structure was begun on the south shore and finally gave the harbour a really satisfactory degree of shelter in 1883, but it suffered repeated storm damage and was never completed; the 1894 OS map shows it some 200 m long, but it had vanished by the 1920s.

**Golf and the Highland Railway**: The quarry was reopened about 1869; when it finally closed in 1912, numerous people emigrated to Canada. Wick golf club was founded in 1870, and laid out its 18-hole course on Ackergill Links, 5 km north of the town. The Sutherland & Caithness (later Highland) Railway reached Wick from the south via Georgemas in 1874, building an engine shed; the line also connected Wick with Thurso. The railway brought city-brewed ales, distributed by Wordie & Co who ran a rail to road cartage depot as early as 1875; this killed the local brewery. But it also allowed speedy transits of iced fish (and of hitherto isolated people) to the south. A new river bridge was built in 1877, at least the fourth erected in the town.

**Fish Gutting not for the Tourist**: In 1886 Barnard noted that between 800 and 1000 boats could still be seen leaving the harbour. Pulteney Distillery was water-powered and family-owned in 1886, using barley from Moray and Ross to make 365,000 litres of Highland malt whisky annually. A public library was commenced, with Carnegie aid, from 1887. The 1891 population was 8500. There were two hotels in Wick by 1894, described by Murray as the *"good but somewhat dear" Station* and the *Caledonian*; but large-scale fish gutting and salting made the town *"not attractive to the tourist"*. A lifeboat station was finally opened in 1895. Pulteneytown remained a separate burgh until 1902. The overfished herring declined rapidly in the early 20$^{th}$ century and by the 1920s only 28 boats remained, mainly in white fishing, with small-scale kippering and boatbuilding. However by then the Claymore milk bottling plant and cheese creamery was open. In 1920–21 Wick went *'dry'* for a time and the pubs were closed; not so Pulteney distillery, which was sold in 1923 to Dewar by James Watson & Co of Dundee. It was, however, mothballed in 1930.

**Taking to the Air and the Airwaves**: Highland Airways of Inverness began flights to Wick and Kirkwall in 1933. Later came routes from Dyce to Wick, Thurso and Orkney. In 1939–40 Wordies carted materials for a new RAF airfield, built on the plateau north of the town; soon after the war it became Wick's civil airport. Despite the fishing decline, some 7500 people still lived in Wick by 1951 and enjoyed typical urban facilities. The distillery was reopened in 1951, and rebuilt in 1959. By contrast the railway engine shed was run down and closed about 1965. About 1964 Grampian Records were set up to make tapes of Scottish dance music; by 1979 they were half owned by London music publishers Campbell Connolly and producing 80,000 recorded cassettes a week with a staff of 35. About 1977 Kestrel Marine leased part of the harbour for an offshore oil supply base.

**Wick in 1978**: In 1978 three builders of wooden boats were still at work, but neither harbour nor town centre seemed very prosperous. Much of the housing was very old, despite some modern development such as the almost new 30-room *Mercury Motor Inn*. The great harbour held a few biggish fishing boats but apart from the oil section showed a distinct lack of investment. The town had three branch banks, a 2-bay fire station, sheriff court, district council office and hospital; there was a good range of shops, including specialists.

**Caithness Glass and New Hospital**: With the provision of an industrial site, the now well-known firm of Caithness Glass started production in 1960, first making paperweights in 1969. It provided 150 jobs by 1979, when they also owned a factory at Oban; they soon opened another at Inveralmond near Perth, and had many overseas markets. In 1991 the firm employed over 300 people in Wick, Oban and Perth, but was then taken over by the Drambuie Group of Edinburgh; their new main factory beside Wick airport was opened in 1992, and glass blowing was open to visitors in 1997. In 1981 Wick was a major local centre with a tourist trade that had developed as far as the rigorous climate would allow; there were five hotels besides the long-established 66-room *Station Hotel*. Wick coastguard station was closed in 1982, but three boatbuilders and two small kippering plants were still at work. By 1985 only about 20 working boats were actually based in Wick, mainly trapping lobsters, but it remained the registration port for ten times as many smaller boats spread along the coast. Noss Head lighthouse was automated in 1987, the year that the new Caithness General Hospital was opened. By that time the distillery was licensed to James & George Stodart, some of its well-recommended output of Pulteney single malt being bottled in Elgin; it is now owned by Inver House.

**Ospreys dive Deep and Ices spread Far**: In 1976 Osprey Electronics leased a factory in Wick to make components for Fortronic of Donibristle in Fife. However, they rapidly became independent makers of instrumentation and underwater television cameras, serving the North Sea oil industry; by 1993, under Norwegian owners, they employed 60 people in Wick. Meantime in 1990 dairy farmer Dan Budge of Hempriggs had moved into the ice cream business, and within three years as Barnes Real Dairy Ice Cream was supplying wholesalers throughout Scotland. Despite the long-term decline in fishing some new housing had been built; the 1991 population was 7681.

**Conferences and Operas, but Few Fish and No Council**: In 1988 *Ackergill Tower* was converted into a 17-room hotel and conference centre; in 1994 it employed 42 people. Its disused former coach-house and stables were converted by its owners John and Arlette Banister into a miniature 90-seat opera house; co-operation with William Wilson's Lyth Arts Centre was intended. Less lucky was Stirkoke House, which in 1994 stood abandoned by its owner. In 1995 printing of the *Northern Times* of Golspie was transferred to rotary presses at Wick. By 1995 the Wick Heritage Centre highlighted the former fishing industry. In 1996 the district council vanished into the vast all-purpose Highland Region, so Wick's role as a centre of independent local government did not quite last 500 years. By then Wick High School had over 900 pupils; a supermarket now stands on the site of a former drill hall. The circuitous rail link survives, though trains to and from the south go via Thurso! There are several fish-related businesses, several in construction and oil-related engineering, Norscot make timber-frame houses, and Caithness Stone still deal in flagstones. Safeway now have a store in the town. Hotels include the long-established 27-roomed *Mackay's*, and the luxurious *Ackergill Tower*; there are also smaller hostelries.

## WIGTOWN & Bladnoch — Map 1, C4

***Galloway small town,*** *pop. 1150* — OS 83: NX 4355

Wigtown lies near the head of a sheltered bay on the coast of Galloway, just west of the estuary of the River Cree. A church was first built there about 550 AD; the name Wigtown might mean *Temple-town, Bay-town* or (less likely) *Wicga's Farm*. In the early 13th century, Devorgilla Balliol founded a Dominican friary. In 1263 Wigtown became the caput of a late sheriffdom embracing the western half of Galloway, and became a Royal Burgh in 1292, but its late 13th century Royal castle has practically vanished. About 1330 the burgh was making some slight contribution to Customs revenue. This ceased after the Black Death, but by 1419 Wigtown had an Earl, and Customs contributions reappeared in the 15th century. Wigtown was linked eastwards by a ferry to Ferrytown of Cree (now Creetown), and in 1441 it was connected with ancient Whithorn by the Bladnoch bridge, spanning the river of that name 1.5 km south of the town. By 1499 Wigtown was trading with Bordeaux, but paid under 1.5% of Scotland's Customs duties in 1535, while it contributed under 1% to burgh taxes; yet in 1560 the burgh was important enough to be represented in Parliament.

**After the Reformation**: From 1583 a parish school was held, and by 1593 Wigtown was the centre of a presbytery; Pont's map of Galloway, made about 1610, showed it as a substantial place, with *'Baldun'* emparked. A whole series of mills lined the banks of the river, from the Newmill near the Stones of Torhouse past Barness mill to a third beside Baldoon; a fourth on the last southern tributary was perhaps Braehead mill. In 1621 the Galloway collection was still contributing a little to non-wine customs duties, but the port was silting up and in 1639 Wigtown ranked a lowly 48th of Scottish burghs in tax rents, last but one of those which rendered returns. In 1655 the Cromwellian Customs official Tucker noted as its sole trade *"there comes sometimes a small boat from England, with salt* *or coals".* But as befitted the county town, however paltry, Wigtown post office was early to open (1705). The Roy map made about 1754 showed a substantial square settlement, from which four roads or tracks radiated, much as today; a *'Ford at Low Water'* led from the shore at Wigtown across the estuary to Ferrytown of Cree. Three mills – Torrhouse, Wake and New – stood west of the town and the 17th century *'Baldune'* (Baldoon) Castle stood alone beside the bridge at Bladnoch.

**Cotton not a Success**: A cotton mill was set up about 1790, and five fairs were scheduled to be held in 1797. Over a thousand people lived in Wigtown in 1799, wrote Heron, *"but it possesses neither manufactures nor trade. Several attempts to establish a branch of the woollen and cotton manufacture have been made, but without much success. A few sloops are here employed for the importing of coals and lime, and exporting of grain".* A small new harbour was built piecemeal from 1788–1825; tiny Wigtown actually became a Port of Registry, with the recognition letters WN. Bladnoch distillery, the most southerly in Scotland, was established in 1817 by John and Thomas McLelland; in 1825 there was also a brewery. The original square once contained the general and cattle markets, for according to Chambers, writing in 1827, *"Wigton derives its only support as a town from its situation amidst fertile fields".* The town had a branch of the British Linen Company's Bank, and also (briefly) a Bank of Scotland branch.

**County Buildings, Railway and Whisky**: The burgh population in 1861 was over 2000, and new County Buildings were erected in 1862. The Wigtownshire Railway was opened in 1875 from Newton Stewart to Wigtown, and was extended to terminate at Whithorn two years later. Wigtown had a goods shed, also used to stable and maintain the makeshift half dozen steam engines that worked the line until the company lost its independence in 1885. The engine shed was moved to Newton Stewart in 1895. The line drained Wigtown rather than stimulating growth, for Newton Stewart had a more strategic location as a service centre. The distillery was enlarged and modernised in 1878, though it remained water-powered; in 1886 its output was about 230,000 litres of Lowland malt a year. At that time Barnard noted *"a beautiful central square, laid out in flower gardens, tennis courts and promenades".* In 1891 the population was only 1450; tree felling in the square was controversial about that time. In 1894 Murray noted the *Galloway Arms* as a *"comfortable"* commercial hotel and Wigtown was still called a *"little seaport town".*

**Cream, Margarine and Wartime Works**: Eventually the county offices were moved to Stranraer. The SCWS Bladnoch creamery was open by about 1900, but the distillery was mothballed in 1938. Two World War II factories built between Wigtown and Newton Stewart had railway sidings. The Baldoon airfield south of the town was served through the station at Kirkinner; afterwards it was retained for private flying. Passenger trains were withdrawn in 1950; by 1951 the population of Wigtown was only some 1600, and its facilities were those of a large village. Beeching closed the railway to freight in 1965 and it was lifted forthwith. However, the distillery reopened in 1956, and was enlarged in the 1960s. The belated Wigtown & Bladnoch golf club, founded in 1960, laid out a 9-hole parkland course, but the harbour had become silted up and derelict by then. The former creamery had changed into an SCWS margarine factory; this appears to have closed by 1975. The Bladnoch distillery passed in turn to Inver House, Bell's and United Distillers, its single malt still known to connoisseurs as a *"memorable dram".*

**Sailing, Flying, Whisky – and Book Town**: Wigtownshire was downgraded to a district of Dumfries & Galloway in 1975. Its erstwhile county town had by then declined to a compact village of unusual appearance, with three hotels and a caravan site. In the 1980s the harbour was cleared out to enable its use by pleasure boats. By 1991 Wigtown's population was 1117. The distillery was closed from 1993 to 1997, but its visitor centre remained open. Meantime by 1995 *Fordbank House* had become a hotel, though the nearby caravan site had closed. By 1995 a little new development was dotted around ancient Wigtown; a butterfly farm was also open by 2000. In that year Wigtown blossomed as Scotland's *'Book Town'*, with several bookshops recently opened, and a resulting doubling in visitors. The extensive GC Book Warehouse is to open in 2001, with up to 40,000 volumes in stock for retail sale.

## WINCHBURGH

**Map 16, C3**

***W. Lothian village,*** *pop. 2550* — OS 65: NT 0874

Winchburgh, whose name implies it was founded by an Anglian named Winca, stands on a plateau about 5 km southwest of South Queensferry. It had an ancient church, 2 km south-east of which was Lord Seton's L-plan tower of Niddry Castle, built by about 1480; in 1568 it briefly sheltered the fleeing Queen Mary. Both these placenames and the road between Edinburgh and Linlithgow appeared on Pont's map of around 1600. The tower of Duntarvie Castle was soon built to the north, but Niddry Castle was abandoned in 1700 when its then owner, the only too successful usurer John Hope, moved to Hopetoun House. The Roy map made about 1754 showed a village, named *'Queensburgh'*, not Winchburgh. By 1791 the Humbie sandstone quarry was open; 80 quarrymen worked there in 1835.

**Canal, Railways and Shale Oil**: The Union Canal, opened in 1822, crossed under the road just west of the village. Then came the Edinburgh & Glasgow Railway, which to maintain a level route excavated massive rock cuttings, passed through the large quarry and tunnelled beneath Winchburgh, which was provided with a station from the line's opening in 1842; it later became part of the North British system. There were two

*Houses at Winchburgh, dating from about 1900; these were some of the best built for workers in the shale-oil industry (and are the only ones surviving in anything like their original condition). (JRH)*

*The Niddry shale-oil works near Winchburgh (one of three near the village), seen in the 1950s. This works had the first successful electric railway in Scotland, opened in 1902; the locomotive seen here was built in the 1940s. In the background is the inclined railway leading to the retorts. The works closed in the early 1960s.* *(Scottish Oils)*

quarries in 1858, but they had flooded by 1869. About 1865 the Dundas Shale-oil Company built a works to distil crude oil. In 1871 the Uphall Mineral Oil Company acquired the Hopetoun shale rights, and built the Niddry Oil Works at Bankhead, 1 km south of the village, to process shale from mines 1 km west of Winchburgh, connected by a mineral line with the Niddry works. When Young's company took over Uphall Oil in 1884, these works were upgraded and renamed Hopetoun. Winchburgh Junction, west of the original station, was created in 1890 when a new line was opened to Dalmeny, enabling trains to run through between Glasgow and Fife across the new Forth Bridge. In 1891 the population of Winchburgh was 424; by 1895 a canal-side inn and a post office were open.

**New Century, New Village**: In 1901 the Oakbank Oil Company built a new village of 230 good houses, the Niddry Castle Rows. The firm's three carefully sited shale mines between Abercorn and Philpstoun, and south of Newton, were linked by a 2'6" gauge railway – the first successful electric railway in Scotland, using overhead wires and trolley locomotives – to their new Niddry Castle oil extraction works immediately east of the village. This was the first all-electric works in the industry. By 1931 the population was almost 1600, but enormous waste shale bings had destroyed the countryside north, south and east of the village by the time the Hopetoun Works closed in 1949. The village population was 2200 in 1951, and had reached a plateau; but the station had already closed and, apart from a little secondary school, Winchburgh still had only the facilities of a small village. The Niddry Castle Oil Works – the last in Scotland to produce shale oil – closed with its associated mines in 1960, leaving the dereliction of the giant bings plus a largely purposeless village.

**New Jobs, New Golf Course and Restored Castle**: Winchburgh lost its post town status about 1973, and by 1976 its secondary school had closed. However its location enabled most of the inhabitants to find work elsewhere in industry, distribution and government services. In 1991 the population of 2535 lived in the modernised rows of this most complete remaining shale industry village, either buying or renting their homes from the council which had acquired them. By 1987 the new 9-hole Niddry Castle golf course adjoined the castle, which was still surrounded by large bings, some by then in the course of reclamation. After 250 years of rooflessness, the castle itself was restored from 1984 to 2000 by Peter Wright. Not all the bings had been reclaimed by 1998, but the oil workers' Institute remains in social use; the reopening of the canal as a through route in 2001 offers additional interest.

## WISHAW & Cambusnethan **Map 16, A5**

***Lanarkshire large town,*** *pop. 30,000*

OS 64/65 or 64/72: NS 7955

A substantial Roman road linked lower Clydeside with the Tweed valley, crossing a triangular plateau north-east of the Clyde and south of the South Calder Water, and skirting the head of the steep defile to the east, later called Garriongill. The medieval Cambusnethan church was built beside the River Clyde 4km to the west, and between there and Garriongill arose the 15th century Cambusnethan House, shown on Pont's very distorted sketch map dated 1596. The area was thickly settled, with about one name per square kilometre. Wishaw and Coltness, already probably lairds' residences, were marked; on the South Calder Water were a mill and adjacent bridge. A parish school was opened in 1627. The Roy map of the 1750s showed the *'Old Roman Way'* still evidently in use between Carluke and Windmillhill (Motherwell). An east–west road linked it with the new Kirkton of Cambusnethan, built 4km east of the old church; and another road paralleled Garriongill between Overtown, the Kirkton, and Hainshaw (Newmains).

**New Mansions and Distillery, Coal and Railways**: In 1819 Robert Lockhart replaced Cambusnethan House with a new mansion called Cambusnethan Priory. Two more new mansions were built beside the South Calder, north-west of the new Kirkton: Coltness House, home of General Sir James Steuart, and Wishaw House, the second seat of Lord Belhaven of Biel; this was enlarged in 1825 to designs by James Gillespie Graham, and in 1858 by William Burn. In 1825 Lord Belhaven set up the Clydesdale distillery, from which grew Wishaw village, taking the Roman road as its main street. The Wishaw & Coltness Railway (W&CR) was opened on the 4'6" *'Scotch'* gauge in 1833, connecting Chapel Colliery 4km to the east of the distillery with the earlier Monkland & Kirkintilloch Railway and passing 1km south-west of Wishaw. A gasworks was established at Wishaw in 1836, and its first post office was open by 1838. It was still a small village in 1841 but soon became linked to the Kirkton of Cambusnethan by a ribbon of roadside development.

**Main Line, Iron and Stone**: When the Caledonian Railway (CR) built its main line, this incorporated the existing W&CR, westwards from Garriongill Junction 2km east of Wishaw. A station, later called Wishaw South, was provided near the village when the line opened in 1848. Mining around Wishaw grew, its coal being favoured for steam raising in the mid 19th century. Then came the rapid growth of iron and steel works at Newmains to the east, and also by the Glasgow Iron & Steel Company at Netherton to the west; they made pig-iron, and later steel by the Bessemer process. Bremner noted a quarry of freestone, which was being used in the erection of Edinburgh's West Meadows area. Wishaw's growing importance as a centre was shown when the *Wishaw Press* was founded as a local newspaper in 1870. In 1880 a new section of the CR with a more convenient station for Wishaw was opened between Law Junction (a mining area east of Garriongill) and Holytown north of Motherwell. Two other lines linked this with the existing railways, making Wishaw a minor junction. Wishaw was extensive enough to justify the existence of sub-post offices by 1886, when the town's early focus, the distillery, employed twenty men making a Lowland malt. In 1891 the population was over 15,000.

**Clothing, Wagons, Carriages and Golf**: In 1894 Murray dismissed Wishaw as being *"surrounded by coal-pits, by which the town is partly undermined"*. Their pitheads actually formed an arc south and west of the town; the ironworks was in operation west of Wishaw Central station, and about then the Clydesdale clothing factory was opened. By the late 19th century R Y Pickering & Co of Wishaw built goods rolling stock, such as dumb-buffered open wagons for the Wemyss Coal Company of Fife, and for the Highland Railway; later they made coal wagons and railway carriages. In 1904 an electric power station was opened. The two adjacent mansions still stood north of the town: Wishaw House to the north-west had a beautiful park, where an 18-hole golf course was laid out in 1897, and due north was J Houldsworth's Coltness in even more extensive policies.

**No Whisky, but Lorries and Trams made**: The Clydesdale distillery was owned by a public company which succumbed to Lloyd George's high taxes; in 1914 it became one of the 5 founder members of Scottish Malt Distillers Ltd. The government suspended whisky production during the war and the distillery was closed by the combine in 1919 and transferred to DCL to become a whisky bond. From 1906 to 1924 Belhaven lorries were made in Wishaw, and Clyde lorries from 1913 to 1932. Being largely a workers' dormitory for the surrounding collieries and iron and steel works, in 1920 Wishaw was incorporated with the even later town of Motherwell into the single large burgh of Motherwell & Wishaw. But Wishaw's steelmaking ended in 1920 (and the ironworks closed in 1930). Pickerings built trains of four-wheel coaches for the winding Balerno branch line as late as 1922, in 1927 some traditional wooden-bodied though luxuriously fitted passenger coaches for the Nitrate Railways of Chile, and in 1928 tram bodies for Glasgow on bogies from Kilmarnock. About 1933 a little-known Wishaw firm, the Atlantic Engine Company, made paraffin-driven engines.

**Steelworks, Housing and Electric Trains**: In 1951, with a population of nearly 32,000, Wishaw was a major local centre. The site of the former Netherton collieries had been developed into a large steelworks. The giant Ravenscraig steelworks *(see Motherwell)* were built between 1955 and 1963 to the west of Wishaw House, which was sadly demolished in 1953; the

*The Excelsior iron and steel works at Wishaw, established in the 1860s by a Black Country ironmaster, with a steam rolling-mill engine brought up from England. This view shows the fly-wheel and gearing of that engine, which worked into the 1960s. (JRH)*

area's deep coal pits had also been exhausted. The grounds of Coltness were taken over for a huge housing development in the years around 1960; by 1972 three-quarters of the houses in the burgh belonged to public authorities. Pickering's carriage and wagon business was still extant until about 1970, but by 1971 Wishaw South station had been closed. However, from 1974 electric trains provided a new service between Lanark and Glasgow, serving Wishaw Central. Wishaw's steelworks was closed about 1980, then being cleared for an industrial estate.

**Pie Cases, Problems and the End of the Priory**: Smith's Industries Wishaw clock factory, which had been a very large concern with 1400 employees, was badly hit by the import of quartz crystal clocks and by the end of 1977 was down to 600 workers. William Waddell Ltd were bakery engineers in Wishaw by 1979, the only firm producing machinery to make pastry cases for Scotch pies – and still doing so! By 1980 Motherwell Bridge Engineering's Special Products Division was located in Wishaw, and about that time the Japanese firm of Daiwa began to manufacture fishing rods and golf clubs from modern graphite compounds on the Netherton industrial estate. In 1981 the old 68-bed hospital was used for geriatric care; by then Cambusnethan Priory had become a hotel – but this ceased to function in 1984, and vandalism and fire led to dereliction.

**Gowkthrapple is No Joke**: A public authority housing estate built in the 1970s about 1.5km south of the town centre took the long-standing but inelegant local name of Gowkthrapple, meaning *'Cuckoo's Gullet'!* In the 1991 census, its 2000 people had Scotland's highest locality density in persons per hectare, the highest percentage of households without a car and the second highest percentage of male unemployment in Scotland, at over 35%. Castlehill was the local primary school.

**Facing up to Ravenscraig's Fate**: Wishaw's population had been rising, and in 1990 a new station was opened to serve Shieldmuir, an area between Wishaw South station and Motherwell, where a new rail-connected postal depot was also constructed in the mid to late 1990s. Between 1985 and 1990 the Wishaw engineering firm of J Martin switched from dependency on the doomed Ravenscraig steelworks to North Sea oil contracts; but it was feared that several other local firms remained vulnerable. The year 1991 saw Wishaw's population approaching 30,000, with high male unemployment. Daiwa then started to expand its sports goods factory to make new top of the market trout rods designed by Harry Jamieson of Nethy Bridge, raising its existing 250 jobs to 300 over the coming few years. By 1992 Allis Mineral Systems had erected new plant.

**After Ravenscraig a New Hospital**: In 1992 Motherwell's Ravenscraig plant was closed by the privatised British Steel, throwing still more local people out of work, and Strathclyde Region, under financial pressure, decided to close Wishaw High School; its listed building was destroyed by fire, consequently being sold as a housing site in 1993. The remaining secondary schools were Coltness High with 860 pupils and St Aidan's High with 1250. Opencast coal working at Greenhead Moss south of Cambusnethan controversially destroyed rare peat habitats on the fringe of the town; the work was complete by 1998. On the up side, plans were announced in 1995 for a new Wishaw General Hospital at Netherton to replace Law Hospital at Carluke. First agreed in principle in 1991, it was now to be controversially financed for the NHS by private capital. Meantime by 1998 Wishaw's old geriatric hospital had been demolished. The new Wishaw General hospital – designed by staff – opened in June 2001, with over 600 beds. Today, major local employers include Fieldings (making school uniforms), Flextronics (in electronics), TFC Cable (electrical assemblies), and structural engineers Bone Steel Ltd.

## WOODHEAD & Gight — Map 10, B2

***Aberdeenshire hamlets,** pop. 300* — OS 29 or 30: NJ 7938

Gight Castle, a 16th century L-plan tower, was built on a bluff overlooking the River Ythan 6km east of Fyvie Castle. On the plateau midway between Gight and Fyvie stands *Woodhead of Fetterletter*, which was a small settlement by 1642, when Gordon supplied Blaeu with information for his atlas. It was evidently a market centre long before it became a burgh of barony in 1685, for in 1723 one William Walker noted *"an old village called Woodhead of Fetterletter, where there is a stone tolbooth, a stone cross, and where, in old times, stood several yearly mercats"*. However, Woodhead still appeared to be a mere hamlet when shown on the Roy map of about 1750. Nearly a century later, in 1846, the mercat cross was rebuilt and markets reinstated; Woodhead was noted by Pratt in 1858 as *"a village with a long-established Episcopal church"*. In the mid 20th century its population of about 375 enjoyed basic services, but by 1981 under 300 people lived there and the school and post office had closed, leaving it entirely dependent on Fyvie and such larger centres as Turriff. There has been little noticeable development since.

## WOODSIDE & Kittybrewster — Map 10, C3

***N-W. areas of Aberdeen,** pop. 23,000* — OS 38: NJ 9209

The Roy map of about 1750 marked the intriguingly named *'Copper Mill'* beside the River Don upstream from Old Aberdeen. A new road was built from Aberdeen over Tyrebagger Hill to Kintore in 1762, and when in 1765 Alexander Carlyle viewed the area west of Old Aberdeen he found it *"full of villages, all the work of 20 years – since before that time the black heath came close to the town"*. Remarkably, the agricultural improvement in the area had been stimulated by industrialists at Old Aberdeen. In the late 18th century *"several new manufactories for spinning flax by machinery were established on the Don near Old Aberdeen"* (Bremner). In 1785 Gordon, Barron & Co built Woodside mill some 1.5km west of Old Aberdeen, originally to spin cotton; from 1787 chlorine was used there in bleaching, using a Swedish discovery.

**Grandhome, Canal, Flax, and Ironfounding**: The enormous Grandhome mill of seven stories which stood almost opposite on the north bank of the river (and took its name from a mansionhouse east of Dyce) was actually built for flax spinning in the 1790s by Alex Smith, a paper maker and a Mr Baird, a silk merchant. The new Grandholm (or Grandhome) bleachfield exceeded 70 acres in extent by 1797. The attendant growth of Woodside as an industrial village seems to have been largely overlooked by historians, who often lump references to Woodside in with Aberdeen, from which it was entirely distinct for over a century. The Aberdeen Canal which opened in 1805 was dug through the area south of the Don en route to Inverurie. The already huge Grandhome mill was extended in 1812 by Leys, Masson & Co, and in 1817 it was said to have nearly 4000 operatives. Three further extensions in the 1820s eventually brought it to 240 spinning frames; it also possessed a bleachworks and the Grandholm Foundry, which in 1835 equipped a mill at Old Rayne. By 1838 the large village of Woodside which had sprung up to accommodate the workers had a post office, and it also acquired an inn.

**The Railway and Kittybrewster**: In mid-century the canal was acquired and closed by the infant Great North of Scotland Railway (GNSR), who infilled its right of way and laid their tracks there. From 1854 the charmingly named Kittybrewster, south-east of Woodside but nearly 2 km from the city, became the inconvenient site of the first Aberdeen terminus of the GNSR, with yards, engine sheds, and workshops where the occasional locomotive was built. From 1855 the line was open to Waterloo Quay (Aberdeen docks), again on the canal alignment. Kittybrewster station was re-sited in 1856 when the Waterloo extension was improved to carry passenger trains. In 1858 a station was opened at Woodside, through which the track was doubled in 1861 as far as Dyce. The Denburn link opened in 1867 to connect Kittybrewster with the main line from the south.

**Textile Trouble, Burgh, Paper and Trams**: In 1851 Lees, Masson & Co still spun flax by steam power at Grandholm, and Milne, Cruden & Co did likewise at Gordon's Mills (and at Spring Gardens in Aberdeen). The Grandhome mill passed to J & J Crombie of Cothal, who converted it to manufacture fine woollens and tweeds. But it seemed that the profits were dissipated, not ploughed back, for in 1864 all three mills were silent, Warden remarking presciently *"and thus it will be everywhere, unless the families of the rising great be trained in habits of industry"*. Woodside became a police burgh in 1868. By 1869 the papermakers Alexander Pirie & Sons of Bucksburn owned a small mill at Woodside, making coarse paper. It appeared that Woodside cotton mill was again in production at that time, and Grandholm mill had been reopened by the Crombies, who employed nearly 600 workers; Haddon & Green employed about 1400 people making carpets and tweeds, split between the Don Mills and a mill at Garlogie, 15 km to the west. In 1874 a privately-owned horse tramway from the city centre reached Kittybrewster.

**Woodside in Aberdeen – engulfed by Sprawl**: In 1887 a new suburban train service was begun, with an additional station opened at Don Street between Woodside and Kittybrewster; a ferry between Gordon's mills and Grandholm works remained open in 1890. In 1891 the city's boundaries were greatly expanded to take in Woodside, and the horse-drawn trams had been extended to Bucksburn by 1894. By then a bridge spanned the river at Woodside – a large but compact village with a post and telegraph office, an inn and the two railway stations. Woodside was still distinct from the city's built-up area which by then had engulfed Kittybrewster, where the large Royal Cornhill Hospital had been built. Woodside quickly lost its separate identity, as urban facilities were provided; Stewart Park was established in 1894 and Westburn Park dates from 1901. In 1898 the city council took over the tramway, and arranged for the Aberdeen Suburban Tramways Company to electrify it in 1899; from 1904 the company operated services between Woodside and Bankhead, which were replaced by buses in 1927.

**Buses take the Train, the Trams and Steam**: In 1902 GNSR locomotive building and repair at Kittybrewster ceased, and was moved to Inverurie. After 1923 Kittybrewster remained the main locomotive running depot in the north-east for their successors the LNER, who built a tall mechanical coaling plant in 1932. The Royal Northern Agricultural Society established its showground at Woodside, and Kittybrewster's Aberdeen & Northern cattle mart was in operation by the 1930s. As urban development consolidated, the substantial Art Deco *Northern Hotel* was built at Kittybrewster in 1937; but in that year growing bus and car competition caused withdrawal of the suburban train services, and Woodside and Don Street stations were closed. However, Woodside mill, by then producing woollens, was still driven by water power until 1965. The trams ceased to run to Woodside in 1958. The Kittybrewster steam locomotive depot was closed in 1961, and livestock movement by rail to Kittybrewster was abandoned in 1967; its passenger station lasted only until about 1970. Retail warehouses were to be built on the Kittybrewster rail yard by 1990.

**Decentralisation, and the Demise of Grandhome Mill**: By 1978 the College of Education had been moved out from the city to Kittybrewster, and from about 1985 the vast Danestone housing estate grew north of the river, bounded to north and west by a former minor road connecting Bridge of Don with North Anderson Drive, but rebuilt by 1985 into a new bypass (by 1999 the A90 trunk road). The opening of the Thainstone cattle market complex at Inverurie about 1990 caused closure of the same company's auction mart at Kittybrewster. In 1991, when the area had some 23,300 residents, the recession sadly compelled the new owners Illingworth Morris of Bradford to close Crombie's historic 200-year old Grandhome Mill, which had already been cut down to 3 storeys after a fire; production and the famous brand name were moved to Langholm. However, in 2000 restoration of the mill seemed likely. The Royal Cornhill Hospital for mental illnesses – which had 700 beds in 1981 – was refurbished in the early 1990s, and from 1995 took in the patients from the doomed Kingseat Hospital at Newmachar. St Machar Academy has a roll of 1140, and the 32-room *Northern Hotel* is 'A' listed.

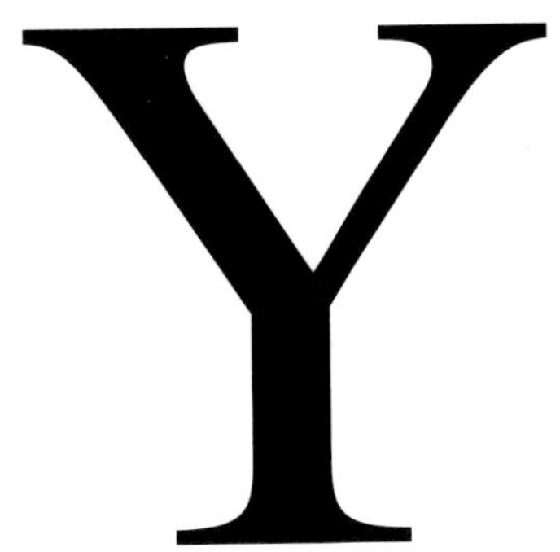

## YARROW, Deuchar & Whitehope

**Map 3, A4**

***Borders settlements,*** *pop. under 100* OS 73: NT 3527

The vast parish of Yarrow is about 27 km in length and contains some 20,000 ha, much of it high hills embracing the long valley of the Yarrow Water. This contains several small settlements, readily confused by strangers (see the two following entries). Standing stones show the great age of the most central of these places, known as Deuchar, the name given to a 16th century tower near *Duchore* Kirk, as Pont who mapped the area about 1600 labelled it. A nearby mill stood in heavily wooded surroundings, later stripped for (and by) sheep. By about 1754, as Roy's map showed, a road followed the north bank of the Yarrow Water past a new Yarrow Kirk in this vicinity. In Yarrow parish was the birthplace in 1749 of Daniel Rutherford, who discovered that plants use carbon dioxide. There was still a mill at Deuchar in 1895 and Whitehope Farm stood beside the kirk; at that time the vast Yarrow parish held only 500 people. In 1951 it still had a population of 400, but by 1991 there were only 191 residents; otherwise – apart from some afforestation – little had outwardly changed at Yarrow in a century.

## YARROW FEUS

**Map 3, A4**

***Small village w. of Selkirk,*** *pop. 200 (area)* OS 73: NT 3426

Above the lengthy but narrow Yarrow Valley stands the prominent 543 metre Ben Ger, to which Gaelic name the Northumbrians added *'Law'* and the Normans prefixed *'Mount'*, hence it now bears the absurd title Mountbenger Law, meaning *'Mountain Mountain* Ger *Mountain'!* Let's get back to Ben Ger. By about 1754, as Roy's map showed, a road followed the north bank of the Yarrow Water past the scattered sites of the later crofts or smallholdings called Yarrow Feus. The *Mountbenger Inn* or *Gordon Arms Inn* at the crossing of the Ettrick to Traquair road 3 km west of Yarrow Feus was open by 1889, and nearby was the Mountbenger primary school. In 1962 Yarrow Feus had a school and also a post office; a third of the population of the parish having vanished in 20 years, primary schooling was centralised there in the mid 1970s. Yarrow Feus consequently kept its post office until about 1990, and also gained a medical practice. The *Gordon Arms Hotel* remains small, with 5 rooms, but like Yarrow primary school it is still open.

## YARROWFORD

**Map 3, A4**

***Borders hamlet,*** *pop. under 100* OS 73: NT 4130

The ancient defensive *'Oldwork'* beside the Yarrow Water was replaced a little upstream by the square 15th century keep of Newark Castle. Reputedly *"the strongest tower in the county"*, it dominated the hill-girt approach from the long, narrow Yarrow valley to Selkirk burgh; the ancient boundary of Yarrow parish excludes areas within 6 km of Selkirk. Newark had a grisly history, and fell into early ruin. By about 1754, as Roy's map showed, a road followed the north bank of the river upstream from the Yarrow Ford 1 km above Newark, where the ancient trackway between Selkirk and Traquair via Minchmoor crossed the river. In 1771 Mungo Park, who was to explore the Niger, was born near Newark Castle. Chambers in the 1820s found Yarrowford – which lies just within Yarrow parish – *"a little village"*; in the 1890s it had a post and telegraph office, a smithy, and to the east the mansionhouse of Broadmeadows, near which Scotland's first youth hostel was opened in 1931. In 1951 Yarrowford had a primary school, and *Broadmeadows Hotel* had 13 rooms. By 1984 the former Yarrowford school had become the village stores and post office, and because of its high fire risk the former hotel nearby functioned only as a pub. There was also a village hall. A detailed survey in 1984 showed that cars were owned by 93% of Yarrowford households, primarily for access to Selkirk, on which the small but then growing village relied; by 1993 even its post office had closed. However, the historic youth hostel is still open seasonally, and well connected by footpaths with the Southern Upland Way.

## YETHOLM (Kirk & Town)

**Map 3, C4**

***Borders twin-villages,*** *pop. 600 (area)* OS 74: NT 8228

Yetholm parish lies in a fold of the Cheviot Hills some 11 km south-east of Kelso, on either side of the upper Bowmont Water, which eventually enters the Tweed through the English River Till; the adjacent settlements of Kirk and Town Yetholm are within 3 km of the long-troubled English border. In the late 15th century Yetholm was a property of the powerful Bothwell family, which may explain why it was the only part of the valley to remain Scottish. There were gypsies in Scotland by 1505, and Kirk Yetholm became their base, because from there they could readily slip across the border whenever this was expedient. Permanent development at Yetholm was problematical until peace came at last in the 1580s, but historians may have overstressed the impact of the troubles, for by the time that Pont mapped Teviotdale around 1600 the area was closely settled, and *'Yettum'* and *'Kirk Yettum'* were adjoined by *'Priorsfyd mill'*. Primside Mill 1.5km to the south was the site of a parish school, opened in 1617. Hoselaw Tower was built some 5km to the north as late as the 17th century, when the habit of building defensible houses persisted in much of Scotland. Town Yetholm became a burgh of barony in 1665.

**Homes for Gypsies and the Road to England**: In the 18th century the Bennets of Grubet obligingly built cottages for the gypsy community at Kirk Yetholm, and a gypsy school was also established. The Roy map made about 1754 used the old spelling *'Yettum'*; mills turned both north and south of Town Yetholm, and there was a *'Wake Mill'* downstream. The sole road through the village followed the Bowmont valley from its head at Cock Law (whence there was a link to Morpeth), through Yetholm to join the Wooler–Kelso road at Mindrum in Northumberland – then the only way by road between Yetholm and the rest of Scotland! Three fairs were scheduled for 1797, though Heron merely mentioned *"the village of Yetholm"* in 1799. Milling led to a brewery which was at work by 1825, though this did not last, and no other industries were established. There was no post office until after 1838. The Yetholms had a population of almost 600 in 1891; the larger place was Town Yetholm, which had the post office, and each settlement possessed an inn.

**Promoting Tourism and serving Walkers**: Although the last so-called monarch of the gypsy tribe died in 1883, a *'Gypsy King'* was crowned at Yetholm as late as 1898 in order to encourage tourism! Yetholm parish held 800 people in 1901 when there were still three mills on the Bowmont Water, but sixty years later all had closed. The twin villages have had about 600 people ever since 1951, but share only the facilities of a small village. A youth hostel had been established by 1963 to serve the north end of the Pennine Way, whose last 3km are in Scotland, and by 1981 no fewer than five small hotels were open in the Yetholms, which had a caravan and camping site by 1983 but remained quiet and remote. A firm of livestock transporters remained at work. By 1998 the extensive late 18th century Yetholm Mill and its farmstead stood sadly derelict. The long distance footpath called *St Cuthbert's Way* follows an Anglo-Scottish east–west course, meeting the long-established Pennine Way at Yetholm, where only two hotels remain open, the *Border* and *Plough*.

## YOKER

**Map 15, B4**

***Eastern part of Clydebank,*** *pop. 20,500*

OS 64: NS 5269

From the 14th century a ferry plied across the tidal River Clyde 9km west of Glasgow, linking Renfrew with Yoker on the north bank, which as late as 1895 was part of Renfrewshire but is now split between Glasgow and Clydebank. *'Yockyrr'* was shown on Pont's map of Lennox, made about 1600. Ferry piers had been built by 1725, and by about 1754 a road joined Glasgow with Dumbarton, crossing *'Yocher Briggs'*. The Yoker distillery was at work by 1770. In 1877 Napier Shanks & Bell established the *'Yoker Old'* shipyard (actually within modern Clydebank), from 1898 named Napier & Miller. In 1882 the Glasgow, Yoker & Clydebank Railway – which ran inland of the main road – was opened by its promoters the North British Railway (NB), with a station at Yoker Mill Road (in Clydebank). The huge 300m-long underwater ledge of the Elderslie Rock, just up-river of the Renfrew ferry, which had restricted the depth of water in the Clyde to 2.5 metres, was finally blasted away in 1886 after 32 years' work to give six metres' clear depth at low water; this boosted the building of larger vessels up-river of Yoker. In 1891 the population was 1256, straddling the county boundary.

**Varied Edwardian Heavy Industry**: In 1896 the Caledonian Railway (CR) opened a duplicate line close alongside the north bank (as the Lanarkshire & Dunbartonshire), giving Yoker its

*Yoker power station, built in 1918 by the Clyde Valley Electric Power Co Ltd. It became a base-load station for the National Grid, and operated until the 1970s.* *(RCAHMS / JRH)*

second station. There was also a post and telegraph office – but most nearby development was in Clydebank. About 1901 Bull's Metal & Marine Company built a non-ferrous foundry beside the ferry terminal, primarily to make ships' propellers, and about 1908 the pump manufacturers Drysdale erected the nearby Bon Accord Works. The first Elderslie dry dock was built in 1904 by the ship repairers Shearer & Co. In 1906 Napier & Miller moved from the Yoker Old shipyard to Old Kilpatrick, to make way for the east end of the new Rothesay Dock, which was served by a new freight branch railway from Clydebank Dock Junction, 1 km to the east of Yoker station on the NB. The Glasgow Motor Lorry Company which was founded at Yoker in 1906 (but renamed Halley Industrial Motors in 1907) built a factory there in the latter year to make steam and petrol engined vehicles, plus its own engines from 1910. By 1914 the firm were well known and large for the period, making lorries and fire appliances and giving rise to the name Halley Street; but from 1914–18 artillery shells largely replaced Halley's vehicle production.

**More Power, but Fewer Lorries and No Whisky**: Yoker Power Station was built in 1918 just downstream of the ferry. The small Blawarthill Hospital in Dyke Road was built in the early 20th century; the vast Knightswood council housing estate around and to the north of it was a Glasgow Corporation development of the late 1920s. Between the wars Halley made commercial vehicle chassis of up to 3.5 tonnes, but were in difficulties by 1927; re-financed as Halley Motors, they survived with falling output until in 1935 the firm was absorbed by Albion *(see Whiteinch)* – the Yoker factory becoming a packing and service depot and ultimately an industrial estate. By then large modern tram *'caurs'* provided a cheap cross-city service to Dalmuir West, Baillieston and Auchenshuggle. The distillery was destroyed by fire in the air raids of March 1941.

**Electric Trains and Exquisite Form**: By the 1950s the area contained some 12,000 people (and railway engine sheds). The trams were sadly abandoned in 1962. The former CR line lost its passenger services when the ex-NB line was electrified around 1960, with the addition of a station named Garscadden (3 km south of the name's original location). Drysdale's pumps ceased trading about 1970 and the power station closed about 1973. Ship-repairing at the Elderslie dockyard ended about 1978, when the yard was taken over by Yarrows. By 1981 Blawarthill hospital was in geriatric use. The Renfrew Ferry which had plied for centuries from Yoker Ferry Road was the last Clyde vehicle ferry service, ending in 1984; a pedestrian ferry still operates. In 1987 Yoker became the control and operations centre for Glasgow's suburban rail services – a carriage washing plant and servicing depot being built at Clydebank Dock Junction. Exquisite Form Brassiere (GB) who made swimwear at Halley Street by 1979, were still producing bras in 1994.

# Bibliography


Adams F (1970) *The Clans, Septs & Regiments of the Scottish Highlands*, Johnston & Bacon, Stirling (8th edition, revised by Sir Thomas Innes)

Adams I H (1978) *The Making of Urban Scotland*, Croom Helm, London

Adamson P and Lamont-Brown R (1981) *Victorian & Edwardian Dundee from Rare Photographs*, Alvie Publications, St Andrews

Anderson A (1986) *The Dean Tavern: A Gothenburg Experiment*, The Dean Tavern Trust, Newtongrange

Anon (1970) *East Kilbride Official Guide*, Burrows, Cheltenham

Automobile Association (1953) *Road Book of Scotland*, AA, London

Automobile Association (1965) *Illustrated Road Book of Scotland*, AA, London, (4th edition)

Ballingall W (1872) *The Shores of Fife*, Edmondston & Douglas, Edinburgh; republished as *The Kingdom of Fife in Days Gone By*, by Lang Syne publishers, Newtongrange, Midlothian

Balneaves E (1977) *The Windswept Isles: Shetland & its People*, John Gifford, London

Barbour J (1375) *The Bruce*: prose translation made in 1907 by G Eyre-Todd; reprinted 1996 by Mercat Press, Edinburgh

Barnard A (1887) *The Whisky Distilleries of the UK*, Harper's Weekly Gazette, London; republished by Mainstream Publishing, Edinburgh, and Lochar Publishing, Moffat, 1987

Barr W W (1972) *Glaswegiana*, Vista, Glasgow

Bede, the Venerable (731) *A History of the English Church and People*, translated by L Sherley-Price, Penguin, Harmondsworth; revised edition, 1968

Beech J (1993) *The Story of Errol Station*, Perth & Kinross District Libraries, Perth

Bennett G P (1980s) *The Great Road between Forth & Tay*, Markinch Printing Company, Markinch, Fife

Bennett G P (1994) *The Water of Leven: Over 250 Years of Power for Local Industry*, unpublished monograph in Kirkcaldy Public Library

Beveridge D (1888) *Between the Ochils and Forth*, Blackwood, Edinburgh

Biddle G (1990) *The Railway Surveyors*, BRB Property Board / Ian Allan, London & Shepperton

Binney M, Harris J & Winnington E (1980) *Lost Houses of Scotland*, Save Britain's Heritage Series

Bird A (1969) *Roads & Vehicles*, Longmans Green & Co, London & Harlow

Black A (1937) *The Story of Tunnels*, Whittlesey House, New York & London

Body G (1971) *British Paddle Steamers*, David & Charles, Newton Abbot

Bolton G D (1953) *Scotland's Western Seaboard*, Oliver & Boyd, Edinburgh

Boswell J (1773) *Journal of a Tour to the Hebrides*, Heinemann, London (1963 reprint)

Bowen D (1990) *Shaking the Iron Universe: British Industry in the 1980s*, Hodder & Stoughton, London

Bray E (1986) *The Discovery of the Hebrides: Voyagers to the Western Isles, 1745–1883*, Collins, London & Glasgow

Breeze D (ed.) (1984) *Studies in Scottish Antiquity*, John Donald, Edinburgh

Bremner D (1869) *The Industries of Scotland – their Rise, Progress and Present Condition*, A & C Black, Edinburgh

Brodie I (1976) *Steamers of the Forth*, David & Charles, Newton Abbot

Brown J M (ed.) (1977) *Scottish Society in the Fifteenth Century*, Edward Arnold, London

Brown P Hume (ed.) (1891) *Early Travellers in Scotland*, republished 1978 by James Thin, Edinburgh

Bruce W S (1980) *The Railways of Fife*, Melven Press, Perth

Burgess R and Kinghorn R (1990) *Moray Coast Railways: Exploring the Remains*, Aberdeen University Press

Butt G and Gordon G (eds) (1985) *Strathclyde: Changing Horizons*, Scottish Academic Press, Edinburgh

CACI (c.1985) *Today's Approach to Market Planning*, CACI, London & Leamington

Cameron A (1995) *Bank of Scotland 1695–1995, A Very Singular Institution*, Mainstream Publishing, Edinburgh

Cameron A D (1994) *The Caledonian Canal*, Canongate Academic, Edinburgh (3rd edition)

Campbell R H (1980) *The Rise and Fall of Scottish Industry 1707–1939*, John Donald, Edinburgh

Campbell R H (1985) *Scotland since 1707: The Rise of an Industrial Society*, John Donald, Edinburgh (2nd edition)

Campbell R H and Dow J B A (1968) *Source Book of Scottish Economic and Social History*, Basil Blackwell, Oxford

Cant M (1984) *Marchmont in Edinburgh*, John Donald, Edinburgh

Cant M (1986, 1987) *Villages of Edinburgh*, John Donald, Edinburgh (2 vols)

Cassells I (1994) *No More Paraffin-Oilers*, Whittles Publishers, Latheronwheel, Caithness (re lighthouses)

Casserley H C (1968) *Britain's Joint Lines*, Ian Allan, Shepperton

Chambers R (1827) *The Picture of Scotland*, William Tait, Edinburgh (2 vols)

Checkland S G (1975) *Scottish Banking, a History 1695–1973*, Collins, Glasgow

Christie G (1955) *Harbours of the Forth*, Christopher Johnson, London

Cobbett W (1833) *Cobbett's Tour in Scotland*, edited by Daniel Green; republished by Aberdeen University Press, 1984

Cochrane H (1975) *Glasgow – the First 800 Years*, City of Glasgow District Council

Crampsey R (1990) *The Scottish Football League – the First 100 Years*, Scottish Football League, Glasgow

Crawford W S (1946) *Nairns 1939–45*, Michael Nairn & Co, Kirkcaldy

Darton M (1990) *The Dictionary of Scottish Place Names*, Lochar Publishing, Moffat

Deans B T (1986) *Green Cars to Hurlford: The Story of Kilmarnock's Municipal Transport*, Scottish Tramway & Transport Society, Glasgow

Defoe D (1724–26) *A Tour through the Whole Island of Great Britain*, G Strahan, London: abridged & edited by P N Furbank and W R Owens, with illustrations selected by A J Coulson, republished 1991 by Yale University Press, New Haven & London

De Mare E (1975) *Bridges of Britain*, Batsford, London (revised edition)

Donaldson G (1983) *Isles of Home: 60 Years of Shetland*, Paul Harris, Edinburgh

Donnachie I (1979) *A History of the Brewing Industry in Scotland*, John Donald, Edinburgh

Donnachie I, Hume J and Moss M (1977) *Historic Industrial Scenes – Scotland*, Moorland Publishing, Hartington, Derbyshire

Donnachie I L and MacLeod I (1974) *Old Galloway*, David and Charles, Newton Abbot

Dorward D (1979) *Scotland's Place-Names*, reprinted by James Thin, Edinburgh (1986)

Dow J L (1975) *Greenock*, Greenock Corporation

Duckham B F (1970) *A History of the Scottish Coal Industry*, David & Charles, Newton Abbot

Duckworth C L D and Langmuir G E (1967) *West Highland Steamers*, T Stephenson & Sons, Prescot, Lancs (3rd edition)

Durie A J (1979) *The Scottish Linen Industry in the 18th Century*, John Donald, Edinburgh

Durie A J (1991) *George Washington Wilson in Dundee & Angus*, AUL Publishing, Aberdeen

Durie A J and Mellor R (1988) *George Washington Wilson and the Scottish Railways*, University of Aberdeen Library

Earnshaw A (1995) *Britain's Railways at War*, Atlantic Transport Publishers, Penryn, Cornwall

Edwards B (1986) *Scottish Seaside Towns*, BBC, London

Elder A (1976) *The Whisky Map of Scotland*, Bartholomew, Edinburgh (also 1991 revised reprint)

Ellis C H (1955) *The North British Railway*, Ian Allan, London

Ellison M H (1989) *Scottish Railway Walks*, Cicerone Press, Milnthorpe, Cumbria

Fawcett R (1994) *Scottish Abbeys and Priories*, Batsford, London

Fenwick H (1978) *Scotland's Abbeys and Cathedrals*, Robert Hale, London

Fenwick H (1986) *Scottish Baronial Houses*, Robert Hale, London

Ferguson D M (1985) *The Wrecks of Scapa Flow*, Orkney Press, Stromness

Fleming J B and Green F H W (1952) 'Some Relations between Country and Towns in Scotland', *Scottish Geographical Magazine*, vol.68 (re Bus Services)

Fontane T (1858) *Across the Tweed: Notes on Travel in Scotland*; translated from the German and republished 1965 by Phoenix House, London

Fraser D (1974) *East Coast Oil Town before 1700*, Standard Press, Montrose (re Montrose)

Frew J (ed.) (1984) *Building for a New Age: The Architects of Victorian and Edwardian St Andrews*, Crawford Centre for the Arts, St Andrews

Gardiner L (1961) *Stage-Coach to John o'Groats*, Hollis & Carter, London

Garmonsway G N (1954) *The Anglo-Saxon Chronicle*, Dent, London (2nd edition)

Geddie J (1894) *Fringes of Fife*, Lang Syne publishers, Newtongrange, Midlothian (reprinted 1982)

Glenrothes Development Corporation (1965) *Glenrothes: A Guide*, Glenrothes DC, Fife

Glover J (1987) *BR Diary 1958–1967*, Ian Allan, Shepperton

Graham D (1993) *Sunset on the Clyde: The Last Summers on the Water*, Neil Wilson, Glasgow

Grant I F (1994) *Everyday Life on an Old Highland Farm*, Shepheard-Walwyn, London (2nd edition 1981)

Grant J S (1977) *Highland Villages*, Robert Hale, London

Gray M (1978) *The Fishing Industries of Scotland 1790–1914*, Oxford University Press

Green S G (1886) *Scottish Pictures*, Religious Tract Society, London

Gulvin C (1984) *The Scottish Hosiery & Knitwear Industry, 1680–1980*, John Donald, Edinburgh

Haldane A R B (1952) *The Drove Roads of Scotland*, David & Charles, Newton Abbot (3rd edition 1973)

Haldane A R B (1962) *New Ways Through the Glens*, David & Charles, Dawlish

Haldane A R B (1971) *Three Centuries of Scottish Posts*, Edinburgh University Press

Halliday R S (1990) *The Disappearing Scottish Colliery*, Scottish Academic Press, Edinburgh

Hart M (1993) *The 100: A Ranking of the Most Influential Persons in History*, Simon & Schuster, London (2nd edition)

Haswell-Smith H (1999) *The Scottish Islands*, Canongate, Edinburgh

Hay G D & Stell G P (1986) *Monuments of Industry: An Illustrated Historical Record*, The Royal Commission on the Ancient and Historical Monuments of Scotland, HMSO

Hayes G (1990) *The Guide to Stationary Steam Engines*, Moorland Publishing, Ashbourne (2nd edition)

Henderson T (1978) *Shetland from Old Photographs*, Shetland Library & Museum, Lerwick

Hendrie W F (1989) *Linlithgow: 600 Years a Royal Burgh*, John Donald, Edinburgh

Henry R et al (1966) *Macduff & its Harbour*, Macduff Town Council

Heron R (1799) *Scotland Delineated*, Bell & Bradfute, Edinburgh (reprinted 1975 by James Thin, Edinburgh)

Hills P (ed.) (1991) *Scots on Scotch*, Mainstream Publishing, Edinburgh

House J (1976) *Pride of Perth: The Story of Arthur Bell & Sons*, Hutchinson Benham, London

Howat P (1980) *The Lochaber Narrow Gauge Railway*; reprinted by Famedram Publishers, Gartocharn

Hume J R (1974) *The Industrial Archaeology of Glasgow*, Blackie, Glasgow & London

Hume J R (1976) *The Industrial Archaeology of Scotland. Vol.1, The Lowlands and Borders*, Batsford, London

Hume J R et al (1990) *Scotland's Industrial Past*, National Museums of Scotland, Edinburgh

Hume J R & Moss MS (2000) *The Making of Scotch Whisky*, Canongate, Edinburgh (2nd edition, revised)

Hutchison J (1986) *Weavers, Miners and the Open Book: A History of Kilsyth*, Kelvinprint, Cumbernauld

Hutton G (1995) *Old Larbert & Stenhousemuir*, Richard Stenlake, Ochiltree, Ayrshire

Hutton G (1995) *Old Perth*, Richard Stenlake, Ochiltree, Ayrshire

Hutton G (1996) *Mining – Ayshire's Lost Industry*, Richard Stenlake, Ochiltree, Ayrshire

Hutton G (1999) *Fife – the Mining Kingdom*, Richard Stenlake, Ochiltree, Ayrshire

Hutton K (ed.) (1987) *Dysart*, Kirkcaldy District Council

Imrie D and Hutchison A (eds) (1989) *Kinglassie: A Village Remembered*, WEA, Edinburgh

Jackson A (1984) *The Symbol Stones of Scotland*, Orkney Press, Kirkwall

Jackson G (1983) *The History and Archaeology of Ports*, World's Work Limited, Tadworth, Surrey

Johnson A (1983) *Roman Forts*, A & C Black, London

Johnston C and Hume J R (1979) *Glasgow Stations*, David & Charles, Newton Abbot

Johnston W & A K (c.1910) *Map of the Railway Systems of Scotland*, W & A K Johnston, Edinburgh & London (several undated editions appeared)

Jones S J (ed.) (1968) *Dundee & District*, British Association for the Advancement of Science

Joyce J (c.1964) *Tramway Heyday*, Ian Allan, London

Keeble D (1976) *Industrial Location & Planning in the UK*, Methuen, London

Keppie L (1986) *Scotland's Roman Remains*, John Donald, Edinburgh

Kerr D (1999) *Shale Oil, Scotland: The World's Pioneering Oil Industry*, (self-published) (2nd edition)

Keys D (1999) *Catastrophe: An Investigation into the Origins of the Modern World*, Century, London

Kirkcaldy Civic Society (1999) *Kirkcaldy Remembered*, Tempus Publishing, Stroud, Glos.

Klapper C (1974) *The Golden Age of Tramways*, David & Charles, Newton Abbot (2nd edition)

Knox J (1786) *A Tour of the Highlands of Scotland and the Hebride Isles: A Report to the British Society for Extending the Fisheries*; reprinted by James Thin, Edinburgh, 1970

Lamb G (1991) *Sky over Scapa 1939–1945*, Birgisey, Birsay, Orkney

Lamont-Brown R and Adamson P (1981) *The Victorian and Edwardian Borderland from Rare Photographs*, Alvie Publications, St Andrews

Larkin E (1992) *An Illustrated History of British Railways Workshops*, Oxford Publishing Company, Sparkford

Lenman B (1975) *From Esk to Tweed: Harbours Ships and Men of the East Coast of Scotland*, Blackie, Glasgow & London

Lenman B (1977) *An Economic History of Modern Scotland*, Batsford, London

Liddell C (1994) *Pitlochry: Heritage of a Highland District*, Perth & Kinross District Libraries

Lindsay M (1980) *Lowland Scottish Villages*, Robert Hale, London

Lindsay M (1987) *Victorian & Edwardian Glasgow from Old Photographs*, Batsford, London

Littlejohn J H (1990) *The Scottish Music Hall 1880–1990*, GC Book Publishers, Wigtown

Lockhart R H B (1937) *My Scottish Youth*, Putnam, London

Lynch M (ed.) (1987) *The Early Modern Town in Scotland*, Croom Helm, London (esp. Chapter 10 by I D White)

Lynch M, Spearman M & Stell G (eds) (1988) *The Scottish Medieval Town*, John Donald, Edinburgh

Lynch M (1991) *Scotland – a New History*, Century, London

Lythe S G E and Butt J (1975) *An Economic History of Scotland 1100–1939*, Blackie, Glasgow & London

McCutcheon C (1994) *Old Airdrie*, Richard Stenlake, Ochiltree

Macdonald A & P (1992) *Granite & Green: Above North-East Scotland*, Mainstream Publishing, Edinburgh

Macgregor D R & Harris R (1974) *Castles of Scotland*, A Collins Map

Macgregor F (1984) *Famous Scots: The Pride of a Small Nation*, Gordon Wright Publishing, Edinburgh

McGregor J A (1982) *All Stations to Mallaig! The West Highland Line Since Nationalisation*, Bradford Barton, Truro

Mackay G (2000) *Scottish Place Names*, Lomond Books, New Lanark

Mackay J (1997) *Sounds out of Silence: a life of Alexander Graham Bell*, Mainstream Publishing, Edinburgh & London

Mackay J A (1978) *Scottish Postmarks from 1693 to the Present Time*, Mackay, Dumfries

McKean C (1984) *The Scottish Thirties – an Architectural Introduction*, Scottish Academic Press, Edinburgh

Mackie J D (1978) *A History of Scotland*, Penguin Books, Harmondsworth (2nd edition, revised & edited by B Lenman and G Parker)

McLean A P (1986) *This Magnificent Line: Story of the Edinburgh–Glasgow Railway*, Lang Syne publishers, Newtongrange, Midlothian

MacLean E (1970) *Bridge of Allan: The Rise of a Village*, Alloa Printing & Publishing Company

McLellan R (1985) *The Isle of Arran*, David & Charles, Newton Abbot (3rd edition)

McMillan A A & Gillanders R J (1997) *Quarries of Scotland*, Technical Advice Note 12, Historic Scotland, Edinburgh

McMillan A A, Gillanders R J & Fairhurst J A (1999) *Building Stones of Edinburgh*, Edinburgh Geological Society (2nd edition)

Macmillan N S C (1970) *The Campbeltown & Machrihanish Light Railway*, David & Charles, Newton Abbot

Macnab P A (1987) *Mull & Iona*, David & Charles, Newton Abbot

McNeill P and Nicholson R (eds) (1975) *An Historical Atlas of Scotland c.400–1600*, University of St Andrews Press

McNeill P G B and MacQueen H L (eds) (1996) *Atlas of Scottish History to 1707*, University of Edinburgh

MacPhail I M M (1974) *The Clydebank Blitz*, Clydebank Town Council

McWilliam C (1975) *Scottish Townscape*, Collins, London

Mair C (1990) *Stirling: The Royal Burgh*, John Donald, Edinburgh

Malcolm D (1992) *Recollections of Paisley*, Richard Stenlake, Glasgow

Manley G (1952) *Climate & the British Scene*, Collins, London

Marshall P (1998) *The Scottish Central Railway: Perth to Stirling*, Oakwood Press, Usk, Mon.

Martin M (1698) *A Voyage to St Kilda*, Brown & Goodwin, London [see Martin (1934) for republication]

Martin M (1703) *A Description of the Western Islands of Scotland*, Andrew Bell, London [see Martin (1934) for republication]

Martin M & Monro D (1934) comprising (1) Martin M (1703) *A Description of the Western Islands of Scotland*; (2) Martin M (1698) *A Voyage to St Kilda*; and (3) Monro D (1549) *A Description of the Western Islands of Scotland*, as printed 1774 for William Auld, Edinburgh; republished in one volume by Eneas Mackay, Stirling

Marwick W H (1964) *Scotland in Modern Times*, Frank Cass, London

Meikle H W (ed.) (1947) *A Description of Scotland & Scottish Life*, Nelson, Edinburgh & London

Miller J (1979) *Caithness*, Skilton & Shaw, London

Minto C F (1990) *Scotland Yesterday*, Batsford, London (2nd edition)

Moncrieff R & A (eds) (1990) *The Annals of Kinross-shire*, Fossoway & District Community Council

Monro D (1549) *A Description of the Western Islands of Scotland*, as printed 1774 for William Auld, Edinburgh [see Martin (1934) for republication]

Morrice P (1983) *The Schweppes Guide to Scotch*, Alphabooks, Sherborne, Dorset

Morris R and F (1983) *Scottish Harbours*, Aletha Press, Everton, Sandy, Beds.

Muckhart & Glendevon Amenity Society (1988) *Muckhart Clackmannanshire: An Illustrated History of the Parish* (self-published)

Muir J (1987) *The Story of my Boyhood and Youth*, Canongate, Edinburgh (first published 1913)

Muir J R (1982) *The Lost Villages of Britain*, Michael Joseph, London

Muir R (1990) *Castles and Strongholds*, Macmillan, London

Muirhead J (1994) *Mills on the River Leven*, Kirkcaldy District Council

Mullay A J (1990) *Rails Across the Border*, Patrick Stephens, Wellingborough

Mullay A J (1991) *Rail Centres: Edinburgh*, Ian Allan, Shepperton

Munn C W (1981) *The Scottish Provincial Banking Companies 1747–1864*, John Donald, Edinburgh

Munro I S (1973) *The Island of Bute*, David & Charles, Newton Abbot

Munro R W (1979) *Scottish Lighthouses*, Thule Press, Stornoway

Murray A (1988) *The Forth Railway Bridge – a Celebration*, Mainstream Publishing, Edinburgh (2nd edition)

Murray J (1894) *Handbook for Scotland*, John Murray, London (Republished 1971 by David & Charles, Newton Abbot)

Naismith R J (1985) *Buildings of the Scottish Countryside*, Victor Gollancz, London

Nelson G (1990) *Highland Bridges*, Aberdeen University Press

New A (1988) *A Guide to the Abbeys of Scotland*, Constable, London

Newton N (1996) *The Life and Times of Inverness*, John Donald, Edinburgh

Nicolaisen W F H (1976) *Scottish Place-Names*, Batsford, London

Nicolson J R (1975) *Shetland*, David & Charles, Newton Abbot (2nd edition)

Nock O S (1963) *The Caledonian Railway*, Ian Allan, London

Nock O S (1965) *The Highland Railway*, Ian Allan, Shepperton

Nock O S (1973) *Underground Railways of the World*, A & C Black, London

Oakley C A (1967) *The Second City*, Blackie, Glasgow & London (first published 1946)

O'Donoghue, Y (1977) *William Roy 1726–1790: Pioneer of the Ordnance Survey*, British Museum, London

Olivier H (1975) *Dam It* (Chapter 2, The North of Scotland Hydro-Electric Scheme) Macmillan SA, Johannesburg

Paget-Tomlinson E (1990) *The Railway Carriers: The History of Wordie & Company*, Terence Dalton

Paterson A J S (1982) *Classic Scottish Paddle Steamers*, David & Charles, Newton Abbot

Paterson L (1988) *Twelve Hundred Miles for Thirty Shillings: Coastal Cruising from the Clyde*, Mainstream Publishing, Edinburgh

Paterson P T (1980) *Bygone Days in Cambusbarron*, Stirling District Libraries

Payne P L (1988) *The Hydro*, Aberdeen University Press

Pearce F W (1987) *Walkerburn: Its Origins and Progress*, Walkerburn Community Council (privately published)

Pennant T (1769) *A Tour of Scotland in 1769*, W Eyres, Warrington (3rd edition); republished 1979 by Melven Press, Perth

Pope R (ed.) (1989) *Atlas of British Social & Economic History*, Routledge, London

Pratt J B (1858) *Buchan*; reprinted by Heritage Press, Turriff

Prebble J (1963) *The Highland Clearances*, Secker & Warburg, London (republished by Penguin 1969)

Price R (1989) *Scotland's Golf Courses*, Aberdeen University Press; reprinted 1992 by Mercat Press, Edinburgh

Pryde G S (1965) *The Burghs of Scotland: A Critical List*, Oxford University Press

Ransome P J G (1984) *The Archaeology of the Transport Revolution 1750–1850*, World's Work Limited, Tadworth, Surrey

Ransome P J G (1989) *Scottish Steam Today*, Richard Drew, Glasgow

Reid J M (1964) *James Lithgow – Master of Work*, Hutchinson, London

Riddell J F (1979) *Clyde Navigation*, John Donald, Edinburgh

Ritchie A (1989) *Picts: An Introduction*, HMSO, Edinburgh

Ritchie A (1993) *Viking Scotland*, Batsford, London, and Historic Scotland

Rolt L T C (1966) *Red for Danger*, Pan Books, London

Roy K (1987) *Travels in a Small Country: A Scottish Journey*, Carrick Publishing, Ayr

Saunders A (1989) *Fortress Britain: Artillery Fortifications in the British Isles and Ireland*, Beaufort Publishing, Liphook, Hants.

Scott J (1927) *History of Tayport*, J & G Innes, Cupar

Scottish Civic Trust (annual) *Buildings at Risk Bulletins*, Scottish Civic Trust, Glasgow

Selman P (ed.) (1988) *Countryside Planning in Practice: The Scottish Experience*, Stirling University Press

Shaw J (1984) *Water Power in Scotland 1550–1870*, John Donald, Edinburgh

Shepherd I A G (1986) *Exploring Scotland's Heritage: Grampian*, HMSO, Edinburgh

Silver O (1987) *The Roads of Fife*, John Donald, Edinburgh

Silver O (1987) 'The Roads of Scotland: From Statute Labour to Tolls', *Scottish Geographical Magazine* vol. 103, no. 3, pp. 141–9

Sinclair O (1989) *Gretna Green: A Romantic History*, Unwin Hyman, London

Smith D J (1989) *Britain's Military Airfields 1939–45*, Patrick Stephens, Wellingborough

Smith D L (1967) *The Dalmellington Iron Company: Its Engines and Men*, David & Charles, Newton Abbot

Smith D L (1969) *The Little Railways of South-West Scotland*, David & Charles, Newton Abbot

Smith D L (1970) *Tales of the Glasgow & South-Western Railway*, David & Charles, Newton Abbot

Smith D L (1976) *Locomotives of the Glasgow & South-Western Railway*, David & Charles, Newton Abbot (Appendix 4, Motive Power Depots)

Smith J S (1986) *George Washington Wilson in Orkney & Shetland*, Kennedy Brothers, Keighley, Yorks.

Smith R (1992) *Catastrophes and Disasters*, Chambers, Edinburgh

Smith R D P (1978) 'The Changing Urban Hierarchy in Scotland', *Regional Studies* vol.12, pp.331–51

Snoddy T G (1968) *Sir John Scot, Lord Scotstarvit: His Life and Times*, Constable, Edinburgh

Somers R (1848) *Letters from the Highlands on the Famine of 1846*, Melven Press, Perth (reprinted 1985)

Stephenson J B (1984) *Ford*, Paul Harris Publishing, Edinburgh

Stephenson J B (1985) *Exploring Scotland's Heritage: The Clyde Estuary & Central Region*, HMSO, Edinburgh

Stevens-Stratten S W (1983) *British Lorries 1945–1983*, Ian Allan, Shepperton

Stevens-Stratten S W (1988) *British Lorries 1900–1945*, Ian Allan, Shepperton

Stone J C (1989) *The Pont Manuscript Maps of Scotland: 16th Century Origins of a Blaeu Atlas*, Map Collector Publications, Tring, Herts

Stone J C (1991) *Illustrated Maps of Scotland from Blaeu's Atlas Novus of the 17th Century*, Studio Editions, London

Strawhorn J (1975) *Ayrshire: The Story of a County*, Ayrshire Archaeological & Natural History Society, Ayr

Tacitus C (1970) *The Agricola and the Germania* (translated from the Latin by H Mattingley and S A Handford), Penguin Books, Harmondsworth

Taylor W (1976) *The Military Roads in Scotland*, David & Charles, Newton Abbot

Thomas D A (1988) *A Companion to the Royal Navy*, Harrap, London

Thomas J (1964) *The Springburn Story: The History of the Scottish Railway Metropolis*, David and Charles, Dawlish

Thomas J (1965) *The West Highland Railway*, David & Charles, Dawlish

Thomas J (1966) *The Callander & Oban Railway*, David & Charles, Newton Abbot

Thomas J (1971) *A Regional History of the Railways of Britain: Vol.6, Scotland – the Lowlands and Borders*, David and Charles, Newton Abbot (revised by A J Paterson 1984)

Thomas J (1977) *The Scottish Railway Book*, David & Charles, Newton Abbot

Thomas J (1977) *The Skye Railway* (updated 1990 by J Farrington), David & Charles, Newton Abbot

Thomas J (1981) *Forgotten Railways: Scotland*, David & Charles, Newton Abbot (2nd edition)

Thomas J & Turnock D (1989) *A Regional History of the Railways of Great Britain: Vol.15, North of Scotland*, David & Charles, Newton Abbot

Thomson D L (1962) *A Handbook of Glasgow Tramways*, Scottish Tramway Museum Society

Trevelyan G M (1926) *History of England*, Longmans Green & Co, London (3rd edition)

Turnock D (1979) *The New Scotland*, David & Charles, Newton Abbot

Turnock D (1982) *Railways in the British Isles: Landscape, Land Use and Society*, A & C Black, London

Twidale G H E and Mack R F (1988) *A Nostalgic Look at Glasgow Trams*, Silver Link Publishing, St Michaels on Wyre, Lancashire

Tyrrell J (1989) *Racecourses on the Flat*, Crowood Press, Ramsbury, Wilts.

Vallance H A (1938) *The Highland Railway* (revised by C R Clinker and republished 1972), Pan Books, London

Vallance H A (1965) *The Great North of Scotland Railway*, (revised by the GNSR Association and republished 1989) David & Charles, Newton Abbot

Various (1987) *The Handbook to Edinburgh*, James Thin, Edinburgh (revised edition)

Waine C V (1980) *Steam Coasters and Short Sea Traders*, Waine Research Publications, Albrighton (2nd edition)

Warden A J (1864) *The Linen Trade*, Longman, London; re-issued by Frank Cass, London, 1967

Warner O (1974) *The Life-boat Service – a History of the Royal National Life-boat Institution 1824–1974*, Cassell, London

Waters F & Grant D (1973) *Thurso Then & Now*, Humphries & Waters, Thurso

Watson H D (1986) *Kilrenny & Cellardyke*, John Donald, Edinburgh

Watters A (1995) *The McIntosh Story*, Kirkcaldy Library

Waugh J L (1923) *Thornhill and its Worthies*, Dinwiddie, Dumfries (3rd edition)

Webster J (1994) *The Flying Scots: A Century of Aviation in Scotland*, The Royal Concert Hall, Glasgow

Webster M S (1958) *John McDouall Stuart*, Melbourne University Press

Weir M (1988) *Ferries in Scotland*, John Donald, Edinburgh

Whittington G and Whyte I D (eds) (1983) *An Historical Geography of Scotland*, Academic Press, London

Whittow J S (1979) *Geology & Scenery in Scotland*, Penguin, Harmondsworth (revised edition)

Wilson G, Ford D et al (2000) *Scotland – Home of Golf*, Pastime Publications, Edinburgh

Wilson J (1973) *Scotland's Malt Whiskies*, Famedram Publishers, Gartocharn

Wilson R (1970) *Scotch: The Formative Years*, Constable, London

Wordsworth D (1805) *A Tour in Scotland in 1803* (reprint of 1894 edition edited by J C Shairp), James Thin, Edinburgh

Worsdall F (1981) *The City that Disappeared: Glasgow's Demolished Architecture*, Richard Drew, Glasgow

Wright G (1985) *The Stone Villages of Britain*, David & Charles, Newton Abbot

Yarwood D (1970) *Robert Adam*, J M Dent & Sons, London

Youngson A J (1973) *After the Forty-Five*, Edinburgh University Press

Ziegler P (1969) *The Black Death*, Collins, London

# INDEX

# DETAILED MAPS

# KEY TO MAPS

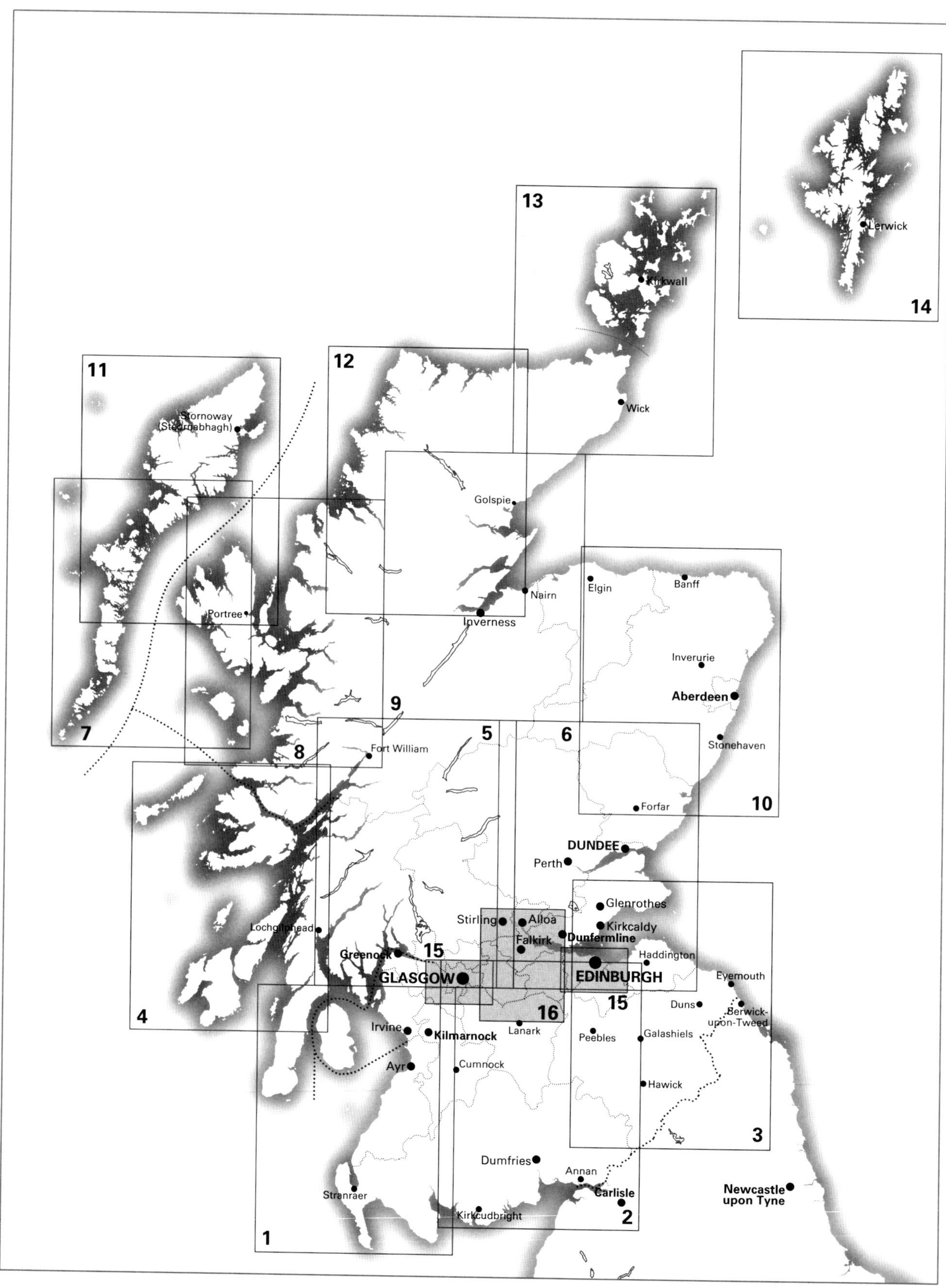

13
14
Lerwick
Kirkwall
11
12
Stornoway
(Steòrnabhagh)
Wick
Golspie
Nairn
Elgin
Banff
Portree
Inverness
Inverurie
Aberdeen
9
7
5
6
Fort William
Stonehaven
8
Forfar
10
DUNDEE
Perth
Glenrothes
Stirling
Alloa
Kirkcaldy
Lochgilphead
Falkirk
Dunfermline
Greenock
15
Haddington
GLASGOW
EDINBURGH
Eyemouth
15
Duns
4
16
Berwick-upon-Tweed
Irvine
Kilmarnock
Lanark
Peebles
Galashiels
Ayr
Cumnock
Hawick
3
Dumfries
Annan
Carlisle
Newcastle upon Tyne
Stranraer
Kirkcudbright
2
1

# Map 1

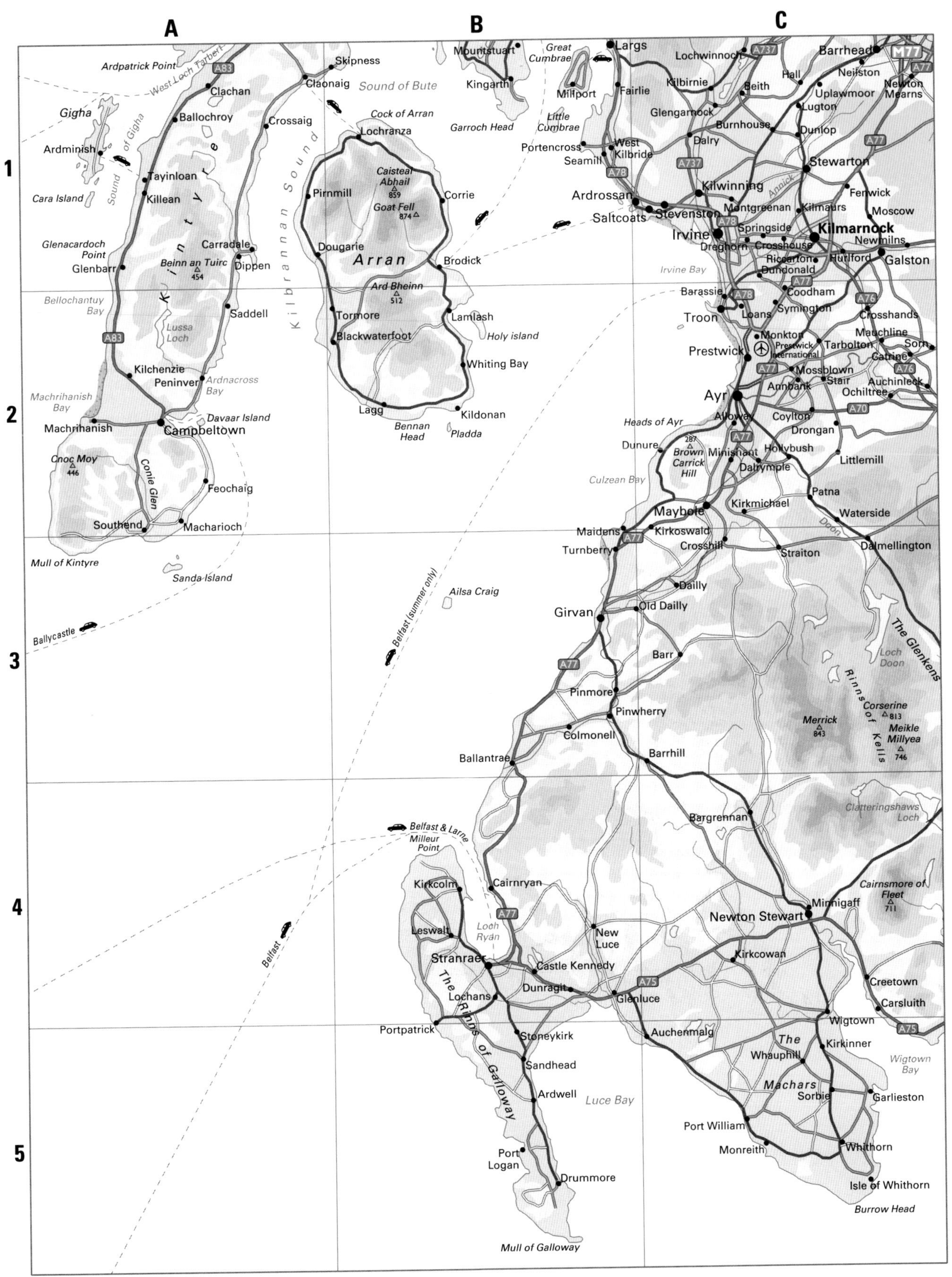

A
B
C
1
2
3
4
5
Ardpatrick Point
West Loch Tarbert
A83
Skipness
Mountstuart
Great Cumbrae
Largs
Lochwinnoch
A737
Barrhead
M77
Clachan
Claonaig
Sound of Bute
Kingarth
Millport
Fairlie
Kilbirnie
Hall
Neilston
Newton Mearns
A77
Gigha
Ballochroy
Crossaig
Cock of Arran
Little Cumbrae
Beith
Uplawmoor
Lugton
Glengarnock
Sound of Gigha
Lochranza
Garroch Head
Burnhouse
Dunlop
Ardminish
Kilbrannan Sound
Portencross
West Kilbride
Dalry
Seamill
A737
Stewarton
A78
Tayinloan
Caisteal Abhail 859
Pirnmill
Corrie
Kilwinning
Fenwick
Cara Island
Killean
Goat Fell 874
Ardrossan
Annick
Montgreenan
Kilmaurs
Moscow
Saltcoats
Stevenston
Springside
Kilmarnock
Glenacardoch Point
Kintyre
Carradale
Dougarie
Irvine
Crosshouse
Newmilns
Dreghorn
Beinn an Tuirc 454
Dippen
Arran
Brodick
Riccarton
Hurlford
Galston
Glenbarr
Dundonald
Irvine Bay
Ard Bheinn 512
A77
Bellochantuy Bay
Barassie
Coodham
A76
Saddell
Tormore
Lamlash
Troon
Loans
Symington
Crosshands
Lussa Loch
Holy island
Monkton
Mauchline
Blackwaterfoot
Prestwick
Prestwick International
Tarbolton
Sorn
Catrine
A83
Kilchenzie
Whiting Bay
Mossblown
A76
Peninver
Ardnacross Bay
Stair
Auchinleck
Machrihanish Bay
Annbank
Ochiltree
Ayr
Lagg
Kildonan
Coylton
A70
Davaar Island
Alloway
Machrihanish
Campbeltown
Bennan Head
Pladda
Heads of Ayr
Drongan
A77
Dunure
287 Brown Carrick Hill
Minishant
Hollybush
Cnoc Moy 446
Littlemill
Dalrymple
Conie Glen
Feochaig
Culzean Bay
Patna
Kirkmichael
Maybole
Waterside
Southend
Macharioch
Maidens
Kirkoswald
Doon
A77
Dalmellington
Crosshill
Straiton
Turnberry
Mull of Kintyre
Sanda Island
Belfast (summer only)
Dailly
Ailsa Craig
Old Dailly
Girvan
The Glenkens
Ballycastle
Loch Doon
Barr
A77
Rinns of Kells
Pinmore
Corserine 813
Pinwherry
Merrick 843
Meikle Millyea 746
Colmonell
Barrhill
Ballantrae
Clatteringshaws Loch
Bargrennan
Belfast & Larne
Milleur Point
Cairnsmore of Fleet 711
Kirkcolm
Cairnryan
Minnigaff
A77
Newton Stewart
Leswalt
Loch Ryan
New Luce
Stranraer
Kirkcowan
Belfast
Castle Kennedy
The Rinns of Galloway
Creetown
Dunragit
A75
Lochans
Glenluce
Carsluith
Wigtown
A75
Portpatrick
Auchenmalg
Stoneykirk
The Machars
Kirkinner
Whauphill
Wigtown Bay
Sandhead
Ardwell
Sorbie
Garlieston
Luce Bay
Port William
Monreith
Whithorn
Port Logan
Drummore
Isle of Whithorn
Burrow Head
Mull of Galloway

# Map 2

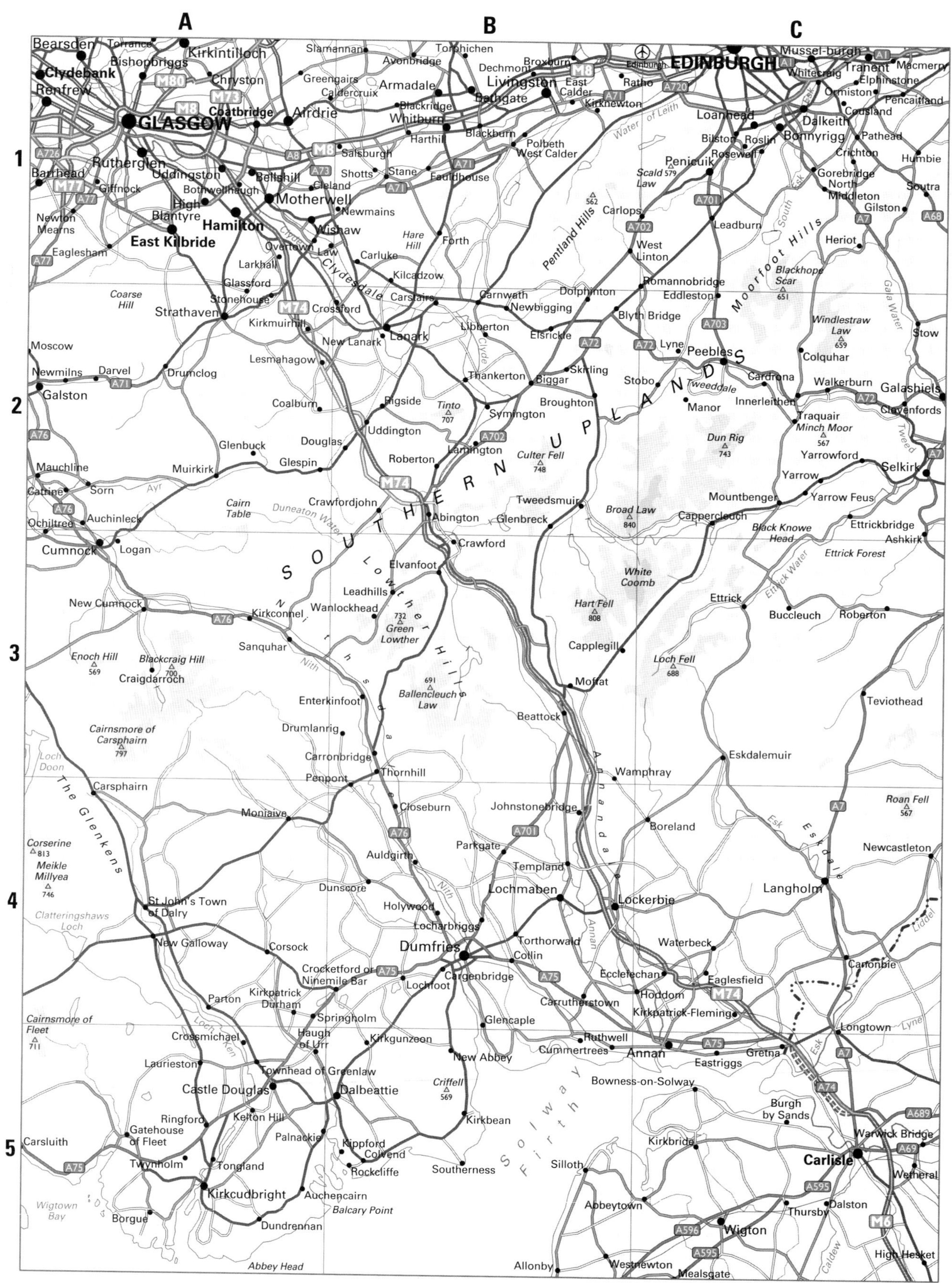

A
B
C
1
2
3
4
5
Bearsden
Torrance
Kirkintilloch
Slamannan
Torphichen
Avonbridge
Dechmont
Broxburn
Edinburgh
EDINBURGH
Mussel-burgh
Tranent
Macmerry
Bishopbriggs
Clydebank
Chryston
Greengairs
Armadale
Livingston
East Calder
Ratho
Whitecraig
Elphinstone
Renfrew
M80
M73
Caldercruix
Bathgate
M8
A71
A720
A1
Ormiston
Pencaitland
Coatbridge
Airdrie
Blackridge
Kirknewton
Water of Leith
Cousland
M8
GLASGOW
Whitburn
Loanhead
Dalkeith
Harthill
Blackburn
Polbeth
West Calder
Bilston
Roslin
Bonnyrigg
Pathead
A726
Salsburgh
Rosewell
Crichton
Rutherglen
M8
A8
A73
A71
Penicuik
Humbie
Barrhead
Uddingston
Bellshill
Shotts
Stane
Fauldhouse
Scald Law
579
Gorebridge
North Middleton
M77
Giffnock
Bothwellhaugh
Cleland
A71
Soutra
A77
High Blantyre
Motherwell
562
Carlops
A701
Gilston
Newton Mearns
Newmains
Pentland Hills
A702
Leadburn
A7
A68
Hamilton
Wishaw
Hare Hill
Heriot
East Kilbride
Overtown
Law
Forth
West Linton
Moorfoot Hills
Eaglesham
Carluke
A77
Larkhall
Clydesdale
Kilcadzow
Blackhope Scar
651
Glassford
Romannobridge
Coarse Hill
Stonehouse
Carstairs
Carnwath
Dolphinton
Eddleston
Gala Water
Strathaven
M74
Crossford
Newbigging
Blyth Bridge
Windlestraw Law
659
Kirkmuirhill
Libberton
A703
Stow
Moscow
New Lanark
Lanark
Clyde
Elsrickle
A72
A72
Lyne
Peebles
Colquhar
Lesmahagow
Newmilns
Darvel
Drumclog
Thankerton
Skirling
Stobo
Cardrona
Galston
A71
Biggar
Tweeddale
Walkerburn
Galashiels
Coalburn
Rigside
Tinto
707
Broughton
Manor
Innerleithen
A72
Clovenfords
A76
Symington
Traquair
Minch Moor
567
Tweed
Glenbuck
Douglas
Uddington
Dun Rig
743
A702
Lamington
Culter Fell
748
Yarrowford
A7
Mauchline
Muirkirk
Glespin
Roberton
Selkirk
Catrine
Sorn
Ayr
M74
Yarrow
Mountbenger
Yarrow Feus
Cairn Table
Crawfordjohn
Tweedsmuir
Broad Law
840
Cappercleuch
A76
Duneaton Water
Auchinleck
Abington
Glenbreck
Black Knowe Head
Ettrickbridge
Ochiltree
Ashkirk
SOUTHERN UPLANDS
Cumnock
Logan
Crawford
Ettrick Forest
Lowther Hills
Elvanfoot
White Coomb
Ettrick Water
Leadhills
New Cumnock
Kirkconnel
Wanlockhead
Ettrick
A76
Hart Fell
808
Buccleuch
Roberton
732
Green Lowther
Nithsdale
Sanquhar
Nith
Capplegill
Enoch Hill
569
Blackcraig Hill
700
Loch Fell
688
Craigdarroch
691
Moffat
Ballencleuch Law
Enterkinfoot
Teviothead
Beattock
Cairnsmore of Carsphairn
797
Drumlanrig
Carronbridge
Eskdalemuir
Loch Doon
Thornhill
Wamphray
Penpont
Carsphairn
The Glenkens
Closeburn
Roan Fell
567
Moniaive
Johnstonebridge
A7
Annandale
Boreland
Esk
Eskdale
Corserine
813
A76
A701
Parkgate
Newcastleton
Meikle Millyea
746
Auldgirth
Templand
Dunscore
Nith
Lochmaben
Langholm
St John's Town of Dalry
Lockerbie
Annan
Holywood
Clatteringshaws Loch
Locharbriggs
Liddel
Corsock
New Galloway
Torthorwald
Waterbeck
Dumfries
Collin
Canonbie
Crocketford or Ninemile Bar
A75
Cargenbridge
A75
Ecclefechan
Lochfoot
Eaglesfield
Parton
Kirkpatrick Durham
Hoddom
M74
Carrutherstown
Springholm
Kirkpatrick-Fleming
Cairnsmore of Fleet
711
Loch Ken
Glencaple
Crossmichael
Haugh of Urr
Longtown
Lyne
Kirkgunzeon
Ruthwell
Esk
Cummertrees
Annan
A75
Gretna
A7
Laurieston
New Abbey
Eastriggs
Townhead of Greenlaw
Criffell
569
Bowness-on-Solway
A74
Castle Douglas
Dalbeattie
Solway Firth
Burgh by Sands
Ringford
Kelton Hill
Kirkbean
A689
Gatehouse of Fleet
Palnackie
Warwick Bridge
Carsluith
Kippford
Colvend
Kirkbride
A69
A75
Twynholm
Tongland
Rockcliffe
Southerness
Silloth
Carlisle
Wetheral
Kirkcudbright
Auchencairn
A595
Wigtown Bay
Balcary Point
Abbeytown
Dalston
Borgue
Thursby
M6
Dundrennan
A596
Wigton
Caldew
A595
High Hesket
Abbey Head
Allonby
Westnewton
Mealsgate

# Map 3

A
B
C
1
2
3
4
5
Monimail
Cupar
Ceres
Pitscottie
Kingsbarns
Auchtermuchty
Ladybank
Strathmiglo
Fife Ness
Kettle
Largoward
Crail
Falkland
Freuchie
Carnbee
Kilrenny
Lundin Links
Anstruther
Kennoway
Markinch
Kilconquhar
Pittenweem
Loch Leven
Leslie
St Monans
Glenrothes
Windygates
Leven
Largo Bay
Elie
Isle of May
Ballingry
Kinglassie
Thornton
Buckhaven
Cardenden
East Wemyss
Kelty
Lochgelly
Templehall
Cowdenbeath
Kirkcaldy
Auchtertool
Firth of Forth
Crossgates
Kinghorn
Aberdour
Burntisland
Bass Rock
Dirleton
North Berwick
Dalgety Bay
Gullane
Inchkeith
Aberlady
Whitekirk
Drem
Cockenzie and Port Seton
Athelstaneford
Tyninghame
Dunbar
East Linton
Cramond
Longniddry
Leith
Tyne
Traprain
Musselburgh
Prestonpans
Spott
Edinburgh
Tranent
Haddington
Stenton
Innerwick
EDINBURGH
Wallyford
Macmerry
Dunglass
Cockburnspath
Whitecraig
Bolton
Garvald
Elphinstone
St Abb's Head
Ormiston
Meikle Black Law
Cousland
Pencaitland
Ecclaw
St Abbs
Water of Leith
Gifford
Coldingham
Loanhead
Dalkeith
Bilston
Roslin
Bonnyrigg
Pathhead
Grantshouse
Eyemouth
Lammer Law
Meikle Says Law
Rosewell
Crichton
Cranshaws
Abbey St Bathans
Ayton
Burnmouth
Penicuik
Humbie
Scald Law
Gorebridge
Auchencrow
Reston
Whiteadder Water
North Middleton
Soutra
Lammermuir Hills
Longformacus
Preston
Chirnside
Foulden
Berwick-upon-Tweed
Gilston
Carlops
Leadburn
Dirrington Great Law
Duns
Heriot
Oxton
Paxton
West Linton
Moorfoot Hills
Gavinton
Blackadder Water
Westruther
Polwarth
Tweedmouth
Romannobridge
Blackhope Scar
Tweed
Eddleston
Lauder
Ladykirk
Scremerston
Houndslow
Norham
Swinton
Holy Island or Lindisfarne
Windlestraw Law
Greenlaw
Gala Water
Stow
Leitholm
Ancroft
Leader Water
Gordon
Eccles
Duddo
Peebles
Colquhar
Hume
Coldstream
Fenwick
Cornhill-on-Tweed
Lowick
Stobo
Cardrona
Earlston
Stichill
Walkerburn
Galashiels
Crookham
Ford
Tweeddale
Manor
Innerleithen
Clovenfords
Smailholm
Flodden
Cockenheugh
Traquair
Old Melrose
Kelso
Milfield
Melrose
Kilham
Belford
Minch Moor
Dun Rig
Newtown St Boswells
Doddington
Dryburgh
Yarrowford
St Boswells
Roxburgh
Heiton
Kirknewton
Chatton
Selkirk
Town Yetholm
Kirk Yetholm
Akeld
Yarrow
Midlem
Wooler
Yarrow Feus
Mountbenger
Nisbet
Eckford
Broad Law
Lilliesleaf
Morebattle
Capperclеuch
Ancrum
Bonjedward
Cateran Hill
Black Knowe Head
Ettrickbridge
Bowmont Water
The Cheviot
Ashkirk
Hassendean
Minto
Jedburgh
Ettrick Forest
Eglingham
Ettrick Water
Kale Water
Teviot
Oxnam
Powburn
Denholm
Hawick
Windy Gyle
Breamish
Ettrick
Glanton
Buccleuch
Roberton
Teviotdale
Camptown
Cheviot Hills
Whittingham
Capplegill
Bonchester Bridge
Chesters
Loch Fell
Southdean
Netherton
Edlingham
Carter Bar
Teviothead
Thropton
Rothbury Forest
Rothbury
Riccarton Junction
Longframlington
Eskdalemuir
Cheviot
Rochester
Redesdale
Otterburn
Roan Fell
Kielder
Elsdon
Esk
Eskdale
Boreland
Liddesdale
Falstone
Newcastleton
Kielder Water (Reservoir)
Rede
Langholm
Bellingham
A91
A92
A90
A902
A1
A720
A68
A701
A702
A7
A697
A703
A72
A696

# Map 4

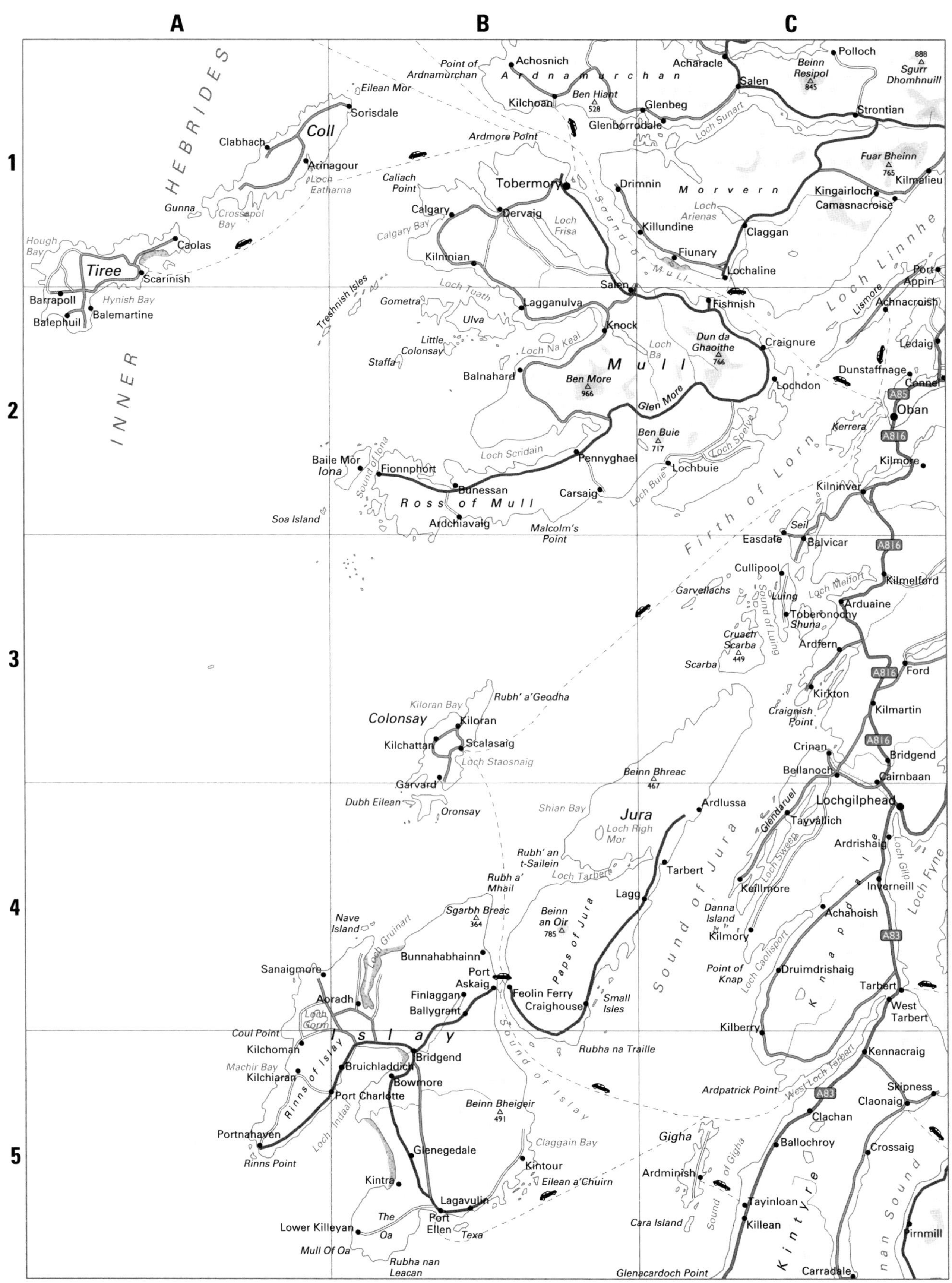
A
B
C
1
2
3
4
5
HEBRIDES
INNER
Coll
Sorisdale
Eilean Mor
Clabhach
Arinagour
Loch Eatharna
Gunna
Crossapol Bay
Hough Bay
Caolas
Tiree
Scarinish
Barrapoll
Hynish Bay
Balemartine
Balephuil
Point of Ardnamurchan
Achosnich
Ardnamurchan
Kilchoan
Ben Hiant
528
Acharacle
Salen
Glenbeg
Glenborrodale
Loch Sunart
Polloch
Beinn Resipol
845
888
Sgurr Dhomhnuill
Strontian
Ardmore Point
Caliach Point
Tobermory
Drimnin
Morvern
Fuar Bheinn
765
Kilmalieu
Kingairloch
Camasnacroise
Calgary
Dervaig
Loch Frisa
Sound of Mull
Loch Arienas
Killundine
Calgary Bay
Claggan
Fiunary
Kilninian
Lochaline
Loch Linnhe
Port Appin
Treshnish Isles
Loch Tuath
Gometra
Lagganulva
Salen
Fishnish
Lismore
Achnacroish
Ulva
Knock
Little Colonsay
Loch Na Keal
Loch Ba
Dun da Ghaoithe
766
Craignure
Ledaig
Staffa
Balnahard
Mull
Ben More
966
Dunstaffnage
Connel
Lochdon
A85
Oban
Glen More
Kerrera
Ben Buie
717
A816
Loch Spelve
Loch Scridain
Baile Mor
Iona
Sound of Iona
Fionnphort
Pennyghael
Lochbuie
Kilmore
Firth of Lorn
Bunessan
Carsaig
Loch Buie
Kilninver
Ross of Mull
Soa Island
Ardchiavaig
Malcolm's Point
Seil
Easdale
Balvicar
A816
Cullipool
Kilmelford
Garvellachs
Luing
Loch Melfort
Sound of Luing
Arduaine
Toberonochy
Shuna
Cruach Scarba
449
Ardfern
Scarba
A816
Ford
Kirkton
Kilmartin
Kiloran Bay
Rubh' a'Geodha
Craignish Point
Colonsay
Kiloran
A816
Kilchattan
Scalasaig
Crinan
Bridgend
Loch Staosnaig
Bellanoch
Cairnbaan
Beinn Bhreac
467
Garvard
Lochgilphead
Dubh Eilean
Oronsay
Shian Bay
Ardlussa
Jura
Glendaruel
Tayvallich
Loch Righ Mor
Ardrishaig
Rubh' an t-Sailein
Sound of Jura
Loch Sween
Loch Gilp
Tarbert
Loch Tarbert
Rubh a' Mhail
Keillmore
Inverneill
Loch Fyne
Lagg
Knapdale
Sgarbh Breac
364
Beinn an Oir
785
Danna Island
Achahoish
Nave Island
Paps of Jura
Kilmory
A83
Loch Gruinart
Point of Knap
Loch Caolisport
Bunnahabhainn
Druimdrishaig
Sanaigmore
Port Askaig
Finlaggan
Feolin Ferry
Small Isles
Tarbert
Aoradh
Ballygrant
Craighouse
West Tarbert
Loch Gorm
Islay
Kilberry
Coul Point
Rubha na Traille
Kilchoman
Bridgend
Kennacraig
Bruichladdich
Sound of Islay
Machir Bay
Kilchiaran
Bowmore
West Loch Tarbert
Rinns of Islay
Ardpatrick Point
Skipness
Port Charlotte
A83
Claonaig
Beinn Bheigeir
491
Clachan
Portnahaven
Gigha
Claggain Bay
Ballochroy
Loch Indaal
Crossaig
Rinns Point
Glenegedale
Sound of Gigha
Kintour
Ardminish
Kintra
Eilean a'Chuirn
Kilbrannan Sound
Lagavulin
Tayinloan
The Oa
Port Ellen
Cara Island
Killean
Lower Killeyan
Texa
Kintyre
Pirnmill
Mull Of Oa
Rubha nan Leacan
Glenacardoch Point
Carradale

# Map 5

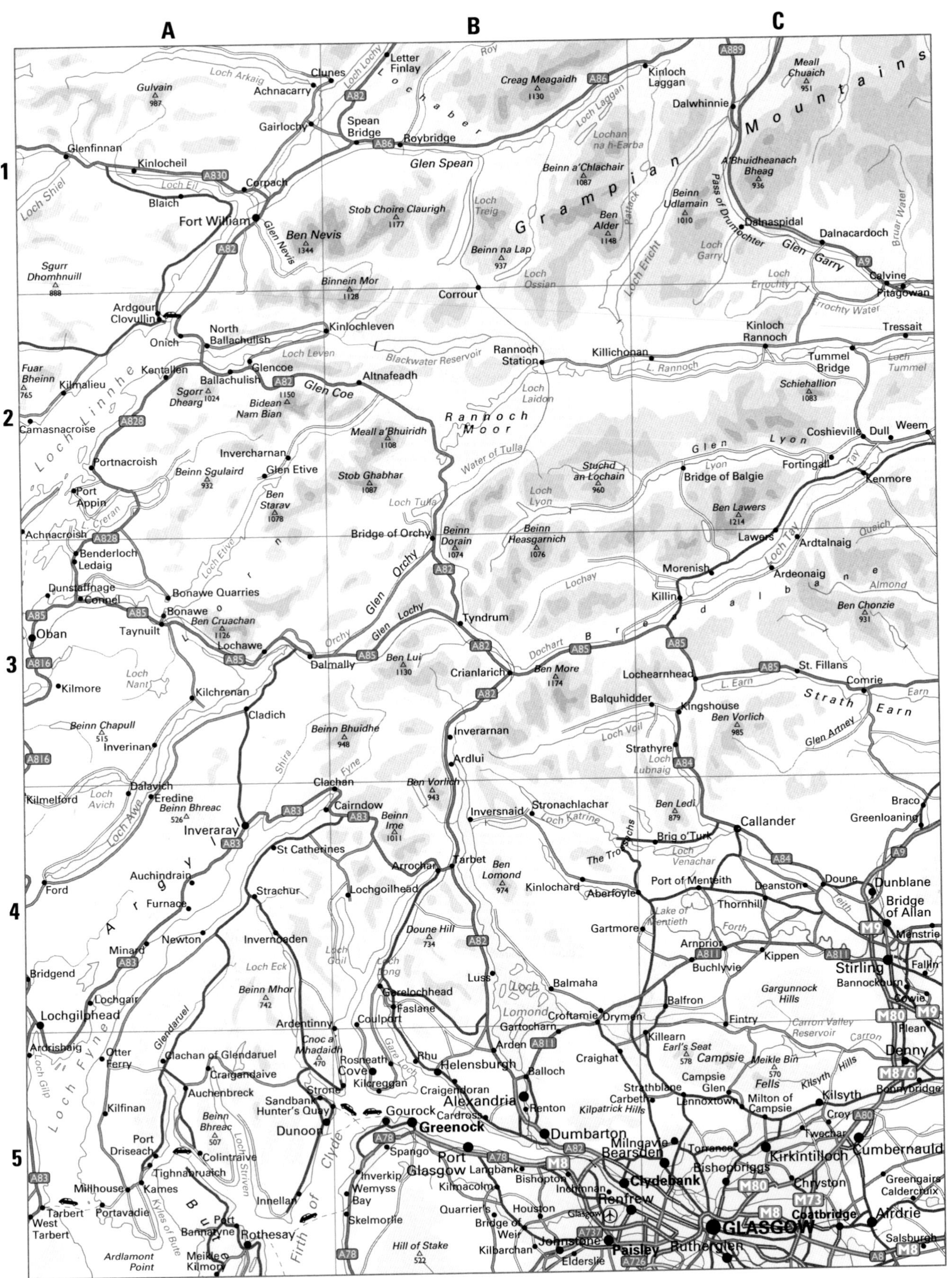

A
B
C
1
2
3
4
5
Fort William
Ben Nevis
Grampian Mountains
Oban
Glasgow
Greenock
Stirling
Inveraray
Callander
Dumbarton
Paisley

# Map 6

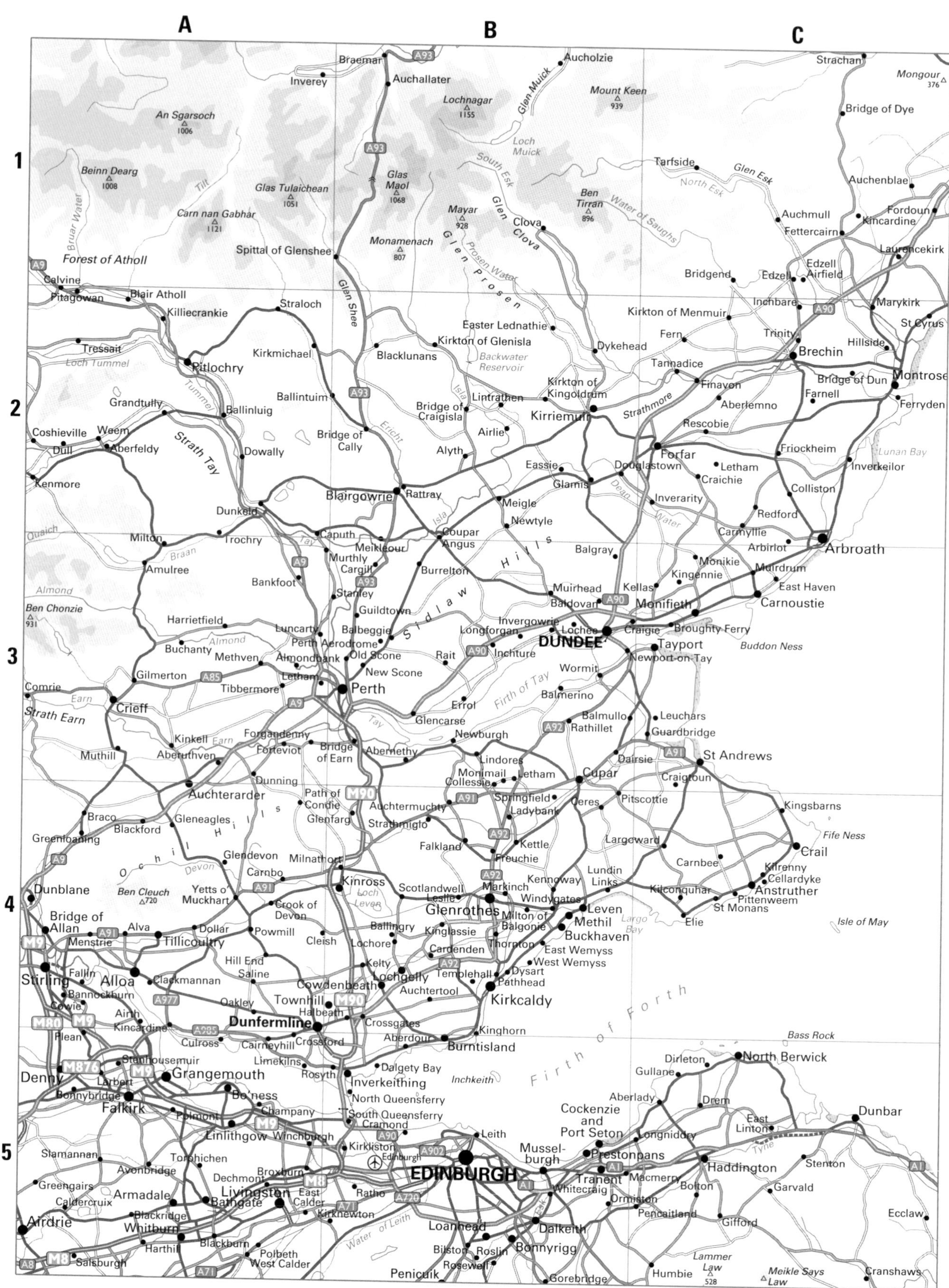

A
B
C
1
2
3
4
5
Braemar
A93
Aucholzie
Strachan
Inverey
Auchallater
Mongour
376
Lochnagar
1155
Glen Muick
Mount Keen
939
Bridge of Dye
An Sgarsoch
1006
Loch Muick
A93
Tarfside
Glen Esk
Beinn Dearg
1008
South Esk
North Esk
Auchenblae
Tilt
Glas Maol
1068
Glas Tulaichean
1051
Ben Tirran
896
Water of Saughs
Fordoun
Bruar Water
Mayar
928
Glen Clova
Clova
Auchmull
Kincardine
Carn nan Gabhar
1121
Fettercairn
Monamenach
807
Glen Prosen
Prosen Water
Laurencekirk
Forest of Atholl
Spittal of Glenshee
Edzell
Edzell Airfield
A9
Calvine
Bridgend
Pitagowan
Blair Atholl
Glen Shee
Straloch
Inchbare
A90
Marykirk
Killiecrankie
Kirkton of Menmuir
St Cyrus
Easter Lednathie
Fern
Trinity
Tressait
Kirkmichael
Blacklunans
Kirkton of Glenisla
Dykehead
Hillside
Loch Tummel
Backwater Reservoir
Brechin
Pitlochry
Tannadice
Bridge of Dun
Montrose
Tummel
Finavon
Kirkton of Kingoldrum
Farnell
Ballintuim
A93
Lintrathen
Strathmore
Aberlemno
Ferryden
Grandtully
Ballinluig
Isla
Bridge of Craigisla
Kirriemuir
Rescobie
Coshieville
Weem
Strath Tay
Bridge of Cally
Ericht
Airlie
Lunan Bay
Dull
Aberfeldy
Dowally
Alyth
Forfar
Friockheim
Eassie
Douglastown
Letham
Inverkeilor
Kenmore
Glamis
Craichie
Colliston
Blairgowrie
Rattray
Dean Water
Inverarity
Meigle
Dunkeld
Isla
Redford
Newtyle
Quaich
Caputh
Coupar Angus
Carmyllie
Milton
Trochry
Meikleour
Sidlaw Hills
Balgray
Arbroath
Braan
Tay
Arbirlot
A9
Murthly
Cargill
Monikie
Amulree
Burrelton
Kingennie
Muirdrum
Bankfoot
A93
East Haven
Almond
Stanley
Muirhead
Kellas
Ben Chonzie
931
Guildtown
Baldovan
A90
Monifieth
Carnoustie
Harrietfield
Invergowrie
Luncarty
Balbeggie
Longforgan
Lochee
Craigie
Broughty Ferry
Almond
Perth Aerodrome
DUNDEE
Tayport
Buchanty
Old Scone
Buddon Ness
Methven
Almondbank
Rait
A90
Inchture
Newport-on-Tay
Gilmerton
A85
Letham
New Scone
Wormit
Comrie
Tibbermore
Perth
Firth of Tay
Earn
Balmerino
Crieff
A9
Errol
Strath Earn
Tay
Glencarse
Balmullo
Leuchars
A92
Rathillet
Guardbridge
Kinkell
Earn
Forgandenny
Newburgh
Forteviot
Bridge of Earn
Abernethy
A91
St Andrews
Muthill
Aberuthven
Lindores
Dairsie
Dunning
Monimail
Letham
Cupar
Collessie
Craigtoun
Path of Condie
M90
Auchterarder
Auchtermuchty
A91
Springfield
Pitscottie
Ceres
Kingsbarns
Gleneagles
Ochil Hills
Ladybank
Braco
Glenfarg
Strathmiglo
Blackford
A92
Fife Ness
Greenloaning
Falkland
Kettle
Largoward
Crail
Glendevon
A9
Devon
Milnathort
Freuchie
Carnbee
Carnbo
A92
Lundin Links
Kilrenny
Dunblane
Kinross
Kennoway
Cellardyke
Ben Cleuch
720
Yetts o' Muckhart
Scotlandwell
Markinch
Anstruther
A91
Loch Leven
Kilconquhar
Muckhart
Leslie
Windygates
Pittenweem
Crook of Devon
Glenrothes
Leven
St Monans
Bridge of Allan
Milton of Balgonie
Methil
Largo Bay
Elie
Isle of May
Alva
A91
Dollar
Ballingry
Kinglassie
Buckhaven
M9
Menstrie
Powmill
Tillicoultry
Cleish
Lochore
Thornton
East Wemyss
Hill End
Cardenden
West Wemyss
Saline
Kelty
A92
Stirling
Fallin
Alloa
Clackmannan
Lochgelly
Templehall
Dysart
Pathhead
Bannockburn
Cowdenbeath
A977
Auchtertool
Cowie
Oakley
Townhill
M90
Kirkcaldy
Firth of Forth
Airth
Halbeath
M80
M9
Kincardine
Dunfermline
Crossgates
A985
Kinghorn
Plean
Culross
Cairneyhill
Crossford
Aberdour
Burntisland
Bass Rock
Stenhousemuir
Limekilns
Dirleton
North Berwick
M876
M9
Dalgety Bay
Larbert
Grangemouth
Rosyth
Gullane
Denny
Inverkeithing
Inchkeith
Bonnybridge
Bo'ness
North Queensferry
Aberlady
Falkirk
Drem
Champany
South Queensferry
Cockenzie and Port Seton
Dunbar
Polmont
Cramond
East Linton
M9
Linlithgow
Winchburgh
Leith
Longniddry
A90
Tyne
Kirkliston
A902
Musselburgh
Prestonpans
Slamannan
Torphichen
Edinburgh
A1
Stenton
Avonbridge
EDINBURGH
Haddington
A1
Dechmont
Broxburn
Tranent
Macmerry
Greengairs
M8
A1
Armadale
Livingston
East Calder
Ratho
Whitecraig
Bolton
Garvald
Caldercruix
Bathgate
A71
A720
Ormiston
Blackridge
Kirknewton
Pencaitland
Ecclaw
Airdrie
Whitburn
Loanhead
Dalkeith
Gifford
Water of Leith
Harthill
Blackburn
Polbeth
Bilston
Roslin
Bonnyrigg
Lammer Law
528
West Calder
Esk
Humbie
Meikle Says Law
Cranshaws
A8
M8
Salsburgh
A71
Penicuik
Rosewell
Gorebridge

# Map 7

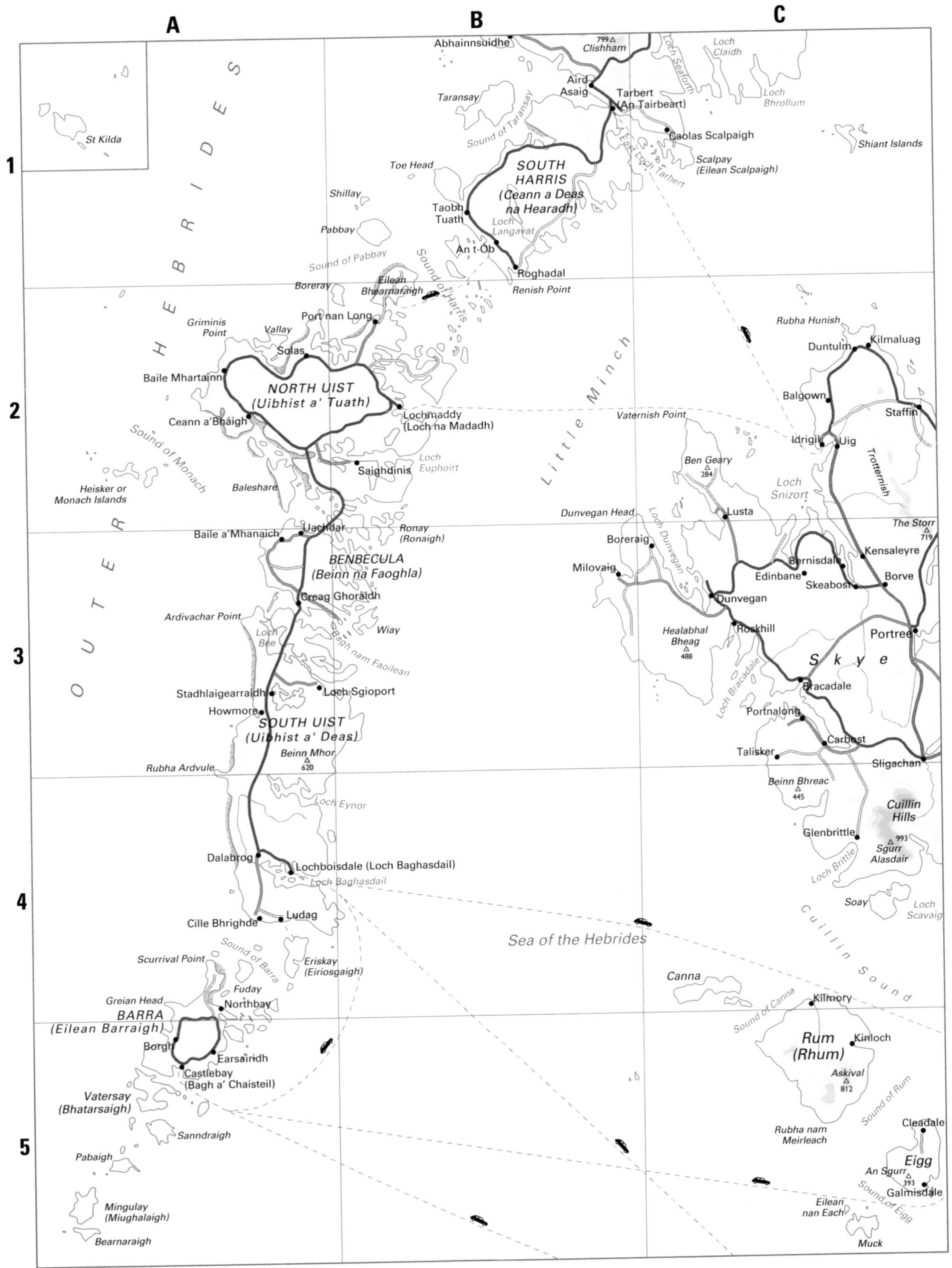

A
B
C
1
2
3
4
5
St Kilda
OUTER HEBRIDES
Abhainnsuidhe
799
Clishham
Loch Seaforth
Loch Claidh
Loch Bhrollum
Aird Asaig
Tarbert
(An Tairbeart)
Taransay
Sound of Taransay
Caolas Scalpaigh
Shiant Islands
East Loch Tarbert
Scalpay
(Eilean Scalpaigh)
Toe Head
SOUTH HARRIS
(Ceann a Deas
na Hearadh)
Shillay
Taobh Tuath
Loch Langavat
Pabbay
An t-Ob
Sound of Pabbay
Sound of Harris
Roghadal
Boreray
Eilean Bhearnaraigh
Renish Point
Griminis Point
Vallay
Port nan Long
Rubha Hunish
Kilmaluag
Duntulm
Solas
Little Minch
Baile Mhartainn
NORTH UIST
(Uibhist a' Tuath)
Balgown
Staffin
Lochmaddy
(Loch na Madadh)
Vaternish Point
Ceann a'Bhàigh
Idrigil
Uig
Sound of Monach
Loch Euphoirt
Saighdinis
Ben Geary
284
Trotternish
Heisker or
Monach Islands
Baleshare
Loch Snizort
Dunvegan Head
Lusta
The Storr
719
Uachdar
Ronay
(Ronaigh)
Baile a'Mhanaich
Boreraig
Loch Dunvegan
BENBECULA
(Beinn na Faoghla)
Kensaleyre
Milovaig
Bernisdale
Edinbane
Borve
Skeabost
Creag Ghoraidh
Dunvegan
Wiay
Ardivachar Point
Loch Bee
Healabhal Bheag
488
Roskhill
Portree
Bagh nam Faoilean
Skye
Loch Bracadale
Bracadale
Stadhlaigearraidh
Loch Sgioport
Howmore
Portnalong
SOUTH UIST
(Uibhist a' Deas)
Carbost
Beinn Mhor
620
Talisker
Sligachan
Rubha Ardvule
Beinn Bhreac
445
Loch Eynor
Cuillin Hills
Glenbrittle
993
Sgurr Alasdair
Dalabrog
Lochboisdale (Loch Baghasdail)
Loch Baghasdail
Loch Brittle
Soay
Loch Scavaig
Ludag
Cille Bhrighde
Sea of the Hebrides
Cuillin Sound
Sound of Barra
Scurrival Point
Eriskay
(Eiriosgaigh)
Canna
Fuday
Greian Head
Northbay
Kilmory
Sound of Canna
BARRA
(Eilean Barraigh)
Rum
(Rhum)
Kinloch
Borgh
Earsairidh
Castlebay
(Bagh a' Chaisteil)
Askival
812
Vatersay
(Bhatarsaigh)
Sound of Rum
Cleadale
Rubha nam Meirleach
Sanndraigh
Eigg
Pabaigh
An Sgurr
393
Galmisdale
Sound of Eigg
Mingulay
(Miughalaigh)
Eilean nan Each
Bearnaraigh
Muck

# Map 8

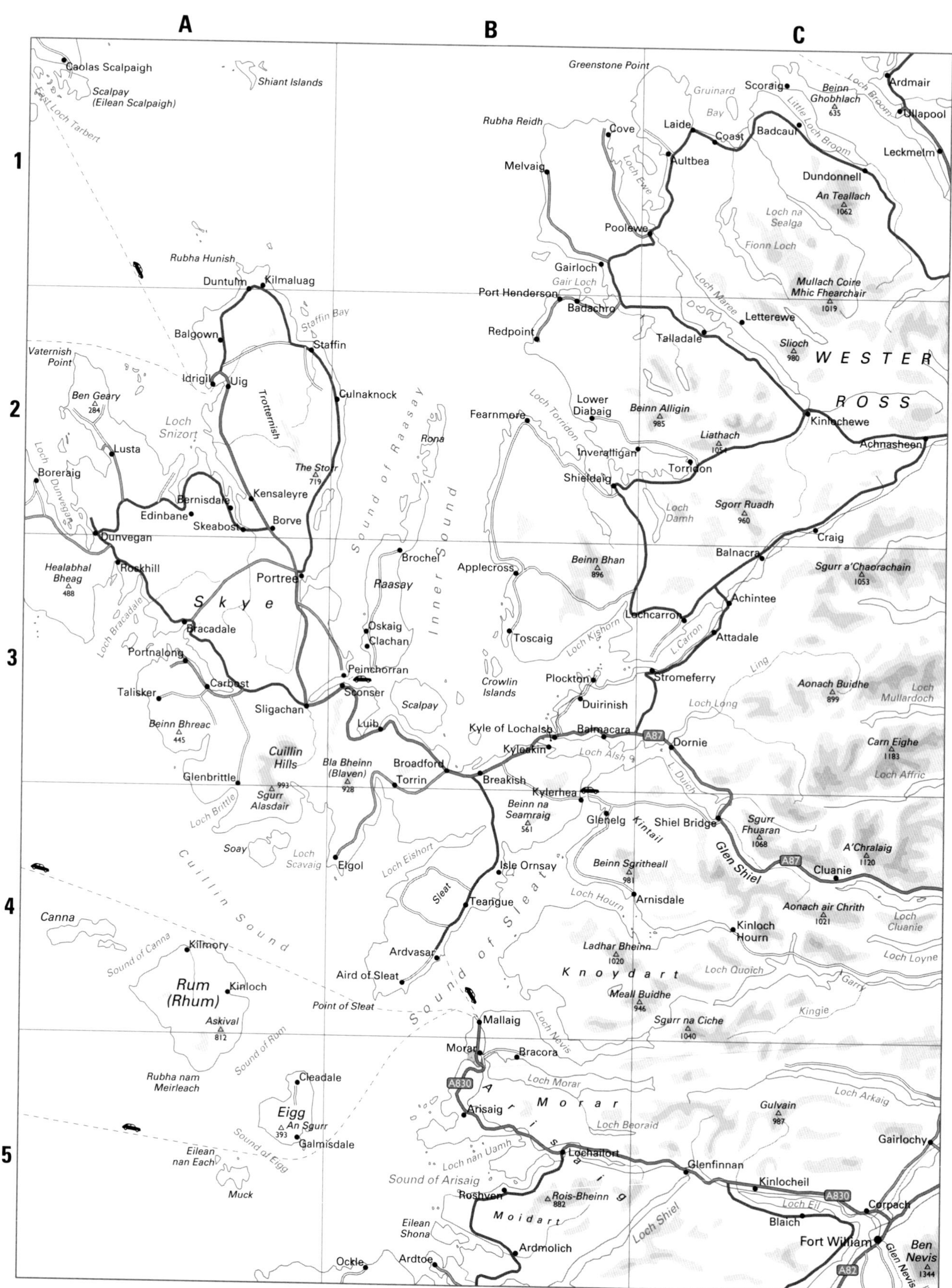
A
B
C
1
2
3
4
5
Caolas Scalpaigh
Scalpay
(Eilean Scalpaigh)
East Loch Tarbert
Shiant Islands
Greenstone Point
Gruinard Bay
Scoraig
Beinn Ghobhlach
635
Ardmair
Loch Broom
Ullapool
Rubha Reidh
Cove
Laide
Coast
Badcaul
Little Loch Broom
Leckmelm
Melvaig
Aultbea
Loch Ewe
Dundonnell
An Teallach
1062
Loch na Sealga
Poolewe
Fionn Loch
Rubha Hunish
Gairloch
Gair Loch
Duntulm
Kilmaluag
Port Henderson
Badachro
Mullach Coire Mhic Fhearchair
1019
Loch Maree
Letterewe
Staffin Bay
Staffin
Balgown
Redpoint
Talladale
Slioch
980
WESTER
ROSS
Vaternish Point
Idrigill
Uig
Trotternish
Ben Geary
284
Loch Snizort
Culnaknock
Sound of Raasay
Fearnmore
Loch Torridon
Lower Diabaig
Beinn Alligin
985
Kinlochewe
Rona
Liathach
1054
Achnasheen
Lusta
Loch Dunvegan
Borereaig
The Storr
719
Inveralligan
Torridon
Shieldaig
Kensaleyre
Bernisdale
Edinbane
Skeabost
Borve
Inner Sound
Loch Damh
Sgorr Ruadh
960
Dunvegan
Craig
Healabhal Bheag
488
Rockhill
Brochel
Applecross
Beinn Bhan
896
Balnacra
Sgurr a'Chaorachain
1053
Portree
Raasay
Skye
Achintee
Bracadale
Loch Bracadale
Oskaig
Clachan
Lochcarron
Toscaig
Loch Kishorn
L. Carron
Attadale
Portnalong
Peinchorran
Crowlin Islands
Plockton
Stromeferry
Ling
Aonach Buidhe
899
Loch Mullardoch
Talisker
Carbost
Sconser
Sligachan
Scalpay
Duirinish
Loch Long
Beinn Bhreac
445
Luib
Kyle of Lochalsh
Balmacara
A87
Dornie
Cuillin Hills
Bla Bheinn
(Blaven)
928
Broadford
Kyleakin
Loch Alsh
Carn Eighe
1183
Glenbrittle
993
Sgurr Alasdair
Torrin
Breakish
L. Duich
Loch Affric
Kylerhea
Beinn na Seamraig
561
Glenelg
Kintail
Shiel Bridge
Sgurr Fhuaran
1068
Loch Brittle
Soay
Loch Scavaig
Elgol
Loch Eishort
Isle Ornsay
Beinn Sgritheall
981
Glen Shiel
A87
Cluanie
A'Chralaig
1120
Cuillin Sound
Sleat
Teangue
Sound of Sleat
Loch Hourn
Arnisdale
Aonach air Chrith
1021
Loch Cluanie
Canna
Kinloch Hourn
Sound of Canna
Kilmory
Ardvasar
Ladhar Bheinn
1020
Loch Loyne
Knoydart
Loch Quoich
Rum
(Rhum)
Kinloch
Aird of Sleat
Garry
Meall Buidhe
946
Point of Sleat
Kingie
Askival
812
Mallaig
Loch Nevis
Sgurr na Ciche
1040
Sound of Rum
Morar
Bracora
Rubha nam Meirleach
Cleadale
A830
Loch Morar
Loch Arkaig
Arisaig
Morar
Gulvain
987
Eigg
An Sgurr
393
Galmisdale
Loch Beoraid
Gairlochy
Sound of Eigg
Eilean nan Each
Loch nan Uamh
Lochailort
Glenfinnan
Sound of Arisaig
Kinlocheil
Muck
Roshven
Rois-Bheinn
882
A830
Corpach
Loch Eil
Loch Shiel
Moidart
Blaich
Eilean Shona
Fort William
Ardmolich
Ben Nevis
1344
Glen Nevis
Ockle
Ardtoe
A82

# Map 9

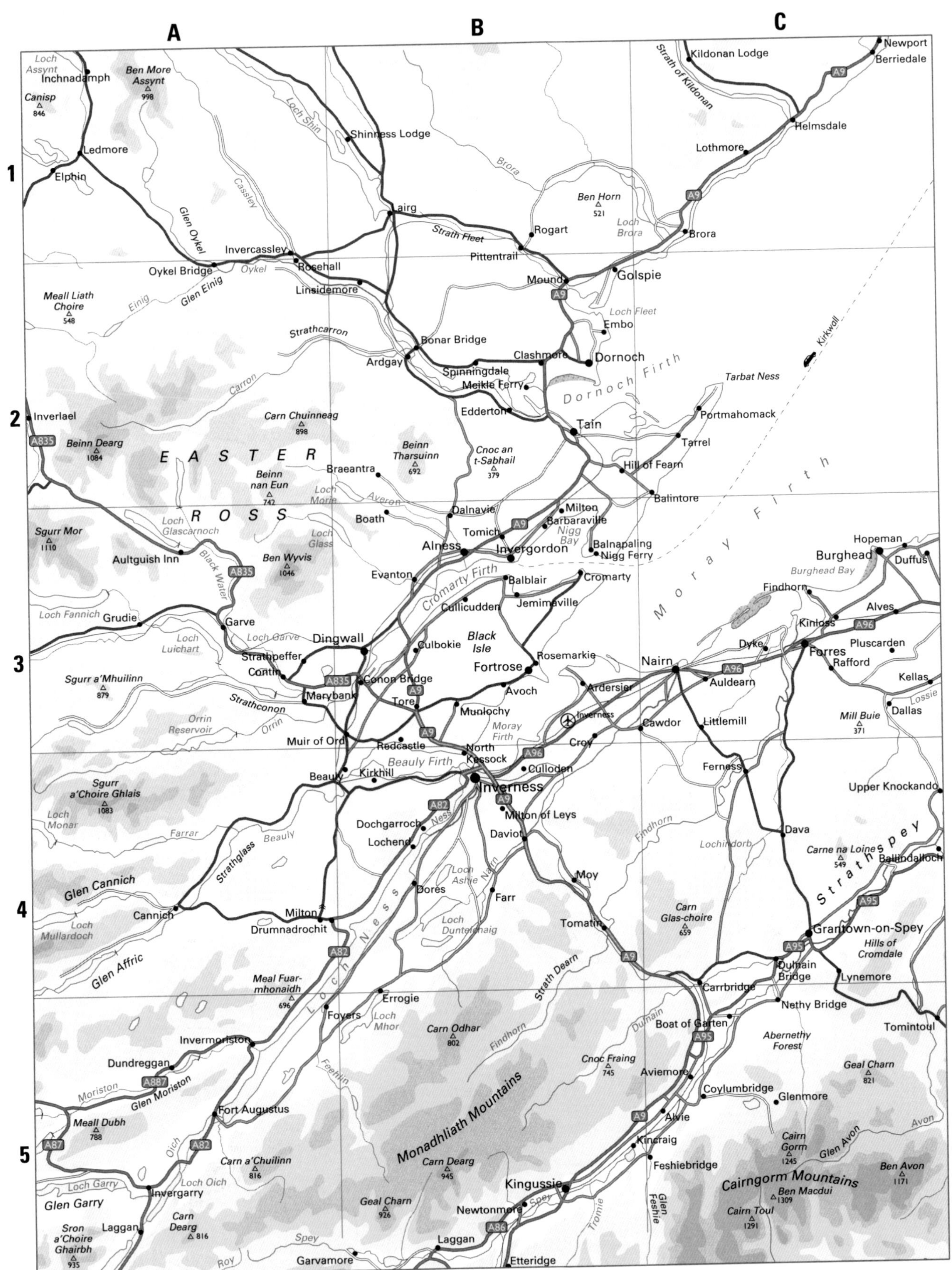
A
B
C
1
2
3
4
5
Inchnadamph
Ben More Assynt
Ledmore
Elphin
Shinness Lodge
Lairg
Kildonan Lodge
Newport
Berriedale
Helmsdale
Lothmore
Ben Horn
Rogart
Brora
Golspie
Mound
Pittentrail
Invercassley
Rosehall
Oykel Bridge
Linsidemore
Bonar Bridge
Ardgay
Embo
Dornoch
Clashmore
Spinningdale
Meikle Ferry
Dornoch Firth
Tarbat Ness
Portmahomack
Edderton
Tain
Tarrel
Hill of Fearn
Balintore
Inverlael
Beinn Dearg
Carn Chuinneag
EASTER ROSS
Beinn Tharsuinn
Cnoc an t-Sabhail
Braeantra
Beinn nan Eun
Boath
Dalnavie
Milton
Barbaraville
Tomich
Alness
Invergordon
Balnapaling
Nigg Ferry
Moray Firth
Sgurr Mor
Aultguish Inn
Ben Wyvis
Evanton
Cromarty Firth
Balblair
Cromarty
Hopeman
Burghead
Duffus
Findhorn
Kinloss
Alves
Forres
Pluscarden
Rafford
Kellas
Dallas
Garve
Grudie
Dingwall
Culbokie
Black Isle
Fortrose
Rosemarkie
Nairn
Auldearn
Dyke
Strathpeffer
Contin
Conon Bridge
Marybank
Tore
Avoch
Munlochy
Ardersier
Cawdor
Littlemill
Sgurr a'Mhuilinn
Muir of Ord
Redcastle
North Kessock
Croy
Beauly
Kirkhill
Inverness
Culloden
Ferness
Upper Knockando
Mill Buie
Sgurr a'Choire Ghlais
Dochgarroch
Lochend
Milton of Leys
Daviot
Dava
Strathspey
Ballindalloch
Carne na Loine
Glen Cannich
Cannich
Strathglass
Dores
Farr
Moy
Milton
Drumnadrochit
Tomatin
Carn Glas-choire
Grantown-on-Spey
Hills of Cromdale
Glen Affric
Loch Ness
Meal Fuar-mhonaidh
Errogie
Foyers
Carrbridge
Dulnain Bridge
Lynemore
Nethy Bridge
Boat of Garten
Tomintoul
Invermoriston
Dundreggan
Glen Moriston
Carn Odhar
Cnoc Fraing
Aviemore
Abernethy Forest
Geal Charn
Coylumbridge
Glenmore
Fort Augustus
Meall Dubh
Monadhliath Mountains
Alvie
Kincraig
Feshiebridge
Cairn Gorm
Glen Avon
Ben Avon
Carn a'Chuilinn
Carn Dearg
Kingussie
Cairngorm Mountains
Ben Macdui
Cairn Toul
Invergarry
Glen Garry
Loch Oich
Geal Charn
Newtonmore
Laggan
Sron a'Choire Ghairbh
Carn Dearg
Laggan
Garvamore
Etteridge
Loch Shin
Strath Fleet
Glen Oykel
Glen Einig
Strathcarron
Strathconon
Orrin Reservoir
Beauly Firth
Loch Mhor
Strath Dearn
Glen Feshie
Kirkwall
A9
A835
A96
A82
A95
A887
A87
A86

# Map 10

A
B
C
1
2
3
4
5
Lossiemouth
Covesea
Duffus
Findochty
Portknockie
Cullen
Sandend
Kingston
Buckie
Spey Bay
Portsoy
Whitehills
Troup Head
Rosehearty
Sandhaven
Fraserburgh
Elgin
A96
Lhanbryde
Portgordon
Fordyce
199
Durn Hill
Kirktown of Deskford
Macduff
Banff
Gardenstown
Pennan
New Aberdour
Mid Ardlaw
Inverallochy
A98
Longmanhill
Memsie
St Combs
Mosstodloch
Fochabers
King Edward
Ladysford
A90
Loch of Strathbeg
Longmorn
Cornhill
Lonmay
Kellas
Spey
Knock Hill
430
Deveron
North Ugie
Old Rattray
Rattray Head
Forgie
Finnygaud
Strichen
Crimond
Newmill
Knock
New Byth
New Pitsligo
New Leeds
Mulben
A95
Aberchirder
St Fergus
Ben Aigan
471
Keith
Turriff
Cuminestown
Fetterangus
Rothes
Isla
Milltown of Rothiemay
Maud
Mintlaw
Longside
Archiestown
Craigellachie
Darra
New Deer
Old Deer
Upper Knockando
Bogniebrae
Peterhead
Aberlour
Drummuir
Stuartfield
Carron
Glendronach
A952
Boddam
Dufftown
Huntly
Auchnagatt
Marypark
Glass
Kirkton of Auchterless
Ballindalloch
Woodhead
Hill of Dudwick
Ben Rinnes
840
Badenscoth
Methlick
174
Hatton
S T R A T H B O G I E
Fyvie
Ythan
Cruden Bay
Fiddich
Culdrain
Glenfoundland
Rothienorman
Toll of Birness
Kirkton of Culsalmond
Bay of Cruden
Bridgend
Glenlivet
Tap o' Noth
563
Tarves
Ellon
Kennethmont
Cook's Cairn
755
Bogie
Old Rayne
Tomnavoulin
Insch
Rhynie
Pitmedden
Collieston
Oldmeldrum
Knockandhu
Oyne
Pitcaple
Auchleven
Urie
Whiterashes
Newburgh
Lumsden
Correen Hills
Carn Mor
804
Ladder Hills
Inverurie
Stromness
Tomintoul
Mossat
Don
Newmachar
Kildrummy
Alford
Hatton of Fintray
Balmedie
Kemnay
Kintore
Potterton
Carn Ealasaid
792
Strathdon
Glenkindie
Monymusk
Aberdeen
Dyce
Muir of Fowlis
Tillyfourie
Blackburn
Lyne of Skene
Cock Bridge
Colnabaichin
A92
Bridge of Don
Dunecht
Bucksburn
Woodside
Mar
Westhill
Kirkton of Skene
Mastrick
Old Aberdeen
Tarland
Morven
871
Lumphanan
Echt
Kingswells
Midmar
Garlogie
Mannofield
Cults
Torphins
Culardoch
900
Cambus o' May
Dinnet
A93
Kincardine O'Neil
Peterculter
Cove Bay
Blairs
Charlestown
Aboyne
Crathie
Ballater
Glen Tanar
Carnferg
525
Portlethen
Marywell
Banchory
Kirkton of Durris
Dee
Strachan
Newtonhill
Netherley
Aucholzie
Muchalls
Mongour
376
Glen Muick
Rickarton
Mount Keen
939
Lochnagar
1155
Bridge of Dye
Stonehaven
Dunnottar
Loch Muick
South Esk
Glas Maol
1068
Tarfside
Glen Esk
Drumlithie
North Esk
Auchenblae
Catterline
Ben Tirran
896
Water of Saughs
Mayar
928
Glen Clova
Auchmull
Fordoun
Kincardine
Roadside of Kinneff
Clova
Fettercairn
Bervie Water
Inverbervie
Monamenach
807
Prosen Water
Laurencekirk
Glen Prosen
Bridgend
Edzell
Edzell Airfield
Gourdon
Inchbare
Marykirk
Johnshaven
Kirkton of Menmuir
Easter Lednathie
St Cyrus
Fern
Trinity
Kirkton of Glenisla
Dykehead
Hillside
Brechin
Backwater Reservoir
Tannadice
Bridge of Dun
Montrose
Kirkton of Kingoldrum
Finavon
Lintrathen
Farnell
Bridge of Craigisla
Strathmore
Aberlemno
Ferryden
Kirriemuir
Airlie
Rescobie
Erricht
Alyth
Forfar
Friockheim
Lunan Bay
Letham
Douglastown
Inverkeilor
Craichie

# Map 11

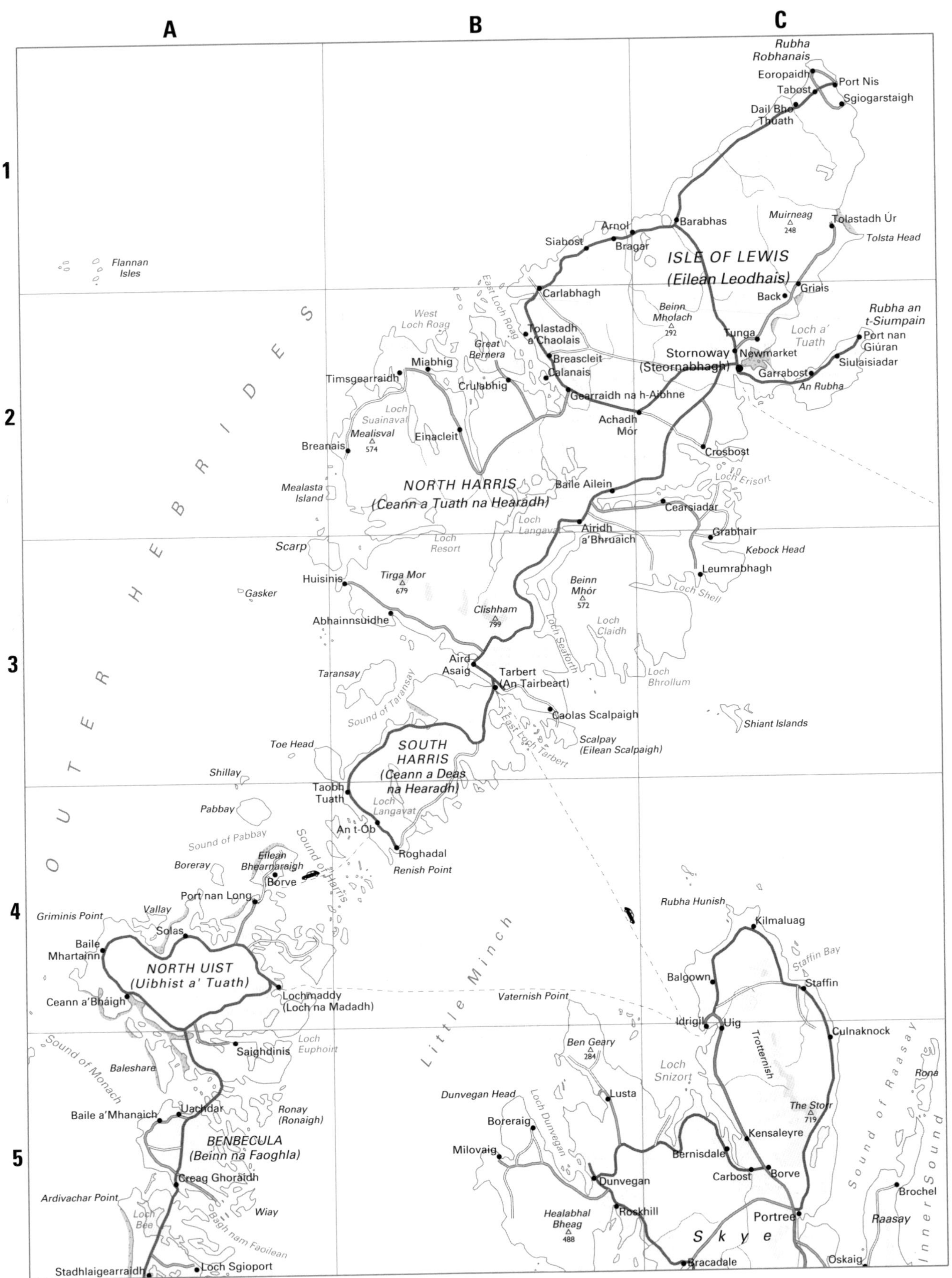
A
B
C
1
2
3
4
5
Rubha Robhanais
Eoropaidh
Port Nis
Tabost
Sgiogarstaigh
Dail Bho Thuath
Barabhas
Muirneag 248
Tolastadh Úr
Tolsta Head
Arnol
Siabost
Bragar
ISLE OF LEWIS
(Eilean Leodhais)
Griais
Back
Flannan Isles
Carlabhagh
Beinn Mholach 292
Rubha an t-Siumpain
Port nan Giúran
Siulaisiadar
Loch a' Tuath
Tunga
Newmarket
Stornoway
(Steornabhagh)
Garrabost
An Rubha
West Loch Roag
East Loch Roag
Tolastadh a' Chaolais
Great Bernera
Breascleit
Calanais
Miabhig
Timsgearraidh
Crulabhig
Gearraidh na h-Aibhne
Achadh Mór
Crosbost
Loch Suainaval
Mealisval 574
Einacleit
Breanais
OUTER HEBRIDES
NORTH HARRIS
(Ceann a Tuath na Hearadh)
Baile Ailein
Loch Erisort
Mealasta Island
Cearsiadar
Loch Langavat
Airidh a' Bhruaich
Grabhair
Kebock Head
Scarp
Loch Resort
Leumrabhagh
Huisinis
Tirga Mor 679
Beinn Mhór 572
Loch Shell
Gasker
Clishham 799
Abhainnsuidhe
Loch Claidh
Loch Seaforth
Aird Asaig
Tarbert
(An Tairbeart)
Loch Bhrollum
Taransay
Sound of Taransay
Caolas Scalpaigh
Shiant Islands
Scalpay
(Eilean Scalpaigh)
East Loch Tarbert
Toe Head
SOUTH HARRIS
(Ceann a Deas na Hearadh)
Shillay
Taobh Tuath
Loch Langavat
Pabbay
Sound of Pabbay
An t-Ob
Roghadal
Renish Point
Boreray
Eilean Bhearnaraigh
Borve
Sound of Harris
Port nan Long
Rubha Hunish
Griminis Point
Vallay
Kilmaluag
Solas
Little Minch
Staffin Bay
Baile Mhartainn
NORTH UIST
(Uibhist a' Tuath)
Balgown
Staffin
Lochmaddy
(Loch na Madadh)
Ceann a'Bhàigh
Vaternish Point
Idrigill
Uig
Culnaknock
Trotternish
Saighdinis
Loch Euphoirt
Sound of Monach
Ben Geary 284
Baleshare
Loch Snizort
Rona
Dunvegan Head
Lusta
The Storr 719
Baile a'Mhanaich
Uachdar
Ronay
(Ronaigh)
BENBECULA
(Beinn na Faoghla)
Boreraig
Loch Dunvegan
Kensaleyre
Sound of Raasay
Milovaig
Bernisdale
Creag Ghoraidh
Carbost
Borve
Dunvegan
Brochel
Ardivachar Point
Loch Bee
Wiay
Bagh nam Faoilean
Healabhal Bheag 488
Rockhill
Portree
Raasay
Skye
Inner Sound
Stadhlaigearraidh
Loch Sgioport
Bracadale
Oskaig

## Map 12

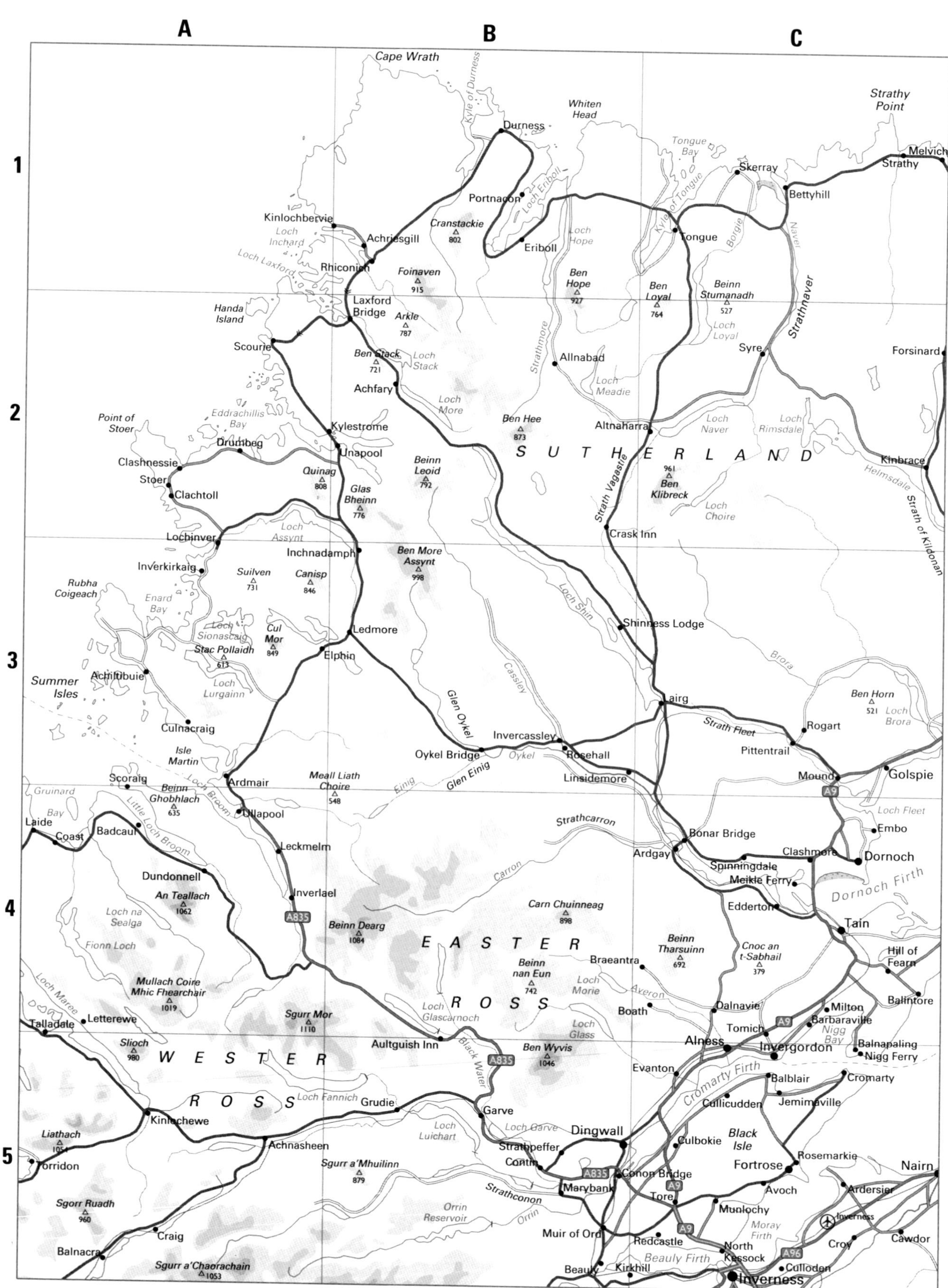
A
B
C
1
2
3
4
5
Cape Wrath
Kyle of Durness
Durness
Whiten Head
Strathy Point
Melvich
Strathy
Tongue Bay
Skerray
Bettyhill
Portnacon
Loch Eriboll
Kyle of Tongue
Tongue
Kinlochbervie
Loch Inchard
Achriesgill
Cranstackie
802
Eriboll
Loch Hope
Borgie
Naver
Loch Laxford
Rhiconich
Foinaven
915
Ben Hope
927
Ben Loyal
764
Beinn Stumanadh
527
Strathnaver
Handa Island
Laxford Bridge
Arkle
787
Loch Loyal
Scourie
Ben Stack
721
Loch Stack
Strathmore
Allnabad
Syre
Forsinard
Achfary
Loch Meadie
Loch More
Point of Stoer
Eddrachillis Bay
Kylestrome
Ben Hee
873
Altnaharra
Loch Naver
Loch Rimsdale
Drumbeg
Unapool
SUTHERLAND
Kinbrace
Clashnessie
Quinag
808
Beinn Leoid
792
961
Ben Klibreck
Helmsdale
Stoer
Clachtoll
Glas Bheinn
776
Strath Vagastie
Loch Choire
Strath of Kildonan
Lochinver
Loch Assynt
Crask Inn
Inchnadamph
Ben More Assynt
998
Inverkirkaig
Suilven
731
Canisp
846
Rubha Coigeach
Enard Bay
Loch Shin
Loch Sionascaig
Cul Mor
849
Ledmore
Shinness Lodge
Stac Pollaidh
613
Elphin
Summer Isles
Achiltibuie
Loch Lurgainn
Cassley
Brora
Glen Oykel
Lairg
Ben Horn
521
Loch Brora
Culnacraig
Strath Fleet
Rogart
Isle Martin
Invercassley
Pittentrail
Oykel Bridge
Oykel
Rosehall
Loch Broom
Meall Liath Choire
548
Einig
Glen Einig
Linsidemore
Mound
Golspie
Scoraig
Ardmair
Gruinard Bay
Beinn Ghobhlach
635
A9
Little Loch Broom
Ullapool
Strathcarron
Loch Fleet
Laide
Coast
Badcaul
Bonar Bridge
Embo
Leckmelm
Ardgay
Clashmore
Dornoch
Dundonnell
Carron
Spinningdale
Meikle Ferry
Dornoch Firth
An Teallach
1062
Inverlael
Carn Chuinneag
898
Edderton
Loch na Sealga
A835
Beinn Dearg
1084
Tain
Fionn Loch
EASTER
Beinn Tharsuinn
692
Cnoc an t-Sabhail
379
Hill of Fearn
Braeantra
Beinn nan Eun
742
Loch Morie
Averon
Mullach Coire Mhic Fhearchair
1019
Loch Maree
ROSS
Balintore
Loch Glascarnoch
Boath
Dalnavie
Milton
Sgurr Mor
1110
A9
Barbaraville
Talladale
Letterewe
Tomich
Loch Glass
Nigg Bay
Alness
Invergordon
Balnapaling
Slioch
980
Aultguish Inn
Black Water
Ben Wyvis
1046
Nigg Ferry
WESTER
A835
Evanton
Cromarty Firth
Balblair
Cromarty
ROSS
Loch Fannich
Grudie
Cullicudden
Jemimaville
Kinlochewe
Garve
Loch Garve
Dingwall
Black Isle
Liathach
1054
Loch Luichart
Strathpeffer
Culbokie
Rosemarkie
Achnasheen
Torridon
Contin
A835
Conon Bridge
Fortrose
Nairn
Sgurr a'Mhuilinn
879
Marybank
A9
Ardersier
Strathconon
Tore
Avoch
Sgorr Ruadh
960
Orrin Reservoir
Orrin
Munlochy
Inverness
Moray Firth
Craig
Muir of Ord
A9
Cawdor
Redcastle
North Kessock
Croy
Balnacra
Beauly Firth
A96
Sgurr a'Chaorachain
1053
Beauly
Kirkhill
Culloden
Inverness

# Map 13

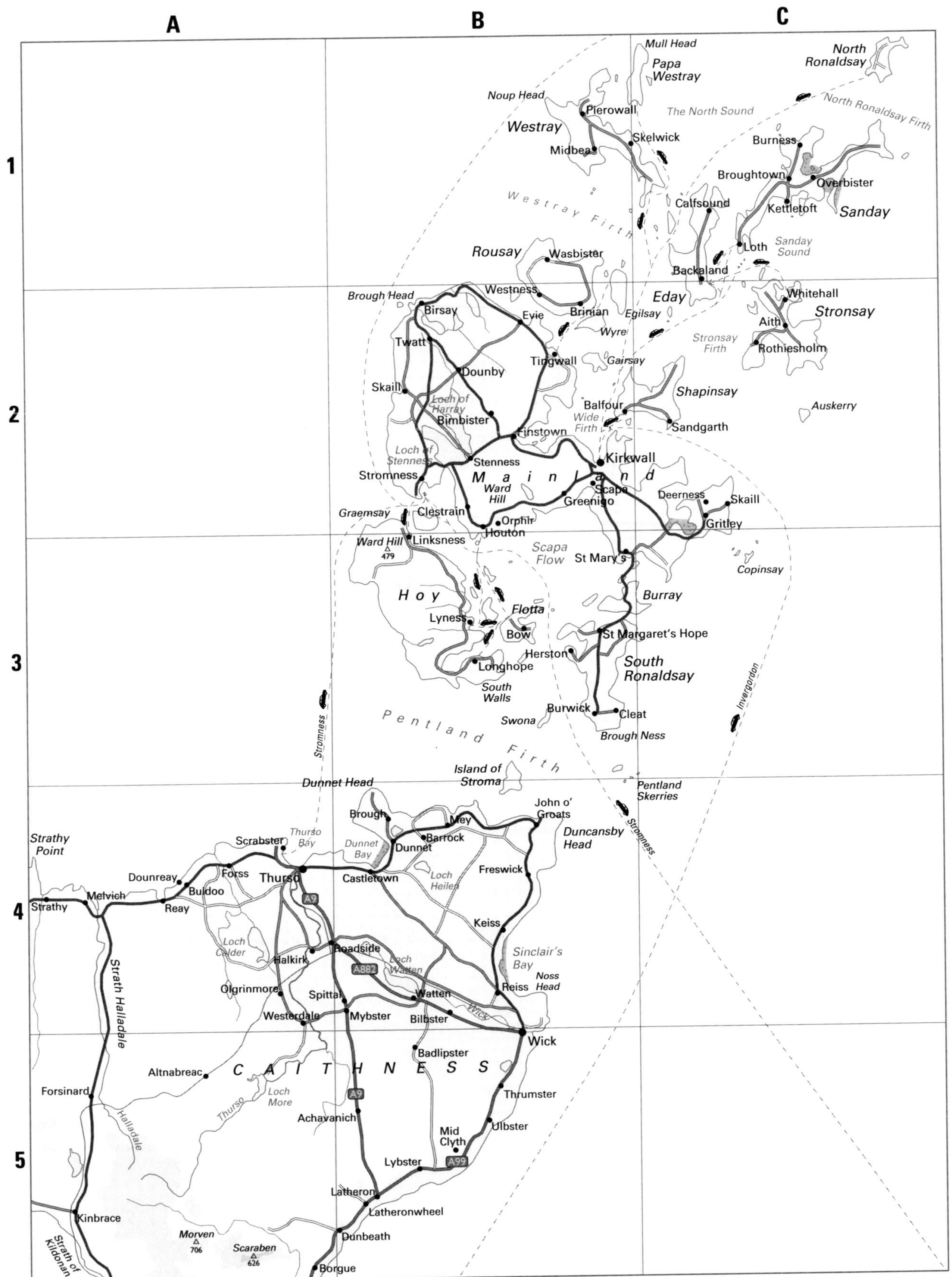
A
B
C
1
2
3
4
5
Mull Head
Papa Westray
North Ronaldsay
Noup Head
Pierowall
The North Sound
North Ronaldsay Firth
Westray
Skelwick
Midbea
Burness
Broughtown
Overbister
Calfsound
Kettletoft
Sanday
Westray Firth
Rousay
Wasbister
Loth
Sanday Sound
Backaland
Westness
Brough Head
Birsay
Eyie
Brinian
Eday
Egilsay
Whitehall
Stronsay
Aith
Wyre
Stronsay Firth
Twatt
Tingwall
Gairsay
Rothiesholm
Dounby
Skaill
Loch of Harray
Shapinsay
Balfour
Auskerry
Bimbister
Wide Firth
Sandgarth
Finstown
Loch of Stenness
Stenness
Kirkwall
Stromness
Mainland
Scapa
Deerness
Skaill
Ward Hill
Greenigo
Graemsay
Clestrain
Orphir
Gritley
Houton
Ward Hill
479
Linksness
Scapa Flow
St Mary's
Copinsay
Hoy
Burray
Flotta
Lyness
Bow
St Margaret's Hope
Herston
Longhope
South Ronaldsay
South Walls
Invergordon
Burwick
Swona
Cleat
Stromness
Pentland Firth
Brough Ness
Island of Stroma
Pentland Skerries
Dunnet Head
John o' Groats
Brough
Mey
Strathy Point
Scrabster
Thurso Bay
Dunnet Bay
Barrock
Dunnet
Duncansby Head
Stromness
Dounreay
Forss
Thurso
Castletown
Loch Heilen
Freswick
Strathy
Melvich
Buldoo
Reay
A9
Keiss
Loch Calder
Halkirk
Roadside
Sinclair's Bay
Strath Halladale
A882
Loch Watten
Noss Head
Olgrinmore
Spittal
Watten
Reiss
Westerdale
Mybster
Bilbster
Wick
Wick
Badlipster
Altnabreac
CAITHNESS
Forsinard
Loch More
Thrumster
Thurso
Halladale
A9
Achavanich
Ulbster
Mid Clyth
Lybster
A99
Latheron
Latheronwheel
Kinbrace
Morven
706
Scaraben
626
Dunbeath
Strath of Kildonan
Borgue

# Map 14

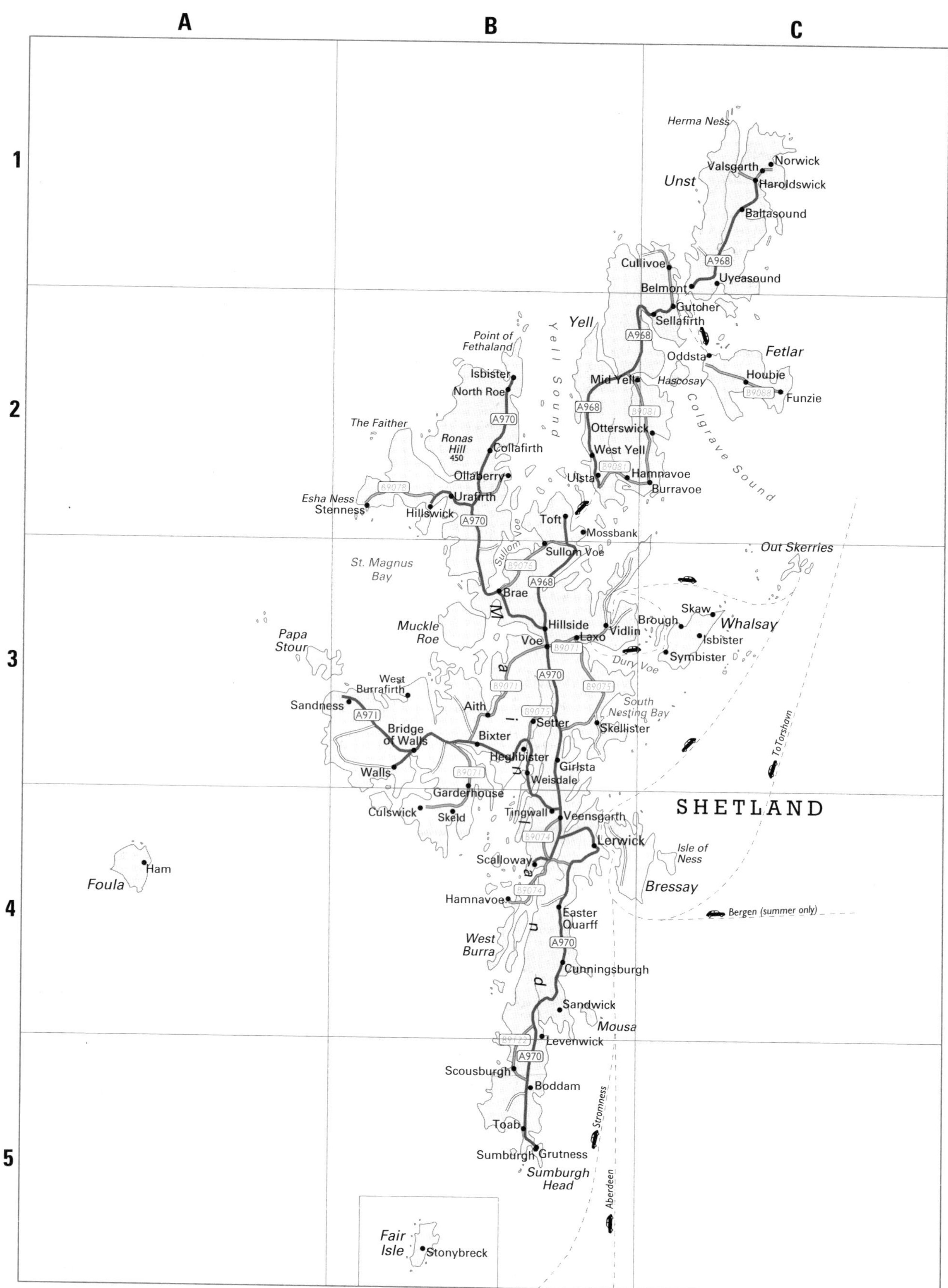
A
B
C
1
2
3
4
5
Herma Ness
Norwick
Valsgarth
Unst
Haroldswick
Baltasound
A968
Cullivoe
Uyeasound
Belmont
Gutcher
Yell
Sellafirth
A968
Fetlar
Oddsta
Point of Fethaland
Yell Sound
Houbie
Isbister
Mid Yell
Hascosay
North Roe
B9088
Funzie
Colgrave Sound
A968
B9081
A970
The Faither
Otterswick
Ronas Hill 450
Collafirth
West Yell
Ollaberry
B9081
Ulsta
Hamnavoe
Burravoe
B9078
Esha Ness
Urafirth
Stenness
Hillswick
A970
Toft
Mossbank
Sullom Voe
Sullom Voe
Out Skerries
St. Magnus Bay
B9076
A968
Brae
Skaw
Brough
Whalsay
Muckle Roe
Hillside
Vidlin
Papa Stour
Laxo
Isbister
Voe
B9071
Symbister
Dury Voe
A970
West Burrafirth
B9071
B9075
South Nesting Bay
Sandness
Aith
A971
B9075
Setter
Skellister
Bridge of Walls
Bixter
Heglibister
To Torshavn
Girlsta
Walls
B9071
Weisdale
Garderhouse
SHETLAND
Culswick
Skeld
Tingwall
Veensgarth
B9074
Lerwick
Isle of Ness
Ham
Scalloway
Foula
Bressay
B9074
Hamnavoe
Easter Quarff
Bergen (summer only)
West Burra
A970
Cunningsburgh
Sandwick
Mousa
B9122
Levenwick
A970
Scousburgh
Boddam
Stromness
Toab
Sumburgh
Grutness
Sumburgh Head
Aberdeen
Fair Isle
Stonybreck

# Map 15

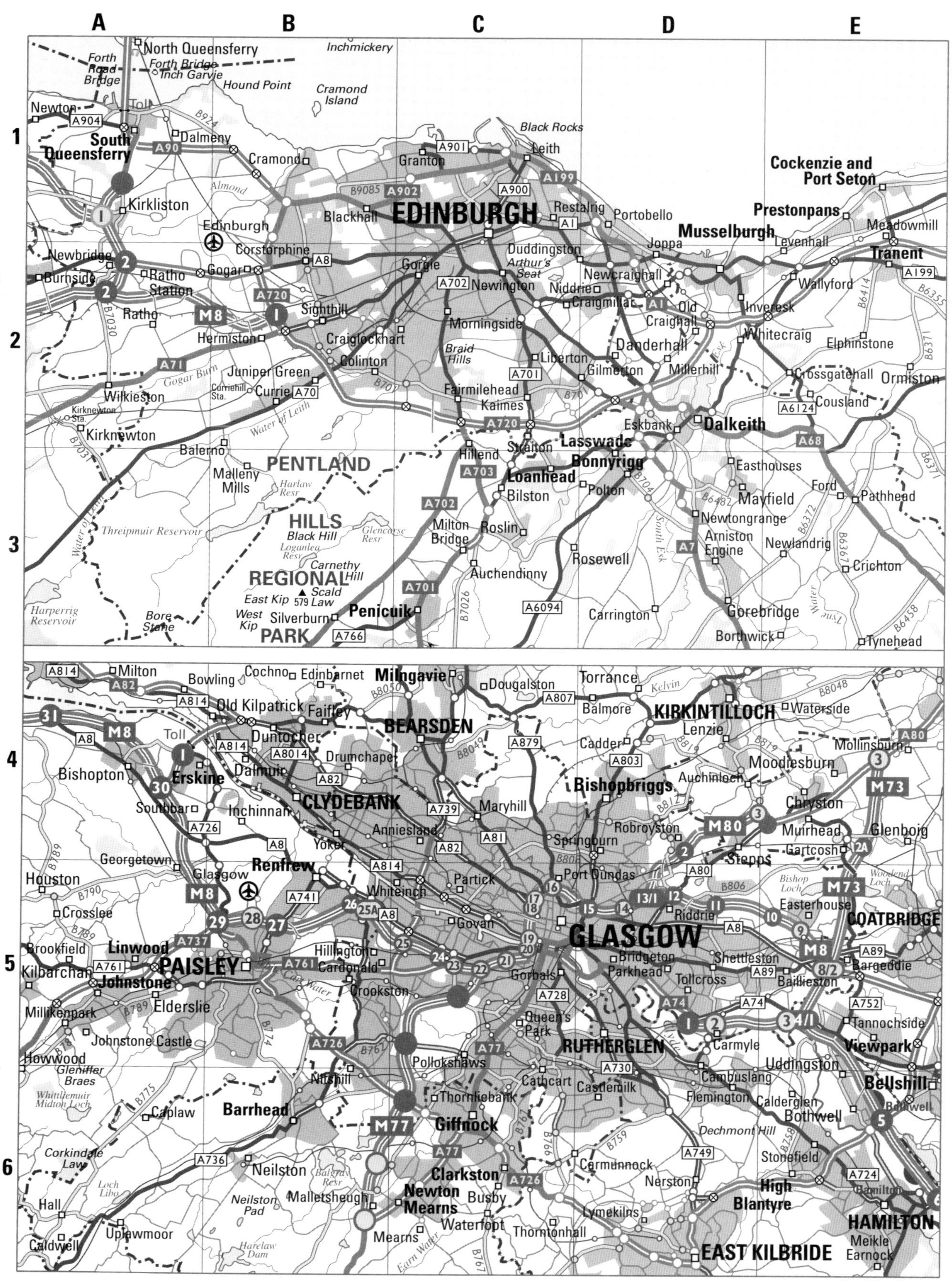

A
B
C
D
E
1
2
3
4
5
6
North Queensferry
Forth Road Bridge
Forth Bridge
Inch Garvie
Inchmickery
Hound Point
Cramond Island
Newton
A904
Toll
South Queensferry
A90
Dalmeny
B924
Cramond
Granton
A901
Black Rocks
Leith
A900
A199
A902
B9085
Kirkliston
Almond
Blackhall
EDINBURGH
Restalrig
A1
Portobello
Edinburgh
Joppa
Musselburgh
Corstorphine
Duddingston
Arthur's Seat
Newbridge
Burnside
Ratho Station
Gogar
A8
Gorgie
A702
Newington
Niddrie
Newcraighall
Ratho
B7030
M8
A720
Sighthill
Craigmillar
Craighall
Old Craighall
Inveresk
Hermiston
Craiglockhart
Morningside
Danderhall
Whitecraig
Colinton
Braid Hills
Liberton
Millerhill
Esk
A71
Gogar Burn
Juniper Green
Currie
Curriehill Sta.
A70
A701
Gilmerton
Wilkieston
Fairmilehead
Kaimes
Kirknewton Sta.
Kirknewton
B7031
Water of Leith
Eskbank
Dalkeith
Balerno
Hillend
Straiton
Lasswade
Bonnyrigg
A703
Loanhead
Malleny Mills
PENTLAND
Harlaw Resr
A702
Bilston
Polton
B704
Threipmuir Reservoir
HILLS
Black Hill
Glencorse Resr
Loganlea Resr
Milton Bridge
Roslin
Carnethy Hill
REGIONAL
Scald Law
579
East Kip
West Kip
A701
Auchendinny
Rosewell
B7026
South Esk
Harperrig Reservoir
Bore Stane
Silverburn
Penicuik
PARK
A766
A6094
Carrington
Cockenzie and Port Seton
Prestonpans
Meadowmill
Levenhall
Tranent
A199
Wallyford
B6414
B6355
Elphinstone
B6371
Crossgatehall
Ormiston
A6124
Cousland
A68
Easthouses
B6482
Mayfield
Ford
Pathhead
Newtongrange
B6372
Arniston Engine
A7
Newlandrig
B6367
Crichton
Gorebridge
Borthwick
B6458
Tynehead
A814
Milton
A82
Bowling
Cochno
Edinbarnet
Milngavie
Dougalston
Torrance
Kelvin
B8048
Old Kilpatrick
Faifley
A807
Balmore
KIRKINTILLOCH
Waterside
M8
Toll
Duntocher
BEARSDEN
Lenzie
A8014
A879
Cadder
A80
Mollinsburn
Bishopton
Erskine
Dalmuir
Drumchapel
A803
Moodiesburn
Bishopbriggs
Auchinloch
M73
Southbar
Inchinnan
CLYDEBANK
A739
Maryhill
Chryston
A726
M80
Robroyston
Muirhead
Glenboig
Anniesland
A81
Springburn
B789
Georgetown
A8
Yoker
A82
Stepps
Gartcosh
Glasgow
Renfrew
A814
Port Dundas
A80
Houston
Partick
B790
Whiteinch
B806
Bishop Loch
Woodend Loch
Crosslee
A741
Riddrie
Easterhouse
Govan
GLASGOW
A8
COATBRIDGE
Brookfield
Linwood
A737
Hillington
Kilbarchan
A761
PAISLEY
Cardonald
Bridgeton
Shettleston
A89
Johnstone
Parkhead
Tollcross
Baillieston
Bargeddie
Cart Water
Crookston
Gorbals
Elderslie
Milliken park
A728
A74
A752
Queen's Park
Tannochside
Johnstone Castle
A726
B767
A77
RUTHERGLEN
Carmyle
Howwood
Pollokshaws
Viewpark
Gleniffer Braes
B774
Nitshill
Cathcart
A730
Castlemilk
Uddingston
Cambuslang
Bellshill
B775
Caplaw
Thornliebank
Barrhead
Flemington
Calderglen
Bothwell
M77
Giffnock
Dechmont Hill
B758
B759
Corkindale Law
A736
Neilston
A77
Clarkston
A749
Stonefield
Cathkin
Carmunnock
A726
Nerston
A724
Loch Libo
Neilston Pad
Malletsheugh
Newton Mearns
Busby
High Blantyre
Hamilton
Hall
Lymekilns
Waterfoot
Thorntonhall
Uplawmoor
Mearns
HAMILTON
Caldwell
Harelaw Dam
Earn Water
B767
EAST KILBRIDE
Meikle Earnock

# Map 16

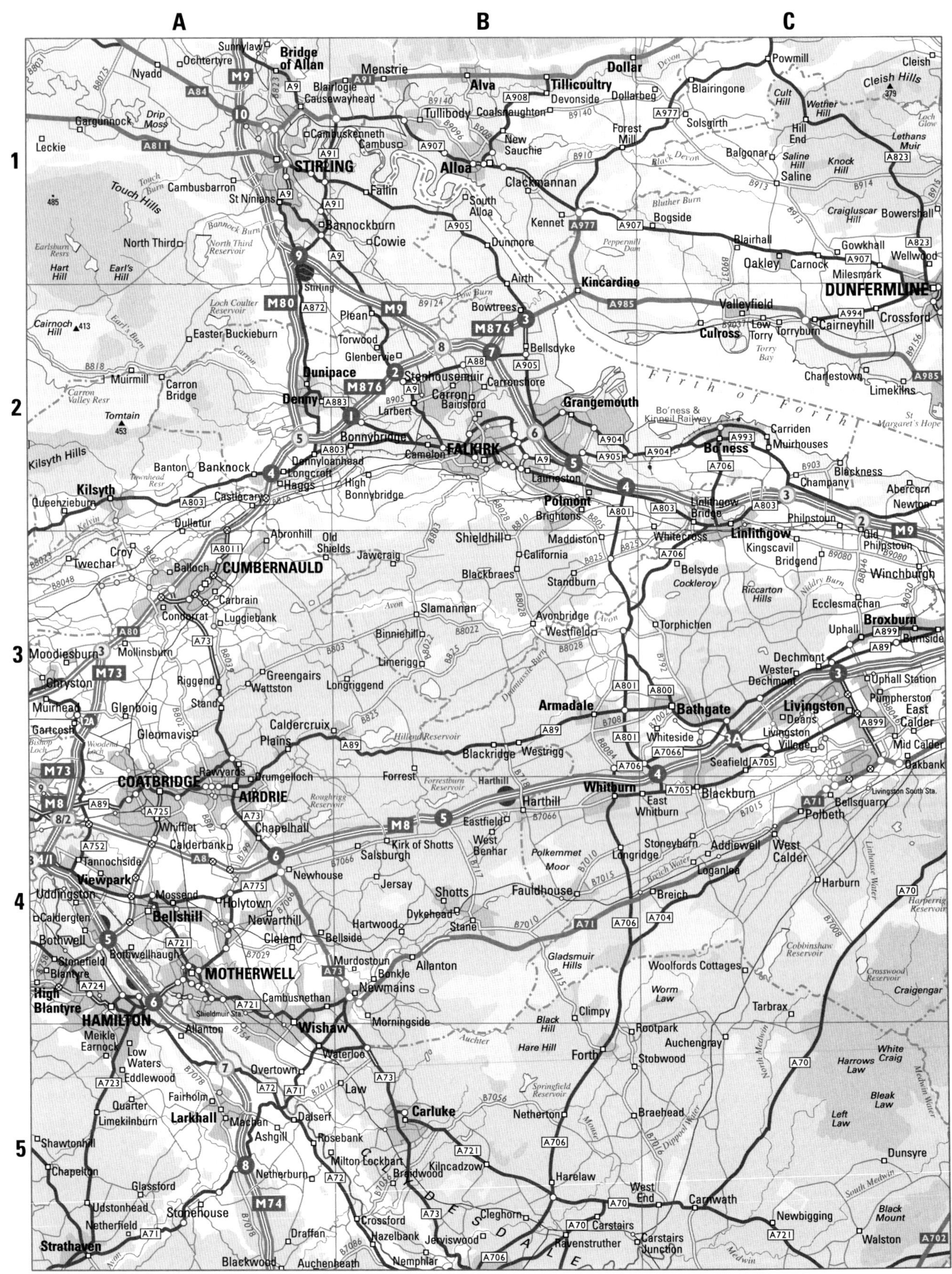

A
B
C
1
2
3
4
5
Sunnylaw
Ochtertyre
Bridge of Allan
Nyadd
M9
Menstrie
Dollar
Powmill
Cleish
Cleish Hills
Alva
Tillicoultry
Blairlogie
Causewayhead
Blairingone
Devonside
Dollarbeg
Cult Hill
Wether Hill
Gargunnock
Drip Moss
Tullibody
Coalsnaughton
Solsgirth
Leckie
Cambuskenneth
Cambus
New Sauchie
Forest Mill
Hill End
Lethans Muir
STIRLING
Alloa
Balgonar
Saline Hill
Knock Hill
Saline
Touch Hills
Cambusbarron
St Ninians
Fallin
Clackmannan
South Alloa
Kennet
Bogside
Craigluscar Hill
Bowershall
Bannockburn
Cowie
Bluther Burn
North Third
North Third Reservoir
Dunmore
Blairhall
Gowkhall
Wellwood
Earlsburn Resrs
Hart Hill
Earl's Hill
Peppermill Dam
Oakley
Carnock
Milesmark
Airth
Kincardine
DUNFERMLINE
Stirling
Loch Coulter Reservoir
Cairnoch Hill
Plean
Bowtrees
Valleyfield
Low Torry
Torryburn
Cairneyhill
Crossford
Easter Buckieburn
Torwood
Culross
Torry Bay
Glenbervie
Bellsdyke
Muirmill
Carron Bridge
Dunipace
Stenhousemuir
Carronshore
Charlestown
Limekilns
Carron Valley Resr
Denny
Larbert
Carron
Bainsford
Grangemouth
Firth of Forth
Tomtain
Bo'ness & Kinneil Railway
Carriden
St Margaret's Hope
Bonnybridge
FALKIRK
Bo'ness
Muirhouses
Kilsyth Hills
Banton
Banknock
Dennyloanhead
Camelon
Longcroft
High Bonnybridge
Haggs
Laurieston
Blackness
Champany
Abercorn
Kilsyth
Queenzieburn
Castlecary
Polmont
Linlithgow Bridge
Newton
Brightons
Philpstoun
Dullatur
Abronhill
Old Shields
Shieldhill
Maddiston
Whitecross
Linlithgow
Old Philpstoun
Croy
Twechar
Jawcraig
California
Kingscavil
Bridgend
Winchburgh
Balloch
CUMBERNAULD
Blackbraes
Standburn
Belsyde
Cockleroy
Riccarton Hills
Carbrain
Ecclesmachan
Condorrat
Luggiebank
Slamannan
Avonbridge
Torphichen
Broxburn
Binniehill
Westfield
Uphall
Moodiesburn
Mollinsburn
Burnside
Limerigg
Dechmont
Wester Dechmont
Chryston
Riggend
Greengairs
Wattston
Longriggend
Uphall Station
Pumpherston
Muirhead
Glenboig
Stand
Armadale
Bathgate
Livingston
Deans
East Calder
Gartcosh
Caldercruix
Whiteside
Livingston Village
Mid Calder
Glenmavis
Plains
Hillend Reservoir
Blackridge
Westrigg
Seafield
Oakbank
Rawyards
Drumgelloch
Forrest
Forrestburn Reservoir
Harthill
COATBRIDGE
AIRDRIE
Roughrigg Reservoir
Whitburn
East Whitburn
Blackburn
Livingston South Sta.
Bellsquarry
Polbeth
Whifflet
Chapelhall
Eastfield
West Benhar
Calderbank
Kirk of Shotts
Salsburgh
Polkemmet Moor
Longridge
Stoneyburn
Addiewell
West Calder
Tannochside
Viewpark
Newhouse
Jersay
Loganlea
Harburn
Uddingston
Mossend
Holytown
Shotts
Fauldhouse
Breich
Calderglen
Bellshill
Newarthill
Hartwood
Dykehead
Stane
Harperrig Reservoir
Bothwell
Cleland
Bellside
Bothwellhaugh
Stonefield
Blantyre
Murdostoun
Allanton
Bonkle
Gladsmuir Hills
Cobbinshaw Reservoir
Woolfords Cottages
Crosswood Reservoir
MOTHERWELL
Newmains
High Blantyre
Cambusnethan
Worm Law
Tarbrax
Craigengar
HAMILTON
Shieldmuir Sta.
Wishaw
Morningside
Climpy
Black Hill
Rootpark
Meikle Earnock
Low Waters
Auchengray
Hare Hill
Forth
Stobwood
White Craig
Harrows Law
Eddlewood
Overtown
Waterloe
Law
Springfield Reservoir
Quarter
Fairholm
Carluke
Netherton
Braehead
Bleak Law
Limekilnburn
Larkhall
Machan
Dalserf
Ashgill
Left Law
Shawtonhill
Rosebank
Dunsyre
Chapelton
Milton Lockhart
Braidwood
Kilncadzow
Harelaw
Glassford
Netherburn
West End
Carnwath
Udstonhead
Stonehouse
Netherfield
Crossford
Cleghorn
Carstairs
Newbigging
Black Mount
Draffan
Hazelbank
Jerviswood
Ravenstruther
Carstairs Junction
Walston
Strathaven
Blackwood
Auchenheath
Nemphlar
CLYDESDALE